HARRAP'S
MINI
French-English
DICTIONARY
DICTIONNAIRE
Anglais-Français

Michael Janes

HARRAP
London

Distributed in the United States by
PRENTICE HALL
New York

Contents/Table des matières

iii

Preface

This dictionary is an entirely new publication designed to provide an up-to-date, practical and concise work of reference giving translations of the most useful French and English vocabulary.

The aim has been to achieve a work of great clarity of equal value to French and to English speakers, whether students, tourists, businessmen or -women or general readers, and to produce a text offering the maximum amount of guidance in pinpointing and understanding translations. Equal importance has been given to the presentation of French and English. Different translations of the same word or phrase are clearly labelled by means of bracketed context indicators and/or style and field labels. A single translation of a word is also often labelled as an additional aid to the user (e.g. **hedgehog** n (animal) hérisson m; **ungainly** a (clumsy) gauche; **béotien, -ienne** nmf (inculte) philistine). The user is helped by having indicators and labels in French in the French section and in English in the English section of the dictionary.

Style and field labels follow bracketed indicators (e.g. **grid** n . . . . (system) El réseau m; **bidule** nm (chose) Fam thingummy). In the event of more than one translation within a grammatical category being qualified by the same style or field label, the label may then precede (see **calé, liquidizer, trucker**).

The user will find in the text important abbreviations, useful geographical information such as names of countries, and a wide coverage of American words and usage. The vocabulary treated includes French and English colloquialisms and slang, and important technical jargon. Comparatives and superlatives of English adjectives are also indicated.

In order to save space, derived words are usually included within the entry of a headword. All such words are highlighted by means of a lozenge. Derivatives may be written in full or abbreviated, as is usually the case for important derived forms (such as English **-ly** or French **-ment**).

An oblique stroke in bold is used to mark the stem of a headword at which point the derived ending is added. A bold dash stands for a headword or the portion of a headword to the left of the oblique stroke (e.g. **awkward** a . . . **◆—ly** adv . . . **◆—ness** n . . . ; **boulevers/er** vt . . . **◆—ant** a . . . **◆—ement** nm).

An oblique stroke within an entry is another space-saving device. It is used to separate non equivalent alternative parts of a phrase or expression matched exactly in French and English (e.g. **les basses/hautes classes** the lower/upper classes is to be understood as: **les basses classes** the lower classes and **les hautes classes** the upper classes; **to give s.o./sth a push** pousser qn/qch as: **to give s.o. a push** pousser qn and **to give sth a push** pousser qch).

A further typographical device, a filled square, may be used to introduce a string of English phrasal verbs (see **come, take**).

In common with other Harrap dictionaries, when a headword appears in an example in the same form, it is represented by its initial letter. This applies whether the headword starts a new line (e.g. **advance** n in a of s.o. avant qn) or applies within an entry, either in full form (e.g. **◆arterial** a a. road route f principale), or in abbreviated form (e.g. (where **◆—ed** stands for **advanced**) **◆—ed** a a. in years âgé).

The pronunciation of both English and French is shown using the latest symbols of the International Phonetic Alphabet. Pronunciation is given for headwords at the start of an entry, and, as an additional help to the user, for a word within an entry where the correct pronunciation may be difficult to derive from the form of the word (e.g. **◆aristocratie** [-asi]; **◆aoûtien, -ienne** [ausjɛ̃, -jɛn]; **◆rabid** ['ræbɪd]; **◆prayer** [preər]).

Stress in English is indicated for headwords and for derived words in which stress differs from that of a headword (e.g. **civilize** ['sɪvɪlaɪz] and **◆civili'zation**). American English pronunciation is listed wherever it is considered to differ substantially from that of British English (e.g. **aristocrat** ['ærɪstəkræt, Am ə'rɪstəkræt], **quinine** ['kwɪnɪn, Am 'kwaɪnaɪn]). American spelling is also given if considered sufficiently different (e.g. **tire** and **tyre, plow** and **plough**).

An original feature of this dictionary is its semantic approach to the order and arrangement of entries. An approach whereby the meaning of words is allowed to influence the structure of entries is felt to be of particular benefit to the user in his or her understanding of language.

Important semantic categories have been indicated by bold Arabic numerals within an entry (see **bolt**, **tail**, **général**) or have been entered as separate headwords (see **bug**[1] and **bug**[2], **draw**[1] and **draw**[2], **start**[1] and **start**[2]). Note that grammatical categories, apart from the first, have been marked by a dash.

Words are entered under the headword from which they are considered to derive (e.g. **approfondi**, abbreviated as ◆—i follows **approfond/ir**; ◆**astronomer** and ◆**astro'nomical** follow **astronomy**). Present and past participles (used adjectivally) are felt to be closely associated in meaning and form with the infinitive from which they derive. They are entered, usually in abbreviated form, within an entry immediately after the infinitive, any other derivatives there may be following in alphabetical order (e.g. **exalt/er** vt . . . ◆—**ant** a . . . ◆—**é** a . . . ◆**exaltation** nf; **accommodat/e** vt . . . ◆—**ing** a . . . ◆**accommo'dation** n; **expir/e** vi . . . ◆—**ed** a . . . ◆**expi'ration** n . . . ◆**expiry** n).

Derived words and compounds are felt to be semantically distinct and are, wherever possible, grouped together alphabetically and listed separately from each other (e.g. **base** n . . . ◆—**less** a . . . ◆—**ness** n . . . ◆**baseball** n . . . ◆**baseboard** n; **bouton** nm . . . ◆**b.-d'or** nm . . . ◆**b.-pression** nf . . . ◆**boutonner** vt . . . ◆**boutonneux**, **-euse** a . . . ◆**boutonnière** nf). Compounds may be listed in the place within an entry where they are felt best to belong by virtue of meaning.

The author wishes to express his gratitude to Monsieur F. Antoine, Mrs H. Curties and Mr S. Fortey for their advice and help, to Mrs R. Hillmore for her assistance with proofreading, and to Mr J.-L. Barbanneau for his support and encouragement.

M. Janes
London, 1988

Préface

Ce dictionnaire entièrement nouveau a pour ambition d'être un ouvrage de référence moderne, pratique et compact, offrant les traductions des termes les plus courants du français comme de l'anglais.

Il veut être un ouvrage qui, par sa grande clarté, soit utile autant au francophone qu'à l'anglophone, pour les études, le tourisme, les affaires aussi bien que pour l'usage courant: il tente de fournir le plus d'indications possible pour aider l'utilisateur à cerner et à comprendre les traductions proposées. On a accordé la même importance à la présentation du français qu'à celle de l'anglais. Les différentes traductions d'un même mot ou d'une même expression sont clairement définies à l'aide d'indications de contexte entre parenthèses et/ou de symboles indiquant le niveau de langue et le domaine d'utilisation. Lorsqu'un mot est accompagné d'une seule traduction, celle-ci est également souvent précédée d'une indication destinée à fournir à l'utilisateur une aide supplémentaire (par exemple **hedgehog** n (*animal*) hérisson m; **ungainly** a (*clumsy*) gauche; **béotien**, **-ienne** nmf (*inculte*) philistine). L'accès à cet ouvrage est facilité par l'utilisation d'indications en français dans la partie français-anglais et en anglais dans la partie anglais-français.

Les indications de niveau de langue et de domaine d'utilisation viennent à la suite de celles entre parenthèses (par exemple **grid** n . . . (*system*) El réseau m; **bidule** nm (*chose*) Fam thingummy). Lorsque plusieurs traductions dans la même catégorie grammaticale sont définies par la même indication, celle-ci peut alors venir en tête (voir **calé**, **liquidizer**, **trucker**).

L'utilisateur trouvera dans cet ouvrage d'importantes abréviations, de précieux éléments de géographie tels que des noms de pays, ainsi qu'une large sélection d'américanismes. Le lexique retenu comprend des mots et des expressions familiers et argotiques, tant en français qu'en anglais, et des termes techniques courants. De plus, les comparatifs et superlatifs des adjectifs anglais sont donnés.

Par souci de concision, les mots dérivés sont généralement donnés dans le corps des articles. Tous ces mots sont repérés par un losange. Les dérivés sont donnés soit sous leur forme complète, soit en abrégé, ce qui est généralement le cas pour les formes dérivées courantes (telles que celles en **-ly** en anglais ou en **-ment** en français).

On utilise une barre oblique pour indiquer le radical d'une entrée à la suite duquel la terminaison d'un dérivé sera ajoutée. Un tiret en gras remplace le mot d'entrée ou la partie de ce mot qui précède la barre oblique (par exemple **awkward** *a* . . . **◆—ly** *adv* . . . **◆—ness** *n* . . . ; **boulevers/er** *vt* . . . **◆—ant** *a* . . . **◆—ement** *nm*).

Toujours par souci de concision, une barre oblique est utilisée dans un article pour éviter la répétition d'un même élément de phrase (par exemple **les basses/hautes classes** the lower/upper classes se lira: **les basses classes** the lower classes et **les hautes classes** the upper classes ; **to give s.o./sth a push** pousser qn/qch se lira: **to give s.o. a push** pousser qn et **to give sth a push** pousser qch).

Enfin, un carré plein peut être utilisé pour introduire une série de verbes à particule en anglais (voir **come**, **take**).

Comme il est d'usage dans les autres dictionnaires Harrap, lorsqu'un mot d'entrée est repris sous la même forme dans un exemple, il est remplacé par sa première lettre. Cela est le cas aussi bien lorsque le mot est au début d'un article (par exemple **advance** *n* in *a*. of s.o.* avant qn) qu'il apparaît dans un article, sous sa forme complète (par exemple **◆arterial** *a* **a. road** route *f* principale) ou en abrégé (par exemple **◆—ed** remplaçant **advanced**) **◆—ed** *a* **a. in years** âgé.

La prononciation de l'anglais comme du français est fournie; elle utilise la notation la plus moderne de l'Alphabet Phonétique International. La phonétique est donnée pour les mots d'entrée au début de l'article, et pour aider l'utilisateur, pour tout mot dans un article dont il pourrait être difficile de déduire la prononciation à partir de l'orthographe (par exemple **◆aristocratie** [-asi]; **◆aoûtien, -ienne** [ausjɛ̃, -jɛn]; **◆rabid** ['ræbɪd]; **◆prayer** [preər]).

En anglais, l'accent tonique est indiqué pour les mots d'entrée et pour les dérivés chaque fois que l'accentuation diffère de celle de l'entrée (par exemple **civilize** et **◆civili'zation**). Les prononciations américaines sont indiquées chaque fois qu'elles diffèrent de façon substantielle de celles de l'anglais britannique (par exemple **aristocrat** ['ærɪstəkræt, *Am* ə'rɪstəkræt], **quinine** ['kwɪniːn, *Am* 'kwaɪnaɪn]). On indique également l'orthographe américaine lorsqu'elle est suffisamment différente de celle de l'anglais britannique (par exemple **tire** et **tyre**, **plow** et **plough**).

Une des caractéristiques originales de ce dictionnaire est son approche sémantique du classement et de l'organisation des articles. On a considéré que cette approche, où le sens des mots détermine pour une part l'organisation des articles, serait d'un grand secours à l'utilisateur en ce qui concerne sa compréhension de la langue.

Les catégories sémantiques importantes sont indiquées dans un article par des chiffres arabes en gras (voir **bolt**, **tail**, **général**) ou sont présentées comme des mots distincts (voir **bug¹** et **bug²**, **draw¹** et **draw²**, **start¹** et **start²**). Les catégories grammaticales autres que la première traitée sont indiquées par un tiret.

Les mots apparaissent sous les mots d'entrée dont ils sont dérivés (par exemple **approfondi**, abrégé en **◆—i** suit **approfond/ir**; **◆astronomer** et **◆astro'nomical** suivent **astronomy**). Les participes présents et passés (utilisés comme adjectifs) sont considérés comme étant étroitement associés par le sens et par la forme à l'infinitif dont ils sont dérivés. Ils sont placés dans l'article, généralement en abrégé, immédiatement après l'infinitif; tous les autres dérivés éventuels apparaissent ensuite par ordre alphabétique (par exemple **exalt/er** *vt* . . . **◆—ant** *a* . . . **◆—é** *a* . . . **◆exaltation** *nf* ; **accommodat/e** *vt* . . . **◆—ing** *a* . . . **◆accommo'dation** *n*; **expir/e** *vi* . . . **◆—ed** *a* . . . **◆expi'ration** *n* . . . **◆expiry** *n*).

Les mots dérivés et les mots composés sont considérés comme étant distincts, du point de vue du sens, et sont, chaque fois que possible, regroupés séparément (par exemple **base** *n* . . . **◆—less** *a* . . . **◆—ness** *n* . . . **◆baseball** *n* . . . **◆baseboard** *n*; **bouton** *nm*. . . **◆b.-d'or** *nm*. . . **◆b.-pression** *nm*. . . **◆boutonner** *vt*. . . **◆boutonneux, -euse** *a* . . . **◆boutonnière** *nf*). Les composés se trouvent placés dans les articles là où leur sens a semblé devoir les appeler.

L'auteur tient à exprimer sa gratitude à Monsieur F. Antoine, à Mrs H. Curties et à Mr S. Fortey pour leurs conseils et leur collaboration, à Mrs R. Hillmore qui a bien voulu nous aider à relire les épreuves, et à Monsieur J.-L. Barbanneau pour son soutien et ses encouragements.

M. Janes
Londres, 1988

Grammar notes

In French, the feminine of an adjective is formed as a rule by adding **e** to the masculine form (e.g. grand, grande; carré, carrée; chevalin, chevaline). If the masculine already ends in **e**, the feminine is the same as the masculine (e.g. utile). Irregular feminine forms of adjectives (e.g. généreux, généreuse; léger, légère; doux; douce) are given in the French-English side of the dictionary. In the English-French side, French adjectives are shown in the masculine form only. Irregular feminines of adjectives are listed in the following way: généreux, -euse; léger, -ère; doux, douce.

To form the plural of a French noun or adjective **s** is usually added to the singular (e.g. arbre, arbres; taxi, taxis; petit, petits). The plural form of a noun ending in **s, x** or **z** (e.g. pois, croix, nez) is the same as that of the singular. Plurals of nouns and adjectives which do not follow these general rules are listed in the French section, including the plurals of French compounds where the formation of the plural involves a change other than the addition of final **s** (e.g. arc-en-ciel, arcs-en-ciel). Those nouns and adjectives where **x** or **aux** is added in the plural are shown in the following way: cerveau, -x; général, -aux.

In English also, **s** is added to form the plural of a noun (e.g. cat, cats; taxi, taxis) but a noun ending in **ch, s, sh, x** or **z** forms its plural by the addition of **es** (e.g. glass, glasses; match, matches. (Note that when **ch** is pronounced [k], the plural is in **s**, e.g. monarch, monarchs.) When a noun ends in **y** preceded by a consonant, **y** is changed to **ies** to form the plural (e.g. army, armies). Irregular English plurals are given in the English-French side, including the plurals of English compounds where the formation of the plural involves a change other than the addition of final **s** (e.g. brother-in-law, brothers-in-law).

English nouns may be used as adjectives. When a French adjective is translated in this way, this use is made clear by the addition of a hyphen following the noun translation (e.g. farm- as a translation of **agricole**).

Most French verbs have regular conjugations though some display spelling anomalies (see French verb conjugations on p (i)). In the French section an asterisk is used to mark an irregular verb, and refers the user to the table of irregular verbs on p (ii).

Most English verbs form their past tense and past participle by adding **ed** to the infinitive (e.g. look, looked) or **d** to an infinitive already ending in **e** (e.g. love, loved). When a verb ends in **y** preceded by a consonant **y** becomes **ied** (e.g. satisfy, satisfied). To form the third person singular of a verb in the present tense **s** is added to the infinitive (e.g. know, knows) but an infinitive in **ch, s, sh, x** or **z** forms its third person singular by the addition of **es** (e.g. dash, dashes). When an infinitive ends in **y** preceded by a consonant, **y** is changed to **ies** to form the third person singular (e.g. satisfy, satisfies).

The English present participle is formed by the addition of **ing** to the infinitive (e.g. look, looking) but final **e** is omitted when an infinitive ends in **e** (e.g. love, loving). When the infinitive ends in a single consonant preceded by a vowel (e.g. tug), the final consonant is usually doubled in the past tense, past and present participles (e.g. tug, tugged, tugging).

Irregular English verb conjugations are given in the English headword list, and a summary of the most important irregular verbs may also be found on p (vii). The doubling of consonants in English verbs is indicated in the text. The latter is shown in the following way: **tug** . . . *vt* (**-gg-**).

Notes sur la grammaire

En français, le féminin d'un adjectif se forme en général en ajoutant e au masculin (par exemple grand, grande; carré, carrée; chevalin, chevaline). Lorsque le masculin se termine déjà par e, le féminin est identique (par exemple utile). Les féminins d'adjectifs qui ne se conforment pas à ces règles (par exemple généreux, généreuse; léger, légère; doux, douce) sont signalés dans la partie français-anglais où ils sont notés comme suit: généreux, -euse; léger, -ère; doux, douce. Dans la partie anglais-français, on ne donne que la forme masculine des adjectifs.

On forme en général le pluriel d'un nom ou d'un adjectif français en ajoutant s au singulier (par exemple arbre, arbres; taxi, taxis; petit, petits). Le pluriel d'un nom se terminant par s, x ou z (par exemple pois, croix, nez) est identique au singulier. Les pluriels des noms et adjectifs qui font exception à ces règles générales sont signalés dans la partie français-anglais, de même que les pluriels des mots composés français dont le passage au pluriel appelle une modification autre que le simple ajout d'un s final (par exemple arc-en-ciel, arcs-en-ciel). Les noms et adjectifs dont le pluriel se forme à l'aide d'un x ou de aux sont notés comme suit: cerveau, -x; général, -aux.

De la même façon, en anglais, on forme le pluriel des noms en ajoutant s (par exemple cat, cats; taxi, taxis) mais on ajoutera es aux noms qui se terminent par ch, s, sh, x ou z (par exemple glass, glasses; match, matches). (Noter cependant que lorsque ch se prononce [k], le pluriel est en s, comme dans monarch, monarchs). Lorsqu'un nom se termine par un y précédé d'une consonne, ce y devient ies au pluriel (par exemple army, armies). Les pluriels irréguliers de l'anglais sont signalés dans la partie anglais-français, de même que les pluriels des mots composés anglais dont le passage au pluriel entraîne une modification autre que le simple ajout d'un s final (par exemple brother-in-law, brothers-in-law).

Les noms anglais peuvent s'utiliser comme adjectifs. Lorsqu'un adjectif français est traduit par un nom, cela est signalé par l'ajout d'un trait d'union à la suite de ce nom (par exemple farm- comme traduction de **agricole**).

La plupart des verbes français ont des conjugaisons régulières; cependant, certains subissent des variations orthographiques (voir: Conjugaisons des verbes français à la page (i)) Dans la partie français-anglais, un astérisque signale un verbe irrégulier et renvoie à la table des verbes irréguliers donnée en page (ii).

En anglais, le passé et le participe passé des verbes se forment dans la plupart des cas en ajoutant ed à l'infinitif (par exemple look, looked) ou seulement d lorsque l'infinitif se termine par un e (par exemple love, loved). Lorsqu'un verbe se termine par un y précédé d'une consonne, ce y devient ied (par exemple satisfy, satisfied). La troisième personne du singulier d'un verbe au présent se forme en ajoutant s à l'infinitif (par exemple know, knows), mais on ajoutera es aux infinitifs qui se terminent par ch, s, sh, x ou z (par exemple dash, dashes). Enfin, lorsqu'un verbe se termine par un y précédé d'une consonne, ce y devient ies à la troisième personne du singulier (par exemple satisfy, satisfies).

Le participe présent en anglais se forme en ajoutant la désinence ing à l'infinitif (par exemple look, looking); lorsqu'un infinitif comporte un e final, celui-ci disparaît (par exemple love, loving). Lorsque l'infinitif se termine par une seule consonne précédée d'une voyelle (par exemple tug), la consonne finale est le plus souvent doublée au passé et aux participes passé et présent (par exemple tug, tugged, tugging).

Les formes des verbes irréguliers anglais sont données dans la partie anglais-français et une liste récapitulative des verbes irréguliers usuels figure en page (vii). Le doublement des consonnes dans les verbes anglais est signalé dans le corps de l'ouvrage; il est noté comme suit: **tug** . . . vt (–gg–).

Abbreviations

Abréviations

adjective	*a*	adjectif
abbreviation	*abbr, abrév*	abréviation
adverb	*adv*	adverbe
agriculture	*Agr*	agriculture
American	*Am*	américain
anatomy	*Anat*	anatomie
architecture	*Archit*	architecture
slang	*Arg*	argot
article	*art*	article
cars, motoring	*Aut*	automobile
auxiliary	*aux*	auxiliaire
aviation, aircraft	*Av*	aviation
biology	*Biol*	biologie
botany	*Bot*	botanique
British	*Br*	britannique
Canadian	*Can*	canadien
carpentry	*Carp*	menuiserie
chemistry	*Ch*	chimie
cinema	*Cin*	cinéma
commerce	*Com*	commerce
conjunction	*conj*	conjonction
cookery	*Culin*	cuisine
definite	*def, déf*	défini
demonstrative	*dem, dém*	démonstratif
economics	*Econ, Écon*	économie
electricity	*El, Él*	électricité
et cetera	*etc*	et cetera
feminine	*f*	féminin
familiar	*Fam*	familier
football	*Fb*	football
figurative	*Fig*	figuré
finance	*Fin*	finance
feminine plural	*fpl*	féminin pluriel
French	*Fr*	français
geography	*Geog, Géog*	géographie
geology	*Geol, Géol*	géologie
geometry	*Geom, Géom*	géométrie
grammar	*Gram*	grammaire
history	*Hist*	histoire
humorous	*Hum*	humoristique
indefinite	*indef, indéf*	indéfini
indicative	*indic*	indicatif
infinitive	*inf*	infinitif
interjection	*int*	interjection
invariable	*inv*	invariable
ironic	*Iron*	ironique
journalism	*Journ*	journalisme
legal, law	*Jur*	juridique
linguistics	*Ling*	linguistique
literary	*Lit, Litt*	littéraire
literature	*Liter, Littér*	littérature

masculine	*m*	masculin
mathematics	*Math*	mathématique
medicine	*Med, Méd*	médecine
carpentry	*Menuis*	menuiserie
meteorology	*Met, Mét*	météorologie
military	*Mil*	militaire
masculine plural	*mpl*	masculin pluriel
music	*Mus*	musique
noun	*n*	nom
nautical	*Nau*	nautique
noun feminine	*nf*	nom féminin
noun masculine	*nm*	nom masculin
noun masculine and feminine	*nmf*	nom masculin et féminin
pejorative	*Pej, Péj*	péjoratif
philosophy	*Phil*	philosophie
photography	*Phot*	photographie
physics	*Phys*	physique
plural	*pl*	pluriel
politics	*Pol*	politique
possessive	*poss*	possessif
past participle	*pp*	participe passé
prefix	*pref, préf*	préfixe
preposition	*prep, prép*	préposition
present participle	*pres p*	participe présent
present tense	*pres t*	temps présent
pronoun	*pron*	pronom
psychology	*Psy*	psychologie
past tense	*pt*	prétérit
	qch	quelque chose
	qn	quelqu'un
registered trademark	®	marque déposée
radio	*Rad*	radio
railway, *Am* railroad	*Rail*	chemin de fer
relative	*rel*	relatif
religion	*Rel*	religion
school	*Sch, Scol*	école
singular	*sing*	singulier
slang	*Sl*	argot
someone	*s.o.*	
sport	*Sp*	sport
something	*sth*	
subjunctive	*sub*	subjonctif
technical	*Tech*	technique
telephone	*Tel, Tél*	téléphone
textiles	*Tex*	industrie textile
theatre	*Th*	théâtre
television	*TV*	télévision
typography, printing	*Typ*	typographie
university	*Univ*	université
United States	*US*	États-Unis
auxiliary verb	*v aux*	verbe auxiliaire
intransitive verb	*vi*	verbe intransitif
impersonal verb	*v imp*	verbe impersonnel
pronominal verb	*vpr*	verbe pronominal
transitive verb	*vt*	verbe transitif
transitive and intransitive verb	*vti*	verbe transitif et intransitif

Pronunciation of French

TABLE OF PHONETIC SYMBOLS

Vowels

[i]	vite, cygne	[y]	cru, sûr
[e]	été, donner	[ø]	feu, meule
[ɛ]	elle, mais	[œ]	œuf, jeune
[a]	chat, fameux	[ə]	le, refaire
[ɑ]	pas, âgé	[ɛ̃]	vin, plein, faim
[ɔ]	donne, fort	[ɑ̃]	enfant, temps
[o]	dos, chaud, peau	[ɔ̃]	mon, nombre
[u]	tout, cour	[œ̃]	lundi, humble

Consonants

[p]	pain, absolu	[z]	cousin, zéro
[b]	beau, abbé	[ʃ]	chose, schéma
[t]	table, nette	[ʒ]	gilet, jeter
[d]	donner, sud	[l]	lait, facile
[k]	camp, képi	[r]	rare, rhume
[g]	garde, second	[m]	mon, flamme
[f]	feu, phrase	[n]	né, canne
[v]	voir, wagon	[ɲ]	campagne
[s]	sou, cire	[ŋ]	jogging
		[']	hanche (*i.e. no liaison or elision*)

Semi-consonants

[j]	piano, voyage
[w]	ouest, noir
[ɥ]	muet, lui

Prononciation de l'anglais

TABLEAU DES SIGNES PHONÉTIQUES

Voyelles et diphtongues

[iː]	bee, police		[ɒ]	lot, what
[ɪə]	beer, real		[ɔː]	all, saw
[ɪ]	bit, added		[ɔɪ]	boil, toy
[e]	bet, said		[əʊ]	low, soap
[eɪ]	date, nail		[ʊ]	put, wool
[eə]	bear, air		[uː]	shoe, too
[æ]	bat, plan		[ʊə]	poor, sure
[aɪ]	fly, life		[ʌ]	cut, some
[ɑː]	art, ask		[ɜː]	burn, learn
[aʊ]	fowl, house		[ə]	china, annoy
			[(ə)]	relation

Consonnes

[p]	pat, top		[ð]	that, breathe
[b]	but, tab		[h]	hat, rehearse
[t]	tap, patter		[l]	lad, all
[d]	dab, sadder		[r]	red, barring
[k]	cat, kite		[ʳ]	better, here (*représente un r*
[g]	go, rogue			*final qui se prononce en*
[f]	fat, phrase			*liaison devant une voyelle,*
[v]	veal, rave			*par exemple 'here is' [hɪəʳɪz])*
[s]	sat, ace		[m]	mat, hammer
[z]	zero, houses		[n]	no, banner
[ʃ]	dish, pressure		[ŋ]	singing, link
[ʒ]	pleasure		[j]	yet, onion
[tʃ]	charm, rich		[w]	wall, quite
[dʒ]	judge, rage		[ˈ]	*marque l'accent tonique;*
[θ]	thatch, breath			*précède la syllabe accentuée*

A

A, a [α] *nm* A, a.

a [a] *voir* avoir.

à [a] *prép* (à + le = au [o], à + les = aux [o]) **1** (*direction: lieu*) to; (*temps*) till, to; **aller à Paris** to go to Paris; **de 3 à 4 h** from 3 till *ou* to 4 (o'clock). **2** (*position: lieu*) at, in; (*surface*) on; **être au bureau/à la ferme/au jardin/à Paris** to be at *ou* in the office/on *ou* at the farm/in the garden/in Paris; **à la maison** at home; **à l'horizon** on the horizon; **à 8 h** at 8 (o'clock); **à mon arrivée** on (my) arrival; **à lundi!** see you (on) Monday! **3** (*description*) **l'homme à la barbe** the man with the beard; **verre à liqueur** liqueur glass. **4** (*attribution*) **donner qch à qn** to give sth to s.o., give s.o. sth. **5** (*devant inf*) **apprendre à lire** to learn to read; **travail à faire** work to do; **maison à vendre** house for sale; **prêt à partir** ready to leave. **6** (*appartenance*) **c'est (son livre) à lui** it's his (book); **c'est à vous de** (*décider, protester etc*) it's up to you to; (*lire, jouer etc*) it's your turn to. **7** (*prix*) for; **pain à 2F** loaf for 2F. **8** (*poids*) by; **vendre au kilo** to sell by the kilo. **9** (*moyen, manière*) **à bicyclette** by bicycle; **à la main** by hand; **à pied** on foot; **au crayon** with a pencil, in pencil; **au galop** at a gallop; **à la française** in the French style *ou* way; **deux à deux** two by two. **10** (*appel*) **au voleur!** (stop) thief!

abaiss/er [abese] *vt* to lower; **a. qn** to humiliate s.o.; **— s'a.** *vpr* (*barrière*) to lower; (*température*) to drop; **s'a. à faire** to stoop to doing. ◆**—ement** [-εsmᾶ] *nm* (*chute*) drop.

abandon [abᾶdɔ̃] *nm* abandonment; surrender; desertion; *Sp* withdrawal; (*naturel*) abandon; (*confiance*) lack of restraint; **à l'a.** in a neglected state. ◆**abandonner** *vt* (*renoncer à*) to give up, abandon; (*droit*) to surrender; (*quitter*) to desert, abandon; **— vi** to give up; *Sp* to withdraw; **— s'a.** *vpr* (*se détendre*) to let oneself go; (*se confier*) to open up; **s'a. à** to give oneself up to, abandon oneself to.

abasourdir [abazurdir] *vt* to stun, astound.

abat-jour [abaʒur] *nm inv* lampshade.

abats [aba] *nmpl* offal; (*de volaille*) giblets.

abattant [abatᾶ] *nm* leaf, flap.

abattis [abati] *nmpl* giblets.

abatt/re* [abatr] *vt* (*mur*) to knock down; (*arbre*) to cut down, fell; (*animal etc*) to slaughter; (*avion*) to shoot down; (*déprimer*) to demoralize; (*épuiser*) to exhaust; **— s'a.** *vpr* (*tomber*) to collapse; (*oiseau*) to swoop down; (*pluie*) to pour down. ◆**—u** *a* (*triste*) dejected, demoralized; (*faible*) at a low ebb. ◆**—age** *nm* felling; slaughter(ing). ◆**—ement** *nm* (*faiblesse*) exhaustion; (*désespoir*) dejection. ◆**abattoir** *nm* slaughterhouse.

abbaye [abei] *nf* abbey.

abbé [abe] *nm* (*chef d'abbaye*) abbot; (*prêtre*) priest. ◆**abbesse** *nf* abbess.

abcès [apsε] *nm* abscess.

abdiquer [abdike] *vti* to abdicate. ◆**abdication** *nf* abdication.

abdomen [abdɔmεn] *nm* abdomen. ◆**abdominal, -aux** *a* abdominal.

abeille [abεj] *nf* bee.

aberrant [aberᾶ] *a* (*idée etc*) ludicrous, absurd. ◆**aberration** *nf* (*égarement*) aberration; (*idée*) ludicrous idea; **dire des aberrations** to talk sheer nonsense.

abhorrer [abɔre] *vt* to abhor, loathe.

abîme [abim] *nm* abyss, chasm, gulf.

abîmer [abime] *vt* to spoil, damage; **— s'a.** *vpr* to get spoilt; **s'a. dans ses pensées** *Litt* to lose oneself in one's thoughts.

abject [abʒεkt] *a* abject, despicable.

abjurer [abʒyre] *vti* to abjure.

ablation [ablasjɔ̃] *nf* (*d'organe*) removal.

ablutions [ablysjɔ̃] *nfpl* ablutions.

abnégation [abnegasjɔ̃] *nf* self-sacrifice, abnegation.

abois (aux) [ozabwa] *adv* at bay.

abolir [abɔlir] *vt* to abolish. ◆**abolition** *nf* abolition.

abominable [abɔminabl] *a* abominable, obnoxious. ◆**abomination** *nf* abomination.

abondant [abɔ̃dᾶ] *a* abundant, plentiful. ◆**abondamment** *adv* abundantly. ◆**abondance** *nf* abundance (**de** of); **en a.** in abundance; **années d'a.** years of plenty. ◆**abonder** *vi* to abound (**en** in).

abonné, -ée [abɔne] *nmf* (*à un journal, au téléphone*) subscriber; *Rail Sp Th* season ticket holder; (*du gaz etc*) consumer.

◆**abonnement** nm subscription; (**carte d'**)a. season ticket. ◆**s'abonner** vpr to subscribe (à to); to buy a season ticket.

abord [abɔr] **1** nm (accès) **d'un a.** facile easy to approach. **2** nm (vue) **au premier a.** at first sight. **3** nmpl (environs) surroundings; **aux abords de** around, nearby. ◆**abordable** a (personne) approachable; (prix, marchandises) affordable.

abord (d') [abɔr] adv (avant tout) first; (au début) at first.

aborder [abɔrde] vi to land; – vt (personne) to approach, accost; (lieu) to approach, reach; (problème) to tackle, approach; (attaquer) Nau to board; (heurter) Nau to run foul of. ◆**abordage** nm (assaut) Nau boarding; (accident) Nau collision.

aborigène [abɔriʒɛn] a & nm aboriginal.

about/ir [abutir] vi to succeed; a. à to end at, lead to, end up in; **n'a. à rien** to come to nothing. ◆**—issants** nmpl voir tenants. ◆**—issement** nm (résultat) outcome; (succès) success.

aboyer [abwaje] vi to bark. ◆**aboiement** nm bark; pl barking.

abrasif, -ive [abrazif, -iv] a & nm abrasive.

abrég/er [abreʒe] vt (récit) to shorten, abridge; (mot) to abbreviate. ◆**—é** nm summary; **en a.** (phrase) in shortened form; (mot) in abbreviated form.

abreuver [abrœve] vt (cheval) to water; – **s'a.** vpr to drink. ◆**abreuvoir** nm (récipient) drinking trough; (lieu) watering place.

abréviation [abrevjasjɔ̃] nf abbreviation.

abri [abri] nm shelter; **à l'a. de** (vent) sheltered from; (besoin) safe from; **sans a.** homeless. ◆**abriter** vt (protéger) to shelter; (loger) to house; – **s'a.** vpr to (take) shelter.

abricot [abriko] nm apricot. ◆**abricotier** nm apricot tree.

abroger [abrɔʒe] vt to abrogate.

abrupt [abrypt] a (versant) sheer; (sentier) steep, abrupt; (personne) abrupt.

abrut/ir [abrytir] vt (alcool) to stupefy (s.o.); (propagande) to brutalize (s.o.); (travail) to leave (s.o.) dazed, wear (s.o.) out. ◆**—i, -ie** nmf idiot; – a idiotic.

absence [apsɑ̃s] nf absence. ◆**absent, -e** a (personne) absent, away; (chose) missing; **air a.** faraway look; – nmf absentee. ◆**absentéisme** nm absenteeism. ◆**s'absenter** vpr to go away.

abside [apsid] nf (d'une église) apse.

absolu [apsɔly] a & nm absolute. ◆**—ment** adv absolutely.

absolution [apsɔlysjɔ̃] nf absolution.

absorb/er [apsɔrbe] vt to absorb. ◆**—ant** a absorbent; **travail a.** absorbing job. ◆**absorption** nf absorption.

absoudre* [apsudr] vt to absolve.

abstenir* (s') [sapstənir] vpr to abstain; **s'a. de** to refrain on abstain from. ◆**abstention** nf abstention.

abstinence [apstinɑ̃s] nf abstinence.

abstraire* [apstrɛr] vt to abstract. ◆**abstrait** a & nm abstract. ◆**abstraction** nf abstraction; **faire a. de** to disregard, leave aside.

absurde [apsyrd] a & nm absurd. ◆**absurdité** nf absurdity; **dire des absurdités** to talk nonsense.

abus [aby] nm abuse, misuse; over-indulgence; (injustice) abuse. ◆**abuser 1** vi to go too far; **a. de** (situation, personne) to take unfair advantage of; (autorité) to abuse, misuse; (friandises) to over-indulge in. **2 s'a.** vpr to be mistaken.

abusif, -ive [abyzif, -iv] a excessive; **emploi a.** Ling improper use, misuse. ◆**—vement** adv Ling improperly.

acabit [akabi] nm **de cet a.** Péj of that ilk ou sort.

acacia [akasja] nm (arbre) acacia.

académie [akademi] nf academy; Univ = (regional) education authority. ◆**académicien, -ienne** nmf academician. ◆**académique** a academic.

acajou [akaʒu] nm mahogany; **cheveux a.** auburn hair.

acariâtre [akarjɑtr] a cantankerous.

accabl/er [akable] vt to overwhelm, overcome; **a. d'injures** to heap insults upon; **accablé de dettes** (over)burdened with debt. ◆**—ement** nm dejection.

accalmie [akalmi] nf lull.

accaparer [akapare] vt to monopolize; (personne) Fam to take up all the time of.

accéder [aksede] vi **a. à** (lieu) to have access to, reach; (pouvoir, trône, demande) to accede to.

accélérer [akselere] vi Aut to accelerate; – vt (travaux etc) to speed up; (allure, pas) to quicken, speed up; – **s'a.** vpr to speed up. ◆**accélérateur** nm Aut accelerator. ◆**accélération** nf acceleration; speeding up.

accent [aksɑ̃] nm accent; (sur une syllabe) stress; **mettre l'a. sur** to stress. ◆**accentuation** nf accentuation. ◆**accentuer** vt to emphasize, accentuate, stress; – **s'a.** vpr to become more pronounced.

accepter [aksɛpte] vt to accept; **a. de faire**

to agree to do. ◆**acceptable** *a* acceptable.
◆**acceptation** *nf* acceptance.

acception [aksεpsjɔ̃] *nf* sense, meaning.

accès [aksε] *nm* access (à to); (*de folie, colère, toux*) fit; (*de fièvre*) attack, bout; *pl* (*routes*) approaches. ◆**accessible** *a* accessible; (*personne*) approachable. ◆**accession** *nf* accession (à to); (à un *traité*) adherence; **a. à la propriété** home ownership.

accessoire [akseswar] *a* secondary; – *nmpl* **Th** props; (*de voiture etc*) accessories; **accessoires de toilette** toilet requisites.

accident [aksidɑ̃] *nm* accident; **a. d'avion/de train** plane/train crash; **par a.** by accident, by chance. ◆**accidenté, -ée** *a* (*terrain*) uneven; (*région*) hilly; (*voiture*) damaged (in an accident); – *nmf* accident victim, casualty. ◆**accidentel, -elle** *a* accidental. ◆**accidentellement** *adv* accidentally, unintentionally.

acclamer [aklame] *vt* to cheer, acclaim. ◆**acclamations** *nfpl* cheers, acclamations.

acclimater [aklimate] *vt*, – **s'a.** *vpr* to acclimatize, *Am* acclimate. ◆**acclimatation** *nf* acclimatization, *Am* acclimation.

accointances [akwɛ̃tɑ̃s] *nfpl* **Péj** contacts.

accolade [akɔlad] *nf* (*embrassade*) embrace; **Typ** brace, bracket.

accoler [akɔle] *vt* to place (side by side) (à against).

accommod/er [akɔmɔde] *vt* to adapt; **Culin** to prepare; **s'a. à** to adapt (oneself) to; **s'a. de** to make the best of. ◆**—ant** *a* accommodating, easy to please. ◆**—ement** *nm* arrangement, compromise.

accompagner [akɔ̃paɲe] *vt* (*personne*) to accompany, go *ou* come with, escort; (*chose*) & **Mus** to accompany; **s'a. de** to be accompanied by, go with. ◆**accompagnateur, -trice** *nmf* **Mus** accompanist; (*d'un groupe*) guide. ◆**accompagnement** *nm* **Mus** accompaniment.

accompl/ir [akɔ̃plir] *vt* to carry out, fulfil, accomplish. ◆**—i** *a* accomplished. ◆**—issement** *nm* fulfilment.

accord [akɔr] *nm* agreement; (*harmonie*) harmony; **Mus** chord; **être d'a.** to agree, be in agreement (**avec** with); **d'a.!** all right! ◆**accorder** *vt* (*donner*) to grant; **Mus** to tune; **Gram** to make agree; – **s'a.** *vpr* to agree; (*s'entendre*) to get along.

accordéon [akɔrdeɔ̃] *nm* accordion; **en a.** (*chaussette etc*) wrinkled.

accoster [akɔste] *vt* to accost; **Nau** to come alongside; – *vi* **Nau** to berth.

accotement [akɔtmɑ̃] *nm* roadside, verge.

accouch/er [akuʃe] *vi* to give birth (**de** to); – *vt* (*enfant*) to deliver. ◆**—ement** *nm* delivery. ◆**—eur** *nm* (*médecin*) obstetrician.

accouder (s') [sakude] *vpr* **s'a. à** *ou* **sur** to lean on (with one's elbows). ◆**accoudoir** *nm* armrest.

accoupl/er [akuple] *vt* to couple; – **s'a.** *vpr* (*animaux*) to mate (à with). ◆**—ement** *nm* coupling; mating.

accourir* [akurir] *vi* to come running, run over.

accoutrement [akutrəmɑ̃] *nm* **Péj** garb, dress.

accoutumer [akutyme] *vt* to accustom; **s'a.** *vpr* to get accustomed (à to); **comme à l'accoutumée** as usual. ◆**accoutumance** *nf* familiarization (à with); **Méd** addiction.

accréditer [akredite] *vt* (*ambassadeur*) to accredit; (*rumeur*) to lend credence to.

accroc [akro] *nm* (*déchirure*) tear; (*difficulté*) hitch, snag.

accroch/er [akrɔʃe] *vt* (*déchirer*) to catch; (*fixer*) to hook; (*suspendre*) to hang up (**on** a hook); (*heurter*) to hit, knock; – *vi* (*affiche etc*) to grab one's attention; – **s'a.** *vpr* (*ne pas céder*) to persevere; (*se disputer*) **Fam** to clash; **s'a. à** (*se cramponner etc*) to cling to; (*s'écorcher*) to catch oneself on. ◆**—age** *nm* **Aut** knock, slight hit; (*friction*) **Fam** clash. ◆**—eur, -euse** *a* (*personne*) tenacious; (*affiche etc*) eyecatching, catchy.

accroître* [akrwatr] *vt* to increase; – **s'a.** *vpr* to increase, grow. ◆**accroissement** *nm* increase; growth.

accroup/ir (s') [sakrupir] *vpr* to squat *ou* crouch (down). ◆**—i** *a* squatting, crouching.

accueil [akœj] *nm* reception, welcome. ◆**accueill/ir*** *vt* to receive, welcome, greet. ◆**—ant** *a* welcoming.

acculer [akyle] *vt* **a. qn à qch** to drive s.o. to *ou* against sth.

accumuler [akymyle] *vt*, – **s'a.** *vpr* to pile up, accumulate. ◆**accumulateur** *nm* accumulator, battery. ◆**accumulation** *nf* accumulation.

accus/er [akyze] *vt* (*dénoncer*) to accuse; (*rendre responsable*) to blame (**de** for); (*révéler*) to show; (*faire ressortir*) to bring out; **a. réception** to acknowledge receipt (**de** of); **a. le coup** to stagger under the blow. ◆**-é, -ée 1** *nmf* accused; (*cour d'assises*) defendant. **2** *a* prominent. ◆**accusateur, -trice** *a* (*regard*) accusing;

(*document*) incriminating; – *nmf* accuser. ◆**accusation** *nf* accusation; *Jur* charge.

acerbe [asɛrb] *a* bitter, caustic.

acéré [asere] *a* sharp.

acétate [acetat] *nm* acetate. ◆**acétique** *a* acetic.

achalandé [aʃalɑ̃de] *a* **bien a.** (*magasin*) well-stocked.

acharn/er (s') [aʃarne] *vpr* **s'a. sur** (*attaquer*) to set upon, lay into; **s'a. contre** (*poursuivre*) to pursue (relentlessly); **s'a. à faire** to struggle to do, try desperately to do. ◆**–é, -ée** *a* relentless; – *nmf* (*du jeu etc*) fanatic. ◆**–ement** *nm* relentlessness.

achat [aʃa] *nm* purchase; *pl* shopping.

acheminer [aʃmine] *vt* to dispatch; – **s'a.** *vpr* **vers** (*lieu*) to head (vers towards).

achet/er [aʃte] *vti* to buy, purchase; **a. à qn** (*vendeur*) to buy from s.o.; (*pour qn*) to buy for s.o. ◆**–eur, -euse** *nm* buyer, purchaser; (*dans un magasin*) shopper.

achever [aʃve] *vt* to finish (off); **a. de faire qch** (*personne*) to finish doing sth; **a. qn** (*tuer*) to finish s.o. off; – **s'a.** *vpr* to end, finish. ◆**achèvement** *nm* completion.

achoppement [aʃɔpmɑ̃] *nm* **pierre d'a.** stumbling block.

acide [asid] *a* acid, sour; – *nm* acid. ◆**acidité** *nf* acidity.

acier [asje] *nm* steel. ◆**aciérie** *nf* steelworks.

acné [akne] *nf* acne.

acolyte [akɔlit] *nm* *Péj* confederate, associate.

acompte [akɔ̃t] *nm* part payment, deposit.

à-côté [akote] *nm* (*d'une question*) side issue; *pl* (*gains*) little extras.

à-coup [aku] *nm* jerk, jolt; **sans à-coups** smoothly; **par à-coups** in fits and starts.

acoustique [akustik] *a* acoustic; – *nf* acoustics.

acquérir* [akerir] *vt* to acquire, gain; (*par achat*) to purchase; **s'a. une réputation**/*etc* to win a reputation/*etc*; **être acquis à** (*idée, parti*) to be a supporter of. ◆**acquéreur** *nm* purchaser. ◆**acquis** *nm* experience. ◆**acquisition** *nf* acquisition; purchase.

acquiesc/er [akjese] *vi* to acquiesce (à to). ◆**–ement** *nm* acquiescence.

acquit [aki] *nm* receipt; **'pour a.'** 'paid'; **par a. de conscience** for conscience sake. ◆**acquitt/er** *vt* to clear, pay; (*accusé*) to acquit; **s'a. de** (*devoir, promesse*) to discharge; **s'a. envers qn** to repay s.o. ◆**–ement** *nm* payment; acquittal; discharge.

âcre [ɑkr] *a* bitter, acrid, pungent.

acrobate [akrɔbat] *nmf* acrobat. ◆**acrobatie(s)** *nf(pl)* acrobatics. ◆**acrobatique** *a* acrobatic.

acrylique [akrilik] *a* & *nm* acrylic.

acte [akt] *nm* act, deed; *Th* act; **un a. de** act of; **a. de naissance** birth certificate; **prendre a. de** to take note of.

acteur, -trice [aktœr, -tris] *nmf* actor, actress.

actif, -ive [aktif, -iv] *a* active; – *nm* *Fin* assets; **à son a.** to one's credit; (*vols, meurtres*) *Hum* to one's name.

action [aksjɔ̃] *nf* action; *Fin* share. ◆**actionnaire** *nmf* shareholder. ◆**actionner** *vt* to set in motion, activate, actuate.

activer [aktive] *vt* to speed up; (*feu*) to boost; – **s'a.** *vpr* to bustle about; (*se dépêcher*) *Fam* to get a move on.

activiste [aktivist] *nmf* activist.

activité [aktivite] *nf* activity; **en a.** (*personne*) fully active; (*volcan*) active.

actuaire [aktɥɛr] *nf* actuary.

actualité [aktɥalite] *nf* (*d'un problème*) topicality; (*évènements*) current events; *pl* *TV Cin* news; **d'a.** topical.

actuel, -elle [aktɥɛl] *a* (*présent*) present; (*contemporain*) topical. ◆**actuellement** *adv* at present, at the present time.

acuité [akɥite] *nf* (*de douleur*) acuteness; (*de vision*) keenness.

acupuncture [akypɔ̃ktyr] *nf* acupuncture. ◆**acupuncteur, -trice** *nmf* acupuncturist.

adage [adaʒ] *nm* (*maxime*) adage.

adapter [adapte] *vt* to adapt; (*ajuster*) to fit (à to); **s'a.** (*s'habituer*) to adapt to; (*tuyau etc*) to fit. ◆**adaptable** *a* adaptable. ◆**adaptateur, -trice** *nmf* adapter. ◆**adaptation** *nf* adaptation.

additif [aditif] *nm* additive.

addition [adisjɔ̃] *nf* addition; (*au restaurant*) bill, *Am* check. ◆**additionnel, -elle** *a* additional. ◆**additionner** *vt* to add (à to); (*nombres*) to add up.

adepte [adɛpt] *nmf* follower.

adéquat [adekwa] *a* appropriate.

adhérer [adere] *vi* **a. à** (*coller*) to adhere ou stick to; (*s'inscrire*) to join; (*pneu etc*) to grip. ◆**adhérence** *nf* (*de pneu*) grip. ◆**adhérent, -ente** *nmf* member.

adhésif, -ive [adezif, -iv] *a* & *nm* adhesive. ◆**adhésion** *nf* membership; (*accord*) support.

adieu, -x [adjø] *int* & *nm* farewell, goodbye.

adipeux, -euse [adipø, -øz] *a* (*tissu*) fatty; (*visage*) fat.

adjacent [adʒasɑ̃] a (contigu) & *Géom* adjacent.

adjectif [adʒɛktif] nm adjective.

adjoindre* [adʒwɛ̃dr] vt (associer) to appoint (s.o.) as an assistant (à to); (ajouter) to add; **s'a. qn** to appoint s.o. ◆**adjoint, -ointe** nmf & a assistant; **a. au maire** deputy mayor.

adjudant [adʒydɑ̃] nm warrant officer.

adjuger [adʒyʒe] vt (accorder) to award; **s'a. qch** *Fam* to grab sth for oneself.

adjurer [adʒyre] vt to beseech, entreat.

admettre* [admɛtr] vt (laisser entrer, accueillir, reconnaître) to admit; (autoriser, tolérer) to allow; (supposer) to admit, grant; (candidat) to pass; **être admis à** (examen) to have passed.

administrer [administre] vt (gérer, donner) to administer. ◆**administrateur, -trice** nmf administrator. ◆**administratif, -ive** a administrative. ◆**administration** nf administration; **l'A.** (service public) government service, the Civil Service.

admirer [admire] vt to admire. ◆**admirable** a admirable. ◆**admirateur, -trice** nmf admirer. ◆**admiratif, -ive** a admiring. ◆**admiration** nf admiration.

admissible [admisibl] a acceptable, admissible; (après un concours) eligible (à for). ◆**admission** nf admission.

adolescent, -ente [adɔlesɑ̃, -ɑ̃t] nmf adolescent, teenager; — a teenage. ◆**adolescence** nf adolescence.

adonner (s') [sadɔne] vpr **s'a. à** (boisson) to take to; (étude) to devote oneself to.

adopter [adɔpte] vt to adopt. ◆**adoptif, -ive** a (fils, patrie) adopted. ◆**adoption** nf adoption; **suisse d'a.** Swiss by adoption.

adorer [adɔre] vt (personne) & *Rel* to worship, adore; (chose) *Fam* to adore, love; **a. faire** to adore ou love doing. ◆**adorable** a adorable. ◆**adoration** nf adoration, worship.

adosser [adose] vt **a. qch à** to lean sth back against; **s'a. à** to lean back against.

adouc/ir [adusir] vt (voix, traits etc) to soften; (boisson) to sweeten; (chagrin) to mitigate, ease; — **s'a.** vpr (temps) to turn milder; (caractère) to mellow. ◆**—issement** nm **a. de la température** milder weather.

adrénaline [adrenalin] nf adrenalin(e).

adresse [adrɛs] nf **1** (domicile) address. **2** (habileté) skill. ◆**adresser** vt (lettre) to send; (compliment, remarque etc) to address; (coup) to direct, aim; (personne) to direct (à to); **a. la parole à** to speak to;

s'a. à to speak to; (aller trouver) to go and see; (bureau) to enquire at; (être destiné à) to be aimed at.

Adriatique [adriatik] nf **l'A.** the Adriatic.

adroit [adrwa] a skilful, clever.

adulation [adylɑsjɔ̃] nf adulation.

adulte [adylt] a & nmf adult, grown-up.

adultère [adyltɛr] a adulterous; — nm adultery.

advenir [advənir] v imp to occur; **a. de** (devenir) to become of; **advienne que pourra** come what may.

adverbe [advɛrb] nm adverb. ◆**adverbial, -aux** a adverbial.

adversaire [advɛrsɛr] nmf opponent, adversary. ◆**adverse** a opposing.

adversité [advɛrsite] nf adversity.

aérer [aere] vt (chambre) to air (out), ventilate; (lit) to air (out); — **s'a.** vpr *Fam* to get some air. ◆**aéré** a airy. ◆**aération** nf ventilation. ◆**aérien, -ienne** a (ligne, attaque etc) air-; (photo) aerial; (câble) overhead; (léger) airy.

aérobic [aerɔbik] nf aerobics.

aéro-club [aerɔklœb] nm flying club. ◆**aérodrome** nm aerodrome. ◆**aérodynamique** a streamlined, aerodynamic. ◆**aérogare** nf air terminal. ◆**aéroglisseur** nm hovercraft. ◆**aérogramme** nm air letter. ◆**aéromodélisme** nm model aircraft building and flying. ◆**aéronautique** nf aeronautics. ◆**aéronavale** nf = *Br* Fleet Air Arm, = *Am* Naval Air Force. ◆**aéroport** nm airport. ◆**aéroporté** a airborne. ◆**aérosol** nm aerosol.

affable [afabl] a affable.

affaiblir [afeblir] vt, — **s'a.** vpr to weaken.

affaire [afɛr] nf (question) matter, affair; (marché) deal; (firme) concern, business; (scandale) affair; (procès) *Jur* case; pl *Com* business; (d'intérêt public, personnel) affairs; (effets) belongings, things; **avoir a. à** to have to deal with; **c'est mon a.** that's my business ou affair ou concern; **faire une bonne a.** to get a good deal, get a bargain; **ça fera l'a.** that will do nicely; **toute une a.** (histoire) quite a business.

affair/er (s') [safere] vpr to busy oneself, run ou bustle about. ◆**—é** a busy. ◆**affairiste** nm (political) racketeer.

affaiss/er (s') [safese] vpr (personne) to collapse; (plancher) to cave in, give way; (sol) to subside, sink. ◆**—ement** [afesmɑ̃] nm (du sol) subsidence.

affaler (s') [safale] vpr to flop down, collapse.

affamé [afame] *a* starving; **a. de** *Fig* hungry for.

affect/er [afɛkte] *vt* (*destiner*) to earmark, assign; (*nommer à un poste*) to post; (*feindre, émouvoir*) to affect. ◆**—é** *a* (*manières, personne*) affected. ◆**affectation** *nf* assignment; posting; (*simulation*) affectation.

affectif, -ive [afɛktif, -iv] *a* emotional.

affection [afɛksjɔ̃] *nf* (*attachement*) affection; (*maladie*) ailment. ◆**affectionn/er** *vt* to be fond of. ◆**—é** *a* loving. ◆**affectueux, -euse** *a* affectionate.

affermir [afɛrmir] *vt* (*autorité*) to strengthen; (*muscles*) to tone up; (*voix*) to steady.

affiche [afiʃ] *nf* poster; *Th* bill. ◆**affich/er** *vt* (*affiche etc*) to post *ou* stick up; *Th* to bill; (*sentiment*) *Péj* to display; **a. qn** *Péj* to parade s.o. ◆**—age** *nm* (bill-)posting; **panneau d'a.** hoarding, *Am* billboard.

affilée (d') [dafile] *adv* (*à la suite*) in a row, at a stretch.

affiler [afile] *vt* to sharpen.

affilier (s') [safilje] *vpr* **s'a. à** to join, become affiliated to. ◆**affiliation** *nf* affiliation.

affiner [afine] *vt* to refine.

affinité [afinite] *nf* affinity.

affirmatif, -ive [afirmatif, -iv] *a* (*ton*) assertive, positive; (*proposition*) affirmative; **il a été a.** he was quite positive; – *nf* **répondre par l'affirmative** to reply in the affirmative.

affirmer [afirme] *vt* to assert; (*proclamer solennellement*) to affirm. ◆**affirmation** *nf* assertion.

affleurer [aflœre] *vi* to appear on the surface.

affliger [afliʒe] *vt* to distress; **affligé de** stricken *ou* afflicted with.

affluence [aflyɑ̃s] *nf* crowd; **heures d'a.** rush hours.

affluent [aflyɑ̃] *nm* tributary.

affluer [aflye] *vi* (*sang*) to flow, rush; (*gens*) to flock. ◆**afflux** *nm* flow; (*arrivée*) influx.

affol/er [afɔle] *vt* to drive out of one's mind; (*effrayer*) to terrify; – **s'a.** *vpr* to panic. ◆**—ement** *nm* panic.

affranch/ir [afrɑ̃ʃir] *vt* (*timbrer*) to stamp; (*émanciper*) to free. ◆**—issement** *nm* **tarifs d'a.** postage.

affréter [afrete] *vt* (*avion*) to charter; (*navire*) to freight.

affreux, -euse [afrø, -øz] *a* hideous, dreadful, ghastly. ◆**affreusement** *adv* dreadfully.

affriolant [afriolɑ̃] *a* enticing.

affront [afrɔ̃] *nm* insult, affront; **faire un a.** à to insult.

affront/er [afrɔ̃te] *vt* to confront, face; (*mauvais temps, difficultés etc*) to brave. ◆**—ement** *nm* confrontation.

affubler [afyble] *vt* *Péj* to dress, rig out (**de** in).

affût [afy] *nm* **à l'a. de** *Fig* on the look-out for.

affûter [afyte] *vt* (*outil*) to sharpen, grind.

Afghanistan [afganistɑ̃] *nm* Afghanistan.

afin [afɛ̃] *prép* **a. de** (+ *inf*) in order to; – *conj* **a. que** (+ *sub*) so that.

Afrique [afrik] *nf* Africa. ◆**africain, -aine** *a & nm* African.

agac/er [agase] *vt* (*personne*) to irritate, annoy. ◆**—ement** *nm* irritation.

âge [ɑʒ] *nm* age; **quel â. as-tu?** how old are you?; **avant l'â.** before one's time; **d'un certain â.** middle-aged; **l'â. adulte** adulthood; **la force de l'â.** the prime of life; **le moyen â.** the Middle Ages. ◆**âgé** *a* elderly; **â. de six ans** six years old; **un enfant â. de six ans** a six-year-old child.

agence [aʒɑ̃s] *nf* agency; (*succursale*) branch office; **a. immobilière** estate agent's office, *Am* real estate office.

agenc/er [aʒɑ̃se] *vt* to arrange; **bien agencé** (*maison etc*) well laid-out; (*phrase*) well put-together. ◆**—ement** *nm* (*de maison etc*) lay-out.

agenda [aʒɛ̃da] *nm* diary, *Am* datebook.

agenouiller (s') [saʒnuje] *vpr* to kneel (down); **être agenouillé** to be kneeling (down).

agent [aʒɑ̃] *nm* agent; **a. (de police)** policeman; **a. de change** stockbroker; **a. immobilier** estate agent, *Am* real estate agent.

aggloméré [aglɔmere] *nm & a* (*bois*) chipboard, fibreboard.

agglomérer (s') [saglɔmere] *vpr* (*s'entasser*) to conglomerate. ◆**agglomération** *nf* conglomeration; (*habitations*) built-up area; (*ville*) town.

aggraver [agrave] *vt* to worsen, aggravate; – **s'a.** *vpr* to worsen. ◆**aggravation** *nf* worsening.

agile [aʒil] *a* agile, nimble. ◆**agilité** *nf* agility, nimbleness.

agir [aʒir] **1** *vi* to act; **a. auprès de** to intercede with. **2 s'agir** *v imp* **il s'agit d'argent**/*etc* it's a question *ou* matter of money/*etc*, it concerns money/*etc*; **de quoi s'agit-il?** what is it?, what's it about?; **il s'agit de se dépêcher**/*etc* we have to

hurry/*etc.* ◆**agissant** *a* active, effective.
◆**agissements** *nmpl Péj* dealings.

agit/er [aʒite] *vt* (*remuer*) to stir; (*secouer*) to shake; (*brandir*) to wave; (*troubler*) to agitate; (*discuter*) to debate; — **s'a.** *vpr* (*enfant*) to fidget; (*peuple*) to stir. ◆—é *a* (*mer*) rough; (*malade*) restless, agitated; (*enfant*) fidgety, restless. ◆**agitateur, -trice** *nmf* (political) agitator. ◆**agitation** *nf* (*de la mer*) roughness; (*d'un malade etc*) restlessness; (*nervosité*) agitation; (*de la rue*) bustle; *Pol* unrest.

agneau, -x [aɲo] *nm* lamb.

agonie [agɔni] *nf* death throes; **être à l'a.** to be suffering the pangs of death. ◆**agoniser** *vi* to be dying.

agrafe [agraf] *nf* hook; (*pour papiers*) staple. ◆**agrafer** *vt* to fasten, hook, do up; (*papiers*) to staple. ◆**agrafeuse** *nf* stapler.

agrand/ir [agrɑ̃dir] *vt* to enlarge; (*grossir*) to magnify; — **s'a.** *vpr* to expand, grow. ◆—**issement** *nm* (*de ville*) expansion; (*de maison*) extension; (*de photo*) enlargement.

agréable [agreabl] *a* pleasant, agreeable, nice. ◆—**ment** [-əmɑ̃] *adv* pleasantly.

agré/er [agree] *vt* to accept; **veuillez a. mes salutations distinguées** (*dans une lettre*) yours faithfully. ◆—é *a* (*fournisseur, centre*) approved.

agrégation [agregasjɔ̃] *nf* competitive examination for recruitment of *lycée* teachers. ◆**agrégé, -ée** *nmf* teacher who has passed the **agrégation**.

agrément [agremɑ̃] *nm* (*attrait*) charm; (*accord*) assent; **voyage d'a.** pleasure trip. ◆**agrémenter** *vt* to embellish; **a. un récit d'anecdotes** to pepper a story with anecdotes.

agrès [agrɛ] *nmpl Nau* tackle, rigging; (*de gymnastique*) apparatus.

agresser [agrese] *vt* to attack. ◆**agresseur** *nm* attacker; (*dans la rue*) mugger; (*dans un conflit*) aggressor. ◆**agressif, -ive** *a* aggressive. ◆**agression** *nf* (*d'un État*) aggression; (*d'un individu*) attack. ◆**agressivité** *nf* aggressiveness.

agricole [agrikɔl] *a* (*peuple*) agricultural, farming; (*ouvrier, machine*) farm. ◆**agriculteur** [agrikyltœr] *nm* farmer. ◆**agriculture** *nf* agriculture, farming.

agripper [agripe] *vt* to clutch, grip; **s'a. à** to cling to, clutch, grip.

agronomie [agrɔnɔmi] *nf* agronomics.

agrumes [agrym] *nmpl* citrus fruit(s).

aguerri [ageri] *a* seasoned, hardened.

aguets (aux) [ozagɛ] *adv* on the look-out.

aguich/er [agiʃe] *vt* to tease, excite. ◆—**ant** *a* enticing.

ah! [a] *int* ah!, oh!

ahur/ir [ayrir] *vt* to astound, bewilder. ◆—**i, -ie** *nmf* idiot.

ai [e] *voir* avoir.

aide [ɛd] *nf* help, assistance, aid; — *nmf* (*personne*) assistant; **à l'a. de** with the help *ou* aid of. ◆**a.-électricien** *nm* electrician's mate. ◆**a.-familiale** *nf* home help. ◆**a.-mémoire** *nm inv Scol* handbook (*of facts etc*).

aider [ɛde] *vt* to help, assist, aid (**à faire** to do); **s'a. de** to make use of.

aïe! [aj] *int* ouch!, ow!

aïeul, -e [ajœl] *nmf* grandfather, grandmother.

aïeux [ajø] *nmpl* forefathers, forebears.

aigle [ɛgl] *nmf* eagle. ◆**aiglon** *nm* eaglet.

aiglefin [ɛglǝfɛ̃] *nm* haddock.

aigre [ɛgr] *a* (*acide*) sour; (*voix, vent, parole*) sharp, cutting. ◆**a.-doux, -douce** *a* bitter-sweet. ◆**aigreur** *nf* sourness; (*de ton*) sharpness; *pl* heartburn.

aigrette [ɛgrɛt] *nf* (*de plumes*) tuft.

aigr/ir (s') [segrir] *vpr* (*vin*) to turn sour; (*caractère*) to sour. ◆—**i** [egri] *a* (*personne*) embittered, bitter.

aigu, -uë [egy] *a* (*crise etc*) acute; (*dents*) sharp, pointed; (*voix*) shrill.

aiguille [egɥij] *nf* (*à coudre, de pin*) needle; (*de montre*) hand; (*de balance*) pointer; **a.** (**rocheuse**) peak.

aiguill/er [egɥije] *vt* (*train*) to shunt, *Am* switch; *Fig* to steer, direct. ◆—**age** *nm* (*appareil*) *Rail* points, *Am* switches. ◆—**eur** *nm Rail* pointsman, *Am* switchman; **a. du ciel** air traffic controller.

aiguillon [egɥijɔ̃] *nm* (*dard*) sting; (*stimulant*) spur. ◆**aiguillonner** *vt* to spur (on), goad.

aiguiser [eg(ɥ)ize] *vt* (*affiler*) to sharpen; (*appétit*) to whet.

ail [aj] *nm* garlic.

aile [ɛl] *nf* wing; (*de moulin à vent*) sail; *Aut* wing, *Am* fender; **battre de l'a.** to be in a bad way; **d'un coup d'a.** (*avion*) in continuous flight. ◆**ailé** [ele] *a* winged. ◆**aileron** *nm* (*de requin*) fin; (*d'avion*) aileron; (*d'oiseau*) pinion. ◆**ailier** [elje] *nm Fb* wing(er).

ailleurs [ajœr] *adv* somewhere else, elsewhere; **partout a.** everywhere else; **d'a.** (*du reste*) besides, anyway; **par a.** (*en outre*) moreover; (*autrement*) otherwise.

ailloli [ajɔli] *nm* garlic mayonnaise.

aimable [ɛmabl] *a* (*complaisant*) kind;

(*sympathique*) likeable, amiable; (*agréable*) pleasant. ◆—ment [-əmɑ̃] *adv* kindly.

aimant [emɑ̃] **1** *nm* magnet. **2** *a* loving. ◆aimanter *vt* to magnetize.

aimer [eme] *vt* (*chérir*) to love; **a. (bien)** (*apprécier*) to like, be fond of; **a. faire** *ou* to like doing *ou* to do; **a. mieux** to prefer; **ils s'aiment** they're in love.

aine [ɛn] *nf* groin.

aîné, -e [ene] *a* (*de deux frères etc*) elder, older; (*de plus de deux*) eldest, oldest; — *nmf* (*enfant*) elder *ou* older (child); eldest *ou* oldest (child); **c'est mon a.** he's my senior.

ainsi [ɛ̃si] *adv* (*comme ça*) (in) this *ou* that way, thus; (*alors*) so; **a. que** as well as; **et a. de suite** and so on; **pour a. dire** so to speak.

air [ɛr] *nm* **1** air; **en plein a.** in the open (air), outdoors; **ficher** *ou* **flanquer en l'a.** *Fam* (*jeter*) to chuck away; (*gâcher*) to mess up, upset; **en l'a.** (*jeter*) (up) in the air; (*paroles, menaces*) empty; (*projets*) uncertain, (up) in the air; **dans l'a.** (*grippe, idées*) about, around. **2** (*expression*) look, appearance; **avoir l'a.** to look, seem; **avoir l'a. de** to look like; **a. de famille** family likeness. **3** (*mélodie*) tune; **a. d'opéra** aria.

aire [ɛr] *nf* (*de stationnement etc*) & *Math* area; (*d'oiseau*) eyrie; **a. de lancement** launching site.

airelle [ɛrɛl] *nf* bilberry, *Am* blueberry.

aisance [ɛzɑ̃s] *nf* (*facilité*) ease; (*prospérité*) easy circumstances, affluence.

aise [ɛz] *nf* **à l'a.** (*dans un vêtement etc*) comfortable; (*dans une situation*) at ease; (*fortuné*) comfortably off; **aimer ses aises** to like one's comforts; **mal à l'a.** uncomfortable, ill at ease. ◆aisé [eze] *a* (*fortuné*) comfortably off; (*naturel*) free and easy; (*facile*) easy. ◆aisément *adv* easily.

aisselle [ɛsɛl] *nf* armpit.

ait [ɛ] *voir* avoir.

ajonc(s) [aʒɔ̃] *nm(pl)* gorse, furze.

ajouré [aʒure] *a* (*dentelle etc*) openwork.

ajourn/er [aʒurne] *vt* to postpone, adjourn. ◆—ement *nm* postponement, adjournment.

ajout [aʒu] *nm* addition. ◆ajouter *vti* to add (à to); **s'a. à** to add to.

ajust/er [aʒyste] *vt* (*pièce, salaires*) to adjust; (*coiffure*) to arrange; (*coup*) to aim; **a. à** (*adapter*) to fit to. ◆—é *a* (*serré*) close-fitting. ◆—ement *nm* adjustment. ◆—eur *nm* (*ouvrier*) fitter.

alaise [alɛz] *nf* (*waterproof*) undersheet.

alambic [alɑ̃bik] *nm* still.

alambiqué [alɑ̃bike] *a* convoluted, over-subtle.

alanguir [alɑ̃gir] *vt* to make languid.

alarme [alarm] *nf* (*signal, inquiétude*) alarm; **jeter l'a.** to cause alarm. ◆alarmer *vt* to alarm; **s'a. de** to become alarmed at.

Albanie [albani] *nf* Albania. ◆albanais, -aise *a & nmf* Albanian.

albâtre [albɑtr] *nm* alabaster.

albatros [albatros] *nm* albatross.

albinos [albinos] *nmf & a inv* albino.

album [albɔm] *nm* (*de timbres etc*) album; (*de dessins*) sketchbook.

alcali [alkali] *nm* alkali. ◆alcalin *a* alkaline.

alchimie [alʃimi] *nf* alchemy.

alcool [alkɔl] *nm* alcohol; (*spiritueux*) spirits; **a. à brûler** methylated spirit(s); **lampe à a.** spirit lamp. ◆alcoolique *a & nmf* alcoholic. ◆alcoolisé *a* (*boisson*) alcoholic. ◆alcoolisme *nm* alcoholism. ◆alcootest® *nm* breath test; (*appareil*) breathalyzer.

alcôve [alkov] *nf* alcove.

aléas [alea] *nmpl* hazards, risks. ◆aléatoire *a* chancy, uncertain; (*sélection*) random.

alentour [alɑ̃tur] *adv* round about, around; **d'a.** surrounding; — *nmpl* surroundings, vicinity; **aux alentours de** in the vicinity of.

alerte [alɛrt] **1** *a* (*leste*) agile, spry; (*éveillé*) alert. **2** *nf* alarm; **en état d'a.** on the alert; **a. aérienne** air-raid warning. ◆alerter *vt* to warn, alert.

alezan, -ane [alzɑ̃ -an] *a & nmf* (*cheval*) chestnut.

algarade [algarad] *nf* (*dispute*) altercation.

algèbre [alʒɛbr] *nf* algebra. ◆algébrique *a* algebraic.

Alger [alʒe] *nm ou f* Algiers.

Algérie [alʒeri] *nf* Algeria. ◆algérien, -ienne *a & nmf* Algerian.

algue(s) [alg] *nf(pl)* seaweed.

alias [aljɑs] *adv* alias.

alibi [alibi] *nm* alibi.

alién/er [aljene] *vt* to alienate; **s'a. qn** to alienate s.o. ◆—é, -ée *nmf* insane person; *Péj* lunatic. ◆aliénation *nf* alienation; *Méd* derangement.

align/er [aliɲe] *vt* to align, line up; **les a.** *Arg* to fork out, pay up; — **s'a.** (*personnes*) to fall into line, line up; *Pol* to align oneself (**sur** with). ◆—ement *nm* alignment.

aliment [alimɑ̃] *nm* food. ◆alimentaire *a* (*industrie, produit etc*) food-. ◆alimentation *nf* feeding; supply(ing); (*régime*) diet, nutrition; (*nourriture*) food; **magasin d'a.** grocer's, grocery store. ◆**alimenter** *vt* (*nourrir*) to feed; (*fournir*) to supply (**en** with); (*débat, feu*) to fuel.

alinéa [alinea] *nm* paragraph.

alité [alite] *a* bedridden.

allaiter [alete] *vti* to (breast)feed.

allant [alɑ̃] *nm* drive, energy, zest.

allécher [aleʃe] *vt* to tempt, entice.

allée [ale] *nf* path, walk, lane; (*de cinéma*) aisle; **allées et venues** comings and goings, running about.

allégation [alegasjɔ̃] *nf* allegation.

alléger [aleʒe] *vt* to alleviate, lighten.

allégorie [alegɔri] *nf* allegory.

allègre [alegr] *a* gay, lively, cheerful. ◆**allégresse** *nf* gladness, rejoicing.

alléguer [alege] *vt* (*excuse etc*) to put forward.

alléluia [aleluja] *nm* hallelujah.

Allemagne [almaɲ] *nf* Germany. ◆**allemand, -ande** *a & nmf* German; – *nm* (*langue*) German.

aller* [ale] **1** *vi* (*aux être*) to go; (*montre etc*) to work, go; **a. à** (*convenir à*) to suit; **a. avec** (*vêtement*) to go with, match; **a. bien/mieux** (*personne*) to be well/better; **il va savoir/venir/***etc* he'll know/come/*etc*, he's going to know/come/*etc*; **il va partir** he's about to leave, he's going to leave; **va voir!** go and see!; **comment vas-tu?, (comment) ça va?** how are you?; **ça va!** all right!, fine!; **ça va (comme ça)?** that's enough!; **allez-y** go on, go ahead; **j'y vais** I'm coming; **allons (donc)!** come on!, come off it!; **allez! au lit!** come on *ou* go on to bed!; **ça va de soi** that's obvious; – **s'en aller** *vpr* to go away; (*tache*) to come out. **2** *nm* outward journey; **a. (simple)** single (ticket), *Am* one-way (ticket); **a. (et) retour** return (ticket), *Am* round-trip (ticket).

allergie [alerʒi] *nf* allergy. ◆**allergique** *a* allergic (**à** to).

alliage [aljaʒ] *nm* alloy.

alliance [aljɑ̃s] *nf* (*anneau*) wedding ring; *Pol* alliance; *Rel* covenant; (*mariage*) marriage.

alli/er [alje] *vt* (*associer*) to combine (**à** with); (*pays*) to ally (**à** with); – **s'a.** *vpr* (*couleurs*) to combine; (*pays*) to become allied (**à** with, to); **s'a. à** (*famille*) to ally oneself with. ◆**—é, -ée** *nmf* ally.

alligator [aligatɔr] *nm* alligator.

allô! [alo] *int Tél* hullo!, hallo!, hello!

allocation [alɔkasjɔ̃] *nf* (*somme*) allowance; **a. (de) chômage** unemployment benefit. ◆**allocataire** *nmf* claimant.

allocution [alɔkysjɔ̃] *nf* (short) speech, address.

allong/er [alɔ̃ʒe] *vt* (*bras*) to stretch out; (*jupe*) to lengthen; (*sauce*) to thin; – *vi* (*jours*) to get longer; – **s'a.** *vpr* to stretch out. ◆**—é** *a* (*oblong*) elongated.

allouer [alwe] *vt* to allocate.

allum/er [alyme] *vt* (*feu, pipe etc*) to light; (*électricité*) to turn *ou* switch on; (*désir, colère*) Fig to kindle; – **s'a.** *vpr* to light up; (*feu, guerre*) to flare up. ◆**—age** *nm* lighting; *Aut* ignition. ◆**allume-gaz** *nm inv* gas lighter. ◆**allumeuse** *nf* (*femme*) teaser.

allumette [alymet] *nf* match.

allure [alyr] *nf* (*vitesse*) pace; (*de véhicule*) speed; (*démarche*) gait, walk; (*maintien*) bearing; (*air*) look; *pl* (*conduite*) ways.

allusion [alyzjɔ̃] *nf* allusion; (*voilée*) hint; **faire a. à** to refer *ou* allude to; to hint at.

almanach [almana] *nm* almanac.

aloi [alwa] *nm* **de bon a.** genuine, worthy.

alors [alɔr] *adv* (*en ce temps-là*) then; (*en ce cas-là*) so, then; **a. que** (*lorsque*) when; (*tandis que*) whereas.

alouette [alwet] *nf* (sky)lark.

alourd/ir [alurdir] *vt* to weigh down; – **s'a.** *vpr* to become heavy *ou* heavier. ◆**—i** *a* heavy.

aloyau [alwajo] *nm* sirloin.

alpaga [alpaga] *nm* (*tissu*) alpaca.

alpage [alpaʒ] *nm* mountain pasture. ◆**Alpes** *nfpl* **les A.** the Alps. ◆**alpestre** *a*, ◆**alpin** *a* alpine. ◆**alpinisme** *nm* mountaineering. ◆**alpiniste** *nmf* mountaineer.

alphabet [alfabe] *nm* alphabet. ◆**alphabétique** *a* alphabetic(al). ◆**alphabétiser** *vt* to teach to read and write.

altercation [alterkasjɔ̃] *nf* altercation.

altér/er [altere] *vt* (*denrée, santé*) to impair, spoil; (*voix, vérité*) to distort; (*monnaie, texte*) to falsify; (*donner soif à*) to make thirsty; – **s'a.** *vpr* (*santé, relations*) to deteriorate. ◆**altération** *nf* deterioration, change (**de** in); (*de visage*) distortion.

alternatif, -ive [alternatif, -iv] *a* alternating. ◆**alternative** *nf* alternative; *pl* alternate periods. ◆**alternativement** *adv* alternately.

altern/er [alterne] *vti* to alternate. ◆**—é** *a* alternate. ◆**alternance** *nf* alternation.

altesse [altes] *nf* (*titre*) Highness.

altier, -ière [altje, -jer] *a* haughty.

altitude [altityd] *nf* altitude, height.

alto [alto] *nm* (*instrument*) viola.

aluminium [alyminjɔm] *nm* aluminium, *Am*

aluminum; **papier a.**, *Fam* **papier alu** tin foil.

alunir [alynir] *vi* to land on the moon.

alvéole [alveɔl] *nf* (*de ruche*) cell; (*dentaire*) socket. ◆**alvéolé** *a* honeycombed.

amabilité [amabilite] *nf* kindness; **faire des amabilités à** to show kindness to.

amadouer [amadwe] *vt* to coax, persuade.

amaigr/ir [amegrir] *vt* to make thin(ner). ◆**—i** *a* thin(ner). ◆**—issant** *a* (*régime*) slimming.

amalgame [amalgam] *nm* amalgam, mixture. ◆**amalgamer** *vt*, **— s'a.** *vpr* to blend, mix, amalgamate.

amande [amɑ̃d] *nf* almond.

amant [amɑ̃] *nm* lover.

amarre [amar] *nf* (*mooring*) rope, hawser; *pl* moorings. ◆**amarrer** *vt* to moor; *Fig* to tie down, make fast.

amas [amɑ] *nm* heap, pile. ◆**amasser** *vt* to pile up; (*richesse, preuves*) to amass, gather; **— s'a.** *vpr* to pile up; (*gens*) to gather.

amateur [amatœr] *nm* (*d'art etc*) lover; *Sp* amateur; (*acheteur*) *Fam* taker; **d'a.** (*talent*) amateur; (*travail*) *Péj* amateurish; **une équipe a.** an amateur team. ◆**amateurisme** *nm Sp* amateurism; *Péj* amateurishness.

amazone [amazon] *nf* horsewoman; **monter en a.** to ride sidesaddle.

ambages (sans) [sɑ̃zɑ̃baʒ] *adv* to the point, in plain language.

ambassade [ɑ̃basad] *nf* embassy. ◆**ambassadeur, -drice** *nmf* ambassador.

ambiance [ɑ̃bjɑ̃s] *nf* atmosphere. ◆**ambiant** *a* surrounding.

ambigu, -guë [ɑ̃bigy] *a* ambiguous. ◆**ambiguïté** [-gɥite] *nf* ambiguity.

ambitieux, -euse [ɑ̃bisjø, -øz] *a* ambitious. ◆**ambition** *nf* ambition. ◆**ambitionner** *vt* to aspire to; **il ambitionne de** his ambition is to.

ambre [ɑ̃br] *nm* (*jaune*) amber; (*gris*) ambergris.

ambulance [ɑ̃bylɑ̃s] *nf* ambulance. ◆**ambulancier, -ière** *nmf* ambulance driver.

ambulant [ɑ̃bylɑ̃] *a* itinerant, travelling.

âme [ɑm] *nf* soul; **â. qui vive** a living soul; **état d'â.** state of mind; **â. sœur** soul mate; **â. damnée** evil henchman, henchman; **avoir charge d'âmes** to be responsible for human life.

améliorer [ameljɔre] *vt*, **— s'a.** *vpr* to improve. ◆**amélioration** *nf* improvement.

amen [amɛn] *adv* amen.

aménag/er [amenaʒe] *vt* (*arranger, installer*) to fit up, fit out (**en** as); (*bateau*) to fit out; (*transformer*) to convert (**en** into); (*construire*) to set up; (*ajuster*) to adjust. ◆**—ement** *nm* fitting up; fitting out; conversion; setting up; adjustment.

amende [amɑ̃d] *nf* fine; **frapper d'une a.** to impose a fine on; **faire a. honorable** to make an apology.

amender [amɑ̃de] *vt Pol* to amend; (*terre*) to improve; **— s'a.** *vpr* to mend *ou* improve one's ways.

amener [amne] *vt* to bring; (*causer*) to bring about; **— s'a.** *vpr Fam* to come along, turn up.

amenuiser (s') [samənɥize] *vpr* to grow smaller, dwindle.

amer, -ère [amɛr] *a* bitter. ◆**amèrement** *adv* bitterly.

Amérique [amerik] *nf* America; **A. du Nord/du Sud** North/South America. ◆**américain, -aine** *a & nmf* American.

amerrir [amerir] *vi* to make a sea landing, (*cabine spatiale*) to splash down.

amertume [amɛrtym] *nf* bitterness.

améthyste [ametist] *nf* amethyst.

ameublement [amœblǝmɑ̃] *nm* furniture.

ameuter [amøte] *vt* (*soulever*) to stir up; (*attrouper*) to gather, muster; (*voisins*) to bring out; **— s'a.** *vpr* to gather, muster.

ami, -e [ami] *nmf* friend; (*des livres, de la nature etc*) lover (**de** of); **petit a.** boyfriend; **petite amie** girlfriend; **— a.** *a* friendly.

amiable (à l') [alamjabl] *a* amicable; **— adv** amicably.

amiante [amjɑ̃t] *nm* asbestos.

amical, -aux [amikal, -o] *a* friendly. ◆**—ement** *adv* in a friendly manner.

amicale [amikal] *nf* association.

amidon [amidɔ̃] *nm* starch. ◆**amidonner** *vt* to starch.

amincir [amɛ̃sir] *vt* to make thin(ner); **— vi** (*personne*) to slim; **— s'a.** *vpr* to become thinner.

amiral, -aux [amiral, -o] *nm* admiral. ◆**amirauté** *nf* admiralty.

amitié [amitje] *nf* friendship; (*amabilité*) kindness; *pl* kind regrds; **prendre en a.** to take a liking to.

ammoniac [amɔnjak] *nm* (*gaz*) ammonia. ◆**ammoniaque** *nf* (*liquide*) ammonia.

amnésie [amnezi] *nf* amnesia.

amnistie [amnisti] *nf* amnesty.

amocher [amɔʃe] *vt Arg* to mess up, bash.

amoindrir [amwɛ̃drir] *vt*, — **s'a.** *vpr* to decrease, diminish.

amoll/ir [amɔlir] *vt* to soften; (*affaiblir*) to weaken. ◆—**issant** *a* enervating.

amonceler [amɔ̃sle] *vt*, — **s'a.** *vpr* to pile up. ◆**amoncellement** *nm* heap, pile.

amont (en) [ɑ̃namɔ̃] *adv* upstream.

amoral, -aux [amɔral, -o] *a* amoral.

amorce [amɔrs] *nf* (*début*) start; *Pêche* bait; (*détonateur*) fuse, detonator; (*de pistolet d'enfant*) cap. ◆**amorcer** *vt* to start; (*hameçon*) to bait; (*pompe*) to prime; — **s'a.** *vpr* to start.

amorphe [amɔrf] *a* listless, apathetic.

amort/ir [amɔrtir] *vt* (*coup*) to cushion, absorb; (*bruit*) to deaden; (*dette*) to pay off; **il a vite amorti sa voiture** his car has been made to pay for itself quickly. ◆—**issement** *nm* *Fin* redemption. ◆—**isseur** *nm* shock absorber.

amour [amur] *nm* love; (*liaison*) romance, love; (*Cupidon*) Cupid; **pour l'a. de** for the sake of; **mon a.** my darling, my love. ◆**a.-propre** *nm* self-respect, self-esteem. ◆**s'amouracher** *vpr Péj* to become infatuated (**de** with). ◆**amoureux, -euse** *nmf* lover; — *a* amorous, loving; **a. de** (*personne*) in love with; (*gloire*) *Fig* enamoured of.

amovible [amɔvibl] *a* removable, detachable.

ampère [ɑ̃pɛr] *nm* *Él* amp(ere).

amphi [ɑ̃fi] *nm* *Univ Fam* lecture hall.

amphibie [ɑ̃fibi] *a* amphibious; — *nm* amphibian.

amphithéâtre [ɑ̃fiteatr] *nm* *Hist* amphitheatre; *Univ* lecture hall.

ample [ɑ̃pl] *a* (*vêtement*) ample, roomy; (*provision*) full; (*vues*) broad. ◆**amplement** *adv* amply, fully; **a. suffisant** ample. ◆**ampleur** *nf* (*de robe*) fullness; (*importance, étendue*) scale, extent; **prendre de l'a.** to grow.

amplifier [ɑ̃plifje] *vt* (*accroître*) to develop; (*exagérer*) to magnify; (*son, courant*) to amplify; — **s'a.** *vpr* to increase. ◆**amplificateur** *nm* amplifier. ◆**amplification** *nf* (*extension*) increase.

amplitude [ɑ̃plityd] *nf* *Fig* magnitude.

ampoule [ɑ̃pul] *nf* (*électrique*) (light) bulb; (*aux pieds etc*) blister; (*de médicament*) phial.

ampoulé [ɑ̃pule] *a* turgid.

amputer [ɑ̃pyte] *vt* **1** (*membre*) to amputate; **a. qn de la jambe** to amputate s.o.'s leg. **2** (*texte*) to curtail, cut (**de** by).

amputation *nf* amputation; curtailment.

amuse-gueule [amyzgœl] *nm inv* cocktail snack, appetizer.

amus/er [amyze] *vt* (*divertir*) to amuse, entertain; (*occuper*) to divert the attention of; — **s'a.** *vpr* to enjoy oneself, have fun; (*en chemin*) to dawdle, loiter; **s'a. avec** to play with; **s'a. à faire** to amuse oneself doing. ◆—**ant** *a* amusing. ◆—**ement** *nm* amusement; (*jeu*) game. ◆**amusette** *nf* frivolous pursuit.

amygdale [amidal] *nf* tonsil.

an [ɑ̃] *nm* year; **il a dix ans** he's ten (years old); **par a.** per annum, per year; **bon a., mal a.** putting the good years and the bad together; **Nouvel A.** New Year.

anachronisme [anakronism] *nm* anachronism.

anagramme [anagram] *nf* anagram.

analogie [analɔʒi] *nf* analogy. ◆**analogue** *a* similar; — *nm* analogue.

analphabète [analfabɛt] *a & nmf* illiterate. ◆**analphabétisme** *nm* illiteracy.

analyse [analiz] *nf* analysis; **a. grammaticale** parsing. ◆**analyser** *vt* to analyse; (*phrase*) to parse. ◆**analytique** *a* analytic(al).

ananas [anana(s)] *nm* pineapple.

anarchie [anarʃi] *nf* anarchy. ◆**anarchique** *a* anarchic. ◆**anarchiste** *nmf* anarchist; — *a* anarchistic.

anathème [anatɛm] *nm* *Rel* anathema.

anatomie [anatɔmi] *nf* anatomy. ◆**anatomique** *a* anatomical.

ancestral, -aux [ɑ̃sɛstral, -o] *a* ancestral.

ancêtre [ɑ̃sɛtr] *nm* ancestor.

anche [ɑ̃ʃ] *nf* *Mus* reed.

anchois [ɑ̃ʃwa] *nm* anchovy.

ancien, -ienne [ɑ̃sjɛ̃, -jɛn] *a* (*vieux*) old; (*meuble*) antique; (*qui n'est plus*) former, ex-, old; (*antique*) ancient; (*dans une fonction*) senior; **a. élève** old boy, *Am* alumnus; **a. combattant** ex-serviceman, *Am* veteran; — *nmf* (*par l'âge*) elder; (*dans une fonction*) senior; **les anciens** (*auteurs, peuples*) the ancients. ◆**anciennement** *adv* formerly. ◆**ancienneté** *nf* age; (*dans une fonction*) seniority.

ancre [ɑ̃kr] *nf* anchor; **jeter l'a.** to (cast) anchor; **lever l'a.** to weigh anchor. ◆**ancrer** *vt* *Nau* to anchor; (*idée*) *Fig* to root, fix; **ancré dans** rooted in.

andouille [ɑ̃duj] *nf* sausage (*made from chitterlings*); **espèce d'a.!** *Fam* (you) nitwit!

âne [ɑn] *nm* (*animal*) donkey, ass; (*personne*) *Péj* ass; **bonnet d'â.** dunce's cap; **dos d'â.** (*d'une route*) hump; **pont en dos d'â.** humpback bridge.

anéant/ir [aneɑ̃tir] *vt* to annihilate, wipe out, destroy; **— s'a.** *vpr* to vanish. ◆**—i** *a* (*épuisé*) exhausted; (*stupéfait*) dismayed; (*accablé*) overwhelmed. ◆**—issement** *nm* annihilation; (*abattement*) dejection.

anecdote [anɛkdɔt] *nf* anecdote. ◆**anecdotique** *a* anecdotal.

anémie [anemi] *nf* an(a)emia. ◆**anémique** *a* an(a)emic. ◆**s'anémier** *vpr* to become an(a)emic.

anémone [anemɔn] *nf* anemone.

ânerie [ɑnri] *nf* stupidity; (*action etc*) stupid thing. ◆**ânesse** *nf* she-ass.

anesthésie [anɛstezi] *nf* an(a)esthesia. **a. générale/locale** general/local an(a)esthetic. ◆**anesthésier** *vt* to an(a)esthetize. ◆**anesthésique** *nm* an(a)esthetic.

anfractuosité [ɑ̃fraktɥozite] *nf* crevice, cleft.

ange [ɑ̃ʒ] *nm* angel; **aux anges** in seventh heaven. ◆**angélique** *a* angelic.

angélus [ɑ̃ʒelys] *nm* Rel angelus.

angine [ɑ̃ʒin] *nf* sore throat; **a. de poitrine** angina (pectoris).

anglais, -aise [ɑ̃glɛ, -ɛz] *a* English; *— nmf* Englishman, Englishwoman; *— nm* (*langue*) English; **filer à l'anglaise** to take French leave.

angle [ɑ̃gl] *nm* (*point de vue*) & *Géom* angle; (*coin*) corner.

Angleterre [ɑ̃glətɛr] *nf* England.

anglican, -ane [ɑ̃glikɑ̃, -an] *a* & *nmf* Anglican.

anglicisme [ɑ̃glisism] *nm* Anglicism. ◆**angliciste** *nmf* English specialist.

anglo- [ɑ̃glo] *préf* Anglo-. ◆**anglo-normand** *a* Anglo-Norman; **îles a.-normandes** Channel Islands. ◆**anglophile** *a* & *nmf* anglophile. ◆**anglophone** *a* English-speaking; *— nmf* English speaker. ◆**anglo-saxon, -onne** *a* & *nmf* Anglo-Saxon.

angoisse [ɑ̃gwas] *nf* anguish. ◆**angoissant** *a* distressing. ◆**angoissé** *a* (*personne*) in anguish; (*geste, cri*) anguished.

angora [ɑ̃gɔra] *nm* (*laine*) angora.

anguille [ɑ̃gij] *nf* eel.

angulaire [ɑ̃gylɛr] *a* **pierre a.** cornerstone. ◆**anguleux, -euse** *a* (*visage*) angular.

anicroche [anikrɔʃ] *nf* hitch, snag.

animal, -aux [animal, -o] *nm* animal; (*personne*) Péj brute, animal; *— a* animal.

animer [anime] *vt* (*inspirer*) to animate; (*encourager*) to spur on; (*débat, groupe*) to

lead; (*soirée*) to enliven; (*regard*) to light up, brighten up; (*mécanisme*) to actuate, drive; **a. la course** *Sp* to set the pace; **animé de** (*sentiment*) prompted by; **— s'a.** *vpr* (*rue etc*) to come to life; (*yeux*) to light up, brighten up. ◆**animé** *a* (*rue*) lively; (*conversation*) animated, lively; (*doué de vie*) animate. ◆**animateur, -trice** *nmf* TV compere, *Am* master of ceremonies, emcee; (*de club*) leader, organizer; (*d'entreprise*) driving force, spirit. ◆**animation** *nf* (*des rues*) activity; (*de réunion*) liveliness; (*de visage*) brightness; *Cin* animation.

animosité [animozite] *nf* animosity.

anis [ani(s)] *nm* (*boisson, parfum*) aniseed. ◆**anisette** *nf* (*liqueur*) anisette.

ankylose [ɑ̃kiloz] *nf* stiffening. ◆**s'ankylos/er** *vpr* to stiffen up. ◆**—é** *a* stiff.

annales [anal] *nfpl* annals.

anneau, -x [ano] *nm* ring; (*de chaîne*) link.

année [ane] *nf* year; **bonne a.!** Happy New Year!

annexe [anɛks] *nf* (*bâtiment*) annex(e); *— a* (*pièces*) appended; **bâtiment a.** annex(e). ◆**annexer** *vt* (*pays*) to annex; (*document*) to append. ◆**annexion** *nf* annexation.

annihiler [aniile] *vt* to destroy, annihilate.

anniversaire [aniverser] *nm* (*d'évènement*) anniversary; (*de naissance*) birthday; *— a* anniversary.

annonce [anɔ̃s] *nf* (*avis*) announcement; (*publicitaire*) advertisement; (*indice*) sign; **petites annonces** classified advertisements, small ads. ◆**annoncer** *vt* (*signaler*) to announce, report; (*être l'indice de*) to indicate; (*vente*) to advertise; **a. le printemps** to herald spring; **s'a. pluvieux/difficile/etc** to look like being rainy/difficult/etc. ◆**annonceur** *nm* advertiser; *Rad TV* announcer.

annonciation [anɔ̃sjasjɔ̃] *nf* Annunciation.

annoter [anɔte] *vt* to annotate. ◆**annotation** *nf* annotation.

annuaire [anɥɛr] *nm* yearbook; (*téléphonique*) directory, phone book.

annuel, -elle [anɥɛl] *a* annual, yearly. ◆**annuellement** *adv* annually. ◆**annuité** *nf* annual instalment.

annulaire [anɥlɛr] *nm* third or third finger.

annuler [anɥle] *vt* (*visite etc*) to cancel; (*mariage*) to annul; (*jugement*) to quash; **— s'a.** *vpr* to cancel each other out. ◆**annulation** *nf* cancellation; annulment; quashing.

anoblir [anɔblir] *vt* to ennoble.

anodin [anɔdɛ̃] a harmless; (*remède*) ineffectual.

anomalie [anɔmali] nf (*irrégularité*) anomaly; (*difformité*) abnormality.

ânonner [anɔne] vt (*en hésitant*) to stumble through; (*d'une voix monotone*) to drone out.

anonymat [anɔnima] nm anonymity; **garder l'a.** to remain anonymous. ◆**anonyme** a & nmf anonymous (person).

anorak [anɔrak] nm anorak.

anorexie [anɔrɛksi] nf anorexia.

anormal, -aux [anɔrmal, -o] a abnormal; (*enfant*) educationally subnormal.

anse [ɑ̃s] nf (*de tasse etc*) handle; (*baie*) cove.

antagonisme [ɑ̃tagɔnism] nm antagonism. ◆**antagoniste** a antagonistic; — nmf antagonist.

antan (d') [dɑ̃tɑ̃] a Litt of yesteryear.

antarctique [ɑ̃tarktik] a antarctic; — nm **l'A.** the Antarctic, Antarctica.

antécédent [ɑ̃tesedɑ̃] nm Gram antecedent; pl past history, antecedents.

antenne [ɑ̃tɛn] nf TV Rad aerial, Am antenna; (*station*) station; (*d'insecte*) antenna, feeler; **a. chirurgicale** surgical outpost; Aut emergency unit; **sur** ou **à l'a.** on the air.

antérieur [ɑ̃terjœr] a (*précédent*) former, previous, earlier; (*placé devant*) front; **membre a.** forelimb; **a. à** prior to. ◆**antérieurement** adv previously. ◆**antériorité** nf precedence.

anthologie [ɑ̃tɔlɔʒi] nf anthology.

anthropologie [ɑ̃trɔpɔlɔʒi] nf anthropology.

anthropophage [ɑ̃trɔpɔfaʒ] nm cannibal. ◆**anthropophagie** nf cannibalism.

antiaérien, -ienne [ɑ̃tiaerjɛ̃, -jɛn] a (*canon*) antiaircraft; (*abri*) air-raid.

antiatomique [ɑ̃tiatɔmik] a **abri a.** fallout shelter.

antibiotique [ɑ̃tibjɔtik] a & nm antibiotic.

antibrouillard [ɑ̃tibrujar] a & nm (*phare*) **a.** fog lamp.

anticancéreux, -euse [ɑ̃tikɑ̃serø, -øz] a **centre a.** cancer hospital.

antichambre [ɑ̃tiʃɑ̃br] nf antechamber, anteroom.

antichoc [ɑ̃tiʃɔk] a inv shockproof.

anticip/er [ɑ̃tisipe] vti a. (**sur**) to anticipate. ◆**-é** a (*retraite etc*) early; (*paiement*) advance; **avec mes remerciements anticipés** thanking you in advance. ◆**anticipation** nf anticipation; **par a.** in advance; **d'a.** (*roman etc*) science-fiction.

anticlérical, -aux [ɑ̃tiklerikal, -o] a anticlerical.

anticonformiste [ɑ̃tikɔ̃fɔrmist] a & nmf nonconformist.

anticonstitutionnel, -elle [ɑ̃tikɔ̃stitysjɔnɛl] a unconstitutional.

anticorps [ɑ̃tikɔr] nm antibody.

anticyclone [ɑ̃tisiklɔn] nm anticyclone.

antidater [ɑ̃tidate] vt to backdate, antedate.

antidémocratique [ɑ̃tidemɔkratik] a undemocratic.

antidérapant [ɑ̃tiderapɑ̃] a non-skid.

antidote [ɑ̃tidɔt] nm antidote.

antigel [ɑ̃tiʒɛl] nm antifreeze.

Antilles [ɑ̃tij] nfpl **les A.** the West Indies. ◆**antillais, -aise** a & nmf West Indian.

antilope [ɑ̃tilɔp] nf antelope.

antimite [ɑ̃timit] a mothproof; — nm mothproofing agent.

antiparasite [ɑ̃tiparazit] a **dispositif a.** Rad suppressor.

antipathie [ɑ̃tipati] nf antipathy. ◆**antipathique** a disagreeable.

antipodes [ɑ̃tipɔd] nmpl **aux a.** (*partir*) to the antipodes; **aux a. de** at the opposite end of the world from; Fig poles apart from.

antique [ɑ̃tik] a ancient. ◆**antiquaire** nmf antique dealer. ◆**antiquité** nf (*temps, ancienneté*) antiquity; (*objet ancien*) antique; pl (*monuments etc*) antiquities.

antirabique [ɑ̃tirabik] a (anti-)rabies.

antisémite [ɑ̃tisemit] a anti-Semitic. ◆**antisémitisme** nm anti-Semitism.

antiseptique [ɑ̃tisɛptik] a & nm antiseptic.

antisudoral, -aux [ɑ̃tisydɔral, -o] nm antiperspirant.

antithèse [ɑ̃titez] nf antithesis.

antivol [ɑ̃tivɔl] nm anti-theft lock ou device.

antonyme [ɑ̃tɔnim] nm antonym.

antre [ɑ̃tr] nm (*de lion etc*) den.

anus [anys] nm anus.

Anvers [ɑ̃vɛr(s)] nm ou f Antwerp.

anxiété [ɑ̃ksjete] nf anxiety. ◆**anxieux, -euse** a anxious; — nmf worrier.

août [u(t)] nm August. ◆**aoûtien, -ienne** [ausjɛ̃, -jɛn] nmf August holidaymaker ou Am vacationer.

apais/er [apeze] vt (*personne*) to appease, calm; (*scrupules, faim*) to appease; (*douleur*) to allay; — **s'a.** vpr (*personne*) to calm down. ◆**-ant** a soothing. ◆**-ements** nmpl reassurances.

apanage [apanaʒ] nm privilege, monopoly (de of).

aparté [aparte] nm Th aside; (*dans une réunion*) private exchange; **en a.** in private.

apartheid [aparted] nm apartheid.

apathie [apati] *nf* apathy. ◆**apathique** *a* apathetic, listless.

apatride [apatrid] *nmf* stateless person.

apercevoir* [apɛrsəvwar] *vt* to see, perceive; (*brièvement*) to catch a glimpse of; **s'a.** de to notice, realize. ◆**aperçu** *nm* overall view, general outline; (*intuition*) insight.

apéritif [aperitif] *nm* aperitif. ◆**apéro** *nm Fam* aperitif.

apesanteur [apazɑ̃tœr] *nf* weightlessness.

à-peu-près [apøprɛ] *nm inv* vague approximation.

apeuré [apœre] *a* frightened, scared.

aphone [afɔn] *a* voiceless.

aphorisme [afɔrism] *nm* aphorism.

aphrodisiaque [afrodizjak] *a* & *nm* aphrodisiac.

aphte [aft] *nm* mouth ulcer. ◆**aphteuse** *af* **fièvre a.** foot-and-mouth disease.

apiculture [apikyltyr] *nf* beekeeping.

apit/oyer [apitwaje] *vt* to move (to pity); **s'a. sur** to pity. ◆**—oiement** *nm* pity, commiseration.

aplanir [aplanir] *vt* (*terrain*) to level; (*difficulté*) to iron out, smooth out.

aplat/ir [aplatir] *vt* to flatten (out); — **s'a.** *vpr* (*s'étendre*) to lie flat; (*s'humilier*) to grovel; (*tomber*) *Fam* to fall flat on one's face; **s'a. contre** to flatten oneself against. ◆**—i** *a* flat. ◆**—issement** *nm* (*état*) flatness.

aplomb [aplɔ̃] *nm* self-possession, self-assurance; *Péj* impudence; **d'a.** (*équilibré*) well-balanced; (*sur ses jambes*) steady; (*bien portant*) in good shape; **tomber d'a.** (*soleil*) to beat down.

apocalypse [apɔkalips] *nf* apocalypse; **d'a.** (*vision etc*) apocalyptic. ◆**apocalyptique** *a* apocalyptic.

apogée [apɔʒe] *nm* apogee; *Fig* peak, apogee.

apolitique [apɔlitik] *a* apolitical.

Apollon [apɔlɔ̃] *nm* Apollo.

apologie [apɔlɔʒi] *nf* defence, vindication. ◆**apologiste** *nmf* apologist.

apoplexie [apɔplɛksi] *nf* apoplexy. ◆**apoplectique** *a* apoplectic.

apostolat [apɔstɔla] *nm* (*prosélytisme*) proselytism; (*mission*) *Fig* calling. ◆**apostolique** *a* apostolic.

apostrophe [apɔstrɔf] *nf* **1** (*signe*) apostrophe. **2** (*interpellation*) sharp *ou* rude remark. ◆**apostropher** *vt* to shout at.

apothéose [apɔteoz] *nf* final triumph, apotheosis.

apôtre [apotr] *nm* apostle.

apparaître* [aparɛtr] *vi* (*se montrer*, *sembler*) to appear.

apparat [apara] *nm* pomp; **d'a.** (*tenue etc*) ceremonial, formal.

appareil [aparɛj] *nm* (*instrument etc*) apparatus; (*électrique*) appliance; *Anat* system; *Tél* telephone; (*avion*) aircraft; (*législatif etc*) *Fig* machinery; **a.** (**photo**) camera; **a.** (**auditif**) hearing aid; **a.** (**dentier**) brace; **qui est à l'a.?** *Tél* who's speaking?

appareiller [apareje] **1** *vi Nau* to get under way. **2** *vt* (*assortir*) to match (up).

apparence [aparɑ̃s] *nf* appearance; (*vestige*) semblance; **en a.** outwardly; **sous l'a. de** under the guise of; **sauver les apparences** to keep up appearances. ◆**apparemment** [-amɑ̃] *adv* apparently. ◆**apparent** *a* apparent; (*ostensible*) visible.

apparent/er (s') [aparɑ̃te] *vpr* (*ressembler*) to be similar *ou* akin (à to). ◆**—é** *a* (*allié*) related; (*semblable*) similar.

appariteur [aparitœr] *nm Univ* porter.

apparition [aparisjɔ̃] *nf* appearance; (*spectre*) apparition.

appartement [apartəmɑ̃] *nm* flat, *Am* apartment.

appartenir* [apartənir] **1** *vi* to belong (à to); **il vous appartient de** it's your responsibility to. **2 s'a.** *vpr* to be one's own master. ◆**appartenance** *nf* membership (à to).

appât [apɑ] *nm* (*amorce*) bait; (*attrait*) lure. ◆**appâter** *vt* (*attirer*) to lure.

appauvrir [apovrir] *vt* to impoverish; — **s'a.** *vpr* to become impoverished *ou* poorer.

appel [apɛl] *nm* (*cri*, *attrait etc*) call; (*demande pressante*) & *Jur* appeal; *Mil* call-up; **faire l'a.** *Scol* to take the register; *Mil* to have a roll call; **faire a. à** to appeal to, call upon; (*requérir*) to call for.

appel/er [aple] *vt* (*personne*, *nom etc*) to call; (*en criant*) to call out to; *Mil* to call up; (*nécessiter*) to call for; **a. à l'aide** to call for help; **en a. à** to appeal to; **il est appelé à** (*de hautes fonctions*) he is marked out for; (*témoigner etc*) he is called upon to; — **s'a.** *vpr* to be called; **il s'appelle Paul** his name is Paul. ◆**—é** *nm Mil* conscript. ◆**appellation** *nf* (*nom*) term; **a. contrôlée** trade name guaranteeing quality of wine.

appendice [apɛ̃dis] *nm* appendix; (*d'animal*) appendage. ◆**appendicite** *nf* appendicitis.

appentis [apɑ̃ti] *nm* (*bâtiment*) lean-to.

appesantir (s') [apəzɑ̃tir] *vpr* to become heavier; **s'a. sur** (*sujet*) to dwell upon.

appétit [apeti] *nm* appetite (**de** for); **mettre**

qn en a. to whet s.o.'s appetite; **bon a.!** enjoy your meal! ◆**appétissant** *a* appetizing.

applaud/ir [aplodir] *vti* to applaud, clap; **a. à** (*approuver*) to applaud. ◆**—issements** *nmpl* applause.

applique [aplik] *nf* wall lamp.

appliqu/er [aplike] *vt* to apply (à to); (*surnom, baiser, gifle*) to give; (*loi, décision*) to put into effect; **s'a. à** (*un travail*) to apply oneself to; (*concerner*) to apply to; **s'a. à faire** to take pains to do. ◆**—é** *a* (*travailleur*) painstaking; (*sciences*) applied. ◆**applicable** *a* applicable. ◆**application** *nf* application.

appoint [apwɛ̃] *nm* contribution; **faire l'a.** to give the correct money *ou* change.

appointements [apwɛ̃tmɑ̃] *nmpl* salary.

appontement [apɔ̃tmɑ̃] *nm* landing stage.

apport [apɔr] *nm* contribution.

apporter [apɔrte] *vt* to bring.

apposer [apoze] *vt Jur* to affix. ◆**apposition** *nf Gram* apposition.

apprécier [apresje] *vt* (*évaluer*) to appraise; (*aimer, percevoir*) to appreciate. ◆**appréciable** *a* appreciable. ◆**appréciation** *nf* appraisal; appreciation.

appréhender [apreɑ̃de] *vt* (*craindre*) to fear; (*arrêter*) to apprehend. ◆**appréhension** *nf* apprehension.

apprendre* [aprɑ̃dr] *vti* (*étudier*) to learn; (*événement, fait*) to hear of, learn of; (*nouvelle*) to hear; **a. à faire** to learn to do; **a. qch à qn** (*enseigner*) to teach s.o. sth; (*informer*) to tell s.o. sth; **a. à qn à faire** to teach s.o. to do; **a. que** to learn that; (*être informé*) to hear that.

apprenti, -ie [aprɑ̃ti] *nmf* apprentice; (*débutant*) novice. ◆**apprentissage** *nm* apprenticeship; **faire l'a. de** *Fig* to learn the experience of.

apprêt/er [aprete] *vt*, **— s'a.** *vpr* to prepare. ◆**—é** *a Fig* affected.

apprivois/er [aprivwaze] *vt* to tame; **— s'a.** *vpr* to become tame. ◆**—é** *a* tame.

approbation [aprɔbasjɔ̃] *nf* approval. ◆**approbateur, -trice** *a* approving.

approche [aprɔʃ] *nf* approach. ◆**approch/er** *vt* (*chaise etc*) to bring up, draw up (**de** to, close to); (*personne*) to approach, come close to; **— vi** to approach, come close(r) *ou* near(er) to; **a. de, s'a. de** to approach, come close(r) *ou* near(er) to. ◆**—ant** *a* similar. ◆**—é** *a* approximate. ◆**—able** *a* approachable.

approfond/ir [aprɔfɔ̃dir] *vt* (*trou etc*) to deepen; (*question*) to go into thoroughly,

(*mystère*) to plumb the depths of. ◆**—i** *a* thorough. ◆**—issement** *nm* deepening; (*examen*) thorough examination.

approprié [aprɔprije] *a* appropriate.

approprier (s') [saprɔprije] *vpr* **s'a. qch** to appropriate sth.

approuver [apruve] *vt* (*autoriser*) to approve; (*apprécier*) to approve of.

approvisionn/er [aprɔvizjɔne] *vt* (*ville etc*) to supply (with provisions); (*magasin*) to stock; **— s'a.** *vpr* to stock up (**de** with), get one's supplies (**de** of). ◆**—ements** *nmpl* stocks, supplies.

approximat/if, -ive [aprɔksimatif, -iv] *a* approximate. ◆**—ivement** *adv* approximately. ◆**approximation** *nf* approximation.

appui [apɥi] *nm* support; (*pour coude etc*) rest; (*de fenêtre*) sill; **à hauteur d'a.** breast-high. ◆**appuie-tête** *nm inv* headrest. ◆**appuyer** *vt* (*soutenir*) to support; (*accentuer*) to stress; **a. qch sur** (*poser*) to lean *ou* rest sth on; (*presser*) to press sth on; **— vi a. sur** to rest on; (*bouton etc*) to press (on); (*mot, élément etc*) to stress; **s'a. sur** to lean on, rest on; (*compter*) to rely on; (*se baser*) to base oneself on.

âpre [ɑpr] *a* harsh, rough; **a. au gain** grasping.

après [aprɛ] *prép* (*temps*) after; (*espace*) beyond; **a. un an** after a year; **a. le pont** beyond the bridge; **a. coup** after the event; **a. avoir mangé** after eating; **a. qu'il t'a vu** after he saw you; **d'a.** (*selon*) according to, from; **— adv** after(wards); **l'année d'a.** the following year; **et a.?** and then what?

après-demain [apredmɛ̃] *adv* the day after tomorrow. ◆**a.-guerre** *nm* post-war period; **d'a.-guerre** post-war. ◆**a.-midi** *nm ou f inv* afternoon. ◆**a.-shampooing** *nm* (hair) conditioner. ◆**a.-ski** *nm* ankle boot, snow boot.

a priori [aprijori] *adv* at the very outset, without going into the matter; **— nm inv** premiss.

à-propos [apropo] *nm* timeliness, aptness.

apte [apt] *a* suited (**à** to), capable (**à** of). ◆**aptitude** *nf* aptitude, capacity (**à, pour** for).

aquarelle [akwarɛl] *nf* watercolour, aquarelle.

aquarium [akwarjɔm] *nm* aquarium.

aquatique [akwatik] *a* aquatic.

aqueduc [akdyk] *nm* aqueduct.

aquilin [akilɛ̃] *a* aquiline.

arabe [arab] *a & nmf* Arab; **— a & nm** (*langue*) Arabic; **chiffres arabes** Arabic

numerals; **désert a.** Arabian desert.
◆**Arabie** *nf* Arabia; **A. Séoudite** Saudi Arabia.

arabesque [arabɛsk] *nf* arabesque.

arable [arabl] *a* arable.

arachide [araʃid] *nf* peanut, groundnut.

araignée [arɛɲe] *nf* spider.

arbalète [arbalɛt] *nf* crossbow.

arbitraire [arbitrɛr] *a* arbitrary.

arbitre [arbitr] *nm Jur* arbitrator; *(maître absolu)* arbiter; *Fb* referee; *Tennis* umpire; **libre a.** free will. ◆**arbitr/er** *vt* to arbitrate; to referee; to umpire. ◆**—age** *nm* arbitration; refereeing; umpiring.

arborer [arbɔre] *vt (insigne, vêtement)* to sport, display.

arbre [arbr] *nm* tree; *Aut* shaft, axle.
◆**arbrisseau, -x** *nm* shrub. ◆**arbuste** *nm* (small) shrub, bush.

arc [ark] *nm (arme)* bow; *(voûte)* arch; *Math* arc; **tir à l'a.** archery. ◆**arcade** *nf* arch(way); *pl* arcade.

arc-boutant [arkbutɑ̃] *nm (pl arcs-boutants)* flying buttress.
◆**s'arc-bouter** *vpr* **s'a. à** *ou* **contre** qch to brace oneself against.

arceau, -x [arso] *nm (de voûte)* arch.

arc-en-ciel [arkɑ̃sjɛl] *nm (pl arcs-en-ciel)* rainbow.

archaïque [arkaik] *a* archaic.

archange [arkɑ̃ʒ] *nm* archangel.

arche [arʃ] *nf (voûte)* arch; **l'a. de Noé** Noah's ark.

archéologie [arkeɔlɔʒi] *nf* arch(a)eology.
◆**archéologue** *nmf* arch(a)eologist.

archer [arʃe] *nm* archer, bowman.

archet [arʃe] *nm Mus* bow.

archétype [arketip] *nm* archetype.

archevêque [arʃəvɛk] *nm* archbishop.

archicomble [arʃikɔ̃bl] *a* jam-packed.

archipel [arʃipɛl] *nm* archipelago.

archiplein [arʃiplɛ̃] *a* chock-full, chock-a-block.

architecte [arʃitɛkt] *nm* architect.
◆**architecture** *nf* architecture.

archives [arʃiv] *nfpl* archives, records.
◆**archiviste** *nmf* archivist.

arctique [arktik] *a* arctic; – *nm* **l'A.** the Arctic.

ardent [ardɑ̃] *a (chaud)* burning, scorching; *(actif, passionné)* ardent, fervent; *(empressé)* eager. ◆**ardemment** [-amɑ̃] *adv* eagerly, fervently. ◆**ardeur** *nf (énergie)* ardour, fervour; *(chaleur)* heat.

ardoise [ardwaz] *nf* slate.

ardu [ardy] *a* arduous, difficult.

are [ar] *nm (mesure)* 100 square metres.

arène [arɛn] *nf Hist* arena; *(pour taureaux)* bullring; *pl Hist* amphitheatre; bullring.

arête [arɛt] *nf (de poisson)* bone; *(de cube etc)* & *Géog* ridge.

argent [arʒɑ̃] *nm (métal)* silver; *(monnaie)* money; **a. comptant** cash. ◆**argenté** *a (plaqué)* silver-plated; *(couleur)* silvery. ◆**argenterie** *nf* silverware.

Argentine [arʒɑ̃tin] *nf* Argentina. ◆**argentin, -ine** *a* & *nmf* Argentinian.

argile [arʒil] *nf* clay. ◆**argileux, -euse** *a* clayey.

argot [argo] *nm* slang. ◆**argotique** *a (terme)* slang.

arguer [argɥe] *vi* **a. de** qch to put forward sth as an argument; **a. que** *(protester)* to protest that. ◆**argumentation** *nf* argumentation, arguments. ◆**argumenter** *vi* to argue.

argument [argymɑ̃] *nm* argument.

argus [argys] *nm* guide to secondhand cars.

argutie [argysi] *nf* specious argument, quibble.

aride [arid] *a* arid, barren.

aristocrate [aristɔkrat] *nmf* aristocrat.
◆**aristocratie** [-asi] *nf* aristocracy.
◆**aristocratique** *a* aristocratic.

arithmétique [aritmetik] *nf* arithmetic; – *a* arithmetical.

arlequin [arləkɛ̃] *nm* harlequin.

armateur [armatœr] *nm* shipowner.

armature [armatyr] *nf (charpente)* framework; *(de lunettes, tente)* frame.

arme [arm] *nf* arm, weapon; **a. à feu** firearm; **carrière des armes** military career.
◆**arm/er** *vt (personne etc)* to arm *(de* with); *(fusil)* to cock; *(appareil photo)* to wind on; *(navire)* to equip; *(béton)* to reinforce; – **s'a.** *vpr* to arm oneself *(de* with). ◆**—ement(s)** *nm(pl)* arms.

armée [arme] *nf* army; **a. active/de métier** regular/professional army; **a. de l'air** air force.

armistice [armistis] *nm* armistice.

armoire [armwar] *nf* cupboard, *Am* closet; *(penderie)* wardrobe, *Am* closet; **a. à pharmacie** medicine cabinet.

armoiries [armwari] *nfpl* (coat of) arms.

armure [armyr] *nf* armour.

armurier [armyrje] *nm* gunsmith.

arôme [arom] *nm* aroma. ◆**aromate** *nm* spice. ◆**aromatique** *a* aromatic.

arpent/er [arpɑ̃te] *vt (terrain)* to survey; *(trottoir etc)* to pace up and down. ◆**—eur** *nm* (land) surveyor.

arqué [arke] *a* arched, curved; *(jambes)* bandy.

arrache-pied (d') [daraʃpje] *adv* unceasingly, relentlessly.

arrach/er [araʃe] *vt* (*clou, dent etc*) to pull out; (*cheveux, page*) to tear out, pull out; (*plante*) to pull up; (*masque*) to tear off, pull off; **a. qch à qn** to snatch sth from s.o.; (*aveu, argent*) to force sth out of s.o.; **a. un bras à qn** (*obus etc*) to blow s.o.'s arm off; **a. qn de son lit** to drag s.o. out of bed. ◆**—age** *nm* (*de plante*) pulling up.

arraisonner [arezɔne] *vt* (*navire*) to board and examine.

arrang/er [arɑ̃ʒe] *vt* (*chambre, visite etc*) to arrange, fix up; (*voiture, texte*) to put right; (*différend*) to settle; **a. qn** (*maltraiter*) *Fam* to fix s.o.; **ça m'arrange** that suits me (fine); **— s'a.** *vpr* (*se réparer*) to be put right; (*se mettre d'accord*) to come to an agreement *ou* arrangement; (*finir bien*) to turn out fine; **s'a. pour faire** to arrange to do, manage to do. ◆**—eant** *a* accommodating. ◆**—ement** *nm* arrangement.

arrestation [arestɑsjɔ̃] *nf* arrest.

arrêt [arɛ] *nm* (*halte, endroit*) stop; (*action*) stopping; *Méd* arrest; *Jur* decree; **temps d'a.** pause; **à l'a.** stationary; **a. de travail** (*grève*) stoppage; (*congé*) sick leave; **sans a.** constantly, non-stop.

arrêté [arete] *nm* order, decision.

arrêt/er [arete] *vt* to stop; (*appréhender*) to arrest; (*regard, jour*) to fix; (*plan*) to draw up; **— vi** to stop; **il n'arrête pas de critiquer**/*etc* he doesn't stop criticizing/*etc*, he's always criticizing/*etc*; **— s'a.** *vpr* to stop; **s'a. de faire** to stop doing. ◆**—é** *a* (*projet*) fixed; (*volonté*) firm.

arrhes [ar] *nfpl Fin* deposit.

arrière [arjɛr] *adv* **en a.** (*marcher*) backwards; (*rester*) behind; (*regarder*) back; **en a. de qn/qch** behind s.o./sth; **— nm** & *a inv* rear, back; **— nm** *Fb* (full) back; **faire marche a.** to reverse, back.

arrière-boutique [arjɛrbutik] *nm* back room (*of a shop*). ◆**a.-garde** *nf* rearguard. ◆**a.-goût** *nm* aftertaste. ◆**a.-grand-mère** *nf* great-grand-mother. ◆**a.-grand-père** *nm* (*pl* **arrière-grands-pères**) great-grand-father. ◆**a.-pays** *nm* hinterland. ◆**a.-pensée** *nf* ulterior motive. ◆**a.-plan** *nm* background. ◆**a.-saison** *nf* end of season, (late) autumn. ◆**a.-train** *nm* hindquarters.

arriéré [arjere] **1** *a* (*enfant*) (mentally) retarded; (*idée*) backward. **2** *nm* (*dette*) arrears.

arrimer [arime] *vt* (*fixer*) to rope down, secure.

arriv/er [arive] *vi* (*aux être*) (*venir*) to arrive, come; (*réussir*) to succeed; (*survenir*) to happen; **a. à** (*atteindre*) to reach; **a. à faire** to manage to do, succeed in doing; **a. à qn** to happen to s.o.; **il m'arrive d'oublier**/*etc* I happen (sometimes) to forget/*etc*, I (sometimes) forget/*etc*; **en a. à faire** to get to the point of doing. ◆**—ant, -ante** *nmf* new arrival. ◆**—ée** *nf* arrival; *Sp* (winning) post. ◆**—age** *nm* consignment. ◆**arriviste** *nmf Péj* social climber, self-seeker.

arrogant [arɔgɑ̃] *a* arrogant. ◆**arrogance** *nf* arrogance.

arroger (s') [sarɔʒe] *vpr* (*droit etc*) to assume (falsely).

arrond/ir [arɔ̃dir] *vt* to make round; (*somme, chiffre*) to round off. ◆**—i** *a* rounded.

arrondissement [arɔ̃dismɑ̃] *nm* (*d'une ville*) district.

arros/er [aroze] *vt* (*terre*) to water; (*repas*) to wash down; (*succès*) to drink to. ◆**—age** *nm* watering; *Fam* booze-up, celebration. ◆**arrosoir** *nm* watering can.

arsenal, -aux [arsənal, -o] *nm Nau* dockyard; *Mil* arsenal.

arsenic [arsənik] *nm* arsenic.

art [ar] *nm* art; **film/critique d'a.** art film/critic; **arts ménagers** domestic science.

artère [artɛr] *nf Anat* artery; *Aut* main road. ◆**artériel, -elle** *a* arterial.

artichaut [artiʃo] *nm* artichoke.

article [artikl] *nm* (*de presse, de commerce*) & *Gram* article; (*dans un contrat, catalogue*) item; **a. de fond** feature (article); **articles de toilette/de voyage** toilet/travel requisites; **à l'a. de la mort** at death's door.

articuler [artikyle] *vt* (*mot etc*) to articulate; **— s'a.** *vpr Anat* to articulate; *Fig* to connect. ◆**articulation** *nf Ling* articulation; *Anat* joint; **a. du doigt** knuckle.

artifice [artifis] *nm* trick, contrivance; **feu d'a.** (*spectacle*) fireworks, firework display.

artificiel, -elle [artifisjɛl] *a* artificial. ◆**artificiellement** *adv* artificially.

artillerie [artijri] *nf* artillery. ◆**artilleur** *nm* gunner.

artisan [artizɑ̃] *nm* craftsman, artisan. ◆**artisanal, -aux** *a* (*métier*) craftsman's. ◆**artisanat** *nm* (*métier*) craftsman's trade; (*classe*) artisan class.

artiste [artist] *nmf* artist; *Th Mus Cin* performer, artist. ◆**artistique** *a* artistic.

as [ɑs] *nm* (*carte, champion*) ace; **a. du volant** crack driver.

ascendant [asɑ̃dɑ̃] a ascending, upward; – nm ascendancy, power; pl ancestors. ◆**ascendance** nf ancestry.

ascenseur [asɑ̃sœr] nm lift, Am elevator.

ascension [asɑ̃sjɔ̃] nf ascent; l'A. Ascension Day.

ascète [aset] nmf ascetic. ◆**ascétique** a ascetic. ◆**ascétisme** nm asceticism.

Asie [azi] nf Asia. ◆**Asiate** nmf Asian. ◆**asiatique** a & nmf Asian, Asiatic.

asile [azil] nm (abri) refuge, shelter; (pour vieillards) home; Pol asylum; a. (d'aliénés) Péj (lunatic) asylum; a. de paix haven of peace.

aspect [aspɛ] nm (vue) sight; (air) appearance; (perspective) & Gram aspect.

asperge [aspɛrʒ] nf asparagus.

asperger [aspɛrʒe] vt to spray, sprinkle (de with).

aspérité [asperite] nf rugged edge, bump.

asphalte [asfalt] nm asphalt.

asphyxie [asfiksi] nf suffocation. ◆**asphyxier** vt to suffocate, asphyxiate.

aspic [aspik] nm (vipère) asp.

aspirant [aspirɑ̃] nm (candidat) candidate.

aspirateur [aspiratœr] nm vacuum cleaner, hoover®; passer (à) l'a. to vacuum, hoover.

aspir/er [aspire] vt (respirer) to breathe in, inhale; (liquide) to suck up; a. à to aspire to. ◆–é a Ling aspirate(d). ◆**aspiration** nf inhaling; suction; (ambition) aspiration.

aspirine [aspirin] nf aspirin.

assagir (s') [sasaʒir] vpr to sober (down), settle down.

assaill/ir [asajir] vt to assault, attack; a. de (questions etc) to assail with. ◆–ant nm assailant, attacker.

assainir [asenir] vt (purifier) to clean up; Fin to stabilize.

assaisonn/er [asɛzɔne] vt to season. ◆–ement nm seasoning.

assassin [asasɛ̃] nm murderer; assassin. ◆**assassinat** nm murder; assassination. ◆**assassiner** vt to murder; (homme politique etc) to assassinate.

assaut [aso] nm assault, onslaught; prendre d'a. to (take by) storm.

assécher [asefe] vt to drain.

assemblée [asɑ̃ble] nf (personnes réunies) gathering; (réunion) meeting; Pol Jur assembly; (de fidèles) Rel congregation.

assembl/er [asɑ̃ble] vt to assemble, put together; – s'a. vpr to assemble, gather. ◆–age nm (montage) assembly; (réunion d'objets) collection.

asséner [asene] vt (coup) to deal, strike.

assentiment [asɑ̃timɑ̃] nm assent, consent.

asseoir* [aswar] vt (personne) to sit (down), seat (sur on); (fondations) to lay; (autorité, réputation) to establish; a. sur (théorie etc) to base on; – s'a. vpr to sit (down).

assermenté [asɛrmɑ̃te] a sworn.

assertion [asɛrsjɔ̃] nf assertion.

asserv/ir [asɛrvir] vt to enslave. ◆–issement nm enslavement.

assez [ase] adv enough; a. de pain/de gens enough bread/people; j'en ai a. I've had enough; a. grand/intelligent/etc (suffisamment) big/clever/etc enough (pour to); a. fatigué/etc (plutôt) fairly ou rather ou quite tired/etc.

assidu [asidy] a (appliqué) assiduous, diligent; a. auprès de attentive to. ◆**assiduité** nf assiduousness, diligence; pl (empressement) attentiveness. ◆**assidûment** adv assiduously.

assiég/er [asjeʒe] vt (ville) to besiege; (guichet) to mob, crowd round; (importuner) to pester, harry; assiégé de (demandes) besieged with; (maux) beset by. ◆–eant, -eante nmf besieger.

assiette [asjɛt] nf 1 (récipient) plate; a. anglaise Culin (assorted) cold meats, Am cold cuts. 2 (à cheval) seat; il n'est pas dans son a. he's feeling out of sorts.

assigner [asiɲe] vt (attribuer) to assign; Jur to summon, subpoena. ◆**assignation** nf Jur subpoena, summons.

assimiler [asimile] vt to assimilate; – s'a. vpr (immigrants) to assimilate, become assimilated (à with). ◆**assimilation** nf assimilation.

assis [asi] a sitting (down), seated; (caractère) settled; (situation) stable, secure.

assise [asiz] nf (base) foundation; pl Jur assizes; Pol congress; cour d'assises court of assizes.

assistance [asistɑ̃s] nf 1 (assemblée) audience; (nombre de personnes présentes) attendance, turn-out. 2 (aide) assistance; l'A. (publique) the child care service; enfant de l'A. child in care. ◆**assist/er** 1 vt (aider) to assist, help. 2 vi a (réunion, cours etc) to attend, be present at; (accident) to witness. ◆–ant, -ante nmf assistant; – nmpl (spectateurs) members of the audience; (témoins) those present; assistante sociale social worker; assistante maternelle mother's help.

associ/er [asɔsje] vt to associate (à with); a. qn à (ses travaux, profits) to involve s.o. in; s'a.à (collaborer) to associate with, become associated with; (aux vues ou au chagrin de qn) to share; (s'harmoniser) to combine with. ◆—é, -ée *nmf* partner, associate; – *a* associate. ◆**association** *nf* association; (*amitié, alliance*) partnership, association.

assoiffé [aswafe] *a* thirsty (**de** for).

assombrir [asɔ̃brir] *vt* (*obscurcir*) to darken; (*attrister*) to cast a cloud over, fill with gloom; – **s'a.** *vpr* to darken; to cloud over.

assomm/er [asɔme] *vt* (*animal*) to stun, brain; (*personne*) to knock unconscious; (*ennuyer*) to bore stiff. ◆—**ant** *a* tiresome, boring.

assomption [asɔ̃psjɔ̃] *nf Rel* Assumption.

assort/ir [asɔrtir] *vt*, – **s'a.** *vpr* to match. ◆—**i** *a* **bien a.** (*magasin*) well-stocked; – *apl* (*objets semblables*) matching; (*fromages etc variés*) assorted; **époux bien assortis** well-matched couple. ◆—**iment** *nm* assortment.

assoup/ir [asupir] *vt* (*personne*) to make drowsy; (*douleur, sentiment etc*) *Fig* to dull; – **s'a.** *vpr* to doze off; *Fig* to subside. ◆—**i** *a* (*personne*) drowsy. ◆—**issement** *nm* drowsiness.

assoupl/ir [asuplir] *vt* (*étoffe, muscles*) to make supple; (*corps*) to limber up; (*caractère*) to soften; (*règles*) to ease, relax. ◆—**issement** *nm* **exercices d'a.** limbering up exercises.

assourd/ir [asurdir] *vt* (*personne*) to deafen; (*son*) to muffle. ◆—**issant** *a* deafening.

assouvir [asuvir] *vt* to appease, satisfy.

assujett/ir [asyʒetir] *vt* (*soumettre*) to subject (**à** to); (*peuple*) to subjugate; (*fixer*) to secure; **s'a. à** to subject oneself to, submit to. ◆—**issant** *a* (*travail*) constraining. ◆—**issement** *nm* subjection; (*contrainte*) constraint.

assumer [asyme] *vt* (*tâche, rôle*) to assume, take on; (*emploi*) to take up, assume; (*remplir*) to fill, hold.

assurance [asyrɑ̃s] *nf* (*aplomb*) (self-)assurance; (*promesse*) assurance; (*contrat*) insurance; **a. au tiers/tous risques** third-party/comprehensive insurance; **assurances sociales =** national insurance, *Am =* social security.

assur/er [asyre] *vt* (*rendre sûr*) to ensure, *Am* make sure; (*par un contrat*) to insure; (*travail etc*) to carry out; (*fixer*) to secure; **a. à qn que** to assure s.o. that; **a. qn de qch, a. qch à qn** to assure s.o. of sth; – **s'a.** *vpr* (*se procurer*) to ensure, secure; (*par un contrat*) to insure oneself, get insured (**contre** against); **s'a. que/de** to make sure that/of. ◆—é, -ée *a* (*succès*) assured, certain; (*pas*) firm, secure; (*air*)

(self-)assured, (self-)confident; – *nmf* policyholder, insured person. ◆—**ément** *adv* certainly, assuredly. ◆**assureur** *nm* insurer.

astérisque [asterisk] *nm* asterisk.

asthme [asm] *nm* asthma. ◆**asthmatique** *a & nmf* asthmatic.

asticot [astiko] *nm* maggot, worm.

astiquer [astike] *vt* to polish.

astre [astr] *nm* star.

astreindre* [astrɛ̃dr] *vt* **a. à** (*discipline*) to compel to accept; **a. à faire** to compel to do. ◆**astreignant** *a* exacting ◆**astreinte** *nf* constraint.

astrologie [astrɔlɔʒi] *nf* astrology. ◆**astrologue** *nm* astrologer.

astronaute [astrɔnot] *nmf* astronaut. ◆**astronautique** *nf* space travel.

astronomie [astrɔnɔmi] *nf* astronomy. ◆**astronome** *nm* astronomer. ◆**astronomique** *a* astronomical.

astuce [astys] *nf* (*pour faire qch*) knack, trick; (*invention*) gadget; (*plaisanterie*) clever joke, wisecrack; (*finesse*) astuteness; **les astuces du métier** the tricks of the trade. ◆**astucieux, -euse** *a* clever, astute.

atelier [atəlje] *nm* (*d'ouvrier*) workshop; (*de peintre*) studio.

atermoyer [atɛrmwaje] *vi* to procrastinate.

athée [ate] *a* atheistic; – *nmf* atheist. ◆**athéisme** *nm* atheism.

Athènes [atɛn] *nm ou f* Athens.

athlète [atlɛt] *nmf* athlete. ◆**athlétique** *a* athletic. ◆**athlétisme** *nm* athletics.

atlantique [atlɑ̃tik] *a* Atlantic; – *nm* **l'A.** the Atlantic.

atlas [atlas] *nm* atlas.

atmosphère [atmɔsfɛr] *nf* atmosphere. ◆**atmosphérique** *a* atmospheric.

atome [atom] *nm* atom. ◆**atomique** [atɔmik] *a* atomic; **bombe a.** atom *ou* atomic bomb.

atomis/er [atɔmize] *vt* (*liquide*) to spray; (*région*) to destroy (*by atomic weapons*). ◆—**eur** *nm* spray.

atone [atɔn] *a* (*personne*) lifeless; (*regard*) vacant.

atours [atur] *nmpl Hum* finery.

atout [atu] *nm* trump card; (*avantage*) *Fig* trump card, asset; **l'a. est cœur** hearts are trumps.

âtre [ɑtr] *nm* (*foyer*) hearth.

atroce [atrɔs] *a* atrocious; (*crime*) heinous, atrocious. ◆**atrocité** *nf* atrociousness; *pl* (*actes*) atrocities.

atrophie [atrɔfi] *nf* atrophy. ◆**atrophié** *a* atrophied.

attabl/er (s') [satable] *vpr* to sit down at the table. ◆—é *a* (*seated*) at the table.

attache [ataʃ] *nf* (*objet*) attachment, fastening; *pl* (*liens*) links.

attach/er [ataʃe] *vt* (*lier*) to tie (up), attach (à to); (*boucler, fixer*) to fasten; **a. du prix/un sens à qch** to attach great value/a meaning to sth; **cette obligation m'attache à lui** this obligation binds me to him; **s'a**. à (*adhérer*) to stick to; (*se lier*) to become attached to; (*se consacrer*) to apply oneself to. ◆—**ant** *a* (*enfant etc*) engaging, appealing. ◆—**é, -ée** *nmf* (*personne*) *Pol Mil* attaché. ◆—**ement** *nm* attachment, affection.

attaque [atak] *nf* attack; **a. aérienne** air raid; **d'a.** in tip-top shape, on top form. ◆**attaqu/er** *vt*, **s'a.** à *vt* to attack; (*difficulté, sujet*) to tackle; – *vi* to attack. ◆—**ant, -ante** *nmf* attacker.

attard/er (s') [satarde] *vpr* (*chez qn*) to linger (on), stay on; (*en chemin*) to loiter, dawdle; **s'a. sur** ou **à** (*détails etc*) to linger over; **s'a. derrière qn** to lag behind s.o. ◆—**é** *a* (*enfant etc*) backward; (*passant*) late.

atteindre* [atɛ̃dr] *vt* (*parvenir à*) to reach; (*idéal*) to attain; (*blesser*) to hit, wound; (*toucher*) to affect; (*offenser*) to hurt, wound; **être atteint de** (*maladie*) to be suffering from.

atteinte [atɛ̃t] *nf* attack; **porter a. à** to attack, undermine; **a. à** (*honneur*) slur on; **hors d'a.** (*objet, personne*) out of reach; (*réputation*) unassailable.

attel/er [atle] *vt* (*bêtes*) to harness, hitch up; (*remorque*) to couple; **s'a. à** (*travail etc*) to apply oneself to. ◆—**age** *nm* harnessing; coupling; (*bêtes*) team.

attenant [atnɑ̃] *a* **a.** (**à**) adjoining.

attend/re [atɑ̃dr] *vt* to wait for, await; (*escompter*) to expect (**de** of, from); **elle attend un bébé** she's expecting a baby; – *vi* to wait; **s'a. à** to expect; **a. d'être informé** to wait to be informed; **a. que qn vienne** to wait for s.o. to come, wait until s.o. comes; **faire a. qn** to keep s.o. waiting; **se faire a.** (*réponse, personne etc*) to be a long time coming; **attends voir** *Fam* let me see; **en attendant** meanwhile; **en attendant que** (+ *sub*) until. ◆—**u** *a* (*avec joie*) eagerly-awaited; (*prévu*) expected; – *prép* considering; **a. que** considering that.

attendr/ir [atɑ̃drir] *vt* (*émouvoir*) to move (to compassion); (*viande*) to tenderize; – **s'a.** *vpr* to be moved (**sur** by). ◆—**i** *a*

compassionate. ◆—**issant** *a* moving. ◆—**issement** *nm* compassion.

attentat [atɑ̃ta] *nm* attempt (*on s.o.'s life*), murder attempt; *Fig* crime, outrage (**à** against); **a. (à la bombe)** (bomb) attack. ◆**attenter** *vi* **a. à** (*la vie de qn*) to make an attempt on; *Fig* to attack.

attente [atɑ̃t] *nf* (*temps*) wait(ing); (*espérance*) expectation(s); **une a. prolongée** a long wait; **être dans l'a. de** to be waiting for; **salle d'a.** waiting room.

attentif, -ive [atɑ̃tif, -iv] *a* (*personne*) attentive; (*travail, examen*) careful; **a. à** (*plaire etc*) anxious to; (*ses devoirs etc*) mindful of. ◆**attentivement** *adv* attentively.

attention [atɑ̃sjɔ̃] *nf* attention; *pl* (*égards*) consideration; **faire** ou **prêter a. à** (*écouter, remarquer*) to pay attention to; **faire a. à/que** (*prendre garde*) to be careful of/that; **a.!** look out!; **be careful!**; **a. à la voiture!** mind ou watch the car! ◆**attentionné** *a* considerate.

atténu/er [atenɥe] *vt* to attenuate, mitigate; – **s'a.** *vpr* to subside. ◆—**antes** *afpl* **circonstances a.** extenuating circumstances.

atterrer [atere] *vt* to dismay.

atterr/ir [aterir] *vi Av* to land. ◆—**issage** *nm Av* landing; **a. forcé** crash ou emergency landing.

attester [ateste] *vt* to testify to; **a. que** to testify that. ◆**attestation** *nf* (*document*) declaration, certificate.

attifer [atife] *vt Fam Péj* to dress up, rig out.

attirail [atiraj] *nm* (*équipement*) *Fam* gear.

attir/er [atire] *vt* (*faire venir*) to attract, draw; (*plaire à*) to attract; (*attention*) to draw (**sur** on); **a. qch à qn** (*causer*) to bring s.o. sth; (*gloire etc*) to win ou earn s.o. sth; **a. dans** (*coin, guet-apens*) to bring into; – **s'a.** *vpr* (*ennuis etc*) to bring upon oneself; (*sympathie de qn*) to win; **a. sur soi** (*colère de qn*) to bring down upon oneself. ◆—**ant** *a* attractive. ◆**attirance** *nf* attraction.

attiser [atize] *vt* (*feu*) to poke; (*sentiment*) *Fig* to rouse.

attitré [atitre] *a* (*représentant*) appointed; (*marchand*) regular.

attitude [atityd] *nf* attitude; (*maintien*) bearing.

attraction [atraksjɔ̃] *nf* attraction.

attrait [atrɛ] *nm* attraction.

attrape [atrap] *nf* trick. ◆**a.-nigaud** *nm* con, trick.

attraper [atrape] *vt* (*ballon, maladie, voleur, train etc*) to catch; (*accent, contravention etc*) to pick up; **se laisser a.** (*duper*) to get taken in *ou* tricked; **se faire a.** (*gronder*) *Fam* to get a telling off. ◆**attrapade** *nf* (*gronderie*) *Fam* telling off.

attrayant [atrɛjɑ̃] *a* attractive.

attribuer [atribɥe] *vt* (*donner*) to assign, allot (à to); (*imputer, reconnaître*) to attribute, ascribe (à to); (*décerner*) to grant, award (à to). ◆**attribuable** *a* attributable. ◆**attribution** *nf* assignment; attribution; (*de prix*) awarding; *pl* (*compétence*) powers.

attribut [atriby] *nm* attribute.

attrister [atriste] *vt* to sadden.

attroup/er [atrupe] *vt*, **— s'a.** *vpr* to gather. ◆**—ement** *nm* gathering, (*disorderly*) crowd.

au [o] *voir* à.

aubaine [obɛn] *nf* (**bonne**) **a.** stroke of good luck, godsend.

aube [ob] *nf* dawn; **dès l'a.** at the crack of dawn.

aubépine [obepin] *nf* hawthorn.

auberge [obɛrʒ] *nf* inn; **a. de jeunesse** youth hostel. ◆**aubergiste** *nmf* innkeeper.

aubergine [obɛrʒin] *nf* aubergine, eggplant.

aucun, -une [okœ̃, -yn] *a* no, not any; **il n'a a. talent** he has no talent, he doesn't have any talent; **a. professeur n'est venu** no teacher has come; *— pron* none, not any; **il n'en a a.** he has none (at all), he doesn't have any (at all); **plus qu'a.** more than any(one); **d'aucuns** some (people). ◆**aucunement** *adv* not at all.

audace [odas] *nf* (*courage*) daring, boldness; (*impudence*) audacity; *pl* daring innovations. ◆**audacieux, -euse** *a* daring, bold.

au-dedans, au-dehors, au-delà *voir* **dedans** etc.

au-dessous [odsu] *adv* (*en bas*) (down) below, underneath; (*moins*) below, under; (*à l'étage inférieur*) downstairs; *— prép* **au-d. de** (*arbre etc*) below, under, beneath; (*âge, prix*) under; (*température*) below; **au-d. de sa tâche** not up to *ou* unequal to one's task.

au-dessus [odsy] *adv* above; over; on top; (*à l'étage supérieur*) upstairs; *— prép* **au-d. de** above; over; (*âge, température, prix*) over; (*posé sur*) on top of.

au-devant [odvɑ̃dɑ̃] *prép* **aller au-d. de** (*personne*) to go to meet; (*danger*) to court; (*désirs de qn*) to anticipate.

audible [odibl] *a* audible.

audience [odjɑ̃s] *nf Jur* hearing; (*entretien*) audience.

audio [odjo] *a inv* (*cassette etc*) audio.

◆**audiophone** *nm* hearing aid.
◆**audio-visuel, -elle** *a* audio-visual.

auditeur, -trice [oditœr, -tris] *nmf Rad* listener; **les auditeurs** the audience; **a. libre** *Univ* auditor, student allowed to attend classes but not to sit examinations. ◆**auditif, -ive** *a* (*nerf*) auditory. ◆**audition** *nf* (*ouïe*) hearing; (*séance d'essai*) *Th* audition; (*séance musicale*) recital. ◆**auditionner** *vti* to audition. ◆**auditoire** *nm* audience. ◆**auditorium** *nm Rad* recording studio (*for recitals*).

auge [oʒ] *nf* (*feeding*) trough.

augmenter [ɔgmɑ̃te] *vt* to increase (**de** by); (*salaire, prix, impôt*) to raise, increase; **a. qn** to give s.o. a rise *ou Am* raise; *— vi* to increase (**de** by); (*prix, population*) to rise, go up. ◆**augmentation** *nf* increase (**de** in, of); **a. de salaire** (pay) rise, *Am* raise; **a. de prix** price rise *ou* increase.

augure [ɔgyr] *nm* (*présage*) omen; (*devin*) oracle; **être de bon/mauvais a.** to be a good/bad omen. ◆**augurer** *vt* to augur, predict.

auguste [ogyst] *a* august.

aujourd'hui [oʒurdɥi] *adv* today; (*actuellement*) nowadays, today; **a. en quinze** two weeks today.

aumône [omon] *nf* alms.

aumônier [omonje] *nm* chaplain.

auparavant [oparavɑ̃] *adv* (*avant*) before(hand); (*d'abord*) first.

auprès de [opreda] *prép* (*assis, situé etc*) by, close to, next to; (*en comparaison de*) compared to; **agir a. de** (*ministre etc*) to use one's influence with; **accès a. de qn** access to s.o.

auquel [okɛl] *voir* **lequel**.

aura, aurait [ora, orɛ] *voir* **avoir**.

auréole [oreol] *nf* (*de saint etc*) halo; (*trace*) ring.

auriculaire [orikyler] *nm* **l'a.** the little finger.

aurore [oror] *nf* dawn, daybreak.

ausculter [oskylte] *vt* (*malade*) to examine (*with a stethoscope*); (*cœur*) to listen to. ◆**auscultation** *nf Méd* auscultation.

auspices [ospis] *nmpl* **sous les a. de** under the auspices of.

aussi [osi] *adv* **1** (*comparaison*) as; **a. sage que** as wise as. **2** (*également*) too, also, as well; **moi a.** so do, can, am *etc* I; **a. bien que** as well as. **3** (*tellement*) so; **un repas a. délicieux** so delicious a meal, such a delicious meal. **4** *conj* (*donc*) therefore.

aussitôt [osito] *adv* immediately, at once; **a. que** as soon as; **a. levé, il partit** as soon as he was up, he left; **a. dit, a. fait** no sooner said than done.

austère [oster] *a* austere. ◆**austérité** *nf* austerity.

austral, *mpl* **-als** [ostral] *a* southern.

Australie [ostrali] *nf* Australia. ◆**australien, -ienne** *a & nmf* Australian.

autant [otɑ̃] *adv* **1 a. de ... que** (*quantité*) as much ... as; (*nombre*) as many ... as; **il a a. d'argent/de pommes que vous** he has as much money/as many apples as you. **2 a.** **de** (*tant de*) so much; (*nombre*) so many; **je n'ai jamais vu a. d'argent/de pommes** I've never seen so much money/so many apples; **pourquoi manges-tu a.?** why are you eating so much? **3 a. que** (*souffrir, lire etc*) as much as; **il lit a. que vous/que possible** he reads as much as you/as possible; **il n'a jamais souffert a.** he's never suffered as *ou* so much; **a. que je sache** as far as I know; **d'a. (plus) que** all the more (so) since; **d'a. moins que** even less since; **a. avouer/etc** we, *etc* might as well confess/*etc*; **en faire/dire a.** to do/say the same; **j'aimerais a. aller au cinéma** I'd just as soon go to the cinema.

autel [otel] *nm* altar.

auteur [otœr] *nm* (*de livre*) author, writer; (*de chanson*) composer; (*de procédé*) originator; (*de crime*) perpetrator; (*d'accident*) cause; **droit d'a.** copyright; **droits d'a.** royalties.

authenticité [otɑ̃tisite] *nf* authenticity. ◆**authentifier** *vt* to authenticate. ◆**authentique** *a* genuine, authentic.

autiste [otist] *a*, **autistique** *a* autistic.

auto [oto] *nf* car; **autos tamponneuses** bumper cars, dodgems.

auto- [oto] *préf* self-.

autobiographie [otobjɔgrafi] *nf* autobiography.

autobus [otobys] *nm* bus.

autocar [otokar] *nm* coach, bus.

autochtone [otɔktɔn] *a & nmf* native.

autocollant [otokɔlɑ̃] *nm* sticker.

autocrate [otokrat] *nm* autocrat. ◆**autocratique** *a* autocratic.

autocuiseur [otokɥizœr] *nm* pressure cooker.

autodéfense [otodefɑ̃s] *nf* self-defence.

autodestruction [otodestryksjɔ̃] *nf* self-destruction.

autodidacte [otodidakt] *a & nmf* self-taught (person).

autodrome [otodrom] *nm* motor-racing track.

auto-école [otoekɔl] *nf* driving school, school of motoring.

autographe [otograf] *nm* autograph.

automate [otomat] *nm* automaton. ◆**automation** *nf* automation. ◆**automatisation** *nf* automation. ◆**automatiser** *vt* to automate.

automatique [otomatik] *a* automatic; *— nm* **l'a. Tél** direct dialling. ◆**—ment** *adv* automatically.

automne [otɔn] *nm* autumn, *Am* fall. ◆**automnal, -aux** *a* autumnal.

automobile [otomobil] *nf & a* (motor)car, *Am* automobile; **l'a. Sp** motoring; **Salon de l'a.** Motor Show; **canot a.** motor boat. ◆**automobiliste** *nmf* motorist.

autonome [otonɔm] *a* (*région etc*) autonomous, self-governing; (*personne*) *Fig* independent. ◆**autonomie** *nf* autonomy.

autopsie [otɔpsi] *nf* autopsy, post-mortem.

autoradio [otoradjo] *nm* car radio.

autorail [otoraj] *nm* railcar.

autoris/er [otorize] *vt* (*habiliter*) to authorize (**à faire** to do); (*permettre*) to permit (**à faire** to do). ◆**—é** *a* (*qualifié*) authoritative. ◆**autorisation** *nf* authorization; permission.

autorité [otorite] *nf* authority. ◆**autoritaire** *a* authoritarian; (*homme, ton*) authoritative.

autoroute [otorut] *nf* motorway, *Am* highway, freeway.

auto-stop [otostɔp] *nm* hitchhiking; **faire de l'a.** to hitchhike. ◆**autostoppeur, -euse** *nmf* hitchhiker.

autour [otur] *adv* around; *— prép* **a. de** around.

autre [otr] *a & pron* other; **un a. livre** another book; **un a.** another (one); **d'autres** others; **as-tu d'autres questions?** have you any other *ou* further questions?; **qn/personne/rien d'a.** s.o./no one/nothing else; **a. chose/part** sth/somewhere else; **qui/quoi d'a.?** who/what else?; **l'un l'a., les uns les autres** each other; **l'un et l'a.** both (of them); **l'un ou l'a.** either (of them); **ni l'un ni l'a.** neither (of them); **les uns ... les autres** some ... others; **nous/vous autres Anglais** we/you English; **d'un moment à l'a.** any moment (now); **... et autres ...** and so on. ◆**autrement** *adv* (*différemment*) differently; (*sinon*) otherwise; (*plus*) far more (**que** than); **pas a. satisfait/etc** not particularly satisfied/*etc*.

autrefois [otrəfwa] *adv* in the past, in days gone by.

Autriche [otriʃ] nf Austria. ◆**autrichien, -ienne** a & nmf Austrian.

autruche [otryʃ] nf ostrich.

autrui [otrɥi] pron others, other people.

auvent [ovɑ̃] nm awning, canopy.

aux [o] voir **à**.

auxiliaire [oksiljɛr] a auxiliary; – nm Gram auxiliary; – nmf (aide) helper, auxiliary.

auxquels, -elles [okɛl] voir **lequel**.

avachir (s') [savaʃir] vpr (soulier, personne) to become flabby ou limp.

avait [avɛ] voir **avoir**.

aval (en) [ɑ̃naval] adv downstream (de from).

avalanche [avalɑ̃ʃ] nf avalanche; Fig flood, avalanche.

avaler [avale] vt to swallow; (livre) to devour; (mots) to mumble; – vi to swallow.

avance [avɑ̃s] nf (marche, progrès) advance; (de coureur, chercheur etc) lead; pl (galantes) advances; **à l'a., d'a., par a.** in advance; **en a.** (arriver, partir) early; (avant l'horaire prévu) ahead (of time); (dans son développement) ahead, in advance; (montre etc) fast; **en a. sur** (qn, son époque etc) ahead of, in advance of; **avoir une heure d'a.** (train etc) to be an hour early.

avanc/er [avɑ̃se] vt (thèse, argent) to advance; (date) to bring forward; (main, chaise) to move forward; (travail) to speed up; – vi to advance, move forward; (montre) to be fast; (faire saillie) to jut out (sur over); **a. en âge** to be getting on (in years); – **s'a.** vpr to advance, move forward; (faire saillie) to jut out. ◆**-é** a advanced; (saison) well advanced. ◆**-ée** nf projection, overhang. ◆**-ement** nm advancement.

avanie [avani] nf affront, insult.

avant [avɑ̃] prép before; **a. de voir** before seeing; **a. qu'il (ne) parte** before he leaves; **a. huit jours** within a week; **a. tout** above all; **a. toute chose** first and foremost; **a. peu** before long; – adv before; **en a.** (mouvement) forward; (en tête) ahead; **en a. de** in front of; **bien a. dans** (creuser etc) very deep(ly) into; **la nuit d'a.** the night before; – nm & a inv front; – nm (joueur) Sp forward.

avantage [avɑ̃taʒ] nm advantage; (bénéfice) Fin benefit; **tu as a. à le faire** it's worth your while to do it; **tirer a. de** to benefit from. ◆**avantager** vt (favoriser) to favour; (faire valoir) to show off to advantage. ◆**avantageux, -euse** a worthwhile, attractive; (flatteur) flattering; Péj conceited; **a. pour qn** advantageous to s.o.

avant-bras [avɑ̃bra] nm inv forearm. ◆**a.-centre** nm Sp centre-forward. ◆**a.-coureur** am **a.-coureur de** (signe) heralding. ◆**a.-dernier, -ière** a & nmf last but one. ◆**a.-garde** nf Mil advance guard; **d'a.-garde** (idée, film etc) avant-garde. ◆**a.-guerre** nm foretaste. ◆**a.-guerre** nm ou f pre-war period; **d'a.-guerre** pre-war. ◆**a.-hier** [avɑ̃tjɛr] adv the day before yesterday. ◆**a.-poste** nm outpost. ◆**a.-première** nf preview. ◆**a.-propos** nm inv foreword. ◆**a.-veille** nf **l'a.-veille** (de) two days before.

avare [avar] a miserly; **a. de** (compliments etc) sparing of; – nmf miser. ◆**avarice** nf avarice.

avarie(s) [avari] nf(pl) damage. ◆**avarié** a (aliment) spoiled, rotting.

avatar [avatar] nm Péj Fam misadventure.

avec [avɛk] prép with; (envers) to(wards); **et a. ça?** (dans un magasin) Fam anything else?; – adv **il est venu a.** (son chapeau etc) Fam he came with it.

avenant [avnɑ̃] a pleasing, attractive; **à l'a.** in keeping (de with).

avènement [avɛnmɑ̃] nm **l'a. de** the coming ou advent of; (roi) the accession of.

avenir [avnir] nm future; **d'a.** (personne, métier) with future prospects; **à l'a.** (désormais) in future.

aventure [avɑ̃tyr] nf adventure; (en amour) affair; **à l'a.** (marcher etc) aimlessly; **dire la bonne a. à qn** to tell s.o.'s fortune. ◆**aventur/er** vt to risk; (remarque) to venture; (réputation) to risk; – **s'a.** vpr to venture (sur on to, **à faire** to do). ◆**-é** a risky. ◆**aventureux, -euse** a (personne, vie) adventurous; (risqué) risky. ◆**aventurier, -ière** nmf Péj adventurer.

avenue [avny] nf avenue.

aver/er (s') [savere] vpr (juste etc) to prove (to be); **il s'avère que** it turns out that. ◆**-é** a established.

averse [avɛrs] nf shower, downpour.

aversion [avɛrsjɔ̃] nf aversion (pour to).

avert/ir [avɛrtir] vt (mettre en garde, menacer) to warn; (informer) to notify, inform. ◆**-i** a informed. ◆**-issement** nm warning; notification; (dans un livre) foreword. ◆**-isseur** nm Aut horn; **a. d'incendie** fire alarm.

aveu, -x [avø] nm confession; **de l'a.** by the admission of.

aveugle [avœgl] a blind; – nmf blind man, blind woman; **les aveugles** the blind. ◆**aveuglément** [-emɑ̃] adv blindly.

◆**aveugl/er** [avœgle] *vt* to blind. ◆**—ement** [-əmɑ̃] *nm* (*égarement*) blindness.

aveuglette (à l') [alavœglɛt] *adv* blindly; **chercher qch à l'a.** to grope for sth.

aviateur, -trice [avjatœr, -tris] *nmf* airman, airwoman. ◆**aviation** *nf* (*industrie, science*) aviation; (*armée de l'air*) air force; (*avions*) aircraft; **l'a.** *Sp* flying; **d'a.** (*terrain, base*) air-.

avide [avid] *a* (*rapace*) greedy (**de** for); **a. d'apprendre**/*etc* (*désireux*) eager to learn/*etc*. ◆**—ment** *adv* greedily. ◆**avidité** *nf* greed.

avilir [avilir] *vt* to degrade, debase.

avion [avjɔ̃] *nm* aircraft, (aero)plane, *Am* airplane; **a. à réaction** jet; **a. de ligne** airliner; **par a.** (*lettre*) airmail; **en a., par a.** (*voyager*) by plane, by air; **aller en a.** to fly.

aviron [avirɔ̃] *nm* oar; **faire de l'a.** to row, practise rowing.

avis [avi] *nm* opinion; *Pol Jur* judgement; (*communiqué*) notice; (*conseil*) & *Fin* advice; **à mon a.** in my opinion, to my mind; **changer d'a.** to change one's mind. ◆**avis/er** [avize] *vt* to advise, inform; (*voir*) to notice; **s'a. de qch** to realize sth suddenly; **s'a. de faire** to venture to do. ◆**—é** *a* prudent, wise; **bien/mal a.** well-/ill-advised.

aviver [avive] *vt* (*couleur*) to bring out; (*douleur*) to sharpen.

avocat, -ate [avɔka, -at] **1** *nmf* barrister, counsel, *Am* attorney, counselor; (*d'une cause*) *Fig* advocate. **2** *nm* (*fruit*) avocado (pear).

avoine [avwan] *nf* oats; **farine d'a.** oatmeal.

avoir* [avwar] **1** *v aux* to have; **je l'ai vu** I've seen him. **2** *vt* (*posséder*) to have; (*obtenir*) to get; (*tromper*) *Fam* to take for a ride; **il a** he has, he's got; **qu'est-ce que tu as?** what's the matter with you?, what's wrong with you?; **j'ai à lui parler** I have to speak

to her; **il n'a qu'à essayer** he only has to try; **a. faim/chaud**/*etc* to be *ou* feel hungry/hot/*etc*; **a. cinq ans**/*etc* to be five (years old)/*etc*; **en a. pour longtemps** to be busy for quite a while; **j'en ai pour dix minutes** this will take me ten minutes; (*ne bougez pas*) I'll be with you in ten minutes; **en a. pour son argent** to get *ou* have one's money's worth; **en a. après** *ou* **contre** to have a grudge against. **3** *v imp* **il y a** there is, *pl* there are; **il y a six ans** six years ago; **il n'y a pas de quoi!** don't mention it!; **qu'est-ce qu'il y a?** what's the matter?, what's wrong? *Fin* credit.

avoisin/er [avwazine] *vt* to border on. ◆**—ant** *a* neighbouring, nearby.

avort/er [avɔrte] *vi* (*projet etc*) *Fig* to miscarry, fail; (**se faire**) **a.** (*femme*) to have *ou* get an abortion. ◆**—ement** *nm* abortion; *Fig* failure. ◆**avorton** *nm* *Péj* runt, puny shrimp.

avou/er [avwe] *vt* to confess, admit (**que** that); **s'a. vaincu** to admit defeat; – *vi* (*coupable*) to confess. ◆**—é** *a* (*ennemi, but*) avowed; – *nm* solicitor, *Am* attorney.

avril [avril] *nm* April; **un poisson d'a.** (*farce*) an April fool joke.

axe [aks] *nm* *Math* axis; (*essieu*) axle; (*d'une politique*) broad direction; **grands axes** (*routes*) main roads. ◆**axer** *vt* to centre; **il est axé sur** his mind is drawn towards.

axiome [aksjom] *nm* axiom.

ayant [ɛjɑ̃] *voir* avoir.

azalée [azale] *nf* (*plante*) azalea.

azimuts [azimyt] *nmpl* **dans tous les a.** *Fam* all over the place, here there and everywhere; **tous a.** (*guerre, publicité etc*) all-out.

azote [azɔt] *nm* nitrogen.

azur [azyr] *nm* azure, (sky) blue; **la Côte d'A.** the (French) Riviera.

azyme [azim] *a* (*pain*) unleavened.

B

B, b [be] *nm* B, b.

babeurre [babœr] *nm* buttermilk.

babill/er [babije] *vi* to prattle, babble. ◆**—age** *nm* prattle, babble.

babines [babin] *nfpl* (*lèvres*) chops, chaps.

babiole [babjɔl] *nf* (*objet*) knick-knack; (*futilité*) trifle.

bâbord [babɔr] *nm* *Nau Av* port (side).

babouin [babwɛ̃] *nm* baboon.

baby-foot [babifut] *nm inv* table *ou* miniature football.

bac [bak] *nm* **1** (*bateau*) ferry(boat). **2** (*cuve*) tank; **b. à glace** ice tray; **b. à laver** washtub. **3** *abrév* = **baccalauréat.**

baccalauréat [bakalɔrea] *nm* school leaving certificate.

bâche [bɑʃ] nf (toile) tarpaulin. ◆**bâcher** vt to cover over (with a tarpaulin).

bachelier, -ière [baʃəlje, -jɛr] nmf holder of the baccalauréat.

bachot [baʃo] nm abrév = **baccalauréat.** ◆**bachoter** vi to cram (for an exam).

bacille [basil] nm bacillus, germ.

bâcler [bɑkle] vt (travail) to dash off carelessly, botch (up).

bactéries [bakteri] nfpl bacteria. ◆**bactériologique** a bacteriological; **la guerre b.** germ warfare.

badaud, -aude [bado, -od] nmf (inquisitive) onlooker, bystander.

baderne [badɛrn] nf **vieille b.** Péj old fogey, old fuddy-duddy.

badigeon [badiʒɔ̃] nm whitewash. ◆**badigeonner** vt (mur) to whitewash, distemper; (écorchure) Méd to paint, coat.

badin [badɛ̃] a (peu sérieux) light-hearted, playful. ◆**badiner** vi to jest, joke; **b. avec** (prendre à la légère) to trifle with. ◆**-age** nm banter, jesting.

badine [badin] nf cane, switch.

bafouer [bafwe] vt to mock ou scoff at.

bafouiller [bafuje] vti to stammer, splutter.

bâfrer [bɑfre] vi Fam to stuff oneself (with food).

bagage [bagaʒ] nm (valise etc) piece of luggage ou baggage; (connaissances) Fig (fund) of knowledge; pl (ensemble des valises) luggage, baggage. ◆**bagagiste** nm baggage handler.

bagarre [bagar] nf brawl. ◆**bagarrer** vi Fam to fight, struggle; — **se b.** vpr to fight, brawl; (se disputer) to quarrel.

bagatelle [bagatɛl] nf trifle, mere bagatelle; **la b. de** Iron the trifling sum of.

bagne [baɲ] nm convict prison; **c'est le b. ici** Fig this place is a real hell hole ou workhouse. ◆**bagnard** nm convict.

bagnole [baɲɔl] nf Fam car; **vieille b.** Fam old banger.

bagou(t) [bagu] nm Fam glibness; **avoir du b.** to have the gift of the gab.

bague [bag] nf (anneau) ring; (de cigare) band. ◆**bagué** a (doigt) ringed.

baguenauder [bagnode] vi, — **se b.** vpr to loaf around, saunter.

baguette [bagɛt] nf (canne) stick; (de chef d'orchestre) baton; (pain) (long thin) loaf, stick of bread; pl (de tambour) drumsticks; (pour manger) chopsticks; **b. (magique)** (magic) wand; **mener à la b.** to rule with an iron hand.

bah! [bɑ] int really!, bah!

bahut [bay] nm (meuble) chest, cabinet; (lycée) Fam school.

baie [be] nf 1 Géog bay. 2 Bot berry. 3 (fenêtre) picture window.

baignade [bɛɲad] nf (bain) bathe, bathing; (endroit) bathing place. ◆**baign/er** vt (immerger) to bathe; (enfant) to bath, Am bathe; **b. les rivages** (mer) to wash the shores; **baigné de** (sueur, lumière) bathed in; (sang) soaked in; — vi **b. dans** (tremper) to soak in; (être imprégné de) to be steeped in; — **se b.** vpr to go swimming ou bathing; (dans une baignoire) to have ou take a bath. ◆**-eur, -euse** 1 nmf bather. 2 nm (poupée) baby doll. ◆**baignoire** nf bath (tub).

bail, pl baux [baj, bo] nm lease. ◆**bailleur** nm Jur lessor; **b. de fonds** financial backer.

bâill/er [bɑje] vi to yawn; (chemise etc) to gape; (porte) to stand ajar. ◆**-ement** nm yawn; gaping.

bâillon [bɑjɔ̃] nm gag. ◆**bâillonner** vt (victime, presse etc) to gag.

bain [bɛ̃] nm bath; (de mer) swim, bathe; **salle de bain(s)** bathroom; **être dans le b.** (au courant) Fam to have got into the swing of things; **petit/grand b.** (piscine) shallow/deep end; **b. de bouche** mouthwash. ◆**b.-marie** nm (pl bains-marie) Culin double boiler.

baïonnette [bajɔnɛt] nf bayonet.

baiser [beze] 1 vt **b. au front/sur la joue** to kiss on the forehead/cheek; — nm kiss; **bons baisers** (dans une lettre) (with) love. 2 vt (duper) Fam to con.

baisse [bɛs] nf fall, drop (de in); **en b.** (température) falling.

baisser [bese] vt (voix, prix etc) to lower, drop; (tête) to bend; (radio, chauffage) to turn down; — vi (prix, niveau etc) to drop, go down; (soleil) to go down, sink; (marée) to go out, ebb; (santé, popularité) to decline; — **se b.** vpr to bend down, stoop.

bajoues [baʒu] nfpl (d'animal, de personne) chops.

bal, pl bals [bal] nm (réunion de grand apparat) ball; (populaire) dance; (lieu) dance hall.

balade [balad] nf walk; (en auto) drive; (excursion) tour. ◆**balader** vt (enfant etc) to take for a walk ou drive; (objet) to trail around; — **se b.** vpr (à pied) to (go for a) walk; (excursionner) to tour (around); **se b. (en voiture)** to go for a drive. ◆**baladeur** nm Walkman®. ◆**baladeuse** nf inspection lamp.

balafre [balafr] nf (blessure) gash, slash;

(*cicatrice*) scar. ◆**balafrer** *vt* to gash, slash; to scar.

balai [balɛ] *nm* broom; **b. mécanique** carpet sweeper; **manche à b.** broomstick; *Av* joystick. ◆**b.-brosse** *nm* (*pl* **balais-brosses**) garden brush *ou* broom (*for scrubbing paving stones*).

balance [balɑ̃s] *nf* (*instrument*) (pair of) scales; (*équilibre*) *Pol Fin* balance; **la B.** (*signe*) Libra; **mettre en b.** to balance, weigh up.

balanc/er [balɑ̃se] *vt* (*bras*) to swing; (*hanches, tête, branches*) to sway; (*lancer*) *Fam* to chuck; (*se débarrasser de*) *Fam* to chuck out; **b. un compte** *Fin* to balance an account; **— se b.** *vpr* (*personne*) to swing (from side to side); (*arbre, bateau etc*) to sway; **je m'en balance!** I couldn't care less! ◆**-é** **a bien b.** (*phrase*) well-balanced; (*personne*) *Fam* well-built. ◆**-ement** *nm* swinging; swaying. ◆**balancier** *nm* (*d'horloge*) pendulum; (*de montre*) balance wheel. ◆**balançoire** *nf* (*escarpolette*) swing; (*bascule*) seesaw.

balayer [baleje] *vt* (*chambre, rue*) to sweep (out *ou* up); (*enlever, chasser*) to sweep away; **le vent balayait la plaine** the wind swept the plain. ◆**balayette** [balɛjɛt] *nf* (hand) brush; (*balai*) short-handled broom. ◆**balayeur, -euse** [balɛjœr, -øz] *nmf* roadsweeper.

balbutier [balbysje] *vti* to stammer.

balcon [balkɔ̃] *nm* balcony; *Th Cin* dress circle.

baldaquin [baldakɛ̃] *nm* (*de lit etc*) canopy.

baleine [balɛn] *nf* (*animal*) whale; (*fanon*) whalebone; (*de parapluie*) rib. ◆**baleinier** *nm* (*navire*) whaler. ◆**baleinière** *nf* whaleboat.

balise [baliz] *nf* *Nau* beacon; *Av* (ground) light; *Aut* road sign. ◆**balis/er** *vt* to mark with beacons *ou* lights; (*route*) to signpost. ◆**-age** *nm* *Nau* beacons; *Av* lighting; *Aut* signposting.

balistique [balistik] *a* ballistic.

balivernes [balivɛrn] *nfpl* balderdash, nonsense.

ballade [balad] *nf* (*légende*) ballad; (*poème court*) &·*Mus* ballade.

ballant [balɑ̃] *a* (*bras, jambes*) dangling.

ballast [balast] *nm* ballast.

balle [bal] *nf* (*de tennis, golf etc*) ball; (*projectile*) bullet; (*paquet*) bale; *pl* (*francs*) *Fam* francs; **se renvoyer la b.** to pass the buck (to each other).

ballet [balɛ] *nm* ballet. ◆**ballerine** *nf* ballerina.

ballon [balɔ̃] *nm* (*jouet d'enfant*) & *Av* balloon; (*sport*) ball; **b. de football** football; **lancer un b. d'essai** *Fig* to put out a feeler. ◆**ballonné** *a* (*ventre*) bloated, swollen. ◆**ballot** *nm* (*paquet*) bundle; (*imbécile*) *Fam* idiot.

ballottage [balɔtaʒ] *nm* (*scrutin*) second ballot (*no candidate having achieved the required number of votes*).

ballotter [balɔte] *vti* to shake (about); **ballotté entre** (*sentiments contraires*) torn between.

balnéaire [balneɛr] *a* **station b.** seaside resort.

balourd, -ourde [balur, -urd] *nmf* (clumsy) oaf. ◆**balourdise** *nf* clumsiness, oafishness; (*gaffe*) blunder.

Baltique [baltik] *nf* **la B.** the Baltic.

balustrade [balystrad] *nf* (hand)rail, railing(s).

bambin [bɑ̃bɛ̃] *nm* tiny tot, toddler.

bambou [bɑ̃bu] *nm* bamboo.

ban [bɑ̃] *nm* (*de tambour*) roll; (*applaudissements*) round of applause; *pl* (*de mariage*) banns; **mettre qn au b. de** to cast s.o. out from, outlaw s.o. from; **un b. pour . . .** three cheers for . . . .

banal, mpl -als [banal] *a* (*fait, accident etc*) commonplace, banal; (*idée, propos*) banal, trite. ◆**banalisé** *a* (*voiture de police*) unmarked. ◆**banalité** *nf* banality; *pl* (*propos*) banalities.

banane [banan] *nf* banana.

banc [bɑ̃] *nm* (*siège, établi*) bench; (*de poissons*) shoal; **b. d'église** pew; **b. d'essai** *Fig* testing ground; **b. de sable** sandbank; **b. des accusés** *Jur* dock.

bancaire [bɑ̃kɛr] *a* (*opération*) banking-; (*chèque*) bank-.

bancal, mpl -als [bɑ̃kal] *a* (*personne*) bandy, bow-legged; (*meuble*) wobbly; (*idée*) shaky.

bande [bɑ̃d] *nf* **1** (*de terrain, papier etc*) strip; (*de film*) reel; (*de journal*) wrapper; (*rayure*) stripe; (*de fréquences*) *Rad* band; (*pansement*) bandage; (*sur la chaussée*) line; **b. magnétique**) tape; **b. vidéo** videotape; **b. sonore** sound track; **b. dessinée** comic strip, strip cartoon; **par la b.** indirectly. **2** (*groupe*) gang, troop, band; (*de chiens*) pack; (*d'oiseaux*) flock; **on a fait b. à part** we split into our own group; **b. d'idiots!** you load of idiots! ◆**bandeau, -x** *nm* (*sur les yeux*) blindfold; (*pour la tête*) headband; (*pansement*) head bandage. ◆**band/er** *vt* (*blessure etc*) to bandage; (*yeux*) to blindfold; (*arc*) to bend; (*muscle*) to tense. ◆**—age** nm (pansement) bandage.

banderole [bɑ̃drɔl] nf (sur mât) pennant, streamer; (sur montants) banner.

bandit [bɑ̃di] nm robber, bandit; (enfant) Fam rascal. ◆**banditisme** nm crime.

bandoulière [bɑ̃duljɛr] nf shoulder strap; **en b.** slung across the shoulder.

banjo [bɑ̃(d)ʒo] nm Mus banjo.

banlieue [bɑ̃ljø] nf suburbs, outskirts; **la grande b.** the outer suburbs; **de b.** (magasin etc) suburban; (train) commuter-. ◆**banlieusard, -arde** nmf (habitant) suburbanite; (voyageur) commuter.

banne [ban] nf (de magasin) awning.

bannière [banjɛr] nf banner.

bann/ir [banir] vt (exiler) to banish; (supprimer) to ban, outlaw. ◆**—issement** nm banishment.

banque [bɑ̃k] nf bank; (activité) banking.

banqueroute [bɑ̃krut] nf (fraudulent) bankruptcy.

banquet [bɑ̃kɛ] nm banquet.

banquette [bɑ̃kɛt] nf (bench) seat.

banquier [bɑ̃kje] nm banker.

banquise [bɑ̃kiz] nf ice floe ou field.

baptême [batɛm] nm christening, baptism; **b. du feu** baptism of fire; **b. de l'air** first flight. ◆**baptiser** vt (enfant) to christen, baptize; (appeler) Fig to christen.

baquet [bakɛ] nm tub, basin.

bar [bar] nm **1** (lieu, comptoir, meuble) bar. **2** (poisson marin) bass.

baragouin [baragwɛ̃] nm gibberish, gabble. ◆**baragouiner** vt (langue) to gabble (a few words of); – vi to gabble away.

baraque [barak] nf hut, shack; (maison) Fam house, place; Péj hovel; (de forain) stall. ◆**—ment** nm (makeshift) huts.

baratin [baratɛ̃] nm Fam sweet talk; Com patter. ◆**baratiner** vt to chat up; Am sweet-talk.

barbare [barbar] a (manières, crime) barbaric; (peuple, invasions) barbarian; – nmf barbarian. ◆**barbarie** nf (cruauté) barbarity. ◆**barbarisme** nm Gram barbarism.

barbe [barb] nf beard; **une b. de trois jours** three days' growth of beard; **se faire la b.** to shave; **à la b. de** under the nose(s) of; **rire dans sa b.** to laugh up one's sleeve; **la b.!** enough!; **quelle b.!** what a drag!; **b. à papa** candyfloss, Am cotton candy.

barbecue [barbəkju] nm barbecue.

barbelé [barbəle] a barbed; – nmpl barbed wire.

barb/er [barbe] vt Fam to bore (stiff); – se

b. vpr to be ou get bored (stiff). ◆**—ant** a Fam boring.

barbiche [barbiʃ] nf goatee (beard).

barbiturique [barbityrik] nm barbiturate.

barbot/er [barbɔte] **1** vi (s'agiter) to splash about, paddle. **2** vt (voler) Fam to filch. ◆**—euse** nf (de bébé) rompers.

barbouill/er [barbuje] vt (salir) to smear; (peindre) to daub; (gribouiller) to scribble; **avoir l'estomac barbouillé** Fam to feel queasy. ◆**—age** nm smear; daub; scribble.

barbu [barby] a bearded.

barda [barda] nm Fam gear; (de soldat) kit.

bardé [barde] a **b. de** (décorations etc) covered with.

barder [barde] v imp ça va b.! Fam there'll be fireworks!

barème [barɛm] nm (des tarifs) table; (des salaires) scale; (livre de comptes) ready reckoner.

baril [bari(l)] nm barrel; **b. de poudre** powder keg.

bariolé [barjɔle] a brightly-coloured.

barman, pl **-men** ou **-mans** [barman, -mɛn] nm barman, Am bartender.

baromètre [barɔmɛtr] nm barometer.

baron, -onne [barɔ̃, -ɔn] nm baron; – nf baroness.

baroque [barɔk] **1** a (idée etc) bizarre, weird. **2** a & nm Archit Mus Liter baroque.

baroud [barud] nm **b. d'honneur** Arg gallant last fight.

barque [bark] nf (small) boat.

barre [bar] nf bar; (trait) line, stroke; Nau helm; **b. de soustraction** minus sign; **b. fixe** Sp horizontal bar. ◆**barreau, -x** (de fenêtre etc) & Jur bar; (d'échelle) rung.

barr/er [bare] **1** vt (route etc) to block (off), close (off); (porte) to bar; (chèque) to cross; (phrase) to cross out; Nau to steer; **b. la route à qn** to bar s.o.'s way; 'rue barrée' 'road closed'. **2 se b.** vpr Arg to hop it, make off. ◆**—age** nm (sur une route) roadblock; (barrière) barrier; (ouvrage hydraulique) dam; (de petite rivière) weir; **le b. d'une rue** the closure of a street; **tir de b.** barrage fire; **b. d'agents** cordon of police. ◆**—eur** nm Sp Nau cox.

barrette [barɛt] nf (pince) (hair)slide, Am barrette.

barricade [barikad] nf barricade. ◆**barricader** vt to barricade; – **se b.** vpr to barricade oneself.

barrière [barjɛr] nf (porte) gate; (clôture) fence; (obstacle, mur) barrier.

barrique [barik] nf (large) barrel.

baryton [baritɔ̃] *nm* baritone.

bas¹, basse [bɑ, bɑs] *a* (*table, prix etc*) low; (*âme, action*) base, mean; (*partie de ville etc*) lower; (*origine*) lowly; **au b. mot** at the very least; **enfant en b. âge** young child; **avoir la vue basse** to be short-sighted; **le b. peuple** *Péj* the lower orders; **coup b.** *Boxe* blow below the belt; — *adv* low; (*parler*) in a whisper, softly; **mettre b.** (*animal*) to give birth; **mettre b. les armes** to lay down one's arms; **jeter b.** to overthrow; **en b.** down (below); (*par l'escalier*) downstairs, down below; **en ou au b. de** at the foot *ou* bottom of; **de haut en b.** from top to bottom; **sauter à b. du lit** to jump out of bed; **à b. les dictateurs/etc!** down with dictators/etc!; — *nm* (*de côte, page etc*) bottom, foot; **du b.** (*tiroir, étagère*) bottom.

bas² [bɑ] *nm* (*chaussette*) stocking; **b. de laine** *Fig* nest egg.

basané [bazane] *a* (*visage etc*) tanned.

bas-bleu [bablø] *nm Péj* bluestocking.

bas-côté [bakote] *nm* (*de route*) roadside, shoulder.

bascule [baskyl] *nf* (*jeu de*) **b.** (game of) seesaw; (*balance à*) **b.** weighing machine; **cheval/fauteuil à b.** rocking horse/chair. ◆**basculer** *vti* (*personne*) to topple over; (*benne*) to tip up.

base [baz] *nf* base; (*principe fondamental*) basis, foundation; **de b.** (*salaire etc*) basic; **produit à b. de lait** milk-based product; **militant de b.** rank-and-file militant. ◆**baser** *vt* to base; **se b. sur** to base oneself on.

bas-fond [bafɔ̃] *nm* (*eau*) shallows; (*terrain*) low ground; *pl* (*population*) *Péj* dregs.

basilic [bazilik] *nm Bot Culin* basil.

basilique [bazilik] *nf* basilica.

basket(-ball) [basket(bol)] *nm* basketball.

basque [bask] **1** *a & nmf* Basque. **2** *nfpl* (*pans de veste*) skirts.

basse [bɑs] **1** *voir* **bas¹**. **2** *nf Mus* bass.

basse-cour [baskur] *nf* (*pl* **basses-cours**) farmyard.

bassement [basmɑ̃] *adv* basely, meanly. ◆**bassesse** *nf* baseness, meanness; (*action*) base *ou* mean act.

bassin [basɛ̃] *nm* (*pièce d'eau*) pond; (*piscine*) pool; (*cuvette*) bowl, basin; (*rade*) dock; *Anat* pelvis; *Géog* basin; **b. houiller** ·coalfield. ◆**bassine** *nf* bowl.

basson [basɔ̃] *nm* (*instrument*) bassoon; (*musicien*) bassoonist.

bastingage [bastɛ̃gaʒ] *nm Nau* bulwarks, rail.

bastion [bastjɔ̃] *nm* bastion.

bastringue [bastrɛ̃g] *nm* (*bal*) *Fam* popular dance hall; (*tapage*) *Arg* shindig, din; (*attirail*) *Arg* paraphernalia.

bas-ventre [bavɑ̃tr] *nm* lower abdomen.

bat [ba] *voir* **battre**.

bât [ba] *nm* packsaddle.

bataclan [bataklɑ̃] *nm Fam* paraphernalia; **et tout le b.** *Fam* and the whole caboodle.

bataille [bataj] *nf* battle; *Cartes* beggar-my-neighbour. ◆**bataill/er** *vi* to fight, battle. ◆**—eur, -euse** *nmf* fighter; — *a* belligerent. ◆**bataillon** *nm* battalion.

bâtard, -arde [batar, -ard] *a & nmf* bastard; **chien b.** mongrel; **œuvre bâtarde** hybrid work.

bateau, -x [bato] *nm* boat; (*grand*) ship. ◆**b.-citerne** *nm* (*pl* **bateaux-citernes**) tanker. ◆**b.-mouche** *nm* (*pl* **bateaux-mouches**) (*sur la Seine*) pleasure boat.

batifoler [batifɔle] *vi Hum* to fool *ou* lark about.

bâtiment [batimɑ̃] *nm* (*édifice*) building; (*navire*) vessel; **le b.** the building, the building trade; **ouvrier du b.** building worker. ◆**bât/ir** *vt* (*construire*) to build; (*coudre*) to baste, tack; **terrain à b.** building site. ◆**—i** *a* **bien b.** well-built; — *nm Menuis* frame, support. ◆**bâtisse** *nf Péj* building. ◆**bâtisseur, -euse** *nm* builder.

bâton [batɔ̃] *nm* (*canne*) stick; (*de maréchal, d'agent*) baton; **b. de rouge** lipstick; **donner des coups de b. à qn** to beat s.o (with a stick); **parler à bâtons rompus** to ramble from one subject to another; **mettre des bâtons dans les roues à qn** to put obstacles in s.o.'s way.

batterie [batri] *nf Mil Aut* battery; **la b.** *Mus* the drums; **b. de cuisine** set of kitchen utensils.

batt/re* [batr] **1** *vt* (*frapper, vaincre*) to beat; (*blé*) to thresh; (*cartes*) to shuffle; (*pays, chemins*) to scour; (*à coups redoublés*) to batter, pound; **b. la mesure** to beat time; **b. à mort** to batter *ou* beat to death; **b. pavillon** to fly a flag; — *vi* to beat; (*porte*) to bang; **b. des mains** to clap (one's hands); **b. des paupières** to blink; **b. des ailes** (*oiseau*) to flap its wings; **le vent fait b. la porte** the wind bangs the door. **2 se b.** *vpr* to fight. ◆**—ant -e** (*pluie*) driving; (*porte*) swing. ◆**—ant** *nm* (*de cloche*) tongue; (*vantail de porte etc*) flap; **porte à deux battants** double door. **3** *nm* (*personne*) fighter. ◆**—u** *a* **chemin ou sentier b.** beaten track. ◆**—age** *nm* (*du blé*) threshing; (*publicité*) *Fam* publicity, hype, ballyhoo. ◆**—ement** nm (de cœur, de tambour) beat; (délai) interval; **battements de cœur** palpitations. ◆**—eur** nm (musicien) percussionist; **b. à œufs** egg beater.

baudet [bodɛ] nm donkey.

baume [bom] nm (résine) & Fig balm.

baux [bo] voir **bail.**

bavard, -arde [bavar, -ard] a (loquace) talkative; (cancanier) gossipy; – nmf chatterbox; gossip. ◆**bavard/er** vi to chat, chatter; (papoter) to gossip; (divulguer) to blab. ◆**—age** nm chatting, chatter(ing); gossip(ing).

bave [bav] nf dribble, slobber; foam; (de limace) slime. ◆**baver** vi to dribble, slobber; (chien enragé) to foam; (encre) to smudge; **en b.** Fam to have a rough time of it. ◆**bavette** nf bib. ◆**baveux, -euse** a (bouche) slobbery; (omelette) runny. ◆**bavoir** nm bib. ◆**bavure** nf smudge; (erreur) blunder; **sans b.** perfect(ly), flawless(ly).

bazar [bazar] nm (magasin, marché) bazaar; (désordre) mess, clutter; (attirail) Fam stuff, gear. ◆**bazarder** vt Fam to sell off, get rid of.

bazooka [bazuka] nm bazooka.

béant [beã] a (plaie) gaping; (gouffre) yawning.

béat [bea] a Péj smug; (heureux) Hum blissful. ◆**béatitude** nf Hum bliss.

beau (or **bel** before vowel or mute h), **belle**, pl **beaux, belles** [bo, bɛl] a (femme, fleur etc) beautiful, attractive; (homme) handsome, good-looking; (voyage, temps etc) fine, lovely; **au b. milieu** right in the middle; **j'ai b. crier/essayer/etc** it's no use (my) shouting/trying/etc; **un b. morceau** a good or sizeable bit; **de plus belle** (recommencer etc) worse than ever; **bel et bien** really; – nm **le b.** the beautiful; **faire le b.** (chien) to sit up and beg; **le plus b. de l'histoire** the best part of the story; – nf (femme) beauty; Sp deciding game.

beaucoup [boku] adv (lire etc) a lot, a great deal; **aimer b.** to like very much; **s'intéresser b. à** to be very interested in; **b. de** (livres etc) many, a lot ou a great deal of; (courage etc) a lot ou a great deal of, much; **pas b. d'argent/etc** not much money/etc; **j'en ai b.** (quantité) I have a lot; (nombre) I have many; **b. plus/moins** much more/less; **many more/fewer; b.** trop much too much; much too many; **de b.** by far; **b. sont . . .** many are . . . .

beau-fils [bofis] nm (pl **beaux-fils**) (d'un

précédent mariage) stepson; (gendre) son-in-law. ◆**b.-frère** nm (pl **beaux-frères**) brother-in-law. ◆**b.-père** nm (pl **beaux-pères**) father-in-law; (parâtre) stepfather.

beauté [bote] nf beauty; **institut** ou **salon de b.** beauty parlour; **en b.** (gagner etc) magnificently; **être en b.** to look one's very best; **de toute b.** beautiful.

beaux-arts [bozar] nmpl fine arts. ◆**b.-parents** nmpl parents-in-law.

bébé [bebe] nm baby; **b.-lion**/etc (pl **bébés-lions**/etc) baby lion/etc.

bébête [bebɛt] a Fam silly.

bec [bɛk] nm (d'oiseau) beak, bill; (de cruche) lip, spout; (de plume) nib; (bouche) Fam mouth; Mus mouthpiece; **coup de b.** peck; **b. de gaz** gas lamp; **clouer le b. à qn** Fam to shut s.o. up; **tomber sur un b.** Fam to come up against a serious snag. ◆**b.-de-cane** nm (pl **becs-de-cane**) door handle.

bécane [bekan] nf Fam bike.

bécarre [bekar] nm Mus natural.

bécasse [bekas] nf (oiseau) woodcock; (personne) Fam simpleton.

bêche [bɛʃ] nf spade. ◆**bêcher** vt **1** (cultiver) to dig. **2** Fig to criticize; (snober) to snub. ◆**bêcheur, -euse** nmf snob.

bécot [beko] nm Fam kiss. ◆**bécoter** vt, – **se b.** vpr Fam to kiss.

becquée [beke] nf beakful; **donner la b. à** (oiseau, enfant) to feed. ◆**becqueter** vt (picorer) to peck (at); (manger) Fam to eat.

bedaine [bədɛn] nf Fam paunch, potbelly.

bedeau, -x [bədo] nm beadle, verger.

bedon [bədõ] nm Fam paunch. ◆**bedonnant** a paunchy, potbellied.

bée [be] a **bouche b.** open-mouthed.

beffroi [befrwa] nm belfry.

bégayer [begeje] vi to stutter, stammer. ◆**bègue** [bɛg] nmf stutterer, stammerer; – a **être b.** to stutter, stammer.

bégueule [begœl] a prudish; – nf prude.

béguin [begɛ̃] nm **avoir le b. pour qn** Fam to have taken a fancy to s.o.

beige [bɛʒ] a & nm beige.

beignet [bɛɲɛ] nm Culin fritter.

bel [bɛl] voir **beau.**

bêler [bele] vi to bleat.

belette [bəlɛt] nf weasel.

Belgique [bɛlʒik] nf Belgium. ◆**belge** a & nmf Belgian.

bélier [belje] nm (animal, machine) ram; **le B.** (signe) Aries.

belle [bɛl] voir **beau.**

belle-fille [bɛlfij] nf (pl **belles-filles**) (d'un

précédent mariage) stepdaughter; (*bru*) daughter-in-law. ◆**b.-mère** *nf* (*pl* **belles-mères**) mother-in-law; (*marâtre*) stepmother. ◆**b.-sœur** *nf* (*pl* **belles-sœurs**) sister-in-law.

belligérant [belizerã] *a* & *nm* belligerent.

belliqueux, -euse [belikø, -øz] *a* warlike; *Fig* aggressive.

belvédère [belvedɛr] *nm* (*sur une route*) viewpoint.

bémol [bemɔl] *nm Mus* flat.

bénédiction [benediksjɔ̃] *nf* blessing, benediction.

bénéfice [benefis] *nm* (*gain*) profit; (*avantage*) benefit; **b.** (**ecclésiastique**) living, benefice. ◆**bénéficiaire** *nmf* beneficiary; – *a* (*marge, solde*) profit-. ◆**bénéficier** *vi* **b. de** to benefit from, have the benefit of. ◆**bénéfique** *a* beneficial.

Bénélux [benelyks] *nm* Benelux.

benêt [bənɛ] *nm* simpleton; – *am* simple-minded.

bénévole [benevɔl] *a* voluntary, unpaid.

bénin, -igne [benɛ̃, -iɲ] *a* (*tumeur, critique*) benign; (*accident*) minor.

bénir [benir] *vt* to bless; (*exalter, remercier*) to give thanks to. ◆**bénit** *a* (*pain*) consecrated; **eau bénite** holy water. ◆**bénitier** [-itje] *nm* (*holy-water*) stoup.

benjamin, -ine [bɛ̃ʒamɛ̃, -in] *nmf* youngest child; *Sp* junior.

benne [bɛn] *nf* (*de grue*) scoop; (*à charbon*) tub, skip; (*de téléphérique*) cable car; **camion à b. basculante** dump truck; **b. à ordures** skip.

béotien, -ienne [beɔsjɛ̃, -jɛn] *nmf* (*inculte*) philistine.

béquille [bekij] *nf* (*canne*) crutch; (*de moto*) stand.

bercail [bɛrkaj] *nm* (*famille etc*) *Hum* fold.

berceau, -x [bɛrso] *nm* cradle.

berc/er [bɛrse] *vt* (*balancer*) to rock; (*apaiser*) to lull; (*leurrer*) to delude (**de** with); **se b. d'illusions** to delude oneself. ◆**-euse** *nf* lullaby.

béret [berɛ] *nm* beret.

berge [bɛrʒ] *nf* (*rivage*) (raised) bank.

berger, -ère [bɛrʒe, -ɛr] **1** *nm* shepherd; **chien (de) b.** sheepdog; – *nf* shepherdess. **2** *nm* **b. allemand** Alsatian (dog), *Am* German shepherd. ◆**bergerie** *nf* sheepfold.

berline [bɛrlin] *nf Aut* (four-door) saloon, *Am* sedan.

berlingot [bɛrlɛ̃go] *nm* (*bonbon aux fruits*) boiled sweet; (*à la menthe*) mint; (*emballage*) (milk) carton.

berlue [bɛrly] *nf* **avoir la b.** to be seeing things.

berne (en) [ãbɛrn] *adv* at half-mast.

berner [bɛrne] *vt* to fool, hoodwink.

besogne [bəzɔɲ] *nf* work, job, task. ◆**besogneux, -euse** *a* needy.

besoin [bazwɛ̃] *nm* need; **avoir b. de** to need; **au b.** if necessary, if need(s) be; **dans le b.** in need, needy.

bestial, -aux [bɛstjal, -o] *a* bestial, brutish. ◆**bestiaux** *nmpl* livestock; (*bovins*) cattle. ◆**bestiole** *nf* (*insecte*) creepy-crawly, bug.

bétail [betaj] *nm* livestock; (*bovins*) cattle.

bête[1] [bɛt] *nf* animal; (*bestiole*) bug, creature; **b. de somme** beast of burden; **b. à bon dieu** ladybird, *Am* ladybug; **b. noire** pet hate, pet peeve; **chercher la petite b.** (*critiquer*) to pick holes.

bête[2] [bɛt] *a* silly, stupid. ◆**bêtement** *adv* stupidly; **tout b.** quite stupidly. ◆**bêtise** [betiz] *nf* silliness, stupidity; (*action, parole*) silly *ou* stupid thing; (*bagatelle*) mere trifle.

béton [betɔ̃] *nm* concrete; **en b.** concrete-; **b. armé** reinforced concrete. ◆**bétonnière** *nf*, ◆**bétonneuse** *nf* cement *ou* concrete mixer.

betterave [bɛtrav] *nf Culin* beetroot, *Am* beet; **b. sucrière** *ou* **à sucre** sugar beet.

beugler [bøgle] *vi* (*taureau*) to bellow; (*vache*) to moo; (*radio*) to blare (out).

beurre [bœr] *nm* butter; **b. d'anchois** anchovy paste. ◆**beurrer** *vt* to butter. ◆**beurrier** *nm* butter dish.

beuverie [bøvri] *nf* drinking session, booze-up.

bévue [bevy] *nf* blunder, mistake.

biais [bjɛ] *nm* (*moyen détourné*) device, expedient; (*aspect*) angle; **regarder de b.** to look at sidelong; **traverser en b.** to cross at an angle. ◆**biaiser** [bjeze] *vi* to prevaricate, hedge.

bibelot [biblo] *nm* curio, trinket.

biberon [bibrɔ̃] *nm* (feeding) bottle.

bible [biblə] *nf* bible; **la B.** the Bible. ◆**biblique** *a* biblical.

bibliobus [biblijɔbys] *nm* mobile library.

bibliographie [biblijɔgrafi] *nf* bibliography.

bibliothèque [biblijɔtɛk] *nf* library; (*meuble*) bookcase; (*à la gare*) bookstall. ◆**bibliothécaire** *nmf* librarian.

bic® [bik] *nm* ballpoint, biro®.

bicarbonate [bikarbɔnat] *nm* bicarbonate.

bicentenaire [bisɑ̃tnɛr] *nm* bicentenary, bicentennial.

biceps [bisɛps] *nm Anat* biceps.

biche [biʃ] *nf* doe, hind; **ma b.** *Fig* my pet.

bichonner [biʃɔne] vt to doll up.

bicoque [bikɔk] nf Péj shack, hovel.

bicyclette [bisiklɛt] nf bicycle, cycle; **la b.** Sp cycling; **aller à b.** to cycle.

bide [bid] nm (ventre) Fam belly; **faire un b.** Arg to flop.

bidet [bide] nm (cuvette) bidet.

bidon [bidɔ̃] **1** nm (d'essence) can; (pour boissons) canteen; (ventre) Fam belly. **2** nm **du b.** Fam rubbish, bluff; – a inv (simulé) Fam fake, phoney. **◆se bidonner** vpr Fam to have a good laugh.

bidonville [bidɔ̃vil] nf shantytown.

bidule [bidyl] nm (chose) Fam thingummy, whatsit.

bielle [bjɛl] nf Aut connecting rod.

bien [bjɛ̃] adv well; **il joue b.** he plays well; **je vais b.** I'm fine ou well; **b. fatigué/souvent/etc** (très) very tired/often/etc; **merci b.!** thanks very much!; **b.! fine!, right!; b. du courage/etc** a lot of courage/etc; **b. des fois/des gens/etc** lots of ou many times/people/etc; **je l'ai b. dit** (intensif) I did say so; **c'est b. compris?** is that quite understood?; **c'est b. toi?** is it really you?; **tu as b. fait** you did right; **c'est b. fait (pour lui)** it serves him right; – a inv (convenable) all right, fine; (agréable) nice, fine; (compétent, bon) good, fine; (à l'aise) comfortable, fine; (beau) attractive; (en forme) well; (moralement) nice; **une fille b.** a nice ou respectable girl; – nm (avantage) good; (capital) possession; **ça te fera du b.** it will do you good; **le b. et le mal** good and evil; **biens de consommation** consumer goods. **◆b.-aimé, -ée** a & nmf beloved. **◆b.-être** nm wellbeing. **◆b.-fondé** nm validity, soundness.

bienfaisance [bjɛ̃fəzɑ̃s] nf benevolence, charity; **de b.** (société etc) benevolent, charitable. **◆bienfaisant** a beneficial.

bienfait [bjɛ̃fɛ] nm (générosité) favour; pl benefits, blessings. **◆bienfaiteur, -trice** nmf benefactor, benefactress.

bienheureux, -euse [bjɛ̃nœrø, -øz] a blessed, blissful.

biennal, -aux [bjenal, -o] a biennial.

bien que [bjɛ̃k(ə)] conj although.

bienséant [bjɛ̃seɑ̃] a proper. **◆bienséance** nf propriety.

bientôt [bjɛ̃to] adv soon; **à b.!** see you soon!; **il est b. dix heures/etc** it's nearly ten o'clock/etc.

bienveillant [bjɛ̃vejɑ̃] a kindly. **◆bienveillance** nf kindliness.

bienvenu, -ue [bjɛ̃vny] a welcome; – nmf

soyez le b.! welcome!; – nf welcome; **souhaiter la bienvenue à** to welcome.

bière [bjɛr] nf **1** (boisson) beer; **b. pression** draught beer. **2** (cercueil) coffin.

biffer [bife] vt to cross ou strike out.

bifteck [biftɛk] nm steak; **gagner son b.** Fam to earn one's (daily) bread.

bifurquer [bifyrke] vi to branch off, fork. **◆bifurcation** nf fork, junction.

bigame [bigam] a bigamous; – nmf bigamist. **◆bigamie** nf bigamy.

bigarré [bigare] a (bariolé) mottled; (hétéroclite) motley, mixed.

bigler [bigle] vi (loucher) Fam to squint; – vti **b. (sur)** (lorgner) Fam to leer at. **◆bigleux, -euse** a Fam cock-eyed.

bigorneau, -x [bigɔrno] nm (coquillage) winkle.

bigot, -ote [bigo, -ɔt] nmf Péj religious bigot; – a over-devout, fanatical.

bigoudi [bigudi] nm (hair)curler ou roller.

bigrement [bigrəmɑ̃] adv Fam awfully.

bijou, -x [biʒu] nm jewel; (ouvrage élégant) Fig gem. **◆bijouterie** nf (commerce) jeweller's shop; (bijoux) jewellery. **◆bijoutier, -ière** nmf jeweller.

bikini [bikini] nm bikini.

bilan [bilɑ̃] nm Fin balance sheet; (résultat) outcome; (d'un accident) (casualty) toll; **b. de santé** checkup; **faire le b.** to make an assessment (de of).

bilboquet [bilbɔkɛ] nm cup-and-ball (game).

bile [bil] nf bile; **se faire de la b.** Fam to worry, fret. **◆bilieux, -euse** a bilious.

bilingue [bilɛ̃g] a bilingual.

billard [bijar] nm (jeu) billiards; (table) billiard table; Méd Fam operating table; **c'est du b.** Fam it's a cinch.

bille [bij] nf (d'un enfant) marble; (de billard) billiard ball; **stylo à b.** ballpoint pen, biro®.

billet [bijɛ] nm ticket; **b. (de banque)** (bank)note, Am bill; **b. aller, b. simple** single ticket, Am one-way ticket; **b. (d')aller et retour** return ticket, Am round trip ticket; **b. doux** love letter.

billion [biljɔ̃] nm billion, Am trillion.

billot [bijo] nm (de bois) block.

bimensuel, -elle [bimɑ̃sɥɛl] a bimonthly, fortnightly.

bimoteur [bimɔtœr] a twin-engined.

binaire [binɛr] a binary.

biner [bine] vt to hoe. **◆binette** nf hoe; (visage) Arg mug, face.

biochimie [bjɔʃimi] nf biochemistry.

biodégradable [bjɔdegradabl] *a* biodegradable.

biographie [bjɔgrafi] *nf* biography. ◆**biographe** *nmf* biographer.

biologie [bjɔlɔʒi] *nf* biology. ◆**biologique** *a* biological.

bip-bip [bipbip] *nm* bleeper.

bipède [biped] *nm* biped.

bique [bik] *nf Fam* nanny-goat.

Birmanie [birmani] *nf* Burma. ◆**birman, -ane** *a* & *nmf* Burmese.

bis¹ [bis] *adv* (*cri*) [bis] encore; *Mus* repeat; **4 bis** (*numéro*) 4A; – *nm Th* encore.

bis², **bise** [bi, biz] *a* greyish-brown.

bisbille [bisbij] *nf* squabble; **en b. avec** *Fam* at loggerheads with.

biscornu [biskɔrny] *a* (*objet*) distorted, misshapen; (*idée*) cranky.

biscotte [biskɔt] *nf* (*pain*) Melba toast; (*biscuit*) rusk, *Am* zwieback.

biscuit [biskɥi] *nm* (*salé*) biscuit, *Am* cracker; (*sucré*) biscuit, *Am* cookie; **b. de Savoie** sponge (cake). ◆**biscuiterie** *nf* biscuit factory.

bise [biz] *nf* **1** (*vent*) north wind. **2** (*baiser*) *Fam* kiss.

biseau, -x [bizo] *nm* bevel.

bison [bizɔ̃] *nm* bison, (American) buffalo.

bisou [bizu] *nm Fam* kiss.

bisser [bise] *vt* (*musicien, acteur*) to encore.

bissextile [bisɛkstil] *af* **année b.** leap year.

bistouri [bisturi] *nm* scalpel, lancet.

bistre [bistr] *a inv* bistre, dark-brown.

bistro(t) [bistro] *nm* bar, café.

bitume [bitym] *nm* (*revêtement*) asphalt.

bivouac [bivwak] *nm Mil* bivouac. ◆**-er** *vi* to bivouac.

bizarre [bizar] *a* peculiar, odd, bizarre. ◆**-ment** *adv* oddly. ◆**bizarrerie** *nf* peculiarity.

blabla(bla) [blabla(bla)] *nm* claptrap, bunkum.

blafard [blafar] *a* pale, pallid.

blague [blag] *nf* **1** (*à tabac*) pouch. **2** (*plaisanterie, farce*) *Fam* joke; *pl* (*absurdités*) *Fam* nonsense; **sans b.!** you're joking! ◆**blagu/er** *vi* to be joking; – *vt* to tease. ◆**-eur, -euse** *nmf* joker.

blair [bler] *nm* (*nez*) *Arg* snout, conk. ◆**blairer** *vt Arg* to stomach.

blaireau, -x [blɛro] *nm* **1** (*animal*) badger. **2** (*brosse*) (shaving) brush.

blâme [blɑm] *nm* (*réprimande*) rebuke; (*reproche*) blame. ◆**blâmable** *a* blameworthy. ◆**blâmer** *vt* to rebuke; to blame.

blanc, blanche [blɑ̃, blɑ̃ʃ] **1** *a* white; (*page etc*) blank; **nuit blanche** sleepless night; **voix blanche** expressionless voice; – *nmf*

(*personne*) white (man *ou* woman); – *nm* (*couleur*) white; (*de poulet*) white meat, breast; (*espace, interligne*) blank; **b. d'œuf** (egg) white; **le b.** (*linge*) whites; **magasin de b.** linen shop; **laisser en b.** to leave blank; **chèque en b.** blank cheque; **cartouche à b.** blank (cartridge); **saigner à b.** to bleed white. **2** *nf Mus* minim, *Am* half-note. ◆**blanchâtre** *a* whitish. ◆**blancheur** *nf* whiteness.

blanchir [blɑ̃ʃir] *vt* to whiten; (*draps*) to launder; (*mur*) to whitewash; *Culin* to blanch; (*argent*) *Fig* to launder; **b. qn** (*disculper*) to clear s.o.; – *vi* to turn white, whiten. ◆**blanchissage** *nm* laundering. ◆**blanchisserie** *nf* (*lieu*) laundry. ◆**blanchisseur, -euse** *nmf* laundryman, laundrywoman.

blanquette [blɑ̃kɛt] *nf* **b. de veau** veal stew in white sauce.

blasé [blɑze] *a* blasé.

blason [blazɔ̃] *nm* (*écu*) coat of arms; (*science*) heraldry.

blasphème [blasfɛm] *nf* blasphemy. ◆**blasphématoire** *a* (*propos*) blasphemous. ◆**blasphémer** *vti* to blaspheme.

blatte [blat] *nf* cockroach.

blazer [blazœr] *nm* blazer.

blé [ble] *nm* wheat; (*argent*) *Arg* bread.

bled [blɛd] *nm Péj Fam* (dump of a) village.

blême [blɛm] *a* sickly pale, wan; **b. de colère** livid with anger.

bless/er [blese] *vt* to injure, hurt; (*avec un couteau, une balle etc*) to wound; (*offenser*) to hurt, offend, wound; **se b. le** *ou* **au bras/etc** to hurt one's arm/*etc*. ◆**-ant** [blesɑ̃] *a* (*parole, personne*) hurtful. ◆**-é, -ée** *nmf* casualty, injured *ou* wounded person. ◆**blessure** *nf* injury; wound.

blet, blette [blɛ, blɛt] *a* (*fruit*) overripe.

bleu [blø] *a* blue; **b. de colère** blue in the face; **steak b.** *Culin* very rare steak; – *nm* (*couleur*) blue; (*contusion*) bruise; (*vêtement*) overalls; (*conscrit*) raw recruit; **bleus de travail** overalls. ◆**bleuir** *vti* to turn blue.

bleuet [bløɛ] *nm* cornflower.

blind/er [blɛ̃de] *vt Mil* to armour(-plate). ◆**-é** (*train etc*) *Mil* armoured; **porte blindée** reinforced steel door; – *nm Mil* armoured vehicle.

bloc [blɔk] *nm* block; (*de pierre*) lump, block; (*de papier*) pad; (*masse compacte*) unit; *Pol* bloc; **en b.** all together *ou* outright; (*serrer etc*) tight, hard; **travailler à b.** *Fam* to work flat out. ◆**b.-notes** (*pl* **blocs-notes**) writing pad.

blocage [blɔkaʒ] *nm* (*des roues*) locking; *Psy* mental block. **b. des prix** price freeze.

blocus [blɔkys] *nm* blockade.

blond, -onde [blɔ̃, -ɔ̃d] *a* fair(-haired); blond; − *nm* fair-haired man; (*couleur*) blond; − *nf* fair-haired woman, blonde; (*bière*) **blonde** lager, pale *ou* light ale. ◆**blondeur** *nf* fairness, blondness.

bloquer [blɔke] *vt* (*obstruer*) to block; (*coincer*) to jam; (*grouper*) to group together; (*ville*) to blockade; (*freins*) to slam *ou* jam on; (*roue*) to lock; (*salaires, prix*) to freeze; **bloqué par la neige/la glace** snowbound/icebound; − **se b.** *vpr* to stick, jam; (*roue*) to lock.

blottir (se) [səblɔtir] *vpr* (*dans un coin etc*) to crouch; (*dans son lit*) to snuggle down; **se b. contre** to huddle *ou* snuggle up to.

blouse [bluz] *nf* (*tablier*) overall, smock; (*corsage*) blouse. ◆**blouson** *nm* (waist-length) jacket.

blue-jean [bludʒin] *nm* jeans, denims.

bluff [blœf] *nm* bluff. ◆**bluffer** *vti* to bluff.

boa [bɔa] *nm* (*serpent, tour de cou*) boa.

bobard [bɔbar] *nm Fam* fib, yarn, tall story.

bobine [bɔbin] *nf* (*de fil, film etc*) reel, spool; (*pour machine à coudre*) bobbin, spool.

bobo [bobo] *nm* (*langage enfantin*) pain; **j'ai b., ça fait b.** it hurts.

bocage [bɔkaʒ] *nm* copse.

bocal, -aux [bɔkal, -o] *nm* glass jar; (*à poissons*) bowl.

bock [bɔk] *nm* (*récipient*) beer glass; (*contenu*) glass of beer.

bœuf, *pl* **-fs** [bœf, bø] *nm* (*animal*) ox (*pl* oxen), bullock; (*viande*) beef.

bohème [bɔɛm] *a & nmf* bohemian. ◆**bohémien, -ienne** *a & nmf* gipsy.

boire* [bwar] *vt* to drink; (*absorber*) to soak up; (*paroles*) *Fig* to take *ou* drink in; **b. un coup** to have a drink; **offrir à b. à qn** to offer s.o. a drink; **b. à petits coups** to sip; − *vi* to drink.

bois¹ [bwa] *voir* **boire**.

bois² [bwa] *nm* (*matière, forêt*) wood; (*de construction*) timber; (*gravure*) woodcut; *pl* (*de cerf*) antlers; *Mus* woodwind instruments; **en ou de b.** wooden; **b. de chauffage** firewood; **b. de lit** bedstead. ◆**boisé** *a* wooded. ◆**boiserie(s)** *nf(pl)* panelling.

boisson [bwasɔ̃] *nf* drink, beverage.

boit [bwa] *voir* **boire**.

boîte [bwat] *nf* box; (*de conserve*) tin, *Am* can; (*de travail*) *Fam* firm; **b. aux ou à lettres** letterbox; **b. de nuit** nightclub; **mettre qn en b.** *Fam* to pull s.o.'s leg. ◆**boîtier** *nm* (*de montre etc*) case.

boiter [bwate] *vi* (*personne*) to limp. ◆**boiteux, -euse** *a* lame; (*meuble*) wobbly; (*projet etc*) *Fig* shaky.

bol [bɔl] *nm* (*récipient*) bowl; **prendre un b. d'air** to get a breath of fresh air; **avoir du b.** *Fam* to be lucky.

bolide [bɔlid] *nm* (*véhicule*) racing car.

Bolivie [bɔlivi] *nf* Bolivia. ◆**bolivien, -ienne** *a & nmf* Bolivian.

bombard/er [bɔ̃barde] *vt* (*ville etc*) to bomb; (*avec des obus*) to shell; **b. qn** *Fam* (*nommer*) to pitchfork s.o. (**à un poste** into a job); **b. de** (*questions*) to bombard with; (*objets*) to pelt with. ◆**-ement** *nm* bombing; shelling. ◆**bombardier** *nm* (*avion*) bomber.

bombe [bɔ̃b] *nf* (*projectile*) bomb; (*atomiseur*) spray; **tomber comme une b.** *Fig* to be a bombshell, be quite unexpected; **faire la b.** *Fam* to have a binge.

bomb/er [bɔ̃be] *vi* (*gonfler*) to bulge; − *vt* **b. la poitrine** to throw out one's chest. **b. qn** (*véhicule etc*) *Fam* to belt along. ◆**-é** *a* (*verre etc*) rounded; (*route*) cambered.

bon¹, bonne¹ [bɔ̃, bɔn] *a* **1** (*satisfaisant etc*) good. **2** (*charitable*) kind, good. **3** (*agréable*) nice, good; **il fait b. se reposer** it's nice *ou* good to rest; **b. anniversaire!** happy birthday! **4** (*qui convient*) right; **c'est le b. clou** it's the right nail. **5** (*approprié, apte*) fit; **b. à manger** fit to eat; **b. pour le service** fit for service; **ce n'est b. à rien** it's useless; **comme b. te semble** as you think fit *ou* best; **c'est b. à savoir** it's worth knowing. **6** (*prudent*) wise, good; **croire b. de** to think it wise *ou* good to. **7** (*compétent*) good; **b. en français** good at French. **8** (*valable*) good; **ce billet est encore b.** this ticket's still good. **9** (*intensif*) **un b. moment** a good while. **10** **à quoi b.?** what's the use *ou* point of good?; **pour de b.** in earnest; **tenir b.** to stand firm; **ah b.?** is that so? **11** − *nm* **du b.** some good; **les bons** the good.

bon² [bɔ̃] *nm* (*billet*) coupon, voucher; (*titre*) *Fin* bond; (*formulaire*) slip.

bonasse [bɔnas] *a* feeble, soft.

bonbon [bɔ̃bɔ̃] *nm* sweet, *Am* candy. ◆**bonbonnière** *nf* sweet box, *Am* candy box.

bonbonne [bɔ̃bɔn] *nf* (*récipient*) demijohn.

bond [bɔ̃] *nm* leap, bound; (*de balle*) bounce; **faire faux b. à qn** to stand s.o. up, let s.o. down (*by not turning up*). ◆**bondir** *vi* to leap, bound.

bonde [bɔ̃d] *nf* (*bouchon*) plug; (*trou*) plughole.

bondé [bɔ̃de] *a* packed, crammed.

bonheur [bɔnœr] *nm* (*chance*) good luck, good fortune; (*félicité*) happiness; **par b.** luckily; **au petit b.** haphazardly.

bonhomie [bɔnɔmi] *nf* good-heartedness.

bonhomme, *pl* **bonshommes** [bɔnɔm, bɔ̃zɔm] **1** *nm* fellow, guy; **b. de neige** snowman; **aller son petit b. de chemin** to go on in one's own sweet way. **2** *a inv* good-hearted.

boniment(s) [bɔnimɑ̃] *nm(pl)* (*bobard*) claptrap; (*baratin*) patter.

bonjour [bɔ̃ʒur] *nm & int* good morning; (*après-midi*) good afternoon; **donner le b. à, dire b. à** to say hello to.

bonne² [bɔn] *nf* (*domestique*) maid; **b. d'enfants** nanny.

bonnement [bɔnmɑ̃] *adv* **tout b.** simply.

bonnet [bɔnɛ] *nm* cap; (*de femme, d'enfant*) bonnet; (*de soutien-gorge*) cup; **gros b.** *Fam* bigshot, bigwig. ◆**bonneterie** *nf* hosiery.

bonsoir [bɔ̃swar] *nm & int* (*en rencontrant qn*) good evening; (*en quittant qn*) goodbye; (*au coucher*) good night.

bonté [bɔ̃te] *nf* kindness, goodness.

bonus [bɔnys] *nm* no claims bonus.

bonze [bɔ̃z] *nm Péj Fam* bigwig.

boom [bum] *nm Écon* boom.

bord [bɔr] *nm* (*rebord*) edge; (*rive*) bank; (*de vêtement*) border; (*de chapeau*) brim; (*de verre*) rim, brim, edge; **au b. de la mer/route** at *ou* by the seaside/roadside; **b. du trottoir** kerb, *Am* curb; **au b. de** (*précipice*) on the brink of; **au b. des larmes** on the verge of tears; **à bord (de)** *Nau Av* on board; **jeter par-dessus b.** to throw overboard. ◆**border** *vt* (*vêtement*) to border, edge; (*lit, personne*) to tuck in; **b. la rue/etc** (*maisons, arbres etc*) to line the street/*etc.* ◆**bordure** *nf* border; **en b.** de bordering on.

bordeaux [bɔrdo] *a inv* maroon.

bordée [bɔrde] *nf* (*salve*) *Nau* broadside; (*d'injures*) *Fig* torrent, volley.

bordel [bɔrdɛl] *nm* **1** *Fam* brothel. **2** (*désordre*) *Fam* mess.

bordereau, -x [bɔrdəro] *nm* (*relevé*) docket, statement; (*formulaire*) note.

borgne [bɔrɲ] *a* (*personne*) one-eyed, blind in one eye; (*hôtel etc*) *Fig* shady.

borne [bɔrn] *nf* (*pierre*) boundary mark; *Él* terminal; *pl* (*limites*) *Fig* bounds; **b. kilométrique** = milestone; **dépasser** *ou* **franchir les bornes** to go too far. ◆**born/er** *vt* (*limiter*) to confine, limit; **se b. à** to confine oneself to. ◆**-é** *a* (*personne*) narrow-minded; (*intelligence*) narrow, limited.

bosquet [bɔskɛ] *nm* grove, thicket, copse.

bosse [bɔs] *nf* (*grosseur dorsale*) hump; (*enflure*) bump, lump; (*de terrain*) hump; **avoir la b. de** *Fam* to have a flair for; **rouler sa b.** *Fam* to knock about the world. ◆**bossu, -ue** *a* hunchbacked; **des b.** hunchback; — *nmf* (*personne*) hunchback.

bosseler [bɔsle] *vt* (*orfèvrerie*) to emboss; (*déformer*) to dent.

bosser [bɔse] *vi Fam* to work (hard).

bot [bo] *am* **pied b.** club foot.

botanique [bɔtanik] *a* botanical; — *nf* botany.

botte [bɔt] *nf* (*chaussure*) boot; (*faisceau*) bunch, bundle. ◆**botter** *vt* (*ballon etc*) *Fam* to boot. ◆**bottier** *nm* bootmaker. ◆**bottillon** *nm*, ◆**bottine** *nf* (ankle) boot.

Bottin® [bɔtɛ̃] *nm* telephone book.

bouc [buk] *nm* billy goat; (*barbe*) goatee; **b. émissaire** scapegoat.

boucan [bukɑ̃] *nm Fam* din, row, racket.

bouche [buʃ] *nf* mouth; **faire la petite** *ou* **fine b.** *Péj* to turn up one's nose; **une fine b.** a gourmet; **b. de métro** métro entrance; **b. d'égout** drain opening, manhole; **b. d'incendie** fire hydrant; **le b.-à-b.** the kiss of life. ◆**bouchée** *nf* mouthful.

bouch/er¹ [buʃe] **1** *vt* (*évier, nez etc*) to block (up), stop up; (*bouteille*) to close, cork; (*vue, rue etc*) to block; **se b. le nez** to hold one's nose. ◆**-é** *a* (*vin*) bottled; (*temps*) overcast; (*personne*) *Fig* stupid, dense. ◆**bouche-trou** *nm* stopgap. ◆**bouchon** *nm* stopper, top; (*de liège*) cork; (*de tube, bidon*) cap, top; *Pêche* float; (*embouteillage*) *Fig* traffic jam.

boucher² [buʃe] *nm* butcher. ◆**boucherie** *nf* butcher's (shop); (*carnage*) butchery.

boucle [bukl] *nf* **1** (*de ceinture*) buckle; (*de fleuve etc*) & *Av* loop; (*de ruban*) bow; **b. d'oreille** earring. **2 b. (de cheveux)** curl. ◆**boucl/er** *vt* **1** to fasten, buckle; (*travail etc*) to finish off; (*enfermer, fermer*) *Fam* to lock up; (*budget*) to balance; (*circuit*) to lap; (*encercler*) to surround, cordon off; **b. la boucle** *Av* to loop the loop; **la b.** *Fam* to shut up. **2** (*cheveux*) to curl; — *vi* to be curly. ◆**-é** *a* (*cheveux*) curly.

bouclier [buklije] *nm* shield.

bouddhiste [budist] *a & nmf* Buddhist.

bouder [bude] *vi* to sulk; — *vt* (*personne, plaisirs etc*) to steer clear of. ◆**bouderie** *nf* sulkiness. ◆**boudeur, -euse** *a* sulky, moody.

boudin [budɛ̃] *nm* black pudding, *Am* blood pudding.

boue [bu] *nf* mud. ◆**boueux, -euse 1** *a*

muddy. **2** *nm* dustman, *Am* garbage collector.

bouée [bwe] *nf* buoy; **b. de sauvetage** lifebuoy.

bouffe [buf] *nf Fam* food, grub, nosh.

bouffée [bufe] *nf* (*de fumée*) puff; (*de parfum*) whiff; (*d'orgueil*) fit; **b. de chaleur** *Méd* hot flush. ◆**bouff/er 1** *vi* to puff out. **2** *vti* (*manger*) *Fam* to eat. ◆**—ant** *a* (*manche*) puff(ed). ◆**bouffi** *a* puffy, bloated.

bouffon, -onne [bufɔ̃, -ɔn] *a* farcical; – *nm* buffoon. ◆**bouffonneries** *nfpl* antics, buffoonery.

bouge [buʒ] *nm* (*bar*) dive; (*taudis*) hovel.

bougeotte [buʒɔt] *nf* **avoir la b.** *Fam* to have the fidgets.

bouger [buʒe] *vi* to move; (*agir*) to stir; (*rétrécir*) to shrink; – *vt* to move; – **se b.** *vpr Fam* to move.

bougie [buʒi] *nf* candle; *Aut* spark(ing) plug. ◆**bougeoir** *nm* candlestick.

bougon, -onne [bugɔ̃, -ɔn] *a Fam* grumpy; – *nmf* grumbler, grouch. ◆**bougonner** *vi Fam* to grumble, grouch.

bougre [bugr] *nm* fellow, bloke; (*enfant*) *Péj* (little) devil. ◆**bougrement** *adv Arg* damned.

bouillabaisse [bujabɛs] *nf* fish soup.

bouillie [buji] *nf* porridge; **en b.** in a mush, mushy.

bouill/ir* [bujir] *vi* to boil; **b. à gros bouillons** to bubble, boil hard; **faire b.** qch to boil sth. ◆**—ant** *a* boiling; **b. de colère**/*etc* seething with anger/*etc*. ◆**bouilloire** *nf* kettle. ◆**bouillon** *nm* (*eau*) broth, stock; (*bulle*) bubble. ◆**bouillonner** *vi* to bubble. ◆**bouillotte** *nf* hot water bottle.

boulanger, -ère [bulɑ̃ʒe, -ɛr] *nmf* baker. ◆**boulangerie** *nf* baker's (shop).

boule [bul] *nf* (*sphère*) ball; *pl* (*jeu*) bowls; **b. de neige** snowball; **faire b. de neige** to snowball; **perdre la b.** *Fam* to go out of one's mind; **se mettre en b.** (*chat etc*) to curl up into a ball; **boules Quiès®** earplugs. ◆**boulet** *nm* (*de forçat*) ball and chain; **b. de canon** cannonball. ◆**boulette** *nf* (*de papier*) pellet; (*de viande*) meatball; (*gaffe*) *Fam* blunder.

bouleau, -x [bulo] *nm* (silver) birch.

bouledogue [buldɔg] *nm* bulldog.

boulevard [bulvar] *nm* boulevard.

boulevers/er [bulverse] *vt* (*déranger*) to turn upside down; (*émouvoir*) to upset deeply, distress; (*vie de qn, pays*) to disrupt. ◆**—ant** *a* upsetting, distressing. ◆**—ement** *nm* upheaval.

boulon [bulɔ̃] *nm* bolt.

boulot, -otte [bulo, -ɔt] **1** *a* dumpy. **2** *nm* (*travail*) *Fam* work.

boum [bum] **1** *int* & *nm* bang. **2** *nf* (*surprise-partie*) *Fam* party.

bouquet [bukɛ] *nm* (*de fleurs*) bunch, bouquet; (*d'arbres*) clump; (*de vin*) bouquet; (*crevette*) prawn; **c'est le b.!** that's the last straw!

bouquin [bukɛ̃] *nm Fam* book. ◆**bouquiner** *vti Fam* to read. ◆**bouquiniste** *nmf* second-hand bookseller.

bourbeux, -euse [burbø, -øz] *a* muddy. ◆**bourbier** *nm* (*lieu, situation*) quagmire, morass.

bourde [burd] *nf* blunder, bloomer.

bourdon [burdɔ̃] *nm* (*insecte*) bumblebee. ◆**bourdonn/er** *vi* to buzz, hum. ◆**—ement** *nm* buzzing, humming.

bourg [bur] *nm* (small) market town. ◆**bourgade** *nf* (large) village.

bourgeois, -oise [burʒwa, -waz] *a* & *nmf* middle-class (person); *Péj* bourgeois. ◆**bourgeoisie** *nf* middle class, bourgeoisie.

bourgeon [burʒɔ̃] *nm* bud. ◆**bourgeonner** *vi* to bud; (*nez*) *Fam* to be pimply.

bourgmestre [burgmɛstr] *nm* (*en Belgique, Suisse*) burgomaster.

bourgogne [burgɔɲ] *nm* (*vin*) Burgundy.

bourlinguer [burlɛ̃ge] *vi* (*voyager*) *Fam* to knock about.

bourrade [burad] *nf* (*du coude*) poke.

bourrasque [burask] *nf* squall.

bourratif, -ive [buratif, -iv] *a* (*aliment*) *Fam* filling, stodgy.

bourreau, -x [buro] *nm* executioner; **b. d'enfants** child batterer; **b. de travail** workaholic.

bourrelet [burlɛ] *nm* weather strip; **b. de graisse** roll of fat, spare tyre.

bourr/er [bure] **1** *vt* to stuff, cram (**full**) (**de** with); (*pipe, coussin*) to fill; **b. de coups** to thrash; **b. le crâne à qn** to brainwash s.o. **2 se b.** *vpr* (*s'enivrer*) *Fam* to get plastered. ◆**—age** *nm* **b. de crâne** brainwashing.

bourrique [burik] *nf* ass.

bourru [bury] *a* surly, rough.

bourse [burs] *nf* (*sac*) purse; *Scol Univ* grant, scholarship; **la B.** the Stock Exchange; **sans b. délier** without spending a penny. ◆**boursier, -ière 1** *a* Stock Exchange. **2** *nmf Scol Univ* grant holder, scholar.

boursouflé [bursufle] *a* (*visage etc*) puffy; (*style*) *Fig* inflated.

bousculer [buskyle] *vt* (*heurter, pousser*) to

jostle; (*presser*) to rush, push; **b. qch** (*renverser*) to knock sth over; **b. les habitudes**/*etc* to turn one's habits/*etc* upside down. ◆**bousculade** *nf* rush, jostling.

bouse [buz] *nf* **b. de vache** cow dung.

bousiller [buzije] *vt Fam* to mess up, wreck.

boussole [busɔl] *nf* compass.

bout [bu] *nm* end; (*de langue, canne, doigt*) tip; (*de papier, pain, ficelle*) bit; **un b. de temps**/*chemin* a little while/way; **au b. d'un moment** after a moment; **à b.** exhausted; **à b. de souffle** out of breath; **à b. de bras** at arm's length; **venir à b. de** (*travail*) to get through; (*adversaire*) to get the better of; **à tout b. de champ** at every turn, every minute; **à b. portant** point-blank.

boutade [butad] *nf* (*plaisanterie*) quip, witticism.

boute-en-train [butɑ̃trɛ̃] *nm inv* (*personne*) live wire.

bouteille [butɛj] *nf* bottle; (*de gaz*) cylinder.

bouteur [butœr] *nm* bulldozer.

boutique [butik] *nf* shop; (*d'un grand couturier*) boutique. ◆**boutiquier, -ière** *nmf Péj* shopkeeper.

boutoir [butwar] *nm* **coup de b.** staggering blow.

bouton [butɔ̃] *nm* (*bourgeon*) bud; (*pustule*) pimple, spot; (*de vêtement*) button; (*poussoir*) (push-)button; (*de porte, de télévision*) knob; **b. de manchette** cuff link. ◆**b.-d'or** *nm* (*pl* **boutons-d'or**) buttercup. ◆**b.-pression** *nm* (*pl* **boutons-pression**) press-stud, *Am* snap. ◆**boutonner** *vt*, **− se b.** *vpr* to button (up). ◆**boutonneux, -euse** *a* pimply, spotty. ◆**boutonnière** *nf* buttonhole.

bouture [butyr] *nf* (*plante*) cutting.

bouvreuil [buvrœj] *nm* (*oiseau*) bullfinch.

bovin [bɔvɛ̃] *a* bovine; − *nmpl* cattle.

bowling [boliŋ] *nm* (tenpin) bowling; (*lieu*) bowling alley.

box, *pl* **boxes** [bɔks] *nm* (*d'écurie*) (loose) box; (*de dortoir*) cubicle; *Jur* dock; *Aut* lockup *ou* individual garage.

boxe [bɔks] *nf* boxing. ◆**boxer** *vi Sp* to box; − *vt Fam* to whack, punch. ◆**boxeur** *nm* boxer.

boyau, -x [bwajo] *nm Anat* gut; (*corde*) catgut; (*de bicyclette*) (racing) tyre *ou Am* tire.

boycott/er [bɔjkɔte] *vt* to boycott. ◆**−age** *nm* boycott.

BP [bepe] *abrév* (*boîte postale*) PO Box.

bracelet [braslɛ] *nm* bracelet, bangle; (*de montre*) strap.

braconner [brakɔne] *vi* to poach. ◆**braconnier** *nm* poacher.

brader [brade] *vt* to sell off cheaply. ◆**braderie** *nf* open-air (clearance) sale.

braguette [bragɛt] *nf* (*de pantalon*) fly, flies.

braille [brɑj] *nm* Braille.

brailler [brɑje] *vti* to bawl. ◆**braillard** *a* bawling.

braire* [brɛr] *vi* (*âne*) to bray.

braise(s) [brɛz] *nf(pl)* embers, live coals. ◆**braiser** [breze] *vt Culin* to braise.

brancard [brɑ̃kar] *nm* (*civière*) stretcher; (*de charrette*) shaft. ◆**brancardier** *nm* stretcher-bearer.

branche [brɑ̃ʃ] *nf* (*d'un arbre, d'une science etc*) branch; (*de compas*) leg; (*de lunettes*) side piece. ◆**branchages** *nmpl* (cut *ou* fallen) branches.

branch/er [brɑ̃ʃe] *vt Él* to plug in; (*installer*) to connect. ◆**−é** *a* (*informé*) *Fam* with it. ◆**−ement** *nm Él* connection.

brandir [brɑ̃dir] *vt* to brandish, flourish.

brandon [brɑ̃dɔ̃] *nm* (*paille, bois*) firebrand.

branle [brɑ̃l] *nm* impetus; **mettre en b.** to set in motion. ◆**b.-bas** *nm inv* turmoil. ◆**branl/er** *vi* to be shaky, shake. ◆**−ant** *a* shaky.

braqu/er [brake] **1** *vt* (*arme etc*) to point, aim; (*yeux*) to fix; **b. qn contre qn** to set *ou* turn s.o. against s.o. **2** *vti Aut* to steer, turn. ◆**−age** *nm Aut* steering; **rayon de b.** turning circle.

bras [brɑ] *nm* arm; **en b. de chemise** in one's shirtsleeves; **b. dessus b. dessous** arm in arm; **sur les b.** *Fig* on one's hands; **son b. droit** *Fig* his right-hand man; **à b. ouverts** with open arms; **à tour de b.** with all one's might; **faire le b. d'honneur** *Fam* to make an obscene gesture; **à b.-le-corps** round the waist. ◆**brassard** *nm* armband. ◆**brassée** *nf* armful. ◆**brassière** *nf* (*de bébé*) vest, *Am* undershirt.

brasier [brɑzje] *nm* inferno, blaze.

brasse [brɑs] *nf* (*nage*) breaststroke; (*mesure*) fathom; **b. papillon** butterfly stroke.

brasser [brase] *vt* to mix; (*bière*) to brew. ◆**brassage** *nm* mixture; brewing. ◆**brasserie** *nf* (*usine*) brewery; (*café*) brasserie. ◆**brasseur** *nm* **b. d'affaires** *Péj* big businessman.

bravache [bravaʃ] *nm* braggart.

bravade [bravad] *nf* **par b.** out of bravado.

brave [brav] *a* & *nm* (*hardi*) brave (man); (*honnête*) good (man). ◆**bravement** *adv* bravely. ◆**braver** *vt* to defy; (*danger*) to brave. ◆**bravoure** *nf* bravery.

bravo [bravo] *int* well done, bravo, good show; – *nm* cheer.

break [brɛk] *nm* estate car, *Am* station wagon.

brebis [brəbi] *nf* ewe; **b. galeuse** black sheep.

brèche [brɛʃ] *nf* breach, gap; **battre en b.** (*attaquer*) to attack (mercilessly).

bredouille [brəduj] *a* **rentrer b.** to come back empty-handed.

bredouiller [brəduje] *vti* to mumble.

bref, brève [brɛf, brɛv] *a* brief, short; – *adv* (*enfin*) **b.** in a word.

breloque [brələk] *nf* charm, trinket.

Brésil [brezil] *nm* Brazil. ◆**brésilien, -ienne** *a* & *nmf* Brazilian.

Bretagne [brətaɲ] *nf* Brittany. ◆**breton, -onne** *a* & *nmf* Breton.

bretelle [brətɛl] *nf* strap; (*voie de raccordement*) *Aut* access road; *pl* (*pour pantalon*) braces, *Am* suspenders.

breuvage [brœvaʒ] *nm* drink, brew.

brève [brɛv] *voir* **bref**.

brevet [brəvɛ] *nm* diploma; **b. (d'invention)** patent. ◆**brevet/er** *vt* to patent. ◆**-é** *a* (*technicien*) qualified.

bréviaire [brevjɛr] *nm* breviary.

bribes [brib] *nfpl* scraps, bits.

bric-à-brac [brikabrak] *nm inv* bric-à-brac, jumble, junk.

brick [brik] *nm* (*de lait, jus d'orange etc*) carton.

bricole [brikɔl] *nf* (*objet, futilité*) trifle. ◆**bricol/er** *vi* to do odd jobs; – *vt* (*réparer*) to patch up; (*fabriquer*) to put together. ◆**-age** *nm* (*petits travaux*) odd jobs; (*passe-temps*) do-it-yourself; **salon/rayon du b.** do-it-yourself exhibition/department. ◆**-eur, -euse** *nmf* handyman, handywoman.

bride [brid] *nf* (*de cheval*) bridle; **à b. abattue** at full gallop. ◆**brider** *vt* (*cheval*) to bridle; (*personne, désir*) to curb; *Culin* to truss; **avoir les yeux bridés** to have slit eyes.

bridge [bridʒ] *nm* (*jeu*) bridge.

brièvement [brijɛvmɑ̃] *adv* briefly. ◆**brièveté** *nf* brevity.

brigade [brigad] *nf* (*de gendarmerie*) squad; *Mil* brigade; **b. des mœurs** vice squad. ◆**brigadier** *nm* police sergeant; *Mil* corporal.

brigand [brigɑ̃] *nm* robber; (*enfant*) rascal.

briguer [brige] *vt* to covet; (*faveurs, suffrages*) to court.

brillant [brijɑ̃] *a* (*luisant*) shining; (*astiqué*) shiny; (*couleur*) bright; (*magnifique*) *Fig* brilliant; – *nm* shine; brightness; *Fig* brilliance; (*diamant*) diamond. ◆**brillamment** *adv* brilliantly.

briller [brije] *vi* to shine; **faire b.** (*meuble*) to polish (up).

brimer [brime] *vt* to bully. ◆**brimade** *nf Scol* bullying, ragging, *Am* hazing; *Fig* vexation.

brin [brɛ̃] *nm* (*d'herbe*) blade; (*de corde, fil*) strand; (*de muguet*) spray; **un b. de** *Fig* a bit of.

brindille [brɛ̃dij] *nf* twig.

bringue [brɛ̃g] *nf* **faire la b.** *Fam* to have a binge.

bringuebaler [brɛ̃gbale] *vi* to wobble about.

brio [brijo] *nm* (*virtuosité*) brilliance.

brioche [brijɔʃ] *nf* **1** brioche (*light sweet bun*). **2** (*ventre*) *Fam* paunch.

brique [brik] *nf* brick. ◆**briquette** *nf* (*aggloméré*) breezeblock.

briquer [brike] *vt* to polish (up).

briquet [brikɛ] *nm* (*cigarette*) lighter.

brise [briz] *nf* breeze.

bris/er [brize] *vt* to break; (*en morceaux*) to smash, break; (*espoir, carrière*) to shatter; (*fatiguer*) to exhaust; **– se b.** *vpr* to break. ◆**-ants** *nmpl* reefs. ◆**brise-lames** *nm inv* breakwater.

britannique [britanik] *a* British; – *nmf* Briton; **les Britanniques** the British.

broc [bro] *nm* pitcher, jug.

brocanteur, -euse [brɔkɑ̃tœr, -øz] *nmf* secondhand dealer (*in furniture etc*).

broche [brɔʃ] *nf Culin* spit; (*bijou*) brooch; *Méd* pin. ◆**brochette** *nf* (*tige*) skewer; (*plat*) kebab.

broché [brɔʃe] *a* **livre b.** paperback.

brochet [brɔʃɛ] *nm* (*poisson*) pike.

brochure [brɔʃyr] *nf* brochure, booklet, pamphlet.

broder [brɔde] *vt* to embroider (**de** with). ◆**broderie** *nf* embroidery.

broncher [brɔ̃ʃe] *vi* (*bouger*) to budge; (*reculer*) to flinch; (*regimber*) to balk.

bronches [brɔ̃ʃ] *nfpl* bronchial tubes. ◆**bronchite** *nf* bronchitis.

bronze [brɔ̃z] *nm* bronze.

bronz/er [brɔ̃ze] *vt* to tan; – *vi*, **– se b.** *vpr* to get (sun)tanned; **se (faire) b.** to sunbathe. ◆**-age** *nm* (sun)tan, sunburn.

brosse [brɔs] *nf* brush; **b. à dents** toothbrush; **cheveux en b.** crew cut. ◆**brosser** *vt* to brush; **b. un tableau de** to give an outline of; **se b. les dents/les cheveux** to brush one's teeth/one's hair.

brouette [bruɛt] *nf* wheelbarrow.

brouhaha [bruaa] *nm* hubbub.

brouillard [brujar] *nm* fog; **il fait du b.** it's foggy.

brouille [bruj] *nf* disagreement, quarrel. ◆**brouiller 1** *vt* (*papiers, idées etc*) to mix up; (*vue*) to blur; (*œufs*) to scramble; *Rad* to jam; **— se b.** *vpr* (*idées*) to be *ou* get confused; (*temps*) to cloud over; (*vue*) to blur. **2** *vt* (*amis*) to cause a split between; **— se b.** *vpr* to fall out (**avec** with). ◆**brouillon, -onne 1** *a* confused. **2** *nm* rough draft.

broussailles [brusaj] *nfpl* brushwood.

brousse [brus] *nf* **la b.** the bush.

brouter [brute] *vti* to graze.

broyer [brwaje] *vt* to grind; (*doigt, bras*) to crush; **b. du noir** to be (down) in the dumps.

bru [bry] *nf* daughter-in-law.

brugnon [bryɲ̃ɔ] *nm* (*fruit*) nectarine.

bruine [brɥin] *nf* drizzle. ◆**bruiner** *v imp* to drizzle.

bruissement [brɥismɑ̃] *nm* (*de feuilles*) rustle, rustling.

bruit [brɥi] *nm* noise, sound; (*nouvelle*) rumour; **faire du b.** to be noisy, make a noise. ◆**bruitage** *nm Cin* sound effects.

brûle-pourpoint (à) [abrylpurpwɛ̃] *adv* point-blank.

brûl/er [bryle] *vt* to use up, burn; (*consommer*) to use up, burn; (*signal, station*) to go through (without stopping); **b. un feu (rouge)** to jump *ou* go through the lights; **ce désir le brûlait** this desire consumed him; **— vi** to burn; **b. (d'envie) de faire** to be burning to do; **ça brûle** (*temps*) it's baking *ou* scorching; **— se b.** *vpr* to burn oneself. ◆**—ant** *a* (*objet, soleil*) burning (hot); (*sujet*) *Fig* red-hot. ◆**—é 1** *nm* **odeur de b.** smell of burning. **2** *a* **cerveau b.**, **tête brûlée** hothead. ◆**brûlure** *nf* burn; **brûlures d'estomac** heartburn.

brume [brym] *nf* mist, haze. ◆**brumeux, -euse** *a* misty, hazy; (*obscur*) *Fig* hazy.

brun, brune [brœ̃, bryn] *a* brown; (*cheveux*) dark, brown; (*personne*) dark-haired; **— nm** (*couleur*) brown; **— nmf** dark-haired person. ◆**brunette** *nf* brunette. ◆**brunir** *vt* (*peau*) to tan; **— vi** to turn brown; (*cheveux*) to go darker.

brushing [brœʃiŋ] *nm* blow-dry.

brusque [brysk] *a* (*manière etc*) abrupt, blunt; (*subit*) sudden, abrupt. ◆**brusquement** *adv* suddenly, abruptly. ◆**brusquer** *vt* to rush. ◆**brusquerie** *nf* abruptness, bluntness.

brut [bryt] *a* (*pétrole*) crude; (*diamant*) rough; (*sucre*) unrefined; (*soie*) raw; (*poids*) & *Fin* gross.

brutal, -aux [brytal, -o] *a* (*violent*) savage, brutal; (*franchise, réponse*) crude, blunt; (*fait*) stark. ◆**brutaliser** *vt* to ill-treat. ◆**brutalité** *nf* (*violence, acte*) brutality. ◆**brute** *nf* brute.

Bruxelles [brysɛl] *nm ou f* Brussels.

bruyant [brɥijɑ̃] *a* noisy. ◆**bruyamment** *adv* noisily.

bruyère [brɥijɛr] *nf* (*plante*) heather; (*terrain*) heath.

bu [by] *voir* **boire**.

buanderie [bɥɑdri] *nf* (*lieu*) laundry.

bûche [byʃ] *nf* log; **ramasser une b.** *Fam* to come a cropper, *Am* take a spill. ◆**bûcher 1** *nm* (*local*) woodshed; (*supplice*) stake. **2** *vt* (*étudier*) *Fam* to slog away at. ◆**bûcheron** *nm* woodcutter, lumberjack.

budget [bydʒɛ] *nm* budget. ◆**budgétaire** *a* budgetary; (*année*) financial.

buée [bɥe] *nf* condensation, mist.

buffet [byfɛ] *nm* (*armoire*) sideboard; (*table, restaurant, repas*) buffet.

buffle [byfl] *nm* buffalo.

buis [bɥi] *nm* (*arbre*) box; (*bois*) boxwood.

buisson [bɥisɔ̃] *nm* bush.

buissonnière [bɥisɔnjɛr] *af* **faire l'école b.** to play truant *ou Am* hookey.

bulbe [bylb] *nm* bulb. ◆**bulbeux, -euse** *a* bulbous.

Bulgarie [bylgari] *nf* Bulgaria. ◆**bulgare** *a* & *nmf* Bulgarian.

bulldozer [byldozœr] *nm* bulldozer.

bulle [byl] *nf* **1** bubble; (*de bande dessinée*) balloon. **2** (*décret du pape*) bull.

bulletin [byltɛ̃] *nm* (*communiqué, revue*) bulletin; (*de la météo*) & *Scol* report; (*de bagages*) ticket, *Am* check; **b. de paie** pay slip; **b. de vote** ballot paper.

buraliste [byralist] *nmf* (*à la poste*) clerk; (*au tabac*) tobacconist.

bureau, -x [byro] *nm* **1** (*table*) desk. **2** (*lieu*) office; (*comité*) board; **b. de change** bureau de change; **b. de location** *Th Cin* box office; **b. de tabac** tobacconist's (shop). ◆**bureaucrate** *nmf* bureaucrat. ◆**bureaucratie** [-asi] *nf* bureaucracy. ◆**bureautique** *nf* office automation.

burette [byrɛt] *nf* oilcan; *Culin* cruet.

burlesque [byrlɛsk] *a* (*idée etc*) ludicrous; (*genre*) burlesque.

bus¹ [bys] *nm Fam* bus.

bus² [by] *voir* **boire**.

busqué [byske] *a* (*nez*) hooked.

buste [byst] *nm* (*torse, sculpture*) bust. ◆**bustier** *nm* long-line bra(ssiere).

but¹ [by(t)] *nm* (*dessein, objectif*) aim, goal;

(*cible*) target; *Fb* goal; **de b. en blanc** point-blank; **aller droit au b.** to go straight to the point; **j'ai pour b. de . . .** my aim is to . . . .

but² [by] *voir* **boire.**

butane [bytan] *nm* (*gaz*) butane.

but/er [byte] **1** *vi* **b. contre** to stumble over; (*difficulté*) *Fig* to come up against. **2 se b.** *vpr* (*s'entêter*) to get obstinate. ◆**-é** *a* obstinate.

butin [bytɛ̃] *nm* loot, booty.

butiner [bytine] *vi* (*abeille*) to gather nectar.

butoir [bytwar] *nm Rail* buffer; (*de porte*) stop(per).

butor [bytɔr] *nm Péj* lout, oaf, boor.

butte [byt] *nf* hillock, mound; **en b. à** (*calomnie etc*) exposed to.

buvable [byvabl] *a* drinkable. ◆**buveur, -euse** *nmf* drinker.

buvard [byvar] *a & nm* (**papier**) **b.** blotting paper.

buvette [byvɛt] *nf* refreshment bar.

C

C, c [se] *nm* C, c

c *abrév* centime.

c' [s] *voir* **ce¹.**

ça [sa] *pron dém* (*abrév de* **cela**) (*pour désigner*) that; (*plus près*) this; (*sujet indéfini*) it, that; **ça m'amuse que . . .** it amuses me that . . . ; **où/quand/comment/etc ça?** where?/when?/how?/*etc*; **ça va (bien)?** how's it going?; **ça va!** fine!, OK!; **ça alors!** (*surprise, indignation*) well I never!, how about that!; **c'est ça** that's right; **et avec ça?** (*dans un magasin*) anything else?

çà [sa] *adv* **çà et là** here and there.

caban [kabɑ̃] *nm* (*veste*) reefer.

cabane [kaban] *nf* hut, cabin; (*à outils*) shed; (*à lapins*) hutch.

cabaret [kabarɛ] *nm* night club, cabaret.

cabas [kabɑ] *nm* shopping bag.

cabillaud [kabijo] *nm* (fresh) cod.

cabine [kabin] *nf Nau Av* cabin; *Tél* phone booth, phone box; (*de camion*) cab; (*d'ascenseur*) car, cage; **c. (de bain)** beach hut; (*à la piscine*) cubicle; **c. (de pilotage)** cockpit; (*d'un grand avion*) flight deck; **c. d'essayage** fitting room; **c. d'aiguillage** signal box.

cabinet [kabinɛ] *nm* (*local*) *Méd* surgery, *Am* office; (*d'avocat*) office, chambers; (*clientèle de médecin ou d'avocat*) practice; *Pol* cabinet; *pl* (*toilettes*) toilet; **c. de toilette** bathroom, toilet; **c. de travail** study.

câble [kabl] *nm* cable; (*cordage*) rope; **la télévision par c.** cable television; **le c.** *TV* cable. ◆**câbler** *vt* (*message*) to cable; **être câblé** *TV* to have cable.

caboche [kabɔʃ] *nf* (*tête*) *Fam* nut, noddle.

cabosser [kabɔse] *vt* to dent.

caboteur [kabɔtœr] *nm* (*bateau*) coaster.

cabotin, -ine [kabɔtɛ̃, -in] *nmf Th* ham actor, ham actress; *Fig* play-actor. ◆**cabotinage** *nm* histrionics, play-acting.

cabrer (se) [səkabre] *vpr* (*cheval*) to rear (up); (*personne*) to rebel.

cabri [kabri] *nm* (*chevreau*) kid.

cabrioles [kabriɔl] *nfpl* **faire des c.** (*sauts*) to cavort, caper.

cabriolet [kabriɔlɛ] *nm Aut* convertible.

cacah(o)uète [kakawɛt] *nf* peanut.

cacao [kakao] *nm* (*boisson*) cocoa.

cacatoès [kakatɔɛs] *nm* cockatoo.

cachalot [kaʃalo] *nm* sperm whale.

cache-cache [kaʃkaʃ] *nm inv* hide-and-seek. ◆**c.-col** *nm inv*, ◆**c.-nez** *nm inv* scarf, muffler. ◆**c.-sexe** *nm inv* G-string.

cachemire [kaʃmir] *nm* (*tissu*) cashmere.

cacher [kaʃe] *vt* to hide, conceal (**à** from); **je ne cache pas que . . .** I don't hide the fact that . . . ; **c. la lumière à qn** to stand in s.o.'s light; **— se c.** *vpr* to hide. ◆**cachette** *nf* hiding place; **en c.** in secret; **en c. de qn** without s.o. knowing.

cachet [kaʃɛ] *nm* (*sceau*) seal; (*de la poste*) postmark; (*comprimé*) tablet; (*d'acteur etc*) fee; *Fig* distinctive character. ◆**cacheter** *vt* to seal.

cachot [kaʃo] *nm* dungeon.

cachotteries [kaʃɔtri] *nfpl* secretiveness; (*petits secrets*) little mysteries. ◆**cachottier, -ière** *a & nmf* secretive (person).

cacophonie [kakɔfɔni] *nf* cacophony.

cactus [kaktys] *nm* cactus.

cadastre [kadastr] *nm* (*registre*) land register.

cadavre [kadavr] *nm* corpse. ◆**cadavéri-**

que *a* (*teint etc*) cadaverous; **rigidité c.** rigor mortis.

caddie® [kadi] *nm* supermarket trolly *ou Am* cart.

cadeau, -x [kado] *nm* present, gift.

cadenas [kadnɑ] *nm* padlock. ◆**cadenasser** *vt* to padlock.

cadence [kadɑ̃s] *nf* rhythm; *Mus* cadence; (*taux, vitesse*) rate; **en c.** in time. ◆**cadencé** *a* rhythmical.

cadet, -ette [kade, -et] *a* (*de deux frères etc*) younger; (*de plus de deux*) youngest; — *nmf* (*enfant*) younger (child); youngest (child); *Sp* junior; **c'est mon c.** he's my junior.

cadran [kadrɑ̃] *nm* (*de téléphone etc*) dial; (*de montre*) face; **c. solaire** sundial; **faire le tour du c.** to sleep round the clock.

cadre [kadr] *nm* **1** (*de photo, vélo etc*) frame; (*décor*) setting; (*sur un imprimé*) box; **dans le c. de** (*limites, contexte*) within the framework *ou* scope of, as part of. **2** (*chef*) *Com* executive, manager; *pl* (*personnel*) *Mil* officers; *Com* management, managers.

cadr/er [kadre] *vi* to tally (**avec** with); — *vt* (*image*) *Cin Phot* to centre. ◆**-eur** *nm* cameraman.

caduc, -uque [kadyk] *a* (*usage*) obsolete; *Bot* deciduous; *Jur* null and void.

cafard, -arde [kafar, -ard] **1** *nmf* (*espion*) sneak. **2** *nm* (*insecte*) cockroach; **avoir le c.** to be in the dumps; **ça me donne le c.** it depresses me. ◆**cafardeux, -euse** *a* (*personne*) in the dumps; (*qui donne le cafard*) depressing.

café [kafe] *nm* coffee; (*bar*) café; **c. au lait, crème** white coffee, coffee with milk; **c. noir, c. nature** black coffee; **tasse de c.** cup of black coffee. ◆**caféine** *nf* caffeine. ◆**cafétéria** *nf* cafeteria. ◆**cafetier** *nm* café owner. ◆**cafetière** *nf* percolator, coffeepot.

cafouiller [kafuje] *vi Fam* to make a mess (of things). ◆**cafouillage** *nm Fam* mess, muddle, snafu.

cage [kaʒ] *nf* cage; (*d'escalier*) well; (*d'ascenseur*) shaft; **c. des buts** *Fb* goal (area).

cageot [kaʒo] *nm* crate.

cagibi [kaʒibi] *nm* (storage) room, cubbyhole.

cagneux, -euse [kaɲø, -øz] *a* knock-kneed.

cagnotte [kaɲɔt] *nf* (*tirelire*) kitty.

cagoule [kagul] *nf* (*de bandit, pénitent*) hood.

cahier [kaje] *nm* (*carnet*) (note)book; *Scol* exercise book.

cahin-caha [kaɛ̃kaa] *adv* **aller c.-caha** to jog along (with ups and downs).

cahot [kao] *nm* jolt, bump. ◆**cahot/er** *vt* to jolt, bump; — *vi* (*véhicule*) to jolt along. ◆**-ant** *a*, ◆**cahoteux, -euse** *a* bumpy.

caïd [kaid] *nm Fam* big shot, leader.

caille [kaj] *nf* (*oiseau*) quail.

cailler [kaje] *vti*, — **se c.** *vpr* (*sang*) to clot, congeal; (*lait*) to curdle; **faire c.** (*lait*) to curdle; **ça caille** *Fam* it's freezing cold. ◆**caillot** *nm* (blood) clot.

caillou, -x [kaju] *nm* stone; (*galet*) pebble. ◆**caillouté** *a* gravelled. ◆**caillouxeux, -euse** *a* stony.

caisse [kɛs] *nf* (*boîte*) case, box; (*cageot*) crate; (*guichet*) cash desk, pay desk; (*de supermarché*) checkout; (*fonds*) fund; (*bureau*) (paying-in) office; *Mus* drum; *Aut* body; **c.** (**enregistreuse**) cash register, till; **c. d'épargne** savings bank; **de c.** (*livre, recettes*) cash-. ◆**caissier, -ière** *nmf* cashier; (*de supermarché*) checkout assistant.

caisson [kɛsɔ̃] *nm* (*de plongeur*) & *Mil* caisson.

cajoler [kaʒɔle] *vt* (*câliner*) to pamper, pet, cosset. ◆**cajolerie(s)** *nf*(*pl*) pampering.

cajou [kaʒu] *nm* (*noix*) cashew.

cake [kɛk] *nm* fruit cake.

calamité [kalamite] *nf* calamity.

calandre [kalɑ̃dr] *nf Aut* radiator grille.

calcaire [kalkɛr] *a* (*terrain*) chalky; (*eau*) hard; — *nm Géol* limestone.

calciné [kalsine] *a* charred, burnt to a cinder.

calcium [kalsjɔm] *nm* calcium.

calcul [kalkyl] *nm* **1** calculation; (*estimation*) calculation, reckoning; (*discipline*) arithmetic; (*différentiel*) calculus. **2** *Méd* stone. ◆**calcul/er** *vt* (*compter*) to calculate, reckon; (*évaluer, combiner*) to calculate. ◆**-é** *a* (*risque etc*) calculated. ◆**calculateur** *nm* calculator, computer. ◆**calculatrice** *nf* (*ordinateur*) calculator.

cale [kal] **1** (*pour maintenir*) wedge. **2** *Nau* hold; **c. sèche** dry dock.

calé [kale] *a Fam* (*instruit*) clever (**en qch** at sth); (*difficile*) tough.

caleçon [kalsɔ̃] *nm* underpants; **c. de bain** bathing trunks.

calembour [kalɑ̃bur] *nm* pun.

calendrier [kalɑ̃drije] *nm* (*mois et jours*) calendar; (*programme*) timetable.

cale-pied [kalpje] *nm* (*de bicyclette*) toeclip.

calepin [kalpɛ̃] *nm* (pocket) notebook.

caler [kale] **1** *vt* (*meuble etc*) to wedge (up); (*appuyer*) to prop (up). **2** *vt* (*moteur*) to stall; – *vi* to stall; (*abandonner*) *Fam* give up.

calfeutrer [kalføtre] *vt* (*avec du bourrelet*) to draughtproof; **se c.** (**chez soi**) to shut oneself away, hole up.

calibre [kalibr] *nm* (*diamètre*) calibre; (*d'œuf*) grade; **de ce c.** (*bêtise etc*) of this degree. ◆**calibrer** *vt* (*œufs*) to grade.

calice [kalis] *nm* (*vase*) *Rel* chalice.

calicot [kaliko] *nm* (*tissu*) calico.

califourchon (à) [akalifurʃɔ̃] *adv* astride; **se mettre à c. sur** to straddle.

câlin [kalɛ̃] *a* endearing, cuddly. ◆**câliner** *vt* (*cajoler*) to make a fuss of; (*caresser*) to cuddle. ◆**câlineries** *nfpl* endearing ways.

calleux, -euse [kalø, -øz] *a* callous, horny.

calligraphie [kaligrafi] *nf* calligraphy.

calme [kalm] *a* calm; (*flegmatique*) calm, cool; (*journée etc*) quiet, calm; – *nm* calm(ness); **du c.!** keep quiet!; (*pas de panique*) keep calm!; **dans le c.** (*travailler, étudier*) in peace and quiet. ◆**calm/er** *vt* (*douleur*) to soothe; (*inquiétude*) to calm; (*ardeur*) to temper; **c. qn** to calm s.o. (down); – **se c.** *vpr* to calm down. ◆**-ant** *nm* sedative; **sous calmants** under sedation.

calomnie [kalɔmni] *nf* slander; (*par écrit*) libel. ◆**calomnier** *vt* to slander; to libel. ◆**calomnieux, -euse** *a* slanderous; libellous.

calorie [kalɔri] *nf* calorie.

calorifère [kalɔrifɛr] *nm* stove.

calorifuge [kalɔrifyʒ] *a* (heat-)insulating. ◆**calorifuger** *vt* to lag.

calot [kalo] *nm* *Mil* forage cap.

calotte [kalɔt] *nf* *Rel* skull cap; (*gifle*) *Fam* slap; **c. glaciaire** icecap.

calque [kalk] *nm* (*dessin*) tracing; (*imitation*) (exact *ou* carbon) copy; (**papier-**)**c.** tracing paper. ◆**calquer** *vt* to trace; to copy; **c. sur** to model on.

calumet [kalyme] *nm* **c. de la paix** peace pipe.

calvaire [kalvɛr] *nm* *Rel* calvary; *Fig* agony.

calvitie [kalvisi] *nf* baldness.

camarade [kamarad] *nmf* friend, chum; *Pol* comrade; **c. de jeu** playmate; **c. d'atelier** workmate. ◆**camaraderie** *nf* friendship, companionship.

cambouis [kɑ̃bwi] *nm* grease, (engine) oil.

cambrer [kɑ̃bre] *vt* to arch; **c. les reins** *ou* **le buste** to throw out one's chest; – **se c.** *vpr* to throw back one's shoulders. ◆**cambrure** *nf* curve; (*de pied*) arch, instep.

cambriol/er [kɑ̃brijɔle] *vt* to burgle, *Am* burglarize. ◆**-age** *nm* burglary. ◆**-eur, -euse** *nmf* burglar.

came [kam] *nf* *Tech* cam; **arbre à cames** camshaft.

camée [kame] *nm* (*pierre*) cameo.

caméléon [kameleɔ̃] *nm* (*reptile*) chameleon.

camélia [kamelja] *nm* *Bot* camellia.

camelot [kamlo] *nm* street hawker. ◆**camelote** *nf* cheap goods, junk.

camembert [kamɑ̃bɛr] *nm* Camembert (cheese).

camer (se) [səkame] *vpr* *Fam* to get high (on drugs).

caméra [kamera] *nf* (TV *ou* film) camera. ◆**caméraman** *nm* (*pl* **-mans** *ou* **-men**) cameraman.

camion [kamjɔ̃] *nm* lorry, *Am* truck. ◆**c.-benne** *nm* (*pl* **camions-bennes**) dustcart, *Am* garbage truck. ◆**c.-citerne** *nm* (*pl* **camions-citernes**) tanker, *Am* tank truck. ◆**camionnage** *nm* (road) haulage, *Am* trucking. ◆**camionnette** *nf* van. ◆**camionneur** *nm* (*entrepreneur*) haulage contractor, *Am* trucker; (*conducteur*) lorry *ou* *Am* truck driver.

camisole [kamizɔl] *nf* **c. de force** straitjacket.

camomille [kamɔmij] *nf* *Bot* camomile; (*tisane*) camomile tea.

camoufl/er [kamufle] *vt* to camouflage. ◆**-age** *nm* camouflage.

camp [kɑ̃] *nm* camp; **feu de c.** campfire; **lit de c.** camp bed; **c. de concentration** concentration camp; **dans mon c.** (*jeu*) on my side; **ficher** *ou* **foutre le c.** *Arg* to clear off. ◆**camp/er** *vi* to camp; – *vt* (*personnage*) to portray (boldly); (*chapeau etc*) to plant boldly; – **se c.** *vpr* to plant oneself (boldly) (**devant** in front of). ◆**-ement** *nm* encampment, camp. ◆**-eur, -euse** *nmf* camper. ◆**camping** *nm* camping; (*terrain*) camp(ing) site. ◆**camping-car** *nm* camper.

campagne [kɑ̃paɲ] *nf* **1** country(side); **à la c.** in the country. **2** (*électorale, militaire etc*) campaign. ◆**campagnard, -arde** *a* country-; – *nm* countryman; – *nf* countrywoman.

campanile [kɑ̃panil] *nm* belltower.

camphre [kɑ̃fr] *nm* camphor.

campus [kɑ̃pys] *nm* *Univ* campus.

camus [kamy] *a* (*personne*) snub-nosed; **nez c.** snub nose.

Canada [kanada] *nm* Canada. ◆**canadien, -ienne** *a & nmf* Canadian; – *nf* fur-lined jacket.

canaille [kanaj] *nf* rogue, scoundrel; – *a* vulgar, cheap.

canal, -aux [kanal, -o] nm (artificiel) canal; (bras de mer) & TV channel; (conduite) & Anat duct; **par le c. de** via, through. ◆**canalisation** nf (de gaz etc) mains. ◆**canaliser** vt (rivière etc) to canalize; (diriger) Fig to channel.

canapé [kanape] nm **1** (siège) sofa, couch, settee. **2** (tranche de pain) canapé.

canard [kanar] nm **1** duck; (mâle) drake. **2** Mus false note. **3** (journal) Péj rag. ◆**canarder** vt (faire feu sur) to fire at or on.

canari [kanari] nm canary.

cancans [kɑ̃kɑ̃] nmpl (malicious) gossip. ◆**cancaner** vi to gossip. ◆**cancanier, -ière** a gossipy.

cancer [kɑ̃sɛr] nm cancer; **le C.** (signe) Cancer. ◆**cancéreux, -euse** a cancerous; – nmf cancer patient. ◆**cancérigène** a carcinogenic. ◆**cancérologue** nmf cancer specialist.

cancre [kɑ̃kr] nm Scol Péj dunce.

cancrelat [kɑ̃krəla] nm cockroach.

candélabre [kɑ̃delabr] nm candelabra.

candeur [kɑ̃dœr] nf innocence, artlessness. ◆**candide** a artless, innocent.

candidat, -ate [kɑ̃dida, -at] nmf candidate; (à un poste) applicant, candidate; **être ou se porter c.** to apply for. ◆**candidature** nf application; Pol candidacy; **poser sa c.** to apply (à for).

cane [kan] nf (female) duck. ◆**caneton** nm duckling.

canette [kanɛt] nf **1** (de bière) (small) bottle. **2** (bobine) spool.

canevas [kanva] nm (toile) canvas; (ébauche) framework, outline.

caniche [kaniʃ] nm poodle.

canicule [kanikyl] nf scorching heat; (période) dog days.

canif [kanif] nm penknife.

canine [kanin] **1** af (espèce, race) canine; **exposition c.** dog show. **2** nf (dent) canine.

caniveau, -x [kanivo] nm gutter (in street).

canne [kan] nf (walking) stick; (à sucre, de bambou) cane; (de roseau) reed; **c. à pêche** fishing rod.

cannelle [kanɛl] nf Bot Culin cinnamon.

cannelure [kanlyr] nf groove; Archit flute.

cannette [kanɛt] nf = **canette**.

cannibale [kanibal] nmf & a cannibal. ◆**cannibalisme** nm cannibalism.

canoë [kanɔe] nm canoe; Sp canoeing. ◆**canoëiste** nmf canoeist.

canon [kanɔ̃] nm **1** (big) gun; Hist cannon; (de fusil etc) barrel; **c. lisse** smooth bore; **chair à c.** cannon fodder. **2** (règle) canon.

◆**canoniser** vt to canonize. ◆**canonnade** nf gunfire. ◆**canonnier** nm gunner.

cañon [kaɲɔ̃] nm canyon.

canot [kano] nm boat; **c. de sauvetage** lifeboat; **c. pneumatique** rubber dinghy. ◆**canot/er** vi to boat, go boating. ◆**—age** nm boating.

cantaloup [kɑ̃talu] nm (melon) cantaloup(e).

cantate [kɑ̃tat] nf Mus cantata.

cantatrice [kɑ̃tatris] nf opera singer.

cantine [kɑ̃tin] nf **1** (réfectoire) canteen; **manger à la c.** Scol to have school dinners. **2** (coffre) tin trunk.

cantique [kɑ̃tik] nm hymn.

canton [kɑ̃tɔ̃] nm (en France) district (division of arrondissement); (en Suisse) canton. ◆**cantonal, -aux** a divisional; cantonal.

cantonade (à la) [alakɑ̃tɔnad] adv (parler etc) to all and sundry, to everyone in general.

cantonn/er [kɑ̃tɔne] vt Mil to billet; (confiner) to confine; – vi Mil to be billeted; **— se c.** vpr to confine oneself (dans to). ◆**—ement** nm (lieu) billet, quarters.

cantonnier [kɑ̃tɔnje] nm road mender.

canular [kanylar] nm practical joke, hoax.

canyon [kaɲɔ̃] nm canyon.

caoutchouc [kautʃu] nm rubber; (élastique) rubber band; pl (chaussures) galoshes; **en c.** (balle etc) rubber-; **c. mousse** foam. ◆**caoutchouter** vt to rubberize. ◆**caoutchouteux, -euse** a rubbery.

CAP [seape] nm abrév (certificat d'aptitude professionnelle) technical and vocational diploma.

cap [kap] nm Géog cape, headland; Nau course; **mettre le c. sur** to steer a course for; **franchir ou doubler le c. de** (difficulté) to get over the worst of; **franchir ou doubler le c. de la trentaine** etc to turn thirty etc.

capable [kapabl] a capable, able; **c. de faire** able to do, capable of doing. ◆**capacité** nf ability, capacity; (contenance) capacity.

cape [kap] nf cape; (grande) cloak.

CAPES [kapɛs] nm abrév (certificat d'aptitude professionnelle à l'enseignement secondaire) teaching diploma.

capillaire [kapilɛr] a (huile, lotion) hair-.

capitaine [kapitɛn] nm captain.

capital, -ale, -aux [kapital, -o] **1** a major, fundamental, chief (peine) capital; (péché) deadly. **2** a (lettre) capital; – nf (lettre, ville) capital. **3** nm & nmpl Fin capital. ◆**capitaliser** vt (accumuler) to build up; – vi to save up. ◆**capitalisme** nm capitalism. ◆**capitaliste** a & nmf capitalist.

capiteux, -euse [kapitø, -øz] a (vin, parfum) heady.

capitonn/er [kapitɔne] vt to pad, upholster. ◆**—age** nm (garniture) padding, upholstery.

capituler [kapityle] vi to surrender, capitulate. ◆**capitulation** nf surrender, capitulation.

caporal, -aux [kapɔral, -o] nm corporal.

capot [kapo] nm Aut bonnet, Am hood.

capote [kapɔt] nf Aut hood, Am (convertible) top; Mil greatcoat; **c. (anglaise)** (préservatif) Fam condom. ◆**capoter** vi Aut Av to overturn.

câpre [kɑpr] nf Bot Culin caper.

caprice [kapris] nm (passing) whim, caprice. ◆**capricieux, -euse** a capricious.

Capricorne [kaprikɔrn] nm **le C.** (signe) Capricorn.

capsule [kapsyl] nf (spatiale) & Méd etc capsule; (de bouteille, pistolet d'enfant) cap.

capter [kapte] vt (faveur etc) to win; (attention) to capture, win; (eau) to draw off; Rad to pick up.

captif, -ive [kaptif, -iv] a & nmf captive. ◆**captiver** vt to captivate, fascinate. ◆**captivité** nf captivity.

capture [kaptyr] nf capture; catch. ◆**capturer** vt (criminel, navire) to capture; (animal) to catch, capture.

capuche [kapyʃ] nf hood. ◆**capuchon** nm hood; (de moine) cowl; (pèlerine) hooded (rain)coat; (de stylo) cap, top.

capucine [kapysin] nf (plante) nasturtium.

caquet [kake] nm (bavardage) cackle. ◆**caquet/er** vi (poule, personne) to cackle. ◆**—age** nm cackle.

car [kar] **1** conj because, for. **2** nm coach, bus, Am bus; **c. de police** police van.

carabine [karabin] nf rifle, carbine; **c. à air comprimé** airgun.

carabiné [karabine] a Fam violent; (punition, amende) very stiff.

caracoler [karakɔle] vi to prance, caper.

caractère [karaktεr] nm **1** (lettre) Typ character; **en petits caractères** in small print; **caractères d'imprimerie** block capitals ou letters; **caractères gras** bold type ou characters. **2** (tempérament, nature) character, nature; (attribut) characteristic; **aucun c. de gravité** no serious element; **son c. inégal** his ou her uneven temper; **avoir bon c.** to be good-natured. ◆**caractériel, -ielle** a (trait, troubles) character-; – a & nmf

disturbed (child). ◆**caractériser** vt to characterize; **se c. par** to be characterized by. ◆**caractéristique** a & nf characteristic.

carafe [karaf] nf decanter, carafe.

carambol/er [karɑ̃bɔle] vt Aut to smash into. ◆**—age** nm pileup, multiple smash-up.

caramel [karamεl] nm caramel; (bonbon dur) toffee.

carapace [karapas] nf (de tortue etc) & Fig shell.

carat [kara] nm carat.

caravane [karavan] nf (dans le désert) caravan; Aut caravan, Am trailer; **c. publicitaire** publicity convoy. ◆**caravaning** n, ◆**caravanage** n caravanning.

carbone [karbɔn] nm carbon; (papier) **c.** carbon (paper). ◆**carboniser** vt to burn (to ashes), char; (substance) Ch to carbonize; **être mort carbonisé** to be burned to death.

carburant [karbyrɑ̃] nm Aut fuel. ◆**carburateur** nm carburettor, Am carburetor.

carcan [karkɑ̃] nm Hist iron collar; (contrainte) Fig yoke.

carcasse [karkas] nf Anat carcass; (d'immeuble etc) frame, shell.

cardiaque [kardjak] a (trouble etc) heart-; **crise c.** heart attack; **arrêt c.** cardiac arrest; – nmf heart patient.

cardinal, -aux [kardinal, -o] **1** a (nombre, point) cardinal. **2** nm Rel cardinal.

Carême [karεm] nm Lent.

carence [karɑ̃s] nf inadequacy, incompetence; Méd deficiency.

carène [karεn] nf Nau hull. ◆**caréné** a Aut Av streamlined.

caresse [karεs] nf caress. ◆**caress/er** [karese] vt (animal, enfant etc) to stroke, pat, fondle; (femme, homme) to caress; (espoir) to cherish. ◆**—ant** a endearing, loving.

cargaison [kargεzɔ̃] nf cargo, freight. ◆**cargo** nm freighter, cargo boat.

caricature [karikatyr] nf caricature. ◆**caricatural, -aux** a ludicrous; **portrait c.** portrait in caricature. ◆**caricaturer** vt to caricature.

carie [kari] nf **la c. (dentaire)** tooth decay; **une c.** a cavity. ◆**carié** a (dent) decayed, bad.

carillon [karijɔ̃] nm (cloches) chimes, peal; (horloge) chiming clock. ◆**carillonner** vi to chime, peal.

carlingue [karlɛ̃g] nf (fuselage) Av cabin.

carnage [karnaʒ] *nm* carnage.

carnassier, -ière [karnasje, -jɛr] *a* carnivorous; − *nm* carnivore.

carnaval, *pl* **-als** [karnaval] *nm* carnival.

carné [karne] *a* (*régime*) meat-.

carnet [karnɛ] *nm* notebook; (*de timbres, chèques, adresses etc*) book; **c. de notes** school report; **c. de route** logbook; **c. de vol** *Av* logbook.

carnivore [karnivɔr] *a* carnivorous; − *nm* carnivore.

carotte [karɔt] *nf* carrot.

carotter [karɔte] *vt Arg* to wangle, cadge (**à qn** from s.o.).

carpe [karp] *nf* carp.

carpette [karpɛt] *nf* rug.

carquois [karkwa] *nm* (*étui*) quiver.

carré [kare] *a* a square; (*en affaires*) *Fig* plain-dealing; − *nm* square; (*de jardin*) patch; *Nau* messroom; **c. de soie** (square) silk scarf.

carreau, -x [karo] *nm* (*vitre*) (window) pane; (*pavé*) tile; (*sol*) tiled floor; *Cartes* diamonds; **à carreaux** (*nappe etc*) check(ed); **se tenir à c.** to watch one's step; **rester sur le c.** to be left for dead; (*candidat*) *Fig* to be left out in the cold. ◆**carrel/er** *vt* to tile. ◆**-age** *nm* (*sol*) tiled floor; (*action*) tiling.

carrefour [karfur] *nm* crossroads.

carrelet [karlɛ] *nm* (*poisson*) plaice, *Am* flounder.

carrément [karemã] *adv* (*dire etc*) straight out, bluntly; (*complètement*) downright, well and truly.

carrer (se) [səkare] *vpr* to settle down firmly.

carrière [karjɛr] *nf* **1** (*terrain*) quarry. **2** (*métier*) career.

carrosse [karɔs] *nm Hist* (horse-drawn) carriage. ◆**carrossable** *a* suitable for vehicles. ◆**carrosserie** *nf Aut* body(work).

carrousel [karuzɛl] *nm* (*tourbillon*) *Fig* whirl, merry-go-round.

carrure [karyr] *nf* breadth of shoulders, build; *Fig* calibre.

cartable [kartabl] *nm Scol* satchel.

carte [kart] *nf* card; (*de lecteur*) ticket; *Géog* map; *Nau* Mét chart; *Culin* menu; *pl* (*jeu*) cards; **c. (postale)** (post)card; **c. à jouer** playing card; **c. de crédit** credit card; **c. des vins** wine list; **c. grise** *Aut* vehicle registration; **c. blanche** *Fig* free hand.

cartel [kartɛl] *nm Écon Pol* cartel.

carter [kartɛr] *nm* (*de moteur*) *Aut* crankcase; (*de bicyclette*) chain guard.

cartilage [kartilaʒ] *nm* cartilage.

carton [kartɔ̃] *nm* cardboard; (*boîte*) cardboard box, carton; (*pour dessin*) portfolio; **en c.-pâte** (*faux*) *Péj* pasteboard; **faire un c. sur** *Fam* to take a potshot at. ◆**cartonn/er** *vt* (*livre*) to case; **livre cartonné** hardback. ◆**-age** *nm* (*emballage*) cardboard package.

cartouche [kartuʃ] *nf* cartridge; (*de cigarettes*) carton; *Phot* cassette. ◆**cartouchière** *nf* (*ceinture*) cartridge belt.

cas [ka] *nm* case; **en tout c.** in any case *ou* event; **en aucun c.** on no account; **en c. de besoin** if need(s) be; **en c. d'accident** in the event of an accident; **en c. d'urgence** in (case of) an emergency; **faire c. de/peu de c.** to set great/little store by; **au c. où elle tomberait** if she should fall; **pour le c. où il pleuvrait** in case it rains.

casanier, -ière [kazanje, -jɛr] *a & nmf* home-loving (person); (*pantouflard*) *Péj* stay-at-home (person).

casaque [kazak] *nf* (*de jockey*) shirt, blouse.

cascade [kaskad] *nf* **1** waterfall; (*série*) *Fig* spate; **en c.** in succession. **2** *Cin* stunt. ◆**cascadeur, -euse** *nmf Cin* stunt man, stunt woman.

case [kaz] *nf* **1** pigeonhole; (*de tiroir*) compartment; (*d'échiquier etc*) square; (*de formulaire*) box. **2** (*hutte*) hut, cabin.

caser [kaze] *vt Fam* (*ranger*) to park, place; **c. qn** (*dans un logement ou un travail*) to find a place for s.o.; (*marier*) to marry s.o. off; − **se c.** *vpr* to settle down.

caserne [kazɛrn] *nf Mil* barracks; **c. de pompiers** fire station.

casier [kazje] *nm* pigeonhole, compartment; (*meuble à clef*) filing cabinet; (*fermant à clef, à consigne automatique*) locker; **c. à bouteilles/à disques** bottle/record rack; **c. judiciaire** criminal record.

casino [kazino] *nm* casino.

casque [kask] *nm* helmet; (*pour cheveux*) (hair) dryer; **c. (à écouteurs)** headphones; **les Casques bleus** the UN peace-keeping force. ◆**casqué** *a* helmeted, wearing a helmet.

casquer [kaske] *vi Fam* to pay up, cough up.

casquette [kaskɛt] *nf* (*coiffure*) cap.

cassation [kasasjɔ̃] *nf* **Cour de c.** supreme court of appeal.

casse[1] [kas] *nf* **1** (*action*) breakage; (*objets*) breakages; (*grabuge*) *Fam* trouble; **mettre à la c.** to scrap; **vendre à la c.** to sell for

scrap. **2** *Typ* case; **bas/haut de c.** lower/upper case.

casse² [kɑs] *nm* (*cambriolage*) *Arg* break-in.

casse-cou [kasku] *nmf inv* (*personne*) *Fam* daredevil. ◆**c.-croûte** *nm inv* snack. ◆**c.-gueule** *nm inv Fam* death trap; — *a inv* perilous. ◆**c.-noisettes** *nm inv*, ◆**c.-noix** *nm inv* nut-cracker(s). ◆**c.-pieds** *nmf inv* (*personne*) *Fam* pain in the neck. ◆**c.-tête** *nm inv* **1** (*massue*) club. **2** (*problème*) headache; (*jeu*) puzzle, brain teaser.

cass/er [kɑse] *vt* to break; (*noix*) to crack; (*annuler*) *Jur* to annul; (*dégrader*) *Mil* to cashier; — *vi*, — **se c.** *vpr* to break; **il me casse la tête** *Fam* he's giving me a headache; **elle me casse les pieds** *Fam* she's getting on my nerves; **se c. la tête** *Fam* to rack one's brains; **se c. la figure à qn** *Fam* to smash s.o.'s face in; **se c. la figure** (*tomber*) *Fam* to come a cropper, *Am* take a spill; **ça ne casse rien** *Fam* it's nothing special; **ça vaut 50F à tout c.** *Fam* it's worth 50F at the very most; **il ne s'est pas cassé** *Iron Fam* he didn't bother himself *ou* exhaust himself. ◆**—ant** *a* (*fragile*) brittle; (*brusque*) *Fam* curt, imperious; (*fatigant*) *Fam* exhausting. ◆**—eur** *nm Aut* breaker, scrap merchant; (*manifestant*) demonstrator who damages property.

casserole [kasrɔl] *nf* (sauce)pan.

cassette [kasɛt] *nf* (*pour magnétophone ou magnétoscope*) cassette; **sur c.** (*film*) on video; **faire une c. de** (*film*) to make a video of.

cassis **1** [kasis] *nm Bot* blackcurrant; (*boisson*) blackcurrant liqueur. **2** [kasi] *nm Aut* dip (across road).

cassoulet [kasule] *nm* stew (of meat and beans).

cassure [kasyr] *nf* (*fissure, rupture*) break; *Géol* fault.

castagnettes [kastaɲɛt] *nfpl* castanets.

caste [kast] *nf* caste; **esprit de c.** class consciousness.

castor [kastɔr] *nm* beaver.

castrer [kastre] *vt* to castrate. ◆**castration** *nf* castration.

cataclysme [kataklism] *nm* cataclysm.

catacombes [katakɔ̃b] *nfpl* catacombs.

catalogue [katalɔg] *nm* catalogue. ◆**cataloguer** *vt* (*livres etc*) to catalogue; **c. qn** *Péj* to categorize s.o.

catalyseur [katalizœr] *nm Ch & Fig* catalyst.

cataphote® [katafɔt] *nm Aut* reflector.

cataplasme [kataplasm] *nm Méd* poultice.

catapulte [katapylt] *nf Hist Av* catapult. ◆**catapulter** *vt* to catapult.

cataracte [katarakt] *nf* **1** *Méd* cataract. **2** (*cascade*) falls, cataract.

catastrophe [katastrɔf] *nf* disaster, catastrophe; **atterrir en c.** to make an emergency landing. ◆**catastrophique** *a* disastrous, catastrophic.

catch [katʃ] *nm* (all-in) wrestling. ◆**catcheur, -euse** *nmf* wrestler.

catéchisme [kateʃism] *nm Rel* catechism.

catégorie [kategɔri] *nf* category. ◆**catégorique** *a* categorical.

cathédrale [katedral] *nf* cathedral.

catholicisme [katɔlisism] *nm* Catholicism. ◆**catholique** *a & nmf* Catholic; **pas (très) c.** (*affaire, personne*) *Fig* shady, doubtful.

catimini (en) [ɑ̃katimini] *adv* on the sly.

cauchemar [koʃmar] *nm* nightmare.

cause [koz] *nf* cause; *Jur* case; **à c. de** because of, on account of; **et pour c.!** for a very good reason!; **pour c. de** on account of; **en connaissance de c.** in full knowledge of the facts; **mettre en c.** (*la bonne foi de qn etc*) (to call into) question; (*personne*) to implicate; **en c.** involved, in question.

caus/er [koze] **1** *vt* (*provoquer*) to cause. **2** *vi* (*bavarder*) to chat (*de* about); (*discourir*) to talk; (*jaser*) to blab. ◆**—ant** *a Fam* chatty, talkative. ◆**causerie** *nf* talk. ◆**causette** *nf* **faire la c.** *Fam* to have a little chat.

caustique [kostik] *a* (*substance, esprit*) caustic.

cauteleux, -euse [kotlø, -øz] *a* wily, sly.

cautériser [koterize] *vt Méd* to cauterize.

caution [kosjɔ̃] *nf* surety; (*pour libérer qn*) *Jur* bail; **sous c.** on bail; **sujet à c.** (*nouvelle etc*) very doubtful. ◆**cautionn/er** *vt* (*approuver*) to sanction. ◆**—ement** *nm* (*garantie*) surety.

cavalcade [kavalkad] *nf Fam* stampede; (*défilé*) cavalcade. ◆**cavale** *nf* **en c.** *Arg* on the run. ◆**cavaler** *vi Fam* to run, rush.

cavalerie [kavalri] *nf Mil* cavalry; (*de cirque*) horses. ◆**cavalier, -ière 1** *nmf* rider; — *nm Mil* trooper, cavalryman; *Échecs* knight; — *nf* (*pour danser*) partner, escort. **3** *a* (*insolent*) offhand.

cave [kav] **1** *nf* cellar, vault. **2** *a* sunken, hollow. ◆**caveau, -x** *nm* (*sépulture*) (burial) vault.

caverne [kavɛrn] *nf* cave, cavern; **homme**

des **cavernes** caveman. ◆**caverneux, -euse** a (voix, rire) hollow, deep-sounding.
caviar [kavjar] nm caviar(e).
cavité [kavite] nf cavity.
CCP [sesepe] nm abrév (Compte chèque postal) PO Giro account, Am Post Office checking account.

ce¹ [s(ə)] (c' before e and é) pron dém 1 it, that; **c'est toi/bon/demain**/etc it's ou that's you/good/tomorrow/etc; **c'est mon médecin** he's my doctor; **ce sont eux qui** ... they are the ones who ...; **c'est à elle de jouer** it's her turn to play; **est-ce que tu viens?** are you coming?; **sur ce** at this point, thereupon. 2 **ce que, ce qui** what; **je sais ce qui est bon/ce que tu veux** I know what is good/what you want; **ce que c'est beau!** how beautiful it is!

ce², **cette**, pl **ces** [s(ə), sɛt, se] (ce becomes **cet** before a vowel or mute h) a dém this, that; pl these, those; (+ -ci) this, pl these; (+ -là) that, pl those; **cet homme** this ou that man; **cet homme-ci** this man; **cet homme-là** that man.
ceci [səsi] pron dém this; **écoutez bien c.** listen to this.
cécité [sesite] nf blindness.
céder [sede] vt to give up (à to); Jur to transfer; **c. le pas à** to give way ou precedence to; – vi (personne) to give way, give in, yield (à to); (branche, chaise etc) to give way.
cédille [sedij] nf Gram cedilla.
cèdre [sɛdr] nm (arbre, bois) cedar.
CEE [seøø] nf abrév (Communauté économique européenne) EEC.
ceindre [sɛ̃dr] vt (épée) Lit to gird on.
ceinture [sɛ̃tyr] nf belt; (de robe de chambre) cord; (taille) Anat waist; (de remparts) Hist girdle; **petite/grande c.** Rail inner/outer circle; **c. de sécurité** Aut Av seatbelt; **c. de sauvetage** lifebelt. ◆**ceinturer** vt to seize round the waist; Rugby to tackle; (ville) to girdle, surround.
cela [s(ə)la] pron dém (pour désigner) that; (sujet indéfini) it, that; **c. m'attriste que** ... it saddens me that ...; **quand/comment/etc c.?** when?/how?/etc; **c'est c.** that is so.
célèbre [selɛbr] a famous. ◆**célébrité** nf fame; (personne) celebrity.
célébrer [selebre] vt to celebrate. ◆**célébration** nf celebration (de of).
céleri [sɛlri] nm (en branches) celery.
céleste [selɛst] a celestial, heavenly.
célibat [seliba] nm celibacy. ◆**célibataire** a (non marié) single, unmarried; (chaste)

celibate; – nm bachelor; – nf unmarried woman, spinster.
celle voir **celui**.
cellier [selje] nm storeroom (for wine etc).
cellophane® [selɔfan] nf cellophane®.
cellule [selyl] nf cell. ◆**cellulaire** a (tissu etc) Biol cell-; **voiture c.** prison van.
celluloïd [selylɔid] nm celluloid.
cellulose [selyloz] nf cellulose.
celtique ou **celte** [sɛltik, sɛlt] a Celtic.
celui, **celle**, pl **ceux**, **celles** [səlɥi, sɛl, sø, sɛl] pron dém 1 the one, pl those, the ones; **c. de Jean** John's (one); **ceux de Jean** John's (ones), those of John. 2 (+ -ci) this one, pl these (ones); (dont on vient de parler) the latter; (+ -là) that one, pl those (ones); the former; **ceux-ci sont gros** these (ones) are big.
cendre [sɑ̃dr] nf ash. ◆**cendré** a ash(-coloured), ashen. ◆**cendrée** nf Sp cinder track.
Cendrillon [sɑ̃drijɔ̃] nm Cinderella.
censé [sɑ̃se] a supposed; **il n'est pas c. le savoir** he's not supposed to know.
censeur [sɑ̃sœr] nm censor; Scol assistant headmaster, vice-principal. ◆**censure** nf **la c.** (examen) censorship; (comité, service) the censor; **motion de c.** Pol censure motion. ◆**censurer** vt (film etc) to censor; (critiquer) & Pol to censure.
cent [sɑ̃] ([sɑ̃t] pl [sɑ̃z] before vowel and mute h except un and onze) a & nm hundred; **c. pages** ou one hundred pages; **deux cents pages** two hundred pages; **deux c. trois pages** two hundred and three pages; **cinq pour c.** five per cent. ◆**centaine** nf **une c.** a hundred (or so); **des centaines de** hundreds of. ◆**centenaire** a & nmf centenarian; – nm (anniversaire) centenary. ◆**centième** a & nmf hundredth; **un c.** a hundredth. ◆**centigrade** a centigrade. ◆**centime** nm centime. ◆**centimètre** nm centimetre; (ruban) tape measure.
central, **-aux** [sɑ̃tral, -o] 1 a central; **pouvoir c.** (power of) central government. 2 nm **c.** (téléphonique) telephone exchange. ◆**centrale** nf (usine) power station. ◆**centraliser** vt to centralize. ◆**centre** nm centre; **c. commercial** shopping centre. ◆**c.-ville** nm inv city ou town centre. ◆**centrer** vt to centre. ◆**centrifuge** a centrifugal. ◆**centrifugeuse** nf liquidizer, juice extractor.
centuple [sɑ̃typl] nm hundredfold; **au c.** a hundredfold. ◆**centupler** vti to increase a hundredfold.

cep [sɛp] nm vine stock. ◆**cépage** nm vine (plant).

cependant [səpɑ̃dɑ̃] conj however, yet.

céramique [seramik] nf (art) ceramics; (matière) ceramic; **de** ou **en c.** ceramic.

cerceau, -x [sɛrso] nm hoop.

cercle [sɛrkl] nm (forme, groupe, étendue) circle; **c. vicieux** vicious circle.

cercueil [sɛrkœj] nm coffin.

céréale [sereal] nf cereal.

cérébral, -aux [serebral, -o] a cerebral.

cérémonie [seremɔni] nf ceremony; **de c.** (tenue etc) ceremonial; **sans c.** (inviter, manger) informally; **faire des cérémonies** Fam to make a lot of fuss; **cérémonial,** pl **-als** nm ceremonial. ◆**cérémonieux, -euse** a ceremonious.

cerf [sɛr] nm deer; (mâle) stag. ◆**cerf-volant** nm (pl **cerfs-volants**) (jouet) kite.

cerise [s(ə)riz] nf cherry. ◆**cerisier** nm cherry tree.

cerne [sɛrn] nm (cercle, marque) ring. ◆**cerner** vt to surround; (problème) to define; **les yeux cernés** with rings under one's eyes.

certain [sɛrtɛ̃] **1** a (sûr) certain, sure; **il est** ou **c'est sûr que tu réussiras** you're certain ou sure to succeed; **je suis c. de réussir** I'm certain ou sure I'll succeed; **être c. de qch** to be certain ou sure of sth. **2** a (imprécis, difficile à fixer) certain; pl certain, some; **un c. temps** a certain (amount of) time; – pron pl some (people), certain people; (choses) some. ◆**certainement** adv certainly. ◆**certes** adv certainly.

certificat [sɛrtifika] nm certificate. ◆**certifier** vt to certify; **je vous certifie que** I assure you that. ◆**-é** a (professeur) qualified.

certitude [sɛrtityd] nf certainty; **avoir la c. que** to be certain that.

cerveau, -x [sɛrvo] nm (organe) brain; (intelligence) mind, brain(s); **rhume de c.** head cold; **fuite des cerveaux** brain drain.

cervelas [sɛrvəla] nm saveloy.

cervelle [sɛrvɛl] nf (substance) brain; Culin brains; **tête sans c.** scatterbrain.

ces voir **ce** 2.

CES [seəɛs] nm abrév (collège d'enseignement secondaire) comprehensive school, Am high school.

césarienne [sezarjɛn] nf Méd Caesarean (section).

cessation [sɛsasjɔ̃] nf (arrêt, fin) suspension.

cesse [sɛs] nf **sans c.** incessantly; **elle n'a**

(**pas**) **eu de c. que je fasse** ... she had no rest until I did ....

cesser [sese] vti to stop; **faire c.** to put a stop ou halt to; **il ne cesse (pas) de parler** he doesn't stop talking. ◆**cessez-le-feu** nm inv ceasefire.

cession [sɛsjɔ̃] nf Jur transfer.

c'est-à-dire [sɛtadir] conj that is (to say), in other words.

cet, cette voir **ce** 2.

ceux voir **celui.**

chacal, pl **-als** [ʃakal] nm jackal.

chacun, -une [ʃakœ̃, -yn] pron each (one), every one; (tout le monde) everyone.

chagrin [ʃagrɛ̃] **1** nm sorrow, grief; **avoir du c.** to be very upset. **2** a Lit doleful. ◆**chagriner** vt to upset, distress.

chahut [ʃay] nm racket, noisy disturbance. ◆**chahut/er** vi to create a racket ou a noisy disturbance; – vt (professeur) to be rowdy with, play up. ◆**—eur, -euse** nmf rowdy.

chai [ʃɛ] nm wine and spirits storehouse.

chaîne [ʃɛn] nf chain; TV channel, network; Géog chain, range; Nau cable; Tex warp; pl (liens) Fig shackles, chains; **c. de montage** assembly line; **travail à la c.** production-line work; **c. haute fidélité,** **c. hi-fi** hi-fi system; **c. de magasins** chain of shops ou Am stores; **collision en c.** Aut multiple collision; **réaction en c.** chain reaction. ◆**chaînette** nf (small) chain. ◆**chaînon** nm (anneau, lien) link.

chair [ʃɛr] nf flesh; (couleur) **c.** flesh-coloured; **en c. et en os** in the flesh; **la c. de poule** goose pimples, gooseflesh; **bien en c.** plump; **c. à saucisses** sausage meat.

chaire [ʃɛr] nf Univ chair; Rel pulpit.

chaise [ʃɛz] nf chair, seat; **c. longue** (siège pliant) deckchair; **c. d'enfant, c. haute** high-chair.

chaland [ʃalɑ̃] nm barge, lighter.

châle [ʃal] nm shawl.

chalet [ʃalɛ] nm chalet.

chaleur [ʃalœr] nf heat; (douce) warmth; (d'un accueil, d'une voix etc) warmth; (des convictions) ardour; (d'une discussion) heat. ◆**chaleureux, -euse** a warm.

challenge [ʃalɑ̃ʒ] nm Sp contest.

chaloupe [ʃalup] nf launch, long boat.

chalumeau, -x [ʃalymo] nm blowlamp, Am blowtorch; Mus pipe.

chalut [ʃaly] nm trawl net, drag net. ◆**chalutier** nm (bateau) trawler.

chamailler (se) [ʃəmaje] vpr to squabble, bicker. ◆**chamailleries** nfpl squabbling, bickering.

chamarré [ʃamare] *a* (*robe etc*) richly coloured; **c. de** (*décorations etc*) Péj bedecked with.

chambard [ʃɑ̃bar] *nm Fam* (*tapage*) rumpus, row. ◆**chambarder** *vt Fam* to turn upside down; **il a tout chambardé dans** he's turned everything upside down in.

chambouler [ʃɑ̃bule] *vt Fam* to make topsy-turvy, turn upside down.

chambre [ʃɑ̃br] *nf* (bed)room; *Pol Jur Tech Anat* chamber; **c. à coucher** bedroom; (*mobilier*) bedroom suite; **c. à air** (*de pneu*) inner tube; **C. des Communes** *Pol* House of Commons; **c. d'ami** guest *ou* spare room; **c. forte** strongroom; **c. noire** *Phot* darkroom; **garder la c.** to stay indoors. ◆**chambrée** *nf Mil* barrack room. ◆**chambrer** *vt* (*vin*) to bring to room temperature.

chameau, -x [ʃamo] *nm* camel.

chamois [ʃamwa] **1** *nm* (*animal*) chamois; **peau de c.** chamois (leather), shammy. **2** *a inv* buff(-coloured).

champ [ʃɑ̃] *nm* field; (*domaine*) *Fig* scope, range; **c. de bataille** battlefield; **c. de courses** racecourse, racetrack; **c. de foire** fairground; **c. de tir** (*terrain*) range; **laisser le c. libre à qn** to leave the field open for s.o. ◆**champêtre** *a* rustic, rural.

champagne [ʃɑ̃paɲ] *nm* champagne; **c. brut** extra-dry champagne.

champignon [ʃɑ̃piɲɔ̃] *nm* **1** *Bot* mushroom; **c. vénéneux** toadstool, poisonous mushroom; **c. atomique** mushroom cloud. **2** *Aut Fam* accelerator pedal.

champion [ʃɑ̃pjɔ̃] *nm* champion. ◆**championnat** *nm* championship.

chance [ʃɑ̃s] *nf* luck; (*probabilité de réussir, occasion*) chance; **avoir de la c.** to be lucky; **tenter** *ou* **courir sa c.** to try one's luck; **c'est une c. que . . .** it's a stroke of luck that . . . ; **mes chances de succès** my chances of success. ◆**chanceux, -euse** *a* lucky.

chancel/er [ʃɑ̃sle] *vi* to stagger, totter; (*courage*) *Fig* to falter. ◆**-ant** *a* (*pas, santé*) faltering, shaky.

chancelier [ʃɑ̃səlje] *nm* chancellor. ◆**chancellerie** *nf* chancellery.

chancre [ʃɑ̃kr] *nm Méd & Fig* canker.

chandail [ʃɑ̃daj] *nm* (thick) sweater, jersey.

chandelier [ʃɑ̃dəlje] *nm* candlestick.

chandelle [ʃɑ̃dɛl] *nf* candle; **voir trente-six chandelles** *Fig* to see stars; **en c.** *Av Sp* straight into the air.

change [ʃɑ̃ʒ] *nm Fin* exchange; **le contrôle des changes** exchange control; **donner le c. à qn** to deceive s.o. ◆**chang/er** *vt* (*modifier, remplacer, échanger*) to change; **c. qn**

en to change s.o. into; **ça la changera de ne pas travailler** it'll be a change for her not to be working; **–** *vi* to change; **c. de voiture/d'adresse/***etc* to change one's car/address/*etc*; **c. de train/de place** to change trains/places; **c. de vitesse/de cap** to change gear/course; **c. de sujet** to change the subject; **– se c.** *vpr* to change (one's clothes). ◆**-eant** *a* (*temps*) changeable; (*humeur*) fickle; (*couleurs*) changing. ◆**-ement** *nm* change; **aimer le c.** to like change. ◆**-eur** *nm* moneychanger; **c. de monnaie** change machine.

chanoine [ʃanwan] *nm* (*personne*) *Rel* canon.

chanson [ʃɑ̃sɔ̃] *nf* song. ◆**chant** *nm* singing; (*chanson*) song; (*hymne*) chant; **c. de Noël** Christmas carol. ◆**chant/er** *vi* to sing; (*psalmodier*) to chant; (*coq*) to crow; **si ça te chante** *Fam* if you feel like it; **faire c. qn** to blackmail s.o.; **–** *vt* to sing; (*glorifier*) to sing of; (*dire*) *Fam* to say. ◆**-ant** *a* (*air, voix*) melodious. ◆**-age** *nm* blackmail. ◆**-eur, -euse** *nm* singer.

chantier [ʃɑ̃tje] *nm* (building) site; (*entrepôt*) builder's yard; **c. naval** shipyard; **mettre un travail en c.** to get a task under way.

chantonner [ʃɑ̃tɔne] *vti* to hum.

chantre [ʃɑ̃tr] *nm Rel* cantor.

chanvre [ʃɑ̃vr] *nm* hemp; **c. indien** (*plante*) cannabis.

chaos [kao] *nm* chaos. ◆**chaotique** *a* chaotic.

chaparder [ʃaparde] *vt Fam* to filch, pinch (à from).

chapeau, -x [ʃapo] *nm* hat; (*de champignon, roue*) cap; **c.!** well done!; **donner un coup de c.** (*pour saluer etc*) to raise one's hat; **c. mou** trilby, *Am* fedora. ◆**chapelier** *nm* hatter.

chapelet [ʃaplɛ] *nm* rosary; **dire son c.** to tell one's beads; **un c. de** (*saucisses, injures etc*) a string of.

chapelle [ʃapɛl] *nf* chapel; **c. ardente** chapel of rest.

chaperon [ʃaprɔ̃] *nm* chaperon(e). ◆**chaperonner** *vt* to chaperon(e).

chapiteau, -x [ʃapito] *nm* (*de cirque*) big top; (*pour expositions etc*) marquee, tent; (*de colonne*) *Archit* capital.

chapitre [ʃapitr] *nm* chapter; **sur le c. de** on the subject of. ◆**chapitrer** *vt* to scold, lecture.

chaque [ʃak] *a* each, every.

char [ʃar] *nm Hist* chariot; (*de carnaval*)

float; *Can Fam* car; **c. à bœufs** oxcart; **c. (d'assaut)** *Mil* tank.

charabia [ʃarabja] *nm Fam* gibberish.

charade [ʃarad] *nf (énigme)* riddle; *(mimée)* charade.

charbon [ʃarbɔ̃] *nm* coal; *(fusain)* charcoal; **c. de bois** charcoal; **sur des charbons ardents** like a cat on hot bricks. ◆**charbonnages** *nmpl* coalmines, collieries. ◆**charbonnier, -ière** *a* coal-; – *nm* coal merchant.

charcuter [ʃarkyte] *vt (opérer) Fam Péj* to cut up (badly).

charcuterie [ʃarkytri] *nf* pork butcher's shop; *(aliment)* cooked (pork) meats. ◆**charcutier, -ière** *nmf* pork butcher.

chardon [ʃardɔ̃] *nm Bot* thistle.

chardonneret [ʃardɔnrɛ] *nm (oiseau)* goldfinch.

charge [ʃarʒ] *nf (poids)* load; *(fardeau)* burden; *Jur Él Mil* charge; *(fonction)* office; *pl Fin* financial obligations; *(dépenses)* expenses; *(de locataire)* (maintenance) charges; **charges sociales** national insurance contributions, *Am* Social Security contributions; **à c.** *(enfant, parent)* dependent; **être à c. à qn** to be a burden to s.o.; **à c. de qn** *(personne)* dependent on s.o.; *(frais)* payable by s.o.; **prendre en c.** to take charge of, take responsibility for.

charg/er [ʃarʒe] *vt* to load; *Él Mil* to charge; *(passager) Fam* to take up; **se c. de** *(enfant, tâche etc)* to take charge of; **c. qn de** *(impôts etc)* to burden s.o. with; *(paquets etc)* to take up with; *(tâche etc)* to entrust s.o. with; **c. qn de faire** to instruct s.o. to do. ◆**-é, -ée** *a (personne, véhicule, arme etc)* loaded; *(journée etc)* heavy, busy; *(langue)* coated; – *a (arbre, navire etc)* laden with; – *nmf* **c. de cours** *Univ* (temporary) lecturer. ◆**-ement** *nm (action)* loading; *(objet)* load. ◆**-eur** *nm (de piles)* charger.

chariot [ʃarjo] *nm (à bagages etc)* trolley, *Am* cart; *(de ferme)* waggon; *(de machine à écrire)* carriage.

charité [ʃarite] *nf (vertu, secours)* charity; *(acte)* act of charity; **faire la c.** to give to charity; **faire la c. à** *(mendiant)* to give to. ◆**charitable** *a* charitable.

charivari [ʃarivari] *nm Fam* hubbub, hullabaloo.

charlatan [ʃarlatɑ̃] *nm* charlatan, quack.

charme [ʃarm] *nm* **1** charm; *(magie)* spell. **2** *(arbre)* hornbeam. ◆**charm/er** *vt* to charm; **je suis charmé de vous voir** I'm delighted to see you. ◆**-ant** *a* charming.

◆**-eur, -euse** *nmf* charmer; – *a* engaging.

charnel, -elle [ʃarnɛl] *a* carnal.

charnier [ʃarnje] *nm* mass grave.

charnière [ʃarnjɛr] *nf* hinge; *Fig* meeting point (**de** between).

charnu [ʃarny] *a* fleshy.

charogne [ʃarɔɲ] *nf* carrion.

charpente [ʃarpɑ̃t] *nf* frame(work); *(de personne)* build. ◆**charpenté** *a* **bien c.** solidly built. ◆**charpenterie** *nf* carpentry. ◆**charpentier** *nm* carpenter.

charpie [ʃarpi] *nf* **mettre en c.** *(déchirer)* & *Fig* to tear to shreds.

charrette [ʃarɛt] *nf* cart. ◆**charretier** *nm* carter. ◆**charrier 1** *vt (transporter)* to cart; *(rivière)* to carry along, wash down *(sand etc)*. **2** *vti (taquiner) Fam* to tease.

charrue [ʃary] *nf* plough, *Am* plow.

charte [ʃart] *nf Pol* charter.

charter [ʃartɛr] *nm Av* charter (flight).

chas [ʃa] *nm* eye *(of a needle)*.

chasse [ʃas] *nf* **1** hunting, hunt; *(poursuite)* chase; *Av* fighter forces; **de c.** *(pilote, avion)* fighter-; **c. sous-marine** underwater (harpoon) fishing; **c. à courre** hunting; **tableau de c.** *(animaux abattus)* bag; **faire la c. à** to hunt down, hunt for; **donner la c. à** to give chase to; **c. à l'homme** manhunt. **2 c. d'eau** toilet flush; **tirer la c.** to flush the toilet.

châsse [ʃas] *nf* shrine.

chassé-croisé [ʃasekrwaze] *nm (pl chassés-croisés) Fig* confused coming(s) and going(s).

chass/er [ʃase] *vt (animal)* to hunt; *(papillon)* to chase; *(faire partir)* to drive out ou off; *(employé)* to dismiss; *(mouche)* to brush away; *(odeur)* to get rid of; – *vi* to hunt; *Aut* to skid. ◆**-eur, -euse** *nm* hunter; – *nm (domestique)* pageboy, bellboy; *Av* fighter; **c. à pied** infantryman. ◆**chasse-neige** *nm inv* snowplough, *Am* snowplow.

châssis [ʃasi] *nm* frame; *Aut* chassis.

chaste [ʃast] *a* chaste, pure. ◆**chasteté** *nf* chastity.

chat, chatte [ʃa, ʃat] *nmf* cat; **un c. dans la gorge** a frog in one's throat; **d'autres chats à fouetter** other fish to fry; **pas un c.** not a soul; **ma (petite) chatte** *Fam* my darling; **c. perché** *(jeu)* tag.

châtaigne [ʃatɛɲ] *nf* chestnut. ◆**châtaignier** *nm* chestnut tree. ◆**châtain** *a inv (chestnut)* brown.

château, -x [ʃato] *nm (forteresse)* castle; *(palais)* palace, stately home; **c. fort** fortified castle; **châteaux en Espagne** *Fig* castles in the air; **c. d'eau** water tower; **c. de cartes** house of cards. ◆**châtelain, -aine** *nmf* lord of the manor, lady of the manor.

châtier [ʃɑtje] *vt Litt* to chastise, castigate; *(style)* to refine.

châtiment [ʃɑtimɑ̃] *nm* punishment.

chaton [ʃatɔ̃] *nm* **1** *(chat)* kitten. **2** *(de bague)* setting, mounting. **3** *Bot* catkin.

chatouill/er [ʃatuje] *vt (exciter, plaire à) Fig* to tickle; *(exciter, plaire à) Fig* to titillate. ◆**—ement** *nm* tickle; *(action)* tickling. ◆**chatouilleux, -euse** *a* ticklish; *(irritable)* touchy.

chatoyer [ʃatwaje] *vi* to glitter, sparkle.

châtrer [ʃɑtre] *vt* to castrate.

chatte [ʃat] *voir* **chat**.

chatteries [ʃatri] *nfpl* cuddles; *(friandises)* delicacies.

chatterton [ʃatɛrtɔn] *nm* adhesive insulating tape.

chaud [ʃo] *a* hot; *(doux)* warm; *(fervent) Fig* warm; **pleurer à chaudes larmes** to cry bitterly; — *nm* heat; warmth; **avoir c.** to be hot; **to be warm**; **il fait c.** it's hot; it's warm; **être au c.** to be in the warm(th); **ça ne me fait ni c. ni froid** it leaves me indifferent. ◆**chaudement** *adv* warmly; *(avec passion)* hotly.

chaudière [ʃodjɛr] *nf* boiler.

chaudron [ʃodrɔ̃] *nm* cauldron.

chauffard [ʃofar] *nm* road hog, reckless driver.

chauff/er [ʃofe] *vt* to heat up, warm up; *(métal etc) Tech* to heat; — *vi* to heat up, warm up; *Aut* to overheat; **ça va c.** *Fam* things are going to hot up; — **se c.** *vpr* to warm oneself up. ◆**—ant** *a (couverture)* electric; *(plaque)* hot-; *(surface)* heating. ◆**—age** *nm* heating. ◆**—eur** *nm* **1** *(de chaudière)* stoker. **2** *Aut* driver; *(employé, domestique)* chauffeur. ◆**chauffe-bain** *nm*, ◆**chauffe-eau** *nm inv* water heater. ◆**chauffe-plats** *nm inv* hotplate.

chaume [ʃom] *nm (tiges coupées)* stubble, straw; *(pour toiture)* thatch; **toit de c.** thatched roof. ◆**chaumière** *nf* thatched cottage.

chaussée [ʃose] *nf* road(way).

chausser [ʃose] *vt (chaussures)* to put on; *(fournir)* to supply in footwear; **c. qn** to put shoes on (to) s.o.; **c. du 40** to take a size 40 shoe; **le soulier te chausse bien** this shoe fits (you) well; — **se c.** *vpr* to put on one's shoes. ◆**chausse-pied** *nm* shoehorn. ◆**chaus-**

sure [ʃo] *nf* shoe; *pl* shoes, footwear; **chaussures à semelles compensées** platform shoes.

chaussette [ʃosɛt] *nf* sock.

chauve [ʃov] *a & nmf* bald (person).

chauve-souris [ʃovsuri] *nf (pl chauves-souris)* *(animal)* bat.

chauvin, -ine [ʃovɛ̃, -in] *a & nmf* chauvinist.

chaux [ʃo] *nf* lime; **blanc de c.** whitewash.

chavirer [ʃavire] *vti Nau* to capsize.

chef [ʃɛf] *nm* **1 de son propre c.** on one's own authority. **2** leader, head; *(de tribu)* chief; *Culin* chef; **en c.** *(commandant, rédacteur)* in chief; **c'est un c.!** *(personne remarquable)* he's an ace!; **c. d'atelier** (shop) foreman; **c. de bande** ringleader, gang leader; **c. d'entreprise** company head; **c. d'équipe** foreman; **c. d'État** head of state; **c. d'état-major** chief of staff; **c. de famille** head of the family; **c. de file** leader; **c. de gare** stationmaster; **c. d'orchestre** conductor. ◆**chef-lieu** *nm (pl chefs-lieux)* chief town *(of a département)*.

chef-d'œuvre [ʃɛdœvr] *nm (pl chefs-d'œuvre)* masterpiece.

chemin [ʃ(ə)mɛ̃] *nm* **1** road, path; *(trajet, direction)* way; **beaucoup de c. à faire** a long way to go; **dix minutes de c.** ten minutes' walk; **se mettre en c.** to start out, set out; **faire du c.** to come a long way; *(idée)* to make considerable headway; **c. faisant** on the way; **à mi-c.** half-way. **2 c. de fer** railway, *Am* railroad. ◆**chemin/er** *vi* to proceed; *(péniblement)* to trudge (along); *(évoluer) Fig* to progress. ◆**—ement** *nm Fig* progress. ◆**cheminot** *nm* railway *ou Am* railroad employee.

cheminée [ʃ(ə)mine] *nf (sur le toit)* chimney; *(de navire)* funnel; *(âtre)* fireplace; *(encadrement)* mantelpiece.

chemise [ʃ(ə)miz] *nf* shirt; *(couverture cartonnée)* folder; **c. de nuit** nightdress. ◆**chemiserie** *nf* men's shirt (and underwear) shop. ◆**chemisette** *nf* short-sleeved shirt. ◆**chemisier** *nm (vêtement)* blouse.

chenal, -aux [ʃənal, -o] *nm* channel.

chenapan [ʃ(ə)napɑ̃] *nm Hum* rogue, scoundrel.

chêne [ʃɛn] *nm (arbre, bois)* oak.

chenet [ʃ(ə)nɛ] *nm* firedog, andiron.

chenil [ʃ(ə)ni(l)] *nm* kennels.

chenille [ʃ(ə)nij] *nf* caterpillar; *(de char) Mil* caterpillar track.

cheptel [ʃɛptɛl] *nm* livestock.

chèque [ʃɛk] *nm* cheque, *Am* check; **c. de voyage** traveller's cheque, *Am* traveler's check. ◆c.-repas nm (pl chèques-repas) luncheon voucher. ◆chéquier nm cheque book, Am checkbook.

cher, chère [ʃɛr] 1 a (aimé) dear (à to); – nmf mon c. my dear fellow; ma chère my dear (woman). 2 a (coûteux) dear, expensive; (quartier, hôtel etc) expensive; la vie chère the high cost of living; payer c. (objet) to pay a lot for; (erreur etc) Fig to pay dearly for. ◆chèrement adv dearly.

cherch/er [ʃɛrʃe] vt to look for, search for; (du secours, la paix etc) to seek; (dans un dictionnaire) to look up; c. ses mots to fumble for one's words; aller c. to (go and) fetch ou get; c. à to attempt to do; tu l'as bien cherché! it's your own fault!, you asked for it! ◆–eur, -euse nmf research worker; c. d'or gold-digger.

chér/ir [ʃerir] vt to cherish. ◆–i, -ie a dearly loved, beloved; – nmf darling.

chérot [ʃero] am Fam pricey.

cherté [ʃɛrte] nf high cost, expensiveness.

chétif, -ive [ʃetif, -iv] a puny; (dérisoire) wretched.

cheval, -aux [ʃ(ə)val, -o] nm horse; c. (vapeur) Aut horsepower; à c. on horseback; faire du c. to go horse riding; à c. sur straddling; à c. sur les principes a stickler for principle; monter sur ses grands chevaux to get excited; c. à bascule rocking horse; c. d'arçons Sp vaulting horse; c. de bataille (dada) hobbyhorse; chevaux de bois (manège) merry-go-round. ◆chevaleresque a chivalrous.

chevalet [ʃ(ə)valɛ] nm knight. ◆chevalin a equine; (boucherie) horse-.

chevalet [ʃ(ə)valɛ] nm easel; Menuis trestle.

chevalière [ʃ(ə)valjɛr] nf signet ring.

chevauchée [ʃ(ə)voʃe] nf (horse) ride.

chevaucher [ʃ(ə)voʃe] vt to straddle; – vi, – se c. vpr to overlap.

chevet [ʃ(ə)vɛ] nm bedhead; table/livre de c. bedside table/book; au c. de at the bedside of.

cheveu, -x [ʃ(ə)vø] nm un c. a hair; les cheveux hair; couper les cheveux en quatre Fig to split hairs; tiré par les cheveux (argument) far-fetched. ◆chevelu a hairy. ◆chevelure nf (head of) hair.

cheville [ʃ(ə)vij] nf Anat ankle; Menuis peg, pin; (pour vis) (wall)plug; c. ouvrière Aut & Fig linchpin; en c. avec Fam in cahoots with. ◆cheviller vt Menuis to peg, pin.

chèvre [ʃɛvr] nf goat; (femelle) nanny-goat. ◆chevreau, -x nm kid.

chèvrefeuille [ʃɛvrəfœj] nm honeysuckle.

chevreuil [ʃəvrœj] nm roe deer; Culin venison.

chevron [ʃəvrɔ̃] nm (poutre) rafter; Mil stripe, chevron; à chevrons (tissu, veste etc) herringbone.

chevronné [ʃəvrɔne] a seasoned, experienced.

chevroter [ʃəvrɔte] vi to quaver, tremble.

chez [ʃe] prép c. qn at s.o.'s house, flat etc; il est c. Jean/c. l'épicier he's at John's (place)/at the grocer's; il va c. Jean/c. l'épicier he's going to John's (place)/to the grocer's; c. moi, c. nous at home; je vais c. moi I'm going home; c. les Suisses/les jeunes among the Swiss/the young; c. Camus in Camus; c. l'homme in man; une habitude c. elle a habit with her; c. Mme Dupont (adresse) care of ou c/o Mme Dupont. ◆c.-soi nm inv un c.-soi a home (of one's own).

chialer [ʃjale] vi (pleurer) Fam to cry.

chic [ʃik] 1 a inv stylish, smart; (gentil) Fam decent, nice; – int c. (alors)! great!; – nm style, elegance. 2 nm avoir le c. pour faire to have the knack of doing.

chicane [ʃikan] 1 nf (querelle) quibble. 2 nfpl (obstacles) zigzag barriers. ◆chicaner vt to quibble with (s.o.); – vi to quibble.

chiche [ʃiʃ] 1 a mean, niggardly; c. de sparing of. 2 int (défi) Fam I bet you I can, etc; c. que je parte sans lui I bet I leave without him.

chichis [ʃiʃi] nmpl faire des c. to make a lot of fuss.

chicorée [ʃikɔre] nf (à café) chicory; (pour salade) endive.

chien [ʃjɛ̃] nm dog; c. d'arrêt pointer, retriever; un mal de c. a hell of a job; temps de c. filthy weather; vie de c. Fig dog's life; entre c. et loup at dusk, in the gloaming. ◆c.-loup nm (pl chiens-loups) wolfhound. ◆chienne nf dog, bitch.

chiendent [ʃjɛ̃dɑ̃] nm Bot couch grass.

chiffon [ʃifɔ̃] nm rag; c. (à poussière) duster. ◆chiffonner vt to crumple; (ennuyer) Fig to bother, distress. ◆chiffonnier nm ragman.

chiffre [ʃifr] nm figure, number; (romain, arabe) numeral; (code) cipher; c. d'affaires Fin turnover. ◆chiffrer vt (montant) to assess, work out; (message) to cipher, code; – vi to mount up; se c. à to amount to, work out at.

chignon [ʃiɲɔ̃] nm bun, chignon.

Chili [ʃili] nm Bot Chile. ◆chilien, -ienne a & nmf Chilean.

chimère [ʃimɛr] *nf* fantasy, (wild) dream. ◆**chimérique** *a* fanciful.

chimie [ʃimi] *nf* chemistry. ◆**chimique** *a* chemical. ◆**chimiste** *nmf* (research) chemist.

chimpanzé [ʃɛ̃pɑ̃ze] *nm* chimpanzee.

Chine [ʃin] *nf* China. ◆**chinois, -oise** *a* & *nmf* Chinese; – *nm* (langue) Chinese. ◆**chinoiser** *vi* to quibble. ◆**chinoiserie** *nf* (objet) Chinese curio; *pl* (bizarreries) Fig weird complications.

chiner [ʃine] *vi* (brocanteur etc) to hunt for bargains.

chiot [ʃjo] *nm* pup(py).

chiper [ʃipe] *vt* Fam to swipe, pinch (à from).

chipie [ʃipi] *nf* vieille c. (femme) Péj old crab.

chipoter [ʃipote] *vi* **1** (manger) to nibble. **2** (chicaner) to quibble.

chips [ʃips] *nmpl* (potato) crisps, *Am* chips.

chiquenaude [ʃiknod] *nf* flick (of the finger).

chiromancie [kirɔmɑ̃si] *nf* palmistry.

chirurgie [ʃiryrʒi] *nf* surgery. ◆**chirurgical, -aux** *a* surgical. ◆**chirurgien** *nm* surgeon.

chlore [klɔr] *nm* chlorine. ◆**chloroforme** *nm* chloroform. ◆**chlorure** *nm* chloride.

choc [ʃɔk] *nm* (heurt) impact, shock; (émotion) & Méd shock; (collision) crash; (des opinions, entre manifestants etc) clash.

chocolat [ʃɔkɔla] *nm* chocolate; **c. à croquer** plain *ou* *Am* bittersweet chocolate; **c. au lait** milk chocolate; **c. glacé** choc-ice; – *a inv* chocolate(-coloured). ◆**chocolaté** *a* chocolate-flavoured.

chœur [kœr] *nm* (chanteurs, nef) Rel choir; (composition musicale) & Fig chorus; **en c.** (all) together, in chorus.

choir [ʃwar] *vi* laisser **c. qn** Fam to turn one's back on s.o.

chois/ir [ʃwazir] *vt* to choose, pick, select. ◆**—i** *a* (œuvres) selected; (terme, langage) well-chosen; (public) select. ◆**choix** *nm* choice; (assortiment) selection; **morceau de c.** choice piece; **au c. du client** according to choice.

choléra [kɔlera] *nm* cholera.

cholestérol [kɔlesterɔl] *nm* cholesterol.

chôm/er [ʃome] *vi* (ouvrier etc) to be unemployed; **jour chômé** (public) holiday. ◆**—age** *nm* unemployment; **en** *ou* **au c.** unemployed; **mettre en c. technique** to lay off, dismiss.

chope [ʃɔp] *nf* beer mug, tankard; (contenu) pint.

choqu/er [ʃɔke] *vt* to offend, shock; (verres) to clink; (commotionner) to shake up. ◆**—ant** *a* shocking, offensive.

choral, mpl -als [kɔral] *a* choral. ◆**chorale** *nf* choral society. ◆**choriste** *nmf* chorister.

chorégraphe [kɔregraf] *nmf* choreographer. ◆**chorégraphie** *nf* choreography.

chose [ʃoz] *nf* thing; **état de choses** state of affairs; **par la force des choses** through force of circumstance; **dis-lui bien des choses de ma part** remember me to him *ou* her; **ce monsieur C.** that Mr What's-his-name; **se sentir tout c.** Fam (décontenancé) to feel all funny; (malade) to feel out of sorts.

chou, -x [ʃu] *nm* cabbage; **choux de Bruxelles** Brussels sprouts; **mon c.!** my pet!; **c. à la crème** cream puff. ◆**c.-fleur** *nm* (*pl* choux-fleurs) cauliflower.

choucas [ʃuka] *nm* jackdaw.

chouchou, -oute [ʃuʃu, -ut] *nmf* (favori) Fam pet, darling. ◆**chouchouter** *vt* to pamper.

choucroute [ʃukrut] *nf* sauerkraut.

chouette [ʃwɛt] **1** *nf* (oiseau) owl. **2** *a* (chic) Fam super, great.

choyer [ʃwaye] *vt* to pet, pamper.

chrétien, -ienne [kretjɛ̃, -jɛn] *a* & *nmf* Christian. ◆**chrétienté** *nf* Christendom. ◆**Christ** [krist] *nm* Christ. ◆**christianisme** *nm* Christianity.

chrome [krom] *nm* chromium, chrome. ◆**chromé** *a* chromium-plated.

chromosome [krɔmozom] *nm* chromosome.

chronique [krɔnik] **1** *a* (malade, chômage etc) chronic. **2** *nf* (annales) chronicle; Journ report, news; (rubrique) column. ◆**chroniqueur** *nm* chronicler; Journ reporter, columnist.

chronologie [krɔnɔlɔʒi] *nf* chronology. ◆**chronologique** *a* chronological.

chronomètre [krɔnɔmɛtr] *nm* stopwatch. ◆**chronométr/er** *vt* Sp to time. ◆**—eur** *nm* Sp timekeeper.

chrysanthème [krizɑ̃tɛm] *nm* chrysanthemum.

chuchot/er [ʃyʃɔte] *vti* to whisper. ◆**—ement** *nm* whisper(ing). ◆**chuchoteries** *nfpl* Fam whispering.

chuinter [ʃwɛ̃te] *vi* (vapeur) to hiss.

chut! [ʃyt] *int* sh!, hush!

chute [ʃyt] *nf* fall; (défaite) (down)fall; **c. d'eau** waterfall; **c. de neige** snowfall; **c. de pluie** rainfall; **c. des cheveux** hair loss. ◆**chuter** *vi* Fam to fall.

Chypre [ʃipr] *nf* Cyprus. ◆**chypriote** *a* & *nmf* Cypriot.

ci [si] **1** *adv* **par-ci par-là** here and there. **2** *pron dém* **comme ci comme ça** so so. **3** *voir* **ce²**, **celui**.

ci-après [siapre] *adv* below, hereafter. ◆**ci-contre** *adv* opposite. ◆**ci-dessous** *adv* below. ◆**ci-dessus** *adv* above. ◆**ci-gît** *adv* here lies (*on gravestones*). ◆**ci-inclus** *a*, ◆**ci-joint** *a* (*inv before n*) (*dans une lettre*) enclosed (herewith).

cible [sibl] *nf* target.

ciboulette [sibulet] *nf Culin* chives.

cicatrice [sikatris] *nf* scar. ◆**cicatriser** *vt*, — **se c.** *vpr* to heal up (*leaving a scar*).

cidre [sidr] *nm* cider.

Cie *abrév* (*compagnie*) Co.

ciel [sjel] *nm* **1** (*pl* **cieux**) sky; **à c. ouvert** (*piscine etc*) open-air; **c. de lit** canopy. **2** (*pl* **cieux** [sjø]) *Rel* heaven; **juste c.!** good heavens!; **sous d'autres cieux** *Hum* in other climes.

cierge [sjerʒ] *nm Rel* candle.

cigale [sigal] *nf* (*insecte*) cicada.

cigare [sigar] *nm* cigar. ◆**cigarette** *nf* cigarette.

cigogne [sigɔɲ] *nf* stork.

cil [sil] *nm* (eye)lash.

cime [sim] *nf* (*d'un arbre*) top; (*d'une montagne*) & *Fig* peak.

ciment [simã] *nm* cement. ◆**cimenter** *vt* to cement.

cimetière [simtjɛr] *nm* cemetery, churchyard; **c. de voitures** scrapyard, breaker's yard, *Am* auto graveyard.

ciné [sine] *nm Fam* cinema. ◆**c.-club** *nm* film society. ◆**cinéaste** *nm* film maker. ◆**cinéphile** *nmf* film buff.

cinéma [sinema] *nm* cinema; **faire du c.** to make films. ◆**cinémascope** *nm* cinemascope. ◆**cinémathèque** *nf* film library; (*salle*) film theatre. ◆**cinématographique** *a* cinema-.

cinglé [sɛgle] *a Fam* crazy.

cingl/er [sɛgle] *vt* to lash. ◆—**ant** *a* (*vent, remarque*) cutting, biting.

cinoche [sinɔʃ] *nm Fam* cinema.

cinq [sɛk] *nm* five; — *a* ([sɛ] *before consonant*) five. ◆**cinquième** *a* & *nmf* fifth; **un c.** a fifth.

cinquante [sɛkãt] *a* & *nm* fifty. ◆**cinquantaine** *nf* about fifty. ◆**cinquantenaire** *a* & *nmf* fifty-year-old (person); — *nm* fiftieth anniversary. ◆**cinquantième** *a* & *nmf* fiftieth.

cintre [sɛtr] *nm* coathanger; *Archit* arch.

◆**cintré** *a* arched; (*veste etc*) tailored, slim-fitting.

cirage [siraʒ] *nm* (shoe) polish.

circoncis [sirkɔsi] *a* circumcised. ◆**circoncision** *nf* circumcision.

circonférence [sirkɔferãs] *nf* circumference.

circonflexe [sirkɔfleks] *a Gram* circumflex.

circonlocution [sirkɔlɔkysjɔ] *nf* circumlocution.

circonscrire [sirkɔskrir] *vt* to circumscribe. ◆**circonscription** *nf* division; **c.** (**électorale**) constituency.

circonspect, -ecte [sirkɔspe(kt), -ɛkt] *a* cautious, circumspect. ◆**circonspection** *nf* caution.

circonstance [sirkɔstãs] *nf* circumstance; **pour/en la c.** for/on this occasion; **de c.** (*habit, parole etc*) appropriate. ◆**circonstancié** *a* detailed. ◆**circonstanciel, -ielle** *a Gram* adverbial.

circonvenir [sirkɔvnir] *vt* to circumvent.

circuit [sirkɥi] *nm Sp Él Fin* circuit; (*périple, voyage, trip*); (*détour*) roundabout way; *pl Él* circuitry. **circuits**.

circulaire [sirkyler] *a* circular; — *nf* (*lettre*) circular. ◆**circulation** *nf* circulation; *Aut* traffic. ◆**circuler** *vi* to circulate; (*véhicule, train*) to move, travel; (*passant*) to walk about; (*rumeur*) to go round, circulate; **faire c.** to circulate; (*piétons etc*) to move on; **circulez!** keep moving!

cire [sir] *nf* wax; (*pour meubles*) polish, wax. ◆**cir/er** *vt* to polish, wax. ◆—**é** *nm* (*vêtement*) oilskin(s). ◆—**eur** *nm* bootblack. ◆—**euse** *nf* (*appareil*) floor polisher. ◆**cireux, -euse** *a* waxy.

cirque [sirk] *nm Th Hist* circus.

cirrhose [siroz] *nf Méd* cirrhosis.

cisaille(s) [sizaj] *nf(pl)* shears. ◆**ciseau, -x** [sizo] *nm* chisel; *pl* scissors. ◆**ciseler** *vt* to chisel.

citadelle [sitadel] *nf* citadel.

cité [site] *nf* city; **c.** (**ouvrière**) housing estate (*for workers*), *Am* housing project *ou* development; **c. universitaire** (students') halls of residence. ◆**citadin, -ine** *nmf* city dweller; — *a* city-, urban.

citer [site] *vt* to quote; *Jur* to summon; *Mil* to mention, cite. ◆**citation** *nf* quotation; *Jur* summons; *Mil* mention, citation.

citerne [sitern] *nf* (*réservoir*) tank.

cithare [sitar] *nf* zither.

citoyen, -enne [sitwajɛ, -ɛn] *nmf* citizen. ◆**citoyenneté** *nf* citizenship.

citron [sitrɔ] *nm* lemon; **c. pressé** (fresh)

lemon juice. ◆**citronnade** nf lemon drink, (still) lemonade.

citrouille [sitruj] nf pumpkin.

civet [sive] nm stew; c. de lièvre jugged hare.

civière [sivjɛr] nf stretcher.

civil [sivil] **1** a (droits, guerre, mariage etc) civil; (non militaire) civilian; (courtois) civil; **année civile** calendar year. **2** nm civilian; **dans le c.** in civilian life; **en c.** (policier) in plain clothes; (soldat) in civilian clothes. ◆**civilité** nf civility.

civiliser [sivilize] vt to civilize; **— se c.** vpr to become civilized. ◆**civilisation** nf civilization.

civique [sivik] a civic; **instruction c.** Scol civics. ◆**civisme** nm civic sense.

clair [klɛr] a (distinct, limpide, évident) clear; (éclairé) light; (pâle) light(-coloured); (sauce, chevelure) thin; **bleu/vert c.** light blue/green; **il fait c.** it's light ou bright; **— adv** (voir) clearly; **— nm c. de lune** moonlight; **le plus c. de** the major ou greater part of; **tirer au c.** (question etc) to clear up. ◆**—ement** adv clearly. ◆**claire-voie (à c.-voie** (barrière) lattice-; (caisse) openwork; (porte) louvre(d).

clairière [klɛrjɛr] nf clearing, glade.

clairon [klɛrɔ̃] nm bugle; (soldat) bugler. ◆**claironner** vt (annoncer) to trumpet forth.

clairsemé [klɛrsəme] a sparse.

clairvoyant [klɛrvwajɑ̃] a (perspicace) clear-sighted. ◆**clairvoyance** nf clear-sightedness.

clam/er [klame] vt to cry out. ◆**—eur** nf clamour, outcry.

clan [klɑ̃] nm clan, clique, set.

clandestin [klɑ̃dɛstɛ̃] a secret, clandestine; (journal, mouvement) underground; **passager c.** stowaway.

clapet [klapɛ] nm Tech valve; (bouche) Arg trap.

clapier [klapje] nm (rabbit) hutch.

clapot/er [klapɔte] vi (vagues) to lap. ◆**—ement** nm, ◆**clapotis** nm lap(ping).

claque [klak] nf smack, slap. ◆**claquer** vt (porte) to smack, bang; (gifler) to smack, slap; (fouet) to crack; (fatiguer) Fam to tire out; (dépenser) Arg to blow; **se c. un muscle** to tear a muscle; **faire c.** (doigts) to snap; (langue) to click; (fouet) to crack; **— vi** (porte) to slam, bang; (drapeau) to flap; (coup de revolver) to ring out; (mourir) Fam to die; (tomber en panne) Fam to break down; **c. des mains** to clap one's hands; **elle claque des dents** her teeth are chattering.

claquemurer (se) [səklakmyre] vpr to shut oneself up, hole up.

claquettes [klakɛt] nfpl tap dancing.

clarifier [klarifje] vt to clarify. ◆**clarification** nf clarification.

clarinette [klarinɛt] nf clarinet.

clarté [klarte] nf light, brightness; (précision) clarity, clearness.

classe [klas] nf class; **aller en c.** to go to school; **c. ouvrière/moyenne** working/middle class; **avoir de la c.** to have class.

class/er [klase] vt to classify, class; (papiers) to file; (candidats) to grade; (affaire) to close; **se c. parmi** to rank ou be classed among; **se c. premier** to come first. ◆**—ement** nm classification; filing; grading; (rang) place; Sp placing. ◆**—eur** nm (meuble) filing cabinet; (portefeuille) (loose leaf) file. ◆**classification** nf classification. ◆**classifier** vt to classify.

classique [klasik] a classical; (typique) classic; **— nm** (œuvre, auteur) classic. ◆**classicisme** nm classicism.

clause [kloz] nf clause.

claustrophobie [klostrɔfɔbi] nf claustrophobia. ◆**claustrophobe** a claustrophobic.

clavecin [klavsɛ̃] nm Mus harpsichord.

clavicule [klavikyl] nf collarbone.

clavier [klavje] nm keyboard.

clé, clef [kle] nf key; (outil) spanner, wrench; Mus clef; **fermer à c.** to lock; **sous c.** under lock and key; **c. de contact** ignition key; **c. de voûte** keystone; **poste/industrie c.** key post/industry; **clés en main** (acheter une maison etc) ready to move in; **prix clés en main** (voiture) on the road price.

clément [klemɑ̃] a (temps) mild, clement; (juge) lenient, clement. ◆**clémence** nf mildness; leniency; clemency.

clémentine [klemɑ̃tin] nf clementine.

clerc [klɛr] nm Rel cleric; (de notaire) clerk. ◆**clergé** nm clergy. ◆**clérical, -aux** a Rel clerical.

cliché [kliʃe] nm Phot negative; Typ plate; (idée) cliché.

client, -ente [klijɑ̃, -ɑ̃t] nmf (de magasin etc) customer; (d'un avocat etc) client; (d'un médecin) patient; (d'hôtel) guest. ◆**clientèle** nf customers, clientele; (d'un avocat) practice, clientele; (d'un médecin) practice, patients; **accorder sa c.** à to give one's custom to.

cligner [kliɲe] vi **c. des yeux** (ouvrir et fermer) to blink; (fermer à demi) to screw up one's eyes; **c. de l'œil** to wink.

◆**clignot/er** vi to blink; (lumière) to flicker; Aut to flash; (étoile) to twinkle. ◆—**ant** nm Aut indicator, Am directional signal.

climat [klima] nm Mét & Fig climate. ◆**climatique** a climatic. ◆**climatisation** nf air-conditioning. ◆**climatiser** vt to air-condition.

clin d'œil [klɛ̃dœj] nm wink; **en un c. d'œil** in the twinkling of an eye.

clinique [klinik] a clinical; – nf (hôpital) (private) clinic.

clinquant [klɛ̃kɑ̃] a tawdry.

clique [klik] nf Péj clique; Mus Mil (drum and bugle) band.

cliqueter [klikte] vi to clink. ◆**cliquetis** nm clink(ing).

clivage [klivaʒ] nm split, division (de in).

cloaque [klɔak] nm cesspool.

clochard, -arde [klɔʃar, -ard] nmf tramp, vagrant.

cloche [klɔʃ] nf 1 bell; **c. à fromage** cheese cover. 2 (personne) Fam idiot, oaf. ◆**clocher** 1 nm bell tower; (en pointe) steeple; **de c.** Fig parochial; **esprit de c.** parochialism. 2 vi to be wrong ou amiss. ◆**clochette** nf (small) bell.

cloche-pied (à) [akloʃpje] adv **sauter à c.-pied** to hop on one foot.

cloison [klwazɔ̃] nf partition; Fig barrier. ◆**cloisonner** vt to partition; (activités etc) Fig to compartmentalize.

cloître [klwatr] nm cloister. ◆**se cloître vpr** to shut oneself away, cloister oneself.

clopin-clopant [klɔpɛ̃klɔpɑ̃] adv **aller c.-clopant** to hobble.

cloque [klɔk] nf blister.

clore [klɔr] vt (débat, lettre) to close. ◆**clos** a (incident etc) closed; (espace) enclosed; – nm (enclosed) field.

clôture [klotyr] nf (barrière) enclosure, fence; (fermeture) closing. ◆**clôturer** vt to enclose; (compte, séance etc) to close.

clou [klu] nm nail; (furoncle) boil; **le c.** (du spectacle) Fam the star attraction; **les clous** (passage) pedestrian crossing; **des clous!** Fam nothing at all! ◆**clouer** vt to nail; **cloué au lit** confined to (one's) bed; **cloué sur place** nailed to the spot; **le bec à qn** Fam to shut s.o. up. ◆**clouté** a (chaussures) hobnailed; (ceinture, pneus) studded; **passage c.** pedestrian crossing, Am crosswalk.

clown [klun] nm clown.

club [klœb] nm (association) club.

cm abrév (centimètre) cm.

co- [kɔ] préf co-.

◆**coaguler** vti, **— se c.** vpr to coagulate.

coaliser (se) [kɔalize] vpr to form a coalition, join forces. ◆**coalition** nf coalition.

coasser [kɔase] vi (grenouille) to croak.

cobaye [kɔbaj] nm (animal) & Fig guinea pig.

cobra [kɔbra] nm (serpent) cobra.

coca [kɔka] nm (Coca-Cola®) coke.

cocagne [kɔkaɲ] nf **pays de c.** dreamland, land of plenty.

cocaïne [kɔkain] nf cocain.

cocarde [kɔkard] nf rosette, cockade; Av roundel. ◆**cocardier, -ière** a Péj flag-waving.

cocasse [kɔkas] a droll, comical. ◆**cocasserie** nf drollery.

coccinelle [kɔksinɛl] nf ladybird, Am ladybug.

cocher¹ [kɔʃe] vt to tick (off), Am to check (off).

cocher² [kɔʃe] nm coachman. ◆**cochère** af **porte c.** main gateway.

cochon, -onne [kɔʃɔ̃, -ɔn] 1 nm pig; (mâle) hog; **c. d'Inde** guinea pig. 2 nmf (personne sale) (dirty) pig; (salaud) swine; – a (histoire, film) dirty, filthy. ◆**cochon-nerie(s)** nf(pl) (obscénité(s)) filth; (pacotille) Fam rubbish.

cocktail [kɔktɛl] nm (boisson) cocktail; (réunion) cocktail party.

coco [kɔko] nm **noix de c.** coconut. ◆**cocotier** nm coconut palm.

cocon [kɔkɔ̃] nm cocoon.

cocorico [kɔkɔriko] int & nm cock-a-doodle-doo; **faire c.** (crier victoire) Fam to give three cheers for France, wave the flag.

cocotte [kɔkɔt] nf (marmite) casserole; **c. minute®** pressure cooker.

cocu [kɔky] nm Fam cuckold.

code [kɔd] nm code; **codes, phares c.** Aut dipped headlights, Am low beams; **C. de la route** Highway Code. ◆**coder** vt to code. ◆**codifier** vt to codify.

coefficient [kɔefisjɑ̃] nm Math coefficient; (d'erreur, de sécurité) Fig margin.

coéquipier, -ière [kɔekipje, -jɛr] nmf team mate.

cœur [kœr] nm heart; Cartes hearts; **au c. de** (ville, hiver etc) in the heart of; **par c.** by heart; **ça me (sou)lève le c.** that turns my stomach; **à c. ouvert** (opération) open-heart; (parler) freely; **avoir mal au c.** to feel sick; **avoir le c. gros ou serré** to have a heavy heart; **ça me tient à c.** that's close to my heart; **avoir bon c.** to be kind-hearted; **de bon c.** (*offrir*) with a good heart, willingly; (*rire*) heartily; **si le c. vous en dit** if you so desire.

coexister [kɔɛgziste] *vi* to coexist. ◆**coexistence** *nf* coexistence.

coffre [kɔfr] *nm* chest; (*de banque*) safe; (*de voiture*) boot, *Am* trunk; (*d'autocar*) luggage ou *Am* baggage compartment. ◆**c.-fort** *nm* (*pl* **coffres-forts**) safe. ◆**coffret** *nm* casket, box.

cogiter [kɔʒite] *vi Iron* to cogitate.

cognac [kɔɲak] *nm* cognac.

cogner [kɔɲe] *vti* to knock; **c. qn** *Arg* (*frapper*) to thump s.o.; (*tabasser*) to beat s.o. up; **se c. la tête/***etc* to knock one's head/*etc.*

cohabiter [kɔabite] *vi* to live together. ◆**cohabitation** *nf* living together; *Pol Fam* power sharing.

cohérent [kɔerɑ̃] *a* coherent. ◆**cohérence** *nf* coherence. ◆**cohésion** *nf* cohesion, cohesiveness.

cohorte [kɔɔrt] *nf* (*groupe*) troop, band, cohort.

cohue [kɔy] *nf* crowd, mob.

coiffe [kwaf] *nf* headdress.

coiff/er [kwafe] *vt* (*chapeau*) to put on, wear; (*surmonter*) *Fig* to cap; (*être à la tête de*) to head; **c. qn** to do s.o.'s hair; **c. qn d'un chapeau** to put a hat on s.o.; — **se c.** *vpr* to do one's hair; **se c. d'un chapeau** to put on a hat. ◆**—eur, -euse¹** *nmf* (*pour hommes*) barber, hairdresser; (*pour dames*) hairdresser. ◆**—euse²** *nf* dressing table. ◆**coiffure** *nf* headgear, hat; (*arrangement*) hairstyle; (*métier*) hairdressing.

coin [kwɛ̃] *nm* (*angle*) corner; (*endroit*) spot; (*de terre, de ciel*) patch; (*cale*) wedge; **du c.** (*magasin etc*) local; **dans le c.** in the (local) area; **au c. du feu** by the fireside; **petit c.** *Fam* loo, *Am* john.

coinc/er [kwɛ̃se] *vt* (*mécanisme, tiroir*) to jam; (*caler*) to wedge; **c. qn** *Fam* to catch s.o., corner s.o.; — **se c.** *vpr* (*mécanisme etc*) to get jammed ou stuck. ◆**—é** *a* (*tiroir etc*) stuck, jammed; (*personne*) *Fam* stuck.

coïncider [kɔɛ̃side] *vi* to coincide. ◆**coïncidence** *nf* coincidence.

coin-coin [kwɛ̃kwɛ̃] *nm inv* (*de canard*) quack.

coing [kwɛ̃] *nm* (*fruit*) quince.

coke [kɔk] *nm* (*combustible*) coke.

col [kɔl] *nm* (*de chemise*) collar; (*de bouteille, & Anat*) neck; *Géog* pass; **c. roulé** polo neck, *Am* turtleneck.

colère [kɔlɛr] *nf* anger; **une c.** (*accès*) a fit of anger; **en c.** angry (**contre** with); **se mettre**

en c. to lose one's temper. ◆**coléreux, -euse** *a*, ◆**colérique** *a* quick-tempered.

colibri [kɔlibri] *nm* hummingbird.

colifichet [kɔlifiʃɛ] *nm* trinket.

colimaçon (en) [ɑ̃kɔlimasɔ̃] *adv* **escalier en c.** spiral staircase.

colin [kɔlɛ̃] *nm* (*poisson*) hake.

colique [kɔlik] *nf* diarrh(o)ea; (*douleur*) stomach pain, colic.

colis [kɔli] *nm* parcel, package.

collabor/er [kɔlabɔre] *vi* collaborate (**avec** with, **à** on); **c. à** (*journal*) to contribute to. ◆**collaborateur, -trice** *nmf* collaborator; contributor. ◆**collaboration** *nf* collaboration; contribution.

collage [kɔlaʒ] *nm* (*œuvre*) collage.

collant [kɔlɑ̃] **1** *a* (*papier*) sticky; (*vêtement*) skin-tight; **être c.** (*importun*) *Fam* to be a pest. **2** *nm* (pair of) tights; (*de danse*) leotard.

collation [kɔlasjɔ̃] *nf* (*repas*) light meal.

colle [kɔl] *nf* (*transparente*) glue; (*blanche*) paste; (*question*) *Fam* poser, teaser; (*interrogation*) *Scol Arg* oral; (*retenue*) *Scol Arg* detention.

collecte [kɔlɛkt] *nf* (*quête*) collection. ◆**collect/er** *vt* to collect. ◆**—eur** *nm* collector; (*égout*) **c.** main sewer.

collectif, -ive [kɔlɛktif, -iv] *a* collective; (*hystérie, démission*) mass-; **billet c.** group ticket. ◆**collectivement** *adv* collectively. ◆**collectivisme** *nm* collectivism. ◆**collectivité** *nf* community, collectivity.

collection [kɔlɛksjɔ̃] *nf* collection. ◆**collectionn/er** *vt* (*timbres etc*) to collect. ◆**—eur, -euse** *nmf* collector.

collège [kɔlɛʒ] *nm* (*secondary*) school, *Am* (high) school; (*électoral, sacré*) college. ◆**collégien** *nm* schoolboy. ◆**collégienne** *nf* schoolgirl.

collègue [kɔlɛg] *nmf* colleague.

coller [kɔle] *vt* (*timbre etc*) to stick; (*à la colle transparente*) to glue; (*à la colle blanche*) to paste; (*affiche*) to stick up; (*papier peint*) to hang; (*mettre*) *Fam* to stick, shove; **c. contre** (*nez, oreille etc*) to press against; **c. qn** (*embarrasser*) *Fam* to stump s.o., catch s.o. out; (*consigner*) *Scol* to keep s.o. in; **être collé à** (*examen*) *Fam* to fail, flunk; **se c. contre** to cling (close) to; **se c. qn/qch** *Fam* to get stuck with s.o./sth.; — *vi* to stick, cling; **c. à** (*s'adapter*) to fit, correspond to; **ça colle!** *Fam* everything's just fine! ◆**colleur, -euse** *nmf* **c. d'affiches** billsticker.

collet [kɔlɛ] *nm* (*lacet*) snare; **prendre qn au c.** to grab s.o. by the scruff of the neck; **elle**

est/ils sont c. she is/they are prim and proper *ou* straight-laced.

collier [kɔlje] *nm (bijou)* necklace; *(de chien, cheval)* & *Tech* collar.

colline [kɔlin] *nf* hill.

collision [kɔlizjɔ̃] *nf (de véhicules)* collision; *(bagarre, conflit)* clash; **entrer en c. avec** to collide with.

colloque [kɔlɔk] *nm* symposium.

collusion [kɔlyzjɔ̃] *nf* collusion.

colmater [kɔlmate] *vt (fuite, fente)* to seal; *(trou)* to fill in; *(brèche)* *Mil* to close, seal.

colombe [kɔlɔ̃b] *nf* dove.

colon [kɔlɔ̃] *nm* settler, colonist; *(enfant)* *child taking part in a holiday camp.* ◆**colonial, -aux** *a* colonial. ◆**colonie** *nf* colony; **c. de vacances** (children's) holiday camp *ou Am* vacation camp.

coloniser [kɔlɔnize] *vt Pol* to colonize; *(peupler)* to settle. ◆**colonisateur, -trice** *a* colonizing; – *nmf* colonizer. ◆**colonisation** *nf* colonization.

côlon [kolɔ̃] *nm Anat* colon.

colonel [kɔlɔnɛl] *nm* colonel.

colonne [kɔlɔn] *nf* column; **c. vertébrale** spine. ◆**colonnade** *nf* colonnade.

color/er [kɔlɔre] *vt* to colour. ◆**—ant** *a* & *nm* colouring. ◆**—é** *a (verre etc)* coloured; *(teint)* ruddy; *(style, foule)* colourful. ◆**coloration** *nf* colouring, colour. ◆**coloriage** *nm* colouring; *(dessin)* coloured drawing. ◆**colorier** *vt (dessin etc)* to colour (in). ◆**coloris** *nm (effet)* colouring; *(nuance)* shade.

colosse [kɔlɔs] *nm* giant, colossus. ◆**colossal, -aux** *a* colossal, gigantic.

colporter [kɔlpɔrte] *vt* to peddle, hawk.

coltiner [kɔltine] *vt (objet lourd)* *Fam* to lug, haul; – **se c.** *vpr (tâche pénible)* *Fam* to take on, tackle.

coma [kɔma] *nm* coma; **dans le c.** in a coma.

combat [kɔ̃ba] *nm* fight; *Mil* combat. ◆**combatif, -ive** *a (personne)* eager to fight; *(instinct, esprit)* fighting. ◆**combatt/re*** *vt* to fight; *(maladie, inflation etc)* to combat, fight; – *vi* to fight. ◆**—ant** *nm* *Mil* combattant; *(bagarreur)* *Fam* brawler; – *a (unité)* fighting.

combien [kɔ̃bjɛ̃] **1** *adv (quantité)* how much; *(nombre)* how many; **c. de** *(temps, argent etc)* how much; *(gens, livres etc)* how many. **2** *adv (à quel point)* how; **tu verras c. il est bête** you'll see how silly he is. **3** *adv (distance)* **c. y a-t-il d'ici à . . . ?** how far is it to . . . ? **4** *nm inv* **le c. sommes-nous?** *(date)* *Fam* what date is it?; **tous les c.?** *(fréquence)* *Fam* how often?

combine [kɔ̃bin] *nf (truc, astuce)* *Fam* trick.

combin/er [kɔ̃bine] *vt (disposer)* to combine; *(calculer)* to devise, plan (out). ◆**—é** *nm (de téléphone)* receiver. ◆**combinaison** *nf* **1** combination; *(manœuvre)* scheme. **2** *(vêtement de femme)* slip; *(de mécanicien)* boiler suit, *Am* overalls; *(de pilote)* flying suit; **c. de ski** ski suit.

comble [kɔ̃bl] **1** *nm* **le c.** *(de la joie etc)* the height of; **pour c.** *(de malheur)* to crown *ou* cap it all; **c'est un *ou* le c.!** that's the limit! **2** *nmpl (mansarde)* attic, loft; **sous les combles** beneath the roof, in the loft *ou* attic. **3** *a (bondé)* packed, full.

combler [kɔ̃ble] *vt (trou, lacune etc)* to fill; *(retard, perte)* to make good; *(vœu)* to fulfil; **c. qn de** *(cadeaux etc)* to lavish on s.o.; *(joie)* to fill s.o. with; **je suis comblé** I'm completely satisfied; **vous me comblez!** you're too good to me!

combustible [kɔ̃bystibl] *nm* fuel; – *a* combustible. ◆**combustion** *nf* combustion.

comédie [kɔmedi] *nf* comedy; *(complication)* *Fam* fuss, palaver; **c. musicale** musical; **jouer la c.** *Fig* to put on an act, play-act; **c'est de la c.** *(c'est faux)* it's a sham. ◆**comédien** *nm Th* & *Fig* actor. ◆**comédienne** *nf Th* & *Fig* actress.

comestible [kɔmestibl] *a* edible; – *nmpl* foods.

comète [kɔmɛt] *nf* comet.

comique [kɔmik] *a (style etc)* *Th* comic; *(amusant)* *Fig* comical, funny; **(auteur) c.** comedy writer; *(acteur)* comic (actor); **le c.** *(genre)* comedy; *Fig* the comical side (of).

comité [kɔmite] *nm* committee; **c. de gestion** board (of management); **en petit c.** in a small group.

commande [kɔmɑ̃d] **1** *nf (achat)* order; **sur c.** to order. **2** *nfpl* **les commandes** *Av Tech* the controls; **tenir les commandes** *(diriger)* *Fig* to have control.

command/er [kɔmɑ̃de] **1** *vt (diriger, exiger, dominer)* to command; *(faire fonctionner)* to control; – *vi* **c. à** *(ses passions etc)* to have control over; **c. à qn de faire** to command s.o. to do. **2** *vt (acheter)* to order. ◆**—ant** *nm Nau* captain; *(grade)* *Mil* major; *(grade)* *Av* squadron leader; **c. de bord** *Av* captain. ◆**—ement** *nm (autorité)* command; *Rel* commandment. ◆**commando** *nm* commando.

commanditaire [kɔmɑ̃diter] *nm Com* sleeping *ou* limited partner, *Am* silent partner.

comme [kɔm] **1** *adv* & *conj* as, like; **un peu**

c. a bit like; **c. moi** like me; **c. cela** like that; **blanc c. neige** (as) white as snow; **c. si** as if; **c. pour faire** as if to do; **c. par hasard** as if by chance; **joli c. tout** *Fam* ever so pretty; **c. ami** as a friend; **c. quoi** (*disant que*) to the effect that; (*ce qui prouve que*) so, which goes to show that; **qu'as-tu c. diplômes?** what do you have in the way of certificates? **2** *adv* (*exclamatif*) **regarde c. il pleut!** look how it's raining!; **c. c'est petit!** isn't it small! **3** *conj* (*temps*) as; (*cause*) as, since; **c. je pars** as I'm leaving; **c. elle entrait** (just) as she was coming in.

commémorer [kɔmemɔre] *vt* to commemorate. ◆**commémoratif, -ive** *a* commemorative. ◆**commémoration** *nf* commemoration.

commenc/er [kɔmɑ̃se] *vti* to begin, start (**à faire** to do, doing; **par** with; **par faire** by doing); **pour c.** to begin with. ◆**—ement** *nm* beginning, start.

comment [kɔmɑ̃] *adv* how; **c. le sais-tu?** how do you know?; **et c.!** and how!; **c.?** (*répétition, surprise*) what?; **c.!** (*indignation*) what!; **c. est-il?** what is he like?; **c. faire?** what's to be done?; **c. t'appelles-tu?** what's your name?; **c. allez-vous?** how are you?

commentaire [kɔmɑ̃tɛr] *nm* (*explications*) commentary; (*remarque*) comment. ◆**commentateur, -trice** *nmf* commentator. ◆**commenter** *vt* to comment (up)on.

commérage(s) [kɔmeraʒ] *nm(pl)* gossip.

commerce [kɔmɛrs] *nm* trade, commerce; (*magasin*) shop, business; **de c.** (*voyageur, maison, tribunal*) commercial; (*navire*) trading; **chambre de c.** chamber of commerce; **faire du c.** to trade; **dans le c.** (*objet*) (on sale) in the shops. ◆**commercer** *vi* to trade. ◆**commerçant, -ante** *nmf* shopkeeper; **c. en gros** wholesale dealer; – *a* (*nation*) trading, mercantile; (*rue, quartier*) shopping-; (*personne*) business-minded. ◆**commercial, -aux** *a* commercial, business-. ◆**commercialiser** *vt* to market.

commère [kɔmɛr] *nf* (*femme*) gossip.

commettre [kɔmɛtr] *vt* (*délit etc*) to commit; (*erreur*) to make.

commis [kɔmi] *nm* (*de magasin*) assistant, *Am* clerk; (*de bureau*) clerk, *Am* clerical worker.

commissaire [kɔmisɛr] *nm* Sp steward; **c.** (**de police**) police superintendent *ou Am* chief; **c. aux comptes** auditor; **c. du bord** *Nau* purser. ◆**c.-priseur** *nm* (*pl* **commissaires-priseurs**) auctioneer. ◆**commis-**

sariat *nm* **c.** (**de police**) (central) police station.

commission [kɔmisjɔ̃] *nf* (*course*) errand; (*message*) message; (*réunion*) commission, committee; (*pourcentage*) *Com* commission (**sur** on); **faire les commissions** to do the shopping. ◆**commissionnaire** *nm* messenger; (*d'hôtel*) commissionaire; *Com* agent.

commod/e [kɔmɔd] **1** *a* (*pratique*) handy; (*simple*) easy; **il n'est pas c.** (*pas aimable*) he's unpleasant; (*difficile*) he's a tough one. **2** *nf* chest of drawers, *Am* dresser. ◆**—ément** *adv* comfortably. ◆**commodité** *nf* convenience.

commotion [kɔmosjɔ̃] *nf* shock; **c.** (**cérébrale**) concussion. ◆**commotionner** *vt* to shake up.

commuer [kɔmɥe] *vt* (*peine*) *Jur* to commute (**en** to).

commun [kɔmœ̃] **1** *a* (*collectif, comparable, habituel*) common; (*frais, cuisine etc*) shared; (*action, démarche etc*) joint; **ami c.** mutual friend; **peu c.** uncommon; **en c.** in common; **transports en c.** public transport; **avoir** *ou* **mettre en c.** to share; **vivre en c.** to live together; **il n'a rien de c. avec** he has nothing in common with. **2** *nm* **le c. des mortels** ordinary mortals. ◆**—ément** [kɔmynemɑ̃] *adv* commonly.

communauté [kɔmynote] *nf* community. ◆**communautaire** *a* community-.

commune [kɔmyn] *nf* (*municipalité française*) commune; **les Communes** *Br Pol* the Commons. ◆**communal, -aux** *a* communal, local, municipal.

communi/er [kɔmynje] *vi* to receive Holy Communion, communicate. ◆**—ant, -ante** *nmf* *Rel* communicant. ◆**communion** *nf* communion; *Rel* (Holy) Communion.

communiqu/er [kɔmynike] *vt* to communicate, pass on; (*mouvement*) to impart, communicate; **se c. à** (*feu, rire*) to spread to; – *vi* (*personne, pièces etc*) to communicate. ◆**—é** *nm* (*avis*) *Pol* communiqué; (*publicitaire*) message; **c. de presse** press release. ◆**communicatif, -ive** *a* communicative; (*contagieux*) infectious. ◆**communication** *nf* communication; **c.** (**téléphonique**) (telephone) call; **mauvaise c.** *Tél* bad line.

communisme [kɔmynism] *nm* communism. ◆**communiste** *a & nmf* communist.

communs [kɔmœ̃] *nmpl* (*bâtiments*) outbuildings.

commutateur [kɔmytatœr] *nm* (*bouton*) *Él* switch.

compact [kɔ̃pakt] *a* dense; (*mécanisme, disque, véhicule*) compact.

compagne [kɔ̃paɲ] *nf* (*camarade*) friend; (*épouse, maîtresse*) companion. ◆**compagnie** *nf* (*présence, société*) & *Com Mil* company; **tenir c. à qn** to keep s.o. company. ◆**compagnon** *nm* companion; (*ouvrier*) workman; **c. de route** travelling companion, fellow traveller; **c. de jeu/de travail** playmate/workmate.

comparaître* [kɔ̃paretr] *vi Jur* to appear (in court) (**devant** before).

compar/er [kɔ̃pare] *vt* to compare; — **se c.** *vpr* to be compared (**à** to). ◆—**é** *a* (*science etc*) comparative. ◆—**able** *a* comparable. ◆**comparaison** *nf* comparison; *Littér* simile. ◆**comparatif, -ive** *a* (*méthode etc*) comparative; — *nm Gram* comparative.

comparse [kɔ̃pars] *nmf Jur* minor accomplice, stooge.

compartiment [kɔ̃partimɑ̃] *nm* compartment. ◆**compartimenter** *vt* to compartmentalize, divide up.

comparution [kɔ̃parysjɔ̃] *nf Jur* appearance (in court).

compas [kɔ̃pa] *nm* **1** (*pour mesurer etc*) (pair of) compasses, *Am* compass. **2** (*boussole*) *Nau* compass.

compassé [kɔ̃pase] *a* (*affecté*) starchy, stiff.

compassion [kɔ̃pasjɔ̃] *nf* compassion.

compatible [kɔ̃patibl] *a* compatible. ◆**compatibilité** *nf* compatibility.

compat/ir [kɔ̃patir] *vi* to sympathize; **c. à** (*la douleur etc de qn*) to share in. ◆—**issant** *a* sympathetic.

compatriote [kɔ̃patrijɔt] *nmf* compatriot.

compenser [kɔ̃pɑ̃se] *vt* to make up for, compensate for; — *vi* to compensate. ◆**compensation** *nf* compensation; **en c.** in compensation for.

compère [kɔ̃per] *nm* accomplice.

compétent [kɔ̃petɑ̃] *a* competent. ◆**compétence** *nf* competence.

compétition [kɔ̃petisjɔ̃] *nf* competition; (*épreuve*) *Sp* event; **de c.** (*esprit, sport*) competitive. ◆**compétitif, -ive** *a* competitive. ◆**compétitivité** *nf* competitiveness.

compiler [kɔ̃pile] *vt* (*documents*) to compile.

complainte [kɔ̃plɛ̃t] *nf* (*chanson*) lament.

complaire (se) [səkɔ̃plɛr] *vpr* **se c. dans qch/à faire** to delight in sth/in doing.

complaisant [kɔ̃plɛzɑ̃] *a* kind, obliging; (*indulgent*) self-indulgent, complacent. ◆**complaisance** *nf* kindness, obligingness; self-indulgence, complacency.

complément [kɔ̃plemɑ̃] *nm* complement; **le c.** (*le reste*) the rest; **un c. d'information** additional information. ◆**complémentaire** *a* complementary; (*détails*) additional.

complet, -ète [kɔ̃plɛ, -ɛt] **1** *a* complete; (*train, hôtel, examen etc*) full; (*aliment*) whole; **au (grand) c.** in full strength. **2** *nm* (*costume*) suit. ◆**complètement** *adv* completely. ◆**compléter** *vt* to complete; (*ajouter à*) to complement; (*somme*) to make up; — **se c.** *vpr* (*caractères*) to complement each other.

complexe [kɔ̃plɛks] **1** *a* complex. **2** *nm* (*sentiment, construction*) complex. ◆**complexé** *a Fam* hung up, inhibited. ◆**complexité** *nf* complexity.

complication [kɔ̃plikasjɔ̃] *nf* complication; (*complexité*) complexity.

complice [kɔ̃plis] *nm* accomplice; — *a* (*regard*) knowing; (*silence, attitude*) conniving; **c. de** *Jur* a party to. ◆**complicité** *nf* complicity.

compliment [kɔ̃plimɑ̃] *nm* compliment; *pl* (*éloges*) compliments; (*félicitations*) congratulations. ◆**complimenter** *vt* to compliment (**sur, pour** on).

compliqu/er [kɔ̃plike] *vt* to complicate; — **se c.** *vpr* (*situation*) to get complicated. ◆—**é** *a* complicated; (*mécanisme etc*) intricate; complicated; (*histoire, problème etc*) involved, complicated.

complot [kɔ̃plo] *nm* plot, conspiracy. ◆**comploter** [kɔ̃plɔte] *vti* to plot (**de faire** to do).

comport/er [kɔ̃pɔrte] **1** *vt* (*impliquer*) to involve, contain; (*comprendre en soi, présenter*) to contain, comprise, have. **2 se c.** *vpr* to behave; (*joueur, voiture*) to perform. ◆—**ement** *nm* behaviour; (*de joueur etc*) performance.

compos/er [kɔ̃poze] *vt* (*former, constituer*) to compose, make up; (*musique, visage*) to compose; (*numéro*) *Tél* to dial; (*texte*) *Typ* to set (up); — *vi Scol* to take an examination; **c. avec** to come to terms with. ◆—**ant** *nm* (*chimique, électronique*) component. ◆—**ante** *nf* (*d'une idée etc*) component. ◆—**é** *a* & *nm* compound. ◆**compositeur, -trice** *nmf Mus* composer; *Typ* typesetter. ◆**composition** *nf* (*action*) composing, making up; *Typ* typesetting; *Mus Littér Ch* composition; *Scol* test, class exam; **c. française** *Scol* French essay *ou* composition.

composter [kɔ̃pɔste] *vt* (*billet*) to cancel, punch.

compote [kɔ̃pɔt] *nf* stewed fruit; **c. de pommes** stewed apples, apple sauce. ◆**compotier** *nm* fruit dish.

compréhensible [kɔ̃preɑ̃sibl] *a* understandable, comprehensible. ◆**compréhensif, -ive** *a* (*personne*) understanding. ◆**compréhension** *nf* understanding, comprehension.

comprendre* [kɔ̃prɑ̃dr] *vt* to understand, comprehend; (*comporter*) to include, comprise; **je n'y comprends rien** I don't understand anything about it; **ça se comprend** that's understandable. ◆**compris** *a* (*inclus*) included (**dans** in); **frais c.** including expenses; **tout c.** (all) inclusive; **y c.** including; **c. entre** (situated) between; (**c'est**) **c.!** it's agreed!

compresse [kɔ̃pres] *nf* Méd compress.

compresseur [kɔ̃prescer] *a* **rouleau c.** steam roller.

comprimer [kɔ̃prime] *vt* to compress; (*colère etc*) to repress; (*dépenses*) to reduce. ◆**—é** *nm* Méd tablet. ◆**compression** *nf* compression; (*du personnel etc*) reduction.

compromettre* [kɔ̃prɔmetr] *vt* to compromise. ◆**compromis** *nm* compromise. ◆**compromission** *nf* compromising action, compromise.

comptable [kɔ̃tabl] *a* (*règles etc*) book-keeping-; — *nmf* bookkeeper; (*expert*) accountant; ◆**comptabilité** *nf* (*comptes*) accounts; (*science*) bookkeeping, accountancy; (*service*) accounts department.

comptant [kɔ̃tɑ̃] *a* **argent c.** (hard) cash; — *adv* **payer c.** to pay (in) cash; (**au**) **c.** (*acheter, vendre*) for cash.

compte [kɔ̃t] *nm* (*comptabilité*) account; (*calcul*) count; (*nombre*) (right) number; **avoir un c. en banque** to have a bank(ing) account; **c. chèque** cheque account, *Am* checking account; **tenir c. de** to take into account; **c. tenu de** considering; **entrer en ligne de c.** to be taken into account; **se rendre c. de** to realize; **rendre c. de** (*exposer*) to report on; (*justifier*) to account for; **c. rendu** report; (*de livre, film*) review; **demander des comptes à** to call to account; **faire le c. de** to count; **à son c.** (*travailler*) for oneself; (*s'installer*) on one's own; **pour le c. de** on behalf of; **pour mon c.** for my part; **sur le c. de qn** about s.o.; **en fin de c.** all things considered; **à bon c.** (*acheter*) cheap(ly); **s'en tirer à bon c.** to get off lightly; **avoir un c. à régler avec qn** to have a score to settle with s.o.; **c. à rebours**

countdown. ◆**c.-gouttes** *nm inv* Méd dropper; **au c.-gouttes** very sparingly. ◆**c.-tours** *nm inv* Aut rev counter.

compt/er [kɔ̃te] *vt* (*calculer*) to count; (*prévoir*) to reckon, allow; (*tenir compte de*) to consider; (*payer*) to pay; **c. faire** to expect to do; (*avoir l'intention de*) to intend to do; **c. qch à qn** (*facturer*) to charge s.o. for sth; **il compte deux ans de service** he has two years' service; **ses jours sont comptés** his *ou* her days are numbered; — *vi* (*calculer, avoir de l'importance*) to count; **c. sur** to rely on; **c. avec** to reckon with; **c. parmi** to be (numbered) among. ◆**—eur** *nm* El meter; **c.** (**de vitesse**) Aut speedometer; **c.** (**kilométrique**) milometer, clock; **c. Geiger** Geiger counter.

comptoir [kɔ̃twar] *nm* 1 (*de magasin*) counter; (*de café*) bar; (*de bureau*) (reception) desk. 2 Com branch, agency.

compulser [kɔ̃pylse] *vt* to examine.

comte [kɔ̃t] *nm* (*noble*) count; *Br* earl. ◆**comté** *nm* county. ◆**comtesse** *nf* countess.

con, conne [kɔ̃, kɔn] *a* (*idiot*) Fam stupid; — *nmf* Fam stupid fool.

concave [kɔ̃kav] *a* concave.

concéder [kɔ̃sede] *vt* to concede, grant (**à** to, **que** that).

concentr/er [kɔ̃sɑ̃tre] *vt* to concentrate; (*attention etc*) to focus, concentrate; — **se c.** *vpr* (*réfléchir*) to concentrate. ◆**—é** *a* (*solution*) concentrated; (*lait*) condensed; (*attentif*) in a state of concentration; — *nm* Ch concentrate; **c. de tomates** tomato purée. ◆**concentration** *nf* concentration.

concentrique [kɔ̃sɑ̃trik] *a* concentric.

concept [kɔ̃sɛpt] *nm* concept. ◆**conception** *nf* (*idée*) & Méd conception.

concern/er [kɔ̃sɛrne] *vt* to concern; **en ce qui me concerne** as far as I'm concerned. ◆**—ant** *prep* concerning.

concert [kɔ̃ser] *nm* Mus concert; (*de louanges*) chorus; **de c.** (*agir*) together, in concert.

concert/er [kɔ̃sɛrte] *vt* to arrange, devise (*in agreement*); — **se c.** *vpr* to consult together. ◆**—é** *a* (*plan*) concerted. ◆**concertation** *nf* (*dialogue*) dialogue.

concession [kɔ̃sesjɔ̃] *nf* concession (**à** to); (*terrain*) plot (of land). ◆**concessionnaire** *nmf* Com (authorized) dealer, agent.

concev/oir* [kɔ̃savwar] 1 *vt* (*imaginer, éprouver, engendrer*) to conceive; (*comprendre*) to understand; **ainsi conçu** (*dépêche etc*) worded as follows. 2 *vi* (*femme*) to conceive. ◆**—able** *a* conceivable.

concierge [kɔ̃sjɛrʒ] *nmf* caretaker, *Am* janitor.

concile [kɔ̃sil] *nm* Rel council.

concili/er [kɔ̃silje] *vt* (*choses*) to reconcile; **se c. l'amitié/etc de qn** to win (over) s.o.'s friendship/*etc*. **◆—ant** *a* conciliatory. **◆conciliateur, -trice** *nmf* conciliator. **◆conciliation** *nf* conciliation.

concis [kɔ̃si] *a* concise, terse. **◆concision** *nf* concision.

concitoyen, -enne [kɔ̃sitwajɛ̃, -ɛn] *nmf* fellow citizen.

conclu/re* [kɔ̃klyr] *vt* (*terminer, régler*) to conclude; **c. que** (*déduire*) to conclude that; – *vi* (*orateur etc*) to conclude; **c. à** to conclude in favour of. **◆—ant** *a* conclusive. **◆conclusion** *nf* conclusion.

concombre [kɔ̃kɔ̃br] *nm* cucumber.

concorde [kɔ̃kɔrd] *nf* concord, harmony. **◆concord/er** *vi* (*faits etc*) to agree; (*caractères*) to match; **c. avec** to match. **◆—ant** *a* in agreement. **◆concordance** *nf* agreement; (*de situations, résultats*) similarity; **c. des temps** *Gram* sequence of tenses.

concourir* [kɔ̃kurir] *vi* (*candidat*) to compete (**pour** for); (*directions*) to converge; **c. à** (*un but*) to contribute to. **◆concours** *nm* Scol Univ competitive examination; (*jeu*) competition; (*aide*) assistance; (*de circonstances*) combination; **c. hippique** horse show.

concret, -ète [kɔ̃krɛ, -ɛt] *a* concrete. **◆concrétiser** *vt* to give concrete form to; **— se c.** *vpr* to materialize.

conçu [kɔ̃sy] *voir* **concevoir**; – *a* **c. pour faire** designed to do; **bien c.** (*maison etc*) well-designed.

concubine [kɔ̃kybin] *nf* (*maîtresse*) concubine. **◆concubinage** *nm* cohabitation; **en c.** as husband and wife.

concurrent, -ente [kɔ̃kyrɑ̃, -ɑ̃t] *nmf* competitor; *Scol Univ* candidate. **◆concurrence** *nf* competition; **faire c. à** to compete with; **jusqu'à c. de** up to the amount of. **◆concurrencer** *vt* to compete with. **◆concurrentiel, -ielle** *a* (*prix etc*) competitive.

condamn/er [kɔ̃dane] *vt* to condemn; *Jur* to sentence (**à** to); (*porte*) to block up, bar; (*pièce*) to keep locked; **c. à une amende** to fine. **◆—é, -ée** *nmf* Jur condemned man, condemned woman; **être c.** (*malade*) to be doomed, be a hopeless case. **◆condamnation** *nf* Jur sentence; (*censure*) condemnation.

condenser [kɔ̃dɑ̃se] *vt*, **— se c.** *vpr* to condense. **◆condensateur** *nm* Él condenser. **◆condensation** *nf* condensation.

condescendre [kɔ̃desɑ̃dr] *vi* to condescend (**à** to). **◆condescendance** *nf* condescension.

condiment [kɔ̃dimã] *nm* condiment.

condisciple [kɔ̃disipl] *nm* Scol classmate, schoolfellow; *Univ* fellow student.

condition [kɔ̃disjɔ̃] *nf* (*état, stipulation, rang*) condition; *pl* (*clauses, tarifs*) Com terms; **à c. de faire, à c. que l'on fasse** providing *ou* provided (that) one does; **mettre en c.** (*endoctriner*) to condition; **sans c.** (*se rendre*) unconditionally. **◆conditionnel, -elle** *a* conditional. **◆conditionn/er** *vt* 1 (*influencer*) to condition. 2 (*article*) Com to package. **◆—é** *a* (*réflexe*) conditioned; **à air c.** (*pièce etc*) air-conditioned. **◆—ement** *nm* conditioning; packaging.

condoléances [kɔ̃doleãs] *nfpl* condolences.

conducteur, -trice [kɔ̃dyktœr, -tris] 1 *nmf* Aut Rail driver. 2 *a & nm* (*corps*) Él conductor; (*fil*) *a.* Él lead (wire).

conduire* [kɔ̃dɥir] 1 *vt* to lead; *Aut* to drive; (*affaire etc*) & Él to conduct; (*eau*) to carry; **c. qn à** (*accompagner*) to take s.o. to. 2 **se c.** *vpr* to behave. **◆conduit** *nm* duct. **◆conduite** *nf* conduct, behaviour; *Aut* driving (**de** of); (*d'entreprise etc*) conduct; (*d'eau, de gaz*) main; **c. à gauche** (*volant*) left-hand drive; **faire un bout de c. à qn** to go with s.o. part of the way; **sous la c. de** under the guidance of.

cône [kon] *nm* cone.

confection [kɔ̃fɛksjɔ̃] *nf* making (**de** of); **vêtements de c.** ready-made clothes; **magasin de c.** ready-made clothing shop. **◆confectionner** *vt* (*gâteau, robe*) to make.

confédération [kɔ̃federasjɔ̃] *nf* confederation. **◆confédéré** *a* confederate.

conférence [kɔ̃ferɑ̃s] *nf* conference; (*exposé*) lecture. **◆conférencier, -ière** *nmf* lecturer. **◆conférer** *vt* (*attribuer, donner*) to confer (**à** on).

confess/er [kɔ̃fese] *vt* to confess; **— se c.** *vpr* Rel to confess (**à** to). **◆—eur** *nm* (*prêtre*) confessor. **◆confession** *nf* confession. **◆confessionnal, -aux** *nm* Rel confessional. **◆confessionnel, -elle** *a* (*école*) Rel denominational.

confettis [kɔ̃feti] *nmpl* confetti.

confiance [kɔ̃fjɑ̃s] *nf* trust, confidence; **faire c. à qn, avoir c. en qn** to trust s.o.; **c. en soi** (self-)confidence; **poste/abus de c.** position/breach of trust; **homme de c.** reliable man; **en toute c.** (*acheter*) quite confidently; **poser la question de c.** *Pol* to ask for a vote of confidence. ◆**confiant** *a* trusting; (*sûr de soi*) confident; **être c. en** ou **dans** to have confidence in.

confidence [kɔ̃fidɑ̃s] *nf* (*secret*) confidence; **en c.** in confidence; **il m'a fait une c.** he confided in me. ◆**confident** *nm* confidant. ◆**confidente** *nf* confidante. ◆**confidentiel, -ielle** *a* confidential.

confier [kɔ̃fje] *vt* **c. à qn** (*enfant, objet*) to give s.o. to look after, entrust s.o. with; **c. un secret/*etc* à qn** to confide a secret/*etc* to s.o.; **— se c.** *vpr* to confide (**à qn** in s.o.).

configuration [kɔ̃figyrasjɔ̃] *nf* configuration.

confin/er [kɔ̃fine] *vt* to confine; **– vi c. à** to border on; **— se c.** *vpr* to confine oneself (**dans** to). ◆**—é** *a* (*atmosphère*) stuffy.

confins [kɔ̃fɛ̃] *nmpl* confines.

confire [kɔ̃fir] *vt* (*cornichon*) to pickle; (*fruit*) to preserve.

confirmer [kɔ̃firme] *vt* to confirm (**que** that); **c. qn dans sa résolution** to confirm s.o.'s resolve. ◆**confirmation** *nf* confirmation.

confiserie [kɔ̃fizri] *nf* (*magasin*) sweet shop, *Am* candy store; *pl* (*produits*) confectionery, sweets, *Am* candy. ◆**confiseur, -euse** *nmf* confectioner.

confisquer [kɔ̃fiske] *vt* to confiscate (**à qn** from s.o.). ◆**confiscation** *nf* confiscation.

confit [kɔ̃fi] *a* **fruits confits** crystallized ou candied fruit. ◆**confiture** *nf* jam, preserves.

conflit [kɔ̃fli] *nm* conflict. ◆**conflictuel, -elle** *a Psy* conflict-provoking.

confluent [kɔ̃flyɑ̃] *nm* (*jonction*) confluence.

confondre [kɔ̃fɔ̃dr] *vt* (*choses, personnes*) to confuse, mix up; (*consterner, étonner*) to confound; (*amalgamer*) to fuse; **c. avec** to mistake for; **— se c.** *vpr* (*s'unir*) to merge; **se c. en excuses** to be very apologetic.

conforme [kɔ̃fɔrm] *a* **c. à** in accordance with; **c. à l'original** (*copie*) true (to the original). ◆**conform/er** *vt* to model, adapt; **— se c.** *vpr* to conform (**à** to). ◆**—ément** *adv* **c. à** in accordance with. ◆**conformisme** *nm* conformity, conformism. ◆**conformiste** *a* & *nmf* conformist. ◆**conformité** *nf* conformity.

confort [kɔ̃fɔr] *nm* comfort. ◆**confortable** *a* comfortable.

confrère [kɔ̃frɛr] *nm* colleague. ◆**confrérie** *nf Rel* brotherhood.

confronter [kɔ̃frɔ̃te] *vt Jur etc* to confront

(**avec** with); (*textes*) to collate; **confronté à** confronted with. ◆**confrontation** *nf* confrontation; collation.

confus [kɔ̃fy] *a* (*esprit, situation, bruit*) confused; (*idée, style*) confused, jumbled, hazy; (*gêné*) embarrassed; **je suis c.!** (*désolé*) I'm terribly sorry!; (*comblé de bienfaits*) I'm overwhelmed! ◆**confusément** *adv* indistinctly, vaguely. ◆**confusion** *nf* confusion; (*gêne, honte*) embarrassment.

congé [kɔ̃ʒe] *nm* leave (of absence); (*avis pour locataire*) notice (to quit); (*pour salarié*) notice (of dismissal); (*vacances*) holiday, *Am* vacation; **c. de maladie** sick leave; **congés payés** holidays with pay, paid holidays; **donner son c. à** (*employé, locataire*) to give notice to; **prendre c. de** to take leave of. ◆**congédier** *vt* (*domestique etc*) to dismiss.

congeler [kɔ̃ʒle] *vt* to freeze. ◆**congélateur** *nm* freezer, deep-freeze. ◆**congélation** *nf* freezing.

congénère [kɔ̃ʒenɛr] *nmf* fellow creature. ◆**congénital, -aux** *a* congenital.

congère [kɔ̃ʒɛr] *nf* snowdrift.

congestion [kɔ̃ʒɛstjɔ̃] *nf* congestion; **c. cérébrale** *Méd* stroke. ◆**congestionn/er** *vt* to congest. ◆**—é** *a* (*visage*) flushed.

Congo [kɔ̃go] *nm* Congo. ◆**congolais, -aise** *a* & *nmf* Congolese.

congratuler [kɔ̃gratyle] *vt Iron* to congratulate.

congrégation [kɔ̃gregasjɔ̃] *nf* (*de prêtres etc*) congregation.

congrès [kɔ̃grɛ] *nm* congress. ◆**congressiste** *nmf* delegate (*to a congress*).

conifère [kɔnifɛr] *nm* conifer.

conique [kɔnik] *a* conic(al), cone-shaped.

conjecture [kɔ̃ʒɛktyr] *nf* conjecture. ◆**conjectural, -aux** *a* conjectural. ◆**conjecturer** *vt* to conjecture, surmise.

conjoint [kɔ̃ʒwɛ̃] **1** *a* (*problèmes, action etc*) joint. **2** *nm* spouse; *pl* husband and wife. ◆**conjointement** *adv* jointly.

conjonction [kɔ̃ʒɔ̃ksjɔ̃] *nf Gram* conjunction.

conjoncture [kɔ̃ʒɔ̃ktyr] *nf* circumstances; *Écon* economic situation. ◆**conjoncturel, -elle** *a* (*prévisions etc*) economic.

conjugal, -aux [kɔ̃ʒygal, -o] *a* conjugal.

conjuguer [kɔ̃ʒyge] *vt* (*verbe*) to conjugate; (*efforts*) to combine; **— se c.** *vpr* (*verbe*) to be conjugated. ◆**conjugaison** *nf Gram* conjugation.

conjur/er [kɔ̃ʒyre] *vt* (*danger*) to avert; (*mauvais sort*) to ward off; **c. qn** (*implorer*) to entreat s.o. (**de faire** to do). ◆**-é, -ée** *nmf* conspirator. ◆**conjuration** *nf* (*complot*) conspiracy.

connaissance [kɔnɛsɑ̃s] *nf* knowledge; (*personne*) acquaintance; *pl* (*science*) knowledge (**en** of); **faire la c. de qn, faire c. avec qn** to make s.o.'s acquaintance, meet s.o.; (*ami, époux etc*) to get to know s.o.; **à ma c.** as far as I know; **avoir c. de** to be aware of; **perdre c.** to lose consciousness, faint; **sans c.** unconscious. ◆**connaisseur** *nm* connoisseur.

connaître [kɔnɛtr] *vt* to know; (*rencontrer*) to meet; (*un succès etc*) to have; (*un malheur etc*) to experience; **faire c.** to make known; — **se c.** *vpr* (*amis etc*) to get to know each other; **nous nous connaissons déjà** we've met before; **s'y c. à** *ou* **en qch** to know (all) about sth; **il ne se connaît plus** he's losing his cool.

connecter [kɔnɛkte] *vt* *Él* to connect. ◆**connexe** *a* (*matières*) allied. ◆**connexion** *nf* *Él* connection.

connerie [kɔnri] *nf* *Fam* (*bêtise*) stupidity; (*action*) stupid thing; *pl* (*paroles*) stupid nonsense.

connivence [kɔnivɑ̃s] *nf* connivance.

connotation [kɔnɔtasjɔ̃] *nf* connotation.

connu *voir* **connaître**; *a* (*célèbre*) well-known.

conquér/ir° [kɔkerir] *vt* (*pays, marché etc*) to conquer. ◆**-ant, -ante** *nmf* conqueror. ◆**conquête** *nf* conquest; **faire la c. de** (*pays, marché etc*) to conquer.

consacrer [kɔsakre] *vt* (*temps, vie etc*) to devote à (à); (*église etc*) *Rel* to consecrate; (*coutume etc*) to establish, sanction, consecrate; **se c. à** to devote oneself to.

conscience [kɔsjɑ̃s] *nf* **1** (*psychologique*) consciousness; **la c. de qch** the awareness *ou* consciousness of sth; **c. de soi** self-awareness; **avoir/prendre c. de** to be/become aware *ou* conscious of; **perdre c.** to lose consciousness. **2** (*morale*) conscience; **avoir mauvaise c.** to have a guilty conscience; **c. professionnelle** conscientiousness. ◆**consciemment** [kɔsjamɑ̃] *adv* consciously. ◆**consciencieux, -euse** *a* conscientious. ◆**conscient** *a* conscious; **c. de** aware *ou* conscious of.

conscrit [kɔskri] *nm* *Mil* conscript. ◆**conscription** *nf* conscription.

consécration [kɔsekrasjɔ̃] *nf* *Rel* consecration; (*confirmation*) sanction, consecration.

consécuti/f, -ive [kɔsekytif, -iv] *a* consecutive; **c. à** following upon. ◆**-vement** *adv* consecutively.

conseil [kɔsɛj] *nm* **1 un c.** a piece of advice, some advice; **des conseils** advice; (**expert-**)**c.** consultant. **2** (*assemblée*) council, committee; **c. d'administration** board of directors; **C. des ministres** *Pol* Cabinet; (*réunion*) Cabinet meeting. ◆**conseiller¹** *vt* (*guider, recommander*) to advise; **c. qch à qn** to recommend sth to s.o.; **c. à qn de faire** to advise s.o. to do. ◆**conseiller², -ère** *nmf* (*expert*) consultant; (*d'un conseil*) councillor.

consent/ir° [kɔsɑ̃tir] *vi* **c. à** to consent to; — *vt* to grant (à to). ◆**-ement** *nm* consent.

conséquence [kɔsekɑ̃s] *nf* consequence; (*conclusion*) conclusion; **en c.** accordingly; **sans c.** (*importance*) of no importance. ◆**conséquent** *a* logical; (*important*) *Fam* important; **par c.** consequently.

conservatoire [kɔservatwar] *nm* academy, school (*of music, drama*).

conserve [kɔserv] *nf* **conserves** tinned *ou* canned food; **de** *ou* **en c.** tinned, canned; **mettre en c.** to tin, can.

conserv/er [kɔserve] *vt* (*ne pas perdre*) to retain, keep; (*fruits, vie, tradition etc*) to preserve; — **se c.** *vpr* (*aliment*) to keep. ◆**-é à bien c.** (*vieillard*) well-preserved. ◆**conservateur, -trice 1** *a* & *nmf* *Pol* Conservative. **2** *nm* (*de musée*) curator; (*de bibliothèque*) (chief) librarian. **3** *nm* (*produit*) *Culin* preservative. ◆**conservation** *nf* (*somme*) deposit; **instinct de c.** survival instinct. ◆**conservatisme** *nm* conservatism.

considér/er [kɔsidere] *vt* to consider (**que** that); (*respecter*) to respect s.o.; **c. comme** to consider to be, regard as; **tout bien considéré** all things considered. ◆**-able** *a* considerable. ◆**considération** *nf* (*motif, examen*) consideration; (*respect*) regard, esteem; *pl* (*remarques*) observations; **prendre en c.** to take into consideration.

consigne [kɔsiɲ] *nf* (*instruction*) orders; *Rail* left-luggage office, *Am* baggage checkroom; *Scol* detention; *Mil* confinement to barracks; (*somme*) deposit; **c. automatique** *Rail* luggage lockers, *Am* baggage lockers. ◆**consignation** *nf* (*somme*) deposit. ◆**consigner** *vt* (*écrire*) to record; (*bouteille etc*) to charge a deposit on; (*bagages*) to deposit in the left-luggage office, *Am* to check; (*élève*) *Scol* to keep in;

(soldat) Mil to confine (to barracks); *(salle)* to seal off, close.

consistant [kɔ̃sistɑ̃] a *(sauce, bouillie)* thick; *(argument, repas)* solid. ◆**consistance** nf *(de liquide)* consistency; **sans c.** *(rumeur)* unfounded; *(esprit)* irresolute.

consister [kɔ̃siste] vi **c. en/dans** to consist of/in; **c. à faire** to consist in doing.

consistoire [kɔ̃sistwar] nm Rel council.

console [kɔ̃sɔl] nf Tech Él console.

consoler [kɔ̃sɔle] vt to console, comfort *(de* for); **se c. de** *(la mort de qn etc)* to get over. ◆**consolation** nf consolation, comfort.

consolider [kɔ̃sɔlide] vt to strengthen, consolidate. ◆**consolidation** nf strengthening, consolidation.

consomm/er [kɔ̃sɔme] vt *(aliment, carburant etc)* to consume; *(crime, œuvre)* Litt to accomplish; – vi *(au café)* to drink; **c. beaucoup/peu** *(véhicule)* to be heavy/light on petrol ou Am gas. ◆**–é 1** a *(achevé)* consummate. **2** nm clear meat soup, consommé. ◆**consommateur, -trice** nmf Com consumer; *(au café)* customer. ◆**consommation** nf consumption; drink; **biens/société de c.** consumer goods/society.

consonance [kɔ̃sɔnɑ̃s] nf Mus consonance; pl *(sons)* sounds.

consonne [kɔ̃sɔn] nf consonant.

consortium [kɔ̃sɔrsjɔm] nm Com consortium.

consorts [kɔ̃sɔr] nmpl **et c.** Péj and people of that ilk.

conspirer [kɔ̃spire] vi **1** to conspire, plot *(contre* against). **2 c. à faire** *(concourir)* to conspire to do. ◆**conspirateur, -trice** nmf conspirator. ◆**conspiration** nf conspiracy.

conspuer [kɔ̃spɥe] vt *(orateur etc)* to boo.

constant, -ante [kɔ̃stɑ̃, -ɑ̃t] a constant; – nf Math constant. ◆**constamment** adv constantly. ◆**constance** nf constancy.

constat [kɔ̃sta] nm *(official)* report; **dresser un c. d'échec** to acknowledge one's failure.

constater [kɔ̃state] vt to note, observe *(que* that); *(vérifier)* to establish; *(enregistrer)* to record; **je ne fais que c.** I'm merely stating a fact. ◆**constatation** nf *(remarque)* observation.

constellation [kɔ̃stelasjɔ̃] nf constellation. ◆**constellé** a **c. de** *(étoiles, joyaux)* studded with.

consterner [kɔ̃stɛrne] vt to distress, dismay. ◆**consternation** nf distress, (profound) dismay.

constip/er [kɔ̃stipe] vt to constipate. ◆**–é**

a constipated; *(gêné)* Fam embarrassed, stiff. ◆**constipation** nf constipation.

constitu/er [kɔ̃stitɥe] vt *(composer)* to make up, constitute; *(être, représenter)* to constitute; *(organiser)* to form; *(instituer)* Jur to appoint; **constitué de** made up of; **se c. prisonnier** to give oneself up. ◆**–ant** a *(éléments)* component, constituent; *(assemblée)* Pol constituent. ◆**constitutif, -ive** a constituent. ◆**constitution** nf *(santé)* & Pol constitution; *(fondation)* formation *(de* of); *(composition)* composition. ◆**constitutionnel, -elle** a constitutional.

constructeur [kɔ̃stryktœr] nm builder; *(fabricant)* maker *(de* of). ◆**constructif, -ive** a constructive. ◆**construction** nf *(de pont etc)* building, construction *(de* of); *(édifice)* building, structure; *(de théorie etc)* & Gram construction; **de c.** *(matériaux, jeu)* building.

construire* [kɔ̃strɥir] vt *(maison, route etc)* to build, construct; *(phrase, théorie etc)* to construct.

consul [kɔ̃syl] nm consul. ◆**consulaire** a consular. ◆**consulat** nm consulate.

consulter [kɔ̃sylte] **1** vt to consult; – **se c.** vpr to consult (each other), confer. **2** vi *(médecin)* to hold surgery, Am hold office hours. ◆**consultatif, -ive** a consultative, advisory. ◆**consultation** nf consultation; **cabinet de c.** Méd surgery, Am office; **heures de c.** Méd surgery hours, Am office hours.

consumer [kɔ̃syme] vt *(détruire, miner)* to consume.

contact [kɔ̃takt] nm contact; *(toucher)* touch; Aut ignition; **être en c. avec** to be in touch ou contact with; **prendre c.** to get in touch *(avec* with); **entrer en c. avec** to come into contact with; **prise de c.** first meeting; **mettre/couper le c.** Aut to switch on/off the ignition. ◆**contacter** vt to contact.

contagieux, -euse [kɔ̃taʒjø, -øz] a *(maladie, rire)* contagious, infectious; **c'est c.** it's catching ou contagious. ◆**contagion** nf Méd contagion, infection; *(de rire etc)* contagiousness.

contaminer [kɔ̃tamine] vt to contaminate. ◆**contamination** nf contamination.

conte [kɔ̃t] nm tale; **c. de fée** fairy tale.

contempler [kɔ̃tɑ̃ple] vt to contemplate, gaze at. ◆**contemplatif, -ive** a contemplative. ◆**contemplation** nf contemplation.

contemporain, -aine [kɔ̃tɑ̃pɔrɛ̃, -ɛn] a & nmf contemporary.

contenance [kɔ̃tnɑ̃s] nf **1** (contenu) capacity. **2** (allure) bearing; **perdre c.** to lose one's composure.

conten/ir* [kɔ̃tnir] vt (renfermer) to contain; (avoir comme capacité) to hold; (contrôler) to hold back, contain; — **se c.** vpr to contain oneself. ◆—**ant** nm container. ◆—**eur** nm (freight) container.

content [kɔ̃tã] **1** a pleased, happy, glad (de faire to do); **c. de qn/qch** pleased ou happy with s.o./sth; **c. de soi** self-satisfied; **non c. d'avoir fait** not content with having done. **2** nm **avoir son c.** to have had one's fill (de of). ◆**content/er** vt to satisfy, please; **se c.** de to be content with, content oneself with. ◆—**ement** nm contentment, satisfaction.

contentieux [kɔ̃tɑ̃sjø] nm (affaires) matters in dispute; (service) legal ou claims department.

contenu [kɔ̃tny] nm (de récipient) contents; (de texte, film etc) content.

cont/er [kɔ̃te] vt (histoire etc) to tell, relate. ◆—**eur, -euse** nmf storyteller.

conteste (sans) [sɑ̃kɔ̃test] adv indisputably.

contest/er [kɔ̃teste] **1** vt (fait etc) to dispute, contest. **2** vi (étudiants etc) to protest; — vt to protest against. ◆—**able** a (théorie etc) controversial. ◆—**able** a debatable. ◆**contestataire** a **étudiant/ ouvrier c.** student/worker protester; — nmf protester. ◆**contestation** nf (discussion) dispute; **faire de la c.** to protest (against the establishment).

contexte [kɔ̃tekst] nm context.

contigu, -uë [kɔ̃tigy] a **c. (à)** (maisons etc) adjoining. ◆**contiguïté** nf close proximity.

continent [kɔ̃tinã] nm continent; (opposé à une île) mainland. ◆**continental, -aux** a continental.

contingent [kɔ̃tɛ̃ʒã] **1** a (accidentel) contingent. **2** nm Mil contingent; (part, quota) quota. ◆**contingences** nfpl contingencies.

continu [kɔ̃tiny] a continuous. ◆**continuel, -elle** a continual, unceasing. ◆**continuellement** adv continually.

continuer [kɔ̃tinɥe] vt to continue, carry on (à ou de faire doing); (prolonger) to continue; — vi to continue, go on. ◆**continuation** nf continuation; **bonne c.!** Fam I hope the rest of it goes well, keep up the good work! ◆**continuité** nf continuity.

contondant [kɔ̃tɔ̃dã] a **instrument c.** Jur blunt instrument.

contorsion [kɔ̃tɔrsjɔ̃] nf contortion. ◆**se**

contorsionner vpr to contort oneself. ◆**contorsionniste** nmf contortionist.

contour [kɔ̃tur] nm outline, contour; pl (de route, rivière) twists, bends. ◆**contourn/er** vt (colline etc) to go round, skirt; (difficulté, loi) to get round. ◆—**é** a (style) convoluted, tortuous.

contraception [kɔ̃trasepsjɔ̃] nf contraception. ◆**contraceptif, -ive** a & nm contraceptive.

contract/er [kɔ̃trakte] vt (muscle, habitude, dette etc) to contract; — **se c.** vpr (cœur etc) to contract. ◆—**é** a (inquiet) tense. ◆**contraction** nf contraction.

contractuel, -elle [kɔ̃traktɥɛl] **1** nmf traffic warden; — nf Am meter maid. **2** a contractual.

contradicteur [kɔ̃tradiktœr] nm contradictor. ◆**contradiction** nf contradiction. ◆**contradictoire** a (propos etc) contradictory; (rapports, théories) conflicting; **débat c.** debate.

contraindre* [kɔ̃trɛ̃dr] vt to compel, force (à faire to do); — **se c.** vpr to compel ou force oneself; (se gêner) to restrain oneself. ◆**contraignant** a constraining, restricting. ◆**contraint** a (air etc) forced, constrained. ◆**contrainte** nf compulsion, constraint; (gêne) constraint, restraint.

contraire [kɔ̃trɛr] a opposite; (défavorable) contrary; **c. à** contrary to; — nm opposite; **(bien) au c.** on the contrary. ◆—**ment** adv **c. à** contrary to.

contrari/er [kɔ̃trarje] vt (projet, action) to thwart; (personne) to annoy. ◆—**ant** a (action etc) annoying; (personne) difficult, perverse. ◆**contrariété** nf annoyance.

contraste [kɔ̃trast] nm contrast. ◆**contraster** vi to contrast (avec with); **faire c.** (mettre en contraste) to contrast.

contrat [kɔ̃tra] nm contract.

contravention [kɔ̃travɑ̃sjɔ̃] nf (amende) Aut fine; (pour stationnement interdit) (parking) ticket; **en c.** contravening the law; **en c. à** in contravention of the law.

contre [kɔ̃tr] **1** prép & adv against; (en échange de) (in exchange) for; **échanger c.** to exchange for; **fâché c.** angry with; **s'abriter c.** to shelter from; **il va s'appuyer c.** he's going to lean against it; **six voix c. deux** six votes to two; **Nîmes c. Arras** Sp Nîmes versus Arras; **un médicament c.** (toux, grippe etc) a medicine for; **par c.** on the other hand; **tout c.** close to ou by. **2** nm (riposte) Sp counter.

contre- [kɔ̃tr] préf counter-.

contre-attaque [kɔ̃tratak] *nf* counterattack. ◆**contre-attaquer** *vt* to counterattack.

contrebalancer [kɔ̃trəbalɑ̃se] *vt* to counterbalance.

contrebande [kɔ̃trəbɑ̃d] *nf* (*fraude*) smuggling, contraband; (*marchandise*) contraband; **de c.** (*tabac etc*) contraband, smuggled; **faire de la c.** to smuggle; **passer qch en c.** to smuggle sth. ◆**contrebandier, -ière** *nmf* smuggler.

contrebas (en) [ɑ̃kɔ̃trəba] *adv & prép* **en c.** (**de**) down below.

contrebasse [kɔ̃trəbas] *nf* Mus doublebass.

contrecarrer [kɔ̃trəkare] *vt* to thwart, frustrate.

contrecœur (à) [akɔ̃trəkœr] *adv* reluctantly.

contrecoup [kɔ̃trəku] *nm* (indirect) effect *ou* consequence; **par c.** as an indirect consequence.

contre-courant (à) [akɔ̃trəkurɑ̃] *adv* against the current.

contredanse [kɔ̃trədɑ̃s] *nf* (*amende*) Aut Fam ticket.

contredire* [kɔ̃trədir] *vt* to contradict; — **se c.** *vpr* to contradict oneself.

contrée [kɔ̃tre] *nf* region, land.

contre-espionnage [kɔ̃trɛspjɔnaʒ] *nm* counterespionage.

contrefaçon [kɔ̃trəfasɔ̃] *nf* counterfeiting, forgery; (*objet imité*) counterfeit, forgery. ◆**contrefaire** *vt* (*parodier*) to mimic; (*déguiser*) to disguise; (*monnaie etc*) to counterfeit, forge.

contreforts [kɔ̃trəfɔr] *nmpl* Géog foothills.

contre-jour (à) [akɔ̃trəʒur] *adv* against the (sun)light.

contremaître [kɔ̃trəmɛtr] *nm* foreman.

contre-offensive [kɔ̃trɔfɑ̃siv] *nf* counteroffensive.

contrepartie [kɔ̃trəparti] *nf* compensation; **en c.** in exchange.

contre-performance [kɔ̃trəperfɔrmɑ̃s] *nf* Sp bad performance.

contre-pied [kɔ̃trəpje] *nm* **le c.-pied d'une opinion/attitude** the (exact) opposite view/attitude; **à c.-pied** Sp on the wrong foot.

contre-plaqué [kɔ̃trəplake] *nm* plywood.

contrepoids [kɔ̃trəpwa] *nm* Tech & Fig counterbalance; **faire c. (à)** to counterbalance.

contrepoint [kɔ̃trəpwɛ̃] *nm* Mus counterpoint.

contrer [kɔ̃tre] *vt* (*personne, attaque*) to counter.

contre-révolution [kɔ̃trərevɔlysjɔ̃] *nf* counter-revolution.

contresens [kɔ̃trəsɑ̃s] *nm* misinterpretation; (*en traduisant*) mistranslation; (*non-sens*) absurdity; **à c.** the wrong way.

contresigner [kɔ̃trəsiɲe] *vt* to countersign.

contretemps [kɔ̃trətɑ̃] *nm* hitch, mishap; **à c.** (*arriver etc*) at the wrong moment.

contre-torpilleur [kɔ̃trətɔrpijœr] *nm* (*navire*) destroyer, torpedo boat.

contrevenir [kɔ̃trəvnir] *vi* **c. à** (*loi etc*) to contravene.

contre-vérité [kɔ̃trəverite] *nf* untruth.

contribu/er [kɔ̃tribɥe] *vi* to contribute (**à** to). ◆**-able** *nmf* taxpayer. ◆**contribution** *nf* contribution; (*impôt*) tax; *pl* (*administration*) tax office; **mettre qn à c.** to use s.o.'s services.

contrit [kɔ̃tri] *a* (*air etc*) contrite. ◆**contrition** *nf* contrition.

contrôle [kɔ̃trol] *nm* (*vérification*) inspection, check(ing) (**de** of); (*des prix, de la qualité*) control; (*maîtrise*) control; (*sur bijou*) hallmark; **un c.** (*examen*) a check (**sur** on); **le c. de soi(-même)** self-control; **le c. des naissances** birth control; **un c. d'identité** an identity check. ◆**contrôl/er** *vt* (*examiner*) to inspect, check; (*maîtrise, surveiller*) to control; — **se c.** *vpr* (*se maîtriser*) to control oneself. ◆**-eur, -euse** *nmf* (*de train*) (ticket) inspector; (*au quai*) ticket collector; (*de bus*) conductor, conductress.

contrordre [kɔ̃trɔrdr] *nm* change of orders.

controverse [kɔ̃trɔvers] *nf* controversy. ◆**controversé** *a* controversial.

contumace (par) [parkɔ̃tymas] *adv* Jur in one's absence, in absentia.

contusion [kɔ̃tyzjɔ̃] *nf* bruise. ◆**contusionner** *vt* to bruise.

convaincre* [kɔ̃vɛ̃kr] *vt* to convince (**de** of); (*accusé*) to prove guilty (**de** of); **c. qn de faire** to persuade s.o. to do. ◆**-ant** *a* convincing. ◆**-u** *a* (*certain*) convinced (**de** of).

convalescent, -ente [kɔ̃valesɑ̃, -ɑ̃t] *nmf* convalescent; — *a* **être c.** to convalesce. ◆**convalescence** *nf* convalescence; **être en c.** to convalesce; **maison de c.** convalescent home.

conven/ir* [kɔ̃vnir] *vi* **c. à** (*être approprié à*) to be suitable for; (*plaire à, aller à*) to suit; **ça convient** (*date etc*) that's suitable; **c. de** (*lieu etc*) to agree upon; (*erreur*) to admit; **c. que** to admit that; **il convient de** it's advisable to; (*selon les usages*) it is proper *ou* fitting to. ◆**-u** *a* (*prix etc*) agreed. ◆**-able** *a* (*approprié, acceptable*) suitable; (*correct*) decent, proper. ◆**-ablement** *adv* suitably; decently. ◆**convenance** *nf* **convenances** (*usages*) convention(s), proprieties; **à sa c.** to one's satisfaction *ou* taste.

convention [kɔ̃vɑ̃sjɔ̃] *nf* (*accord*) agreement, convention; (*règle*) & *Am Pol* convention; **c. collective** collective bargaining; **de c.** (*sentiment etc*) conventional. ◆**conventionné** *a* (*prix, tarif*) regulated (by voluntary agreement); **médecin c.** = National Health Service doctor (*bound by agreement with the State*). ◆**conventionnel, -elle** *a* conventional.

convergent [kɔ̃vɛrʒɑ̃] *a* converging, convergent. ◆**convergence** *nf* convergence. ◆**converger** *vi* to converge.

converser [kɔ̃vɛrse] *vi* to converse. ◆**conversation** *nf* conversation.

conversion [kɔ̃vɛrsjɔ̃] *nf* conversion. ◆**convert/ir** *vt* to convert (**à** to, **en** into); **— se c.** *vpr* to be converted, convert. ◆**-i, -ie** *nmf* convert. ◆**convertible** *a* convertible; **—** *nm* (*canapé*) bed settee.

convexe [kɔ̃vɛks] *a* convex.

conviction [kɔ̃viksjɔ̃] *nf* (*certitude, croyance*) conviction; **pièce à c.** *Jur* exhibit.

convier [kɔ̃vje] *vt* to invite (**à une soirée**/*etc* to a party/*etc*, **à faire** to do).

convive [kɔ̃viv] *nmf* guest (*at table*).

convoi [kɔ̃vwa] *nm* (*véhicules, personnes etc*) convoy; *Rail* train; **c.** (**funèbre**) funeral procession. ◆**convoy/er** *vt* to escort. ◆**-eur** *nm Nau* escort ship; **c. de fonds** security guard.

convoiter [kɔ̃vwate] *vt* to desire, envy, covet. ◆**convoitise** *nf* desire, envy.

convoquer [kɔ̃voke] *vt* (*candidats, membres etc*) to summon *ou* invite (to attend); (*assemblée*) to convene, summon; **c. à** to summon *ou* invite to. ◆**convocation** *nf* (*action*) summoning; convening; (*ordre*) summons (to attend); (*lettre*) (written) notice (to attend).

convulser [kɔ̃vylse] *vt* to convulse. ◆**convulsif, -ive** *a* convulsive. ◆**convulsion** *nf* convulsion.

coopérer [kɔɔpere] *vi* to co-operate (**à** in, **avec** with). ◆**coopératif, -ive** *a* co-operative; **—** *nf* co-operative (society). ◆**coopération** *nf* co-operation.

coopter [kɔɔpte] *vt* to co-opt.

coordonn/er [kɔɔrdɔne] *vt* to co-ordinate. ◆**-ées** *nfpl Math* co-ordinates; (*adresse,*

téléphone) *Fam* particulars, details. ◆**coordination** *nf* co-ordination.

copain [kɔpɛ̃] *nm Fam* (*camarade*) pal; (*petit ami*) boyfriend; **être c. avec** to be pals with.

copeau, -x [kɔpo] *nm* (*de bois*) shaving.

copie [kɔpi] *nf* copy; (*devoir, examen*) *Scol* paper. ◆**copier** *vti* to copy; *Scol* to copy, crib (**sur** from). ◆**copieur, -euse** *nmf* (*élève etc*) copycat, copier.

copieux, -euse [kɔpjø, -øz] *a* copious, plentiful.

copilote [kɔpilɔt] *nm* co-pilot.

copine [kɔpin] *nf Fam* (*camarade*) pal; (*petite amie*) girlfriend; **être c. avec** to be pals with.

copropriété [kɔprɔprijete] *nf* joint ownership; (*immeuble en*) **c.** block of flats in joint ownership, *Am* condominium.

copulation [kɔpylɑsjɔ̃] *nf* copulation.

coq [kɔk] *nm* cock, rooster; **c. au vin** coq au vin (*chicken cooked in wine*); **passer du c. à l'âne** to jump from one subject to another.

coque [kɔk] *nf* **1** (*de noix*) shell; (*mollusque*) cockle; **œuf à la c.** boiled egg. **2** *Nau* hull.

coquelicot [kɔkliko] *nm* poppy.

coqueluche [kɔklyʃ] *nf Méd* whooping-cough; **la c. de** *Fig* the darling of.

coquet, -ette [kɔkɛ, -ɛt] *a* (*chic*) smart; (*joli*) pretty; (*provocant*) coquettish, flirtatious; (*somme*) *Fam* tidy; **—** *nf* coquette, flirt. ◆**coquetterie** *nf* (*élégance*) smartness; (*goût de la toilette*) dress sense; (*galanterie*) coquetry.

coquetier [kɔktje] *nm* egg cup.

coquille [kɔkij] *nf* shell; *Typ* misprint; **c. Saint-Jacques** scallop. ◆**coquillage** *nm* (*mollusque*) shellfish; (*coquille*) shell.

coquin, -ine [kɔkɛ̃, -in] *nmf* rascal; **—** *a* mischievous, rascally; (*histoire etc*) naughty.

cor [kɔr] *nm Mus* horn; **c. (au pied)** corn; **réclamer** *ou* **demander à c. et à cri** to clamour for.

corail, -aux [kɔraj, -o] *nm* coral.

Coran [kɔrɑ̃] *nm* **le C.** the Koran.

corbeau, -x [kɔrbo] *nm* crow; (**grand**) **c.** raven.

corbeille [kɔrbɛj] *nf* basket; **c. à papier** waste paper basket.

corbillard [kɔrbijar] *nm* hearse.

corde [kɔrd] *nf* rope; (*plus mince*) (fine) cord; (*de raquette, violon etc*) string; **c.** (**raide**) (*d'acrobate*) tightrope; **instrument à cordes** *Mus* string(ed) instrument; **c. à linge** washing (*ou* clothes) line; **c. à sauter** skipping rope, *Am* jump rope; **usé jusqu'à**

la c. threadbare; **cordes vocales** vocal cords; **prendre un virage à la c.** *Aut* to hug a bend; **pas dans mes cordes** *Fam* not my line. ◆**cordage** *nm Nau* rope. ◆**cordée** *nf* roped (climbing) party. ◆**cordelette** *nf* (fine) cord. ◆**corder** *vt* (*raquette*) to string. ◆**cordon** *nm* (*de tablier, sac etc*) string; (*de soulier*) lace; (*de rideau*) cord, rope; (*d'agents de police*) cordon; (*décoration*) ribbon, sash; (*ombilical*) *Anat* cord. ◆**c.-bleu** *nm* (*pl* **cordons-bleus**) cordon bleu (cook), first-class cook.

cordial, -aux [kɔrdjal, -o] *a* cordial, warm; − *nm Méd* cordial. ◆**cordialité** *nf* cordiality.

cordonnier [kɔrdɔnje] *nm* shoe repairer, cobbler. ◆**cordonnerie** *nf* shoe repairer's shop.

Corée [kɔre] *a* Korea. ◆**coréen, -enne** *a* & *nmf* Korean.

coriace [kɔrjas] *a* (*aliment, personne*) tough.

corne [kɔrn] *nf* (*de chèvre etc*) horn; (*de cerf*) antler; (*matière, instrument*) horn; (*angle, pli*) corner.

cornée [kɔrne] *nf Anat* cornea.

corneille [kɔrnɛj] *nf* crow.

cornemuse [kɔrnəmyz] *nf* bagpipes.

corner [kɔrne] **1** *vt* (*page*) to turn down the corner of, dog-ear. **2** *vi* (*véhicule*) to sound its horn. **3** [kɔrner] *nm Fb* corner.

cornet [kɔrnɛ] *nm* **1 c.** (**à pistons**) *Mus* cornet. **2** (*de glace*) cornet, cone; **c.** (**de papier**) (paper) cone.

corniaud [kɔrnjo] *nm* (*chien*) mongrel; (*imbécile*) *Fam* drip, twit.

corniche [kɔrniʃ] *nf Archit* cornice; (*route*) cliff road.

cornichon [kɔrniʃɔ̃] *nm* (*concombre*) gherkin; (*niais*) *Fam* clot, twit.

cornu [kɔrny] *a* (*diable etc*) horned.

corollaire [kɔrɔlɛr] *nm* corollary.

corporation [kɔrpɔrasjɔ̃] *nf* trade association, professional body.

corps [kɔr] *nm Anat Ch Fig etc* body; *Mil Pol* corps; **c. électoral** electorate; **c. enseignant** teaching profession; **c. d'armée** army corps; **garde du c.** bodyguard; **un c. de bâtiment** a main building; **c. et âme** body and soul; **lutter c. à c.** to fight hand-to-hand; **à son c. défendant** under protest; **prendre c.** (*projet*) to take shape; **donner c. à** (*rumeur, idée*) to give substance to; **faire c. avec** to form a part of, belong with; **perdu c. et biens** *Nau* lost with all hands; **esprit de c.** corporate spirit. ◆**corporel, -elle** *a* bodily; (*châtiment*) corporal.

corpulent [kɔrpylɑ̃] *a* stout, corpulent. ◆**corpulence** *nf* stoutness, corpulence.

corpus [kɔrpys] *nm Ling* corpus.

correct [kɔrɛkt] *a* (*exact*) correct; (*bienséant, honnête*) proper, correct; (*passable*) adequate. ◆−**ement** *adv* correctly; properly; adequately. ◆**correcteur, -trice 1** *a* (*verres*) corrective. **2** *nmf Scol* examiner; *Typ* proofreader. ◆**correctif, -ive** *a* & *nm* corrective.

correction [kɔrɛksjɔ̃] *nf* (*rectification etc*) correction; (*punition*) thrashing; (*exactitude, bienséance*) correctness; **la c. de** (*devoirs, examen*) the marking of; **c. d'épreuves** *Typ* proofreading. ◆**correctionnel, -elle** *a* **tribunal c.,** − *nf* magistrates' court, *Am* police court.

corrélation [kɔrelasjɔ̃] *nf* correlation.

correspond/re [kɔrɛspɔ̃dr] **1** *vi* (*s'accorder*) to correspond (à to, with); (*chambres etc*) to communicate; **c. avec** *Rail* to connect with; − **se c.** *vpr* (*idées etc*) to correspond; (*chambres etc*) to communicate. **2** *vi* (*écrire*) to correspond (**avec** with). ◆−**ant, -ante** *a* corresponding; − *nmf* correspondent; (*d'un élève, d'un adolescent*) pen friend; *Tél* caller. ◆**correspondance** *nf* correspondence; (*de train, d'autocar*) connection, *Am* transfer.

corrida [kɔrida] *nf* bullfight.

corridor [kɔridɔr] *nm* corridor.

corrig/er [kɔriʒe] *vt* (*texte, injustice etc*) to correct; (*épreuve*) *Typ* to read; (*devoir*) *Scol* to mark, correct; (*châtier*) to beat, punish; **c. qn de** (*défaut*) to cure s.o. of; **se c. de** to cure oneself of. ◆−**é** *nm Scol* model (answer), correct version, key. ◆**corroborer** [kɔrɔbɔre] *vt* to corroborate.

corroder [kɔrɔde] *vt* to corrode. ◆**corrosif, -ive** *a* corrosive. ◆**corrosion** *nf* corrosion.

corromp/re* [kɔrɔ̃pr] *vt* to corrupt; (*soudoyer*) to bribe; (*aliment, eau*) to taint. ◆−**u** *a* corrupt; (*altéré*) tainted. ◆**corruption** *nf* (*dépravation*) corruption; (*de juge etc*) bribery.

corsage [kɔrsaʒ] *nm* (*chemisier*) blouse; (*de robe*) bodice.

corsaire [kɔrsɛr] *nm* (*marin*) *Hist* privateer.

Corse [kɔrs] *nf* Corsica. ◆**corse** *a* & *nmf* Corsican.

cors/er [kɔrse] *vt* (*récit, action*) to heighten; **l'affaire se corse** things are hotting up. ◆−**é** *a* (*vin*) full-bodied; (*café*) strong; (*sauce, histoire*) spicy; (*problème*) tough; (*addition de restaurant*) steep.

corset [kɔrsɛ] *nm* corset.

cortège [kɔrtɛʒ] nm (défilé) procession; (suite) retinue; **c. officiel** (automobiles) motorcade.

corvée [kɔrve] nf chore, drudgery; Mil fatigue (duty).

cosaque [kɔzak] nm Cossack.

cosmopolite [kɔsmɔpɔlit] a cosmopolitan.

cosmos [kɔsmɔs] nm (univers) cosmos; (espace) outer space. ◆**cosmique** a cosmic. ◆**cosmonaute** nmf cosmonaut.

cosse [kɔs] nf (de pois etc) pod.

cossu [kɔsy] a (personne) well-to-do; (maison etc) opulent.

costaud [kɔsto] a Fam brawny, beefy; – nm Fam strong man.

costume [kɔstym] nm (pièces d'habillement) costume, dress; (complet) suit. ◆**costum/er** vt **c. qn** to dress s.o. up (en as). ◆**-é** a bal **c.** fancy-dress ball.

cote [kɔt] nf (marque de classement) mark, letter, number; (tableau de valeurs) (official) listing; (des valeurs boursières) quotation; (évaluation, popularité) rating; (de cheval) odds (de on); **c. d'alerte** danger level.

côte [kot] nf **1** Anat rib; (de mouton) chop; (de veau) cutlet. à **côtes** (étoffe) ribbed; **c. à c.** side by side; **se tenir les côtes** to split one's sides (laughing). **2** (montée) hill; (versant) hillside. **3** (littoral) coast.

côté [kote] nm side; (direction) way; **de l'autre c.** on the other side (de of); (direction) the other way; **de ce c.** (passer) this way; **du c. de** (vers, près de) towards; **de c.** (se jeter, mettre de l'argent etc) to one side; (regarder) sideways, to one side; à **c.** close by, nearby; (pièce) in the other room; (maison) next door; **la maison d'à c.** the house next door; à **c. de** next to, beside; (comparaison) compared to; **passer à c.** (balle) to fall wide (de of); **venir de tous côtés** to come from all directions; **d'un c.** on the one hand; **de mon c.** for my part; à **mes côtés** by my side; **laisser de c.** (travail) to neglect; (du) **c. argent**/etc Fam as regards money/etc, moneywise/etc; **le bon c.** (d'une affaire) the bright side (de of).

coteau, -x [kɔto] nm (small) hill; (versant) hillside.

côtelé [kotle] a (étoffe) ribbed; **velours c.** cord(uroy).

côtelette [kotlet] nf (d'agneau, de porc) chop; (de veau) cutlet.

cot/er [kɔte] vt (valeur boursière) to quote. ◆**-é** a **bien c.** highly rated.

coterie [kɔtri] nf Péj set, clique.

côtier, -ière [kotje, -jɛr] a coastal; (pêche) inshore.

cotiser [kɔtize] vi to contribute (à to, **pour** towards); **c. (à)** (club) to subscribe (to); — **se c.** vpr to club together (**pour acheter** to buy). ◆**cotisation** nf (de club) dues, subscription; (de pension etc) contribution(s).

coton [kɔtɔ̃] nm cotton; **c. (hydrophile)** cottonwool, Am (absorbent) cotton. ◆**cotonnade** nf cotton (fabric). ◆**cotonnier, -ière** a (industrie) cotton-.

côtoyer [kotwaje] vt (route, rivière) to run along, skirt; (la misère, la folie etc) Fig to be ou come close to; **c. qn** (fréquenter) to rub shoulders with s.o.

cou [ku] nm neck; **sauter au c. de qn** to throw one's arms around s.o.; **jusqu'au c.** Fig up to one's eyes ou ears.

couche [kuʃ] nf **1** (épaisseur) layer; (de peinture) coat; Géol stratum; **couches sociales** social strata. **2** (linge de bébé) nappy, Am diaper. **3** (linge de bébé) to have a miscarriage; **les couches** Méd confinement. **couch/er** [kuʃe] vt to put to bed; (héberger) to put up; (allonger) to lay (down ou out); (blé) to flatten; **c. (par écrit)** to put down (in writing); **c. qn en joue** to aim at s.o.; — vi to sleep (avec with); — **se c.** vpr to go to bed; (s'allonger) to lie flat ou down; (soleil) to set, go down; — nm (moment) bedtime; **c. de soleil** sunset. ◆**-ant** a (soleil) setting; — nm (aspect) sunset; **le c.** (ouest) west. ◆**-é** a être **c.** to be in bed; (étendu) to be lying (down). ◆**-age** nm sleeping (situation); (matériel) bedding; **sac de c.** sleeping bag. ◆**couchette** nf Rail sleeping berth, couchette; Nau bunk.

couci-couça [kusikusa] adv Fam so-so.

coucou [kuku] nm (oiseau) cuckoo; (pendule) cuckoo clock; Bot cowslip.

coude [kud] nm elbow; (de chemin, rivière) bend; **se serrer** ou **se tenir les coudes** to help one another, stick together; **c. à c.** side by side; **coup de c.** poke ou dig (with one's elbow), nudge; **pousser du c.** to nudge. ◆**coudoyer** vt to rub shoulders with.

cou-de-pied [kudpje] nm (pl **cous-de-pied**) instep.

coudre* [kudr] vti to sew.

couenne [kwan] nf (pork) crackling.

couette [kwet] nf (édredon) duvet, continental quilt.

couffin [kufɛ̃] nm (de bébé) Moses basket, Am bassinet.

couic! [kwik] *int* eek!, squeak! ◆**couiner** *vi Fam* to squeal; (*pleurer*) to whine.

couillon [kujɔ̃] *nm* (*idiot*) *Arg* drip, cretin.

coul/er¹ [kule] *vi* (*eau etc*) to flow; (*robinet, nez, stylo*) to run; (*fuir*) to leak; **c. de source** *Fig* to follow naturally; **faire c. le sang** to cause bloodshed; − *vt* (*métal, statue*) to cast; (*vie*) *Fig* to pass, lead; (*glisser*) to slip; **se c. dans** (*passer*) to slip into; **se la c. douce** to have things easy. ◆**—ant** (*style*) flowing; (*caractère*) easygoing. ◆**—ée** *nf* (*de métal*) casting; **c. de lave** lava flow. ◆**—age** *nm* (*de métal, statue*) casting; (*gaspillage*) *Fam* wastage.

couler² [kule] *vi* (*bateau, nageur*) to sink; **c. à pic** to sink to the bottom; − *vt* to sink; (*discréditer*) *Fig* to discredit.

couleur [kulœr] *nf* colour; (*colorant*) paint; *Cartes* suit; *pl* (*teint, carnation*) colour; **c. chair** flesh-coloured; **de c.** (*homme, habit etc*) coloured; **en couleurs** (*photo, télévision*) colour-; **téléviseur c.** colour TV set; **haut en c.** colourful; **sous c. de faire** while pretending to do.

couleuvre [kulœvr] *nf* (grass) snake.

coulisse [kulis] *nf* **1** (*de porte*) runner; **à c.** (*porte etc*) sliding. **2 dans les coulisses** *Th* in the wings, backstage; **dans la c.** (*caché*) *Fig* behind the scenes. ◆**coulissant** *a* (*porte etc*) sliding.

couloir [kulwar] *nm* corridor; (*de circulation*) & *Sp* lane; (*dans un bus*) gangway.

coup [ku] *nm* blow, knock; (*léger*) tap, touch; (*choc moral*) blow; (*de fusil etc*) shot; (*de crayon, d'horloge*) & *Sp* stroke; (*aux échecs etc*) move; (*fois*) *Fam* time; **donner des coups à** to hit; **c. de brosse** brush(-up) to; **c. de chiffon** wipe (with a rag); **c. de sonnette** ring (on a bell); **c. de dents** bite; **c. de chance** stroke of luck; **c. d'État** coup; **c. dur** *Fam* nasty blow; **sale c.** dirty trick; **mauvais c.** piece of mischief; **c. franc** *Fb* free kick; **tenter le c.** *Fam* to have a go *ou* try; **réussir son c.** to bring it off; **faire les quatre cents coups** to get into all kinds of mischief; **tenir le c.** to hold out; **avoir/attraper le c.** to have/get the knack; **sous le c. de** (*émotion etc*) under the influence of; **il est dans le c.** *Fam* he's in the know; **après c.** after the event, afterwards; **sur le c. de midi** on the stroke of twelve; **sur le c.** (*alors*) at the time; **tué sur le c.** killed outright; **à c. sûr** for sure; **c. sur c.** (*à la suite*) one after the other, in quick succession; **tout à c., tout d'un c.** suddenly; **à tout c.** at every go; **d'un seul c.** in one go; **du premier c.** at the first go; **du c.**

suddenly; (*de ce fait*) as a result; **pour le c.** this time. ◆**c.-de-poing** *nm* (*pl coups-de-poing*) ◆**c.-de-poing** (*américain*) knuckle-duster.

coupable [kupabl] *a* guilty (**de** of); (*plaisir, désir*) sinful; **déclarer c.** *Jur* to convict; − *nmf* guilty person, culprit.

coupe [kup] *nf* **1** *Sp* cup; (*à fruits*) dish; (*à boire*) goblet, glass. **2** (*de vêtement etc*) cut; *Géom* section; **c. de cheveux** haircut. ◆**coup/er** *vt* to cut; (*arbre*) to cut down; (*vivres etc*) & *Tél* to cut off; (*courant etc*) to switch off; (*voyage*) to break (off); (*faim, souffle etc*) to take away; (*vin*) to water down; (*morceler*) to cut up; (*croiser*) to cut across; **c. la parole à** to cut short; − *vi* to cut; **c.** (*à corvée*) *Fam* to get out of; **ne coupez pas!** *Tél* hold the line!; − **se c.** *vpr* (*routes*) to intersect; (*se trahir*) to give oneself away; **se c. au doigt** to cut one's finger. ◆**—ant** *a* sharp; − *nm* (*tranchant*) edge. ◆**—é** *nm Aut* coupé.

coupe-circuit [kupsirkɥi] *nm inv Él* cutout, circuit breaker. ◆**c.-file** *nm inv* (*carte*) official pass. ◆**c.-gorge** *nm inv* cut-throat alley. ◆**c.-ongles** *nm inv* (*finger nail*) clippers. ◆**c.-papier** *nm inv* paper knife.

couperet [kupre] *nm* (*meat*) chopper; (*de guillotine*) blade.

couperosé [kuproze] *a* (*visage*) blotchy.

couple [kupl] *nm* pair, couple. ◆**coupler** *vt* to couple, connect.

couplet [kuple] *nm* verse.

coupole [kupol] *nf* dome.

coupon [kupɔ̃] *nm* (*tissu*) remnant, oddment; (*pour la confection d'un vêtement*) length; (*ticket, titre*) coupon; **c. réponse** reply coupon.

coupure [kupyr] *nf* cut; (*de journal*) cutting, *Am* clipping; (*billet*) banknote.

cour [kur] *nf* **1** court(yard); (*de gare*) forecourt; **c. de récréation** *Scol* playground. **2** (*de roi*) & *Jur* court. **3** (*de femme, d'homme*) courtship; **faire la c. à qn** to court s.o., woo s.o.

courage [kuraʒ] *nm* courage; (*zèle*) spirit; **perdre c.** to lose heart *ou* courage; **s'armer de c.** to pluck up courage; **bon c.!** keep your chin up! ◆**courageux, -euse** *a* courageous; (*énergique*) spirited.

couramment [kuramɑ̃] *adv* (*parler*) fluently; (*souvent*) frequently.

courant [kurɑ̃] **1** *a* (*fréquent*) common; (*compte, année, langage*) current; (*eau*) running; (*modèle, taille*) standard; (*affaires*) routine; **le dix/etc c.** *Com* the tenth/etc inst(ant). **2** *nm* (*de l'eau, élec-*

trique) current; **c. d'air** draught; **coupure de c.** *El* power cut; **dans le c. de** (*mois etc*) during the course of; **être/mettre au c.** to know/tell (**de** about); **au c.** (*à jour*) up to date.

courbature [kurbatyr] *nf* (muscular) ache. ◆**courbaturé** *a* aching (all over).

courbe [kurb] *a* curved; — *nf* curve. ◆**courber** *vti* to bend; — **se c.** *vpr* to bend (over).

courge [kurʒ] *nf* marrow, *Am* squash. ◆**courgette** *nf* courgette, *Am* zucchini.

cour/ir* [kurir] *vi* to run; (*se hâter*) to rush; (*à bicyclette, en auto*) to race; **en courant** (*vite*) in a rush; **le bruit court que**— there's a rumour going around that ...; **faire c.** (*nouvelle*) to spread; **il court encore** (*voleur*) he's still at large; — *vt* (*risque*) to run; (*épreuve sportive*) to run (in); (*danger*) to face, court; (*rues, monde*) to roam; (*magasins, cafés*) to go round; (*filles*) to run after. ◆**-eur** *nm Sp etc* runner; (*cycliste*) cyclist; *Aut* racing driver; (*galant*) *Péj* womanizer.

couronne [kuron] *nf* (*de roi, dent*) crown; (*funéraire*) wreath. ◆**couronn/er** *vt* to crown; (*auteur, ouvrage*) to award a prize to. ◆**-é** *a* (*tête*) crowned; (*ouvrage*) prize-. ◆**-ement** *nm* (*sacre*) coronation; *Fig* crowning achievement.

courrier [kurje] *nm* post, mail; (*transport*) postal *ou* mail service; (*article*) *Journ* column; **par retour du c.** by return of post, *Am* by return mail.

courroie [kurwa] *nf* (*attache*) strap; (*de transmission*) *Tech* belt.

courroux [kuru] *nm Litt* wrath.

cours [kur] *nm* **1** (*de maladie, rivière, astre, pensées etc*) course; (*cote*) rate, price; **c. d'eau** river, stream; **suivre son c.** (*déroulement*) to follow its course; **avoir c.** (*monnaie*) to be legal tender; (*théorie*) to be current; **en c.** (*travail*) in progress; (*année*) current; (*affaires*) outstanding; **en c. de route** on the way; **au c. de** during; **donner libre c. à** to give free rein to. **2** (*leçon*) class; (*série de leçons*) course; (*conférence*) lecture; (*établissement*) school; (*manuel*) textbook; **c. magistral** lecture. **3** (*allée*) avenue.

course [kurs] *nf* **1** (*action*) run(ning); (*épreuve de vitesse*) *& Fig* race; (*trajet*) journey, run; (*excursion*) hike; (*de projectile etc*) path, flight; *pl* (*de chevaux*) races; **il n'est plus dans la c.** *Fig* he's out of touch; **cheval de c.** racehorse; **voiture de c.** racing car. **2** (*commission*) errand; *pl* (*achats*)

shopping; **faire une c.** to run an errand; **faire les courses** to do the shopping.

coursier, -ière [kursje, -jɛr] *nm* messenger.

court [kur] **1** *a* short; **c'est un peu c.** *Fam* that's not very much; — *adv* short; **couper c.** (*entretien*) to cut short; **tout c.** quite simply; **à c. de** (*argent etc*) short of; **pris de c.** caught unawares. **2** *nm* Tennis court. ◆**c.-bouillon** *nm* (*pl* **courts-bouillons**) court-bouillon (*spiced water for cooking fish*). ◆**c.-circuit** *nm* (*pl* **courts-circuits**) *El* short circuit. ◆**c.-circuiter** *vt* to short-circuit.

courtier, -ière [kurtje, -jɛr] *nmf* broker. ◆**courtage** *nm* brokerage.

courtisan [kurtizɑ̃] *nm Hist* courtier. ◆**courtisane** *nf Hist* courtesan. ◆**courtiser** *vt* to court.

courtois [kurtwa] *a* courteous. ◆**courtoisie** *nf* courtesy.

couru [kury] *a* (*spectacle, lieu*) popular; **c'est c.** (**d'avance**) *Fam* it's a sure thing.

couscous [kuskus] *nm Culin* couscous.

cousin, -ine [kuzɛ̃, -in] *nmf* cousin. **2** *nm* (*insecte*) gnat, midge.

coussin [kusɛ̃] *nm* cushion.

cousu [kuzy] *a* sewn; **c. main** handsewn.

coût [ku] *nm* cost. ◆**coût/er** *vti* to cost; **ça coûte combien?** how much is it?, how much does it cost?; **ça lui en coûte de faire** it pains him *ou* her to do; **coûte que coûte** at all costs; **les yeux de la tête** to cost the earth. ◆**-ant** *a* **à prix c.** cost price. ◆**coûteux, -euse** *a* costly, expensive.

couteau, -x [kuto] *nm* knife; **coup de c.** stab; **à couteaux tirés** at daggers drawn (**avec** with); **visage en lame de c.** hatchet face; **retourner le c. dans la plaie** *Fig* to rub it in.

coutume [kutym] *nf* custom; **avoir c. de faire** to be accustomed to doing; **comme de c.** as usual; **plus que de c.** more than is customary. ◆**coutumier, -ière** *a* customary.

couture [kutyr] *nf* sewing, needlework; (*métier*) dressmaking; (*raccord*) seam; **maison de c.** fashion house. ◆**couturier** *nm* fashion designer. ◆**couturière** *nf* dressmaker.

couvent [kuvɑ̃] *nm* (*pour religieuses*) convent; (*pour moines*) monastery; (*pensionnat*) convent school.

couv/er [kuve] *vt* (*œufs*) to sit on, hatch; (*projet*) *Fig* to hatch; (*rhume etc*) to be getting; **c. qn** to pamper s.o.; **c. des yeux** (*convoiter*) to look at enviously; — *vi* (*poule*) to brood; (*mal*) to be brewing;

(*feu*) to smoulder. ◆—**ée** *nf* (*petits*) brood; (*œufs*) clutch. ◆**couveuse** *nf* (*pour nouveaux-nés, œufs*) incubator.

couvercle [kuvɛrkl] *nm* lid, cover.

couvert [kuvɛr] **1** *nm* (*cuiller, fourchette, couteau*) (set of) cutlery; (*au restaurant*) cover charge; **mettre le c.** to lay the table; **table de cinq couverts** table set for five. **2** *nm* **sous (le) c. de** (*apparence*) under cover of; **se mettre à c.** to take cover. **3** *a* covered (**de** with, in); (*ciel*) overcast. ◆**couverture** *nf* (*de lit*) blanket, cover; (*de livre etc*) & *Fin Mil* cover; (*de toit*) roofing; **c. chauffante** electric blanket; **c. de voyage** travelling rug.

couvre-chef [kuvrəʃɛf] *nm* *Hum* headgear. ◆**c.-feu** *nm* (*pl* -**x**) curfew. ◆**c.-lit** *nm* bedspread. ◆**c.-pied** *nm* quilt.

couvr/ir [kuvrir] *vt* to cover (**de** with); (*voix*) to drown; — **se c.** *vpr* (*se vêtir*) to cover up, wrap up; (*se coiffer*) to cover one's head; (*ciel*) to cloud over. ◆—**eur** *nm* roofer.

cow-boy [kɔbɔj] *nm* cowboy.

crabe [krab] *nm* crab.

crac! [krak] *int* (*rupture*) snap!; (*choc*) bang!, smash!

crach/er [kraʃe] *vi* to spit; (*stylo*) to splutter; (*radio*) to crackle; — *vt* to spit (out); **c. sur qch** (*dédaigner*) *Fam* to turn one's nose up at sth. ◆—**é** *a* **c'est son portrait tout c.** *Fam* that's the spitting image of him *ou* her. ◆**crachat** *nm* spit, spittle.

crachin [kraʃɛ̃] *nm* (fine) drizzle.

crack [krak] *nm* *Fam* ace, wizard, real champ.

craie [krɛ] *nf* chalk.

craindre* [krɛ̃dr] *vt* (*personne, mort, douleur etc*) to be afraid of, fear, dread; (*chaleur etc*) to be sensitive to; **c. de faire** to be afraid of doing, dread doing; **je crains qu'elle ne vienne** I'm afraid *ou* I dread (that) she might come; **c. pour qch** to fear for sth; **ne craignez rien** have no fear. ◆**crainte** *nf* fear, dread; **de c. de faire** for fear of doing; **de c. que** (+ *sub*) for fear that. ◆**craintif, -ive** *a* timid.

cramoisi [kramwazi] *a* crimson.

crampe [krɑ̃p] *nf* *Méd* cramp.

crampon [krɑ̃pɔ̃] **1** *nm* (*personne*) *Fam* leech, hanger-on. **2** *nmpl* (*de chaussures*) studs.

cramponner (se) [səkrɑ̃pɔne] *vpr* **se c. à** to hold on to, cling to.

cran [krɑ̃] *nm* **1** (*entaille*) notch; (*de ceinture*) hole; **c. d'arrêt** catch; **couteau à c. d'arrêt** flick-knife, *Am* switchblade; **c. de**

sûreté safety catch. **2** (*de cheveux*) wave. **3** (*audace*) *Fam* pluck, guts. **4** **à c.** (*excédé*) *Fam* on edge.

crâne [krɑn] *nm* skull; (*tête*) *Fam* head. ◆**crânienne** *af* **boîte c.** cranium, brain pan.

crâner [krɑne] *vi* *Péj* to show off, swagger.

crapaud [krapo] *nm* toad.

crapule [krapyl] *nf* villain, (filthy) scoundrel. ◆**crapuleux, -euse** *a* vile, sordid.

craqueler [krakle] *vt*, — **se c.** *vpr* to crack.

craqu/er [krake] *vi* (*branche*) to snap; (*chaussure*) to creak; (*bois sec*) to crack; (*sous la dent*) to crunch; (*se déchirer*) to split, rip; (*projet, entreprise etc*) to come apart at the seams, crumble; (*personne*) to break down, reach breaking point; — *vt* (*faire*) **c.** (*allumette*) to strike. ◆—**ement** *nm* snapping *ou* creaking *ou* cracking (sound).

crasse [kras] **1** *a* (*ignorance*) crass. **2** *nf* filth. ◆**crasseux, -euse** *a* filthy.

cratère [kratɛr] *nm* crater.

cravache [kravaʃ] *nf* horsewhip, riding crop.

cravate [kravat] *nf* (*autour du cou*) tie. ◆**cravaté** *a* wearing a tie.

crawl [krol] *nm* (*nage*) crawl. ◆**crawlé** *a* **dos c.** backstroke.

crayeux, -euse [krɛjø, -øz] *a* chalky.

crayon [krɛjɔ̃] *nm* (*en bois*) pencil; (*de couleur*) crayon; **c. à bille** ballpoint (pen). ◆**crayonner** *vt* to pencil.

créance [kreɑ̃s] *nf* **1** *Fin Jur* claim (for money). **2** **lettres de c.** *Pol* credentials. ◆**créancier, -ière** *nf* creditor.

créateur, -trice [kreatœr, -tris] *nmf* creator; — *a* creative; **esprit c.** creativeness. ◆**créatif, -ive** *a* creative. ◆**création** *nf* creation. ◆**créativité** *nf* creativity. ◆**créature** *nf* (*être*) creature.

crécelle [kresɛl] *nf* (*de supporter*) rattle.

crèche [krɛʃ] *nf* (*de Noël*) *Rel* crib, manger; *Scol* day nursery, crèche. ◆**crécher** *vi* (*loger*) *Arg* to bed down, hang out.

crédible [kredibl] *a* credible. ◆**crédibilité** *nf* credibility.

crédit [kredi] *nm* (*influence*) & *Fin* credit; *pl* (*sommes*) funds; **à c.** (*acheter*) on credit, on hire purchase; **faire c.** *Fin* to give credit (à to). ◆**créditer** *vt* *Fin* to credit (**de** with). ◆**créditeur, -euse** (*solde, compte*) credit-; **son compte est c.** his account is in credit, he is in credit.

credo [kredo] *nm* creed.

crédule [kredyl] *a* credulous. ◆**crédulité** *nf* credulity.

créer [kree] *vt* to create.

crémaillère [kremajɛr] *nf* **pendre la c.** to have a house-warming (party).

crématoire [krematwar] *a* **four c.** crematorium. ◆**crémation** *nf* cremation.

crème [krɛm] *nf* cream; (*dessert*) cream dessert; **café c.** white coffee, coffee with cream ou milk; **c.** Chantilly whipped cream; **c. glacée** ice cream; **c. à raser** shaving cream; **c. anglaise** custard; – *a inv* cream(-coloured); – *nm* (*café*) white coffee. ◆**crémerie** *nf* (*magasin*) dairy (shop). ◆**crémeux, -euse** *a* creamy. ◆**crémier, -ière** *nmf* dairyman, dairywoman.

créneau, -x [kreno] *nm Hist* crenellation; (*trou*) Fig slot, gap; *Écon* market opportunity, niche; **faire un c.** *Aut* to park between two vehicles.

créole [kreɔl] *nmf* Creole; – *nm Ling* Creole.

crêpe [krɛp] **1** *nf Culin* pancake. **2** *nm* (*tissu*) crepe; (*caoutchouc*) crepe (rubber). ◆**crêperie** *nf* pancake bar.

crépi [krepi] *a* & *nm* roughcast.

crépit/er [krepite] *vi* to crackle. ◆**-ement** *nm* crackling (sound).

crépu [krepy] *a* (*cheveux, personne*) frizzy.

crépuscule [krepyskyl] *nm* twilight, dusk. ◆**crépusculaire** *a* (*lueur etc*) twilight-, dusk-.

crescendo [kreʃɛndo] *adv* & *nm inv* crescendo.

cresson [kresɔ̃] *nm* (water) cress.

crête [krɛt] *nf* (*d'oiseau, de vague, de montagne*) crest; **c. de coq** cockscomb.

Crète [krɛt] *nf* Crete.

crétin, -ine [kretɛ̃, -in] *nmf* cretin; – *a* cretinous.

creus/er [krøze] **1** *vt* (*terre, sol*) to dig (a hole ou holes in); (*trou, puits*) to dig; (*évider*) to hollow (out); (*idée*) Fig to go deeply into; **c. l'estomac** to whet the appetite. **2 se c.** *vpr* (*joues etc*) to become hollow; (*abîme*) Fig to form; **se c. la tête** ou **la cervelle** to rack one's brains. ◆**-é** *a* **c. de rides** (*visage*) furrowed with wrinkles.

creuset [krøze] *nm* (*récipient*) crucible; (*lieu*) Fig melting pot.

creux, -euse [krø, -øz] *a* (*tube, joues, paroles etc*) hollow; (*estomac*) empty; (*sans activité*) slack; **assiette creuse** soup plate; – *nm* hollow; (*de l'estomac*) pit; (*moment*) slack period; **c. des reins** small of the back.

crevaison [krəvɛzɔ̃] *nf* puncture.

crevasse [krəvas] *nf* crevice, crack; (*de glacier*) crevasse; *pl* (*aux mains*) chaps.

◆**crevasser** *vt*, – **se c.** *vpr* to crack; (*peau*) to chap.

crève [krɛv] *nf* (*rhume*) Fam bad cold.

crev/er [krəve] *vi* (*bulle etc*) to burst; (*pneu*) to puncture, burst; (*mourir*) Fam to die, drop dead; **c. d'orgueil** to be bursting with pride; **c. de rire** Fam to split one's sides; **c. d'ennui/de froid** Fam to be bored/to freeze to death; **c. de faim** Fam to be starving; – *vt* to burst; (*œil*) to put ou knock out; **c. qn** Fam to wear ou knock s.o. out; **ça (vous) crève les yeux** Fam it's staring you in the face; **c. le cœur** to be heartbreaking. ◆**-ant** *a* (*fatigant*) Fam exhausting; (*drôle*) Arg hilarious, killing. ◆**-é** *a* (*fatigué*) Fam worn ou knocked out; (*mort*) Fam dead. ◆**crève-cœur** *nm inv* heartbreak.

crevette [krəvɛt] *nf* (*grise*) shrimp; (*rose*) prawn.

cri [kri] *nm* (*de joie, surprise*) cry, shout; (*de peur*) scream; (*de douleur, d'alarme*) cry; (*appel*) call, cry; **c. de guerre** war cry; **un chapeau/etc dernier c.** the latest hat/etc. ◆**criard** *a* (*enfant*) bawling; (*son*) screeching; (*couleur*) gaudy, showy.

criant [krijɑ̃] *a* (*injustice etc*) glaring.

crible [kribl] *nm* sieve, riddle. ◆**cribler** *vt* to sift; **criblé de** (*balles, dettes etc*) riddled with.

cric [krik] *nm* (*instrument*) Aut jack.

cricket [krikɛt] *nm Sp* cricket.

crier [krije] *vi* to shout (out), cry (out); (*de peur*) to scream; (*oiseau*) to chirp; (*grincer*) to creak, squeak; **c. au scandale**/*etc* to proclaim sth to be a scandal/*etc*; **c. après qn** Fam to shout at s.o.; – *vt* (*injure, ordre*) to shout (out); (*son innocence etc*) to proclaim; **c. vengeance** to cry out for vengeance. ◆**crieur, -euse** *nmf* **c. de journaux** newspaper seller.

crime [krim] *nm* crime; (*assassinat*) murder. ◆**criminalité** *nf* crime (in general), criminal practice. ◆**criminel, -elle** *a* criminal; – *nmf* criminal; (*assassin*) murderer.

crin [krɛ̃] *nm* horsehair; **c. végétal** vegetable fibre; **à tous crins** (*pacifiste etc*) out-and-out. ◆**crinière** *nf* mane.

crique [krik] *nf* creek, cove.

criquet [krikɛ] *nm* locust.

crise [kriz] *nf* crisis; (*accès*) attack; (*de colère*) fit; (*pénurie*) shortage; **c. de conscience** (moral) dilemma.

crisp/er [krispe] *vt* (*muscle*) to tense; (*visage*) to make tense; (*poing*) to clench; **c. qn** Fam to aggravate s.o.; **se c. sur** (*main*) to grip tightly. ◆**-ant** *a* aggravating. ◆**-é**

a (*personne*) tense. ◆**crispation** *nf* (*agacement*) aggravation.

crisser [krise] *vi* (*pneu, roue*) to screech; (*neige*) to crunch.

cristal, -aux [kristal, -o] *nm* crystal; *pl* (*objets*) crystal(ware); (*pour nettoyer*) washing soda. ◆**cristallin** *a* (*eau, son*) crystal-clear. ◆**cristalliser** *vti*, **– se c.** *vpr* to crystallize.

critère [kriter] *nm* criterion.

critérium [kriterjɔm] *nm* (*épreuve*) Sp eliminating heat.

critique [kritik] *a* critical; – *nf* (*reproche*) criticism; (*analyse de film, livre etc*) review; (*de texte*) critique; **faire la c. de** (*film etc*) to review; **affronter la c.** to confront the critics; – *nm* critic. ◆**critiqu/er** *vt* to criticize. ◆**–able** *a* open to criticism.

croasser [krɔase] *vi* (*corbeau*) to caw.

croc [kro] *nm* (*crochet*) hook; (*dent*) fang. ◆**c.-en-jambe** (*pl* **crocs-en-jambe**) = **croche-pied.**

croche [krɔʃ] *nf Mus* quaver, *Am* eighth (note).

croche-pied [krɔʃpje] *nm* **faire un c.-pied à qn** to trip s.o. up.

crochet [krɔʃɛ] *nm* (*pour accrocher*) & *Boxe* hook; (*aiguille*) crochet hook; (*travail*) crochet; (*clef*) picklock; *Typ* (*square*) bracket; **faire qch au c.** to crochet sth; **faire un c.** (*route*) to make a sudden turn; (*personne*) to make a detour *ou* side trip; (*pour éviter*) to swerve; **vivre aux crochets de qn** *Fam* to sponge off *ou* on s.o. ◆**crocheter** *vt* (*serrure*) to pick. ◆**crochu** *a* (*nez*) hooked.

crocodile [krɔkɔdil] *nm* crocodile.

crocus [krɔkys] *nm Bot* crocus.

croire* [krwar] *vt* to believe; (*estimer*) to think, believe (**que** that); **j'ai cru la voir** I thought I saw her; **je crois que oui** I think *ou* believe so; **je n'en crois pas mes yeux** I can't believe my eyes; **à l'en c.** according to him; **il se croit malin/quelque chose** he thinks he's smart/quite something; – *vi* to believe (**à, en** in).

croisé¹ [krwaze] *nm Hist* crusader. ◆**croisade** *nf* crusade.

crois/er [krwaze] *vt* to cross; (*bras*) to fold, cross; **c. qn** to pass *ou* meet s.o.; – *vi* (*veston*) to fold over; *Nau* to cruise; – **se c.** *vpr* (*voitures etc*) to pass *ou* meet (each other); (*routes etc*) to cross; (*lettres*) to cross in the post. ◆**–é², -ée** *a* (*bras*) folded, crossed; (*veston*) double-breasted; **mots croisés** crossword; **tirs croisés** crossfire; **race croisée** crossbreed; – *nf* (*fenêtre*)

casement; **croisée des chemins** crossroads. ◆**–ement** *nm* (*action*) crossing; (*de routes*) crossroads, intersection; (*de véhicules*) passing. ◆**–eur** *nm* (*navire de guerre*) cruiser. ◆**croisière** *nf* cruise; **vitesse de c.** *Nau Av* & *Fig* cruising speed.

croître* [krwatr] *vi* (*plante etc*) to grow; (*augmenter*) to grow, increase; (*lune*) to wax. ◆**croissant 1** *a* (*nombre etc*) growing. **2** *nm* crescent; (*pâtisserie*) croissant. ◆**croissance** *nf* growth.

croix [krwa] *nf* cross.

croque-mitaine [krɔkmiten] *nm* bogeyman. ◆**c.-monsieur** *nm inv* toasted cheese and ham sandwich. ◆**c.-mort** *nm Fam* undertaker's assistant.

croqu/er [krɔke] **1** *vt* (*manger*) to crunch; – *vi* (*fruit etc*) to be crunchy, crunch. **2** *vt* (*peindre*) to sketch; **joli à c.** pretty as a picture. ◆**–ant** *a* (*biscuit etc*) crunchy. ◆**croquette** *nf Culin* croquette.

croquet [krɔke] *nm Sp* croquet.

croquis [krɔki] *nm* sketch.

crosse [krɔs] *nf* (*d'évêque*) crook; (*de fusil*) butt; (*de hockey*) stick.

crotte [krɔt] *nf* (*de lapin etc*) mess, droppings. ◆**crottin** *nm* (*horse*) dung.

crotté [krɔte] *a* (*bottes etc*) muddy.

croul/er [krule] *vi* (*édifice, projet etc*) to crumble, collapse; **c. sous une charge** (*porteur etc*) to totter beneath a burden; **faire c.** (*immeuble etc*) to bring down. ◆**–ant** *a* (*mur etc*) tottering; – *nm* (*vieux*) *Fam* old-timer.

croupe [krup] *nf* (*de cheval*) rump; **monter en c.** (*à cheval*) to ride pillion. ◆**croupion** *nm* (*de poulet*) parson's nose.

croupier [krupje] *nm* (*au casino*) croupier.

croupir [krupir] *vi* (*eau*) to stagnate, become foul; **c. dans** (*le vice etc*) to wallow in; **eau croupie** stagnant water.

croustill/er [krustije] *vi* to be crusty; to be crunchy. ◆**–ant** *a* (*pain*) crusty; (*biscuit*) crunchy; (*histoire*) *Fig* spicy, juicy.

croûte [krut] *nf* (*de pain etc*) crust; (*de fromage*) rind; (*de plaie*) scab; **casser la c.** *Fam* to have a snack; **gagner sa c.** *Fam* to earn one's bread and butter. ◆**croûton** *nm* crust (*at end of loaf*); *pl* (*avec soupe*) croûtons.

croyable [krwajabl] *a* credible, believable. ◆**croyance** *nf* belief (**à, en** in). ◆**croyant, -ante** *a* **être c.** to be a believer; – *nmf* believer.

CRS [seɛrɛs] *nmpl abrév* (*Compagnies républicaines de sécurité*) French state security police, riot police.

cru[1] [kry] *voir* **croire.**

cru[2] [kry] **1** *a* (*aliment etc*) raw; (*lumière*) glaring; (*propos*) crude; **monter à c.** to ride bareback. **2** *nm* (*vignoble*) vineyard; **un grand c.** (*vin*) a vintage wine; **vin du c.** local wine.

cruauté [kryote] *nf* cruelty (**envers** to).

cruche [kryʃ] *nf* pitcher, jug.

crucial, -aux [krysjal, -o] *a* crucial.

crucifier [krysifje] *vt* to crucify. ◆**crucifix** [krysifi] *nm* crucifix. ◆**crucifixion** *nf* crucifixion.

crudité [krydite] *nf* (*grossièreté*) crudeness; *pl Culin* assorted raw vegetables.

crue [kry] *nf* (*cours d'eau*) swelling, flood; **en c.** in spate.

cruel, -elle [kryɛl] *a* cruel (**envers, avec** to).

crûment [krymɑ̃] *adv* crudely.

crustacés [krystase] *nmpl* shellfish, crustaceans.

crypte [kript] *nf* crypt.

Cuba [kyba] *nm* Cuba. ◆**cubain, -aine** *a* & *nmf* Cuban.

cube [kyb] *nm* cube; *pl* (*jeu*) building blocks; – *a* (*mètre etc*) cubic. ◆**cubique** *a* cubic.

cueillir* [kœjir] *vt* to gather, pick; (*baiser*) to snatch; (*voleur*) *Fam* to pick up, run in. ◆**cueillette** *nf* gathering, picking; (*fruits cueillis*) harvest.

cuiller, cuillère [kɥijɛr] *nf* spoon; **petite c., c. à café** teaspoon; **c. à soupe** table spoon. ◆**cuillerée** *nf* spoonful.

cuir [kɥir] *nm* leather; (*peau épaisse d'un animal vivant*) hide; **c. chevelu** scalp.

cuirasse [kɥiras] *nf Hist* breastplate. ◆**se cuirass/er** *vpr* to steel oneself (**contre** against). ◆**-é** *nm* battleship.

cuire* [kɥir] *vt* to cook; (*à l'eau*) to boil; (*porcelaine*) to bake, fire; (*au four*) to bake; (*viande*) to roast; – *vi* to cook; to boil; to bake; to roast; (*soleil*) to bake, boil; **faire c.** to cook. ◆**cuisant** *a* (*affront, blessure etc*) stinging. ◆**cuisson** *nm* cooking; (*de porcelaine*) baking, firing.

cuisine [kɥizin] *nf* (*pièce*) kitchen; (*art*) cooking, cuisine, cookery; (*aliments*) cooking; (*intrigues*) *Péj* scheming; **faire la c.** to cook, do the cooking; **livre de c.** cook(ery) book; **haute c.** high-class cooking. ◆**cuisiner** *vti* to cook; **c. qn** (*interroger*) *Fam* to grill s.o. ◆**cuisinier, -ière** *nmf* cook; – *nf* (*appareil*) cooker, stove, *Am* range.

cuisse [kɥis] *nf* thigh; (*de poulet, mouton*) leg.

cuit [kɥi] **1** *voir* **cuire;** – *a* cooked; **bien c.**

well done *ou* cooked. **2** *a* (*pris*) *Fam* done for.

cuite [kɥit] *nf* **prendre une c.** *Fam* to get plastered *ou* drunk.

cuivre [kɥivr] *nm* (*rouge*) copper; (*jaune*) brass; *pl* (*ustensiles*) & *Mus* brass. ◆**cuivré** *a* copper-coloured, coppery.

cul [ky] *nm* (*derrière*) *Fam* backside; (*de bouteille etc*) bottom. ◆**c.-de-jatte** *nm* (*pl* **culs-de-jatte**) legless cripple. ◆**c.-de-sac** *nm* (*pl* **culs-de-sac**) dead end, cul-de-sac.

culasse [kylas] *nf Aut* cylinder head; (*d'une arme à feu*) breech.

culbute [kylbyt] *nf* (*cabriole*) somersault; (*chute*) (*backward*) tumble; **faire une c.** to somersault; to tumble. ◆**culbuter** *vi* to tumble over (*backwards*); – *vt* (*personne, chaise*) to knock over.

culinaire [kyliner] *a* (*art*) culinary; (*recette*) cooking.

culmin/er [kylmine] *vi* (*montagne*) to reach its highest point, peak (**à at**); (*colère*) *Fig* to reach a peak. ◆**-ant** *a* **point c.** (*de réussite, montagne etc*) peak.

culot [kylo] *nm* **1** (*aplomb*) *Fam* nerve, cheek. **2** (*d'ampoule, de lampe etc*) base. ◆**culotté** *a* **être c.** *Fam* to have plenty of nerve *ou* cheek.

culotte [kylɔt] *nf Sp* (*pair of*) shorts; (*de femme*) (*pair of*) knickers *ou Am* panties; **culottes (courtes)** (*de jeune garçon*) short trousers *ou Am* pants; **c. de cheval** riding breeches.

culpabilité [kylpabilite] *nf* guilt.

culte [kylt] *nm* (*hommage*) *Rel* worship, cult; (*pratique*) *Rel* religion; (*service protestant*) service; (*admiration*) *Fig* cult.

cultiv/er [kyltive] *vt* (*terre*) to farm, cultivate; (*plantes*) to grow, cultivate; (*goût, relations etc*) to cultivate; – **se c.** *vpr* to cultivate one's mind. ◆**-é** *a* (*esprit, personne*) cultured, cultivated. ◆**cultivateur, -trice** *nmf* farmer. ◆**culture** *nf* (*action*) farming, cultivation; (*agriculture*) farming; (*horticulture*) growing, cultivation; (*éducation, civilisation*) culture; *pl* (*terres*) fields (*under cultivation*); (*plantes*) crops; **c. générale** general knowledge. ◆**culturel, -elle** *a* cultural.

cumin [kymɛ̃] *nm Bot Culin* caraway.

cumul [kymyl] *nm* **c. de fonctions** plurality of offices. ◆**cumulatif, -ive** *a* cumulative. ◆**cumuler** *vt* **c. deux fonctions** to hold two offices (*at the same time*).

cupide [kypid] *a* avaricious. ◆**cupidité** *nf* avarice, cupidity.

Cupidon [kypidɔ̃] *nm* Cupid.

cure [kyr] *nf* **1** (course of) treatment, cure. **2** (*fonction*) office (of a parish priest); (*résidence*) presbytery. ◆**curable** *a* curable. ◆**curé** *nm* (parish) priest.

curer [kyre] *vt* to clean out; **se c. le nez/ les dents** to pick one's nose/teeth. ◆**curedent** *nm* toothpick. ◆**cure-ongles** *nm inv* nail cleaner. ◆**cure-pipe** *nm* pipe cleaner.

curieux, -euse [kyrjø, -øz] *a* (*bizarre*) curious; (*indiscret*) inquisitive, curious (**de** about); **c. de savoir** curious to know; – *nmf* inquisitive *ou* curious person; (*badaud*) onlooker. ◆**curieusement** *adv* curiously. ◆**curiosité** *nf* (*de personne, forme etc*) curiosity; (*chose*) curiosity; (*spectacle*) unusual sight.

curriculum (vitæ) [kyrikylɔm(vite)] *nm inv* curriculum (vitae), *Am* résumé.

curseur [kyrsœr] *nm* (*d'un ordinateur*) cursor.

cutané [kytane] *a* (*affection etc*) skin-. ◆**cuti-(réaction)** *nf* skin test.

cuve [kyv] *nf* vat; (*réservoir*) & *Phot* tank. ◆**cuvée** *nf* (*récolte de vin*) vintage.

◆**cuver** *vt* **c. son vin** *Fam* to sleep it off. ◆**cuvette** *nf* (*récipient*) & *Géog* basin, bowl; (*des cabinets*) pan, bowl.

cyanure [sjanyr] *nm* cyanide.

cybernétique [sibɛrnetik] *nf* cybernetics.

cycle [sikl] *nm* **1** (*série, révolution*) cycle. **2** (*bicyclette*) cycle. ◆**cyclable** *a* (*piste*) cycle-. ◆**cyclique** *a* cyclic(al). ◆**cyclisme** *nm Sp* cycling. ◆**cycliste** *nmf* cyclist; – *a* (*course*) cycle-; (*champion*) cycling; **coureur c.** racing cyclist. ◆**cyclomoteur** *nm* moped.

cyclone [siklon] *nm* cyclone.

cygne [siɲ] *nm* swan; **chant du c.** *Fig* swan song.

cylindre [silɛ̃dr] *nm* cylinder; (*de rouleau compresseur*) roller. ◆**cylindrée** *nf Aut* (engine) capacity. ◆**cylindrique** *a* cylindrical.

cymbale [sɛ̃bal] *nf* cymbal.

cynique [sinik] *a* cynical; – *nmf* cynic. ◆**cynisme** *nm* cynicism.

cyprès [siprɛ] *nm* (*arbre*) cypress.

cypriote [siprijɔt] *a* & *nmf* Cypriot.

cytise [sitiz] *nf Bot* laburnum.

D

D, d [de] *nm* D, d.
d' [d] *voir* de [1,2].

d'abord [dabɔr] *adv* (*en premier lieu*) first; (*au début*) at first.

dactylo [daktilo] *nf* (*personne*) typist; (*action*) typing. ◆**dactylographie** *nf* typing. ◆**dactylographier** *vt* to type.

dada [dada] *nm* (*manie*) hobby horse, pet subject.

dadais [dadɛ] *nm* (**grand**) **d.** big oaf.

dahlia [dalja] *nm* dahlia.

daigner [deɲe] *vt* **d. faire** to condescend *ou* deign to do.

daim [dɛ̃] *nm* fallow deer; (*mâle*) buck; (*cuir*) suede.

dais [dɛ] *nm* (*de lit, feuillage etc*) canopy.

dalle [dal] *nf* paving stone; (*funèbre*) (flat) gravestone. ◆**dallage** *nm* (*action, surface*) paving. ◆**dallé** *a* (*pièce, cour etc*) paved.

daltonien, -ienne [daltɔnjɛ̃, -jɛn] *a* & *n* colour-blind (person). ◆**daltonisme** *nm* colour blindness.

dame [dam] *nf* **1** lady; (*mariée*) married lady. **2** *Échecs Cartes* queen; (*au jeu de dames*) king; (**jeu de**) **dames** draughts, *Am*

checkers. ◆**damer** *vt* (*au jeu de dames*) to crown; **d. le pion à qn** to outsmart s.o. ◆**damier** *nm* draughtboard, *Am* checkerboard.

damner [dane] *vt* to damn; **faire d.** *Fam* to torment, drive mad; **– se d.** *vpr* to be damned. ◆**damnation** *nf* damnation.

dancing [dɑ̃siŋ] *nm* dance hall.

dandiner (se) [sədɑ̃dine] *vpr* to waddle.

dandy [dɑ̃di] *nm* dandy.

Danemark [danmark] *nm* Denmark. ◆**danois, -oise** *a* Danish; – *nmf* Dane; – *nm* (*langue*) Danish.

danger [dɑ̃ʒe] *nm* danger; **en d.** in danger *ou* jeopardy; **mettre en d.** to endanger, jeopardize; **en cas de d.** in an emergency; **en d. de mort** in peril of death; **'d. de mort'** (*panneau*) 'danger'; **sans d.** (*se promener etc*) safely; **être sans d.** to be safe; **pas de d.!** *Fam* no way!, no fear! ◆**dangereux, -euse** *a* dangerous (**pour** to). ◆**dangereusement** *adv* dangerously.

dans [dɑ̃] *prép* in; (*changement de lieu*) into; (*à l'intérieur de*) inside, within; **entrer d.** to go in(to); **d. Paris** in Paris, within Paris;

d. un rayon de within (a radius of); **boire/prendre/***etc* **d.** to drink/take/*etc* from *ou* out of; **marcher d. les rues** (*à travers*) to walk through *ou* about the streets; **d. ces circonstances** under *ou* in these circumstances; **d. deux jours/***etc* (*temps futur*) in two days/*etc*, in two days'/*etc* time; **d. les dix francs/***etc* (*quantité*) about ten francs/*etc*.

danse [dɑ̃s] *nf* dance; (*art*) dancing. ◆**dans/er** *vti* to dance; **faire d. l'anse du panier** (*domestique*) to fiddle on the shopping money. ◆**—eur, -euse** *nmf* dancer; **en danseuse** (*cycliste*) standing on the pedals.

dard [dar] *nm* (*d'abeille etc*) sting; (*de serpent*) tongue. ◆**darder** *vt* (*flèche*) to shoot; (*regard*) to flash, dart; **le soleil dardait ses rayons** the sun cast down its burning rays.

dare-dare [dardar] *adv Fam* at *ou* on the double.

date [dat] *nf* date; **de vieille d.** (*amitié etc*) (of) long-standing; **faire d.** (*événement*) to mark an important date, be epoch-making; **en d. du . . .** dated the . . . ; **d. limite** deadline. ◆**datation** *nf* dating. ◆**dater** *vt* (*lettre etc*) to date; *– vi* (*être dépassé*) to be dated; **d. de** to date back to, date from; **à d. de** as from. ◆**dateur** *nm* (*de montre*) date indicator; *– a & nm* (*tampon*) date stamp.

datte [dat] *nf* (*fruit*) date. ◆**dattier** *nm* date palm.

daube [dob] *nf* **bœuf en d.** braised beef stew.

dauphin [dofɛ̃] *nm* (*mammifère marin*) dolphin.

davantage [davɑ̃taʒ] *adv* (*quantité*) more; (*temps*) longer; **d. de temps/***etc* more time/*etc*; **d. de** more; longer than.

de¹ [d(ə)] (**d'** before a vowel or mute h; **de + le = du, de + les = des**) *prép* **1** (*complément d'un nom*) of; **les rayons du soleil** the rays of the sun, the sun's rays; **la ville de Paris** the town of Paris; **le livre de Paul** Paul's book; **un pont de fer** an iron bridge; **le train de Londres** the London train; **une augmentation/diminution de** an increase/decrease in. **2** (*complément d'un adjectif*) **digne de** worthy of; **heureux de partir** happy to leave; **content de qch** pleased with sth. **3** (*complément d'un verbe*) **parler de** to speak of *ou* about; **se souvenir de** to remember; **décider de faire** to decide to do; **traiter de lâche** to call a coward. **4** (*provenance*: *lieu & temps*) from; **venir/dater de** to come/date from; **mes amis du village** my friends from the village, my village friends; **le train de Londres** the train from London. **5** (*agent*) **accompagné de** accompanied by. **6** (*moyen*) **armé de** armed with; **se nourrir de** to live on. **7** (*manière*) **d'une voix douce** in *ou* with a gentle voice. **8** (*cause*) **puni de** punished for; **mourir de faim** to die of hunger. **9** (*temps*) **travailler de nuit** to work by night; **six heures du matin** six o'clock in the morning. **10** (*mesure*) **avoir six mètres de haut, être haut de six mètres** to be six metres high; **retarder de deux heures** to delay by two hours; **homme de trente ans** thirty-year-old man; **gagner cent francs de l'heure** to earn one hundred francs an hour.

de² [d(ə)] *art partitif* some; **elle boit du vin** she drinks (some) wine; **il ne boit pas de vin** (*négation*) he doesn't drink (any) wine; **des fleurs** (some) flowers; **de jolies fleurs** (some) pretty flowers; **d'agréables soirées** (some) pleasant evenings; **il y en a six de tués** (*avec un nombre*) six are killed.

dé [de] *nm* (*à jouer*) dice; (*à coudre*) thimble; **les dés** the dice; (*jeu*) dice; **les dés sont jetés** *Fig* the die is cast; **couper en dés** *Culin* to dice.

déambuler [deɑ̃byle] *vi* to stroll, saunter.

débâcle [debɑkl] *nf Mil* rout; (*ruine*) *Fig* downfall; (*des glaces*) *Géog* breaking up.

déball/er [debale] *vt* to unpack; (*étaler*) to display. ◆**—age** *nm* unpacking; display.

débandade [debɑ̃dad] *nf* (*mad*) rush, stampede; *Mil* rout; **à la d.** in confusion; **tout va à la d.** everything's going to rack and ruin.

débaptiser [debatize] *vt* (*rue*) to rename.

débarbouiller [debarbuje] *vt* **d. qn** to wash s.o.'s face; **se d.** to wash one's face.

débarcadère [debarkader] *nm* landing stage, quay.

débardeur [debardœr] *nm* **1** (*docker*) stevedore. **2** (*vêtement*) slipover, *Am* (*sweater*) vest.

débarqu/er [debarke] *vt* (*passagers*) to land; (*marchandises*) to unload; **d. qn** (*congédier*) *Fam* to sack s.o.; *– vi* (*passagers*) to disembark, land; (*arriver naïf*) *Fam* not to be quite with it; **d. chez qn** *Fam* to turn up suddenly at s.o.'s place. ◆**—ement** *nm* landing; unloading; *Mil* landing.

débarras [debara] *nm* lumber room, *Am* storeroom; **bon d.!** *Fam* good riddance! ◆**débarrasser** *vt* (*voie, table etc*) to clear (**de** of); **d. qn de** (*ennemi, soucis etc*) to rid s.o. of; (*manteau etc*) to relieve s.o. of; **se d. de** to get rid of, rid oneself of.

débat [deba] *nm* discussion, debate; *pl Pol Jur* proceedings. ◆**débattre*** *vt* to discuss, debate; **— se d.** *vpr* to struggle *ou* fight (to get free), put up a fight.

débauche [deboʃ] *nf* debauchery; **une d. de** *Fig* a wealth *ou* profusion of. ◆**débauch/er** *vt* **d. qn** (*détourner*) *Fam* to entice s.o. away from work; (*licencier*) to dismiss s.o., lay s.o. off. ◆**—é, —ée** *a* (*libertin*) debauched, profligate; **—** *nmf* debauchee, profligate.

débile [debil] *a* (*esprit, enfant etc*) weak, feeble; *Péj Fam* idiotic; **—** *nmf Péj Fam* idiot, moron. ◆**débilité** *nf* debility, weakness; *pl* (*niaiseries*) *Fam* sheer nonsense. ◆**débiliter** *vt* to debilitate, weaken.

débiner [debine] **1** *vt* (*décrier*) *Fam* to run down. **2 se d.** *vpr* (*s'enfuir*) *Arg* to hop it, bolt.

débit [debi] *nm* **1** (*vente*) turnover, sales; (*de fleuve*) (rate of) flow; (*d'un orateur*) delivery; **d. de tabac** tobacconist's shop, *Am* tobacco store; **d. de boissons** bar, café. **2** (*compte*) *Fin* debit. ◆**débiter** *vt* **1** (*découper*) to cut up, slice up (**en** into); (*vendre*) to sell; (*fournir*) to yield; (*dire*) *Péj* to utter, spout. **2** *Fin* to debit. ◆**débiteur, -trice** *nmf* debtor; **—** *a* (*solde, compte*) debit-; **son compte est d.** his account is in debit, he is in debit.

déblais [deblɛ] *nmpl* (*terre*) earth; (*décombres*) rubble. ◆**déblayer** *vt* (*terrain, décombres*) to clear.

débloquer [deblɔke] **1** *vt* (*machine*) to unjam; (*crédits, freins, compte*) to release; (*prix*) to decontrol. **2** *vi* (*divaguer*) *Fam* to talk through one's hat, talk nonsense.

déboires [debwar] *nmpl* disappointments, setbacks.

déboît/er [debwate] **1** *vt* (*tuyau*) to disconnect; (*os*) *Méd* to dislocate. **2** *vi Aut* to pull out, change lanes. ◆**—ement** *nm Méd* dislocation.

débonnaire [debɔnɛr] *a* good-natured, easy-going.

débord/er [debɔrde] *vi* (*fleuve, liquide*) to overflow; (*en bouillant*) to boil over; **d. de** (*vie, joie etc*) *Fig* to be overflowing *ou* bubbling over with; **l'eau déborde du vase** the water is running over the top of the vase *ou* is overflowing the vase; **—** *vt* (*dépasser*) to go *ou* extend beyond; (*faire saillie*) to stick out from; *Mil Sp* to outflank; **débordé de travail/de visites** snowed under with work/visits.

◆**—ement** *nm* overflowing; (*de joie, activité*) outburst.

débouch/er [debuʃe] **1** *vt* (*bouteille*) to open, uncork; (*lavabo, tuyau*) to clear, unblock. **2** *vi* (*surgir*) to emerge, come out (**de** from); **d. sur** (*rue*) to lead out onto, lead into; *Fig* to lead up to. ◆**—é** *nm* (*carrière*) & *Géog* opening; (*de rue*) exit; (*marché*) *Com* outlet.

débouler [debule] *vi* (*arriver*) *Fam* to burst in, turn up.

déboulonner [debulɔne] *vt* to unbolt; **d. qn** *Fam* (*renvoyer*) to sack *ou* fire s.o.; (*discréditer*) to bring s.o. down.

débours [debur] *nmpl* expenses. ◆**débourser** *vt* to pay out.

debout [d(ə)bu] *adv* standing (up); **mettre d.** (*planche etc*) to stand up, put upright; **se mettre d.** to stand *ou* get up; **se tenir** *ou* **rester d.** (*personne*) to stand (up), remain standing (up); **rester d.** (*édifice etc*) to remain standing; **être d.** (*levé*) to be up (and about); **d.!** get up!; **ça ne tient pas d.** (*théorie etc*) that doesn't hold water *ou* make sense.

déboutonner [debutɔne] *vt* to unbutton, undo; **— se d.** *vpr* (*personne*) to undo one's buttons.

débraillé [debraje] *a* (*tenue etc*) slovenly, sloppy; **—** *nm* slovenliness, sloppiness.

débrancher [debrɑ̃ʃe] *vt El* to unplug, disconnect.

débrayer [debreje] *vi* **1** *Aut* to declutch, release the clutch. **2** (*se mettre en grève*) to stop work. ◆**débrayage** (*grève*) strike, walk-out.

débridé [debride] *a* (*effréné*) unbridled.

débris [debri] *nmpl* fragments, scraps; (*restes*) remains; (*détritus*) rubbish, debris.

débrouiller [debruje] **1** *vt* (*écheveau etc*) to unravel, disentangle; (*affaire*) to sort out. **2 se d.** *vpr* to manage, get by, make out; **se d. pour faire** to manage (somehow) to do. ◆**débrouillard** *a* smart, resourceful. ◆**débrouillardise** *nf* smartness, resourcefulness.

débroussailler [debrusaje] *vt* (*chemin*) to clear (of brushwood); (*problème*) *Fig* to clarify.

débusquer [debyske] *vt* (*gibier, personne*) to drive out, dislodge.

début [deby] *nm* start, beginning; **au d.** at the beginning; **faire ses débuts** (*sur la scène etc*) to make one's debut. ◆**début/er** *vi* to start, begin; (*dans une carrière*) to start out in life; (*sur la scène etc*) to make one's début. ◆—ant, -ante *nmf* beginner; – *a* novice.

déca [deka] *nm Fam* decaffeinated coffee.

deçà (en) [ãd(ə)sa] *adv* (on) this side; – *prép* en d. de (on) this side of; *(succès, prix etc) Fig* short of.

décacheter [dekaʃte] *vt (lettre etc)* to open, unseal.

décade [dekad] *nf (dix jours)* period of ten days; *(décennie)* decade.

décadent [dekadã] *a* decadent. ◆**décadence** *nf* decay, decadence.

décaféiné [dekafeine] *a* decaffeinated.

décalaminer [dekalamine] *vt (moteur)* Aut to decoke, decarbonize.

décalcomanie [dekalkɔmani] *nf (image)* transfer, Am decal.

décal/er [dekale] *vt* **1** *(avancer)* to shift; *(départ, repas)* to shift (the time of). **2** *(ôter les cales de)* to unwedge. ◆—age *nm (écart)* gap, discrepancy; **d. horaire** time difference.

décalque [dekalk] *nm* tracing. ◆**décalquer** *vt (dessin)* to trace.

décamper [dekãpe] *vi* to make off, clear off.

décanter [dekãte] *vt (liquide)* to settle, clarify; **d. ses idées** to clarify one's ideas; **— se d.** *vpr (idées, situation)* to become clearer, settle.

décap/er [dekape] *vt (métal)* to clean, scrape down; *(surface peinte)* to strip. ◆—ant *nm* cleaning agent; *(pour enlever la peinture)* paint stripper. ◆—eur *nm* **d. thermique** hot-air paint stripper.

décapiter [dekapite] *vt* to decapitate, behead.

décapotable [dekapɔtabl] *a (voiture)* convertible.

décapsul/er [dekapsyle] *vt* **d. une bouteille** to take the cap ou top off a bottle. ◆—eur *nm* bottle-opener.

décarcasser (se) [sədekarkase] *vpr Fam* to flog oneself to death *(pour faire* doing).

décathlon [dekatlɔ̃] *nm Sp* decathlon.

décati [dekati] *a* worn out, decrepit.

décavé [dekave] *a Fam* ruined.

décéd/er [desede] *vi* to die. ◆—é *a* deceased.

déceler [desle] *vt (trouver)* to detect, uncover; *(révéler)* to reveal.

décembre [desãbr] *nm* December.

décennie [deseni] *nf* decade.

décent [desã] *a (bienséant, acceptable)* decent. ◆**décemment** [-amã] *adv* decently. ◆**décence** *nf* decency.

décentraliser [desãtralize] *vt* to decentral-

ize. ◆**décentralisation** *nf* decentralization.

déception [desɛpsjɔ̃] *nf* disappointment. ◆**décevoir*** *vt* to disappoint. ◆**décevant** *a* disappointing.

décerner [deserne] *vt (prix etc)* to award; *(mandat d'arrêt etc)* Jur to issue.

décès [desɛ] *nm* death.

déchaîn/er [deʃene] *vt (colère, violence)* to unleash, let loose; **d. l'enthousiasme/les rires** to set off wild enthusiasm/a storm of laughter; **— se d.** *vpr (tempête, rires)* to break out; *(foule)* to run amok ou riot; *(colère, personne)* to explode. ◆—é *a (foule, flots)* wild, raging. ◆—ement [-ɛnmã] *nm (de rires, de haine etc)* outburst; *(de violence)* outbreak, eruption; **le d. de la tempête** the raging of the storm.

déchanter [deʃãte] *vi Fam* to become disillusioned; *(changer de ton)* to change one's tune.

décharge [deʃarʒ] *nf Jur* discharge; **d. (publique)** *(rubbish)* dump ou tip, Am *(garbage)* dump; **d. (électrique)** (electrical) discharge, shock; **recevoir une d. (électrique)** to get a shock; **à la d. de qn** in s.o.'s defence. ◆**décharg/er** *vt* to unload; *(batterie)* El to discharge; *(accusé)* Jur to discharge, exonerate; **d. qn de** *(travail etc)* to relieve s.o. of; **d. sur qn** *(son arme)* to fire at s.o.; *(sa colère)* to vent on s.o.; **— se d.** *vpr (batterie)* to go flat; **se d. sur qn du soin de faire qch** to unload onto s.o. the job of doing sth. ◆—ement *nm* unloading.

décharné [deʃarne] *a* skinny, bony.

déchausser (se) [sədeʃose] *vpr* **d. qn** to take s.o.'s shoes off; **se d.** to take one's shoes off; *(dent)* to get loose.

dèche [dɛʃ] *nf* **être dans la d.** Arg to be flat broke.

déchéance [deʃeãs] *nf (déclin)* decline, decay, degradation.

déchet [deʃɛ] *nm* **déchets** *(résidus)* scraps, waste; **il y a du d.** there's some waste ou wastage.

déchiffrer [deʃifre] *vt (message)* to decipher; *(mauvaise écriture)* to make out, decipher.

déchiqueter [deʃikte] *vt* to tear to shreds, cut to bits. ◆—é *a (drapeau etc)* (all) in shreds; *(côte)* jagged.

déchir/er [deʃire] *vt* to tear (up), rip (up); *(vêtement)* to tear ou rip; *(ouvrir)* to tear ou rip open; *(pays, groupe)* to tear apart; **d. l'air** *(bruit)* to rend the air; **ce bruit me déchire les oreilles** this noise is ear-splitting; **— se d.** *vpr (robe etc)* to tear, to rip. ◆**—ant** a (navrant) heart-breaking; (aigu) ear-splitting. ◆**—ement** nm (souffrance) heartbreak; pl (divisions) Pol deep rifts. ◆**déchirure** nf tear, rip; d. musculaire torn muscle.

déchoir [defwar] vi to lose prestige. ◆**déchu** a (ange) fallen; être d. de (ses droits etc) to have forfeited.

décibel [desibɛl] nm decibel.

décid/er [deside] vt (envoi, opération) to decide on; d. que to decide that; d. qn à faire to persuade s.o. to do; — vi d. de (destin de qn) to decide; (voyage etc) to decide on; d. de faire to decide to do; — se d. vpr (question) to be decided; se d. à faire to make up one's mind to do; se d. pour qch to decide on sth ou in favour of sth. ◆**—é** a (air, ton) determined, decided; (net, pas douteux) decided; c'est d. it's settled; être d. à faire to be decided about doing ou determined to do. ◆**—ément** adv undoubtedly.

décilitre [desilitr] nm decilitre.

décimal, -aux [desimal, -o] a decimal. ◆**décimale** nf decimal.

décimer [desime] vt to decimate.

décimètre [desimɛtr] nm decimetre; double d. ruler.

décisif, -ive [desizif, -iv] a decisive; (moment) crucial. ◆**décision** nf decision; (fermeté) determination.

déclamer [deklame] vt to declaim; Péj to spout. ◆**déclamatoire** a Péj bombastic.

déclarer [deklare] vt to declare (que that); (décès, vol etc) to notify; (coupable) to convict, find guilty; d. la guerre to declare war (à on); — se d. vpr (s'expliquer) to declare one's views; (incendie, maladie) to break out; se d. contre to come out against. ◆**déclaration** nf declaration; (de décès etc) notification; (commentaire) statement, comment; d. de revenus tax return.

déclench/er [deklɑ̃ʃe] vt (mécanisme) to set ou trigger off, release; (attaque) to launch; (provoquer) to trigger off, spark off; d. le travail Méd to induce labour; — se d. vpr (sonnerie) to go off; (attaque, grève) to start. ◆**—ement** nm (d'un appareil) release.

déclic [deklik] nm (mécanisme) catch, trigger; (bruit) click.

déclin [deklɛ̃] nm decline; (du jour) close; (de la lune) wane. ◆**décliner 1** vi (refuser) to decline. **2** vt (réciter) to state. **3** vi (forces etc) to decline, wane; (jour) to draw to a close.

déclivité [deklivite] nf slope.

décocher [dekɔʃe] vt (flèche) to shoot, fire; (coup) to let fly, aim; (regard) to flash.

décoder [dekɔde] vt (message) to decode.

décoiffer [dekwafe] vt d. qn to mess up s.o.'s hair.

décoincer [dekwɛ̃se] vt (engrenage) to unjam.

décoll/er [dekɔle] **1** vi (avion etc) to take off; elle ne décolle pas d'ici Fam she won't leave ou budge. **2** vt (timbre etc) to unstick; — se d. vpr to come unstuck. ◆**—age** nm Av takeoff.

décolleté [dekɔlte] a (robe) low-cut; — nm (de robe) low neckline; (de femme) bare neck and shoulders.

décoloniser [dekɔlɔnize] vt to decolonize. ◆**décolonisation** nf decolonization.

décolor/er [dekɔlɔre] vt to discolour, fade; (cheveux) to bleach. ◆**—ant** nm bleach. ◆**décoloration** nf discolo(u)ration; bleaching.

décombres [dekɔ̃br] nmpl ruins, rubble, debris.

décommander [dekɔmɑ̃de] vt (marchandises, invitation) to cancel; (invités) to put off; — se d. vpr to cancel (one's appointment).

décomposer [dekɔ̃poze] vt to decompose; (visage) to distort; — se d. vpr (pourrir) to decompose; (visage) to become distorted. ◆**décomposition** nf decomposition.

décompresser [dekɔ̃prese] vi Psy Fam to unwind.

décompression [dekɔ̃presjɔ̃] nf decompression.

décompte [dekɔ̃t] nm deduction; (détail) breakdown. ◆**décompter** vt to deduct.

déconcerter [dekɔ̃sɛrte] vt to disconcert.

déconfit [dekɔ̃fi] a downcast. ◆**déconfiture** nf (state of) collapse ou defeat; (faillite) Fam financial ruin.

décongeler [dekɔ̃ʒle] vt (aliment) to thaw, defrost.

décongestionner [dekɔ̃ʒɛstjɔne] vt (rue) & Méd to relieve congestion in.

déconnecter [dekɔnɛkte] vt Él & Fig to disconnect.

déconner [dekɔne] vi (divaguer) Fam to talk nonsense.

déconseiller [dekɔ̃seje] vt d. qch à qn to advise s.o. against sth; d. à qn de faire to advise s.o. against doing; c'est déconseillé it is inadvisable.

déconsidérer [dekɔ̃sidere] vt to discredit.

décontaminer [dekɔ̃tamine] vt to decontaminate.

décontenancer [dekɔ̃tnɑse] vt to disconcert; **— se d.** vpr to lose one's composure, become flustered.

décontracter [dekɔ̃trakte] vt, **— se d.** vpr to relax. ◆**décontraction** nf relaxation.

déconvenue [dekɔ̃vny] nf disappointment.

décor [dekɔr] nm Th scenery, decor; Cin set; (paysage) scenery; (d'intérieur) decoration; (cadre, ambiance) setting; **entrer dans le d.** (véhicule) Fam to run off the road.

décorer [dekɔre] vt (maison, soldat etc) to decorate (de with). ◆**décorateur, -trice** nmf (interior) decorator; Th stage designer; Cin set designer. ◆**décoratif, -ive** a decorative. ◆**décoration** nf decoration.

décortiquer [dekɔrtike] vt (graine) to husk; (homard etc) to shell; (texte) Fam to take to pieces, dissect.

découcher [dekuʃe] vi to stay out all night.

découdre [dekudr] vt to unstitch; **— vi en d.** Fam to fight it out; **— se d.** vpr to come unstitched.

découler [dekule] vi **d. de** to follow from.

découp/er [dekupe] vt (poulet etc) to carve; (article etc) Journ to cut out; **se d. sur** to stand out against. ◆**—é a** (côte) jagged. ◆**—age** nm carving; cutting out; (image) cut-out. ◆**découpure** nf (contour) jagged outline; (morceau) piece cut out, cut-out.

découplé [dekuple] a **bien d.** (personne) well-built, strapping.

décourag/er [dekuraʒe] vt (dissuader) to discourage (de from); (démoraliser) to dishearten, discourage; **— se d.** vpr to get discouraged ou disheartened. ◆**—ement** nm discouragement.

décousu [dekuzy] a (propos, idées) disconnected.

découvrir* [dekuvrir] vt (trésor, terre etc) to discover; (secret, vérité etc) to find out, discover; (casserole etc) to take the lid off; (dévoiler) to disclose (à to); (dénuder) to uncover, expose; (voir) to perceive; **d. que** to discover ou find out that; **— se d.** vpr (se dénuder) to uncover oneself; (enlever son chapeau) to take one's hat off; (ciel) to clear (up). ◆**découvert 1** a (terrain) open; (tête etc) bare; **à d.** exposed, unprotected; **agir à d.** to act openly. **2** nm (d'un compte) Fin overdraft. ◆**découverte** nf discovery; **partir** ou **aller à la d. de** to go in search of.

décrasser [dekrase] vt (éduquer) to take the rough edges off.

décrépit [dekrepi] a (vieillard) decrepit.

◆**décrépitude** nf (des institutions etc) decay.

décret [dekre] nm decree. ◆**décréter** vt to order, decree.

décrier [dekrije] vt to run down, disparage.

décrire* [dekrir] vt to describe.

décroch/er [dekrɔʃe] **1** vt (détacher) to unhook; (tableau) to take down; (obtenir) Fam to get, land; **d. (le téléphone)** to pick up the phone. **2** vi Fam (abandonner) to give up; (perdre le fil) to be unable to follow, lose track. ◆**—é a** (téléphone) off the hook.

décroître* [dekrwatr] vi (mortalité etc) to decrease, decline; (eaux) to subside; (jours) to draw in. ◆**décroissance** nf decrease, decline (de in, of).

décrotter [dekrɔte] vt (chaussures) to clean ou scrape (the mud off). ◆**décrottoir** nm shoe scraper.

décrypter [dekripte] vt (message) to decipher, decode.

déçu [desy] voir **décevoir**; **– a** disappointed.

déculotter (se) [sedekylɔte] vpr to take off one's trousers ou Am pants. ◆**déculottée** nf Fam thrashing.

décupler [dekyple] vti to increase tenfold.

dédaign/er [dedɛɲe] vt (personne, richesse etc) to scorn, despise; (repas) to turn up one's nose at; (offre) to spurn; (ne pas tenir compte de) to disregard. ◆**dédaigneux, -euse** a scornful, disdainful (de of). ◆**dédain** nm scorn, disdain (pour, de for).

dédale [dedal] nm maze, labyrinth.

dedans [d(ə)dɑ̃] adv inside; **de d.** from (the) inside, from within; **en d.** on the inside; **au-d. (de), au d. (de)** inside; **au-d. ou au d. de lui-même** inwardly; **tomber d.** (trou) to fall in (it); **donner d.** (être dupé) Fam to fall in; **mettre d.** Fam (en prison) to put inside; (tromper) to take in; **je me suis fait rentrer d.** (accident de voiture) Fam someone went ou crashed into me; **– nm le d.** the inside.

dédicace [dedikas] nf dedication, inscription. ◆**dédicacer** vt (livre etc) to dedicate, inscribe (à to).

dédier [dedje] vt to dedicate.

dédire (se) [sədedir] vpr to go back on one's word; **se d. de** (promesse etc) to go back on. ◆**dédit** [dedi] (somme) Com forfeit, penalty.

dédommag/er [dedɔmaʒe] vt to compensate (de for). ◆**—ement** nm compensation.

dédouaner [dedwane] vt (marchandises) to clear through customs; **d. qn** to restore s.o.'s prestige.

dédoubl/er [deduble] vt (classe etc) to split into two; **d. un train** to run an extra train; **— se d.** vpr to be in two places at once. ◆**—ement** nm **d. de la personnalité** Psy split personality.

déduire* [dedɥir] vt (retirer) to deduct (de from); (conclure) to deduce (de from). ◆**déductible** a (frais) deductible, allowable. ◆**déduction** nf (raisonnement) & Com deduction.

déesse [dees] nf goddess.

défaill/ir* [defajir] vi (s'évanouir) to faint; (forces) to fail, flag; **sans d.** without flinching. ◆**—ant** a (personne) faint; (témoin) Jur defaulting. ◆**défaillance** nf (évanouissement) fainting fit; (faiblesse) weakness; (panne) fault; **une d. de mémoire** a lapse of memory.

défaire* [defɛr] vt (nœud etc) to undo, untie; (bagages) to unpack; (installation) to take down; (coiffure) to mess up; — **se d.** vpr (nœud etc) to come undone ou untied; **se d. de** to get rid of. ◆**défait** a (lit) unmade; (visage) drawn; (armée) defeated. ◆**défaite** nf defeat. ◆**défaitisme** nm defeatism.

défalquer [defalke] vt (frais) to deduct (de from).

défaut [defo] nm (faiblesse) fault, shortcoming, failing, defect; (de diamant etc) flaw; (désavantage) drawback; (contumace) Jur default; **le d. de la cuirasse** the chink in the armour; **faire d.** to be lacking; **le temps me fait d.** I lack time; **à d. de** for want of; **en d.** at fault; **prendre qn en d.** to catch s.o. out; **ou, à d. ....** or, failing that ....

défaveur [defavœr] nf disfavour. ◆**défavorable** a unfavourable (à to). ◆**défavoriser** vt to put at a disadvantage, be unfair to.

défection [defɛksjɔ̃] nf defection, desertion; **faire d.** to desert; (ne pas venir) to fail to turn up.

défectueux, -euse [defɛktɥø, -øz] a faulty, defective. ◆**défectuosité** nf defectiveness; (défaut) defect (de in).

défendre [defɑ̃dr] **1** vt (protéger) to defend; — **se d.** vpr to defend oneself; **se d. de** (pluie etc) to protect oneself from; **se d. de faire** (s'empêcher de) to refrain from doing; **je me défends** (bien) Fam I can hold my own. **2** vt **d. à qn de faire** (interdire) to forbid s.o. to do, not allow s.o. to do; **d. qch à qn** to forbid s.o. sth. ◆**défendable** a defensible.

défense [defɑ̃s] nf **1** (protection) defence, Am defense; **sans d.** defenceless. **2**

(interdiction) **'d. de fumer'** 'no smoking'; **'d. d'entrer'** 'no entry', 'no admittance'. **3** (d'éléphant) tusk. ◆**défenseur** nm defender; (des faibles) protector, defender. ◆**défensif, -ive** a defensive; — nf **sur la défensive** on the defensive.

déférent [deferɑ̃] a deferential. ◆**déférence** nf deference.

déférer [defere] **1** vt (coupable) Jur to refer (à to). **2** vi **d. à l'avis de qn** to defer to s.o.'s opinion.

déferler [defɛrle] vi (vagues) to break; (haine etc) to erupt; **d. dans** ou **sur** (foule) to surge ou sweep into.

défi [defi] nm challenge; **lancer un d. à qn** to challenge s.o.; **mettre qn au d. de faire** to defy ou dare ou challenge s.o. to do.

déficient [defisjɑ̃] a Méd deficient. ◆**déficience** nf Méd deficiency.

déficit [defisit] nm deficit. ◆**déficitaire** a (budget etc) in deficit; (récolte etc) Fig short, insufficient.

défier¹ [defje] vt (provoquer) to challenge (à to); (braver) to defy; **d. qn de faire** ou challenge s.o. to do.

défier² (se) [sədefje] vpr **se d. de** Litt to distrust. ◆**défiance** nf distrust (de of). ◆**défiant** a distrustful (à l'égard de of).

défigur/er [defigyre] vt (visage) to disfigure; (vérité etc) to distort, distortion. ◆**—ement** nm disfigurement; distortion.

défil/er [defile] vi (manifestants) to march (devant past); Mil to march ou file past; (paysage, jours) to pass by; (visiteurs) to keep coming and going, stream in and out; (images) Cin to flash by (on the screen); — **se d.** vpr Fam (s'éloigner) to sneak off; (éviter d'agir) to cop out. ◆**—é** nm **1** (cortège) procession; (de manifestants) march; Mil parade, march past; (de visiteurs) stream, succession. **2** Géog gorge, pass.

défin/ir [definir] vt to define. ◆**—i** a (article) Gram definite. ◆**définition** nf definition; (de mots croisés) clue.

définitif, -ive [definitif, -iv] a final, definitive; — nf **en définitive** in the final analysis, finally. ◆**définitivement** adv (partir) permanently, for good; (exclure) definitively.

déflagration [deflagrɑsjɔ̃] nf explosion.

déflation [deflɑsjɔ̃] nf Écon deflation.

déflorer [deflore] vt (idée, sujet) to spoil the freshness of.

défonc/er [defɔ̃se] **1** vt (porte, mur etc) to smash in ou down; (trottoir, route etc) to dig up, break up. **2 se d.** vpr (drogué) Fam to get high (à on). ◆—é a 1 (route) full of potholes, bumpy. 2 (drogué) Fam high.

déform/er [defɔrme] vt (objet) to put ou knock out of shape; (doigt, main) to deform; (faits, image etc) to distort; (goût) to corrupt; — **se d.** vpr to lose its shape. ◆—é a (dos) misshapen; (corps etc) deformed, misshapen; **chaussée déformée** uneven road surface. ◆**déformation** nf distortion; corruption; (de membre) deformity; **c'est de la d. professionnelle** it's an occupational hazard, it's a case of being conditioned by one's job.

défouler (se) [sədefule] vpr Fam to let off steam.

défraíchir (se) [sədefreʃir] vpr (étoffe etc) to lose its freshness, become faded.

défrayer [defreje] vt **d. qn** to pay ou defray s.o.'s expenses; **d. la chronique** to be the talk of the town.

défricher [defriʃe] vt (terrain) to clear (for cultivation); (sujet etc) Fig to open up.

défriser [defrize] vt (cheveux) to straighten; **d. qn** (contrarier) Fam to ruffle ou annoy s.o.

défroisser [defrwase] vt (papier) to smooth out.

défroqué [defrɔke] a (prêtre) defrocked.

défunt, -unte [defœ̃, -œ̃t] a (mort) departed; **son d. mari** her late husband; — nmf **le d., la défunte** the deceased, the departed.

dégag/er [degaʒe] vt (lieu, table) to clear (de of); (objet en gage) to redeem; (odeur) to give off; (chaleur) to give out; (responsabilité) to disclaim; (idée, conclusion) to bring out; **d. qn de** (promesse) to release s.o. from; (décombres) to free s.o. from, pull s.o. out of; **cette robe dégage la taille** this dress leaves the waist free and easy; — vi Fb to clear the ball (down the pitch); **d.!** clear the way!; — **se d.** vpr (rue, ciel) to clear; **se d. de** (personne) to release oneself from (promise); to get free from, free oneself from (rubble); **se d. de** (odeur) to issue ou emanate from (vérité, impression) to emerge from. ◆—é a (ciel) clear; (ton, allure) easy-going, casual; (vue) open. ◆—ement nm 1 (action) clearing; redemption; (d'odeur) emanation; (de chaleur) emission; release; freeing; Fb clearance, kick; **itinéraire de d.** Aut relief road. 2 (espace libre) clearing; (de maison) passage.

dégaíner [degene] vti (arme) to draw.

dégarnir [degarnir] vt to clear, empty; (arbre, compte) to strip; — **se d.** vpr (crâne) to go bald; (salle) to clear, empty. ◆—i a

(salle) empty, bare; (tête) balding; **front d.** receding hairline.

dégâts [dega] nmpl damage; **limiter les d.** Fig to prevent matters getting worse.

dégel [deʒɛl] nm thaw. ◆**dégeler** vt to thaw (out); (crédits) to unfreeze; — vi to thaw (out); — v imp to thaw; — **se d.** vpr (personne, situation) to thaw (out).

dégénér/er [deʒenere] vi to degenerate (en into). ◆—é, -ée a & nmf degenerate. ◆**dégénérescence** nf degeneration.

dégingandé [deʒɛ̃gɑ̃de] a gangling, lanky.

dégivrer [deʒivre] vt Aut Av to de-ice; (réfrigérateur) to defrost.

déglingu/er (se) [sədeglɛ̃ge] vpr Fam to fall to bits. ◆—é a falling to bits, in bits.

dégobiller [degɔbije] vt Fam to spew up.

dégonfl/er [degɔ̃fle] vt (pneu etc) to deflate, let down; — **se d.** vpr (flancher) Fam to chicken out, get cold feet. ◆—é, -ée a (pneu) flat; (lâche) Fam chicken, yellow; — nmf Fam yellow belly.

dégorger [degɔrʒe] vi (se déverser) to discharge (dans into); **faire d.** (escargots) Culin to cover with salt.

dégot(t)er [degɔte] vt Fam to find, turn up.

dégouliner [deguline] vi to trickle, drip, run.

dégourd/ir [degurdir] vt (doigts etc) to take the numbness out of; **d. qn** Fig to smarten ou wise s.o. up, sharpen s.o.'s wits; — **se d.** vpr to smarten up, wise up; **se d. les jambes** to stretch one's legs. ◆—i a (malin) smart, sharp.

dégoût [degu] nm disgust; **le d. de** (la vie, les gens etc) disgust for; **avoir un ou du d. pour qch** to have a (strong) dislike ou distaste for sth. ◆**dégoût/er** vt to disgust; **d. qn de qch** to put s.o. off sth; **se d. de** to take a (strong) dislike to, become disgusted with. ◆—ant a disgusting. ◆—é a disgusted; **être d. de** to be sick of ou disgusted with ou by ou at; **elle est partie dégoûtée** she left in disgust; **il n'est pas d.** (difficile) he's not too fussy; **faire le d.** to be fussy.

dégrad/er [degrade] vt 1 (avilir) to degrade; (mur etc) to deface, damage; — **se d.** vpr (s'avilir) to degrade oneself; (édifice, situation) to deteriorate. 2 vt (couleur) to shade off. ◆—ant a degrading. ◆—é nm (de couleur) shading off, gradation. ◆**dégradation** nf (de drogué etc) & Ch degradation; (de situation etc) deterioration; pl (dégâts) damage.

dégrafer [degrafe] vt (vêtement) to unfasten, unhook.

dégraisser [degrese] vt 1 (bœuf) to take the

fat off; (*bouillon*) to skim. **2** (*entreprise*) *Fam* to slim down, trim down the size of (*by laying off workers*).

degré [dəgre] *nm* **1** degree; **enseignement du premier/second d.** primary/secondary education; **au plus haut d.** (*avare etc*) extremely. **2** (*gradin*) Litt step.

dégrever [degrəve] *vt* (*contribuable*) to reduce the tax burden on.

dégriffé [degrife] *a* **vêtement d.** unlabelled designer garment.

dégringoler [degrɛ̃gɔle] *vi* to tumble (down); **faire d. qch** to topple sth over; — *vt* (*escalier*) to rush down. ◆**dégringolade** *nf* tumble.

dégriser [degrize] *vt* **d. qn** to sober s.o. (up).

dégrossir [degrosir] *vt* (*travail*) to rough out; **d. qn** to refine s.o.

déguerpir [degerpir] *vi* to clear off *ou* out.

dégueulasse [degœlas] *a Fam* lousy, disgusting.

dégueuler [degœle] *vi* (*vomir*) *Arg* to puke.

déguis/er [degize] *vt* (*pour tromper*) to disguise; **d. qn en** (*costumer*) to dress s.o. up as, disguise s.o. as; — **se d.** *vpr* to dress oneself up, disguise oneself (**en** as). ◆**—ement** *nm* disguise; (*de bal costumé etc*) fancy dress.

déguster [degyste] **1** *vt* (*goûter*) to taste, sample; (*apprécier*) to relish. **2** *vi* (*subir des coups*) *Fam* to cop it, get a good hiding. ◆**dégustation** *nf* tasting, sampling.

déhancher (se) [sədeɑ̃ʃe] *vpr* (*femme etc*) to sway *ou* wiggle one's hips; (*boiteux*) to walk lop-sided.

dehors [dəɔr] *adv* out(side); (*à l'air*) outdoors, outside; **en d.** on the outside; **en d. de** outside; (*excepté*) apart from; **en d. de la ville/fenêtre** out of town/the window; **au-d. (de), au d. (de)** outside; **déjeuner/jeter/etc d.** to lunch/throw/*etc* out; — *nm* (*extérieur*) outside; *pl* (*aspect*) outward appearance.

déjà [deʒa] *adv* already; **est-il d. parti?** has he left yet *ou* already?; **elle l'a d. vu** she's seen it before, she's already seen it; **c'est d. pas mal** that's not bad at all!; **quand partez-vous, d.?** when are you leaving, again?

déjeuner [deʒœne] *vi* (*à midi*) to (have) lunch; (*le matin*) to (have) breakfast; — *nm* lunch; **petit d.** breakfast.

déjouer [deʒwe] *vt* (*intrigue etc*) to thwart, foil.

déjuger (se) [sədeʒyʒe] *vpr* to go back on one's opinion *ou* decision.

delà [d(ə)la] *adv* **au-d. (de), au d. (de), par-d.,**

par d. beyond; **au-d. du pont/***etc* beyond *ou* past the bridge/*etc*; — *nm* **l'au-d.** the (world) beyond.

délabr/er (se) [sədelabre] *vpr* (*édifice*) to become dilapidated, fall into disrepair; (*santé*) to become impaired. ◆**—ement** *nm* dilapidation, disrepair; impaired state.

délacer [delase] *vt* (*chaussures*) to undo.

délai [dele] *nm* time limit; (*répit, sursis*) extra time, extension; **dans un d. de dix jours** within ten days; **sans d.** without delay; **à bref d.** at short notice; **dans les plus brefs délais** as soon as possible; **dernier d.** final date.

délaisser [delese] *vt* to forsake, desert, abandon; (*négliger*) to neglect.

délass/er [delase] *vt*, — **se d.** *vpr* to relax. ◆**—ement** *nm* relaxation, diversion.

délateur, -trice [delatœr, -tris] *nmf* informer.

délavé [delave] *a* (*tissu, jean*) faded; (*ciel*) watery; (*terre*) waterlogged.

délayer [deleje] *vt* (*mélanger*) to mix (with liquid); (*discours, texte*) *Fig* to pad out, drag out.

delco [dɛlko] *nm Aut* distributor.

délect/er (se) [sədelɛkte] *vpr* **se d. de qch/à faire** to (take) delight in sth/in doing. ◆**—able** *a* delectable. ◆**délectation** *nf* delight.

délégu/er [delege] *vt* to delegate (**à** to). ◆**—é, -ée** *nmf* delegate. ◆**délégation** *nf* delegation.

délest/er [deleste] *vt* *Él* to cut the power from; **d. qn de** (*voler à qn*) *Fam* to relieve s.o. of. ◆**—age** *nm* *Aut* relief; **itinéraire de d.** alternative route (*to relieve congestion*).

délibér/er [delibere] *vi* (*réfléchir*) to deliberate (**sur** upon); (*se consulter*) to confer, deliberate (**de** about). ◆**—é** (*résolu*) determined; (*intentionnel*) deliberate; **de propos d.** deliberately. ◆**—ément** *adv* (*à dessein*) deliberately. ◆**délibération** *nf*

délicat [delika] *a* (*santé, travail etc*) delicate; (*question*) tricky, delicate; (*geste*) tactful; (*conscience*) scrupulous; (*exigeant*) particular. ◆**délicatement** *adv* delicately; tactfully. ◆**délicatesse** *nf* delicacy; tact(fulness); scrupulousness.

délice [delis] *nm* delight; — *nfpl* delights. ◆**délicieux, -euse** *a* (*mets, fruit etc*) delicious; (*endroit, parfum etc*) delightful.

délié [delje] **1** *a* (*esprit*) sharp; (*doigts*) nimble; (*mince*) slender. **2** *nm* (*d'une lettre*) (thin) upstroke.

délier [delje] *vt* to untie, undo; (*langue*) *Fig*

to loosen; **d. qn de** to release s.o. from; — **se d.** *vpr* (*paquet etc*) to come undone *ou* untied.

délimiter [delimite] *vt* to mark off, delimit; (*définir*) to define. ◆**délimitation** *nf* demarcation, delimitation; definition.

délinquant, -ante [delɛ̃kā, -āt] *a* & *nmf* delinquent. ◆**délinquance** *nf* delinquency.

délire [delir] *nm Méd* delirium; (*exaltation*) *Fig* frenzy. ◆**délir/er** *vi Méd* to be delirious; (*dire n'importe quoi*) *Fig* to rave; **d. de** (*joie etc*) to be wild with. ◆**-ant** *a* (*malade*) delirious; (*joie*) frenzied, wild; (*déraisonnable*) utterly absurd.

délit [deli] *nm* offence, misdemeanour.

délivrer [delivre] *vt* **1** (*prisonnier*) to release, deliver; (*ville*) to deliver; **d. qn de** (*souci etc*) to rid s.o. of. **2** (*billet, diplôme etc*) to issue. ◆**délivrance** *nf* release; deliverance; issue; (*soulagement*) relief.

déloger [delɔʒe] *vi* to move out; — *vt* to force *ou* drive out; *Mil* to dislodge.

déloyal, -aux [delwajal, -o] *a* disloyal; (*concurrence*) unfair. ◆**déloyauté** *nf* disloyalty; unfairness; (*action*) disloyal act.

delta [dɛlta] *nm* (*de fleuve*) delta.

deltaplane® [dɛltaplan] *nm* (*engin*) hangglider; **faire du d.** to practise hanggliding.

déluge [delyʒ] *nm* flood; (*de pluie*) downpour; (*de compliments, coups*) shower.

déluré [delyre] *a* (*malin*) smart, sharp; (*fille*) *Péj* brazen.

démagogie [demagɔʒi] *nf* demagogy. ◆**démagogue** *nmf* demagogue.

demain [d(ə)mɛ̃] *adv* tomorrow; **à d.!** see you tomorrow!; **ce n'est pas d. la veille** *Fam* that won't happen for a while yet.

demande [d(ə)mād] *nf* request; (*d'emploi*) application; (*de renseignements*) inquiry; *Écon* demand; (*question*) question; **d. en mariage** proposal (of marriage); **demandes d'emploi** *Journ* situations wanted. ◆**demander** *vt* to ask for; (*emploi*) to apply for; (*autorisation*) to request, ask for; (*charité*) to beg for; (*prix*) to charge; (*nécessiter, exiger*) to require; **d. un nom/le chemin/l'heure** to ask a name/the way/the time; **d. qch à qn** to ask s.o. for sth; **d. à qn de faire** to ask s.o. to do; **d. si/où** to ask *ou* inquire whether/where; **on te demande!** you're wanted!; **ça demande du temps/une heure** it takes time/an hour; **d. en mariage** to propose (marriage) to; — **se d.** *vpr* to wonder, ask oneself (*pourquoi why*, *si if*).

démanger [demāʒe] *vti* to itch; **son bras le** *ou* **lui démange** his arm itches; **ça me démange de ...** *Fig* I'm itching to .... ◆**démangeaison** *nf* itch; **avoir des démangeaisons** to be itching; **j'ai une d. au bras** my arm's itching.

démanteler [demātle] *vt* (*bâtiment*) to demolish; (*organisation*) to break up.

démantibuler [demātibyle] *vt* (*mécanisme etc*) *Fam* to pull to pieces.

démaquill/er (se) [sədemakije] *vpr* to take off one's make-up. ◆**-ant** *nm* make-up remover.

démarcation [demarkasjɔ̃] *nf* demarcation.

démarche [demarʃ] *nf* walk, step, gait; (*de pensée*) process; **faire des démarches** to take the necessary steps (**pour faire** to do).

démarcheur, -euse [demarʃœr, -øz] *nmf Pol* canvasser; *Com* door-to-door salesman *ou* saleswoman.

démarqu/er [demarke] *vt* (*prix*) to mark down; **se d. de** *Fig* to dissociate oneself from.

démarr/er [demare] *vi* (*moteur*) *Aut* to start (up); (*partir*) *Aut* to move *ou* drive off; (*entreprise etc*) *Fig* to get off the ground; — *vt* (*commencer*) *Fam* to start. ◆**-age** *nm* *Aut* start; **d. en côte** hill start. ◆**-eur** *nm* *Aut* starter.

démasquer [demaske] *vt* to unmask.

démêl/er [demele] *vt* to disentangle; (*discerner*) to fathom. ◆**-é** *nm* (*dispute*) squabble; *pl* (*ennuis*) trouble (**avec** with).

démembrer [demābre] *vt* (*pays etc*) to dismember.

déménag/er [demenaʒe] *vi* to move (out), move house; — *vt* (*meubles*) to (re)move. ◆**-ement** *nm* move, moving (house); (*de meubles*) removal, moving (of); **voiture de d.** removal van, *Am* moving van. ◆**-eur** *nm* removal man, *Am* (furniture) mover.

démener (se) [sədemne] *vpr* to fling oneself about; **se d. pour faire** to spare no effort to do.

dément, -ente [demā, -āt] *a* insane; (*génial*) *Iron* fantastic; — *nmf* lunatic. ◆**démence** *nf* insanity. ◆**démentiel, -ielle** *a* insane.

dément/ir [demātir] *vt* (*infirmer*) to belie; (*nouvelle, faits etc*) to deny; **d. qn** to give the lie to s.o. ◆**-i** *nm* denial.

démerder (se) [sədemɛrde] *vpr* (*se débrouiller*) *Arg* to manage (by oneself).

démesure [deməzyr] *nf* excess. ◆**démesuré** *a* excessive, inordinate.

démettre [demɛtr] *vt* **1** (*os*) to dislocate; **d. le pied** to dislocate one's foot. **2 d. qn de**

to dismiss s.o. from; **se d. de ses fonctions** to resign one's office.

demeurant (au) [odəmœrɑ̃] *adv* for all that, after all.

demeure [dəmœr] *nf* **1** dwelling (place), residence. **2 mettre qn en d. de faire** to summon *ou* instruct s.o. to do. ◆**demeur/er** *vi* **1** (*aux* être) (*rester*) to remain; **en d. là** (*affaire etc*) to rest there. **2** (*aux* avoir) (*habiter*) to live, reside. ◆**—é** *a Fam* (mentally) retarded.

demi, -ie [d(ə)mi] *a* half; **d.-journée** half-day; **une heure et demie** an hour and a half; (*horloge*) half past one; *– adv* (à) **d. plein** half-full; **à d. nu** half-naked; **ouvrir à d.** to open halfway; **faire les choses à d.** to do things by halves; *– nmf* (*moitié*) half; *– nm* (*verre*) (half-pint) glass of beer; *Fb* half-back; *– nf* (à *l'horloge*) half-hour.

demi-cercle [d(ə)misɛrkl] *nm* semicircle. ◆**d.-douzaine** *nf* **une d.-douzaine** (de) a half-dozen, half a dozen. ◆**d.-finale** *nf Sp* semifinal. ◆**d.-frère** *nm* stepbrother. ◆**d.-heure** *nf* **une d.-heure** a half-hour, half an hour. ◆**d.-mesure** *nf* half-measure. ◆**d.-mot** *nm* **tu comprendras à d.-mot** you'll understand without my having to spell it out. ◆**d.-pension** *nf* half-board. ◆**d.-pensionnaire** *nmf* day boarder, *Am* day student. ◆**d.-saison** *nf* **de d.-saison** (*vêtement*) between seasons. ◆**d.-sel** *a inv* (*beurre*) slightly salted; (*fromage*) ◆**d.-sel** cream cheese. ◆**d.-sœur** *nf* stepsister. ◆**d.-tarif** *nm & a inv* (*billet*) (à) **d.-tarif** half-price. ◆**d.-tour** *nm* about turn, *Am* about face; *Aut* U-turn; **faire d.-tour** to turn back.

démission [demisjɔ̃] *nf* resignation. ◆**démissionnaire** *a* (*ministre etc*) outgoing. ◆**démissionner** *vi* to resign.

démobiliser [demɔbilize] *vt* to demobilize. ◆**démobilisation** *nf* demobilization.

démocrate [demɔkrat] *nmf* democrat; *– a* democratic. ◆**démocratie** [-asi] *nf* democracy. ◆**démocratique** *a* democratic.

démod/er (se) [sədemɔde] *vpr* to go out of fashion. ◆**—é** *a* old-fashioned.

démographie [demɔgrafi] *nf* demography.

demoiselle [d(ə)mwazɛl] *nf* (*célibataire*) spinster, single woman; (*jeune fille*) young lady; **d. d'honneur** (à *un mariage*) bridesmaid; (*de reine*) maid of honour.

démolir [demɔlir] *vt* (*maison, jouet etc*) to demolish; (*projet etc*) to shatter; **d. qn** (*battre, discréditer*) *Fam* to tear s.o. to

pieces. ◆**démolition** *nf* demolition; **en d.** being demolished.

démon [demɔ̃] *nm* demon; **petit d.** (*enfant*) little devil. ◆**démoniaque** *a* devilish, fiendish.

démonstrateur, -trice [demɔ̃stratœr, -tris] *nmf* (*dans un magasin etc*) demonstrator. ◆**démonstratif, -ive** *a* demonstrative. ◆**démonstration** *nf* demonstration; **d. de force** show of force.

démonter [demɔ̃te] *vt* (*assemblage*) to dismantle, take apart; (*installation*) to take down; **d. qn** (*troubler*) *Fig* to disconcert s.o.; **une mer démontée** a stormy sea; **— se d.** *vpr* to come apart; (*installation*) to come down; (*personne*) to be put out *ou* disconcerted.

démontrer [demɔ̃tre] *vt* to demonstrate, show.

démoraliser [demɔralize] *vt* to demoralize; **— se d.** *vpr* to become demoralized. ◆**démoralisation** *nf* demoralization.

démordre [demɔrdr] *vi* **il ne démordra pas de** (*son opinion etc*) he won't budge from.

démouler [demule] *vt* (*gâteau*) to turn out (*from its mould*).

démunir [demynir] *vt* **d. qn de** to deprive s.o. of; **se d. de** to part with.

démystifier [demistifje] *vt* (*public etc*) to disabuse; (*idée etc*) to debunk.

dénationaliser [denasjɔnalize] *vt* to denationalize.

dénatur/er [denatyre] *vt* (*propos, faits etc*) to misrepresent, distort. ◆**—é** *a* (*goût, père etc*) unnatural.

dénégation [denegasjɔ̃] *nf* denial.

déneiger [deneʒe] *vt* to clear of snow.

dénicher [denife] *vt* (*trouver*) to dig up, turn up; (*ennemi, fugitif*) to hunt out, flush out.

dénier [denje] *vt* to deny; (*responsabilité*) to disclaim, deny; **d. qch à qn** to deny s.o. sth.

dénigr/er [denigre] *vt* to denigrate, disparage. ◆**—ement** *nm* denigration, disparagement.

dénivellation [denivelasjɔ̃] *nf* unevenness; (*pente*) gradient; *pl* (*accidents*) bumps.

dénombrer [denɔ̃bre] *vt* to count, number.

dénomm/er [denɔme] *vt* to name. ◆**—é, -ée** *nmf* **un d. Dupont** a man named Dupont. ◆**dénomination** *nf* designation, name.

dénonc/er [denɔ̃se] *vt* (*injustice etc*) to denounce (à qn to); **d. qn** to inform on s.o., denounce s.o. (à to); *Scol* to tell on s.o. (à to); **— se d.** *vpr* to give oneself up (à to). ◆**dénonciateur, -trice** *nmf* informer. ◆**dénonciation** *nf* denunciation.

dénoter [denɔte] vt to denote.

dénouer [denwe] vt (nœud, corde) to undo, untie; (cheveux) to undo; (situation, intrigue) to unravel; (problème, crise) to clear up; **— se d.** vpr (nœud) to come undone ou untied; (cheveux) to come undone. ◆**dénouement** nm outcome, ending; Th dénouement.

dénoyauter [denwajote] vt (prune etc) to stone, Am to pit.

denrée [dɑ̃re] nf food(stuff); **denrées alimentaires** foodstuffs.

dense [dɑ̃s] a dense. ◆**densité** nf density.

dent [dɑ̃] nf tooth; (de roue) cog; (de fourche) prong; (de timbre-poste) perforation; **d. de sagesse** wisdom tooth; **rien à se mettre sous la d.** nothing to eat; **manger à belles dents/du bout des dents** to eat whole-heartedly/half-heartedly; **faire ses dents** (enfant) to be teething; **coup de d.** bite; **sur les dents** (surmené) exhausted; (énervé) on edge; **avoir une d. contre qn** to have it in for s.o. ◆**dentaire** a dental. ◆**dentée** af **roue d.** cogwheel. ◆**dentier** nm denture(s), (set of) false teeth. ◆**dentifrice** nm toothpaste. ◆**dentiste** nmf dentist; **chirurgien d.** dental surgeon. ◆**dentition** nf (dents) (set of) teeth.

dentelé [dɑ̃tle] a (côte) jagged; (feuille) serrated. ◆**dentelure** nf jagged outline ou edge.

dentelle [dɑ̃tɛl] nf lace.

dénud/er [denyde] vt to (lay) bare. ◆**—é** a bare.

dénué [denɥe] a **d. de** devoid of, without.

dénuement [denymɑ̃] nm destitution; **dans le d.** poverty-stricken.

déodorant [deɔdɔrɑ̃] nm deodorant.

dépann/er [depane] vt (mécanisme) to get going (again), repair; **d. qn** Fam to help s.o. out. ◆**—age** nm (emergency) repair; **voiture/service de d.** breakdown vehicle/service. ◆**—eur** nm repairman; Aut breakdown mechanic. ◆**—euse** nf (voiture) Aut breakdown lorry, Am wrecker, tow truck.

dépareillé [depareje] a (chaussure etc) odd, not matching; (collection) incomplete.

déparer [depare] vt to mar, spoil.

départ [depar] nm departure; (début) start, beginning; Sp start; **point/ligne de d.** starting point/post; **au d.** at the outset, at the start; **au d. de Paris/etc** (excursion etc) departing from Paris/etc.

départager [departaʒe] vt (concurrents) to decide between; **d. les votes** to give the casting vote.

département [departəmɑ̃] nm department.

◆**départemental, -aux** a departmental; **route départementale** secondary road.

départir (se) [sədepartir] vpr **se d. de** (attitude) to depart from, abandon.

dépass/er [depase] vt (durée, attente etc) to go beyond, exceed; (endroit) to go past, go beyond; (véhicule, bicyclette etc) to overtake, pass; (pouvoir) to go beyond, overstep; **d. qn** (en hauteur) to be taller than s.o.; (surclasser) to be ahead of s.o.; pass. **dépasse** Fig that's (quite) beyond me; **—** (jupon, clou etc) to stick out, show. ◆**—é** a (démodé) outdated; (incapable) unable to cope. ◆**—ement** nm Aut overtaking, passing.

dépays/er [depeize] vt to disorientate, Am disorient. ◆**—ement** nm disorientation; (changement) change of scenery.

dépecer [depase] vt (animal) to cut up, carve up.

dépêche [depɛʃ] nf telegram; (diplomatique) dispatch. ◆**dépêcher** vt to dispatch; **— se d.** vpr to hurry (up).

dépeign/er [depene] vt **d. qn** to make s.o.'s hair untidy. ◆**—é** a **être d.** to have untidy hair; **sortir d.** to go out with untidy hair.

dépeindre* [depɛ̃dr] vt to depict, describe.

dépenaillé [depɑ̃naje] a in tatters ou rags.

dépend/re [depɑ̃dr] 1 vi to depend (de on); **d. de** (appartenir à) to belong to; (être soumis à) to be dependent on; **ça dépend de toi** that depends on you, that's up to you. 2 vt (décrocher) to take down. ◆**—ant** a dependent (de on). ◆**dépendance** nf dependence; **sous la d. de qn** under s.o.'s domination. 2 nfpl (bâtiments) outbuildings.

dépens [depɑ̃] nmpl Jur costs; **aux d. de** at the expense of; **apprendre à ses d.** to learn to one's cost.

dépense [depɑ̃s] nf (action) spending; (frais) expense, expenditure; (d'électricité etc) consumption; (physique) exertion. ◆**dépenser** vt (argent) to spend; (électricité etc) to use; (forces) to exert; (énergie) to expend; **— se d.** vpr to exert oneself. ◆**dépensier, -ière** a wasteful, extravagant.

déperdition [deperdisjɔ̃] nf (de chaleur etc) loss.

dépér/ir [deperir] vi (personne) to waste away; (plante) to wither; (santé etc) to decline. ◆**—issement** nm (baisse) decline.

dépêtrer [depetre] vt to extricate; **— se d.** vpr to extricate oneself (**de** from).

dépeupl/er [depœple] vt to depopulate. ◆**—ement** nm depopulation.

dépilatoire [depilatwar] nm hair-remover.

dépist/er [depiste] vt (criminel etc) to track down; (maladie, fraude) to detect. ◆**—age** nm Méd detection.

dépit [depi] nm resentment, chagrin; **en d.** in spite of. ◆**dépiter** vt to vex, chagrin; **— se d.** vpr to feel resentment ou chagrin.

déplac/er [deplase] vt to shift, move; (fonctionnaire) to transfer; **— se d.** vpr to move (about); (voyager) to get about, travel (about). ◆**—é** a (mal à propos) out of place; **personne déplacée** (réfugié) displaced person. ◆**—ement** nm (voyage) (business ou professional) trip; (d'ouragan, de troupes) movement; **les déplacements** (voyages) travel(ling); **frais de d.** travelling expenses.

déplaire* [depler] vi **d. à qn** to displease s.o.; **cet aliment lui déplaît** he ou she dislikes this food; **n'en déplaise à l'on** with all due respect to; **– v imp il me déplaît de faire** I dislike doing, it displeases me to do; **— se d.** vpr to dislike it. ◆**déplaisant** a unpleasant, displeasing. ◆**déplaisir** nm displeasure.

dépli/er [deplije] vt to open out, unfold. ◆**—ant** nm (prospectus) leaflet.

déplor/er [deplɔre] vt (regretter) to deplore; (la mort de qn) to mourn (over), lament (over); **d. qn** to mourn (for) s.o.; **d. que** (+ sub) to deplore the fact that, regret that). ◆**—able** a deplorable, lamentable.

déployer [deplwaje] vt (ailes) to spread; (journal, carte) to unfold, spread (out); (objets, courage etc) to display; (troupes) to deploy; **— se d.** vpr (drapeau) to unfurl. ◆**déploiement** nm (démonstration) display; Mil deployment.

dépoli [depɔli] a **verre d.** frosted glass.

déport/er [depɔrte] vt **1** (exiler) Hist to deport (to a penal colony); (dans un camp de concentration) Hist to send to a concentration camp, deport. **2** (dévier) to veer ou carry (off course). ◆**—é, -ée** nmf deportee; (concentration camp) inmate. ◆**déportation** nf deportation; internment (in a concentration camp).

dépos/er [depoze] vt (poser) to put down; (laisser) to leave; (argent, lie) to deposit; (plainte) to lodge; (armes) to lay down; (gerbe) to lay; (ordures) to dump; (marque de fabrique) to register; (projet de loi) to introduce; (souverain) to depose; **d. qn** Aut to drop s.o (off), put s.o. off; **d. son bilan** Fin to go into liquidation, file for bankruptcy; **– vi** Jur to testify; (liquide) to leave a deposit; **— se d.** vpr (poussière, lie) to

settle. ◆**dépositaire** nmf Fin agent; (de secret) custodian. ◆**déposition** nf Jur statement; (de souverain) deposing.

déposséder [deposede] vt to deprive, dispossess (**de** of).

dépôt [depo] nm (d'ordures etc) dumping, (lieu) dump; (de gerbe) laying; (d'autobus, de trains) depot; (entrepôt) warehouse; (argent) deposit; (de vin) deposit, sediment; **d. (calcaire)** (de chaudière etc) deposit; **laisser qch à qn en d.** to give s.o. sth for safekeeping ou in trust.

dépotoir [depɔtwar] nm rubbish dump, Am garbage dump.

dépouille [depuj] nf hide, skin; (de serpent) slough; pl (butin) spoils; **d. (mortelle)** mortal remains. ◆**dépouill/er** vt (animal) to skin, flay; (analyser) to go through, analyse; **d. de** (dégarnir) to strip of; (déposséder) to deprive of; **se d. de** to rid ou divest oneself of, cast off; **d. un scrutin** to count votes. ◆**—é** a (arbre) bare; (style) austere, spare; **d. de** bereft of. ◆**—ement** nm (de document etc) analysis; (privation) deprivation; (sobriété) austerity; **d. du scrutin** counting of the votes.

dépourvu [depurvy] a **d. de** devoid of; **prendre qn au d.** to catch s.o. unawares ou off his guard.

dépraver [deprave] vt to deprave. ◆**dépravation** nf depravity.

déprécier [depresje] vt (dénigrer) to disparage; (monnaie, immeuble etc) to depreciate; **— se d.** vpr (baisser) to depreciate, lose (its) value. ◆**dépréciation** nf depreciation.

déprédations [depredasjɔ̃] nfpl damage, ravages.

dépression [depresjɔ̃] nf depression; **zone de d.** trough of low pressure; **d. nerveuse** nervous breakdown; **d. économique** slump. ◆**dépressif, -ive** a depressive. ◆**déprime** nf la d. (dépression) Fam the blues. ◆**déprim/er** vt to depress. ◆**—é** a depressed.

depuis [dəpɥi] prép since; **d. lundi** since Monday; **d. qu'elle est partie** since she left; **j'habite ici d. un mois** I've been living here for a month; **d. quand êtes-vous là?** how long have you been here?; **d. peu/longtemps** for a short/long time; **d. Paris jusqu'à Londres** from Paris to London; **– adv** since (then), ever since.

députation [depytasjɔ̃] nf (groupe) deputation, delegation; **candidat à la d.** parliamentary candidate. ◆**député** nm dele-

gate, deputy; (*au parlement*) deputy, = *Br*
MP, = *Am* congressman, congresswoman.

déracin/er [derasine] *vt* (*personne, arbre
etc*) to uproot; (*préjugés etc*) to eradicate,
root out. ◆**—ement** *nm* uprooting; eradi-
cation.

déraill/er [deraje] *vi* **1** (*train*) to jump the
rails, be derailed; **faire d.** to derail. **2**
(*divaguer*) *Fam* to drivel, talk through one's
hat. ◆**—ement** *nm* (*de train*) derailment.
◆**—eur** *nm* (*de bicyclette*) derailleur (gear
change).

déraisonnable [derezɔnabl] *a* unreasonable. ◆**déraisonner** *vi* to talk nonsense.

dérang/er [derɑ̃ʒe] *vt* (*affaires*) to disturb,
upset; (*estomac*) to upset; (*projets etc*) to mess
up, upset; (*vêtements*) to mess up; (*cerveau,
esprit*) to derange; **d. qn** to disturb *ou*
bother *ou* trouble s.o.; **je viendrai si ça ne te
dérange pas** I'll come if that doesn't put
you out *ou* if that's not imposing; **ça vous
dérange si je fume?** do you mind if I
smoke?; **— se d.** *vpr* to put oneself to a lot
of trouble (**pour faire** to do), (*se déplacer*) to
move; **ne te dérange pas!** don't trouble
yourself!, don't bother! ◆**—ement** *nm*
(*gêne*) bother, inconvenience; (*désordre*)
disorder; **en d.** (*téléphone etc*) out of order.

dérap/er [derape] *vi* to skid. ◆**—age** *nm*
skid; (*des prix, de l'inflation*) *Fig* loss of
control (**de** over).

dératé [derate] *nm* **courir comme un d.** to
run like mad.

dérégl/er [deregle] *vt* (*mécanisme*) to put
out of order; (*estomac, habitudes*) to upset;
(*esprit*) to unsettle; **— se d.** *vpr* (*montre,
appareil*) to go wrong. ◆**—é** *a* out of
order; (*vie, mœurs*) dissolute, wild; (*imagination*) wild. ◆**dérèglement** *nm* (*de
mécanisme*) breakdown; (*d'esprit*) disorder; (*d'estomac*) upset.

dérider [deride] *vt*, **— se d.** *vpr* to cheer up.

dérision [derizjɔ̃] *nf* derision, mockery;
tourner en d. to mock, deride; **par d.** deri-
sively; **de d.** derisive. ◆**dérisoire** *a* ridiculous, derisory, derisive.

dérive [deriv] *nf Nau* drift; **partir à la d.**
(*navire*) to drift out to sea; **aller à la d.**
(*navire*) to drift *ou* to go adrift; (*entreprise etc*) *Fig* to
drift (towards ruin). ◆**dériv/er** *vi Nau Av*
to drift; **d. de** (*venir*) to derive from, be
derived from; *— vt* (*cours d'eau*) to divert;
Ling to derive (**from** from). ◆**—é** *nm Ling Ch*
derivative; (*produit*) by-product. ◆**dériv-
atif** *nm* distraction (**à** from). ◆**dérivation** *nf* (*de cours d'eau*) diversion; *Ling*
derivation; (*déviation routière*) bypass.

dermatologie [dermatɔlɔʒi] *nf* dermatology.

dernier -ière [dernje, -jɛr] *a* last; (*nouvelles,
mode*) latest; (*étage*) top; (*degré*) highest;
(*qualité*) lowest; **le d. rang** the back *ou* last
row; **ces derniers mois** these past few
months, these last *ou* final months; **de la
dernière importance** of the utmost importance; **en d.** last; *– nmf* last (person *ou* last
one); **ce d.** (*de deux*) the latter; (*de
plusieurs*) the last-mentioned; **être le d. de
la classe** to be (at) the bottom of the class;
le d. des derniers the lowest of the low; **le d.
de mes soucis** the least of my worries.
◆**d.-né**, ◆**dernière-née** *nmf* youngest
(child). ◆**dernièrement** *adv* recently.

dérob/er [derɔbe] *vt* (*voler*) to steal (**à**
from); (*cacher*) to hide (**à** from); **— se d.**
vpr to get out of one's obligations;
(*s'éloigner*) to slip away; (*éviter de répondre*) to dodge the issue; **se d. à** (*obligations*)
to shirk, get out of; (*regards*) to hide from;
ses jambes se sont dérobées sous lui his legs
gave way beneath him. ◆**—é** *a* (*porte etc*)
hidden, secret; **à la dérobée** on the sly,
stealthily. ◆**dérobade** *nf* dodge, evasion.

déroger [derɔʒe] *vi* **d. à une règle/**etc to
depart from a rule/etc. ◆**dérogation** *nf*
exemption, (special) dispensation.

dérouiller [deruje] *vt* **d. qn** (*battre*) *Arg* to
thrash *ou* thump s.o.; **se d. les jambes** *Fam*
to stretch one's legs.

dérouler [derule] *vt* (*carte etc*) to unroll;
(*film*) to unwind; **— se d.** *vpr* (*événement*)
to take place, pass off; (*paysage, souvenirs*)
to unfold; (*récit*) to develop. ◆**—ement**
nm (*d'une action*) unfolding, development;
(*cours*) course;

dérouter [derute] *vt* (*avion, navire*) to divert,
reroute; (*candidat etc*) to baffle; (*poursuivant*) to throw off the scent.

derrick [derik] *nm* derrick.

derrière [derjɛr] *prep & adv* behind; **d. moi**
behind me, *Am* in back of me; **assis d.**
(*dans une voiture*) sitting in the back; **d.**
(*roue*) back, rear; (*pattes*) hind; **par d.**
(*attaquer*) from behind, from the rear; *–
nm* (*de maison etc*) back, rear; (*fesses*)
behind, bottom.

des [de] *voir* **le** [1, 2].

dès [dɛ] *prep* from; **d. cette époque** (as) from
that time, from that time on; **d. le début**
(right) from the start; **d. son enfance** since
ou from (his *ou* her) childhood; **d. le**

sixième siècle as early as *ou* as far back as the sixth century; **d. l'aube** at (the crack of) dawn; **d. qu'elle viendra** as soon as she comes.

désabusé [dezabyze] *a* disenchanted, disillusioned.

désaccord [dezakɔr] *nm* disagreement. ◆**désaccordé** *a Mus* out of tune.

désaccoutumer (se) [sǝdezakutyme] *vpr* **se d. de** to lose the habit of.

désaffecté [dezafɛkte] *a (école etc)* disused.

désaffection [dezafɛksjɔ̃] *nf* loss of affection, disaffection (**pour** for).

désagréable [dezagreabl] *a* unpleasant, disagreeable. ◆**-ment** [-ǝmɑ̃] *adv* unpleasantly.

désagréger [dezagreʒe] *vt,* **— se d.** *vpr* to disintegrate, break up. ◆**désagrégation** *nf* disintegration.

désagrément [dezagremɑ̃] *nm* annoyance, trouble.

désaltérer [dezaltere] *vt* **d. qn** to quench s.o.'s thirst; **se d.** to quench one's thirst. ◆**-ant** a thirst-quenching.

désamorcer [dezamɔrse] *vt (obus, situation)* to defuse.

désappointer [dezapwɛte] *vt* to disappoint.

désapprouver [dezapruve] *vt* to disapprove of; **–** *vi* to disapprove. ◆**désapprobateur, -trice** *a* disapproving. ◆**désapprobation** *nf* disapproval.

désarçonner [dezarsɔne] *vt (jockey)* to throw, unseat; *(déconcerter) Fig* to nonpluss, throw.

désarmer [dezarme] *vt (émouvoir) & Mil* to disarm; **–** *vi Mil* to disarm; *(céder)* to let up. ◆**-ant** *a (charme etc)* disarming. ◆**-é** *a (sans défense)* unarmed; *Fig* helpless. ◆**-ement** *nm (de nation)* disarmament.

désarroi [dezarwa] *nm (angoisse)* distress.

désarticuler [dezartikyle] *vt (membre)* to dislocate.

désastre [dezastr] *nm* disaster. ◆**désastreux, -euse** *a* disastrous.

désavantage [dezavɑ̃taʒ] *nm* disadvantage, handicap; *(inconvénient)* drawback, disadvantage. ◆**désavantager** *vt* to put at a disadvantage, handicap. ◆**désavantageux, -euse** *a* disadvantageous.

désaveu, -x [dezavø] *nm* repudiation. ◆**désavouer** *vt (livre, personne etc)* to disown, repudiate.

désaxé, -ée [dezakse] *a & nmf* unbalanced (person).

desceller [desele] *vt (pierre etc)* to loosen; **— se d.** *vpr* to come loose.

descendre [desɑ̃dr] *vi (aux être)* to come *ou* go down, descend **(de** from); *(d'un train etc)* to get off *ou* out, alight **(de** from); *(d'un arbre)* to climb down **(de** from); *(nuit, thermomètre)* to fall; *(marée)* to go out; **d. à** *(une bassesse)* to stoop to; **d. à l'hôtel** to put up at a hotel; **d. de** *(être issu de)* to be descended from; **d. de cheval** to dismount; **d. en courant/flânant**/*etc* to run/stroll/*etc* down; **–** *vt (aux avoir) (escalier etc)* to come *ou* go down, descend; *(objets)* to bring *ou* take down; *(avion)* to bring *ou* shoot down; **d. qn** *(tuer) Fam* to bump s.o. off. ◆**-ant, -ante 1** *a* descending; *(marée)* outgoing. **2** *nmf (personne)* descendant. ◆**descendance** *nf (enfants)* descendants; *(origine)* descent.

descente [desɑ̃t] *nf (action)* descent; *(irruption)* raid **(dans** upon); *(en parachute)* drop; *(pente)* slope; **la d. des bagages** bringing *ou* taking down the luggage; **il fut accueilli à sa d. d'avion** he was met as he got off the plane; **d. à skis** downhill run; **d. de lit** *(tapis)* bedside rug.

descriptif, -ive [dɛskriptif, -iv] *a* descriptive. ◆**description** *nf* description.

déségrégation [desegregasjɔ̃] *nf* desegregation.

désemparé [dezɑ̃pare] *a* distraught, at a loss; *(navire)* crippled.

désemplir [dezɑ̃plir] *vi* **ce magasin**/*etc* **ne désemplit pas** this shop/*etc* is always crowded.

désenchant/er [dezɑ̃ʃɑ̃te] *vt* to disenchant. ◆**-ement** *nm* disenchantment.

désencombrer [dezɑ̃kɔ̃bre] *vt (passage etc)* to clear.

désenfler [dezɑ̃fle] *vi* to go down, become less swollen.

déséquilibre [dezekilibr] *nm (inégalité)* imbalance; *(mental)* unbalance; **en d.** *(meuble etc)* unsteady. ◆**déséquilibrer** *vt* to throw off balance; *(esprit, personne) Fig* to unbalance.

désert [dezɛr] *a* deserted; **île déserte** desert island; **–** *nm* desert, wilderness. ◆**désertique** *a (région etc)* desert-.

déserter [dezɛrte] *vti* to desert. ◆**déserteur** *nm Mil* deserter. ◆**désertion** *nf* desertion.

désespér/er [dezɛspere] *vi* to despair **(de** of); **–** *vt* to drive to despair; **— se d.** *vpr* to (be in) despair. ◆**-ant** *a (enfant etc)* that drives one to despair, hopeless. ◆**-é, -ée** *a (personne)* in despair, despairing; *(cas, situation)* desperate, hopeless; *(efforts, cris)* desperate; **–** *nmf (suicidé)* person driven to despair *ou* desperation. ◆—**ément** *adv* desperately. ◆**désespoir** *nm* despair; **au d.** in despair; **en d. de cause** in desperation, as a (desperate) last resort.

déshabiller [dezabije] *vt* to undress, strip; — **se d.** *vpr* to get undressed, undress.

déshabituer [dezabitɥe] *vt* **d. qn de** to break s.o. of the habit of.

désherb/er [dezɛrbe] *vti* to weed. ◆—**ant** *nm* weed killer.

déshérit/er [dezerite] *vt* to disinherit. ◆—**é** *a* (*pauvre*) underprivileged; (*laid*) ill-favoured.

déshonneur [dezɔnœr] *nm* dishonour, disgrace. ◆**déshonor/er** *vt* to disgrace, dishonour. ◆—**ant** *a* dishonourable.

déshydrater [dezidrate] *vt* to dehydrate; — **se d.** *vpr* to become dehydrated.

désigner [deziɲe] *vt* (*montrer*) to point to, point out; (*élire*) to appoint, designate; (*signifier*) to indicate, designate; **ses qualités le désignent pour** his qualities mark him out for. ◆**désignation** *nf* designation.

désillusion [dezilyzjɔ̃] *nf* disillusion(ment). ◆**désillusionner** *vt* to disillusion.

désincarné [dezɛ̃karne] *a* (*esprit*) disembodied.

désinence [dezinɑ̃s] *nf Gram* ending.

désinfect/er [dezɛ̃fɛkte] *vt* to disinfect. ◆—**ant** *nm* & *a* disinfectant. ◆**désinfection** *nf* disinfection.

désinformation [dezɛ̃fɔrmasjɔ̃] *nf Pol* misinformation.

désintégrer (se) [sədezɛ̃tegre] *vpr* to disintegrate. ◆**désintégration** *nf* disintegration.

désintéress/er (se) [sədezɛ̃terese] *vpr* **se d. de** to lose interest in, take no further interest in. ◆—**é** *a* (*altruiste*) disinterested. ◆—**ement** [-ɛsmɑ̃] *nm* (*altruisme*) disinterestedness. ◆**désintérêt** *nm* lack of interest.

désintoxiquer [dezɛ̃tɔksike] *vt* (*alcoolique, drogué*) to cure.

désinvolte [dezɛ̃vɔlt] *a* (*dégagé*) easy-going, casual; (*insolent*) offhand, casual. ◆**désinvolture** *nf* casualness; offhandedness.

désir [dezir] *nm* desire, wish. ◆**désirable** *a* desirable. ◆**désirer** *vt* to want, desire; (*convoiter*) to desire; **je désire venir** I would like to come, I wish *ou* want to come; **je désire que tu viennes** I want you to come; **ça laisse à d.** it leaves something *ou* a lot to be desired. ◆**désireux, -euse** *a* **d. de faire** anxious *ou* eager to do, desirous of doing.

désist/er (se) [sədeziste] *vpr* (*candidat etc*) to withdraw. ◆—**ement** *nm* withdrawal.

désobé/ir [dezɔbeir] *vi* to disobey; **d. à qn** to disobey s.o. ◆—**issant** *a* disobedient. ◆**désobéissance** *nf* disobedience (à to).

désobligeant [dezɔbliʒɑ̃] *a* disagreeable, unkind.

désodorisant [dezɔdɔrizɑ̃] *nm* air freshener.

désœuvré [dezœvre] *a* idle, unoccupied. ◆**désœuvrement** *nm* idleness.

désol/er [dezɔle] *vt* to distress, upset (very much); — **se d.** *vpr* to be distressed *ou* upset (**de** at). ◆—**ant** *a* distressing, upsetting. ◆—**é** *a* (*région*) desolate; (*affligé*) distressed; **être d.** (*navré*) to be sorry (**que** (+ *sub*) that, **de faire** to do). ◆**désolation** *nf* (*peine*) distress, grief.

désolidariser (se) [sədesɔlidarize] *vpr* to dissociate oneself (**de** from).

désopilant [dezɔpilɑ̃] *a* hilarious, screamingly funny.

désordre [dezɔrdr] *nm* (*de papiers, affaires, idées*) mess, muddle, disorder; (*de cheveux, pièce*) untidiness; *Méd* disorder; *pl* (*émeutes*) disorder, unrest; **en d.** untidy, messy. ◆**désordonné** *a* (*personne, chambre*) untidy, messy.

désorganiser [dezɔrganize] *vt* to disorganize. ◆**désorganisation** *nf* disorganization.

désorienter [dezɔrjɑ̃te] *vt* **d. qn** to disorientate *ou Am* disorient s.o., make s.o. lose his bearings; (*déconcerter*) to bewilder s.o. ◆**désorientation** *nf* disorientation.

désormais [dezɔrmɛ] *adv* from now on, in future, henceforth.

désosser [dezɔse] *vt* (*viande*) to bone.

despote [dɛspɔt] *nm* despot. ◆**despotique** *a* despotic. ◆**despotisme** *nm* despotism.

desquels, desquelles [dekɛl] *voir* lequel.

dessaisir (se) [sədesezir] *vpr* **se d. de qch** to part with sth, relinquish sth.

dessaler [desale] *vt* (*poisson etc*) to remove the salt from (*by smoking*).

dessécher [deseʃe] *vt* (*végétation*) to dry up, wither; (*gorge, bouche*) to dry, parch; (*fruits*) to desiccate, dry; (*cœur*) to harden; — **se d.** *vpr* (*plante*) to wither, dry up; (*peau*) to dry (up), get dry; (*maigrir*) to waste away.

dessein [desɛ̃] *nm* aim, design; **dans le d. de faire** with the aim of doing; **à d.** intentionally.

desserrer [desere] *vt* (*ceinture etc*) to loosen, slacken; (*poing*) to open, unclench;

(*frein*) to release; **il n'a pas desserré les dents** he didn't open his mouth; **— se d.** *vpr* to come loose.

dessert [desɛr] *nm* dessert, sweet.

desserte [desɛrt] *nf* **assurer la d. de** (*village etc*) to provide a (bus *ou* train) service to. ◆**desservir** *vt* **1** (*table*) to clear (away). **2 d. qn** to harm s.o., do s.o. a disservice. **3 l'autobus/etc dessert ce village** the bus/*etc* provides a service to *ou* stops at this village; **ce quartier est bien desservi** this district is well served by public transport.

dessin [desɛ̃] *nm* drawing; (*rapide*) sketch; (*motif*) design, pattern; (*contour*) outline; **d. animé** *Cin* cartoon; **d. humoristique** *Journ* cartoon; **école de d.** art school; **planche à d.** drawing board. ◆**dessinateur, -trice** *nmf* drawer; sketcher; **d. humoristique** cartoonist; **d. de modes** dress designer; **d. industriel** draughtsman, *Am* draftsman. ◆**dessiner** *vt* to draw; (*rapidement*) to sketch; (*meuble, robe etc*) to design; (*indiquer*) to outline, trace; **d. (bien) la taille** (*vêtement*) to show off the figure; **— se d.** *vpr* (*colline etc*) to stand out, be outlined; (*projet*) to take shape.

dessoûler [desule] *vti Fam* to sober up.

dessous [d(ə)su] *adv* under(neath), beneath, below; **en d.** (*sous*) under(neath); (*agir*) *Fig* in an underhand way; **vêtement de d.** undergarment; **drap de d.** bottom sheet; **— *nm*** underneath; *pl* (*vêtements*) underclothes; **d. de table** backhander, bribe; **les gens du d.** the people downstairs *ou* below; **avoir le d.** to be defeated, get the worst of it. ◆**d.-de-plat** *nm inv* table mat.

dessus [d(ə)sy] *adv* (*marcher, écrire*) on it; (*monter*) on top (of it), on it; (*lancer, passer*) over it; **de d. la table** off *ou* from the table; **vêtement de d.** outer garment; **drap de d.** top sheet; **par-d.** (*sauter etc*) over (it); **par-d. tout** above all; **— *nm*** top; (*de chaussure*) upper; **avoir le d.** to have the upper hand, get the best of it; **les gens du d.** the people upstairs *ou* above. ◆**d.-de-lit** *nm inv* bedspread.

déstabiliser [destabilize] *vt* to destabilize.

destin [destɛ̃] *nm* fate, destiny. ◆**destinée** *nf* fate, destiny (*of an individual*).

destin/er [destine] *vt* **d. qch à qn** to intend *ou* mean sth for s.o.; **d. qn à** (*carrière, fonction*) to intend *ou* destine s.o. for; **se d. à** (*carrière etc*) to intend *ou* mean to take up; **destiné à mourir/etc** (*condamné*) destined *ou* fated to die/*etc*. ◆**destinataire** *nmf* addressee. ◆**destination** *nf* (*usage*)

purpose; (*lieu*) destination; **à d. de** (*train etc*) (going) to, (bound) for.

destituer [destitɥe] *vt* (*fonctionnaire etc*) to dismiss (from office). ◆**destitution** *nf* dismissal.

destructeur, -trice [destryktœr, -tris] *a* destructive; **— *nmf*** (*personne*) destroyer. ◆**destructif, -ive** *a* destructive. ◆**destruction** *nf* destruction.

désuet, -ète [desɥɛ, -ɛt] *a* antiquated, obsolete.

désunir [dezynir] *vt* (*famille etc*) to divide, disunite. ◆**désunion** *nf* disunity, dissension.

détach/er[1] [detaʃe] *vt* (*ceinture, vêtement*) to undo; (*nœud*) to untie, undo; (*personne, mains*) to untie; (*ôter*) to take off, detach; (*mots*) to pronounce clearly; **d. qn** (*libérer*) to let s.o. loose; (*affecter*) to transfer s.o. (on assignment) (**à** to); **d. les yeux de qn/qch** to take one's eyes off s.o./sth; **— se d.** *vpr* (*chien, prisonnier*) to break loose; (*se dénouer*) to come undone; **se d.** (**de qch**) (*fragment*) to come off (sth); **se d.** (**de amis**) to break away from, grow apart from; **se d.** (**sur**) (*ressortir*) to stand out (against). ◆**-é à 1** (*nœud*) loose, undone. **2** (*air, ton etc*) detached. ◆**-ement** *nm* **1** (*indifférence*) detachment. **2** (*de fonctionnaire*) (temporary) transfer; *Mil* detachment.

détach/er[2] [detaʃe] *vt* (*linge etc*) to remove the spots *ou* stains from. ◆**-ant** *nm* stain remover.

détail [detaj] *nm* **1** detail; **en d.** in detail; **le d. de** (*dépenses etc*) a detailing *ou* breakdown of. **2 de d.** (*magasin, prix*) retail; **vendre au d.** to sell retail; (*par petites quantités*) to sell separately; **faire le d.** to retail to the public. ◆**détaill/er** *vt* **1** (*vendre*) to sell in small quantities *ou* separately; (*au détail*) (to) sell retail. **2** (*énumérer*) to detail. ◆**-ant, -ante** *nmf* retailer. ◆**-é à** (*récit etc*) detailed.

détaler [detale] *vi Fam* to run off, make tracks.

détartrer [detartre] *vt* (*chaudière, dents etc*) to scale.

détaxer [detakse] *vt* (*denrée etc*) to reduce the tax on; (*supprimer*) to take the tax off; **produit détaxé** duty-free article.

détecter [detekte] *vt* to detect. ◆**détecteur** *nm* (*appareil*) detector. ◆**détection** *nf* detection.

détective [detɛktiv] *nm* **d. (privé)** (private) detective.

déteindre[*] [detɛ̃dr] *vi* (*couleur ou étoffe au lavage*) to run; (*au soleil*) to fade; **ton**

tablier bleu a déteint sur ma chemise the blue of your apron has come off on(to) my shirt; **d. sur qn** (*influencer*) to leave one's mark on s.o.

dételer [detle] *vt* (*chevaux*) to unhitch, unharness.

détend/re [detɑ̃dr] *vt* (*arc etc*) to slacken, relax; (*situation, atmosphère*) to ease; **d. qn** to relax s.o.; **— se d.** *vpr* to slacken, get slack; to ease; (*se reposer*) to relax; (*rapports*) to become less strained. **◆—u** *a* (*visage, atmosphère*) relaxed; (*ressort, câble*) slack. **◆détente** *nf* **1** (*d'arc*) slackening; (*de relations*) easing of tension, *Pol* détente; (*repos*) relaxation; (*saut*) leap, spring. **2** (*gâchette*) trigger.

déten/ir* [detnir] *vt* to hold; (*secret, objet volé*) to be in possession of; (*prisonnier*) to hold, detain. **◆—u, -ue** *nmf* prisoner. **◆détenteur, -trice** *nmf* (*de record etc*) holder. **◆détention** *nf* (*d'armes*) possession; (*captivité*) detention; **d. préventive** *Jur* custody.

détergent [detɛrʒɑ̃] *nm* detergent.

détériorer [deterjɔre] *vt* (*abîmer*) to damage; **— se d.** *vpr* (*empirer*) to deteriorate. **◆détérioration** *nf* damage (de to); (*d'une situation etc*) deterioration (**de** in).

détermin/er [detɛrmine] *vt* (*préciser*) to determine; (*causer*) to bring about; **d. qn à faire** to induce s.o. to do, make s.o. do; **se d. à faire** to resolve *ou* determine to do. **◆—ant** *a* (*motif*) determining, deciding; (*rôle*) decisive. **◆—é** *a* (*précis*) specific; (*résolu*) determined. **◆détermination** *nf* (*fermeté*) determination; (*résolution*) resolve.

déterrer [detere] *vt* to dig up, unearth.

détest/er [detɛste] *vt* to hate, detest; **d. faire** to hate doing *ou* to do, detest doing. **◆—able** *a* awful, foul.

détonateur [detɔnatœr] *nm* detonator. **◆détonation** *nf* explosion, blast.

détonner [detɔne] *vi* (*contraster*) to jar, be out of place.

détour [detur] *nm* (*de route etc*) bend, curve; (*crochet*) detour; **sans d.** (*parler*) without beating about the bush; **faire des détours** (*route*) to wind.

détourn/er [deturne] *vt* (*fleuve, convoi etc*) to divert; (*tête*) to turn (away); (*coups*) to ward off; (*conversation, sens*) to change; (*fonds*) to embezzle, misappropriate; (*avion*) to hijack; **d. qn de** (*son devoir, ses amis*) to take *ou* turn s.o. away from; (*sa route*) to lead s.o. away from; (*projet*) to talk s.o. out of; **d. les yeux** to look away,

avert one's eyes; **— se d.** *vpr* to turn aside *ou* away; **se d. de** (*chemin*) to wander *ou* stray from. **◆—é** *a* (*chemin, moyen*) roundabout, indirect. **◆—ement** *nm* (*de cours d'eau*) diversion; **d.** (**d'avion**) hijack(ing); **d.** (**de fonds**) embezzlement.

détraqu/er [detrake] *vt* (*mécanisme*) to break, put out of order; — **se d.** *vpr* (*machine*) to go wrong; **se d. l'estomac** to upset one's stomach; **se d. la santé** to ruin one's health. **◆—é, -ée** *a* out of order; (*cerveau*) deranged; — *nmf* crazy *ou* deranged person.

détremper [detrɑ̃pe] *vt* to soak, saturate.

détresse [detrɛs] *nf* distress; **en d.** (*navire, âme*) in distress; **dans la d.** (*misère*) in (great) distress.

détriment de (au) [odetrimɑ̃də] *prép* to the detriment of.

détritus [detritys] *nmpl* refuse, rubbish.

détroit [detrwa] *nm Géog* strait(s), sound.

détromper [detrɔ̃pe] *vt* **d. qn** to undeceive s.o., put s.o. right; **détrompez-vous!** don't you believe it!

détrôner [detrone] *vt* (*souverain*) to dethrone; (*supplanter*) to supersede, oust.

détrousser [detruse] *vt* (*voyageur etc*) to rob.

détruire* [detrɥir] *vt* (*ravager, tuer*) to destroy; (*projet, santé*) to ruin, wreck, destroy.

dette [dɛt] *nf* debt; **faire des dettes** to run *ou* get into debt; **avoir des dettes** to be in debt.

deuil [dœj] *nm* (*affliction, vêtements*) mourning; (*mort de qn*) bereavement; **porter le d., être en d.** to be in mourning.

deux [dø] *a* & *nm* two; **d. fois** twice, two times; **tous** (**les**) **d.** both; **en moins de d.** *Fam* in no time. **◆d.-pièces** *nm inv* (*vêtement*) two-piece; (*appartement*) two-roomed flat *ou Am* apartment. **◆d.-points** *nm inv Gram* colon. **◆d.-roues** *nm inv* two-wheeled vehicle. **◆d.-temps** *nm inv* two-stroke (engine).

deuxième [døzjɛm] *a* & *nmf* second. **◆—ment** *adv* secondly.

dévaler [devale] *vt* (*escalier etc*) to hurtle *ou* race *ou* rush down; — *vi* (*tomber*) to tumble down, come tumbling down.

dévaliser [devalize] *vt* (*détrousser*) to clean out, strip, rob (of everything).

dévaloriser [devalɔrize] **1** *vt*, **— se d.** *vpr* (*monnaie*) to depreciate. **2** *vt* (*humilier etc*) to devalue, disparage. **◆dévalorisation** *nf* (*de monnaie*) depreciation.

dévaluer [devalɥe] *vt* (*monnaie*) & *Fig* to devalue. **◆dévaluation** *nf* devaluation.

devancer [d(ə)vɑ̃se] vt to get ou be ahead of; (question etc) to anticipate, forestall; (surpasser) to outstrip; **tu m'as devancé** (action) you did it before me; (lieu) you got there before me. ◆**devancier, -ière** nmf predecessor.

devant [d(ə)vɑ̃] prép & adv in front (of); **d.** (**l'hôtel**/etc) in front (of the hotel/etc); **marcher d.** (**qn**) to walk in front (of s.o.) ou ahead (of s.o.); **passer d.** (**l'église**/etc) to go past (the church/etc); **assis d.** (dans une voiture) sitting in the front; **l'avenir est d. toi** the future is ahead of you; **loin d.** a long way ahead ou in front; **d. le danger** (confronté à) in the face of danger; **mes yeux/la loi** before my eyes/the law; — nm front; **de d.** (roue, porte) front; **patte de d.** foreleg; **par d.** from ou at the front; **prendre les devants** (action) to take the initiative. ◆**devanture** nf (vitrine) shop window; (façade) shop front.

dévaster [devaste] vt (ruiner) to devastate. ◆**dévastation** nf devastation.

déveine [devɛn] nf Fam tough ou bad luck.

développ/er [devlɔpe] vt to develop; Phot to develop, process; — **se d.** vpr to develop. ◆**—ement** nm development; Phot developing, processing; **les pays en voie de d.** the developing countries.

devenir* [dəvnir] vi (aux être) to become; (vieux, difficile etc) to get, grow, become; (rouge, bleu etc) to turn, go, become; **d. un papillon/un homme**/etc to grow into a butterfly/a man/etc; **qu'est-il devenu?** what's become of him ou it?, where's he ou it got to?; **qu'est-ce que tu deviens?** Fam how are you doing?

dévergond/er (se) [sədevergɔ̃de] vpr to fall into dissolute ways. ◆**—é** a dissolute, licentious.

déverser [devɛrse] vt (liquide, rancune) to pour out; (bombes, ordures) to dump; — **se d.** vpr (liquide) to empty, pour out (dans into).

dévêtir [devetir] vt, — **se d.** vpr Litt to undress.

dévier [devje] vt (circulation, conversation) to divert; (coup, rayons) to deflect; — vi (de ses principes etc) to deviate (de from); (de sa route) to veer (off course). ◆**déviation** nf deflection, deviation; (chemin) bypass; (itinéraire provisoire) diversion.

deviner [d(ə)vine] vt to guess (que that); (avenir) to predict; **d. (le jeu de) qn** to see through s.o. ◆**devinette** nf riddle.

devis [d(ə)vi] nm estimate (of cost of work to be done).

dévisager [deviza͜ʒe] vt **d. qn** to stare at s.o.

devise [d(ə)viz] nf (légende) motto; pl (monnaie) (foreign) currency.

dévisser [devise] vt to unscrew, undo; — **se d.** vpr (bouchon etc) to come undone.

dévoiler [devwale] vt (révéler) to disclose; (statue) to unveil; — **se d.** vpr (mystère) to come to light.

devoir*[1] [d(ə)vwar] v aux **1** (nécessité) **je dois refuser** I must refuse, I have (got) to refuse; **j'ai dû refuser** I had to refuse. **2** (forte probabilité) **il doit être tard** it must be late; **elle a dû oublier** she must have forgotten; **il ne doit pas être bête** he can't be stupid. **3** (obligation) **tu dois l'aider** you should help her, you ought to help her; **il aurait dû venir** he should have come, he ought to have come; **vous devriez rester** you should stay, you ought to stay. **4** (supposition) **elle doit venir** she should be coming, she's supposed to be coming, she's due to come; **le train devait arriver à midi** the train was due (to arrive) at noon; **je devais le voir** I was (due) to see him.

devoir*[2] [d(ə)vwar] **1** vt to owe; **d. qch à qn** to owe s.o. sth, owe sth to s.o.; **l'argent qu'on m'est dû** the money due to ou owing to me, the money owed (to) me; **se d. à** to have to devote oneself to; **comme il se doit** as is proper. **2** nm duty; Scol exercise; **devoir(s)** (travail à faire à la maison) Scol homework; **présenter ses devoirs à qn** to pay one's respects to s.o.

dévolu [devɔly] **1** a **d. à qn** (pouvoirs, tâche) vested in s.o., allotted to s.o. **2** nm **jeter son d. sur** to set one's heart on.

dévor/er [devɔre] vt (manger) to gobble up, devour; (incendie) to engulf, devour; (tourmenter, lire) to devour. ◆**—ant** a (faim) ravenous; (passion) devouring.

dévot, -ote [devo, -ɔt] a & nmf devout ou pious (person). ◆**dévotion** nf devotion.

dévou/er (se) [sadevwe] vpr (à une tâche) to dedicate oneself, devote oneself (à to); **se d.** (**pour qn**) (se sacrifier) to sacrifice oneself (for s.o.). ◆**—é** a (ami, femme etc) devoted (à qn to s.o.); (domestique, soldat etc) dedicated. ◆**—ement** [-umɑ̃] nm devotion, dedication; (de héros) devotion to duty.

dévoyé, -ée [devwaje] a & nmf delinquent.

dextérité [dɛksterite] nf dexterity, skill.

diabète [djabɛt] nm Méd diabetes. ◆**diabétique** a & nmf diabetic.

diable [djɑbl] nm devil; **d.!** heavens!; **où/pourquoi/que d.?** where/why/what the devil?; **un bruit/vent**/etc **du d.** the devil of a noise/wind/*etc*; **à la d.** anyhow; **habiter au d.** to live miles from anywhere. ◆**diablerie** *nf* devilment, mischief. ◆**diablesse** *nf* **c'est une d.** *Fam* she's a devil. ◆**diablotin** *nm* (*enfant*) little devil. ◆**diabolique** *a* diabolical, devilish.

diabolo [djabɔlo] *nm* (*boisson*) lemonade *ou Am* lemon soda flavoured with syrup.

diacre [djakr] *nm Rel* deacon.

diadème [djadɛm] *nm* diadem.

diagnostic [djagnɔstik] *nm* diagnosis. ◆**diagnostiquer** *vt* to diagnose.

diagonal, -aux [djagɔnal, -o] *a* diagonal. ◆**diagonale** *nf* diagonal (line); **en d.** diagonally.

diagramme [djagram] *nm* (*schéma*) diagram; (*courbe*) graph.

dialecte [djalɛkt] *nm* dialect.

dialogue [djalɔg] *nm* conversation; *Pol Cin Th Littér* dialogue. ◆**dialoguer** *vi* to have a conversation *ou* dialogue.

dialyse [djaliz] *nf Méd* dialysis.

diamant [djamā] *nm* diamond.

diamètre [djamɛtr] *nm* diameter. ◆**diamétralement** *adv* **d. opposés** (*avis etc*) diametrically opposed, poles apart.

diapason [djapazɔ̃] *nm Mus* tuning fork; **être/se mettre au d.** de *Fig* to be/get in tune with.

diaphragme [djafragm] *nm* diaphragm.

diapositive, *Fam* **diapo** [djapozitiv, djapo] *nf* (*colour*) slide, transparency.

diarrhée [djare] *nf* diarrh(o)ea.

diatribe [djatrib] *nf* diatribe.

dictateur [diktatœr] *nm* dictator. ◆**dictatorial, -aux** *a* dictatorial. ◆**dictature** *nf* dictatorship.

dict/er [dikte] *vt* to dictate (à to). ◆**-ée** *nf* dictation. ◆**dictaphone**® *nm* dictaphone®.

diction [diksjɔ̃] *nf* diction, elocution.

dictionnaire [diksjɔner] *nm* dictionary.

dicton [diktɔ̃] *nm* saying, adage, dictum.

didactique [didaktik] *a* didactic.

dièse [djez] *a* & *nm Mus* sharp.

diesel [djezɛl] *a* & *nm* (*moteur*) **d.** diesel (engine).

diète [djɛt] *nf* (*jeûne*) starvation diet; **à la d.** on a starvation diet. ◆**diététicien, -ienne** *nmf* dietician. ◆**diététique** *nf* dietetics; — *a* (*magasin de*) health-; **aliment** *ou* **produit d.** health food.

dieu, -x [djø] *nm* god; **D.** God; **D. merci!** thank God!, thank goodness!

diffamer [difame] *vt* (*en paroles*) to slander; (*par écrit*) to libel. ◆**diffamation** *nf* defamation; (*en paroles*) slander; (*par écrit*)

libel; **campagne de d.** smear campaign. ◆**diffamatoire** *a* slanderous; libellous.

différent [diferā] *a* different; *pl* (*divers*) different, various; **d. de** different from *ou* to, unlike. ◆**différemment** [-amā] *adv* differently (**de** from, to). ◆**différence** *nf* difference (**de** in); **à la d. de** unlike; **faire la d. entre** to make a distinction between.

différencier [diferāsje] *vt* to differentiate (**de** from); — **se d.** *vpr* to differ (**de** from).

différend [diferā] *nm* difference (of opinion).

différentiel, -ielle [diferāsjɛl] *a* differential.

différ/er [difere] **1** *vi* to differ (**de** from). **2** *vt* (*remettre*) to postpone, defer. ◆**-é** *nm* **en d.** (*émission*) (pre)recorded.

difficile [difisil] *a* difficult; (*exigeant*) fussy, particular, hard *ou* difficult to please; **c'est d. à faire** it's hard *ou* difficult to do; **il (nous) est d. de faire ça** it's hard *ou* difficult (for us) to do that. ◆**-ment** *adv* with difficulty; **d. lisible** not easily read. ◆**difficulté** *nf* difficulty (**à faire** in doing); **en d.** in a difficult situation.

difforme [diform] *a* deformed, misshapen. ◆**difformité** *nf* deformity.

diffus [dify] *a* (*lumière, style*) diffuse.

diffuser [difyze] *vt* (*émission, nouvelle etc*) to broadcast; (*lumière, chaleur*) *Phys* to diffuse; (*livre*) to distribute. ◆**diffusion** *nf* broadcasting; (*de connaissances*) & *Phys* diffusion; (*de livre*) distribution.

digérer [diʒere] *vt* to digest; (*endurer*) *Fam* to stomach; — *vi* to digest. ◆**digeste** *a*, ◆**digestible** *a* digestible. ◆**digestif, -ive** *a* digestive; — *nm* after-dinner liqueur. ◆**digestion** *nf* digestion.

digitale [diʒital] *af* **empreinte d.** fingerprint.

digne [diɲ] *a* - (*fier*) dignified; (*honnête*) worthy; **d. de** qn worthy of s.o.; **d. d'admiration/etc** worthy of *ou* deserving of admiration/*etc*; **d. de foi** reliable. ◆**dignement** *adv* with dignity. ◆**dignitaire** *nm* dignitary. ◆**dignité** *nf* dignity.

digression [digresjɔ̃] *nf* digression.

digue [dig] *nf* dyke, dike.

dilapider [dilapide] *vt* to squander, waste.

dilater [dilate] *vt*, — **se d.** *vpr* to dilate, expand. ◆**dilatation** *nf* dilation, expansion.

dilatoire [dilatwar] *a* **manœuvre** *ou* **moyen d.** delaying tactic.

dilemme [dilɛm] *nm* dilemma.

dilettante [diletāt] *nmf Péj* dabbler, amateur.

diligent [diliʒā] *a* (*prompt*) speedy and efficient; (*soin*) diligent. ◆**diligence** *nf* **1** (*célérité*) speedy efficiency; **faire d.** to make haste. **2** (*véhicule*) *Hist* stagecoach.

diluer [dilɥe] *vt* to dilute. ◆**dilution** *nf* dilution.

diluvienne [dilyvjɛn] *af* **pluie d.** torrential rain.

dimanche [dimɑ̃ʃ] *nm* Sunday.

dimension [dimɑ̃sjɔ̃] *nf* dimension; **à deux dimensions** two-dimensional.

diminuer [diminɥe] *vt* to reduce, decrease; (*frais*) to cut down (on); reduce; (*mérite*, *forces*) to diminish, lessen, reduce; **d. qn** (*rabaisser*) to diminish s.o., lessen s.o.; — *vi* (*réserves*, *nombre*) to decrease, diminish; (*jours*) to get shorter, draw in; (*prix*) to drop, decrease. ◆**diminutif, -ive** *a* & *nm Gram* diminutive; — *nm* (*prénom*) nickname. ◆**diminution** *nf* reduction, decrease (**de** in).

dinde [dɛ̃d] *nf* turkey (hen), *Culin* turkey. ◆**dindon** *nm* turkey (cock).

dîner [dine] *vi* to have dinner, dine; (*au Canada, en Belgique etc*) to (have) lunch; — *nm* dinner; lunch; (*soirée*) dinner party. ◆**dînette** *nf* (*jouet*) doll's dinner service; (*jeu*) doll's dinner party. ◆**dîneur, -euse** *nmf* diner.

dingue [dɛ̃g] *a Fam* nuts, screwy, crazy; — *nmf* Fam nutcase.

dinosaure [dinozor] *nm* dinosaur.

diocèse [djosɛz] *nm Rel* diocese.

diphtérie [difteri] *nf* diphtheria.

diphtongue [diftɔ̃g] *nf Ling* diphthong.

diplomate [diplomat] *nm Pol* diplomat; — *nmf* (*négociateur*) diplomatist; — *a* (*habile*, *plein de tact*) diplomatic. ◆**diplomatie** [-asi] *nf* (*tact*) & *Pol* diplomacy; (*carrière*) diplomatic service. ◆**diplomatique** *a Pol* diplomatic.

diplôme [diplom] *nm* certificate, diploma; *Univ* degree. ◆**diplômé, -ée** *a* & *nmf* qualified (person); **être d. (de)** *Univ* to be a graduate (of).

dire* [dir] *vt* (*mot, avis etc*) to say; (*vérité*, *secret, heure etc*) to tell; (*penser*) to think (**de** of; about); **d. des bêtises** to talk nonsense; **elle dit que tu mens** she says (that) you're lying; **d. qch à qn** to tell s.o. sth, say sth to s.o.; **d. à qn que** to tell s.o. that, say to s.o. that; **d. à qn de faire** to tell s.o. to do; **dit-il** he said; **dit-on** they say; **d. que oui/non** to say yes/no; **d. du mal/du bien de** to speak ill/well of; **on dirait un château** it looks like a castle; **on dirait du Mozart** it sounds like Mozart; **on dirait du cabillaud** it tastes like cod; **on dirait que il** would seem that; **ça ne me dit rien** (*envie*) I don't feel like *ou* fancy that; (*souvenir*) it doesn't ring a bell; **ça vous dit de rester?** do you feel like staying?; **dites donc!** I say!; **ça va sans d.** that goes without saying; **autrement dit** in other words; **c'est beaucoup d.** that's going too far; **à l'heure dite** at the agreed time; **à vrai d.** to tell the truth; **il se dit malade**/*etc* he says he's ill/*etc*; **ça ne se dit pas** that's not said; – *nm* **au d.** de according to; **les dires de** (*déclarations*) the statements of.

direct [dirɛkt] *a* direct; (*chemin*) straight, direct; (*manière*) straightforward, direct; **train d.** through train, non-stop train; – *nm* **en d.** (*émission*) live; **un d. du gauche** *Boxe* a straight left. ◆**-ement** *adv* directly; (*immédiatement*) straight (away), directly.

directeur, -trice [dirɛktœr, -tris] *nmf* director; (*d'entreprise*) manager(ess), director; (*de journal*) editor; *Scol* headmaster, headmistress; – *a* (*principe*) guiding; **idées** *ou* **lignes directrices** guiding lines.

direction [dirɛksjɔ̃] *nf* **1** (*de société*) running, management; (*de club*) leadership, running; (*d'études*) supervision; (*mécanisme*) *Aut* steering; **avoir la d. de** to be in charge of; **sous la d. de** (*orchestre*) conducted by; **la d.** (*équipe dirigeante*) the management; **une d.** (*fonction*) *Com* a directorship; *Scol* a headmastership; *Journ* an editorship. **2** (*sens*) direction; **en d. de** (*train*) (going) to, for.

directive [dirɛktiv] *nf* directive, instruction.

dirig/er [diriʒe] *vt* (*société*) to run, manage, direct; (*débat, cheval*) to lead; (*véhicule*) to steer; (*orchestre*) to conduct; (*études*) to supervise, direct; (*conscience*) to guide; (*orienter*) to turn (**vers towards**); (*arme*, *lumière*) to point, direct (**vers towards**); **se d. vers** (*lieu, objet*) to make one's way towards, head *ou* make for; (*dans une carrière*) to turn towards. ◆**-eant** *a* (*classe*) ruling; – *nm* (*de pays, club*) leader; (*d'entreprise*) manager. ◆**-é** *a* (*économie*) planned. ◆**-eable** *a* & *nm* (*ballon*) airship. ◆**dirigisme** *nm Écon* state control.

dis [di] *voir* **dire**.

discern/er [disɛrne] *vt* (*voir*) to make out, discern; (*différencier*) to distinguish. ◆**-ement** *nm* discernment, discrimination.

disciple [disipl] *nm* disciple, follower.

discipline [disiplin] *nf* (*règle, matière*) discipline. ◆**disciplinaire** *a* disciplinary. ◆**disciplin/er** *vt* (*contrôler, éduquer*) to discipline; — **se d.** *vpr* to discipline oneself. ◆**—é** a well-disciplined.

disco [disko] *a* Fam disco; **aller en d.** to go to a disco.

discontinu [diskɔ̃tiny] *a* (*ligne*) discontinuous; (*bruit etc*) intermittent. ◆**discontinuer** *vi* sans d. without stopping.

disconvenir [diskɔ̃vnir] *vi* **je n'en disconviens pas** I don't deny it.

discorde [diskɔrd] *nf* discord. ◆**discordance** *nf* (*de caractères*) clash, conflict; (*de son*) discord. ◆**discordant** *a* (*son*) discordant; (*témoignages*) conflicting; (*couleurs*) clashing.

discothèque [diskɔtɛk] *nf* record library; (*club*) discotheque.

discours [diskur] *nm* speech; (*écrit littéraire*) discourse. ◆**discourir** *vi* Péj to speechify, ramble on.

discourtois [diskurtwa] *a* discourteous.

discrédit [diskredi] *nm* disrepute, discredit. ◆**discréditer** *vt* to discredit, bring into disrepute; — **se d.** *vpr* (*personne*) to become discredited.

discret, -ète [diskrɛ, -ɛt] *a* (*personne, manière etc*) discreet; (*vêtement*) simple. ◆**discrètement** *adv* discreetly; (*s'habiller*) simply. ◆**discrétion** *nf* discretion; **vin/etc à d.** as much wine/etc as one wants. ◆**discrétionnaire** *a* discretionary.

discrimination [diskriminasjɔ̃] *nf* (*ségrégation*) discrimination. ◆**discriminatoire** *a* discriminatory.

disculper [diskylpe] *vt* to exonerate (*de* from).

discussion [diskysjɔ̃] *nf* discussion; (*conversation*) talk; (*querelle*) argument; **pas de d.!** no argument! ◆**discuter** *vt* to discuss; (*familièrement*) to talk over; (*contester*) to question; **ça peut se d., ça se discute** that's arguable; — *vi* (*parler*) to talk (*de* about, **avec** with); (*répliquer*) to argue; **d. de** *ou* **sur qch** to discuss sth. ◆**—é** a (*auteur*) much discussed *ou* debated; (*théorie, question*) disputed, controversial. ◆**—able** *a* arguable, debatable.

disette [dizɛt] *nf* food shortage.

diseuse [dizœz] *nf* **d. de bonne aventure** fortune-teller.

disgrâce [disgras] *nf* disgrace, disfavour. ◆**disgracier** *vt* to disgrace.

disgracieux, -euse [disgrasjø, -øz] *a* ungainly.

disjoindre [disʒwɛ̃dr] *vt* (*questions*) to treat separately. ◆**disjoint** *a* (*questions*) unconnected, separate. ◆**disjoncteur** *nm* Él circuit breaker.

disloquer [dislɔke] *vt* (*membre*) to dislocate; (*meuble, machine*) to break up; — **se d.** *vpr* (*cortège*) to break up; (*meuble etc*) to fall apart; **se d. le bras** (*dislocate one's arm*. ◆**dislocation** *nf* (*de membre*) dislocation.

dispar/aître [disparɛtr] *vi* to disappear; (*être porté manquant*) to be missing; (*mourir*) to die; **d. en mer** to be lost at sea; **faire d.** to remove, get rid of. ◆**—u, -ue** *a* (*soldat etc*) missing, lost; — *nmf* (*absent*) missing person; (*mort*) departed, (*être porté* **d.** to be reported missing. ◆**disparition** *nf* disappearance; (*mort*) death.

disparate [disparat] *a* ill-assorted.

disparité [disparite] *nf* disparity (**entre, de** between).

dispendieux, -euse [dispɑ̃djø, -øz] *a* expensive, costly.

dispensaire [dispɑ̃sɛr] *nm* community health centre.

dispense [dispɑ̃s] *nf* exemption; **d. d'âge** waiving of the age limit. ◆**dispenser** *vt* (*soins, bienfaits etc*) to dispense; **d. qn de** (*obligation*) to exempt *ou* excuse s.o. from; **je vous dispense de** (*vos réflexions etc*) I can dispense with; **se d. de faire** to spare oneself the bother of doing.

disperser [disperse] *vt* to disperse, scatter; (*efforts*) to dissipate; — **se d.** *vpr* (*foule*) to disperse; **elle se disperse trop** she tries to do too many things at once. ◆**dispersion** *nf* (*d'une armée etc*) dispersal, dispersion.

disponible [disponibl] *a* available; (*place*) spare, available; (*esprit*) alert. ◆**disponibilité** *nf* availability; *pl* Fin available funds.

dispos [dispo] *a* fit, in fine fettle; **frais et d.** refreshed.

dispos/er [dispoze] *vt* to arrange; (*troupes*) Mil to dispose; **d. qn à** (*la bonne humeur etc*) to dispose *ou* incline s.o. towards; **se d. à faire** to prepare to do; — *vi* **d. de qch** to have sth at one's disposal; (*utiliser*) to make use of sth; **d. de qn** Péj to take advantage of s.o., abuse s.o. ◆**—é** *a* **bien/mal d.** in a good/bad mood; **bien d. envers** well-disposed towards; **d. à faire** prepared *ou* disposed to do. ◆**disposition** *nf* arrangement; (*de troupes*) disposition; (*de maison, page*) layout; (*humeur*) frame of mind; (*tendance*) tendency, (pre)disposition (**à** to); (*clause*) Jur provision; *pl* (*aptitudes*) ability, aptitude (**pour** for); **à la d. de qn** at s.o.'s disposal; **prendre ses ou des dispositions** (*préparatifs*) to make arrangements, prepare; (*pour l'avenir*) to make provision; **dans de bonnes disposi-tions à l'égard de** well-disposed towards.

dispositif [dispozitif] *nm* (*mécanisme*) device; **d. de défense** *Mil* defence system; **d. antiparasite** *Él* suppressor.

disproportion [disproporsjɔ̃] *nf* disproportion. ◆**disproportionné** *a* disproportionate.

dispute [dispyt] *nf* quarrel. ◆**disputer** *vt* (*match*) to play; (*terrain*, *droit etc*) to contest, dispute; (*rallye*) to compete in; **d. qch à qn** (*prix*, *première place etc*) to fight with s.o. for *ou* over sth, contend with s.o. for sth; **d. qn** (*gronder*) *Fam* to tell s.o. off; **— se d.** *vpr* to quarrel (**avec** with); (*match*) to take place; **se d. qch** to fight over sth.

disqualifier [diskalifje] *vt* to disqualify; **— se d.** *vpr Fig* to become discredited. ◆**disqualification** *nf Sp* disqualification.

disque [disk] *nm Mus* record; *Sp* discus; (*cercle*, *objet*) disk; *Am* disk; (*pour ordinateur*) disk. ◆**disquaire** *nmf* record dealer. ◆**disquette** *nf* (*pour ordinateur*) floppy disk.

dissection [discksjɔ̃] *nf* dissection.

dissemblable [disɑ̃mblabl] *a* dissimilar (**à** to).

disséminer [disemine] *vt* (*graines*, *mines etc*) to scatter; (*idées*) *Fig* to disseminate. ◆**dissémination** *nf* scattering; (*d'idées*) *Fig* dissemination.

dissension [disɑ̃sjɔ̃] *nf* dissension.

disséquer [diseke] *vt* to dissect.

disserter [diserte] *vi* **d. sur** to comment upon, discuss. ◆**dissertation** *nf Scol* essay.

dissident, -ente [disidɑ̃, -ɑ̃t] *a & nmf* dissident. ◆**dissidence** *nf* dissidence.

dissimuler [disimyle] *vt* (*cacher*) to conceal, hide (**à** from); **— vi** (*feindre*) to pretend; **— se d.** *vpr* to hide, conceal oneself. ◆**-é** *a* (*enfant*) *Péj* secretive. ◆**dissimulation** *nf* concealment; (*duplicité*) deceit.

dissiper [disipe] *vt* (*brouillard*, *craintes*) to dispel; (*fortune*) to squander, dissipate; **d. qn** to lead s.o. astray, distract s.o.; **— se d.** *vpr* (*brume*) to clear, lift; (*craintes*) to disappear; (*élève*) to misbehave. ◆**-é** *a* (*élève*) unruly; (*vie*) dissipated. ◆**dissipa-tion** *nf* (*de brouillard*) clearing; (*indiscipline*) misbehaviour; (*débauche*) *Litt* dissipation.

dissocier [disɔsje] *vt* to dissociate (**de** from).

dissolu [disɔly] *a* (*vie etc*) dissolute.

dissoudre* [disudr] *vt*, **— se d.** *vpr* to

dissolve. ◆**dissolution** *nf* dissolution. ◆**dissolvant** *a & nm* solvent; (*pour vernis à ongles*) nail polish remover.

dissuader [disɥade] *vt* to dissuade, deter (**de qch** from sth, **de faire** from doing). ◆**dissuasif, -ive** *a* (*effet*) deterrent; **être d.** *Fig* to be a deterrent. ◆**dissuasion** *nf* dissuasion; **force de d.** *Mil* deterrent.

distant [distɑ̃] *a* distant; (*personne*) aloof, distant; **d. de dix kilomètres** (*éloigné*) ten kilometres away; (*à intervalles*) ten kilometres apart. ◆**distance** *nf* distance; **à deux mètres de d.** two metres apart; **à d.** at *ou* from a distance; **garder ses distances** to keep one's distance. ◆**distancer** *vt* to leave behind, outstrip.

distendre [distɑ̃dr] *vt*, **— se d.** *vpr* to distend.

distiller [distile] *vt* to distil. ◆**distillation** *nf* distillation. ◆**distillerie** *nf* (*lieu*) distillery.

distinct, -incte [distɛ̃, -ɛ̃kt] *a* (*différent*) distinct, separate (**de** from); (*net*) clear, distinct. ◆**distinctement** *adv* distinctly, clearly. ◆**distinctif, -ive** *a* distinctive. ◆**distinction** *nf* (*différence*, *raffinement*) distinction.

distingu/er [distɛ̃ge] *vt* (*différencier*) to distinguish; (*voir*) to make out; (*choisir*) to single out; **d. le blé de l'orge** to tell wheat from barley, distinguish between wheat and barley; **— se d.** *vpr* (*s'illustrer*) to distinguish oneself; **se d. de** (*différer*) to be distinguishable from; **se d. par** (*sa gaieté*, *beauté etc*) to be conspicuous for. ◆**-é** *a* (*bien élevé*, *éminent*) distinguished; **senti-ments distingués** (*formule épistolaire*) *Com* yours faithfully.

distorsion [distɔrsjɔ̃] *nf* (*du corps*, *d'une image etc*) distortion.

distraction [distraksjɔ̃] *nf* amusement, distraction; (*étourderie*) (fit of) absent-mindedness. ◆**distraire*** *vt* (*divertir*) to entertain, amuse; (*détourner*) to distract s.o. (**de** from); **— se d.** *vpr* to amuse oneself, enjoy oneself. ◆**dis-trait** *a* absent-minded. ◆**distraitement** *adv* absent-mindedly. ◆**distrayant** *a* entertaining.

distribuer [distribɥe] *vt* (*répartir*) to distribute; (*donner*) to give *ou* hand out, distribute; (*courrier*) to deliver; (*eau*) to supply; (*cartes*) to deal; **bien distribué** (*appartement*) well-arranged. ◆**distri-buteur** *nm Aut Cin* distributor; **d.** (*automa-tique*) vending machine; **d. de billets** *Rail* ticket machine; (*de billets de banque*) cash dispenser *ou* machine. ◆**distribution** nf distribution; (*du courrier*) delivery; (*de l'eau*) supply; (*acteurs*) Th Cin cast; **d. des prix** prize giving.

district [distrikt] nm district.

dit [di] *voir* **dire**; – a (*convenu*) agreed; (*surnommé*) called.

dites [dit] *voir* **dire**.

divaguer [divage] vi (*dérailler*) to rave, talk drivel. ◆**divagations** nfpl ravings.

divan [divã] nm divan, couch.

divergent [diverʒã] a diverging, divergent. ◆**divergence** nf divergence. ◆**diverger** vi to diverge (**de** from).

divers, -erses [diver, -ers] apl (*distincts*) varied, diverse; **d. groupes** (*plusieurs*) various *ou* sundry groups. ◆**diversement** adv in various ways. ◆**diversifier** vt to diversify; **– se d.** vpr Écon to diversify. ◆**diversité** nf diversity.

diversion [diversjɔ̃] nf diversion.

divert/ir [divertir] vt to amuse, entertain; **– se d.** vpr to enjoy oneself, amuse oneself. ◆**–issement** nm amusement, entertainment.

dividende [dividãd] nm Math Fin dividend.

divin [divɛ̃] a divine. ◆**divinité** nf divinity.

diviser [divize] vt, **– se d.** vpr to divide (**en** into). ◆**divisible** a divisible. ◆**division** nf division.

divorce [divɔrs] nm divorce. ◆**divorc/er** vi to get *ou* be divorced, divorce; **d. d'avec qn** to divorce s.o. ◆**–é, -ée** a divorced (**d'avec** from); **–** nmf divorcee.

divulguer [divylge] vt to divulge. ◆**divulgation** nf divulgence.

dix [dis] ([dis] *before consonant*, [diz] *before vowel*) a & nm ten. ◆**dixième** [dizjɛm] a & nmf tenth; **un d.** a tenth. ◆**dix-huit** [dizɥit] a & nm eighteeen. ◆**dix-huitième** a & nmf eighteenth. ◆**dix-neuf** [diznœf] a & nm nineteen. ◆**dix-neuvième** a & nmf nineteenth. ◆**dix-sept** [disset] a & nm seventeen. ◆**dix-septième** a & nmf seventeenth.

dizaine [dizen] nf about ten.

docile [dɔsil] a submissive, docile. ◆**docilité** nf submissiveness, docility.

dock [dɔk] nm Nau dock. ◆**docker** [dɔker] nm docker.

docteur [dɔktœr] nm Méd Univ doctor (ès, en of). ◆**doctorat** nm doctorate, = PhD (ès, en in).

doctrine [dɔktrin] nf doctrine. ◆**doctrinaire** a & nmf Péj doctrinaire.

document [dɔkymã] nm document. ◆**documentaire** a documentary; – nm (*film*) documentary. ◆**documentaliste** nmf information officer.

document/er [dɔkymãte] vt (*informer*) to document; **– se d.** vpr to collect material *ou* information. ◆**–é a** (**bien** *ou* **très**) **d.** (*personne*) well-informed. ◆**documentation** nf (*documents*) documentation, Com literature; (*renseignements*) information.

dodeliner [dɔdline] vi **d. de la tête** to nod (one's head).

dodo [dodo] nm (*langage enfantin*) **faire d.** to sleep; **aller au d.** to go to bye-byes.

dodu [dɔdy] a chubby, plump.

dogme [dɔgm] nm dogma. ◆**dogmatique** a dogmatic. ◆**dogmatisme** nm dogmatism.

dogue [dɔg] nm (*chien*) mastiff.

doigt [dwa] nm finger; **d. de pied** toe; **à deux doigts de** within an ace of; **montrer du d.** to point (to); **savoir sur le bout du d.** to have at one's finger tips. ◆**doigté** nm Mus fingering, touch; (*savoir-faire*) tact, expertise. ◆**doigtier** nm fingerstall.

dois, doit [dwa] *voir* **devoir** [1,2].

doléances [dɔleãs] nfpl (*plaintes*) grievances.

dollar [dɔlar] nm dollar.

domaine [dɔmɛn] nm (*terres*) estate, domain; (*sphère*) province, domain.

dôme [dom] nm dome.

domestique [dɔmestik] a (*animal*) domestic(ated); (*de la famille*) family-, domestic; (*ménager*) domestic, household; – nmf servant. ◆**domestiquer** vt to domesticate.

domicile [dɔmisil] nm home; Jur abode; **travailler à d.** to work at home; **livrer à d.** (*pain etc*) to deliver (to the house). ◆**domicilié** a resident (**à, chez** at).

domin/er [dɔmine] vt to dominate; (*situation, sentiment*) to master, dominate; (*être supérieur à*) to surpass, outclass; (*tour, rocher*) to tower above, dominate (*valley, building etc*); – vi (*être le plus fort*) to be dominant, dominate; (*être le plus important*) to predominate; **– se d.** vpr to control oneself. ◆**–ant a** a dominant. ◆**–ante** nf dominant feature; Mus dominant. ◆**dominateur, -trice** a domineering. ◆**domination** nf domination.

dominicain, -aine [dɔminikɛ̃, -en] a & nmf Rel Dominican.

dominical, -aux [dɔminikal, -o] a (*repos*) Sunday-.

domino [dɔmino] nm domino; pl (*jeu*) dominoes.

dommage [dɔmaʒ] nm **1** (**c'est**) **d.!** it's a

pity *ou* a shame! (*que* that); **quel d.!** what a pity *ou* a shame! **2** (*tort*) prejudice, harm; *pl* (*dégâts*) damage; **dommages-intérêts** *Jur* damages.

dompt/er [dɔ̃te] *vt* (*animal*) to tame; (*passions, rebelles*) to subdue. ◆**—eur, -euse** *nmf* (*de lions*) lion tamer.

don [dɔ̃] *nm* (*cadeau, aptitude*) gift; (*aumône*) donation; **le d. du sang/etc** (the) giving of blood/*etc*; **faire d. de** to give; **avoir le d. de** (*le chic pour*) to have the knack of. ◆**donateur, -trice** *nmf* Jur donor. ◆**donation** *nf* Jur donation.

donc [dɔ̃(k)] *conj* so, then; (*par conséquent*) so, therefore; (*intensif*) will you sit down!, sit down then!; **qui/quoi d.?** who?/what?; **allons d.!** come on!

donjon [dɔ̃ʒɔ̃] *nm* (*de château*) keep.

donne [dɔn] *nf* Cartes deal.

donner [dɔne] *vt* to give; (*récolte, résultat*) to produce; (*sa place*) to give up; (*pièce, film*) to put on; (*cartes*) to deal; **d. un coup à** to hit, give a blow to; **d. le bonjour à qn** to say hello to s.o.; **d. à réparer** to take (in) to be repaired; **d. raison à qn** to say s.o. is right; **ça donne soif/faim** it makes you thirsty/hungry; **je lui donne trente ans** I'd say *ou* guess he *ou* she was thirty; **ça n'a rien donné** (*efforts*) it hasn't got us anywhere; **c'est donné** *Fam* it's dirt cheap; **étant donné** (*la situation etc*) considering, in view of; **étant donné que** seeing (that), considering (that); **à un moment donné** at some stage; **— vi d. sur** (*fenêtre*) to look out onto, overlook; (*porte*) to open onto; **d. dans** (*piège*) to fall into; **d. de la tête contre** to hit one's head against; **— se d.** *vpr* (*se consacrer*) to devote oneself (**à** to); **se d. du mal** to go to a lot of trouble (**pour faire** to do); **s'en d. à cœur joie** to have a whale of a time, enjoy oneself to the full. ◆**données** *nfpl* (*information*) data; (*de problème*) (known) facts; (*d'un roman*) basic elements. ◆**donneur, -euse** *nmf* giver; (*de sang, d'organe*) donor; Cartes dealer.

dont [dɔ̃] *pron rel* (= de qui, duquel, de quoi *etc*) (*personne*) of whom; (*chose*) of which; (*appartenance: personne*) whose, of whom; (*appartenance: chose*) of which, whose; **une mère d. le fils est ill**; **la fille d. il est fier** the daughter he is proud of *ou* of whom he is proud; **les outils d. j'ai besoin** the tools I need; **la façon d. elle joue** the way (in which) she plays; **voici ce d. il s'agit** here's what it's about.

doper [dɔpe] *vt* (*cheval, sportif*) to dope; —

se d. *vpr* to dope oneself. ◆**doping** *nm* (*action*) doping; (*substance*) dope.

dorénavant [dɔrenavɑ̃] *adv* henceforth.

dor/er [dɔre] *vt* (*objet*) to gild; **d. la pilule** *Fig* to sugar the pill; **se (faire) d. au soleil** to bask in the sun; — *vi* Culin to brown. ◆**—é** a (*objet*) gilt; (*couleur*) golden; — *nm* (*couche*) gilt. ◆**dorure** *nf* gilding.

dorloter [dɔrlɔte] *vt* to pamper, coddle.

dormir* [dɔrmir] *vi* to sleep; (*être endormi*) to be asleep; (*argent*) to lie idle; **histoire à d. debout** tall story, cock-and-bull story; **eau dormante** stagnant water. ◆**dortoir** *nm* dormitory.

dos [do] *nm* back; (*de nez*) bridge; (*de livre*) spine; **voir qn de d.** to have a back view of s.o.; **à d. de chameau** (riding) on a camel; **'voir au d.'** (*verso*) 'see over'; **j'en ai plein le d.** *Fam* I'm sick of it; **mettre qch sur le d. de qn** (*accusation*) to pin sth on s.o. ◆**dossard** *nm* Sp number (*fixed on back*). ◆**dossier** *nm* **1** (*de siège*) back. **2** (*papiers, compte rendu*) file, dossier; (*classeur*) folder, file.

dose [doz] *nf* dose; (*quantité administrée*) dosage. ◆**dos/er** *vt* (*remède*) to measure out the dose of; (*équilibrer*) to strike the correct balance between. ◆**—age** *nm* measuring out (*of dose*); (*équilibre*) balance; **faire le d. de = doser.** ◆**—eur** *nm* **bouchon d.** measuring cap.

dot [dɔt] *nf* dowry.

doter [dɔte] *vt* (*hôpital etc*) to endow; **d. de** (*matériel*) to equip with; (*qualité*) Fig to endow with. ◆**dotation** *nf* endowment; equipping.

douane [dwan] *nf* customs. ◆**douanier, -ière** *nm* customs officer; — *a* (*union etc*) customs-.

double [dubl] *a* double; (*rôle, avantage etc*) twofold, double; — *adv* double; — *nm* (*de personne*) double; (*copie*) copy, duplicate; (*de timbre*) swap, duplicate; **le d. (de)** (*quantité*) twice as much (as). ◆**doublage** *nm* (*de film*) dubbing. ◆**doublement** *adv* doubly; — *nm* doubling. ◆**doubler 1** *vt* (*augmenter*) to double; (*vêtement*) to line; (*film*) to dub; (*acteur*) to stand in for; (*classe*) Scol to repeat; (*cap*) Nau to round; **se d. de** to be coupled with; — *vi* (*augmenter*) to double. **2** *vti* Aut to overtake, pass. ◆**doublure** *nf* (*étoffe*) lining; Th understudy; Cin stand-in, double.

douce [dus] *voir* **doux.** ◆**doucement** *adv* (*délicatement*) gently; (*à voix basse*) softly; (*sans bruit*) quietly; (*lentement*) slowly; (*sans à-coups*) smoothly; (*assez bien*) *Fam* so-so. ◆**douceur** nf (de miel etc) sweetness; (de personne, pente etc) gentleness; (de peau etc) softness; (de temps etc) mildness; pl (sucreries) sweets, Am candies; **en d.** (démarrer etc) smoothly.

douche [duʃ] nf shower. ◆**doucher** vt **d. qn** to give s.o. a shower; — **se d.** vpr to take ou have a shower.

doué [dwe] a gifted, talented (en at); (intelligent) clever; **d. de** gifted with; **il est d. pour** he has a gift ou talent for.

douille [duj] nf (d'ampoule) El socket; (de cartouche) case.

douillet, -ette [duje, -et] a (lit etc) soft, cosy, snug; **il est d.** (délicat) Péj he's soft.

douleur [dulœr] nf (mal) pain; (chagrin) sorrow, grief. ◆**douloureux, -euse** a (maladie, membre, décision, perte etc) painful.

doute [dut] nm doubt; pl (méfiance) doubts, misgivings; **sans d.** no doubt, probably; **sans aucun d.** without (any ou a) doubt; **mettre en d.** to cast doubt on; **dans le d.** uncertain, doubtful; **ça ne fait pas de d.** there is no doubt about it. ◆**douter** vi to doubt; **d. de qch/qn** to doubt sth/s.o.; **d. que** (+ sub) to doubt whether ou that; **se d. de qch** to suspect sth; **je m'en doute** I suspect so, I would think so. ◆**douteux, -euse** a doubtful; (louche, médiocre) dubious; **il est d. que** (+ sub) it's doubtful whether ou that.

douve(s) [duv] nf(pl) (de château) moat.

Douvres [duvr] nm ou f Dover.

doux, douce [du, dus] a (miel, son etc) sweet; (personne, pente etc) gentle; (peau, lumière, drogue etc) soft; (émotion, souvenir etc) pleasant; (temps, climat) mild; **en douce** on the quiet.

douze [duz] a & nm twelve. ◆**douzaine** nf (douze) dozen; (environ) about twelve; **une d. d'œufs/etc** a dozen eggs/etc. ◆**douzième** a & nmf twelfth; **un d.** a twelfth.

doyen, -enne [dwajɛ̃, -ɛn] nmf Rel Univ dean; **d. (d'âge)** oldest person.

draconien, -ienne [drakɔnjɛ̃, -jɛn] a (mesures) drastic.

dragée [draʒe] nf sugared almond; **tenir la d. haute à qn** (tenir tête à qn) to stand up to s.o.

dragon [dragɔ̃] nm (animal) dragon; Mil Hist dragoon.

drague [drag] nf (appareil) dredge; (filet) drag net. ◆**draguer** vt **1** (rivière etc) to dredge. **2** Arg (racoler) to try and pick up;

(faire du baratin à) to chat up, Am smooth-talk.

drainer [drene] vt to drain.

drame [dram] nm drama; (catastrophe) tragedy. ◆**dramatique** a dramatic; **critique d.** drama critic; **auteur d.** playwright, dramatist; **film d.** drama. ◆**dramatiser** vt (exagérer) to dramatize. ◆**dramaturge** nmf dramatist.

drap [dra] nm (de lit) sheet; (tissu) cloth; **dans de beaux draps** Fig in a fine mess.

drapeau, -x [drapo] nm flag; **être sous les drapeaux** Mil to be in the services.

draper [drape] vt to drape (**de** with). ◆**draperie** nf (étoffe) drapery.

dresser [drese] **1** vt (échelle, statue) to put up, erect; (piège) to lay, set; (oreille) to prick up; (liste) to draw up, make out; — **se d.** vpr (personne) to stand up; (statue, montagne) to rise up, stand; **se d. contre** (abus) to stand up against. **2** vt (animal) to train; (personne) Péj to drill, teach. ◆**dressage** nm training. ◆**dresseur, -euse** nmf trainer.

dribbler [drible] vti Fb to dribble.

drogue [drɔg] nf (médicament) Péj drug; **une d.** (stupéfiant) a drug; **la d.** drugs, dope. ◆**droguer** vt (victime) to drug; (malade) to dose up; — **se d.** vpr to take drugs, be on drugs; (malade) to dose oneself up. ◆**-é, -ée** nmf drug addict.

droguerie [drɔgri] nf hardware shop ou Am store. ◆**droguiste** nmf owner of a droguerie.

droit¹ [drwa] nm (privilège) right; (d'inscription etc) fee(s), dues; pl (de douane) duty; **le d.** (science juridique) law; **avoir d. à** to be entitled to; **avoir le d. de faire** to be entitled to do, have the right to do; **à bon d.** rightly. **d. d'entrée** entrance fee.

droit² [drwa] a (ligne, route etc) straight; (personne, mur etc) upright, straight; (angle) right; (veston) single-breasted; (honnête) Fig upright; — adv straight; **tout d.** straight ou right ahead. ◆**droite¹** nf (ligne) straight line.

droit³ [drwa] a (côté, bras etc) right; — nm (coup) Boxe right. ◆**droite²** nf **la d.** (côté) the right (side); Pol the right (wing); **à d.** (tourner) (to the) right; (rouler, se tenir) on the right(-hand) side; **de d.** (fenêtre etc) right-hand; (politique, candidat) rightwing; **à d. de** on ou to the right of; **à d. et à gauche** (voyager etc) here, there and everywhere. ◆**droitier, -ière** a & nmf right-handed one. ◆**droiture** nf uprightness.

drôle [drol] a funny; **d. d'air/de type** funny look/fellow. ◆**—ment** adv funnily; (*extrêmement*) Fam dreadfully.

dromadaire [drɔmadɛr] nm dromedary.

dru [dry] a (*herbe etc*) thick, dense; – adv **tomber d.** (*pluie*) to pour down heavily; **pousser d.** to grow thick(ly).

du [dy] = **de + le**.

dû, due [dy] a **d. à** (*accident etc*) due to; – nm due; (*argent*) dues.

dualité [dɥalite] nf duality.

dubitatif, -ive [dybitatif, -iv] a (*regard etc*) dubious.

duc [dyk] nm duke. ◆**duché** nm duchy. ◆**duchesse** nf duchess.

duel [dɥɛl] nm duel.

dûment [dymɑ̃] adv duly.

dune [dyn] nf (sand) dune.

duo [dɥo] nm Mus duet; (*couple*) Hum duo.

dupe [dyp] nf dupe, fool; – a **d. de** duped by, fooled by. ◆**duper** vt to fool, dupe.

duplex [dypleks] nm split-level flat, Am duplex; (*émission en*) **d.** Tél link-up.

duplicata [dyplikata] nm inv duplicate.

duplicateur [dyplikatœr] nm (*machine*) duplicator.

duplicité [dyplisite] nf duplicity, deceit.

dur [dyr] a (*substance*) hard; (*difficile*) hard, tough; (*viande*) tough; (*hiver, leçon, ton*) harsh; (*personne*) hard, harsh; (*brosse, carton*) stiff; (*œuf*) hard-boiled; **d. d'oreille** hard of hearing; **d. à cuire** Fam hard-bitten, tough; – adv (*travailler*) hard; – nm Fam tough guy. ◆**durement** adv harshly. ◆**dureté** nf hardness; harshness; toughness.

durant [dyrɑ̃] prép during.

durc/ir [dyrsir] vti, – **se d.** vpr to harden. ◆**—issement** nm hardening.

durée [dyre] nf (*de film, événement*) length; (*période*) duration; (*de pile*) Él life; **de longue d.** (*disque*) long-playing. ◆**dur/er** vi to last; **ça dure depuis . . .** it's been going on for . . . . ◆**—able** a durable, lasting.

durillon [dyrijɔ̃] nm callus.

duvet [dyvɛ] nm **1** (*d'oiseau, de visage*) down. **2** (*sac*) sleeping bag. ◆**duveté** a, ◆**duveteux, -euse** a downy.

dynamique [dinamik] a dynamic; – nf (*force*) Fig dynamic force, thrust. ◆**dynamisme** nm dynamism.

dynamite [dinamit] nf dynamite. ◆**dynamiter** vt to dynamite.

dynamo [dinamo] nf dynamo.

dynastie [dinasti] nf dynasty.

dysenterie [disɑ̃tri] nf Méd dysentery.

dyslexique [disleksik] a & nmf dyslexic.

E

E, e [ə, ø] nm E, e.

eau, -x [o] nf water; **il est tombé beaucoup d'e.** a lot of rain fell; **e. douce** (*non salée*) fresh water; (*du robinet*) soft water; **e. salée** salt water; **e. de Cologne** eau de Cologne; **e. de toilette** toilet water; **grandes eaux** (*d'un parc*) ornamental fountains; **tomber à l'e.** (*projet*) to fall through; **ça lui fait venir l'e. à la bouche** it makes his *ou* her mouth water; **tout en e.** sweating; **prendre l'e.** (*chaussure*) to take water, leak. ◆**e.-de-vie** nf (pl **eaux-de-vie**) brandy. ◆**e.-forte** nf (pl **eaux-fortes**) (*gravure*) etching.

ébah/ir [ebair] vt to astound, dumbfound, amaze. ◆**—issement** nm amazement.

ébattre (s') [sebatr] vpr to frolic, frisk about. ◆**ébats** nmpl frolics.

ébauche [eboʃ] nf (*esquisse*) (rough) outline, (rough) sketch; (*début*) beginnings. ◆**ébaucher** vt (*projet, tableau, œuvre*) to sketch out, outline; **e. un sourire** to give a faint smile; – **s'é.** vpr to take shape.

ébène [ebɛn] nf (*bois*) ebony.

ébéniste [ebenist] nm cabinet-maker. ◆**ébénisterie** nf cabinet-making.

éberlué [eberlɥe] a Fam dumbfounded.

éblou/ir [ebluir] vt to dazzle. ◆**—issement** nm (*aveuglement*) dazzling, dazzle; (*émerveillement*) feeling of wonder; (*malaise*) fit of dizziness.

éboueur [ebwœr] nm dustman, Am garbage collector.

ébouillanter [ebujɑ̃te] vt to scald; – **s'é.** vpr to scald oneself.

éboul/er (s') [sebule] vpr (*falaise etc*) to crumble; (*terre, roches*) to fall. ◆**—ement** nm landslide. ◆**éboulis** nm (mass of) fallen debris.

ébouriffant [eburifɑ̃] a Fam astounding.

ébouriffer [eburife] vt (*cheveux*) to dishevel, ruffle, tousle.

ébranl/er [ebrɑ̃le] vt (mur, confiance etc) to shake; (santé) to weaken, affect; (personne) to shake, shatter; — **s'é.** vpr (train, cortège etc) to move off. ◆**—ement** nm (secousse) shaking, shock; (nerveux) shock.

ébrécher [ebreʃe] vt (assiette) to chip; (lame) to nick. ◆**ébréchure** nf chip; nick.

ébriété [ebrijete] nf drunkenness.

ébrouer (s') [sebrue] vpr (cheval) to snort; (personne) to shake oneself (about).

ébruiter [ebrɥite] vt (nouvelle etc) to make known, divulge.

ébullition [ebylisjɔ̃] nf boiling; **être en é.** (eau) to be boiling; (ville) Fig to be in turmoil.

écaille [ekɑj] nf 1 (de poisson) scale; (de tortue, d'huître) shell; (résine synthétique) tortoise-shell. 2 (de peinture) flake. ◆**écailler** 1 vt (poisson) to scale; (huître) to shell. 2 **s'é.** (peinture) to flake (off), peel.

écarlate [ekarlat] a & nf scarlet.

écarquiller [ekarkije] vt **é. les yeux** to open one's eyes wide.

écart [ekar] nm (intervalle) gap, distance; (mouvement, embardée) swerve; (différence) difference (**de** in, **entre** between); **écarts** (de conduite, langage etc) lapses in; **le grand é.** (de gymnaste) the splits; **à l'é.** out of the way; Fig to keep s.o. out of things; **à l'é.** de away from, clear of. ◆**écart/er** vt (objets) to move away from each other, move apart; (jambes) to spread, open; (rideaux) to draw (aside), open; (crainte, idée) to brush aside, dismiss; (carte) to discard; **é. qch de qch** to move sth away from sth; **é. qn de** (éloigner) to keep s.o. out of; (exclure) to keep s.o. out of; — **s'é.** vpr (s'éloigner) to move away (**de** from); (se séparer) to move aside (**de** from); **s'é. de** (sujet, bonne route) to stray from ou deviate from. ◆**—é** a (endroit) remote; **les jambes écartées** with legs (wide) apart. ◆**—ement** nm (espace) gap, distance (**de** between).

écartelé [ekartəle] a (tiraillé) torn between.

ecchymose [ekimoz] nf bruise.

ecclésiastique [eklezjastik] a ecclesiastical; — nm ecclesiastic, clergyman.

écervelé, -ée [esɛrvəle] a scatterbrained; — nmf scatterbrain.

échafaud [eʃafo] nm (pour exécution) scaffold.

échafaudage [eʃafodaʒ] nm (construction) scaffold(ing); (tas) heap; (système) Fig fabric. ◆**échafauder** vi to put up scaffolding ou a scaffold; — vt (projet etc) to put together, think up.

échalas [eʃala] nm **grand é.** tall skinny person.

échalote [eʃalɔt] nf Bot Culin shallot, scallion.

échancré [eʃɑ̃kre] a (encolure) V-shaped, scooped. ◆**échancrure** nf (de robe) opening.

échange [eʃɑ̃ʒ] nm exchange; **en é.** in exchange (**de** for). ◆**échanger** vt to exchange (**contre** for). ◆**échangeur** nm (intersection) Aut interchange.

échantillon [eʃɑ̃tijɔ̃] nm sample. ◆**échantillonnage** nm (collection) range (of samples).

échappatoire [eʃapatwar] nf evasion, way out.

échapp/er [eʃape] vi **é. à qn** to escape from s.o.; **é. à la mort/un danger/etc** to escape death/a danger/etc; **ce nom m'échappe** that name escapes me; **ça lui a échappé (des mains)** it slipped out of his ou her hands; **laisser é.** (cri) to let out; (objet, occasion) to let slip; **l'é. belle** to have a close shave; **ça m'a échappé** (je n'ai pas compris) I didn't catch it; — **s'é.** vpr (s'enfuir) to escape (**de** from); (s'éclipser) to slip away; Sp to break away; (gaz, eau) to escape, come out. ◆**-é, -ée** nmf runaway. ◆**-ée** nf Sp breakaway; (vue) vista. ◆**-ement** nm **tuyau d'é.** Aut exhaust pipe; **pot d'é.** Aut silencer, Am muffler.

écharde [eʃard] nf (de bois) splinter.

écharpe [eʃarp] nf scarf; (de maire) sash; **en é.** (bras) in a sling; **prendre en é.** Aut to hit sideways.

écharper [eʃarpe] vt **é. qn** to cut s.o. to bits.

échasse [eʃas] nf (bâton) stilt. ◆**échassier** nm wading bird.

échauder [eʃode] vt **être échaudé, se faire é.** (déçu) Fam to be taught a lesson.

échauffer [eʃofe] vt (moteur) to overheat; (esprit) to excite; — **s'é.** vpr (discussion) & Sp to warm up.

échauffourée [eʃofure] nf (bagarre) clash, brawl, skirmish.

échéance [eʃeɑ̃s] nf Com date (due), expiry ou Am expiration date; (paiement) payment (due); (obligation) commitment; **à brève/longue é.** (projet, emprunt) short-/long-term.

échéant (le cas) [ləkazeʃeɑ̃] adv if the occasion should arise, possibly.

échec [eʃɛk] nm 1 (insuccès) failure; **faire é. à** (inflation etc) to hold in check. 2 **les**

échecs (jeu) chess; **en é.** in check; **é.!** check!; **é. et mat!** checkmate!

échelle [eʃɛl] nf 1 (marches) ladder; **faire la courte é. à qn** to give s.o. a leg up. 2 (mesure, dimension) scale; **à l'é.** nationale on a national scale. ◆**échelon** nm (d'échelle) rung; (de fonctionnaire) grade; (dans une organisation) echelon; **à l'é. régional/national** on a regional/national level. ◆**échelonner** vt (paiements) to space out, space out; — **s'é.** vpr to be spread out.

écheveau, -x [eʃvo] nm (de laine) skein; Fig muddle, tangle.

échevelé [eʃəvle] a (ébouriffé) dishevelled; (course, danse etc) Fig wild.

échine [eʃin] nf Anat backbone, spine.

échiner (s') [eʃine] vpr (s'évertuer) Fam to knock oneself out (à faire doing).

échiquier [eʃikje] nm (tableau) chessboard.

écho [eko] nm (d'un son) echo; (réponse) response; pl Journ gossip (items), local news; **avoir des échos de** to hear some news about; **se faire l'é. de** (opinions etc) to echo. ◆**échotier, -ière** nmf Journ gossip columnist.

échographie [ekografi] nf (ultrasound) scan; **passer une é.** (femme enceinte) to have a scan.

échoir* [eʃwar] vi (terme) to expire; **é. à** (part) to fall to s.o.

échouer [eʃwe] vi to fail; **é. à** (examen) to fail. 2 vi, — **s'é.** vpr (navire) to run aground.

éclabousser [eklabuse] vt to splash, spatter (de with); (salir) Fig to tarnish the image of. ◆**éclaboussure** nf splash, spatter.

éclair [eklɛr] 1 nm (lumière) flash; **un é.** Mét a flash of lightning. 2 nm (gâteau) éclair. 3 a inv (visite, raid) lightning.

éclaircir [eklɛrsir] vt (couleur etc) to lighten, make lighter; (sauce) to thin out; (question, mystère) to clear up, clarify; — **s'é.** vpr (ciel) to clear (up); (idées) to become clear(er); (devenir moins dense) to thin out; **s'é. la voix** to clear one's throat. ◆**—ie** nf (dans le ciel) clear patch; (durée) sunny spell. ◆**—issement** nm (explication) clarification.

éclairer [eklɛre] vt (pièce etc) to light (up); (situation) Fig to throw light on; **é. qn** (avec une lampe etc) to give s.o. some light; (informer) Fig to enlighten s.o.; — vi (lampe) to give light; — **s'é.** vpr (visage) to light up, brighten up; (question, situation) to become clear(er); **s'é. à la bougie** to use candlelight. ◆**—é** a (averti) enlightened; **bien/mal é.** (illuminé) well/badly lit.

◆**—age** nm (de pièce etc) light(ing); (point de vue) Fig light.

◆**—eur, -euse** [eklɛrœr, -øz] nm Mil scout; — nmf (boy) scout, girl guide.

éclat [ekla] nm 1 (de la lumière) brightness; (de phare) Aut glare; (du feu) blaze; (splendeur) brilliance, radiance; (de la jeunesse) bloom; (de diamant) glitter, sparkle. 2 (fragment de verre ou de bois) splinter; (de rire, colère) (out)burst; **é. d'obus** shrapnel; **éclats de voix** noisy outbursts, shouts. ◆**éclat/er** vi (pneu, obus etc) to burst; (pétard, bombe) to go off, explode; (verre) to shatter, break into pieces; (guerre, incendie) to break out; (orage, scandale) to break; (parti) to break up; **é. de rire** to burst out laughing; **é. en sanglots** to burst into tears. ◆**—ant** a (lumière, couleur, succès) brilliant; (bruit) thunderous; (vérité) blinding; (beauté) radiant. ◆**—ement** nm (de pneu etc) bursting; (de bombe etc) explosion; (de parti) break-up.

éclectique [eklɛktik] a eclectic.

éclipse [eklips] nf (du soleil) & Fig eclipse. ◆**éclipser** vt to eclipse; — **s'é.** vpr (soleil) to be eclipsed; (partir) Fam to slip away.

éclopé, -ée [eklope] a & nmf limping ou lame (person).

éclore [eklɔr] vi (œuf) to hatch; (fleur) to open (out), blossom. ◆**éclosion** nf hatching; opening, blossoming.

écluse [eklyz] nf Nau lock.

écœurer [ekœre] vt (aliment etc) to make (s.o.) feel sick; (au moral) to sicken, nauseate. ◆**—ement** nm (répugnance) nausea, disgust.

école [ekɔl] nf school; (militaire) academy; **aller à l'é.** to go to school; **é. de danse/dessin** dancing/art school; **faire é.** to gain a following; **les grandes écoles** universities establishments giving high-level professional training; **é. normale** teachers' training college. ◆**écolier, -ière** nmf schoolboy, schoolgirl.

écologie [ekɔlɔʒi] nf ecology. ◆**écologique** a ecological. ◆**écologiste** nmf Pol environmentalist.

éconduire [ekɔ̃dɥir] vt (repousser) to reject.

économe [ekɔnɔm] 1 a thrifty, economical. 2 nmf (de collège etc) bursar, steward. ◆**économie** nf (activité économique, vertu) economy; pl (pécule) savings; **une é. de** (gain) a saving; **faire une é. de temps** to save time; **faire des économies** to save (up); **é. politique** economics. ◆**économique** a 1 (doctrine etc) economic; **science é.** economics. 2 (bon marché, *avantageux*) economical. ◆**économiquement** *adv* economically. ◆**économiser** *vt* (*forces, argent, énergie etc*) to save; – *vi* to economize (**sur** on). ◆**économiste** *nmf* economist.

écoper [ekɔpe] **1** *vt* (*bateau*) to bail out, bale out. **2** *vi Fam* to cop it; **é. (de)** (*punition*) to cop, get.

écorce [ekɔrs] *nf* (*d'arbre*) bark; (*de fruit*) peel, skin; **l'é. terrestre** the earth's crust.

écorcher [ekɔrʃe] *vt* (*animal*) to skin, flay; (*érafler*) to graze; (*client*) *Fam* to fleece; (*langue étrangère*) *Fam* to murder; **é. les oreilles** to grate on one's ears; – **s'é.** *vpr* to graze oneself. ◆**écorchure** *nf* graze.

Écosse [ekɔs] *nf* Scotland. ◆**écossais, -aise** *a* Scottish; (*tissu*) tartan; (*whisky*) Scotch; – *nmf* Scot.

écosser [ekɔse] *vt* (*pois*) to shell.

écot [eko] *nm* (*quote-part*) share.

écoul/er [ekule] **1** *vt* (*se débarrasser de*) to dispose of; (*produits*) *Com* to sell (off), clear. **2 s'é.** *vpr* (*eau*) to flow out, run out; (*temps*) to pass, elapse; (*foule*) to disperse. ◆**-é** *a* (*années etc*) past. ◆**-ement** *nm* **1** (*de liquide, véhicules*) flow; (*de temps*) passage. **2** (*débit*) *Com* sale, selling.

écourter [ekurte] *vt* (*séjour, discours etc*) to cut short; (*texte, tige etc*) to shorten.

écoute [ekut] *nf* listening; **à l'é.** *Rad* tuned in, listening in (**de** to); **être aux écoutes** (*attentif*) to keep one's ears open (**de** for). ◆**écout/er** *vt* to listen to; (*radio*) to listen (**in**) to; – *vi* to listen; (*aux portes etc*) to eavesdrop, listen; **si je m'écoutais** if I did what I wanted. ◆**-eur** *nm* (*de téléphone*) earpiece; *pl* (*casque*) headphones, earphones.

écrabouiller [ekrabuje] *vt Fam* to crush to a pulp.

écran [ekrã] *nm* screen; **le petit é.** television.

écras/er [ekraze] *vt* (*broyer*) to crush; (*fruit, insecte*) to squash, crush; (*cigarette*) to put out; (*tuer*) *Aut* to run over; (*vaincre*) to beat (hollow), crush; (*dominer*) to outstrip; **écrasé de** (*travail, douleur*) overwhelmed with; **se faire é.** *Aut* to get run over; – **s'é.** *vpr* (*avion, voiture*) to crash (**contre** into); **s'é. dans** (*foule*) to crush ou squash into. ◆**-ant** *a* (*victoire, nombre, chaleur*) overwhelming. ◆**-é** *a* (*nez*) snub. ◆**-ement** *nm* crushing.

écrémer [ekreme] *vt* (*lait*) to skim, cream; (*collection etc*) *Fig* to cream off the best from.

écrevisse [ekrəvis] *nf* (*crustacé*) crayfish.

écrier (s') [ekrije] *vpr* to cry out, exclaim (**que** that).

écrin [ekrɛ̃] *nm* (jewel) case.

écrire [ekrir] *vt* to write; (*noter*) to write (down); (*orthographier*) to spell; **é. à la machine** to type; – *vi* to write; – **s'é.** *vpr* (*mot*) to be spelt. ◆**écrit** *nm* written document, paper; (*examen*) *Scol* written paper; *pl* (*œuvres*) writings; **par é.** in writing. ◆**écriteau, -x** *nm* notice, sign. ◆**écriture** *nf* (*système*) writing; (*personnelle*) (hand)writing; *pl Com* accounts; **l'É.** *Rel* the Scripture(s). ◆**écrivain** *nm* author, writer.

écrou [ekru] *nm Tech* nut.

écrouer [ekrue] *vt* to imprison.

écroul/er (s') [ekrule] *vpr* (*édifice, projet etc*) to collapse; (*blessé etc*) to slump down, collapse. ◆**-ement** *nm* collapse.

écru [ekry] *a* **toile é.** unbleached linen; **soie é.** raw silk.

écueil [ekœj] *nm* (*rocher*) reef; (*obstacle*) *Fig* pitfall.

écuelle [ekɥɛl] *nf* (*bol*) bowl.

éculé [ekyle] *a* (*chaussure*) worn out at the heel; *Fig* hackneyed.

écume [ekym] *nf* (*de mer, bave d'animal etc*) foam; *Culin* scum. ◆**écumer** *vt Culin* to skim; (*piller*) to plunder; – *vi* to foam (**de rage** with anger). ◆**écumoire** *nf Culin* skimmer.

écureuil [ekyrœj] *nm* squirrel.

écurie [ekyri] *nf* stable.

écusson [ekysɔ̃] *nm* (*emblème d'étoffe*) badge.

écuyer, -ère [ekɥije, -ɛr] *nmf* (*cavalier*) (horse) rider, equestrian.

eczéma [ɛgzema] *nm Méd* eczema.

édenté [edãte] *a* toothless.

édicter [edikte] *vt* to enact, decree.

édifice [edifis] *nm* building, edifice; (*ensemble organisé*) *Fig* edifice. ◆**édification** *nf* construction; edification; enlightenment. ◆**édifier** *vt* (*bâtiment*) to construct, erect; (*théorie*) to construct; **é. qn** (*moralement*) to edify s.o.; (*détromper*) *Iron* to enlighten s.o.

Édimbourg [edɛ̃bur] *nm ou f* Edinburgh.

édit [edi] *nm Hist* edict.

éditer [edite] *vt* (*publier*) to publish; (*annoter*) to edit. ◆**éditeur, -trice** *nmf* publisher; editor. ◆**édition** *nf* (*livre, journal*) edition; (*diffusion, métier*) publishing. ◆**éditorial, -aux** *nm* (*article*) editorial.

édredon [edrədɔ̃] *nm* eiderdown.

éducation [edykasjɔ̃] *nf* (*enseignement*) education; (*façon d'élever*) upbringing, education; **avoir de l'é.** to have good manners, be well-bred. ◆**éducateur, -trice** *nmf* educator. ◆**éducatif, -ive** *a* educational. ◆**éduquer** *vt* (*à l'école*) to educate (*s.o.*); (*à la maison*) to bring (*s.o.*) up, educate (*s.o.*) (*à faire* to do); (*esprit*) to educate, train.

effac/er [efase] *vt* (*gommer*) to rub out, erase; (*en lavant*) to wash out; (*avec un chiffon*) to wipe away; (*souvenir*) Fig to blot out, erase. ◆**—é é** *a* (*modeste*) self-effacing. — **s'e.** *vpr* (*souvenir, couleur etc*) to fade; (*se placer en retrait*) to step ou draw aside. ◆**—ement** *nm* (*modestie*) self-effacement.

effar/er [efare] *vt* to scare, alarm. ◆**—ement** *nm* alarm.

effaroucher [efaruʃe] *vt* to scare away, frighten away.

effectif, -ive [efɛktif, -iv] **1** *a* (*réel*) effective, real. **2** *nm* (*nombre*) (total) strength; (*de classe*) *Scol* size, total number; *pl* (*employés*) & *Mil* manpower. ◆**effectivement** *adv* (*en effet*) actually, effectively, indeed.

effectuer [efɛktɥe] *vt* (*expérience etc*) to carry out; (*paiement, trajet etc*) to make.

efféminé [efemine] *a* effeminate.

effervescent [efɛrvesɑ̃] *a* (*mélange, jeunesse*) effervescent. ◆**effervescence** *nf* (*exaltation*) excitement, effervescence; (*de liquide*) effervescence.

effet [efɛ] *nm* **1** (*résultat*) effect; (*impression*) impression, effect (**sur** on); **faire de l'e.** (*remède etc*) to be effective; **rester sans e.** to have no effect; **à cet e.** to this end, for this purpose; **en e.** indeed, in fact; **il me fait l'e. d'être fatigué** he seems to me to be tired; **sous l'e. de la colère** (*agir*) in anger, out of anger. **2 e.** de commerce bill, draft.

effets [efɛ] *nmpl* (*vêtements*) clothes, things.

efficace [efikas] *a* (*mesure etc*) effective; (*personne*) efficient. ◆**efficacité** *nf* effectiveness, efficiency.

effigie [efiʒi] *nf* effigy.

effilé [efile] *a* tapering, slender.

effilocher (s') [sefiloʃe] *vpr* to fray.

efflanqué [eflɑ̃ke] *a* emaciated.

effleurer [eflœre] *vt* (*frôler*) to skim, touch lightly; (*égratigner*) to graze; (*question*) Fig to touch on; **e. qn** (*pensée etc*) to cross s.o.'s mind.

effondr/er (s') [sefɔ̃dre] *vpr* (*projet, édifice, personne*) to collapse; (*toit*) to cave in, collapse. ◆**—ement** *nm* collapse; *Com* (*abattement*) dejection.

efforcer (s') [seforse] *vpr* **s'e. de faire** to try (hard) ou endeavour ou strive to do.

effort [efɔr] *nm* effort; **sans e.** (*réussir etc*) effortlessly; (*réussite etc*) effortless.

effraction [efraksjɔ̃] *nf* **pénétrer par e.** (*cambrioleur*) to break in; **vol avec e.** housebreaking.

effranger (s') [sefrɑ̃ʒe] *vpr* to fray.

effray/er [efreje] *vt* to frighten, scare; — **s'e.** *vpr* to be frightened ou scared. ◆**—ant** *a* frightening, scary.

effréné [efrene] *a* unrestrained, wild.

effriter [efrite] *vt*, — **s'e.** *vpr* to crumble (away).

effroi [efrwa] *nm* (*frayeur*) dread. ◆**effroyable** *a* dreadful, appalling. ◆**effroyablement** *adv* dreadfully.

effronté [efrɔ̃te] *a* (*enfant etc*) cheeky, brazen; (*mensonge*) shameless. ◆**effronterie** *nf* effrontery.

effusion [efyzjɔ̃] *nf* **1 e.** de sang bloodshed. **2** (*manifestation*) effusion; **avec e.** effusively.

égailler (s') [segaje] *vpr* to disperse.

égal, -ale, -aux [egal, -o] *a* equal (**à** to); (*uniforme, régulier*) even; **ça m'est é.** I don't care, it's all the same to me; — *nmf* (*personne*) equal; **traiter qn d'é. à é.** ou **en é.** to treat s.o. as an equal; **sans é.** without match. ◆**—ement** *adv* (*au même degré*) equally; (*aussi*) also, as well. ◆**égaler** *vt* to equal, match (**en** in); (*en quantité*) *Math* to equal. ◆**égalisation** *nf* *Sp* equalization; levelling. ◆**égaliser** *vt* to equalize; (*terrain*) to level; — *vi* *Sp* to equalize. ◆**égalitaire** *a* egalitarian. ◆**égalité** *nf* equality; (*régularité*) evenness; **à é.** (*de score*) *Sp* equal (on points); **signe d'é.** *Math* equals sign.

égard [egar] *nm* **à l'é. de** (*concernant*) with respect ou regard to; (*envers*) towards; **avoir des égards pour** to have respect ou consideration for; **à cet é.** in this respect; **à certains égards** in some respects.

égarer [egare] *vt* (*objet*) to mislay; **é. qn** (*dérouter*) to mislead s.o.; (*aveugler, troubler*) to lead s.o. astray, misguide s.o.; — **s'é.** *vpr* to lose one's way, get lost; (*objet*) to get mislaid, go astray; (*esprit*) to wander.

égayer [egeje] *vt* (*pièce*) to brighten up; **é. qn** (*réconforter, amuser*) to cheer s.o. up; — **s'é.** *vpr* (*par la moquerie*) to be amused.

égide [eʒid] *nf* **sous l'é. de** under the aegis of.

églantier [eglɑ̃tje] *nm* (*arbre*) wild rose. ◆**églantine** *nf* (*fleur*) wild rose.

église [egliz] *nf* church.

égocentrique [egɔsɑ̃trik] *a* egocentric.

égoïne [egɔin] *nf* (*scie*) é. hand saw.

égoïsme [egɔism] *nm* selfishness, egoism. ◆**égoïste** *a* selfish, egoistic(al); – *nmf* egoist.

égorger [egɔrʒe] *vt* to cut ou slit the throat of.

égosiller (s') [segozije] *vpr* to scream one's head off, bawl out.

égotisme [egotism] *nm* egotism.

égout [egu] *nm* sewer; **eaux d'é.** sewage.

égoutter [egute] *vt* (*vaisselle*) to drain; (*légumes*) to strain, drain; – *vi*, – **s'é.** *vpr* to drain; to strain; (*linge*) to drip. ◆**égouttoir** *nm* (*panier*) (dish) drainer.

égratigner [egratiɲe] *vt* to scratch. ◆**égratignure** *nf* scratch.

égrener [egrane] *vt* (*raisins*) to pick off; (*épis*) to shell; **é. son chapelet** *Rel* to count one's beads.

Égypte [eʒipt] *nf* Egypt. ◆**égyptien, -ienne** [-sjɛ̃, -sjɛn] *a & nmf* Egyptian.

eh! [e] *int* hey!; **eh bien!** well!

éhonté [eɔ̃te] *a* shameless; **mensonge é.** barefaced lie.

éjecter [eʒɛkte] *vt* to eject. ◆**éjectable** *a* **siège é.** *Av* ejector seat. ◆**éjection** *nf* ejection.

élaborer [elabɔre] *vt* (*système etc*) to elaborate. ◆**élaboration** *nf* elaboration.

élaguer [elage] *vt* (*arbre, texte etc*) to prune.

élan [elɑ̃] *nm* **1** (*vitesse*) momentum, impetus; (*impulsion*) impulse; (*fougue*) fervour, spirit; **prendre son é.** *Sp* to take a run (up); **d'un seul é.** in one bound. **2** (*animal*) elk.

élanc/er [elɑ̃se] **1** *vi* (*dent etc*) to give shooting pains. **2 s'é.** *vpr* (*bondir*) to leap ou rush (forward); **s'é. vers le ciel** (*tour*) to soar up (high) into the sky. ◆**—é** *a* (*personne, taille etc*) slender. ◆**—ement** *nm* shooting pain.

élargir [elarʒir] **1** *vt* (*chemin*) to widen; (*esprit, débat*) to broaden; – **s'é.** *vpr* (*sentier etc*) to widen out. **2** *vt* (*prisonnier*) to free.

élastique [elastik] *a* (*objet, caractère*) elastic; (*règlement, notion*) flexible, supple; – *nm* (*tissu*) elastic; (*lien*) elastic ou rubber band. ◆**élasticité** *nf* elasticity.

élection [elɛksjɔ̃] *nf* election; **é. partielle** by-election. ◆**électeur, -trice** *nmf* voter, elector. ◆**électoral, -aux** *a* (*campagne, réunion*) election-; **collège é.** electoral college. ◆**électorat** *nm* (*électeurs*) electorate, voters.

électricien [elɛktrisjɛ̃] *nm* electrician. ◆**électricité** *nf* electricity; **coupure d'é.** power cut. ◆**électrifier** *vt* *Rail* to electrify. ◆**électrique** *a* (*pendule, décharge*) electric; (*courant, fil*) electric(al); (*phénomène, effet*) *Fig* electric. ◆**électriser** *vt* (*animer*) *Fig* to electrify. ◆**électrocuter** *vt* to electrocute.

électrode [elɛktrɔd] *nf* *Él* electrode.

électrogène [elɛktrɔʒɛn] *a* **groupe é.** *Él* generator.

électroménager [elɛktrɔmenaʒe] *am* **appareil é.** household electrical appliance.

électron [elɛktrɔ̃] *nm* electron. ◆**électronicien, -ienne** *nmf* electronics engineer. ◆**électronique** *a* electronic; (*microscope*) electron-; – *nf* electronics.

électrophone [elɛktrɔfɔn] *nm* record player.

élégant [elegɑ̃] *a* (*style, mobilier, solution etc*) elegant; (*bien habillé*) smart, elegant. ◆**élégamment** *adv* elegantly; smartly. ◆**élégance** *nf* elegance.

élégie [eleʒi] *nf* elegy.

élément [elemɑ̃] *nm* (*composante, personne*) & *Ch* element; (*de meuble*) unit; (*d'ensemble*) *Math* member; (*de notions*) rudiments, elements; **dans son é.** (*milieu*) in one's element. ◆**élémentaire** *a* elementary.

éléphant [elefɑ̃] *nm* elephant. ◆**éléphantesque** *a* (*énorme*) *Fam* elephantine.

élévateur [elevatœr] *am* **chariot é.** forklift truck.

élévation [elevasjɔ̃] *nf* raising; *Géom* elevation; **é. de** (*hausse*) rise in.

élève [elɛv] *nmf* *Scol* pupil.

élev/er [elve] *vt* (*prix, objection, voix etc*) to raise; (*enfant*) to bring up, raise; (*animal*) to breed, rear; (*âme*) to uplift, raise; – **s'é.** *vpr* (*prix, montagne, ton, avion etc*) to rise; **s'é. à** (*prix etc*) to amount to; **s'é. contre** to rise up against. ◆**—é** *a* (*haut*) high; (*noble*) noble; **bien/mal é.** well-/bad-mannered. ◆**—age** *nm* (*de bovins*) cattle rearing; **l'é. de** the breeding ou rearing of. ◆**—eur, -euse** *nmf* breeder.

élider [elide] *vt Ling* to elide.

éligible [eliʒibl] *a* *Pol* eligible (à for).

élimé [elime] *a* (*tissu*) threadbare, worn thin.

éliminer [elimine] *vt* to eliminate. ◆**élimination** *nf* elimination. ◆**éliminatoire** *a & nf* (*épreuve*) é. *Sp* heat, qualifying round.

élire* [elir] *vt Pol* to elect (à to).

élision [elizjɔ̃] *nf Ling* elision.

élite [elit] *nf* elite (**de** of); **d'é.** (*chef, sujet etc*) top-notch.

elle [ɛl] *pron* **1** (*sujet*) she; (*chose, animal*) it;

pl they; **e. est** she is; it is; **elles sont** they are. **2** (*complément*) her; (*chose, animal*) it; *pl* them; them; for her; **pour elles** for them; **plus grande qu'e./qu'elles** taller than her/them. ◆**e.-même** *pron* herself; (*chose, animal*) itself; *pl* themselves.

ellipse [elips] *nf Géom* ellipse. ◆**elliptique** *a* elliptical.

élocution [elɔkysjɔ̃] *nf* diction; **défaut d'é.** speech defect.

éloge [elɔʒ] *nm* praise; (*panégyrique*) eulogy; **faire l'é. de** to praise. ◆**élogieux, -euse** *a* laudatory.

éloign/er [elwaɲe] *vt* (*chose, personne*) to move *ou* take away (**de** from); (*clients*) to keep away; (*crainte, idée*) to get rid of, banish; (*date*) to put off; **é. qn de** (*sujet, but*) to take *ou* get s.o. away from; **— s'é.** (*partir*) to move *ou* go away (**de** from); (*dans le passé*) to become (more) remote; **s'é. de** (*sujet, but*) to get away from. ◆**-é** *a* far-off, remote, distant; (*parent*) distant; **é. de** (*village, maison etc*) far (away) from; (*très différent*) far removed from. ◆**-ement** *nm* remoteness, distance; (*absence*) separation (**de** from); **avec l'é.** (*avec le recul*) with time.

élongation [elɔ̃gasjɔ̃] *nf Méd* pulled muscle.

éloquent [elɔkɑ̃] *a* eloquent. ◆**éloquence** *nf* eloquence.

élu, -ue [ely] *voir* **élire**; **— *nmf Pol* elected member *ou* representative; **les élus** *Rel* the chosen, the elect.

élucider [elyside] *vt* to elucidate. ◆**élucidation** *nf* elucidation.

éluder [elyde] *vt* to elude, evade.

émacié [emasje] *a* emaciated.

émail, -aux [emaj, -o] *nm* enamel; **en é.** enamel-. ◆**émailler** *vt* to enamel.

émaillé [emaje] *a* **é. de fautes/etc** (*texte*) peppered with errors/*etc*.

émanciper [emɑ̃sipe] *vt* (*femmes*) to emancipate; **— s'é.** *vpr* to become emancipated. ◆**émancipation** *nf* emancipation.

émaner [emane] *vi* to emanate. ◆**émanation** *nf* emanation; **une é. de** *Fig* a product of.

emball/er [ɑ̃bale] **1** *vt* (*dans une caisse etc*) to pack; (*dans du papier*) to wrap (up). **2** *vt* (*moteur*) to race; **e. qn** (*passionner*) *Fam* to enthuse s.o., thrill; **— s'e.** *vpr* (*personne*) *Fam* to get carried away; (*cheval*) to bolt; (*moteur*) to race. ◆**-é** *a Fam* enthusiastic. ◆**-age** *nm* (*action*) *s* packing; wrapping; (*caisse*) packaging; (*papier*) wrapping (paper). ◆**-ement** *nm Fam* (sudden) enthusiasm.

embarcadère [ɑ̃barkadɛr] *nm* landing place, quay.

embarcation [ɑ̃barkasjɔ̃] *nf* (small) boat.

embardée [ɑ̃barde] *nf Aut* (sudden) swerve; **faire une e.** to swerve.

embargo [ɑ̃bargo] *nm* embargo.

embarqu/er [ɑ̃barke] *vt* (*passagers*) to embark, take on board; (*marchandises*) to load (up); (*voler*) *Fam* to walk off with; (*prisonnier*) *Fam* to cart off; **e. qn dans** (*affaire*) *Fam* to involve s.o. in, launch s.o. into; **— vi, — s'e.** *vpr* to embark, (go on) board; **s'e. dans** (*aventure etc*) *Fam* to embark on. ◆**-ement** *nm* (*de passagers*) boarding.

embarras [ɑ̃bara] *nm* (*malaise, gêne*) embarrassment; (*difficulté*) difficulty, trouble; (*obstacle*) obstacle; **dans l'e.** in difficulty; **faire des e.** (*chichis*) to make a fuss. ◆**embarrass/er** *vt* (*obstruer*) to clutter, encumber; **e. qn** to be in s.o.'s way; (*déconcerter*) to embarrass s.o., bother s.o.; **s'e. de** to burden oneself with; (*se soucier*) to bother oneself about. ◆**-ant** *a* (*paquet*) cumbersome; (*question*) embarrassing.

embauche [ɑ̃boʃ] *nf* (*action*) hiring; (*travail*) work. ◆**embaucher** *vt* (*ouvrier*) to hire, take on.

embaumer [ɑ̃bome] **1** *vt* (*cadavre*) to embalm. **2** *vt* (*parfumer*) to give a sweet smell to; **— vi** to smell sweet.

embell/ir [ɑ̃belir] *vt* (*texte, vérité*) to embellish; **e. qn** to make s.o. attractive. ◆**-issement** *nm* (*de ville etc*) improvement, embellishment.

embêt/er [ɑ̃bete] *vt Fam* (*contrarier, taquiner*) to annoy, bother; (*raser*) to bore; **— s'e.** *vpr Fam* to get bored. ◆**-ant** *a Fam* annoying; boring. ◆**-ement** [-ɛtmɑ̃] *nm Fam* **un e.** (some) trouble *ou* bother; **des embêtements** trouble(s), bother.

emblée (d') [dɑ̃ble] *adv* right away.

emblème [ɑ̃blɛm] *nm* emblem.

embobiner [ɑ̃bɔbine] *vt* (*tromper*) *Fam* to hoodwink.

emboîter [ɑ̃bwate] *vt*, **— s'e.** *vpr* (*pièces*) to fit into each other, fit together; **e. le pas à qn** to follow on s.o.'s heels; (*imiter*) *Fig* to follow in s.o.'s footsteps.

embonpoint [ɑ̃bɔ̃pwɛ̃] *nm* plumpness.

embouchure [ɑ̃buʃyr] *nf* (*de cours d'eau*) mouth; *Mus* mouthpiece.

embourber (s') [sɑ̃burbe] *vpr* (*véhicule*) & *Fig* to get bogged down.

embourgeoiser (s') [sɑ̃burʒwaze] *vpr* to become middle-class.

embout [ãbu] nm (de canne) tip, end piece; (de seringue) nozzle.

embouteill/er [ãbuteje] vt Aut to jam, congest. ◆**-age** nm traffic jam.

emboutir [ãbutir] vt (voiture) to bash ou crash into; (métal) to stamp, emboss.

embranch/er (s') [sãbrãʃe] vpr (voie) to branch off. ◆**-ement** nm (de voie) junction, fork; (de règne animal) branch.

embras/er [ãbraze] vt to set ablaze; — **s'e.** vpr (prendre feu) to flare up. ◆**-ement** nm (troubles) flare-up.

embrass/er [ãbrase] vt (adopter, contenir) to embrace; **e. qn** to kiss s.o.; (serrer) to embrace ou hug s.o.; — **s'e.** vpr to kiss (each other). ◆**embrassade** nf embrace, hug.

embrasure [ãbrazyr] nf (de fenêtre, porte) opening.

embray/er [ãbreje] vi to let in ou engage the clutch. ◆**-age** nm (mécanisme, pédale) Aut clutch.

embrigader [ãbrigade] vt to recruit.

embrocher [ãbrɔʃe] vt Culin & Fig to skewer.

embrouiller [ãbruje] vt (fils) to tangle (up); (papiers etc) to muddle up, mix up; **e. qn** to confuse s.o., get s.o. muddled; — **s'e.** vpr to get confused ou muddled (dans in, with). ◆**embrouillamini** nm Fam muddle, mix-up. ◆**embrouillement** nm confusion, muddle.

embroussaillé [ãbrusaje] a (barbe, chemin) bushy.

embruns [ãbrœ̃] nmpl (sea) spray.

embryon [ãbrijɔ̃] nm embryo. ◆**embryonnaire** a Méd & Fig embryonic.

embûches [ãbyʃ] nfpl (difficultés) traps, pitfalls.

embuer [ãbɥe] vt (vitre, yeux) to mist up.

embusquer (s') [sãbyske] vpr to lie in ambush. ◆**embuscade** nf ambush.

éméché [emeʃe] a (ivre) Fam tipsy.

émeraude [emrod] nf emerald.

émerger [emerʒe] vi to emerge (de from).

émeri [emri] nm toile (d')é. emery cloth.

émerveill/er [emerveje] vt to amaze; — **s'é.** vpr to marvel, to be filled with wonder (de at). ◆**-ement** nm wonder, amazement.

émett/re* [emetr] vt (lumière, son etc) to give out, emit; Rad to transmit, broadcast; (cri) to utter; (opinion, vœu) to express; (timbre-poste, monnaie) to issue; (chèque) to draw; (emprunt) Com to float. ◆**-eur** nm (poste) é. Rad transmitter.

émeute [emøt] nf riot. ◆**émeutier, -ière** nmf rioter.

émietter [emjete] vt, — **s'é.** vpr (pain etc) to crumble.

émigr/er [emigre] vi (personne) to emigrate. ◆**-ant, -ante** nmf emigrant. ◆**-é, -ée** nmf exile, émigré. ◆**émigration** nf emigration.

éminent [eminã] a eminent. ◆**éminemment** [-amã] adv eminently. ◆**éminence** nf 1 (colline) hillock. 2 son É. Rel his Eminence.

émissaire [emiser] nm emissary.

émission [emisjɔ̃] nf (programme) TV Rad broadcast; (action) emission (de of); (de programme) TV Rad transmission; (de timbre-poste, monnaie) issue.

emmagasiner [ãmagazine] vt to store (up).

emmanchure [ãmãʃyr] nf (de vêtement) arm hole.

emmêler [ãmele] vt to tangle (up).

emménag/er [ãmenaʒe] vi (dans un logement) to move in; **e. dans** to move into. ◆**-ement** nm moving in.

emmener [ãmne] vt to take (à to); (prisonnier) to take away; **e. qn faire une promenade** to take s.o. for a walk.

emmerd/er [ãmerde] vt Arg to annoy, bug; (raser) to bore stiff; — **s'e.** vpr Arg to get bored stiff. ◆**-ement** nm Arg bother, trouble. ◆**-eur, -euse** nmf (personne) Arg pain in the neck.

emmitoufler (s') [sãmitufle] vpr to wrap (oneself) up.

emmurer [ãmyre] vt (personne) to wall in.

émoi [emwa] nm excitement; **en é.** agog, excited.

émoluments [emɔlymã] nmpl remuneration.

émotion [emosjɔ̃] nf (trouble) excitement; (sentiment) emotion; (peur) a scare. ◆**émotif, -ive** a emotional. ◆**émotionné** a Fam upset.

émouss/er [emuse] vt (pointe) to blunt; (sentiment) to dull. ◆**-é** a (pointe) blunt; (sentiment) dulled.

émouv/oir* [emuvwar] vt (affecter) to move, touch; — **s'é.** vpr to be moved ou touched. ◆**-ant** a moving, touching.

empailler [ãpaje] vt (animal) to stuff.

empaler (s') [sãpale] vpr to impale oneself.

empaqueter [ãpakte] vt to pack(age).

emparer (s') [sãpare] vpr **s'e. de** to seize, take hold of.

empât/er (s') [sãpate] vpr to fill out, get fat(ter). ◆**-é** a fleshy, fat.

empêch/er [ãpeʃe] vt to prevent, stop; **e. qn de faire** to prevent ou stop s.o. (from) doing; **n'empêche qu'il a raison** Fam all the same she's right; **n'empêche!** *Fam* all the same!; **elle ne peut pas s'e.** de rire she can't help laughing. **◆—ement** [-ɛʃmɑ̃] *nm* difficulty, hitch; **avoir un e.** to be unavoidably detained.

empereur [ɑ̃prœr] *nm* emperor.

empeser [ɑ̃pəze] *vt* to starch.

empester [ɑ̃pɛste] *vt* (*pièce*) to make stink, stink out; (*tabac etc*) to stink of; **e. qn** to stink s.o. out; – *vi* to stink.

empêtrer (s') [sɑ̃petre] *vpr* to get entangled (**dans** in).

emphase [ɑ̃faz] *nf* pomposity. **◆emphatique** *a* pompous.

empiéter [ɑ̃pjete] *vi* **e. sur** to encroach upon. **◆empiétement** *nm* encroachment.

empiffrer (s') [sɑ̃pifre] *vpr Fam* to gorge *ou* stuff oneself (**de** with).

empil/er [ɑ̃pile] *vt*, **– s'e.** *vpr* to pile up (**sur** on); **s'e. dans** (*personnes*) to pile into (*building, car etc*). **◆—ement** *nm* (*tas*) pile.

empire [ɑ̃pir] *nm* (*territoires*) empire; (*autorité*) hold, influence; **sous l'e. de** (*peur etc*) in the grip of.

empirer [ɑ̃pire] *vi* to worsen, get worse.

empirique [ɑ̃pirik] *a* empirical. **◆empirisme** *nm* empiricism.

emplacement [ɑ̃plasmɑ̃] *nm* site, location; (*de stationnement*) place.

emplâtre [ɑ̃platr] *nm* (*onguent*) *Méd* plaster.

emplette [ɑ̃plɛt] *nf* purchase; *pl* shopping.

emplir [ɑ̃plir] *vt*, **– s'e.** *vpr* to fill (**de** with).

emploi [ɑ̃plwa] *nm* **1** (*usage*) use; **e. du temps** timetable; **mode d'e.** directions (for use). **2** (*travail*) job, position, employment; **l'e.** (*travail*) *Écon Pol* employment; **sans e.** unemployed. **◆employ/er** *vt* (*utiliser*) to use; **e. qn** (*occuper*) to employ s.o.; **– s'e.** *vpr* (*expression etc*) to be used; **s'e. à faire** to devote oneself to doing. **◆—é, -ée** *nmf* employee; (*de bureau, banque*) clerk, employee; (*des postes/etc*) postal/etc worker; **e. de magasin** shop assistant, *Am* sales clerk. **◆employeur, -euse** *nmf* employer.

empocher [ɑ̃pɔʃe] *vt* (*argent*) to pocket.

empoigner [ɑ̃pwaɲe] *vt* (*saisir*) to grab, grasp; **– s'e.** *vpr* to come to blows, fight. **◆empoignade** *nf* (*querelle*) fight.

empoisonn/er [ɑ̃pwazɔne] *vt* (*personne, aliment, atmosphère*) to poison; (*empester*) to stink out; (*gâter, altérer*) to trouble, bedevil; **e. qn** (*embêter*) *Fam* to get on s.o.'s nerves; **– s'e.** *vpr* (*par accident*) to be poisoned; (*volontairement*) to poison oneself. **◆—ant** *a* (*embêtant*) *Fam* irritating.

◆—ement *nm* poisoning; (*ennui*) *Fam* problem, trouble.

emport/er [ɑ̃pɔrte] *vt* (*prendre*) to take (away) (**avec soi** with one); (*enlever*) to take away; (*prix, trophée*) to carry off; (*décision*) to carry; (*entraîner*) to carry along *ou* away; (*par le vent*) to blow off *ou* away; (*par les vagues*) to sweep away; (*par la maladie*) to carry off; **l'e. sur qn** to get the upper hand over s.o.; **se laisser e.** *Fig* to get carried away (**par** by); **– s'e.** *vpr* to lose one's temper (**contre** with). **◆—é** *a* (*caractère*) hot-tempered. **◆—ement** *nm* anger; *pl* fits of anger.

empoté [ɑ̃pɔte] *a Fam* clumsy.

empourprer (s') [sɑ̃purpre] *vpr* to turn crimson.

empreint [ɑ̃prɛ̃] *a* **e. de** stamped with, heavy with.

empreinte [ɑ̃prɛ̃t] *nf* (*marque*) & *Fig* mark, stamp; **e. digitale** fingerprint; **e. des pas** footprint.

empress/er (s') [sɑ̃prese] *vpr* **s'e. de faire** to hasten to do; **s'e. auprès de qn** to busy oneself with s.o., be attentive to s.o.; **s'e. autour de qn** to rush around s.o. **◆—é** *a* eager, attentive; **e. à faire** eager to do. **◆—ement** [-ɛsmɑ̃] *nm* (*hâte*) eagerness; (*auprès de qn*) attentiveness.

emprise [ɑ̃priz] *nf* ascendancy, hold (**sur** over).

emprisonn/er [ɑ̃prizɔne] *vt* & *Jur* to imprison; (*enfermer*) *Fig* to confine. **◆—ement** *nm* imprisonment.

emprunt [ɑ̃prœ̃] *nm* (*argent*) *Com* loan; (*mot*) *Ling* borrowed word; **un e. à** *Ling* a borrowing from; **l'e. de qch** the borrowing of sth; **d'e.** borrowed; **nom d'e.** assumed name. **◆emprunt/er** *vt* (*obtenir*) to borrow (**à qn** from s.o.); (*route etc*) to use; (*nom*) to assume; **e. à** (*tirer de*) to derive *ou* borrow from. **◆—é** *a* (*gêné*) ill-at-ease.

empuantir [ɑ̃pɥɑ̃tir] *vt* to make stink, stink out.

ému [emy] *voir* **émouvoir**; – *a* (*attendri*) moved; (*apeuré*) nervous; (*attristé*) upset; **une voix émue** a voice charged with emotion.

émulation [emylasjɔ̃] *nf* emulation.

émule [emyl] *nmf* imitator, follower.

en¹ [ɑ̃] *prép* **1** (*lieu*) in; (*direction*) to; **être en ville/en France** to be in town/in France; **aller en ville/en France** to go to town/to France. **2** (*temps*) in; **en été** in summer; **en février** in February; **d'heure en heure** from hour to hour. **3** (*moyen, état etc*) by; in; at; on; **en avion** by plane; **en groupe**

in a group; **en mer** at sea; **en guerre** at war; **en fleur** in flower; **en congé** on leave; **en vain** in vain. **4** (*matière*) in; **en bois** wooden, in wood; **chemise en nylon** nylon shirt; **c'est en or** it's (made of) gold. **5** (*comme*) **en cadeau** as a present; **en ami** as a friend. **6** (+ *participe présent*) **en mangeant/chantant/etc** while eating/singing/etc; **en apprenant que** ... on hearing that ...; **en souriant** smiling, with a smile; **en ne disant rien** by saying nothing; **sortir en courant** to run out. **7** (*transformation*) into; **traduire en** to translate into.

en² [ɑ̃] *pron & adv* **1** (= *de là*) from there; **j'en viens** I've just come from there. **2** (= *de ça, lui, eux etc*) **il en est content** he's pleased with it *ou* him *ou* them; **en parler** to talk about it; **en mourir** to die of *ou* from it; **elle m'en frappa** she struck me with it. **3** (*partitif*) some; **j'en ai** I have some; **en veux-tu?** do you want some *ou* any?; **je t'en supplie** I beg you (to).

encadr/er [ɑ̃kɑdre] *vt* (*tableau*) to frame; (*entourer d'un trait*) to box in; (*troupes, étudiants*) to supervise, train; (*prisonnier, accusé*) to flank. **◆—ement** *nm* (*action*) framing; supervision; (*de porte, photo*) frame; (*décor*) setting; (*personnel*) training and supervisory staff.

encaissé [ɑ̃kese] *a* (*vallée*) deep.

encaiss/er [ɑ̃kese] *vt* (*argent, loyer etc*) to collect; (*effet, chèque*) Com to cash; (*coup*) Fam to take; **je ne peux pas l'e.** Fam I can't stand him *ou* her. **◆—encaissement** *nm* (*de loyer etc*) collection; (*de chèque*) cashing.

encapuchonné [ɑ̃kapyʃɔne] *a* hooded.

encart [ɑ̃kar] *nm* (*feuille*) insert. **◆—encarter** *vt* to insert.

en-cas [ɑ̃kɑ] *nm inv* (*repas*) snack.

encastrer [ɑ̃kastre] *vt* to build in (**dans** into), embed (**dans** into).

encaustique [ɑ̃kostik] *nf* (wax) polish. **◆—encaustiquer** *vt* to wax, polish.

enceinte [ɑ̃sɛ̃t] **1** *af* (*femme*) pregnant; **e. de six mois/etc** six months/etc pregnant. **2** *nf* (*muraille*) (surrounding) wall; (*espace*) enclosure; **e. acoustique** (loud)speakers.

encens [ɑ̃sɑ̃] *nm* incense. **◆—encensoir** *nm* Rel censer.

encercler [ɑ̃serkle] *vt* to surround, encircle.

enchaîn/er [ɑ̃ʃene] *vt* (*animal*) to chain (up); (*prisonnier*) to put in chains, chain (up); (*assembler*) to link (up), connect; — *vi* (*continuer à parler*) to continue; — **s'e.** *vpr* (*idées etc*) to be linked (up). **◆—enchaînement** *nm* (*succession*) chain, series; (*liaison*) link(ing) (**de** between, of).

enchant/er [ɑ̃ʃɑ̃te] *vt* (*ravir*) to delight, enchant; (*ensorceler*) to bewitch, enchant. **◆—é** *a* (*ravi*) delighted (**de** with, **que** + *sub*) that); **e. de faire votre connaissance!** pleased to meet you! **◆—ement** *nm* delight; enchantment; **comme par e.** as if by magic. **◆—eur** *a* delightful, enchanting; — *nm* (*sorcier*) magician.

enchâsser [ɑ̃ʃɑse] *vt* (*diamant*) to set, embed.

enchère [ɑ̃ʃɛr] *nf* (*offre*) bid; **vente aux enchères** auction; **mettre aux enchères** (put up for) auction. **◆—enchér/ir** *vi* **e. sur qn** to outbid s.o. **◆—isseur** *nm* bidder.

enchevêtrer [ɑ̃ʃvetre] *vt* to (en)tangle; — **s'e.** *vpr* to get entangled (**dans** in). **◆—enchevêtrement** *nm* tangle, entanglement.

enclave [ɑ̃klav] *nf* enclave. **◆—enclaver** *vt* to enclose (completely).

enclencher [ɑ̃klɑ̃ʃe] *vt* Tech to engage.

enclin [ɑ̃klɛ̃] *am* **e. à** inclined *ou* prone to.

enclore [ɑ̃klɔr] *vt* (*terrain*) to enclose. **◆—enclos** *nm* (*terrain, clôture*) enclosure.

enclume [ɑ̃klym] *nf* anvil.

encoche [ɑ̃kɔʃ] *nf* notch, nick (**à** in).

encoignure [ɑ̃kwaɲyr] *nf* corner.

encoller [ɑ̃kɔle] *vt* to paste.

encolure [ɑ̃kɔlyr] *nf* (*de cheval, vêtement*) neck; (*tour du cou*) collar (size).

encombre (sans) [sɑ̃zɑ̃kɔ̃br] *adv* without a hitch.

encombr/er [ɑ̃kɔ̃bre] *vt* (*couloir, pièce etc*) to clutter up (**de** with); (*rue*) to congest, clog (**de** with); **e. qn** to hamper s.o.; — **s'e. de** to burden *ou* saddle oneself with. **◆—ant** *a* (*paquet*) bulky, cumbersome; (*présence*) awkward. **◆—é** *a* (*profession, marché*) overcrowded, saturated. **◆—ement** *nm* (*embarras*) clutter; Aut traffic jam; (*volume*) bulk(iness).

encontre de (à l') [alɑ̃kɔ̃trədə] *adv* against; (*contrairement à*) contrary to.

encore [ɑ̃kɔr] *adv* **1** (*toujours*) still; **tu es e. là?** are you still here? **2** (*avec négation*) yet; **pas e.** not yet; **ne pars pas e.** don't go yet; **je ne suis pas e. prêt** I'm not ready yet, I'm still not ready. **3** (*de nouveau*) again; **essaie e.** try again. **4** (*de plus*) **e. un café** another coffee, one more coffee; **e. une fois** (once) again, once more; **e. un** another (one), one more; **e. du pain** (some) more bread; **que veut-il e.?** what else *ou* more does he want?; **e. quelque chose** something else; **qui/quoi e.?** who/what else?; **chante e.** sing some more. **5** (*avec comparatif*) even, still; **e. mieux** even better, better still. **6** (*aussi*) also. **7 si e.** (*si seulement*) if only; **et e.!** (*à peine*) if that!, only just! **8 e. que** (+ *sub*) although.

encourag/er [ɑ̃kuraʒe] *vt* to encourage (à faire to do). ◆**—eant** a encouraging. ◆**—ement** *nm* encouragement.

encourir* [ɑ̃kurir] *vt* (*amende etc*) to incur.

encrasser [ɑ̃krase] *vt* to clog up (with dirt).

encre [ɑ̃kr] *nf* ink; **e. de Chine** Indian ink; **e. sympathique** invisible ink. ◆**encrier** *nm* inkwell, inkpot.

encroûter (s') [sɑ̃krute] *vpr Péj* to get set in one's ways; **s'e. dans** (*habitude*) to get stuck in.

encyclique [ɑ̃siklik] *nf Rel* encyclical.

encyclopédie [ɑ̃siklɔpedi] *nf* encyclop(a)edia. ◆**encyclopédique** a encyclop(a)edic.

endémique [ɑ̃demik] a endemic.

endetter [ɑ̃dete] *vt* **e. qn** to get s.o. into debt; **— s'e.** *vpr* to get into debt. ◆**endettement** *nm* (*dettes*) debts.

endeuiller [ɑ̃dœje] *vt* to plunge into mourning.

endiablé [ɑ̃djable] a (*rythme etc*) frantic, wild.

endiguer [ɑ̃dige] *vt* (*fleuve*) to dam (up); (*réprimer*) Fig to stem.

endimanché [ɑ̃dimɑ̃ʃe] a in one's Sunday best.

endive [ɑ̃div] *nf* chicory, endive.

endoctrin/er [ɑ̃dɔktrine] *vt* to indoctrinate. ◆**—ement** *nm* indoctrination.

endolori [ɑ̃dɔlɔri] a painful, aching.

endommager [ɑ̃dɔmaʒe] *vt* to damage.

endorm/ir* [ɑ̃dɔrmir] *vt* (*enfant, patient*) to put to sleep; (*ennuyer*) to send to sleep; (*soupçons etc*) to lull; (*douleur*) to deaden; **— s'e.** *vpr* to fall asleep, go to sleep. ◆**—i** a asleep, sleeping; (*indolent*) Fam sluggish.

endosser [ɑ̃dose] *vt* (*vêtement*) to put on, don; (*responsabilité*) to assume; (*chèque*) to endorse.

endroit [ɑ̃drwa] *nm* **1** place, spot; (*de film, livre*) part, place. **2** (*de tissu*) right side; **à l'e.** (*vêtement*) right side out, the right way round.

enduire* [ɑ̃dɥir] *vt* to smear, coat (de with). ◆**enduit** *nm* coating; (*de mur*) plaster.

endurant [ɑ̃dyrɑ̃] a hardy, tough. ◆**endurance** *nf* endurance.

endurc/ir [ɑ̃dyrsir] *vt* to harden; **s'e. à** (*personne*) to become hardened to (*pain etc*). ◆**—i** a hardened; (*célibataire*) confirmed. ◆**—issement** *nm* hardening.

endurer [ɑ̃dyre] *vt* to endure, bear.

énergie [enerʒi] *nf* energy; **avec é.** (*protester*

etc) forcefully. ◆**énergétique** a (*ressources etc*) energy-. ◆**énergique** a (*dynamique*) energetic; (*remède*) powerful; (*mesure, ton*) forceful. ◆**énergiquement** adv (*protester etc*) energetically.

énergumène [energymεn] *nmf Péj* rowdy character.

énerv/er [enerve] *vt* **é. qn** (*irriter*) to get on s.o.'s nerves; (*rendre énervé*) to make s.o. nervous; **— s'é.** *vpr* to get worked up. ◆**—é** a on edge, irritated. ◆**—ement** *nm* irritation, nervousness.

enfant [ɑ̃fɑ̃] *nmf* child (*pl* children); **e. en bas âge** infant; **un e. de** (*originaire*) a native of; **attendre un e.** to expect a baby *ou* a child; **e. trouvé** foundling; **e. de chœur** Rel altar boy; **e. prodige** child prodigy; **e. prodigue** prodigal son; **bon e.** (*caractère*) good natured. ◆**enfance** *nf* childhood; **première e.** infancy, early childhood; **dans son e.** (*science etc*) in its infancy. ◆**enfanter** *vt* to give birth to; **— vi** to give birth. ◆**enfantillage** *nm* childishness. ◆**enfantin** a (*voix, joie*) childlike; (*langage, jeu*) children's; (*puéril*) childish; (*simple*) easy.

enfer [ɑ̃fεr] *nm* hell; **d'e.** (*vision, bruit*) infernal; **feu d'e.** roaring fire; **à un train d'e.** at breakneck speed.

enfermer [ɑ̃fεrme] *vt* (*personne etc*) to shut up, lock up; (*objet précieux*) to lock up, shut away; (*jardin*) to enclose; **s'e. dans** (*chambre etc*) to shut *ou* lock oneself (up) in; (*attitude etc*) Fig to maintain stubbornly.

enferrer (s') [sɑ̃fεre] *vpr* **s'e. dans** to get caught up in.

enfiévré [ɑ̃fjevre] a (*surexcité*) feverish.

enfiler [ɑ̃file] *vt* (*aiguille*) to thread; (*perles etc*) to string; (*vêtement*) Fam to slip on, pull on; (*rue, couloir*) to take; **s'e. dans** (*rue etc*) to take. ◆**enfilade** *nf* (*série*) row, string.

enfin [ɑ̃fε̃] adv (à la fin) finally, at last; (*en dernier lieu*) lastly; (*en somme*) in a word; (*conclusion résignée*) well; **e. bref** (*en somme*) Fam in a word; **il est grand, e. pas trop petit** he's tall – well, not too short anyhow; **mais e.** but; (*mais*) **e.!** for heaven's sake!

enflamm/er [ɑ̃flame] *vt* to set fire to, ignite; (*allumette*) to light; (*irriter*) Méd to inflame; (*imagination, colère*) to excite, inflame; **— s'e.** *vpr* to catch fire, ignite; **s'e. de colère** to flare up. ◆**—é** a (*discours*) fiery.

enfler [ɑ̃fle] vt to swell; (voix) to raise; — vi Méd to swell (up). ◆**enflure** nf swelling.

enfonc/er [ɑ̃fɔ̃se] vt (clou etc) to knock in, drive in; (chapeau) to push ou force down; (porte, voiture) to smash in; e. dans (couteau, mains etc) to plunge into; — vi, — s'e. vpr (s'enliser) to sink (dans into); s'e. dans (pénétrer) to plunge into, disappear (deep) into. ◆—é a (yeux) sunken.

enfouir [ɑ̃fwir] vt to bury.

enfourcher [ɑ̃furʃe] vt (cheval etc) to mount, bestride.

enfourner [ɑ̃furne] vt to put in the oven.

enfreindre* [ɑ̃frɛ̃dr] vt to infringe.

enfuir* (s') [sɑ̃fɥir] vpr to run away ou off, flee (de from).

enfumer [ɑ̃fyme] vt (pièce) to fill with smoke; (personne) to smoke out.

engag/er [ɑ̃gaʒe] vt (bijou etc) to pawn; (parole) to pledge; (discussion, combat) to start; (clef etc) to insert (dans into); (capitaux) to tie up, invest; e. la bataille avec to join battle with; e. qn (lier) to bind s.o., commit s.o.; (embaucher) to hire s.o., engage s.o.; e. qn dans (affaire etc) to involve s.o. in; e. qn à faire (exhorter) to urge s.o. to do; — s'e. vpr (s'inscrire) Mil to enlist; Sp to enter; (au service d'une cause) to commit oneself; (action) to start; s'e. à faire to commit oneself to doing, undertake to do; s'e. dans (voie) to enter, get involved in. ◆—eant a engaging, inviting. ◆—é a (écrivain etc) committed. ◆—ement nm (promesse) commitment; (commencement) start; (de recrues) Mil enlistment; (inscription) Sp entry; (combat) Mil engagement; prendre l'e. de to undertake to.

engelure [ɑ̃ʒlyr] nf chilblain.

engendrer [ɑ̃ʒɑ̃dre] vt (procréer) to beget; (causer) to generate, engender.

engin [ɑ̃ʒɛ̃] nm machine, device; (projectile) missile; e. explosif explosive device.

englober [ɑ̃glɔbe] vt to include, embrace.

engloutir [ɑ̃glutir] vt (avaler) to wolf (down), gobble (up); (faire sombrer ou disparaître) to engulf.

engorger [ɑ̃gɔrʒe] vt to block up, clog.

engouement [ɑ̃gumɑ̃] nm craze.

engouffrer [ɑ̃gufre] vt (avaler) to wolf (down); (fortune) to consume; s'e. dans to sweep ou rush into.

engourd/ir [ɑ̃gurdir] vt (membre) to numb; (esprit) to dull; — s'e. vpr to go numb; to become dull. ◆—issement nm numbness; dullness.

engrais [ɑ̃grɛ] nm (naturel) manure; (chimique) fertilizer.

engraisser [ɑ̃grese] vt (animal) to fatten (up); — vi, — s'e. vpr to get fat, put on weight.

engrenage [ɑ̃grənaʒ] nm Tech gears; Fig mesh, chain, web.

engueuler [ɑ̃gœle] vt e. qn Fam to swear at s.o., give s.o. hell. ◆**engueulade** nf Fam (réprimande) dressing-down, severe talking-to; (dispute) slanging match, row.

enhardir [ɑ̃ardir] vt to make bolder; s'e. à faire to make bold to do.

énième [enjɛm] a Fam umpteenth, nth.

énigme [enigm] nf enigma, riddle. ◆**énigmatique** a enigmatic.

enivrer [ɑ̃nivre] vt (soûler, troubler) to intoxicate; — s'e. vpr to get drunk (de on).

enjamber [ɑ̃ʒɑ̃be] vt to step over; (pont etc) to span (river etc). ◆**enjambée** nf stride.

enjeu, -x [ɑ̃ʒø] nm (mise) stake(s).

enjoindre [ɑ̃ʒwɛ̃dr] vt e. à qn de faire Litt to order s.o. to do.

enjôler [ɑ̃ʒole] vt to wheedle, coax.

enjoliv/er [ɑ̃ʒolive] vt to embellish. ◆—eur nm Aut hubcap.

enjoué [ɑ̃ʒwe] a playful. ◆**enjouement** nm playfulness.

enlacer [ɑ̃lase] vt to entwine; (serrer dans ses bras) to clasp.

enlaidir [ɑ̃ledir] vt to make ugly; — vi to grow ugly.

enlev/er [ɑ̃lve] vt to take away ou off, remove (à qn from s.o.); (ordures) to collect; (vêtement) to take off, remove; (tache) to take out, lift, remove; (enfant etc) to kidnap, abduct; — s'e. vpr (tache) to come out; (vernis) to come off. ◆—é a (scène, danse etc) well-rendered. ◆**enlèvement** nm kidnapping, abduction; (d'un objet) removal; (des ordures) collection.

enliser (s') [sɑ̃lize] vpr (véhicule) & Fig to get bogged down (dans in).

enneigé [ɑ̃neʒe] a snow-covered. ◆**enneigement** nm snow coverage; bulletin d'e. snow report.

ennemi, -ie [enmi] nmf enemy; — a (personne) hostile (de to); (pays etc) enemy-.

ennui [ɑ̃nɥi] nm boredom; (mélancolie) weariness; un e. (tracas) (some) trouble ou bother; des ennuis trouble(s), bother; l'e., c'est que . . . the annoying thing is that . . . .

ennuy/er [ɑ̃nɥije] vt (agacer) to annoy, bother; (préoccuper) to bother; (fatiguer) to bore; — s'e. vpr to get bored. ◆—é a (air) bored; **je suis e.** that annoys ou bothers me. ◆**ennuyeux, -euse** a (fastidieux) boring; (contrariant) annoying.

énonc/er [enɔ̃se] vt to state, express. ◆—**é** nm (de texte) wording, terms; (phrase) Ling utterance.

enorgueillir [ɑ̃nɔrgœjir] vt to make proud; **s'e. de** to pride oneself on.

énorme [enɔrm] a enormous, huge, tremendous. ◆**énormément** adv enormously, tremendously; **e. de** an enormous ou tremendous amount of. ◆**énormité** nf (dimension) enormity; (faute) (enormous) blunder.

enquérir (s') [sɑ̃kerir] vpr **s'e. de** to inquire about.

enquête [ɑ̃kɛt] nf (de police etc) investigation; (judiciaire, administrative) inquiry; (sondage) survey. ◆**enquêter** vi (police etc) to investigate; **e. sur** (crime) to investigate. ◆**enquêteur, -euse** nmf investigator.

enquiquiner [ɑ̃kikine] vt Fam to annoy, bug.

enraciner (s') [sɑ̃rasine] vpr to take root; **enraciné dans** (personne, souvenir) rooted in; **bien enraciné** (préjugé etc) deep-rooted.

enrag/er [ɑ̃raʒe] vi **e. de faire** to be furious about doing; **faire e. qn** to get on s.o.'s nerves. ◆—**eant** a infuriating. ◆—**é** a (chien) rabid, mad; (joueur etc) Fam fanatical (de about); **rendre/devenir e.** (furieux) to make/become furious.

enrayer [ɑ̃reje] vt (maladie etc) to check; — **s'e.** vpr (fusil) to jam.

enregistr/er [ɑ̃rʒistre] vt **1** (inscrire) to record; (sur registre) to register; (constater) to note, register; **(faire) e.** (bagages) to register, Am check. **2** (musique, émission etc) to record. ◆—**ement** nm (des bagages) registration, Am checking; (d'un acte) registration; (sur bande etc) recording. ◆—**eur, -euse** a (appareil) recording-; **caisse enregistreuse** cash register.

enrhumer [ɑ̃ryme] vt **e. qn** to give s.o. a cold; **être enrhumé** to have a cold; — **s'e.** vpr to catch a cold.

enrich/ir [ɑ̃riʃir] vt to enrich (de with); — **s'e.** vpr (personne) to get rich. ◆—**issement** nm enrichment.

enrober [ɑ̃rɔbe] vt to coat (de in); **enrobé de chocolat** chocolate-coated.

enrôl/er [ɑ̃role] vt, — **s'e.** vpr to enlist. ◆—**ement** nm enlistment.

enrou/er (s') [sɑ̃rwe] vpr to get hoarse. ◆—**é** a hoarse. ◆—**ement** [ɑ̃rumɑ̃] nm hoarseness.

enrouler [ɑ̃rule] vt (fil etc) to wind; (tapis, cordage) to roll up; **s'e. dans** (couvertures) to roll ou wrap oneself up in; **s'e. sur ou autour de qch** to wind round sth.

ensabler [ɑ̃sable] vt, — **s'e.** vpr (port) to silt up.

ensanglanté [ɑ̃sɑ̃glɑ̃te] a bloodstained.

enseigne [ɑ̃sɛɲ] **1** nf (de magasin etc) sign; **e. lumineuse** neon sign; **logés à la même e.** Fig in the same boat. **2** nm **e. de vaisseau** lieutenant, Am ensign.

enseign/er [ɑ̃seɲe] vt to teach; **e. qch à qn** to teach s.o. sth; — vi to teach. ◆—**ant, -ante** [-ɑ̃, -ɑ̃t] a (corps) teaching-; — nmf teacher. ◆—**ement** [-ɛɲmɑ̃] nm education; (action, métier) teaching.

ensemble [ɑ̃sɑ̃bl] **1** adv together. **2** nm (d'objets) group, set; Math set; Mus ensemble; (mobilier) suite; (vêtement féminin) outfit; (harmonie) unity; **l'e. du personnel** the whole (of the) staff; **l'e. des enseignants** all (of) the teachers; **dans l'e.** on the whole; **d'e.** (vue etc) general; **grand e.** (quartier) housing complex ou Am development; (ville) = new town, = Am planned community. ◆**ensemblier** nm (interior) decorator.

ensemencer [ɑ̃səmɑ̃se] vt (terre) to sow.

ensevelir [ɑ̃səvlir] vt to bury.

ensoleillé [ɑ̃sɔleje] a (endroit, journée) sunny.

ensommeillé [ɑ̃sɔmeje] a sleepy.

ensorceler [ɑ̃sɔrsəle] vt (envoûter, séduire) to bewitch. ◆**ensorcellement** nm (séduction) spell.

ensuite [ɑ̃sɥit] adv (puis) next, then; (plus tard) afterwards.

ensuivre* (s') [sɑ̃sɥivr] vpr to follow, ensue; — v imp **il s'ensuit que** it follows that.

entacher [ɑ̃taʃe] vt (honneur etc) to sully, taint.

entaille [ɑ̃taj] nf (fente) notch; (blessure) gash, slash. ◆**entailler** vt to notch; to gash, slash.

entame [ɑ̃tam] nf first slice.

entamer [ɑ̃tame] vt (pain, peau etc) to cut (into); (bouteille, boîte etc) to start (on); (négociations etc) to enter into, start; (sujet) to broach; (capital) to break ou eat into; (métal, plastique) to damage; (résolution, réputation) to shake.

entass/er [ɑ̃tase] vt, — **s'e.** vpr (objets) to pile up, heap up; **(s')e. dans** (passagers etc) to crowd ou pack ou pile into; **ils s'entassaient sur la plage** they were crowded ou packed (together) on the beach.

◆**—ement** *nm* (*tas*) pile, heap; (*de gens*) crowding.

entend/re [ɑ̃tɑ̃dr] *vt* to hear; (*comprendre*) to understand; (*vouloir*) to intend, mean; **e. parler de** to hear of; **e. dire que** to hear (it said) that; **e. raison** to listen to reason; **laisser e. à qn que** to understand that; **— s'e.** *vpr* (*être entendu*) to be heard; (*être compris*) to be understood; **s'e.** (**sur**) (*être d'accord*) to agree (on); **s'e.** (**avec qn**) (*s'accorder*) to get on (with s.o.); **on ne s'entend plus!** (*à cause du bruit etc*) we can't hear ourselves speak!; **il s'y entend** (*est expert*) he knows all about that. ◆**—u** *a* (*convenu*) agreed; (*compris*) understood; (*sourire, air*) knowing; **e.!** all right!; **bien e.** of course. ◆**—ement** *nm* (*faculté*) understanding. ◆**entente** *nf* (*accord*) agreement, understanding; (**bonne**) **e.** (*amitié*) good relationship, harmony.

entériner [ɑ̃terine] *vt* to ratify.

enterrer [ɑ̃tere] *vt* (*mettre en ou sous terre*) to bury; (*projet*) *Fig* to scrap. ◆**enterrement** *nm* burial; (*funérailles*) funeral.

entêtant [ɑ̃tetɑ̃] *a* (*enivrant*) heady.

en-tête [ɑ̃tɛt] *nm* (*de papier*) heading; **papier à en-tête** headed paper.

entêt/er (s') [sɑ̃tete] *vpr* to persist (**à faire** in doing). ◆**—é** *a* (*têtu*) stubborn; (*persévérant*) persistent. ◆**—ement** [ɑ̃tɛtmɑ̃] *nm* stubbornness; (*à faire qch*) persistence.

enthousiasme [ɑ̃tuzjasm] *nm* enthusiasm. ◆**enthousiasmer** *vt* to fill with enthusiasm, enthuse; **s'e. pour** to be *ou* get enthusiastic over, enthuse over. ◆**enthousiaste** *a* enthusiastic.

enticher (s') [sɑ̃tiʃe] *vpr* **s'e. de** to become infatuated with.

entier, -ière [ɑ̃tje, -jɛr] **1** *a* (*total*) whole, entire; (*absolu*) absolute, complete, entire; (*intact*) intact; **payer place entière** to pay full price; **le pays tout e.** the whole *ou* entire country; **— nm** (*unité*) whole; **en e., dans son e.** in its entirety, completely. **2** *a* (*caractère, personne*) unyielding. ◆**entièrement** *adv* entirely.

entité [ɑ̃tite] *nf* entity.

entonner [ɑ̃tone] *vt* (*air*) to start singing.

entonnoir [ɑ̃tonwar] *nm* (*ustensile*) funnel.

entorse [ɑ̃tɔrs] *nf* *Méd* sprain; **e. à** (*règlement*) infringement of.

entortill/er [ɑ̃tɔrtije] *vt* **e. qch autour de qch** (*papier etc*) to wrap sth around sth; **e. qn** *Fam* to dupe s.o., get round s.o.; **— s'e.** *vpr* (*lierre etc*) to wind, twist. ◆**—é** *a* (*phrase etc*) convoluted.

entour/er [ɑ̃ture] *vt* to surround (**de** with); (*envelopper*) to wrap (**de** in); **e. qn de ses bras** to put one's arms round s.o.; **s'e. de** to surround oneself with. ◆**—age** *nm* (*proches*) circle of family and friends.

entourloupette [ɑ̃turlupɛt] *nf* *Fam* nasty trick.

entracte [ɑ̃trakt] *nm* *Th* interval, *Am* intermission.

entraide [ɑ̃trɛd] *nf* mutual aid. ◆**s'entraider** [sɑ̃trede] *vpr* to help each other.

entrailles [ɑ̃traj] *nfpl* entrails.

entrain [ɑ̃trɛ̃] *nm* spirit, liveliness; **plein d'e.** lively.

entraîn/er [ɑ̃trene] **1** *vt* (*charrier*) to sweep *ou* carry away; (*roue*) *Tech* to drive; (*causer*) to bring about; (*impliquer*) to entail, involve; **e. qn** (*emmener*) to lead *ou* draw s.o. (*away*); (*de force*) to drag s.o. (*away*); (*attirer*) *Péj* to lure s.o.; (*charmer*) to carry s.o. away; **e. qn à faire** (*amener*) to lead s.o. to do. **2** *vt* (*athlète, cheval etc*) to train (**à** for); **— s'e.** *vpr* to train oneself; *Sp* to train. ◆**—ant** [-ɑ̃nɑ̃] *a* (*musique*) captivating. ◆**—ement** [-ɛnmɑ̃] *nm* **1** *Sp* training. **2** *Tech* drive; (*élan*) impulse. ◆**—eur** [-ɛnœr] *nm* (*instructeur*) *Sp* trainer, coach; (*de cheval*) trainer.

entrave [ɑ̃trav] *nf* (*obstacle*) *Fig* hindrance (**à** to). ◆**entraver** *vt* to hinder, hamper.

entre [ɑ̃tr(ə)] *prép* between; (*parmi*) among(st); **l'un d'e. vous** one of you; (*soit dit*) **e. nous** between you and me; **se dévorer e. eux** (*réciprocité*) to devour each other; **e. deux âges** middle-aged; **e. autres** among other things; **e. les mains de** in the hands of.

entrebâill/er [ɑ̃trəbaje] *vt* (*porte*) to open slightly. ◆**—é** *a* ajar, slightly open. ◆**—eur** *nm* **e.** (**de porte**) door chain.

entrechoquer (s') [sɑ̃trəʃɔke] *vpr* (*bouteilles etc*) to knock against each other, chink.

entrecôte [ɑ̃trəkot] *nf* (*boned*) rib steak.

entrecouper [ɑ̃trəkupe] *vt* (*entremêler*) to punctuate (**de** with), intersperse (**de** with).

entrecroiser [ɑ̃trəkrwaze] *vt*, **— s'e.** *vpr* (*fils*) to interlace; (*routes*) to intersect.

entre-deux-guerres [ɑ̃trədøgɛr] *nm inv* inter-war period.

entrée [ɑ̃tre] *nf* (*action*) entry, entrance; (*porte*) entrance; (*accès*) entry, admission (**de** to); (*vestibule*) entrance hall, entry; (*billet*) ticket (of admission); *Culin* first course, entrée; (*mot dans un dictionnaire etc*) entry; (*processus informatique*) input; **à son e.** as he *ou* she came in; **'e. interdite'** 'no entry', 'no admittance'; **'e. libre'** 'admission free'; **e. en matière** (*d'un discours*) opening.

entrefaites (sur ces) [syrsezɑ̃trəfɛt] *adv* at that moment.

entrefilet [ɑ̃trəfilɛ] *nm Journ* (news) item.

entrejambes [ɑ̃trəʒɑ̃b] *nm inv* (*de pantalon*) crutch, crotch.

entrelacer [ɑ̃trəlase] *vt*, **— s'e.** *vpr* to intertwine.

entremêler [ɑ̃trəmele] *vt*, **— s'e.** *vpr* to intermingle.

entremets [ɑ̃trəmɛ] *nm* (*plat*) sweet, dessert.

entremetteur, -euse [ɑ̃trəmɛtœr, -øz] *nmf Péj* go-between.

entremise [ɑ̃trəmiz] *nf* intervention; **par l'e. de qn** through s.o.

entreposer [ɑ̃trəpoze] *vt* to store; *Jur* to bond. ◆**entrepôt** *nm* warehouse; (*de la douane*) *Jur* bonded warehouse.

entreprendre* [ɑ̃trəprɑ̃dr] *vt* (*travail, voyage etc*) to start on, undertake; **e. de faire** to undertake to do. ◆**entreprenant** *a* enterprising; (*galant*) brash, forward. ◆**entrepreneur** *nm* (*en bâtiment*) (building) contractor. ◆**entreprise** *nf* **1** (*opération*) undertaking. **2** (*firme*) company, firm.

entrer [ɑ̃tre] *vi* (*aux* **être**) (*aller*) to go in, enter; (*venir*) to come in, enter; **e. dans** to go into; (*carrière*) to enter, go into; (*club*) to join, enter; (*détail, question*) to go *ou* enter into; (*pièce*) to come *ou* go into, enter; (*arbre etc*) *Aut* to crash into; **e. en action** to go *ou* get into action; **e. en ébullition** to start boiling; **entrez!** come in!; **faire/laisser e. qn** to show/let s.o. in.

entresol [ɑ̃trəsɔl] *nm* mezzanine (floor).

entre-temps [ɑ̃trətɑ̃] *adv* meanwhile.

entretenir* [ɑ̃trətnir] *vt* **1** (*voiture, maison etc*) to maintain; (*relations, souvenir*) to keep up; (*famille*) to keep, maintain; (*sentiment*) to entertain; **e. sa forme/sa santé** to keep fit/healthy; **s'e. de** to talk to s.o. about; **s'e. de** to talk about (**avec** with). ◆**—u** *a* (*femme*) kept. ◆**entretien** *nm* **1** (*de route, maison etc*) maintenance, upkeep; (*subsistance*) keep. **2** (*dialogue*) conversation; (*entrevue*) interview.

entre-tuer (s') [sɑ̃trətɥe] *vpr* to kill each other.

entrevoir* [ɑ̃trəvwar] *vt* (*rapidement*) to catch a glimpse of; (*pressentir*) to (fore)see.

entrevue [ɑ̃trəvy] *nf* interview.

entrouvrir* [ɑ̃truvrir] *vt*, **— s'e.** *vpr* to half-open. ◆**entrouvert** *a* (*porte, fenêtre*) ajar, half-open.

énumérer [enymere] *vt* to enumerate, list. ◆**énumération** *nf* enumeration.

envahir [ɑ̃vair] *vt* to invade; (*herbe etc*) to overrun; **e. qn** (*doute, peur etc*) to overcome s.o. ◆**—issant** *a* (*voisin etc*) intrusive. ◆**—issement** *nm* invasion. ◆**—isseur** *nm* invader.

enveloppe [ɑ̃vlɔp] *nf* (*pli*) envelope; (*de colis*) wrapping; (*de pneu*) casing; (*d'oreiller*) cover; (*apparence*) *Fig* exterior; **mettre sous e.** to put into an envelope. ◆**envelopper** *vt* to wrap (up); **e. la ville** (*brouillard etc*) to envelop the town; **enveloppé de mystère** shrouded *ou* enveloped in mystery; **— s'e.** *vpr* to wrap oneself (up) (**dans** in). ◆**—ant** *a* (*séduisant*) captivating.

envenimer [ɑ̃vnime] *vt* (*plaie*) to make septic; (*querelle*) *Fig* to envenom; **— s'e.** *vpr* to turn septic; *Fig* to become envenomed.

envergure [ɑ̃vɛrgyr] *nf* **1** (*d'avion, d'oiseau*) wingspan. **2** (*de personne*) calibre; (*ampleur*) scope, importance; **de grande e.** wide-ranging, far-reaching.

envers [ɑ̃vɛr] **1** *prép* towards, *Am* toward(s). **2** *nm* (*de tissu*) wrong side; (*de médaille*) reverse side; **à l'e.** (*chaussette*) inside out; (*pantalon*) back to front; (*à contresens, de travers*) the wrong way; (*à en désordre*) upside down.

envie [ɑ̃vi] *nf* **1** (*jalousie*) envy; (*désir*) longing, desire; **avoir e. de qch** to want sth; **j'ai e. de faire** I feel like doing, I would like to do; **elle meurt d'e. de faire** she's dying *ou* longing to do. **2** (*peau autour des ongles*) hangnail. ◆**envier** *vt* to envy (**qch à qn** s.o. sth). ◆**envieux, -euse** *a* & *nmf* envious (person); **faire des envieux** to cause envy.

environ [ɑ̃virɔ̃] *adv* (*à peu près*) about; **— nmpl** outskirts, surroundings; **aux environs de** (*Paris, Noël, dix francs etc*) around, in the vicinity of. ◆**environner** *vt* to surround. ◆**—ant** *a* surrounding. ◆**—ement** *nm* environment.

envisager [ɑ̃vizaʒe] *vt* to consider; (*imaginer comme possible*) to envisage, *Am* envision, consider; **e. de faire** to consider *ou* contemplate doing. ◆**—eable** *a* thinkable.

envoi [ɑ̃vwa] *nm* (*action*) dispatch, sending; (*paquet*) consignment; **coup d'e.** *Fb* kick-off.

envol [ɑ̃vɔl] *nm* (*d'oiseau*) taking flight; (*d'avion*) take-off; **piste d'e.** *Av* runway. ◆**s'envoler** *vi* (*oiseau*) to fly away; (*avion*) to take off; (*emporté par le vent*) to blow away; (*espoir*) *Fig* to vanish. ◆**—ée** *nf* (*élan*) *Fig* flight.

envoût/er [ɑ̃vute] *vt* to bewitch. ◆**—ement** *nm* bewitchment.

envoy/er* [ɑ̃vwaje] *vt* to send; (*pierre*) to throw; (*gifle*) to give; **e. chercher qn** to send for s.o.; **— s'e.** *vpr Fam* (*travail etc*) to take on, do; (*repas etc*) to put *ou* stash away. ◆**—é, —ée** *nmf* envoy; *Journ* correspondent. ◆**—eur** *nm* sender.

épagneul, -eule [epaɲœl] *nmf* spaniel.

épais, -aisse [epɛ, -ɛs] *a* thick; (*personne*) thick-set; (*esprit*) dull. ◆**épaisseur** *nf* thickness; (*dimension*) depth. ◆**épaissir** *vt* to thicken; — *vi*, — **s'é.** *vpr* to thicken; (*grossir*) to fill out; **le mystère s'épaissit** the mystery is deepening.

épanch/er [epɑ̃ʃe] *vt* (*cœur*) *Fig* to pour out; — **s'é.** *vpr* (*parler*) to pour out one's heart, unbosom oneself. ◆**—ement** *nm* (*aveu*) outpouring; *Méd* effusion.

épanou/ir (s') [sepanwir] *vpr* (*fleur*) to open out; (*personne*) *Fig* to fulfil oneself, blossom (out); (*visage*) to beam. ◆**—i** *a* (*fleur, personne*) in full bloom; (*visage*) beaming. ◆**—issement** *nm* (*éclat*) full bloom; (*de la personnalité*) fulfilment.

épargne [eparɲ] *nf* saving (**de** of); (*qualité, vertu*) thrift; (*sommes d'argent*) savings. ◆**épargn/er** *vt* (*ennemi etc*) to spare; (*denrée rare etc*) to be sparing with; (*argent, temps*) to save; **e. qch à qn** (*ennuis, chagrin etc*) to spare s.o. sth. ◆**—ant, -ante** *nmf* saver.

éparpiller [eparpije] *vt*, — **s'é.** *vpr* to scatter; (*efforts*) to dissipate. ◆**épars** *a* scattered.

épaté [epate] *a* (*nez*) flat. ◆**épatement** *nm* flatness.

épat/er [epate] *vt Fam* to stun, astound. ◆**—ant** *a Fam* stunning, marvellous.

épaule [epol] *nf* shoulder. ◆**épauler** *vt* (*fusil*) to raise (to one's shoulder); **é. qn** (*aider*) to back s.o. up.

épave [epav] *nf* (*bateau, personne*) wreck; *pl* (*débris*) *Nau* (pieces of) wreckage.

épée [epe] *nf* sword; **un coup d'é.** a sword thrust.

épeler [eple] *vt* (*mot*) to spell.

éperdu [eperdy] *a* frantic, wild (**de** with); (*regard*) distraught. ◆**—ment** *adv* (*aimer*) madly; **elle s'en moque e.** she couldn't care less.

éperon [eprɔ̃] *nm* (*de cavalier, coq*) spur. ◆**éperonner** (*cheval, personne*) to spur (on).

épervier [epɛrvje] *nm* sparrowhawk.

éphémère [efemɛr] *a* short-lived, ephemeral, transient.

épi [epi] *nm* (*de blé etc*) ear; (*mèche de cheveux*) tuft of hair.

épice [epis] *nf Culin* spice. ◆**épic/er** *vt* to spice. ◆**—é** *a* (*plat, récit etc*) spicy.

épicier, -ière [episje, -jɛr] *nmf* grocer. ◆**épicerie** *nf* (*magasin*) grocer's (shop); (*produits*) groceries.

épidémie [epidemi] *nf* epidemic. ◆**épidémique** *a* epidemic.

épiderme [epidɛrm] *nm Anat* skin.

épier [epje] *vt* (*observer*) to watch closely; (*occasion*) to watch out for; **é. qn** to spy on s.o.

épilepsie [epilɛpsi] *nf* epilepsy. ◆**épileptique** *a* & *nmf* epileptic.

épiler [epile] *vt* (*jambe*) to remove unwanted hair from; (*sourcil*) to pluck.

épilogue [epilog] *nm* epilogue.

épinard [epinar] *nm* (*plante*) spinach; *pl* (*feuilles*) *Culin* spinach.

épine [epin] *nf* **1** (*de buisson*) thorn; (*d'animal*) spine, prickle. **2** **é. dorsale** *Anat* spine. ◆**épineux, -euse** *a* (*tige, question*) thorny.

épingle [epɛ̃gl] *nf* pin; **é. de nourrice, é. de sûreté** safety pin; **é. à linge** clothes peg, *Am* clothes pin; **virage en é. à cheveux** hairpin bend; **tiré à quatre épingles** very spruce. ◆**épingler** *vt* to pin; **é. qn** (*arrêter*) *Fam* to nab s.o.

épique [epik] *a* epic.

épiscopal, -aux [episkɔpal, -o] *a* episcopal.

épisode [epizod] *nm* episode; **film à épisodes** serial. ◆**épisodique** *a* occasional, episodic; (*accessoire*) minor.

épitaphe [epitaf] *nf* epitaph.

épithète [epitɛt] *nf* epithet; *Gram* attribute.

épître [epitr] *nf* epistle.

éploré [eplore] *a* (*personne, air*) tearful.

éplucher [eplyʃe] *vt* (*pommes de terre*) to peel; (*salade*) to clean, pare; (*texte*) *Fig* to dissect. ◆**épluchure** *nf* peeling.

éponge [epɔ̃ʒ] *nf* sponge. ◆**éponger** *vt* (*liquide*) to sponge up, mop up; (*carrelage*) to sponge (down), mop; (*dette etc*) *Fin* to absorb; **s'é. le front** to mop one's brow.

épopée [epɔpe] *nf* epic.

époque [epɔk] *nf* (*date*) time, period; (*historique*) age; **meubles d'é.** period furniture; **à l'é.** at the time.

épouse [epuz] *nf* wife, *Jur* spouse.

épouser [epuze] *vt* **1 é. qn** to marry s.o. **2** (*opinion etc*) to espouse; (*forme*) to assume, adopt.

épousseter [epuste] *vt* to dust.

époustoufler [epustufle] vt Fam to astound.

épouvantail [epuvɑ̃taj] nm (à oiseaux) scarecrow.

épouvante [epuvɑ̃t] nf (peur) terror; (appréhension) dread; **d'é.** (film etc) horror-. ◆**épouvant/er** to terrify. ◆**–able** a terrifying; (très mauvais) appalling.

époux [epu] nm husband, Jur spouse; pl husband and wife.

éprendre (**s'**) [seprɑ̃dr] vpr **s'é. de qn** to fall in love with s.o. ◆**épris** a in love (de with).

épreuve [eprœv] nf (essai, examen) test; Sp event, heat; Phot print; Typ proof; (malheur) ordeal, trial; **mettre à l'é.** to put to the test. ◆**éprouv/er** [epruve] vt to test, try; (sentiment etc) to experience, feel; **é. qn** (mettre à l'épreuve) to put s.o. to the test; (faire souffrir) to distress s.o. ◆**–ant** a (pénible) trying. ◆**–é** a (sûr) well-tried.

éprouvette [epruvɛt] nf test tube; **bébé é.** test tube baby.

épuis/er [epɥize] vt (personne, provisions, sujet) to exhaust; — **s'é.** vpr (réserves, patience) to run out; **s'é. à faire** to exhaust oneself doing. ◆**–ant** a exhausting. ◆**–é** a exhausted; (édition) out of print; (marchandise) out of stock. ◆**–ement** nm exhaustion.

épuisette [epɥizɛt] nf fishing net (on pole).

épurer [epyre] vt to purify; (personnel etc) to purge; (goût) to refine. ◆**épuration** nf purification; purging; refining.

équateur [ekwatœr] nm equator; **sous l'é.** at ou on the equator. ◆**équatorial, -aux** a equatorial.

équation [ekwasjɔ̃] nf Math equation.

équerre [ekɛr] nf **é.** (à dessiner) setsquare, Am triangle; **d'é.** straight, square.

équestre [ekɛstr] a (figure etc) equestrian; (exercices etc) horseriding-.

équilibre [ekilibr] nm balance; **tenir ou mettre en é.** to balance (sur on); **se tenir en é.** to (keep one's) balance; **perdre l'é.** to lose one's balance. ◆**équilibrer** vt (charge, budget etc) to balance; — **s'é.** vpr (équipes etc) to (counter)balance each other; (comptes) to balance.

équinoxe [ekinɔks] nm equinox.

équipage [ekipaʒ] nm Nau Av crew.

équipe [ekip] nf team; (d'ouvriers) gang; **é. de nuit** night shift; **é. de secours** search party; **faire é. avec** to team up with. ◆**équipier, -ière** nmf team member.

équipée [ekipe] nf escapade.

équip/er [ekipe] vt to equip (de with); — **s'é.** vpr to equip oneself. ◆**–ement** nm equipment; (de camping, ski etc) gear, equipment.

équitation [ekitasjɔ̃] nf (horse) riding.

équité [ekite] nf fairness. ◆**équitable** a fair, equitable. ◆**équitablement** adv fairly.

équivalent [ekivalɑ̃] a & nm equivalent. ◆**équivalence** nf equivalence. ◆**équivaloir** vi **é. à** to be equivalent to.

équivoque [ekivɔk] a (ambigu) equivocal; (douteux) dubious; − nf ambiguity.

érable [erabl] nm (arbre, bois) maple.

érafler [erafle] vt to graze, scratch. ◆**éraflure** nf graze, scratch.

éraillée [eraje] af (voix) rasping.

ère [er] nf era.

érection [erɛksjɔ̃] nf (de monument etc) erection.

éreinter [erɛ̃te] vt (fatiguer) to exhaust; (critiquer) to tear to pieces, slate, slam.

ergot [ergo] nm (de coq) spur.

ergoter [ergɔte] vi to quibble, cavil.

ériger [eriʒe] vt to erect; **s'é. en** to set oneself up as.

ermite [ermit] nm hermit.

érosion [erozjɔ̃] nf erosion. ◆**éroder** vt to erode.

érotique [erɔtik] a erotic. ◆**érotisme** nm eroticism.

err/er [ere] vi to wander, roam. ◆**–ant** a wandering, roving; (animal) stray.

erreur [erœr] nf (faute) error, mistake; (action blâmable, opinion fausse) error; **par e.** by mistake, in error; **dans l'e.** mistaken. ◆**erroné** a erroneous.

ersatz [erzats] nm substitute.

éructer [erykte] vi Litt to belch.

érudit, -ite [erydi, -it] a scholarly, erudite; − nmf scholar. ◆**érudition** nf scholarship, erudition.

éruption [erypsjɔ̃] nf (de volcan, colère) eruption (de of); Méd rash.

es voir **être**.

ès [ɛs] prép of; **licencié/docteur ès lettres** = BA/PhD.

escabeau, -x [eskabo] nm stepladder, (pair of) steps; (tabouret) stool.

escadre [eskadr] nf Nau Av fleet, squadron. ◆**escadrille** nf (unité) Av flight. ◆**escadron** nm squadron.

escalade [eskalad] nf climbing; (de prix) & Mil escalation. ◆**escalader** vt to climb, scale.

escale [eskal] nf Av stop(over); Nau port of call; **faire e. à** Av to stop (over) at; Nau to put in at; **vol sans e.** non-stop flight.

escalier [eskalje] nm staircase, stairs; **e. mé-**

canique *ou* **roulant** escalator; **e. de secours** fire escape.

escalope [ɛskalɔp] *nf Culin* escalope.

escamot/er [ɛskamɔte] *vt* (*faire disparaître*) to make vanish; (*esquiver*) to dodge. ◆**—able** *a Av Tech* retractable.

escapade [ɛskapad] *nf* (*excursion*) jaunt; **faire une e.** to run off.

escargot [ɛskargo] *nm* snail.

escarmouche [ɛskarmuʃ] *nf* skirmish.

escarpé [ɛskarpe] *a* steep. ◆**escarpement** *nm* (*côte*) steep slope.

escarpin [ɛskarpɛ̃] *nm* (*soulier*) pump, court shoe.

escient [ɛsjɑ̃] *nm* **à bon e.** discerningly, wisely.

esclaffer (s') [sɛsklafe] *vpr* to roar with laughter.

esclandre [ɛsklɑ̃dr] *nm* (noisy) scene.

esclave [ɛsklav] *nmf* slave; **être l'e. de** to be a slave to. ◆**esclavage** *nm* slavery.

escompte [ɛskɔ̃t] *nm* discount; **taux d'e.** bank rate. ◆**escompter** *vt* 1 (*espérer*) to anticipate (**faire doing**), expect (**faire** to do). 2 *Com* to discount.

escorte [ɛskɔrt] *nf Mil Nau etc* escort. ◆**escorter** *vt* to escort.

escouade [ɛskwad] *nf* (*petite troupe*) squad.

escrime [ɛskrim] *nf Sp* fencing. ◆**escrimeur, -euse** *nmf* fencer.

escrimer (s') [sɛskrime] *vpr* to slave away (**à faire** at doing).

escroc [ɛskro] *nm* swindler, crook. ◆**escroquer** *vt* **e. qn** to swindle s.o.; **e. qch à qn** to swindle s.o. out of sth. ◆**escroquerie** *nf* swindling; **une e.** a swindle.

espace [ɛspas] *nm* space; **e. vert** garden, park. ◆**espacer** *vt* to space out; **espacés d'un mètre** (spaced out) one metre apart; **s'e.** (*maisons, visites etc*) to become less frequent.

espadon [ɛspadɔ̃] *nm* swordfish.

espadrille [ɛspadrij] *nf* rope-soled sandal.

Espagne [ɛspaɲ] *nf* Spain. ◆**espagnol, -ole** *a* Spanish; — *nmf* Spaniard; — *nm* (*langue*) Spanish.

espèce [ɛspɛs] 1 *nf* (*race*) species; (*genre*) kind, sort; **c'est une e. d'idiot** he's a silly fool; **e. d'idiot!/de maladroit!**/*etc* (you) silly fool!/oaf!/*etc*. 2 *nfpl* (*argent*) **en espèces** in cash.

espérance [ɛsperɑ̃s] *nf* hope; **avoir des espérances** to have expectations; **e. de vie** life expectancy. ◆**espérer** *vt* to hope for; **e. que** to hope that; **e. faire** to hope to do; — *vi* to hope; **e. en qn/qch** to trust in s.o./sth.

espiègle [ɛspjɛgl] *a* mischievous. ◆**es-**

pièglerie *nf* mischievousness; (*farce*) mischievous trick.

espion, -onne [ɛspjɔ̃, -ɔn] *nmf* spy. ◆**espionnage** *nm* espionage, spying. ◆**espionner** *vt* to spy on; — *vi* to spy.

esplanade [ɛsplanad] *nf* esplanade.

espoir [ɛspwar] *nm* hope; **avoir de l'e.** to have hope(s); **sans e.** (*cas etc*) hopeless.

esprit [ɛspri] *nm* (*attitude, fantôme*) spirit; (*intellect*) mind; (*humour*) wit; (*être humain*) person; **avoir de l'e.** to be witty; **cette idée m'est venue à l'e.** this idea crossed my mind.

esquimau, -aude, -aux [ɛskimo, -od, -o] 1 *a* & *nmf* Eskimo. 2 *nm* (*glace*) choc-ice (*on a stick*).

esquinter [ɛskɛ̃te] *vt Fam* (*voiture etc*) to damage, bash; (*critiquer*) to slam, pan (*author, film etc*); **s'e. la santé** to damage one's health; **s'e. à faire** (*se fatiguer*) to wear oneself out doing.

esquisse [ɛskis] *nf* (*croquis, plan*) sketch. ◆**esquisser** *vt* to sketch; **e. un geste** to make a (slight) gesture.

esquive [ɛskiv] *nf Boxe* dodge; **e. de** (*question*) dodging of, evasion of. ◆**esquiver** *vt* (*coup, problème*) to dodge; — **s'e.** *vpr* to slip away.

essai [ɛse] *nm* (*épreuve*) test, trial; (*tentative*) try, attempt; *Rugby* try; *Littér* essay; **à l'e.** (*objet*) *Com* on trial, on approval; **pilote d'e.** test pilot; **période d'e.** trial period.

essaim [ɛsɛ̃] *nm* swarm (**of bees etc**).

essayer [ɛseje] *vt* to try (**de faire** to do); (*vêtement*) to try on; (*méthode*) to try (out); **s'e. à qch/à faire** to try one's hand at sth/at doing. ◆**essayage** *nm* (*de costume*) fitting.

essence [ɛsɑ̃s] *nf* 1 (*extrait*) *Ch Culin* essence; *Aut* petrol, *Am* gas; **poste d'e.** filling station. 2 *Phil* essence. 3 (*d'arbres*) species. ◆**essentiel, -ielle** *a* essential (**à, pour** for); — *nm* **l'e.** the main thing *ou* point; (*quantité*) the main part (**de** of). ◆**essentiellement** *adv* essentially.

essieu, -x [ɛsjø] *nm* axle.

essor [ɛsɔr] *nm* (*de pays, d'entreprise etc*) development, rise, expansion; **en plein e.** (*industrie etc*) booming.

essor/er [ɛsɔre] *vt* (*linge*) to wring; (*dans une essoreuse*) to spin-dry; (*dans une machine à laver*) to spin. ◆**—euse** *nf* (*à main*) wringer; (*électrique*) spin dryer.

essouffler [ɛsufle] *vt* to make (s.o.) out of breath; — **s'e.** (*subir*) to suffer. ◆**es-**

essuyer [ɛsɥije] 1 *vt* to wipe; — **s'e.** *vpr* to wipe oneself. 2 *vt* (*subir*) to suffer. ◆**es-**

suie-glace nm inv windscreen wiper, Am windshield wiper. ◆**essuie-mains** nm inv (hand) towel.

est¹ [ε] voir **être**.

est² [εst] nm east; – a inv (côte) east(ern); **d'e.** (vent) east(erly); **de l'e.** eastern; Allemagne **de l'E.** East Germany. ◆**e.-allemand, -ande** a & nmf East German.

estafilade [εstafilad] nf gash, slash.

estampe [εstãp] nf (gravure) print.

estamper [εstãpe] vt (rouler) Fam to swindle.

estampille [εstãpij] nf mark, stamp.

esthète [εstεt] nmf aesthete, Am esthete. ◆**esthétique** a aesthetic, Am esthetic.

esthéticienne [εstetisjεn] nf beautician.

estime [εstim] nf esteem, regard. ◆**estim/er** [εstime] vt (objet) to value; (juger) to consider (que that); (calculer) to estimate; (apprécier) to appreciate; **e. qn** to have high regard for s.o., esteem s.o.; **s'e. heureux/etc** to consider oneself happy/etc. ◆**–able** a respectable. ◆**estimation** nf (de mobilier etc) valuation; (calcul) estimation.

estival, -aux [εstival, -o] a (période etc) summer-. ◆**estivant, -ante** nmf holidaymaker, Am vacationer.

estomac [εstɔma] nm stomach.

estomaquer [εstɔmake] vt Fam to flabbergast.

estomper [εstɔpe] vt (rendre flou) to blur; – **s'e.** vpr to become blurred.

estrade [εstrad] nf (tribune) platform.

estropi/er [εstrɔpje] vt to cripple, maim. ◆**–é, -ée** nmf cripple.

estuaire [εstɥεr] nm estuary.

esturgeon [εstyrʒɔ̃] nm (poisson) sturgeon.

et [e] conj and; **vingt et un/etc** twenty-one/etc.

étable [etabl] nf cowshed.

établi [etabli] nm Menuis (work)bench.

établ/ir [etablir] vt to establish; (installer) to set up; (plan, chèque, liste) to draw up; – **s'é.** vpr (habiter) to settle; (épicier etc) to set up shop as, set (oneself) up as. ◆**–issement** nm (action, bâtiment, institution) establishment; Com firm, establishment; **é. scolaire** school.

étage [etaʒ] nm (d'immeuble) floor, storey, Am story; (de fusée etc) stage; **à l'é.** upstairs; **au premier é.** on the first ou Am second floor. ◆**étager (s')** (rochers, maisons etc) to range above one another.

étagère [etaʒεr] nf shelf; (meuble) shelving unit.

étai [etε] nm Tech prop, stay.

étain [etε̃] nm (métal) tin; (de gobelet etc) pewter.

était [etε] voir **être**.

étal, pl étals [etal] nm (au marché) stall.

étalage [etalaʒ] nm display; (vitrine) display window; **faire é. de** to make a show ou display of. ◆**étalagiste** nmf window dresser.

étaler [etale] vt (disposer) to lay out; (luxe etc) & Com to display; (crème, beurre etc) to spread; (vacances) to stagger; – **s'é.** vpr (s'affaler) to sprawl; (tomber) Fam to fall flat; (luxe etc) **s'é. sur** (congés, paiements etc) to be spread over.

étalon [etalɔ̃] nm 1 (cheval) stallion. 2 (modèle) standard.

étanche [etãʃ] a watertight; (montre) waterproof.

étancher [etãʃe] vt (sang) to stop the flow of; (soif) to quench, slake.

étang [etã] nm pond.

étant [etã] voir **être**.

étape [etap] nf (de voyage etc) stage; (lieu) stop(over); **faire é.** à to stop off ou over at.

état [eta] nm 1 (condition, manière d'être) state; (registre, liste) statement, list; **en bon é.** in good condition; **en é. de faire** in a position to do; **é. d'esprit** state ou frame of mind; **é. d'âme** mood; **é. civil** civil status (birth, marriage, death etc); **é. de choses** situation, state of affairs; **à l'é. brut** in a raw state; **de son é.** (métier) by trade; **faire é. de** (mention) to mention, put forward. **2 É.** (nation) State; **homme d'É.** statesman. ◆**étatisé** a state-controlled, state-owned. **état-major** [etamaʒɔr] nm (pl états-majors) (d'un parti etc) senior staff.

États-Unis [etazyni] nmpl É.-Unis (**d'Amérique**) United States (of America).

étau, -x [eto] nm Tech vice, Am vise.

étayer [eteje] vt to prop up, support.

été¹ [ete] nm summer.

été² [ete] voir **être**.

éteindre* [etε̃dr] vt (feu, cigarette etc) to put out, extinguish; (lampe etc) to turn ou switch off; (dette, espoir) to extinguish; – vi to switch off; – **s'é.** vpr (feu) to go out; (personne) to pass away; (race) to die out. ◆**éteint** a (feu) out; (volcan, race, amour) extinct; (voix) faint.

étendard [etãdar] nm (drapeau) standard.

étend/re [etãdr] vt (nappe) to spread (out); (beurre) to spread; (linge) to hang out; (agrandir) to extend; **é. le bras/etc** to stretch out one's arm/etc; **é. qn** to stretch s.o. out; – **s'é.** vpr (personne) to stretch (oneself) out; (*plaine etc*) to stretch; (*feu*) to spread; (*pouvoir*) to extend; **s'é. sur** (*sujet*) to dwell on. ◆—**u** (*à, forêt, vocabulaire etc*) extensive; (*personne*) stretched out. ◆—**ue** (*d'importance*) extent; (*surface*) expanse; (*d'eau*) expanse, stretch.

éternel, -elle [eternɛl] *a* eternal. ◆**éternellement** *adv* eternally, for ever. ◆**éterniser** *vt* to perpetuate; — **s'é.** *vpr* (*débat etc*) to drag on endlessly; (*visiteur etc*) to stay for ever. ◆**éternité** *nf* eternity.

éternu/er [etɛrnɥe] *vi* to sneeze. ◆—**ement** [-ymã] *nm* sneeze.

êtes [ɛt] *voir* être.

éther [etɛr] *nm* ether.

Éthiopie [etjɔpi] *nf* Ethiopia. ◆**éthiopien, -ienne** *a & nmf* Ethiopian.

éthique [etik] *a* ethical; — *nf Phil* ethics; **l'é. puritaine**/*etc* the Puritan/*etc* ethic.

ethnie [etni] *nf* ethnic group. ◆**ethnique** *a* ethnic.

étinceler [etɛ̃sle] *vi* to sparkle. ◆**étincelle** *nf* spark. ◆**étincellement** *nm* sparkle.

étioler (s') [setjɔle] *vpr* to wilt, wither.

étiqueter [etikte] *vt* to label. ◆**étiquette** *nf* **1** (*marque*) label. **2** (*protocole*) (diplomatic *ou* court) etiquette.

étirer [etire] *vt* to stretch; — **s'é.** *vpr* to stretch (oneself).

étoffe [etɔf] *nf* material, cloth, fabric; (*de héros etc*) *Fig* stuff (de *of*).

étoffer *vt*, — **s'é.** *vpr* to fill out.

étoile [etwal] *nf* **1** star; **à la belle é.** in the open. **2 é. de mer** starfish. ◆**étoilé** *a* (*ciel, nuit*) starry; (*vitre*) cracked (*star-shaped*); **é. de** (*rubis etc*) studded with; **la bannière étoilée** *Am* the Star-Spangled Banner.

étonn/er [etɔne] *vt* to surprise, astonish; — **s'é.** to be surprised *ou* astonished (de *qch* at sth, que (+ *sub*) that). ◆—**ant** *a* (*ahurissant*) surprising; (*remarquable*) amazing. ◆—**ement** *nm* surprise, astonishment.

étouff/er [etufe] *vt* (*tuer*) to suffocate, smother; (*bruit*) to muffle; (*feu*) to smother; (*révolte, sentiment*) to stifle; (*scandale*) to hush up; **é. qn** (*chaleur*) to stifle s.o.; (*aliment, colère*) to choke s.o.; — *vi* to suffocate; **on étouffe!** it's stifling!; **é. de colère** to choke with anger. — **s'é.** *vpr* (*en mangeant*) to choke, gag (sur, avec *on*); (*mourir*) to suffocate. ◆—**ant** *a* (*air*) stifling. ◆—**ement** *nm Méd* suffocation.

étourdi, -ie [eturdi] *a* thoughtless; — *nmf* scatterbrain. ◆**étourderie** *nf* thoughtlessness; **une é.** (*faute*) a thoughtless blunder.

étourd/ir [eturdir] *vt* to stun, daze; (*vertige,*

vin) to make dizzy; (*abrutir*) to deafen. ◆—**issant** *a* (*bruit*) deafening; (*remarquable*) stunning. ◆—**issement** *nm* dizziness; (*syncope*) dizzy spell.

étourneau, -x [eturno] *nm* starling.

étrange [etrɑ̃ʒ] *a* strange, odd. ◆—**ment** *adv* strangely, oddly. ◆**étrangeté** *nf* strangeness, oddness.

étranger, -ère [etrɑ̃ʒe, -ɛr] *a* (*d'un autre pays*) foreign; (*non familier*) strange (à *to*); **il m'est é.** he's unknown to me; — *nmf* foreigner; (*inconnu*) stranger; **à l'é.** abroad; **de l'é.** from abroad.

étrangl/er [etrɑ̃gle] *vt* **é. qn** (*tuer*) to strangle s.o.; (*col, aliment*) to choke s.o.; — **s'é.** *vpr* (*de colère, en mangeant etc*) to choke. ◆—**é** *a* (*voix*) choking; (*passage*) constricted. ◆—**ement** *nm* (*d'une victime*) strangulation. ◆—**eur, -euse** *nmf* strangler.

être* [ɛtr] **1** *vi* to be; **il est tailleur** he's a tailor; **est-ce qu'elle vient?** is she coming?; **il vient, n'est-ce pas?** he's coming, isn't he?; **est-ce qu'il aime le thé?** does he like tea?; **nous sommes dix** there are ten of us; **nous sommes le dix** today is the tenth (of the month); **où en es-tu?** how far have you got?; **il a été à Paris** (*est allé*) he's been to Paris; **elle est de Paris** she's from Paris; **elle est de la famille** she's one of the family; **c'est à faire tout de suite** it must be done straight away; **c'est à lui** it's his; **cela étant** that being so. **2** *v aux* (*avec venir, partir etc*) to have; **elle est déjà arrivée** she has already arrived. **3** *nm* (*personne*) being; **ê. humain** human being; **les êtres chers** the loved ones.

étreindre [etrɛ̃dr] *vt* to grip; (*ami*) to embrace. ◆**étreinte** *nf* grip; (*amoureuse etc*) embrace.

étrenner [etrene] *vt* to use *ou* wear for the first time.

étrennes [etrɛn] *nfpl* New Year gift; (*gratification*) = Christmas box *ou* tip.

étrier [etrije] *nm* stirrup.

étriper (s') [setripe] *vpr Fam* to fight (each other) to the kill.

étriqué [etrike] *a* (*vêtement*) tight, skimpy; (*esprit, vie*) narrow.

étroit [etrwa] *a* narrow; (*vêtement*) tight; (*parenté, collaboration etc*) close; (*discipline*) strict; **être à l'é.** to be cramped. ◆**étroitement** *adv* (*surveiller etc*) closely. ◆**étroitesse** *nf* narrowness; closeness; **é. d'esprit** narrow-mindedness.

étude [etyd] *nf* **1** (*action, ouvrage*) study; (*salle*) *Scol* study room; **à l'é.** (*projet*) under consideration; **faire des études de** (*médecine etc*) to study. **2** (*de notaire etc*) office. ◆**étudiant, -ante** *nmf* & a student. ◆**étudier** *vti* to study.

étui [etɥi] *nm* (*à lunettes, à cigarettes etc*) case; (*de revolver*) holster.

étymologie [etimɔlɔʒi] *nf* etymology.

eu, eue [y] *voir* avoir.

eucalyptus [økaliptys] *nm* (*arbre*) eucalyptus.

Eucharistie [økaristi] *nf* Rel Eucharist.

euh! [ø] *int* hem!, er!, well!

euphémisme [øfemism] *nm* euphemism.

euphorie [øfɔri] *nf* euphoria. ◆**euphorique** a euphoric.

eurent [yr] *voir* avoir.

euro- [øro] *préf* Euro-.

Europe [ørɔp] *nf* Europe. ◆**européen, -enne** a & *nmf* European.

eut [y] *voir* avoir.

euthanasie [øtanazi] *nf* euthanasia.

eux [ø] *pron* (*sujet*) they; (*complément*) them; (*réfléchi, emphase*) themselves. ◆**eux-mêmes** *pron* themselves.

évacuer [evakɥe] *vt* to evacuate; (*liquide*) to drain off. ◆**évacuation** *nf* evacuation.

évad/er (s') [evade] *vpr* to escape (**de** from). ◆**-é, -ée** *nmf* escaped prisoner.

évaluer [evalɥe] *vt* (*chiffre, foule etc*) to estimate; (*meuble etc*) to value. ◆**évaluation** *nf* estimation; valuation.

évangile [evɑ̃ʒil] *nm* gospel; **É.** Gospel. ◆**évangélique** a evangelical.

évanou/ir (s') [evanwir] *vpr* Méd to black out, faint; (*espoir, crainte etc*) to vanish. ◆**-I** a Méd unconscious. ◆**-issement** *nm* (*syncope*) blackout, fainting fit; (*disparition*) vanishing.

évaporer (s') [evapore] *vpr* Ch to evaporate; (*disparaître*) Fam to vanish into thin air. ◆**évaporation** *nf* evaporation.

évasif, -ive [evazif, -iv] a evasive.

évasion [evazjɔ̃] *nf* escape (**d'un lieu** from a place, **devant un danger**/*etc* from a danger/*etc*; (*hors de la réalité*) escapism; **é. fiscale** tax evasion.

évêché [eveʃe] *nm* (*territoire*) bishopric, see.

éveil [evɛj] *nm* awakening; **en é.** on the alert; **donner l'é. à** to alert.

éveill/er [eveje] *vt* (*susciter*) to arouse; **é. qn** to awake(n) s.o.; **— s'é.** *vpr* to awake(n) (**à** to); (*sentiment, idée*) to be aroused. ◆**-é** a awake; (*vif*) lively, alert.

événement [evenmã] *nm* event.

éventail [evãtaj] *nm* **1** (*instrument portatif*) fan; **en é.** (*orteils*) spread out. **2** (*choix*) range.

évent/er [evãte] *vt* **1** (*secret*) to discover. **2**

é. qn to fan s.o. **3 s'é.** *vpr* (*bière, vin etc*) to turn stale. ◆**-é a** (*bière, vin etc*) stale.

éventrer [evãtre] *vt* (*animal etc*) to disembowel; (*sac*) to rip open.

éventuel, -elle [evãtɥɛl] a a possible. ◆**éventuellement** adv possibly. ◆**éventualité** *nf* possibility; **dans l'é. de** in the event of.

évêque [evɛk] *nm* bishop.

évertuer (s') [severtɥe] *vpr* **s'é. à faire** to do one's utmost to do, struggle to do.

éviction [eviksjɔ̃] *nf* (*de concurrent etc*) & Pol ousting.

évident [evidã] a obvious, evident (**que** that). ◆**évidemment** [-amã] adv certainly, obviously. ◆**évidence** *nf* obviousness; **une é.** an obvious fact; **nier l'é.** to deny the obvious; **être en é.** to be conspicuous *ou* in evidence; **mettre en é.** (*fait*) to underline.

évider [evide] *vt* to hollow out.

évier [evje] *nm* (kitchen) sink.

évincer [evɛ̃se] *vt* (*concurrent etc*) & Pol to oust.

éviter [evite] *vt* to avoid (**de faire** doing); **é. qch à qn** to spare s.o. s.th.

évolu/er [evɔlɥe] *vi* **1** (*changer*) to develop, change; (*société, idée, situation*) to evolve. **2** (*se déplacer*) to move; Mil to manœuvre, Am maneuver. ◆**-é a** (*pays*) advanced; (*personne*) enlightened. ◆**évolution** *nf* **1** (*changement*) development; evolution. **2** (*d'un danseur etc*) & Mil movement.

évoquer [evoke] *vt* to evoke, call to mind. ◆**évocateur, -trice** a evocative. ◆**évocation** *nf* evocation, recalling.

ex [ɛks] *nmf* (*mari, femme*) Fam ex.

ex- [ɛks] *préf* ex-; **ex-mari** ex-husband.

exacerber [ɛgzasɛrbe] *vt* (*douleur etc*) to exacerbate.

exact [ɛgzakt] a (*précis*) exact, accurate; (*juste, vrai*) correct, exact, right; (*ponctuel*) punctual. ◆**exactement** adv exactly. ◆**exactitude** *nf* exactness; accuracy; correctness; punctuality.

exaction [ɛgzaksjɔ̃] *nf* exaction.

ex aequo [ɛgzeko] adv **être classés ex ae.** Sp to tie, be equally placed.

exagér/er [ɛgzaʒere] *vt* to exaggerate; **— vi** (*parler*) to exaggerate; (*agir*) to overdo it, go too far. ◆**-é a** excessive. ◆**-ément** adv excessively. ◆**exagération** *nf* exaggeration; (*excès*) excessiveness.

exalt/er [ɛgzalte] *vt* (*glorifier*) to exalt; (*animer*) to fire, stir. ◆**-ant** a stirring. ◆**-é, -ée** a (*sentiment*) impassioned,

wild; – *nmf Péj* fanatic. ◆**exaltation** *nf*
(*délire*) elation, excitement.

examen [ɛgzamɛ̃] *nm* examination; *Scol* ex-
am(ination); **e. blanc** *Scol* mock ex-
am(ination). ◆**examinateur, -trice** *nmf*
Scol examiner. ◆**examiner** *vt* (*considérer,
regarder*) to examine.

exaspérer [ɛgzaspere] *vt* (*énerver*) to aggravate, exasperate. ◆**exaspération** *nf* exasperation, aggravation.

exaucer [ɛgzose] *vt* (*désir*) to grant; **e. qn** to
grant s.o.'s wish(es).

excavation [ɛkskavasjɔ̃] *nf* (*trou*) hollow.

excéder [ɛksede] *vt* **1** (*dépasser*) to exceed. **2**
é. qn (*fatiguer, énerver*) to exasperate s.o.
◆**excédent** *nm* surplus, excess; **e. de**
bagages excess luggage *ou Am* baggage.
◆**excédentaire** *a* (*poids etc*) excess-.

excellent [ɛksɛlɑ̃] *a* excellent. ◆**excellence** *nf* **1** excellence; **par e.** above all else
ou all others. **2 E.** (*titre*) Excellency.
◆**exceller** *vi* to excel (**en qch** in sth, **à faire**
in doing).

excentrique [ɛksɑ̃trik] **1** *a & nmf* (*original*)
eccentric. **2** *a* (*quartier*) remote. ◆**excentricité** *nf* (*bizarrerie*) eccentricity.

excepté [ɛksɛpte] *prép* except. ◆**excepter**
vt to except. ◆**exception** *nf* exception; **à**
l'e. de except (for), with the exception of;
faire e. to be an exception. ◆**exceptionnel, -elle** *a* exceptional. ◆**exceptionnellement** *adv* exceptionally.

excès [ɛksɛ] *nm* excess; (*de table*)
over-eating; **e. de vitesse** *Aut* speeding.
◆**excessif, -ive** *a* excessive. ◆**excessivement** *adv* excessively.

excit/er [ɛksite] *vt* (*faire naître*) to excite,
rouse, stir; **e. qn** (*mettre en colère*) to provoke s.o.; (*agacer*) to annoy s.o.; (*enthousiasmer*) to thrill s.o., excite s.o.; **e. qn à**
faire to incite s.o. to do; – **s'e.** *vpr*
(*nerveux, enthousiaste*) to get excited.
◆**—ant** *a* exciting; – *nm* stimulant. ◆**—é**
a excited. ◆**—able** *a* excitable. ◆**excitation** *nf* (*agitation*) excitement; **e. à** (*haine
etc*) incitement to.

exclamer (s') [ɛksklame] *vpr* to exclaim.
◆**exclamatif, -ive** *a* exclamatory. ◆**exclamation** *nf* exclamation.

excl/ure* [ɛksklyr] *vt* (*écarter*) to exclude
(**de** from); (*chasser*) to expel (**de** from); **e.**
qch (*rendre impossible*) to preclude sth.
◆**—u** *a* (*solution etc*) out of the question;
(*avec une date*) exclusive. ◆**exclusif, -ive**
a (*droit, modèle, préoccupation*) exclusive.
◆**exclusion** *nf* exclusion. ◆**exclusivement** *adv* exclusively. ◆**exclusivité** *nf*

Com exclusive rights; **en e.** (*film*) having an
exclusive showing (**à** at).

excommunier [ɛkskɔmynje] *vt* to excommunicate. ◆**excommunication** *nf* excommunication.

excrément(s) [ɛkskremɑ̃] *nm(pl)* excrement.

excroissance [ɛkskrwasɑ̃s] *nf* (out)growth.

excursion [ɛkskyrsjɔ̃] *nf* outing, excursion,
tour; (*à pied*) hike.

excuse [ɛkskyz] *nf* (*prétexte*) excuse; *pl* (*regrets*) apology; **des excuses** an apology;
faire des excuses to apologize (**à** to); **toutes
mes excuses** (my) sincere apologies.
◆**excuser** *vt* (*justifier, pardonner*) to excuse (**qn d'avoir fait, qn de faire** s.o. for doing); – **s'e.** *vpr* to apologize (**de** for, **auprès**
de to); **excusez-moi!, je m'excuse!** excuse
me!

exécrer [ɛgzekre] *vt* to loathe. ◆**exécrable**
a atrocious.

exécut/er [ɛgzekyte] *vt* **1** (*projet, tâche etc*)
to carry out, execute; (*statue, broderie etc*)
to produce; (*jouer*) *Mus* to perform. **2 e. qn**
(*tuer*) to execute s.o. **3 s'e.** *vpr* to comply.
◆**—ant, -ante** *nmf Mus* performer.
◆**—able** *a* practicable. ◆**exécutif** *am*
(*pouvoir*) executive; – *nm* l'e. Pol the executive. ◆**exécution** *nf* **1** carrying out, execution; production; performance. **2** (*mise
à mort*) execution.

exemple [ɛgzɑ̃pl] *nm* example; **par e.** for example, for instance; (*ça*) **par e.!** *Fam* good
heavens!; **donner l'e.** to set an example (**à**
to). ◆**exemplaire 1** *a* exemplary. **2** *nm*
(*livre etc*) copy.

exempt [ɛgzɑ̃] *a* **e. de** (*dispensé de*) exempt
from; (*sans*) free from. ◆**exempter** *vt* to
exempt (**de** from). ◆**exemption** *nf* exemption.

exercer [ɛgzɛrse] *vt* (*muscles, droits*) to exercise; (*autorité, influence*) to exert (**sur** over);
(*métier*) to carry on, work at; (*profession*)
to practise; **e. qn à** (*couture etc*) to train s.o.
in; **e. qn à faire** to train s.o. to do; – *vi*
(*médecin*) to practise; – **s'e.** *vpr* (*influence
etc*) to be exerted; **s'e. à qch** (*sportif etc*) to
practise (sth); **s'e. à faire** to practise doing.
◆**exercice** *nm* (*physique etc*) & *Scol* exercise; *Mil* drill, exercise; (*de métier*) practice; **l'e. de** (*pouvoir etc*) the exercise of; **en**
e. (*fonctionnaire*) in office; (*médecin*) in
practice; **faire de l'e., prendre de l'e.** to
(take) exercise.

exhaler [ɛgzale] *vt* (*odeur etc*) to give off.

exhaustif, -ive [ɛgzostif, -iv] *a* exhaustive.

exhiber [ɛgzibe] *vt* to exhibit, show.

◆**exhibition** nf exhibition. ◆**exhibitionniste** nmf exhibitionist.

exhorter [εgzɔrte] vt to urge, exhort (**à faire** to do).

exhumer [εgzyme] vt (cadavre) to exhume; (vestiges) to dig up.

exiger [εgziʒe] vt to demand, require (de from, **que** + sub that). ◆**exigeant** a demanding, exacting. ◆**exigence** nf demand, requirement; **d'une grande e.** very demanding.

exigu, -uë [εgzigy] a (appartement etc) cramped, tiny. ◆**exiguïté** nf crampedness.

exil [εgzil] nm (expulsion) exile. ◆**exil/er** to exile; — **s'e.** vpr to go into exile. ◆**-é, -ée** nmf (personne) exile.

existence [εgzistɑ̃s] nf existence. ◆**existentialisme** nm existentialism. ◆**exist/er** vi to exist; – v imp **il existe** . . . (sing) there is . . . ; (pl) there are . . . . ◆**-ant** a existing.

exode [εgzɔd] nm exodus.

exonérer [εgzɔnere] vt to exempt (**de** from). ◆**exonération** nf exemption.

exorbitant [εgzɔrbitɑ̃] a exorbitant.

exorciser [εgzɔrsize] vt to exorcize. ◆**exorcisme** nm exorcism.

exotique [εgzɔtik] a exotic. ◆**exotisme** nm exoticism.

expansif, -ive [εkspɑ̃sif, -iv] a expansive, effusive.

expansion [εkspɑ̃sjɔ̃] nf Com Phys Pol expansion; **en (pleine) e.** (fast ou rapidly) expanding.

expatri/er (s') [εkspatrije] vpr to leave one's country. ◆**-é, -ée** a & nmf expatriate.

expectative [εkspεktativ] nf **être dans l'e.** to be waiting to see what happens.

expédient [εkspedjɑ̃] nm (moyen) expedient.

expédier [εkspedje] vt **1** (envoyer) to send off. **2** (affaires, client) to dispose of quickly, dispatch. ◆**expéditeur, -trice** nmf sender. ◆**expéditif, -ive** a expeditious, quick. ◆**expédition** nf **1** (envoi) dispatch. **2** (voyage) expedition.

expérience [εksperjɑ̃s] nf (pratique, connaissance) experience; (scientifique) experiment; **faire l'e. de qch** to experience sth. ◆**expérimental, -aux** a experimental. ◆**expérimentation** nf experimentation. ◆**expériment/er** vt Phys Ch to try out, experiment with; – vi to experiment. ◆**-é** a experienced.

expert [εkspεr] a expert, skilled (**en** in); –

nm expert; (d'assurances) valuer. ◆**e.comptable** nm (pl **experts-comptables**) = chartered accountant, = Am certified public accountant. ◆**expertise** nf (évaluation) (expert) appraisal; (compétence) expertise.

expier [εkspje] vt (péchés, crime) to expiate, atone for. ◆**expiation** nf expiation (**de** of).

expirer [εkspire] **1** vti to breathe out. **2** vi (mourir) to pass away; (finir, cesser) to expire. ◆**-ant** a dying. ◆**expiration** nf (échéance) expiry, Am expiration.

explicite [εksplisit] a explicit. ◆**-ment** adv explicitly.

expliquer [εksplike] vt to explain (**à** to); – **s'e.** vpr to explain oneself; (discuter) to talk things over, have it out (**avec** with); **s'e. qch** (comprendre) to understand sth; **ça s'explique** that is understandable. ◆**explicable** a understandable. ◆**explicatif, -ive** a explanatory. ◆**explication** nf explanation; (mise au point) discussion.

exploit [εksplwa] nm exploit, feat.

exploit/er [εksplwate] vt **1** (champs) to farm; (ferme, entreprise) to run; (mine) to work; (situation) Fig to exploit. **2** (abuser de) Péj to exploit (s.o.). ◆**-ant, -ante** nmf farmer. ◆**exploitation** nf **1** Péj exploitation. **2** farming; running; working; (entreprise) concern; (agricole) farm.

explorer [εksplɔre] vt to explore. ◆**explorateur, -trice** nmf explorer. ◆**exploration** nf exploration.

exploser [εksploze] vi (gaz etc) to explode; (bombe) to blow up, explode; **e. (de colère)** Fam to explode, blow up; **faire e.** (bombe) to explode. ◆**explosif, -ive** a & nm explosive. ◆**explosion** nf explosion; (de colère, joie) outburst.

exporter [εkspɔrte] vt to export (**vers** to, **de** from). ◆**exportateur, -trice** nmf exporter; – a exporting. ◆**exportation** nf (produit) export; (action) export(ation), exporting.

expos/er [εkspoze] vt (présenter, soumettre) & Phot to expose (**à** to); (marchandises) to display; (tableau etc) to exhibit; (idée, théorie) to set out; (vie, réputation) to risk, endanger; **s'e. à** to expose oneself to. ◆**-ant, -ante** nmf exhibitor. ◆**-é 1** a **bien e.** (édifice) having a good exposure; **e. au sud** facing south. **2** nm (compte rendu) account (**de** of); (discours) talk; Scol paper. ◆**exposition** nf (de marchandises etc) display; (salon) exhibition; (au danger etc) &

Phot exposure (à to); (*de maison etc*) aspect.

exprès [ekspre] *adv* on purpose, intentionally; (*spécialement*) specially.

exprès[2], **-esse** [ekspres] **1** *a* (*ordre, condition*) express. **2** *a inv* **lettre/colis** e. express letter/parcel. ◆**expressément** *adv* expressly.

express [ekspres] *a* & *nm inv* (*train*) express; (*café*) espresso.

expressif, -ive [ekspresif, -iv] *a* expressive. ◆**expression** *nf* (*phrase, mine etc*) expression. ◆**exprimer** *vt* to express; **— s'e.** *vpr* to express oneself.

exproprier [eksproprije] *vt* to seize the property of by compulsory purchase.

expulser [ekspylse] *vt* to expel (*de* from); (*joueur*) *Sp* to send off; (*locataire*) to evict. ◆**expulsion** *nf* expulsion; eviction; sending off.

expurger [ekspyrʒe] *vt* to expurgate.

exquis [ekski] *a* exquisite.

extase [ekstaz] *nf* ecstasy, rapture. ◆**s'extasi/er** *vpr* to be in raptures (**sur** over, about). ◆**—é** *a* ecstatic.

extensible [ekstãsibl] *a* expandable. ◆**extension** *nf* extension; (*essor*) expansion.

exténuer [ekstenɥe] *vt* (*fatiguer*) to exhaust.

extérieur [eksterjœr] *a* (*monde etc*) outside; (*surface*) outer; (*signe*) outward, external; (*politique*) foreign; **e.** à external to; **—** *nm* outside, exterior; **à l'e.** (**de**) outside; **à l'e.** (*match*) away; **en e.** *Cin* on location. ◆**—ement** *adv* externally; (*en apparence*) outwardly. ◆**extérioriser** *vt* to express.

exterminer [ekstermine] *vt* to exterminate, wipe out. ◆**extermination** *nf* extermination.

externe [ekstern] **1** *a* external. **2** *nmf* *Scol* day pupil; *Méd* non-resident hospital doctor, *Am* intern.

extincteur [ekstẽktœr] *nm* fire extinguisher. ◆**extinction** *nf* (*de feu*) extinguishing; (*de voix*) loss; (*de race*) extinction.

extirper [ekstirpe] *vt* to eradicate.

extorquer [ekstorke] *vt* to extort (à from). ◆**extorsion** *nf* extortion.

extra [ekstra] **1** *a inv* (*très bon*) *Fam* top-quality. **2** *nm inv* *Culin* (extra-special) treat; (*serviteur*) extra hand *ou* help.

extra- [ekstra] *préf* extra-. ◆**e.-fin** *a* extra-fine. ◆**e.-fort** *a* extra-strong.

extradition [ekstradisjɔ̃] *nf* extradition. ◆**extrader** *vt* to extradite.

extraire* [ekstrer] *vt* to extract (**de** from); (*charbon*) to mine. ◆**extraction** *nf* extraction. ◆**extrait** *nm* extract; **un e. de naissance** (a copy of one's) birth certificate.

extraordinaire [ekstraordiner] *a* extraordinary. ◆**—ment** *adv* exceptionally; (*très, bizarrement*) extraordinarily.

extravagant [ekstravagã] *a* extravagant. ◆**extravagance** *nf* extravagance.

extrême [ekstrem] *a* extreme; **—** *nm* extreme; **pousser à l'e.** to take *ou* carry to extremes. ◆**—ment** *adv* extremely. ◆**extrémiste** *a* & *nmf* extremist. ◆**extrémité** *nf* (*bout*) extremity, end; *pl* (*excès*) extremes.

exubérant [egzyberã] *a* exuberant. ◆**exubérance** *nf* exuberance.

exulter [egzylte] *vi* to exult, rejoice. ◆**exultation** *nf* exultation.

F

F, f [ef] *nm* F, f.

F *abrév* **franc(s)**.

fable [fɑbl] *nf* fable.

fabrique [fabrik] *nf* factory; **marque de f.** trade mark.

fabriquer [fabrike] *vt* (*objet*) to make; (*industriellement*) to manufacture; (*récit*) *Péj* to fabricate, make up; **qu'est-ce qu'il fabrique?** *Fam* what's he up to? ◆**fabricant, -ante** *nmf* manufacturer. ◆**fabrication** *nf* manufacture; (*artisanale*) making; **de f. française** of French make.

fabuleux, -euse [fabylø, -øz] *a* (*légendaire, incroyable*) fabulous.

fac [fak] *nf* *Univ* *Fam* = **faculté 2**.

façade [fasad] *nf* (*de bâtiment*) front, façade; (*apparence*) *Fig* pretence, façade; **de f.** (*luxe etc*) sham.

face [fas] *nf* face; (*de cube etc*) side; (*de monnaie*) head; **de f.** (*photo*) full-face; (*vue*) front; **faire f. à** (*situation etc*) to face, face up to; **en f.** opposite; **en f. de** opposite, facing; (*en présence de*) in front of; **en f. d'un problème, f. à un problème** in the face of a problem, faced with a problem; **f. à** (*vis-à-vis de*) facing; **regarder qn en f.** to look s.o. in the face; **à f.** face to face; **un f. à f.** *TV* a face to face encounter; **sauver/perdre la f.** to save/lose face.

facétie [fasesi] *nf* joke, jest. ◆**facétieux, -euse** [-esjø, -øz] *a* (*personne*) facetious.

facette [faset] *nf* (*de diamant, problème etc*) facet.

fâch/er [faʃe] *vt* to anger; — **se f.** *vpr* to get angry or annoyed (**contre** with); **se f. avec qn** (*se brouiller*) to fall out with s.o. ◆**—é** *a* (*air*) angry; (*amis*) on bad terms; **f. avec** *ou* **contre qn** angry *ou* annoyed with s.o.; **f. de qch** sorry about sth. ◆**fâcherie** *nf* quarrel. ◆**fâcheux, -euse** *a* (*nouvelle etc*) unfortunate.

facho [faʃo] *a* & *nmf Fam* fascist.

facile [fasil] *a* easy; (*caractère, humeur*) easygoing; (*banal*) *Péj* facile; **c'est f. à faire** it's easy to do; **il est f. de faire ça** it's easy to do that; **f. à vivre** easy to get along with, easygoing. ◆**—ment** *adv* easily. ◆**facilité** *nf* (*simplicité*) easiness; (*aisance*) ease; **facilités de paiement** *Com* easy terms; **avoir de la f.** to be gifted; **avoir toutes facilités pour** to have every facility *ou* opportunity to. ◆**faciliter** *vt* to facilitate, make easier.

façon [fasɔ̃] *nf* **1** way; **la f. dont elle parle** the way (in which) she talks; **f. (d'agir)** behaviour; **je n'aime pas ses façons** I don't like his *ou* her manners *ou* ways; **une f. de parler** a manner of speaking; **à la f. de** in the fashion of; **de toute f.** anyway, anyhow; **de f. à** so as to; **de f. générale** generally speaking; **à ma f.** my way, (in) my own way; **faire des façons** to make a fuss; **table f. chêne** imitation oak table. **2** (*coupe de vêtement*) cut, style. ◆**façonner** *vt* (*travailler, former*) to fashion, shape; (*fabriquer*) to manufacture.

facteur [faktœr] *nm* **1** postman, *Am* mailman. **2** (*élément*) factor. ◆**factrice** *nf Fam* postwoman.

factice [faktis] *a* false, artificial; (*diamant*) imitation-.

faction [faksjɔ̃] *nf* **1** (*groupe*) *Pol* faction. **2** **de f.** *Mil* on guard (duty), on sentry duty.

facture [faktyr] *nf Com* invoice, bill. ◆**facturer** *vt* to invoice, bill.

facultatif, -ive [fakyltatif, -iv] *a* optional; **arrêt f.** request stop.

faculté [fakylte] *nf* **1** (*aptitude*) faculty; (*possibilité*) freedom (**de faire** to do); **une f. de travail** a capacity for work. **2** *Univ* faculty; **à la f.** *Fam* at university, *Am* at school.

fadaises [fadɛz] *nfpl* twaddle, nonsense.

fade [fad] *a* insipid. ◆**fadasse** *a Fam* wishy-washy.

fagot [fago] *nm* bundle (of firewood).

fagoter [fagote] *vt Péj* to dress, rig out.

faible [fɛbl] *a* weak, feeble; (*bruit, voix*) faint; (*vent, quantité, chances*) slight; (*revenus*) small; **f. en anglais** poor at English/*etc*; — *nm* (*personne*) weakling; **les faibles** the weak; **avoir un f. pour** to have a weakness *ou* a soft spot for. ◆**faiblement** *adv* weakly; (*légèrement*) slightly; (*éclairer, parler*) faintly. ◆**faiblesse** *nf* weakness, feebleness; faintness; slightness; smallness; (*défaut, syncope*) weakness. ◆**faiblir** *vi* (*forces*) to weaken; (*courage, vue*) to fail; (*vent*) to slacken.

faïence [fajɑ̃s] *nf* (*matière*) earthenware; *pl* (*objets*) crockery, earthenware.

faille [faj] *nf Géol* fault; *Fig* flaw.

faillible [fajibl] *a* fallible.

faillir* [fajir] *vi* **1 il a failli tomber** he almost *ou* nearly fell. **2 f. à** (*devoir*) to fail in.

faillite [fajit] *nf Com* bankruptcy; *Fig* failure; **faire f.** to go bankrupt.

faim [fɛ̃] *nf* hunger; **avoir f.** to be hungry; **donner f. à qn** to make s.o. hungry; **manger à sa f.** to eat one's fill; **mourir de f.** to die of starvation; (*avoir très faim*) *Fig* to be starving.

fainéant, -ante [feneɑ̃, -ɑ̃t] *a* idle; — *nmf* idler. ◆**fainéanter** *vi* to idle. ◆**fainéantise** *nf* idleness.

faire* [fɛr] **1** *vt* (*bruit, pain, faute etc*) to make; (*devoir, dégâts, ménage etc*) to do; (*rêve, chute*) to have; (*sourire, grognement*) to give; (*promenade, sieste*) to have, take; (*guerre*) to wage, make; **ça fait dix mètres de large** (*mesure*) it's ten metres wide; **2 et 2 font 4** 2 and 2 are 4; **ça fait dix francs** that is *ou* comes to ten francs; **qu'a-t-il fait (de)?** what's he done (with)?; **que f.?** what's to be done?; **f. du tennis/du piano/***etc* to play tennis/the piano/*etc*; **f. l'idiot** to act *ou* play the fool; **ça ne fait rien** that doesn't matter; **comment as-tu fait pour . . . ?** how did you manage to . . . ?; **il ne fait que travailler** he does nothing but work, he keeps on working; **je ne fais que d'arriver** I've just arrived; **oui, fit-elle** yes, she said. **2** *vi* (*agir*) to do; (*paraître*) to look; **faire vieux** he looks old; **il fera un bon médecin** he'll make *ou* be a good doctor; **elle ferait bien de partir** she'd do well to leave. **3** *v imp* **il fait beau/froid/***etc* it's fine/cold/*etc*; **quel temps fait-il?** what's the weather like?; **ça fait deux ans que je ne l'ai pas vu** I haven't seen him for two years, it's (been) two years since I saw him. **4** v aux (+ inf): **f. construire une maison** to have ou get a house built (**à qn, par qn** by s.o.); **f. crier/souffrir/**etc **qn** to make s.o. shout/suffer/etc; **se f. couper les cheveux** to have one's hair cut; **se f. craindre/obéir/**etc to make oneself feared/obeyed/etc; **se f. tuer/renverser/**etc to get ou be killed/knocked down/etc. **5 se f.** vpr (fabrication) to be made; (activité) to be done; **se f. des illusions** to have illusions; **se f. des amis** to make friends; **se f. vieux/**etc (devenir) to get old/etc; **il se fait tard** it's getting late; **comment se fait-il que?** how is it that?; **se f. à** to get used to, adjust to; **ne t'en fais pas!** don't worry!

faire-part [fɛrpar] nm inv (de mariage etc) announcement.

faisable [fəzabl] a feasible.

faisan [fəzɑ̃] nm (oiseau) pheasant.

faisandé [fəzɑ̃de] a (gibier) high.

faisceau, -x [fɛso] nm (lumineux) beam; (de tiges etc) bundle.

fait [fɛ] **1** voir **faire**; — a (fromage) ripe; (homme) grown; (yeux) made up; (ongles) polished; **tout f.** ready made; **bien f.** (jambes, corps etc) shapely; **c'est bien f.!** it serves you right! **2** nm event, occurrence; (donnée, réalité) fact; **prendre sur le f.** to catch in the act; **du f. de** on account of; **divers** Journ (miscellaneous) news item; **au f.** (à propos) by the way; **aller au f.** to get to the point; **faits et gestes** actions; **en f.** in fact; **en f. de** in the matter of.

faîte [fɛt] nm (haut) top; (apogée) Fig height.

faites [fɛt] voir **faire**.

faitout [fɛtu] nm stewing pot, casserole.

falaise [falɛz] nf cliff.

falloir* [falwar] **1** v imp **il faut qch/qn** I, you, we etc need sth/s.o.; **il lui faut un stylo** he ou she needs a pen; **il faut partir/**etc I, you, we etc have to go/etc; **il faut que je parte** I have to go; **il faudrait qu'elle reste** she ought to stay; **il faut un jour** it takes a day (**pour faire** to do); **comme il faut** proper(ly); **s'il le faut** if need be. **2 s'en f.** v imp **peu s'en est fallu qu'il ne pleure** he almost cried; **tant s'en faut** far from it.

falsifier [falsifje] vt (texte etc) to falsify. ◆**falsification** nf falsification.

famé (mal) [malfame] a of ill repute.

famélique [famelik] a ill-fed, starving.

fameux, -euse [famø, -øz] a famous; (excellent) Fam first-class; **pas f.** Fam not much good.

familial, -aux [familjal, -o] a family-.

familier, -ière [familje, -jɛr] a (bien connu) familiar (**à** to); (amical) friendly, informal; (locution) colloquial, familiar; **f. avec qn** (over)familiar with s.o.; — nm (de club etc) regular visitor. ◆**familiariser** vt to familiarize (**avec** with); — **se f.** vpr to familiarize oneself (**avec** with). ◆**familiarité** nf familiarity; pl Péj liberties. ◆**familièrement** adv familiarly; (parler) informally.

famille [famij] nf family; **en f.** (dîner etc) with one's family; **un père de f.** a family man.

famine [famin] nf famine.

fan [fan] nm (admirateur) Fam fan.

fana [fana] nmf Fam fan; **être f. de** to be crazy about.

fanal, -aux [fanal, -o] nm lantern, light.

fanatique [fanatik] a fanatical; — nmf fanatic. ◆**fanatisme** nm fanaticism.

fan/er (se) [səfane] vpr (fleur, beauté) to fade. ◆**-é** a faded.

fanfare [fɑ̃far] nf (orchestre) brass band; (air, musique) fanfare.

fanfaron, -onne [fɑ̃farɔ̃, -ɔn] a boastful; — nmf braggart.

fange [fɑ̃ʒ] nf Litt mud, mire.

fanion [fanjɔ̃] nm (drapeau) pennant.

fantaisie [fɑ̃tezi] nf (caprice) fancy, whim; (imagination) imagination, fantasy; (de) f. (bouton etc) fancy. ◆**fantaisiste** a (pas sérieux) fanciful; (irrégulier) unorthodox.

fantasme [fɑ̃tasm] nm Psy fantasy. ◆**fantasmer** vi to fantasize (**sur** about).

fantasque [fɑ̃task] a whimsical.

fantassin [fɑ̃tasɛ̃] nm Mil infantryman.

fantastique [fɑ̃tastik] a (imaginaire, excellent) fantastic.

fantoche [fɑ̃tɔʃ] nm & a puppet.

fantôme [fɑ̃tom] nm ghost, phantom; — a (ville, train) ghost-; (firme) bogus.

faon [fɑ̃] nm (animal) fawn.

faramineux, -euse [faraminø, -øz] a Fam fantastic.

farce¹ [fars] nf practical joke, prank; Th farce; **magasin de farces et attrapes** joke shop. ◆**farceur, -euse** nmf (blagueur) wag, joker.

farce² [fars] nf Culin stuffing. ◆**farcir** vt **1** Culin to stuff. **2** **se f. qn/qch** Fam to put up with s.o./sth.

fard [far] nm make-up. ◆**farder** vt (vérité) to camouflage; — **se f.** vpr (se maquiller) to make up.

fardeau, -x [fardo] nm burden, load.

farfelu, -ue [farfəly] a Fam crazy, bizarre; — nmf Fam weirdo.

farine [farin] nf (de blé) flour; **f. d'avoine**

oatmeal. ◆**farineux, -euse** *a Péj* floury, powdery.

farouche [faruʃ] *a* **1** (*timide*) shy, unsociable; (*animal*) easily scared. **2** (*violent, acharné*) fierce. ◆**—ment** *adv* fiercely.

fart [far(t)] *nm* (ski) wax. ◆**farter** *vt* (*skis*) to wax.

fascicule [fasikyl] *nm* volume.

fasciner [fasine] *vt* to fascinate. ◆**fascination** *nf* fascination.

fascisme [faʃism] *nm* fascism. ◆**fasciste** *a & nmf* fascist.

fasse(nt) [fas] *voir* **faire**.

faste [fast] *nm* ostentation, display.

fastidieux, -euse [fastidjø, -øz] *a* tedious, dull.

fatal [fatal] *a* (*mortel*) fatal; (*inévitable*) inevitable; (*moment, ton*) fateful; **c'est f.!** it was bound to happen! ◆**—ement** *adv* inevitably. ◆**fataliste** *a* fatalistic; – *nmf* fatalist. ◆**fatalité** *nf* (*destin*) fate. ◆**fatidique** *a* (*jour, date*) fateful.

fatigue [fatig] *nf* tiredness, fatigue, weariness. ◆**fatigant** *a* (*épuisant*) tiring; (*ennuyeux*) tiresome. ◆**fatigu/er** *vt* to tire, fatigue; (*yeux*) to strain; (*importuner*) to annoy; (*raser*) to bore; – *vi* (*moteur*) to strain; – **se f.** *vpr* (*se lasser*) to get tired, tire (**de** of); (*travailler*) to tire oneself out (**à faire** doing). ◆**-é** *a* tired, weary (**de** of).

fatras [fatra] *nm* jumble, muddle.

faubourg [fobur] *nm* suburb. ◆**faubourien, -ienne** *a* (*accent etc*) suburban, common.

fauché [foʃe] *a* (*sans argent*) *Fam* broke.

fauch/er [foʃe] *vt* **1** (*herbe*) to mow; (*blé*) to reap; (*abattre, renverser*) *Fig* to mow down. **2** (*voler*) *Fam* to snatch, pinch. ◆**—euse** *nf* (*machine*) reaper.

faucille [fosij] *nf* (*instrument*) sickle.

faucon [fokõ] *nm* (*oiseau*) falcon, hawk; (*personne*) *Fig* hawk.

faudra, faudrait [fodra, fodrε] *voir* **falloir**.

faufiler (se) [səfofile] *vpr* to edge *ou* inch one's way (**dans** through, into; **entre** between).

faune [fon] *nf* wildlife, fauna; (*gens*) *Péj* set.

faussaire [foser] *nm* (*faux-monnayeur*) forger.

fausse [fos] *voir* **faux¹**. ◆**faussement** *adv* falsely.

fausser [fose] *vt* (*sens, réalité etc*) to distort; (*clé etc*) to buckle; **f. compagnie à qn** to give s.o. the slip.

fausseté [foste] *nf* (*d'un raisonnement etc*) falseness; (*hypocrisie*) duplicity.

faut [fo] *voir* **falloir**.

faute [fot] *nf* (*erreur*) mistake; (*responsabilité*) fault; (*délit*) offence; (*péché*) sin; *Fb* foul; **c'est la f.** it's your fault, you're to blame; **f. de temps/etc** for lack of time/*etc*; **f. de mieux** for want of anything better; **en f.** at fault; **sans f.** without fail. ◆**fautif, -ive** *a* (*coupable*) at fault; (*erroné*) faulty.

fauteuil [fotœj] *nm* armchair; (*de président*) chair; **f. d'orchestre** *Th* seat in the stalls; **f. roulant** wheelchair; **f. pivotant** swivel chair.

fauteur [fotœr] *nm* **f. de troubles** troublemaker.

fauve [fov] **1** *a & nm* (*couleur*) fawn. **2** *nm* wild beast; **chasse aux fauves** big game hunting.

faux¹, fausse [fo, fos] *a* (*inauthentique*) false; (*pas vrai*) untrue, false; (*pas exact*) wrong; (*monnaie*) counterfeit, forged; (*bijou, marbre*) imitation-, fake; (*voix*) out of tune; (*col*) detachable; – *adv* (*chanter*) out of tune; – *nm* (*contrefaçon*) forgery; **le f.** the false, the untrue. ◆**f.-filet** *nm Culin* sirloin. ◆**f.-fuyant** *nm* subterfuge. ◆**f.-monnayeur** *nm* counterfeiter.

faux² [fo] *nf* (*instrument*) scythe.

faveur [favœr] *nf* favour; **en f. de** (*au profit de*) in favour of; **de f.** (*billet*) complimentary; (*traitement, régime*) preferential. ◆**favorable** *a* favourable (**à** to). ◆**favori, -ite** *a & nmf* favourite. ◆**favoriser** *vt* to favour. ◆**favoritisme** *nm* favouritism.

favoris [favɔri] *nmpl* sideburns, side whiskers.

fébrile [febril] *a* feverish. ◆**fébrilité** *nf* feverishness.

fécond [fekõ] *a* (*femme, idée etc*) fertile. ◆**féconder** *vt* to fertilize. ◆**fécondité** *nf* fertility.

fécule [fekyl] *nf* starch. ◆**féculents** *nmpl* (*aliments*) carbohydrates.

fédéral, -aux [federal, -o] *a* federal. ◆**fédération** *nf* federation. ◆**fédérer** *vt* to federate.

fée [fe] *nf* fairy. ◆**féerie** *nf Th* fantasy extravaganza; *Fig* fairy-like spectacle. ◆**féerique** *a* fairy(-like), magical.

feindre* [fɛ̃dr] *vt* to feign, sham; **f. de faire** to pretend to do. ◆**feint** *a* feigned, sham. ◆**feinte** *nf* sham, pretence; *Boxe Mil* feint.

fêler [fele] *vt*, – **se f.** *vpr* (*tasse*) to crack. ◆**fêlure** *nf* crack.

félicité [felisite] *nf* bliss, felicity.

féliciter [felisite] *vt* to congratulate (**qn de** *ou* **sur** s.o. on); **se f. de** to congratulate oneself on. ◆**félicitations** *nfpl* congratulations (**pour** on).

félin [felɛ̃] a & *nm* feline.

femelle [fəmɛl] a & *nf* (*animal*) female.

féminin [feminɛ̃] a (*prénom, hormone etc*) female; (*trait, intuition etc*) & *Gram* feminine; (*mode, revue, équipe etc*) women's. ◆**féministe** a & *nmf* feminist. ◆**féminité** *nf* femininity.

femme [fam] *nf* woman; (*épouse*) wife; **f. médecin** woman doctor; **f. de chambre** (chamber)maid; **f. de ménage** cleaning lady, maid; **bonne f.** *Fam* woman.

fémur [femyr] *nm* thighbone, femur.

fendiller (se) [səfɑ̃dije] *vpr* to crack.

fendre [fɑ̃dr] *vt* (*bois etc*) to split; (*foule*) to force one's way through; (*onde, air*) to cleave; (*cœur*) *Fig* to break, rend; **— se f.** *vpr* (*se fissurer*) to crack.

fenêtre [f(ə)nɛtr] *nf* window.

fenouil [fənuj] *nm Bot Culin* fennel.

fente [fɑ̃t] *nf* (*de tirelire, palissade, jupe etc*) slit; (*de rocher*) split, crack.

féodal, -aux [feodal, -o] a feudal.

fer [fɛr] *nm* iron; (*partie métallique de qch*) metal (part); **de f., en f.** (*outil etc*) iron-; **fil de f.** wire; **f. à cheval** horseshoe; **f.** (**à repasser**) iron; **f. à friser** curling tongs; **f. de lance** *Fig* spearhead; **de f.** (*santé*) *Fig* cast-iron; (*main, volonté*) *Fig* iron-. ◆**fer-blanc** *nm* (*pl* **fers-blancs**) tin(-plate).

fera, ferait [fəra, fərɛ] *voir* **faire**.

férié [ferje] a **jour f.** (public) holiday.

ferme[1] [fɛrm] *nf* farm; (*maison*) farm(house).

ferme[2] [fɛrm] a (*beurre, décision etc*) firm; (*autoritaire*) firm (**avec** with); (*pas, voix*) steady; (*pâte*) stiff; **— adv** (*travailler, boire*) hard; (*discuter*) keenly; **tenir f.** to stand firm *ou* fast. ◆**—ment** [-əmɑ̃] *adv* firmly.

ferment [fɛrmɑ̃] *nm* ferment. ◆**fermentation** *nf* fermentation. ◆**fermenter** *vi* to ferment.

ferm/er [fɛrme] *vt* to close, shut; (*gaz, radio etc*) to turn *ou* switch off; (*passage*) to block; (*vêtement*) to do up; (**à clef**) to lock; **f. la marche** to bring up the rear; **— vi**, **— se f.** *vpr* to close, shut. ◆**—é** a (*porte, magasin etc*) closed, shut; (*route, circuit etc*) closed; (*gaz etc*) off. ◆**fermeture** *nf* closing, closure; (*heure*) closing time; (*mécanisme*) catch; **f. éclair**® zip (fastener), *Am* zipper. ◆**fermoir** *nm* clasp, (snap) fastener.

fermeté [fɛrməte] *nf* firmness; (*de geste, voix*) steadiness.

fermier, -ière [fɛrmje, -jɛr] *nmf* farmer; **— a** (*poulet, produit*) farm-.

féroce [ferɔs] a fierce, ferocious. ◆**férocité** *nf* ferocity, fierceness.

ferraille [fɛraj] *nf* scrap-iron; **mettre à la f.** to scrap. ◆**ferrailleur** *nm* scrap-iron merchant.

ferré [fere] a **1** (*canne*) metal-tipped; **voie ferrée** railway, *Am* railroad; (*rails*) track. **2** (*calé*) *Fam* well up (**en** in, **sur** on).

ferrer [fere] *vt* (*cheval*) to shoe.

ferronnerie [fɛrɔnri] *nf* ironwork.

ferroviaire [fɛrɔvjɛr] a (*compagnie etc*) railway-, *Am* railroad-.

ferry-boat [feribot] *nm* ferry.

fertile [fɛrtil] a (*terre, imagination*) fertile; **f. en incidents** eventful. ◆**fertiliser** *vt* to fertilize. ◆**fertilité** *nf* fertility.

fervent, -ente [fɛrvɑ̃, -ɑ̃t] a fervent; **— *nmf*** devotee (**de** of). ◆**ferveur** *nf* fervour.

fesse [fɛs] *nf* buttock; **les fesses** one's behind. ◆**fessée** *nf* spanking.

festin [fɛstɛ̃] *nm* (*banquet*) feast.

festival, pl -als [fɛstival] *nm Mus Cin* festival.

festivités [fɛstivite] *nfpl* festivities.

festoyer [fɛstwaje] *vi* to feast, carouse.

fête [fɛt] *nf* (*civile*) holiday; (*religieuse*) feast; (*entre amis*) party; **f. du village** village fair *ou* fête; **f. de famille** family celebration; **c'est sa f.** it's his *ou* her saint's day; **f. des Mères** Mother's Day; **jour de f.** (public) holiday; **faire la f.** to make merry, revel; **air de f.** festive air. ◆**fêter** *vt* (*événement*) to celebrate.

fétiche [fetiʃ] *nm* (*objet de culte*) fetish; (*mascotte*) *Fig* mascot.

fétide [fetid] a fetid, stinking.

feu[1], **-x** [fø] *nm* fire; (*lumière*) *Aut Nau Av* light; (*de réchaud*) burner; (*de dispute*) *Fig* heat; *pl* (*de signalisation*) traffic lights; **feux de position** *Aut* parking lights; **feux de croisement** *Aut* dipped headlights, *Am* low beams; **f. rouge** *Aut* (*lumière*) red light; (*objet*) traffic lights; **tous feux éteints** *Aut* without lights; **mettre le f. à** to set fire to; **en f.** on fire, ablaze; **avez-vous du f.?** have you got a light?; **donner le f. vert** to give the go-ahead (**à** to); **ne pas faire long f.** not to last very long; **à f. doux** *Culin* on a low light; **au f.!** (there's a) fire!; **f.! *Mil* fire!; **coup de f.** (*bruit*) gunshot; **feux croisés** *Mil* crossfire.

feu[2] [fø] a *inv* late; **f. ma tante** my late aunt.

feuille [fœj] *nf* leaf; (*de papier etc*) sheet; (*de température*) chart; *Journ* newssheet; **f. d'impôt** tax form *ou* return; **f. de paye** pay slip. ◆**feuillage** nm foliage. ◆**feuillet** nm (de livre) leaf. ◆**feuilleter** vt (livre) to flip ou leaf through; **pâte feuilletée** puff ou flaky pastry. ◆**feuilleton** nm (roman, film etc) serial. ◆**feuillu** a leafy.

feutre [føtr] nm felt; (chapeau) felt hat; **crayon f.** felt-tip(ped) pen. ◆**feutré** a (bruit) muffled; **à pas feutrés** silently.

fève [fɛv] nf bean.

février [fevrije] nm February.

fiable [fjabl] a reliable. ◆**fiabilité** nf reliability.

fiacre [fjakr] nm Hist hackney carriage.

fianc/er (se) [səfjɑ̃se] vpr to become engaged (avec to). ◆**—é** nm fiancé; **un f. engaged couple.** ◆**—ée** nf fiancée. ◆**fiançailles** nfpl engagement.

fiasco [fjasko] nm fiasco; **faire f.** to be a fiasco.

fibre [fibr] nf fibre; **f. (alimentaire)** roughage, (dietary) fibre; **f. de verre** fibreglass.

ficelle [fisɛl] nf 1 string; **connaître les ficelles** (d'un métier etc) to known the ropes. 2 (pain) long thin loaf. ◆**ficeler** vt to tie up.

fiche [fiʃ] nf 1 (carte) index ou record card; (papier) slip, form; **f. technique** data record. 2 El (broche) pin; (prise) plug. ◆**fichier** nm card index, file.

fiche(r) [fiʃ(e)] vt (pp fichu) Fam (faire) to do; (donner) to give; (jeter) to throw; (mettre) to put; **f. le camp** to clear off; **fiche-moi la paix!** leave me alone!; **se f. de qn** to make fun of s.o.; **je m'en fiche!** I don't give a damn!

ficher [fiʃe] vt 1 (enfoncer) to drive in. 2 (renseignement, personne) to put on file.

fichu [fiʃy] 1 a Fam (mauvais) lousy, rotten; (capable) able (de faire to do); **il est f.,** he's had it, he's done for; **mal f.** (malade) not well. 2 nm (head) scarf.

fictif, -ive [fiktif, -iv] a fictitious. ◆**fiction** nf fiction.

fidèle [fidɛl] a faithful (à to); – nmf faithful supporter; (client) regular customer; **les fidèles** (croyants) the faithful; (à l'église) the congregation. ◆**—ment** adv faithfully. ◆**fidélité** nf fidelity, faithfulness.

fief [fjɛf] nm (spécialité, chasse gardée) domain.

fiel [fjɛl] nm gall.

fier (se) [səfje] vpr se f. à to trust.

fier, fière [fjɛr] a proud (de of); **un f. culot** Péj a rare cheek. ◆**fièrement** adv proudly. ◆**fierté** nf pride.

fièvre [fjɛvr] nf (maladie) fever; (agitation) frenzy; **avoir de la f.** to have a temperature ou a fever. ◆**fiévreux, -euse** a feverish.

fig/er [fiʒe] vt (sang, sauce etc) to congeal; **f. qn** (paralyser) Fig to freeze s.o.; – vi (liquide) to congeal; – se f. vpr (personne) Fig to freeze. ◆**—é** a (locution) set, fixed; (regard) frozen; (société) petrified.

fignol/er [fiɲɔle] vt Fam to round off meticulously, refine. ◆**—é** a Fam meticulous.

figue [fig] nf fig; **mi-f., mi-raisin** (accueil etc) neither good nor bad, mixed. ◆**figuier** nm fig tree.

figurant, -ante [figyrɑ̃, -ɑ̃t] nmf Cin Th extra.

figure [figyr] nf 1 (visage) face. 2 (personnage) & Géom figure; (de livre) figure, illustration; **faire f. de riche/d'imbécile/etc** to look rich/a fool/etc. ◆**figurine** nf statuette.

figur/er [figyre] vt to represent; – vi to appear, figure; – **se f.** vpr to imagine; **figurez-vous que . . . ?** would you believe that . . . ? ◆**—é** a (sens) figurative; – nm **au f.** figuratively.

fil [fil] nm 1 (de coton, pensée etc) thread; (lin) linen; **f. dentaire** dental floss; **de f. en aiguille** bit by bit. 2 (métallique) wire; **f. de fer** wire; **f. à plomb** plumbline; **au bout du f.** Tél on the line; **passer un coup de f. à qn** Tél to give s.o. a ring ou a call. 3 (de couteau) edge. 4 **au f. de l'eau/des jours** with the current/the passing of time.

filament [filamɑ̃] nm El filament.

filandreux, -euse [filɑ̃drø, -øz] a (phrase) long-winded.

filante [filɑ̃t] af **étoile f.** shooting star.

file [fil] nf 1 line; (couloir) Aut lane; **f. d'attente** queue, Am line; **en f. (indienne)** in single file; **chef de f.** leader; **(se) mettre en f.** to line up.

filer [file] 1 vt (coton etc) to spin. 2 vt **f. qn** (suivre) to shadow s.o., tail s.o. 3 vt Fam **f. qch à qn** (objet) to slip s.o. sth; **f. un coup de pied/etc à qn** to give s.o. a kick/etc. 4 vi (partir) to shoot off, bolt; (aller vite) to speed along; (temps) to fly; (bas, collant) to ladder, run; (liquide) to trickle, run; **filez!** hop it!; **f. entre les doigts de qn** to slip through s.o.'s fingers; **f. doux** to be obedient. ◆**filature** nf 1 (usine) textile mill. 2 (de policiers etc) shadowing; **prendre en f.** to shadow.

filet [filɛ] nm 1 (de pêche) & Sp net; (à bagages) Rail (luggage) rack; **f. (à provisions)** string ou net bag (for shopping). 2 (d'eau) trickle. 3 (de poisson, viande) fillet.

filial, -aux [filjal, -o] a filial.

filiale [filjal] nf subsidiary (company).

filiation [filjasjɔ̃] *nf* relationship.

filière [filjɛr] *nf* (*de drogue*) network; **suivre la f.** (*pour obtenir qch*) to go through the official channels; (*employé*) to work one's way up.

filigrane [filigran] *nm* (*de papier*) watermark.

filin [filɛ̃] *nm* Nau rope.

fille [fij] *nf* **1** girl; **petite f.** (little *ou* young) girl; **jeune f.** girl, young lady; **vieille f.** *Péj* old maid; **f. (publique)** *Péj* prostitute. **2** (*parenté*) daughter, girl. ◆**-f.-mère** *nf* (*pl* **filles-mères**) *Péj* unmarried mother. ◆**fillette** *nf* little girl.

filleul [fijœl] *nm* godson. ◆**filleule** *nf* goddaughter.

film [film] *nm* film, movie; (*pellicule*) film; **f. muet/parlant** silent/talking film *ou* movie; **le f. des événements** the sequence of events. ◆**filmer** *vt* (*personne, scène*) to film.

filon [filɔ̃] *nm* Géol seam; **trouver le (bon) f.** to strike it lucky.

filou [filu] *nm* rogue, crook.

fils [fis] *nm* son; **Dupont f.** Dupont junior.

filtre [filtr] *nm* filter; **(à bout) f.** (*cigarette*) (filter-)tipped; **(bout) f.** filter tip. ◆**filtrer** *vt* to filter; (*personne, nouvelles*) to scrutinize; – *vi* to filter (through).

fin [fɛ̃] **1** *nf* end; (*but*) end, aim; **mettre f. à** to put an end *ou* a stop to; **prendre f.** to come to an end; **tirer à sa f.** to draw to an end *ou* a close; **sans f.** endless; **à la f.** in the end; **arrêtez, à la f.!** stop, for heaven's sake!; **f. de semaine** weekend; **f. mai** at the end of May; **à cette f.** to this end. **2** *a* (*pointe, travail, tissu etc*) fine; (*taille, tranche*) thin; (*plat*) delicate, choice; (*esprit, oreille*) sharp; (*observation*) sharp, fine; (*gourmet*) discerning; (*rusé*) shrewd; (*intelligent*) clever; **au f. fond de** in the depths of; – *adv* (*couper, moudre*) finely; (*écrire*) small.

final, -aux *ou* **-als** [final, -o] *a* final; – *nm* *Mus* finale. ◆**finale** *nf* Sp final; *Gram* final syllable; – *nm* *Mus* finale. ◆**finalement** *adv* finally; (*en somme*) after all. ◆**finaliste** *nmf* Sp finalist.

finance [finɑ̃s] *nf* finance. ◆**financ/er** *vt* to finance. ◆**-ement** *nm* financing. ◆**financier, -ière** *a* financial; – *nm* financier. ◆**financièrement** *adv* financially.

fine [fin] *nf* liqueur brandy.

finement [finmɑ̃] *adv* (*broder, couper etc*) finely; (*agir*) cleverly.

finesse [fines] *nf* (*de pointe etc*) fineness; (*de taille etc*) thinness; (*de plat*) delicacy; (*d'esprit, de goût*) finesse; *pl* (*de langue*) niceties.

fin/ir [finir] *vt* to finish; (*discours, vie*) to end, finish; – *vi* to finish, end; **f. de faire** to finish doing; (*cesser*) to stop doing; **f. par faire** to end up *ou* finish up doing; **f. par qch** to finish (up) *ou* end (up) with sth; **en f. avec** to put an end to, finish with; **elle n'en finit pas** there's no end to it, she goes on and on. ◆**-i** *a* (*produit*) finished; (*univers etc*) & *Math* finite; **c'est f.** it's over *ou* finished; **il est f.** (*fichu*) he's done for *ou* finished; – *nm* (*poli*) finish. ◆**-issant** *a* (*siècle*) declining. ◆**finish** *nm* Sp finish. ◆**finition** *nf* (*action*) Tech finishing; (*résultat*) finish.

Finlande [fɛ̃lɑ̃d] *nf* Finland. ◆**finlandais, -aise** *a* Finnish; – *nmf* Finn. ◆**finnois, -oise** *a* Finnish; – *nm* Finn; – *nm* (*langue*) Finnish.

fiole [fjɔl] *nf* phial, flask.

firme [firm] *nf* (*entreprise*) Com firm.

fisc [fisk] *nm* tax authorities; – Inland Revenue; – *Am* Internal Revenue. ◆**fiscal, -aux** *a* fiscal, tax-. ◆**fiscalité** *nf* tax system; (*charges*) taxation.

fission [fisjɔ̃] *nf* Phys fission.

fissure [fisyr] *nf* split, crack, fissure. ◆**se fissurer** *vpr* to split, crack.

fiston [fistɔ̃] *nm* Fam son, sonny.

fixe [fiks] *a* fixed; (*prix, heure*) set, fixed; **idée f.** obsession; **regard f.** stare; **être au beau f.** *Mét* to be set fair; – *nm* (*paie*) fixed salary. ◆**-ment** [-əmɑ̃] *adv* **regarder f.** to stare at. ◆**fixer** *vt* (*attacher*) to fix (à to); (*choix*) to settle; (*règle, date etc*) to decide, fix; **f. (du regard)** to stare at; **f. qn sur** to inform s.o. clearly about; **être fixé** (*décidé*) to be decided; **comme ça on est fixé!** (*renseigné*) we've got the picture!; – **se f.** *vpr* (*regard*) to become fixed; (*s'établir*) to settle. ◆**fixateur** *nm* Phot fixer; (*pour cheveux*) setting lotion. ◆**fixation** *nf* (*action*) fixing; (*dispositif*) fastening, binding; *Psy* fixation.

flacon [flakɔ̃] *nm* bottle, flask.

flageoler [flaʒɔle] *vi* to shake, tremble.

flageolet [flaʒɔlɛ] *nm* Bot Culin (dwarf) kidney bean.

flagrant [flagrɑ̃] *a* (*injustice etc*) flagrant, glaring; **pris en f. délit** caught in the act *ou* red-handed.

flair [flɛr] *nm* **1** (*d'un chien etc*) (sense of) smell, scent. **2** (*clairvoyance*) intuition, flair. ◆**flairer** *vt* to sniff at, smell; (*discerner*) Fig to smell, sense.

flamand, -ande [flamɑ̃, -ɑ̃d] *a* Flemish; – *nmf* Fleming; – *nm* (*langue*) Flemish.

flamant [flamɑ̃] *nm* (*oiseau*) flamingo.

flambant [flãbã] *adv* f. neuf brand new.

flambeau, -x [flãbo] *nm* torch.

flamb/er [flãbe] **1** *vi* to burn, blaze; – *vt* (*aiguille*) Méd to sterilize; (*poulet*) to singe. **2** *vi* (*jouer*) Fam to gamble for big money. ◆**—é a** (*ruiné*) Fam done for. ◆**—ée** *nf* blaze; (*de colère, des prix etc*) Fig surge; (*de violence*) flare-up, eruption. ◆**—eur** *nm* Fam big gambler. ◆**flamboyer** *vi* to blaze, flame.

flamme [flam] *nf* flame; (*ardeur*) Fig fire; **en flammes** on fire. ◆**flammèche** *nf* spark.

flan [flã] *nm* **1** Culin custard tart *ou* pie. **2 au f.** Fam on the off chance, on the spur of the moment.

flanc [flã] *nm* side; (*d'une armée, volcan, animal*) flank; **tirer au f.** Arg to shirk, idle.

flancher [flãʃe] *vi* Fam to give in, weaken.

Flandre(s) [flãdr] *nf(pl)* Flanders.

flanelle [flanɛl] *nf* (*tissu*) flannel.

flâner [flãne] *vi* to stroll, dawdle. ◆**flânerie** *nf* (*action*) strolling; (*promenade*) stroll.

flanquer [flãke] *vt* **1** to flank (**de** with). **2** Fam (*jeter*) to chuck; (*donner*) to give; **f. qn à la porte** to throw s.o. out.

flaque [flak] *nf* puddle, pool.

flash, *pl* **flashes** [flaʃ] *nm* **1** Phot (*éclair*) flashlight; (*dispositif*) flash(gun). **2** TV Rad (*news*)flash.

flasque [flask] *a* flabby, floppy.

flatt/er [flate] *vt* to flatter; **se f. d'être malin/de réussir** to flatter oneself on being smart/on being able to succeed. ◆**—é a** flattered (**de qch** by sth, **de faire** to do, **que** that). ◆**flatterie** *nf* flattery. ◆**flatteur, -euse** *nmf* flatterer; – *a* flattering.

fléau, -x [fleo] *nm* **1** (*calamité*) scourge; (*personne, chose*) bane, plague. **2** Agr flail.

flèche [flɛʃ] *nf* arrow; (*d'église*) spire; **monter en f.** (*prix*) to (sky)rocket, shoot ahead. ◆**flécher** [fleʃe] *vt* to signpost (with arrows). ◆**fléchette** *nf* dart; *pl* (*jeu*) darts.

fléchir [fleʃir] *vt* (*membre*) to flex, bend; **f. qn** Fig to move s.o., persuade s.o.; – *vi* (*membre*) to bend; (*poutre*) to sag; (*faiblir*) to give way; (*baisser*) to fall off.

flegme [flɛgm] *nm* composure. ◆**flegmatique** *a* phlegmatic, stolid.

flemme [flɛm] *nf* Fam laziness; **il a la f.** he can't be bothered, he's just too lazy. ◆**flemmard, -arde** *a* Fam lazy; – *nmf* Fam lazybones.

flétrir [fletrir] **1** *vt*, – **se f.** *vpr* to wither. **2** *vt* (*blâmer*) to stigmatize, brand.

fleur [flœr] *nf* flower; (*d'arbre, d'arbuste*) blossom; **en f.** in flower, in bloom; in blos-

som; **à** *ou* **dans la f. de l'âge** in the prime of life; **à f. d'eau** just above the water; **à fleurs** (*tissu*) floral. ◆**fleur/ir** *vi* to flower, bloom; (*arbre etc*) to blossom; (*art, commerce etc*) Fig to flourish; – *vt* (*table etc*) to decorate with flowers. ◆**—i a** (*fleur, jardin*) in bloom; (*tissu*) flowered, floral; (*teint*) florid; (*style*) flowery, florid. ◆**fleuriste** *nmf* florist.

fleuve [flœv] *nm* river.

flexible [flɛksibl] *a* flexible, pliable. ◆**flexibilité** *nf* flexibility.

flexion [flɛksjɔ̃] *nf* **1** Anat flexion, flexing. **2** Gram inflexion.

flic [flik] *nm* Fam cop, policeman.

flinguer [flɛ̃ge] *vt* **f. qn** Arg to shoot s.o.

flipper [flipœr] *nm* (*jeu*) pinball.

flirt [flœrt] *nm* (*rapports*) flirtation; (*personne*) flirt. ◆**flirter** *vi* to flirt (**avec** with). ◆**flirteur, -euse** *a* flirtatious; – *nmf* flirt.

flocon [flɔkɔ̃] *nm* (*de neige*) flake; (*de laine*) flock; **flocons d'avoine** Culin porridge oats. ◆**floconneux, -euse** *a* fluffy.

floraison [flɔrɛzɔ̃] *nf* flowering; **en pleine f.** in full bloom. ◆**floral, -aux** *a* floral. ◆**floralies** *nfpl* flower show.

flore [flɔr] *nf* flora.

florissant [flɔrisã] *a* flourishing.

flot [flo] *nm* (*de souvenirs, larmes*) flood, stream; (*marée*) floodtide; (*de mer*) waves; (*de lac*) waters; **à flots** in abundance; **à f.** (*bateau, personne*) afloat; **mettre à f.** (*bateau, firme*) to launch; **remettre qn à f.** to restore s.o.'s fortunes.

flotte [flɔt] *nf* **1** Nau Av fleet. **2** Fam (*pluie*) rain; (*eau*) water. ◆**flottille** *nf* Nau flotilla.

flott/er [flɔte] *vi* to float; (*drapeau*) to fly; (*cheveux*) to flow; (*pensées*) to drift; (*pleuvoir*) Fam to rain. ◆**—ant** *a* **1** (*bois, dette etc*) floating; (*vêtement*) flowing, loose. **2** (*esprit*) indecisive. ◆**—ement** *nm* (*hésitation*) indecision. ◆**—eur** *nm* Pêche etc float.

flou [flu] *a* (*photo*) fuzzy, blurred; (*idée*) hazy, fuzzy; – *nm* fuzziness.

fluctuant [flyktɥã] *a* (*prix, opinions*) fluctuating. ◆**fluctuations** *nfpl* fluctuation(s) (**de** in).

fluet, -ette [flɥɛ, -ɛt] *a* thin, slender.

fluide [flɥid] *a* (*liquide*) & Fig fluid; – *nm* (*liquide*) fluid. ◆**fluidité** *nf* fluidity.

fluorescent [flɥɔresã] *a* fluorescent.

flûte [flyt] **1** *nf* Mus flute. **2** *nf* (*verre*) champagne glass. **3** *int* heck!, darn!, dash it! ◆**flûté a** (*voix*) piping. ◆**flûtiste** *nmf* flautist, Am flutist.

fluvial, -aux [flyvjal, -o] *a* river-, fluvial.

flux [fly] *nm* (*abondance*) flow; **f. et reflux** ebb and flow.

focal, -aux [fɔkal, -o] *a* focal. ◆**focaliser** *vt* (*intérêt etc*) to focus.

fœtus [fetys] *nm* foetus, *Am* fetus.

foi [fwa] *nf* faith; **sur la f. de** on the strength of; **agir de bonne/mauvaise f.** to act in good/bad faith; **ma f., oui!** yes, indeed!

foie [fwa] *nm* liver.

foin [fwɛ̃] *nm* hay; **faire du f.** (*scandale*) *Fam* to make a stink.

foire [fwar] *nf* fair; **faire la f.** *Fam* to go on a binge, have a ball.

fois [fwa] *nf* time; **une f.** once; **deux f.** twice, two times; **chaque f. que** each time (that), whenever; **une f. qu'il sera arrivé** (*dès que*) once he has arrived; **à la f.** at the same time, at once; **à la f. riche et heureux** both rich and happy; **une autre f.** (*elle fera attention etc*) next time; **des f.** *Fam* sometimes; **non mais des f.!** *Fam* you must be joking!; **une f. pour toutes, une bonne f.** once and for all.

foison [fwazɔ̃] *nf* **à f.** in plenty. ◆**foisonner** *vi* to abound (**de, en** in). ◆**—ement** *nm* abundance.

fol [fɔl] *voir* **fou.**

folâtre [fɔlɑtr] *a* playful. ◆**folâtrer** *vi* to romp, frolic.

folichon, -onne [fɔliʃɔ̃, -ɔn] *a* **pas f.** not very funny, not much fun.

folie [fɔli] *nf* madness, insanity; **faire une f.** to do a foolish thing; (*dépense*) to be wildly extravagant; **aimer qn à la f.** to be madly in love with s.o.

folklore [fɔlklɔr] *nm* folklore. ◆**folklorique** *a* (*danse etc*) folk-; (*pas sérieux*) *Fam* lightweight, trivial, silly.

folle [fɔl] *voir* **fou.** ◆**follement** *adv* madly.

fomenter [fɔmɑ̃te] *vt* (*révolte etc*) to foment.

foncé [fɔ̃se] *a* (*couleur*) dark.

foncer [fɔ̃se] **1** *vi* (*aller vite*) to tear *ou* charge along; **f. sur qn** to charge into *ou* at s.o. **2** *vti* (*couleur*) to darken.

foncier, -ière [fɔ̃sje, -jɛr] *a* **1** fundamental, basic. **2** (*propriété*) landed. ◆**foncièrement** *adv* fundamentally.

fonction [fɔ̃ksjɔ̃] *nf* (*rôle*) & *Math* function; (*emploi*) office, function, duty; **f. publique** civil service; **faire f. de** (*personne*) to act as; (*objet*) to serve *ou* act as; **en f. de** according to. ◆**fonctionnaire** *nmf* civil servant. ◆**fonctionnel, -elle** *a* functional. ◆**fonctionner** *vi* (*machine etc*) to work, operate, function; (*organisation*) to function; **faire f.** to operate, work. ◆**—ement** *nm* working.

fond [fɔ̃] *nm* (*de boîte, jardin, vallée etc*) bottom; (*de salle, armoire etc*) back; (*de culotte*) seat; (*de problème, débat etc*) essence; (*arrière-plan*) background; (*contenu*) content; (*du désespoir*) *Fig* depths; **au f. de** at the bottom of; at the back of; **fonds de verre** dregs; **f. de teint** foundation cream; **f. sonore** background music; **un f. de bon sens** a stock of good sense; **au f.** basically, in essence; **à f.** (*connaître etc*) thoroughly; **de f. en comble** from top to bottom; **de f.** (*course*) long-distance; (*bruit*) background-.

fondamental, -aux [fɔ̃damɑ̃tal, -o] *a* fundamental, basic.

fond/er [fɔ̃de] *vt* (*ville etc*) to found; (*commerce*) to set up; (*famille*) to start; (**se**) **f. sur** to base (oneself) on; **être fondé à croire**/*etc* to be justified in thinking/*etc*; **bien fondé** well-founded. ◆**—ement** *nm* foundation. ◆**fondateur, -trice** *nmf* founder; – *a* (*membre*) founding, founder-. ◆**fondation** *nf* (*création, œuvre*) foundation (**de** of).

fond/re [fɔ̃dr] *vt* to melt; (*métal*) to smelt; (*cloche*) to cast; (*amalgamer*) *Fig* to fuse (**avec** with); **faire f.** (*dissoudre*) to dissolve; – *vi* to melt; (*se dissoudre*) to dissolve; **f. en larmes** to burst into tears; **f. sur** to swoop on; – **se f.** *vpr* to merge, fuse. ◆**—ant** *a* (*fruit*) which melts in the mouth. ◆**—u** *nm* **f. enchaîné** *Cin* dissolve. ◆**—ue** *nf* *Culin* fondue. ◆**fonderie** *nf* (*usine*) smelting works, foundry.

fonds [fɔ̃] **1** *nm* **f.** (*de commerce*) a business. **2** *nmpl* (*argent*) funds. **3** *nm* (*culturel etc*) *Fig* fund.

font [fɔ̃] *voir* **faire.**

fontaine [fɔ̃tɛn] *nf* (*construction*) fountain; (*source*) spring.

fonte [fɔ̃t] *nf* **1** (*des neiges*) melting; (*d'acier*) smelting. **2** (*fer*) cast iron; **en f.** (*poêle etc*) cast-iron.

fonts [fɔ̃] *nmpl* **f. baptismaux** *Rel* font.

football [futbol] *nm* football, soccer. ◆**footballeur, -euse** *nmf* footballer.

footing [futiŋ] *nm* *Sp* jogging, jog-trotting.

forage [fɔraʒ] *nm* drilling, boring.

forain [fɔrɛ̃] *a* (*marchand*) itinerant; **fête foraine** (fun)fair.

forçat [fɔrsa] *nm* (*prisonnier*) convict.

force [fɔrs] *nf* force; (*physique, morale*) strength; (*atomique etc*) power; **de toutes ses forces** with all one's strength; **les forces armées** the armed forces; **de f.** by force, forcibly; **en f.** (*attaquer, venir*) in force; **cas de f. majeure** circumstances beyond one's control; **dans la f. de l'âge** in the prime of life; **à f. de** through sheer force of, by dint of. ◆**forc/er** vt (*porte, fruits etc*) to force; (*attention*) to force, compel; (*voix*) to strain; (*sens*) to stretch; **f. qn à faire** to force *ou* compel s.o. to do; – vi (*y aller trop fort*) to overdo it; – **se f.** vpr to force oneself (**à faire** to do). ◆**-é** a forced (**de faire** to do); **un sourire f.** a forced smile; **c'est f.** *Fam* it's inevitable *ou* obvious. ◆**-ément** adv inevitably, obviously; **pas f.** not necessarily.

forcené, -ée [fɔrsəne] a frantic, frenzied; – nmf madman, madwoman.

forceps [fɔrsɛps] nm forceps.

forcir [fɔrsir] vi (*grossir*) to fill out.

forer [fɔre] vt to drill, bore. ◆**foret** nm drill.

forêt [fɔrɛ] nf forest. ◆**forestier, -ière** a forest-; – nm (*garde*) f. forester, *Am* (forest) ranger.

forfait [fɔrfɛ] nm **1** (*prix*) all-inclusive price; **travailler à f.** to work for a lump sum. **2** **déclarer f.** *Sp* to withdraw from the game. **3** (*crime*) *Litt* heinous crime. ◆**forfaitaire** a **prix f.** all-inclusive price.

forge [fɔrʒ] nf forge. ◆**forg/er** vt (*métal, liens etc*) to forge; (*inventer*) to make up. ◆**-é** a **fer f.** wrought iron. ◆**forgeron** nm (black)smith.

formaliser (se) [səfɔrmalize] vpr to take offence (**de** at).

formalité [fɔrmalite] nf formality.

format [fɔrma] nm format, size.

forme [fɔrm] nf (*contour*) shape, form; (*manière, genre*) form; pl (*de femme, d'homme*) figure; **en f. de** in the form of; **en f. d'aiguille/de poire/etc** needle-/pear-/etc shaped; **dans les formes** in due form; **en (pleine) f.** in good shape *ou* form, on form; **prendre f.** to take shape. ◆**formateur, -trice** a formative. ◆**formation** nf formation; (*éducation*) education, training. ◆**formel, -elle** a (*structure, logique etc*) formal; (*démenti*) categorical, formal; (*preuve*) positive, formal. ◆**formellement** adv (*interdire*) strictly. ◆**form/er** vt (*groupe, caractère etc*) to form; (*apprenti etc*) to train; – **se f.** vpr (*apparaître*) to form; (*institution*) to be formed. ◆**-é** a (*personne*) fully-formed.

formidable [fɔrmidabl] a tremendous.

formule [fɔrmyl] nf **1** formula; (*phrase*) (set) expression; (*méthode*) method; **f. de politesse** polite expression. **2** (*feuille*) form. ◆**formulaire** nm (*feuille*) form. ◆**formulation** nf formulation. ◆**formuler** vt to formulate.

fort¹ [fɔr] a strong; (*pluie, mer*) heavy;

(*voix*) loud; (*fièvre*) high; (*femme, homme*) large; (*élève*) bright; (*pente*) steep; (*ville*) fortified; (*chances*) good; **f. en** (*maths etc*) good at; **c'est plus f. qu'elle** she can't help it; **c'est un peu f.** *Fam* that's a bit much; **à plus forte raison** all the more reason; – adv **1** (*frapper*) hard; (*pleuvoir*) hard, heavily; (*parler*) loud; (*serrer*) tight; **sentir f.** to have a strong smell. **2** (*très*) *Vieilli* very; (*beaucoup*) *Litt* very much; – nm **son f.** one's strong point; **les forts** the strong; **au plus f. de** in the thick of. ◆**fortement** adv greatly; (*frapper*) hard.

fort² [fɔr] nm *Hist Mil* fort. ◆**forteresse** nf fortress.

fortifi/er [fɔrtifje] vt to strengthen, fortify; – **se f.** vpr (*malade*) to fortify oneself. ◆**-ant** nm *Méd* tonic. ◆**-é** a (*ville, camp*) fortified. ◆**fortification** nf fortification.

fortuit [fɔrtɥi] a (*rencontre etc*) chance-, fortuitous. ◆**fortuitement** adv by chance.

fortune [fɔrtyn] nf (*argent, hasard*) fortune; **avoir de la f.** to have (private) means; **faire f.** to make one's fortune; **de f.** (*moyens etc*) makeshift; **dîner à la f. du pot** to take pot luck. ◆**fortuné** a (*riche*) well-to-do.

forum [fɔrɔm] nm forum.

fosse [fos] nf (*trou*) pit; (*tombe*) grave; **f. d'aisances** cesspool.

fossé [fose] nm ditch; (*douve*) moat; (*dissentiment*) *Fig* gulf, gap.

fossette [fosɛt] nf dimple.

fossile [fɔsil] nm & a fossil.

fossoyeur [fɔswajœr] nm gravedigger.

fou (*or* **fol** *before vowel or mute h*), **folle** [fu, fɔl] a (*personne, projet etc*) mad, insane, crazy; (*envie*) wild, mad; (*espoir*) foolish; (*rire*) uncontrollable; (*cheval, camion*) runaway; (*succès, temps*) tremendous; **f. à lier** raving mad; **f. de** (*musique, personne etc*) mad *ou* wild *ou* crazy about; **f. de joie** wild with joy; – nmf madman, madwoman; – nm (*bouffon*) jester; *Échecs* bishop; **faire le f.** to play the fool.

foudre [fudr] nf **la f.** lightning; **coup de f.** *Fig* love at first sight. ◆**foudroy/er** vt to strike by lightning; *Él* to electrocute; (*malheur etc*) *Fig* to strike (*s.o.*) down. ◆**-ant** a (*succès, vitesse etc*) staggering. ◆**-é** a (*stupéfait*) thunderstruck.

fouet [fwɛ] nm whip; *Culin* (egg) whisk. ◆**fouetter** vt to whip; (*œufs*) to whisk; (*pluie etc*) to lash (*face, windows etc*); **crème fouettée** whipped cream.

fougère [fuʒɛr] nf fern.

fougue [fug] *nf* fire, ardour. ◆**fougueux, -euse** *a* fiery, ardent.

fouille [fuj] *nf* 1 (*archéologique*) excavation, dig. 2 (*de personne, bagages etc*) search. ◆**fouiller** 1 *vti* (*creuser*) to dig. 2 *vt* (*personne, maison etc*) to search; – *vi* **f. dans** (*tiroir etc*) to rummage *ou* search through. **fouillis** [fuji] *nm* jumble.

fouine [fwin] *nf* (*animal*) stone marten.

fouin/er [fwine] *vi Fam* to nose about. ◆**—eur, -euse** *a Fam* nosy; – *nmf Fam* nosy parker.

foulard [fular] *nm* (head) scarf.

foule [ful] *nf* crowd; **en f.** in mass; **une f. de** (*objets etc*) a mass of; **un bain de f.** a walkabout.

foulée [fule] *nf Sp* stride; **dans la f. Fam** at one and the same time.

fouler [fule] *vt* to press; (*sol*) to tread; **f. aux pieds** to trample on; **se f. la cheville/***etc* to sprain one's ankle/*etc*; **il ne se foule pas (la rate)** *Fam* he doesn't exactly exert himself. ◆**foulure** *nf* sprain.

four [fur] *nm* 1 oven; (*de potier etc*) kiln. 2 **petit f.** (*gâteau*) (small) fancy cake. 3 *Th Cin* flop; **faire un f.** to flop.

fourbe [furb] *a* deceitful; – *nmf* cheat. ◆**fourberie** *nf* deceit.

fourbi [furbi] *nm* (*choses*) *Fam* stuff, gear, rubbish.

fourbu [furby] *a* (*fatigué*) dead beat.

fourche [furʃ] *nf* fork; **f. à foin** pitchfork. ◆**fourchette** *nf* 1 *Culin* fork. 2 (*de salaires etc*) *Écon* bracket. ◆**fourchu** *a* forked.

fourgon [furgɔ̃] *nm* (*camion*) van; (*mortuaire*) hearse; *Rail* luggage van, *Am* baggage car. ◆**fourgonnette** *nf* (small) van.

fourmi [furmi] *nf* 1 (*insecte*) ant. 2 **avoir des fourmis** *Méd* to have pins and needles (**dans** in). ◆**fourmilière** *nf* anthill. ◆**fourmiller** *vi* to teem, swarm (**de** with). 2 *Méd* to tingle.

fournaise [furnɛz] *nf* (*chambre etc*) *Fig* furnace.

fourneau, -x [furno] *nm* (*poêle*) stove; (*four*) furnace; **haut f.** blast furnace.

fournée [furne] *nf* (*de pain, gens*) batch.

fourn/ir [furnir] *vt* to supply, provide; (*effort*) to make; **f. qch à qn** to supply s.o. with sth; – *vi* **f. à** (*besoin etc*) to provide for; – **se f.** *vpr* to get one's supplies (**chez** from), shop (**chez** at). ◆**—i** *a* (*barbe*) bushy; **bien f.** (*boutique*) well-stocked. ◆**fournisseur** *nm* (*commerçant*) supplier. ◆**fourniture** *nf* (*action*) supply(ing) (**de** of); *pl* (*objets*) supplies.

fourrage [furaʒ] *nm* fodder.

fourrager [furaʒe] *vi Fam* to rummage (**dans** in, through).

fourreau, -x [furo] *nm* (*gaine*) sheath.

fourr/er [fure] 1 *vt Culin* to fill, stuff; (*vêtement*) to fur-line. 2 *vt Fam* (*mettre*) to stick; (*flanquer*) to chuck; **f. qch dans la tête de qn** to knock sth into s.o.'s head; **f. son nez dans** to poke one's nose into; – **se f.** *vpr* to put *ou* stick oneself (**dans** in). ◆**—é 1** *a* (*gant etc*) fur-lined; (*bonbon etc*) jam- *ou* cream-filled; **coup f.** (*traîtrise*) stab in the back. 2 *nm Bot* thicket. ◆**—eur** *nm* furrier. ◆**fourrure** *nf* (*pour vêtement etc, de chat etc*) fur.

fourre-tout [furtu] *nm inv* (*pièce*) junk room; (*sac*) holdall, *Am* carryall.

fourrière [furjɛr] *nf* (*lieu*) pound.

fourvoyer (se) [səfurvwaje] *vpr* to go astray.

foutre* [futr] *vt Arg* = **fiche(r).** ◆**foutu** *a Arg* = **fichu.** ◆**foutaise** *nf Arg* rubbish, rot.

foyer [fwaje] *nm* (*domicile*) home; (*d'étudiants etc*) hostel; (*âtre*) hearth; (*lieu de réunion*) club; *Th* foyer; *Géom Phys* focus; **f. de** (*maladie etc*) seat of; (*énergie, lumière*) source of; **fonder un f.** to start a family.

fracas [fraka] *nm* din; (*d'un objet qui tombe*) crash. ◆**fracass/er** *vt*, – **se f.** *vpr* to smash. ◆**—ant** *a* (*nouvelle, film etc*) sensational.

fraction [fraksjɔ̃] *nf* fraction. ◆**fractionner** *vt*, – **se f.** *vpr* to split (up).

fracture [fraktyr] *nf* fracture; **se faire une f. au bras/***etc* to fracture one's arm/*etc*. ◆**fracturer** *vt* (*porte etc*) to break (open); **se f. la jambe/***etc* to fracture one's leg/*etc*.

fragile [fraʒil] *a* (*verre, santé etc*) fragile; (*enfant etc*) frail; (*équilibre*) shaky. ◆**fragilité** *nf* fragility; (*d'un enfant etc*) frailty.

fragment [fragmã] *nm* fragment. ◆**fragmentaire** *a* fragmentary, fragmented. ◆**fragmentation** *nf* fragmentation. ◆**fragmenter** *vt* to fragment, divide.

frais¹, fraîche [frɛ, frɛʃ] *a* (*poisson, souvenir etc*) fresh; (*temps*) cool, fresh, (*plutôt désagréable*) chilly; (*œufs*) new-laid, fresh; (*boisson*) cold, cool; (*peinture*) wet; (*date*) recent; **boire f.** to drink something cold *ou* cool; **servir f.** (*vin etc*) to serve chilled; – *nm* **prendre le f.** to get some fresh air; **il fait f.** it's cool; (*froid*) it's chilly; **mettre au f.** to put in a cool place. ◆**fraîchement** *adv* 1 (*récemment*) freshly. 2 (*accueillir etc*) coolly. ◆**fraîcheur** *nf* freshness; coolness;

chilliness. ◆**fraîchir** vi (temps) to get cooler ou chillier, freshen.

frais² [frɛ] nmpl expenses; (droits) fees; **à mes f.** at my expense; **faire des f.** to go to some expense; **faire les f.** to bear the cost (**de** of); **j'en ai été pour mes f.** I wasted my time and effort; **faux f.** incidental expenses; **f. généraux** running expenses, overheads.

fraise [frɛz] nf **1** (fruit) strawberry. **2** (de dentiste) drill. ◆**fraisier** nm (plante) strawberry plant.

framboise [frãbwaz] nf raspberry. ◆**framboisier** nm raspberry cane.

franc¹, franche [frã, frãʃ] a **1** (personne, réponse etc) frank; (visage, gaieté) open; (net) clear; (cassure, coupe) clean; (vrai) Péj downright. **2** (zone) free; **coup f.** Fb free kick; **f. de port** carriage paid. ◆**franchement** adv (honnêtement) frankly; (sans ambiguïté) clearly; (vraiment) really. ◆**franchise** nf **1** frankness; openness; **en toute f.** quite frankly. **2** (exemption) Com exemption; **en f.** (produit) duty-free; '**f. postale**' 'official paid'. **3** (permis de vendre) Com franchise.

franc² [frã] nm (monnaie) franc.

France [frãs] nf France. ◆**français, -aise** a French; – nmf Frenchman, Frenchwoman; **les F.** the French; – nm (langue) French.

franch/ir [frãʃir] vt (fossé) to jump (over), clear; (frontière, seuil etc) to cross; (porte) to go through; (distance) to cover; (limites) to exceed; (mur du son) to break (through), go through. ◆**-issable** a (rivière, col) passable.

franc-maçon [frãmasɔ̃] nm (pl francs-maçons) Freemason. ◆**franc-maçonnerie** nf Freemasonry.

franco [frãko] adv carriage paid.

franco- [frãko] préf Franco-.

francophile [frãkɔfil] a & nmf francophile. ◆**francophone** a French-speaking; – nmf French speaker. ◆**francophonie** nf **la f.** the French-speaking community.

frange [frãʒ] nf (de vêtement etc) fringe; (de cheveux) fringe, Am bangs.

frangin [frãʒɛ̃] nm Fam brother. ◆**frangine** nf Fam sister.

franquette (à la bonne) [alabɔnfrãkɛt] adv without ceremony.

frappe [frap] nf **1** (dactylographie) typing; (de dactylo etc) touch; **faute de f.** typing error. **2 force de f.** Mil strike force. ◆**frapp/er** vt (battre) to strike, hit; (monnaie) to mint; **f. qn** (surprendre, affecter) to

strike s.o.; (impôt, mesure etc) to hit s.o.; **frappé de** (horreur etc) stricken with; **frappé de panique** panic-stricken; – vi (à la porte etc) to knock, bang (à at); **f. du pied** to stamp (one's foot); – **se f.** vpr (se tracasser) to worry. ◆**-ant** a striking. ◆**-é** a (vin) chilled.

frasque [frask] nf prank, escapade.

fraternel, -elle [fratɛrnɛl] a fraternal, brotherly. ◆**fraterniser** vi to fraternize (**avec** with). ◆**fraternité** nf fraternity, brotherhood.

fraude [frod] nf Jur fraud; (à un examen) cheating; **passer qch en f.** to smuggle sth; **prendre qn en f.** to catch s.o. cheating. ◆**fraud/er** vt to defraud; – vi Jur to commit fraud; (à un examen) to cheat (à in); **f. sur** (poids etc) to cheat on ou over. ◆**-eur, -euse** nmf Jur defrauder. ◆**frauduleux, -euse** a fraudulent.

frayer [freje] vt (voie etc) to clear; **se f. un passage** to clear a way, force one's way (à travers, dans through).

frayeur [frejœr] nf fear, fright.

fredaine [frədɛn] nf prank, escapade.

fredonner [frədɔne] vt to hum.

freezer [frizœr] nm (de réfrigérateur) freezer.

frégate [fregat] nf (navire) frigate.

frein [frɛ̃] nm brake; **donner un coup de f.** to brake; **mettre un f. à** Fig to put a curb on. ◆**frein/er** vi Aut to brake; – vt (gêner) Fig to check, curb. ◆**-age** nm Aut braking.

frelaté [frəlate] a (vin etc) & Fig adulterated.

frêle [frɛl] a frail, fragile.

frelon [frəlɔ̃] nm (guêpe) hornet.

frémir [fremir] vi to shake, shudder (**de** with); (feuille) to quiver; (eau chaude) to simmer.

frêne [frɛn] nm (arbre, bois) ash.

frénésie [frenezi] nf frenzy. ◆**frénétique** a frenzied, frantic.

fréquent [frekã] a frequent. ◆**fréquemment** [-amã] adv frequently. ◆**fréquence** nf frequency.

fréquent/er [frekãte] vt (lieu) to visit, frequent; (école, église) to attend; **f. qn** to see ou visit s.o.; – **se f.** vpr (fille et garçon) to see each other, go out together; (voisins) to see each other socially. ◆**-é** a **très f.** (lieu) very busy. ◆**fréquentable** a **peu f.** (personne, endroit) not very commendable. ◆**fréquentation** nf visiting; pl (personnes) company.

frère [frɛr] nm brother.

fresque [frɛsk] nf (œuvre peinte) fresco.

fret [frɛ] nm freight.

frétiller [fretije] *vi* (*poisson*) to wriggle; **f. de** (*impatience*) to quiver with; **f. de joie** to tingle with excitement.

fretin [frətɛ̃] *nm* **menu f.** small fry.

friable [frijabl] *a* crumbly.

friand [frijɑ̃] *a* **f. de** fond of, partial to. ◆**friandises** *nfpl* sweet stuff, sweets, *Am* candies.

fric [frik] *nm* (*argent*) *Fam* cash, dough.

fric-frac [frikfrak] *nm* (*cambriolage*) *Fam* break-in.

friche [friʃ] *adv* fallow.

friction [friksjɔ̃] *nf* **1** massage, rub(-down); (*de cheveux*) friction. **2** (*désaccord*) friction. ◆**frictionner** *vt* to rub (down).

frigidaire® [friʒidɛr] *nm* fridge. ◆**frigo** *nm Fam* fridge. ◆**frigorifié** *a* (*personne*) *Fam* very cold. ◆**frigorifique** *a* (*vitrine*) refrigerated; (*wagon*) refrigerator-.

frigide [friʒid] *a* frigid. ◆**frigidité** *nf* frigidity.

frileux, -euse [frilø, -øz] *a* sensitive to cold, chilly.

frime [frim] *nf Fam* sham, show.

frimousse [frimus] *nf Fam* little face.

fringale [frɛ̃gal] *nf Fam* raging appetite.

fringant [frɛ̃gɑ̃] *a* (*allure etc*) dashing.

fringues [frɛ̃g] *nfpl* (*vêtements*) *Fam* togs, clothes.

frip/er [fripe] *vt* to crumple; **— se f.** *vpr* to get crumpled. ◆**-é** *a* (*visage*) crumpled, wrinkled.

fripier, -ière [fripje, -jɛr] *nmf* secondhand clothes dealer.

fripon, -onne [fripɔ̃, -ɔn] *nmf* rascal; **—** *a* rascally.

fripouille [fripuj] *nf* rogue, scoundrel.

frire* [frir] *vti* to fry; **faire f.** to fry.

frise [friz] *nf Archit* frieze.

fris/er [frize] **1** *vt* (*cheveux*) to curl, wave; **f. qn** to curl ou wave s.o.'s hair. **2** *vt* (*effleurer*) to skim; (*accident etc*) to be within an ace of; **f. la trentaine** to be close on thirty. ◆**-é** *a* curly. ◆**frisette** *nf* ringlet, little curl.

frisquet [friskɛ] *am* chilly, coldish.

frisson [frisɔ̃] *nm* shiver; shudder; **donner le f. à qn** to give s.o. the creeps ou shivers. ◆**frissonner** *vi* (*de froid*) to shiver; (*de peur etc*) to shudder (**de** with).

frit [fri] *voir* **frire; —** *a* (*poisson etc*) fried. ◆**frites** *nfpl* chips, *Am* French fries. ◆**friteuse** *nf* (*deep*) fryer. ◆**friture** *nf* (*matière*) (frying) oil ou fat; (*aliment*) fried fish; (*bruit*) *Rad Tél* crackling.

frivole [frivɔl] *a* frivolous. ◆**frivolité** *nf* fri-

froid [frwa] *a* cold; **garder la tête froide** to keep a cool head; **—** *nm* cold; **avoir/prendre f.** to be/catch cold; **il fait f.** it's cold; **coup de f.** *Méd* chill; **jeter un f.** to cast a chill (**dans** over); **démarrer à f.** *Aut* to start (from) cold; **être en f.** to be on bad terms (**avec** with). ◆**froidement** *adv* coldly. ◆**froideur** *nf* (*de sentiment, personne etc*) coldness.

froisser [frwase] **1** *vt*, **— se f.** *vpr* (*tissu etc*) to crumple, rumple; **se f. un muscle** to strain a muscle. **2** *vt* **f. qn** to offend s.o.; **se f.** to take offence (**de** at).

frôler [frole] *vt* (*toucher*) to brush against, touch lightly; (*raser*) to skim; (*la mort etc*) to come within an ace of.

fromage [frɔmaʒ] *nm* cheese; **f. blanc** soft white cheese. ◆**fromager, -ère** *a* (*industrie*) cheese-; **—** *nm* (*fabricant*) cheesemaker. ◆**fromagerie** *nf* cheese dairy.

froment [frɔmɑ̃] *nm* wheat.

fronce [frɔ̃s] *nf* (*pli dans un tissu*) gather, fold. ◆**fronc/er** *vt* **1** (*étoffe*) to gather. **2 f. les sourcils** to frown. ◆**-ement f. de sourcils** frown.

fronde [frɔ̃d] *nf* **1** (*arme*) sling. **2** (*sédition*) revolt.

front [frɔ̃] *nm* forehead, brow; *Mil Pol* front; **de f.** (*heurter*) head-on; (*côte à côte*) abreast; (*à la fois*) (all) at once; **faire f. à** to face.

frontière [frɔ̃tjɛr] *nf* border, frontier; **—** *a inv* **ville/***etc* **f.** border town/*etc*. ◆**frontalier, -ière** *a* border-, frontier-.

fronton [frɔ̃tɔ̃] *nm Archit* pediment.

frott/er [frɔte] *vt* to rub; (*astiquer*) to rub (up), shine; (*plancher*) to scrub; (*allumette*) to strike; **se f. à qn** (*défier*) to meddle with s.o., provoke s.o.; **—** *vi* to rub; (*nettoyer, laver*) to scrub. ◆**-ement** *nm* rubbing; *Tech* friction.

froufrou(s) [frufru] *nm(pl)* (*bruit*) rustling.

frousse [frus] *nf Fam* funk, fear; **avoir la f.** to be scared. ◆**froussard, -arde** *nmf Fam* coward.

fructifier [fryktifje] *vi* (*arbre, capital*) to bear fruit. ◆**fructueux, -euse** *a* (*profitable*) fruitful.

frugal, -aux [frygal, -o] *a* frugal. ◆**frugalité** *nf* frugality.

fruit [frɥi] *nm* fruit; **des fruits, les fruits** fruit; **porter f.** to bear fruit; **fruits de mer** seafood; **avec f.** fruitfully. ◆**fruité** *a* fruity. ◆**fruitier, -ière** *a* (*arbre*) fruit-; **—** *nmf* fruiterer.

frusques [frysk] *nfpl* (*vêtements*) *Fam* togs, clothes.

fruste [fryst] a (personne) rough.

frustr/er [frystre] vt f. qn to frustrate s.o.; f. qn de to deprive s.o. of. ◆—é a frustrated. ◆frustration nf frustration.

fuel [fjul] nm (fuel) oil.

fugace [fygas] a fleeting.

fugitif, -ive [fyʒitif, -iv] 1 nmf runaway, fugitive. 2 a (passager) fleeting.

fugue [fyg] nf 1 Mus fugue. 2 (absence) flight; **faire une f.** to run away.

fuir* [fɥir] vi to flee, run away; (temps) to fly; (gaz, robinet, stylo etc) to leak; – vt (éviter) to shun, avoid. ◆**fuite** nf (évasion) flight (de from); (de gaz etc) leak(age); (de documents) leak; **en f.** on the run; **prendre la f.** to take flight; **f. des cerveaux** brain drain; **délit de f.** Aut hit-and-run offence.

fulgurant [fylgyrã] a (regard) flashing; (vitesse) lightning-; (idée) spectacular, striking.

fulminer [fylmine] vi (personne) to thunder forth (**contre** against).

fumée [fyme] nf smoke; (vapeur) steam, fumes; pl (de vin) fumes. ◆**fum/er** vi to smoke; (liquide brûlant) to steam; (rager) Fam to fume; – vt to smoke. ◆—é a (poisson, verre etc) smoked. ◆—**eur, -euse** nmf smoker; **compartiment fumeurs** Rail smoking compartment. ◆**fume-cigarette** nm inv cigarette holder.

fumet [fymɛ] nm aroma, smell.

fumeux, -euse [fymø, -øz] a (idée etc) hazy, woolly.

fumier [fymje] nm manure, dung; (tas) dunghill.

fumigation [fymigasjɔ̃] nf fumigation.

fumigène [fymiʒɛn] a (bombe, grenade etc) smoke-.

fumiste [fymist] nmf (étudiant etc) time-waster, good-for-nothing. ◆**fumisterie** nf Fam farce, con.

funambule [fynãbyl] nmf tightrope walker.

funèbre [fynɛbr] a (service, marche etc) funeral-; (lugubre) gloomy. ◆**funérailles** nfpl funeral. ◆**funéraire** a (frais, salon etc) funeral-.

funeste [fynɛst] a (désastreux) catastrophic.

funiculaire [fynikylɛr] nm funicular.

fur et à mesure (au) [ofyreamzyr] adv as one goes along, progressively; **au f. et à m. que** as.

furent [fyr] voir être.

furet [fyrɛ] nm (animal) ferret. ◆**furet/er** vi to ferret about. ◆—**eur, -euse** a inquisitive, prying; – nmf inquisitive person.

fureur [fyrœr] nf (violence) fury; (colère) rage, fury; (passion) passion (de for); **en f.** furious; **faire f.** (mode etc) to be all the rage. ◆**furibond** a furious. ◆**furie** nf (colère, mégère) fury. ◆**furieux, -euse** a (violent, en colère) furious (**contre** with, at); (vent) raging; (coup) Fig tremendous.

furoncle [fyrɔ̃kl] nm Méd boil.

furtif, -ive [fyrtif, -iv] a furtive, stealthy.

fusain [fyzɛ̃] nm 1 (crayon, dessin) charcoal. 2 Bot spindle tree.

fuseau, -x [fyzo] nm 1 Tex spindle; **en f.** (jambes) spindly. 2 **f. horaire** time zone. 3 (pantalon) ski pants. ◆**fuselé** a slender.

fusée [fyze] nf rocket; (d'obus) fuse; **f. éclairante** flare.

fuselage [fyzlaʒ] nm Av fuselage.

fuser [fyze] vi (rires etc) to burst forth.

fusible [fyzibl] nm Él fuse.

fusil [fyzi] nm rifle, gun; (de chasse) shot-gun; **coup de f.** gunshot, report; **un bon f.** (personne) a good shot. ◆**fusillade** nf (tirs) gunfire; (exécution) shooting. ◆**fusiller** vt (exécuter) to shoot; **f. qn du regard** to glare at s.o.

fusion [fyzjɔ̃] nf 1 melting; Phys Biol fusion; **point de f.** melting point; **en f.** (métal) molten. 2 (union) fusion; Com merger. ◆**fusionner** vti Com to merge.

fut [fy] voir être.

fût [fy] nm 1 (tonneau) barrel, cask. 2 (d'arbre) trunk. ◆**futaie** nf timber forest.

futé [fyte] a cunning, smart.

futile [fytil] a (propos, prétexte etc) frivolous, futile; (personne) frivolous; (tentative, action) futile. ◆**futilité** nf futility; pl (bagatelles) trifles.

futur, -ure [fytyr] a future; **future mère** mother-to-be; – nmf **f. (mari)** husband-to-be; **future (épouse)** wife-to-be; – nm future.

fuyant [fɥijã] voir fuir; – a (front, ligne) receding; (personne) evasive. ◆**fuyard** nm (soldat) runaway, deserter.

G

G, g [ʒe] nm G, g.
gabardine [gabardin] nf (tissu, imperméable) gabardine.
gabarit [gabari] nm (de véhicule etc) size, dimension.
gâcher [gɑʃe] vt **1** (gâter) to spoil; (occasion, argent) to waste; (vie, travail) to mess up. **2** (plâtre) to mix. ◆**gâchis** nm (désordre) mess; (gaspillage) waste.
gâchette [gɑʃɛt] nf (d'arme à feu) trigger; **une fine g.** (personne) Fig a marksman.
gadget [gadʒɛt] nm gadget.
gadoue [gadu] nf (boue) dirt, sludge; (neige) slush.
gaffe [gaf] nf (bévue) Fam blunder, gaffe. ◆**gaff/er** vi to blunder. ◆**—eur, -euse** nmf blunderer.
gag [gag] nm (effet comique) Cin Th (sight) gag.
gaga [gaga] a Fam senile, gaga.
gage [gaʒ] **1** nm (promesse) pledge; (témoignage) proof; (caution) security; **mettre en g.** to pawn. **2** nmpl (salaire) pay; **tueur à gages** hired killer, hitman.
gager [gaʒe] vt **g. que** Litt to wager that. ◆**gageure** [gaʒyr] nf Litt (impossible) wager.
gagn/er [gɑɲe] **1** vt (par le travail) to earn; (mériter) to earn. **2** vt (par le jeu) to win; (réputation, estime etc) Fig to win, gain; **g. qn** to win s.o. over (à to); **g. une heure/etc** (économiser) to save an hour/etc; **g. du temps** (temporiser) to gain time; **du terrain/du poids** to gain ground/weight; — vi (vainqueur) to win; **g. à être connu** to be well worth getting to know. **3** vt (atteindre) to reach; **g. qn** (sommeil, faim etc) to overcome s.o.; — vi (incendie etc) to spread, gain. ◆**—ant, -ante** a (billet, cheval) winning; — nmf winner. ◆**gagne-pain** nm inv (emploi) job, livelihood.
gai [ge] a (personne, air etc) cheerful, gay, jolly; (ivre) merry, tipsy; (couleur, pièce) bright, cheerful. ◆**gaiement** adv cheerfully, gaily. ◆**gaieté** nf (de personne etc) gaiety, cheerfulness, jollity.
gaillard [gajar] a vigorous; (grivois) coarse; — nm (robuste) strapping fellow; (type) Fam fellow. ◆**gaillarde** nf Péj brazen wench.

gain [gɛ̃] nm (profit) gain, profit; (avantage) Fig advantage; pl (salaire) earnings; (au jeu) winnings; **un g. de temps** a saving of time.
gaine [gɛn] nf **1** (sous-vêtement) girdle. **2** (étui) sheath.
gala [gala] nm official reception, gala.
galant [galɑ̃] a (homme) gallant; (ton, propos) Hum amorous; – nm suitor. ◆**galanterie** nf (courtoisie) gallantry.
galaxie [galaksi] nf galaxy.
galbe [galb] nm curve, contour. ◆**galbé** a (jambes) shapely.
gale [gal] nf **la g.** Méd the itch, scabies; (d'un chien) mange; **une (mauvaise) g.** (personne) Fam a pest.
galère [galɛr] nf (navire) Hist galley. ◆**galérien** nm Hist & Fig galley slave.
galerie [galri] nf **1** (passage, magasin etc) gallery; Th balcony. **2** Aut roof rack.
galet [galɛ] nm pebble, stone; pl shingle, pebbles.
galette [galɛt] nf **1** round, flat, flaky cake; (crêpe) pancake. **2** (argent) Fam dough, money.
galeux, -euse [galø, -øz] a (chien) mangy.
galimatias [galimatja] nm gibberish.
Galles [gal] nfpl **pays de G.** Wales. ◆**gallois, -oise** a Welsh; – nm (langue) Welsh; – nmf Welshman, Welshwoman.
gallicisme [galisism] nm (mot etc) gallicism.
galon [galɔ̃] nm (ruban) braid; (signe) Mil stripe; **prendre du g.** Mil & Fig to get promoted.
galop [galo] nm gallop; **aller au g.** to gallop; **g. d'essai** Fig trial run. ◆**galopade** nf (ruée) stampede. ◆**galop/er** vi (cheval) to gallop; (personne) to rush. ◆**—ant** a (inflation etc) Fig galloping.
galopin [galopɛ̃] nm urchin, rascal.
galvaniser [galvanize] vt (métal) & Fig to galvanize.
galvauder [galvode] vt (talent, avantage etc) to debase, misuse.
gambade [gɑ̃bad] nf leap, caper. ◆**gambader** vi to leap ou frisk about.
gambas [gɑ̃bas] nfpl scampi.
gamelle [gamɛl] nf (de soldat) mess tin; (de campeur) billy(can).
gamin, -ine [gamɛ̃, -in] nmf (enfant) Fam

kid; – *a* playful, naughty. ◆**gaminerie** *nf*
playfulness; (*acte*) naughty prank.
gamme [gam] *nf Mus* scale; (*série*) range.
gammée [game] *af* **croix g.** swastika.
gang [gɑ̃g] *nm* (*de malfaiteurs*) gang.
◆**gangster** *nm* gangster.
gangrène [gɑ̃grɛn] *nf* gangrene. ◆**se gan-
grener** [səgɑ̃grəne] *vpr Méd* to become
gangrenous.
gangue [gɑ̃g] *nf* (*enveloppe*) *Fig Péj* outer
crust.
gant [gɑ̃] *nm* glove; **g. de toilette** face cloth,
cloth glove (*for washing*); **jeter/relever le
g.** *Fig* to throw down/take up the gauntlet;
boîte à gants glove compartment. ◆**ganté**
a (*main*) gloved; (*personne*) wearing gloves.
garage [garaʒ] *nm Aut* garage; **voie de g.**
Rail siding; *Fig* dead end. ◆**garagiste**
nmf garage owner.
garant, -ante [garɑ̃, -ɑ̃t] *nmf* (*personne*) *Jur*
guarantor; **se porter g. de** to guarantee,
vouch for; – *nm* (*garantie*) guarantee.
◆**garantie** *nf* guarantee; (*caution*) security; (*protection*) *Fig* safeguard; **garantie(s)**
(*de police d'assurance*) cover. ◆**garantir** *vt*
to guarantee (**contre** against); **g. (à qn) que**
to guarantee (s.o.) that; **g. de** (*protéger*) to
protect from.
garce [gars] *nf Péj Fam* bitch.
garçon [garsɔ̃] *nm* boy, lad; (*jeune homme*)
young man; (*célibataire*) bachelor; **g. de
café**) waiter; **g. d'honneur** (*d'un mariage*)
best man; **g. manqué** tomboy; **de g.** (*comportement*) boyish. ◆**garçonnet** *nm* little
boy. ◆**garçonnière** *nf* bachelor flat *ou
Am* apartment.
garde [gard] **1** *nm* (*gardien*) guard; *Mil*
guardsman; **g. champêtre** rural policeman;
g. du corps bodyguard; **G. des Sceaux** Justice Minister. **2** *nf* (*d'enfants, de bagages
etc*) care, custody (**de** of); **avoir la g. de** to
be in charge of; **faire bonne g.** to keep a
close watch; **prendre g.** to pay attention (**à
qch** to sth), be careful (**à qch** of sth); **prendre g. de ne pas faire** to be careful not to
do; **mettre en g.** to warn (**contre** against);
mise en g. warning; **de g.** on duty; (*soldat*)
on guard duty; **monter la g.** to stand on
guard; **sur ses gardes** on one's
guard; **g. à vue** (*police*) custody; **chien de g.**
watchdog. **3** *nf* (*escorte, soldats*) guard.
garde-à-vous [gardavu] *nm inv Mil* (position of) attention. ◆**g.-boue** *nm inv* mudguard, *Am* fender. ◆**g.-chasse** *nm* (*pl
gardes-chasses*) gamekeeper. ◆**g.-côte**
nm (*personne*) coastguard. ◆**g.-fou** *nm*
railing(s), parapet. ◆**g.-malade** *nmf* (*pl*

gardes-malades) nurse. ◆**g.-manger** *nm
inv* (*armoire*) food safe; (*pièce*) larder.
◆**g.-robe** *nf* (*habits, armoire*) wardrobe.
garder [garde] *vt* (*maintenir, conserver, mettre de côté*) to keep; (*vêtement*) to keep on;
(*surveiller*) to watch (over); (*défendre*) to
guard; (*enfant*) to look after, watch; (*habitude*) to keep up; **g. qn** (*retenir*) to keep;
g. la chambre to keep to one's room; **g. le lit**
to stay in bed; – **se g.** *vpr* (*aliment*) to
keep; **se g. de qch** (*éviter*) to beware of sth;
se g. de faire to take care not to do.
◆**garderie** *nf* day nursery. ◆**gardeuse**
nf **g. d'enfants** babysitter.
gardien, -ienne [gardjɛ̃, -jɛn] *nmf* (*d'immeuble, d'hôtel*) caretaker; (*de prison*)
(prison) guard, warder; (*de zoo, parc*) keeper;
(*de musée*) attendant; **g. de but** *Fb* goalkeeper; **gardienne d'enfants** child minder;
g. de nuit night watchman; **g. de la paix**
policeman; **g. de** (*libertés etc*) *Fig* guardian
of; – *am* **ange g.** guardian angel.
gare [gar] **1** *nf Rail* station; **g. routière** bus
ou coach station. **2** *int* **g. à** watch *ou* look
out for; **g. à toi!** watch *ou* look out!; **sans
crier g.** without warning.
garer [gare] *vt* (*voiture etc*) to park; (*au garage*) to garage; – **se g.** *vpr* (*se protéger*) to
get out of the way (**de** of); *Aut* to park.
gargariser (se) [səgargarize] *vpr* to gargle.
◆**gargarisme** *nm* gargle.
gargote [gargɔt] *nf* cheap eating house.
gargouille [garguj] *nf Archit* gargoyle.
◆**gargouiller** *vi* (*fontaine, eau*) to
gurgle; (*ventre*) to rumble. ◆**gargouillis**
nm gurgling; rumbling.
garnement [garnəmɑ̃] *nm* rascal, urchin.
garn/ir [garnir] *vt* (*équiper*) to furnish, fit
out (**de** with); (*magasin*) to stock; (*tissu*) to
line; (*orner*) to adorn (**de** with); (*enjoliver*)
to trim (**de** with); (*couvrir*) to cover; *Culin*
to garnish; – **se g.** *vpr* (*lieu*) to fill (up) (**de**
with). ◆–**i** *a* (*plat*) served with vegetables; **bien g.** (*portefeuille*) *Fig* well-lined.
◆**garniture** *nf Culin* garnish, trimmings;
pl Aut fittings, upholstery; **g. de lit** bed
linen.
garnison [garnizɔ̃] *nf Mil* garrison.
gars [gɑ] *nm Fam* fellow, guy.
gas-oil [gazwal] *nm* diesel (oil).
gaspill/er [gaspije] *vt* to waste. ◆–**age** *nm*
waste.
gastrique [gastrik] *a* gastric. ◆**gastro-
nome** *nm* gourmet. ◆**gastronomie** *nf*
gastronomy.
gâteau, -x [gɑto] *nm* cake; **g. de riz** rice
pudding; **g. sec** (*sweet*) biscuit, *Am* cookie;

c'était du g. (*facile*) *Fam* it was a piece of cake.

gât/er [gate] *vt* to spoil; (*plaisir, vue*) to mar, spoil; **— se g.** *vpr* (*aliment, dent*) to go bad; (*temps, situation*) to get worse; (*relations*) to turn sour. **◆—é** *a* (*dent, fruit etc*) bad. **◆gâteries** *nfpl* (*cadeaux*) treats.

gâteux, -euse [gatø, -øz] *a* senile, soft in the head.

gauche¹ [goʃ] *a* (*côté, main etc*) left; — *nf* la g. (*côté*) the left (side); *Pol* the left (wing); **à g.** (*tourner etc*) (to the) left; (*marcher, se tenir*) on the left(-hand) side; **de g.** (*fenêtre etc*) left-hand; (*parti, politique etc*) left-wing; **à g. de** on ou to the left. **◆gaucher, -ère** *a & nmf* left-handed (person). **◆gauchisant** *a Pol* leftish. **◆gauchiste** *a & nmf Pol* (extreme) leftist.

gauche² [goʃ] *a* (*maladroit*) awkward. **◆—ment** *adv* awkwardly. **◆gaucherie** *nf* awkwardness; (*acte*) blunder.

gauchir [goʃir] *vti* to warp.

gaufre [gofr] *nf Culin* waffle. **◆gaufrette** *nf* wafer (biscuit).

gaule [gol] *nf* long pole; *Pêche* fishing rod.

Gaule [gol] *nf* (*pays*) *Hist* Gaul. **◆gaulois** *a* Gallic; (*propos etc*) *Fig* broad, earthy; — *nmpl* **les G.** *Hist* the Gauls. **◆gauloiserie** *nf* broad joke.

gausser (se) [sogose] *vpr Litt* to poke fun (de at).

gaver [gave] *vt* (*animal*) to force-feed; (*personne*) *Fig* to cram (de with); **— se g.** *vpr* to gorge ou stuff oneself (de with).

gaz [gaz] *nm inv* gas; *usine* à g. gasworks; **chambre/réchaud à g.** gas chamber/stove; **avoir des g.** to have wind ou flatulence.

gaze [gaz] *nf* (*tissu*) gauze.

gazelle [gazɛl] *nf* (*animal*) gazelle.

gazer [gaze] **1** *vi Aut Fam* to whizz along; **ça gaze!** everything's just fine! **2** *vt Mil* to gas.

gazette [gazɛt] *nf Journ* newspaper.

gazeux, -euse [gazø, -øz] *a* (*état*) gaseous; (*boisson, eau*) fizzy. **◆gazomètre** *nm* gasometer.

gazinière [gazinjɛr] *nf* gas cooker ou *Am* stove.

gazole [gazɔl] *nm* diesel (oil).

gazon [gazɔ̃] *nm* grass, lawn.

gazouiller [gazuje] *vi* (*oiseau*) to chirp; (*bébé, ruisseau*) to babble. **◆gazouillis** *nm* chirping; babbling.

geai [ʒɛ] *nm* (*oiseau*) jay.

géant, -ante [ʒeɑ̃, -ɑ̃t] *a & nmf* giant.

Geiger [ʒeʒɛr] *nm* **compteur G.** Geiger counter.

geindre [ʒɛ̃dr] *vi* to whine, whimper.

gel [ʒɛl] *nm* **1** (*temps, glace*) frost; (*de crédits*) *Econ* freezing. **2** (*substance*) gel. **◆gel/er** *vti* to freeze; **on gèle ici** it's freezing here; **— v imp il gèle** it's freezing. **◆—é** *a* frozen; (*doigts*) *Méd* frostbitten. **◆—ée** *nf* frost; *Culin* jelly, *Am* jello; **g. blanche** ground frost.

gélatine [ʒelatin] *nf* gelatin(e).

gélule [ʒelyl] *nf* (*médicament*) capsule.

Gémeaux [ʒemo] *nmpl* **les G.** (*signe*) Gemini.

gém/ir [ʒemir] *vi* to groan, moan. **◆—issement** *nm* groan, moan.

gencive [ʒɑ̃siv] *nf Anat* gum.

gendarme [ʒɑ̃darm] *nm* gendarme, policeman (*soldier performing police duties*). **◆gendarmerie** *nf* police force; (*local*) police headquarters.

gendre [ʒɑ̃dr] *nm* son-in-law.

gène [ʒɛn] *nm Biol* gene.

gêne [ʒɛn] *nf* (*trouble physique*) discomfort; (*confusion*) embarrassment; (*dérangement*) bother, trouble; **dans la g.** *Fin* in financial difficulties. **◆gên/er** *vt* (*déranger, irriter*) to bother, annoy; (*troubler*) to embarrass; (*mouvement, action*) to hamper, hinder; (*circulation*) *Aut* to hold up, block; **g. qn** (*vêtement*) to be uncomfortable on s.o.; (*par sa présence*) to be in s.o.'s way; **ça ne me gêne pas** I don't mind (si if); **— se g.** *vpr* (*se déranger*) to put oneself out; **ne te gêne pas pour moi!** don't mind me! **◆—ant** *a* (*objet*) cumbersome; (*présence, situation*) awkward; (*personne*) annoying. **◆—é** *a* (*intimidé*) embarrassed; (*mal à l'aise*) uneasy, awkward; (*silence, sourire*) awkward; (*sans argent*) short of money.

généalogie [ʒenealɔʒi] *nf* genealogy. **◆généalogique** *a* genealogical; **arbre g.** family tree.

général, -aux [ʒeneral, -o] **1** *a* (*global, commun*) general; **en g.** in general. **2** *nm* (*officier*) *Mil* general. **◆générale** *nf Th* dress rehearsal. **◆généralement** *adv* generally; **g. parlant** broadly ou generally speaking. **◆généralisation** *nf* generalization. **◆généraliser** *vti* to generalize; **— se g.** *vpr* to become general ou widespread. **◆généraliste** *nmf Méd* general practitioner, GP. **◆généralité** *nf* generality; **la g. de** the majority of.

générateur [ʒeneratœr] *nm*, **◆génératrice** *nf El* generator.

génération [ʒenerasjɔ̃] *nf* generation.

généreux, -euse [ʒenerø, -øz] *a* generous (de with). **◆généreusement** *adv* generously. **◆générosité** *nf* generosity.

générique [ʒenerik] nm Cin credits.

genèse [ʒənɛz] nf genesis.

genêt [ʒəne] nm (arbrisseau) broom.

génétique [ʒenetik] nf genetics; – a genetic.

Genève [ʒənɛv] nm ou f Geneva.

génie [ʒeni] nm 1 (aptitude, personne) genius; **avoir le g. pour faire/de qch** to have a genius for doing/for sth. 2 (lutin) genie, spirit. 3 **g. civil** civil engineering; **g. militaire** engineering corps. ◆**génial, -aux** a (personne, invention) brilliant; (formidable) Fam fantastic.

génisse [ʒenis] nf (vache) heifer.

génital, -aux [ʒenital, -o] a genital; **organes génitaux** genitals.

génocide [ʒenɔsid] nm genocide.

genou, -x [ʒ(ə)nu] nm knee; **être à genoux** to be kneeling (down); **se mettre à genoux** to kneel (down); **prendre qn sur ses genoux** to take s.o. on one's lap ou knee. ◆**genouillère** nf Fb etc knee pad.

genre [ʒɑ̃r] nm 1 (espèce) kind, sort; (attitude) manner, way; **g. humain** mankind; **g. de vie** way of life. 2 Littér Cin genre; Gram gender; Biol genus.

gens [ʒɑ̃] nmpl ou nfpl people; **jeunes g.** young people; (hommes) young men.

gentil, -ille [ʒɑ̃ti, -ij] a (agréable) nice, pleasant; (aimable) kind, nice; (mignon) pretty; **g. avec qn** nice ou kind to s.o.; **sois g.** (sage) be good. ◆**gentillesse** nf kindness; **avoir la g. de faire** to be kind enough to do. ◆**gentiment** adv (aimablement) kindly; (sagement) nicely.

gentilhomme, pl **gentilshommes** [ʒɑ̃tijɔm, ʒɑ̃tizɔm] nm (noble) Hist gentleman.

géographie [ʒeɔgrafi] nf geography. ◆**géographique** a geographical.

geôlier, -ière [ʒolje, -jɛr] nmf jailer, gaoler.

géologie [ʒeɔlɔʒi] nf geology. ◆**géologique** a geological. ◆**géologue** nmf geologist.

géomètre [ʒeɔmɛtr] nm (arpenteur) surveyor.

géométrie [ʒeɔmetri] nf geometry. ◆**géométrique** a geometric(al).

géranium [ʒeranjɔm] nm Bot geranium.

gérant, -ante [ʒerɑ̃, -ɑ̃t] nmf manager, manageress; **g. d'immeubles** landlord's agent. ◆**gérance** nf (gestion) management.

gerbe [ʒɛrb] nf (de blé) sheaf; (de fleurs) bunch; (d'eau) spray; (d'étincelles) shower.

gercer [ʒɛrse] vti, – **se g.** vpr (peau, lèvres) to chap, crack. ◆**gerçure** nf chap, crack.

gérer [ʒere] vt (fonds, commerce etc) to manage.

germain [ʒɛrmɛ̃] a **cousin g.** first cousin.

germanique [ʒɛrmanik] a Germanic.

germe [ʒɛrm] nm Méd Biol germ; Bot shoot; (d'une idée) Fig seed, germ. ◆**germer** vi Bot & Fig to germinate.

gésir [ʒezir] vi (être étendu) Litt to lie; **il gît/gisait** he is/was lying; **ci-gît** here lies.

gestation [ʒɛstasjɔ̃] nf gestation.

geste [ʒɛst] nm gesture; **ne pas faire un g.** (ne pas bouger) not to make a move. ◆**gesticuler** vi to gesticulate.

gestion [ʒɛstjɔ̃] nf (action) management, administration. ◆**gestionnaire** nmf administrator.

geyser [ʒezɛr] nm Géol geyser.

ghetto [geto] nm ghetto.

gibecière [ʒibsjɛr] nf shoulder bag.

gibier [ʒibje] nm (animaux, oiseaux) game.

giboulée [ʒibule] nf shower, downpour.

gicl/er [ʒikle] vi (liquide) to spurt, squirt; (boue) to splash; **faire g.** to spurt, squirt. ◆**-ée** nf jet, spurt. ◆**-eur** nm (de carburateur) Aut jet.

gifle [ʒifl] nf slap (in the face). ◆**gifler** vt **g. qn** to slap s.o., slap s.o.'s face.

gigantesque [ʒigɑ̃tɛsk] a gigantic.

gigogne [ʒigɔɲ] a **table g.** nest of tables.

gigot [ʒigo] nm leg of mutton ou lamb.

gigoter [ʒigɔte] vi Fam to kick, wriggle.

gilet [ʒile] nm waistcoat, Am vest; (cardigan) cardigan; **g. (de corps)** vest, Am undershirt; **g. pare-balles** bulletproof jacket ou Am vest; **g. de sauvetage** life jacket.

gin [dʒin] nm (eau-de-vie) gin.

gingembre [ʒɛ̃ʒɑ̃br] nm Bot Culin ginger.

girafe [ʒiraf] nf giraffe.

giratoire [ʒiratwar] a **sens g.** Aut roundabout, Am traffic circle.

girl [gœrl] nf (danseuse) chorus girl.

girofle [ʒirɔfl] nm **clou de g.** Bot clove.

giroflée [ʒirɔfle] nf Bot wall flower.

girouette [ʒirwɛt] nf weathercock, weather vane.

gisement [ʒizmɑ̃] nm (de minerai, pétrole) Géol deposit.

gitan, -ane [ʒitɑ̃, -an] nmf (Spanish) gipsy.

gîte [ʒit] nm (abri) resting place.

gîter [ʒite] vi (navire) to list.

givre [ʒivr] nm (hoar)frost. ◆**se givrer** vpr (pare-brise etc) to ice up, frost up. ◆**givré** a frost-covered.

glabre [glabr] a (visage) smooth.

glace [glas] nf 1 (eau gelée) ice; (crème glacée) ice cream. 2 (vitre) window; (miroir) mirror; (verre) plate glass.

glacer [glase] **1** vt (sang) Fig to chill; **g. qn** (transir, paralyser) to chill s.o.; **– se g.** vpr (eau) to freeze. **2** vt (gâteau) to ice, (au jus) to glaze; (papier) to glaze. ◆**glaçant** a (attitude etc) chilling, icy. ◆**glacé** a **1** (eau, main, pièce) ice-cold, icy; (vent) freezing, icy; (accueil) Fig icy, chilly. **2** (thé) iced; (fruit, marron) candied; (papier) glazed. ◆**glaçage** nm (de gâteau etc) icing. ◆**glacial, -aux** a icy. ◆**glacier** nm **1** Géol glacier. **2** (vendeur) ice-cream man. ◆**glacière** nf (boîte, endroit) icebox. ◆**glaçon** nm Culin ice cube; Géol block of ice; (sur le toit) icicle.

glaïeul [glajœl] nm Bot gladiolus.

glaires [glɛr] nfpl Méd phlegm.

glaise [glɛz] nf clay.

gland [glɑ̃] nm **1** Bot acorn. **2** (pompon) Tex tassel.

glande [glɑ̃d] nf gland.

glander [glɑ̃de] vi Arg to fritter away one's time.

glaner [glane] vt (blé, renseignement etc) to glean.

glapir [glapir] vi to yelp, yap.

glas [glɑ] nm (de cloche) knell.

glauque [glok] a sea-green.

gliss/er [glise] vi (involontairement) to slip; (patiner, coulisser) to slide; (sur l'eau) to glide; **g. sur** (sujet) to slide ou gloss over; **ça glisse** it's slippery; **– vt** (introduire) to slip (dans into); (murmurer) to whisper; **se g. dans/sous** to slip into/under. ◆**–ant** a slippery. ◆**glissade** nf (involontaire) slip; (volontaire) slide. ◆**glissement** nm (de sens) Ling shift; **g. à gauche** Pol swing ou shift to the left; **g. de terrain** Géol landslide. ◆**glissière** nf groove; **porte à g.** sliding door; **fermeture à g.** zip (fastener), Am zipper.

global, -aux [glɔbal, -o] a total, global; **somme globale** lump sum. ◆**–ement** adv collectively, as a whole.

globe [glɔb] nm globe; **g. de l'œil** eyeball.

globule [glɔbyl] nm (du sang) corpuscle.

gloire [glwar] nf (renommée, louange, mérite) glory; (personne célèbre) celebrity; **se faire g. de** to glory in; **à la g. de** in praise of. ◆**glorieux, -euse** a (plein de gloire) glorious. ◆**glorifier** vt to glorify; **se g. de** to glory in.

glossaire [glɔsɛr] nm glossary.

glouglou [gluglu] nm (de liquide) gurgle. ◆**glouglouter** vi to gurgle.

glouss/er [gluse] vi (poule) to cluck; (personne) to chuckle. ◆**–ement** nm cluck; chuckle.

glouton, -onne [glutɔ̃, -ɔn] a greedy, gluttonous; **– nmf** glutton. ◆**gloutonnerie** nf gluttony.

gluant [glyɑ̃] a sticky.

glucose [glykoz] nm glucose.

glycérine [gliserin] nf glycerin(e).

glycine [glisin] nf Bot wisteria.

gnome [gnom] nm (nain) gnome.

gnon [nɔ̃] nm Arg blow, punch.

goal [gol] nm Fb goalkeeper.

gobelet [gɔblɛ] nm tumbler; (de plastique, papier) cup.

gober [gɔbe] vt (œuf, mouche etc) to swallow (whole); (propos) Fig to swallow.

godasse [gɔdas] nf Fam shoe.

godet [gɔdɛ] nm (récipient) pot; (verre) Arg drink.

goéland [gɔelɑ̃] nm (sea)gull.

gogo [gɔgo] nm (homme naïf) Fam sucker.

gogo (à) [agogo] adv Fam galore.

goguenard [gɔgnar] a mocking.

goguette (en) [ɑ̃gɔgɛt] adv Fam on the spree.

goinfre [gwɛ̃fr] nm (glouton) Fam pig, guzzler. ◆**se goinfrer** vpr Fam to stuff oneself (de with).

golf [gɔlf] nm golf; (terrain) golf course. ◆**golfeur, -euse** nmf golfer.

golfe [gɔlf] nm gulf, bay.

gomme [gɔm] nf **1** (substance) gum. **2** (à effacer) rubber, Am eraser. ◆**gommé** a (papier) gummed. ◆**gommer** vt (effacer) to rub out, erase.

gomme (à la) [alagɔm] adv Fam useless.

gond [gɔ̃] nm (de porte etc) hinge.

gondole [gɔ̃dɔl] nf (bateau) gondola. ◆**gondolier** nm gondolier.

gondoler [gɔ̃dɔle] **1** vi, **– se g.** vpr (planche) to warp. **2 se g.** vpr (rire) Fam to split one's sides.

gonfl/er [gɔ̃fle] vt to swell; (pneu) to inflate, pump up; (en soufflant) to blow up; (poitrine) to swell out; (grossir) Fig to inflate; **– vi, – se g.** vpr to swell; **se g. de** (orgueil, émotion) to swell with; **être** Fam (courageux) to have plenty of pluck; (insolent) to have plenty of nerve. ◆**–able** a inflatable. ◆**–ement** nm swelling. ◆**–eur** nm (air) pump.

gong [gɔ̃g] nm gong.

gorge [gɔrʒ] nf **1** throat; (seins) Litt bust. **2** Géog gorge. ◆**gorg/er** vt (remplir) (de with); **se g. de** to stuff ou gorge oneself with. ◆**–é** a **de** (saturé) gorged with. ◆**–ée** nf mouthful; **petite g.** sip; **d'une seule g.** in ou at one gulp.

gorille [gɔrij] *nm* **1** (*animal*) gorilla. **2** (*garde du corps*) *Fam* bodyguard.

gosier [gozje] *nm* throat, windpipe.

gosse [gɔs] *nmf* (*enfant*) *Fam* kid, youngster.

gothique [gɔtik] *a* & *nm* Gothic.

gouache [gwaʃ] *nf* (*peinture*) gouache.

goudron [gudrɔ̃] *nm* tar. ◆**goudronner** *vt* to tar.

gouffre [gufr] *nm* gulf, chasm.

goujat [guʒa] *nm* churl, lout.

goulasch [gulaʃ] *nf Culin* goulash.

goulot [gulo] *nm* (*de bouteille*) neck; **boire au g.** to drink from the bottle.

goulu, -ue [guly] *a* greedy; – *nmf* glutton. ◆**goulûment** *adv* greedily.

goupille [gupij] *nf* (*cheville*) pin.

goupiller [gupije] *vt* (*arranger*) *Fam* to work out, arrange.

gourde [gurd] *nf* **1** (*à eau*) water bottle, flask. **2** (*personne*) *Péj Fam* chump, oaf.

gourdin [gurdɛ̃] *nm* club, cudgel.

gourer (se) [səgure] *vpr Fam* to make a mistake.

gourmand, -ande [gurmã, -ãd] *a* fond of eating, *Péj* greedy; **g. de** fond of; **être g. de sucreries**) to have a sweet tooth; – *nmf* hearty eater, *Péj* glutton. ◆**gourmandise** *nf* good eating, *Péj* gluttony; *pl* (*mets*) delicacies.

gourmet [gurmɛ] *nm* gourmet, epicure.

gourmette [gurmɛt] *nf* chain *ou* identity bracelet.

gousse [gus] *nf* **g. d'ail** clove of garlic.

goût [gu] *nm* taste; **de bon g.** in good taste; **prendre g. à qch** to take a liking to sth; **par g.** from *ou* by choice; **sans g.** tasteless. ◆**goûter** *vt* (*aliment*) to taste; (*apprécier*) to relish, enjoy; **g. à qch** to taste (a little of) sth; **g. de** (*pour la première fois*) to try out, taste; – *vi* to have a snack, have tea; – *nm* snack, tea.

goutte [gut] *nf* **1** drop. **couler g. à g.** to drip. **2** (*maladie*) gout. ◆**g.-à-goutte** *nm inv Méd* drip. ◆**gouttelette** *nf* droplet. ◆**goutter** *vi* (*eau, robinet, nez*) to drip (**de** from).

gouttière [gutjɛr] *nf* (*d'un toit*) gutter.

gouvernail [guvɛrnaj] *nm* (*pale*) rudder; (*barre*) helm.

gouvernante [guvɛrnãt] *nf* governess.

gouvernement [guvɛrnəmã] *nm* government. ◆**gouvernemental, -aux** *a* (*parti, politique etc*) government-.

gouvern/er [guvɛrne] *vti Pol* & *Fig* to govern, rule. ◆**-ants** *nmpl* rulers. ◆**-eur** *nm* governor.

grabuge [graby3] *nm* **du g.** (*querelle*) *Fam* a rumpus.

grâce [gras] **1** *nf* (*charme*) & *Rel* grace; (*avantage*) favour; (*miséricorde*) mercy; **crier g.** to cry for mercy; **de bonne/mauvaise g.** with good/bad grace; **donner le coup de g. à** to finish off; **faire g. de qch à qn** to spare s.o. sth. **2** *prép* **g. à** thanks to. ◆**gracier** *vt* (*condamné*) to pardon.

gracieux, -euse [grasjø, -øz] *a* **1** (*élégant*) graceful; (*aimable*) gracious. **2** (*gratuit*) gratuitous; **à titre g.** free (of charge). ◆**gracieusement** *adv* gracefully; graciously; free (of charge).

gracile [grasil] *a Litt* slender.

gradation [gradasjɔ̃] *nf* gradation.

grade [grad] *nm Mil* rank; **monter en g.** to be promoted. ◆**gradé** *nm Mil* non-commissioned officer.

gradin [gradɛ̃] *nm Th etc* row of seats, tier.

graduel, -elle [gradɥɛl] *a* gradual.

graduer [gradɥe] *vt* (*règle*) to graduate; (*exercices*) to grade, make gradually more difficult.

graffiti [grafiti] *nmpl* graffiti.

grain [grɛ̃] *nm* **1** (*de blé etc*) & *Fig* grain; (*de café*) bean; (*de chapelet*) bead; (*de poussière*) speck; *pl* (*céréales*) grain; **le g.** (*de cuir, papier*) the grain; **g. de beauté** mole; (*sur le visage*) beauty spot; **g. de raisin** grape. **2** *Mét* shower.

graine [grɛn] *nf* seed; **mauvaise g.** (*enfant*) *Péj* bad lot, rotten egg.

graisse [grɛs] *nf* fat; (*lubrifiant*) grease. ◆**graissage** *nm Aut* lubrication. ◆**graisser** *vt* to grease. ◆**graisseux, -euse** *a* (*vêtement etc*) greasy, oily; (*bourrelets, tissu*) fatty.

grammaire [gramɛr] *nf* grammar. ◆**grammatical, -aux** *a* grammatical.

gramme [gram] *nm* gram(me).

grand, grande [grã, grãd] *a* big, large; (*en hauteur*) tall; (*mérite, âge, chaleur, ami etc*) great; (*bruit*) loud, great; (*différence*) wide, great, big; (*adulte, mûr, plus âgé*) grown up, big; (*officier, maître*) great; (*âme*) noble; **g. frère/etc** (*plus âgé*) big brother/etc; **le g. air** the open air; **il est g. temps** it's high time (**que** that); – *adv* **g. ouvert** (*yeux, fenêtre*) wide-open; **ouvrir g.** to open wide; **en g.** on a grand *ou* large scale; – *nm Scol* senior; (*adulte*) grown-up; **les quatre Grands** *Pol* The Big Four. ◆**grandement** *adv* (*beaucoup*) greatly; (*généreusement*) grandly; **avoir g. de quoi vivre** to have plenty to live on. ◆**grandeur** *nf* (*importance, gloire*) greatness; (*dimension*) size, magni-

tude; (*majesté, splendeur*) grandeur; **g. na-ture** life-size; **g. d'âme** generosity.
grand-chose [grɑ̃ʃoz] *pron* **pas g.-chose** not much. **◆g.-mère** *nf* (*pl* **grands-mères**) grandmother. **◆grands-parents** *nmpl* grandparents. **◆g.-père** *nm* (*pl* **grands-pères**) grandfather.
Grande-Bretagne [grɑ̃dbrətaɲ] *nf* Great Britain.
grandiose [grɑ̃djoz] *a* grandiose, grand.
grandir [grɑ̃dir] *vi* to grow; (*bruit*) to grow louder; — *vt* (*grossir*) to magnify; **g. qn** (*faire paraître plus grand*) to make s.o. seem taller.
grange [grɑ̃ʒ] *nf* barn.
granit(e) [granit] *nm* granite.
graphique [grafik] *a* (*signe, art*) graphic; — *nm* graph.
grappe [grap] *nf* (*de fruits etc*) cluster; **g. de raisin** bunch of grapes.
grappin [grapɛ̃] *nm* **mettre le g. sur** *Fam* to grab hold of.
gras, grasse [grɑ, grɑs] *a* (*personne, ventre etc*) fat; (*aliment*) fatty; (*graisseux*) greasy, oily; (*caractère*) *Typ* bold, heavy; (*plante, contour*) thick; (*rire*) throaty, deep; (*toux*) loose, phlegmy; (*récompense*) rich; **matières grasses** fat; **foie g.** Culin foie gras, fattened goose liver; — *nm* (*de viande*) fat. **◆grassement** *adv* (*abondamment*) handsomely. **◆grassouillet, -ette** *a* plump.
gratifier [gratifje] *vt* **g. qn de** to present *ou* favour s.o. with. **◆gratification** *nf* (*prime*) bonus.
gratin [gratɛ̃] *nm* **1 au g.** Culin baked with breadcrumbs and grated cheese. **2** (*élite*) *Fam* upper crust.
gratis [gratis] *adv* Fam free (of charge), gratis.
gratitude [gratityd] *nf* gratitude.
gratte-ciel [gratsjɛl] *nm inv* skyscraper.
gratte-papier [gratpapje] *nm* (*employé*) *Péj* pen-pusher.
gratter [grate] *vt* (*avec un outil etc*) to scrape; (*avec les ongles, les griffes etc*) to scratch; (*boue*) to scrape off; (*effacer*) to scratch out; **ça me gratte** *Fam* it itches, I have an itch; — *vi* (*à la porte etc*) to scratch; (*tissu*) to be scratchy; — **se g.** *vpr* to scratch oneself. **◆grattoir** *nm* scraper.
gratuit [gratɥi] *a* (*billet etc*) free; (*hypothèse, acte*) gratuitous. **◆gratuité** *nf* **la g. de l'enseignement**/*etc* free education/*etc*. **◆gratuitement** *adv* free (of charge); gratuitously.
gravats [grava] *nmpl* rubble, debris.
grave [grav] *a* serious; (*juge, visage*) grave,

solemn; (*voix*) deep, low; (*accent*) Gram grave; **ce n'est pas g.!** it's not important! **◆—ment** *adv* (*malade, menacé*) seriously; (*dignement*) gravely.
grav/er [grave] *vt* (*sur métal etc*) to engrave; (*sur bois*) to carve; (*disque*) to cut; (*dans sa mémoire*) to imprint, engrave. **◆—eur** *nm* engraver.
gravier [gravje] *nm* gravel. **◆gravillon** *nm* gravel; *pl* gravel, (loose) chippings.
gravir [gravir] *vt* to climb (*with effort*).
gravité [gravite] *nf* **1** (*de situation etc*) seriousness; (*solennité*) gravity. **2** Phys gravity.
graviter [gravite] *vi* to revolve (*autour de* around). **◆gravitation** *nf* gravitation.
gravure [gravyr] *nf* (*action, art*) engraving; (*à l'eau forte*) etching; (*estampe*) print; (*de disque*) recording; **g. sur bois** (*objet*) woodcut.
gré [gre] *nm* **à son g.** (*goût*) to his *ou* her taste; (*désir*) as he *ou* she pleases; **de bon g.** willingly; **contre le g. de** against the will of; **bon g. mal g.** willy-nilly; **au g. de** (*vent etc*) at the mercy of.
Grèce [grɛs] *nf* Greece. **◆grec, grecque** *a* & *nmf* Greek; — *nm* (*langue*) Greek.
greffe [grɛf] **1** *nf* (*de peau*) & Bot graft; (*d'organe*) transplant; — *nm* Jur record office. **◆greffer** *vt* (*peau etc*) & Bot to graft (*à* on to); (*organe*) to transplant. **◆greffier** *nm* clerk (of the court). **◆greffon** *nm* (*de peau*) & Bot graft.
grégaire [greger] *a* (*instinct*) gregarious.
grêle [grɛl] **1** *nf* Mét & Fig hail. **2** *a* (*fin*) spindly, (very) slender *ou* thin. **◆grêler** *v imp* to hail. **◆grêlon** *nm* hailstone.
grêlé [grele] *a* (*visage*) pockmarked.
grelot [grəlo] *nm* (small round) bell.
grelotter [grələte] *vi* to shiver (**de** with).
grenade [grənad] *nf* **1** Bot pomegranate. **2** (*projectile*) Mil grenade. **◆grenadine** *nf* pomegranate syrup, grenadine.
grenat [grəna] *a inv* (*couleur*) dark red.
grenier [grənje] *nm* attic; Agr granary.
grenouille [grənuj] *nf* frog.
grès [grɛ] *nm* (*roche*) sandstone; (*poterie*) stoneware.
grésiller [grezije] *vi* Culin to sizzle; Rad to crackle.
grève [grɛv] *nf* **1** strike; **g. de la faim** hunger strike; **g. du zèle** work-to-rule, Am rule-book slow-down; **g. perlée** go-slow, Am slow-down (strike); **g. sauvage/sur le tas** wildcat/sit-down strike; **g. tournante** strike by rota. **2** (*de mer*) shore; (*de rivière*) bank. **◆gréviste** *nmf* striker.

gribouiller [gribuje] *vti* to scribble. ◆**gribouillis** *nm* scribble.

grief [grijɛf] *nm* (*plainte*) grievance.

grièvement [grijɛvmɑ̃] *adv* g. blessé seriously *ou* badly injured.

griffe [grif] *nf* **1** (*ongle*) claw; **sous la g. de qn** (*pouvoir*) in s.o.'s clutches. **2** (*de couturier*) (designer) label; (*tampon*) printed signature; (*d'auteur*) *Fig* mark, stamp. ◆**griffé** *a* (*vêtement*) designer-. ◆**griffer** *vt* to scratch, claw.

griffonn/er [grifone] *vt* to scrawl, scribble. ◆**—age** *nm* scrawl, scribble.

grignoter [griɲɔte] *vti* to nibble.

gril [gril] *nm* *Culin* grill, grid(iron). ◆**grillade** [grijad] *nf* (*viande*) grill. ◆**grille-pain** *nm inv* toaster. ◆**griller** *vt* (*viande*) to grill, broil; (*pain*) to toast; (*café*) to roast; (*ampoule*) *El* to blow; (*brûler*) to scorch; (*cigarette*) *Fam* to smoke; **g. un feu rouge** *Aut Fam* to drive through *ou* jump a red light; *– vi* **mettre à g.** to put on the grill; **on grille ici** *Fam* it's scorching; **g. de faire** to be itching to do.

grille [grij] *nf* (*clôture*) railings; (*porte*) (iron) gate; (*de fourneau, foyer*) grate; (*de radiateur*) *Aut* grid, grille; (*des salaires*) *Fig* scale; *pl* (*de prison*) bars, grating; **g. (des horaires)** schedule. ◆**grillage** *nm* wire netting.

grillon [grijɔ̃] *nm* (*insecte*) cricket.

grimace [grimas] *nf* (*pour faire rire*) (funny) face, grimace; (*de dégoût, douleur*) grimace. ◆**grimacer** *vi* to grimace (**de** with).

grimer [grime] *vt*, **– se g.** *vpr* (*acteur*) to make up.

grimp/er [grɛ̃pe] *vi* to climb (**à qch** up sth); (*prix*) *Fam* to rocket; *– vt* to climb. ◆**—ant** *a* (*plante*) climbing.

grinc/er [grɛ̃se] *vi* to grate, creak; **g. des dents** to grind *ou* gnash one's teeth. ◆**—ement** *nm* grating; grinding.

grincheux, -euse [grɛ̃ʃø, -øz] *a* grumpy, peevish.

gringalet [grɛ̃gale] *nm* (*homme*) *Péj* puny runt, weakling.

grippe [grip] *nf* **1** (*maladie*) flu, influenza. **2** **prendre qch/qn en g.** to take a strong dislike to sth/s.o. ◆**grippé** *a* être g. to have (the) flu.

gripper [gripe] *vi*, **– se g.** *vpr* (*moteur*) to seize up.

grippe-sou [gripsu] *nm* skinflint, miser.

gris [gri] *a* grey, *Am* gray; (*temps*) dull, grey; (*ivre*) tipsy; *– nm* grey. ◆**grisaille** *nf* (*de vie*) dullness, greyness, *Am* grayness. ◆**grisâtre** *a* greyish, *Am* grayish.

◆**griser** *vt* (*vin etc*) to make (s.o.) tipsy, intoxicate (s.o.); (*air vif, succès*) to exhilarate (s.o.). ◆**griserie** *nf* intoxication; exhilaration. ◆**grisonn/er** *vi* (*cheveux, personne*) to go grey. ◆**—ant** *a* greying.

grisou [grizu] *nm* (*gaz*) firedamp.

grive [griv] *nf* (*oiseau*) thrush.

grivois [grivwa] *a* bawdy. ◆**grivoiserie** *nf* (*propos*) bawdy talk.

Groenland [grɔɛnlɑ̃d] *nm* Greenland.

grog [grɔg] *nm* (*boisson*) grog, toddy.

grogn/er [grɔɲe] *vi* to growl, grumble (**contre** at); (*cochon*) to grunt. ◆**—ement** *nm* growl, grumble; grunt. ◆**grognon, -onne** *a* grumpy, peevish.

grommeler [grɔmle] *vti* to grumble, mutter.

gronder [grɔ̃de] *vi* (*chien*) to growl; (*tonnerre*) to rumble; *– vt* (*réprimander*) to scold. ◆**grondement** *nm* growl; rumble. ◆**gronderie** *nf* scolding.

gros, grosse [gro, gros] *a* big; (*gras*) fat; (*épais*) thick; (*effort, progrès*) great; (*fortune, somme*) large; (*bruit*) loud; (*averse, mer, rhume*) heavy; (*faute*) serious, gross; (*traits, laine, fil*) coarse; **g. mot** swear word; *– adv* **gagner g.** to earn big money; **risquer g.** to take a big risk; **en g.** (*globalement*) roughly; (*écrire*) in big letters; (*vendre*) in bulk, wholesale; *– nmf* (*personne*) fat man, fat woman; *– nm* **le g. de** the bulk of; **de g.** (*maison, prix*) wholesale.

groseille [grozɛj] *nf* (white *ou* red) currant; **g. à maquereau** gooseberry.

grossesse [grosɛs] *nf* pregnancy.

grosseur [grosœr] *nf* **1** (*volume*) size; (*obésité*) weight. **2** (*tumeur*) *Méd* lump.

grossier, -ière [grosje, -jɛr] *a* (*matière, tissu, traits*) coarse, rough; (*idée, solution*) rough, crude; (*instrument*) crude; (*erreur*) gross; (*personne, manières*) coarse, uncouth, rude; **être g. envers** (*insolent*) to be rude to. ◆**grossièrement** *adv* (*calculer*) roughly; (*se tromper*) grossly; (*répondre*) coarsely, rudely. ◆**grossièreté** *nf* coarseness; roughness; (*insolence*) rudeness; (*mot*) rude word.

gross/ir [grosir] *vi* (*personne*) to put on weight; (*fleuve*) to swell; (*nombre, bosse, foule*) to swell, get bigger; (*bruit*) to get louder; *– vt* to swell; (*exagérer*) *Fig* to magnify; *– vti* (*verre, loupe etc*) to magnify; **verre grossissant** magnifying glass. ◆**—issement** *nm* increase in weight; swelling, increase in size; (*de microscope etc*) magnification.

grossiste [grosist] *nmf* *Com* wholesaler.

grosso modo [grosomɔdo] *adv* (*en gros*) roughly.

grotesque [grɔtɛsk] *a* (*risible*) ludicrous, grotesque.

grotte [grɔt] *nf* grotto.

grouill/er [gruje] **1** *vi* (*rue, fourmis, foule etc*) to be swarming (**de** with). **2 se g.** *vpr* (*se hâter*) *Arg* to step on it. ◆**—ant** *a* swarming (**de** with).

groupe [grup] *nm* group; **g. scolaire** (*bâtiments*) school block. ◆**groupement** *nm* (*action*) grouping; (*groupe*) group. ◆**grouper** *vt* to group (together); **— se g.** *vpr* to band together, group (together).

grue [gry] *nf* (*machine, oiseau*) crane.

grumeau, -x [grymo] *nm* (*dans une sauce etc*) lump. ◆**grumeleux, -euse** *a* lumpy.

gruyère [gryjɛr] *nm* gruyère (cheese).

gué [ge] *nm* ford; **passer à g.** to ford.

guenilles [gənij] *nfpl* rags (and tatters).

guenon [gənɔ̃] *nf* female monkey.

guépard [gepar] *nm* cheetah.

guêpe [gɛp] *nf* wasp. ◆**guêpier** *nm* (*nid*) wasp's nest; (*piège*) *Fig* trap.

guère [gɛr] *adv* (**ne**) **. . . g.** hardly, scarcely; **il ne sort g.** he hardly *ou* scarcely goes out.

guéridon [geridɔ̃] *nm* pedestal table.

guérilla [gerija] *nf* guerrilla warfare. ◆**guérillero** *nm* guerrilla.

guér/ir [gerir] *vt* (*personne, maladie*) to cure (**de** of); (*blessure*) to heal; **—** *vi* to recover; (*blessure*) to heal; (*rhume*) to get better; **g. de** (*fièvre etc*) to get over, recover from. ◆**—i** a cured, better, well. ◆**guérison** *nf* (*de personne*) recovery; (*de maladie*) cure; (*de blessure*) healing. ◆**guérisseur, -euse** *nmf* faith healer.

guérite [gerit] *nf Mil* sentry box.

guerre [gɛr] *nf* war; (*chimique etc*) warfare; **en g.** at war (**avec** with); **faire la g.** to wage *ou* make war (**à** on, against); **g. d'usure** war of attrition; **conseil de g.** court-martial. ◆**guerrier, -ière** *a* (*chant, danse*) war-; (*nation*) war-like; **—** *nmf* warrior. ◆**guerroyer** *vi Litt* to war.

guet [gɛ] *nm* **faire le g.** to be on the look-out. ◆**guett/er** *vt* to be on the look-out for,

watch (out) for; (*gibier*) to lie in wait for. ◆**—eur** *nm* (*soldat*) look-out.

guet-apens [gɛtapɑ̃] *nm inv* ambush.

guêtre [gɛtr] *nf* gaiter.

gueule [gœl] *nf* (*d'animal, de canon*) mouth; (*de personne*) *Fam* mouth; (*figure*) *Fam* face; **avoir la g. de bois** *Fam* to have a hangover; **faire la g.** *Fam* to sulk. ◆**gueuler** *vti* to bawl (out). ◆**gueuleton** *nm* (*repas*) *Fam* blow-out, feast.

gui [gi] *nm Bot* mistletoe.

guichet [giʃɛ] *nm* (*de gare, cinéma etc*) ticket office; (*de banque etc*) window; *Th* box office, ticket office; **à guichets fermés** *Th Sp* with all tickets sold in advance. ◆**guichetier, -ière** *nmf* (*à la poste etc*) counter clerk; (*à la gare*) ticket office clerk.

guide [gid] **1** *nm* (*personne, livre etc*) guide. **2** *nf* (*éclaireuse*) (girl) guide. **3** *nfpl* (*rênes*) reins. ◆**guider** *vt* to guide; **se g. sur** to guide oneself by.

guidon [gidɔ̃] *nm* (*de bicyclette etc*) handlebar(s).

guigne [giɲ] *nf* (*malchance*) *Fam* bad luck.

guignol [giɲɔl] *nm* (*spectacle*) = Punch and Judy show.

guillemets [gijmɛ] *nmpl Typ* inverted commas, quotation marks.

guilleret, -ette [gijrɛ, -ɛt] *a* lively, perky.

guillotine [gijɔtin] *nf* guillotine.

guimauve [gimov] *nf Bot Culin* marshmallow.

guimbarde [gɛ̃bard] *nf* (*voiture*) *Fam* old banger, *Am* (old) wreck.

guindé [gɛ̃de] *a* (*affecté*) stiff, stilted, stuck-up.

guingois (de) [dəgɛ̃gwa] *adv* askew.

guirlande [girlɑ̃d] *nf* garland, wreath.

guise [giz] *nf* **n'en faire qu'à sa g.** to do as one pleases; **en g. de** by way of.

guitare [gitar] *nf* guitar. ◆**guitariste** *nmf* guitarist.

guttural, -aux [gytyral, -o] *a* guttural.

gymnase [ʒimnɑz] *nm* gymnasium. ◆**gymnaste** *nmf* gymnast. ◆**gymnastique** *nf* gymnastics.

gynécologie [ʒinekɔlɔʒi] *nf* gynaecology, *Am* gynecology. ◆**gynécologue** *nmf* gynaecologist, *Am* gynecologist.

H

H, h [aʃ] *nm* H, h; **l'heure H** zero hour; **bombe H** H-bomb.

ha! [ʼa] *int* ah!, oh!; **ha, ha!** (*rire*) ha-ha!

habile [abil] *a* clever, skilful (**à qch** at sth, **à faire** at doing). ◆**habilement** *adv* cleverly, skilfully. ◆**habileté** *nf* skill, ability.

habill/er [abije] *vt* to dress (**de** in); (*fournir en vêtements*) to clothe; (*couvrir*) to cover (**de** with); **h. qn en soldat**/*etc* (*déguiser*) to dress s.o. up as a soldier/*etc*; — **s'h.** *vpr* to dress (oneself), get dressed; (*avec élégance, se déguiser*) to dress up. ◆**—é** *a* dressed (**de** in); (*costume, robe*) smart, dressy. ◆**—ement** *nm* (*vêtements*) clothing, clothes.

habit [abi] *nm* costume, outfit; (*tenue de soirée*) evening dress, tails; *pl* (*vêtements*) clothes.

habit/er [abite] *vi* to live (**à, en, dans** in); — *vt* (*maison, région*) to live in; (*planète*) to inhabit. ◆**—ant, -ante** *nmf* (*de pays etc*) inhabitant; (*de maison*) resident, occupant. ◆**—é** *a* (*région*) inhabited; (*maison*) occupied. ◆**—able** *a* (in)habitable. ◆**habitat** *nm* (*d'animal, de plante*) habitat; (*conditions*) housing, living conditions. ◆**habitation** *nf* house, dwelling; (*action de résider*) living.

habitude [abityd] *nf* habit; **avoir l'h. de qch** to be used to sth; **avoir l'h. de faire** to be used to doing, be in the habit of doing; **prendre l'h. de faire** to get into the habit of doing; **d'h.** usually; **comme d'h.** as usual. ◆**habituel, -elle** *a* usual, customary. ◆**habituellement** *adv* usually. ◆**habitu/er** *vt* **h. qn à** to accustom s.o. to; **être habitué à** to be used to *ou* accustomed to; — **s'h.** *vpr* to get accustomed (**à** to). ◆**—é, -ée** *nmf* regular (customer *ou* visitor).

hache [aʃ] *nf* axe, *Am* ax. ◆**hachette** *nf* hatchet.

hach/er [aʃe] *vt* (*au couteau*) to chop (up); (*avec un appareil*) to mince, *Am* grind; (*déchiqueter*) to cut to pieces. ◆**—é** *a* **1** (*viande*) minced, *Am* ground; chopped. **2** (*style*) staccato, broken. ◆**hachis** *nm* (*viande*) mince, minced *ou Am* ground meat. ◆**hachoir** *nm* (*couteau*) chopper; (*appareil*) mincer, *Am* grinder.

hagard [agar] *a* wild-looking, frantic.

haie [ˈɛ] *nf* (*clôture*) *Bot* hedge; (*rangée*) row; (*de coureur*) *Sp* hurdle; (*de chevaux*) *Sp* fence, hurdle; **course de haies** (*coureurs*) hurdle race; (*chevaux*) steeplechase.

haillons [ajɔ̃] *nmpl* rags (and tatters).

haine [ˈɛn] *nf* hatred, hate. ◆**haineux, -euse** *a* full of hatred.

haïr* [ˈair] *vt* to hate. ◆**haïssable** *a* hateful, detestable.

hâle [ˈɑl] *nm* suntan. ◆**hâlé** *a* (*par le soleil*) suntanned; (*par l'air*) weather-beaten.

haleine [alɛn] *nf* breath; **hors d'h.** out of breath; **perdre h.** to get out of breath; **reprendre h.** to get one's breath back, catch one's breath; **de longue h.** (*travail*) long-term; **tenir en h.** to hold in suspense.

hal/er [ˈale] *vt* *Nau* to tow. ◆**—age** *nm* towing; **chemin de h.** towpath.

halet/er [ˈalte] *vi* to pant, gasp. ◆**—ant** *a* panting, gasping.

hall [ˈol] *nm* (*de gare*) main hall, concourse; (*d'hôtel*) lobby, hall; (*de maison*) hall(way).

halle [ˈal] *nf* (covered) market; **les halles** the central food market.

hallucination [alysinasjɔ̃] *nf* hallucination. ◆**hallucinant** *a* extraordinary.

halo [ˈalo] *nm* (*auréole*) halo.

halte [ˈalt] *nf* (*arrêt*) stop, *Mil* halt; (*lieu*) stopping place, *Mil* halting place; **faire h.** to stop; — *int* stop!, *Mil* halt!

haltère [altɛr] *nm* (*poids*) *Sp* dumbbell. ◆**haltérophilie** *nf* weight lifting.

hamac [ˈamak] *nm* hammock.

hameau, -x [ˈamo] *nm* hamlet.

hameçon [amsɔ̃] *nm* (fish) hook; **mordre à l'h.** *Pêche & Fig* to rise to *ou* swallow the bait.

hamster [ˈamster] *nm* hamster.

hanche [ˈɑ̃ʃ] *nf* *Anat* hip.

hand(-)ball [ˈadbal] *nm* *Sp* handball.

handicap [ˈɑdikap] *nm* (*désavantage*) & *Sp* handicap. ◆**handicap/er** *vt* to handicap. ◆**—é, -ée** *a & nmf* handicapped (person); **h. moteur** spastic.

hangar [ˈɑ̃gar] *nm* (*entrepôt*) shed; (*pour avions*) hangar.

hanneton [ˈantɔ̃] *nm* (*insecte*) cockchafer.

hanter [ˈɑ̃te] *vt* to haunt.

hantise [ˈɑ̃tiz] *nf* **la h. de** an obsession with.

happer ['ape] vt (saisir) to catch, snatch; (par la gueule) to snap up.

haras ['arɑ] nm stud farm.

harasser [arase] vt to exhaust.

harceler ['arsəle] vt to harass, torment (de with). ◆**harcèlement** nm harassment.

hardi ['ardi] a bold, daring. ◆**—ment** adv boldly. ◆**hardiesse** nf boldness, daring; **une h.** (action) Litt an audacity.

harem ['arɛm] nm harem.

hareng ['arɑ̃] nm herring.

hargne ['arɲ] nf aggressive bad temper. ◆**hargneux, -euse** a bad-tempered, aggressive.

haricot ['ariko] nm (blanc) (haricot) bean; (vert) French bean, green bean.

harmonica [armɔnika] nm harmonica, mouthorgan.

harmonie [armɔni] nf harmony. ◆**harmonieux, -euse** a harmonious. ◆**harmonique** a & nm Mus harmonic. ◆**harmoniser** vt, — **s'h.** vpr to harmonize. ◆**harmonium** nm Mus harmonium.

harnacher [arnaʃe] vt (cheval etc) to harness. ◆**harnais** nm (de cheval, bébé) harness.

harpe ['arp] nf harp. ◆**harpiste** nmf harpist.

harpon ['arpɔ̃] nm harpoon. ◆**harponner** vt (baleine) to harpoon; **h. qn** (arrêter) Fam to waylay s.o.

hasard ['azar] nm **le h.** chance; **un h.** (coïncidence) a coincidence; **un heureux h.** a stroke of luck; **un malheureux h.** a rotten piece of luck; **par h.** by chance; **si par h.** if by any chance; **au h.** at random, haphazardly; **à tout h.** just in case; **les hasards de** (risques) the hazards of. ◆**hasard/er** vt (remarque, démarche) to venture, hazard; (vie, réputation) to risk; **se h. dans** to venture into; **se h. à faire** to risk doing, venture to do. ◆**—é** a, ◆**hasardeux, -euse** a risky, hazardous.

haschisch ['aʃiʃ] nm hashish.

hâte ['ɑt] nf haste, speed; (impatience) eagerness; **en h., à la h.** hurriedly, in a hurry, in haste; **avoir h. de faire** (désireux) to be eager to do, be in a hurry to do. ◆**hâter** vt (pas, départ etc) to hasten; — **se h.** vpr to hurry, make haste (**de faire** to do). ◆**hâtif, -ive** a hasty, hurried; (développement) precocious; (fruit) early.

hausse ['os] nf rise (**de** in); **en h.** rising. ◆**hausser** vt (prix, voix etc) to raise; (épaules) to shrug; **se h. sur la pointe des pieds** to stand on tip-toe.

haut ['o] a high; (de taille) tall; (classes) up-

per; higher; (fonctionnaire etc) high-ranking; **le h. Rhin** the upper Rhine; **la haute couture** high fashion; **à haute voix** aloud, in a loud voice; **h. de 5 mètres** 5 metres high ou tall; — adv (voler, viser etc) high (up); (estimer) highly; (parler) loud, loudly; **tout h.** (lire, penser) aloud, out loud; **h. placé** (personne) in a high position; **plus h.** (dans un texte) above, further back; — nm (partie haute) top; **en h.** at the top of, on top; **en h.** (loger) upstairs; (regarder) up; (mettre) on (the) top; **d'en h.** (de la partie haute, du ciel etc) from high up, from up above; **avoir 5 mètres de h.** to be 5 metres high ou tall; **des hauts et des bas** Fig ups and downs.

hautain ['otɛ̃] a haughty.

hautbois ['obwa] nm Mus oboe.

haut-de-forme ['odfɔrm] nm (pl hauts-de-forme) top hat.

hautement ['otmɑ̃] adv (tout à fait, très) highly. ◆**hauteur** nf height; Géog hill; (orgueil) Péj haughtiness; Mus pitch; **à la h. de** (objet) level with; (rue) opposite; (situation) Fig equal to; **il n'est pas à la h.** he isn't up to it; saut en h. Sp high jump.

haut-le-cœur ['olkœr] nm inv **avoir des h.-le-cœur** to retch, gag.

haut-le-corps ['olkɔr] nm inv (sursaut) sudden start, jump.

haut-parleur ['oparlœr] nm loudspeaker.

hâve ['ɑv] a gaunt, emaciated.

havre ['ɑvr] nm (refuge) Litt haven.

Haye (La) [la'ɛ] nf The Hague.

hayon ['ɛjɔ̃] nm (porte) Aut tailgate, hatchback.

hé ! [e] int (là) (appel) hey !; **hé ! hé !** well, well!

hebdomadaire [ɛbdɔmadɛr] a weekly; — nm (publication) weekly.

héberg/er [ebɛrʒe] vt to put up, accommodate. ◆**—ement** nm accommodation; **centre d'h.** shelter.

hébété [ebete] a dazed, stupefied.

hébreu, -x [ebrø] am Hebrew; — nm (langue) Hebrew. ◆**hébraïque** a Hebrew.

hécatombe [ekatɔ̃b] nf (great) slaughter.

hectare [ɛktar] nm hectare (= 2.47 acres).

hégémonie [eʒemɔni] nf hegemony, supremacy.

hein ! [ɛ̃] int (surprise, interrogation etc) eh!

hélas ! ['elɑs] int alas!, unfortunately.

héler ['ele] vt (taxi etc) to hail.

hélice [elis] nf Av Nau propeller.

hélicoptère [elikɔptɛr] nm helicopter. ◆**héliport** nm heliport.

hellénique [elenik] a Hellenic, Greek.

helvétique [ɛlvetik] a Swiss.

hem! [ɛm] int (a)hem!, hm!

hémicycle [emisikl] nm semicircle; *Pol Fig* French National Assembly.

hémisphère [emisfɛr] nm hemisphere.

hémorragie [emɔraʒi] nf *Méd* h(a)emorrhage; (*de capitaux*) *Com* outflow, drain.

hémorroïdes [emɔrɔid] nfpl piles, h(a)emorrhoids.

henn/ir [enir] vi (*cheval*) to neigh. ◆**—issement** nm neigh.

hep! [ɛp] int hey!, hey there!

hépatite [epatit] nf hepatitis.

herbe [ɛrb] nf grass; (*médicinale etc*) herb; **mauvaise h.** weed; **fines herbes** *Culin* herbs; **en h.** (*blés*) green; (*poète etc*) *Fig* budding. ◆**herbage** nm grassland. ◆**herbeux, -euse** a grassy. ◆**herbicide** nm weed killer. ◆**herbivore** a grass-eating, herbivorous. ◆**herbu** a grassy.

hercule [ɛrkyl] nm Hercules, strong man. ◆**herculéen, -enne** a herculean.

hérédité [eredite] nf heredity. ◆**héréditaire** a hereditary.

hérésie [erezi] nf heresy. ◆**hérétique** a heretical; – nmf heretic.

hériss/er ['erise] vt (*poils*) to bristle (up); **h. qn** (*irriter*) to ruffle s.o., ruffle s.o.'s feathers; – **se h.** vpr to bristle (up); to get ruffled. ◆**—é** a (*cheveux*) bristly; (*cactus*) prickly; **h. de** bristling with.

hérisson ['erisɔ̃] nm (*animal*) hedgehog.

hérit/er [erite] vti to inherit (**qch de qn** sth from s.o.); **h. de qch** to inherit sth. ◆**—age** nm (*biens*) inheritance; (*culturel, politique etc*) *Fig* heritage. ◆**héritier** nm heir. ◆**héritière** nf heiress.

hermétique [ɛrmetik] a hermetically sealed, airtight; (*obscur*) *Fig* impenetrable. ◆**—ment** adv hermetically.

hermine [ɛrmin] nf (*animal, fourrure*) ermine.

hernie ['erni] nf *Méd* hernia, rupture; (*de pneu*) swelling.

héron ['erɔ̃] nm (*oiseau*) heron.

héros ['ero] nm hero. ◆**héroïne** [erɔin] nf 1 (*femme*) heroine. 2 (*stupéfiant*) heroin. ◆**héroïque** [erɔik] a heroic. ◆**héroïsme** [erɔism] nm heroism.

hésit/er [ezite] vi to hesitate (**sur** over, about; **à faire** to do); (*en parlant*) to falter, hesitate. ◆**—ant** a (*personne*) hesitant; (*pas, voix*) faltering, unsteady, wavering. ◆**hésitation** nf hesitation; **avec h.** hesitantly.

hétéroclite [eterɔklit] a (*disparate*) motley.

hétérogène [eterɔʒɛn] a heterogeneous.

hêtre ['ɛtr] nm (*arbre, bois*) beech.

heu! [ø] int (*hésitation*) er!

heure [œr] nf (*mesure*) hour; (*moment*) time; **quelle h. est-il?** what time is it?; **il est six heures** it's six (o'clock); **six heures moins cinq** five to six; **six heures cinq** five past *ou Am* after six; **à l'h.** (*arriver*) on time; (*être payé*) by the hour; **dix kilomètres à l'h.** ten kilometres an hour; **à l'h. qu'il est** (by) now; **de dernière h.** (*nouvelle*) last minute; **de bonne h.** early; **à une h. avancée** at a late hour, late at night; **tout à l'h.** (*futur*) in a few moments, later; (*passé*) a moment ago; **à toute h.** (*continuellement*) at all hours; **faire des heures supplémentaires** to work *ou* do overtime; **heures creuses** off-peak *ou* slack periods; **l'h. d'affluence**, **l'h. de pointe** (*circulation etc*) rush hour; (*dans les magasins*) peak period; **l'h. de pointe** (*électricité etc*) peak period.

heureux, -euse [œrø, -øz] a happy; (*chanceux*) lucky, fortunate; (*issue, changement*) successful; (*expression, choix*) apt; **h. de qch/de voir qn** (*satisfait*) happy *ou* pleased *ou* glad about sth/to see s.o.; – adv (*vivre, mourir*) happily. ◆**heureusement** adv (*par chance*) fortunately, luckily, happily (*pour* for); (*avec succès*) successfully; (*exprimer*) aptly.

heurt ['œr] nm bump, knock; (*d'opinions etc*) *Fig* clash; **sans heurts** smoothly. ◆**heurt/er** vt (*cogner*) to knock, bump, hit (*contre* against); (*mur, piéton*) to bump into, hit; **h. qn** (*choquer*) to offend s.o., upset s.o.; – **se h. à** to bump into, hit; (*difficultés*) *Fig* to come up against. ◆**—é** a (*couleurs, tons*) clashing; (*style, rythme*) jerky. ◆**heurtoir** nm (door) knocker.

hexagone [ɛgzagɔn] nm hexagon; **l'H.** *Fig* France. ◆**hexagonal, -aux** a hexagonal; *Fig Fam* French.

hiatus [jatys] nm *Fig* hiatus, gap.

hiberner [ibɛrne] vi to hibernate. ◆**hibernation** nf hibernation.

hibou, -x ['ibu] nm owl.

hic ['ik] nm **voilà le h.** *Fam* that's the snag.

hideux, -euse ['idø, -øz] a hideous.

hier [(i)jɛr] adv & nm yesterday; **h. soir** last *ou* yesterday night, yesterday evening; **elle n'est pas née d'h.** *Fig* she wasn't born yesterday.

hiérarchie ['jerarʃi] nf hierarchy. ◆**hiérarchique** a (*ordre*) hierarchical; **par la voie h.** through the official channels. ◆**hiérarchiser** vt (*emploi, valeurs*) to grade.

hi-fi ['ifi] a inv & nf inv *Fam* hi-fi.

hilare [ilar] *a* merry. ◆**hilarant** *a* (*drôle*) hilarious. ◆**hilarité** *nf* (sudden) laughter.

hindou, -oue [ɛ̃du] *a & nmf* Hindu.

hippie [ipi] *nmf* hippie.

hippique [ipik] *a* **un concours h.** a horse show, a show-jumping event. ◆**hippodrome** *nm* racecourse, racetrack (*for horses*).

hippopotame [ipɔpɔtam] *nm* hippopotamus.

hirondelle [irɔ̃dɛl] *nf* (*oiseau*) swallow.

hirsute [irsyt] *a* (*personne, barbe*) unkempt, shaggy.

hispanique [ispanik] *a* Spanish, Hispanic.

hisser ['ise] *vt* (*voile, fardeau etc*) to hoist, raise; — **se h.** *vpr* to raise (up).

histoire [istwar] *nf* (*science, événements*) history; (*récit, mensonge*) story; (*affaire*) *Fam* business, matter; *pl* (*ennuis*) trouble; (*façons, chichis*) fuss; **toute une h.** (*problème*) quite a lot of trouble; (*chichis*) quite a lot of fuss; **h. de voir**/*etc* (so as) to see/etc; **h. de rire** for (the sake of) a laugh; **sans histoires** (*voyage etc*) uneventful. ◆**historien, -ienne** *nmf* historian. ◆**historique** *a* historical; (*lieu, événement*) historic; — *nm* **faire l'h. de** to give an historical account of.

hiver [iver] *nm* winter. ◆**hivernal, -aux** *a* (*froid etc*) winter.

HLM ['aʃɛlɛm] *nm ou f abrév* (*habitation à loyer modéré*) = council flats, *Am* = low-rent apartment building (*sponsored by government*).

hoch/er ['ɔʃe] *vt* **h. la tête** (*pour dire oui*) to nod one's head; (*pour dire non*) to shake one's head. ◆**—ement** *nm* **h. de tête** nod; shake of the head.

hochet ['ɔʃɛ] *nm* (*jouet*) rattle.

hockey ['ɔkɛ] *nm* hockey; **h. sur glace** ice hockey.

holà! ['ɔla] *int* (*arrêtez*) hold on!, stop!; (*pour appeler*) hallo!; — *nm inv* **mettre le h.** à to put a stop to.

hold-up ['ɔldœp] *nm inv* (*attaque*) holdup, stick-up.

Hollande ['ɔlɑ̃d] *nf* Holland. ◆**hollandais, -aise** *a* Dutch; — *nmf* Dutchman, Dutchwoman; — *nm* (*langue*) Dutch.

holocauste [ɔlɔkost] *nm* (*massacre*) holocaust.

homard [ɔmar] *nm* lobster.

homélie [ɔmeli] *nf* homily.

homéopathie [ɔmeɔpati] *nf* hom(o)eopathy.

homicide [ɔmisid] *nm* murder, homicide; **h. involontaire** manslaughter.

hommage [ɔmaʒ] *nm* tribute, homage (à to); *pl* (*civilités*) respects; **rendre h. à** to pay (a) tribute to, pay homage to.

homme [ɔm] *nm* man; **l'h.** (*espèce*) man(kind); **des vêtements d'h.** men's clothes; **d'h. à h.** man to man; **l'h. de la rue** *Fig* the man in the street; **h. d'affaires** businessman. ◆**h.-grenouille** *nm* (*pl* **hommes-grenouilles**) frogman.

homogène [ɔmɔʒɛn] *a* homogeneous. ◆**homogénéité** *nf* homogeneity.

homologue [ɔmɔlɔg] *a* equivalent (**de** to); — *nmf* counterpart, opposite number.

homologuer [ɔmɔlɔge] *vt* to approve *ou* recognize officially, validate.

homonyme [ɔmɔnim] *nm* (*personne, lieu*) namesake.

homosexuel, -elle [ɔmɔsɛksɥɛl] *a & nmf* homosexual. ◆**homosexualité** *nf* homosexuality.

Hongrie ['ɔ̃gri] *nf* Hungary. ◆**hongrois, -oise** *a & nmf* Hungarian; — *nm* (*langue*) Hungarian.

honnête [ɔnɛt] *a* (*intègre*) honest; (*satisfaisant, passable*) decent, fair. ◆**honnêtement** *adv* honestly; decently. ◆**honnêteté** *nf* honesty.

honneur [ɔnœr] *nm* (*dignité, faveur*) honour; (*mérite*) credit; **en l'h. de** in honour of; **faire h. à** (*sa famille etc*) to be a credit to; (*par sa présence*) to do honour to; (*promesse etc*) to honour; (*repas*) to do justice to; **en h.** (*roman etc*) in vogue; **invité d'h.** guest of honour; **membre d'h.** honorary member; **avoir la place d'h.** to have pride of place *ou* the place of honour. ◆**honorabilité** *nf* respectability. ◆**honorable** *a* honourable; (*résultat, salaire etc*) *Fig* respectable. ◆**honoraire 1** *a* (*membre*) honorary. **2** *nmpl* (*d'avocat etc*) fees. ◆**honorer** *vt* to honour (**de** with); **h. qn** (*conduite etc*) to do credit to s.o.; **s'h. d'être** to pride oneself *ou* itself on being. ◆**honorifique** *a* (*titre*) honorary.

honte ['ɔ̃t] *nf* shame; **avoir h.** to be *ou* feel ashamed (**de qch/de faire** of sth/to do, of doing); **faire h. à** to put to shame; **fausse h.** self-consciousness. ◆**honteux, -euse** *a* (*déshonorant*) shameful; (*penaud*) ashamed, shamefaced; **être h. de** to be ashamed of. ◆**honteusement** *adv* shamefully.

hop! ['ɔp] *int* **allez, h.!** jump!, move!

hôpital, -aux [ɔpital, -o] *nm* hospital; **à l'h.** in hospital, *Am* in the hospital.

hoquet ['ɔkɛ] *nm* hiccup; **le h.** (the) hiccups. ◆**hoqueter** *vi* to hiccup.

horaire [ɔrɛr] *a* (*salaire etc*) hourly; (*vitesse*) per hour; – *nm* timetable, schedule.

horde [ɔrd] *nf* (*troupe*) Péj horde.

horizon [ɔrizɔ̃] *nm* horizon; (*vue, paysage*) view; **à l'h.** on the horizon.

horizontal, -aux [ɔrizɔ̃tal, -o] *a* horizontal. ◆**—ement** *adv* horizontally.

horloge [ɔrlɔʒ] *nf* clock. ◆**horloger, -ère** *nmf* watchmaker. ◆**horlogerie** *nf* (*magasin*) watchmaker's (shop); (*industrie*) watchmaking.

hormis [ɔrmi] *prép* Litt save, except (for).

hormone [ɔrmɔn] *nf* hormone. ◆**hormonal, -aux** *a* (*traitement etc*) hormone-.

horoscope [ɔrɔskɔp] *nm* horoscope.

horreur [ɔrœr] *nf* horror; *pl* (*propos*) horrible things; **faire h. à** to disgust; **avoir h. de** to hate, loathe. ◆**horrible** *a* horrible, awful. ◆**horriblement** *adv* horribly. ◆**horrifiant** *a* horrifying, horrific. ◆**horrifié** *a* horrified.

horripiler [ɔripile] *vt* to exasperate.

hors [ɔr] *prép* **h. de** (*maison, boîte etc*) outside, out of; (*danger, haleine etc*) Fig out of; **h. de doute** beyond doubt; **h. de soi** (*furieux*) beside oneself; **être h. jeu** Fb to be offside. ◆**h.-bord** *nm inv* speedboat; **moteur h.-bord** outboard motor. ◆**h.-concours** *a inv* non-competing. ◆**h.-d'œuvre** *nm inv* Culin starter, hors-d'œuvre. ◆**h.-jeu** *nm inv* Fb offside. ◆**h.-la-loi** *nm inv* outlaw. ◆**h.-taxe** *a inv* (*magasin, objet*) duty-free.

hortensia [ɔrtɑ̃sja] *nm* (*arbrisseau*) hydrangea.

horticole [ɔrtikɔl] *a* horticultural. ◆**horticulteur, -trice** *nmf* horticulturalist. ◆**horticulture** *nf* horticulture.

hospice [ɔspis] *nm* (*pour vieillards*) geriatric hospital.

hospitalier, -ière [ɔspitalje, -jɛr] *a* **1** (*accueillant*) hospitable. **2** (*personnel etc*) Méd hospital-. ◆**hospitaliser** *vt* to hospitalize. ◆**hospitalité** *nf* hospitality.

hostie [ɔsti] *nf* (*pain*) Rel host.

hostile [ɔstil] *a* hostile (**à** à, towards). ◆**hostilité** *nf* hostility (**envers** to, towards); *pl* Mil hostilities.

hôte [ot] *nm* (*maître*) host. *nmf* (*invité*) guest. ◆**hôtesse** *nf* hostess; **h. (de l'air)** (air) hostess.

hôtel [otel] *nm* hotel; **h. particulier** mansion, town house; **h. de ville** town hall; **h. des ventes** auction rooms. ◆**hôtelier, -ière** *nmf* hotel-keeper, hotelier; – *a* (*industrie etc*) hotel-. ◆**hôtellerie** *nf* **1** (*auberge*) inn, hostelry. **2** (*métier*) hotel trade.

hotte [ɔt] *nf* **1** (*panier*) basket (*carried on back*). **2** (*de cheminée etc*) hood.

houblon [ublɔ̃] *nm* **le h.** Bot hops.

houille [uj] *nf* coal; **h. blanche** hydro-electric power. ◆**houiller, -ère** *a* (*bassin, industrie*) coal-; – *nf* coalmine, colliery.

houle [ul] *nf* (*de mer*) swell, surge. ◆**houleux, -euse** *a* (*mer*) rough; (*réunion etc*) Fig stormy.

houppette [upɛt] *nf* powder puff.

hourra ['ura] *nm* & *int* hurray, hurrah.

houspiller [uspije] *vt* to scold, upbraid.

housse [us] *nf* (*protective*) cover.

houx [u] *nm* holly.

hublot [yblo] *nm* Nau Av porthole.

huche [yʃ] *nf* **h. à pain** bread box *ou* chest.

hue! [y] *int* gee up! (*to horse*).

huer ['ɥe] *vt* to boo. ◆**huées** *nfpl* boos.

huile [ɥil] *nf* **1** oil; **peinture à l'h.** oil painting. **2** (*personnage*) Fam big shot. ◆**huiler** *vt* to oil. ◆**huileux, -euse** *a* oily.

huis [ɥi] *nm* **à h. clos** Jur in camera.

huissier [ɥisje] *nm* (*introducteur*) usher; (*officier*) Jur bailiff.

huit [ɥit] *a* (['ɥi] *before consonant*) eight; **h. jours a week**; – *nm* eight. ◆**huitaine** *nf* (*about*) eight; (*semaine*) week. ◆**huitième** *a* & *nmf* eighth; **un h.** an eighth.

huître [ɥitr] *nf* oyster.

hululer [ylyle] *vi* (*hibou*) to hoot.

humain [ymɛ̃] *a* human; (*compatissant*) humane; – *nmpl* humans. ◆**humainement** *adv* (*possible etc*) humanly; (*avec humanité*) humanely. ◆**humaniser** *vt* (*prison, ville etc*) to humanize, make more humane. ◆**humanitaire** *a* humanitarian. ◆**humanité** *nf* (*genre humain, sentiment*) humanity.

humble [œ̃bl] *a* humble. ◆**humblement** *adv* humbly.

humecter [ymɛkte] *vt* to moisten, damp(en).

humer ['yme] *vt* (*respirer*) to breathe in; (*sentir*) to smell.

humeur [ymœr] *nf* (*caprice*) mood, humour; (*caractère*) temperament; (*irritation*) bad temper; **bonne h.** (*gaieté*) good humour; **de bonne/mauvaise h.** in a good/bad mood *ou* humour; **égalité d'h.** evenness of temper.

humide [ymid] *a* damp, wet; (*saison, route*) wet; (*main, yeux*) moist; **climat/temps h.** (*chaud*) humid climate/weather; (*froid, pluvieux*) damp *ou* wet climate/weather. ◆**humidifier** *vt* to humidify. ◆**humidité** *nf* humidity; (*plutôt froide*) damp(ness); (*vapeur*) moisture.

humili/er [ymilje] *vt* to humiliate, humble.

◆—ant a humiliating. ◆humiliation nf humiliation. ◆humilité nf humility.

humour [ymur] nm humour; avoir de l'h. ou beaucoup d'h. ou le sens de l'h. to have a sense of humour. ◆humoriste nmf humorist. ◆humoristique a (livre, ton etc) humorous.

huppé ['ype] a (riche) Fam high-class, posh.

hurl/er ['yrle] vi (loup, vent) to howl; (personne) to scream, yell; (− vt (slogans, injures etc) to scream, yell. ◆—ement nm howl; scream, yell.

hurluberlu [yrlyberly] nm (personne) scatterbrain.

hutte ['yt] nf hut.

hybride [ibrid] a & nm hybrid.

hydrater [idrate] vt (peau) to moisturize; crème hydratante moisturizing cream.

hydraulique [idrolik] a hydraulic.

hydravion [idravjɔ̃] nm seaplane.

hydro-électrique [idroelɛktrik] a hydroelectric.

hydrogène [idrɔʒɛn] nm Ch hydrogen.

hydrophile [idrɔfil] a coton h. cotton wool, Am (absorbent) cotton.

hyène [jɛn] nf (animal) hyena.

hygiaphone [iʒjafɔn] nm (hygienic) grill.

hygiène [iʒjɛn] nf hygiene. ◆hygiénique a hygienic; (promenade) healthy; (serviette, conditions) sanitary; papier h. toilet paper.

hymne [imn] nm Rel Littér hymn; h. national national anthem.

hyper- [iper] préf hyper-.

hypermarché [ipermarʃe] nm hypermarket.

hypertension [ipertɑ̃sjɔ̃] nf high blood pressure.

hypnose [ipnoz] nf hypnosis. ◆hypnotique a hypnotic. ◆hypnotiser vt to hypnotize. ◆hypnotiseur nm hypnotist. ◆hypnotisme nm hypnotism.

hypocrisie [ipɔkrizi] nf hypocrisy. ◆hypocrite a hypocritical; − nmf hypocrite.

hypodermique [ipɔdermik] a hypodermic.

hypothèque [ipɔtɛk] nf mortgage. ◆hypothéquer (maison, avenir) to mortgage.

hypothèse [ipɔtɛz] nf assumption; (en sciences) hypothesis; dans l'h. où ... supposing (that) .... ◆hypothétique a hypothetical.

hystérie [isteri] nf hysteria. ◆hystérique a hysterical.

I

I, i [i] nm I, i.

iceberg [isbɛrg] nm iceberg.

ici [isi] adv here; par i. (passer) this way; (habiter) around here, hereabouts; jusqu'i. (temps) up to now; (lieu) as far as this ou here; d'i. à mardi by Tuesday, between now and Tuesday; d'i. à une semaine within a week; d'i. peu before long; i. Dupont Tél this is Dupont, Dupont here; je ne suis pas d'i. I'm a stranger around here; les gens d'i. the people (from) around here, the locals. ◆i.-bas adv on earth.

icône [ikon] nf Rel icon.

idéal, -aux [ideal, -o] a & nm ideal; l'i. (valeurs spirituelles) ideals; c'est l'i. Fam that's the ideal thing. ◆idéalement adv ideally. ◆idéaliser vt to idealize. ◆idéalisme nm idealism. ◆idéaliste a idealistic; − nmf idealist.

idée [ide] nf idea (de of, que that); changer d'i. to change one's mind; il m'est venu à l'i. que it occurred to me that; se faire une i. de (rêve) to imagine; (concept) to get ou have

an idea of; avoir dans l'i. de faire to have it in mind to do; i. fixe obsession.

idem [idɛm] adv ditto.

identifier [idɑ̃tifje] vt to identify (à, avec with). ◆identification nf identification. ◆identique a identical (à to, with). ◆identité nf identity; carte d'i identity card.

idéologie [ideɔlɔʒi] nf ideology. ◆idéologique a ideological.

idiome [idjom] nm (langue) idiom. ◆idiomatique a idiomatic.

idiot, -ote [idjo, -ɔt] a idiotic, silly; − nmf idiot. ◆idiotement adv idiotically. ◆idiotie [-osi] nf (état) idiocy; une i. an idiotic ou silly thing.

idole [idɔl] nm idol. ◆idolâtrer vt to idolize.

idylle [idil] nf (amourette) romance.

idyllique [idilik] a (merveilleux) idyllic.

if [if] nm yew (tree).

igloo [iglu] nm igloo.

ignare [iɲar] a Péj ignorant; − nmf ignoramus.

ignifugé [iɲifyʒe] a fireproof(ed).

ignoble [iɲɔbl] a vile, revolting.

ignorant [iɲɔrɑ̃] a ignorant (**de** of). **◆ignorance** nf ignorance. **◆ignor/er** vt not to know, be ignorant of; **j'ignore si** I don't know if; **i. qn** (être indifférent à) to ignore s.o., cold-shoulder s.o. **◆—é a** (inconnu) unknown.

il [il] pron (personne) he; (chose, animal) it; **il est he is**; **it is**; **il pleut** it's raining; **il est vrai que** it's true that; **il y a** there is; pl there are; **il y a six ans** (temps écoulé) six years ago; **il y a une heure qu'il travaille** (durée) he's been working for an hour; **qu'est-ce qu'il y a?** what's the matter?, what's wrong?; **il n'y a pas de quoi!** don't mention it!; **il doit/peut y avoir** there must/may be.

île [il] nf island; **les îles Britanniques** the British Isles.

illégal, -aux [ilegal, -o] a illegal. **◆illégalité** nf illegality.

illégitime [ileʒitim] a (enfant, revendication) illegitimate; (non fondé) unfounded.

illettré, -ée [iletre] a & nmf illiterate.

illicite [ilisit] a unlawful, illicit.

illico [iliko] adv **i. (presto)** Fam straightaway.

illimité [ilimite] a unlimited.

illisible [ilizibl] a (écriture) illegible; (livre) unreadable.

illogique [ilɔʒik] a illogical.

illumin/er [ilymine] vt to light up, illuminate; **— s'i.** vpr (visage, personne, ciel) to light up. **◆—é a** (monument) floodlit, lit up. **◆illumination** nf (action, lumière) illumination.

illusion [ilyzjɔ̃] nf illusion (sur about); **se faire des illusions** to delude oneself. **◆s'illusionner** vpr to delude oneself (sur about). **◆illusionniste** nmf conjurer. **◆illusoire** a illusory, illusive.

illustre [ilystr] a famous, illustrious.

illustr/er [ilystre] vt (d'images, par des exemples) to illustrate (**de** with); **— s'i.** vpr to become famous. **◆—é a** (livre, magazine) illustrated; **— nm** (périodique) comic. **◆illustration** nf illustration.

îlot [ilo] nm **1** (île) small island. **2** (maisons) block.

ils [il] pron they; **ils sont** they are.

image [imaʒ] nf picture; (ressemblance, symbole) image; (dans une glace) reflection; **i. de marque** (de firme etc) (public) image. **◆imagé a** (style) colourful, full of imagery.

imagination [imaʒinasjɔ̃] nf imagination; pl (chimères) imaginings.

imaginer [imaʒine] vt (envisager, supposer) to imagine; (inventer) to devise; **— s'i.** (se figurer) to imagine (**que** that); (se voir) to imagine oneself. **◆imaginable** a imaginable. **◆imaginaire** a imaginary. **◆imaginatif, -ive** a imaginative.

imbattable [ɛ̃batabl] a unbeatable.

imbécile [ɛ̃besil] a idiotic; **— nmf** imbecile, idiot. **◆imbécillité** nf (état) imbecility; **une i.** (action, parole) an idiotic thing.

imbiber [ɛ̃bibe] vt to soak (**de** with, in); **— s'i.** vpr to become soaked.

imbriquer (s') [sɛ̃brike] vpr (questions etc) to overlap, be bound up with each other.

imbroglio [ɛ̃brɔljo] nm muddle, foul-up.

imbu [ɛ̃by] a **i. de** imbued with.

imbuvable [ɛ̃byvabl] a undrinkable; (personne) Fig insufferable.

imiter [imite] vt to imitate; (contrefaire) to forge; **i. qn** (pour rire) to mimic s.o., take s.o. off; (faire comme) to do the same as s.o., follow suit. **◆imitateur, -trice** nmf imitator; (artiste) Th impersonator, mimic. **◆imitatif, -ive** a imitative. **◆imitation** nf imitation.

immaculé [imakyle] a (sans tache, sans péché) immaculate.

immangeable [ɛ̃mɑ̃ʒabl] a inedible.

immanquable [ɛ̃mɑ̃kabl] a inevitable.

immatriculer [imatrikyle] vt to register; **se faire i.** to register. **◆immatriculation** nf registration.

immédiat [imedja] a immediate; **— nm dans l'i.** for the time being. **◆immédiatement** adv immediately.

immense [imɑ̃s] a immense, vast. **◆immensément** adv immensely. **◆immensité** nf immensity, vastness.

immerger [imerʒe] vt to immerse, put under water; **— s'i.** vpr (sous-marin) to submerge. **◆immersion** nf immersion; submersion.

immettable [ɛ̃mɛtabl] a (vêtement) unfit to be worn.

immeuble [imœbl] nm building; (d'habitation) block of flats, Am apartment building; (de bureaux) office block.

immigr/er [imigre] vi to immigrate. **◆—ant, -ante** nmf immigrant. **◆—é, -ée** a & nmf immigrant. **◆immigration** nf immigration.

imminent [iminɑ̃] a imminent. **◆imminence** nf imminence.

immiscer (s') [simise] vpr to interfere (dans in).

immobile [imɔbil] a still, motionless. **◆immobiliser** vt to immobilize; (arrêter) to stop; **— s'i.** *vpr* to stop, come to a standstill. ◆**immobilité** *nf* stillness; *(inactivité)* immobility.

immobilier, -ière [iməbilje, -jɛr] *a (vente)* property-; *(société)* construction-; **agent i.** estate agent, *Am* real estate agent.

immodéré [imɔdere] *a* immoderate.

immonde [imɔ̃d] *a* filthy. ◆**immondices** *nfpl* refuse, rubbish.

immoral, -aux [imɔral, -o] *a* immoral. ◆**immoralité** *nf* immorality.

immortel, -elle [imɔrtɛl] *a* immortal. ◆**immortaliser** *vt* to immortalize. ◆**immortalité** *nf* immortality.

immuable [imɥabl] *a* immutable, unchanging.

immuniser [imynize] *vt* to immunize **(contre** against); **immunisé contre** *(à l'abri de)* *Méd* & *Fig* immune to *ou* from. ◆**immunitaire** *(déficience etc)* *Méd* immune. ◆**immunité** *nf* immunity.

impact [ɛ̃pakt] *nm* impact **(sur** on).

impair [ɛ̃pɛr] **1** *a (nombre)* odd, uneven. **2** *nm (gaffe)* blunder.

imparable [ɛ̃parabl] *a (coup etc)* unavoidable.

impardonnable [ɛ̃pardɔnabl] *a* unforgivable.

imparfait [ɛ̃parfɛ] **1** *a (connaissance etc)* imperfect. **2** *nm (temps)* *Gram* imperfect.

impartial, -aux [ɛ̃parsjal, -o] *a* impartial, unbiased. ◆**impartialité** *nf* impartiality.

impartir [ɛ̃partir] *vt* to grant (à to).

impasse [ɛ̃pas] *nf (rue)* dead end, blind alley; *(situation)* *Fig* impasse; **dans l'i.** *(négociations)* in deadlock.

impassible [ɛ̃pasibl] *a* impassive, unmoved. ◆**impassibilité** *nf* impassiveness.

impatient [ɛ̃pasjɑ̃] *a* impatient; **i. de faire** eager *ou* impatient to do. ◆**impatiemment** [-amã] *adv* impatiently. ◆**impatience** *nf* impatience. ◆**impatienter** *vt* to annoy, make impatient; **— s'i.** *vpr* to get impatient.

impayable [ɛ̃pɛjabl] *a (comique)* *Fam* hilarious, priceless.

impayé [ɛ̃pɛje] *a* unpaid.

impeccable [ɛ̃pekabl] *a* impeccable, immaculate. ◆**—ment** [-amã] *adv* impeccably, immaculately.

impénétrable [ɛ̃penetrabl] *a (forêt, mystère etc)* impenetrable.

impénitent [ɛ̃penitã] *a* unrepentant.

impensable [ɛ̃pãsabl] *a* unthinkable.

imper [ɛ̃pɛr] *nm* *Fam* raincoat, mac.

impératif, -ive [ɛ̃peratif, -iv] *a (consigne,*

ton) imperative; **—** *nm (mode)* *Gram* imperative.

impératrice [ɛ̃peratris] *nf* empress.

imperceptible [ɛ̃persɛptibl] *a* imperceptible (à to).

imperfection [ɛ̃perfɛksjɔ̃] *nf* imperfection.

impérial, -aux [ɛ̃perjal, -o] *a* imperial. ◆**impérialisme** *nm* imperialism.

impériale [ɛ̃perjal] *nf (d'autobus)* top deck.

impérieux, -euse [ɛ̃perjø, -øz] *a (autoritaire)* imperious; *(besoin)* pressing, imperative.

imperméable [ɛ̃permeabl] **1** *a* impervious (à to); *(manteau, tissu)* waterproof. **2** *nm* raincoat, mackintosh. ◆**imperméabilisé** *a* waterproof.

impersonnel, -elle [ɛ̃persɔnɛl] *a* impersonal.

impertinent [ɛ̃pɛrtinɑ̃] *a* impertinent **(envers** to). ◆**impertinence** *nf* impertinence.

imperturbable [ɛ̃pɛrtyrbabl] *a* unruffled, imperturbable.

impétueux, -euse [ɛ̃petɥø, -øz] *a* impetuous. ◆**impétuosité** *nf* impetuosity.

impitoyable [ɛ̃pitwajabl] *a* ruthless, pitiless, merciless.

implacable [ɛ̃plakabl] *a* implacable, relentless.

implanter [ɛ̃plãte] *vt (industrie, mode etc)* to establish; **— s'i.** *vpr* to become established. ◆**implantation** *nf* establishment.

implicite [ɛ̃plisit] *a* implicit. ◆**—ment** *adv* implicitly.

impliquer [ɛ̃plike] *vt (entraîner)* to imply; **i. que** *(supposer)* to imply that; **i. qn** *(engager)* to implicate s.o. **(dans** in). ◆**implication** *nf (conséquence, participation)* implication.

implorer [ɛ̃plɔre] *vt* to implore **(qn de faire** s.o. to do).

impoli [ɛ̃pɔli] *a* impolite, rude. ◆**impolitesse** *nf* impoliteness; **une i.** an act of rudeness.

impopulaire [ɛ̃pɔpylɛr] *a* unpopular.

important [ɛ̃pɔrtɑ̃] *a (personnage, événement etc)* important; *(quantité, somme etc)* considerable, big, great; **—** *nm* **l'i., c'est de ... the** important thing is to .... ◆**importance** *nf (gravité etc)* significance; *(taille)* size; *(de dégâts)* extent; **ça n'a pas d'i.** it doesn't matter.

importer [ɛ̃pɔrte] **1** *v imp* to matter, be important (à to); **il importe de faire** it's important to do; **peu importe, n'importe** it doesn't matter; **n'importe qui/quoi/ où/quand/comment** anyone/anything/ anywhere/any time/anyhow. **2** *vt (marchandises etc)* to import **(de** from). ◆**im-**

portateur, -trice nmf importer; – a importing. **◆importation** nf (objet) import; (action) import(ing), importation; **d'i.** (article) imported.

importun, -une [ɛ̃pɔrtœ̃, -yn] a a troublesome, intrusive; – nmf nuisance, intruder. **◆importuner** vt to inconvenience, trouble.

impos/er [ɛ̃poze] 1 vt to impose, enforce (à on); (exiger) to demand; (respect) to command; – vi **en i. à qn** to impress s.o., command respect from s.o.; – **s'i.** vpr (chez qn) Péj to impose; (s'affirmer) to assert oneself, compel recognition; (aller de soi) to stand out; (être nécessaire) to be essential. 2 vt Fin to tax. **◆–ant** a imposing. **◆–able** a Fin taxable. **◆imposition** nf Fin taxation.

impossible [ɛ̃pɔsibl] a impossible (à faire to do); **il (nous) est i.** de faire it is impossible (for us) to do; **il est i. que** (+ sub) it is impossible that; **ça m'est i.** I cannot possibly; – nm **faire l'i.** to do the impossible. **◆impossibilité** nf impossibility.

imposteur [ɛ̃pɔstœr] nm impostor. **◆imposture** nf deception.

impôt [ɛ̃po] nm tax; pl (contributions) (income) tax, taxes; **i. sur le revenu** income tax.

impotent, -ente [ɛ̃pɔtɑ̃, -ɑ̃t] a crippled, disabled; – nmf cripple, invalid.

impraticable [ɛ̃pratikabl] a (projet etc) impracticable; (chemin etc) impassable.

imprécis [ɛ̃presi] a imprecise. **◆imprécision** nf lack of precision.

imprégner [ɛ̃preɲe] vt to saturate, impregnate (de with); – **s'i.** vpr to become saturated ou impregnated (de with); **imprégné de** (idées) imbued ou infused with. **◆imprégnation** nf saturation.

imprenable [ɛ̃prənabl] a Mil impregnable.

impresario [ɛ̃presarjo] nm (business) manager, impresario.

impression [ɛ̃presjɔ̃] nf 1 impression; **avoir l'i. que** to have the feeling ou impression that; **être sous l'impression que** under the impression that; **faire une bonne i. à qn** to make a good impression on s.o. 2 Typ printing. **impressionn/er** [ɛ̃presjɔne] vt (influencer) to impress; (émouvoir, troubler) to make a strong impression on. **◆–ant** a impressive. **◆–able** a impressionable.

imprévisible [ɛ̃previzibl] a unforeseeable. **◆imprévoyance** nf lack of foresight. **◆imprévoyant** a shortsighted. **◆imprévu** a unexpected, unforeseen; – nm **en cas d'i.** in case of anything unexpected.

imprim/er [ɛ̃prime] vt 1 (livre etc) to print;

(trace) to impress (dans in); (cachet) to stamp. 2 (communiquer) Tech to impart (à to). **◆–ante** nf (d'ordinateur) printer. **◆–é** nm (formulaire) printed form; – nm(pl) (par la poste) printed matter. **◆imprimerie** nf (technique) printing; (lieu) printing works. **◆imprimeur** nm printer.

improbable [ɛ̃prɔbabl] a improbable, unlikely. **◆improbabilité** nf improbability, unlikelihood.

impromptu [ɛ̃prɔ̃pty] a & adv impromptu.

impropre [ɛ̃prɔpr] a inappropriate; **i. à qch** unfit for sth. **◆impropriété** nf (incorrection) Ling impropriety.

improviser [ɛ̃prɔvize] vti to improvise. **◆improvisation** nf improvisation.

improviste (à l') [alɛ̃prɔvist] adv unexpectedly; **une visite à l'i.** an unexpected visit; **prendre qn à l'i.** to catch s.o. unawares.

imprudent [ɛ̃prydɑ̃] a (personne, action) careless, rash; **il est i. de it** is unwise to. **◆imprudemment** [-amɑ̃] adv carelessly. **◆imprudence** nf carelessness; **une i.** an act of carelessness.

impudent [ɛ̃pydɑ̃] a impudent **◆impudence** nf impudence.

impudique [ɛ̃pydik] a lewd.

impuissant [ɛ̃pɥisɑ̃] a helpless; Méd impotent; **i. à faire** powerless to do. **◆impuissance** nf helplessness; Méd impotence.

impulsif, -ive [ɛ̃pylsif, -iv] a impulsive. **◆impulsion** nf impulse; **donner une i. à** (élan) Fig to give an impetus ou impulse to.

impunément [ɛ̃pynemɑ̃] adv with impunity. **◆impuni** a unpunished.

impur [ɛ̃pyr] a impure. **◆impureté** nf impurity.

imputer [ɛ̃pyte] vt to attribute, impute (à to); (affecter) Fin to charge (à to). **◆imputable** a attributable (à to). **◆imputation** nf Jur accusation.

inabordable [inabɔrdabl] a (lieu) inaccessible; (personne) unapproachable; (prix) prohibitive.

inacceptable [inaksɛptabl] a unacceptable.

inaccessible [inaksesibl] a inaccessible.

inaccoutumé [inakutyme] a unusual, unaccustomed.

inachevé [inaʃve] a unfinished.

inactif, -ive [inaktif, -iv] a inactive. **◆inaction** nf inactivity, inaction. **◆inactivité** nf inactivity.

inadapté, -ée [inadapte] a & nmf maladjusted (person). **◆inadaptation** nf maladjustment.

inadmissible [inadmisibl] a unacceptable, inadmissible.

inadvertance (par) [parinadvertãs] adv inadvertently.

inaltérable [inalterabl] a (couleur) fast; (sentiment) unchanging.

inamical, -aux [inamikal, -o] a unfriendly.

inanimé [inanime] a (mort) lifeless; (évanoui) unconscious; (matière) inanimate.

inanité [inanite] nf (vanité) futility.

inanition [inanisjõ] nf **mourir d'i.** to die of starvation.

inaperçu [inapersy] a **passer i.** to go unnoticed.

inapplicable [inaplikabl] a inapplicable (à to).

inappliqué [inaplike] a (élève etc) inattentive.

inappréciable [inapresjabl] a invaluable.

inapte [inapt] a unsuited (à qch to sth), inept (à qch at sth); Mil unfit ◆**inaptitude** nf ineptitude, incapacity.

inarticulé [inartikyle] a (son) inarticulate.

inattaquable [inatakabl] a unassailable.

inattendu [inatãdy] a unexpected.

inattentif, -ive [inatãtif, -iv] a inattentive, careless; **i. à** (soucis, danger etc) heedless of. ◆**inattention** nf lack of attention; **dans un moment d'i.** in a moment of distraction.

inaudible [inodibl] a inaudible.

inaugurer [inogyre] vt (politique, édifice) to inaugurate; (école, congrès) to open, inaugurate; (statue) to unveil. ◆**inaugural, -aux** a inaugural. ◆**inauguration** nf inauguration; opening; unveiling.

inauthentique [inotãtik] a not authentic.

inavouable [inavwabl] a shameful.

incalculable [ẽkalkylabl] a incalculable.

incandescent [ẽkãdesã] a incandescent.

incapable [ẽkapabl] a incapable; **i. de faire** unable to do, incapable of doing; — nmf (personne) incompetent. ◆**incapacité** nf incapacity, inability (**de faire** to do); Méd disability, incapacity.

incarcérer [ẽkarsere] vt to incarcerate. ◆**incarcération** nf incarceration.

incarné [ẽkarne] a (ongle) ingrown.

incarner [ẽkarne] vt to embody, incarnate. ◆**incarnation** nf embodiment, incarnation.

incartade [ẽkartad] nf indiscretion, prank.

incassable [ẽkasabl] a unbreakable.

incendie [ẽsãdi] nm fire; (guerre) Fig conflagration. ◆**incendiaire** nmf arsonist; — a (bombe) incendiary; (discours) inflammatory. ◆**incendier** vt to set fire to, set on fire.

incertain [ẽsertẽ] a uncertain; (temps) unsettled; (entreprise) chancy; (contour) indistinct. ◆**incertitude** nf uncertainty.

incessamment [ẽsesamã] adv without delay, shortly.

incessant [ẽsesã] a incessant.

inceste [ẽsest] nm incest. ◆**incestueux, -euse** a incestuous.

inchangé [ẽ∫ãʒe] a unchanged.

incidence [ẽsidãs] nf (influence) effect.

incident [ẽsidã] nm incident; (accroc) hitch.

incinérer [ẽsinere] vt (ordures) to incinerate; (cadavre) to cremate. ◆**incinération** nf incineration; cremation.

inciser [ẽsize] vt to make an incision in. ◆**incision** nf (entaille) incision.

incisif, -ive¹ [ẽsizif, -iv] a incisive, sharp.

incisive² [ẽsiziv] nf (dent) incisor.

inciter [ẽsite] vt to urge, incite (**à faire** to do). ◆**incitation** nf incitement (**à** to).

incliner [ẽkline] vt (courber) to bend; (pencher) to tilt, incline; **i. la tête** (approuver) to nod one's head; (révérence) to bow (one's head); **i. qn à faire** to make s.o. inclined to do, incline s.o. to do; — vi **i. à** to be inclined towards; — **s'i.** vpr (se courber) to bow (down); (s'avouer vaincu) to admit defeat; (chemin) to slope down. ◆**inclinaison** nf incline, slope. ◆**inclination** nf (goût) inclination; (de tête) nod, (révérence) bow.

incl/ure° [ẽklyr] vt to include; (enfermer) to enclose. ◆**—us** a included; **du quatre jusqu'au dix mai i.** from the fourth to the tenth of May inclusive; **jusqu'à lundi i.** up to and including (next) Monday. ◆**inclusion** nf inclusion. ◆**inclusivement** adv inclusively.

incognito [ẽkɔɲito] adv incognito.

incohérent [ẽkɔerã] a incoherent. ◆**incohérence** nf incoherence.

incollable [ẽkɔlabl] a Fam infallible, unable to be caught out.

incolore [ẽkɔlɔr] a colourless; (verre, vernis) clear.

incomber [ẽkɔbe] vi **i. à qn** (devoir) to fall to s.o.; **il lui incombe de faire** it's his ou her duty ou responsiblity to do.

incommode [ẽkɔmɔd] a awkward. ◆**incommodité** nf awkwardness.

incommod/er [ẽkɔmɔde] vt to bother, annoy. ◆**—ant** a annoying.

incomparable [ẽkɔparabl] a incomparable.

incompatible [ẽkɔpatibl] a incompatible, inconsistent (**avec** with). ◆**incompatibilité** nf incompatibility, inconsistency.

incompétent [ɛ̃kɔpetɑ̃] a incompetent. ◆**incompétence** nf incompetence.

incomplet, -ète [ɛ̃kɔplɛ, -ɛt] a incomplete; (fragmentaire) scrappy, sketchy.

incompréhensible [ɛ̃kɔpreɑsibl] a incomprehensible. ◆**incompréhensif, -ive** a uncomprehending, lacking understanding. ◆**incompréhension** nf lack of understanding. ◆**incompris** a misunderstood.

inconcevable [ɛ̃kɔsvabl] a inconceivable.

inconciliable [ɛ̃kɔsiljabl] a irreconcilable.

inconditionnel, -elle [ɛ̃kɔdisjɔnɛl] a unconditional.

inconfort [ɛ̃kɔfɔr] nm lack of comfort. ◆**inconfortable** a uncomfortable.

incongru [ɛ̃kɔgry] a unseemly, incongruous.

inconnu, -ue [ɛ̃kɔny] a unknown (à to); – nmf (étranger) stranger; (auteur) unknown; – nm l'i. the unknown; – nf Math unknown (quantity).

inconscient [ɛ̃kɔsjɑ̃] a unconscious (de of); (irréfléchi) thoughtless, senseless; – nm l'i. Psy the unconscious. ◆**inconsciemment** [-amɑ̃] adv unconsciously. ◆**inconscience** nf (physique) unconsciousness; (irréflexion) utter thoughtlessness.

inconséquence [ɛ̃kɔsekɑ̃s] nf inconsistency.

inconsidéré [ɛ̃kɔsidere] a thoughtless.

inconsolable [ɛ̃kɔsɔlabl] a inconsolable.

inconstant [ɛ̃kɔstɑ̃] a fickle. ◆**inconstance** nf fickleness.

incontestable [ɛ̃kɔtɛstabl] a undeniable, indisputable. ◆**incontesté** a undisputed.

incontinent [ɛ̃kɔtinɑ̃] a incontinent.

incontrôlable [ɛ̃kɔtrole] a unchecked. ◆**incontrôlable** a unverifiable.

inconvenant [ɛ̃kɔvnɑ̃] a improper. ◆**inconvenance** nf impropriety.

inconvénient [ɛ̃kɔvenjɑ̃] nm (désavantage) drawback; (risque) risk; (objection) objection.

incorporer [ɛ̃kɔrpɔre] vt (introduire, admettre) to incorporate (dans into); (ingrédient) to blend (à with); Mil to enrol. ◆**incorporation** nf incorporation (de of); Mil enrolment.

incorrect [ɛ̃kɔrɛkt] a (inexact) incorrect; (inconvenant) improper; (grossier) impolite. ◆**incorrection** nf (faute) impropriety, error; (inconvenance) impropriety; une i. (grossièreté) an impolite word ou act.

incorrigible [ɛ̃kɔriʒibl] a incorrigible.

incorruptible [ɛ̃kɔryptibl] a incorruptible.

incrédule [ɛ̃kredyl] a incredulous. ◆**incrédulité** nf disbelief, incredulity.

increvable [ɛ̃krəvabl] a (robuste) Fam tireless.

incriminer [ɛ̃krimine] vt to incriminate.

incroyable [ɛ̃krwajabl] a incredible, unbelievable. ◆**incroyablement** adv incredibly. ◆**incroyant, -ante** a unbelieving; – nmf unbeliever.

incrusté [ɛ̃kryste] a (de tartre) encrusted; i. de (orné) inlaid with. ◆**incrustation** nf (ornement) inlay; (action) inlaying.

incruster (s') [sɛ̃kryste] vpr (chez qn) Fig to dig oneself in, be difficult to get rid of.

incubation [ɛ̃kybasjɔ̃] nf incubation.

inculp/er [ɛ̃kylpe] vt Jur to charge (de with), indict (de for). ◆**-é, -ée** nmf l'i. the accused. ◆**inculpation** nf charge, indictment.

inculquer [ɛ̃kylke] vt to instil (à into).

inculte [ɛ̃kylt] a (terre) uncultivated; (personne) uneducated.

incurable [ɛ̃kyrabl] a incurable.

incursion [ɛ̃kyrsjɔ̃] nf incursion, inroad (dans into).

incurver [ɛ̃kyrve] vt to curve.

Inde [ɛ̃d] nf India.

indécent [ɛ̃desɑ̃] a indecent. ◆**indécemment** [-amɑ̃] adv indecently. ◆**indécence** nf indecency.

indéchiffrable [ɛ̃deʃifrabl] a undecipherable.

indécis [ɛ̃desi] a (victoire, résultat) undecided; (indistinct) vague; être i. (hésiter) to be undecided; (de tempérament) to be indecisive ou irresolute. ◆**indécision** nf indecisiveness, indecision.

indéfectible [ɛ̃defɛktibl] a unfailing.

indéfendable [ɛ̃defɑ̃dabl] a indefensible.

indéfini [ɛ̃defini] a (indéterminé) indefinite; (imprécis) undefined. ◆**indéfiniment** adv indefinitely. ◆**indéfinissable** a indefinable.

indéformable [ɛ̃defɔrmabl] a (vêtement) which keeps its shape.

indélébile [ɛ̃delebil] a (encre, souvenir) indelible.

indélicat [ɛ̃delika] a (grossier) indelicate; (malhonnête) unscrupulous.

indemne [ɛ̃dɛmn] a unhurt, unscathed.

indemniser [ɛ̃dɛmnize] vt to indemnify, compensate (de for). ◆**indemnisation** nf compensation. ◆**indemnité** nf (dédommagement) indemnity; (allocation) allowance.

indémontable [ɛ̃demɔ̃tabl] a that cannot be taken apart.

indéniable [ɛ̃denjabl] a undeniable.

indépendant [ɛ̃depɑ̃dɑ̃] a independent (de

of); (*chambre*) self-contained; (*journaliste*) freelance. ◆**indépendamment** *adv* independently (**de** of); **i. de** (*sans aucun égard à*) apart from. ◆**indépendance** *nf* independence.

indescriptible [ɛ̃dɛskriptibl] *a* indescribable.

indésirable [ɛ̃dezirabl] *a* & *nmf* undesirable.

indestructible [ɛ̃dɛstryktibl] *a* indestructible.

indéterminé [ɛ̃detɛrmine] *a* indeterminate. ◆**indétermination** *nf* (*doute*) indecision.

index [ɛ̃dɛks] *nm* (*liste*) index; *Anat* forefinger, index finger.

indexer [ɛ̃dɛkse] *vt Écon* to index-link, tie (**sur** to).

indicateur, -trice [ɛ̃dikatœr, -tris] **1** *nm* (*espion*) (police) informer. **2** *nm Rail* guide, timetable; *Tech* indicator, gauge. **3** *a* **poteau** i. signpost. ◆**indicatif, -ive 1** *a* indicative (**de** of); – *nm Mus* signature tune; *Tél* dialling code, *Am* area code. **2** *nm* (*mode*) *Gram* indicative. ◆**indication** *nf* indication (**de** of); (*renseignement*) (piece of) information; (*directive*) instruction.

indice [ɛ̃dis] *nm* (*indication*) sign; (*dans une enquête*) *Jur* clue; (*des prix*) index; (*de salaire*) grade; **i. d'écoute** *TV Rad* rating.

indien, -ienne [ɛ̃djɛ̃, -jɛn] *a* & *nmf* Indian.

indifférent [ɛ̃diferɑ̃] *a* indifferent (**à** to); **ça m'est i.** that's all the same to me. ◆**indifféremment** [-amɑ̃] *adv* indifferently. ◆**indifférence** *nf* indifference (**à** to).

indigène [ɛ̃diʒɛn] *a* & *nmf* native.

indigent [ɛ̃diʒɑ̃] *a* (very) poor. ◆**indigence** *nf* poverty.

indigeste [ɛ̃diʒɛst] *a* indigestible. ◆**indigestion** *nf* (attack of) indigestion.

indigne [ɛ̃diɲ] *a* (*personne*) unworthy; (*chose*) shameful; **i. de qn/qch** unworthy of s.o./sth. ◆**indignité** *nf* unworthiness; **une i.** (*honte*) an indignity.

indigner [ɛ̃diɲe] *vt* **i. qn** to make s.o. indignant; – **s'i.** *vpr* to be *ou* become indignant (**de** at). ◆**indignation** *nf* indignation.

indigo [ɛ̃digo] *nm* & *a inv* (*couleur*) indigo.

indiqu/er [ɛ̃dike] *vt* (*montrer*) to show, indicate; (*dire*) to point out, tell; (*recommander*) to recommend; **i. du doigt** to point to *ou* at. ◆**-é** *a* (*heure*) appointed; (*conseillé*) recommended; (*adéquat*) appropriate.

indirect [ɛ̃dirɛkt] *a* indirect. ◆**-ement** *adv* indirectly.

indiscipline [ɛ̃disiplin] *nf* lack of discipline. ◆**indiscipliné** *a* unruly.

indiscret, -ète [ɛ̃diskrɛ, -ɛt] *a* (*indélicat*) indiscreet, tactless; (*curieux*) *Péj* inquisitive, prying. ◆**indiscrétion** *nf* indiscretion.

indiscutable [ɛ̃diskytabl] *a* indisputable.

indispensable [ɛ̃dispɑ̃sabl] *a* indispensable, essential.

indispos/er [ɛ̃dispoze] *vt* (*incommoder*) to make unwell, upset; **i. qn** (*contre soi*) (*mécontenter*) to antagonize s.o. ◆**-é** *a* (*malade*) indisposed, unwell. ◆**indisposition** *nf* indisposition.

indissoluble [ɛ̃disɔlybl] *a* (*liens etc*) solid, indissoluble.

indistinct, -incte [ɛ̃distɛ̃(kt), -ɛ̃kt] *a* indistinct. ◆**-ement** [-ɛ̃ktəmɑ̃] *adv* indistinctly; (*également*) without distinction.

individu [ɛ̃dividy] *nm* individual. ◆**individualiser** *vt* to individualize. ◆**individualiste** *a* individualistic; – *nmf* individualist. ◆**individualité** *nf* (*originalité*) individuality. ◆**individuel, -elle** *a* individual. ◆**individuellement** *adv* individually.

indivisible [ɛ̃divizibl] *a* indivisible.

Indochine [ɛ̃dɔʃin] *nf* Indo-China.

indolent [ɛ̃dɔlɑ̃] *a* indolent. ◆**indolence** *nf* indolence.

indolore [ɛ̃dɔlɔr] *a* painless.

indomptable [ɛ̃dɔ̃tabl] *a* (*énergie, volonté*) indomitable. ◆**indompté** *a* (*animal*) untamed.

Indonésie [ɛ̃dɔnezi] *nf* Indonesia.

indubitable [ɛ̃dybitabl] *a* beyond doubt.

indue [ɛ̃dy] *af* **à une heure i.** at an ungodly hour.

induire* [ɛ̃dɥir] *vt* **i. qn en erreur** to lead s.o. astray.

indulgent [ɛ̃dylʒɑ̃] *a* indulgent (**envers** to, **avec** with). ◆**indulgence** *nf* indulgence.

industrie [ɛ̃dystri] *nf* industry. ◆**industrialisé** *a* industrialized. ◆**industriel, -elle** *a* industrial; – *nmf* industrialist.

inébranlable [inebrɑ̃labl] *a* (*certitude, personne*) unshakeable, unwavering.

inédit [inedi] *a* (*texte*) unpublished; (*nouveau*) *Fig* original.

ineffable [inefabl] *a Litt* inexpressible, ineffable.

inefficace [inefikas] *a* (*mesure, effort etc*) ineffective, ineffectual; (*personne*) inefficient. ◆**inefficacité** *nf* ineffectiveness; inefficiency.

inégal, -aux [inegal, -o] *a* unequal; (*sol, humeur*) uneven. ◆**inégalable** *a* incomparable. ◆**inégalé** *a* unequalled. ◆**inégalité** *nf* (*morale*) inequality; (*physique*) difference; (*irrégularité*) unevenness; *pl* (*bosses*) bumps.

inélégant [inelegã] *a* coarse, inelegant.

inéligible [ineliʒibl] *a* (*candidat*) ineligible.

inéluctable [inelyktabl] *a* inescapable.

inepte [inɛpt] *a* absurd, inept. ◆**ineptie** [-si] *nf* absurdity, ineptitude.

inépuisable [inepɥizabl] *a* inexhaustible.

inerte [inɛrt] *a* inert; (*corps*) lifeless. ◆**inertie** [-si] *nf* inertia.

inespéré [inɛspere] *a* unhoped-for.

inestimable [inɛstimabl] *a* priceless.

inévitable [inevitabl] *a* inevitable, unavoidable.

inexact [inɛgzakt] *a* (*erroné*) inaccurate, inexact; **c'est i.!** it's incorrect! ◆**inexactitude** *nf* inaccuracy, inexactitude; (*manque de ponctualité*) lack of punctuality.

inexcusable [inɛkskyzabl] *a* inexcusable.

inexistant [inɛgzistã] *a* non-existent.

inexorable [inɛgzorabl] *a* inexorable.

inexpérience [inɛksperjãs] *nf* inexperience. ◆**inexpérimenté** *a* (*personne*) inexperienced; (*machine, arme*) untested.

inexplicable [inɛksplikabl] *a* inexplicable. ◆**inexpliqué** *a* unexplained.

inexploré [inɛksplore] *a* unexplored.

inexpressif, -ive [inɛkspresif, -iv] *a* expressionless.

inexprimable [inɛksprimabl] *a* inexpressible.

inextricable [inɛkstrikabl] *a* inextricable.

infaillible [ɛ̃fajibl] *a* infallible. ◆**infaillibilité** *nf* infallibility.

infaisable [ɛ̃fəzabl] *a* (*travail etc*) that cannot be done.

infamant [ɛ̃famã] *a* ignominious.

infâme [ɛ̃fam] *a* (*odieux*) vile, infamous; (*taudis*) squalid. ◆**infamie** *nf* infamy.

infanterie [ɛ̃fãtri] *nf* infantry.

infantile [ɛ̃fãtil] *a* (*maladie, réaction*) infantile.

infarctus [ɛ̃farktys] *nm* **un i.** *Méd* a coronary.

infatigable [ɛ̃fatigabl] *a* tireless, indefatigable.

infect [ɛ̃fɛkt] *a* (*puant*) foul; (*mauvais*) lousy, vile.

infecter [ɛ̃fɛkte] **1** *vt* (*air*) to contaminate, foul. **2** *vt Méd* to infect; — **s'i.** *vpr* to get infected. ◆**infectieux, -euse** *a* infectious. ◆**infection** *nf* **1** *Méd* infection. **2** (*odeur*) stench.

inférer [ɛ̃fere] *vt* (*conclure*) to infer (**de** from, **que** that).

inférieur, -eure [ɛ̃ferjœr] *a* (*partie*) lower; (*qualité, personne*) inferior; **à l'étage i.** on

the floor below; **i. à** inferior to; (*plus petit que*) smaller than; — *nmf* (*personne*) *Péj* inferior. ◆**infériorité** *nf* inferiority.

infernal, -aux [ɛ̃fɛrnal, -o] *a* infernal.

infester [ɛ̃fɛste] *vt* to infest, overrun (**de** with). ◆**-é** *a* **i. de requins/de fourmis**/etc shark-/ant-/etc infested.

infidèle [ɛ̃fidɛl] *a* unfaithful (**à** to). ◆**infidélité** *nf* unfaithfulness; **une i.** (*acte*) an infidelity.

infiltrer (s') [sɛ̃filtre] *vpr* (*liquide*) to seep or percolate (through) (**dans** into); (*lumière*) to filter (through) (**dans** into); **s'i. dans** (*groupe, esprit*) *Fig* to infiltrate. ◆**infiltration** *nf* (*de personne, idée, liquide*) infiltration.

infime [ɛ̃fim] *a* (*très petit*) tiny; (*personne*) *Péj* lowly.

infini [ɛ̃fini] *a* infinite; — *nm Math Phot* infinity; *Phil* infinite; **à l'i.** (*beaucoup*) ad infinitum, endlessly; *Math* to infinity. ◆**infiniment** *adv* infinitely; (*regretter, remercier*) very much. ◆**infinité** *nf* **une i. de** an infinite amount of.

infinitif [ɛ̃finitif] *nm Gram* infinitive.

infirme [ɛ̃firm] *a* disabled, crippled; — *nmf* disabled person. ◆**infirmité** *nf* disability.

infirmer [ɛ̃firme] *vt* to invalidate.

infirmerie [ɛ̃firmari] *nf* infirmary, sickbay. ◆**infirmier** *nm* male nurse. ◆**infirmière** *nf* nurse.

inflammable [ɛ̃flamabl] *a* (in)flammable.

inflammation [ɛ̃flamasjɔ̃] *nf Méd* inflammation.

inflation [ɛ̃flasjɔ̃] *nf Écon* inflation. ◆**inflationniste** *a Écon* inflationary.

infléchir [ɛ̃fleʃir] *vt* (*courber*) to inflect, bend; (*modifier*) to shift. ◆**inflexion** *nf* bend; (*de voix*) tone, inflexion; **une i. de la tête** a nod.

inflexible [ɛ̃flɛksibl] *a* inflexible.

infliger [ɛ̃fliʒe] *vt* to inflict (**à** on); (*amende*) to impose (**à** on).

influence [ɛ̃flyãs] *nf* influence. ◆**influencer** *vt* to influence. ◆**influençable** *a* easily influenced. ◆**influent** *a* influential. ◆**influer** *vi* **i. sur** to influence.

information [ɛ̃fɔrmasjɔ̃] *nf* information; (*nouvelle*) piece of news; (*enquête*) *Jur* inquiry; *pl* information; *Journ Rad TV* news.

informatique [ɛ̃fɔrmatik] *nf* (*science*) computer science; (*technique*) data processing. ◆**informaticien, -ienne** *nmf* computer scientist. ◆**informatiser** *vt* to computerize.

informe [ɛ̃fɔrm] *a* shapeless.

informer [ɛ̃fɔrme] *vt* to inform (**de** of, about;

que that); — **s'i.** *vpr* to inquire (**de** about; **si** if, whether). ◆**informateur, -trice** *nmf* informant.

infortune [ɛ̃fɔrtyn] *nf* misfortune. ◆**infortuné** *a* ill-fated, hapless.

infraction [ɛ̃fraksjɔ̃] *nf* (*délit*) offence; **i. à** breach of, infringement of.

infranchissable [ɛ̃frɑ̃ʃisabl] *a* (*mur, fleuve*) impassable; (*fig*) insuperable.

infrarouge [ɛ̃fraruʒ] *a* infrared.

infroissable [ɛ̃frwasabl] *a* crease-resistant.

infructueux, -euse [ɛ̃fryktɥø, -øz] *a* fruitless.

infuser [ɛ̃fyze] *vt* (**faire**) **i.** (*thé*) to infuse. ◆**infusion** *nf* (*tisane*) (herb *ou* herbal) tea, infusion.

ingénier (s') [sɛ̃ʒenje] *vpr* to exercise one's wits (**à faire** in order to do).

ingénieur [ɛ̃ʒenjœr] *nm* engineer. ◆**ingénierie** [-iri] *nf* engineering.

ingénieux, -euse [ɛ̃ʒenjø, -øz] *a* ingenious. ◆**ingéniosité** *nf* ingenuity.

ingénu [ɛ̃ʒeny] *a* artless, naïve.

ingérer (s') [sɛ̃ʒere] *vpr* to interfere (**dans** in). ◆**ingérence** *nf* interference.

ingrat [ɛ̃gra] *a* (*personne*) ungrateful (**envers** to); (*sol*) barren; (*tâche*) thankless; (*visage, physique*) unattractive; (*âge*) awkward. ◆**ingratitude** *nf* ingratitude.

ingrédient [ɛ̃gredjɑ̃] *nm* ingredient.

inguérissable [ɛ̃gerisabl] *a* incurable.

ingurgiter [ɛ̃gyrʒite] *vt* to gulp down.

inhabitable [inabitabl] *a* uninhabitable. ◆**inhabité** *a* uninhabited.

inhabituel, -elle [inabitɥɛl] *a* unusual.

inhalateur [inalatœr] *nm* Méd inhaler. ◆**inhalation** *nf* inhalation; **faire des inhalations** to inhale.

inhérent [inerɑ̃] *a* inherent (**à** in).

inhibé [inibe] *a* inhibited. ◆**inhibition** *nf* inhibition.

inhospitalier, -ière [inɔspitalje, -jɛr] *a* inhospitable.

inhumain [inymɛ̃] *a* (*cruel, terrible*) inhuman.

inhumer [inyme] *vt* to bury, inter. ◆**inhumation** *nf* burial.

inimaginable [inimaʒinabl] *a* unimaginable.

inimitable [inimitabl] *a* inimitable.

inimitié [inimitje] *nf* enmity.

ininflammable [inɛ̃flamabl] *a* (*tissu etc*) non-flammable.

inintelligent [inɛ̃teliʒɑ̃] *a* unintelligent.

inintelligible [inɛ̃teliʒibl] *a* unintelligible.

inintéressant [inɛ̃teresɑ̃] *a* uninteresting.

ininterrompu [inɛ̃terɔ̃py] *a* uninterrupted, continuous.

inique [inik] *a* iniquitous. ◆**iniquité** *nf* iniquity.

initial, -aux [inisjal, -o] *a* initial. ◆**initiale** *nf* (*lettre*) initial. ◆**initialement** *adv* initially.

initiative [inisjativ] *nf* **1** initiative. **2** syndicat **d'i.** tourist office.

initi/er [inisje] *vt* to initiate (**à** into); **s'i. à** (*art, science*) to become acquainted with *ou* initiated into. ◆**-é, -ée** *nmf* initiate; **les initiés** the initiated. ◆**initiateur, -trice** *nmf* initiator. ◆**initiation** *nf* initiation.

injecter [ɛ̃ʒɛkte] *vt* to inject; **injecté de sang** bloodshot. ◆**injection** *nf* injection.

injonction [ɛ̃ʒɔ̃ksjɔ̃] *nf* order, injunction.

injure [ɛ̃ʒyr] *nf* insult; *pl* abuse, insults. ◆**injurier** *vt* to abuse, insult, swear at. ◆**injurieux, -euse** *a* abusive, insulting (**pour** to).

injuste [ɛ̃ʒyst] *a* (*contraire à la justice*) unjust; (*partial*) unfair. ◆**injustice** *nf* injustice.

injustifiable [ɛ̃ʒystifjabl] *a* unjustifiable. ◆**injustifié** *a* unjustified.

inlassable [ɛ̃lasabl] *a* untiring.

inné [ine] *a* innate, inborn.

innocent, -ente [inɔsɑ̃, -ɑ̃t] *a* innocent (**de** of); — *nmf* Jur innocent person; (*idiot*) simpleton. ◆**innocemment** [-amɑ̃] *adv* innocently. ◆**innocence** *nf* innocence. ◆**innocenter** *vt* **i. qn** to clear s.o. (**de** of).

innombrable [inɔ̃brabl] *a* innumerable.

innommable [inɔmabl] *a* (*dégoûtant*) unspeakable, foul.

innover [inɔve] *vi* to innovate. ◆**innovateur, -trice** *nmf* innovator. ◆**innovation** *nf* innovation.

inoccupé [inɔkype] *a* unoccupied.

inoculer [inɔkyle] *vt* **i. qch à qn** to infect *ou* inoculate s.o. with sth. ◆**inoculation** *nf* (*vaccination*) inoculation.

inodore [inɔdɔr] *a* odourless.

inoffensif, -ive [inɔfɑ̃sif, -iv] *a* harmless, inoffensive.

inonder [inɔ̃de] *vt* to flood, inundate; (*mouiller*) to soak; (*envahir*) inundated with; **inondé de soleil** bathed in sunlight. ◆**inondable** *a* (*chaussée etc*) liable to flooding. ◆**inondation** *nf* flood; (*action*) flooding (**de** of).

inopérant [inɔperɑ̃] *a* inoperative.

inopiné [inɔpine] *a* unexpected.

inopportun [inɔpɔrtœ̃] *a* inopportune.

inoubliable [inubljabl] *a* unforgettable.

inouï [inwi] *a* incredible, extraordinary.

inox [inɔks] *nm* stainless steel; **en i.** (*couteau etc*) stainless-steel. ◆**inoxydable** *a* (*couteau etc*) stainless-steel; **acier i.** stainless steel.

inqualifiable [ɛ̃kalifjabl] *a* (*indigne*) unspeakable.

inquiet, -iète [ɛ̃kjɛ, -jɛt] *a* anxious, worried (**about**). ◆**inquiét/er** *vt* (*préoccuper*) to worry; (*police*) to bother, harass (*suspect etc*); — **s'i.** *vpr* to worry (**de** about). ◆—**ant** *a* worrying. ◆**inquiétude** *nf* anxiety, concern, worry.

inquisiteur, -trice [ɛ̃kizitœr, -tris] *a* (*regard*) *Péj* inquisitive. ◆**inquisition** *nf* inquisition.

insaisissable [ɛ̃sɛzisabl] *a* elusive.

insalubre [ɛ̃salybr] *a* unhealthy, insalubrious.

insanités [ɛ̃sanite] *nfpl* (*idioties*) absurdities.

insatiable [ɛ̃sasjabl] *a* insatiable.

insatisfait [ɛ̃satisfɛ] *a* unsatisfied, dissatisfied.

inscrire* [ɛ̃skrir] *vt* to write *ou* put down; (*sur un registre*) to register; (*graver*) to inscribe; **i. qn** to enrol s.o.; — **s'i.** *vpr* to enrol (**à** at); **s'i. à** (*parti, club*) to join, enrol in; (*examen*) to enter *ou* enrol *ou* register for; **s'i. dans (le cadre de)** to be part of; **s'i. en faux contre** to deny absolutely. ◆**inscription** *nf* writing down; enrolment; registration; (*de médaille, sur écriteau etc*) inscription; **frais d'i.** *Univ* tuition fees.

insecte [ɛ̃sɛkt] *nm* insect. ◆**insecticide** *nm* insecticide.

insécurité [ɛ̃sekyrite] *nf* insecurity.

insémination [ɛ̃seminasjɔ̃] *nf Méd* insemination.

insensé [ɛ̃sɑ̃se] *a* senseless, absurd.

insensible [ɛ̃sɑ̃sibl] *a* (*indifférent*) insensitive (**à** to); (*graduel*) imperceptible, very slight. ◆**insensiblement** *adv* imperceptibly. ◆**insensibilité** *nf* insensitivity.

inséparable [ɛ̃separabl] *a* inseparable (**de** from).

insérer [ɛ̃sere] *vt* to insert (**dans** into, in); **s'i. dans** (*programme etc*) to be part of. ◆**insertion** *nf* insertion.

insidieux, -euse [ɛ̃sidjø, -øz] *a* insidious.

insigne [ɛ̃siɲ] *nm* badge, emblem; *pl* (*de maire etc*) insignia.

insignifiant [ɛ̃siɲifjɑ̃] *a* insignificant, unimportant. ◆**insignifiance** *nf* insignificance.

insinuer [ɛ̃sinɥe] *vt Péj* to insinuate (**que** that); — **s'i.** *vpr* to insinuate oneself (**dans** into). ◆**insinuation** *nf* insinuation.

insipide [ɛ̃sipid] *a* insipid.

insist/er [ɛ̃siste] *vi* to insist (**pour faire** on doing); (*continuer*) *Fam* to persevere; **i. sur** (*détail, syllabe etc*) to stress; **i. pour que** (+ *sub*) to insist that. ◆—**ant** *a* insistent, persistent. ◆**insistance** *nf* insistence, persistence.

insolation [ɛ̃sɔlasjɔ̃] *nf Méd* sunstroke.

insolent [ɛ̃sɔlɑ̃] *a* (*impoli*) insolent; (*luxe*) indecent. ◆**insolence** *nf* insolence.

insolite [ɛ̃sɔlit] *a* unusual, strange.

insoluble [ɛ̃sɔlybl] *a* insoluble.

insolvable [ɛ̃sɔlvabl] *a Fin* insolvent.

insomnie [ɛ̃sɔmni] *nf* insomnia; *pl* (*periods of*) insomnia; **nuit d'i.** sleepless night. ◆**insomniaque** *nmf* insomniac.

insondable [ɛ̃sɔ̃dabl] *a* unfathomable.

insonoriser [ɛ̃sɔnɔrize] *vt* to soundproof, insulate. ◆**insonorisation** *nf* soundproofing, insulation.

insouciant [ɛ̃susjɑ̃] *a* carefree; **i. de** unconcerned about. ◆**insouciance** *nf* carefree attitude, lack of concern.

insoumis [ɛ̃sumi] *a* rebellious. ◆**insoumission** *nf* rebelliousness.

insoupçonnable [ɛ̃supsɔnabl] *a* beyond suspicion. ◆**insoupçonné** *a* unsuspected.

insoutenable [ɛ̃sutnabl] *a* unbearable; (*théorie*) untenable.

inspecter [ɛ̃spɛkte] *vt* to inspect. ◆**inspecteur, -trice** *nmf* inspector. ◆**inspection** *nf* inspection.

inspir/er [ɛ̃spire] **1** *vt* to inspire; **i. qch à qn** to inspire s.o. with sth; **s'i. de** to take one's inspiration from. **2** *vi Méd* to breathe in. ◆—**é** *a* inspired; **être bien i. de faire** to have the good idea to do. ◆**inspiration** *nf* **1** inspiration. **2** *Méd* breathing in.

instable [ɛ̃stabl] *a* (*meuble*) unsteady, shaky; (*temps*) unsettled; (*caractère, situation*) unstable. ◆**instabilité** *nf* unsteadiness; instability.

installer [ɛ̃stale] *vt* (*équiper*) to fit out, fix up; (*appareil, meuble etc*) to install, put in; (*étagère*) to put up; **i. qn dans** (*une fonction, un logement*) to install s.o. (**dans** in); — **s'i.** *vpr* (*s'asseoir, s'établir*) to settle (down); (*médecin etc*) to set oneself up; **s'i. dans** (*maison, hôtel*) to move into. ◆**installateur** *nm* fitter. ◆**installation** *nf* fitting out; installation; putting in; moving in; *pl* (*appareils*) fittings; (*bâtiments*) facilities.

instance [ɛ̃stɑ̃s] **1** *nf* (*juridiction, autorité*) authority; **tribunal de première i.** ≃ magistrates' court; **en i. de** (*divorce, départ*) in the process of. **2** *nfpl* (*prières*) insistence, entreaties.

instant [ɛstɑ̃] *nm* moment, instant; **à l'i.** a moment ago; **pour l'i.** for the moment. ◆**instantané** *a* instantaneous; **café i.** instant coffee; — *nm Phot* snapshot.

instaurer [ɛstɔre] *vt* to found, set up.

instigateur, -trice [ɛstigatœr, -tris] *nmf* instigator. ◆**instigation** *nf* instigation.

instinct [ɛstɛ̃] *nm* instinct; **d'i.** instinctively, by instinct. ◆**instinctif, -ive** *a* instinctive.

instituer [ɛstitɥe] *vt* (*règle, régime*) to establish, institute.

institut [ɛstity] *nm* institute; **i. de beauté** beauty salon *ou* parlour; **i. universitaire de technologie** polytechnic, technical college.

instituteur, -trice [ɛstitytœr, -tris] *nmf* primary school teacher.

institution [ɛstitysjɔ̃] *nf* (*règle, organisation, structure etc*) institution; *Scol* private school. ◆**institutionnel, -elle** *a* institutional.

instructif, -ive [ɛstryktif, -iv] *a* instructive.

instruction [ɛstryksjɔ̃] *nf* education, schooling; *Mil* training; *Jur* investigation; (*document*) directive; *pl* (*ordres*) instructions. ◆**instructeur** *nm* (*moniteur*) & *Mil* instructor.

instruire* [ɛstrɥir] *vt* to teach, educate; *Mil* to train; *Jur* to investigate; **i. qn de** to inform *ou* instruct s.o. of; — **s'i.** *vpr* to educate oneself; **s'i. de** to inquire about. ◆**instruit** *a* educated.

instrument [ɛstrymɑ̃] *nm* instrument; (*outil*) implement, tool. ◆**instrumental, -aux** *a Mus* instrumental. ◆**instrumentiste** *nmf Mus* instrumentalist.

insu de (à l') [aɛsyd(ə)] *prép* without the knowledge of.

insuccès [ɛsyksɛ] *nm* failure.

insuffisant [ɛsyfizɑ̃] *a* (*en qualité*) inadequate; (*en quantité*) insufficient, inadequate. ◆**insuffisance** *nf* inadequacy.

insulaire [ɛsyler] *a* insular; – *nmf* islander.

insuline [ɛsylin] *nf Méd* insulin.

insulte [ɛsylt] *nf* insult (à to). ◆**insulter** *vt* to insult.

insupportable [ɛsyportabl] *a* unbearable.

insurg/er (s') [sɛsyrʒe] *vpr* to rise (up), rebel (**contre** against). ◆**-é, -ée** *nmf* a insurgent, rebel. ◆**insurrection** *nf* insurrection, uprising.

insurmontable [ɛsyrmɔ̃tabl] *a* insurmountable, insuperable.

intact [ɛtakt] *a* intact.

intangible [ɛtɑ̃ʒibl] *a* intangible.

intarissable [ɛtarisabl] *a* inexhaustible.

intégral, -aux [ɛtegral, -o] *a* full, complete; (*édition*) unabridged. ◆**intégralement** *adv* in full, fully. ◆**intégralité** *nf* whole (**de** of); **dans son i.** in full.

intègre [ɛtɛgr] *a* upright, honest. ◆**intégrité** *nf* integrity.

intégr/er [ɛtegre] *vt* to integrate (**dans** in); – **s'i.** *vpr* to become integrated, adapt. ◆**-ante** *af* **faire partie i. de** to be part and parcel of. ◆**intégration** *nf* integration.

intellectuel, -elle [ɛtelɛktɥel] *a* & *nmf* intellectual.

intelligent [ɛteliʒɑ̃] *a* intelligent, clever. ◆**intelligemment** [-amɑ̃] *adv* intelligently. ◆**intelligence** *nf* (*faculté*) intelligence; *pl Mil Pol* secret relations; **avoir l'i. de qch** (*compréhension*) to have an understanding of sth; **d'i. avec qn** in complicity with s.o. ◆**intelligentsia** [-dʒentsja] *nf* intelligentsia.

intelligible [ɛteliʒibl] *a* intelligible. ◆**intelligibilité** *nf* intelligibility.

intempérance [ɛtɑ̃perɑ̃s] *nf* intemperance.

intempéries [ɛtɑ̃peri] *nfpl* **les i.** the elements, bad weather.

intempestif, -ive [ɛtɑ̃pestif, -iv] *a* untimely.

intenable [ɛtnabl] *a* (*position*) untenable; (*enfant*) unruly, uncontrollable.

intendant, -ante [ɛtɑ̃dɑ̃, -ɑ̃t] *nmf Scol* bursar. ◆**intendance** *nf Scol* bursar's office.

intense [ɛtɑ̃s] *a* intense; (*circulation, trafic*) heavy. ◆**intensément** *adv* intensely. ◆**intensif, -ive** *a* intensive. ◆**intensifier** *vt*, – **s'i.** *vpr* to intensify. ◆**intensité** *nf* intensity.

intenter [ɛtɑ̃te] *vt* **i. un procès à** *Jur* to institute proceedings against.

intention [ɛtɑ̃sjɔ̃] *nf* intention; *Jur* intent; **avoir l'i. de faire** to intend to do; **à l'i. de qn** for s.o.; **à votre i.** for you. ◆**intentionné** *a* **bien i.** well-intentioned. ◆**intentionnel, -elle** *a* intentional, wilful. ◆**intentionnellement** *adv* intentionally.

inter- [ɛter] *préf* inter-.

interaction [ɛteraksjɔ̃] *nf* interaction.

intercaler [ɛterkale] *vt* to insert.

intercéder [ɛtersede] *vt* to intercede (**auprès de** with).

intercepter [ɛtersepte] *vt* to intercept. ◆**interception** *nf* interception.

interchangeable [ɛterʃɑ̃ʒabl] *a* interchangeable.

interclasse [ɛterklɑs] *nm Scol* break (between classes).

intercontinental, -aux [ɛterkɔ̃tinɑ̃tal, -o] *a* intercontinental.

interdépendant [ɛ̃terdepɑ̃dɑ̃] *a* interdependent.

interd/ire* [ɛ̃terdir] *vt* to forbid, not to allow (**qch à qn** s.o. sth); (*meeting, film etc*) to ban; **i. à qn de faire** (*médecin, père etc*) not to allow s.o. to do, forbid s.o. to do; (*attitude, santé etc*) to prevent s.o. from doing, not allow s.o. to do. ◆**—it à i.** forbidden, not allowed; **il est i.** de it is forbidden to; **'stationnement i.'** 'no parking'. **2** (*étonné*) nonplussed. ◆**interdiction** *nf* ban (**de** on); **'i. de fumer'** 'no smoking'.

intéress/er [ɛ̃terese] *vt* to interest; (*concerner*) to concern; **s'i. à** to take an interest in, be interested in. ◆**—ant** *a* (*captivant*) interesting; (*affaire, prix etc*) attractive, worthwhile. ◆**—é, —ée** *a* (*avide*) self-interested; (*motif*) selfish; (*concerné*) concerned; **—nmf i.** the interested party.

intérêt [ɛ̃tere] *nm* interest; *Péj* self-interest; *pl Fin* interest; **tu as i. à faire** it would pay you to do, you'd do well to do; **des intérêts dans** *Com* an interest *ou* stake in.

interface [ɛ̃terfas] *nf Tech* interface.

intérieur [ɛ̃terjœr] *a* (*cour, paroi*) inner, interior; (*poche*) inside; (*vie, sentiment*) inner, inward; (*mer*) inland; (*politique, vol*) internal, domestic; **—** *nm* (*de boîte etc*) inside (**de** of); (*de maison*) interior, inside; (*de pays*) interior; **à l'i.** (**de**) inside; **d'i.** (*vêtement, jeux*) indoor; **femme d'i.** home-loving woman; **ministère de l'I.** Home Office, *Am* Department of the Interior. ◆**—ement** *adv* (*dans le cœur*) inwardly.

intérim [ɛ̃terim] *nm* **pendant l'i.** in the interim; **assurer l'i.** to deputize (**de** for); **ministre/etc par i.** acting minister/etc. ◆**intérimaire** *a* temporary, interim; **—** *nmf* (*fonctionnaire*) deputy; (*secrétaire*) temporary.

interligne [ɛ̃terliɲ] *nm Typ* space (between the lines).

interlocuteur, -trice [ɛ̃terlɔkytœr, -tris] *nmf Pol* negotiator; **mon i.** the person I am, was *etc* speaking to.

interloqué [ɛ̃terlɔke] *a* dumbfounded.

interlude [ɛ̃terlyd] *nm Mus TV* interlude.

intermède [ɛ̃termɛd] *nm* (*interruption*) & *Th* interlude.

intermédiaire [ɛ̃termedjɛr] *a* intermediate; **—** *nmf* intermediary; **par l'i. de** through (the medium of).

interminable [ɛ̃terminabl] *a* endless, interminable.

intermittent, -ente [ɛ̃termitɑ̃] *a* intermittent. ◆**intermittence** *nf* **par i.** intermittently.

international, -aux [ɛ̃ternasjɔnal, -o] *a* in-

ternational; **—** *nm* (*joueur*) *Sp* international.

interne [ɛ̃tern] **1** *a* (*douleur etc*) internal; (*oreille*) inner. **2** *nmf Scol* boarder; **i.** (*des hôpitaux*) houseman, *Am* intern. ◆**internat** *nm* (*école*) boarding school.

intern/er [ɛ̃terne] *vt* (*réfugié*) to intern; (*aliéné*) to confine. ◆**—ement** *nm* internment; confinement.

interpeller [ɛ̃terpele] *vt* to shout at, address sharply; (*dans une réunion*) to question, (*interrompre*) to heckle; (*arrêter*) *Jur* to take in for questioning. ◆**interpellation** *nf* sharp address; questioning; heckling; (*de police*) arrest.

interphone [ɛ̃terfɔn] *nm* intercom.

interplanétaire [ɛ̃terplaneter] *a* interplanetary.

interpoler [ɛ̃terpɔle] *vt* to interpolate.

interposer (s') [sɛ̃terpoze] *vpr* (*dans une dispute etc*) to intervene (**dans** in); **s'i. entre** to come between.

interprète [ɛ̃terpret] *nmf Ling* interpreter; (*chanteur*) singer; *Th Mus* performer; (*porte-parole*) spokesman, spokeswoman; **faire l'i.** *Ling* to interpret. ◆**interprétariat** *nm* (*métier*) *Ling* interpreting. ◆**interprétation** *nf* interpretation; *Th Mus* performance. ◆**interpréter** *vt* (*expliquer*) to interpret; (*chanter*) to sing; (*jouer*) *Th* to play, perform; (*exécuter*) *Mus* to perform.

interroger [ɛ̃terɔʒe] *vt* to question; *Jur* to interrogate; (*faits*) to examine. ◆**interrogateur, -trice** *a* (*air*) questioning; **—** *nmf Scol* examiner. ◆**interrogatif, -ive** *a & nm Gram* interrogative. ◆**interrogation** *nf* question; (*action*) questioning; (*épreuve*) *Scol* test. ◆**interrogatoire** *nm Jur* interrogation.

interrompre* [ɛ̃terɔ̃pr] *vt* to interrupt, break off; **i. qn** to interrupt s.o.; **— s'i.** *vpr* (*personne*) to break off, stop. ◆**interrupteur** *nm* (*bouton*) *Él* switch. ◆**interruption** *nf* interruption; (*des hostilités, du courant*) break (**de** in).

intersection [ɛ̃terseksjɔ̃] *nf* intersection.

interstice [ɛ̃terstis] *nm* crack, chink.

interurbain [ɛ̃teryrbɛ̃] *a & nm* (*téléphone*) **i.** long-distance telephone service.

intervalle [ɛ̃terval] *nm* (*écart*) space, gap; (*temps*) interval; **dans l'i.** (*entretemps*) in the meantime.

intervenir* [ɛ̃tervənir] *vi* (*s'interposer, agir*) to intervene; (*survenir*) to occur; (*opérer*) *Méd* to operate; **être intervenu** (*accord*) to be reached. ◆**intervention** *nf* intervention; **i.** (*chirurgicale*) operation.

intervertir [ɛ̃tɛrvɛrtir] *vt* to invert. ◆**interversion** *nf* inversion.

interview [ɛ̃tɛrvju] *nf Journ TV* interview. ◆**interviewer** [-vjuve] *vt* to interview.

intestin [ɛ̃tɛstɛ̃] *nm* intestine, bowel. ◆**intestinal, -aux** *a* intestinal, bowel-.

intime [ɛ̃tim] *a* intimate; (*ami*) close, intimate; (*vie, fête, journal*) private; (*pièce, coin*) cosy; (*cérémonie*) quiet; — *nmf* close *ou* intimate friend. ◆—**ment** *adv* intimately. ◆**intimité** *nf* intimacy; privacy; cosiness; **dans l'i.** (*mariage etc*) in private.

intimider [ɛ̃timide] *vt* to intimidate, frighten. ◆**intimidation** *nf* intimidation.

intituler [ɛ̃tityle] *vt* to entitle; — **s'i.** *vpr* to be entitled.

intolérable [ɛ̃tɔlerabl] *a* intolerable (**que** that). ◆**intolérance** *nf* intolerance. ◆**intolérant** *a* intolerant (**de** of).

intonation [ɛ̃tɔnasjɔ̃] *nf Ling* intonation; (*ton*) tone.

intoxiqu/er [ɛ̃tɔksike] *vt* (*empoisonner*) to poison; *Psy Pol* to brainwash; — **s'i.** *vpr* to be *ou* become poisoned. ◆—**é, -ée** *nmf* addict. ◆**intoxication** *nf* poisoning; *Psy Pol* brainwashing.

intra- [ɛ̃tra] *préf* intra-.

intraduisible [ɛ̃tradɥizibl] *a* untranslatable.

intraitable [ɛ̃trɛtabl] *a* uncompromising.

intransigeant [ɛ̃trɑ̃ziʒɑ̃] *a* intransigent. ◆**intransigeance** *nf* intransigence.

intransitif, -ive [ɛ̃trɑ̃zitif, -iv] *a & nm Gram* intransitive.

intraveineux, -euse [ɛ̃travɛnø, -øz] *a Méd* intravenous.

intrépide [ɛ̃trepid] *a* (*courageux*) fearless, intrepid; (*obstiné*) headstrong. ◆**intrépidité** *nf* fearlessness.

intrigue [ɛ̃trig] *nf* intrigue; *Th Cin Littér* plot. ◆**intrigant, -ante** *nmf* schemer. ◆**intriguer 1** *vi* to scheme, intrigue. **2** *vt* **i. qn** (*intéresser*) to intrigue s.o., puzzle s.o.

intrinsèque [ɛ̃trɛ̃sɛk] *a* intrinsic. ◆—**ment** *adv* intrinsically.

introduire* [ɛ̃trodɥir] *vt* (*présenter*) to introduce, bring in; (*insérer*) to insert (**dans** into), put in (**dans** to); (*faire entrer*) to show (s.o.) in; **s'i. dans** to get into. ◆**introduction** *nf* (*texte, action*) introduction.

introspectif, -ive [ɛ̃trospɛktif, -iv] *a* introspective. ◆**introspection** *nf* introspection.

introuvable [ɛ̃truvabl] *a* that cannot be found anywhere.

introverti, -ie [ɛ̃trovɛrti] *nmf* introvert.

intrus, -use [ɛ̃try, -yz] *nmf* intruder. ◆**intrusion** *nf* intrusion (**dans** into).

intuition [ɛ̃tɥisjɔ̃] *nf* intuition. ◆**intuitif, -ive** *a* intuitive.

inusable [inyzabl] *a Fam* hard-wearing.

inusité [inyzite] *a Gram* unused.

inutile [inytil] *a* unnecessary, useless; **c'est i. de crier** it's pointless *ou* useless to shout. ◆**inutilement** *adv* (*vainement*) needlessly. ◆**inutilité** *nf* uselessness.

inutilisable [inytilizabl] *a* unusable. ◆**inutilisé** *a* unused.

invalider [ɛ̃valide] *vt* to invalidate.

invariable [ɛ̃varjabl] *a* invariable. ◆—**ment** [-əmɑ̃] *adv* invariably.

invasion [ɛ̃vazjɔ̃] *nf* invasion.

invective [ɛ̃vɛktiv] *nf* invective. ◆**invectiver** *vt* to abuse; — *vi* **i. contre** to inveigh against.

invendable [ɛ̃vɑ̃dabl] *a* unsaleable. ◆**invendu** *a* unsold.

inventaire [ɛ̃vɑ̃tɛr] *nm* (*liste*) *Com* inventory; (*étude*) *Fig* survey; **faire l'i.** *Com* to do the stocktaking (**de** of).

inventer [ɛ̃vɑ̃te] *vt* (*découvrir*) to invent; (*imaginer*) to make up. ◆**inventeur, -trice** *nmf* inventor. ◆**inventif, -ive** *a* inventive. ◆**invention** *nf* invention.

inverse [ɛ̃vɛrs] *a* (*sens*) opposite; (*ordre*) reverse; *Math* inverse; — *nm* **l'i.** the reverse, the opposite. ◆**inversement** *adv* conversely. ◆**inverser** *vt* (*ordre*) to reverse. ◆**inversion** *nf Gram Anat etc* inversion.

investigation [ɛ̃vɛstigasjɔ̃] *nf* investigation.

invest/ir [ɛ̃vɛstir] **1** *vti Com* to invest (**dans** in). **2** *vt* **i. qn de** (*fonction etc*) to invest s.o. with. ◆—**issement** *nm Com* investment. ◆**investiture** *nf Pol* nomination.

invétéré [ɛ̃vetere] *a* inveterate.

invincible [ɛ̃vɛ̃sibl] *a* invincible.

invisible [ɛ̃vizibl] *a* invisible.

invit/er [ɛ̃vite] *vt* to invite; **i. qn à faire** to invite *ou* ask s.o. to do; (*inciter*) to tempt s.o. to do. ◆—**é, -ée** *nmf* guest. ◆**invitation** *nf* invitation.

invivable [ɛ̃vivabl] *a* unbearable.

involontaire [ɛ̃vɔlɔ̃tɛr] *a* involuntary. ◆—**ment** *adv* accidentally, involuntarily.

invoquer [ɛ̃vɔke] *vt* (*argument etc*) to put forward; (*appeler*) to invoke, call upon. ◆**invocation** *nf* invocation (**à** to).

invraisemblable [ɛ̃vrɛsɑ̃blabl] *a* incredible; (*improbable*) improbable. ◆**invraisemblance** *nf* improbability.

invulnérable [ɛ̃vylnerabl] *a* invulnerable.

iode [jɔd] *nm* **teinture d'i.** *Méd* iodine.

ira, irait [ira, irɛ] *voir* **aller 1.**

Irak [irak] *nm* Iraq. ◆**irakien, -ienne** *a & nmf* Iraqi.

Iran [irɑ̃] nm Iran. ◆**iranien, -ienne** a & nmf Iranian.

irascible [irasibl] a irascible.

iris [iris] nm Anat Bot iris.

Irlande [irlɑ̃d] nf Ireland. ◆**irlandais, -aise** a Irish; – nmf Irishman, Irishwoman; – nm (langue) Irish.

ironie [irɔni] nf irony. ◆**ironique** a ironic(al).

irradier [iradje] vt to irradiate.

irraisonné [irɛzɔne] a irrational.

irréconciliable [irekɔ̃siljabl] a irreconcilable.

irrécusable [irekyzabl] a irrefutable.

irréel, -elle [ireɛl] a unreal.

irréfléchi [irefleʃi] a thoughtless, unthinking.

irréfutable [irefytabl] a irrefutable.

irrégulier, -ière [iregylje, -jɛr] a irregular. ◆**irrégularité** nf irregularity.

irrémédiable [iremedjabl] a irreparable.

irremplaçable [irɑ̃plasabl] a irreplaceable.

irréparable [ireparabl] a (véhicule etc) beyond repair; (tort, perte) irreparable.

irrépressible [irepresibl] a (rires etc) irrepressible.

irréprochable [ireprɔʃabl] a beyond reproach, irreproachable.

irrésistible [irezistibl] a (personne, charme etc) irresistible.

irrésolu [irezɔly] a irresolute.

irrespirable [irespirabl] a unbreathable; Fig stifling.

irresponsable [irɛspɔ̃sabl] a (personne) irresponsible.

irrévérencieux, -euse [ireverɑ̃sjø, -øz] a irreverent.

irréversible [ireversibl] a irreversible.

irrévocable [irevɔkabl] a irrevocable.

irriguer [irige] vt to irrigate. ◆**irrigation** nf irrigation.

irrit/er [irite] vt to irritate; – **s'i.** vpr to get angry (de, contre at). ◆**—ant** a irritating; – nm irritation. ◆**irritable** a irritable. ◆**irritation** nf (colère) & Méd irritation.

irruption [irypsjɔ̃] nf faire i. dans to burst into.

islam [islam] nm Islam. ◆**islamique** a Islamic.

Islande [islɑ̃d] nf Iceland. ◆**islandais, -aise** a Icelandic.

isol/er [izɔle] vt to isolate (de from); (contre le froid etc) & Él to insulate; – **s'i.** vpr to cut oneself off, isolate oneself. ◆**—ant** a insulating; – nm insulating material. ◆**—é** a isolated; (écarté) remote, isolated; **i. de** cut off ou isolated from. ◆**isolation** nf insulation. ◆**isolement** nm isolation. ◆**isolément** adv in isolation, singly. ◆**isoloir** nm polling booth.

isorel® [izɔrɛl] nm hardboard.

Israël [israɛl] nm Israel. ◆**israélien, -ienne** a & nmf Israeli. ◆**israélite** a Jewish; – nm Jew; – nf Jewess.

issu [isy] a être i. de to come from.

issue [isy] nf (sortie) exit, way out; (solution) Fig way out; (résultat) outcome; **à l'i. de** at the close of; **rue** etc **sans i.** dead end; **situation** etc **sans i.** Fig dead end.

isthme [ism] nm Géog isthmus.

Italie [itali] nf Italy. ◆**italien, -ienne** a & nmf Italian; – nm (langue) Italian.

italique [italik] a Typ italic; – nm italics.

itinéraire [itinerɛr] nm itinerary, route.

itinérant [itinerɑ̃] a itinerant.

IVG [iveʒe] nf abrév (interruption volontaire de grossesse) (voluntary) abortion.

ivoire [ivwar] nm ivory.

ivre [ivr] a drunk (de with). ◆**ivresse** nf drunkenness; **en état d'i.** under the influence of drink. ◆**ivrogne** nmf drunk(ard).

J

J, j [ʒi] nm J, j; **le jour J.** D-day.

j' [ʒ] voir **je**.

jacasser [ʒakase] vi (personne, pie) to chatter.

jachère (en) [ɑ̃ʒaʃɛr] adv (champ etc) fallow.

jacinthe [ʒasɛ̃t] nf hyacinth.

jacousi [ʒakuzi] nm (baignoire, piscine) jacuzzi.

jade [ʒad] nm (pierre) jade.

jadis [ʒadis] adv at one time, once.

jaguar [ʒagwar] nm (animal) jaguar.

jaill/ir [ʒajir] vi (liquide) to spurt (out), gush (out); (lumière) to flash, stream; (cri) to burst out; (vérité) to burst forth; (étincelle) to fly out. ◆**—issement** nm (de liquide) gush.

jais [ʒɛ] nm (noir) de j. jet-black.

jalon [ʒalɔ̃] nm (piquet) marker; **poser les jalons** Fig to prepare the way (**de** for). ◆**jalonner** vt to mark (out); (border) to line.

jaloux, -ouse [ʒalu, -uz] a jealous (**de** of). ◆**jalouser** vt to envy. ◆**jalousie** nf 1 jealousy. 2 (persienne) venetian blind.

Jamaïque [ʒamaik] nf Jamaica.

jamais [ʒamɛ] adv 1 (négatif) never; **sans** je **sortir** without ever going out; **elle ne sort** je she never goes out. 2 (positif) ever; **à (tout)** j. for ever; **si** j. if ever.

jambe [ʒɑ̃b] nf leg; **à toutes jambes** as fast as one can; **prendre ses jambes à son cou** to take to one's heels.

jambon [ʒɑ̃bɔ̃] nm Culin ham. ◆**jambonneau, -x** nm knuckle of ham.

jante [ʒɑ̃t] nf (de roue) rim.

janvier [ʒɑ̃vje] nm January.

Japon [ʒapɔ̃] nm Japan. ◆**japonais, -aise** a nm nf Japanese; – & nm (langue) Japanese.

japp/er [ʒape] vi (chien etc) to yap, yelp. ◆**-ement** nm yap, yelp.

jaquette [ʒakɛt] nf (d'homme) tailcoat, morning coat; (de femme, livre) jacket.

jardin [ʒardɛ̃] nm garden; **j. d'enfants** kindergarten, playschool; **j. public** park; (plus petit) gardens. ◆**jardinage** nm gardening. ◆**jardiner** vi to do the garden, be gardening. ◆**jardinerie** nf garden centre. ◆**jardinier** nm gardener. ◆**jardinière** nf (personne) gardener; (caisse à fleurs) window box; **j. de légumes** Culin mixed vegetable dish; **j. d'enfants** kindergarten teacher.

jargon [ʒargɔ̃] nm jargon.

jarret [ʒarɛ] nm Anat back of the knee.

jarretelle [ʒartɛl] nf (de gaine) suspender, Am garter. ◆**jarretière** nf (autour de la jambe) garter.

jaser [ʒaze] vi (bavarder) to jabber.

jasmin [ʒasmɛ̃] nm Bot jasmine.

jatte [ʒat] nf (bol) bowl.

jauge [ʒoʒ] nf 1 (instrument) gauge. 2 (capacité) capacity; Nau tonnage. ◆**jauger** vt (personne) Litt to size up.

jaune [ʒon] 1 a yellow; – nm (couleur) yellow; **j. d'œuf** (egg) yolk. 2 nm (ouvrier) Péj blackleg, scab. ◆**jaunâtre** a yellowish. ◆**jaunir** vti to (turn) yellow. ◆**jaunisse** nf Méd jaundice.

Javel (eau de) [odʒavɛl] nf bleach. ◆**javelliser** vt to chlorinate.

javelot [ʒavlo] nm javelin.

jazz [dʒaz] nm jazz.

je [ʒ(ə)] pron (j' before vowel or mute h) I; **je suis** I am.

jean [dʒin] nm (pair of) jeans.

jeep [dʒip] nf jeep.

je-m'en-fichisme [ʒmɑ̃fiʃism] nm inv Fam couldn't-care-less attitude.

jérémiades [ʒeremjad] nfpl Fam lamentations.

jerrycan [(d)ʒerikɑ̃] nm jerry can.

jersey [ʒɛrzɛ] nm (tissu) jersey.

Jersey [ʒɛrzɛ] nf Jersey.

jésuite [ʒezɥit] nm Jesuit.

Jésus [ʒezy] nm Jesus; **J.-Christ** Jesus Christ.

jet [ʒɛ] nm throw; (de vapeur) burst, gush; (de lumière) flash; **j. d'eau** fountain; **premier j.** (ébauche) first draft; **d'un seul j.** in one go.

jetée [ʒ(ə)te] nf pier, jetty.

jeter [ʒ(ə)te] vt to throw (**à** to, **dans** into); (mettre à la poubelle) to throw away; (ancre, regard, sort) to cast; (bases) to lay; (cri, son) to let out, utter; (éclat, lueur) to throw out, give out; (noter) to jot down; **j. un coup d'œil sur** ou **à** to have ou take a look at; (rapidement) to glance at; – **se** j. vpr to throw oneself; **se j. sur** to fall on, pounce on; **se j. contre** (véhicule) to crash into; **se j. dans** (fleuve) to flow into. ◆**jetable** a (rasoir etc) disposable.

jeton [ʒ(ə)tɔ̃] nm (pièce) token; (pour compter) counter; (à la roulette) chip.

jeu, -x [ʒø] nm 1 game; (amusement) play; (d'argent) gambling; Th acting; Mus playing; **j. de mots** play on words, pun; **jeux de société** parlour ou party games; **j. télévisé** television quiz; **maison de jeux** gambling club; **en j.** (en cause) at stake; (forces etc) at work; **entrer en j.** to come into play. 2 (série complète) set; (de cartes) pack, deck, Am deck; (cartes en main) hand; **j. d'échecs** chess set. 3 (de ressort, verrou) Tech play.

jeudi [ʒødi] nm Thursday.

jeun (à) [aʒœ̃] adv on an empty stomach; **être à j.** to have eaten no food.

jeune [ʒœn] a young; (inexpérimenté) inexperienced; **Dupont j.** Dupont junior; **d'allure j.** young-looking; **jeunes gens** young people; – nmf young person; **les jeunes** young people. ◆**jeunesse** nf youth; (apparence) youthfulness; **la** j. (jeunes) the young, youth.

jeûne [ʒøn] nm fast; (action) fasting. ◆**jeûner** vi to fast.

joaillier, -ière [ʒoaje, -jɛr] nmf jeweller.

◆**joaillerie** nf jewellery; (magasin) jewellery shop.

jockey [ʒɔkɛ] nm jockey.

jogging [dʒɔgiŋ] nm Sp jogging; (chaussure) running ou jogging shoe; **faire du j.** to jog.

joie [ʒwa] nf joy, delight; **feu de j.** bonfire.

joindre* [ʒwɛ̃dr] vt (mettre ensemble, relier) to join; (efforts) to combine; (insérer dans une enveloppe) to enclose (à with); (ajouter) to add (à to); (qn) (contacter) to get in touch with s.o.; **j. les deux bouts** Fig to make ends meet; **se j. à** (se mettre avec, participer à) to join. ◆**joint** a (efforts) joint, combined; − nm Tech joint; (de robinet) washer. ◆**jointure** nf Anat joint.

joker [ʒɔkɛr] nm Cartes joker.

joli [ʒɔli] a nice, lovely; (femme, enfant) pretty. ◆**-ment** adv nicely; (très, beaucoup) awfully.

jonc [ʒɔ̃] nm Bot (bul)rush.

joncher [ʒɔ̃ʃe] vt to litter (de with); **jonché de** strewn ou littered with.

jonction [ʒɔ̃ksjɔ̃] nf (de tubes, routes etc) junction.

jongl/er [ʒɔ̃gle] vi to juggle. ◆**-eur, -euse** nmf juggler.

jonquille [ʒɔ̃kij] nf daffodil.

Jordanie [ʒɔrdani] nf Jordan.

joue [ʒu] nf Anat cheek; **coucher qn en j.** to aim (a gun) at s.o.

jouer [ʒwe] vi to play; Th to act; (au tiercé etc) to gamble, bet; (à la Bourse) to gamble; (entrer en jeu) to come into play; (être important) to count; (fonctionner) to work; **j. au tennis/aux cartes/etc** to play tennis/cards/etc; **j. du piano/du violon/etc** to play the piano/violin/etc; **j. des coudes** to use one's elbows; − vt (musique, tour, jeu) to play; (risquer) to gamble, bet (sur on); (cheval) to bet on; (personnage, rôle) Th to play; (pièce) Th to perform, put on; (film) to show, put on; **j. gros jeu** to play for high stakes; **se j. de** to scoff at; (difficultés) to make light of. ◆**jouet** nm toy; **le j. de qn** Fig s.o.'s plaything. ◆**joueur, -euse** nmf player; (au tiercé etc) gambler; **beau j., bon j.**, good loser.

joufflu [ʒufly] a (visage) chubby; (enfant) chubby-cheeked.

joug [ʒu] nm Agr & Fig yoke.

jouir [ʒwir] vi **1 j. de** (savourer, avoir) to enjoy. **2** (éprouver le plaisir sexuel) to come. ◆**jouissance** nf enjoyment; (usage) Jur use.

joujou, -x [ʒuʒu] nm Fam toy.

jour [ʒur] nm day; (lumière) (day)light;

(ouverture) gap, opening; (aspect) Fig light; **il fait j.** it's (day)light; **grand j., plein j.** broad daylight; **de nos jours** nowadays, these days; **au j. le j.** from day to day; **du j. au lendemain** overnight; **mettre à j.** to bring up to date; **mettre au j.** to bring into the open; **se faire j.** to come to light; **donner le j. à** to give birth to; **le j. de l'An** New Year's day. ◆**journalier, -ière** a daily. ◆**journée** nf day; **pendant la j.** during the day(time); **toute la j.** all day (long). ◆**journellement** adv daily.

journal, -aux [ʒurnal, -o] nm (news)paper; (spécialisé) journal; (intime) diary; **j. (parlé)** Rad news bulletin; **j. de bord** Nau logbook. ◆**journalisme** nm journalism. ◆**journaliste** nmf journalist. ◆**journalistique** a (style etc) journalistic.

jovial, -aux [ʒɔvjal, -o] a jovial, jolly. ◆**jovialité** nf jollity.

joyau, -aux [ʒwajo] nm jewel.

joyeux, -euse [ʒwajø, -øz] a merry, happy, joyful; **j. anniversaire!** happy birthday!; **j. Noël!** merry ou happy Christmas!

jubilé [ʒybile] nm (golden) jubilee.

jubiler [ʒybile] vi to be jubilant. ◆**jubilation** nf jubilation.

jucher [ʒyʃe] vt, − **se j.** vpr to perch (sur on).

judaïque [ʒydaik] a Jewish. ◆**judaïsme** nm Judaism.

judas [ʒyda] nm (de porte) peephole, spy hole.

judiciaire [ʒydisjɛr] a judicial, legal.

judicieux, -euse [ʒydisjø, -øz] a sensible, judicious.

judo [ʒydo] nm judo. ◆**judoka** nmf judo expert.

juge [ʒyʒ] nm judge; Sp referee, umpire; **j. d'instruction** examining magistrate; **j. de paix** Justice of the Peace; **j. de touche** Fb linesman. ◆**juger** vt (personne, question etc) to judge; (affaire) Jur to try; (estimer) to consider (que that); **j. qn** Jur to try s.o.; − vi **j. de** to judge; **jugez de ma surprise/etc** imagine my surprise/etc. ◆**jugement** nm judg(e)ment; (verdict) Jur sentence; **passer en j.** Jur to stand trial. ◆**jugeote** nf Fam commonsense.

jugé (au) [oʒyʒe] adv by guesswork.

juguler [ʒygyle] vt to check, suppress.

juif, juive [ʒɥif, ʒɥiv] a Jewish; − nm Jew; − nf Jew(ess).

juillet [ʒɥijɛ] nm July.

juin [ʒɥɛ̃] nm June.

jumeau, -elle, pl -eaux, -elles [ʒymo, -ɛl] a (frères, lits etc) twin; − nmf twin. **2** nfpl (*longue-vue*) binoculars; **jumelles de théâtre** opera glasses. ◆**jumel/er** *vt* (*villes*) to twin. ◆**—age** *nm* twinning.

jument [ʒymɑ̃] *nf* (*cheval*) mare.

jungle [ʒœ̃ɡl] *nf* jungle.

junior [ʒynjɔr] *nm* & *a* (*inv au sing*) *Sp* junior.

junte [ʒœ̃t] *nf* *Pol* junta.

jupe [ʒyp] *nf* skirt. ◆**jupon** *nm* petticoat.

jurer [ʒyre] **1** *vi* (*blasphémer*) to swear. **2** *vt* (*promettre*) to swear (**que** that, **de faire** to do); – *vi* **j. de qch** to swear to sth. **3** *vi* (*contraster*) to clash (**avec** with). ◆**juré** *a* (*ennemi*) sworn; – *nm* *Jur* juror. ◆**juron** *nm* swearword, oath.

juridiction [ʒyridiksjɔ̃] *nf* jurisdiction.

juridique [ʒyridik] *a* legal. ◆**juriste** *nmf* legal expert, jurist.

jury [ʒyri] *nm* *Jur* jury; (*de concours*) panel (of judges), jury.

jus [ʒy] *nm* (*des fruits etc*) juice; (*de viande*) gravy; (*café*) *Fam* coffee; (*électricité*) *Fam* power.

jusque [ʒysk] *prép* **jusqu'à** (*espace*) as far as, (right) up to; (*temps*) until, (up) till, to; (*même*) even; **jusqu'à dix francs**/*etc* (*limite*) up to ten francs/*etc*; **jusqu'ici** as far as (*espace*) or up till now (*temps*); **jusqu'en mai**/*etc* until May/*etc*; **jusqu'où?** how far?; **j. dans**/ **sous**/*etc* right into/under/*etc*; **j. chez moi** as far as my place; (*temps*) up till now; **en avoir j.-là** *Fam* to be fed up; – *conj* **jusqu'à ce qu'il vienne** until he comes.

juste [ʒyst] *a* (*équitable*) fair, just; (*légitime*) just; (*calcul, raisonnement*) correct, right, accurate; (*remarque*) sound; (*oreille*) good; (*voix*) *Mus* true; (*vêtement*) tight; **un peu j.** (*quantité, repas etc*) barely enough; **très j.!** quite so *ou* right!; **à 3 heures j.** on the stroke of 3; – *adv* (*deviner, compter*) correctly, right, accurately; (*chanter*) in tune; (*exactement, seulement*) just; **au j.** exactly; **tout j.** (*à peine, seulement*) only just; **c'était j.!** (*il était temps*) it was a near thing!; **un peu j.** (*mesurer, compter*) a bit on the short side; – *nm* (*homme*) just man. ◆**justement** *adv* precisely, exactly, just; (*avec justesse ou justice*) justly. ◆**justesse** *nf* (*exactitude*) accuracy; **de j.** (*éviter, gagner etc*) just.

justice [ʒystis] *nf* justice; (*organisation, autorités*) law; **en toute j.** in all fairness; **rendre j. à** to do justice to. ◆**justicier, -ière** *nmf* dispenser of justice.

justifier [ʒystifje] *vt* to justify; – *vi* **j. de** to prove; – **se j.** *vpr* *Jur* to clear oneself (**de** of); (*attitude etc*) to be justified. ◆**justifiable** *a* justifiable. ◆**justificatif, -ive** *a* **document j.** supporting document, proof. ◆**justification** *nf* justification; (*preuve*) proof.

jute [ʒyt] *nm* (*fibre*) jute.

juteux, -euse [ʒytø, -øz] *a* juicy.

juvénile [ʒyvenil] *a* youthful.

juxtaposer [ʒykstapoze] *vt* to juxtapose. ◆**juxtaposition** *nf* juxtaposition.

K

K, k [ka] *nm* K, k.

kaki [kaki] *a inv* & *nm* khaki.

kaléidoscope [kaleidɔskɔp] *nm* kaleidoscope.

kangourou [kɑ̃ɡuru] *nm* **1** (*animal*) kangaroo. **2**® (*porte-bébé*) baby sling.

karaté [karate] *nm* *Sp* karate.

kart [kart] *nm* *Sp* (go-)kart, go-cart. ◆**karting** [-iŋ] *nm* *Sp* (go-)karting.

kascher [kaʃɛr] *a inv Rel* kosher.

kayac [kajak] *nm* (*bateau*) *Sp* canoe.

képi [kepi] *nm* (*coiffure*) *Mil* kepi.

kermesse [kɛrmɛs] *nf* charity fête; (*en Belgique etc*) village fair.

kérosène [kerozɛn] *nm* kerosene, aviation fuel.

kibboutz [kibuts] *nm* kibbutz.

kidnapp/er [kidnape] *vt* to kidnap. ◆**—eur, -euse** *nmf* kidnapper.

kilo(gramme) [kilo, kilɔɡram] *nm* kilo(gramme).

kilomètre [kilɔmɛtr] *nm* kilometre. ◆**kilométrage** *nm* *Aut* = mileage. ◆**kilométrique** *a* **borne k.** = milestone.

kilowatt [kilɔwat] *nm* kilowatt.

kimono [kimɔno] *nm* (*tunique*) kimono.

kinésithérapie [kineziterapi] *nf* physiotherapy. ◆**kinésithérapeute** *nmf* physiotherapist.

kiosque [kjɔsk] *nm* (*à journaux*) kiosk, stall; **k. à musique** bandstand.

kit [kit] *nm* (*meuble etc prêt à monter*) kit; **en k.** in kit form, ready to assemble.

klaxon® [klaksɔn] *nm Aut* horn. ◆**klaxonner** *vi* to hoot, *Am* honk.

km *abrév* (*kilomètre*) km.

k.-o. [kao] *a inv* **mettre k.-o.** *Boxe* to knock out.

kyrielle [kirjɛl] *nf* **une k. de** a long string of.

kyste [kist] *nm Méd* cyst.

L

L, l [ɛl] *nm* L, l.

l', la [l, la] *voir le.*

là [la] **1** *adv* there; (*chez soi*) in, home; **je reste là** I'll stay here; **c'est là que** *ou* **où** that's where; **c'est là ton erreur** that's *ou* there's your mistake; **là où il est** where he is; **à cinq mètres de là** five metres away; **de là son échec** (*cause*) hence his *ou* her failure; **jusque-là** (*lieu*) as far as that; **passe par là** go that way. **2** *adv* (*temps*) then; **jusque-là** up till then. **3** *int* **là, là!** (*pour rassurer*) there, there!; **alors là!** well!; **oh là là!** oh dear! **4** *voir* **ce**², **celui.**

là-bas [labɑ] *adv* over there.

label [label] *nm Com* label, mark (*of quality, origin etc*).

labeur [labœr] *nm Litt* toil.

labo [labo] *nm Fam* lab. ◆**laboratoire** *nm* laboratory; **l. de langues** language laboratory.

laborieux, -euse [labɔrjø, -øz] *a* (*pénible*) laborious; (*personne*) industrious; **les classes laborieuses** the working classes.

labour [labur] *nm* ploughing, *Am* plowing, digging over. ◆**labour/er** *vt* (*avec charrue*) to plough, *Am* plow; (*avec bêche*) to dig over; (*visage etc*) *Fig* to furrow. ◆**-eur** *nm* ploughman, *Am* plowman.

labyrinthe [labirɛ̃t] *nm* maze, labyrinth.

lac [lak] *nm* lake.

lacer [lase] *vt* to lace (up). ◆**lacet** *nm* **1** (*shoe- ou boot-*)lace. **2** (*de route*) twist, zigzag; **route en l.** winding *ou* zigzag road.

lacérer [lasere] *vt* (*papier etc*) to tear; (*visage etc*) to lacerate.

lâche [lɑʃ] **1** *a* cowardly; — *nmf* coward. **2** *a* (*détendu*) loose, slack. ◆**lâchement** *adv* in a cowardly manner. ◆**lâcheté** *nf* cowardice; **une l.** (*action*) a cowardly act.

lâch/er [lɑʃe] *vt* (*main, objet etc*) to let go of; (*bombe, pigeon*) to release; (*place, études*) to give up; (*juron*) to utter, let slip; (*secret*) to let out; **l. qn** (*laisser tranquille*) to leave s.o. (alone); (*abandonner*) *Fam* to drop s.o.; **l. prise** to let go; — *vi* (*corde*) to give way; — *nm* release. ◆**-eur, -euse** *nmf Fam* deserter.

kyrielle [kirjɛl] *nf* **une k. de** a long string of.

kyste [kist] *nm Méd* cyst.

laconique [lakɔnik] *a* laconic.

lacrymogène [lakrimɔʒɛn] *a* **gaz l.** tear gas.

lacté [lakte] *a* (*régime*) milk-; **la Voie lactée** the Milky Way.

lacune [lakyn] *nf* gap, deficiency.

lad [lad] *nm* stable boy, groom.

là-dedans [lad(ə)dɑ̃] *adv* (*lieu*) in there, inside. ◆**là-dessous** *adv* underneath. ◆**là-dessus** *adv* on it, on that; (*monter*) on top; (*alors*) thereupon. ◆**là-haut** *adv* up there; (*à l'étage*) upstairs.

lagon [lagɔ̃] *nm* (small) lagoon. ◆**lagune** *nf* lagoon.

laid [lɛ] *a* ugly; (*ignoble*) wretched. ◆**laideur** *nf* ugliness.

laine [lɛn] *nf* wool; **de l., en l.** woollen. ◆**lainage** *nm* (*vêtement*) woollen garment, woolly; (*étoffe*) woollen material; *pl* (*vêtements, objets fabriqués*) woollens. ◆**laineux, -euse** *a* woolly.

laïque [laik] *a* (*vie*) secular; (*habit, tribunal*) lay; — *nmf* (*non-prêtre*) layman, laywoman.

laisse [lɛs] *nf* lead, leash; **en l.** on a lead *ou* leash.

laisser [lese] *vt* to leave; **l. qn partir/ entrer/etc** (*permettre*) to let s.o. go/come in/etc; **l. qch à qn** (*confier, donner*) to let s.o. have sth, leave sth with s.o.; (*vendre*) to let s.o. have sth; **laissez-moi le temps de le faire** give me *ou* leave me time to do it; **se l. aller/faire** to let oneself go/be pushed around. ◆**laissé(e)-pour-compte** *nmf* (*personne*) misfit, reject. ◆**laisser-aller** *nm inv* carelessness, slovenliness; ◆**laissez-passer** *nm inv* (*sauf-conduit*) pass.

lait [lɛ] *nm* milk; **frère/sœur de l.** foster-brother/-sister; **dent de l.** milk tooth. ◆**laitage** *nm* milk product *ou* food. ◆**laiterie** *nf* dairy. ◆**laiteux, -euse** *a* milky. ◆**laitier, -ière** *a* (*produits*) dairy-; — *nm* (*livreur*) milkman; (*vendeur*) dairyman; — *nf* dairywoman.

laiton [lɛtɔ̃] *nm* brass.

laitue [lety] nf lettuce.

laïus [lajys] nm Fam speech.

lama [lama] nm (animal) llama.

lambeau, -x [lɑ̃bo] nm shred, bit; **mettre en lambeaux** to tear to shreds; **tomber en lambeaux** to fall to bits.

lambin, -ine [lɑ̃bɛ̃, -in] nmf dawdler. **◆lambiner** vi to dawdle.

lambris [lɑ̃bri] nm panelling. **◆lambrisser** vt to panel.

lame [lam] nf **1** (de couteau, rasoir etc) blade; (de métal) strip, plate; **l. de parquet** floorboard. **2** (vague) wave; **l. de fond** ground swell.

lamelle [lamɛl] nf (thin strip; **l. de verre** (pour microscope) slide.

lamenter (se) [səlamɑ̃te] vpr to moan, lament; **se l. sur** to lament (over). **◆lamentable** a (mauvais) deplorable; (voix, cri) mournful. **◆lamentation** nf lament(ation).

laminé [lamine] a (métal) laminated.

lampadaire [lɑ̃padɛr] nm standard lamp; (de rue) street lamp.

lampe [lɑ̃p] nf lamp; (au néon) light; (de vieille radio) valve, Am (vacuum) tube; **l. de poche** torch, Am flashlight.

lampée [lɑ̃pe] nf Fam gulp.

lampion [lɑ̃pjɔ̃] nm Chinese lantern.

lance [lɑ̃s] nf spear; (de tournoi) Hist lance; (extrémité de tuyau) nozzle; **l. d'incendie** fire hose.

lance-flammes [lɑ̃sflam] nm inv flame thrower. **◆l.-pierres** nm inv catapult. **◆l.-roquettes** nm inv rocket launcher.

lanc/er [lɑ̃se] vt (jeter) to throw (à to); (avec force) to hurl; (navire, mode, acteur, idée) to launch; (regard) to cast (à at); (moteur) to start; (ultimatum) to issue; (bombe) to drop; (gifle) to give; (cri) to utter; — **se l.** vpr (se précipiter) to rush; **se l. dans** (aventure, discussion) to launch into; — nm un l. a throw; **le l. de** the throwing of. **◆—ée** nf momentum. **◆—ement** nm Sp throwing; (de fusée, navire etc) launch(ing).

lancinant [lɑ̃sinɑ̃] a (douleur) shooting; (obsédant) haunting.

landau [lɑ̃do] nm (pl -s) pram, Am baby carriage.

lande [lɑ̃d] nf moor, heath.

langage [lɑ̃gaʒ] nm (système, faculté d'expression) language; **l. machine** computer language.

lange [lɑ̃ʒ] nm (baby) blanket. **◆langer** vt (bébé) to change.

langouste [lɑ̃gust] nf (spiny) lobster.

◆langoustine nf (Dublin) prawn, Norway lobster.

langue [lɑ̃g] nf Anat tongue; Ling language; **de l.** anglaise/française English-/French-speaking; **l. maternelle** mother tongue; **mauvaise l.** (personne) gossip. **◆languette** nf (patte) tongue.

langueur [lɑ̃gœr] nf languor. **◆langu/ir** vi to languish (après for, after); (conversation) to flag. **◆—issant** a languid; (conversation) flagging.

lanière [lanjɛr] nf strap; (d'étoffe) strip.

lanterne [lɑ̃tɛrn] nf lantern; (électrique) lamp; pl Aut sidelights.

lanterner [lɑ̃tɛrne] vi to loiter.

lapalissade [lapalisad] nf statement of the obvious, truism.

laper [lape] vt (boire) to lap up; — vi to lap.

lapider [lapide] vt to stone.

lapin [lapɛ̃] nm rabbit; **mon (petit) l.!** my dear!; **poser un l. à qn** Fam to stand s.o. up.

laps [laps] nm **un l. de temps** a lapse of time.

lapsus [lapsys] nm slip (of the tongue).

laquais [lakɛ] nm Hist & Fig lackey.

laque [lak] nf lacquer; **l. à cheveux** hair spray, (hair) lacquer. **◆laquer** vt to lacquer.

laquelle [lakɛl] voir **lequel**.

larbin [larbɛ̃] nm Fam flunkey.

lard [lar] nm (fumé) bacon; (gras) (pig's) fat. **◆lardon** nm Culin strip of bacon ou fat.

large [larʒ] a wide, broad; (vêtement) loose; (idées, esprit) broad; (grand) large; (généreux) liberal; **l. d'esprit** broad-minded; **l. de six mètres** six metres wide; — adv (calculer) liberally, broadly; — nm breadth, width; **avoir six mètres de l.** to be six metres wide; **le l.** (mer) the open sea; **au l. de Cherbourg** Nau off Cherbourg; **être au l.** to have lots of room; **avoir l. le temps** to have plenty of time, have ample time. **◆largesse** nf liberality. **◆largeur** nf width, breadth; (d'esprit) breadth.

larguer [large] vt (bombe, parachutiste) to drop; **l. qn** (se débarrasser de) to drop s.o.; **l. les amarres** Nau to cast off.

larme [larm] nf tear; (goutte) Fam drop; **en larmes** in tears; **rire aux larmes** to laugh till one cries. **◆larmoyer** vi (yeux) to water.

larve [larv] nf (d'insecte) larva, grub.

larvé [larve] a latent, underlying.

larynx [larɛ̃ks] nm Anat larynx. **◆laryngite** nf Méd laryngitis.

las, lasse [lɑ, lɑs] a tired, weary (de of).

◆**lasser** vt to tire, weary; **se l. de** to tire of.
◆**lassitude** nf tiredness, weariness.

lascar [laskar] nm Fam (clever) fellow.

lascif, -ive [lasif, -iv] a lascivious.

laser [lazɛr] nm laser.

lasso [laso] nm lasso.

latent [latɑ̃] a latent.

latéral, -aux [lateral, -o] a lateral, side-.

latin, -ine [latɛ̃, -in] a & nmf Latin; − nm (langue) Latin.

latitude [latityd] nf Géog & Fig latitude.

latrines [latrin] nfpl latrines.

latte [lat] nf slat, lath; (de plancher) board.

lauréat, -ate [lɔrea, -at] nmf (prize)winner; − a prize-winning.

laurier [lɔrje] nm Bot laurel, bay; **du l.** Culin bay leaves.

lavabo [lavabo] nm washbasin, sink; pl (cabinet) toilet(s), Am washroom.

lavande [lavɑ̃d] nf lavender.

lave [lav] nf Géol lava.

lave-auto [lavoto] nm car wash. ◆**l.-glace** nm windscreen ou Am windshield washer. ◆**l.-linge** nm washing machine. ◆**l.-vaisselle** nm dishwasher.

laver [lave] vt to wash; **l. qn de** (soupçon etc) to clear s.o. of; − **se l.** vpr to wash (oneself), Am wash up; **se l. les mains** to wash one's hands (Fig **de** of). ◆**lavable** a washable. ◆**lavage** nm washing; **l. de cerveau** Psy brainwashing. ◆**laverie** nf (automatique) launderette, Am laundromat. ◆**lavette** nf dish cloth; (homme) Péj drip. ◆**laveur** nm **l. de carreaux** window cleaner ou Am washer. ◆**lavoir** nm (bâtiment) washhouse.

laxatif, -ive [laksatif, -iv] nm & a Méd laxative.

laxisme [laksism] nm permissiveness, laxity. ◆**laxiste** a permissive, lax.

layette [lɛjɛt] nf baby clothes, layette.

le, la, pl **les** [l(ə), la, le] (le & la become l' before a vowel or mute h) **1** art déf (à + le = au, à + les = aux; de + le = du, de + les = des); **le garçon** the boy; **la fille** the girl; **venez, les enfants!** come children!; **les petits/rouges/etc** the little ones/red ones/etc; **mon ami le plus intime** my closest friend. **2** (généralisation, abstraction) **la beauté** beauty; **la France** France; **les Français** the French; **les hommes** men; **aimer le café** to like coffee. **3** (possession) **il ouvrit la bouche** he opened his mouth; **se blesser au pied** to hurt one's foot; **avoir les cheveux blonds** to have blond hair. **4** (mesure) **dix francs le kilo** ten francs a kilo. **5** (temps) **elle vient le lundi** she comes on Monday(s);

elle passe le soir she comes over in the evening(s); **l'an prochain** next year; **une fois l'an** once a year. **6** pron (homme) him; (femme) her; (chose, animal) it; pl them; **je la vois** I see her; I see it; **je le vois** I see him; I see it; **je les vois** I see them; **es-tu fatigué?** − **je le suis** are you tired? − I am; **je le crois** I think so.

leader [lidœr] nm Pol leader.

lécher [leʃe] vt to lick; **se l. les doigts** to lick one's fingers. ◆**lèche-vitrines** nm **faire du l.-vitrines** to go window-shopping.

leçon [ləsɔ̃] nf lesson; **faire la l. à qn** to lecture s.o.

lecteur, -trice [lɛktœr, -tris] nmf reader; Univ (foreign language) assistant; **l. de cassettes** cassette player. ◆**lecture** nf reading; pl (livres) books; **faire de la l. à qn** to read to s.o.; **de la l.** some reading matter.

légal, -aux [legal, -o] a legal; (médecine) forensic. ◆**légalement** adv legally. ◆**légaliser** vt to legalize. ◆**légalité** nf legality (de of); **respecter la l.** to respect the law.

légation [legasjɔ̃] nf Pol legation.

légende [leʒɑ̃d] nf **1** (histoire, fable) legend. **2** (de plan, carte) key, legend; (de photo) caption. ◆**légendaire** a legendary.

léger, -ère [leʒe, -ɛr] a light; (bruit, faute, fièvre etc) slight; (café, thé, argument) weak; (bière, tabac) mild; (frivole) frivolous; (irréfléchi) careless; **à la légère** (agir) rashly. ◆**légèrement** adv lightly; (un peu) slightly; (à la légère) rashly. ◆**légèreté** nf lightness; frivolity.

légiférer [leʒifere] vi to legislate.

légion [leʒjɔ̃] nf Mil & Fig legion. ◆**légionnaire** nm (de la Légion étrangère) legionnaire.

législatif, -ive [leʒislatif, -iv] a legislative; (élections) parliamentary. ◆**législation** nf legislation. ◆**législature** nf (période) Pol term of office.

légitime [leʒitim] a (action, enfant etc) legitimate; **en état de l. défense** acting in self-defence. ◆**légitimité** nf legitimacy.

legs [leg] nm Jur legacy, bequest; (héritage) Fig legacy. ◆**léguer** vt to bequeath (à to).

légume [legym] **1** nm vegetable. **2** nf **grosse l.** (personne) Fam bigwig.

lendemain [lɑ̃dmɛ̃] nm **le l.** the next day; (avenir) Fig the future; **le l. de** the day after; **le l. matin** the next morning.

lent [lɑ̃] a slow. ◆**lentement** adv slowly. ◆**lenteur** nf slowness.

lentille [lɑ̃tij] nf **1** Bot Culin lentil. **2** (verre) lens.

léopard [leɔpar] nm leopard.

lèpre [lɛpr] *nf* leprosy. ◆**lépreux, -euse** *a* leprous; – *nmf* leper.

lequel, laquelle, *pl* **lesquels, lesquelles** [ləkɛl, lakɛl, lekɛl] (+ **à** = **auquel, à laquelle, auxquel(le)s;** + **de** = **duquel, de laquelle, desquel(le)s**) *pron* (*chose, animal*) which; (*personne*) who, (*indirect*) whom; (*interrogatif*) which (one); **dans l.** in which; **parmi lesquels** (*choses, animaux*) among which; (*personnes*) among whom; **l. préférez-vous?** which (one) do you prefer?

les [le] *voir* **le.**

lesbienne [lɛsbjɛn] *nf* & *af* lesbian.

léser [leze] *vt* (*personne*) *Jur* to wrong.

lésiner [lezine] *vi* to be stingy (**sur** with).

lésion [lezjɔ̃] *nf* *Méd* lesion.

lessive [lesiv] *nf* (*produit*) washing powder; (*linge*) washing; **faire la l.** to do the wash(ing). ◆**lessiver** *vt* to scrub, wash. ◆**-é** *a* *Fam* (*fatigué*) washed-out; (*ruiné*) washed-up. ◆**-euse** *nf* (*laundry*) boiler.

lest [lɛst] *nm* ballast. ◆**lester** *vt* to ballast, weight down; (*remplir*) *Fam* to overload.

leste [lɛst] *a* (*agile*) nimble; (*grivois*) coarse.

léthargie [letarʒi] *nf* lethargy. ◆**léthargique** *a* lethargic.

lettre [lɛtr] *nf* (*missive, caractère*) letter; **en toutes lettres** (*mot*) in full; (*nombre*) in words; **les lettres** (*discipline*) *Univ* arts; **homme de lettres** man of letters. ◆**lettré, -ée** *a* well-read; – *nmf* scholar.

leucémie [løsemi] *nf* leuk(a)emia.

leur [lœr] 1 *a poss* their; **l. chat** their cat; **leurs voitures** their cars; – *pron poss* **le l., la l., les leurs** theirs. 2 *pron inv* (*indirect*) to them; **il l. est facile de . . .** it's easy for them to . . . .

leurre [lœr] *nm* illusion; (*tromperie*) trickery. ◆**leurrer** *vt* to delude.

lever [l(ə)ve] *vt* to lift (up), raise; (*blocus, interdiction*) to lift; (*séance*) to close; (*camp*) to strike; (*plan*) to draw up; (*impôts, armée*) to levy; **l. les yeux** to look up; – *vi* (*pâte*) to rise; (*blé*) to come up; – **se l.** *vpr* to get up; (*soleil, rideau*) to rise; (*jour*) to break; (*brume*) to clear, lift; – *nm* **l. du soleil** sunrise; **le l. du rideau** *Th* the curtain. ◆**-ant** *a* (*soleil*) rising; – *nm* **le l.** the east. ◆**-ée** *nf* **être l.** (*debout*) to be up. ◆**-ée** *nf* (*d'interdiction*) lifting; (*d'impôts*) levying; (*du courrier*) collection; **l. de boucliers** public outcry.

levier [ləvje] *nm* lever; (*pour soulever*) crowbar.

lèvre [lɛvr] *nf* lip; **du bout des lèvres** half-heartedly, grudgingly.

lévrier [levrije] *nm* greyhound.

levure [ləvyr] *nf* yeast.

lexique [lɛksik] *nm* vocabulary, glossary.

lézard [lezar] *nm* lizard.

lézarde [lezard] *nf* crack, split. ◆**lézarder** 1 *vi* *Fam* to bask in the sun. 2 **se l.** *vpr* to crack, split.

liaison [ljɛzɔ̃] *nf* (*rapport*) connection; (*routière etc*) link; *Gram Mil* liaison; **l. (amoureuse)** love affair; **en l. avec qn** in contact with s.o.

liane [ljan] *nf* *Bot* jungle vine.

liant [ljɑ̃] *a* sociable.

liasse [ljas] *nf* bundle.

Liban [libɑ̃] *nm* Lebanon. ◆**libanais, -aise** *a* & *nmf* Lebanese.

libell/er [libele] *vt* (*contrat etc*) to word, draw up; (*chèque*) to make out. ◆**-é** *nm* wording.

libellule [libelyl] *nf* dragonfly.

libéral, -ale, -aux [liberal, -o] *a* & *nmf* liberal. ◆**libéraliser** *vt* to liberalize. ◆**libéralisme** *nm* liberalism. ◆**libéralité** *nf* liberality; (*don*) liberal gift.

libér/er [libere] *vt* (*prisonnier etc*) to (set) free, release; (*pays, esprit*) to liberate (**de** from); **l. qn de** to free s.o. of *ou* from; – **se l.** *vpr* to get free, free oneself (**de** of, from). ◆**libérateur, -trice** *a* (*sentiment etc*) liberating; – *nmf* liberator. ◆**libération** *nf* freeing, release; liberation; **l. conditionnelle** *Jur* parole. ◆**liberté** *nf* freedom, liberty; **en l. provisoire** *Jur* on bail; **mettre en l.** to free, release; **mise en l.** release.

libraire [librɛr] *nmf* bookseller. ◆**librairie** *nf* (*magasin*) bookshop.

libre [libr] *a* free (**de qch** from sth, **de faire** to do); (*voie, route*) clear; (*place*) vacant, free; (*école*) private and religious); **l. penseur** freethinker. ◆**l.-échange** *nm* *Écon* free trade. ◆**l.-service** *nm* (*pl* **libres-services**) (*système, magasin etc*) self-service. ◆**librement** *adv* freely.

Libye [libi] *nf* Libya. ◆**libyen, -enne** *a* & *nmf* Libyan.

licence [lisɑ̃s] *nf* *Sp Com Littér* licence; *Univ* (bachelor's) degree; **l. ès lettres/sciences** arts/science degree, = BA/BSc, = *Am* BA/BS. ◆**licencié, -ée** *a* & *nmf* graduate; **l. ès lettres/sciences** bachelor of arts/science = BA/BSc = *Am* BA/BS.

licencier [lisɑ̃sje] *vt* (*ouvrier*) to lay off, dismiss. ◆**licenciement** *nm* dismissal.

licite [lisit] *a* licit, lawful.

licorne [likɔrn] *nf* unicorn.

lie [li] *nf* dregs.

liège [ljɛʒ] *nm* (*matériau*) cork.

lien [ljɛ̃] *nm* (*rapport*) link, connection; (*de*

parenté tie, bond; (*attache, ficelle*) tie. ◆**lier** vt (*attacher*) to tie (up), bind; (*relier*) to link (up), connect; (*conversation, amitié*) to strike up; **l. qn** (*unir, engager*) to bind s.o.; **— se l.** vpr (*idées etc*) to connect, link together; **se l. avec qn** to make friends with s.o.; **amis très liés** very close friends.

lierre [ljɛr] nm ivy.

lieu, -x [ljø] nm place; (*d'un accident*) scene; **les lieux** (*locaux*) the premises; **sur les lieux** on the spot; **avoir l.** to take place, be held; **au l. de** instead of; **avoir l. de faire** (*des raisons*) to have good reason to do; **en premier l.** in the first place, firstly; **en dernier l.** lastly; **l. commun** commonplace. ◆**l.-dit** nm (pl lieux-dits) Géog locality.

lieue [ljø] nf (*mesure*) Hist league.

lieutenant [ljøtnã] nm lieutenant.

lièvre [ljɛvr] nm hare.

ligament [ligamã] nm ligament.

ligne [liɲ] nf (*trait, règle, contour, transport*) line; (*belle silhouette de femme etc*) figure; (*rangée*) row, line; **(se) mettre en l.** to line up; **en l.** Tél connected, through; **entrer en l. de compte** to be of consequence, count; **faire entrer en l. de compte** to take into account; **grande l.** Rail main line; **les grandes lignes** Fig the broad outline; **pilote de l.** airline pilot; **à la l.** Gram new paragraph.

lignée [liɲe] nf line, ancestry.

ligoter [ligɔte] vt to tie up.

ligue [lig] nf (*alliance*) league. ◆**se liguer** vpr to join together, gang up (*contre* against).

lilas [lila] nm lilac; – a inv (*couleur*) lilac.

limace [limas] nf (*mollusque*) slug.

limaille [limɑj] nf filings.

limande [limãd] nf (*poisson*) dab.

lime [lim] nf (*outil*) file. ◆**limer** vt to file.

limier [limje] nm (*chien*) bloodhound.

limite [limit] nf limit; (*de propriété, jardin etc*) boundary; pl Fb boundary lines; **dépasser la l.** to go beyond the bounds; – a (*cas*) extreme; (*vitesse, prix, âge etc*) maximum; **date l.** latest date, deadline; **date l. de vente** Com sell-by date. ◆**limitatif, -ive** a restrictive. ◆**limitation** nf limitation; (*de vitesse*) limit. ◆**limiter** vt to limit, restrict; (*délimiter*) to border; **se l. à faire** to limit ou restrict oneself to doing.

limoger [limɔʒe] vt (*destituer*) to dismiss.

limonade [limɔnad] nf (*eau, explication*) fizzy) lemonade.

limpide [lɛ̃pid] a (*eau, explication*) (crystal) clear. ◆**limpidité** nf clearness.

lin [lɛ̃] nm Bot flax; (*tissu*) linen; **huile de l.** linseed oil.

linceul [lɛ̃sœl] nm shroud.

linéaire [lineɛr] a linear.

linge [lɛ̃ʒ] nm (*pièces de tissu*) linen; (*à laver*) washing, linen; (*torchon*) cloth; **l. (de corps)** underwear. ◆**lingerie** nf (*de femmes*) underwear; (*local*) linen room.

lingot [lɛ̃go] nm ingot.

linguiste [lɛ̃gɥist] nmf linguist. ◆**linguistique** a linguistic; – nf linguistics.

lino [lino] nm lino. ◆**linoléum** nm linoleum.

linotte [linɔt] nf (*oiseau*) linnet; **tête de l.** Fig scatterbrain.

lion [ljɔ̃] nm lion. ◆**lionceau, -x** nm lion cub. ◆**lionne** nf lioness.

liquéfier [likefje] vt, **— se l.** vpr to liquefy.

liqueur [likœr] nf liqueur.

liquide [likid] a liquid; **argent l.** ready cash; – nm liquid; **du l.** (*argent*) ready cash.

liquider [likide] vt (*dette, stock etc*) to liquidate; (*affaire, travail*) to wind up, finish off; **l. qn** (*tuer*) Fam to liquidate s.o. ◆**liquidation** nf liquidation; winding up; (*vente*) (clearance) sale.

lire¹ * [lir] vti to read.

lire² [lir] nf (*monnaie*) lira.

lis¹ [lis] nm (*plante, fleur*) lily.

lis², lisent [li, liz] voir **lire¹**.

liseron [lizrɔ̃] nm Bot convolvulus.

lisible [lizibl] a (*écriture*) legible; (*livre*) readable. ◆**lisiblement** adv legibly.

lisière [lizjɛr] nf edge, border.

lisse [lis] a smooth. ◆**lisser** vt to smooth; (*plumes*) to preen.

liste [list] nf list; **l. électorale** register of electors, electoral roll; **sur la l. rouge** Tél ex-directory, Am unlisted.

lit¹ [li] nm bed; **l. d'enfant** cot, Am crib; **lits superposés** bunk beds; **garder le l.** to stay in bed. ◆**literie** nf bedding, bed clothes.

lit² [li] voir **lire¹**.

litanie [litani] **1** nf (*énumération*) long list (*de of*). **2** nfpl (*prière*) Rel litany.

litière [litjɛr] nf (*couche de paille*) litter.

litige [litiʒ] nm dispute; Jur litigation. ◆**litigieux, -euse** a contentious.

litre [litr] nm litre.

littéraire [literɛr] a literary. ◆**littérature** nf literature.

littéral, -aux [literal, -o] a literal. ◆**—ement** adv literally.

littoral, -aux [litɔral, -o] a coastal; – nm coast(line).

liturgie [lityrʒi] nf liturgy. ◆**liturgique** a liturgical.

livide [livid] a (*bleuâtre*) livid; (*pâle*) (ghastly) pale, pallid.

livre¹ [livr] nm book; **l. de bord** Nau logbook; **l. de poche** paperback (book); **le l., l'industrie du l.** the book industry. **2** nf (monnaie, poids) pound. ◆**livresque** a (savoir) Péj bookish. ◆**livret** nm (registre) book; Mus libretto; **l. scolaire** school report book; **l. de famille** family registration book; **l. de caisse d'épargne** bankbook, passbook.

livrée [livre] nf (uniforme) livery.

livrer [livre] vt (marchandises) to deliver (à to); (secret) to give away; **l. qn à** (la police etc) to give s.o. up ou over to; **l. bataille** to do ou join battle; — **se l.** vpr (se rendre) to give oneself up (à to); (se confier) to confide (à in); **se l. à** (habitude, excès etc) to indulge in; (tâche) to devote oneself to; (désespoir, destin) to abandon oneself to. ◆**livraison** nf delivery. ◆**livreur, -euse** nmf delivery man, delivery woman.

lobe [lɔb] nm Anat lobe.

local, -aux [lɔkal, -o] **1** a local. **2** nm & nmpl (pièce, bâtiment) premises. ◆**localement** adv locally. ◆**localiser** vt (déterminer) to locate; (limiter) to localize. ◆**localité** nf locality.

locataire [lɔkatɛr] nmf tenant; (hôte payant) lodger.

location [lɔkasjɔ̃] nf (de maison etc) renting; (à bail) leasing; (de voiture) hiring; (réservation) booking; (par propriétaire) renting (out), letting; leasing (out); hiring (out); (loyer) rental; (bail) lease; **bureau de l.** booking office; **en l.** on hire.

lock-out [lɔkawt] nm inv (industriel) lock-out.

locomotion [lɔkɔmosjɔ̃] nf locomotion. ◆**locomotive** nf locomotive, engine.

locuteur [lɔkytœr] nm Ling speaker. ◆**locution** nf phrase, idiom; Gram phrase.

logarithme [lɔgaritm] nm logarithm.

loge [lɔʒ] nf (de concierge) lodge; (d'acteur) dressing-room; (de spectateur) Th box.

log/er [lɔʒe] vt (recevoir, mettre) to accommodate, house; (héberger) to put up; **être logé et nourri** to have board and lodging; — vi (à l'hôtel etc) to put up, lodge; (habiter) to live; (trouver à) **se l.** to find somewhere to live; (temporairement) to find somewhere to stay; **se l. dans** (balle) to lodge (itself) in. ◆—**eable** a habitable. ◆—**ement** nm accommodation, lodging; (habitat) housing; (appartement) lodgings, flat, Am apartment; (maison) dwelling. ◆—**eur, -euse** nmf landlord, landlady.

logiciel [lɔʒisjɛl] nm (d'un ordinateur) software inv.

logique [lɔʒik] a logical; — nf logic. ◆—**ment** adv logically.

logistique [lɔʒistik] nf logistics.

logo [lɔgo] nm logo.

loi [lwa] nf law; Pol act; **projet de l.** Pol bill; **faire la l.** to lay down the law (à to).

loin [lwɛ̃] adv far (away ou off); **Boston est l. (de Paris)** Boston is a long way away (from Paris); **plus l.** further, farther; (ci-après) further on; **l. de là** Fig far from it; **au l.** in the distance, far away; **de l.** from a distance; (de beaucoup) by far; **de l. en l.** every so often. ◆**lointain** a distant, far-off; — nm dans le l. in the distance.

loir [lwar] nm (animal) dormouse.

loisir [lwazir] nm **le l. de faire** the time to do; **moment de l.** moment of leisure; **loisirs** (temps libre) spare time, leisure (time); (distractions) spare-time ou leisure activities.

Londres [lɔ̃dr] nm ou f London. ◆**londonien, -ienne** a London-; — nmf Londoner.

long, longue [lɔ̃, lɔ̃g] a long; **être l. (à faire)** to be a long time ou slow (in doing); **l. de deux mètres** two metres long; — nm avoir **deux mètres de l.** to be two metres long; **tomber de tout son l.** to fall flat; **(tout) le l. de** (espace) all along; **tout le l. de** (temps) throughout; **de l. en large** (marcher etc) up and down; **en l. et en large** thoroughly; **en l.** lengthwise; **à la longue** in the long run. ◆**l.-courrier** nm Av long-distance airliner. ◆**longue-vue** nf (pl longues-vues) telescope.

longer [lɔ̃ʒe] vt to pass ou go along; (forêt, mer) to skirt; (mur) to hug.

longévité [lɔ̃ʒevite] nf longevity.

longitude [lɔ̃ʒityd] nf longitude.

longtemps [lɔ̃tɑ̃] adv (for) a long time; **trop/avant l.** too/before long; **aussi l. que** as long as.

longue [lɔ̃g] voir **long**. ◆**longuement** adv at length. ◆**longuet, -ette** a Fam (fairly) lengthy. ◆**longueur** nf length; pl (de texte, film) over-long passages; **saut en l.** Sp long jump; **à l. de journée** all day long; **l. d'onde** Rad & Fig wavelength.

lopin [lɔpɛ̃] nm **l. de terre** plot ou patch of land.

loquace [lɔkas] a loquacious.

loque [lɔk] **1** nfpl rags. **2** nf **l. (humaine)** (personne) human wreck.

loquet [lɔkɛ] nm latch.

lorgner [lɔrɲe] vt (regarder, convoiter) to eye.

lors [lɔr] adv **l. de** at the time of; **depuis l.,**

dès l. from then on; **dès l. que** (*puisque*) since.

losange [lɔzɑ̃ʒ] *nm Géom* diamond, lozenge.

lot [lo] *nm* **1** (*de loterie*) prize; **gros l.** top prize, jackpot. **2** (*portion, destin*) lot. ◆**loterie** *nf* lottery, raffle. ◆**lotir** *vt* (*terrain*) to divide into lots; **bien loti** *Fig* favoured by fortune. ◆**lotissement** *nm* (*terrain*) building plot; (*habitations*) housing estate *ou* development.

lotion [losjɔ̃] *nf* lotion.

loto [loto] *nm* (*jeu*) lotto.

louche [luʃ] **1** *a* (*suspect*) shady, fishy. **2** *nf Culin* ladle.

loucher [luʃe] *vi* to squint; **l. sur** *Fam* to eye.

louer [lwe] *vt* **1** (*prendre en location*) to rent (*house, flat etc*); (*à bail*) to lease; (*voiture*) to hire, rent; (*réserver*) to book; (*donner en location*) to rent (out), let; to lease (out); to hire (out); **maison/chambre à l.** house/room to let. **2** (*exalter*) to praise (**de** for); **se l. de** to be highly satisfied with. ◆**louable** *a* praiseworthy, laudable. ◆**louange** *nf* praise; **à la l. de** in praise of.

loufoque [lufɔk] *a* (*fou*) *Fam* nutty, crazy.

loukoum [lukum] *nm* Turkish delight.

loup [lu] *nm* wolf; **avoir une faim de l.** to be ravenous. ◆**l.-garou** *nm* (*pl* **loups-garous**) werewolf.

loupe [lup] *nf* magnifying glass.

louper [lupe] *vt Fam* (*train etc*) to miss; (*examen*) to fail; (*travail*) to mess up.

lourd [lur] *a* heavy (*Fig* **de** with); (*temps, chaleur*) close, sultry; (*faute*) gross; (*tâche*) arduous; (*esprit*) dull; **– ** *adv* **peser l.** (*malle etc*) to be heavy. ◆**lourdaud, -aude** *a* loutish, oafish; **– ** *nmf* lout, oaf. ◆**lourdement** *adv* heavily. ◆**lourdeur** *nf* heaviness; (*de temps*) closeness; (*d'esprit*) dullness.

loutre [lutr] *nf* otter.

louve [luv] *nf* she-wolf. ◆**louveteau, -x** *nm* (*scout*) cub (scout).

louvoyer [luvwaje] *vi* (*tergiverser*) to hedge, be evasive.

loyal, -aux [lwajal, -o] *a* (*fidèle*) loyal (**envers** to); (*honnête*) honest, fair (**envers** to). ◆**loyalement** *adv* loyally; fairly. ◆**loyauté** *nf* loyalty; honesty, fairness.

loyer [lwaje] *nm* rent.

lu [ly] *voir* **lire** [1].

lubie [lybi] *nf* whim.

lubrifi/er [lybrifje] *vt* to lubricate. ◆**—ant** *nm* lubricant.

lubrique [lybrik] *a* lewd, lustful.

lucarne [lykarn] *nf* (*ouverture*) skylight; (*fenêtre*) dormer window.

lucide [lysid] *a* lucid. ◆**lucidité** *nf* lucidity.

lucratif, -ive [lykratif, -iv] *a* lucrative.

lueur [lɥœr] *nf* (*lumière*) & *Fig* glimmer.

luge [lyʒ] *nf* toboggan, sledge.

lugubre [lygybr] *a* gloomy, lugubrious.

lui [lɥi] **1** *pron mf* (*complément indirect*) (to) him; (*femme*) (to) her; (*chose, animal*) (to) it; **je le lui ai montré** I showed it to him *ou* to her, I showed it to him *ou* her it; **il lui est facile de ...** it's easy for him *ou* her to .... **2** *pron m* (*complément direct*) him; (*chose, animal*) it; (*sujet emphatique*) he; **pour lui** for him; **plus grand que lui** taller than him; **il ne pense qu'à lui** he only thinks of himself. ◆**lui-même** *pron* himself; (*chose, animal*) itself.

luire* [lɥir] *vi* to shine, gleam. ◆**luisant** *a* (*métal etc*) shiny.

lumbago [lɔ̃bago] *nm* lumbago.

lumière [lymjɛr] *nf* light; **à la l. de** by the light of; (*grâce à*) *Fig* in the light of; **faire toute la l. sur** *Fig* to clear up; **mettre en l.** to bring to light. ◆**luminaire** *nm* (*appareil*) lighting appliance. ◆**lumineux, -euse** *a* (*idée, ciel etc*) bright, brilliant; (*ondes, source etc*) light-; (*cadran, corps etc*) *Tech* luminous.

lunaire [lynɛr] *a* lunar; **clarté l.** light *ou* brightness of the moon.

lunatique [lynatik] *a* temperamental.

lunch [lœ̃ʃ, lœ̃tʃ] *nm* buffet lunch, snack.

lundi [lœ̃di] *nm* Monday.

lune [lyn] *nf* moon; **l. de miel** honeymoon.

lunette [lynɛt] *nf* **1** **lunettes** glasses, spectacles; (*de protection, de plongée*) goggles; **lunettes de soleil** sunglasses. **2** (*astronomique*) telescope; **l. arrière** *Aut* rear window.

lurette [lyrɛt] *nf* **il y a belle l.** a long time ago.

luron [lyrɔ̃] *nm* **gai l.** gay fellow.

lustre [lystr] *nm* (*éclairage*) chandelier; (*éclat*) lustre. ◆**lustré** *a* (*par l'usure*) shiny.

luth [lyt] *nm Mus* lute.

lutin [lytɛ̃] *nm* elf, imp, goblin.

lutte [lyt] *nf* fight, struggle; *Sp* wrestling; **l. des classes** class warfare *ou* struggle. ◆**lutter** *vi* to fight, struggle; *Sp* to wrestle. ◆**lutteur, -euse** *nmf* fighter; *Sp* wrestler.

luxe [lyks] *nm* luxury; **un l. de** a wealth of; **de l.** (*article*) luxury-; (*modèle*) de luxe. ◆**luxueux, -euse** *a* luxurious.

Luxembourg [lyksãbur] *nm* Luxembourg.

luxure [lyksyr] *nf* lewdness, lust.

luxuriant [lyksyrjã] *a* luxuriant.

luzerne [lyzɛrn] *nf Bot* lucerne, *Am* alfalfa.

lycée [lise] *nm* (secondary) school, *Am* high school. ◆**lycéen, -enne** *nmf* pupil (*at lycée*).

lymphatique [lɛ̃fatik] *a* (*apathique*) sluggish.

lynch/er [lɛ̃ʃe] *vt* to lynch. ◆**—age** *nm* lynching.

lynx [lɛ̃ks] *nm* (*animal*) lynx.

lyre [lir] *nf Mus Hist* lyre.

lyrique [lirik] *a* (*poème etc*) lyric; (*passionné*) *Fig* lyrical. ◆**lyrisme** *nm* lyricism.

lys [lis] *nm* (*plante, fleur*) lily.

M

M, m [ɛm] *nm* M, m.

m *abrév* (*mètre*) metre.

M [məsjø] *abrév* = **Monsieur**.

m' [m] *voir* **me**.

ma [ma] *voir* **mon**.

macabre [makabr] *a* macabre, gruesome.

macadam [makadam] *nm* (*goudron*) tarmac.

macaron [makarɔ̃] *nm* (*gâteau*) macaroon; (*insigne*) (round) badge.

macaroni(s) [makarɔni] *nm*(*pl*) macaroni.

macédoine [masedwan] *nf* **m.** (**de légumes**) mixed vegetables; **m.** (**de fruits**) fruit salad.

macérer [masere] *vti Culin* to soak. ◆**macération** *nf* soaking.

mâcher [mɑʃe] *vt* to chew; **il ne mâche pas ses mots** he doesn't mince matters *ou* his words.

machiavélique [makjavelik] *a* Machiavellian.

machin [maʃɛ̃] *nm Fam* (*chose*) thing, what's-it; (*personne*) what's-his-name.

machinal, -aux [maʃinal, -o] *a* (*involontaire*) unconscious, mechanical. ◆**—ement** *adv* unconsciously, mechanically.

machination [maʃinasjɔ̃] *nf* machination.

machine [maʃin] *nf* (*appareil, avion, système etc*) machine; (*locomotive, moteur*) engine; *pl Tech* machines, (heavy) machinery; **m. à coudre** sewing machine; **m. à écrire** typewriter; **m. à laver** washing machine. ◆**machinerie** *nf Nau* engine room. ◆**machiniste** *nm Th* stage-hand.

macho [matʃo] *nm* macho *m*; – *a* (*f inv*) (*attitude etc*) macho.

mâchoire [mɑʃwar] *nf* jaw.

mâchonner [mɑʃɔne] *vt* to chew, munch.

maçon [masɔ̃] *nm* builder; bricklayer; mason. ◆**maçonnerie** *nf* (*travaux*) building work; (*ouvrage de briques*) brickwork; (*de pierres*) masonry, stonework.

maculer [makyle] *vt* to stain (**de** with).

Madagascar [madagaskar] *nf* Madagascar.

madame, pl mesdames [madam, medam] *nf* madam; **oui m.** yes (madam); **bonjour mesdames** good morning (ladies); **Madame ou Mme Legras** Mrs Legras; **Madame** (*sur une lettre*) *Com* Dear Madam.

madeleine [madlɛn] *nf* (small) sponge cake.

mademoiselle, pl mesdemoiselles [madmwazɛl, medmwazɛl] *nf* miss; **oui m.** yes (miss); **bonjour mesdemoiselles** good morning (ladies); **Mademoiselle ou Mlle Legras** Miss Legras; **Mademoiselle** (*sur une lettre*) *Com* Dear Madam.

madère [madɛr] *nm* (*vin*) Madeira.

madone [madɔn] *nf Rel* madonna.

madrier [madrije] *nm* (*poutre*) beam.

maestro [maɛstro] *nm* Mus maestro.

maf(f)ia [mafja] *nf* Mafia.

magasin [magazɛ̃] *nm* shop, *Am* store; (*entrepôt*) warehouse; (*d'arme*) & *Phot* magazine; **grand m.** department store. ◆**magasinier** *nm* warehouseman.

magazine [magazin] *nm* (*revue*) magazine.

magie [maʒi] *nf* magic. ◆**magicien, -ienne** *nmf* magician. ◆**magique** *a* (*baguette, mot*) magic; (*mystérieux, enchanteur*) magical.

magistral, -aux [maʒistral, -o] *a* masterly, magnificent. ◆**—ement** *adv* magnificently.

magistrat [maʒistra] *nm* magistrate. ◆**magistrature** *nf* judiciary, magistracy.

magnanime [maɲanim] *a* magnanimous.

magnat [maɲa] *nm* tycoon, magnate.

magner (se) [səmaɲe] *vpr Fam* to hurry up.

magnésium [maɲezjɔm] *nm* magnesium.

magnétique [maɲetik] *a* magnetic. ◆**magnétiser** *vt* to magnetize. ◆**magnétisme** *nm* magnetism.

magnétophone [maɲetɔfɔn] *nm* (*Fam* **magnéto**) tape recorder; **m. à cassettes** cassette recorder. ◆**magnétoscope** *nm* video (cassette) recorder.

magnifique [maɲifik] *a* magnificent. ◆**magnificence** *nf* magnificence. ◆**magnifiquement** *adv* magnificently.

magnolia [maɲɔlja] *nm* (*arbre*) magnolia.

magot [mago] *nm* (*économies*) nest egg, hoard.

magouille(s) [maguj] *nf(pl)* *Pol Fam* fiddling, graft.

mai [mɛ] *nm* May.

maigre [mɛgr] *a* thin, lean; (*viande*) lean; (*fromage, yaourt*) low-fat; (*repas, salaire, espoir*) meagre; **faire m.** to abstain from meat ◆**maigrement** *adv* (*chichement*) meagrely. ◆**maigreur** *nf* thinness; (*de viande*) leanness; (*médiocrité*) *Fig* meagreness. ◆**maigrichon, -onne** *a* & *nmf* skinny (person). ◆**maigrir** *vi* to get thin(ner); – *vt* to make thin(ner).

maille [maj] *nf* (*de tricot*) stitch; (*de filet*) mesh; **m. filée** (*de bas*) run, ladder. ◆**maillon** *nm* (*de chaîne*) link.

maillet [majɛ] *nm* (*outil*) mallet.

maillot [majo] *nm* (*de sportif*) jersey; (*de danseur*) leotard, tights; **m. (de corps)** vest, *Am* undershirt; **m. (de bain)** (*de femme*) swimsuit; (*d'homme*) (swimming) trunks.

main [mɛ̃] *nf* hand; **tenir à la m.** to hold in one's hand; **à la m.** (*livrer, faire etc*) by hand; **la m. dans la m.** hand in hand; **haut les mains!** hands up!; **donner un coup de m. à qn** to lend s.o. a (helping) hand; **coup de m.** (*habileté*) knack; **sous la m.** at hand, handy; **en venir aux mains** to come to blows; **avoir la m. heureuse** to be lucky, have a lucky streak; **mettre la dernière m. à** to put the finishing touches to; **en m. propre** (*remettre qch*) in person; **attaque/vol à m. armée** armed attack/robbery; **homme de m.** henchman, hired man; **m. courante** handrail; **prêter m.-forte à** to lend assistance to. ◆**m.-d'œuvre** *nf* (*pl* **mains-d'œuvre**) (*travail*) manpower, labour; (*salariés*) labour *ou* work force.

maint [mɛ̃] *a Litt* many a; **maintes fois, à maintes reprises** many a time.

maintenant [mɛ̃tnɑ̃] *adv* now; (*de nos jours*) nowadays; **m. que** that; **dès m.** from now on.

maintenir* [mɛ̃tnir] *vt* (*conserver*) to keep, maintain; (*retenir*) to hold, keep; (*affirmer*) to maintain (**que** that); – **se m.** *vpr* (*durer*) to be maintained; (*rester*) to keep; (*malade, vieillard*) to hold one's own. ◆**maintien** *nm* (*action*) maintenance (**de** of); (*allure*) bearing.

maire [mɛr] *nm* mayor. ◆**mairie** *nf* town hall; (*administration*) town council.

mais [mɛ] *conj* but; **m. oui, m. si** yes of course; **m. non** definitely not.

maïs [mais] *nm* (*céréale*) maize, *Am* corn; **farine de m.** cornflour, *Am* cornstarch.

maison [mɛzɔ̃] *nf* (*bâtiment*) house; (*immeuble*) building; (*chez-soi, asile*) home; *Com* firm; (*famille*) household; **à la m.** at home; (*rentrer, aller*) home; – *a inv* (*pâté, tartes etc*) homemade; **m. de la culture** arts *ou* cultural centre; **m. d'étudiants** student hostel; **m. des jeunes** youth club; **m. de repos** rest home; **m. de retraite** old people's home. ◆**maisonnée** *nf* household. ◆**maisonnette** *nf* small house.

maître [mɛtr] *nm* master; **se rendre m. de** (*incendie*) to master, control; (*pays*) to conquer; **être m. de** (*situation etc*) to be in control of, be master of; **m. de soi** in control of oneself; **m. d'école** teacher; **m. d'hôtel** (*restaurant*) head waiter; **m. de maison** host; **m. chanteur** blackmailer; **m. nageur** (*sauveteur*) swimming instructor (and lifeguard). ◆**maîtresse** *nf* mistress; **m. d'école** teacher; **m. de maison** hostess; (*ménagère*) housewife; **être m. de** (*situation etc*) to be in control of; – *af* (*idée, poutre*) main; (*carte*) master.

maîtrise [mɛtriz] *nf* (*habileté, contrôle*) mastery (**de** of); (*grade*) *Univ* master's degree (**de** in); **m. (de soi)** self-control. ◆**maîtriser** *vt* (*émotion*) to master, control; (*sujet*) to master; (*incendie*) to (bring under) control; **m. qn** to subdue s.o.; – **se m.** *vpr* to control oneself.

majesté [maʒɛste] *nf* majesty; **Votre M.** (*titre*) Your Majesty. ◆**majestueux, -euse** *a* majestic, stately.

majeur [maʒœr] **1** *a* (*primordial*) & *Mus* major; **être m.** *Jur* to be of age; **la majeure partie de** most of; **en majeure partie** for the most part. **2** *nm* (*doigt*) middle finger.

majorer [maʒɔre] *vt* to raise, increase. ◆**majoration** *nf* (*hausse*) increase (**de** in).

majorette [maʒɔrɛt] *nf* (drum) majorette.

majorité [maʒɔrite] *nf* majority (**de** of); (*âge*) *Jur* coming of age, majority; (*gouvernement*) party in office, government; **en m.** in the *ou* a majority; (*pour la plupart*) in the main. ◆**majoritaire** *a* (*vote etc*) majority-; **être m.** to be in the *ou* a majority; **être m. aux élections** to win the elections.

Majorque [maʒɔrk] *nf* Majorca.

majuscule [maʒyskyl] *a* capital; – *nf* capital letter.

mal, maux [mal, mo] **1** *nm Phil Rel* evil;

(*dommage*) harm; (*douleur*) pain; (*maladie*) illness; (*malheur*) misfortune; **dire du m. de** to speak ill of; **m. de dents** toothache; **m. de gorge** sore throat; **m. de tête** headache; **m. de ventre** stomachache; **m. de mer** seasickness; **m. du pays** homesickness; **avoir le m. du pays**/*etc* to be homesick/*etc*; **avoir m. à la tête/à la gorge**/*etc* to have a headache/sore throat/*etc*; **ça (me) fait m., j'ai m.** it hurts me; **faire du m. à** to harm, hurt; **avoir du m. à faire** to have trouble (in) doing; **se donner du m. pour faire** to go to a lot of trouble to do. **2** *adv* (*travailler etc*) badly; (*entendre, comprendre*) not too well; **aller m.** (*projet etc*) to be going badly; (*personne*) *Méd* to be bad or ill; **m. (à l'aise)** uncomfortable; **se trouver m.** to (feel) faint; **(ce n'est) pas m.** (*mauvais*) (that's) not bad; **pas m.** (*beaucoup*) *Fam* quite a lot (de of); **c'est m. de jurer**/*etc* (*moralement*) it's wrong to swear/*etc*; **de m. en pis** from bad to worse; **m. renseigner/interpréter/** *etc* to misinform/misinterpret/*etc*.

malade [malad] *a* ill, sick; (*arbre, dent*) diseased; (*estomac, jambe*) bad; **être m. du foie/cœur** to have a bad liver/heart; — *nmf* sick person; (*à l'hôpital, d'un médecin*) patient; **les malades** the sick. ◆**maladie** *nf* illness, sickness, disease. ◆**maladif, -ive** *a* (*personne*) sickly; (*morbide*) morbid.

maladroit [maladrwa] *a* (*malhabile*) clumsy, awkward; (*indélicat*) tactless. ◆**maladresse** *nf* clumsiness, awkwardness; (*bévue*) blunder.

malaise [malɛz] *nm* (*angoisse*) uneasiness, malaise; (*indisposition*) faintness, dizziness; **avoir un m.** to feel faint *ou* dizzy.

malaisé [maleze] *a* difficult.

Malaisie [malɛzi] *nf* Malaysia.

malaria [malarja] *nf* malaria.

malavisé [malavize] *a* ill-advised (**de faire** to do).

malax/er [malakse] *vt* (*pétrir*) to knead; (*mélanger*) to mix. ◆**—eur** *nm Tech* mixer.

malchance [malʃɑ̃s] *nf* bad luck; **une m.** (*mésaventure*) a mishap. ◆**malchanceux, -euse** *a* unlucky.

malcommode [malkɔmɔd] *a* awkward.

mâle [mal] *a* male; (*viril*) manly; — *nm* male.

malédiction [malediksjɔ̃] *nf* curse.

maléfice [malefis] *nm* evil spell. ◆**maléfique** *a* baleful, evil.

malencontreux, -euse [malɑ̃kɔ̃trø, -øz] *a* unfortunate.

malentendant, -ante [malɑ̃tɑ̃dɑ̃, -ɑ̃t] *nmf* person who is hard of hearing.

malentendu [malɑ̃tɑ̃dy] *nm* misunderstanding.

malfaçon [malfasɔ̃] *nf* defect.

malfaisant [malfəzɑ̃] *a* evil, harmful.

malfaiteur [malfɛtœr] *nm* criminal.

malformation [malfɔrmasjɔ̃] *nf* malformation.

malgré [malgre] *prép* in spite of; **m. tout** for all that, after all; **m. soi** (*à contrecœur*) reluctantly.

malhabile [malabil] *a* clumsy.

malheur [malœr] *nm* (*événement*) misfortune; (*accident*) mishap; (*malchance*) bad luck, misfortune; **par m.** unfortunately. ◆**malheureusement** *adv* unfortunately. ◆**malheureux, -euse** *a* (*misérable, insignifiant*) wretched, miserable; (*fâcheux*) unfortunate; (*malchanceux*) unlucky, unfortunate; — *nmf* (*infortuné*) (poor) wretch; (*indigent*) needy person.

malhonnête [malɔnɛt] *a* dishonest. ◆**malhonnêteté** *nf* dishonesty; **une m.** (*action*) a dishonest act.

malice [malis] *nf* mischievousness. ◆**malicieux, -euse** *a* mischievous.

malin, -igne [malɛ̃, -iɲ] *a* (*astucieux*) smart, clever; (*plaisir*) malicious; (*tumeur*) *Méd* malignant. ◆**malignité** *nf* (*méchanceté*) malignity; *Méd* malignancy.

malingre [malɛ̃gr] *a* puny, sickly.

malintentionné [malɛ̃tɑ̃sjɔne] *a* ill-intentioned (**à l'égard de** towards).

malle [mal] *nf* (*coffre*) trunk; (*de véhicule*) boot, *Am* trunk. ◆**mallette** *nf* small suitcase; (*pour documents*) attaché case.

malléable [maleabl] *a* malleable.

malmener [malməne] *vt* to manhandle, treat badly.

malodorant [malɔdɔrɑ̃] *a* smelly.

malotru, -ue [malɔtry] *nmf* boor, lout.

malpoli [malpɔli] *a* impolite.

malpropre [malprɔpr] *a* (*sale*) dirty. ◆**malpropreté** *nf* dirtiness.

malsain [malsɛ̃] *a* unhealthy, wholesome.

malséant [malseɑ̃] *a* unseemly.

malt [malt] *nm* malt.

Malte [malt] *nf* Malta. ◆**maltais, -aise** *a* & *nmf* Maltese.

maltraiter [maltrete] *vt* to ill-treat.

malveillant [malvejɑ̃] *a* malevolent. ◆**malveillance** *nf* malevolence, ill will.

malvenu [malvəny] *a* (*déplacé*) uncalled-for.

maman [mamɑ̃] *nf* mum(my), *Am* mom(my).

mamelle [mamɛl] *nf* (*d'animal*) teat; (*de*

vache) udder. ◆**mamelon** *nm* **1** (*de femme*) nipple. **2** (*colline*) hillock.

mamie [mami] *nf Fam* granny, grandma.

mammifère [mamifɛr] *nm* mammal.

manche [mɑ̃ʃ] **1** *nf* (*de vêtement*) sleeve; *Sp Cartes* round; **la M.** *Géog* the Channel. **2** *nm* (*d'outil etc*) handle; **m. à balai** broomstick; (*d'avion, d'ordinateur*) joystick. ◆**manchette** *nf* **1** (*de chemise etc*) cuff. **2** *Journ* headline. ◆**manchon** (*fourrure*) muff.

manchot, -ote [mɑ̃ʃo, -ɔt] **1** *a & nmf* one-armed *ou* one-handed (person). **2** *nm* (*oiseau*) penguin.

mandarin [mɑ̃darɛ̃] *nm* (*lettré influent*) *Univ Péj* mandarin.

mandarine [mɑ̃darin] *nf* (*fruit*) tangerine, mandarin (orange).

mandat [mɑ̃da] *nm* **1** (*postal*) money order. **2** *Pol* mandate; *Jur* power of attorney; **m. d'arrêt** warrant (for s.o.'s arrest). ◆**mandataire** *nmf* (*délégué*) representative, proxy. ◆**mandater** *vt* to delegate; *Pol* to give a mandate to.

manège [manɛʒ] *nm* **1** (*à la foire*) merry-go-round, roundabout; (*lieu*) riding-school; (*piste*) ring, manège; (*exercice*) horsemanship. **2** (*intrigue*) wiles, trickery.

manette [manɛt] *nf* lever, handle.

manger [mɑ̃ʒe] *vt* to eat; (*essence, électricité*) *Fig* to guzzle; (*fortune*) to eat up; (*corroder*) to eat into; **donner à m.** to feed; – *vi* to eat; **trouver à bien ici** the food is good here; **m. à sa faim** to have enough to eat; – *nm* food. ◆**mangeable** *a* eatable. ◆**mangeaille** *nf Péj* (bad) food. ◆**mangeoire** *nf* (*feeding*) trough. ◆**mangeur, -euse** *nmf* eater.

mangue [mɑ̃g] *nf* (*fruit*) mango.

manie [mani] *nf* mania, craze (**de** for). ◆**maniaque** *a* finicky, fussy; – *nmf* fusspot, **un m. de la propreté**/etc a maniac for cleanliness/etc.

manier [manje] *vt* to handle; **se m. bien** (*véhicule etc*) to handle well. ◆**maniabilité** *nf* (*de véhicule etc*) manoeuvrability. ◆**maniable** *a* easy to handle. ◆**maniement** *nm* handling; **m. d'armes** *Mil* drill.

manière [manjɛr] *nf* way, manner; *pl* (*politesse*) manners; **de toute m.** anyway, anyhow; **de m. à faire** so as to do; **à ma m.** my way, (in) my own way; **de cette m.** (in) this way; **la m. dont elle parle** the way (in which) she talks; **d'une m. générale** generally speaking; **faire des manières** (*chichis*) to make a fuss; (*être affecté*) to put on airs. ◆**maniéré** *a* affected; (*style*) mannered.

manif [manif] *nf Fam* demo.

manifeste [manifɛst] **1** *a* (*évident*) manifest, obvious. **2** *nm Pol* manifesto.

manifester [manifɛste] **1** *vt* to show, manifest; – **se m.** *vpr* (*apparaître*) to appear; (*sentiment, maladie etc*) to show *ou* manifest itself. **2** *vi Pol* to demonstrate. ◆**manifestant, -ante** *nmf* demonstrator. ◆**manifestation** *nf* **1** (*expression*) expression, manifestation; (*action*) manoeuvring; (*apparition*) appearance. **2** *Pol* demonstration; (*réunion, fête*) event.

manigance [manigɑ̃s] *nf* little scheme. ◆**manigancer** *vt* to plot.

manipuler [manipyle] *vt* (*manier*) to handle; (*faits, électeurs*) *Péj* to manipulate. ◆**manipulation** *nf* (*maniement*) handling; *Péj* manipulation (**de** of); *pl Pol Péj* manipulation.

manivelle [manivɛl] *nf Aut* crank.

mannequin [mankɛ̃] *nm* (*femme, homme*) (fashion) model; (*statue*) dummy.

manœuvre [manœvr] **1** *nm* (*ouvrier*) labourer. **2** *nf* (*opération*) & *Mil* manoeuvre, *Am* maneuver; (*action*) manoeuvring; (*intrigue*) scheme. ◆**manœuvrer** *vt* (*véhicule, personne etc*) to manoeuvre, *Am* maneuver; (*machine*) to operate; – *vi* to manoeuvre, *Am* maneuver.

manoir [manwar] *nm* manor house.

manque [mɑ̃k] *nm* lack (**de** of); (*lacune*) gap; *pl* (*défauts*) shortcomings; **m. à gagner** loss of profit. ◆**manqu/er** *vt* (*chance, cible etc*) to miss; (*ne pas réussir*) to make a mess of, ruin; (*examen*) to fail; – *vi* (*faire défaut*) to be short *ou* lacking; (*être absent*) to be absent (**à** from); (*être en moins*) to be missing *ou* short; (*défaillir, échouer*) to fail; **m. de** (*pain, argent etc*) to be short of; (*attention, cohérence*) to lack; **ça manque de sel**/etc it lacks salt/etc, there isn't any salt/etc; **m. à** (*son devoir*) to fail in; (*sa parole*) to break; **le temps lui manque** he's short of time, he has no time; **elle/cela lui manque** he misses her/that; **je ne manquerai pas de venir** I won't fail to come; **ne manquez pas de venir** don't forget to come; **elle a manqué (de) tomber** (*faillir*) she nearly fell; – *v imp* **il manque/il nous manque dix tasses** there are/we are ten cups short. ◆**–ant** *a* missing. ◆**–é** *a* (*médecin, pilote etc*) failed; (*livre*) unsuccessful. ◆**–ement** *nm* breach (**à** of).

mansarde [mɑ̃sard] *nf* attic.

manteau, -x [mɑ̃to] *nm* coat.

manucure [manykyr] *nmf* manicurist. ◆**manucurer** *vt Fam* to manicure.

manuel, -elle [manɥɛl] **1** a (travail etc) manual. **2** nm (livre) handbook, manual.

manufacture [manyfaktyr] nf factory. ◆**manufacturé** a (produit) manufactured.

manuscrit [manyskri] nm manuscript; (tapé à la machine) typescript.

manutention [manytɑ̃sjɔ̃] nf Com handling (of stores). ◆**manutentionnaire** nmf packer.

mappemonde [mapmɔ̃d] nf map of the world; (sphère) Fam globe.

maquereau, -x [makro] nm (poisson) mackerel.

maquette [makɛt] nf (scale) model.

maquill/er [makije] vt (visage) to make up; (voiture etc) Péj to tamper with; (vérité etc) Péj to fake; — **se m.** to make (oneself) up. ◆**—age** nm (fard) make-up.

maquis [maki] nm Bot scrub, bush; Mil Hist maquis.

maraîcher, -ère [mareʃe, -ɛʃer] nmf market gardener, Am truck farmer.

marais [mare] nm marsh, bog; **m. salant** saltworks, saltern.

marasme [marasm] nm Écon stagnation.

marathon [maratɔ̃] nm marathon.

maraudeur, -euse [marodœr, -øz] nmf petty thief.

marbre [marbr] nm marble. ◆**marbrier** nm (funéraire) monumental mason.

marc [mar] nm (eau-de-vie) marc, brandy; **m. (de café)** coffee grounds.

marchand, -ande [marʃɑ̃, -ɑ̃d] nmf trader, shopkeeper; (de vins, charbon) merchant; (de cycles, meubles) dealer; **m. de bonbons** confectioner; **m. de couleurs** hardware merchant ou dealer; **m. de journaux** (dans la rue) newsvendor; (dans un magasin) newsagent, Am news dealer; **m. de légumes** greengrocer; **m. de poissons** fishmonger; − a (valeur) market; (prix) trade-. ◆**marchandise(s)** nf(pl) goods, merchandise.

marchand/er [marʃɑ̃de] vi to haggle, bargain; − vt (objet) to haggle over. ◆**—age** nm haggling, bargaining.

marche [marʃ] nf **1** (d'escalier) step, stair. **2** (démarche, trajet) walk; Mil Mus march; (pas) pace; (de train, véhicule) movement; (de maladie, d'événement) progress, course; **la m.** (action) Sp walking; **faire m. arrière** Aut to reverse; **la bonne m. de** (opération, machine) the smooth running of; **un train/véhicule en m.** a moving train/ vehicle; **mettre qch en m.** to start sth (up). ◆**marcher** vi (à pied) to walk; Mil to

march; (poser le pied) to tread, step; (train, véhicule etc) to run, go, move; (fonctionner) to go, work, run; (prospérer) to go well; **faire m.** (machine) to work; (entreprise) to run; (personne) Fam to kid; **ça marche?** Fam how's it going?; **elle va m.** (accepter) Fam she'll go along (with it). ◆**marcheur, -euse** nmf walker.

marché [marʃe] nm (lieu) market; (contrat) deal; **faire son ou le m.** to do one's shopping (in the market); **être bon m.** to be cheap; **voiture(s)/etc bon m.** cheap car(s)/ etc; **vendre (à) bon m.** to sell cheap(ly); **c'est meilleur m.** it's cheaper; **par-dessus le m.** Fig into the bargain; **au m. noir** on the black market; **le M. commun** the Common Market.

marchepied [marʃəpje] nm (de train, bus) step(s); (de voiture) running board.

mardi [mardi] nm Tuesday; **M. gras** Shrove Tuesday.

mare [mar] nf (flaque) pool; (étang) pond.

marécage [marekaʒ] nm swamp, marsh. ◆**marécageux, -euse** a marshy, swampy.

maréchal, -aux [mareʃal, -o] nm Fr Mil marshal. ◆**m.-ferrant** nm (pl maréchaux-ferrants) blacksmith.

marée [mare] nf tide; (poissons) fresh (sea) fish; **m. noire** oil slick.

marelle [marɛl] nf (jeu) hopscotch.

margarine [margarin] nf margarine.

marge [marʒ] nf margin; **en m. de** (en dehors de) on the periphery of, on the fringe(s) of; **m. de sécurité** safety margin. ◆**marginal, -ale, -aux** a (secondaire, asocial) marginal; − nmf misfit, dropout; (bizarre) weirdo.

marguerite [margərit] nf (fleur) marguerite, daisy.

mari [mari] nm husband.

mariage [marjaʒ] nm marriage; (cérémonie) wedding; (mélange) Fig blend, marriage; **demande en m.** proposal of (marriage). ◆**mari/er** vt (couleurs) to blend; **m. qn** (maire, prêtre etc) to marry s.o.; **m. qn avec** to marry s.o. (off) to; − **se m.** vpr to get married, marry; **se m. avec qn** to marry s.o., get married to s.o. ◆**—é a** married; − nm (bride)groom; **les mariés** the bride and (bride)groom; **les jeunes mariés** the newly-weds. ◆**—ée** nf bride.

marijuana [mariʒɥana] nf marijuana.

marin [marɛ̃] a (air, sel etc) sea-; (flore) marine; (mille) nautical; (costume) sailor-; − nm seaman, sailor. ◆**marine** nf m. (de guerre) navy; **m. marchande** merchant navy; **(bleu) m.** (couleur) navy (blue).

marina [marina] *nf* marina.

mariner [marine] *vti* Culin to marinate.

marionnette [marjɔnɛt] *nf* puppet; (*à fils*) marionette.

maritalement [maritalmã] *adv* vivre m. to live together (as husband and wife).

maritime [maritim] *a* (*droit, province, climat etc*) maritime; (*port*) sea-; (*gare*) harbour-; (*chantier*) naval; (*agent*) shipping-.

marjolaine [marʒɔlɛn] *nf* (*aromate*) marjoram.

mark [mark] *nm* (*monnaie*) mark.

marmaille [marmɑj] *nf* (*enfants*) Fam kids.

marmelade [marmɔlad] *nf* m. (**de fruits**) stewed fruit; **en m.** Culin Fig in a mush.

marmite [marmit] *nf* (cooking) pot.

marmonner [marmɔne] *vti* to mutter.

marmot [marmo] *nm* (*enfant*) Fam kid.

marmotter [marmɔte] *vti* to mumble.

Maroc [marɔk] *nm* Morocco. **◆marocain, -aine** *a* & *nmf* Moroccan.

maroquinerie [marɔkinri] *nf* (*magasin*) leather goods shop. **◆maroquinier** *nm* leather dealer.

marotte [marɔt] *nf* (*dada*) Fam fad, craze.

marque [mark] *nf* (*trace, signe*) mark; (*de fabricant*) make, brand; (*points*) Sp score; **m. de fabrique** trademark; **m. déposée** registered trademark; **la m. de** (*preuve*) the stamp of; **de m.** (*hôte, visiteur*) distinguished; (*produit*) of quality. **◆marqu/er** *vt* (*par une marque etc*) to mark; (*écrire*) to note down; (*indiquer*) to show, mark; (*point, but*) Sp to score; **m. qn** Sp to mark s.o.; **m. les points** Sp to keep (the) score; **m. le coup** to mark the event; – *vi* (*trace*) to leave a mark; (*date, événement*) to stand out; Sp to score. **◆—ant** *a* (*remarquable*) outstanding. **◆—é** *a* (*différence, accent etc*) marked, pronounced. **◆—eur** *nm* (*crayon*) marker.

marquis [marki] *nm* marquis. **◆marquise** *nf* **1** marchioness. **2** (*auvent*) glass canopy.

marraine [marɛn] *nf* godmother.

marre [mar] *nf* en avoir m. Fam to be fed up (de with).

marr/er (se) [səmare] *vpr* Fam to have a good laugh. **◆—ant** *a* Fam hilarious, funny.

marron[1] [marɔ̃] **1** *nm* chestnut; (*couleur*) (chestnut) brown; **m. (d'Inde)** horse chestnut; – *a inv* (*couleur*) (chestnut) brown. **2** *nm* (*coup*) Fam punch, clout. **◆marronnier** *nm* (horse) chestnut tree.

marron[2], -onne [marɔ̃, -ɔn] *a* (*médecin etc*) bogus.

mars [mars] *nm* March.

marsouin [marswɛ̃] *nm* porpoise.

marteau, -x [marto] *nm* hammer; (*de porte*) (door)knocker; **m. piqueur, m. pneumatique** pneumatic drill. **◆marteler** *vt* to hammer. **◆martèlement** *nm* hammering.

martial, -aux [marsjal, -o] *a* martial; **cour martiale** court-martial; **loi martiale** martial law.

martien, -ienne [marsjɛ̃, -jɛn] *nmf* & *a* Martian.

martinet [martinɛ] *nm* (*fouet*) (small) whip.

martin-pêcheur [martɛ̃pɛʃœr] *nm* (*pl* martins-pêcheurs) (*oiseau*) kingfisher.

martyr, -yre[1] [martir] *nmf* (*personne*) martyr; **enfant m.** battered child. **◆martyre[2]** *nm* (*souffrance*) martyrdom. **◆martyriser** *vt* to torture; (*enfant*) to batter.

marxisme [marksism] *nm* Marxism. **◆marxiste** *a* & *nmf* Marxist.

mascara [maskara] *nm* mascara.

mascarade [maskarad] *nf* masquerade.

mascotte [maskɔt] *nf* mascot.

masculin [maskylɛ̃] *a* male; (*viril*) masculine, manly; Gram masculine; (*vêtement, équipe*) men's; – *nm* Gram masculine. **◆masculinité** *nf* masculinity.

masochisme [mazɔism] *nm* masochism. **◆masochiste** *nmf* masochist; – *a* masochistic.

masque [mask] *nm* mask. **◆masquer** *vt* (*dissimuler*) to mask (à from); (*cacher à la vue*) to block off.

massacre [masakr] *nm* massacre, slaughter. **◆massacr/er** *vt* to massacre, slaughter; (*abîmer*) Fam to ruin. **◆—ant** *a* (*humeur*) excruciating.

massage [masaʒ] *nm* massage.

masse [mas] *nf* **1** (*volume*) mass; (*gros morceau, majorité*) bulk (**de** of); **en m.** (*venir, vendre*) in large numbers; **départ en m.** mass *ou* wholesale departure; **manifestation de m.** mass demonstration; **la m.** (*foule*) the masses; **les masses** (*peuple*) the masses; **une m. de** (*tas*) a mass of; **des masses de** Fam masses of. **2** (*outil*) sledgehammer. **3** Él carth, Am ground. **◆mass/er 1** *vt*, – **se m.** *vpr* (*gens*) to mass. **2** *vt* (*frotter*) to massage. **◆—eur** *nm* masseur. **◆—euse** *nf* masseuse.

massif, -ive [masif, -iv] *a* **1** massive; (*départs etc*) mass-; (*or, chêne etc*) solid. **2** *nm* (*d'arbres, de fleurs*) clump; Géog massif. **◆massivement** *adv* (*en masse*) in large numbers.

massue [masy] *nf* (*bâton*) club.

mastic [mastik] *nm* (*pour vitres*) putty; (*pour bois*) filler; **m. (silicone)** mastic.

◆**mastiquer** vt 1 (vitre) to putty; (porte) to mastic; (bois) to fill. 2 (mâcher) to chew, masticate.

mastoc [mastɔk] a inv Péj Fam massive.

mastodonte [mastodɔ̃t] nm (personne) Péj monster; (véhicule) juggernaut.

masturber (se) [səmastyrbe] vpr to masturbate. ◆**masturbation** nf masturbation.

masure [mazyr] nf tumbledown house.

mat [mat] 1 a (papier, couleur) mat(t); (bruit) dull. 2 a inv & nm Échecs (check)mate; **faire ou mettre m.** to (check)mate.

mât [ma] nm (de navire) mast; (poteau) pole.

match [matʃ] nm Sp match, Am game; **m. nul** tie, draw.

matelas [matla] nm mattress; **m. pneumatique** air bed. ◆**matelassé** a (meuble) padded; (tissu) quilted.

matelot [matlo] nm sailor, seaman.

mater [mate] vt (enfant, passion etc) to subdue.

matérialiser [materjalize] vt, — **se m.** vpr to materialize. ◆**matérialisation** nf materialization.

matérialisme [materjalism] nm materialism. ◆**matérialiste** a materialistic; – nmf materialist.

matériaux [materjo] nmpl (building) materials; (de roman, enquête etc) material.

matériel, -ielle [materjɛl] 1 a material; (personne) Péj materialistic; (financier) financial; (pratique) practical. 2 nm equipment, material(s); (d'un ordinateur) hardware inv. ◆**matériellement** adv materially; **m. impossible** physically impossible.

maternel, -elle [maternɛl] a motherly, maternal; (parenté, réprimande) maternal; – nf (école) maternelle nursery school. ◆**materner** vt to mother. ◆**maternité** nf (état) motherhood, maternity; (hôpital) maternity hospital ou unit; (grossesse) pregnancy; **de m.** (congé, allocation) maternity-.

mathématique [matematik] a mathematical; – nfpl mathematics. ◆**mathématicien, -ienne** nmf mathematician. ◆**maths** [mat] nfpl Fam maths, Am math.

matière [matjɛr] nf (sujet) & Scol subject; (de livre) subject matter; **une m., la m., des matières** (substance(s)) matter; **m. première** raw material; **en m. d'art**/etc as regards art/etc, in art/etc; **s'y connaître en m. de** to be experienced in.

matin [matɛ̃] nm morning; **de grand m., de bon m., au petit m.** very early (in the morn-

ing); **le m.** (chaque matin) in the morning; **à sept heures du m.** at seven in the morning; **tous les mardis m.** every Tuesday morning. ◆**matinal, -aux** a (personne) early; (fleur, soleil etc) morning-. ◆**matinée** nf morning; Th matinée; **faire la grasse m.** to sleep late, lie in.

matou [matu] nm tomcat.

matraque [matrak] nf (de policier) truncheon, Am billy (club); (de malfaiteur) cosh, club. ◆**matraqu/er** vt (frapper) to club; (publicité etc) to plug (away) at. ◆**-age** nm (publicitaire) plugging, publicity build-up.

matrice [matris] nf 1 Anat womb. 2 Tech matrix.

matricule [matrikyl] nm (registration) number; – a (livret, numéro) registration-.

matrimonial, -aux [matrimɔnjal, -o] a matrimonial.

mâture [matyr] nf Nau masts.

maturité [matyrite] nf maturity. ◆**maturation** nf maturing.

maudire* [modir] vt to curse. ◆**maudit** a (sacré) (ac)cursed, damned.

maugréer [mogree] vi to growl, grumble (contre at).

mausolée [mozole] nm mausoleum.

maussade [mosad] a (personne etc) glum, sullen; (temps) gloomy.

mauvais [move] a bad; (méchant, malveillant) evil, wicked; (mal choisi) wrong; (mer) rough; **plus m.** worse; **le plus m.** the worst; **il fait m.** the weather's bad; **ça sent m.** it smells bad; (fig) bad ou bad; **mauvaise santé** ill ou bad ou poor health; – nm **le bon et le m.** the good and the bad.

mauve [mov] a & nm (couleur) mauve.

mauviette* [movjɛt] nf personne Péj weakling.

maux [mo] voir **mal**.

maxime [maksim] nf maxim.

maximum [maksimɔm] nm maximum; **le m. de** (force etc) the maximum (amount of); **au m.** as much as possible; (tout au plus) at most; – a maximum; **la température m.** maximum temperature. ◆**maximal, -aux** a maximum.

mayonnaise [majɔnɛz] nf mayonnaise.

mazout [mazut] nm (fuel) oil.

me [m(ə)] (**m'** before vowel or mute h) pron 1 (complément direct) me; **il me voit** he sees me. 2 (indirect) (to) me; **elle me parle** she speaks to me; **tu me l'as dit** you told me. 3 (réfléchi) myself; **je me lave** I wash myself.

méandres [meɑ̃dr] nmpl meander(ing)s.

mec [mɛk] nm (individu) Arg guy, bloke.

mécanique [mekanik] a mechanical; (jouet) clockwork-; – nf (science) mechanics; (mécanisme) mechanism. ◆**mécanicien** nm mechanic; Rail train driver. ◆**mécanisme** nm mechanism.

mécaniser [mekanize] vt to mechanize. ◆**mécanisation** nf mechanization.

mécène [mesɛn] nm patron (of the arts).

méchant [meʃɑ̃] a (cruel) malicious, wicked, evil; (désagréable) nasty; (enfant) naughty; (chien) vicious; **ce n'est pas m.** (grave) Fam it's nothing much. ◆**méchamment** adv (cruellement) maliciously; (très) Fam terribly. ◆**méchanceté** nf malice, wickedness; **une m.** (acte) a malicious act; (parole) a malicious word.

mèche [mɛʃ] nf **1** (de cheveux) lock; pl (reflets) highlights. **2** (de bougie) wick; (de pétard) fuse; (de perceuse) drill, bit. **3 de m. avec qn** (complicité) Fam in collusion ou cahoots with s.o.

méconn/aître* [mekɔnɛtr] vt to ignore; (méjuger) to fail to appreciate. ◆**—u** a unrecognized. ◆**—aissable** a unrecognizable.

mécontent [mekɔ̃tɑ̃] a dissatisfied, discontented (**de** with). ◆**mécontent/er** vt to displease, dissatisfy. ◆**—ement** nm dissatisfaction, discontent.

médaille [medaj] nf (décoration) Sp medal; (pieuse) medallion; (pour chien) name tag; **être m. d'or/d'argent** Sp to be a gold/silver medallist. ◆**médaillé, -ée** nmf medal holder. ◆**médaillon** nm (bijou) locket, medallion; (ornement) Archit medallion.

médecin [medsɛ̃] nm doctor, physician. ◆**médecine** nf medicine; **étudiant en m.** medical student. ◆**médical, -aux** a medical. ◆**médicament** nm medicine. ◆**médicinal, -aux** a medicinal. ◆**médico-légal, -aux** a (laboratoire) forensic.

médias [medja] nmpl (mass) media. ◆**médiatique** a media-.

médiateur, -trice [medjatœr, -tris] nmf mediator; – a mediating. ◆**médiation** nf mediation.

médiéval, -aux [medjeval, -o] a medi(a)eval.

médiocre [medjɔkr] a mediocre, second-rate. ◆**médiocrement** adv (pas très) not very; (pas très bien) not very well. ◆**médiocrité** nf mediocrity.

médire* [medir] vi **m. de** to speak ill of, slander. ◆**médisance(s)** nf(pl) malicious gossip, slander; **une m.** a piece of malicious gossip.

méditer [medite] vt (conseil etc) to meditate on; **m. de faire** to consider doing; – vi to meditate (**sur** on). ◆**méditatif, -ive** a meditative. ◆**méditation** nf meditation.

Méditerranée [mediterane] nf **la M.** the Mediterranean. ◆**méditerranéen, -enne** a Mediterranean.

médium [medjɔm] nm (spirite) medium.

méduse [medyz] nf jellyfish.

méduser [medyze] vt to stun, dumbfound.

meeting [mitiŋ] nm Pol Sp meeting, rally.

méfait [mefɛ] nm Jur misdeed; pl (dégâts) ravages.

méfi/er (se) [səmefje] vpr **se m. de** to distrust, mistrust; (faire attention à) to watch out for, beware of; **méfie-toi!** watch out!, beware!; **je me méfie** I'm distrustful ou suspicious. ◆**—ant** a distrustful, suspicious. ◆**méfiance** nf distrust, mistrust.

mégalomane [megaloman] nmf megalomaniac. ◆**mégalomanie** nf megalomania.

mégaphone [megafon] nm loudhailer.

mégarde (par) [parmegard] adv inadvertently, by mistake.

mégère [meʒɛr] nf (femme) Péj shrew.

mégot [mego] nm Fam cigarette end ou butt.

meilleur, -eure [mejœr] a better (**que** than); **le m. moment/résultat/etc** the best moment/result/etc; – nmf **le m., la meilleure** the best (one).

mélancolie [melɑ̃kɔli] nf melancholy, gloom. ◆**mélancolique** a melancholy, gloomy.

mélange [melɑ̃ʒ] nm mixture, blend; (opération) mixing. ◆**mélanger** vt (mêler) to mix; (brouiller) to mix (up), muddle; – **se m.** vpr to mix; (idées etc) to get mixed (up) ou muddled.

mélasse [melas] nf treacle, Am molasses.

mêl/er [mele] vt to mix, mingle (**à** with); (qualités, thèmes) to combine; (brouiller) to mix (up), muddle; **m. qn à** (impliquer) to involve s.o. in; – **se m.** vpr to mix, mingle (**à** with); **se m. à** (la foule etc) to join; **se m. de** (s'ingérer dans) to meddle in; **mêle-toi de ce qui te regarde!** mind your own business! ◆**—ée** a mixed (**de** with). ◆**—ée** nf (bataille) rough-and-tumble; Rugby scrum(mage).

méli-mélo [melimelo] nm (pl mélis-mélos) Fam muddle.

mélodie [melɔdi] nf melody. ◆**mélodieux, -euse** a melodious. ◆**mélodique** a Mus melodic. ◆**mélomane** nmf music lover.

mélodrame [melɔdram] *nm* melodrama.
◆**mélodramatique** *a* melodramatic.

melon [m(ə)lɔ̃] *nm* **1** (*fruit*) melon. **2** (*chapeau*) m. bowler (hat).

membrane [mɑ̃bran] *nf* membrane.

membre [mɑ̃br] *nm* **1** *Anat* limb. **2** (*d'un groupe*) member.

même [mɛm] **1** *a* (*identique*) same; **en m. temps** at the same time (**que** as); **ce livre/ etc m.** (*exact*) this very book/*etc*; **il est la bonté m.** he is kindness itself; **lui-m./vous-m./etc** himself/yourself/*etc*; – *pron* **le m., la m.** the same (one); **j'ai les mêmes** I have the same (ones). **2** *adv* (*y compris, aussi*) even; **m. si** even if; **tout de m., quand m.** all the same; **de m.** likewise; **de m. que** just as; **ici m.** in this very place; **à m. de** in a position to; **à m. le sol** on the ground; **à m. la bouteille** from the bottle.

mémento [memɛ̃to] *nm* (*aide-mémoire*) handbook; (*agenda*) notebook.

mémoire [memwar] **1** *nf* memory; **de m. d'homme** in living memory; **à la m. de** in memory of. **2** *nm* (*requête*) petition; *Univ* memoir; *pl Littér* memoirs. ◆**mémorable** *a* memorable. ◆**mémorandum** [memɔrɑ̃dɔm] *nm Pol Com* memorandum. ◆**mémorial, -aux** *nm* (*monument*) memorial.

menace [mənas] *nf* threat, menace. ◆**mena/cer** *vt* to threaten (**de faire** to do). ◆**–çant** *a* threatening.

ménage [menaʒ] *nm* (*entretien*) housekeeping; (*couple*) couple, household; **faire le m.** to do the housework; **faire bon m. avec** to get on happily with. ◆**ménager¹, -ère** *a* (*appareil*) domestic, household-; **travaux ménagers** housework; – *nf* (*femme*) housewife.

ménag/er² [menaʒe] *vt* (*arranger*) to prepare *ou* arrange (carefully); (*épargner*) to use sparingly, be careful with; (*fenêtre, escalier etc*) to build; **m. qn** to treat *ou* handle s.o. gently *ou* carefully. ◆**–ement** *nm* (*soin*) care.

ménagerie [menaʒri] *nf* menagerie.

mendier [mɑ̃dje] *vi* to beg; – *vt* to beg for. ◆**mendiant, -ante** *nmf* beggar. ◆**mendicité** *nf* begging.

menées [məne] *nfpl* schemings, intrigues.

men/er [məne] *vt* (*personne, vie etc*) to lead; (*lutte, enquête, tâche etc*) to carry out; (*affaires*) to run; (*bateau*) to command; **m. qn à** (*accompagner, transporter*) to take s.o. to; **m. à bien** *Fig* to carry through; – *vi Sp* to lead. ◆**–eur, -euse** *nmf* (*de révolte*) (ring)leader.

méningite [menɛ̃ʒit] *nf Méd* meningitis.

ménopause [menɔpoz] *nf* menopause.

menottes [mənɔt] *nfpl* handcuffs.

mensonge [mɑ̃sɔ̃ʒ] *nm* lie; (*action*) lying. ◆**mensonger, -ère** *a* untrue, false.

menstruation [mɑ̃stryasjɔ̃] *nf* menstruation.

mensuel, -elle [mɑ̃sɥɛl] *a* monthly; – *nm* (*revue*) monthly. ◆**mensualité** *nf* monthly payment. ◆**mensuellement** *adv* monthly.

mensurations [mɑ̃syrasjɔ̃] *nfpl* measurements.

mental, -aux [mɑ̃tal, -o] *a* mental. ◆**mentalité** *nf* mentality.

menthe [mɑ̃t] *nf* mint.

mention [mɑ̃sjɔ̃] *nf* mention, reference; (*annotation*) comment; **m. bien** *Scol Univ* distinction; **faire m. de** to mention. ◆**mentionner** *vt* to mention.

ment/ir* [mɑ̃tir] *vi* to lie, tell lies *ou* a lie (**à** to). ◆**–eur, -euse** *nmf* liar; – *a* lying.

menton [mɑ̃tɔ̃] *nm* chin.

menu [məny] **1** *a* (*petit*) tiny; (*mince*) slender, fine; (*peu important*) minor, petty; – *adv* (*hacher*) small, finely; – *nm* **par le m.** in detail. **2** *nm* (*carte*) *Culin* menu.

menuisier [mənɥizje] *nm* carpenter, joiner. ◆**menuiserie** *nf* carpentry, joinery; (*ouvrage*) woodwork.

méprendre (se) [səmeprɑ̃dr] *vpr* **se m. sur** to be mistaken about. ◆**méprise** *nf* mistake.

mépris [mepri] *nm* contempt (**de** of, for), scorn (**de** for); **au m. de** without regard to. ◆**mépris/er** *vt* to despise, scorn. ◆**–ant** *a* scornful, contemptuous. ◆**–able** *a* despicable.

mer [mɛr] *nf* sea; (*marée*) tide; **en m.** at sea; **par m.** by sea; **aller à la m.** to go to the seaside; **un homme à la m.!** man overboard!

mercantile [mɛrkɑ̃til] *a Péj* money-grabbing.

mercenaire [mɛrsəner] *a & nm* mercenary.

mercerie [mɛrsəri] *nf* (*magasin*) haberdasher's, *Am* notions store. ◆**mercier, -ière** *nmf* haberdasher, *Am* notions merchant.

merci [mɛrsi] **1** *int & nm* thank you, thanks (**de, pour** for); (**non) m.!** no, thank you! **2** *nf* **à la m. de** at the mercy of.

mercredi [mɛrkrədi] *nm* Wednesday.

mercure [mɛrkyr] *nm* mercury.

merde! [mɛrd] *int Fam* (bloody) hell!

mère [mɛr] *nf* mother; **m. de famille** mother (of a family); **la m. Dubois** *Fam* old Mrs Dubois; **maison m.** *Com* parent firm.

méridien [meridjɛ̃] *nm* meridian.

méridional, -ale, -aux [meridjɔnal, -o] *a* southern; – *nmf* southerner.

meringue [mərɛ̃g] *nf* (*gâteau*) meringue.

merisier [mərizje] *nm* (*bois*) cherry.

mérite [merit] *nm* merit; **homme de m.** (*valeur*) man of worth. ◆**mérit/er** *vt* (*être digne de*) to deserve; (*valoir*) to be worth; **m. de réussir/***etc* to deserve to succeed/*etc.* ◆—**ant** *a* deserving. ◆**méritoire** *a* commendable.

merlan [mɛrlɑ̃] *nm* (*poisson*) whiting.

merle [mɛrl] *nm* blackbird.

merveille [mɛrvɛj] *nf* wonder, marvel; **à m.** wonderfully (well). ◆**merveilleusement** *adv* wonderfully. ◆**merveilleux, -euse** *a* wonderful, marvellous; – *nm* **le m.** (*surnaturel*) the supernatural.

mes [me] *voir* **mon.**

mésange [mezɑ̃ʒ] *nf* (*oiseau*) tit.

mésaventure [mezavɑ̃tyr] *nf* misfortune, misadventure.

mesdames [medam] *voir* **madame.**

mesdemoiselles [medmwazɛl] *voir* **mademoiselle.**

mésentente [mezɑ̃tɑ̃t] *nf* misunderstanding.

mesquin [mɛskɛ̃] *a* mean, petty. ◆**mesquinerie** *nf* meanness, pettiness; **une m.** an act of meanness.

mess [mɛs] *nm inv* Mil mess.

message [mesaʒ] *nm* message. ◆**messager, -ère** *nmf* messenger.

messageries [mesaʒri] *nfpl* Com courier service.

messe [mɛs] *nf* Rel mass.

Messie [mesi] *nm* Messiah.

messieurs [mesjø] *voir* **monsieur.**

mesure [mzyr] *nf* (*évaluation, dimension*) measurement; (*quantité, disposition*) measure; (*retenue*) moderation; (*cadence*) Mus time, beat; **fait sur m.** made to measure; **à m. que** as, as fast as; **dans la m. où** in so far as; **dans une certaine m.** to a certain extent; **en m. de** able to, in a position to; **dépasser la m.** to exceed the bounds. ◆**mesur/er** *vt* to measure; (*juger, estimer*) to calculate, assess, measure; (*argent, temps*) to ration (out); **m. 1 mètre 83** (*personne*) to be six feet tall; (*objet*) to measure six feet; **se m. à** *ou* **avec qn** Fig to pit oneself against s.o. ◆—**é** *a* (*pas, ton*) measured; (*personne*) moderate.

met [me] *voir* **mettre.**

métal, -aux [metal, -o] *nm* metal. ◆**métallique** *a* (*objet*) metal-; (*éclat, reflet, couleur*) metallic. ◆**métallisé** *a* (*peinture*) metallic.

métallo [metalo] *nm* Fam steelworker. ◆**métallurgie** *nf* (*industrie*) steel industry; (*science*) metallurgy. ◆**métallurgique** *a* **usine m.** steelworks. ◆**métallurgiste** *a* & *nm* (*ouvrier*) m. steelworker.

métamorphose [metamɔrfoz] *nf* metamorphosis. ◆**métamorphoser** *vt*, – **se m.** *vpr* to transform (**en** into).

métaphore [metafɔr] *nf* metaphor. ◆**métaphorique** *a* metaphorical.

métaphysique [metafizik] *a* metaphysical.

météo [meteo] *nf* (*bulletin*) weather forecast.

météore [meteɔr] *nm* meteor. ◆**météorite** *nm* meteorite.

météorologie [meteɔrɔlɔʒi] *nf* (*science*) meteorology; (*service*) weather bureau. ◆**météorologique** *a* meteorological; (*bulletin, station, carte*) weather-.

méthode [metɔd] *nf* method; (*livre*) course. ◆**méthodique** *a* methodical.

méticuleux, -euse [metikylø, -øz] *a* meticulous.

métier [metje] *nm* **1** (*travail*) job; (*manuel*) trade; (*intellectuel*) profession; (*habileté*) professional skill; **homme de m.** specialist. **2 m. (à tisser)** loom.

métis, -isse [metis] *a* & *nmf* half-caste.

mètre [mɛtr] *nm* (*mesure*) metre; (*règle*) (metre) rule; **m. (à ruban)** tape measure. ◆**métr/er** *vt* (*terrain*) to survey. ◆—**age** *nm* **1** surveying. **2** (*tissu*) length; (*de film*) footage; **long m.** (*film*) full length film; **court m.** (*film*) short film. ◆—**eur** *nm* quantity surveyor. ◆**métrique** *a* metric.

métro [metro] *nm* underground, *Am* subway.

métropole [metrɔpɔl] *nf* (*ville*) metropolis; (*pays*) mother country. ◆**métropolitain** *a* metropolitan.

mets [me] *nm* (*aliment*) dish.

mett/re* [mɛtr] **1** *vt* to put; (*table*) to lay; (*vêtement, lunettes*) to put on, wear; (*chauffage, radio etc*) to put on, switch on; (*réveil*) to set (à for); (*dépenser*) to spend (**pour une robe/***etc* on a dress/*etc*); **m. dix heures/***etc* **à venir** (*consacrer*) to take ten hours/*etc* coming *ou* to come; **m. à l'aise** (*rassurer*) to put *ou* set at ease; (*dans un fauteuil etc*) to make comfortable; **m. en colère** to make angry; **m. en liberté** to free; **mettons que** (+ *sub*) let's suppose that; – **se m.** *vpr* (*se placer*) to put oneself; (*debout*) to stand; (*assis*) to sit; (*objet*) to be put, go; **se m. en short/pyjama/***etc* to get into one's shorts/pyjamas/*etc*; **se m. en rapport avec** to get in touch with; **se m. à** (*endroit*) to go to; (*travail*) to set oneself to, start; **se m. à faire** to start doing; **se m. à table** to sit (down) at the table; **se m. à l'aise** to make oneself comfortable; **se m. au beau/froid** (*temps*) to turn fine/cold. ◆—**able** *a* wearable. ◆—**eur** *nm* **m. en scène** *Th* producer; *Cin* director.

meuble [mœbl] *nm* piece of furniture; *pl* furniture. ◆**meubl/er** *vt* to furnish; (*remplir*) *Fig* to fill. ◆—**é** *nm* furnished flat *ou Am* apartment.

meugl/er [møgle] *vi* to moo, low. ◆—**ement(s)** *nm(pl)* mooing.

meule [møl] *nf* **1** (*de foin*) haystack. **2** (*pour moudre*) millstone.

meunier, -ière [mønje, -jɛr] *nmf* miller.

meurt [mœr] *voir* **mourir.**

meurtre [mœrtr] *nm* murder. ◆**meurtrier, -ière** *nmf* murderer; – *a* deadly, murderous.

meurtrir [mœrtrir] *vt* to bruise. ◆**meurtrissure** *nf* bruise.

meute [møt] *nf* (*de chiens, de créanciers etc*) pack.

Mexique [mɛksik] *nm* Mexico. ◆**mexicain, -aine** *a & nmf* Mexican.

mi- [mi] *préf* **la mi-mars**/*etc* mid March/*etc*; **à mi-distance** mid-distance, midway.

miaou [mjau] *int* (*cri du chat*) miaow.

◆**miaul/er** [mjole] *vi* to miaow, mew. ◆—**ement(s)** *nm(pl)* miaowing, mewing.

mi-bas [miba] *nm inv* knee sock.

miche [miʃ] *nf* round loaf.

mi-chemin (à) [amiʃmɛ̃] *adv* halfway.

mi-clos [miklo] *a* half-closed.

micmac [mikmak] *nm* (*manigance*) *Fam* intrigue.

mi-corps (à) [amikɔr] *adv* (up) to the waist.

mi-côte (à) [amikot] *adv* halfway up *ou* down (the hill).

micro [mikro] *nm* microphone, mike. ◆**microphone** *nm* microphone.

micro- [mikro] *préf* micro-.

microbe [mikrɔb] *nm* germ, microbe.

microcosme [mikrɔkɔsm] *nm* microcosm.

microfilm [mikrɔfilm] *nm* microfilm.

micro-onde [mikrɔɔd] *nf* microwave; **four à micro-ondes** microwave oven.

microscope [mikrɔskɔp] *nm* microscope. ◆**microscopique** *a* microscopic.

midi [midi] *nm* **1** (*heure*) midday, noon, twelve o'clock; (*heure du déjeuner*) lunchtime. **2** (*sud*) south; **le M.** the south of France.

mie [mi] *nf* soft bread, crumb.

miel [mjɛl] *nm* honey. ◆**mielleux, -euse** *a* (*parole, personne*) unctuous.

mien, mienne [mjɛ̃, mjɛn] *pron poss* **le m., la mienne** mine, my one; **les miens, les miennes** mine, my ones; **les miens** my two; – *nmpl* **les miens** (*amis etc*) my (own) people.

miette [mjɛt] *nf* (*de pain, de bon sens etc*) crumb; **réduire en miettes** to smash to pieces.

mieux [mjø] *adv & a inv* better (**que** than); (*plus à l'aise*) more comfortable; (*plus beau*) better-looking; **le m., la m., les m.** (*convenir, être etc*) the best; (*de deux*) the better; **le m. serait de à...**; the best thing would be to...; **de m. en m.** better and better; **tu ferais m. de partir** you had better leave; **je ne demande pas m.** there's nothing I'd like better (**que de faire** than to do); – *nm* (*amélioration*) improvement; **faire de son m.** to do one's best.

mièvre [mjɛvr] *a* (*douceureux*) *Péj* mannered, wishy-washy.

mignon, -onne [miɲɔ̃, -ɔn] *a* (*charmant*) cute; (*agréable*) nice.

migraine [migrɛn] *nf* headache; *Méd* migraine.

migration [migrasjɔ̃] *nf* migration. ◆**migrant, -ante** *a & nmf* (*travailleur*) migrant worker, migrant.

mijoter [miʒɔte] *vt Culin* to cook (lovingly); (*lentement*) to simmer; (*complot*) *Fig Fam* to brew; – *vi* to simmer.

mil [mil] *nm inv* (*dans les dates*) a *ou* one thousand; **l'an deux m.** the year two thousand.

milice [milis] *nf* militia. ◆**milicien** *nm* militiaman.

milieu, -x [miljø] *nm* (*centre*) middle; (*cadre, groupe social*) environment; (*entre extrêmes*) middle course; (*espace*) *Phys* medium; *pl* (*groupes, littéraires etc*) circles; **au m. de** in the middle of; **au m. du danger** in the midst of danger; **le juste m.** the happy medium; **le m.** (*de malfaiteurs*) the underworld.

militaire [militɛr] *a* military; – *nm* serviceman; (*dans l'armée de terre*) soldier.

milit/er [milite] *vi* (*personne*) to be a militant; (*arguments etc*) to militate (**pour** in favour of). ◆—**ant, -ante** *a & nmf* militant.

mille [mil] **1** *a & nm inv* a *ou* one thousand; **m. hommes**/*etc* a *ou* one thousand men/*etc*; **deux m.** two thousand; **mettre dans le m.** to hit the bull's-eye. **2** *nm* (*mesure*) mile. ◆**m.-pattes** *nm inv* (*insecte*) centipede.

◆**millième** a & nmf thousandth; **un m.** a thousandth. ◆**millier** nm thousand; **un m. (de)** a thousand or so.

millefeuille [milfœj] nm (gâteau) cream slice.

millénaire [milenɛr] nm millennium.

millésime [milezim] nm date (on coins, wine etc).

millet [mijɛ] nm Bot millet.

milli- [mili] préf milli-.

milliard [miljar] nm thousand million, Am billion. ◆**milliardaire** a & nmf multimillionaire.

millimètre [milimɛtr] nm millimetre.

million [miljɔ̃] nm million; **un m. de livres/etc** a million pounds/etc; **deux millions** two million. ◆**millionième** a & nmf millionth. ◆**millionnaire** nmf millionaire.

mime [mim] nmf (acteur) mime; **le m.** (art) mime. ◆**mimer** vti to mime. ◆**mimique** nf (mine) (funny) face; (gestes) signs, sign language.

mimosa [mimoza] nm (arbre, fleur) mimosa.

minable [minabl] a (médiocre) pathetic; (lieu, personne) shabby.

minaret [minarɛ] nm (de mosquée) minaret.

minauder [minode] vi to simper, make a show of affectation.

mince [mɛ̃s] **1** a thin; (élancé) slim; (insignifiant) slim, paltry. **2** int m. (alors)! oh heck!, blast (it)! ◆**minceur** nf thinness; slimness. ◆**mincir** vi to grow slim.

mine [min] nf **1** appearance; (physionomie) look; **avoir bonne/mauvaise m.** (santé) to look well/ill; **faire m. de faire** to appear to do, make as if to do. **2** (d'or, de charbon etc) & Fig mine; **m. de charbon** coalmine. **3** (de crayon) lead. **4** (engin explosif) mine. ◆**miner** vt **1** (saper) to undermine. **2** (garnir d'explosifs) to mine.

minerai [minrɛ] nm ore.

minéral, -aux [mineral, -o] a & nm mineral. ◆**minéralogique** [mineralɔʒik] a **numéro m.** Aut registration ou Am license number.

minet, -ette [minɛ, -ɛt] nmf **1** (chat) puss. **2** (personne) Fam fashion-conscious young man ou woman.

mineur, -eure [minœr] **1** nm (ouvrier) miner. **2** a (jeune, secondaire) & Mus minor; – nmf Jur minor. ◆**minier, -ière** a (industrie) mining-.

mini- [mini] préf mini-.

miniature [minjatyr] nf miniature; – a inv (train etc) miniature-.

minibus [minibys] nm minibus.

minime [minim] a trifling, minor, minimal. ◆**minimiser** vt to minimize.

minimum [minimɔm] nm minimum; **le m. de** (force etc) the minimum (amount of); **au (grand) m.** at the very least; **la température m.** the minimum temperature. ◆**minimal, -aux** a minimum, minimal.

ministre [ministr] nm Pol Rel minister; **m. de l'Intérieur** = Home Secretary, Am Secretary of the Interior. ◆**ministère** nm ministry; (gouvernement) cabinet; **m. de l'Intérieur** = Home Office, Am Department of the Interior. ◆**ministériel, -ielle** a ministerial; (crise, remaniement) cabinet-.

minorer [minɔre] vt to reduce.

minorité [minɔrite] nf minority; **en m.** in the ou a minority. ◆**minoritaire** a (parti etc) minority-; **être m.** to be in the ou a minority.

Minorque [minɔrk] nf Minorca.

minuit [minɥi] nm midnight, twelve o'clock.

minus [minys] nm (individu) Péj Fam moron.

minuscule [minyskyl] **1** a (petit) tiny, minute. **2** a & nf (lettre) m. small letter.

minute [minyt] nf minute; **à la m.** (tout de suite) this (very) minute; **d'une m. à l'autre** any minute (now); – à **l'm** aliments ou plats **m.** convenience food(s). ◆**minuter** vt to time. ◆**minuterie** nf time switch.

minutie [minysi] nf meticulousness. ◆**minutieux, -euse** a meticulous.

mioche [mjɔʃ] nmf (enfant) Fam kid, youngster.

miracle [mirakl] nm miracle; **par m.** miraculously. ◆**miraculeux, -euse** a miraculous.

mirador [miradɔr] nm Mil watchtower.

mirage [miraʒ] nm mirage.

mirifique [mirifik] a Hum fabulous.

mirobolant [mirɔbɔlɑ̃] a Fam fantastic.

miroir [mirwar] nm mirror. ◆**miroiter** vi to gleam, shimmer.

mis [mi] voir **mettre**; – a **bien m.** (vêtu) well dressed.

misanthrope [mizɑ̃trɔp] nmf misanthropist; – a misanthropic.

mise [miz] nf **1** (action de mettre) putting; **m. en service** putting into service; **m. en marche** starting up; **m. à la retraite** pensioning off; **m. à feu** (de fusée) blast-off; **m. en scène** Th production; Cin direction. **2** (argent) stake. **3** (tenue) attire. ◆**miser** vt (argent) to stake (sur on); – vi **m. sur** (cheval) to back; (compter sur) to bank on.

misère [mizɛr] nf (grinding) poverty; (malheur) misery; (bagatelle) trifle. ◆**mi-**

sérable a miserable, wretched; (*indigent*) poor, destitute; (*logement, quartier*) seedy, slummy; – *nmf* (*poor*) wretch; (*indigent*) pauper. ◆**miséreux, -euse** a destitute; – *nmf* pauper.

miséricorde [mizerikɔrd] *nf* mercy. ◆**miséricordieux, -euse** a merciful.

misogyne [mizɔʒin] *nmf* misogynist.

missile [misil] *nm* (*fusée*) missile.

mission [misjɔ̃] *nf* (*tâche*) task. ◆**missionnaire** *nm & a* missionary.

missive [misiv] *nf* (*lettre*) missive.

mistral [mistral] *nm inv* (*vent*) mistral.

mite [mit] *nf* (*clothes*) moth; (*du fromage etc*) mite. ◆**mité** a moth-eaten.

mi-temps [mitɑ̃] *nf* (*pause*) *Sp* half-time; (*période*) *Sp* half; **à mi-t.** (*travailler etc*) part-time.

miteux, -euse a [mitø, -øz] a shabby.

mitigé [mitiʒe] a (*zèle etc*) moderate, lukewarm; (*mêlé*) *Fam* mixed.

mitraille [mitraj] *nf* gunfire. ◆**mitrailler** *vt* to machinegun; (*photographier*) *Fam* to click ou snap away at. ◆**mitraillette** *nf* submachine gun. ◆**mitrailleur à fusil m.** machinegun. ◆**mitrailleuse** *nf* machinegun.

mi-voix (à) [amivwa] *adv* in an undertone.

mixe(u)r [miksœr] *nm* (*pour mélanger*) (food) mixer.

mixte [mikst] a mixed; (*école*) co-educational, mixed; (*tribunal*) joint.

mixture [mikstyr] *nf* (*boisson*) *Péj* mixture.

Mlle [madmwazɛl] *abrév* = **Mademoiselle**.

MM [mesjø] *abrév* = **Messieurs**.

mm *abrév* (*millimètre*) mm.

Mme [madam] *abrév* = **Madame**.

mobile [mɔbil] **1** a (*pièce etc*) moving; (*personne*) mobile; (*feuillets*) detachable, loose; (*reflets*) changing; **échelle m.** sliding scale; **fête m.** move(e)able feast; – *nm* (*œuvre d'art*) mobile. **2** *nm* (*motif*) motive (de for). ◆**mobilité** *nf* mobility.

mobilier [mɔbilje] *nm* furniture.

mobiliser [mɔbilize] *vti* to mobilize. ◆**mobilisation** *nf* mobilization.

mobylette [mɔbilɛt] *nf* moped.

mocassin [mɔkasɛ̃] *nm* (*chaussure*) moccasin.

moche [mɔʃ] a *Fam* (*laid*) ugly; (*mauvais, peu gentil*) lousy, rotten.

modalité [mɔdalite] *nf* method (de of).

mode [mɔd] **1** *nf* fashion; (*industrie*) fashion trade; **à la m.** in fashion, fashionable; **passé de m.** out of fashion; **à la m. de** in the manner of. **2** *nm* mode, method; **m. d'emploi**

directions (for use); **m. de vie** way of life. **3** *nm Gram* mood.

modèle [mɔdɛl] *nm* (*schéma, exemple, personne*) model; **m.** (*réduit*) (scale) model; – a (*élève etc*) model-. ◆**model/er** *vt* to model (sur on); **se m. sur** to model oneself on. ◆**—age** *nm* (*de statue etc*) modelling. ◆**modéliste** *nmf Tex* stylist, designer.

modéré [mɔdere] a moderate. ◆**—ment** *adv* moderately.

modérer [mɔdere] *vt* to moderate, restrain; (*vitesse, allure*) to reduce; – **se m.** *vpr* to restrain oneself. ◆**modérateur, -trice** a moderating; – *nmf* moderator. ◆**modération** *nf* moderation, restraint; reduction; **avec m.** in moderation.

moderne [mɔdern] a modern; – *nm* **le m.** (*mobilier*) modern furniture. ◆**modernisation** *nf* modernization. ◆**moderniser** *vt*, – **se m.** *vpr* to modernize. ◆**modernisme** *nm* modernism.

modeste [mɔdest] a modest. ◆**modestement** *adv* modestly. ◆**modestie** *nf* modesty.

modifier [mɔdifje] *vt* to modify, alter; – **se m.** *vpr* to alter. ◆**modification** *nf* modification, alteration.

modique [mɔdik] a (*salaire, prix*) modest. ◆**modicité** *nf* modesty.

module [mɔdyl] *nm* module.

moduler [mɔdyle] *vt* to modulate. ◆**modulation** *nf* modulation.

moelle [mwal] *nf Anat* marrow; **m. épinière** spinal cord.

moelleux, -euse a [mwalø, -øz] a soft; (*voix, vin*) mellow.

mœurs [mœr(s)] *nfpl* (*morale*) morals; (*habitudes*) habits, customs.

mohair [mɔɛr] *nm* mohair.

moi [mwa] *pron* **1** (*complément direct*) me; **laissez-moi** leave me; **pour moi** for me. **2** (*indirect*) (to) me; **montrez-le-moi** show it to me, show me. **3** (*sujet*) I; **moi, je veux** I want. ◆**moi** *nm inv Psy* self, ego. ◆**moi-même** *pron* myself.

moignon [mwaɲɔ̃] *nm* stump.

moindre [mwɛ̃dr] a **être m.** (*moins grand*) to be less; **le m. doute/etc** the slightest ou least doubt/etc; **le m.** (*de mes problèmes etc*) the least (de of); (*de deux problèmes etc*) the lesser (de of).

moine [mwan] *nm* monk, friar.

moineau, -x [mwano] *nm* sparrow.

moins [mwɛ̃] **1** *adv* (*[mwɛz] before vowel*) less (que than); **m. de** (*temps, zèle etc*) less (que than), not so much (que as); (*gens, livres etc*) fewer (que than), not so many (que as); (cent francs etc) less than; **m. froid/grand**/etc not as cold/big/etc (que as); **de m. en m.** less and less; **le m., la m., les m.** (travailler etc) the least; **le m. grand** the smallest; **au m., du m.** at least; **en m.** (qui manque) missing; **dix ans**/etc **de m.** ten years/etc less; **en m.** (personne, objet) less; (personnes, objets) fewer; **les m. de vingt ans** those under twenty, the under-twenties; **à m. que** (+ sub) unless. **2** prép Math minus; **deux heures m. cinq** five to two; **il fait m. dix (degrés)** it's minus ten (degrees).

mois [mwa] nm month; **au m. de juin**/etc in (the month of) June/etc.

mois/ir [mwazir] vi to go mouldy; (attendre) Fig to hang about. **◆—i** a mouldy; — nm mould, mildew; **sentir le m.** to smell musty. **◆moisissure** nf mould, mildew.

moisson [mwasɔ̃] nf harvest. **◆moissonner** vt to harvest. **◆moissonneuse-batteuse** nf (pl moissonneuses-batteuses) combine-harvester.

moite [mwat] a sticky, moist. **◆moiteur** nf stickiness, moistness.

moitié [mwatje] nf half; **la m. de la pomme**/etc half (of) the apple/etc; **à m.** (remplir etc) halfway; **à m. fermé/cru**/etc half closed/raw/etc; **à m. prix** (for ou at) half-price; **de m.** by half; **m.-moitié** Fam so-so; **partager m.-moitié** Fam to split fifty-fifty.

moka [mɔka] nm (café) mocha.

mol [mɔl] voir mou.

molaire [mɔlɛr] nf (dent) molar.

molécule [mɔlekyl] nf molecule.

moleskine [mɔlɛskin] nf imitation leather.

molester [mɔlɛste] vt to manhandle.

molette [mɔlɛt] nf **clé à m.** adjustable wrench ou spanner.

mollasse [mɔlas] a Péj flabby.

molle [mɔl] voir mou. **◆mollement** adv feebly; (paresseusement) lazily. **◆mollesse** nf softness; (faiblesse) feebleness. **◆mollir** vi to go soft; (courage) to flag.

mollet [mɔlɛ] **1** a **œuf m.** soft-boiled egg. **2** nm (de jambe) calf.

mollusque [mɔlysk] nm mollusc.

môme [mom] nmf (enfant) Fam kid.

moment [mɔmɑ̃] nm (instant) moment; (période) time; **en ce m.** at the moment; **par moments** at times; **au m. de partir** when just about to leave; **au m. où** when, just as; **du m. que** (puisque) seeing that. **◆momentané** a momentary. **◆momentanément** adv temporarily, for the moment.

momie [mɔmi] nf (cadavre) mummy.

mon, ma, pl **mes** [mɔ̃, ma, me] (**ma** becomes **mon** [mɔ̃n] before a vowel or mute h) a poss my; **mon père** my father; **ma mère** my mother; **mon ami(e)** my friend.

Monaco [mɔnako] nf Monaco.

monarque [mɔnark] nm monarch. **◆monarchie** nf monarchy. **◆monarchique** a monarchic.

monastère [mɔnastɛr] nm monastery.

monceau, -x [mɔ̃so] nm heap, pile.

monde [mɔ̃d] nm world; (milieu social) set; **du m.** (gens) people; (beaucoup) a lot of people; **un m. fou** a tremendous crowd; **le (grand) m.** (high) society; **le m. entier** the whole world; **tout le m.** everybody; **mettre au m.** to give birth to; **pas le moins du m.!** not in the least ou slightest! **◆mondain, -aine** a (vie, réunion etc) society-. **◆mondanités** nfpl (événements) social events. **◆mondial, -aux** a (renommée etc) world-; (crise) worldwide. **◆mondialement** adv (the whole) world over.

monégasque [mɔnegask] a & nmf Monegasque.

monétaire [mɔnetɛr] a monetary.

mongolien, -ienne [mɔ̃gɔljɛ̃, -jɛn] a & nmf Méd mongol.

moniteur, -trice [mɔnitœr, -tris] nmf **1** instructor; (de colonie de vacances) assistant, Am camp counselor. **2** (écran) Tech monitor.

monnaie [mɔnɛ] nf (devise) currency, money; (appoint, pièces) change; **pièce de m.** coin; **(petite) m.** (small) change; **faire de la m.** to get change; **faire de la m. à qn** to give s.o. change (**sur un billet** for a note); **c'est m. courante** it's very frequent; **Hôtel de la M.** mint. **◆monnayer** vt (talent etc) to cash in on; (bien, titre) Com to convert into cash.

mono [mɔno] a inv (disque etc) mono.

mono- [mɔno] préf mono-.

monocle [mɔnɔkl] nm monocle.

monologue [mɔnɔlɔg] nm monologue.

monoplace [mɔnɔplas] a & nmf (avion, voiture) single-seater.

monopole [mɔnɔpɔl] nm monopoly. **◆monopoliser** vt to monopolize.

monosyllabe [mɔnɔsilab] nm monosyllable. **◆monosyllabique** a monosyllabic.

monotone [mɔnɔtɔn] a monotonous. **◆monotonie** nf monotony.

monseigneur [mɔ̃sɛɲœr] nm (évêque) His ou Your Grace; (prince) His ou Your Highness.

monsieur, pl **messieurs** [məsjø, mesjø] nm gentleman; **oui m.** yes; (avec déférence) yes sir; **oui messieurs** yes (gentlemen); **M. Legras** Mr Legras; **Messieurs** *ou* **MM Legras** Messrs Legras; **tu vois ce m.?** do you see that man *ou* gentleman?; **Monsieur** *(sur une lettre)* Com Dear Sir.

monstre [mɔ̃str] *nm* monster; – *a (énorme) Fam* colossal. ◆**monstrueux, -euse** *a (abominable, énorme)* monstrous. ◆**monstruosité** *nf (horreur)* monstrosity.

mont [mɔ̃] *nm (montagne)* mount.

montagne [mɔ̃taɲ] *nf* mountain; **la m.** *(zone)* the mountains; **montagnes russes** *Fig* roller coaster. ◆**montagnard, -arde** *nmf* mountain dweller; – *a (peuple)* mountain-. ◆**montagneux, -euse** *a* mountainous.

mont-de-piété [mɔ̃dpjete] *nm (pl monts-de-piété)* pawnshop.

monte-charge [mɔ̃tʃarʒ] *nm inv* service lift *ou Am* elevator.

mont/er [mɔ̃te] *vi (aux être) (personne)* to go *ou* come up; *(s'élever)* to go up; *(grimper)* to climb up; *(sur onto)* to go up, rise; *(prix)* to go up, rise; *(marée)* to come in; *(avion)* to climb; **m. dans un véhicule** to get in(to) a vehicle; **m. dans un train** to get on(to) a train; **m. sur** *(échelle etc)* to climb up; *(trône)* to ascend; **m. en courant/etc** to run/etc up; **m. (à cheval)** *Sp* to ride (a horse); **m. en graine** *(salade etc)* to go to seed; – *vt (aux avoir) (côte etc)* to climb (up); *(objets)* to bring *ou* take up; *(cheval)* to ride; *(tente, affaire)* to set up; *(machine)* to assemble; *(bijou)* to set, mount; *(complot, démonstration)* to mount; *(pièce)* Th to stage, mount; **m. l'escalier** to go up *ou* come upstairs *ou* up the stairs; **faire m.** *(visiteur etc)* to show up; **m. qn contre qn** to set s.o. against s.o.; – **se m.** *vpr (s'irriter) Fam* to get angry; **se m. à** *(frais)* to amount to. ◆**-ant 1** *a (chemin)* uphill; *(mouvement)* upward; *(marée)* rising; *(col)* stand-up; *(robe)* high-necked; **chaussure montante** boot. **2** *nm (somme)* amount. **3** *nm (de barrière)* post; *(d'échelle)* upright. ◆**-é** *a (police)* mounted. ◆**-ée** *nf* ascent, climb; *(de prix, des eaux)* rise; *(chemin)* slope. ◆**-age** *nm Tech* assembling, assembly; *Cin* editing. ◆**-eur, -euse** *nmf Tech* fitter; *Cin* editor.

montre [mɔ̃tr] *nf* **1** watch; **course contre la m.** race against time. **2 faire m. de** to show. ◆**m.-bracelet** *nf (pl montres-bracelets)* wristwatch.

Montréal [mɔ̃real] *nm ou f* Montreal.

montrer [mɔ̃tre] *vt* to show (à to); **m. du doigt** to point to; **m. à qn à faire qch** to show s.o. how to do sth; – **se m.** *vpr* to show oneself, appear; *(s'avérer)* to turn out to be; **se m. courageux/etc** *(être)* to be courageous/etc.

monture [mɔ̃tyr] *nf* **1** *(cheval)* mount. **2** *(de lunettes)* frame; *(de bijou)* setting.

monument [mɔnymã] *nm* monument; **m. aux morts** war memorial. ◆**monumental, -aux** *a (imposant, énorme etc)* monumental.

moquer (se) [səmɔke] *vpr* **se m. de** *(allure etc)* to make fun of; *(personne)* to make a fool of, make fun of; **je m'en moque!** *Fam* I couldn't care less! ◆**moquerie** *nf* mockery. ◆**moqueur, -euse** *a* mocking.

moquette [mɔkɛt] *nf* fitted carpet(s), wall-to-wall carpeting.

moral, -aux [mɔral, -o] *a* moral; – *nm* **le m.** spirits, morale. ◆**morale** *nf (principes)* morals; *(code)* moral code; *(d'histoire etc)* moral; **faire la m. à qn** to lecture s.o. ◆**moralement** *adv* morally. ◆**moraliser** *vi* to moralize. ◆**moraliste** *nmf* moralist. ◆**moralité** *nf (mœurs)* morality; *(de fable, récit etc)* moral.

moratoire [mɔratwar] *nm* moratorium.

morbide [mɔrbid] *a* morbid.

morceau, -x [mɔrso] *nm* piece, bit; *(de sucre)* lump; *(de viande)* Culin cut; *(extrait) Littér* extract. ◆**morceler** *vt (terrain)* to divide up.

mordiller [mɔrdije] *vt* to nibble.

mord/re [mɔrdr] *vti* to bite; **ça mord** *Pêche* I have a bite. ◆**-ant 1** *a (voix, manière)* scathing; *(froid)* biting; *(personne, ironie)* caustic. **2** *nm (énergie)* punch. ◆**-u, -ue** *nmf* **un m. du jazz/etc** *Fam* a jazz/etc fan.

morfondre (se) [səmɔrfɔ̃dr] *vpr* to get bored (waiting), mope (about).

morgue [mɔrg] *nf (lieu)* mortuary, morgue.

moribond, -onde [mɔribɔ̃, -ɔ̃d] *a & nmf* dying *ou* moribund (person).

morne [mɔrn] *a* dismal, gloomy, dull.

morose [mɔroz] *a* morose, sullen.

morphine [mɔrfin] *nf* morphine.

mors [mɔr] *nm (de harnais)* bit.

morse [mɔrs] *nm* **1** Morse (code). **2** *(animal)* walrus.

morsure [mɔrsyr] *nf* bite.

mort¹ [mɔr] *nf* death; **mettre à m.** to put to death; **silence de m.** dead silence. ◆**mortalité** *nf* death rate, mortality. ◆**mortel, -elle** *a (hommes, ennemi, danger etc)* mortal; *(accident)* fatal; *(chaleur)* deadly; *(pâleur)* deathly; – *nmf* mortal. ◆**mortellement** *adv (blessé)* fatally.

mort², **morte** [mɔr, mɔrt] *a (personne, plante, ville etc)* dead; **m. de fatigue** dead tired; **m. de froid** numb with cold; **m. de peur** frightened to death; – *nmf* dead man, dead woman; **les morts the dead; de nombreux morts** (*victimes*) many deaths *ou* casualties; **le jour** *ou* **la fête des Morts** All Souls' Day. ◆**morte-saison** *nf* off season. ◆**mort-né** a (*enfant*) & *Fig* stillborn.

mortier [mɔrtje] *nm* mortar.

mortifier [mɔrtifje] *vt* to mortify.

mortuaire [mɔrtɥɛr] *a* (*avis, rites etc*) death-, funeral.

morue [mɔry] *nf* cod.

morve [mɔrv] *nf* (nasal) mucus. ◆**morveux, -euse** a (*enfant*) snotty (-nosed).

mosaïque [mɔzaik] *nf* mosaic.

Moscou [mɔsku] *nm ou f* Moscow.

mosquée [mɔske] *nf* mosque.

mot [mo] *nm* word; **envoyer un m. à** to drop a line to; **m. à** *ou* **pour m.** word for word; **bon m.** witticism; **mots croisés** crossword (puzzle); **m. d'ordre** *Pol* resolution, order; (*slogan*) watchword; **m. de passe** password.

motard [mɔtar] *nm Fam* motorcyclist.

motel [mɔtɛl] *nm* motel.

moteur[1] [mɔtœr] *nm* (*de véhicule etc*) engine, motor; *Él* motor.

moteur[2], **-trice** [mɔtœr, -tris] *a* (*force*) driving-; (*nerf, muscle*) motor.

motif [mɔtif] *nm* **1** reason, motive. **2** (*dessin*) pattern.

motion [mɔsjɔ̃] *nf Pol* motion; **on a voté une m. de censure** a vote of no confidence was given.

motiver [mɔtive] *vt* (*inciter, causer*) to motivate; (*justifier*) to justify. ◆**motivation** *nf* motivation.

moto [mɔto] *nf* motorcycle, motorbike. ◆**motocycliste** *nmf* motorcyclist.

motorisé [mɔtɔrize] *a* motorized.

motte [mɔt] *nf* (*de terre*) clod, lump; (*de beurre*) block.

mou (*or* **mol** before vowel or mute h), **molle** [mu, mɔl] *a* (*faible, sans énergie*) feeble; – *nm* **avoir du m.** (*cordage*) to be slack.

mouchard, -arde [muʃar, -ard] *nmf Péj* informer. ◆**moucharder** *vt* **m. qn** *Fam* to inform on s.o.

mouche [muʃ] *nf* (*insecte*) fly; **prendre la m.** (*se fâcher*) to go into a huff; **faire m.** to hit the bull's-eye. ◆**moucheron** (*insecte*) midge.

moucher [muʃe] *vt* **m. qn** to wipe s.o.'s nose; **se m.** to blow one's nose.

moucheté [muʃte] *a* speckled, spotted.

mouchoir [muʃwar] *nm* handkerchief; (*en papier*) tissue.

moudre* [mudr] *vt* (*café, blé*) to grind.

moue [mu] *nf* long face, pout; **faire la m.** to pout, pull a (long) face.

mouette [mwɛt] *nf* (sea)gull.

moufle [mufl] *nf* (gant) mitt(en).

mouill/er [muje] **1** *vt* to wet, make wet; **se faire m.** to get wet; – **se m.** *vpr* to get (oneself) wet; (*se compromettre*) *Fam* to get involved (*by taking risks*). **2** *vt* **m. l'ancre** *Nau* to (drop) anchor; – *vi* to anchor. ◆**-é** a wet (**de** with). ◆**-age** *nm* (*action*) *Nau* anchoring; (*lieu*) anchorage.

moule[1] [mul] *nm* mould, *Am* mold; **m. à gâteaux** cake tin. ◆**mouler** *vt* to mould, *Am* mold; (*statue*) to cast; **m. qn** (*vêtement*) to fit s.o. tightly. ◆**-ant** *a* (*vêtement*) tight-fitting. ◆**-age** *nm* moulding; casting; (*objet*) cast. ◆**moulure** *nf Archit* moulding.

moule[2] [mul] *nf* (*mollusque*) mussel.

moulin [mulɛ̃] *nm* mill; (*moteur*) *Fam* engine; **m. à vent** windmill; **m. à café** coffee-grinder.

moulinet [mulinɛ] *nm* **1** (*de canne à pêche*) reel. **2** (*de bâton*) twirl.

moulu [muly] *voir* **moudre**; – *a* (*café*) ground; (*éreinté*) *Fam* dead tired.

mour/ir* [murir] *vi* (aux être) to die (**de**, from); **m. de froid** to die of exposure; **m. d'ennui/de fatigue** *Fig* to be dead bored/tired; **m. de peur** *Fig* to be frightened to death; **s'ennuyer à m.** to be bored to death; – **se m.** *vpr* to be dying. ◆**-ant, -ante** *a* dying; (*voix*) faint; – *nmf* dying person.

mousquetaire [muskətɛr] *nm Mil Hist* musketeer.

mousse [mus] **1** *nf* (*Bot* moss. **2** *nf* (*écume*) froth, foam; (*de bière*) froth; (*de savon*) lather; **m. à raser** shaving foam. **3** *nf Culin* mousse. **4** *nm Nau* ship's boy. ◆**mousser** *vi* (*bière etc*) to froth; (*savon*) to lather; (*eau savonneuse*) to foam. ◆**mousseux, -euse** a frothy; (*vin*) sparkling; – *nm* sparkling wine. ◆**moussu** *a* mossy.

mousseline [muslin] *nf* (*coton*) muslin.

mousson [musɔ̃] *nf* (*vent*) monsoon.

moustache [mustaʃ] *nf* moustache, *Am* mustache; *pl* (*de chat etc*) whiskers. ◆**moustachu** *a* wearing a moustache.

moustique [mustik] *nm* mosquito. ◆**moustiquaire** *nf* mosquito net; (*en métal*) screen.

moutard [mutar] *nm* (*enfant*) *Arg* kid.

moutarde [mutard] *nf* mustard.

mouton [mutɔ̃] *nm* sheep; (*viande*) mutton;

pl (sur la mer) white horses; *(poussière)* bits of dust; **peau de m.** sheepskin.

mouvement [muvmã] *nm (geste, déplacement, groupe etc)* & *Mus* movement; *(de colère)* outburst; *(impulsion)* impulse; **en m.** in motion. ◆**mouvementé** *a (animé)* lively, exciting; *(séance, vie etc)* eventful.

mouv/oir° [muvwar] *vi,* — **se m.** *vpr* to move; **mû par** *(mécanisme)* driven by. ◆—**ant** *a (changeant)* changing; **sables mouvants** quicksands.

moyen¹, -enne [mwajɛ̃, -ɛn] *a* average; *(format, entreprise etc)* medium(-sized); *(solution)* intermediate, middle; — *nf* average; *(dans un examen)* pass mark; *(dans un devoir)* half marks; **la moyenne d'âge** the average age; **en moyenne** on average. ◆**moyennement** *adv* averagely, moderately.

moyen² [mwajɛ̃] *nm (procédé, façon)* means, way **(de faire of doing, to do);** *pl (capacités)* ability, powers; *(argent, ressources)* means; **au m. de by means of; il n'y a pas m. de faire** it's not possible to do; **je n'ai pas les moyens** *(argent)* I can't afford it; **par mes propres moyens** under my own steam.

moyennant [mwajɛnã] *prép (pour)* (in return) for; *(avec)* with.

moyeu, -x [mwajø] *nm (de roue)* hub.

mucosités [mykozite] *nfpl* mucus.

mue [my] *nf* moulting; breaking of the voice. ◆**muer** [mɥe] *vi (animal)* to moult; *(voix)* to break; **se m. en** to become transformed into.

muet, -ette [mɥɛ, -ɛt] *a (infirme)* dumb; *(de surprise etc)* speechless; *(film, reproche etc)* silent; *Gram* mute; — *nmf* dumb person.

mufle [myfl] *nm* 1 *(d'animal)* nose, muzzle. 2 *(individu) Péj* lout.

mug/ir [myʒir] *vi (vache)* to moo; *(bœuf)* to bellow; *(vent) Fig* to roar. ◆—**issement(s)** *nm(pl)* moo(ing); bellow(ing); roar(ing).

muguet [mygɛ] *nm* lily of the valley.

mule [myl] *nf* 1 *(pantoufle)* mule. 2 *(animal)* (she-)mule. ◆**mulet¹** *nm* (he-)mule.

mulet² [mylɛ] *nm (poisson)* mullet.

multi- [mylti] *préf* multi-.

multicolore [myltikɔlɔr] *a* multicoloured.

multinationale [myltinasjɔnal] *nf* multinational.

multiple [myltipl] *a (nombreux)* numerous; *(ayant des formes variées)* multiple; — *nm Math* multiple. ◆**multiplication** *nf* multiplication; *(augmentation)* increase. ◆**multiplicité** *nf* multiplicity. ◆**multiplier** *vt* to

multiply; — **se m.** *vpr* to increase; *(se reproduire)* to multiply.

multitude [myltityd] *nf* multitude.

municipal, -aux [mynisipal, -o] *a* municipal; **conseil m.** town council. ◆**municipalité** *nf (corps)* town council; *(commune)* municipality.

munir [mynir] *vt* **m. de** to provide *ou* equip with; — **se m. de** to provide oneself with; **muni de** *(papiers, arme etc)* in possession of.

munitions [mynisjɔ̃] *nfpl* ammunition.

muqueuse [mykøz] *nf* mucous membrane.

mur [myr] *nm* wall; **m. du son** sound barrier; **au pied du m.** *Fig* with one's back to the wall. ◆**muraille** *nf* (high) wall. ◆**mural, -aux** *a (carte etc)* wall-; **peinture murale** mural (painting). ◆**murer** *vt (porte)* to wall up; **m. qn** to wall s.o. in.

mûr [myr] *a (fruit, projet etc)* ripe; *(âge, homme)* mature. ◆**mûrement** *adv (réfléchir)* carefully. ◆**mûrir** *vti (fruit)* to ripen; *(personne, projet)* to mature.

muret [myrɛ] *nm* low wall.

murmure [myrmyr] *nm* murmur. ◆**murmurer** *vti* to murmur.

musc [mysk] *nm (parfum)* musk.

muscade [myskad] *nf* nutmeg.

muscle [myskl] *nm* muscle. ◆**musclé** *a (bras)* brawny, muscular. ◆**musculaire** *a (tissu, système etc)* muscular. ◆**musculature** *nf* muscles.

museau, -x [myzo] *nm (de chien etc)* muzzle; *(de porc)* snout. ◆**museler** *vt (animal, presse etc)* to muzzle. ◆**muselière** *nf (appareil)* muzzle.

musée [myze] *nm* museum; **m. de peinture** (public) art gallery. ◆**muséum** *nm* (natural history) museum.

musette [myzɛt] *nf (d'ouvrier)* duffel bag, kit bag.

music-hall [myzikol] *nm* variety theatre.

musique [myzik] *nf* music; *(fanfare) Mil* band. ◆**musical, -aux** *a* musical. ◆**musicien, -ienne** *nmf* musician; — *a* **être très/assez m.** to be very/quite musical.

musulman, -ane [myzylmã, -an] *a* & *nmf* Moslem, Muslim.

muter [myte] *vt (employé)* to transfer. ◆**mutation** *nf* 1 transfer. 2 *Biol* mutation.

mutil/er [mytile] *vt* to mutilate, maim; **être mutilé** to be disabled. ◆-**é, -ée** *nmf* **m. de guerre/du travail** disabled ex-serviceman/ worker. ◆**mutilation** *nf* mutilation.

mutin [mytɛ̃] **1** *a (espiègle)* saucy. **2** *nm (rebelle)* mutineer. ◆**se mutin/er** *vpr* to mutiny. ◆-**é** *a* mutinous. ◆**mutinerie** *nf* mutiny.

mutisme [mytism] nm (stubborn) silence.
mutualité [mytɥalite] nf mutual insurance. ◆**mutualiste** nmf member of a friendly ou Am benefit society. ◆**mutuelle**¹ nf friendly society, Am benefit society.
mutuel, -elle² [mytɥel] a (réciproque) mutual. ◆**mutuellement** adv (l'un l'autre) each other (mutually).
myope [mjɔp] a & nmf shortsighted (person). ◆**myopie** nf shortsightedness.
myosotis [mjozotis] nm Bot forget-me-not.
myrtille [mirtij] nf Bot bilberry.

mystère [mister] nm mystery. ◆**mystérieux, -euse** a mysterious.
mystifier [mistifje] vt to fool, deceive, hoax. ◆**mystification** nf hoax.
mystique [mistik] a mystic(al); – nmf (personne) mystic; – nf mystique (de of). ◆**mysticisme** nm mysticism.
mythe [mit] nm myth. ◆**mythique** a mythical. ◆**mythologie** nf mythology. ◆**mythologique** a mythological.
mythomane [mitɔman] nmf compulsive liar.

N

N, n [ɛn] nm N, n.
n' [n] voir **ne**.
nabot [nabo] nm Péj midget.
nacelle [nasɛl] nf (de ballon) car, gondola; (de landau) carriage, carrycot.
nacre [nakr] nf mother-of-pearl. ◆**nacré** a pearly.
nage [naʒ] nf (swimming) stroke; **n. libre** freestyle; **traverser à la n.** to swim across; **en n.** Fig sweating. ◆**nager** vi to swim; (flotter) to float; **je nage dans le bonheur** my happiness knows no bounds; **je nage complètement** (je suis perdu) Fam I'm all at sea; – vt (crawl etc) to swim. ◆**nageur, -euse** nmf swimmer.
nageoire [naʒwar] nf (de poisson) fin; (de phoque) flipper.
naguère [nagɛr] adv Litt not long ago.
naïf, -ïve [naif, -iv] a simple, naïve; – nmf (jobard) simpleton.
nain, naine [nɛ̃, nɛn] nmf dwarf; – a (arbre, haricot) dwarf-.
naissance [nɛsɑ̃s] nf birth; (de bras, cou) base; **donner n. à** Fig to give rise to; **de n.** from birth.
naître* [nɛtr] vi to be born; (jour) to dawn; (sentiment, difficulté) to arise (de from); **faire n.** (soupçon, industrie etc) to give rise to, create. ◆**naissant** a (amitié etc) incipient.
naïveté [naivte] nf simplicity, naïveté.
nant/ir [nɑ̃tir] vt n. de to provide with. ◆**—i** a & nmpl (riche) affluent.
naphtaline [naftalin] nf mothballs.
nappe [nap] nf **1** (de) table cloth. **2** (d'eau) sheet; (de gaz, pétrole) layer; (de brouillard) blanket. ◆**napperon** nm (soft) table mat; (pour vase etc) (soft) mat, cloth.

narcotique [narkɔtik] a & nm narcotic.
narguer [narge] vt to flout, mock.
narine [narin] nf nostril.
narquois [narkwa] a sneering.
narration [narasjɔ̃] nf (récit, acte, art) narration. ◆**narrateur, -trice** nmf narrator.
nasal, -aux [nazal, -o] a nasal.
naseau, -x [nazo] nm (de cheval) nostril.
nasiller [nazije] vi (personne) to speak with a twang; (micro, radio) to crackle. ◆**nasillard** a (voix) nasal; (micro etc) crackling.
natal, mpl -als [natal] a (pays etc) native; **sa maison natale** the house where he ou she was born. ◆**natalité** nf birthrate.
natation [natasjɔ̃] nf swimming.
natif, -ive [natif, -iv] a & nmf native; **être n. de** to be a native of.
nation [nasjɔ̃] nf nation; **les Nations Unies** the United Nations. ◆**national, -aux** a national; ◆**nationale** nf (route) trunk road, Am highway. ◆**nationaliser** vt to nationalize. ◆**nationaliste** a Péj nationalistic; – nmf nationalist. ◆**nationalité** nf nationality.
nativité [nativite] nf Rel nativity.
natte [nat] nf **1** (de cheveux) plait, Am braid. **2** (tapis) mat, (piece of) matting. ◆**natt/er** vt to plait, Am braid. ◆**—age** n (matière) matting.
naturaliser [natyralize] vt (personne) Pol to naturalize. ◆**naturalisation** nf naturalization.
nature [natyr] nf (monde naturel, caractère) nature; **de toute n.** of every kind; **être de n. à** to be likely to; **payer en n.** Fin to pay in kind; **n. morte** (tableau) still life; **plus grand que n.** larger than life; – a inv (omelette, yaourt etc) plain; (café) black. ◆**natura-**

liste *nmf* naturalist. ◆**naturiste** *nmf* nudist, naturist.

naturel, -elle [natyrɛl] *a* natural; **mort naturelle** death from natural causes; – *nm* (*caractère*) nature; (*simplicité*) naturalness. ◆**naturellement** *adv* naturally.

naufrage [nofraʒ] *nm* (ship)wreck; (*ruine*) *Litt Fig* ruin; **faire n.** to be (ship)wrecked. ◆**naufragé, -ée** *a* & *nmf* shipwrecked (person).

nausée [noze] *nf* nausea, sickness. ◆**nauséabond** *a* nauseating, sickening.

nautique [notik] *a* nautical; (*sports, ski*) water-.

naval, mpl -als [naval] *a* naval; **constructions navales** shipbuilding.

navet [navɛ] *nm* **1** *Bot Culin* turnip. **2** (*film etc*) *Péj* flop, dud.

navette [navɛt] *nf* (*transport*) shuttle (service); **faire la n.** (*véhicule, personne etc*) to shuttle back and forth (**entre** between); **n. spatiale** space shuttle.

naviguer [navige] *vi* (*bateau*) to sail; (*piloter, voler*) to navigate. ◆**navigabilité** *nf* (*de bateau*) seaworthiness; (*d'avion*) airworthiness. ◆**navigable** *a* (*fleuve*) navigable. ◆**navigant** *a* **personnel n.** *Av Nau* crew. ◆**navigateur** *nm* *Av* navigator. ◆**navigation** *nf* (*pilotage*) navigation; (*trafic*) *Nau* shipping.

navire [navir] *nm* ship.

navr/er [navre] *vt* to upset (greatly), grieve. ◆**-ant** *a* upsetting. ◆**-é** *a* (*air*) grieved; **je suis n.** I'm (terribly) sorry (**de faire** to do).

nazi, -ie [nazi] *a* & *nmf Pol Hist* Nazi.

ne [n(ə)] (**n'** *before vowel or mute h; used to form negative verb with* **pas, jamais, que** *etc*) *adv* **1** (+ **pas**) not; **elle ne boit pas she** doesn't drink; **il n'ose (pas)** he doesn't dare; **n'importe** it doesn't matter. **2** (*with* **craindre, avoir peur** *etc*) **je crains qu'il ne parte** I'm afraid he'll leave.

né [ne] *a* born; **il est né** he was born; **née Dupont** née Dupont.

néanmoins [neɑ̃mwɛ] *adv* nevertheless, nonetheless.

néant [neɑ̃] *nm* nothingness, void; (*sur un formulaire*) = none.

nébuleux, -euse [nebylø, -øz] *a* hazy, nebulous.

nécessaire [nesesɛr] *a* necessary; (*inéluctable*) unavoidable; – *nm* **le n.** (*biens*) the necessities; **le strict n.** the bare necessities; **n. de couture** sewing box, workbox; **n. de toilette** sponge bag, dressing case; **faire le n.** to do what's necessary *ou* the necessary. ◆**né-**

cessairement *adv* necessarily; (*échouer etc*) inevitably. ◆**nécessité** *nf* necessity. ◆**nécessiter** *vt* to necessitate, require. ◆**nécessiteux, -euse** *a* needy.

nécrologie [nekrɔlɔʒi] *nf* obituary.

nectarine [nɛktarin] *nf* (*fruit*) nectarine.

néerlandais, -aise [neɛrlɑ̃dɛ, -ɛz] *a* Dutch; – *nmf* Dutchman, Dutchwoman; – *nm* (*langue*) Dutch.

nef [nɛf] *nf* (*d'église*) nave.

néfaste [nefast] *a* (*influence etc*) harmful (**à** to).

négatif, -ive [negatif, -iv] *a* negative; – *nm Phot* negative; – *nf* **répondre par la négative** to answer in the negative. ◆**négation** *nf* negation, denial (**de** of); *Gram* negation; (*mot*) negative.

négligeable [negliʒabl] *a* negligible.

négligent [negliʒɑ̃] *a* negligent, careless. ◆**négligemment** [-amɑ̃] *adv* negligently, carelessly. ◆**négligence** *nf* negligence, carelessness; (*faute*) (careless) error.

néglig/er [negliʒe] *vt* (*personne, conseil, travail etc*) to neglect; **n. de faire** to neglect to do; – **se n.** *vpr* (*négliger sa tenue ou sa santé*) to neglect oneself. ◆**-é** *a* (*tenue*) untidy, neglected; (*travail*) careless; – *nm* (*de tenue*) untidiness; (*vêtement*) negligee.

négoci/er [negosje] *vti Fin Pol* to negotiate. ◆**-ant, -ante** *nmf* merchant, trader. ◆**-able** *a Fin* negotiable. ◆**négociateur, -trice** *nmf* negotiator. ◆**négociation** *nf* negotiation.

nègre [nɛgr] **1** *a* (*art, sculpture etc*) Negro. **2** *nm* (*écrivain*) ghost writer.

neige [nɛʒ] *nf* snow; **n. fondue** sleet; **n. carbonique** dry ice. ◆**neiger** *v imp* to snow. ◆**neigeux, -euse** *a* snowy.

nénuphar [nenyfar] *nm* water lily.

néo [neo] *préf* neo-.

néon [neɔ̃] *nm* (*gaz*) neon; **au n.** (*éclairage etc*) neon-.

néophyte [neɔfit] *nmf* novice.

néo-zélandais, -aise [neozelɑ̃dɛ, -ɛz] *a* (*peuple etc*) New Zealand-; – *nmf* New Zealander.

nerf [nɛr] *nm Anat* nerve; (*vigueur*) *Fam* to have guts; **du n.!, un peu de n.!** buck up!; **ça me porte** *ou* **me tape sur les nerfs** it gets on my nerves; **être sur les nerfs** *Fig* to be keyed up *ou* het up. ◆**nerveux, -euse** *a* nervous; (*centre, cellule*) nerve-. ◆**nervosité** *nf* nervousness.

nervure [nɛrvyr] *nf* (*de feuille*) vein.

nescafé [nɛskafe] *nm* instant coffee.

n'est-ce pas? [nɛspa] *adv* isn't he?, don't

you? *etc*; **il fait beau, n'est-ce pas?** the weather's fine, isn't it?

net, nette [nɛt] **1** *a* (*conscience, idée, image, refus*) clear; (*coupure, linge*) clean; (*soigné*) neat; (*copie*) fair; – *adv* (*s'arrêter*) short, dead; (*tuer*) outright; (*parler*) plainly; (*refuser*) flat(ly); (*casser, couper*) clean. **2** *a* (*poids, prix etc*) Com net(t). ◆**nettement** *adv* clearly, plainly; (*sensiblement*) markedly. ◆**netteté** *nf* clearness; (*de travail*) neatness.

nettoyer [netwaje] *vt* to clean (up); (*plaie*) to cleanse, clean (up); (*vider, ruiner*) Fam to clean out. ◆**nettoiement** *nm* cleaning; **service du n.** refuse *ou* Am garbage collection. ◆**nettoyage** *nm* cleaning; **n. à sec** dry cleaning.

neuf[1], **neuve** [nœf, nœv] *a* new; **quoi de n.?** what's new(s)?; – *nm* **il y a du n.** there's been something new; **remettre à n.** to make as good as new.

neuf[2] [nœf] *a* & *nm* [nœv] *before* **heures** & **ans**) nine. ◆**neuvième** *a* & *nmf* ninth.

neurasthénique [nørastenik] *a* depressed.

neutre [nøtr] **1** *a* (*pays, personne etc*) neutral; – *nm* El neutral. **2** *a* & *nm* Gram neuter. ◆**neutraliser** *vt* to neutralize. ◆**neutralité** *nf* neutrality.

neveu, -x [nəvø] *nm* nephew.

névralgie [nevralʒi] *nf* headache; Méd neuralgia. ◆**névralgique** *a* **centre n.** Fig nerve centre.

névrose [nevroz] *nf* neurosis. ◆**névrosé, -ée** *a* & *nmf* neurotic.

nez [ne] *nm* nose; **n. à n.** face to face (**avec** with); **au n. de qn** (*rire etc*) in s.o.'s face; **mettre le n. dehors** Fam to stick one's nose outside.

ni [ni] *conj* **ni ... ni** (+ *ne*) neither ... nor; **il n'a ni faim ni soif** he's neither hungry nor thirsty; **sans manger ni boire** without eating or drinking; **ni l'un(e) ni l'autre** neither (of them).

niais, -aise [njɛ, -ɛz] *a* silly, simple; – *nmf* simpleton. ◆**niaiserie** *nf* silliness; *pl* (*paroles*) nonsense.

niche [niʃ] *nf* (*de chien*) kennel; (*cavité*) niche, recess.

nich/er [niʃe] *vi* (*oiseau*) to nest; (*loger*) Fam to hang out; – **se n.** *vpr* (*oiseau*) to nest; (*se cacher*) to hide oneself. ◆**-ée** *nf* (*oiseaux, enfants*) brood; (*chiens*) litter.

nickel [nikɛl] *nm* (*métal*) nickel.

nicotine [nikɔtin] *nf* nicotine.

nid [ni] *nm* nest; **n. de poules** Aut pothole.

nièce [njɛs] *nf* niece.

nième [ɛnjɛm] *a* nth.

nier [nje] *vt* to deny (**que** that); – *vi* Jur to deny the charge.

nigaud, -aude [nigo, -od] *a* silly; – *nmf* silly fool.

Nigéria [niʒerja] *nm ou f* Nigeria.

n'importe [nɛ̃pɔrt] *voir* **importer 1.**

nippon, -one *ou* **-onne** [nipɔ̃, -ɔn] *a* Japanese.

niveau, -x [nivo] *nm* (*hauteur*) level; (*degré, compétence*) standard, level; **n. de vie** standard of living; **n. à bulle (d'air)** spirit level; **au n. de qn** (*élève etc*) up to s.o.'s standard. ◆**niveler** *vt* (*surface*) to level; (*fortunes etc*) to even (up).

noble [nɔbl] *a* noble; – *nmf* nobleman, noblewoman. ◆**noblement** *adv* nobly. ◆**noblesse** *nf* (*caractère, classe*) nobility.

noce(s) [nɔs] *nf(pl)* wedding; **faire la noce** Fam to have a good time, make merry; **noces d'argent/d'or** silver/golden wedding. ◆**noceur, -euse** *nmf* Fam fast liver, reveller.

nocif, -ive [nɔsif, -iv] *a* harmful. ◆**nocivité** *nf* harmfulness.

noctambule [nɔktɑ̃byl] *nmf* (*personne*) night bird *ou* prowler. ◆**nocturne** *a* nocturnal, night-; – *nm* (*de magasins etc*) late night opening; (**match en n.**) Sp floodlit match, *Am* night game.

Noël [nɔɛl] *nm* Christmas; **le père N.** Father Christmas, Santa Claus.

nœud [nø] *nm* **1** knot; (*ruban*) bow; **le n. du problème**/*etc* the crux of the problem/*etc*; **n. coulant** noose, slipknot; **n. papillon** bow tie. **2** (*mesure*) Nau knot.

noir, noire [nwar] *a* black; (*nuit, lunettes etc*) dark; (*idées*) gloomy; (*âme, crime*) vile; (*misère*) dire; **roman n.** thriller; **film n.** film noir; **il fait n.** it's dark; – *nm* (*couleur*) black; (*obscurité*) dark; **N.** (*homme*) black; **vendre au n.** to sell on the black market; – *nf Mus* crotchet, *Am* quarter note; **Noire** (*femme*) black. ◆**noirceur** *nf* blackness; (*d'une action etc*) vileness. ◆**noircir** *vt* to blacken; – *vi*, – **se n.** *vpr* to turn black.

noisette [nwazɛt] *nf* hazelnut. ◆**noisetier** *nm* hazel (tree).

noix [nwa] *nf* (*du noyer*) walnut; **n. de coco** coconut; **n. du Brésil** Brazil nut; **n. de beurre** knob of butter; **à la n.** Fam trashy, awful.

nom [nɔ̃] *nm* name; Gram noun; **n. de famille** surname; **n. de jeune fille** maiden name; **n. propre** Gram proper noun; **au n. de qn** on s.o.'s behalf; **sans n.** (*anonyme*) nameless; (*vil*) vile; **n. d'un chien!** Fam oh hell!

nomade [nɔmad] *a* nomadic; – *nmf* nomad.

nombre [nɔ̃br] *nm* number; **ils sont au** *ou* **du n. de** (*parmi*) they're among; **ils sont au n. de dix** there are ten of them; **elle est au n. de** she's one of; **le plus grand n. de** the majority of. ◆**nombreux, -euse** *a* (*amis, livres etc*) numerous; (*famille, collection etc*) large; **peu n.** few; **venir n.** to come in large numbers.

nombril [nɔ̃bri] *nm* navel.

nominal, -aux [nɔminal, -o] *a* nominal. ◆**nomination** *nf* appointment, nomination.

nommer [nɔme] *vt* (*appeler*) to name; **n. qn** (*désigner*) to appoint s.o. (**à un poste/***etc* to a post/*etc*); **n. qn président/lauréat** to nominate s.o. chairman/prizewinner; – **se n.** *vpr* (*s'appeler*) to be called. ◆**nommément** *adv* by name.

non [nɔ̃] *adv* & *nm inv* no; **n.!** no!; **tu viens ou n.?** are you coming or not?; **n. seulement** not only; **n. (pas) que** (+ *sub*) . . . not that . . . ; **c'est bien, n.?** *Fam* it's all right, isn't it?; **je crois que n.** I don't think so; **(ni) moi n. plus** neither do, am, can *etc* I; **une place n. réservée** an unreserved seat.

non- [nɔ̃] *préf* non-.

nonante [nɔnɑ̃t] *a* (*en Belgique, en Suisse*) ninety.

nonchalant [nɔ̃ʃalɑ̃] *a* nonchalant, apathetic. ◆**nonchalance** *nf* nonchalance, apathy.

non-conformiste [nɔ̃kɔ̃fɔrmist] *a* & *nmf* nonconformist.

non-fumeur, -euse [nɔ̃fymœr, -øz] *nmf* non-smoker.

non-sens [nɔ̃sɑ̃s] *nm inv* absurdity.

nord [nɔr] *nm* north; **au n. de** north of; du **n.** (*vent, direction*) northerly; (*ville*) northern; (*gens*) from *ou* in the north; **Amérique/Afrique du N.** North America/Africa; **l'Europe du N.** Northern Europe; – *a inv* (*côte*) north(ern). ◆**n.-africain, -aine** *a* & *nmf* North African. ◆**n.-américain, -aine** *a* & *nmf* North American. ◆**n.-est** *nm* & *a inv* north-east. ◆**n.-ouest** *nm* & *a inv* north-west.

nordique [nɔrdik] *a* & *nmf* Scandinavian.

normal, -aux [nɔrmal, -o] *a* normal. ◆**normale** *nf* norm, normality; **au-dessus de la n.** above normal. ◆**normalement** *adv* normally. ◆**normaliser** *vt* (*uniformiser*) to standardize; (*relations etc*) to normalize.

normand, -ande [nɔrmɑ̃, -ɑ̃d] *a* & *nmf* Norman. ◆**Normandie** *nf* Normandy.

norme [nɔrm] *nf* norm.

Norvège [nɔrvɛʒ] *nf* Norway. ◆**norvégien, -ienne** *a* & *nmf* Norwegian; – *nm* (*langue*) Norwegian.

nos [no] *voir* **notre**.

nostalgie [nɔstalʒi] *nf* nostalgia. ◆**nostalgique** *a* nostalgic.

notable [nɔtabl] *a* (*fait etc*) notable; – *nm* (*personne*) notable. ◆**—ment** [-əmɑ̃] *adv* (*sensiblement*) notably.

notaire [nɔtɛr] *nm* solicitor, notary.

notamment [nɔtamɑ̃] *adv* notably.

note [nɔt] *nf* (*remarque etc*) & *Mus* note; (*chiffrée*) *Scol* mark, *Am* grade; (*compte, facture*) bill, *Am* check; **prendre n. de** to make a note of. ◆**notation** *nf* notation; *Scol* marking. ◆**noter** *vt* (*prendre note de*) to note; (*remarquer*) to note, notice; (*écrire*) to note down; (*devoir etc*) *Scol* to mark, *Am* grade; **être bien noté** (*personne*) to be highly rated.

notice [nɔtis] *nf* (*résumé, préface*) note; (*mode d'emploi*) instructions.

notifier [nɔtifje] *vt* **n. qch à qn** to notify s.o. of sth.

notion [nɔsjɔ̃] *nf* notion, idea; *pl* (*éléments*) rudiments.

notoire [nɔtwar] *a* (*criminel, bêtise*) notorious; (*fait*) well-known. ◆**notoriété** *nf* (*renom*) fame; (*de fait*) general recognition.

notre, pl nos [nɔtr, no] *a poss our*. ◆**nôtre** *pron poss* **le** *ou* **la n., les nôtres** ours; – *nmpl* **les nôtres** (*parents etc*) our (own) people.

nouer [nwe] *vt* to tie, knot; (*amitié, conversation*) to strike up; **avoir la gorge nouée** to have a lump in one's throat. ◆**noueux, -euse** *a* (*bois*) knotty; (*doigts*) gnarled.

nougat [nuga] *nm* nougat.

nouille [nuj] *nf* (*idiot*) *Fam* drip.

nouilles [nuj] *nfpl* noodles.

nounours [nunurs] *nm* teddy bear.

nourrice [nuris] *nf* (*assistante maternelle*) child minder, nurse; (*qui allaite*) wet nurse; **mettre en n.** to put out to nurse.

nourr/ir [nurir] *vt* (*alimenter, faire vivre*) to feed; (*espoir etc*) *Fig* to nourish; (*esprit*) to enrich; **se n. de** to feed on; – *vi* (*aliment*) to be nourishing. ◆**—issant** *a* nourishing. ◆**nourriture** *nf* food.

nourrisson [nurisɔ̃] *nm* infant.

nous [nu] *pron* **1** (*sujet*) we; **n. sommes** we are. **2** (*complément direct*) us; **il n.** connaît he knows us. **3** (*indirect*) (to) us; **il n. l'a donné** he gave it to us, he gave us it. **4** (*réfléchi*) ourselves; **n. n. lavons** we wash ourselves. **5** (*réciproque*) each other;

n. n. détestons we hate each other. ◆**n.-mêmes** pron ourselves.

nouveau (or **nouvel** before vowel or mute h), **nouvelle**¹, pl **nouveaux, nouvelles** [nuvo, nuvɛl] a new; — nmf Scol new boy, new girl; — nm **du n.** something new; **de n.,** **à n.** again. ◆**n.-né, -ée** a & nmf new-born (baby). ◆**n.-venu** nm, ◆**nouvelle-venue** nf newcomer. ◆**nouveauté** nf newness, novelty; pl (livres) new books; (disques) new releases; (vêtements) new fashions; **une n.** (objet) a novelty.

nouvelle² [nuvɛl] nf **1 nouvelle(s)** news; **une n.** a piece of news. **2** Littér short story.

Nouvelle-Zélande [nuvɛlzelɑ̃d] nf New Zealand.

novateur, -trice [nɔvatœr, -tris] nmf innovator.

novembre [nɔvɑ̃br] nm November.

novice [nɔvis] nmf novice; — a inexperienced.

noyau, -x [nwajo] nm (de fruit) stone, Am pit; (d'atome, de cellule) nucleus; (groupe) group; **un n. d'opposants** a hard core of opponents.

noyaut/er [nwajote] vt Pol to infiltrate. ◆**—age** nm infiltration.

noy/er¹ [nwaje] vt (personne etc) to drown; (terres) to flood; — **se n.** vpr to drown; (se suicider) to drown oneself; **se n. dans le détail** to get bogged down in details. ◆**—é, -ée** nmf (mort) drowned person; — a (être n. (perdu) Fig to be out of one's depth. ◆**noyade** nf drowning.

noyer² [nwaje] nm (arbre) walnut tree.

nu [ny] a (personne, vérité) naked; (mains, chambre) bare; **tout nu** (stark) naked, (in the) nude; **voir à l'œil nu** to see with the naked eye; **mettre à nu** (exposer) to lay bare; **se mettre nu** to strip off; **tête nue,** **nu-tête** bare-headed; — nm (femme, homme, œuvre) nude.

nuage [nɥaʒ] nm cloud; **un n. de lait** Fig a dash of milk. ◆**nuageux, -euse** a (ciel) cloudy.

nuance [nɥɑ̃s] nf (de sens) nuance; (de couleurs) shade, nuance; (de regret) tinge, nuance. ◆**nuanc/er** vt (teintes) to blend,

shade; (pensée) to qualify. ◆**—é** a (jugement) qualified.

nucléaire [nykleɛr] a nuclear.

nudisme [nydism] nm nudism. ◆**nudiste** nmf nudist. ◆**nudité** nf nudity, nakedness; (de mur etc) bareness.

nuée [nɥe] nf **une n. de** (foule) a host of; (groupe compact) a cloud of.

nues [ny] nfpl **porter qn aux n.** to praise s.o. to the skies.

nuire* [nɥir] vi **n. à** (personne, intérêts etc) to harm. ◆**nuisible** a harmful.

nuit [nɥi] nf night; (obscurité) dark(ness); **il fait n.** it's dark; **avant la n.** before nightfall; **la n.** (se promener etc) at night; **cette** **n.** (aujourd'hui) tonight; (hier) last night. ◆**nuitée** nf overnight stay (in hotel etc).

nul, nulle [nyl] a **1** (risque etc) non-existent, nil; (médiocre) useless, hopeless; (non valable) Jur null (and void); **faire match n.** Sp to tie, draw. **2** a (aucun) no; **de nulle importance** of no importance; **sans n. doute** without any doubt; **nulle part** nowhere; — pron m (aucun) no one. ◆**nullard, -arde** nmf Fam useless person. ◆**nullement** adv not at all. ◆**nullité** nf (d'un élève etc) uselessness; (personne) useless person.

numéraire [nymerɛr] nm cash, currency.

numéral, -aux [nymeral, -o] a & nm numeral. ◆**numérique** a (numerical); (montre etc) digital.

numéro [nymero] nm (de journal) issue, number; (au cirque) act; **un n. de** **danse/de chant** a dance/song number; **quel n.!** (personne) Fam what a character!; **n. vert** Tél = Freefone®, = Am tollfree number. ◆**numérot/er** vt (pages, sièges) to number. ◆**—age** nm numbering.

nu-pieds [nypje] nmpl open sandals.

nuptial, -aux [nypsjal, -o] a (chambre) bridal; (anneau, cérémonie) wedding-.

nuque [nyk] nf back ou nape of the neck.

nurse [nœrs] nf nanny, (children's) nurse.

nutritif, -ive [nytritif, -iv] a nutritious, nutritive. ◆**nutrition** nf nutrition.

nylon [nilɔ̃] nm (fibre) nylon.

nymphe [nɛ̃f] nf nymph. ◆**nymphomane** nf Péj nymphomaniac.

O

O, o [o] *nm* O, o.

oasis [ɔazis] *nf* oasis.

obédience [ɔbedjɑ̃s] *nf Pol* allegiance.

obé/ir [ɔbeir] *vi* to obey; **o. à qn/qch** to obey s.o./sth; **être obéi** to be obeyed (**à** to). ◆**—issant** *a* obedient. ◆**obéissance** *nf* obedience (**à** to).

obélisque [ɔbelisk] *nm (monument)* obelisk.

obèse [ɔbɛz] *a & nmf* obese (person). ◆**obésité** *nf* obesity.

objecter [ɔbʒɛkte] *vt (prétexte)* to put forward, plead; **o. que** to object that; **on lui objecta son jeune âge** they objected that he *ou* she was too young. ◆**objecteur** *nm* **o. de conscience** conscientious objector. ◆**objection** *nf* objection.

objectif, -ive [ɔbʒɛktif, -iv] **1** *a (opinion etc)* objective. **2** *nm (but)* objective; *Phot* lens. ◆**objectivement** *adv* objectively. ◆**objectivité** *nf* objectivity.

objet [ɔbʒɛ] *nm (chose, sujet, but)* object; *(de toilette)* article; **faire l'o. de** *(étude, critiques etc)* to be the subject of; *(soins, surveillance)* to be given, receive; **objets trouvés** *(bureau)* lost property, *Am* lost and found.

obligation [ɔbligasjɔ̃] *nf (devoir, lieu, nécessité)* obligation; *Fin* bond. ◆**obligatoire** *a* compulsory, obligatory; *(inévitable)* *Fam* inevitable. ◆**obligatoirement** *adv (fatalement)* inevitably; **tu dois o. le faire** you have to do it.

oblig/er [ɔbliʒe] *vt* **1** *(contraindre)* to compel, oblige (**à faire** to do); *(engager)* to bind; **être obligé de faire** to have to do, be compelled *ou* obliged to do. **2** *(rendre service à)* to oblige; **être obligé à qn de qch** to be obliged to s.o. for sth. ◆**—eant** *a* obliging, kind. ◆**—é** *a (obligatoire)* necessary; *(fatal)* *Fam* inevitable. ◆**obligeamment** [-amɑ̃] *adv* obligingly. ◆**obligeance** *nf* kindness.

oblique [ɔblik] *a* oblique; **regard o.** sidelong glance; **en o.** at an (oblique) angle. ◆**obliquer** *vi (véhicule etc)* to turn off.

oblitérer [ɔblitere] *vt (timbre)* to cancel; *(billet, carte)* to stamp; **timbre oblitéré** *(non neuf)* used stamp. ◆**oblitération** *nf* cancellation; stamping.

oblong, -ongue [ɔblɔ̃, -ɔ̃g] *a* oblong.

obnubilé [ɔbnybile] *a (obsédé)* obsessed (**par** with).

obscène [ɔpsɛn] *a* obscene. ◆**obscénité** *nf* obscenity.

obscur [ɔpskyr] *a (noir)* dark; *(peu clair, inconnu, humble)* obscure. ◆**obscurcir** *vt (chambre etc)* to darken; *(rendre peu intelligible)* to obscure *(text, ideas etc)*; **— s'o.** *vpr (ciel)* to cloud over, darken; *(vue)* to become dim. ◆**obscurément** *adv* obscurely. ◆**obscurité** *nf* dark(ness); *(de texte, d'acteur etc)* obscurity.

obséd/er [ɔpsede] *vt* to obsess, haunt. ◆**—ant** *a* haunting, obsessive. ◆**-é, -ée** *nmf* maniac (**de** for); **o. sexuel** sex maniac.

obsèques [ɔpsɛk] *nfpl* funeral.

obséquieux, -euse [ɔpsekjø, -øz] *a* obsequious.

observer [ɔpserve] *vt (regarder)* to observe, watch; *(remarquer, respecter)* to observe; **faire o. qch à qn** *(signaler)* to point sth out to s.o. ◆**observateur, -trice** *a* observant; **— *nmf*** observer. ◆**observation** *nf (examen, remarque)* observation; *(reproche)* (critical) remark, rebuke; *(de règle etc)* observance; **en o.** *(malade)* under observation. ◆**observatoire** *nm* observatory; *(colline etc)* *Fig & Mil* observation post.

obsession [ɔpsesjɔ̃] *nf* obsession. ◆**obsessif, -ive** *a (peur etc)* obsessive. ◆**obsessionnel, -elle** *a Psy* obsessive.

obstacle [ɔpstakl] *nm* obstacle; **faire o. à** to stand in the way of.

obstétrique [ɔpstetrik] *nf Méd* obstetrics.

obstin/er (s') [ɔpstine] *vpr* to be obstinate *ou* persistent; **s'o. à faire** to persist in doing. ◆**—é** *a* stubborn, obstinate, persistent. ◆**obstination** *nf* stubbornness, obstinacy, persistence.

obstruction [ɔpstryksjɔ̃] *nf Méd Pol Sp* obstruction; **faire de l'o.** *Pol Sp* to be obstructive. ◆**obstruer** *vt* to obstruct.

obtempérer [ɔptɑ̃pere] *vi* to obey an injunction; **o. à** to obey.

obtenir* [ɔptənir] *vt* to get, obtain, secure. ◆**obtention** *nf* obtaining, obtention.

obturer [ɔptyre] *vt (trou etc)* to stop *ou* close up. ◆**obturateur** *nm Phot* shutter; *Tech* valve.

obtus [ɔpty] *a (angle, esprit)* obtuse.

obus [ɔby] nm Mil shell.

occasion [ɔkazjɔ̃] nf 1 (chance) opportunity, chance (**de faire** to do); (circonstance) occasion; **à l'o.** on occasion, when the occasion arises; **à l'o. de** on the occasion of. 2 Com (marché avantageux) bargain; (objet non neuf) second-hand buy; **d'o.** second-hand, used. ◆**occasionner** vt to cause; **o. qch à qn** to cause s.o. sth.

occident [ɔksidɑ̃] nm **l'O.** Pol the West. ◆**occidental, -aux** a Géog Pol western; — nmpl **les occidentaux** Pol Westerners. ◆**occidentalisé** a Pol Westernized.

occulte [ɔkylt] a occult.

occup/er [ɔkype] vt (maison, pays, usine etc) to occupy; (place, temps) to take up, occupy; (poste) to hold, occupy; **o. qn** (absorber) to occupy s.o., keep s.o. busy; (ouvrier etc) to employ s.o.; — **s'o.** vpr to keep (oneself) busy (**à faire** doing); **s'o. de** (affaire, problème etc) to deal with; (politique) to be engaged in; **s'o. de qn** (malade etc) to take care of s.o.; (client) to see to s.o., deal with s.o.; **ne t'en occupe pas!** (ne t'en fais pas) don't worry!; (ne t'en mêle pas) mind your own business! ◆**—ant, -ante** a (armée) occupying; — nmf (habitant) occupant; — nm Mil forces of occupation, occupier. ◆**—é** a busy (**à faire** doing); (place, maison etc) occupied; (ligne) Tél engaged, Am busy; (taxi) hired. ◆**occupation** nf (activité, travail etc) occupation; **l'o. de** (action) the occupation of.

occurrence [ɔkyrɑ̃s] nf Ling occurrence; **en l'o.** in the circumstances, as it happens ou happened.

océan [ɔseɑ̃] nm ocean. ◆**océanique** a oceanic.

ocre [ɔkr] nm & a inv (couleur) ochre.

octave [ɔktav] nf Mus octave.

octobre [ɔktɔbr] nm October.

octogénaire [ɔktɔʒenɛr] nmf octogenarian.

octogone [ɔktɔgɔn] nm octagon. ◆**octogonal, -aux** a octagonal.

octroi [ɔktrwa] nm Litt granting. ◆**octroyer** vt Litt to grant (**à** to).

oculaire [ɔkylɛr] a **témoin o.** eyewitness; **globe o.** eyeball. ◆**oculiste** nmf eye specialist.

ode [ɔd] nf (poème) ode.

odeur [ɔdœr] nf smell, odour; (de fleur) scent. ◆**odorant** a sweet-smelling. ◆**odorat** nm sense of smell.

odieux, -euse [ɔdjø, -øz] a odious, obnoxious.

œcuménique [ekymenik] a Rel (o)ecumenical.

œil, pl **yeux** [œj, jø] nm eye; **sous mes yeux** before my very eyes; **lever/baisser les yeux** to look up/down; **fermer l'o.** (dormir) to shut one's eyes; **fermer les yeux sur** to turn a blind eye to; **ouvre l'o.!** keep your eyes open!; **coup d'o.** (regard) glance, look; **jeter un coup d'o. sur** to (have a) look ou glance at; **à vue d'o.** visibly; **faire les gros yeux à** to scowl at; **avoir à l'o.** (surveiller) to keep an eye on; **à l'o.** (gratuitement) Fam free; **faire de l'o. à** Fam to make eyes at; **o. au beurre noir** Fig black eye; **mon o.!** Fam (incrédulité) my foot!; (refus) no way!, no chance!

œillade [œjad] nf (clin d'œil) wink.

œillères [œjɛr] nfpl (de cheval) & Fig blinkers, Am blinders.

œillet [œjɛ] nm 1 Bot carnation. 2 (trou de ceinture) eyelet.

œuf, pl **œufs** [œf, ø] nm egg; pl (de poisson) (hard) roe; **o. sur le plat** fried egg; **étouffer qch dans l'o.** Fig to nip ou stifle sth in the bud.

œuvre [œvr] nf (travail, acte, livre etc) work; **o. (de charité)** (organisation) charity; **l'o. de** (production artistique etc) the works of; **mettre en o.** (employer) to make use of; **mettre tout en o.** to do everything possible (**pour faire** to do). ◆**œuvrer** vi Litt to work.

offense [ɔfɑ̃s] nf insult; Rel transgression. ◆**offens/er** vt to offend; **s'o. de** to take offence at. ◆**—ant, -ante** a offensive.

offensif, -ive [ɔfɑ̃sif, -iv] a offensive; — nf (attaque) offensive; (du froid) onslaught.

offert [ɔfɛr] voir **offrir**.

office [ɔfis] 1 nm (fonction) office; (bureau) office, bureau; **d'o.** (être promu etc) automatically; **faire o. de** to serve as; **ses bons offices** (service) one's good offices. 2 nm Rel service. 3 nm ou f (pièce pour provisions) pantry.

officiel, -ielle [ɔfisjɛl] a (acte etc) official; — nm (personnage) official. ◆**officiellement** adv officially. ◆**officieux, -euse** a unofficial.

officier [ɔfisje] 1 vi Rel to officiate. 2 nm (dans l'armée etc) officer.

offre [ɔfr] nf offer; (aux enchères) bid; **l'o. et la demande** Écon supply and demand; **offres d'emploi** Journ situations vacant. ◆**offrande** nf offering.

offr/ir [ɔfrir] vt (proposer, présenter) to offer (**de faire** to do); (donner en cadeau) to give; (démission) to tender, offer; **je lui ai offert de le loger** I offered to put him up; — **s'o.** vpr (cadeau etc) to treat oneself to; (se _proposer_) to offer oneself (**comme** as); **s'o. à faire** to offer _ou_ volunteer to do; **s'o. (aux yeux)** (_vue etc_) to present itself. **◆—ant** _nm_ **au plus o.** to the highest bidder.

offusquer [ɔfyske] _vt_ to offend, shock; **s'o. de** to take offence at.

ogive [ɔʒiv] _nf_ (_de fusée_) nose cone; **o. nucléaire** nuclear warhead.

ogre [ɔgr] _nm_ ogre.

oh! [o] _int_ oh!, o!

ohé! [ɔe] _int_ hey (there)!

oie [wa] _nf_ goose.

oignon [ɔɲɔ̃] _nm_ (_légume_) onion; (_de tulipe, lis etc_) bulb; **occupe-toi de tes oignons!** _Fam_ mind your own business!

oiseau, -x [wazo] _nm_ bird; **à vol d'o.** as the crow flies; **drôle d'o.** (_individu_) _Péj_ odd fish, _Am_ oddball; **o. rare** (_personne étonnante_) _Iron_ rare bird, perfect gem.

oiseux, -euse [wazø, -øz] _a_ (_futile_) idle, vain.

oisif, -ive [wazif, -iv] _a_ (_inactif_) idle; – _nmf_ idler. **◆oisiveté** _nf_ idleness.

oléoduc [ɔleɔdyk] _nm_ oil pipeline.

olive [ɔliv] _nf_ (_fruit_) olive; **huile d'o.** olive oil; – _a inv_ (_couleur_) (**vert) o.** olive (green). **◆olivier** (_arbre_) olive tree.

olympique [ɔlɛ̃pik] _a_ (_jeux, record etc_) Olympic.

ombilical, -aux [ɔ̃bilikal, -o] _a_ (_cordon_) umbilical.

ombrage [ɔ̃braʒ] _nm_ **1** (_ombre_) shade. **2 prendre o. de** (_jalousie, dépit_) to take umbrage at. **◆ombrag/er** _vt_ to give shade to. **◆—é** _a_ shady. **◆ombrageux, -euse** _a_ (_caractère, personne_) touchy.

ombre [ɔ̃br] _nf_ (_d'arbre etc_) shade; (_de personne, objet_) shadow; **l'o. d'un doute** Fig the shadow of a doubt; **l'o. de** (_remords, reproche etc_) the trace of; **30° à l'o.** 30° in the shade; **dans l'o.** (_comploter, travailler etc_) in secret.

ombrelle [ɔ̃brɛl] _nf_ sunshade, parasol.

omelette [ɔmlɛt] _nf_ omelet(te); **o. au fromage/etc** cheese/_etc_ omelet(te).

omettre* [ɔmɛtr] _vt_ to omit (**de faire** to do). **◆omission** _nf_ omission.

omni- [ɔmni] _préf_ omni-. **◆omnipotent** _a_ omnipotent.

omnibus [ɔmnibys] _a_ & _nm_ (**train**) _o._ slow train (_stopping at all stations_).

omoplate [ɔmɔplat] _nf_ shoulder blade.

on [ɔ̃] (_sometimes_ **l'on** [lɔ̃]) _pron_ (_les gens_) they, people; (_nous_) we, one; (_vous_) you, one; **on dit** they say, people say, it is said; **on frappe** (_quelqu'un_) someone's knocking;

on me l'a donné it was given to me, I was given it.

once [ɔ̃s] _nf_ (_mesure_) & _Fig_ ounce.

oncle [ɔ̃kl] _nm_ uncle.

onctueux, -euse [ɔ̃ktɥø, -øz] _a_ (_liquide, crème_) creamy; (_manières, paroles_) _Fig_ smooth.

onde [ɔ̃d] _nf_ _Phys Rad_ wave; **grandes ondes** long wave; **ondes courtes/moyennes** short/medium wave; **sur les ondes** (_sur l'antenne_) on the radio.

ondée [ɔ̃de] _nf_ (_pluie_) (sudden) shower.

on-dit [ɔ̃di] _nm inv_ rumour, hearsay.

ondoyer [ɔ̃dwaje] _vi_ to undulate. **◆ondulation** _nf_ undulation; (_de cheveux_) wave. **◆ondul/er** _vi_ to undulate; (_cheveux_) to be wavy. **◆—é** _a_ wavy.

onéreux, -euse [ɔnerø, -øz] _a_ costly.

ongle [ɔ̃gl] _nm_ (finger) nail.

onglet [ɔ̃glɛ] _nm_ (_entaille de canif etc_) (nail) groove.

ont [ɔ̃] _voir_ avoir.

ONU [ɔny] _nf abrév_ (_Organisation des nations unies_) UN.

onyx [ɔniks] _nm_ (_pierre précieuse_) onyx.

onze [ɔ̃z] _a_ & _nm_ eleven. **◆onzième** _a_ & _nmf_ eleventh.

opale [ɔpal] _nf_ (_pierre_) opal.

opaque [ɔpak] _a_ opaque. **◆opacité** _nf_ opacity.

opéra [ɔpera] _nm_ (_ouvrage, art_) opera; (_édifice_) opera house. **◆opérette** _nf_ operetta.

opér/er [ɔpere] _vt_ (_exécuter_) to carry out; (_choix_) to make; – _vi_ (_agir_) to work, act; (_procéder_) to proceed; – **s'o.** _vpr_ (_se produire_) to take place. **◆—ant** _a_ (_efficace_) operative. **◆—é, -ée** _nmf_ _Méd_ patient (_operated on_). **◆opérateur, -trice** _nmf_ (_de prise de vues_) _Cin_ cameraman; (_sur machine_) operator. **◆opération** _nf_ (_acte_) & _Méd Mil Math etc_ operation; _Fin_ deal. **◆opérationnel, -elle** _a_ operational. **◆opératoire** _a_ _Méd_ operative; **bloc o.** operating _ou_ surgical wing.

opiner [ɔpine] _vi_ **o.** (_de la tête ou du chef_) to nod assent.

opiniâtre [ɔpinjɑtr] _a_ stubborn, obstinate. **◆opiniâtreté** _nf_ stubbornness, obstinacy.

opinion [ɔpinjɔ̃] _nf_ opinion (**sur** about, on).

opium [ɔpjɔm] _nm_ opium.

opportun [ɔpɔrtɛ̃] _a_ opportune, timely. **◆opportunément** _adv_ opportunely.

◆**opportunisme** *nm* opportunism. ◆**opportunité** *nf* timeliness.

oppos/er [ɔpoze] *vt* (*argument, résistance*) to put up (**à** against); (*équipes, rivaux*) to bring together, set against each other; (*objets*) to place opposite each other; (*couleurs*) to contrast; **o. qch à qch** (*objet*) to place sth opposite sth; **o. qn à qn** to set s.o. against s.o.; **match qui oppose ...** match between ... ; **— s'o.** *vpr* (*couleurs*) to contrast; (*équipes*) to confront each other; **s'o. à** (*mesure, personne etc*) to oppose, be opposed to; **je m'y oppose** I'm opposed to it, I oppose. ◆**—ant, -ante** *a* (*opposing*); — *nmf* opponent. ◆**—é** *a* (*direction etc*) opposite; (*intérêts, équipe*) opposing; (*opinions*) opposite, opposing; (*couleurs*) contrasting; **être o. à** to be opposed to; — *nm* **l'o.** the opposite (**de** of); **à l'o.** (*côté*) on the opposite side (**de** from, to); **à l'o. de** (*contrairement à*) contrary to. ◆**opposition** *nf* opposition; **faire o. à** to oppose; **par o. à** as opposed to.

oppress/er [ɔprese] *vt* (*gêner*) to oppress. ◆**—ant** *a* oppressive. ◆**—eur** *nm Pol* oppressor. ◆**oppressif, -ive** *a* (*loi etc*) oppressive. ◆**oppression** *nf* oppression. ◆**opprim/er** *vt* (*tyranniser*) to oppress. ◆**—és** *nmpl* **les o.** the oppressed.

opter [ɔpte] *vi* **o. pour** to opt for.

opticien, -ienne [ɔptisjɛ̃, -jɛn] *nmf* optician.

optimisme [ɔptimism] *nm* optimism. ◆**optimiste** *a* optimistic; — *nmf* optimist.

optimum [ɔptimɔm] *nm & a* optimum; **la température o.** the optimum temperature. ◆**optimal, -aux** *a* optimal.

option [ɔpsjɔ̃] *nf* (*choix*) option; (*chose*) optional extra.

optique [ɔptik] *a* (*verre*) optical; — *nf* optics; (*aspect*) perspective; **d'o.** (*illusion, instrument etc*) optical.

opulent [ɔpylɑ̃] *a* opulent. ◆**opulence** *nf* opulence.

or [ɔr] **1** *nm* gold; **en or** (*chaîne etc*) gold-; **d'or** (*cheveux, âge, règle*) golden; (*cœur*) of gold; **mine d'or** *Géol* goldmine; (*fortune*) *Fig* goldmine; **affaire en or** (*achat*) bargain; (*commerce*) *Fig* goldmine; **or noir** (*pétrole*) *Fig* black gold. **2** *conj* (*alors, cependant*) now, well.

oracle [ɔrakl] *nm* oracle.

orage [ɔraʒ] *nm* (thunder)storm. ◆**orageux, -euse** *a* stormy.

oraison [ɔrɛzɔ̃] *nf* prayer; **o. funèbre** funeral oration.

oral, -aux [ɔral, -o] *a* oral; — *nm* (*examen*) *Scol* oral.

orange [ɔrɑ̃ʒ] *nf* (*fruit*) orange; **o. pressée** (fresh) orange juice; — *a & nm* (*couleur*) orange. ◆**orangé** *a & nm* (*couleur*) orange. ◆**orangeade** *nf* orangeade. ◆**oranger** *nm* orange tree.

orang-outan(g) [ɔrɑ̃utɑ̃] *nm* (*pl* **orangs-outan(g)s**) orang-outang.

orateur [ɔratœr] *nm* speaker, orator.

orbite [ɔrbit] *nf* (*d'astre etc*) & *Anat* orbit; (*d'œil*) socket; **mettre sur o.** (*fusée etc*) to put into orbit.

orchestre [ɔrkɛstr] *nm* (*classique*) orchestra; (*moderne*) band; (*places*) *Th* stalls, *Am* orchestra. ◆**orchestrer** *vt* (*organiser*) & *Mus* to orchestrate.

orchidée [ɔrkide] *nf* orchid.

ordinaire [ɔrdinɛr] *a* (*habituel, normal*) ordinary, *Am* regular; (*médiocre*) ordinary, average; **d'o., à l'o.** usually; **comme d'o., comme à l'o.** as usual; **de l'essence o.** two-star (petrol), *Am* regular. ◆**—ment** *adv* usually.

ordinal, -aux [ɔrdinal, -o] *a* (*nombre*) ordinal.

ordinateur [ɔrdinatœr] *nm* computer.

ordination [ɔrdinasjɔ̃] *nf Rel* ordination.

ordonnance [ɔrdɔnɑ̃s] *nf* **1** (*de médecin*) prescription. **2** (*décret*) *Jur* order, ruling. **3** (*disposition*) arrangement. **4** (*soldat*) orderly.

ordonn/er [ɔrdɔne] *vt* **1** (*enjoindre*) to order (**que** (+ *sub*) that); **o. à qn de faire** to order s.o. to do. **2** (*agencer*) to arrange, order. **3** (*médicament etc*) to prescribe. **4** (*prêtre*) to ordain. ◆**—é** *a* (*personne, maison etc*) orderly.

ordre [ɔrdr] *nm* (*commandement, structure, association etc*) order; (*absence de désordre*) tidiness (*of room, person etc*); **en o.** (*chambre etc*) tidy; **mettre en o., mettre de l'o. dans** to tidy (up); **de premier o.** first-rate; **o.** (*public*) (law and) order; **par o. d'âge** in order of age; **à l'o. du jour** (*au programme*) on the agenda; (*d'actualité*) of topical interest; **les forces de l'o.** the police; **jusqu'à nouvel o.** until further notice; **de l'o. de** (*environ*) of the order of.

ordure [ɔrdyr] *nf* filth, muck; *pl* (*débris*) refuse, rubbish, *Am* garbage. ◆**ordurier, -ière** *a* (*plaisanterie etc*) lewd.

oreille [ɔrɛj] *nf* ear; **être tout oreilles** to be all ears; **faire la sourde o.** to turn a deaf ear; **casser les oreilles à qn** to deafen s.o.

oreiller [ɔreje] *nm* pillow.

oreillons [ɔrɛjɔ̃] *nmpl Méd* mumps.

ores (d') [dɔr] *adv* **d'ores et déjà** [dɔrzedeʒa] henceforth.

orfèvre [ɔrfɛvr] nm goldsmith, silversmith. ◆**orfèvrerie** nf (magasin) goldsmith's or silversmith's shop; (objets) gold or silver plate.

organe [ɔrgan] nm Anat & Fig organ; (porte-parole) mouthpiece. ◆**organique** a organic. ◆**organisme** nm 1 (corps) body; Anat Biol organism. 2 (bureaux etc) organization.

organisation [ɔrganizasjɔ̃] nf (arrangement, association) organization.

organis/er [ɔrganize] vt to organize; **— s'o.** vpr to organize oneself, get organized. ◆**—é** a (esprit, groupe etc) organized. ◆**organisateur, -trice** nmf organizer.

organiste [ɔrganist] nmf Mus organist.

orgasme [ɔrgasm] nm orgasm.

orge [ɔrʒ] nf barley.

orgie [ɔrʒi] nf orgy.

orgue [ɔrg] nm Mus organ; **o. de Barbarie** barrel organ; **— nfpl** organ; **grandes orgues** great organ.

orgueil [ɔrgœj] nm pride. ◆**orgueilleux, -euse** a proud.

orient [ɔrjɑ̃] nm l'O. the Orient, the East; **Moyen-O., Proche-O.** Middle East; **Extrême-O.** Far East. ◆**oriental, -ale, -aux** a eastern; (de l'Orient) oriental; **— nmf** oriental.

orient/er [ɔrjɑ̃te] vt (lampe, antenne etc) to position, direct; (voyageur, élève etc) to direct; (maison) to orientate, Am orient; **— s'o.** vpr to find one's bearings or direction; **s'o. vers** (carrière etc) to move towards. ◆**—é** a (ouvrage, film etc) slanted. ◆**orientable** a (lampe etc) adjustable, flexible; (bras de machine) movable. ◆**orientation** nf direction; (action) positioning, directing; (de maison) aspect, orientation; (tendance) Pol Littér etc trend; **o. professionnelle** vocational guidance.

orifice [ɔrifis] nm opening, orifice.

originaire [ɔriʒinɛr] a **être o. de** (natif) to be a native of.

original, -ale, -aux [ɔriʒinal, -o] 1 a (idée, artiste, version etc) original; **— nm** (modèle) original. 2 a & nmf (bizarre) eccentric. ◆**originalité** nf originality; eccentricity.

origine [ɔriʒin] nf origin; **à l'o.** originally; **d'o.** (pneu etc) original; **pays d'o.** country of origin. ◆**originel, -elle** a (sens, péché, habitant etc) original.

orme [ɔrm] nm (arbre, bois) elm.

ornement [ɔrnəmɑ̃] nm ornament. ◆**ornemental, -aux** a ornamental. ◆**ornementation** nf ornamentation. ◆**ornementé** a

adorned, ornamented (de with). ◆**orn/er** vt to decorate, adorn (de with). ◆**—é** a (style etc) ornate.

ornière [ɔrnjɛr] nf (sillon) & Fig rut.

orphelin, -ine [ɔrfəlɛ̃, -in] nmf orphan; **—** a orphaned. ◆**orphelinat** nm orphanage.

orteil [ɔrtɛj] nm toe; **gros o.** big toe.

orthodoxe [ɔrtɔdɔks] a orthodox; **— nmpl les orthodoxes** the orthodox. ◆**orthodoxie** nf orthodoxy.

orthographe [ɔrtɔgraf] nf spelling. ◆**orthographier** vt (mot) to spell.

orthopédie [ɔrtɔpedi] nf orthop(a)edics.

ortie [ɔrti] nf nettle.

os [ɔs, pl o ou ɔs] nm bone; **trempé jusqu'aux os** soaked to the skin; **tomber sur un os** (difficulté) Fam to hit a snag.

OS [ɔɛs] abrév **= ouvrier spécialisé.**

oscar [ɔskar] nm Cin Oscar.

osciller [ɔsile] vi Tech to oscillate; (se balancer) to swing, sway; (hésiter) to waver; (varier) to fluctuate; (flamme) to flicker. ◆**oscillation** nf Tech oscillation; (de l'opinion) fluctuation.

oseille [ozɛj] nf 1 Bot Culin sorrel. 2 (argent) Arg dough.

os/er [oze] vti to dare; **o. faire** to dare to do. ◆**—é** a bold, daring.

osier [ozje] nm (branches) wicker.

ossature [ɔsatyr] nf (du corps) frame; (de bâtiment) & Fig framework. ◆**osselets** nmpl (jeu) jacks, knucklebones. ◆**ossements** nmpl (de cadavres) bones. ◆**osseux, -euse** a (tissu) bone-; (maigre) bony.

ostensible [ɔstɑ̃sibl] a conspicuous.

ostentation [ɔstɑ̃tasjɔ̃] nf ostentation.

otage [ɔtaʒ] nm hostage; **prendre qn en o.** to take s.o. hostage.

OTAN [ɔtɑ̃] nf abrév (Organisation du traité de l'Atlantique Nord) NATO.

otarie [ɔtari] nf (animal) sea lion.

ôter [ote] vt to remove, take away (à qn from s.o.); (vêtement) to take off, remove; (déduire) to take (away); **ôte-toi de là!** Fam get out of the way!

otite [ɔtit] nf ear infection.

oto-rhino [ɔtɔrino] nmf Méd Fam ear, nose and throat specialist.

ou [u] conj or; **ou bien** or else; **ou elle ou moi** either her or me.

où [u] adv & pron where; **le jour où** the day when, the day on which; **la table où** the table on which; **l'état où** the condition in which; **par où?** which way?; **d'où?** where from?; **d'où ma surprise**/*etc* (*conséquence*) hence my surprise/*etc*; **le pays d'où** the country from which; **où qu'il soit** wherever he may be.

ouate [wat] *nf Méd* cotton wool, *Am* absorbent cotton.

oubli [ubli] *nm* (*défaut*) forgetfulness; **l'o. de qch** forgetting sth; **un o.** a lapse of memory; (*omission*) an oversight; **tomber dans l'o.** to fall into oblivion. ◆**oublier** *vt* to forget (**de faire** to do); (*faute, problème*) to overlook; — **s'o.** *vpr* (*traditions etc*) to be forgotten; (*personne*) *Fig* to forget oneself. ◆**oublieux, -euse** *a* forgetful (**de** of).

oubliettes [ublijɛt] *nfpl* (*de château*) dungeon.

ouest [wɛst] *nm* west; **à l'o.** de west of; **d'o.** (*vent*) west(erly); **de l'o.** western; **Allemagne de l'O.** West Germany; **l'Europe de l'O.** Western Europe; – *a inv* (*côte*) west(ern). ◆**o.-allemand, -ande** *a & nmf* West German.

ouf! [uf] *int* (*soulagement*) ah!, phew!

oui [wi] *adv & nm inv* yes; **o.!** yes!; **les o.** (*votes*) the ayes; **tu viens, o.?** come on, will you?; **je crois que o.** I think so; **si o.** if so.

ouï-dire [widir] *nm inv* hearsay.

ouïe [wi] *nf* hearing; **être tout o.** *Fam* to be all ears.

ouïe?! [uj] *int* ouch!

ouïes [wi] *nfpl* (*de poisson*) gills.

ouille! [uj] *int* ouch!

ouragan [uragɑ̃] *nm* hurricane.

ourler [urle] *vt* to hem. ◆**ourlet** *nm* hem.

ours [urs] *nm* bear; **o. blanc/gris** polar/grizzly bear.

oursin [ursɛ̃] *nm* (*animal*) sea urchin.

ouste! [ust] *int Fam* scram!

outil [uti] *nm* tool. ◆**outiller** *vt* to equip. ◆**-age** *nm* tools; (*d'une usine*) equipment.

outrage [utraʒ] *nm* insult (**à** to). ◆**outrager** *vt* to insult, offend. ◆**-eant** *a* insulting, offensive.

outrance [utrɑ̃s] *nf* (*excès*) excess; **à o.** (*travailler etc*) to excess; **guerre à o.** all-out war. ◆**outrancier, -ière** *a* excessive.

outre [utr] *prép* besides; – *adv* **en o.** besides, moreover; **o. mesure** inordinately; **passer o.** to take no notice (**à** of). ◆**o.-Manche**

adv across the Channel. ◆**o.-mer** *adv* overseas; **d'o.-mer** (*peuple*) overseas.

outrepasser [utrəpase] *vt* (*limite etc*) to go beyond, exceed.

outr/er [utre] *vt* to exaggerate, overdo; **o. qn** (*indigner*) to outrage s.o. ◆**-é** *a* (*excessif*) exaggerated; (*révolté*) outraged.

outsider [awtsajdœr] *nm Sp* outsider.

ouvert [uvɛr] *voir* **ouvrir**; – *a* open; (*robinet, gaz etc*) on; **à bras ouverts** with open arms. ◆**ouvertement** *adv* openly. ◆**ouverture** *nf* opening; (*trou*) hole; (*avance*) & *Mus* overture; (*d'objectif*) *Phot* aperture; **o. d'esprit** open-mindedness.

ouvrable [uvrabl] *a* **jour o.** working day.

ouvrage [uvraʒ] *nm* (*travail, objet, livre*) work; (*couture*) (needle)work; **un o.** (*travail*) a piece of work. ◆**ouvragé** *a* (*bijou etc*) finely worked.

ouvreuse [uvrøz] *nf Cin* usherette.

ouvrier, -ière [uvrije, -jɛr] *nmf* worker; **o. agricole** farm labourer; **o. qualifié/spécialisé** skilled/unskilled worker; – *a* (*législation etc*) industrial; (*quartier, éducation*) working-class; **classe ouvrière** working class.

ouvrir* [uvrir] *vt* to open (up); (*gaz, radio etc*) to turn on, switch on; (*inaugurer*) to open; (*hostilités*) to begin; (*appétit*) to whet; (*liste, procession*) to head; – *vi* to open; (*ouvrir la porte*) to open (up); – **s'o.** *vpr* (*porte, boîte etc*) to open (up); **s'o. la jambe** to cut one's leg open; **s'o. à qn** *Fig* to open one's heart to s.o. (**de qch** about sth). ◆**ouvre-boîtes** *nm inv* tin opener, *Am* can-opener. ◆**ouvre-bouteilles** *nm inv* bottle opener.

ovaire [ovɛr] *nm Anat* ovary.

ovale [oval] *a & nm* oval.

ovation [ovasjɔ̃] *nf* (*standing*) ovation.

OVNI [ɔvni] *nm abrév* (*objet volant non identifié*) UFO.

oxyde [ɔksid] *nm Ch* oxide; **o. de carbone** carbon monoxide. ◆**oxyder** *vt*, – **s'o.** *vpr* to oxidize.

oxygène [ɔksiʒɛn] *nm* oxygen; **à o.** (*masque, tente*) oxygen-. ◆**oxygén/er** *vt* (*cheveux*) to bleach; – **s'o.** *vpr Fam* to breathe *ou* get some fresh air. ◆**-ée** *a* **eau o.** (hydrogen) peroxide.

P

P, p [pe] *nm* P, p.

pachyderme [paʃidɛrm] *nm* elephant.

pacifier [pasifje] *vt* to pacify. ◆**pacification** *nf* pacification. ◆**pacifique 1** *a* (*non violent, non militaire*) peaceful; (*caractère, personne*) peaceable.

paître* [pɛtr] *vi* to graze; **envoyer p.** *Fig* to send packing.

paix [pɛ] *nf* peace; (*traité*) *Pol* peace treaty; **en p.** in peace; (*avec sa conscience*) at peace (*avec* with); **avoir la p.** to have (some) peace and quiet.

Pakistan [pakistã] *nm* Pakistan. ◆**pakistanais, -aise** *a & nmf* Pakistani.

palabres [palabr] *nmpl* palaver.

palace [palas] *nm* luxury hotel.

palais [palɛ] *nm* **1** (*château*) palace; **P. de justice** law courts; **p. des sports** sports stadium *ou* centre. **2** *Anat* palate.

palan [palã] *nm* (*de navire etc*) hoist.

pâle [pɑl] *a* pale.

palet [palɛ] *nm* (*hockey sur glace*) puck.

paletot [palto] *nm* (*knitted*) cardigan.

palette [palɛt] *nf* **1** (*de peintre*) palette. **2** (*support pour marchandises*) pallet.

pâleur [pɑlœr] *nf* paleness, pallor. ◆**pâlir** *vi* to go *ou* turn pale (**de** with).

palier [palje] *nm* **1** (*d'escalier*) landing; **être voisins de p.** to live on the same floor. **2** (*niveau*) level; (*phase de stabilité*) plateau; **par paliers** (*étapes*) in stages.

palissade [palisad] *nf* fence (of stakes).

pallier [palje] *vt* (*difficultés etc*) to alleviate. ◆**palliatif** *nm* palliative.

palmarès [palmarɛs] *nm* prize list; (*des chansons*) hit-parade.

palme [palm] *nf* **1** palm (leaf); (*symbole*) *Fig* palm. **2** (*de nageur*) flipper. ◆**palmier** *nm* palm (tree).

palmé [palme] *a* (*patte, pied*) webbed.

palombe [palɔ̃b] *nf* wood pigeon.

pâlot, -otte [pɑlo, -ɔt] *a* pale.

palourde [palurd] *nf* (*mollusque*) clam.

palp/er [palpe] *vt* to feel, finger. ◆**—able** *a* tangible.

palpit/er [palpite] *vi* (*frémir*) to quiver; (*cœur*) to palpitate, throb. ◆**—ant** *a* (*récit etc*) thrilling. ◆**palpitations** *nfpl* quivering; palpitations.

pâmer (se) [səpame] *vpr* **se p. de** (*joie etc*) to be paralysed *ou* ecstatic with.

pamphlet [pɑ̃flɛ] *nm* lampoon.

pamplemousse [pɑ̃pləmus] *nm* grapefruit.

pachyderme [paʃidɛrm] *nm* elephant.

pacifier [pasifje] *vt* to pacify. ◆**pacification** *nf* pacification. ◆**pacifique 1** *a* (*non violent, non militaire*) peaceful; (*personne, peuple*) peace-loving. **2** *a* (*côte etc*) Pacific; **Océan P.** Pacific Ocean; — *nm* **le P.** the Pacific. ◆**pacifiste** *a & nmf* pacifist.

pack [pak] *nm* (*de lait etc*) carton.

pacotille [pakɔtij] *nf* (*camelote*) trash.

pacte [pakt] *nm* pact. ◆**pactiser** *vi* **p. avec qn** *Péj* to be in league with s.o.

paf! [paf] **1** *int* bang!, wallop! **2** *a inv* (*ivre*) *Fam* sozzled, plastered.

pagaie [pagɛ] *nf* paddle. ◆**pagayer** *vi* (*ramer*) to paddle.

pagaïe, pagaille [pagaj] *nf* (*désordre*) *Fam* mess, shambles; **en p.** *Fam* in a mess; **avoir des livres/etc en p.** *Fam* to have loads of books/etc.

paganisme [paganism] *nm* paganism.

page [paʒ] **1** *nf* (*de livre etc*) page; **à la p.** (*personne*) *Fig* up-to-date. **2** *nm* (*à la cour*) *Hist* page (boy).

pagne [paɲ] *nm* loincloth.

pagode [pagɔd] *nf* pagoda.

paie [pɛ] *nf* pay, wages. ◆**paiement** *nm* payment.

païen, -enne [pajɛ̃, -ɛn] *a & nmf* pagan, heathen.

paillasson [pajasɔ̃] *nm* (door)mat.

paille [paj] *nf* straw; (*pour boire*) (drinking) straw; **homme de p.** *Fig* stooge, man of straw; **tirer à la courte p.** to draw lots; **sur la p.** *Fig* penniless; **feu de p.** *Fig* flash in the pan. ◆**paillasse** *nf* **1** (*matelas*) straw mattress. **2** (*d'un évier*) draining-board.

paillette [pajɛt] *nf* (*d'habit*) sequin; *pl* (*de lessive, savon*) flakes; (*d'or*) *Géol* gold dust.

pain [pɛ̃] *nm* bread; **un p.** a loaf (of bread); **p. grillé** toast; **p. complet** wholemeal bread; **p. d'épice** gingerbread; **petit p.** roll; **p. de savon/de cire** bar of soap/wax; **avoir du p. sur la planche** (*travail*) *Fig* to have a lot on one's plate.

pair [pɛr] **1** *a* (*numéro*) even. **2** *nm* (*personne*) peer; **hors (de) p.** unrivalled, without equal; **aller de p.** to go hand in hand (**avec** with); **au p.** (*étudiante etc*) au pair; **travailler au p.** to work as an au pair.

pan [pɑ̃] **1** nm (de chemise) tail; (de ciel) patch; **p. de mur** section of wall. **2** int bang!

pan- [pɑ̃, pan] préf Pan-.

panacée [panase] nf panacea.

panache [panaʃ] nm (plumet) plume; **avoir du p.** (fière allure) to have panache; **un p. de fumée** a plume of smoke.

panaché [panaʃe] **1** a (bigarré, hétéroclite) motley. **2** a & nm (demi) **p.** shandy; **bière panachée** shandy.

pancarte [pɑ̃kart] nf sign, notice; (de manifestant) placard.

pancréas [pɑ̃kreas] nm Anat pancreas.

panda [pɑ̃da] nm (animal) panda.

pané [pane] a Culin breaded.

panier [panje] nm (ustensile, contenu) basket; **p. à salade** salad basket; (voiture) Fam police van, prison van. ◆**p.-repas** nm (pl paniers-repas) packed lunch.

panique [panik] nf panic; **pris de p.** panic-stricken; – a **peur p.** panic fear. ◆**paniqu/er** vi to panic. ◆**-é** a panic-stricken.

panne [pan] nf breakdown; **tomber en p.** to break down; **être en p.** to have broken down; **p. d'électricité** power cut, blackout; **avoir une p. sèche** to run out of petrol ou Am gas.

panneau, -x [pano] nm **1** (écriteau) sign, notice, board; **p. (de signalisation)** traffic ou road sign; **p. (d'affichage)** (publicité) hoarding, Am billboard. **2** (de porte etc) panel. ◆**panonceau, -x** nm (enseigne) sign.

panoplie [panɔpli] nf **1** (jouet) outfit. **2** (gamme, arsenal) (wide) range, assortment.

panorama [panɔrama] nm panorama. ◆**panoramique** a panoramic.

panse [pɑ̃s] nf Fam paunch, belly. ◆**pansu** a potbellied.

pans/er [pɑ̃se] vt (plaie, main etc) to dress, bandage; (personne) to dress the wound(s) of, bandage (up); (cheval) to groom. ◆**-ement** nm (bande) bandage, dressing; **p. adhésif** sticking plaster, Am Band-Aid®.

pantalon [pɑ̃talɔ̃] nm (pair of) trousers ou Am pants; **deux pantalons** two pairs of trousers ou Am pants; **en p.** in trousers, Am pants.

pantelant [pɑ̃tlɑ̃] a gasping.

panthère [pɑ̃tɛr] nf (animal) panther.

pantin [pɑ̃tɛ̃] nm (jouet) jumping jack; (personne) Péj puppet.

pantois [pɑ̃twa] a flabbergasted.

pantoufle [pɑ̃tufl] nf slipper. ◆**pantou-**

flard, -arde nmf Fam stay-at-home, Am homebody.

paon [pɑ̃] nm peacock.

papa [papa] nm dad(dy); **de p.** (désuet) Péj outdated; **fils à p.** Péj rich man's son, daddy's boy.

pape [pap] nm pope. ◆**papauté** nf papacy.

paperasse(s) [papras] nf(pl) Péj (official) papers. ◆**paperasserie** nf Péj (official) papers; (procédure) red tape.

papeterie [papetri] nf (magasin) stationer's shop; (articles) stationery; (fabrique) paper mill. ◆**papetier, -ière** nmf stationer.

papi [papi] nm Fam grand(d)ad.

papier [papje] nm (matière) paper; **un p.** (feuille) a piece ou sheet of paper; (formulaire) a form; Journ an article; **en p.** (sac etc) paper-; **papiers (d'identité)** (identity) papers; **p. à lettres** writing paper; **du p. journal** (some) newspaper; **p. peint** wallpaper; **p. de verre** sandpaper.

papillon [papijɔ̃] nm **1** (insecte) butterfly; (écrou) butterfly nut, Am wing nut; **p. (de nuit)** moth. **2** (contravention) (parking) ticket.

papot/er [papote] vi to prattle. ◆**-age(s)** nm(pl) prattle.

paprika [paprika] nm (poudre) Culin paprika.

papy [papi] nm Fam grand(d)ad.

Pâque [pak] nf la **P.** Rel Passover.

paquebot [pakbo] nm Nau liner.

pâquerette [pakrɛt] nf daisy.

Pâques [pak] nm & nfpl Easter.

paquet [pakɛ] nm (de sucre, bonbons etc) packet; (colis) package; (de cigarettes) pack(et); (de cartes) pack.

par [par] prép **1** (agent, manière, moyen) by; **choisi/frappé/etc p.** chosen/hit/etc by; **p. erreur** by mistake; **p. mer** by sea; **p. le train** by train; **p. la force/le travail/etc** by ou through force/work/etc; **apprendre p. un voisin** to learn from ou through a neighbour; **commencer/s'ouvrir p. qch** (récit etc) to begin/open with sth; **p. malchance** unfortunately. **2** (lieu) through; **p. la porte/le tunnel/etc** through ou by the door/tunnel/etc; **regarder/jeter p. la fenêtre** to look/throw out (of) the window; **p. les rues** through the streets; **p. ici/là** (aller) this/that way; (habiter) around here/there. **3** (motif) out of, from; **p. respect/pitié/etc** out of ou from respect/pity/etc. **4** (temps) on; **p. un jour d'hiver/etc** on a winter's day/etc; **p. le passé** in the past; **p. ce froid** in this cold. **5** (distributif) **dix fois p.** an ten times a ou per year; **deux p. deux** two by two; **p. deux fois** twice. **6** (*trop*) **p. trop ai-mable**/*etc* far too kind/*etc*.

para [para] *nm* Mil Fam para(trooper).

para- [para] *préf* para-.

parabole [parabɔl] *nf* **1** (*récit*) parable. **2** Math parabola.

parachever [paraʃ(ə)ve] *vt* to perfect.

parachute [paraʃyt] *nf* parachute. ◆**parachuter** *vt* to parachute; (*nommer*) Fam to pitchfork (**à un poste** into). ◆**parachutisme** *nm* parachute jumping. ◆**parachutiste** *nmf* parachutist; Mil paratrooper.

parade [parad] *nf* **1** (*étalage*) show, parade; (*spectacle*) & Mil parade. **2** Boxe Escrime parry; (*riposte*) Fig reply. ◆**parader** *vi* to parade, show off.

paradis [paradi] *nm* paradise, heaven. ◆**paradisiaque** (*endroit etc*) Fig heavenly.

paradoxe [paradɔks] *nm* paradox. ◆**paradoxalement** *adv* paradoxically.

parafe [paraf] *voir* **paraphe**. ◆**parafer** *voir* **parapher**.

paraffine [parafin] *nf* paraffin (wax).

parages [paraʒ] *nmpl* region, area (**de** of); **dans ces p.** in these parts.

paragraphe [paragraf] *nm* paragraph.

paraître* [parɛtr] **1** *vi* (*se montrer*) to appear; (*sembler*) to seem, look, appear; – *v imp* **il paraît qu'il va partir** it appears *ou* seems (that) he's leaving. **2** *vi* (*livre*) to be published, come out; **faire p.** to bring out.

parallèle [paralɛl] **1** *a* (*comparable*) & Math parallel (**à** with, to); (*marché*) Com unofficial. **2** *nm* (*comparaison*) & Géog parallel. ◆**—ment** *adv* **p. à** parallel to.

paralyser [paralize] *vt* to paralyse, Am paralyze. ◆**paralysie** *nf* paralysis. ◆**paralytique** *a* & *nmf* paralytic.

paramètre [parametr] *nm* parameter.

paranoïa [paranɔja] *nf* paranoia. ◆**paranoïaque** *a* & *nmf* paranoid.

parapet [parapɛ] *nm* parapet.

paraphe [paraf] *nm* initials, signature; (*traits*) flourish. ◆**parapher** *vt* to initial, sign.

paraphrase [parafraz] *nf* paraphrase. ◆**paraphraser** *vt* to paraphrase.

parapluie [paraplɥi] *nm* umbrella.

parasite [parazit] *nm* (*personne, organisme*) parasite; *pl* Rad interference; – *a* parasitic(al).

parasol [parasɔl] *nm* parasol, sunshade.

paratonnerre [paratɔnɛr] *nm* lightning conductor *ou* Am rod.

paravent [paravã] *nm* (folding) screen.

parc [park] *nm* **1** park; (*de château*) grounds. **2** (*de bébé*) (play) pen; (*à moutons, à bétail*) pen; **p. (de stationnement)** car park, Am parking lot; **p. à huîtres** oyster bed.

parcelle [parsɛl] *nf* fragment, particle; (*terrain*) plot; (*de vérité*) Fig grain.

parce que [parsk(ə)] *conj* because.

parchemin [parʃəmɛ̃] *nm* parchment.

parcimonie [parsimɔni] *nf* **avec p.** parsimoniously. ◆**parcimonieux, -euse** *a* parsimonious.

par-ci par-là [parsiparla] *adv* here, there and everywhere.

parcmètre [parkmetr] *nm* parking meter.

parcourir* [parkurir] *vt* (*région*) to travel through, tour, scour; (*distance*) to cover; (*texte*) to glance through. ◆**parcours** *nm* (*itinéraire*) route; (*de fleuve*) & Sp course; (*voyage*) trip, journey.

par-delà [pard(ə)la] *voir* **delà**.

par-derrière [pardɛrjɛr] *voir* **derrière**.

par-dessous [pard(ə)su] *prép* & *adv* under(neath).

pardessus [pard(ə)sy] *nm* overcoat.

par-dessus [pard(ə)sy] *prép* & *adv* over (the top of); **p.-dessus tout** above all.

par-devant [pard(ə)vã] *voir* **devant**.

pardon [pardɔ̃] *nm* forgiveness, pardon; **p.?** (*pour demander*) excuse me?, Am pardon me?; **p.!** (*je le regrette*) sorry!; **demander p.** to apologize (**à** to). ◆**pardonn/er** *vt* to forgive; **p. qch à qn** *ou* **p. à qn d'avoir fait qch** to forgive s.o. for sth/for doing sth. ◆**—able** *a* forgivable.

pare-balles [parbal] *a inv* **gilet p.-balles** bulletproof jacket *ou* Am vest.

pare-brise [parbriz] *nm inv* Aut windscreen, Am windshield.

pare-chocs [parʃɔk] *nm inv* Aut bumper.

pareil, -eille [parɛj] *a* similar; **p. à** the same as, similar to; **être pareils** to be the same, be similar *ou* alike; **un p. désordre**/*etc* such a mess/*etc*; **en p. cas** in such a case; – *nmf* (*personne*) equal; **rendre la pareille à qn** to treat s.o. the same way; **sans p.** unparalleled, unique; – *adv* Fam the same. ◆**pareillement** *adv* in the same way; (*aussi*) likewise.

parement [parmã] *nm* (*de pierre, de vêtement*) facing.

parent, -ente [parã, -ãt] *nmf* relation, relative; – *nmpl* (*père et mère*) parents; – *a* related (**de** to). ◆**parenté** *nf* (*rapport*) relationship, kinship.

parenthèse [parãtɛz] *nf* (*signe*) bracket, parenthesis; (*digression*) digression.

parer [pare] **1** vt (coup) to parry, ward off; − vi p. à to be prepared for. **2** vt (orner) to adorn (**de** with).

paresse [pares] nf laziness, idleness. ◆**paresser** vi to laze (about). ◆**paresseux, -euse** a lazy, idle; − nmf lazybones.

parfaire [parfer] vt to perfect. ◆**parfait** a perfect; **p.!** excellent!; − nm Gram perfect (tense). ◆**parfaitement** adv perfectly; (certainement) certainly.

parfois [parfwa] adv sometimes.

parfum [parfɛ̃] nm (odeur) fragrance, scent; (goût) flavour; (liquide) perfume, scent. ◆**parfum/er** vt to perfume, scent; (glace, crème etc) to flavour (**à** with); − **se p.** vpr to put on perfume; (habituellement) to wear perfume. ◆**-é** a (savon, mouchoir) scented; **p. au café**/etc coffee-/etc flavoured. ◆**parfumerie** nf (magasin) perfume shop.

pari [pari] nm bet, wager; pl Sp betting, bets; **p. mutuel urbain** = the tote, Am pari-mutuel. ◆**parier** vti to bet (**sur** on, **que** that). ◆**parieur, -euse** nmf Sp better, punter.

Paris [pari] nm ou f Paris. ◆**parisien, -ienne** a (accent etc) Parisian, Paris-; − nmf Parisian.

parité [parite] nf parity.

parjure [parʒyr] nm perjury; − nmf perjurer. ◆**se parjurer** vpr to perjure oneself.

parka [parka] nm parka.

parking [parkiŋ] nm (lieu) car park, Am parking lot.

par-là [parla] adv voir **par-ci**.

parlement [parləmɑ̃] nm parliament. ◆**parlementaire** a parliamentary; − nmf member of parliament. ◆**parlementer** vi to parley, negotiate.

parl/er [parle] vi to talk, speak (**de** about, of; **à** to); **tu parles!** Fam you must be joking!; **sans p. de** . . . not to mention . . . ; − vt (langue) to speak; **p. affaires**/etc to talk business/etc; − **se p.** vpr (langue) to be spoken; − nm speech; (régional) dialect. ◆**-ant** a (film) talking; (regard etc) eloquent. ◆**-é** a (langue) spoken.

parloir [parlwar] nm (de couvent, prison) visiting room.

parmi [parmi] prép among(st).

parodie [parɔdi] nf parody. ◆**parodier** vt to parody.

paroi [parwa] nf wall; (de maison) inside wall; (de rocher) (rock) face.

paroisse [parwas] nf parish. ◆**paroissial,**

-aux a (registre, activité etc) parish-. ◆**paroissien, -ienne** nmf parishioner.

parole [parɔl] nf (mot, promesse) word; (faculté, langage) speech; **adresser la p. à** to speak to; **prendre la p.** to speak, make a speech; **demander la p.** to ask to speak; **perdre la p.** to lose one's tongue.

paroxysme [parɔksism] nm (de douleur etc) height.

parpaing [parpɛ̃] nm concrete block, breezeblock.

parqu/er [parke] vt (bœufs) to pen; (gens) to herd together, confine; (véhicule) to park; − **se p.** vpr Aut to park.

parquet [parke] nm **1** (parquet) floor(ing). **2** Jur Public Prosecutor's office.

parrain [parɛ̃] nm Rel godfather; (répondant) sponsor. ◆**parrain/er** vt to sponsor. ◆**-age** nm sponsorship.

pars, part [par] voir **partir**.

parsemer [parsəme] vt to strew, dot (**de** with).

part² [par] nf (portion) share, part; **prendre p. à** (activité) to take part in; (la joie etc de qn) to share; **de toutes parts** from ou on all sides; **de p. et d'autre** on both sides; **d'une p.,** . . . **d'autre p.** on the one hand, . . . on the other hand; **d'autre p.** (d'ailleurs) moreover; **pour ma p.** as far as I'm concerned; **de la p. de** (provenance) from; **c'est de la p. de qui?** Tél who's speaking?; **faire p. de qch à qn** to inform s.o. of sth; **quelque p.** somewhere; **nulle p.** nowhere; **autre p.** somewhere else; **à p.** (séparément) apart; (mettre, prendre) aside; (excepté) except from; **un cas/une place**/etc **à p.** a separate ou special case/place/etc; **membre à p. entière** full member.

partage [partaʒ] nm dividing, division; (participation) sharing; (distribution) sharing out; (sort) Fig lot. ◆**partag/er** vt (repas, frais, joie etc) to share (**avec** with); (diviser) to divide (up); (distribuer) to share out; − **se p.** vpr (bénéfices etc) to share (between themselves etc); **se p. entre** to divide one's time between. ◆**-é** a (avis etc) divided; **p. entre** (sentiments) torn between.

partance (en) [ɑ̃partɑ̃s] adv (train etc) about to depart (**pour** for).

partant [partɑ̃] nm (coureur, cheval) Sp starter.

partenaire [partəner] nmf (époux etc) & Sp Pol partner.

parterre [parter] nm **1** (de jardin etc) flower bed. **2** Th stalls, Am orchestra.

parti [parti] nm Pol party; (époux) match; **prendre un p.** to make a decision, follow a course; **prendre p. pour** to side with; **tirer p. de** to turn to (good) account; **p. pris** (*préjugé*) prejudice; **être de p. pris** to be prejudiced (**contre** against).

partial, -aux [parsjal, -o] *a* biased. ◆**partialité** *nf* bias.

participe [partisip] *nm* Gram participle.

particip/er [partisipe] *vi* **p. à** (*activité, jeu etc*) to take part in, participate in; (*frais, joie etc*) to share (in). ◆**—ant, -ante** *nmf* participant. ◆**participation** *nf* participation; sharing; (*d'un acteur*) appearance; collaboration; **p. (aux frais)** (*contribution*) share (in the expenses).

particule [partikyl] *nf* particle.

particulier, -ière [partikylje, -jɛr] *a* (*spécial, spécifique*) particular; (*privé*) private; (*bizarre*) peculiar; **p. à** peculiar to; **en p.** (*surtout*) in particular; (*séparément*) in private; — *nm* private individual *ou* citizen. ◆**particularité** *nf* peculiarity. ◆**particulièrement** *adv* particularly; **tout p.** especially.

partie [parti] *nf* part; (*de cartes, de tennis etc*) game; (*de chasse, de plaisir*) & *Jur* party; (*métier*) line, field; **en p.** partly, in part; **en grande p.** mainly; **faire p. de** to be part of; (*adhérer à*) to belong to; (*comité*) to be on. ◆**partiel, -ielle** *a* partial; — *nm* (*examen*) *Univ* term exam. ◆**partiellement** *adv* partially.

part/ir* [partir] *vi* (*aux être*) (*aller, disparaître*) to go; (*s'en aller*) to leave, go (off); (*se mettre en route*) to set off; (*s'éloigner*) to go (away); (*moteur*) to start; (*fusil, coup de feu*) to go off; (*flèche*) to shoot off; (*bouton*) to come off; (*tache*) to come out; **p. de** (*commencer par*) to start (off) with; **ça part du cœur** it comes from the heart; **à p. de** (*date, prix*) from. ◆**—i** *a* **bien p.** off to a good start.

partisan [partizã] *nm* follower, supporter; *Mil* partisan; — *a* (*esprit*) *Péj* partisan; **être p. de qch** *ou* **de faire** to be in favour of sth/of doing.

partition [partisjɔ̃] *nf* Mus score.

partout [partu] *adv* everywhere; **p. où tu vas ou iras** everywhere *ou* wherever you go; **p. sur la table/etc** all over the table/etc.

paru [pary] *voir* **paraître**. ◆**parution** *nf* (*de livre etc*) publication.

parure [paryr] *nf* (*toilette*) finery; (*bijoux*) jewellery.

parven/ir* [parvənir] *vi* (*aux être*) **p. à** (*lieu*) to reach; (*fortune, ses fins*) to achieve; **p. à faire** to manage to do. ◆**—u, -ue** *nmf* Péj upstart.

parvis [parvi] *nm* square (*in front of church etc*).

pas¹ [pa] *adv* (*négatif*) not; (*ne*) . . . **p.** not; **je ne sais p.** I do not *ou* don't know; **p. de pain/de café/etc** no bread/coffee/etc; **p. encore** not yet; **p. du tout** not at all.

pas² [pa] *nm* **1** step, pace; (*allure*) pace; (*bruit*) footstep; (*trace*) footprint; **à deux p.** (**de**) close by; **revenir sur ses p.** to go back on one's tracks; **au p.** at a walking pace; **rouler au p.** (*véhicule*) to go dead slow(ly); **au p.** (*cadencé*) in step; **faire les cent p.** to walk up and down; **faux p.** stumble; (*faute*) *Fig* blunder; **le p. de la porte** the doorstep. **2** (*de vis*) thread. **3** *Géog* straits; **le p. de Calais** the Straits of Dover.

pascal [paskal] *a* (*semaine, messe etc*) Easter-.

passable [pɑsabl] *a* acceptable, tolerable; **mention p.** *Scol Univ* pass. ◆**—ment** [-əmã] *adv* acceptably; (*beaucoup*) quite a lot.

passage [pɑsaʒ] *nm* (*action*) passing, passage; (*traversée*) *Nau* crossing, passage; (*extrait*) passage; (*couloir*) passage(way); (*droit*) right of way; (*venue*) arrival; (*chemin*) path; **p. clouté** *ou* **pour piétons** (pedestrian) crossing; **obstruer le p.** to block the way; **p. souterrain** subway, *Am* underpass; **p. à niveau** level crossing, *Am* grade crossing; **'p. interdit'** 'no thoroughfare'; **'cédez le p.'** *Aut* 'give way', *Am* 'yield'; **être de p.** to be passing through (**à Paris/etc** Paris/etc); **hôte de p.** passing guest. ◆**passager, -ère 1** *nmf* passenger; **p. clandestin** stowaway. **2** *a* (*de courte durée*) passing, temporary. ◆**passagèrement** *adv* temporarily.

passant, -ante [pɑsɑ̃, -ɑ̃t] *a* (*rue*) busy; — *nmf* passer-by. **2** *nm* (*de ceinture etc*) loop.

passe [pɑs] *nf* *Sp* pass; **mot de p.** password; **en p. de faire** on the road to doing; **une mauvaise p.** *Fig* a bad patch.

passe-montagne [pɑsmɔ̃taɲ] *nm* balaclava.

passe-partout [pɑspartu] *nm inv* (*clé*) master key; — *a inv* (*compliment, phrase*) all-purpose.

passe-passe [pɑspɑs] *nm inv* **tour de p.-passe** conjuring trick.

passe-plat [pɑspla] *nm* service hatch.

passeport [pɑspɔr] *nm* passport.

passer [pɑse] *vi* (*aux être ou avoir*) (*aller, venir*) to pass (**à** to); (*facteur, laitier*) to come; (*temps*) to pass (by), go by; (*courant*) to flow; (*film, programme*) to be shown, be on; (*loi*) to be passed; (*douleur, mode*) to pass; (*couleur*) to fade; **p. devant** (*maison etc*) to go past *ou* by (house (by); **p. à ou par Paris** to pass through Paris; **p. à la radio** to come *ou* go on the radio; **p. à l'ennemi/à la caisse** to go over to the enemy/the cash desk; **laisser p.** (*personne, lumière*) to let in *ou* through; (*occasion*) to let slip; **p. prendre** to pick up, fetch; **p. voir qn** to drop in on s.o.; **p. pour** (*riche etc*) to be taken for; **faire p. qn pour** to pass s.o. off as; **p. sur** (*détail etc*) to overlook, pass over; **p. capitaine/etc** to be promoted captain/*etc*; **p. en** (*seconde etc*) *Scol* to pass up into; *Aut* to change up to; **ça passe** (*c'est passable*) that'll do; **en passant** (*dire qch*) in passing; – *vt* (*aux avoir*) (*frontière etc*) to pass, cross; (*maison etc*) to pass, go past; (*donner*) to pass, hand (à to); (*mettre*) to put; (*vêtement etc*) to overlook; (*temps*) to spend, pass (à faire doing); (*disque*) to play, put on; (*film, programme*) to show, put on; (*loi, motion*) to pass; (*chemise*) to slip on; (*examen*) to take, sit (for); (*thé*) to strain; (*café*) to filter; (*commande*) to place; (*accord*) to conclude; (*colère*) to vent (**sur** on); (*limites*) to go beyond; (*visite médicale*) to go through; **p. (son tour)** to pass; **p. qch à qn** (*caprice etc*) to grant s.o. sth; (*pardonner*) to excuse s.o. sth; **je vous passe ...** *Tél* I'm putting you through to ...; **p. un coup d'éponge/etc à qch** to go over sth with a sponge/*etc*; – **se p.** *vpr* (*se produire*) to take place, happen; (*douleur*) to pass, go (away); **se p. de** to do *ou* go without; **se p. de commentaires** to need no comment; **ça s'est bien passé** it went off all right. ◆**passé 1** *a* (*temps etc*) past; (*couleur*) faded; **la semaine passée** last week; **dix heures passées** after *ou* gone ten (o'clock); **être passé** (*personne*) to have been (and gone); (*orage*) to be over; **avoir vingt ans passés** to be over twenty; – *nm* (*temps, vie passée*) past; *Gram* past (tense). **2** *prép* after; **p. huit heures** after eight (o'clock).

passerelle [pasrɛl] *nf* (*pont*) footbridge; (*voie d'accès*) *Nau Av* gangway.

passe-temps [pastɑ̃] *nm inv* pastime.

passeur, -euse [pasœr, -øz] *nmf* **1** *Nau* ferryman, ferrywoman. **2** (*contrebandier*) smuggler.

passible [pasibl] *a* **p. de** (*peine*) *Jur* liable to.

passif, -ive [pasif, -iv] **1** *a* (*rôle, personne etc*) passive; – *nm Gram* passive. **2** *nm Com* liabilities. ◆**passivité** *nf* passiveness, passivity.

passion [pasjɔ̃] *nf* passion; **avoir la p. des**

voitures/d'écrire/etc to have a passion *ou* a great love for cars/writing/*etc*. ◆**passionnel, -elle** *a* (*crime*) of passion. ◆**passionn/er** *vt* to thrill, fascinate; **se p.** **pour** to have a passion for. ◆**—ant** *a* thrilling. ◆**—é, -ée** *a* passionate; **p. de qch** passionately fond of sth; – *nmf* **fan** (**de** of). ◆**—ément** *adv* passionately.

passoire [paswar] *nf* (*pour liquides*) sieve; (*à thé*) strainer; (*à légumes*) colander.

pastel [pastɛl] *nm* pastel; **au p.** (*dessin*) pastel-; – *a inv* (*ton*) pastel.

pastèque [pastɛk] *nf* watermelon.

pasteur [pastœr] *nm Rel* pastor.

pasteurisé [pastœrize] *a* (*lait, beurre etc*) pasteurized.

pastiche [pastiʃ] *nm* pastiche.

pastille [pastij] *nf* pastille, lozenge.

pastis [pastis] *nm* aniseed liqueur, pastis.

pastoral, -aux [pastɔral, -o] *a* pastoral.

patate [patat] *nf Fam* spud, potato.

patatras! [patatra] *int* crash!

pataud [pato] *a* clumsy, lumpish.

patauger [patɔʒe] *vi* (*marcher*) to wade (*in the mud etc*); (*barboter*) to splash about; (*s'empêtrer*) *Fig* to flounder. ◆**pataugeoire** *nf* paddling pool.

patchwork [patʃwœrk] *nm* patchwork.

pâte [pɑt] *nf* (*substance*) paste; (*à pain, à gâteau*) dough; (*à tarte*) pastry; **pâtes** (*alimentaires*) pasta; **p. à modeler** plasticine®, modelling clay; **p. à frire** batter; **p. dentifrice** toothpaste.

pâté [pɑte] *nm* **1** (*charcuterie*) pâté; **p.** (**en croûte**) meat pie. **2 p.** (**de sable**) sand castle; **p. de maisons** block of houses. **3** (*tache d'encre*) (ink) blot.

pâtée [pɑte] *nf* (*pour chien, volaille etc*) mash.

patelin [patlɛ̃] *nm Fam* village.

patent [patɑ̃] *a* patent, obvious.

patère [patɛr] *nf* (coat) peg.

paternel, -elle [patɛrnɛl] *a* (*amour etc*) fatherly, paternal; (*parenté, réprimande*) paternal. ◆**paternité** *nf* (*état*) paternity, fatherhood; (*de livre*) authorship.

pâteux, -euse [pɑtø, -øz] *a* (*substance*) doughy, pasty; (*style*) woolly; **avoir la bouche** *ou* **la langue pâteuse** (*après s'être enivré*) to have a mouth full of cotton wool *ou* *Am* cotton.

pathétique [patetik] *a* moving; – *nm* pathos.

pathologie [patɔlɔʒi] *nf* pathology. ◆**pathologique** *a* pathological.

patient, -ente [pasjɑ̃, -ɑ̃t] **1** *a* patient. **2** *nmf Méd* patient. ◆**patiemment** [-amɑ̃] *adv* patiently. ◆**patience** *nf* patience; **prendre p.** to have patience; **perdre p.** to lose patience. ◆**patienter** *vi* to wait (patiently).

patin [patɛ̃] *nm* skate; (*pour le parquet*) cloth pad (*used for walking*); **p. à roulettes** ice/roller skate. ◆**patin/er** *vi Sp* to skate; (*véhicule, embrayage*) to slip. ◆**-age** *nm Sp* skating; **p. artistique** figure skating. ◆**-eur, -euse** *nmf Sp* skater. ◆**patinoire** *nf* (*piste*) *Sp* & *Fig* skating rink, ice rink.

patine [patin] *nf* patina.

patio [patjo] *nm* patio.

pâtir [pɑtir] *vi* **p. de** to suffer from.

pâtisserie [pɑtisri] *nf* pastry, cake; (*magasin*) cake shop; (*art*) cake *ou* pastry making. ◆**pâtissier, -ière** *nmf* pastrycook and cake shop owner.

patois [patwa] *nm Ling* patois.

patraque [patrak] *a* (*malade*) *Fam* under the weather.

patriarche [patrijarʃ] *nm* patriarch.

patrie [patri] *nf* (*native*) country; (*ville*) birth place. ◆**patriote** *nmf* patriot; – *a* (*personne*) patriotic. ◆**patriotique** *a* (*chant etc*) patriotic. ◆**patriotisme** *nm* patriotism.

patrimoine [patrimwan] *nm* (*biens*) & *Fig* heritage.

patron, -onne [patrɔ̃, -ɔn] 1 *nmf* (*chef*) employer, boss; (*propriétaire*) owner (**de** of); (*gérant*) manager, manageress; (*de bar*) landlord, landlady. 2 *nmf Rel* patron saint. 3 *nm* (*modèle de papier*) *Tex* pattern. ◆**patronage** *nm* 1 (*protection*) patronage. 2 (*centre*) youth club. ◆**patronal, -aux** *a* (*syndicat etc*) employers'. ◆**patronat** *nm* employers. ◆**patronner** *vt* to sponsor.

patrouille [patruj] *nf* patrol. ◆**patrouiller** *vi* to patrol. ◆**-eur** *nm* (*navire*) patrol boat.

patte [pat] *nf* 1 (*membre*) leg; (*de chat, chien*) paw; (*main*) *Fam* hand; **à quatre pattes** on all fours. 2 (*de poche*) flap; (*languette*) tongue.

pattes [pat] *nfpl* (*favoris*) sideboards, *Am* sideburns.

pâture [pɑtyr] *nf* (*nourriture*) food; (*intellectuelle*) *Fig* fodder. ◆**pâturage** *nm* pasture.

paume [pom] *nf* (*de main*) palm.

paum/er [pome] *vt Fam* to lose; **un coin ou trou paumé** (*sans attrait*) a dump. ◆**-é, -ée** *nmf* (*malheureux*) *Fam* down-and-out, loser.

paupière [popjɛr] *nf* eyelid.

pause [poz] *nf* (*arrêt*) break; (*dans le discours etc*) pause.

pauvre [povr] *a* poor; (*terre*) impoverished, poor; **p. en** (*calories etc*) low in; (*ressources etc*) low on; – *nmf* (*indigent, malheureux*) poor man, poor woman; **les pauvres** the poor. ◆**pauvrement** *adv* poorly. ◆**pauvreté** *nf* (*besoin*) poverty; (*insuffisance*) poorness.

pavaner (se) [səpavane] *vpr* to strut (about).

pav/er [pave] *vt* to pave. ◆**-é** *nm* **un p.** a paving stone; (*rond, de vieille chaussée*) a cobblestone; **sur le p.** *Fig* on the streets. ◆**-age** *nm* (*travail, revêtement*) paving.

pavillon [pavijɔ̃] *nm* 1 (*maison*) house; (*de chasse*) lodge; (*d'hôpital*) ward; (*d'exposition*) pavilion. 2 (*drapeau*) flag.

pavoiser [pavwaze] *vt* to deck out with flags; – *vi* (*exulter*) *Fig* to rejoice.

pavot [pavo] *nm* (*cultivé*) poppy.

pay/er [peje] *vt* (*personne, somme*) to pay; (*service, objet, faute*) to pay for; (*récompenser*) to repay; **p. qch à qn** (*offrir en cadeau*) *Fam* to treat s.o. to sth; **p. qn pour faire** to pay s.o. to do *ou* for doing; – *vi* (*personne, métier, crime*) to pay; **se p. qch** (*s'acheter*) *Fam* to treat oneself to sth; **se p. la tête de qn** *Fam* to make fun of s.o. ◆**-ant** [pejɑ̃] *a* (*hôte, spectateur*) who pays, paying; (*place, entrée*) that one has to pay for; (*rentable*) worthwhile. ◆**payable** *a* payable. ◆**paye** *nf* pay, wages. ◆**payement** *nm* payment.

pays [pei] *nm* country; (*région*) region; (*village*) village; **p. des rêves/du soleil** land of dreams/sun; **du p.** (*vin, gens etc*) local.

paysage [peizaʒ] *nm* landscape, scenery.

paysan, -anne [peizɑ̃, -an] *nmf* (*small*) farmer; (*rustre*) *Péj* peasant; – *a* country-; (*monde*) farming.

Pays-Bas [peiba] *nmpl* **les P.-Bas** the Netherlands.

PCV [peseve] *abrév* (*paiement contre vérification*) **téléphoner en PCV** to reverse the charges, *Am* call collect.

PDG [pedeʒe] *abrév* = **président directeur général**.

péage [peaʒ] *nm* (*droit*) toll; (*lieu*) tollgate.

peau, -x [po] *nf* skin; (*de fruit*) peel, skin; (*cuir*) hide, skin; (*fourrure*) pelt; **dans la p. de qn** *Fig* in s.o.'s shoes; **faire p. neuve** *Fig* to turn over a new leaf. ◆**P.-Rouge** *nmf* (*pl* **Peaux-Rouges**) (Red) Indian.

pêche¹ [pɛʃ] *nf* (*activité*) fishing; (*poissons*) catch; **p.** (**à la ligne**) angling; **aller à la p.** to go fishing. ◆**pêcher**¹ *vi* to fish; – *vt* (*chercher à prendre*) to fish for; (*attraper*) to catch; (dénicher) Fam to dig up. ◆**pêcheur** nm fisherman; angler.

pêche² [pɛʃ] nf (fruit) peach. ◆**pêcher²** nm (arbre) peach tree.

péché [peʃe] nm sin. ◆**péch/er** vi to sin; **p. par orgueil**/etc to be too proud/etc. ◆**-eur, -eresse** nmf sinner.

pectoraux [pɛktɔro] nmpl (muscles) chest muscles.

pécule [pekyl] nm **un p.** (économies) (some) savings, a nest egg.

pécuniaire [pekynjɛr] a monetary.

pédagogie [pedagɔʒi] nf (science) education, teaching methods. ◆**pédagogique** a educational. ◆**pédagogue** nmf teacher.

pédale [pedal] nf **1** pedal; **p. de frein** footbrake (pedal). **2** (homosexuel) Péj Fam pansy, queer. ◆**pédaler** vi to pedal.

pédalo [pedalo] nm pedal boat, pedalo.

pédant, -ante [pedɑ̃, -ɑ̃t] nmf pedant; – a pedantic. ◆**pédantisme** nm pedantry.

pédé [pede] nm (homosexuel) Péj Fam queer.

pédiatre [pedjatr] nmf Méd p(a)ediatrician.

pédicure [pedikyr] nmf chiropodist.

pedigree [pedigre] nm (de chien, cheval etc) pedigree.

pègre [pɛgr] nf **la p.** the (criminal) underworld.

peigne [pɛɲ] nm comb; **passer au p. fin** Fig to go through with a fine toothcomb; **un coup de p.** (action) a comb. ◆**peigner** vt (cheveux) to comb; **p. qn** to comb s.o.'s hair; – **se p.** vpr to comb one's hair.

peignoir [pɛɲwar] nm dressing gown, Am bathrobe; **p. (de bain)** bathrobe.

peinard [penar] a Arg quiet (and easy).

peindre* [pɛ̃dr] vt to paint; (décrire) Fig to depict, paint; **p. en bleu**/etc to paint blue/etc; – vi to paint.

peine [pɛn] nf **1** (châtiment) punishment; **p. de mort** death penalty ou sentence; **p. de prison** prison sentence; **'défense d'entrer sous p. d'amende'** 'trespassers will be fined'. **2** (chagrin) sorrow, grief; **avoir de la p.** to be upset ou sad; **faire de la p. à** to upset, cause pain ou sorrow to. **3** (effort, difficulté) trouble; **se donner de la p. ou beaucoup de p.** to go to a lot of trouble (**pour faire** to do); **avec p.** with difficulty; **ça vaut la p. d'attendre**/etc it's worth (while) waiting/etc; **ce n'est pas** ou **ça ne vaut pas la p.** it's not worth while ou worth it; **ce n'est pas la p.** it's not worth while ou not worth bothering. ◆**peiner 1** vt to upset, grieve. **2** vi to labour, struggle.

peine (à) [apen] adv hardly, scarcely.

peintre [pɛ̃tr] nm painter; **p. (en bâtiment)** (house) painter, (painter and) decorator. ◆**peinture** nf (tableau, activité) painting; (couleur) paint; **'p. fraîche'** 'wet paint'. ◆**peinturlurer** vt Fam to daub with colour; **se p. (le visage)** to paint one's face.

péjoratif, -ive [peʒɔratif, -iv] a pejorative, derogatory.

pékinois [pekinwa] nm (chien) pekin(g)ese.

pelage [pəlaʒ] nm (d'animal) coat, fur.

pelé [pəle] a bare.

pêle-mêle [pɛlmɛl] adv in disorder.

peler [pəle] vt (fruit) to peel; **se p. facilement** (fruit) to peel easily; – vi (peau bronzée) to peel.

pèlerin [pɛlrɛ̃] nm pilgrim. ◆**pèlerinage** nm pilgrimage.

pèlerine [pɛlrin] nf (manteau) cape.

pélican [pelikɑ̃] nm (oiseau) pelican.

pelisse [pəlis] nf fur-lined coat.

pelle [pɛl] nf shovel; (d'enfant) spade; **p. à poussière** dustpan; **ramasser** ou **prendre une p.** (tomber) Fam to come a cropper, Am take a spill; **à la p.** (argent etc) Fam galore. ◆**pelletée** nf shovelful. ◆**pelleteuse** nf Tech mechanical shovel, excavator.

pellicule [pelikyl] nf Phot film; (couche) film, layer; pl Méd dandruff.

pelote [pəlɔt] nf (de laine) ball; (à épingles) pincushion; **p. (basque)** Sp pelota.

peloter [pəlɔte] vt (palper) Fam to paw.

peloton [pəlɔtɔ̃] nm **1** (coureurs) Sp pack, main body. **2** Mil squad; **p. d'exécution** firing squad. **3** (de ficelle) ball.

pelotonner (se) [səpəlɔtɔne] vpr to curl up (into a ball).

pelouse [pluz] nf lawn; Sp enclosure.

peluche [plyʃ] nf (tissu) plush; pl (flocons) fluff, lint; **une p.** (flocon) a bit of fluff ou lint; **jouet en p.** soft toy; **chien**/etc **en p.** (jouet) furry dog/etc; **ours en p.** teddy bear. ◆**pelucher** vi to get fluffy ou linty. ◆**pelucheux, -euse** a fluffy, linty.

pelure [plyr] nf (épluchure) peeling; **une p.** (piece of) peeling.

pénal, -aux [penal, -o] a (droit, code etc) penal. ◆**pénalisation** nf Sp penalty. ◆**pénaliser** vt Sp Jur to penalize (**pour** for). ◆**pénalité** nf Jur Rugby penalty.

penalty, pl -ties [penalti, -iz] nm Fb penalty.

penaud [pəno] a sheepish.

penchant [pɑ̃ʃɑ̃] nm (faible) liking (**pour** for); (tendance) inclination (**à qch** towards sth).

pench/er [pɑ̃ʃe] vt (objet) to tilt; (tête) to lean; – vi (arbre etc) to lean (over); **p. pour** Fig to be inclined towards; – **se p.** vpr to lean (forward); **se p. par** (fenêtre) to lean out of; **se p. sur** (*problème etc*) to examine. ◆**—é** *a* leaning.

pendaison [pɑ̃dɛzɔ̃] *nf* hanging.

pendant¹ [pɑ̃dɑ̃] *prép* (*au cours de*) during; **p. la nuit** during the night; **p. deux mois** (*pour une période de*) for two months; **p. que** while, whilst.

pendentif [pɑ̃dɑ̃tif] *nm* (*collier*) pendant.

penderie [pɑ̃dri] *nf* wardrobe.

pend/re [pɑ̃dr] *vti* to hang (à from); **— se p.** *vpr* (*se tuer*) to hang oneself; (*se suspendre*) to hang (à from). ◆**—ant²** *a* **1** hanging; (*langue*) hanging out; (*joues*) sagging; (*question*) Fig pending. **2** *nm* **p. (d'oreille)** drop earring. **3** *nm* **le p. de** the companion piece to. ◆**—u, -ue** *a* (*objet*) hanging (à from); **— pendu** hanged man, hanged woman.

pendule [pɑ̃dyl] **1** *nf* clock. **2** *nm* (*balancier*) & Fig pendulum. ◆**pendulette** *nf* small clock.

pénétr/er [penetre] *vi* **p. dans** to enter; (*profondément*) to penetrate (into); **— vt** (*substance, mystère etc*) to penetrate; **se p. de** (*idée*) to become convinced of. ◆**—ant** *a* (*esprit, froid etc*) penetrating, keen. ◆**pénétration** *nf* penetration.

pénible [penibl] *a* (*difficile*) difficult; (*douloureux*) painful, distressing; (*ennuyeux*) tiresome; (*agaçant*) annoying. ◆**—ment** [-əmɑ̃] *adv* with difficulty; (*avec douleur*) painfully.

péniche [peniʃ] *nf* barge; **p. de débarquement** Mil landing craft.

pénicilline [penisilin] *nf* penicillin.

péninsule [penɛ̃syl] *nf* peninsula. ◆**péninsulaire** *a* peninsular.

pénis [penis] *nm* penis.

pénitence [penitɑ̃s] *nf* (*punition*) punishment; (*peine*) Rel penance; (*regret*) penitence. ◆**pénitent, -ente** *nmf* Rel penitent.

pénitencier [penitɑ̃sje] *nm* prison. ◆**pénitentiaire** *a* (*régime etc*) prison-.

pénombre [penɔ̃br] *nf* half-light, darkness.

pensée [pɑ̃se] *nf* **1** thought. **2** (*fleur*) pansy. ◆**pens/er** *vi* to think (à of, about); **p. à qch/à faire qch** (*ne pas oublier*) to remember sth/to do sth; **p. à tout** (*prévoir*) to think of everything; **penses-tu!** you must be joking!, not at all!; **— vt** to think (*que* that); (*concevoir*) to think out; (*imaginer*) to imagine (*que* that); **je pensais rester** (*intention*) I was thinking of staying, I thought I'd stay; **je pense réussir** (*espoir*) I hope to succeed; **que pensez-vous de . . . ?** what do you think of *ou* about . . . ?; **p. du bien de** to think highly of. ◆**—ant** *a* **bien p.** Péj or-

thodox. ◆**—eur** *nm* thinker. ◆**pensif, -ive** *a* thoughtful, pensive.

pension [pɑ̃sjɔ̃] *nf* **1** boarding school; (*somme, repas*) board; **être en p.** to board, be a boarder (**chez** with); **p. (de famille)** guesthouse, boarding house; **p. complète** full board. **2** (*allocation*) pension; **p. alimentaire** maintenance allowance. ◆**pensionnaire** *nmf* (*élève*) boarder; (*d'hôtel*) resident; (*de famille*) lodger. ◆**pensionnat** *nm* boarding school; (*élèves*) boarders. ◆**pensionné, -ée** *nmf* pensioner.

pentagone [pɛ̃tagon] *nm* **le P.** Am Pol the Pentagon.

pentathlon [pɛ̃tatlɔ̃] *nm* Sp pentathlon.

pente [pɑ̃t] *nf* slope; **être en p.** to slope, be sloping.

Pentecôte [pɑ̃tkot] *nf* Whitsun, Am Pentecost.

pénurie [penyri] *nf* scarcity, shortage (**de** of).

pépère [peper] **1** *nm* Fam grand(d)ad. **2** *a* (*tranquille*) Fam quiet and easy.

pépier [pepje] *vi* (*oiseau*) to cheep, chirp.

pépin [pepɛ̃] *nm* **1** (*de fruit*) pip, Am pit. **2** (*ennui*) Fam hitch, bother. **3** (*parapluie*) Fam brolly.

pépinière [pepinjɛr] *nf Bot* nursery.

pépite [pepit] *nf* (*gold*) nugget.

péquenaud, -aude [pekno, -od] *nmf* Péj Arg peasant, bumpkin.

perçant [pɛrsɑ̃] *a* (*cri, froid*) piercing; (*yeux*) sharp, keen.

percée [pɛrse] *nf* (*dans une forêt*) opening; (*avance technologique, attaque militaire*) breakthrough.

perce-neige [pɛrsnɛʒ] *nm ou f inv Bot* snowdrop.

perce-oreille [pɛrsɔrɛj] *nm* (*insecte*) earwig.

percepteur [pɛrsɛptœr] *nm* tax collector. ◆**perceptible** *a* perceptible (**à** to), noticeable. ◆**perception** *nf* **1** (*bureau*) tax office; (*d'impôt*) collection. **2** (*sensation*) perception.

perc/er [pɛrse] *vt* (*trouer*) to pierce; (*avec perceuse*) to drill (a hole in); (*trou, ouverture*) to make, drill; (*mystère etc*) to uncover; **p. une dent** (*bébé*) to cut a tooth; **— vi** (*soleil, ennemi, sentiment*) to break *ou* come through; (*abcès*) to burst. ◆**—euse** *nf* drill.

percevoir* [pɛrsəvwar] *vt* **1** (*sensation*) to perceive; (*son*) to hear. **2** (*impôt*) to collect.

perche [pɛrʃ] *nf* **1** (*bâton*) pole; **saut à la p.** pole-vaulting. **2** (*poisson*) perch.

perch/er [pɛrʃe] *vi* (*oiseau*) to perch; (*volailles*) to roost; (*loger*) Fam to hang out; **—**

vt (*placer*) *Fam* to perch; **— se p.** *vpr* (*oiseau, personne*) to perch. **◆—é** *a* perched. **◆perchoir** *nm* perch; (*de volailles*) roost.

percolateur [pɛrkɔlatœr] *nm* (*de restaurant*) percolator.

percussion [pɛrkysjɔ̃] *nf Mus* percussion.

percutant [pɛrkytɑ̃] *a Fig* powerful.

percuter [pɛrkyte] *vt* (*véhicule*) to crash into; **—** *vi* **p. contre** to crash into.

perd/re [pɛrdr] *vt* to lose; (*gaspiller*) to waste; (*ruiner*) to ruin; (*habitude*) to get out of; **p. de vue** to lose sight of; **—** *vi* to lose; (*récipient, tuyau*) to leak; **j'y perds** I lose out, I lose on the deal; **— se p.** *vpr* (*s'égarer*) to get lost; (*dans les détails*) to lose oneself; (*disparaître*) to disappear; **je m'y perds** I'm lost *ou* confused. **◆—ant, -ante** *a* (*billet*) losing; *— nmf* loser. **◆—u** *a* lost; wasted; (*malade*) finished; (*lieu*) isolated, in the middle of nowhere; **à ses moments perdus** in one's spare time; **une balle perdue** a stray bullet; **c'est du temps p.** it's a waste of time. **◆perdition (en)** *adv* (*navire*) in distress.

perdrix [pɛrdri] *nf* partridge. **◆perdreau, -x** *nm* young partridge.

père [pɛr] *nm* father; **Dupont p.** Dupont senior; **le p. Jean** *Fam* old John.

péremptoire [perɑ̃ptwar] *a* peremptory.

perfection [pɛrfɛksjɔ̃] *nf* perfection. **◆perfectionn/er** *vt* to improve, perfect; **se p. en anglais**/*etc* to improve one's English/*etc*. **◆—é** *a* (*machine etc*) advanced. **◆—ement** *nm* improvement (de in, par rapport à on); **cours de p.** advanced *ou* refresher course. **◆perfectionniste** *nmf* perfectionist.

perfide [pɛrfid] *a Litt* treacherous, perfidious. **◆perfidie** *nf Litt* treachery.

perforer [pɛrfɔre] *vt* (*pneu, intestin etc*) to perforate; (*billet, carte*) to punch; **carte perforée** punch card. **◆perforateur** *nm* (*appareil*) drill. **◆perforation** *nf* perforation; (*trou*) punched hole. **◆perforatrice** *nf* (*pour cartes*) *Tech* (card) punch. **◆perforeuse** *nf* (paper) punch.

performance [pɛrfɔrmɑ̃s] *nf* (*d'athlète, de machine etc*) performance. **◆performant** *a* (highly) efficient.

péricliter [periklite] *vi* to go to rack and ruin.

péril [peril] *nm* peril; **à tes risques et périls at your own risk. **◆périlleux, -euse** *a* perilous; **saut p.** somersault (*in mid air*).

périm/er [perime] *vi,* **— se p.** *vpr* laisser

(**se**) **p.** (*billet*) to allow to expire. **◆—é** *a* expired; (*désuet*) outdated.

périmètre [perimɛtr] *nm* perimeter.

période [perjɔd] *nf* period. **◆périodique** *a* periodic; *— nm* (*revue*) periodical.

péripétie [peripesi] *nf* (unexpected) event.

périphérie [periferi] *nf* (*limite*) periphery; (*banlieue*) outskirts. **◆périphérique** *a* (*quartier*) outlying, peripheral; *— nm* (*boulevard*) **p.** (motorway) ring road, *Am* beltway.

périphrase [perifraz] *nf* circumlocution.

périple [peripl] *nm* trip, tour.

pér/ir [perir] *vi* to perish, die. **◆—issable** *a* (*denrée*) perishable.

périscope [periskɔp] *nm* periscope.

perle [pɛrl] *nf* (*bijou*) pearl; (*de bois, verre etc*) bead; (*personne*) *Fig* gem, pearl; (*erreur*) *Iron* howler, gem. **◆perler** *vi* (*sueur*) to form beads; **grève perlée** go-slow, *Am* slow-down strike.

permanent, -ente [pɛrmanɑ̃, -ɑ̃t] **1** *a* permanent; (*spectacle*) *Cin* continuous; (*comité*) standing. **2** *nf* (*coiffure*) perm. **◆permanence** *nf* permanence; (*service, bureau*) duty office; (*salle*) *Scol* study room; **être de p.** to be on duty; **en p.** permanently.

perméable [pɛrmeabl] *a* permeable.

permettre* [pɛrmɛtr] *vt* to allow, permit; **p. à qn de faire** (*permission, possibilité*) to allow *ou* permit s.o. to do; **permettez!** excuse me!; **vous permettez?** may I?; **se p. de faire** to allow oneself to do, take the liberty to do; **se p. qch** (*se payer*) to afford sth. **◆permis** *a* allowed, permitted; *— nm* (*autorisation*) permit, licence; **p. de conduire** (*carte*) driving licence, *Am* driver's license; **p. de travail** work permit. **◆permission** *nf* permission; (*congé*) *Mil* leave; **demander la p.** to ask (for) permission (**de faire** to do).

permuter [pɛrmyte] *vt* to change round *ou* over, permutate. **◆permutation** *nf* permutation.

pernicieux, -euse [pɛrnisjø, -øz] *a* (*nocif*) & *Méd* pernicious.

pérorer [perɔre] *vi Péj* to speechify.

Pérou [peru] *nm* Peru.

perpendiculaire [pɛrpɑ̃dikylɛr] *a & nf* perpendicular (à to).

perpétrer [pɛrpetre] *vt* (*crime*) to perpetrate.

perpétuel, -elle [pɛrpetɥɛl] *a* perpetual; (*fonction, rente*) for life. **◆perpétuellement** *adv* perpetually. **◆perpétuer** *vt* to perpetuate. ◆**perpétuité (à)** adv in perpetuity; (condamné) for life.

perplexe [perpleks] a perplexed, puzzled. ◆**perplexité** nf perplexity.

perquisition [perkizisjɔ̃] nf (house) search (by police). ◆**perquisitionner** vti to search.

perron [perɔ̃] nm (front) steps.

perroquet [perɔkɛ] nm parrot.

perruche [peryʃ] nf budgerigar, Am parakeet.

perruque [peryk] nf wig.

persan [persɑ̃] a (langue, tapis, chat) Persian; – nm (langue) Persian.

persécut/er [persekyte] vt (tourmenter) to persecute; (importuner) to harass. ◆**persécuteur, -trice** nmf persecutor. ◆**persécution** nf persecution.

persévér/er [persevere] vi to persevere (dans in). ◆**—ant** a persevering. ◆**persévérance** nf perseverance.

persienne [persjɛn] nf (outside) shutter.

persil [persi] nm parsley.

persist/er [persiste] vi to persist (à faire in doing). ◆**—ant** a persistent; à feuilles persistantes (arbre etc) evergreen. ◆**persistance** nf persistence.

personnage [persɔnaʒ] nm (célébrité) (important) person; Th Littér character.

personnaliser [persɔnalize] vt to personalize; (voiture) to customize.

personnalité [persɔnalite] nf (individualité, personnage) personality.

personne [persɔn] 1 nf person; pl people; grande p. grown-up; adult; jolie p. pretty girl ou woman; en p. in person. 2 pron (négatif) nobody, no one; ne . . . p. nobody, no one; je ne vois p. I don't see anybody ou anyone; mieux que p. better than anybody ou anyone.

personnel, -elle [persɔnɛl] 1 a personal; (joueur, jeu) individualistic. 2 nm staff, personnel. ◆**personnellement** adv personally.

personnifier [persɔnifje] vt to personify. ◆**personnification** nf personification.

perspective [perspektiv] nf (art) perspective; (point de vue) Fig viewpoint, perspective; (de paysage etc) view; (possibilité, espérance) prospect; en p. Fig in view, in prospect.

perspicace [perspikas] a shrewd. ◆**perspicacité** nf shrewdness.

persuader [persɥade] vt to persuade (qn de faire s.o. to do); se p. que to be convinced that. ◆**persuasif, -ive** a persuasive.

◆**persuasion** nf persuasion; (croyance) conviction.

perte [pert] nf loss; (gaspillage) waste (de temps/d'argent of time/money); (ruine) ruin; à p. de vue as far as the eye can see; vendre à p. to sell at a loss.

pertinent [pertinɑ̃] a relevant, pertinent. ◆**pertinence** nf relevance.

perturb/er [pertyrbe] vt (trafic, cérémonie etc) to disrupt; (ordre public, personne) to disturb. ◆**—é a** (troublé) Fam perturbed. ◆**perturbateur, -trice** a (élément) disruptive; – nmf trouble-maker. ◆**perturbation** nf disruption; (crise) upheaval.

péruvien, -ienne [peryvjɛ̃, -jɛn] a & nmf Peruvian.

pervenche [pervɑ̃ʃ] nf Bot periwinkle.

pervers [perver] a wicked, perverse; (dépravé) perverted. ◆**perversion** nf perversion. ◆**perversité** nf perversity. ◆**pervertir** vt to pervert. ◆**-i, -ie** nmf pervert.

pesant [pəzɑ̃] a heavy, weighty; – nm valoir son p. d'or to be worth one's weight in gold. ◆**pesamment** adv heavily. ◆**pesanteur** nf heaviness; (force) Phys gravity.

pes/er [pəze] vt to weigh; – vi to weigh; p. lourd to be heavy; (argument etc) Fig to carry (a lot of) weight; p. sur (appuyer) to bear down upon; (influer) to bear upon; p. sur qn (menace) to hang over s.o.; p. sur l'estomac to lie (heavily) on the stomach. ◆**—ée** nf weighing; Boxe weigh-in; (effort) pressure. ◆**—age** nm weighing. ◆**pèse-bébé** nm (baby) scales. ◆**pèse-personne** nm (bathroom) scales.

pessimisme [pesimism] nm pessimism. ◆**pessimiste** a pessimistic; – nmf pessimist.

peste [pest] nf Méd plague; (personne, enfant) Fig pest.

pester [peste] vi to curse; p. contre qch/qn to curse sth/s.o.

pestilentiel, -ielle [pestilɑ̃sjɛl] a fetid, stinking.

pétale [petal] nm petal.

pétanque [petɑ̃k] nf (jeu) bowls.

pétarades [petarad] nfpl (de moto etc) backfiring. ◆**pétarader** vi to backfire.

pétard [petar] nm (explosif) firecracker, banger.

péter [pete] vi Fam (éclater) to go bang ou pop; (se rompre) to snap.

pétill/er [petije] vi (eau, champagne) to sparkle, fizz; (bois, feu) to crackle; (yeux) to sparkle. ◆**—ant** a (eau, vin, regard) sparkling.

petit, -ite [p(ə)ti, -it] *a* small, little; (*de taille*) short; (*bruit, espoir, coup*) slight; (*jeune*) young, small; (*mesquin, insignifiant*) petty; **tout p.** tiny; **un bon p. travail** a nice little job; **un p. Français** a (little) French boy; — *nmf* (little) boy, (little) girl; (*personne*) small person; *Scol* junior; *pl* (*d'animal*) young; (*de chien*) pups, young; (*de chat*) kittens, young; — *adv* **p. à p.** little by little. ◆**p.-bourgeois** *a* Péj middle-class. ◆**p.-suisse** *nm* soft cheese (*for dessert*). ◆**petitement** *adv* (*chichement*) shabbily, poorly. ◆**petitesse** *nf* (*de taille*) smallness; (*mesquinerie*) pettiness.

petit-fils [p(ə)tifis] *nm* (*pl* petits-fils) grandson, grandchild. ◆**petite-fille** *nf* (*pl* petites-filles) granddaughter, grandchild. ◆**petits-enfants** *nmpl* grandchildren.

pétition [petisjɔ̃] *nf* petition.

pétrifier [petrifje] *vt* (*de peur, d'émoi etc*) to petrify.

pétrin [petrɛ̃] *nm* (*situation*) Fam fix; **dans le p.** in a fix.

pétrir [petrir] *vt* to knead.

pétrole [petrɔl] *nm* oil, petroleum; **p.** (*lampant*) paraffin, *Am* kerosene; **nappe de p.** (*sur la mer*) oil slick. ◆**pétrolier, -ière** *a* (*industrie*) oil-; — *nm* (*navire*) oil tanker. ◆**pétrolifère** *a* **gisement p.** oil field.

pétulant [petylɑ̃] *a* exuberant.

pétunia [petynja] *nm* Bot petunia.

peu [pø] *adv* (*lire, manger etc*) not much, little; **elle mange p.** she doesn't eat much, she eats little; **un p.** (*lire, surpris etc*) a little, a bit; **p. de sel/de temps/***etc* not much salt/time/*etc*, little salt/time/*etc*; **un p. de fromage/***etc* a little cheese/*etc*, a bit of cheese/*etc*; **le p. de fromage que j'ai** the little cheese I have; **p. de gens/de livres/***etc* few people/books/*etc*, not many people/ books/*etc*; **p. sont . . .** few are . . . ; **un (tout) petit p.** a (tiny) little bit; **p. intéressant/souvent/***etc* not very interesting/often/*etc*; **p. de chose** not much; **p. à p.** gradually, little by little; **à p.** près more or less; **p. après/avant** shortly after/before.

peuplade [pœplad] *nf* tribe.

peuple [pœpl] *nm* (*nation, masse*) people; **les gens du p.** the common people. ◆**peupl/er** *vt* to populate, people. ◆**—é** *a* (*quartier etc*) populated (**de** with).

peuplier [pøplije] *nm* (*arbre, bois*) poplar.

peur [pœr] *nf* fear; **avoir p.** to be afraid *ou* frightened *ou* scared (**de** of); **faire p. à** to frighten; scare; **de p. que** (+ *sub*) for fear that; **de p. de faire** for fear of doing.

◆**peureux, -euse** *a* fearful, easily frightened.

peut, peux [pø] *voir* **pouvoir 1.**

peut-être [pøtɛtr] *adv* perhaps, maybe; **p.-être qu'il viendra** perhaps *ou* maybe he'll come.

phallique [falik] *a* a phallic. ◆**phallocrate** *nm* Péj male chauvinist.

phare [far] *nm* Nau lighthouse; *Aut* headlight, headlamp; **rouler pleins phares** *Aut* to drive on full headlights; **faire un appel de phares** *Aut* to flash one's lights.

pharmacie [farmasi] *nf* chemist's shop, *Am* drugstore; (*science*) pharmacy; (*armoire*) medicine cabinet. ◆**pharmaceutique** *a* pharmaceutical. ◆**pharmacien, -ienne** *nmf* chemist, pharmacist, *Am* druggist.

pharynx [farɛ̃ks] *nm* Anat pharynx.

phase [faz] *nf* phase.

phénomène [fenɔmɛn] *nm* phenomenon; (*personne*) Fam eccentric. ◆**phénoménal, -aux** *a* phenomenal.

philanthrope [filɑ̃trɔp] *nmf* philanthropist. ◆**philanthropique** *a* philanthropic.

philatélie [filateli] *nf* philately, stamp collecting. ◆**philatélique** *a* philatelic. ◆**philatéliste** *nmf* philatelist, stamp collector.

philharmonique [filarmɔnik] *a* philharmonic.

Philippines [filipin] *nfpl* **les P.** the Philippines.

philosophe [filɔzɔf] *nmf* philosopher; — *a* (*sage, résigné*) philosophical. ◆**philosopher** *vi* to philosophize (**sur** about). ◆**philosophie** *nf* philosophy. ◆**philosophique** *a* philosophical.

phobie [fɔbi] *nf* phobia.

phonétique [fɔnetik] *a* phonetic; — *nf* phonetics.

phonographe [fɔnɔgraf] *nm* gramophone, *Am* phonograph.

phoque [fɔk] *nm* (*animal marin*) seal.

phosphate [fɔsfat] *nm* Ch phosphate.

phosphore [fɔsfɔr] *nm* Ch phosphorus.

photo [foto] *nf* photo; (*art*) photography; **prendre une p. de, prendre en p.** to take a photo of; — *a inv* **appareil p.** camera. ◆**photocopie** *nf* photocopy. ◆**photocopier** *vt* to photocopy. ◆**photocopieur** *nm*, ◆**photocopieuse** *nf* (*machine*) photocopier. ◆**photogénique** *a* photogenic. ◆**photographe** *nmf* photographer. ◆**photographie** *nf* (*art*) photography; (*image*) photograph. ◆**photographier** *vt* to photograph. ◆**photographique** *a* photographic. ◆**photomaton**® *nm (appareil)* photo booth.

phrase [fraz] *nf (mots)* sentence.

physicien, -ienne [fizisjɛ̃, -jɛn] *nmf* physicist.

physiologie [fizjɔlɔʒi] *nf* physiology. ◆**physiologique** *a* physiological.

physionomie [fizjɔnɔmi] *nf* face.

physique [fizik] **1** *a (corps, aspect)* physique; **au p.** physically. **2** *nf (science)* physics. ◆—**ment** *adv* physically.

piaffer [pjafe] *vi (cheval)* to stamp; **p. d'impatience** *Fig* to fidget impatiently.

piailler [pjɑje] *vi (oiseau)* to cheep; *(enfant) Fam* to squeal.

piano [pjano] *nm* piano; **p. droit/à queue** upright/grand piano. ◆**pianiste** *nmf* pianist.

piaule [pjol] *nf (chambre) Arg* room, pad.

pic [pik] *nm* **1** *(cime)* peak. **2** *(outil)* pick(axe); **p. à glace** ice pick. **3** *(oiseau)* woodpecker.

pic (à) [pik] *adv (verticalement)* sheer; **couler à p.** to sink to the bottom; **arriver à p.** *Fig* to arrive in the nick of time.

pichet [piʃɛ] *nm* jug, pitcher.

pickpocket [pikpɔkɛt] *nm* pickpocket.

pick-up [pikœp] *nm inv (camionnette)* pick-up truck.

picorer [pikɔre] *vti* to peck.

picoter [pikɔte] *vt (yeux)* to make smart; *(jambes)* to make tingle; **les yeux me picotent** my eyes are smarting.

pie [pi] *nf* **1** *(oiseau)* magpie. **2** *a inv (couleur)* piebald.

pièce [pjɛs] *nf* **1** *(de maison etc)* room. **2** *(morceau, objet etc)* piece; *(de pantalon)* patch; *(écrit) & Jur* document; **p. de monnaie** coin; **p. (de théâtre)** play; **p. (d'artillerie)** gun; **p. d'identité** proof of identity, identity card; **p. d'eau** pool, pond; **pièces détachées** *ou* **de rechange** *(de véhicule etc)* spare parts; **cinq dollars/etc (la) p.** five dollars/etc each; **travailler à la p.** to do piecework.

pied [pje] *nm* foot; *(de meuble)* leg; *(de verre, lampe)* base; *Phot* stand; **un p. de salade** a head of lettuce; **à p.** on foot; **aller à p.** to walk, go on foot; **au p. de** at the foot *ou* bottom of; **au p. de la lettre** *Fig* literally; **avoir p.** *(nageur)* to have a footing, touch the bottom; **coup de p.** kick; **donner un coup de p.** to kick (à qn s.o.); **sur p.** *(debout, levé)* up and about; **sur ses pieds** *(malade guéri)* up and about; **sur un p. d'égalité** on an equal footing; **comme un p.** *(mal) Fam* dreadfully; **faire un p. de nez** to thumb one's nose (à at); **mettre sur p.** *(projet)* to set up. ◆**p.-noir** *nmf (pl* **pieds-noirs)** Algerian Frenchman *ou* Frenchwoman.

piédestal, -aux [pjedestal, -o] *nm* pedestal.

piège [pjɛʒ] *nm (pour animal) & Fig* trap. ◆**piéger** *vt (animal)* to trap; *(voiture etc)* to booby-trap; **engin piégé** booby trap; **lettre/colis/voiture piégé(e)** letter/parcel/car bomb.

pierre [pjɛr] *nf* stone; *(précieuse)* gem, stone; **p. à briquet** flint; **geler à p. fendre** to freeze (rock) hard. ◆**pierreries** *nfpl* gems, precious stones. ◆**pierreux, -euse** *a* stony.

piété [pjete] *nf* piety.

piétiner [pjetine] *vt (fouler aux pieds)* to trample (on); – *vi* to stamp (one's feet); *(marcher sur place)* to mark time; *(ne pas avancer) Fig* to make no headway.

piéton¹ [pjetɔ̃] *nm* pedestrian. ◆**piéton², -onne** *a*, ◆**piétonnier, -ière** *a (rue etc)* pedestrian.

piètre [pjɛtr] *a* wretched, poor.

pieu, -x [pjø] *nm* **1** *(piquet)* post, stake. **2** *(lit) Fam* bed.

pieuvre [pjœvr] *nf* octopus.

pieux, -euse [pjø, -øz] *a* pious.

pif [pif] *nm (nez) Fam* nose. ◆**pifomètre (au)** *adv (sans calcul) Fam* at a rough guess.

pigeon [piʒɔ̃] *nm* pigeon; *(personne) Fam* dupe; **p. voyageur** carrier pigeon. ◆**pigeonner** *vt (voler) Fam* to rip off.

piger [piʒe] *vti Fam* to understand.

pigment [pigmɑ̃] *nm* pigment.

pignon [piɲɔ̃] *nm (de maison etc)* gable.

pile [pil] *nf* **1** *El* battery; *(atomique)* pile; **radio à piles** battery radio. **2** *nf (tas)* pile; **en p.** in a pile. **3** *nf (de pont)* pier. **4** *nf* **p. (ou face)?** heads *ou* tails?; **jouer à p. ou face** to toss up. **5** *adv* **s'arrêter p.** to stop short *ou* dead; **à deux heures p.** on the dot of two.

piler [pile] **1** *vt (amandes)* to grind; *(ail)* to crush. **2** *vi (en voiture)* to stop dead. ◆**pilonner** *vt Mil* to bombard, shell.

pilier [pilje] *nm* pillar.

pilon [pilɔ̃] *nm (de poulet)* drumstick.

piller [pije] *vti* to loot, pillage. ◆**pillage** *nm* looting, pillage. ◆**pillard, -arde** *nmf* looter.

pilori [pilɔri] *nm* **mettre au p.** *Fig* to pillory.

pilote [pilɔt] *nm Av Nau* pilot; *(de voiture, char)* driver; *(guide) Fig* guide; – *a* **usine(-)/etc** *Fig* factory/plan. ◆**pilot/er** *vt Av* to fly, pilot; *Nau* to pilot; **p. qn** to show s.o. around. ◆—**age** *nm* piloting; **école de p.** flying school; **poste de p.** cockpit.

pilotis [piloti] *nm* (*pieux*) *Archit* piles.

pilule [pilyl] *nf* pill; **prendre la p.** (*femme*) to be on the pill; **se mettre à/arrêter la p.** to go on/off the pill.

piment [pimɑ̃] *nm* pimento, pepper. ◆**pimenté** *a Culin & Fig* spicy.

pimpant [pɛ̃pɑ̃] *a* spruce.

pin [pɛ̃] *nm* (*bois, arbre*) pine; **pomme de p.** pine cone.

pinailler [pinɑje] *vi Fam* to quibble, split hairs.

pinard [pinar] *nm* (*vin*) *Fam* wine.

pince [pɛ̃s] *nf* (*outil*) pliers; *Méd* forceps; (*de cycliste*) clip; (*levier*) crowbar; *pl* (*de crabe*) pincers; **p. (à linge)** (*clothes*) peg *ou* *Am* pin; **p. (à épiler)** tweezers; **p. (à sucre)** sugar tongs; **p. à cheveux** hairgrip. ◆**pinc/er** *vt* to pinch; (*corde*) *Mus* to pluck; (*arrêter*) *Jur* to nab s.o., pinch s.o.; **se p. le doigt** to get one's finger caught (**dans** in). ◆**-é** *a* (*air*) stiff, constrained. ◆**-ée** *nf* (*de sel etc*) pinch (**de** of). ◆**pincettes** *nfpl* (*fire*) tongs; (*d'horloger*) tweezers. ◆**pinçon** *nm* pinch (mark).

pinceau, -x [pɛ̃so] *nm* (paint)brush.

pince-sans-rire [pɛ̃sɑ̃rir] *nm* person of dry humour.

pinède [pinɛd] *nf* pine forest.

pingouin [pɛ̃gwɛ̃] *nm* auk, penguin.

ping-pong [piŋpɔ̃g] *nm* ping-pong.

pingre [pɛ̃gr] *a* stingy; – *nmf* skinflint.

pinson [pɛ̃sɔ̃] *nm* (*oiseau*) chaffinch.

pintade [pɛ̃tad] *nf* guinea fowl.

pin-up [pinœp] *nf inv* (*fille*) pinup.

pioche [pjɔʃ] *nf* pick(axe). ◆**piocher** *vti* (*creuser*) to dig (with a pick).

pion [pjɔ̃] *nm* **1** (*au jeu de dames*) piece; *Échecs & Fig* pawn. **2** *Scol* master (in charge of discipline).

pionnier [pjɔnje] *nm* pioneer.

pipe [pip] *nf* (*de fumeur*) pipe; **fumer la p.** to smoke a pipe.

pipeau, -x [pipo] *nm* (*flûte*) pipe.

pipe-line [piplin] *nm* pipeline.

pipi [pipi] *nm* **faire p.** *Fam* to go for a pee.

pique [pik] **1** *nm* (*couleur*) *Cartes* spades. **2** *nf* (*arme*) pike. **3** *nf* (*allusion*) cutting remark.

pique-assiette [pikasjɛt] *nmf inv* scrounger.

pique-nique [piknik] *nm* picnic. ◆**pique-niquer** *vi* to picnic.

piqu/er [pike] *vt* (*entamer, percer*) to prick; (*langue, yeux*) to sting; (*curiosité*) to rouse; (*coudre*) to (machine-)stitch; (*édredon, couvre-lit*) to quilt; (*crise de nerfs*) to have;

(*maladie*) to get; **p. qn** (*abeille*) to sting s.o.; (*serpent*) to bite s.o.; *Méd* to give s.o. an injection; **p. qch dans** (*enfoncer*) to stick sth into; **p. qch** (*arrêter*) *Jur* to nab s.o., pinch s.o.; **p. qch** (*voler*) *Fam* to pinch sth; **p. une colère** to fly into a rage; **p. une tête** to plunge headlong; – *vi* (*avion*) to dive; (*moutarde etc*) to be hot; – **se p.** *vpr* to prick oneself; **se p. de faire qch** to pride oneself on being able to do sth. ◆**-ant** *a* (*épine*) prickly; (*froid*) biting; (*sauce, goût*) pungent, piquant; (*mot*) cutting; (*détail*) spicy; – *nm Bot* prickle, thorn; (*d'animal*) spine, prickle. ◆**-é** *a* (*meuble*) worm-eaten; (*fou*) *Fam* crazy; – *nm Av* (*nose*)dive; **descente en p.** *Av* nosedive. ◆**-eur, -euse** *nmf* (*sur machine à coudre*) machinist. ◆**piqûre** *nf* (*d'épingle*) prick; (*d'abeille*) sting; (*de serpent*) bite; (*trou*) hole; *Méd* injection; (*point*) stitch.

piquet [pikɛ] *nm* **1** (*pieu*) stake, picket; (*de tente*) peg. **2 p. (de grève)** picket (line), strike picket. **3 au p.** *Scol* in the corner.

piqueté [pikte] *a* **p. de** dotted with.

pirate [pirat] *nm* pirate; **p. de l'air** hijacker; – *a* (*radio, bateau*) pirate-. ◆**piraterie** *nf* piracy; (*acte*) act of piracy; **p. (aérienne)** hijacking.

pire [pir] *a* worse (**que** than); **le p. moment/résultat/etc** the worst moment/result/etc; – *nmf* **le ou la p.** the worst (one); **le p. de tout** the worst (thing) of all; **au p.** at (the very) worst; **s'attendre au p.** to expect the (very) worst.

pirogue [pirɔg] *nf* canoe, dugout.

pis [pi] **1** *nm* (*de vache*) udder. **2** *a inv & adv* *Litt* worse; **de mal en p.** from bad to worse; – *nm* **le p.** *Litt* the worst.

pis-aller [pizale] *nm inv* (*personne, solution*) stopgap.

piscine [pisin] *nf* swimming pool.

pissenlit [pisɑ̃li] *nm* dandelion.

pistache [pistaʃ] *nf* (*fruit, parfum*) pistachio.

piste [pist] *nf* (*trace de personne ou d'animal*) track, trail; *Sp* track, racetrack; (*de magnétophone*) track; *Av* runway; (*de cirque*) ring; (*de patinage*) rink; (*pour chevaux*) racecourse, racetrack; **p. cyclable** cycle track, *Am* bicycle path; **p. de danse** dance floor; **p. de ski** ski run; **tour de p.** *Sp* lap.

pistolet [pistɔlɛ] *nm* gun, pistol; (*de peintre*) spray gun.

piston [pistɔ̃] *nm* **1** *Aut* piston. **2 avoir du p.** (*appui*) to have connections. ◆**pistonner** *vt* (*appuyer*) to pull strings for.

pitié [pitje] *nf* pity; **j'ai p. de lui, il me fait p.** I pity him. I feel sorry for him. ◆**piteux, -euse** *a Iron* pitiful. ◆**pitoyable** *a* pitiful.

piton [pitɔ̃] *nm* **1** (*à crochet*) hook. **2** *Géog* peak.

pitre [pitr] *nm* clown. ◆**pitrerie(s)** *nf(pl)* clowning.

pittoresque [pitɔresk] *a* picturesque.

pivert [piver] *nm* (*oiseau*) woodpecker.

pivoine [pivwan] *nf Bot* peony.

pivot [pivo] *nm* pivot; (*personne*) *Fig* linchpin, mainspring. ◆**pivoter** *vi* (*personne*) to swing round; (*fauteuil*) to swivel; (*porte*) to revolve.

pizza [pidza] *nf* pizza. ◆**pizzeria** *nf* pizza parlour.

placage [plakaʒ] *nm* (*revêtement*) facing; (*en bois*) veneer.

placard [plakar] *nm* **1** (*armoire*) cupboard, *Am* closet. **2** (*pancarte*) poster. ◆**placarder** *vt* (*affiche*) to post (up); (*mur*) to cover with posters.

place [plas] *nf* (*endroit, rang*) & *Géom* place; (*occupée par qn ou qch*) room; (*lieu public*) square; (*siège*) seat, place; (*prix d'un trajet*) *Aut* fare; (*emploi*) job, position; **p. (de parking)** (parking) space; **p. (financière)** (*financière*) market; **à la p.** (*échange*) instead of (**de** of); **à votre p.** in your place; **sur p.** on the spot; **en p.** (*objet*) in place; **ne pas tenir en p.** to be unable to keep still; **mettre en p.** to install, set up; **faire p. à** to give way to; **changer qch de p.** to move sth.

plac/er [plase] *vt* (*mettre*) to put, place; (*situer*) to place, position; (*invité, spectateur*) to seat; (*argent*) to invest, place (**dans** in); (*vendre*) to place, sell; **un mot** to get a word in edgeways *ou Am* edgewise; **— se p.** *vpr* (*personne*) to take up a position, place oneself; (*objet*) to be put *ou* placed; (*cheval, coureur*) to be placed; **se p. troisième/etc** *Sp* to come *ou* be third/etc. ◆**-é** *a* (*objet*) & *Sp* placed; **bien/mal p. pour faire** in a good/bad position to do; **les gens haut placés** people in high places. ◆**-ement** *nm* (*d'argent*) investment.

placide [plasid] *a* placid.

plafond [plafɔ̃] *nm* ceiling. ◆**plafonnier** *nm Aut* roof light.

plage [plaʒ] *nf* **1** beach; (*ville*) (seaside) resort. **2** (*sur disque*) track. **3 p. arrière** *Aut* parcel shelf.

plagiat [plaʒja] *nm* plagiarism. ◆**plagier** *vt* to plagiarize.

plaid [plɛd] *nm* travelling rug.

plaider [plede] *vti Jur* to plead. ◆**plaideur,**

-euse *nmf* litigant. ◆**plaidoirie** *nf Jur* speech (for the defence). ◆**plaidoyer** *nm* plea.

plaie [plɛ] *nf* (*blessure*) wound; (*coupure*) cut; (*corvée, personne*) *Fig* nuisance.

plaignant, -ante [plɛɲɑ̃, -ɑ̃t] *nmf Jur* plaintiff.

plaindre* [plɛ̃dr] **1** *vt* to feel sorry for, pity. **2 se p.** *vpr* (*protester*) to complain (**de** about, **que** that); (*souffrir*) to complain (**de** of *ou* about). ◆**plainte** *nf* complaint; (*cri*) moan, groan. ◆**plaintif, -ive** *a* sorrowful, plaintive.

plaine [plɛn] *nf Géog* plain.

plaire* [plɛr] *vi* & *v imp* **p. à** to please; **elle lui plaît** he likes her, she pleases him; **ça me plaît** I like it; **il me plaît de faire** I like doing; **s'il vous** *ou* **te plaît** please; **— se p.** *vpr* (*à Paris etc*) to like *ou* enjoy it; (*l'un l'autre*) to like each other.

plaisance [plɛzɑ̃s] *nf* **bateau de p.** pleasure boat; **navigation de p.** yachting.

plaisant [plɛzɑ̃] *a* (*drôle*) amusing; (*agréable*) pleasing; **— mauvais p.** *Péj* joker. ◆**plaisanter** *vi* to joke, jest; **p. avec qch** to trifle with sth; **— vt** to tease. ◆**plaisanterie** *nf* joke, jest; (*bagatelle*) trifle; **par p.** for a joke. ◆**plaisantin** *nm Péj* joker.

plaisir [plezir] *nm* pleasure; **faire p. à** to please; **faites-moi le p. de . . .** would you be good enough to . . . ; **pour le p.** for fun, for the fun of it; **au p. (de vous revoir)** see you again sometime.

plan [plɑ̃] **1** *nm* (*projet, dessin*) plan; (*de ville*) map; (*niveau*) *Géom* plane; **au premier p.** in the foreground; **gros p.** *Phot Cin* close-up; **sur le p. politique/etc** from the political/etc viewpoint, politically/etc; **de premier p.** (*question etc*) major; **p. d'eau** stretch of water; **laisser en p.** (*abandonner*) to ditch. **2** *a* (*plat*) even, flat.

planche [plɑ̃ʃ] *nf* **1** board, plank; **p. à repasser/à dessin** ironing/drawing board; **p. (à roulettes)** skateboard; **p. (de surf)** surfboard; **p. (à voile)** sailboard; **faire de la p. (à voile)** to go windsurfing; **faire la p.** to float on one's back. **2** (*illustration*) plate. **3** (*de légumes*) bed, plot.

plancher [plɑ̃ʃe] *nm* floor.

plan/er [plane] *vi* (*oiseau*) to glide, hover; (*avion*) to glide; **p. sur qn** (*mystère, danger*) to hang over s.o.; **vol plané** glide. ◆**-eur** *nm* (*avion*) glider.

planète [planɛt] *nf* planet. ◆**planétaire** *a* planetary. ◆**planétarium** *nm* planetarium.

planifier [planifje] *vt Écon* to plan. ◆**pla-**

nification nf Écon planning. ◆**planning** nm (industriel, commercial) planning; **p familial** family planning.

planque [plɑ̃k] nf 1 (travail) Fam cushy job. 2 (lieu) Fam hideout. ◆**planquer** vt, — **se p.** vpr Fam to hide.

plant [plɑ̃] nm (plante) seedling; (de légumes etc) bed.

plante [plɑ̃t] nf 1 Bot plant; **p. d'appartement** house plant; **jardin des plantes** botanical gardens. 2 **p. des pieds** sole (of the foot). ◆**plant/er** vt (arbre, plante etc) to plant; (clou, couteau) to drive in; (tente, drapeau, échelle) to put up; (mettre) to put (**sur** on, **contre** against); (regard) to fix (**sur** on); **p. là qn** to leave s.o. standing; **se p. devant** to plant oneself in front of. ◆—**é** a (immobile) standing; **bien p.** (personne) sturdy. ◆**plantation** nf (action) planting; (terrain) bed; (de café, d'arbres etc) plantation. ◆**planteur** nm plantation owner.

planton [plɑ̃tɔ̃] nm Mil orderly.

plantureux, -euse [plɑ̃tyrø, -øz] a (repas etc) abundant.

plaque [plak] nf plate; (de verre, métal) sheet, plate; (de verglas) sheet; (de marbre) slab; (de chocolat) bar; (commémorative) plaque; (tache) Méd blotch; **p. chauffante** Culin hotplate; **p. tournante** (carrefour) Fig centre; **p. minéralogique**, **p. d'immatriculation** Aut number ou Am license plate; **p. dentaire** (dental) plaque. ◆**plaqu/er** vt (métal, bijou) to plate; (bois) to veneer; (cheveux) to plaster (down); Rugby to tackle; (aplatir) to flatten (**contre** against); (abandonner) Fam to give (sth) up; **p. qn** Fam to ditch s.o.; **se p. contre** to flatten oneself against. ◆—**é** a (bijou) plated; **p. or** gold-plated; — nm **p. or** gold plate. ◆—**age** nm Rugby tackle.

plasma [plasma] nm Méd plasma.

plastic [plastik] nm plastic explosive. ◆**plastiquer** vt to blow up.

plastique [plastik] a (art, substance) plastic; **matière p.** plastic; — nm (matière) plastic; **en p.** (bouteille etc) plastic.

plastron [plastrɔ̃] nm shirtfront.

plat [pla] 1 a flat; (mer) calm, smooth; (fade) flat, dull; **à fond p.** flat-bottomed; **à p. ventre** flat on one's face; **à p.** (pneu, batterie) flat; (déprimé, épuisé) Fam low; **poser à p.** to put ou lay (down) flat; **tomber à p.** to fall down flat; **assiette plate** dinner plate; **calme p.** dead calm; — nm (de la main) flat. 2 nm (récipient, mets) dish; (partie du repas) course; **'p. du jour'** (au restaurant) 'today's special'.

platane [platan] nm plane tree.

plateau, -x [plato] nm (pour servir) tray; (de balance) pan; (de tourne-disque) turntable; (plate-forme) Cin TV set; Th stage; Géog plateau; **p. à fromages** cheeseboard.

plate-bande [platbɑ̃d] nf (pl **plates-bandes**) flower bed.

plate-forme [platfɔrm] nf (pl **plates-formes**) platform; **p.-forme pétrolière** oil rig.

platine [platin] 1 nm (métal) platinum. 2 nf (d'électrophone) deck. ◆**platiné** a (cheveux) platinum, platinum-blond(e).

platitude [platityd] nf platitude.

plâtre [plɑtr] nm (matière) plaster; **un p.** Méd a plaster cast; **dans le p.** Méd in plaster; **les plâtres** (d'une maison etc) the plasterwork; **p. à mouler** plaster of Paris. ◆**plâtr/er** vt (mur) to plaster; (membre) to put in plaster. ◆—**age** nm plastering. ◆**plâtrier** nm plasterer.

plausible [plozibl] a plausible.

plébiscite [plebisit] nm plebiscite.

plein [plɛ̃] a (rempli, complet) full; (paroi) solid; (ivre) Fam tight; **p. de** full of; **en pleine mer** on the open sea; **en p. visage/**etc right in the middle of the face/etc; **en p. jour** in broad daylight; — prép & adv **des billes p. les poches** pockets full of marbles; **du chocolat p. la figure** chocolate all over one's face; **p. de lettres/d'argent/**etc (beaucoup de) Fam lots of letters/money/etc; **à p.** (travailler) to full capacity; — nm **faire le p.** Aut to fill up (the tank); **battre son p.** (fête) to be in full swing. ◆**pleinement** adv fully.

pléonasme [pleɔnasm] nm (expression) redundancy.

pléthore [pletɔr] nf plethora.

pleurer [plœre] vi to cry, weep (**sur** over); — vt (regretter) to mourn (for). ◆**pleureur** a **saule p.** weeping willow. ◆**pleurnicher** vi to snivel, grizzle. ◆**pleurs (en)** adv in tears.

pleurésie [plœrezi] nf Méd pleurisy.

pleuvoir* [pløvwar] v imp to rain; **il pleut** it's raining; — vi (coups etc) to rain down (**sur** on).

pli [pli] nm 1 (de papier etc) fold; (de jupe, robe) pleat; (de pantalon, de bouche) crease; (de bras) bend; (faux) p. crease; **mise en plis** (coiffure) set. 2 (enveloppe) Com envelope, letter; **sous p. séparé** under separate cover. 3 Cartes trick. 4 (habitude) habit; **prendre le p. de faire** to get into the habit of doing. ◆**plier** vt to fold; (courber) to bend; **p. qn à** to submit to to; — vi (branche) to bend; — **se p.** vpr (lit, chaise *etc*) to fold (up); **se p. à** to submit to, give in to. **◆—ant** *a* (*chaise etc*) folding; (*parapluie*) telescopic; – *nm* folding stool. **◆—able** *a* pliable. **◆—age** *nm* (*manière*) fold; (*action*) folding.

plinthe [plɛ̃t] *nf* skirting board, *Am* baseboard.

pliss/er [plise] *vt* (*jupe, robe*) to pleat; (*froisser*) to crease; (*lèvres*) to pucker; (*front*) to wrinkle, crease; (*yeux*) to screw up. **◆—é** *nm* pleating, pleats.

plomb [plɔ̃] *nm* (*métal*) lead; (*fusible*) fuse; (*poids pour rideau etc*) lead weight; *pl* (*de chasse*) lead shot, buckshot; **de p.** (*tuyau etc*) lead-; (*sommeil*) *Fig* heavy; (*soleil*) blazing; (*ciel*) leaden. **◆plomb/er** *vt* (*dent*) to fill; (*colis*) to seal (with lead). **◆—é** *a* (*teint*) leaden. **◆—age** *nm* (*de dent*) filling.

plombier [plɔ̃bje] *nm* plumber. **◆plomberie** *nf* (*métier, installations*) plumbing.

plong/er [plɔ̃ʒe] *vi* (*personne, avion etc*) to dive, plunge; (*route, regard*) *Fig* to plunge; – *vt* (*mettre, enfoncer*) to plunge, thrust (*dans* into); **se p. dans** (*lecture etc*) to immerse oneself in. **◆—eant** *a* (*décolleté*) plunging; (*vue*) bird's-eye-. **◆—é a p. dans** (*lecture etc*) immersed ou deep in. **◆—ée** *nf* diving; (*de sous-marin*) submersion; **en p.** (*sous-marin*) submerged. **◆plongeoir** *nm* diving board. **◆plongeon** *nm* dive. **◆plongeur, -euse** *nmf* diver; (*employé de restaurant*) dishwasher.

plouf [pluf] *nm & int* splash.

ployer [plwaje] *vti* to bend.

plu [ply] *voir* **plaire, pleuvoir.**

pluie [plɥi] *nf* rain; **une p.** (*averse*) & *Fig* a shower; **sous la p.** in the rain.

plume [plym] *nf* **1** (*d'oiseau*) feather. **2** (*pour écrire*) *Hist* quill pen; (*pointe en acier*) (pen) nib; **stylo à p.** (fountain) pen; **vivre de sa p.** *Fig* to live by one's pen. **◆plumage** *nm* plumage. **◆plumeau, -x** *nm* feather duster. **◆plumer** *vt* (*volaille*) to pluck; **p. qn** (*voler*) *Fig* to fleece s.o. **◆plumet** *nm* plume. **◆plumier** *nm* pencil box, pen box.

plupart (la) [laplypar] *nf* most; **la p. des cas/etc** most cases/*etc*; **la p. du temps** most of the time; **la p. d'entre eux** most of them; **pour la p.** mostly.

pluriel, -ielle [plyrjɛl] *a & nm Gram* plural; **au p.** (*nom*) plural, in the plural.

plus¹ [ply] ([plyz] *before vowel*, [plys] *in end position*) **1** *adv comparatif* (*travailler etc*) more (*que* than); **p. d'un kilo/de dix/etc** (*quantité, nombre*) more than a kilo/ten/

etc; **p. de thé/etc** (*davantage*) more tea/*etc*; **p. beau/rapidement/etc** more beautiful/rapidly/*etc* (*que* than); **p. tard** later; **p. petit** smaller; **de p. en p.** more and more; **de p. en p. vite** quicker and quicker; **p. il crie p. il s'enroue** the more he shouts the more hoarse he gets; **p. ou moins** more or less; **en p.** in addition (**de** to); **de p.** more (**que** than); (*en outre*) moreover; **les enfants (âgés) de p. de dix ans** children over ten; **j'ai dix ans de p. qu'elle** I'm ten years older than her; **il est p. de cinq heures** it's after five (o'clock). **2** *adv superlatif* **le p.** (*travailler etc*) (the) most; **le p. beau/etc** the most beautiful/*etc*; (*de deux*) the more beautiful/*etc*; **le p. grand/etc** the biggest/*etc*; (*de deux*) the bigger/*etc*; **j'ai le p. de livres** I have (the) most books; **j'en ai le p.** I have (the) most; (**tout**) **au p.** at (the very) most.

plus² [ply] *adv de négation* **p. de** (*pain, argent etc*) no more; **il n'a p. de pain** he has no more bread; (*ne*) he doesn't have any more bread; **tu n'es p. jeune** you're no longer young, you're not young any more ou any longer; **elle ne le fait p.** she no longer does it, she doesn't do it any more ou any longer; **je ne la reverrai p.** I won't see her again.

plus³ [plys] *prép* plus; **deux p. deux font quatre** two plus two are four; **il fait p. deux (degrés)** it's two degrees above freezing; – *nm* **le signe p.** the plus sign.

plusieurs [plyzjœr] *a & pron* several.

plus-value [plyvaly] *nf* (*bénéfice*) profit.

plutonium [plytɔnjɔm] *nm* plutonium.

plutôt [plyto] *adv* rather (**que** than).

pluvieux, -euse [plyvjø, -øz] *a* rainy, wet.

PMU [peemy] *abrév* = **pari mutuel urbain.**

pneu [pnø] *nm* (*pl* -**s**) **1** (*de roue*) tyre, *Am* tire. **2** (*lettre*) express letter. **◆pneumatique 1** *a* (*matelas etc*) inflatable; **marteau p.** pneumatic drill. **2** *nm* = **pneu.**

pneumonie [pnømɔni] *nf* pneumonia.

poche [pɔʃ] *nf* pocket; (*de kangourou etc*) pouch; (*sac en papier etc*) bag; *pl* (*sous les yeux*) bags; **livre de p.** paperback; **faire des poches** (*pantalon*) to be baggy; **j'ai un franc en p.** I have one franc on me. **◆pochette** *nf* (*sac*) bag, envelope; (*d'allumettes*) book; (*de disque*) sleeve, jacket; (*mouchoir*) pocket handkerchief; (*sac à main*) (clutch) bag.

poch/er [pɔʃe] *vt* **1 p. l'œil à qn** to give s.o. a black eye. **2** (*œufs*) to poach. **◆—é** *a* **œil p.** black eye.

podium [pɔdjɔm] *nm Sp* rostrum, podium.

poêle [pwal] **1** *nm* stove. **2** *nf* **p. (à frire)** frying pan.

poème [pɔɛm] *nm* poem. **◆poésie** *nf* poetry; **une p.** (*poème*) a piece of poetry. **◆poète** *nm* poet; – a **femme p.** poetess. **◆poétique** a poetic.

pognon [pɔɲ5] *nm* (*argent*) *Fam* dough.

poids [pwa] *nm* weight; **au p.** by weight; **de p.** (*influent*) influential; **p. lourd** (heavy) lorry *ou Am* truck; **lancer le p.** *Sp* to put *ou* hurl the shot.

poignant [pwaɲɑ̃] a (*souvenir etc*) poignant. **poignard** [pwaɲar] *nm* dagger; **coup de p.** stab. **◆poignarder** *vt* to stab.

poigne [pwaɲ] *nf* (*étreinte*) grip.

poignée [pwaɲe] *nf* (*quantité*) handful (**de** of); (*de porte, casserole etc*) handle; (*d'épée*) hilt; **p. de main** handshake; **donner une p. de main à** to shake hands with.

poignet [pwaɲɛ] *nm* wrist; (*de chemise*) cuff.

poil [pwal] *nm* hair; (*pelage*) coat, fur; (*de brosse*) bristle; (*de tapis*) pile; (*d'étoffe*) nap; **à p.** (*nu*) *Arg* (stark) naked; **au p.** (*travail etc*) *Arg* top-rate; **de bon/mauvais p.** *Fam* in a good/bad mood; **de tout p.** of all kinds. **◆poilu** a hairy.

poinçon [pwɛ̃s5] *nm* (*outil*) awl, bradawl; (*marque de bijou etc*) hallmark. **◆poinçonner** *vt* (*bijou*) to hallmark; (*billet*) to punch. **◆poinçonneuse** *nf* (*machine*) punch.

poindre [pwɛ̃dr] *vi* (*jour*) *Litt* to dawn.

poing [pwɛ̃] *nm* fist; **coup de p.** punch.

point¹ [pwɛ̃] *nm* (*lieu, question, degré, score etc*) point; (*sur i, à l'horizon etc*) dot; (*tache*) spot; (*note*) *Scol* mark; (*de couture*) stitch; **sur le p. de faire** about to do, on the point of doing; **p.** (*final*) full stop, period; **p. d'exclamation** exclamation mark *ou Am* point; **p. d'interrogation** question mark; **p. de vue** point of view, viewpoint; (*endroit*) viewing point; **à p.** (*nommé*) (*arriver etc*) at the right moment; **à p.** (*rôti etc*) medium (cooked); (*steak*) medium rare; **mal en p.** in bad shape; **mettre au p.** *Phot* to focus; *Aut* to tune; (*technique etc*) to elaborate, perfect; (*éclaircir*) *Fig* to clarify, clear up; **mise au p.** focusing; tuning, tune-up; elaboration; *Fig* clarification; **faire le p.** *Fig* to take stock, sum up; **p. mort** *Aut* neutral; **au p. mort** *Fig* at a standstill; **p. noir** *Aut* (*accident*) black spot; **p. du jour** daybreak; **p. de côté** (*douleur*) stitch (in one's side). **◆p.-virgule** *nm* (*pl* **points-virgules**) semicolon.

point² [pwɛ̃] *adv Litt* = **pas**¹.

pointe [pwɛ̃t] *nf* (*extrémité*) point, tip; (*pour grille*) spike; (*clou*) nail; *Géog* headland; (*maximum*) *Fig* peak; **une p. de** (*soupçon, nuance*) a touch of; **sur la p. des pieds** on

tiptoe; **en p.** pointed; **de p.** (*technique etc*) latest, most advanced; **à la p. de** (*progrès etc*) *Fig* in *ou* at the forefront of.

point/er [pwɛ̃te] **1** *vt* (*cocher*) to tick (off), *Am* check (off). **2** *vt* (*braquer, diriger*) to point (**sur, vers**). **3** *vti* (*employé*) to clock in, (*à la sortie*) to clock out; **— se p.** *vpr* (*arriver*) *Fam* to show up. **4** *vi* (*bourgeon etc*) to appear; **p. vers** to point upwards towards. **◆—age** *nm* (*de personnel*) clocking in; clocking out.

pointillé [pwɛ̃tije] *nm* dotted line; – a dotted.

pointilleux, -euse [pwɛ̃tijø, -øz] a fussy, particular.

pointu [pwɛ̃ty] a (*en pointe*) pointed; (*voix*) shrill.

pointure [pwɛ̃tyr] *nf* (*de chaussure, gant*) size.

poire [pwar] *nf* **1** (*fruit*) pear. **2** (*figure*) *Fam* mug. **3** (*personne*) *Fam* sucker. **◆poirier** *nm* pear tree.

poireau, -x [pwaro] *nm* leek.

poireauter [pwarote] *vi* (*attendre*) *Fam* to kick one's heels.

pois [pwa] *nm* (*légume*) pea; (*dessin*) (polka) dot; **petits p.** (garden) peas; **p. chiche** chickpea; **à p.** (*vêtement*) spotted, dotted.

poison [pwaz5] *nm* (*substance*) poison.

poisse [pwas] *nf Fam* bad luck.

poisseux, -euse [pwasø, -øz] a sticky.

poisson [pwas5] *nm* fish; **p. rouge** goldfish; **les Poissons** (*signe*) Pisces. **◆poissonnerie** *nf* fish shop. **◆poissonnier, -ière** *nmf* fishmonger.

poitrine [pwatrin] *nf Anat* chest; (*seins*) breast, bosom; (*de veau, mouton*) *Culin* breast.

poivre [pwavr] *nm* pepper. **◆poivr/er** *vt* to pepper. **◆—é** a *Culin* peppery; (*plaisanterie*) *Fig* spicy. **◆poivrier** *nm Bot* pepper plant; (*ustensile*) pepperpot. **◆poivrière** *nf* pepperpot.

poivron [pwavr5] *nm* pepper, capsicum.

poivrot, -ote [pwavro, -ɔt] *nmf Fam* drunk(ard).

poker [pɔkɛr] *nm Cartes* poker.

polar [pɔlar] *nm* (*roman*) *Fam* whodunit.

polariser [pɔlarize] *vt* to polarize.

pôle [pol] *nm Géog* pole; **p. Nord/Sud** North/South Pole. **◆polaire** a polar.

polémique [pɔlemik] a controversial, polemical; – *nf* controversy, polemic.

poli [pɔli] **1** a (*courtois*) polite (**avec** to, with). **2** a (*lisse, brillant*) polished; – *nm* (*aspect*) polish. **◆—ment** *adv* politely.

police [pɔlis] *nf* **1** police; **faire** *ou* **assurer la**

p. to maintain order (dans in); **p. secours** emergency services; **p. mondaine** *ou* **des mœurs** = vice squad. **2** p. (**d'assurance**) (insurance) policy. ◆**policier** *a* (*enquête, état*) police-; **roman p.** detective novel; – *nm* policeman, detective.

polichinelle [pɔliʃinɛl] *nf* secret de p. open secret.

polio [pɔljo] *nf* (*maladie*) polio; – *nmf* (*personne*) polio victim. ◆**poliomyélite** [-ɔmjelit] *nf* poliomyelitis.

polir [pɔlir] *vt* (*substance dure, style*) to polish.

polisson, -onne [pɔlisɔ̃, -ɔn] *a* naughty; – *nmf* rascal.

politesse [pɔlites] *nf* politeness; **une p.** (*parole*) a polite word; (*action*) an act of politeness.

politique [pɔlitik] *a* political; **homme p.** politician; – *nf* (*science, activité*) politics; (*mesures, manières de gouverner*) Pol policies; **une p.** (*tactique*) a policy. ◆**politicien, -ienne** *nmf* *Péj* politician. ◆**politiser** *vt* to politicize.

pollen [pɔlɛn] *nm* pollen.

polluer [pɔlɥe] *vt* to pollute. ◆**polluant** *nm* pollutant. ◆**pollution** *nf* pollution.

polo [pɔlo] *nm* **1** (*chemise*) sweat shirt. **2** *Sp* polo.

polochon [pɔlɔʃɔ̃] *nm* (*traversin*) *Fam* bolster.

Pologne [pɔlɔɲ] *nf* Poland. ◆**polonais, -aise** *a* Polish; – *nmf* Pole; – *nm* (*langue*) Polish.

poltron, -onne [pɔltrɔ̃, -ɔn] *a* cowardly; – *nmf* coward.

polycopi/er [pɔlikɔpje] *vt* to mimeograph, duplicate. ◆**-é** *nm* *Univ* mimeographed copy (*of lecture etc*).

polyester [pɔliɛstɛr] *nm* polyester.

Polynésie [pɔlinezi] *nf* Polynesia.

polyvalent [pɔlivalɑ̃] *a* (*rôle*) multi-purpose, varied; (*professeur, ouvrier*) all-round; **école polyvalente, lycée p.** comprehensive school.

pommade [pɔmad] *nf* ointment.

pomme [pɔm] *nf* **1** apple; **p. d'Adam** *Anat* Adam's apple. **2** (*d'arrosoir*) rose. **3 p. de terre** potato; **pommes vapeur** steamed potatoes; **pommes frites** chips, *Am* French fries; **pommes chips** potato crisps *ou* *Am* chips. ◆**pommier** *nm* apple tree.

pommette [pɔmɛt] *nf* cheekbone.

pompe [pɔ̃p] **1** *nf* pump; **p. à essence** petrol *ou* *Am* gas station; **p. à incendie** fire engine; **coup de p.** *Fam* tired feeling. **2** *nf* (*chaussure*) *Fam* shoe. **3** *nf* (*en gymnastique*)

press-up, *Am* push-up. **4** *nfpl* **pompes funèbres** undertaker's; **entrepreneur des pompes funèbres** undertaker. **5** *nf* **p. anti-sèche** *Scol* crib. **6** *nf* (*splendeur*) pomp. ◆**pomper** *vt* to pump; (*évacuer*) to pump out (**de** of); (*absorber*) to soak up; (*épuiser*) *Fam* to tire out; – *vi* to pump. ◆**pompeux, -euse** *a* pompous. ◆**pompier 1** *nm* fireman; **voiture des pompiers** fire engine. **2** *a* (*emphatique*) pompous. ◆**pompiste** *nmf* *Aut* pump attendant.

pompon [pɔ̃pɔ̃] *nm* (*ornement*) pompon. ◆**pomponner** *vt* to doll up.

ponce [pɔ̃s] *nf* (**pierre**) **p.** pumice (stone). ◆**poncer** *vt* to rub down, sand. ◆**ponceuse** *nf* (*machine*) sander.

ponctuation [pɔ̃ktɥasjɔ̃] *nf* punctuation. ◆**ponctuer** *vt* to punctuate (**de** with).

ponctuel, -elle [pɔ̃ktɥɛl] *a* (*à l'heure*) punctual; (*unique*) *Fig* one-off, *Am* one-of-a-kind. ◆**ponctualité** *nf* punctuality.

pondéré [pɔ̃dere] *a* level-headed. ◆**pondération** *nf* level-headedness.

pondre [pɔ̃dr] *vt* (*œuf*) to lay; (*livre, discours*) *Péj Fam* to produce; – *vi* (*poule*) to lay.

poney [pɔnɛ] *nm* pony.

pont [pɔ̃] *nm* bridge; (*de bateau*) deck; **p.** (**de graissage**) *Aut* ramp; **faire le p.** *Fig* to take the intervening day's *ou* days off (*between two holidays*); **p. aérien** airlift. ◆**p.-levis** *nm* (*pl* **ponts-levis**) drawbridge.

ponte [pɔ̃t] **1** *nf* (*d'œufs*) laying. **2** *nm* (*personne*) *Fam* bigwig.

pontife [pɔ̃tif] *nm* **1** (*souverain*) **p.** pope. **2** (*ponte*) *Fam* bigshot. ◆**pontifical, -aux** *a* papal, pontifical.

pop [pɔp] *nm* & *a inv* *Mus* pop.

popote [pɔpɔt] *nf* (*cuisine*) *Fam* cooking.

populace [pɔpylas] *nf* *Péj* rabble.

populaire [pɔpylɛr] *a* (*personne, tradition, gouvernement etc*) popular; (*quartier, milieu*) lower-class; (*expression*) colloquial; (*art*) folk-. ◆**populariser** *vt* to popularize. ◆**popularité** *nf* popularity (**auprès de** with).

population [pɔpylasjɔ̃] *nf* population. ◆**populeux, -euse** *a* populous, crowded.

porc [pɔr] *nm* pig; (*viande*) pork; (*personne*) *Péj* swine.

porcelaine [pɔrsəlɛn] *nf* china, porcelain.

porc-épic [pɔrkepik] *nm* (*pl* **porcs-épics**) (*animal*) porcupine.

porche [pɔrʃ] *nm* porch.

porcherie [pɔrʃəri] *nf* pigsty.

pore [pɔr] *nm* pore. ◆**poreux, -euse** *a* porous.

pornographie [pɔrnɔgrafi] *nf* pornography. ◆**pornographique** *a* (*Fam* **porno**) pornographic.

port [pɔr] *nm* **1** port, harbour; **arriver à bon p.** to arrive safely. **2** (*d'armes*) carrying; (*de barbe*) wearing; (*prix*) carriage, postage; (*attitude*) bearing.

portable [pɔrtabl] *a* (*robe etc*) wearable; (*portatif*) portable.

portail [pɔrtaj] *nm* (*de cathédrale etc*) portal.

portant [pɔrtɑ̃] *a* **bien p.** in good health.

portatif, -ive [pɔrtatif, -iv] *a* portable.

porte [pɔrt] *nf* door, (*passage*) doorway; (*de jardin*) gate. (*passage*) gateway; (*de ville*) entrance, *Hist* gate; **p. (d'embarquement)** *Av* (departure) gate; **Alger, p. de . . .** Algiers, gateway to . . . ; **p. d'entrée** front door; **mettre à la p.** (*jeter dehors*) to throw out; (*employé*) to sack. ◆**p.-fenêtre** *nf* (*pl* **portes-fenêtres**) French window.

porte-à-faux [pɔrtafo] *nm inv* **en p.-à-faux** (*en déséquilibre*) unstable.

porte-avions [pɔrtavjɔ̃] *nm inv* aircraft carrier. ◆**p.-bagages** *nm inv* luggage rack. ◆**p.-bébé** *nm* (*nacelle*) carrycot, *Am* baby basket; (*kangourou®*) baby sling. ◆**p.-bonheur** *nm inv* (*fétiche*) (lucky) charm. ◆**p.-cartes** *nm inv* card holder ou case. ◆**p.-clés** *nm inv* key ring. ◆**p.-documents** *nm inv* briefcase. ◆**p.-drapeau, -x** *nm Mil* standard bearer. ◆**p.-jarretelles** *nm inv* suspender ou *Am* garter belt. ◆**p.-monnaie** *nm inv* purse. ◆**p.-parapluie** *nm inv* umbrella stand. ◆**p.-plume** *nm inv* pen (*for dipping in ink*). ◆**p.-revues** *nm inv* newspaper rack. ◆**p.-savon** *nm* soapdish. ◆**p.-serviettes** *nm inv* towel rail. ◆**p.-voix** *nm inv* megaphone.

portée [pɔrte] *nf* **1** (*de fusil etc*) range; **à la p. de qn** within reach of s.o.; (*richesse, plaisir etc*) *Fig* within s.o.'s grasp; **à p. de la main** within (easy) reach; **à p. de voix** within earshot; **hors de p.** out of reach. **2** (*animaux*) litter. **3** (*importance, effet*) significance, import. **4** *Mus* stave.

portefeuille [pɔrtəfœj] *nm* wallet; *Pol Com* portfolio.

portemanteau, -x [pɔrtmɑ̃to] *nm* (*sur pied*) hatstand; (*barre*) hat ou coat peg.

porte-parole [pɔrtparɔl] *nm inv* (*homme*) spokesman; (*femme*) spokeswoman (**de** for, of).

port/er [pɔrte] *vt* to carry; (*vêtement, lunettes, barbe etc*) to wear; (*trace, responsabilité, fruits etc*) to bear; (*regard*) to cast; (*attaque*) to make (**contre** against); (*coup*) to strike; (*sentiment*) to have (**à** for); (*inscrire*) to enter, write down; **p.** (*amener*) to bring ou take sth to; **p. qn à faire** (*pousser*) to lead ou prompt s.o. to do; **p. bonheur/malheur** to bring good/bad luck; **se faire p. malade** to report sick; – *vi* (*voix*) to carry; (*canon*) to fire; (*vue*) to extend; **p. (juste)** (*coup*) to hit the mark; (*mot, reproche*) to hit home; **p. sur** (*reposer sur*) to rest on; (*concerner*) to bear on; (*accent*) to fall on; (*heurter*) to strike; – **se p.** *vpr* (*vêtement*) to be worn; **se p. bien/mal** to be well/ill; **comment te portes-tu?** how are you?; **se p. candidat** to stand as a candidate. ◆**-ant** *a* **bien p.** in good health. ◆**-é** *a* **p. à croire/etc** inclined to believe/etc; **p. sur qch** fond of sth. ◆**-eur, -euse** *nm Rail* porter; – *nmf Méd* carrier; (*de nouvelles, chèque*) bearer; **mère porteuse** surrogate mother.

portier [pɔrtje] *nm* doorkeeper, porter. ◆**portière** *nf* (*de véhicule, train*) door. ◆**portillon** *nm* gate.

portion [pɔrsjɔ̃] *nf* (*part, partie*) portion; (*de nourriture*) helping, portion.

portique [pɔrtik] *nm* **1** *Archit* portico. **2** (*de balançoire etc*) crossbar, frame.

porto [pɔrto] *nm* (*vin*) port.

portrait [pɔrtrɛ] *nm* portrait; **être le p. de** (*son père etc*) to be the image of; **faire un p.** to paint ou draw a portrait of (**de** of); **p. en pied** full-length portrait. ◆**p.-robot** *nm* (*pl* **portraits-robots**) identikit (picture), photofit.

portuaire [pɔrtɥer] *a* (*installations etc*) harbour-.

Portugal [pɔrtygal] *nm* Portugal. ◆**portugais, -aise** *a* & *nmf* Portuguese; – *nm* (*langue*) Portuguese.

pose [poz] *nf* **1** (*installation*) putting up; putting in; laying. **2** (*attitude de modèle, affectation*) pose; (*temps*) *Phot* exposure. ◆**pos/er** *vt* to put (down); (*papier peint, rideaux*) to put up; (*sonnette, chauffage*) to put in; (*mine, moquette, fondations*) to lay; (*question*) to ask (**à qn** s.o.); (*principe, conditions*) to lay down; **p. sa candidature** to apply, put in one's application (**à** for); **ça pose la question de . . .** it poses the question of . . . ; – *vi* (*modèle etc*) to pose (**pour** for); – **se p.** *vpr* (*oiseau, avion*) to land; (*problème, question*) to arise; **se p.** (*yeux*) to fix on; **se p. en chef/etc** to set oneself up as ou pose as a leader/etc; **la question se pose!** this question should be asked! ◆**-é** *a* (*calme*) calm, staid.

◆—ément adv calmly. **◆—eur, -euse** nmf Péj poseur.

positif, -ive [pozitif, -iv] a positive. **◆positivement** adv positively.

position [pozisjɔ̃] nf (attitude, emplacement, opinion etc) position; **prendre p.** Fig to take a stand (**contre** against); **prise de p.** stand.

posologie [pozɔlɔʒi] nf (de médicament) dosage.

posséder [posede] vt to possess; (maison etc) to own, possess; (bien connaître) to master. **◆possesseur** nm possessor; owner. **◆possessif, -ive** a (personne, adjectif etc) possessive; – nm Gram possessive. **◆possession** nf possession; **en p.** in possession of; **prendre p. de** to take possession of.

possible [posibl] a possible (**à faire** to do); **il (nous) est p. de le faire** it is possible (for us) to do it; **il est p. que** (+ sub) it is possible that; **le plus tôt** etc **p.** as soon/etc as possible; **autant que p.** as much ou as many as possible; **– nm faire son p.** to do one's utmost (**pour faire** to do); **dans la mesure du p.** as far as possible. **◆possibilité** nf possibility.

post- [post] préf post-.

postdater [postdate] vt to postdate.

poste [post] **1** nf (service) post, mail; (local) post office; **bureau de p.** post office; **Postes (et Télécommunications)** (administration) Post Office; **par la p.** by post, by mail; **p. aérienne** airmail; **mettre à la p.** to post, mail. **2** nm (lieu, emploi) post; **p. de secours** first aid post; **p. de police** police station; **p. d'essence** petrol ou Am gas station; **p. d'incendie** fire hydrant; **p. d'aiguillage** signal box ou Am tower. **3** nm (appareil) Rad TV set; Tél extension (number). **◆postal, -aux** a postal; **boîte postale** PO Box; **code p.** postcode, Am zip code. **◆poster 1** vt à qn (placer) Mil to post s.o. **2** vt (lettre) to post, mail. **3** [poster] nm poster.

postérieur [posterjœr] **1** a (document etc) later; **p. à** after. **2** nm (derrière) Fam posterior.

postérité [posterite] nf posterity.

posthume [postym] a posthumous; **à titre p.** posthumously.

postiche [postiʃ] a (barbe etc) false.

postier, -ière [postje, -jɛr] nmf postal worker.

postillonner [postijɔne] vi to sputter.

post-scriptum [postskriptɔm] nm inv postscript.

postul/er [postyle] vt **1** (emploi) to apply

for. **2** (poser) Math to postulate. **◆—ant, -ante** nmf applicant.

posture [postyr] nf posture.

pot [po] nm **1** pot; (à confiture) jar, pot; (à lait) jug; (à bière) mug; (de crème, yaourt) carton; **p. de chambre** chamber pot; **p. de fleurs** flower pot; **prendre un p.** (verre) Fam to have a drink. **2** (chance) Fam luck; **avoir du p.** to be lucky.

potable [potabl] a drinkable; (passable) Fam tolerable; **'eau p.'** 'drinking water'.

potage [potaʒ] nm soup.

potager, -ère [potaʒe, -ɛr] a (jardin) vegetable-; **plante potagère** vegetable; – nm vegetable garden.

potasser [potase] vt (examen) to cram for; – vi to cram.

pot-au-feu [potofø] nm inv (plat) beef stew.

pot-de-vin [podvɛ̃] nm (pl pots-de-vin) bribe.

pote [pot] nm (ami) Fam pal, buddy.

poteau, -x [poto] nm pole; (télégraphique) pole; **p. d'arrivée** Sp winning post.

potelé [potle] a plump, chubby.

potence [potɑ̃s] nf (gibet) gallows.

potentiel, -ielle [potɑ̃sjɛl] a & nm potential.

poterie [potri] nf (art) pottery; **une p.** a piece of pottery; **des poteries** (objets) pottery. **◆potier** nm potter.

potin [potɛ̃] **1** nmpl (cancans) gossip. **2** nm (bruit) Fam row.

potion [posjɔ̃] nf potion.

potiron [potirɔ̃] nm pumpkin.

pot-pourri [popuri] nm (pl pots-pourris) Mus medley.

pou, -x [pu] nm louse; **poux** lice.

poubelle [pubɛl] nf dustbin, Am garbage can.

pouce [pus] nm **1** thumb; **un coup de p.** Fam a helping hand. **2** (mesure) Hist & Fig inch.

poudre [pudr] nf powder; **p. (à canon)** (explosif) gunpowder; **en p.** (lait) powdered; (chocolat) drinking; **sucre en p.** castor ou caster sugar. **◆poudrer** vt to powder; – **se p.** vpr (femme) to powder one's nose. **◆poudreux, -euse** a powdery, dusty. **◆poudrier** nm (powder) compact. **◆poudrière** nf (powder) magazine; (région) Fig powder keg.

pouf [puf] **1** int thump! **2** nm (siège) pouf(fe).

pouffer [pufe] vi **p. (de rire)** to burst out laughing, guffaw.

pouilleux, -euse [pujø, -øz] a (sordide) miserable; (mendiant) lousy.

poulain [pulɛ̃] nm (cheval) foal; **le p. de qn** Fig s.o.'s protégé.

poule [pul] *nf* **1** hen, *Culin* fowl; **être p. mouillée** (*lâche*) to be chicken; **oui, ma p.!** *Fam* yes, my pet! **2** (*femme*) *Péj* tart. ◆**poulailler** *nm* **1** (hen) coop. **2 le p.** *Th Fam* the gods, the gallery. ◆**poulet** *nm* **1** (*poule, coq*) *Culin* chicken. **2** (*policier*) *Fam* cop.

pouliche [puliʃ] *nf* (*jument*) filly.

poulie [puli] *nf* pulley.

poulpe [pulp] *nm* octopus.

pouls [pu] *nm Méd* pulse.

poumon [pumɔ̃] *nm* lung; **à pleins poumons** (*respirer*) deeply; (*crier*) loudly; **p. d'acier** iron lung.

poupe [pup] *nf Nau* stern, poop.

poupée [pupe] *nf* doll.

poupin [pupɛ̃] *a* **visage p.** baby face.

poupon [pupɔ̃] *nm* (*bébé*) baby; (*poupée*) doll.

pour [pur] **1** *prép* for; **p. toi/moi/**etc for you/me/*etc*; **faites-le p. lui** do it for him, do it for his sake; **partir p.** (*Paris etc*) to leave for; **elle va partir p. cinq ans** she's leaving for five years; **p. femme/base/**etc as a wife/basis/*etc*; **p. moi, p. ma part** (*quant à moi*) as for me; **dix p. cent** ten per cent; **gentil p.** kind to; **elle est p.** she's in favour; **p. faire** (in order) to do, so as to do; **p. que tu saches** so (that) you may know; **p. quoi faire?** what for?; **trop petit/poli/**etc **p. faire** too small/polite/*etc* to do; **assez grand/**etc **p. faire** big enough to do; **p. cela** for that reason; **jour p. jour/heure p. heure** to the day/hour; **p. intelligent/**etc **qu'il soit** however clever/*etc* he may be; **ce n'est pas p. me plaire** it doesn't exactly please me; **acheter p. cinq francs de bonbons** to buy five francs' worth of sweets. **2** *nm* **le p. et le contre** the pros and cons.

pourboire [purbwar] *nm* (*argent*) tip.

pourcentage [pursɑ̃taʒ] *nm* percentage.

pourchasser [purʃase] *vt* to pursue.

pourparlers [purparle] *nmpl* negotiations, talks.

pourpre [purpr] *a & nm* purple.

pourquoi [purkwa] *adv & conj* why; **p. pas?** why not?; **—** *nm inv* reason (**de** for); **le p. et le comment** the whys and wherefores.

pourra, pourrait [pura, purɛ] *voir* **pouvoir** 1.

pourrir [purir] *vi*, **— se p.** *vpr* to rot; **—** *vt* to rot; **p. qn** to corrupt s.o. ◆**pourri** *a* (*fruit, temps, personne etc*) rotten. ◆**pourriture** *nf* rot, rottenness; (*personne*) *Péj* swine.

poursuite [pursɥit] **1** *nf* chase, pursuit; (*du bonheur, de créancier*) pursuit (**de** of); (*continuation*) continuation; **se mettre à la p. de** to go in pursuit of. **2** *nfpl Jur* legal proceed-

ings (**contre** against). ◆**poursuiv/re***¹* **1** *vt* (*courir après*) to chase, pursue; (*harceler, relancer*) to hound, pursue; (*obséder*) to haunt; (*but, idéal etc*) to pursue. **2** *vt* **p. qn** *Jur* (*au criminel*) to prosecute s.o.; (*au civil*) to sue s.o. **3** *vt* (*lecture, voyage etc*) to continue (with), carry on (with), pursue; **— vi, — se p.** *vpr* to continue, go on. ◆**—ant, -ante** *nmf* pursuer.

pourtant [purtɑ̃] *adv* yet, nevertheless.

pourtour [purtur] *nm* perimeter.

pourvoir* [purvwar] *vt* to provide (**de** with); **être pourvu de** to have, be provided with; **— vi p. à** (*besoins etc*) to provide for. ◆**pourvoyeur, -euse** *nmf* supplier.

pourvu que [purvykə] *conj* (*condition*) provided *ou* providing (that); **p. qu'elle soit là** (*souhait*) I only hope (that) she's there.

pousse [pus] *nf* **1** (*bourgeon*) shoot, sprout. **2** (*croissance*) growth.

pousse-café [puskafe] *nm inv* after-dinner liqueur.

pouss/er [puse] **1** *vt* to push; (*du coude*) to nudge, poke; (*véhicule, machine*) to drive hard; (*recherches*) to pursue; (*cri*) to utter; (*soupir*) to heave; **p. qn à faire** to urge s.o. to do; **p. qn à bout** to push s.o. to his limits; **p. trop loin** (*gentillesse etc*) to carry too far; **p. à la perfection** to bring to perfection; **— vi** to push; **p. jusqu'à Paris/**etc to push on as far as Paris/*etc*; **— se p.** *vpr* (*se déplacer*) to move up *ou* over. **2** *vi* (*croître*) to grow; **faire p.** (*plante, barbe etc*) to grow. ◆**—é** *a* (*travail, études*) advanced. ◆**—ée** *nf* (*pression*) pressure; (*coup*) push; (*d'ennemi*) thrust, push; (*de fièvre etc*) outbreak; (*de l'inflation*) upsurge. ◆**poussette** *nf* pushchair, *Am* stroller; **p. canne** (baby) buggy, *Am* (collapsible) stroller; **p. de marché** shopping trolley *ou Am* cart. ◆**poussoir** *nm* (push) button.

poussière [pusjɛr] *nf* dust; **dix francs et des poussières** *Fam* a bit over ten francs. ◆**poussiéreux, -euse** *a* dusty.

poussif, -ive [pusif, -iv] *a* short-winded, puffing.

poussin [pusɛ̃] *nm* (*poulet*) chick.

poutre [putr] *nf* (*en bois*) beam; (*en acier*) girder. ◆**poutrelle** *nf* girder.

pouvoir* [puvwar] **1** *v aux* (*capacité*) to be able, can; (*permission, éventualité*) may, can; **je peux deviner** I can guess, I'm able to guess; **tu peux entrer** you may *ou* can come in; **il peut être malade** he may *ou* might be ill; **elle pourrait/**etc **venir** she might/could come; **j'ai pu l'obtenir** I managed to get it; **j'aurais pu l'obtenir** I could have got it *ou Am* gotten it; **je n'en peux plus** I'm utterly exhausted; – *v imp* **il peut neiger** it may snow; **– se p.** *vpr* **il se peut qu'elle parte** (it's possible that) she might leave. **2** *nm* (*capacité, autorité*) power; (*procuration*) power of attorney; **les pouvoirs publics** the authorities; **au p.** Pol in power; **en son p.** in one's power (**de faire** to do).

poux [pu] *voir* pou.

pragmatique [pragmatik] *a* pragmatic.

prairie [prɛr] *nf* (*mollusque*) clam.

prairie [preri] *nf* meadow.

praline [pralin] *nf* sugared almond. ◆**praliné** *a* (*glace*) praline-flavoured.

praticable [pratikabl] *a* (*projet, chemin*) practicable.

praticien, -ienne [pratisjɛ̃, -jɛn] *nmf* practitioner.

pratique [pratik] **1** *a* (*connaissance, personne, instrument etc*) practical. **2** *nf* (*exercice, procédé*) practice; (*expérience*) practical experience; **la p. de la natation/du golf/etc** swimming/golfing/etc; **mettre en p.** to put into practice; **en p.** (*en réalité*) in practice. ◆**pratiqu/er** *vt* (*art etc*) to practise; (*football*) to play, practise; (*trou, route*) to make; (*opération*) to carry out; **p. la natation** to go swimming; – *vi* to practise. ◆**–ant, -ante** *a Rel* practising; – *nmf* churchgoer.

pratiquement [pratikmã] *adv* (*presque*) practically; (*en réalité*) in practice.

pré [pre] *nm* meadow.

pré- [pre] *préf* pre-.

préalable [prealabl] *a* previous, preliminary; **p. à** prior to; – *nm* precondition, prerequisite; **au p.** beforehand. ◆**–ment** [-əmã] *adv* beforehand.

préambule [preãbyl] *nm* (*de loi*) preamble; Fig prelude (**à** to).

préau, -x [preo] *nm* Scol covered playground.

préavis [preavi] *nm* (*de congé etc*) (advance) notice (**de** of).

précaire [preker] *a* precarious.

précaution [prekosjã] *nf* (*mesure*) precaution; (*prudence*) caution; **par p.** as a precaution. ◆**précautionneux, -euse** *a* cautious.

précédent, -ente [presedã, -ãt] **1** *a* previous, preceding, earlier; – *nmf* previous one. **2** *nm* (*fait, exemple*) a precedent; **sans p.** unprecedented. ◆**précédemment** [-amã] *adv* previously. ◆**précéder** *vti* to precede; **faire p. qch de qch** to precede sth by sth.

précepte [presept] *nm* precept.

précepteur, -trice [preseptœr, -tris] *nmf* (private) tutor.

prêcher [prefe] *vti* to preach; **p. qn** Rel & Fig to preach to s.o.

précieux, -euse [presjø, -øz] *a* precious.

précipice [presipis] *nm* abyss, chasm.

précipit/er [presipite] *vt* (*jeter*) to throw, hurl; (*plonger*) to plunge (**dans** into); (*hâter*) to hasten; **– se p.** *vpr* (*se jeter*) to throw ou hurl oneself; (*foncer*) to rush (**à, sur** on to); (*s'accélérer*) to speed up. ◆**–é** *a* hasty. ◆**précipitamment** *adv* hastily. ◆**précipitation 1** *nf* haste. **2** *nfpl* (*pluie*) precipitation.

précis [presi] **1** *a* precise; (*idée, mécanisme*) accurate, precise; **à deux heures précises** at two o'clock sharp ou precisely. **2** *nm* (*résumé*) summary; (*manuel*) handbook. ◆**précisément** *adv* precisely. ◆**préciser** *vt* to specify (**que** that); **– se p.** *vpr* to become clear(er). ◆**précision** *nf* precision; accuracy; (*détail*) detail; (*explication*) explanation.

précoce [prekɔs] *a* (*fruit, mariage, mort etc*) early; (*personne*) precocious. ◆**précocité** *nf* precociousness; earliness.

préconçu [prekɔ̃sy] *a* preconceived.

préconiser [prekɔnize] *vt* to advocate (**que** that).

précurseur [prekyrsœr] *nm* forerunner, precursor; – *a* **un signe p. de qch** a sign heralding sth.

prédécesseur [predesesœr] *nm* predecessor.

prédestiné [predestine] *a* fated, predestined (**à faire** to do).

prédicateur [predikatœr] *nm* preacher.

prédilection [predileksjã] *nf* (special) liking; **de p.** favourite.

prédire* [predir] *vt* to predict (**que** that). ◆**prédiction** *nf* prediction.

prédisposer [predispoze] *vt* to predispose (**à qch** to sth, **à faire** to do). ◆**prédisposition** *nf* predisposition.

prédominer [predomine] *vi* to predominate. ◆**–ant** *a* predominant. ◆**prédominance** *nf* predominance.

préfabriqué [prefabrike] *a* prefabricated.

préface [prefas] *nf* preface. ◆**préfacer** *vt* to preface.

préfér/er [prefere] *vt* to prefer (**à** to); **p. faire** to prefer to do. ◆**–é, -ée** *a* & *nmf* favourite. ◆**–able** *a* preferable (**à** to). ◆**préférence** *nf* preference; **de p.** preferably; **de p. à** in preference to. ◆**préférentiel, -ielle** *a* preferential.

préfet [prefɛ] nm prefect, *chief administrator in a department*; **p. de police** prefect of police, *Paris chief of police.* ◆**préfecture** nf prefecture; **p. de police** Paris police headquarters.

préfixe [prefiks] nm prefix.

préhistoire [preistwar] nf prehistory. ◆**préhistorique** a prehistoric.

préjudice [preʒydis] nm Jur prejudice, harm; **porter p. à** to prejudice, harm. ◆**préjudiciable** a prejudicial (à to).

préjugé [preʒyʒe] nm (parti pris) prejudice; **avoir un p.** ou **des préjugés** to be prejudiced (**contre** against).

prélasser (se) [səprelase] vpr to loll (about), lounge (about).

prélat [prela] nm Rel prelate.

prélever [prelve] vt (échantillon) to take (**sur** from); (somme) to deduct (**sur** from). ◆**prélèvement** nm taking; deduction; **p. de sang** blood sample; **p. automatique** Fin standing order.

préliminaire [preliminer] a preliminary; – nmpl preliminaries.

prélude [prelyd] nm prelude (à to).

prématuré [prematyre] a premature; – nm (bébé) premature baby. ◆—ment adv prematurely, too soon.

préméditer [premedite] vt to premeditate. ◆**préméditation** nf Jur premeditation.

premier, -ière [prəmje, -jɛr] a first; (enfance) early; (page) Journ front, first; (qualité, nécessité, importance) prime; (état) original; (notion, cause) basic; (danseuse, rôle) leading; (inférieur) bottom; (supérieur) top; **nombre p.** Math prime number; **le p. rang** the front ou first row; **à la première occasion** at the earliest opportunity; **P. ministre** Prime Minister, Premier; – nmf first (one); **arriver le p.** ou **en p.** to arrive first; **être le p. de la classe** to be (at the) top of the class; – nm (date) first; (étage) first ou Am second floor; **le p. de l'an** New Year's Day; – nf Th Cin première; Rail first class; Scol = sixth form, Am = twelfth grade; Aut first (gear); (événement historique) first. ◆**premier-né** nm, ◆**première-née** nf first-born (child). ◆**premièrement** adv firstly.

prémisse [premis] nf premiss.

prémonition [premɔnisjɔ̃] nf premonition.

prémunir [premynir] vt to safeguard (**contre** against).

prénatal, mpl -als [prenatal] a antenatal, Am prenatal.

prendre* [prɑ̃dr] vt to take (**à qn** from s.o.); (attraper) to catch, get; (voyager par) to take, travel by; (acheter) to get; (douche, bain) to take, have; (repas) to have; (nouvelles) to take; (temps, heure) to take (up); (pensionnaire) to take (in); (ton, air) to put on; (engager) to take on; (s.o.) (on); (chercher) to pick up, get; **p. qn pour** (un autre) to (mis)take s.o. for; (considérer) to take s.o. for; **p. qn** (doute etc) to seize s.o.; **p. feu** to catch fire; **p. de la place** to take up room; **p. du poids/de la vitesse** to put on weight/speed; **à tout p.** on the whole; **qu'est-ce qui te prend?** what's got ou Am gotten into you?; – vi (feu) to catch; (gelée, ciment) to set; (greffe, vaccin) to take; (mode) to catch on; – **se p.** vpr (objet) to be taken; (s'accrocher) to get caught; (eau) to freeze; **se p. pour un génie/etc** to think one is a genius/etc; **s'y p.** to go ou set about it; **s'en p. à** (critiquer, attaquer) to attack; (accuser) to blame; **se p. à faire** to begin to do. ◆**prenant** a (travail, film etc) engrossing; (voix) engaging. ◆**preneur, -euse** nmf taker, buyer.

prénom [prenɔ̃] nm first name. ◆**prénommer** vt to name; **il se prénomme Louis** his first name is Louis.

préoccuper [preɔkype] vt (inquiéter) to worry; (absorber) to preoccupy; **se p. de** to be worried about; to be preoccupied about. ◆—ant a worrying. ◆—é a worried. ◆**préoccupation** nf worry; (idée, problème) preoccupation.

préparer [prepare] vt to prepare; (repas etc) to get ready, prepare; (examen) to study for, prepare (for); **p. qch à qn** to prepare sth for s.o.; **p. qn à** (examen) to prepare ou coach s.o. for; – **se p.** vpr to get (oneself) ready, prepare oneself (à **qch** for sth); (orage) to brew, threaten. ◆**préparatifs** nmpl preparations (**de** for). ◆**préparation** nf preparation. ◆**préparatoire** a preparatory.

prépondérant [prepɔ̃derɑ̃] a dominant. ◆**prépondérance** nf dominance.

préposer [prepoze] vt **p. qn à** to put s.o. in charge of. ◆—é, -ée nmf employee; (facteur) postman, postwoman.

préposition [prepozisjɔ̃] nf preposition.

préretraite [prerətrɛt] nf early retirement.

prérogative [prerɔgativ] nf prerogative.

près [prɛ] adv **p. de** (qn/qch) near (to), close to; **p. de deux ans/etc** (presque) nearly two years/etc; **p. de partir/etc** about to leave/etc; **tout p.** nearby (**de qn/qch** s.o./sth), close by (**de qn/qch** s.o./sth); **de p.** (lire, examiner, suivre) closely; **à peu de chose p.** almost; **à cela p.** except for that; **voici le**

chiffre à un franc p. here is the figure give or take a franc; **calculer au franc p.** to calculate to the nearest franc.

présage [prezaʒ] *nm* omen, foreboding. ◆**présager** *vt* to forebode.

presbyte [prɛsbit] *a* & *nmf* long-sighted (person). ◆**presbytie** [-bisi] *nf* long-sightedness.

presbytère [prɛsbitɛr] *nm* Rel presbytery.

préscolaire [preskɔlɛr] *a* (âge etc) pre-school.

prescrire* [prɛskrir] *vt* to prescribe. ◆**prescription** *nf* (instruction) & Jur prescription.

préséance [preseɑ̃s] *nf* precedence (**sur** over).

présent¹ [prezɑ̃] **1** *a* (non absent) present; **les personnes présentes** those present. **2** *a* (actuel) present; – *nm* (temps) present; Gram present (tense); **à p.** now, at present; **dès à p.** from now on. ◆**présence** *nf* presence; (à l'école, au bureau etc) attendance (à at); **feuille de p.** attendance sheet; **faire acte de p.** to put in an appearance; **en p.** (personnes) face to face; **en p. de** in the presence of; **p. d'esprit** presence of mind.

présent² [prezɑ̃] *nm* (cadeau) present.

présent/er [prezɑ̃te] *vt* (offrir, exposer, animer etc) to present; (montrer) to show, present; **p. qn à qn** to introduce *ou* present s.o. to; **– se p.** *vpr* to introduce *ou* present oneself (à to); (chez qn) to show up; (occasion etc) to arise; **se p. à** (examen) to sit for; (élections) to stand in *ou* at, run in (emploi) to apply for; (autorités) to report to; **ça se présente bien** it looks promising. ◆**–able** *a* presentable. ◆**présentateur, -trice** *nmf* TV announcer, presenter. ◆**présentation** *nf* presentation; introduction. ◆**présentoir** *nm* (étagère) (display) stand.

préserver [prezɛrve] *vt* to protect, preserve (**de** from). ◆**préservatif** *nm* sheath, condom. ◆**préservation** *nf* protection, preservation.

présidence [prezidɑ̃s] *nf* (de nation) presidency; (de firme etc) chairmanship. ◆**président, -ente** *nmf* (de nation) president; (de réunion, firme) chairman, chairwoman; **p. directeur général** chairman and managing director, Am chief executive officer. ◆**présidentiel, -ielle** *a* presidential.

présider [prezide] *vt* (réunion) to preside at *ou* over, chair; – *vi* to preside. ◆**présomption** [prezɔ̃psjɔ̃] *nf* (conjecture, suffisance) presumption.

présomptueux, -euse [prezɔ̃ptɥø, -øz] *a* presumptuous.

presque [prɛsk(ə)] *adv* almost, nearly; **p. jamais/rien** hardly ever/anything.

presqu'île [prɛskil] *nf* peninsula.

presse [prɛs] *nf* (journaux, appareil) press; Typ (printing) press; **de p.** (conférence, agence) press-.

presse-citron [prɛssitrɔ̃] *nm inv* lemon squeezer. ◆**p.-papiers** *nm inv* paperweight. ◆**p.-purée** *nm inv* (potato) masher.

pressentir* [prɛsɑ̃tir] *vt* (deviner) to sense (que that). ◆**pressentiment** *nm* foreboding, presentiment.

press/er [prese] *vt* (serrer) to press, press; (bouton) to press; (fruit) to squeeze; (départ etc) to hasten; **p. qn** to hurry s.o. (**de faire** to do); (assaillir) to harass s.o. (**de questions** with questions); **p. le pas** to speed up; – *vi* (temps) to be pressing *ou* urgent; **rien ne presse** there's no hurry; **– se p.** *vpr* (se grouper) to crowd, swarm; (se serrer) to squeeze (together); (se hâter) to hurry; **presse-toi** (**de partir**) hurry up (**and go**). ◆**–ant** *a* pressing, urgent. ◆**–é** *a* (personne) in a hurry; (air) hurried; (travail) pressing, urgent. ◆**pressing** [-iŋ] *nm* (magasin) dry cleaner's. ◆**pressoir** *nm* (wine) press.

pression [presjɔ̃] *nf* pressure; **faire p. sur qn** to put pressure on s.o., pressurize s.o.; **bière (à la) p.** draught beer; – *nm* (bouton-)**p.** press-stud, Am snap.

pressuriser [presyrize] *vt* Av to pressurize.

prestance [prestɑ̃s] *nf* (imposing) presence.

prestation [prestasjɔ̃] *nf* **1** (allocation) allowance, benefit. **2** (performance) performance.

prestidigitateur, -trice [prestidiʒitatœr, -tris] *nmf* conjurer. ◆**prestidigitation** *nf* conjuring.

prestige [prestiʒ] *nm* prestige. ◆**prestigieux, -euse** *a* prestigious.

presto [prɛsto] *adv* Fam *voir* illico.

présumer [prezyme] *vt* to presume (**que** that).

présupposer [presypoze] *vt* to presuppose (**que** that).

prêt¹ [prɛ] *a* (préparé, disposé) ready (**à faire** to do, **à qch** for sth). ◆**p.-à-porter** [prɛtaporte] *nm inv* ready-to-wear clothes.

prêt² [prɛ] *nm* (emprunt) loan. ◆**p.-logement** *nm* (pl prêts-logement) mortgage.

prétend/re [pretɑ̃dr] *vt* to claim (**que** that); (vouloir) to intend (**faire** to do); **p.**

être/savoir to claim to be/to know; **elle se prétend riche** she claims to be rich; – *vi* **p. à** (*titre etc*) to lay claim to. ◆**—ant** *nm* (*amoureux*) suitor. ◆**—u** a so-called. ◆**—ument** *adv* supposedly.

prétentieux, -euse [pretɑ̃sjø, -øz] *a* & *nmf* pretentious (person). ◆**prétention** *nf* (*vanité*) pretension; (*revendication, ambition*) claim.

prêt/er [prete] *vt* (*argent, objet*) to lend (à to); (*aide, concours*) to give (à to); (*attribuer*) to attribute (à to); **p. attention** to pay attention (à to); **p. serment** to take an oath; – *vi* **p. à** (*phrase etc*) to lend itself to; **se p. à** (*consentir à*) to agree to; (*sujet etc*) to lend itself to. ◆**—eur, -euse** *nmf* (*d'argent*) lender; **p. sur gages** pawnbroker.

prétexte [pretɛkst] *nm* pretext, excuse; **sous p. de/que** on the pretext of/that. ◆**prétexter** *vt* to plead (that).

prêtre [prɛtr] *nm* priest; **grand p.** high priest.

preuve [prœv] *nf* proof, evidence; **faire p. de** to show; **faire ses preuves** (*personne*) to prove oneself; (*méthode*) to prove itself.

prévaloir [prevalwar] *vi* to prevail (**contre** against, **sur** over).

prévenant [prevnɑ̃] *a* considerate. ◆**prévenance(s)** *nf* (*pl*) (*gentillesse*) consideration.

préven/ir* [prevnir] *vt* **1** (*avertir*) to warn (que that); (*aviser*) to inform (que that). **2** (*désir, question*) to anticipate; (*malheur*) to avert. ◆**—u, -ue 1** *nmf* Jur defendant, accused. **2** *a* prejudiced (**contre** against). ◆**préventif, -ive** *a* preventive. ◆**prévention** *nf* **1** prevention; **p. routière** road safety. **2** (*opinion*) prejudice.

prévoir* [prevwar] *vt* (*anticiper*) to foresee (que that); (*prédire*) forecast (que that); (*temps*) Mét to forecast; (*projeter, organiser*) to plan (for); (*réserver, préparer*) to allow, provide. ◆**—u** *a* (*conditions*) laid down; **un repas est p.** a meal is provided; **au moment p.** at the appointed time; **comme p.** as planned, as expected; **p. pour** (*véhicule, appareil etc*) designed for. ◆**prévisible** *a* foreseeable. ◆**prévision** *nf* (*opinion*) & Mét forecast; **en p. de** in expectation of.

prévoyant [prevwajɑ̃] *a* (*personne*) provident. ◆**prévoyance** *nf* foresight; **société de p.** provident society.

prier [prije] **1** *vi* Rel to pray; – *vt* **p. Dieu pour qu'il nous accorde qch** to pray (to God) for sth. **2** *vt* **p. qn de faire** to ask ou request s.o. to do; (*implorer*) to beg s.o. to do; **je vous en prie** (*faites donc, allez-y*)

please; (*en réponse à 'merci'*) don't mention it; **je vous prie** please; **se faire p.** to wait to be asked. ◆**prière** *nf* Rel prayer; (*demande*) request; **p. de répondre**/*etc* please answer/*etc*.

primaire [primɛr] *a* primary.

prime [prim] **1** *nf* (*d'employé*) bonus; (*d'État*) subsidy; (*cadeau*) Com free gift; **p. (d'assurance)** (insurance) premium. **2** *a* **de p. abord** at the very first glance.

primé [prime] *a* (*animal*) prize-winning.

primer [prime] *vi* to excel, prevail; – *vt* to prevail over.

primeurs [primœr] *nfpl* early fruit and vegetables.

primevère [primvɛr] *nf* (*à fleurs jaunes*) primrose.

primitif, -ive [primitif, -iv] *a* (*art, société etc*) primitive; (*état, sens*) original; – *nm* (*artiste*) primitive. ◆**primitivement** *adv* originally.

primo [primo] *adv* first(ly).

primordial, -aux [primɔrdjal, -o] *a* vital (**de faire** to do).

prince [prɛ̃s] *nm* prince. ◆**princesse** *nf* princess. ◆**princier, -ière** *a* princely. ◆**principauté** *nf* principality.

principal, -aux [prɛ̃sipal, -o] *a* main, chief, principal; – *nm* (*de collège*) Scol principal; **le p.** (*essentiel*) the main ou chief thing. ◆**—ement** *adv* mainly.

principe [prɛ̃sip] *nm* principle; **par p.** on principle; **en p.** theoretically, in principle; (*normalement*) as a rule.

printemps [prɛ̃tɑ̃] *nm* (*saison*) spring. ◆**printanier, -ière** *a* (*temps etc*) spring-, spring-like.

priorité [priorite] *nf* priority; **la p.** Aut the right of way; **la p. à droite** Aut right of way to traffic coming from the right; **'cédez la p.'** Aut 'give way', Am 'yield'; **en p.** as a matter of priority. ◆**prioritaire** *a* (*industrie etc*) priority-; **être p.** to have priority; Aut to have the right of way.

pris [pri] *voir* **prendre**; – *a* (*place*) taken; (*crème, ciment*) set; (*eau*) frozen; (*gorge*) infected; (*nez*) congested; **être (très) p.** (*occupé*) to be (very) busy; **p. de** (*peur, panique*) stricken with.

prise [priz] *voir* **prendre**; – *nf* taking; (*manière d'empoigner*) grip, hold; (*de ville*) capture, taking; (*objet saisi*) catch; (*de tabac*) pinch; **p. (de courant)** *Él* (*mâle*) plug; (*femelle*) socket; **p. multiple** *Él* adaptor; **p. d'air** air vent; **p. de conscience** awareness; **p. de contact** first meeting; **p. de position** Fig stand; **p. de sang** blood test; **p.**

de son (sound) recording; **p. de vue(s)** *Cin Phot* (action) shooting; (résultat) shot; **aux prises avec** at grips with.

priser [prize] **1** vt tabac à p. snuff; – vi to take snuff. **2** vt (estimer) to prize.

prisme [prism] nm prism.

prison [prizɔ̃] nf prison, jail, gaol; (réclusion) imprisonment; **mettre en p.** to imprison, put in prison. **◆prisonnier, -ière** nmf prisoner; **faire qn p.** to take s.o. prisoner.

privé [prive] a private; **en p.** (seul à seul) in private; – nm **dans le p.** in private life; *Com Fam* in the private sector.

priver [prive] vt to deprive (**de** of); **se p. de** to deprive oneself of, do without. **◆privation** nf deprivation (**de** of); pl (sacrifices) hardships.

privilège [privilɛʒ] nm privilege. **◆privilégié, -ée** a & nmf privileged (person).

prix [pri] nm **1** (d'un objet, du succès etc) price; **à tout p.** at all costs; **à aucun p.** on no account; **hors (de) p.** exorbitant; **attacher du p. à** to attach importance to; **menu à p. fixe** set price menu. **2** (récompense) prize.

pro- [pro] préf pro-.

probable [prɔbabl] a probable, likely; **peu p.** unlikely. **◆probabilité** nf probability, likelihood; **selon toute p.** in all probability. **◆probablement** adv probably.

probant [prɔbɑ̃] a conclusive.

probité [prɔbite] nf (honnêteté) integrity.

problème [prɔblɛm] nm problem. **◆problématique** a doubtful, problematic.

procéd/er [prɔsede] vi (agir) to proceed; (se conduire) to behave; **p. à** (enquête etc) to carry out. **◆‒é** nm process; (conduite) behaviour. **◆procédure** nf procedure; *Jur* proceedings.

procès [prɔsɛ] nm (criminel) trial; (civil) lawsuit; **faire un p. à** to take to court.

processeur [prɔsesœr] nm (d'ordinateur) processor.

procession [prɔsesjɔ̃] nf procession.

processus [prɔsesys] nm process.

procès-verbal, -aux [prɔsɛvɛrbal, -o] nm (de réunion) minutes; (constat) *Jur* report; (contravention) fine, ticket.

prochain, -aine [prɔʃɛ̃, -ɛn] **1** a next; (avenir) near; (parent) close; (mort, arrivée) impending; (mariage) forthcoming; **un jour p.** one day soon; – nf **à la prochaine!** *Fam* see you soon!; **à la prochaine (station)** at the next stop. **2** nm (semblable) fellow (man). **◆prochainement** adv shortly, soon.

proche [prɔʃ] a (espace) near, close; (temps) close (at hand); (parent, ami) close; (avenir) near; **p. de** near (to), close to; **une maison/etc** p. a house/etc nearby ou close by; – nmpl close relations.

proclamer [prɔklame] vt to proclaim, declare (**que** that); **p. roi** to proclaim king. **◆proclamation** nf proclamation, declaration.

procréer [prɔkree] vt to procreate. **◆procréation** nf procreation.

procuration [prɔkyrasjɔ̃] nf power of attorney; **par p.** (voter) by proxy.

procurer [prɔkyre] vt **p. qch à qn** (personne) to obtain sth for s.o.; (occasion etc) to afford s.o. sth; **se p. qch** to obtain sth.

procureur [prɔkyrœr] nm = *Br* public prosecutor; = *Am* district attorney.

prodige [prɔdiʒ] nm (miracle) wonder; (personne) prodigy. **◆prodigieux, -euse** a prodigious, extraordinary.

prodigue [prɔdig] a (dépenser) wasteful, prodigal. **◆prodiguer** vt to lavish (**à qn** s.o.).

production [prɔdyksjɔ̃] nf production; (de la terre) yield. **◆producteur, -trice** nmf *Com Cin* producer; – a producing; **pays p. de pétrole** oil-producing country. **◆productif, -ive** a (terre, réunion etc) productive. **◆productivité** nf productivity.

produire* [prɔdɥir] **1** vt (fabriquer, présenter etc) to produce; (causer) to bring about, produce. **2 se p.** vpr (événement etc) to happen, occur. **◆produit** nm (article etc) product; (pour la vaisselle) liquid; (d'une vente, d'une collecte) proceeds; pl (de la terre) produce; **p. (chimique)** chemical; **p. de beauté** cosmetic.

proéminent [prɔeminɑ̃] a prominent.

prof [prɔf] nm *Fam* = **professeur**.

profane [prɔfan] **1** nmf lay person. **2** a (art etc) secular.

profaner [prɔfane] vt to profane, desecrate. **◆profanation** nf profanation, desecration.

proférer [prɔfere] vt to utter.

professer [prɔfese] vt to profess (**que** that).

professeur [prɔfesœr] nm teacher; *Univ* lecturer, *Am* professor; (titulaire d'une chaire) *Univ* professor.

profession [prɔfesjɔ̃] nf **1** occupation, vocation; (libérale) profession; (manuelle) trade; **de p.** (chanteur etc) professional, by profession. **2 p. de foi** *Fig* declaration of principles. **◆professionnel, -elle** a professional; (école) vocational, trade-; – nmf (non amateur) professional.

profil [prɔfil] nm (de personne, objet) profile;

de p. in profile. ◆**profiler** vt to outline, profile; — se p. vpr to be outlined ou profiled (sur against).

profit [prɔfi] nm profit; (avantage) advantage, profit; **vendre à p.** to sell at a profit; **tirer p. de** to benefit by, profit by; **au p. de** for the benefit of. ◆**profitable** a profitable (à to). ◆**profiter** vi p. **de** to take advantage of; **p. à qn** to profit s.o.; **p. (bien)** (enfant) Fam to thrive. ◆**profiteur, -euse** nmf Péj profiteer.

profond [prɔfɔ̃] a deep; (esprit, joie, erreur etc) profound, great; (cause) underlying; **p. de deux mètres** two metres deep; — adv (pénétrer etc) deep; — nm **au plus p. de** in the depths of. ◆**profondément** adv deeply; (dormir) soundly; (triste, souhaiter) profoundly; (extrêmement) thoroughly. ◆**profondeur** nf depth; profoundness; (de of) depths; **en p.** (étudier etc) in depth; **à six mètres de p.** at a depth of six metres.

profusion [prɔfyzjɔ̃] nf profusion; **à p.** in profusion.

progéniture [prɔʒenityr] nf Hum offspring.

progiciel [prɔʒisjɛl] nm (pour ordinateur) (software) package.

programme [prɔgram] nm programme, Am program; (d'une matière) Scol syllabus; (d'ordinateur) program; **p. (d'études)** (d'une école) curriculum. ◆**programmation** nf programming. ◆**programmer** vt Cin Rad TV to programme, Am program; (ordinateur) to program. ◆**programmeur, -euse** nmf (computer) programmer.

progrès [prɔgrɛ] nm & nmpl progress; **faire des p.** to make (good) progress. ◆**progresser** vi to progress. ◆**progressif, -ive** a progressive. ◆**progression** nf progression. ◆**progressiste** a & nmf Pol progressive. ◆**progressivement** adv progressively, gradually.

prohiber [prɔibe] vt to prohibit, forbid. ◆**prohibitif, -ive** a prohibitive. ◆**prohibition** nf prohibition.

proie [prwa] nf prey; **être en p. à** to be (a) prey to, be tortured by.

projecteur [prɔʒɛktœr] nm (de monument) floodlight; (de prison) & Mil searchlight; Th spot(light); Cin projector.

projectile [prɔʒɛktil] nm missile.

projet [prɔʒɛ] nm plan; (ébauche) draft; (entreprise, étude) project.

projeter [prɔʒte] vt **1** (lancer) to hurl, project. **2** (film, ombre) to project; (lumière) to flash. **3** (voyage, fête etc) to plan; **p. de faire** to plan to do. ◆**projection** nf (lancement)

hurling, projection; (de film, d'ombre) projection; (séance) showing.

prolétaire [prɔleter] nmf proletarian. ◆**prolétariat** nm proletariat. ◆**prolétarien, -ienne** a proletarian.

proliférer [prɔlifere] vi to proliferate. ◆**prolifération** nf proliferation.

prolifique [prɔlifik] a prolific.

prolixe [prɔliks] a verbose, wordy.

prologue [prɔlɔg] nm prologue (de, à to).

prolonger [prɔlɔ̃ʒe] vt to prolong, extend; — se p. vpr (séance, rue, effet) to continue. ◆**prolongateur** nm (rallonge) El extension cord. ◆**prolongation** nf extension; pl Fb extra time. ◆**prolongement** nm extension.

promenade [prɔmnad] nf (à pied) walk; (en voiture) ride, drive; (en vélo, à cheval) ride; (action) Sp walking; (lieu) walk, promenade; **faire une p.** = se promener. ◆**promener** vt to take for a walk ou ride; (visiteur) to take ou show around; **p. qch sur qch** (main, regard) to run sth over sth; **envoyer p.** Fam to send packing; — se p. vpr (à pied) to (go for a) walk; (en voiture) to (go for a) ride ou drive. ◆**promeneur, -euse** nmf walker, stroller.

promesse [prɔmɛs] nf promise. ◆**promett/re** vt to promise (qch à qn s.o. sth); **p. de faire** to promise to do; **c'est promis** it's a promise; — vi **p. (beaucoup)** Fig to be promising; **se p. qch** to promise oneself sth; **se p. de faire** to resolve to do. ◆**—eur, -euse** a promising.

promontoire [prɔmɔ̃twar] nm Géog headland.

promoteur [prɔmɔtœr] nm (immobilier) property developer.

promotion [prɔmosjɔ̃] nf **1** promotion; **en p.** Com on (special) offer. **2** (candidats) Univ year. ◆**promouvoir**[*] vt (personne, produit etc) to promote; **être promu** (employé) to be promoted (à to).

prompt [prɔ̃] a swift, prompt, quick. ◆**promptitude** nf swiftness, promptness.

promulguer [prɔmylge] vt to promulgate.

prôner [prone] vt (vanter) to extol; (préconiser) to advocate.

pronom [prɔnɔ̃] nm Gram pronoun. ◆**pronominal, -aux** a pronominal.

prononc/er [prɔnɔ̃se] vt (articuler) to pronounce; (dire) to utter; (discours) to deliver; (jugement) Jur to pronounce, pass; — vi Jur Ling to pronounce; — se p. vpr (mot) to be pronounced; (personne) to reach a decision (sur about, on); **se p. pour** to come out in favour of. ◆**—é a** (visible) pronounced, marked. ◆**prononciation** nf pronunciation.

pronostic [prɔnɔstik] nm (prévision) & Sp forecast. ◆**pronostiquer** vt to forecast.

propagande [prɔpagɑ̃d] nf propaganda. ◆**propagandiste** nmf propagandist.

propager [prɔpaʒe] vt, — **se p.** vpr to spread. ◆**propagation** nf spread(ing).

propension [prɔpɑ̃sjɔ̃] nf propensity (à qch for sth, à faire to do).

prophète [prɔfɛt] nm prophet. ◆**prophétie** [-fesi] nf prophecy. ◆**prophétique** a prophetic. ◆**prophétiser** vti to prophesy.

propice [prɔpis] a favourable à.

proportion [prɔpɔrsjɔ̃] nf proportion; Math ratio; **en p. de** in proportion to; **hors de p.** out of proportion (**avec** to). ◆**proportionnel, -elle** a proportional (à to). ◆**proportionn/er** vt to proportion (à to); **—é** a proportionate (à to); **bien p.** well ou nicely proportioned.

propos [prɔpo] **1** nmpl (paroles) remarks, utterances. **2** nm (intention) purpose. **3** nm (sujet) subject; **à p. de** about; **à p. de rien** for no reason; **à tout p.** for no reason, at every turn. **4** adv **à p.** (arriver etc) at the right time; **à p.!** by the way!; **juger à p. de faire** to consider it fit to do.

proposer [prɔpoze] vt (suggérer) to suggest, propose (**qch à qn** sth to s.o., **que** (+ sub) that); (offrir) to offer (**qch à qn** s.o. sth, **de faire** to do); (candidat) to put forward, propose; **je te propose de rester** I suggest (that) you stay; **se p. pour faire** to offer to do; **se p. faire** to propose ou mean to do. ◆**proposition** nf suggestion, proposal; (de paix) proposal, (affirmation) proposition; Gram clause.

propre[1] [prɔpr] a clean; (soigné) neat; (honnête) decent; — nm **mettre qch au p.** to make a fair copy of sth. ◆**proprement**[1] adv (avec propreté) cleanly; (avec netteté) neatly; (comme il faut) decently. ◆**propreté** nf cleanliness; (netteté) neatness.

propre[2] [prɔpr] **1** a (à soi) own; **mon p. argent** my own money; **ses propres mots** his very ou his own words. **2** a (qui convient) right, proper; **p. à** (attribut, caractère etc) peculiar to; (approprié) well-suited to; **p. à faire** likely to do; **sens p.** literal meaning; **nom p.** proper noun; — nm **le p. de** (qualité) the distinctive quality of; **au p.** (au sens propre) literally. ◆**proprement**[2] adv (strictement) strictly; **à p. parler** strictly speaking; **le village/etc p. dit** the village/etc proper ou itself.

propriété [prɔprijete] nf **1** (bien) property;

(droit) ownership, property. **2** (qualité) property. **3** (de mot) suitability. ◆**propriétaire** nmf owner; (d'hôtel) proprietor, owner; (qui loue) landlord, landlady; **p. foncier** landowner.

propulser [prɔpylse] vt (faire avancer, projeter) to propel. ◆**propulsion** nf propulsion.

prosaïque [prɔzaik] a prosaic, pedestrian.

proscrire* [prɔskrir] vt to proscribe, banish. ◆**proscrit, -ite** nmf (personne) exile. ◆**proscription** nf banishment.

prose [proz] nf prose.

prospecter [prɔspɛkte] vt (sol) to prospect; (pétrole) to prospect for; (région) Com to canvass. ◆**prospecteur, -trice** nmf prospector. ◆**prospection** nf prospecting; Com canvassing.

prospectus [prɔspɛktys] nm leaflet, prospectus.

prospère [prɔspɛr] a (florissant) thriving, prosperous; (riche) prosperous. ◆**prospérer** vi to thrive, flourish, prosper. ◆**prospérité** nf prosperity.

prostate [prɔstat] nf Anat prostate (gland).

prosterner (se) [səprɔstɛrne] vpr to prostrate oneself (**devant** before). ◆**—é** a prostrate. ◆**—ement** nm prostration.

prostituer [prɔstitɥe] vt to prostitute; — **se p.** vpr to prostitute oneself. ◆**prostituée** nf prostitute. ◆**prostitution** nf prostitution.

prostré [prɔstre] a (accablé) prostrate. ◆**prostration** nf prostration.

protagoniste [prɔtagɔnist] nmf protagonist.

protecteur, -trice [prɔtɛktœr, -tris] nmf protector; (mécène) patron; — a (geste etc) & Écon protective; (ton, air) Péj patronizing. ◆**protection** nf protection; (mécénat) patronage; **de p.** (écran etc) protective. ◆**protectionnisme** nm Écon protectionism.

protég/er [prɔteʒe] vt to protect (**de** from, **contre** against); (appuyer) Fig to patronize; — **se p.** vpr to protect oneself. ◆**—é** nm protégé. ◆**—ée** nf protégée. ◆**protège-cahier** nm exercise book cover.

protéine [prɔtein] nf protein.

protestant, -ante [prɔtɛstɑ̃, -ɑ̃t] a & nmf Protestant. ◆**protestantisme** nm Protestantism.

protester [prɔtɛste] vi to protest (**contre** against); **p. de** (son innocence etc) to protest; — vt to protest (**que** that). ◆**protestation** nf protest (**contre** against); pl (d'amitié) protestations (**de** of).

prothèse [prɔtɛz] *nf* **(appareil de)** p. *(membre)* artificial limb; *(dents)* false teeth.

protocole [prɔtɔkɔl] *nm* protocol.

prototype [prɔtɔtip] *nm* prototype.

protubérance [prɔtyberɑ̃s] *nf* protuberance. ◆**protubérant** *a (yeux)* bulging; *(menton)* protruding.

proue [pru] *nf Nau* prow, bow(s).

prouesse [prues] *nf* feat, exploit.

prouver [pruve] *vt* to prove *(que* that).

Provence [prɔvɑ̃s] *nf* Provence. ◆**provençal, -ale, -aux** *a & nm* Provençal.

provenir* [prɔvnir] *vi* p. de to come from. ◆**provenance** *nf* origin; **en p. de** from.

proverbe [prɔvɛrb] *nm* proverb. ◆**proverbial, -aux** *a* proverbial.

providence [prɔvidɑ̃s] *nf* providence. ◆**providentiel, -ielle** *a* providential.

province [prɔvɛ̃s] *nf* province; la p. the provinces; **en p.** in the provinces; **de p.** *(ville etc)* provincial. ◆**provincial, -ale, -aux** *a & nmf* provincial.

proviseur [prɔvizœr] *nm (de lycée)* headmaster.

provision [prɔvizjɔ̃] *nf* 1 *(réserve)* supply, stock; *pl (achats)* shopping; *(vivres)* provisions: **panier/sac à provisions** shopping basket/bag. 2 *(acompte)* advance payment; **chèque sans p.** dud cheque.

provisoire [prɔvizwar] *a* temporary, provisional. ◆**—ment** *adv* temporarily, provisionally.

provoquer [prɔvɔke] *vt* 1 *(causer)* to bring about, provoke; *(désir)* to arouse. 2 *(défier)* to provoke *(s.o.)*. ◆**provocant** *a* provocative. ◆**provocateur** *nm* troublemaker. ◆**provocation** *nf* provocation.

proxénète [prɔksenɛt] *nm* pimp.

proximité [prɔksimite] *nf* closeness, proximity; **à p.** close by; **à p. de** close to.

prude [pryd] *a* prudish; – *nf* prude.

prudent [prydɑ̃] *a (circonspect)* cautious, careful; *(sage)* sensible. ◆**prudemment** [-amɑ̃] *adv* cautiously, carefully; *(sagement)* sensibly. ◆**prudence** *nf* caution, care, prudence; *(sagesse)* wisdom; **par p.** as a precaution.

prune [pryn] *nf (fruit)* plum. ◆**pruneau, -x** *nm* prune. ◆**prunelle** *nf* 1 *(fruit)* sloe. 2 *(de l'œil)* pupil. ◆**prunier** *nm* plum tree.

P.-S. [pees] *abrév (post-scriptum)* PS.

psaume [psom] *nm* psalm.

pseudo- [psødo] *préf* pseudo-.

pseudonyme [psødɔnim] *nm* pseudonym.

psychanalyse [psikanaliz] *nf* psychoanalysis. ◆**psychanalyste** *nmf* psychoanalyst.

psychiatre [psikjatr] *nmf* psychiatrist. ◆**psychiatrie** *nf* psychiatry. ◆**psychiatrique** *a* psychiatric.

psychique [psiʃik] *a* mental, psychic.

psycho [psiko] *préf* psycho-.

psychologie [psikɔlɔʒi] *nf* psychology. ◆**psychologique** *a* psychological. ◆**psychologue** *nmf* psychologist.

psychose [psikoz] *nf* psychosis.

PTT [petete] *nfpl (Postes, Télégraphes, Téléphones)* Post Office, = GPO.

pu [py] *voir* **pouvoir 1**.

puant [pɥɑ̃] *a* stinking. ◆**puanteur** *nf* stink, stench.

pub [pyb] *nf Fam (réclame)* advertising; *(annonce)* ad.

puberté [pybɛrte] *nf* puberty.

public, -ique [pyblik] *a* public; **dette publique** national debt; – *nm* public; *(de spectacle)* audience; **le grand p.** the general public; **en p.** in public. ◆**publiquement** *adv* publicly.

publication [pyblikasjɔ̃] *nf (action, livre etc)* publication. ◆**publier** *vt* to publish.

publicité [pyblisite] *nf* publicity *(pour* for); *(réclame)* advertising, publicity; *(annonce)* advertisement; *Rad TV* commercial. ◆**publicitaire** *a (agence, film)* publicity-, advertising-.

puce [pys] *nf* 1 flea; **le marché aux puces, les puces** the flea market. 2 *(d'un ordinateur)* chip, microchip.

puceron [pysrɔ̃] *nm* greenfly.

pudeur [pydœr] *nf (sense of)* modesty; **attentat à la p.** *Jur* indecency. ◆**pudibond** *a* prudish. ◆**pudique** *a* modest.

puer [pɥe] *vi* to stink; – *vt* to stink of.

puériculture [pɥerikyltyr] *nf* infant care, child care. ◆**puéricultrice** *nf* children's nurse.

puéril [pɥeril] *a* puerile. ◆**puérilité** *nf* puerility.

puis [pɥi] *adv* then; **et p. quoi?** and so what?

puiser [pɥize] *vt* to draw, take *(dans* from); – *vi* p. dans to dip into.

puisque [pɥisk(ə)] *conj* since, as.

puissant [pɥisɑ̃] *a* powerful. ◆**puissamment** *adv* powerfully. ◆**puissance** *nf (force, nation)* & *Math Tech* power; **en p.** *(talent, danger etc)* potential.

puits [pɥi] *nm* well; *(de mine)* shaft.

pull-(over) [pyl(ɔvɛr)] *nm* pullover, sweater.

pulluler [pylyle] *vi* Péj to swarm.

pulmonaire [pylmɔnɛr] *a (congestion, maladie)* of the lungs, lung-.

pulpe [pylp] *nf* (*de fruits*) pulp.

pulsation [pylsɑsjɔ̃] *nf* (heart)beat.

pulvériser [pylverize] *vt* (*broyer*) & *Fig* to pulverize; (*liquide*) to spray. ◆**pulvérisateur** *nm* spray, atomizer. ◆**pulvérisation** *nf* (*de liquide*) spraying.

punaise [pynεz] *nf* **1** (*insecte*) bug. **2** (*clou*) drawing pin, *Am* thumbtack. ◆**punaiser** *vt* (*fixer*) to pin (up).

punch 1 [pɔ̃ʃ] *nm* **1** (*boisson*) punch. **2** [pœnʃ] (*énergie*) punch.

punir [pynir] *vt* to punish. ◆**punissable** *a* punishable (**de** by). ◆**punition** *nf* punishment.

pupille [pypij] **1** *nf* (*de l'œil*) pupil. **2** *nmf* (*enfant sous tutelle*) ward.

pupitre [pypitr] *nm* (*d'écolier*) desk; (*d'orateur*) lectern; **p. à musique** music stand.

pur [pyr] *a* pure; (*alcool*) neat, straight. ◆**purement** *adv* purely. ◆**pureté** *nf* purity.

purée [pyre] *nf* purée; **p. (de pommes de terre)** mashed potatoes, mash.

purgatoire [pyrgatwar] *nm* purgatory.

purge [pyrʒ] *nf Pol Méd* purge.

purger [pyrʒe] *vt* **1** (*conduite*) *Tech* to drain, clear. **2** (*peine*) *Jur* to serve.

purifier [pyrifje] *vt* to purify. ◆**purification** *nf* purification.

purin [pyrɛ̃] *nm* liquid manure.

puriste [pyrist] *nmf Gram* purist.

puritain, -aine [pyritɛ̃, -ɛn] *a* & *nmf* puritan.

pur-sang [pyrsɑ̃] *nm inv* (*cheval*) thoroughbred.

pus 1 [py] *nm* (*liquide*) pus, matter.

pus 2, put [py] *voir* **pouvoir 1**.

putain [pytɛ̃] *nf Péj Fam* whore.

putois [pytwa] *nm* (*animal*) polecat.

putréfier [pytrefje] *vt*, — **se p.** *vpr* to putrefy. ◆**putréfaction** *nf* putrefaction.

puzzle [pœzl] *nm* (jigsaw) puzzle, jigsaw.

p.-v. [peve] *nm inv* (*procès-verbal*) (traffic) fine.

PVC [pevese] *nm* (*plastique*) PVC.

pygmée [pigme] *nm* pygmy.

pyjama [piʒama] *nm* pyjamas, *Am* pajamas; **un p.** a pair of pyjamas *ou Am* pajamas; **de p.** (*veste, pantalon*) pyjama-, *Am* pajama-.

pylône [pilon] *nm* pylon.

pyramide [piramid] *nf* pyramid.

Pyrénées [pirene] *nfpl* **les P.** the Pyrenees.

pyromane [pirɔman] *nmf* arsonist, firebug.

python [pitɔ̃] *nm* (*serpent*) python.

Q

Q, q [ky] *nm* Q, q.

QI [kyi] *nm inv abrév* (*quotient intellectuel*) IQ.

qu' [k] *voir* **que**.

quadrill/er [kadrije] *vt* (*troupes, police*) to be positioned throughout, comb, cover (*town etc*). ◆**—é** *a* (*papier*) squared. ◆**—age** *nm* (*lignes*) squares.

quadrupède [k(w)adryped] *nm* quadruped.

quadruple [k(w)adrypl] *a* **q. de** fourfold; — *nm* **le q.** four times as much as. ◆**quadrupl/er** *vti* to quadruple. ◆**—és, -ées** *nmfpl* quadruplets, quads.

quai [ke] *nm Nau* quay; (*pour marchandises*) wharf; (*de fleuve*) embankment, bank; *Rail* platform.

qualification [kalifikɑsjɔ̃] *nf* **1** description. **2** (*action*) *Sp* qualifying, qualification. ◆**qualificatif** *nm* (*mot*) term. ◆**qualifi/er 1** *vt* (*décrire*) to describe (**de** as); **se faire q. de menteur**/*etc* to be called a liar/*etc*. **2** *vt* (*rendre apte*) & *Sp* to qualify

(**pour qch** for sth, **pour faire** to do); — **se q.** *vpr Sp* to qualify (**pour** for). **3** *vt Gram* to qualify. ◆**—é** *a* qualified (**pour faire** to do); (*ouvrier, main-d'œuvre*) skilled.

qualité [kalite] *nf* quality; (*condition sociale etc*) occupation, status; **produit**/*etc* **de q.** high-quality product/*etc*; **en sa q. de** in one's capacity as. ◆**qualitatif, -ive** *a* qualitative.

quand [kɑ̃] *conj* & *adv* when; **q. je viendrai** when I come; **c'est pour q.?** (*réunion, mariage*) when is it?; **q. bien même vous le feriez** even if you did it; **q. même** all the same.

quant (à) [kɑ̃ta] *prép* as for.

quantité [kɑ̃tite] *nf* quantity; **une q., des quantités** (*beaucoup*) a lot (**de** of); **en q.** (*abondamment*) in plenty. ◆**quantifier** *vt* to quantify. ◆**quantitatif, -ive** *a* quantitative.

quarante [karɑ̃t] *a* & *nm* forty. ◆**quarantaine** *nf* **1 une q. (de)** (*nombre*) (about) forty; **avoir la q.** (*âge*) to be about forty. **2** *Méd* quarantine; **mettre en q.** *Méd* to quarantine; *Fig* to send to Coventry, *Am* give the silent treatment to. ◆**quarantième** *a & nmf* fortieth.

quart [kar] *nm* **1** quarter; **q. (de litre)** quarter litre, quarter of a litre; **q. d'heure** quarter of an hour; **un mauvais q. d'heure** *Fig* a trying time; **une heure et q.** an hour and a quarter; **il est une heure et q.** it's a quarter past *ou Am* after one; **une heure moins le q.** a quarter to one. **2** *Nau* watch; **de q.** on watch.

quartette [kwartɛt] *nm* (jazz) quartet(te).

quartier [kartje] **1** *nm* neighbourhood, district; (*chinois etc*) quarter; **de q.** (*cinéma etc*) local; **les gens du q.** the local people. **2** *nm* (*de pomme, lune*) quarter; (*d'orange*) segment. **3** *nm* (*pl*) **quartier(s)** *Mil* quarters; **q. général** headquarters.

quartz [kwarts] *nm* quartz; **montre**/*etc* **à q.** quartz watch/*etc*.

quasi [kazi] *adv* almost. ◆**quasi-** *préf* near; **q.-obscurité** near darkness. ◆**quasiment** *adv* almost.

quatorze [katɔrz] *a & nm* fourteen. ◆**quatorzième** *a & nmf* fourteenth.

quatre [katr] *a & nm* four; **se mettre en q.** to go out of one's way (**pour faire** to do); **son q. heures** (*goûter*) one's afternoon snack; **un de ces q.** *Fam* some day soon. ◆**quatrième** *a & nmf* fourth. ◆**quatrièmement** *adv* fourthly.

quatre-vingt(s) [katrəvɛ̃] *a & nm* eighty; **q.-vingts ans** eighty years; **q.-vingt-un** eighty-one. ◆**q.-vingt-dix** *a & nm* ninety.

quatuor [kwatɥɔr] *nm* *Mus* quartet(te).

que [k(ə)] (**qu'** *before a vowel or mute h*) **1** *conj* that; **je pense qu'elle restera** I think (that) she'll stay; **qu'elle vienne ou non** whether she comes or not; **qu'il s'en aille!** let him leave!; **ça fait un an q. je suis là** I've been here for a year; **ça fait un an q. je suis parti** I left a year ago. **2** (*ne*) . . . **q.** only; **tu n'as qu'un franc** you only have one franc. **3** (*comparaison*) than; (*avec aussi, même, tel, autant*) as; **plus/moins âgé q. lui** older/younger than him; **aussi sage/**etc **q.** as wise/*etc* as; **le même q.** the same as. **4** *adv* (*ce*) **qu'il est bête!** (*comme*) how silly he is!; **q. de gens!** (*combien*) what a lot of people! **5** *pron rel* (*chose*) that, which; (*personne*) that, whom; (*temps*) when; **le livre q. j'ai** the book (that *ou* which) I have; **l'ami q. j'ai** the friend (that *ou* whom) I have; **un jour/mois/**etc **q.** one day/month/*etc* when. **6** *pron interrogatif* what; **q. fait-il?**,

qu'est-ce qu'il fait? what is he doing?; **qu'est-ce qui est dans ta poche?** what's in your pocket?; **q. préférez-vous?** which do you prefer?

Québec [kebɛk] *nm* **le Q.** Quebec.

quel, quelle [kɛl] **1** *a interrogatif* what, which; (*qui*) who; **q. livre/acteur?** what *ou* which book/actor?; **q. livre/acteur préférez-vous?** which *ou* what book/actor do you prefer?; **q. est cet homme?** who is that man?; **je sais q. est ton but** I know what your aim is; (*personne*) whoever it *ou* he may be; – *pron interrogatif* which (one); **q. est le meilleur?** which (one) is the best? **2** *a exclamatif* **q. idiot!** what a fool!; **q. joli bébé!** what a pretty baby!

quelconque [kɛlkɔ̃k] *a* **1** any, some (or other); **une raison q.** any reason (whatever *ou* at all), some reason (or other). **2** (*banal*) ordinary.

quelque [kɛlk(ə)] **1** *a* some; **q. jour** some day; **quelques femmes** a few women, some women; **les quelques amies qu'elle a** the few friends she has. **2** *adv* (*environ*) about, some; **et q.** *Fam* and a bit; **q. grand qu'il soit** however tall he may be; **q. numéro qu'elle choisisse** whichever number she chooses; **q. peu** somewhat. **3** *pron* **q. chose** something; (*interrogation*) anything, something; **il y a q. chose** *Fig* there's something the matter with him; **q. chose d'autre** something else; **q. chose de grand/**etc something big/*etc*. **4** *adv* **q. part** somewhere; (*interrogation*) anywhere, somewhere.

quelquefois [kɛlkəfwa] *adv* sometimes.

quelques-uns, -unes [kɛlkəzœ̃, -yn] *pron* some.

quelqu'un [kɛlkœ̃] *pron* someone, somebody; (*interrogation*) anyone, anybody; someone, somebody; **q. d'intelligent/**etc someone clever/*etc*.

quémander [kemɑ̃de] *vt* to beg for.

qu'en-dira-t-on [kɑ̃diratɔ̃] *nm inv* (*propos*) gossip.

quenelle [kənɛl] *nf Culin* quenelle, fish *ou* meat roll.

querelle [kərɛl] *nf* quarrel, dispute. ◆**se quereller** *vpr* to quarrel. ◆**querelleur, -euse** *a* quarrelsome.

question [kɛstjɔ̃] *nf* question; (*affaire, problème*) matter, issue, question; **il est q. de** it's a question *ou* question of (**faire** doing); (*on projette de*) there's some question of (**faire** doing); **il n'en est pas q.** there's no question of it, it's out of the question; **en q.** in question; **hors de q.** out of the question;

(re)mettre en q. to (call in) question.
◆questionner *vt* to question (sur about).
quête [kɛt] *nf* 1 (collecte) collection. 2 (recherche) quest (de for); en q. de in quest *ou* search of. ◆quêter *vt* to seek, beg for; − *vi* to collect money.
queue [kø] *nf* 1 (d'animal) tail; (de fleur) stalk, stem; (de fruit) stalk; (de poêle) handle; (de comète) trail; (de robe) train; (de cortège, train) rear; q. de cheval (coiffure) ponytail; faire une q. de poisson *Aut* to cut in (à qn in front of s.o.); à la q. (de classe) at the bottom of; à la q. leu leu (marcher) in single file. 2 (file) queue, *Am* line; faire la q. to queue up, *Am* line up. 3 (de billard) cue. ◆q.-de-pie *nf* (*pl* queues-de-pie) (habit) tails.
qui [ki] *pron* (personne) who, that; (interrogatif) who; (après prép) whom; (chose) which, that; l'homme q. the man who *ou* that; la maison q. the house which *ou* that; q.? who?; q. (est-ce q.) est là? who's there?; q. désirez-vous voir?, q. est-ce que vous désirez voir? who(m) do you want to see?; sans q. without whom; la femme de q. je parle the woman I'm talking about *ou* about whom I'm talking; l'ami sur l'aide de q. je compte the friend on whose help I rely; q. que vous soyez whoever you are, whoever you may be; q. que ce soit anyone (at all); à q. est ce livre? whose book is this?
quiche [kiʃ] *nf* (tarte) quiche.
quiconque [kikɔ̃k] *pron* (celui qui) whoever; (n'importe qui) anyone.
quignon [kiɲɔ̃] *nm* chunk (of bread).
quille [kij] *nf* 1 (de navire) keel. 2 (de jeu) skittle; *pl* (jeu) skittles, ninepins. 3 (jambe) *Fam* leg.
quincaillier, -ière [kɛ̃kaje, -jɛr] hardware dealer, ironmonger. ◆quincaillerie *nf* hardware; (magasin) hardware shop.
quinine [kinin] *nf* Méd quinine.
quinquennal, -aux [kɛ̃kenal, -o] *a* (plan) five-year.
quinte [kɛ̃t] *nf* Méd coughing fit.

quintessence [kɛ̃tesɑ̃s] *nf* quintessence.
quintette [kɛ̃tɛt] *nm* Mus quintet(te).
quintuple [kɛ̃typl] *a* q. de fivefold; − *nm* le q. de five times as much as. ◆quintupl/er *vti* to increase fivefold. ◆−és, -ées *nmfpl* (enfants) quintuplets, quins.
quinze [kɛ̃z] *a* & *nm* fifteen; q. jours two weeks, fortnight. ◆quinzaine *nf* une q. (de) (nombre) (about) fifteen; q. (de jours) two weeks, fortnight. ◆quinzième *a* & *nmf* fifteenth.
quiproquo [kiprɔko] *nm* misunderstanding.
quittance [kitɑ̃s] *nf* receipt.
quitte [kit] *a* quits, even (envers with); q. à faire even if it means doing; en être q. pour une amende/etc to (be lucky enough to) get off with a fine/etc.
quitter [kite] *vt* to leave; (ôter) to take off; − *vi* ne quittez pas! *Tél* hold the line!, hold on!; − se q. *vpr* (se séparer) to part.
qui-vive (sur le) [syrləkiviv] *adv* on the alert.
quoi [kwa] *pron* what; (après prép) which; à q. penses-tu? what are you thinking about?; après q. after which; ce à q. je m'attendais what I was expecting; de q. manger/etc (assez) enough to eat/etc; de q. couper/écrire/etc (instrument) something to cut/write/etc with; de q. que je dise whatever I say; q. que ce soit anything (at all); q. qu'il en soit be that as it may; il n'y a pas de q.! (en réponse à 'merci') don't mention it!; q.? what?; c'est un idiot, q.! (non traduit) *Fam* he's a fool!
quoique [kwak(ə)] *conj* (+ sub) (al)though.
quolibet [kɔlibe] *nm* Litt gibe.
quorum [k(w)ɔrɔm] *nm* quorum.
quota [k(w)ɔta] *nm* quota.
quote-part [kɔtpar] *nf* (*pl* quotes-parts) share.
quotidien, -ienne [kɔtidjɛ̃, -jɛn] *a* (journalier) daily; (banal) everyday; − *nm* daily (paper). ◆quotidiennement *adv* daily.
quotient [kɔsjɑ̃] *nm* quotient.

R

R, r [ɛr] *nm* R, r.
rabâch/er [rabɑʃe] *vt* to repeat endlessly; − *vi* to repeat oneself ◆−age *nm* endless repetition.
rabais [rabɛ] *nm* (price) reduction, discount; au r. (acheter) cheap, at a reduction.
rabaisser [rabese] *vt* (dénigrer) to belittle, humble; r. à (ravaler) to reduce to.
rabat-joie [rabaʒwa] *nm inv* killjoy.

rabattre [rabatr] vt (baisser) to put ou pull down; (refermer) to close (down); (replier) to fold down ou over; (déduire) Aut to cut in; **en r.** (prétentieux) Fig to climb down (from one's high horse); **— se r.** vpr (se refermer) to close; (après avoir doublé) Aut to cut in (devant in front of); **se r. sur** Fig to fall back on.

rabbin [rabɛ̃] nm rabbi; **grand r.** chief rabbi.

rabibocher [rabibɔʃe] vt (réconcilier) Fam to patch it up between; **— se r.** vpr Fam to patch it up.

rabiot [rabjo] nm (surplus) Fam extra (helping); **faire du r.** Fam to work extra time.

râble [rabl] a stocky, thickset.

rabot [rabo] nm (outil) plane. **◆raboter** vt to plane.

raboteux, -euse [rabotø, -øz] a uneven, rough.

rabougri [rabugri] a (personne, plante) stunted.

rabrouer [rabrue] vt to snub, rebuff.

racaille [rakaj] nf rabble, riffraff.

raccommod/er [rakɔmɔde] **1** vt to mend; (chaussette) to darn. **2** vt (réconcilier) Fam to reconcile; **— se r.** vpr Fam to make it up (avec with). **◆—age** nm mending; darning.

raccompagner [rakɔ̃paɲe] vt to see ou take back (home); **r. à la porte** to see to the door, see out.

raccord [rakɔr] nm (dispositif) connection; (de papier peint) join; **r. (de peinture)** touch-up. **◆raccord/er** vt, **— se r.** vpr to connect (up), join (up) (à with, to). **◆—ement** nm (action, résultat) connection.

raccourc/ir [rakursir] vt to shorten; **— vi** to get shorter; (au lavage) to shrink. **◆—i** nm **1** (chemin) short cut. **2 en r.** (histoire etc) in a nutshell.

raccroc (par) [parrakro] adv by a (lucky) chance.

raccrocher [rakrɔʃe] vt to hang back up; (récepteur) Tél to put down; (relier) to connect (à with, to); (client) to accost; **se r. à** to hold on to, cling to; (se rapporter à) to link (up) with; **— vi** Tél to hang up, ring off.

race [ras] nf (groupe ethnique) race; (animale) breed; (famille) stock; (engeance) Péj breed; **de r.** (chien) pedigree-; (cheval) thoroughbred. **◆racé** a (chien) pedigree-; (cheval) thoroughbred; (personne) distinguished. **◆racial, -aux** a racial. **◆racisme** nm racism, racialism. **◆raciste** a & nmf racist, racialist.

rachat [raʃa] nm Com repurchase; (de firme)

take-over; Rel redemption. **◆racheter** vt to buy back; (objet d'occasion) to buy; (nouvel article) to buy another; (firme) to take over, buy out; (pécheur, dette) to redeem; (compenser) to make up for; **r. des chaussettes/du pain/etc** to buy (some) more socks/bread/etc; **— se r.** vpr to make amends, redeem oneself.

racine [rasin] nf (de plante, personne etc) & Math root; **prendre r.** (plante) & Fig to take root.

racket [raket] nm (association) racket; (activité) racketeering.

raclée [rakle] nf Fam hiding, thrashing.

racler [rakle] vt to scrape; (enlever) to scrape off; **se r. la gorge** to clear one's throat. **◆raclette** nf scraper; (à vitres) squeegee. **◆racloir** nm scraper. **◆raclures** nfpl (déchets) scrapings.

racol/er [rakɔle] vt (prostituée) to solicit (s.o.); (vendeur etc) to tout for (s.o.), solicit (s.o.). **◆—age** nm soliciting; touting. **◆—eur, -euse** nmf tout.

raconter [rakɔ̃te] vt (histoire) to tell, relate; (décrire) to describe; **r. qch à qn** (vacances etc) to tell s.o. about sth; **r. à qn que** to tell s.o. that, say to s.o. that. **◆racontars** nmpl gossip, stories.

racornir [rakɔrnir] vt to harden; **— se r.** vpr to get hard.

radar [radar] nm radar; **contrôle r.** (pour véhicules etc) radar control. **◆radariste** nmf radar operator.

rade [rad] nf **1** Nau (natural) harbour. **2** **laisser en r.** to leave stranded, abandon; **rester en r.** to be left behind.

radeau, -x [rado] nm raft.

radiateur [radjatœr] nm (à eau) & Aut radiator; (électrique, à gaz) heater.

radiation [radjasjɔ̃] nf **1** Phys radiation. **2** (suppression) removal (de from).

radical, -ale, -aux [radikal, -o] a radical; **— nm** Ling stem; **— nmf** Pol radical.

radier [radje] vt to strike ou cross off (de from).

radieux, -euse [radjø, -øz] a (personne, visage) radiant, beaming; (soleil) brilliant; (temps) glorious.

radin, -ine [radɛ̃, -in] a Fam stingy; **— nmf** Fam skinflint.

radio [radjo] **1** nf radio; (poste) radio (set); **à la r.** on the radio. **2** nf (photo) Méd X-ray; **passer ou faire une r.** to be X-rayed, have an X-ray. **3** nm (opérateur) radio operator. **◆radioactif, -ive** a radioactive. **◆radioactivité** nf radioactivity. **◆radiodiffuser** vt to broadcast (on the radio). **◆radio-**

diffusion nf broadcasting. ◆**radio-graphie** nf (photo) X-ray; (technique) radiography. ◆**radiographier** vt to X-ray. ◆**radiologie** nf Méd radiology. ◆**radiologue** nmf (technicien) radiographer; (médecin) radiologist. ◆**radiophonique** a (programme) radio-. ◆**radiotélévisé** a broadcast on radio and television.

radis [radi] nm radish; **r. noir** horseradish.

radot/er [radɔte] vi to drivel (on), ramble (on). ◆—**age** nm (propos) drivel.

radouc/ir (se) [saradusir] vpr to calm down; (temps) to become milder. ◆—**issement** nm r. (du temps) milder weather.

rafale [rafal] nf (vent) gust, squall; (de mitrailleuse) burst; (de balles) hail.

raffermir [rafɛrmir] vt to strengthen; (muscles etc) to tone up; — **se r.** vpr to become stronger.

raffin/er [rafine] vt (pétrole, sucre, manières) to refine. ◆—**é** a refined. ◆—**age** nm (du pétrole, sucre) refining. ◆—**ement** nm (de personne) refinement. ◆**raffinerie** nf refinery.

raffoler [rafole] vi **r. de** (aimer) to be very fond of, be mad ou wild about.

raffut [rafy] nm Fam din, row.

rafiot [rafjo] nm (bateau) Péj (old) tub.

rafistoler [rafistɔle] vt Fam to patch up.

rafle [rafl] nf (police) raid.

rafler [rafle] vt (enlever) Fam to swipe, make off with.

rafraîch/ir [rafreʃir] vt to cool (down); (remettre à neuf) to brighten up; (mémoire, personne) to refresh; — vi **mettre à r.** Culin to chill; — **se r.** vpr to refresh oneself; (se laver) to freshen (oneself) up; (temps) to get cooler. ◆—**issant** a refreshing. ◆—**issement** nm **1** (de température) cooling. **2** (boisson) cold drink; pl (fruits, glaces etc) refreshments.

ragaillardir [ragajardir] vt to buck up.

rage [raʒ] nf **1** (colère) rage; **r. de dents** violent toothache; **faire r.** (incendie, tempête) to rage. **2** (maladie) rabies. ◆**rager** vi (personne) Fam to rage, fume. ◆**rageant** a Fam infuriating. ◆**rageur, -euse** a bad-tempered, furious.

ragots [rago] nmpl Fam gossip.

ragoût [ragu] nm Culin stew.

ragoûtant [ragutã] a **peu r.** (mets, personne) unsavoury.

raid [rɛd] nm (incursion, attaque) Mil Av raid.

raide [rɛd] a (rigide, guindé) stiff; (côte) steep; (cheveux) straight; (corde etc) tight; **c'est r.!** (exagéré) Fam it's a bit stiff ou

much!; — adv (grimper) steeply; **tomber r. mort** to drop dead. ◆**raideur** nf stiffness; steepness. ◆**raidillon** nm (pente) short steep rise. ◆**raidir** vt, — **se r.** vpr to stiffen; (corde) to tighten; (position) to harden; **se r. contre** Fig to steel oneself against.

raie [rɛ] nf **1** (trait) line; (de couleur) stripe; (de cheveux) parting, Am part. **2** (poisson) skate, ray.

rail [raj] nm (barre) rail; **le r.** (transport) rail.

railler [raje] vt to mock, make fun of. ◆**raillerie** nf gibe, mocking remark. ◆**railleur, -euse** a mocking.

rainure [renyr] nf groove.

raisin [rezɛ̃] nm raisin(s) grapes; **grain de r.** grape; **manger du r. ou des raisins** to eat grapes; **r. sec** raisin.

raison [rezɔ̃] nf **1** (faculté, motif) reason; **entendre r.** to listen to reason; **la r. pour laquelle je . . .** the reason (why ou that) I . . . ; **pour raisons de famille/de santé/etc** for family/health/etc reasons; **en r. de** (cause) on account of; **à r. de** (proportion) at the rate of; **avoir r. de qn/de qch** to get the better of s.o./sth; **mariage de r.** marriage of convenience; **à plus forte r.** all the more so; **de plus** all the more reason (**pour faire** to do, for doing). **2** avoir r. to be right (**de faire** to do, in doing); **donner r. à qn** to agree with s.o.; (événement etc) to prove s.o. right; **avec r.** rightly. ◆**raisonnable** a reasonable. ◆**raisonnablement** adv reasonably.

raisonn/er [rezɔne] vi (penser) to reason; (discuter) to argue; — vt **r. qn** to reason with s.o. ◆—**é** a (projet) well-thought-out. ◆—**ement** nm (faculté, activité) reasoning; (propositions) argument. ◆—**eur, -euse** a Péj argumentative; — nmf Péj arguer.

rajeun/ir [raʒœnir] vt to make (feel ou look) younger; (personnel) to infuse new blood into; (moderniser) to modernize; (personne âgée) Méd to rejuvenate; — vi to get ou feel ou look younger. ◆—**issant** a Méd rejuvenating. ◆—**issement** nm Méd rejuvenation; **le r. de la population** the population getting younger.

rajout [raʒu] nm addition. ◆**rajouter** vt to add (à to); **en r.** Fig to overdo it.

rajuster [raʒyste] vt (mécanisme) to readjust; (lunettes, vêtements) to straighten, adjust; (cheveux) to rearrange; — **se r.** vpr to straighten ou tidy oneself up.

râle [rɑl] nm (de blessé) groan; (de mourant) death rattle. ◆**râler** vi (blessé) to groan; (mourant) to give the death rattle; (proteser) *Fam* to grouse, moan. ◆**râleur, -euse** *nmf Fam* grouser, moaner.

ralentir [ralɑ̃tir] *vti*, — **se r.** *vpr* to slow down. ◆—**i** *nm Cin TV* slow motion; **au r.** (*filmer, travailler*) in slow motion; (*vivre*) at a slower pace; **tourner au r.** (*moteur, usine*) to idle, tick over, *Am* turn over.

rallier [ralje] *vt* (*rassembler*) to rally; (*rejoindre*) to rejoin; **r. qn à** (*convertir*) to win s.o. over to; — **se r.** *vpr* (*se regrouper*) to rally; **se r. à** (*point de vue*) to come over ou round to.

rallonge [ralɔ̃ʒ] *nf* (*de table*) extension; (*fil électrique*) extension (lead); **une r. (de)** (*supplément*) *Fam* (some) extra. ◆**rallonger** *vti* to lengthen.

rallumer [ralyme] *vt* to light again, relight; (*lampe*) to switch on again; (*conflit, haine*) to rekindle; — **se r.** *vpr* (*guerre, incendie*) to flare up again.

rallye [rali] *nm Sp Aut* rally.

ramage [ramaʒ] **1** *nm* (*d'oiseaux*) song, warbling. **2** *nmpl* (*dessin*) foliage.

ramass/er [ramase] **1** *vt* (*prendre par terre, réunir*) to pick up; (*ordures, copies*) to collect, pick up; (*fruits, coquillages*) to gather; (*rhume, amende*) *Fam* to pick up, get; **r. une bûche** ou **une pelle** *Fam* to come a cropper, *Am* take a spill. **2 se r.** *vpr* (*se pelotonner*) to curl up. ◆—**é** *a* (*trapu*) squat, stocky; (*recroquevillé*) huddled; (*concis*) compact. ◆—**age** *nm* picking up; collection; gathering; **r. scolaire** school bus service.

ramassis [ramasi] *nm* **r. de** (*voyous etc*) *Péj* bunch of.

rambarde [rɑ̃bard] *nf* guardrail.

rame [ram] *nf* **1** (*aviron*) oar. **2** (*de métro*) train. **3** (*de papier*) ream. ◆**ramer** *vi* to row. ◆**rameur, -euse** *nmf* rower.

rameau, -x [ramo] *nm* branch; **les Rameaux** *Rel* Palm Sunday.

ramener [ramne] *vt* to bring ou take back; (*paix, calme, ordre etc*) to restore, bring back; (*remettre en place*) to put back; **r. à** (*réduire à*) to reduce to; **r. à la vie** to bring back to life; — **se r.** *vpr* (*arriver*) *Fam* to turn up; **se r. à** (*problème etc*) to boil down to.

ramier [ramje] *nm* (**pigeon**) **r.** wood pigeon.

ramification [ramifikasjɔ̃] *nf* ramification.

ramoll/ir [ramɔlir] *vt*, — **se r.** *vpr* to soften. ◆—**i** *a* soft; (*personne*) soft-headed.

ramon/er [ramɔne] *vt* (*cheminée*) to sweep. ◆—**age** *nm* (chimney) sweeping. ◆—**eur** *nm* (chimney)sweep.

rampe [rɑ̃p] *nf* **1** (*pente*) ramp, slope; **r. de lancement** (*de fusées etc*) launch(ing) pad. **2**

(*d'escalier*) banister(s). **3** (*projecteurs*) *Th* footlights.

ramper [rɑ̃pe] *vi* to crawl; (*plante*) to creep; **r. devant** *Fig* to cringe ou crawl to.

rancard [rɑ̃kar] *nm Fam* (*rendez-vous*) date; (*renseignement*) tip.

rancart [rɑ̃kar] *nm* **mettre au r.** *Fam* to throw out, scrap.

rance [rɑ̃s] *a* rancid. ◆**rancir** *vi* to turn rancid.

ranch [rɑ̃tʃ] *nm* ranch.

rancœur [rɑ̃kœr] *nf* rancour, resentment.

rançon [rɑ̃sɔ̃] *nf* ransom; **la r. de** (*inconvénient*) the price of (*success, fame etc*). ◆**rançonner** *vt* to hold to ransom.

rancune [rɑ̃kyn] *nf* grudge; **garder r. à qn** to bear s.o. a grudge; **sans r.!** no hard feelings! ◆**rancunier, -ière** *a* vindictive, resentful.

randonnée [rɑ̃dɔne] *nf* (*à pied*) walk, hike; (*en voiture*) drive, ride; (*en vélo*) ride.

rang [rɑ̃] *nm* (*rangée*) row, line; (*condition, grade, classement*) rank; **les rangs** (*hommes*) *Mil* the ranks (**de** of); **les rangs de ses ennemis** (*nombre*) *Fig* the ranks of his enemies; **se mettre en rang(s)** to line up (**par trois**/*etc* in threes/*etc*); **par r. de** in order of. ◆**rangée** *nf* row, line.

rang/er [rɑ̃ʒe] *vt* (*papiers, vaisselle etc*) to put away; (*chambre etc*) to tidy (up); (*chiffres, mots*) to arrange; (*voiture*) to park; **parmi** (*auteur etc*) to rank among; — **se r.** *vpr* (*élèves etc*) to line up; (*s'écarter*) to stand aside; (*voiture*) to pull over; (*s'assagir*) to settle down; **se r. à** (*avis de qn*) to fall in with. ◆—**é** *a* (*chambre etc*) tidy; (*personne*) steady; (*bataille*) pitched. ◆—**ement** *nm* putting away; (*de chambre etc*) tidying (up); (*espace*) storage space.

ranimer [ranime] *vt* (*réanimer, revigorer*) to revive; (*encourager*) to spur on; (*feu, querelle*) to rekindle.

rapace [rapas] **1** *a* (*avide*) grasping. **2** *nm* (*oiseau*) bird of prey.

rapatrier [rapatrije] *vt* to repatriate. ◆**rapatriement** *nm* repatriation.

râpe [rɑp] *nf Culin* grater; shredder; (*lime*) rasp. ◆**râp/er** *vt* (*fromage*) to grate; (*carottes etc*) to shred; (*finement*) to grate; (*bois*) to rasp. ◆—**é 1** *a* (*fromage*) grated; — *nm* grated cheese. **2** *a* (*vêtement*) threadbare.

rapetisser [raptise] *vt* to make (look) smaller; (*vêtement*) to shorten; — *vi* to get smaller; (*au lavage*) to shrink; (*jours*) to get shorter.

râpeux, -euse [rɑpø, -øz] *a* rough.

raphia [rafja] *nm* raffia.

rapide [rapid] *a* fast, quick, rapid; (*pente*) steep; — *nm* (*train*) express (train); (*de fleuve*) rapid. ◆**—ment** *adv* fast, quickly, rapidly. ◆**rapidité** *nf* speed, rapidity.

rapiécer [rapjese] *vt* to patch (up).

rappel [rapɛl] *nm* (*de diplomate etc*) recall; (*évocation, souvenir*) reminder; (*paiement*) back pay; *pl* Th curtain calls; (*vaccination de*) r. Méd booster; **r. à l'ordre** call to order. ◆**rappeler** (*pour faire revenir*) & Tél to call back; (*diplomate, souvenir*) to recall; **r. qch à qn** (*redire*) to remind s.o. of sth; — *vi* Tél to call back; — **se r.** (*histoire, personne etc*) to remember, recall, recollect.

rappliquer [raplike] *vi* (*arriver*) Fam to show up.

rapport [rapɔr] *nm* **1** (*lien*) connection, link; *pl* (*entre personnes*) relations; **rapports** (**sexuels**) (sexual) intercourse; **par r. à** compared to *ou* with; (*envers*) towards; **se mettre en r. avec qn** to get in touch with s.o.; **en r. avec** in keeping with; **sous le r. de** from the point of view of. **2** (*revenu*) Com return, yield. **3** (*récit*) report. ◆**rapporter 1** *vt* (*ramener*) to bring *ou* take back; (*ajouter*) to add; — *vi* (*chien*) to retrieve. **2** *vt* (*récit*) to report; (*mot célèbre*) to repeat; — *vi* (*moucharder*) Fam to tell tales. **3** *vt* (*profit*) Com to bring in, yield; — *vi* (*investissement*) Com to bring in a good return. **4** *vt* **r. qch à** (*rattacher*) to relate sth to; **se r. à** to relate to, be connected with; **s'en r. à** to rely on. ◆**rapporteur, -euse 1** *nmf* (*mouchard*) telltale. **2** *nm* Jur reporter. **3** *nm* Géom protractor.

rapproch/er [raprɔʃe] *vt* to bring closer (*de* to); (*chaise*) to pull up (*de* to); (*réconcilier*) to bring together; (*réunir*) to join; (*comparer*) to compare; — **se r.** *vpr* to come *ou* get closer (*de* to); (*se réconcilier*) to come together, be reconciled; (*ressembler*) to be close (*de* to). ◆**—é** *a* close, near; (*yeux*) close-set; (*fréquent*) frequent. ◆**—ement** *nm* (*réconciliation*) reconciliation; (*rapport*) connection; (*comparaison*) comparison.

rapt [rapt] *nm* (*d'enfant*) abduction.

raquette [rakɛt] *nf* (*de tennis*) racket; (*de ping-pong*) bat.

rare [rar] *a* rare; (*argent, main-d'œuvre etc*) scarce; (*barbe, herbe*) sparse; **il est r. que** (+ *sub*) it's seldom *ou* rare that. ◆**se raréfier** *vpr* (*denrées etc*) to get scarce. ◆**rarement** *adv* rarely, seldom. ◆**rareté** *nf* rarity; scarcity; **une r.** (*objet*) a rarity.

ras [rɑ] *a* (*cheveux*) close-cropped; (*herbe, poil*) short; (*mesure*) full; **en rase campagne** in (the) open country; **à r. de** very close to; **à r. bord** (*remplir*) to the brim; **en avoir r. le bol** Fam to be fed up (**de** with); **pull** (**au**) **r. du cou** *ou* **à col r.** crew-neck(ed) pullover; — *adv* short.

ras/er [rɑze] **1** *vt* (*menton, personne*) to shave; (*barbe, moustache*) to shave off; — **se r.** *vpr* to (have a) shave. **2** *vt* (*démolir*) to raze, knock down. **3** *vt* (*frôler*) to skim, brush. **4** *vt* (*ennuyer*) Fam to bore. ◆**—ant** *a* Fam boring. ◆**—é** *a* **bien r.** clean-shaven; **mal r.** unshaven. ◆**—age** *nm* shaving. ◆**—eur, -euse** *nmf* Fam bore. ◆**rasoir 1** *nm* shaver. **2** *a inv* Fam boring.

rassasier [rasazje] *vti* to satisfy; **être rassasié** to have had enough (**de** of).

rassembler [rasɑ̃ble] *vt* to gather (together), assemble; (*courage*) to summon up, muster; — **se r.** *vpr* to gather, assemble. ◆**rassemblement** *nm* (*action, gens*) gathering.

rasseoir * (**se**) [səraswar] *vpr* to sit down again.

rassis, *f* **rassie** [rasi] *a* (*pain, brioche etc*) stale. ◆**rassir** *vti* to turn stale.

rassurer [rasyre] *vt* to reassure; **rassure-toi** set your mind at rest, don't worry. ◆**—ant** *a* (*nouvelle*) reassuring, comforting.

rat [ra] *nm* rat; **r. de bibliothèque** Fig bookworm.

ratatiner (**se**) [səratatine] *vpr* to shrivel (up); (*vieillard*) to become wizened.

rate [rat] *nf* Anat spleen.

râteau, -x [rɑto] *nm* (*outil*) rake.

râtelier [rɑtəlje] *nm* **1** (*support pour outils, armes etc*) rack. **2** (*dentier*) Fam set of false teeth.

rat/er [rate] *vt* (*bus, cible, occasion etc*) to miss; (*gâcher*) to spoil, ruin; (*vie*) to waste; (*examen*) to fail; — *vi* (*projet etc*) to fail; (*pistolet*) to misfire. ◆**—é, -ée 1** *nmf* (*personne*) failure. **2** *nmpl* **avoir des ratés** Aut to backfire. ◆**—age** *nm* (*échec*) Fam failure.

ratifier [ratifje] *vt* to ratify. ◆**ratification** *nf* ratification.

ration [rasjɔ̃] *nf* ration; **r. de** Fig share of. ◆**rationn/er** *vt* (*vivres, personne*) to ration. ◆**—ement** *nm* rationing.

rationaliser [rasjɔnalize] *vt* to rationalize. ◆**rationalisation** *nf* rationalization.

rationnel, -elle [rasjɔnɛl] *a* (*pensée, méthode*) rational.

ratisser [ratise] *vt* **1** (*allée etc*) to rake; (*feuilles etc*) to rake up. **2** (*fouiller*) to comb. **r. qn** (*au jeu*) Fam to clean s.o. out.

raton [ratɔ̃] *nm* **r. laveur** rac(c)oon.

rattach/er [rataʃe] *vt* to tie up again; (*in-*

corporer, joindre) to join (à to); (*idée, question*) to link (à to); **r. qn à** (*son pays etc*) to bind s.o. to; **se r. à** to be linked to. ◆**—ement** *nm* (*annexion*) joining (à to).

rattrap/er [ratrape] *vt* to catch; (*prisonnier etc*) to recapture; (*erreur, temps perdu*) to make up for; **r. qn** (*rejoindre*) to catch up with s.o., catch s.o. up; **— se r.** *vpr* to catch up; (*se dédommager, prendre une compensation*) to make up for it; **se r. à** (*branche etc*) to catch hold of. ◆**—age** *nm* **cours de r.** *Scol* remedial classes; **r. des prix/salaires** adjustment of prices/wages (*to the cost of living*).

rature [ratyr] *nf* deletion. ◆**raturer** *vt* to delete, cross out.

rauque [rok] *a* (*voix*) hoarse, raucous.

ravages [ravaʒ] *nmpl* devastation; (*de la maladie, du temps*) ravages; **faire des r.** to wreak havoc. ◆**ravager** *vt* to devastate, ravage.

raval/er [ravale] *vt* **1** (*façade etc*) to clean (and restore). **2** (*salive, sanglots*) to swallow. **3** (*avilir*) *Litt* to lower. ◆**—ement** *nm* (*de façade etc*) cleaning (and restoration).

ravi [ravi] *a* delighted (**de** with, **de faire** to do).

ravier [ravje] *nm* hors-d'œuvre dish.

ravigoter [ravigɔte] *vt* *Fam* to buck up.

ravin [ravɛ̃] *nm* ravine, gully.

ravioli [ravjɔli] *nmpl* ravioli.

rav/ir [ravir] *vt* **1** to delight; **à r.** (*chanter etc*) delightfully. **2** (*emporter*) to snatch (à from). ◆**—issant** *a* delightful, lovely. ◆**ravisseur, -euse** *nmf* kidnapper.

raviser (se) [səravize] *vpr* to change one's mind.

ravitaill/er [ravitaje] *vt* to provide with supplies, supply; (*avion*) to refuel; **— se r.** *vpr* to stock up (with supplies). ◆**—ement** *nm* supplying; refuelling; (*denrées*) supplies; **aller au r.** (*faire des courses*) *Fam* to stock up, get stocks in.

raviver [ravive] *vt* (*feu, sentiment*) to revive; (*couleurs*) to brighten up.

ray/er [reje] *vt* (*érafler*) to scratch; (*mot etc*) to cross out; **r. qn de** (*liste*) to cross off or strike s.o. off. ◆**—é** *a* scratched; (*tissu*) striped; (*papier*) lined, ruled. ◆**rayure** *nf* scratch; (*bande*) stripe; **à rayures** striped.

rayon [rɛjɔ̃] *nm* **1** (*de lumière, soleil etc*) *Phys* ray; (*de cercle*) radius; (*de roue*) spoke; (*d'espoir*) *Fig* ray; **r. X** X-ray; **r. d'action** range; **dans un r. de** within a radius of. **2** (*planche*) shelf; (*de magasin*) department. **3** (*de ruche*) honeycomb. ◆**rayonnage** *nm* shelving, shelves.

rayonn/er [rɛjɔne] *vi* to radiate; (*dans une région*) to travel around (*from a central base*); **r. de joie** to beam with joy. ◆**—ant** *a* (*visage etc*) radiant; (*de*) radiant, beaming (**de** with). ◆**—ement** *nm* (*éclat*) radiance; (*influence*) influence; (*radiation*) radiation.

raz-de-marée [rɑdmare] *nm inv* tidal wave; (*bouleversement*) *Fig* upheaval; **r. de-marée électoral** landslide.

razzia [ra(d)zja] *nf* **faire une r. sur** (*tout enlever sur*) *Fam* to raid.

re- [r(ə)] *préf* re-.

ré- [re] *préf* re-.

réabonn/er (se) [səreabɔne] *vpr* to renew one's subscription (à to). ◆**—ement** *nm* renewal of subscription.

réacteur [reaktœr] *nm* (*d'avion*) jet engine; (*nucléaire*) reactor.

réaction [reaksjɔ̃] *nf* reaction; **r. en chaîne** chain reaction; **avion à r.** jet (aircraft); **moteur à r.** jet engine. ◆**réactionnaire** *a* & *nmf* reactionary.

réadapter [readapte] *vt*, **— se r.** *vpr* to readjust (à to). ◆**réadaptation** *nf* readjustment.

réaffirmer [reafirme] *vt* to reaffirm.

réagir [reaʒir] *vi* to react (**contre** against, **à** to); (*se secouer*) *Fig* to shake oneself out of it.

réalis/er [realize] *vt* (*projet etc*) to carry out, realize; (*ambition, rêve*) to fulfil; (*achat, bénéfice, vente*) to make; (*film*) to direct; (*capital*) *Com* to realize; (*se rendre compte*) to realize (**que** that); **— se r.** *vpr* (*vœu*) to come true; (*projet*) to be carried out; (*personne*) to fulfil oneself. ◆**—able** *a* (*plan*) workable; (*rêve*) attainable. ◆**réalisateur, -trice** *nmf* *Cin TV* director. ◆**réalisation** *nf* realization; (*de rêve*) fulfilment; *Cin TV* direction; (*œuvre*) achievement.

réalisme [realism] *nm* realism. ◆**réaliste** *a* realistic; — *nmf* realist.

réalité [realite] *nf* reality; **en r.** (in actual) fact, in reality.

réanimer [reanime] *vt* *Méd* to resuscitate. ◆**réanimation** *nf* resuscitation; (*service de*) **r.** intensive care unit.

réapparaître [reaparetr] *vi* to reappear. ◆**réapparition** *nf* reappearance.

réarmer [rearme] *vt* (*fusil etc*) to reload; — *vi*, **— se r.** *vpr* (*pays*) to rearm. ◆**réarmement** *nm* rearmament.

rébarbatif, -ive [rebarbatif, -iv] *a* forbidding, off-putting.

rebâtir [r(ə)bɑtir] *vt* to rebuild.

rebattu [r(ə)baty] *a* (*sujet*) hackneyed.

rebelle [rəbɛl] *a* rebellious; (*troupes*) rebel-; (*fièvre*) stubborn; (*mèche*) unruly; **r. à** resistant to; — *nmf* rebel. ◆**se rebeller** *vpr* to rebel (**contre** against). ◆**rébellion** *nf* rebellion.

rebiffer (se) [sərə)bife] *vpr Fam* to rebel.

rebond [rəbɔ̃] *nm* bounce; (*par ricochet*) rebound. ◆**rebondir** *vi* to bounce; to rebound; (*faire*) **r.** (*affaire, discussion etc*) to get going again. ◆**rebondissement** *nm* new development (**de** in).

rebondi [r(ə)bɔ̃di] *a* chubby, rounded.

rebord [r(ə)bɔr] *nm* edge; (*de plat etc*) rim; (*de vêtement*) hem; **r. de (la) fenêtre** windowsill, window ledge.

reboucher [r(ə)buʃe] *vt* (*flacon*) to put the top back on.

rebours (à) [ar(ə)bur] *adv* the wrong way.

rebrousse-poil (à) [arbruspwal] *adv* **prendre qn à r.-poil** *Fig* to rub s.o. up the wrong way.

rebrousser [r(ə)bruse] *vt* **r. chemin** to turn back.

rebuffade [rəbyfad] *nf Litt* rebuff.

rébus [rebys] *nm* (*jeu*) rebus.

rebut [rəby] *nm* **mettre au r.** to throw out, scrap; **le r. de la société** *Péj* the dregs of society.

rebut/er [r(ə)byte] *vt* (*décourager*) to put off; (*choquer*) to repel. ◆**-ant** *a* offputting; (*choquant*) repellent.

récalcitrant [rekalsitrɑ̃] *a* recalcitrant.

recaler [r(ə)kale] *vt* **r. qn** *Scol Fam* to fail s.o., flunk s.o.; **être recalé, se faire r.** *Scol Fam* to fail, flunk.

récapituler [rekapityle] *vti* to recapitulate. ◆**récapitulation** *nf* recapitulation.

recel [rəsɛl] *nm* receiving stolen goods, fencing; harbouring. ◆**receler** *vt* (*mystère, secret etc*) to contain; (*objet volé*) to receive; (*malfaiteur*) to harbour. ◆**receleur, -euse** *nmf* receiver (*of stolen goods*), fence.

recens/er [r(ə)sɑ̃se] *vt* (*population*) to take a census of; (*inventorier*) to make an inventory of. ◆**-ement** *nm* census; inventory.

récent [resɑ̃] *a* recent. ◆**récemment** [-amɑ̃] *adv* recently.

récépissé [resepise] *nm* (*reçu*) receipt.

récepteur [reseptœr] *nm Tél Rad* receiver. ◆**réceptif, -ive** *a* receptive (**à** to). ◆**réception** *nf* (*accueil, soirée*) & *Rad* reception; (*de lettre etc*) *Com* receipt; (*d'hôtel etc*) reception (desk). ◆**réceptionniste** *nmf* receptionist.

récession [resesjɔ̃] *nf Écon* recession.

recette [r(ə)sɛt] *nf* **1** *Culin* & *Fig* recipe. **2**

(*argent, bénéfice*) takings; (*bureau*) tax office; **recettes** (*rentrées*) *Com* receipts; **faire r.** *Fig* to be a success.

recev/oir* [rəsvwar] *vt* to receive; (*obtenir*) to get, receive; (*accueillir*) to welcome; (*accepter*) to accept; **être reçu (à)** (*examen*) to pass; **être reçu premier** to come first; — *vi* to receive guests *ou* visitors *ou* *Méd* patients. ◆**-able** *a* (*excuse etc*) admissible. ◆**-eur, -euse** *nmf* (*d'autobus*) (bus) conductor, (bus) conductress; (*des impôts*) tax collector; (*des postes*) postmaster, postmistress.

rechange (de) [dər(ə)ʃɑ̃ʒ] *a* (*pièce, outil etc*) spare; (*solution etc*) alternative; **vêtements/chaussures de r.** a change of clothes/shoes.

rechapé [r(ə)ʃape] *a* **pneu r.** retread.

réchapper [reʃape] *vi* **r. de** *ou* **à** (*accident etc*) to come through.

recharge [r(ə)ʃarʒ] *nf* (*de stylo etc*) refill. ◆**recharger** *vt* (*camion, fusil*) to reload; (*briquet, stylo etc*) to refill; (*batterie*) to recharge.

réchaud [reʃo] *nm* (portable) stove.

réchauff/er [reʃofe] *vt* (*personne, aliment etc*) to warm up; — **se r.** *vpr* to warm oneself up; (*temps*) to get warmer. ◆**-é** *nm* **du r.** *Fig Péj* old hat. ◆**-ement** *nm* (*de température*) rise (**de** in).

rêche [rɛʃ] *a* rough, harsh.

recherche [r(ə)ʃɛrʃ] *nf* **1** search, quest (**de** for); **à la r.** **de** in search of. **2** **la r., des recherches** (*scientifique etc*) research (**sur** on, into); **faire des recherches** to research; (*enquête*) to make investigations. **3** (*raffinement*) studied elegance; *Péj* affectation. ◆**recherch/er** *vt* to search *ou* hunt for; (*cause, faveur, perfection*) to seek. ◆**-é** *a* **1** (*très demandé*) in great demand; (*rare*) much sought-after; **r. pour meurtre** wanted for murder. **2** (*élégant*) elegant; *Péj* affected.

rechigner [r(ə)ʃiɲe] *vi* (*renâcler*) to jib (**à qch** at sth, **à faire** at doing).

rechute [r(ə)ʃyt] *nf Méd* relapse. ◆**rechuter** *vi Méd* to (have a) relapse.

récidive [residiv] *nf Jur* further offence; *Méd* recurrence (**de** of). ◆**récidiver** *vi Jur* to commit a further offence; (*maladie*) to recur. ◆**récidiviste** *nmf Jur* further offender.

récif [resif] *nm* reef.

récipient [resipjɑ̃] *nm* container, receptacle.

réciproque [resiprɔk] *a* mutual, reciprocal; — *nf* (*inverse*) opposite; **rendre la r. à qn** to get even with s.o. ◆**réciprocité** *nf* reciprocity. ◆**réciproquement** adv (l'un l'autre) each other; **et r.** and vice versa.

récit [resi] nm (compte rendu) account; (histoire) story.

récital, pl **-als** [resital] nm Mus recital.

réciter [resite] vt to recite. ◆**récitation** nf recitation.

réclame [reklam] nf advertising; (annonce) advertisement; **en r.** Com on (special) offer; – a inv **prix r.** (special) offer price; **vente r.** (bargain) sale.

réclamer [reklame] vt (demander, nécessiter) to demand, call for; (revendiquer) to claim; – vi to complain; **se r. de qn** to invoke s.o.'s authority. ◆**réclamation** nf complaint; pl (bureau) complaints department.

reclasser [r(ə)klɑse] vt (fiches etc) to reclassify.

reclus, -use [rəkly, -yz] a (vie) cloistered; – nmf recluse.

réclusion [reklyzjɔ̃] nf imprisonment (with hard labour); **r. à perpétuité** life imprisonment.

recoiffer (se) [sər(ə)kwafe] vpr (se peigner) to do ou comb one's hair.

recoin [rəkwɛ̃] nm nook, recess.

recoller [r(ə)kɔle] vt (objet cassé) to stick together again; (enveloppe) to stick back down.

récolte [rekɔlt] nf (action) harvest; (produits) crop, harvest; (collection) Fig crop. ◆**récolter** vt to harvest, gather (in); (recueillir) Fig to collect, gather; (coups) Fam to get.

recommand/er [r(ə)kɔmɑ̃de] **1** vt (appuyer, conseiller) to recommend; **r. à qn de faire** to recommend s.o. to do. **2** (lettre etc) to register. **3** vt **r. à (âme)** to commend to. **4 se r.** vpr **se r. de qn** to invoke s.o.'s authority. ◆**-é** nm **en r.** (envoyer) by registered post. ◆**-able** a **peu r.** not very commendable. ◆**recommandation** nf **1** (appui, conseil, louange) recommendation. **2** (de lettre etc) registration.

recommenc/er [r(ə)kɔmɑ̃se] vti to start ou begin again. ◆**-ement** nm (reprise) renewal (**de** of).

récompense [rekɔ̃pɑ̃s] nf reward (**de** for); (prix) award; **en r. de** in return for. ◆**récompenser** vt to reward (**de, pour** for).

réconcilier [rekɔ̃silje] vt to reconcile; – **se r.** vpr to become reconciled, make it up (**avec** with). ◆**réconciliation** nf reconciliation.

reconduire* [r(ə)kɔ̃dɥir] vt **1 r. qn** to see ou take s.o. back; (à la porte) to show s.o. out. **2** (mesures etc) to renew. ◆**reconduction** nf renewal.

réconfort [rekɔ̃fɔr] nm comfort. ◆**réconfort/er** vt to comfort; (revigorer) to fortify. ◆**-ant** a comforting; (boisson etc) fortifying.

reconnaissant [r(ə)kɔnɛsɑ̃] a grateful, thankful (**à qn de qch** to s.o. for sth). ◆**reconnaissance¹** nf (gratitude) gratitude.

reconnaître* [r(ə)kɔnɛtr] vt to recognize (**à qch** by sth); (admettre) to acknowledge, admit (**que** that); (terrain) Mil to reconnoitre; **être reconnu coupable** to be found guilty; – **se r.** vpr (s'orienter) to find one's bearings; **se r. coupable** to admit one's guilt. ◆**reconnu** a (chef, fait) acknowledged, recognized. ◆**reconnaissable** a recognizable (**à qch** by sth). ◆**reconnaissance²** nf recognition; (aveu) acknowledgement; Mil reconnaissance; **r. de dette** IOU.

reconsidérer [r(ə)kɔ̃sidere] vt to reconsider.

reconstituant [r(ə)kɔ̃stitɥɑ̃] adj (aliment, régime) restorative.

reconstituer [r(ə)kɔ̃stitɥe] vt (armée, parti) to constitute; (crime, quartier) to reconstruct; (faits) to piece together; (fortune) to build up again. ◆**reconstitution** nf constitution; reconstruction.

reconstruire* [r(ə)kɔ̃strɥir] vt (ville, fortune) to rebuild. ◆**reconstruction** nf rebuilding.

reconvertir [r(ə)kɔ̃vɛrtir] **1** vt (bâtiment etc) to reconvert. **2 se r.** vpr to take up a new form of employment. ◆**reconversion** nf reconversion.

recopier [r(ə)kɔpje] vt to copy out.

recoucher (se) [sər(ə)kuʃe] vpr to go back to bed.

recoudre* [r(ə)kudr] vt (bouton) to sew back on.

recoup/er [r(ə)kupe] vt (témoignage etc) to tally with, confirm; – **se r.** vpr to tally, match ou tie up. ◆**-ement** nm crosscheck(ing).

recourbé [r(ə)kurbe] a curved; (nez) hooked.

recours [r(ə)kur] nm recourse (**à** to); Jur appeal; **avoir r. à** to resort to; (personne) to turn to; **notre dernier r.** our last resort. ◆**recourir*** vi **r. à** to resort to; (personne) to turn to.

recouvrer [r(ə)kuvre] vt (argent, santé) to recover.

recouvrir* [r(ə)kuvrir] vt (livre, meuble, sol etc) to cover; (de nouveau) to recover; (cacher) Fig to conceal, mask.

récréation [rekreasjɔ̃] nf recreation; (temps) Scol break, playtime.

récriminer [rekrimine] vi to complain bitterly (contre about). ◆**récrimination** nf (bitter) complaint.

récrire [rekrir] vt (lettre etc) to rewrite.

recroqueviller (se) [sər(ə)krɔkvije] vpr (papier, personne etc) to curl up.

recrudescence [rəkrydesɑ̃s] nf new outbreak (de of).

recrue [rəkry] nf recruit. ◆**recrut/er** vt to recruit. ◆**—ement** nm recruitment.

rectangle [rɛktɑ̃gl] nm rectangle. ◆**rectangulaire** a rectangular.

rectifier [rɛktifje] vt (erreur etc) to correct, rectify; (ajuster) to adjust. ◆**rectificatif** nm (document) amendment, correction. ◆**rectification** nf correction, rectification.

recto [rɛkto] nm front (of the page).

reçu [r(ə)sy] voir **recevoir**; — a (usages etc) accepted; (idée) conventional, received; (candidat) successful; — nm (écrit) Com receipt.

recueil [r(ə)kœj] nm (ouvrage) collection (de of).

recueill/ir* [r(ə)kœjir] 1 vt to collect, gather; (suffrages) to win, get; (prendre chez soi) to take in. 2 se r. vpr to meditate; (devant un monument) to stand in silence. ◆**—i** a (air) meditative. ◆**—ement** nm meditation.

recul [r(ə)kyl] nm (d'armée, de négociateur, de maladie) retreat; (éloignement) distance; (déclin) decline; (mouvement de) r. (de véhicule) backward movement; **avoir un mouvement de r.** (personne) to recoil; **phare de r.** Aut reversing light. ◆**reculade** nf Péj retreat. ◆**recul/er** vi to move ou step back; Aut to reverse; (armée) to retreat; (épidémie, glacier) to recede, retreat; (renoncer) to back down, retreat; (diminuer) to decline; **r. devant** Fig to recoil ou shrink from; — vt to move ou push back; (différer) to postpone. ◆**—é** a (endroit, temps) remote.

reculons (à) [arkylɔ̃] adv backwards.

récupérer [rekypere] vt to recover, get back; (ferraille etc) to salvage; (heures) to make up; (mouvement, personne etc) Pol Péj to take over, convert; — vi to recuperate, recover. ◆**récupération** nf recovery; salvage; recuperation.

récurer [rekyre] vt (casserole etc) to scour; **poudre à r.** scouring powder.

récuser [rekyze] vt to challenge; — se r. vpr to decline to give an opinion.

recycl/er [r(ə)sikle] vt (reconvertir) to retrain (s.o.); (matériaux) to recycle; — se r. vpr to retrain. ◆**—age** nm retraining; recycling.

rédacteur, -trice [redaktœr, -tris] nmf writer; (de chronique) Journ editor; (de dictionnaire etc) compiler; **r. en chef** Journ editor(-in-chief). ◆**rédaction** nf (action) writing; (de contrat) drawing up; (devoir) Scol essay, composition; (rédacteurs) Journ editorial staff; (bureaux) Journ editorial offices.

reddition [redisjɔ̃] nf surrender.

redemander [rədmɑ̃de] vt (pain etc) to ask for more; **r. qch à qn** to ask s.o. for sth back.

rédemption [redɑ̃psjɔ̃] nf Rel redemption.

redescendre [r(ə)desɑ̃dr] vi (aux être) to come ou go back down; — vt (aux avoir) (objet) to bring ou take back down.

redevable [rədvabl] a **être r. de qch à qn** (argent) to owe s.o. sth; Fig to be indebted to s.o. for sth.

redevance [rədvɑ̃s] nf (taxe) TV licence fee; Tél rental charge.

redevenir [rədvənir] vi (aux être) to become again.

rédiger [rediʒe] vt to write; (contrat) to draw up; (dictionnaire etc) to compile.

redire* [r(ə)dir] 1 vt to repeat. 2 vi **avoir** ou **trouver à r. à qch** to find fault with sth. ◆**redite** nf (pointless) repetition.

redondant [r(ə)dɔ̃dɑ̃] a (style) redundant.

redonner [r(ə)dɔne] vt to give back; (de nouveau) to give more.

redoubl/er [r(ə)duble] vti **1** to increase; **r. de patience**/etc to be much more patient/etc; **à coups redoublés** (frapper) harder and harder. **2 r. (une classe)** Scol to repeat a year ou Am a grade. ◆**—ant, -ante** nmf pupil repeating a year ou Am a grade. ◆**—ement** nm increase (de in); repeating a year ou Am a grade.

redout/er [r(ə)dute] vt to dread (**de faire** doing). ◆**—able** a formidable, fearsome.

redress/er [r(ə)drese] vt to straighten (out); (économie, mât, situation, tort) to right; — se r. vpr (se mettre assis) to sit up; (debout) to stand up; (pays, situation etc) to right itself. ◆**—ement** [-ɛsmɑ̃] nm (essor) recovery.

réduction [redyksjɔ̃] nf reduction (**de** in); **en r.** (copie, modèle etc) small-scale.

réduire* [redɥir] vt to reduce (**à** to, **de** by); **r. qn à** (contraindre à) to reduce s.o. to (silence, inaction etc); **se r. à** (se ramener à) to come down to, amount to; **se r. en cendres**/etc to be reduced to ashes/etc; – vi (faire) **r.** (sauce) to reduce, boil down. ◆**réduit 1** a (prix, vitesse) reduced; (moyens) limited; (à petite échelle) small-scale. **2** nm (pièce) Péj cubbyhole; (recoin) recess.

réécrire [reekrir] vt (texte) to rewrite.

rééduquer [reedyke] vt (membre) Méd to re-educate; **r. qn** to rehabilitate s.o., re-educate s.o. ◆**rééducation** nf re-education; rehabilitation.

réel, -elle [reel] a real; **le r.** reality. ◆**réellement** adv really.

réélire [reelir] vt to re-elect.

réexpédier [reekspedje] vt (lettre etc) to forward; (à l'envoyeur) to return.

refaire* [r(ə)fɛr] vt to do again, redo; (erreur, voyage) to make again; (réparer) to do up, redo; (duper) Fam to take in. ◆**réfection** nf repair(ing).

réfectoire [refɛktwar] nm refectory.

référendum [referɑ̃dɔm] nm referendum.

référer [refere] vi **en r. à** to refer the matter to; – **se r.** vpr **se r. à** to refer to. ◆**référence** nf reference.

refermer [r(ə)fɛrme] vt, – **se r.** vpr to close ou shut (again).

refiler [r(ə)file] vt (donner) Fam to palm off (à on).

réfléchir [refleʃir] **1** vt (image) to reflect; – **se r.** vpr to be reflected. **2** vi (penser) to think (**à, sur** about); – vt **r. que** to realize that. ◆**-i** a (personne) thoughtful, reflective; (action, décision) carefully thought-out; (verbe) Gram reflexive. ◆**réflecteur** nm reflector. ◆**réflexion** nf **1** (de lumière etc) reflection. **2** (méditation) thought, reflection; (remarque) remark; **à la r., r. faite** on second thoughts ou Am thought, on reflection.

reflet [r(ə)flɛ] nm (image) & Fig reflection; (lumière) glint; (couleur) tint. ◆**refléter** vt (image, sentiment etc) to reflect; – **se r.** vpr to be reflected.

réflexe [reflɛks] nm & a reflex.

refluer [r(ə)flye] vi (eaux) to ebb, flow back; (foule) to surge back. ◆**reflux** nm ebb; backward surge.

réforme nf **1** (changement) reform. **2** (de soldat) discharge. ◆**réformateur, -trice** nmf reformer. ◆**réformer 1** vt to reform;

– **se r.** vpr to mend one's ways. **2** vt (soldat) to invalid out, discharge.

refouler [r(ə)fule] vt to force ou drive back; (sentiment) to repress; (larmes) to hold back. ◆**-é** a (personne) Psy repressed. ◆**-ement** nm Psy repression.

réfractaire [refrakter] a **r.** à resistant to.

refrain [r(ə)frɛ̃] nm (de chanson) refrain, chorus; (rengaine) Fig tune.

refréner [r(ə)frene] vt to curb, check.

réfrigérer [refriʒere] vt to refrigerate. ◆**-ant** a (accueil, air) Fam icy. ◆**réfrigérateur** nm refrigerator. ◆**réfrigération** nf refrigeration.

refroidir [r(ə)frwadir] vt to cool (down); (décourager) Fig to put off; (ardeur) to dampen, cool; – vi to get cold, cool down; – **se r.** vpr Méd to catch cold; (temps) to get cold; (ardeur) to cool (off). ◆**-issement** nm cooling; (rhume) chill; **r. de la température** fall in the temperature.

refuge [r(ə)fyʒ] nm refuge; (pour piétons) (traffic) island; (de montagne) (mountain) hut. ◆**se réfugier** vpr to take refuge. ◆**-é, -ée** nmf refugee.

refus [r(ə)fy] nm refusal; **ce n'est pas de r.** Fam I won't say no. ◆**refuser** vt to refuse (**qch à qn** s.o. sth, **de faire** to do); (offre, invitation) to turn down, refuse; (client) to turn away, refuse; (candidat) to fail; – **se r.** vpr (plaisir etc) to deny oneself; **se r. à** (évidence etc) to refuse to accept, reject; **se r. à croire**/etc to refuse to believe/etc.

réfuter [refyte] vt to refute.

regagner [r(ə)gaɲe] vt (récupérer) to regain; (revenir à) to get back to. ◆**regain** nm **r. de** (retour) renewal of.

régal [regal] nm, pl **-als** treat. ◆**régaler** vt to treat to a delicious meal; **r. de** to treat to; – **se r.** vpr to have a delicious meal.

regard [r(ə)gar] nm (coup d'œil, expression) look; (fixe) stare, gaze; **chercher du r.** to look (a)round for; **attirer les regards** to attract attention; **jeter un r. sur** to glance at. **2 au r. de** in regard to; **en r.** compared with. ◆**regarder 1** vt to look at; (fixement) to stare at, gaze at; (observer) to watch; (considérer) to consider, regard (**comme** as); **r. qn faire** to watch s.o. do; – vi to look; to stare, gaze; to watch; **r. à** (dépense, qualité etc) to pay attention to; **r. vers** (maison etc) to face; – **se r.** vpr (personnes) to look at each other. **2** vt (concerner) to concern. ◆**-ant** a (économe) careful (with money).

régates [regat] nfpl regatta.

régence [reʒɑ̃s] nf regency.

régénérer [reʒenere] vt to regenerate.

régenter [reʒɑ̃te] vt to rule over.

régie [reʒi] nf (entreprise) state-owned company; Th stage management; Cin TV production department.

regimber [r(ə)ʒɛ̃be] vi to balk (**contre** at).

régime [reʒim] nm **1** system; Pol régime. **2** Méd diet; **se mettre au r.** to go on a diet; **suivre un r.** to be on a diet. **3** (de moteur) speed; **à ce r.** Fig at this rate. **4** (de bananes, dattes) bunch.

régiment [reʒimɑ̃] nm Mil regiment; **un r. de** (quantité) Fig a host of.

région [reʒjɔ̃] nf region. area. ◆**régional, -aux** a regional.

régir [reʒir] vt (déterminer) to govern.

régisseur [reʒisœr] nm (de propriété) steward; Th stage manager; Cin assistant director.

registre [rəʒistr] nm register.

règle [rɛgl] **1** nf (principe) rule; **en r.** (papiers d'identité etc) in order; **être/se mettre en r. avec qn** to be/put oneself right with s.o.; **en r. générale** as a (general) rule. **2** nf (instrument) ruler; **r. à calcul** slide rule. **3** nfpl (menstruation) period.

règlement [rɛgləmɑ̃] nm **1** (arrêté) regulation; (règles) regulations. **2** (de conflit, problème etc) settling; (paiement) payment; **r. de comptes** Fig (violent) settling of scores. ◆**réglementaire** a in accordance with the regulations; (tenue) Mil regulation-. ◆**réglementation** nf **1** (action) regulation. **2** (règles) regulations. ◆**réglementer** vt to regulate.

régler [regle] **1** vt (conflit, problème etc) to settle; (mécanisme) to regulate, adjust; (moteur) to tune; (papier) to rule; **se r. sur** to model oneself on. **2** vti (payer) to pay; **r. qn** to settle up with s.o.; **r. son compte à** Fig to settle old scores with. ◆**réglé** a (vie) ordered; (papier) ruled. ◆**réglable** a (siège etc) adjustable; (de moteur) tuning. ◆**réglage** nm adjustment; (de moteur) tuning.

réglisse [reglis] nf liquorice, Am licorice.

règne [rɛɲ] nm reign; (animal, minéral, végétal) kingdom. ◆**régner** vi to reign; (prédominer) to prevail; **faire r. l'ordre** to maintain (law and) order.

regorger [r(ə)gɔrʒe] vi **r. de** to be overflowing with.

régresser [regrese] vi to regress. ◆**régression** nf regression; **en r.** on the decline.

regret [r(ə)grɛ] nm regret; **à r.** with regret; **avoir le r.** or **être au r. de faire** to be sorry to do. ◆**regrett/er** vt to regret; **r. qn** to miss s.o.; **je regrette** I'm sorry; **r. que** (+ sub) to

be sorry that, regret that. ◆**—able** a regrettable.

regrouper [r(ə)grupe] vt, **— se r.** vpr to gather together.

régulariser [regylarize] vt (situation) to regularize.

régulation [regylasjɔ̃] nf (action) regulation.

régulier, -ière [regylje, -jɛr] a regular; (progrès, vie, vitesse) steady; (légal) legal; (honnête) honest. ◆**régularité** nf regularity; steadiness; legality. ◆**régulièrement** adv regularly; (normalement) normally.

réhabiliter [reabilite] vt (dans l'estime publique) to rehabilitate.

réhabituer (se) [sareabitɥe] vpr **se r. à qch/à faire qch** to get used to sth/to doing sth again.

rehausser [raose] vt to raise; (faire valoir) to enhance.

réimpression [reɛ̃presjɔ̃] nf (livre) reprint.

rein [rɛ̃] nm kidney; pl (dos) (small of the) back; **r. artificiel** Méd kidney machine.

reine [rɛn] nf queen.

reine-claude [rɛnklod] nf greengage.

réintégrer [reɛ̃tegre] vt **1** (fonctionnaire etc) to reinstate. **2** (lieu) to return to. ◆**réintégration** nf reinstatement.

réitérer [reitere] vt to repeat.

rejaillir [r(ə)ʒajir] vi to spurt (up ou out); **r. sur** Fig to rebound on.

rejet [r(ə)ʒɛ] nm **1** (refus) & Méd rejection. **2** Bot shoot. ◆**rejeter** vt to throw back; (épave) to cast up; (vomir) to bring up; (refuser) & Méd to reject; **r. une erreur/etc sur qn** to put the blame for a mistake/etc on s.o.

rejeton [r(ə)ʒtɔ̃] nm (enfant) Fam kid.

rejoindre* [r(ə)ʒwɛ̃dr] vt (famille, régiment) to rejoin, get ou go back to; (lieu) to get back to; (route, rue) to join; **r. qn** to join ou meet s.o.; (rattraper) to catch up with s.o.; **— se r.** vpr (personnes) to meet; (routes, rues) to join, meet.

réjou/ir [reʒwir] vt to delight; **— se r.** vpr to be delighted (**de** at, **de faire** to do). ◆**—i** a (air) joyful. ◆**—issant** a cheering. ◆**réjouissance** nf rejoicing; pl festivities, rejoicings.

relâche [r(ə)lɑʃ] nf Th Cin (temporary) closure; **faire r.** (théâtre, cinéma) to close; (bateau) to put in (**dans un port** at a port); **sans r.** without a break.

relâch/er [r(ə)lɑʃe] vt to slacken; (discipline, étreinte) to relax; **r. qn** to release s.o.; **— se r.** vpr to slacken; (discipline) to become lax. **2** vi (bateau) to put in. ◆**—é** a lax.

◆**—ement** nm (de corde etc) slackness; (de discipline) slackening.

relais [r(ə)lɛ] nm Él Rad TV relay; (course de) r. Sp relay (race); **r. routier** transport café, Am truck stop (café); **prendre le r.** to take over (de from).

relance [r(ə)lɑ̃s] nf (reprise) revival. ◆**relancer** vt to throw back; (moteur) to restart; (industrie etc) to put back on its feet; **r. qn** (solliciter) to pester s.o.

relater [r(ə)late] vt to relate (**que** that).

relatif, -ive [r(ə)latif, -iv] a relative (**à** to). ◆**relativement** adv relatively; **r. à** compared to, relative to.

relation [r(ə)lasjɔ̃] nf (rapport) relation(ship); (ami) acquaintance; **avoir des relations** (amis influents) to have connections; **entrer/être en relations avec** to come into/be in contact with; **relations internationales**/etc international/etc relations.

relax(e) [rəlaks] a Fam relaxed, informal.

relaxer (se) [sər(ə)lakse] vpr to relax. ◆**relaxation** nf relaxation.

relayer [r(ə)leje] vt to relieve, take over from; (émission) to relay; — **se r.** vpr to take (it in) turns (**pour faire** to do); Sp to take over from one another.

reléguer [r(ə)lege] vt to relegate (**à** to).

relent [rəlɑ̃] nm stench, smell.

relève [r(ə)lɛv] nf (remplacement) relief; **prendre la r.** to take over (de from).

relev/er [rəlve] vt to raise; (ramasser) to pick up; (chaise etc) to put up straight; (personne tombée) to help up; (col) to turn up; (manches) to roll up; (copier) to note down; (traces) to find; (relayer) to relieve; (rehausser) to enhance; (sauce) to season; (faute) to pick up out; (compteur) to read; (défi) to accept; (économie, pays) to put back on its feet; (mur) to rebuild; **r. qn de** (fonctions) to relieve s.o. of; — **v r. de** (dépendre de) to come under; (maladie) to get over; — **se r.** vpr (personne) to get up; **se r. de** (malheur) to recover from; (ruines) to rise from. ◆**—é** nm list; (de dépenses) statement; (de compteur) reading; **r. de compte** (bank) statement. ◆**relèvement** nm (d'économie, de pays) recovery.

relief [rəljɛf] **1** nm (forme, ouvrage) relief; **en r.** (cinéma) three-D; (livre) pop-up; **mettre en r.** Fig to highlight. **2** nmpl (de repas) remains.

relier [rəlje] vt to link, connect (**à** to); (ensemble) to link (together); (livre) to bind.

religion [r(ə)liʒjɔ̃] nf religion; (foi) faith. ◆**religieux, -euse 1** a religious; **mariage**

r. church wedding; — nm monk; — nf nun. **2** nf Culin cream bun.

reliquat [r(ə)lika] nm (de dette etc) remainder.

relique [r(ə)lik] nf relic.

relire* [r(ə)lir] vt to reread.

reliure [rəljyr] nf (couverture de livre) binding; (art) bookbinding.

reluire [r(ə)lɥir] vi to shine, gleam; **faire r.** (polir) to shine (up). ◆**reluisant** a shiny; **peu r.** Fig far from brilliant.

reluquer [r(ə)lyke] vt Fig to eye (up).

remâcher [r(ə)maʃe] vt Fig to brood over.

remanier [r(ə)manje] vt (texte) to revise; (ministère) to reshuffle. ◆**remaniement** nm revision; reshuffle.

remarier (se) [sər(ə)marje] vpr to remarry.

remarque [r(ə)mark] nf remark; (annotation) note; **je lui en ai fait la r.** I remarked on it to him ou her. ◆**remarquable** a remarkable (**par** for). ◆**remarquablement** adv remarkably. ◆**remarquer** vt **1** (apercevoir) to notice (**que** that); **faire r.** to point out (**à** to, **que** that); **se faire r.** to attract attention; **remarque!** mind (you)! **2** (dire) to remark (**que** that).

rembarrer [rɑ̃bare] vt to rebuff, snub.

remblai [rɑ̃blɛ] nm (terres) embankment. ◆**remblayer** vt (route) to bank up; (trou) to fill in.

rembourr/er [rɑ̃bure] vt (matelas etc) to stuff, pad; (vêtement) to pad. ◆**—age** nm (action, matière) stuffing; padding.

rembourser [rɑ̃burse] vt to pay back, repay; (billet) to refund. ◆**remboursement** nm repayment; refund; **envoi contre r.** cash on delivery.

remède [r(ə)mɛd] nm remedy, cure; (médicament) medicine. ◆**remédier** vi **r. à** to remedy.

remémorer (se) [sər(ə)memɔre] vpr (histoire etc) to recollect.

remercier [r(ə)mɛrsje] vt **1** to thank (**de qch, pour qch**, for sth); **je vous remercie d'être venu** thank you for coming; **je vous remercie** (non merci) no thank you. **2** (congédier) to dismiss. ◆**remerciements** nmpl thanks.

remettre* [r(ə)mɛtr] vt to put back, replace; (vêtement) to put back on; (donner) to hand over (**à** to); (restituer) to give back (**à** to); (démission, devoir) to hand in; (différer) to postpone (**à** until); (ajouter) to add more ou another; (peine) Jur to remit; (guérir) to restore to health; (reconnaître) to place, remember; **r. en cause** ou **question** to call into question; **r. en état** to repair; **r. ça** Fam to start again; **se r. à** (*activité*) to go back to; **se r. à faire** to start to do again; **se r. de** (*chagrin, maladie*) to recover from, get over; **s'en r. à** to rely on. ◆**remise** *nf* **1** (*de lettre etc*) delivery; (*de peine*) Jur remission; (*ajournement*) postponement; **r. en cause** *ou* **question** calling into question; **r. en état** repair(ing). **2** (*rabais*) discount. ◆(*local*) shed; Aut garage. ◆**remiser** *vt* to put away.

réminiscences [reminisãs] *nfpl* (*vague*) recollections, reminiscences.

rémission [remisjɔ̃] *nf* Jur Rel Méd remission; **sans r.** (*travailler etc*) relentlessly.

remmener [rɑ̃mne] *vt* to take back.

remonte-pente [r(ə)mɔ̃tpɑ̃t] *nm* ski lift.

remont/er [r(ə)mɔ̃te] *vi* (*aux* **être**) to come *ou* go back up; (*niveau, prix*) to rise again, go back up; (*dans le temps*) to go back (**à** to); **r. dans** (*voiture*) to go *ou* get back in(to); (*bus, train*) to go *ou* get back on(to); **r. sur** (*cheval, vélo*) to remount; — *vt* (*aux* **avoir**) (*escalier, pente*) to come *ou* go back up; (*porter*) to bring *ou* take back up; (*montre*) to wind up; (*relever*) to raise; (*col*) to turn up; (*objet démonté*) to reassemble; (*garde-robe etc*) to restock; **r. qn** (*ragaillardir*) to buck s.o. up; **r. le moral à qn** to cheer s.o. up. ◆**—ant** *a* (*boisson*) fortifying; — *nm* Méd tonic. ◆**—ée** *nf* (*de pente etc*) ascent; (*d'eau, de prix*) rise. **2 r. mécanique** ski lift. ◆**remontoir** *nm* (*de mécanisme, montre*) winder.

remontrance [r(ə)mɔ̃trãs] *nf* reprimand; **faire des remontrances à** to reprimand, remonstrate with.

remontrer [r(ə)mɔ̃tre] *vt* **en r. à qn** to prove one's superiority over s.o.

remords [r(ə)mɔr] *nm & nmpl* remorse; **avoir des r.** to feel remorse.

remorque [r(ə)mɔrk] *nf* Aut trailer; (*câble de*) **r.** towrope; **prendre en r.** to tow; **en r.** on tow; **en r.** (*voiture, bateau*) to tow. ◆**remorquer** *vt* (*voiture, bateau*) to tow. ◆**remorqueur** *nm* tug(boat).

remous [r(ə)mu] *nm* eddy; (*de foule*) bustle; (*agitation*) Fig turmoil.

rempart [rɑ̃par] *nm* rampart.

remplacer [rɑ̃plase] *vt* to replace (**par** with, by); (*succéder à*) to take over from; (*temporairement*) to stand in for. ◆**remplaçant, -ante** *nmf* (*personne*) replacement; (*enseignant*) supply teacher; Sp reserve. ◆**remplacement** *nm* (*action*) replacement; **assurer le r. de qn** to stand in for s.o.; **en r.** (*en remplaçant*).

rempl/ir [rɑ̃plir] *vt* to fill (up) (**de** with); (*fiche etc*) to fill in *ou* out; (*condition, de-*

voir, tâche) to fulfil; (*fonctions*) to perform; — *se r.* *vpr* to fill (up). ◆**—i** *a* full (**de** of). ◆**remplissage** *nm* filling; (*verbiage*) Péj padding.

remporter [rɑ̃pɔrte] *vt* **1** (*objet*) to take back. **2** (*prix, victoire*) to win; (*succès*) to achieve.

remu/er [r(ə)mɥe] *vt* (*déplacer, émouvoir*) to move; (*café etc*) to stir; (*terre*) to turn over; (*salade*) to toss; — *vi* to move; (*gigoter*) to fidget; (*se rebeller*) to stir; — *se r.* *vpr* to move; (*se démener*) to exert oneself. ◆**—ant** *a* (*enfant*) restless, fidgety. ◆**remue-ménage** *nm inv* commotion.

rémunérer [remynere] *vt* (*personne*) to pay; (*travail*) to pay for. ◆**rémunérateur, -trice** *a* remunerative. ◆**rémunération** *nf* payment (**de** for).

renâcler [r(ə)nakle] *vi* **1** (*cheval*) to snort. **2 r. à** to jib at, balk at.

renaître [r(ə)nɛtr] *vi* (*fleur*) to grow again; (*espoir, industrie*) to revive. ◆**renaissance** *nf* rebirth, renaissance.

renard [r(ə)nar] *nm* fox.

renchérir [rɑ̃ʃerir] *vi* **r. sur** *ou* **sur ce que qn dit**/*etc* to go further than s.o. in what one says/*etc*.

rencontre [rɑ̃kɔ̃tr] *nf* meeting; (*inattendue*) & Mil encounter; Sp match, Am game; (*de routes*) junction; **aller à la r. de** to go to meet. ◆**rencontrer** *vt* to meet; (*difficultés*) to come up against, encounter; (*trouver*) to come across, find; (*heurter*) to hit; (*équipe*) Sp to play; — *se r.* *vpr* to meet.

rendez-vous [rɑ̃devu] *nm inv* appointment; (*d'amoureux*) date; (*lieu*) meeting place; **donner r.-vous à qn, prendre r.-vous avec qn** to make an appointment with.

rendormir (**se**) [sərɑ̃dɔrmir] *vpr* to go back to sleep.

rend/re [rɑ̃dr] *vt* (*restituer*) to give back, return; (*hommage*) to pay; (*invitation*) to return; (*santé*) to restore; (*monnaie, son*) to give; (*justice*) to dispense; (*jugement*) to pronounce, give; (*armes*) to surrender; (*exprimer, traduire*) to render; (*vomir*) to bring up; **r. célèbre**/**plus grand**/**possible**/*etc* to make famous/bigger/possible/*etc*; — *vi* (*arbre, terre*) to yield; (*vomir*) to be sick; — *se r.* *vpr* (*capituler*) to surrender (**à** to); (*aller*) to go (**à** to); **se r. à** (*évidence, ordres*) to submit to; **se r. malade**/**utile**/*etc* to make oneself ill/useful/*etc*. ◆**—u** *a* (*fatigué*) exhausted; **être r.** (*arrivé*) to have arrived. ◆**rendement** *nm* Agr Fin yield; (*de personne, machine*) output.

renégat, -ate [rənega, -at] *nmf* renegade.

rênes [rɛn] *nfpl* reins.

renferm/er [rɑ̃fɛrme] *vt* to contain; **— se r.** *vpr* **se r. (en soi-même)** to withdraw into oneself. ◆**—é** 1 *a* (*personne*) withdrawn. 2 *nm* **sentir le r.** (*chambre etc*) to smell stuffy.

renflé [rɑ̃fle] *a* bulging. ◆**renflement** *nm* bulge.

renflouer [rɑ̃flue] *vt* (*navire*) & *Com* to refloat.

renfoncement [rɑ̃fɔ̃smɑ̃] *nm* recess; **dans le r. d'une porte** in a doorway.

renforcer [rɑ̃fɔrse] *vt* to reinforce, strengthen. ◆**renforcement** *nm* reinforcement, strengthening. ◆**renfort** *nm* **des renforts** *Mil* reinforcements; **à grand r. de** *Fig* with a great deal of.

renfrogn/er (se) [sərɑ̃frɔɲe] *vpr* to scowl. ◆**—é** *a* scowling, sullen.

rengaine [rɑ̃gɛn] *nf* **la même r.** *Fig Péj* the same old song *ou* story.

rengorger (se) [sərɑ̃gɔrʒe] *vpr* to give oneself airs.

renier [rənje] *vt* (*ami, pays etc*) to disown; (*foi, opinion*) to renounce. ◆**reniement** *nm* disowning; renunciation.

renifler [r(ə)nifle] *vti* to sniff. ◆**reniflement** *nm* sniff.

renne [rɛn] *nm* reindeer.

renom [rənɔ̃] *nm* renown; (*réputation*) reputation (**de** for). ◆**renommé** *a* famous, renowned (**pour** for). ◆**renommée** *nf* fame, renown; (*réputation*) reputation.

renoncer [r(ə)nɔ̃se] *vi* **r. à** to give up, abandon; **r. à faire** to give up (the idea of) doing. ◆**renoncement** *nm*, ◆**renonciation** *nf* renunciation (**à** of).

renouer [rənwe] *vt* (*lacet etc*) to retie. 2 (*reprendre*) to renew; **— vi r. avec qch** (*mode, tradition etc*) to revive sth; **r. avec qn** to take up with s.o. again.

renouveau, -x [r(ə)nuvo] *nm* revival.

renouveler [r(ə)nuvle] *vt* to renew; (*action, erreur, question*) to repeat; **— se r.** *vpr* (*incident*) to recur, happen again; (*cellules, sang*) to be renewed. ◆**renouvelable** *a* renewable. ◆**renouvellement** *nm* renewal.

rénover [renɔve] *vt* (*institution, méthode*) to reform; (*édifice, meuble etc*) to renovate. ◆**rénovation** *nf* reform; renovation.

renseign/er [rɑ̃sɛɲe] *vt* to inform, give information to (**sur** about); **— se r.** *vpr* to inquire, make inquiries, find out (**sur** about). ◆**—ement** *nm* (piece of) information; *pl* information; *Tél* directory inquiries, *Am* information; *Mil* intelligence;

prendre *ou* **demander des reseignements** to make inquiries.

rentable [rɑ̃tabl] *a* profitable. ◆**rentabilité** *nf* profitability.

rente [rɑ̃t] *nf* (*private income*); (*pension*) pension; **avoir des rentes** to have private means. ◆**rentier, -ière** *nmf* person of private means.

rentr/er [rɑ̃tre] *vi* (*aux être*) to go *ou* come back, return; (*chez soi*) to go *ou* come (back) home; (*entrer*) to go *ou* come in; (*entrer de nouveau*) to go *ou* come back in; (*école*) to start again; (*argent*) to come in; **r. dans** (*entrer dans*) to go *ou* come into; (*entrer de nouveau dans*) to go *ou* come back into; (*famille, pays*) to return to; (*ses frais*) to get back; (*catégorie*) to come under; (*heurter*) to crash into; (*s'emboîter dans*) to fit into; **r. (en classe)** to start school again; **je lui suis rentré dedans** (*frapper*) *Fam* I laid into him *ou* her; **— vt** (*aux avoir*) to bring *ou* take in; (*voiture*) to put away; (*chemise*) to tuck in; (*griffes*) to draw in. ◆**—é** *a* (*colère*) suppressed; (*yeux*) sunken. ◆**—ée** *nf* 1 (*retour*) return; (*de parlement*) reassembly; (*d'acteur*) comeback; **r. (des classes)** beginning of term *ou* of the school year. 2 (*des foins etc*) bringing in; (*d'impôt*) collection; *pl* (*argent*) receipts.

renverse (à la) [alarɑ̃vɛrs] *adv* (*tomber*) backwards, on one's back.

renvers/er [rɑ̃vɛrse] *vt* (*mettre à l'envers*) to turn upside down; (*faire tomber*) to knock over *ou* down; (*piéton*) to knock down, run over; (*liquide*) to spill, knock over; (*courant, ordre*) to reverse; (*gouvernement*) to overturn, overthrow; (*projet*) to upset; (*tête*) to tip back; **— se r.** *vpr* (*en arrière*) to lean back; (*bouteille, vase etc*) to fall over. ◆**—ant** *a* (*nouvelle etc*) astounding. ◆**—ement** *nm* (*d'ordre, de situation*) reversal; (*de gouvernement*) overthrow.

renvoi [rɑ̃vwa] *nm* 1 return; dismissal; expulsion; postponement; (*dans un livre*) reference. 2 (*rot*) belch, burp. ◆**renvoyer*** *vt* to send back, return; (*importun*) to send away; (*employé*) to dismiss; (*élève*) to expel; (*balle etc*) to throw back; (*ajourner*) to postpone (**à** until); (*lumière, image etc*) to reflect; **r. qn à** (*adresser à*) to refer s.o. to.

réorganiser [reɔrganize] *vt* to reorganize.

réouverture [reuvɛrtyr] *nf* reopening.

repaire [r(ə)pɛr] *nm* den.

repaître (se) [sərəpɛtr] *vpr* **se r. de** (*sang*) *Fig* to wallow in.

répand/re [repɑ̃dr] *vt* (*liquide*) to spill;

(idées, joie, nouvelle) to spread; *(fumée, odeur)* to give off; *(chargement, lumière, larmes, sang)* to shed; *(gravillons etc)* to scatter; *(dons)* to lavish; **— se r.** *vpr (nouvelle, peur etc)* to spread; *(liquide)* to spill; **se r. dans** *(fumée, odeur)* to spread through; *(louanges etc)* to pour forth praise/etc. ◆**—u** *a (opinion, usage)* widespread; *(épars)* scattered.

reparaître [r(ə)parɛtr] *vi* to reappear.

réparer [repare] *vt* to repair, mend; *(forces, santé)* to restore; *(faute)* to make amends for; *(perte)* to make good; *(erreur)* to put right. ◆**réparable** *a (montre etc)* repairable. ◆**réparateur, -trice** *nmf* repairer; *— a (sommeil)* refreshing. ◆**réparation** *nf* repair(ing); *(compensation)* amends, compensation *(de* for); *pl Mil Hist* reparations; **en r.** under repair.

reparler [r(ə)parle] *vi* **r. de** to talk about again.

repartie [reparti] *nf (réponse vive)* repartee.

repartir* [r(ə)partir] *vi (aux être)* to set off again; *(s'en retourner)* to go back; *(reprendre)* to start again; **r. à** *ou* **de zéro** to go back to square one.

répartir [repartir] *vt* to distribute; *(partager)* to share (out); *(classer)* to divide (up); *(étaler dans le temps)* to spread (out) *(sur* over). ◆**répartition** *nf* distribution; sharing; division.

repas [r(ə)pɑ] *nm* meal; **prendre un r.** to have *ou* eat a meal.

repass/er [r(ə)pɑse] *vi* to come *ou* go back; *— vt (traverser)* to go back over; *(examen)* to resit; *(leçon, rôle)* to go over; *(film)* to show again; *(maladie, travail)* to pass on *(à* to). **2** *vt (linge)* to iron. **3** *vt (couteau)* to sharpen. ◆**—age** *nm* ironing.

repêcher [r(ə)peʃe] *vt* to fish out; *(candidat)* Fam to allow to pass.

repenser [r(ə)pɑse] *vt* to rethink.

repentir [r(ə)pɑtir] *nm* repentance. ◆**se repentir*** *vpr Rel* to repent *(de* of); **se r. de** *(regretter)* to regret, be sorry for. ◆**repentant** *a*, ◆**repenti** *a* repentant.

répercuter [reperkyte] *vt (son)* to echo; **— se r.** *vpr* to echo, reverberate; **se r.** *sur Fig* to have repercussions on. ◆**répercussion** *nf* repercussion.

repère [r(ə)pɛr] *nm (guide)* mark; *(jalon)* marker; **point de r.** *(espace, temps)* landmark, point of reference. ◆**repérer** *vt* to locate; *(personnne)* Fam to spot; **— se r.** *vpr* to get one's bearings.

répertoire [repɛrtwar] *nm* **1** index; *(carnet)* indexed notebook; **r. d'adresses** address

book. **2** *Th* repertoire. ◆**répertorier** *vt* to index.

répéter [repete] *vti* to repeat; *Th* to rehearse; **— se r.** *vpr (radoter)* to repeat oneself; *(se reproduire)* to repeat itself. ◆**répétitif, -ive** *a* repetitive. ◆**répétition** *nf* repetition; *Th* rehearsal; **r. générale** *Th* (final) dress rehearsal.

repiquer [r(ə)pike] *vt* **1** *(plante)* to plant out. **2** *(disque)* to tape, record (on tape).

répit [repi] *nm* rest, respite; **sans r.** ceaselessly.

replacer [r(ə)plase] *vt* to replace, put back.

repli [r(ə)pli] *nm* fold; withdrawal; *pl (de l'âme)* recesses. ◆**replier 1** *vt* to fold (up); *(siège)* to fold up; *(couteau, couverture)* to fold back; *(ailes, jambes)* to tuck in; **— se r.** *vpr (siège)* to fold up; *(couteau, couverture)* to fold back. **2** *vt, —* **se r.** *vpr Mil* to withdraw; **se r. sur soi-même** to withdraw into oneself.

réplique [replik] *nf* **1** *(réponse)* reply; *(riposte)* retort; *Th* lines; **pas de r.!** no answering back!; **sans r.** *(argument)* irrefutable. **2** *(copie)* replica. ◆**répliquer** *vt* to reply (que that); *(riposter)* to retort (que that); *— vi (être impertinent)* to answer back.

répond/re [repɔdr] *vi* to answer, reply; *(être impertinent)* to answer back; *(réagir)* to respond *(à* to); **r. à qn** to answer s.o., reply to s.o.; *(avec impertinence)* to answer s.o. back; **r. à** *(lettre, objection, question)* to answer, reply to; *(salut)* to return; *(besoin)* to meet, answer; *(correspond à)* to correspond to; **r. de** *(garantir)* to answer for *(s.o., sth)*; *— vt (remarque etc)* to answer *ou* reply with; **r. que** to answer *ou* reply that. ◆**—ant, -ante** *nmf* guarantor. **2** *nm* **avoir du r.** to have money behind one. ◆**—eur** *nm Tél* answering machine. ◆**réponse** *nf* answer, reply; *(réaction)* response *(à* to); **en r. à** in answer *ou* reply *ou* response to.

reporter¹ [r(ə)porte] *vt* to take back; *(différer)* to postpone, put off *(à* until); *(transcrire, transférer)* to transfer *(sur* to); *(somme)* Com to carry forward *(sur* to); **se r. à** *(texte etc)* to refer to; *(en esprit)* to go *ou* think back to. ◆**report** *nm* postponement; transfer; *Com* carrying forward. ◆**reportage** *nm* (news) report, article; *(en direct)* commentary; *(métier)* reporting.

reporter² [r(ə)portɛr] *nm* reporter.

repos [r(ə)po] *nm* rest; *(tranquillité)* peace (and quiet); *(de l'esprit)* peace of mind; **r.!** *Mil* at ease!; **jour de r.** day off; **de tout r.** *(situation etc)* safe. ◆**repos/er 1** *vt (objet)* to put back down; *(problème, question)* to raise again. **2** vt (délasser) to rest, relax; **r. sa tête sur** (appuyer) to rest one's head on; – vi (être enterré ou étendu) to rest, lie; **r. sur** (bâtiment) to be built on; (théorie etc) to be based on, rest on; **laisser r.** (vin) to allow to settle; **— se r.** vpr to rest; **se r. sur qn** to rely on s.o. ◆**—ant** a relaxing, restful. ◆**—é** a rested, fresh.

repouss/er [r(ə)puse] **1** vt to push back; (écarter) to push away; (attaque, ennemi) to repulse; (importun etc) to turn away, repulse; (dégoûter) to repel; (décliner) to reject; (différer) to put off, postpone. **2** vi (cheveux, feuilles) to grow again. ◆**—ant** a repulsive, repellent.

répréhensible [repreãsibl] a reprehensible, blameworthy.

reprendre* [r(ə)prãdr] vt (objet) to take back; (évadé, ville) to recapture; (passer prendre) to pick up again; (souffle) to get back; (activité) to resume, take up again; (texte) to go back over; (vêtement) to alter; (histoire, refrain) to take up; (pièce) Th to put on again; (blâmer) to admonish; (corriger) to correct; **r. de la viande/un œuf/etc** to take (some) more meat/another egg/etc; **r. ses esprits** to come round; **r. des forces** to recover one's strength; – vi (recommencer) to resume; (affaires) to pick up again; (dire) to go on, continue; **— se r.** vpr (se ressaisir) to take a hold on oneself; (se corriger) to correct oneself; **s'y r. à deux/plusieurs fois** to have another go/several goes (at it).

représailles [r(ə)prezaj] nfpl reprisals, retaliation.

représent/er [r(ə)prezãte] vt to represent; (jouer) Th to perform; **— se r.** vpr (s'imaginer) to imagine. ◆**—ant, -ante** nmf representative; **r. de commerce** (travelling) salesman ou saleswoman, sales representative. ◆**représentatif, -ive** a representative (de of). ◆**représentation** nf representation; Th performance.

répression [represjɔ̃] nf suppression, repression; (mesures de contrôle) Pol repression. ◆**répressif, -ive** a repressive. ◆**réprimer** vt (sentiment, révolte etc) to suppress, repress.

réprimande [reprimãd] nf reprimand. ◆**réprimander** vt to reprimand.

repris [r(ə)pri] nm **r. de justice** hardened criminal.

reprise [r(ə)priz] nf (de ville) Mil recapture; (recommencement) resumption; (de pièce de théâtre, de coutume) revival; Rad TV repeat; (de tissu) mend, repair; Boxe round;

(essor) Com recovery, revival; (d'un locataire) money for fittings; (de marchandise) taking back; (pour nouvel achat) part exchange, trade-in; pl Aut acceleration; **à plusieurs reprises** on several occasions. ◆**repriser** vt (chaussette etc) to mend, darn.

réprobation [reprobasjɔ̃] nf disapproval. ◆**réprobateur, -trice** a disapproving.

reproche [r(ə)prɔʃ] nm reproach; **faire des reproches à qn** to reproach s.o.; **sans r.** beyond reproach. ◆**reprocher** vt **r. qch à qn** to reproach ou blame s.o. for sth; **r. qch à qch** to have sth against sth; **n'avoir rien à se r.** to have nothing to reproach ou blame oneself for.

reproduire* [r(ə)prɔdɥir] **1** vt (son, modèle etc) to reproduce; **— se r.** vpr Biol Bot to reproduce. **2** se r. vpr (incident etc) to happen again, recur. ◆**reproducteur, -trice** a reproductive. ◆**reproduction** nf (de son etc) & Biol Bot reproduction.

réprouver [repruve] vt to disapprove of, condemn.

reptile [reptil] nm reptile.

repu [rəpy] a (rassasié) satiated.

république [repyblik] nf republic. ◆**républicain, -aine** a & nmf republican.

répudier [repydje] vt to repudiate.

répugnant [repynã] a repugnant, loathsome. ◆**répugnance** nf repugnance, loathing (pour for); (manque d'enthousiasme) reluctance. ◆**répugner** vi **r. à qn** to be repugnant to s.o.; **r. à faire** to be loath to do.

répulsion [repylsjɔ̃] nf repulsion.

réputation [repytasjɔ̃] nf reputation; **avoir la r. d'être franc** to have a reputation for frankness ou for being frank. ◆**réputé** a (célèbre) renowned (pour for); **r. pour être** (considéré comme) reputed to be.

requérir [rəkerir] vt (nécessiter) to demand, require; (peine) Jur to call for. ◆**requête** nf request; Jur petition. ◆**requis** a required.

requiem [rekɥijem] nm inv requiem.

requin [r(ə)kɛ̃] nm (poisson) & Fig shark.

réquisition [rekizisjɔ̃] nf requisition. ◆**réquisitionner** vt to requisition, commandeer.

réquisitoire [rekizitwar] nm (critique) indictment (contre of).

rescapé, -ée [reskape] a surviving; – nmf survivor.

rescousse (à la) [alareskus] adv to the rescue.

réseau, -x [rezo] *nm* network; **r. d'espionnage** spy ring *ou* network.

réserve [rezɛrv] *nf* **1** (*restriction, doute*) reservation; (*réticence*) reserve; **sans r.** (*admiration etc*) unqualified; **sous r. de** subject to; **sous toutes réserves** without guarantee. **2** (*provision*) reserve; (*entrepôt*) storeroom; (*de bibliothèque*) stacks; **la r.** *Mil* the reserve; **les réserves** (*soldats*) the reserves; **en r.** in reserve. **3** (*de chasse, pêche*) preserve; (*indienne*) reservation; **r. naturelle** nature reserve.

réserv/er [rezɛrve] *vt* to reserve; (*garder*) to keep, save; (*marchandises*) to put aside (**à** for); (*place, table*) to book, reserve; (*sort, surprise etc*) to hold in store (**à** for); **se r. pour** to save oneself for; **se r. de faire** to reserve the right to do. ◆**—é** *a* (*personne, place*) reserved; (*prudent*) guarded. ◆**réservation** *nf* reservation, booking. ◆**réservoir** *nm* (*lac*) reservoir; (*citerne, cuve*) tank; **r. d'essence** *Aut* petrol *ou* Am gas tank.

résidence [rezidɑ̃s] *nf* residence; **r. secondaire** second home; **r. universitaire** hall of residence. ◆**résident, -ente** *nmf* (*foreign*) resident. ◆**résidentiel, -ielle** *a* (*quartier*) residential. ◆**résider** *vi* to be resident (**à, en, dans** in); **r. dans** (*consister dans*) to lie in.

résidu [rezidy] *nm* residue.

résigner (se) [sərezine] *vpr* to resign oneself (**à qch** to sth, **à faire** to doing). ◆**résignation** *nf* resignation.

résilier [rezilje] *vt* (*contrat*) to terminate. ◆**résiliation** *nf* termination.

résille [rezij] *nf* (*pour cheveux*) hairnet.

résine [rezin] *nf* resin.

résistance [rezistɑ̃s] *nf* resistance (**à** to); (*conducteur*) *Él* (heating) element; **plat de r.** main dish. ◆**résist/er** *vi* **r. à** to resist; (*chaleur, fatigue, souffrance*) to withstand; (*examen*) to stand up to. ◆**—ant, -ante** *a* tough, strong; **r. à la chaleur** heat-resistant; **r. au choc** shockproof; **—** *nmf* *Mil Hist* Resistance fighter.

résolu [rezɔly] *voir* **résoudre**; **—** *a* resolute, determined; **r. à faire** resolved *ou* determined to do. ◆**—ment** *adv* resolutely. ◆**résolution** *nf* (*décision*) resolution; (*fermeté*) determination.

résonance [rezɔnɑ̃s] *nf* resonance.

résonner [rezɔne] *vi* to resound (**de** with); (*salle, voix*) to echo.

résorber [rezɔrbe] *vt* (*chômage*) to reduce; (*excédent*) to absorb; **— se r.** *vpr* to be re-

duced; to be absorbed. ◆**résorption** *nf* reduction; absorption.

résoudre* [rezudr] *vt* (*problème*) to solve; (*difficulté*) to resolve; **r. de faire** to decide *ou* resolve to do; **se r. à faire** to decide *ou* resolve to do; (*se résigner*) to bring oneself to do.

respect [rɛspɛ] *nm* respect (**pour, de** for); **mes respects à** my regards *ou* respects to; **tenir qn en r.** to hold s.o. in check. ◆**respectabilité** *nf* respectability. ◆**respectable** *a* (*honorable, important*) respectable. ◆**respecter** *vt* to respect; **qui se respecte** self-respecting. ◆**respectueux, -euse** *a* respectful (**envers** to, **de** of).

respectif, -ive [rɛspɛktif, -iv] *a* respective. ◆**respectivement** *adv* respectively.

respirer [rɛspire] *vi* to breathe; (*reprendre haleine*) to get one's breath (back); (*être soulagé*) to breathe again; **—** *vt* to breathe (in); (*exprimer*) *Fig* to exude. ◆**respiration** *nf* breathing; (*haleine*) breath; **r. artificielle** *Méd* artificial respiration. ◆**respiratoire** *a* breathing-, respiratory.

resplend/ir [rɛsplɑ̃dir] *vi* to shine; (*visage*) to glow (**de** with). ◆**—issant** *a* radiant.

responsable [rɛspɔ̃sabl] *a* responsible (**de qch** for sth, **devant qn** to s.o.); **—** *nmf* (*chef*) person in charge; (*dans une organisation*) official; (*coupable*) person responsible (**de** for). ◆**responsabilité** *nf* responsibility; (*légale*) liability.

resquiller [rɛskije] *vi* (*au cinéma, dans le métro etc*) to avoid paying; (*sans attendre*) to jump the queue, *Am* cut in (line).

ressaisir (se) [sər(ə)sezir] *vpr* to pull oneself together.

ressasser [r(ə)sase] *vt* (*ruminer*) to keep going over; (*répéter*) to keep trotting out.

ressemblance [r(ə)sɑ̃blɑ̃s] *nf* resemblance, likeness. ◆**ressembl/er** *vi* **r. à** to resemble, look *ou* be like; **cela ne lui ressemble pas** (*ce n'est pas son genre*) that's not like him *ou* her; **— se r.** to look *ou* be alike. ◆**—ant** *a* **portrait r.** good likeness.

ressentiment [r(ə)sɑ̃timɑ̃] *nm* resentment.

ressentir* [r(ə)sɑ̃tir] *vt* to feel; **se r. de** to feel *ou* show the effects of.

resserre [r(ə)sɛr] *nf* storeroom; (*remise*) shed.

resserrer [r(ə)sere] *vt* (*nœud, boulon etc*) to tighten; (*contracter*) to close (up), contract; (*liens*) *Fig* to strengthen; **— se r.** *vpr* to tighten; (*amitié*) to become closer; (*se contracter*) to close (up), contract; (*route etc*) to narrow.

resservir [r(ə)sɛrvir] **1** *vi* (*outil etc*) to come

in useful (again). **2 se r.** *vpr* **se r. de** (*plat etc*) to have another helping of.

ressort [r(ə)sɔr] *nm* **1** *Tech* spring. **2** (*énergie*) spirit. **3 du r.** within the competence of; **en dernier r.** (*décider etc*) in the last resort, as a last resort.

ressortir¹ * [r(ə)sɔrtir] *vi* (*aux* **être**) **1** to go *ou* come back out. **2** (*se voir*) to stand out; **faire r.** to bring out; **il ressort de** (*résulte*) it emerges from.

ressortir² [r(ə)sɔrtir] *vi* (*conjugated like* **finir**) **r. à** to fall within the scope of.

ressortissant, -ante [r(ə)sɔrtisã, -ãt] *nmf* (*citoyen*) national.

ressource [r(ə)surs] **1** *nfpl* (*moyens*) resources; (*argent*) means, resources. **2** *nf* (*recours*) recourse; (*possibilité*) possibility (**de faire** of doing); **dernière r.** last resort.

ressusciter [resysite] *vi* to rise from the dead; (*malade, pays*) to recover, revive; – *vt* (*mort*) to raise; (*malade, mode*) to revive.

restaurant [rɛstɔrã] *nm* restaurant.

restaurer [rɛstɔre] **1** *vt* (*réparer, rétablir*) to restore. **2 se r.** *vpr* to have sth to eat. ◆**restaurateur, -trice** *nmf* **1** (*de tableaux*) restorer. **2** (*hôtelier, hôtelière*) restaurant owner. ◆**restauration** *nf* **1** restoration. **2** (*hôtellerie*) catering.

reste [rɛst] *nm* rest, remainder (**de** of); *Math* remainder; *pl* remains (**de** of); (*de repas*) leftovers; **un r. de fromage/etc** some left-over cheese/*etc*; **au r., du r.** moreover, besides.

rester [rɛste] *vi* (*aux* **être**) to stay, remain; (*calme, jeune etc*) to keep, stay, remain; (*subsister*) to remain, be left; **il reste du pain/etc** there's some bread/*etc* left (over); **il me reste une minute/etc** I have one minute/*etc* left; **l'argent qui lui reste** the money *he ou* she has left; **reste à savoir** it remains to be seen; **il me reste deux choses à faire** I still have two things to do; **il me reste à vous remercier** it remains for me to thank you; **en r. à** to stop at; **restons-en là** let's leave it at that. ◆**restant** *a* remaining; **poste restante** poste restante, *Am* general delivery; – *nm* **le r.** the rest, the remainder; **un r. de viande/etc** some left-over meat/*etc*.

restituer [rɛstitɥe] *vt* **1** (*rendre*) to return, restore (**à** to). **2** (*son*) to reproduce; (*énergie*) to release. ◆**restitution** *nf* return.

restreindre * [rɛstrɛ̃dr] *vt* to restrict, limit (**à** to); – **se r.** *vpr* to decrease; (*faire des économies*) to cut back *ou* down. ◆**restreint** *a* limited, restricted (**à** to). ◆**restrictif, -ive**

a restrictive. ◆**restriction** *nf* restriction; **sans r.** unreservedly.

résultat [rezylta] *nm* result; (*conséquence*) outcome, result; **avoir qch pour r.** to result in sth. ◆**résulter** *vi* **r. de** to result from.

résum/er [rezyme] *vt* to summarize; (*récapituler*) to sum up; – **se r.** *vpr* (*orateur*) to sum up; **se r. à** (*se réduire à*) to boil down to. ◆**-é** *nm* summary; **en r.** in short; (*en récapitulant*) to sum up.

résurrection [rezyrɛksjɔ̃] *nf* resurrection.

rétabl/ir [retablir] *vt* to restore; (*malade*) to re-establish; (*malade*) to restore to health; (*employé*) to reinstate; – **se r.** *vpr* to be restored; (*malade*) to recover. ◆**-issement** *nm* restoring; re-establishment; *Méd* recovery.

retaper [r(ə)tape] *vt* (*maison, voiture etc*) to do up; (*lit*) to straighten; (*malade*) *Fam* to buck up.

retard [r(ə)tar] *nm* lateness; (*sur un programme etc*) delay; (*infériorité*) backwardness; **en r.** late; (*retardé*) backward; **en r. dans qch** behind in sth; **en r. sur qn/qch** behind s.o./sth; **rattraper** *ou* **combler son r.** to catch up; **avoir du r.** to be late; (*sur un programme*) to be behind (schedule); (*montre*) to be slow; **avoir une heure de r.** to be an hour late; **prendre du r.** (*montre*) to lose (time); **sans r.** without delay. ◆**retardataire** *a* (*arrivant*) late; **enfant r.** *Méd* slow learner; – *nmf* latecomer. ◆**retardement** *nm* **à r.** delayed-action; **bombe à r.** time bomb.

retard/er [r(ə)tarde] *vt* to delay; (*date, départ, montre*) to put back; **r. qn** (*dans une activité*) to put back; – *vi* (*montre*) to be slow; **r. de cinq minutes** to be five minutes slow; **r.** (*sur son temps*) (*personne*) to be behind the times. ◆**-é, -ée** *a* (*enfant*) backward; – *nmf* backward child.

retenir * [rətnir] *vt* (*empêcher d'agir, contenir*) to hold back; (*attention, souffle*) to hold; (*réserver*) to book; (*se souvenir de*) to remember; (*fixer*) to hold (in place), secure; (*déduire*) to take off; (*candidature, proposition*) to accept; (*chiffre*) *Math* to carry; (*chaleur, odeur*) to retain; (*invité, suspect etc*) to detain, keep; **r. qn prisonnier** to keep *ou* hold s.o. prisoner; **r. qn de faire** to stop s.o. (from) doing; – **se r.** *vpr* (*se contenir*) to restrain oneself; **se r. de faire** to stop oneself (from) doing; **se r. à** to cling to. ◆**retenue** *nf* **1** (*modération*) restraint. **2** (*de salaire*) deduction, stoppage; (*chiffre*) *Math* figure carried over. **3** *Scol* detention; **en r.** in detention.

retent/ir [r(ə)tɑ̃tir] *vi* to ring (out) (**de** with). ◆**—issant** *a* resounding; (*scandale*) major. ◆**—issement** *nm* (*effet*) effect; **avoir un grand r.** (*film etc*) to create a stir.

réticent [retisɑ̃] *a* (*réservé*) reticent; (*hésitant*) reluctant. ◆**réticence** *nf* reticence; reluctance.

rétine [retin] *nf Anat* retina.

retir/er [r(ə)tire] *vt* to withdraw; (*sortir*) to take out; (*ôter*) to take off; (*éloigner*) to take away; (*reprendre*) to pick up; (*offre, plainte*) to take back, withdraw; **r. qch à qn** (*permis etc*) to take sth away from s.o.; **r. qch de** (*gagner*) to derive sth from; **— se r.** *vpr* to withdraw, retire (**de** from); (*mer*) to ebb. ◆**—é** *a* (*lieu, vie*) secluded.

retomber [r(ə)tɔ̃be] *vi* to fall; (*de nouveau*) to fall again; (*pendre*) to hang (down); (*après un saut etc*) to land; (*intérêt*) to slacken; **r. dans** (*erreur, situation*) to fall ou sink back into; **r. sur qn** (*frais, responsabilité*) to fall on s.o. ◆**retombées** *nfpl* (*radioactives*) fallout.

rétorquer [retɔrke] *vt* **r. que** to retort that.

retors [rətɔr] *a* wily, crafty.

rétorsion [retɔrsjɔ̃] *nf Pol* retaliation; **mesure de r.** reprisal.

retouche [r(ə)tuʃ] *nf* touching up; alteration. ◆**retoucher** *vt* (*photo, tableau*) to touch up, retouch; (*texte, vêtement*) to alter.

retour [r(ə)tur] *nm* return; (*de fortune*) reversal; **être de r.** to be back (**de** from); **en r.** (*en échange*) in return; **par r. (du courrier)** by return of (post), *Am* by return mail; **à mon retour** when I get ou get back (**de** from); **r. en arrière** flashback; **r. de flamme** *Fig* backlash; **match r.** return match ou *Am* game.

retourner [r(ə)turne] *vt* (*aux* avoir) (*tableau etc*) to turn round; (*matelas, steak etc*) to turn over; (*foin, terre etc*) to turn; (*vêtement, sac etc*) to turn inside out; (*maison*) to turn upside down; (*compliment, lettre*) to return; **r. qn** (*bouleverser*) *Fam* to upset s.o., shake s.o.; **r. contre qn** (*argument*) to turn against s.o.; (*arme*) to turn on s.o.; **de quoi il retourne** what it's about; **— vi** (*aux* être) to go back, return; **— se r.** *vpr* (*pour regarder*) to turn round, look back; (*sur le dos*) to turn over ou round; (*dans son lit*) to toss and turn; (*voiture*) to overturn; **s'en r.** to go back; **se r. contre** *Fig* to turn against.

retracer [r(ə)trase] *vt* (*histoire etc*) to retrace.

rétracter [retrakte] *vt*, **— se r.** *vpr* to retract. ◆**rétractation** *nf* (*désaveu*) retraction.

retrait [r(ə)trɛ] *nm* withdrawal; (*de bagages, billets*) collection; (*de mer*) ebb(ing); **en r.** (*maison etc*) set back.

retraite [r(ə)trɛt] *nf* **1** (*d'employé*) retirement; (*pension*) (retirement) pension; (*refuge*) retreat, refuge; **r. anticipée** early retirement; **prendre sa r.** to retire; **à la r.** retired; **mettre à la r.** to pension off. **2** *Mil* retreat; **r. aux flambeaux** torchlight tattoo. ◆**retraité, -ée** *a* retired; **— *nmf*** senior citizen, (old age) pensioner.

retrancher [r(ə)trɑ̃ʃe] **1** *vt* (*mot, passage etc*) to cut (**de** from); (*argent, quantité*) to deduct (**de** from). **2** **se r.** *vpr* (*soldat, gangster etc*) to entrench oneself; **se r. dans/derrière** *Fig* to take refuge in/behind.

retransmettre [r(ə)trɑ̃smɛtr] *vt* to broadcast. ◆**retransmission** *nf* broadcast.

rétréc/ir [retresir] *vt* to narrow; (*vêtement*) to take in; **— vi**, **— se r.** *vpr* (*au lavage*) to shrink; (*rue etc*) to narrow. ◆**—i** *a* (*esprit, rue*) narrow.

rétribuer [retribɥe] *vt* to pay, remunerate; (*travail*) to pay for. ◆**rétribution** *nf* payment, remuneration.

rétro [retro] *a inv* (*mode etc*) which harks back to the past, retro.

rétro- [retro] *préf* retro-. ◆**rétroactif, -ive** *a* retroactive.

rétrograde [retrograd] *a* retrograde. ◆**rétrograder** *vi* (*reculer*) to move back; (*civilisation etc*) to go backwards; *Aut* to change down; **— vt** (*fonctionnaire, officier*) to demote.

rétrospectif, -ive [retrospektif, -iv] *a* (*sentiment etc*) retrospective; **— *nf*** (*de films, tableaux*) retrospective. ◆**rétrospectivement** *adv* in retrospect.

retrouss/er [r(ə)truse] *vt* (*jupe etc*) to hitch ou tuck up; (*manches*) to roll up ◆**—é** *a* (*nez*) snub, turned-up.

retrouver [r(ə)truve] *vt* to find (again); (*rejoindre*) to meet (again); (*forces, santé*) to regain; (*découvrir*) to rediscover; (*se rappeler*) to recall; **— se r.** *vpr* (*chose*) to be found (again); (*se trouver*) to find oneself (back); (*se rencontrer*) to meet (again); **s'y r.** (*s'orienter*) to find one's bearings ou way. ◆**retrouvailles** *nfpl* reunion.

rétroviseur [retrovizœr] *nm Aut* (rear-view) mirror.

réunion [reynjɔ̃] *nf* (*séance*) meeting; (*d'objets*) collection, gathering; (*d'éléments divers*) combination; (*jonction*) joining. ◆**réunir** *vt* to collect, gather; (*relier*) to join; (*convoquer*) to call together, assemble; (*rapprocher*) to bring together; (*qua-*

lités, *tendances*) to combine. ◆**réunis** *apl*
(*éléments*) combined.

réuss/ir [reysir] *vi* to succeed, be successful
(**à faire** in doing); (*plante*) to thrive; **r. à**
(*examen*) to pass; **r. à qn** to work (out) well
for s.o.; (*aliment, climat*) to agree with s.o.;
– vt to make a success of. ◆**—i** a successful. ◆**réussite** *nf* **1** success. **2 faire des**
réussites *Cartes* to play patience.

revaloir [r(ə)valwar] *vt* **je vous le revaudrai**
(*en bien ou en mal*) I'll pay you back.

revaloriser [r(ə)valɔrize] *vt* (*salaire*) to
raise. ◆**revalorisation** *nf* raising.

revanche [r(ə)vɑ̃ʃ] *nf* revenge; *Sp* return
game; **en r.** on the other hand.

rêve [rɛv] *nm* dream; **faire un r.** to have a
dream; **maison/voiture/***etc* **de r.** dream
house/car/*etc*. ◆**rêvasser** *vi* to daydream.

revêche [rəvɛʃ] *a* bad-tempered, surly.

réveil [revɛj] *nm* waking (up); *Fig* awakening; (*pendule*) alarm (clock). ◆**réveill/er**
vt (*personne*) to wake (up); (*sentiment, souvenir*) *Fig* to revive, awaken; **— se r.** *vpr* to
wake (up); *Fig* to revive, awaken. ◆**—é** *a*
awake. ◆**réveille-matin** *nm inv* alarm
(clock).

réveillon [revɛjɔ̃] *nm* (*repas*) midnight supper (*on Christmas Eve or New Year's Eve*).
◆**réveillonner** *vi* to take part in a *réveillon*.

révéler [revele] *vt* to reveal (**que** that); **— se**
r. to be revealed; **se r. facile/***etc* to turn out
to be easy/*etc*. ◆**révélateur, -trice** *a* re-
vealing; **r. de** indicative of. ◆**révélation**
nf revelation.

revenant [rəvnɑ̃] *nm* ghost.

revendiquer [r(ə)vɑ̃dike] *vt* to claim; (*exiger*) to demand. ◆**revendicatif, -ive** *a*
(*mouvement etc*) protest-. ◆**revendication** *nf* claim; demand; (*action*) claiming;
demanding.

revendre [r(ə)vɑ̃dr] *vt* to resell; **avoir (de)**
qch à r. to have sth to spare. ◆**revendeur,
-euse** *nmf* retailer; (*d'occasion*) second-
hand dealer; (*de drogue*) drug pusher; **r.
de billets** ticket tout. ◆**revente** *nf* resale.

revenir* [rəvnir] *vi* (*aux être*) to come back,
return; (*date*) to come round again; (*mot*)
to come *ou* crop up; (*coûter*) to cost (**à qn**
s.o.); **r. à** (*activité, sujet*) to go back to, return to; (*se résumer à*) to boil down to; **r. à**
qn (*forces, mémoire*) to come back to s.o.,
return to s.o.; (*honneur*) to fall to s.o.; **r. à
soi** to come to *ou* round; **r. de** (*maladie,
surprise*) to get over; **r. sur** (*décision,
promesse*) to go back on; (*passé, question*)

to go back over; **r. sur ses pas** to retrace
one's steps; **faire r.** (*aliment*) to brown.

revenu [rəvny] *nm* income (**de** from); (*d'un
État*) revenue (**de** from); **déclaration de
revenus** tax return.

rêv/er [reve] *vi* to dream (**de** of, **de faire** of
doing); *– vt* to dream (**que** that); (*désirer*)
to dream of. ◆**—é** *a* ideal.

réverbération [reverberasjɔ̃] *nf* (*de lumière*)
reflection; (*de son*) reverberation.

révérence [reverɑ̃s] *nf* reverence; (*salut
d'homme*) bow; (*salut de femme*) curts(e)y;
faire une r. to bow; to curts(e)y. ◆**révérer**
vt to revere.

révérend, -ende [reverɑ̃, -ɑ̃d] *a & nm Rel*
reverend.

rêverie [rɛvri] *nf* daydream; (*activité*)
daydreaming.

revers [r(ə)vɛr] *nm* (*côté*) reverse; *Tennis*
backhand; (*de veste*) lapel; (*de pantalon*)
turn-up; *Am* cuff; (*d'étoffe*) wrong side;
(*coup du sort*) setback, reverse; **r. de main**
(*coup*) backhander; **le r. de la médaille** *Fig*
the other side of the coin.

réversible [reversibl] *a* reversible.

revêtir* [r(ə)vetir] *vt* to cover (**de** with);
(*habit*) to put on; (*caractère, forme*) to assume; (*route*) to surface; **r. qn** (*habiller*) to
dress s.o. (**de** in); **r. de** (*signature*) to provide with. ◆**revêtement** *nm* (*surface*) covering; (*de route*) surface.

rêveur, -euse [rɛvœr, -øz] *a* dreamy; *– nmf*
dreamer.

revient [rəvjɛ̃] *nm* **prix de r.** cost price.

revigorer [r(ə)vigɔre] *vt* (*personne*) to revive.

revirement [r(ə)virmɑ̃] *nm* (*changement*)
about-turn, *Am* about-face; (*de situation,
d'opinion, de politique*) reversal.

réviser [revize] *vt* (*notes, texte*) to revise;
(*jugement, règlement etc*) to review; (*machine, voiture*) to overhaul, service. ◆**révision** *nf* revision; review; overhaul, service.

revivre* [r(ə)vivr] *vi* to live again; **faire r.** to
revive; *– vt* (*incident etc*) to relive.

révocation [revɔkasjɔ̃] *nf* **1** (*de contrat etc*)
revocation. **2** (*de fonctionnaire*) dismissal.

revoici [r(ə)vwasi] *prép* **me r.** here I am
again.

revoilà [r(ə)vwala] *prép* **la r.** there she is
again.

revoir* [r(ə)vwar] *vt* to see (again); (*texte*)
to revise; **au r.** goodbye.

révolte [revɔlt] *nf* revolt. ◆**révolt/er 1** *vt* to
revolt, incense. **2 se r.** *vpr* to revolt, rebel
(**contre** against). ◆**—ant** *a* (*honteux*) revolting. ◆**—é, -ée** *nmf* rebel.

révolu [revɔly] a (*époque*) past; **avoir trente ans révolus** to be over thirty (years of age).

révolution [revɔlysjɔ̃] nf (*changement, rotation*) revolution. ◆**révolutionnaire** a & nmf revolutionary. ◆**révolutionner** vt to revolutionize; (*émouvoir*) Fig to shake up.

revolver [revɔlvɛr] nm (*revolver*) gun.

révoquer [revɔke] vt 1 (*contrat etc*) to revoke. 2 (*fonctionnaire*) to dismiss.

revue [r(ə)vy] nf 1 (*examen*) & Mil review; **passer en r.** to review. 2 (*de music-hall*) variety show. 3 (*magazine*) magazine; (*spécialisée*) journal.

rez-de-chaussée [redʃose] nm inv ground floor, Am first floor.

rhabiller (se) [sərabije] vpr to get dressed again.

rhapsodie [rapsɔdi] nf rhapsody.

rhétorique [retɔrik] nf rhetoric.

Rhin [rɛ̃] nm **le R.** the Rhine.

rhinocéros [rinɔserɔs] nm rhinoceros.

rhododendron [rɔdɔdɛ̃drɔ̃] nm rhododendron.

rhubarbe [rybarb] nf rhubarb.

rhum [rɔm] nm rum.

rhumatisme [rymatism] nm Méd rheumatism; **avoir des rhumatismes** to have rheumatism. ◆**rhumatisant, -ante** a & nmf rheumatic. ◆**rhumatismal, -aux** a (*douleur*) rheumatic.

rhume [rym] nm cold; **r. de cerveau** head cold; **r. des foins** hay fever.

riant [rjɑ̃] a cheerful, smiling.

ricaner [rikane] vi (*sarcastiquement*) to snigger; (*bêtement*) to giggle.

riche [riʃ] a rich; (*personne, pays*) rich, wealthy; **r. en** (*minérai, vitamines etc*) rich in; — nmf rich ou wealthy person; **les riches** the rich. ◆**—ment** (*vêtu, illustré etc*) richly. ◆**richesse** nf wealth; (*d'étoffe, de sol, vocabulaire*) richness; pl (*trésor*) riches; (*ressources*) wealth.

ricin [risɛ̃] nm **huile de r.** castor oil.

ricocher [rikɔʃe] vi to ricochet, rebound. ◆**ricochet** nm ricochet, rebound; **par r.** Fig as an indirect result.

rictus [riktys] nm grin, grimace.

ride [rid] nf wrinkle; ripple. ◆**rider** vt (*visage*) to wrinkle; (*eau*) to ripple; — **se r.** vpr to wrinkle.

rideau, -x [rido] nm curtain; (*métallique*) shutter; (*écran*) Fig screen (**de** of); **le r. de fer** Pol the Iron Curtain.

ridicule [ridikyl] a ridiculous, ludicrous; — nm (*moquerie*) ridicule; (*défaut*) absurdity; (*de situation etc*) ridiculousness; **tourner en r.** to ridicule. ◆**ridiculiser** vt to ridicule.

rien [rjɛ̃] pron nothing; **il ne sait r.** he knows nothing, he doesn't know anything; **r. du tout** nothing at all; **r. d'autre/de bon/etc** nothing else/good/etc; **r. de tel** nothing like it; **de r.!** (*je vous en prie*) don't mention it!; **ça ne fait r.** it doesn't matter; **en moins de r.** in no time; **trois fois r.** (*chose insignifiante*) next to nothing; **pour r.** (*à bas prix*) for next to nothing; **il n'en est r.** (*ce n'est pas vrai*) nothing of the kind; — nm trifle, (mere) nothing; **un r. de** a hint ou touch of; **en un r. de temps** (*vite*) in no time; **un r. trop petit/etc** just a bit too small/etc.

rieur, -euse [rjœr, -øz] a cheerful.

riflard [riflar] nm Fam brolly, umbrella.

rigide [riʒid] a rigid; (*carton, muscle*) stiff; (*personne*) Fig inflexible; (*éducation*) strict. ◆**rigidité** nf rigidity; stiffness; inflexibility; strictness.

rigole [rigɔl] nf (*conduit*) channel; (*filet d'eau*) rivulet.

rigoler [rigɔle] vi Fam to laugh; (*s'amuser*) to have fun ou a laugh; (*plaisanter*) to joke (**avec** about). ◆**rigolade** nf Fam fun; (*chose ridicule*) joke; **prendre qch à la r.** to make a joke out of sth. ◆**rigolo, -ote** a Fam funny; — nmf Fam joker.

rigueur [rigœr] nf rigour; harshness; strictness; (*précision*) precision; **être de r.** to be the rule; **à la r.** if absolutely necessary, at ou Am in a pinch; **tenir r. à qn de qch** Fig to hold sth against s.o. ◆**rigoureux, -euse** a rigorous; (*climat, punition*) harsh; (*personne, morale, sens*) strict.

rillettes [rijɛt] nfpl potted minced pork.

rime [rim] nf rhyme. ◆**rimer** vi to rhyme (**avec** with); **ça ne rime à rien** it makes no sense.

rincer [rɛ̃se] vt to rinse (out). ◆**rinçage** nm rinsing; (*opération*) rinse.

ring [riŋ] nm (boxing) ring.

ringard [rɛ̃gar] a (*démodé*) Fam unfashionable, fuddy-duddy.

ripaille [ripaj] nf Fam feast.

riposte [ripɔst] nf (*réponse*) retort; (*attaque*) counter(attack). ◆**riposter** vi to retort; **r. à** (*attaque*) to counter; (*insulte*) to reply to; — vt **r. que** to retort that.

rire* [rir] vi to laugh (**de** at); (*s'amuser*) to have a good time; (*plaisanter*) to joke; **faire qch pour r.** to do sth for a laugh ou a joke; **se r. de qch** to laugh sth off; — nm laugh; pl laughter; **le r.** (*activité*) laughter. ◆**risée** nf mockery; **être la r.** de to be the laughing stock of. ◆**risible** a laughable.

ris [ri] nm **r. de veau** Culin (calf) sweetbread.

risque [risk] *nm* risk; **r. du métier** occupational hazard; **au r. de qch/de faire** at the risk of sth/of doing; **à vos risques et périls** at your own risk; **assurance tous risques** comprehensive insurance. ◆**risquer** *vt* to risk; (*question, regard*) to venture, hazard; **r. de faire** to stand a good chance of doing; **se r. à faire** to dare to do; **se r. dans** to venture into. ◆**risqué** *a* risky; (*plaisanterie*) daring, risqué.

ristourne [risturn] *nf* discount.

rite [rit] *nm* rite; (*habitude*) *Fig* ritual. ◆**rituel, -elle** *a & nm* ritual.

rivage [rivaʒ] *nm* shore.

rival, -ale, -aux [rival, -o] *a & nmf* rival. ◆**rivaliser** *vi* to compete (**avec** with, **de** in). ◆**rivalité** *nf* rivalry.

rive [riv] *nf* (*de fleuve*) bank; (*de lac*) shore.

rivé [rive] *a* **r. à** (*chaise etc*) *Fig* riveted to; **r. sur** *Fig* riveted on. ◆**rivet** *nm* (*tige*) rivet. ◆**riveter** *vt* to rivet (together).

riverain, -aine [rivrɛ̃, -ɛn] *a* riverside; lakeside; – *nmf* riverside resident; (*de lac*) lakeside resident; (*de rue*) resident.

rivière [rivjɛr] *nf* river.

rixe [riks] *nf* brawl, scuffle.

riz [ri] *nm* rice; **r. au lait** rice pudding. ◆**rizière** *nf* paddy (field), ricefield.

RN *abrév* = **route nationale**.

robe [rɔb] *nf* (*de femme*) dress; (*d'ecclésiastique, de juge*) robe; (*de professeur*) gown; (*pelage*) coat; **r. de soirée** ou **du soir** evening dress ou gown; **r. de grossesse/de mariée** maternity/wedding dress; **r. de chambre** dressing gown; **r. chasuble** pinafore (dress).

robinet [rɔbinɛ] *nm* tap, *Am* faucet; **eau du r.** tap water.

robot [rɔbo] *nm* robot; **r. ménager** food processor, liquidizer.

robuste [rɔbyst] *a* robust. ◆**robustesse** *nf* robustness.

roc [rɔk] *nm* rock.

rocaille [rɔkaj] *nf* (*terrain*) rocky ground; (*de jardin*) rockery. ◆**rocailleux, -euse** *a* rocky, stony; (*voix*) harsh.

rocambolesque [rɔkɑ̃bɔlɛsk] *a* (*aventure etc*) fantastic.

roche [rɔʃ] *nf*, **rocher** [rɔʃe] *nm* (*bloc, substance*) rock. ◆**rocheux, -euse** *a* rocky.

rock [rɔk] *nm* (*musique*) rock; – *a inv* (*chanteur etc*) rock-.

rod/er [rɔde] *vt* (*moteur, voiture*) to run in, *Am* break in; **être rodé** (*personne*) *Fig* to have got ou *Am* gotten the hang of things. ◆**—age** *nm* running in, *Am* breaking in.

rôd/er [rode] *vi* to roam (about); (*suspect*)

to prowl (about). ◆**—eur, -euse** *nmf* prowler.

rogne [rɔɲ] *nf* *Fam* anger; **en r.** in a temper.

rogner [rɔɲe] *vt* to trim, clip; (*réduire*) to cut; – *vi* **r. sur** (*réduire*) to cut down on. ◆**rognures** *nfpl* clippings, trimmings.

rognon [rɔɲɔ̃] *nm* *Culin* kidney.

roi [rwa] *nm* king; **fête** ou **jour des rois** Twelfth Night.

roitelet [rwatlɛ] *nm* (*oiseau*) wren.

rôle [rol] *nm* role, part; **à tour de r.** in turn.

romain, -aine [rɔmɛ̃, -ɛn] **1** *a & nmf* Roman. **2** *nf* (*laitue*) cos (lettuce), *Am* romaine.

roman [rɔmɑ̃] **1** *nm* novel; (*histoire*) *Fig* story; **r.-fleuve** saga. **2** *a* (*langue*) Romance; *Archit* Romanesque. ◆**romancé** *a* (*histoire*) fictional. ◆**romancier, -ière** *nmf* novelist.

romanesque [rɔmanɛsk] *a* romantic; (*incroyable*) fantastic.

romanichel, -elle [rɔmaniʃɛl] *nmf* gipsy.

romantique [rɔmɑ̃tik] *a* romantic. ◆**romantisme** *nm* romanticism.

romarin [rɔmarɛ̃] *nm* *Bot Culin* rosemary.

romp/re* [rɔ̃pr] *vt* to break; (*pourparlers, relations*) to break off; (*digue*) to burst; – *vi* to break (*Fig* avec with); to burst; (*fiancés*) to break it off; – **se r.** *vpr* to break; to burst. ◆**—u** *a* **1** (*fatigué*) exhausted. **2 r. à** (*expérimenté*) experienced in.

romsteck [rɔmstɛk] *nm* rump steak.

ronces [rɔ̃s] *nfpl* (*branches*) brambles.

ronchonner [rɔ̃ʃɔne] *vi* *Fam* to grouse, grumble.

rond, ronde [rɔ̃, rɔ̃d] *a* round; (*gras*) plump; (*honnête*) straight; (*ivre*) *Fam* tight; **dix francs tout r.** ten francs exactly; – *adv* **tourner r.** (*machine etc*) to run smoothly; – *nm* (*objet*) ring; (*cercle*) circle; (*tranche*) slice; *pl* (*argent*) *Fam* money; **r. de serviette** napkin ring; **en r.** (*s'asseoir etc*) in a ring ou circle; **tourner en r.** (*toupie etc*) *Fig* to go round and round. ◆**r.-de-cuir** *nm* (*pl* **ronds-de-cuir**) *Péj* pen pusher. ◆**r.-point** *nm* (*pl* **ronds-points**) *Aut* roundabout, *Am* traffic circle. ◆**ronde** *nf* (*tour de surveillance*) round; (*de policier*) beat; (*danse*) round (dance); (*note*) *Mus* semibreve, *Am* whole note; **à la r.** around; (*boire*) in turn. ◆**rondelet, -ette** *a* chubby; (*somme*) *Fig* tidy. ◆**rondelle** *nf* (*tranche*) slice; *Tech* washer. ◆**rondement** *adv* (*efficacement*) briskly; (*franchement*) straight. ◆**rondeur** *nf* roundness; (*du corps*) plumpness. ◆**rondin** *nm* log.

ronéotyper [rɔneɔtipe] *vt* to duplicate, roneo.

ronflant [rɔ̃flɑ̃] *a* (*langage etc*) *Péj* high-flown; (*feu*) roaring.

ronfler [rɔ̃fle] *vi* (*personne*) to snore; (*moteur*) to hum. ◆**ronflement** *nm* snore, snoring; hum(ming).

rong/er [rɔ̃ʒe] *vt* to gnaw (at); (*ver, mer, rouille*) to eat into (*sth*); (*maladie*) to consume s.o.; **se r. les ongles** to bite one's nails; **se r. les sangs** (*s'inquiéter*) to worry oneself sick. ◆**—eur** *nm* (*animal*) rodent.

ronron [rɔ̃rɔ̃] *nm*, **ronronnement** [rɔ̃rɔnmɑ̃] *nm* purr(ing). ◆**ronronner** *vi* to purr.

roquette [rɔkɛt] *nf Mil* rocket.

rosbif [rɔsbif] *nm* **du r.** (*rôti*) roast beef; (*à rôtir*) roasting beef; **un r.** a joint of roast *ou* roasting beef.

rose [roz] **1** *nf* (*fleur*) rose. **2** *a* (*couleur*) pink; (*situation, teint*) rosy; — *nm* pink. ◆**rosé** *a* pinkish; & – *a & nm* (*vin*) rosé. ◆**rosette** *nf* (*d'un officier*) rosette; (*nœud*) bow. ◆**rosier** *nm* rose bush.

roseau, -x [rozo] *nm* (*plante*) reed.

rosée [roze] *nf* dew.

rosse [rɔs] *a & nf Fam* nasty (person).

ross/er [rɔse] *vt Fam* to thrash. ◆**—ée** *nf Fam* thrashing.

rossignol [rɔsiɲɔl] *nm* **1** (*oiseau*) nightingale. **2** (*crochet*) picklock.

rot [ro] *nm Fam* burp, belch. ◆**roter** *vi Fam* to burp, belch.

rotation [rɔtasjɔ̃] *nf* rotation; (*de stock*) turnover. ◆**rotatif, -ive** *a* rotary; — *nf* rotary press.

rotin [rɔtɛ̃] *nm* rattan, cane.

rôt/ir [rotir] *vti*, — **se r.** *vpr* to roast; **faire r.** to roast. ◆**—i** *nm* **du r.** roasting meat; (*cuit*) roast meat; **un r.** a joint; **r. de bœuf/de porc** (joint of) roast beef/pork. ◆**rôtissoire** *nf* (roasting) spit.

rotule [rɔtyl] *nf* kneecap.

roturier, -ière [rɔtyrje, -jɛr] *nmf* commoner.

rouage [rwaʒ] *nm* (*de montre etc*) (working) part; (*d'organisation etc*) *Fig* cog.

roublard [rublar] *a* wily, foxy.

rouble [rubl] *nm* (*monnaie*) r(o)uble.

roucouler [rukule] *vi* (*oiseau, amoureux*) to coo.

roue [ru] *nf* wheel; **r.** (**dentée**) cog(wheel); **faire la r.** (*paon*) to spread its tail; (*se pavaner*) *Fig* to strut; **faire r. libre** *Aut* to freewheel.

roué, -ée [rwe] *a & nmf* sly *ou* calculating (person).

rouer [rwe] *vt* **r. qn de coups** to beat s.o. black and blue.

rouet [rwɛ] *nm* spinning wheel.

rouge [ruʒ] *a* red; (*fer*) red-hot; — *nm* (*couleur*) red; (*vin*) Fam red wine; **r.** (**à lèvres**) lipstick; **r.** (**à joues**) rouge; **le feu est au r.** *Aut* (the) traffic lights are red; — *nmf* (*personne*) *Pol* Red. ◆**r.-gorge** *nm* (*pl* **rouges-gorges**) robin. ◆**rougeâtre** *a* reddish. ◆**rougeaud** *a* red-faced. ◆**rougeoyer** *vi* to glow (red). ◆**rougeur** *nf* redness; (*due à la gêne ou à la honte*) blush(ing); *pl Méd* red spots *ou* blotches. ◆**rougir** *vti* to redden, turn red; — *vi* (*de gêne, de honte*) to blush (**de** with); (*de colère, de joie*) to flush (**de** with).

rougeole [ruʒɔl] *nf* measles.

rouget [ruʒɛ] *nm* (*poisson*) mullet.

rouille [ruj] *nf* rust; — *a inv* (*couleur*) rust-coloured. ◆**rouill/er** *vi* to rust; — **se r.** *vpr* to rust; (*esprit, sportif etc*) *Fig* to get rusty. ◆**-é** *a* rusty.

roul/er [rule] *vt* to roll; (*brouette, meuble*) to wheel, push; (*crêpe, ficelle, manches etc*) to roll up; **r. qn** (*duper*) *Fam* to cheat s.o.; — *vi* to roll; (*train, voiture*) to go, travel; (*conducteur*) to drive; **r. sur** (*conversation*) to turn on; **ça roule!** *Fam* everything's fine!; — **se r.** *vpr* to roll; **se r. dans** (*couverture etc*) to roll oneself (up) in. ◆**—ant** *a* (*escalier, trottoir*) moving; (*meuble*) on wheels. ◆**roulé** *nm* (*gâteau*) Swiss roll. ◆**rouleau, -x** *nm* (*outil, vague*) roller; (*de papier, pellicule etc*) roll; **r. à pâtisserie** rolling pin; **r. compresseur** steamroller. ◆**roulement** *nm* (*bruit*) rumbling, rumble; (*de tambour, de tonnerre, d'yeux*) roll; (*ordre*) rotation; **par r.** in rotation; **r. à billes** *Tech* ball bearing. ◆**roulette** *nf* (*de meuble*) castor; (*de dentiste*) drill; (*jeu*) roulette. ◆**roulis** *nm* (*de navire*) roll(ing).

roulotte [rulɔt] *nf* (*de gitan*) caravan.

Roumanie [rumani] *nf* Romania. ◆**roumain, -aine** *a & nmf* Romanian; — *nm* (*langue*) Romanian.

round [rawnd, rund] *nm Boxe* round.

roupiller [rupije] *vi Fam* to kip, sleep.

rouquin, -ine [rukɛ̃, -in] *a Fam* red-haired; — *nmf Fam* redhead.

rouspét/er [ruspete] *vi Fam* to grumble, complain. ◆**-eur, -euse** *nmf* grumbler.

rousse [rus] *voir* **roux**.

rousseur [rusœr] *nf* redness; **tache de r.** freckle. ◆**roussir** *vt* (*brûler*) to singe, scorch; — *vi* (*feuilles*) to turn brown; **faire r.** *Culin* to brown.

route [rut] *nf* road (**to**); (*itinéraire*) way,

route; (*aérienne, maritime*) route; (*chemin*) *Fig* path, way; **r. nationale/départementale** main/secondary road; **grande r., grand-r.** main road; **code de la r.** Highway Code; **en r.** on the way, en route; **en r.!** let's go!; **par la r.** by road; **sur la bonne r.** *Fig* on the right track; **mettre en r.** (*voiture etc*) to start (up); **se mettre en r.** to set out (**pour** for); **une heure de r.** *Aut* an hour's drive; **bonne r.!** have a good trip! ◆**routier, -ière** *a* (*carte etc*) road-; – *nm* (*camionneur*) (long distance) lorry *ou Am* truck driver; (*restaurant*) transport café, *Am* truck stop.

routine [rutin] *nf* routine; **de r.** (*contrôle etc*) routine-. ◆**routinier, -ière** *a* (*travail etc*) routine-; (*personne*) addicted to routine.

rouvrir° [ruvrir] *vti*, – **se r.** *vpr* to reopen.

roux, rousse [ru, rus] *a* (*cheveux*) red, ginger; (*personne*) red-haired; – *nmf* redhead.

royal, -aux [rwajal, -o] *a* royal; (*cadeau, festin etc*) fit for a king; (*salaire*) princely. ◆**royalement** *adv* (*traiter*) royally. ◆**royaliste** *a & nmf* royalist. ◆**royaume** *nm* kingdom. ◆**Royaume-Uni** *nm* United Kingdom. ◆**royauté** *nf* (*monarchie*) monarchy.

ruade [rɥad] *nf* (*d'âne etc*) kick.

ruban [rybɑ̃] *nm* ribbon; (*d'acier, de chapeau*) band; **r. adhésif** adhesive *ou* sticky tape.

rubéole [rybeɔl] *nf* German measles, rubella.

rubis [rybi] *nm* (*pierre*) ruby; (*de montre*) jewel.

rubrique [rybrik] *nf* (*article*) *Journ* column; (*catégorie, titre*) heading.

ruche [ryʃ] *nf* (bee)hive.

rude [ryd] *a* (*grossier*) crude; (*rêche*) rough; (*pénible*) tough; (*hiver, voix*) harsh; (*remarquable*) *Fam* tremendous. ◆**—ment** *adv* (*parler, traiter*) harshly; (*frapper, tomber*) hard; (*très*) *Fam* awfully. ◆**rudesse** *nf* harshness. ◆**rudoyer** *vt* to treat harshly.

rudiments [rydimɑ̃] *nmpl* rudiments. ◆**rudimentaire** *a* rudimentary.

rue [ry] *nf* street; **être à la r.** (*sans domicile*) to be on the streets. ◆**ruelle** *nf* alley(way).

ruer [rɥe] **1** *vi* (*cheval*) to kick (out). **2 se r.** *vpr* (*foncer*) to rush, fling oneself (**sur** at). ◆**ruée** *nf* rush.

rugby [rygbi] *nm* rugby. ◆**rugbyman**, *pl* **-men** [rygbiman, -mɛn] *nm* rugby player.

rug/ir [ryʒir] *vi* to roar. ◆**—issement** *nm* roar.

rugueux, -euse [rygø, -øz] *a* rough. ◆**rugosité** *nf* roughness; *pl* (*aspérités*) roughness.

ruine [rɥin] *nf* (*décombres*) & *Fig* ruin; **en r.** (*édifice*) in ruins; **tomber en r.** to fall into ruin. ◆**ruiner** *vt* to ruin; – **se r.** *vpr* (*en dépensant*) to ruin oneself. ◆**ruineux, -euse** *a* (*goûts, projet*) ruinously expensive; (*dépense*) ruinous.

ruisseau, -x [rɥiso] *nm* stream; (*caniveau*) gutter. ◆**ruisseler** *vi* to stream (**de** with).

rumeur [rymœr] *nf* (*protestation*) clamour; (*murmure*) murmur; (*nouvelle*) rumour.

ruminer [rymine] *vt* (*méditer*) to ponder on, ruminate over.

rumsteak [rɔmstɛk] *nm* rump steak.

rupture [ryptyr] *nf* break(ing); (*de fiançailles, relations*) breaking off; (*de pourparlers*) breakdown (**de** in); (*brouille*) break (up), split; (*de contrat*) breach; (*d'organe*) *Méd* rupture.

rural, -aux [ryral, -o] *a* rural, country-; – *nmpl* country people.

ruse [ryz] *nf* (*subterfuge*) trick; **la r.** (*habileté*) cunning; (*fourberie*) trickery. ◆**rusé, -ée** *a & nmf* crafty *ou* cunning (person). ◆**ruser** *vi* to resort to trickery.

Russie [rysi] *nf* Russia. ◆**russe** *a & nmf* Russian; – *nm* (*langue*) Russian.

rustique [rystik] *a* (*meuble*) rustic.

rustre [rystr] *nm* lout, churl.

rutabaga [rytabaga] *nm* (*racine*) swede, *Am* rutabaga.

rutilant [rytilɑ̃] *a* a gleaming, glittering.

rythme [ritm] *nm* rhythm; (*de travail*) rate, tempo; (*de la vie*) pace; **au r. de trois par jour** *at a ou* the rate of three a day. ◆**rythmé** *a*, ◆**rythmique** *a* rhythmic(al).

S

S, s [ɛs] *nm* S, s.

s' [s] *voir* **se, si.**

sa [sa] *voir* **son** [2].

SA *abrév* (*société anonyme*) *Com* plc, *Am* Inc.

sabbat [saba] *nm* (Jewish) Sabbath.

◆**sabbatique** a (*année etc*) Univ sabbatical.

sable [sabl] nm sand; **sables mouvants** quicksand(s). ◆**sabler** vt (*route*) to sand. ◆**sableux, -euse** a (*eau*) sandy. ◆**sablier** nm hourglass; Culin egg timer. ◆**sablière** nf (*carrière*) sandpit. ◆**sablonneux, -euse** a (*terrain*) sandy.

sablé [sable] nm shortbread biscuit ou Am cookie.

saborder [saborde] vt (*navire*) to scuttle; (*entreprise*) Fig to shut down.

sabot [sabo] nm **1** (*de cheval etc*) hoof. **2** (*chaussure*) clog. **3** (*de frein*) Aut shoe; **s. (de Denver)** Aut (wheel) clamp.

sabot/er [sabote] vt to sabotage; (*bâcler*) to botch. ◆**-age** nm sabotage; **un s.** an act of sabotage. ◆**-eur, -euse** nmf saboteur.

sabre [sabr] nm sabre, sword.

sabrer [sabre] vt (*élève, candidat*) Fam to give a thoroughly bad mark to.

sac [sak] nm **1** bag; (*grand et en toile*) sack; **s. (à main)** handbag; **s. à dos** rucksack. **2** **mettre à s.** (*ville*) Mil to sack.

saccade [sakad] nf jerk, jolt; **par saccades** jerkily, in fits and starts. ◆**saccadé** a (*geste, style*) jerky.

saccager [sakaʒe] vt (*ville, région*) Mil to sack; (*bouleverser*) Fig to turn upside down.

saccharine [sakarin] nf saccharin.

sacerdoce [saserdɔs] nm (*fonction*) Rel priesthood; Fig vocation.

sachet [saʃɛ] nm (*small*) bag; (*de lavande etc*) sachet; **s. de thé** teabag.

sacoche [sakɔʃ] nf bag; (*de vélo, moto*) saddlebag; Scol satchel.

sacquer [sake] vt Fam (*renvoyer*) to sack; (*élève*) to give a thoroughly bad mark to.

sacre [sakr] nm (*d'évêque*) consecration; (*de roi*) coronation. ◆**sacrer** vt (*évêque*) to consecrate; (*roi*) to crown.

sacré [sakre] a (*saint*) sacred; (*maudit*) Fam damned. ◆**-ment** adv Fam (*très*) damn(ed); (*beaucoup*) a hell of a lot.

sacrement [sakrəmã] nm Rel sacrament.

sacrifice [sakrifis] nm sacrifice. ◆**sacrifier** vt to sacrifice (à to, pour for); — vi **s.** à (*mode etc*) to pander to; — **se s.** vpr to sacrifice oneself (à, pour).

sacrilège [sakrilɛʒ] nm sacrilege; — a sacrilegious.

sacristie [sakristi] nf vestry.

sacro-saint [sakrosɛ̃] a Iron sacrosanct.

sadisme [sadism] nm sadism. ◆**sadique** a sadistic; — nmf sadist.

safari [safari] nm safari; **faire un s.** to be ou go on safari.

safran [safrɑ̃] nm saffron.

sagace [sagas] a shrewd, sagacious.

sage [saʒ] a wise; (*enfant*) well-behaved, good; (*modéré*) moderate; — nm wise man, sage. ◆**sagement** adv wisely; (*avec calme*) quietly. ◆**sagesse** nf wisdom; good behaviour; moderation.

sage-femme [saʒfam] nf (*pl* sages-femmes) midwife.

Sagittaire [saʒitɛr] nm le S. (*signe*) Sagittarius.

Sahara [saara] nm le S. the Sahara (desert).

saign/er [seɲe] vti to bleed. ◆**-ant** [seɲɑ̃] a (*viande*) Culin rare, underdone. ◆**-ée** nf **1** Méd bleeding, blood-letting; (*perte*) Fig heavy loss. **2** **la s. du bras** Anat the bend of the arm. ◆**saignement** nm bleeding; **s. de nez** nosebleed.

saillant [sajɑ̃] a projecting, jutting out; (*trait etc*) Fig salient. ◆**saillie** nf projection; **en s., faisant s.** projecting.

sain [sɛ̃] a healthy; (*moralement*) sane; (*jugement*) sound; (*nourriture*) wholesome, healthy; **s. et sauf** safe and sound, unhurt. ◆**sainement** adv (*vivre*) healthily; (*raisonner*) sanely.

saindoux [sɛ̃du] nm lard.

saint, sainte [sɛ̃, sɛ̃t] a holy; (*personne*) saintly; **s. Jean** Saint John; **sainte nitouche** Iron little innocent; **la Sainte Vierge** the Blessed Virgin; — nmf saint. ◆**s.-bernard** nm (*chien*) St Bernard. ◆**S.-Esprit** nm Holy Spirit. ◆**S.-Siège** nm Holy See. ◆**S.-Sylvestre** nf New Year's Eve.

sais [sɛ] voir **savoir**.

saisie [sezi] nf Jur seizure; **s. de données** data capture ou entry.

sais/ir [sezir] **1** vt to grab (hold of), seize; (*occasion*) & Jur to seize; (*comprendre*) to understand, grasp; (*frapper*) Fig to strike; **se s.** de to grab (hold of), seize. **2** vt (*viande*) Culin to fry briskly. ◆**-i** a **s.** de (*joie, peur etc*) overcome by. ◆**-issant** a (*film etc*) gripping; (*contraste, ressemblance*) striking. ◆**-issement** nm (*émotion*) shock.

saison [sezɔ̃] nf season; **en/hors s.** in/out of season; **en pleine ou haute s.** in (the) high season; **en basse s.** in the low season. ◆**saisonnier, -ière** a seasonal.

sait [sɛ] voir **savoir**.

salade [salad] nf **1** (*laitue*) lettuce; **s. (verte)** (*green*) salad; **s. de fruits/de tomates/etc** fruit/tomato/etc salad. **2** nf (*désordre*) Fam mess. **3** nfpl (*mensonges*) Fam stories, nonsense. ◆**saladier** nm salad bowl.

salaire [saler] *nm* wage(s), salary.

salaison [salezɔ̃] *nf Culin* salting; *pl* (*denrées*) salt(ed) meat *ou* fish.

salamandre [salamɑ̃dr] *nf* (*animal*) salamander.

salami [salami] *nm Culin* salami.

salarial, -aux [salarjal, -o] *a* (*accord etc*) wage-. ◆**salarié, -ée** *a* wage-earning; – *nmf* wage earner.

salaud [salo] *nm Arg Péj* bastard, swine.

sale [sal] *a* dirty; (*dégoûtant*) filthy; (*mauvais*) nasty; (*couleur*) dirty. ◆**salement** *adv* (*se conduire, manger*) disgustingly. ◆**saleté** *nf* dirtiness; filthiness; (*crasse*) dirt, filth; (*action*) dirty trick; (*camelote*) *Fam* rubbish, junk; *pl* (*détritus*) mess, dirt; (*obscénités*) filth. ◆**salir** *vt* to (make) dirty; (*réputation*) *Fig* to sully, tarnish; – **se s.** *vpr* to get dirty. ◆**salissant** *a* (*métier*) dirty, messy; (*étoffe*) easily dirtied. ◆**salissure** *nf* (*tache*) dirty mark.

sal/er [sale] *vt Culin* to salt. ◆**—é a 1** (*eau*) salt-; (*saveur*) salty; (*denrées*) salted; (*grivois*) *Fig* spicy. **2** (*excessif*) *Fam* steep. ◆**salière** *nf* saltcellar.

salive [saliv] *nf* saliva. ◆**saliver** *vi* to salivate.

salle [sal] *nf* room; (*très grande, publique*) hall; (*d'hôpital*) ward; (*public*) *Th* house, audience; **s. à manger** dining room; **s. d'eau** washroom, shower room; **s. d'exposition** *Com* showroom; **s. de jeux** (*pour enfants*) games room; (*avec machines à sous*) amusement arcade; **s. d'opération** *Méd* operating theatre.

salon [salɔ̃] *nm* sitting room, lounge; (*exposition*) show; **s. de beauté/de coiffure** beauty/hairdressing salon; **s. de thé** tearoom(s).

salope [salɔp] *nf* (*femme*) *Arg Péj* bitch, cow. ◆**saloperie** *nf Arg* (*action*) dirty trick; (*camelote*) rubbish, junk; **des saloperies** (*propos*) filth.

salopette [salɔpɛt] *nf* dungarees; (*d'ouvrier*) overalls.

salsifis [salsifi] *nm Bot Culin* salsify.

saltimbanque [saltɛ̃bɑ̃k] *nmf* (*travelling*) acrobat.

salubre [salybr] *a* healthy, salubrious. ◆**salubrité** *nf* healthiness; **s. publique** public health.

saluer [salɥe] *vt* to greet; (*en partant*) to take one's leave; (*de la main*) to wave to; (*de la tête*) to nod to; *Mil* to salute; **s. qn comme** *Fig* to hail s.o. as. ◆**salut 1** *nm* greeting; wave; nod; *Mil* salute; – *int Fam* hello!, hi!; (*au revoir*) bye! **2** *nm* (*de peuple etc*) salvation; (*sauvegarde*) safety. ◆**salutation** *nf* greeting.

salutaire [salyter] *a* salutary.

salve [salv] *nf* salvo.

samedi [samdi] *nm* Saturday.

SAMU [samy] *nm abrév* (*service d'assistance médicale d'urgence*) emergency medical service.

sanatorium [sanatɔrjɔm] *nm* sanatorium.

sanctifier [sɑ̃ktifje] *vt* to sanctify.

sanction [sɑ̃ksjɔ̃] *nf* (*approbation, peine*) sanction. ◆**sanctionner** *vt* (*confirmer, approuver*) to sanction; (*punir*) to punish.

sanctuaire [sɑ̃ktɥɛr] *nm Rel* sanctuary.

sandale [sɑ̃dal] *nf* sandal.

sandwich [sɑ̃dwitʃ] *nm* sandwich.

sang [sɑ̃] *nm* blood; **coup de s.** *Méd* stroke. ◆**sanglant** *a* bloody; (*critique, reproche*) scathing. ◆**sanguin, -ine 1** *a* (*vaisseau etc*) blood-; (*tempérament*) full-blooded. **2** *nf* (*fruit*) blood orange. ◆**sanguinaire** *a* blood-thirsty.

sang-froid [sɑ̃frwa] *nm* self-control, calm; **avec s.-froid** calmly; **de s.-froid** (*tuer*) in cold blood.

sangle [sɑ̃gl] *nf* (*de selle, parachute*) strap.

sanglier [sɑ̃glije] *nm* wild boar.

sanglot [sɑ̃glo] *nm* sob. ◆**sangloter** *vi* to sob.

sangsue [sɑ̃sy] *nf* leech.

sanitaire [saniter] *a* health-; (*conditions*) sanitary; (*personnel*) medical; (*appareils etc*) bathroom-, sanitary.

sans [sɑ̃] ([sɑ̃z] *before vowel and mute h*) *prép* without; **s. faire** without doing; **ça va s. dire** that goes without saying; **s. qu'il le sache** without him *ou* his knowing; **s. cela, s. quoi** otherwise; **s. plus** (*but*) no more than that; **s. exception/faute** without exception/fail; **s. importance/travail** unimportant/unemployed; **s. argent/manches** penniless/sleeveless. ◆**s.-abri** *nm inv* homeless person; **les s.-abri** the homeless. ◆**s.-gêne** *a inv* inconsiderate; – *nm inv* inconsiderateness. ◆**s.-travail** *nmf inv* unemployed person.

santé [sɑ̃te] *nf* health; **en bonne/mauvaise s.** in good/bad health, well/not well; (**à votre**) **s.!** (*en trinquant*) your health!, cheers!; **maison de s.** nursing home.

saoul [su] = **soûl**.

saper [sape] *vt* to undermine.

sapeur-pompier [sapœrpɔ̃pje] *nm* (*pl* **sapeurs-pompiers**) fireman.

saphir [safir] *nm* (*pierre*) sapphire; (*d'électrophone*) sapphire, stylus.

sapin [sapɛ̃] nm (arbre, bois) fir; **s. de Noël** Christmas tree.

sarbacane [sarbakan] nf (jouet) peashooter.

sarcasme [sarkasm] nm sarcasm; **un s.** a piece of sarcasm. ◆**sarcastique** a sarcastic.

sarcler [sarkle] vt (jardin etc) to weed.

Sardaigne [sardɛɲ] nf Sardinia.

sardine [sardin] nf sardine.

sardonique [sardɔnik] a sardonic.

SARL abrév (société à responsabilité limitée) Ltd, Am Inc.

sarment [sarmɑ̃] nm vine shoot.

sarrasin [sarazɛ̃] nm buckwheat.

sas [sɑ(s)] nm (pièce étanche) Nau Av airlock.

Satan [satɑ̃] nm Satan. ◆**satané** a (maudit) blasted. ◆**satanique** a satanic.

satellite [satelit] nm satellite; **pays s.** Pol satellite (country).

satiété [sasjete] nf **à s.** (boire, manger) one's fill; (répéter) ad nauseam.

satin [satɛ̃] nm satin. ◆**satiné** a satiny, silky.

satire [satir] nf satire (contre on). ◆**satirique** a satiric(al).

satisfaction [satisfaksjɔ̃] nf satisfaction. ◆**satisfaire*** vt to satisfy; − vi **s. à** (conditions, engagement etc) to fulfil. ◆**satisfaisant** a (acceptable) satisfactory. ◆**satisfait** a satisfied, content (de with).

saturateur [satyratœr] nm (de radiateur) humidifier.

saturer [satyre] vt to saturate (de with).

satyre [satir] nm Fam sex fiend.

sauce [sos] nf sauce; (jus de viande) gravy; **s. tomate** tomato sauce. ◆**saucière** nf sauce boat; gravy boat.

saucisse [sosis] nf sausage. ◆**saucisson** nm (cold) sausage.

sauf¹ [sof] prép except (que that); **s. avis contraire** unless you hear otherwise; **s. erreur** barring error.

sauf², sauve [sof, sov] a (honneur) intact, saved; **avoir la vie sauve** to be unharmed. ◆**sauf-conduit** nm (document) safeconduct.

sauge [soʒ] nf Bot Culin sage.

saugrenu [sogrəny] a preposterous.

saule [sol] nm willow; **s. pleureur** weeping willow.

saumâtre [somatr] a (eau) briny, brackish.

saumon [somɔ̃] nm salmon; − a inv (couleur) salmon (pink).

saumure [somyr] nf (pickling) brine.

sauna [sona] nm sauna.

saupoudrer [sopudre] vt (couvrir) to sprinkle (de with).

saur [sor] am **hareng s.** smoked herring, kipper.

saut [so] nm jump, leap; **faire un s.** to jump, leap; **faire un s. chez qn** (visite) to pop round to s.o.'s; **au s. du lit** on getting out of bed; **s. à la corde** skipping, Am jumping rope. ◆**sauter** vi to jump, leap; (bombe) to go off, explode; (poudrière etc) to go up, blow up; (fusible) to blow; (se détacher) to come off; **faire s.** (détruire) to blow up; (arracher) to tear off; (casser) to break; (renvoyer) Fam to get rid of, fire; (fusible) to blow; Culin to sauté; **s. à la corde** to skip, Am jump rope; **ça saute aux yeux** it's obvious; − vt (franchir) to jump (over); (mot, classe, repas) to skip. ◆**sautemouton** nm (jeu) leapfrog. ◆**sautiller** vi to hop. ◆**sautoir** nm Sp jumping area.

sauté [sote] a & nm Culin sauté. ◆**sauteuse** nf (shallow) pan.

sauterelle [sotrɛl] nf grasshopper.

sautes [sot] nfpl (d'humeur, de température) sudden changes (de in).

sauvage [sovaʒ] a (primitif, cruel) savage; (farouche) unsociable, shy; (illégal) unauthorized; − nmf unsociable person; (brute) savage. ◆**sauvagerie** nf unsociability; (cruauté) savagery.

sauve [sov] a voir **sauf²**.

sauvegarde [sovgard] nf safeguard (contre against). ◆**sauvegarder** vt to safeguard.

sauver [sove] 1 vt to save; (d'un danger) to rescue (de from); (matériel) to salvage; **la vie à qn** to save s.o.'s life. **2 se s.** vpr (s'enfuir) to run away ou off; (partir) Fam to get off, go. ◆**sauve-qui-peut** nm inv stampede. ◆**sauvetage** nm rescue; **canot de s.** lifeboat; **ceinture de s.** life belt; **radeau de s.** life raft. ◆**sauveteur** nm rescuer. ◆**sauveur** nm saviour.

sauvette (à la) [alasovɛt] adv **vendre à la s.** to hawk illicitly (on the streets).

savant [savɑ̃] a learned, scholarly; (manœuvre etc) masterly, clever; − nm scientist. ◆**savamment** adv learnedly; (avec habileté) cleverly, skilfully.

savate [savat] nf old shoe ou slipper.

saveur [savœr] nf (goût) flavour; (piment) Fig savour.

savoir* [savwar] vt to know; (nouvelle) to know, have heard; **j'ai su la nouvelle** I heard ou got to know the news; **s. lire/ nager/etc** (pouvoir) to know how to read/swim/etc; **faire s. à qn que** to inform ou tell s.o. that; **à s.** (c'est-à-dire) that is,

namely; **je ne saurais pas** I could not, I cannot; **(pas) que je sache** (not) as far as I know; **je n'en sais rien** I have no idea, I don't know; **un je ne sais quoi** a something or other; – *nm* (*culture*) learning, knowledge.
◆**s.-faire** *nm inv* know-how, ability.
◆**s.-vivre** *nm inv* good manners.

savon [savɔ̃] *nm* **1** soap; (*morceau*) bar of soap. **2 passer un s. à qn** (*réprimander*) *Fam* to give s.o. a dressing-down *ou* a talking-to.
◆**savonner** *vt* to soap. ◆**savonnette** *nf* bar of soap. ◆**savonneux, -euse** *a* soapy.

savourer [savure] *vt* to savour, relish.
◆**savoureux, -euse** *a* tasty; (*histoire etc*) *Fig* juicy.

saxophone [saksɔfɔn] *nm* saxophone.

sbire [sbir] *nm* (*homme de main*) *Péj* henchman.

scabreux, -euse [skabrø, -øz] *a* obscene.

scalpel [skalpɛl] *nm* scalpel.

scandale [skɑ̃dal] *nm* scandal; (*tapage*) uproar; **faire s.** (*livre etc*) to scandalize people; **faire un s.** to make a scene. ◆**scandaleux, -euse** *a* scandalous, outrageous. ◆**scandaleusement** *adv* outrageously. ◆**scandaliser** *vt* to scandalize, shock; — **se s.** *vpr* to be shocked *ou* scandalized (**de** by, **que** (+ *sub*) that).

scander [skɑ̃de] *vt* (*vers*) to scan; (*slogan*) to chant.

Scandinavie [skɑ̃dinavi] *nf* Scandinavia. ◆**scandinave** *a* & *nmf* Scandinavian.

scanner [skanɛr] *nm* (*appareil*) *Méd* scanner.

scaphandre [skafɑ̃dr] *nm* (*de plongeur*) diving suit; (*de cosmonaute*) spacesuit; **s. autonome** aqualung. ◆**scaphandrier** *nm* diver.

scarabée [skarabe] *nm* beetle.

scarlatine [skarlatin] *nf* scarlet fever.

scarole [skarɔl] *nf* endive.

sceau, -x [so] *nm* (*cachet, cire*) seal.
◆**scell/er** *vt* **1** (*document etc*) to seal. **2** (*fixer*) *Tech* to cement. ◆**-és** *nmpl* (*cachets de cire*) seals.

scélérat, -ate [selera, -at] *nmf* scoundrel.

scel-o-frais® [selofrɛ] *nm* clingfilm, *Am* plastic wrap.

scénario [senarjo] *nm* (*déroulement*) *Fig* scenario; (*esquisse*) *Cin* scenario; (*dialogues etc*) screenplay. ◆**scénariste** *nmf* *Cin* scriptwriter.

scène [sɛn] *nf* **1** *Th* scene; (*estrade, art*) stage; (*action*) action; **mettre en s.** (*pièce, film*) to direct. **2** (*dispute*) scene; **faire une s.**

(à qn) to make *ou* create a scene; **s. de ménage** domestic quarrel.

scepticisme [septisism] *nm* scepticism, *Am* skepticism. ◆**sceptique** *a* sceptical, *Am* skeptical; – *nmf* sceptic, *Am* skeptic.

scheik [ʃɛk] *nm* sheikh.

schéma [ʃema] *nm* diagram; *Fig* outline.
◆**schématique** *a* diagrammatic; (*succinct*) *Péj* sketchy. ◆**schématiser** *vt* to represent diagrammatically; (*simplifier*) *Péj* to oversimplify.

schizophrène [skizɔfrɛn] *a* & *nmf* schizophrenic.

sciatique [sjatik] *nf Méd* sciatica.

scie [si] *nf* (*outil*) saw. ◆**scier** *vt* to saw.
◆**scierie** *nf* sawmill.

sciemment [sjamɑ̃] *adv* knowingly.

science [sjɑ̃s] *nf* science; (*savoir*) knowledge; (*habileté*) skill; **sciences humaines** social science(s); **étudier les sciences** to study science. ◆**s.-fiction** *nf* science fiction.
◆**scientifique** *a* scientific; – *nmf* scientist.

scinder [sɛ̃de] *vt*, — **se s.** *vpr* to divide, split.

scintill/er [sɛ̃tije] *vi* to sparkle, glitter; (*étoiles*) to twinkle. ◆**-ement** *nm* sparkling; twinkling.

scission [sisjɔ̃] *nf* (*de parti etc*) split (**de** in).

sciure [sjyr] *nf* sawdust.

sclérose [skleroz] *nf Méd* sclerosis; *Fig* ossification; **s. en plaques** multiple sclerosis.
◆**sclérosé** *a* (*société etc*) *Fig* ossified.

scolaire [skɔlɛr] *a* school-. ◆**scolariser** *vt* (*pays*) to provide with schools; (*enfant*) to send to school, put in school. ◆**scolarité** *nf* schooling.

scooter [skutɛr] *nm* (*motor*) scooter.

score [skɔr] *nm* *Sp* score.

scories [skɔri] *nfpl* (*résidu*) slag.

scorpion [skɔrpjɔ̃] *nm* scorpion; **le S.** (*signe*) Scorpio.

scotch [skɔtʃ] *nm* **1** (*boisson*) Scotch, whisky. **2**® (*ruban adhésif*) sellotape®, *Am* scotch (tape)®. ◆**scotcher** *vt* to sellotape, *Am* to tape.

scout [skut] *a* & *nm* scout. ◆**scoutisme** *nm* scout movement, scouting.

script [skript] *nm* (*écriture*) printing.

scrupule [skrypyl] *nm* scruple; **sans scrupules** unscrupulous; (*agir*) unscrupulously. ◆**scrupuleux, -euse** *a* scrupulous. ◆**scrupuleusement** *adv* scrupulously.

scruter [skryte] *vt* to examine, scrutinize.

scrutin [skrytɛ̃] *nm* (*vote*) ballot; (*opérations électorales*) poll(ing).

sculpter [skylte] *vt* to sculpt(ure), carve.

◆**sculpteur** *nm* sculptor. ◆**sculptural, -aux** *a* (*beauté*) statuesque. ◆**sculpture** *nf* (*art, œuvre*) sculpture; **s. sur bois** woodcarving.

se [s(ə)] (**s'** *before vowel or mute h*) *pron* **1** (*complément direct*) himself; (*sujet femelle*) herself; (*non humain*) itself; (*indéfini*) oneself; *pl* themselves; **il se lave**. he washes himself. **2** (*indirect*) to himself; to herself; to itself; to oneself; **se dire** to say to oneself; **elle se dit** she says to herself. **3** (*réciproque*) (to) each other, (to) one another; **ils s'aiment** they love each other *ou* one another; **ils** *ou* **elles se parlent** they speak to each other *ou* one another. **4** (*passif*) **ça se fait** that is done; **ça se vend bien** it sells well. **5** (*possessif*) **il se lave les mains** he washes his hands.

séance [seɑ̃s] *nf* **1** (*d'assemblée etc*) session, sitting; (*de travail etc*) session; **s. (de pose)** (*chez un peintre*) sitting. **2** *Cin Th* show, performance. **3 s. tenante** at once.

séant [seɑ̃] **1** *a* (*convenable*) seemly, proper. **2** *nm* **se mettre sur son s.** to sit up.

seau, -x [so] *nm* bucket, pail.

sec, sèche [sek, sɛʃ] *a* dry; (*fruits, légumes*) dried; (*ton*) curt, harsh; (*maigre*) spare; (*cœur*) *Fig* hard; **coup s.** sharp blow, tap; **bruit s.** (*rupture*) snap; – *adv* (*frapper, pleuvoir*) hard; (*boire*) neat, straight; – *nm* **à s.** dried up, dry; (*sans argent*) *Fam* broke; **au s.** in a dry place. ◆**séch/er¹** *vti* to dry; – **se s.** *vpr* to dry oneself. **2** (*cours*) *Scol Fam* to skip; – *vi* (*ignorer*) *Scol Fam* to be stumped. ◆**-age** *nm* drying. ◆**sécheresse** *nf* dryness; (*de ton*) curtness; *Mét* drought. ◆**séchoir** *nm* (*appareil*) drier; **s. à linge** clotheshorse.

sécateur [sekatœr] *nm* pruning shears, secateurs.

sécession [sesesjɔ̃] *nf* secession; **faire s.** to secede.

sèche [sɛʃ] *voir* **sec**. ◆**sèche-cheveux** *nm inv* hair drier. ◆**sèche-linge** *nm inv* tumble drier.

second, -onde¹ [sgɔ̃, -ɔ̃d] *a & nmf* second; **de seconde main** second-hand; – *nm* (*adjoint*) second in command; (*étage*) second floor, *Am* third floor; *nm* *Rail* second class; *Scol* = fifth form, *Am* = eleventh grade; (*vitesse*) *Aut* second (gear). ◆**secondaire** *a* secondary.

seconde² [sgɔ̃d] *nf* (*instant*) second.

seconder [sgɔ̃de] *vt* to assist.

secouer [s(ə)kwe] *vt* to shake; (*paresse, poussière*) to shake off; **s. qn** (*maladie, nouvelle etc*) to shake s.o. up; **s. qch de qch**

(*enlever*) to shake sth out of sth; – **se s.** *vpr* (*faire un effort*) *Fam* to shake oneself out of it.

secour/ir [skurir] *vt* to assist, help. ◆**-able** *a* (*personne*) helpful. ◆**secourisme** *nm* first aid. ◆**secouriste** *nmf* first-aid worker.

secours [s(ə)kur] *nm* assistance, help; (*aux indigents*) aid, relief; **le s., les s.** *Mil* relief; (*premiers*) **s.** *Méd* first aid; **au s.!** help!; **porter s. à qn** to give s.o. assistance *ou* help; **de s.** (*sortie*) emergency-; (*équipe*) rescue-; (*roue*) spare.

secousse [s(ə)kus] *nf* jolt, jerk; (*psychologique*) shock; *Géol* tremor.

secret, -ète [sǝkre, -ɛt] *a* secret; (*cachottier*) secretive; – *nm* secret; (*discrétion*) secrecy; **en s.** in secret, secretly; **dans le s.** (*au courant*) in on the secret.

secrétaire [sǝkreter] **1** *nmf* secretary; **s. d'État** Secretary of State; **s. de mairie** town clerk; **s. de rédaction** subeditor. **2** *nm* (*meuble*) writing desk. ◆**secrétariat** *nm* (*bureau*) secretary's office; (*d'organisation internationale*) secretariat; (*métier*) secretarial work; **de s.** (*école, travail*) secretarial.

sécréter [sekrete] *vt* *Méd Biol* to secrete. ◆**sécrétion** *nf* secretion.

secte [sɛkt] *nf* sect. ◆**sectaire** *a & nmf* *Péj* sectarian.

secteur [sɛktœr] *nm* *Mil Com* sector; (*de ville*) district; (*domaine*) *Fig* area; (*de réseau*) *Él* supply area; (*ligne*) *Él* mains.

section [sɛksjɔ̃] *nf* section; (*de ligne d'autobus*) fare stage; *Mil* platoon. ◆**sectionner** *vt* to divide (into sections); (*artère, doigt*) to sever.

séculaire [sekyler] *a* (*tradition etc*) age-old.

secundo [s(ə)gɔ̃do] *adv* secondly.

sécurité [sekyrite] *nf* (*tranquillité*) security; (*matérielle*) safety; **s. routière** road safety; **s. sociale** = social services *ou* security; **de s.** (*dispositif, ceinture, marge etc*) safety-; **en s.** secure; safe. ◆**sécuriser** *vt* to reassure, make feel (emotionally) secure.

sédatif [sedatif] *nm* sedative.

sédentaire [sedɑ̃ter] *a* sedentary.

sédiment [sedimɑ̃] *nm* sediment.

séditieux, -euse [sedisjø, -øz] *a* seditious. ◆**sédition** *nf* sedition.

séduire* [sedɥir] *vt* to charm, attract; (*plaire à*) to appeal to; (*abuser de*) to seduce. ◆**séduisant** *a* attractive. ◆**séducteur, -trice** *a* seductive; – *nmf* seducer. ◆**séduction** *nf* attraction.

segment [sɛgmɑ̃] *nm* segment.

ségrégation [segregasjɔ̃] *nf* segregation.

seiche [sɛʃ] *nf* cuttlefish.

seigle [sɛgl] *nm* rye.

seigneur [sɛɲœr] *nm Hist* lord; **S.** *Rel* Lord.

sein [sɛ̃] *nm* (*mamelle, poitrine*) breast; *Fig* bosom; **bout de s.** nipple; **au s. de** (*parti etc*) within; (*bonheur etc*) in the midst of.

Seine [sɛn] *nf* la **S.** the Seine.

séisme [seism] *nm* earthquake.

seize [sɛz] *a & nm* sixteen. ◆**seizième** *a & nmf* sixteenth.

séjour [seʒur] *nm* stay; (*salle de*) **s.** living room. ◆**séjourner** *vi* to stay.

sel [sɛl] *nm* salt; (*piquant*) *Fig* spice; (*humour*) wit; *pl Méd* (smelling) salts; **sels de bain** bath salts.

sélect [selɛkt] *a Fam* select.

sélectif, -ive [selɛktif, -iv] *a* selective. ◆**sélection** *nf* selection. ◆**sélectionner** *vt* to select.

self(-service) [sɛlf(sɛrvis)] *nm* self-service restaurant *ou* shop.

selle [sɛl] 1 *nf* (*de cheval*) saddle. **2** *nfpl* les **selles** *Méd* bowel movements, stools. ◆**seller** *vt* (*cheval*) to saddle.

sellette [sɛlɛt] *nf* **sur la s.** (*personne*) under examination, in the hot seat.

selon [s(ə)lɔ̃] *prép* according to (**que** whether); **c'est s.** *Fam* it (all) depends.

Seltz (eau de) [odsɛls] *nf* soda (water).

semailles [s(ə)maj] *nfpl* (*travail*) sowing; (*période*) seedtime.

semaine [s(ə)mɛn] *nf* week; **en s.** (*opposé à week-end*) in the week.

sémantique [semɑ̃tik] *a* semantic; – *nf* semantics.

sémaphore [semafɔr] *nm* (*appareil*) *Rail Nau* semaphore.

semblable [sɑ̃blabl] *a* similar (**à** to); **être semblables** to be alike *ou* similar; **de semblables propos/etc** (*tels*) such remarks/etc; – *nm* fellow (creature); **toi et tes semblables** you and your kind.

semblant [sɑ̃blɑ̃] *nm* **faire s.** to pretend (**de faire** to do); **un s.** de a semblance of.

sembler [sɑ̃ble] *vi* to seem; (**il (me) semble vieux** he seems *ou* looks old (to me); **s. être/faire** to seem to be/to do; – *v imp* **il semble que** (+ *sub ou indic*) it seems that, it looks as if; **il me semble que** it seems to me that, I think that.

semelle [s(ə)mɛl] *nf* (*de chaussure*) sole; (*intérieure*) insole.

semer [s(ə)me] *vt* 1 (*graines*) to sow; (*jeter*) *Fig* to strew; (*répandre*) to spread; **semé de** *Fig* strewn with, dotted with. **2** (*concurrent, poursuivant*) to shake off. ◆**semence** *nf*

seed; (*clou*) tack. ◆**semeur, -euse** *nmf* sower (**de** of).

semestre [s(ə)mɛstr] *nm* half-year; *Univ* semester. ◆**semestriel, -ielle** *a* half-yearly.

semi- [səmi] *préf* semi-.

séminaire [seminɛr] *nm* **1** *Univ* seminar. **2** *Rel* seminary.

semi-remorque [səmirəmɔrk] *nm* (*camion*) articulated lorry, *Am* semi(trailer).

semis [s(ə)mi] *nm* sowing; (*terrain*) seedbed; (*plant*) seedling.

sémite [semit] *a* Semitic; – *nmf* Semite. ◆**sémitique** *a* (*langue*) Semitic.

semonce [səmɔ̃s] *nf* reprimand; **coup de s.** *Nau* warning shot.

semoule [s(ə)mul] *nf* semolina.

sempiternel, -elle [sɑ̃pitɛrnɛl] *a* endless, ceaseless.

sénat [sena] *nm Pol* senate. ◆**sénateur** *nm Pol* senator.

sénile [senil] *a* senile. ◆**sénilité** *nf* senility.

sens [sɑ̃s] *nm* **1** (*faculté, raison*) sense; (*signification*) meaning, sense; **à mon s.** to my mind; **s. commun** commonsense; **s. de l'humour** sense of humour; **ça n'a pas de s.** that doesn't make sense. **2** (*direction*) direction; **s. giratoire** *Aut* roundabout, *Am* traffic circle, rotary; **s. interdit** *ou* **unique** (*rue*) one-way street; **'s. interdit'** 'no entry'; **à s. unique** (*rue*) one-way; **s. dessus dessous** [sɑ̃dsydsu] upside down; **dans le s./le s. inverse des aiguilles d'une montre** clockwise/anticlockwise, *Am* counterclockwise.

sensation [sɑ̃sasjɔ̃] *nf* sensation, feeling; **faire s.** to cause *ou* create a sensation; **à s.** (*film etc*) *Péj* sensational. ◆**sensationnel, -elle** *a Fig* sensational.

sensé [sɑ̃se] *a* sensible.

sensible [sɑ̃sibl] *a* sensitive (**à** to); (*douloureux*) tender, sore; (*perceptible*) perceptible; (*progrès etc*) appreciable. ◆**sensiblement** *adv* (*notablement*) appreciably; (*à peu près*) more or less. ◆**sensibiliser** *vt* **s. qn à** (*problème etc*) to make s.o. alive to *ou* aware of. ◆**sensibilité** *nf* sensitivity.

sensoriel, -ielle [sɑ̃sɔrjɛl] *a* sensory.

sensuel, -elle [sɑ̃syɛl] *a* (*sexuel*) sensual; (*musique, couleur etc*) sensuous. ◆**sensualité** *nf* sensuality; sensuousness.

sentence [sɑ̃tɑ̃s] *nf* **1** *Jur* sentence. **2** (*maxime*) maxim.

senteur [sɑ̃tœr] *nf* (*odeur*) scent.

sentier [sɑ̃tje] *nm* path.

sentiment [sɑ̃timɑ̃] *nm* feeling; **avoir le s. de** (*apprécier*) to be aware of; **faire du s.** to be sentimental. ◆**sentimental, -aux** *a* senti-

mental; (*amoureux*) love-. ◆**sentimentalité** *nf* sentimentality.

sentinelle [sɑ̃tinɛl] *nf* sentry.

sentir* [sɑ̃tir] *vt* to feel; (*odeur*) to smell; (*goût*) to taste; (*racisme etc*) to smack of; (*connaître*) to sense, be conscious of; **s. le moisi/le parfum/***etc* to smell musty/of perfume/*etc*; **s. le poisson/***etc* (*avoir le goût de*) to taste of fish/*etc*; **je ne peux pas le s.** (*supporter*) *Fam* I can't bear ou stand him; **se faire s.** (*effet etc*) to make itself felt; **se s. fatigué/humilié/***etc* to feel tired/humiliated/*etc*; – *vi* to smell.

séparation [separasjɔ̃] *nf* separation; (*en deux*) division, split; (*départ*) parting. ◆**séparer** *vt* to separate (**de** from); (*diviser en deux*) to divide, split (up); (*cheveux*) to part; – **se s.** *vpr* (*se quitter*) to part; (*adversaires, époux*) to separate; (*assemblée, cortège*) to disperse, break up; (*se détacher*) to split off; **se s. de** (*objet aimé, chien etc*) to part with. ◆**séparé** *a* (*distinct*) separate; (*époux*) separated (**de** from). ◆**séparément** *adv* separately.

sept [sɛt] *a & nm* seven. ◆**septième** *a & nmf* seventh; **un s.** a seventh.

septante [sɛptɑ̃t] *a & nm* (*en Belgique, Suisse*) seventy.

septembre [sɛptɑ̃br] *nm* September.

septennat [sɛptena] *nm Pol* seven-year term (of office).

septentrional, -aux [sɛptɑ̃trijɔnal, -o] *a* northern.

sépulcre [sepylkr] *nm Rel* sepulchre.

sépulture [sepyltyr] *nf* burial; (*lieu*) burial place.

séquelles [sekɛl] *nfpl* (*de maladie*) after-effects; (*de guerre*) aftermath.

séquence [sekɑ̃s] *nf Mus Cartes Cin* sequence.

séquestrer [sekɛstre] *vt* to confine (illegally), lock up.

sera, serait [s(ə)ra, s(ə)rɛ] *voir* **être**.

serein [sərɛ̃] *a* serene. ◆**sérénité** *nf* serenity.

sérénade [serenad] *nf* serenade.

sergent [sɛrʒɑ̃] *nm Mil* sergeant.

série [seri] *nf* series; (*ensemble*) set; **s. noire** *Fig* string *ou* series of disasters; **de s.** (*article etc*) standard; **fabrication en s.** mass production; **fins de s.** *Com* oddments; **hors s.** *Fig* outstanding.

sérieux, -euse [serjø, -øz] *a* (*personne, maladie, doute etc*) serious; (*de bonne foi*) genuine, serious; (*digne de foi, fiable*) reliable; (*bénéfices*) substantial; **de sérieuses chances de . . .** a good chance of . . . ; –

nm seriousness; (*fiabilité*) reliability; **prendre au s.** to take seriously; **garder son s.** to keep a straight face; **manquer de s.** (*travailleur*) to lack application. ◆**sérieusement** *adv* seriously; (*travailler*) conscientiously.

serin [s(ə)rɛ̃] *nm* canary.

seriner [s(ə)rine] *vt* **s. qch à qn** to repeat sth to s.o. over and over again.

seringue [s(ə)rɛ̃g] *nf* syringe.

serment [sɛrmɑ̃] *nm* (*affirmation solennelle*) oath; (*promesse*) pledge; **prêter s.** to take an oath; **faire le s. de faire** to swear to do; **sous s.** *Jur* on *ou* under oath.

sermon [sɛrmɔ̃] *nm Rel* sermon; (*discours*) *Péj* lecture. ◆**sermonner** *vt* (*faire la morale à*) to lecture.

serpe [sɛrp] *nf* bill(hook).

serpent [sɛrpɑ̃] *nm* snake; **s. à sonnette** rattlesnake.

serpenter [sɛrpɑ̃te] *vi* (*sentier etc*) to meander.

serpentin [sɛrpɑ̃tɛ̃] *nm* (*ruban*) streamer.

serpillière [sɛrpijɛr] *nf* floor cloth.

serre [sɛr] **1** *nf* greenhouse. **2** *nfpl* (*d'oiseau*) claws, talons.

serre-livres [sɛrlivr] *nm inv* bookend. ◆**s.-tête** *nm inv* (*bandeau*) headband.

serr/er [sere] *vt* (*saisir, tenir*) to grip, clasp; (*presser*) to squeeze, press; (*corde, nœud, vis*) to tighten; (*poing*) to clench; (*taille*) to hug; (*pieds*) to pinch; (*frein*) to apply, put on; (*rapprocher*) to close up; (*rangs*) *Mil* to close; **s. la main à** to shake hands with; **s. les dents** *Fig* to grit one's teeth; **s. qn** (*embrasser*) to hug s.o.; (*vêtement*) to be too tight for s.o.; **s. qn de près** (*talonner*) to be close behind s.o.; – *vi* **s. à droite** *Aut* to keep (to the) right; – **se s.** *vpr* (*se rapprocher*) to squeeze up *ou* together; **se s. contre** to squeeze up against. ◆**-é** *a* (*budget, nœud, vêtement*) tight; (*gens*) packed (together); (*mailles, lutte*) close; (*rangs*) serried; (*dense*) dense, thick; (*cœur*) *Fig* heavy; **avoir la gorge serrée** *Fig* to have a lump in one's throat.

serrure [sɛryr] *nf* lock. ◆**serrurier** *nm* locksmith.

sertir [sɛrtir] *vt* (*diamant etc*) to set.

sérum [serɔm] *nm* serum.

servante [sɛrvɑ̃t] *nf* (*maid*)servant.

serveur, -euse [sɛrvœr, -øz] *nmf* waiter, waitress; (*au bar*) barman, barmaid.

serviable [sɛrvjabl] *a* helpful, obliging. ◆**serviabilité** *nf* helpfulness.

service [sɛrvis] *nm* service; (*fonction, travail*) duty; (*pourboire*) service (charge); (*département*) *Com* department; *Tennis* serve, service; **un s.** (*aide*) a favour; **rendre s.** to be of service (**à qn** to s.o.), help (**à qn** s.o.); **rendre un mauvais s. à qn** to do s.o. a disservice; **ça pourrait rendre s.** *Fam* that might come in useful; **s. (non) compris** service (not) included; **s. après-vente** *Com* aftersales (service); **s. d'ordre** (*policiers*) police; **être de s.** to be on duty; **s. à café/à thé** coffee/tea service *ou* set; **à votre s.!** at your service!

serviette [sɛʀvjɛt] *nf* **1** towel; **s. de bain/de toilette** bath/hand towel; **s. hygiénique** sanitary towel; **s. (de table)** serviette, napkin. **2** (*sac*) briefcase.

servile [sɛʀvil] *a* servile; (*imitation*) slavish. **◆servilité** *nf* servility; slavishness.

servir* [sɛʀviʀ] **1** *vt* to serve (**qch à qn** s.o. with sth, to s.o.); (*convive*) to wait on; **– vi** to serve; **— se s.** *vpr* (*à table*) to help oneself (**de** to). **2** *vi* (*être utile*) to be useful, serve; **s. à qch/à faire** (*objet*) to be used for sth/to do *ou* for doing; **ça ne sert à rien** it's useless, it's no good *ou* use (**de faire** doing); **à quoi ça sert de protester/etc** what's the use *ou* good of protesting/*etc*; **s. de qch** (*objet*) to be used for sth, serve as sth; **ça me sert à faire/de qch** I use it to do *ou* for doing/as sth; **s. à qn de guide/etc** to act as a guide/*etc* to s.o. **3 se s.** *vpr* **se s. de** (*utiliser*) to use.

serviteur [sɛʀvitœʀ] *nm* servant. **◆servitude** *nf* (*esclavage*) servitude; (*contrainte*) *Fig* constraint.

ses [se] *voir* **son²**.

session [sesjɔ̃] *nf* session.

set [sɛt] *nm* **1** *Tennis* set. **2 s. (de table)** (*napperon*) place mat.

seuil [sœj] *nm* doorstep; (*entrée*) doorway; (*limite*) *Fig* threshold; **au s. de** *Fig* on the threshold of.

seul, seule [sœl] **1** *a* (*sans compagnie*) alone; **tout s.** all alone, by oneself, on one's own; **se sentir s.** to feel lonely *ou* alone; **– adv** (*tout*) **s.** (*agir, vivre*) by oneself, on one's own; (*parler*) to oneself; **s. à s.** (*parler*) in private. **2** *a* (*unique*) only; **la seule femme/etc** the only woman/*etc*; **un s. chat/etc** only one cat/*etc*; **une seule fois** only once; **pas un s. livre/etc** not a single book/*etc*; **seuls les garçons . . . , les garçons seuls . . .** only the boys . . . : **–** *nmf* **la, le seul** the only one; **un s., une seule** only one, one only; **pas un s.** (**non plus**) not a single one. **◆seulement** *adv* only; **non s. . . . mais . . .** not only . . . but (also) . . . ; **pas s.** (*même*) not even; **sans s. faire** without even doing.

sève [sɛv] *nf Bot & Fig* sap.

sévère [sevɛʀ] *a* severe; (*parents, professeur*) strict. **◆—ment** *adv* severely; (*élever*) strictly. **◆sévérité** *nf* severity; strictness.

sévices [sevis] *nmpl* brutality.

sévir [seviʀ] *vi* (*fléau*) *Fig* to rage; **s. contre** to deal severely with.

sevrer [səvʀe] *vt* (*enfant*) to wean; **s. de** (*priver*) *Fig* to deprive of.

sexe [sɛks] *nm* (*catégorie, sexualité*) sex; (*organes*) genitals; **l'autre s.** the opposite sex. **◆sexiste** *a & nmf* sexist. **◆sexualité** *nf* sexuality. **◆sexuel, -elle** *a* sexual; (*éducation, acte*) sex-.

sextuor [sɛkstɥɔʀ] *nm* sextet.

seyant [sejɑ̃] *a* (*vêtement*) becoming.

shampooing [ʃɑ̃pwɛ] *nm* shampoo; **s. colorant** rinse; **faire un s. à qn** to shampoo s.o.'s hair.

shérif [ʃeʀif] *nm Am* sheriff.

shooter [ʃute] *vti Fb* to shoot.

short [ʃɔʀt] *nm* (pair of) shorts.

si [si] **1** (= **s'** [s] *before* **il, ils**) *conj* if; **s'il vient** if he comes; **si j'étais roi** if I were *ou* was king; **je me demande si** I wonder whether *ou* if; **si on restait?** (*suggestion*) what if we stayed?; **si je dis ça, c'est que . . .** I say this because . . . ; **si ce n'est** (*sinon*) if not; **si oui** if so. **2** *adv* (*tellement*) so; **si riche que toi/que tu crois** not as rich as you/as you think; **un si bon dîner** such a good dinner; **si grand qu'il soit** however big he may be; **si bien que** with the result that. **3** *adv* (*après négative*) yes; **tu ne viens pas? – si!** you're not coming? – yes (I am)!

siamois [sjamwa] *a* Siamese; **frères s., sœurs siamoises** Siamese twins.

Sicile [sisil] *nf* Sicily.

SIDA [sida] *nm Méd* AIDS. **◆sidéen, -enne** *nmf* AIDS sufferer.

sidérer [sideʀe] *vt Fam* to flabbergast.

sidérurgie [sideʀyʀʒi] *nf* iron and steel industry.

siècle [sjɛkl] *nm* century; (*époque*) age.

siège [sjɛʒ] *nm* **1** (*meuble, centre*) & *Pol* seat; (*d'autorité, de parti etc*) headquarters; **s. (social)** (*d'entreprise*) head office. **2** *Mil* siege; **mettre le s. devant** to lay siege to. **◆siéger** *vi Pol* to sit.

sien, sienne [sjɛ̃, sjɛn] *pron poss* **le s., la sienne,** les siens(ne)s his; (*de femme*) hers; (*de chose*) its; **les deux siens** his *ou* her two; **–** *nmpl* **les siens** (*amis etc*) one's (own) people.

sieste [sjɛst] *nf* siesta; **faire la s.** to have *ou* take a nap.

siffler [sifle] *vi* to whistle; (*avec un sifflet*) to

blow one's whistle; (*gaz, serpent*) to hiss; (*en respirant*) to wheeze; – *vt* (*chanson*) to whistle; (*chien*) to whistle to; (*faute, fin de match* Sp) to blow one's whistle for; (*acteur, pièce*) to boo; (*boisson*) Fam to knock back. ◆**sifflement** *nm* whistling, whistle; hiss(ing). ◆**sifflet** *nm* (*instrument*) whistle; *pl* Th booing, boos; (**coup de) s.** *nm* whistle. ◆**siffloter** *vti* to whistle.

sigle [sigl] *nm* (*initiales*) abbreviation; (*prononcé comme un mot*) acronym.

signal, -aux [sinal, -o] *nm* signal; **s. d'alarme** *Rail* communication cord; **signaux routiers** road signs. ◆**signal/er 1** *vt* (*faire remarquer*) to point out (**à qn** to s.o., **que** that); (*annoncer, indiquer*) to indicate, signal; (*dénoncer à la police etc*) to report (**à** to). **2 se s.** *vpr* **se s. par** to distinguish oneself by. ◆**—ement** *nm* (*de personne*) description, particulars. ◆**signalisation** *nf* signalling; *Aut* signposting; **s. (routière)** (*signaux*) road signs.

signature [sinatyr] *nf* signature; (*action*) signing. ◆**signataire** *nmf* signatory. ◆**signer 1** *vt* to sign. **2 se s.** *vpr Rel* to cross oneself.

signe [sin] *nm* (*indice*) sign, indication; **s. particulier/de ponctuation** distinguishing/punctuation mark; **faire s. à qn** (*geste*) to motion to *ou* beckon s.o. (**de faire** to do); (*contacter*) to get in touch with s.o.; **faire s. que oui** to nod (one's head); **faire s. que non** to shake one's head.

signet [sinɛ] *nm* bookmark.

signification [sinifikasjɔ̃] *nf* meaning. ◆**significatif, -ive** *a* significant, meaningful; **s. de** indicative of. ◆**signifier** *vt* to mean, signify (**que** that); (*faire connaître*) to make sth known to s.o., signify sth to s.o.

silence [silɑ̃s] *nm* silence; *Mus* rest; **en s.** in silence; **garder le s.** to keep quiet *ou* silent (**sur** about). ◆**silencieux, -euse 1** *a* silent. **2** *nm Aut* silencer, *Am* muffler; (*d'arme*) silencer. ◆**silencieusement** *adv* silently.

silex [silɛks] *nm* (*roche*) flint.

silhouette [silwɛt] *nf* outline; (*en noir*) silhouette; (*ligne du corps*) figure.

silicium [silisjɔm] *nm* silicon. ◆**silicone** *nf* silicone.

sillage [sijaʒ] *nm* (*de bateau*) wake; **dans le s. de** *Fig* in the wake of.

sillon [sijɔ̃] *nm* furrow; (*de disque*) groove.

sillonner [sijɔne] *vt* (*traverser*) to cross; (*en tous sens*) to criss-cross.

silo [silo] *nm* silo.

simagrées [simagre] *nfpl* airs (and graces); (*cérémonies*) fuss.

similaire [similɛr] *a* similar. ◆**similitude** *nf* similarity.

similicuir [similikɥir] *nm* imitation leather.

simple [sɛ̃pl] *a* simple; (*non multiple*) single; (*employé, particulier*) ordinary; – *nmf* **s. d'esprit** simpleton; – *nm Tennis* singles. ◆**simplement** *adv* simply. ◆**simplet, -ette** *a* (*personne*) a bit simple. ◆**simplicité** *nf* simplicity. ◆**simplification** *nf* simplification. ◆**simplifier** *vt* to simplify. ◆**simpliste** *a* simplistic.

simulacre [simylakr] *nm* **un s. de** a pretence of.

simuler [simyle] *vt* to simulate; (*feindre*) to feign. ◆**simulateur, -trice** *nmf* (*hypocrite*) shammer; (*tire-au-flanc*) & *Mil* malingerer. **2** *nm* (*appareil*) simulator. ◆**simulation** *nf* simulation; feigning.

simultané [simyltane] *a* simultaneous. ◆**—ment** *adv* simultaneously.

sincère [sɛ̃sɛr] *a* sincere. ◆**sincèrement** *adv* sincerely. ◆**sincérité** *nf* sincerity.

sinécure [sinekyr] *nf* sinecure.

singe [sɛ̃ʒ] *nm* monkey, ape. ◆**singer** *vt* (*imiter*) to ape, mimic. ◆**singeries** *nfpl* antics, clowning.

singulariser (se) [səsɛ̃gylarize] *vpr* to draw attention to oneself.

singulier, -ière [sɛ̃gylje, -jɛr] **1** *a* peculiar, odd. **2** *a* & *nm Gram* singular. ◆**singularité** *nf* peculiarity. ◆**singulièrement** *adv* (*notamment*) particularly; (*beaucoup*) extremely.

sinistre [sinistr] **1** *a* (*effrayant*) sinister. **2** *nm* disaster; (*incendie*) fire; (*dommage*) *Jur* damage. ◆**sinistré, -ée** *a* (*population, région*) disaster-stricken; – *nmf* disaster victim.

sinon [sinɔ̃] *conj* (*autrement*) otherwise, or else; (*sauf*) except (**que** that); (*si ce n'est*) if not.

sinueux, -euse [sinɥø, -øz] *a* winding. ◆**sinuosités** *nfpl* twists (and turns).

sinus [sinys] *nm inv Anat* sinus.

siphon [sifɔ̃] *nm* siphon; (*d'évier*) trap, U-bend.

sirène [sirɛn] *nf* **1** (*d'usine etc*) siren. **2** (*femme*) mermaid.

sirop [siro] *nm* (*à diluer, boisson*) (fruit) cordial; **s. contre la toux** cough mixture *ou* syrup.

siroter [sirɔte] *vt Fam* to sip (at).

sis [si] *a Jur* situated.

sismique [sismik] *a* seismic; **secousse s.** earth tremor.

site [sit] *nm* (*endroit*) site; (*environnement*) setting; (*pittoresque*) beauty spot; **s.** (*touristique*) (*monument etc*) place of interest.

sitôt [sito] *adv* s. que as soon as; **s. levée, elle partit** as soon as she was up, she left; **s. après** immediately after; **pas de s.** not for some time.

situation [situɑsjɔ̃] *nf* situation, position; (*emploi*) position; **s. de famille** marital status. ◆**situ/er** *vt* to situate, locate; — **se s.** *vpr* (*se trouver*) to be situated. ◆**—é a** (*maison etc*) situated.

six [sis] ([si] *before consonant*, [siz] *before vowel*) *a & nm* six. ◆**sixième** *a & nmf* sixth; **un s.** a sixth.

sketch [skɛtʃ] *nm* (*pl* **sketches**) *Th* sketch.

ski [ski] *nm* (*objet*) ski; (*sport*) skiing; **faire du s.** to ski; **s. nautique** water skiing. ◆**ski/er** *vi* to ski. ◆**—eur, -euse** skier.

slalom [slalɔm] *nm Sp* slalom.

slave [slav] *a* Slav; (*langue*) Slavonic; — *nmf* Slav.

slip [slip] *nm* (*d'homme*) briefs, (under)pants; (*de femme*) panties, pants, knickers; **s. de bain** (swimming) trunks; (*d'un bikini*) briefs.

slogan [slɔgɑ̃] *nm* slogan.

SMIC [smik] *nm abrév* (*salaire minimum interprofessionnel de croissance*) minimum wage.

smoking [smɔkiŋ] *nm* (*veston, costume*) dinner jacket, *Am* tuxedo.

snack(-bar) [snak(bar)] *nm* snack bar.

SNCF [ɛsɛnseɛf] *nf abrév* (*Société nationale des Chemins de fer français*) French railways.

snob [snɔb] *nmf* snob; — *a* snobbish. ◆**snober** *vt* s. qn to snub s.o. ◆**snobisme** *nm* snobbery.

sobre [sɔbr] *a* sober. ◆**sobriété** *nf* sobriety.

sobriquet [sɔbrikɛ] *nm* nickname.

sociable [sɔsjabl] *a* sociable. ◆**sociabilité** *nf* sociability.

social, -aux [sɔsjal, -o] *a* social. ◆**socialisme** *nm* socialism. ◆**socialiste** *a & nmf* socialist.

société [sɔsjete] *nf* society; (*compagnie*) *& Com* company; **s. anonyme** *Com* (public) limited company, *Am* incorporated company. ◆**sociétaire** *nmf* (*d'une association*) member.

sociologie [sɔsjɔlɔʒi] *nf* sociology.

◆**sociologique** *a* sociological. ◆**sociologue** *nmf* sociologist.

socle [sɔkl] *nm* (*de statue, colonne*) plinth, pedestal; (*de lampe*) base.

socquette [sɔkɛt] *nf* ankle sock.

soda [sɔda] *nm* (*à l'orange etc*) fizzy drink, *Am* soda (pop).

sœur [sœr] *nf* sister; *Rel* nun, sister.

sofa [sɔfa] *nm* sofa, settee.

soi [swa] *pron* oneself; **chacun pour s.** every man for himself; **en s.** in itself; **cela va de s.** it's self-evident (que that); **amour/ conscience de s.** self-love/-awareness. ◆**s.-même** *pron* oneself.

soi-disant [swadizɑ̃] *a inv* so-called; — *adv* supposedly.

soie [swa] *nf* **1** silk. **2** (*de porc etc*) bristle. ◆**soierie** *nf* (*tissu*) silk.

soif [swaf] *nf* thirst (*Fig* de for); **avoir s.** to be thirsty; **donner s. à qn** to make s.o. thirsty.

soign/er [swaɲe] *vt* to look after, take care of; (*malade*) to tend, nurse; (*maladie*) to treat; (*détails, présentation, travail*) to take care over; **se faire s.** to have (medical) treatment; — **se s.** *vpr* to take care of oneself, look after oneself. ◆**—é a** (*personne*) well-groomed; (*travail*) neat, tidy; (*travail*) careful. ◆**soigneux, -euse** *a* careful (**de** with); (*propre*) tidy, neat. ◆**soigneusement** *adv* carefully.

soin [swɛ̃] *nm* care; (*ordre*) tidiness, neatness; *pl* care; *Méd* treatment; **avoir** *ou* **prendre s. de qch/de faire** to take care of sth/to do; **les premiers soins** first aid; **soins de beauté** beauty care *ou* treatment; **aux bons soins de** (*sur lettre*) care of, c/o; **avec s.** carefully, with care.

soir [swar] *nm* evening; **le s.** (*chaque soir*) in the evening; **à neuf heures du s.** at nine in the evening; **du s.** (*repas, robe etc*) evening-. ◆**soirée** *nf* evening; (*réunion*) party; **s. dansante** dance.

soit 1 [swa] *voir* **être. 2** [swa] *conj* (*à savoir*) that is (to say); **s. . . . s. . . .** either . . . or . . . . **3** [swat] *adv* (*oui*) very well.

soixante [swasɑ̃t] *a & nm* sixty. ◆**soixantaine** *nf* une s. (de) (*nombre*) (about) sixty; **avoir la s.** (*âge*) to be about sixty. ◆**soixante-dix** *a & nm* seventy. ◆**soixante-dixième** *a & nmf* seventieth. ◆**soixantième** *a & nmf* sixtieth.

soja [sɔʒa] *nm* (*plante*) soya; **graine de s.** soya bean; **germes** *ou* **pousses de s.** beansprouts.

sol [sɔl] *nm* ground; (*plancher*) floor; (*matière, territoire*) soil.

solaire [sɔlɛr] *a* solar; (*chaleur, rayons*) sun's; (*crème, filtre*) sun-; (*lotion, huile*) suntan-.

soldat [sɔlda] *nm* soldier; **simple s.** private.

solde [sɔld] **1** *nm* (*de compte, à payer*) balance. **2 en s.** (*acheter*) at sale price, *Am* on sale; *pl* (*marchandises*) sale goods; (*vente*) (clearance) sale(s).(3) *nf Mil* pay; **à la s. de** *Fig Péj* in s.o.'s pay. ◆**sold/er 1** *vt* (*compte*) to pay the balance of; (*articles*) to sell off, clear. **2** *vt* (*compte*) to pay the balance. **3 se s.** *vpr* **se s. par** (*un échec, une défaite etc*) to end in. ◆**—é** *a* (*article etc*) reduced. ◆**solderie** *nf* discount ou reject shop.

sole [sɔl] *nf* (*poisson*) sole.

soleil [sɔlɛj] *nm* sun; (*chaleur, lumière*) sunshine; (*fleur*) sunflower; **au s.** in the sun; **il fait (du) s.** it's sunny, the sun's shining; **prendre un bain de s.** to sunbathe; **coup de s.** *Méd* sunburn.

solennel, -elle [sɔlanɛl] *a* solemn. ◆**solennellement** *adv* solemnly. ◆**solennité** *nf* solemnity.

solex® [sɔlɛks] *nm* moped.

solfège [sɔlfɛʒ] *nm* rudiments of music.

solidaire [sɔlidɛr] *a* **être s.** (*ouvriers etc*) to be as one, show solidarity (**de** with); (*pièce de machine*) to be interdependent (**de** with). ◆**solidairement** *adv* jointly. ◆**se solidariser** *vpr* to show solidarity (**avec** with). ◆**solidarité** *nf* solidarity; (*d'éléments*) interdependence.

solide [sɔlid] *a* (*voiture, nourriture, caractère etc*) & *Ch* solid; (*argument, qualité, raison*) sound; (*vigoureux*) robust; — *nm Ch* solid. ◆**solidement** *adv* solidly. ◆**se solidifier** *vpr* to solidify. ◆**solidité** *nf* solidity; (*d'argument etc*) soundness.

soliste [sɔlist] *nmf Mus* soloist.

solitaire [sɔlitɛr] *a* solitary; — *nmf* loner; (*ermite*) recluse, hermit; **en s.** on one's own. ◆**solitude** *nf* solitude.

solive [sɔliv] *nf* joist, beam.

solliciter [sɔlisite] *vt* (*audience, emploi etc*) to seek; (*tenter*) to tempt, entice; **s. qn** (*faire appel à*) to appeal to s.o. (**de faire** to do); **être (très) sollicité** (*personne*) to be in (great) demand. ◆**sollicitation** *nf* (*demande*) appeal; (*tentation*) temptation.

sollicitude [sɔlisityd] *nf* solicitude, concern.

solo [sɔlo] *a inv* & *nm Mus* solo.

solstice [sɔlstis] *nm* solstice.

soluble [sɔlybl] *a* (*substance, problème*) soluble; **café s.** instant coffee. ◆**solution** *nf* (*d'un problème etc*) & *Ch* solution (**de** to).

solvable [sɔlvabl] *a Fin* solvent. ◆**solvabilité** *nf Fin* solvency.

solvant [sɔlvā] *nm Ch* solvent.

sombre [sɔbr] *a* dark; (*triste*) sombre, gloomy; **il fait s.** it's dark.

sombrer [sɔbre] *vi* (*bateau*) to sink, founder; **s. dans** (*folie, sommeil etc*) to sink into.

sommaire [sɔmɛr] *a* summary; (*repas, tenue*) scant; — *nm* summary, synopsis.

sommation [sɔmasjɔ̃] *nf Jur* (*de sentinelle etc*) warning.

somme [sɔm] **1** *nf* sum; **faire la s. de** to add up; **en s., s. toute** in short. **2** *nm* (*sommeil*) nap; **faire un s.** to have ou take a nap.

sommeil [sɔmɛj] *nm* sleep; (*envie de dormir*) sleepiness, drowsiness; **avoir s.** to be ou feel sleepy ou drowsy. ◆**sommeiller** *vi* to doze; (*faculté, qualité*) *Fig* to slumber.

sommelier [sɔmalje] *nm* wine waiter.

sommer [sɔme] *vt* **s. qn de faire** (*enjoindre*) & *Jur* to summon s.o. to do.

sommes [sɔm] *voir* **être**.

sommet [sɔmɛ] *nm* top; (*de montagne*) summit, top; (*de la gloire etc*) *Fig* height, summit; **conférence au s.** summit (conference).

sommier [sɔmje] *nm* (*de lit*) base; **s. à ressorts** spring base.

sommité [sɔmite] *nf* leading light, top person (**de** in).

somnambule [sɔmnãbyl] *nmf* sleepwalker; **être s.** to sleepwalk. ◆**somnambulisme** *nm* sleepwalking.

somnifère [sɔmnifɛr] *nm* sleeping pill.

somnolence [sɔmnɔlãs] *nf* drowsiness, sleepiness. ◆**somnolent** *a* drowsy, sleepy. ◆**somnoler** *vi* to doze, drowse.

somptueux, -euse [sɔptɥø, -øz] *a* sumptuous, magnificent. ◆**somptuosité** *nf* sumptuousness, magnificence.

son¹ [sɔ̃] *nm* **1** (*bruit*) sound. **2** (*de grains*) bran.

son², sa, *pl* **ses** [sɔ̃, sa, se] (*sa* becomes **son** [sɔn] *before a vowel or mute h*) *a poss* his; (*de femme*) her; (*de chose*) its; (*indéfini*) one's; **son père** his ou her ou one's father; **sa durée** its duration.

sonate [sɔnat] *nf Mus* sonata.

sonde [sɔd] *nf Géol* drill; *Nau* sounding line; *Méd* probe; (*pour l'alimentation*) (feeding) tube; **s. spatiale** *Av* space probe. ◆**sondage** *nm* sounding; drilling; probing; **s. (d'opinion)** opinion poll. ◆**sonder** *vt* (*rivière etc*) to sound; (*terrain*) to drill; *Av* & *Méd* to probe; (*personne, l'opinion*) *Fig* to sound out.

songe [sɔ̃ʒ] *nm* dream.

song/er [sɔ̃ʒe] *vi* **s. à qch/à faire** to think of sth/of doing; — *vt* **s. que** to consider ou think that. ◆**—eur, -euse** a thoughtful, pensive.

sonner vi to ring; (cor, cloches etc) to sound; **midi a sonné** it has struck twelve; — vt to ring; (domestique) to ring for; (cor etc) to sound; (l'heure) to strike; (assommer) to knock out. ◆**sonnantes** afpl **à cinq heures s.** on the stroke of five/etc. ◆**sonné** a **1** trois/etc **heures sonnées** gone ou past three/etc o'clock. **2** (fou) crazy. ◆**sonnerie** nf (son) ring(ing); (de cor etc) sound; (appareil) bell. ◆**sonnette** nf bell; **s. d'alarme** alarm (bell); **coup de s.** ring.

sonnet [sɔnɛ] nm (poème) sonnet.

sonore [sɔnɔr] a (rire) loud; (salle, voix) resonant; (effet, film, ondes etc) sound-. ◆**sonorisation** nf (matériel) sound equipment ou system. ◆**sonoriser** vt (film) to add sound to; (salle) to wire for sound. ◆**sonorité** nf (de salle) acoustics, resonance; (de violon etc) tone.

sont [sɔ̃] voir **être**.

sophistiqué [sɔfistike] a sophisticated.

soporifique [sɔpɔrifik] a (médicament, discours etc) soporific.

soprano [sɔprano] nmf (personne) Mus soprano; — nm (voix) soprano.

sorbet [sɔrbɛ] nm Culin water ice, sorbet.

sorcellerie [sɔrsɛlri] nf witchcraft, sorcery. ◆**sorcier** nm sorcerer. ◆**sorcière** nf witch; **chasse aux sorcières** Pol witch-hunt.

sordide [sɔrdid] a (acte, affaire etc) sordid; (maison etc) squalid.

sornettes [sɔrnɛt] nfpl (propos) Péj twaddle.

sort [sɔr] nm **1** (destin, hasard) fate; (condition) lot. **2** (maléfice) spell.

sorte [sɔrt] nf sort, kind (de of); **en quelque s.** as it were, in a way; **de (telle) s. que** so that, in such a way that; **de la s.** (de cette façon) in that way; **faire en s. que** (+ sub) to see to it that.

sortie [sɔrti] nf **1** departure, exit; (de scène) exit; (promenade) walk; (porte) exit, way out; (de livre, modèle) Com appearance; (de disque, film) release; (d'ordinateur) output; pl (argent) outgoings; **à la s. de l'école** (moment) when school comes out; **l'heure de la s.** de qn the time at which s.o. leaves; **première s.** (de convalescent etc) first time out. **2 s. de bain** (peignoir) bathrobe.

sortilège [sɔrtilɛʒ] nm (magic) spell.

sort/ir [sɔrtir] vi (aux **être**) to go out, leave; (venir) to come out; (pour s'amuser) to go out; (film, bourgeon etc) to come out; (numéro gagnant) to come up; **s. de** (endroit) to leave; (sujet) to stray from;

(université) to be a graduate of; (famille, milieu) to come from; (légalité, limites) to go beyond; (compétence) to be outside; (gonds, rails) to come off; **s. de l'ordinaire** to be out of the ordinary; **s. de table** to leave the table; **s. de terre** (plante, fondations) to come up; **s. indemne** to escape unhurt (de from); — vt (aux **avoir**) to take out (de of); (film, modèle, livre etc) Com to bring out; (dire) Fam to come out with; (expulser) Fam to throw out; **s'en s., se s. d'affaire** to pull ou come through, get out of trouble. ◆**—ant** a (numéro) winning; (député etc) Pol outgoing. ◆**—able** a (personne) presentable.

sosie [sozi] nm (de personne) double.

sot, sotte [so, sɔt] a foolish; — nmf fool. ◆**sottement** adv foolishly. ◆**sottise** nf foolishness; (action, parole) foolish thing; pl (injures) Fam insults; **faire des sottises** (enfant) to be naughty, misbehave.

sou [su] nm sous (argent) money; **elle n'a pas un ou le s.** she doesn't have a penny, she's penniless; **pas un s. de** (bon sens etc) not an ounce of; **appareil ou machine à sous** fruit machine, one-armed bandit.

soubresaut [subraso] nm (sursaut) (sudden) start.

souche [suʃ] nf (d'arbre) stump; (de carnet) stub, counterfoil; (famille, de vigne) stock.

souci [susi] nm (inquiétude) worry, concern; (préoccupation) concern; **se faire du s.** to be worried, worry; **ça lui donne du s.** it worries him ou her. ◆**se soucier** vpr **se s. de** to be concerned ou worried about. ◆**soucieux, -euse** a concerned, worried (**de qch** about sth); **se plaire/etc** anxious to please/etc.

soucoupe [sukup] nf saucer; **s. volante** flying saucer.

soudain [sudɛ̃] a sudden; — adv suddenly. ◆**soudainement** adv suddenly. ◆**soudaineté** nf suddenness.

Soudan [sudã] nm Sudan.

soude [sud] nf Ch soda; **cristaux de s.** washing soda.

souder [sude] vt to solder; (par soudure autogène) to weld; (groupes etc) Fig to unite (closely); — **se s.** vpr (os) to knit (together). ◆**soudure** nf soldering; (métal) solder; **s. (autogène)** welding.

soudoyer [sudwaje] vt to bribe.

souffle [sufl] nm puff, blow; (haleine) breath; (respiration) breathing; (de bombe etc) blast; (inspiration) Fig inspiration; **s. (d'air)** breath of air. ◆**souffler** vi to blow; (haleter) to puff; **laisser s. qn** (reprendre haleine) to let s.o. get his breath back; — vt

soufflé [sufle] *nm Culin* soufflé.

souffrance [sufrɑ̃s] *nf* 1 suffering. 2 en s. (*colis etc*) unclaimed; (*affaire*) in abeyance. **souffreteux, -euse** [sufrətø, -øz] *a* sickly. **souffr/ir*** [sufrir] 1 *vi* to suffer; **s. de** to suffer from; (*gorge, pieds etc*) to have trouble with; **faire s. qn** (*physiquement*) to hurt s.o.; (*moralement*) to make s.o. suffer, hurt s.o. 2 *vt* (*endurer*) to suffer; **je ne peux pas le s.** I can't bear him. 3 *vt* (*exception*) to admit of. **—ant** *a* unwell.

soufre [sufr] *nm* sulphur, *Am* sulfur.

souhait [swɛ] *nm* wish; **à vos souhaits!** (*après un éternuement*) bless you!; **à s.** perfectly. **souhait/er** [swete] *vt* (*bonheur etc*) to wish for; (*chance etc*) to wish s.o. sth; **faire s.** to hope to do; **s. que** (+ *sub*) to hope that. **—able** *a* desirable.

souiller [suje] *vt* to soil, dirty; (*déshonorer*) *Fig* to sully.

soûl [su] 1 *a* drunk. 2 *nm* **tout son s.** (*boire etc*) to one's heart's content. **soûler** *vt* to make drunk; **— se s.** *vpr* to get drunk.

soulager [sulaʒe] *vt* to relieve (**de** of). **soulagement** *nm* relief.

soulever [sulve] *vt* to raise, lift (up); (*l'opinion, le peuple*) to stir up; (*poussière, question*) to raise; (*sentiment*) to arouse; **cela me soulève le cœur** it makes me feel sick, it turns my stomach; **— se s.** *vpr* (*malade etc*) to lift oneself (up); (*se révolter*) to rise (up). **soulèvement** *nm* (*révolte*) (up)rising.

soulier [sulje] *nm* shoe.

souligner [suliɲe] *vt* (*d'un trait*) to underline; (*accentuer, faire remarquer*) to emphasize, underline; **s. que** to emphasize that.

soumettre* [sumɛtr] 1 *vt* (*pays, rebelles*) to subjugate, subdue; **s. à** (*assujettir*) to subject to; **— se s.** *vpr* to submit (**à** to). 2 *vt* (*présenter*) to submit (**à** to). **soumis** *a* (*docile*) submissive; **s. à** subject to. **soumission** *nf* 1 submission; (*docilité*) submissiveness. 2 (*offre*) *Com* tender.

soupape [supap] *nf* valve.

soupçon [supsɔ̃] *nm* suspicion; **un s. de** (*quantité*) *Fig* a hint *ou* touch of. **soupçonner** *vt* to suspect (**de** of, **d'avoir fait** of

doing, **que** that). **soupçonneux, -euse** *a* suspicious.

soupe [sup] *nf* soup. **soupière** *nf* (*soup*) tureen.

soupente [supɑ̃t] *nf* (*sous le toit*) loft.

souper [supe] *nm* supper; **— vi** to have supper.

soupeser [supəze] *vt* (*objet dans la main*) to feel the weight of; (*arguments etc*) *Fig* to weigh up.

soupir [supir] *nm* sigh. **soupir/er** *vi* to sigh; **s. après** to yearn for. **—ant** *nm* (*amoureux*) suitor.

soupirail, -aux [supiraj, -o] *nm* basement window.

souple [supl] *a* (*personne, esprit, règlement*) flexible; (*cuir, membre, corps*) supple. **souplesse** *nf* flexibility; suppleness.

source [surs] *nf* 1 (*point d'eau*) spring; **eau de s.** spring water; **prendre sa s.** (*rivière*) to rise (**à, dans** in). 2 (*origine*) source; **de s. sûre** on good authority.

sourcil [sursi] *nm* eyebrow. **sourciller** *vi* **ne pas s.** *Fig* not to bat an eyelid.

sourd, sourde [sur, surd] 1 *a* deaf (*Fig* **à** to); **— nmf** deaf person. 2 *a* (*bruit, douleur*) dull; (*caché*) secret. **s.-muet** (*pl* **sourds-muets**), **sourde-muette** (*pl* **sourdes-muettes**) *a* deaf and dumb; **— nmf** deaf mute.

sourdine [surdin] *nf* (*dispositif*) *Mus* mute; **en s.** *Fig* quietly, secretly.

souricière [surisjɛr] *nf* mousetrap; *Fig* trap.

sourire* [surir] *vi* to smile (**à** at); **s. à qn** (*fortune*) to smile on s.o.; **— nm** smile; **faire un s. à qn** to give s.o. a smile.

souris [suri] *nf* mouse.

sournois [surnwa] *a* sly, underhand. **sournoisement** *adv* slyly. **sournoiserie** *nf* slyness.

sous [su] *prép* (*position*) under(neath), beneath; (*rang*) under; **s. la pluie** in the rain; **s. cet angle** from that angle *ou* point of view; **s. le nom de** under the name of; **s. Charles X** under Charles X; **s. peu** (*bientôt*) shortly.

sous- [su] *préf* (*subordination, subdivision*) sub-; (*insuffisance*) under-.

sous-alimenté [suzalimɑ̃te] *a* undernourished. **sous-alimentation** *nf* undernourishment.

sous-bois [subwa] *nm* undergrowth.

sous-chef [suʃɛf] *nmf* second-in-command.

souscrire* [suskrir] *vi* **s. à** (*payer, approuver*) to subscribe to. **souscription** *nf* subscription.

sous-développé [sudevlɔpe] a (*pays*) underdeveloped.

sous-directeur, -trice [sudirεktœr, -tris] nmf assistant manager, assistant manageress.

sous-entend/re [suzɑ̃tɑ̃dr] vt to imply. ◆—**u** nm insinuation.

sous-estimer [suzεstime] vt to underestimate.

sous-jacent [suʒasɑ̃] a underlying.

sous-louer [sulwe] vt (*appartement*) to sublet.

sous-main [sumɛ̃] nm inv desk pad.

sous-marin, -ine [sumarɛ̃] a underwater; plongée sous-marine skin diving; – nm submarine.

sous-officier [suzɔfisje] nm noncommissioned officer.

sous-payer [supeje] vt (*ouvrier etc*) to underpay.

sous-produit [suprɔdɥi] nm by-product.

soussigné, -ée [susine] a & nmf undersigned; je s. I the undersigned.

sous-sol [susɔl] nm basement; *Géol* subsoil.

sous-titre [sutitr] nm subtitle. ◆**sous-titrer** vt (*film*) to subtitle.

soustraire* [sustrεr] vt to remove; *Math* to subtract, take away (de from); s. qn à (*danger etc*) to shield ou protect s.o. from; se s. à to escape from; (*devoir, obligation*) to avoid. ◆**soustraction** nf *Math* subtraction.

sous-trait/er [sutrete] vi *Com* to subcontract. ◆—**ant** nm subcontractor.

sous-verre [suvεr] nm inv (*encadrement*) (frameless) glass mount.

sous-vêtement [suvεtmɑ̃] nm undergarment; *pl* underwear.

soutane [sutan] nf (*de prêtre*) cassock.

soute [sut] nf (*magasin*) *Nau* hold.

souten/ir* [sutnir] vt to support, hold up; (*droits, opinion*) to uphold, maintain; (*candidat etc*) to back, support; (*malade*) to sustain; (*effort, intérêt*) to sustain, keep up; (*thèse*) to defend; (*résister à*) to withstand; s. que to maintain that; – se s. vpr (*blessé etc*) to hold oneself up; (*se maintenir, durer*) to be sustained. ◆—**u** a (*attention, effort*) sustained; (*style*) lofty. ◆**soutien** nm support; (*personne*) supporter; s. de famille breadwinner. ◆**soutien-gorge** nm (*pl* soutiens-gorge) bra.

souterrain [sutrɛ̃] a underground; – nm underground passage.

soutirer [sutire] vt s. qch à qn to extract ou get sth from s.o.

souvenir [suvnir] nm memory, recollection;

(*objet*) memento; (*cadeau*) keepsake; (*pour touristes*) souvenir; en s. de in memory of; mon bon s. à (give) my regards to. ◆**se souvenir*** vpr se s. de to remember, recall; se s. que to remember ou recall that.

souvent [suvɑ̃] adv often; peu s. seldom; le plus s. more often than not, most often.

souverain, -aine [suvrɛ̃, -εn] a sovereign; (*extrême*) *Péj* supreme; – nmf sovereign. ◆**souveraineté** nf sovereignty.

soviétique [sɔvjetik] a Soviet; l'Union s. the Soviet Union; – nmf Soviet citizen.

soyeux, -euse [swajø, -øz] a silky.

spacieux, -euse [spasjø, -øz] a spacious, roomy.

spaghetti(s) [spageti] nmpl spaghetti.

sparadrap [sparadra] nm *Méd* sticking plaster, *Am* adhesive tape.

spasme [spasm] nm spasm. ◆**spasmodique** a spasmodic.

spatial, -aux [spasjal, -o] a (*vol etc*) space-; engin s. spaceship, spacecraft.

spatule [spatyl] nf spatula.

speaker [spikœr] nm, **speakerine** [spikrin] nf *Rad TV* announcer.

spécial, -aux [spesjal, -o] a special; (*bizarre*) peculiar. ◆**spécialement** adv especially, particularly; (*exprès*) specially.

spécialiser (se) [saspesjalize] vpr to specialize (dans in). ◆**spécialisation** nf specialization. ◆**spécialiste** nmf specialist. ◆**spécialité** nf speciality, *Am* specialty.

spécifier [spesifje] vt to specify (que that).

spécifique [spesifik] a *Phys Ch* specific.

spécimen [spesimεn] nm specimen; (*livre etc*) specimen copy.

spectacle [spεktakl] nm 1 (*vue*) spectacle, sight; se donner en s. *Péj* to make an exhibition of oneself. 2 (*représentation*) show; le s. (*industrie*) show business. ◆**spectateur, -trice** nmf *Sp* spectator; (*témoin*) onlooker, witness; *pl Th Cin* audience.

spectaculaire [spεktakylεr] a spectacular.

spectre [spεktr] nm 1 (*fantôme*) spectre, ghost. 2 (*solaire*) spectrum.

spéculer [spekyle] vi *Fin Phil* to speculate; s. sur (*tabler sur*) to bank ou rely on. ◆**spéculateur, -trice** nmf speculator. ◆**spéculatif, -ive** a *Fin Phil* speculative. ◆**spéculation** nf *Fin Phil* speculation.

spéléologie [speleɔlɔʒi] nf (*activité*) potholing, caving, *Am* spelunking. ◆**spéléologue** nmf potholer, *Am* spelunker.

sperme [spεrm] nm sperm, semen.

sphère [sfεr] nf (*boule, domaine*) sphere. ◆**sphérique** a spherical.

sphinx [sfɛ̃ks] nm sphinx.

spirale 275 stop

spirale [spiral] *nf* spiral.

spirite [spirit] *nmf* spiritualist. ◆spiritisme *nm* spiritualism.

spirituel, -elle [spiritɥɛl] *a* 1 (*amusant*) witty. 2 (*pouvoir, vie etc*) spiritual.

spiritueux [spiritɥø] *nmpl* (*boissons*) spirits.

splendide [splɑ̃did] *a* (*merveilleux, riche, beau*) splendid. ◆splendeur *nf* splendour.

spongieux, -euse [spɔ̃ʒjø, -øz] *a* spongy.

spontané [spɔ̃tane] *a* spontaneous. ◆spontanéité *nf* spontaneity. ◆spontanément *adv* spontaneously.

sporadique [spɔradik] *a* sporadic.

sport [spɔr] *nm* sport; faire du s. to play sport *ou Am* sports; (de) s. (*chaussures, vêtements*) casual, sports; voiture/veste de s. sports car/jacket. ◆sportif, -ive *a* (*attitude, personne*) sporting; (*association, journal, résultats*) sports, sporting; (*allure*) athletic; – *nm* sportsman, *nf* sportswoman. ◆sportivité *nf* (*esprit*) sportsmanship.

spot [spɔt] *nm* 1 (*lampe*) spot(light). 2 s. (*publicitaire*) *Rad TV* commercial.

sprint [sprint] *nm Sp* sprint. ◆sprint/er *vi* to sprint; – *nm* [-œr] sprinter. ◆-euse *nf* sprinter.

square [skwar] *nm* public garden.

squelette [skəlɛt] *nm* skeleton. ◆squelettique *a* (*personne, maigreur*) skeleton-like; (*exposé*) sketchy.

stable [stabl] *a* stable. ◆stabilisateur *nm* stabilizer. ◆stabiliser *vt* to stabilize; – se s. *vpr* to stabilize. ◆stabilité *nf* stability.

stade [stad] *nm* 1 *Sp* stadium. 2 (*phase*) stage.

stage [staʒ] *nm* training period; (*cours*) (training) course. ◆stagiaire *a* & *nmf* trainee.

stagner [stagne] *vi* to stagnate. ◆stagnant *a* stagnant. ◆stagnation *nf* stagnation.

stalle [stal] *nf* (*box*) & *Rel* stall.

stand [stɑ̃d] *nm* (*d'exposition etc*) stand, stall; s. de ravitaillement *Sp* pit; s. de tir (*de foire*) shooting range; *Mil* firing range.

standard [stɑ̃dar] 1 *nm Tél* switchboard. 2 *a inv* (*modèle etc*) standard. ◆standardiser *vt* to standardize. ◆standardiste *nmf* (switchboard) operator.

standing [stɑ̃diŋ] *nm* standing, status; de (grand) s. (*immeuble*) luxury-.

starter [starter] *nm* 1 *Aut* choke. 2 *Sp* starter.

station [stasjɔ̃] *nf* (*de métro, d'observation etc*) & *Rad* station; (*de ski*) resort; (*d'autobus*) stop; s. de taxis taxi rank, *Am*

taxi stand; s. debout standing (position); s. (thermale) spa. ◆s.-service *nf* (*pl stations-service*) *Aut* service station.

stationnaire [stasjɔnɛr] *vi a* stationary.

stationn/er [stasjɔne] *vi* (*se garer*) to park; (*être garé*) to be parked. ◆-ement *nm* parking.

statique [statik] *a* static.

statistique [statistik] *nf* (*donnée*) statistic; la s. (*techniques*) statistics; – *a* statistical.

statue [staty] *nf* statue. ◆statuette *nf* statuette.

statuer [statɥe] *vi* s. sur *Jur* to rule on.

statu quo [statykwo] *nm inv* status quo.

stature [statyr] *nf* stature.

statut [staty] *nm* 1 (*position*) status. 2 *pl* (*règles*) statutes. ◆statutaire *a* statutory.

steak [stɛk] *nm* steak.

stencil [stɛnsil] *nm* stencil.

sténo [steno] *nf* (*personne*) stenographer; (*sténographie*) shorthand, stenography; prendre en s. to take down in shorthand. ◆sténodactylo *nf* shorthand typist, *Am* stenographer. ◆sténographie *nf* shorthand, stenography.

stéréo [stereo] *nf* stereo; – *a inv* (*disque etc*) stereo. ◆stéréophonique *a* stereophonic.

stéréotype [stereotip] *nm* stereotype. ◆stéréotypé *a* stereotyped.

stérile [steril] *a* sterile; (*terre*) barren. ◆stérilisation *nf* sterilization. ◆stériliser *vt* to sterilize. ◆stérilité *nf* sterility; (*de terre*) barrenness.

stérilet [sterilɛ] *nm* IUD, coil.

stéthoscope [stetɔskɔp] *nm* stethoscope.

steward [stiwart] *nm Av Nau* steward.

stigmate [stigmat] *nm Fig* mark, stigma (de of). ◆stigmatiser *vt* (*dénoncer*) to stigmatize.

stimul/er [stimyle] *vt* to stimulate. ◆-ant *nm Fig* stimulus; *Méd* stimulant. ◆stimulateur *nm* s. cardiaque pacemaker. ◆stimulation *nf* stimulation.

stimulus [stimylys] *nm* (*pl* stimuli [-li]) (*physiologique*) stimulus.

stipuler [stipyle] *vt* to stipulate (que that). ◆stipulation *nf* stipulation.

stock [stɔk] *nm Com* & *Fig* stock (de of). ◆stock/er *vt* (*keep in*) stock. ◆-age *nm* stocking.

stoïque [stɔik] *a* stoic(al). ◆stoïcisme *nm* stoicism.

stop [stɔp] 1 *int* stop; – *nm* (*panneau*) *Aut* stop sign; (*feu arrière*) *Aut* brake light. 2 *nm* faire du s. *Fam* to hitchhike. ◆stopp/er 1 *vti* to stop. 2 *vt* (*vêtement*) to mend (invisibly). ◆**—age** nm (invisible) mending.

store [stɔr] nm blind, Am (window) shade; (de magasin) awning.

strabisme [strabism] nm squint.

strapontin [strapɔ̃tɛ̃] nm tip-up seat.

stratagème [strataʒɛm] nm stratagem, ploy.

stratège [stratɛʒ] nm strategist. ◆**stratégie** nf strategy. ◆**stratégique** a strategic.

stress [strɛs] nm inv Méd Psy stress. ◆**stressant** a stressful. ◆**stressé** a under stress.

strict [strikt] a strict; (langue, tenue, vérité) plain; (droit) basic; **le s. minimum/nécessaire** the bare minimum/necessities. ◆**strictement** adv strictly; (vêtu) plainly.

strident [stridɑ̃] a strident, shrill.

strie [stri] nf streak; (sillon) groove. ◆**strier** vt to streak.

strip-tease [striptiz] nm striptease. ◆**strip-teaseuse** nf stripper.

strophe [strɔf] nf stanza, verse.

structure [stryktyr] nf structure. ◆**structural, -aux** a structural. ◆**structurer** vt to structure.

stuc [styk] nm stucco.

studieux, -euse [stydjø, -øz] a studious; (vacances etc) devoted to study.

studio [stydjo] nm (de peintre) & Cin TV studio; (logement) studio flat ou Am apartment.

stupéfait [stypefɛ] a amazed, astounded (de at, by). ◆**stupéfaction** nf amazement. ◆**stupéfi/er** vt to amaze, astound. ◆**—ant** a amazing, astounding. 2 nm drug, narcotic. ◆**stupeur** nf 1 (étonnement) amazement. 2 (inertie) stupor.

stupide [stypid] a stupid. ◆**stupidement** adv stupidly. ◆**stupidité** nf stupidity; (action, parole) stupid thing.

style [stil] nm style; **de s.** (meuble) period-. ◆**stylisé** a stylized. ◆**styliste** nmf (de mode etc) designer. ◆**stylistique** a stylistic.

stylé [stile] a well-trained.

stylo [stilo] nm pen; **s. à bille** ballpoint (pen), biro®; **s. à encre** fountain pen.

su [sy] voir savoir.

suave [sɥav] a (odeur, voix) sweet.

subalterne [sybaltɛrn] a & nmf subordinate.

subconscient [sypkɔ̃sjɑ̃] a & nm subconscious.

subdiviser [sybdivize] vt to subdivide (en into). ◆**subdivision** nf subdivision.

subir [sybir] vt to undergo; (conséquences, défaite, perte, tortures) to suffer; (influence) to be under; **s. qn** (supporter) Fam to put up with s.o.

subit [sybi] a sudden. ◆**subitement** adv suddenly.

subjectif, -ive [sybʒɛktif, -iv] a subjective. ◆**subjectivement** adv subjectively. ◆**subjectivité** nf subjectivity.

subjonctif [sybʒɔ̃ktif] nm Gram subjunctive.

subjuguer [sybʒyge] vt to subjugate; (envoûter) to captivate.

sublime [syblim] a & nm sublime.

sublimer [syblime] vt Psy to sublimate.

submerger [sybmɛrʒe] vt to submerge; (envahir) Fig to overwhelm; **submergé de** (travail etc) overwhelmed with; **submergé par** (ennemi, foule) swamped by. ◆**submersible** nm submarine.

subordonn/er [sybɔrdɔne] vt to subordinate (à to). ◆**—é, -ée** a subordinate (à to); **être s. à** (dépendre de) to depend on; — nmf subordinate. ◆**subordination** nf subordination.

subreptice [sybrɛptis] a surreptitious.

subside [sypsid] nm grant, subsidy.

subsidiaire [sybsidjɛr] a subsidiary; **question s.** (de concours) deciding question.

subsister [sybziste] vi (rester) to remain; (vivre) to get by, subsist; (doutes, souvenirs etc) to linger (on), subsist. ◆**subsistance** nf subsistence.

substance [sypstɑ̃s] nf substance; **en s.** Fig in essence. ◆**substantiel, -ielle** a substantial.

substantif [sypstɑ̃tif] nm Gram noun, substantive.

substituer [sypstitɥe] vt to substitute (à for); **se s. à qn** to take the place of s.o., substitute for s.o.; (représenter) to substitute for s.o. ◆**substitution** nf substitution.

subterfuge [sypterfyʒ] nm subterfuge.

subtil [syptil] a subtle. ◆**subtilité** nf subtlety.

subtiliser [syptilize] vt (dérober) Fam to make off with.

subvenir* [sybvənir] vi **s. à** (besoins, frais) to meet.

subvention [sybvɑ̃sjɔ̃] nf subsidy. ◆**subventionner** vt to subsidize.

subversif, -ive [sybvɛrsif, -iv] a subversive. ◆**subversion** nf subversion.

suc [syk] nm (gastrique, de fruit) juice; (de plante) sap.

succédané [syksedane] *nm* substitute (**de** for).

succéder [syksede] *vi* **s. à qn** to succeed s.o.; **s. à qch** to follow sth, come after sth; **— se s.** *vpr* to succeed one another; to follow one another. ◆**successeur** *nm* successor. ◆**successif, -ive** *a* successive. ◆**successivement** *adv* successively. ◆**succession** *nf* **1** succession (**de** of, **à** to); **prendre la s. de qn** to succeed s.o. **2** (*patrimoine*) *Jur* inheritance, estate.

succès [syksɛ] *nm* success; **s. de librairie** (*livre*) best-seller; **avoir du s.** to be successful, be a success; **à s.** (*auteur, film etc*) successful; **avec s.** successfully.

succinct [syksɛ̃] *a* succinct, brief.

succion [sy(k)sjɔ̃] *nf* suction.

succomber [sykɔ̃be] *vi* **1** (*mourir*) to die. **2 s. à** (*céder à*) to succumb to, give in to.

succulent [sykylɑ̃] *a* succulent.

succursale [sykyrsal] *nf Com* branch; **magasin à succursales multiples** chain ou multiple store.

sucer [syse] *vt* to suck. ◆**sucette** *nf* lollipop; (*tétine*) dummy, comforter, *Am* pacifier.

sucre [sykr] *nm* sugar; (*morceau*) sugar lump; **s. cristallisé** granulated sugar; **s. en morceaux** lump sugar; **s. en poudre**, **semoule** caster sugar, *Am* finely ground sugar; **s. d'orge** barley sugar. ◆**sucr/er** *vt* to sugar, sweeten. ◆**—é** *a* sweet, sugary; (*artificiellement*) sweetened; (*douceureux*) *Fig* sugary, syrupy. ◆**sucrerie 1** *nf* (*usine*) sugar refinery. **2** *nfpl* (*bonbons*) sweets, *Am* candy. ◆**sucrier, -ière** *a* (*industrie*) sugar-; *— nm* (*récipient*) sugar bowl.

sud [syd] *nm* south; **au s. de** south of; **du s.** (*vent, direction*) southerly; (*ville*) southern; (*gens*) from *ou* in the south; **Amérique/Afrique du S.** South America/Africa; **l'Europe du S.** Southern Europe; *— a inv* (*côte*) south(ern). ◆**s.-africain, -aine** *a* & *nmf* South African. ◆**s.-américain** *a* & *nmf* South American. ◆**s.-est** *nm* & *a inv* south-east. ◆**s.-ouest** *nm* & *a inv* south-west.

Suède [sɥɛd] *nf* Sweden. ◆**suédois, -oise** *a* Swedish; *— nmf* Swede; *— nm* (*langue*) Swedish.

suer [sɥe] *vi* (*personne, mur etc*) to sweat; **faire s. qn** *Fam* to get on s.o.'s nerves; **se faire s.** *Fam* to be bored stiff; *— vt* (*sang etc*) to sweat. ◆**sueur** *nf* sweat; **(tout) en s.** sweating.

suffire* [syfir] *vi* to be enough *ou* sufficient, suffice (**à** for); **ça suffit!** that's enough!; **il**

suffit de faire one only has to do; **il suffit d'une goutte/etc pour faire** a drop/*etc* is enough to do; **il ne me suffit pas de faire** I'm not satisfied with doing; *— se s.* *vpr* **se s. (à soi-même)** to be self-sufficient. ◆**suffisant** *a* **1** sufficient, adequate. **2** (*vaniteux*) conceited. ◆**suffisamment** *adv* sufficiently; **s. de** sufficient, enough. ◆**suffisance** *nf* (*vanité*) conceit.

suffixe [syfiks] *nm Gram* suffix.

suffoquer [syfɔke] *vti* to choke, suffocate. ◆**suffocant** *a* stifling, suffocating. ◆**suffocation** *nf* suffocation; (*sensation*) feeling of suffocation.

suffrage [syfraʒ] *nm Pol* (*voix*) vote; (*droit*) suffrage.

suggérer [sygʒere] *vt* (*proposer*) to suggest (**de faire** doing, **que** (+ *sub*) that); (*évoquer*) to suggest. ◆**suggestif, -ive** *a* suggestive. ◆**suggestion** *nf* suggestion.

suicide [sɥisid] *nm* suicide. ◆**suicidaire** *a* suicidal. ◆**se suicid/er** *vpr* to commit suicide. ◆**—é, -ée** *nmf* suicide (victim).

suie [sɥi] *nf* soot.

suif [sɥif] *nm* tallow.

suinter [sɥɛ̃te] *vi* to ooze, seep. ◆**suintement** *nm* oozing, seeping.

suis [sɥi] *voir* être, suivre.

Suisse [sɥis] *nf* Switzerland. ◆**suisse** *a* & *nmf* Swiss. ◆**Suissesse** *nf* Swiss (woman *ou* girl).

suite [sɥit] *nf* (*reste*) rest; (*continuation*) continuation; (*de film, roman*) sequel; (*série*) series, sequence; (*appartement, escorte*) & *Mus* suite; (*cohérence*) order; *pl* (*résultats*) consequences; (*séquelles*) effects; **attendre la s.** to wait and see what happens next; **donner s. à** (*demande etc*) to follow up; **faire s. (à)** to follow; **prendre la s. de qn** to take over from s.o.; **par la s.** afterwards; **par s. de** as a result of; **à la s.** one after another; **à la s. de** (*derrière*) behind; (*événement, maladie etc*) as a result of; **de s.** in succession.

suiv/re* [sɥivr] *vt* to follow; (*accompagner*) to go with, accompany; (*classe*) *Scol* to attend, go to; (*malade*) to treat; **s. (des yeux ou du regard)** to watch; **s. son chemin** to go on one's way; **se s.** to follow each other; *— vi* to follow; **faire s.** (*courrier*) to forward; **'à s.'** 'to be continued'; **comme suit** as follows. ◆**—ant¹, -ante** *a* next, following; (*ci-après*) following; *— nmf* next (one); **au s.!** next!, the next person! ◆**—ant²** *prép* (*selon*) according to. ◆**—i** *a* (*régulier*) regular, steady; (*cohérent*) coherent; (*article*)

Com regularly on sale; **peu/très s.** (*cours*) poorly/well attended.

sujet¹, -ette [syʒɛ, -ɛt] *a* **s. à** (*maladie etc*) subject *ou* liable to; – *nmf* (*personne*) *Pol* subject.

sujet² [syʒɛ] *nm* **1** (*question*) & *Gram* subject; (*d'examen*) question; **au s. de** about; **à quel s.?** about what? **2** (*raison*) cause; **avoir s. de faire** to have (good) cause *ou* (good) reason to do. **3** *nm* (*individu*) subject; **un mauvais s.** (*garçon*) a rotten egg.

sulfurique [sylfyrik] *a* (*acide*) sulphuric, *Am* sulfuric.

sultan [syltã] *nm* sultan.

summum [sɔmɔm] *nm* (*comble*) *Fig* height.

super [sypɛr] **1** *a* (*bon*) *Fam* great. **2** *nm* (*supercarburant*) *Fam* four-star (petrol), *Am* premium *ou* hi-test gas.

superbe [sypɛrb] *a* superb.

supercarburant [sypɛrkarbyrã] *nm* high-octane petrol *ou Am* gasoline.

supercherie [sypɛrʃəri] *nf* deception.

superficie [sypɛrfisi] *nf* surface; (*dimensions*) area. ◆**superficiel, -ielle** *a* superficial. ◆**superficiellement** *adv* superficially.

superflu [sypɛrfly] *a* superfluous.

super-grand [sypɛrgrã] *nm Pol Fam* superpower.

supérieur, -eure [sypɛrjœr] *a* (*étages, partie etc*) upper; (*qualité, air, ton*) superior; (*études*) higher; **à l'étage s.** on the floor above; **s. à** (*meilleur que*) superior to, better than; (*plus grand que*) above, greater than; – *nmf* superior. ◆**supériorité** *nf* superiority.

superlatif, -ive [sypɛrlatif, -iv] *a* & *nm Gram* superlative.

supermarché [sypɛrmarʃe] *nm* supermarket.

superposer [sypɛrpoze] *vt* (*objets*) to put on top of each other; (*images etc*) to superimpose.

superproduction [sypɛrprɔdyksjɔ̃] *nf* (*film*) blockbuster.

superpuissance [sypɛrpɥisãs] *nf Pol* superpower.

supersonique [sypɛrsɔnik] *a* supersonic.

superstitieux, -euse [sypɛrstisjø, -øz] *a* superstitious. ◆**superstition** *nf* superstition.

superviser [sypɛrvize] *vt* to supervise.

supplanter [syplãte] *vt* to take the place of.

suppléer [syplee] *vt* (*remplacer*) to replace; (*compenser*) to make up for; – *vi* **s. à** (*compenser*) to make up for. ◆**—ant, -ante**

a & *nmf* (*personne*) substitute, replacement; (*professeur*) **s.** supply teacher.

supplément [syplemã] *nm* (*argent*) extra charge, supplement; (*de livre, revue*) supplement; **en s.** extra; **un s. de** (*information, travail etc*) extra, additional. ◆**supplémentaire** *a* extra, additional.

supplice [syplis] *nm* torture; **au s.** *Fig* on the rack. ◆**supplicier** *vt* to torture.

suppli/er [syplie] *vt* **s. qn de faire** to beg *ou* implore s.o. to do; **je vous en supplie!** I beg *ou* implore you! ◆**—ant, -ante** *a* (*regard etc*) imploring. ◆**supplication** *nf* plea, entreaty.

support [sypɔr] *nm* **1** support; (*d'instrument etc*) stand. **2** (*moyen*) *Fig* medium; **s. audio-visuel** audio-visual aid.

support/er¹ [sypɔrte] *vt* to bear, endure; (*frais*) to bear; (*affront etc*) to suffer; (*résister à*) to withstand; (*soutenir*) to support. ◆**—able** *a* bearable; (*excusable, passable*) tolerable.

supporter² [sypɔrter] *nm Sp* supporter.

supposer [sypoze] *vt* to suppose, assume (*que* that); (*impliquer*) to imply (*que* that); **à s.** *ou* **en supposant que** (+ *sub*) supposing (that). ◆**supposition** *nf* supposition, assumption.

suppositoire [sypozitwar] *nm Méd* suppository.

supprimer [syprime] *vt* to remove, get rid of; (*institution, loi*) to abolish; (*journal etc*) to suppress; (*mot, passage*) to cut, delete; (*train etc*) to cancel; (*tuer*) to do away with; **s. qch à qn** to take sth away from s.o. ◆**suppression** *nf* removal; abolition; suppression; cutting; cancellation.

suprématie [sypremasi] *nf* supremacy. ◆**suprême** *a* supreme.

sur [syr] *prép* on, upon; (*par-dessus*) over; (*au sujet de*) on, about; **s. les trois heures** at about three o'clock; **six s. dix** six out of ten; **un jour s. deux** every other day; **coup s. coup** blow after *ou* upon blow; **six mètres s. dix** six metres by ten; **mettre/monter/etc s.** to put/climb/etc on (to); **aller/tourner/etc s.** to go/turn/etc towards; **s. ce** after which, and then; (*maintenant*) and now.

sur- [syr] *préf* over-.

sûr [syr] *a* sure, certain (**de of**, **que** that); (*digne de confiance*) reliable; (*avenir*) secure; (*lieu*) safe; (*main*) steady; (*goût*) unerring; (*jugement*) sound; **s. de soi** self-assured; **bien s.!** of course!

surabondant [syrabɔdã] *a* over-abundant.

suranné [syrane] *a* outmoded.

surboum [syrbum] *nf Fam* party.

surcharge [syrʃarʒ] nf **1** overloading; (poids) extra load; **s. de travail** extra work; **en s.** (passagers etc) extra. **2** (correction de texte etc) alteration; (de timbre-poste) surcharge. ◆**surcharger** vt (voiture, personne etc) to overload (**de** with).

surchauffer [syrʃofe] vt to overheat.

surchoix [syrʃwa] a inv Com top-quality.

surclasser [syrklase] vt to outclass.

surcroît [syrkrwa] nm increase (**de** in); **de s., par s.** in addition.

surdité [syrdite] nf deafness.

surdoué, -ée [syrdwe] nmf child who has a genius-level IQ.

surélever [syrelve] vt to raise (the height of).

sûrement [syrmɑ̃] adv certainly; (sans danger) safely.

surenchère [syrɑ̃ʃɛr] nf Com higher bid; **s. électorale** Fig bidding for votes. ◆**surenchérir** vi to bid higher (**sur** than).

surestimer [syrɛstime] vt to overestimate; (peinture etc) to overvalue.

sûreté [syrte] nf safety; (de l'état) security; (garantie) surety; (de geste) sureness; (de jugement) soundness; **être en s.** to be safe; **mettre en s.** to put in a safe place; **de s.** (épingle, soupape etc) safety-.

surexcité [syrɛksite] a overexcited.

surf [sœrf] nm Sp surfing; **faire du s.** to surf, go surfing.

surface [syrfas] nf surface; (dimensions) (surface) area; **faire s.** (sous-marin etc) to surface; (**magasin à**) **grande s.** hypermarket.

surfait [syrfɛ] a overrated.

surgelé [syrʒəle] a (deep-)frozen; – nmpl (deep-)frozen foods.

surgir [syrʒir] vi to appear suddenly (**de** from); (conflit, problème) to arise.

surhomme [syrɔm] nm superman. ◆**surhumain** a superhuman.

sur-le-champ [syrləʃɑ̃] adv immediately.

surlendemain [syrlɑ̃dmɛ̃] nm **le s.** two days later; **le s. de** two days after.

surmen/er [syrmane] vt, – **se s.** vpr to overwork. ◆**-age** nm overwork.

surmonter [syrmɔ̃te] vt **1** (obstacle, peur etc) to overcome, get over. **2** (être placé sur) to be on top of, top.

surnager [syrnaʒe] vi to float.

surnaturel, -elle [syrnatyrɛl] a & nm supernatural.

surnom [syrnɔ̃] nm nickname. ◆**surnommer** vt to nickname.

surnombre [syrnɔ̃br] nm **en s.** too many; **je suis en s.** I am one too many.

surpasser [syrpase] vt to surpass (**en** in); – **se s.** vpr to surpass oneself.

surpeuplé [syrpœple] a overpopulated.

surplomb [syrplɔ̃] nm **en s.** overhanging. ◆**surplomber** vti to overhang.

surplus [syrply] nm surplus; pl Com surplus (stock).

surprendre* [syrprɑ̃dr] vt (étonner, prendre sur le fait) to surprise; (secret) to discover; (conversation) to overhear; **se s. à faire** to find oneself doing. ◆**surprenant** a surprising. ◆**surpris** a surprised (**de** at, **que** (+ sub) that). ◆**surprise** nf surprise. ◆**surprise-partie** nf (pl **surprises-parties**) party.

surréaliste [syrealist] a (bizarre) Fam surrealistic.

sursaut [syrso] nm (sudden) start ou jump; **en s.** with a start; **s. de** (énergie etc) burst of. ◆**sursauter** vi to start, jump.

sursis [syrsi] nm Mil deferment; (répit) reprieve; **un an** (**de prison**) **avec s.** a one-year suspended sentence.

surtaxe [syrtaks] nf surcharge.

surtout [syrtu] adv especially; (avant tout) above all; **s. pas** certainly not; **s. que** especially as ou since.

surveill/er [syrveje] vt (garder) to watch, keep an eye on; (épier) to watch; (contrôler) to supervise; **s. son langage/sa santé** Fig to watch one's language/health; – **se s.** vpr to watch oneself. ◆**-ant, -ante** nmf (de lycée) supervisor (in charge of discipline); (de prison) warder; (de chantier) supervisor; **s. de plage** lifeguard. ◆**surveillance** nf watch (**sur** over); (de travaux, d'ouvriers) supervision; (de la police) surveillance, observation.

survenir* [syrvanir] vi to occur; (personne) to turn up.

survêtement [syrvɛtmɑ̃] nm Sp tracksuit.

survie [syrvi] nf survival. ◆**surviv/re*** vi to survive (**à qch** sth); **s. à qn** to outlive s.o., survive s.o. ◆**-ant, -ante** nmf survivor. ◆**survivance** nf (chose) survival, relic.

survol [syrvɔl] nm **le s. de** flying over; (question) Fig the overview of. ◆**survoler** vt (en avion) to fly over; (question) Fig to go over (quickly).

survolté [syrvɔlte] a (surexcité) worked up.

susceptible [sysɛptibl] a **1** (ombrageux) touchy, sensitive. **2 s. de** (interprétations etc) open to; **s. de faire** likely ou liable to do; (capable) able to do. ◆**susceptibilité** nf touchiness, sensitiveness.

susciter [syste] vt (sentiment) to arouse; (ennuis, obstacles etc) to create.

suspect, -ecte [syspɛ(kt), -ɛkt] *a* suspicious, suspect; **s. de** suspected of; – *nmf* suspect. **◆suspecter** *vt* to suspect (**de qch** of sth, **de faire** of doing); (*bonne foi etc*) to question, suspect, doubt.

suspend/re [syspɑ̃dr] *vt* **1** (*destituer, différer, interrompre*) to suspend. **2** (*fixer*) to hang (up) (**à** on); **se s. à** to hang from. **◆—u** *a* **s. à** hanging from; **pont s.** suspension bridge. **◆suspension** *nf* **1** (*d'hostilités, d'employé etc*) & *Aut* suspension; **points de s.** *Gram* dots, suspension points. **2** (*lustre*) hanging lamp.

suspens (en) [ɑ̃syspɑ̃] **1** (*affaire, travail*) in abeyance. **2** (*dans l'incertitude*) in suspense.

suspense [syspɛns] *nm* suspense; **film à s.** thriller, suspense film.

suspicion [syspisjɔ̃] *nf* suspicion.

susurrer [sysyre] *vti* to murmur.

suture [sytyr] *nf* Méd stitching; **point de s.** stitch. **◆suturer** *vt* to stitch up.

svelte [svɛlt] *a* slender. **◆sveltesse** *nf* slenderness.

SVP *abrév* (*s'il vous plaît*) please.

syllabe [silab] *nf* syllable.

symbole [sɛ̃bɔl] *nm* symbol. **◆symbolique** *a* symbolic; (*salaire*) nominal. **◆symboliser** *vt* to symbolize. **◆symbolisme** *nm* symbolism.

symétrie [simetri] *nf* symmetry. **◆symétrique** *a* symmetrical.

sympa [sɛ̃pa] *a inv* Fam = **sympathique**.

sympathie [sɛ̃pati] *nf* liking, affection; (*affinité*) affinity; (*condoléances*) sympathy; **avoir de la s. pour qn** to be fond of s.o. **◆sympathique** *a* nice, pleasant; (*accueil, geste*) friendly. **◆sympathis/er** *vi* to get

on well (**avec** with). **◆—ant, -ante** *nmf* Pol sympathizer.

symphonie [sɛ̃fɔni] *nf* symphony. **◆symphonique** *a* symphonic; (*orchestre*) symphony-.

symposium [sɛ̃pozjɔm] *nm* symposium.

symptôme [sɛ̃ptom] *nm* symptom. **◆symptomatique** *a* symptomatic (**de** of).

synagogue [sinagɔg] *nf* synagogue.

synchroniser [sɛ̃krɔnize] *vt* to synchronize.

syncope [sɛ̃kɔp] *nf* Méd blackout; **tomber en s.** to black out.

syndicat [sɛ̃dika] *nm* **1** (*d'employés, d'ouvriers*) trade union; (*de patrons etc*) association. **2 s. d'initiative** tourist (information) office. **◆syndical, -aux** *a* (*réunion etc*) (trade) union-. **◆syndicalisme** *nm* trade unionism. **◆syndicaliste** *nmf* trade unionist; – *a* (trade) union-. **◆syndiqu/er** *vt* to unionize; – **se s.** *vpr* (*adhérer*) to join a trade union. **◆—é, -ée** *nmf* (trade) union member.

syndrome [sɛ̃drom] *nm* Méd & Fig syndrome.

synode [sinɔd] *nm* Rel synod.

synonyme [sinɔnim] *a* synonymous (**de** with); – *nm* synonym.

syntaxe [sɛ̃taks] *nf* Gram syntax.

synthèse [sɛ̃tɛz] *nf* synthesis. **◆synthétique** *a* synthetic.

syphilis [sifilis] *nf* syphilis.

Syrie [siri] *nf* Syria. **◆syrien, -ienne** *a* & *nmf* Syrian.

système [sistɛm] *nm* (*structure, réseau etc*) & *Anat* system; **le s. D** Fam resourcefulness. **◆systématique** *a* systematic; (*soutien*) unconditional. **◆systématiquement** *adv* systematically.

T

T, t [te] *nm* T, t.

t' [t] *voir* **te**.

ta [ta] *voir* **ton** [1].

tabac [taba] **1** *nm* tobacco; (*magasin*) tobacconist's (shop), *Am* tobacco store; **t. (à priser)** snuff. **2** *Fam* **passer à t.** to beat up; **passage à t.** beating up. **3** *a inv* (*couleur*) buff. **◆tabatière** *nf* (*boîte*) snuffbox.

tabasser [tabase] *vt* Fam to beat up.

table [tabl] *nf* **1** (*meuble*) table; (*nourriture*) fare; **t. de jeu/de nuit/d'opération** card/bedside/operating table; **t. basse** coffee

table; **t. à repasser** ironing board; **t. roulante** (tea) trolley, *Am* (serving) cart; **mettre/débarrasser la t.** to lay ou set/clear the table; **être à t.** to be sitting at the table; **à t.!** (*food's*) ready!; **faire t. rase** Fig to make a clean sweep (**de** of); **mettre sur t. d'écoute** (*téléphone*) to tap. **2** (*liste*) table; **t. des matières** table of contents.

tableau, -x [tablo] *nm* **1** (*peinture*) picture, painting; (*image, description*) picture; Th scene; **t. de maître** (*peinture*) old master. **2** (*panneau*) board; Rail train-indicator;

(liste) list; *(graphique)* chart; **t. (noir)** (black)board; **t. d'affichage** notice board, *Am* bulletin board; **t. de bord** *Aut* dashboard; **t. de contrôle** *Tech* control panel.

tabler [table] *vi* **t. sur** to count *ou* rely on.

tablette [tablet] *nf (d'armoire, de lavabo)* shelf; *(de cheminée)* mantelpiece; *(de chocolat)* bar, slab.

tablier [tablije] *nm* **1** *(vêtement)* apron; *(d'écolier)* smock; **rendre son t.** *(démissionner)* to give notice. **2** *(de pont)* roadway.

tabou [tabu] *a & nm* taboo.

tabouret [taburɛ] *nm* stool.

tabulateur [tabylatœr] *nm (de machine à écrire etc)* tabulator.

tac [tak] *nm* **répondre du t. au t.** to give tit for tat.

tache [taʃ] *nf* spot, mark; *(salissure)* stain; **faire t.** *(détonner)* *Péj* to jar, stand out; **faire t. d'huile** *Fig* to spread. ◆**tacher** *vt*, **— se t.** *vpr (tissu etc)* to stain; **—** *vi (vin etc)* to stain. ◆**tacheté** a speckled, spotted.

tâche [taʃ] *nf* task, job; **travailler à la t.** to do piecework.

tâcher [taʃe] *vi* **t. de faire** to try *ou* endeavour to do.

tâcheron [taʃrɔ̃] *nm* drudge.

tacite [tasit] *a* tacit. ◆**—ment** *adv* tacitly.

taciturne [tasityrn] *a* taciturn.

tacot [tako] *nm (voiture) Fam* (old) wreck, banger.

tact [takt] *nm* tact.

tactile [taktil] *a* tactile.

tactique [taktik] *a* tactical; **—** *nf* **la t.** tactics; **une t.** a tactic.

Tahiti [taiti] *nm* Tahiti. ◆**tahitien, -ienne** [taisjɛ̃, -jɛn] *a & nmf* Tahitian.

taie [tɛ] *nf* **t. d'oreiller** pillowcase, pillowslip.

taillade [tajad] *nf* gash, slash. ◆**taillader** *vt* to gash, slash.

taille¹ [taj] *nf* **1** *(stature)* height; *(dimension, mesure commerciale)* size; **de haute t.** *(personne)* tall; **de petite t.** short; **de t. moyenne** *(objet, personne)* medium-sized; **être de t. à faire** *Fig* to be capable of doing; **de t.** *(erreur, objet) Fam* enormous. **2** *Anat* waist; **tour de t.** waist measurement.

taille² [taj] *nf* cutting; cutting out; trimming; pruning; *(forme)* shape. ◆**taill/er** *vt* to cut; *(vêtement)* to cut out; *(haie, barbe)* to trim; *(arbre)* to prune; *(crayon)* to sharpen. **2 se t.** *vpr (partir) Arg* to clear off. ◆**—é** a **t. en athlète** */etc* built like an athlete*/etc*; **t. pour faire** *Fig* cut out for doing. ◆**—euses** *afpl* autos **s.** dodgems, bumper cars.

taille-crayon(s) [tajkrɛjɔ̃] *nm inv* pencil-sharpener. ◆**t.-haies** *nm inv* (garden) shears; *(électrique)* hedge trimmer.

tailleur [tɑjœr] *nm* **1** *(personne)* tailor. **2** *(costume féminin)* suit.

taillis [taji] *nm* copse, coppice.

tain [tɛ̃] *nm (de glace)* silvering; **glace sans t.** two-way mirror.

taire* [ter] *vt* to say nothing about; **—** *vi* **faire t. qn** to silence s.o. **— se t.** *vpr (rester silencieux)* to keep quiet **(sur qch** about sth); *(cesser de parler)* to fall silent, shut up; **tais-toi!** be *ou* keep quiet!, shut up!

talc [talk] *nm* talcum powder.

talent [talɑ̃] *nm* talent; **avoir du t. pour** to have a talent for. ◆**talentueux, -euse** *a* talented.

taler [tale] *vt (fruit)* to bruise.

talion [taljɔ̃] *nm* **la loi du t.** *(vengeance)* an eye for an eye.

talisman [talismɑ̃] *nm* talisman.

talkie-walkie [talkiwalki] *nm (poste)* walkie-talkie.

taloche [talɔʃ] *nf (gifle) Fam* clout, smack.

talon [talɔ̃] *nm* **1** heel; **(chaussures à) talons hauts** high heels, high-heeled shoes. **2** *(de chèque, carnet)* stub, counterfoil; *(bout de pain)* crust; *(de jambon)* heel. ◆**talonner** *vt (fugitif etc)* to follow on the heels of; *(ballon) Rugby* to heel; *(harceler) Fig* to hound, dog.

talus [taly] *nm* slope, embankment.

tambour [tɑ̃bur] *nm* **1** *(de machine etc)* & *Mus* drum; *(personne)* drummer. **2** *(porte)* revolving door. ◆**tambourin** *nm* tambourine. ◆**tambouriner** *vi (avec les doigts etc)* to drum **(sur** on).

tamis [tami] *nm* sieve. ◆**tamiser** *vt* to sift; *(lumière)* to filter, subdue.

Tamise [tamiz] *nf* **la T.** the Thames.

tampon [tɑ̃pɔ̃] *nm* **1** *(bouchon)* plug, stopper; *(d'ouate)* wad, pad; *Méd* swab; **t. hygiénique** *ou* **périodique** tampon; **t. à récurer** scouring pad. **2** *(de train etc)* & *Fig* buffer; **état t.** buffer state. **3** *(marque, instrument)* stamp; **t. buvard** blotter; **t. encreur** ink(ing) pad. ◆**tamponn/er** *vt (visage etc)* to dab; *(plaie)* to swab. **2** *vt (train, voiture)* to crash into; **— se t.** *vpr* to crash into each other. **3** *vt (lettre, document)* to stamp. ◆**—euses** *afpl* autos **s.** dodgems, bumper cars.

tam-tam [tamtam] *nm (tambour)* tom-tom.

tandem [tɑ̃dɛm] *nm* **1** *(bicyclette)* tandem. **2** *(duo) Fig* duo, pair; **en t.** *(travailler etc)* in tandem.

tandis que [tɑ̃di(ə)] *conj (pendant que)* while; *(contraste)* whereas, while.

tangent [tɑ̃ʒɑ̃] *a* **1** *Géom* tangential **(à** to).

2 (*juste*) *Fam* touch and go, close. ◆**tangente** *nf Géom* tangent.

tangible [tɑ̃ʒibl] *a* tangible.

tango [tɑ̃go] *nm* tango.

tang/uer [tɑ̃ge] *vi* (*bateau, avion*) to pitch. ◆**-age** *nm* pitching.

tanière [tanjɛr] *nf* den, lair.

tank [tɑ̃k] *nm Mil* tank.

tanker [tɑ̃kɛr] *nm* (*navire*) tanker.

tann/er [tane] *vt* (*cuir*) to tan. ◆**-é** *a* (*visage*) weather-beaten, tanned.

tant [tɑ̃] *adv* so much (*que* that); **t. de** (*pain, temps etc*) so much (*que* that); (*gens, choses etc*) so many (*que* that); **t. de fois** so often, so many times; **t. que** (*autant que*) as much as; (*aussi fort que*) as hard as; (*aussi longtemps que*) as long as; **t. mieux!** good!, I'm glad!; **t. pis!** too bad!, pity!; **t. soit peu** (*even*) remotely *ou* slightly; **un t. soit peu** somewhat; **t. s'en faut** far from it; **t. bien que mal** more or less, so-so.

tante [tɑ̃t] *nf* aunt.

tantinet [tɑ̃tinɛ] *nm & adv* **un t.** a tiny bit (**de** of).

tantôt [tɑ̃to] *adv* **1 t. . . . t.** sometimes . . . sometimes, now . . . now. **2** (*cet après-midi*) this afternoon.

taon [tɑ̃] *nm* horsefly, gadfly.

tapage [tapaʒ] *nm* din, uproar. ◆**tapageur, -euse** *a* **1** (*bruyant*) rowdy. **2** (*criard*) flashy.

tape [tap] *nf* slap. ◆**tap/er 1** *vt* (*enfant, cuisse*) to slap; (*table*) to bang; **t. qn** (*emprunter de l'argent à qn*) *Fam* to touch s.o., tap s.o. (**de** for); – *vi* (*soleil*) to beat down; **t. sur qch** to bang on sth; **t. à la porte** to bang on the door; **t. sur qn** (*critiquer*) *Fam* to run s.o. down, knock s.o.; **t. sur les nerfs de qn** *Fam* to get on s.o.'s nerves; **t. dans** (*provisions etc*) to dig into; **t. du pied** to stamp one's foot; **t. dans l'œil à qn** *Fam* to take s.o.'s fancy; – **se t.** *vpr* (*travail*) *Fam* to do, take on; (*repas, vin*) *Fam* to put away. **2** *vti* (*écrire à la machine*) to type. ◆**-ant** *a* à midi **t.** at twelve sharp; **à huit heures tapant(es)** at eight sharp. ◆**-eur, -euse** *nmf Fam* person who borrows money.

tape-à-l'œil [tapalœj] *a inv* flashy, gaudy.

tapée [tape] *nf* **une t. de** *Fam* a load of.

tapioca [tapjoka] *nm* tapioca.

tapir (se) [sətapir] *vpr* to crouch (**down**). ◆**tapi** *a* crouching, crouched.

tapis [tapi] *nm* carpet; **t. de bain** bathmat; **t. roulant** (*pour marchandises*) conveyor belt; (*pour personnes*) moving pavement *ou* Am

sidewalk; **t. de sol** groundsheet; **t. de table** table cover; **envoyer qn au t.** (*abattre*) to floor s.o.; **mettre sur le t.** (*sujet*) to bring up for discussion. ◆**t.-brosse** *nm* doormat.

tapisser [tapise] *vt* (*mur*) to (wall)paper; to hang with tapestry; (*recouvrir*) *Fig* to cover. ◆**tapisserie** *nf* (*tenture*) tapestry; (*papier peint*) wallpaper. ◆**tapissier, -ière** *nmf* (*qui pose des tissus etc*) upholsterer; **t.(-décorateur)** interior decorator.

tapoter [tapote] *vt* to tap; (*joue*) to pat; – *vi* **t. sur** to tap on.

taquin, -ine [takɛ̃, -in] *a* (*fond of*) teasing; – *nmf* tease(r). ◆**taquiner** *vt* to tease; (*inquiéter, agacer*) to bother. ◆**taquinerie(s)** *nf(pl)* teasing.

tarabiscoté [tarabiskɔte] *a* over-elaborate.

tarabuster [tarabyste] *vt* (*idée etc*) to trouble (*s.o.*).

tard [tar] *adv* late; **plus t.** later (on); **au plus t.** at the latest; **sur le t.** late in life. ◆**tarder** *vi* (*lettre, saison*) to be a long time coming; **il a fait t.** to take one's time doing; (*différer*) to delay (in) doing; **ne tardez pas** (*agissez tout de suite*) don't delay; **elle ne va pas t.** she won't be long; **sans t.** without delay; **il me tarde de faire** I long to do. ◆**tardif, -ive** *a* late; (*regrets*) belated. ◆**tardivement** *adv* late.

tare [tar] *nf* **1** (*poids*) tare. **2** (*défaut*) *Fig* defect. ◆**taré** *a* (*corrompu*) corrupt; *Méd* defective; (*fou*) *Fam* mad, idiotic.

targuer (se) [sətarge] *vpr* **se t. de qch/de faire** to boast about sth/about doing.

tarif [tarif] *nm* (*prix*) rate; *Aut Rail* fare; (*tableau*) price list, tariff. ◆**tarification** *nf* (*price*) fixing.

tarir [tarir] *vti*, – **se t.** *vpr* (*fleuve etc*) & *Fig* to dry up; **ne pas t. d'éloges sur qn** to rave about s.o.

tartare [tartar] *a* **sauce t.** tartar sauce.

tarte [tart] **1** *nf* tart, flan, *Am* (open) pie. **2** *a inv Fam* (*sot*) silly; (*laid*) ugly. ◆**tartelette** *nf* (small) tart.

tartine [tartin] *nf* slice of bread; **t. (de beurre/de confiture)** slice of bread and butter/jam. ◆**tartiner** *vt* (*beurre*) to spread; **fromage à t.** cheese spread.

tartre [tartr] *nm* (*de bouilloire*) scale, fur; (*de dents*) tartar.

tas [tɑ] *nm* pile, heap; **un** *ou* **des t. de** (*beaucoup*) *Fam* lots of; **mettre en t.** to pile *ou* heap up; **former qn sur le t.** (*au travail*) to train s.o. on the job.

tasse [tas] *nf* cup; **t. à café** coffee cup; **t. à thé** teacup; **boire la t.** *Fam* to swallow a mouthful (*when swimming*).

tasser [tɑse] vt to pack, squeeze (**dans** into); (terre) to pack down; **un café**/etc **bien tassé** (fort) a good strong coffee/etc; **— se t.** vpr (se voûter) to become bowed; (se serrer) to squeeze up; (sol) to sink, collapse; **ça va se t.** (s'arranger) Fam things will pan out (all right).

tâter [tɑte] vt to feel; (sonder) Fig to sound out; **— vi t. de** (métier, prison) to have a taste of, experience; **— se t.** vpr (hésiter) to be in ou of two minds. ◆**tâtonn/er** vi to grope about, feel one's way. ◆**—ement** nm **par t.** (procéder) by trial and error. ◆**tâtons (à)** adv avancer à t. to feel one's way (along); **chercher à t.** to grope for.

tatillon, -onne [tatijɔ̃, -ɔn] a finicky.

tatou/er [tatwe] vt (corps, dessin) to tattoo. ◆**—age** nm (dessin) tattoo; (action) tattooing.

taudis [todi] nm slum, hovel.

taule [tol] nf (prison) Fam nick, jug, Am can.

taupe [top] nf (animal, espion) mole. ◆**taupinière** nf molehill.

taureau, -x [tɔro] nm bull; **le T.** (signe) Taurus. ◆**tauromachie** nf bull-fighting.

taux [to] nm rate; **t. d'alcool/de cholestérol**/etc alcohol/cholesterol/etc level.

taverne [tavɛrn] nf tavern.

taxe [taks] nf (prix) official price; (impôt) tax; (douanière) duty; **t. de séjour** tourist tax; **t. à la valeur ajoutée** value-added tax. ◆**taxation** nf fixing of the price (**de** of); taxation (**de** of). ◆**taxer** vt 1 (produit) to fix the price of; (objet de luxe etc) to tax. **2 t. qn** to accuse s.o. of.

taxi [taksi] nm taxi.

taxiphone [taksifɔn] nm pay phone.

Tchécoslovaquie [tʃekɔslɔvaki] nf Czechoslovakia. ◆**tchèque** a & nmf Czech; **—** (langue) Czech.

te [t(ə)] (**t'** before vowel or mute h) pron 1 (complément direct) you; **je te vois** I see you. 2 (indirect) (to) you; **il te parle** he speaks to you; **elle te l'a dit** she told you. 3 (réfléchi) yourself; **tu te laves** you wash yourself.

technicien, -ienne [tɛknisjɛ̃, -jɛn] nmf technician. ◆**technique** a technical; **—** nf technique. ◆**techniquement** adv technically. ◆**technocrate** nm technocrat. ◆**technologie** nf technology. ◆**technologique** a technological.

teck [tɛk] nm (bois) teak.

teckel [tekɛl] nm (chien) dachshund.

tee-shirt [tiʃœrt] nm tee-shirt.

teindre* [tɛdr] vt to dye; **— se t.** vpr to dye

one's hair. ◆**teinture** nf dyeing; (produit) dye. ◆**teinturerie** nf (boutique) (dry) cleaner's. ◆**teinturier, -ière** nmf dry cleaner.

teint [tɛ̃] nm 1 (de visage) complexion. 2 **bon ou grand t.** (tissu) colourfast; **bon t.** (catholique etc) Fig staunch.

teinte [tɛ̃t] nf shade, tint; **une t. de** (dose) Fig a tinge of. ◆**teinter** vt to tint; (bois) to stain; **se t. de** (remarque, ciel) Fig to be tinged with.

tel, telle [tɛl] a such; **un t. homme/livre**/etc such a man/book/etc; **un t. intérêt**/etc such interest/etc; **de tels mots**/etc such words/etc; **t. que** such as, like; **t. que je l'ai laissé** just as I left it; **laissez-le t. quel** leave it just as it is; **en tant que t., comme t.** as such; **t. ou t.** such and such; **rien de t. que ...** (there's) nothing like ...; **rien de t.** nothing like it; **Monsieur Un t.** Mr So-and-so; **t. père t. fils** like father like son.

télé [tele] nf (téléviseur) Fam TV, telly; **à la t.** on TV, on the telly; **regarder la t.** to watch TV ou the telly.

télé- [tele] préf tele-.

télébenne [teleben] nf, **télécabine** [telekabin] nf (cabine, système) cable car.

télécommande [telekɔmɑ̃d] nf remote control. ◆**télécommander** vt to operate by remote control.

télécommunications [telekɔmynikɑsjɔ̃] nfpl telecommunications.

téléfilm [telefilm] nm TV film.

télégramme [telegram] nm telegram.

télégraphe [telegraf] nm telegraph. ◆**télégraphie** nf telegraphy. ◆**télégraphier** vt (message) to wire, cable (que that). ◆**télégraphique** a (fil, poteau) telegraph-; (style) Fig telegraphic. ◆**télégraphiste** nm (messager) telegraph boy.

téléguid/er [telegide] vt to radio-control. ◆**—age** nm radio-control.

télématique [telematik] nf telematics, computer communications.

télépathie [telepati] nf telepathy.

téléphérique [teleferik] nm (système) cable car, cableway.

téléphone [telefɔn] nm (tele)phone; **coup de t.** (phone) call; **passer un coup de t. à qn** to give s.o. a call ou a ring; **au t.** on the (tele)phone; **avoir le t.** to be on the (tele)phone; **par le t. arabe** Fig on the grapevine. ◆**téléphoner** vt (nouvelle etc) to (tele)phone (**à** to); **— vi** to (tele)phone; **t. à qn** to (tele)phone s.o., call s.o. (up). ◆**téléphonique** a (appel etc) (tele)phone-, telephone-. ◆**téléphoniste** nf operator, telephonist.

télescope [telɛskɔp] *nm* telescope. ◆**télescopique** *a* telescopic.

télescop/er [telɛskɔpe] *vt Aut Rail* to smash into; **se t.** to smash into each other. ◆**-age** *nm* smash.

téléscripteur [teleskriptœr] *nm* (*appareil*) teleprinter.

télésiège [telesjɛʒ] *nm* chair lift.

téléski [teleski] *nm* ski tow.

téléspectateur, -trice [telespɛktatœr, -tris] *nmf* (television) viewer.

téléviser [televize] *vt* to televise; **journal télévisé** television news. ◆**téléviseur** *nm* television (set). ◆**télévision** *nf* television; **à la t.** on (the) television; **regarder la t.** to watch (the) television; **de t.** (*programme etc*) television-.

télex [telɛks] *nm* (*service, message*) telex.

telle [tɛl] *voir* **tel**.

tellement [tɛlmã] *adv* (*si*) so; (*tant*) so much; **t. grand/etc que** so big/etc that; **crier/etc t. que** to shout/etc so much; **t. de** (*travail etc*) so much; (*soucis etc*) so many; **personne ne peut le supporter, t. il est bavard** nobody can stand him, he's so talkative; **tu aimes ça? - pas t.** do you like it? - not much *ou* a lot.

téméraire [temerɛr] *a* rash, reckless. ◆**témérité** *nf* rashness, recklessness.

témoign/er [temwaɲe] **1** *vi Jur* to testify (**contre** against); **t. de qch** (*personne, attitude etc*) to testify to sth; **–** *vt* **t. que** *Jur* to testify that. **2** *vt* (*gratitude etc*) to show (**à qn** (to) s.o.). ◆**-age** *nm* **1** testimony, evidence; (*récit*) account; **faux t.** (*délit*) Jur perjury. **2** (*d'affection etc*) Fig token, sign (**de** of); **en t. de** as a token *ou* sign of.

témoin [temwɛ̃] **1** *nm* witness; **t. oculaire** eyewitness; **être t. de** (*accident etc*) to witness; **–** *a* **appartement t.** show flat *ou* Am apartment. **2** *nm* Sp baton.

tempe [tãp] *nf* Anat temple.

tempérament [tãperamã] *nm* **1** (*caractère*) temperament; (*physique*) constitution. **2** **acheter à t.** to buy on hire purchase *ou* Am on the installment plan.

tempérance [tãperãs] *nf* temperance.

température [tãperatyr] *nf* temperature; **avoir** *ou* **faire de la t.** Méd to have a temperature.

tempér/er [tãpere] *vt* Litt to temper. ◆**-é** *a* (*climat, zone*) temperate.

tempête [tãpɛt] *nf* storm; **t. de neige** snowstorm, blizzard.

tempêter [tãpete] *vi* (*crier*) to storm, rage (**contre** against).

temple [tãpl] *nm* Rel temple; (*protestant*) church.

tempo [tɛmpo] *nm* tempo.

temporaire [tãpɔrɛr] *a* temporary. ◆**-ment** *adv* temporarily.

temporel, -elle [tãpɔrɛl] *a* temporal.

temporiser [tãpɔrize] *vi* to procrastinate, play for time.

temps¹ [tã] *nm* (*durée, période, moment*) time; *Gram* tense; (*étape*) stage; **t. d'arrêt** pause, break; **en t. de guerre** in time of war, in wartime; **avoir/trouver le t.** to have/find (the) time (**de faire** to do); **il est t.** it is time (**de faire** to do); **il était t.!** it was about time (too)!; **pendant un t.** for a while *ou* time; **ces derniers t.** lately; **de t. en t.** [dətãzãtã], **de t. à autre** [dətãzaotr] from time to time, now and again; **en t. utile** [ãtãzytil] in good *ou* due time; **en même t.** at the same time (**que** as); **à t.** (*arriver*) in time; **à plein t.** (*travailler etc*) full-time; **à t. partiel** (*travailler etc*) part-time; **dans le t.** (*autrefois*) once, at one time; **avec le t.** (*à la longue*) in time; **tout le t.** all the time; **du t. de** in the time of; **de mon t.** in my time; **à quatre t.** (*moteur*) four-stroke.

temps² [tã] *nm* (*atmosphérique*) weather; **il fait beau/mauvais t.** the weather's fine/bad; **quel t. fait-il?** what's the weather like?

tenable [tanabl] *a* bearable.

tenace [tanas] *a* stubborn, tenacious. ◆**ténacité** *nf* stubbornness, tenacity.

tenailler [tanaje] *vt* (*faim, remords*) to rack, torture (s.o.).

tenailles [tanaj] *nfpl* (*outil*) pincers.

tenancier, -ière [tanãsje, -jɛr] *nmf* (*d'hôtel etc*) manager, manageress.

tenant, -ante [tanã, -ãt] *nmf* (*de titre*) Sp holder. **2** *nm* (*partisan*) supporter (**de** of).

tenants [tanã] *nmpl* **les t. et les aboutissants** (*d'une question etc*) the ins and outs (**de** of).

tendance [tãdãs] *nf* (*penchant*) tendency; (*évolution*) trend (**à** towards); **avoir t. à faire** to have a tendency to do, tend to do.

tendancieux, -euse [tãdãsjø, -øz] *a* Péj tendentious.

tendeur [tãdœr] *nm* (*pour arrimer des bagages*) elastic strap.

tendon [tãdɔ̃] *nm* Anat tendon, sinew.

tend/re¹ [tãdr] **1** *vt* to stretch; (*main*) to hold out (**à qn** to s.o.); (*bras, jambe*) to stretch out; (*cou*) to strain, crane; (*muscle*) to tense, flex; (*arc*) to bend; (*piège*) to lay, set; (*filet*) to spread; (*tapisserie*) to hang; **t. qch à qn** to hold out sth to s.o.; **t. l'oreille** Fig to prick up one's ears; **– se t.** *vpr* (*rap-*

ports) to become strained. **2** *vi* **t.** à qch/à faire to tend towards sth/to do. ◆—**u** *a* (*corde*) tight, taut; (*personne, situation*) tense; (*rapports*) strained; (*main*) outstretched.

tendre² [tɑ̃dr] *a* **1** (*viande*) tender; (*peau*) delicate, tender; (*bois, couleur*) soft. **2** (*affectueux*) loving, tender. ◆—**ment** [-əmɑ̃] *adv* lovingly, tenderly. ◆**tendresse** *nf* (*affection*) affection, tenderness. ◆**tendreté** *nf* (*de viande*) tenderness.

ténèbres [tenɛbr] *nfpl* darkness, gloom. ◆**ténébreux, -euse** *a* dark, gloomy; (*mystérieux*) mysterious.

teneur [tənœr] *nf* (*de lettre etc*) content; **t. en alcool**/*etc* alcohol/*etc* content (of).

tenir* [tənir] *vt* (*à la main etc*) to hold; (*pari, promesse*) to keep; (*hôtel*) to run, keep; (*comptes etc*) to keep; (*propos*) to utter; (*rôle*) to play; **t. propre/chaud**/*etc* to keep clean/hot/*etc*; **je le tiens!** (*je l'ai attrapé*) I've got him!; **je le tiens de** (*fait etc*) I got it from; (*caractère héréditaire*) I inherited it from; **t. pour** to regard as; **t. sa droite** *Aut* to keep to the right; **t. la route** (*voiture*) to hold the road; — *vi* (*nœud etc*) to hold; (*coiffure, neige*) to last, hold; (*offre*) to stand; (*résister*) to hold out; **t. à** (*personne, jouet etc*) to be attached to, be fond of; (*la vie*) to value; (*provenir*) to stem from; **t. à faire** to be anxious to do; **t. dans qch** (*être contenu*) to fit into sth; **t. de qn** to take after s.o.; **tenez!** (*prenez*) here (you are)!; **tiens!** (*surprise*) hey!, well!; — *v imp* **il ne tient qu'à vous** it's up to you (**de faire** to do); — **se t.** *vpr* (*rester*) to keep, remain; (*avoir lieu*) to be held; **se t.** (*debout*) to stand (up); **se t. droit** to stand up or sit up straight; **se t. par la main** to hold hands; **se t. à** to hold on to; **se t. bien** to behave oneself; **tout se tient** *Fig* it all hangs together; **s'en t. à** (*se limiter à*) to stick to; **savoir à quoi s'en t.** to know what's what.

tennis [tenis] *nm* tennis; (*terrain*) tennis court; **t. de table** table tennis; — *nfpl* (*chaussures*) plimsolls, pumps, *Am* sneakers.

ténor [tenɔr] *nm* *Mus* tenor.

tension [tɑ̃sjɔ̃] *nf* tension; **t.** (**artérielle**) blood pressure; **t. d'esprit** concentration; **avoir de la t.** *Méd* to have high blood pressure.

tentacule [tɑ̃takyl] *nm* tentacle.

tente [tɑ̃t] *nf* tent.

tenter¹ [tɑ̃te] *vt* (*essayer*) to try; **t. de faire** to try *ou* attempt to do. ◆**tentative** *nf* attempt; **t. de suicide** suicide attempt.

tent/er² [tɑ̃te] *vt* (*allécher*) to tempt; **tenté de faire** tempted to do. ◆—**ant** *a* tempting. ◆**tentation** *nf* temptation.

tenture [tɑ̃tyr] *nf* (*wall*) hanging; (*de porte*) drape, curtain.

tenu [təny] *voir* **tenir**; — *a* **t. de faire** obliged to do; **bien/mal t.** (*maison etc*) well/badly kept.

ténu [teny] *a* (*fil etc*) fine; (*soupçon, différence*) tenuous; (*voix*) thin.

tenue [təny] *nf* **1** (*vêtements*) clothes, outfit; (*aspect*) appearance; **t. de combat** *Mil* combat dress; **t. de soirée** (*smoking*) evening dress. **2** (*conduite*) (good) behaviour; (*maintien*) posture; **manquer de t.** to lack (good) manners. **3** (*de maison, hôtel*) running; (*de comptes*) *Com* keeping. **4 t. de route** *Aut* road-holding.

ter [tɛr] *a* **1** (*numéro*) 4B.

térébenthine [terebɑ̃tin] *nf* turpentine.

tergal® [tergal] *nm* Terylene®, *Am* Dacron®.

tergiverser [tɛrʒiverse] *vi* to procrastinate.

terme [tɛrm] *nm* **1** (*mot*) term. **2** (*loyer*) rent; (*jour*) rent day; (*période*) rental period. **3** (*date limite*) time (limit), date; (*fin*) end; **mettre un t. à** to put an end to; **à court/long t.** (*projet etc*) short-/long-term; **être né avant/à t.** to be born prematurely/at (full) term. **4 moyen t.** (*solution*) middle course. **5 en bons/mauvais termes** on good/bad terms (**avec qn** with s.o.).

terminer [tɛrmine] *vt* (*achever*) to finish, complete; (*lettre, phrase, débat, soirée*) to end; — **se t.** *vpr* to end (**par** with, **en** in). ◆**terminaison** *nf* *Gram* ending. ◆**terminal, -aux** **1** *a* final; (*phase*) *Méd* terminal; — *a* &/*cl* (*classe*) **terminale** *Scol* = sixth form, *Am* = twelfth grade. **2** *nm* (*d'ordinateur, pétrolier*) terminal.

terminologie [tɛrminɔlɔʒi] *nf* terminology.

terminus [tɛrminys] *nm* terminus.

termite [tɛrmit] *nm* (*insecte*) termite.

terne [tɛrn] *a* (*couleur, journée etc*) dull, drab; (*personne*) dull. ◆**ternir** *vt* (*métal, réputation*) to tarnish; (*miroir, meuble*) to dull; — **se t.** *vpr* (*métal*) to tarnish.

terrain [tɛrɛ̃] *nm* (*sol*) **a** *Fig* ground; (*étendue*) land; *Mil Géol* terrain; (*à bâtir*) plot, site; **un t.** a piece of land; **t. d'aviation** airfield; **t. de camping** campsite; **t. de football/rugby** football/rugby pitch; **t. de golf** golf course; **t. de jeu** playground; **t. de sport** sports ground, playing field; **t. vague** waste ground, *Am* vacant lot; **céder/gagner/perdre du t.** *Mil* & *Fig* to give/

lose ground; **tout t., tous terrains** (*véhicule*) all-purpose.

terrasse [teras] *nf* **1** terrace; (*toit*) terrace (roof). **2** (*de café*) pavement *ou Am* sidewalk area; **à la t.** outside.

terrassement [terasmã] *nm* (*travail*) excavation.

terrasser [terase] *vt* (*adversaire*) to floor, knock down; (*accabler*) *Fig* to overcome.

terrassier [terasje] *nm* labourer, navvy.

terre [tɛr] *nf* (*matière*) earth; (*sol*) ground; (*opposé à mer, étendue*) land; *pl* (*domaine*) land, estate; (*le monde*) the earth; **la t.** (*le monde*) the earth; **la T.** (*planète*) Earth; **à** *ou* **par t.** (*poser, tomber*) to the ground; **par t.** (*assis, couché*) on the ground; **aller à t.** *Nau* to go ashore; **sous t.** underground; **t. cuite** (baked) clay, earthenware; **en t. cuite** (*poterie*) clay-. ◆**t.-à-terre** *a inv* down-to-earth. ◆**t.-plein** *nm* (*earth*) platform; (*au milieu de la route*) central reservation, *Am* median strip. ◆**terrestre** *a* (*vie, joies*) earthly; (*animaux, transport*) land-; **la surface t.** the earth's surface; **globe t.** (terrestrial) globe. ◆**terreux, -euse** *a* (*goût*) earthy; (*sale*) grubby; (*couleur*) dull; (*teint*) ashen. ◆**terrien, -ienne** *a* land-owning; – *nmf* (*habitant de la terre*) earth dweller, earthling; **propriétaire t.** landowner; – *nmf* (*habitant de la terre*) earth dweller, earthling.

terreau [tero] *nm* compost.

terrer (se) [sətere] *vpr* (*fugitif, animal*) to hide, go to ground *ou* earth.

terreur [tɛrœr] *nf* terror; **t. de** fear of. ◆**terrible** *a* terrible; (*formidable*) *Fam* terrific. ◆**terriblement** *adv* (*extrêmement*) terribly. ◆**terrifier** *vt* to terrify. ◆**-ant** *a* terrifying; (*extraordinaire*) incredible.

terrier [tɛrje] *nm* **1** (*de lapin etc*) burrow. **2** (*chien*) terrier.

terrine [tɛrin] *nf* (*récipient*) *Culin* terrine; (*pâté*) pâté.

territoire [tɛritwar] *nm* territory. ◆**territorial, -aux** *a* territorial.

terroir [tɛrwar] *nm* (*sol*) soil; (*région*) region; **du t.** (*accent etc*) rural.

terroriser [tɛrɔrize] *vt* to terrorize. ◆**terrorisme** *nm* terrorism. ◆**terroriste** *a & nmf* terrorist.

tertiaire [tɛrsjɛr] *a* tertiary.

tertre [tɛrtr] *nm* hillock, mound.

tes [te] *voir* **ton**[1].

tesson [tesõ] *nm* **t. de bouteille** piece of broken bottle.

test [tɛst] *nm* test. ◆**tester** *vt* (*élève, produit*) to test.

testament [tɛstamã] *nm* **1** *Jur* will; (*œuvre*) *Fig* testament. **2** **Ancien/Nouveau T.** *Rel* Old/New Testament.

testicule [tɛstikyl] *nm Anat* testicle.

tétanos [tetanos] *nm Méd* tetanus.

têtard [tɛtar] *nm* tadpole.

tête [tɛt] *nf* head; (*figure*) face; (*cheveux*) (head of) hair; (*cerveau*) brain; (*cime*) top; (*de clou, cortège, lit*) head; (*de page, liste*) top, head; (*coup*) *Fb* header; **t. nucléaire** nuclear warhead; **tenir t. à** (*s'opposer à*) to stand up to; **en t.** *Sp* in the lead; **t. nue** bare-headed; **tu n'as pas de t.!** you're a scatterbrain!; **faire la t.** (*bouder*) to sulk; **faire une t.** *Fb* to head the ball; **avoir/faire une drôle de t.** to have/give a funny look; **perdre la t.** *Fig* to lose one's head; **tomber la t. la première** to fall headlong *ou* head first; **calculer qch de t.** to work sth out in one's head; **se mettre dans la t. de faire** to get it into one's head to do; **à t. reposée** at one's leisure; **à la t. de** (*entreprise, parti*) at the head of; (*classe*) *Scol* at the top of; **de la t. aux pieds** from head *ou* top to toe; **en t.** *Sp* in the lead. ◆**t.-à-queue** *nm inv* **faire un t.-à-queue** *Aut* to spin right round. ◆**t.-à-tête** *adv* (**en**) **t.-à-tête** (*seul*) in private, alone together; – *nm inv* tête-à-tête. ◆**t.-bêche** *adv* head to tail.

têt/er [tete] *vt* (*lait, biberon etc*) to suck; **t. sa mère** (*bébé*) to suck, feed; – *vi* **donner à t. à** to feed, suckle. ◆**-ée** *nf* (*de bébé*) feed. ◆**tétine** *nf* **1** (*de biberon*) teat, *Am* nipple; (*sucette*) dummy, *Am* pacifier. **2** (*de vache*) udder. ◆**téton** *nm Fam* breast.

têtu [tety] *a* stubborn, obstinate.

texte [tɛkst] *nm* text; *Th* lines; text; (*de devoir*) *Scol* subject; (*morceau choisi*) *Littér* passage. ◆**textuel, -elle** *a* (*traduction*) literal.

textile [tɛkstil] *a & nm* textile.

texture [tɛkstyr] *nf* texture.

TGV [teʒeve] *abrév* = **train à grande vitesse**.

Thaïlande [tailãd] *nf* Thailand. ◆**thaïlandais, -aise** *a & nmf* Thai.

thé [te] *nm* (*boisson, réunion*) tea. ◆**théière** *nf* teapot.

théâtre [teatr] *nm* (*art, lieu*) theatre; (*œuvres*) drama; (*d'un crime*) *Fig* scene; (*des opérations*) *Mil* theatre; **faire du t.** to act. ◆**théâtral, -aux** *a* theatrical.

thème [tɛm] *nm* theme; (*traduction*) *Scol* translation, prose.

théologie [teɔlɔʒi] *nf* theology. ◆**théologien** *nm* theologian. ◆**théologique** *a* theological.

théorème [teɔrɛm] *nm* theorem.

théorie [teɔri] *nf* theory; **en t.** in theory.

◆**théoricien, -ienne** *nmf* theorist, theoretician. ◆**théorique** *a* theoretical. ◆**théoriquement** *adv* theoretically.

thérapeutique [terapøtik] *a* therapeutic; – *nf* (*traitement*) therapy. ◆**thérapie** *nf Psy* therapy.

thermal, -aux [tɛrmal, -o] *a* **station thermale** spa; **eaux thermales** hot springs.

thermique [tɛrmik] *a* (*énergie, unité*) thermal.

thermomètre [tɛrmɔmɛtr] *nm* thermometer.

thermonucléaire [tɛrmɔnykleɛr] *a* thermonuclear.

thermos® [tɛrmɔs] *nm ou f* Thermos (flask)®, vacuum flask.

thermostat [tɛrmɔsta] *nm* thermostat.

thèse [tɛz] *nf* (*proposition, ouvrage*) thesis.

thon [tɔ̃] *nm* tuna (fish).

thorax [tɔraks] *nm Anat* thorax.

thym [tɛ̃] *nm Bot Culin* thyme.

thyroïde [tirɔid] *a & nf Anat* thyroid.

tibia [tibja] *nm* shin bone, tibia.

tic [tik] *nm* (*contraction*) tic, twitch; (*manie*) *Fig* mannerism.

ticket [tikɛ] *nm* ticket; **t. de quai** *Rail* platform ticket.

tic(-)tac [tiktak] *int & nm inv* tick-tock.

tiède [tjɛd] *a* (*luke*)warm, tepid; (*climat, vent*) mild; (*accueil, partisan*) half-hearted. ◆**tiédeur** *nf* (*luke*)warmness, tepidness; mildness; half-heartedness. ◆**tiédir** *vt* to cool (down); (*chauffer*) to warm (up); – *vi* to cool (down); to warm up.

tien, tienne [tjɛ̃, tjɛn] *pron poss* **le t., la tienne, les tien(ne)s** yours; **les deux tiens** your two; – *nmpl* **les tiens** (*amis etc*) your (own) people.

tiens, tient [tjɛ̃] *voir* **tenir**.

tiercé [tjɛrse] *nm* (*pari*) place betting (on horses); **gagner au t.** to win on the races.

tiers, tierce [tjɛr, tjɛrs] *a* a third; – *nm* (*fraction*) third; (*personne*) third party; **assurance au t.** third-party insurance. ◆**T.-Monde** *nm* Third World.

tige [tiʒ] *nf* (*de plante*) stem, stalk; (*de botte*) leg; (*barre*) rod.

tignasse [tiɲas] *nf* mop of hair.

tigre [tigr] *nm* tiger. ◆**tigresse** *nf* tigress.

tigré [tigre] *a* (*tacheté*) spotted; (*rayé*) striped.

tilleul [tijœl] *nm* lime (tree), linden (tree); (*infusion*) lime (blossom) tea.

timbale [tɛ̃bal] *nf* **1** (*gobelet*) (metal) tumbler. **2** *Mus* kettledrum.

timbre [tɛ̃br] *nm* **1** (*marque, tampon, vignette*) stamp; (*cachet de la poste*) post-

mark. **2** (*sonnette*) bell. **3** (*d'instrument, de voix*) tone (quality). ◆**t.-poste** *nm* (*pl* **timbres-poste**) (postage) stamp. ◆**timbr/er** *vt* (*affranchir*) to stamp (*letter*); (*marquer*) to stamp (*document*). ◆**-é** *a* **1** (*voix*) sonorous. **2** (*fou*) *Fam* crazy.

timide [timid] *a* (*gêné*) shy, timid; (*timoré*) timid. ◆**-ment** *adv* shyly; timidly. ◆**timidité** *nf* shyness; timidity.

timonier [timɔnje] *nm Nau* helmsman.

timoré [timɔre] *a* timorous, fearful.

tintamarre [tɛ̃tamar] *nm* din, racket.

tint/er [tɛ̃te] *vi* (*cloche*) to ring, toll; (*clés, monnaie*) to jingle; (*verres*) to chink. ◆**-ement(s)** *nm(pl)* ringing; jingling; chinking.

tique [tik] *nf* (*insecte*) tick.

tiquer [tike] *vi* (*personne*) to wince.

tir [tir] *nm* (*sport*) shooting; (*action*) firing, shooting; (*feu, rafale*) fire; *Fb* shot; **t. (forain), (stand de) t.** shooting *ou* rifle range; **t. à l'arc** archery; **ligne de t.** line of fire.

tirade [tirad] *nf Th & Fig* monologue.

tirail/er [tirɑje] **1** *vt* to pull (away) at; (*harceler*) *Fig* to pester, plague; **tiraillé entre** (*possibilités etc*) torn between. **2** *vi* (*au fusil*) to shoot wildly. ◆**-ement** *nm* **1** (*conflit*) conflict (**entre** between). **2** (*crampe*) *Méd* cramp.

tire [tir] *nf* **vol à la t.** *Fam* pickpocketing.

tire-au-flanc [tiroflɑ̃] *nm inv* (*paresseux*) shirker. ◆**t.-bouchon** *nm* corkscrew. ◆**t.-d'aile (à)** *adv* swiftly.

tirelire [tirlir] *nf* moneybox, *Am* coin bank.

tir/er [tire] *vt* to pull; (*langue*) to stick out; (*trait, conclusion, rideaux*) to draw; (*chapeau*) to raise; (*balle, canon*) to fire, shoot; (*gibier*) to shoot; *Typ Phot* to print; **t. de** (*sortir*) to take *ou* pull *ou* draw out of; (*obtenir*) to get from; (*nom, origine*) to derive from; (*produit*) to extract from; **t. qn de** (*danger, lit*) to get s.o. out of; – *vi* to pull (**sur** on, at); (*faire feu*) to fire, shoot (**sur** at); *Fb* to shoot; (*cheminée*) to draw; **t. sur** (*couleur*) to verge on; **t. au sort** to draw lots; **t. à sa fin** to draw to a close; – **se t.** *vpr* (*partir*) *Fam* to beat it; **se t. de** (*problème, travail*) to cope with; (*danger, situation*) to get out of; **se t. d'affaire** to get out of trouble; **s'en t.** *Fam* (*en réchapper*) to come *ou* pull through; (*réussir*) to get along. ◆**-é** *a* (*traits, visage*) drawn; **t. par les cheveux** *Fig* far-fetched. ◆**-age** *nm* **1** (*action*) *Typ Phot* printing; (*édition*) edition; (*quantité*) (print) run; (*de journal*) circulation. **2** (*de loterie*) draw; **t. au sort**

drawing of lots. **3** (de cheminée) draught.
◆**—eur** nm gunman; **t. d'élite** marksman;
un bon/mauvais t. a good/bad shot.
◆**—euse** nf **t. de cartes** fortune-teller.

tiret [tirɛ] nm (trait) dash.

tiroir [tirwar] nm (de commode etc) drawer.
◆**t.-caisse** nm (pl **tiroirs-caisses**) (cash)
till.

tisane [tizan] nf herb(al) tea.

tison [tizɔ̃] nm (fire)brand, ember. ◆**tisonner** vt (feu) to poke. ◆**tisonnier** nm
poker.

tiss/er [tise] vt to weave. ◆**—age** nm (action) weaving. ◆**tisserand, -ande** nmf
weaver.

tissu [tisy] nm fabric, material, cloth; Biol
tissue; **un t. de** (mensonges etc) a web of; **le
t. social** the fabric of society, the social
fabric; **du t.-éponge** (terry) towelling.

titre [titr] nm (nom, qualité) title; Com bond;
(diplôme) qualification; pl (droits) claims (à
to); (gros) Journ headline; **t. de propriété**
title deed; **t. de transport** ticket; **à quel t.?**
(pour quelle raison) on what grounds?; **à ce
t.** (en cette qualité) as such; (pour cette
raison) therefore; **à aucun t.** on no account;
au même t. in the same way (**que** as); **à t.
d'exemple/d'ami** as an example/friend; **à t.
exceptionnel** exceptionally; **à t. privé** in
a private capacity; **à juste t.** rightly.
◆**titr/er** vt (film) to title; Journ to run as a
headline. ◆**—é** (personne) titled. ◆**titulaire** a (professeur) staff-, full; **être t. de**
(permis etc) to be the holder of; (poste) to
hold; — nmf (de permis, poste) holder (**de**
of). ◆**titulariser** vt (fonctionnaire) to give
tenure to.

tituber [titybe] vi to reel, stagger.

toast [tost] nm **1** (pain grillé) piece ou slice
of toast. **2** (allocution) toast; **porter un t. à**
to drink (a toast) to.

toboggan [tɔbɔgɑ̃] nm **1** (pente) slide;
(traîneau) toboggan. **2** Aut flyover, Am
overpass.

toc [tɔk] **1** int **t. t.!** knock knock! **2** nm **du t.**
(camelote) rubbish, trash; **en t.** (bijou) imi-
tation-.

tocsin [tɔksɛ̃] nm alarm (bell).

tohu-bohu [tɔyboy] nm (bruit) hubbub,
commotion; (confusion) hurly-burly.

toi [twa] pron **1** (complément) you; **c'est
toi** it's you; **avec t.** with you. **2** (sujet) you; **t., tu
peux** you may. **3** (réfléchi) **assieds-t.** sit
(yourself) down; **dépêche-t.** hurry up.
◆**t.-même** pron yourself.

toile [twal] nf **1** cloth; (à voile) canvas; (à
draps) linen; **une t.** a piece of cloth ou can-

vas ou linen; **t. de jute** hessian; **drap de t.**
linen sheet; **t. de fond** Th & Fig backcloth.
2 (tableau) canvas, painting. **3 t. d'araignée**
cobweb, (spider's) web.

toilette [twalɛt] nf (action) wash(ing); (vêtements) outfit, clothes; **articles de t.** toiletries; **cabinet de t.** washroom; **eau/savon/
trousse de t.** toilet water/soap/bag; **table
de t.** dressing table; **faire sa t.** to wash (and
dress); **les toilettes** (W-C) the toilet(s);
aller aux toilettes to go to the toilet.

toiser [twaze] vt to eye scornfully.

toison [twazɔ̃] nf (de mouton) fleece.

toit [twa] nm roof; **t. ouvrant** Aut sunroof.
◆**toiture** nf roof(ing).

tôle [tol] nf **la t.** sheet metal; **une t.** a steel ou
metal sheet; **t. ondulée** corrugated iron.

tolér/er [tɔlere] vt (permettre) to tolerate,
allow; (supporter) to tolerate, bear; (à la
douane) to allow. ◆**—ant** a tolerant (à
l'égard de of). ◆**—able** a tolerable.
◆**tolérance** nf tolerance; (à la douane) allowance.

tollé [tɔle] nm outcry.

tomate [tɔmat] nf tomato; **sauce t.** tomato
sauce.

tombe [tɔ̃b] nf grave; (avec monument)
tomb. ◆**tombale** af **pierre t.** gravestone,
tombstone. ◆**tombeau, -x** nm tomb.

tomb/er [tɔ̃be] vi (aux être) to fall; (température) to drop, fall; (vent) to drop (off);
(cheveux, robe) to hang down; **t. malade** to
fall ill; **t.** (par terre) to fall down; **faire t.**
(personne) to knock over; (gouvernement,
prix) to bring down; **laisser t.** (objet) to
drop; (personne, projet etc) Fig to drop,
give up; **tu m'as laissé t. hier** Fig you let me
down yesterday; **se laisser t. dans un fauteuil** to drop into an armchair; **tu tombes
bien/mal** Fig you've come at the right/
wrong time; **t. de fatigue** ou **de sommeil** to
be ready to drop; **t. un lundi** to fall on a
Monday; **t. sur** (trouver) to come across.
◆**—ée** nf **t. de la nuit** nightfall.

tombereau, -x [tɔ̃bro] nm (charrette) tip
cart.

tombola [tɔ̃bɔla] nf raffle.

tome [tɔm] nm (livre) volume.

ton¹, ta, pl **tes** [tɔ̃, ta, te] (**ta** becomes **ton**
[tɔ̃n] before a vowel or mute h) a poss your; **ton
père** your father; **ta mère** your mother; **ton
ami(e)** your friend.

ton² [tɔ̃] nm tone; (de couleur) shade, tone;
(gamme) Mus key; (hauteur de son) & Ling
pitch; **de bon t.** (goût) in good taste; **donner
le t.** Fig to set the tone. ◆**tonalité** nf (de

radio etc) tone; *Tél* dialling tone, *Am* dial tone.

tond/re [tɔ̃dr] *vt* 1 (*mouton*) to shear; (*cheveux*) to clip, crop; (*gazon*) to mow. 2 t. qn (*escroquer*) *Fam* to fleece s.o. ◆—**euse** *nf* shears; (*à cheveux*) clippers; t. (à gazon) (lawn)mower.

tonifi/er [tɔnifje] *vt* (*muscles, peau*) to tone up; (*esprit, personne*) to invigorate. ◆—**ant** *a* (*activité, climat* etc) invigorating.

tonique [tɔnik] 1 *a* (*accent*) *Ling* tonic. 2 *a* (*froid, effet, vin*) tonic, invigorating; — *nm Méd* tonic.

tonitruant [tɔnitryɑ̃] *a* (*voix*) *Fam* booming.

tonnage [tɔnaʒ] *nm Nau* tonnage.

tonne [tɔn] *nf* (*poids*) metric ton, tonne; **des tonnes de** (*beaucoup*) *Fam* tons of.

tonneau, -x [tɔno] *nm* 1 (*récipient*) barrel, cask. 2 (*manœuvre*) *Av* roll; **faire un t.** *Aut* to roll over. 3 (*poids*) *Nau* ton. ◆**tonnelet** *nm* keg.

tonnelle [tɔnɛl] *nf* arbour, bower.

tonner [tɔne] *vi* (*canons*) to thunder; (*crier*) *Fig* to thunder, rage (**contre** against); — *v imp* **il tonne** it's thundering. ◆**tonnerre** *nm* thunder; **coup de t.** thunderclap; *Fig* bombshell, thunderbolt; **du t.** (*excellent*) *Fam* terrific.

tonte [tɔ̃t] *nf* (*de moutons*) shearing; (*de gazon*) mowing.

tonton [tɔ̃tɔ̃] *nm Fam* uncle.

tonus [tɔnys] *nm* (*énergie*) energy, vitality.

top [tɔp] *nm* (*signal sonore*) *Rad* stroke.

topaze [tɔpaz] *nf* (*pierre*) topaz.

topinambour [tɔpinɑ̃bur] *nm* Jerusalem artichoke.

topo [tɔpo] *nm* (*exposé*) *Fam* talk, speech.

topographie [tɔpɔgrafi] *nf* topography.

toque [tɔk] *nf* (*de fourrure*) fur hat; (*de juge, jockey*) cap; (*de cuisinier*) hat.

toqu/er (se) [sɔtɔke] *vpr* **se t. de qn** *Fam* to become infatuated with s.o. ◆—**é** *a* (*fou*) *Fam* crazy. ◆**toquade** *nf Fam* (*pour qch*) craze (**pour** for); (*pour qn*) infatuation (**pour** with).

torche [tɔrʃ] *nf* (*flambeau*) torch; **t. électrique** torch, *Am* flashlight.

torcher [tɔrʃe] *vt* 1 (*travail*) to skimp. 2 (*essuyer*) *Fam* to wipe.

torchon [tɔrʃɔ̃] *nm* (*à vaisselle*) tea towel, *Am* dish towel; (*de ménage*) duster, cloth.

tord/re [tɔrdr] *vt* to twist; (*linge, cou*) to wring; (*barre*) to bend; **se t. la cheville/le pied/le dos** to twist *ou* sprain one's ankle/foot/back; — **se t.** *vpr* to twist; (*barre*) to bend; **se t. de douleur** to writhe with pain; **se t. (de rire)** to split one's sides

(laughing). ◆—**ant** *a* (*drôle*) *Fam* hilarious. ◆—**u** *a* twisted; (*esprit*) warped.

tornade [tɔrnad] *nf* tornado.

torpeur [tɔrpœr] *nf* lethargy, torpor.

torpille [tɔrpij] *nf* torpedo. ◆**torpill/er** *vt Mil & Fig* to torpedo. ◆—**eur** *nm* torpedo boat.

torréfier [tɔrefje] *vt* (*café*) to roast.

torrent [tɔrɑ̃] *nm* (*ruisseau*) torrent; **un t. de** (*injures, larmes*) a flood of; **il pleut à torrents** it's pouring (down). ◆**torrentiel, -ielle** *a* (*pluie*) torrential.

torride [tɔrid] *a* (*chaleur* etc) torrid, scorching.

torsade [tɔrsad] *nf* (*de cheveux*) twist, coil. ◆**torsader** *vt* to twist (together).

torse [tɔrs] *nm Anat* chest; (*statue*) torso.

torsion [tɔrsjɔ̃] *nf* twisting; *Phys Tech* torsion.

tort [tɔr] *nm* (*dommage*) wrong; (*défaut*) fault; **avoir t.** to be wrong (**de faire** to do, in doing); **tu as t. de fumer!** you shouldn't smoke!; **être dans son t.** *ou* **en t.** to be in the wrong; **donner t. à qn** (*accuser*) to blame s.o.; (*faits* etc) to prove s.o. wrong; **faire du t. à qn** to harm *ou* wrong s.o.; **à t.** wrongly; **à t. et à travers** wildly, indiscriminately; **à t. ou à raison** rightly or wrongly.

torticolis [tɔrtikɔli] *nm* stiff neck.

tortill/er [tɔrtije] *vt* to twist, twirl; (*moustache*) to twist; (*tripoter*) to twiddle with; — **se t.** *vpr* (*ver, personne*) to wriggle; (*en dansant, des hanches*) to wiggle. ◆—**ement** *nm* wriggling, wiggling.

tortionnaire [tɔrsjɔnɛr] *nm* torturer.

tortue [tɔrty] *nf* tortoise; (*marine*) turtle; **quelle t.!** *Fig* what a slowcoach *ou Am* slowpoke!

tortueux, -euse [tɔrtɥø, -øz] *a* tortuous.

torture [tɔrtyr] *nf* torture. ◆**torturer** *vt* to torture; **se t. les méninges** to rack one's brains.

tôt [to] *adv* early; **au plus t.** at the earliest; **le plus t. possible** as soon as possible; **t. ou tard** sooner or later; **je n'étais pas plus t. sorti que . . .** no sooner had I gone out than . . . .

total, -aux [tɔtal, -o] *a* & *nm* total; **au t.** all in all, in total; (*somme toute*) all in all. ◆**totalement** *adv* totally, completely. ◆**totaliser** *vt* to total. ◆**totalité** *nf* entirety; **la t.** de all of; **en t.** entirely. ◆**totalitaire** *a Pol* totalitarian.

toubib [tubib] *nm* (*médecin*) *Fam* doctor.

touche [tuʃ] *nf* (*de peintre*) touch; *Pêche* bite; (*clavier*) key; **une t. de** (*un peu de*) a touch *ou* hint of; **(ligne de)** t. Fb Rugby touchline.

touche-à-tout [tuʃatu] **1** *a & nmf inv* (*qui touche*) meddlesome (person). **2** *nmf inv* (*qui se disperse*) dabbler.

touch/er [tuʃe] *vt* to touch; (*paie*) to draw; (*chèque*) to cash; (*cible*) to hit; (*émouvoir*) to touch, move; (*concerner*) to affect; **t. qn** (*contacter*) to get in touch with s.o., reach s.o.; – *vi* **t. à** to touch; (*sujet*) to broach; (*but, fin*) to approach; – **se t.** *vpr* (*lignes etc*) to touch; – *nm* (*sens*) touch; **au t.** to the touch. ◆—**ant** *a* (*émouvant*) touching, moving.

touffe [tuf] *nf* (*de cheveux, d'herbe*) tuft; (*de plantes*) cluster. ◆**touffu** *a* (*barbe, haie*) thick, bushy; (*livre*) Fig heavy.

toujours [tuʒur] *adv* always; (*encore*) still; **pour t.** for ever; **essaie t.!** (*quand même*) try anyhow!; **t. est-il que . . .** the fact remains that . . . .

toupet [tupɛ] *nm* (*audace*) Fam cheek, nerve.

toupie [tupi] *nf* (spinning) top.

tour [tur] *nf* **1** Archit tower; (*immeuble*) tower block, high-rise. **2** Échecs rook, castle.

tour [tur] *nm* **1** (*mouvement, ordre, tournure*) turn; (*artifice*) trick; (*excursion*) trip, outing; (*à pied*) stroll, walk; (*en voiture*) drive; **t. de phrase** turn of phrase; **t. de piste** Sp lap; **t. de cartes** card trick; **t. d'horizon** survey; *ou* size; **de dix mètres de t.** ten metres round; **faire le t. de** to go round; (*question, situation*) to review; **faire un t.** (*à pied*) to go for a stroll *ou* walk; (*en voiture*) to go for a drive; (*voyage*) to go on a trip; **faire *ou* jouer un t. à qn** to play a trick on s.o.; **c'est mon t.** it's my turn; **à qui le tour?** whose turn (is it)?; **à son t.** in (one's) turn; **à t. de rôle** in turn; **à t. à t.** in turn, by turns. **2** Tech lathe; (*de potier*) wheel.

tourbe [turb] *nf* peat. ◆**tourbière** *nf* peat bog.

tourbillon [turbijɔ̃] *nm* (*de vent*) whirlwind; (*d'eau*) whirlpool; (*de neige, sable*) eddy; (*tournoiement*) Fig whirl, swirl. ◆**tourbillonner** *vi* to whirl, swirl; to eddy.

tourelle [turɛl] *nf* turret.

tourisme [turism] *nm* tourism; **faire du t.** to do some sightseeing *ou* touring; **agence/office de t.** tourist agency/office. ◆**touriste** *nmf* tourist. ◆**touristique** *a* (*guide, menu etc*) tourist-; **route t., circuit t.** scenic route.

tourment [turmã] *nm* torment. ◆**tour-**

ment/er *vt* to torment; – **se t.** *vpr* to worry (oneself). ◆—**é** *a* (*mer, vie*) turbulent, stormy; (*sol*) rough, uneven; (*expression, visage*) anguished.

tourmente [turmãt] *nf* (*troubles*) turmoil.

tourne-disque [turnǝdisk] *nm* record player.

tournée [turne] *nf* **1** (*de livreur etc*) round; (*théâtrale*) tour; **faire la t. de** (*magasins etc*) to make the rounds of, go round. **2** (*de boissons*) round.

tourn/er [turne] *vt* to turn; (*film*) to shoot, make; (*difficulté*) to get round; **t. en ridicule** to ridicule; – *vi* to turn; (*tête, toupie*) to spin; (*Terre*) to revolve, turn; (*moteur*) to run, go; (*usine*) to run; (*lait, vinaigre*) to go off; Cin to shoot; **t. autour de** (*objet*) to go round; (*maison, personne*) to hang around; (*question*) to centre on; **t. bien/mal** (*évoluer*) to turn out well/badly; **t. au froid** (*temps*) to turn cold; **t. à l'aigre** (*ton, conversation etc*) to turn nasty *ou* sour; **t. de l'œil** Fam to faint; – **se t.** *vpr* to turn (*vers* to, towards). ◆—**ant 1** *a* **pont t.** swing bridge. **2** *nm* (*virage*) bend, turning; (*moment*) Fig turning point. ◆—**age** *nm* Cin shooting, filming. ◆—**eur** *nm* (*ouvrier*) turner. ◆**tournoyer** *vi* to spin (round), whirl.

◆**tournure** *nf* (*expression*) turn of phrase; **t. d'esprit** way of thinking; **t. des événements** turn of events; **prendre t.** (*forme*) to take shape.

tournesol [turnǝsɔl] *nm* sunflower.

tournevis [turnǝvis] *nm* screwdriver.

tourniquet [turnikɛ] *nm* **1** (*barrière*) turnstile. **2** (*pour arroser*) sprinkler.

tournoi [turnwa] *nm* Sp & Hist tournament.

tourte [turt] *nf* pie.

tourterelle [turtǝrɛl] *nf* turtledove.

Toussaint [tusɛ̃] *nf* All Saints' Day.

tousser [tuse] *vi* to cough.

tout, toute, *pl* **tous, toutes** [tu, tut, tu, tut] **1** *a* all; **tous les livres/etc** all the books/etc; **t. l'argent/le village/etc** the whole (of the) money/village/etc, all the money/village/etc; **toute la nuit** all night, the whole (of the) night; **tous (les) deux** both; **tous (les) trois** all three; **t. un problème** quite a problem. **2** *a* (*chaque*) every, each; (*n'importe quel*) any; **tous les ans/jours/etc** every *ou* each year/day/etc; **tous les deux/trois mois/etc** every second/third month/etc; **tous les cinq mètres** every five metres; **t. homme** [tutɔm] every *ou* any man; **à toute heure** at any time. **3** *pron pl* (**tous** = [tus]) all; **ils sont tous là, tous sont là** they're all there. **4** *pron m sing* **tout** everything;

dépenser t. to spend everything, spend it all; **t. ce que** everything that, all that; **en** t. *(au total)* in all. **5** *adv (tout à fait)* quite; *(très)* very; **t. petit** very small; **t. neuf** brand new; **t. simplement** quite simply; **t. seul** all alone; **t. droit** straight ahead; **t. autour** all around, right round; **t. au début** right at the beginning; **t. premier** the very first; **t. au moins/plus** at the very least/most; **t. en chantant/***etc* while singing/*etc*; **t. rusé qu'il est** however sly he may be; **t. à coup** suddenly, all of a sudden; **t. à fait** completely, quite; **t. de même** all the same; *(indignation)* really!; **t. de suite** at once. **6** *nm* **le** t., **le** t. **est** *(l'important)* the main thing is (**que**, **de faire** to do); **pas du t.** not at all; **rien du t.** nothing at all; **du t. au t.** *(changer)* entirely, completely. ◆**t.-puissant, toute-puissante** *a* all-powerful.

tout-à-l'égout [tutalegu] *nm inv* mains drainage.

toutefois [tutfwa] *adv* nevertheless, however.

toutou [tutu] *nm (chien) Fam* doggie.

toux [tu] *nf* cough.

toxicomane [toksikɔman] *nmf* drug addict. ◆**toxicomanie** *nf* drug addiction. ◆**toxine** *nf* toxin. ◆**toxique** *a* toxic.

trac [trak] *nm* **le** t. *(peur)* the jitters; *(de candidat)* exam nerves; *Th* stage fright.

tracas [traka] *nm* worry. ◆**tracasser** *vt*, **— se** t. *vpr* to worry. ◆**tracasseries** *nfpl* annoyances. ◆**tracassier, -ière** *a* irksome.

trace [tras] *nf (quantité, tache, vestige)* trace; *(marque)* mark; *(de fugitif etc)* trail; *pl (de bête, de pneus)* tracks; **traces de pas** footprints; **suivre les traces de qn** *Fig* to follow in s.o.'s footsteps.

trac/er [trase] *vt* *(dessiner)* to draw; *(écrire)* to trace; **t. une route** to mark out a route; *(frayer)* to open up a route. ◆**—é** *nm* *(plan)* layout; *(ligne)* line.

trachée [traʃe] *nf Anat* windpipe.

tract [trakt] *nm* leaflet.

tractations [traktasjɔ̃] *nfpl Péj* dealings.

tracter [trakte] *vt (caravane etc)* to tow. ◆**tracteur** *nm (véhicule)* tractor.

traction [traksjɔ̃] *nf Tech* traction; *Sp* pull-up; **t. arrière/avant** *Aut* rear-/front-wheel drive.

tradition [tradisjɔ̃] *nf* tradition. ◆**traditionnel, -elle** *a* traditional.

traduire* [tradɥir] *vt* **1** to translate *(de* from, *in* into); *(exprimer) Fig* to express. **2** **t. qn en justice** to bring s.o. before the courts. ◆**traducteur, -trice** *nmf* translator. ◆**traduction** *nf* translation. ◆**traduisible** *a* translatable.

trafic [trafik] *nm* **1** *Aut Rail etc* traffic. **2** *Com Péj* traffic, trade; **faire du** t. to traffic, trade; **faire le** t. **de** to traffic in, trade in. ◆**trafiqu/er** *vi (produit) Fam* to tamper with. ◆**—ant, -ante** *nmf* trafficker, dealer; **t. d'armes/de drogue** arms/drug trafficker *or* dealer.

tragédie [traʒedi] *nf Th & Fig* tragedy. ◆**tragique** *a* tragic. ◆**tragiquement** *adv* tragically.

trahir [trair] *vt* to betray; *(secret etc)* to betray, give away; *(forces)* to fail *(s.o.)*; **— se** t. *vpr* to give oneself away, betray oneself. ◆**trahison** *nf* betrayal; *(crime) Pol* treason.

train [trɛ̃] *nm* **1** *(locomotive, transport, jouet)* train; **t. à grande vitesse** high-speed train; **t. couchettes** sleeper; **t. auto-couchettes** *(car)* sleeper. **2** **en** t. *(forme)* on form; **se mettre en** t. to get (oneself) into shape. **3** **être en** t. **de faire** to be (busy) doing; **mettre qch en** t. to get sth going, start sth off. **4** *(allure)* pace; **t. de vie** life style. **5** *(de pneus)* set; *(de péniches, véhicules)* string. **6** **t. d'atterrissage** *Av* undercarriage.

traine [tren] *nf* **1** *(de robe)* train. **2 à la** t. *(en arrière)* lagging behind.

traineau, -x [treno] *nm* sledge, sleigh, *Am* sled.

trainée [trene] *nf* **1** *(de substance)* trail, streak; *(bande)* streak; **se répandre comme une** t. **de poudre** *(vite)* to spread like wildfire. **2** *(prostituée) Arg* tart.

trainer [trene] *vt* to drag; *(mots)* to drawl; **(faire)** t. **en longueur** *(faire durer)* to drag out; **—** *vi (jouets, papiers etc)* to lie around; *(subsister)* to linger on; *(s'attarder)* to lag behind, dawdle; *(errer)* to hang around; **t. (par terre)** *(robe etc)* to trail (on the ground); **t. (en longueur)** *(durer)* to drag on; **— se** t. *vpr (avancer)* to drag oneself (along); *(par terre)* to crawl; *(durer)* to drag on. ◆**traïnant** *a (voix)* drawling. ◆**trainailler** *vi Fam* **= trainasser.** ◆**traïnard, -arde** *nmf* slowcoach, *Am* slowpoke. ◆**traïnasser** *vi Fam* to dawdle; *(errer)* to hang around.

train-train [trɛ̃trɛ̃] *nm* routine.

traire* [trɛr] *vt (vache)* to milk.

trait [trɛ] *nm* **1** line; *(en dessinant)* stroke; *(caractéristique)* feature, trait; *pl (du visage)* features; **t. d'union** hyphen; *(intermédiaire) Fig* link; **d'un** t. *(boire)* in one gulp, in one go; **à grands traits** in outline; **t. de** (*esprit, génie*) flash of; (*bravoure*) act of; **avoir t. à** (*se rapporter à*) to relate to. **2 cheval de t.** draught horse.

traite [tʀɛt] *nf* **1** (*de vache*) milking. **2** *Com* bill, draft. **3 d'une (seule) t.** (*sans interruption*) in one go. **4 t. des Noirs** slave trade; **t. des blanches** white slave trade.

traité [tʀete] *nm* **1** *Pol* treaty. **2** (*ouvrage*) treatise (**sur** on).

trait/er [tʀete] *vt* (*se comporter envers*) & *Méd* to treat; (*problème, sujet*) to deal with; (*marché*) *Com* to negotiate; (*matériau, produit*) to treat, process; **t. qn de lâche/etc** to call s.o. a coward/*etc*; — *vi* to negotiate, deal (**avec** with); **t. de** (*sujet*) to deal with. ◆—**ant** [-etɑ̃] *a* **médecin t.** regular doctor. ◆—**ement** [-etmɑ̃] *nm* **1** treatment; **mauvais traitements** rough treatment; **t. de données/de texte** data/word processing; **machine de t. de texte** word processor. **2** (*gains*) salary.

traiteur [tʀetœʀ] *nm* (*fournisseur*) caterer; **chez le t.** (*magasin*) at the delicatessen.

traître [tʀɛtʀ] *nm* traitor; **en t.** treacherously; — *a* (*dangereux*) treacherous; **être t. à** to be a traitor to. ◆**traîtrise** *nf* treachery.

trajectoire [tʀaʒɛktwaʀ] *nf* path, trajectory.

trajet [tʀaʒɛ] *nm* journey, trip; (*distance*) distance; (*itinéraire*) route.

trame [tʀam] *nf* **1** (*de récit etc*) framework. **2** (*de tissu*) weft.

tramer [tʀame] *vt* (*évasion etc*) to plot; (*complot*) to hatch.

trampoline [tʀɑ̃polin] *nm* trampoline.

tram(way) [tʀam(wɛ)] *nm* tram, *Am* streetcar.

tranche [tʀɑ̃ʃ] *nf* (*morceau coupé*) slice; (*bord*) edge; (*partie*) portion; (*de salaire, impôts*) bracket; **t. d'âge** age bracket.

tranchée [tʀɑ̃ʃe] *nf* trench.

tranch/er [tʀɑ̃ʃe] *vt* **1** to cut. **2** *vt* (*difficulté, question*) to settle; — *vi* (*décider*) to decide. **3** *vi* (*contraster*) to contrast (**avec, sur** with). ◆—**ant** **1** *a* (*couteau*) sharp; — *nm* (*cutting*) edge. **2** *a* (*péremptoire*) trenchant, cutting. ◆—**é** *a* (*couleurs*) distinct; (*opinion*) clear-cut.

tranquille [tʀɑ̃kil] *a* quiet; (*mer*) calm, still; (*conscience*) clear; (*esprit*) easy; (*certain*) *Fam* confident; **je suis t.** (*rassuré*) my mind is at rest; **soyez t.** don't worry; **laisser t.** to leave me alone. ◆**tranquillement** *adv* calmly. ◆**tranquilliser** *vt* to reassure; **tranquillisez-vous** set your mind at rest. ◆—**ant** *nm* *Méd* tranquillizer. ◆**tranquil-**

lité *nf* (peace and) quiet; (*d'esprit*) peace of mind.

trans- [tʀɑ̃z, tʀɑ̃s] *préf* trans-.

transaction [tʀɑ̃zaksjɔ̃] *nf* **1** (*compromis*) compromise. **2** *Com* transaction.

transatlantique [tʀɑ̃zatlɑ̃tik] *a* transatlantic; — *nm* (*paquebot*) transatlantic liner; (*chaise*) deckchair.

transcend/er [tʀɑ̃sɑ̃de] *vt* to transcend. ◆—**ant** *a* transcendent.

transcrire* [tʀɑ̃skʀiʀ] *vt* to transcribe. ◆**transcription** *nf* transcription; (*document*) transcript.

transe [tʀɑ̃s] *nf* **en t.** (*mystique*) in a trance; (*excité*) very exited.

transférer [tʀɑ̃sfeʀe] *vt* to transfer (**à** to). ◆**transfert** *nm* transfer.

transfigurer [tʀɑ̃sfigyʀe] *vt* to transform, transfigure.

transformer [tʀɑ̃sfɔʀme] *vt* to transform, change; (*maison, matière première*) to convert; (*robe etc*) to alter; (*essai*) *Rugby* to convert; **t. en** to turn into; — **se t.** *vpr* to change, be transformed (**en** into). ◆**transformateur** *nm* *Él* transformer. ◆**transformation** *nf* transformation, change; conversion.

transfuge [tʀɑ̃sfyʒ] *nm* *Mil* renegade; — *nmf* *Pol* renegade.

transfusion [tʀɑ̃sfyzjɔ̃] *nf* **t.** (**sanguine**) (blood) transfusion.

transgresser [tʀɑ̃sgʀese] *vt* (*loi, ordre*) to disobey.

transi [tʀɑ̃zi] *a* (*personne*) numb with cold; **t. de peur** paralysed by fear.

transiger [tʀɑ̃ziʒe] *vi* to compromise.

transistor [tʀɑ̃zistɔʀ] *nm* (*dispositif, poste*) transistor. ◆**transistorisé** *a* (*téléviseur etc*) transistorized.

transit [tʀɑ̃zit] *nm* transit; **en t.** in transit. ◆**transiter** *vt* (**faire**) **t.** to send in transit; — *vi* to be in transit.

transitif, -ive [tʀɑ̃zitif, -iv] *a* *Gram* transitive.

transition [tʀɑ̃zisjɔ̃] *nf* transition. ◆**transitoire** *a* (*qui passe*) transient; (*provisoire*) transitional.

transmettre* [tʀɑ̃smɛtʀ] *vt* (*héritage, message etc*) to pass on (**à** to); *Phys Tech* to transmit; *Rad TV* to broadcast, transmit. ◆**transmetteur** *nm* (*appareil*) transmitter, transmitting device. ◆**transmission** *nf* transmission; passing on.

transparaître* [tʀɑ̃spaʀɛtʀ] *vi* to show (through).

transparent [tʀɑ̃spaʀɑ̃] *a* transparent. ◆**transparence** *nf* transparency.

transpercer [trãsperse] *vt* to pierce, go through.

transpirer [trãspire] *vi* (*suer*) to perspire; (*information*) *Fig* to leak out. ◆**transpiration** *nf* perspiration.

transplanter [trãsplãte] *vt* (*organe, plante etc*) to transplant. ◆**transplantation** *nf* transplantation; (*greffe*) *Méd* transplant.

transport [trãspɔr] *nm* **1** (*action*) transport, transportation (**de** *of*); *pl* (*moyens*) transport; **moyen de t.** means of transport; **transports en commun** public transport. **2** (*émotion*) *Litt* rapture. ◆**transporter 1** *vt* (*véhicule, train*) to transport, convey; (*à la main*) to carry, take; **t. d'urgence à l'hôpital** to rush to hospital; **— se t.** *vpr* (*aller*) to take oneself (**à** *to*). **2** *vt Litt* to enrapture. ◆**transporteur** *nm* **t. (routier)** haulier, *Am* trucker.

transposer [trãspoze] *vt* to transpose. ◆**transposition** *nf* transposition.

transvaser [trãsvaze] *vt* (*vin*) to decant.

transversal, -aux [trãsversal, -o] *a* (*barre, rue etc*) cross-, transverse.

trapèze [trapɛz] *nm* (*au cirque*) trapeze. ◆**trapéziste** *nmf* trapeze artist.

trappe [trap] *nf* (*dans le plancher*) trap door.

trappeur [trapœr] *nm* (*chasseur*) trapper.

trapu [trapy] *a* **1** (*personne*) stocky, thickset. **2** (*problème etc*) *Fam* tough.

traquenard [traknar] *nm* trap.

traquer [trake] *vt* to track *ou* hunt (down).

traumatis/er [tromatize] *vt* to traumatize. ◆**—ant** *a* traumatic. ◆**traumatisme** *nm* (*choc*) trauma.

travail, -aux [travaj, -o] *nm* (*activité, lieu*) work; (*emploi, tâche*) job; (*façonnage*) working (**de** *of*); (*ouvrage, étude*) work, publication; *Écon Méd* labour; *pl* work; (*dans la rue*) roadworks; (*aménagement*) alterations; **travaux forcés** hard labour; **travaux ménagers** housework; **travaux pratiques** *Scol Univ* practical work; **travaux publics** public works; **t. au noir** moonlighting; **en t.** (*femme*) *Méd* in labour.

travaill/er [travaje] **1** *vi* to work (**à qch** *at ou* on sth); **— *vt** (*discipline, rôle, style*) to work on; (*façonner*) to work; (*inquiéter*) to worry; **t. la terre** to work the land. **2** *vi* (*bois*) to warp. ◆**—é** *a* (*style*) elaborate. ◆**—eur, -euse** *a* hard-working; **— *nmf** worker ◆**travailliste** *a Pol* Labour-; **— *nmf Pol** member of the Labour party.

travers [traver] **1** *prép & adv* **à t.** through; **en t. (de)** across. **2** *adv* **de t.** (*chapeau, nez etc*) crooked; (*comprendre*) badly; (*regarder*) askance; **aller de t.** *Fig* to go

wrong; **j'ai avalé de t.** it went down the wrong way. **3** *nm* (*défaut*) failing.

traverse [travers] *nf* **1** *Rail* sleeper, *Am* tie. **2** **chemin de t.** short cut.

travers/er [traverse] *vt* to cross, go across; (*foule, période, mur*) to go through. ◆**—ée** *nf* (*action, trajet*) crossing.

traversin [traversē] *nm* (*coussin*) bolster.

travest/ir [travestir] *vt* to disguise; (*pensée, vérité*) to misrepresent. ◆**—i** *nm Th* female impersonator; (*homosexuel*) transvestite. ◆**—issement** *nm* disguise; misrepresentation.

trébucher [trebyʃe] *vi* to stumble (**sur** *over*); **faire t.** to trip (up).

trèfle [trefl] *nm* **1** (*plante*) clover. **2** (*couleur*) *Cartes* clubs.

treille [trej] *nf* climbing vine.

treillis [treji] *nm* **1** lattice(work); (*en métal*) wire mesh. **2** (*tenue militaire*) combat uniform.

treize [trez] *a & nm inv* thirteen. ◆**treizième** *a & nmf* thirteenth.

tréma [trema] *nm Gram* di(a)eresis.

trembl/er [trãble] *vi* to tremble, shake; (*de froid, peur*) to tremble (**de** *with*); (*flamme, lumière*) to flicker; (*voix*) to tremble, quaver; (*avoir peur*) to be afraid (**que** *+ sub* that, **de faire** *to do*); **t. pour qn** to fear for s.o. ◆**—ement** *nm* (*action, frisson*) trembling; **t. de terre** earthquake. ◆**trembloter** *vi* to quiver.

trémousser (se) [sɔtremuse] *vpr* to wriggle (about).

trempe [trãp] *nf* (*caractère*) stamp; **un homme de sa t.** a man of his stamp.

tremper [trãpe] **1** *vt* to soak, drench; (*plonger*) to dip (**dans** *in*); **— *vi** to soak; **faire t.** to soak; **— se t.** *vpr* (*se baigner*) to take a dip. **2** *vt* (*acier*) to temper. **3** *vi* **t. dans** (*participer*) *Péj* to be mixed up in. ◆**trempette** *nf* **faire t.** (*se baigner*) to take a dip.

tremplin [trãplē] *nm Natation & Fig* springboard.

trente [trãt] *a & nm* thirty; **un t.-trois tours** (*disque*) an LP. ◆**trentaine** *nf* **une t. (de)** (*nombre*) (about) thirty; **avoir la t.** (*âge*) to be about thirty. ◆**trentième** *a & nmf* thirtieth.

trépidant [trepidã] *a* (*vie etc*) hectic.

trépied [trepje] *nm* tripod.

trépigner [trepiɲe] *vi* to stamp (one's feet).

très [tre] *adv* ([trez] *before vowel or mute h*) very; (*avec adjectif*) much; **t. aimé/critiqué/etc.** much liked/criticized/*etc.*

trésor [trezɔr] *nm* treasure; **le T. (public)**

(service) public revenue (department); (finances) public funds; **des trésors de** Fig a treasure house of. ◆**trésorerie** nf (bureaux d'un club etc) accounts department; (capitaux) funds; (gestion) accounting. ◆**trésorier, -ière** nmf treasurer.

tressaill/ir* [tresajir] vi (sursauter) to jump, start; (frémir) to shake, quiver; (de joie, peur) to tremble (with). ◆**—ement** nm start; quiver; trembling.

tressauter [tresote] vi (sursauter) to start, jump.

tresse [tres] nf (cordon) braid; (cheveux) plait, Am braid. ◆**tresser** vt to braid; to plait.

tréteau, -x [treto] nm trestle.

treuil [trœj] nm winch, windlass.

trêve [trɛv] nf Mil truce; (répit) Fig respite.

tri [tri] nm sorting (out); **faire le** t. **de** to sort (out); (centre de) t. (des postes) sorting office. ◆**triage** nm sorting (out).

triangle [trijɑ̃gl] nm triangle. ◆**triangulaire** a triangular.

tribord [tribɔr] nm Nau Av starboard.

tribu [triby] nf tribe. ◆**tribal, -aux** a tribal.

tribulations [tribylasjɔ̃] nfpl tribulations.

tribunal, -aux [tribynal, -o] nm Jur court; (militaire) tribunal.

tribune [tribyn] nf 1 (de salle publique etc) gallery; (de stade) (grand)stand; (d'orateur) rostrum. 2 t. **libre** (dans un journal) open forum.

tribut [triby] nm tribute (à to).

tributaire [tribytɛr] a t. **de** Fig dependent on.

tricher [trife] vi to cheat. ◆**tricherie** nf cheating, trickery; **une** t. a piece of trickery. ◆**tricheur, -euse** nmf cheat, Am cheater.

tricolore [trikɔlɔr] a 1 (cocarde etc) red, white and blue; **le drapeau/l'équipe** t. the French flag/team. 2 **feu** t. traffic lights.

tricot [triko] nm (activité, ouvrage) knitting; (chandail) jumper, sweater; **un** t. (ouvrage) a piece of knitting; **en** t. knitted; t. **de corps** vest, Am undershirt. ◆**tricoter** vti to knit.

tricycle [trisikl] nm tricycle.

trier [trije] vt (séparer) to sort (out); (choisir) to pick ou sort out.

trilogie [trilɔʒi] nf trilogy.

trimbal(l)er [trɛ̃bale] vt Fam to cart about, drag around; **— se** t. vpr Fam to trail around.

trimer [trime] vi Fam to slave (away), toil.

trimestre [trimɛstr] nm (période) Com quarter; Scol term. ◆**trimestriel, -ielle** a (revue) quarterly; (bulletin) Scol end-of-term.

tringle [trɛ̃gl] nf rail, rod; t. **à rideaux** curtain rail ou rod.

Trinité [trinite] nf **la** T. (fête) Trinity; (dogme) the Trinity.

trinquer [trɛ̃ke] vi to chink glasses; t. **à** to drink to.

trio [trijo] nm (groupe) & Mus trio.

triomphe [trijɔ̃f] nm triumph (sur over); **porter qn en** t. to carry s.o. shoulder-high. ◆**triomphal, -aux** a triumphal. ◆**triomph/er** vi to triumph (de over); (jubiler) to be jubilant. ◆**—ant** a triumphant.

tripes [trip] nfpl (intestins) Fam guts; Culin tripe. ◆**tripier, -ière** nmf tripe butcher.

triple [tripl] a treble, triple; **— nm le** t. three times as much (**de** as). ◆**tripl/er** vti to treble, triple. ◆**—és, -ées** nmfpl (enfants) triplets.

tripot [tripo] nm (café etc) Péj gambling den.

tripoter [tripɔte] vt to fiddle about ou mess about with; **— vi** to fiddle ou mess about.

trique [trik] nf cudgel, stick.

triste [trist] a sad; (couleur, temps, rue) gloomy, dreary; (lamentable) unfortunate, sorry. ◆**tristement** adv sadly. ◆**tristesse** nf sadness; gloom, dreariness.

triturer [trityre] vt (manipuler) to manipulate.

trivial, -aux [trivjal, -o] a coarse, vulgar. ◆**trivialité** nf coarseness, vulgarity.

troc [trɔk] nm exchange, barter.

troène [trɔɛn] nm (arbuste) privet.

trognon [trɔɲɔ̃] nm (de pomme, poire) core; (de chou) stump.

trois [trwa] a & nm three. ◆**troisième** a & nmf third. ◆**troisièmement** adv thirdly.

trolley(bus) [trɔlɛ(bys)] nm trolley(bus).

trombe [trɔ̃b] nf t. **d'eau** (pluie) rainstorm, downpour; **en** t. (entrer etc) Fig like a whirlwind.

trombone [trɔ̃bɔn] nm 1 Mus trombone. 2 (agrafe) paper clip.

trompe [trɔ̃p] nf 1 (d'éléphant) trunk; (d'insecte) proboscis. 2 Mus horn.

tromper [trɔ̃pe] vt to deceive, mislead; (escroquer) to cheat; (échapper à) to elude; (être infidèle à) to be unfaithful to; **— se** t. vpr to be mistaken, make a mistake; **se** t. **de route/de train/etc** to take the wrong road/train/etc; **se** t. **de date/de jour/etc** to get the date/day/etc wrong. ◆**tromperie** nf deceit, deception. ◆**trompeur, -euse** a (apparences etc) deceptive, misleading; (personne) deceitful.

trompette [trɔ̃pɛt] nf trumpet. ◆**trompettiste** nmf trumpet player.

tronc [trɔ̃] nm **1** Bot Anat trunk. **2** Rel collection box.

tronçon [trɔ̃sɔ̃] nm section. ◆**tronçonn/er** vt to cut (into sections). ◆**-euse** nf chain saw.

trône [tron] nm throne. ◆**trôner** vi (vase, personne etc) Fig to occupy the place of honour.

tronquer [trɔ̃ke] vt to truncate; (texte etc) to curtail.

trop [tro] adv too; too much; too many; t. dur/far/loin/etc too hard/far/etc; t. fatigué too tired, overtired; boire/lire/etc t. to drink/read/etc too much; t. de sel/etc (quantité) too much salt/etc; t. de gens/etc (nombre) too many people/etc; du fromage/etc de en t. (quantité) too much cheese/etc; des œufs/etc de ou en t. (nombre) too many eggs/etc; un franc/verre/etc de t. ou en t. one franc/glass/etc too many; se sentir de t. Fig to feel in the way.

trophée [trofe] nm trophy.

tropique [trɔpik] nm tropic. ◆**tropical, -aux** a tropical.

trop-plein [troplɛ̃] nm (dispositif, liquide) overflow; (surabondance) Fig excess.

troquer [trɔke] vt to exchange (contre for).

trot [tro] nm trot; aller à t. to trot; au t. (sans traîner) Fam at the double. ◆**trott/er** [trɔte] vi (cheval etc) to trot; (personne) to scurry (along).

trotteuse [trɔtøz] nf (de montre) second hand.

trottiner [trɔtine] vi (personne) to patter (along).

trottinette [trɔtinet] nf (jouet) scooter.

trottoir [trɔtwar] nm pavement, Am sidewalk; t. roulant moving walkway, travolator.

trou [tru] nm hole; (d'aiguille) eye; (manque) Fig gap (dans in); (village) Péj hole, dump; t. d'homme (ouverture) manhole; t. de (la) serrure keyhole; t. (de mémoire) Fig lapse (of memory).

trouble [trubl] **1** a (liquide) cloudy; (image) blurred; (affaire) shady; voir t. to see blurred. **2** nm (émoi, émotion) agitation; (désarroi) distress; (désordre) confusion; pl Méd trouble; (révolte) disturbances, troubles. ◆**troubl/er** vt to disturb; (liquide) to make cloudy; (projet) to upset; (esprit) to unsettle; (vue) to blur; (inquiéter) to trouble; — se t. vpr (liquide) to become cloudy; (candidat etc) to become flustered. ◆**-ant** a (détail etc) disquieting. ◆**trouble-fête** nmf inv killjoy, spoilsport.

trou/er [true] vt to make a hole ou holes in;

(silence, ténèbres) to cut through. ◆**-ée** nf gap; (brèche) Mil breach.

trouille [truj] nf avoir la t. Fam to have the jitters, be scared. ◆**trouillard** a (poltron) Fam chicken.

troupe [trup] nf Mil troop; (groupe) group; Th company, troupe; la t., les troupes (armée) the troops.

troupeau, -x [trupo] nm (de vaches) & Fig Péj herd; (de moutons, d'oies) flock.

trousse [trus] nf **1** (étui) case, kit; (d'écolier) pencil case; t. à outils toolkit; t. à pharmacie first-aid kit. **2** nfpl aux trousses de qn Fig on s.o.'s heels.

trousseau, -x [truso] nm **1** (de clés) bunch. **2** (de mariée) trousseau.

trouver [truve] vt to find; aller/venir t. qn to go/come and see s.o.; je trouve que (je pense que) I think that; comment la trouvez-vous? what do you think of her?; — se t. vpr to be; (être situé) to be situated; (se sentir) to feel; (dans une situation) to find oneself; se t. mal (s'évanouir) to faint; il se trouve que it happens that. ◆**trouvaille** nf (lucky) find.

truand [tryɑ̃] nm crook.

truc [tryk] nm **1** (astuce) trick; (moyen) way; avoir/trouver le t. to have/get the knack (pour faire of doing). **2** (chose) Fam thing. ◆**-age** nm = truquage.

truchement [tryʃmɑ̃] nm par le t. de qn through (the intermediary of) s.o.

truculent [trykylɑ̃] a (langage, personnage) colourful.

truelle [tryɛl] nf trowel.

truffe [tryf] nf **1** (champignon) truffle. **2** (de chien) nose.

truff/er [tryfe] vt (remplir) to stuff (de with). ◆**-é** a (pâté etc) Culin with truffles.

truie [trɥi] nf (animal) sow.

truite [trɥit] nf trout.

truqu/er [tryke] vt (photo etc) to fake; (élections, match) to rig, fix. ◆**-é** a (photo etc) fake-; (élections, match) rigged, fixed; (scène) Cin trick-. ◆**-age** nm Cin (special) effect; (action) faking; rigging.

trust [trœst] nm Com (cartel) trust; (entreprise) corporation.

tsar [dzar] nm tsar, czar.

TSF [teɛsɛf] nf abrév (télégraphie sans fil) wireless, radio.

tsigane [tsigan] a & nmf (Hungarian) gipsy.

TSVP [teɛsvepe] abrév (tournez s'il vous plaît) PTO.

TTC [tetese] abrév (toutes taxes comprises) inclusive of tax.

tu[1] [ty] pron you (familiar form of address).

tu² [ty] *voir* **taire.**

tuba [tyba] *nm* **1** *Mus* tuba. **2** *Sp* snorkel.

tube [tyb] *nm* **1** tube; (*de canalisation*) pipe. **2** (*chanson, disque*) *Fam* hit. ◆**tubulaire** *a* tubular.

tuberculeux, -euse [tybɛrkylø, -øz] *a* tubercular; **être t.** to have tuberculosis *ou* TB. ◆**tuberculose** *nf* tuberculosis, TB.

tue-mouches [tymuʃ] *a inv* **papier t.-mouches** flypaper. ◆**t.-tête (à)** *adv* at the top of one's voice.

tu/er [tɥe] *vt* to kill; (*d'un coup de feu*) to shoot (dead), kill; (*épuiser*) *Fig* to wear out; **— se t.** *vpr* to kill oneself; to shoot oneself; (*dans un accident*) to be killed; **se t. à faire** *Fig* to wear oneself out doing. **—ant** *a* (*fatigant*) exhausting. ◆**tuerie** *nf* slaughter. ◆**tueur, -euse** *nmf* killer.

tuile [tɥil] *nf* **1** tile. **2** (*malchance*) *Fam* (stroke of) bad luck.

tulipe [tylip] *nf* tulip.

tuméfié [tymefje] *a* swollen.

tumeur [tymœr] *nf* tumour, growth.

tumulte [tymylt] *nm* commotion; (*désordre*) turmoil. ◆**tumultueux, -euse** *a* turbulent.

tunique [tynik] *nf* tunic.

Tunisie [tynizi] *nf* Tunisia. ◆**tunisien, -ienne** *a & nmf* Tunisian.

tunnel [tynɛl] *nm* tunnel.

turban [tyrbɑ̃] *nm* turban.

turbine [tyrbin] *nf* turbine.

turbulences [tyrbylɑ̃s] *nfpl Phys Av* turbulence.

turbulent [tyrbylɑ̃] *a* (*enfant etc*) boisterous, turbulent.

turfiste [tyrfist] *nmf* racegoer, punter.

Turquie [tyrki] *nf* Turkey. ◆**turc, turque** *a* Turkish; *— nmf* Turk; *— nm* (*langue*) Turkish.

turquoise [tyrkwaz] *a inv* turquoise.

tuteur, -trice [tytœr, -tris] **1** *nmf Jur* guardian. **2** *nm* (*bâton*) stake, prop. ◆**tutelle** *nf* *Jur* guardianship; *Fig* protection.

tutoyer [tytwaje] *vt* to address familiarly (*using tu*). ◆**tutoiement** *nm* familiar address, use of *tu*.

tutu [tyty] *nm* ballet skirt, tutu.

tuyau, -x [tɥijo] *nm* **1** pipe; **t. d'arrosage** hose(pipe); **t. de cheminée** flue; **t. d'échappement** *Aut* exhaust (pipe). **2** (*renseignement*) *Fam* tip. ◆**tuyauter** *vt* **t. qn** (*conseiller*) *Fam* to give s.o. a tip. ◆**tuyauterie** *nf* (*tuyaux*) piping.

TVA [tevea] *nf abrév* (*taxe à la valeur ajoutée*) VAT.

tympan [tɛ̃pɑ̃] *nm* eardrum.

type [tip] *nm* (*modèle*) type; (*traits*) features; (*individu*) *Fam* fellow, guy, bloke; **le t. même de** *Fig* the very model of; *— a inv* (*professeur etc*) typical. ◆**typique** *a* typical (**de** of). ◆**typiquement** *adv* typically.

typhoïde [tifɔid] *nf Méd* typhoid (fever).

typhon [tifɔ̃] *nm Mét* typhoon.

typographe [tipɔgraf] *nmf* typographer. ◆**typographie** *nf* typography, printing. ◆**typographique** *a* typographical, printing.

tyran [tirɑ̃] *nm* tyrant. ◆**tyrannie** *nf* tyranny. ◆**tyrannique** *a* tyrannical. ◆**tyranniser** *vt* to tyrannize.

tzigane [dzigan] *a & nmf* (Hungarian) gipsy.

U

U, u [y] *nm* U, u.

ulcère [ylsɛr] *nm* ulcer, sore.

ulcérer [ylsere] *vt* (*blesser, irriter*) to embitter.

ultérieur [ylterjœr] *a* later. ◆**—ement** *adv* later.

ultimatum [yltimatɔm] *nm* ultimatum.

ultime [yltim] *a* final, last.

ultra- [yltra] *préf* ultra-. ◆**u.-secret, -ète** *a* (*document*) top-secret.

ultramoderne [yltramɔdɛrn] *a* ultramodern.

ultraviolet, -ette [yltravjɔle, -ɛt] *a* ultraviolet.

un, une [œ̃, yn] **1** *art indéf* a, (*devant voyelle*) an; **une page** a page; **un ange** [œ̃nɑ̃ʒ] an angel. **2** *a* one; **la page un** page one; **un kilo** one kilo; **un type** (*un quelconque*) some *ou* a fellow. **3** *pron & nmf* one; **l'un** one; **les uns** some; **le numéro un** number one; **j'en ai un** I have one; **l'un d'eux** one of them; **la une** *Journ* page one.

unanime [ynanim] *a* unanimous. ◆**unanimité** *nf* unanimity; **à l'u.** unanimously.

uni [yni] *a* united; (*famille etc*) close; (*surface*) smooth; (*couleur, étoffe*) plain.

unième [ynjɛm] *a* (*après un numéral*) (-)first; **trente et u.** thirty-first; **cent u.** hundred and first.

unifier [ynifje] *vt* to unify. ◆**unification** *nf* unification.

uniforme [yniform] **1** *a* (*régulier*) uniform. **2** *nm* (*vêtement*) uniform. ◆**uniformément** *adv* uniformly. ◆**uniformiser** *vt* to standardize. ◆**uniformité** *nf* uniformity.

unijambiste [yniʒãbist] *a & nmf* one-legged (man *ou* woman).

unilatéral, -aux [ynilateral, -o] *a* unilateral; (*stationnement*) on one side of the road only.

union [ynjõ] *nf* union; (*association*) association; (*entente*) unity. ◆**unir** *vt* to unite, join (together); **u. la force au courage**/*etc* to combine strength with courage/*etc*; **— s'u.** *vpr* to unite; (*se marier*) to be joined together; (*se joindre*) to join (together).

unique [ynik] *a* **1** (*fille, fils*) only; (*espoir, souci etc*) only, sole; (*prix, salaire, voie*) single, one; **son seul et u. souci** his *ou* her one and only worry. **2** (*incomparable*) unique. ◆**uniquement** *adv* only, solely.

unisexe [yniseks] *a inv* (*vêtements etc*) unisex.

unisson (à l') [alynisõ] *adv* in unison (de with).

unité [ynite] *nf* (*élément, grandeur*) & Mil unit; (*cohésion, harmonie*) unity. ◆**unitaire** *a* (*prix*) per unit.

univers [ynivɛr] *nm* universe.

universel, -elle [ynivɛrsɛl] *a* universal. ◆**universellement** *adv* universally. ◆**universalité** *nf* universality.

université [ynivɛrsite] *nf* university; **à l'u.** at university. ◆**universitaire** *a* university-; *– nmf* academic.

uranium [yranjɔm] *nm* uranium.

urbain [yrbɛ̃] *a* urban, town-, city-. ◆**urbaniser** *vt* to urbanize, build up. ◆**urbanisme** *nm* town planning, *Am* city planning. ◆**urbaniste** *nmf* town planner, *Am* city planner.

urgent [yrʒã] *a* urgent, pressing. ◆**urgence** *nf* (*cas*) emergency; (*de décision, tâche etc*) urgency; **d'u.** (*mesures etc*) emergency-; **état d'u.** *Pol* state of emergency; **faire qch d'u.** to do sth urgently.

urine [yrin] *nf* urine. ◆**uriner** *vi* to urinate. ◆**urinoir** *nm* (public) urinal.

urne [yrn] *nf* **1** (*électorale*) ballot box; **aller aux urnes** to go to the polls. **2** (*vase*) urn.

URSS [yrs] *nf abrév* (*Union des Républiques Socialistes Soviétiques*) USSR.

usage [yzaʒ] *nm* use; *Ling* usage; (*habitude*) custom; **faire u. de** to make use of; **faire de l'u.** (*vêtement etc*) to wear well; **d'u.** (*habituel*) customary; **à l'u. de** for (the use of); **hors d'u.** no longer usable. ◆**usagé** *a* worn; (*d'occasion*) used. ◆**usager** *nm* user. ◆**us/er** *vt* (*vêtement, personne*) to wear out; (*consommer*) to use (up); (*santé*) to ruin; *– vi* **u. de** to use; **— s'u.** *vpr* (*tissu, machine*) to wear out; (*personne*) to wear oneself out. ◆**—é** *a* (*tissu etc*) worn (out); (*sujet etc*) well-worn; (*personne*) worn out.

usine [yzin] *nf* factory; (*à gaz, de métallurgie*) works.

usiner [yzine] *vt* (*pièce*) *Tech* to machine.

usité, -e [yzite] *a* commonly used.

ustensile [ystãsil] *nm* utensil.

usuel, -elle [yzɥɛl] *a* everyday, ordinary; *– nmpl* (*livres*) reference books.

usure [yzyr] *nf* (*détérioration*) wear (and tear); (*intérêt*) usury; **avoir qn à l'u.** *Fig* to wear s.o. down (in the end).

usurier, -ière [yzyrje, -jɛr] *nmf* usurer.

usurper [yzyrpe] *vt* to usurp.

utérus [yterys] *nm Anat* womb, uterus.

utile [ytil] *a* useful (à to). ◆**utilement** *adv* usefully.

utiliser [ytilize] *vt* to use, utilize. ◆**utilisable** *a* usable. ◆**utilisateur, -trice** *nmf* user. ◆**utilisation** *nf* use. ◆**utilité** *nf* use(fulness); **d'une grande u.** very useful.

utilitaire [ytiliter] *a* utilitarian; (*véhicule*) utility-.

utopie [ytɔpi] *nf* (*idéal*) utopia; (*projet, idée*) utopian plan *ou* idea. ◆**utopique** *a* utopian.

V

V, v [ve] *nm* V, v.

va [va] *voir* **aller 1**.

vacances [vakãs] *nfpl* holiday(s), *Am* vaca-

tion; **en v.** on holiday, *Am* on vacation; **prendre ses v.** to take one's holiday(s) *ou Am* vacation; **les grandes v.** the summer

holidays *ou Am* vacation. ◆**vacancier, -ière** *nmf* holidaymaker, *Am* vacationer.

vacant [vakã] *a* vacant. ◆**vacance** *nf (poste)* vacancy.

vacarme [vakarm] *nm* din, uproar.

vaccin [vaksɛ̃] *nm* vaccine; **faire un v. à** to vaccinate. ◆**vaccination** *nf* vaccination. ◆**vacciner** *vt* to vaccinate.

vache [vaʃ] **1** *nf* cow; **v.** laitière dairy cow. **2** *nf (peau de)* **v.** *(personne) Fam* swine; − *a (méchant) Fam* nasty. ◆**vachement** *adv Fam (très)* damned; *(beaucoup)* a hell of a lot. ◆**vacherie** *nf Fam (action, parole)* nasty thing; *(caractère)* nastiness.

vacill/er [vasije] *vi* to sway, wobble; *(flamme, lumière)* to flicker; *(jugement, mémoire etc)* to falter, waver. ◆−**ant** *a (démarche, mémoire)* shaky; *(lumière etc)* flickering.

vadrouille [vadruj] *nf* **en v.** *Fam* roaming *ou* wandering about. ◆**vadrouiller** *vi Fam* to roam *ou* wander about.

va-et-vient [vaevjɛ̃] *nm inv (mouvement)* movement to and fro; *(de personnes)* comings and goings.

vagabond, -onde [vagabɔ̃, -ɔ̃d] *a* wandering; − *nmf (clochard)* vagrant, tramp. ◆**vagabond/er** *vi* to roam *ou* wander about; *(pensée)* to wander. ◆−**age** *nm* wandering; *Jur* vagrancy.

vagin [vaʒɛ̃] *nm* vagina.

vagir [vaʒir] *vi (bébé)* to cry, wail.

vague [vag] **1** *a* vague; *(regard)* vacant; *(souvenir)* dim, vague; − *nm* vagueness; **regarder dans le v.** to gaze into space, gaze vacantly; **rester dans le v.** *(être évasif)* to keep it vague. **2** *nf (de mer)* & *Fig* wave; **v. de chaleur** heat wave; **v. de froid** cold snap *ou* spell; **v. de fond** *(dans l'opinion) Fig* tidal wave. ◆**vaguement** *adv* vaguely.

vaillant [vajã] *a* brave, valiant; *(vigoureux)* healthy. ◆**vaillamment** *adv* bravely, valiantly. ◆**vaillance** *nf* bravery.

vain [vɛ̃] *a* **1** *(futile)* vain, futile; *(mots, promesse)* empty; **en v.** in vain, vainly. **2** *(vaniteux)* vain. ◆**vainement** *adv* in vain, vainly.

vainc/re* [vɛ̃kr] *vt* to defeat, beat; *(surmonter)* to overcome. ◆−**u, -ue** *nmf* defeated man *ou* woman; *Sp* loser. ◆**vainqueur** *nm* victor; *Sp* winner; − *am* victorious.

vaisseau, -x [vɛso] *nm* **1** *Anat Bot* vessel. **2** *(bateau)* ship, vessel; **v. spatial** spaceship.

vaisselle [vɛsɛl] *nf* crockery; *(à laver)* washing-up; **faire la v.** to do the washing-up, do *ou* wash the dishes.

val, *pl* **vals** *ou* **vaux** [val, vo] *nm* valley.

valable [valabl] *a (billet, motif etc)* valid; *(remarquable, rentable) Fam* worthwhile.

valet [valɛ] *nm* **1** *Cartes* jack. **2** **v.** (de chambre) valet, manservant; **v. de ferme** farmhand.

valeur [valœr] *nf* value; *(mérite)* worth; *(poids)* importance, weight; *pl (titres) Com* stocks and shares; **la v. de** *(quantité)* the equivalent of; **avoir de la v.** to be valuable; **mettre en v.** *(faire ressortir)* to highlight; **de v.** *(personne)* of merit, able; **objets de v.** valuables.

valide [valid] *a* **1** *(personne)* fit, able-bodied; *(population)* able-bodied. **2** *(billet etc)* valid. ◆**valider** *vt* to validate. ◆**validité** *nf* validity.

valise [valiz] *nf* (suit)case; **v. diplomatique** diplomatic bag *ou Am* pouch; **faire ses valises** to pack (one's bags).

vallée [vale] *nf* valley. ◆**vallon** *nm* (small) valley. ◆**vallonné** *a (région etc)* undulating.

valoir* [valwar] *vi* to be worth; *(s'appliquer)* to apply **(pour** to); **v. mille francs/cher/etc** to be worth a thousand francs/a lot/etc; **un vélo vaut bien une auto** a bicycle is as good as a car; **il vaut mieux rester** it's better to stay; **il vaut mieux que j'attende** I'd better wait; **ça ne vaut rien** it's worthless, it's no good; **ça vaut le coup** *Fam ou* **la peine** it's worthwhile **(de faire** doing); **faire v.** *(faire ressortir)* to highlight, set off; *(argument)* to put forward; *(droit)* to assert; − *vt* **v. qch à qn** to bring *ou* get s.o. sth; − **se v.** *vpr (objets, personnes)* to be as good as each other; **ça se vaut** *Fam* it's all the same.

valse [vals] *nf* waltz. ◆**valser** *vi* to waltz.

valve [valv] *nf (clapet)* valve. ◆**valvule** *nf (du cœur)* valve.

vampire [vɑ̃pir] *nm* vampire.

vandale [vɑ̃dal] *nmf* vandal. ◆**vandalisme** *nm* vandalism.

vanille [vanij] *nf* vanilla; **glace/etc à la v.** vanilla ice cream/etc. ◆**vanillé** *a* vanilla-flavoured.

vanité [vanite] *nf* vanity. ◆**vaniteux, -euse** *a* vain, conceited.

vanne [van] *nf* **1** *(d'écluse)* sluice (gate), floodgate. **2** *(remarque) Fam* dig, gibe.

vanné [vane] *a (fatigué) Fam* dead beat.

vannerie [vanri] *nf (fabrication, objets)* basketwork, basketry.

vantail, -aux [vɑ̃taj, -o] *nm (de porte)* leaf.

vanter [vɑ̃te] *vt* to praise; − **se v.** *vpr* to boast, brag **(de** about, of). ◆**vantard, -arde** *a* boastful; − *nmf* boaster, braggart,

◆**vantardise** *nf* boastfulness; (*propos*) boast.

va-nu-pieds [vanypje] *nmf inv* tramp, beggar.

vapeur [vapœr] *nf* (*brume, émanation*) vapour; **v. (d'eau)** steam; **cuire à la v. to** steam; **bateau à v.** steamship. ◆**vaporeux, -euse** *a* hazy, misty; (*tissu*) translucent, diaphanous.

vaporiser [vaporize] *vt* to spray. ◆**vaporisateur** *nm* (*appareil*) spray.

vaquer [vake] *vi* **v. à** to attend to.

varappe [varap] *nf* rock-climbing.

varech [varɛk] *nm* wrack, seaweed.

vareuse [varøz] *nf* (*d'uniforme*) tunic.

varicelle [varisɛl] *nf* chicken pox.

varices [varis] *nfpl* varicose veins.

vari/er [varje] *vti* to vary (from). ◆—**é** *a* (*diversifié*) varied; (*divers*) various. ◆—**able** *a* variable; (*humeur, temps*) changeable. ◆**variante** *nf* variant. ◆**variation** *nf* variation. ◆**variété** *nf* variety; **spectacle de variétés** *Th* variety show.

variole [varjɔl] *nf* smallpox.

vas [va] *voir* **aller 1.**

vase [vaz] **1** *nm* vase. **2** *nf* (*boue*) silt, mud.

vaseline [vazlin] *nf* Vaseline®.

vaseux, -euse [vazø, -øz] *a* **1** (*boueux*) silty, muddy. **2** (*fatigué*) off colour. **3** (*idées etc*) woolly, hazy.

vasistas [vazista] *nm* (*dans une porte ou une fenêtre*) hinged panel.

vaste [vast] *a* vast, huge.

Vatican [vatikã] *nm* Vatican.

va-tout [vatu] *nm inv* **jouer son v.-tout** to stake one's all.

vaudeville [vodvil] *nm Th* light comedy.

vau-l'eau (à) [avolo] *adv* **aller à v.-l'eau** to go to rack and ruin.

vaurien, -ienne [vorjɛ̃, -jɛn] *nmf* good-for-nothing.

vautour [votur] *nm* vulture.

vautrer (se) [səvotre] *vpr* to sprawl; **se v. dans** (*boue, vice*) to wallow in.

va-vite (à la) [alavit] *adv Fam* in a hurry.

veau, -x [vo] *nm* (*animal*) calf; (*viande*) veal; (*cuir*) calf(skin).

vécu [veky] *voir* **vivre**; – *a* (*histoire etc*) real(-life), true.

vedette [vədɛt] *nf* **1** *Cin TV* star; **avoir la v.** (*artiste*) to head the bill; **en v.** (*personne*) in the limelight; (*objet*) in a prominent position. **2** (*canot*) motor boat, launch.

végétal, -aux [veʒetal, -o] *a* (*huile, règne*) vegetable-; – *nm* plant. ◆**végétarien,**

-**ienne** *a* & *nmf* vegetarian. ◆**végétation 1** *nf* vegetation. **2** *nfpl Méd* adenoids.

végéter [veʒete] *vi* (*personne*) *Péj* to vegetate.

véhément [veemã] *a* vehement. ◆**véhémence** *nf* vehemence.

véhicule [veikyl] *nm* vehicle. ◆**véhiculer** *vt* to convey.

veille [vɛj] *nf* **1** **la v. (de)** (*jour précédent*) the day before; **à la v. de** (*événement*) on the eve of; **la v. de Noël** Christmas Eve. **2** (*état*) wakefulness; *pl* vigils.

veill/er [veje] *vi* to stay up *ou* awake; (*sentinelle etc*) to be on watch; **v. à qch** to attend to sth, see to sth; **v. à ce que** (+ *sub*) to make sure that; **v. sur qn** to watch over s.o.; – *vt* (*malade*) to sit with, watch over. ◆—**ée** *nf* (*soirée*) evening; (*réunion*) evening get-together; (*mortuaire*) vigil. ◆—**eur** *nm* **v. de nuit** night watchman. ◆—**euse** *nf* (*lampe*) night light; (*de voiture*) sidelight; (*de réchaud*) pilot light.

veine [vɛn] *nf* **1** *Anat Bot Géol* vein. **2** (*chance*) *Fam* luck; **avoir de la v.** to be lucky; **une v.** a piece *ou* stroke of luck. ◆**veinard, -arde** *nmf Fam* lucky devil; – *a Fam* lucky.

vêler [vele] *vi* (*vache*) to calve.

vélin [velɛ̃] *nm* (*papier, peau*) vellum.

velléité [veleite] *nf* vague desire.

vélo [velo] *nm* bike, bicycle; (*activité*) cycling; **faire du v.** to cycle, go cycling. ◆**vélodrome** *nm Sp* velodrome, cycle track. ◆**vélomoteur** *nm* (lightweight) motorcycle.

velours [v(ə)lur] *nm* velvet; **v. côtelé** corduroy, cord. ◆**velouté** *a* soft, velvety; (*au goût*) mellow, smooth; – *nm* smoothness; **v. d'asperges/etc** (*potage*) cream of asparagus/etc soup.

velu [vəly] *a* hairy.

venaison [vənɛzɔ̃] *nf* venison.

vénal, -aux [venal, -o] *a* mercenary, venal.

vendange(s) [vãdãʒ] *nf*(*pl*) grape harvest, vintage. ◆**vendanger** *vi* to pick the grapes. ◆**vendangeur, -euse** *nmf* grapepicker.

vendetta [vãdeta] *nf* vendetta.

vend/re [vãdr] *vt* to sell; **v. qch à qn** to sell s.o. sth, sell sth to s.o.; **v. qn** (*trahir*) to sell s.o. out; **à v.** (*maison etc*) for sale; – **se v.** *vpr* to be sold; **ça se vend bien** it sells well. ◆—**eur, -euse** *nmf* (*de magasin*) sales *ou* shop assistant, *Am* sales clerk; (*marchand*) salesman, saleswoman; *Jur* vendor, seller.

vendredi [vãdrədi] *nm* Friday; **V. saint** Good Friday.

vénéneux, -euse [venenø, -øz] a poisonous.

vénérable [venerabl] a venerable. ◆**vénérer** vt to venerate.

vénérien, -ienne [venerjɛ̃, -jɛn] a Méd venereal.

venger [vɑ̃ʒe] vt to avenge; — **se v.** vpr to take (one's) revenge, avenge oneself (**de qn** on s.o., **de qch** for sth). ◆**vengeance** nf revenge, vengeance. ◆**vengeur, -eresse** a vengeful; – nmf avenger.

venin [venɛ̃] nm (substance) & Fig venom. ◆**venimeux, -euse** a poisonous, venomous; (haineux) Fig venomous.

venir* [v(ə)nir] vi (aux être) to come (**de** from); **v. faire** to come to do; **viens/venais me voir** come and ou to see me; **je viens/venais d'arriver** I've/I'd just arrived; **en v. à** (conclusion etc) to come to; **où veux-tu en v.?** what are you driving ou getting at?; **d'où vient que...?** how is it that...?; **s'il venait à faire** (éventualité) if he happened to do; **les jours/etc qui viennent** the coming days/etc; **une idée m'est venue** an idea occurred to me; **faire v.** to send for, get.

vent [vɑ̃] nm wind; **il fait ou il y a du v.** it's windy; **coup de v.** gust of wind; **avoir v. de** (connaissance) to get wind of; **dans le v.** (à la mode) Fam trendy, with it.

vente [vɑ̃t] nf sale; **v. (aux enchères)** auction (sale); **v. de charité** bazaar, charity sale; **en v.** (disponible) on sale; **point de v.** sales ou retail outlet; **prix de v.** selling price; **salle des ventes** auction room.

ventilateur [vɑ̃tilatœr] nm (électrique) & Aut fan; (dans un mur) ventilator. ◆**ventilation** nf ventilation. ◆**ventiler** vt to ventilate.

ventouse [vɑ̃tuz] nf (pour fixer) suction grip; **à v.** (crochet, fléchette) suction-.

ventre [vɑ̃tr] nm belly, stomach; (utérus) womb; (de cruche etc) bulge; **avoir/prendre du v.** to have/get a paunch; **à plat v.** flat on one's face. ◆**ventru** a (personne) pot-bellied; (objet) bulging.

ventriloque [vɑ̃trilɔk] nmf ventriloquist.

venu, -ue¹ [v(ə)ny] voir **venir**; – nmf **nouveau v., nouvelle venue** newcomer; **premier v.** anyone; – a **bien v.** (à propos) timely; **mal v.** untimely; **être bien/mal v. de faire** to have good grounds/no grounds for doing.

venue² [v(ə)ny] nf (arrivée) coming.

vêpres [vɛpr] nfpl Rel vespers.

ver [vɛr] nm worm; (larve) grub; (de fruits, fromage etc) maggot; **v. luisant** glow-worm;

v. à soie silkworm; **v. solitaire** tapeworm; **v. de terre** earthworm.

véracité [verasite] nf truthfulness, veracity.

véranda [verɑ̃da] nf veranda(h).

verbe [vɛrb] nm Gram verb. ◆**verbal, -aux** a (promesse, expression etc) verbal.
◆**verbiage** nm verbiage.

verdâtre [vɛrdɑtr] a greenish.

verdeur [vɛrdœr] nf (de fruit, vin) tartness; (de vieillard) sprightliness; (de langage) crudeness.

verdict [vɛrdikt] nm verdict.

verdir [vɛrdir] vti to turn green.
◆**verdoyant** a green, verdant. ◆**verdure** nf (arbres etc) greenery.

véreux, -euse [verø, -øz] a (fruit etc) wormy, maggoty; (malhonnête) Fig dubious, shady.

verge [vɛrʒ] nf Anat penis.

verger [vɛrʒe] nm orchard.

vergetures [vɛrʒətyr] nfpl stretch marks.

verglas [vɛrgla] nm (black) ice, Am sleet.
◆**verglacé** a (route) icy.

vergogne (sans) [sɑ̃vɛrgɔɲ] a shameless; – adv shamelessly.

véridique [veridik] a truthful.

vérifier [verifje] vt to check, verify; (confirmer) to confirm; (comptes) to audit. ◆**vérifiable** a verifiable. ◆**vérification** nf verification; confirmation; audit(ing).

vérité [verite] nf truth; (de personnage, tableau etc) trueness to life; (sincérité) sincerity; **en v.** in fact. ◆**véritable** a true, real; (non imité) real, genuine; (exactement nommé) veritable, real. ◆**véritablement** adv really.

vermeil, -eille [vɛrmɛj] a bright red, vermilion.

vermicelle(s) [vɛrmisɛl] nm(pl) Culin vermicelli.

vermine [vɛrmin] nf (insectes, racaille) vermine.

vermoulu [vɛrmuly] a worm-eaten.

vermouth [vɛrmut] nm vermouth.

verni [vɛrni] a (chanceux) Fam lucky.

vernir [vɛrnir] vt to varnish; (poterie) to glaze. ◆**vernis** nm varnish; glaze; (apparence) Fig veneer; **v. à ongles** nail polish ou varnish. ◆**vernissage** nm (d'exposition de peinture) first day. ◆**vernisser** vt (poterie) to glaze.

verra, verrait [vɛra, vɛrɛ] voir **voir**.

verre [vɛr] nm (substance, récipient) glass; **boire ou prendre un v.** to have a drink; **v. à bière/à vin** beer/wine glass; **v. de contact**

contact lens. ◆**verrerie** nf (objets) glassware. ◆**verrière** nf (toit) glass roof..

verrou [veru] nm bolt; **fermer au v.** to bolt; **sous les verrous** behind bars. ◆**verrouiller** vt to bolt.

verrue [very] nf wart.

vers [ver] prép (direction) towards, toward; (approximation) around, about.

vers² [ver] nm (d'un poème) line; pl (poésie) verse.

versant [versã] nm slope, side.

versatile [versatil] a fickle, volatile.

verse (à) [avers] adv in torrents; **pleuvoir à v.** to pour (down).

versé [verse] a **v. dans** (well-)versed in.

Verseau [verso] nm **le V.** (signe) Aquarius.

vers/er [verse] **1** vt to pour; (larmes, sang) to shed. **2** vt (argent) to pay. **3** vi (basculer) to overturn. ◆**—ement** nm payment. ◆**—eur** a **bec v.** spout.

verset [verse] nm Rel verse.

version [versjɔ̃] nf version; (traduction) Scol translation, unseen.

verso [verso] nm back (of the page); **'voir au v.'** 'see overleaf'.

vert [ver] a green; (pas mûr) unripe; (vin) young; (vieillard) Fig sprightly; – nm green.

vert-de-gris [verdəgri] nm inv verdigris.

vertèbre [vertebr] nf vertebra.

vertement [vertəmã] adv (réprimander etc) sharply.

vertical, -ale, -aux [vertikal, -o] a & nf vertical; **à la verticale** vertically. ◆**verticalement** adv vertically.

vertige [vertiʒ] nm (feeling of) dizziness ou giddiness; (peur de tomber dans le vide) vertigo; pl dizzy spells; **avoir le v.** to feel dizzy ou giddy. ◆**vertigineux, -euse** a (hauteur) giddy, dizzy; (très grand) Fig staggering.

vertu [verty] nf virtue; **en v. de** in accordance with. ◆**vertueux, -euse** a virtuous.

verve [verv] nf (d'orateur etc) brilliance.

verveine [verven] nf (plante) verbena.

vésicule [vezikyl] nf **v. biliaire** gall bladder.

vessie [vesi] nf bladder.

veste [vest] nf jacket, coat.

vestiaire [vestjer] nm cloakroom, Am locker room; (meuble métallique) locker.

vestibule [vestibyl] nm (entrance) hall.

vestiges [vestiʒ] nmpl (restes, ruines) remains; (traces) traces, vestiges.

vestimentaire [vestimãter] a (dépense) clothing-; (détail) of dress.

veston [vestɔ̃] nm (suit) jacket.

vêtement [vetmã] nm garment, article of clothing; pl clothes; **du v.** (industrie, commerce) clothing-; **vêtements de sport** sportswear.

vétéran [veterã] nm veteran.

vétérinaire [veteriner] a veterinary; – nmf vet, veterinary surgeon, Am veterinarian.

vétille [vetij] nf trifle, triviality.

vêt/ir* [vetir] vt, – **se v.** vpr to dress. ◆**—u** a dressed (de in).

veto [veto] nm inv veto; **mettre ou opposer son v.** à to veto.

vétuste [vetyst] a dilapidated.

veuf, veuve [vœf, vœv] a widowed; – nm widower; – nf widow.

veuille [vœj] voir vouloir.

veule [vøl] a feeble. ◆**veulerie** nf feebleness.

veut, veux [vø] voir vouloir.

vex/er [vekse] vt to upset, hurt; – **se v.** vpr to be ou get upset (de at). ◆**—ant** a hurtful; (contrariant) annoying. ◆**vexation** nf humiliation.

viable [vjabl] a (enfant, entreprise etc) viable. ◆**viabilité** nf viability.

viaduc [vjadyk] nm viaduct.

viager, -ère [vjaʒe, -ɛr] a **rente viagère** life annuity; – nm life annuity.

viande [vjãd] nf meat.

vibrer [vibre] vi to vibrate; (être ému) to thrill (de with); **faire v.** (auditoire etc) to thrill. ◆**vibrant** a (émouvant) emotional; (voix, son) resonant, vibrant. ◆**vibration** nf vibration. ◆**vibromasseur** nm (appareil) vibrator.

vicaire [viker] nm curate.

vice [vis] nm vice; (défectuosité) defect.

vice- [vis] préf vice-.

vice versa [vis(e)versa] adv vice versa.

vicier [visje] vt to taint, pollute.

vicieux, -euse [visjø, -øz] a depraved; – nmf pervert. **2** a **cercle v.** vicious circle.

vicinal, -aux [visinal, -o] a **chemin v.** byroad, minor road.

vicissitudes [visisityd] nfpl vicissitudes.

vicomte [vikɔ̃t] nm viscount. ◆**vicomtesse** nf viscountess.

victime [viktim] nf victim; (d'un accident) casualty; **être v. de** to be the victim of.

victoire [viktwar] nf victory; Sp win. ◆**victorieux, -euse** a victorious; (équipe) winning.

victuailles [viktɥaj] nfpl provisions.

vidange [vidãʒ] nf emptying, draining; Aut oil change; (dispositif) waste outlet. ◆**vidanger** vt to empty, drain.

vide [vid] a empty; – nm emptiness, void; (absence d'air) vacuum; (gouffre etc) drop;

vidéo [video] *a inv* video. ◆**vidéocassette** *nf* video (cassette).

vide-ordures [vidɔrdyr] *nm inv* (refuse) chute. ◆**vide-poches** *nm inv Aut* glove compartment.

vid/er [vide] *vt* to empty; (*lieu*) to vacate; (*poisson, volaille*) *Culin* to gut; (*querelle*) to settle; **v. qn** *Fam* (*chasser*) to throw s.o. out; (*épuiser*) to tire s.o. out; **— se v.** *vpr* to empty. ◆**—é a** (*fatigué*) *Fam* exhausted. ◆**—eur** *nm* (*de boîte de nuit*) bouncer.

vie [vi] *nf* life; (*durée*) lifetime; **coût de la v.** cost of living; **gagner sa v.** to earn one's living *ou* livelihood; **en v.** living; **à v., pour la v.** for life; **donner la v. à** to give birth to; **avoir la v. dure** (*préjugés etc*) to die hard; **jamais de la v.!** not on your life!, never!

vieill/ir [vjejir] *vi* to grow old; (*changer*) to age; (*théorie, mot*) to become old-fashioned; **— vt v. qn** (*vêtement etc*) to age s.o. ◆**—i a** (*démodé*) old-fashioned. ◆**—issant** *a* ageing. ◆**—issement** *nm* ageing.

viens, vient [vjɛ̃] *voir* **venir**.

vierge [vjɛrʒ] *nf* virgin; **la V.** (*signe*) Virgo; **— a** (*femme, neige etc*) virgin; (*feuille de papier, film*) blank; **être v.** (*femme, homme*) to be a virgin.

Viêt-nam [vjetnam] *nm* Vietnam. ◆**vietnamien, -ienne** *a & nmf* Vietnamese.

vieux (*ou* **vieil** *before vowel or mute h*), **vieille** [vjø, vjej] *a* old; **être v. jeu** (*a inv*) to be old-fashioned; **v. garçon** bachelor; **vieille fille** *Péj* old maid; **— nm** old man; *pl* old people; **mon v.** (*mon cher*) *Fam* old boy, old man; **— nf** old woman; **ma vieille** (*ma chère*) *Fam* old girl. ◆**vieillard** *nm* old man. ◆**vieillerie** *nf* (*objet*) old thing; (*idée*) old idea. ◆**vieillesse** *nf* old age. ◆**vieillot** *a* antiquated.

vif, vive [vif, viv] *a* (*enfant, mouvement*) lively; (*alerte*) alert, sharp; (*intelligence, intérêt, vent*) keen; (*couleur, lumière*) bright; (*froid*) biting; (*pas*) quick, brisk; (*impression, imagination, style*) vivid; (*parole*) sharp; (*regret, satisfaction, succès etc*) great; (*coléreux*) quick-tempered; **brûler/ enterrer qn v.** to burn/bury s.o. alive; **— nm le v. du sujet** the heart of the matter; **à v.** (*plaie*) open; **piqué au v.** (*vexé*) cut to the quick.

vigie [viʒi] *nf* (*matelot*) lookout; (*poste*) lookout post.

vigilant [viʒilɑ̃] *a* vigilant. ◆**vigilance** *nf* vigilance.

vigile [viʒil] *nm* (*gardien*) watchman; (*de nuit*) night watchman.

vigne [viɲ] *nf* (*plante*) vine; (*plantation*) vineyard. ◆**vigneron, -onne** *nmf* wine grower. ◆**vignoble** *nm* vineyard; (*région*) vineyards.

vignette [viɲɛt] *nf Aut* road tax sticker; (*de médicament*) price label (*for reimbursement by Social Security*).

vigueur [vigœr] *nf* vigour; **entrer/être en v.** (*loi*) to come into/be in force. ◆**vigoureux, -euse** *a* (*personne, style etc*) vigorous; (*bras*) sturdy.

vilain *a* (*laid*) ugly; (*mauvais*) nasty; (*enfant*) naughty.

villa [villa] *nf* (detached) house.

village [vilaʒ] *nm* village. ◆**villageois, -oise** *a* village-; — *nmf* villager.

ville [vil] *nf* town; (*grande*) city; **aller/être en v.** to go into/be in town; **v. d'eaux** spa (town).

villégiature [vileʒjatyr] *nf* **lieu de v.** (holiday) resort.

vin [vɛ̃] *nm* wine; **v. ordinaire** *ou* **table wine**; **v. d'honneur** reception (*in honour of s.o.*). ◆**vinicole** *a* (*région*) wine-growing; (*industrie*) wine-.

vinaigre [vinɛgr] *nm* vinegar. ◆**vinaigré** *a* seasoned with vinegar. ◆**vinaigrette** *nf* (*sauce*) vinaigrette, French dressing, *Am* Italian dressing.

vindicatif, -ive [vɛ̃dikatif, -iv] *a* vindictive.

vingt [vɛ̃] ([vɛ̃t] *before vowel or mute h and in numbers 22–29*) *a & nm* twenty; **v. et un** twenty-one. ◆**vingtaine** *nf* **une v. (de)** (*nombre*) about twenty; **avoir la v.** (*âge*) to be about twenty. ◆**vingtième** *a & nmf* twentieth.

vinyle [vinil] *nm* vinyl.

viol [vjɔl] *nm* rape; (*de loi, lieu*) violation. ◆**violation** *nf* violation. ◆**violenter** *vt* to rape. ◆**violer** *vt* (*femme*) to rape; (*loi, lieu*) to violate. ◆**violeur** *nm* rapist.

violent [vjɔlɑ̃] *a* violent; (*remède*) drastic. ◆**violemment**[-amɑ̃] *adv* violently. ◆**violence** *nf* violence; (*acte*) act of violence.

violet, -ette [vjɔlɛ, -ɛt] **1** *a & nm* (*couleur*) purple, violet. **2** *nf* (*fleur*) violet. ◆**violacé** *a* purplish.

violon [vjɔlɔ̃] *nm* violin. ◆**violoncelle** *nm* cello. ◆**violoncelliste** *nmf* cellist. ◆**violoniste** *nmf* violinist.

vipère [vipɛr] *nf* viper, adder.

virage [viraʒ] *nm* (*de route*) bend; (*de véhicule*) turn; (*revirement*) *Fig* change of course. **◆vir/er 1** *vi* to turn, veer; (*sur soi*) to turn round; **v. au bleu**/*etc* to turn blue/*etc.* **2** *vt* (*expulser*) *Fam* to throw out. **3** *vt* (*somme*) *Fin* to transfer (**à** to). **◆—ement** *nm Fin* (*bank ou credit*) transfer.

virée [vire] *nf Fam* trip, outing.

virevolter [virvɔlte] *vi* to spin round.

virginité [virʒinite] *nf* virginity.

virgule [virgyl] *nf Gram* comma; *Math* (decimal) point; **2 v. 5** 2 point 5.

viril [viril] *a* virile, manly; (*attribut, force*) male. **◆virilité** *nf* virility, manliness.

virtuel, -elle [virtɥɛl] *a* potential.

virtuose [virtɥoz] *nmf* virtuoso. **◆virtuosité** *nf* virtuosity.

virulent [virylɑ̃] *a* virulent. **◆virulence** *nf* virulence.

virus [virys] *nm* virus.

vis¹ [vi] *voir* **vivre, voir.**

vis² [vis] *nf* screw.

visa [viza] *nm* (*timbre*) stamp, stamped signature; (*de passeport*) visa; **v. de censure** (*d'un film*) certificate.

visage [vizaʒ] *nm* face.

vis-à-vis [vizavi] *prép* **v.-à-vis de** opposite; (*à l'égard de*) with respect to; (*envers*) towards; (*comparé à*) compared to; **–** *nm* (*personne*) person opposite; (*bois, maison etc*) opposite view.

viscères [viser] *nmpl* intestines. **◆viscéral, -aux** *a* (*haine etc*) *Fig* deeply felt.

viscosité [viskozite] *nf* viscosity.

viser [vize] **1** *vi* to aim (**à** at); **v. à faire** to do; **–** *vt* (*cible*) to aim at; (*concerner*) to be aimed at. **2** *vt* (*passeport, document*) to stamp. **◆visées** *nfpl* (*desseins*) *Fig* aims; **avoir des visées sur** to have designs on. **◆viseur** *nm Phot* viewfinder; (*d'arme*) sight.

visible [vizibl] *a* visible. **◆visiblement** *adv* visibly. **◆visibilité** *nf* visibility.

visière [vizjer] *nf* (*de casquette*) peak; (*en plastique etc*) eyeshade; (*de casque*) visor.

vision [vizjɔ̃] *nf* (*conception, image*) vision; (*sens*) (eye)sight, vision; **avoir des visions** *Fam* to be seeing things. **◆visionnaire** *a* & *nmf* visionary. **◆visionner** *vt Cin* to view. **◆visionneuse** *nf* (*pour diapositives*) viewer.

visite [vizit] *nf* visit; (*personne*) visitor; (*examen*) inspection; **rendre v. à, faire une v. à** to visit; **v.** (**à domicile**) *Méd* call, visit; **v.** (**médicale**) medical examination; **v. guidée** guided tour; **de v.** (*carte, heures*) visiting-. **◆visiter** *vt* to visit; (*examiner*) to inspect. **◆visiteur, -euse** *nmf* visitor.

vison [vizɔ̃] *nm* mink.

visqueux, -euse [viskø, -øz] *a* viscous; (*surface*) sticky; (*répugnant*) *Fig* slimy.

visser [vise] *vt* to screw on.

visuel, -elle [vizɥɛl] *a* visual.

vit [vi] *voir* **vivre, voir.**

vital, -aux [vital, -o] *a* vital. **◆vitalité** *nf* vitality.

vitamine [vitamin] *nf* vitamin. **◆vitaminé** *a* (*biscuits etc*) vitamin-enriched.

vite [vit] *adv* quickly, fast; (*tôt*) soon; **v.!** quick(ly)! **◆vitesse** *nf* speed; (*régime*) *Aut* gear; **boîte de vitesses** gearbox; **à toute v.** at top *ou* full speed; **v. de pointe** top speed; **en v.** quickly.

viticole [vitikɔl] *a* (*région*) wine-growing; (*industrie*) wine-. **◆viticulteur** *nm* wine grower. **◆viticulture** *nf* wine growing.

vitre [vitr] *nf* (*de véhicule*) window. **◆vitrage** *nm* (*vitres*) windows. **◆vitrail, -aux** *nm* stained-glass window. **◆vitré** *a* glass-, glazed. **◆vitreux, -euse** *a* (*regard, yeux*) *Fig* glassy. **◆vitrier** *nm* glazier.

vitrine [vitrin] *nf* (*de magasin*) (shop) window; (*meuble*) showcase, display cabinet.

vitriol [vitrijɔl] *nm Ch* & *Fig* vitriol.

vivable [vivabl] *a* (*personne*) easy to live with; (*endroit*) fit to live in.

vivace [vivas] *a* (*plante*) perennial; (*haine*) *Fig* inveterate.

vivacité [vivasite] *nf* liveliness; (*de l'air, d'émotion*) keenness; (*agilité*) quickness; (*de couleur, d'impression, de style*) vividness; (*emportement*) petulance; **v. d'esprit** quick-wittedness.

vivant [vivɑ̃] *a* (*en vie*) alive, living; (*être, matière, preuve*) living; (*conversation, enfant, récit, rue*) lively; **langue vivante** modern language; **–** *nm* **de son v.** in one's lifetime; **bon v.** jovial fellow; **les vivants** the living.

vivats [viva] *nmpl* cheers.

vive¹ [viv] *voir* **vif.**

vive² [viv] *int* **v. le roi**/*etc!* long live the king/*etc!*; **v. les vacances!** hurray for the holidays!

vivement [vivmɑ̃] *adv* quickly, briskly; (*répliquer*) sharply; (*sentir*) keenly; (*regretter*) deeply; **v. demain!** roll on tomorrow!, I can hardly wait for tomorrow!; **v. que** (**+ sub**) I'll be glad when.

vivier [vivje] *nm* fish pond.

vivifier [vivifje] *vt* to invigorate.

vivisection [vivisɛksjɔ̃] *nf* vivisection.

vivre* [vivr] **1** *vi* to live; **elle vit encore** she's still alive *ou* living; **faire v.** (*famille etc*) to support; **v. vieux** to live to be old; **difficile/facile à v.** hard/easy to get on with; **manière de v.** way of life; **v. de** (*fruits etc*) to live on; (*travail etc*) to live by; **avoir de quoi v.** to have enough to live on; **vivent les vacances!** hurray for the holidays!; — *vt* (*vie*) to live; (*aventure, époque*) to live through; (*éprouver*) to experience. **2** *nmpl* food, supplies. ◆**vivoter** *vi* to jog along, get by.

vlan! [vlɑ̃] *int* bang!, wham!

vocable [vɔkabl] *nm* term, word.

vocabulaire [vɔkabylɛr] *nm* vocabulary.

vocal, -aux [vɔkal, -o] *a* (*cordes, musique*) vocal.

vocation [vɔkasjɔ̃] *nf* vocation, calling.

vociférer [vɔsifere] *vti* to shout angrily. ◆**vocifération** *nf* angry shout.

vodka [vɔdka] *nf* vodka.

vœu, -x [vø] *nm* (*souhait*) wish; (*promesse*) vow; **faire le v. de faire** to (make a) vow to do; **tous mes vœux!** (my) best wishes!

vogue [vɔg] *nf* fashion, vogue; **en v.** in fashion, in vogue.

voici [vwasi] *prép* here is, this is; *pl* here are, these are; **me v.** here I am; **le v.** here he is! sad now; **v. dix ans** *etc* ten years *etc* ago; **v. dix ans que** it's ten years since.

voie [vwa] *nf* (*route*) road; (*rails*) track, line; (*partie de route*) lane; (*chemin*) way; (*moyen*) means, way; (*de communication*) line; (*diplomatique*) channels; (*quai*) Rail platform; **en v. de** in the process of; **en v. de développement** (*pays*) developing; **v. publique** public highway; **v. navigable** waterway; **v. sans issue** cul-de-sac, dead end; **préparer la v.** Fig to pave the way; **sur la (bonne) v.** on the right track.

voilà [vwala] *prép* there is, that is; *pl* there are, those are; **les v.** there they are; **v., j'arrive!** all right, I'm coming!; **le v. parti** he has left now; **v. dix ans** *etc* ten years *etc* ago; **v. dix ans que** it's ten years since.

voile[1] [vwal] *nm* (*étoffe qui cache, coiffure etc*) & Fig veil; (*tissu fin*) net curtain. ◆**voil/er**[1] *vt* (*visage, vérité etc*) to veil; — **se v.** *vpr* (*personne*) to wear a veil; (*ciel, regard*) to cloud over. ◆**—é** *a* (*femme, allusion*) veiled; (*terne*) dull; (*photo*) hazy.

voile[2] [vwal] *nf* (*de bateau*) sail; (*activité*) sailing; **bateau à voiles** sailing boat, *Am* sailboat; **faire de la v.** to sail, go sailing. ◆**voilier** *nm* sailing ship; (*de plaisance*) sailing boat, *Am* sailboat. ◆**voilure** *nf* Nau sails.

voiler[2] [vwale] *vt*, — **se v.** *vpr* (*roue*) to buckle.

voir* [vwar] *vti* to see; **faire ou laisser v. qch**

to show sth; **fais v.** let me see, show me; **v. qn faire** to see s.o. do or doing; **voyons!** (*sois raisonnable*) come on!; **y v. clair** (*comprendre*) to see clearly; **je ne peux pas la v.** (*supporter*) Fam I can't stand (the sight of) her; **v. venir** (*attendre*) to wait and see; **on verra bien** (*attendons*) we'll see; **ça n'a rien à v. avec** that's got nothing to do with; — **se v.** *vpr* to see oneself; (*se fréquenter*) to see each other; (*objet, attitude etc*) to be seen; (*reprise, tache*) to show; **ça se voit** that's obvious.

voire [vwar] *adv* indeed.

voirie [vwari] *nf* (*enlèvement des ordures*) refuse collection; (*routes*) public highways.

voisin, -ine [vwazɛ̃, -in] *a* (*pays, village etc*) neighbouring; (*maison, pièce*) next (**de** to); (*idée, état etc*) similar (**de** to); — *nmf* neighbour. ◆**voisinage** *nm* (*quartier, voisins*) neighbourhood; (*proximité*) proximity. ◆**voisiner** *vi* **v. avec** to be side by side with.

voiture [vwatyr] *nf* Aut car; Rail carriage, coach, *Am* car; (*charrette*) cart; **v. (à cheval)** (horse-drawn) carriage; **v. de course/ de tourisme** racing/private car; **v. d'enfant** pram, *Am* baby carriage; **en v.!** Rail all aboard!

voix [vwa] *nf* voice; (*suffrage*) vote; **à v. basse** in a whisper; **à portée de v.** within earshot; **avoir v. au chapitre** Fig to have a say.

vol [vɔl] *nm* **1** (*d'avion, d'oiseau*) flight; (*groupe d'oiseaux*) flock, flight; **v. libre** hang gliding; **v. à voile** gliding. **2** (*délit*) theft; (*hold-up*) robbery; **v. à l'étalage** shoplifting; **c'est du v.!** (*trop cher*) it's daylight robbery!

volage [vɔlaʒ] *a* flighty, fickle.

volaille [vɔlaj] *nf* **la v.** (*oiseaux*) poultry; **une v.** (*oiseau*) a fowl. ◆**volailler** *nm* poulterer.

volatile [vɔlatil] *nm* (*oiseau domestique*) fowl.

volatiliser (se) [səvɔlatilize] *vpr* (*disparaître*) to vanish (into thin air).

vol-au-vent [vɔlovɑ̃] *nm inv* Culin vol-au-vent.

volcan [vɔlkɑ̃] *nm* volcano. ◆**volcanique** *a* volcanic.

voler [vɔle] **1** *vi* (*oiseau, avion etc*) to fly; (*courir*) Fig to rush. **2** *vt* (*dérober*) to steal (**à** from); **v. qn** to rob s.o.; — *vi* to steal. ◆**volant 1** *a* (*tapis etc*) flying; **feuille volante** loose sheet. **2** *nm* Aut (steering) wheel; (*objet*) shuttlecock; (*de jupe*) flounce. ◆**volée** *nf* flight; (*groupe d'oiseaux*) flock, flight; (*de coups, flèches etc*) volley; (*suite de* coups) thrashing; **lancer à toute v.** to throw as hard as one can; **sonner à toute v.** to peal ou ring out. ◆**voleter** vi to flutter. ◆**voleur, -euse** nmf thief; **au v.!** stop thief! ; – a thieving.

volet [vɔlɛ] nm **1** (de fenêtre) shutter. **2** (de programme, reportage etc) section, part. **volière** [vɔljɛr] nf aviary.

volley(-ball) [vɔlɛ(bol)] nm volleyball. ◆**volleyeur, -euse** nmf volleyball player.

volonté [vɔlɔ̃te] nf (faculté, intention) will; (désir) wish; Phil Psy free will; **elle a de la v.** she has willpower; **bonne v.** goodwill; **mauvaise v.** ill will; **à v.** at will; (quantité) as much as desired. ◆**volontaire** a (délibéré, qui agit librement) voluntary; (opiniâtre) wilful, Am willful; – nmf volunteer. ◆**volontairement** adv voluntarily; (exprès) deliberately. ◆**volontiers** [-tje] adv willingly, gladly; (habituellement) readily; **v.!** (oui) I'd love to!

volt [vɔlt] nm El volt. ◆**voltage** nm voltage. **volte-face** [vɔltafas] nf inv about turn, Am about-face; **faire v.-face** to turn round.

voltige [vɔltiʒ] nf acrobatics. **voltiger** [vɔltiʒe] vi to flutter.

volubile [vɔlybil] a (bavard) loquacious, voluble.

volume [vɔlym] nm (capacité, intensité, tome) volume. ◆**volumineux, -euse** a bulky, voluminous.

volupté [vɔlypte] nf sensual pleasure. ◆**voluptueux, -euse** a voluptuous.

vom/ir [vɔmir] vt to vomit, bring up; (exécrer) Fig to loathe; – vi to vomit, be sick. ◆**—i** nm Fam vomit. ◆**—issement** nm (action) vomiting. ◆**vomitif, -ive** a Fam nauseating.

vont [vɔ̃] voir **aller 1.**

vorace [vɔras] a (appétit, lecteur etc) voracious.

vos [vo] voir **votre.**

vote [vɔt] nm (action) vote, voting; (suffrage) vote; (de loi) passing; **bureau de v.** polling station. ◆**voter** vi to vote; – vt (loi) to pass; (crédits) to vote. ◆**votant, -ante** nmf voter.

votre, pl vos [vɔtr, vo] a poss your. ◆**vôtre** pron poss **le** ou **la v., les vôtres** yours; **à la v.!** (toast) cheers!; – nmpl **les vôtres** (parents etc) your (own) people.

vouer [vwe] vt (promettre) to vow (à to); (consacrer) to dedicate (à to); (condamner) to doom (à to); **se v. à** to dedicate oneself to.

vouloir* [vulwar] vt to want (**faire** to do); **je veux qu'il parte** I want him to go; **v. dire** to

mean (**que** that); **je voudrais rester** I'd like to stay; **je voudrais un pain** I'd like a loaf of bread; **voulez-vous me suivre** will you follow me; **si tu veux** if you like ou wish; **en v. à qn d'avoir fait qch** to hold it against s.o. for doing sth; **l'usage veut que . . .** (+ sub) custom requires that . . . ; **v. du bien à qn** to wish s.o. well; **je veux bien** I don't mind (**faire** doing); **que voulez-vous!** (résignation) what can you expect!; **sans le v.** unintentionally; **ça ne veut pas bouger** it won't move; **ne pas v. de qch/de qn** not to want sth/s.o.; **veuillez attendre** kindly wait. ◆**voulu** a (requis) required; (délibéré) deliberate, intentional.

vous [vu] pron **1** (sujet, complément direct) you; **v. êtes** you are; **il v. connaît** he knows you. **2** (complément indirect) (to) you; **il v. l'a donné** he gave it to you, he gave you it. **3** (réfléchi) yourself, pl yourselves; **v. v. lavez** you wash yourself; you wash yourselves. **4** (réciproque) each other; **v. v. aimez** you love each other. ◆**v.-même** pron yourself. ◆**v.-mêmes** pron pl yourselves.

voûte [vut] nf (plafond) vault; (porche) arch(way). ◆**voûté** (à personne) bent, stooped.

vouvoyer [vuvwaje] vt to address formally (using vous).

voyage [vwajaʒ] nm trip, journey; (par mer) voyage; **aimer les voyages** to like travelling; **faire un v., partir en v.** to go on a trip; **être en v.** to be (away) travelling; **de v.** (compagnon etc) travelling-; **bon v.!** have a pleasant trip!; **v. de noces** honeymoon; **v. organisé** (package) tour. ◆**voyager** vi to travel. ◆**voyageur, -euse** nmf traveller; (passager) passenger; **v. de commerce** commercial traveller. ◆**voyagiste** nm tour operator.

voyant [vwajɑ̃] **1** a gaudy, loud. **2** nm (signal) (warning) light; (d'appareil électrique) pilot light.

voyante [vwajɑ̃t] nf clairvoyant.

voyelle [vwajɛl] nf vowel.

voyeur, -euse [vwajœr, -øz] nmf peeping Tom, voyeur.

voyou [vwaju] nm hooligan, hoodlum.

vrac (en) [ɑ̃vrak] adv (en désordre) haphazardly; (au poids) loose, unpackaged.

vrai [vrɛ] a true; (réel) real; (authentique) genuine; – adv **dire v.** to be right (in what one says); – nm (vérité) truth. ◆**—ment** adv really.

vraisemblable [vrɛsɑ̃blabl] a (probable) likely, probable; (plausible) plausible. ◆**vraisemblablement** adv probably.

◆**vraisemblance** *nf* likelihood; plausibility.

vrille [vrij] *nf* **1** (*outil*) gimlet. **2** *Av* (tail)spin.

vromb/ir [vrɔ̃bir] *vi* to hum. ◆**—issement** *nm* hum(ming).

vu [vy] **1** *voir* **voir**; – **a bien vu** well thought of; **mal vu** frowned upon. **2** *prép* in view of; **vu que** seeing that.

vue [vy] *nf* (*spectacle*) sight; (*sens*) (eye)sight; (*panorama, photo, idée*) view; **en v.** (*proche*) in sight; (*en évidence*) on view; (*personne*) *Fig* in the public eye; **avoir en v.** to have in mind; **à v.** (*tirer*) on sight; (*payable*) at sight; **à première v.** at first sight; **de v.** (*connaître*) by sight; **en v. de faire** with a view to doing.

vulgaire [vylgɛr] *a* (*grossier*) vulgar, coarse; (*ordinaire*) common. ◆**—ment** *adv* vulgarly, coarsely; (*appeler*) commonly. ◆**vulgariser** *vt* to popularize. ◆**vulgarité** *nf* vulgarity, coarseness.

vulnérable [vylnerabl] *a* vulnerable. ◆**vulnérabilité** *nf* vulnerability.

W

W, w [dubləve] *nm* W, w.

wagon [vagɔ̃] *nm* Rail (*de voyageurs*) carriage, coach, *Am* car; (*de marchandises*) wag(g)on, truck, *Am* freight car. ◆**w.-lit** *nm* (*pl* **wagons-lits**) sleeping car, sleeper. ◆**w.-restaurant** *nm* (*pl* **wagons-restaurants**) dining car, diner. ◆**wagonnet** *nm* (small) wagon *ou* truck.

wallon, -onne [walɔ̃, -ɔn] *a* & *nmf* Walloon.

waters [water] *nmpl* toilet.

watt [wat] *nm* *Él* watt.

w-c [(dublə)vese] *nmpl* toilet.

week-end [wikɛnd] *nm* weekend.

western [wɛstɛrn] *nm* Cin western.

whisky, *pl* -ies [wiski] *nm* whisky, *Am* whiskey.

X

X, x [iks] *nm* X, x; **rayon X** X-ray.

xénophobe [ksenɔfɔb] *a* xenophobic; – *nmf* xenophobe. ◆**xénophobie** *nf* xeno-phobia.

xérès [gzeres] *nm* sherry.

xylophone [ksilɔfɔn] *nm* xylophone.

Y

Y, y¹ [igrɛk] *nm* Y, y.

y² [i] **1** *adv* there; (*dedans*) in it; *pl* in them; (*dessus*) on it; *pl* on them; **elle y vivra** she'll live there; **j'y entrai** I entered (it); **allons-y** let's go; **j'y suis!** (*je comprends*) now I get it!; **je n'y suis pour rien** I have nothing to do with me, that's nothing to do with me. **2** *pron* (= *à cela*) **j'y pense** I think of it; **je m'y attendais** I was expecting it; **ça y est!** that's it!

yacht [jɔt] *nm* yacht.

yaourt [jaur(t)] *nm* yog(h)urt.

yeux [jø] *voir* **œil**.

yiddish [(j)idiʃ] *nm* & *a* Yiddish.

yoga [jɔga] *nm* yoga.

yog(h)ourt [jɔgur(t)] *nm* *voir* **yaourt**.

Yougoslavie [jugɔslavi] *nf* Yugoslavia. ◆**yougoslave** *a* & *nmf* Yugoslav(ian).

yo-yo [jɔjo] *nm inv* yoyo.

Z

Z, z [zɛd] *nm* Z, z.
zèbre [zɛbr] *nm* zebra. ◆**zébré** *a* striped, streaked (**de** with).
zèle [zɛl] *nm* zeal; **faire du z.** to overdo it. ◆**zélé** *a* zealous.
zénith [zenit] *nm* zenith.
zéro [zero] *nm* (*chiffre*) nought, zero; (*dans un numéro*) 0 [əu]; (*température*) zero; (*rien*) nothing; (*personne*) *Fig* nobody, nonentity; **deux buts à z.** *Fb* two nil, *Am* two zero; **partir de z.** to start from scratch.
zeste [zɛst] *nm* **un z. de citron** (a piece of) lemon peel.
zézayer [zezeje] *vi* to lisp.
zibeline [ziblin] *nf* (*animal*) sable.

zigzag [zigzag] *nm* zigzag; **en z.** (*route etc*) zigzag(ging); ◆**zigzaguer** *vi* to zigzag.
zinc [zɛ̃g] *nm* (*métal*) zinc; (*comptoir*) *Fam* bar.
zizanie [zizani] *nf* discord.
zodiaque [zɔdjak] *nm* zodiac.
zona [zona] *nm* *Méd* shingles.
zone [zon] *nf* zone, area; (*domaine*) *Fig* sphere; (*faubourgs misérables*) shanty town; **z. bleue** restricted parking zone; **z. industrielle** trading estate, *Am* industrial park.
zoo [zo(o)] *nm* zoo. ◆**zoologie** [zɔɔlɔʒi] *nf* zoology. ◆**zoologique** *a* zoological; **jardin** *ou* **parc z.** zoo.
zoom [zum] *nm* (*objectif*) zoom lens.
zut! [zyt] *int* *Fam* bother!, heck!

French verb conjugations

REGULAR VERBS

	-ER Verbs	-IR Verbs	-RE Verbs
Infinitive	donn/er	fin/ir	vend/re
1 Present	je donne	je finis	je vends
	tu donnes	tu finis	tu vends
	il donne	il finit	il vend
	nous donnons	nous finissons	nous vendons
	vous donnez	vous finissez	vous vendez
	ils donnent	ils finissent	ils vendent
2 Imperfect	je donnais	je finissais	je vendais
	tu donnais	tu finissais	tu vendais
	il donnait	il finissait	il vendait
	nous donnions	nous finissions	nous vendions
	vous donniez	vous finissiez	vous vendiez
	ils donnaient	ils finissaient	ils vendaient
3 Past historic	je donnai	je finis	je vendis
	tu donnas	tu finis	tu vendis
	il donna	il finit	il vendit
	nous donnâmes	nous finîmes	nous vendîmes
	vous donnâtes	vous finîtes	vous vendîtes
	ils donnèrent	ils finirent	ils vendirent
4 Future	je donnerai	je finirai	je vendrai
	tu donneras	tu finiras	tu vendras
	il donnera	il finira	il vendra
	nous donnerons	nous finirons	nous vendrons
	vous donnerez	vous finirez	vous vendrez
	ils donneront	ils finiront	ils vendront
5 Subjunctive	je donne	je finisse	je vende
	tu donnes	tu finisses	tu vendes
	il donne	il finisse	il vende
	nous donnions	nous finissions	nous vendions
	vous donniez	vous finissiez	vous vendiez
	ils donnent	ils finissent	ils vendent
6 Imperative	donne	finis	vends
	donnons	finissons	vendons
	donnez	finissez	vendez
7 Present participle	donnant	finissant	vendant
8 Past participle	donné	fini	vendu

SPELLING ANOMALIES OF -ER VERBS

Verbs in **-ger** (e.g. **manger**) take an extra e before endings beginning with **o** or **a**: *Present* je mange, nous mangeons; *Imperfect* je mangeais, nous mangions; *Past historic* je mangeai, nous mangeâmes; *Present participle* mangeant. Verbs in **-cer** (e.g. **commencer**) change **c** to **ç** before endings beginning with **o** or **a**: *Present* je commence, nous commençons; *Imperfect* je commençais, nous commencions; *Past historic* je commençai, nous commençâmes; *Present participle* commençant. Verbs containing mute **e** in their penultimate syllable fall into two groups. In the first (e.g. **mener**, **peser**, **lever**), e becomes è before an unpronounced syllable in the present and subjunctive, and in the future and conditional tenses (e.g. je mène, ils mèneront). The second group contains most verbs ending in **-eler** and **-eter** (e.g. **appeler**, **jeter**). These verbs change l to ll and t to tt before an unpronounced syllable (e.g. j'appelle, ils appelleront; je jette, ils jetteront). However, the following verbs in **-eler** and **-eter** fall into the first group in which e changes to è before mute e (e.g. je modèle, ils modèleront; j'achète, ils achèteront): **celer**, **ciseler**, **démanteler**, **geler**, **marteler**, **modeler**, **peler**; **acheter**, **crocheter**, **fureter**, **haleter**. Derived verbs (e.g. **dégeler**, **racheter**) are conjugated in the same way. Verbs containing e acute in their penultimate syllable change é to è before the unpronounced endings of the present and subjunctive only (e.g. je cède but je céderai). Verbs in **-yer** (e.g. **essuyer**) change y to i before an unpronounced syllable in the present and subjunctive, and in the future and conditional tenses (e.g. j'essuie, ils essuieront). In verbs in **-ayer** (e.g. **balayer**), y may be retained before mute e (e.g. je balaie or balaye, ils balaieront or balayeront).

IRREGULAR VERBS

Listed below are those verbs considered to be the most useful. Forms and tenses not given are fully derivable. Note that the endings of the past historic fall into three categories, the 'a' and 'i' categories shown at *donner*, and at *finir* and *vendre*, and the 'u' category which has the following endings: -us, -ut, -ûmes, -ûtes, -urent. Most of the verbs listed below form their past historic with 'u'. The imperfect may usually be formed by adding -ais, -ait, -ions, -iez, -aient to the stem of the first person plural of the present tense, e.g. 'je buvais' etc may be derived from 'nous buvons' (stem 'buv-' and ending '-ons'); similarly, the present participle may generally be formed by substituting -ant for -ons (e.g. buvant). The future may usually be formed by adding -ai, -as, -a, -ons, -ez, -ont to the infinitive or to an infinitive without final 'e' where the ending is -re (e.g. conduire). The imperative usually has the same forms as the second persons singular and plural and first person plural of the present tense.

1 = Present   2 = Imperfect   3 = Past historic   4 = Future
5 = Subjunctive   6 = Imperative   7 = Present participle
8 = Past participle   n = nous   v = vous   †verbs conjugated with **être** only.

abattre	*like* **battre**
absoudre	1 j'absous, n absolvons 2 j'absolvais
	3 j'absolus *(rarely used)* 5 j'absolve 7 absolvant
	8 absous, absoute
†s'abstenir	*like* **tenir**
abstraire	1 j'abstrais, n abstrayons 2 j'abstrayais 3 *none* 5 j'abstraie
	7 abstrayant 8 abstrait
accourir	*like* **courir**
accroître	*like* **croître** *except* 8 accru
accueillir	*like* **cueillir**
acquérir	1 j'acquiers, n acquérons 2 j'acquérais 3 j'acquis
	4 j'acquerrai 5 j'acquière 7 acquérant 8 acquis
adjoindre	*like* **atteindre**
admettre	*like* **mettre**
†aller	1 je vais, tu vas, il va, n allons, v allez, ils vont 4 j'irai
	5 j'aille, nous allions, ils aillent 6 va, allons, allez *(but note* vas-y*)*
apercevoir	*like* **recevoir**
apparaître	*like* **connaître**
appartenir	*like* **tenir**
apprendre	*like* **prendre**
asseoir	1 j'assieds, n asseyons, ils asseyent 2 j'asseyais 3 j'assis
	4 j'assiérai 5 j'asseye 7 asseyant 8 assis

astreindre	*like* **atteindre**
atteindre	1 j'atteins, n atteignons, ils atteignent 2 j'atteignais
	3 j'atteignis 4 j'atteindrai 5 j'atteigne 7 atteignant
	8 atteint
avoir	1 j'ai, tu as, il a, n avons, v avez, ils ont 2 j'avais 3 j'eus
	4 j'aurai 5 j'aie, il ait, n ayons, ils aient 6 aie, ayons, ayez
	7 ayant 8 eu
battre	1 je bats, n battons 5 je batte
boire	1 je bois, n buvons, ils boivent 2 je buvais 3 je bus
	5 je boive, n buvons 7 buvant 8 bu
bouillir	1 je bous, n bouillons, ils bouillent 2 je bouillais
	3 *not used* 5 je bouille 7 bouillant
braire	(*defective*) 1 il brait, ils braient 4 il braira, ils brairont
combattre	*like* **battre**
commettre	*like* **mettre**
comparaître	*like* **connaître**
comprendre	*like* **prendre**
compromettre	*like* **mettre**
concevoir	*like* **recevoir**
conclure	1 je conclus, n concluons, ils concluent 5 je conclue
concourir	*like* **courir**
conduire	1 je conduis, n conduisons 3 je conduisis 5 je conduise
	8 conduit
connaître	1 je connais, il connaît, n connaissons 3 je connus
	5 je connaisse 7 connaissant 8 connu
conquérir	*like* **acquérir**
consentir	*like* **mentir**
construire	*like* **conduire**
contenir	*like* **tenir**
contraindre	*like* **atteindre**
contredire	*like* **dire** *except* 1 v contredisez
convaincre	*like* **vaincre**
convenir	*like* **tenir**
corrompre	*like* **rompre**
coudre	1 je couds, n cousons, ils cousent 3 je cousis 5 je couse
	7 cousant 8 cousu
courir	1 je cours, n courons 3 je courus 4 je courrai 5 je coure
	8 couru
couvrir	1 je couvre, n couvrons 2 je couvrais 5 je couvre 8 couvert
craindre	*like* **atteindre**
croire	1 je crois, n croyons, ils croient 2 je croyais 3 je crus
	5 je croie, n croyions 7 croyant 8 cru
croître	1 je crois, il croît, n croissons 2 je croissais 3 je crûs
	5 je croisse 7 croissant 8 crû, crue
cueillir	1 je cueille, n cueillons 2 je cueillais 4 je cueillerai
	5 je cueille 7 cueillant
cuire	1 je cuis, n cuisons 2 je cuisais 3 je cuisis 5 je cuise
	7 cuisant 8 cuit
débattre	*like* **battre**
décevoir	*like* **recevoir**
découvrir	*like* **couvrir**
décrire	*like* **écrire**
décroître	*like* **croître** *except* 8 décru
déduire	*like* **conduire**
défaillir	1 je défaille, n défaillons 2 je défaillais 3 je défaillis
	5 je défaille 7 défaillant 8 défailli

défaire	*like* **faire**
dépeindre	*like* **atteindre**
déplaire	*like* **plaire**
déteindre	*like* **atteindre**
détenir	*like* **tenir**
détruire	*like* **conduire**
†**devenir**	*like* **tenir**
devoir	1 je dois, n devons, ils doivent 2 je devais 3 je dus 4 je devrai 5 je doive, n devions 6 *not used* 7 devant 8 dû, due, *pl* dus, dues
dire	1 je dis, n disons, v dites 2 je disais 3 je dis 5 je dise 7 disant 8 dit
disparaître	*like* **connaître**
dissoudre	*like* **absoudre**
distraire	*like* **abstraire**
dormir	*like* **mentir**
†**échoir**	(*defective*) 1 il échoit 3 il échut, ils échurent 4 il échoira 7 échéant 8 échu
écrire	1 j'écris, n écrivons 2 j'écrivais 3 j'écrivis 5 j'écrive 7 écrivant 8 écrit
élire	*like* **lire**
émettre	*like* **mettre**
émouvoir	*like* **mouvoir** *except* 8 ému
encourir	*like* **courir**
endormir	*like* **mentir**
enduire	*like* **conduire**
enfreindre	*like* **atteindre**
†**s'enfuir**	*like* **fuir**
†**s'ensuivre**	*like* **suivre** (*but third person only*)
entreprendre	*like* **prendre**
entretenir	*like* **tenir**
entrevoir	*like* **voir**
entrouvrir	*like* **couvrir**
envoyer	4 j'enverrai
†**s'éprendre**	*like* **prendre**
éteindre	*like* **atteindre**
être	1 je suis, tu es, il est, n sommes, v êtes, ils sont 2 j'étais 3 je fus 4 je serai 5 je sois, n soyons, ils soient 6 sois, soyons, soyez 7 étant 8 été
exclure	*like* **conclure**
extraire	*like* **abstraire**
faillir	(*defective*) 3 je faillis 4 je faillirai 8 failli
faire	1 je fais, n faisons, v faites, ils font 2 je faisais 3 je fis 4 je ferai 5 je fasse 7 faisant 8 fait
falloir	(*impersonal*) 1 il faut 2 il fallait 3 il fallut 4 il faudra 5 il faille 6 *none* 7 *none* 8 fallu
feindre	*like* **atteindre**
foutre	1 je fous, n foutons 2 je foutais 3 *none* 5 je foute 7 foutant 8 foutu
frire	(*defective*) 1 je fris, tu fris, il frit 4 je frirai (*rare*) 6 fris (*rare*) 8 frit (*for other persons and tenses use* faire frire)
fuir	1 je fuis, n fuyons, ils fuient 2 je fuyais 3 je fuis 5 je fuie 7 fuyant 8 fui
haïr	1 je hais, il hait, n haïssons
inclure	*like* **conclure**
induire	*like* **conduire**
inscrire	*like* **écrire**

(iv)

instruire	*like* **conduire**
interdire	*like* **dire** *except* 1 v interdisez
interrompre	*like* **rompre**
intervenir	*like* **tenir**
introduire	*like* **conduire**
joindre	*like* **atteindre**
lire	1 je lis, n lisons 2 je lisais 3 je lus 5 je lise 7 lisant 8 lu
luire	*like* **nuire**
maintenir	*like* **tenir**
maudire	1 je maudis, n maudissons 2 je maudissais 3 je maudis 4 je maudirai 5 je maudisse 7 maudissant 8 maudit
méconnaître	*like* **connaître**
médire	*like* **dire** *except* 1 v médisez
mentir	1 je mens, n mentons 2 je mentais 5 je mente 7 mentant
mettre	1 je mets, n mettons 2 je mettais 3 je mis 5 je mette 7 mettant 8 mis
moudre	1 je mouds, n moulons 2 je moulais 3 je moulus 5 je moule 7 moulant 8 moulu
†mourir	1 je meurs, n mourons, ils meurent 2 je mourais 3 je mourus 4 je mourrai 5 je meure, n mourions 7 mourant 8 mort
mouvoir	1 je meus, n mouvons, ils meuvent 2 je mouvais 3 je mus (*rare*) 4 je mouvrai 5 je meuve, n mouvions 8 mû, mue, *pl* mus, mues
†naître	1 je nais, il naît, n naissons 2 je naissais 3 je naquis 4 je naîtrai 5 je naisse 7 naissant 8 né
nuire	1 je nuis, n nuisons 2 je nuisais 3 je nuisis 5 je nuise 7 nuisant 8 nui
obtenir	*like* **tenir**
offrir	*like* **couvrir**
omettre	*like* **mettre**
ouvrir	*like* **couvrir**
paître	(*defective*) 1 il paît 2 il paissait 3 *none* 4 il paîtra 5 il paisse 7 paissant 8 *none*
paraître	*like* **connaître**
parcourir	*like* **courir**
†partir	*like* **mentir**
†parvenir	*like* **tenir**
peindre	*like* **atteindre**
percevoir	*like* **recevoir**
permettre	*like* **mettre**
plaindre	*like* **atteindre**
plaire	1 je plais, n plaisons 2 je plaisais 3 je plus 5 je plaise 7 plaisant 8 plu
pleuvoir	(*impersonal*) 1 il pleut 2 il pleuvait 3 il plut 4 il pleuvra 5 il pleuve 6 *none* 7 pleuvant 8 plu
poursuivre	*like* **suivre**
pourvoir	*like* **voir** *except* 4 je pourvoirai
pouvoir	1 je peux *or* je puis, tu peux, il peut, n pouvons, ils peuvent 2 je pouvais 3 je pus 4 je pourrai 5 je puisse 6 *not used* 7 pouvant 8 pu
prédire	*like* **dire** *except* 1 v prédisez
prendre	1 je prends, n prenons, ils prennent 2 je prenais 3 je pris 5 je prenne 7 prenant 8 pris
prescrire	*like* **écrire**
pressentir	*like* **mentir**

prévenir	*like* tenir
prévoir	*like* voir *except* 4 je prévoirai
produire	*like* conduire
promettre	*like* mettre
promouvoir	*like* mouvoir *except* 8 promu
proscrire	*like* écrire
†provenir	*like* tenir
rabattre	*like* battre
rasseoir	*like* asseoir
recevoir	1 je reçois, n recevons, ils reçoivent 2 je recevais 3 je reçus
	4 je recevrai 5 je reçoive, n recevions, ils reçoivent 7 recevant
	8 reçu
reconnaître	*like* connaître
reconduire	*like* conduire
reconstruire	*like* conduire
recoudre	*like* coudre
recourir	*like* courir
recouvrir	*like* couvrir
recueillir	*like* cueillir
†redevenir	*like* tenir
redire	*like* dire
réduire	*like* conduire
refaire	*like* faire
rejoindre	*like* atteindre
relire	*like* lire
remettre	*like* mettre
†renaître	*like* naître
rendormir	*like* mentir
renvoyer	*like* envoyer
†repartir	*like* mentir
repentir	*like* mentir
reprendre	*like* prendre
reproduire	*like* conduire
résoudre	1 je résous, n résolvons 2 je résolvais 3 je résolus
	5 je résolve 7 résolvant 8 résolu
ressentir	*like* mentir
ressortir	*like* mentir
restreindre	*like* atteindre
retenir	*like* tenir
†revenir	*like* tenir
revêtir	*like* vêtir
revivre	*like* vivre
revoir	*like* voir
rire	1 je ris, n rions 2 je riais 3 je ris 5 je rie, n riions
	7 riant 8 ri
rompre	*regular except* 1 il rompt
rouvrir	*like* couvrir
satisfaire	*like* faire
savoir	1 je sais, n savons, ils savent 2 je savais 3 je sus 4 je saurai
	5 je sache 6 sache, sachons, sachez 7 sachant 8 su
séduire	*like* conduire
sentir	*like* mentir
servir	*like* mentir
sortir	*like* mentir
souffrir	*like* couvrir
soumettre	*like* mettre
sourire	*like* rire

souscrire	*like* **écrire**
soustraire	*like* **abstraire**
soutenir	*like* **tenir**
†**se souvenir**	*like* **tenir**
subvenir	*like* **tenir**
suffire	1 je suffis, n suffisons 2 je suffisais 3 je suffis 5 je suffise 7 suffisant 8 suffi
suivre	1 je suis, n suivons 2 je suivais 3 je suivis 5 je suive 7 suivant 8 suivi
surprendre	*like* **prendre**
†**survenir**	*like* **tenir**
survivre	*like* **vivre**
taire	1 je tais, n taisons 2 je taisais 3 je tus 5 je taise 7 taisant 8 tu
teindre	*like* **atteindre**
tenir	1 je tiens, n tenons, ils tiennent 2 je tenais 3 je tins, tu tins, il tint, n tînmes, v tîntes, ils tinrent 4 je tiendrai 5 je tienne 7 tenant 8 tenu
traduire	*like* **conduire**
traire	*like* **abstraire**
transcrire	*like* **écrire**
transmettre	*like* **mettre**
transparaître	*like* **connaître**
tressaillir	*like* **défaillir**
vaincre	1 je vaincs, il vainc, n vainquons 2 je vainquais 3 je vainquis 5 je vainque 7 vainquant 8 vaincu
valoir	1 je vaux, n valons 2 je valais 3 je valus 4 je vaudrai 5 je vaille 6 *not used* 7 valant 8 valu
†**venir**	*like* **tenir**
vêtir	1 je vêts, n vêtons 2 je vêtais 5 je vête 7 vêtant 8 vêtu
vivre	1 je vis, n vivons 2 je vivais 3 je vécus 5 je vive 7 vivant 8 vécu
voir	1 je vois, n voyons 2 je voyais 3 je vis 4 je verrai 5 je voie, n voyions 7 voyant 8 vu
vouloir	1 je veux, n voulons, ils veulent 2 je voulais 3 je voulus 4 je voudrai 5 je veuille 6 veuille, veuillons, veuillez 7 voulant 8 voulu.

Verbes anglais irréguliers

Infinitif	Prétérit	Participe passé
arise	arose	arisen
be	was, were	been
bear	bore	borne
beat	beat	beaten
become	became	become
begin	began	begun
bend	bent	bent
bet	bet, betted	bet, betted
bid	bade, bid	bidden, bid
bind	bound	bound
bite	bit	bitten
bleed	bled	bled
blow	blew	blown
break	broke	broken
breed	bred	bred

bring	brought	brought
broadcast	broadcast	broadcast
build	built	built
burn	burnt, burned	burnt, burned
burst	burst	burst
buy	bought	bought
cast	cast	cast
catch	caught	caught
choose	chose	chosen
cling	clung	clung
come	came	come
cost	cost	cost
creep	crept	crept
cut	cut	cut
deal	dealt	dealt
dig	dug	dug
dive	dived, *Am* dove	dived
do	did	done
draw	drew	drawn
dream	dreamed, dreamt	dreamed, dreamt
drink	drank	drunk
drive	drove	driven
dwell	dwelt	dwelt
eat	ate [et, *Am* eɪt]	eaten
fall	fell	fallen
feed	fed	fed
feel	felt	felt
fight	fought	fought
find	found	found
fling	flung	flung
fly	flew	flown
forbid	forbad(e)	forbidden
forecast	forecast	forecast
foresee	foresaw	foreseen
forget	forgot	forgotten
forgive	forgave	forgiven
forsake	forsook (*rare*)	forsaken
freeze	froze	frozen
get	got	got, *Am* gotten
give	gave	given
go	went	gone
grind	ground	ground
grow	grew	grown
hang	hung, hanged	hung, hanged
have	had	had
hear	heard	heard
hide	hid	hidden
hit	hit	hit
hold	held	held
hurt	hurt	hurt
keep	kept	kept
kneel	knelt, kneeled	knelt, kneeled
know	knew	known
lay	laid	laid
lead	led	led
lean	leant, leaned	leant, leaned
leap	leapt, leaped	leapt, leaped

(viii)

learn	learnt, learned	learnt, learned
leave	left	left
lend	lent	lent
let	let	let
lie	lay	lain
light	lit, lighted	lit, lighted
lose	lost	lost
make	made	made
mean	meant	meant
meet	met	met
mislay	mislaid	mislaid
mislead	misled	misled
misunderstand	misunderstood	misunderstood
mow	mowed	mown, mowed
overcome	overcame	overcome
pay	paid	paid
put	put	put
quit	quit, quitted	quit, quitted
read	read [red]	read [red]
rid	rid	rid
ride	rode	ridden
ring	rang	rung
rise	rose	risen
run	ran	run
saw	sawed	sawn, sawed
say	said	said
see	saw	seen
seek	sought	sought
sell	sold	sold
send	sent	sent
set	set	set
sew	sewed	sewn, sewed
shake	shook	shaken
shed	shed	shed
shine	shone ([ʃɒn, *Am* ʃəʊn])	shone ([ʃɒn, *Am* ʃəʊn])
shoot	shot	shot
show	showed	shown, showed
shrink	shrank	shrunk, shrunken
shut	shut	shut
sing	sang	sung
sink	sank	sunk
sit	sat	sat
sleep	slept	slept
slide	slid	slid
sling	slung	slung
slit	slit	slit
smell	smelt, smelled	smelt, smelled
sow	sowed	sown, sowed
speak	spoke	spoken
speed	sped, speeded	sped, speeded
spell	spelt, spelled	spelt, spelled
spend	spent	spent
spill	spilt, spilled	spilt, spilled
spin	spun	spun
spit	spat, spit	spat, spit
split	split	split
spoil	spoilt, spoiled	spoilt, spoiled

spread	spread	spread
spring	sprang	sprung
stand	stood	stood
steal	stole	stolen
stick	stuck	stuck
sting	stung	stung
stink	stank, stunk	stunk
stride	strode	stridden (*rare*)
strike	struck	struck
string	strung	strung
strive	strove	striven
swear	swore	sworn
sweep	swept	swept
swell	swelled	swollen, swelled
swim	swam	swum
swing	swung	swung
take	took	taken
teach	taught	taught
tear	tore	torn
tell	told	told
think	thought	thought
throw	threw	thrown
thrust	thrust	thrust
tread	trod	trodden
undergo	underwent	undergone
understand	understood	understood
undertake	undertook	undertaken
upset	upset	upset
wake	woke	woken
wear	wore	worn
weave	wove	woven
weep	wept	wept
win	won	won
wind	wound	wound
withdraw	withdrew	withdrawn
withhold	withheld	withheld
withstand	withstood	withstood
wring	wrung	wrung
write	wrote	written

Numerals

Les nombres

Cardinal numbers

Les nombres cardinaux

nought	0	zéro
one	1	un
two	2	deux
three	3	trois
four	4	quatre
five	5	cinq
six	6	six
seven	7	sept
eight	8	huit
nine	9	neuf
ten	10	dix

eleven	11	onze
twelve	12	douze
thirteen	13	treize
fourteen	14	quatorze
fifteen	15	quinze
sixteen	16	seize
seventeen	17	dix-sept
eighteen	18	dix-huit
nineteen	19	dix-neuf
twenty	20	vingt
twenty-one	21	vingt et un
twenty-two	22	vingt-deux
thirty	30	trente
forty	40	quarante
fifty	50	cinquante
sixty	60	soixante
seventy	70	soixante-dix
seventy-five	75	soixante-quinze
eighty	80	quatre-vingts
eighty-one	81	quatre-vingt-un
ninety	90	quatre-vingt-dix
ninety-one	91	quatre-vingt-onze
a *or* one hundred	100	cent
a hundred and one	101	cent un
a hundred and two	102	cent deux
a hundred and fifty	150	cent cinquante
two hundred	200	deux cents
two hundred and one	201	deux cent un
two hundred and two	202	deux cent deux
a *or* one thousand	1,000 (1 000)	mille
a thousand and one	1,001 (1 001)	mille un
a thousand and two	1,002 (1 002)	mille deux
two thousand	2,000 (2 000)	deux mille
a *or* one million	1,000,000 (1 000 000)	un million

Ordinal numbers

Les nombres ordinaux

first	1st	1er	premier
second	2nd	2e	deuxième
third	3rd	3e	troisième
fourth	4th	4e	quatrième
fifth	5th	5e	cinquième
sixth	6th	6e	sixième
seventh	7th	7e	septième
eighth	8th	8e	huitième
ninth	9th	9e	neuvième
tenth	10th	10e	dixième
eleventh	11th	11e	onzième
twelfth	12th	12e	douzième
thirteenth	13th	13e	treizième
fourteenth	14th	14e	quatorzième
fifteenth	15th	15e	quinzième
twentieth	20th	20e	vingtième
twenty-first	21st	21e	vingt et unième
twenty-second	22nd	22e	vingt deuxième
thirtieth	30th	30e	trentième

Examples of usage	Exemples d'emplois
three (times) out of ten	*trois (fois) sur dix*
ten at a time, in *or* by tens, ten by ten	*dix par dix, dix à dix*
the ten of us/you, we ten/you ten	*nous dix/vous dix*
all ten of them *or* us *or* you	*tous les dix, toutes les dix*
there are ten of us/them	*nous sommes dix/elles sont dix*
(between) the ten of them	*à eux dix, à elles dix*
ten of them came/were living together	*ils sont venus/ils vivaient à dix*
page ten	*page dix*
Charles the Tenth	*Charles Dix*
to live at number ten	*habiter au (numéro) dix*
to be the tenth to arrive/to leave	*arriver/partir le dixième*
to come tenth, be tenth *(in a race)*	*arriver dixième, être dixième*
it's the tenth (today)	*nous sommes le dix (aujourd'hui)*
the tenth of May, May the tenth, *Am* May tenth	*le dix mai*
to arrive/be paid/*etc* on the tenth	*arriver/être payé/etc le dix*
to arrive/be paid/*etc* on the tenth of May *or* on May the tenth *or Am* on May tenth	*arriver/être payé/etc le dix mai*
by the tenth, before the tenth	*avant le dix, pour le dix*
it's ten (o'clock)	*il est dix heures*
it's half past ten	*il est dix heures et demie*
ten past ten, *Am* ten after ten	*dix heures dix*
ten to ten	*dix heures moins dix*
by ten (o'clock), before ten (o'clock)	*pour dix heures, avant dix heures*
to be ten (years old)	*avoir dix ans*
a child of ten, a ten-year-old (child)	*un enfant de dix ans*

Days and months | Les jours et les mois

Monday *lundi*; Tuesday *mardi*; Wednesday *mercredi*; Thursday *jeudi*; Friday *vendredi*; Saturday *samedi*; Sunday *dimanche*

January *janvier*; February *février*; March *mars*; April *avril*; May *mai*; June *juin*; July *juillet*; August *août*; September *septembre*; October *octobre*; November *novembre*; December *décembre*

Examples of usage	Exemples d'emplois
on Monday (*e.g.* he arrives on Monday)	*lundi (par exemple il arrive lundi)*
(on) Mondays	*le lundi*
see you on Monday!	*à lundi!*
by Monday, before Monday	*avant lundi, pour lundi*
Monday morning/evening	*lundi matin/soir*
a week/two weeks on Monday, *Am* a week/two weeks from Monday	*lundi en huit/en quinze*
it's Monday (today)	*nous sommes (aujourd'hui) lundi*
Monday the tenth of May, Monday May the tenth, *Am* Monday May tenth	*(le) lundi dix mai*
on Monday the tenth of May, on Monday May the tenth *or Am* May tenth	*le lundi dix mai*
tomorrow is Tuesday	*demain c'est mardi*
in May	*en mai, au mois de mai*
every May, each May	*tous les ans en mai, chaque année en mai*
by May, before May	*avant mai, pour mai*

A

A, a [eɪ] n A, a m; **5A** (number) 5 bis; **A1** (dinner date) Fam super, superbe; **to go from A to B** aller du point A au point B.

a [ə, stressed eɪ] (before vowel or mute h an [ən, stressed æn]) indef art **1** un, une; **a man** un homme; **an apple** une pomme. **2** (= def art in Fr) **six pence a kilo** six pence le kilo; **50 km an hour** 50 km à l'heure; **I have a broken arm** j'ai le bras cassé. **3** (art omitted in Fr) **he's a doctor** il est médecin; **Caen, a town in Normandy** Caen, ville de Normandie; **what a man!** quel homme! **4** (a certain) **a Mr Smith** un certain M. Smith. **5** (time) **twice a month** deux fois par mois. **6** (some) **to make a noise/a fuss** faire du bruit/des histoires.

aback [əˈbæk] adv **taken a.** déconcerté.

abandon [əˈbændən] **1** vt abandonner. **2** n (freedom of manner) laisser-aller m, abandon m. ◆**—ment** n abandon m.

abase [əˈbeɪs] vt **to a. oneself** s'humilier, s'abaisser.

abashed [əˈbæʃt] a confus, gêné.

abate [əˈbeɪt] vi (of storm, pain) se calmer; (of flood) baisser; – vt diminuer, réduire. ◆**—ment** n diminution f, réduction f.

abbey [ˈæbɪ] n abbaye f.

abbot [ˈæbət] n abbé m. ◆**abbess** n abbesse f.

abbreviate [əˈbriːvɪeɪt] vt abréger. ◆**abbreviˈation** n abréviation f.

abdicate [ˈæbdɪkeɪt] vti abdiquer. ◆**abdiˈcation** n abdication f.

abdomen [ˈæbdəmən] n abdomen m. ◆**abˈdominal** a abdominal.

abduct [æbˈdʌkt] vt Jur enlever. ◆**abduction** n enlèvement m, rapt m.

aberration [æbəˈreɪʃ(ə)n] n (folly, lapse) aberration f.

abet [əˈbet] vt (-tt-) **to aid and a. s.o.** être le complice de qn.

abeyance [əˈbeɪəns] n **in a.** (matter) en suspens.

abhor [əbˈhɔːr] vt (-rr-) avoir horreur de, exécrer. ◆**abhorrent** a exécrable. ◆**abhorrence** n horreur f.

abide [əˈbaɪd] **1** vi **to a. by** (promise etc) rester fidèle à. **2** vt supporter; **I can't a. him** je ne peux pas le supporter.

ability [əˈbɪlətɪ] n capacité f (**to do** pour faire), aptitude f (**to do** à faire); **to the best of my a.** de mon mieux.

abject [ˈæbdʒekt] a abject; **a. poverty** la misère.

ablaze [əˈbleɪz] a en feu; **a. with** (light) resplendissant de; (anger) enflammé de.

able [ˈeɪb(ə)l] a (-er, -est) capable, compétent; **to be a.** to do être capable de faire, pouvoir faire; **to be a. to swim/drive** savoir nager/conduire. ◆**a.-ˈbodied** a robuste. ◆**ably** adv habilement.

ablutions [əˈbluːʃ(ə)nz] npl ablutions fpl.

abnormal [æbˈnɔːm(ə)l] a anormal. ◆**abnorˈmality** n anomalie f; (of body) difformité f. ◆**abnormally** adv Fig exceptionnellement.

aboard [əˈbɔːd] adv Nau à bord; **all a.** Rail en voiture; – prep **a. the ship** à bord du navire; **a. the train** dans le train.

abode [əˈbəʊd] n (house) Lit demeure f; Jur domicile m.

abolish [əˈbɒlɪʃ] vt supprimer, abolir. ◆**aboˈlition** n suppression f, abolition f.

abominable [əˈbɒmɪnəb(ə)l] a abominable. ◆**abomiˈnation** n abomination f.

aboriginal [æbəˈrɪdʒən(ə)l] a & n aborigène (m). ◆**aborigines** npl aborigènes mpl.

abort [əˈbɔːt] vt Med faire avorter; (space flight, computer program) abandonner; – vi Med & Fig avorter. ◆**abortion** n avortement m; **to have an a.** se faire avorter. ◆**abortive** a (plan etc) manqué, avorté.

abound [əˈbaʊnd] vi abonder (**in, with** en).

about [əˈbaʊt] adv **1** (approximately) à peu près, environ; (**at**) **a. two o'clock** vers deux heures. **2** (here and there) çà et là, ici et là; (ideas, flu) Fig dans l'air; (rumour) en circulation; **to look a.** regarder autour; **to follow a.** suivre partout; **to bustle a.** s'affairer; **there are lots a.** il y en a beaucoup; (**out and**) **a.** (after illness) sur pied, guéri; (**up and**) **a.** (out of bed) levé, debout; **a. turn, a. face** Mil demi-tour m; Fig volte-face f inv; – prep **1** (around) **a. the garden** autour du jardin; **a. the streets** par ou dans les rues. **2** (near to) **a. here** par ici. **3** (concerning) au sujet de; **to talk a.** parler de; **a book a.** un livre sur; **what's it (all) a.?** de quoi s'agit-il?; **while you're a.** it pendant que vous y êtes; **what** or **how a. me?** et moi alors?; **what** or **how a. a drink?** que dirais-tu de prendre un verre? **4** (+ *inf*) **a.** to do sur le point de faire; **I was a.** to say j'étais sur le point de dire, j'allais dire.

above [ə'bʌv] *adv* au-dessus; (*in book*) ci-dessus; **from a.** d'en haut; **floor a.** étage *m* supérieur *ou* du dessus; – *prep* au-dessus de; **a. all** par-dessus tout, surtout; **a. the bridge** (*on river*) en amont du pont; **he's a. me** (*in rank*) c'est mon supérieur; **a. lying** incapable de mentir; **a. asking** trop fier pour demander. ◆**a.-'mentioned** *a* susmentionné. ◆**aboveboard** *a* ouvert, honnête; – *adv* sans tricherie, cartes sur table.

abrasion [ə'breɪʒ(ə)n] *n* frottement *m*; *Med* écorchure *f*. ◆**abrasive** *a* (*substance*) abrasif; (*rough*) *Fig* rude, dur; (*irritating*) agaçant; – *n* abrasif *m*.

abreast [ə'brest] *adv* côte à côte, de front; **four a.** par rangs de quatre; **to keep a. of** or **with** se tenir au courant de.

abridge [ə'brɪdʒ] *vt* (*book etc*) abréger. ◆**abridg(e)ment** *n* abrégement *m* (of de); (*abridged version*) abrégé *m*.

abroad [ə'brɔːd] *adv* **1** (*in* or *to a foreign country*) à l'étranger; **from a.** de l'étranger. **2** (*over a wide area*) de tous côtés; **rumour a.** bruit *m* qui court.

abrogate ['æbrəgeɪt] *vt* abroger.

abrupt [ə'brʌpt] *a* (*sudden*) brusque; (*person*) brusque, abrupt; (*slope, style*) abrupt. ◆**-ly** *adv* (*suddenly*) brusquement; (*rudely*) avec brusquerie.

abscess ['æbses] *n* abcès *m*.

abscond [əb'skɒnd] *vi* *Jur* s'enfuir.

absence ['æbsəns] *n* absence *f*; **in the a. of sth** à défaut de qch, faute de qch; **a. of mind** distraction *f*.

absent ['æbsənt] *a* absent (**from** de); (*look*) distrait; – [æb'sent] *vt* **to a. oneself** s'absenter. ◆**a.-'minded** *a* distrait. ◆**a.-'mindedness** *n* distraction *f*. ◆**absen'tee** *n* absent, -ente *mf*. ◆**absen'teeism** *n* absentéisme *m*.

absolute ['æbsəluːt] *a* absolu; (*proof etc*) indiscutable; (*coward etc*) parfait, véritable. ◆**-ly** *adv* absolument; (*forbidden*) formellement.

absolve [əb'zɒlv] *vt* *Rel Jur* absoudre; **to a. from** (*vow*) libérer de. ◆**absolution** [æbsə'luːʃ(ə)n] *n* absolution *f*.

absorb [əb'zɔːb] *vt* absorber; (*shock*) amortir; **to become absorbed in** (*work*) s'absorber dans. ◆**-ing** *a* (*work*)

absorbant; (*book, film*) prenant. ◆**absorbent** *a & n* absorbant (*m*); **a. cotton** *Am* coton *m* hydrophile. ◆**absorber** *n* **shock a.** *Aut* amortisseur *m*. ◆**absorption** *n* absorption *f*.

abstain [əb'steɪn] *vi* s'abstenir (**from** de). ◆**abstemious** *a* sobre, frugal. ◆**absten-tion** *n* abstention *f*. ◆**abstinence** *n* abstinence *f*.

abstract ['æbstrækt] **1** *a & n* abstrait (*m*). **2** *n* (*summary*) résumé *m*. **3** [əb'strækt] *vt* (*remove*) retirer; (*notion*) abstraire. ◆**ab'straction** *n* (*idea*) abstraction *f*; (*absent-mindedness*) distraction *f*.

abstruse [əb'struːs] *a* obscur.

absurd [əb'sɜːd] *a* absurde, ridicule. ◆**absurdity** *n* absurdité *f*. ◆**absurdly** *adv* absurdement.

abundant [ə'bʌndənt] *a* abondant. ◆**abundance** *n* abondance *f*. ◆**abun-dantly** *adv* **a. clear** tout à fait clair.

abuse [ə'bjuːs] *n* (*abusing*) abus *m* (**of** de); (*curses*) injures *fpl*; – [ə'bjuːz] *vt* (*misuse*) abuser de; (*malign*) dire du mal de; (*insult*) injurier. ◆**abusive** *a* injurieux.

abysmal [ə'bɪzm(ə)l] *a* (*bad*) *Fam* désas-treux, exécrable.

abyss [ə'bɪs] *n* abîme *m*.

acacia [ə'keɪʃə] *n* (*tree*) acacia *m*.

academic [ækə'demɪk] *a* universitaire; (*scholarly*) érudit, intellectuel; (*issue etc*) *Pej* théorique; (*style, art*) académique; – *n* (*teacher*) *Univ* universitaire *mf*. ◆**academy** [ə'kædəmɪ] *n* (*society*) académie *f*; *Mil Mus* école *f*. ◆**acade'mician** *n* académicien, -ienne *mf*.

accede [ək'siːd] *vi* **to a. to** (*request, throne, position*) accéder à.

accelerate [ək'seləreɪt] *vt* accélérer; – *vi* s'accélérer; *Aut* accélérer. ◆**accele-'ration** *n* accélération *f*. ◆**accelerator** *n* *Aut* accélérateur *m*.

accent ['æksənt] *n* accent *m*; – [æk'sent] *vt* accentuer. ◆**accentuate** [æk'sentʃueɪt] *vt* accentuer.

accept [ək'sept] *vt* accepter. ◆**-ed** *a* (*opin-ion etc*) reçu, admis. ◆**acceptable** *a* (*worth accepting, tolerable*) acceptable. ◆**acceptance** *n* acceptation *f*; (*approval, favour*) accueil *m* favorable.

access ['ækses] *n* accès *m* (**to sth** à qch, **to s.o.** auprès de qn). ◆**ac'cessible** *a* accessible.

accession [æk'seʃ(ə)n] *n* accession *f* (**to** à); (*increase*) augmentation *f*; (*sth added*) nouvelle acquisition *f*.

accessory [ək'sesərɪ] **1** n (person) Jur complice mf. **2** npl (objects) accessoires mpl.

accident ['æksɪdənt] n accident m; by a. (by chance) par accident; (unintentionally) accidentellement, sans le vouloir. ◆**a.-prone** a prédisposé aux accidents. ◆**acci'dental** a accidentel, fortuit. ◆**acci'dentally** adv accidentellement, par mégarde; (by chance) par accident.

acclaim [ə'kleɪm] vt acclamer; **to a.** king proclamer roi. ◆**accla'mation** n acclamation(s) f(pl), louange(s) f(pl).

acclimate ['ækləmeɪt] vti Am = acclimatize. ◆**a'cclimatize** vt acclimater; – vi s'acclimater. ◆**accli'mation** n Am, ◆**acclimati'zation** n acclimatisation f.

accolade ['ækəleɪd] n (praise) Fig louange f.

accommodat/e [ə'kɒmədeɪt] vt (of house) loger, recevoir; (have room for) avoir dela place pour (mettre); (adapt) adapter (to à); (supply) fournir (s.o. with sth qch à qn); (oblige) rendre service à; (reconcile) concilier; **to a. oneself to** s'accomoder à. ◆**—ing** a accommodant, obligeant. ◆**accommo'dation** n **1** (lodging) logement m; (rented room or rooms) chambre(s) f(pl); pl (in hotel) Am chambre(s) f(pl). **2** (compromise) compromis m, accommodement m.

accompany [ə'kʌmpənɪ] vt accompagner. ◆**accompaniment** n accompagnement m. ◆**accompanist** n Mus accompagnateur, -trice mf.

accomplice [ə'kʌmplɪs] n complice mf.

accomplish [ə'kʌmplɪʃ] vt (task, duty) accomplir; (aim) réaliser. ◆**—ed** a accompli. ◆**—ment** n accomplissement m; (of aim) réalisation f; (thing achieved) réalisation f; pl (skills) talents mpl.

accord [ə'kɔːd] **1** n accord m; **of my own a.** volontairement, de mon plein gré; – vi concorder. **2** vt (grant) accorder. ◆**accordance** n **in a. with** conformément à.

according to [ə'kɔːdɪŋtuː] prep selon, d'après, suivant. ◆**accordingly** adv en conséquence.

accordion [ə'kɔːdɪən] n accordéon m.

accost [ə'kɒst] vt accoster, aborder.

account [ə'kaʊnt] **1** n Com compte m; pl comptabilité f, comptes mpl; **accounts department** comptabilité f; **to take into a.** tenir compte de; **ten pounds on a.** un acompte de dix livres; **of some a.** d'une certaine importance; **on a. of** à cause de; **on**

no a. en aucun cas. **2** n (report) compte rendu m, bilan m; (explanation) explication f; **by all accounts** au dire de tous; **to give a good a. of oneself** s'en tirer à son avantage; – vi **to a. for** (explain) expliquer; (give reckoning of) rendre compte de. **3** vt **to a. oneself lucky/etc** (explanation) se considérer heureux/etc. ◆**accountable** a responsable (for à, devant); (explainable) explicable.

accountant [ə'kaʊntənt] n comptable mf. ◆**accountancy** n comptabilité f.

accoutrements [ə'kuːtrəmənts] (Am **accouterments** [ə'kuːtərmənts]) npl équipement m.

accredit [ə'kredɪt] vt (ambassador) accréditer; **to a. s.o. with sth** attribuer qch à qn.

accrue [ə'kruː] vi (of interest) Fin s'accumuler; **to a. to** (of advantage etc) revenir à.

accumulate [ə'kjuːmjʊleɪt] vt accumuler, amasser; – vi s'accumuler. ◆**accumu'lation** n accumulation f; (mass) amas m. ◆**accumulator** n El accumulateur m.

accurate ['ækjʊrət] a exact, précis. ◆**accuracy** n exactitude f, précision f. ◆**accurately** adv avec précision.

accursed [ə'kɜːsɪd] a maudit, exécrable.

accus/e [ə'kjuːz] vt accuser (of de). ◆**—ed** n **the a.** Jur l'inculpé, -ée mf, l'accusé, -ée mf. ◆**—ing** a accusateur. ◆**accu'sation** n accusation f.

accustom [ə'kʌstəm] vt habituer, accoutumer. ◆**—ed** a habitué (to sth à qch, to doing à faire); **to get a.** to s'habituer à, s'accoutumer à.

ace [eɪs] n (card, person) as m.

acetate ['æsɪteɪt] n acétate m.

acetic [ə'siːtɪk] a acétique.

ache [eɪk] n douleur f, mal m; **to have an a. in one's arm** avoir mal au bras; – vi faire mal; **my head aches** ma tête me fait mal; **it makes my heart a.** cela me serre le cœur; **to be aching to do** brûler de faire. ◆**aching** a douloureux.

achieve [ə'tʃiːv] vt accomplir, réaliser; (success, aim) atteindre; (victory) remporter. ◆**—ment** n accomplissement m, réalisation f; (of de); (feat) réalisation f, exploit m.

acid ['æsɪd] a & n acide (m). ◆**a'cidity** n acidité f.

acknowledge [ək'nɒlɪdʒ] vt reconnaître (as pour); (greeting) répondre à; **to a.** (receipt of) accuser réception de; **to a. defeat** s'avouer vaincu. ◆**—ment** n reconnaissance f; (of letter) accusé m de réception; (receipt) reçu m, récépissé m.

acme ['ækmɪ] n sommet m, comble m.

acne ['æknɪ] n acné f.

acorn ['eɪkɔːn] n Bot gland m.

acoustic [ə'kuːstɪk] a acoustique; – npl acoustique f.

acquaint [ə'kweɪnt] vt **to a. s.o. with sth** informer qn de qch; **to be acquainted with** (person) connaître; (fact) savoir; **we are acquainted** on se connaît. ◆**acquaintance** n (person, knowledge) connaissance f.

acquiesce [ækwɪ'es] vi acquiescer (**in** à). ◆**acquiescence** n acquiescement m.

acquire [ə'kwaɪər] vt acquérir; (taste) prendre (**for** à); (friends) se faire; **aquired taste** goût m qui s'acquiert. ◆**acqui'sition** n acquisition f. ◆**acquisitive** a avide, cupide.

acquit [ə'kwɪt] vt (-tt-) **to a. s.o. (of a crime)** acquitter qn. ◆**acquittal** n acquittement m.

acre ['eɪkər] n acre f (= 0,4 hectare). ◆**acreage** n superficie f.

acrid ['ækrɪd] a (smell, manner etc) âcre.

acrimonious [ækrɪ'məʊnɪəs] a acerbe.

acrobat ['ækrəbæt] n acrobate mf. ◆**acro-'batic** a acrobatique; – npl acrobatie(s) f(pl).

acronym ['ækrənɪm] n sigle m.

across [ə'krɒs] adv & prep (from side to side (of)) d'un côté à l'autre (de); (on the other side (of)) de l'autre côté (de); (crossways) en travers (de); **to be a kilometre/etc a.** (wide) avoir un kilomètre/etc de large; **to walk or go a.** (street etc) traverser; **to come a.** (person) rencontrer (par hasard), tomber sur; (thing) trouver (par hasard); **to get sth a.** to s.o. faire comprendre qch à qn.

acrostic [ə'krɒstɪk] n acrostiche m.

acrylic [ə'krɪlɪk] a & n acrylique (m).

act [ækt] 1 n (deed) acte m; a. (of parliament) loi f; **caught in the a.** pris sur le fait; **a. of walking** action f de marcher; **an a. of folly** une folie. 2 n (of play) Th acte m; (turn) Th numéro m; **in on the a.** Fam dans le coup; **to put on an a.** Fam jouer la comédie; – vi (part) Th jouer; **to a. the fool** faire l'idiot; – vi Th Cin jouer; (pretend) jouer la comédie. 3 vi (do sth, behave) agir; (function) fonctionner; **to a. as** (secretary etc) faire office de; (of object) servir de; **to a. (up)on** (affect) agir sur; (advice) suivre; **to a. on behalf of** représenter; **to a. up** (of person, machine) Fam faire des siennes. ◆**—ing 1** a (manager etc) intérimaire, provisoire. **2** n (of play) représentation f; (actor's art) jeu m; (career) théâtre m.

action ['ækʃ(ə)n] n action f; Mil combat m; Jur procès m, action f; **to take a.** prendre des mesures; **to put into a.** (plan) exécuter; **out of a.** hors d'usage, hors (de) service; (person) hors de combat; **killed in a.** mort au champ d'honneur; **to take industrial a.** se mettre en grève.

active ['æktɪv] a actif; (interest) vif; (volcano) en activité. ◆**activate** vt Ch activer; (mechanism) actionner. ◆**activist** n activiste mf. ◆**activity** n activité f; (in street) mouvement m.

actor ['æktər] n acteur m. ◆**actress** n actrice f.

actual ['æktʃʊəl] a réel, véritable; (example) concret; **the a. book** le livre même; **in a. fact** en réalité, effectivement. ◆**—ly** adv (truly) réellement; (in fact) en réalité, en fait.

actuary ['æktʃʊərɪ] n actuaire mf.

actuate ['æktʃʊeɪt] vt (person) animer; (machine) actionner.

acumen ['ækjumen, Am ə'kjuːmən] n perspicacité f, finesse f.

acupuncture ['ækjʊpʌŋktʃər] n acupuncture f.

acute [ə'kjuːt] a aigu; (anxiety, emotion) vif, profond; (observer) perspicace; (shortage) grave. ◆**—ly** adv (to suffer, feel) vivement, profondément. ◆**—ness** n acuité f; perspicacité f.

ad [æd] n Fam pub f; (private, in newspaper) annonce f; **small ad** petite annonce.

AD [eɪ'diː] abbr (anno Domini) après Jésus-Christ.

adage ['ædɪdʒ] n adage m.

Adam ['ædəm] n **A.'s apple** pomme f d'Adam.

adamant ['ædəmənt] a inflexible.

adapt [ə'dæpt] vt adapter (**to** à); **to a.** (oneself) s'adapter. ◆**adaptable** a (person) capable de s'adapter, adaptable. ◆**adaptor** n (device) adaptateur m; (plug) prise f multiple. ◆**adap'tation** n adaptation f.

add [æd] vt ajouter (**to** à, **that** que); **to a. (up** or **together)** (total) additionner; **to a.** in inclure; – vi **to a. to** (increase) augmenter; **to a. up to** (total) s'élever à; (mean) signifier; **it all adds up** Fam ça s'explique. ◆**a'ddendum**, pl **-da** n supplément m. ◆**adding machine** n machine f à calculer. ◆**a'ddition** n addition f; augmentation f; **in a.** de plus; **in a. to** en plus de. ◆**a'dditional** a supplémentaire. ◆**a'dditionally** adv de plus. ◆**additive** n additif m.

adder ['ædər] n vipère f.

addict ['ædɪkt] *n* intoxiqué, -ée *mf*; **jazz/sport** a. fanatique *mf* du jazz/du sport; **drug a.** drogué, -ée *mf.* ◆a'**ddicted** *a* **to be a. to** *(study, drink)* s'adonner à; *(music)* se passionner pour; *(to have the habit of)* avoir la manie de; **a. to cigarettes** drogué par la cigarette. ◆a'**ddiction** *n* *(habit)* manie *f*; *(dependency)* Med dépendance *f*; **drug a.** toxicomanie *f.* ◆a'**ddictive** *a* qui crée une dépendance.

address [ə'dres, *Am* 'ædres] *n* *(on letter etc)* adresse *f*; *(speech)* allocution *f*; **form of a.** formule *f* de politesse; – [ə'dres] *(person)* s'adresser à; *(audience)* parler devant; *(words, speech)* adresser (**to** à); *(letter)* mettre l'adresse sur; **a. to s.o.** *(send, intend for)* adresser à qn. ◆**addressee** [ædre'siː] *n* destinataire *mf.*

adenoids ['ædɪnɔɪdz] *npl* végétations *fpl* (adénoïdes).

adept ['ædept, *Am* ə'dept] *a* expert (**in, at** à).

adequate ['ædɪkwət] *a* *(quantity)* suffisant; *(acceptable)* convenable; *(person, performance)* compétent. ◆**adequacy** *n* *(of person)* compétence *f*; **to doubt the a. of sth** douter que qch soit suffisant. ◆**adequately** *adv* suffisamment; convenablement.

adhere [əd'hɪər] *vi* **to a. to** adhérer à; *(decision)* s'en tenir à; *(rule)* respecter. ◆**adherence** *n*, ◆**adhesion** *n* *(grip)* adhérence *f*; *(support)* Fig adhésion *f.* ◆**adhesive** *a & n* adhésif *(m).*

ad infinitum [ædɪnfɪ'naɪtəm] *adv* à l'infini.

adjacent [ə'dʒeɪsənt] *a* *(house, angle etc)* adjacent (**to** à).

adjective ['ædʒɪktɪv] *n* adjectif *m.*

adjoin [ə'dʒɔɪn] *vt* avoisiner. ◆**—ing** *a* avoisinant, voisin.

adjourn [ə'dʒɜːn] *vt* *(postpone)* ajourner; *(session)* lever, suspendre; – *vi* lever la séance; **to a. to** *(go)* passer à. ◆**—ment** *n* ajournement *m*; suspension *f* (de séance), levée *f* de séance.

adjudicate [ə'dʒuːdɪkeɪt] *vti* juger. ◆**adjudi'cation** *n* jugement *m.* ◆**adjudicator** *n* juge *m*, arbitre *m.*

adjust [ə'dʒʌst] *vt* Tech régler, ajuster; *(prices)* (r)ajuster; *(arrange)* arranger; **to a.** *(oneself)* **to** s'adapter à. ◆**—able** *a* réglable. ◆**—ment** *n* Tech réglage *m*; *(of person)* adaptation *f*; *(of prices)* rajustement *m.*

ad-lib [æd'lɪb] *vi* (**-bb-**) improviser; – *a (joke etc)* improvisé.

administer [əd'mɪnɪstər] **1** *vt* *(manage, dispense)* administrer (**to** à). **2** *vi* **to a. to**

pourvoir à. ◆**admini'stration** *n* administration *f*; *(ministry)* gouvernement *m.* ◆**admini'strative** *a* administratif. ◆**administrator** *n* administrateur, -trice *mf.*

admiral ['ædmərəl] *n* amiral *m.*

admir/e [əd'maɪər] *vt* admirer. ◆**—ing** *a* admiratif. ◆**—er** *n* admirateur, -trice *mf.* ◆'**admirable** *a* admirable. ◆admi'**ration** *n* admiration *f.*

admit [əd'mɪt] *vt* (**-tt-**) *(let in)* laisser entrer; *(accept)* admettre; *(acknowledge)* reconnaître, avouer; – *vi* **a. to sth** *(confess)* avouer qch; **to a. of** permettre. ◆**admittedly** *adv* c'est vrai (que). ◆**admissible** *a* admissible. ◆**admission** *n* *(entry to theatre etc)* entrée *f* (**to** à, de); *(to club, school)* admission *f*; *(acknowledgement)* aveu *m*; **a. (charge)** *(price m d')*entrée *f.* ◆**admittance** *n* entrée *f*; '**no a.**' 'entrée interdite'.

admonish [əd'mɒnɪʃ] *vt* *(reprove)* réprimander; *(warn)* avertir.

ado [ə'duː] *n* **without further a.** sans (faire) plus de façons.

adolescent [ædə'lesənt] *n* adolescent, -ente *mf.* ◆**adolescence** *n* adolescence *f.*

adopt [ə'dɒpt] *vt* *(child, method, attitude etc)* adopter; *(candidate)* Pol choisir. ◆**—ed** *a (child)* adoptif; *(country)* d'adoption. ◆**adoption** *n* adoption *f.* ◆**adoptive** *a (parent)* adoptif.

adore [ə'dɔːr] *vt* adorer; **he adores being flattered** il adore qu'on le flatte. ◆**adorable** *a* adorable. ◆ado'**ration** *n* adoration *f.*

adorn [ə'dɔːn] *vt* *(room, book)* orner; *(person, dress)* parer. ◆**—ment** *n* ornement *m*; parure *f.*

adrenalin(e) [ə'drenəlɪn] *n* adrénaline *f.*

Adriatic [eɪdrɪ'ætɪk] *n* **the A.** l'Adriatique *f.*

adrift [ə'drɪft] *a & adv* Nau à la dérive; **to come a.** *(of rope, collar etc)* se détacher; **to turn s.o. a.** Fig abandonner qn à son sort.

adroit [ə'drɔɪt] *a* adroit, habile.

adulation [ædjʊ'leɪʃ(ə)n] *n* adulation *f.*

adult ['ædʌlt] *a & n* adulte *(mf).* ◆**adulthood** *n* âge *m* adulte.

adulterate [ə'dʌltəreɪt] *vt* *(food)* altérer.

adultery [ə'dʌltərɪ] *n* adultère *m.* ◆**adulterous** *a* adultère.

advanc/e [əd'vɑːns] *n* *(movement, money)* avance *f*; *(of science)* progrès *mpl*; *pl (of friendship, love)* avances *fpl*; **in a.** à l'avance, d'avance; *(to arrive)* en avance; **in a. of s.o.** avant qn; – *a (payment)* anticipé; **a. booking** réservation *f*; **a. guard** avant-garde *f*; – *vt (put forward, lend)* avancer; (*science, work*) faire avancer; – *vi* (*go forward, progress*) avancer; (*towards s.o.*) s'avancer, avancer. **◆—ed** *a* avancé; (*studies*) supérieur; **a. in years** âgé. **◆—ement** *n* (*progress, promotion*) avancement *m*.

advantage [əd'vɑːntidʒ] *n* avantage *m* (**over** sur); **to take a.** of profiter de; (*person*) tromper, exploiter; (*woman*) séduire; **to show (off) to a.** faire valoir. **◆advan-'tageous** *a* avantageux (**to**, pour), profitable.

advent ['ædvent] *n* arrivée *f*, avènement *m*; **A. Rel** l'Avent *m*.

adventure [əd'ventʃər] *n* aventure *f*; – *a* (*film etc*) d'aventures. **◆adventurer** *n* aventurier, -ière *mf*. **◆adventurous** *a* aventureux.

adverb ['ædvɜːb] *n* adverbe *m*.

adversary ['ædvəsərɪ] *n* adversaire *mf*.

adverse ['ædvɜːs] *a* hostile, défavorable. **◆ad'versity** *n* adversité *f*.

advert ['ædvɜːt] *n* Fam pub *f*; (*private, in newspaper*) annonce *f*.

advertis/e ['ædvətaɪz] *vt* (*goods*) faire de la publicité pour; (*make known*) annoncer; – *vi* faire de la publicité; **to a. (for s.o.)** mettre une annonce (pour chercher qn). **◆—er** *n* annonceur *m*. **◆—ement** [əd'vɜːtɪsmənt, *Am* ædvə'taɪzmənt] *n* publicité *f*; (*private or classified in newspaper*) annonce *f*; (*poster*) affiche *f*; **classified a.** petite annonce; **the advertisements** *TV* la publicité.

advice [əd'vaɪs] *n* conseil(s) *m*(*pl*); *Com* avis *m*; **a piece of a.** un conseil.

advis/e [əd'vaɪz] *vt* (*counsel*) conseiller; (*recommend*) recommander; (*notify*) informer; **to a. s.o. to do** conseiller à qn de faire; **to a. against** déconseiller. **◆—ed** *a* **well-a.** (*action*) prudent. **◆—able** *a* (*wise*) prudent (**to do de faire**); (*act*) à conseiller. **◆—edly** [-ɪdlɪ] *adv* après réflexion. **◆—er** *n* conseiller, -ère *mf*. **◆advisory** *a* consultatif.

advocate 1 ['ædvəkət] *n* (*of cause*) défenseur *m*, avocat, -ate *mf*; *Jur* avocat *m*. **2** ['ædvəkeɪt] *vt* préconiser, recommander.

aegis ['iːdʒɪs] *n* **under the a. of** sous l'égide de.

aeon ['iːən] *n* éternité *f*.

aerial ['eərɪəl] *n* antenne *f*; – *a* aérien.

aerobatics [eərə'bætɪks] *npl* acrobatie *f* aérienne. **◆ae'robics** *npl* aérobic *f*. **◆'aerodrome** *n* aérodrome *m*. **◆aero-dy'namic** *a* aérodynamique. **◆aero-'nautics** *npl* aéronautique *f*. **◆'aeroplane**

n avion *m*. **◆'aerosol** *n* aérosol *m*. **◆'aerospace** *a* (*industry*) aérospatial.

aesthetic [iːs'θetɪk, *Am* es'θetɪk] *a* esthé-tique.

afar [ə'fɑːr] *adv* **from a.** de loin.

affable ['æfəb(ə)l] *a* affable, aimable.

affair [ə'feər] *n* (*matter, concern*) affaire *f*; (*love*) **a.** liaison *f*; **state of affairs** état *m* de choses.

affect [ə'fekt] *vt* (*move, feign*) affecter; (*concern*) toucher, affecter; (*harm*) nuire à; (*be fond of*) affectionner. **◆—ed** *a* (*manner*) affecté; (*by disease*) atteint. **◆affec'tation** *n* affectation *f*.

affection [ə'fekʃ(ə)n] *n* affection *f* (**for** pour). **◆affectionate** *a* affectueux, aimant. **◆affectionately** *adv* affectueuse-ment.

affiliate [ə'fɪlɪeɪt] *vt* affilier; **to be affiliated** s'affilier (**to** à); **affiliated company** filiale *f*. **◆affili'ation** *n* affiliation *f*; *pl* (*political*) attaches *fpl*.

affinity [ə'fɪnɪtɪ] *n* affinité *f*.

affirm [ə'fɜːm] *vt* affirmer. **◆affir'mation** *n* affirmation *f*. **◆affirmative** *a* affirmatif; – *n* affirmative *f*.

affix [ə'fɪks] *vt* apposer.

afflict [ə'flɪkt] *vt* affliger (**with** de). **◆afflic-tion** *n* (*misery*) affliction *f*; (*disorder*) infirmité *f*.

affluent ['æflʊənt] *a* riche; **a. society** société *f* d'abondance. **◆affluence** *n* richesse *f*.

afford [ə'fɔːd] *vt* **1** (*pay for*) avoir les moyens d'acheter, pouvoir se payer; (*time*) pouvoir trouver; **I can a. to wait** je peux me permet-tre d'attendre. **2** (*provide*) fournir, donner; **to a. s.o. sth** fournir qch à qn.

affray [ə'freɪ] *n* *Jur* rixe *f*, bagarre *f*.

affront [ə'frʌnt] *n* affront *m*; – *vt* faire un affront à.

Afghanistan [æf'gænɪstɑːn] *n* Afghanistan *m*. **◆'Afghan** *a* & *n* afghan, -ane (*mf*).

afield [ə'fiːld] *adv* **further a.** plus loin; **too far a.** trop loin.

afloat [ə'fləʊt] *adv* (*ship, swimmer, business*) à flot; (*awash*) submergé; **life a.** la vie sur l'eau.

afoot [ə'fʊt] *adv* **there's sth a.** il se trame qch; **there's a plan a.** to on prépare un projet pour.

aforementioned [ə'fɔːmenʃənd] *a* susmen-tionné.

afraid [ə'freɪd] *a* **to be a.** avoir peur (**of, to** de; **that que**); **to make s.o. afraid** faire peur à qn; **he's a.** (**that**) **she may be ill** il a peur qu'elle (ne) soit malade; **I'm a. he's out** (*I regret to say*) je regrette, il est sorti.

afresh [əˈfreʃ] *adv* de nouveau.

Africa [ˈæfrɪkə] *n* Afrique *f*. ◆**African** *a & n* africain, -aine (*mf*).

after [ˈɑːftər] *adv* (*month*) suivant, le mois d'après; – *prep* après; **a. all** après tout; **a. eating** après avoir mangé; **day a. day** jour après jour; **page a. page** page sur page; **time a. time** bien des fois; **a. you!** je vous en prie!; **ten a. four** *Am* quatre heures dix; **to be a. sth/s.o.** (*seek*) chercher qch/qn; – *conj* après que; **a. he saw you** après qu'il t'a vu. ◆**aftercare** *n Med* soins *mpl* postopératoires; *Jur* surveillance *f*. ◆**aftereffects** *npl* suites *fpl*, séquelles *fpl*. ◆**afterlife** *n* vie *f* future. ◆**aftermath** [-mɑːθ] *n* suites *fpl*. ◆**after'noon** *n* après-midi *m or f inv*; **in the a.** l'après-midi; **good a.!** (*hello*) bonjour!; (*goodbye*) au revoir! ◆**after'noons** *adv Am* l'après-midi. ◆**aftersales (service)** *n* service *m* après-vente. ◆**aftershave (lotion)** *n* lotion *f* après-rasage. ◆**aftertaste** *n* arrière-goût *m*. ◆**afterthought** *n* réflexion *f* après coup. ◆**afterward(s)** *adv* après, plus tard.

afters [ˈɑːftəz] *npl Fam* dessert *m*.

again [əˈgen, əˈgeɪn] *adv* de nouveau, encore une fois; (*furthermore*) en outre; **to do a.** refaire; **to go down/up a.** redescendre/remonter; **never a.** plus jamais; **half as much a.** moitié plus; **a. and a., time and (time) a.** maintes fois; **what's his name a.?** comment s'appelle-t-il déjà?

against [əˈgenst, əˈgeɪnst] *prep* contre; **to go or be a.** s'opposer à; **a law a. drinking** une loi qui interdit de boire; **his age is a. him** son âge lui est défavorable; **a. a background of** sur (un) fond de; **a. the light** à contre-jour; **a. the law** illégal; **a. the rules** interdit, contraire aux règlements.

age [eɪdʒ] *n* (*lifespan, period*) âge *m*; (*old*) vieillesse *f*; **the Middle Ages** le moyen âge; **what a. are you?**, **what's your a.?** quel âge as-tu?; **five years of a.** âgé de cinq ans; **to be of a.** être majeur; **under a.** trop jeune, mineur; **to wait (for) ages** *Fam* attendre une éternité; **a. group** tranche *f* d'âge; – *vti* (*pres p* **ag(e)ing**) vieillir. ◆**a.-old** *a* séculaire. ◆**aged** *a* [eɪdʒd] **a. ten** âgé de dix ans; [ˈeɪdʒɪd] vieux, âgé; **the a.** les personnes *fpl* âgées. ◆**ageless** *a* toujours jeune.

agenda [əˈdʒendə] *n* ordre du jour.

agent [ˈeɪdʒənt] *n* agent *m*; (*dealer*) Com concessionnaire *mf*. ◆**agency** *n* **1** (*office*) agence *f*. **2 through the a. of s.o.** par l'intermédiaire de qn.

agglomeration [əglɒməˈreɪʃ(ə)n] *n* agglomération *f*.

aggravate [ˈægrəveɪt] *vt* (*make worse*) aggraver; **to a. s.o.** *Fam* exaspérer qn. ◆**aggra'vation** *n* aggravation *f*; *Fam* exaspération *f*; (*bother*) *Fam* ennui(s) *m(pl)*.

aggregate [ˈægrɪgət] *a* global; – *n* (*total*) ensemble *m*.

aggression [əˈgreʃ(ə)n] *n* agression *f*. ◆**aggressive** *a* agressif. ◆**aggressiveness** *n* agressivité *f*. ◆**aggressor** *n* agresseur *m*.

aggrieved [əˈgriːvd] *a* (*offended*) blessé, froissé; (*tone*) peiné.

aghast [əˈgɑːst] *a* consterné, horrifié.

agile [ˈædʒaɪl, *Am* ˈædʒ(ə)l] *a* agile. ◆**a'gility** *n* agilité *f*.

agitate [ˈædʒɪteɪt] *vt* (*worry, shake*) agiter; – *vi* **to a. for** *Pol* faire campagne pour. ◆**agi'tation** *n* (*anxiety, unrest*) agitation *f*. ◆**agitator** *n* agitateur, -trice *mf*.

aglow [əˈgləʊ] *a* **to be a.** briller (**with** de).

agnostic [ægˈnɒstɪk] *a & n* agnostique (*mf*).

ago [əˈgəʊ] *adv* **a year a.** il y a un an; **how long a.?** il y a combien de temps (de cela)?; **as long a. as 1800** en 1800.

agog [əˈgɒg] *a* (*excited*) en émoi; (*eager*) impatient.

agony [ˈægənɪ] *n* (*pain*) douleur *f* atroce; (*anguish*) angoisse *f*; **to be in a.** souffrir horriblement; **a. column** *Journ* courrier *m* du cœur. ◆**agonize** *vi* se faire beaucoup de souci. ◆**agonized** *a* (*look*) angoissé; (*cry*) de douleur. ◆**agonizing** *a* (*pain*) atroce; (*situation*) angoissant.

agree [əˈgriː] *vi* (*come to terms*) se mettre d'accord, s'accorder; (*be in agreement*) être d'accord, s'accorder (**with** avec); (*of facts, dates etc*) concorder; *Gram* s'accorder; **to a. upon** (*decide*) convenir de; **to a. to sth/to doing** consentir à qch/à faire; **it doesn't a. with me** (*food, climate*) ça ne me réussit pas; – *vt* (*figures*) faire concorder; (*accounts*) Com approuver; **to a. to do** accepter de faire; **to a. that** (*admit*) admettre que. ◆**agreed** *a* (*time, place*) convenu; **we are a.** nous sommes d'accord; **a.!** entendu! ◆**agreeable** *a* **1** (*pleasant*) agréable. **2 to be a.** (*agree*) être d'accord; **to be a. to sth** consentir à qch. ◆**agreement** *n* accord *m*; *Pol Com* convention *f*, accord *m*; **in a. with** d'accord avec.

agriculture [ˈægrɪkʌltʃər] *n* agriculture *f*. ◆**agri'cultural** *a* agricole.

aground [əˈgraʊnd] *adv* **to run a.** *Nau* (s')échouer.

ah! [ɑː] *int* ah!

ahead [əˈhed] *adv* (*in space*) en avant; (*leading*) en tête; (*in the future*) dans l'avenir; **a.** (*of time or of schedule*) en avance (sur l'horaire); **one hour/etc a.** une heure/etc d'avance (of sur); **a. of** (*space*) devant; (*time, progress*) en avance sur; **to go a.** (*advance*) avancer; (*continue*) continuer; (*start*) commencer; **go a.!** allez-y!; **to go a. with** (*task*) poursuivre; **to get a.** prendre de l'avance; (*succeed*) réussir; **to think a.** penser à l'avenir; **straight a.** tout droit.

aid [eid] *n* (*help*) aide *f*; (*apparatus*) support *m*, moyen *m*; **with the a. of** (*a stick etc*) à l'aide de; **in a. of** (*charity etc*) au profit de; **what's this in a. of?** *Fam* quel est le but de tout ça?, ça sert à quoi?; – *vt* aider (**to do** à faire).

aide [eid] *n Pol* aide *mf*.

AIDS [eidz] *n Med* SIDA *m*.

ail [eil] *vt* **what ails you?** de quoi souffrez-vous? ◆**—ing** *a* souffrant, malade. ◆**—ment** *n* maladie *f*.

aim [eim] *n* but *m*; **to take a.** viser; **with the a. of** dans le but de; – *vt* (*gun*) braquer, diriger (**at** sur); (*lamp*) diriger (**at** vers); (*stone*) lancer (**at** à vers); (*blow, remark*) décocher (**at** à); – *vi* viser; **to a. at s.o.** viser qn; **to a. to do** *or* **at doing** avoir l'intention de faire. ◆**—less** *a*, ◆**—lessly** *adv* sans but.

air [eər] **1** *n* air *m*; **in the open a.** en plein air; **by a.** (*to travel*) en or par avion; (*letter, freight*) par avion; **to be up** *or* **go on the a.** (*person*) passer à l'antenne; (*programme*) être diffusé; (**up**) **in the a.** (*to throw*) en l'air; (*plan*) incertain, en l'air; **there's sth in the a.** *Fig* il se prépare qch; – *a* (*raid, base etc*) aérien; **a. force/hostess** armée *f*/hôtesse *f* de l'air; **a. terminal** aérogare *f*; – *vt* (*room*) aérer; (*views*) exposer; **airing cupboard** armoire *f* sèche-linge. **2** *n* (*appearance, tune*) air *m*; **to put on airs** se donner des airs; **with an a. of sadness/etc** d'un air triste/etc.

airborne [ˈeəbɔːn] *a* (*in course of flight*); (*troops*) aéroporté; **to become a.** (*of aircraft*) décoller. ◆**airbridge** *n* pont *m* aérien. ◆**air-conditioned** *a* climatisé. ◆**air-conditioner** *n* climatiseur *m*. ◆**air-craft** *n inv* avion(s) *m(pl)*; **a. carrier** porte-avions *m inv*. ◆**aircrew** *n Av* équipage *m* ◆**airfield** *n* terrain *m* d'aviation. ◆**airgun** *n* carabine *f* à air comprimé. ◆**airletter** *n* aérogramme. *m* ◆**airlift** *n* pont *m* aérien; – *vt* transporter par avion. ◆**airline** *n* ligne *f* aérienne. ◆**airliner** *n*

avion *m* de ligne. ◆**airlock** *n* (*chamber*) *Nau Av* sas *m*; (*in pipe*) bouchon *m*. ◆**airmail** *n* poste *f* aérienne; **by a.** par avion. ◆**airman** *n* (*pl* **-men**) aviateur *m*. ◆**airplane** *n Am* avion *m*. ◆**airpocket** *n* trou *m* d'air. ◆**airport** *n* aéroport *m*. ◆**airship** *n* dirigeable *m*. ◆**airsickness** *n* mal *m* de l'air. ◆**airstrip** *n* terrain *m* d'atterrissage. ◆**airtight** *a* hermétique. ◆**airway** *n* (*route*) couloir *m* aérien. ◆**airworthy** *a* en état de navigation.

airy [ˈeəri] *a* (**-ier, -iest**) (*room*) bien aéré; (*promise*) vain; (*step*) léger. ◆**a.-fairy** *a Fam* farfelu. ◆**airily** *adv* (*not seriously*) d'un ton léger.

aisle [ail] *n* couloir *m*; (*of church*) nef *f* latérale.

aitch [eitʃ] *n* (*letter*) h *m*.

ajar [əˈdʒɑːr] *a & adv* (*door*) entrouvert.

akin [əˈkin] *a* **a. (to)** apparenté (à).

alabaster [ˈæləbɑːstər] *n* albâtre *m*.

alacrity [əˈlækriti] *n* empressement *m*.

à la mode [ælæˈməud] *a Culin Am* avec de la crème glacée.

alarm [əˈlɑːm] *n* (*warning, fear*) alarme *f*; (*apparatus*) sonnerie *f* (d'alarme); **false a.** fausse alerte *f*; **a. (clock)** réveil *m*, réveille-matin *m inv*; – *vt* (*frighten*) alarmer. ◆**alarmist** *n* alarmiste *m*.

alas! [əˈlæs] *int* hélas!

albatross [ˈælbətrɒs] *n* albatros *m*.

albeit [ɔːlˈbiːt] *conj Lit* quoique.

albino [ælˈbiːnəu, *Am* ælˈbainəu] *n* (*pl* -**os**) albinos *mf*.

album [ˈælbəm] *n* (*book, record*) album *m*.

alchemy [ˈælkəmi] *n* alchimie *f*. ◆**alchemist** *n* alchimiste *m*.

alcohol [ˈælkəhɒl] *n* alcool *m*. ◆**alco'holic** *a* (*person*) alcoolique; (*drink*) alcoolisé; – *n* (*person*) alcoolique *mf*. ◆**alcoholism** *n* alcoolisme *m*.

alcove [ˈælkəuv] *n* alcôve *f*.

alderman [ˈɔːldəmən] *n* (*pl* -**men**) conseiller, -ère *mf* municipal(e).

ale [eil] *n* bière *f*.

alert [əˈlɜːt] *a* (*watchful*) vigilant; (*sharp, awake*) éveillé; – *n* alerte *f*; **on the a.** sur le qui-vive; – *vt* alerter. ◆**—ness** *n* vigilance *f*.

alfalfa [ælˈfælfə] *n Am* luzerne *f*.

algebra [ˈældʒibrə] *n* algèbre *f*. ◆**alge'braic** *a* algébrique.

Algeria [ælˈdʒiəriə] *n* Algérie *f*. ◆**Algerian** *a & n* algérien, -ienne (*mf*).

alias [ˈeiliəs] *adv* alias; – *n* nom *m* d'emprunt.

alibi [ˈælibai] *n* alibi *m*.

alien ['eɪliən] *a* étranger (**to** à); – *n* étranger, -ère *mf*. ◆**alienate** *vt* aliéner; **to a. s.o.** (*make unfriendly*) s'aliéner qn.

alight [ə'laɪt] **1** *a* (*fire*) allumé; (*building*) en feu; (*face*) éclairé; **to set a.** mettre le feu à. **2** *vi* descendre (**from** de); (*of bird*) se poser.

align [ə'laɪn] *vt* aligner. ◆**—ment** *n* alignement *m*.

alike [ə'laɪk] **1** *a* (*people, things*) semblables, pareils; **to look** *or* **be a.** se ressembler. **2** *adv* de la même manière; **summer and winter a.** été comme hiver.

alimony ['ælɪmənɪ, *Am* 'ælɪməʊnɪ] *n Jur* pension *f* alimentaire.

alive [ə'laɪv] *a* vivant, en vie; **a. to** conscient de; **a. with** grouillant de; **burnt a.** brûlé vif; **anyone a.** n'importe qui; **to keep a.** (*custom, memory*) entretenir, perpétuer; **a. and kicking** *Fam* plein de vie; **look a.!** *Fam* active-toi!

all [ɔːl] *a* tout, toute, *pl* tous, toutes; **a. day** toute la journée; **a. (the) men** tous les hommes; **with a. speed** à toute vitesse; **for a. her wealth** malgré toute sa fortune; – *pron* tous *mpl*, toutes *fpl*; (*everything*) tout; **a. will die** tous mourront; **my sisters are a. here** toutes mes sœurs sont ici; **he ate it a., he ate a. of it** il a tout mangé; **a. (that) he has** tout ce qu'il a; **a. in a.** à tout prendre; **in a., a. told** en tout; **a. but impossible**/*etc* presque impossible/*etc*; **anything a.** à quoi que ce soit; **if there's any wind at a.** s'il y a le moindre vent; **not at a.** pas du tout; (*after 'thank you'*) il n'y a pas de quoi; **a. of us** nous tous; **take a. of it** prends (le) tout; – *adv* tout; **a. alone** tout seul; **a. bad** entièrement mauvais; **a. over** (*everywhere*) partout; (*finished*) fini; **a. right** (très) bien; **he's a. right** (*not harmed*) il est sain et sauf; (*healthy*) il va bien; **a. too soon** bien trop tôt; **six a.** *Fb* six buts partout; **a. there** *Fam* éveillé, intelligent; **not a. there** *Fam* simple d'esprit; **a. in** *Fam* épuisé; **a.-in price** prix global; – *n* **my a.** tout ce que j'ai. ◆**a.-'clear** *n Mil* fin *f* d'alerte. ◆**a.-'day** *a* (*party*) qui dure toute la nuit; (*shop*) ouvert toute la nuit. ◆**a.-out** *a* (*effort*) violent; (*war, strike*) tous azimuts. ◆**a.-'powerful** *a* tout-puissant. ◆**a.-purpose** *a* (*tool*) universel. ◆**a.-round** *a* complet. ◆**a.-'rounder** *n* personne *f* qui fait de tout. ◆**a.-time** *a* (*record*) jamais atteint; **to reach an a.-time low/high** arriver au point le plus bas/le plus haut.

allay [ə'leɪ] *vt* calmer, apaiser.

alleg/e [ə'ledʒ] *vt* prétendre. ◆**—ed** *a* (*so-called*) prétendu; (*author, culprit*) présumé; **he is a. to be** on prétend qu'il est. ◆**—edly** [-ɪdlɪ] *adv* d'après ce qu'on dit. ◆**alle'gation** *n* allégation *f*.

allegiance [ə'liːdʒəns] *n* fidélité *f* (**to** à).

allegory ['ælɪgərɪ, *Am* 'æləgɔːrɪ] *n* allégorie *f*. ◆**alle'gorical** *a* allégorique.

allergy ['ælədʒɪ] *n* allergie *f*. ◆**a'llergic** *a* allergique (**to** à).

alleviate [ə'liːvɪeɪt] *vt* alléger.

alley ['ælɪ] *n* ruelle *f*; (*in park*) allée *f*; **blind a.** impasse *f*; **that's up my a.** *Fam* c'est mon truc. ◆**alleyway** *n* ruelle *f*.

alliance [ə'laɪəns] *n* alliance *f*.

allied ['ælaɪd] *a* (*country*) allié; (*matters*) connexe.

alligator ['ælɪgeɪtər] *n* alligator *m*.

allocate ['æləkeɪt] *vt* (*assign*) attribuer, allouer (**to** à); (*distribute*) répartir. ◆**allo-'cation** *n* attribution *f*.

allot [ə'lɒt] *vt* (**-tt-**) (*assign*) attribuer; (*distribute*) répartir. ◆**—ment** *n* attribution *f*; (*share*) partage *m*; (*land*) lopin *m* de terre (loué pour la culture).

allow [ə'laʊ] **1** *vt* permettre; (*grant*) accorder; (*a request*) accéder à; (*deduct*) *Com* déduire; (*add*) *Com* ajouter; **to a. s.o. to do** permettre à qn de faire, autoriser qn à faire; **a. me!** permettez(-moi)!; **not allowed** interdit; **you're not allowed to go on** vous interdit de partir. **2** *vi* **a. for** tenir compte de. ◆**—able** *a* (*acceptable*) admissible; (*expense*) déductible.

allowance [ə'laʊəns] *n* allocation *f*; (*for travel, housing, food*) indemnité *f*; (*for duty-free goods*) tolérance *f*; (*tax-free amount*) abattement *m*; **to make allowance(s) for** (*person*) être indulgent envers; (*thing*) tenir compte de.

alloy ['ælɔɪ] *n* alliage *m*.

allude [ə'luːd] *vi* **to a.** to faire allusion à. ◆**allusion** *n* allusion *f*.

allure [ə'lʊər] *vt* attirer.

ally ['ælaɪ] *n* allié, -ée *mf*; – [ə'laɪ] *vt* (*country, person*) allier.

almanac ['ɔːlmənæk] *n* almanach *m*.

almighty [ɔːl'maɪtɪ] **1** *a* tout-puissant; **the A.** le Tout-Puissant. **2** *a* (*great*) *Fam* terrible, formidable.

almond ['ɑːmənd] *n* amande *f*.

almost ['ɔːlməʊst] *adv* presque; **he a. fell**/*etc* il a failli tomber/*etc*.

alms [ɑːmz] *npl* aumône *f*.

alone [ə'ləʊn] *a & adv* seul; **an expert a. can ... seul** un expert peut ... ; **I did it (all) a.** je l'ai fait à moi (tout) seul, je l'ai fait (tout) seul; **to leave** or **let a.** (*person*) laisser tranquille or en paix; (*thing*) ne pas toucher à.

along [ə'lɒŋ] *prep* (**all**) **a.** (tout) le long de; **to go** or **walk a.** (*street*) passer par; **a. here** par ici; **a. with** avec; – *adv* **all a.** d'un bout à l'autre; (*time*) dès le début; **come a.!** venez!; **move a.!** avancez!

alongside [əlɒŋ'saɪd] *prep* & *adv* à côté (de); **to come a.** *Nau* accoster; **a. the kerb** le long du trottoir.

aloof [ə'luːf] *a* distant; – *adv* à distance; **to keep a.** garder ses distances (**from** par rapport à). **◆—ness** *n* réserve *f*.

aloud [ə'laud] *adv* à haute voix.

alphabet ['ælfəbet] *n* alphabet *m*. **◆alpha'betical** *a* alphabétique.

Alps [ælps] *npl* **the A.** les Alpes *fpl*. **◆alpine** *a* (*club, range etc*) alpin; (*scenery*) alpestre.

already [ɔːl'redɪ] *adv* déjà.

alright [ɔːl'raɪt] *adv* Fam = **all right**.

Alsatian [æl'seɪʃ(ə)n] *n* (*dog*) berger *m* allemand, chien-loup *m*.

also ['ɔːlsəu] *adv* aussi, également. **◆a.-ran** *n* (*person*) Fig perdant, -ante *mf*.

altar ['ɔːltər] *n* autel *m*.

alter ['ɔːltər] *vt* changer, modifier; (*clothing*) retoucher; – *vi* changer. **◆alte'ration** *n* changement *m*, modification *f*; retouche *f*.

altercation [ɔːltə'keɪʃ(ə)n] *n* altercation *f*.

alternat/e [ɔːl'tɜːnət] *a* alterné; **on a. days** tous les deux jours; **a. laughter and tears** des rires et des larmes qui se succèdent; – [ˈɔːltəneɪt] *vi* alterner (**with** avec); – *vt* faire alterner. **◆—ing** *a* (*current*) El alternatif. **◆—ely** *adv* alternativement. **◆alter'nation** *n* alternance *f*.

alternative [ɔːl'tɜːnətɪv] *a* **an a. way/etc** une autre façon/*etc*; **a. answers/etc** (*différentes*). – *n* (*choice*) alternative *f*. **◆—ly** *adv* comme alternative; **or a.** (*or else*) ou bien.

although [ɔːl'ðəu] *adv* bien que, quoique (+ *sub*).

altitude ['æltɪtjuːd] *n* altitude *f*.

altogether [ɔːltə'geðər] *adv* (*completely*) tout à fait; (*on the whole*) somme toute; **how much a.?** combien en tout?

aluminium [ælju'mɪnjəm] (*Am* **aluminum** [ə'luːmɪnəm]) *n* aluminium *m*.

alumnus [ə'lʌmnəs], *pl* **-ni** [-naɪ] *n* Am ancien(ne) élève *mf*, ancien(ne) étudiant, -ante *mf*.

always ['ɔːlweɪz] *adv* toujours; **he's a. criticizing** il est toujours à critiquer.

am [æm, *unstressed* əm] *see* **be**.

a.m. [eɪ'em] *adv* du matin.

amalgam [ə'mælgəm] *n* amalgame *m*. **◆a'malgamate** *vt* amalgamer; (*society*) Com fusionner; – *vi* s'amalgamer; fusionner.

amass [ə'mæs] *vt* (*riches*) amasser.

amateur ['æmətər] *n* amateur *m*; – *a* (*interest, sports*) d'amateur; **a. painter/**etc peintre/*etc* amateur. **◆amateurish** *a* (*work*) Pej d'amateur; (*person*) Pej maladroit, malhabile. **◆amateurism** *n* amateurisme *m*.

amaz/e [ə'meɪz] *vt* stupéfier, étonner. **◆—ed** *a* stupéfait (**at sth** de qch), étonné (**at sth** par or de qch); **a. at seeing/**etc stupéfait or étonné de voir/*etc*. **◆—ing** *a* stupéfiant; Fam extraordinaire. **◆—ingly** *adv* extraordinairement; (*miraculously*) par miracle. **◆amazement** *n* stupéfaction *f*.

ambassador [æm'bæsədər] *n* ambassadeur *m*; (*woman*) ambassadrice *f*.

amber ['æmbər] *n* ambre *m*; **a.** (**light**) Aut (feu *m*) orange *m*.

ambidextrous [æmbɪ'dekstrəs] *a* ambidextre.

ambiguous [æm'bɪgjuəs] *a* ambigu. **◆ambi'guity** *n* ambiguïté *f*.

ambition [æm'bɪʃ(ə)n] *n* ambition *f*. **◆ambitious** *a* ambitieux.

ambivalent [æm'bɪvələnt] *a* ambigu, équivoque.

amble ['æmb(ə)l] *vi* marcher d'un pas tranquille.

ambulance ['æmbjuləns] *n* ambulance *f*; **a. man** ambulancier *m*.

ambush ['æmbuʃ] *n* guet-apens *m*, embuscade *f*; – *vt* prendre en embuscade.

amen [ɑː'men, eɪ'men] *int* amen.

amenable [ə'miːnəb(ə)l] *a* docile; **a. to** (*responsive to*) sensible à; **a. to reason** raisonnable.

amend [ə'mend] *vt* (*text*) modifier; (*conduct*) corriger; Pol amender. **◆—ment** *n* Pol amendement *m*.

amends [ə'mendz] *npl* **to make a. for** réparer; **to make a.** réparer son erreur.

amenities [ə'miːnɪtɪz, Am ə'menɪtɪz] *npl* (*pleasant things*) agréments *mpl*; (*of sports club etc*) équipement *m*; (*of town*) aménagements *mpl*.

America [ə'merɪkə] *n* Amérique *f*; North/South A. Amérique du Nord/du Sud. **◆American** *a* & *n* américain, -aine (*mf*). **◆Americanism** *n* américanisme *m*.

amethyst ['æməθɪst] *n* améthyste *f*.

amiable ['eɪmɪəb(ə)l] *a* aimable.

amicab/le ['æmɪkəb(ə)l] *a* amical. **◆—ly** *adv* amicalement; Jur à l'amiable.

amid(st) [ə'mɪd(st)] *prep* au milieu de, parmi.

amiss [ə'mɪs] *adv & a* mal (à propos); **sth is a.** (*wrong*) qch ne va pas; **that wouldn't come a.** ça ne ferait pas de mal; **to take a.** prendre en mauvaise part.

ammonia [ə'məʊnɪə] *n* (*gas*) ammoniac *m*; (*liquid*) ammoniaque *f*.

ammunition [æmjʊ'nɪʃ(ə)n] *n* munitions *fpl*.

amnesia [æm'niːzjə] *n* amnésie *f*.

amnesty [æm'nəstɪ] *n* amnistie *f*.

amok [ə'mɒk] *adv* **to run a.** se déchaîner, s'emballer.

among(st) [ə'mʌŋ(st)] *prep* parmi, entre; **a. themselves/friends** entre eux/amis; **a. the French/etc** (*group*) chez les Français/etc; **a. the crowd** dans *or* parmi la foule.

amoral [eɪ'mɒrəl] *a* amoral.

amorous [æmərəs] *a* amoureux.

amount [ə'maʊnt] **1** *n* quantité *f*; (*sum of money*) somme *f*; (*total of bill etc*) montant *m*; (*scope, size*) importance *f*. **2** *vi* **to a. to** s'élever à; (*mean*) *Fig* signifier; **it amounts to the same thing** ça revient au même.

amp(ere) [æmp(eər)] *n El* ampère *m*.

amphibian [æm'fɪbɪən] *n & a* amphibie (*m*). ◆**amphibious** *a* amphibie.

amphitheatre [æmfɪθɪətər] *n* amphithéâtre *m*.

ample [æmp(ə)l] *a* (*roomy*) ample; (*enough*) largement assez de; (*reasons, means*) solides; **you have a. time** tu as largement le temps. ◆**amply** *adv* largement, amplement.

amplify [æmplɪfaɪ] *vt* amplifier. ◆**amplifier** *n El* amplificateur *m*.

amputate [æmpjʊteɪt] *vt* amputer. ◆**ampu'tation** *n* amputation *f*.

amuck [ə'mʌk] *adv see* **amok**.

amulet [æmjʊlət] *n* amulette *f*.

amus/e [ə'mjuːz] *vt* amuser, divertir; **to keep s.o. amused** amuser qn. ◆**-ing** *a* amusant. ◆**-ement** *n* amusement *m*, divertissement *m*; (*pastime*) distraction *f*; **a. arcade** salle *f* de jeux.

an [æn, *unstressed* ən] *see* **a**.

anachronism [ə'nækrənɪz(ə)m] *n* anachronisme *m*.

an(a)emia [ə'niːmɪə] *n* anémie *f*. ◆**an(a)emic** *a* anémique.

an(a)esthesia [ænɪs'θiːzɪə] *n* anesthésie *f*. ◆**an(a)esthetic** [ænɪs'θetɪk] *n* (*substance*) anesthésique *m*; **under the a.** sous anesthésie; **general/local a.** anesthésie *f* générale/locale. ◆**an(a)esthetize** [ə'niːsθɪtaɪz] *vt* anesthésier.

anagram [ænəgræm] *n* anagramme *f*.

analogy [ə'nælədʒɪ] *n* analogie *f*. ◆**analogous** *a* analogue (**to** à).

analyse [ænəlaɪz] *vt* analyser. ◆**analysis**, *pl* **-yses** [ə'næləsɪs, -ɪsiːz] *n* analyse *f*. ◆**analyst** *n* analyste *mf*. ◆**ana'lytical** *a* analytique.

anarchy [ænəkɪ] *n* anarchie *f*. ◆**a'narchic** *a* anarchique. ◆**anarchist** *n* anarchiste *mf*.

anathema [ə'næθəmə] *n Rel* anathème *m*; **it is (an) a. to me** j'ai une sainte horreur de cela.

anatomy [ə'nætəmɪ] *n* anatomie *f*. ◆**ana'tomical** *a* anatomique.

ancestor [ænsestər] *n* ancêtre *m*. ◆**an'cestral** *a* ancestral. ◆**ancestry** *n* (*lineage*) ascendance *f*; (*ancestors*) ancêtres *mpl*.

anchor [æŋkər] *n* ancre *f*; **to weigh a.** lever l'ancre; – *vt* (*ship*) mettre à l'ancre; – *vi* jeter l'ancre, mouiller. ◆**-ed** *a* à l'ancre. ◆**-age** *n* mouillage *m*.

anchovy [æntʃəvɪ, *Am* æn'tʃəʊvɪ] *n* anchois *m*.

ancient [eɪnʃənt] *a* ancien; (*pre-medieval*) antique; (*person*) *Hum* vétuste.

ancillary [æn'sɪlərɪ] *a* auxiliaire.

and [ænd, *unstressed* ən(d)] *conj* et; **a knife a. fork** un couteau et une fourchette; **two hundred a. two** deux cent deux; **better a. better** de mieux en mieux; **go a. see** va voir.

anecdote [ænɪkdəʊt] *n* anecdote *f*.

anemone [ə'nemənɪ] *n* anémone *f*.

anew [ə'njuː] *adv Lit* de *or* à nouveau.

angel [eɪndʒəl] *n* ange *m*. ◆**an'gelic** *a* angélique.

anger [æŋgər] *n* colère *f*; **in a., out of a.** sous le coup de la colère; – *vt* mettre en colère, fâcher.

angl/e [æŋg(ə)l] **1** *n* angle *m*; **at an a.** en biais. **2** *vi* (*to fish*) pêcher à la ligne; **to a. for** *Fig* quêter. ◆**-er** *n* pêcheur, -euse *mf* à la ligne. ◆**-ing** *n* pêche *f* à la ligne.

Anglican [æŋglɪkən] *a & n* anglican, -ane (*mf*).

anglicism [æŋglɪsɪz(ə)m] *n* anglicisme *m*.

Anglo- [æŋgləʊ] *pref* anglo-. ◆**Anglo-'Saxon** *a & n* anglo-saxon, -onne (*mf*).

angora [æŋ'gɔːrə] *n* (*wool*) angora *m*.

angry [æŋgrɪ] *a* (**-ier, -iest**) (*person, look*) fâché; (*letter*) indigné; **to get a.** se fâcher, se mettre en colère (**with** contre). ◆**angrily** *adv* en colère; (*to speak*) avec colère.

anguish [æŋgwɪʃ] *n* angoisse *f*. ◆**-ed** *a* angoissé.

angular [æŋgjʊlər] *a* (*face*) anguleux.

animal ['ænɪməl] a animal; – n animal m, bête f.

animate ['ænɪmeɪt] vt animer; **to become animated** s'animer; – ['ænɪmət] a (alive) animé. ◆**ani'mation** n animation f.

animosity [ænɪ'mɒsɪtɪ] n animosité f.

aniseed ['ænɪsiːd] n Culin anis m.

ankle ['æŋk(ə)l] n cheville f; **a. sock** socquette f.

annals ['æn(ə)lz] npl annales fpl.

annex [ə'neks] vt annexer.

annex(e) ['æneks] n (building) annexe f. ◆annex'ation n annexion f.

annihilate [ə'naɪəleɪt] vt anéantir, annihiler. ◆annihi'lation n anéantissement m.

anniversary [ænɪ'vɜːsərɪ] n (of event) anniversaire m, commémoration f.

annotate ['ænəteɪt] vt annoter. ◆anno'tation n annotation f.

announc/e [ə'naʊns] vt annoncer; (birth, marriage) faire part de. ◆**—ement** n annonce f; (of birth, marriage) avis m; (private letter) faire-part m inv. ◆**—er** n TV speaker m, speakerine f.

annoy [ə'nɔɪ] vt (inconvenience) ennuyer, gêner; (irritate) agacer, contrarier. ◆**—ed** a contrarié, fâché; **to get a.** se fâcher (with contre). ◆**—ing** a ennuyeux, contrariant. ◆annoyance n contrariété f, ennui m.

annual ['ænjʊəl] a annuel; – n (book) annuaire m. ◆**—ly** adv annuellement.

annuity [ə'njuːɪtɪ] n (of retired person) pension f viagère.

annul [ə'nʌl] vt (-ll-) annuler. ◆**—ment** n annulation f.

anoint [ə'nɔɪnt] vt oindre (with de). ◆**—ed** a oint.

anomalous [ə'nɒmələs] a anormal. ◆anomaly n anomalie f.

anon [ə'nɒn] adv Hum tout à l'heure.

anonymous [ə'nɒnɪməs] a anonyme; **to remain a.** garder l'anonymat. ◆ano'nymity n anonymat m.

anorak ['ænəræk] n anorak m.

anorexia [ænə'reksɪə] n anorexie f.

another [ə'nʌðər] a & pron un(e) autre; **a. man** un autre homme; **a. month** (additional) encore un mois, un autre mois; **a. ten** encore dix; **one a.** l'un(e) l'autre, pl les un(e)s les autres; **they love one a.** ils s'aiment (l'un l'autre).

answer ['ɑːnsər] n réponse f; (to problem) solution f (to de); (reason) explication f; – vt (person, question, phone etc) répondre à; (word) répondre; (problem) résoudre; (prayer, wish) exaucer; **to a. the bell** or **the door** ouvrir la porte; – vi répondre; **to a.**

back rèpliquer, répondre; **to a. for** (s.o., sth) répondre de. ◆**—able** a responsable (for sth de qch, to s.o. devant qn).

ant [ænt] n fourmi f. ◆**anthill** n fourmilière f.

antagonism [æn'tægənɪz(ə)m] n antagonisme m; (hostility) hostilité f. ◆**antagonist** n antagoniste mf. ◆**antago'nistic** a antagoniste; (hostile) hostile. ◆**antagonize** vt provoquer (l'hostilité de).

antarctic [æn'tɑːktɪk] a antarctique; – n **the A.** l'Antarctique m.

antecedent [æntɪ'siːd(ə)nt] n antécédent m.

antechamber ['æntɪtʃeɪmbər] n antichambre f.

antedate ['æntɪdeɪt] vt (letter) antidater.

antelope ['æntɪləʊp] n antilope f.

antenatal [æntɪ'neɪt(ə)l] a prénatal.

antenna¹, pl **-ae** [æn'tenə, -iː] n (of insect etc) antenne f.

antenna² [æn'tenə] n (pl **-as**) (aerial) Am antenne f.

anteroom ['æntɪrʊm] n antichambre f.

anthem ['ænθəm] n **national a.** hymne m national.

anthology [æn'θɒlədʒɪ] n anthologie f.

anthropology [ænθrə'pɒlədʒɪ] n anthropologie f.

anti- ['ænti, Am 'æntaɪ] pref anti-; **to be a. sth** Fam être contre qch. ◆**anti'aircraft** a antiaérien. ◆**antibi'otic** a & n antibiotique (m). ◆**antibody** n anticorps m. ◆**anti'climax** n chute f dans l'ordinaire; (let-down) déception f. ◆**anti'clockwise** adv dans le sens inverse des aiguilles d'une montre. ◆**anti'cyclone** n anticyclone m. ◆**antidote** n antidote m. ◆**antifreeze** n Aut antigel m. ◆**anti'histamine** n Med antihistaminique m. ◆**anti'perspirant** n antisudoral m. ◆**anti-Se'mitic** a antisémite. ◆**anti-'Semitism** n antisémitisme m. ◆**anti'septic** a & n antiseptique (m). ◆**anti'social** a (misfit) asocial; (measure, principles) antisocial; (unsociable) insociable.

anticipate [æn'tɪsɪpeɪt] vt (foresee) prévoir; (forestall) devancer; (expect) s'attendre à; (the future) anticiper sur. ◆**antici'pation** n prévision f; (expectation) attente f; **in a.** of en prévision de, dans l'attente de; **in a.** (to thank s.o., pay etc) d'avance.

antics ['æntɪks] npl bouffonneries fpl.

antipathy [æn'tɪpəθɪ] n antipathie f.

antipodes [æn'tɪpədiːz] npl antipodes mpl.

antiquarian [æntɪ'kweərɪən] a **a. bookseller**

libraire *mf* spécialisé(e) dans le livre ancien.

antiquated ['æntɪkweɪtɪd] *a* vieilli; (*person*) vieux jeu *inv*.

antique [æn'tiːk] *a* (*furniture etc*) ancien; (*of Greek etc antiquity*) antique; **a. dealer** antiquaire *mf*; **a. shop** magasin *m* d'antiquités; – *n* objet *m* ancien *or* d'époque, antiquité *f*. ◆**antiquity** *n* (*period etc*) antiquité *f*.

antithesis, *pl* **-eses** [æn'tɪθəsɪs, -ɪsiːz] *n* antithèse *f*.

antler ['æntlər] *n* (*tine*) andouiller *m*; *pl* bois *mpl*.

antonym ['æntənɪm] *n* antonyme *m*.

Antwerp ['æntwɜːp] *n* Anvers *m or f*.

anus ['eɪnəs] *n* anus *m*.

anvil ['ænvɪl] *n* enclume *f*.

anxiety [æŋ'zaɪətɪ] *n* (*worry*) inquiétude *f* (*about* au sujet de); (*fear*) anxiété *f*; (*eagerness*) impatience *f* (*for* de).

anxious ['æŋkʃəs] *a* (*worried*) inquiet (*about* de, pour); (*troubled*) anxieux; (*causing worry*) inquiétant; (*eager*) impatient (*to do* de faire); **I'm a. (that) he should go** je tiens beaucoup à ce qu'il parte. ◆**-ly** *adv* avec inquiétude; (*to wait etc*) impatiemment.

any ['enɪ] *a* **1** (*interrogative*) du, de la, des; **have you a. milk/tickets?** avez-vous du lait/des billets?; **is there a man** (*at all*) **who ...?** y a-t-il un homme (quelconque) qui ...? **2** (*negative*) de; (*not any at all*) aucun; **he hasn't a. milk/tickets** il n'a pas de lait/de billets; **there isn't a. proof** il n'y a aucune preuve. **3** (*no matter which*) n'importe quel. **4** (*every*) tout; **at a. hour** à toute heure; **in a. case, at a. rate** de toute façon; – *pron* **1** (*no matter which one*) n'importe lequel; (*somebody*) quelqu'un; **if a. of you** si l'un d'entre vous, si quelqu'un parmi vous; **more than a.** plus que aucun. **2** (*quantity*) en; **have you a.?** en as-tu?; **I don't see a.** je n'en vois pas; – *adv* (*usually not translated*) (*not*) **a.** further/happier/*etc* (pas) plus loin/plus heureux/*etc*; **I don't see her a. more** je ne la vois plus, je ne la vois plus; **a. more tea?** (*a little*) encore du thé?, encore un peu de thé?; **a. better?** (*un peu*) mieux?

anybody ['enɪbɒdɪ] *pron* **1** (*somebody*) quelqu'un; **do you see a.?** vois-tu quelqu'un?; **more than a.** plus que aucun. **2** (*negative*) personne; **he doesn't know a.** il ne connaît personne. **3** (*no matter who*) n'importe qui; **a. would think that ...** on croirait que ....

anyhow ['enɪhaʊ] *adv* (*at any rate*) de toute façon; (*badly*) n'importe comment; **to**

leave sth a. (*in confusion*) laisser qch sens dessus dessous.

anyone ['enɪwʌn] *pron* = **anybody**.

anyplace ['enɪpleɪs] *adv Am* = **anywhere**.

anything ['enɪθɪŋ] *pron* **1** (*something*) quelque chose; **can you see a.?** voyez-vous quelque chose? **2** (*negative*) rien; **he doesn't do a.** il ne fait rien; **without a.** sans rien. **3** (*everything*) tout; **a. you like** (*tout*) ce que tu veux; **like a.** (*to work etc*) *Fam* comme un fou. **4** (*no matter what*) **a.** (**at all**) n'importe quoi.

anyway ['enɪweɪ] *adv* (*at any rate*) de toute façon.

anywhere ['enɪweər] *adv* **1** (*no matter where*) n'importe où. **2** (*everywhere*) partout; **a. you go** partout où vous allez, où que vous alliez; **a. you like** là où tu veux. **3** (*somewhere*) quelque part; **is he going a.?** va-t-il quelque part? **4** (*negative*) nulle part; **he doesn't go a.** il ne va nulle part; **without a. to put it** sans un endroit où le mettre.

apace [ə'peɪs] *adv* rapidement.

apart [ə'pɑːt] *adv* (*to or at one side*) à part; **to tear a.** (*to pieces*) mettre en pièces; **we kept them a.** (*separate*) on les tenait séparés; **with legs (wide) a.** les jambes écartées; **they are a metre a.** ils se trouvent à un mètre l'un de l'autre; **a. from** (*except for*) à part; **to take a.** démonter; **to come a.** (*of two objects*) se séparer; (*of knot etc*) se défaire; **to tell a.** distinguer entre; **worlds a.** (*very different*) diamétralement opposé.

apartheid [ə'pɑːteɪt] *n* apartheid *m*.

apartment [ə'pɑːtmənt] *n* (*flat*) *Am* appartement *m*; (*room*) chambre *f*; **a. house** *Am* immeuble *m* (*d'habitation*).

apathy ['æpəθɪ] *n* apathie *f*. ◆**apa'thetic** *a* apathique.

ape [eɪp] *n* singe *m*; – *vt* (*imitate*) singer.

aperitif [ə'perətɪf] *n* apéritif *m*.

aperture ['æpətʃʊər] *n* ouverture *f*.

apex ['eɪpeks] *n Geom & Fig* sommet *m*.

aphorism ['æfərɪz(ə)m] *n* aphorisme *m*.

aphrodisiac [æfrə'dɪzɪæk] *a & n* aphrodisiaque (*m*).

apiece [ə'piːs] *adv* chacun; **a pound a.** une livre (la) pièce *or* chacun.

apish ['eɪpɪʃ] *a* simiesque; (*imitative*) imitateur.

apocalypse [ə'pɒkəlɪps] *n* apocalypse *f*. ◆**apoca'lyptic** *a* apocalyptique.

apocryphal [ə'pɒkrɪfəl] *a* apocryphe.

apogee ['æpədʒiː] *n* apogée *m*.

apologetic [əpɒlə'dʒetɪk] *a* (*letter*) plein d'excuses; **to be a. about** s'excuser de. ◆**apologetically** *adv* en s'excusant.

apology [əˈpɒlədʒɪ] n excuses fpl; **an a. for a dinner** Fam Pej un dîner minable. ◆**apologist** n apologiste mf. ◆**apologize** vi s'excuser (for de); **to a. to s.o.** faire ses excuses à qn (for pour).

apoplexy [ˈæpəpleksɪ] n apoplexie f. ◆**apoˈplectic** a & n apoplectique (mf).

apostle [əˈpɒs(ə)l] n apôtre m.

apostrophe [əˈpɒstrəfɪ] n apostrophe f.

appal [əˈpɔːl] (Am **appall**) vt (**-ll-**) épouvanter. ◆**appalling** a épouvantable.

apparatus [æpəˈreɪtəs, Am -ˈrætəs] n (equipment, organization) appareil m; (in gym) agrès mpl.

apparel [əˈpærəl] n habit m, habillement m.

apparent [əˈpærənt] a (obvious, seeming) apparent; **it's a. that** il est évident que. ◆**-ly** adv apparemment.

apparition [æpəˈrɪʃ(ə)n] n apparition f.

appeal [əˈpiːl] n (call) appel m; (entreaty) supplication f; (charm) attrait m; (interest) intérêt m; Jur appel m; – vt **to a. to** (s.o., s.o.'s kindness) faire appel à; **to a. to s.o.** (attract) plaire à qn, séduire qn; (interest) intéresser qn; **to a. to s.o. for sth** demander qch à qn; **to a. to s.o. to do** supplier qn de faire; – vi Jur faire appel. ◆**-ing** a (begging) suppliant; (attractive) séduisant.

appear [əˈpɪər] vi (become visible) apparaître; (present oneself) se présenter; (seem, be published) paraître; (act) Th jouer; Jur comparaître; **it appears that** (it seems) il semble que (+ sub or indic); (it is rumoured) il paraîtrait que (+ indic). ◆**appearance** n (act) apparition f; (look) apparence f, aspect m; (of book) parution f; **to put in an a.** faire acte de présence.

appease [əˈpiːz] vt apaiser; (curiosity) satisfaire.

append [əˈpend] vt joindre, ajouter (to à). ◆**-age** n Anat appendice m.

appendix, pl **-ixes** or **-ices** [əˈpendɪks, -ɪksɪz, -ɪsiːz] n (of book) & Anat appendice m. ◆**appendicitis** [əpendɪˈsaɪtɪs] n appendicite f.

appertain [æpəˈteɪn] vi **to a. to** se rapporter to.

appetite [ˈæpɪtaɪt] n appétit m; **to take away s.o.'s a.** couper l'appétit à qn. ◆**appetizer** n (drink) apéritif m; (food) amuse-gueule m inv. ◆**appetizing** a appétissante.

applaud [əˈplɔːd] vt (clap) applaudir; (approve of) approuver, applaudir à; – vi applaudir. ◆**applause** n applaudissements mpl.

apple [ˈæp(ə)l] n pomme f; **stewed apples**, **sauce** compote f de pommes; **eating/**cooking a.** pomme f à couteau/à cuire; **a. pie** tarte f aux pommes; **a. core** trognon m de pomme; **a. tree** pommier m.

appliance [əˈplaɪəns] n appareil m.

apply [əˈplaɪ] 1 vt (put, carry out etc) appliquer; (brake) Aut appuyer sur; **to a. oneself to** s'appliquer à. 2 vi (be relevant) s'appliquer (to à); **to a. for** (job) poser sa candidature à, postuler; **to a. to s.o.** (ask) s'adresser à qn (for pour). ◆**applied** a (maths etc) appliqué. ◆**applicable** a applicable (to à). ◆**applicant** n candidat, -ate mf (for à). ◆**appliˈcation** n application f; (request) demande f; (for job) candidature f; (for membership) demande f d'adhésion or d'inscription; **a. (form)** (job) formulaire m de candidature; (club) formulaire m d'inscription or d'adhésion.

appoint [əˈpɔɪnt] vt (person) nommer (to sth à qch, **to do** pour faire); (time etc) désigner, fixer; **at the appointed time** à l'heure dite; **well-appointed** bien équipé. ◆**-ment** n nomination f; (meeting) rendez-vous m inv; (post) place f, situation f.

apportion [əˈpɔːʃ(ə)n] vt répartir.

apposite [ˈæpəzɪt] a juste, à propos.

appraise [əˈpreɪz] vt évaluer. ◆**appraisal** n évaluation f.

appreciate [əˈpriːʃɪeɪt] 1 vt (enjoy, value, assess) apprécier; (understand) comprendre; (be grateful for) être reconnaissant de. 2 vi prendre de la valeur. ◆**appreciable** a appréciable, sensible. ◆**appreciˈation** n 1 (judgement) appréciation f; (gratitude) reconnaissance f. 2 (rise in value) plus-value f. ◆**appreciative** a (grateful) reconnaissant (of de); (laudatory) élogieux; **to be a. of** (enjoy) apprécier.

apprehend [æprɪˈhend] vt (seize, arrest) appréhender. ◆**apprehension** n (fear) appréhension f. ◆**apprehensive** a inquiet (about de, au sujet de); **to be a. of** redouter.

apprentice [əˈprentɪs] n apprenti, -ie mf; – vt mettre en apprentissage (to chez). ◆**apprenticeship** n apprentissage m.

approach [əˈprəʊtʃ] vt (draw near to) s'approcher de (qn, feu, porte etc); (age, result, town) approcher de; (subject) aborder; (accost) aborder (qn); **to a. s.o. about** parler à qn de; – vi (of person, vehicle) s'approcher; (of date etc) approcher; – n approche f; (method) façon f de s'y prendre; (path) voie f d'accès m; **a. to** (question) manière f d'aborder; **to make approaches to** faire des avances à.

◆—**able** a (place) accessible; (person) abordable.
appropriate 1 [ə'prəʊprɪət] a (place, tools, clothes etc) approprié, adéquat; (remark, time) opportun; **a. to** or **for** propre à, approprié à. **2** [ə'prəʊprɪeɪt] vt (set aside) affecter; (steal) s'approprier. ◆—**ly** adv convenablement.
approv/e [ə'pruːv] vt approuver; **to a. of sth** approuver qch; **I don't a. of him** il ne me plaît pas, je ne l'apprécie pas; **I a. of his going** je trouve bon qu'il y aille; **I a. of her having accepted** je l'approuve d'avoir accepté. ◆—**ing** a approbateur. ◆**approval** n approbation f; **on a.** (goods) Com à l'essai.
approximate [ə'prɒksɪmət] a approximatif; – [ə'prɒksɪmeɪt] vi **to a. to** se rapprocher de. ◆—**ly** adv à peu près, approximativement. ◆**approxi'mation** n approximation f.
apricot ['eɪprɪkɒt] n abricot m.
April ['eɪprəl] n avril m; **to make an A. fool of** faire un poisson d'avril à.
apron ['eɪprən] n (garment) tablier m.
apse [æps] n (of church) abside f.
apt [æpt] a (suitable) convenable; (remark, reply) juste; (word, name) bien choisi; (student) doué, intelligent; **to be a. to** avoir tendance à; **a. at sth** habile à qch. ◆**aptitude** n aptitude f (for à, pour). ◆**aptly** adv convenablement; **a. named** qui porte bien son nom.
aqualung ['ækwəlʌŋ] n scaphandre m autonome.
aquarium [ə'kweərɪəm] n aquarium m.
Aquarius [ə'kweərɪəs] n (sign) le Verseau.
aquatic [ə'kwætɪk] a (plant etc) aquatique; (sport) nautique.
aqueduct ['ækwɪdʌkt] n aqueduc m.
aquiline ['ækwɪlaɪn] a (nose, profile) aquilin.
Arab ['ærəb] a & n arabe (mf). ◆**Arabian** [ə'reɪbɪən] a arabe. ◆**Arabic** a & n (language) arabe (m); **A. numerals** chiffres mpl arabes.
arabesque [ærə'besk] n (decoration) arabesque f.
arable ['ærəb(ə)l] a (land) arable.
arbiter ['ɑːbɪtər] n arbitre m. ◆**arbitrate** vti arbitrer. ◆**arbi'tration** n arbitrage m; **to go to a.** soumettre la question à l'arbitrage. ◆**arbitrator** n (in dispute) médiateur, -trice mf.
arbitrary ['ɑːbɪtrərɪ] a arbitraire.
arbour ['ɑːbər] n tonnelle f, charmille f.
arc [ɑːk] n (of circle) arc m.

arcade [ɑː'keɪd] n (market) passage m couvert.
arch [ɑːtʃ] n (of bridge) arche f; Archit voûte f, arc m; (of foot) cambrure f; – vt (one's back etc) arquer, courber. ◆**archway** n passage m voûté, voûte f.
arch- [ɑːtʃ] pref (villain etc) achevé; **a. enemy** ennemi m numéro un.
arch(a)eology [ɑːkɪ'ɒlədʒɪ] n archéologie f. ◆**arch(a)eologist** n archéologue mf.
archaic [ɑː'keɪɪk] a archaïque.
archangel ['ɑːkeɪndʒəl] n archange m.
archbishop [ɑːtʃ'bɪʃəp] n archevêque m.
archer ['ɑːtʃər] n archer m. ◆**archery** n tir m à l'arc.
archetype ['ɑːkɪtaɪp] n archétype m.
archipelago [ɑːkɪ'peləgəʊ] n (pl -oes or -os) archipel m.
architect ['ɑːkɪtekt] n architecte m. ◆**architecture** n architecture f.
archives ['ɑːkaɪvz] npl archives fpl. ◆**archivist** n archiviste mf.
arctic ['ɑːktɪk] a arctique; (weather) polaire, glacial; – n the A. l'Arctique m.
ardent ['ɑːdənt] a ardent. ◆—**ly** adv ardemment. ◆**ardour** n ardeur f.
arduous ['ɑːdjʊəs] a ardu.
are [ɑːr] see be.
area ['eərɪə] n Math superficie f; Geog région f; (of town) quartier m; Mil zone f; (domain) Fig domaine m, secteur m, terrain m; built-up a. agglomération f; parking a. aire f de stationnement; a. code Tel Am indicatif m.
arena [ə'riːnə] n Hist & Fig arène f.
Argentina [ɑːdʒən'tiːnə] n Argentine f. ◆**Argentine** ['ɑːdʒəntaɪn] a & n, ◆**Argentinian** a & n argentin, -ine (mf).
argu/e ['ɑːgjuː] vi (quarrel) se disputer (with avec, about au sujet de); (reason) raisonner (with avec, about sur); to a. in favour of plaider pour; – vt (matter) discuter; to a. that (maintain) soutenir que. ◆—**able** ['ɑːgjʊəb(ə)l] a discutable. ◆—**ably** adv on pourrait soutenir que. ◆—**ment** n (quarrel) dispute f; (reasoning) argument m; (debate) discussion f; to have an a. se disputer. ◆**argu'mentative** a raisonneur.
aria ['ɑːrɪə] n Mus air m (d'opéra).
arid ['ærɪd] a aride.
Aries ['eəriːz] n (sign) le Bélier.
arise [ə'raɪz] vi (pt arose, pp arisen) (of problem, opportunity etc) se présenter; (of cry, objection) s'élever; (result) résulter (from de); (get up) Lit se lever.
aristocracy [ærɪ'stɒkrəsɪ] n aristocratie f. ◆**aristocrat** ['ærɪstəkræt, Am ə'rɪstəkræt]

n aristocrate *mf*. ◆**aristo'cratic** *a* aristocratique.

arithmetic [ə'rɪθmətɪk] *n* arithmétique *f*.

ark [ɑːk] *n* Noah's a. l'arche *f* de Noé.

arm [ɑːm] **1** *n* bras *m*; **a. in a.** bras dessus bras dessous; **with open arms** à bras ouverts. **2** *n* (*weapon*) arme *f*; **arms race** course *f* aux armements; – *vt* armer (**with** de). ◆**armament** *n* armement *m*. ◆**armband** *n* brassard *m*. ◆**armchair** *n* fauteuil *m*. ◆**armful** *n* brassée *f*. ◆**armhole** *n* emmanchure *f*. ◆**armpit** *n* aisselle *f*. ◆**armrest** *n* accoudoir *m*.

armadillo [ɑːmə'dɪləʊ] *n* (*pl* -os) tatou *m*.

armistice ['ɑːmɪstɪs] *n* armistice *m*.

armour ['ɑːmər] *n* (*of knight etc*) armure *f*; (*of tank etc*) blindage *m*. ◆**armoured** *a*, ◆**armour-plated** *a* blindé. ◆**armoury** *n* arsenal *m*.

army ['ɑːmɪ] *n* armée *f*; – *a* (*uniform etc*) militaire; **to join the a.** s'engager; **regular a.** armée *f* active.

aroma [ə'rəʊmə] *n* arôme *m*. ◆**aro'matic** *a* aromatique.

arose [ə'rəʊz] *see* **arise**.

around [ə'raʊnd] *prep* autour de; (*approximately*) environ, autour de; **to go a. the world** faire le tour du monde; – *adv* autour; **all a.** tout autour; **to follow a.** suivre partout; **to rush a.** courir çà et là; **here and there;** **he's still a.** il est encore là; **there's a lot of flu a.** il y a pas mal de grippes dans l'air; **up and a.** (*after illness*) *Am* sur pied, guéri.

arouse [ə'raʊz] *vt* éveiller, susciter; (*sexually*) exciter; **to a. from sleep** tirer du sommeil.

arrange [ə'reɪndʒ] *vt* arranger; (*time, meeting*) fixer; **it was arranged that** il était convenu que; **to a. to do** s'arranger pour faire. ◆**-ment** *n* (*layout, agreement*) arrangement *m*; *pl* (*preparations*) préparatifs *mpl*; (*plans*) projets *mpl*; **to make arrangements to** s'arranger pour.

array [ə'reɪ] *n* (*display*) étalage *m*. ◆**arrayed** *a* (*dressed*) *Lit* (re)vêtu (**in** de).

arrears [ə'rɪəz] *npl* (*payment*) arriéré *m*; **to be in a.** avoir des arriérés.

arrest [ə'rest] *vt* arrêter; – *n Jur* arrestation *f*; **under a.** en état d'arrestation; **cardiac a.** arrêt *m* du cœur. ◆**-ing** *a* (*striking*) *Fig* frappant.

arrive [ə'raɪv] *vi* arriver. ◆**arrival** *n* arrivée *f*; **new a.** nouveau venu *m*, nouvelle venue *f*; (*baby*) nouveau-né. ◆**née** *mf*.

arrogant ['ærəgənt] *a* arrogant. ◆**arro-**

gance *n* arrogance *f*. ◆**arrogantly** *adv* avec arrogance.

arrow ['ærəʊ] *n* flèche *f*.

arsenal ['ɑːsən(ə)l] *n* arsenal *m*.

arsenic ['ɑːsnɪk] *n* arsenic *m*.

arson ['ɑːs(ə)n] *n* incendie *m* volontaire. ◆**arsonist** *n* incendiaire *mf*.

art [ɑːt] *n* art *m*; (*cunning*) artifice *m*; **work of a.** œuvre *f* d'art; **fine arts** beaux-arts *mpl*; **faculty of arts** *Univ* faculté *f* des lettres; **a. school** école *f* des beaux-arts.

artefact ['ɑːtɪfækt] *n* objet *m* fabriqué.

artery ['ɑːtərɪ] *n* *Anat Aut* artère *f*. ◆**ar'terial** *a* *Anat* artériel; **a. road** route *f* principale.

artful ['ɑːtfəl] *a* rusé, astucieux. ◆**-ly** *adv* astucieusement.

arthritis [ɑː'θraɪtɪs] *n* arthrite *f*.

artichoke ['ɑːtɪtʃəʊk] *n* (*globe*) a. artichaut *m*; **Jerusalem a.** topinambour *m*.

article ['ɑːtɪk(ə)l] *n* (*object, clause*) & *Journ Gram* article *m*; **a. of clothing** vêtement *m*; **articles of value** objets *mpl* de valeur; **leading a.** *Journ* éditorial *m*.

articulate [ɑː'tɪkjʊlət] *a* (*sound*) net, distinct; (*person*) qui s'exprime clairement; – [ɑː'tɪkjʊleɪt] *vti* (*speak*) articuler. ◆**-ed** *a* **a. lorry** semi-remorque *m*. ◆**articu'lation** *n* articulation *f*.

artifact ['ɑːtɪfækt] *n* objet *m* fabriqué.

artifice ['ɑːtɪfɪs] *n* artifice *m*.

artificial [ɑːtɪ'fɪʃ(ə)l] *a* artificiel. ◆**artifici'ality** *n* caractère *m* artificiel. ◆**artificially** *adv* artificiellement.

artillery [ɑː'tɪlərɪ] *n* artillerie *f*.

artisan ['ɑːtɪzæn] *n* artisan *m*.

artist ['ɑːtɪst] *n* (*actor, painter etc*) artiste *mf*. ◆**artiste** [ɑː'tiːst] *n* *Th Mus* artiste *m*. ◆**ar'tistic** *a* (*sense, treasure etc*) artistique; (*person*) artiste. ◆**artistry** *n* art *m*.

artless ['ɑːtləs] *a* naturel, naïf.

arty ['ɑːtɪ] *a* *Pej* du genre artiste.

as [æz, *unstressed* əz] *adv* & *conj* **1** (*manner etc*) comme; **as you like** comme tu veux; **such as** comme, tel que; **as much or as hard as I can** (autant que je peux; **as it is** (*this being the case*) les choses étant ainsi; (*to leave it*) comme ça, tel quel; **it's late as it is** il est déjà tard; **as if, as though** comme si. **2** (*comparison*) **as tall as you** aussi grand que vous; **is he as tall as you?** est-il aussi *or* si grand que vous?; **as white as a sheet** blanc comme un linge; **as much or as hard as you** autant que vous; **the same as** le même que; **twice as big as** deux fois plus grand que. **3** (*concessive*) **(as) clever as he is** si *or* aussi intelligent qu'il soit. **4** (*capacity*) **as a**

teacher comme professeur, en tant que or en qualité de professeur; **to act as a father** agir en père. **5** (*reason*) puisque, comme; **as it's late** puisqu'il est tard, comme il est tard. **6** (*time*) **as I left** comme je partais; **as one grows older** à mesure que l'on vieillit; **as he slept** pendant qu'il dormait; **one day as . . .** un jour que . . . ; **as from, as of** (*time*) à partir de. **7** (*concerning*) **as for that, as to that** quant à cela. **8** (+ *inf*) **so as to** de manière à; **so stupid as to** assez bête pour.

asbestos [æs'bestəs] *n* amiante *f*.

ascend [ə'send] *vi* monter; – *vt* (*throne*) monter sur; (*stairs*) monter; (*mountain*) faire l'ascension de. **◆ascent** *n* ascension *f* (de); (*slope*) côte *f*.

ascertain [æsə'tein] *vt* (*discover*) découvrir; (*check*) s'assurer de.

ascetic [ə'setik] *a* ascétique; – *n* ascète *mf*.

ascribe [ə'skraib] *vt* attribuer (to à).

ash [æʃ] *n* **1** (*of cigarette etc*) cendre *f*; A. Wednesday mercredi *m* des Cendres. **2** (*tree*) frêne *m*. **◆ashen** *a* (*pale grey*) cendré; (*face*) pâle. **◆ashcan** *n Am* poubelle *f*. **◆ashtray** *n* cendrier *m*.

ashamed [ə'feimd] *a* honteux; **to be a. of** avoir honte de; **to be a. (of oneself)** avoir honte.

ashore [ə'ʃɔːr] *adv* **to go a.** débarquer; **to put s.o.** débarquer qn.

Asia ['eiʃə] *n* Asie *f*. **◆Asian** *a* asiatique; – *n* Asiatique *mf*, Asiate *mf*.

aside [ə'said] **1** *adv* de côté; **to draw a.** (*curtain*) écarter; **to take** or **draw s.o. a.** prendre qn à part; **to step a.** s'écarter; **a. from** en dehors de. **2** *n Th* aparté *m*.

asinine ['æsinain] *a* stupide, idiot.

ask [ɑːsk] *vt* demander; (*a question*) poser; (*invite*) inviter; **to a. s.o. (for) sth** demander qch à qn; **to a. s.o. to do** demander à qn de faire; – *vi* demander; **to a. for sth/s.o.** demander qch/qn; **to a. for sth back** redemander qch; **to a. about sth** se renseigner sur qch; **to a. after** or **about s.o.** demander des nouvelles de qn; **to a. s.o. about** interroger qn sur; **asking price** prix *m* demandé.

askance [ə'skæns] *adv* **to look a.** at regarder avec méfiance.

askew [ə'skjuː] *adv* de biais, de travers.

aslant [ə'slɑːnt] *adv* de travers.

asleep [ə'sliːp] *a* endormi; (*arm, leg*) engourdi; **to be a.** dormir; **to fall a.** s'endormir.

asp [æsp] *n* (*snake*) aspic *m*.

asparagus [ə'spærəgəs] *n* (*plant*) asperge *f*; (*shoots*) *Culin* asperges *fpl*.

aspect ['æspekt] *n* aspect *m*; (*of house*) orientation *f*.

aspersions [ə'spɜːʃ(ə)nz] *npl* **to cast a. on** dénigrer.

asphalt ['æsfælt, *Am* 'æsfɔːlt] *n* asphalte *m*; – *vt* asphalter.

asphyxia [æs'fiksiə] *n* asphyxie *f*. **◆asphyxiate** *vt* asphyxier. **◆asphyxi'ation** *n* asphyxie *f*.

aspire [ə'spaiər] *vi* **to a. to** aspirer à. **◆aspi'ration** *n* aspiration *f*.

aspirin ['æsprin] *n* aspirine *f*.

ass [æs] *n* (*animal*) âne *m*; (*person*) *Fam* imbécile *mf*, âne *m*; **she-a.** ânesse *f*.

assail [ə'seil] *vt* assaillir (**with** de). **◆assailant** *n* agresseur *m*.

assassin [ə'sæsin] *n Pol* assassin *m*. **◆assassinate** *vt Pol* assassiner. **◆assassi'nation** *n Pol* assassinat *m*.

assault [ə'sɔːlt] *n Mil* assaut *m*; *Jur* agression *f*; – *vt Jur* agresser; (*woman*) violenter.

assemble [ə'semb(ə)l] *vt* (*objects, ideas*) assembler; (*people*) rassembler; (*machine*) monter; – *vi* se rassembler. **◆assembly** *n* (*meeting*) assemblée *f*; *Tech* montage *m*, assemblage *m*; *Sch* rassemblement *m*; **a. line** (*in factory*) chaîne *f* de montage.

assent [ə'sent] *n* assentiment *m*; – *vi* consentir (to à).

assert [ə'sɜːt] *vt* affirmer (**that** que); (*rights*) revendiquer; **to a. oneself** s'affirmer. **◆assertion** *n* affirmation *f*; revendication *f*. **◆assertive** *a* affirmatif; *Pej* autoritaire.

assess [ə'ses] *vt* (*estimate, evaluate*) évaluer; (*decide amount of*) fixer le montant de; (*person*) juger. **◆—ment** *n* évaluation *f*; jugement *m*. **◆assessor** *n* (*valuer*) expert *m*.

asset ['æset] *n* atout *m*, avantage *m*; *pl Com* biens *mpl*, avoir *m*.

assiduous [ə'sidjuəs] *a* assidu.

assign [ə'sain] *vt* (*allocate*) assigner; (*day etc*) fixer; (*appoint*) nommer (**to** à). **◆—ment** *n* (*task*) mission *f*; *Sch* devoirs *mpl*.

assimilate [ə'simileit] *vt* assimiler; – *vi* s'assimiler. **◆assimi'lation** *n* assimilation *f*.

assist [ə'sist] *vti* aider (**in doing, to do** à faire). **◆assistance** *n* aide *f*; **to be of a. to s.o.** aider qn. **◆assistant** *n* assistant, -ante *mf*; (*in shop*) vendeur, -euse *mf*; – *a* adjoint.

assizes [ə'saiziz] *npl Jur* assises *fpl*.

associate [ə'səuʃieit] *vt* associer (**with** à, **avec**); – *vi* **to a. with s.o.** fréquenter qn; **to**

a. (oneself) with (in business venture) s'associer à or avec; — (with) a. se associé, -ée (mf). ◆associ'ation n association f; pl (memories) souvenirs mpl.

assort/ed [ə'sɔːtɪd] a (different) variés; (foods) assortis; well-a. bien assorti. ◆—ment n assortiment m.

assuage [ə'sweɪdʒ] vt apaiser, adoucir.

assum/e [ə'sjuːm] vt 1 (take on) prendre; (responsibility, role) assumer; (attitude, name) adopter. 2 (suppose) présumer (that que). ◆—ed a (feigned) faux; a. name nom m d'emprunt. ◆assumption n (supposition) supposition f.

assur/e [ə'ʃuər] vt assurer. ◆—edly [-ɪdlɪ] adv assurément. ◆assurance n assurance f.

asterisk ['æstərɪsk] n astérisque m.

astern [ə'stɜːn] adv Nau à l'arrière.

asthma ['æsmə] n asthme m. ◆asth'matic a & n asthmatique (mf).

astir [ə'stɜːr] a (excited) en émoi; (out of bed) debout.

astonish [ə'stɒnɪʃ] vt étonner; to be astonished s'étonner (at sth de qch). ◆—ing a étonnant. ◆—ingly adv étonnamment. ◆—ment n étonnement m.

astound [ə'staund] vt stupéfier, étonner. ◆—ing a stupéfiant.

astray [ə'streɪ] adv to go a. s'égarer; to lead a. égarer.

astride [ə'straɪd] adv à califourchon; — prep à cheval sur.

astringent [ə'strɪndʒənt] a (harsh) sévère.

astrology [ə'strɒlədʒɪ] n astrologie f. ◆astrologer n astrologue m.

astronaut ['æstrənɔːt] n astronaute mf.

astronomy [ə'strɒnəmɪ] n astronomie f. ◆astronomer n astronome m. ◆astro-'nomical a astronomique.

astute [ə'stjuːt] a (crafty) rusé; (clever) astucieux.

asunder [ə'sʌndər] adv (to pieces) en pièces; (in two) en deux.

asylum [ə'saɪləm] n asile m; lunatic a. Pej maison f de fous, asile m d'aliénés.

at [æt, unstressed ət] prep 1 à; at the end à la fin; at work au travail; at six (o'clock) à six heures. 2 chez; at the doctor's chez le médecin; at home chez soi, à la maison. ◆at-home f n réception f. 3 en; at sea en mer; at war en guerre; good at (geography etc) fort en. 4 contre; angry at fâché contre. 5 sur; to shoot at tirer sur; at my request sur ma demande. 6 de; to laugh at rire de; surprised at surpris de. 7 (au)près de; at the window (au)près de la fenêtre. 8 par; to

come in at the door entrer par la porte; six at a time six par six. 9 at night la nuit; to look at regarder; not at all pas du tout; (after 'thank you') pas de quoi!; nothing at all rien du tout; to be (hard) at it être très occupé, travailler dur; he's always (on) at me Fam il est toujours après moi.

ate [et, Am eɪt] see eat.

atheism ['eɪθɪɪz(ə)m] n athéisme m. ◆atheist n athée mf.

Athens ['æθɪnz] n Athènes m or f.

athlete ['æθliːt] n athlète mf; a.'s foot Med mycose f. ◆ath'letic a athlétique; a. meeting réunion f sportive. ◆ath'letics npl athlétisme m.

atishoo! [ə'tɪʃuː] (Am atchoo [ə'tʃuː]) int atchoum!

Atlantic [ət'læntɪk] a atlantique; — n the A. l'Atlantique m.

atlas ['ætləs] n atlas m.

atmosphere ['ætməsfɪər] n atmosphère f. ◆atmos'pheric a atmosphérique.

atom ['ætəm] n atome m; a. bomb bombe f atomique. ◆a'tomic a atomique. ◆atomizer n atomiseur m.

atone [ə'təʊn] vi to a. for expier. ◆—ment n expiation f (for de).

atrocious [ə'trəʊʃəs] a atroce. ◆atrocity n atrocité f.

atrophy ['ætrəfɪ] vi s'atrophier.

attach [ə'tætʃ] vt attacher (to à); (document) joindre (to à); attached to (fond of) attaché à. ◆—ment n (affection) attachement m; (fastener) attache f; (tool) accessoire m.

attaché [ə'tæʃeɪ] n 1 Pol attaché, -ée mf. 2 a. case attaché-case m.

attack [ə'tæk] n Mil Med & Fig attaque f; (of fever) accès m; (on s.o.'s life) attentat m; heart a. crise f cardiaque; — vt attaquer; (problem, plan) s'attaquer à; — vi attaquer. ◆—er n agresseur m.

attain [ə'teɪn] vt parvenir à, atteindre, réaliser. ◆—able a accessible. ◆—ment n (of ambition, aim etc) réalisation f (of de); pl (skills) talents mpl.

attempt [ə'tempt] n tentative f; to make an a. to essayer or tenter de; a. on (record) tentative pour battre; a. on s.o.'s life attentat m contre qn; — vt tenter; (task) entreprendre; to a. to do essayer or tenter de faire; attempted murder tentative de meurtre.

attend [ə'tend] vt (match etc) assister à; (course) suivre; (school, church) aller à; (wait on, serve) servir; (escort) accompagner; (patient) soigner; — vi assister; to a. to (pay attention to) prêter attention à;

(*take care of*) s'occuper de. ◆—ed *a*
well-a. (*course*) très suivi; (*meeting*) où il y a
du monde. ◆attendance *n* présence *f* (at
à); (*people*) assistance *f*; school a. scolarité
f; in a. de service. ◆attendant 1 *n*
employé, -ée *mf*; (*in museum*) gardien,
-ienne *mf*; *pl* (*of prince, king etc*) suite *f*. 2 *a*
(*fact*) concomitant.

attention [ə'tenʃ(ə)n] *n* attention *f*; to pay a.
prêter *or* faire attention (to à); a.! *Mil*
garde-à-vous!; to stand at a. *Mil* être au
garde-à-vous; a. to detail minutie *f*.
◆attentive *a* (*heedful*) attentif (to à);
(*thoughtful*) attentionné (to pour).
◆attentively *adv* avec attention, attentivement.

attenuate [ə'tenjʊeɪt] *vt* atténuer.

attest [ə'test] *vti* to a. (to) témoigner de.

attic ['ætɪk] *n* grenier *m*.

attire [ə'taɪər] *n Lit* vêtements *mpl*.

attitude ['ætɪtjuːd] *n* attitude *f*.

attorney [ə'tɜːnɪ] *n* (*lawyer*) *Am* avocat *m*;
district a. *Am* = procureur *m* (de la République).

attract [ə'trækt] *vt* attirer. ◆attraction *n*
attraction *f*; (*charm, appeal*) attrait *m*.
◆attractive *a* (*price etc*) intéressant; (*girl*)
belle, jolie; (*boy*) beau; (*manners*)
attrayant.

attribut/e 1 ['ætrɪbjuːt] *n* (*quality*) attribut
m. 2 [ə'trɪbjuːt] *vt* (*ascribe*) attribuer (to à).
◆—able *a* attribuable (to à).

attrition [ə'trɪʃ(ə)n] *n* war of a. guerre *f*
d'usure.

attuned [ə'tjuːnd] *a* a. to (*of ideas, trends etc*)
en accord avec; (*used to*) habitué à.

atypical [eɪ'tɪpɪk(ə)l] *a* peu typique.

aubergine ['əʊbəʒiːn] *n* aubergine *f*.

auburn ['ɔːbən] *a* (*hair*) châtain roux.

auction ['ɔːkʃən] *n* vente *f* (aux enchères); —
vt to a. (off) vendre (aux enchères).
◆auctio'neer *n* commissaire-priseur *m*,
adjudicateur, -trice *mf*.

audacious [ɔː'deɪʃəs] *a* audacieux.
◆audacity *n* audace *f*.

audib/le ['ɔːdɪb(ə)l] *a* perceptible, audible.
◆—ly *adv* distinctement.

audience ['ɔːdɪəns] *n* assistance *f*, public *m*;
(*of speaker, musician*) auditoire *m*; *Th Cin*
spectateurs *mpl*; *Rad* auditeurs *mpl*; (*interview*) audience *f*.

audio ['ɔːdɪəʊ] *a* (*cassette, system etc*) audio
inv. ◆audiotypist *n* dactylo *f* au
magnétophone, audiotypiste *mf*.
◆audio-'visual *a* audio-visuel.

audit ['ɔːdɪt] *vt* (*accounts*) vérifier; — *n* vérifi-

cation *f* (des comptes). ◆auditor *n*
commissaire *m* aux comptes.

audition [ɔː'dɪʃ(ə)n] *n* audition *f*; — *vti* auditionner.

auditorium [ɔːdɪ'tɔːrɪəm] *n* salle *f* (de spectacle, concert etc).

augment [ɔːg'ment] *vt* augmenter (with, by
de).

augur ['ɔːgər] *vt* présager; — *vi* to a. well être
de bon augure.

august [ɔː'gʌst] *a* auguste.

August ['ɔːgəst] *n* août *m*.

aunt [ɑːnt] *n* tante *f*. ◆auntie *or* aunty *n*
Fam tata *f*.

au pair [əʊ'peər] *adv* au pair; — *n* au p. (girl)
jeune fille *f* au pair.

aura ['ɔːrə] *n* émanation *f*, aura *f*; (*of place*)
atmosphère *f*.

auspices ['ɔːspɪsɪz] *npl* auspices *mpl*.

auspicious [ɔː'spɪʃəs] *a* favorable.

austere [ɔː'stɪər] *a* austère. ◆austerity *n*
austérité *f*.

Australia [ɒ'streɪlɪə] *n* Australie *f*. ◆Aus-
tralian *a* & *n* australien, -ienne (*mf*).

Austria ['ɒstrɪə] *n* Autriche *f*. ◆Austrian *a*
& *n* autrichien, -ienne (*mf*).

authentic [ɔː'θentɪk] *a* authentique.
◆authenticate *vt* authentifier.
◆authen'ticity *n* authenticité *f*.

author ['ɔːθər] *n* auteur *m*. ◆authoress *n*
femme *f* auteur. ◆authorship *n* (*of book
etc*) paternité *f*.

authority [ɔː'θɒrɪtɪ] *n* autorité *f*; (*permission*)
autorisation *f* (to do de faire); to be in a. (*in
charge*) être responsable. ◆authori-
'tarian *a* & *n* autoritaire (*mf*).
◆authoritative *a* (*report*) autorisé; (*tone,
person*) autoritaire.

authorize ['ɔːθəraɪz] *vt* autoriser (to do à
faire). ◆authori'zation *n* autorisation *f*.

autistic [ɔː'tɪstɪk] *a* autiste, autistique.

autobiography [ɔːtəbaɪ'ɒgrəfɪ] *n* autobiographie *f*.

autocrat ['ɔːtəkræt] *n* autocrate *m*. ◆auto-
'cratic *a* autocratique.

autograph ['ɔːtəɡrɑːf] *n* autographe *m*; — *vt*
dédicacer (for à).

automat ['ɔːtəmæt] *n Am* cafétéria *f* à
distributeurs automatiques.

automate ['ɔːtəmeɪt] *vt* automatiser.
◆auto'mation *n* automatisation *f*, automation *f*.

automatic [ɔːtə'mætɪk] *a* automatique.
◆automatically *adv* automatiquement.

automaton [ɔː'tɒmətən] *n* automate *m*.

automobile ['ɔːtəməbiːl] *n Am* auto(mobile)
f.

autonomous [ɔːˈtɒnəməs] a autonome. ◆**autonomy** n autonomie f.

autopsy [ˈɔːtɒpsɪ] n autopsie f.

autumn [ˈɔːtəm] n automne m. ◆**autumnal** [ɔːˈtʌmnəl] a automnal.

auxiliary [ɔːgˈzɪljərɪ] a & n auxiliaire (mf); a. (verb) (verbe m) auxiliaire m.

avail [əˈveɪl] 1 vt to a. oneself of profiter de, tirer parti de. 2 n to no a. en vain; of no a. inutile.

available [əˈveɪləb(ə)l] a (thing, means etc) disponible; (person) libre, disponible; (valid) valable; a. to all (goal etc) accessible à tous. ◆**availa'bility** n disponibilité f; validité f; accessibilité f.

avalanche [ˈævəlɑːnʃ] n avalanche f.

avarice [ˈævərɪs] n avarice f. ◆**ava'ricious** a avare.

avenge [əˈvendʒ] vt venger; to a. oneself se venger (on de).

avenue [ˈævənjuː] n avenue f; (way to a result) Fig voie f.

average [ˈævərɪdʒ] n moyenne f; on a. en moyenne; − a moyen; − vt (do) faire en moyenne; (reach) atteindre la moyenne de; (figures) faire la moyenne de.

averse [əˈvɜːs] a to be a. to doing répugner à faire. ◆**aversion** n (dislike) aversion f, répugnance f.

avert [əˈvɜːt] vt (prevent) éviter; (turn away) détourner (from de).

aviary [ˈeɪvɪərɪ] n volière f.

aviation [eɪvɪˈeɪʃ(ə)n] n aviation f. ◆**'aviator** n aviateur, -trice mf.

avid [ˈævɪd] a avide (for de).

avocado [ævəˈkɑːdəu] n (pl -os) a. (pear) avocat m.

avoid [əˈvɔɪd] vt éviter; to a. doing éviter de faire. ◆**-able** a évitable. ◆**avoidance** n his a. of (danger etc) son désir m d'éviter; tax a. évasion f fiscale.

avowed [əˈvaud] a (enemy) déclaré, avoué.

await [əˈweɪt] vt attendre.

awake [əˈweɪk] vi (pt awoke, pp awoken) s'éveiller; − vt (person, hope etc) éveiller; − a réveillé, éveillé; (wide-)a. éveillé; to keep s.o. a. empêcher qn de dormir, tenir qn éveillé; he's (still) a. il ne dort pas (encore); a. to (conscious of) conscient de. ◆**awaken 1** vti = **awake. 2** vt to a. s.o. to sth faire prendre conscience de qch à qn. ◆**awakening** n réveil m.

award [əˈwɔːd] vt (money) attribuer; (prize) décerner, attribuer; (damages) accorder; − n (prize) prix m, récompense f; (scholarship) bourse f.

aware [əˈweər] a avisé, informé; a. of (conscious) conscient de; (informed) au courant de; to become a. of prendre conscience de. ◆**-ness** n conscience f.

awash [əˈwɒʃ] a inondé (with de).

away [əˈweɪ] adv 1 (distant) loin; (far) a. au loin, très loin; 5 km a. à 5 km (de distance). 2 (absent) parti, absent; a. with you! va-t-en!; to drive a. partir (en voiture); to look a. détourner les yeux; to work/talk/ etc a. travailler/parler/etc sans relâche; to fade/melt a. disparaître/fondre complètement. 3 to play a. Sp jouer à l'extérieur.

awe [ɔː] n crainte f (mêlée de respect); to be in a. of s.o. éprouver de la crainte envers qn. ◆**a.-inspiring** a, ◆**awesome** a (impressive) imposant; (frightening) effrayant.

awful [ˈɔːfəl] a affreux; (terrifying) épouvantable; (ill) malade; an a. lot of Fam un nombre incroyable de; I feel a. (about it) j'ai vraiment honte. ◆**-ly** adv affreusement; (very) Fam terriblement; thanks a. merci infiniment.

awhile [əˈwaɪl] adv quelque temps; (to stay, wait) un peu.

awkward [ˈɔːkwəd] a 1 (clumsy) maladroit; (age) ingrat. 2 (difficult) difficile; (cumbersome) gênant; (tool) peu commode; (time) inopportun; (silence) gêné. ◆**-ly** adv maladroitement; (speak) d'un ton gêné; (placed) à un endroit difficile. ◆**-ness** n maladresse f; difficulté f; (discomfort) gêne f.

awning [ˈɔːnɪŋ] n auvent m; (over shop) store m; (glass canopy) marquise f.

awoke(n) [əˈwəuk(ən)] see **awake**.

awry [əˈraɪ] adv to go a. (of plan etc) mal tourner.

axe [æks] (Am **ax**) n hache f; (reduction) Fig coupe f sombre; − vt réduire; (eliminate) supprimer.

axiom [ˈæksɪəm] n axiome m.

axis, pl **axes** [ˈæksɪs, ˈæksiːz] n axe m.

axle [ˈæks(ə)l] n essieu m.

ay(e) [aɪ] 1 adv oui. 2 n the ayes (votes) les voix fpl pour.

azalea [əˈzeɪlɪə] n (plant) azalée f.

B

B, b [biː] *n* B, b *m*; **2B** (*number*) 2 ter.
BA *abbr* = **Bachelor of Arts.**
babble ['bæb(ə)l] *vi* (*of baby, stream*) gazouiller; (*mumble*) bredouiller; – *vt* to b. (**out**) bredouiller; – *n inv* gazouillement *m*, gazouillis *m*; (*of voices*) rumeur *f*.
babe [beɪb] *n* **1** petit(e) enfant *mf*, bébé *m*. **2** (*girl*) Sl pépée *f*.
baboon [bə'buːn] *n* babouin *m*.
baby ['beɪbɪ] *n* **1** bébé *m*; – *a* (*clothes etc*) de bébé; **b. boy** petit garçon *m*; **b. girl** petite fille *f*; **b. carriage** Am voiture *f* d'enfant; **b. sling** kangourou® *m*, porte-bébé *m*; **b. tiger**/*etc* bébé-tigre/*etc m*; **b. face** visage *m* poupin. **2** *n* Sl (*girl*) pépée *f*; (*girlfriend*) copine *f*. **3** *vt* Fam dorloter. ◆**b.-batterer** *n* bourreau *m* d'enfants. ◆**b.-minder** *n* gardien, -ienne *mf* d'enfants. ◆**b.-sit** *vi* (*pt & pp* -sat, *pres p* -sitting) garder les enfants, faire du baby-sitting. ◆**b.-sitter** *n* baby-sitter *mf*. ◆**b.-snatching** *n* rapt *m* d'enfant. ◆**b.-walker** *n* trotteur *m*, youpala®*m*.
babyish ['beɪbɪʃ] *a* Pej de bébé; (*puerile*) enfantin.
bachelor ['bætʃələr] *n* **1** célibataire *m*; **b. flat** garçonnière *f*. **2 B. of Arts/of Science** licencié -ée *mf* ès lettres/ès sciences.
back [bæk] *n* (*of person, animal*) dos *m*; (*of chair*) dossier *m*; (*of hand*) revers *m*; (*of house*) derrière *m*, arrière *m*; (*of room*) fond *m*; (*of page*) verso *m*,(*of fabric*) envers *m*; Fb arrière *m*; **at the b. of** (*book*) à la fin de; (*car*) à l'arrière de; **at the b. of one's mind** derrière la tête; **b. to front** devant derrière, à l'envers; **to get s.o.'s b. up** Fam irriter qn; **in b. of** Am derrière; – *a* arrière *inv*, de derrière; (*taxes*) arriéré; **b. door** porte *f* de derrière; **b. room** pièce *f* du fond; **b. end of** bus) arrière *m*; **b. street** rue *f* écartée; **b. number** vieux numéro *m*; **b. pay** rappel *m* de salaire; **b. tooth** molaire *f*; – *adv* en arrière; **b.** loin derrière; **far b.** in the past à une époque reculée; **to stand b.** (*of house*) être en retrait (**from** par rapport à); **to go b. and forth** aller et venir; **to come b.** revenir; **he's b.** il est de retour, il est rentré *ou* revenu; **a month b.** il y a un mois; **the trip there and b.** le voyage aller et retour; – *vt* Com financer; (*horse etc*) parier sur, jouer;

(*car*) faire reculer; (*wall*) renforcer; **to b. s.o (up)** (*support*) appuyer qn; – *vi* (*move backwards*) reculer; **to b. down** se dégonfler; **to b. out** (*withdraw*) se retirer; Aut sortir en marche arrière; **to b. on to** (*of window etc*) donner par derrière sur; **to b. up** Aut faire marche arrière. ◆**–ing** *n* (*aid*) soutien *m*; (*material*) support *m*, renfort *m*. ◆**–er** *n* (*supporter*) partisan *m*; Sp parieur, -euse *mf*; Fin bailleur *m* de fonds.
backache ['bækeɪk] *n* mal *m* aux reins. ◆**back'bencher** *n* Pol membre *m* sans portefeuille. ◆**backbiting** *n* médisance *f*. ◆**backbreaking** *a* éreintant. ◆**backcloth** *n* toile *f* de fond. ◆**backchat** *n* impertinence *f*. ◆**back'date** *vt* (*cheque*) antidater. ◆**back'handed** *a* (*compliment*) équivoque. ◆**backhander** *n* revers *m*; (*bribe*) Fam pot-de-vin *m*. ◆**backrest** *n* dossier *m*. ◆**backside** *n* (*buttocks*) Fam derrière *m*. ◆**back'stage** *adv* dans les coulisses. ◆**backstroke** *n* Sp dos *m* crawlé. ◆**backtrack** *vi* rebrousser chemin. ◆**backup** *n* appui *m*; (*tailback*) Am embouteillage *m*; **b. lights** Aut feux *mpl* de recul. ◆**backwater** *n* (*place*) trou *m* perdu. ◆**backwoods** *npl* forêts *f* vierges. ◆**back'yard** *n* arrière-cour *f*; Am jardin *m* (à l'arrière d'une maison).
backbone ['bækbəʊn] *n* colonne *f* vertébrale; (*of fish*) grande arête *f*; (*main support*) pivot *m*.
backfire [bæk'faɪər] *vi* Aut pétarader; (*of plot etc*) Fig échouer.
backgammon ['bækgæmən] *n* trictrac *m*.
background ['bækgraʊnd] *n* fond *m*, arrière-plan *m*; (*events*) Fig antécédents *mpl*; (*education*) formation *f*; (*environment*) milieu *m*; (*conditions*) Pol climat *m*, contexte *m*; **to keep s.o. in the b.** tenir qn à l'écart; **b. music** musique *f* de fond.
backlash ['bæklæʃ] *n* choc *m* en retour, retour *m* de flamme.
backlog ['bæklɒg] *n* (*of work*) arrière *m*.
backward ['bækwəd] *a* (*glance etc*) en arrière; (*retarded*) arriéré; **b. in doing** lent à faire; – *adv* = **backwards**. ◆**–ness** *n* (*of country etc*) retard *m*. ◆**backwards** *adv* en arrière; (*to walk*) à reculons; (*to fall*) à la

renverse; **to move b.** reculer; **to go b. and forwards** aller et venir.

bacon ['beɪkən] n lard m; (in rashers) bacon m; **b. and eggs** œufs mpl au jambon.

bacteria [bæk'tɪərɪə] npl bactéries fpl.

bad [bæd] a (**worse**, **worst**) mauvais; (wicked) méchant; (sad) triste; (accident, wound etc) grave; (tooth) carié; (arm, leg) malade; (pain) violent; (air) vicié; **b. language** gros mots mpl; **it's b. to think that . . .** ce n'est pas bien de penser que . . . ; **to feel b.** Med se sentir mal; **I feel b. about it** ça m'a chagriné; **things are b.** ça va mal; **she's not b.!** elle n'est pas mal!; **to go b.** se gâter; (of milk) tourner; **in a b. way** mal en point; (ill) très mal; (in trouble) dans le pétrin; **too b.!** tant pis! ◆**b.-'mannered** a mal élevé. ◆**b.-'tempered** a grincheux. ◆**badly** adv mal; (hurt) grièvement; **b. affected/shaken** très touché/bouleversé; **to be b. mistaken** se tromper lourdement; **b. off** dans la gêne; **to be b. off for** manquer de; **to want b.** avoir grande envie de.

badge [bædʒ] n (of policeman etc) plaque f; (bearing slogan or joke) badge m.

badger ['bædʒər] **1** n (animal) blaireau m. **2** vt importuner.

badminton ['bædmɪntən] n badminton m.

baffle ['bæf(ə)l] vt (person) déconcerter, dérouter.

bag [bæg] **1** n sac m; pl (luggage) valises fpl, bagages mpl; (under the eyes) poches fpl; **bags of** Fam (lots of) beaucoup de; **an old b.** une vieille taupe; **in the b.** Fam dans la poche. **2** vt (-gg-) (take, steal) Fam piquer, s'adjuger; (animal) Sp tuer.

baggage ['bægɪdʒ] n bagages mpl; Mil équipement m; **b. car** Am fourgon m; **b. room** Am consigne f.

baggy ['bægɪ] a (-ier, -iest) (clothing) trop ample; (trousers) faisant des poches.

bagpipes ['bægpaɪps] npl cornemuse f.

Bahamas [bə'hɑːməz] npl the B. les Bahamas fpl.

bail [beɪl] **1** n Jur caution f; **on b.** en liberté provisoire; – vt **to b. (out)** fournir une caution pour; **to b. out** (ship) écoper; (person, company) Fig tirer d'embarras. **2** vi **to b. out** Am Av sauter (en parachute).

bailiff ['beɪlɪf] n Jur huissier m; (of landowner) régisseur m.

bait [beɪt] **1** n amorce f, appât m; – vt (fishing hook) amorcer. **2** vt (annoy) asticoter, tourmenter.

baize [beɪz] n green b. (on card table etc) tapis m vert.

bak/e [beɪk] vt (faire) cuire (au four); – vi

(of cook) faire de la pâtisserie or du pain; (of cake etc) cuire (au four); **we're** or **it's baking** Fam on cuit. ◆**-ed** a (potatoes) au four; **b. beans** haricots mpl blancs (à la tomate). ◆**-ing** n cuisson f; **b. powder** levure f (chimique). ◆**-er** n boulanger, -ère mf. ◆**bakery** n boulangerie f.

balaclava [bælə'klɑːvə] n **b. (helmet)** passe-montagne m.

balance ['bæləns] n (scales) & Econ Pol Com balance f; (equilibrium) équilibre m; (of account) Com solde m; (remainder) reste m; **to strike a b.** trouver le juste milieu; **sense of b.** sens de la mesure; **in the balance** incertain; **on b.** à tout prendre; **b. sheet** bilan m; – vt tenir or mettre en équilibre (on sur); (budget, account) équilibrer; (compare) mettre en balance, peser; **to b. (out)** (compensate for) compenser; **to b. (oneself)** se tenir en équilibre; – vi (of accounts) être en équilibre, s'équilibrer.

balcony ['bælkənɪ] n balcon m.

bald [bɔːld] a (-er, -est) chauve; (statement) brutal; (tyre) lisse; **b. patch** or **spot** tonsure f. ◆**b.-'headed** a chauve. ◆**balding** a to **be b.** perdre ses cheveux. ◆**baldness** n calvitie f.

balderdash ['bɔːldədæʃ] n balivernes fpl.

bale [beɪl] **1** n (of cotton etc) balle f. **2** vi **to b. out** Av sauter (en parachute).

baleful ['beɪlfʊl] a sinistre, funeste.

balk [bɔːk] vi reculer (at devant), regimber (at contre).

ball [bɔːl] n balle f; (inflated) Fb Rugby etc ballon m; Billiards bille f; (of string, wool) pelote f; (sphere) boule f; (of meat or fish) Culin boulette f; **on the b.** (alert) Fam éveillé; **he's on the b.** (efficient, knowledgeable) Fam il connaît son affaire, il est au point; **b. bearing** roulement m à billes; **b. game** Am partie f de baseball; **it's a whole new b. game** or **a different b. game** Am Fig c'est une tout autre affaire. ◆**ballcock** n robinet m à flotteur. ◆**ballpoint** n stylo m à bille.

ball² [bɔːl] n (dance) bal m. ◆**ballroom** n salle f de danse.

ballad ['bæləd] n Liter ballade f; Mus romance f.

ballast ['bæləst] n lest m; – vt lester.

ballet ['bæleɪ] n ballet m. ◆**balle'rina** n ballerine f.

ballistic [bə'lɪstɪk] a **b. missile** engin m balistique.

balloon [bə'luːn] n ballon m; Met ballon-sonde m.

ballot ['bælət] *n* (*voting*) scrutin *m*; **b.** (**paper**) bulletin *m* de vote; **b. box** urne *f*; – *vt* (*members*) consulter (par un scrutin).

ballyhoo [bælɪ'huː] *n Fam* battage *m* (publicitaire).

balm [bɑːm] *n* (*liquid, comfort*) baume *m*. ◆**balmy** *a* (-ier, -iest) **1** (*air*) *Lit* embaumé. **2** (*crazy*) *Fam* dingue, timbré.

baloney [bə'ləʊnɪ] *n Sl* foutaises *fpl*.

Baltic ['bɔːltɪk] *n* the **B.** la Baltique.

balustrade ['bæləstreɪd] *n* balustrade *f*.

bamboo [bæm'buː] *n* bambou *m*.

bamboozle [bæm'buːz(ə)l] *vt* (*cheat*) *Fam* embobiner.

ban [bæn] *n* interdiction *f*; – (-nn-) interdire; **to b. from** (*club etc*) exclure de; **to ban s.o. from doing** interdire à qn de faire.

banal [bə'nɑːl, *Am* 'beɪn(ə)l] *a* banal. ◆**ba'nality** *n* banalité *f*.

banana [bə'nɑːnə] *n* banane *f*.

band [bænd] *n* **1** (*strip*) bande *f*; (*of hat*) ruban *m*; **rubber** *or* **elastic b.** élastique *m*. **2** (*group*) bande *f*; *Mus* (*petit*) orchestre *m*; *Mil* fanfare *f*; – *vi* **to b. together** former une bande, se grouper. ◆**bandstand** *n* kiosque *m* à musique. ◆**bandwagon** *n* to **jump on the b.** *Fig* suivre le mouvement.

bandage ['bændɪdʒ] *n* (*strip*) bande *f*; (*for wound*) pansement *m*; (*for holding in place*) bandage *m*; – *vt* **to b. (up)** (*arm, leg*) bander; (*wound*) mettre un pansement sur.

Band-Aid® ['bændeɪd] *n* pansement *m* adhésif.

bandit ['bændɪt] *n* bandit *m*. ◆**banditry** *n* banditisme *m*.

bandy ['bændɪ] **1** *a* (-ier, -iest) (*person*) bancal; (*legs*) arqué. ◆**b.-'legged** *a* bancal. **2** *vt* **to b. about** (*story etc*) faire circuler, propager.

bane [beɪn] *n Lit* fléau *m*. ◆**baneful** *a* funeste.

bang [bæŋ] *n* **1** (*hit, noise*) coup *m* (violent); (*of gun etc*) détonation *f*; (*of door*) claquement *m*; – *vt* cogner, frapper; (*door*) (faire) claquer; **to b. one's head** se cogner la tête; – *vi* cogner, frapper; (*of door*) claquer; (*of gun*) détoner; (*of firework*) éclater; **to b. down** (*lid*) rabattre (violemment); **to b. into** sth heurter qch; – *int* vlan!, pan!; **to go (off)** b. éclater. **2** *adv* (*exactly*) *Fam* exactement; **b. in the middle** en plein milieu; **b. on six** à six heures tapantes.

banger ['bæŋər] *n* **1** *Culin Fam* saucisse *f*. **2** (*firecracker*) pétard *m*. **3** *old b.* (*car*) *Fam* tacot *m*, guimbarde *f*.

bangle ['bæŋg(ə)l] *n* bracelet *m* (rigide).

bangs [bæŋz] *npl* (*of hair*) *Am* frange *f*.

banish ['bænɪʃ] *vt* bannir.

banister ['bænɪstər] *n* **banister(s)** rampe *f* (d'escalier).

banjo ['bændʒəʊ] *n* (*pl* -os *or* -oes) banjo *m*.

bank [bæŋk] **1** *n* (*of river*) bord *m*, rive *f*; (*raised*) berge *f*; (*of earth*) talus *m*; (*of sand*) banc *m*; **the Left B.** (*in Paris*) la Rive gauche; – *vt* **to b. (up)** (*earth etc*) amonceler. **2** *vt* couvrir. **3** *n Com* banque *f*; **b. account** compte *m* en banque; **b. card** carte *f* d'identité bancaire; **b. holiday** jour *m* férié; **b. note** billet *m* de banque; **b. rate** taux *m* d'escompte; – *vt* (*money*) mettre en banque; – *vi* avoir un compte en banque (**with** à). **3** *vi Av* virer. **4** *vi* **to b. on** **s.o./sth** (*rely on*) compter sur qn/qch. ◆**-ing** *a* bancaire; – *n* (*activity, profession*) la banque. ◆**-er** *n* banquier *m*.

bankrupt ['bæŋkrʌpt] *a* **to go b.** faire faillite; **b. of** (*ideas*) *Fig* dénué de; – *vt* mettre en faillite. ◆**bankruptcy** *n* faillite *f*.

banner ['bænər] *n* (*at rallies etc*) banderole *f*; (*flag*) & *Fig* bannière *f*.

banns [bænz] *npl* bans *mpl*.

banquet ['bæŋkwɪt] *n* banquet *m*.

banter ['bæntər] *vti* plaisanter; – *n* plaisanterie *f*. ◆**-ing** *a* (*tone, air*) plaisantin.

baptism ['bæptɪzəm] *n* baptême *m*. ◆**bap'tize** *vt* baptiser.

bar [bɑːr] *n* **1** barre *f*; (*of gold*) lingot *m*; (*of chocolate*) tablette *f*; (*on window*) & *Jur* barreau *m*; **b. of soap** savonnette *f*; **behind bars** *Jur* sous les verrous; **to b. s.o.** *Fig* faire obstacle à. **2** *n* (*pub*) bar *m*; (*counter*) comptoir *m*. **3** *n* (*group of notes*) *Mus* mesure *f*. **4** *vt* (-rr-) (*way etc*) bloquer, barrer; (*window*) griller. **5** *vt* (*prohibit*) interdire (**s.o. from doing** à qn de faire); (*exclude*) exclure (**from** à). **6** *prep* sauf. ◆**barmaid** *n* serveuse *f* de bar. ◆**barman** *n*, ◆**bartender** *n* barman *m*.

Barbados [bɑː'beɪdɒs] *n* Barbade *f*.

barbarian [bɑː'beərɪən] *n* barbare *mf*. ◆**barbaric** *a* barbare. ◆**barbarity** *n* barbarie *f*.

barbecue ['bɑːbɪkjuː] *n* barbecue *m*; – *vt* griller (au barbecue).

barbed [bɑːbd] *a* **b. wire** fil *m* de fer barbelé; (*fence*) barbelés *mpl*.

barber ['bɑːbər] *n* coiffeur *m* (*pour hommes*).

barbiturate [bɑː'bɪtjʊrət] *n* barbiturique *m*.

bare [beər] *a* (-er, -est) nu; (*tree, field etc*) dénudé; (*cupboard*) vide; (*mere*) simple; **the b. necessities** le strict nécessaire; **with his b. hands** à mains nues; – *vt* mettre à nu.

◆—**ness** n (of person) nudité f.
◆**bareback** a to ride b. monter à cru.
◆**barefaced** a (lie) éhonté. ◆**barefoot**
adv nu-pieds; – a aux pieds nus. ◆**bare-
'headed** a & adv nu-tête inv.

barely ['beəlɪ] adv (scarcely) à peine, tout
juste.

bargain ['bɑːɡɪn] n (deal) marché m, affaire
f; a (good) b. (cheap buy) une occasion, une
bonne affaire; **it's a b.!** (agreed) c'est
entendu!; **into the b.** par-dessus le marché;
b. price prix m exceptionnel; **b. counter**
rayon m des soldes; – vi (negotiate)
négocier; (haggle) marchander; **to b. for** or
on sth Fig s'attendre à qch. ◆—**ing** n
négociations fpl; marchandage m.

barge [bɑːdʒ] **1** n chaland m, péniche f. **2** vi
to b. in (enter a room) faire irruption;
(interrupt) interrompre; **to b. into** (hit) se
cogner contre.

baritone ['bærɪtəun] n (voice, singer)
baryton m.

bark [bɑːk] **1** n (of tree) écorce f. **2** vi (of dog
etc) aboyer; – n aboiement m. ◆—**ing** n
aboiements mpl.

barley ['bɑːlɪ] n orge f; **b. sugar** sucre m
d'orge.

barmy ['bɑːmɪ] a (-ier, -iest) Fam dingue,
timbré.

barn [bɑːn] n (for crops etc) grange f; (for
horses) écurie f; (for cattle) étable f.
◆**barnyard** n basse-cour f.

barometer [bə'rɒmɪtər] n baromètre m.

baron ['bærən] n baron m; (industrialist) Fig
magnat m. ◆**baroness** n baronne f.

baroque [bə'rɒk, Am bə'rəuk] a & n Archit
Mus baroque (m).

barracks ['bærəks] npl caserne f.

barrage ['bærɑːʒ, Am bə'rɑːʒ] n (barrier)
barrage m; **a b. of** (questions etc) un feu
roulant de.

barrel ['bærəl] n **1** (cask) tonneau m; (of oil)
baril m. **2** (of gun) canon m. **3** **b. organ**
orgue m de Barbarie.

barren ['bærən] a stérile; (style) Fig aride.

barrette [bə'ret] n (hair slide) Am barrette f.

barricade ['bærɪkeɪd] n barricade f; – vt
barricader; **to b. oneself (in)** se barricader.

barrier ['bærɪər] n barrière f; Fig obstacle m,
barrière f; (ticket) b. Rail portillon m;
sound b. mur m du son.

barring ['bɑːrɪŋ] prep sauf, excepté.

barrister ['bærɪstər] n avocat m.

barrow ['bærəu] n charrette f or voiture f à
bras; (wheelbarrow) brouette f.

barter ['bɑːtər] vt troquer, échanger (for
contre); – n troc m, échange m.

base [beɪs] **1** n (bottom, main ingredient)
base f; (of lamp, fort) pied m. **2** (military)
base f; (of army) base f. **3** vt baser, fonder (on sur); **based in** or **on**
London basé à Londres. **4** a (dishonourable)
bas, ignoble; (metal) vil. ◆—**less** a sans
fondement. ◆—**ness** n bassesse f.
◆**baseball** n base-ball m. ◆**baseboard**
n Am plinthe f.

basement ['beɪsmənt] n sous-sol m.

bash [bæʃ] n Fam (bang) coup m; **to have a
b.** (try) essayer un coup; – vt Fam (hit)
cogner; **to b. (about)** (ill-treat) malmener;
to b. s.o. up tabasser qn; **to b. in** or **down**
(door etc) défoncer. ◆—**ing** n (thrashing)
Fam raclée f.

bashful ['bæʃfəl] a timide.

basic ['beɪsɪk] a fondamental; (pay etc) de
base; – n **the basics** Fam l'essentiel m.
◆—**ally** [-klɪ] adv au fond.

basil ['bæz(ə)l] n Bot Culin basilic m.

basilica [bə'zɪlɪkə] n basilique f.

basin ['beɪs(ə)n] n bassin m, bassine f; (for
soup, food) bol m; (of river) bassin m;
(portable washbasin) cuvette f; (sink)
lavabo m.

basis, pl **-ses** ['beɪsɪs, -siːz] n base f; **on the
b. of** d'après; **on that b.** dans ces conditions; **on a weekly/etc b.** chaque
semaine/etc.

bask [bɑːsk] vi se chauffer.

basket ['bɑːskɪt] n panier m; (for bread,
laundry, litter) corbeille f. ◆**basketball** n
basket(-ball) m.

Basque [bæsk] a & n basque (mf).

bass¹ [beɪs] n Mus basse f; – a (note, voice)
bas.

bass² [bæs] n (sea fish) bar m; (fresh-water)
perche f.

bassinet [bæsɪ'net] n (cradle) Am couffin m.

bastard ['bɑːstəd] **1** n & a bâtard, -arde
(mf). **2** n Pej Sl salaud m, salope f.

baste [beɪst] vt **1** (fabric) bâtir. **2** Culin
arroser.

bastion ['bæstɪən] n bastion m.

bat [bæt] n **1** (animal) chauve-souris f. **2** n
Cricket batte f; Table Tennis raquette f; **off
my own b.** de ma propre initiative; – vt
(-tt-) (ball) frapper. **3** vt **she didn't b. an
eyelid** elle n'a pas sourcillé.

batch [bætʃ] n (of people) groupe m; (of
letters) paquet m; (of books) lot m; (of
loaves) fournée f; (of papers) liasse f.

bated ['beɪtɪd] a **with b. breath** en retenant
son souffle.

bath [bɑːθ] n (pl **-s** [bɑːðz]) bain m; (tub)
baignoire f; **swimming baths** piscine f; – vt
baigner; – vi prendre un bain.

◆**bathrobe** n peignoir m (de bain); Am robe f de chambre. ◆**bathroom** n salle f de bain(s); (toilet) Am toilettes fpl. ◆**bathtub** n baignoire f.

bath/e [beɪð] vt baigner; (wound) laver; – vi se baigner; Am prendre un bain; – n bain m (de mer), baignade f. ◆**—ing** n baignade(s) f(pl); **b. costume** or **suit** maillot m de bain.

baton ['bætən, Am bə'tɒn] n Mus Mil bâton m; (truncheon) matraque f.

battalion [bə'tæljən] n bataillon m.

batter ['bætər] **1** n pâte f à frire. **2** vt battre, frapper; (baby) martyriser; Mil pilonner; **to b. down** (door) défoncer. ◆**—ed** a (car, hat) cabossé; (house) délabré; (face) meurtri; (wife) battu. ◆**—ing** n **to take a b.** Fig souffrir beaucoup.

battery ['bætərɪ] n Mil El Aut Agr batterie f; (in radio etc) pile f.

battle ['bæt(ə)l] n bataille f; (struggle) Fig lutte f; **that's half the b.** Fam c'est ça le secret de la victoire; **b. dress** tenue f de campagne; – vi se battre, lutter. ◆**battlefield** n champ m de bataille. ◆**battleship** n cuirassé m.

battlements ['bæt(ə)lmənts] npl (indentations) créneaux mpl; (wall) remparts mpl.

batty ['bætɪ] a (-ier, -iest) Sl dingue, toqué.

baulk [bɔːk] vi reculer (**at** devant), regimber (at contre).

bawdy ['bɔːdɪ] a (-ier, -iest) paillard, grossier.

bawl [bɔːl] vti **to b. (out)** beugler, brailler; **to b. s.o. out** Am Sl engueuler qn.

bay [beɪ] **1** n Geog Archit baie f. **2** n Bot laurier m. **3** n (for loading etc) aire f. **4** n (of dog) aboiement m; **at b.** aux abois; **to hold at b.** tenir à distance; – vi aboyer. **5** a (horse) bai.

bayonet ['beɪənɪt] n baïonnette f.

bazaar [bə'zɑːr] n (market, shop) bazar m; (charity sale) vente f de charité.

bazooka [bə'zuːkə] n bazooka m.

BC [biː'siː] abbr (before Christ) avant Jésus-Christ.

be [biː] vi (pres t **am, are, is;** pt **was, were;** pp **been;** pres p **being**) **1** être; **it is green/small** c'est vert/petit; **she's a doctor** elle est médecin; **he's an Englishman** c'est un Anglais; **it's 3 (o'clock)** il est trois heures; **it's the sixth of May** c'est or nous sommes le six mai. **2** avoir; **to be hot/right/lucky** avoir chaud/raison/de la chance; **my feet are cold** j'ai froid aux pieds; **he's 20 (age)** il a 20 ans; **to be 2 metres high** avoir 2 mètres de haut; **to be 6 feet tall** mesurer 1,80 m. **3**

(health) aller; **how are you?** comment vas-tu? **4** (place, situation) se trouver, être; **she's in York** elle se trouve or elle est à York. **5** (exist) être; **the best painter there is** le meilleur peintre qui soit; **leave me be** laissez-moi (tranquille); **that may be** cela se peut. **6** (go, come) **I've been to see her** je suis allé or j'ai été la voir; **he's (already) been** il est (déjà) venu. **7** (weather) & Math faire; **it's fine** il fait beau; **2 and 2 are 4** 2 et 2 font 4. **8** (cost) coûter, faire; **it's 20 pence** ça coûte 20 pence; **how much is it?** ça fait combien?, c'est combien? **9** (auxiliary) **I am/was doing** je fais/faisais; **I'm listening to the radio** (in the process of) je suis en train d'écouter la radio; **she's been there some time** elle est là depuis longtemps; **he was killed** il a été tué, on l'a tué; **I've been waiting (for) two hours** j'attends depuis deux heures; **it is said** on dit; **to be pitied** à plaindre; **isn't it?, aren't you?** n'est-ce pas?, non?; **I am!, he is!** etc oui! **10** (+ inf) **he is to come** (must) il doit venir; **he's shortly to go** (intends to) il va bientôt partir. **11 there is** or **are** il y a; (pointing) voilà; **here is** or **are** voici.

beach [biːtʃ] n plage f. ◆**beachcomber** n (person) ramasseur, -euse mf d'épaves.

beacon ['biːkən] n Nau Av balise f; (lighthouse) phare m.

bead [biːd] n (small sphere, drop of liquid) perle f; (of rosary) grain m; (of sweat) goutte f; **(string of) beads** collier m.

beak [biːk] n bec m.

beaker ['biːkər] n gobelet m.

beam [biːm] **1** n (of wood) poutre f. **2** n (of light) rayon m; (of headlight, torch) faisceau m (lumineux); – vi rayonner; (of person) Fig sourire largement. **3** vt Rad diffuser. ◆**—ing** a (radiant) radieux.

bean [biːn] n haricot m; (of coffee) grain m; (broad) fève f; **to be full of beans** Fam déborder d'entrain. ◆**beanshoots** npl, ◆**beansprouts** npl germes mpl de soja.

bear[1] [beər] n (animal) ours m.

bear[2] [beər] vt (pt **bore,** pp **borne**) (carry, show) porter; (endure) supporter; (resemblance) offrir; (comparison) soutenir; (responsibility) assumer; (child) donner naissance à; **to b. in mind** tenir compte de; **to b. out** corroborer; **to b. left/etc** (turn) tourner à gauche/etc; **to b. north/etc** (go) aller en direction du nord/etc; **to b. (up)on** (relate to) se rapporter à; **to b. heavily on** (of burden) Fig peser sur; **to b. with** être indulgent envers, être patient avec; **to bring to b.** (one's energies) consacrer (**on** à);

(*pressure*) exercer (**on** sur); **to b. up** ne pas se décourager, tenir le coup; **b. up!** du courage! ◆—**ing** n (*posture, conduct*) maintien m; (*relationship, relevance*) relation f (**on** avec); *Nau Av* position f; **to get one's bearings** s'orienter. ◆—**able** a supportable. ◆—**er** n porteur, -euse mf.

beard [biəd] n barbe f. ◆**bearded** a barbu.

beast [biːst] n bête f, animal m; (*person*) brute f. ◆**beastly** a *Fam* (*bad*) vilain, infect; (*spiteful*) méchant; – adv *Fam* terriblement.

beat [biːt] n (*of heart, drum*) battement m; (*of policeman*) ronde f; *Mus* mesure f, rythme m; – vt (*pt* **beat,** *pp* **beaten**) battre; (*defeat*) vaincre; **that beats me** *Fam* ça me dépasse; **to b. s.o. to it** devancer qn; **b. it!** *Sl* fichez le camp!; **to b. back** or **off** repousser; **to b. down** (*price*) faire baisser; **to b. in** or **down** (*door*) défoncer; **to b. out** (*rhythm*) marquer; (*tune*) jouer; **to b. s.o. up** tabasser qn; – vi battre; (*at door*) frapper (**at** à); **to b. about** or **around the bush** tourner autour du pot; **to b. down** (*of rain*) tomber à verse; (*of sun*) taper. ◆—**ing** n (*blows, defeat*) raclée f. ◆—**er** n (*for eggs*) batteur m.

beauty ['bjuːti] n (*quality, woman*) beauté f; **it's a b.!** c'est une merveille!; **the b. of it is ...** le plus beau, c'est que ...; **b. parlour** institut m de beauté; **b. spot** (*on skin*) grain m de beauté; (*in countryside*) site m pittoresque. ◆**beau'tician** n esthéticienne f. ◆**beautiful** a (*très*) beau; (*superb*) merveilleux. ◆**beautifully** adv merveilleusement.

beaver ['biːvər] n castor m; – vi **to b. away** travailler dur (**at** sth à qch).

because [bi'kɒz] conj parce que; **b. of** à cause de.

beck [bek] n **at s.o.'s b. and call** aux ordres de qn.

beckon ['bekən] vti **to b.** (**to**) **s.o.** faire signe à qn (**to do** de faire).

become [bi'kʌm] **1** vi (*pt* **became,** *pp* **become**) devenir; **to b. a painter** devenir peintre; **to b. thin** maigrir; **to b. worried** commencer à s'inquiéter; **what has b. of her?** qu'est-elle devenue? **2** vt **that becomes her** ce chapeau lui sied or lui va. ◆—**ing** a (*clothes*) seyant; (*modesty*) bienséant.

bed [bed] n lit m; *Geol* couche f; (*of vegetables*) carré m; (*of sea*) fond m; (*flower bed*) parterre m; **to go to b.** (aller) se coucher; **in b.** couché; **to get out of b.** se lever; **b. and**

breakfast (*in hotel etc*) chambre f avec petit déjeuner; **b. settee** (canapé m) convertible m; **air b.** matelas m pneumatique; – vt (**-dd-**) **to b.** (**out**) (*plant*) repiquer; – vi **to b. down** se coucher. ◆**bedding** n literie f. ◆**bedbug** n punaise f. ◆**bedclothes** npl couvertures fpl et draps mpl. ◆**bedridden** a alité. ◆**bedroom** n chambre f à coucher. ◆**bedside** n chevet m; – a (*lamp, book, table*) de chevet. ◆**bed'sitter** n, *Fam* ◆**bedsit** n chambre f meublée. ◆**bedspread** n dessus-de-lit m inv. ◆**bedtime** n heure f du coucher.

bedeck [bi'dek] vt orner (**with** de).

bedevil [bi'dev(ə)l] vt (**-ll-**, *Am* **-l-**) (*plague*) tourmenter; (*confuse*) embrouiller; **bedevilled by** (*problems etc*) perturbé par, empoisonné par.

bedlam ['bedləm] n (*noise*) *Fam* chahut m.

bedraggled [bi'dræg(ə)ld] a (*clothes, person*) débraillé.

bee [biː] n abeille f. ◆**beehive** n ruche f. ◆**beekeeping** n apiculture f. ◆**beeline** n **to make a b. for** aller droit vers.

beech [biːtʃ] n (*tree, wood*) hêtre m.

beef [biːf] n **1** bœuf m. **2** vi (*complain*) *Sl* rouspéter. ◆**beefburger** n hamburger m. ◆**beefy** a (**-ier, -iest**) *Fam* musclé, costaud.

beer [biər] n bière f; **b. glass** chope f. ◆**beery** a (*room, person*) qui sent la bière.

beet [biːt] n betterave f (à sucre); *Am* = **beetroot.** ◆**beetroot** n betterave f (potagère).

beetle ['biːt(ə)l] n **1** cafard m, scarabée m. **2** vi **to b. off** *Fam* se sauver.

befall [bi'fɔːl] vt (*pt* **befell,** *pp* **befallen**) arriver à.

befit [bi'fit] vt (**-tt-**) convenir à.

before [bi'fɔːr] adv avant; (*already*) déjà; (*in front*) devant; **the month b.** le mois d'avant or précédent; **the day b.** la veille; **I've never done it b.** je ne l'ai jamais (encore) fait; – prep (*time*) avant; (*place*) devant; **the year b. last** il y a deux ans; – conj avant que (+ ne + *sub*), avant de (+ *inf*); **b. he goes** avant qu'il (ne) parte; **b. going** avant de partir. ◆**beforehand** adv à l'avance, avant.

befriend [bi'frend] vt offrir son amitié à, aider.

befuddled [bi'fʌd(ə)ld] a (*drunk*) ivre.

beg [beg] vt (**-gg-**) **to b.** (**for**) solliciter, demander; (*bread, money*) mendier; **to b. s.o. to do** prier or supplier qn de faire; **I b. to** je me permets de; **to b. the question** esquiver la question; – vi mendier;

(*entreat*) supplier; **to go begging** (*of food, articles*) ne pas trouver d'amateurs. ◆**beggar** *n* mendiant, -ante *mf*; (*person*) *Sl* individu *m*; **lucky b.** veinard, -arde *mf*. ◆**beggarly** *a* misérable.

beget [bɪ'get] *vt* (*pt* begot, *pp* begotten, *pres p* begetting) engendrer.

begin [bɪ'gɪn] *vt* (*pt* began, *pp* begun, *pres p* beginning) commencer; (*fashion, campaign*) lancer; (*bottle, sandwich*) entamer; (*conversation*) engager; **to b. doing** *or* **to do** commencer *or* se mettre à faire; — *vi* commencer (**with** par, **by doing** par faire); **to b. with** commencer qch; **beginning from** à partir de (qn); **to b. with** (*first*) d'abord. ◆**—ning** *n* commencement *m*, début *m*. ◆**—ner** *n* débutant, -ante *mf*.

begrudge [bɪ'grʌdʒ] *vt* (*give unwillingly*) donner à contrecœur; (*envy*) envier (**s.o. sth** qch à qn); (*reproach*) reprocher (**s.o. sth** qch à qn); **to b. doing** faire à contrecœur.

behalf [bɪ'hɑːf] *n* **on b.** de, pour, au nom de, de la part de; (*in the interest of*) en faveur de, pour.

behave [bɪ'heɪv] *vi* se conduire; (*of machine*) fonctionner; **to b.** (**oneself**) se tenir bien; (*of child*) être sage. ◆**behaviour** *n* conduite *f*, comportement *m*; **to be on one's best b.** se conduire de son mieux.

behead [bɪ'hed] *vt* décapiter.

behest [bɪ'hest] *n* *Lit* ordre *m*.

behind [bɪ'haɪnd] **1** *prep* derrière; (*more backward than, late according to*) en retard sur; — *adv* derrière; (*late*) en retard (**with**, **in** dans). **2** *n* (*buttocks*) *Fam* derrière *m*. ◆**behindhand** *adv* en retard.

beholden [bɪ'həʊldən] *a* redevable (**to à, for** de).

beige [beɪʒ] *a & n* beige (*m*).

being ['biːɪŋ] *n* (*person, life*) être *m*; **to come into b.** naître, être créé.

belated [bɪ'leɪtɪd] *a* tardif.

belch [beltʃ] **1** *vi* (*of person*) faire un renvoi, éructer; — *n* renvoi *m*. **2** *vt* **to b. (out)** (*smoke*) vomir.

beleaguered [bɪ'liːgəd] *a* (*besieged*) assiégé.

belfry ['belfrɪ] *n* beffroi *m*, clocher *m*.

Belgium ['beldʒəm] *n* Belgique *f*. ◆**Belgian** ['beldʒən] *a & n* belge (*mf*).

belie [bɪ'laɪ] *vt* démentir.

belief [bɪ'liːf] *n* (*believing, thing believed*) croyance *f* (**in** s.o. en qn, **in sth** à *or* en qch); (*trust*) confiance *f*, foi *f*; (*faith*) *Rel* foi *f* (**in** en).

believ/e [bɪ'liːv] *vti* croire (**in** God/s.o. en Dieu/qn); **I b. so** je crois que oui; **I b. I'm right** je crois avoir raison; **to b.**

in doing croire qu'il faut faire; **he doesn't b. in smoking** il désapprouve que l'on fume. ◆**—able** *a* croyable. ◆**—er** *n Rel* croyant, -ante *mf*; **b. in** (*supporter*) partisan, -ane *mf* de.

belittle [bɪ'lɪt(ə)l] *vt* déprécier.

bell [bel] *n* cloche *f*; (*small*) clochette *f*; (*in phone*) sonnerie *f*; (*on door, bicycle*) sonnette *f*; (*on dog*) grelot *m*. ◆**bellboy** *n*, ◆**bellhop** *n Am* groom *m*.

belle [bel] *n* (*woman*) beauté *f*, belle *f*.

belligerent [bɪ'lɪdʒərənt] *a & n* belligérant, -ante (*mf*).

bellow ['beləʊ] *vi* beugler, mugir.

bellows ['beləʊz] *npl* (**pair of) b.** soufflet *m*.

belly ['belɪ] *n* ventre *m*; **b. button** *Sl* nombril *m*. ◆**bellyache** *n* mal *m* au ventre; — *vi* rouspéter. ◆**bellyful** *n* **to have a b.** *Sl* en avoir plein le dos.

belong [bɪ'lɒŋ] *vi* appartenir (**to** à); **to b. to** (*club*) être membre de; **the cup belongs here** la tasse se range ici. ◆**—ings** *npl* affaires *fpl*.

beloved [bɪ'lʌvɪd] *a & n* bien-aimé, -ée (*mf*).

below [bɪ'ləʊ] *prep* (*lower than*) au-dessous de; (*under*) sous, au-dessous de; (*unworthy of*) *Fig* indigne de; — *adv* en dessous; **see b.** (*in book etc*) voir ci-dessous.

belt [belt] **1** *n* ceinture *f*; (*area*) zone *f*, région *f*; *Tech* courroie *f*. **2** *vt* (*hit*) *Sl* rosser. **3** *vi* **to b. (along)** (*rush*) *Sl* filer à toute allure; **b. up!** (*shut up*) *Sl* boucle-la!

bemoan [bɪ'məʊn] *vt* déplorer.

bench [bentʃ] *n* (*seat*) banc *m*; (*work table*) établi *m*, banc *m*; **the B.** *Jur* la magistrature (*assise*); (*court*) le tribunal.

bend [bend] *n* courbe *f*; (*in river, pipe*) coude *m*; (*in road*) *Aut* virage *m*; (*of arm, knee*) pli *m*; **round the b.** (*mad*) *Sl* tordu; — *vt* (*pt & pp* bent) courber; (*leg, arm*) plier; (*direct*) diriger; **to b. the rules** faire une entorse au règlement; — *vi* (*of branch*) plier, être courbé; (*of road*) tourner; **to b. (down)** se courber; **to b. (over** *or* **forward)** se pencher; **to b. to** (*s.o.'s will*) se soumettre à.

beneath [bɪ'niːθ] *prep* au-dessous de, sous; (*unworthy of*) indigne de; — *adv* (au-)dessous.

benediction [benɪ'dɪkʃ(ə)n] *n* bénédiction *f*.

benefactor ['benɪfæktər] *n* bienfaiteur *m*. ◆**benefactress** *n* bienfaitrice *f*.

beneficial [benɪ'fɪʃəl] *a* bénéfique.

beneficiary [benɪ'fɪʃərɪ] *n* bénéficiaire *mf*.

benefit ['benɪfɪt] *n* (*advantage*) avantage *m*; (*money*) allocation *f*; *pl* (*of science, education etc*) bienfaits *mpl*; **to s.o.'s b.** dans l'intérêt de qn; **for your (own) b.** pour vous,

pour votre bien; **to be of b.** faire du bien (**to** à); **to give s.o. the b.** of the doubt accorder à qn le bénéfice du doute; **b. concert**/*etc* concert/*etc* m de bienfaisance; – *vt* faire du bien à; (*be useful to*) profiter à; – *vi* gagner (**from doing** à faire); **you'll b.** **from** or **by the rest** le repos vous fera du bien.
Benelux ['beniləks] *n* Bénélux *m*.
benevolent [bɪ'nevələnt] *a* bienveillant. ◆**benevolence** *n* bienveillance *f*.
benign [bɪ'naɪn] *a* bienveillant, bénin; (*climate*) doux; (*tumour*) bénin.
bent [bent] **1** *a* (*nail, mind*) tordu; (*dishonest*) *Sl* corrompu; **b. on doing** résolu à faire. **2** *n* (*talent*) aptitude *f* (**for** pour); (*inclination, liking*) penchant *m*, goût *m* (**for** pour).
bequeath [bɪ'kwiːð] *vt* léguer (**to** à). ◆**bequest** *n* legs *m*.
bereaved [bɪ'riːvd] *a* endeuillé; – *n* **the b.** la famille, la femme *etc* du disparu. ◆**bereavement** *n* deuil *m*.
bereft [bɪ'reft] *a* **b. of** dénué de.
beret ['bereɪ, Am bə'reɪ] *n* béret *m*.
berk [bɜːk] *n* Sl imbécile *m*.
Bermuda [bə'mjuːdə] *n* Bermudes *fpl*.
berry ['berɪ] *n* baie *f*.
berserk [bə'zɜːk] *a* **to go b.** devenir fou, se déchaîner.
berth [bɜːθ] *n* (*in ship, train*) couchette *f*; (*anchorage*) mouillage *m*; – *vi* (*of ship*) mouiller.
beseech [bɪ'siːtʃ] *vt* (*pt & pp* **besought** or **beseeched**) *Lit* implorer (**to do** de faire).
beset [bɪ'set] *vt* (*pt & pp* **beset,** *pres p* **besetting**) assaillir (*qn*); **b. with obstacles**/*etc* semé or hérissé d'obstacles/*etc*.
beside [bɪ'saɪd] *prep* à côté de; **that's b. the point** ça n'a rien à voir; **b. oneself** (*angry, excited*) hors de soi.
besides [bɪ'saɪdz] *prep* (*in addition to*) en plus de; (*except*) excepté; **there are ten of us b.** Paul nous sommes dix sans compter Paul; – *adv* (*in addition*) de plus; (*moreover*) d'ailleurs.
besiege [bɪ'siːdʒ] *vt* (*of soldiers, crowd*) assiéger; (*annoy*) *Fig* assaillir (**with** de).
besotted [bɪ'sɒtɪd] *a* (*drunk*) abruti; **b. with** (*infatuated*) entiché de.
bespatter [bɪ'spætər] *vt* éclabousser (**with** de).
bespectacled [bɪ'spektɪk(ə)ld] *a* à lunettes.
bespoke [bɪ'spəʊk] *a* (*tailor*) à façon.
best [best] *a* meilleur; **the b. page in the book** la meilleure page du livre; **the b. part of** (*most*) la plus grande partie de; **the b. thing** le mieux; **b. man** (*at wedding*) témoin *m*, garçon *m* d'honneur; – *n* **the b.** (*one*) le

meilleur, la meilleure; **it's for the b.** c'est pour le mieux; **at b.** au mieux; **to do one's b.** faire de son mieux; **to look one's b.,** be at one's b. être à son avantage; **to the b. of my knowledge** autant que je sais; **to make the b. of** (*accept*) s'accommoder de; **to get the b. of it** avoir le dessus; **in one's Sunday b.** endimanché; **all the b.!** portez-vous bien!; (*in letter*) amicalement; – *adv* (**the**) **b.** (*to play etc*) le mieux; **the b. loved** le plus aimé; **to think it b. to** juger prudent de. ◆**b.-'seller** *n* (*book*) best-seller *m*.
bestow [bɪ'stəʊ] *vt* accorder, conférer (**on** à).
bet [bet] *n* pari *m*; – *vti* (*pt & pp* **bet** or **betted,** *pres p* **betting**) parier (**on** sur, **that** que); **you b.!** *Fam* (*of course*) tu parles! ◆**betting** *n* pari(s) *m*(*pl*); **b. shop** or **office** bureau *m* du pari mutuel.
betoken [bɪ'təʊkən] *vt* *Lit* annoncer.
betray [bɪ'treɪ] *vt* trahir; **to b. to s.o.** (*give away to*) livrer à qn. ◆**betrayal** *n* (*disloyalty*) trahison *f*; (*disclosure*) révélation *f*.
better ['betər] *a* meilleur (**than** que); **she's** (**much**) **b.** *Med* elle va (bien) mieux; **he's b. than** (*at games*) il joue mieux que; (*at maths etc*) il est plus fort que; **that's b.** c'est mieux; **to get b.** (*recover*) se remettre; (*improve*) s'améliorer; **it's b. to go** il vaut mieux partir; **the b. part of** (*most*) la plus grande partie de; – *adv* mieux; **I had b. go** il vaut mieux que je parte; **so much the b.,** **all the b.** tant mieux (**for** pour); – *n* to **get the b. of s.o.** l'emporter sur qn; **change for the b.** amélioration *f*; **one's betters** ses supérieurs *mpl*; – *vt* (*improve*) améliorer; (*outdo*) dépasser; **to b. oneself** améliorer sa condition. ◆**—ment** *n* amélioration *f*.
between [bɪ'twiːn] *prep* entre; **we did it b.** (**the two of**) **us** nous l'avons fait à nous deux; **b. you and me** entre nous; **in b.** entre; – *adv* **in b.** (*space*) au milieu, entre les deux; (*time*) dans l'intervalle.
bevel ['bev(ə)l] *n* (*edge*) biseau *m*.
beverage ['bevərɪdʒ] *n* boisson *f*.
bevy ['bevɪ] *n* (*of girls*) essaim *m*, bande *f*.
beware [bɪ'weər] *vi* **to b. of** (*s.o., sth*) se méfier de, prendre garde à; **b.!** méfiez-vous!, prenez garde!; **b. of falling**/*etc* prenez garde de (ne pas) tomber/*etc*; **'b. of the trains'** 'attention aux trains'.
bewilder [bɪ'wɪldər] *vt* dérouter, rendre perplexe. ◆**—ment** *n* confusion *f*.
bewitch [bɪ'wɪtʃ] *vt* enchanter. ◆**—ing** *a* enchanteur.
beyond [bɪ'jɒnd] *prep* (*further than*) au-delà

de; (*reach, doubt*) hors de; (*except*) sauf; **b. a year**/*etc* (*longer than*) plus d'un an/*etc*; **b. belief** incroyable; **b. his** *or* **her means** au-dessus de ses moyens; **it's b. me** ça me dépasse; – *adv* (*further*) au-delà.

bias ['baɪəs] **1** *n* penchant *m* (*towards* pour); (*prejudice*) préjugé *m*, parti pris *m*; – *vt* (**-ss-** *or* **-s-**) influencer. **2** *n* **cut on the b.** (*fabric*) coupé dans le biais. ◆**bias(s)ed** *a* partial; **to be b. against** avoir des préjugés contre.

bib [bɪb] *n* (*baby's*) bavoir *m*.

bible ['baɪb(ə)l] *n* bible *f*; **the B.** la Bible. ◆**biblical** ['bɪblɪk(ə)l] *a* biblique.

bibliography [bɪblɪ'ɒɡrəfɪ] *n* bibliographie *f*.

bicarbonate [baɪ'kɑːbənət] *n* bicarbonate *m*.

bicentenary [baɪsen'tiːnərɪ] *n*, ◆**bicentennial** *n* bicentenaire *m*.

biceps ['baɪseps] *n Anat* biceps *m*.

bicker ['bɪkər] *vi* se chamailler. ◆**—ing** *n* chamailleries *fpl*.

bicycle ['baɪsɪk(ə)l] *n* bicyclette *f*; – *vi* faire de la bicyclette.

bid¹ [bɪd] *vt* (*pt & pp* **bid,** *pres p* **bidding**) offrir, faire une offre de; – *vi* faire une offre (**for** pour); **to b. for** *Fig* tenter d'obtenir; – *n* (*at auction*) offre *f*, enchère *f*; (*tender*) *Com* soumission *f*; (*attempt*) tentative *f*. ◆**—ding¹** *n* enchères *fpl*. ◆**—der** *n* enchérisseur *m*; soumissionnaire *mf*; **to the highest b.** au plus offrant.

bid² [bɪd] *vt* (*pt* **bade** [bæd], *pp* **bidden** *or* **bid,** *pres p* **bidding**) (*command*) commander (**s.o. to do** à qn de faire); (*say*) dire. ◆**—ding²** *n* ordre(s) *m(pl)*.

bide [baɪd] *vt* **to b. one's time** attendre le bon moment.

bier [bɪər] *n* (*for coffin*) brancards *mpl*.

bifocals [baɪ'fəʊkəlz] *npl* verres *mpl* à double foyer.

big [bɪɡ] *a* (**bigger, biggest**) grand, gros; (*in age, generous*) grand; (*in bulk, amount*) gros; **b. deal!** *Am Fam* (bon) et alors!; **b. mouth** *Fam* grande gueule *f*; **b. toe** gros orteil *m*; – *adv* **to do things b.** *Fam* faire grand; **to talk b.** fanfaronner. ◆**bighead** *n*, ◆**big'headed** *a* prétentieux, -euse (*mf*). ◆**big-'hearted** *a* généreux. ◆**big-shot** *n*, ◆**bigwig** *n Fam* gros bonnet *m*. ◆**big-time** *a Fam* important.

bigamy ['bɪɡəmɪ] *n* bigamie *f*. ◆**bigamist** *n* bigame *mf*. ◆**bigamous** *a* bigame.

bigot ['bɪɡət] *n* fanatique *mf*; *Rel* bigot, -ote *mf*. ◆**bigoted** *a* fanatique; *Rel* bigot.

bike [baɪk] *n Fam* vélo *m*; – *vi Fam* aller à vélo.

bikini [bɪ'kiːnɪ] *n* bikini *m*.

bilberry ['bɪlbərɪ] *n* myrtille *f*.

bile [baɪl] *n* bile *f*. ◆**bilious** ['bɪlɪəs] *a* bilieux.

bilge [bɪldʒ] *n* (*nonsense*) *Sl* foutaises *fpl*.

bilingual [baɪ'lɪŋɡwəl] *a* bilingue.

bill [bɪl] **1** *n* (*of bird*) bec *m*. **2** *n* (*invoice*) facture *f*, note *f*; (*in restaurant*) addition *f*; (*in hotel*) note *f*; (*draft*) *Com* effet *m*; (*of sale*) acte *m*; (*banknote*) *Am* billet *m*; (*law*) *Pol* projet *m* de loi; (*poster*) affiche *f*; **b. of fare** menu *m*; **b. of rights** déclaration *f* des droits; – *vt Th* mettre à l'affiche, annoncer; **to b. s.o.** *Com* envoyer la facture à qn. ◆**billboard** *n* panneau *m* d'affichage. ◆**billfold** *n* *Am* portefeuille *m*.

billet ['bɪlɪt] *vt Mil* cantonner; – *n* cantonnement *m*.

billiard ['bɪljəd] *a* (*table etc*) de billard. ◆**billiards** *npl* (jeu *m* de) billard *m*.

billion ['bɪljən] *n* billion *m*; *Am* milliard *m*.

billow ['bɪləʊ] *n* flot *m*; – *vi* (*of sea*) se soulever; (*of smoke*) tourbillonner.

billy-goat ['bɪlɪɡəʊt] *n* bouc *m*.

bimonthly [baɪ'mʌnθlɪ] *a* (*fortnightly*) bimensuel; (*every two months*) bimestriel.

bin [bɪn] *n* boîte *f*; (*for bread*) coffre *m*, huche *f*; (*for litter*) boîte *f* à ordures, poubelle *f*.

binary ['baɪnərɪ] *a* binaire.

bind [baɪnd] **1** *vt* (*pt & pp* **bound**) lier; (*fasten*) attacher, lier; (*book*) relier; (*fabric, hem*) border; **to b. s.o. to do** *Jur* obliger *or* astreindre qn à faire. **2** *n* (*bore*) *Fam* plaie *f*. ◆**—ing** *a* (*contract*) irrévocable; **to be b. on s.o.** *Jur* lier qn. **2** *n* (*of book*) reliure *f*. ◆**—er** *n* (*for papers*) classeur *m*.

binge [bɪndʒ] *n* **to go on a b.** *Sl* faire la bringue.

bingo ['bɪŋɡəʊ] *n* loto *m*.

binoculars [bɪ'nɒkjʊləz] *npl* jumelles *fpl*.

biochemistry [baɪəʊ'kemɪstrɪ] *n* biochimie *f*.

biodegradable [baɪəʊdɪ'ɡreɪdəb(ə)l] *a* biodégradable.

biography [baɪ'ɒɡrəfɪ] *n* biographie *f*. ◆**biographer** *n* biographe *mf*.

biology [baɪ'ɒlədʒɪ] *n* biologie *f*. ◆**biological** *a* biologique.

birch [bɜːtʃ] *n* **1** (*tree*) bouleau *m*. **2** (*whip*) verge *f*; – *vt* fouetter.

bird [bɜːd] *n* oiseau *m*; (*fowl*) *Culin* volaille *f*; (*girl*) *Sl* poulette *f*, nana *f*; **b.'s-eye view**

perspective *f* à vol d'oiseau; *Fig* vue *f* d'ensemble. ◆**birdseed** *n* grains *mpl* de millet.

biro® ['baɪərəʊ] *n* (*pl* -**os**) stylo *m* à bille, bic® *m*.

birth [bɜːθ] *n* naissance *f*; **to give b. to** donner naissance à; **b. certificate** acte *m* de naissance; **b. control** limitation *f* des naissances. ◆**birthday** *n* anniversaire *m*; **happy b.!** bon anniversaire! ◆**birthplace** *n* lieu *m* de naissance; (*house*) maison *f* natale. ◆**birthrate** *n* (taux *m* de) natalité *f*. ◆**birthright** *n* droit *m* (qu'on a dès sa naissance), patrimoine *m*.

biscuit ['bɪskɪt] *n* biscuit *m*, gâteau *m* sec; *Am* petit pain *m* au lait.

bishop ['bɪʃəp] *n* évêque *m*; (*in chess*) fou *m*.

bison ['baɪs(ə)n] *n* *inv* bison *m*.

bit¹ [bɪt] *n* 1 morceau *m*; (*of string, time*) bout *m*; **a b.** (*a little*) un peu; **a tiny b.** un tout petit peu; **quite a b.** (*very*) très; (*much*) beaucoup; **not a b.** pas du tout; **a b. of luck** une chance; **b. by b.** petit à petit; **in bits (and pieces)** en morceaux; **to come to bits** se démonter. **2** (*coin*) pièce *f*. **3** (*of horse*) mors *m*. **4** (*of drill*) mèche *f*. **5** (*computer information*) bit *m*.

bit² [bɪt] *see* **bite**.

bitch [bɪtʃ] **1** *n* chienne *f*; (*woman*) *Pej Fam* garce *f*. **2** *vi* (*complain*) *Fam* râler. ◆**bitchy** *a* (-ier, -iest) *Fam* vache.

bit/e [baɪt] *n* (*wound*) morsure *f*; (*from insect*) piqûre *f*; *Fishing* touche *f*; (*mouthful*) bouchée *f*; (*of style etc*) *Fig* mordant *m*; **a b. to eat** un morceau à manger; — *vti* (*pt* **bit**, *pp* **bitten**) mordre; (*of insect*) piquer, mordre; **to b. one's nails** se ronger les ongles; **to b. on sth** mordre qch; **to b. sth off** arracher qch d'un coup de dent(s). ◆**-ing** *a* mordant; (*wind*) cinglant.

bitter ['bɪtər] **1** *a* (*person, taste, irony etc*) amer; (*cold, wind*) glacial, âpre; (*criticism*) acerbe; (*shock, fate*) cruel; (*conflict*) violent. **2** *n* bière *f* (pression). ◆**-ness** *n* amertume *f*; âpreté *f*; violence *f*. ◆**bitter-sweet** *a* aigre-doux.

bivouac ['bɪvʊæk] *n* *Mil* bivouac *m*; – *vi* (-ck-) bivouaquer.

bizarre [bɪ'zɑːr] *a* bizarre.

blab [blæb] *vi* (-bb-) jaser. ◆**blabber** *vi* jaser. ◆**blabbermouth** *n* jaseur, -euse *mf*.

black [blæk] *a* (-er, -est) noir; **b. eye** œil *m* au beurre noir; **to give s.o. a b. eye** pocher l'œil à qn; **b. and blue** (*bruised*) couvert de bleus; **b. sheep** *Fig* brebis *f* galeuse; **b. ice** verglas *m*; **b. pudding** boudin *m*; – *n* (*colour*) noir *m*; (*Negro*) Noir, -e *mf*; – *vt*

noircir; (*refuse to deal with*) boycotter; – *vi* **to b. out** (*faint*) s'évanouir. ◆**blacken** *vti* noircir. ◆**blackish** *a* noirâtre. ◆**blackness** *n* noirceur *f*; (*of night*) obscurité *f*.

blackberry ['blækbərɪ] *n* mûre *f*. ◆**blackbird** *n* merle *m*. ◆**blackboard** *n* tableau *m* (noir). ◆**black'currant** *n* cassis *m*. ◆**blackleg** *n* (*strike breaker*) jaune *m*. ◆**blacklist** *n* liste *f* noire; – *vt* mettre sur la liste noire. ◆**blackmail** *n* chantage *m*; – *vt* faire chanter. ◆**blackmailer** *n* maître chanteur *m*. ◆**blackout** *n* panne *f* d'électricité; (*during war*) *Mil* black-out *m*; *Med* syncope *f*; (*news*) **b.** black-out *m*. ◆**blacksmith** *n* forgeron *m*.

blackguard ['blægɑːd, -gəd] *n* canaille *f*.

bladder ['blædər] *n* vessie *f*.

blade [bleɪd] *n* lame *f*; (*of grass*) brin *m*; (*of windscreen wiper*) caoutchouc *m*.

blame [bleɪm] *vt* accuser; (*censure*) blâmer; **to b. sth on s.o.** *or* **s.o. for sth** rejeter la responsabilité de qch sur qn; **to b. s.o. for sth** (*reproach*) reprocher qch à qn; **you're to b.** c'est ta faute; – *n* faute *f*; (*censure*) blâme *m*. ◆**-less** *a* irréprochable.

blanch [blɑːntʃ] *vt* (*vegetables*) blanchir; – *vi* (*turn pale with fear etc*) blêmir.

blancmange [blə'mɒnʒ] *n* blanc-manger *m*.

bland [blænd] *a* (-er, -est) doux; (*food*) fade.

blank [blæŋk] *a* (*paper, page*) blanc, vierge; (*cheque*) en blanc; (*look, mind*) vide; (*puzzled*) ébahi; (*refusal*) absolu; – *a* & *n* **b. (space)** blanc *m*; **b. (cartridge)** cartouche *f* à blanc; **my mind's a b.** j'ai la tête vide. ◆**blankly** *adv* sans expression.

blanket ['blæŋkɪt] **1** *n* couverture *f*; (*of snow etc*) *Fig* couche *f*; – *vt* (*cover*) *Fig* recouvrir. **2** *a* (*term etc*) général. ◆**-ing** (*blankets*) couvertures *fpl*.

blare [bleər] *n* (*noise*) beuglement *m*; (*of trumpet*) sonnerie *f*; – *vi* **to b. (out)** (*of radio*) beugler; (*of music, car horn*) retentir.

blarney ['blɑːnɪ] *n Fam* boniment(s) *m(pl)*.

blasé ['blɑːzeɪ] *a* blasé.

blaspheme [blæs'fiːm] *vti* blasphémer. ◆**'blasphemous** *a* blasphématoire; (*person*) blasphémateur. ◆**'blasphemy** *n* blasphème *m*.

blast [blɑːst] **1** *n* explosion *f*; (*air from explosion*) souffle *m*; (*of wind*) rafale *f*, coup *m*; (*of trumpet*) sonnerie *f*; **(at) full b.** (*loud*) à plein volume; (*fast*) à pleine vitesse; **b. furnace** haut fourneau *m*; – *vt* (*blow up*) faire sauter; (*hopes*) *Fig* détruire; **to b. s.o.** *Fam* réprimander qn. **2** *int* zut!, merde! ◆**—ed** a Fam fichu. ◆**blast-off** n (of spacecraft) mise f à feu.

blatant ['bleɪtənt] a (obvious) flagrant, criant; (shameless) éhonté.

blaz/e [bleɪz] **1** n (fire) flamme f, feu m; (conflagration) incendie m; (splendour) Fig éclat m; **b. of light** torrent m de lumière; – vi (of fire) flamber; (of sun, colour, eyes) flamboyer. **2** vt **to b. a trail** marquer la voie. ◆**—ing** a (burning) en feu; (sun) brûlant; (argument) Fig violent.

blazer ['bleɪzər] n blazer m.

bleach [bliːtʃ] n décolorant m; (household detergent) eau f de Javel; – vt (hair) décolorer, oxygéner; (linen) blanchir.

bleak [bliːk] a (-er, -est) (appearance, future etc) morne; (countryside) désolé.

bleary ['bliəri] a (eyes) troubles, voilés.

bleat [bliːt] vi bêler.

bleed [bliːd] vti (pt & pp bled) saigner; **to b. to death** perdre tout son sang. ◆**—ing** a (wound) saignant; (bloody) Sl foutu.

bleep [bliːp] n signal m, bip m; – vt appeler au bip-bip. ◆**bleeper** n bip-bip m.

blemish ['blemɪʃ] n (fault) défaut m; (on fruit, reputation) tache f; – vt (reputation) ternir.

blend [blend] n mélange m; – vt mélanger; – vi se mélanger; (go together) se marier (with avec). ◆**—er** n Culin mixer m.

bless [bles] vt bénir; **to be blessed with** le bonheur de posséder; **b. you!** (sneezing) à vos souhaits! ◆**—ed** [-ɪd] a saint, béni; (happy) Rel bienheureux; (blasted) Fam fichu, sacré. ◆**—ing** n bénédiction f; (divine favour) grâce f; (benefit) bienfait m; **what a b. that . . .** quelle chance que . . . .

blew [bluː] see **blow 1**.

blight [blaɪt] n (on plants) rouille f; (scourge) Fig fléau m; **to be** or **cast a b. on** avoir une influence néfaste sur; **urban b.** (area) quartier m délabré; (condition) délabrement m (de quartier). ◆**blighter** n Pej Fam type m.

blimey! ['blaɪmɪ] int Fam zut!, mince!

blimp [blɪmp] n dirigeable m.

blind [blaɪnd] **1** a aveugle; **b. person** aveugle mf; **b. in one eye** borgne; **he's b. to** (fault) il ne voit pas; **to turn a b. eye to** fermer les yeux sur; **b. alley** impasse f; – n **the b.** les aveugles mpl; – vt aveugler. **2** n (on window) store m; (deception) feinte f. ◆**—ly** adv aveuglément. ◆**—ness** n cécité f; Fig aveuglement m. ◆**blinders** npl Am œillères fpl. ◆**blindfold** n bandeau m; – vt bander les yeux à; – adv les yeux bandés.

blink [blɪŋk] vi cligner des yeux; (of eyes)

cligner; (of light) clignoter; – vt **to b. one's eyes** cligner des yeux; – n clignement m; **on the b.** (machine) Fam détraqué. ◆**—ing** a (bloody) Fam sacré. ◆**blinkers** npl (for horse) œillères fpl; (indicators) Aut clignotants mpl.

bliss [blɪs] n félicité f. ◆**blissful** a (happy) très joyeux; (wonderful) merveilleux. ◆**blissfully** adv (happy, unaware) parfaitement.

blister ['blɪstər] n (on skin) ampoule f; – vi se couvrir d'ampoules.

blithe [blaɪð] a joyeux.

blitz [blɪts] n (attack) Av raid m éclair; (bombing) bombardement m aérien; Fig Fam offensive f; – vt bombarder.

blizzard ['blɪzəd] n tempête f de neige.

bloat [bləʊt] vt gonfler.

bloater ['bləʊtər] n hareng m saur.

blob [blɒb] n (of water) (grosse) goutte f; (of ink, colour) tache f.

bloc [blɒk] n Pol bloc m.

block [blɒk] n (of stone etc) bloc m; (of buildings) pâté m (de maisons); (in pipe) obstruction f; (mental) blocage m; **b. of flats** immeuble m; **b. away** Am une rue plus loin; **school b.** groupe m scolaire; **b. capitals** or **letters** majuscules fpl. **2** vt (obstruct) bloquer; (pipe) boucher, bloquer; (one's view) boucher; **to b. off** (road) barrer; (light) intercepter; **to b. up** (pipe, hole) bloquer. ◆**blo'ckade** n blocus m; – vt bloquer. ◆**blockage** n obstruction f. ◆**blockbuster** n Cin superproduction f, film m à grand spectacle. ◆**blockhead** n imbécile mf.

bloke [bləʊk] n Fam type m.

blond [blɒnd] a & n blond (m). ◆**blonde** a & n blonde (f).

blood [blʌd] n sang m; – a (group, orange etc) sanguin; (donor, bath etc) de sang; (poisoning etc) du sang; **b. pressure** tension f (artérielle); **high b. pressure** (hyper)tension f. ◆**bloodcurdling** a à vous tourner le sang. ◆**bloodhound** n (dog, detective) limier m. ◆**bloodletting** n saignée f. ◆**bloodshed** n effusion f de sang. ◆**bloodshot** a (eye) injecté de sang. ◆**bloodsucker** n (insect, person) sangsue f. ◆**bloodthirsty** a sanguinaire.

bloody ['blʌdɪ] **1** a (-ier, -iest) sanglant. **2** a (blasted) Fam sacré; – adv Fam vachement. ◆**b.-'minded** a hargneux, pas commode.

bloom [bluːm] n fleur f; **in b.** en fleur(s); – vi fleurir; (of person) Fig s'épanouir. ◆**—ing**

a **1** (*in bloom*) en fleur(s); (*thriving*) florissant. **2** (*blinking*) *Fam* fichu.

bloomer ['blu:mər] *n Fam* (*mistake*) gaffe *f*.

blossom ['blɒsəm] *n* fleur(s) *f(pl)*; – *vi* fleurir; **to b. (out)** (*of person*) s'épanouir; **to b. (out) into** devenir.

blot [blɒt] *n* tache *f*; – *vt* (*-tt-*) tacher; (*dry*) sécher; **to b. out** (*word*) rayer; (*memory*) effacer. ◆**blotting** *a* **b. paper** (papier *m*) buvard *m*. ◆**blotter** *n* buvard *m*.

blotch [blɒtʃ] *n* tache *f*. ◆**blotchy** *a* (*-ier, -iest*) couvert de taches; (*face*) marbré.

blouse [blauz, *Am* blaus] *n* chemisier *m*.

blow¹ [bləu] *vt* (*pt* **blew**, *pp* **blown**) (*of wind*) pousser (*un navire etc*), chasser (*la pluie etc*); (*smoke, glass*) souffler; (*bubbles*) faire; (*trumpet*) souffler dans; (*fuse*) faire sauter; (*kiss*) envoyer (**to** à); (*money*) *Fam* claquer; **to b. one's nose** se moucher; **to b. a whistle** siffler; **to b. away** (*of wind*) emporter; **to b. down** (*chimney etc*) faire tomber; **to b. off** (*hat etc*) emporter; (*arm*) arracher; **to b. out** (*candle*) souffler; (*cheeks*) gonfler; **to b. up** (*building etc*) faire sauter; (*tyre*) gonfler; (*photo*) agrandir; – *vi* (*of wind*) souffler; (*of fuse*) sauter; (*of papers etc*) s'éparpiller; **b.!** *Fam* zut!; **to b. down** (*fall*) tomber; **to b. off** *or* **away** s'envoler; **to b. out** (*of light*) s'éteindre; **to b. over** (*pass*) passer; **to b. up** (*explode*) exploser. ◆**blow-dry** *n* brushing *m*. ◆**blowlamp** *n* chalumeau *m*. ◆**blowout** *n* (*of tyre*) éclatement *m*; (*meal*) *Sl* gueuleton *m*. ◆**blowtorch** *n Am* chalumeau *m*. ◆**blow-up** *n Phot* agrandissement *m*.

blow² [bləu] *n* coup *m*; **to come to blows** en venir aux mains.

blowy ['bləui] *a* **it's b.** *Fam* il y a du vent.

blowzy ['blauzi] *a* **b. woman** (*slovenly*) *Fam* femme *f* débraillée.

blubber ['blʌbər] *n* graisse *f* (de baleine).

bludgeon ['blʌdʒən] *n* gourdin *m*; – *vt* matraquer.

blue [blu:] *a* (**bluer, bluest**) bleu; **to feel b.** *Fam* avoir le cafard; **b. film** film *m* porno; – *n* bleu *m*; **the blues** (*depression*) *Fam* le cafard; *Mus* le blues. ◆**bluebell** *n* jacinthe *f* des bois. ◆**blueberry** *n* airelle *f*. ◆**bluebottle** *n* mouche *f* à viande. ◆**blueprint** *n* Fig plan *m* (de travail).

bluff [blʌf] **1** *a* (*person*) brusque, direct. **2** *vti* bluffer; – *n* bluff *m*.

blunder ['blʌndər] **1** *n* (*mistake*) bévue *f*, gaffe *f*; – *vi* faire une bévue. **2** *vi* (*move awkwardly*) avancer à tâtons. ◆**-ing** *a* maladroit; – *n* maladresse *f*.

blunt [blʌnt] *a* (**-er, -est**) (*edge*) émoussé; (*pencil*) épointé; (*person*) brusque; (*speech*) franc; – *vt* émousser; épointer. ◆**-ly** *adv* carrément. ◆**-ness** *n* Fig brusquerie *f*; (*of speech*) franchise *f*.

blur [blɜːr] *n* tache *f* floue, contour *m* imprécis; – *vt* (*-rr-*) estomper, rendre flou; (*judgment*) *Fig* troubler. ◆**blurred** *a* (*image*) flou, estompé.

blurb [blɜːb] *n Fam* résumé *m* publicitaire, laïus *m*.

blurt [blɜːt] *vt* **to b. (out)** laisser échapper, lâcher.

blush [blʌʃ] *vi* rougir (**at, with** de); – *n* rougeur *f*; **with a b.** en rougissant.

bluster ['blʌstər] *vi* (*of person*) tempêter; (*of wind*) faire rage. ◆**blustery** *a* (*weather*) de grand vent, à bourrasques.

boa ['bəuə] *n* (*snake*) boa *m*.

boar [bɔːr] *n* (*wild*) **b.** sanglier *m*.

board¹ [bɔːd] *n* (*piece of wood*) planche *f*; (*for notices, games etc*) tableau *m*; (*cardboard*) carton *m*; (*committee*) conseil *m*, commission *f*; **b. (of directors)** conseil *m* d'administration; **on b.** *Nau Av* à bord (de); **B. of Trade** *Br Pol* ministère *m* du Commerce; **across the b.** (*pay rise*) général; **to go by the b.** (*of plan*) être abandonné. **2** *vt Nau Av* monter à bord de; (*bus, train*) monter dans; **to b. up** (*door*) boucher. ◆**-ing** *n Nau Av* embarquement *m*. ◆**boardwalk** *n Am* promenade *f*.

board² [bɔːd] *n* (*food*) pension *f*; **b. and lodging, bed and b.** (chambre *f* avec) pension *f*; – *vi* (*lodge*) être en pension (**with** chez); **boarding house** pension *f* (de famille); **boarding school** pensionnat *m*. ◆**-er** *n* pensionnaire *m f*.

boast [bəust] *vi* se vanter (**about, of** de); – *vt* se glorifier de; **to b. that one can do . . .** se vanter de (pouvoir) faire . . .; – *n* vantardise *f*. ◆**-ing** *n* vantardise *f*. ◆**boastful** *a* vantard. ◆**boastfully** *adv* en se vantant.

boat [bəut] *n* bateau *m*; (*small*) barque *f*, canot *m*; (*liner*) paquebot *m*; **in the same b.** Fig logé à la même enseigne; **b. race** course *f* d'aviron. ◆**-ing** *n* canotage *m*; **b. trip** excursion *f* en bateau.

boatswain ['bəus(ə)n] *n* maître *m* d'équipage.

bob [bɒb] *vi* (*-bb-*) **to b. (up and down)** (*on water*) danser sur l'eau.

bobbin ['bɒbin] *n* bobine *f*.

bobby ['bɒbi] *n* **1** (*policeman*) *Fam* flic *m*, agent *m*. **2 b. pin** *Am* pince *f* à cheveux.

bode [bəʊd] vi **to b. well/ill** être de bon/mauvais augure.

bodice ['bɒdɪs] n corsage m.

body ['bɒdɪ] n corps m; (of vehicle) carrosserie f; (quantity) masse f; (institution) organisme m; **the main b. of** le gros de; **b. building** culturisme m. ◆**bodily** a physique; (need) matériel; – adv physiquement; (as a whole) tout entier. ◆**bodyguard** n garde m du corps, gorille m. ◆**bodywork** n carrosserie f.

boffin ['bɒfɪn] n Fam chercheur, -euse mf scientifique.

bog [bɒg] n marécage m; – vt **to get bogged down** s'enliser. ◆**boggy** a (-ier, -iest) marécageux.

bogey ['bəʊgɪ] n spectre m; **b. man** croque-mitaine m.

boggle ['bɒg(ə)l] vi **the mind boggles** cela confond l'imagination.

bogus ['bəʊgəs] a faux.

bohemian [bəʊ'hiːmɪən] a & n (artist etc) bohème (mf).

boil [bɔɪl] n Med furoncle m, clou m. **2** vi bouillir; **to b. away** (until dry) s'évaporer; (on and on) bouillir sans arrêt; **to b. down to** Fig se ramener à; **to b. over** (of milk, emotions etc) déborder; – vt **to b. (up)** faire bouillir; – n **to be on the b., come to the b.** bouillir; **to bring to the b.** amener à ébullition. ◆**-ed** a (beef) bouilli; (potato) cuit à l'eau; **b. egg** œuf m à la coque. ◆**-ing** n ébullition f; **at b. point** à ébullition; – a & adv **b. (hot)** bouillant; **it's b. (hot)** (weather) il fait une chaleur infernale. ◆**-er** n chaudière f; **b. suit** bleu m (de travail).

boisterous ['bɔɪstərəs] a (noisy) tapageur; (child) turbulent; (meeting) houleux.

bold [bəʊld] a (-er, -est) hardi; **b. type** caractères mpl gras. ◆**-ness** n hardiesse f.

Bolivia [bə'lɪvɪə] n Bolivie f. ◆**Bolivian** a & n bolivien, -ienne (mf).

bollard ['bɒləd, 'bɒlɑːd] n Aut borne f.

boloney [bə'ləʊnɪ] n Sl foutaises fpl.

bolster ['bəʊlstər] **1** n (pillow) traversin m, polochon m. **2** vt **to b. (up)** (support) soutenir.

bolt [bəʊlt] **1** n (on door etc) verrou m; (for nut) boulon m; – vt (door) verrouiller. **2** n (dash) fuite f, ruée f; – vi (dash) se précipiter; (flee) détaler; (of horse) s'emballer. **3** n **b.** (of lightning) éclair m. **4** vt (food) engloutir. **5** adv **b. upright** tout droit.

bomb [bɒm] n bombe f; **letter b.** lettre f piégée; **b. disposal** désamorçage m; – vt bombarder. ◆**-ing** n bombardement m.

◆**-er** n (aircraft) bombardier m; (terrorist) plastiqueur m. ◆**bombshell** n **to come as a b.** tomber comme une bombe. ◆**bombsite** n terrain m vague, lieu m bombardé.

bombard [bɒm'bɑːd] vt bombarder (with de). ◆**-ment** n bombardement m.

bona fide [bəʊnə'faɪdɪ, Am -'faɪd] a sérieux, de bonne foi.

bonanza [bə'nænzə] n Fig mine f d'or.

bond [bɒnd] **1** n (agreement, promise) engagement m; (link) lien m; Com bon m, obligation f; (adhesion) adhérence f. **2** vt (goods) entreposer.

bondage ['bɒndɪdʒ] n esclavage m.

bone [bəʊn] **1** n os m; (of fish) arête f; **b. of contention** pomme f de discorde; **b. china** porcelaine f tendre; – vt (meat etc) désosser. **2** vi **to b. up on** (subject) Am Fam bûcher. ◆**bony** a (-ier, -iest) (thin) osseux, maigre; (fish) plein d'arêtes.

bone-dry [bəʊn'draɪ] a tout à fait sec. ◆**b.-idle** a paresseux comme une couleuvre.

bonfire ['bɒnfaɪər] n (for celebration) feu m de joie; (for dead leaves) feu m (de jardin).

bonkers ['bɒŋkəz] a (crazy) Fam dingue.

bonnet ['bɒnɪt] n (hat) bonnet m; Aut capot m.

bonus ['bəʊnəs] n prime f; **no claims b.** Aut bonus m.

boo [buː] **1** int hou! **2** vti huer; – npl huées fpl.

boob [buːb] n (mistake) gaffe f; – vi Sl gaffer.

booby-trap ['buːbɪtræp] n engin m piégé; – vt (-pp-) piéger.

book [bʊk] **1** n livre m; (of tickets) carnet m; (record) registre m; pl (accounts) comptes mpl; (exercise) **b.** cahier m. **2** vt **to b. (up)** (seat etc) réserver, retenir; **to b. s.o.** Jur donner un procès-verbal à qn; **to b. (down)** inscrire; (fully) **booked (up)** (hotel, concert) complet; (person) pris; – vi **to b. (up)** réserver des places; **to b. in** (in hotel) signer le registre. ◆**-ing** n réservation f; **b. clerk** guichetier, -ière mf; **b. office** bureau m de location, guichet m. ◆**-able** a (seat) qu'on peut réserver. ◆**bookish** a (word, theory) livresque; (person) studieux.

bookbinding ['bʊkbaɪndɪŋ] n reliure f. ◆**bookcase** n bibliothèque f. ◆**bookend** n serre-livres m inv. ◆**bookkeeper** n comptable mf. ◆**bookkeeping** n comptabilité f. ◆**booklet** n brochure f. ◆**book-lover** n bibliophile m. ◆**bookmaker** n bookmaker m. ◆**bookmark** n

boom [buːm] **1** *vi* (*of thunder, gun etc*) gronder; – *n* grondement *m*; **sonic b.** bang *m*. **2** *n Econ* expansion *f*, essor *m*, boom *m*.

boomerang ['buːməraŋ] *n* boomerang *m*.

boon [buːn] *n* aubaine *f*, avantage *m*.

boor [buər] *n* rustre *m*. ◆**boorish** *a* rustre.

boost [buːst] *vt* (*push*) donner une poussée à; (*increase*) augmenter; (*product*) faire de la réclame pour; (*economy*) stimuler; (*morale*) remonter; – *n* **to give a b. to** = **to boost**. ◆**–er** *n* **b.** (**injection**) piqûre *f* de rappel.

boot [buːt] **1** *n* (*shoe*) botte *f*; (**ankle**) **b.** bottillon *m*; (**knee**) **b.** bottine *f*; **to get the b.** *Fam* être mis à la porte; **b. polish** cirage *m*; – *vt* (*kick*) donner un coup *or* des coups de pied à; **to b. out** mettre à la porte. **2** *n Aut* coffre *m*. **3** *n* **to b.** en plus. ◆**bootblack** *n* cireur *m*. ◆**boo'tee** *n* (*of baby*) chausson *m*.

booth [buːð, buːθ] *n Tel* cabine *f*; (*at fair*) baraque *f*.

booty ['buːtɪ] *n* (*stolen goods*) butin *m*.

booz/e [buːz] *n Fam* alcool *m*, boisson(s) *f(pl)*; (*drinking bout*) beuverie *f*; – *vi Fam* boire (beaucoup). ◆**–er** *n Fam* (*person*) buveur, -euse *mf*; (*place*) bistrot *m*.

border ['bɔːdər] *n* (*of country*) & *Fig* frontière *f*; (*edge*) bord *m*; (*of garden etc*) bordure *f*; – *a* (*town*) frontière *inv*; (*incident*) de frontière; – *vt* (*street*) border; **to b.** (**on**) (*country*) toucher à; **to b.** (**up**)**on** (*resemble*) être voisin de. ◆**borderland** *n* pays *m* frontière. ◆**borderline** *n* frontière *f*; **b. case** cas *m* limite.

bor/e¹ [bɔːr] **1** *vt* (*weary*) ennuyer; **to be bored** s'ennuyer; – *n* (*person*) raseur, -euse *mf*; (*thing*) ennui *m*. **2** *vt Tech* forer, creuser; (*hole*) percer; – *vi* forer. **3** *n* (*of gun*) calibre *m*. ◆**–ing** *a* ennuyeux. ◆**boredom** *n* ennui *m*.

bore² [bɔːr] *see* **bear**².

born [bɔːn] *a* né; **to be b.** naître; **he was b.** il est né.

borne [bɔːn] *see* **bear**².

borough ['bʌrə] *n* (*town*) municipalité *f*; (*part of town*) arrondissement *m*.

borrow ['bɒrəʊ] *vt* emprunter (**from** à). ◆**–ing** *n* emprunt *m*.

Borstal ['bɔːst(ə)l] *n* maison *f* d'éducation surveillée.

bosom ['buzəm] *n* (*chest*) & *Fig* sein *m*; **b. friend** ami, -ie *mf* intime.

boss [bɒs] *n Fam* patron, -onne *mf*, chef *m*; – *vt Fam* diriger; **to b. s.o. around** *or* **about** régenter qn. ◆**bossy** *a* (**-ier, -iest**) *Fam* autoritaire.

boss-eyed ['bɒsaɪd] *a* **to be b.-eyed** loucher.

bosun ['bəʊs(ə)n] *n* maître *m* d'équipage.

botany ['bɒtənɪ] *n* botanique *f*. ◆**bo'tanical** *a* botanique. ◆**botanist** *n* botaniste *mf*.

botch [bɒtʃ] *vt* **to b.** (**up**) (*spoil*) bâcler; (*repair*) rafistoler.

both [bəʊθ] *a* les deux, l'un(e) et l'autre; – *pron* tous *or* toutes (les) deux, l'un(e) et l'autre; **b. of us** nous deux; – *adv* (*at the same time*) à la fois; **b. you and I** vous et moi.

bother ['bɒðər] *vt* (*annoy, worry*) ennuyer; (*disturb*) déranger; (*pester*) importuner; **I can't be bothered!** je n'en ai pas envie!, ça m'embête!; – *vi* **to b. about** (*worry about*) se préoccuper de; (*deal with*) s'occuper de; **to b. doing** *or* **to do** se donner la peine de faire; – *n* (*trouble*) ennui *m*; (*effort*) peine *f*; (*inconvenience*) dérangement *m*; **b.!** zut alors!

bottle ['bɒt(ə)l] *n* bouteille *f*; (*small*) flacon *m*; (*wide-mouthed*) bocal *m*; (*for baby*) biberon *m*; (*hot-water*) **b.** bouillotte *f*; **b. opener** ouvre-bouteilles *m inv*; – *vt* mettre en bouteille; **to b. up** (*feeling*) contenir. ◆**b.-feed** *vt* (*pt & pp* **-fed**) nourrir au biberon. ◆**bottleneck** *n* (*in road*) goulot *m* d'étranglement; (*traffic holdup*) bouchon *m*.

bottom ['bɒtəm] *n* (*of sea, hole, box*) fond *m*; (*of page, hill etc*) bas *m*; (*buttocks*) *Fam* derrière *m*; (*of table*) bout *m*; **to be** (**at the**) **b. of the class** être le dernier de la classe; – *a* (*part, shelf*) inférieur, du bas; **b. floor** rez-de-chaussée *m*; **b. gear** première vitesse *f*. ◆**–less** *a* insondable.

bough [baʊ] *n Lit* rameau *m*.

bought [bɔːt] *see* **buy**.

boulder ['bəʊldər] *n* rocher *m*.

boulevard ['buːləvaːd] *n* boulevard *m*.

bounc/e [baʊns] **1** *vi* (*of ball*) rebondir; (*of person*) faire des bonds; **to b. into** bondir dans; – *vt* faire rebondir; – *n* (re)bond *m*. **2** *vi* (*of cheque*) *Fam* être sans provision, être en bois. ◆**–ing** *a* (*baby*) robuste. ◆**–er** *n* (*at club etc*) *Fam* videur *m*.

bound¹ [baʊnd] *a* **b. to do** (*obliged*) obligé de faire; (*certain*) sûr de faire; **it's b. to happen** ça arrivera sûrement; **to be b. for**

être en route pour. **2** *n* (*leap*) bond *m*; – *vi* bondir.

bound² [baʊnd] *see* **bind 1**; – *a* **b. up with** (*connected*) lié à.

bounds [baʊndz] *npl* limites *fpl*; **out of b.** (*place*) interdit. ◆**boundary** *n* limite *f*. ◆**bounded** *a* **b. by** limité par. ◆**boundless** *a* sans bornes.

bountiful ['baʊntɪfəl] *a* généreux.

bounty ['baʊntɪ] *n* (*reward*) prime *f*.

bouquet [bəʊ'keɪ] *n* (*of flowers, wine*) bouquet *m*.

bourbon ['bɜːbən] *n* (*whisky*) *Am* bourbon *m*.

bout [baʊt] *n* période *f*; *Med* accès *m*, crise *f*; *Boxing* combat *m*; (*session*) séance *f*.

boutique [buː'tiːk] *n* boutique *f* (*de mode*).

bow¹ [bəʊ] *n* (*weapon*) arc *m*; *Mus* archet *m*; (*knot*) nœud *m*; **b. tie** nœud *m* papillon. ◆**b.-'legged** *a* aux jambes arquées.

bow² [baʊ] **1** *n* révérence *f*; (*nod*) salut *m*; – *vt* courber, incliner; – *vi* s'incliner (**to** devant); (*nod*) incliner la tête; **to b. down** (*submit*) s'incliner. **2** *n* *Nau* proue *f*.

bowels ['baʊəlz] *npl* intestins *mpl*; (*of earth*) *Fig* entrailles *fpl*.

bowl [bəʊl] **1** *n* (*for food*) bol *m*; (*basin*) & *Geog* cuvette *f*; (*for sugar*) sucrier *m*; (*for salad*) saladier *m*; (*for fruit*) corbeille *f*, coupe *f*. **2** *vi* *Sp* boules *fpl*. **3** *vi* *Cricket* lancer la balle; **to b. along** *Aut* rouler vite; – *vt* (*ball*) *Cricket* servir; **to b. s.o. over** (*knock down*) renverser qn; (*astound*) bouleverser qn. ◆**—ing** *n* (*tenpin*) bowling *m*; **b. alley** bowling *m*. ◆**—er¹** *n* *Cricket* lanceur, -euse *mf*.

bowler² ['bəʊlər] *n* **b.** (**hat**) (*chapeau m*) melon *m*.

box [bɒks] **1** *n* boîte *f*; (*large*) caisse *f*; (*of cardboard*) carton *m*; *Th* loge *f*; *Jur* barre *f*, banc *m*; (*for horse*) box *m*; *TV Fam* télé *f*; **b. office** bureau *m* de location, guichet *m*; **b. room** (*lumber room*) débarras *m*; (*bedroom*) petite chambre (*carrée*); – *vt* **to b. (up)** mettre en boîte; **to b. in** (*enclose*) enfermer. **2** *vti* *Boxing* boxer; **to b. s.o.'s ears** gifler qn. ◆**—ing** *n* **1** boxe *f*; **b. ring** ring *m*. **2 B. Day** le lendemain de Noël. ◆**—er** *n* boxeur *m*. ◆**boxcar** *n* *Rail Am* wagon *m* couvert. ◆**boxwood** *n* buis *m*.

boy [bɔɪ] *n* garçon *m*; **English b.** jeune Anglais *m*; **old b.** *Sch* ancien élève *m*; **yes, old b.!** oui, mon vieux!; **the boys** (*pals*) *Fam* les copains *mpl*; **my dear b.** mon cher ami; **oh b.!** *Am* mon Dieu! ◆**boyfriend** *n* petit ami *m*. ◆**boyhood** *n* enfance *f*. ◆**boyish** *a* de garçon; *Pej* puéril.

boycott ['bɔɪkɒt] *vt* boycotter; – *n* boycottage *m*.

bra [brɑː] *n* soutien-gorge *m*.

brac/e [breɪs] *n* (*for fastening*) attache *f*; (*dental*) appareil *m*; *pl* (*trouser straps*) bretelles *fpl*; – *vt* (*fix*) attacher; (*press*) appuyer; **to b. oneself for** (*news, shock*) se préparer à. ◆**—ing** *a* (*air etc*) fortifiant.

bracelet ['breɪslɪt] *n* bracelet *m*.

bracken ['brækən] *n* fougère *f*.

bracket ['brækɪt] *n* *Tech* support *m*, tasseau *m*; (*round sign*) *Typ* parenthèse *f*; (*square*) *Typ* crochet *m*; *Fig* groupe *m*, tranche *f*; – *vt* mettre entre parenthèses or crochets; **to b. together** *Fig* mettre dans le même groupe.

bradawl ['brædɔːl] *n* poinçon *m*.

brag [bræg] *vi* (**-gg-**) se vanter (**about, of** de). ◆**—ging** *n* vantardise *f*. ◆**braggart** *n* vantard, -arde *mf*.

braid [breɪd] *n* (*hair*) tresser; (*trim*) galonner; – *n* tresse *f*; galon *m*.

Braille [breɪl] *n* braille *m*.

brain [breɪn] *n* cerveau *m*; (*of bird etc*) & *Pej* cervelle *f*; – *a* (*operation, death*) cérébral; – *vt Fam* assommer; **to have brains** (*sense*) avoir de l'intelligence; **b. drain** fuite *f* des cerveaux. ◆**brainchild** *n* invention *f* personnelle. ◆**brainstorm** *n* *Psy Fig* aberration *f*; *Am* idée *f* géniale. ◆**brainwash** *vt* faire un lavage de cerveau à. ◆**brainwave** *n* idée *f* géniale.

brainy ['breɪnɪ] *a* (**-ier, -iest**) *Fam* intelligent.

braise [breɪz] *vt* *Culin* braiser.

brak/e [breɪk] *vi* freiner; – *n* frein *m*; **b. light** *Aut* stop *m*. ◆**—ing** *n* freinage *m*.

bramble ['bræmb(ə)l] *n* ronce *f*.

bran [bræn] *n* *Bot* son *m*.

branch [brɑːntʃ] *n* branche *f*; (*of road*) embranchement *m*; (*of store etc*) succursale *f*; **b. office** succursale *f*; – *vi* **to b. off** (*of road*) bifurquer; **to b. out** (*of family, tree*) se ramifier; *Fig* étendre ses activités.

brand [brænd] *n* (*trademark, stigma & on cattle*) marque *f*; – *vt* (*mark*) marquer; (*stigmatize*) flétrir; **to be branded as** avoir la réputation de.

brandish ['brændɪʃ] *vt* brandir.

brand-new [brænd'njuː] *a* tout neuf, flambant neuf.

brandy ['brændɪ] *n* cognac *m*; (*made with pears etc*) eau-de-vie *f*.

brash [bræʃ] *a* effronté, fougueux.

brass [brɑːs] *n* cuivre *m*; (*instruments*) *Mus* cuivres *mpl*; **the top b.** (*officers, executives*) *Fam* les huiles *fpl*; **b. band** fanfare *f*.

brassiere ['bræzɪər, *Am* brə'zɪər] *n* soutien-gorge *m*.

brat [bræt] *n Pej* môme *mf*, gosse *mf*; (*badly behaved*) galopin *m*.

bravado [brə'vɑːdəʊ] *n* bravade *f*.

brave [breɪv] *a* (-er, -est) courageux, brave; – *n* (*Red Indian*) guerrier *m* (indien), brave *m*; – *vt* braver. ◆**bravery** *n* courage *m*.

bravo! ['brɑːvəʊ] *int* bravo!

brawl [brɔːl] *n* (*fight*) bagarre *f*; – *vi* se bagarrer. ◆**-ing** *a* bagarreur.

brawn [brɔːn] *n* muscles *mpl*. ◆**brawny** *a* (-ier, -iest) musclé.

bray [breɪ] *vi* (*of ass*) braire.

brazen ['breɪz(ə)n] *a* (*shameless*) effronté; – *vt* to b. it out payer d'audace, faire front.

Brazil [brə'zɪl] *n* Brésil *m*. ◆**Brazilian** *a* & *n* brésilien, -ienne (*mf*).

breach [briːtʃ] **1** *n* violation *f*, infraction *f*; (*of contract*) rupture *f*; (*of trust*) abus *m*; – *vt* (*law, code*) violer. **2** *n* (*gap*) brèche *f*; – *vt* (*wall etc*) ouvrir une brèche dans.

bread [bred] *n inv* pain *m*; (*money*) *Sl* blé *m*, fric *m*; **loaf of b.** pain *m*; (*slice or piece of*) **b. and butter** tartine *f*; **b. and butter** (*job*) *Fig* gagne-pain *m*. ◆**breadbin** *n* 1 coffre *m* à pain. ◆**breadbox** *n Am* coffre *m* à pain. ◆**breadboard** *n* planche *f* à pain. ◆**breadcrumb** *n* miette *f* (de pain); *pl Culin* chapelure *f*. ◆**breadline** *n* on the b. indigent. ◆**breadwinner** *n* soutien *m* de famille.

breadth [bretθ] *n* largeur *f*.

break [breɪk] *vt* (*pt* broke, *pp* broken) casser; (*into pieces*) briser; (*silence, vow etc*) rompre; (*strike, heart, ice etc*) briser; (*record*) *Sp* battre; (*law*) violer; (*one's word*) manquer à; (*journey*) interrompre; (*sound barrier*) franchir; (*a fall*) amortir; (*news*) révéler (to à); **to b.** (*oneself of*) (*habit*) se débarrasser de; **to b. open** (*safe*) percer; **to b. new ground** innover; – *vi* se casser; se briser; se rompre; (*of voice*) s'altérer; (*of boy's voice*) muer; (*of weather*) se gâter; (*of news*) éclater; (*of day*) se lever; (*of wave*) déferler; **to b. free** se libérer; **to b. loose** s'échapper; **to b. with s.o.** rompre avec qn; – *n* cassure *f*; (*in relationship, continuity etc*) rupture *f*; (*in journey*) interruption *f*; (*rest*) repos *m*; (*for tea*) pause *f*; *Sch* récréation *f*; (*change*) *Met* changement *m*; **a lucky b.** *Fam* une chance. ◆**-ing** *a* **b. point** *Tech* point *m* de rupture; **at b. point** (*patience*) à bout; (*person*) sur le point de craquer, à bout. ◆**-able** *a* cassable. ◆**-age** *n* casse *f*; *pl* (*things broken*) la casse. ◆**-er** *n* (*wave*) brisant *m*; (*dealer*)

Aut casseur *m*. ■ **to b. away** *vi* se détacher; – *vt* détacher. ◆**breakaway** *a* (*group*) dissident; **to b. down** *vt* (*door*) enfoncer; (*resistance*) briser; (*analyse*) analyser; – *vi* *Aut Tech* tomber en panne; (*of negotiations etc*) échouer; (*collapse*) s'effondrer. ◆**breakdown** *n* panne *f*; analyse *f*; (*in talks*) rupture *f*; (*nervous*) dépression *f*; – *a* (*service*) *Aut* de dépannage; **b. lorry** dépanneuse *f*; **to b. in** *vi* interrompre; (*of burglar*) entrer par effraction; – *vt* (*door*) enfoncer; (*horse*) dresser; (*vehicle*) *Am* roder. ◆**break-in** *n* cambriolage *m*; **to b. into** *vt* (*safe*) forcer; (*start*) entamer; **to b. off** *vt* détacher; (*relations*) rompre; – *vi* se détacher; (*stop*) s'arrêter; **to b. off with** rompre avec; **to b. out** *vi* éclater; (*escape*) s'échapper; **to b. out in** (*pimples*) avoir une poussée de; **to b. through** *vi* (*of sun*) & *Mil* percer; – *vt* (*defences*) percer. ◆**breakthrough** *n Fig* percée *f*, découverte *f*; **to b. up** *vt* mettre en morceaux; (*marriage*) briser; (*fight*) mettre fin à; – *vi* (*end*) prendre fin; (*of group*) se disperser; (*of marriage*) se briser; *Sch* partir en vacances. ◆**breakup** *n* fin *f*; (*in friendship, marriage*) rupture *f*.

breakfast ['brekfəst] *n* petit déjeuner *m*.

breakwater ['breɪkwɔːtər] *n* brise-lames *m inv*.

breast [brest] *n* sein *m*; (*chest*) poitrine *f*. ◆**b.-feed** *vt* (*pt* & *pp* -fed) allaiter. ◆**breaststroke** *n* (*swimming*) brasse *f*.

breath [breθ] *n* haleine *f*, souffle *m*; (*of air*) souffle *m*; **under one's b.** tout bas; **one's last b.** son dernier soupir; **out of b.** à bout de souffle; **to get a b. of air** prendre l'air; **to take a deep b.** respirer profondément. ◆**breathalyser** *n* alcootest®. ◆**breathless** *a* haletant. ◆**breathtaking** *a* sensationnel.

breath/e [briːð] *vti* respirer; **to b. in** aspirer; **to b. out** expirer; **to b. air into sth** souffler dans qch; – *vt* (*a sigh*) pousser; (*a word*) dire. ◆**-ing** *n* respiration *f*; **b. space** moment *m* de repos. ◆**-er** *n Fam* moment *m* de repos; **to go for a b.** sortir prendre l'air.

bred [bred] *see* breed 1; – *a* well-b. bien élevé.

breeches ['brɪtʃɪz] *npl* culotte *f*.

breed [briːd] **1** *vt* (*pt* & *pp* bred) (*animals*) élever; (*cause*) *Fig* engendrer; – *vi* (*of animals*) se reproduire. **2** *n* race *f*, espèce *f*. ◆**-ing** *n* élevage *m*; reproduction *f*; *Fig* éducation *f*. ◆**-er** *n* éleveur, -euse *mf*.

breeze [briːz] *n* brise *f*. ◆**breezy** *a* (-ier,

-iest) 1 (*weather, day*) frais, venteux. **2** (*cheerful*) jovial; (*relaxed*) décontracté.

breezeblock ['briːzblɒk] *n* parpaing *m*, briquette *f*.

brevity ['brevɪtɪ] *n* brièveté *f*.

brew [bruː] *vt* (*beer*) brasser; (*trouble, plot*) préparer; **to b. tea** préparer du thé; (*infuse*) (faire) infuser du thé; – *vi* (*beer*) fermenter; (*of tea*) infuser; (*of storm, trouble*) se préparer; – *n* (*drink*) breuvage *m*; (*of tea*) infusion *f*. ◆**-er** *n* brasseur *m*. ◆**brewery** *n* brasserie *f*.

bribe [braɪb] *n* pot-de-vin *m*; – *vt* soudoyer, corrompre. ◆**bribery** *n* corruption *f*.

brick [brɪk] *n* brique *f*; (*child's*) cube *m*; **to drop a b.** *Fam* faire une gaffe; – *vt* **to b. up** (*gap, door*) murer. ◆**bricklayer** *n* maçon *m*. ◆**brickwork** *n* ouvrage *m* en briques; (*bricks*) briques *fpl*.

bridal ['braɪd(ə)l] *a* (*ceremony*) nuptial; **b. gown** robe *f* de mariée.

bride [braɪd] *n* mariée *f*; **the b. and groom** les mariés *mpl*. ◆**bridegroom** *n* marié *m*. ◆**bridesmaid** *n* demoiselle *f* d'honneur.

bridge [brɪdʒ] **1** *n* pont *m*; (*of nose*) arête *f*; (*false tooth*) bridge *m*; – *vt* **to b. a gap** combler une lacune. **2** *n* *Cards* bridge *m*.

bridle ['braɪd(ə)l] *n* (*for horse*) bride *f*; – *vt* (*horse, instinct etc*) brider; **b. path** allée *f* cavalière.

brief [briːf] **1** *a* (**-er, -est**) bref; **in b.** en résumé. **2** *n* *Jur* dossier *m*; (*instructions*) *Mil* instructions *fpl*, *Fig* tâche *f*, fonctions *fpl*; – *vt* donner des instructions à; (*inform*) mettre au courant (**on** de). **3** *npl* (*underpants*) slip *m*. ◆**-ing** *n* *Mil* Pol instructions *fpl*, *Av* briefing *m*. ◆**-ly** *adv* (*quickly*) en vitesse; (*to say*) brièvement.

brigade [brɪ'geɪd] *n* brigade *f*. ◆**briga'dier** *n* général *m* de brigade.

bright [braɪt] *a* (**-er, -est**) brillant, vif; (*weather, room*) clair; (*clever*) intelligent; (*happy, future*) joyeux, brillant, prometteur; (*idea*) génial; **b. interval** *Met* éclaircie *f*; – *adv* **b. and early** (*to get up*) de bonne heure. ◆**-ly** *adv* brillamment. ◆**-ness** *n* éclat *m*; (*of person*) intelligence *f*. ◆**brighten** *vt* **to b. (up)** (*person, room*) égayer; – *vi* **to b. (up)** (*of weather*) s'éclaircir; (*of face*) s'éclairer.

brilliant ['brɪljənt] *a* (*light*) éclatant; (*very clever*) brillant. ◆**brilliance** *n* éclat *m*; (*of person*) grande intelligence *f*.

brim [brɪm] *n* bord *m*; – *vi* (**-mm-**) **to b. over** déborder (**with** de).

brine [braɪn] *n* *Culin* saumure *f*.

bring [brɪŋ] *vt* (*pt & pp* brought) (*person, vehicle etc*) amener; (*thing*) apporter; (*to cause*) amener; (*action*) *Jur* intenter; **to b. along** or **over** or **round** amener; apporter; **to b. back** ramener; rapporter; (*memories*) rappeler; **to b. sth up/down** monter/descendre qch; **to b. sth in/out** rentrer/sortir qch; **to b. sth to** (*perfection, a peak etc*) porter qch à; **to b. sth to an end** mettre fin à; **to b. to mind** rappeler; **to b. sth on oneself** s'attirer qch; **to b. oneself to do** se résoudre à faire; **to b. about** provoquer, amener; **to b. down** (*overthrow*) faire tomber; (*reduce*) réduire; (*shoot down*) abattre; **to b. forward** (*in time or space*) avancer; (*witness*) produire; **to b. in** (*person*) faire entrer or venir; (*introduce*) introduire; (*income*) *Com* rapporter; **to b. off** (*task*) mener à bien; **to b. out** (*person*) faire sortir; (*meaning*) faire ressortir; (*book*) publier; (*product*) lancer; **to b. over** (*to convert to*) convertir à; **to b. round** *Med* ranimer; (*convert*) convertir (**to** à); **to b. s.o. to** *Med* ranimer qn; **to b. together** mettre en contact; (*reconcile*) réconcilier; **to b. up** (*child etc*) élever; (*question*) soulever; (*subject*) mentionner; (*vomit*) vomir.

brink [brɪŋk] *n* bord *m*.

brisk [brɪsk] *a* (**-er, -est**) vif; (*trade*) actif; **at a b. pace** d'un bon pas; (*to walk*) d'un bon pas. ◆**-ly** *adv* vivement; (*to walk*) d'un bon pas. ◆**-ness** *n* vivacité *f*.

bristle ['brɪs(ə)l] *n* poil *m*; – *vi* se hérisser. ◆**-ing** *a* **b. with** (*difficulties*) hérissé de.

Britain ['brɪt(ə)n] *n* Grande-Bretagne *f*. ◆**British** *a* britannique; – *n* **the B.** les Britanniques *mpl*. ◆**Briton** *n* Britannique *mf*.

Brittany ['brɪtənɪ] *n* Bretagne *f*.

brittle ['brɪt(ə)l] *a* cassant, fragile.

broach [brəʊtʃ] *vt* (*topic*) entamer.

broad¹ [brɔːd] *a* (**-er, -est**) (*wide*) large; (*outline*) grand, général; (*accent*) prononcé; **in b. daylight** en plein jour; **b. bean** fève *f*; **b. jump** *Sp Am* saut *m* en longueur. ◆**b.-'minded** *a* à l'esprit large. ◆**b.-'shouldered** *a* large d'épaules. ◆**broaden** *vt* élargir; – *vi* s'élargir. ◆**broadly** *adv* **b.** (**speaking**) en gros, grosso modo.

broad² [brɔːd] *n* (*woman*) *Am Sl* nana *f*.

broadcast ['brɔːdkɑːst] *vt* (*pt & pp* broadcast) *Rad & Fig* diffuser; *TV* téléviser; – *vi* (*of station*) émettre; (*of person*) parler à la radio or à la télévision; – *a* (radio)diffusé; télévisé; – *n* émission *f*. ◆**-ing** *n* radiodiffusion *f*; télévision *f*.

broccoli [ˈbrɒkəli] *n inv* brocoli *m*.

brochure [ˈbrəʊʃər] *n* brochure *f*, dépliant *m*.

brogue [brəʊg] *n Ling* accent *m* irlandais.

broil [brɔɪl] *vti* griller. ◆—**er** *n* poulet *m* (à rôtir); (*apparatus*) gril *m*.

broke [brəʊk] **1** *see* break. **2** *a* (*penniless*) fauché. ◆**broken** *see* break; — *a* (*ground*) accidenté; (*spirit*) abattu; (*man, voice, line*) brisé; **b. English** mauvais anglais *m*; **b. home** foyer *m* brisé. ◆**broken-'down** *a* (*machine etc*) (tout) déglingué, détraqué.

brolly [ˈbrɒli] *n* (*umbrella*) *Fam* pépin *m*.

bronchitis [brɒŋˈkaɪtɪs] *n* bronchite *f*.

bronze [brɒnz] *n* bronze *m*; — *a* (*statue etc*) en bronze.

brooch [brəʊtʃ] *n* (*ornament*) broche *f*.

brood [bruːd] **1** *n* couvée *f*, nichée *f*; — *vi* (*of bird*) couver. **2** *vi* méditer tristement (**over**, **on** sur); **to b. over** (*a plan*) ruminer. ◆**broody** *a* (**-ier, -iest**) (*person*) maussade, rêveur; (*woman*) *Fam* qui a envie d'avoir un enfant.

brook [brʊk] **1** *n* ruisseau *m*. **2** *vt* souffrir, tolérer.

broom [bruːm] *n* **1** (*for sweeping*) balai *m*. **2** *Bot* genêt *m*. ◆**broomstick** *n* manche *m* à balai.

Bros *abbr* (*Brothers*) Frères *mpl*.

broth [brɒθ] *n* bouillon *m*.

brothel [ˈbrɒθ(ə)l] *n* maison *f* close, bordel *m*.

brother [ˈbrʌðər] *n* frère *m*. ◆**b.-in-law** *n* (*pl* **brothers-in-law**) beau-frère *m*. ◆**brotherhood** *n* fraternité *f*. ◆**brotherly** *a* fraternel.

brow [braʊ] *n* (*forehead*) front *m*; (*of hill*) sommet *m*.

browbeat [ˈbraʊbiːt] *vt* (*pt* **-beat**, *pp* **-beaten**) intimider.

brown [braʊn] *a* (**-er, -est**) brun; (*reddish*) marron; (*hair*) châtain; (*tanned*) bronzé; — *n* brun *m*; marron *m*; — *vt* brunir; *Culin* faire dorer; **to be browned off** *Fam* en avoir marre. ◆**brownish** *a* brunâtre.

Brownie [ˈbraʊni] *n* **1** (*girl scout*) jeannette *f*. **2 b.** *Culin Am* petit gâteau *m* au chocolat.

browse [braʊz] *vi* (*in shop*) regarder; (*in bookshop*) feuilleter des livres; (*of animal*) brouter; **to b. through** (*book*) feuilleter.

bruis/e [bruːz] *vt* contusionner, meurtrir; (*fruit, heart*) meurtrir; — *n* bleu *m*, contusion *f*. ◆—**ed** *a* couvert de bleus.

brunch [brʌntʃ] *n* repas *m* mixte (*petit déjeuner pris comme déjeuner*).

brunette [bruːˈnet] *n* brunette *f*.

brunt [brʌnt] *n* **to bear the b. of** (*attack etc*) subir le plus gros de.

brush [brʌʃ] *n* brosse *f*; (*for shaving*) blaireau *m*; (*little broom*) balayette *f*; (*action*) coup *m* de brosse; (*fight*) accrochage *m*; — *vt* (*teeth, hair etc*) brosser; (*clothes*) donner un coup de brosse à; **to b. aside** écarter; **to b. away** *or* **off** enlever; **to b. up** (*on*) (*language*) se remettre à; — *vi* **to b. against** effleurer. ◆**b.-off** *n Fam* **to give s.o. the b.-off** envoyer promener qn. ◆**b.-up** *n* coup *m* de brosse. ◆**brushwood** *n* broussailles *fpl*.

brusque [bruːsk] *a* brusque.

Brussels [ˈbrʌs(ə)lz] *n* Bruxelles *m or f*; **B. sprouts** choux *mpl* de Bruxelles.

brutal [ˈbruːt(ə)l] *a* brutal. ◆**bru'tality** *n* brutalité *f*.

brute [bruːt] *n* (*animal, person*) brute *f*; — *a* **by b. force** par la force.

BSc, *Am* **BS** *abbr* = **Bachelor of Science.**

bubble [ˈbʌb(ə)l] *n* (*of air, soap etc*) bulle *f*; (*in boiling liquid*) bouillon *m*; **b. and squeak** *Fam* friture *f* de purée et de viande réchauffées; **b. bath** bain *m* moussant; **b. gum** chewing-gum *m*; — *vi* bouillonner; **to b. over** déborder (**with** de). ◆**bubbly** *n Hum Fam* champagne *m*.

buck [bʌk] *n* **1** *Am Fam* dollar *m*. **2** *n* (*animal*) mâle *m*. **3** *vt* **to b. up** remonter le moral à; — *vi* **to b. up** prendre courage; (*hurry*) se grouiller. ◆**buckshot** *n inv* du gros plomb *m*. ◆**buck'tooth** *n* (*pl* **-teeth**) dent *f* saillante.

bucket [ˈbʌkɪt] *n* seau *m*.

buckle [ˈbʌk(ə)l] **1** *n* boucle *f*; — *vt* boucler. **2** *vti* (*warp*) voiler, gauchir. **3** *vi* **to b. down to** (*task*) s'atteler à.

bud [bʌd] *n* (*of tree*) bourgeon *m*; (*of flower*) bouton *m*; — *vi* (**-dd-**) bourgeonner; pousser des boutons. ◆**budding** *a* (*talent*) naissant; (*doctor etc*) en herbe.

Buddhist [ˈbʊdɪst] *a & n* bouddhiste (*mf*).

buddy [ˈbʌdi] *n Am Fam* copain *m*, pote *m*.

budge [bʌdʒ] *vi* bouger; — *vt* faire bouger.

budgerigar [ˈbʌdʒərɪgɑːr] *n* perruche *f*.

budget [ˈbʌdʒɪt] *n* budget *m*; — *vi* dresser un budget; **to b.** for inscrire au budget. ◆**budgetary** *a* budgétaire.

budgie [ˈbʌdʒi] *n Fam* perruche *f*.

buff [bʌf] **1** *a* **b.(-coloured)** chamois *inv*. **2** *n* jazz/etc **b.** *Fam* fana(tique) *mf* du jazz/etc. **3** *n* **in the b.** *Fam* tout nu.

buffalo [ˈbʌfələʊ] *n* (*pl* **-oes** *or* **-o**) buffle *m*; (*American*) **b.** bison *m*.

buffer [ˈbʌfər] *n* (*on train*) tampon *m*; (*at end of track*) butoir *m*; **b. state** état *m* tampon.

buffet 1 ['bʌfit] vt frapper; (of waves) battre; (of wind, rain) cingler (qn). **2** ['bufei] n (table, meal, café) buffet m; **cold b.** viandes fpl froides.

buffoon [bə'fuːn] n bouffon m.

bug 1 ['bʌg] **1** n punaise f; (any insect) Fam bestiole f; Med Fam microbe m, virus m; **the travel b.** (urge) le désir de voyager. **2** n Fam (in machine) défaut m; (in computer program) erreur f. **3** n (apparatus) Fam micro m; – vt (-gg-) (room) Fam installer des micros dans.

bug 2 [bʌg] vt (-gg-) (annoy) Am Fam embêter.

bugbear ['bʌgbeər] n (worry) cauchemar m.

buggy ['bʌgɪ] n (baby b.) (pushchair) poussette f; (folding) poussette-canne f; (pram) Am landau m.

bugle ['bjuːg(ə)l] n clairon m. ◆**bugler** n (person) clairon m.

build [bɪld] **1** n (of person) carrure f. **2** vt (pt & pp built) construire; (house, town) construire, bâtir; **to b. in** (cupboard etc) encastrer; – vi bâtir, construire. ◆**built-in** a (cupboard etc) encastré; (element of machine etc) incorporé; (innate) Fig inné. **3 to b. up** vt (reputation) bâtir; (increase) augmenter; (accumulate) accumuler; (business) monter; (speed, one's strength) prendre; – vi augmenter, monter; s'accumuler. ◆**build-up** n montée f; accumulation f; Mil concentration f; Journ publicité f. ◆**built-up** a urbanisé; **b.-up area** agglomération f.

builder ['bɪldər] n maçon m; (contractor) entrepreneur m; (of cars etc) constructeur m; (labourer) ouvrier m.

building ['bɪldɪŋ] n bâtiment m; (flats, offices) immeuble m; (action) construction f; **b. society** caisse f d'épargne-logement, = société f de crédit immobilier.

bulb [bʌlb] n Bot bulbe m, oignon m; El ampoule f. ◆**bulbous** a bulbeux.

Bulgaria [bʌl'geərɪə] n Bulgarie f. ◆**Bulgarian** a & n bulgare (mf).

bulg/e [bʌldʒ] vi to b. (out) se renfler, bomber; (of eyes) sortir de la tête; – n renflement m; (increase) Fam augmentation f. ◆**-ing** a renflé, bombé; (eyes) protubérant; (bag) gonflé (with de).

bulk [bʌlk] n inv grosseur f, volume m; **the b. of** (most) la majeure partie de; **in b.** (to buy, sell) en gros. ◆**bulky** a (-ier, -iest) gros, volumineux.

bull [bul] n **1** taureau m. **2** (nonsense) Fam foutaises fpl. ◆**bullfight** n corrida f.

◆**bullfighter** n matador m. ◆**bullring** n arène f.

bulldog ['buldɒg] n bouledogue m; **b. clip** pince f (à dessin).

bulldoze ['buldəuz] vt passer au bull-dozer. ◆**-er** n bulldozer m, bouteur m.

bullet ['bulit] n balle f. ◆**bulletproof** a (jacket, Am vest) pare-balles inv; (car) blindé.

bulletin ['bulətin] n bulletin m.

bullion ['buljən] n or m or argent m en lingots.

bullock ['bulək] n bœuf m.

bull's-eye ['bulzaɪ] n (of target) centre m; **to hit the b.-eye** faire mouche.

bully ['bulɪ] n (grosse) brute f, tyran m; – vt brutaliser; (persecute) tyranniser; **to b. into doing** forcer à faire.

bulwark ['bulwək] n rempart m.

bum [bʌm] **1** n (loafer) Am Fam clochard m; – vi (-mm-) **to b.** (around) se balader. **2** vt (-mm-) **to b. sth off s.o.** (cadge) Am Fam taper qn de qch. **3** n (buttocks) Fam derrière m.

bumblebee ['bʌmb(ə)lbiː] n bourdon m.

bumf [bʌmf] n Pej Sl paperasses fpl.

bump [bʌmp] vt (of car etc) heurter; **to b. one's head/knee** se cogner la tête/le genou; **to b. into** se cogner contre; (of car) rentrer dans; (meet) Fam tomber sur; **to b. off** (kill) Sl liquider; **to b. up** Fam augmenter; – vi **to b. along** (on rough road) Aut cahoter; – n (impact) choc m; (jerk) cahot m; (on road, body) bosse f. ◆**-er** n (of car etc) pare-chocs m inv; **a** (crop etc) exceptionnel; **b. cars** autos fpl tamponneuses. ◆**bumpy** a (-ier, -iest) (road, ride) cahoteux.

bumpkin ['bʌmpkɪn] n rustre m.

bumptious ['bʌmpʃəs] a prétentieux.

bun [bʌn] n **1** Culin petit pain m au lait. **2** (of hair) chignon m.

bunch [bʌntʃ] n (of flowers) bouquet m; (of keys) trousseau m; (of bananas) régime m; (of people) bande f; **b. of grapes** grappe f de raisin; **a b. of** (mass) Fam un tas de.

bundle ['bʌnd(ə)l] **1** n paquet m; (of papers) liasse f; (of firewood) fagot m. **2** vt (put) fourrer; (push) pousser (into dans); **to b. (up)** mettre en paquet; **to b. s.o. off** expédier qn; – vi **to b. (oneself) up** se couvrir (bien).

bung [bʌŋ] n **1** (stopper) bonde f; – vt **to b. up** (stop up) boucher. **2** vt (toss) Fam balancer, jeter.

bungalow ['bʌŋgələu] n bungalow m.

bungl/e ['bʌŋg(ə)l] vt gâcher; – vi travailler

mal. ◆—ing n gâchis m; — a (clumsy) maladroit.

bunion ['bʌnjən] n (on toe) oignon m.

bunk [bʌŋk] n 1 Rail Nau couchette f; b. beds lits mpl superposés. 2 Sl = bunkum. ◆bunkum n Sl foutaises fpl.

bunker ['bʌŋkər] n Mil Golf bunker m; (coalstore in garden) coffre m.

bunny ['bʌnɪ] n Fam Jeannot m lapin.

buoy [bɔɪ] n bouée f; — vt to b. up (support) Fig soutenir.

buoyant ['bɔɪənt] a Fig gai, optimiste; (market) Fin ferme.

burden ['bɜːd(ə)n] n fardeau m; (of tax) poids m; — vt charger, accabler (with de).

bureau, pl -eaux ['bjʊərəʊ, -əʊz] n (office) bureau m; (desk) secrétaire m. ◆bureaucracy [bjʊə'rɒkrəsɪ] n bureaucratie f. ◆bureaucrat ['bjʊərəkræt] n bureaucrate mf.

burger ['bɜːgər] n Fam hamburger m.

burglar ['bɜːglər] n cambrioleur, -euse mf; b. alarm sonnerie f d'alarme. ◆burglarize vt Am cambrioler. ◆burglary n cambriolage m. ◆burgle vt cambrioler.

burial ['berɪəl] n enterrement m; — a (service) funèbre; b. ground cimetière m.

burlap ['bɜːlæp] n Am toile f à sac.

burlesque [bɜː'lesk] n parodie f; Th Am revue f.

burly ['bɜːlɪ] a (-ier, -iest) costaud.

Burma ['bɜːmə] n Birmanie f. ◆Bur'mese a & n birman, -ane (mf).

burn [bɜːn] n brûlure f; — vt (pt & pp burned or burnt) brûler; to b. down or off or up brûler; burnt alive brûlé vif; — vi brûler; to b. down (of house) brûler (complètement), être réduit en cendres; to b. out (of fire) s'éteindre; (of fuse) sauter. ◆—ing a en feu; (fire) allumé; (topic, fever etc) Fig brûlant; — n smell of b. odeur f de brûlé. ◆—er n (of stove) brûleur m.

burp [bɜːp] n Fam rot m; — vi Fam roter.

burrow ['bʌrəʊ] n (hole) terrier m; — vti creuser.

bursar ['bɜːsər] n (in school) intendant, -ante mf.

bursary ['bɜːsərɪ] n (grant) bourse f.

burst [bɜːst] n éclatement m, explosion f; (of laughter) éclat m; (of applause) salve f; (of thunder) coup m; (surge) élan m; (fit) accès m; (burst water pipe) Fam tuyau m crevé; — vi (pt & pp burst) (of balloon, tyre, boil etc) crever; (of bomb etc) éclater; to b. into (room) faire irruption dans; to b. into tears fondre en larmes; to b. into flames prendre feu, s'embraser; to b. open s'ouvrir avec

force; to b. out laughing éclater de rire; — vt crever, faire éclater; (rupture) rompre; to b. open ouvrir avec force. ◆—ing a (full) plein à craquer (with de); b. with (joy) débordant de; to be b. to do mourir d'envie de faire.

bury ['berɪ] vt (dead person) enterrer; (hide) enfouir; (plunge, absorb) plonger.

bus [bʌs] n (auto)bus m; (long-distance) (auto)car m; — a (driver, ticket etc) d'autobus; d'autocar; b. shelter abribus m; b. station gare f routière; b. stop arrêt m d'autobus; — vt (-ss-) (children) transporter (en bus) à l'école. ◆bussing n Sch ramassage m scolaire.

bush [bʊʃ] n buisson m; (of hair) tignasse f; the b. (land) la brousse. ◆bushy a (-ier, -iest) (hair, tail etc) broussailleux.

bushed [bʊʃt] a (tired) Fam crevé.

business ['bɪznɪs] n affaires fpl, commerce m; (shop) commerce m; (task, concern, matter) affaire f; the textile b. le textile; big b. Fam les grosses entreprises fpl commerciales; on b. (to travel) pour affaires; it's your b. to... c'est à vous de...; you have no b. to... vous n'avez pas le droit de...; that's none of your b.! ça ne vous regarde pas!; to mean b. Fam ne pas plaisanter; — a (commercial; (meeting, trip) d'affaires; b. hours (office) heures fpl de travail; (shop) heures fpl d'ouverture. ◆businesslike a sérieux, pratique. ◆businessman n (pl -men) homme m d'affaires. ◆businesswoman n (pl -women) femme f d'affaires.

busker ['bʌskər] n musicien, -ienne mf des rues.

bust [bʌst] n 1 (sculpture) buste m; (woman's breasts) poitrine f. 2 a (broken) Fam fichu; to go b. (bankrupt) faire faillite; — vti (pt & pp bust or busted) Fam to burst & to break. ◆b.-up n Fam (quarrel) engueulade f; (breakup) rupture f.

bustl/e ['bʌs(ə)l] vi to b. (about) s'affairer; — n activité f, branle-bas m. ◆—ing a (street) bruyant.

bus/y ['bɪzɪ] a (-ier, -iest) occupé (doing à faire); (active) actif; (day) chargé; (street) animé; (line) Tel Am occupé; to be b. doing (in the process of) être en train de faire; — vt to b. oneself s'occuper (with sth à qch, doing à faire). ◆—ily adv activement. ◆busybody n to be a b. faire la mouche du coche.

but [bʌt, unstressed bət] 1 conj mais. 2 prep (except) sauf; b. for that sans cela; b. for him sans lui; no one b. you personne d'autre que toi. **3** *adv* (*only*) ne . . . que, seulement.

butane ['bjuːteɪn] *n* (*gas*) butane *m*.

butcher ['butʃər] *n* boucher *m*; **b.'s shop** boucherie *f*; – *vt* (*people*) massacrer; (*animal*) abattre. ◆**butchery** massacre *m* (*of* de).

butler ['bʌtlər] *n* maître *m* d'hôtel.

butt [bʌt] *n* (*of cigarette*) mégot *m*; (*of gun*) crosse *f*; (*buttocks*) *Am Fam* derrière *m*. **b. for ridicule** objet *m* de risée. **2** *vi* **to b.** interrompre, intervenir.

butter ['bʌtər] *n* beurre *m*; **b. bean** haricot *m* blanc; **b. dish** beurrier *m*; – *vt* beurrer; **to b. s.o. up** *Fam* flatter qn. ◆**buttercup** *n* bouton-d'or *m*. ◆**buttermilk** *n* lait *m* de beurre.

butterfly ['bʌtərflaɪ] *n* papillon *m*; **to have butterflies** *Fam* avoir le trac; **b. stroke** *Swimming* brasse *f* papillon.

buttock ['bʌtək] *n* fesse *f*.

button ['bʌtən] *n* bouton *m*; – *vt* **to b. (up)** boutonner; – *vi* **to b. up** (*of garment*) se boutonner. ◆**buttonhole** *n* boutonnière *f*; (*flower*) fleur *f*. **2** *vt* (*person*) *Fam* accrocher.

buttress ['bʌtris] *n Archit* contrefort *m*; **flying b.** arc-boutant *m*; – *vt* (*story etc*) (*support*) *Archit & Fig* soutenir.

buxom ['bʌksəm] *a* (*woman*) bien en chair.

buy [baɪ] *vt* (*pt & pp* **bought**) acheter (**from** s.o. à qn, **for** s.o. à *or* pour qn); (*story etc*) *Am Fam* avaler, croire; **to b. back** racheter; **to b. over** (*bribe*) corrompre; **to b. up** acheter en bloc; – *n* **a good b.** une bonne affaire. ◆**-er** *n* acheteur, -euse *mf*.

buzz [bʌz] **1** *vi* bourdonner; **to b. off** *Fam* décamper; – *n* bourdonnement *m*. **2** *vt* (*building etc*) *Av* raser. **3** *vt* **to b. s.o.** *Tel*

appeler qn; – *n Tel Fam* coup *m* de fil. ◆**-er** *n* interphone *m*; (*of bell, clock*) sonnerie *f*; (*hooter*) sirène *f*.

by [baɪ] *prep* **1** (*agent, manner*) par; **hit/chosen/etc** by frappé/choisi/etc par; **surrounded/followed/etc** by entouré/suivi/ etc de; **by doing** en faisant; **by sea** par mer; **by mistake** par erreur; **by car** en voiture; **by bicycle** à bicyclette; **by moonlight** au clair de lune; **one by one** un à un; **day by day** de jour en jour; **by day/night** de jour/de nuit; **by** *sight/far* de vue/loin; **by the door** (*through*) par la porte; (*all*) **by oneself** tout seul. **2** (*next to*) à côté de; (*near*) près de; **by the lake/sea** au bord du lac/de la mer; **to pass by the bank** passer devant la banque. **3** (*before in time*) avant; **by Monday** avant lundi, d'ici lundi; **by now** à cette heure-ci, déjà; **by yesterday** (*dès*) hier. **4** (*amount, measurement*) à; **by the kilo** au kilo; **taller by a metre** plus grand d'un mètre; **paid by the hour** payé à l'heure. **5** (*according to*) d'après; – *adv* **close by** tout près; **to go by, pass by** passer; **to put by** mettre de côté; **by and by** bientôt; **by and large** en gros. ◆**by-election** *n* élection *f* partielle. ◆**by-law** *n* arrêté *m*; (*of organization*) statut *m*. ◆**by-product** *n* sous-produit *m*. ◆**by-road** *n* chemin *m* de traverse.

bye(-bye)! [baɪ('baɪ)] *int Fam* salut!, au revoir!

bygone ['baɪgɒn] *a* in b. days jadis.

bypass ['baɪpɑːs] *n* déviation *f* (routière), dérivation *f*; – *vt* contourner; (*ignore*) *Fig* éviter de passer par.

bystander ['baɪstændər] *n* spectateur, -trice *mf*; (*in street*) badaud, -aude *mf*.

byword ['baɪwɜːd] *n* **a b. for** *Pej* un synonyme de.

C

C, c [siː] *n* C, c *m*.

c *abbr* = **cent.**

cab [kæb] *n* taxi *m*; (*horse-drawn*) *Hist* fiacre *m*; (*of train driver etc*) cabine *f*. ◆**cabby** *n Fam* (chauffeur *m* de) taxi *m*; *Hist* cocher *m*.

cabaret ['kæbəreɪ] *n* (*show*) spectacle *m*; (*place*) cabaret *m*.

cabbage ['kæbɪdʒ] *n* chou *m*.

cabin ['kæbɪn] *n Nau Rail* cabine *f*; (*hut*) cabane *f*, case *f*; **c. boy** mousse *m*.

cabinet ['kæbɪnɪt] **1** *n* (*cupboard*) armoire *f*; (*for display*) vitrine *f*; (*filing*) **c.** classeur *m* (de bureau). **2** *n Pol* cabinet *m*; – *a* ministériel; **c. minister** ministre *m*. ◆**c.-maker** *n* ébéniste *m*.

cable ['keɪb(ə)l] *n* câble *m*; **c. car** (*with overhead cable*) téléphérique *m*; *Rail* funiculaire *m*; **c. television** la télévision par câble; **to have c.** *Fam* avoir le câble; – *vt* (*message etc*) câbler (**to** à).

caboose [kə'buːs] n Rail Am fourgon m (de queue).

cache [kæʃ] n (place) cachette f; **an arms' c.** des armes cachées, une cache d'armes.

cachet ['kæʃeɪ] n (mark, character etc) cachet m.

cackle ['kækəl] vi (of hen) caqueter; (laugh) glousser; – n caquet m; gloussement m.

cacophony [kə'kɒfənɪ] n cacophonie f.

cactus, pl -ti or -tuses ['kæktəs, -taɪ, -təsɪz] n cactus m.

cad [kæd] n Old-fashioned Pej goujat m.

cadaverous [kə'dævərəs] a cadavérique.

caddie ['kædɪ] n Golf caddie m.

caddy ['kædɪ] n (tea) c. boîte f à thé.

cadence ['keɪdəns] n Mus cadence f.

cadet [kə'det] n Mil élève m officier.

cadge [kædʒ] vi (beg) Pej quémander; – vt (meal) se faire payer (off s.o. par qn); to c. money from or off s.o. taper qn.

Caesarean [sɪ'zeərɪən] n c. (section) Med césarienne f.

café ['kæfeɪ] n café(-restaurant) m. ◆**cafeteria** [kæfɪ'tɪərɪə] n cafétéria f.

caffeine ['kæfiːn] n caféine f.

cage [keɪdʒ] n cage f; – vt to c. (up) mettre en cage.

cagey ['keɪdʒɪ] a Fam peu communicatif (about à l'égard de).

cahoots [kə'huːts] n in c. Sl de mèche, en cheville (with avec).

cajole [kə'dʒəul] vt amadouer, enjôler.

cak/e [keɪk] 1 n gâteau m; (small) pâtisserie f; c. of soap savonnette f. 2 vi (harden) durcir; – vt (cover) couvrir (with de). ◆**-ed** a (mud) séché.

calamine ['kæləmaɪn] n c. (lotion) lotion f apaisante (à la calamine).

calamity [kə'læmɪtɪ] n calamité f. ◆**calamitous** a désastreux.

calcium ['kælsɪəm] n calcium m.

calculat/e ['kælkjuleɪt] vti calculer; to c. that Fam supposer que; to c. on compter sur. ◆**-ing** a (shrewd) calculateur. ◆**calcu'lation** n calcul m. ◆**calculator** n calculatrice f; (pocket) calculatrice (de poche). ◆**calculus** n Math Med calcul m.

calendar ['kælɪndər] n calendrier m; (directory) annuaire m.

calf [kɑːf] n (pl calves) 1 (animal) veau m. 2 Anat mollet m.

calibre ['kælɪbər] n calibre m. ◆**calibrate** vt calibrer.

calico ['kælɪkəʊ] n (pl -oes or -os) (fabric) calicot m; (printed) Am indienne f.

call [kɔːl] n appel m; (shout) cri m; (vocation) vocation f; (visit) visite f; (telephone) c. communication f, appel m téléphonique; to make a c. Tel téléphoner (to à); on c. de garde; no c. to do aucune raison de faire; there's no c. for that article Com cet article n'est pas très demandé; c. box cabine f (téléphonique); – vt appeler; (wake up) réveiller; (person to meeting) convoquer (to à); (attention) attirer (to sur); (truce) demander; (consider) considérer; he's called David il s'appelle David; to c. a meeting convoquer une assemblée; to c. s.o. a liar/etc qualifier or traiter qn de menteur/etc; to c. into question mettre en question; let's c. it a day Fam on va s'arrêter là, ça suffit; to c. sth (out) (shout) crier qch; – vi appeler; to c. (out) (cry out) crier; to c. (in or round or by or over) (visit) passer. ■ to c. back vti rappeler; to c. for vt (require) demander; (summon) appeler; (collect) passer prendre; to c. in vt faire venir or entrer; (police) appeler; (recall) rappeler, faire rentrer; – vi to c. in on s.o. passer chez qn. ◆**call-in** a (programme) Rad à ligne ouverte; to c. off vt (cancel) annuler; (dog) rappeler; to c. out vt (doctor) appeler; (workers) donner une consigne de grève à; – vi to c. out for demander à haute voix; to c. up vt Mil Tel appeler; (memories) évoquer. ◆**call-up** n Mil appel m, mobilisation f; to c. (up)on vi (visit) passer voir, passer chez; (invoke) invoquer; to c. (up)on s.o. to do inviter qn à faire; (urge) sommer qn de faire. ◆**calling** n vocation f; c. card Am carte f de visite. ◆**caller** n visiteur, -euse mf; Tel correspondant, -ante mf.

calligraphy [kə'lɪgrəfɪ] n calligraphie f.

callous ['kæləs] a 1 cruel, insensible. 2 (skin) calleux. ◆**callus** n durillon m, cal m.

callow ['kæləʊ] a inexpérimenté.

calm [kɑːm] a (-er, -est) calme, tranquille; keep c.! (don't panic) du calme!; – n calme m; – vt to c. (down) calmer; – vi to c. down se calmer. ◆**-ly** adv calmement. ◆**-ness** n calme m.

calorie ['kælərɪ] n calorie f.

calumny ['kæləmnɪ] n calomnie f.

calvary ['kælvərɪ] n Rel calvaire m.

calve [kɑːv] vi (of cow) vêler.

camber ['kæmbər] n (in road) bombement m.

came [keɪm] see come.

camel ['kæməl] n chameau m.

camellia [kə'miːlɪə] n Bot camélia m.

cameo ['kæmɪəʊ] n camée m.

camera ['kæmrə] n appareil(-photo) m; TV Cin caméra f. ◆cameraman n (pl -men) caméraman m.

camomile ['kæməmaɪl] n Bot camomille f.

camouflage ['kæməflɑːʒ] n camouflage m; – vt camoufler.

camp¹ [kæmp] n camp m, campement m; c. bed lit m de camp; – vi to c. (out) camper. ◆–ing n Sp camping m; c. site n (terrain m de) camping m. ◆–er n (person) campeur, -euse mf; (vehicle) camping-car m. ◆campfire n feu m de camp. ◆campsite n camping m.

camp² [kæmp] a (affected) affecté, exagéré (de façon à provoquer le rire).

campaign [kæm'peɪn] n Pol Mil Journ etc campagne f; – vi faire campagne. ◆–er n militant, -ante mf (for pour).

campus ['kæmpəs] n Univ campus m.

can¹ [kæn, unstressed kən] v aux (pres t can; pt could) (be able to) pouvoir; (know how to) savoir; if I c. si je peux; she c. swim elle sait nager; if I could swim si je savais nager; he could do it tomorrow il pourrait le faire demain; he couldn't help me il ne pouvait pas m'aider; he could have done it il aurait pu le faire; you could be wrong (possibility) tu as peut-être tort; he can't be old (probability) il ne doit pas être vieux; c. I come in? (permission) puis-je entrer?; you can't or c. not come tu ne peux pas venir; I c. see je vois.

can² [kæn] n (for water etc) bidon m; (tin for food) boîte f; – vt (-nn-) mettre en boîte. ◆canned a en boîte, en conserve; c. food conserves fpl. ◆can-opener n ouvre-boîtes m inv.

Canada ['kænədə] n Canada m. ◆Canadian [kə'neɪdɪən] a & n canadien, -ienne (mf).

canal [kə'næl] n canal m.

canary [kə'neərɪ] n canari m, serin m.

cancan ['kænkæn] n french-cancan m.

cancel ['kænsəl] vt (-ll-, Am -l-) annuler; (goods, taxi, appointment) décommander; (word, paragraph etc) biffer; (train) supprimer; (stamp) oblitérer; to c. a ticket (with date) composter un billet; (punch) poinçonner un billet; to c. each other out s'annuler. ◆cance'llation n annulation f; suppression f; oblitération f.

cancer ['kænsər] n cancer m; C. (sign) le Cancer; c. patient cancéreux, -euse mf. ◆cancerous a cancéreux.

candelabra [kændɪ'lɑːbrə] n candélabra m.

candid ['kændɪd] a franc, sincère. ◆candour n franchise f, sincérité f.

candidate ['kændɪdeɪt] n candidat, -ate mf. ◆candidacy n, ◆candidature n candidature f.

candle ['kænd(ə)l] n bougie f; (tallow) chandelle f; Rel cierge m; c. grease suif m. ◆candlelight n by c. à la (lueur d'une) bougie; to have dinner by c. dîner aux chandelles. ◆candlestick n bougeoir m; (tall) chandelier m.

candy ['kændɪ] n Am bonbon(s) m(pl); (sugar) c. sucre m candi; c. store Am confiserie f. ◆candied a (fruit) confit, glacé. ◆candyfloss n barbe f à papa.

cane [keɪn] n (stick) canne f; (for basket) rotin m; Sch baguette f; – vt (punish) Sch fouetter.

canine ['keɪnaɪn] 1 a canin. 2 n (tooth) canine f.

canister ['kænɪstər] n boîte f (en métal).

canker ['kænkər] n (in disease) & Fig chancre m.

cannabis ['kænəbɪs] n (plant) chanvre m indien; (drug) haschisch m.

cannibal ['kænɪbəl] n & a cannibale (mf).

cannon ['kænən] n (pl -s or inv) canon m. ◆cannonball n boulet m (de canon).

cannot ['kænɒt] = can not.

canny ['kænɪ] a (-ier, -iest) rusé, malin.

canoe [kə'nuː] n canoë m, kayak m; – vi faire du canoë ou du kayak. ◆–ing n to go c. Sp faire du canoë ou du kayak. ◆canoeist n canoëiste mf.

canon ['kænən] n (law) canon m; (clergyman) chanoine m. ◆canonize vt Rel canoniser.

canopy ['kænəpɪ] n (over bed, altar etc) dais m; (hood of pram) capote f; (awning) auvent m; (made of glass) marquise f; (of sky) Fig voûte f.

cant [kænt] n (jargon) jargon m.

can't [kɑːnt] = can not.

cantaloup(e) ['kæntəluːp, Am -loʊp] n (melon) cantaloup m.

cantankerous [kæn'tæŋkərəs] a grincheux, acariâtre.

cantata [kæn'tɑːtə] n Mus cantate f.

canteen [kæn'tiːn] n (place) cantine f; (flask) gourde f; c. of cutlery ménagère f.

canter ['kæntər] n petit galop m; – vi aller au petit galop.

cantor ['kæntər] n Rel chantre m, maître m de chapelle.

canvas ['kænvəs] n (grosse) toile f; (for embroidery) canevas m.

canvass ['kænvəs] vt (an area) faire du démarchage dans; (opinions) sonder; to c.

s.o. *Pol* solliciter des voix de qn; *Com* solliciter des commandes de qn. ◆**—ing** n *Com* démarchage m, prospection f; *Pol* démarchage m (électoral). ◆**—er** n *Pol* agent m électoral; *Com* démarcheur, -euse mf.

canyon ['kænjən] n cañon m, canyon m.

cap[1] [kæp] n 1 (hat) casquette f; (for shower etc) & Nau bonnet m; Mil képi m. 2 (of bottle, tube, valve) bouchon m; (of milk or beer bottle) capsule f; (of pen) capuchon m. 3 (of child's gun) amorce f, capsule f. 4 (Dutch) Cap (contraceptive) diaphragme m.

cap[2] [kæp] n (-pp-) (outdo) surpasser; to c. it all pour comble; capped with (covered) coiffé de.

capable ['keɪpəb(ə)l] a (person) capable (of sth de qch, of doing de faire); competent. c. of (thing) susceptible de. ◆**capa'bility** n capacité f. ◆**capably** adv avec compétence.

capacity [kə'pæsɪtɪ] n (of container) capacité f, contenance f; (ability) aptitude f, capacité f; (output) rendement m; in my c. as en ma qualité de; in an advisory/etc c. à titre consultatif/etc; filled to c. absolument plein, comble; c. audience salle f comble.

cape [keɪp] n 1 (cloak) cape f; (of cyclist) pèlerine f. 2 Geog cap m; C. Town Le Cap.

caper ['keɪpər] 1 vi (jump about) gambader. 2 n (activity) Sl affaire f; (prank) Fam farce f; (trip) Fam virée f. 3 n Bot Culin câpre f.

capital ['kæpɪtəl] 1 a (punishment, letter, importance) capital; – n c. (city) capitale f; c. (letter) majuscule f, capitale f. 2 n (money) capital m, capitaux mpl. ◆**capitalism** n capitalisme m. ◆**capitalist** a & n capitaliste (mf). ◆**capitalize** vi to c. on tirer parti de.

capitulate [kə'pɪtʃʊleɪt] vi capituler. ◆**capitu'lation** n capitulation f.

caprice [kə'priːs] n caprice m. ◆**capricious** [kə'prɪʃəs] a capricieux.

Capricorn ['kæprɪkɔːn] n (sign) le Capricorne.

capsize [kæp'saɪz] vi Nau chavirer; – vt (faire) chavirer.

capsule ['kæpsəl, 'kæpsjuːl] n (medicine, of spaceship etc) capsule f.

captain ['kæptɪn] n capitaine m; – vt Nau commander; Sp être le capitaine de.

caption ['kæpʃ(ə)n] n Cin Journ sous-titre m; (under illustration) légende f.

captivate ['kæptɪveɪt] vt captiver.

captive ['kæptɪv] n captif, -ive mf, prisonnier, -ière mf. ◆**cap'tivity** n captivité f.

capture ['kæptʃər] n capture f; – vt (person, animal) prendre, capturer; (town) prendre; (attention) capter; (represent in words, on film etc) rendre, reproduire.

car [kɑːr] n voiture f, auto(mobile) f; Rail wagon m; – a (industry) automobile; c. ferry ferry-boat m; c. park parking m; c. radio autoradio m; c. wash (action) lavage m automatique; (machine) lave-auto m. ◆**carfare** n Am frais mpl de voyage. ◆**carport** n auvent m (pour voiture). ◆**carsick** a to be c. être malade en voiture.

carafe [kə'ræf] n carafe f.

caramel ['kærəməl] n (flavouring, toffee) caramel m.

carat ['kærət] n carat m.

caravan ['kærəvæn] n (in desert) & Aut caravane f; (horse-drawn) roulotte f; c. site camping m pour caravanes.

caraway ['kærəweɪ] n Bot Culin cumin m, carvi m.

carbohydrates [kɑːbə'haɪdreɪts] npl (in diet) féculents mpl.

carbon ['kɑːbən] n carbone m; c. copy double m (au carbone); Fig réplique f, double m; c. paper (papier m) carbone m.

carbuncle ['kɑːbʌŋk(ə)l] n Med furoncle m, clou m.

carburettor [kɑːbjʊ'retər] (Am **carburetor** ['kɑːbəreɪtər]) n carburateur m.

carcass ['kɑːkəs] n (body, framework) carcasse f.

carcinogenic [kɑːsɪnə'dʒenɪk] a cancérigène.

card [kɑːd] n carte f; (cardboard) carton m; (index) c. fiche f; c. index fichier m; c. table table f de jeu; to play cards jouer aux cartes; on or Am in the cards Fam très vraisemblable; to get one's cards (be dismissed) Fam être renvoyé. ◆**cardboard** n carton m. ◆**cardsharp** n tricheur, -euse mf.

cardiac ['kɑːdɪæk] a cardiaque.

cardigan ['kɑːdɪgən] n cardigan m, gilet m.

cardinal ['kɑːdɪn(ə)l] 1 a (number etc) cardinal. 2 n (priest) cardinal m.

care [keər] 1 vi to c. about (feel concern about) se soucier de, s'intéresser à; I don't c. ça m'est égal; I couldn't c. less Fam je m'en fiche; who cares? qu'est-ce que ça fait? 2 vi (like) aimer, vouloir; would you c. to try? voulez-vous essayer?, aimeriez-vous essayer?; I don't c. for it (music etc) je n'aime pas tellement ça; to c. for (a drink, a change etc) avoir envie de; to c. about or for s.o. avoir de la sympathie pour qn; to c. for

career [kəˈrɪər] **1** n carrière f; – a (diplomat etc) de carrière. **2** vi to c. along aller à toute vitesse.

careful [ˈkeəf(ə)l] a (diligent) soigneux (about, of de); (cautious) prudent; a. (with money) regardant; to be c. of or with (heed) faire attention à. **◆—ly** adv avec soin; prudemment. **◆careless** a négligent; (thoughtless) irréfléchi; (inattentive) inattentif (of à). **◆carelessness** n négligence f, manque m de soin.

caress [kəˈres] n caresse f; – vt (stroke) caresser; (kiss) embrasser.

cargo [ˈkɑːgəʊ] n (pl -oes, Am -os) cargaison f; c. boat cargo m.

Caribbean [kærɪˈbiːən, Am kəˈrɪbɪən] a caraïbe; – n the C. (Islands) les Antilles fpl.

caricature [ˈkærɪkətʃʊər] n caricature f; – vt caricaturer.

caring [ˈkeərɪŋ] a (loving) aimant; (understanding) compréhensif; – n affection f.

carnage [ˈkɑːnɪdʒ] n carnage m.

carnal [ˈkɑːn(ə)l] a charnel, sexuel.

carnation [kɑːˈneɪʃən] n œillet m.

carnival [ˈkɑːnɪvəl] n carnaval m.

carnivore [ˈkɑːnɪvɔːr] n carnivore m. **◆carnivorous** a carnivore.

carol [ˈkærəl] n chant m (de Noël).

carouse [kəˈraʊz] vi faire la fête.

carp [kɑːp] **1** n (fish) carpe f. **2** vi critiquer; to c. at critiquer.

carpenter [ˈkɑːpɪntər] n (for house building) charpentier m; (light woodwork) menuisier m. **◆carpentry** n charpenterie f; menuiserie f.

carpet [ˈkɑːpɪt] n tapis m; (fitted) moquette f; c. sweeper balai m mécanique; – vt recouvrir d'un tapis or d'une moquette; (of snow etc) Fig tapisser. **◆—ing** n (carpets) tapis mpl; moquette f.

carriage [ˈkærɪdʒ] n (horse-drawn) voiture f, équipage m; Rail voiture f; Com transport m; (bearing of person) port m; (of typewriter) chariot m; c. paid port payé. **◆carriageway** n (of road) chaussée f.

carrier [ˈkærɪər] n Com entreprise f de transports; Med porteur, -euse mf; c. (bag) sac m (en plastique); c. pigeon pigeon m voyageur.

carrion [ˈkærɪən] n charogne f.

carrot [ˈkærət] n carotte f.

carry [ˈkærɪ] vt porter; (goods) transporter; (by wind) emporter; (involve) comporter; (interest) Com produire; (extend) faire passer; (win) remporter; (authority) avoir; (child) Med attendre; (motion) Pol faire passer, voter; (self) soutenir; Math retenir; to c. too far pousser trop loin; to c. oneself se comporter; – vi (of sound) porter. ■ to c. away vt emporter; Fig transporter; to be or get carried away (excited) s'emballer; to c. back vt (thing) rapporter; (person) ramener; (in thought) reporter; to c. off vt emporter; (kidnap) enlever; (prize) remporter; to c. it off réussir; to c. on vt continuer; (conduct) diriger, mener; (sustain) soutenir; – vi continuer (doing à faire); (behave) Pej se conduire (mal); (complain) se plaindre; to c. on with sth continuer qch; to c. on about (talk) causer de. **◆carryings-on** npl Pej activités fpl; (behaviour) Pej façons fpl; to c. out vt (plan etc) exécuter, réaliser; (repair etc) effectuer; (duty) accomplir; (meal) Am emporter; to c. through vt (plan etc) mener à bonne fin.

carrycot [ˈkærɪkɒt] n Am fourre-tout m inv. **◆carrycot** n (nacelle f) porte-bébé m.

cart [kɑːt] **1** n charrette f (handcart) voiture f à bras. **2** vt (goods, people) transporter; to c. (around) Fam trimbal(l)er; to c. away emporter. **◆carthorse** n cheval m de trait.

cartel [kɑːˈtel] n Econ Pol cartel m.

cartilage [ˈkɑːtɪlɪdʒ] n cartilage m.

carton [ˈkɑːtən] n (box) carton m; (of milk, fruit juice etc) brick m, pack m; (of cigarettes) cartouche f; (of cream) pot m.

cartoon [kɑːˈtuːn] n Journ dessin m (humoristique); Cin dessin m animé; (strip) c. bande f dessinée. **◆cartoonist** n Journ dessinateur, -trice mf (humoristique).

cartridge [ˈkɑːtrɪdʒ] n (of firearm, pen, camera, tape deck) cartouche f; (of record player) cellule f; c. belt cartouchière f.

carv/e [kɑːv] vt (cut) tailler (out of dans); (sculpt) sculpter; (initials etc) graver; to c. (up) (meat) découper; to c. up (country) dépecer, morceler; to c. out sth for oneself (career etc) se tailler qch. **◆—ing** n (wood) c. sculpture f (sur bois).

cascade [kæsˈkeɪd] n (of rocks) chute f; (of

blows) déluge m; (of lace) flot m; – vi tomber; (hang) pendre.

case [keɪs] n **1** (instance) & Med cas m; Jur affaire f; Phil arguments mpl; **in any c.** en tout cas; **in c. it rains** au cas où il pleuvrait; **in c. of** en cas de; **(just) in c.** à tout hasard. **2** (bag) valise f; (crate) caisse f; (for pen, glasses, camera, violin, cigarettes) étui m; (for jewels) coffret m. ◆**casing** n (covering) enveloppe f.

cash [kæʃ] n argent m; **to pay (in) c.** (not by cheque) payer en espèces or à liquide; **to pay c. (down)** payer comptant; **c. price** prix m (au) comptant; **c. box** caisse f; **c. desk** caisse f; **c. register** caisse f enregistreuse; – vt (banknote) changer; **to c. a cheque** (of person) encaisser un chèque; (of bank) payer un chèque; **to c. in on** Fam profiter de. ◆**ca'shier 1** n caissier, -ière mf. **2** vt (dismiss) Mil casser.

cashew ['kæʃuː] n (nut) cajou m.

cashmere ['kæʃmɪər] n cachemire m.

casino [kə'siːnəʊ] n (pl -os) casino m.

cask [kɑːsk] n fût m, tonneau m. ◆**casket** n (box) coffret m; (coffin) cercueil m.

casserole ['kæsərəʊl] n (covered dish) cocotte f; (stew) ragoût m en cocotte.

cassette [kə'set] n cassette f; Phot cartouche f; **c. player** lecteur m de cassettes; **c. recorder** magnétophone m à cassettes.

cassock ['kæsək] n soutane f.

cast [kɑːst] **1** n Th acteurs mpl; (list) Th distribution f; (mould) moulage m; (of dice) coup m; Med plâtre m; (squint) léger strabisme m; **c. of mind** tournure f d'esprit. **2** vt (pt & pp **cast**) (throw) jeter; (light, shadow) projeter; (blame) rejeter; (glance) jeter; (doubt) exprimer; (lose) perdre; (metal) couler; (role) Th distribuer; (actor) donner un rôle à; **to c. one's mind back** to reporter en arrière; **to c. a vote** voter; **to c. aside** rejeter; **to c. off** (chains etc) se libérer de; (shed, lose) se dépouiller de; Fig abandonner. **3** vi **to c. off** Nau appareiller. **4** n c. **iron** fonte f. ◆**c.-'iron** a (pan etc) en fonte; (will etc) Fig de fer, solide.

castaway ['kɑːstəweɪ] n naufragé, -ée mf.

caste [kɑːst] n caste f.

caster ['kɑːstər] n (wheel) roulette f; **c. sugar** sucre m en poudre.

castle ['kɑːs(ə)l] n château m; (in chess) tour f.

castoffs ['kɑːstɒfs] npl vieux vêtements mpl.

castor ['kɑːstər] n (wheel) roulette f; **c. oil** huile f de ricin; **c. sugar** sucre m en poudre.

castrate [kæ'streɪt] vt châtrer. ◆**castration** n castration f.

casual ['kæʒjʊəl] a (meeting) fortuit; (remark) fait en passant; (stroll) sans but; (offhand) désinvolte, insouciant; (worker) temporaire; (work) irrégulier; **c. clothes** vêtements mpl sport; **a c. acquaintance** quelqu'un que l'on connaît un peu. ◆**-ly** adv par hasard; (informally) avec désinvolture; (to remark) en passant.

casualty ['kæʒjʊəltɪ] n (dead) mort m, morte f; (wounded) blessé, -ée mf; (accident victim) accidenté, -ée mf; **casualties** morts et blessés mpl; Mil pertes fpl; **c. department** Med service m des accidentés.

cat [kæt] n chat m, chatte f; **c. burglar** monte-en-l'air m inv; **c.'s eyes®** cataphotes® mpl, clous mpl. ◆**catcall** n sifflet m, huée f.

cataclysm ['kætəklɪzəm] n cataclysme m.

catalogue ['kætəlɒg] (Am **catalog**) n catalogue m; – vt cataloguer.

catalyst ['kætəlɪst] n Ch & Fig catalyseur m.

catapult ['kætəpʌlt] n lance-pierres m inv; Hist Av catapulte f; – vt catapulter.

cataract ['kætərækt] n (waterfall) & Med cataracte f.

catarrh [kə'tɑːr] n catarrhe m, rhume m.

catastrophe [kə'tæstrəfɪ] n catastrophe f. ◆**cata'strophic** a catastrophique.

catch [kætʃ] vt (pt & pp **caught**) (ball, thief, illness etc) attraper; (grab) prendre, saisir; (surprise) (surprendre); (understand) saisir; (train etc) attraper, (réussir à) prendre; (attention) attirer; (of nail etc) accrocher; (finger etc) se prendre (in dans); **to c. sight of** apercevoir; **to c. fire** prendre feu; **to c. s.o. (in)** Fam trouver qn (chez soi); **to c. one's breath** (rest a while) reprendre haleine; (stop breathing) retenir son souffle; **I didn't c. the train/etc** j'ai manqué le train/etc; **to c. s.o. out** prendre qn en défaut; **to c. s.o. up** rattraper qn; – vi (of fire) prendre; **her skirt (got) caught in the door** sa jupe s'est prise or coincée dans la porte; **to c. on** prendre, devenir populaire; (understand) saisir; **to c. up** se rattraper; **to c. up with s.o.** rattraper qn; – n capture f, prise f; (trick, snare) piège m; (on door) loquet m. ◆**-ing** a contagieux. ◆**catchphrase** n, ◆**catchword** n slogan m.

catchy ['kætʃɪ] a (-ier, -iest) (tune) Fam facile à retenir.

catechism ['kætɪkɪzəm] n Rel catéchisme m.

category ['kætɪgərɪ] n catégorie f. ◆**cate-**

'gorical *a* catégorique. ◆**categorize** *vt* classer (par catégories).

cater ['keɪtər] *vi* s'occuper de la nourriture; **to c. for** *or* **to** (*need, taste*) satisfaire; (*readership*) *Journ* s'adresser à. ◆**-ing** *n* restauration *f*. ◆**-er** *n* traiteur *m*.

caterpillar ['kætəpɪlər] *n* chenille *f*.

catgut ['kætgʌt] *n* (*cord*) boyau *m*.

cathedral [kə'θiːdrəl] *n* cathédrale *f*.

catholic ['kæθlɪk] **1** *a* & *n* **C.** catholique (*mf*). **2** *a* (*taste*) universel; (*view*) libéral. ◆**Ca'tholicism** *n* catholicisme *m*.

cattle ['kæt(ə)l] *npl* bétail *m*, bestiaux *mpl*.

catty ['kætɪ] *a* (**-ier, -iest**) *Fam* rosse, méchant.

caucus ['kɔːkəs] *n* *Pol* *Am* comité *m* électoral.

caught [kɔːt] *see* **catch**.

cauldron ['kɔːldrən] *n* chaudron *m*.

cauliflower ['kɒlɪflaʊər] *n* chou-fleur *m*.

cause [kɔːz] *n* cause *f*; (*reason*) raison *f*; **c. for complaint** sujet *m* de plainte; — *vt* causer, occasionner; (*trouble*) créer, causer (**for** à); **to c. sth to move**/etc faire bouger/etc qch.

causeway ['kɔːzweɪ] *n* chaussée *f*.

caustic ['kɔːstɪk] *a* (*remark, substance*) caustique.

cauterize ['kɔːtəraɪz] *vt* *Med* cautériser.

caution ['kɔːʃ(ə)n] *n* (*care*) prudence *f*, précaution *f*; (*warning*) avertissement *m*; — *vt* (*warn*) avertir; **to c. s.o. against sth** mettre qn en garde contre qch. ◆**cautionary** *a* (*tale*) moral. ◆**cautious** *a* prudent, circonspect. ◆**cautiously** *adv* prudemment.

cavalcade ['kævəlkeɪd] *n* (*procession*) cavalcade *f*.

cavalier [kævə'lɪər] **1** *a* (*selfish*) cavalier. **2** *n* (*horseman, knight*) *Hist* cavalier *m*.

cavalry ['kævəlrɪ] *n* cavalerie *f*.

cave [keɪv] **1** *n* caverne *f*, grotte *f*. **2** *vi* **to c. in** (*fall in*) s'effondrer. ◆**caveman** *n* (*pl* **-men**) homme *m* des cavernes. ◆**cavern** ['kævən] *n* caverne *f*.

caviar(e) ['kævɪɑːr] *n* caviar *m*.

cavity ['kævɪtɪ] *n* cavité *f*.

cavort [kə'vɔːt] *vi* *Fam* cabrioler; **to c. naked**/etc se balader tout nu/etc.

cease [siːs] *vti* cesser (**doing** de faire). ◆**c.-fire** *n* cessez-le-feu *m* *inv*. ◆**ceaseless** *a* incessant. ◆**ceaselessly** *adv* sans cesse.

cedar ['siːdər] *n* (*tree, wood*) cèdre *m*.

cedilla [sɪ'dɪlə] *n* *Gram* cédille *f*.

ceiling ['siːlɪŋ] *n* (*of room, on wages etc*) plafond *m*.

celebrat/e ['selɪbreɪt] *vt* (*event*) fêter; (*mass, s.o.'s merits etc*) célébrer; — *vi* faire la fête; **we should c. (that)!** il faut fêter ça! ◆**-ed** *a* célèbre. ◆**cele'bration** *n* fête *f*; **the c. of** (*marriage etc*) la célébration de. ◆**ce'lebrity** *n* (*person*) célébrité *f*.

celery ['selərɪ] *n* céleri *m*.

celibate ['selɪbət] *a* (*abstaining from sex*) célibataire; (*monk etc*) abstinent. ◆**celibacy** *n* (*of young person etc*) célibat *m*; (*of monk etc*) abstinence *f*.

cell [sel] *n* cellule *f*; *El* élément *m*. ◆**cellular** *a* cellulaire; **c. blanket** couverture *f* en cellular.

cellar ['selər] *n* cave *f*.

cello ['tʃeləʊ] *n* (*pl* **-os**) violoncelle *m*. ◆**cellist** *n* violoncelliste *mf*.

cellophane® ['seləfeɪn] *n* cellophane® *f*.

celluloid ['seljʊlɔɪd] *n* celluloïd *m*.

cellulose ['seljʊləʊs] *n* cellulose *f*.

Celsius ['selsɪəs] *a* Celsius *inv*.

Celt [kelt] *n* Celte *mf*. ◆**Celtic** *a* celtique, celte.

cement [sɪ'ment] *n* ciment *m*; **c. mixer** bétonnière *f*; — *vt* cimenter.

cemetery ['semətrɪ, *Am* 'seməterɪ] *n* cimetière *m*.

cenotaph ['senətɑːf] *n* cénotaphe *m*.

censor ['sensər] *n* censeur *m*; — *vt* (*film etc*) censurer. ◆**censorship** *n* censure *f*.

censure ['senʃər] *vt* blâmer; *Pol* censurer; — *n* blâme *m*; **c. motion, vote of c.** motion *f* de censure.

census ['sensəs] *n* recensement *m*.

cent [sent] *n* (*coin*) cent *m*; **per c.** pour cent.

centenary [sen'tiːnərɪ, *Am* sen'tenərɪ] *n* centenaire *m*.

centigrade ['sentɪgreɪd] *a* centigrade *m*.

centimetre ['sentɪmiːtər] *n* centimètre *m*.

centipede ['sentɪpiːd] *n* mille-pattes *m* *inv*.

centre ['sentər] *n* centre *m*; **c. forward** *Fb* avant-centre *m*; — *vt* centrer; — *vi* **to c. on** (*of thoughts*) se concentrer sur; (*of question*) tourner autour de. ◆**central** *a* central. ◆**centralize** *vt* centraliser. ◆**centrifugal** [sen'trɪfjʊgəl] *a* centrifuge.

century ['sentʃərɪ] *n* siècle *m*; (*score*) *Sp* cent points *mpl*.

ceramic [sə'ræmɪk] *a* (*tile etc*) de *or* en céramique; — *npl* (*objects*) céramiques *fpl*; (*art*) céramique *f*.

cereal ['sɪərɪəl] *n* céréale *f*.

cerebral ['serɪbrəl, *Am* sə'riːbrəl] *a* cérébral.

ceremony ['serɪmənɪ] *n* (*event*) cérémonie *f*; **to stand on c.** faire des cérémonies *or* des façons. ◆**cere'monial** *a* de cérémonie; —

n cérémonial *m*. ◆**cere'monious** *a* cérémonieux.

certain ['sɜːtən] *a* (*particular, some*) certain; (*sure*) sûr, certain; **she's c. to come, she'll come for c.** c'est certain *or* sûr qu'elle viendra; **I'm not c. what to do** je ne sais pas très bien ce qu'il faut faire; **to be c. of sth/that** être certain de qch/que; **for c.** (*to say, know*) avec certitude; **be c. to go!** vas-y sans faute!; **to make c. of** (*fact*) s'assurer de; (*seat etc*) s'assurer. ◆**-ly** *adv* certainement; (*yes*) bien sûr; (*without fail*) sans faute, (*without any doubt*) sans aucun doute. ◆**certainty** *n* certitude *f*.

certificate [sə'tɪfɪkɪt] *n* certificat *m*; *Univ* diplôme *m*.

certify ['sɜːtɪfaɪ] *vt* certifier; **to c. (insane)** déclarer dément; – *vi* **to c. to sth** attester qch.

cervix ['sɜːvɪks] *n* col *m* de l'utérus.

cesspool ['sespuːl] *n* fosse *f* d'aisances; *Fig* cloaque *f*.

chafe [tʃeɪf] *vt* (*skin*) *Lit* frotter.

chaff [tʃæf] *vt* (*tease*) taquiner.

chaffinch ['tʃæfɪntʃ] *n* (*bird*) pinson *m*.

chagrin ['ʃægrɪn, *Am* ʃə'grɪn] *n* contrariété *f*; – *vt* contrarier.

chain [tʃeɪn] *n* (*of rings, mountains*) chaîne *f*; (*of ideas, events*) enchaînement *m*, suite *f*; (*of lavatory*) chasse *f* d'eau; **c. reaction** réaction *f* en chaîne; **to be a c.-smoker**, **to c.-smoke** fumer cigarette sur cigarette, fumer comme un pompier; **c. saw** tronçonneuse *f*; **c. store** magasin *m* à succursales multiples; – *vt* **to c. (down)** enchaîner; **to c. (up)** (*dog*) mettre à l'attache.

chair [tʃeər] *n* chaise *f*; (*armchair*) fauteuil *m*; *Univ* chaire *f*; **the c.** (*office*) la présidence; **c. lift** télésiège *m*; – *vt* (*meeting*) présider. ◆**chairman** *n* (*pl* **-men**) président, -ente *mf*. ◆**chairmanship** *n* présidence *f*.

chalet ['ʃæleɪ] *n* chalet *m*.

chalk [tʃɔːk] *n* craie *f*; **not by a long c.** loin de là, tant s'en faut; – *vt* marquer *or* écrire à la craie; **to c. up** (*success*) *Fig* remporter. ◆**chalky** *a* (**-ier, -iest**) crayeux.

challenge ['tʃælɪndʒ] *n* défi *m*; (*task*) gageure *f*; *Mil* sommation *f*; **c. for** (*bid*) tentative *f* d'obtenir; – *vt* défier (**s.o. to do** qn de faire); (*dispute*) contester; **to c. s.o. to a game** inviter qn à jouer; **to c. s.o. to a duel** provoquer qn en duel. ◆**-ing** *a* (*job*) exigeant; (*book*) stimulant. ◆**-er** *n* *Sp* challenger *m*.

chamber ['tʃeɪmbər] *n* chambre *f*; (*of judge*) cabinet *m*; – *a* (*music, orchestra*) de cham-

bre; **c. pot** pot *m* de chambre. ◆**chambermaid** *n* femme *f* de chambre.

chameleon [kə'miːliən] *n* (*reptile*) caméléon *m*.

chamois ['ʃæmɪ] *n* **c. (leather)** peau *f* de chamois.

champagne [ʃæm'peɪn] *n* champagne *m*.

champion ['tʃæmpiən] *n* champion, -onne *mf*; **c. skier** champion, -onne du ski; – *vt* (*support*) se faire le champion de. ◆**championship** *n* *Sp* championnat *m*.

chance [tʃɑːns] *n* (*luck*) hasard *m*; (*possibility*) chances *fpl*, possibilité *f*; (*opportunity*) occasion *f*; (*risk*) risque *m*; **by c.** par hasard; **by any c.** (*possibly*) par hasard; **on the off c. (that) you could help me** au cas où tu pourrais m'aider; – *a* (*remark*) fait au hasard; (*occurrence*) accidentel; – *vt* **to c. doing** prendre le risque de faire; **to c. to find/***etc* trouver/*etc* par hasard; **to c. it** risquer le coup; – *v imp* **it chanced that** (*happened*) il s'est trouvé que.

chancel ['tʃɑːnsəl] *n* (*in church*) chœur *m*.

chancellor ['tʃɑːnsələr] *n* *Pol Jur* chancelier *m*. ◆**chancellery** *n* chancellerie *f*.

chandelier [ʃændə'lɪər] *n* lustre *m*.

change [tʃeɪndʒ] *n* changement *m*; (*money*) monnaie *f*; **for a c.** pour changer; **it makes a c. from** ça change de; **to have a c. of heart** changer d'avis; **a c. of clothes** des vêtements de rechange; – *vt* (*modify*) changer; (*exchange*) échanger (**for** contre); (*money*) changer; (*transform*) transformer (**into** en); **to change trains/one's skirt/***etc* changer de train/de jupe/*etc*; **to c. gear** *Aut* changer de vitesse; **to c. the subject** changer de sujet; – *vi* (*alter*) changer; (*change clothes*) se changer; **to c. over** passer. ◆**-ing** *n* (*of guard*) relève *f*; **c. room** vestiaire *m*. ◆**changeable** *a* (*weather, mood etc*) changeant, variable. ◆**changeless** *a* immuable. ◆**changeover** *n* passage *m* (**from** de, **to** à).

channel ['tʃæn(ə)l] *n* (*navigable*) chenal *m*; *TV* chaîne *f*, canal *m*; (*groove*) rainure *f*; *Fig* direction *f*; **through the c. of** par le canal de; **the C.** *Geog* la Manche; **the C. Islands** les îles anglo-normandes; – *vt* (**-ll-**, *Am* **-l-**) (*energies, crowd etc*) canaliser (**into** vers).

chant [tʃɑːnt] *n* (*of demonstrators*) chant *m* scandé; *Rel* psalmodie *f*; – *vt* (*slogan*) scander; – *vi* scander des slogans.

chaos ['keɪɒs] *n* chaos *m*. ◆**cha'otic** *a* chaotique.

chap [tʃæp] **1** *n* (*fellow*) *Fam* type *m*; **old c.!**

mon vieux! **2** n (*on skin*) gerçure f; – vi (**-pp-**) se gercer; – vt gercer.

chapel ['tʃæp(ə)l] n chapelle f; (*non-conformist church*) temple m.

chaperon(e) ['ʃæpərəʊn] n chaperon m; – vt chaperonner.

chaplain ['tʃæplɪn] n aumônier m.

chapter ['tʃæptər] n chapitre m.

char [tʃɑːr] **1** n (**-rr-**) (*convert to carbon*) carboniser; (*scorch*) brûler légèrement. **2** n *Fam* femme f de ménage; – vi to go charring *Fam* faire des ménages. **3** n (*tea*) *Sl* thé m.

character ['kærɪktər] n (*of person, place etc*) & *Typ* caractère m; (*in book, film*) personnage m; (*strange person*) numéro m; Th actor acteur m de genre. **◆characteristic** a & n caractéristique (f). **◆characteristically** adv typiquement. **◆characterize** vt caractériser.

charade [ʃəˈrɑːd] n (*game*) charade f (mimée); (*travesty*) parodie f, comédie f.

charcoal ['tʃɑːkəʊl] n charbon m (de bois); (*crayon*) fusain m, charbon m.

charge [tʃɑːdʒ] n (*in battle*) Mil charge f; Jur accusation f; (*cost*) prix m; (*responsibility*) responsabilité f, charge f; (*care*) garde f; pl (*expenses*) frais mpl; **there's a c.** (**for it**) c'est payant; **free of c.** gratuit; **extra c.** supplément m; **to take c. of** prendre en charge; **to be in c. of** (*child etc*) avoir la garde de; (*office etc*) être responsable de; **the person in c.** le *or* la responsable; **who's in c. here?** qui commande ici?; – vt Mil El charger; Jur accuser, inculper; **to c. s.o.** Com faire payer qn; **to c. (up) to** Com mettre sur le compte de; **how much do you c.?** combien demandez-vous?; – vi (*rush*) se précipiter; **c.!** Mil chargez! **◆-able** a. to aux frais de. **◆charger** n (*for battery*) chargeur m.

chariot ['tʃærɪət] n Mil char m.

charisma [kəˈrɪzmə] n magnétisme m.

charity ['tʃærɪtɪ] n (*kindness, alms*) charité f; (*society*) fondation f *or* œuvre f charitable; **to give to c.** faire la charité. **◆charitable** a charitable.

charlady ['tʃɑːleɪdɪ] n femme f de ménage.

charlatan ['ʃɑːlətən] n charlatan m.

charm [tʃɑːm] n (*attractiveness, spell*) charme m; (*trinket*) amulette f; – vt charmer. **◆-ing** a charmant. **◆-ingly** adv d'une façon charmante.

chart [tʃɑːt] n (*map*) carte f; (*graph*) graphique m, tableau m; (**pop**) **charts** hit-parade m; **flow c.** organigramme m; –

vt (*route*) porter sur la carte; (*figures*) faire le graphique de; (*of graph*) montrer.

charter ['tʃɑːtər] n (*document*) charte f; (*aircraft*) charter m; **the c. of** (*hiring*) l'affrètement m de; **c. flight** charter m; – vt (*aircraft etc*) affréter. **◆-ed a c. accountant** expert-comptable m.

charwoman ['tʃɑːwʊmən] n (pl **-women**) femme f de ménage.

chary ['tʃeərɪ] a (**-ier, -iest**) (*cautious*) prudent.

chase [tʃeɪs] n poursuite f, chasse f; **to give c.** se lancer à la poursuite (**to** de); – vt poursuivre; **to c. away** *or* **off** chasser; **to c. sth up** *Fam* essayer d'obtenir qch, rechercher qch; – vi **to c. after** courir après.

chasm ['kæzəm] n abîme m, gouffre m.

chassis ['ʃæsɪ, *Am* 'tʃæsɪ] n *Aut* châssis m.

chaste [tʃeɪst] a chaste. **◆chastity** n chasteté f.

chasten ['tʃeɪs(ə)n] vt (*punish*) châtier; (*cause to improve*) faire se corriger, assagir. **◆-ing** a (*experience*) instructif.

chastise [tʃæ'staɪz] vt punir.

chat [tʃæt] n causette f; **to have a c.** bavarder; – vi (**-tt-**) causer, bavarder; – vt **to c. up** *Fam* baratiner, draguer. **◆chatty** a (**-ier, -iest**) (*person*) bavard; (*style*) familier; (*text*) plein de bavardages.

chatter ['tʃætər] vi (*of birds, monkeys*) jacasser; **his teeth are chattering** il claque des dents; – n bavardage m; jacassement m. **◆chatterbox** n bavard, -arde mf.

chauffeur ['ʃəʊfər] n chauffeur m (de maître).

chauvinist ['ʃəʊvɪnɪst] n & a chauvin, -ine (mf); **male c.** *Pej* phallocrate m.

cheap [tʃiːp] a (**-er, -est**) bon marché inv, pas cher; (*rate etc*) réduit; (*worthless*) sans valeur; (*superficial*) facile; (*mean, petty*) mesquin; **cheaper** moins cher, meilleur marché; – adv (*to buy*) (à) bon marché, au rabais; (*to feel*) humilié. **◆cheapen** vt Fig déprécier. **◆cheaply** adv (à) bon marché. **◆cheapness** n bas prix m; Fig mesquinerie f.

cheat [tʃiːt] vt (*deceive*) tromper; (*defraud*) frauder; **to c. s.o. out of sth** escroquer qch à qn; **to c. on** (*wife, husband*) faire une infidélité *or* des infidélités à; – vi tricher; (*defraud*) frauder; – n (*at games etc*) tricheur, -euse mf; (*crook*) escroc m. **◆-ing** n (*deceit*) tromperie f; (*trickery*) tricherie f. **◆-er** n *Am* = **cheat**.

check¹ [tʃek] vt (*examine*) vérifier; (*inspect*) contrôler; (*tick*) cocher, pointer; (*stop*) arrêter, enrayer; (*restrain*) contenir, maîtriser; (*rebuke*) réprimander; (*baggage*) *Am* mettre à la consigne; **to c. in** (*luggage*) *Av* enregistrer; **to c. sth out** confirmer qch; – *vi* vérifier; **to c. in** (*at hotel etc*) signer le registre; (*arrive at hotel*) arriver; (*at airport*) se présenter (à l'enregistrement), enregistrer ses bagages; **to c. on sth** vérifier qch; **to c. out** (*at hotel etc*) régler sa note; **to c. up** vérifier, se renseigner; – *n* vérification *f*; contrôle *m*; (*halt*) arrêt *m*; *Chess* échec *m*; (*curb*) frein *m*; (*tick*) = croix *f*; (*receipt*) *Am* reçu *m*; (*bill in restaurant etc*) *Am* addition *f*; (*cheque*) *Am* chèque *m*. ◆**c.-in** *n Av* enregistrement *m* (des bagages). ◆**checking account** *n Am* compte *m* courant. ◆**checkmate** *n Chess* échec et mat *m*. ◆**checkout** *n* (*in supermarket*) caisse *f*. ◆**checkpoint** *n* contrôle *m*. ◆**checkroom** *n Am* vestiaire *m*; (*left-luggage office*) *Am* consigne *f*. ◆**checkup** *n* bilan *m* de santé.

check² [tʃek] *n* (*pattern*) carreaux *mpl*; – *a* à carreaux. ◆**checked** *a* à carreaux.

checkered ['tʃekəd] *a Am* = **chequered**.

checkers ['tʃekəz] *npl Am* jeu *m* de dames.

cheddar ['tʃedər] *n* (*cheese*) cheddar *m*.

cheek [tʃiːk] *n* joue *f*; (*impudence*) *Fig* culot *m*. ◆**cheekbone** *n* pommette *f*. ◆**cheeky** *a* (-**ier**, -**iest**) (*person, reply etc*) effronté.

cheep [tʃiːp] *vi* (*of bird*) piailler.

cheer¹ [tʃiər] *n* **cheers** (*shouts*) acclamations *fpl*; **cheers!** *Fam* à votre santé! – *vt* (*applaud*) acclamer; **to c. on** encourager; **to c. (up)** donner du courage à; (*amuse*) égayer; – *vi* applaudir; **to c. up** prendre courage; s'égayer; **c. up!** (du) courage! ◆**—ing** *n* (*shouts*) acclamations *fpl*; – *a* (*encouraging*) réjouissant.

cheer² [tʃiər] *n* (*gaiety*) joie *f*; **good c.** (*food*) la bonne chère. ◆**cheerful** *a* gai. ◆**cheerfully** *adv* gaiement. ◆**cheerless** *a* morne.

cheerio! [tʃiəriˈəu] *int* salut!, au revoir!

cheese [tʃiːz] *n* fromage *m*. ◆**cheeseburger** *n* cheeseburger *m*. ◆**cheesecake** *n* tarte *f* au fromage blanc. ◆**cheesed** *a* **to be c. (off)** *Fam* en avoir marre (**with** de). ◆**cheesy** *a* (-**ier**, -**iest**) (*shabby, bad*) *Am Fam* miteux.

cheetah ['tʃiːtə] *n* guépard *m*.

chef [ʃef] *n Culin* chef *m*.

chemistry ['kemistri] *n* chimie *f*. ◆**chemical** *a* chimique; – *n* produit *m* chimique. ◆**chemist** *n* (*dispensing*) pharmacien,

-ienne *mf*; (*scientist*) chimiste *mf*; **chemist('s)** (*shop*) pharmacie *f*.

cheque [tʃek] *n* chèque *m*. ◆**chequebook** *n* carnet *m* de chèques.

chequered ['tʃekəd] *a* (*pattern*) à carreaux; (*career etc*) qui connaît des hauts et des bas.

cherish ['tʃeriʃ] *vt* (*person*) chérir; (*hope*) nourrir, caresser.

cherry ['tʃeri] *n* cerise *f*; – *a* cerise *inv*; **c. brandy** cherry *m*.

chess [tʃes] *n* échecs *mpl*. ◆**chessboard** *n* échiquier *m*.

chest [tʃest] *n* **1** *Anat* poitrine *f*. **2** (*box*) coffre *m*; **c. of drawers** commode *f*.

chestnut ['tʃestnʌt] *n* châtaigne *f*, marron *m*; – *a* (*hair*) châtain; **c. tree** châtaignier *m*.

chew [tʃuː] *vt* **to c. (up)** mâcher; **to c. over** *Fig* ruminer; – *vi* mastiquer; **chewing gum** chewing-gum *m*.

chick [tʃik] *n* poussin *m*; (*girl*) *Fam* nana *f*. ◆**chicken 1** *n* poulet *m*; *pl* (*poultry*) volaille *f*; **it's c. feed** *Fam* c'est deux fois rien, c'est une bagatelle. **2** *a Fam* froussard; – *vi* **to c. out** *Fam* se dégonfler. ◆**chickenpox** *n* varicelle *f*.

chickpea ['tʃikpiː] *n* pois *m* chiche.

chicory ['tʃikəri] *n* (*in coffee etc*) chicorée *f*; (*for salad*) endive *f*.

chide [tʃaid] *vt* gronder.

chief [tʃiːf] *n* chef *m*; (*boss*) *Fam* patron *m*, chef *m*; **in c.** (*commander, editor*) en chef; – *a* (*main, highest in rank*) principal. ◆**—ly** *adv* principalement, surtout. ◆**chieftain** *n* (*of clan etc*) chef *m*.

chilblain ['tʃilblein] *n* engelure *f*.

child, *pl* **children** [tʃaild, 'tʃildrən] *n* enfant *mf*; **c. care** *or* **welfare** protection *f* de l'enfance; **child's play** *Fig* jeu *m* d'enfant; **c. minder** gardien, -ienne *d*'enfants. ◆**childbearing** *n* (*act*) accouchement *m*; (*motherhood*) maternité *f*. ◆**childbirth** *n* accouchement *m*, couches *fpl*. ◆**childhood** *n* enfance *f*. ◆**childish** *a* puéril, enfantin. ◆**childishness** *n* puérilité *f*. ◆**childlike** *a* naïf, innocent.

chill [tʃil] *n* froid *m*; (*coldness in feelings*) froideur *f*; *Med* refroidissement *m*; **to catch a c.** prendre froid; – *vt* (*wine, melon*) faire rafraîchir; (*meat, food*) réfrigérer; **to c. s.o.** (*with fear, cold etc*) faire frissonner qn (**with** de); **to be chilled to the bone** être transi. ◆**—ed** *a* (*wine*) frais. ◆**chilly** *a* (-**ier**, -**iest**) froid; (*sensitive to cold*) frileux; **it's c.** il fait (un peu) froid.

chilli ['tʃili] *n* (*pl* -**ies**) piment *m* (de Cayenne).

chime [tʃaɪm] vi (of bell) carillonner; (of clock) sonner; **to c. in** (interrupt) interrompre; – n carillon m; sonnerie f.

chimney ['tʃɪmnɪ] n cheminée f. ◆**chimneypot** n tuyau m de cheminée. ◆**chimneysweep** n ramoneur m.

chimpanzee [tʃɪmpæn'ziː] n chimpanzé m.

chin [tʃɪn] n menton m.

china ['tʃaɪnə] n inv porcelaine f; – a en porcelaine. ◆**chinaware** n (objects) porcelaine f.

China ['tʃaɪnə] n Chine f. ◆**Chi'nese** a & n chinois, -oise (mf); – n (language) chinois m.

chink [tʃɪŋk] **1** n (slit) fente f. **2** vi tinter; – vt faire tinter; – n tintement m.

chip [tʃɪp] vt (-pp-) (cup etc) ébrécher; (table etc) écorner; (paint) écailler; (cut) tailler; – vi **to c. in** Fam contribuer; – n (splinter) éclat m; (break) ébréchure f; écornure f; (microchip) puce f; (counter) jeton m; pl (French fries) frites fpl; (crisps) Am chips mpl. ◆**chipboard** n (bois m) aggloméré m. ◆**chippings** npl road or loose c. gravillons mpl.

chiropodist [kɪ'rɒpədɪst] n pédicure mf.

chirp [tʃɜːp] vi (of bird) pépier; – n pépiement m.

chirpy ['tʃɜːpɪ] a (-ier, -iest) gai, plein d'entrain.

chisel ['tʃɪz(ə)l] n ciseau m; – vt (-ll-, Am -l-) ciseler.

chit [tʃɪt] n (paper) note f, billet m.

chitchat ['tʃɪttʃæt] n bavardage m.

chivalry ['ʃɪvəlrɪ] n (practices etc) chevalerie f; (courtesy) galanterie f. ◆**chivalrous** a (man) galant.

chives [tʃaɪvz] npl ciboulette f.

chloride ['klɔːraɪd] n chlorure m. ◆**chlorine** n chlore m. ◆**chloroform** n chloroforme m.

choc-ice ['tʃɒkaɪs] n (ice cream) esquimau m.

chock [tʃɒk] n (wedge) cale f; – vt caler. **chock-a-block** [tʃɒkə'blɒk] a, **◆c.-'full** a Fam archiplein.

chocolate ['tʃɒklɪt] n chocolat m; **milk c.** chocolat au lait; **plain** or Am **bittersweet c.** chocolat à croquer; – a (cake) au chocolat; (colour) chocolat inv.

choice [tʃɔɪs] n choix m; **from c., out of c.** de son propre choix; – a (goods) de choix.

choir ['kwaɪər] n chœur m. ◆**choirboy** n jeune choriste m.

chok/e [tʃəʊk] **1** vt (person) étrangler, étouffer; (clog) boucher, engorger; **to c. back** (sobs etc) étouffer; – vi s'étran-

gler, étouffer; **to c. on** (fish bone etc) s'étrangler avec. **2** n Aut starter m. ◆**—er** n (scarf) foulard m; (necklace) collier m (de chien).

cholera ['kɒlərə] n choléra m.

cholesterol [kə'lestərɒl] n cholestérol m.

choose [tʃuːz] vt (pt chose, pp chosen) choisir (**to do** de faire); **to c. to do** (decide) juger bon de faire; – vi choisir; **as I/you/etc c.** comme il me/vous/etc plaît. ◆**choos(e)y** a (-sier, -siest) difficile (about sur).

chop [tʃɒp] **1** n (of lamb, pork) côtelette f; **to lick one's chops** Fig s'en lécher les babines; **to get the c.** Sl être flanqué à la porte. **2** vt (-pp-) couper (à la hache); (food) hacher; **to c. down** (tree) abattre; **to c. off** trancher; **to c. up** hacher. **3** vti (-pp-) **to c. and change** changer constamment d'idées, de projets etc. ◆**chopper** n hachoir m; Sl hélicoptère m. ◆**choppy** a (sea) agité.

chopsticks ['tʃɒpstɪks] npl Culin baguettes fpl.

choral ['kɔːrəl] a choral; **c. society** chorale f. ◆**chorister** ['kɒrɪstər] n choriste mf.

chord [kɔːd] n Mus accord m.

chore [tʃɔːr] n travail m (routinier); (unpleasant) corvée f; pl (domestic) travaux mpl du ménage.

choreographer [kɒrɪ'ɒgrəfər] n chorégraphe mf.

chortle ['tʃɔːt(ə)l] vi glousser; – n gloussement m.

chorus ['kɔːrəs] n chœur m; (dancers) Th troupe f; (of song) refrain m; **c. girl** girl f.

chose, chosen [tʃəʊz, 'tʃəʊz(ə)n] see **choose.**

chowder ['tʃaʊdər] n Am soupe f aux poissons.

Christ [kraɪst] n Christ m. ◆**Christian** ['krɪstʃən] a & n chrétien, -ienne (mf); **C. name** prénom m. ◆**Christi'anity** n christianisme m.

christen ['krɪs(ə)n] vt (name) & Rel baptiser. ◆**—ing** n baptême m.

Christmas ['krɪsməs] n Noël m; **at C. (time)** à (la) Noël; **Merry** or **Happy C.** Joyeux Noël; **Father C.** le père Noël; – a (tree, card, day, party etc) de Noël; **C. box** étrennes fpl.

chrome [krəʊm] n, ◆**chromium** n chrome m.

chromosome ['krəʊməsəʊm] n chromosome m.

chronic ['krɒnɪk] a (disease, state etc) chronique; (bad) Sl atroce.

chronicle ['krɒnɪk(ə)l] n chronique f; – vt faire la chronique de.

chronology [krə'nɒlədʒɪ] n chronologie f.
◆**chrono'logical** a chronologique.

chronometer [krə'nɒmɪtər] n chronomètre m.

chrysanthemum [krɪ'sænθəməm] n chrysanthème m.

chubby ['tʃʌbɪ] a (-ier, -iest) (body) dodu; (cheeks) rebondi. ◆**c.-'cheeked** a joufflu.

chuck [tʃʌk] vt Fam jeter, lancer; **to c. (in)** or **(up)** (give up) Fam laisser tomber; **to c. away** Fam balancer; (money) gaspiller; **to c. out** Fam balancer.

chuckle ['tʃʌk(ə)l] vi glousser, rire; – n gloussement m.

chuffed [tʃʌft] a Sl bien content; (displeased) Iron Sl pas heureux.

chug [tʃʌg] vi (-gg-) **to c. along** (of vehicle) avancer lentement (en faisant teuf-teuf).

chum [tʃʌm] n Fam copain m. ◆**chummy** a (-ier, -iest) Fam amical; **c. with** copain avec.

chump [tʃʌmp] n (fool) crétin, -ine mf.

chunk [tʃʌŋk] n (gros) morceau m. ◆**chunky** a (-ier, -iest) (person) Fam trapu; (coat, material etc) de grosse laine.

church [tʃɜːtʃ] n église f; (service) office m; (Catholic) messe f; **c. hall** salle f paroissiale. ◆**churchgoer** n pratiquant, -ante mf. ◆**churchyard** n cimetière m.

churlish ['tʃɜːlɪʃ] a (rude) grossier; (bad-tempered) hargneux.

churn [tʃɜːn] **1** n (for making butter) baratte f; (milk can) bidon m. **2** vt **to c. out** Pej produire (en série).

chute [ʃuːt] n glissière f; (in playground, pool) toboggan m; (for refuse) vide-ordures m inv.

chutney ['tʃʌtnɪ] n condiment m épicé (à base de fruits).

cider ['saɪdər] n cidre m.

cigar [sɪ'gɑːr] n cigare m. ◆**ciga'rette** n cigarette f; **c. end** mégot m; **c. holder** fume-cigarette m inv; **c. lighter** briquet m.

cinch [sɪntʃ] n **it's a c.** Fam (easy) c'est facile; (sure) c'est (sûr et) certain.

cinder ['sɪndər] n cendre f; **c. track** Sp cendrée f.

Cinderella [sɪndə'relə] n Liter Cendrillon f; Fig parent m pauvre.

cine-camera ['sɪnɪkæmərə] n caméra f.

cinema ['sɪnəmə] n cinéma m. ◆**cinema-goer** n cinéphile m. ◆**cinemascope** n cinémascope m.

cinnamon ['sɪnəmən] n Bot Culin cannelle f.

cipher ['saɪfər] n (code, number) chiffre m; (zero, person) Fig zéro m.

circle ['sɜːk(ə)l] n (shape, group, range etc)

cercle m; (around eyes) cerne m; Th balcon m; (of milieux) milieux m; pl (move round) faire le tour de; (word etc) entourer d'un cercle; – vi (of aircraft, bird etc) décrire des cercles. ◆**circular** a circulaire; – n (letter) circulaire f; (advertisement) prospectus m. ◆**circulate** vi circuler; – vt faire circuler. ◆**circu'lation** n circulation f; Journ tirage m; **in c.** (person) Fam dans le circuit.

circuit ['sɜːkɪt] n circuit m; Jur Th tournée f; **c. breaker** El disjoncteur m. ◆**circuitous** [sɜː'kjuːɪtəs] a (route, means) indirect. ◆**circuitry** n El circuits mpl.

circumcised ['sɜːkəmsaɪzd] a circoncis. ◆**circum'cision** n circoncision f.

circumference [sɜː'kʌmfərəns] n circonférence f.

circumflex ['sɜːkəmfleks] n circonflexe m.

circumscribe ['sɜːkəmskraɪb] vt circonscrire.

circumspect ['sɜːkəmspekt] a circonspect.

circumstance ['sɜːkəmstəns] n circonstance f; pl Com situation f; financière; **in** or **under no circumstances** en aucun cas. ◆**circum'stantial** a (evidence) Jur indirect.

circus ['sɜːkəs] n Th Hist cirque m.

cirrhosis [sɪ'rəʊsɪs] n Med cirrhose f.

cistern ['sɪstən] n (in house) réservoir m (d'eau).

citadel ['sɪtəd(ə)l] n citadelle f.

cite [saɪt] vt citer. ◆**citation** [saɪ'teɪʃ(ə)n] n citation f.

citizen ['sɪtɪz(ə)n] n Pol Jur citoyen, -enne mf; (of town) habitant, -ante mf; **Citizens' Band** Rad la CB. ◆**citizenship** n citoyenneté f.

citrus ['sɪtrəs] a **c. fruit(s)** agrumes mpl.

city ['sɪtɪ] n (grande) ville f, cité f; **c. dweller** citadin, -ine mf; **c. centre** centre-ville m inv; **c. hall** Am hôtel m de ville; **c. page** Journ rubrique f financière.

civic ['sɪvɪk] a (duty) civique; (centre) administratif; (authorities) municipal; – npl (social science) instruction f civique.

civil ['sɪv(ə)l] a **1** (rights, war, marriage etc) civil; **c. defence** défense f passive; **c. servant** fonctionnaire m; **c. service** fonction f publique. **2** (polite) civil. ◆**ci'vilian** a & n civil, -ile (mf). ◆**ci'vility** n civilité f. ◆**civilize** ['sɪvɪlaɪz] vt civiliser. ◆**civili'zation** n civilisation f.

civvies ['sɪvɪz] npl **in c.** Sl (habillé) en civil.

clad [klæd] a vêtu (**in** de).

claim [kleɪm] vt (one's due etc) revendiquer, réclamer; (require) réclamer; **to c. that**

(*assert*) prétendre que; – *n* (*demand*) prétention *f*, revendication *f*; (*statement*) affirmation *f*; (*complaint*) réclamation *f*; (*right*) droit *m*; (*land*) concession *f*; (*insurance*) c. demande d'indemnité; **to lay c. to** prétendre à. ◆**claimant** *n* allocataire *mf*.

clairvoyant [kleə'vɔɪənt] *n* voyant, -ante *f*.

clam [klæm] *n* (*shellfish*) praire *f*.

clamber ['klæmbər] *vi* **to c. (up)** grimper; **to c. up** (*stairs*) grimper; (*mountain*) gravir.

clammy ['klæmɪ] *a* (*hands etc*) moite (et froid).

clamour ['klæmər] *n* clameur *f*; – *vi* vociférer (**against** contre); **to c. for** demander à grands cris.

clamp [klæmp] *n* crampon *m*; *Carp* serre-joint(s) *m*; (*wheel*) c. *Aut* sabot *m* (de Denver); – *vt* serrer; – *vi* **to c. down** sévir (**on** contre). ◆**clampdown** *n* (*limitation*) *Fam* coup *m* d'arrêt, restriction *f*.

clan [klæn] *n* clan *m*.

clandestine [klæn'destɪn] *a* clandestin.

clang [klæŋ] *n* son *m* métallique. ◆**clanger** *n Sl* gaffe *f*; **to drop a c.** faire une gaffe.

clap [klæp] **1** *vti* (*-pp-*) (*applaud*) applaudir; **to c. (one's hands)** battre des mains; – *n* battement *m* (des mains); (*on back*) tape *f*; (*of thunder*) coup *m*. **2** *vt* (*-pp-*) (*put*) fourrer. ◆**clapped-'out** *a* (*car, person*) *Sl* crevé. ◆**clapping** *n* applaudissements *mpl*. ◆**claptrap** *n* (*nonsense*) *Fam* boniment *m*.

claret ['klærət] *n* (*wine*) bordeaux *m* rouge.

clarify ['klærɪfaɪ] *vt* clarifier. ◆**clarifi-'cation** *n* clarification *f*.

clarinet [klærɪ'net] *n* clarinette *f*.

clarity ['klærɪtɪ] *n* (*of water, expression etc*) clarté *f*.

clash [klæʃ] *vi* (*of plates, pans*) s'entrechoquer; (*of interests, armies*) se heurter; (*of colours*) jurer (**with** avec); (*of people*) se bagarrer; (*coincide*) tomber en même temps (**with** que); – *n* (*noise*) choc *m*, heurt *m*; (*of interests*) conflit *m*; (*of events*) coïncidence *f*.

clasp [klɑːsp] *vt* (*hold*) serrer; **to c. one's hands** joindre les mains; – *n* (*fastener*) fermoir *m*; (*of belt*) boucle *f*.

class [klɑːs] *n* classe *f*; (*lesson*) cours *m*; (*grade*) *Univ* mention *f*; **the c. of 1987** *Am* la promotion de 1987; – *vt* classer. ◆**classmate** *n* camarade *mf* de classe. ◆**classroom** *n* (*salle f de*) classe *f*.

classic ['klæsɪk] *a* classique; – *n* (*writer, work etc*) classique *m*; **to study classics**

étudier les humanités *fpl*. ◆**classical** *a* classique. ◆**classicism** *n* classicisme *m*.

classify ['klæsɪfaɪ] *vt* classer, classifier. ◆**—ied** *a* (*information*) secret. ◆**classifi-'cation** *n* classification *f*.

classy ['klɑːsɪ] *a* (*-ier, -iest*) *Fam* chic *inv*.

clatter ['klætər] *n* bruit *m*, fracas *m*.

clause [klɔːz] *n* *Jur* clause *f*; *Gram* proposition *f*.

claustrophobia [klɔːstrə'fəʊbɪə] *n* claustrophobie *f*. ◆**claustrophobic** *a* claustrophobe.

claw [klɔː] *n* (*of cat, sparrow etc*) griffe *f*; (*of eagle*) serre *f*; (*of lobster*) pince *f*; – *vt* (*scratch*) griffer; **to c. back** (*money etc*) *Pej Fam* repiquer, récupérer.

clay [kleɪ] *n* argile *f*.

clean [kliːn] *a* (*-er, -est*) propre; (*clear-cut*) net; (*fair*) *Sp* loyal; (*joke*) non paillard; (*record*) *Jur* vierge; **c. living** vie *f* saine; **to make a c. breast of it** tout avouer; – *adv* (*utterly*) complètement, carrément; **to break c.** se casser net; **to cut c.** couper net; – *n* **to give sth a c.** nettoyer qch; – *vt* nettoyer; (*wash*) laver; (*wipe*) essuyer; **to c. one's teeth** se brosser or se laver les dents; **to c. out** nettoyer; (*empty*) *Fig* vider; **to c. up** nettoyer; (*reform*) *Fig* épurer; – *vi* **to c. (up)** faire le nettoyage. ◆**—ing** *n* nettoyage *m*; (*housework*) ménage *m*; **c. woman** femme *f* de ménage. ◆**—er** *n* (*woman*) femme *f* de ménage; (*dry*) **c.** teinturier, -ière *mf*. ◆**—ly** *adv* (*to break, cut*) net. ◆**—ness** *n* propreté *f*. ◆**clean-'cut** *a* net. ◆**clean-'living** *a* honnête, chaste. ◆**clean-'shaven** *a* rasé (de près). ◆**clean-up** *n* *Fig* épuration *f*.

cleanliness ['klenlɪnɪs] *n* propreté *f*.

cleanse [klenz] *vt* nettoyer; (*soul, person etc*) *Fig* purifier. ◆**—ing** *a* **c. cream** crème *f* démaquillante. ◆**—er** *n* (*cream, lotion*) démaquillant *m*.

clear [klɪər] *a* (*-er, -est*) (*water, sound etc*) clair; (*glass*) transparent; (*outline, photo*) net, clair; (*mind*) lucide; (*road*) libre, dégagé; (*profit*) net; (*obvious*) évident, clair; (*certain*) certain; (*complete*) entier; **to be c. of** (*free of*) être libre de; (*out of*) être hors de; **to make oneself c.** se faire comprendre; **c. conscience** conscience *f* nette *or* tranquille; – *adv* (*quite*) complètement; **c. of** (*away from*) à l'écart de; **to keep** *or* **steer c. of** se tenir à l'écart de; **to get c. of** (*away from*) s'éloigner de; – *vt* (*path, place, table*) débarrasser, dégager; (*land*) défricher; (*fence*) franchir (sans toucher); (*obstacle*) éviter; (*person*) *Jur* disculper;

(*cheque*) compenser; (*goods, debts*) liquider; (*through customs*) dédouaner; (*for security etc*) autoriser; **to c. s.o. of** (*suspicion*) laver qn de; **to c. one's throat** s'éclaircir la gorge; – *vi* **to c. (up)** (*of weather*) s'éclaircir, (*of fog*) se dissiper. ■ **to c. away** *vt* (*remove*) enlever; – *vi* (*of fog*) se dissiper; **to c. off** *vi* (*leave*) *Fam* filer; – *vt* (*table*) débarrasser; **to c. out** *vt* (*empty*) vider; (*clean*) nettoyer; (*remove*) enlever; **to c. up** *vt* (*mystery etc*) éclaircir; – *vti* (*tidy*) ranger. ◆**—ing** *n* (*in woods*) clairière *f*. ◆**—ly** *adv* clairement; (*to understand*) bien, clairement; (*obviously*) évidemment. ◆**—ness** *n* (*of sound*) clarté *f*, netteté *f*; (*of mind*) lucidité *f*. ◆**clearance** *n* (*sale*) soldes *mpl*; (*space*) dégagement *m*; (*permission*) autorisation *f*; (*of cheque*) compensation *f*. ◆**clear-'cut** *a* net. ◆**clear-'headed** *a* lucide.

clearway ['klıƏweı] *n* route *f* à stationnement interdit.

cleavage ['kliːvıdʒ] *n* (*split*) clivage *m*; (*of woman*) *Fam* naissance *f* des seins.

cleft [kleft] *a* (*palate*) fendu; (*stick*) fourchu; – *n* fissure *f*.

clement ['klemƏnt] *a* clément. ◆**clemency** *n* clémence *f*.

clementine ['klemƏntaɪn] *n* clémentine *f*.

clench [klentʃ] *vt* (*press*) serrer.

clergy ['klɜːdʒɪ] *n* clergé *m*. ◆**clergyman** *n* (*pl* **-men**) ecclésiastique *m*.

cleric ['klerɪk] *n* *Rel* clerc *m*. ◆**clerical** *a* (*job*) d'employé; (*work*) de bureau; (*error*) d'écriture; *Rel* clérical.

clerk [klɑːk, *Am* klɜːk] *n* employé, -ée *mf* (de bureau); *Jur* clerc *m*; (*in store*) *Am* vendeur, -euse *mf*; **c. of the court** *Jur* greffier *m*.

clever ['klevƏr] *a* (**-er, -est**) intelligent; (*smart, shrewd*) astucieux; (*skilful*) habile (**at** sth à qch, **at doing** à faire); (*ingenious*) ingénieux; (*gifted*) doué; **c. at** (*English etc*) fort en; **c. with one's hands** habile *or* adroit de ses mains. ◆**—ly** *adv* intelligemment, astucieusement; habilement. ◆**—ness** *n* intelligence *f*; astuce *f*; habileté *f*.

cliché ['kliːʃeɪ] *n* (*idea*) cliché *m*.

click [klɪk] 1 *n* déclic *m*, bruit *m* sec; – *vi* faire un déclic; (*of lovers etc*) *Fam* se plaire du premier coup; **it clicked** (*I realized*) *Fam* j'ai compris tout à coup. 2 *vt* **to c. one's heels** *Mil* claquer des talons.

client ['klaɪƏnt] *n* client, -ente *mf*. ◆**clientele** [kliːƏn'tel] *n* clientèle *f*.

cliff [klɪf] *n* falaise *f*.

climate ['klaɪmɪt] *n* *Met* & *Fig* climat *m*; **c. of opinion** opinion *f* générale. ◆**cli'matic** *a* climatique.

climax ['klaɪmæks] *n* point *m* culminant; (*sexual*) orgasme *m*; – *vi* atteindre son point culminant.

climb [klaɪm] *vt* **to c. (up)** (*steps*) monter, gravir; (*hill, mountain*) gravir, faire l'ascension de; (*tree, ladder*) monter à, grimper à; **to c. (over)** (*wall*) escalader; **to c. down (from)** descendre de; – *vi* **to c. (up)** monter; (*of plant*) grimper; **to c. down** descendre; (*back down*) *Fig* en rabattre; – *n* montée *f*. ◆**—ing** *n* montée *f*; (*mountain*) **c.** alpinisme *m*. ◆**—er** *n* grimpeur, -euse *mf*; *Sp* alpiniste *mf*; *Bot* plante *f* grimpante; **social c.** arriviste *mf*.

clinch [klɪntʃ] *vt* (*deal, bargain*) conclure; (*argument*) consolider.

cling [klɪŋ] *vi* (*pt* & *pp* **clung**) se cramponner, s'accrocher (**to** à); (*stick*) adhérer (**to** à). ◆**—ing** *a* (*clothes*) collant. ◆**clingfilm** *n* scel-o-frais®*m*, film *m* étirable.

clinic ['klɪnɪk] *n* (*private*) clinique *f*; (*health centre*) centre *m* médical. ◆**clinical** *a* *Med* clinique; *Fig* scientifique, objectif.

clink [klɪŋk] *vi* tinter; – *vt* faire tinter; – *n* tintement *m*.

clip [klɪp] 1 *vt* (**-pp-**) (*cut*) couper; (*sheep*) tondre; (*hedge*) tailler; (*ticket*) poinçonner; **to c. sth out of** (*newspaper etc*) découper qch dans. 2 *n* (*for paper*) attache *f*, trombone *m*; (*of brooch, of cyclist, for hair*) pince *f*; – *vt* (**-pp-**) **to c. (on)** attacher. 3 *n* (*of film*) extrait *m*; (*blow*) *Fam* taloche *f*. ◆**clipping** *n* *Journ* coupure *f*. ◆**clippers** *npl* (*for hair*) tondeuse *f*; (*for nails*) pince *f* à ongles; (*pocket-sized, for finger nails*) coupe-ongles *m* inv.

clique [kliːk] *n* *Pej* clique *f*. ◆**cliquey** *a* *Pej* exclusif.

cloak [kləʊk] *n* (grande) cape *f*; *Fig* manteau *m*; **c. and dagger** (*film etc*) d'espionnage. ◆**cloakroom** *n* vestiaire *m*; (*for luggage*) *Rail* consigne *f*; (*lavatory*) toilettes *fpl*.

clobber ['klɒbƏr] 1 *vt* (*hit*) *Sl* rosser. 2 *n* (*clothes*) *Sl* affaires *fpl*.

clock [klɒk] *n* (*large*) horloge *f*; (*small*) pendule *f*; *Aut* compteur *m*; **against the c.** *Fig* contre la montre; **round the c.** *Fig* vingt-quatre heures sur vingt-quatre; **c. tower** clocher *m*; – *vt* *Sp* chronométrer; **to c. up** (*miles*) *Aut* *Fam* faire; **to c. in** *or* **out** (*of worker*) pointer. ◆**clockwise** *adv* dans le sens des aiguilles d'une montre. ◆**clockwork** *a* mécanique; *Fig* régulier;

– n to go like c. aller comme sur des roulettes.

clod [klɒd] n **1** (of earth) motte f. **2** (oaf) Fam balourd, -ourde mf.

clog [klɒg] **1** n (shoe) sabot m. **2** vt (-gg-) to c. (up) (obstruct) boucher.

cloister ['klɔɪstər] n cloître m; – vt cloîtrer.

close¹ [kləʊs] a (-er, -est) (place, relative etc) proche (to de); (collaboration, resemblance, connection) étroit; (friend etc) intime; (order, contest) serré; (study) rigoureux; (atmosphere) Met lourd; (vowel) fermé; **c. to** (near) près de, proche de; **c. to tears** au bord des larmes; **to have a c. shave** or **call** l'échapper belle; – adv **c. (by), c. at hand** (tout) près; **c. to** près de; **c. behind** juste derrière; **c. on** (almost) Fam pas loin de; **c. together** (to stand) serrés; **to follow c.** suivre de près; – n (enclosed area) enceinte f. ◆**c.-'cropped** a (hair) (coupé) ras. ◆**c.-'knit** a très uni. ◆**c.-up** n gros plan m.

close² [kləʊz] n fin f, conclusion f; **to bring to a c.** mettre fin à; **to draw to a c.** tirer à sa fin; – vt fermer; (discussion) terminer, clore; (opening) boucher; (road) barrer; (gap) réduire; (deal) conclure; **to c. the meeting** lever la séance; **to c. ranks** serrer les rangs; **to c. in** (enclose) enfermer; **to c. up** fermer; – vi se fermer; (end) se terminer; **to c. (up)** (of shop) fermer; (of wound) se refermer; **to c. in** (approach) approcher; **to c. in on s.o.** se rapprocher de qn. ◆ **to c. down** vti (close for good) fermer (définitivement); – vi TV terminer les émissions. ◆**c.-down** n fermeture f (définitive); TV fin f (des émissions). ◆**closing** n fermeture f; (of session) clôture f; – a final; **c. time** heure f de fermeture. ◆**closure** ['kləʊʒər] n fermeture f.

closely ['kləʊslɪ] adv (to link, guard) étroitement; (to follow) de près; (to listen) attentivement; **c. contested** très disputé; **to hold s.o. c.** tenir qn contre soi. ◆**closeness** n proximité f; (of collaboration etc) étroitesse f; (of friendship) intimité f; (of weather) lourdeur f.

closet ['klɒzɪt] n (cupboard) Am placard m; (wardrobe) Am penderie f.

clot [klɒt] n **1** (of blood) caillot m; – vt (-tt-) (blood) coaguler; – vi (of blood) se coaguler. **2** n (person) Fam imbécile mf.

cloth [klɒθ] n tissu m, étoffe f; (of linen) toile f; (woollen) drap m; (for dusting) chiffon m; (for dishes) torchon m; (tablecloth) nappe f.

cloth/e [kləʊð] vt habiller, vêtir (in de). ◆**—ing** n habillement m; (clothes) vêtements mpl; **an article of c.** un vêtement.

clothes [kləʊðz] npl vêtements mpl; **to put one's c. on** s'habiller; **c. shop** magasin m d'habillement; **c. brush** brosse f à habits; **c. peg, Am c. pin** pince f à linge; **c. line** corde f à linge.

cloud [klaʊd] n nuage m; (of arrows, insects) Fig nuée f; – vt (mind, issue) obscurcir; (window) embuer; – vi **to c. (over)** (of sky) se couvrir. ◆**cloudburst** n averse f. ◆**cloudy** a (-ier, -iest) (weather) couvert, nuageux; (liquid) trouble.

clout [klaʊt] **1** n (blow) Fam taloche f; – vt Fam flanquer une taloche à, talocher. **2** n Pol Fam influence f, pouvoir m.

clove [kləʊv] n clou m de girofle; **c. of garlic** gousse f d'ail.

clover ['kləʊvər] n trèfle m.

clown [klaʊn] n clown m; – vi **to c. (around)** faire le clown.

cloying ['klɔɪɪŋ] a écœurant.

club [klʌb] n **1** (weapon) matraque f, massue f; (golf) c. (stick) club m; – vt (-bb-) matraquer. **2** n (society) club m, cercle m; – vi (-bb-) to c. together se cotiser (to buy pour acheter). **3** n & npl Cards trèfle m. ◆**clubhouse** n pavillon m.

clubfoot ['klʌbfʊt] n pied m bot. ◆**club-'footed** a pied bot inv.

cluck [klʌk] vi (of hen) glousser.

clue [kluː] n indice m; (of crossword) définition f; (to mystery) clef f; **I don't have a c.** Fam je n'en ai pas la moindre idée. ◆**clueless** a Fam stupide.

clump [klʌmp] n (of flowers, trees) massif m.

clumsy ['klʌmzɪ] a (-ier, -iest) maladroit; (shape) lourd; (tool) peu commode. ◆**clumsily** adv maladroitement. ◆**clumsiness** n maladresse f.

clung [klʌŋ] see cling.

cluster ['klʌstər] n groupe m; (of flowers) grappe f; (of stars) amas m; – vi se grouper.

clutch [klʌtʃ] **1** vt (hold tight) serrer, étreindre; (cling to) se cramponner à; (grasp) saisir; – vi **to c. at** essayer de saisir; – n étreinte f. **2** n (apparatus) Aut embrayage m; (pedal) pédale f d'embrayage. **3** npl **s.o.'s clutches** (power) les griffes fpl de qn.

clutter ['klʌtər] n (objects) fouillis m, désordre m; – vt **to c. (up)** encombrer (with de).

cm abbr (centimetre) cm.

co- [kəʊ] pref co-.

Co abbr (company) Cie.

coach [kəʊtʃ] **1** n (horse-drawn) carrosse m; Rail voiture f, wagon m; Aut autocar m. **2** n (person) Sch répétiteur, -trice mf; Sp entraîneur *m*; – *vt* (*pupil*) donner des leçons (particulières) à; (*sportsman etc*) entraîner; **to c. s.o. for** (*exam*) préparer qn à. ◆**coachman** *n* (*pl* -**men**) cocher *m*.

coagulate [kəʊˈægjʊlett] *vi* (*of blood*) se coaguler; – *vt* coaguler.

coal [kəʊl] *n* charbon *m*; *Geol* houille *f*; – *a* (*basin etc*) houiller; (*merchant, fire*) de charbon; (*cellar, bucket*) à charbon. ◆**coalfield** *n* bassin *m* houiller. ◆**coalmine** *n* mine *f* de charbon.

coalition [kəʊəˈlɪʃ(ə)n] *n* coalition *f*.

coarse [kɔːs] *a* (-**er**, -**est**) (*person, manners*) grossier, vulgaire; (*surface*) rude; (*fabric*) grossier; (*salt*) gros; (*accent*) commun, vulgaire. ◆**ness** *n* grossièreté *f*; vulgarité *f*.

coast [kəʊst] *n* côte *f*; – *vi* (**down** *or* **along**) (*of vehicle etc*) descendre en roue libre. ◆**coastal** *a* côtier. ◆**coaster** *n* (*ship*) caboteur *m*; (*for glass etc*) dessous *m* de verre, rond *m*. ◆**coastguard** *n* (*person*) garde *m* maritime, garde-côte *m*. ◆**coastline** *n* littoral *m*.

coat [kəʊt] *n* manteau *m*; (*overcoat*) pardessus *m*; (*jacket*) veste *f*; (*of animal*) pelage *m*; (*of paint*) couche *f*; **c. of arms** blason *m*, armoiries *fpl*; **c. hanger** cintre *m*; – *vt* couvrir, enduire (**with de**); (*with chocolate*) enrober (**with de**). ◆**ed** *a* **c. tongue** langue *f* chargée. ◆**ing** *n* couche *f*.

coax [kəʊks] *vt* amadouer, cajoler; **to c. s.o. to do** *or* **into doing** amadouer qn pour qu'il fasse. ◆**ing** *n* cajoleries *fpl*.

cob [kɒb] *n* **corn on the c.** épi *m* de maïs.

cobble [ˈkɒb(ə)l] *n* pavé *m*; – *vt* **to c. together** (*text etc*) *Fam* bricoler. ◆**cobbled** *a* pavé. ◆**cobblestone** *n* pavé *m*.

cobbler [ˈkɒblər] *n* cordonnier *m*.

cobra [ˈkəʊbrə] *n* (*snake*) cobra *m*.

cobweb [ˈkɒbweb] *n* toile *f* d'araignée.

cocaine [kəʊˈkeɪn] *n* cocaïne *f*.

cock [kɒk] **1** *n* (*rooster*) coq *m*; (*male bird*) (*oiseau m*) mâle *m*. **2** *vt* (*gun*) armer; **to c. (up)** (*ears*) dresser. ◆**c.-a-doodle-'doo** *n* & *int* cocorico (*m*). ◆**c.-and-'bull story** *n* histoire *f* à dormir debout.

cockatoo [kɒkəˈtuː] *n* (*bird*) cacatoès *m*.

cocker [ˈkɒkər] *n* **c. (spaniel)** cocker *m*.

cockerel [ˈkɒkərəl] *n* jeune coq *m*, coquelet *m*.

cock-eyed [kɒkˈaɪd] *a Fam* **1** (*cross-eyed*) bigleux. **2** (*crooked*) de travers. **3** (*crazy*) absurde, stupide.

cockle [ˈkɒk(ə)l] *n* (*shellfish*) coque *f*.

cockney [ˈkɒknɪ] *a* & *n* cockney (*mf*).

cockpit [ˈkɒkpɪt] *n Av* poste *m* de pilotage.

cockroach [ˈkɒkrəʊtʃ] *n* (*beetle*) cafard *m*.

cocksure [kɒkˈʃʊər] *a Fam* trop sûr de soi.

cocktail [ˈkɒkteɪl] *n* (*drink*) cocktail *m*; (*fruit*) **c.** macédoine *f* (de fruits); **c. party** cocktail *m*; **prawn c.** crevettes *fpl* à la mayonnaise.

cocky [ˈkɒkɪ] *a* (-**ier**, -**iest**) *Fam* trop sûr de soi, arrogant.

cocoa [ˈkəʊkəʊ] *n* cacao *m*.

coconut [ˈkəʊkənʌt] *n* noix *f* de coco; **c. palm** cocotier *m*.

cocoon [kəˈkuːn] *n* cocon *m*.

cod [kɒd] *n* morue *f*; (*bought fresh*) cabillaud *m*. ◆**c.-liver 'oil** *n* huile *f* de foie de morue.

COD [siːəʊˈdiː] *abbr* (*cash on delivery*) livraison *f* contre remboursement.

coddle [ˈkɒd(ə)l] *vt* dorloter.

code [kəʊd] *n* code *m*; – *vt* coder. ◆**ing** *n* codage *m*. ◆**codify** *vt* codifier.

co-educational [kəʊedjuˈkeɪʃən(ə)l] *a* (*school, teaching*) mixte.

coefficient [kəʊɪˈfɪʃənt] *n Math* coefficient *m*.

coerce [kəʊˈɜːs] *vt* contraindre. ◆**coercion** *n* contrainte *f*.

coexist [kəʊɪɡˈzɪst] *vi* coexister. ◆**coexistence** *n* coexistence *f*.

coffee [ˈkɒfɪ] *n* café *m*; **white c.** café *m* au lait; (*ordered in restaurant etc*) (café) *m* crème *m*; **black c.** café *m* noir, café nature; **c. bar, c. house** café *m*, cafétéria *f*; **c. break** pause-café *f*; **c. table** table *f* basse. ◆**coffeepot** *n* cafetière *f*.

coffers [ˈkɒfəz] *npl* (*funds*) coffres *mpl*.

coffin [ˈkɒfɪn] *n* cercueil *m*.

cog [kɒɡ] *n Tech* dent *f*; (*person*) *Fig* rouage *m*.

cogent [ˈkəʊdʒənt] *a* (*reason, argument*) puissant, convaincant.

cogitate [ˈkɒdʒɪteɪt] *vi Iron* cogiter.

cognac [ˈkɒnjæk] *n* cognac *m*.

cohabit [kəʊˈhæbɪt] *vi* (*of unmarried people*) vivre en concubinage.

coherent [kəʊˈhɪərənt] *a* cohérent; (*speech*) compréhensible. ◆**cohesion** *n* cohésion *f*. ◆**cohesive** *a* cohésif.

cohort [ˈkəʊhɔːt] *n* (*group*) cohorte *f*.

coil [kɔɪl] *n* (*of wire etc*) rouleau *m*; *El* bobine *f*; (*contraceptive*) stérilet *m*; – *vt* (*rope, hair*) enrouler; – *vi* (*of snake etc*) s'enrouler.

coin [kɔɪn] *n* pièce *f* (de monnaie); (*currency*) monnaie *f*; – *vt* (*money*) frapper; (*word*) *Fig* inventer, forger; **to c. a phrase** pour ainsi dire. ◆**c.-operated** *a* automatique. ◆**coinage** n (coins) monnaie f; Fig invention f.

coincide [kəʊɪnˈsaɪd] vi coïncider (**with** avec). ◆**co'incidence** n coïncidence f. ◆**coinci'dental** a fortuit; **it's c.** c'est une coïncidence.

coke [kəʊk] n **1** (fuel) coke m. **2** (Coca-Cola®) coca m.

colander [ˈkʌləndər] n (for vegetables etc) passoire f.

cold [kəʊld] n froid m; Med rhume m; **to catch c.** prendre froid; **out in the c.** Fig abandonné, en carafe; – a (-**er**, -**est**) froid; **to be** or **feel c.** (of person) avoir froid; **my hands are c.** j'ai les mains froides; **it's c.** (of weather) il fait froid; **to get c.** (of weather) se refroidir; (of food) refroidir; **to get c. feet** Fam se dégonfler; **in c. blood** de sang-froid; **c. cream** crème f de beauté; **c. meats**, Am **c. cuts** Culin assiette f anglaise. ◆**c.-'blooded** a (person) cruel, insensible; (act) de sang-froid. ◆**c.-'shoulder** vt snober. ◆**coldly** adv avec froideur. ◆**coldness** n froideur f.

coleslaw [ˈkəʊlslɔː] n salade f de chou cru.

colic [ˈkɒlɪk] n Med coliques fpl.

collaborate [kəˈlæbəreɪt] vi collaborer (**on** à). ◆**collabo'ration** n collaboration f. ◆**collaborator** n collaborateur, -trice mf.

collage [ˈkɒlɑːʒ] n (picture) collage m.

collapse [kəˈlæps] vi (fall) s'effondrer, s'écrouler; (of government) tomber; (faint) Med se trouver mal; – n effondrement m, écroulement m; (of government) chute f. ◆**collapsible** a (chair etc) pliant.

collar [ˈkɒlər] n (on garment) col m; (of dog) collier m; **to seize by the c.** saisir au collet; – vt Fam saisir (qn) au collet; Fig Fam retenir (qn); (take, steal) Sl piquer. ◆**collarbone** n clavicule f.

collate [kəˈleɪt] vt collationner, comparer (**with** avec).

colleague [ˈkɒliːg] n collègue mf, confrère m.

collect [kəˈlekt] vt (pick up) ramasser; (gather) rassembler, recueillir; (taxes) percevoir; (rent, money) encaisser; (stamps etc as hobby) collectionner; (fetch, call for) (passer) prendre; – vi (of dust) s'accumuler; (of people) se rassembler; **to c. for** (in street, church) quêter pour; – adv **to call** or **phone c.** Am téléphoner en PCV. ◆**collection** [kəˈlekʃ(ə)n] n ramassage m; (of taxes) perception f; (of objects) collection f; (of poems) recueil m; (of money in church etc) quête f; (of mail) levée f. ◆**collective** a collectif. ◆**collectively** adv

collectivement. ◆**collector** n (of stamps etc) collectionneur, -euse mf.

college [ˈkɒlɪdʒ] n Pol Rel Sch collège m; (university) université f; Mus conservatoire m; **teachers' training c.** école f normale; **art c.** école f des beaux-arts; **agricultural c.** institut m d'agronomie, lycée m agricole.

collide [kəˈlaɪd] vi entrer en collision (**with** avec), se heurter (**with** à). ◆**collision** n collision f; Fig conflit m, collision f.

colliery [ˈkɒliəri] n houillère f.

colloquial [kəˈləʊkwiəl] a (word etc) familier. ◆**colloquialism** n expression f familière.

collusion [kəˈluːʒ(ə)n] n collusion f.

collywobbles [ˈkɒliwɒb(ə)lz] npl **to have the c.** (feel nervous) Fam avoir la frousse.

cologne [kəˈləʊn] n eau f de Cologne.

colon [ˈkəʊlən] n **1** Gram deux-points m inv. **2** Anat côlon m.

colonel [ˈkɜːn(ə)l] n colonel m.

colony [ˈkɒləni] n colonie f. ◆**colonial** [kəˈləʊniəl] a colonial. ◆**coloni'zation** n colonisation f. ◆**colonize** vt coloniser.

colossal [kəˈlɒs(ə)l] a colossal.

colour [ˈkʌlər] n couleur f; – a (photo, television) en couleurs; (television set) couleur inv; (problem) racial; **c. supplement** Journ supplément m illustré; **off c.** (not well) mal fichu; (improper) scabreux; – vt colorer; **to c. (in)** (drawing) colorier. ◆—**ed** a (person, pencil) de couleur; (glass, water) coloré. ◆—**ing** n coloration f; (with crayons) coloriage m; (hue, effect) coloris m; (matter) colorant m. ◆**colour-blind** a daltonien. ◆**colourful** a (crowd, story) coloré; (person) pittoresque.

colt [kəʊlt] n (horse) poulain m.

column [ˈkɒləm] n colonne f. ◆**columnist** n Journ chroniqueur m; **gossip c.** échotier, -ière mf.

coma [ˈkəʊmə] n coma m; **in a c.** dans le coma.

comb [kəʊm] n peigne m; – vt peigner; (search) Fig ratisser; **to c. one's hair** se peigner; **to c. out** (hair) démêler.

combat [ˈkɒmbæt] n combat m; – vti combattre (**for** pour). ◆**combatant** n combattant, -ante mf.

combine¹ [kəmˈbaɪn] vt unir, joindre (**with** à); (elements, sounds) combiner; (qualities, efforts) allier, joindre; – vi s'unir; **everything combined to** .... tout s'est ligué pour .... ◆—**ed** a (effort) conjugué; **c. wealth/etc** (of people) richesses/etc réunies; **c. forces** Mil forces fpl alliées. ◆**combi'nation** n combinaison f; (of *qualities*) réunion *f*; (*of events*) concours *m*; **in c. with** en association avec.

combine² ['kɒmbaɪn] *n Com* cartel *m*; **c. harvester** *Agr* moissonneuse-batteuse *f*.

combustion [kəm'bʌstʃ(ə)n] *n* combustion *f*.

come [kʌm] *vi* (*pt* **came**, *pp* **come**) venir (**from** de, **to** à); (*arrive*) arriver, venir; (*happen*) arriver; **c. and see me** viens me voir; **I've just c. from** j'arrive de; **to c. for** venir chercher; **to c. home** rentrer; **coming!** j'arrive!; **c. now!** voyons!; **to c. as a surprise** (**to**) surprendre; **to c. near** *or* **close to doing** faillir faire; **to c. on page 2** se trouver à la page 2; **nothing came of it** ça n'a abouti à rien; **to c. to** (*decision*) parvenir à; **to c. to an end** toucher à sa fin; **to c. true** se réaliser; **c. May/***etc** *Fam* au mai/*etc*; **the life to c.** la vie future; **how c. that...?** *Fam* comment se fait-il que...? ■ **to c. about** *vi* (*happen*) se faire, arriver; **to c. across** *vi* (*of speech*) faire de l'effet; (*of feelings*) se montrer; – *vt* (*thing, person*) tomber sur; **to c. along** *vi* venir (**with** avec); (*progress*) avancer; **c. along!** allons!; **to c. at** (*attack*) attaquer; **to c. away** *vi* (*leave, come off*) partir; **to c. back** *vi* revenir; (*return home*) rentrer; ◆**come-back** *n* retour *m*; *Th Pol* rentrée *f*; (*retort*) réplique *f*; **to c. by** *vt* (*obtain*) obtenir; (*find*) trouver; **to c. down** *vi* descendre; (*of rain, price*) tomber; ◆**comedown** *n Fam* humiliation *f*; **to c. forward** *vi* (*make oneself known, volunteer*) se présenter; **to c. forward with** offrir, suggérer; **to c. in** *vi* entrer; (*of tide*) monter; (*of train, athlete*) arriver; *Pol* arriver au pouvoir; (*of clothes*) devenir à la mode, se faire beaucoup; (*of money*) rentrer; **to c. in for** recevoir; **to c. into** (*money*) hériter de; **to c. off** *vi* se détacher, partir; (*succeed*) réussir; (*happen*) avoir lieu; (*fare, manage*) s'en tirer; – *vt* (*fall from*) tomber de; (*get down from*) descendre de; **to c. on** *vi* (*follow*) suivre; (*progress*) avancer; (*start*) commencer; (*arrive*) arriver; (*of play*) être joué; **c. on!** allez!; **to c. out** *vi* sortir; (*of sun, book*) paraître; (*of stain*) s'enlever, partir; (*of secret*) être révélé; (*of photo*) réussir; **to c. out (on strike)** se mettre en grève; **to c. over** *vi* (*visit*) venir, passer; **to c. over funny** *or* **peculiar** se trouver mal; – *vt* (*take hold of*) saisir (*qn*); **to c. round** *vi* (*visit*) venir, passer; (*recur*) revenir; (*regain consciousness*) revenir à soi; **to c. through** *vi* (*survive*) s'en tirer; – *vt* se tirer indemne de; **to c. to** *vi* (*regain consciousness*) revenir à soi; (*amount to*) *Com* revenir à, faire; **to c. under** *vi* être classé sous; (*s.o.'s influence*) tomber sous; **to c. up** *vi* (*rise*) monter; (*of plant*) sortir; (*of question, job*) se présenter; **to c. up against** (*wall, problem*) se heurter à; **to c. up to** (*reach*) arriver jusqu'à; (*one's hopes*) répondre à; **to c. up with** (*idea, money*) trouver; **to c. upon** *vt* (*book, reference etc*) tomber sur. ◆**coming** *a* (*future*) à venir; – *n Rel* avènement *m*; **comings and goings** allées *fpl* et venues.

comedy ['kɒmɪdɪ] *n* comédie *f*. ◆**co'median** *n* (*actor* *m*) comique *m*, actrice *f* comique.

comet ['kɒmɪt] *n* comète *f*.

comeuppance [kʌm'ʌpəns] *n* **he got his c.** *Pej Fam* il n'a eu que ce qu'il mérite.

comfort ['kʌmfət] *n* confort *m*; (*consolation*) réconfort *m*, consolation *f*; (*peace of mind*) tranquillité *f* d'esprit; **to like one's comforts** aimer ses aises *fpl*; **c. station** *Am* toilettes *fpl*; – *vt* consoler; (*cheer*) réconforter. ◆**—able** *a* (*chair, house etc*) confortable; (*rich*) aisé; **he's c.** (*in chair etc*) il est à l'aise, il est bien; **make yourself c.** mets-toi à l'aise. ◆**—ably** *adv* **c. off** (*rich*) à l'aise. ◆**—er** *n* (*baby's dummy*) sucette *f*; (*quilt*) *Am* édredon *m*. ◆**comfy** *a* (**-ier, -iest**) (*chair etc*) *Fam* confortable; **I'm c.** je suis bien.

comic ['kɒmɪk] *a* comique; – *n* (*actor*) comique *m*; (*actress*) actrice *f* comique; (*magazine*) illustré *m*; **c. strip** bande *f* dessinée. ◆**comical** *a* comique, drôle.

comma ['kɒmə] *n Gram* virgule *f*.

command [kə'mɑːnd] *vt* (*order*) commander (**s.o. to do** à qn de faire); (*control, dominate*) commander (*régiment, vallée etc*); (*be able to use*) disposer de; (*respect*) imposer (**from** à); (*require*) exiger; – *vi* commander; – *n* ordre *m*; (*power*) commandement *m*; (*troops*) troupes *fpl*; (*mastery*) maîtrise *f* (**of** de); **at one's c.** (*disposal*) à sa disposition; **to be in c. (of)** (*ship, army etc*) commander; (*situation*) être maître (de). ◆**—ing** *a* (*authoritative*) imposant; (*position*) dominant; **c. officer** commandant *m*. ◆**—er** *n* chef *m*; *Mil* commandant *m*. ◆**—ment** *n Rel* commandement *m*.

commandant ['kɒməndænt] *n Mil* commandant *m* (*d'un camp etc*). ◆**comman'deer** *vt* réquisitionner.

commando [kə'mɑːndəʊ] *n* (*pl* **-os** *or* **-oes**) *Mil* commando *m*.

commemorate [kə'meməreɪt] *vt* commémorer. ◆**commemo'ration** *n* commémoration f. ◆**commemorative** a commémoratif.

commence [kə'mens] vti commencer (**doing** à faire). ◆**—ment** n commencement m; Univ Am remise f des diplômes.

commend [kə'mend] vt (praise) louer; (recommend) recommander; (entrust) confier (**to** à). ◆**—able** a louable. ◆**commen'dation** n éloge m.

commensurate [kə'menʃərət] a proportionné (**to, with** à).

comment ['kɒment] n commentaire m, remarque f; – vi faire des commentaires or des remarques (**on** sur); **to c. on** (text, event, news item) commenter; **to c. that** remarquer que. ◆**commentary** n commentaire m; (**live**) **c.** TV Rad reportage m. ◆**commentate** vi TV Rad faire un reportage (**on** sur). ◆**commentator** n TV Rad reporter m, commentateur, -trice mf.

commerce ['kɒmɜːs] n commerce m. ◆**co'mmercial 1** a commercial; (street) commerçant; (traveller) de commerce. **2** n (advertisement) TV publicité f; **the commercials** TV la publicité. ◆**co'mmercialize** vt (event) Pej transformer en une affaire de gros sous.

commiserate [kə'mɪzəreɪt] vi **to c. with s.o.** s'apitoyer sur le sort de qn. ◆**commise'ration** n commisération f.

commission [kə'mɪʃ(ə)n] n (fee, group) commission f; (order for work) commande f; **out of c.** hors service; **to get one's c.** Mil être nommé officier; – vt (artist) passer une commande à; (book) commander; Mil nommer (qn) officier; **to c. to do** charger de faire. ◆**commissio'naire** n (in hotel etc) commissionnaire m. ◆**commissioner** n Pol commissaire m; (**police**) **c.** préfet m (de police).

commit [kə'mɪt] vt (-tt-) (crime) commettre; (entrust) confier (**to** à); **to c. suicide** se suicider; **to c. to memory** apprendre par cœur; **to c. to prison** incarcérer; **to c. oneself** s'engager (**to** à); (compromise oneself) se compromettre. ◆**—ment** n obligation f; (promise) engagement m.

committee [kə'mɪtɪ] n comité m.

commodity [kə'mɒdɪtɪ] n produit m, article m.

common ['kɒmən] **1** a (-er, -est) (shared, vulgar) commun; (frequent) courant, fréquent, commun; **the c. man** l'homme m du commun; **in c.** (shared) en commun (**with** avec); **to have nothing in c.** n'avoir rien de commun (**with** avec); **in c. with** (like) comme; **c. law** droit m coutumier; **C.**

Market Marché m commun; **c. room** salle f commune; **c. or garden** ordinaire. **2** n (land) terrain m communal; **House of Commons** Pol Chambre f des Communes; **the Commons** Pol les Communes fpl. ◆**—er** n roturier, -ière mf. ◆**—ly** adv (generally) communément; (vulgarly) d'une façon commune. ◆**—ness** n fréquence f; (vulgarity) vulgarité f. ◆**commonplace** a banal; – n banalité f. ◆**common'sense** n sens m commun; – a sensé.

Commonwealth ['kɒmənwelθ] n **the C.** le Commonwealth.

commotion [kə'məʊʃ(ə)n] n agitation f.

communal [kə'mjuːn(ə)l] a (of the community) communautaire; (shared) commun. ◆**—ly** adv en communauté; (to live) en communauté.

commune 1 ['kɒmjuːn] n (district) commune f; (group) communauté f. **2** [kə'mjuːn] vi Rel & Fig communier (**with** avec). ◆**co'mmunion** n communion f; (**Holy**) **C.** communion f.

communicate [kə'mjuːnɪkeɪt] vt communiquer; (illness) transmettre; – vi (of person, rooms etc) communiquer. ◆**communi'cation** n communication f; **c. cord** Rail signal m d'alarme. ◆**communicative** a communicatif. ◆**communiqué** n Pol communiqué m.

communism ['kɒmjunɪz(ə)m] n communisme m. ◆**communist** a & n communiste (mf).

community [kə'mjuːnɪtɪ] n communauté f; – a (rights, life etc) communautaire; **the student c.** les étudiants mpl; **c. centre** centre m socio-culturel; **c. worker** animateur, -trice mf socio-culturel(le).

commute [kə'mjuːt] **1** vt Jur commuer (**to** en). **2** vi (travel) faire la navette (**to work** pour se rendre à son travail). ◆**—ing** n trajets mpl journaliers. ◆**—er** n banlieusard, -arde mf; **c. train** train m de banlieue.

compact 1 [kəm'pækt] a (car, crowd, substance) compact; (style) condensé; **c. disc** ['kɒmpækt] disque m compact. **2** ['kɒmpækt] n (for face powder) poudrier m.

companion [kəm'pænjən] n (person) compagnon m, compagne f; (handbook) manuel m. ◆**companionship** n camaraderie f.

company ['kʌmpənɪ] n (fellowship, firm) compagnie f; (guests) invités, -ées mfpl; **to keep s.o. c.** tenir compagnie à qn; **to keep good c.** avoir de bonnes fréquentations; **he's good c.** c'est un bon compagnon.

compar/e [kəm'peər] vt comparer; **compared to** or **with** en comparaison de; – vi être comparable, se comparer (**with** à). ◆**–able** ['kɒmpərəb(ə)l] a comparable. ◆**comparative** a comparatif; (relative) relatif. ◆**comparatively** adv relativement. ◆**comparison** n comparaison f (**between** entre; **with** à, avec).

compartment [kəm'pɑːtmənt] n compartiment m. ◆**compart'mentalize** vt compartimenter.

compass ['kʌmpəs] n 1 (for navigation) boussole f; Nau compas m; (range) Fig portée f. 2 (for measuring etc) Am compas m; (**pair of**) **compasses** compas m.

compassion [kəm'pæʃ(ə)n] n compassion f. ◆**compassionate** a compatissant; **on c. grounds** pour raisons de famille.

compatible [kəm'pætɪb(ə)l] a ◆**compati'bility** n compatibilité f.

compatriot [kəm'pætrɪət, kəm'peɪtrɪət] n compatriote mf.

compel [kəm'pel] vt (**-ll-**) contraindre (**to do** à faire); (respect etc) imposer (**from** à); **compelled to do** contraint de faire. ◆**compelling** a irrésistible.

compendium [kəm'pendɪəm] n abrégé m.

compensate ['kɒmpənseɪt] vt **to s.o.** (with payment, recompense) dédommager qn (**for** de); **to c. for sth** (make up for) compenser qch; – vi compenser. ◆**compen'sation** n (financial) dédommagement m; (consolation) compensation f, dédommagement m; **in c. for** en compensation de.

compère ['kɒmpeər] n TV Rad animateur, -trice mf, présentateur, -trice mf; – vt (a show) animer, présenter.

compete [kəm'piːt] vi prendre part (**in** à), concourir (**in** à); (vie) rivaliser (**with** avec); Com faire concurrence (**with** à); **to c. for** (prize etc) concourir pour; **to c. in a rally** courir dans un rallye.

competent ['kɒmpɪtənt] a (capable) compétent (**to do** pour faire); (sufficient) suffisant. ◆**–ly** adv avec compétence. ◆**competence** n compétence f.

competition [kɒmpə'tɪʃ(ə)n] n (rivalry) compétition f, concurrence f; (contest) un concours; Sp une compétition. ◆**com-'petitive** a (price, market) compétitif; (selection) par concours; (person) aimant la compétition; **c. exam(ination)** concours m. ◆**com'petitor** n concurrent, -ente mf.

compil/e [kəm'paɪl] vt (dictionary) rédiger; (list) dresser; (documents) compiler. ◆**–er** n rédacteur, -trice mf.

complacent [kəm'pleɪsənt] a content de

soi. ◆**complacence** n, ◆**complacency** n autosatisfaction f, contentement m de soi.

complain [kəm'pleɪn] vi se plaindre (**of, about** de; **that** que). ◆**complaint** n plainte f; Com réclamation f; Med maladie f; (**cause for**) **c.** sujet m de plainte.

complement ['kɒmplɪmənt] n complément m; – ['kɒmplɪment] vt compléter. ◆**comple-'mentary** a complémentaire.

complete [kəm'pliːt] a (total) complet; (finished) achevé; (downright) Pej parfait; – vt (add sth missing) compléter; (finish) achever; (a form) remplir. ◆**–ly** adv complètement. ◆**completion** n achèvement m, réalisation f.

complex ['kɒmpleks] 1 a complexe. 2 n (feeling, buildings) complexe m; **housing c.** grand ensemble m. ◆**com'plexity** n complexité f.

complexion [kəm'plekʃ(ə)n] n (of the face) teint m; Fig caractère m.

compliance [kəm'plaɪəns] n (agreement) conformité f (**with** avec).

complicat/e ['kɒmplɪkeɪt] vt compliquer. ◆**–ed** a compliqué. ◆**compli'cation** n complication f.

complicity [kəm'plɪsɪtɪ] n complicité f.

compliment ['kɒmplɪmənt] n compliment m; pl (of author) hommages mpl; **compliments of the season** meilleurs vœux pour Noël et la nouvelle année; – ['kɒmplɪment] vt complimenter. ◆**compli'mentary** a 1 (flattering) flatteur. 2 (free) à titre gracieux; (ticket) de faveur.

comply [kəm'plaɪ] vi obéir (**with** à); (request) accéder à.

component [kəm'pəʊnənt] a (part) constituant; – n (chemical, electronic) composant m; Tech pièce f; (element) Fig composante f.

compos/e [kəm'pəʊz] vt composer; **to c. oneself** se calmer. ◆**–ed** a calme. ◆**–er** n Mus compositeur, -trice mf. ◆**compo-'sition** n Mus Liter Ch composition f; Sch rédaction f. ◆**composure** n calme m, sang-froid m.

compost ['kɒmpɒst, Am 'kɒmpəʊst] n compost m.

compound 1 ['kɒmpaʊnd] n (substance, word) composé m; (area) enclos m; – a Ch composé; (sentence, number) complexe. 2 [kəm'paʊnd] vt Ch compliquer; (increase) Fig aggraver.

comprehend [kɒmprɪ'hend] vt comprendre. ◆**comprehensible** a compréhensible. ◆**comprehension** n compréhension *f.* ◆**comprehensive** *a* complet; (*knowledge*) étendu; (*view, measure*) d'ensemble; (*insurance*) tous-risques *inv*; – *a* & *n* **c. (school)** = collège *m* d'enseignement secondaire.

compress [kəm'pres] *vt* comprimer; (*ideas etc*) *Fig* condenser. ◆**compression** *n* compression *f*; condensation *f*.

comprise [kəm'praɪz] *vt* comprendre, englober.

compromise ['kɒmprəmaɪz] *vt* compromettre; – *vi* accepter un compromis; – *n* compromis *m*; – *a* (*solution*) de compromis.

compulsion [kəm'pʌlʃ(ə)n] *n* contrainte *f*. ◆**compulsive** *a* (*behaviour*) *Psy* compulsif; (*smoker, gambler*) invétéré; **c. liar** mythomane *mf*.

compulsory [kəm'pʌlsərɪ] *a* obligatoire.

compunction [kəm'pʌŋkʃ(ə)n] *n* scrupule *m.*

comput/e [kəm'pjuːt] *vt* calculer. ◆**—ing** *n* informatique *f.* ◆**computer** *n* ordinateur *m*; – *a* (*system*) informatique; (*course*) d'informatique; **c. operator** opérateur, -trice *mf* sur ordinateur; **c. science** informatique *f*; **c. scientist** informaticien, -ienne *mf.* ◆**computerize** *vt* informatiser.

comrade ['kɒmreɪd] *n* camarade *mf.* ◆**comradeship** *n* camaraderie *f.*

con [kɒn] *vt* (**-nn-**) *Sl* rouler, escroquer; **to be conned** se faire avoir ou rouler; – *n Sl* escroquerie *f*; **c. man** escroc *m.*

concave ['kɒnkeɪv] *a* concave.

conceal [kən'siːl] *vt* (*hide*) dissimuler (**from s.o.** à qn); (*plan etc*) tenir secret. ◆**—ment** *n* dissimulation *f.*

concede [kən'siːd] *vt* concéder (**to** à, **that** que); – *vi* céder.

conceit [kən'siːt] *n* vanité *f.* ◆**conceited** *a* vaniteux. ◆**conceitedly** *adv* avec vanité.

conceiv/e [kən'siːv] *vt* (*idea, child etc*) concevoir; – *vi* (*of woman*) concevoir; **to c. of** concevoir. ◆**—able** *a* concevable, envisageable. ◆**—ably** *adv* **yes, c.** oui, c'est concevable.

concentrate ['kɒnsəntreɪt] *vt* concentrer; – *vi* se concentrer (**on** sur); **to c. on doing** s'appliquer à faire. ◆**concen'tration** *n* concentration *f*; **c. camp** camp *m* de concentration.

concentric [kən'sentrɪk] *a* concentrique.

concept ['kɒnsept] *n* concept *m.* ◆**con-'ception** *n* (*idea*) & *Med* conception *f.*

concern [kən'sɜːn] *vt* concerner; **to c. oneself with, be concerned with** s'occuper de; **to be concerned about** s'inquiéter de; –

n (*matter*) affaire *f*; (*anxiety*) inquiétude *f*; (*share*) *Com* intérêt(s) *m*(*pl*) (**in** dans); (*business*) **c.** entreprise *f.* ◆**—ed** *a* (*anxious*) inquiet; **the department c.** le service compétent; **the main person c.** le principal intéressé. ◆**—ing** *prep* en ce qui concerne.

concert ['kɒnsət] *n* concert *m*; **in c.** (*together*) de concert (**with** avec). ◆**c.-goer** *n* habitué, -ée *mf* des concerts. ◆**con'certed** *a* (*effort*) concerté.

concertina [kɒnsə'tiːnə] *n* concertina *m*; **c. crash** *Aut* carambolage *m.*

concession [kən'seʃ(ə)n] *n* concession *f* (**to** à).

conciliate [kən'sɪlɪeɪt] *vt* **to c. s.o.** (*win over*) se concilier qn; (*soothe*) apaiser qn. ◆**concili'ation** *n* conciliation *f*; apaisement *m.* ◆**conciliatory** [kən'sɪlɪətərɪ, *Am* -tɔːrɪ] *a* conciliant.

concise [kən'saɪs] *a* concis. ◆**—ly** *adv* avec concision. ◆**—ness** *n*, ◆**concision** *n* concision *f.*

conclud/e [kən'kluːd] *vt* (*end, settle*) conclure; **to c. that** (*infer*) conclure que; – *vi* (*of event etc*) se terminer (**with** par); (*of speaker*) conclure. ◆**—ing** *a* final. ◆**conclusion** *n* conclusion *f*; **in c.** pour conclure. ◆**conclusive** *a* concluant. ◆**conclusively** *adv* de manière concluante.

concoct [kən'kɒkt] *vt* *Culin Pej* concocter, confectionner; (*scheme*) *Fig* combiner. ◆**concoction** *n* (*substance*) *Pej* mixture *f*; (*act*) confection *f*; *Fig* combinaison *f.*

concord ['kɒŋkɔːd] *n* concorde *f.*

concourse ['kɒŋkɔːs] *n* (*hall*) *Am* hall *m*; *Rail* hall *m*, salle *f* des pas perdus.

concrete ['kɒŋkriːt] **1** *a* (*real, positive*) concret. **2** *n* béton *m*; – *a* en béton; **c. mixer** bétonnière *f*, bétonneuse *f.*

concur [kən'kɜːr] *vi* (**-rr-**) **1** (*agree*) être d'accord (**with** avec). **2** **to c. to** (*contribute*) concourir à.

concurrent [kən'kʌrənt] *a* simultané. ◆**—ly** *adv* simultanément.

concussion [kən'kʌʃ(ə)n] *n Med* commotion *f* (*cérébrale*).

condemn [kən'dem] *vt* condamner; (*building*) déclarer inhabitable. ◆**condem-'nation** *n* condamnation *f.*

condense [kən'dens] *vt* condenser; – *vi* se condenser. ◆**conden'sation** *n* condensation *f* (**of** de); (*mist*) buée *f.*

condescend [kɒndɪ'send] *vi* condescendre (**to do** à faire). ◆**condescension** *n* condescendance *f.*

condiment ['kɒndɪmənt] *n* condiment *m.*

condition [kənˈdɪʃ(ə)n] **1** n (*stipulation, circumstance, rank*) condition f; (*state*) état m, condition f; **on c. that one does** à condition de faire, à condition que l'on fasse; **in/out of c.** en bonne/mauvaise forme. **2** vt (*action etc*) déterminer, conditionner; **to c. s.o.** Psy conditionner qn (**into doing** à faire). ◆**conditional** a conditionnel; **to be c. upon** dépendre de. ◆**conditioner** n (*hair*) après-shampooing m.

condo [ˈkɒndəʊ] n abbr (pl -os) Am = **condominium**.

condolences [kənˈdəʊlənsɪz] npl condoléances fpl.

condom [ˈkɒndəm] n préservatif m, capote f (anglaise).

condominium [kɒndəˈmɪnɪəm] n Am (*building*) (immeuble m en) copropriété f; (*apartment*) appartement m dans un copropriété.

condone [kənˈdəʊn] vt (*forgive*) pardonner; (*overlook*) fermer les yeux sur.

conducive [kənˈdjuːsɪv] a **c. to** favorable à.

conduct [ˈkɒndʌkt] n (*behaviour, directing*) conduite f; – [kənˈdʌkt] vt (*lead*) conduire, mener; (*orchestra*) diriger; (*electricity etc*) conduire; **to c. oneself** se conduire. ◆—**ed** a (*visit*) guidé; **c. tour** excursion f accompagnée. ◆**conductor** n Mus chef m d'orchestre; (*on bus*) receveur m; Rail Am chef m de train; (*metal, cable etc*) conducteur m. ◆**conductress** n (*on bus*) receveuse f.

cone [kəʊn] n cône m; (*of ice cream*) cornet m; (*paper*) c. cornet m (de papier); **traffic c.** cône m de chantier.

confectioner [kənˈfekʃənər] n (*sweets*) confiseur, -euse mf; (*of cakes*) pâtissier, -ière mf. ◆**confectionery** n (*sweets*) confiserie f; (*cakes*) pâtisserie f.

confederate [kənˈfedərət] a confédéré; – n (*accomplice*) complice mf, acolyte m. ◆**confederacy** n, ◆**confede'ration** n confédération f.

confer [kənˈfɜːr] **1** vt (**-rr-**) (*grant*) conférer (**on** à); (*degree*) Univ remettre. **2** vi (**-rr-**) (*talk together*) conférer, se consulter.

conference [ˈkɒnfərəns] n conférence f; (*scientific etc*) congrès m.

confess [kənˈfes] **1** vt avouer, confesser (**that que, to** à); – vi avouer; **to c.** (**to** à) (*crime etc*) avouer, confesser. **2** vt Rel confesser; – vi se confesser. ◆**confession** n aveu m, confession f; Rel confession f. ◆**confessional** n Rel confessionnal m.

confetti [kənˈfetɪ] n confettis mpl.

confide [kənˈfaɪd] vt confier (**to** à, **that** que);

– vi **to c. in** (*talk to*) se confier à. ◆**confidant, -ante** [-ænt] n confident, -ente mf. ◆**confidence** n (*trust*) confiance f; (*secret*) confidence f; (*self-*)**c.** confiance f en soi; **in c.** en confidence; **motion of no c.** Pol motion f de censure; **c. trick** escroquerie f; **c. trickster** escroc m. ◆**confident** a sûr, assuré; (*self-*)**c.** sûr de soi. ◆**confidential** a confidentiel; (*secretary*) particulier. ◆**confidentially** adv en confidence. ◆**confidently** adv avec confiance.

configuration [kənfɪgjʊˈreɪʃ(ə)n] n configuration f.

confine [kənˈfaɪn] vt enfermer, confiner (**to, in** dans); (*limit*) limiter (**to** à); **to c. oneself to doing** se limiter à faire. ◆—**ed** a (*atmosphere*) confiné; (*space*) réduit; **c. to bed** obligé de garder le lit. ◆—**ment** n Med couches fpl; Jur emprisonnement m. ◆**confines** npl limites fpl, confins mpl.

confirm [kənˈfɜːm] vt confirmer (**that** que); (*strengthen*) raffermir. ◆—**ed** a (*bachelor*) endurci; (*smoker, habit*) invétéré. ◆**confir'mation** n confirmation f; raffermissement m.

confiscate [ˈkɒnfɪskeɪt] vt confisquer (**from** s.o. à qn). ◆**confis'cation** n confiscation f.

conflagration [kɒnfləˈgreɪʃ(ə)n] n (*grand*) incendie m, brasier m.

conflict [ˈkɒnflɪkt] n conflit m; – [kənˈflɪkt] vi être en contradiction, être incompatible (**with** avec); (*of dates, events, TV programmes*) tomber en même temps (**with** que). ◆—**ing** a (*views, theories etc*) contradictoires; (*dates*) incompatibles.

confluence [ˈkɒnfluːəns] n (*of rivers*) confluent m.

conform [kənˈfɔːm] vi se conformer (**to, with** à); (*of ideas etc*) être en conformité. ◆**conformist** a & n conformiste (mf). ◆**conformity** n (*likeness*) conformité f; Pej conformisme m.

confound [kənˈfaʊnd] vt confondre; **c. him!** que le diable l'emporte! ◆—**ed** a (*damned*) Fam sacré.

confront [kənˈfrʌnt] vt (*danger*) affronter; (*problems*) faire face à; **to c. s.o.** (*be face to face with*) se trouver en face de qn; (*oppose*) s'opposer à qn; **to c. s.o. with** (*person*) confronter qn avec; (*thing*) mettre qn en présence de. ◆**confron'tation** n confrontation f.

confuse [kənˈfjuːz] vt (*perplex*) confondre; (*muddle*) embrouiller; **to c. with** (*mistake for*) confondre avec. ◆—**ed** a (*situation,* *noises etc*) confus; **to be c.** (*of person*) s'y perdre; **to get c.** s'embrouiller. ◆**-ing** *a* difficile à comprendre, déroutant. ◆**confusion** *n* confusion *f*; **in c.** en désordre.

congeal [kən'dʒiːl] *vt* figer; – *vi* (se) figer.

congenial [kən'dʒiːnɪəl] *a* sympathique.

congenital [kən'dʒenɪtəl] *a* congénital.

congested [kən'dʒestɪd] *a* (*street*) encombré; (*town*) surpeuplé; *Med* congestionné. ◆**congestion** *n* (*traffic*) encombrement(s) *m(pl)*; (*overcrowding*) surpeuplement *m*; *Med* congestion *f*.

Congo ['kɒŋgəʊ] *n* Congo *m*.

congratulate [kən'grætjʊleɪt] *vt* féliciter (**s.o. on sth** qn de qch). ◆**congratu'lations** *npl* félicitations *fpl* (**on** pour). ◆**congratu'latory** *a* (*telegram etc*) de félicitations.

congregate ['kɒŋgrɪgeɪt] *vi* se rassembler. ◆**congre'gation** *n* (*worshippers*) assemblée *f*, fidèles *mfpl*.

congress ['kɒŋgres] *n* congrès *m*; **C.** *Pol Am* le Congrès. ◆**Congressman** *n* (*pl* -men) *Am* membre *m* du Congrès. ◆**Con'gressional** *a Am* du Congrès.

conic(al) ['kɒnɪk(ə)l] *a* conique.

conifer ['kɒnɪfər] *n* (*tree*) conifère *m*.

conjecture [kən'dʒektʃər] *n* conjecture *f*; – *vt* conjecturer; – *vi* faire des conjectures. ◆**conjectural** *a* conjectural.

conjugal ['kɒndʒʊgəl] *a* conjugal.

conjugate ['kɒndʒʊgeɪt] *vt* (*verb*) conjuguer. ◆**conju'gation** *n Gram* conjugaison *f*.

conjunction [kən'dʒʌŋkʃ(ə)n] *n Gram* conjonction *f*; **in c. with** conjointement avec.

conjur/e ['kʌndʒər] *vt* **to c. (up)** (*by magic*) faire apparaître; **to c. up** (*memories etc*) *Fig* évoquer. ◆**-ing** *n* prestidigitation *f*. ◆**-er** *n* prestidigitateur, -trice *mf*.

conk [kɒŋk] **1** *n* (*nose*) *Sl* pif *m*. **2 to c. out** (*break down*) *Fam* claquer, tomber en panne.

conker ['kɒŋkər] *n* (*horse-chestnut fruit*) *Fam* marron *m* (d'Inde).

connect [kə'nekt] *vt* relier (**with, to** à); (*telephone, stove etc*) brancher; **to c. with** *Tel* mettre en communication avec; (*in memory*) associer avec; – *vi* **to be connected** (*of events etc*) être relié; **to c. with** (*of train, bus*) assurer la correspondance avec. ◆**-ed** *a* (*facts etc*) lié, connexe; (*speech*) suivi; **to be c. with** (*have dealings with*) être lié à; (*have to do with, relate to*) avoir rapport à; (*by marriage*) être allié à. ◆**connection** *n* (*link*) rapport *m*, relation *f* (**with** avec); (*train, bus etc*) correspondance *f*; (*phone call*) communication *f*; (*between pipes etc*) *Tech* raccord *m*; *pl* (*contacts*) relations *fpl*; **in c. with** à propos de.

connive [kə'naɪv] *vi* **to c. at** fermer les yeux sur; **to c. to do** se mettre de connivence pour (faire (**with** avec); **to c. together** agir en complicité. ◆**connivance** *n* connivence *f*.

connoisseur [kɒnə'sɜːr] *n* connaisseur *m*.

connotation [kɒnə'teɪʃ(ə)n] *n* connotation *f*.

conquer ['kɒŋkər] *vt* (*country, freedom etc*) conquérir; (*enemy, habit*) vaincre. ◆**-ing** *a* victorieux. ◆**conqueror** *n* conquérant, -ante *mf*, vainqueur *m*. ◆**conquest** *n* conquête *f*.

cons [kɒnz] *npl* **the pros and (the) c.** le pour et le contre.

conscience ['kɒnʃəns] *n* conscience *f*. ◆**c.-stricken** *a* pris de remords.

conscientious [kɒnʃɪ'enʃəs] *a* consciencieux; **c. objector** objecteur *m* de conscience. ◆**-ness** *n* application *f*, sérieux *m*.

conscious ['kɒnʃəs] *a* conscient (**of sth** de qch); (*intentional*) délibéré; *Med* conscient; **to be c. of doing** avoir conscience de faire. ◆**-ly** *adv* (*knowingly*) consciemment. ◆**-ness** *n* conscience *f* (**of** de); *Med* connaissance *f*.

conscript ['kɒnskrɪpt] *n Mil* conscrit *m*; – [kən'skrɪpt] *vt* enrôler (par conscription). ◆**con'scription** *n* conscription *f*.

consecrate ['kɒnsɪkreɪt] *vt* (*church etc*) *Rel* consacrer. ◆**conse'cration** *n* consécration *f*.

consecutive [kən'sekjʊtɪv] *a* consécutif. ◆**-ly** *adv* consécutivement.

consensus [kən'sensəs] *n* consensus *m*, accord *m* (général).

consent [kən'sent] *vi* consentir (**to** à); – *n* consentement *m*; **by common c.** de l'aveu de tous; **by mutual c.** d'un commun accord.

consequence ['kɒnsɪkwəns] *n* (*result*) conséquence *f*; (*importance*) importance *f*, conséquence *f*. ◆**consequently** *adv* par conséquent.

conservative [kən'sɜːvətɪv] **1** *a* (*estimate*) modeste; (*view*) traditionnel. **2** *a & n* **C.** *Pol* conservateur, -trice (*mf*). ◆**conservatism** *n* (*in behaviour*) & *Pol Rel* conservatisme *m*.

conservatoire [kən'sɜːvətwɑːr] *n Mus* conservatoire *m*.

conservatory [kən'sɜːvətrɪ] *n* (*greenhouse*) serre *f*.

conserve [kən'sɜːv] *vt* préserver, conserver;

(one's strength) ménager; **to c. energy** faire des économies d'énergie. ◆**conser'vation** n (energy-saving) économies fpl d'énergie; (of nature) protection f de l'environnement; Phys conservation f.

consider [kənˈsɪdər] vt considérer; (take into account) tenir compte de; **I'll c. it** j'y réfléchirai; **to c. doing** envisager de faire; **to c. that** estimer or considérer que; **he's or she's being considered (for the job)** sa candidature est à l'étude; **all things considered** en fin de compte. ◆**as prep** (all things considered) étant donné, vu. ◆**-able** a (large) considérable; (much) beaucoup de. ◆**-ably** adv beaucoup de, considérablement. ◆**consideration** n (thought, thoughtfulness, reason) considération f; **under c.** à l'étude; **out of c. for** par égard pour; **to take into c.** prendre en considération.

considerate [kənˈsɪdərət] a plein d'égards (to pour), attentionné (to à l'égard de).

consign [kənˈsaɪn] vt (send) expédier; (give, entrust) confier (to à). ◆**-ment** n (act) expédition f; (goods) arrivage m.

consist [kənˈsɪst] vi consister (of en, in dans, in doing à faire).

consistent [kənˈsɪstənt] a logique, conséquent; (coherent) cohérent; (friend) fidèle; **c. with** compatible avec, conforme à. ◆**-ly** adv (logically) avec logique; (always) constamment. ◆**consistency** n 1 logique f; cohérence f. 2 (of liquid etc) consistance f.

console¹ [kənˈsəʊl] vt consoler. ◆**consolation** n consolation f; **c. prize** prix m de consolation.

console² [ˈkɒnsəʊl] n (control desk) Tech console f.

consolidate [kənˈsɒlɪdeɪt] vt consolider; — vi se consolider. ◆**consolidation** n consolidation f.

consonant [ˈkɒnsənənt] n consonne f.

consort 1 [ˈkɒnsɔːt] n époux m, épouse f; **prince c.** prince m consort. **2** [kənˈsɔːt] vi to **c. with** Pej fréquenter.

consortium [kənˈsɔːtɪəm] n Com consortium m.

conspicuous [kənˈspɪkjʊəs] a visible, en évidence; (striking) remarquable, manifeste; (showy) voyant; **to be c. by one's absence** briller par son absence; **to make oneself c.** se faire remarquer. ◆**-ly** adv visiblement.

conspire [kənˈspaɪər] vi 1 (plot) conspirer (against contre); **to c. to do** comploter de faire. 2 **to c. to do** (of events) conspirer à faire. ◆**conspiracy** n conspiration f.

constable [ˈkʌnstəb(ə)l] n (police) **c.** agent m (de police). ◆**con'stabulary** n la police.

constant [ˈkɒnstənt] a (frequent) incessant; (unchanging) constant; (faithful) fidèle. ◆**constancy** n constance f. ◆**constantly** adv constamment, sans cesse.

constellation [kɒnstəˈleɪʃ(ə)n] n constellation f.

consternation [kɒnstəˈneɪʃ(ə)n] n consternation f.

constipate [ˈkɒnstɪpeɪt] vt constiper. ◆**consti'pation** n constipation f.

constituent [kənˈstɪtjʊənt] **1** a (element etc) constituant, constitutif. **2** n Pol électeur, -trice mf. ◆**constituency** n circonscription f électorale; (voters) électeurs mpl.

constitute [ˈkɒnstɪtjuːt] vt constituer. ◆**consti'tution** n (of person etc) & Pol constitution f. ◆**consti'tutional** a Pol constitutionnel.

constrain [kənˈstreɪn] vt contraindre.

constrict [kənˈstrɪkt] vt (tighten, narrow) resserrer; (movement) gêner. ◆**con'striction** n resserrement m.

construct [kənˈstrʌkt] vt construire. ◆**construction** n construction f; **under c.** en construction. ◆**constructive** a constructif.

construe [kənˈstruː] vt interpréter, comprendre.

consul [ˈkɒnsəl] n consul m. ◆**consular** a consulaire. ◆**consulate** n consulat m.

consult [kənˈsʌlt] vt consulter; — vi to **c. with** discuter avec, conférer avec. ◆**-ing** a (room) Med de consultation; (physician) consultant. ◆**consultancy** n c. (firm) Com cabinet m d'experts-conseils; **c. fee** honoraires mpl de conseils. ◆**consultant** n conseiller, -ère mf; Med spécialiste mf; (financial, legal) conseil m, expert-conseil m; — a (engineer etc) consultant. ◆**consul'tation** n consultation f. ◆**consultative** a consultatif.

consum/e [kənˈsjuːm] vt (food, supplies etc) consommer; (of fire, grief, hate) consumer. ◆**-ing** a (ambition) brûlant. ◆**-er** n consommateur, -trice mf; **c. goods/society** biens mpl/société f de consommation. ◆**con'sumption** n consommation f (of de).

consummate [ˈkɒnsəmət] a (perfect) consommé.

contact [ˈkɒntækt] n contact m; (person) relation f; **in c. with** en contact avec; **c. lenses** lentilles fpl or verres mpl de contact; — vt se mettre en contact avec, contacter.

contagious [kənˈteɪdʒəs] a contagieux.

contain [kənˈteɪn] vt (enclose, hold back) contenir; **to c. oneself** se contenir. ◆**—er** n récipient m; (for transporting freight) conteneur m, container m.

contaminate [kənˈtæmɪneɪt] vt contaminer. ◆**contami'nation** n contamination f.

contemplate [ˈkɒntəmpleɪt] vt (look at) contempler; (consider) envisager (doing de faire). ◆**contem'plation** n contemplation f; **in c.** en prévision de.

contemporary [kənˈtempərərɪ] a contemporain (with de); – n (person) contemporain, -aine mf.

contempt [kənˈtempt] n mépris m; **to hold in c.** mépriser. ◆**contemptible** a méprisable. ◆**contemptuous** a dédaigneux (of de).

contend [kənˈtend] **1** vi **to c. with** (problem) faire face à; (person) avoir affaire à; (compete) rivaliser avec; (struggle) se battre avec. **2** vt **to c. that** (claim) soutenir que. ◆**—er** n concurrent, -ente mf. ◆**contention** n **1** (argument) dispute f. **2** (claim) affirmation f. ◆**contentious** a (issue) litigieux.

content¹ [kənˈtent] a satisfait (with de); **he's c. to do** il ne demande pas mieux que de faire. ◆**—ed** a satisfait. ◆**—ment** n contentement m.

content² [ˈkɒntent] n (of text, film etc) contenu m; pl (of container) contenu m; **(table of) contents** (of book) table f des matières; **alcoholic/iron/etc c.** teneur f en alcool/fer/etc.

contest [kənˈtest] vt (dispute) contester; (fight for) disputer; – [ˈkɒntest] n (competition) concours m; (fight) lutte f; Boxing combat m. ◆**con'testant** n concurrent, -ente mf; (in fight) adversaire mf.

context [ˈkɒntekst] n contexte m.

continent [ˈkɒntɪnənt] n continent m; **the C.** l'Europe f (continentale). ◆**conti'nental** a continental; européen; **c. breakfast** petit déjeuner m à la française.

contingent [kənˈtɪndʒənt] **1** a (accidental) contingent; **to be c. upon** dépendre de. **2** nm Mil contingent m. ◆**contingency** n éventualité f; **c. plan** plan m d'urgence.

continu/e [kənˈtɪnjuː] vt continuer (**to do** or **doing** à or de faire); (resume) reprendre; **to c. (with)** (work, speech etc) poursuivre, continuer; – vi continuer; (resume) reprendre; **to c. in** (job) garder. ◆**—ed** a (interest, attention etc) soutenu, assidu; (presence) continu(el); **to be c.** (of story) à suivre. ◆**continual** a continuel. ◆**continually**

adv continuellement. ◆**continuance** n continuation f. ◆**continu'ation** n continuation f; (resumption) reprise f; (new episode) suite f. ◆**continuity** [kɒntɪˈnjuːɪtɪ] n continuité f. ◆**continuous** a continu; Cin performance Cin spectacle m permanent. ◆**continuously** adv sans interruption.

contort [kənˈtɔːt] vt (twist) tordre; **to c. oneself** se contorsionner. ◆**contortion** n contorsion f. ◆**contortionist** n (acrobat) contorsionniste mf.

contour [ˈkɒntuər] n contour m.

contraband [ˈkɒntrəbænd] n contrebande f.

contraception [kɒntrəˈsepʃ(ə)n] n contraception f. ◆**contraceptive** a & n contraceptif (m).

contract 1 [ˈkɒntrækt] n contrat m; **c. work** travail m en sous-traitance; – vt **to c. out of** (agreement etc) se dégager de. **2** [kənˈtrækt] vt (habit, debt, muscle etc) contracter; – vi (of heart etc) se contracter. ◆**con'traction** n (of muscle, word) contraction f. ◆**con'tractor** n entrepreneur m.

contradict [kɒntrəˈdɪkt] vt contredire; (belie) démentir. ◆**contradiction** n contradiction f. ◆**contradictory** a contradictoire.

contralto [kənˈtræltəʊ] n (pl -os) contralto m.

contraption [kənˈtræpʃ(ə)n] n Fam machin m, engin m.

contrary [ˈkɒntrərɪ] a contraire (**to** à); – adv **c. to** contrairement à; – n contraire m; **on the c.** au contraire; **unless you, I etc hear to the c.** sauf avis contraire; **she said nothing to the c.** elle n'a rien dit contre. **2** [kənˈtreərɪ] a (obstinate) entêté, difficile.

contrast 1 [ˈkɒntrɑːst] n contraste m; **in c. to** par opposition à. **2** [kənˈtrɑːst] vi contraster (with avec); – vt faire contraster, mettre en contraste. ◆**—ing** a (colours etc) opposés.

contravene [kɒntrəˈviːn] vt (law) enfreindre. ◆**contravention** n **in c. of** en contravention de.

contribute [kənˈtrɪbjuːt] vt donner, fournir (**to** à); (article) écrire (**to** pour); **to c. money** to contribuer à, verser de l'argent à; – vi **to c. to** contribuer à; (publication) collaborer à. ◆**contri'bution** n contribution f; (to pension fund etc) cotisation(s) f(pl); Journ article m. ◆**contributor** n Journ collaborateur, -trice mf; (of money) donateur, -trice mf. ◆**contributory** a **a c. factor** un facteur qui a contribué (**in** à).

contrite [kənˈtraɪt] a contrit. ◆**contrition** n contrition f.

contriv/e [kənˈtraɪv] vt inventer; **to c. to do**

trouver moyen de faire. ◆—ed *a* artificiel.
◆**contrivance** *n* (*device*) dispositif *m*;
(*scheme*) invention *f*.

control [kən'trəʊl] *vt* (-ll-) (*business, organization*) diriger; (*traffic*) régler; (*prices, quality*) contrôler; (*emotion, reaction*) maîtriser, contrôler; (*disease*) enrayer; (*situation*) être maître de; **to c. oneself** se contrôler; – *n* (*authority*) autorité *f* (**over** sur); (*of traffic*) réglementation *f*; (*of prices etc*) contrôle *m*; (*of emotion etc*) maîtrise *f*, *pl* (*of train etc*) commandes *fpl*; (*knobs*) TV Rad boutons *mpl*; **the c. of** (*fires etc*) la lutte contre; (**self-)c.** le contrôle de soi-même; **to keep s.o. under c.** tenir qn; **everything is under c.** tout est en ordre; **in c.** of maître de; **to lose c. of** (*situation, vehicle*) perdre le contrôle de; **out of c.** (*situation, crowd*) difficilement maîtrisable; **c. tower** *Av* tour *f* de contrôle. ◆**controller** *n* **air traffic c.** aiguilleur *m* du ciel.

controversy ['kɒntrəvɜːsɪ] *n* controverse *f*. ◆**contro'versial** *a* (*book, author*) contesté, discuté; (*doubtful*) discutable.

conundrum [kə'nʌndrəm] *n* devinette *f*, énigme *f*; (*mystery*) énigme *f*.

conurbation [kɒnɜː'beɪʃ(ə)n] *n* agglomération *f*, conurbation *f*.

convalesce [kɒnvə'les] *vi* être en convalescence. ◆**convalescence** *n* convalescence *f*. ◆**convalescent** *n* convalescent, -ente *mf*; **c. home** maison *f* de convalescence.

convector [kən'vektər] *n* radiateur *m* à convection.

convene [kən'viːn] *vt* convoquer; – *vi* se réunir.

convenient [kən'viːnɪənt] *a* commode, pratique; (*well-situated*) bien situé (**for the shops**/*etc* par rapport aux magasins/*etc*); (*moment*) convenable, opportun; **to be c. (for)** (*suit*) convenir (à). ◆—**ly** *adv* (*to arrive*) à propos; **c. situated** bien situé. ◆**convenience** *n* commodité *f*; (*comfort*) confort *m*; (*advantage*) avantage *m*; **to** *or* **at one's c.** à sa convenance; **c. food(s)** plats *mpl* *or* aliments *mpl* minute; **(public) conveniences** toilettes *fpl*.

convent ['kɒnvənt] *n* couvent *m*.

convention [kən'venʃ(ə)n] *n* (*agreement*) & *Am Pol* convention *f*; (*custom*) usage *m*, convention *f*; (*meeting*) Pol assemblée *f*. ◆**conventional** *a* conventionnel.

converge [kən'vɜːdʒ] *vi* converger. ◆—**ing** *a* convergent. ◆**convergence** *n* convergence *f*.

conversant [kən'vɜːsənt] *a* **to be c. with**

(*custom etc*) connaître; (*fact*) savoir; (*cars etc*) s'y connaître en.

conversation [kɒnvə'seɪʃ(ə)n] *n* conversation *f*. ◆**conversational** *a* (*tone*) de la conversation; (*person*) loquace. ◆**conversationalist** *n* causeur, -euse *mf*.

converse [kən'vɜːs] *vi* s'entretenir (**with** avec). **2** ['kɒnvɜːs] *a* & *n* inverse (*m*). ◆**con'versely** *adv* inversement.

convert [kən'vɜːt] *vt* (*change*) convertir (**into** en); (*building*) aménager (**into** en); **to c. s.o.** convertir qn (**to** à); – ['kɒnvɜːt] *n* converti, -ie *mf*. ◆**con'version** *n* conversion *f*; aménagement *m*. ◆**con'vertible** *a* convertible; – *n* (*car*) (voiture *f*) décapotable *f*.

convex ['kɒnveks] *a* convexe.

convey [kən'veɪ] *vt* (*goods, people*) transporter; (*sound, message, order*) transmettre; (*idea*) communiquer; (*evoke*) évoquer; (*water etc through pipes*) amener. ◆**conveyance** *n* transport *m*; *Aut* véhicule *m*. ◆**conveyor** *a* **c. belt** tapis *m* roulant.

convict ['kɒnvɪkt] *n* forçat *m*; – [kən'vɪkt] *vt* déclarer coupable, condamner. ◆**con'viction** *n* Jur condamnation *f*; (*belief*) conviction *f*; **to carry c.** (*of argument etc*) être convaincant.

convince [kən'vɪns] *vt* convaincre, persuader. ◆—**ing** *a* convaincant. ◆—**ingly** *adv* de façon convaincante.

convivial [kən'vɪvɪəl] *a* joyeux, gai; (*person*) bon vivant.

convoke [kən'vəʊk] *vt* (*meeting etc*) convoquer.

convoluted [kɒnvə'luːtɪd] *a* (*argument, style*) compliqué, tarabiscoté.

convoy ['kɒnvɔɪ] *n* (*ships, cars, people*) convoi *m*.

convulse [kən'vʌls] *vt* bouleverser, ébranler; (*face*) contracter. ◆**convulsion** *n* convulsion *f*. ◆**convulsive** *a* convulsif.

coo [kuː] *vi* (*of dove*) roucouler.

cook [kʊk] *vt* (faire) cuire; (*accounts*) Fam truquer; **to c. up** Fam inventer; – *vi* (*of food*) cuire; (*of person*) faire la cuisine; **what's cooking?** Fam qu'est-ce qui se passe?; – *n* (*person*) cuisinier, -ière *mf*. ◆—**ing** *n* cuisine *f*; **c. apple** pomme *f* à cuire. ◆—**er** *n* (*stove*) cuisinière *f*; (*apple*) pomme *f* à cuire. ◆**cookbook** *n* livre *m* de cuisine. ◆**cookery** *n* cuisine *f*; **c. book** livre *m* de cuisine.

cookie ['kʊkɪ] *Am* biscuit *m*, gâteau *m* sec.

cool [kuːl] *a* (**-er, -est**) (*weather, place etc*) frais; (*manner, person*) calme; (*reception etc*) froid; (*impertinent*) Fam effronté; **I feel**

c. j'ai (un peu) froid; **a c. drink** une boisson fraîche; **a c. £50** la coquette somme de 50 livres; – n (of evening) fraîcheur f; **to keep (in the) c.** tenir au frais; **to keep/lose one's c.** garder/perdre son sang-froid; – vi **to c. (down)** refroidir, rafraîchir; – vi **to c. (down or off)** (of enthusiasm) se refroidir; (of anger, angry person) se calmer; (of hot liquid) refroidir; **to c. off** (refresh oneself by drinking, bathing etc) se rafraîchir; **to c. off towards s.o.** se refroidir envers qn. ◆**—ing** n (of air, passion etc) refroidissement m. ◆**—er** n (for food) glacière f. ◆**—ly** adv calmement; (to welcome) froidement; (boldly) effrontément. ◆**—ness** n fraîcheur f; (unfriendliness) froideur f. ◆**cool-'headed** a calme.

coop [kuːp] **1** n (for chickens) poulailler m. **2** vt **to c. up** (person) enfermer.

co-op ['kəʊɒp] n Am appartement m en copropriété.

co-operate [kəʊ'ɒpəreɪt] vi coopérer (**in** à, **with** avec). ◆**co-ope'ration** n coopération f. ◆**co-operative** a coopératif; – n coopérative f.

co-opt [kəʊ'ɒpt] vt coopter.

co-ordinate [kəʊ'ɔːdɪneɪt] vt coordonner. ◆**co-ordinates** [kəʊ'ɔːdɪnəts] npl Math coordonnées fpl; (clothes) coordonnés mpl. ◆**co-ordi'nation** n coordination f.

cop [kɒp] **1** n (policeman) Fam flic m. **2** vt (-pp-) (catch) Sl piquer. **3** vi (-pp-) **to c. out** Sl se défiler, éviter ses responsabilités.

cope [kəʊp] vi **to c. with** s'occuper de; (problem) faire face à; (to be able to) **c.** (savoir) se débrouiller.

co-pilot ['kəʊpaɪlət] n copilote m.

copious ['kəʊpɪəs] a copieux.

copper ['kɒpər] n **1** cuivre m; pl (coins) petite monnaie f. **2** (policeman) Fam flic m.

coppice ['kɒpɪs], **copse** [kɒps] n taillis m.

copulate ['kɒpjʊleɪt] vi s'accoupler. ◆**copu'lation** n copulation f.

copy ['kɒpɪ] n copie f; (of book etc) exemplaire m; Phot épreuve f; – vti copier; – vt **to c. out** or **down** (re)copier. ◆**copyright** n copyright m.

coral ['kɒrəl] n corail m; **c. reef** récif m de corail.

cord [kɔːd] n **1** (of curtain, pyjamas etc) cordon m; El cordon m électrique; **vocal cords** cordes fpl vocales. **2** npl Fam velours m, pantalon m en velours (côtelé).

cordial ['kɔːdɪəl] a **1** (friendly) cordial. **2** n (fruit) c. sirop m.

cordon ['kɔːdən] n cordon m; – vt **to c. off** (place) boucler, interdire l'accès à.

corduroy ['kɔːdərɔɪ] n (fabric) velours m côtelé; pl pantalon m en velours (côtelé), velours m.

core [kɔːr] n (of fruit) trognon m; (of problem) cœur m; (group of people) & Geol El noyau m; – vt (apple) vider. ◆**corer** n vide-pomme m.

cork [kɔːk] n liège m; (for bottle) bouchon m; – vt **to c. (up)** (bottle) boucher. ◆**corkscrew** n tire-bouchon m.

corn [kɔːn] n **1** (wheat) blé m; (maize) Am maïs m; (seed) grain m; **c. on the cob** épi m de maïs. **2** (hard skin) cor m. ◆**corned beef** corned-beef m, singe m. ◆**cornflakes** npl céréales fpl. ◆**cornflour** n farine f de maïs, maïzena® f. ◆**cornflower** n bleuet m. ◆**cornstarch** n Am = cornflour.

cornea ['kɔːnɪə] n Anat cornée f.

corner ['kɔːnər] n **1** coin m; (of street, room) coin m, angle m; (bend in road) virage m; Fb corner m; **in a (tight) c.** dans une situation difficile. **2** vt (animal, enemy etc) acculer; (person in corridor etc) Fig coincer, accrocher; (market) Com accaparer; – vi Aut prendre un virage. ◆**cornerstone** n pierre f angulaire.

cornet ['kɔːnɪt] n (of ice cream etc) & Mus cornet m.

Cornwall ['kɔːnwəl] n Cornouailles fpl. ◆**Cornish** a de Cornouailles.

corny ['kɔːnɪ] a (-ier, -iest) (joke etc) rebattu.

corollary [kə'rɒlərɪ, Am 'kɒrələrɪ] n corollaire m.

coronary ['kɒrənərɪ] n Med infarctus m.

coronation [kɒrə'neɪʃ(ə)n] n couronnement m, sacre m.

coroner ['kɒrənər] n Jur coroner m.

corporal ['kɔːpərəl] n **1** Mil caporal(-chef) m. **2** a **c. punishment** châtiment m corporel.

corporation [kɔːpə'reɪʃ(ə)n] n (business) société f commerciale; (of town) conseil m municipal. ◆**corporate** a collectif; **c. body** corps m constitué.

corps [kɔːr, pl kɔːz] n Mil Pol corps m.

corpse [kɔːps] n cadavre m.

corpulent ['kɔːpjʊlənt] a corpulent. ◆**corpulence** n corpulence f.

corpus ['kɔːpəs] n Ling corpus m.

corpuscle ['kɔːpʌs(ə)l] n Med globule m.

corral [kə'ræl] n Am corral m.

correct [kə'rekt] a (right, accurate) exact, correct; (proper) correct; **he's c.** il a raison; – vt corriger. ◆**—ly** adv correctement.

◆**—ness** n (accuracy, propriety) correction f. ◆**correction** n correction f. ◆**corrective** a (act, measure) rectificatif.

correlate ['kɒrəleɪt] vi correspondre (**with** à); – vt faire correspondre. ◆**corre'lation** n corrélation f.

correspond [kɒrɪ'spɒnd] vi **1** (agree, be similar) correspondre (**to** à, **with** avec). **2** (by letter) correspondre (**with** avec). ◆**—ing** a (matching) correspondant; (similar) semblable. ◆**correspondence** n correspondance f; **c. course** cours m par correspondance. ◆**correspondent** n correspondant, -ante mf; Journ envoyé, -ée mf.

corridor ['kɒrɪdɔːr] n couloir m, corridor m.

corroborate [kə'rɒbəreɪt] vt corroborer.

corrode [kə'rəʊd] vt ronger, corroder; – vi se corroder. ◆**corrosion** n corrosion f. ◆**corrosive** a corrosif.

corrugated ['kɒrəgeɪtɪd] a (cardboard) ondulé; **c. iron** tôle f ondulée.

corrupt [kə'rʌpt] vt corrompre; – a corrompu. ◆**corruption** n corruption f.

corset ['kɔːsɪt] n (boned) corset m; (elasticated) gaine f.

Corsica ['kɔːsɪkə] n Corse f.

cos [kɒs] n **c. (lettuce)** (laitue f) romaine f.

cosh [kɒʃ] n matraque f; – vt matraquer.

cosiness ['kəʊzɪnəs] n intimité f, confort m.

cosmetic [kɒz'metɪk] n produit m de beauté; – a esthétique; Fig superficiel.

cosmopolitan [kɒzmə'pɒlɪtən] a & n cosmopolite (mf).

cosmos ['kɒzmɒs] n cosmos m. ◆**cosmic** a cosmique. ◆**cosmonaut** n cosmonaute mf.

Cossack ['kɒsæk] n cosaque m.

cosset ['kɒsɪt] vt choyer.

cost [kɒst] vti (pt & pp **cost**) coûter; **how much does it c.?** ça coûte or ça vaut combien?; **to c. the earth** Fam coûter les yeux de la tête; – n coût m, prix m; **at great c.** à grands frais; **to my c.** à mes dépens; **at any c., at all costs** à tout prix; **at c. price** au prix coûtant. ◆**c.-effective** a rentable. ◆**costly** a (-ier, -iest) (expensive) coûteux; (valuable) précieux.

co-star ['kəʊstɑːr] n Cin Th partenaire mf.

costume ['kɒstjuːm] n costume m; (woman's suit) tailleur m; (swimming) maillot m (de bain); **c. jewellery** bijoux mpl de fantaisie.

cosy ['kəʊzɪ] **1** a (-ier, -iest) douillet, intime; **make yourself (nice and) c.** mets-toi à l'aise; **we're c. on est bien ici. 2** n (tea) c. couvre-théière m.

cot [kɒt] n lit m d'enfant; (camp bed) Am lit m de camp.

cottage ['kɒtɪdʒ] n petite maison f de campagne; (thatched) c. chaumière f; **c. cheese** fromage m blanc (maigre); **c. industry** travail m à domicile (activité artisanale).

cotton ['kɒtən] **1** n coton m; (yarn) fil m (de coton); **absorbent c.** Am, **c. wool** coton m hydrophile, ouate f; **c. candy** Am barbe f à papa. **2** vi **to c. on (to)** Sl piger.

couch [kaʊtʃ] **1** n canapé m. **2** vt (express) formuler.

couchette [kuː'ʃet] n Rail couchette f.

cough [kɒf] **1** n toux f; **c. mixture** sirop m contre la toux; – vi tousser; – vt **to c. up** (blood) cracher. **2** vt **to c. up** (money) Sl cracher; – vi **to c. up** Sl payer, casquer.

could [kʊd, unstressed kəd] see can[1].

couldn't ['kʊd(ə)nt] = could not.

council ['kaʊns(ə)l] n conseil m; **c. flat/house** appartement m/maison f loué(e) à la municipalité, HLM m or f. ◆**councillor** n conseiller, -ère mf; (town) **c.** conseiller m municipal.

counsel ['kaʊnsəl] n (advice) conseil m; Jur avocat, -ate mf; – vt (-ll-, Am -l-) conseiller (s.o. to do à qn de faire). ◆**counsellor** n conseiller, -ère mf.

count[1] [kaʊnt] vt (find number of, include) compter; (deem) considérer; **not counting Paul** sans compter Paul; **to c. in** (include) inclure; **to c. out** exclure; (money) compter; – vi (calculate, be important) compter; **to c. against s.o.** être un désavantage pour qn, jouer contre qn; **to c. on s.o.** (rely on) compter sur qn; **to c. on doing** compter faire; – n compte m; Jur chef m (d'accusation); **he's lost c. of the books he has** il ne sait plus combien il a de livres. ◆**countdown** n compte m à rebours.

count[2] [kaʊnt] n (title) comte m.

countenance ['kaʊntɪnəns] **1** n (face) mine f, expression f. **2** vt (allow) tolérer; (approve) approuver.

counter ['kaʊntər] **1** n (in shop, bar etc) comptoir m; (in bank etc) guichet m; **under the c.** Fig clandestinement, au marché noir; **over the c.** (to obtain medicine) sans ordonnance. **2** n (in games) jeton m. **3** n Tech compteur m. **4** adv **c. to** à l'encontre de. **5** vt (plan) contrarier; (insult) riposter à; (blow) parer; – vi riposter (**with** par).

counter- ['kaʊntər] pref contre-.

counterattack ['kaʊntərətæk] n contre-attaque f; – vi contre-attaquer.

counterbalance ['kaʊntəbæləns] n contrepoids m; – vt contrebalancer.

counterclockwise [kauntə'klɒkwaɪz] *a* & *adv Am* dans le sens inverse des aiguilles d'une montre.

counterfeit ['kauntəfɪt] *a* faux; – *n* contrefaçon *f*, faux *m*; – *vt* contrefaire.

counterfoil ['kauntəfɔɪl] *n* souche *f*.

counterpart ['kauntəpɑːt] *n* (*thing*) équivalent *m*; (*person*) homologue *mf*.

counterpoint ['kauntəpɔɪnt] *n Mus* contrepoint *m*.

counterproductive [kauntəprə'dʌktɪv] *a* (*action*) inefficace, qui produit l'effet contraire.

countersign ['kauntəsaɪn] *vt* contresigner.

countess ['kauntɪs] *n* comtesse *f*.

countless ['kauntləs] *a* innombrable.

countrified ['kʌntrɪfaɪd] *a* rustique.

country ['kʌntrɪ] *n* pays *m*; (*region*) région *f*, pays *m*; (*homeland*) patrie *f*; (*opposed to town*) campagne *f*; – *a* (*house etc*) de campagne; **c. dancing** la danse folklorique. ◆**countryman** *n* (*pl* **-men**) (*fellow*) *c.* compatriote *m*. ◆**countryside** *n* campagne *f*.

county ['kauntɪ] *n* comté *m*; **c. seat** *Am*, **c. town** chef-lieu *m*.

coup [kuː], *pl* **kuz**] *n Pol* coup *m* d'État.

couple ['kʌp(ə)l] **1** *n* (*of people, animals*) couple *m*; **a c.** of deux ou trois; (*a few*) quelques. **2** *vt* (*connect*) accoupler. **3** *vi* (*mate*) s'accoupler.

coupon ['kuːpɒn] *n* (*voucher*) bon *m*; (*ticket*) coupon *m*.

courage ['kʌrɪdʒ] *n* courage *m*. ◆**courageous** [kə'reɪdʒəs] *a* courageux.

courgette [kuə'ʒet] *n* courgette *f*.

courier ['kurɪər] *n* (*for tourists*) guide *m*; (*messenger*) messager *m*; **c. service** service *m* de messagerie.

course [kɔːs] **1** *n* (*duration, movement*) cours *m*; (*of ship*) route *f*; (*of river*) cours *m*; (*way*) Fig route *f*, chemin *m*; (*means*) moyen *m*; (*of action*) ligne *f* de conduite; (*option*) parti *m*; **your best c. is to** . . . le mieux c'est de . . . ; **as a matter of c.** normalement; **in (the) c. of** time avec le temps, à la longue; **in due c.** en temps utile. **2** *n Sch Univ* cours *m*; **c. of lectures** série *f* de conférences; **c.** (*of treatment*) *Med* traitement *m*. **3** *n Culin* plat *m*; **first c.** entrée *f*, hors-d'œuvre *m*. **4** *n* (*racecourse*) champ *m* de courses; (*golf*) c. terrain *m* (de golf). **5** *adv* **of c.!** bien sûr!, mais oui!; **of c. not!** bien sûr que non!

court [kɔːt] **1** *n* (*of monarch*) cour *f*; *Jur* cour *f*, tribunal *m*; *Tennis* court *m*; **c. of enquiry** commission *f* d'enquête; **high c.** cour *f* suprême; **to take to c.** poursuivre en

justice; **c. shoe** escarpin *m*. **2** *vt* (*woman*) faire la cour à; (*danger, support*) rechercher. ◆**-ing** *a* (*couple*) d'amoureux; **they are c.** ils sortent ensemble. ◆**courthouse** *n* palais *m* de justice. ◆**courtier** *n Hist* courtisan *m*. ◆**courtroom** *n* salle *f* du tribunal. ◆**courtship** *n* (*act, period of time*) cour *f*. ◆**courtyard** *n* cour *f*.

courteous ['kɜːtɪəs] *a* poli, courtois. ◆**courtesy** *n* politesse *f*, courtoisie *f*.

court-martial [kɔːt'mɑːʃəl] *n* conseil *m* de guerre; – *vt* (**-ll-**) faire passer en conseil de guerre.

cousin ['kʌz(ə)n] *n* cousin, -ine *mf*.

cove [kəuv] *n* (*bay*) *Geog* anse *f*.

covenant ['kʌvənənt] *n Jur* convention *f*; *Rel* alliance *f*.

Coventry ['kɒvəntrɪ] *n* **to send s.o. to C.** *Fig* mettre qn en quarantaine.

cover ['kʌvər] *n* (*lid*) couvercle *m*; (*of book*) & *Fin* couverture *f*; (*for furniture, typewriter*) housse *f*; (*bedspread*) dessus-de-lit *m*; **the covers** (*blankets*) les couvertures *fpl*; **to take c.** se mettre à l'abri; **c. charge** (*in restaurant*) couvert *m*; **c. note** certificat *m* provisoire d'assurance; **under separate c.** (*letter*) sous pli séparé; – *vt* couvrir; (*protect*) protéger, couvrir; (*distance*) parcourir, couvrir; (*include*) englober, recouvrir; (*treat*) traiter; (*event*) *Journ TV Rad* couvrir, faire le reportage de; (*aim gun at*) tenir en joue; (*insure*) assurer; **to c.** over recouvrir; **to c. up** recouvrir; (*truth, tracks*) dissimuler; (*scandal*) étouffer, camoufler; – *vi* **to c. up** se couvrir; **to c. up for** s.o. couvrir qn. ◆**c.-up** *n* tentative *f* pour étouffer *or* camoufler une affaire. ◆**covering** *n* (*wrapping*) enveloppe *f*; (*layer*) couche *f*; **c. letter** lettre *f* jointe (*à un document*).

coveralls ['kʌvərɔːlz] *npl Am* bleus *mpl* de travail.

covert ['kəuvət, 'kʌvət] *a* secret.

covet ['kʌvɪt] *vt* convoiter. ◆**covetous** *a* avide.

cow [kau] **1** *n* vache *f*; (*of elephant etc*) femelle *f*; (*nasty woman*) *Fam* chameau *m*. **2** *vt* (*person*) intimider. ◆**cowboy** *n* cow-boy *m*. ◆**cowhand** *n* vacher, -ère *mf*. ◆**cowshed** *n* étable *f*.

coward ['kauəd] *n* lâche *mf*. ◆**-ly** *a* lâche. ◆**cowardice** *n* lâcheté *f*.

cower ['kauər] *vi* (*crouch*) se tapir; (*with fear*) *Fig* reculer (par peur).

cowslip ['kauslɪp] *n Bot* coucou *m*.

cox [kɒks] vt Nau barrer; – n barreur, -euse mf.

coy [kɔɪ] a (-er, -est) qui fait son or sa timide. ◆**coyness** n timidité f feinte.

coyote [kaɪˈəʊtɪ] n (wolf) Am coyote m.

cozy [ˈkəʊzɪ] Am = cosy.

crab [kræb] **1** n crabe m. **2** n c. apple pomme f sauvage. **3** vi (-bb-) (complain) Fam rouspéter. ◆**crabbed** a (person) grincheux.

crack [kræk] n (fissure) fente f; (in glass etc) fêlure f; (in skin) crevasse f; (snapping noise) craquement m; (of whip) claquement m; (blow) coup m; (joke) Fam plaisanterie f (at aux dépens de); **to have a c. at doing** Fam essayer de faire; **at the c. of dawn** au point du jour; – vt (glass, ice) fêler; (nut) casser; (ground, skin) crevasser; (whip) faire claquer; (joke) lancer; (problem) résoudre; (code) déchiffrer; (safe) percer; **it's not as hard as it's cracked up to be** ce n'est pas aussi dur qu'on le dit; – vi se fêler; se crevasser; (of branch, wood) craquer; **to get cracking** (get to work) Fam s'y mettre; (hurry) se grouiller; **to c. down on** sévir contre; **to c. up** (mentally) Fam craquer. ◆**c.-up** n Fam dépression f nerveuse; (crash) Am Fam accident m. ◆**cracked** a (crazy) Fam fou. ◆**cracker** n **1** (cake) biscuit m (salé). **2** (firework) pétard m; **Christmas c.** diablotin m. **3** **she's a c.** Fam elle est sensationnelle. ◆**crackers** a (mad) Sl cinglé. ◆**crackpot** a Fam fou; – n fou m, folle f.

crack [kræk] a (first-rate) de premier ordre; **c. shot** tireur m d'élite.

crackle [ˈkræk(ə)l] vi crépiter; (of sth frying) Culin grésiller; – n crépitement m; grésillement m.

cradle [ˈkreɪd(ə)l] n berceau m; – vt bercer.

craft [krɑːft] **1** n (skill) art m; (job) métier m (artisanal); – vt façonner. **2** n (cunning) ruse f. **3** n inv (boat) bateau m. ◆**craftsman** n (pl -men) artisan m. ◆**craftsmanship** n (skill) art m; **a piece of c.** un beau travail, une belle pièce. ◆**crafty** a (-ier, -iest) astucieux, Pej rusé.

crag [kræg] n rocher m à pic. ◆**craggy** a (rock) à pic; (face) rude.

cram [kræm] vt (-mm-) **to c. into** (force) fourrer dans; **to c. with** (fill) bourrer de; – vi **to c. into** (of people) s'entasser dans; **to c. (for an exam)** bachoter.

cramp [kræmp] n Med crampe f (in à). ◆**cramped** a (in a room or one's clothes) à l'étroit; **in c. conditions** à l'étroit.

cranberry [ˈkrænbərɪ] n Bot canneberge f.

crane [kreɪn] **1** n (bird) & Tech grue f. **2** vt **to c. one's neck** tendre le cou.

crank [kræŋk] **1** n (person) Fam excentrique mf; (fanatic) fanatique mf. **2** n (handle) Tech manivelle f; – vt **to c. (up)** (vehicle) faire démarrer à la manivelle. ◆**cranky** a (-ier, -iest) excentrique; (bad-tempered) Am grincheux.

crannies [ˈkrænɪz] npl **nooks and c.** coins et recoins mpl.

craps [kræps] n **to shoot c.** Am jouer aux dés.

crash [kræʃ] n accident m; (of firm) faillite f; (noise) fracas m; (of thunder) coup m; **c. course/diet** cours m/régime m intensif; **c. helmet** casque m (anti-choc); **c. landing** atterrissage m en catastrophe; – int (of fallen object) patatras!; – vt (car) avoir un accident avec; **to c. one's car into** faire rentrer sa voiture dans; – vi Aut Av s'écraser; **to c. into** rentrer dans; **the cars crashed (into each other)** les voitures se sont percutées or carambolées; **to c. (down)** tomber; (break) se casser; (of roof) s'effondrer. ◆**c.-land** vi atterrir en catastrophe.

crass [kræs] a grossier; (stupidity) crasse.

crate [kreɪt] n caisse f, cageot m.

crater [ˈkreɪtər] n cratère m; (bomb) entonnoir m.

cravat [krəˈvæt] n foulard m (autour du cou).

crav/e [kreɪv] vt **to c. (for)** éprouver un grand besoin de; (mercy) implorer. ◆**—ing** n désir m, grand besoin m (for de).

craven [ˈkreɪvən] a Pej lâche.

crawl [krɔːl] vi ramper; (of child) se traîner (à quatre pattes); Aut avancer au pas; **to be crawling with** grouiller de; – n Swimming crawl m; **to move at a c.** Aut avancer au pas.

crayfish [ˈkreɪfɪʃ] n inv écrevisse f.

crayon [ˈkreɪən] n crayon m, pastel m.

craze [kreɪz] n manie f (for de), engouement m (for pour). ◆**crazed** a affolé.

crazy [ˈkreɪzɪ] a (-ier, -iest) fou; **c. about sth** fana de qch; **c. about s.o.** fou de qn; **c. paving** dallage m irrégulier. ◆**craziness** n folie f.

creak [kriːk] vi (of hinge) grincer; (of timber) craquer. ◆**creaky** a grinçant; qui craque.

cream [kriːm] n crème f; (élite) Fig crème f; gratin m; – a (cake) à la crème; **c.(-coloured)** crème inv; **c. cheese** fromage m blanc; (of milk) écrémer; **to c. off** Fig écrémer. ◆**creamy** a (-ier, -iest) crémeux.

crease [kriːs] vt froisser, plisser; – vi se froisser; – n pli m; (accidental) (faux) pli m. ◆**c.-resistant** a infroissable.

create [kriːˈeɪt] *vt* créer; *(impression, noise)* faire. ◆**creation** *n* création *f*. ◆**creative** *a* créateur, créatif. ◆**creativeness** *n* créativité *f*. ◆**crea'tivity** *n* créativité *f*. ◆**creator** *n* créateur, -trice *mf*.

creature [ˈkriːtʃər] *n* animal *m*, bête *f*; *(person)* créature *f*; **one's c. comforts** ses aises *fpl*.

crèche [kreʃ] *n (nursery)* crèche *f*; *(manger) Rel Am* crèche *f*.

credence [ˈkriːdəns] *n* **to give** *or* **lend c. to** ajouter foi à.

credentials [krɪˈdenʃəlz] *npl* références *fpl*; *(identity)* pièces *fpl* d'identité; *(of diplomat)* lettres *fpl* de créance.

credible [ˈkredɪb(ə)l] *a* croyable; *(politician, information)* crédible. ◆**credi'bility** *n* crédibilité *f*.

credit [ˈkredɪt] *n (influence, belief)* & *Fin* crédit *m*; *(merit)* mérite *m*; *Univ* unité *f* de valeur; *f* *Cin* générique *m*; **to give c. to** *(person) Fin* faire crédit à; *Fig* reconnaître le mérite de; *(statement)* ajouter foi à; **to be a c. to** faire honneur à; **on c.** à crédit. ■ *n. (account)* créditeur; **to one's c.** *Fig* à son actif; – *a (balance)* créditeur; **c. card** carte *f* de crédit; **c. facilities** facilités *fpl* de paiement; – *vt (believe)* croire; *Fin* créditer *(s.o. with sth* qn de qch); **to c. s.o. with** *(qualities)* attribuer à qn. ◆**creditable** *a* honorable. ◆**creditor** *n* créancier, -ière *mf*. ◆**creditworthy** *a* solvable.

credulous [ˈkredjʊləs] *a* crédule.

creed [kriːd] *n* credo *m*.

creek [kriːk] *n (bay)* crique *f*; *(stream) Am* ruisseau *m*; **up the c.** *(in trouble) Sl* dans le pétrin.

creep [kriːp] **1** *vi (pt & pp* **crept**) ramper; *(silently)* se glisser *(furtivement)*; *(slowly)* avancer lentement; **it makes my flesh c.** ça me donne la chair de poule. **2** *n (person) Sl* salaud *m*; **it gives me the creeps** *Fam* ça me fait froid dans le dos. ◆**creepy** *a (*-ier, -iest*) Fam* terrifiant; *(nasty) Fam* vilain. ◆**creepy-'crawly** *n Fam, Am* ◆**creepy-'crawler** *n Fam* bestiole *f*.

cremate [krɪˈmeɪt] *vt* incinérer. ◆**crema'tion** *n* crémation *f*. ◆**crema'torium** *n* crématorium *m*. ◆**'crematory** *n Am* crématorium *m*.

Creole [ˈkriːəʊl] *n* créole *mf*; *Ling* créole *m*.

crêpe [kreɪp] *n (fabric)* crêpe *m*; **c. (rubber)** crêpe *m*; **c. paper** papier *m* crépon.

crept [krept] *see* **creep 1**.

crescendo [krɪˈʃendəʊ] *n (pl* -os*)* crescendo *m inv*.

crescent [ˈkres(ə)nt] *n* croissant *m*; *(street) Fig* rue *f* (en demi-lune).

cress [kres] *n* cresson *m*.

crest [krest] *n (of bird, wave, mountain)* crête *f*; *(of hill)* sommet *m*; *(on seal, letters etc)* armoiries *fpl*.

Crete [kriːt] *n* Crète *f*.

cretin [ˈkretɪn, *Am* ˈkriːt(ə)n] *n* crétin, -ine *mf*. ◆**cretinous** *a* crétin.

crevasse [krɪˈvæs] *n (in ice) Geol* crevasse *f*.

crevice [ˈkrevɪs] *n (crack)* crevasse *f*, fente *f*.

crew [kruː] *n Nau Av* équipage *m*; *(gang)* équipe *f*; **c. cut** (coupe *f* en) brosse *f*. ◆**c.-neck(ed)** *a* à col ras.

crib [krɪb] **1** *n (cradle)* berceau *m*; *(cot) Am* lit *m* d'enfant; *Rel* crèche *f*. **2** *n (copy)* plagiat *m*; *Sch* traduction *f*; *(list of answers) Sch* pompe *f* anti-sèche; – *vti* (*-bb-*) copier.

crick [krɪk] *n* **c. in the neck** torticolis *m*; **c. in the back** tour *m* de reins.

cricket [ˈkrɪkɪt] *n* **1** *(game)* cricket *m*. **2** *(insect)* grillon *m*. ◆**cricketer** *n* joueur, -euse *mf* de cricket.

crikey! [ˈkraɪkɪ] *int Sl* zut (alors)!

crime [kraɪm] *n* crime *m*; *(not serious)* délit *m*; *(criminal practice)* criminalité *f*. ◆**criminal** *a & n* criminel, -elle *(mf)*.

crimson [ˈkrɪmz(ə)n] *a & n* cramoisi *(m)*.

cring/e [krɪndʒ] *vi* reculer *(from* devant*)*; *Fig* s'humilier *(to, before* devant*)*. ◆**-ing** *a Fig* servile.

crinkle [ˈkrɪŋk(ə)l] *vt* froisser; – *vi* se froisser; – *n* fronce *f*. ◆**crinkly** *a* froissé; *(hair)* frisé.

crippl/e [ˈkrɪp(ə)l] *n (lame)* estropié, -ée *mf*; *(disabled)* infirme *mf*; – *vt* estropier; *(disable)* rendre infirme; *(nation etc) Fig* paralyser. ◆**-ed** *a* estropié; infirme; *(ship)* désemparé; **c. with** *(rheumatism, pains)* perclus de. ◆**-ing** *a (tax)* écrasant.

crisis, *pl* **-ses** [ˈkraɪsɪs, -siːz] *n* crise *f*.

crisp [krɪsp] **1** *a (*-er, -est*) (biscuit)* croustillant; *(apple etc)* croquant; *(snow)* craquant; *(air, style)* vif. **2** *npl (potato)* **crisps** (pommes *fpl*) chips *mpl*. ◆**crispbread** *n* pain *m* suédois.

criss-cross [ˈkrɪskrɒs] *a (lines)* entrecroisés; *(muddled)* enchevêtrés; – *vi* s'entrecroiser; – *vt* sillonner (en tous sens).

criterion, *pl* **-ia** [kraɪˈtɪərɪən, -ɪə] *n* critère *m*.

critic [ˈkrɪtɪk] *n* critique *m*. ◆**critical** *a* critique. ◆**critically** *adv (to examine etc)* en critique; *(harshly)* sévèrement; *(ill)* gravement. ◆**criticism** *n* critique *f*. ◆**criticize** *vti* critiquer. ◆**cri'tique** *n (essay etc)* critique *f*.

croak [krəʊk] vi (of frog) croasser; – n croassement m.

crochet ['krəʊʃeɪ] vt faire au crochet; – vi faire du crochet; – n (travail m au) crochet m; **c. hook** crochet m.

crock [krɒk] n **a c., an (old) c.** Fam (person) un croulant; (car) un tacot.

crockery ['krɒkərɪ] n (cups etc) vaisselle f.

crocodile ['krɒkədaɪl] n crocodile m.

crocus ['krəʊkəs] n crocus m.

crony ['krəʊnɪ] n Pej Fam copain m, copine f.

crook [krʊk] n **1** (thief) escroc m. **2** (shepherd's stick) houlette f.

crooked ['krʊkɪd] a courbé; (path) tortueux; (hat, picture) de travers; (deal, person) malhonnête; – adv de travers. ◆**-ly** adv de travers.

croon [kruːn] vti chanter (à voix basse).

crop [krɒp] **1** n (harvest) récolte f; (produce) culture f; (of questions etc) Fig série f; (of people) groupe m. **2** vt (**-pp-**) (hair) couper (ras); – n **c. of hair** chevelure f. **3** vi (**-pp-**) to **c. up** se présenter, survenir. ◆**cropper** n **to come a c.** Sl (fall) ramasser une pelle; (fail) échouer.

croquet ['krəʊkeɪ] n (game) croquet m.

croquette [krəʊ'ket] n Culin croquette f.

cross[1] [krɒs] **1** n croix f; **a c. between** (animal) un croisement entre or de. **2** vt traverser; (threshold, barrier) franchir; (legs, animals) croiser; (thwart) contrecarrer; (cheque) barrer; **to c. off** or **out** rayer; **it never crossed my mind that . . .** il ne m'est pas venu à l'esprit que . . . ; **crossed lines** Tel lignes fpl embrouillées; – vi (of paths) se croiser; **to c. (over)** traverser. ◆**-ing** n Nau traversée f; (pedestrian) passage m clouté. ◆**cross-breed** n métis, -isse mf, hybride m. ◆**c.-'country** a à travers champs; **c.-country race** cross(-country) m. ◆**c.-exami'nation** n contre-interrogatoire m. ◆**c.-e'xamine** vt interroger. ◆**c.-eyed** a qui louche. ◆**c.-'legged** a & adv les jambes croisées. ◆**c.-'purposes** npl **to be at c.-purposes** se comprendre mal. ◆**c.-'reference** n renvoi m. ◆**c.-section** n coupe f transversale; Fig échantillon m.

cross[2] [krɒs] a (angry) fâché (**with** contre). ◆**-ly** adv d'un air fâché.

crossbow ['krɒsbəʊ] n arbalète f.

crosscheck ['krɒs'tʃek] n contre-épreuve f; – vt vérifier.

crossfire ['krɒsfaɪər] n feux mpl croisés.

crossroads ['krɒsrəʊdz] n carrefour m.

crosswalk ['krɒswɔːk] n Am passage m clouté.

crossword ['krɒswɜːd] n **c. (puzzle)** mots mpl croisés.

crotch [krɒtʃ] n (of garment) entre-jambes m inv.

crotchet ['krɒtʃɪt] n Mus noire f.

crotchety ['krɒtʃɪtɪ] a grincheux.

crouch [kraʊtʃ] vi **to c. (down)** s'accroupir, se tapir. ◆**-ing** a accroupi, tapi.

croupier ['kruːpɪər] n (in casino) croupier m.

crow [krəʊ] **1** n corbeau m, corneille f; **as the c. flies** à vol d'oiseau; **c.'s nest** Nau nid m de pie. **2** vi (of cock) chanter; (boast) Fig se vanter (**about** de). ◆**crowbar** n levier m.

crowd [kraʊd] n foule f; (particular group) bande f; (of things) Fam masse f; **quite a c.** beaucoup de monde; – vt (fill) remplir; (of people) s'entasser dans; **to c. round s.o.** se presser autour de qn; **to c. together** se serrer; – vt (fill) remplir; **to c. into** (press) entasser dans; **don't c. me!** Fam ne me bouscule pas! ◆**-ed** a plein (**with** de); (train etc) bondé, plein; (city) encombré; **it's very c.!** il y a beaucoup de monde!

crown [kraʊn] n (of king, tooth) couronne f; (of head, hill) sommet m; **c.** court cour f d'assises; **C. jewels**, joyaux mpl de la Couronne; – vt couronner. ◆**-ing** a (glory etc) suprême; **c. achievement** couronnement m.

crucial ['kruːʃəl] a crucial.

crucify ['kruːsɪfaɪ] vt crucifier. ◆**crucifix** ['kruːsɪfɪks] n crucifix m. ◆**cruci'fixion** n crucifixion f.

crude [kruːd] a (**-er**, **-est**) (oil, fact) brut; (manners, person) grossier; (language, light) cru; (painting, work) rudimentaire. ◆**-ly** adv (to say, order etc) crûment. ◆**-ness** n grossièreté f; crudité f; état m rudimentaire.

cruel [krʊəl] a (**crueller**, **cruellest**) cruel. ◆**cruelty** n cruauté f; **an act of c.** une cruauté.

cruet ['kruːɪt] n **c. (stand)** salière f, poivrière f et huilier m.

cruis/e [kruːz] vi Nau croiser; Aut rouler; Av voler; (of taxi) marauder; (of tourists) faire une croisière; – n croisière f. ◆**-ing** a **c. speed** Nau Av & Fig vitesse f de croisière. ◆**-er** n Nau croiseur m.

crumb [krʌm] n miette f; (of comfort) Fig brin m; **crumbs!** Hum Fam zut!

crumble ['krʌmb(ə)l] vt (bread) émietter; – vi (collapse) s'effondrer; **to c. (away)** (in small pieces) & Fig s'effriter. ◆**crumbly** a friable.

crummy ['krʌmɪ] a (**-ier**, **-iest**) Fam moche, minable.

crumpet ['krʌmpɪt] n Culin petite crêpe f grillée (servie beurrée).

crumple ['krʌmp(ə)l] vt froisser; – vi se froisser.

crunch [krʌntʃ] 1 vt (food) croquer; – vi (of snow) craquer. 2 n the c. Fam le moment critique. ◆**crunchy** a (-ier, -iest) (apple etc) croquant.

crusade [kruː'seɪd] n Hist & Fig croisade f; – vi faire une croisade. ◆**crusader** n Hist croisé m; Fig militant, -ante mf.

crush [krʌʃ] 1 n (crowd) cohue f; (rush) bousculade f; to have a c. on s.o. Fam avoir le béguin pour qn. 2 vt écraser; (hope) détruire; (clothes) froisser; (cram) entasser (into dans). ◆**–ing** a (defeat) écrasant.

crust [krʌst] n croûte f. ◆**crusty** a (-ier, -iest) (bread) croustillant.

crutch [krʌtʃ] n 1 Med béquille f. 2 (crotch) entre-jambes m inv.

crux [krʌks] n the c. of (problem, matter) le nœud de.

cry [kraɪ] n (shout) cri m; to have a c. Fam pleurer; – vi (weep) pleurer; to c. (out) pousser un cri, crier; (exclaim) s'écrier; to c. (out) for demander à grands cris; to be crying out for avoir grand besoin de; to c. off (withdraw) abandonner; to c. off (sth) se désintéresser (de qch); to c. over pleurer (sur); – vt (shout) crier. ◆**–ing** a (need etc) très grand; a c. shame une véritable honte; – n cris mpl; (weeping) pleurs mpl.

crypt [krɪpt] n crypte f.

cryptic ['krɪptɪk] a secret, énigmatique.

crystal ['krɪst(ə)l] n cristal m. ◆**c.-'clear** a (water, sound) cristallin; Fig clair comme le jour or l'eau de roche. ◆**crystallize** vt cristalliser; – vi (se) cristalliser.

cub [kʌb] n 1 (of animal) petit m. 2 (scout) louveteau m.

Cuba ['kjuːbə] n Cuba m. ◆**Cuban** a & n cubain, -aine (mf).

cubbyhole ['kʌbɪhəʊl] n cagibi m.

cube [kjuːb] n cube m; (of meat etc) dé m. ◆**cubic** a (shape) cubique; (metre etc) cube; c. capacity volume m; Aut cylindrée f.

cubicle ['kjuːbɪk(ə)l] n (for changing) cabine f; (in hospital) box m.

cuckoo ['kʊkuː] 1 n (bird) coucou m; c. clock coucou m. 2 a (stupid) Sl cinglé.

cucumber ['kjuːkʌmbər] n concombre m.

cuddle ['kʌd(ə)l] vt (hug) serrer (dans ses bras); (caress) câliner; – vi (of lovers) se serrer; to (kiss and) c. s'embrasser; to c. up to (huddle) se serrer or se blottir contre; – n

caresse f. ◆**cuddly** a (-ier, -iest) a câlin, caressant; (toy) doux, en peluche.

cudgel ['kʌdʒəl] n trique f, gourdin m.

cue [kjuː] n 1 Th réplique f; (signal) signal m. 2 (billiard) c. queue f (de billard).

cuff [kʌf] 1 n (of shirt etc) poignet m, manchette f; (of trousers) Am revers m; off the c. Fig impromptu; c. link bouton m de manchette. 2 vt (strike) gifler.

cul-de-sac ['kʌldəsæk] n impasse f, cul-de-sac m.

culinary ['kʌlɪnərɪ] a culinaire.

cull [kʌl] vt choisir; (animals) abattre sélectivement.

culminate ['kʌlmɪneɪt] vi to c. in finir par. ◆**culmi'nation** n point m culminant.

culprit ['kʌlprɪt] n coupable mf.

cult [kʌlt] n culte m.

cultivate ['kʌltɪveɪt] vt (land, mind etc) cultiver. ◆**–ed** a cultivé. ◆**culti'vation** n culture f; land or fields under c. cultures fpl.

culture ['kʌltʃər] n culture f. ◆**cultural** a culturel. ◆**cultured** a cultivé.

cumbersome ['kʌmbəsəm] a encombrant.

cumulative ['kjuːmjʊlətɪv] a cumulatif; c. effect (long-term) effet m or résultat m à long terme.

cunning ['kʌnɪŋ] a astucieux; Pej rusé; – n astuce f; ruse f. ◆**–ly** adv avec astuce; avec ruse.

cup [kʌp] n tasse f; (goblet, prize) coupe f; that's my c. of tea Fam c'est à mon goût; c. final Fb finale f de la coupe. ◆**c.-tie** n Fb match m éliminatoire. ◆**cupful** n tasse f.

cupboard ['kʌbəd] n armoire f; (built-in) placard m.

Cupid ['kjuːpɪd] n Cupidon m.

cupola ['kjuːpələ] n Archit coupole f.

cuppa ['kʌpə] n Fam tasse f de thé.

curate ['kjʊərɪt] n vicaire m.

curator [kjʊə'reɪtər] n (of museum) conservateur m.

curb [kɜːb] n 1 (kerb) Am bord m du trottoir. 2 vt (feelings) refréner, freiner; (ambitions) modérer; (expenses) limiter; – n frein m; to put a c. on mettre un frein à.

curdle ['kɜːd(ə)l] vt cailler; – vi se cailler; (of blood) Fig se figer.

curds [kɜːdz] npl lait m caillé. ◆**curd cheese** n fromage m blanc (maigre).

cure [kjʊər] vt guérir (of de); (poverty) Fig éliminer; – n remède m (for contre); (recovery) guérison f; rest c. cure f de repos. 2 vt Culin (smoke) fumer; (salt) saler; (dry) sécher. ◆**curable** a guérissable, curable. ◆**curative** a curatif.

curfew ['kɜːfjuː] n couvre-feu m.

curio ['kjʊərɪəʊ] n (pl **-os**) bibelot m, curiosité f.

curious ['kjʊərɪəs] a (odd) curieux; (inquisitive) curieux (**about** de); **c. to know** curieux de savoir. ◆**-ly** adv (oddly) curieusement. ◆**curi'osity** n curiosité f.

curl [kɜːl] **1** vti (hair) boucler, friser; – n boucle f; (of smoke) Fig spirale f. **2** vi **to c. up** (shrivel) se racornir; **to c. oneself up** (into a ball) se pelotonner. ◆**-er** n bigoudi m. ◆**curly** a (-ier, -iest) bouclé, frisé.

currant ['kʌrənt] n (fruit) groseille f; (dried grape) raisin m de Corinthe.

currency ['kʌrənsɪ] n (money) monnaie f; (acceptance) Fig cours m; (**foreign**) **c.** devises fpl (étrangères).

current ['kʌrənt] **1** a (fashion, trend etc) actuel; (opinion, use, phrase) courant; (year, month) en cours, courant; **c. affairs** questions fpl d'actualité; **c. events** actualité f; **the c. issue** (of magazine etc) le dernier numéro. **2** n (of river, air) & El courant m. ◆**-ly** adv actuellement, à présent.

curriculum, pl **-la** [kə'rɪkjʊləm, -lə] n programme m (scolaire); **c. (vitae)** curriculum (vitae) m inv.

curry ['kʌrɪ] **1** n Culin curry m, cari m. **2** vt **to c. favour with** s'insinuer dans les bonnes grâces de.

curs/e [kɜːs] n malédiction f; (swearword) juron m; (bane) Fig fléau m; – vt maudire; **cursed with** (blindness etc) affligé de; – vi (swear) jurer. ◆**-ed** [-ɪd] a Fam maudit.

cursor ['kɜːsər] n (on computer screen) curseur m.

cursory ['kɜːsərɪ] a (too) rapide, superficiel.

curt [kɜːt] a brusque. ◆**-ly** adv d'un ton brusque. ◆**-ness** n brusquerie f.

curtail [kɜː'teɪl] vt écourter, raccourcir; (expenses) réduire. ◆**-ment** n raccourcissement m; réduction f.

curtain ['kɜːt(ə)n] n rideau m; **c. call** Th rappel m.

curts(e)y ['kɜːtsɪ] n révérence f; – vi faire une révérence.

curve [kɜːv] n courbe f; (in road) Am virage m; pl (of woman) Fam rondeurs fpl; – vt courber; – vi se courber; (of road) tourner, faire une courbe.

cushion ['kʊʃən] n coussin m; – vt (shock) Fig amortir. ◆**cushioned** a (seat) rembourré; **c. against** Fig protégé contre.

cushy ['kʊʃɪ] a (-ier, -iest) (job, life) Fam pépère, facile.

custard ['kʌstəd] n crème f anglaise; (when set) crème f renversée.

custodian [kʌ'stəʊdɪən] n gardien, -ienne mf.

custody ['kʌstədɪ] n (care) garde f; **to take into c.** Jur mettre en détention préventive. ◆**cu'stodial** a **c. sentence** peine f de prison.

custom ['kʌstəm] n coutume f; (patronage) Com clientèle f. ◆**customary** a habituel, coutumier; **it is c. to** il est d'usage de. ◆**custom-built** a, ◆**customized** a (car etc) (fait) sur commande.

customer ['kʌstəmər] n client, -ente mf; Pej individu m.

customs ['kʌstəmz] n & npl (**the**) **c.** la douane; **c. (duties)** droits mpl de douane; **c. officer** douanier m; **c. union** union f douanière.

cut [kʌt] n coupure f; (stroke) coup m; (of clothes, hair) coupe f; (in salary) réduction f; (of meat) morceau m; – vt (pt & pp **cut**, pres p **cutting**) couper; (meat) découper; (glass, tree) tailler; (record) graver; (hay) faucher; (profits, prices etc) réduire; (tooth) percer; (corner) Aut prendre à la corde; **to c. open** ouvrir (au couteau etc); **to c. short** (visit) abréger; – vi (of person, scissors) couper; (of material) se couper; **to c. into** (cake) entamer. ■ **to c. away** vt (remove) enlever; **to c. back (on)** vti réduire. ◆**cutback** n réduction f; **to c. down** vt (tree) abattre, couper; **to c. down (on)** vti réduire; **to c. in** vi interrompre; Aut faire une queue de poisson (on s.o. à qn); **to c. off** vt couper; (isolate) isoler; **to c. out** vi (of engine) Aut caler; – vt (article) découper; (garment) tailler; (remove) enlever; (leave out, get rid of) Fam supprimer; **to c. out drinking** (stop) Fam s'arrêter de boire; **c. it out!** Fam ça suffit!; **c. out to be a doctor/etc** fait pour être médecin/etc. ◆**cutout** n (picture) découpage m; El coupe-circuit m inv; **to c. up** vt couper (en morceaux); (meat) découper; **c. up about** démoralisé par. ◆**cutting** n coupe f; (of diamond) taille f; (article) Journ coupure f; (plant) bouture f; Cin montage m; – a (wind, word) cinglant; **c. edge** tranchant m.

cute [kjuːt] a (-er, -est) Fam (pretty) mignon; (shrewd) astucieux.

cuticle ['kjuːtɪk(ə)l] n petites peaux fpl (de l'ongle).

cutlery ['kʌtlərɪ] n couverts mpl.

cutlet ['kʌtlɪt] n (of veal etc) côtelette f.

cut-price [kʌt'praɪs] a à prix réduit.

cutthroat ['kʌtθrəʊt] n assassin m; – a (competition) impitoyable.

cv [si'vi:] *n abbr* curriculum (vitae) *m inv.*

cyanide ['saɪənaɪd] *n* cyanure *m.*

cybernetics [saɪbə'netɪks] *n* cybernétique *f.*

cycle ['saɪk(ə)l] **1** *n* bicyclette *f*, vélo *m*; – *a (path, track)* cyclable; *(race)* cycliste; – *vi* aller à bicyclette (**to** à); *Sp* faire de la bicyclette. **2** *n (series, period)* cycle *m.* ◆**cycling** *n* cyclisme *m*; – *a (champion)* cycliste. ◆**cyclist** *n* cycliste *mf.* ◆**cyclic(al)** ['sɪklɪk(ə)l] *a* cyclique.

cyclone ['saɪkləun] *n* cyclone *m.*

cylinder ['sɪlɪndər] *n* cylindre *m.* ◆**cylindrical** *a* cylindrique.

cymbal ['sɪmbəl] *n* cymbale *f.*

cynic ['sɪnɪk] *n* cynique *mf.* ◆**cynical** *a* cynique. ◆**cynicism** *n* cynisme *m.*

cypress ['saɪprəs] *n (tree)* cyprès *m.*

Cyprus ['saɪprəs] *n* Chypre *f.* ◆**Cypriot** ['sɪprɪət] *a & n* cypriote (*mf*).

cyst [sɪst] *n Med* kyste *m.*

czar [zɑːr] *n* tsar *m.*

Czech [tʃek] *a & n* tchèque (*mf*). ◆**Czecho'slovak** *a & n* tchécoslovaque (*mf*). ◆**Czechoslo'vakia** *n* Tchécoslovaquie *f.* ◆**Czechoslo'vakian** *a & n* tchécoslovaque (*mf*).

D

D, d [di:] *n* D, d *m.* ◆**D.-day** *n* le jour J.

dab [dæb] *n* a d. of un petit peu de; – *vt* (-**bb**-) *(wound, brow etc)* tamponner; **to d. sth on sth** appliquer qch (à petits coups) sur qch.

dabble ['dæb(ə)l] *vi* to d. in s'occuper *or* se mêler un peu de.

dad [dæd] *n Fam* papa *m.* ◆**daddy** *n Fam* papa *m*; **d. longlegs** *(cranefly)* tipule *f*; *(spider) Am* faucheur *m.*

daffodil ['dæfədɪl] *n* jonquille *f.*

daft [dɑːft] *a* (-**er**, -**est**) *Fam* idiot, bête.

dagger ['dægər] *n* poignard *m*; **at daggers drawn** à couteaux tirés (**with** avec).

dahlia ['deɪljə, *Am* 'dæljə] *n* dahlia *m.*

daily ['deɪlɪ] *a* quotidien, journalier; *(wage)* journalier; – *adv* quotidiennement; – *n* d. (**paper**) quotidien *m*; **d.** (**help**) *(cleaning woman)* femme *f* de ménage.

dainty ['deɪntɪ] *a* (-**ier**, -**iest**) délicat; *(pretty)* mignon; *(tasteful)* élégant. ◆**daintily** *adv* délicatement; élégamment.

dairy ['deərɪ] *n (on farm)* laiterie *f*; *(shop)* crèmerie *f*; – *a (produce, cow etc)* laitier. ◆**dairyman** *n (pl* -**men***)* laitier *m.* ◆**dairywoman** *n (pl* -**women***)* laitière *f.*

daisy ['deɪzɪ] *n* pâquerette *f.*

dale [deɪl] *n Geog Lit* vallée *f.*

dally ['dælɪ] *vi* musarder, lanterner.

dam [dæm] *n (wall)* barrage *m*; – *vt* (-**mm**-) *(river)* barrer.

damage ['dæmɪdʒ] *n* dégâts *mpl*, dommages *mpl*; *(harm) Fig* préjudice *m*; *pl Jur* dommages-intérêts *mpl*; – *vt (spoil)* abîmer; *(material object)* endommager, abîmer; *(harm) Fig* nuire à. ◆**-ing** *a* préjudiciable (**to** à).

dame [deɪm] *n Lit* dame *f*; *Am Sl* nana *f*, fille *f.*

damn [dæm] *vt (condemn, doom)* condamner; *Rel* damner; *(curse)* maudire; **d. him!** *Fam* qu'il aille au diable!; – *int* **d.** (**it**)! *Fam* zut!, merde!; – *n* **he doesn't care a d.** *Fam* il s'en fiche pas mal; – *a Fam* fichu, sacré; – *adv Fam* sacrément; **d. all** rien du tout. ◆**-ed 1** *a (soul)* damné. **2** *Fam* = **damn** *a & adv.* ◆**-ing** *a (evidence etc)* accablant. ◆**dam'nation** *n* damnation *f.*

damp [dæmp] *a* (-**er**, -**est**) humide; *(skin)* moite; – *n* humidité *f.* ◆**damp(en)** *vt* humecter; **to d. (down)** *(zeal)* refroidir; *(ambition)* étouffer. ◆**damper** *n* **to put a d. on** jeter un froid sur. ◆**dampness** *n* humidité *f.*

damsel ['dæmzəl] *n Lit & Hum* demoiselle *f.*

damson ['dæmzən] *n* prune *f* de Damas.

danc/e [dɑːns] *n* danse *f*; *(social event)* bal *m*; **d. hall** dancing *m*; – *vi* danser; **to d. for joy** sauter de joie; – *vt (polka etc)* danser. ◆**-ing** *n* danse *f*; **d. partner** cavalier, -ière *mf.* ◆**-er** *n* danseur, -euse *mf.*

dandelion ['dændɪlaɪən] *n* pissenlit *m.*

dandruff ['dændrʌf] *n* pellicules *fpl.*

dandy ['dændɪ] **1** *n* dandy *m.* **2** *a (very good) Am Fam* formidable.

Dane [deɪn] *n* Danois, -oise *mf.*

danger ['deɪndʒər] *n (peril)* danger *m* (**to** pour); *(risk)* risque *m*; **in d.** en danger; **in d. of** *(threatened by)* menacé de; **to be in d. of falling***/etc* risquer de tomber/*etc*; **on the d. list** *Med* dans un état critique; **d. signal** signal *m* d'alarme; **d. zone** zone *f* dangereuse. ◆**dangerous** *a (place, illness,*

person etc) dangereux (**to** pour).
◆**dangerously** *adv* dangereusement; (*ill*) gravement.

dangle ['dæŋg(ə)l] *vt* balancer; (*prospect*) *Fig* faire miroiter (**before** s.o. aux yeux de qn); – *vi* (*hang*) pendre; (*swing*) se balancer.

Danish ['deɪnɪʃ] *a* danois; – *n* (*language*) danois *m*.

dank [dæŋk] *a* (-er, -est) humide (et froid).

dapper ['dæpər] *a* pimpant, fringant.

dappled ['dæp(ə)ld] *a* pommelé, tacheté.

dar/e [deər] *vt* oser (**do** faire); **she d. not come** elle n'ose pas venir; **he doesn't d. (to) go** il n'ose pas y aller; **if you d. (to)** si tu l'oses, si tu oses le faire; **I d. say he tried** il a sans doute essayé, je suppose qu'il a essayé; **to d. s.o. to do** défier qn de faire. ◆**-ing** *a* audacieux; – *n* audace *f*. ◆**daredevil** *n* casse-cou *m inv*, risque-tout *m inv*.

dark [dɑːk] *a* (-er, -est) obscur, noir, sombre; (*colour*) foncé, sombre; (*skin*) brun, foncé; (*hair*) brun, noir, foncé; (*eyes*) foncé; (*gloomy*) sombre; **it's d.** il fait nuit *or* noir; **to keep sth d.** tenir qch secret; **d. glasses** lunettes *fpl* noires; – *n* noir *m*, obscurité *f*; **after d.** après la tombée de la nuit; **to keep s.o. in the d.** laisser qn dans l'ignorance (**about** de). ◆**d.-'haired** *a* aux cheveux bruns. ◆**d.-'skinned** *a* brun; (*race*) de couleur. ◆**darken** *vt* assombrir, obscurcir; (*colour*) foncer; – *vi* s'assombrir; (*of colour*) foncer. ◆**darkness** *n* obscurité *f*, noir *m*.

darkroom ['dɑːkruːm] *n Phot* chambre *f* noire.

darling ['dɑːlɪŋ] *n* (*favourite*) chouchou, -oute *mf*; (**my**) **d.** (mon) chéri, (ma) chérie; **he's a d.** c'est un amour; **be a d.!** sois un ange!; – *a* chéri; (*delightful*) *Fam* adorable.

darn [dɑːn] **1** *vt* (*socks*) repriser. **2** *int* **d. it!** bon sang! ◆**-ing** *n* reprise *f*; – *a* (*needle, wool*) à repriser.

dart [dɑːt] **1** *vi* se précipiter, s'élancer (**for** vers); **to make a d.** se précipiter (**for** vers). *Sp* fléchette *f*; *pl* (*game*) fléchettes *fpl*. ◆**dartboard** *n Sp* cible *f*.

dash [dæʃ] **1** *n* (*run, rush*) ruée *f*; **to make a d.** se précipiter (**for** vers); – *vi* se précipiter; (*of waves*) se briser (**against** contre); **to d. off** *or* **away** partir *or* filer en vitesse; – *vt* jeter (avec force); (*shatter*) briser; **d. (it)!** *Fam* zut!; **to d. off** (*letter*) faire en vitesse. **2** *n* (*stroke*) trait *m*; *Typ* tiret *m*. ◆**-ing** *a* (*person*) sémillant.

dashboard ['dæʃbɔːd] *n Aut* tableau *m* de bord.

data ['deɪtə] *npl* données *fpl*; **d. processing** informatique *f*.

date¹ [deɪt] *n* date *f*; (*on coin*) millésime *m*; (*meeting*) *Fam* rendez-vous *m inv*; (*person*) *Fam* copain, -ine *mf* (*avec qui on a un rendez-vous*); **up to d.** moderne; (*information*) à jour; (*well-informed*) au courant (**on** de); **out of d.** (*old-fashioned*) démodé; (*expired*) périmé; **to d.** à ce jour, jusqu'ici; **d. stamp** (*object*) (tampon *m*) dateur *m*; (*mark*) cachet *m*; – *vt* (*letter etc*) dater; (*girl, boy*) *Fam* sortir avec; – *vi* (*become out of date*) dater; **to d. back to, to d. from** dater de. ◆**dated** *a* démodé.

date² [deɪt] *n Bot* datte *f*.

datebook ['deɪtbʊk] *n Am* agenda *m*.

daub [dɔːb] *vt* barbouiller (**with** de).

daughter ['dɔːtər] *n* fille *f*. ◆**d.-in-law** *n* (*pl* **daughters-in-law**) belle-fille *f*, bru *f*.

daunt [dɔːnt] *vt* décourager, rebuter. ◆**-less** *a* intrépide.

dawdl/e ['dɔːd(ə)l] *vi* traîner, lambiner. ◆**-er** *n* traînard, -arde *mf*.

dawn [dɔːn] *n* aube *f*, aurore *f*; – *vi* (*of day*) poindre; (*of new era, idea*) naître, voir le jour; **it dawned upon him that . . .** il lui est venu à l'esprit que . . . . ◆**-ing** *a* naissant.

day [deɪ] *n* jour *m*; (*working period, whole day long*) journée *f*; *pl* (*period*) époque *f*, temps *mpl*; **all d. (long)** toute la journée; **what d. is it?** quel jour sommes-nous?; **the following** *or* **next d.** le lendemain; **the d. before** la veille; **the d. before yesterday** avant-hier; **the d. after tomorrow** après-demain; **to the d.** jour pour jour; **d. boarder** demi-pensionnaire *mf*; **d. nursery** crèche *f*; **d. return** *Rail* aller et retour *m* (*pour une journée*); **d. tripper** excursionniste *mf* ◆**d.-to-'d.** *a* journalier; **on a d.-to-day basis** (*every day*) journellement. ◆**daybreak** *n* point *m* du jour. ◆**daydream** *n* rêverie *f*; – *vi* rêvasser. ◆**daylight** *n* (lumière *f* du) jour *m*; (*dawn*) point *m* du jour; **it's d.** il fait jour. ◆**daytime** *n* journée *f*.

daze [deɪz] *vt* (*with drugs etc*) hébéter; (*by blow*) étourdir; – *n* in **a d.** étourdi; hébété.

dazzle ['dæz(ə)l] *vt* éblouir; – *n* éblouissement *m*.

deacon ['diːkən] *n Rel* diacre *m*.

dead [ded] *a* mort; (*numb*) engourdi; (*party etc*) qui manque de vie, mortel; (*telephone*) sans tonalité; **in (the) d. centre** au beau milieu; **to be a d. loss** (*person*) *Fam* n'être bon à rien; **it's a d. loss** *Fam* ça ne vaut rien; **d. silence** un silence de mort; **a d. stop** un arrêt complet; **d. end** (*street*) & *Fig* impasse *f*; **d.-end job** un travail sans avenir; – *adv* (*completely*) absolument; (*very*) très; **d. beat** *Fam* éreinté; **d. drunk** *Fam* ivre mort; **to stop d.** s'arrêter net; – *n* **the d.** les morts *mpl*; **in the d. of** (*night, winter*) au cœur de. ◆**—ly** a (**-ier, -iest**) (*enemy, silence, paleness*) mortel; (*weapon*) meurtrier; **d. sins** péchés *mpl* capitaux; – *adv* mortellement. ◆**deadbeat** *n Am Fam* parasite *m*. ◆**deadline** *n* date *f* limite; (*hour*) heure *f* limite. ◆**deadlock** *n Fig* impasse *f*. ◆**deadpan** a (*face*) figé, impassible.

deaden ['ded(ə)n] *vt* (*shock*) amortir; (*pain*) calmer; (*feeling*) émousser.

deaf [def] a sourd (**to** à); **d. and dumb** sourd-muet; **d. in one ear** sourd d'une oreille; **the d.** les sourds *mpl*. ◆**d.-aid** *n* audiophone *m*, prothèse *f* auditive. ◆**deafen** *vt* assourdir. ◆**deafness** *n* surdité *f*.

deal[1] [diːl] **1** *n* **a good** *or* **great d.** beaucoup (**of** de). **2** *n Com* marché *m*, affaire *f*; *Cards* donne *f*; **fair d.** traitement *m* *or* arrangement *m* équitable; **it's a d.** d'accord; **big d.!** *Iron* la belle affaire! **3** *vt* (*pt & pp* **dealt** [delt]) (*blow*) porter; **to d.** (**out**) (*cards*) donner; (*money*) distribuer. **4** *vi* (*trade*) traiter (**with** avec qn); **to d. in** faire le commerce de; **to d. with** (*take care of*) s'occuper de; (*concern*) traiter de, parler de; **I can d. with him** (*handle*) je sais m'y prendre avec lui. ◆**—ings** *npl* relations *fpl* (**with** avec); *Com* transactions *fpl*. ◆**—er** *n* marchand, -ande *mf* (**in** de); (*agent*) dépositaire *mf*; (*for cars*) concessionnaire *mf*; (*in drugs*) *Sl* revendeur, -euse *mf* de drogues; *Cards* donneur, -euse *mf*.

deal[2] [diːl] *n* (*wood*) sapin *m*.

dean [diːn] *n Rel Univ* doyen *m*.

dear [dɪər] a (**-er, -est**) (*loved, precious, expensive*) cher; (*price*) élevé; **D. Sir** (*in letter*) *Com* Monsieur; **D. Uncle** (mon) cher oncle; **oh d.!** oh là là!, oh mon Dieu!; – *n* (**my**) **d.** (*darling*) (mon) chéri, (ma) chérie; (*friend*) mon cher, ma chère; **she's a d.** c'est un amour; **be a d.!** sois un ange!; – *adv* (*to cost, pay*) cher. ◆**—ly** *adv* tendrement; (*very much*) beaucoup; **to pay d. for sth** payer qch cher.

dearth [dɜːθ] *n* manque *m*, pénurie *f*.

death [deθ] *n* mort *f*; **to put to d.** mettre à mort; **to be bored to d.** s'ennuyer à mourir;

to be burnt to d. mourir carbonisé; **to be sick to d.** en avoir vraiment marre; **many deaths** (*people killed*) de nombreux morts *mpl*; – *a* (*march*) funèbre; (*mask*) mortuaire; **d. certificate** acte *m* de décès; **d. duty** droits *mpl* de succession; **d. penalty** *or* **sentence** peine *f* de mort; **d. rate** mortalité *f*; **it's a d. trap** il y a un danger de mort. ◆**deathbed** *n* lit *m* de mort. ◆**deathblow** *n* coup *m* mortel. ◆**deathly** a mortel, de mort; – *adv* **d. pale** d'une pâleur mortelle.

debar [dɪˈbɑːr] *vt* (**-rr-**) exclure; **to d. from doing** interdire de faire.

debase [dɪˈbeɪs] *vt* (*person*) avilir; (*reputation, talents*) galvauder; (*coinage*) altérer.

debat/e [dɪˈbeɪt] *vti* discuter; **to d.** (**with oneself**) **whether to leave**/*etc* se demander si on doit partir/*etc*; – *n* débat *m*, discussion *f*. ◆**—able** a discutable, contestable.

debauch [dɪˈbɔːtʃ] *vt* corrompre, débaucher. ◆**debauchery** *n* débauche *f*. ◆**debility** *n* faiblesse *f*, débilité *f*.

debilitate [dɪˈbɪlɪteɪt] *vt* débiliter.

debit ['debɪt] *n* débit *m*; **in d.** (*account*) débiteur; – *a* (*balance*) *Fin* débiteur; – *vt* débiter (**s.o. with sth** qch de qn).

debonair [debəˈneər] a jovial; (*charming*) charmant; (*polite*) poli.

debris ['debriː] *n* débris *mpl*.

debt [det] *n* dette *f*; **to be in d.** avoir des dettes; **to be £50 in d.** devoir 50 livres; **to run** *or* **get into d.** faire des dettes. ◆**debtor** *n* débiteur, -trice *mf*.

debunk [diːˈbʌŋk] *vt Fam* démystifier.

debut ['deɪbjuː] *n Th* début *m*.

decade ['dekeɪd] *n* décennie *f*.

decadent ['dekədənt] a décadent. ◆**decadence** *n* décadence *f*.

decaffeinated [diːˈkæfɪneɪtɪd] a décaféiné.

decal ['diːkæl] *n Am* décalcomanie *f*.

decant [dɪˈkænt] *vt* (*wine*) décanter. ◆**—er** *n* carafe *f*.

decapitate [dɪˈkæpɪteɪt] *vt* décapiter.

decathlon [dɪˈkæθlɒn] *n Sp* décathlon *m*.

decay [dɪˈkeɪ] *vi* (*go bad*) se gâter; (*rot*) pourrir; (*of tooth*) se carier, se gâter; (*of building*) tomber en ruine; (*decline*) *Fig* décliner; – *n* pourriture *f*, décomposition *f*; (*of tooth*) carie(s) *f*(*pl*); (*of nation*) décadence *f*; **to fall into d.** (*of building*) tomber en ruine. ◆**—ing** a (*nation*) décadent; (*meat, fruit etc*) pourrissant.

deceased [dɪˈsiːst] a décédé, défunt; – *n* **the d.** le défunt, la défunte; *pl* les défunt(e)s.

deceit [dɪˈsiːt] *n* tromperie *f*. ◆**deceitful** a

trompeur. ◆**deceitfully** adv avec duplicité.

deceive [dɪ'siːv] vti tromper; **to d. oneself** se faire des illusions.

December [dɪ'sembər] n décembre m.

decent ['diːsənt] a (respectable) convenable, décent; (good) Fam bon; (kind) Fam gentil; **that was d. (of you)** c'était chic de ta part. ◆**decency** n décence f; (kindness) Fam gentillesse f. ◆**decently** adv décemment.

decentralize [diː'sentrəlaɪz] vt décentraliser. ◆**decentrali'zation** n décentralisation f.

deception [dɪ'sepʃ(ə)n] n tromperie f. ◆**deceptive** a trompeur.

decibel ['desɪbel] n décibel m.

decid/e [dɪ'saɪd] vt (question etc) régler, décider; (s.o.'s career, fate etc) décider de; **to d. to do** décider de faire; **to d. that** décider que; **to d. s.o. to do** décider qn à faire; − vi (make decisions) décider; (make up one's mind) se décider (on doing à faire); **to d. on sth** décider de qch, se décider à qch; (choose) se décider pour qch. ◆−**ed** a (firm) décidé, résolu; (clear) net. ◆−**edly** adv résolument; nettement. ◆−**ing** a (factor etc) décisif.

decimal ['desɪməl] a décimal; **d. point** virgule f; − n décimale f. ◆**decimali-'zation** n décimalisation f.

decimate ['desɪmeɪt] vt décimer.

decipher [dɪ'saɪfər] vt déchiffrer.

decision [dɪ'sɪʒ(ə)n] n décision f. ◆**decisive** [dɪ'saɪsɪv] a (defeat, tone etc) décisif; (victory) net, incontestable. ◆**decisively** adv (to state) avec décision; (to win) nettement, incontestablement.

deck [dek] **1** n Nau pont m; **top d.** (of bus) impériale f. **2** n **d. of cards** jeu m de cartes. **3** n (of record player) platine f. **4** vt (out) (adorn) orner. ◆**deckchair** n chaise f longue.

declare [dɪ'kleər] vt déclarer (that que); (verdict, result) proclamer. ◆**decla'ration** n déclaration f; proclamation f.

declin/e [dɪ'klaɪn] **1** vi (deteriorate) décliner; (of birthrate, price etc) baisser; **to d. in importance** perdre de l'importance; − n déclin m; (fall) baisse f. **2** vt (refuse) décliner, refuser; **to d. to do** refuser de faire. ◆−**ing** a **one's d. years** ses dernières années.

decode [diː'kəʊd] vt (message) décoder.

decompose [diːkəm'pəʊz] vt décomposer; − vi se décomposer. ◆**decompo-'sition** n décomposition f.

decompression [diːkəm'preʃ(ə)n] n décompression f.

decontaminate [diːkən'tæmɪneɪt] vt décontaminer.

decor ['deɪkɔːr] n décor m.

decorat/e ['dekəreɪt] vt (cake, house, soldier) décorer (**with** de); (paint etc) peindre (et tapisser); (hat, skirt etc) orner (**with** de). ◆−**ing** n interior d. décoration f d'intérieurs. ◆**deco'ration** n décoration f. ◆**decorative** a décoratif. ◆**decorator** n (house painter etc) peintre m décorateur; (interior) d. ensemblier m, décorateur, -trice mf.

decorum [dɪ'kɔːrəm] n bienséances fpl.

decoy ['diːkɔɪ] n (artificial bird) appeau m; (police) d. policier m en civil.

decreas/e [dɪ'kriːs] vti diminuer; − ['diːkriːs] n diminution f (**in** de). ◆−**ing** a (number etc) décroissant. ◆−**ingly** adv de moins en moins.

decree [dɪ'kriː] n Pol Rel décret m; Jur jugement m; (municipal) arrêté m; − vt (pt & pp **decreed**) décréter.

decrepit [dɪ'krepɪt] a (building) en ruine; (person) décrépit.

decry [dɪ'kraɪ] vt décrier.

dedicat/e ['dedɪkeɪt] vt (devote) consacrer (**to** à); (book) dédier (**to** à); **to d. oneself to** se consacrer à. ◆**dedi'cation** n (in book) dédicace f; (devotion) dévouement m.

deduce [dɪ'djuːs] vt (conclude) déduire (**from** de, **that** que).

deduct [dɪ'dʌkt] vt (subtract) déduire, retrancher (**from** de); (from wage, account) prélever (**from** sur). ◆**deductible** a à déduire (**from** de); (expenses) déductible. ◆**deduction** n (inference) & Com déduction f.

deed [diːd] n action f, acte m; (feat) exploit m; Jur acte m (notarié).

deem [diːm] vt juger, estimer.

deep [diːp] a (-er, -est) profond; (snow) épais; (voice) grave; (note) Mus bas; (person) insondable; **to be six metres/etc d.** avoir six mètres/etc de profondeur; **d. in thought** absorbé or plongé dans ses pensées; **the d. end** (in swimming pool) le grand bain; **d. red** rouge foncé; − adv (to breathe) profondément; **d. into the night** tard dans la nuit; − n the d. l'océan m. ◆−**ly** adv (grateful, to regret etc) profondément. ◆**deep-'freeze** vt surgeler; − n congélateur m. ◆**d.-'fryer** n friteuse f. ◆**d.-'rooted** a, ◆**d.-'seated** a bien ancré, profond. ◆**d.-'set** a (eyes) enfoncés.

deepen ['diːpən] vt approfondir; (increase) augmenter; – vi devenir plus profond; (of mystery) s'épaissir. ◆**-ing** a grandissant.

deer [dɪər] n inv cerf m.

deface [dɪ'feɪs] vt (damage) dégrader; (daub) barbouiller.

defamation [defə'meɪʃ(ə)n] n diffamation f. ◆**de'famatory** a diffamatoire.

default [dɪ'fɔːlt] n by d. Jur par défaut; to win by d. gagner par forfait; – vi Jur faire défaut; **to d. on one's payments** Fin être en rupture de paiement.

defeat [dɪ'fiːt] vt battre, vaincre; (plan) faire échouer; – n défaite f; (of plan) échec m. ◆**defeatism** n défaitisme m.

defect 1 ['diːfekt] n défaut m. **2** [dɪ'fekt] vi Pol déserter, faire défection; **to d. to** (the West, the enemy) passer à. ◆**de'fection** n défection f. ◆**de'fective** a défectueux; Med déficient. ◆**de'fector** n transfuge mf.

defence [dɪ'fens] (Am **defense**) n défense f; **the body's defences** les défenses de l'organisme (against contre); **in his d.** Jur à sa décharge, pour le défendre. ◆**defenceless** a sans défense. ◆**defensible** a défendable. ◆**defensive** a défensif; – n **on the d.** sur la défensive.

defend [dɪ'fend] vt défendre. ◆**defendant** n (accused) Jur prévenu, -ue mf. ◆**defender** n défenseur m; (of title) Sp détenteur, -trice mf.

defer [dɪ'fɜːr] **1** vt (-rr-) (postpone) différer, reporter. **2** vi (-rr-) **to d. to** (yield) déférer à. ◆**-ment** n report m.

deference ['defərəns] n déférence f. ◆**defe'rential** a déférent, plein de déférence.

defiant [dɪ'faɪənt] a (tone etc) de défi; (person) rebelle. ◆**defiance** n (resistance) défi m (of à); **in d. of** (contempt) au mépris de. ◆**defiantly** adv d'un air de défi.

deficient [dɪ'fɪʃənt] a insuffisant; Med déficient; **to be d. in** manquer de. ◆**deficiency** n manque m; (flaw) défaut m; Med carence f; (mental) déficience f.

deficit ['defɪsɪt] n déficit m.

defile [dɪ'faɪl] vt souiller, salir. ◆**defi'nition** n définition f.

define [dɪ'faɪn] vt définir.

definite ['defɪnɪt] a (date, plan) précis, déterminé; (obvious) net, évident; (firm) ferme; (certain) certain; **d. article** Gram article m défini. ◆**-ly** adv certainement; (appreciably) nettement; (to say) catégoriquement.

definitive [dɪ'fɪnɪtɪv] a définitif.

deflate [dɪ'fleɪt] vt (tyre) dégonfler. ◆**deflation** n dégonflement m; Econ déflation f.

deflect [dɪ'flekt] vt faire dévier; – vi dévier.

deform [dɪ'fɔːm] vt déformer. ◆**-ed** a (body) difforme. ◆**deformity** n difformité f.

defraud [dɪ'frɔːd] vt (customs, State etc) frauder; **to d. s.o. of sth** escroquer qch à qn.

defray [dɪ'freɪ] vt (expenses) payer.

defrost [dɪ'frɒst] vt (fridge) dégivrer; (food) décongeler.

deft [deft] a adroit (with de). ◆**-ness** n adresse f.

defunct [dɪ'fʌŋkt] a défunt.

defuse [diː'fjuːz] vt (bomb, conflict) désamorcer.

defy [dɪ'faɪ] vt (person, death etc) défier; (effort, description) résister à; **to d. s.o. to do** défier qn de faire.

degenerate [dɪ'dʒenəreɪt] vi dégénérer (into en); – [dɪ'dʒenərət] a & n dégénéré, -ée (mf). ◆**degene'ration** n dégénérescence f.

degrade [dɪ'greɪd] vt dégrader. ◆**degradation** [degrə'deɪʃ(ə)n] n Mil Ch dégradation f; (of person) déchéance f.

degree [dɪ'griː] n **1** degré m; **not in the slightest d.** pas du tout; **to such a d.** à tel point (that que). **2** Univ diplôme m; (Bachelor's) licence f; (Master's) maîtrise f; (PhD) doctorat m.

dehumanize [diː'hjuːmənaɪz] vt déshumaniser.

dehydrate [diːhaɪ'dreɪt] vt déshydrater.

de-ice [diː'aɪs] vt Av Aut dégivrer.

deign [deɪn] vt daigner (**to do** faire).

deity ['diːɪtɪ] n dieu m.

dejected [dɪ'dʒektɪd] a abattu, découragé. ◆**dejection** n abattement m.

dekko ['dekəʊ] n Sl coup m d'œil.

delay [dɪ'leɪ] vt retarder; (payment) différer; – vi (be slow) tarder (**doing** à faire); (linger) s'attarder; – n (lateness) retard m; (waiting period) délai m; **without d.** sans tarder. ◆**delayed-'action** a (bomb) à retardement. ◆**delaying** a **d. tactics** moyens mpl dilatoires.

delectable [dɪ'lektəb(ə)l] a délectable.

delegate 1 ['delɪgeɪt] vt déléguer (**to** à). **2** ['delɪgət] n délégué, -ée mf. ◆**dele'gation** n délégation f.

delete [dɪ'liːt] vt rayer, supprimer. ◆**deletion** n (thing deleted) rature f; (act) suppression f.

deleterious [delɪ'tɪərɪəs] a néfaste.

deliberate¹ [dɪ'lɪbəreɪt] vi délibérer; – vt délibérer sur.

deliberate² [dɪ'lɪbərət] a (intentional) délibéré; (cautious) réfléchi; (slow) mesuré.

◆—ly adv (intentionally) exprès, délibérément; (to walk) avec mesure. **◆delibe-'ration** n délibération f.

delicate ['delɪkət] a délicat. **◆delicacy** n délicatesse f; Culin mets m délicat, gourmandise f. **◆delicately** adv délicatement. **◆delica'tessen** n (shop) épicerie f fine, traiteur m.

delicious [dɪ'lɪʃəs] a délicieux.

delight [dɪ'laɪt] n délice m, grand plaisir m, joie f; pl (pleasures, things) délices fpl; **to be the d. of** faire les délices de; **to take d. in sth/in doing** se délecter de qch/à faire; — vt réjouir; — vi se délecter (in doing à faire). **◆—ed** a ravi, enchanté (with sth de qch, to do de faire, that que). **◆delightful** a charmant; (meal, perfume, sensation) délicieux. **◆delightfully** adv avec beaucoup de charme; (wonderfully) merveilleusement.

delineate [dɪ'lɪnɪeɪt] vt (outline) esquisser; (portray) décrire.

delinquent [dɪ'lɪŋkwənt] a & n délinquant, -ante (mf). **◆delinquency** n délinquance f.

delirious [dɪ'lɪərɪəs] a délirant; **to be d.** avoir le délire, délirer. **◆delirium** n Med délire m.

deliver [dɪ'lɪvər] vt **1** (goods, milk etc) livrer; (letters) distribuer; (hand over) remettre (to à). **2** (rescue) délivrer (from de). **3** (give birth to) mettre au monde, accoucher de; **to d. a woman('s baby)** accoucher une femme. **4** (speech) prononcer; (ultimatum, warning) lancer; (blow) porter. **◆deliverance** n délivrance f. **◆delivery** n **1** livraison f; distribution f; remise f. **2** Med accouchement m. **3** (speaking) débit m. **◆deliveryman** n (pl -men) livreur m.

delta ['deltə] n (of river) delta m.

delude [dɪ'luːd] vt tromper; **to d. oneself** se faire des illusions. **◆delusion** n illusion f; Psy aberration f mentale.

deluge ['deljuːdʒ] n (of water, questions etc) déluge m; — vt inonder (with de).

de luxe [dɪ'lʌks] a de luxe.

delve [delv] vi **to d. into** (question, past) fouiller; (books) fouiller dans.

demagogue ['deməgɒg] n démagogue mf.

demand [dɪ'mɑːnd] vt exiger (sth from s.o. qch de qn), réclamer (sth from s.o. qch à qn); (rights, more pay) revendiquer; **to d. that** exiger que; **to d. to know** insister pour savoir; — n exigence f; (claim) revendication f, réclamation f; (request) & Econ demande f; **in great d.** très demandé; **to**

make demands on s.o. exiger beaucoup de qn. **◆—ing** a exigeant.

demarcation [diːmɑː'keɪʃ(ə)n] n démarcation f.

demean [dɪ'miːn] vt **to d. oneself** s'abaisser, s'avilir.

demeanour [dɪ'miːnər] n (behaviour) comportement m.

demented [dɪ'mentɪd] a dément.

demerara [demə'reərə] n **d. (sugar)** cassonade f, sucre m roux.

demise [dɪ'maɪz] n (death) décès m; Fig disparition f.

demo ['deməu] n (pl -os) (demonstration) Fam manif f.

demobilize [diː'məubɪlaɪz] vt démobiliser.

democracy [dɪ'mɒkrəsɪ] n démocratie f. **◆democrat** ['deməkræt] n démocrate mf. **◆demo'cratic** a démocratique; (person) démocrate.

demography [dɪ'mɒgrəfɪ] n démographie f.

demolish [dɪ'mɒlɪʃ] vt démolir. **◆demo-'lition** n démolition f.

demon ['diːmən] n démon m.

demonstrate ['demənstreɪt] vt démontrer; (machine) faire une démonstration de; — vi Pol manifester. **◆demon'stration** n démonstration f; Pol manifestation f. **◆de'monstrative** a démonstratif. **◆demonstrator** n Pol manifestant, -ante mf; (in shop etc) démonstrateur, -trice mf.

demoralize [dɪ'mɒrəlaɪz] vt démoraliser.

demote [dɪ'məut] vt rétrograder.

demure [dɪ'mjuər] a sage, réservé.

den [den] n antre m, tanière f.

denationalize [diː'næʃ(ə)nəlaɪz] vt dénationaliser.

denial [dɪ'naɪəl] n (of truth etc) dénégation f; (of rumour) démenti m; (of authority) rejet m; **to issue a d.** publier un démenti.

denigrate ['denɪgreɪt] vt dénigrer.

denim ['denɪm] n (toile f) coton m; pl (jeans) (blue-)jean m.

denizen ['denɪz(ə)n] n habitant, -ante mf.

Denmark ['denmɑːk] n Danemark m.

denomination [dɪnɒmɪ'neɪʃ(ə)n] n confession f, religion f; (sect) secte m; (of coin, banknote) valeur f; Math unité f. **◆denominational** a (school) confessionnel.

denote [dɪ'nəut] vt dénoter.

denounce [dɪ'nauns] vt (person, injustice etc) dénoncer (to à); **to d. s.o. as a spy/etc** accuser qn publiquement d'être un espion/etc. **◆denunci'ation** n dénonciation f; accusation f publique.

dense [dens] a (-er, -est) dense; (stupid)

Fam lourd, bête. ◆—**ly** *adv* d. populated/*etc* très peuplé/*etc.* ◆**density** *n* densité *f*.

dent [dent] *n* (*in metal*) bosselure *f*; (*in car*) bosse *f*, gnon *m*; **full of dents** (*car*) cabossé; **to make a d. in one's savings** taper dans ses économies; *vt* cabosser, bosseler.

dental ['dent(ə)l] *a* dentaire; **d. surgeon** chirurgien *m* dentiste. ◆**dentist** *n* dentiste *mf*. ◆**dentistry** *n* médecine *f* dentaire; **school of d.** école *f* dentaire. ◆**dentures** *npl* dentier *m*.

deny [dɪ'naɪ] *vt* nier (**doing** avoir fait, **that** que); (*rumour*) démentir; (*authority*) rejeter; (*disown*) renier; **to d. s.o. sth** refuser qch à qn.

deodorant [diː'əʊdərənt] *n* déodorant *m*.

depart [dɪ'pɑːt] *vi* partir; (*deviate*) s'écarter (**from** de); – *vt* **to d. this world** *Lit* quitter ce monde. ◆—**ed** *a & n* (*dead*) défunt, -unte (*mf*). ◆**departure** *n* départ *m*; **a d. from** (*custom, rule*) un écart par rapport à, une entorse à; **to be a new d. for** constituer une nouvelle voie pour.

department [dɪ'pɑːtmənt] *n* département *m*; (*in office*) service *m*; (*in shop*) rayon *m*; *Univ* section *f*, département *m*; **that's your d.** (*sphere*) c'est ton rayon; **d. store** grand magasin *m*. ◆**depart'mental** *a* **d. manager** (*office*) chef *m* de service; (*shop*) chef *m* de rayon.

depend [dɪ'pend] *vi* dépendre (**on, upon** de); **to d. (up)on** (*rely on*) compter sur (**for sth** pour qch); **you can d. on it!** tu peux en être sûr! ◆—**able** *a* (*person, information etc*) sûr; (*machine*) fiable, sûr. ◆**dependant** *n* personne *f* à charge. ◆**dependence** *n* dépendance *f*. ◆**dependency** *n* (*country*) dépendance *f*. ◆**dependent** *a* dépendant (**on, upon** de); (*relative*) à charge; **to be d. (up)on** dépendre de.

depict [dɪ'pɪkt] *vt* (*describe*) dépeindre; (*pictorially*) représenter. ◆**depiction** *n* peinture *f*, représentation *f*.

deplete [dɪ'pliːt] *vt* (*use up*) épuiser; (*reduce*) réduire. ◆**depletion** *n* épuisement *m*; réduction *f*.

deplor/e [dɪ'plɔː] *vt* déplorer. ◆—**able** *a* déplorable.

deploy [dɪ'plɔɪ] *vt* (*troops etc*) déployer.

depopulate [diː'pɒpjʊleɪt] *vt* dépeupler. ◆**depopu'lation** *n* dépeuplement *m*.

deport [dɪ'pɔːt] *vt Pol Jur* expulser; (*to concentration camp etc*) *Hist* déporter. ◆**depor'tation** *n* expulsion *f*; déportation *f*.

deportment [dɪ'pɔːtmənt] *n* maintien *m*.

depose [dɪ'pəʊz] *vt* (*king etc*) déposer.

deposit [dɪ'pɒzɪt] *vt* (*object, money etc*) déposer; – *n* (*in bank, wine*) & *Ch* dépôt *m*; (*part payment*) acompte *m*; (*against damage*) caution *f*; (*on bottle*) consigne *f*; **d. account** *Fin* compte *m* d'épargne. ◆—**or** *n* déposant, -ante *mf*, épargnant, -ante *mf*.

depot ['depəʊ, *Am* 'diːpəʊ] *n* dépôt *m*; (*station*) *Rail Am* gare *f*; (**bus**) **d.** *Am* gare *f* routière.

deprave [dɪ'preɪv] *vt* dépraver. ◆**depravity** *n* dépravation *f*.

deprecate ['deprəkeɪt] *vt* désapprouver.

depreciate [dɪ'priːʃɪeɪt] *vt* (*reduce in value*) déprécier; – *vi* se déprécier. ◆**depreci'ation** *n* dépréciation *f*.

depress [dɪ'pres] *vt* (*discourage*) déprimer; (*push down*) appuyer sur. ◆—**ed** *a* déprimé; (*in decline*) en déclin; (*in crisis*) en crise; **to get d.** se décourager. ◆**depression** *n* dépression *f*.

depriv/e [dɪ'praɪv] *vt* priver (**of** de). ◆—**ed** *a* (*child etc*) déshérité. ◆**depri'vation** *n* privation *f*; (*loss*) perte *f*.

depth [depθ] *n* profondeur *f*; (*of snow*) épaisseur *f*; (*of interest*) intensité *f*; **in the depths of** (*forest, despair*) au plus profond de; (*winter*) au cœur de; **to get out of one's d.** *Fig* perdre pied, nager; **in d.** en profondeur.

deputize ['depjʊtaɪz] *vi* assurer l'intérim (**for** de); – *vt* **to d.** (**s.o. to do** qn pour faire). ◆**depu'tation** *n* députation *f*. ◆**deputy** *n* (*replacement*) suppléant, -ante *mf*; (*assistant*) adjoint, -ointe *mf*; **d.** (**sheriff**) *Am* shérif *m* adjoint; **d. chairman** vice-président, -ente *mf*.

derailed [dɪ'reɪld] *a* **to be d.** (*of train*) dérailler. ◆**derailment** *n* déraillement *m*.

deranged [dɪ'reɪndʒd] *a* (*person, mind*) dérangé.

derelict ['derɪlɪkt] *a* à l'abandon, abandonné.

deride [dɪ'raɪd] *vt* tourner en dérision. ◆**derision** *n* dérision *f*. ◆**derisive** *a* (*laughter etc*) moqueur; (*amount*) dérisoire. ◆**derisory** *a* dérisoire.

derive [dɪ'raɪv] *vt* **to d. from** (*pleasure, profit etc*) tirer de; *Ling* dériver de; **to be derived from** dériver de, provenir de; – *vi* **to d. from** dériver de. ◆**deri'vation** *n Ling* dérivation *f*. ◆**derivative** *a & n Ling Ch* dérivé (*m*).

dermatology [dɜːmə'tɒlədʒɪ] *n* dermatologie *f*.

derogatory [dɪ'rɒɡət(ə)rɪ] *a* (*word*) péjoratif; (*remark*) désobligeant (**to** pour).

derrick ['derɪk] n (over oil well) derrick m.

derv [dɜːv] n gazole m, gas-oil m.

descend [dɪ'send] vi descendre (from de); (of rain) tomber; **to d. upon** (attack) faire une descente sur, tomber sur; (of tourists) envahir; – vt (stairs) descendre; **to be descended from** descendre de. ◆**-ing** a (order) décroissant. ◆**descendant** n descendant, -ante f. ◆**descent** n 1 descente f; (into crime) chute f. 2 (ancestry) souche f, origine f.

describe [dɪ'skraɪb] vt décrire. ◆**description** n description f; (on passport) signalement m; **of every d.** de toutes sortes. ◆**descriptive** a descriptif.

desecrate ['desɪkreɪt] vt profaner. ◆**desecration** n profanation f.

desegregate [diː'segrɪgeɪt] vt supprimer la ségrégation raciale dans. ◆**desegregation** n déségrégation f.

desert[1] ['dezət] n désert m; – a désertique; **d. island** île f déserte.

desert[2] [dɪ'zɜːt] vt déserter, abandonner; **to d. s.o.** (of luck etc) abandonner qn; – vi Mil déserter. ◆**-ed** a (place) désert. ◆**-er** n Mil déserteur m. ◆**desertion** n désertion f; (by spouse) abandon m (du domicile conjugal).

deserts [dɪ'zɜːts] n **one's just d.** ce qu'on mérite.

deserv/e [dɪ'zɜːv] vt mériter (**to do** de faire). ◆**-ing** a (person) méritant; (act, cause) louable, méritoire; **d. of** digne de. ◆**-edly** [-ɪdlɪ] adv à juste titre.

desiccated ['desɪkeɪtɪd] a (des)séché.

design [dɪ'zaɪn] vt (car, furniture etc) dessiner; (dress) créer, dessiner; (devise) concevoir (**for s.o.** pour qn, **to do** pour faire); **well designed** bien conçu; – n (aim) dessein m, intention f; (sketch) plan m, dessin m; (of dress, car) modèle m, (planning) conception f, création f; (pattern) motif m, dessin m; **industrial d.** dessin m industriel; **by d.** intentionnellement; **to have designs on** avoir des desseins sur. ◆**-er** n dessinateur, -trice mf; **d. clothes** vêtements mpl griffés.

designate ['dezɪgneɪt] vt désigner. ◆**designation** n désignation f.

desir/e [dɪ'zaɪər] n désir m; **I've no d.** to je n'ai aucune envie de; – vt désirer (**to do** faire). ◆**-able** a désirable; **d. property**/etc (in advertising) (très) belle propriété/etc.

desk [desk] n Sch pupitre m; (in office) bureau m; (in shop) caisse f; (reception) **d.** réception f; **the news d.** Journ le service des

informations; – a (job) de bureau; **d. clerk** (in hotel) Am réceptionniste mf.

desolate ['desələt] a (deserted) désolé; (in ruins) dévasté; (dreary, bleak) morne, triste. ◆**desolation** n (ruin) dévastation f; (emptiness) solitude f.

despair [dɪ'speər] n désespoir m; **to drive s.o. to d.** désespérer qn; **in d.** au désespoir; – vi désespérer (**of s.o.** de qn, **of doing** de faire). ◆**-ing** a désespéré. ◆**desperate** a désespéré; (criminal) capable de tout; (serious) grave; **to be d. for** (money, love etc) avoir désespérément besoin de; (a cigarette, baby etc) mourir d'envie d'avoir. ◆**desperately** adv (ill) gravement; (in love) éperdument. ◆**desperation** n désespoir m; **in d.** (as a last resort) en désespoir de cause.

despatch [dɪ'spætʃ] see **dispatch**.

desperado [despə'rɑːdəʊ] n (pl -oes or -os) criminel m.

despise [dɪ'spaɪz] vt mépriser. ◆**despicable** a ignoble, méprisable.

despite [dɪ'spaɪt] prep malgré.

despondent [dɪ'spɒndənt] a découragé. ◆**despondency** n découragement m.

despot ['despɒt] n despote m. ◆**despotism** n despotisme m.

dessert [dɪ'zɜːt] n dessert m. ◆**dessertspoon** n cuiller f à dessert.

destabilize [diː'steɪbəlaɪz] vt déstabiliser.

destination [destɪ'neɪʃ(ə)n] n destination f.

destine ['destɪn] vt destiner (**for** à, **to do** faire); **it was destined to happen** ça devait arriver. ◆**destiny** n destin m; (fate of individual) destinée f.

destitute ['destɪtjuːt] a (poor) indigent; **d. of** (lacking in) dénué de. ◆**destitution** n dénuement m.

destroy [dɪ'strɔɪ] vt détruire; (horse etc) abattre. ◆**-er** n (person) destructeur, -trice mf; (ship) contre-torpilleur m. ◆**destruct** vt Mil détruire. ◆**destruction** n destruction f. ◆**destructive** a (person, war) destructeur; (power) destructif.

detach [dɪ'tætʃ] vt détacher (**from** de). ◆**-ed** a (indifferent) détaché; (view) désintéressé; **d. house** maison f individuelle. ◆**-able** a (lining) amovible. ◆**-ment** n (attitude) & Mil détachement m; **the d. of** (action) la séparation de.

detail ['diːteɪl, Am dɪ'teɪl] **1** n détail m; **in d.** en détail; – vt raconter or exposer en détail or par le menu, détailler. **2** vt Mil détacher (**to do** pour faire); – n détachement m. ◆**-ed** a (account etc) détaillé.

detain [dɪ'teɪn] vt retenir; (imprison) détenir.

◆**detai'nee** n Pol Jur détenu, -ue mf.
◆**detention** n Jur détention f; Sch retenue f.

detect [dɪ'tekt] vt découvrir; (perceive) distinguer; (identify) identifier; (mine) détecter; (illness) dépister. ◆**detection** n découverte f; identification f; détection f; dépistage m. ◆**detector** n détecteur m.

detective [dɪ'tektɪv] n agent m de la Sûreté, policier m (en civil); (private) détective m; − a (film etc) policier; story roman m policier; **d. constable** = inspecteur m de police.

deter [dɪ'tɜːr] vt (-rr-) to d. s.o. dissuader or décourager qn (from doing de faire, from sth de qch).

detergent [dɪ'tɜːdʒənt] n détergent m.

deteriorate [dɪ'tɪərɪəreɪt] vi se détériorer; (of morals) dégénérer. ◆**deterio'ration** n détérioration f; dégénérescence f.

determin/e [dɪ'tɜːmɪn] vt déterminer; (price) fixer; to d. s.o. to do décider qn à faire; to d. that décider que; to d. to do se déterminer à faire. ◆**-ed** a (look, quantity) déterminé; to d. to do or on doing décidé à faire; I'm d. she'll succeed je suis bien décidé à ce qu'elle réussisse.

deterrent [dɪ'terənt, Am dɪ'tɜːrənt] n Mil force f de dissuasion; to be a d. Fig être dissuasif.

detest [dɪ'test] vt détester (doing faire). ◆**-able** a détestable.

detonate [detɪneɪt] vt faire détoner or exploser; − vi détoner. ◆**deto'nation** n détonation f. ◆**detonator** n détonateur m.

detour [dɪtuːər] n détour m.

detract [dɪ'trækt] vi to d. from (make less) diminuer. ◆**detractor** n détracteur, -trice mf.

detriment [detrɪmənt] n détriment m. ◆**detri'mental** a préjudiciable (to à).

devalue [diː'væljuː] vt (money) & Fig dévaluer. ◆**devalu'ation** n dévaluation f.

devastat/e [devəsteɪt] vt (lay waste) dévaster; (opponent) anéantir; (person) Fig foudroyer. ◆**-ing** a (storm etc) dévastateur; (overwhelming) confondant, accablant; (charm) irrésistible.

develop [dɪ'veləp] vt développer; (area, land) mettre en valeur; (habit, illness) contracter; (talent) manifester; Phot développer; to d. a liking for prendre goût à; − vi se développer; (of event) se produire; to d. into devenir. ◆**-ing** a (country) en voie de développement; − n Phot développement m. ◆**-er** n (property) d. promoteur m (de construction).

◆**-ment** n développement m; (of land) mise f en valeur; (housing) d. lotissement m; (large) grand ensemble m; **a (new) d.** (in situation) un fait nouveau.

deviate [diːvɪeɪt] vi dévier (from de); to d. from the norm s'écarter de la norme. ◆**deviant** a anormal. ◆**devi'ation** n déviation f.

device [dɪ'vaɪs] n dispositif m, engin m; (scheme) procédé m; **left to one's own devices** livré à soi-même.

devil [devəl] n diable m; a or the d. of a problem Fam un problème épouvantable; a or the d. of a noise Fam un bruit infernal; I had a or the d. of a job Fam j'ai eu un mal fou (doing, to do à faire); what/where/why the d.? Fam que/où/pourquoi diable?; like the d. (to run etc) comme un fou. ◆**devilish** a diabolique. ◆**devilry** n (mischief) diablerie f.

devious [diːvɪəs] a (mind, behaviour) tortueux; he's d. il a l'esprit tortueux. ◆**-ness** n (of person) esprit m tortueux.

devise [dɪ'vaɪz] vt (plan) combiner; (plot) tramer; (invent) inventer.

devitalize [diː'vaɪtəlaɪz] vt rendre exsangue, affaiblir.

devoid [dɪ'vɔɪd] a **d. of** dénué or dépourvu de; (guilt) exempt de.

devolution [diːvəluː'ʃ(ə)n] n Pol décentralisation f; the d. of (power) la délégation de.

devolve [dɪ'vɒlv] vi to d. upon incomber à.

devot/e [dɪ'vəʊt] vt consacrer (to à). ◆**-ed** a dévoué; (admirer) fervent. ◆**-edly** adv avec dévouement. ◆**devo'tee** n Sp Mus passionné, -ée mf. ◆**devotion** n dévouement m; (religious) dévotion f; pl (prayers) dévotions fpl.

devour [dɪ'vaʊər] vt (eat, engulf, read etc) dévorer.

devout [dɪ'vaʊt] a dévot, pieux; (supporter, prayer) fervent.

dew [djuː] n rosée f. ◆**dewdrop** n goutte f de rosée.

dext(e)rous [dekst(ə)rəs] a adroit, habile. ◆**dex'terity** n adresse f, dextérité f.

diabetes [daɪə'biːtiːz] n Med diabète m. ◆**diabetic** a & n diabétique (mf).

diabolical [daɪə'bɒlɪk(ə)l] a diabolique; (bad) épouvantable.

diadem [daɪədem] n diadème m.

diagnosis, pl -oses [daɪəg'nəʊsɪs, -əʊsiːz] n diagnostic m. ◆**'diagnose** vt diagnostiquer.

diagonal [daɪ'ægən(ə)l] a diagonal; − n (line) diagonale f. ◆**-ly** adv en diagonale.

diagram [daɪəgræm] n schéma m,

diagramme *m*; *Geom* figure *f.* ◆**diagra'mmatic** *a* schématique.

dial ['daɪəl] *n* cadran *m*; — *vt* (-ll-, *Am* -l-) (*number*) *Tel* composer; (*person*) appeler; **to d. s.o. direct** appeler qn par l'automatique; **d. tone** *Am* tonalité *f.* ◆**dialling** *a* **d. code** indicatif *m*; **d. tone** tonalité *f.*

dialect ['daɪəlekt] *n* (*regional*) dialecte *m*; (*rural*) patois *m.*

dialogue ['daɪəlɒg] (*Am* **dialog**) *n* dialogue *m.*

dialysis, pl -yses [daɪˈælɪsɪs, -ɪsiːz] *n* *Med* dialyse *f.*

diameter [daɪˈæmɪtər] *n* diamètre *m.* ◆**dia'metrically** *adv* (*opposed*) diamétralement.

diamond ['daɪəmənd] **1** *n* (*stone*) diamant *m*; (*shape*) losange *m*; (*baseball*) *Am* terrain *m* (de baseball); **d. necklace/**etc rivière *f*/etc de diamants. **2** *n* & *npl* Cards carreau *m.*

diaper ['daɪəpər] *n* (*for baby*) *Am* couche *f.*

diaphragm ['daɪəfræm] *n* diaphragme *m.*

diarr(o)ea [daɪəˈriːə] *n* diarrhée *f.*

diary ['daɪərɪ] *n* (*calendar*) agenda *m*; (*private*) journal *m* (intime).

dice [daɪs] *n inv* dé *m* (à jouer); — *vt* Culin couper en dés.

dicey ['daɪsɪ] *a* (**-ier, -iest**) *Fam* risqué.

dichotomy [daɪˈkɒtəmɪ] *n* dichotomie *f.*

dickens ['dɪkɪnz] *n* **where/why/what the d.?** *Fam* où/pourquoi/que diable?

dictate [dɪkˈteɪt] *vt* dicter (**to** à); — *vi* dicter; **to d. to s.o.** (*order around*) régenter qn. ◆**dictation** *n* dictée *f.* ◆**'dictaphone®** *n* dictaphone® *m.*

dictates ['dɪkteɪts] *npl* préceptes *mpl*; **the d. of conscience** la voix de la conscience.

dictator [dɪkˈteɪtər] *n* dictateur *m.* ◆**dicta'torial** *a* dictatorial. ◆**dictatorship** *n* dictature *f.*

diction ['dɪkʃ(ə)n] *n* langage *m*; (*way of speaking*) diction *f.*

dictionary ['dɪkʃənərɪ] *n* dictionnaire *m.*

dictum ['dɪktəm] *n* dicton *m.*

did [dɪd] *see* **do**.

diddle ['dɪd(ə)l] *vt* *Sl* rouler; **to d. s.o. out of sth** carotter qch à qn; **to get diddled out of sth** se faire refaire de qch.

die [daɪ] **1** *vi* (*pt* & *pp* **died**, *pres p* **dying**) mourir (**of, from** de); **to be dying to do** mourir d'envie de faire; **to be dying for sth** *Fam* mourir d'une envie folle de qch; **to d. away** (*of noise*) mourir; **to d. down** (*of fire*) mourir; (*of storm*) se calmer; **to d. off** mourir (les uns après les autres); **to d. out** (*of custom*) mourir. **2** *n* (*in engraving*) coin *m*; *Tech* matrice *f*; **the d. is cast** *Fig* les dés sont jetés.

diehard ['daɪhɑːd] *n* réactionnaire *mf.*

diesel ['diːz(ə)l] *a* & *n* **d. (engine)** (moteur *m*) diesel *m*; **d. (oil)** gazole *m.*

diet ['daɪət] *n* (*for slimming etc*) régime *m*; (*usual food*) alimentation *f*; **to go on a d.** faire un régime; — *vi* suivre un régime. ◆**dietary** *a* diététique; **d. fibre** fibre(s) *f(pl)* alimentaire(s). ◆**die'tician** *n* diététicien, -ienne *mf.*

differ ['dɪfər] *vi* différer (**from** de); (*disagree*) ne pas être d'accord (**from** avec). ◆**difference** *n* différence *f* (**in** de); (*in age, weight etc*) écart *m*, différence *f*; (*of opinion*) différend *m*; **it makes no d.** ça n'a pas d'importance; **it makes no d. to me** ça m'est égal; **to make a d. in sth** changer qch. ◆**different** *a* différent (**from, to** de); (*another*) autre; (*various*) différents, divers. ◆**diffe'rential** *a* différentiel; — *n Econ* écarts *mpl* salariaux. ◆**diffe'rentiate** *vt* différencier (**from** de); **to d. (between)** faire la différence entre. ◆**differently** *adv* différemment (**from, to** de), autrement (**from, to** que).

difficult ['dɪfɪkəlt] *a* difficile (**to do** à faire); **it's d. for us to . . .** il nous est difficile de . . .; **the d. thing is to . . .** le plus difficile est de . . . . ◆**difficulty** *n* difficulté *f*; **to have d. doing** avoir du mal à faire; **to be in d.** avoir des difficultés; **d. with** des ennuis *mpl* avec.

diffident ['dɪfɪdənt] *a* (*person*) qui manque d'assurance; (*smile, tone*) mal assuré. ◆**diffidence** *n* manque *m* d'assurance.

diffuse [dɪˈfjuːz] *vt* (*spread*) diffuser; — [dɪˈfjuːs] *a* (*spread out, wordy*) diffus. ◆**diffusion** *n* diffusion *f.*

dig [dɪg] *vt* (*pt* & *pp* **dug**, *pres p* **digging**) (*ground*) bêcher; (*hole, grave etc*) creuser; (*understand*) *Sl* piger; (*appreciate*) *Sl* aimer; **to d. sth into** (*thrust*) enfoncer qch dans; **to d. out** (*animal, fact*) déterrer; (*accident victim*) dégager; (*find*) *Fam* dénicher; **to d. up** déterrer; (*weed*) arracher; (*earth*) retourner; (*street*) piocher; — *vi* creuser; (*of pig*) fouiller; **to d. (oneself) in** *Mil* se retrancher; **to d. in** (*eat*) *Fam* manger; **to d. into** (*s.o.'s past*) fouiller dans; (*meal*) *Fam* attaquer; — *n* (*with spade*) coup *m* de bêche; (*push*) coup *m* de poing or de coude; (*remark*) *Fam* coup *m* de griffe. ◆**digger** *n* (*machine*) pelleteuse *f.*

digest [daɪˈdʒest] *vti* digérer; — ['daɪdʒest] *n Journ* condensé *m.* ◆**digestible** *a* digeste.

◆**digestion** *n* digestion *f*. ◆**digestive** *a* digestif.

digit ['dɪdʒɪt] *n* (*number*) chiffre *m*. ◆**digital** *a* (*watch, keyboard etc*) numérique.

dignified ['dɪgnɪfaɪd] *a* digne, qui a de la dignité. ◆**dignify** *vt* donner de la dignité à; **to d. with the name of** honorer du nom de. ◆**dignitary** *n* dignitaire *m*. ◆**dignity** *n* dignité *f*.

digress [daɪ'gres] *vi* faire une digression; **to d. from** s'écarter de. ◆**digression** *n* digression *f*.

digs [dɪgz] *npl Fam* chambre *f* (meublée), logement *m*.

dilapidated [dɪ'læpɪdeɪtɪd] *a* (*house*) délabré. ◆**dilapi'dation** *n* délabrement *m*.

dilate [daɪ'leɪt] *vt* dilater; − *vi* se dilater. ◆**dilation** *n* dilatation *f*.

dilemma [daɪ'lemə] *n* dilemme *m*.

dilettante [dɪlɪ'tæntɪ] *n* dilettante *mf*.

diligent ['dɪlɪdʒənt] *a* assidu, appliqué; **to be d. in doing sth** faire qch avec zèle. ◆**diligence** *n* zèle *m*, assiduité *f*.

dilly-dally [dɪlɪ'dælɪ] *vi Fam* (*dawdle*) lambiner, lanterner; (*hesitate*) tergiverser.

dilute [daɪ'luːt] *vt* diluer; − *a* dilué.

dim [dɪm] *a* (**dimmer, dimmest**) (*feeble*) faible; (*colour*) terne; (*room*) sombre; (*memory, outline*) vague; (*person*) stupide; − *vt* (**-mm-**) (*light*) baisser, réduire; (*glory*) ternir; (*memory*) estomper. ◆**-ly** *adv* faiblement; (*vaguely*) vaguement. ◆**-ness** *n* faiblesse *f*; (*of memory etc*) vague *m*; (*of room*) pénombre *f*. ◆**dimwit** *n* idiot, -ote *mf*. ◆**dim'witted** *a* idiot.

dime [daɪm] *n* (*US & Can coin*) (pièce *f* de) dix cents *mpl*; **a d. store** = un Prisunic®, un Monoprix®.

dimension [daɪ'menʃ(ə)n] *n* dimension *f*; (*extent*) *Fig* étendue *f*. ◆**dimensional** *a* **two-d.** à deux dimensions.

diminish [dɪ'mɪnɪʃ] *vti* diminuer. ◆**-ing** *a* qui diminue.

diminutive [dɪ'mɪnjʊtɪv] **1** *a* (*tiny*) minuscule. **2** *a & n Gram* diminutif (*m*).

dimple ['dɪmp(ə)l] *n* fossette *f*. ◆**dimpled** *a* (*chin, cheek*) à fossettes.

din [dɪn] **1** *n* (*noise*) vacarme *m*. **2** *vt* (**-nn-**) **to d. into s.o. that** rabâcher à qn que.

din/e [daɪn] *vi* dîner (**off, on** de); **to d. out** dîner en ville. ◆**-ing** *a* **d. car** *Rail* wagon-restaurant *m*; **d. room** salle *f* à manger. ◆**-er** *n* dîneur, -euse *mf*; *Rail* wagon-restaurant *m*; (*short-order restaurant*) *Am* petit restaurant *m*.

◆**ding(dong)!** ['dɪŋ(dɒŋ)] *int* (*of bell*) dring!, ding (dong)!

dinghy ['dɪŋgɪ] *n* petit canot *m*, youyou *m*; (**rubber**) **d.** canot *m* pneumatique.

dingy ['dɪndʒɪ] *a* (**-ier, -iest**) (*dirty*) malpropre; (*colour*) terne. ◆**dinginess** *n* malpropreté *f*.

dinner ['dɪnər] *n* (*evening meal*) dîner *m*; (*lunch*) déjeuner *m*; (*for dog, cat*) pâtée *f*; **to have d.** dîner; **to have s.o. to d.** avoir qn à dîner; **d. dance** dîner-dansant *m*; **d. jacket** smoking *m*; **d. party** dîner *m* (à la maison); **d. plate** grande assiette *f*; **d. service**, **d. set** service *m* de table.

dinosaur ['daɪnəsɔːr] *n* dinosaure *m*.

dint [dɪnt] *n* **by d. of** à force de.

diocese ['daɪəsɪs] *n Rel* diocèse *m*.

dip [dɪp] *vt* (**-pp-**) plonger; (*into liquid*) tremper, plonger; **to d. one's headlights** se mettre en code; − *vi* (*of sun etc*) baisser; (*of road*) plonger; **to d. into** (*pocket, savings*) puiser dans; (*book*) feuilleter; − *n* (*in road*) déclivité *f*; (*for food*) sauce *f*; **to go for a d.** faire trempette.

diphtheria [dɪp'θɪərɪə] *n* diphtérie *f*.

diphthong ['dɪfθɒŋ] *n Ling* diphtongue *f*.

diploma [dɪ'pləʊmə] *n* diplôme *m*.

diplomacy [dɪ'pləʊməsɪ] *n* (*tact*) & *Pol* diplomatie *f*. ◆**'diplomat** *n* diplomate *mf*. ◆**diplo'matic** *a* diplomatique; **to be d.** (*tactful*) *Fig* être diplomate.

dipper ['dɪpər] *n* **the big d.** (*at fairground*) les montagnes *fpl* russes.

dire ['daɪər] *a* affreux; (*poverty, need*) extrême.

direct [daɪ'rekt] **1** *a* (*result, flight, person etc*) direct; (*danger*) immédiat; − *adv* directement. **2** *vt* (*work, one's steps, one's attention*) diriger; (*letter, remark*) adresser (**to** à); (*efforts*) orienter (**to, towards** vers); (*film*) réaliser; (*play*) mettre en scène; **to d. s.o. to** (*place*) indiquer à qn le chemin de; **to d. s.o. to do** charger qn de faire. ◆**direction** *n* direction *f*, sens *m*; (*management*) direction *f*; (*of film*) réalisation *f*; (*of play*) mise *f* en scène; *pl* (*orders*) indications *fpl*; **directions (for use)** mode *m* d'emploi; **in the opposite d.** en sens inverse. ◆**directive** [dɪ'rektɪv] *n* directive *f*. ◆**directly** *adv* (*without detour*) directement; (*at once*) tout de suite; (*to speak*) franchement; − *conj Fam* aussitôt que. ◆**directness** *n* (*of reply*) franchise *f*. ◆**director** *n* directeur, -trice *mf*; (*of film*) réalisateur, -trice *mf*; (*of play*) metteur en scène. ◆**directorship** *n Com* poste *m* de directeur.

directory [daɪ'rektərɪ] *n Tel* annuaire *m*; (*of*

streets) guide m; (*of addresses*) répertoire m; **d. enquiries** Tel renseignements mpl.

dirge [dɜːdʒ] n chant m funèbre.

dirt [dɜːt] n saleté f; (*filth*) ordure f; (*mud*) boue f; (*earth*) terre f; (*talk*) Fig obscénité(s) f(pl); **d. cheap** Fam très bon marché; **d. road** chemin m de terre; **d. track** Sp cendrée f. ◆**dirty** a (-ier, -iest) sale; (*job*) salissant; (*obscene, unpleasant*) sale; (*word*) grossier, obscène; **to get d.** se salir; **to get sth d.** salir qch; **a d. joke** une histoire cochonne; **a d. trick** un sale tour; **a d. old man** un vieux cochon; – adv (*to fight*) déloyalement; – vt salir; (*machine*) encrasser; – vi se salir.

disabl/e [dɪsˈeɪb(ə)l] vt rendre infirme; (*maim*) mutiler. ◆**—ed** a infirme, handicapé; (*maimed*) mutilé; – n **the d.** les infirmes mpl, les handicapés mpl. ◆**disa'bility** n infirmité f; Fig désavantage m.

disadvantage [dɪsədˈvɑːntɪdʒ] n désavantage m; – vt désavantager.

disaffected [dɪsəˈfektɪd] a mécontent. ◆**disaffection** n désaffection f (**for** pour).

disagree [dɪsəˈɡriː] vi ne pas être d'accord, être en désaccord (**with** avec); (*of figures*) ne pas concorder; **to d. with** (*of food etc*) ne pas réussir à. ◆**—able** a désagréable. ◆**—ment** n désaccord m; (*quarrel*) différend m.

disallow [dɪsəˈlaʊ] vt rejeter.

disappear [dɪsəˈpɪər] vi disparaître. ◆**disappearance** n disparition f.

disappoint [dɪsəˈpɔɪnt] vt décevoir; **I'm disappointed with it** ça m'a déçu. ◆**—ing** a décevant. ◆**—ment** n déception f.

disapprov/e [dɪsəˈpruːv] vi **to d. of s.o./sth** désapprouver qn/qch; **I d.** je suis contre. ◆**—ing** a (*look etc*) désapprobateur. ◆**disapproval** n désapprobation f.

disarm [dɪsˈɑːm] vti désarmer. ◆**disarma'ment** n désarmement m.

disarray [dɪsəˈreɪ] n (*disorder*) désordre m; (*distress*) désarroi m.

disaster [dɪˈzɑːstər] n désastre m, catastrophe f; **d. area** région f sinistrée. ◆**d.-stricken** a sinistré. ◆**disastrous** a désastreux.

disband [dɪsˈbænd] vt disperser; – vi se disperser.

disbelief [dɪsbəˈliːf] n incrédulité f.

disc [dɪsk] (*Am* **disk**) n disque m; **identity d.** plaque f d'identité; **d. jockey** animateur, -trice mf de variétés etc, disc-jockey m.

discard [dɪsˈkɑːd] vt (*get rid of*) se débarrasser de; (*plan, hope etc*) Fig abandonner.

discern [dɪˈsɜːn] vt discerner. ◆**—ing** a

(*person*) averti, sagace. ◆**—ible** a perceptible. ◆**—ment** n discernement m.

discharge [dɪsˈtʃɑːdʒ] vt (*gun, accused person*) décharger; (*liquid*) déverser; (*patient, employee*) renvoyer; (*soldier*) libérer; (*unfit soldier*) réformer; (*one's duty*) accomplir; – vi (*of wound*) suppurer; – [ˈdɪstʃɑːdʒ] n (*of gun*) & El décharge f; (*of liquid*) & Med écoulement m; (*dismissal*) renvoi m; (*freeing*) libération f; (*of unfit soldier*) réforme f.

disciple [dɪˈsaɪp(ə)l] n disciple m.

discipline [ˈdɪsɪplɪn] n (*behaviour, subject*) discipline f; – vt (*control*) discipliner; (*punish*) punir. ◆**disci'plinarian** n partisan, -ane mf de la discipline; **to be a (strict) d.** être très à cheval sur la discipline. ◆**disci'plinary** a disciplinaire.

disclaim [dɪsˈkleɪm] vt désavouer; (*responsibility*) (dé)nier.

disclose [dɪsˈkləʊz] vt révéler, divulguer. ◆**disclosure** n révélation f.

disco [ˈdɪskəʊ] n (pl -os) Fam disco(thèque) f.

discolour [dɪsˈkʌlər] vt décolorer; (*teeth*) jaunir; – vi se décolorer; jaunir. ◆**discolo(u)ration** n décoloration f; jaunissement m.

discomfort [dɪsˈkʌmfət] n (*physical, mental*) malaise m, gêne f; (*hardship*) inconvénient m.

disconcert [dɪskənˈsɜːt] vt déconcerter.

disconnect [dɪskəˈnekt] vt (*unfasten etc*) détacher; (*unplug*) débrancher; (*wires*) El déconnecter; (*gas, telephone etc*) couper. ◆**—ed** a (*speech*) décousu.

discontent [dɪskənˈtent] n mécontentement m. ◆**discontented** a mécontent.

discontinu/e [dɪskənˈtɪnjuː] vt cesser, interrompre. ◆**—ed** a (*article*) Com qui ne se fait plus.

discord [ˈdɪskɔːd] n discorde f; Mus dissonance f.

discotheque [ˈdɪskətek] n (*club*) discothèque f.

discount 1 [ˈdɪskaʊnt] n (*on article*) remise f; (*on account paid early*) escompte m; **at a d.** (*to buy, sell*) au rabais; **d. store** solderie f. **2** [dɪsˈkaʊnt] vt (*story etc*) ne pas tenir compte de.

discourage [dɪsˈkʌrɪdʒ] vt décourager; **to get discouraged** se décourager. ◆**—ment** n découragement m.

discourse [ˈdɪskɔːs] n discours m.

discourteous [dɪsˈkɜːtɪəs] a impoli, discourtois. ◆**discourtesy** n impolitesse f.

discover [dɪsˈkʌvər] vt découvrir. ◆**discovery** n découverte f.

discredit [dɪs'kredɪt] vt (cast slur on) discréditer; (refuse to believe) ne pas croire; – n discrédit m. ◆—**able** a indigne.

discreet [dɪs'kriːt] a (careful) prudent, avisé; (unassuming, reserved etc) discret. ◆**discretion** n prudence f; discrétion f; **I'll use my own d.** je ferai comme bon me semblera. ◆**discretionary** a discrétionnaire.

discrepancy [dɪs'krepənsɪ] n divergence f, contradiction f (**between** entre).

discriminat/e [dɪs'krɪmɪneɪt] vi **to d. between** distinguer entre; **to d. against** établir une discrimination contre; – vt **to d. sth/s.o. from** distinguer qch/qn de. ◆—**ing** a (person) averti, sagace; (ear) fin. ◆**discrimi'nation** n (judgement) discernement m; (distinction) distinction f; (partiality) discrimination f. ◆**dis-criminatory** [-ətərɪ] a discriminatoire.

discus [dɪskəs] n Sp disque m.

discuss [dɪs'kʌs] vt (talk about) discuter de; (examine in detail) discuter. ◆**discussion** n discussion f; **under d.** (matter etc) en question, en discussion.

disdain [dɪs'deɪn] vt dédaigner; – n dédain m. ◆**disdainful** a dédaigneux; **to be d. of** dédaigner.

disease [dɪ'ziːz] n maladie f. ◆**diseased** a malade.

disembark [dɪsɪm'bɑːk] vti débarquer. ◆**disembar'kation** n débarquement m.

disembodied [dɪsɪm'bɒdɪd] a désincarné.

disembowel [dɪsɪm'baʊəl] vt (-ll-, Am -l-) éventrer.

disenchant [dɪsɪn'tʃɑːnt] vt désenchanter. ◆—**ment** n désenchantement m.

disengage [dɪsɪn'geɪdʒ] vt (object) dégager; (troops) désengager.

disentangle [dɪsɪn'tæŋg(ə)l] vt démêler; **to d. oneself from** se dégager de.

disfavour [dɪs'feɪvər] n défaveur f.

disfigure [dɪs'fɪgər] vt défigurer. ◆—**ment** n défigurement m.

disgorge [dɪs'gɔːdʒ] vt (food) vomir.

disgrac/e [dɪs'greɪs] n (shame) honte f (**to** à); (disfavour) disgrâce f; – vt déshonorer, faire honte à. ◆—**ed** a (politician etc) disgracié. ◆**disgraceful** a honteux (**of s.o.** de la part de qn). ◆**disgracefully** adv honteusement.

disgruntled [dɪs'grʌnt(ə)ld] a mécontent.

disguise [dɪs'gaɪz] vt déguiser (**as** en); – n déguisement m; **in d.** déguisé.

disgust [dɪs'gʌst] n dégoût m (**for, at, with** pour); **in d.** dégoûté; – vt dégoûter, écœurer. ◆—**ed** a dégoûté (**at, by, with** de); **to be d. with s.o.** (annoyed) être fâché contre qn; **d.**

to hear that ... indigné d'apprendre que .... ◆—**ing** a dégoûtant, écœurant. ◆—**ingly** adv d'une façon dégoûtante.

dish [dɪʃ] **1** n (container) plat m; (food) mets m, plat m; **the dishes** la vaisselle; **she's a (real) d.** Sl c'est un beau brin de fille. **2** vt **to d. out** distribuer; **to d. out** or **up** (food) servir. ◆**dishcloth** n (for washing) lavette f; (for drying) torchon m. ◆**dishpan** n Am bassine f (à vaisselle). ◆**dishwasher** n lave-vaisselle m inv.

disharmony [dɪs'hɑːmənɪ] n désaccord m; Mus dissonance f.

dishearten [dɪs'hɑːt(ə)n] vt décourager.

dishevelled [dɪ'ʃev(ə)ld] a hirsute, échevelé.

dishonest [dɪs'ɒnɪst] a malhonnête; (insincere) de mauvaise foi. ◆**dishonesty** n malhonnêteté f; mauvaise foi f.

dishonour [dɪs'ɒnər] n déshonneur m; – vt déshonorer; (cheque) refuser d'honorer. ◆—**able** a peu honorable. ◆—**ably** adv avec déshonneur.

dishy [dɪʃɪ] a (-ier, -iest) (woman, man) Sl beau, sexy, qui a du chien.

disillusion [dɪsɪ'luːʒ(ə)n] vt désillusionner; – n désillusion f. ◆—**ment** n désillusion f.

disincentive [dɪsɪn'sentɪv] n mesure f dissuasive; **to be a d. to** décourager qn; **it's a d. to work/invest/etc** cela n'encourage pas à travailler/investir/etc.

disinclined [dɪsɪn'klaɪnd] a peu disposé (**to** à). ◆**disincli'nation** n répugnance f.

disinfect [dɪsɪn'fekt] vt désinfecter. ◆**dis-infectant** a & n désinfectant (m). ◆**dis-infection** n désinfection f.

disinherit [dɪsɪn'herɪt] vt déshériter.

disintegrate [dɪs'ɪntɪgreɪt] vi se désintégrer; – vt désintégrer. ◆**disinte'gration** n désintégration f.

disinterested [dɪs'ɪntrɪstɪd] a (impartial) désintéressé; (uninterested) Fam indifférent (**in** à).

disjointed [dɪs'dʒɔɪntɪd] a décousu.

disk [dɪsk] n **1** Am = **disc. 2** (magnetic) d. (of computer) disque m (magnétique).

dislike [dɪs'laɪk] vt ne pas aimer (**doing** faire); **he doesn't d. it** ça ne lui déplaît pas; – n aversion f (**for, of** pour); **to take a d. to** (person, thing) prendre en grippe; **our likes and dislikes** nos goûts et dégoûts mpl.

dislocate [dɪsləʊkeɪt] vt (limb) disloquer; Fig désorganiser. ◆**dislo'cation** n dislocation f.

dislodge [dɪs'lɒdʒ] vt faire bouger, déplacer; (enemy) déloger.

disloyal [dɪs'lɔɪəl] a déloyal. ◆**disloyalty** n déloyauté f.

dismal ['dɪzməl] *a* morne, triste. ◆**—ly** *adv* (*to fail, behave*) lamentablement.

dismantle [dɪs'mænt(ə)l] *vt* (*machine etc*) démonter; (*organization*) démanteler.

dismay [dɪs'meɪ] *vt* consterner; – *n* consternation *f*.

dismember [dɪs'membər] *vt* (*country etc*) démembrer.

dismiss [dɪs'mɪs] *vt* congédier, renvoyer (*from* de); (*official*) destituer; (*appeal*) Jur rejeter; (*thought etc*) Fig écarter; **d.!** Mil rompez!; (*class*) **d.!** *Sch* vous pouvez partir. ◆**dismissal** *n* renvoi *m*; destitution *f*.

dismount [dɪs'maunt] *vi* descendre (*from* de); – *vt* (*rider*) démonter, désarçonner.

disobey [dɪsə'beɪ] *vt* désobéir à; – *vi* désobéir. ◆**disobedience** *n* désobéissance *f*. ◆**disobedient** *a* désobéissant.

disorder [dɪs'ɔːdər] *n* (*confusion*) désordre *m*; (*riots*) désordres *mpl*; **disorder(s)** *Med* troubles *mpl*. ◆**disorderly** *a* (*meeting etc*) désordonné.

disorganize [dɪs'ɔːɡənaɪz] *vt* désorganiser.

disorientate [dɪs'ɔːrɪənteɪt] (*Am* **disorient** [dɪs'ɔːrɪənt]) *vt* désorienter.

disown [dɪs'əun] *vt* désavouer, renier.

disparage [dɪs'pærɪdʒ] *vt* dénigrer. ◆**—ing** *a* peu flatteur.

disparate ['dɪspərət] *a* disparate. ◆**disparity** *n* disparité *f* (*between* entre, de).

dispassionate [dɪs'pæʃənət] *a* (*unemotional*) calme; (*not biased*) impartial.

dispatch [dɪs'pætʃ] *vt* (*letter, work*) expédier; (*troops, messenger*) envoyer; – *n* expédition *f* (*of* de); *Journ Mil* dépêche *f*; **d. rider** Mil *etc* courrier *m*.

dispel [dɪs'pel] *vt* (**-ll-**) dissiper.

dispensary [dɪs'pensərɪ] *n* (*in hospital*) pharmacie *f*; (*in chemist's shop*) officine *f*.

dispense [dɪs'pens] **1** *vt* (*give out*) distribuer; (*justice*) administrer; (*medicine*) préparer. **2** *vi* **to d. with** (*do without*) se passer de; **to d. with the need for** rendre superflu. ◆**dispen'sation** *n* distribution *f*; **special d.** (*exemption*) dérogation *f*. ◆**dispenser** *n* (*device*) distributeur *m*; **cash d.** distributeur *m* de billets.

disperse [dɪs'pɜːs] *vt* disperser; – *vi* se disperser. ◆**dispersal** *n*, ◆**dispersion** *n* dispersion *f*.

dispirited [dɪs'pɪrɪtɪd] *a* découragé.

displace [dɪs'pleɪs] *vt* (*bone, furniture, refugees*) déplacer; (*replace*) supplanter.

display [dɪs'pleɪ] *vt* montrer; (*notice, electronic data etc*) afficher; (*painting, goods*) exposer; (*courage etc*) faire preuve de; – *n*

(*in shop*) étalage *m*; (*of force*) déploiement *m*; (*of anger etc*) manifestation *f*; (*of paintings*) exposition *f*; (*of luxury*) étalage *m*; Mil parade *f*; (*of electronic data*) affichage *m*; **d. unit** (*of computer*) moniteur *m*; **on d.** exposé; **air d.** fête *f* aéronautique.

displeas/e [dɪs'pliːz] *vt* déplaire à. ◆**—ed** *a* mécontent (*with* de). ◆**—ing** *a* désagréable. ◆**displeasure** *n* mécontentement *m*.

dispos/e [dɪs'pəuz] *vt* disposer (**s.o. to do** qn à faire); – *vi* **to d. of** (*get rid of*) se débarrasser de; (*one's time, money*) disposer de; (*sell*) vendre; (*matter*) expédier, liquider; (*kill*) liquider. ◆**—ed** *a* disposé (**to do** à faire); **well-d. towards** bien disposé envers. ◆**—able** *a* (*plate etc*) à jeter, jetable; (*income*) disponible. ◆**disposal** *n* (*sale*) vente *f*; (*of waste*) évacuation *f*; **at the d. of** à la disposition de. ◆**dispo'sition** *n* (*placing*) disposition *f*; (*character*) naturel *m*; (*readiness*) inclination *f*.

dispossess [dɪspə'zes] *vt* déposséder (**of** de).

disproportion [dɪsprə'pɔːʃ(ə)n] *n* disproportion *f*. ◆**disproportionate** *a* disproportionné.

disprove [dɪs'pruːv] *vt* réfuter.

dispute [dɪs'pjuːt] *n* discussion *f*; (*quarrel*) dispute *f*; *Pol* conflit *m*; *Jur* litige *m*; **beyond d.** incontestable; **in d.** (*matter*) en litige; (*territory*) contesté; – *vt* (*claim etc*) contester; (*discuss*) discuter.

disqualify [dɪs'kwɒlɪfaɪ] *vt* (*make unfit*) rendre inapte (*from* à); *Sp* disqualifier; **to d. from driving** retirer le permis à. ◆**disquali'fication** *n* *Sp* disqualification *f*.

disregard [dɪsrɪ'ɡɑːd] *vt* ne tenir aucun compte de; – *n* indifférence *f* (*for* à); (*law*) désobéissance *f* (*for* à).

disrepair [dɪsrɪ'peər] *n* **in (a state of) d.** en mauvais état.

disreputable [dɪs'repjutəb(ə)l] *a* peu recommandable; (*behaviour*) honteux.

disrepute [dɪsrɪ'pjuːt] *n* discrédit *m*; **to bring into d.** jeter le discrédit sur.

disrespect [dɪsrɪ'spekt] *n* manque *m* de respect. ◆**disrespectful** *a* irrespectueux (**to** envers).

disrupt [dɪs'rʌpt] *vt* perturber; (*communications*) interrompre; (*plan*) déranger. ◆**disruption** *n* perturbation *f*; interruption *f*;

dérangement *m.* ◆**disruptive** *a* (*element etc*) perturbateur.

dissatisfied [dɪ'sætɪsfaɪd] *a* mécontent (**with** de). ◆**dissatis'faction** *n* mécontentement *m.*

dissect [daɪ'sekt] *vt* disséquer. ◆**dissection** *n* dissection *f.*

disseminate [dɪ'semɪneɪt] *vt* disséminer.

dissension [dɪ'senʃ(ə)n] *n* dissension *f.*

dissent [dɪ'sent] *vi* différer (d'opinion) (**from sth** à l'égard de qch); – *n* dissentiment *m.* ◆**-ing** *a* dissident.

dissertation [dɪsə'teɪʃ(ə)n] *n Univ* mémoire *m.*

dissident ['dɪsɪdənt] *a & n* dissident, -ente (*mf*). ◆**dissidence** *n* dissidence *f.*

dissimilar [dɪ'sɪmɪlər] *a* dissemblable (**to** à).

dissipate ['dɪsɪpeɪt] *vt* dissiper; (*energy*) gaspiller. ◆**dissi'pation** *n* dissipation *f*; gaspillage *m.*

dissociate [dɪ'səʊʃɪeɪt] *vt* dissocier (**from** de).

dissolute ['dɪsəluːt] *a* (*life, person*) dissolu.

dissolve [dɪ'zɒlv] *vt* dissoudre; – *vi* se dissoudre. ◆**disso'lution** *n* dissolution *f.*

dissuade [dɪ'sweɪd] *vt* dissuader (**from doing** de faire); **to d. s.o. from sth** détourner qn de qch. ◆**dissuasion** *n* dissuasion *f.*

distance ['dɪstəns] *n* distance *f*; **in the d.** au loin; **from a d.** de loin; **at a d.** à quelque distance; **it's within walking d.** on peut y aller à pied; **to keep one's d.** garder ses distances. ◆**distant** *a* éloigné, lointain; (*relative*) éloigné; (*reserved*) distant; **5 km d. from** (à une distance de) 5 km de. ◆**distantly** *adv* **we're d. related** nous sommes parents éloignés.

distaste [dɪs'teɪst] *n* aversion *f* (**for** pour). ◆**distasteful** *a* désagréable, déplaisant.

distemper [dɪs'tempər] **1** *n* (*paint*) badigeon *m*; – *vt* badigeonner. **2** *n* (*in dogs*) maladie *f.*

distend [dɪs'tend] *vt* distendre; – *vi* se distendre.

distil [dɪs'tɪl] *vt* (**-ll-**) distiller. ◆**distillation** *n* distillation *f.* ◆**distillery** *n* distillerie *f.*

distinct [dɪs'tɪŋkt] *a* **1** (*voice, light etc*) distinct; (*definite, marked*) net, marqué; (*promise*) formel. **2** (*different*) distinct (**from** de). ◆**distinction** *n* distinction *f*; *Univ* mention *f* très bien; **of d.** (*singer, writer etc*) de marque. ◆**distinctive** *a* distinctif. ◆**distinctively** *adv* distinctement; (*to stipulate, forbid*) formellement; (*noticeably*) nettement, sensiblement; **d. possible** tout à fait possible.

distinguish [dɪs'tɪŋgwɪʃ] *vti* distinguer (**from** de, **between** entre); **to d. oneself** se distinguer (**as** en tant que). ◆**-ed** *a* distingué. ◆**-ing** *a* **d. mark** signe *m* particulier; (*discernible*) visible. ◆**-able** *a* qu'on peut distinguer; (*discernible*) visible.

distort [dɪs'tɔːt] *vt* déformer. ◆**-ed** *a* (*false*) faux. ◆**distortion** *n El Med* distorsion *f*; (*of truth*) déformation *f.*

distract [dɪs'trækt] *vt* distraire (**from** de). ◆**-ed** *a* (*troubled*) préoccupé; (*mad with worry*) éperdu. ◆**-ing** *a* (*noise etc*) gênant. ◆**distraction** *n* (*lack of attention, amusement*) distraction *f*; **to drive to d.** rendre fou.

distraught [dɪs'trɔːt] *a* éperdu, affolé.

distress [dɪs'tres] *n* (*pain*) douleur *f*; (*anguish*) chagrin *m*; (*misfortune, danger*) détresse *f*; **in d.** (*ship, soul*) en détresse; **in (great) d.** (*poverty*) dans la détresse; – *vt* affliger, peiner. ◆**-ing** *a* affligeant, pénible.

distribute [dɪs'trɪbjuːt] *vt* distribuer; (*spread evenly*) répartir. ◆**distri'bution** *n* distribution *f*; répartition *f.* ◆**distributor** *n Aut Cin* distributeur *m*; (*of goods*) *Com* concessionnaire *mf.*

district ['dɪstrɪkt] *n* région *f*; (*of town*) quartier *m*; (*administrative*) arrondissement *m*; **d. attorney** *Am* = procureur *m* (de la République); **d. nurse** infirmière *f* visiteuse.

distrust [dɪs'trʌst] *vt* se méfier de; – *n* méfiance *f* (**of** de). ◆**distrustful** *a* méfiant; **to be d.** of se méfier de.

disturb [dɪs'tɜːb] *vt* (*sleep, water*) troubler; (*papers, belongings*) déranger; **to d. s.o.** (*bother*) déranger qn; (*alarm, worry*) troubler qn. ◆**-ed** *a* (*person etc*) *Psy* troublé. ◆**-ing** *a* (*worrying*) inquiétant; (*annoying, irksome*) gênant. ◆**disturbance** *n* (*noise*) tapage *m*; *Pol* troubles *mpl.*

disunity [dɪs'juːnɪtɪ] *n* désunion *f.*

disuse [dɪs'juːs] *n* **to fall into d.** tomber en désuétude. ◆**disused** [-'juːzd] *a* désaffecté.

ditch [dɪtʃ] **1** *n* fossé *m.* **2** *vt Fam* se débarrasser de.

dither ['dɪðər] *vi Fam* hésiter, tergiverser; **to d. (around)** (*waste time*) tourner en rond.

ditto ['dɪtəʊ] *adv* idem.

divan [dɪ'væn] *n* divan *m.*

div/e [daɪv] **1** *vi* (*pt* **dived**, *Am* **dove** [dəʊv]) plonger; (*rush*) se précipiter, se jeter; **to d. for** (*pearls*) pêcher; – *n* plongeon *m*; (*of submarine*) plongée *f*; (*of aircraft*) piqué *m.* **2** *n* (*bar, club*) *Pej* boui-boui *m.* ◆**-ing** *n* (*underwater*) plongée *f* sous-marine; **d. suit** scaphandre *m*; **d. board** plongeoir *m*. **◆−er** *n* plongeur, -euse *mf*; (*in suit*) scaphandrier *m*.

diverge [daɪ'vɜːdʒ] *vi* diverger (**from** de). **◆divergence** *n* divergence *f*. **◆divergent** *a* divergent.

diverse [daɪ'vɜːs] *a* divers. **◆diversify** *vt* diversifier; − *vi Econ* se diversifier. **◆diversity** *n* diversité *f*.

divert [daɪ'vɜːt] *vt* détourner (**from** de); (*traffic*) dévier; (*aircraft*) dérouter; (*amuse*) divertir. **◆diversion** *n Aut* déviation *f*; (*amusement*) divertissement *m*; *Mil* diversion *f*.

divest [daɪ'vest] *vt* **to d. of** (*power, rights*) priver de.

divid/e [dɪ'vaɪd] *vt* diviser (**into** en); **to d. (off) from** séparer de; **to d. up** (*money*) partager; **to d. one's time between** partager son temps entre; − *vi* se diviser. **◆−ed** *a* (*opinion*) partagé. **◆−ing** *a* **d. line** ligne *f* de démarcation.

dividend ['dɪvɪdend] *n Math Fin* dividende *m*.

divine [dɪ'vaɪn] *a* divin. **◆divinity** *n* (*quality, deity*) divinité *f*; (*study*) théologie *f*.

division [dɪ'vɪʒ(ə)n] *n* division *f*; (*dividing object*) séparation *f*. **◆divisible** *a* divisible. **◆divisive** [-'vaɪsɪv] *a* qui sème la zizanie.

divorc/e [dɪ'vɔːs] *n* divorce *m*; − *vt* (*spouse*) divorcer d'avec; *Fig* séparer; − *vi* divorcer. **◆−ed** *a* divorcé (**from** d'avec); **to get d.** divorcer. **◆divorcee** [dɪvɔː'siː, *Am* dɪvɔr'seɪ] *n* divorcé, -ée *mf*.

divulge [daɪ'vʌldʒ] *vt* divulguer.

DIY [diːaɪ'waɪ] *n abbr* (*do-it-yourself*) bricolage *m*.

dizzy ['dɪzɪ] *a* (**-ier, -iest**) (*heights*) vertigineux; **to feel d.** avoir le vertige; **to make s.o. (feel) d.** donner le vertige à qn. **◆dizziness** *n* vertige *m*.

DJ [diː'dʒeɪ] *abbr* = **disc jockey**.

do [duː] **1** *v aux* (*3rd person sing pres t* **does**; *pt* **did**; *pp* **done**; *pres p* **doing**) **do you know?** savez-vous?; **est-ce que vous savez?**; **I do not** *or* **don't see** je ne vois pas; **he did say so** (*emphasis*) il l'a bien dit; **do stay here** reste donc; **you know him, don't you?** tu le connais, n'est-ce pas?; **better than I do** mieux que je ne le fais; **neither do I** moi non plus; **so do I** moi aussi; **oh, does he?** (*surprise*) ah oui?; **don't!** non! **2** *vt* faire; **to do nothing but sleep** ne faire que dormir; **what does she do?** (*in general*), **what is she doing?** (*now*) qu'est-ce qu'elle fait?, que

fait-elle?; **what have you done (with)** ...? qu'as-tu fait (de) ...?; **well done** (*congratulations*) bravo!; *Culin* bien cuit; **it's over and done (with)** c'est fini; **that'll do me** (*suit*) ça fera mon affaire; **I've been done** (*cheated*) *Fam* je me suis fait avoir; **I'll do you!** *Fam* je t'aurai!; **to do s.o. out of sth** escroquer qch à qn; **he's hard done by** on le traite durement; **I'm done (in)** (*tired*) *Sl* je suis claqué *or* vanné; **he's done for** *Fam* il est fichu; **to do in** (*kill*) *Sl* supprimer; **to do out** (*clean*) nettoyer; **to do over** (*redecorate*) refaire; **to do up** (*coat, button*) boutonner; (*zip*) fermer; (*house*) refaire; (*goods*) emballer; **do yourself up (well)!** (*wrap up*) couvre-toi (bien)! **3** *vi* (*get along*) aller, marcher; (*suit*) faire l'affaire, convenir; (*be enough*) suffire; (*finish*) finir; **how do you do?** (*introduction*) enchanté; (*greeting*) bonjour; **he did well** *or* **right to leave** il a bien fait de partir; **do as I do** fais comme moi; **to make do** se débrouiller; **to do away with sth/s.o.** supprimer qch/qn; **I could do with** (*need, want*) j'aimerais bien (avoir *or* prendre); **to do without sth/s.o.** se passer de qch/qn; **to have to do with** (*relate to*) avoir à voir avec; (*concern*) concerner; **anything doing?** *Fam* est-ce qu'il se passe quelque chose? **4** *n* (*pl* **dos** *or* **do's**) (*party*) soirée *f*, fête *f*; **the do's and don'ts** ce qu'il faut faire ou ne pas faire.

docile ['dəʊsaɪl] *a* docile.

dock [dɒk] **1** *n Nau* dock *m*; − *vi* (*in port*) relâcher; (*at quayside*) se mettre à quai; (*of spacecraft*) s'arrimer. **2** *n Jur* banc *m* des accusés. **3** *vt* (*wages*) rogner; **to d. sth from** (*wages*) retenir qch sur. **◆−er** *n* docker *m*. **◆dockyard** *n* chantier *m* naval.

docket ['dɒkɪt] *n* fiche *f*, bordereau *m*.

doctor ['dɒktər] **1** *n Med* médecin *m*, docteur *m*; *Univ* docteur *m*. **2** *vt* (*text, food*) altérer; (*cat*) *Fam* châtrer. **◆doctorate** *n* doctorat *m* (**in** ès, en).

doctrine ['dɒktrɪn] *n* doctrine *f*. **◆doctrinaire** *a* & *n Pej* doctrinaire (*mf*).

document ['dɒkjʊmənt] *n* document *m*; − ['dɒkjʊment] *vt* (*inform*) documenter; (*report in detail*) *TV Journ* accorder une large place à. **◆docu'mentary** *a* & *n* documentaire (*m*).

doddering ['dɒdərɪŋ] *a* (*senile*) gâteux; (*shaky*) branlant.

dodge [dɒdʒ] *vt* (*question, acquaintance etc*) esquiver; (*pursuer*) échapper à; (*tax*) éviter de payer; − *vi* faire un saut (de côté); **to d. out of sight** s'esquiver; **to d. through**

(*crowd*) se faufiler dans; – *n* mouvement *m* de côté; (*trick*) Fig truc *m*, tour *m*.

dodgems ['dɒdʒəmz] *npl* autos *fpl* tamponneuses.

dodgy ['dɒdʒɪ] *a* (**-ier, -iest**) Fam (*tricky*) délicat; (*dubious*) douteux; (*unreliable*) peu sûr.

doe [dəʊ] *n* (*deer*) biche *f*.

doer ['duːər] *n* Fam personne *f* dynamique.

does [dʌz] *see* do.

dog [dɒg] **1** *n* chien *m*; (*person*) Pej type *m*. **d. biscuit** biscuit *m or* croquette *f* pour chien; **d. collar** Fam col *m* de pasteur; **d. days** canicule *f*. **2** *vt* (**-gg-**) (*follow*) poursuivre. ◆**d.-eared** *a* (*page etc*) écorné. ◆**d.-'tired** *a* Fam claqué, crevé. ◆**doggy** *n* Fam toutou *m*; **d. bag** (*in restaurant*) Am petit sac *m* pour emporter les restes.

dogged ['dɒgɪd] *a* obstiné. ◆**–ly** *adv* obstinément.

dogma ['dɒgmə] *n* dogme *m*. ◆**dog'matic** *a* dogmatique. ◆**dogmatism** *n* dogmatisme *m*.

dogsbody ['dɒgzbɒdɪ] *n* Pej factotum *m*, sous-fifre *m*.

doily ['dɔɪlɪ] *n* napperon *m*.

doing ['duːɪŋ] *n* that's your d. c'est toi qui as fait ça; **doings** Fam activités *fpl*, occupations *fpl*.

do-it-yourself [duːɪtjə'self] *n* bricolage *m*; – *a* (*store, book*) de bricolage.

doldrums ['dɒldrəmz] *npl* to be in the d. (*of person*) avoir le cafard; (*of business*) être en plein marasme.

dole [dəʊl] **1** *n* **d. (money)** allocation *f* de chômage; **to go on the d.** s'inscrire au chômage. **2** *vt* to **d. out** distribuer au compte-gouttes.

doleful ['dəʊlfʊl] *a* morne, triste.

doll [dɒl] *n* poupée *f*; (*girl*) Fam nana *f*; **doll's house**, Am **dollhouse** maison *f* de poupée. **2** *vt* to **d. up** Fam bichonner.

dollar ['dɒlər] *n* dollar *m*.

dollop ['dɒləp] *n* (*of food*) Pej gros morceau *m*.

dolphin ['dɒlfɪn] *n* (*sea animal*) dauphin *m*.

domain [dəʊ'meɪn] *n* (*land, sphere*) domaine *m*.

dome [dəʊm] *n* dôme *m*, coupole *f*.

domestic [də'mestɪk] *a* familial, domestique; (*animal*) domestique; (*trade, flight*) intérieur; (*product*) national; **d. science** arts *mpl* ménagers; **d. servant** domestique *mf*. ◆**domesticated** *a* habitué à la vie du foyer; (*animal*) domestiqué.

domicile ['dɒmɪsaɪl] *n* domicile *m*.

dominant ['dɒmɪnənt] *a* dominant;

(*person*) dominateur. ◆**dominance** *n* prédominance *f*. ◆**dominate** *vti* dominer. ◆**domi'nation** *n* domination *f*. ◆**domi-'neering** *a* dominateur.

dominion [də'mɪnjən] *n* domination *f*; (*land*) territoire *m*; Br Pol dominion *m*.

domino ['dɒmɪnəʊ] *n* (*pl* **-oes**) domino *m*; *pl* (*game*) dominos *mpl*.

don [dɒn] **1** *n* Br Univ professeur *m*. **2** *vt* (**-nn-**) revêtir.

donate [dəʊ'neɪt] *vt* faire don de; (*blood*) donner; – *vi* donner. ◆**donation** *n* don *m*.

done [dʌn] *see* do.

donkey ['dɒŋkɪ] *n* âne *m*; **for d.'s years** Fam depuis belle lurette, depuis un siècle; **d. work** travail *m* ingrat.

donor ['dəʊnər] *n* (*of blood, organ*) donneur, -euse *mf*.

doodle ['duːd(ə)l] *vi* griffonner.

doom [duːm] *n* ruine *f*; (*fate*) destin *m*; (*gloom*) Fam tristesse *f*; – *vt* condamner, destiner (**to** à); **to be doomed (to failure)** être voué à l'échec.

door [dɔːr] *n* porte *f*; (*of vehicle, train*) portière *f*, porte *f*; **out of doors** dehors; **d.-to-door salesman** démarcheur *m*. ◆**doorbell** *n* sonnette *f*. ◆**doorknob** *n* poignée *f* de porte. ◆**doorknocker** *n* marteau *m*. ◆**doorman** *n* (*pl* **-men**) (*of hotel etc*) portier *m*, concierge *m*. ◆**doormat** *n* paillasson *m*. ◆**doorstep** *n* seuil *m*. ◆**doorstop(per)** *n* butoir *m* (de porte). ◆**doorway** *n* in the d. dans l'encadrement de la porte.

dope [dəʊp] **1** *n* Fam drogue *f*; (*for horse, athlete*) doping *m*; – *vt* doper. **2** *n* (*information*) Fam tuyaux *mpl*. **3** *n* (*idiot*) Fam imbécile *mf*. ◆**dopey** *a* (**-ier, -iest**) Fam (*stupid*) abruti; (*sleepy*) endormi; (*drugged*) drogué, camé.

dormant ['dɔːmənt] *a* (*volcano, matter*) en sommeil; (*passion*) endormi.

dormer ['dɔːmər] *n* **d. (window)** lucarne *f*.

dormitory ['dɔːmɪtrɪ, Am 'dɔːmɪtɔːrɪ] *n* dortoir *m*; Am résidence *f* (universitaire).

dormouse, *pl* **-mice** ['dɔːmaʊs, -maɪs] *n* loir *m*.

dos/e [dəʊs] *n* dose *f*; (*of hard work*) Fig période *f*; (*of illness*) attaque *f*; – *vt* to **d. oneself (up)** se bourrer de médicaments. ◆**–age** *n* (*amount*) dose *f*.

dosshouse ['dɒshaʊs] *n* Sl asile *m* (de nuit).

dossier ['dɒsɪeɪ] *n* (*papers*) dossier *m*.

dot [dɒt] *n* point *m*; **polka d.** pois *m*; **on the d.** Fam à l'heure pile; – *vt* (**-tt-**) (*an i*) mettre un point sur. ◆**dotted** *a* d. line pointillé *m*; **d. with** parsemé de.

dot/e ['dəʊt] *vi* **to d. on** être gaga de. ◆**—ing** *a* affectueux; **her d. husband/father** son mari/père qui lui passe tout.

dotty ['dɒtɪ] *a* (**-ier, -iest**) *Fam* cinglé, toqué.

double ['dʌb(ə)l] *a* double; **d. bed** un grand lit; **a d. room** une chambre pour deux personnes; **d. 's'** deux 's'; **d.** deux fois six; **d. three four two** (*phone number*) trente-trois quarante-deux; — *adv* deux fois; (*to fold*) en deux; **he earns d. what I earn** il gagne le double de moi ou deux fois plus que moi; **to see d.** voir double; — *n* double *m*; (*person*) double *m*, sosie *m*; (*stand-in*) *Cin* doublure *f*; **on** *or* **at the d.** au pas de course; — *vt* doubler; **to d. back** *or* **over** replier; — *vi* doubler; **to d. back** (*of person*) revenir en arrière; **to d. up** (*with pain, laughter*) être plié en deux. ◆**d.-'barrelled** *a* (*gun*) à deux canons; (*name*) à rallonges. ◆**d.-'bass** *n Mus* contrebasse *f*. ◆**d.-'breasted** *a* (*jacket*) croisé. ◆**d.-'cross** *vt* tromper. ◆**d.-'dealing** *n* double jeu *m*. ◆**d.-'decker (bus)** *n* autobus *m* à impériale. ◆**d.-'door** *n* porte *f* à deux battants. ◆**d.-'dutch** *n Fam* baragouin *m*. ◆**d.-'glazing** *n* (*window*) double vitrage *m*, double(s) fenêtre(s) *f*(*pl*). ◆**d.-'parking** *n* stationnement *m* en double file. ◆**d.-'quick** *adv* en vitesse.

doubly ['dʌblɪ] *adv* doublement.

doubt [daʊt] *n* doute *m*; **to be in d. about** avoir des doutes sur; **I have no d. about it** je n'en doute pas; **no d.** (*probably*) sans doute; **in d.** (*result, career etc*) dans la balance; — *vt* douter de; **to d. whether** *or* **that** *or* **if** douter que (+ *sub*). ◆**doubtful** *a* douteux; **to be d. about sth** avoir des doutes sur qch; **it's d. whether** *or* **that il est douteux que** (+ *sub*). ◆**doubtless** *adv* sans doute.

dough [dəʊ] *n* pâte *f*; (*money*) *Fam* fric *m*, blé *m*. ◆**doughnut** *n* beignet *m* (rond).

dour ['dʊər] *a* austère.

douse [daʊs] *vt* arroser, tremper; (*light*) *Fam* éteindre.

dove¹ [dʌv] *n* colombe *f*. ◆**dovecote** [-kɒt] *n* colombier *m*.

dove² [dəʊv] *Am see* dive 1.

Dover ['dəʊvər] *n* Douvres *m* or *f*.

dovetail ['dʌvteɪl] **1** *n Carp* queue *f* d'aronde. **2** *vi* (*fit*) *Fig* concorder.

dowdy ['daʊdɪ] *a* (**-ier, -iest**) peu élégant, sans chic.

down¹ [daʊn] *adv* en bas; (*to the ground*) par terre, à terre; (*of sun*) couché; (*of blind,

temperature) baissé; (*out of bed*) descendu; (*of tyre*) dégonflé, (*worn*) usé; **d.** (*in writing*) inscrit; (*lie*) **d.!** (*to dog*) couché!; **to come** *or* **go d.** descendre; **to come d. from** (*place*) arriver de; **to fall d.** tomber (par terre); **d. there** *or* **here** en bas; **d. with traitors/etc!** à bas les traîtres/etc!; **d. with** (**the**) **flu** grippé; **to feel d.** (*depressed*) *Fam* avoir le cafard; **d. to** (*in series, numbers, dates etc*) jusqu'à; **d. payment** acompte *m*; **d. under** aux antipodes, en Australie; **d. at heel**, *Am* **d. at the heels** miteux; — *prep* (*at bottom of*) en bas de; (*from top to bottom of*) du haut en bas de; (*along*) le long de; **to go d.** (*hill etc*) descendre; **to live d. the street** habiter plus loin dans la rue; — *vt* (*shoot down*) abattre; (*knock down*) terrasser; **to d. a drink** vider un verre. ◆**down-and-'out** *a* **to be d.** être sur le pavé; — *n* clochard, -arde *mf*. ◆**downbeat** *a* (*gloomy*) *Fam* pessimiste. ◆**downcast** *a* découragé. ◆**downfall** *n* chute *f*. ◆**downgrade** *vt* (*job etc*) déclasser; (*person*) rétrograder. ◆**down'hearted** *a* découragé. ◆**down'hill** *adv* en pente; **to go d.** descendre; *Fig* être sur le déclin. ◆**downmarket** *a Com* bas de gamme. ◆**downpour** *n* averse *f*, pluie *f* torrentielle. ◆**downright** *a* (*rogue etc*) véritable; (*refusal etc*) catégorique; **a d. nerve** *or* **cheek** un sacré culot; — *adv* (*rude etc*) franchement. ◆**'downstairs** *a* (*room, neighbours*) d'en bas; (*on the ground floor*) du rez-de-chaussée; — [daʊn'steəz] *adv* en bas; au rez-de-chaussée; **to come** *or* **go d.** descendre l'escalier. ◆**down'stream** *adv* en aval. ◆**down-to-'earth** *a* terre-à-terre *inv*. ◆**down'town** *adv* en ville; **d. Chicago/etc** le centre de Chicago/etc. ◆**downtrodden** *a* opprimé. ◆**downward** *a* vers le bas; (*path*) qui descend; (*trend*) à la baisse. ◆**downward(s)** *adv* vers le bas.

down² [daʊn] *n* (*on bird, person etc*) duvet *m*.

downs [daʊnz] *npl* collines *fpl*.

dowry ['daʊərɪ] *n* dot *f*.

doze [dəʊz] *n* petit somme *m*; — *vi* sommeiller; **to d. off** s'assoupir. ◆**dozy** *a* (**-ier, -iest**) assoupi; (*silly*) *Fam* bête, gourde.

dozen ['dʌz(ə)n] *n* douzaine *f*; **a d.** (*eggs, books etc*) une douzaine de; **dozens of** *Fig* des dizaines de.

Dr *abbr* (*Doctor*) Docteur.

drab [dræb] *a* terne; (*weather*) gris. ◆**—ness** *n* caractère *m* terne; (*of weather*) grisaille *f*.

draconian [drəˈkəʊnɪən] *a* draconien.

draft [drɑːft] **1** n (outline) ébauche f; (of letter etc) brouillon m; (bill) Com traite f; – vt to d. (out) (sketch out) faire le brouillon de; (write out) rédiger. **2** n Mil Am conscription f; (men) contingent m; – vt (conscript) appeler (sous les drapeaux). **3** n Am = draught.

draftsman ['drɑːftsmən] n = draughtsman.

drag [dræg] vt (-gg-) traîner, tirer; (river) draguer; **to d. sth from s.o.** (confession etc) arracher qch à qn; **to d. along** (en)traîner; **to d. s.o. away from** arracher qn à; **to d. s.o. into** entraîner qn dans; – vi traîner; **to d. on** or **out** (last a long time) se prolonger; – n Fam (tedium) corvée f; (person) raseur, -euse mf; (on cigarette) bouffée f (**on** de); **in d.** (clothing) en travesti.

dragon ['drægən] n dragon m. ◆**dragonfly** n libellule f.

drain [dreɪn] n (sewer) égout m; (pipe, channel) canal m; (outside house) puisard m; (in street) bouche f d'égout; **it's (gone) down the d.** (wasted) Fam c'est fichu; **to be a d. on** (resources, patience) épuiser; – vt (land) drainer; (glass, tank) vider; (vegetables) égoutter; (resources) épuiser; **to d. (off)** (liquid) faire écouler; **to d. of** (deprive of) priver de; – vi **to d. (off)** (of liquid) s'écouler; **to d. away** (of strength) s'épuiser; **draining board** paillasse f. ◆**—age** n (act) drainage m; (sewers) système m d'égouts. ◆**—er** n (board) paillasse f; (rack, basket) égouttoir m. ◆**drainboard** n Am paillasse f. ◆**drainpipe** n tuyau m d'évacuation.

drake [dreɪk] n canard m (mâle).

dram [dræm] n (drink) Fam goutte f.

drama ['drɑːmə] n (event) drame m; (dramatic plays) théâtre m. ◆**d. critic** critique m dramatique. ◆**dra'matic** a dramatique; (very great, striking) spectaculaire. ◆**dra'matically** adv (to change, drop etc) de façon spectaculaire. ◆**dra'matics** n théâtre m. ◆**dramatist** ['dræmətɪst] n dramaturge m. ◆**dramatize** vt (exaggerate) dramatiser; (novel etc) adapter (pour la scène or l'écran).

drank [dræŋk] see **drink**.

drap/e [dreɪp] vt draper (**with** de); (wall) tapisser (de tentures); – npl tentures fpl; (heavy curtains) Am rideaux mpl. ◆**—er** n marchand, -ande mf de nouveautés.

drastic ['dræstɪk] a radical, sévère; (reduction) massif. ◆**drastically** adv radicalement.

draught [drɑːft] n courant m d'air; (for fire) tirage m; pl (game) dames fpl; – a (horse) de trait; (beer) (à la) pression. **d. excluder**

bourrelet m (de porte, de fenêtre). ◆**draughtboard** n damier m. ◆**draughty** a (-ier, -iest) (room) plein de courants d'air.

draughtsman ['drɑːftsmən] n (pl -men) dessinateur, -trice mf (industriel(le) or technique).

draw [drɔː] **1** n (of lottery) tirage m au sort; Sp match m nul; (attraction) attraction f; – vt (pt **drew**, pp **drawn**) (pull) tirer; (pass) passer (**over** sur, **into** dans); (prize) gagner; (applause) provoquer; (money from bank) retirer (**from**, **out of** de); (salary) toucher; (attract) attirer; (well-water, comfort) puiser (**from** dans); **to d. a smile** faire sourire (**from** s.o. à qn); **to d. a bath** faire couler un bain; **to d. sth to a close** mettre fin à qch; **to d. a match** Sp faire match nul; **to d. in** (claws) rentrer; – vt **to d. out** (money) retirer; (meeting) prolonger; **to d. up** (chair) approcher; (contract, list, plan) dresser, rédiger; **to d. (up)on** (savings) puiser dans; – vi (enter) entrer (**into** dans); (arrive) arriver; **to d. near (to)** s'approcher (de); (of time) approcher (de); **to d. to a close** tirer à sa fin; **to d. aside** (step aside) s'écarter; **to d. away** (go away) s'éloigner; **to d. back** (recoil) reculer; **to d. in** (of days) diminuer; **to d. on** (of time) s'avancer; **to d. up** (of vehicle) s'arrêter. ◆**drawback** n inconvénient m. ◆**drawbridge** n pont-levis m.

draw [drɔː] **2** vt (pt **drew**, pp **drawn**) (picture) dessiner; (circle) tracer; (parallel, distinction) Fig faire (entre); – vi (as artist) dessiner. ◆**—ing** n dessin m; **d. board** planche f à dessin; **d. pin** punaise f; **d. room** salon m.

drawer [drɔːr] **1** n (in furniture) tiroir m. **2** npl (women's knickers) culotte f.

drawl [drɔːl] vi parler d'une voix traînante; – n voix f traînante.

drawn [drɔːn] see **draw**[1,2]; – a (face) tiré, crispé. **d. match** or **game** match m nul.

dread [dred] vt redouter (**doing** de faire); – n crainte f, terreur f. ◆**dreadful** a épouvantable; (child) insupportable; (ill) malade; **I feel d. (about it)** j'ai vraiment honte. ◆**dreadfully** adv terriblement; **to be** or **feel d. sorry** regretter infiniment.

dream [driːm] vti (pt & pp **dreamed** or **dreamt** [dremt]) rêver; (imagine) songer (**of** à, **that** que); **I wouldn't d. of it!** (il n'en est) pas question!; **to d. sth up** imaginer qch; – n rêve m; (wonderful thing or person) Fam merveille f; **to have a d.** faire un rêve (**about** de); **to have dreams of** rêver de; **a d. house**/etc une maison/etc de rêve; **a d.**

world un monde imaginaire. ◆**—er** n rêveur, -euse mf. ◆**dreamy** a (-ier, -iest) rêveur.

dreary ['drɪərɪ] a (-ier, -iest) (gloomy) morne; (monotonous) monotone; (boring) ennuyeux.

dredge/e [dredʒ] vt (river etc) draguer; — n drague f. ◆**—er** n 1 (ship) dragueur m. 2 Culin saupoudreuse f.

dregs [dregz] npl the d. (in liquid, of society) la lie.

drench [drentʃ] vt tremper; to get drenched se faire tremper (jusqu'aux os).

dress [dres] 1 n (woman's garment) robe f; (style of dressing) tenue f; d. circle Th (premier) balcon m; d. designer dessinateur, -trice mf de mode; (well-known) couturier m; d. rehearsal (répétition f) générale f; d. shirt chemise f de soirée. 2 vt (clothe) habiller; (adorn) orner; (salad) assaisonner; (wound) panser; (skins, chicken) préparer; to get dressed s'habiller; dressed for tennis/etc en tenue de tennis/etc; — vi s'habiller; to d. up (smartly) bien s'habiller; (in disguise) se déguiser (as en). ◆**—ing** n Med pansement m; (seasoning) Culin assaisonnement m; to give s.o. a d.-down passer un savon à qn; d. gown robe f de chambre; (of boxer) peignoir m; d. room Th loge f; d. table coiffeuse f. ◆**—er** n 1 (furniture) vaisselier m; Am coiffeuse f. 2 she's a good d. elle s'habille toujours bien. ◆**dressmaker** n couturière f. ◆**dressmaking** n couture f.

dressy ['dresɪ] a (-ier, -iest) (smart) chic inv; (too) d. trop habillé.

drew [druː] see draw[1,2].

dribble ['drɪb(ə)l] vi (of baby) baver; (of liquid) tomber goutte à goutte; Sp dribbler; — vt laisser tomber goutte à goutte; (ball) Sp dribbler.

dribs [drɪbz] npl in d. and drabs par petites quantités; (to arrive) par petits groupes.

dried [draɪd] a (fruit) sec; (milk) en poudre; (flowers) séché.

drier ['draɪər] n = dryer.

drift [drɪft] vi être emporté par le vent or le courant; (of ship) dériver; Fig aller à la dérive; (of snow) s'amonceler; to d. about (aimlessly) se promener sans but, traînailler; to d. apart (of husband and wife) devenir des étrangers l'un pour l'autre; to d. into/towards glisser dans/vers; — n mouvement m; (direction) sens m; (of events) cours m; (of snow) amoncellement m, congère f; (meaning) sens m général.

◆**—er** n (aimless person) paumé, -ée mf. ◆**driftwood** n bois m flotté.

drill [drɪl] 1 n (tool) perceuse f; (bit) mèche f; (for rock) foreuse f; (for tooth) fraise f; (pneumatic) marteau m pneumatique; — vt percer; (tooth) fraiser; (oil well) forer; — vi to d. for oil faire de la recherche pétrolière. 2 n Mil Sch exercice(s) m(pl); (procedure) Fig marche f à suivre; — vt faire faire l'exercice; — vt faire faire l'exercice à.

drink [drɪŋk] n boisson f; (glass of sth) verre m; to give s.o. a d. donner (quelque chose) à boire à qn; — vt (pt drank, pp drunk) boire; to d. oneself to death se tuer à force de boire; to d. down or up boire; — vi boire (out of dans); to d. up finir son verre; to d. to boire à la santé de. ◆**—ing** n (water) potable; (song) à boire; d. bout beuverie f; d. fountain fontaine f publique, borne-fontaine f; d. trough abreuvoir m. ◆**—able** a (fit for drinking) potable; (palatable) buvable. ◆**—er** n buveur, -euse mf.

drip [drɪp] vi (-pp-) dégouliner, dégoutter; (of washing, vegetables) s'égoutter; (of tap) fuir; — vt (paint etc) laisser couler; — n (drop) goutte f; (sound) bruit m de goutte; (fool) Fam nouille f. ◆**d.-dry** a (shirt etc) sans repassage. ◆**dripping** n (Am drippings) Culin graisse f; — a & adv d. (wet) dégoulinant.

drive/e [draɪv] n promenade f en voiture; (energy) énergie f; Psy instinct m; Pol campagne f; (road to private house) allée f; an hour's d. une heure de voiture; left-hand d. Aut (véhicule m à) conduite f à gauche; front-wheel d. Aut traction f avant; — vt (pt drove, pp driven) (vehicle, train, passenger) conduire; (machine) actionner; to d. (away or out) (chase away) chasser; to d. s.o. to do pousser qn à faire; to d. to despair réduire au désespoir; to d. mad or crazy rendre fou; to d. the rain/smoke against (of wind) rabattre la pluie/fumée contre; to d. back (enemy etc) repousser; (passenger) Aut ramener (en voiture); to d. in (thrust) enfoncer; to d. s.o. hard surmener qn; he drives a Ford il a une Ford; — vi (drive a car) conduire; to d. (along) (go, run) Aut rouler; to d. on the left rouler à gauche; to d. away or off Aut partir; to d. back Aut revenir; to d. on Aut continuer; to d. to Aut aller (en voiture) à; to d. up Aut arriver; what are you driving at? Fig où veux-tu en venir? ◆**—ing** 1 n conduite f; d. lesson leçon f de conduite; d. licence, d. test permis m de conduire; d. school auto-école

f. **2** a (forceful) d. force force f agissante; **d. rain** pluie f battante. ◆**–er** n (of car) conducteur, -trice mf; (of taxi, lorry) chauffeur m, conducteur, -trice mf; (train) de mécanicien m; **she's a good d.** elle conduit bien; **driver's license** Am permis m de conduire.

drivel ['drɪv(ə)l] vi (-ll-, Am -l-) radoter; – n radotage m.

drizzle ['drɪz(ə)l] n bruine f, crachin m; – vi bruiner. ◆**drizzly** a (weather) de bruine; **it's d.** il bruine.

droll [drəʊl] a drôle, comique.

dromedary ['drɒmədərɪ, Am 'drɒmɪderɪ] n dromadaire m.

drone [drəʊn] **1** n (bee) abeille f mâle. **2** n (hum) bourdonnement m; (purr) ronronnement m; Fig débit m monotone; – vi (of bee) bourdonner; (of engine) ronronner; **to d. (on)** Fig parler d'une voix monotone.

drool [druːl] vi (slaver) baver; Fig radoter; **to d. over** Fig s'extasier devant.

droop [druːp] vi (of head) pencher; (of eyelid) tomber; (of flower) se faner.

drop [drɒp] **1** n (of liquid) goutte f. **2** n (fall) baisse f, chute f (**in** de); (slope) descente f; (distance of fall) hauteur f (de chute); (jump) Av saut m; – vt (-pp-) laisser tomber; (price, voice) baisser; (bomb) larguer; (passenger, goods) Aut déposer; Nau débarquer; (letter) envoyer (**to** à); (put) mettre; (omit) omettre; (remark) laisser échapper; (get rid of) supprimer; (habit) abandonner; (team member) Sp écarter; **to d. s.o. off** Aut déposer qn; **to d. a line** écrire un petit mot (**to** à); **to d. a hint** faire une allusion; **to d. a hint that** laisser entendre que; **to d. one's h's** ne pas aspirer les h; **to d. a word in s.o.'s ear** glisser un mot à l'oreille de qn; – vi (fall) tomber; (of person) (se laisser) tomber; (of price) baisser; (of conversation) cesser; **he's ready to d.** Fam il tombe de fatigue; **let it d.!** Fam laisse tomber!; **to d. across** or **in** passer (chez qn); **to d. away** (diminish) diminuer; **to d. back** or **behind** rester en arrière, se laisser distancer; **to d. off** (fall asleep) s'endormir; (fall off) tomber; (of interest, sales etc) diminuer. ◆**d.-off** n (decrease) diminution f (**in** de); **to d. out** (fall out) tomber; (withdraw) cesser; (socially) se mettre en marge de la société; Sch Univ laisser tomber ses études. ◆**d.-out** n marginal, -ale mf; Univ étudiant, -ante mf qui abandonne ses études. ◆**droppings** npl (of animal) crottes fpl; (of bird) fiente f.

dross [drɒs] n déchets mpl.

drought [draʊt] n sécheresse f.

drove [drəʊv] see **drive**.

droves [drəʊvz] npl (of people) foules fpl; **in d.** en foule.

drown [draʊn] vi se noyer; – vt noyer; **to d. oneself, be drowned** se noyer. ◆**–ing** a qui se noie; – n (death) noyade f.

drowse [draʊz] vi somnoler. ◆**drows/y** a (-ier, -iest) somnolent; **to feel d.** avoir sommeil; **to make s.o. (feel) d.** assoupir qn. ◆**–ily** adv d'un air somnolent. ◆**–iness** n somnolence f.

drubbing ['drʌbɪŋ] n (beating) raclée f.

drudge [drʌdʒ] n bête f de somme, esclave mf du travail; – vi travailler dur. ◆**drudgery** n corvée(s) f(pl), travail m ingrat.

drug [drʌg] n Med médicament m, drogue f; (narcotic) stupéfiant m, drogue f; Fig drogue f; drugs (dope in general) la drogue; **to be on drugs, take drugs** se droguer; **d. addict** drogué, -ée mf; **d. addiction** toxicomanie f; **d. taking** usage m de la drogue; – vt (-gg-) droguer; (drink) mêler un somnifère à. ◆**druggist** n Am pharmacien, -ienne mf, droguiste mf. ◆**drugstore** n Am drugstore m.

drum [drʌm] n Mus tambour m; (for oil) bidon m; **the big d.** Mus la grosse caisse; **the drums** Mus la batterie; – vi (-mm-) Mil battre du tambour; (with fingers) tambouriner; – vt **to d. sth into s.o.** Fig rabâcher qch à qn; **to d. up** (support, interest) susciter; **to d. up business** or **custom** attirer les clients. ◆**drummer** n (joueur, -euse mf de) tambour m; (in pop or jazz group) batteur m. ◆**drumstick** n Mus baguette f de tambour; (of chicken) pilon m, cuisse f.

drunk [drʌŋk] see **drink**; – a ivre; **d. with** Fig ivre de; **to get d.** s'enivrer; – n ivrogne mf, pochard, -arde mf. ◆**drunkard** n ivrogne mf. ◆**drunken** a (quarrel) d'ivrogne; (person) ivrogne; (driver) ivre; **d. driving** conduite f en état d'ivresse. ◆**drunkenness** n (state) ivresse f; (habit) ivrognerie f.

dry [draɪ] a (drier, driest) sec; (well, river) à sec; (day) sans pluie; (toast) sans beurre; (wit) caustique; (subject, book) aride; **on d. land** sur la terre ferme; **to keep sth d.** tenir qch au sec; **to wipe d.** essuyer; **to run d.** se tarir; **to feel** or **be d.** Fam avoir soif; **d. dock** cale f sèche; **d. goods store** Am magasin m de nouveautés; – vt (dishes etc) essuyer; **to d. off** or **up** sécher; – vi sécher; **to d. off** sécher; **to d. up** sécher; (run dry) se tarir; **d. up!** Fam tais-toi! ◆**–ing** n séchage m; essuyage m. ◆**–er** n (for hair, *clothes*) sécher m; (*helmet-style for hair*) casque m. ◆**—ness** n sécheresse f; (*of wit*) causticité f; (*of book*) aridité f. ◆**dry-'clean** vt nettoyer à sec. ◆**dry-'cleaner** n teinturier, -ière mf.

dual ['djuːəl] a double; **d. carriageway** route f à deux voies (séparées). ◆**du'ality** n dualité f.

dub [dʌb] vt (**-bb-**) **1** (*film*) doubler. **2** (*nickname*) surnommer. ◆**dubbing** n Cin doublage m.

dubious ['djuːbɪəs] a (*offer, person etc*) douteux; **I'm d. about going** or **whether to go** je me demande si je dois y aller; **to be d. about sth** douter de qch.

duchess ['dʌtʃɪs] n duchesse f. ◆**duchy** n duché m.

duck [dʌk] **1** n canard m. **2** vi se baisser (vivement); — vt (*head*) baisser; **to d. s.o.** plonger qn dans l'eau. ◆**—ing** n bain m forcé. ◆**duckling** n caneton m.

duct [dʌkt] n Anat Tech conduit m.

dud [dʌd] a Fam (*bomb*) non éclaté; (*coin*) faux; (*cheque*) en bois; (*watch etc*) qui ne marche pas; — n (*person*) zéro m, type m nul.

dude [duːd] n Am Fam dandy m; **d. ranch** ranch(-hôtel) m.

due[1] [djuː] a (*money, sum*) dû (**to** à); (*rent, bill*) à payer; (*respect*) qu'on doit (**to** à); (*fitting*) qui convient; **to fall d.** échoir; **she's d. for** (*a rise etc*) elle doit or devrait recevoir; **he's d. (to arrive)** (*is awaited*) il doit être là-bas; **in d. course** (*at proper time*) en temps utile; (*finally*) à la longue; **d. to** (*attributable to*) dû à; (*because of*) à cause de; (*thanks to*) grâce à; — n dû m; pl droits mpl; **to give s.o. his d.** admettre que qn a raison.

due[2] [djuː] adv (tout) droit; **d. north/south** plein nord/sud.

duel ['djuːəl] n duel m; — vi (**-ll-**, Am **-l-**) se battre en duel.

duet [djuː'et] n duo m.

duffel, duffle ['dʌf(ə)l] a **d. bag** sac m de marin; **d. coat** duffel-coat m.

dug [dʌg] see **dig**. ◆**dugout** n **1** Mil abri m souterrain. **2** (*canoe*) pirogue f.

duke [djuːk] n duc m.

dull [dʌl] a (**-er, -est**) (*boring*) ennuyeux; (*colour, character*) terne; (*weather*) maussade; (*mind*) lourd, borné; (*sound, ache*) sourd; (*edge, blade*) émoussé; (*hearing, sight*) faible; — vt (*senses*) émousser; (*sound, pain*) amortir; (*colour*) ternir;

(*mind*) engourdir. ◆**—ness** n (*of mind*) lourdeur f d'esprit; (*tedium*) monotonie f; (*of colour*) manque m d'éclat.

duly ['djuːlɪ] adv (*properly*) comme il convient (convenait etc); (*in fact*) en effet; (*in due time*) en temps utile.

dumb [dʌm] a (**-er, -est**) muet; (*stupid*) Fam idiot, bête. ◆**—ness** n mutisme m; bêtise f. ◆**dumbbell** n (*weight*) haltère m. ◆**dumbwaiter** n (*lift for food*) monte-plats m inv.

dumbfound [dʌm'faʊnd] vt sidérer, ahurir.

dummy ['dʌmɪ] **1** n (*of baby*) sucette f; (*of dressmaker*) mannequin m; (*of book*) maquette f; (*of ventriloquist*) pantin m; (*fool*) Fam idiot, -ote mf. **2** a factice, faux; **d. run** (*on car etc*) essai m.

dump [dʌmp] vt (*rubbish*) déposer; **to d. (down)** déposer; **to d. s.o.** (*ditch*) Fam plaquer qn; — n (*for ammunition*) Mil dépôt m; (*dirty or dull town*) Fam trou m; (*house, slum*) Fam baraque f; (*rubbish*) dépôt m d'ordures; (*place*) dépôt m d'ordures, décharge f; **to be (down) in the dumps** Fam avoir le cafard; **d. truck = dumper**. ◆**—er** n **d. (truck)** camion m à benne basculante.

dumpling ['dʌmplɪŋ] n Culin boulette f (de pâte).

dumpy ['dʌmpɪ] a (**-ier, -iest**) (*person*) boulot, gros et court.

dunce [dʌns] n cancre m, âne m.

dune [djuːn] n dune f.

dung [dʌŋ] n crotte f; (*of cattle*) bouse f; (*manure*) fumier m.

dungarees [dʌŋɡə'riːz] npl (*of child, workman*) salopette f; (*jeans*) Am jean m.

dungeon ['dʌndʒən] n cachot m.

dunk [dʌŋk] vt (*bread, biscuit etc*) tremper.

dupe [djuːp] vt duper; — n dupe f.

duplex ['duːpleks] n (*apartment*) Am duplex m.

duplicate ['djuːplɪkeɪt] vt (*key, map*) faire un double de; (*on machine*) polycopier; — ['djuːplɪkət] n double m; **in d.** en deux exemplaires; **a d. copy**/etc une copie/etc en double; **a d. key** un double de la clef. ◆**dupli'cation** n (*on machine*) polycopie f; (*of effort*) répétition f. ◆**duplicator** n duplicateur m.

duplicity [djuː'plɪsɪtɪ] n duplicité f.

durable ['djuːərəb(ə)l] a (*shoes etc*) résistant; (*friendship, love*) durable. ◆**dura'bility** n résistance f; durabilité f.

duration [djuə'reɪʃ(ə)n] n durée f.

duress [dju'res] n **under d.** sous la contrainte.

during ['djuərɪŋ] prep pendant, durant.

dusk [dʌsk] n (twilight) crépuscule m.
dusky ['dʌskɪ] a (-ier, -iest) (complexion) foncé.
dust [dʌst] n poussière f; **d. cover** (for furniture) housse f; (for book) jaquette f; d. **jacket** n jaquette f; – vt épousseter; (sprinkle) saupoudrer (**with** de). ◆**—er** n chiffon m. ◆**dustbin** n poubelle f. ◆**dustcart** n camion-benne m. ◆**dustman** n (pl -**men**) éboueur m, boueux m. ◆**dustpan** n petite pelle f (à poussière).
dusty ['dʌstɪ] a (-ier, -iest) poussiéreux.
Dutch [dʌtʃ] a néerlandais, hollandais; **D. cheese** hollande m; **to go D.** partager les frais (**with** avec); – n (language) hollandais m. ◆**Dutchman** n (pl -**men**) Hollandais m. ◆**Dutchwoman** n (pl -**women**) Hollandaise f.
duty ['djuːtɪ] n devoir m; (tax) droit m; pl (responsibilities) fonctions fpl; **on d.** Mil de service; (doctor etc) de garde; Sch de permanence; **off d.** libre. ◆**d.-'free** a (goods, shop) hors-taxe inv. ◆**dutiful** a respectueux, obéissant; (worker) consciencieux.
dwarf [dwɔːf] n nain m, naine f; – vt (of building, person etc) rapetisser, écraser.

dwell [dwel] vi (pt & pp **dwelt**) demeurer; **to d. (up)on** (think about) penser sans cesse à; (speak about) parler sans cesse de, s'étendre sur; (insist on) appuyer sur. ◆**—ing** n habitation f. ◆**—er** n habitant, -ante m.
dwindl/e ['dwɪnd(ə)l] vt diminuer (peu à peu). ◆**—ing** a (interest etc) décroissant.
dye [daɪ] n teinture f; – vt teindre; **to d. green/etc** teindre en vert/etc. ◆**dyeing** n teinture f; (industry) teinturerie f. ◆**dyer** n teinturier, -ière mf.
dying ['daɪɪŋ] see **die 1**; – a mourant, moribond; (custom) qui se perd; (day, words) dernier; – n (death) mort f.
dyke [daɪk] n (wall) digue f; (ditch) fossé m.
dynamic [daɪ'næmɪk] a dynamique. ◆**'dynamism** n dynamisme m.
dynamite ['daɪnəmaɪt] n dynamite f; – vt dynamiter.
dynamo ['daɪnəməʊ] n (pl -**os**) dynamo f.
dynasty ['dɪnəstɪ, Am 'daɪnəstɪ] n dynastie f.
dysentery ['dɪsəntrɪ] n Med dysenterie f.
dyslexic [dɪs'leksɪk] a & n dyslexique (mf).

E

E, e [iː] n E, e m.
each [iːtʃ] a chaque; – pron chacun, -une; **e. one** chacun, -une; **e. other** l'un(e) l'autre, pl les un(e)s les autres; **to see e. other** se voir (l'un(e) l'autre); **e. of us** chacun, -une d'entre nous.
eager ['iːgər] a impatient (**to do** de faire); (enthusiastic) ardent, passionné; **to be e. for** désirer vivement; **e. for** (money) avide de; **e. to help** empressé (à aider); **to be e. to do** (want) avoir envie de faire. ◆**—ly** adv (to await) avec impatience; (to work, serve) avec empressement. ◆**—ness** n impatience f (**to do** de faire); (zeal) empressement m (**to do** à faire); (greed) avidité f.
eagle ['iːg(ə)l] n aigle m. ◆**e.-'eyed** a au regard d'aigle.
ear¹ [ɪər] n oreille f; **all ears** Fam tout ouïe; **up to one's ears in work** débordé de travail; **to play it by e.** Fam agir selon la situation; **thick e.** Fam gifle f. ◆**earache** n mal d'oreille. ◆**eardrum** n tympan m. ◆**earmuffs** npl serre-tête m inv (pour protéger les oreilles), protège-oreilles m inv. ◆**earphones** npl casque m. ◆**earpiece** n écouteur m. ◆**earplug** n (to keep out noise) boule f Quiès®. ◆**earring** n boucle f d'oreille. ◆**earshot** n **within e.** à portée de voix. ◆**ear-splitting** a assourdissant.
ear² [ɪər] n (of corn) épi m.
earl [ɜːl] n comte m.
early ['ɜːlɪ] a (-ier, -iest) (first) premier; (fruit, season) précoce; (death) prématuré; (age) jeune; (painting, work) de jeunesse; (reply) rapide; (return, retirement) anticipé; (ancient) ancien; **it's e.** (looking at time) il est tôt; **it's too e. to get up/etc** il est trop tôt pour se lever/etc; **to be e.** (ahead of time) arriver de bonne heure or en avance; (in getting up) être matinal; **in e. times** jadis; **in e. summer** au début de l'été; **one's e. life** sa jeunesse; – adv tôt, de bonne heure; (ahead of time) en avance; (to die) prématurément; **as e. as possible** le plus tôt possible; **earlier (on)** plus tôt; **at**

the earliest au plus tôt; **as e. as yesterday** déjà hier. ◆**e.-'warning system** *n* dispositif *m* de première alerte.

earmark ['ɪəmɑːk] *vt (funds)* assigner (**for** à).

earn [ɜːn] *vt* gagner; *(interest)* *Fin* rapporter. ◆**—ings** *npl (wages)* rémunérations *fpl*; *(profits)* bénéfices *mpl*.

earnest ['ɜːnɪst] *a (sincere)* sincère; – *n* **in e.** sérieusement; **it's raining in e.** il pleut pour de bon; **he's in e.** il est sérieux. ◆**—ness** *n* sérieux *m*; sincérité *f*.

earth [ɜːθ] *n (world, ground)* terre *f*; *El* terre *f*, masse *f*; **to fall to e.** tomber à or par terre; **nothing/nobody on e.** rien/personne au monde; **where/what on e.?** où/que diable? ◆**earthly** *a (possessions etc)* terrestre; **not an e. chance** *Fam* pas la moindre chance; **for no e. reason** *Fam* sans la moindre raison. ◆**earthy** *a (terreux; (person)* *Fig* terre-à-terre *inv*. ◆**earthquake** *n* tremblement *m* de terre. ◆**earthworks** *npl (excavations)* terrassements *mpl*. ◆**earthworm** *n* ver *m* de terre.

earthenware ['ɜːθənwɛər] *n* faïence *f*; – *a* en faïence.

earwig ['ɪəwɪg] *n (insect)* perce-oreille *m*.

ease [iːz] **1** *n (physical)* bien-être *m*; *(mental)* tranquillité *f*; *(facility)* facilité *f*; *(ill)* at e. *(in situation)* (mal) à l'aise; **at e.** *(of mind)* tranquille; **(stand) at e.!** *Mil* repos!; **with e.** facilement. **2** *vt (pain)* soulager; *(mind)* calmer; *(tension)* diminuer; *(loosen)* relâcher; **to e. off/along** enlever/déplacer doucement; **to e. oneself through** se glisser par; – *vi* **to e. (off** or **up)** *(of situation)* se détendre; *(of pressure)* diminuer; *(of demand)* baisser; *(of pain)* se calmer; *(not work so hard)* se relâcher. ◆**easily** *adv* facilement; **e. the best/**etc de loin le meilleur/etc; **that could e. be** ça pourrait bien être. ◆**easiness** *n* aisance *f*.

easel ['iːz(ə)l] *n* chevalet *m*.

east [iːst] *n* est *m*; **Middle/Far E.** Moyen-/Extrême-Orient *m*; – *a (coast)* est *inv*; *(wind)* d'est; **E. Africa** Afrique *f* orientale; **E. Germany** Allemagne *f* de l'Est; – *adv* à l'est, vers l'est. ◆**eastbound** *a (carriageway)* est *inv*; *(traffic)* en direction de l'est. ◆**easterly** *a (point)* est *inv*; *(direction)* de l'est; *(wind)* d'est. ◆**eastern** *a (coast)* est *inv*; **E. France** l'Est *m* de la France; **E. Europe** Europe *f* de l'Est. ◆**easterner** *n* habitant, -ante *mf* de l'Est. ◆**eastward(s)** *a & adv* vers l'est.

Easter ['iːstər] *n* Pâques *m sing* or *fpl*; **E. week** semaine *f* pascale; **Happy E.!** joyeuses Pâques!

easy ['iːzɪ] *a (-ier, -iest)* facile; *(manners)* naturel; *(life)* tranquille; *(pace)* modéré; **to feel e. in one's mind** être tranquille; **to be an e. first** *Sp* être bon premier; **I'm e.** *Fam* ça m'est égal; **e. chair** fauteuil *m (*rembourré); – *adv* doucement; **go e. on** *(sugar etc)* vas-y doucement or mollo avec; *(person)* ne sois pas trop dur avec or envers; **take it e.** *(rest)* repose-toi; *(work less)* ne te fatigue pas; *(calm down)* calme-toi; *(go slow)* ne te presse pas. ◆**easy'going** *a (carefree)* insouciant; *(easy to get on with)* traitable.

eat [iːt] *vt (pt* **ate** [et, *Am* eit], *pp* **eaten** ['iːt(ə)n]); manger; *(meal)* prendre; *(one's words)* *Fig* ravaler; **to e. breakfast** or **lunch** déjeuner; **what's eating you?** *SI* qu'est-ce qui te tracasse?; **to e. up** *(finish)* finir; **eaten up with** *(envy)* dévoré de; – *vi* manger; **to e. into** *(of acid)* ronger; **to e. out** *(lunch)* déjeuner dehors; *(dinner)* dîner dehors. ◆**—ing** *a* **e. apple** pomme *f* à couteau; **e. place** restaurant *m*. ◆**—able** *a* mangeable. ◆**—er** *n* **big e.** gros mangeur *m*, grosse mangeuse *f*.

eau de Cologne [əʊdəkə'ləʊn] *n* eau de Cologne.

eaves [iːvz] *npl* avant-toit *m*. ◆**eavesdrop** *vt* (-pp-) **to e. (on)** écouter (de façon indiscrète). ◆**eavesdropper** *n* oreille *f* indiscrète.

ebb [eb] *n* reflux *m*; **e. and flow** le flux et le reflux; **e. tide** marée *f* descendante; **at a low e.** *Fig* très bas; – *vi* refluer; **to e. (away)** *(of strength etc)* *Fig* décliner.

ebony ['ebənɪ] *n (wood)* ébène *f*.

ebullient [ɪ'bʌlɪənt] *a* exubérant.

eccentric [ɪk'sentrɪk] *a & n* excentrique *(mf)*. ◆**eccen'tricity** *n* excentricité *f*.

ecclesiastic [ɪkliːzɪ'æstɪk] *a & n* ecclésiastique *(m)*. ◆**ecclesiastical** *a* ecclésiastique.

echelon ['eʃəlɒn] *n (of organization)* échelon *m*.

echo ['ekəʊ] *n (pl* -oes*)* écho *m*; – *vt (sound)* répercuter; *(repeat)* *Fig* répéter; – *vi* **the explosion/**etc **echoed** l'écho de l'explosion/etc se répercuta; **to e. with the sound of** résonner de l'écho de.

éclair [eɪ'klɛər] *n (cake)* éclair *m*.

eclectic [ɪ'klektɪk] *a* éclectique.

eclipse [ɪ'klɪps] *n (of sun etc)* & *Fig* éclipse *f*; – *vt* éclipser.

ecology [ɪ'kɒlədʒɪ] *n* écologie *f*. ◆**eco'logical** *a* écologique.

economic [iːkə'nɒmɪk] *a* économique; *(profitable)* rentable. ◆**economical** *a* économique; (*thrifty*) économe. **◆economically** *adv* économiquement. **◆economics** *n* (*science f*) économie *f*; (*profitability*) aspect *m* financier.

economy [ɪ'kɒnəmɪ] *n* (*saving, system, thrift*) économie *f*; **e. class** *Av* classe *f* touriste. **◆economist** *n* économiste *mf*. **◆economize** *vti* économiser (**on** sur).

ecstasy ['ekstəsɪ] *n* extase *f*. **◆ecstatic** *a* extasié; **to be e. about** s'extasier sur. **◆ec'statically** *adv* avec extase.

ecumenical [iːkjuˈmenɪk(ə)l] *a* œcuménique.

eczema ['eksɪmə] *n Med* eczéma *m*.

eddy ['edɪ] *n* tourbillon *m*, remous *m*.

edge [edʒ] *n* bord *m*; (*of forest*) lisière *f*; (*of town*) abords *mpl*; (*of page*) marge *f*; (*of knife etc*) tranchant *m*, fil *m*; **on e.** (*person*) énervé; (*nerves*) tendu; **to set s.o.'s teeth on e.** (*irritate s.o.*) crisper qn, faire grincer les dents à qn; **to have the e. or a slight e.** Fig être légèrement supérieur (**over, on** à); – *vt* (*clothing etc*) border (**with** de); – *vti* **to e.** (**oneself**) **into** (*move*) se glisser dans; **to e.** (**oneself**) **forward** avancer doucement. **◆—ing** *n* (*border*) bordure *f*. **◆edgeways** *adv* de côté; **to get a word in e.** Fam placer un mot.

edgy ['edʒɪ] *a* (**-ier, -iest**) énervé. **◆edginess** *n* nervosité *f*.

edible ['edɪb(ə)l] *a* (*mushroom, berry etc*) comestible; (*meal, food*) mangeable.

edict ['iːdɪkt] *n* décret *m*; *Hist* édit *m*.

edifice ['edɪfɪs] *n* (*building, organization*) édifice *m*.

edify ['edɪfaɪ] *vt* (*improve the mind of*) édifier.

Edinburgh ['edɪnb(ə)rə] *n* Édimbourg *m or f*.

edit ['edɪt] *vt* (*newspaper etc*) diriger; (*article etc*) mettre au point; (*film*) monter; (*annotate*) éditer; (*compile*) rédiger; **to e.** (**out**) (*cut out*) couper. **◆editor** *n* (*of review*) directeur, -trice *mf*; (*compiler*) rédacteur, -trice *mf*; *TV Rad* réalisateur, -trice *mf*; **sports e.** *Journ* rédacteur *m* sportif, rédactrice *f* sportive; **the e.** (**in chief**) *of* (*newspaper*) le rédacteur *m* en chef. **◆edi'torial** *a* de la rédaction; **e. staff** rédaction *f*; – *n* éditorial *m*.

edition [ɪ'dɪʃ(ə)n] *n* édition *f*.

educat/e ['edjukeɪt] *vt* (*family, children*) éduquer; (*pupil*) instruire; (*mind*) former, éduquer; **to be educated at** faire ses études à. **◆—ed** *a* (*voice*) cultivé; (**well-**)**e.** (*person*) instruit. **◆edu'cation** *n* éducation *f*; (*teaching*) instruction *f*, enseigne-

ment *m*; (*training*) formation *f*; (*subject*) *Univ* pédagogie *f*. **◆edu'cational** *a* (*establishment*) d'enseignement; (*method*) pédagogique; (*game*) éducatif; (*supplies*) scolaire. **◆edu'cationally** *adv* du point de vue de l'éducation. **◆educator** *n* éducateur, -trice *mf*.

EEC [iːiː'siː] *n abbr* (*European Economic Community*) CEE *f*.

eel [iːl] *n* anguille *f*.

eerie ['ɪərɪ] *a* (**-ier, -iest**) sinistre, étrange.

efface [ɪ'feɪs] *vt* effacer.

effect [ɪ'fekt] **1** *n* (*result, impression*) effet *m* (**on** sur); *pl* (*goods*) biens *mpl*; **to no e.** en vain; **in e.** en fait; **to put into e.** mettre en application, faire entrer en vigueur; **to come into e., take e.** entrer en vigueur; **to take e.** (*of drug etc*) agir; **to have an e.** (*of medicine etc*) faire de l'effet; **to have no e.** rester sans effet; **to this e.** (*in this meaning*) dans ce sens; **to the e. that** (*saying that*) comme quoi. **2** *vt* (*carry out*) effectuer, réaliser.

effective [ɪ'fektɪv] *a* (*efficient*) efficace; (*actual*) effectif; (*striking*) frappant; **to become e.** (*of law*) prendre effet. **◆—ly** *adv* efficacement; (*in effect*) effectivement. **◆—ness** *n* efficacité *f*; (*quality*) effet *m* frappant.

effeminate [ɪ'femɪnət] *a* efféminé.

effervescent [efə'ves(ə)nt] *a* (*mixture, youth*) effervescent; (*drink*) gazeux. **◆effervesce** *vi* (*of drink*) pétiller. **◆effervescence** *n* (*excitement*) & *Ch* effervescence *f*; pétillement *m*.

effete [ɪ'fiːt] *a* (*feeble*) mou, faible; (*decadent*) décadent.

efficient [ɪ'fɪʃ(ə)nt] *a* (*method*) efficace; (*person*) compétent, efficace; (*organization*) efficace, performant; (*machine*) performant, à haut rendement. **◆efficiency** *n* efficacité *f*; compétence *f*; performances *fpl*. **◆efficiently** *adv* efficacement; avec compétence; **to work e.** (*of machine*) bien fonctionner.

effigy ['efɪdʒɪ] *n* effigie *f*.

effort ['efət] *n* effort *m*; **to make an e.** faire un effort (**to** pour); **it isn't worth the e.** ça ne *or* n'en vaut pas la peine; **his** *or* **her latest e.** Fam ses dernières tentatives. **◆—less** *a* (*victory etc*) facile. **◆—lessly** *adv* facilement, sans effort.

effrontery [ɪ'frʌntərɪ] *n* effronterie *f*.

effusive [ɪ'fjuːsɪv] *a* (*person*) expansif; (*thanks, excuses*) sans fin. **◆—ly** *adv* avec effusion.

e.g. [iː'dʒiː] *abbr (exempli gratia)* par exemple.

egalitarian [ɪgælɪ'teərɪən] *a (society etc)* égalitaire.

egg¹ [eg] *n* œuf *m*; **e. timer** sablier *m*; **e. whisk** fouet *m* (à œufs). ◆**eggcup** *n* coquetier *m*. ◆**egghead** *n Pej* intellectuel, -elle *mf*. ◆**eggplant** *n* aubergine *f*. ◆**eggshell** *n* coquille *f*.

egg² [eg] *vt* **to e. on** *(encourage)* inciter (**to do** à faire).

ego ['iːgəu] *n (pl* **-os)** the **e.** *Psy* le moi. ◆**ego'centric** *a* égocentrique. ◆**egoism** *n* égoïsme *m*. ◆**egoist** *n* égoïste *mf*. ◆**ego'istic(al)** *a* égoïste. ◆**egotism** *n* égotisme *m*.

Egypt ['iːdʒɪpt] *n* Égypte *f*. ◆**E'gyptian** *a & n* égyptien, -ienne *(mf)*.

eh? [eɪ] *int Fam* hein?

eiderdown ['aɪdədaun] *n* édredon *m*.

eight [eɪt] *a & n* huit *(m)*. ◆**eigh'teen** *a & n* dix-huit *(m)*. ◆**eigh'teenth** *a & n* dix-huitième *(mf)*. ◆**eighth** *a & n* huitième *(mf)*; **an e.** un huitième. ◆**eightieth** *a & n* quatre-vingtième *(mf)*. ◆**eighty** *a & n* quatre-vingts *(m)*; **e.-one** quatre-vingt-un.

Eire ['eərə] *n* République *f* d'Irlande.

either ['aɪðər] **1** *a & pron (one or other)* l'un(e) ou l'autre; *(with negative)* ni l'un(e) ni l'autre; *(each)* chaque; **on e.** side de chaque côté, des deux côtés. **2** *adv* **she can't swim e.** elle ne sait pas nager non plus; **I don't e.** (ni) moi non plus; **not so far off e.** *(moreover)* pas si loin d'ailleurs. **3** *conj* **e. . . . or** ou (bien) . . . ou (bien), soit . . . soit; *(with negative)* ni . . . ni.

eject [iː'dʒekt] *vt* expulser; *Tech* éjecter. ◆**ejector** *a* **e. seat** *Av* siège *m* éjectable.

eke [iːk] *vt* **to e. out** *(income etc)* faire durer; **to e. out a living** gagner (difficilement) sa vie.

elaborate [ɪ'læbərət] *a* compliqué, détaillé; *(preparation)* minutieux; *(style)* recherché; *(meal)* raffiné; — [ɪ'læbəreɪt] *vt (theory etc)* élaborer; — *vi* entrer dans les détails (**on** de). ◆**—ly** *adv (to plan)* minutieusement; *(to decorate)* avec recherche. ◆**elabo'ration** *n* élaboration *f*.

elapse [ɪ'læps] *vi* s'écouler.

elastic [ɪ'læstɪk] *a (object, character)* élastique; **e. band** élastique *m*; — *n (fabric)* élastique *m*. ◆**ela'sticity** *n* élasticité *f*.

elated [ɪ'leɪtɪd] *a* transporté de joie. ◆**elation** *n* exaltation *f*.

elbow ['elbəu] *n* coude *m*; **e. grease** *Fam* huile *f* de coude; **to have enough e. room** avoir assez de place; — *vt* **to e. one's way** se frayer un chemin (à coups de coude) *(through* à travers).

elder¹ ['eldər] *a & n (of two people)* aîné, -ée *(mf)*. ◆**elderly** *a* assez âgé, entre deux âges. ◆**eldest** *a & n* aîné, -ée *(mf)*; **his or her e. brother** l'aîné de ses frères.

elder² ['eldər] *n (tree)* sureau *m*.

elect [ɪ'lekt] *vt Pol* élire (**to** à); **to e. to do** choisir de faire; — *a* **the president/etc e.** le président/*etc* désigné. ◆**election** *n* élection *f*; **general e.** élections *fpl* législatives; — *a (campaign)* électoral; *(day, results)* du scrutin, des élections. ◆**electio'neering** *n* campagne *f* électorale. ◆**elective** *a (course) Am* facultatif. ◆**electoral** *a* électoral. ◆**electorate** *n* électorat *m*.

electric [ɪ'lektrɪk] *a* électrique; **e. blanket** couverture *f* chauffante; **e. shock** décharge *f* électrique; **e. shock treatment** électrochoc *m*. ◆**electrical** *a* électrique; **e. engineer** ingénieur *m* électricien. ◆**elec'trician** *n* électricien *m*. ◆**elec'tricity** *n* électricité *f*. ◆**electrify** *vt Rail* électrifier; *(excite) Fig* électriser. ◆**electrocute** *vt* électrocuter.

electrode [ɪ'lektrəud] *n El* électrode *f*.

electron [ɪ'lektrɒn] *n* électron *m*; — *a (microscope)* électronique. ◆**elec'tronic** *a* électronique. ◆**elec'tronics** *n* électronique *f*.

elegant ['elɪgənt] *a* élégant. ◆**elegance** *n* élégance *f*. ◆**elegantly** *adv* avec élégance, élégamment.

elegy ['elədʒɪ] *n* élégie *f*.

element ['elɪmənt] *n (component, environment)* élément *m*; *(of heater)* résistance *f*; **an e. of truth** un grain or une part de vérité; **the human/chance e.** le facteur humain/chance; **in one's e.** dans son élément. ◆**ele'mental** *a* élémentaire. ◆**ele'mentary** *a* élémentaire; *(school) Am* primaire; **e. courtesy** la courtoisie la plus élémentaire.

elephant ['elɪfənt] *n* éléphant *m*. ◆**ele'phantine** [elɪ'fæntaɪn] *a (large)* éléphantesque; *(clumsy)* gauche.

elevate ['elɪveɪt] *vt* élever (**to** à). ◆**ele-'vation** *n* élévation *f* (**of** de); *(height)* altitude *f*. ◆**elevator** *n Am* ascenseur *m*.

eleven [ɪ'lev(ə)n] *a & n* onze *(m)*. ◆**elevenses** [ɪ'lev(ə)nzɪz] *n Fam* pause-café *f (vers onze heures du matin)*. ◆**eleventh** *a & n* onzième *(mf)*.

elf [elf] *n (pl* **elves)** lutin *m*.

elicit [ɪ'lɪsɪt] *vt* tirer, obtenir (**from** de).

elide [ɪ'laɪd] *vt Ling* élider. ◆**elision** *n* élision *f*.

eligible ['elɪdʒəb(ə)l] a (*for post etc*) admissible (**for** à); (*for political office*) éligible (**for** à); **to be e. for** (*entitled to*) avoir droit à; **an e. young man** (*suitable as husband*) un beau parti. ◆**eligi'bility** n admissibilité f; Pol éligibilité f.

eliminate [ɪ'lɪmɪneɪt] vt éliminer (**from** de). ◆**elimi'nation** n élimination f.

elite [eɪ'liːt] n élite f (**of** de).

elk [elk] n (*animal*) élan m.

ellipse [ɪ'lɪps] n Geom ellipse f. ◆**elliptical** a elliptique.

elm [elm] n (*tree, wood*) orme m.

elocution [elə'kjuːʃ(ə)n] n élocution f.

elongate ['iːlɒŋgeɪt] vt allonger. ◆**elon'gation** n allongement m.

elope [ɪ'ləʊp] vi (*of lovers*) s'enfuir (**with** avec). ◆**—ment** n fugue f (amoureuse).

eloquent ['eləkwənt] a éloquent. ◆**elo'quence** n éloquence f.

else [els] adv ailleurs; **someone e.** quelqu'un d'autre; **everybody e.** tout le monde à part moi, vous *etc*, tous les autres; **nobody/nothing e.** personne/rien d'autre; **something e.** autre chose; **something** or **anything e.?** encore quelque chose?; **somewhere e.** ailleurs, autre part; **who e.?** qui encore?, qui d'autre?; **how e.?** de quelle autre façon?; **or e.** ou bien, sinon. ◆**elsewhere** adv ailleurs; **e. in the town** dans une autre partie de la ville.

elucidate [ɪ'luːsɪdeɪt] vt élucider.

elude [ɪ'luːd] vt (*enemy*) échapper à; (*question*) éluder; (*obligation*) se dérober à; (*blow*) esquiver. ◆**elusive** a (*enemy, aims*) insaisissable; (*reply*) évasif.

emaciated [ɪ'meɪsɪeɪtɪd] a émacié.

emanate ['eməneɪt] vi émaner (**from** de).

emancipate [ɪ'mænsɪpeɪt] vt (*women*) émanciper. ◆**emanci'pation** n émancipation f.

embalm [ɪm'bɑːm] vt (*dead body*) embaumer.

embankment [ɪm'bæŋkmənt] n (*of path etc*) talus m; (*of river*) berge f.

embargo [ɪm'bɑːgəʊ] n (pl -oes) embargo m.

embark [ɪm'bɑːk] vt embarquer; – vi (s')embarquer; **to e. on** (*start*) commencer, entamer; (*launch into*) se lancer dans, s'embarquer dans. ◆**embar'kation** n embarquement m.

embarrass [ɪm'bærəs] vt embarrasser, gêner. ◆**—ing** a (*question etc*) embarrassant. ◆**—ment** n embarras m, gêne f; (*financial*) embarras mpl.

embassy ['embəsɪ] n ambassade f.

embattled [ɪm'bæt(ə)ld] a (*political party, person etc*) assiégé de toutes parts; (*attitude*) belliqueux.

embedded [ɪm'bedɪd] a (*stick, bullet*) enfoncé; (*jewel*) & Ling enchâssé; (*in one's memory*) gravé; (*in stone*) scellé.

embellish [ɪm'belɪʃ] vt embellir. ◆**—ment** n embellissement m.

embers ['embəz] npl braise f, charbons mpl ardents.

embezzl/e [ɪm'bez(ə)l] vt (*money*) détourner. ◆**—ement** n détournement m de fonds. ◆**—er** n escroc m, voleur m.

embitter [ɪm'bɪtər] vt (*person*) aigrir; (*situation*) envenimer.

emblem ['embləm] n emblème m.

embody [ɪm'bɒdɪ] vt (*express*) exprimer; (*represent*) incarner; (*include*) réunir. ◆**embodiment** n incarnation f (**of** de).

emboss [ɪm'bɒs] vt (*metal*) emboutir; (*paper*) gaufrer, emboutir. ◆**—ed** a en relief.

embrace [ɪm'breɪs] vt étreindre, embrasser; (*include, adopt*) embrasser; – vi s'étreindre, s'embrasser; – n étreinte f.

embroider [ɪm'brɔɪdər] vt (*cloth*) broder; (*story, facts*) Fig enjoliver. ◆**embroidery** n broderie f.

embroil [ɪm'brɔɪl] vt **to e. s.o. in** mêler qn à.

embryo ['embrɪəʊ] n (pl -os) embryon m. ◆**embry'onic** a Med & Fig embryonnaire.

emcee [em'siː] n Am présentateur, -trice mf.

emend [ɪ'mend] vt (*text*) corriger.

emerald ['emərəld] n émeraude f.

emerge [ɪ'mɜːdʒ] vi apparaître (**from** de); (*from hole etc*) sortir; (*of truth, from water*) émerger; (*of nation*) naître; **it emerges that** il apparaît que. ◆**emergence** n apparition f.

emergency [ɪ'mɜːdʒənsɪ] n (*case*) urgence f; (*crisis*) crise f; (*contingency*) éventualité f; **in an e.** en cas d'urgence; – a (*measure etc*) d'urgence; (*exit, brake*) de secours; (*ward, services*) Med des urgences; **e. landing** atterrissage m forcé; **e. powers** Pol pouvoirs mpl extraordinaires.

emery ['emərɪ] a **e. cloth** toile f (d')émeri.

emigrant ['emɪgrənt] n émigrant, -ante mf. ◆**emigrate** vi émigrer. ◆**emi'gration** n émigration f.

eminent ['emɪnənt] a éminent. ◆**eminence** n distinction f; **his E.** Rel son Éminence f. ◆**eminently** adv hautement, remarquablement.

emissary ['emɪsərɪ] n émissaire m.

emit [ɪ'mɪt] vt (-tt-) (*light, heat etc*) émettre;

(*smell*) dégager. ◆**emission** n émission f; dégagement m.

emotion [ɪ'məʊʃ(ə)n] n (*strength of feeling*) émotion f; (*joy, love etc*) sentiment m. ◆**emotional** a (*person, reaction*) émotif; (*story, speech*) émouvant; (*moment*) d'émotion intense; (*state*) Psy émotionnel. ◆**emotionally** adv (*to say*) avec émotion; **to be e. unstable** avoir des troubles émotifs. ◆**emotive** a (*person*) émotif; (*word*) affectif; **an e. issue** une question sensible.

emperor ['empərər] n empereur m.

emphasize ['emfəsaɪz] vt souligner (**that** que); (*word, fact*) appuyer or insister sur, souligner. ◆**emphasis** n Ling accent m (tonique); (*insistence*) insistance f; **to lay** or **put e. on** mettre l'accent sur. ◆**em'phatic** a (*person, refusal*) catégorique; (*forceful*) énergique; **to be e. about** insister sur. ◆**em'phatically** adv catégoriquement; énergiquement; **e. no!** absolument pas!

empire ['empaɪər] n empire m.

empirical [em'pɪrɪk(ə)l] a empirique. ◆**empiricism** n empirisme m.

employ [ɪm'plɔɪ] vt (*person, means*) employer; – n **in the e. of** au service de. ◆**employee** [ɪm'plɔɪiː, emplɔ'iː] n employé, -ée mf. ◆**employer** n patron, -onne mf. ◆**employment** n emploi m; **place of e.** lieu m de travail; **in the e. of** employé par; **e. agency** bureau m de placement.

empower [ɪm'paʊər] vt autoriser (**to do** à faire).

empress ['emprɪs] n impératrice f.

empt/y ['emptɪ] a (-ier, -iest) vide; (*threat, promise etc*) vain; (*stomach*) creux; **on an e. stomach** à jeun; **to return/etc e.-handed** revenir/*etc* les mains vides; – npl (*bottles*) bouteilles fpl vides; – vt **to e. (out)** (*box, pocket, liquid etc*) vider; (*vehicle*) décharger; (*objects in box etc*) sortir (**from, out of** de); – vi se vider; (*of river*) se jeter (**into** dans). ◆**-iness** n vide m.

emulate ['emjʊleɪt] vt imiter. ◆**emu'lation** n émulation f.

emulsion [ɪ'mʌlʃ(ə)n] n (*paint*) peinture f (mate); Phot émulsion f.

enable [ɪ'neɪb(ə)l] vt **to e. s.o. to do** permettre à qn de faire.

enact [ɪn'ækt] vt (*law*) promulguer; (*part of play*) jouer.

enamel [ɪ'næm(ə)l] n émail m; – a en émail; – vt (-ll-, Am -l-) émailler.

enamoured [ɪn'æməd] a **e. of** (*thing*) séduit par; (*person*) amoureux de.

encamp [ɪn'kæmp] vi camper. ◆**-ment** n campement m.

encapsulate [ɪn'kæpsjʊleɪt] vt Fig résumer.

encase [ɪn'keɪs] vt recouvrir (**in** de).

enchant [ɪn'tʃɑːnt] vt enchanter. ◆**-ing** a enchanteur. ◆**-ment** n enchantement m.

encircle [ɪn'sɜːk(ə)l] vt entourer; Mil encercler. ◆**-ment** n encerclement m.

enclave ['enkleɪv] n enclave f.

enclos/e [ɪn'kləʊz] vt (*send with letter*) joindre (**in, with** à); (*fence off*) clôturer; **to e. with** (*a fence, wall*) entourer de. ◆**-ed** a (*space*) clos; (*cheque etc*) ci-joint; (*market*) couvert. ◆**enclosure** n Com pièce f jointe; (*fence, place*) enceinte f.

encompass [ɪn'kʌmpəs] vt (*surround*) entourer; (*include*) inclure.

encore ['ɒŋkɔːr] int & n bis (m); – vt bisser.

encounter [ɪn'kaʊntər] vt rencontrer; – n rencontre f.

encourage [ɪn'kʌrɪdʒ] vt encourager (**to do** à faire). ◆**-ment** n encouragement m.

encroach [ɪn'krəʊtʃ] vi empiéter (**on, upon** sur); **to e. on the land** (*of sea*) gagner du terrain. ◆**-ment** n empiétement m.

encumber [ɪn'kʌmbər] vt encombrer (**with** de). ◆**encum'brance** n embarras m.

encyclical [ɪn'sɪklɪk(ə)l] n Rel encyclique f.

encyclop(a)edia [ɪnsaɪklə'piːdɪə] n encyclopédie f. ◆**encyclop(a)edic** a encyclopédique.

end [end] n (*of street, object etc*) bout m, extrémité f; (*of time, meeting, book etc*) fin f; (*purpose*) but m, fin f; **at an e.** (*discussion etc*) fini; (*period*) écoulé; (*patience*) à bout; **in the e.** à la fin; **to come to an e.** prendre fin; **to put an end to, bring to an e.** mettre fin à; **there's no e. to it** ça n'en finit plus; **no e. of** Fam beaucoup de; **six days on e.** six jours d'affilée; **for days on e.** pendant des jours (et des jours); (*standing*) **on e.** (*box etc*) debout; (*hair*) hérissé; – a (*row, house*) dernier; **e. product** Com produit m fini; Fig résultat m; – vt finir, terminer, achever (**with** par); (*rumour, speculation*) mettre fin à; – vi finir, se terminer, s'achever; **to e. in failure** se solder par un échec; **to e. in a point** finir en pointe; **to e. up doing** finir par faire; **to e. up in** (*London etc*) se retrouver à; **he ended up in prison/a doctor** il a fini en prison/par devenir médecin.

endanger [ɪn'deɪndʒər] vt mettre en danger.

endear [ɪn'dɪər] vt faire aimer or apprécier (**to** de); **that's what endears him to me** c'est cela qui me plaît en lui. ◆**-ing** a attachant, sympathique. ◆**-ment** n parole *f* tendre; **term of e.** terme *m* d'affection.

endeavour [ɪn'devər] *vi* s'efforcer (**to do de** faire); – *n* effort *m* (**to do** pour faire).

ending ['endɪŋ] *n* fin *f*; (*outcome*) issue *f*; *Ling* terminaison *f*. **◆endless** *a* (*speech, series etc*) interminable; (*patience*) infini; (*countless*) innombrable. **◆endlessly** *adv* interminablement.

endive ['endɪv, *Am* 'endaɪv] *n Bot* Culin (*curly*) chicorée *f*; (*smooth*) endive *f*.

endorse [ɪn'dɔːs] *vt* (*cheque etc*) endosser; (*action*) approuver; (*claim*) appuyer. **◆—ment** *n* (*on driving licence*) contravention *f*.

endow [ɪn'daʊ] *vt* (*institution*) doter (**with** de); (*chair, hospital bed*) fonder; **endowed with** (*person*) *Fig* doté de. **◆—ment** *n* dotation *f*; fondation *f*.

endur/e [ɪn'djʊər] **1** *vt* (*bear*) supporter (**doing** de faire). **2** *vi* (*last*) durer. **◆—ing** *a* durable. **◆—able** *a* supportable. **◆endurance** *n* endurance *f*, résistance *f*.

enemy ['enəmɪ] *n* ennemi, -ie *mf*; – *a* (*army, tank etc*) ennemi.

energy ['enədʒɪ] *n* énergie *f*; (*crisis, resources etc*) énergétique. **◆ener'getic** *a* énergique; **to feel e.** se sentir en pleine forme. **◆ener'getically** *adv* énergiquement.

enforc/e [ɪn'fɔːs] *vt* (*law*) faire respecter; (*discipline*) imposer (**on** à). **◆—ed** *a* (*rest, silence etc*) forcé.

engag/e [ɪn'geɪdʒ] *vt* (*take on*) engager, prendre; **to e. s.o. in conversation** engager la conversation avec qn; **to e. the clutch** *Aut* embrayer; – *vi* **to e. in** (*launch into*) se lancer dans; (*be involved into*) être mêlé à. **◆—ed** *a* **1** (*person, toilet*) & *Tel* occupé; **e. in doing** occupé à faire; **to be e. in business**/*etc* être dans les affaires/*etc.* **2** (*betrothed*) fiancé; **to get e.** se fiancer. **◆—ing** *a* (*smile*) engageant. **◆—ement** *n* (*agreement to marry*) fiançailles *fpl*; (*meeting*) rendez-vous *m inv*; (*undertaking*) engagement *m*; **to have a prior e.** (*be busy*) être déjà pris, ne pas être libre; **e. ring** bague *f* de fiançailles.

engender [ɪn'dʒendər] *vt* (*produce*) engendrer.

engine ['endʒɪn] *n Aut* moteur *m*; *Rail* locomotive *f*; *Nau* machine *f*; **e. driver** mécanicien *m*.

engineer [endʒɪ'nɪər] **1** *n* ingénieur *m*; (*repairer*) dépanneur *m*; *Rail Am* mécanicien *m*; **civil e.** ingénieur *m* des travaux publics; **mechanical e.** ingénieur *m*

mécanicien. **2** *vt* (*arrange secretly*) machiner. **◆—ing** *n* ingénierie *f*; (**civil) e.** génie *m* civil, travaux *mpl* publics; (**mechanical) e.** mécanique *f*; **e. factory** atelier *m* de construction mécanique.

England ['ɪŋglənd] *n* Angleterre *f*. **◆English** *a* anglais; **the E. Channel** la Manche; **the E.** les Anglais *mpl*; – *n* (*language*) anglais *m*. **◆Englishman** *n* (*pl* **-men**) Anglais *m*. **◆English-speaking** *a* anglophone. **◆Englishwoman** *n* (*pl* **-women**) Anglaise *f*.

engrav/e [ɪn'greɪv] *vt* graver. **◆—ing** *n* gravure *f*. **◆—er** *n* graveur *m*.

engrossed [ɪn'grəʊst] *a* absorbé (**in** par).

engulf [ɪn'gʌlf] *vt* engloutir.

enhance [ɪn'hɑːns] *vt* (*beauty etc*) rehausser; (*value*) augmenter.

enigma [ɪ'nɪgmə] *n* énigme *f*. **◆enig'matic** *a* énigmatique.

enjoy [ɪn'dʒɔɪ] *vt* aimer (**doing** faire); (*meal*) apprécier; (*income, standard of living etc*) jouir de; **to e. the evening** passer une bonne soirée; **to e. oneself** s'amuser; **to e. being in London**/*etc* se plaire à Londres/*etc.* **◆—able** *a* agréable. **◆—ably** *adv* agréablement. **◆—ment** *n* plaisir *m*.

enlarge [ɪn'lɑːdʒ] *vt* agrandir; – *vi* s'agrandir; **to e. (up)on** (*say more about*) s'étendre sur. **◆—ment** *n* agrandissement *m*.

enlighten [ɪn'laɪt(ə)n] *vt* éclairer (**s.o. on** or **about sth** qn sur qch). **◆—ing** *a* instructif. **◆—ment** *n* (*explanations*) éclaircissements *mpl*; **an age of e.** une époque éclairée.

enlist [ɪn'lɪst] *vi* (*in the army etc*) s'engager; – *vt* (*recruit*) engager; (*supporter*) recruter; (*support*) obtenir. **◆—ment** *n* engagement *m*; recrutement *m*.

enliven [ɪn'laɪv(ə)n] *vt* (*meeting, people etc*) égayer, animer.

enmeshed [ɪn'meʃt] *a* empêtré (**in** dans).

enmity ['enmɪtɪ] *n* inimitié *f* (**between** entre).

enormous [ɪ'nɔːməs] *a* énorme; (*explosion*) terrible; (*success*) fou. **◆enormity** *n* (*vastness, extent*) énormité *f*; (*atrocity*) atrocité *f*. **◆enormously** *adv* (*very much*) énormément; (*very*) extrêmement.

enough [ɪ'nʌf] *a* & *n* assez (*de*); **e. time/cups**/*etc* assez de temps/de tasses/*etc*; **to have e. to live on** avoir de quoi vivre; **to have e. to drink** avoir assez à boire; **to have had e. of** *Pej* en avoir assez de; **it's e. for me to see that** . . . il me suffit de voir que . . . ; **that's e.** ça suffit, c'est assez; – *adv* assez, suffisamment (**to** pour); **strangely e., he left** chose curieuse, il est parti.

enquire [ɪnˈkwaɪər] *vi* = **inquire**.

enquiry [ɪnˈkwaɪərɪ] *n* = **inquiry**.

enrage [ɪnˈreɪdʒ] *vt* mettre en rage.

enrapture [ɪnˈræptʃər] *vt* ravir.

enrich [ɪnˈrɪtʃ] *vt* enrichir; (*soil*) fertiliser. ◆**—ment** *n* enrichissement *m*.

enrol [ɪnˈrəʊl] (*Am* **enroll**) *vi* (**-ll-**) s'inscrire (**in, for** à); — *vt* inscrire. ◆**—ment** *n* inscription *f*; (*people enrolled*) effectif *m*.

ensconced [ɪnˈskɒnst] *a* bien installé (**in** dans).

ensemble [ɒnˈsɒmb(ə)l] *n* (*clothes*) & *Mus* ensemble *m*.

ensign [ˈensən] *n* (*flag*) pavillon *m*; (*rank*) *Am Nau* enseigne *m* de vaisseau.

enslave [ɪnˈsleɪv] *vt* asservir.

ensu/e [ɪnˈsjuː] *vi* s'ensuivre. ◆**—ing** *a* (*day, year etc*) suivant; (*event*) qui s'ensuit.

ensure [ɪnˈʃʊər] *vt* assurer; **to e. that** (*make sure*) s'assurer que.

entail [ɪnˈteɪl] *vt* (*imply, involve*) entraîner, impliquer.

entangle [ɪnˈtæŋg(ə)l] *vt* emmêler, enchevêtrer; **to get entangled** s'empêtrer. ◆**—ment** *n* enchevêtrement *m*; **an e. with** (*police*) des démêlés *mpl* avec.

enter [ˈentər] *vt* (*room, vehicle, army etc*) entrer dans; (*road*) s'engager dans; (*university*) s'inscrire à; (*write down*) inscrire (**in** dans, **on** sur); (*in ledger*) porter (**in** sur); **to e. s.o. for** (*exam*) inscrire qn à; **to e. a painting/etc in** (*competition*) présenter un tableau/etc à; **it didn't e. my head** ça ne m'est pas venu à l'esprit (**that** que); — *vi* entrer; **to e. for** (*race, exam*) s'inscrire pour; **to e. into** (*plans*) entrer dans; (*conversation, relations*) entrer en; **you don't e. into it** tu n'y es pour rien; **to e. into or upon** (*career*) entrer dans; (*negotiations*) entamer; (*agreement*) conclure.

enterpris/e [ˈentəpraɪz] *n* (*undertaking, firm*) entreprise *f*; (*spirit*) *Fig* initiative *f*. ◆**—ing** *a* (*a person*) plein d'initiative; (*attempt*) hardi.

entertain [entəˈteɪn] *vt* amuser, distraire; (*guest*) recevoir; (*idea, possibility*) envisager; (*hope*) chérir; **to e. s.o. to a meal** recevoir qn à dîner; — *vi* (*receive guests*) recevoir. ◆**—ing** *a* amusant. ◆**—er** *n* artiste *mf*. ◆**—ment** *n* amusement *m*, distraction *f*; (*show*) spectacle *m*.

enthral(l) [ɪnˈθrɔːl] *vt* (**-ll-**) (*delight*) captiver.

enthuse [ɪnˈθjuːz] *vi* **to e. over** *Fam* s'emballer pour. ◆**enthusiasm** *n* enthousiasme *m*. ◆**enthusiast** *n* enthousiaste

mf; *jazz/etc* e. passionné, -ée *mf* du jazz/etc. ◆**enthusi'astic** *a* enthousiaste; (*golfer etc*) passionné; **to be e. about** (*hobby*) être passionné de; **he was e. about** *or* **over** (*gift etc*) il a été emballé par; **to get e.** s'emballer (**about** pour). ◆**enthusi'astically** *adv* avec enthousiasme.

entic/e [ɪnˈtaɪs] *vt* attirer (par la ruse); **to e. to do** entraîner (par la ruse) à faire. ◆**—ing** *a* séduisant, alléchant. ◆**—ement** *n* (*bait*) attrait *m*.

entire [ɪnˈtaɪər] *a* entier. ◆**—ly** *adv* tout à fait, entièrement. ◆**entirety** [ɪnˈtaɪərətɪ] *n* intégralité *f*; **in its e.** en entier.

entitl/e [ɪnˈtaɪt(ə)l] *vt* **to e. s.o. to do** donner à qn le droit de faire; **to e. s.o. to sth** donner à qn (le droit à qch; **that entitles me to believe that ...** ça m'autorise à croire que ... . ◆**—ed** *a* (*book*) intitulé; **to be e.** to do avoir le droit de faire; **to be e. to sth** avoir droit à qch. ◆**—ment** *n* one's **e.** son dû.

entity [ˈentɪtɪ] *n* entité *f*.

entourage [ˈɒntʊrɑːʒ] *n* entourage *m*.

entrails [ˈentreɪlz] *npl* entrailles *fpl*.

entrance 1 [ˈentrəns] *n* entrée *f* (**to** de); (*to university etc*) admission *f* (**to** à); **e. examination** examen *m* d'entrée. **2** [ɪnˈtrɑːns] *vt* *Fig* transporter, ravir.

entrant [ˈentrənt] *n* (*in race*) concurrent, -ente *mf*; (*for exam*) candidat, -ate *mf*.

entreat [ɪnˈtriːt] *vt* supplier, implorer (**to do** de faire). ◆**entreaty** *n* supplication *f*.

entrée [ˈɒntreɪ] *n* *Culin* entrée *f*; (*main dish*) *Am* plat *m* principal.

entrench [ɪnˈtrentʃ] *vt* **to e. oneself** *Mil* & *Fig* se retrancher.

entrust [ɪnˈtrʌst] *vt* confier (**to** à); **to e. s.o. with sth** confier qch à qn.

entry [ˈentrɪ] *n* (*way in, action*) entrée *f*; (*in ledger*) écriture *f*; (*term in dictionary or logbook*) entrée *f*; (*competitor*) *Sp* concurrent, -ente *mf*; (*thing to be judged in competition*) objet *m* (*or* œuvre *f* *or* projet *m*) soumis à un jury; **e. form** feuille *f* d'inscription; '**no e.**' (*on door etc*) 'entrée interdite'; (*road sign*) 'sens interdit'.

entwine [ɪnˈtwaɪn] *vt* entrelacer.

enumerate [ɪˈnjuːmərət] *vt* énumérer. ◆**enume'ration** *n* énumération *f*.

enunciate [ɪˈnʌnsɪeɪt] *vt* (*word*) articuler; (*theory*) énoncer. ◆**enunci'ation** *n* articulation *f*; énonciation *f*.

envelop [ɪnˈveləp] *vt* envelopper (**in fog/mystery/etc** de brouillard/mystère/etc).

envelope [ˈenvələʊp] *n* enveloppe *f*.

envious [ˈenvɪəs] *a* envieux (**of sth** de qch);

e. of s.o. jaloux de qn. ◆**enviable** a enviable. ◆**enviously** adv avec envie.

environment [ɪnˈvaɪərənmənt] n milieu m; (cultural, natural) environnement m. ◆**environ'mental** a du milieu; de l'environnement. ◆**environ'mentalist** n écologiste mf.

envisage [ɪnˈvɪzɪdʒ] vt (imagine) envisager; (foresee) prévoir.

envision [ɪnˈvɪʒ(ə)n] vt Am = **envisage.**

envoy [ˈenvɔɪ] n Pol envoyé, -ée mf.

envy [ˈenvɪ] n envie f; – vt envier (s.o. sth qch à qn).

ephemeral [ɪˈfemərəl] a éphémère.

epic [ˈepɪk] a épique; – n épopée f; (screen) e. film m à grand spectacle.

epidemic [epɪˈdemɪk] n épidémie f; – a épidémique.

epilepsy [ˈepɪlepsɪ] n épilepsie f. ◆**epi'leptic** a & n épileptique (mf).

epilogue [ˈepɪlɒg] n épilogue m.

episode [ˈepɪsəʊd] n épisode m. ◆**episodic** [epɪˈsɒdɪk] a épisodique.

epistle [ɪˈpɪs(ə)l] n épître f.

epitaph [ˈepɪtɑːf] n épitaphe f.

epithet [ˈepɪθet] n épithète f.

epitome [ɪˈpɪtəmɪ] n the e. of l'exemple même de, l'incarnation de. ◆**epitomize** vt incarner.

epoch [ˈiːpɒk] n époque f. ◆**e.-making** a (event) qui fait date.

equal [ˈiːkwəl] a égal (to à); with e. hostility avec la même hostilité; on an e. footing sur un pied d'égalité (with avec); to be e. to égaler; e. to (task, situation) à la hauteur de; – n égal, -ale mf; to treat s.o. as an e. traiter qn en égal or d'égal à égal; he doesn't have his e. il n'a pas son pareil; – vt (-ll-, Am -l-) égaler (in beauty/etc en beauté/etc); equals sign Math signe m d'égalité. ◆**e'quality** n égalité f. ◆**equalize** vt égaliser; – vi Sp égaliser. ◆**equally** adv (to an equal degree, also) également; (to divide) en parts égales; he's as stupid (just as) il est tout aussi bête.

equanimity [ekwəˈnɪmɪtɪ] n égalité f d'humeur.

equate [ɪˈkweɪt] vt mettre sur le même pied (with que), assimiler (with à).

equation [ɪˈkweɪʒ(ə)n] n Math équation f.

equator [ɪˈkweɪtər] n équateur m; at or on the e. sous l'équateur. ◆**equatorial** [ekwəˈtɔːrɪəl] a équatorial.

equestrian [ɪˈkwestrɪən] a équestre.

equilibrium [iːkwɪˈlɪbrɪəm] n équilibre m.

equinox [ˈiːkwɪnɒks] n équinoxe m.

equip [ɪˈkwɪp] vt (-pp-) équiper (with de);

(well-)equipped with pourvu de; (well-)equipped to do compétent pour faire. ◆**—ment** n équipement m, matériel m.

equity [ˈekwɪtɪ] n (fairness) équité f; pl Com actions fpl. ◆**equitable** a équitable.

equivalent [ɪˈkwɪvələnt] a & n équivalent (m). ◆**equivalence** n équivalence f.

equivocal [ɪˈkwɪvək(ə)l] a équivoque.

era [ˈɪərə, Am ˈerə] n époque f; (historical, geological) ère f.

eradicate [ɪˈrædɪkeɪt] vt supprimer; (evil, prejudice) extirper.

erase [ɪˈreɪz, Am ɪˈreɪs] vt effacer. ◆**eraser** n (rubber) gomme f. ◆**erasure** n rature f.

erect [ɪˈrekt] 1 a (upright) (bien) droit. 2 vt (build) construire; (statue, monument) ériger; (scaffolding) monter; (tent) dresser. ◆**erection** n construction f; érection f; montage m; dressage m.

ermine [ˈɜːmɪn] n (animal, fur) hermine f.

erode [ɪˈrəʊd] vt éroder; (confidence etc) Fig miner, ronger. ◆**erosion** n érosion f.

erotic [ɪˈrɒtɪk] a érotique. ◆**eroticism** n érotisme m.

err [ɜːr] vi (be wrong) se tromper; (sin) pécher.

errand [ˈerənd] n commission f, course f; e. boy garçon m de courses.

erratic [ɪˈrætɪk] a (conduct etc) irrégulier; (person) lunatique.

error [ˈerər] n (mistake) erreur f, faute f; (wrongdoing) erreur f; in e. par erreur. ◆**erroneous** [ɪˈrəʊnɪəs] a erroné.

erudite [ˈerʊdaɪt, Am ˈerjʊdaɪt] a érudit, savant. ◆**eru'dition** n érudition f.

erupt [ɪˈrʌpt] vi (of volcano) entrer en éruption; (of pimples) apparaître; (of war, violence) éclater. ◆**eruption** n (of volcano, pimples, anger) éruption f (of de); (of violence) flambée f.

escalate [ˈeskəleɪt] vi (of war, violence) s'intensifier; (of prices) monter en flèche; – vt intensifier. ◆**esca'lation** n escalade f.

escalator [ˈeskəleɪtər] n escalier m roulant.

escapade [ˈeskəpeɪd] n (prank) frasque f.

escape [ɪˈskeɪp] vi (of gas, animal etc) s'échapper; (of prisoner) s'évader, s'échapper; to e. from (person) échapper à; (place, object) s'échapper de; escaped prisoner évadé, -ée mf; – vt (death) échapper à; (punishment) éviter; that name escapes me ce nom m'échappe; to e. notice passer inaperçu; – n (of gas etc) fuite f; (of person) évasion f, fuite f; to have a lucky or narrow e. l'échapper belle. ◆**escapism** n évasion f (hors de la réalité). ◆**escapist** a (film etc) d'évasion.

eschew [ɪ'stʃuː] vt éviter, fuir.

escort ['eskɔːt] n Mil Nau escorte f; (of woman) cavalier m; – [ɪ'skɔːt] vt escorter.

Eskimo ['eskɪməʊ] n (pl -os) Esquimau, -aude mf; – a esquimau.

esoteric [esəʊ'terɪk] a obscur, ésotérique.

especial [ɪ'speʃəl] a particulier. ◆**—ly** adv (in particular) particulièrement; (for particular purpose) (tout) exprès; **e. as** d'autant plus que.

espionage ['espɪənɑːʒ] n espionnage m.

esplanade ['espləneɪd] n esplanade f.

espouse [ɪ'spaʊz] vt (a cause) épouser.

espresso [e'spresəʊ] n (pl -os) (café m) express m.

Esq [ɪ'skwaɪər] abbr (esquire) **J. Smith Esq** (on envelope) Monsieur J. Smith.

essay ['eseɪ] n (attempt) & Liter essai m; Sch rédaction f; Univ dissertation f.

essence ['esəns] n Phil Ch essence f; Culin extrait m, essence f; (main point) essentiel m (of de); **in e.** essentiellement.

essential [ɪ'senʃ(ə)l] a (principal) essentiel; (necessary) indispensable, essentiel; **it's e. that** il est indispensable que (+ sub); – npl **the essentials** l'essentiel m (of de); (of grammar) les éléments mpl. ◆**—ly** adv essentiellement.

establish [ɪ'stæblɪʃ] vt établir; (state, society) fonder. ◆**—ed** a (well-)e. (firm) solide; (fact) reconnu; (reputation) établi; **she's (well-)e.** elle a une réputation établie. ◆**—ment** n (institution, firm) établissement m; **the e. of** l'établissement de; la fondation de; **the E.** les classes fpl dirigeantes.

estate [ɪ'steɪt] n (land) terre(s) f(pl), propriété f; (possessions) Jur fortune f; (of deceased person) succession f; **housing e.** lotissement m; (workers') cité f (ouvrière); **industrial e.** complexe m industriel; **e. agency** agence f immobilière; **e. agent** agent m immobilier; **e. car** break m; **e. tax** Am droits mpl de succession.

esteem [ɪ'stiːm] vt estimer; **highly esteemed** très estimé; – n estime f.

esthetic [es'θetɪk] a Am esthétique.

estimate ['estɪmeɪt] vt (value) estimer, évaluer; (consider) estimer (that que); – ['estɪmət] n (assessment) évaluation f, estimation f; (judgement) évaluation f; (price for work to be done) devis m; **rough e.** chiffre m approximatif. ◆**esti'mation** n jugement m; (esteem) estime f; **in my e.** à mon avis.

estranged [ɪ'streɪndʒd] a **to become e.** (of couple) se séparer.

estuary ['estjʊərɪ] n estuaire m.

etc [et'setərə] adv etc.

etch [etʃ] vti graver à l'eau forte. ◆**—ing** n (picture) eau-forte f.

eternal [ɪ'tɜːn(ə)l] a éternel. ◆**eternally** adv éternellement. ◆**eternity** n éternité f.

ether ['iːθər] n éther m. ◆**e'thereal** a éthéré.

ethic ['eθɪk] n éthique f. ◆**ethics** n (moral standards) moralité f; (study) Phil éthique f. ◆**ethical** a moral, éthique.

Ethiopia [iːθɪ'əʊpɪə] n Éthiopie f. ◆**Ethiopian** a & n éthiopien, -ienne (mf).

ethnic ['eθnɪk] a ethnique.

ethos ['iːθɒs] n génie m.

etiquette ['etɪket] n (rules) bienséances fpl; (diplomatic) protocole m, étiquette f; **professional e.** déontologie f.

etymology [etɪ'mɒlədʒɪ] n étymologie f.

eucalyptus [juːkə'lɪptəs] n (tree) eucalyptus m.

eulogy ['juːlədʒɪ] n panégyrique m, éloge m.

euphemism ['juːfəmɪz(ə)m] n euphémisme m.

euphoria [juː'fɔːrɪə] n euphorie f. ◆**euphoric** a euphorique.

Euro- ['jʊərəʊ] pref euro-.

Europe ['jʊərəp] n Europe f. ◆**Euro'pean** a & n européen, -éenne (mf).

euthanasia [juːθə'neɪzɪə] n euthanasie f.

evacuate [ɪ'vækjʊeɪt] vt évacuer. ◆**evacu-'ation** n évacuation f.

evade [ɪ'veɪd] vt éviter, esquiver; (pursuer, tax) échapper à; (law, question) éluder.

evaluate [ɪ'væljʊeɪt] vt évaluer (at à). ◆**evalu'ation** n évaluation f.

evangelical [iːvæn'dʒelɪk(ə)l] a Rel évangélique.

evaporate [ɪ'væpəreɪt] vi s'évaporer; (of hopes) s'évanouir. ◆**—ed** a **e. milk** lait m concentré. ◆**evapo'ration** n évaporation f.

evasion [ɪ'veɪʒ(ə)n] n **e. of** (pursuer etc) fuite f devant; (question) esquive f de; **tax e.** évasion f fiscale. ◆**evasive** a évasif.

eve [iːv] n **the e. of** la veille de.

even ['iːv(ə)n] **1** a (flat) uni, égal, lisse; (equal) égal; (regular) régulier; (number) pair; **to get e. with s.o.** se venger de; **I'll get e. with him (for that)** je lui revaudrai ça; **we're e.** (quits) nous sommes quittes; (in score) nous sommes à égalité; **to break e.** Fin s'y retrouver; – vt **to e. (out or up)** égaliser. **2** adv même; **e. better/more** encore mieux/plus; **e. if or though** même si; **e. so** quand même. ◆**—ly** adv de manière égale; (regularly) régulièrement. ◆**—ness** n (of *surface, temper*) égalité *f*; (*of movement etc*) régularité *f*. ◆**even-'tempered** *a* de caractère égal.

evening ['iːvnɪŋ] *n* soir *m*; (*duration of evening, event*) soirée *f*; **in the e.**, *Am* **evenings** le soir; **at seven in the e.** à sept heures du soir; **every Tuesday e.** tous les mardis soir; **all e. (long)** toute la soirée *f*; **e.** (*newspaper edition*) du soir; **e. performance** *Th* soirée *f*; **e. dress** tenue *f* de soirée; (*of woman*) robe *f* du soir *or* de soirée.

event [ɪ'vent] *n* événement *m*; *Sp* épreuve *f*; **in the e. of death** en cas de décès; **in any e.** en tout cas; **after the e.** après coup. ◆**eventful** *a* (*journey etc*) mouvementé; (*occasion*) mémorable.

eventual [ɪ'ventʃʊəl] *a* final, définitif. ◆**eventu'ality** *n* éventualité *f*. ◆**eventually** *adv* finalement, à la fin; (*some day or other*) un jour ou l'autre; (*after all*) en fin de compte.

ever ['evər] *adv* jamais; **has he e. seen it?** l'a-t-il jamais vu?; **more than e.** plus que jamais; **nothing e.** jamais rien; **hardly e.** presque jamais; **e. ready** toujours prêt; **the first e.** le tout premier; **e. since** (*that event etc*) depuis; **e. since then** depuis lors, dès lors; (*for e.*) (*for always*) pour toujours; (*continually*) sans cesse; **the best son e.** le meilleur fils du monde; **e. so sorry/happy/***etc* *Fam* vraiment désolé/heureux/*etc*; **thank you e. so much** *Fam* merci mille fois; **it's e. such a pity** *Fam* c'est vraiment dommage; **why e. not?** pourquoi pas donc? ◆**evergreen** *n* arbre *m* à feuilles persistantes. ◆**ever'lasting** *a* éternel. ◆**ever-'more** *adv* **for e.** à (tout) jamais.

every ['evrɪ] *a* chaque; **e. child** chaque enfant, tous les enfants; **e. time** chaque fois (**that** que); **e. one** chacun; **e. single one** (sans exception) tous; **to have e. confidence in** avoir pleine confiance en; **e. second** *or* **other day** tous les deux jours; **her e. gesture** ses moindres gestes; **e. bit as big** tout aussi grand (**as** que); **e. so often, e. now and then** de temps en temps. ◆**everybody** *pron* tout le monde; **e. in turn** chacun à son tour. ◆**everyday** *a* (*happening, life etc*) de tous les jours; (*banal*) banal; **in e. use** d'usage courant. ◆**everyone** *pron* = everybody. ◆**everyplace** *adv* *Am* = everywhere. ◆**everything** *pron* tout; **e. I have** tout ce que j'ai. ◆**everywhere** *adv* partout; **e. she goes** où qu'elle aille, partout où elle va.

evict [ɪ'vɪkt] *vt* expulser (**from** de). ◆**eviction** *n* expulsion *f*.

evidence ['evɪdəns] *n* (*proof*) preuve(s)

f(*pl*); (*testimony*) témoignage *m*; (*obviousness*) évidence *f*; **to give e.** témoigner (**against** contre); **e. of** (*wear etc*) des signes *mpl* de; **e.** (*noticeable*) (bien) en vue. ◆**evident** *a* évident (**that** que); **it is e. from ... il** apparaît de ... (**that** que). ◆**evidently** *adv* (*obviously*) évidemment; (*apparently*) apparemment.

evil ['iːv(ə)l] *a* (*spell, influence, person*) malfaisant; (*deed, advice, system*) mauvais; (*consequence*) funeste; – *n* mal *m*; **to speak e.** dire du mal (**about, of** de).

evince [ɪ'vɪns] *vt* manifester.

evoke [ɪ'vəʊk] *vt* (*recall, conjure up*) évoquer; (*admiration*) susciter. ◆**evocative** *a* évocateur.

evolution [iːvə'luːʃ(ə)n] *n* évolution *f*. ◆**evolve** *vi* (*of society, idea etc*) évoluer; (*of plan*) se développer; – *vt* (*system etc*) développer.

ewe [juː] *n* brebis *f*.

ex- [eks] *n* (*former spouse*) *Fam* ex *mf*.

ex- [eks] *pref* ex-; **ex-wife** ex-femme *f*.

exacerbate [ɪk'sæsəbeɪt] *vt* (*pain*) exacerber.

exact [ɪg'zækt] *a* (*accurate, precise etc*) exact; **to be (more) e. about** préciser. **2** *vt* (*demand*) exiger (**from** de); (*money*) extorquer (**from** à). ◆—**ing** *a* exigeant. ◆—**ly** *adv* exactement; **it's e. 5 o'clock** il est 5 heures juste. ◆—**ness** *n* exactitude *f*.

exaggerate [ɪg'zædʒəreɪt] *vt* exagérer; (*in one's own mind*) s'exagérer; – *vi* exagérer. ◆**exagge'ration** *n* exagération *f*.

exalt [ɪg'zɔːlt] *vt* (*praise*) exalter. ◆—**ed** *a* (*position, rank*) élevé. ◆**exal'tation** *n* exaltation *f*.

exam [ɪg'zæm] *n Univ Sch Fam* examen *m*.

examine [ɪg'zæmɪn] *vt* examiner; (*accounts, luggage*) vérifier; (*passport*) contrôler; (*orally*) interroger (*témoin, élève*). ◆**exami'nation** *n* (*inspection*) & *Univ Sch* examen *m*; (*of accounts etc*) vérification *f*; (*of passport*) contrôle *m*; **class e.** *Sch* composition *f*. ◆**examiner** *n Sch* examinateur, -trice *mf*.

example [ɪg'zɑːmp(ə)l] *n* exemple *m*; **for e.** par exemple; **to set a good/bad e.** donner le bon/mauvais exemple (**to** à); **to make an e. of** punir pour l'exemple.

exasperate [ɪg'zɑːspəreɪt] *vt* exaspérer; **to get exasperated** s'exaspérer (**at** de). ◆**exaspe'ration** *n* exaspération *f*.

excavate ['ekskəveɪt] *vt* (*dig*) creuser; (*for relics etc*) fouiller; (*uncover*) déterrer. ◆**exca'vation** *n Tech* creusement *m*; (*archeological*) fouille *f*.

exceed [ɪkˈsiːd] vt dépasser, excéder. ◆**—ingly** adv extrêmement.

excel [ɪkˈsel] vi (-ll-) exceller (**in** sth en qch, **in doing** à faire); – vt surpasser.

Excellency [ˈeksələnsɪ] n (title) Excellence f.

excellent [ˈeksələnt] a excellent. ◆**excellence** n excellence f. ◆**excellently** adv parfaitement, admirablement.

except [ɪkˈsept] prep sauf, excepté; **e. for** à part; **e. that** à part le fait que, sauf que; **e. if** sauf si; **to do nothing e. wait** ne rien faire sinon attendre; – vt excepter. ◆**exception** n exception f; **with the e. of** à l'exception de; **to take e. to** (object to) désapprouver; (be hurt by) s'offenser de. ◆**exceptional** a exceptionnel. ◆**exceptionally** adv exceptionnellement.

excerpt [ˈeksɜːpt] n (from film, book etc) extrait m.

excess [ˈekses] n excès m; (surplus) Com excédent m; **one's excesses** ses excès mpl; **to e. à l'excès; an e. of** (details) un luxe de; – a (weight etc) excédentaire, en trop; **e. fare** supplément m (de billet); **e. luggage** excédent m de bagages. ◆**ex'cessive** a excessif. ◆**ex'cessively** adv (too, too much) excessivement; (very) extrêmement.

exchange [ɪksˈtʃeɪndʒ] vt (addresses, blows etc) échanger (**for** contre); – n échange m; Fin change m; (telephone) central m (téléphonique); **in e.** en échange (**for** de).

Exchequer [ɪksˈtʃekər] n Chancellor of the E. = ministre m des Finances.

excise [ˈeksaɪz] n taxe f (**on** sur).

excit/e [ɪkˈsaɪt] vt (agitate, provoke, stimulate) exciter; (enthuse) enthousiasmer, exciter. ◆**—ed** a excité; (laughter) énervé; **to get e.** (nervous, angry, enthusiastic) s'exciter; **to be e. about** (new car, news) se réjouir de; **to be e. about the holidays** être surexcité à l'idée de partir en vacances. ◆**—ing** a (book, adventure) passionnant. ◆**—able** a excitable. ◆**—edly** adv avec agitation; (to wait, jump about) dans un état de surexcitation. ◆**—ement** n agitation f, excitation f, fièvre f; (emotion) vive émotion f; (adventure) aventure f; **great e.** surexcitation f.

exclaim [ɪkˈskleɪm] vti s'exclamer, s'écrier (**that** que). ◆**excla'mation** n exclamation f; **e. mark** or Am **point** point m d'exclamation.

exclude [ɪksˈkluːd] vt exclure (**from** de); (name from list) écarter (**from** de). ◆**exclusion** n exclusion f. ◆**exclusive** a (right, interest, design) exclusif; (club, group) fermé; (interview) en exclusivité; **e.**

of wine/etc vin/etc non compris. ◆**exclusively** adv exclusivement.

excommunicate [ekskəˈmjuːnɪkeɪt] vt excommunier.

excrement [ˈekskrəmənt] n excrément(s) m(pl).

excruciating [ɪkˈskruːʃɪeɪtɪŋ] a insupportable, atroce.

excursion [ɪkˈskɜːʃ(ə)n] n excursion f.

excuse [ɪkˈskjuːz] vt (justify, forgive) excuser (**s.o. for doing** qn d'avoir fait, qn de faire); (exempt) dispenser (**from** de); **e. me for asking** permettez-moi de demander; **e. me!** excusez-moi!, pardon!; **you're excused** tu peux t'en aller or sortir; – [ɪkˈskjuːs] n excuse f; **it was an e. for** cela a servi de prétexte à.

ex-directory [eksdəˈrektərɪ] a Tel sur la liste rouge.

execute [ˈeksɪkjuːt] vt (criminal, order, plan etc) exécuter. ◆**exe'cution** n exécution f. ◆**exe'cutioner** n bourreau m.

executive [ɪgˈzekjʊtɪv] a (power) exécutif; (ability) d'exécution; (job) de cadre; (car, plane) de direction; – n (person) cadre m; (board, committee) bureau m; **the e.** Pol l'exécutif m; (senior) **e.** cadre m supérieur; **junior e.** jeune cadre m; **business e.** directeur m commercial.

exemplary [ɪgˈzemplərɪ] a exemplaire. ◆**exemplify** vt illustrer.

exempt [ɪgˈzempt] a exempt (**from** de); – vt exempter (**from** de). ◆**exemption** n exemption f.

exercise [ˈeksəsaɪz] n (of power etc) & Sch Sp Mil exercice m; pl Univ Am cérémonies fpl; **e. book** cahier m; – vt exercer; (troops) faire faire l'exercice à; (dog, horse etc) promener; (tact, judgement etc) faire preuve de; (rights) faire valoir, exercer; – vi (take exercise) prendre de l'exercice.

exert [ɪgˈzɜːt] vt exercer; (force) employer; **to e. oneself** (physically) se dépenser; **he never exerts himself** (takes the trouble) il ne se fatigue jamais; **to e. oneself to do** (try hard) s'efforcer de faire. ◆**exertion** n effort m; (of force) emploi m.

exhale [eksˈheɪl] vt (breathe out) expirer; (give off) exhaler; – vi exhaler.

exhaust [ɪgˈzɔːst] **1** vt (use up, tire) épuiser; **to become exhausted** s'épuiser. **2** n **e.** (pipe) Aut pot m or tuyau m d'échappement. ◆**—ing** a épuisant. ◆**exhaustion** n épuisement m. ◆**exhaustive** a (study etc) complet; (research) approfondi.

exhibit [ɪgˈzɪbɪt] vt (put on display) exposer; (ticket, courage etc) montrer; – n objet m exposé; *Jur* pièce *f* à conviction. ◆**exhi'bition** *n* exposition *f*; **an e.** of (*display*) une démonstration de; **to make an e.** (*of display*) **of oneself** se donner en spectacle. ◆**exhi'bitionist** *n* exhibitionniste *mf*. ◆**exhibitor** *n* exposant, -ante *mf*.

exhilarate [ɪg'zɪləreɪt] *vt* stimuler; (*of air*) vivifier; (*elate*) rendre fou de joie. ◆**exhila'ration** *n* liesse *f*, joie *f*.

exhort [ɪg'zɔːt] *vt* exhorter (**to do** à faire, **to sth** à qch).

exhume [eks'hjuːm] *vt* exhumer.

exile ['egzaɪl] *vt* exiler; – *n* (*absence*) exil *m*; (*person*) exilé, -ée *mf*.

exist [ɪg'zɪst] *vi* exister; (*live*) vivre (**on** de); (**to continue**) **to e.** subsister; **the notion exists that . . .** il existe une notion selon laquelle . . . . ◆**-ing** *a* (*law*) existant; (*circumstances*) actuel. ◆**existence** *n* existence *f*; **to come into e.** être créé; **to be in e.** exister. ◆**exi'stentialism** *n* existentialisme *m*.

exit ['eksɪt, 'egzɪt] *n* (*action*) sortie *f*; (*door, window*) sortie *f*, issue *f*; – *vi Th* sortir.

exodus ['eksədəs] *n inv* exode *m*.

exonerate [ɪg'zɒnəreɪt] *vt* (*from blame*) disculper (**from** de).

exorbitant [ɪg'zɔːbɪtənt] *a* exorbitant. ◆**-ly** *adv* démesurément.

exorcize ['eksɔːsaɪz] *vt* exorciser. ◆**exorcism** *n* exorcisme *m*.

exotic [ɪg'zɒtɪk] *a* exotique.

expand [ɪk'spænd] *vt* (*one's fortune, knowledge etc*) étendre; (*trade, ideas*) développer; (*production*) augmenter; (*gas, metal*) dilater; – *vi* s'étendre; se développer; augmenter; se dilater; **to e. on** développer ses idées sur; (*fast or rapidly*) **expanding sector/etc** *Com* secteur/*etc* en (pleine) expansion. ◆**expansion** *n Com Phys Pol* expansion *f*; développement *m*; augmentation *f*; dilatation *f*. ◆**expansionism** *n* expansionnisme *m*.

expanse [ɪk'spæns] *n* étendue *f*.

expansive [ɪk'spænsɪv] *a* expansif. ◆**-ly** *adv* avec effusion.

expatriate [eks'pætrɪət, *Am* eks'peɪtrɪət] *a & n* expatrié, -ée (*mf*).

expect [ɪk'spekt] *vt* (*anticipate*) s'attendre à, attendre, escompter; (*think*) penser (**that** que); (*suppose*) supposer (**that** que); (*await*) attendre; **to e. sth from s.o./sth** attendre qch de qn/qch; **to e. to do** compter faire; **to e. that** (*anticipate*) s'attendre à ce que (+ *sub*); **I e. you to come** (*want*) je te demande de venir; **it was expected** c'était prévu (**that** que); **she's expecting a baby** elle attend un bébé. ◆**expectancy** *n* attente *f*; **life e.** espérance *f* de vie. ◆**expectant** *a* (*crowd*) qui attend; **e. mother** future mère *f*. ◆**expec'tation** *n* attente *f*; **to come up to s.o.'s expectations** répondre à l'attente de qn.

expedient [ɪks'piːdɪənt] *a* avantageux; (*suitable*) opportun; – *n* (*resource*) expédient *m*.

expedite ['ekspədaɪt] *vt* (*hasten*) accélérer; (*task*) expédier.

expedition [ekspɪ'dɪʃ(ə)n] *n* expédition *f*.

expel [ɪk'spel] *vt* (**-ll-**) expulser (**from** de); (*from school*) renvoyer; (*enemy*) chasser.

expend [ɪk'spend] *vt* (*energy, money*) dépenser; (*resources*) épuiser. ◆**-able** *a* (*object*) remplaçable; (*troops*) sacrifiable. ◆**expenditure** *n* (*money spent*) dépenses *fpl*; **an e. of** (*time, money*) une dépense de.

expense [ɪk'spens] *n* frais *mpl*, dépense *f*; *pl Fin* frais *mpl*; **business/travelling expenses** frais *mpl* généraux/de déplacement; **to go to some e.** faire des frais; **at s.o.'s e.** aux dépens de qn; **an e. account** une *or* sa note de frais (professionnels).

expensive [ɪk'spensɪv] *a* (*goods etc*) cher, coûteux; (*hotel etc*) cher; (*tastes*) dispendieux; **to be e.** coûter cher; **an e. mistake** une faute qui coûte cher. ◆**-ly** *adv* à grands frais.

experienc/e [ɪk'spɪərɪəns] *n* (*knowledge, skill, event*) expérience *f*; **from** *or* **by e.** par expérience; **he's had e.** of (*work etc*) il a déjà fait; (*grief etc*) il a déjà éprouvé; **I've had e. of driving** j'ai déjà conduit; **terrible experiences** de rudes épreuves *fpl*; **unforgettable e.** moment *m* inoubliable; – *vt* (*undergo*) connaître, subir; (*remorse, difficulty*) éprouver; (*joy*) ressentir. ◆**-ed** *a* (*person*) expérimenté; (*eye, ear*) exercé; **to be e. in** s'y connaître en (matière de).

experiment [ɪk'sperɪmənt] *n* expérience *f*; – [ɪk'sperɪment] *vi* faire une expérience *or* des expériences; **to e. with sth** *Phys Ch* expérimenter qch. ◆**experi'mental** *a* expérimental; **e. period** période *f* d'expérimentation.

expert ['ekspɜːt] *n* expert *m* (**on, in** en); spécialiste *mf* (**on, in** de); – *a* expert (**in sth** en qch, **in** *or* **at doing** à faire); (*advice*) d'un expert, d'expert; (*eye*) connaisseur; **e. touch** doigté *m*, grande habileté *f*. ◆**exper'tise** *n* compétence *f* (**in** en). ◆**expertly** *adv* habilement.

expiate ['ekspɪeɪt] *vt* (*sins*) expier.

expir/e [ɪk'spaɪər] *vi* expirer. ◆**-ed** *a*

(*ticket, passport etc*) périmé. ◆**ex'piration** *n Am.* ◆**expiry** *n* expiration *f.*

explain [ɪk'spleɪn] *vt* expliquer (**to** à, **that** que); (*reasons*) exposer; (*mystery*) éclaircir; **e. yourself!** explique-toi!; **to e. away** justifier. ◆**-able** *a* explicable. ◆**expla-'nation** *n* explication *f.* ◆**explanatory** *a* explicatif.

expletive [ɪk'spliːtɪv, *Am* 'eksplətɪv] *n* (*oath*) juron *m.*

explicit [ɪk'splɪsɪt] *a* explicite. ◆**-ly** *adv* explicitement.

explode [ɪk'spləʊd] *vi* exploser; **to e. with laughter** *Fig* éclater de rire; – *vt* faire exploser; (*theory*) *Fig* démythifier, discréditer.

exploit 1 [ɪk'splɔɪt] *vt* (*person, land etc*) exploiter. **2** ['eksplɔɪt] *n* (*feat*) exploit *m.* ◆**exploi'tation** *n* exploitation *f.*

explore [ɪk'splɔːr] *vt* explorer; (*possibilities*) examiner. ◆**explo'ration** *n* exploration *f.* ◆**exploratory** *a* d'exploration; (*talks, step etc*) préliminaire, exploratoire; **e. operation** *Med* sondage *m.* ◆**explorer** *n* explorateur, -trice *mf.*

explosion [ɪk'spləʊʒ(ə)n] *n* explosion *f.* ◆**explosive** *a* (*weapon, question*) explosif; (*mixture, gas*) détonant; – *n* explosif *m.*

exponent [ɪk'spəʊnənt] *n* (*of opinion, theory etc*) interprète *m* (**of** de).

export ['ekspɔːt] *n* exportation *f*; – *a* (*goods etc*) d'exportation; – [ɪk'spɔːt] *vt* exporter (**to** vers, **from** de). ◆**expor'tation** *n* exportation *f.* ◆**ex'porter** *n* exportateur, -trice *mf*; (*country*) pays *m* exportateur.

expose [ɪk'spəʊz] *vt* (*leave uncovered, describe*) & *Phot* exposer; (*wire*) dénuder; (*plot, scandal etc*) révéler, dévoiler; (*crook etc*) démasquer; **to e. to** (*subject to*) exposer à; **to e. oneself** *Jur* commettre un attentat à la pudeur. ◆**expo'sition** *n* exposition *f.* ◆**exposure** *n* exposition *f* (**to** à); (*of plot etc*) révélation *f*; (*of house etc*) exposition *f*; *Phot* pose *f*; **to die of e.** mourir de froid.

expound [ɪk'spaʊnd] *vt* (*theory etc*) exposer.

express [ɪk'spres] **1** *vt* exprimer; (*proposition*) énoncer; **to e. oneself** s'exprimer. **2** *a* (*order*) exprès, formel; (*intention*) explicite; (*purpose*) seul; (*letter, delivery*) exprès *inv*; (*train*) rapide, express *inv*; – *adv* (*to send*) par exprès; – *n* (*train*) rapide *m*, express *m inv.* ◆**expression** *n* (*phrase, look etc*) expression *f*; **an e. of** (*gratitude, affection etc*) un témoignage de. ◆**expressive** *a* expressif. ◆**expressly** *adv* expressément. ◆**expressway** *n Am* autoroute *f.*

expulsion [ɪk'spʌlʃ(ə)n] *n* expulsion *f*; (*from school*) renvoi *m.*

expurgate ['ekspɜːgeɪt] *vt* expurger.

exquisite [ɪk'skwɪzɪt] *a* exquis. ◆**-ly** *adv* d'une façon exquise.

ex-serviceman [eks'sɜːvɪsmən] *n* (*pl* **-men**) ancien combattant *m.*

extant ['ekstənt, ek'stænt] *a* existant.

extend [ɪk'stend] *vt* (*arm, business*) étendre; (*line, visit, meeting*) prolonger (**by** de); (*hand*) tendre (**to s.o.** à qn); (*house*) agrandir; (*knowledge*) élargir; (*time limit*) reculer; (*help, thanks*) offrir (**to** à); **to e. an invitation to** faire une invitation à; – *vi* (*of wall, plain etc*) s'étendre (**to** jusqu'à); (*in time*) se prolonger; **to e. to s.o.** (*of joy etc*) gagner qn. ◆**extension** *n* (*in space*) prolongement *m*; (*in time*) prolongation *f*; (*of powers, measure, meaning, strike*) extension *f*; (*for table, wire*) rallonge *f*; (*to building*) agrandissement(s) *m(pl)*; (*of telephone*) appareil *m* supplémentaire; (*of office telephone*) poste *m*; **an e. (of time)** un délai. ◆**extensive** *a* étendu, vaste; (*repairs, damage*) important; (*use*) courant. ◆**extensively** *adv* (*very much*) beaucoup, considérablement; **e. used** largement répandu.

extent [ɪk'stent] *n* (*scope*) étendue *f*; (*size*) importance *f*; (*degree*) mesure *f*; **to a large/certain e.** dans une large/certaine mesure; **to such an e. that** à tel point que.

extenuating [ɪk'stenjʊeɪtɪŋ] *a* **e. circumstances** circonstances *fpl* atténuantes.

exterior [ɪks'tɪərɪər] *a & n* extérieur (*m*).

exterminate [ɪk'stɜːmɪneɪt] *vt* (*people etc*) exterminer; (*disease*) supprimer; (*evil*) extirper. ◆**extermi'nation** *n* extermination *f*; suppression *f.*

external [ek'stɜːn(ə)l] *a* (*influence, trade etc*) extérieur; **for e. use** (*medicine*) à usage externe; **e. affairs** *Pol* affaires *fpl* étrangères. ◆**-ly** *adv* extérieurement.

extinct [ɪk'stɪŋkt] *a* (*volcano, love*) éteint; (*species, animal*) disparu. ◆**extinction** *n* extinction *f*; disparition *f.*

extinguish [ɪk'stɪŋgwɪʃ] *vt* éteindre. ◆**-er** *n* (*fire*) **e.** extincteur *m.*

extol [ɪk'stəʊl] *vt* (**-ll-**) exalter, louer.

extort [ɪk'stɔːt] *vt* (*money*) extorquer (**from** à); (*consent*) arracher (**from** à). ◆**extortion** *n Jur* extorsion *f* de fonds; **it's (sheer) e.!** c'est du vol! ◆**extortionate** *a* exorbitant.

extra ['ekstrə] *a* (*additional*) supplémentaire; **one e. glass** un verre de *or* en plus, encore un verre; **(any) e. bread?**

encore du pain?; **to be e.** (*spare*) être en trop; (*cost more*) être en supplément; (*of postage*) être en sus; **wine is 3 francs e.** il y a un supplément de 3F pour le vin; **e. care** un soin tout particulier; **e. charge** or **portion** supplément *m*; **e. time** *Fb* prolongation *f*; – *adv* **e. big**/*etc* plus grand/*etc* que d'habitude; – *n* (*perk*) à-côté *m*; *Cin Th* figurant, -ante *mf*; *pl* (*expenses*) frais *mpl* supplémentaires; **an optional e.** (*for car etc*) un accessoire en option.

extra- ['ekstrə] *pref* extra-. ◆**e.-'dry** *a* (*champagne*) brut. ◆**e.-'fine** *a* extra-fin. ◆**e.-'strong** *a* extra-fort.

extract [ɪk'strækt] *vt* extraire (**from** de); (*tooth*) arracher; (*promise*) arracher, soutirer (**from** à); (*money*) soutirer (**from** à); – ['ekstrækt] *n* (*of book etc*) & *Culin Ch* extrait *m*. ◆**ex'traction** *n* extraction *f*; arrachement *m*; (*descent*) origine *f*.

extra-curricular [ekstrəkə'rɪkjulər] *a* (*activities etc*) en dehors des heures de cours, extrascolaire.

extradite ['ekstrədaɪt] *vt* extrader. ◆**extra-'dition** *n* extradition *f*.

extramarital [ekstrə'mærɪt(ə)l] *a* en dehors du mariage, extra-conjugal.

extramural [ekstrə'mjuərəl] *a* (*studies*) hors faculté.

extraneous [ɪk'streɪnɪəs] *a* (*detail etc*) accessoire.

extraordinary [ɪk'strɔːdən(ə)rɪ] *a* (*strange, exceptional*) extraordinaire.

extra-special [ekstrə'speʃəl] *a* (*occasion*) très spécial; (*care*) tout particulier.

extravagant [ɪk'strævəgənt] *a* (*behaviour, idea etc*) extravagant; (*claim*) exagéré; (*wasteful with money*) dépensier, prodigue. ◆**extravagance** *n* extravagance *f*; prodigalité *f*; (*thing bought*) folle dépense *f*.

extravaganza [ɪkstrævə'gænzə] *n* *Mus Liter* & *Fig* fantaisie *f*.

extreme [ɪk'striːm] *a* (*exceptional, furthest*) extrême; (*danger, poverty*) très grand; (*praise*) outré; **at the e. end** à l'extrémité; **of**

e. importance de première importance; – *n* (*furthest degree*) extrême *m*; **to carry** or **take to extremes** pousser à l'extrême; **extremes of temperature** températures *fpl* extrêmes; **extremes of climate** excès *mpl* du climat. ◆**extremely** *adv* extrêmement. ◆**extremist** *a* & *n* extrémiste (*mf*). ◆**extremity** [ɪk'stremɪtɪ] *n* extrémité *f*.

extricate ['ekstrɪkeɪt] *vt* dégager (**from** de); **to e. oneself from** (*difficulty*) se tirer de.

extrovert ['ekstrəvɜːt] *n* extraverti, -ie *mf*.

exuberant [ɪg'zjuːbərənt] *a* exubérant. ◆**exuberance** *n* exubérance *f*.

exude [ɪg'zjuːd] *vt* (*charm, honesty etc*) *Fig* respirer.

exultation [egzʌl'teɪʃ(ə)n] *n* exultation *f*.

eye[1] [aɪ] *n* œil *m* (*pl* yeux); **before my very eyes** sous mes yeux; **all the eyes** être tout yeux; **as far as the e. can see** à perte de vue; **up to one's eyes in debt** endetté jusqu'au cou; **up to one's eyes in work** débordé de travail; **to have an e. on** (*house, car*) avoir en vue; **to keep an e. on** surveiller; **to make eyes at** *Fam* faire de l'œil à; **to lay** or **set eyes on** voir, apercevoir; **to take one's eyes off s.o./sth** quitter qn/qch des yeux; **to catch the e.** attirer l'œil, accrocher le regard; **keep an e. out!, keep your eyes open!** ouvre l'œil!, sois vigilant!; **we don't see e. to e.** nous n'avons pas le même point de vue; **e. shadow** fard *m* à paupières; **to be an e.-opener for s.o.** *Fam* être une révélation pour qn. ◆**eyeball** *n* globe *m* oculaire. ◆**eyebrow** *n* sourcil *m*. ◆**eye-catching** *a* (*title etc*) accrocheur. ◆**eyeglass** *n* monocle *m*. ◆**eyeglasses** *npl* (*spectacles*) *Am* lunettes *fpl*. ◆**eyelash** *n* cil *m*. ◆**eyelid** *n* paupière *f*. ◆**eyeliner** *n* eye-liner *m*. ◆**eyesight** *n* vue *f*. ◆**eyesore** *n* (*building etc*) horreur *f*. ◆**eyestrain** *n* **to have e.** avoir les yeux qui tirent. ◆**eyewash** *n* (*nonsense*) *Fam* sottises *fpl*. ◆**eyewitness** *n* témoin *m* oculaire.

eye[2] [aɪ] *vt* reluquer, regarder.

F

F, f [ef] *n* F, f *m*.

fable ['feɪb(ə)l] *n* fable *f*.

fabric ['fæbrɪk] *n* (*cloth*) tissu *m*, étoffe *f*; (*of building*) structure *f*; **the f. of society** le tissu

social.

fabricate ['fæbrɪkeɪt] *vt* (*invent, make*) fabriquer. ◆**fabri'cation** *n* fabrication *f*.

fabulous ['fæbjuləs] *a* (*incredible, legendary*) fabuleux; (*wonderful*) *Fam* formidable.

façade [fə'sɑːd] *n* *Archit & Fig* façade *f*.

face [feɪs] *n* visage *m*, figure *f*; (*expression*) mine *f*; (*of clock*) cadran *m*; (*of building*) façade *f*; (*of cliff*) paroi *f*; (*of the earth*) surface *f*; **she laughed in my f.** elle m'a ri au nez; **to show one's f.** se montrer; **f. down(wards)** (*person*) face contre terre; (*thing*) tourné à l'envers; **f. to f.** face à face; **in the f. of** devant; (*despite*) en dépit de; **to save/lose f.** sauver/perdre la face; **to make** *or* **pull faces** faire des grimaces; **to tell s.o. sth to his f.** dire qch à qn tout cru; **f. powder** poudre *f* de riz; **f. value** (*of stamp etc*) valeur *f*; **to take sth at f. value** prendre qch au pied de la lettre; – *vt* (*danger, enemy etc*) faire face à; (*accept*) accepter; (*look in the face*) regarder (*qn*) bien en face; **to f., be facing** (*be opposite*) être en face de; (*window etc*) donner sur; **faced with** (*prospect, problem*) face à, devant; (*defeat*) menacé par; (*bill*) contraint à payer; **he can't f. leaving** il n'a pas le courage de partir; – *vi* (*of house*) être orienté (**north**/*etc* au nord/*etc*); (*of person*) se tourner (**towards** vers); **to f. up to** (*danger*) faire face à; (*fact*) accepter; **about f.!** *Am Mil* demi-tour! ◆**facecloth** *n* gant *m* de toilette. ◆**facelift** *n* *Med* lifting *m*; (*of building*) ravalement *m*.

faceless ['feɪsləs] *a* anonyme.

facet ['fæsɪt] *n* (*of problem, diamond etc*) facette *f*.

facetious [fə'siːʃəs] *a* (*person*) facétieux; (*remark*) plaisant.

facial ['feɪʃ(ə)l] *a* du visage; *Med* facial; – *n* soin *m* du visage.

facile ['fæsaɪl, *Am* 'fæs(ə)l] *a* facile, superficiel.

facilitate [fə'sɪlɪteɪt] *vt* faciliter. ◆**facility** *n* (*ease*) facilité *f*; (*possibilities*) facilités *fpl*; (*for sports*) équipements *mpl*; (*in harbour, airport etc*) installations *fpl*; (*means*) moyens *mpl*, ressources *fpl*; **special facilities** (*conditions*) conditions *fpl* spéciales (**for** pour).

facing ['feɪsɪŋ] *n* (*of dress etc*) parement *m*.

fact [fækt] *n* fait *m*; **as a matter of f., in f.** en fait; **the facts of life** les choses *fpl* de la vie; **is that a f.?** c'est vrai?; **f. and fiction** le réel et l'imaginaire.

faction ['fækʃ(ə)n] *n* (*group*) *Pol* faction *f*.

factor ['fæktər] *n* (*element*) facteur *m*.

factory ['fækt(ə)rɪ] *n* (*large*) usine *f*; (*small*)

fabrique *f*; **arms/porcelain f.** manufacture *f* d'armes/de porcelaine.

factual ['fæktʃʊəl] *a* objectif, basé sur les faits, factuel; (*error*) de fait.

faculty ['fæk(ə)ltɪ] *n* (*aptitude*) & *Univ* faculté *f*.

fad [fæd] *n* (*personal habit*) marotte *f*; (*fashion*) folie *f*, mode *f* (**for** de).

fade [feɪd] *vi* (*of flower*) se faner; (*of light*) baisser; (*of colour*) passer; (*of fabric*) se décolorer; **to f. (away)** (*of memory, smile*) s'effacer; (*of sound*) s'affaiblir; (*of person*) dépérir; – *vt* (*fabric*) décolorer.

fag [fæg] *n* **1** (*cigarette*) *Fam* clope *m*, tige *f*; **f. end** mégot *m*. **2** (*male homosexual*) *Am Sl* pédé *m*.

fagged [fægd] *a* **f. (out)** (*tired*) *Sl* claqué.

faggot ['fægət] *n* **1** *Culin* boulette *f* (de viande). **2** (*male homosexual*) *Am Sl* pédé *m*.

fail [feɪl] *vi* (*of person, plan etc*) échouer; (*of business*) faire faillite; (*of light, health, sight*) baisser; (*of memory, strength*) défaillir; (*of brakes*) *Aut* lâcher; (*run short*) manquer; (*of gas, electricity*) être coupé; (*of engine*) tomber en panne; **to f. in** (*one's duty*) manquer à; (*exam*) échouer à; – *vt* (*exam*) échouer à; (*candidate*) refuser, recaler; **to f. s.o.** (*let down*) laisser tomber qn, décevoir qn; (*of words*) manquer à qn; **to f. to do** (*omit*) manquer de faire; (*not be able*) ne pas arriver à faire; **I f. to see** je ne vois pas; – *adv* **without f.** à coup sûr, sans faute. ◆**-ed** *a* (*attempt, poet*) manqué. ◆**-ing** *n* (*fault*) défaut *m*; – *prep* à défaut de; **f. this, f. that** à défaut. ◆**failure** *n* échec *m*; (*of business*) faillite *f*; (*of engine, machine*) panne *f*; (*of gas etc*) coupure *f*, panne *f*; (*person*) raté, -ée *mf*; **f. to do** (*inability*) incapacité *f* de faire; **her f. to leave** le fait qu'elle n'est pas partie; **to end in f.** se solder par un échec; **heart f.** arrêt *m* du cœur.

faint [feɪnt] *a* (**-er, -est**) léger; (*voice*) faible; (*colour*) pâle; (*idea*) vague; **I haven't the faintest idea** je n'en ai pas la moindre idée. **2** *a* *Med* défaillant (**with** de); **to f. I** se trouver mal, défaillir; – *vi* s'évanouir (**from** de); **fainting fit** évanouissement *m*. ◆**-ly** *adv* (*weakly*) faiblement; (*slightly*) légèrement. ◆**-ness** *n* légèreté *f*; faiblesse *f*. ◆**faint-'hearted** *a* timoré, timide.

fair[1] [feər] *n* foire *f*; (*for charity*) fête *f*; (*funfair*) fête *f* foraine; (*larger*) parc *m* d'attractions. ◆**fairground** *n* champ *m* de foire.

fair² [feər] **1** a (-er, -est) (equitable) juste, équitable; (game, fight) loyal; **f. (and square)** honnête(ment); **f. play** fair-play m inv; **that's not f. play!** ce n'est pas du jeu!; **that's not f. to him** ce n'est pas juste pour lui; **f. enough!** très bien!; – adv (to play) loyalement. **2** a (rather good) passable, assez bon; (amount, warning) raisonnable; **a f. amount (of)** pas mal (of); **f. copy** copie f au propre. **3** a (wind) favorable; (weather) beau. **◆—ly** adv **1** (to treat) équitablement; (to get) honnêtement. **2** (rather) assez, plutôt; **f. sure** presque sûr. **◆—ness¹** n justice f; (of decision) équité f; **in all f.** en toute justice. **◆fair-'minded** a impartial. **◆fair-'sized** a assez grand.

fair³ [feər] n (hair, person) blond; (complexion, skin) clair. **◆—ness²** n (of hair) blond m; (of skin) blancheur f. **◆fair-'haired** a blond. **◆fair-'skinned** a à la peau claire.

fairy [feəri] n fée f; **f. lights** guirlande f multicolore; **f. tale** conte m de fées.

faith [feiθ] n foi f; **to have f. in s.o.** avoir confiance en qn; **to put one's f. in** (justice, medicine etc) se fier à; **in good/bad f.** de bonne/mauvaise foi; **f. healer** guérisseur, -euse mf. **◆faithful** a fidèle. **◆faithfully** adv fidèlement; **yours f.** (in letter) Com veuillez agréer l'expression de mes salutations distinguées. **◆faithfulness** n fidélité f. **◆faithless** a déloyal, infidèle.

fake [feik] n (painting, document etc) faux m; (person) imposteur m; – vt (document, signature etc) falsifier, maquiller; (election) truquer; **to f. death** faire semblant d'être mort; – vi (pretend) faire semblant; – a faux; (elections) truqué.

falcon ['fɔːlkən] n faucon m.

fall [fɔːl] n chute f; (in price, demand etc) baisse f; (waterfall) chutes fpl (d'eau); **the f.** Am l'automne m; – vi (pt fell, pp fallen) tomber; (of building) s'effondrer; **her face fell** Fig son visage se rembrunit; **to f. into** tomber dans; (habit) Fig prendre; **to f. off a bicycle/etc** tomber d'une bicyclette/etc; **to f. off** or **down a ladder** tomber (en bas) d'une échelle; **to fall on s.o.** (of onus) retomber sur qn; **to f. on a Monday/etc** (of event) tomber un lundi/etc; **to f. over sth** tomber en butant contre qch; **to f. short of** (expectation) ne pas répondre à; **to f. short of being** être loin d'être; **to f. victim** devenir victime (to de); **to f. asleep** s'endormir; **to f. ill** tomber malade; **to f. due** échoir. **◆to f. apart** (of mechanism) tomber en morceaux; Fig se désagréger; **to f. away** (come off) se détacher, tomber; (of numbers) diminuer; **to f. back on** (as last resort) se rabattre sur; **to f. behind** rester en arrière; (in work) prendre du retard; **to f. down** tomber; (of building) s'effondrer; **to f. for** Fam (person) tomber amoureux de; (trick) se laisser prendre à; **to f. in** (collapse) s'écrouler; **f. in with** (tally with) cadrer avec; (agree to) accepter; **to f. off** (come off) se détacher, tomber; (of numbers) diminuer. **◆falling-'off** n diminution f; **to f. out with** (quarrel with) se brouiller avec; **to f. over** tomber; (of table, vase) se renverser; **to f. through** (of plan) tomber à l'eau, échouer. **◆fallen** a tombé; (angel, woman) déchu; **f. leaf** feuille f morte. **◆fallout** n (radioactive) retombées fpl.

fallacious [fə'leiʃəs] a faux. **◆fallacy** ['fæləsi] n erreur f; Phil faux raisonnement m.

fallible ['fæləb(ə)l] a faillible.

fallow ['fæləʊ] a (land) en jachère.

false [fɔːls] a faux; **a f. bottom** un double fond. **◆falsehood** n mensonge m; **truth and f.** le vrai et le faux. **◆falseness** n fausseté f. **◆falsify** vt falsifier.

falter ['fɔːltər] vi (of step, resolution) chanceler; (of voice, speaker) hésiter; (of courage) vaciller.

fame [feim] n renommée f; (glory) gloire f. **◆famed** a renommé.

familiar [fə'miljər] a (task, atmosphere etc) familier; (event) habituel; **f. with s.o.** (too friendly) familier avec qn; **to be f. with** (know) connaître; **I'm f. with her voice** je connais bien sa voix, sa voix m'est familière; **to make oneself f. with** se familiariser avec; **he looks f. (to me)** je l'ai déjà vu (quelque part). **◆famili'arity** n familiarité f (with avec); (of event, sight etc) caractère m familier. **◆familiarize** vt familiariser (with avec); **to f. oneself with** se familiariser avec.

family ['fæmɪlɪ] n famille f; – a (name, doctor etc) de famille; (planning, problem) familial; (tree) généalogique; **f. man** père m de famille.

famine ['fæmɪn] n famine f.

famished ['fæmɪʃt] a affamé.

famous ['feiməs] a célèbre (for par, pour). **◆—ly** adv (very well) Fam rudement bien.

fan [fæn] **1** n (hand-held) éventail m; (mechanical) ventilateur m; **f. heater** radiateur m soufflant; – vt (-nn-) (person etc) éventer; (fire, quarrel) attiser. **2** n (of person) admirateur, -trice mf, fan m; Sp supporter *m*; **to be a jazz/sports f.** être passionné *or* mordu de jazz/de sport.

fanatic [fə'nætɪk] *n* fanatique *mf*. ◆**fanatical** *a* fanatique. ◆**fanaticism** *n* fanatisme *m*.

fancy ['fænsɪ] **1** *n* (*whim, imagination*) fantaisie *f*; (*liking*) goût *m*; **to take a f. to s.o.** se prendre d'affection pour qn; **I took a f. to it, it took my f.** j'en ai eu envie; **when the f. takes me** quand ça me chante; – *a* (*hat, button etc*) fantaisie *inv*; (*idea*) fantaisiste; (*price*) exorbitant; (*car*) de luxe; (*house, restaurant*) chic; **f. dress** (*costume*) travesti *m*; **f.-dress ball** bal *m* masqué. **2** *vt* (*imagine*) se figurer (**that** que); (*think*) croire (**that** que); (*want*) avoir envie de; (*like*) aimer; **f. that!** tiens (donc)!; **he fancies her** *Fam* elle lui plaît; **to f. oneself** as se prendre pour; **she fancies herself!** elle se prend pour qn! ◆**fancier** *n* **horse/etc f.** amateur *m* de chevaux/*etc*. ◆**fanciful** *a* fantaisiste.

fanfare ['fænfeər] *n* (*of trumpets*) fanfare *f*.

fang [fæŋ] *n* (*of dog etc*) croc *m*; (*of snake*) crochet *m*.

fantastic [fæn'tæstɪk] *a* fantastique; **a f. idea** (*absurd*) une idée aberrante.

fantasy ['fæntəsɪ] *n* (*imagination*) fantaisie *f*; *Psy* fantasme *m*. ◆**fantasize** *vi* fantasmer (**about** sur).

far [faɪr] *adv* (**farther** *or* **further, farthest** *or* **furthest**) (*distance*) loin; **f. bigger/more expensive/etc** (*much*) beaucoup plus grand/plus cher/*etc* (**than** que); **f. more** beaucoup plus; **f. advanced** très avancé; **how f. is it to . . . ?** combien y a-t-il d'ici à . . . ?; **is it f. to . . . ?** sommes-nous, suis-je *etc* loin de . . . ?; **how f. are you going?** jusqu'où vas-tu?; **how f. has he got with?** (*plans, work etc*) où en est-il de?; **so f.** (*time*) jusqu'ici; (*place*) jusque-là; **as f. as** (*place*) jusqu'à; **as f. or so f. as I know** autant que je sache; **as f. or so f. as I'm concerned** en ce qui me concerne; **as f. back as 1820** dès 1820; **f. from doing** loin de faire; **f. from it!** loin de là!; **f. away** *or* **off** au loin; **to be (too) f. away** être (trop) loin (**from** de); **f. and wide** partout; **by f.** de loin; **f. into the night** très avant dans la nuit; – *a* (*side, end*) autre; **it's a f. cry from** on est loin de. ◆**faraway** *a* lointain; (*look*) distrait, dans le vague. ◆**far-'fetched** *a* forcé, exagéré. ◆**f.-'flung** *a* (*widespread*) vaste. ◆**f.-'off** *a* lointain. ◆**f.-'reaching** *a* de grande portée. ◆**f.-'sighted** *a* clairvoyant.

farce [faɪs] *n* farce *f*. ◆**farcical** *a* grotesque, ridicule.

fare [feər] **1** *n* (*price*) prix *m* du billet; (*ticket*) billet *m*; (*taxi passenger*) client, -ente *mf*. **2** *n* (*food*) chère *f*, nourriture *f*; **prison f.** régime *m* de prison; **bill of f.** menu *m*. **3** *vi* (*manage*) se débrouiller; **how did she f.?** comment ça s'est passé (pour elle)?

farewell [feə'wel] *n & int* adieu (*m*); – *a* (*party etc*) d'adieu.

farm [faɪm] *n* ferme *f*; – *a* (*worker, produce etc*) agricole; **f. land** terres *fpl* cultivées; – *vt* cultiver; – *vi* être agriculteur. ◆—**ing** *n* agriculture *f*; (*breeding*) élevage *m*; **dairy f.** industrie *f* laitière. ◆—**er** *n* fermier, -ière *mf*, agriculteur *m*. ◆**farmhand** *n* ouvrier, -ière *mf* agricole. ◆**farmhouse** *n* ferme *f*. ◆**farmyard** *n* basse-cour *f*.

farther ['faɪðər] *adv* plus loin; **nothing is f. from** (*my mind, the truth etc*) rien n'est plus éloigné de; **f. forward** plus avancé; **to get f. away** s'éloigner; – *a* (*end*) autre. ◆**farthest** *a* le plus éloigné; – *adv* le plus loin.

fascinate ['fæsɪneɪt] *vt* fasciner. ◆**fasci-'nation** *n* fascination *f*.

fascism ['fæʃɪz(ə)m] *n* fascisme *m*. ◆**fascist** *a & n* fasciste (*mf*).

fashion ['fæʃ(ə)n] **1** *n* (*style in clothes etc*) mode *f*; **in f.** à la mode; **out of f.** démodé; **f. designer** (*grand*) couturier *m*; **f. house** maison *f* de couture; **f. show** présentation *f* de collections. **2** *n* (*manner*) façon *f*; (*custom*) habitude *f*; **after a f.** tant bien que mal, plus au moins. **3** *vt* (*make*) façonner. ◆—**able** *a* à la mode; (*place*) chic *inv*; **it's f. to do** il est de bon ton de faire. ◆—**ably** *adv* (*dressed etc*) à la mode.

fast [faɪst] **1** *a* (**-er, -est**) rapide; **to be f.** (*of clock*) avancer (**by** de); **f. colour** couleur *f* grand teint *inv*; **f. living** vie *f* dissolue; – *adv* (*quickly*) vite; (*firmly*) ferme, bien; **how f.?** à quelle vitesse?; **f. asleep** profondément endormi. **2** *vi* (*go without food*) jeûner; – *n* jeûne *m*.

fasten ['faɪs(ə)n] *vt* attacher (**to** à); (*door, window*) fermer (bien); **to f. down** *or* **up** attacher; – *vi* (*of dress etc*) s'attacher; (*of door, window*) se fermer. ◆—**er** *n*, ◆—**ing** *n* (*clip*) attache *f*; (*of garment*) fermeture *f*; (*of bag*) fermoir *m*; (*hook*) agrafe *f*.

fastidious [fə'stɪdɪəs] *a* difficile (à contenter), exigeant.

fat [fæt] **1** *n* graisse *f*; (*on meat*) gras *m*; **vegetable f.** huile *f* végétale. **2** *a* (**fatter, fattest**) gras; (*cheek, salary, volume*) gros; **to get f.** grossir; **that's a f. lot of good** *or* **use!** *Iron*

Fam ça va vraiment servir (à quelque chose)! ◆**fathead** *n* imbécile *mf*.

fatal ['feɪt(ə)l] *a* mortel; (*error, blow etc*) *Fig* fatal. ◆**-ly** *adv* (*wounded*) mortellement.

fatality [fə'tælɪtɪ] *n* **1** (*person killed*) victime *f*. **2** (*of event*) fatalité *f*.

fate [feɪt] *n* destin *m*, sort *m*; one's f. son sort. ◆**fated** *a* **f. to do** destiné à faire; **our meeting/his death/etc** was f. notre rencontre/sa mort/*etc* devait arriver. ◆**fateful** *a* (*important*) fatal, décisif; (*prophetic*) fatidique; (*disastrous*) néfaste.

father ['fɑːðər] *n* père *m*; — *vt* engendrer; (*idea*) *Fig* inventer. ◆**-in-law** *n* (*pl* **fathers-in-law**) beau-père *m*. ◆**fatherhood** *n* paternité *f*. ◆**fatherland** *n* patrie *f*. ◆**fatherly** *a* paternel.

fathom ['fæðəm] **1** *n* *Nau* brasse *f* (= 1,8 m). **2** *vt* **to f. (out)** (*understand*) comprendre.

fatigue [fə'tiːg] **1** *n* fatigue *f*; — *vt* fatiguer. **2** *n* **f.** (*duty*) *Mil* corvée *f*.

fatness ['fætnɪs] *n* corpulence *f*. ◆**fatten** *vt* engraisser. ◆**fattening** *a* qui fait grossir. ◆**fatty** *a* (**-ier, -iest**) (*food*) gras; (*tissue*) *Med* adipeux; — *n* (*person*) *Fam* gros lard *m*.

fatuous ['fætjʊəs] *a* stupide.

faucet ['fɔːsɪt] *n* (*tap*) *Am* robinet *m*.

fault [fɔːlt] *n* (*blame*) faute *f*; (*failing, defect*) défaut *m*; (*mistake*) erreur *f*; *Geol* faille *f*; **to find f. (with)** critiquer; **he's at f.** c'est sa faute, il est fautif; **his** *or* **her memory is at f.** sa mémoire lui fait défaut; — *vt* **to f. s.o./sth** trouver des défauts chez qn/à qch. ◆**f.-finding** *a* critique, chicanier. ◆**faultless** *a* irréprochable. ◆**faulty** *a* (**-ier, -iest**) défectueux.

fauna ['fɔːnə] *n* (*animals*) faune *f*.

favour ['feɪvər] *n* (*approval, advantage*) faveur *f*; (*act of kindness*) service *m*; **to do s.o. a f.** rendre service à qn; **in f.** (*person*) bien vu; (*fashion*) en vogue; **it's in her f. to do** elle a intérêt à faire; **in f. of** (*for the sake of*) au profit de, en faveur de; **to be in f. of** (*support*) être pour, être partisan de; (*prefer*) préférer; — *vt* (*encourage*) favoriser; (*support*) être partisan de; (*prefer*) préférer; **he favoured me with a visit** il a eu la gentillesse de me rendre visite. ◆**-able** *a* favorable (**to** à). ◆**favourite** *a* favori, préféré; — *n* favori, -ite *mf*. ◆**favouritism** *n* favoritisme *m*.

fawn [fɔːn] **1** *n* (*deer*) faon *m*; — *n* *a* (*colour*) fauve *m*. **2** *vi* **to f. (up)on** flatter, flagorner.

fear [fɪər] *n* crainte *f*, peur *f*; **for f. of** de peur de; **for f. that** de peur que (+ *ne* + *sub*);

there's no f. of his going il ne risque pas d'y aller; **there are fears** (that) **he might leave** on craint qu'il ne parte; — *vt* craindre; **I f.** (that) **he might leave** je crains qu'il ne parte; **to f. for** (*one's life etc*) craindre pour. ◆**fearful** *a* (*frightful*) affreux; (*timid*) peureux. ◆**fearless** *a* intrépide. ◆**fearlessness** *n* intrépidité *f*. ◆**fearsome** *a* redoutable.

feasible ['fiːzəb(ə)l] *a* (*practicable*) faisable; (*theory, explanation etc*) plausible. ◆**feasi'bility** *n* possibilité *f* (**of doing** de faire); plausibilité *f*.

feast [fiːst] *n* festin *m*, banquet *m*; *Rel* fête *f*; — *vi* banqueter; **to f. on** (*cakes etc*) se régaler de.

feat [fiːt] *n* exploit *m*, tour *m* de force; **f. of skill** tour *m* d'adresse.

feather ['feðər] **1** *n* plume *f*; **f. duster** plumeau *m*. **2** *vt* **to f. one's nest** (*enrich oneself*) faire sa pelote.

feature ['fiːtʃər] **1** *n* (*of face, person*) trait *m*; (*of thing, place, machine*) caractéristique *f*; **f. (article)** article *m* de fond; **f. (film)** grand film *m*; **to be a regular f.** (*in newspaper*) paraître régulièrement. **2** *vt* représenter (*as comme*); *Journ Cin* présenter; **a film featuring Chaplin** un film avec Charlot en vedette; — *vi* (*appear*) figurer (**in** dans).

February ['febrʊərɪ] *n* février *m*.

fed [fed] *see* **feed**; — *a* **to be f. up** *Fam* en avoir marre (**with** de).

federal ['fedərəl] *a* fédéral. ◆**federate** *vt* fédérer. ◆**fede'ration** *n* fédération *f*.

fee [fiː] *n* (*price*) prix *m*; (*sum*) somme *f*; **fee(s)** (*professional*) honoraires *mpl*; (*of artist*) cachet *m*; (*for registration*) droits *mpl*; **tuition fees** frais *mpl* de scolarité; **entrance f.** droit *m* d'entrée; **membership fee(s)** cotisation *f*; **f.-paying school** école *f* privée.

feeble ['fiːb(ə)l] *a* (**-er, -est**) faible; (*excuse*) pauvre. ◆**f.-'minded** *a* imbécile.

feed [fiːd] *n* (*food*) nourriture *f*; (*baby's breast feed*) tétée *f*; (*baby's bottle feed*) biberon *m*; — *vt* (*pt & pp* **fed**) donner à manger à, nourrir; (*breast-feed*) allaiter (*un bébé*); (*bottle-feed*) donner le biberon à (*un bébé*); (*machine*) *Tech* alimenter; — *vi* (*eat*) manger; **to f. on** se nourrir de. ◆**-ing** *n* alimentation *f*. ◆**feedback** *n* réaction(s) *f(pl)*.

feel [fiːl] *n* (*touch*) toucher *m*; (*sensation*) sensation *f*; — *vt* (*pt & pp* **felt**) (*be aware of*) sentir; (*experience*) éprouver, ressentir; (*touch*) tâter, palper; (*think*) avoir l'impression (**that** que); **to f. one's way**

avancer à tâtons; – *vi* (*tired, old etc*) se sentir; **to f. (about)** (*grope*) tâtonner; (*in pocket etc*) fouiller; **it feels hard** c'est dur (au toucher); **I f. sure** je suis sûr (**that** que); **I f. hot/sleepy/hungry** j'ai chaud/ sommeil/faim; **she feels better** elle va mieux; **to f. like** (*want*) avoir envie de; **to f. as if** avoir l'impression que; **it feels like cotton** on dirait du coton; **what do you f. about . . . ?** que pensez-vous de . . . ?; **I f. bad about it** ça m'ennuie, ça me fait de la peine; **what does it f. like?** quelle impression ça (te) fait?; **to f. for** (*look for*) chercher; (*pity*) éprouver de la pitié pour; **to f. up to doing** être (assez) en forme pour faire. **◆–ing** *n* (*emotion, impression*) sentiment *m*; (*physical*) sensation *f*; **a f. for** (*person*) de la sympathie pour; (*music*) une appréciation de; **bad f.** animosité *f*. **◆–er** *n* (*of snail etc*) antenne *f*; **to put out a f.** *Fig* lancer un ballon d'essai.

feet [fiit] *see* **foot**[1].

feign [fein] *vt* feindre, simuler.

feint [feint] *n Mil Boxing* feinte *f*.

feisty ['faisti] *a* (**-ier, -iest**) (*lively*) *Am Fam* plein d'entrain.

felicitous [fə'lisitəs] *a* heureux.

feline ['fiilain] *a* félin.

fell [fel] 1 *see* **fall**. 2 *vt* (*tree etc*) abattre.

fellow ['feləu] *n* 1 (*man, boy*) garçon *m*, type *m*; **an old f.** un vieux; **poor f.!** pauvre malheureux! 2 (*comrade*) compagnon *m*, compagne *f*; **f. being** *or* **man** semblable *m*; **f. countryman, f. countrywoman** compatriote *mf*; **f. passenger** compagnon *m* de voyage, compagne *f* de voyage. 3 (*of society*) membre *m*. **◆fellowship** *n* camaraderie *f*; (*group*) association *f*; (*membership*) qualité *f* de membre; (*grant*) bourse *f* universitaire.

felony ['feləni] *n* crime *m*.

felt[1] [felt] *see* **feel**.

felt[2] [felt] *n* feutre *m*; **f.-tip(ped) pen** crayon *m* feutre.

female ['fiimeil] *a* (*animal etc*) femelle; (*quality, name, voice etc*) féminin; (*vote*) des femmes; **f. student** étudiante *f*; – *n* (*woman*) femme *f*; (*animal*) femelle *f*.

feminine ['feminin] *a* féminin. **◆femi'ninity** *n* féminité *f*. **◆feminist** *a & n* féministe (*mf*).

fenc/e [fens] 1 *n* barrière *f*, clôture *f*; *Sp* obstacle *m*; – *vt* **to f. (in)** clôturer. 2 *vi* (*with sword*) *Sp* faire de l'escrime. 3 *n* (*criminal*) *Fam* receleur, -euse *mf*. **◆–ing** *n Sp* escrime *f*.

fend [fend] 1 *vi* **to f. for oneself** se débrouil-

ler. 2 *vt* **to f. off** (*blow etc*) parer, éviter. **◆–er** *n* 1 (*for fire*) garde-feu *m inv*. 2 (*on car*) *Am* aile *f*.

fennel ['fen(ə)l] *n Bot Culin* fenouil *m*.

ferment ['fɜiment] *n* ferment *m*; *Fig* effervescence *f*; – [fə'ment] *vi* fermenter. **◆fermen'tation** *n* fermentation *f*.

fern [fɜin] *n* fougère *f*.

ferocious [fə'rəuʃəs] *a* féroce. **◆ferocity** *n* férocité *f*.

ferret ['ferit] *n* (*animal*) furet *m*; – *vi* **to f. about** (*pry*) fureter; – *vt* **to f. out** dénicher.

Ferris wheel ['feriswiil] *n* (*at funfair*) grande roue *f*.

ferry ['feri] *n* ferry-boat *m*; (*small, for river*) bac *m*; – *vt* transporter.

fertile ['fɜitail, *Am* 'fɜit(ə)l] *a* (*land, imagination*) fertile; (*person, creature*) fécond. **◆fer'tility** *n* fertilité *f*; fécondité *f*. **◆fertilize** *vt* (*land*) fertiliser; (*egg, animal etc*) féconder. **◆fertilizer** *n* engrais *m*.

fervent ['fɜiv(ə)nt] *a* fervent. **◆fervour** *n* ferveur *f*.

fester ['festər] *vi* (*of wound*) suppurer; (*of anger etc*) *Fig* couver.

festival ['festiv(ə)l] *n Mus Cin* festival *m*; *Rel* fête *f*. **◆festive** *a* (*atmosphere, clothes*) de fête; (*mood*) joyeux; **f. season** période *f* des fêtes. **◆fe'stivities** *npl* réjouissances *fpl*, festivités *fpl*.

festoon [fe'stuin] *vt* **to f. with** orner de.

fetch [fetʃ] *vt* 1 (*person*) amener; (*object*) apporter; **to (go and) f.** aller chercher; **to f. in** rentrer; **to f. out** sortir. 2 (*be sold for*) rapporter (**ten pounds**/*etc* dix livres/*etc*); (*price*) atteindre. **◆–ing** *a* (*smile etc*) charmant, séduisant.

fête [feit] *n* fête *f*; – *vt* fêter.

fetid ['fetid] *a* fétide.

fetish ['fetiʃ] *n* (*magical object*) fétiche *m*; **to make a f. of** *Fig* être obsédé par.

fetter ['fetər] *vt* (*hinder*) entraver.

fettle ['fet(ə)l] *n* **in fine f.** en pleine forme.

fetus ['fiitəs] *n Am* fœtus *m*.

feud [fjuid] *n* querelle *f*, dissension *f*.

feudal ['fjuid(ə)l] *a* féodal.

fever ['fiivər] *n* fièvre *f*; **to have a f.** (*temperature*) avoir de la fièvre. **◆feverish** *a* (*person, activity*) fiévreux.

few [fjui] *a & pron* peu (de); **f. towns**/*etc* peu de villes/*etc*; **a f. towns**/*etc* quelques villes/*etc*; **f. of them** peu d'entre eux; **a f.** quelques-un(e)s (de); **a f. of us** quelques-uns d'entre nous; **one of the f. books** l'un des rares livres; **quite a f., a good f.** bon nombre (de); **a f. more books**/*etc* encore quelques livres/*etc*; **f. and far between** rares (et espacés); **f. came** peu sont venus; **to be f.** être peu nombreux; **every f. days** tous les trois ou quatre jours. ◆**fewer** a & pron moins (de) (**than** que); **to be f.** être moins nombreux (**than** que); **no f. than** pas moins de. ◆**fewest** a & pron le moins (de).

fiancé(e) [fɪˈɒnseɪ] n fiancé, -ée mf.

fiasco [fɪˈæskəʊ] n (pl -os, Am -oes) fiasco m.

fib [fɪb] n Fam blague f, bobard m; – vi (-bb-) Fam raconter des blagues. ◆**fibber** n Fam blagueur, -euse mf.

fibre [ˈfaɪbər] n fibre f; Fig caractère m. ◆**fibreglass** n fibre f de verre.

fickle [ˈfɪk(ə)l] a inconstant.

fiction [ˈfɪkʃ(ə)n] n fiction f; (works of) f. romans mpl. ◆**fictional** a, ◆**fic'titious** a fictif.

fiddl/e [ˈfɪd(ə)l] **1** n (violin) Fam violon m; – vi Fam jouer du violon. **2** vi Fam **to f. about** (waste time) traînailler, glandouiller; **to f. with** (watch, pen etc) tripoter; (cars etc) bricoler. **3** n (dishonesty) Fam combine f, fraude f; – vi (swindle) Fam faire de la fraude; – vt (accounts etc) Fam falsifier. ◆**-ing** a (petty) insignifiant. ◆**-er** n **1** Fam joueur, -euse mf de violon. **2** (swindler) Sl combinard, -arde mf. ◆**fiddly** a (task) délicat.

fidelity [fɪˈdelɪtɪ] n fidélité f (**to** à).

fidget [ˈfɪdʒɪt] vi **to f.** (about) gigoter, se trémousser; **to f.** (about) with tripoter; – n personne f qui ne tient pas en place. ◆**fidgety** a agité, remuant.

field [fiːld] n champ m; Sp terrain m; (sphere) domaine m; **to have a f. day** (a good day) s'en donner à cœur joie; **f. glasses** jumelles fpl; **f. marshal** maréchal m.

fiend [fiːnd] n démon m; a jazz/etc f. Fam un(e) passionné, -ée de jazz/etc; (sex) f. Fam satyre m. ◆**fiendish** a diabolique.

fierce [fɪəs] a (-er, -est) féroce; (wind, attack) furieux. ◆**-ness** n férocité f; fureur f.

fiery [ˈfaɪərɪ] a (-ier, -iest) (person, speech) fougueux; (sun, eyes) ardent.

fiesta [fɪˈestə] n fiesta f.

fifteen [fɪfˈtiːn] a & n quinze (m). ◆**fifteenth** a & n quinzième (mf). ◆**fifth** a & n cinquième (mf); **a f.** un cinquième. ◆**fiftieth** a & n cinquantième (mf). ◆**fifty** a & n cinquante (m).

fig [fɪg] n figue f; **f. tree** figuier m.

fight [faɪt] n bagarre f, rixe f; Mil Boxing combat m; (struggle) lutte f; (quarrel) dispute f; (spirit) combativité f; **to put up a (good) f.** bien se défendre; – vi (pt & pp

fought) se battre (**against** contre); Mil se battre, combattre; (struggle) lutter; (quarrel) se disputer; **to f. back** se défendre; **to f. over sth** se disputer qch; – vt se battre avec (s.o. etc); (evil) lutter contre, combattre; **to f. a battle** livrer bataille; **to f. back** (tears) refouler; **to f. off** (attacker, attack) repousser; (illness) lutter contre; **to f. it out** se bagarrer. ◆**-ing** n Mil combat(s) m(pl); – a (person) combatif; (troops) de combat. ◆**-er** n combattant, -ante mf; Boxing boxeur m; Fig battant m, lutteur, -euse mf; (aircraft) chasseur m.

figment [ˈfɪgmənt] n a f. of one's imagination une création de son esprit.

figurative [ˈfɪgjʊrətɪv] a (meaning) figuré; (art) figuratif. ◆**-ly** adv au figuré.

figure¹ [ˈfɪgər, Am ˈfɪgjər] n **1** (numeral) chiffre m; (price) prix m; pl (arithmetic) calcul m. **2** (shape) forme f; (outlined shape) silhouette f; (of woman) ligne f; **she has a nice f.** elle est bien faite. **3** (diagram) & Liter figure f; **a f. of speech** une figure de rhétorique; Fig une façon de parler; **f. of eight**, Am **f. eight** huit m; **f. skating** patinage m artistique. **4** (important person) figure f, personnage m. ◆**figurehead** n Nau figure f de proue; (person) Fig potiche f.

figure² [ˈfɪgər, Am ˈfɪgjər] **1** vt (imagine) (s')imaginer; (guess) penser (**that** que); **to f. out** arriver à comprendre; (problem) résoudre; – vi (make sense) s'expliquer; **to f. on doing** Am compter faire. **2** vi (appear) figurer (**on** sur).

filament [ˈfɪləmənt] n filament m.

filch [fɪltʃ] vt (steal) voler (**from** à).

fil/e [faɪl] **1** n (tool) lime f; – vt **to f.** (down) limer. **2** n (folder, information) dossier m; (loose-leaf) classeur m; (for card index, computer data) fichier m; – vt (claim, application) déposer; **to f.** (away) classer. **3** n **in single f.** en file; – vi **to f. in/out** entrer/sortir à la queue leu leu; **to f. past** (coffin etc) défiler devant. ◆**-ing** **1** a **f. clerk** documentaliste mf; **f. cabinet** classeur m. **2** npl (particles) limaille f.

fill [fɪl] vt remplir (**with** de); (tooth) plomber; (sail) gonfler; (need) répondre à; **to f. in** (form) remplir; (hole) combler; (door) condamner; **to f. s.o. in on** Fam mettre qn au courant de; **to f. up** (glass etc) remplir; **to f. up or out** (form) remplir; – vi **to f. up** (with fuel) faire le plein; – n **to eat one's f.** manger à sa faim; **to have had one's f. of** Pej en avoir assez de. ◆**-ing** a *(meal etc)* substantiel, nourrissant; – *n (in tooth)* plombage *m*; *Culin* garniture *f*; **f. station** poste *m* d'essence. ◆**—er** *n (for cracks in wood)* mastic *m*.

fillet ['fɪlɪt, *Am* fɪ'leɪ] *n Culin* filet *m*; – *vt (pt & pp Am* [fɪ'leɪd]) *(fish)* découper en filets; *(meat)* désosser.

fillip ['fɪlɪp] *n (stimulus)* coup *m* de fouet.

filly ['fɪlɪ] *n (horse)* pouliche *f*.

film [fɪlm] *n* film *m*; *(layer)* & *Phot* pellicule *f*; – *a (festival)* du film; *(studio, technician, critic)* de cinéma; **f. fan** *or* **buff** cinéphile *mf*; **f. library** cinémathèque *f*; **f. star** vedette *f* (de cinéma); – *vt* filmer.

filter ['fɪltər] *n* filtre *m*; *(traffic sign)* flèche *f*; **f. lane** *Aut* couloir *m* de tourne; **f. tip** (bout *m*) filtre *m*; **f.-tipped cigarette** cigarette *f* (à bout) filtre; – *vt* filtrer; – *vi* filtrer **(through sth** à travers qch); **to f. through** filtrer.

filth [fɪlθ] *n* saleté *f*; *(obscenities)* *Fig* saletés *fpl*. ◆**filthy** *a (-ier, -iest) (hands etc)* sale; *(language)* obscène; *(habit)* dégoûtant; **f. weather** un temps infect, un sale temps.

fin [fɪn] *n (of fish, seal)* nageoire *f*; *(of shark)* aileron *m*.

final ['faɪn(ə)l] *a* dernier; *(decision)* définitif; *(cause)* final; – *n Sp* finale *f*; *pl Univ* examens *mpl* de dernière année. ◆**finalist** *n Sp* finaliste *mf*. ◆**finalize** *vt (plan)* mettre au point; *(date)* fixer (définitivement). ◆**finally** *adv (lastly)* enfin, en dernier lieu; *(eventually)* finalement, enfin; *(once and for all)* définitivement.

finale [fɪ'nɑːlɪ] *n Mus* finale *m*.

finance ['faɪnæns] *n* finance *f*; – *a (company, page)* financier; – *vt* financer. ◆**fi'nancial** *a* financier; **f. year** année *f* budgétaire. ◆**fi'nancially** *adv* financièrement. ◆**fi'nancier** *n (grand)* financier *m*.

find [faɪnd] *n (discovery)* trouvaille *f*; – *vt (pt & pp* **found**) trouver; *(sth or s.o. lost)* retrouver; *(difficulty)* éprouver (**in doing** à faire); **I f. that** je trouve que; **£20 all found** 20 livres logé et nourri; **to f. s.o. guilty** *Jur* prononcer qn coupable; **to f. one's feet** *(settle in)* s'adapter; **to f. oneself** *(to be)* se trouver. ■ **to f. out** *vt (information etc)* découvrir; *(person)* démasquer; – *vi (enquire)* se renseigner (**about** sur); **to f. out about** *(discover)* découvrir. ◆**—ings** *npl* conclusions *fpl*.

fine [faɪn] *n (money)* amende *f*; *Aut* contravention *f*; – *vt* **to f. s.o.** *(£10/etc)* infliger une amende qch (de dix livres/*etc*) à qn.

fine [faɪn] 1 *a (-er, -est) (thin, small, not coarse)* fin; *(gold)* pur; *(feeling)* délicat;

(distinction) subtil; – *adv (to cut, write)* menu. **2** *a (-er, -est) (beautiful)* beau; *(good)* bon; *(excellent)* excellent; **to be f.** *(in good health)* aller bien; – *adv (well)* très bien. ◆**—ly** *adv (dressed)* magnifiquement; *(chopped)* menu; *(embroidered, ground)* finement.

finery ['faɪnərɪ] *n (clothes)* parure *f*, belle toilette *f*.

finesse [fɪ'nes] *n (skill, tact)* doigté *m*; *(refinement)* finesse *f*.

finger ['fɪŋgər] *n* doigt *m*; **little f.** auriculaire *m*, petit doigt *m*; **middle f.** majeur *m*; **f. mark** trace *f* de doigt; – *vt* toucher (des doigts), palper. ◆**—ing** *n Mus* doigté *m*. ◆**fingernail** *n* ongle *m*. ◆**fingerprint** *n* empreinte *f* digitale. ◆**fingerstall** *n* doigtier *m*. ◆**fingertip** *n* bout *m* du doigt.

finicky ['fɪnɪkɪ] *a (precise)* méticuleux; *(difficult)* difficile **(about** sur).

finish ['fɪnɪʃ] *n (end)* fin *f*; *Sp* arrivée *f*; *(of article, car etc)* finition *f*; **paint with a matt f.** peinture *f* mate; – *vt* **to f.** *(off or* **up)** finir, terminer; **to f. doing** finir de faire; **to f. s.o. off** *(kill)* achever qn; – *vi (of meeting etc)* finir, se terminer; *(of person)* finir, terminer; **to f. first** terminer premier; *(in race)* arriver premier; **to have finished with** *(object)* ne plus avoir besoin de; *(situation, person)* en avoir fini avec; **to f. off or up** *(of person)* finir, terminer; **to f. up** *(end up)* se retrouver à; **to f. up doing** finir par faire; **finishing school** institution *f* pour jeunes filles; **finishing touch** touche *f* finale. ◆**—ed** *a (ended, done for)* fini.

finite ['faɪnaɪt] *a* fini.

Finland ['fɪnlənd] *n* Finlande *f*. ◆**Finn** *n* Finlandais, -aise *mf*, Finnois, -oise *mf*. ◆**Finnish** *a* finlandais, finnois; – *n (language)* finnois *m*.

fir [fɜːr] *n (tree, wood)* sapin *m*.

fire [faɪər] *n* feu *m*; *(accidental)* incendie *m*; *(electric)* radiateur *m*; **on f.** en feu; **(there's a) f.!** au feu!; **f.!** *Mil* feu!; **f. alarm** avertisseur *m* d'incendie; **f. brigade**, *Am* **f. department** pompiers *mpl*; **f. engine** *(vehicle)* voiture *f* de pompiers; *(machine)* pompe *f* à incendie; **f. escape** escalier *m* de secours; **f. station** caserne *f* de pompiers. ◆**firearm** *n* arme *f* à feu. ◆**firebug** *n* pyromane *mf*. ◆**firecracker** *n Am* pétard *m*. ◆**fireguard** *n* garde-feu *m inv*. ◆**fireman** *n (pl* **-men)** *(sapeur-)pompier m*. ◆**fireplace** *n* cheminée *f*. ◆**fireproof** *a (door)* ignifugé, anti-incendie. ◆**fireside** *n* coin *m* du feu; **f. chair** fauteuil *m*. ◆**firewood** *n* bois *m* de chauffage.

◆**firework** n feu m d'artifice; **a f. display, fireworks,** un feu d'artifice.

fire² ['faɪər] 1 vt (cannon) tirer; (pottery) cuire; (imagination) enflammer; **to f. a gun** tirer un coup de fusil; **to f. questions at** bombarder de questions; **to f. s.o.** (dismiss) Fam renvoyer qn; – vi tirer (at sur); **f. away!** Fam vas-y, parle!; **firing squad** peloton m d'exécution; **in** or **Am on the firing line** en butte aux attaques.

firm [fɜːm] 1 n Com maison f, firme f. 2 a (-er, -est) (earth, decision etc) ferme; (strict) ferme (with avec); (faith) solide; (character) résolu. ◆**-ly** adv fermement; (to speak) d'une voix ferme. ◆**-ness** n fermeté f; (of faith) solidité f.

first [fɜːst] a premier; **I'll do it f. thing in the morning** je le ferai dès le matin, sans faute; **f. cousin** cousin, -ine mf germain(e); – adv d'abord, premièrement; (for the first time) pour la première fois; **f. of all** tout d'abord; **at f.** d'abord; **to come f.** (in race) arriver premier; (in exam) être le premier; – n premier, -ière mf; Univ = licence f avec mention très bien; **from the f.** dès le début; **f. aid** premiers soins mpl or secours mpl; (gear) Aut première f. ◆**f.-'class** a (ticket etc) de première (classe); (mail) ordinaire; – adv (to travel) en première. ◆**f.-'hand** a & adv de première main; **to have (had) f.-hand experience of** avoir fait l'expérience personnelle de. ◆**f.-'rate** a excellent. ◆**firstly** adv premièrement.

fiscal ['fɪsk(ə)l] a fiscal.

fish [fɪʃ] n (pl inv or **-es** [-ɪz]) poisson m; **f. market** marché m aux poissons; **f. bone** arête f; **f. bowl** bocal m; **f. fingers,** Am **f. sticks** Culin bâtonnets mpl de poisson; **f. shop** poissonnerie f; – vi pêcher; **f. for** (salmon etc) pêcher; (compliment etc) Fig chercher; – vt to **f. out** (from water) repêcher; (from pocket etc) Fig sortir. ◆**-ing** n pêche f; **to go f.** aller à la pêche; **f. net** (of fisherman) filet m (de pêche); (of angler) épuisette f; **f. rod** canne f à pêche. ◆**fisherman** n (pl **-men**) pêcheur m. ◆**fishmonger** n poissonnier, -ière mf. ◆**fishy** a (-ier, -iest) (smell) de poisson; Fig Pej louche.

fission ['fɪʃ(ə)n] n Phys fission f.

fissure ['fɪʃər] n fissure f.

fist [fɪst] n poing m. ◆**fistful** n poignée f.

fit¹ [fɪt] 1 a (fitter, fittest) (suited) propre, bon (for à); (fitting) convenable; (worthy) digne (for de); (able) capable (for de, to do faire); (healthy) en bonne santé; **f. to eat** bon à manger, mangeable; **to see f. to do**

juger à propos de faire; **as you see f.** comme bon vous semble; **f. to drop** Fam prêt à tomber; **to keep f.** se maintenir en forme. 2 vt (-tt-) (of coat etc) aller (bien) à (qn), être à la taille de (qn); (match) répondre à; (equal) égaler; (suit) convenir à; **to f. sth on s.o.** (garment) ajuster qch à qn; **to f. sth (on) to sth** (put) poser qch sur qch; (adjust) adapter qch à qch; (fix) fixer qch à qch; **to f. (out** or **up) with** (house, ship etc) équiper de; **to f. (in)** (window) poser; **to f. in** (object) faire entrer; (patient, customer) prendre; **to f. (in)** (key) aller dans la serrure; – vi (of clothes) aller (bien) à (qn); **this shirt fits** (fits me) cette chemise me va (bien); **to f. (in)** (go in) entrer, aller; (of facts, plans) s'accorder, cadrer (with avec); **he doesn't f. in** il ne peut pas s'intégrer; – n **a good f.** (dress etc) à la bonne taille; **a close** or **tight f.** ajusté. ◆**fitted** a (cupboard) encastré; (garment) ajusté; **f. carpet** moquette f; **f. (kitchen) units** éléments mpl de cuisine. ◆**fitting** 1 a (suitable) convenable. 2 n (of clothes) essayage m; **f. room** salon m d'essayage; (booth) cabine f d'essayage. 3 npl (in house etc) installations fpl. ◆**fitment** n (furniture) meuble m encastré; (accessory) Tech accessoire m. ◆**fitness** n (of remark etc) à-propos m; (for job) aptitudes fpl (for pour); Med santé f. ◆**fitter** n Tech monteur, -euse mf.

fit² [fɪt] n Med & Fig accès m, crise f; **in fits and starts** par à-coups. ◆**fitful** a (sleep) agité.

five [faɪv] a & n cinq (m). ◆**fiver** n Fam billet m de cinq livres.

fix [fɪks] 1 vt (make firm, decide) fixer; (tie with rope) attacher; (mend) réparer; (deal with) arranger; (prepare, cook) Am préparer, faire; (in s.o.'s mind) graver (in dans); (conduct fraudulently) truquer; (bribe) acheter; (hopes, ambitions) mettre (on en); **to f. s.o.** (punish) Fam régler son compte à qn; **to f. (on)** (lid etc) mettre en place; **to f. up** arranger; **to f. s.o. up with sth** (job etc) procurer qch à qn. 2 n Av Nau position f; (injection) Sl piqûre f; **in a f.** Fam dans le pétrin. ◆**-ed** a (idea, price etc) fixe; (resolution) inébranlable; **how's he f. for . . . ?** Fam (cash etc) a-t-il assez de . . . ?; (tomorrow etc) qu'est-ce qu'il fait pour . . . ? ◆**fixings** npl Culin Am garniture f. ◆**fix'ation** n fixation f. ◆**fixer** n (schemer) Fam combinard, -arde mf. ◆**fixture** 1 n Sp match m (prévu). 2 npl (in house) meubles mpl fixes, installations fpl.

fizz [fɪz] vi (of champagne) pétiller; (of gas) siffler. ◆**fizzy** a (-ier, -iest) pétillant.

fizzle ['fɪz(ə)l] vi (hiss) siffler; (of liquid) pétiller; to f. out (of firework) rater, faire long feu; (of plan) Fig tomber à l'eau; (of custom) disparaître.

flabbergasted ['flæbəgɑːstɪd] a Fam sidéré.

flabby ['flæbɪ] a (-ier, -iest) (skin, character, person) mou, flasque.

flag [flæg] 1 n drapeau m; Nau pavillon m; (for charity) insigne m; f. stop Am arrêt m facultatif; − vt (-gg-) to f. down (taxi) faire signe à. 2 vi (-gg-) (of plant) dépérir; (of conversation) languir; (of worker) fléchir. ◆**flagpole** n mât m.

flagrant ['fleɪgrənt] a flagrant.

flagstone ['flægstəʊn] n dalle f.

flair [fleər] n (intuition) flair m; to have a f. for (natural talent) avoir un don pour.

flake [fleɪk] n (of snow etc) flocon m; (of metal, soap) paillette f; − vi to f. (off) (of paint) s'écailler. ◆**flaky** a f. pastry pâte f feuilletée.

flamboyant [flæm'bɔɪənt] a (person, manner) extravagant.

flame [fleɪm] n flamme f; to go up in flames s'enflammer; − vi to f. (up) (of fire, house) flamber. ◆**−ing** a 1 (sun) flamboyant. 2 (damn) Fam fichu.

flamingo [flə'mɪŋgəʊ] n (pl -os or -oes) (bird) flamant m.

flammable ['flæməb(ə)l] a inflammable.

flan [flæn] n tarte f.

flank [flæŋk] n flanc m; − vt flanquer (with de).

flannel ['flænəl] n (cloth) flanelle f; (face) f. gant m de toilette, carré-éponge m. ◆**flanne'lette** n pilou m, finette f.

flap [flæp] 1 vi (-pp-) (of wings, sail, shutter etc) battre; − vt to f. its wings (of bird) battre des ailes; − n battement m. 2 n (of pocket, envelope) rabat m; (of table) abattant m; (of door) battant m.

flare [fleər] n (light) éclat m; Mil fusée f éclairante; (for runway) balise f; − vi (blaze) flamber; (shine) briller; to f. up (of fire) s'enflammer; (of region) s'embraser; (of war) éclater; (get angry) s'emporter. ◆**f.-up** n (of violence, fire) flambée f; (of region) embrasement m. ◆**flared** a (skirt) évasé; (trousers) à pattes d'éléphant.

flash [flæʃ] n (of light) éclat m; (of anger, genius) éclair m; Phot flash m; f. of lightning éclair m; news f. flash m; in a f. en un clin d'œil; − vi (shine) briller; (on and off) clignoter; to f. past (rush) Fig passer

comme un éclair; − vt (aim) diriger (on, at sur); (a light) projeter; (a glance) jeter; to f. (around) (flaunt) étaler; to f. one's headlights faire un appel de phares. ◆**flashback** n retour m en arrière. ◆**flashlight** n lampe f électrique or de poche; Phot flash m.

flashy ['flæʃɪ] a (-ier, -iest) a voyant, tape-à-l'œil inv.

flask [flɑːsk] n thermos® m or f inv; Ch flacon m; (phial) fiole f.

flat[1] [flæt] a (flatter, flattest) plat; (tyre, battery) à plat; (nose) aplati; (beer) éventé; (refusal) net; (rate, fare) fixe; (voice) Mus faux; (razed to the ground) rasé; to put sth (down) à plat; f. (on one's face) à plat ventre; to fall f. Fig tomber à plat; to be f.-footed avoir les pieds plats; − adv (to say) carrément; (to sing) faux; f. broke Fam complètement fauché; in two minutes f. en deux minutes pile; to f. out (to work) d'arrache-pied; (to run) à toute vitesse; − n (of hand) plat m; (puncture) Aut crevaison f; Mus bémol m. ◆**−ly** adv (to deny etc) catégoriquement. ◆**−ness** n (of surface) égalité f. ◆**flatten** vt (crops) coucher; (town) raser; to f. (out) (metal etc) aplatir.

flat[2] [flæt] n (rooms) appartement m.

flatter ['flætər] vt flatter; (of clothes) avantager (qn). ◆**−ing** a flatteur; (of clothes) avantageux. ◆**−er** n flatteur, -euse mf. ◆**flattery** n flatterie f.

flatulence ['flætjʊləns] n to have f. avoir des gaz.

flaunt [flɔːnt] vt (show off) faire étalage de; (defy) Am narguer, défier.

flautist ['flɔːtɪst] n flûtiste mf.

flavour ['fleɪvər] n (taste) goût m, saveur f; (of ice cream, sweet etc) parfum m; − vt (food) assaisonner; (sauce) relever; (ice cream etc) parfumer (with à). ◆**−ing** n assaisonnement m; (in cake) parfum m.

flaw [flɔː] n défaut m. ◆**flawed** a imparfait. ◆**flawless** a parfait.

flax [flæks] n lin m. ◆**flaxen** a de lin.

flay [fleɪ] vt (animal) écorcher; (criticize) Fig éreinter.

flea [fliː] n puce f; f. market marché m aux puces. ◆**fleapit** n Fam cinéma m miteux.

fleck [flek] n (mark) petite tache f.

fledgling ['fledʒlɪŋ] n (novice) blanc-bec m.

flee [fliː] vi (pt & pp fled) fuir, s'enfuir, se sauver; − vt (place) s'enfuir de; (danger etc) fuir.

fleece [fliːs] 1 n (sheep's coat) toison f. 2 vt (rob) voler.

fleet [fliːt] n (of ships) flotte f; **a f. of cars** un parc automobile.

fleeting ['fliːtɪŋ] a (visit, moment) bref; (beauty) éphémère.

Flemish ['flemɪʃ] a flamand; – n (language) flamand m.

flesh [fleʃ] n chair f; **her (own) f. and blood** la chair de sa chair; **in the f.** en chair et en os; **f. wound** blessure f superficielle. ◆**fleshy** a (-ier, -iest) charnu.

flew [fluː] see fly².

flex [fleks] vt (limb) fléchir; (muscle) faire jouer, bander. **2** n (wire) fil m (souple); (for telephone) cordon m.

flexible ['fleksɪb(ə)l] a flexible, souple. ◆**flexi'bility** n flexibilité f.

flick [flɪk] vt donner un petit coup à; **to f. off** (remove) enlever (d'une chiquenaude); – vi **to f. over** or **through** (pages) feuilleter; – n petit coup m; (with finger) chiquenaude f; **f. knife** couteau m à cran d'arrêt.

flicker ['flɪkər] vi (of flame, light) vaciller; (of needle) osciller; – n vacillement m; **f. of light** lueur f.

flier ['flaɪər] n **1** (person) aviateur, -trice mf. **2** (handbill) Am prospectus m, Pol tract m.

flies [flaɪz] npl (on trousers) braguette f.

flight [flaɪt] n **1** (of bird, aircraft etc) vol m; (of bullet) trajectoire f; (of imagination) élan m; (floor, storey) étage m; **f. of stairs** escalier m; **f. deck** cabine f de pilotage. **2** (fleeing) fuite f (from de); **to take f.** prendre la fuite.

flighty ['flaɪtɪ] a (-ier, -iest) inconstant, volage.

flimsy ['flɪmzɪ] a (-ier, -iest) (cloth, structure etc) (trop) léger or mince; (excuse) mince, frivole.

flinch [flɪntʃ] vi (with pain) tressaillir; **to f. from** (duty etc) se dérober à; **without flinching** (complaining) sans broncher.

fling [flɪŋ] **1** vt (pt & pp flung) jeter, lancer; **to f. open** (door etc) ouvrir brutalement. **2** n **to have one's** or **a f.** (indulge oneself) s'en donner à cœur joie.

flint [flɪnt] n silex m; (for cigarette lighter) pierre f.

flip [flɪp] **1** vt (-pp-) (with finger) donner une chiquenaude à; – vi **to f. through** (book etc) feuilleter; – n chiquenaude f; **the f. side** (of record) la face deux. **2** a (cheeky) Am Fam effronté.

flip-flops ['flɪpflɒps] npl tongs fpl.

flippant ['flɪpənt] a irrévérencieux; (off-hand) désinvolte.

flipper ['flɪpər] n (of seal) nageoire f; (of swimmer) palme f.

flipping ['flɪpɪŋ] a Fam sacré; – adv Fam sacrément, bougrement.

flirt [flɜːt] vi flirter (with avec); – n flirteur, -euse mf. ◆**flir'tation** n flirt m. ◆**flir'tatious** a flirteur.

flit [flɪt] vi (-tt-) (fly) voltiger; **to f. in and out** (of person) Fig entrer et sortir (rapidement).

float [fləʊt] n Fishing flotteur m; (in parade) char m; – vi flotter (on sur); **to f. down the river** descendre la rivière; – vt (boat, currency) faire flotter; (loan) Com émettre. ◆—**ing** a (wood, debt etc) flottant; (population) instable; (voters) indécis.

flock [flɒk] n (of sheep etc) troupeau m; (of birds) volée f; Rel Hum ouailles fpl; (of tourists etc) foule f; – vi venir en foule; **to f. round s.o.** s'attrouper autour de qn.

floe [fləʊ] n (ice) f. banquise f.

flog [flɒg] vt (-gg-) **1** (beat) flageller. **2** (sell) Sl vendre. ◆**flogging** n flagellation f.

flood [flʌd] n inondation f; (of letters, tears etc) Fig flot m, déluge m, torrent m; – vt (field etc) inonder (with de); (river) faire déborder; **to f. (out)** (house) inonder; – vi (of building) être inondé; (of river) déborder; (of people, money) affluer; **to f. into** (of tourists etc) envahir. ◆—**ing** n inondation f. ◆**floodgate** n (in water) vanne f.

floodlight ['flʌdlaɪt] n projecteur m; – vt (pt & pp floodlit) illuminer; **floodlit match** Sp (match m en) nocturne m.

floor [flɔːr] **1** n (ground) sol m; (wooden etc in building) plancher m; (for dancing) piste f (de danse); **on the f.** par terre; **first f.** premier étage m; (ground floor) Am rez-de-chaussée m inv; **f. polish** encaustique f; **f. show** spectacle m (de cabaret). **2** vt (knock down) terrasser; (puzzle) stupéfier. ◆**floorboard** n planche f.

flop [flɒp] **1** vi (-pp-) **to f. down** (collapse) s'effondrer; **to f. about** s'agiter mollement. **2** vi (-pp-) Fam échouer; (of play, film etc) faire un four; – n Fam échec m, fiasco m; Th Cin four m.

floppy ['flɒpɪ] a (-ier, -iest) (soft) mou; (clothes) (trop) large; (ears) pendant; **f. disk** (of computer) disquette f.

flora ['flɔːrə] n (plants) flore f. ◆**floral** a floral; (material) à fleurs.

florid ['flɒrɪd] a (style) fleuri; (complexion) rougeaud, fleuri.

florist ['flɒrɪst] n fleuriste mf.

floss [flɒs] n (dental) f. fil m (de soie) dentaire.

flotilla [flə'tɪlə] n Nau flottille f.

flounce [flaʊns] n (frill on dress etc) volant m.

flounder ['flaʊndər] **1** vi (in water etc) patauger (avec effort), se débattre; (in speech) hésiter, patauger. **2** n (fish) carrelet m.

flour ['flaʊər] n farine f.

flourish ['flʌrɪʃ] **1** vi (of person, business, plant etc) prospérer; (of the arts) fleurir. **2** vt (wave) brandir. **3** n (decoration) fioriture f; Mus fanfare f. ◆**—ing** a prospère, florissant.

flout [flaʊt] vt narguer, braver.

flow [fləʊ] vi couler; (of current) El circuler; (of hair, clothes) flotter; (of traffic) s'écouler; **to f. in** (of people, money) affluer; **to f. back** refluer; **to f. into the sea** se jeter dans la mer; – n (of river) courant m; (of tide) flux m; (of blood) & El circulation f; (of traffic, liquid) écoulement m; (of words) Fig flot m. ◆**—ing** a (movement) gracieux; (style) coulant; (beard) flottant.

flower ['flaʊər] n fleur f; **f. bed** plate-bande f; **f. shop** (boutique f de) fleuriste mf; **f. show** floralies fpl; – vi fleurir. ◆**—ed** a (dress) à fleurs. ◆**—ing** n floraison f; – a (in bloom) en fleurs; (with flowers) à fleurs. ◆**flowery** a (style etc) fleuri; (material) à fleurs.

flown [fləʊn] see **fly** [2].

flu [fluː] n (influenza) Fam grippe f.

fluctuate ['flʌktjʊeɪt] vi varier. ◆**fluctu-ation(s)** n(pl) (in prices etc) fluctuations fpl (in de).

flue [fluː] n (of chimney) conduit m.

fluent ['fluːənt] a (style) aisé; **to be f., be a f. speaker** s'exprimer avec facilité; **he's f. in Russian, his Russian is f.** il parle couramment le russe. ◆**fluency** n facilité f. ◆**fluently** adv avec facilité; (to speak) Ling couramment.

fluff [flʌf] **1** n (down) duvet m; (of material) peluche f(pl); (on floor) moutons mpl. **2** vt (bungle) Fam rater. ◆**fluffy** a (-ier, -iest) (bird etc) duveteux; (material) pelucheux; (toy) en peluche; (hair) bouffant.

fluid ['fluːɪd] a fluide; (plans) flexible, non arrêté; – n fluide m, liquide m.

fluke [fluːk] n Fam coup m de chance; **by a f.** par raccroc.

flummox ['flʌməks] vt Fam désorienter, dérouter.

flung [flʌŋ] see **fling** [1].

flunk [flʌŋk] vi (in exam) Am Fam être collé; – vt Am Fam (pupil) coller; (exam) être collé à; (school) laisser tomber.

flunk(e)y ['flʌŋkɪ] n Pej larbin m.

fluorescent [flʊə'res(ə)nt] a fluorescent.

fluoride ['flʊəraɪd] n (in water, toothpaste) fluor m.

flurry ['flʌrɪ] n **1** (of activity) poussée f. **2** (of snow) rafale f.

flush [flʌʃ] **1** n (of blood) flux m; (blush) rougeur f; (of youth, beauty) éclat m; (of victory) ivresse f; – vi (blush) rougir. **2** vt **to f. (out)** (clean) nettoyer à grande eau; **to f. the pan** or **the toilet** tirer la chasse d'eau; **to s.o. out** (chase away) faire sortir qn (from de). **3** a (level) de niveau (with de); **f. (with money)** Fam bourré de fric. ◆**—ed** a (cheeks etc) rouge; **f. with** (success) ivre de.

fluster ['flʌstər] vt énerver; **to get flustered** s'énerver.

flute [fluːt] n flûte f. ◆**flutist** n Am flûtiste mf.

flutter ['flʌtər] **1** vi voltiger; (of wing) battre; (of flag) flotter (mollement); (of heart) palpiter; **to f. about** (of person) papillonner; – vt **to f. its wings** battre des ailes. **2** n **to have a f.** (bet) Fam parier.

flux [flʌks] n changement m continuel.

fly [1] [flaɪ] n (insect) mouche f; **f. swatter** (instrument) tapette f. ◆**flypaper** n papier m tue-mouches.

fly [2] [flaɪ] vi (pt **flew**, pp **flown**) (of bird, aircraft etc) voler; (of passenger) aller en avion; (of time) passer vite; (of flag) flotter; (flee) fuir; **to f. away** or **off** s'envoler; **to f. out** Av partir en avion; (from room) sortir à toute vitesse; **I must f.!** il faut que je file!; **to f. at s.o.** (attack) sauter sur qn; – vt (aircraft) piloter; (passengers) transporter (par avion); (airline) voyager par; (flag) arborer; (kite) faire voler; **to f. the French flag** battre pavillon français; **to f. across** or **over** survoler. **3** n (flight) vol m; (air travel) aviation f; **to like to f.** aimer l'avion; – a (personnel, saucer etc) volant; (visit) éclair inv; **with f. colours** (to succeed) haut la main; **a f. start** un très bon départ; **f. time** (length) Av durée f du vol; **ten hours'/etc f. time** dix heures/etc de vol. ◆**—er** n = **flier**. ◆**flyby** n Av Am défilé m aérien. ◆**fly-by-night** a (firm) véreux. ◆**flyover** n (bridge) toboggan m. ◆**flypast** n Av défilé m aérien.

fly [3] [flaɪ] n (on trousers) braguette f.

foal [fəʊl] n poulain m.

foam [fəʊm] n (on sea, mouth) écume f; (on beer) mousse f; **f. rubber** caoutchouc m mousse; **f. (rubber) mattress** or matelas m/etc mousse; – vi (of sea, mouth) écumer; (of beer, mouth) mousser.

fob [fɔb] *vt* (**-bb-**) to f. sth off on s.o., f. s.o. off with sth, refiler qch à qn.

focal ['fəʊk(ə)l] *a* focal; **f. point** point *m* central. ◆**focus** n foyer *m*; (*of attention, interest*) centre *m*; **in f.** au point; — *vt Phot* mettre au point; (*light*) faire converger; (*efforts, attention*) concentrer (**on** sur); — *vi* (*converge*) converger (**on** sur); **to f. one's eyes** (**on**) fixer les yeux sur; **to f. on** (*direct one's attention to*) se concentrer sur.

fodder ['fɔdər] *n* fourrage *m*.

foe [fəʊ] *n* ennemi, -ie *mf*.

foetus ['fiːtəs] *n* fœtus *m*.

fog [fɔg] *n* brouillard *m*, brume *f*; — *vt* (**-gg-**) (*issue*) *Fig* embrouiller. ◆**fogbound** *a* bloqué par le brouillard. ◆**foghorn** *n* corne *f* de brume; (*voice*) *Pej* voix *f* tonitruante. ◆**foglamp** *n* (phare *m*) anti-brouillard *m*. ◆**foggy** (**-ier, -iest**) (*day*) de brouillard; **it's f.** il fait du brouillard; **f. weather** brouillard *m*; **she hasn't the foggiest** (**idea**) *Fam* elle n'en a pas la moindre idée.

fog(e)y ['fəʊgɪ] *n* **old f.** vieille baderne *f*.

foible ['fɔɪb(ə)l] *n* petit défaut *m*.

foil [fɔɪl] **1** *n* feuille *f* de métal; *Culin* papier *m* alu(minium). **2** *n* (*contrasting person*) repoussoir *m*. **3** *vt* (*plans etc*) déjouer.

foist [fɔɪst] *vt* **to f. sth on s.o.** (*fob off*) refiler qch à qn; **to f. oneself on s.o.** s'imposer à qn.

fold¹ [fəʊld] *n* pli *m*; — *vt* plier; (*wrap*) envelopper (**in** dans); **to f. away** or **down** or **up** plier; **to f. back** or **over** replier; **to f. one's arms** (se) croiser les bras; — *vi* (*of chair etc*) se plier; (*of business* *Fam* s'écrouler; **to f. away** or **down** or **up** (*of chair etc*) se plier; **to f. back** or **over** (*of blanket etc*) se replier. ◆**—ing** *a* (*chair etc*) pliant. ◆**—er** *n* (*file holder*) chemise *f*; (*pamphlet*) dépliant *m*.

fold² [fəʊld] *n* (*for sheep*) parc *m* à moutons; *Rel Fig* bercail *m*.

-fold [fəʊld] *suffix* **tenfold** *a* par dix; — *adv* dix fois.

foliage ['fəʊlɪɪdʒ] *n* feuillage *m*.

folk [fəʊk] **1** *n* gens *mpl* or *fpl*; *pl* gens *mpl* or *fpl*; (*parents*) *Fam* parents *mpl*; **hello folks!** *Fam* salut tout le monde!; **old f.** like **it** les vieux l'apprécient. **2** *a* (*dance etc*) folklorique; **f. music** (*contemporary*) (musique *f*) folk *m*. ◆**folklore** *n* folklore *m*.

follow ['fɔləʊ] *vt* suivre; (*career*) poursuivre; **followed by** suivi de; **to f. suit** *Fig* en faire autant; **to f. s.o. around** suivre qn partout; **to f. through** (*idea etc*) poursuivre

jusqu'au bout; **to f. up** (*suggestion, case*) suivre; (*advantage*) exploiter; (*letter*) donner suite à; (*remark*) faire suivre (**with** de); — *vi* **to f.** (**on**) suivre; **it follows that** il s'ensuit que; **that doesn't f.** ce n'est pas logique. ◆**—ing 1** *a* suivant; — *prep* à la suite de. **2** *n* (*supporters*) partisans *mpl*; **to have a large f.** avoir de nombreux partisans; (*of serial, fashion*) être très suivi. ◆**—er** *n* partisan *m*. ◆**follow-up** *n* suite *f*; (*letter*) rappel *m*.

folly ['fɔlɪ] *n* folie *f*, sottise *f*.

foment [fəʊ'ment] *vt* (*revolt etc*) fomenter.

fond [fɔnd] *a* (**-er, -est**) (*loving*) tendre, affectueux; (*doting*) indulgent; (*wish, ambition*) naïf; **to be** (*very*) **f. of** aimer (beaucoup). ◆**—ly** *adv* tendrement. ◆**—ness** *n* (*for things*) prédilection *f* (**for** pour); (*for people*) affection *f* (**for** pour).

fondle ['fɔnd(ə)l] *vt* caresser.

food [fuːd] *n* nourriture *f*; (*particular substance*) aliment *m*; (*cooking*) cuisine *f*; (*for cats, pigs*) pâtée *f*; (*for plants*) engrais *m*; *pl* (*foodstuffs*) aliments *mpl*; — *a* (*needs etc*) alimentaire; **a fast f. shop** un fast-food; **f. poisoning** intoxication *f* alimentaire; **f. value** valeur *f* nutritive. ◆**foodstuffs** *npl* denrées *fpl* or produits *mpl* alimentaires.

fool [fuːl] *n* imbécile *mf*, idiot, -ote *mf*, sot, sotte *mf*; (*silly f.!* espèce d'imbécile!); **to make a f. of** (*ridicule*) ridiculiser; (*trick*) duper; **to be f. enough to do** être assez stupide pour faire; **to play the f.** faire l'imbécile; — *vt* (*trick*) duper; — *vi* **to f.** (*about* or *around*) faire l'imbécile; (*waste time*) perdre son temps; **to f. around** (*make love*) *Am Fam* faire l'amour (**with** avec). ◆**foolish** *a* bête, idiot. ◆**foolishly** *adv* bêtement. ◆**foolishness** *n* bêtise *f*, sottise *f*. ◆**foolproof** *a* (*scheme etc*) infaillible.

foolhardy ['fuːlhɑːdɪ] *a* téméraire. ◆**foolhardiness** *n* témérité *f*.

foot¹, *pl* **feet** [fut, fiːt] *n* pied *m*; (*of animal*) patte *f*; (*measure*) pied *m* (= 30,48 cm); **at the f. of** (*page, stairs*) au bas de; (*table*) au bout de; **on f.** à pied; **on one's feet** (*standing*) debout; (*recovered*) *Med* sur pied; **f. brake** *Aut* frein *m* au plancher; **f.-and-mouth disease** fièvre *f* aphteuse. ◆**footbridge** *n* passerelle *f*. ◆**foothills** *npl* contreforts *mpl*. ◆**foothold** *n* prise *f* (de pied); *Fig* position *f*; **to gain a f.** prendre pied. ◆**footlights** *npl* *Th* rampe *f*. ◆**footloose** *a* libre de toute attache. ◆**footman** *n* (*pl* **-men**) valet *m* de pied. ◆**footmark** *n* empreinte *f* (de pied). ◆**footnote** *n* note *f* au bas de la page; *Fig* post-scriptum m. ◆**footpath** n sentier m; (at roadside) chemin m (piétonnier). ◆**footstep** n pas m; to follow in s.o.'s footsteps suivre les traces de qn. ◆**footwear** n chaussures fpl.

foot² [fut] vt (bill) payer.

football ['futbɔːl] n (game) football m; (ball) ballon m. ◆**footballer** n joueur, -euse mf de football.

footing ['futɪŋ] n prise f (de pied); Fig position f; on a war f. sur le pied de guerre; on an equal f. sur un pied d'égalité.

for [fɔr, unstressed fər] **1** prep pour; (in exchange for) contre; (for a distance of) pendant; (in spite of) malgré; f. you/me/etc pour toi/moi/etc; what f. pourquoi?; what's it f.? ça sert à quoi?; for example par exemple; f. love par amour; f. sale à vendre; to swim f. (towards) nager vers; a train f. un train à destination de or en direction de; the road f. London la route (en direction) de Londres; fit f. eating bon à manger; eager f. avide de; to look f. chercher; to come f. dinner venir dîner; to sell £7 vendre sept livres; what's the Russian f. 'book'? comment dit-on 'livre' en russe?; but f. her sans elle; he was away f. a month (throughout) il a été absent pendant un mois; he won't be back f. a month il ne sera pas de retour avant un mois; he's been here f. a month (he's still here) il est ici depuis un mois; I haven't seen him f. ten years voilà dix ans que je ne l'ai vu; it's easy f. her to do it il lui est facile de le faire; it's f. you to say c'est à toi de dire; f. that to be done pour que ça soit fait. **2** conj (because) car.

forage ['fɒrɪdʒ] vt to f. (about) fourrager (for pour trouver).

foray ['fɒreɪ] n incursion f.

forbearance [fɔːˈbeərəns] n patience f.

forbid [fəˈbɪd] vt (pt forbad(e), pp forbidden, pres p forbidding) interdire, défendre (s.o. to do à qn de faire); to f. s.o. sth interdire or défendre qch à qn. ◆**forbidden** a (fruit etc) défendu; she is f. to leave il lui est interdit de partir. ◆**forbidding** a menaçant, sinistre.

force [fɔːs] n force f; the (armed) forces Mil les forces armées; by (sheer) f. de force; in f. (rule) en vigueur; (in great numbers) en grand nombre, en force; − vt contraindre, forcer (to do à faire); (impose) imposer (on à); (push) pousser; (lock) forcer; (confession) arracher (from à); to f. back (enemy etc) faire reculer; (repress) refouler; to f. down (aircraft) forcer à atterrir; to f. out

faire sortir de force. ◆**forced** a forcé (to do de faire); a f. smile un sourire forcé. ◆**force-feed** vt (pt & pp f.-fed) nourrir de force. ◆**forceful** a énergique, puissant. ◆**forcefully** adv avec force, énergiquement. ◆**forcible** a de force; (forceful) énergique. ◆**forcibly** adv (by force) de force.

forceps ['fɔːseps] n forceps m.

ford [fɔːd] n gué m; − vt (river etc) passer à gué.

fore [fɔr] n to come to the f. se mettre en évidence.

forearm ['fɔːrɑːm] n avant-bras m inv.

forebod/e [fɔːˈbəʊd] vt (be a warning of) présager. ◆**-ing** n (feeling) pressentiment m.

forecast ['fɔːkɑːst] vt (pt & pp forecast) prévoir; − n prévision f; Met prévisions fpl; Sp pronostic m.

forecourt ['fɔːkɔːt] n avant-cour f; (of filling station) aire f (de service), devant m.

forefathers ['fɔːfɑːðəz] npl aïeux mpl.

forefinger ['fɔːfɪŋgər] n index m.

forefront ['fɔːfrʌnt] n in the f. of au premier rang de.

forego [fɔːˈgəʊ] vt (pp foregone) renoncer à. ◆**'foregone** a it's a f. conclusion c'est couru d'avance.

foregoing [fɔːˈgəʊɪŋ] a précédent.

foreground ['fɔːɡraʊnd] n premier plan m.

forehead ['fɒrɪd, 'fɔːhed] n (brow) front m.

foreign ['fɒrən] a étranger; (trade) extérieur; (travel, correspondent) à l'étranger; (produce) de l'étranger; F. Minister ministre m des Affaires étrangères. ◆**foreigner** n étranger, -ère mf.

foreman ['fɔːmən] n (pl -men) (worker) contremaître m; (of jury) président m.

foremost ['fɔːməʊst] **1** a principal. **2** adv first and f. tout d'abord.

forensic [fəˈrensɪk] a (medicine) légal; (laboratory) médico-légal.

forerunner ['fɔːrʌnər] n précurseur m.

foresee [fɔːˈsiː] vt (pt foresaw, pp foreseen) prévoir. ◆**-able** a prévisible.

foreshadow [fɔːˈʃædəʊ] vt présager.

foresight ['fɔːsaɪt] n prévoyance f.

forest ['fɒrɪst] n forêt f. ◆**forester** n (garde m) forestier m.

forestall [fɔːˈstɔːl] vt devancer.

foretaste ['fɔːteɪst] n avant-goût m.

foretell [fɔːˈtel] vt (pt & pp foretold) prédire.

forethought ['fɔːθɔːt] n prévoyance f.

forever [fəˈrevər] adv (for always) pour toujours; (continually) sans cesse.

forewarn [fɔːˈwɔːn] vt avertir.

foreword ['fɔːwɜːd] n avant-propos m inv.

forfeit ['fɔːfɪt] vt (lose) perdre; – n (penalty) peine f; (in game) gage m.

forge [fɔːdʒ] 1 vt (signature, money) contrefaire; (document) falsifier. 2 vt (friendship, bond) forger. 3 vi to f. ahead (progress) aller de l'avant. 4 vt (metal) forger; – n forge f. ◆—er n (of banknotes etc) faussaire m. ◆forgery n faux m, contrefaçon f.

forget [fə'get] vt (pt forgot, pp forgotten, pres p forgetting) oublier (to do faire); f. it! Fam (when thanked) pas de quoi!; (it doesn't matter) peu importe!; to f. oneself s'oublier; – vi oublier; to f. about oublier. ◆f.-me-not n Bot myosotis m. ◆forgetful a to be f. (of) oublier, être oublieux (de). ◆forgetfulness n manque m de mémoire; (carelessness) négligence f; in a moment of f. dans un moment d'oubli.

forgiv/e [fə'gɪv] vt (pt forgave, pp forgiven) pardonner (s.o. sth qch à qn). ◆—ing a indulgent. ◆forgiveness n pardon m; (compassion) clémence f.

forgo [fɔː'gəu] vt (pp forgone) renoncer à.

fork [fɔːk] 1 n (for eating) fourchette f; (for garden etc) fourche f. 2 vi (of road) bifurquer; to f. left (in vehicle) prendre à gauche; – n bifurcation f, fourche f. 3 vt to f. out (money) Fam allonger; – vi to f. out (pay) Fam casquer. ◆—ed a fourchu. ◆forklift truck n chariot m élévateur.

forlorn [fə'lɔːn] a (forsaken) abandonné; (unhappy) triste, affligé.

form [fɔːm] 1 n (shape, type, style) forme f; (document) formulaire m; Sch classe f; it's good f. c'est ce qui se fait; in the f. of en forme de; a f. of speech une façon de parler; on f., in good f. (en pleine) forme; – vt (group, character etc) former; (clay) façonner; (habit) contracter; (an opinion) se former; (constitute) constituer, former; to f. part of faire partie de; – vi (appear) se former. ◆for'mation n formation f. ◆formative a formateur.

formal ['fɔːm(ə)l] a (person, tone etc) cérémonieux; (stuffy) Pej compassé; (official) officiel; (in due form) en bonne et due forme; (denial, structure, logic) formel; (resemblance) extérieur; f. dress tenue f ou habit m de cérémonie; f. education éducation f scolaire. ◆for'mality n cérémonie f; (requirement) formalité f. ◆formally adv (to declare etc) officiellement; f. dressed en tenue de cérémonie.

format ['fɔːmæt] n format m.

former ['fɔːmər] 1 a (previous) ancien; (situ-

ation) antérieur; her f. husband son ex-mari m; in f. days autrefois. 2 a (of two) premier; – pron the f. celui-là, celle-là, le premier, la première. 2.

formidable ['fɔːmɪdəb(ə)l] a effroyable, terrible.

formula ['fɔːmjulə] n 1 (pl -as or -ae [-iː]) formule f. 2 (pl -as) (baby's feed) Am mélange m lacté. ◆formulate vt formuler. ◆formu'lation n formulation f.

forsake [fə'seɪk] vt (pt forsook, pp forsaken) abandonner.

fort [fɔːt] n Hist Mil fort m; to hold the f. (in s.o.'s absence) Fam prendre la relève.

forte ['fɔːteɪ, Am fɔːt] n (strong point) fort m.

forth [fɔːθ] adv en avant; from this day f. désormais; and so f. et ainsi de suite.

forthcoming [fɔːθ'kʌmɪŋ] a 1 (event) à venir; (book, film) qui va sortir; my f. book mon prochain livre. 2 (available) disponible. 3 (open) communicatif; (helpful) serviable.

forthright ['fɔːθraɪt] a direct, franc.

forthwith [fɔːθ'wɪθ] adv sur-le-champ.

fortieth ['fɔːtɪəθ] a & n quarantième (mf).

fortify ['fɔːtɪfaɪ] vt (strengthen) fortifier; to f. s.o. (of food, drink etc) réconforter qn, remonter qn. ◆fortifi'cation n fortification f.

fortitude ['fɔːtɪtjuːd] n courage m (moral).

fortnight ['fɔːtnaɪt] n quinze jours mpl, quinzaine f. ◆—ly adv bimensuel; – adv tous les quinze jours.

fortress ['fɔːtrɪs] n forteresse f.

fortuitous [fɔː'tjuːɪtəs] a fortuit.

fortunate ['fɔːtʃ(ə)nɪt] a (choice, event etc) heureux; to be f. (of person) avoir de la chance; it's f. (for her) that c'est heureux (pour elle) que. ◆—ly adv heureusement.

fortune ['fɔːtʃuːn] n (wealth) fortune f; (luck) chance f; (chance) sort m, hasard m, fortune f; to have the good f. to avoir la chance ou le bonheur de; to tell s.o.'s f. dire la bonne aventure à qn; to make one's f. faire fortune. ◆f.-teller n diseur, -euse mf de bonne aventure.

forty ['fɔːtɪ] a & n quarante (m).

forum ['fɔːrəm] n forum m.

forward ['fɔːwəd] adv forward(s) en avant; to go f. avancer; from this time f. désormais; – a (movement) en avant; (gears) Aut avant inv; (child) Fig précoce; (pert) effronté; – n Fb avant m; – vt (letter) faire suivre; (goods) expédier. ◆—ness n précocité f; effronterie f. ◆forward-looking a tourné vers l'avenir.

fossil ['fɒs(ə)l] n & a fossile (m).

foster ['fɒstər] **1** vt encourager; (hope) nourrir. **2** vt (child) élever; – a (child, family) adoptif.

fought [fɔːt] see **fight.**

foul [faul] **1** a (-er, -est) infect; (air) vicié; (breath) fétide; (language) grossier; (action, place) immonde; **to be f.-mouthed** avoir un langage grossier. **2** n Sp coup m irrégulier; Fb faute f; – a **f. play** Sp jeu m irrégulier; Jur acte m criminel. **3** vt **to f. (up)** salir; (air) vicier; (drain) encrasser; **to f. up** (life, plans) Fam gâcher. ◆**f.-up** n (in system) Fam raté m.

found[1] [faund] see **find.**

found[2] [faund] vt (town, opinion etc) fonder (on sur). ◆**—er**[1] n fondateur, -trice m. ◆**foun'dation** n fondation f; (basis) Fig base f, fondement m; **without f.** sans fondement; **f. cream** fond m de teint.

founder[2] ['faundər] vi (of ship) sombrer.

foundry ['faundrɪ] n fonderie f.

fountain ['fauntɪn] n fontaine f; **f. pen** stylo(-plume) m.

four [fɔːr] a & n quatre (m); **on all fours** à quatre pattes; **the Big F.** Pol les quatre Grands; **f.-letter word** = mot m de cinq lettres. ◆**fourfold** a quadruple; – adv au quadruple. ◆**foursome** n deux couples mpl. ◆**four'teen** a & n quatorze (m). ◆**fourth** a & n quatrième (mf).

fowl [faul] n (hens) volaille f; **a f.** une volaille.

fox [fɒks] **1** n renard m. **2** vt (puzzle) mystifier; (trick) tromper. ◆**foxy** a (sly) rusé, futé.

foxglove ['fɒksglʌv] n Bot digitale f.

foyer ['fɔɪeɪ] n Th foyer m; (in hotel) hall m.

fraction ['frækʃ(ə)n] n fraction f. ◆**fractionally** adv un tout petit peu.

fractious ['frækʃəs] a grincheux.

fracture ['fræktʃər] n fracture f; – vt fracturer; **to f. one's leg/etc** se fracturer la jambe/etc; – vi se fracturer.

fragile ['frædʒaɪl, Am 'frædʒ(ə)l] a fragile. ◆**fra'gility** n fragilité f.

fragment ['frægmənt] n fragment m, morceau m. ◆**frag'mented** a, ◆**fragmentary** a fragmentaire.

fragrant ['freɪgrənt] a parfumé. ◆**fragrance** n parfum m.

frail [freɪl] a (-er, -est) (person) frêle, fragile; (hope, health) fragile. ◆**frailty** n fragilité f.

frame [freɪm] **1** n (of person, building) charpente f; (of picture, bicycle) cadre m; (of window, car) châssis m; (of spectacles) monture f; **f. of mind** humeur f; – vt (picture) encadrer; (proposals etc) Fig

formuler. **2** vt **to f. s.o.** Fam monter un coup contre qn. ◆**f.-up** n Fam coup m monté. ◆**framework** n structure f; **(with)in the f. of** (context) dans le cadre de.

franc [fræŋk] n franc m.

France [frɑːns] n France f.

franchise ['fræntʃaɪz] **1** n Pol droit m de vote. **2** (right to sell product) Com franchise f.

Franco- ['fræŋkəʊ] pref franco-.

frank [fræŋk] **1** a (-er, -est) (honest) franc. **2** vt (letter) affranchir. ◆**—ly** adv franchement. ◆**—ness** n franchise f.

frankfurter ['fræŋkfɜːtər] n saucisse f de Francfort.

frantic ['fræntɪk] a (activity, shout) frénétique; (rush, desire) effréné; (person) hors de soi; **f. with joy** fou de joie. ◆**frantically** adv comme un fou.

fraternal [frə'tɜːn(ə)l] a fraternel. ◆**fraternity** n (bond) fraternité f; (society) & Univ Am confrérie f. ◆**fraternize** ['frætənaɪz] vi fraterniser (with avec).

fraud [frɔːd] n **1** Jur fraude f. **2** (person) imposteur m. ◆**fraudulent** a frauduleux.

fraught [frɔːt] a **f. with** plein de, chargé de; **to be f.** (of situation) être tendu; (of person) Fam être contrarié.

fray [freɪ] **1** vt (garment) effilocher; (rope) user; – vi s'effilocher; s'user. **2** n (fight) rixe f. ◆**—ed** a (nerves) Fig tendu.

freak [friːk] n (person) phénomène m, monstre m; **a jazz/etc f.** Fam une(e) fana de jazz/etc; – a (result, weather etc) anormal. ◆**freakish** a anormal.

freckle ['frek(ə)l] n tache f de rousseur. ◆**freckled** a couvert de taches de rousseur.

free [friː] a (freer, freest) (at liberty, not occupied) libre; (gratis) gratuit; (lavish) généreux (with de); **to get f.** se libérer; **f. to do** libre de faire; **to let s.o. go f.** relâcher qn; **f. of charge** gratuit; **f. of** (without) sans; **f. of s.o.** (rid of) débarrassé de qn; **to have a f. hand** Fig avoir carte blanche (**to do** pour faire); **f. and easy** décontracté; **f. trade** libre-échange m; **f. speech** liberté f d'expression; **f. kick** Fb coup m franc; **f.-range egg** œuf m de ferme; – adv (of charge) gratuitement; – vt (pt & pp freed) (prisoner etc) libérer; (trapped person, road) dégager; (country) affranchir, libérer; (untie) détacher. ◆**Freefone®** Tel = numéro m vert. ◆**free-for-'all** n mêlée f générale. ◆**freehold** n propriété f foncière libre. ◆**freelance** a indépendant; – n collaborateur, -trice mf indépendant(e). ◆**freeloader** n (sponger) Am parasite m. ◆**Freemason** n franc-maçon m. ◆**Freemasonry** n franc-maçonnerie f. ◆**freestyle** n Swimming nage f libre. ◆**free'thinker** n libre penseur, -euse mf. ◆**freeway** n Am autoroute f.

freedom ['friːdəm] n liberté f; **f. from** (worry, responsibility) absence f de.

freely ['friːli] adv (to speak, circulate etc) librement; (to give) libéralement.

freez/e [friːz] vi (pt **froze**, pp **frozen**) geler; (of smile) Fig se figer; Culin se congeler; **to f. to death** mourir de froid; **to f. up** or **over** geler; (of windscreen) se givrer; - vt geler; (credits, river) geler; congeler, surgeler; (prices, wages) bloquer; **frozen food** surgelés mpl; - n Met gel m; (of prices etc) blocage m. ◆**-ing** a (weather etc) glacial; (hands, person) gelé; **it's f. on gèle**; **- n below f.** au-dessous de zéro. ◆**-er** n (deep-freeze) congélateur m; (in fridge) freezer m.

freight [freit] n (goods, price) fret m; (transport) transport m; **f. train** Am train m de marchandises; - vt (ship) affréter. ◆**-er** n (ship) cargo m.

French [frentʃ] a français; (teacher) de français; (embassy) de France; **F. fries** Am frites fpl; **the F.** les Français mpl; - n (language) français m. ◆**Frenchman** n (pl -men) Français m. ◆**French-speaking** a francophone. ◆**Frenchwoman** n (pl -women) Française f.

frenzy ['frenzi] n frénésie f. ◆**frenzied** a (shouts etc) frénétique; (person) effréné; (attack) violent.

frequent ['friːkwənt] a fréquent; (visitor) habitué, -ée mf (to de); - [frɪ'kwent] vt fréquenter. ◆**frequency** n fréquence f. ◆**frequently** adv fréquemment.

fresco ['freskəʊ] n (pl -oes or -os) fresque f.

fresh [freʃ] 1 a (-er, -est) frais; (new) nouveau; (impudent) Fam culotté; **to get some f. air** prendre le frais; **f. water** eau f douce. **2** adv **f. from** fraîchement arrivé de; **f. out of**, **f. from** (university) frais émoulu de. ◆**freshen** 1 vi (of wind) fraîchir. **2** vi **to f. up** faire un brin de toilette; - vt **to f. up** (house etc) retaper; **to f. s.o. up** (of bath) rafraîchir qn. ◆**freshener** n air f. désodorisant m. ◆**freshman** n (pl -men) étudiant, -ante mf de première année. ◆**freshness** n fraîcheur f; (cheek) Fam culot m.

fret [fret] vi (-tt-) (worry) se faire du souci, s'en faire; (of baby) pleurer. ◆**fretful** a (baby etc) grognon.

friar ['fraɪər] n frère m, moine m.

friction ['frɪkʃ(ə)n] n friction f.

Friday ['fraɪdɪ] n vendredi m.

fridge [frɪdʒ] n Fam frigo m.

fried [fraɪd] pt & pp of fry; - a (fish etc) frit; **f. egg** œuf m sur le plat. ◆**frier** n (pan) friteuse f.

friend [frend] n ami, -ie mf; (from school, work) camarade mf; **to be friends with** être ami avec; **to make friends** se lier d'amitié (avec). ◆**friendly** a (-ier, -iest) amical; (child, animal) gentil, affectueux; (kind) gentil; **some f. advice** un conseil d'ami; **to be f. with** être ami avec. ◆**friendship** n amitié f.

frieze [friːz] n Archit frise f.

frigate ['frɪgət] n (ship) frégate f.

fright [fraɪt] n peur f; (person, hat etc) Fig Fam horreur f; **to have a f.** avoir peur; **to give s.o. a f.** faire peur à qn. ◆**frighten** vt effrayer, faire peur à; **to f. away** or **off** (animal) effaroucher; (person) chasser. ◆**frightened** a effrayé; **to be f.** avoir peur (of de). ◆**frightening** a effrayant. ◆**frightful** a affreux. ◆**frightfully** adv (ugly, late) affreusement; (kind, glad) terriblement.

frigid ['frɪdʒɪd] a (air, greeting etc) froid; Psy frigide.

frill [frɪl] n Tex volant m; pl (fuss) Fig manières fpl, chichis mpl; (useless embellishments) fioritures fpl, superflu m; **no frills** (spartan) spartiate.

fringe [frɪndʒ] **1** n (of hair, clothes etc) frange f. **2** n (of forest) lisière f; **on the fringe(s) of society** en marge de la société; - a (group, theatre) marginal; **f. benefits** avantages mpl divers.

frisk [frɪsk] **1** vt (search) fouiller (au corps). **2** vi **to f.** (about) gambader. ◆**frisky** a (-ier, -iest) a vif.

fritter ['frɪtər] **1** vt **to f. away** (waste) gaspiller. **2** n Culin beignet m.

frivolous ['frɪvələs] a frivole. ◆**fri'volity** n frivolité f.

frizzy ['frɪzɪ] a (hair) crépu.

fro [frəʊ] adv **to go to and f.** aller et venir.

frock [frɒk] n (dress) robe f; (of monk) froc m.

frog [frɒg] n grenouille f; **a f. in one's throat** Fig un chat dans la gorge. ◆**frogman** n (pl -men) homme-grenouille m.

frolic ['frɒlɪk] vi (pt & pp **frolicked**) **to f.** (about) gambader; - npl (capers) ébats mpl; (pranks) gamineries fpl.

from [frɒm, unstressed frəm] prep **1** de; **a letter f.** une lettre de; **to suffer f.** souffrir de;

where are you f.? d'où êtes-vous?; a train f. un train en provenance de; to be ten metres (away) f. the house être à dix mètres de la maison. 2 (time onwards) à partir de, dès, depuis; f. today (on), as f. today à partir d'aujourd'hui, dès aujourd'hui; f. her childhood dès or depuis son enfance. 3 (numbers, prices onwards) à partir de; f. five francs à partir de cinq francs. 4 (away from) à; to take/hide/borrow f. prendre/cacher/emprunter à. 5 (out of) dans; sur; to take f. (box) prendre dans; (table) prendre sur; to drink f. a cup/etc boire dans une tasse/etc; to drink (straight) f. the bottle boire à (même) la bouteille. 6 (according to) d'après; f. what I saw d'après ce que j'ai vu. 7 (cause) par; f. conviction/habit/etc par conviction/habitude/ etc. 8 (on the part of, on behalf of) de la part de; tell her f. me dis-lui de ma part.

front [frʌnt] n (of garment, building) devant m; (of boat, car) avant m; (of crowd) premier rang m; (of book) début m; Mil Pol Met front m; (beach) front m or bord m de mer; (appearance) Fig façade f; **in f. (of)** devant; **in f.** (ahead) en avant; Sp en tête; **in the f.** (of vehicle) à l'avant; (of house) devant; – a (tooth etc) de devant; (part, wheel, car seat) avant inv; (row, page) premier; (view) de face; **f. door** porte f d'entrée; **f. line** Mil front m; **f. room** (lounge) salon m; **f. runner** Fig favori, -ite mf; **f.-wheel drive** (on vehicle) traction f avant; – vi to f. on to or (of windows etc) donner sur. ◆**frontage** n façade f. ◆**frontal** a (attack) de front.

frontier ['frʌntɪər] n frontière f; – a (town, post) frontière inv.

frost [frɒst] n gel m, gelée f; (frozen drops on glass, grass etc) gelée f blanche, givre m; – vi to f. up (of windscreen etc) se givrer. ◆**frostbite** n gelure f. ◆**frostbitten** a gelé. ◆**frosty** a (-ier, -iest) glacial; (window) givré; **it's f.** il gèle.

frosted ['frɒstɪd] a (glass) dépoli.

frosting ['frɒstɪŋ] n (icing) Culin glaçage m.

froth [frɒθ] n mousse f; – vi mousser. ◆**frothy** a (-ier, -iest) (beer etc) mousseux.

frown [fraʊn] n froncement m de sourcils; – vi froncer les sourcils; to f. (up)on Fig désapprouver.

froze, frozen ['frəʊz, 'frəʊz(ə)n] see freeze.

frugal ['fruːg(ə)l] a (meal) frugal; (thrifty) parcimonieux. ◆**-ly** adv parcimonieusement.

fruit [fruːt] n fruit m; (some) f. (one item) un fruit; (more than one) des fruits; – a

(basket) à fruits; (drink) aux fruits; (salad) de fruits; **f. tree** arbre m fruitier. ◆**fruitcake** n cake m. ◆**fruiterer** n fruitier, -ière mf. ◆**fruitful** a (meeting, career etc) fructueux, fécond. ◆**fruitless** a stérile. ◆**fruity** a (-ier, -iest) a fruité, de fruit; (joke) Fig corsé.

fruition [fruːˈɪʃ(ə)n] n **to come to f.** se réaliser.

frumpish ['frʌmpɪʃ] a, **frumpy** ['frʌmpɪ] a Fam (mal) fagoté.

frustrat/e [frʌˈstreɪt] vt (person) frustrer; (plans) faire échouer. ◆**-ed** a (mentally, sexually) frustré; (effort) vain. ◆**-ing** a irritant. ◆**fruˈstration** n frustration f; (disappointment) déception f.

fry [fraɪ] 1 vt (faire) frire; – vi frire. 2 n small f. menu fretin m. ◆**-ing** n friture f; **f. pan** poêle f (à frire). ◆**-er** n (pan) friteuse f.

ft abbr (measure) = foot, feet.

fuddled ['fʌd(ə)ld] a (drunk) gris; (confused) embrouillé.

fuddy-duddy ['fʌdɪdʌdɪ] n **he's an old f.-duddy** Fam il est vieux jeu.

fudge [fʌdʒ] 1 n (sweet) caramel m mou. 2 vt to f. the issue refuser d'aborder le problème.

fuel [fjʊəl] n combustible m; Aut carburant m; **f. (oil)** mazout m; – vt (-ll-, Am -l-) (stove) alimenter; (ship) ravitailler (en combustible); (s.o.'s anger etc) attiser.

fugitive ['fjuːdʒɪtɪv] n fugitif, -ive mf.

fugue [fjuːg] n Mus fugue f.

fulfil, Am **fulfill** [fʊlˈfɪl] vt (-ll-) (ambition, dream) accomplir, réaliser; (condition, duty) remplir; (desire) satisfaire; **to f. oneself** s'épanouir. ◆**fulfilling** a satisfaisant. ◆**fulfilment** n, Am ◆**fulfillment** n accomplissement m, réalisation f; (feeling) satisfaction f.

full [fʊl] a (-er, -est) plein (of de); (bus, theatre, meal) complet; (life, day) bien rempli; (skirt) ample; (hour) entier; (member) à part entière; **the f. price** le prix fort; **to pay (the) f. fare** payer plein tarif; **to be f. (up)** (of person) Fam n'avoir plus faim; (of hotel) être complet; **f. facts** tous les faits; **at f. speed** à toute vitesse; **f. name** (on form) nom et prénom; **f. stop** Gram point m; – adv **to know f. well** savoir fort bien; **f. in the face** (to hit etc) en pleine figure; – n **in f.** (text) intégral; (to publish, read) intégralement; (to write one's name) en toutes lettres; **to the f.** (completely) tout à fait. ◆**fullness** n (of details) abondance *f.; (of dress)* ampleur *f.* ◆**fully** *adv* entièrement; *(at least)* au moins.

full-back ['fʊlbæk] *n Fb* arrière *m.* ◆**f.-'grown** *a* adulte; *(foetus)* arrivé à terme. ◆**f.-'length** *a (film)* de long métrage; *(portrait)* en pied; *(dress)* long. ◆**f.-'scale** *a (model etc)* grandeur nature *inv*; *(operation etc) Fig* de grande envergure. ◆**f.-'sized** *a (model)* grandeur nature *inv.* ◆**f.-'time** *a & adv* à plein temps.

fully-fledged, *Am* **full-fledged** [fʊl(ɪ)'fledʒd] *a (engineer etc)* diplômé; *(member)* à part entière. ◆**f.-formed** *a (baby etc)* formé. ◆**f.-grown** *a* = **full-grown**.

fulsome ['fʊlsəm] *a (praise etc)* excessif.

fumble ['fʌmb(ə)l] *vi* to f. *(about) (grope)* tâtonner; *(search)* fouiller *(for* pour trouver)* to f. *(about)* with tripoter.

fume [fjuːm] *vi (give off fumes)* fumer; *(of person) Fig* rager; *– npl* émanations *fpl*; *(from car exhaust)* gaz *m inv.*

fumigate ['fjuːmɪgeɪt] *vt* désinfecter (par fumigation).

fun [fʌn] *n* amusement *m*; to be (good) f. être très amusant; to have (some) f. s'amuser; to make f. of, poke f. at se moquer de; for f., for the f. of it pour le plaisir.

function ['fʌŋkʃ(ə)n] *n* **1** *(role, duty) & Math* fonction *f*; *(meeting)* réunion *f*; *(ceremony)* cérémonie *f* (publique). **2** *vi (work)* fonctionner. ◆**functional** *a* fonctionnel.

fund [fʌnd] *n (for pension, relief etc) Fin* caisse *f*; *(of knowledge etc) Fig* fond *m*; *pl (money resources)* fonds *mpl*; *(for special purpose)* crédits *mpl*; *– vt (with money)* fournir des fonds *or* des crédits à.

fundamental [fʌndə'ment(ə)l] *a* fondamental; *– npl* principes *mpl* essentiels.

funeral ['fjuːnərəl] *n* enterrement *m*; *(grandiose)* funérailles *fpl*; *– a (service, march)* funèbre; *(expenses, parlour)* funéraire.

funfair ['fʌnfeər] *n* fête *f* foraine; *(larger)* parc *m* d'attractions.

fungus, *pl* **-gi** ['fʌŋgəs, -gaɪ] *n Bot* champignon *m*; *(mould)* moisissure *f.*

funicular [fjuː'nɪkjʊlər] *n* funiculaire *m.*

funk [fʌŋk] *n* to be in a f. *(afraid) Fam* avoir la frousse; *(depressed, sulking) Am Fam* faire la gueule.

funnel ['fʌn(ə)l] *n* **1** *(of ship)* cheminée *f.* **2** *(tube for pouring)* entonnoir *m.*

funny ['fʌnɪ] *a* (**-ier, -iest**) *(amusing)* drôle; *(strange)* bizarre; **a f. idea** une drôle d'idée; **there's some f. business going on** il y a quelque chose de louche; **to feel f.** ne pas se sentir très bien. ◆**funnily** *adv* drôlement; bizarrement; **f. enough . . .** chose bizarre . . . .

fur [fɜːr] *n* **1** *(of animal)* poil *m*, pelage *m*; *(for wearing etc)* fourrure *f.* **2** *n (in kettle)* dépôt *m* (de tartre); *– vi* **(-rr-)** to f. (up) s'entartrer.

furious ['fjʊərɪəs] *a (violent, angry)* furieux **(with,** at contre); *(pace, speed)* fou. ◆**-ly** *adv* furieusement; *(to drive, rush)* à une allure folle.

furnace ['fɜːnɪs] *n (forge)* fourneau *m*; *(room etc) Fig* fournaise *f.*

furnish ['fɜːnɪʃ] *vt* **1** *(room)* meubler. **2** *(supply)* fournir **(s.o. with sth** qch à qn). ◆**-ings** *npl* ameublement *m.*

furniture ['fɜːnɪtʃər] *n* meubles *mpl*; **a piece of f.** un meuble.

furrier ['fʌrɪər] *n* fourreur *m.*

furrow ['fʌrəʊ] *n (on brow) & Agr* sillon *m.*

furry ['fɜːrɪ] *a (animal)* à poil; *(toy)* en peluche.

further ['fɜːðər] **1** *adv & a* = **farther. 2** *adv (more)* davantage, plus; *(besides)* en outre; *– a (additional)* supplémentaire; *(education)* post-scolaire; **f. details** de plus amples détails; **a f. case/etc** *(another)* un autre cas/etc; **without f. delay** sans plus attendre. **3** *vt (cause, research etc)* promouvoir. ◆**furthermore** *adv* en outre. ◆**furthest** *a & adv* = **farthest.**

furtive ['fɜːtɪv] *a* furtif.

fury ['fjʊərɪ] *n (violence, anger)* fureur *f.*

fuse [fjuːz] **1** *vti (melt) Tech* fondre; *Fig* fusionner. **2** *vt* to f. the lights *etc* faire sauter les plombs; *– vi* the lights *etc* have fused les plombs ont sauté; *– n (wire) El* fusible *m*, plomb *m.* **3** *n (of bomb)* amorce *f.* ◆**fused** *a (plug) El* avec fusible incorporé. ◆**fusion** *n (union) & Phys Biol* fusion *f.*

fuselage ['fjuːzəlɑːʒ] *n Av* fuselage *m.*

fuss [fʌs] *n* façons *fpl*, histoires *fpl*, chichis *mpl*; *(noise)* agitation *f*; **what a (lot of) f.!** quelle histoire!; **to kick up** *or* **make a f.** faire des histoires; **to make a f. of** être aux petits soins pour; *– vi* faire des chichis; *(worry)* se tracasser **(about** pour); *(rush about)* s'agiter; **to f. over s.o.** être aux petits soins pour qn. ◆**fusspot** *n, Am* ◆**fussbudget** *n Fam* enquiquineur, -euse *mf.* ◆**fussy** *a* (**-ier, -iest**) méticuleux **(about** sur); *(difficult)* difficile **(about** sur).

fusty ['fʌstɪ] *a* (**-ier, -iest**) *(smell)* de renfermé.

futile ['fjuːtaɪl, *Am* 'fjuːt(ə)l] *a* futile, vain. ◆**fu'tility** *n* futilité *f.*

future ['fjuːtʃər] n avenir m; Gram futur m; **in f.** (from now on) à l'avenir; **in the f.** (one day) un jour (futur); – a futur, à venir; (date) ultérieur.

fuzz [fʌz] n **1** (down) Fam duvet m. **2 the f.** (police) Sl les flics mpl. ◆**fuzzy** a (-ier, -iest) (hair) crépu; (picture, idea) flou.

G

G, g [dʒiː] n G, g m. ◆**G.-string** n (cloth) cache-sexe m inv.

gab [gæb] n **to have the gift of the g.** Fam avoir du bagou(t).

gabardine [gæbə'diːn] n (material, coat) gabardine f.

gabble ['gæb(ə)l] vi (chatter) jacasser; (indistinctly) bredouiller; – n baragouin m.

gable ['geɪb(ə)l] n Archit pignon m.

gad [gæd] vi (-dd-) **to g. about** se balader, vadrouiller.

gadget ['gædʒɪt] n gadget m.

Gaelic ['geɪlɪk, 'gælɪk] a & n gaélique (m).

gaffe [gæf] n (blunder) gaffe f, bévue f.

gag [gæg] n **1** (over mouth) bâillon m; – vt (-gg-) (victim, press etc) bâillonner. **2** n (joke) plaisanterie f; Cin Th gag m. **3** vi (-gg-) (choke) Am s'étouffer (**on** avec).

gaggle ['gæg(ə)l] n (of geese) troupeau m.

gaiety ['geɪtɪ] n gaieté f; (of colour) éclat m. ◆**gaily** adv gaiement.

gain [geɪn] vt (obtain, win) gagner; (objective) atteindre; (experience, reputation) acquérir; (popularity) gagner en; **to g. speed/weight** prendre de la vitesse/du poids; – vi (of watch) avancer; **to g. in strength** gagner en force; **to g. on** (catch up with) rattraper; – n (increase) augmentation f (**in**); (profit) Com bénéfice m, gain m; Fig avantage m. ◆**gainful** a profitable; (employment) rémunéré.

gainsay [geɪn'seɪ] vt (pt & pp gainsaid [-sed]) (person) contredire; (facts) nier.

gait [geɪt] n (walk) démarche f.

gala ['gɑːlə, 'geɪlə] n gala m, fête f; **swimming g.** concours m de natation.

galaxy ['gæləksɪ] n galaxie f.

gale [geɪl] n grand vent m, rafale f (de vent).

gall [gɔːl] **1** n Med bile f; (bitterness) Fig fiel m; (cheek) Fam effronterie f; **g. bladder** vésicule f biliaire. **2** vt (vex) blesser, froisser.

gallant ['gælənt] a (brave) courageux; (splendid) magnifique; (chivalrous) galant. ◆**gallantry** n (bravery) courage m.

galleon ['gælɪən] n (ship) Hist galion m.

gallery ['gælərɪ] n (room etc) galerie f; (for public, press) tribune f; **art g.** (private) galerie f d'art; (public) musée m d'art.

galley ['gælɪ] n (ship) Hist galère f; (kitchen) Nau Av cuisine f.

Gallic ['gælɪk] a (French) français. ◆**gallicism** n (word etc) gallicisme m.

gallivant ['gælɪvænt] vi **to g.** (**about**) Fam courir, vadrouiller.

gallon ['gælən] n gallon m (Br = 4,5 litres, Am = 3,8 litres).

gallop ['gæləp] n galop m; – vi (gallop) galoper; **to g. away** (rush) Fig partir au galop or en vitesse. ◆**-ing** a (inflation etc) Fig galopant.

gallows ['gæləʊz] npl potence f.

gallstone ['gɔːlstəʊn] n Med calcul m biliaire.

galore [gə'lɔːr] adv à gogo, en abondance.

galoshes [gə'lɒʃɪz] npl (shoes) caoutchoucs mpl.

galvanize ['gælvənaɪz] vt (metal) & Fig galvaniser.

gambit ['gæmbɪt] n opening g. Fig manœuvre f stratégique.

gambl/e ['gæmb(ə)l] vi jouer (**on** sur, **with** avec); **to g. on** (count on) miser sur; – vt (wager) jouer; **to g.** (**away**) (lose) perdre (au jeu); – n (bet) & Fig coup m risqué. ◆**-ing** n jeu m. ◆**-er** n joueur, -euse mf.

game [geɪm] **1** n jeu m; (of football, cricket etc) match m; (of tennis, chess, cards) partie f; **to have a g. of** jouer un match de; (faire une partie de; **games** Sch le sport; **games teacher** professeur m d'éducation physique. **2** n (animals, birds) gibier m; **to be fair g. for** Fig être une proie idéale pour. **3** a (brave) courageux; **g. for** (willing) prêt à. **4** a (leg) estropié; **to have a g. leg** être boiteux. ◆**gamekeeper** n garde-chasse m.

gammon ['gæmən] n (ham) jambon m fumé.

gammy ['gæmɪ] a Fam = game 4.

gamut ['gæmət] n Mus & Fig gamme f.

gang [gæŋ] n bande f; (of workers) équipe f; (of crooks) gang m; – vi **to g. up on or**

against se liguer contre. ◆**gangster** n gangster m.

gangling ['gæŋglɪŋ] a dégingandé.

gangrene ['gæŋgriːn] n gangrène f.

gangway ['gæŋweɪ] n passage m; (in train) couloir m; (in bus, cinema, theatre) allée f; (footbridge) Av Nau passerelle f; g.! dégagez!

gaol [dʒeɪl] n & vt = **jail.**

gap [gæp] n (empty space) trou m, vide m; (breach) trou m; (in time) intervalle m; (in knowledge) lacune f; **the g. between** (divergence) l'écart m entre.

gap/e [geɪp] vi (stare) rester or être bouche bée; **to g. at** regarder bouche bée. ◆**-ing** a (chasm, wound) béant.

garage ['gærɑː(d)ʒ, 'gærɪdʒ, Am gə'rɑːʒ] n garage m; – vt mettre au garage.

garb [gɑːb] n (clothes) costume m.

garbage ['gɑːbɪdʒ] n ordures fpl; **g. can** Am poubelle f; **g. collector** or **man** Am éboueur m; **g. truck** Am camion-benne m.

garble ['gɑːb(ə)l] vt (words etc) déformer, embrouiller.

garden ['gɑːd(ə)n] n jardin m; **the gardens** (park) le parc; **g. centre** (store) jardinerie f; (nursery) pépinière f; **g. party** garden-party f; **g. produce** produits mpl maraîchers; – vi **to be gardening** jardiner. ◆**-ing** n jardinage m. ◆**-er** n jardinier, -ière mf.

gargle ['gɑːg(ə)l] vi se gargariser; – n gargarisme m.

gargoyle ['gɑːgɔɪl] n Archit gargouille f.

garish ['geərɪʃ, Am 'gærɪʃ] a voyant, criard.

garland ['gɑːlənd] n guirlande f.

garlic ['gɑːlɪk] n ail m; **g. sausage** saucisson m à l'ail.

garment ['gɑːmənt] n vêtement m.

garnish ['gɑːnɪʃ] vt garnir (with); – n garniture f.

garret ['gærət] n mansarde f.

garrison ['gærɪsən] n Mil garnison f.

garrulous ['gærələs] a (talkative) loquace.

garter ['gɑːtər] n (round leg) jarretière f; (attached to belt) Am jarretelle f; (for men) fixe-chaussette m.

gas [gæs] 1 n gaz m inv; (gasoline) Am essence f; Med Am anesthésie f au masque; – a (meter, mask, chamber) à gaz; (pipe) de gaz; (industry) du gaz; (heating) au gaz; **g. fire** or **heater** appareil m de chauffage à gaz; **g. station** Am poste m d'essence; **g. stove** (portable) réchaud m à gaz; (large) cuisinière f à gaz; – vt (-ss-) (poison) asphyxier; Mil gazer. 2 vi (-ss-) (talk) Fam bavarder; – n **for a g.** (fun) Am Fam pour rire. ◆**gasbag** n Fam commère

f. ◆**gasman** n (pl -men) employé m du gaz. ◆**gasoline** n Am essence f. ◆**gasworks** n usine f à gaz.

gash [gæʃ] n entaille f; – vt entailler.

gasp [gɑːsp] 1 vi **to g. (for breath)** haleter; – n halètement m. 2 vi **to g. with** or **in surprise/**etc avoir le souffle coupé de surprise/etc; – vt (say gasping) hoqueter; – n a **g. of surprise/**etc un hoquet de surprise/etc.

gassy ['gæsɪ] a (-ier, -iest) (drink) gazeux.

gastric ['gæstrɪk] a (juices, ulcer) gastrique. ◆**ga'stronomy** n gastronomie f.

gate [geɪt] n (of castle, airport etc) porte f; (at level crossing, field etc) barrière f; (metal) grille f; (in Paris Metro) portillon m. ◆**gateway** n **the g. to success/**etc le chemin du succès/etc.

gâteau, pl **-eaux** ['gætəʊ, -əʊz] n Culin gros gâteau m à la crème.

gatecrash ['geɪtkræʃ] vti **to g. (a party)** s'inviter de force à (une réception).

gather ['gæðər] vt (people, objects) rassembler; (pick up) ramasser; (flowers) cueillir; (information) recueillir; (understand) comprendre; (skirt, material) froncer; **I g. that . . .** (infer) je crois comprendre que . . . ; **to g. speed** prendre de la vitesse; **to g. in** (crops, harvest) rentrer; (essays, exam papers) ramasser; **to g. up** (strength) rassembler; (papers) ramasser; – vi (of people) se rassembler, s'assembler, s'amasser; (of clouds) se former; (of dust) s'accumuler; **to g. round** s'approcher; **to g. round s.o.** entourer qn. ◆**-ing** n (group) réunion f.

gaudy ['gɔːdɪ] a (-ier, -iest) voyant, criard.

gauge [geɪdʒ] n (instrument) jauge f, indicateur m; Rail écartement m; **to be a g. of sth** Fig permettre de jauger qch; – vt (measure) mesurer; (estimate) évaluer, jauger.

gaunt [gɔːnt] a (thin) décharné.

gauntlet ['gɔːntlɪt] n gant m; **to run the g. of** Fig essuyer (le feu de).

gauze [gɔːz] n (fabric) gaze f.

gave [geɪv] see **give.**

gawk [gɔːk] vi **to g. (at)** regarder bouche bée.

gawp [gɔːp] vi = **gawk.**

gay [geɪ] a (-er, -est) **1** (cheerful) gai, joyeux; (colour) vif, gai. **2** Fam homo(sexuel), gay inv.

gaze [geɪz] n regard m (fixe); – vi regarder; **to g. at** regarder (fixement).

gazelle [gə'zel] n (animal) gazelle f.

gazette [gə'zet] n journal m officiel.

GB [dʒiːˈbiː] *abbr* (*Great Britain*) Grande-Bretagne *f*.

GCSE [dʒiːsiːesˈiː] *abbr* (*General Certificate of Secondary Education*) = baccalauréat *m*.

gear [gɪər] **1** *n* matériel *m*, équipement *m*; (*belongings*) affaires *fpl*; (*clothes*) *Fam* vêtements *mpl* (à la mode); (*toothed wheels*) *Tech* engrenage *m*; (*speed*) *Aut* vitesse *f*; **in g.** *Aut* en prise; **not in g.** *Aut* au point mort; **g. lever**, *Am* **g. shift** levier *m* de (changement de) vitesse. **2** *vt* (*adapt*) adapter (**to** à); **geared (up) to do** prêt à faire; **to g. oneself up for** se préparer pour. ◆**gearbox** *n* boîte *f* de vitesses.

gee! [dʒiː] *int Am Fam* ça alors!

geese [giːs] *see* **goose**.

geezer [ˈgiːzər] *n Hum Sl* type *m*.

Geiger counter [ˈgaɪgəkaʊntər] *n* compteur *m* Geiger.

gel [dʒel] *n* (*substance*) gel *m*.

gelatin(e) [ˈdʒelətɪn, *Am* -tən] *n* gélatine *f*.

gelignite [ˈdʒelɪgnaɪt] *n* dynamite *f* (au nitrate de soude).

gem [dʒem] *n* pierre *f* précieuse; (*person or thing of value*) *Fig* perle *f*; (*error*) *Iron* perle *f*.

Gemini [ˈdʒemɪnaɪ] *n* (*sign*) les Gémeaux *mpl*.

gen [dʒen] *n* (*information*) *Sl* coordonnées *fpl*; − *vi* (-nn-) **to g. up on** *Sl* se rancarder sur.

gender [ˈdʒendər] *n Gram* genre *m*; (*of person*) sexe *m*.

gene [dʒiːn] *n Biol* gène *m*.

genealogy [dʒiːnɪˈælədʒɪ] *n* généalogie *f*.

general [ˈdʒenərəl] **1** *a* général; **in g.** en général; **the g. public** le (grand) public; **for g. use** à l'usage du public; **a g. favourite** aimé or apprécié de tous; **g. delivery** *Am* poste *f* restante; **to be g.** (*widespread*) être très répandu. **2** *n* (*officer*) *Mil* général *m*. ◆**gene'rality** *n* généralité *f*. ◆**generali'zation** *n* généralisation *f*. ◆**generalize** *vti* généraliser. ◆**generally** *adv* généralement; **g. speaking** en général, généralement parlant.

generate [ˈdʒenəreɪt] *vt* (*heat*) produire; (*fear, hope etc*) *Ling* engendrer. ◆**gene'ration** *n* génération *f*; **the g. of** (*heat*) la production de; **g. gap** conflit *m* des générations. ◆**generator** *n El* groupe *m* électrogène, génératrice *f*.

generous [ˈdʒenərəs] *a* généreux (**with** de); (*helping, meal etc*) copieux. ◆**gene'rosity** *n* générosité *f*. ◆**generously** *adv* généreusement; (*to serve s.o.*) copieusement.

genesis [ˈdʒenəsɪs] *n* genèse *f*.

genetic [dʒɪˈnetɪk] *a* génétique. ◆**genetics** *n* génétique *f*.

Geneva [dʒɪˈniːvə] *n* Genève *m or f*.

genial [ˈdʒiːnɪəl] *a* (*kind*) affable; (*cheerful*) jovial.

genie [ˈdʒiːnɪ] *n* (*goblin*) génie *m*.

genital [ˈdʒenɪt(ə)l] *a* génital; − *npl* organes *mpl* génitaux.

genius [ˈdʒiːnɪəs] *n* (*ability, person*) génie *m*; **to have a g. for doing/for sth** avoir le génie pour faire/de qch.

genocide [ˈdʒenəsaɪd] *n* génocide *m*.

gent [dʒent] *n Fam* monsieur *m*; **gents' shoes** *Com* chaussures *fpl* pour hommes; **the gents** *Fam* les toilettes *fpl* (pour hommes).

genteel [dʒenˈtiːl] *a Iron* distingué.

gentle [ˈdʒent(ə)l] *a* (**-er, -est**) (*person, sound, slope etc*) doux; (*hint, reminder*) discret; (*touch*) léger; (*pace*) mesuré; (*exercise, progress*) modéré; (*birth*) noble. ◆**gentleman** *n* (*pl* **-men**) monsieur *m*; (*well-bred*) gentleman *m*, monsieur *m* bien élevé. ◆**gentlemanly** *a* distingué, bien élevé. ◆**gentleness** *n* douceur *f*. ◆**gently** *adv* doucement; (*to remind*) discrètement; (*smoothly*) en douceur.

genuine [ˈdʒenjuɪn] *a* (*authentic*) véritable, authentique; (*sincere*) sincère, vrai. ◆**-ly** *adv* authentiquement; sincèrement. ◆**-ness** *n* authenticité *f*; sincérité *f*.

geography [dʒɪˈɒgrəfɪ] *n* géographie *f*. ◆**geo'graphical** *a* géographique.

geology [dʒɪˈɒlədʒɪ] *n* géologie *f*. ◆**geo'logical** *a* géologique. ◆**geologist** *n* géologue *mf*.

geometry [dʒɪˈɒmɪtrɪ] *n* géométrie *f*. ◆**geo'metric(al)** *a* géométrique.

geranium [dʒɪˈreɪnɪəm] *n Bot* géranium *m*.

geriatric [dʒerɪˈætrɪk] *a* (*hospital*) du troisième âge; **g. ward** service *m* de gériatrie.

germ [dʒɜːm] *n Biol* & *Fig* germe *m*; *Med* microbe *m*; **g. warfare** guerre *f* bactériologique.

German [ˈdʒɜːmən] *a* & *n* allemand, -ande (*mf*); **G. measles** *Med* rubéole *f*; **G. shepherd** (*dog*) *Am* berger *m* allemand; − *n* (*language*) allemand *m*. ◆**Ger'manic** *a* germanique.

Germany [ˈdʒɜːmənɪ] *n* Allemagne *f*; **West G.** Allemagne de l'Ouest.

germinate [ˈdʒɜːmɪneɪt] *vi Bot* & *Fig* germer.

gestation [dʒeˈsteɪʃ(ə)n] *n* gestation *f*.

gesture [ˈdʒestʃər] *n* geste *m*; − *vi* **to g. to**

s.o. to do faire signe à qn de faire. ◆ge'sticulate vi gesticuler.

get [get] 1 vt (pt & pp got, pp Am gotten, pres p getting) (obtain) obtenir, avoir; (find) trouver; (buy) acheter, prendre; (receive) recevoir, avoir; (catch) attraper, prendre; (seize) prendre, saisir; (fetch) aller chercher (qn, qch); (put) mettre; (derive) tirer (from de); (understand) comprendre, saisir; (prepare) préparer; (lead) mener; (target) atteindre, avoir; (reputation) se faire; (annoy) Fam ennuyer; **I have got, Am I have gotten** j'ai; **to g. s.o. to do sth** faire faire qch à qn; **to g. sth built/etc** faire construire/etc qch; **to g. things going** or **started** faire démarrer les choses. 2 vi (go) aller; (arrive) arriver (to à); (become) devenir, se faire; **to g. caught/run over/etc** se faire prendre/écraser/etc; **to g. married** se marier; **to g. dressed/washed** s'habiller/se laver; **where have you got** or **Am gotten to?** où en es-tu?; **you've got to stay** (must) tu dois rester; **to g. to do** (succeed in doing) parvenir à faire; **to g. working** se mettre à travailler. ■ **to g. about** or **(a)round** vi se déplacer; (of news) circuler; **to g. across** vt (road) traverser; (person) faire traverser; (message) communiquer; – vi traverser; (of speaker) se faire comprendre; **to g. across to s.o. that** faire comprendre à qn que; **to g. along** vi (leave) se sauver; (manage) se débrouiller; (progress) avancer; (be on good terms) s'entendre (with avec); **to g. at** vt (reach) parvenir à, atteindre; (taunt) s'en prendre à; **what is he getting at?** où veut-il en venir?; **to g. away** vi (leave) partir, s'en aller; (escape) s'échapper; **there's no getting away from it** il faut le reconnaître, c'est comme ça. ◆**getaway** n (escape) fuite f; **to g. back** vt (recover) récupérer; (replace) remettre; – vi (return) revenir, retourner; **to g. back at, g. one's own back at** (punish) se venger de; **g. back!** (move back) reculez!; **to g. by** vi (pass) passer; (manage) se débrouiller; **to g. down** vi (go down) descendre (from de); – vt (bring down) descendre (from de); (write) noter; (depress) Fam déprimer; **to g. down to** (task, work) se mettre à; **to g. in** vt (bicycle, washing etc) rentrer; (buy) acheter; (summon) faire venir; **to g. in a car/etc** monter dans une voiture/etc; – vi (enter) entrer; (come home) rentrer; (enter vehicle or train) monter; (of plane, train) arriver; (of candidate) Pol être élu; **to g. into** vt entrer dans; (vehicle, train) monter dans;

(habit) prendre; **to g. into bed/a rage** se mettre au lit/en colère; **to g. into trouble** avoir des ennuis; **to g. off** vi (leave) partir; (from vehicle or train) descendre (from de); (escape) s'en tirer; (finish work) sortir; (be acquitted) Jur être acquitté; – vt (remove) enlever; (despatch) expédier; Jur faire acquitter (qn); **to g. off (from) a chair** se lever d'une chaise; **to g. off doing** Fam se dispenser de faire; **to g. on** vt (shoes, clothes) mettre; (bus, train) monter dans; – vi (progress) marcher, avancer; (continue) continuer; (succeed) réussir; (enter bus or train) monter; **s'entendre (with avec); how are you getting on?** comment ça va?; **to g. on to s.o.** (telephone) toucher qn, contacter qn; **to g. on with** (task) continuer; **to g. out** vi sortir; (from vehicle or train) descendre (from, of de); **to g. out of** (obligation) échapper à; (trouble) se tirer de; (habit) perdre; – vt (remove) enlever; (bring out) sortir (qch), faire sortir (qn); **to g. over** vt (road) traverser; (obstacle) surmonter; (fence) franchir; (illness) se remettre de; (surprise) revenir de; (ideas) communiquer; **let's g. it over with** finissons-en; – vi (cross) traverser; **to g. round** vt (obstacle) contourner; (person) entortiller; – vi **to g. round to doing** en venir à faire; **to g. through** vi (pass) passer; (finish) finir; (pass exam) être reçu; – vt (hole etc) passer par; (task, meal) venir à bout de; (exam) être reçu à; **g. me through to your boss** (on the telephone) passe-moi ton patron; **to g. together** vi (of people) se rassembler. ◆**g.-together** n réunion f; **to g. up** vi (rise) se lever (from de); (on ladder, in book) en arriver à; (mischief, trouble etc) faire; – vt (ladder, stairs etc) monter; (party, group) organiser; **to g. sth up** (bring up) monter qch. ◆**g.-up** n (clothes) Fam accoutrement m.

geyser ['giːzər] n 1 (water heater) chauffe-eau m inv. 2 Geol geyser m.

Ghana ['gɑːnə] n Ghana m.

ghastly ['gɑːstlɪ] a (-ier, -iest) (pale) blême, pâle; (horrible) affreux.

gherkin ['gɜːkɪn] n cornichon m.

ghetto ['getəʊ] n (pl -os) ghetto m.

ghost [gəʊst] n fantôme m; **not the g. of a chance** pas l'ombre d'une chance; – a (story) de fantôme; (ship) fantôme; (town) mort. ◆**-ly** a spectral.

ghoulish ['guːlɪʃ] a morbide.

giant ['dʒaɪənt] *n* géant *m*; – *a* géant, gigantesque; (*steps*) de géant; (*packet etc*) Com géant.

gibberish ['dʒɪbərɪʃ] *n* baragouin *m*.

gibe [dʒaɪb] *vi* railler; **to g.** at railler; – *n* raillerie *f*.

giblets ['dʒɪblɪts] *npl* (*of fowl*) abats *mpl*.

giddy ['gɪdɪ] *a* (**-ier, -iest**) (*heights*) vertigineux; **to feel g.** avoir le vertige; **to make g.** donner le vertige à. ◆**giddiness** *n* vertige *m*.

gift [gɪft] *n* cadeau *m*; (*talent*) & *Jur* don *m*; **g. voucher** chèque-cadeau *m*. ◆**gifted** *a* doué (**with de, for** pour). ◆**giftwrapped** *a* en paquet-cadeau.

gig [gɪg] *n* *Mus Fam* engagement *m*, séance *f*.

gigantic [dʒaɪˈgæntɪk] *a* gigantesque.

giggle ['gɪg(ə)l] *vi* rire (sottement); – *n* petit rire *m* sot; **to have the giggles** avoir le fou rire.

gild [gɪld] *vt* dorer. ◆**gilt** *a* doré; – *n* dorure *f*.

gills [gɪlz] *npl* (*of fish*) ouïes *fpl*.

gimmick ['gɪmɪk] *n* (*trick, object*) truc *m*.

gin [dʒɪn] *n* (*drink*) gin *m*.

ginger ['dʒɪndʒər] **1** *a* (*hair*) roux. **2** *n* *Bot Culin* gingembre *m*; **g. beer** boisson *f* gazeuse au gingembre. ◆**gingerbread** *n* pain *m* d'épice.

gingerly ['dʒɪndʒəlɪ] *adv* avec précaution.

gipsy ['dʒɪpsɪ] *n* bohémien, -ienne *mf*; (*Central European*) Tsigane *mf*; (*music*) tsigane.

giraffe [dʒɪˈrɑːf, dʒɪˈræf] *n* girafe *f*.

girder ['gɜːdər] *n* (*metal beam*) poutre *f*.

girdle ['gɜːd(ə)l] *n* (*belt*) ceinture *f*; (*corset*) gaine *f*.

girl [gɜːl] *n* (*young*) fille *f*; (*daughter*) fille *f*; (*servant*) bonne *f*; (*sweetheart*) *Fam* petite amie *f*; **English g.** jeune Anglaise *f*; **g. guide** éclaireuse *f*. ◆**girlfriend** *n* amie *f*; (*of boy*) petite amie *f*. ◆**girlish** *a* de (jeune) fille.

girth [gɜːθ] *n* (*measure*) circonférence *f*; (*of waist*) tour *m*.

gist [dʒɪst] *n* **to get the g.** of comprendre l'essentiel de.

give [gɪv] *vt* (*pt* **gave**, *pp* **given**) donner (**to** à); (*help, support*) prêter; (*gesture, pleasure*) faire; (*a sigh*) pousser; (*a look*) jeter; (*a blow*) porter; **g. me York 234** passez-moi le 234 à York; **she doesn't g. a damn** *Fam* elle s'en fiche; **to g. way** (*yield, break*) céder (**to** à); (*collapse*) s'effondrer; *Aut* céder la priorité (**to** à). ■ **to g. away** *vt* (*prize*) distribuer; (*money*) donner; (*facts*) révéler; (*betray*) trahir (*qn*);

to g. back *vt* (*return*) rendre; **to g. in** *vi* (*surrender*) céder (**to** à); – *vt* (*hand in*) remettre; **to g. off** *vt* (*smell, heat*) dégager; **to g. out** *vt* distribuer; – *vi* (*of supplies, patience*) s'épuiser; (*of engine*) rendre l'âme; **to g. over** *vt* (*devote*) donner, consacrer (**to** à); **to g. oneself over to** s'adonner à; – *vi* **g. over!** (*stop*) *Fam* arrête!; **to g. up** *vi* abandonner, renoncer; – *vt* abandonner, renoncer à; (*seat*) céder (**to** à); (*prisoner*) livrer (**to** à); (*patient*) condamner; **to g. up smoking** cesser de fumer. ◆**given** *a* (*fixed*) donné; **to be g. to doing** (*prone to do*) avoir l'habitude de faire; **g. your age** (*in view of*) étant donné votre âge; **g. that** étant donné que. ◆**giver** *n* donateur, -trice *mf*.

glacier ['glæsɪər, *Am* 'gleɪʃər] *n* glacier *m*.

glad [glæd] *a* (*person*) content (**of, about** de). ◆**gladden** *vt* réjouir. ◆**gladly** *adv* (*willingly*) volontiers.

glade [gleɪd] *n* clairière *f*.

gladiolus, *pl* **-i** [glædɪˈəʊləs, -aɪ] *n* *Bot* glaïeul *m*.

glamour ['glæmər] *n* (*charm*) enchantement *m*; (*splendour*) éclat *m*. ◆**glamorize** *vt* montrer sous un jour séduisant. ◆**glamorous** *a* séduisant.

glance [glɑːns] **1** *n* coup *m* d'œil; – *vi* jeter un coup d'œil (**at** à, sur). **2** *vt* **to g. off sth** (*of bullet*) ricocher sur qch.

gland [glænd] *n* glande *f*. ◆**glandular** *a* **g. fever** *Med* mononucléose *f* infectieuse.

glar/e [gleər] **1** *vi* **to g. at s.o.** foudroyer qn (du regard); – *n* regard *m* furieux. **2** *n* (*of sun*) briller d'un éclat aveuglant; – *n* éclat *m* aveuglant. ◆**-ing** *a* (*sun*) aveuglant; (*eyes*) furieux; (*injustice*) flagrant; **a g. mistake** une faute grossière.

glass [glɑːs] *n* verre *m*; (*mirror*) miroir *m*, glace *f*; *pl* (*spectacles*) lunettes *fpl*; **a pane of g.** une vitre, un carreau; **g.** (*door*) vitré; (*industry*) du verre. ◆**glassful** *n* (plein) verre *m*.

glaze [gleɪz] *vt* (*door*) vitrer; (*pottery*) vernisser; (*paper*) glacer; – *n* (*on pottery*) vernis *m*; (*on paper*) glacé *m*. ◆**glazier** *n* vitrier *m*.

gleam [gliːm] *n* lueur *f*; – *vi* (re)luire.

glean [gliːn] *vt* (*grain, information etc*) glaner.

glee [gliː] *n* joie *f*. ◆**gleeful** *a* joyeux.

glen [glen] *n* vallon *m*.

glib [glɪb] *a* (*person*) qui a la parole facile; (*speech*) facile, peu sincère. ◆**-ly** *adv* (*to say*) peu sincèrement.

glid/e [glaɪd] *vi* glisser; (*of vehicle*) avancer

silencieusement; (of aircraft, bird) planer. ◆**—ing** n Av Sp vol m à voile. ◆**—er** n Av planeur m.

glimmer ['glımər] vi luire (faiblement); – n (light, of hope etc) lueur f; (faible) lueur f.

glimpse [glımps] n aperçu m; **to catch** or **get a g.** of entrevoir.

glint [glınt] vi (shine with flashes) briller; – n éclair m; (in eye) étincelle f.

glisten ['glıs(ə)n] vi (of wet surface) briller; (of water) miroiter.

glitter ['glıtər] vi scintiller, briller; – n scintillement m.

gloat [gləʊt] vi jubiler (**over** à la vue de).

globe [gləʊb] n globe m. ◆**global** a (comprehensive) global; (universal) universel, mondial.

gloom [gluːm] n (darkness) obscurité f; (sadness) Fig tristesse f. ◆**gloomy** a (-ier, -iest) (dark, dismal) sombre, triste; (sad) Fig triste; (pessimistic) pessimiste.

glory ['glɔːrı] n gloire f; **in all one's g.** Fig dans toute sa splendeur; **to be in one's g.** (very happy) Fam être à son affaire; – vi to **g. in** se glorifier de. ◆**glorify** vt (praise) glorifier; **it's a glorified barn**/etc ce n'est guère plus qu'une grange/etc. ◆**glorious** a (full of glory) glorieux; (splendid, enjoyable) magnifique.

gloss [glɒs] 1 n (shine) brillant m; **g. paint** peinture f brillante; **g. finish** brillant m. 2 n (note) glose f, commentaire m. 3 vt to **g. over** (minimize) glisser sur; (conceal) dissimuler. ◆**glossy** a (-ier, -iest) brillant; (paper) glacé; (magazine) de luxe.

glossary ['glɒsərı] n glossaire m.

glove [glʌv] n gant m; **g. compartment** Aut (shelf) vide-poches m inv; (enclosed) boîte f à gants. ◆**gloved** a **a g. hand** une main gantée.

glow [gləʊ] vi (of sky, fire) rougeoyer; (of lamp) luire; (of eyes, person) Fig rayonner (with de); – n rougeoiement m; (of colour) éclat m; (of lamp) lueur f. ◆**—ing** a (account, terms etc) très favorable, enthousiaste. ◆**glow-worm** n ver m luisant.

glucose ['gluːkəʊs] n glucose m.

glue [gluː] n colle f; – vt coller (**to**, **on** à). ◆**glued** a **g. to** (eyes) Fam fixés or rivés sur; **to be g. to** (television) Fam être cloué devant.

glum [glʌm] a (glummer, glummest) triste.

glut [glʌt] vt (-tt-) (overfill) rassasier; (market) Com surcharger (**with** de); – n (of produce, oil etc) Com surplus m (of de).

glutton ['glʌt(ə)n] n glouton, -onne mf; **g. for work** bourreau m de travail; **g. for**

punishment masochiste mf. ◆**gluttony** n gloutonnerie f.

glycerin(e) ['glısəriːn] n glycérine f.

GMT [dʒiːem'tiː] abbr (Greenwich Mean Time) GMT.

gnarled [nɑːld] a noueux.

gnash [næʃ] vt to **g. one's teeth** grincer des dents.

gnat [næt] n (insect) cousin m.

gnaw [nɔː] vti to **g. (at)** ronger.

gnome [nəʊm] n (little man) gnome m.

go [gəʊ] **1** vi (3rd person sing pres t **goes**; pt **went**; pp **gone**; pres p **going**) aller (**to** à, **from** de); (depart) partir, s'en aller; (disappear) disparaître; (be sold) se vendre; (function) marcher, fonctionner; (progress) aller, marcher; (become) devenir; (be) être; (of time) passer; (of hearing, strength) baisser; (of rope) céder; (of fuse) sauter; (of material) s'user; **to go well/badly** (of event) se passer bien/mal; **she's going to do** (is about to, intends to) elle va faire; **it's all gone** (finished) il n'y en a plus; **to go and get** (fetch) aller chercher; **to go and see** aller voir; **to go riding/sailing/on a trip**/etc faire du cheval/de la voile/un voyage/etc; **to let go of** lâcher; **to go to** (doctor, lawyer etc) aller voir; **to get things going** faire démarrer les choses; **is there any beer going?** (available) y a-t-il de la bière?; **it goes to show that . . .** ça sert à montrer que . . . ; **two hours**/etc **to go** (still left) encore deux heures/etc. **2** n (pl **goes**) (energy) dynamisme m; (attempt) coup m; **to have a go at** (doing) sth essayer de (faire) qch; **at one go** d'un seul coup; **on the go** en mouvement, actif; **to make a go of** (make a success of) réussir. ■ **to go about** or **(a)round** vi se déplacer; (of news, rumour) circuler; **to go about** vt (one's duties etc) s'occuper de; **to know how to go about it** savoir s'y prendre; **to go across** vt traverser; – vi (cross) traverser; (go) aller (**to** à); **to go across to s.o.('s)** faire un saut chez qn; **to go after** vt (follow) suivre; (job) viser; **to go against** vt (of result) être défavorable à; (s.o.'s wishes) aller contre; (harm) nuire à; **to go ahead** vi aller de l'avant; **to go ahead with** (plan etc) poursuivre; **go ahead!** allez-y! ◆**go-ahead** a dynamique; – n **to get the go-ahead** avoir le feu vert; **to go along** vi aller, avancer; **to go along with** (agree) être d'accord avec; **to go away** vi partir, s'en aller; **to go back** vi retourner, revenir; (in time) remonter; (step back, retreat) reculer; **to go back on** (promise) revenir sur; **to go by** vi passer; – vt (act according to) se fonder sur; (*judge from*) juger d'après; (*instruction*) suivre; **to go down** *vi* descendre; (*fall down*) tomber; (*of ship*) couler; (*of sun*) se coucher; (*of storm*) s'apaiser; (*of temperature, price etc*) baisser; (*of tyre*) se dégonfler; **to go down well** (*of speech etc*) être bien reçu; **to go down with** (*illness*) attraper; – *vt* **to go down the stairs/street** descendre l'escalier/la rue; **to go for** *vt* (*fetch*) aller chercher; (*attack*) attaquer; (*like*) *Fam* aimer beaucoup; **to go forward(s)** *vi* avancer; **to go in** *vi* (r)entrer; (*of sun*) se cacher; **to go in for** (*exam*) se présenter à; (*hobby, sport*) faire; (*career*) entrer dans; (*like*) *Fam* aimer beaucoup; – *vt* **to go in a room/etc** entrer dans une pièce/*etc*; **to go into** *vt* (*room etc*) entrer dans; (*question*) examiner; **to go off** *vi* (*leave*) partir; (*go bad*) se gâter; (*of effect*) passer; (*of alarm*) se déclencher; (*of event*) se passer; – *vt* (*one's food*) perdre le goût de; **to go on** *vi* continuer (**doing** à faire); (*travel*) poursuivre sa route; (*happen*) se passer; (*last*) durer; (*of time*) passer; **to go on at** (*nag*) *Fam* s'en prendre à; **to go on about** *Fam* parler sans cesse de; **to go out** *vi* sortir; (*of light, fire*) s'éteindre; (*of tide*) descendre; (*of newspaper, product*) être distribué (**to** à); (*depart*) partir; **to go out to work** travailler (au dehors); **to go over** *vi* (*go*) aller (**to** à); (*cross over*) traverser; (*to enemy*) passer (**to** à); **to go over to s.o.('s)** faire un saut chez qn; – *vt* examiner; (*speech*) revoir; (*in one's mind*) repasser; (*touch up*) retoucher; (*overhaul*) réviser (*véhicule, montre*); **to go round** *vi* (*turn*) tourner; (*make a detour*) faire le tour; (*be sufficient*) suffire; **to go round to s.o.('s)** passer chez qn, faire un saut chez qn; **enough to go round** assez pour tout le monde; – *vt* **to go round a corner** tourner un coin; **to go through** *vi* passer; (*of deal*) être conclu; – *vt* (*undergo, endure*) subir; (*examine*) examiner; (*search*) fouiller; (*spend*) dépenser; (*wear out*) user; (*perform*) accomplir; **to go through with** (*carry out*) réaliser, aller jusqu'au bout de; **to go under** *vi* (*of ship, person, firm*) couler; **to go up** *vi* monter; (*explode*) sauter; – *vt* **to go up the stairs/street** monter l'escalier/la rue; **to go without** *vt* se passer de.

goad [gəud] *n* aiguillon *m*; – *vt* **to g. (on)** aiguillonner.

goal [gəul] *n* but *m*. ◆**goalkeeper** *n Fb* gardien *m* de but, goal *m*. ◆**goalpost** *n Fb* poteau *m* de but.

goat [gəut] *n* chèvre *f*; **to get s.o.'s g.** *Fam*

énerver qn. ◆**goa'tee** *n* (*beard*) barbiche *f.*

gobble ['gɒb(ə)l] *vt* **to g. (up)** engloutir, engouffrer.

go-between ['gəubitwiːn] *n* intermédiaire *mf*.

goblet ['gɒblit] *n* verre *m* à pied.

goblin ['gɒblin] *n* (*evil spirit*) lutin *m*.

god [gɒd] *n* dieu *m*; **G.** Dieu *m*; **the gods** *Th Fam* le poulailler. ◆**g.-fearing** *a* croyant. ◆**g.-forsaken** *a* (*place*) perdu, misérable. ◆**goddess** *n* déesse *f*. ◆**godly** *a* dévot.

godchild ['gɒdtʃaild] *n* (*pl* **-children**) filleul, -eule *mf*. ◆**goddaughter** *n* filleule *f*. ◆**godfather** *n* parrain *m*. ◆**godmother** *n* marraine *f*. ◆**godson** *n* filleul *m*.

goddam(n) ['gɒdæm] *a Am Fam* foutu.

godsend ['gɒdsend] *n* aubaine *f*.

goes [gəuz] *see* **go** 1.

goggle ['gɒg(ə)l] 1 *vi* **to g. at** regarder en roulant de gros yeux. 2 *npl* (*spectacles*) lunettes *fpl* (protectrices). ◆**g.-'eyed** *a* aux yeux saillants.

going ['gəuiŋ] 1 *n* (*departure*) départ *m*; (*speed*) allure *f*; (*conditions*) conditions *fpl*; **it's hard g.** c'est difficile. 2 *a* **the g. price** le prix pratiqué (**for** pour); **a g. concern** une entreprise qui marche bien. ◆**goings-'on** *npl Pej* activités *fpl*.

go-kart ['gəukaːt] *n Sp* kart *m*.

gold [gəuld] *n* or *m*; – *a* (*watch etc*) en or; (*coin, dust*) d'or. ◆**golden** *a* (*made of gold*) d'or; (*in colour*) doré, d'or; (*opportunity*) excellent. ◆**goldmine** *n* mine *f* d'or. ◆**gold-'plated** *a* plaqué or. ◆**goldsmith** *n* orfèvre *m*.

goldfinch ['gəuldfintʃ] *n* (*bird*) chardonneret *m*.

goldfish ['gəuldfiʃ] *n* poisson *m* rouge.

golf [gɒlf] *n* golf *m*. ◆**golfer** *n* golfeur, -euse *mf*.

golly! ['gɒli] *int* (**by**) **g.!** *Fam* mince (alors)!

gondola ['gɒndələ] *n* (*boat*) gondole *f*. ◆**gondo'lier** *n* gondolier *m*.

gone [gɒn] *see* **go** 1; – *a* **it's g. two** *Fam* il est plus de deux heures. ◆**goner** *n* **to be a g.** *Sl* être fichu.

gong [gɒŋ] *n* gong *m*.

good [gud] *a* (**better**, **best**) bon; (*kind*) gentil; (*weather*) beau; (*pleasant*) bon, agréable; (*well-behaved*) sage; **be g. enough to...** ayez la gentillesse de...; **my g. friend** mon cher ami; **a g. chap** *or* fellow un brave type; **g. and strong** bien fort; **a g. (long) walk** une bonne promenade; **very g.!** (*all right*) très bien!; **that's g. of you** c'est gentil de ta part; **to feel g.** se sentir bien;

that isn't g. enough (*bad*) ça ne va pas; (*not sufficient*) ça ne suffit pas; **it's g. for us** ça nous fait du bien; **g. at** (*French etc*) Sch bon or fort en; **to be g. with** (*children*) savoir s'y prendre avec; **it's a g. thing (that)** . . . heureusement que . . . ; **a g. many, a g. deal (of)** beaucoup (de); **as g. as** (*almost*) pratiquement; **g. afternoon**, **g. morning** bonjour; (*on leaving someone*) au revoir; **g. evening** bonsoir; **g. night** bonsoir; (*before going to bed*) bonne nuit; **to make g.** *vi* (*succeed*) réussir; – *vt* (*loss*) compenser; (*damage*) réparer; **G. Friday** Vendredi m Saint; – (*in virtue*) bien m; **for her g.** pour son bien; **there's some g. in him** il a du bon; **it's no g. crying/shouting/etc** ça ne sert à rien de pleurer/crier/etc; **that's no g.** (*worthless*) ça ne vaut rien; (*bad*) ça ne va pas; **what's the g.?** à quoi bon?; **for g.** (*to leave, give up etc*) pour de bon.
◆**g.-for-nothing** *a & n* propre à rien (*mf*).
◆**g.-'humoured** *a* de bonne humeur.
◆**g.-'looking** *a* beau. ◆**goodness** *n* bonté *f*; **my g.!** mon Dieu! ◆**good'will** *n* bonne volonté *f*; (*zeal*) zèle m.

goodbye [gud'baɪ] *int & n* au revoir (*m inv*).

goodly ['gudlɪ] *a* (*size, number*) grand.

goods [gudz] *npl* marchandises *fpl*; (*articles for sale*) articles *mpl*.

gooey ['guːɪ] *a* Fam gluant, poisseux.

goof [guːf] *vi* **to g. (up)** (*blunder*) Am faire une gaffe.

goon [guːn] *n* Fam idiot, -ote *mf*.

goose, *pl* **geese** [guːs, giːs] *n* oie *f*; **g. pimples** *or* **bumps** chair *f* de poule. ◆**gooseflesh** *n* chair *f* de poule.

gooseberry ['guzbərɪ, Am 'guːsbərɪ] *n* groseille *f* à maquereau.

gorge [gɔːdʒ] **1** *n* (*ravine*) gorge *f*. **2** *vt* (*food*) engloutir; **to g. oneself** s'empiffrer (**on** de).

gorgeous ['gɔːdʒəs] *a* magnifique.

gorilla [gə'rɪlə] *n* gorille m.

gormless ['gɔːmləs] *a* Fam stupide.

gorse [gɔːs] *n inv* ajonc(s) m(*pl*).

gory ['gɔːrɪ] *a* (**-ier, -iest**) (*bloody*) sanglant; (*details*) Fig horrible.

gosh [gɒʃ] *int* Fam mince (alors)!

go-slow [gəʊ'sləʊ] *n* (*strike*) grève *f* perlée.

gospel ['gɒspəl] *n* évangile m.

gossip ['gɒsɪp] *n* (*talk*) bavardage(s) m(*pl*); (*malicious*) cancan(s) m(*pl*); (*person*) commère *f*; **g. column** Journ échos *mpl*; – *vi* bavarder; (*maliciously*) cancaner. ◆**—ing** *a*, ◆**gossipy** *a* bavard, cancanier.

got, *Am* **gotten** [gɒt, 'gɒt(ə)n] *see* **get**.

Gothic ['gɒθɪk] *a & n* gothique (m).

gouge [gaʊdʒ] *vt* **to g. out** (*eye*) crever.

goulash ['guːlæʃ] *n* Culin goulasch *f*.

gourmet ['guəmeɪ] *n* gourmet m.

gout [gaʊt] *n* Med goutte *f*.

govern ['gʌv(ə)n] *vt* (*rule*) gouverner; (*city*) administrer; (*business*) gérer; (*emotion*) maîtriser, gouverner; (*influence*) déterminer; – *vi* Pol gouverner; **governing body** conseil m d'administration. ◆**governess** *n* gouvernante *f*. ◆**government** *n* gouvernement m; (*local*) administration *f*; – *a* (*department, policy etc*) gouvernemental; (*loan*) d'État. ◆**govern'mental** *a* gouvernemental. ◆**governor** *n* gouverneur m; (*of school*) administrateur, -trice *mf*; (*of prison*) directeur, -trice *mf*.

gown [gaʊn] *n* (*dress*) robe *f*; (*of judge, lecturer*) toge *f*.

GP [dʒiː'piː] *n abbr* (*general practitioner*) (*médecin m*) généraliste m.

GPO [dʒiːpiː'əʊ] *abbr* (*General Post Office*) = PTT *fpl*.

grab [græb] *vt* (**-bb-**) **to g.** (*hold of*) saisir, agripper; **to g. sth from s.o.** arracher qch à qn.

grace [greɪs] *n* (*charm, goodwill etc*) grâce *f*; Rel grâce *f*; (*extension of time*) délai m de grâce; **to say g.** dire le bénédicité. **2** *vt* (*adorn*) orner; (*honour*) honorer (**with** de). ◆**graceful** *a* gracieux. ◆**gracious** *a* (*kind*) aimable, gracieux (**to** envers); (*elegant*) élégant; **good g.!** Fam bonté divine!

gradation [grə'deɪʃ(ə)n, Am greɪ'deɪʃ(ə)n] *n* gradation *f*.

grade [greɪd] *n* catégorie *f*; Mil Math grade m; (*of milk*) qualité *f*; (*of eggs*) calibre m; (*level*) niveau m; (*mark*) Sch Univ note *f*; (*class*) Am Sch classe *f*; **g. school** Am école *f* primaire; **g. crossing** Am passage m à niveau; – *vt* (*classify*) classer; (*colours etc*) graduer; (*paper*) Sch Univ noter.

gradient ['greɪdɪənt] *n* (*slope*) inclinaison *f*.

gradual ['grædʒʊəl] *a* progressif, graduel; (*slope*) doux. ◆**—ly** *adv* progressivement, peu à peu.

graduat/e ['grædʒʊeɪt] *vi* Univ obtenir son diplôme; Am Sch obtenir son baccalauréat; **to g. from** sortir de; – *vt* (*mark with degrees*) graduer; – ['grædʒʊət] *n* diplômé, -ée *mf*, licencié, -ée *mf*. ◆**—ed** *a* (*tube etc*) gradué; **to be g.** Am Sch Univ = **to graduate**. ◆**graduation** *n* Univ remise *f* des diplômes.

graffiti [grə'fiːtɪ] *npl* graffiti *mpl*.

graft [grɑːft] *n* Med Bot greffe *f*; – *vt* greffer (**on to** à).

grain [greɪn] *n* (*seed, particle*) grain m;

(*seeds*) grain(s) *m(pl)*; (*in cloth*) fil *m*; (*in wood*) fibre *f*; (*in leather, paper*) grain *m*; (*of truth*) Fig once *f*.

gram(me) ['græm] *n* gramme *m*.

grammar ['græmər] *n* grammaire *f*; **g. school** lycée *m*. ◆**gra'mmatical** *a* grammatical.

gramophone ['græməfəun] *n* phonographe *m*.

granary ['grænəri] *n* Agr grenier *m*; **g. loaf** pain *m* complet.

grand [grænd] **1** *a* (**-er, -est**) magnifique, grand; (*style*) grandiose; (*concert, duke*) grand; (*piano*) à queue; (*wonderful*) Fam magnifique. **2** *n inv Am Sl* mille dollars *mpl*; *Br Sl* mille livres *fpl*. ◆**grandeur** ['grændʒər] *n* magnificence *f*; (*of person, country*) grandeur *f*.

grandchild ['græntʃaild] *n* (*pl* **-children**) petit(e)-enfant *mf*. ◆**grand(d)ad** *n* Fam pépé *m*, papi *m*. ◆**granddaughter** *n* petite-fille *f*. ◆**grandfather** *n* grand-père *m*. ◆**grandmother** *n* grand-mère *f*. ◆**grandparents** *npl* grands-parents *mpl*. ◆**grandson** *n* petit-fils *m*.

grandstand ['grændstænd] *n* Sp tribune *f*.

grange [greɪndʒ] *n* (*house*) manoir *m*.

granite ['grænɪt] *n* granit(e) *m*.

granny ['græni] *n* Fam mamie *f*.

grant [grɑːnt] **1** *vt* accorder (**to** à); (*request*) accéder à; (*prayer*) exaucer; (*admit*) admettre (**that** que); **to take for granted** (*event*) considérer comme allant de soi; (*person*) considérer comme faisant partie du décor; **I take (it) for granted that** . . . je présume que . . . . **2** *n* subvention *f*, allocation *f*; *Univ* bourse *f*.

granule ['grænjuːl] *n* granule *m*. ◆**granulated** *a* **g. sugar** sucre *m* cristallisé.

grape [greɪp] *n* grain *m* de raisin; *pl* le raisin, les raisins *mpl*; **to eat grapes** manger du raisin *or* des raisins; **g. harvest** vendange *f*. ◆**grapefruit** *n* pamplemousse *m*. ◆**grapevine** *n* **on the g.** Fig par le téléphone arabe.

graph [græf, grɑːf] *n* graphique *m*, courbe *f*; **g. paper** papier *m* millimétré.

graphic ['græfɪk] *a* graphique; (*description*) Fig explicite, vivant. ◆**graphically** *adv* (*to describe*) explicitement.

grapple ['græp(ə)l] *vi* **to g. with** (*person, problem etc*) se colleter avec.

grasp [grɑːsp] *vt* (*seize, understand*) saisir; – *n* (*firm hold*) prise *f*; (*understanding*) compréhension *f*; (*knowledge*) connaissance *f*; **to have a strong g.** (*strength of hand*) avoir de la poigne; **within s.o.'s g.**

(*reach*) à la portée de qn. ◆**—ing** *a* (*greedy*) rapace.

grass [grɑːs] *n* herbe *f*; (*lawn*) gazon *m*; **the g. roots** Pol la base. ◆**grasshopper** *n* sauterelle *f*. ◆**grassland** *n* prairie *f*. ◆**grassy** *a* herbeux.

grate [greɪt] **1** *n* (*for fireplace*) grille *f* de foyer. **2** *vt* Culin râper. **3** *vi* (*of sound*) grincer (**on** sur); **to g. on the ears** écorcher les oreilles; **to g. on s.o.'s nerves** taper sur les nerfs de qn. ◆**—ing 1** *a* (*sound*) grinçant; *Fig* irritant. **2** *n* (*bars*) grille *f*. ◆**—er** *n* Culin râpe *f*.

grateful ['greɪtfəl] *a* reconnaissant (**to** à, **for** de); (*words, letter*) de remerciement; (*friend, attitude*) plein de reconnaissance; **I'm g. (to you) for your help** je vous suis reconnaissant de votre aide; **I'd be g. if you'd be quieter** j'aimerais bien que tu fasses moins de bruit; **g. thanks** mes sincères remerciements. ◆**—ly** *adv* avec reconnaissance.

gratif/y ['grætɪfaɪ] *vt* (*whim*) satisfaire; **to s.o.** faire plaisir à qn. ◆**—ied** *a* très content (**with** *or* **at** sth de qch, **to do** de faire). ◆**—ying** *a* très satisfaisant; **it's g. to** . . . ça fait plaisir de . . . . ◆**gratifi'cation** *n* satisfaction *f*.

gratis ['grætɪs, 'greɪtɪs] *adv* gratis.

gratitude ['grætɪtjuːd] *n* reconnaissance *f*, gratitude *f* (**for** de).

gratuitous [grə'tjuːɪtəs] *a* (*act etc*) gratuit.

gratuity [grə'tjuːɪti] *n* (*tip*) pourboire *m*.

grave¹ [greɪv] *n* tombe *f*; **g. digger** fossoyeur *m*. ◆**gravestone** *n* pierre *f* tombale. ◆**graveyard** *n* cimetière *m*; **auto g.** Am Fam cimetière *m* de voitures.

grave² [greɪv] *a* (**-er, -est**) (*serious*) grave. ◆**—ly** *adv* gravement; (*concerned, displeased*) extrêmement.

gravel ['græv(ə)l] *n* gravier *m*.

gravitate ['grævɪteɪt] *vi* **to g. towards** (*be drawn towards*) être attiré vers; (*move towards*) se diriger vers. ◆**gravi'tation** *n* gravitation *f*.

gravity ['grævɪti] *n* **1** (*seriousness*) gravité *f*. **2** Phys pesanteur *f*, gravité *f*.

gravy ['greɪvi] *n* jus *m* de viande.

gray [greɪ] Am = **grey**.

graze [greɪz] **1** *vi* (*of cattle*) paître. **2** *vt* (*scrape*) écorcher; (*touch lightly*) frôler, effleurer; – *n* (*wound*) écorchure *f*.

grease [griːs] *n* graisse *f*; – *vt* graisser. ◆**greaseproof** *a* & *n* (*paper*) papier *m* sulfurisé. ◆**greasy** *a* (**-ier, -iest**) graisseux; (*hair*) gras; (*road*) glissant.

great [greɪt] *a* (**-er, -est**) grand; (*effort, heat,* *parcel*) gros, grand; (*excellent*) magnifique, merveilleux; **to g. at** (*English, tennis etc*) être doué pour; **a g. deal** or **number (of)** beaucoup (de); **a g. many** beaucoup (de); **a g. opinion of** une haute opinion de; **a very g. age** un âge très avancé; **the greatest team**/*etc* (*best*) la meilleure équipe/*etc*; **Greater London** le grand Londres. ◆**g.-'grandfather** *n* arrière-grand-père *m.* ◆**g.-'grandmother** *n* arrière-grand-mère *f.* ◆**greatly** *adv* (*much*) beaucoup; (*very*) très, bien; **I g. prefer** je préfère de beaucoup. ◆**greatness** *n* (*in size, importance*) grandeur *f*; (*in degree*) intensité *f.*

Great Britain [greit'brit(ə)n] *n* Grande-Bretagne *f.*

Greece [griːs] *n* Grèce *f.* ◆**Greek** *a* grec; – *n* Grec *m*, Grecque *f*; (*language*) grec *m.*

greed [griːd] *n* avidité *f* (**for** de); (*for food*) gourmandise *f.* ◆**greed/y** *a* (**-ier, -iest**) avide (**for** de); (*for food*) glouton, gourmand. ◆**-ily** *adv* avidement; (*to eat*) gloutonnement. ◆**-iness** *n* = **greed.**

green [griːn] *a* (**-er, -est**) vert; (*pale*) blême, vert; (*immature*) *Fig* naïf, vert; **to turn** or **go g.** verdir; **the g. belt** (*land*) la ceinture verte; **the g. light** *Fig* (*feu*) vert; **to have g. fingers** or *Am* **a g. thumb** avoir la main verte; **g. with envy** *Fig* vert de jalousie; – *n* (*colour*) vert *m*; (*lawn*) pelouse *f*; (*village square*) place *f* gazonnée; *pl Culin* légumes *mpl* verts. ◆**greenery** *n* (*plants, leaves*) verdure *f.* ◆**greenfly** *n* puceron *m* (*des plantes*). ◆**greengrocer** *n* marchand, -ande *mf* de légumes. ◆**greenhouse** *n* serre *f.* ◆**greenish** *a* verdâtre. ◆**greenness** *n* (*colour*) vert *m*; (*greenery*) verdure *f.*

greengage ['griːngeɪdʒ] *n* (*plum*) reine-claude *f.*

Greenland ['griːnlənd] *n* Groenland *m.*

greet [griːt] *vt* saluer, accueillir; **to g. s.o.** (*of sight*) s'offrir aux regards de qn. ◆**-ing** *n* salutation *f*; (*welcome*) accueil *m*; *pl* (*for birthday, festival*) vœux *mpl*; **send my greetings to . . .** envoie mon bon souvenir à . . . ; **greetings card** carte *f* de vœux.

gregarious [grɪ'geərɪəs] *a* (*person*) sociable; (*instinct*) grégaire.

gremlin ['gremlɪn] *n* *Fam* petit diable *m.*

grenade [grə'neɪd] *n* (*bomb*) grenade *f.*

grew [gruː] *see* **grow.**

grey [greɪ] *a* (**-er, -est**) gris; (*outlook*) *Fig* sombre; **to be going g.** grisonner; – *vi* **to be greying** être grisonnant. ◆**g.-'haired** *a* aux cheveux gris. ◆**greyhound** *n* lévrier *m.* ◆**greyish** *a* grisâtre.

grid [grɪd] *n* (*grating*) grille *f*; (*system*) *El* réseau *m*; *Culin* gril *m.* ◆**gridiron** *n Culin* gril *m.*

griddle ['grɪd(ə)l] *n* (*on stove*) plaque *f* à griller.

grief [griːf] *n* chagrin *m*, douleur *f*; **to come to g.** avoir des ennuis; (*of driver, pilot etc*) avoir un accident; (*of plan*) échouer; **good g.!** ciel!, bon sang!

grieve [griːv] *vt* peiner, affliger; – *vi* s'affliger (**over** de); **to g. for s.o.** pleurer qn. ◆**grievance** *n* grief *m*; *pl* (*complaints*) doléances *fpl.*

grievous ['griːvəs] *a* (*serious*) très grave.

grill [grɪl] **1** *n* (*utensil*) gril *m*; (*dish*) grillade *f*; – *vti* griller. **2** *vt* (*question*) *Fam* cuisiner.

grille [grɪl] *n* (*metal bars*) grille *f*; (*radiator*) **g.** *Aut* calandre *f.*

grim [grɪm] *a* (**grimmer, grimmest**) sinistre; (*face*) sévère; (*truth*) brutal; (*bad*) *Fam* (*plutôt*) affreux; **g. determination** une volonté inflexible. ◆**-ly** *adv* (*to look at*) sévèrement.

grimace ['grɪməs] *n* grimace *f*; – *vi* grimacer.

grime [graɪm] *n* saleté *f.* ◆**grimy** *a* (**-ier, -iest**) sale.

grin [grɪn] *vi* (**-nn-**) avoir un large sourire; (*with pain*) avoir un rictus; – *n* large sourire *m*; rictus *m.*

grind [graɪnd] **1** *vt* (*pt & pp* **ground**) moudre; (*blade, tool*) aiguiser; (*handle*) tourner; (*oppress*) *Fig* écraser; **to g. one's teeth** grincer des dents; – *vi* **to g. to a halt** s'arrêter (*progressivement*). **2** *n Fam* corvée *f*, travail *m* long et monotone. ◆**-ing** *a* **g. poverty** la misère noire. ◆**-er** *n* **coffee g.** moulin *m* à café.

grip [grɪp] *vt* (**-pp-**) (*seize*) saisir; (*hold*) tenir serré; (*of story*) *Fig* empoigner (*qn*); **to g. the road** (*of tyres*) adhérer à la route; – *vi* (*of brakes*) mordre; – *n* (*hold*) prise *f*; (*hand clasp*) poigne *f*; **get a g. on yourself!** secoue-toi!; **to get to grips with** (*problem*) s'attaquer à; **in the g. of** en proie à. ◆**gripping** *a* (*book, film etc*) prenant.

gripe [graɪp] *vi* (*complain*) *Sl* rouspéter.

grisly ['grɪzlɪ] *a* (*gruesome*) horrible.

gristle ['grɪs(ə)l] *n Culin* cartilage *m.*

grit [grɪt] **1** *n* (*sand*) sable *m*; (*gravel*) gravillon *m*; – *vt* (**-tt-**) (*road*) sabler. **2** *n* (*pluck*) *Fam* cran *m.* **3** *vt* (**-tt-**) **to g. one's teeth** serrer les dents.

grizzle ['grɪz(ə)l] *vi Fam* pleurnicher. ◆**grizzly** *a* **1** (*child*) *Fam* pleurnicheur. **2** (*bear*) gris.

groan [grəʊn] *vi* (*with pain*) gémir;

(*complain*) grogner, gémir; − *n* gémissement *m*; grognement *m*.

grocer ['grəʊsər] *n* épicier, -ière *mf*; **grocer's (shop)** épicerie *f*. ◆**grocery** *n* (*shop*) épicerie *f*; *pl* (*food*) épicerie *f*.

grog [grɒg] *n* (*drink*) grog *m*.

groggy ['grɒgɪ] *a* (*-ier, -iest*) (*weak*) faible; (*shaky on one's feet*) pas solide sur les jambes.

groin [grɔɪn] *n* Anat aine *f*.

groom [gruːm] 1 *n* (*bridegroom*) marié *m*. 2 *n* (*for horses*) lad *m*; − *vt* (*horse*) panser; to g. s.o. for (*job*) Fig préparer qn pour; **well groomed** (*person*) très soigné.

groove [gruːv] *n* (*for sliding door etc*) rainure *f*; (*in record*) sillon *m*.

grope [grəʊp] *vi* to g. (*about*) tâtonner; to g. for chercher à tâtons.

gross [grəʊs] 1 *a* (*-er, -est*) (*coarse*) grossier; (*error*) gros, grossier; (*injustice*) flagrant. 2 *a* (*weight, income*) Com brut; − *vt* faire une recette brute de. 3 *n* (*number*) grosse *f*. ◆**—ly** *adv* grossièrement; (*very*) énormément, extrêmement.

grotesque [grəʊ'tesk] *a* (*ludicrous, strange*) grotesque; (*frightening*) monstrueux.

grotto ['grɒtəʊ] *n* (*pl* -oes *or* -os) grotte *f*.

grotty ['grɒtɪ] *a* (*-ier, -iest*) Fam affreux, moche.

ground[1] [graʊnd] 1 *n* terre *f*, sol *m*; (*area for camping, football etc*) & Fig terrain *m*; (*estate*) terres *fpl*; (*earth*) El Am terre *f*, masse *f*; (*background*) fond *m*; *pl* (*reasons*) raisons *fpl*, motifs *mpl*; (*gardens*) parc *m*; **on the g.** (*lying etc*) par terre; **to lose g.** perdre du terrain; **g. floor** rez-de-chaussée *m* inv; **g. frost** gelée *f* blanche. 2 *vt* (*aircraft*) bloquer *or* retenir au sol. ◆**—ing** *n* connaissances *fpl* (de fond) (**in** en). ◆**groundless** *a* sans fondement. ◆**groundnut** *n* arachide *f*. ◆**groundsheet** *n* tapis *m* de sol. ◆**groundswell** *n* lame *f* de fond. ◆**groundwork** *n* préparation *f*.

ground[2] [graʊnd] *see* grind 1; − *a* (*coffee*) moulu; − *npl* (*coffee*) grounds marc *m* (de café).

group [gruːp] *n* groupe *m*; − *vt* to g. (**together**) grouper; − *vi* se grouper. ◆**—ing** *n* (*group*) groupe *m*.

grouse [graʊs] 1 *n inv* (*bird*) coq *m* de bruyère. 2 *vi* (*complain*) Fam rouspéter.

grove [grəʊv] *n* bocage *m*.

grovel ['grɒv(ə)l] *vi* (*-ll-, Am -l-*) Pej ramper, s'aplatir (**to s.o.** devant qn).

grow [grəʊ] *vi* (*pt* grew, *pp* grown) (*of person*) grandir; (*of plant, hair*) pousser;

(*increase*) augmenter, grandir, croître; (*expand*) s'agrandir; to g. fat(ter) grossir; to g. to like finir par aimer; to g. into devenir; to g. on s.o. (*of book, music etc*) plaire progressivement à qn; to g. out of (*one's clothes*) devenir trop grand pour; (*a habit*) perdre; to g. up devenir adulte; **when I g. up** quand je serai grand; − *vt* (*plant, crops*) cultiver, faire pousser; (*beard, hair*) laisser pousser. ◆**—ing** *a* (*child*) qui grandit; (*number*) grandissant. ◆**grown** *a* (*full-grown*) adulte. ◆**grown-up** *n* grande personne *f*, adulte *mf*; − *a* (*ideas etc*) d'adulte. ◆**grower** *n* (*person*) cultivateur, -trice *mf*.

growl [graʊl] *vi* grogner (**at** contre); − *n* grognement *m*.

growth [grəʊθ] *n* croissance *f*; (*increase*) augmentation *f* (**in** de); (*of hair*) pousse *f*; (*beard*) barbe *f*; Med tumeur *f* (**on** à).

grub [grʌb] *n* (*food*) Fam bouffe *f*.

grubby ['grʌbɪ] *a* (*-ier, -iest*) sale.

grudge [grʌdʒ] 1 *vt* (*give*) donner à contrecœur; (*reproach*) reprocher (**s.o. sth** qch à qn); to g. doing faire à contrecœur. 2 *n* rancune *f*; **to have a g. against** en vouloir à. ◆**—ing** *a* peu généreux. ◆**—ingly** *adv* à contrecœur.

gruelling, *Am* **grueling** ['gruːəlɪŋ] *a* (*day, detail etc*) éprouvant, atroce.

gruesome ['gruːsəm] *a* horrible.

gruff [grʌf] *a* (*-er, -est*) (*voice, person*) bourru.

grumble ['grʌmb(ə)l] *vi* (*complain*) grogner (**about, at** contre), se plaindre (**about, at** de).

grumpy ['grʌmpɪ] *a* (*-ier, -iest*) grincheux.

grunt [grʌnt] *vti* grogner; − *n* grognement *m*.

guarantee [gærən'tiː] *n* garantie *f*; − *vt* garantir (**against** contre); (*vouch for*) se porter garant de; to g. (**s.o.**) that certifier *or* garantir (à qn) que. ◆**guarantor** *n* garant, -ante *mf*.

guard [gɑːd] *n* (*vigilance, group of soldiers etc*) garde *f*; (*individual person*) garde *m*; Rail chef *m* de train; **to keep a g. on** surveiller; **under g.** sous surveillance; **on one's g.** sur ses gardes; **to catch s.o. off his g.** prendre qn au dépourvu; **on g. (duty)** de garde; **to stand g.** monter la garde; − *vt* (*protect*) protéger (**against** contre); (*watch over*) surveiller, garder; − *vi* to g. against (*protect oneself*) se prémunir contre; (*prevent*) empêcher; **to g. against doing** se garder de faire. ◆**—ed** *a* (*cautious*) prudent.

◆**guardian** *n* gardien, -ienne *mf*; *(of child)* Jur tuteur, -trice *mf*.

guerrilla [gə'rɪlə] *n (person)* guérillero *m*; g. **warfare** guérilla *f*.

guess [ges] *n* conjecture *f*; *(intuition)* intuition *f*; *(estimate)* estimation *f*; **to make a g.** (essayer de) deviner; **an educated** *or* **informed g.** une conjecture fondée; − *vt* deviner (**that** que); *(estimate)* estimer; *(suppose)* Am supposer (**that** que); *(think)* Am croire (**that** que); − *vi* deviner; **I g. (so)** Am je suppose; je crois. ◆**guesswork** *n* hypothèse *f*; **by g.** au jugé.

guest [gest] *n* invité, -ée *mf*; *(in hotel)* client, -ente *mf*; *(at meal)* convive *mf*; − *a (speaker, singer etc)* invité. ◆**guesthouse** *n* pension *f* de famille. ◆**guestroom** *n* chambre *f* d'ami.

guffaw [gʌ'fɔ:] *vi* rire bruyamment.

guidance ['gaɪdəns] *n (advice)* conseils *mpl*.

guid/e [gaɪd] *n (person, book etc)* guide *m*; *(indication)* indication *f*; *(girl)* g. éclaireuse *f*; **dog** chien *m* d'aveugle; **g. book** guide *m*; − *vt (lead)* guider. ◆**−ed** *a (missile, rocket)* téléguidé; **g. tour** visite *f* guidée. ◆**−ing** *a (principle)* directeur. ◆**guidelines** *npl* lignes *fpl* directrices, indications *fpl* à suivre.

guild [gɪld] *n* association *f*; Hist corporation *f*.

guile [gaɪl] *n (deceit)* ruse *f*.

guillotine ['gɪlətiːn] *n* guillotine *f*; *(for paper)* massicot *m*.

guilt [gɪlt] *n* culpabilité *f*. ◆**guilty** *a* (-ier, -iest) coupable; **g. person** coupable *mf*; **to find s.o. g.** déclarer qn coupable.

guinea pig ['gɪnɪpɪg] *n (animal)* & Fig cobaye *m*.

guise [gaɪz] *n* **under the g. of** sous l'apparence de.

guitar [gɪ'tɑ:r] *n* guitare *f*. ◆**guitarist** *n* guitariste *mf*.

gulf [gʌlf] *n (in sea)* golfe *m*; *(chasm)* gouffre *m*; **a g. between** Fig un abîme entre.

gull [gʌl] *n (bird)* mouette *f*.

gullet ['gʌlɪt] *n* gosier *m*.

gullible ['gʌlɪb(ə)l] *a* crédule.

gully ['gʌlɪ] *n (valley)* ravine *f*; *(drain)* rigole *f*.

gulp [gʌlp] **1** *vt* **to g. (down)** avaler (vite); − *n (of drink)* gorgée *f*, lampée *f*; **in** *or* **at one**

g. d'une seule gorgée. **2** *vi (with emotion)* avoir la gorge serrée; − *n* serrement *m* de gorge.

gum¹ [gʌm] *n* Anat gencive *f*. ◆**gumboil** *n* abcès *m* (dentaire).

gum² [gʌm] **1** *n (glue from tree)* gomme *f*; *(any glue)* colle *f*; − *vt* (**-mm-**) coller. **2** *n (for chewing)* chewing-gum *m*.

gumption ['gʌmpʃ(ə)n] *n* Fam *(courage)* initiative *f*; *(commonsense)* jugeote *f*.

gun [gʌn] *n* pistolet *m*, revolver *m*; *(cannon)* canon *m*; − *vt* (**-nn-**) **to g. down** abattre. ◆**gunfight** *n* échange *m* de coups de feu. ◆**gunfire** *n* coups *mpl* de feu; Mil tir *m* d'artillerie. ◆**gunman** *n (pl* **-men)** bandit *m* armé. ◆**gunner** *n* Mil artilleur *m*. ◆**gunpoint** *n* **at g.** sous la menace d'un pistolet *or* d'une arme. ◆**gunpowder** *n* poudre *f* à canon. ◆**gunshot** *n* coup *m* de feu; **g. wound** blessure *f* par balle.

gurgle ['gɜ:g(ə)l] *vi (of water)* glouglouter; − *n* glouglou *m*.

guru ['guːruː] *n (leader)* Fam gourou *m*.

gush [gʌʃ] *vi* jaillir (**out of** de); − *n* jaillissement *m*.

gust [gʌst] *n (of smoke)* bouffée *f*; **g. (of wind)** rafale *f* (de vent). ◆**gusty** *a* (**-ier, -iest**) *(weather)* venteux; *(day)* de vent.

gusto ['gʌstəʊ] *n* **with g.** avec entrain.

gut [gʌt] **1** *n* Anat intestin *m*; *(catgut)* boyau *m*; *pl* Fam *(innards)* ventre *m*, tripes *fpl*; *(pluck)* cran *m*, tripes *fpl*; **he hates your guts** Fam il ne peut pas te sentir. **2** *vt* (**-tt-**) *(of fire)* dévaster.

gutter ['gʌtər] *n (on roof)* gouttière *f*; *(in street)* caniveau *m*.

guttural ['gʌtərəl] *a* guttural.

guy [gaɪ] *n (fellow)* Fam type *m*.

guzzle ['gʌz(ə)l] *vi (eat)* bâfrer; − *vt (eat)* engloutir; *(drink)* siffler.

gym [dʒɪm] *n* gym(nastique) *f*; *(gymnasium)* gymnase *m*; **g. shoes** tennis *fpl*. ◆**gymnasium** *n* gymnase *m*. ◆**gymnast** *n* gymnaste *mf*. ◆**gym'nastics** *n* gymnastique *f*.

gynaecology, Am **gynecology** [gaɪn-ɪ'kɒlədʒɪ] *n* gynécologie *f*. ◆**gynae-cologist** *n*, Am ◆**gynecologist** *n* gynécologue *mf*.

gypsy ['dʒɪpsɪ] = gipsy.

gyrate [dʒaɪ'reɪt] *vi* tournoyer.

H

H, h [eɪtʃ] n H, h m; **H bomb** bombe f H.

haberdasher ['hæbədæʃər] n mercier, -ière mf; *(men's outfitter)* Am chemisier m. ◆**haberdashery** n mercerie f; Am chemiserie f.

habit ['hæbɪt] n **1** habitude f; **to be in/get into the h.** of doing avoir/prendre l'habitude de faire; **to make a h.** of doing avoir pour habitude de faire. **2** *(addiction) Med* accoutumance f; **a h.-forming drug** une drogue qui crée une accoutumance. **3** *(costume) Rel* habit m. ◆**ha'bitual** a habituel; *(smoker, drinker etc)* invétéré. ◆**ha'bitually** adv habituellement.

habitable ['hæbɪtəb(ə)l] a habitable. ◆**habitat** n *(of animal, plant)* habitat m. ◆**habi'tation** n habitation f; **fit for h.** habitable.

hack [hæk] **1** vt *(cut)* tailler, hacher. **2** n *(old horse)* rosse f; *(hired)* cheval m de louage; **h. (writer)** Pej écrivaillon m.

hackney ['hæknɪ] a **h. carriage** Hist fiacre m.

hackneyed ['hæknɪd] a *(saying)* rebattu, banal.

had [hæd] see have.

haddock ['hædək] n *(fish)* aiglefin m; **smoked h.** haddock m.

haemorrhage ['hemərɪdʒ] n Med hémorragie f.

haemorrhoids ['hemərɔɪdz] npl hémorroïdes fpl.

hag [hæg] n *(woman)* Pej (vieille) sorcière f.

haggard ['hægəd] a *(person, face)* hâve, émacié.

haggl/e ['hæg(ə)l] vi marchander; **to h. over** *(thing)* marchander; *(price)* débattre, discuter. ◆**-ing** n marchandage m.

Hague (The) [ðə'heɪg] n La Haye.

ha-ha! [haː'haː] int *(laughter)* ha, ha!

hail [heɪl] n Met & Fig grêle f; – v imp Met grêler; **it's hailing** il grêle. ◆**hailstone** n grêlon m.

hail [heɪl] **1** vt *(greet)* saluer; *(taxi)* héler. **2** vi **to h. from** *(of person)* être originaire de; *(of ship etc)* être en provenance de.

hair [heər] n *(on head)* cheveux mpl; *(on body, of animal)* poils mpl; **a h.** *(on head)* un cheveu; *(on body, of animal)* un poil; **by a hair's breadth** de justesse; **long/red/etc haired** aux cheveux longs/roux/etc; **h.**

cream brillantine f; **h. dryer** sèche-cheveux m inv; **h. spray** *(bombe f de)* laque f. ◆**hairbrush** n brosse f à cheveux. ◆**haircut** n coupe f de cheveux; **to have a h.** se faire couper les cheveux. ◆**hairdo** n *(pl -dos)* Fam coiffure f. ◆**hairdresser** n coiffeur, -euse mf. ◆**hairgrip** n pince f à cheveux. ◆**hairnet** n résille f. ◆**hairpiece** n postiche m. ◆**hairpin** n épingle f à cheveux; **h. bend** Aut virage m en épingle à cheveux. ◆**hair-raising** a à faire dresser les cheveux sur la tête. ◆**hair-splitting** n ergotage m. ◆**hairstyle** n coiffure f.

hairy ['heərɪ] a *(-ier, -iest)* *(person, animal, body)* poilu; *(unpleasant, frightening) Fam* effroyable.

hake [heɪk] n *(fish)* colin m.

hale [heɪl] a **h. and hearty** vigoureux.

half [hɑːf] n *(pl halves)* moitié f, demi, -ie mf; *(of match)* Sp mi-temps f; **h. (of) the apple/etc** la moitié de la pomme/etc; **ten and a h.** dix et demi; **ten and a h. weeks** dix semaines et demie; **to cut in h.** couper en deux; **to go halves with** partager les frais avec; – a demi; **h. a day, a h.-day** une demi-journée; **at h. price** à moitié prix; **h. man h. beast** mi-homme mi-bête; **h. sleeves** manches fpl mi-longues; – adv *(dressed, full etc)* à demi, à moitié; *(almost)* presque; **h. asleep** à moitié endormi; **h. past one** une heure et demie; **he isn't h. lazy/etc** Fam il est rudement paresseux/etc; **h. as much as** moitié moins que; **h. as much again** moitié plus.

half-back ['hɑːfbæk] n Fb demi m. ◆**h.-'baked** a *(idea) Fam* à la manque, à la noix. ◆**h.-breed** n, ◆**h.-caste** n Pej métis, -isse mf. ◆**h.-(a-)'dozen** n demi-douzaine f. ◆**h.-'hearted** a *(person, manner)* peu enthousiaste; *(effort)* timide. ◆**h.-'hour** n demi-heure f. ◆**h.-light** n demi-jour m. ◆**h.-'mast** n at **h.-mast** *(flag)* en berne. ◆**h.-'open** a entrouvert. ◆**h.-'term** n Sch petites vacances fpl, congé m de demi-trimestre. ◆**h.-'time** n Sp mi-temps f. ◆**half'way** adv *(between places)* à mi-chemin *(between* entre); **to fill/etc h.** remplir/etc à moitié; **h. through**

(book) à la moitié de. ◆**h.-wit** *n*, ◆**h.-'witted** *a* imbécile *(mf)*.

halibut ['hælɪbət] *n (fish)* flétan *m*.

hall [hɔːl] *n (room)* salle *f*; *(house entrance)* entrée *f*, vestibule *m*; *(of hotel)* hall *m*; *(mansion)* manoir *m*; *(for meals) Univ* réfectoire *m*; **h. of residence** *Univ* pavillon *m* universitaire; **halls of residence** *Univ* cité *f* universitaire; **lecture h.** *Univ* amphithéâtre *m*. ◆**hallmark** *n (on silver or gold)* poinçon *m*; *Fig* sceau *m*. ◆**hallstand** *n* portemanteau *m*. ◆**hallway** *n* entrée *f*, vestibule *m*.

hallelujah [hælɪ'luːjə] *n & int* alléluia *(m)*.

hallo! [hə'ləu] *int (greeting)* bonjour!; *Tel* allô!; *(surprise)* tiens!

hallow ['hæləu] *vt* sanctifier.

Hallowe'en [hæləu'iːn] *n* la veille de la Toussaint.

hallucination [həluːsɪ'neɪʃ(ə)n] *n* hallucination *f*.

halo ['heɪləu] *n (pl -oes or -os)* auréole *f*, halo *m*.

halt [hɔːlt] *n* halte *f*; **to call a h.** to mettre fin à; **to come to a h.** s'arrêter; – *vi* faire halte; – *int Mil* halte! ◆**—ing** *a (voice)* hésitant.

halve [hɑːv] *vt (time, expense)* réduire de moitié; *(cake, number etc)* diviser en deux.

ham [hæm] *n* **1** jambon *m*; **h. and eggs** œufs *mpl* au jambon. **2** *(actor) Th Pej* cabotin, -ine *mf*. ◆**h.-'fisted** *a Fam* maladroit.

hamburger ['hæmbɜːgər] *n* hamburger *m*.

hamlet ['hæmlɪt] *n* hameau *m*.

hammer ['hæmər] *n* marteau *m*; – *vt (metal, table)* marteler; *(nail)* enfoncer (**into** dans); *(defeat) Fam* battre à plate(s) couture(s); *(criticize) Fam* démolir; **to h. out** *(agreement)* mettre au point; – *vi* frapper (au marteau). ◆**—ing** *n (defeat) Fam* raclée *f*, défaite *f*.

hammock ['hæmək] *n* hamac *m*.

hamper ['hæmpər] **1** *vt* gêner. **2** *n (basket)* panier *m*; *(laundry basket) Am* panier *m* à linge.

hamster ['hæmstər] *n* hamster *m*.

hand [hænd] *n* **1** main *f*; **to hold in one's h.** tenir à la main; **by h.** *(to deliver etc)* à la main; **at** *or* **to h.** *(within reach)* sous la main, à portée de la main; **(close) at h.** *(person etc)* tout près; *(day etc)* proche; **in h.** *(situation)* bien en main; *(matter)* en question; *(money)* disponible; **on h.** *(ready for use)* disponible; **to have s.o. on one's hands** *Fig* avoir qn sur les bras; **on the right h.** du côté droit (**of** de); **on the one h....** d'une part...; **on the other h....** d'autre part...; **hands up!** *(in attack)* haut les

mains!; *Sch* levez la main!; **hands off!** pas touche!, bas les pattes!; **my hands are full** *Fig* je suis très occupé; **to give s.o. a hand** *(help)* h. donner un coup de main à qn; **to get out of h.** *(of person)* devenir impossible; *(of situation)* devenir incontrôlable; **h. in h.** la main dans la main; **h. in h. with** *(together with) Fig* de pair avec; **at first h.** de première main; **to win hands down** gagner haut la main; – *a (luggage etc)* à main. **2** *n (worker)* ouvrier, -ière *mf*; *(of clock)* aiguille *f*; *Cards* jeu *m*; *(writing)* écriture *f*. ◆**handbag** *n* sac *m* à main. ◆**handbook** *n (manual)* manuel *m*; *(guide)* guide *m*. ◆**handbrake** *n* frein *m* à main. ◆**handbrush** *n* balayette *f*. ◆**handcuff** *vt* passer les menottes à. ◆**handcuffs** *npl* menottes *fpl*. ◆**hand'made** *a* fait à la main. ◆**hand'picked** *a Fig* trié sur le volet. ◆**handrail** *n (on stairs)* rampe *f*. ◆**handshake** *n* poignée *f* de main. ◆**handwriting** *n* écriture *f*. ◆**hand'written** *a* écrit à la main.

hand [hænd] *vt (give)* donner (**to** à); **to h. down** *(bring down)* descendre; *(knowledge, heirloom)* transmettre (**to** à); **to h. in** remettre; **to h. out** distribuer; **to h. over** remettre; *(power)* transmettre; **to h. round** *(cakes)* passer. ◆**handout** *n (leaflet)* prospectus *m*; *(money)* aumône *f*.

handful ['hændful] *n (bunch, group)* poignée *f*; **(quite) a h.** *(difficult) Fig* difficile.

handicap ['hændɪkæp] *n (disadvantage)* & *Sp* handicap *m*; – *vt (-pp-)* handicaper. ◆**handicapped** *a (disabled)* handicapé.

handicraft ['hændɪkrɑːft] *n* artisanat *m* d'art. ◆**handiwork** *n* artisanat *m* d'art; *(action) Fig* ouvrage *m*.

handkerchief ['hæŋkətʃɪf] *n (pl -fs)* mouchoir *m*; *(for neck)* foulard *m*.

handle ['hænd(ə)l] *n* **1** *(of door)* poignée *f*; *(of knife)* manche *m*; *(of bucket)* anse *f*; *(of saucepan)* queue *f*; *(of pump)* bras *m*. **2** *vt (manipulate)* manier; *(touch)* toucher à; *(ship, vehicle)* manœuvrer; *(deal with)* s'occuper de; *(difficult child etc)* s'y prendre avec; – *vi* **h. well** *(of machine)* être facile à manier.

handlebars ['hænd(ə)lbɑːz] *npl* guidon *m*.

handsome ['hænsəm] *a (person, building etc)* beau; *(gift)* généreux; *(profit, sum)* considérable. ◆**—ly** *adv (generously)* généreusement.

handy ['hændɪ] *a (-ier, -iest) (convenient, practical)* commode, pratique; *(skilful)* habile (**at doing** à faire); *(useful)* utile; *(near)* proche, accessible; **to come in h.** se révéler utile; **to keep h.** avoir sous la main. ◆**handyman** n (pl **-men**) (DIY enthusiast) bricoleur m.

hang¹ [hæŋ] **1** vt (pt & pp **hung**) suspendre (**on**, from à); (on hook) accrocher (**on**, from à); suspendre; (wallpaper) poser; (let dangle) laisser pendre (**from**, out of de); **to h. with** (decorate with) orner de; **to h. out** (washing) étendre; (flag) arborer; **to h. up** (picture etc) accrocher; – vi (dangle) pendre; (of threat) planer; (of fog, smoke) flotter; **to h. about** (loiter) traîner, rôder; (wait) Fam attendre; **to h. down** (dangle) pendre; (of hair) tomber; **to h. on** (hold out) résister; (wait) Fam attendre; **to h. on to** (cling to) ne pas lâcher; (keep) garder; **to h. out** (of tongue, shirt) pendre; (live) Sl crécher; **to h. together** (of facts) se tenir; (of plan) tenir debout; **to h. up** Tel raccrocher. **2** n **to get the h. of sth** Fam arriver à comprendre qch; **to get the h. of doing** Fam trouver le truc pour faire. ◆**—ing¹** n suspension f; – a suspendu (**from** à); (leg, arm) pendant; **h. on** (wall) accroché à. ◆**hang-glider** n delta-plane® m. ◆**hang-gliding** n vol m libre. ◆**hangnail** n petites peaux fpl. ◆**hangover** n Fam gueule f de bois. ◆**hangup** n Fam complexe m.

hang² [hæŋ] vt (pt & pp **hanged**) (criminal) pendre (**for** pour); – vi (of criminal) être pendu. ◆**—ing²** n Jur pendaison f. ◆**hangman** n (pl **-men**) bourreau m.

hangar ['hæŋər] n Av hangar m.

hanger ['hæŋər] n (coat) **h.** cintre m. ◆**hanger-'on** n (pl hangers-on) (person) Pej parasite m.

hanker ['hæŋkər] vi **to h. after** or **for** avoir envie de. ◆**—ing** n (forte) envie f, (vif) désir m.

hankie, hanky ['hæŋkɪ] n Fam mouchoir m.

hanky-panky ['hæŋkɪ'pæŋkɪ] n inv Fam (deceit) manigances fpl, magouilles fpl; (sexual behaviour) papouilles fpl, pelotage m.

haphazard [hæp'hæzəd] a au hasard, au petit bonheur; (selection, arrangement) aléatoire. ◆**—ly** adv au hasard.

hapless ['hæpləs] a Lit infortuné.

happen ['hæpən] vi arriver, se passer, se produire; **to h. to s.o./sth** arriver à qn/qch; **it (so) happens that I know, I h. to know** il se trouve que je le sais; **do you h. to have . . . ?** est-ce que par hasard vous avez . . . ?; **whatever happens** quoi qu'il arrive. ◆**—ing** n évènement m.

happy ['hæpɪ] a (-ier, -iest) heureux (**to do** de faire, **about sth** de qch); **I'm not (too** or **very) h. about (doing) it** ça ne me plaît pas beaucoup (de le faire); **H. New Year!** bonne année!; **H. Christmas!** joyeux Noël! ◆**h.-go-'lucky** a insouciant. ◆**happily** adv (contentedly) tranquillement; (joyously) joyeusement; (fortunately) heureusement. ◆**happiness** n bonheur m.

harass ['hærəs, Am hə'ræs] vt harceler. ◆**—ment** n harcèlement m.

harbour ['hɑːbər] **1** n port m. **2** vt (shelter) héberger; (criminal) cacher, abriter; (fear, secret) nourrir.

hard [hɑːd] a (-er, -est) (not soft, severe) dur; (difficult) difficile, dur; (study) assidu; (fact) brutal; (drink) alcoolisé; (water) calcaire; **h. drinker/worker** gros buveur m/travailleur m; **a h. frost** une forte gelée; **to be h. on** or **to s.o.** être dur avec qn; **to find it h. to sleep**/etc avoir du mal à dormir/etc; **h. labour** Jur travaux mpl forcés; **h. cash** espèces fpl; **h. core** (group) noyau m; **h. of hearing** malentendant; **h. up** (broke) Fam fauché; **to be h. up for** manquer de; – adv (-er, -est) (to work) dur; (to pull) fort; (to hit, freeze) dur, fort; (to study) assidûment; (to think) sérieusement; (to rain) à verse; (badly) mal; **h. by** tout près; **h. done by** traité injustement.

hard-and-fast [hɑːdən(d)'fɑːst] a (rule) strict. ◆**'hardback** n livre m relié. ◆**'hardboard** n Isorel® m. ◆**hard-'boiled** a (egg) dur. ◆**hard-'core** a (rigid) Pej inflexible. ◆**hard-'headed** a réaliste. ◆**hard-'wearing** a résistant. ◆**hard-'working** a travailleur.

harden ['hɑːd(ə)n] vti durcir; **to h. oneself to** s'endurcir à. ◆**—ed** a (criminal) endurci.

hardly ['hɑːdlɪ] adv à peine; **he h. talks** il parle à peine, il ne parle guère; **h. ever** presque jamais.

hardness ['hɑːdnɪs] n dureté f.

hardship ['hɑːdʃɪp] n (ordeal) épreuve(s) f(pl); (deprivation) privation(s) f(pl).

hardware ['hɑːdweər] n inv quincaillerie f; (of computer) & Mil matériel m.

hardy ['hɑːdɪ] a (-ier, -iest) (person, plant) résistant.

hare [heər] n lièvre m. ◆**h.-brained** a (person) écervelé; (scheme) insensé.

harem [hɑː'riːm] n harem m.

hark [hɑːk] vi Lit écouter; **to h. back to** (subject etc) Fam revenir sur.

harm [hɑːm] n (hurt) mal m; (prejudice) tort m; **he means (us) no h.** il ne nous veut pas de mal; **she'll come to no h.** il ne lui arrivera rien; – vt (hurt) faire du mal à; (prejudice)

nuire à, faire du tort à; (object) endommager, abîmer. ◆**harmful** a nuisible.
◆**harmless** a (person, treatment) inoffensif; (hobby, act) innocent; (gas, fumes etc) qui n'est pas nuisible, inoffensif.

harmonica [hɑːˈmɒnɪkə] n harmonica m.

harmony [ˈhɑːmənɪ] n harmonie f. ◆har'**monic** a & n Mus harmonique (m). ◆har'**monious** a harmonieux. ◆har'**monium** n Mus harmonium m. ◆**harmonize** vt harmoniser; – vi s'harmoniser.

harness [ˈhɑːnɪs] n (for horse, baby) harnais m; – vt (horse) harnacher; (energy etc) Fig exploiter.

harp [hɑːp] 1 n Mus harpe f. 2 vt to h. on (about) sth Fam rabâcher qch. ◆**harpist** n harpiste mf.

harpoon [hɑːˈpuːn] n harpon m; – vt (whale) harponner.

harpsichord [ˈhɑːpsɪkɔːd] n Mus clavecin m.

harrowing [ˈhærəʊɪŋ] a (tale, memory) poignant; (cry, sight) déchirant.

harsh [hɑːʃ] a (-er, -est) (severe) dur, sévère; (sound, taste) âpre; (surface) rugueux; (fabric) rêche. ◆**-ly** adv durement, sévèrement. ◆**-ness** n dureté f, sévérité f; âpreté f; rugosité f.

harvest [ˈhɑːvɪst] n moisson f, récolte f; (of people, objects) Fig ribambelle f; – vt moissonner, récolter.

has [hæz] see **have**. ◆**has-been** n Fam personne f finie.

hash [hæʃ] 1 n Culin hachis m; – vt to h. (up) hacher. 2 n (mess) Fam gâchis m. 3 n (hashish) Fam hasch m, H m.

hashish [ˈhæʃiːʃ] n haschisch m.

hassle [ˈhæs(ə)l] n Fam (trouble) histoires fpl; (bother) mal m, peine f.

haste [heɪst] n hâte f; in h. à la hâte; to make h. se hâter. ◆**hasten** vi se hâter (to do de faire); – vt hâter. ◆**hasty** a (-ier, -iest) (sudden) précipité; (visit) rapide; (decision, work) hâtif. ◆**hastily** adv (quickly) en hâte; (too quickly) hâtivement.

hat [hæt] n chapeau m; that's old h. Fam (old-fashioned) c'est vieux jeu; (stale) c'est vieux comme les rues; to score or get a h. trick Sp réussir trois coups consécutifs.

hatch [hætʃ] 1 vi (of chick, egg) éclore; – vt faire éclore; (plot) Fig tramer. 2 n (in kitchen wall) passe-plats m inv.

hatchback [ˈhætʃbæk] n (door) hayon m; (car) trois-portes f inv, cinq-portes f inv.

hatchet [ˈhætʃɪt] n hachette f.

hate [heɪt] vt détester, haïr; to h. doing or to

do détester faire; **I h.** to say it ça me gêne de le dire; – n haine f; **pet h.** Fam bête f noire. ◆**hateful** a haïssable. ◆**hatred** n haine f.

haughty [ˈhɔːtɪ] a (-ier, -iest) hautain. ◆**haughtily** adv avec hauteur.

haul [hɔːl] 1 vt (pull) tirer, traîner; (goods) camionner. 2 n (fish) prise f; (of thief) butin m; **a long h.** (trip) un long voyage. ◆**haulage** n camionnage m. ◆**hauler** n Am, ◆**haulier** n transporteur m routier.

haunt [hɔːnt] 1 vt hanter. 2 n endroit m favori; (of criminal) repaire m. ◆**-ing** a (music, memory) obsédant.

have [hæv] 1 (3rd person sing pres t **has**; pt & pp **had**; pres p **having**) vt avoir; (get) recevoir, avoir; (meal, shower etc) prendre; **he has got, he has** il a; **to h. a walk/dream/etc** faire une promenade/un rêve/etc; **to h. a drink** prendre or boire un verre; **to h. a wash** se laver; **to h. a holiday** (spend) passer des vacances; **will you h. . . . ?** (a cake, some tea etc) est-ce que tu veux . . . ?; **to let s.o. h. sth** donner qch à qn; **to h. it from s.o. that** tenir de qn que; **he had me by the hair** il me tenait par les cheveux; **I won't h. this** (allow) je ne tolérerai pas ça; **you've had it!** Fam tu es fichu!; **to h. on** (clothes) porter; **to have sth on** (be busy) être pris; **to h. s.o. over** inviter qn chez soi. 2 v aux avoir; (with monter, sortir etc & pronominal verbs) être; **to h. decided/been** avoir décidé/été; **to h. gone** être allé; **to h. cut oneself** s'être coupé; **I've just done it** je viens de le faire; **to h. to do** (must) devoir faire; **I've got to go, I h. to go** je dois partir, je suis obligé de partir, il faut que je parte; **I don't h. to go** je ne suis pas obligé de partir; **to h. sth done** (get sth done) faire faire qch; **he's had his suitcase brought up** il a fait monter sa valise; **I've had my car stolen** on m'a volé mon auto; **she's had her hair cut** elle s'est fait couper les cheveux; **I've been doing it for months** je le fais depuis des mois; **haven't I?, hasn't she?** etc n'est-ce pas?; **no I haven't!** non!; **yes I h.!** si!; **after he had eaten, he left** après avoir mangé, il partit. 3 npl **the haves and (the) have-nots** les riches mpl et les pauvres mpl.

haven [ˈheɪv(ə)n] n refuge m, havre m.

haversack [ˈhævəsæk] n (shoulder bag) musette f.

havoc [ˈhævək] n ravages mpl.

hawk [hɔːk] 1 n (bird) & Pol faucon m. 2 vt (goods) colporter. ◆**-er** n colporteur, -euse mf.

hawthorn [ˈhɔːθɔːn] n aubépine f.

hay [heɪ] *n* foin *m*; **h. fever** rhume *m* des foins. ◆**haystack** *n* meule *f* de foin.

haywire ['heɪwaɪər] *a* **to go h.** (*of machine*) se détraquer; (*of scheme, plan*) mal tourner.

hazard ['hæzəd] *n* risque *m*; **health h.** risque *m* pour la santé; **it's a fire h.** ça risque de provoquer un incendie; – *vt* (*guess, remark etc*) hasarder, risquer. ◆**hazardous** *a* hasardeux.

haze [heɪz] *n* brume *f*; **in a h.** (*person*) *Fig* dans le brouillard. ◆**hazy** *a* (**-ier, -iest**) (*weather*) brumeux; (*sun*) voilé; (*photo, idea*) flou; **I'm h. about my plans** je ne suis pas sûr de mes projets.

hazel ['heɪz(ə)l] *n* (*bush*) noisetier *m*; – *a* (*eyes*) noisette *inv*. ◆**hazelnut** *n* noisette *f*.

he [hiː] *pron* il; (*stressed*) lui; **he wants** il veut; **he's a happy man** c'est un homme heureux; **if I were he** si j'étais lui; **he and I** lui et moi; – *n* mâle *m*; **he-bear** ours *m* mâle.

head [hed] **1** *n* (*of person, hammer etc*) tête *f*; (*of page*) haut *m*; (*of bed*) chevet *m*, tête *f*; (*of arrow*) pointe *f*; (*of beer*) mousse *f*; (*leader*) chef *m*; (*subject heading*) rubrique *f*; **h. of hair** chevelure *f*; **h. cold** rhume *m* de cerveau; **it didn't enter my h.** ça ne m'est pas venu à l'esprit (*that* que); **to take it into one's h. to** se mettre en tête de faire; **the h.** *Sch* = **the headmaster**; = **the headmistress**; **to shout one's h. off** *Fam* crier à tue-tête; **to have a good h. for business** avoir le sens des affaires; **at the h. of** (*in charge of*) à la tête de; **at the h. of the table** au haut bout de la table; **at the h. of the list** en tête de liste; **it's above my h.** ça me dépasse; **to keep one's h.** garder son sang-froid; **to go off one's h.** devenir fou; **it's coming to a h.** (*of situation*) ça devient critique; **heads or tails?** pile ou face?; **per h., a h.** (*each*) par personne. **2** *a* principal; (*gardener*) en chef; **h. waiter** maître *m* d'hôtel; **a h. start** une grosse avance. **3** *vt* (*group, firm*) être à la tête de; (*list, poll*) être en tête de; (*vehicle*) diriger (*towards* vers); **to h. the ball** *Fb* faire une tête; **to h. off** (*person*) détourner de son chemin; (*prevent*) empêcher; **to be headed for** *Am* = **to h. for**; – *vi* **to h. for, to be heading for** (*place*) se diriger vers; (*ruin etc*) *Fig* aller à. ◆**-ed** *a* (*paper*) à en-tête. ◆**-ing** *n* (*of chapter, page etc*) titre *m*; (*of subject*) rubrique *f*; (*printed on letter etc*) en-tête *m*. ◆**-er** *n* *Fb* coup *m* de tête.

headache ['hedeɪk] *n* mal *m* de tête; (*difficulty, person*) *Fig* problème *m*. ◆**head-dress** *n* (*ornamental*) coiffe *f*.

◆**headlamp** *n*, ◆**headlight** *n* *Aut* phare *m*. ◆**headline** *n* (*of newspaper*) manchette *f*; *pl* (gros) titres *mpl*; *Rad TV* (grands) titres *mpl*. ◆**headlong** *adv* (*to fall*) la tête la première; (*to rush*) tête baissée. ◆**head'master** *n* *Sch* directeur *m*; (*of lycée*) proviseur *m*. ◆**head'mistress** *n* *Sch* directrice *f*; (*of lycée*) proviseur *m*. ◆**head-'on** *adv* & *a* (*to collide, collision*) de plein fouet. ◆**headphones** *npl* casque *m* (à écouteurs). ◆**headquarters** *npl* *Com Pol* siège *m* (central); *Mil* quartier *m* général. ◆**headrest** *n* appuie-tête *m inv*. ◆**headscarf** *n* (*pl* **-scarves**) foulard *m*. ◆**headstrong** *a* têtu. ◆**headway** *n* progrès *mpl*.

heady ['hedɪ] *a* (**-ier, -iest**) (*wine etc*) capiteux; (*action, speech*) emporté.

heal [hiːl] *vi* **h. (up)** (*of wound*) se cicatriser; – *vt* (*wound*) cicatriser, guérir; (*person, sorrow*) guérir. ◆**-er** *n* guérisseur, -euse *mf*.

health [helθ] *n* santé *f*; **h. food** aliment *m* naturel; **h. food shop** *or* *Am* **store** magasin *m* diététique; **h. resort** station *f* climatique; **the H. Service** = la Sécurité Sociale. ◆**healthful** *a* (*climate*) sain. ◆**healthy** *a* (**-ier, -iest**) (*person*) en bonne santé, sain; (*food, attitude etc*) sain; (*appetite*) bon, robuste.

heap [hiːp] *n* tas *m*; **heaps of** *Fam* des tas de; **to have heaps of time** *Fam* avoir largement le temps; – *vt* entasser, empiler; **to h. on s.o.** (*gifts, praise*) couvrir qn de; (*work*) accabler qn de. ◆**-ed** *a* **h. spoonful** grosse cuillerée *f*. ◆**-ing** *a* **h. spoonful** *Am* grosse cuillerée *f*.

hear [hɪər] *vt* (*pt & pp* **heard** [hɜːd]) entendre; (*listen to*) écouter; (*learn*) apprendre (*that* que); **I heard him coming** je l'ai entendu venir; **to h. it said that** entendre dire que; **have you heard the news?** connais-tu la nouvelle?; **I've heard that . . .** on m'a dit que . . . ; j'ai appris que . . . ; **h. out** écouter jusqu'au bout; **h.,** **h.!** bravo!; – *vi* entendre; (*get news*) recevoir *or* avoir des nouvelles (*from* de); **I've heard of** *or* **about him** j'ai entendu parler de lui; **she wouldn't h. of it** elle ne voulait pas en entendre parler; **I wouldn't h. of it!** pas question! ◆**-ing** *n* (*sense*) ouïe *f*; *Jur* audition *f*; **h. aid** appareil *m* auditif. ◆**hearsay** *n* ouï-dire *m inv*.

hearse [hɜːs] *n* corbillard *m*.

heart [hɑːt] *n* cœur *m*; *pl* *Cards* cœur *m*; (*off*) **by h.** par cœur; **to lose h.** perdre courage; **to one's h.'s content** tout son

saoul or content; **at h.** au fond; **his h. is set
on it** il le veut à tout prix, il y tient; **his h. is
set on doing it** il veut le faire à tout prix, il
tient à le faire; **h. disease** maladie f de
cœur; **h. attack** crise f cardiaque.
◆**heartache** n chagrin m. ◆**heartbeat** n
battement m de cœur. ◆**heartbreaking** a
navrant. ◆**heartbroken** a navré, au cœur
brisé. ◆**heartburn** n Med brûlures fpl
d'estomac. ◆**heartthrob** n (man) Fam
idole f.

hearten ['hɑːt(ə)n] vt encourager. ◆**–ing** a
encourageant.

hearth [hɑːθ] n foyer m.

hearty ['hɑːtɪ] a (**-ier, -iest**) (meal, appetite)
gros. ◆**heartily** adv (to eat) avec appétit;
(to laugh) de tout son cœur; (absolutely)
absolument.

heat [hiːt] **1** n chaleur f; (of oven) température f; (heating) chauffage m; **in the h. of**
(argument etc) dans le feu de; (the day) au
plus chaud de; **at low h., on a low h.** Culin à
feu doux; **h. wave** vague f de chaleur; – vti
to h. (up) chauffer. **2** n (in race, competition)
éliminatoire f; **it was a dead h.** ils sont
arrivés ex aequo. ◆**–ed** a (swimming
pool) chauffé; (argument) passionné.
◆**–edly** adv avec passion. ◆**–ing** n
chauffage m. ◆**–er** n radiateur m, appareil
m de chauffage; **water h.** chauffe-eau m inv.

heath [hiːθ] n (place, land) lande f.

heathen ['hiːð(ə)n] a & n païen, -enne (mf).

heather ['heðər] n (plant) bruyère f.

heave [hiːv] vt (lift) soulever; (pull) tirer;
(drag) traîner; (throw) Fam lancer; (a sigh)
pousser; – vi (of stomach, chest) se
soulever; (retch) Fam avoir des
haut-le-cœur; – n (effort) effort m (pour
soulever etc).

heaven ['hev(ə)n] n ciel m, paradis m; **h.
knows when** Fam Dieu sait quand; **good
heavens!** Fam mon Dieu!; **it was h.** Fam
c'était divin. ◆**–ly** a céleste; (pleasing)
Fam divin.

heavy ['hevɪ] a (**-ier, -iest**) lourd; (weight etc)
lourd, pesant; (work, cold etc) gros; (blow)
violent; (concentration, rain) fort; (traffic)
dense; (smoker, drinker) grand; (film, text)
difficile; **a h. day** une journée chargée; **h.
casualties** de nombreuses victimes; **to be h.
on petrol** or Am **gas** Aut consommer
beaucoup; **it's h. going** c'est difficile.
◆**heavily** adv (to walk, tax etc) lourdement; (to breathe) péniblement; (to smoke,
drink) beaucoup; (underlined) fortement;
(involved) très; **to rain h.** pleuvoir à verse.
◆**heaviness** n pesanteur f, lourdeur f.

◆**heavyweight** n Boxing poids m lourd;
Fig personnage m important.

Hebrew ['hiːbruː] a hébreu (m only),
hébraïque; – n (language) hébreu m.

heck [hek] int Fam zut!; – n = **hell** in
expressions.

heckl/e ['hek(ə)l] vt interpeller, interrompre. ◆**–ing** n interpellations fpl. ◆**–er** n
interpellateur, -trice mf.

hectic ['hektɪk] a (activity) fiévreux;
(period) très agité; (trip) mouvementé; **h.
life** vie f trépidante.

hedge [hedʒ] **1** n Bot haie f. **2** vi (answer
evasively) ne pas se mouiller, éviter de se
compromettre. ◆**hedgerow** n Bot haie f.

hedgehog ['hedʒhɒg] n (animal) hérisson
m.

heed [hiːd] vt faire attention à; – n to pay h.
to faire attention à. ◆**–less** a h. of
(danger etc) inattentif à.

heel [hiːl] n **1** talon m; **down at h.,** Am down
at the heels (shabby) miteux; **h. bar** cordonnerie f express; (on sign) 'talon minute'. **2**
(person) Am Fam salaud m.

hefty ['heftɪ] a (**-ier, -iest**) (large, heavy) gros;
(person) costaud.

heifer ['hefər] n (cow) génisse f.

height [haɪt] n hauteur f; (of person) taille f;
(of mountain) altitude f; **the h. of** (glory,
success, fame) le sommet de, l'apogée m de;
(folly, pain) le comble de; **at the h. of**
(summer, storm) au cœur de. ◆**heighten**
vt (raise) rehausser; (tension, interest) Fig
augmenter.

heinous ['heɪnəs] a (crime etc) atroce.

heir [eər] n héritier m. ◆**heiress** n héritière
f. ◆**heirloom** n héritage m, bijou m ou
meuble m de famille.

heist [haɪst] n Am Sl hold-up m inv.

held [held] see hold.

helicopter ['helɪkɒptər] n hélicoptère m.
◆**heliport** n héliport m.

hell [hel] n enfer m; **a h. of a lot** (very much)
Fam énormément, vachement; **a h. of a lot
of** (very many, very much) Fam énormément de; **a h. of a nice guy** Fam un type
super; **what the h. are you doing?** Fam
qu'est-ce que tu fous?; **to h. with him** Fam
qu'il aille se faire voir!; **h.!** Fam zut!; **to be
h.-bent on** Fam être acharné à. ◆**hellish** a
diabolique.

hello! [hə'ləʊ] int = hallo.

helm [helm] n Nau barre f.

helmet ['helmɪt] n casque m.

help [help] n aide f, secours m; (cleaning
woman) femme f de ménage; (office or shop
workers) employés, -ées mfpl; **with the h. of**

(*stick etc*) à l'aide de; **to cry** or **shout for h.** crier au secours; **h.!** au secours!; – *vt* aider (**do, to do** à faire); **to h. s.o. to soup**/*etc* (*serve*) servir du potage/*etc* à qn; **to h. out** aider; **to h. up** aider à monter; **to h. oneself** se servir (**to** de); **I can't h. laughing**/*etc* je ne peux m'empêcher de rire/*etc*; **he can't h. being blind**/*etc* ce n'est pas sa faute s'il est aveugle/*etc*; **it can't be helped** on n'y peut rien; – *vi* to h. (out) aider. ◆–**ing** *n* (*serving*) portion *f*. ◆–**er** *n* assistant, -ante *mf*. ◆**helpful** *a* (*useful*) utile; (*obliging*) serviable. ◆**helpless** *a* (*powerless*) impuissant; (*baby*) désarmé; (*disabled*) impotent. ◆**helplessly** *adv* (*to struggle*) en vain.

helter-skelter [heltə'skeltər] **1** *adv* à la débandade. **2** *n* (*slide*) toboggan *m*.

hem [hem] *n* ourlet *m*; – *vt* (**-mm-**) (*garment*) ourler; **to h. in** *Fig* enfermer, cerner.

hemisphere ['hemisfiər] *n* hémisphère *m*.

hemorrhage ['hemərɪdʒ] *n Med* hémorragie *f*.

hemorrhoids ['hemərɔɪdz] *npl* hémorroïdes *fpl*.

hemp [hemp] *n* chanvre *m*.

hen [hen] *n* poule *f*; **h.'s bird** oiseau *m* femelle. ◆**henpecked** *a* (*husband*) harcelé or dominé par sa femme.

hence [hens] *adv* **1** (*therefore*) d'où. **2** (*from now*) **ten years**/*etc* d'ici dix ans/*etc*. ◆**henceforth** *adv* désormais.

henchman ['hentʃmən] *n* (*pl* **-men**) *Pej* acolyte *m*.

hepatitis [hepə'taɪtɪs] *n* hépatite *f*.

her [hɜːr] **1** *pron* la, l'; (*after prep etc*) elle; (**to) h.** (*indirect*) lui; **I see h.** je la vois; **I saw h.** je l'ai vue; **I give** (**to**) **h.** je lui donne; **with h.** avec elle. **2** *poss a* son, sa, *pl* ses.

herald ['herəld] *vt* annoncer.

heraldry ['herəldrɪ] *n* héraldique *f*.

herb [hɜːb, *Am* ɜːb] *n* herbe *f*; *pl Culin* fines herbes *fpl*. ◆**herbal** *a* **h. tea** infusion *f* (d'herbes).

Hercules ['hɜːkjʊliːz] *n* (*strong man*) hercule *m*.

herd [hɜːd] *n* troupeau *m*; – *vti* **to h. together** (se) rassembler (en troupeau).

here [hɪər] **1** *adv* ici; (*then*) alors; **h. is, h. are** voici; **h. he is** le voici; **h. she is** la voici; **this man h.** cet homme-ci; **I won't be h. tomorrow** je ne serai pas là demain; **h. and there** çà et là; **h. you are!** (*take this*) tenez!; **h.'s to you!** (*toast*) à ta tienne! **2** *int* (*calling s.o.'s attention*) holà!, écoutez!; (*giving s.o. sth*) tenez! ◆**herea'bouts** *adv* par ici. ◆**here-**

'after *adv* après; (*in book*) ci-après. ◆**here'by** *adv* (*to declare*) par le présent acte. ◆**here'with** *adv* (*with letter*) *Com* ci-joint.

heredity [hɪ'redɪtɪ] *n* hérédité *f*. ◆**hereditary** *a* héréditaire.

heresy ['herəsɪ] *n* hérésie *f*. ◆**heretic** *n* hérétique *mf*. ◆**he'retical** *a* hérétique.

heritage ['herɪtɪdʒ] *n* héritage *m*.

hermetically [hɜː'metɪklɪ] *adv* hermétiquement.

hermit ['hɜːmɪt] *n* solitaire *mf*, ermite *m*.

hernia ['hɜːnɪə] *n Med* hernie *f*.

hero ['hɪərəʊ] *n* (*pl* **-oes**) héros *m*. ◆**he'roic** *a* héroïque. ◆**he'roics** *npl Pej* grandiloquence *f*. ◆**heroine** ['herəʊɪn] *n* héroïne *f*. ◆**heroism** ['herəʊɪz(ə)m] *n* héroïsme *m*.

heroin ['herəʊɪn] *n* (*drug*) héroïne *f*.

heron ['herən] *n* (*bird*) héron *m*.

herring ['herɪŋ] *n* hareng *m*; **a red h.** *Fig* une diversion.

hers [hɜːz] *poss pron* le sien, la sienne, *pl* les sien(ne)s; **this hat is h.** ce chapeau est à elle or est le sien; **a friend of h.** une amie à elle.

her'self *pron* elle-même; (*reflexive*) se, s'; (*after prep*) elle; **she cut h.** elle s'est coupée; **she thinks of h.** elle pense à elle.

hesitate ['hezɪteɪt] *vi* hésiter (**over, about** sur; **to do** à faire). ◆**hesitant** *a* hésitant. ◆**hesitantly** *adv* avec hésitation. ◆**hesi'tation** *n* hésitation *f*.

hessian ['hesɪən] *n* toile *f* de jute.

heterogeneous [het(ə)rəʊ'dʒiːnɪəs] *a* hétérogène.

het up [het'ʌp] *a Fam* énervé.

hew [hjuː] *vt* (*pp* **hewn** or **hewed**) tailler.

hexagon ['heksəgən] *n* hexagone *m*. ◆**hex'agonal** *a* hexagonal.

hey! [heɪ] *int* hé!, holà!

heyday ['heɪdeɪ] *n* (*of person*) apogée *m*, zénith *m*; (*of thing*) âge *m* d'or.

hi! [haɪ] *int Am Fam* salut!

hiatus [haɪ'eɪtəs] *n* (*gap*) hiatus *m*.

hibernate ['haɪbəneɪt] *vi* hiberner. ◆**hiber-'nation** *n* hibernation *f*.

hiccough, hiccup ['hɪkʌp] *n* hoquet *m*; (**the**) **hiccoughs, (the) hiccups** le hoquet; – *vi* hoqueter.

hick [hɪk] *n* (*peasant*) *Am Sl Pej* plouc *mf*.

hide¹ [haɪd] *vt* (*pt* **hid**, *pp* **hidden**) cacher, dissimuler (**from** à); – *vi* to h. (away or out) se cacher (**from** de). ◆**h.-and-'seek** *n* cache-cache *m inv*. ◆**h.-out** *n* cachette *f*. ◆**hiding 1** *n* **to go into h.** se cacher; **h. place** cachette *f*. **2** *a* **good h.** (*thrashing*) *Fam* une bonne volée or correction.

hide² [haɪd] n (skin) peau f.

hideous ['hɪdɪəs] a horrible; (person, sight, crime) hideux. ◆**-ly** adv (badly, very) horriblement.

hierarchy ['haɪərɑːkɪ] n hiérarchie f.

hi-fi ['haɪfaɪ] n hi-fi f inv; (system) chaîne f hi-fi; – a hi-fi inv.

high [haɪ] a (-er, -est) haut; (speed) grand; (price) élevé; (fever) fort, gros; (colour, complexion) vif; (idea, number) grand, élevé; (meat, game) faisandé; (on drugs) Fam défoncé; **to be five metres h.** être haut de cinq mètres, avoir cinq mètres de haut; **it is h. time that** il est grand temps que (+ sub); **h. jump** Sp saut m en hauteur; **h. noon** plein midi m; **h.** = **college** m d'enseignement secondaire; **h. spirits** entrain m; **h. spot** (of visit, day) point m culminant; (of show) clou m; **h. street** grand-rue f; **h. summer** le cœur de l'été; **h. table** table f d'honneur; **h. and mighty** arrogant; **to leave s.o. h. and dry** Fam laisser qn en plan; – adv **h. (up)** (fly, throw etc) haut; **to aim h.** viser haut; – n **on h.** en haut; **a new h., an all-time h.** (peak) Fig un nouveau record. ◆**-er** a supérieur (than à). ◆**-ly** adv hautement, fortement; (interesting) très; (paid) très bien; (to recommend) chaudement; **to speak h. of** dire beaucoup de bien de; **h. strung** nerveux. ◆**-ness** n H. (title) Altesse f.

highbrow ['haɪbraʊ] a & n intellectuel, -elle (mf).

high-chair ['haɪtʃeər] n chaise f haute. ◆**h.-'class** a (service) de premier ordre; (building) de luxe; (person) raffiné. ◆**h.-'flown** a (language) ampoulé. ◆**h.-'handed** a tyrannique. ◆**h.-'minded** a à l'âme noble. ◆**h.-'pitched** a (sound) aigu. ◆**h.-'powered** a (person) très dynamique. ◆**h.-rise** a **h.-rise flats** tour f. ◆**h.-'speed** a ultra-rapide. ◆**h.-'strung** a Am nerveux. ◆**h.-'up** a (person) haut placé.

highlands ['haɪləndz] npl régions fpl montagneuses.

highlight ['haɪlaɪt] n (of visit, day) point m culminant; (of show) clou m; (in hair) reflet m; – vt souligner.

highroad ['haɪrəʊd] n grand-route f.

highway ['haɪweɪ] n grande route f; Am autoroute f; **public h.** voie f publique; **h. code** code m de la route.

hijack ['haɪdʒæk] vt (aircraft, vehicle) détourner. ◆**-ing** n

détournement m. ◆**-er** n Av pirate m de l'air.

hik/e [haɪk] 1 n excursion f à pied; – vi marcher à pied. 2 vt (price) Am Fam augmenter; – n Am Fam hausse f. ◆**-er** n excursionniste f.

hilarious [hɪ'leərɪəs] a (funny) désopilant.

hill [hɪl] n colline f; (small) coteau m; (slope) pente f. ◆**hillbilly** n Am Fam péquenaud, -aude mf. ◆**hillside** n coteau m; **on the h.** à flanc de coteau. ◆**hilly** a (-ier, -iest) accidenté.

hilt [hɪlt] n (of sword) poignée f; **to the h.** Fig au maximum.

him [hɪm] pron le, l'; (after prep etc) lui; **(to) h.** (indirect) lui; **I see h.** je le vois; **I saw h.** je l'ai vu; **I give (to) h.** je lui donne; **with h.** avec lui. ◆**him'self** pron lui-même; (reflexive) se, s'; (after prep) lui; **he cut h.** il s'est coupé; **he thinks of h.** il pense à lui.

hind [haɪnd] a de derrière, postérieur. ◆**hindquarters** npl arrière-train m.

hinder ['hɪndər] vt (obstruct) gêner; (prevent) empêcher (**from doing** de faire). ◆**hindrance** n gêne f.

hindsight ['haɪndsaɪt] n **with h.** rétrospectivement.

Hindu ['hɪnduː] a & n hindou, -oue (mf).

hing/e [hɪndʒ] 1 n (of box, stamp) charnière f; (of door) gond m, charnière f. 2 vi **to h. on** (depend on) dépendre de. ◆**-ed** a à charnière(s).

hint [hɪnt] n indication f; (insinuation) allusion f; (trace) trace f; (advice) conseils mpl; **to drop a h.** faire une allusion; – vt laisser entendre (**that** que); – vi **to h. at** faire allusion à.

hip [hɪp] n Anat hanche f.

hippie ['hɪpɪ] n hippie mf.

hippopotamus [hɪpə'pɒtəməs] n hippopotame m.

hire ['haɪər] vt (vehicle etc) louer; (person) engager; **to h. out** donner en location, louer; – n location f; (of boat, horse) louage m; **for h.** à louer; **on h.** en location; **h. purchase** vente f à crédit, location-vente f; **on h. purchase** à crédit.

his [hɪz] 1 poss a son, sa, pl ses. 2 poss pron le sien, la sienne, pl les sien(ne)s; **this hat is h.** ce chapeau est à lui or est le sien; **a friend of h.** un ami à lui.

Hispanic [hɪs'pænɪk] a & n Am hispano-américain, -aine (mf).

hiss [hɪs] vti siffler; – n sifflement m; pl Th sifflets mpl. ◆**-ing** n sifflement(s) m(pl).

history ['hɪstərɪ] n (study, events) histoire f; **it will make h.** or **go down in h.** ça va faire date; **your medical h.** vos antécédents médicaux. ◆**hi'storian** n historien, -ienne mf. ◆**hi'storic(al)** a historique.

histrionic [histrɪ'ɒnɪk] a Pej théâtral; – npl attitudes fpl théâtrales.

hit [hɪt] vti (pt & pp hit, pres p hitting) (strike) frapper; (knock against) & Aut heurter; (reach) atteindre; (affect) toucher, affecter; (find) trouver, rencontrer; **to h. the head-lines** Fam faire les gros titres; **to h. back** rendre coup pour coup; (verbally, militarily etc) riposter; **to h. it off** Fam s'entendre bien (with avec); **to h. out (at)** Fam attaquer; **to h. (up)on** (find) tomber sur; – n (blow) coup m; (success) coup m réussi; Th succès m; h. (song) chanson f à succès; **to make a h. with** Fam avoir un succès avec; **h.-and-run driver** chauffard m (qui prend la fuite). ◆**h.-or-'miss** a (chancy, random) aléatoire.

hitch [hɪtʃ] **1** n (snag) anicroche f, os m, problème m. **2** vt (fasten) accrocher (**to** à). **3** vti **to h. (a lift or a ride)** Fam faire du stop (**to** jusqu'à). ◆**hitchhike** vi faire de l'auto-stop (**to** jusqu'à). ◆**hitchhiking** n auto-stop m. ◆**hitchhiker** n auto-stoppeur, -euse mf.

hitherto [hɪðə'tuː] adv jusqu'ici.

hive [haɪv] **1** n ruche f. **2** vt **to h. off** (industry) dénationaliser.

hoard [hɔːd] n réserve f; (of money) trésor m; – vt amasser. ◆—**ing** n (fence) panneau m d'affichage.

hoarfrost ['hɔːfrɒst] n givre m.

hoarse [hɔːs] a (-er, -est) (person, voice) enroué. ◆—**ness** n enrouement m.

hoax [həʊks] n canular m; – vt faire un canular à, mystifier.

hob [hɒb] n (on stove) plaque f chauffante.

hobble ['hɒb(ə)l] vi (walk) clopiner.

hobby ['hɒbɪ] n passe-temps m inv; **my h.** mon passe-temps favori. ◆**hobbyhorse** n (favourite subject) dada m.

hobnob ['hɒbnɒb] vi (-bb-) **to h. with** frayer avec.

hobo ['həʊbəʊ] n (pl -oes or -os) Am vagabond m.

hock [hɒk] vt (pawn) Fam mettre au clou; – n **in h.** Fam au clou.

hockey ['hɒkɪ] n hockey m; **ice h.** hockey sur glace.

hocus-pocus [həʊkəs'pəʊkəs] n (talk) charabia m; (deception) tromperie f.

hodgepodge ['hɒdʒpɒdʒ] n fatras m.

hoe [həʊ] n binette f, houe f; – vt biner.

hog [hɒg] **1** n (pig) cochon m, porc m; **road h.** Fig chauffard m. **2** n **to go the whole h.**

Fam aller jusqu'au bout. **3** vt (-gg-) Fam monopoliser, garder pour soi.

hoist [hɔɪst] vt hisser; – n Tech palan m.

hold [həʊld] n (grip) prise f; (of ship) cale f; (of aircraft) soute f; **to get h. of** (grab) saisir; (contact) joindre; (find) trouver; **to get a h. of oneself** se maîtriser; – vt (pt & pp held) tenir; (breath, interest, heat, attention) retenir; (a post) occuper; (a record) posséder; (contain) contenir; (maintain, believe) maintenir (that que); (ceremony, mass) célébrer; (keep) garder; **to h. hands** se tenir par la main; **to h. one's own** se débrouiller; (of sick person) se maintenir; **h. the line!** Tel ne quittez pas!; **h. it!** (stay still) ne bouge pas!; **to be held** (of event) avoir lieu; **to h. back** (crowd, tears) contenir; (hide) cacher (from à); **to h. down** (job) occuper; (keep) garder; (person on ground) maintenir au sol; **to h. in** (stomach) rentrer; **to h. off** (enemy) tenir à distance; **to h. on** (keep in place) tenir en place (son chapeau etc); **to h. out** (offer) offrir; (arm) étendre; **to h. over** (postpone) remettre; **to h. together** (nation, group) assurer l'union de; **to h. up** (raise) lever; (support) soutenir; (delay) retarder; (bank) attaquer (à main armée); – vi (of nail, rope) tenir; (of weather) se maintenir; **to h. (good)** (of argument) valoir (for pour); **to h. forth** (talk) Pej disserter; **if the rain holds off** s'il ne pleut pas; **to h. on** (endure) tenir bon; (wait) attendre; **h. on!** Tel ne quittez pas!; **to h. onto** (cling to) tenir bon; (keep) garder; **h. on (tight)!** tenez bon!; **to h. out** (resist) résister; (last) durer. ◆**holdall** n (bag) fourre-tout m inv. ◆**holdup** n (attack) hold-up m inv; (traffic jam) bouchon m; (delay) retard m.

holder ['həʊldər] n (of post, passport) titulaire mf; (of record, card) détenteur, -trice mf; (container) support m.

holdings ['həʊldɪŋz] npl Fin possessions fpl.

hole [həʊl] n trou m; (town etc) Fam bled m, trou m; (room) Fam baraque f; – vt trouer; – vi **to h. up** (hide) Fam se terrer.

holiday ['hɒlɪdeɪ] n (rest) vacances fpl; **holiday(s)** (from work, school etc) vacances fpl; **a h.** (day off) un congé; **a (public or bank) h.,** Am **a legal h.** un jour férié; **on h.** en vacances; **holidays with pay** congés mpl payés; – a (camp, clothes etc) de vacances; **in h. mood** d'humeur folâtre. ◆**holiday-maker** n vacancier, -ière mf.

holiness ['həʊlɪnəs] n sainteté f.

Holland ['hɒlənd] n Hollande f.

hollow ['hɒləu] *a* creux; (*victory*) faux; (*promise*) vain; – *n* creux *m*; – *vt* **to h. out** creuser.

holly ['hɒlɪ] *n* houx *m*.

holocaust ['hɒləkɔːst] *n* (*massacre*) holocauste *m*.

holster ['həulstər] *n* étui *m* de revolver.

holy ['həulɪ] *a* (-ier, -iest) saint; (*bread, water*) bénit; (*ground*) sacré.

homage ['hɒmɪdʒ] *n* hommage *m*.

home[1] [həum] *n* maison *f*; (*country*) pays *m* (natal); (*for soldiers*) foyer *m*; **(at) h.** à la maison, chez soi; **to feel at h.** se sentir à l'aise; **to play at h.** Fb jouer à domicile; **far from h.** loin de chez soi; **a broken h.** un foyer désuni; **a good h.** une bonne famille; **to make one's h. in** s'installer à; **my h. is here** j'habite ici; – *adv* à la maison, chez soi; **to go** *or* **come h.** rentrer; **to be h.** rentré; **to drive h.** ramener (qn) (en voiture); (*nail*) enfoncer; **to bring sth h. to s.o.** Fig faire voir qch à qn; (*a life, pleasures etc*) de famille; Pol national; (*cooking, help*) familial; (*visit, match*) à domicile. **h. economics** économie *f* domestique; **h. town** (*birth place*) ville *f* natale; **h. rule** Pol autonomie *f*; **H. Office** = ministère *m* de l'Intérieur; **H. Secretary** = ministre *m* de l'Intérieur. ◆**homecoming** *n* retour *m* au foyer. ◆**home′grown** *a* Bot du jardin; Pol du pays. ◆**homeland** *n* patrie *f*. ◆**homeloving** *a* casanier. ◆**home′made** *a* (fait à la) maison *inv*. ◆**homework** *n* Sch devoir(s) *m(pl)*.

home[2] [həum] *vi* **to h. in on** se diriger automatiquement sur.

homeless ['həumlɪs] *a* sans abri; – *n* **the h.** les sans-abri *m inv*.

homely ['həumlɪ] *a* (-ier, -iest) (*simple*) simple; (*comfortable*) accueillant; (*ugly*) Am laid.

homesick ['həumsɪk] *a* nostalgique; **to be h.** avoir le mal du pays. ◆**-ness** *n* nostalgie *f*, mal *m* du pays.

homeward ['həumwəd] *a* (*trip*) de retour; – *adv* **h. bound** sur le chemin de retour.

homey ['həumɪ] *a* (-ier, -iest) Am Fam accueillant.

homicide ['hɒmɪsaɪd] *n* homicide *m*.

homily ['hɒmɪlɪ] *n* homélie *f*.

homogeneous [həumə′dʒiːnɪəs] *a* homogène.

homosexual [həumə′seksjuəl] *a* & *n* homosexuel, -elle (*mf*). ◆**homosexu′ality** *n* homosexualité *f*.

honest ['ɒnɪst] *a* honnête; (*frank*) franc (*with* avec); (*profit, money*) honnêtement gagné; **the h. truth** la pure vérité; **to be (quite) h.** ... pour être franc .... ◆**honesty** *n* honnêteté *f*; franchise *f*; (*of report, text*) exactitude *f*.

honey ['hʌnɪ] *n* miel *m*; (*person*) Fam chéri, -ie *mf*. ◆**honeycomb** *n* rayon *m* de miel. ◆**honeymoon** *n* (*occasion*) lune *f* de miel; (*trip*) voyage *m* de noces. ◆**honeysuckle** *n* Bot chèvrefeuille *m*.

honk [hɒŋk] *n* Aut klaxonner; – *n* coup *m* de klaxon®.

honour ['ɒnər] *n* honneur *m*; **in h. of** en l'honneur de; **an honours degree** Univ = une licence; – *vt* honorer (**with** de). ◆**honorary** *a* (*member*) honoraire; (*title*) honorifique. ◆**honourable** *a* honorable.

hood [hud] *n* **1** capuchon *m*; (*mask of robber*) cagoule *f*; (*soft car or pram roof*) capote *f*; (*bonnet*) Aut capot *m*; (*above stove*) hotte *f*. **2** (*hoodlum*) Am Sl gangster *m*. ◆**hooded** *a* (*person*) encapuchonné; (*coat*) à capuchon.

hoodlum ['huːdləm] *n* Fam (*hooligan*) voyou *m*; (*gangster*) gangster *m*.

hoodwink ['hudwɪŋk] *vt* tromper, duper.

hoof, *pl* **-fs, -ves** [huf, -fs, -vz] (*Am* [huf, -fs, huvz]) *n* sabot *m*.

hoo-ha ['huːhɑː] *n* Fam tumulte *m*.

hook [huk] *n* crochet *m*; (*on clothes*) agrafe *f*; Fishing hameçon *m*; **off the h.** (*phone*) décroché; **to let** *or* **get s.o. off the h.** tirer qn d'affaire; – *vt* **to h.** (**on** *or* **up**) accrocher (**to** à). ◆**-ed** *a* (*nose, beak*) recourbé; (*person*) entiché (**on** de); Fam (*chess etc*) enragé de; (*person*) entiché de; **to be h. on drugs** Fam ne plus pouvoir se passer de la drogue. ◆**-er** *n* Am Sl prostituée *f*.

hook(e)y ['hukɪ] *n* **to play h.** Am Fam faire l'école buissonnière.

hooligan ['huːlɪgən] *n* vandale *m*, voyou *m*. ◆**hooliganism** *n* vandalisme *m*.

hoop [huːp] *n* cerceau *m*; (*of barrel*) cercle *m*.

hoot [huːt] **1** *vi* Aut klaxonner; (*of train*) siffler; (*of owl*) hululer; – *n* Aut coup *m* de klaxon®. **2** *vti* (*jeer*) huer; – *n* huée *f*. ◆**-er** *n* Aut klaxon®·m; (*of factory*) sirène *f*.

hoover® ['huːvər] *n* aspirateur *m*; – *vt* Fam passer à l'aspirateur.

hop [hɒp] *vi* (-pp-) (*of person*) sauter (à cloche-pied); (*of animal*) sauter; (*of bird*) sautiller; **h. it!** (*in car*) montez!; **to h. on a bus** monter dans un autobus; **to h. on a plane** attraper un vol; – *vt* **h. it!** Fam fiche le camp!; – *n* (*leap*) saut *m*; Av étape *f*.

hope [həup] *n* espoir *m*, espérance *f*; – *vi*

espérer; **to h. for** (*desire*) espérer; (*expect*) attendre; **I h. so/not** j'espère que oui/non; – *vt* espérer (**to do** faire, **that** que). ◆**hopeful** *a* (*person*) optimiste, plein d'espoir; (*promising*) prometteur; (*encouraging*) encourageant; **to be h. that** avoir bon espoir que. ◆**hopefully** *adv* avec optimisme; (*one hopes*) on espère (que). ◆**hopeless** *a* désespéré, sans espoir; (*useless, bad*) nul; (*liar*) invétéré. ◆**hopelessly** *adv* sans espoir; (*extremely*) complètement; (*in love*) éperdument.

hops [hɒps] *npl Bot* houblon *m*.

hopscotch ['hɒpskɒtʃ] *n* (*game*) marelle *f*.

horde [hɔːd] *n* horde *f*, foule *f*.

horizon [həˈraɪz(ə)n] *n* horizon *m*; **on the h.** à l'horizon.

horizontal [hɒrɪˈzɒnt(ə)l] *a* horizontal. ◆**—ly** *adv* horizontalement.

hormone ['hɔːməʊn] *n* hormone *f*.

horn [hɔːn] *1 n* (*of animal*) corne *f*; *Mus* cor *m*; *Aut* klaxon® *m*. *2 vi* **to h. in** *Am Fam* dire son mot, interrompre.

hornet ['hɔːnɪt] *n* (*insect*) frelon *m*.

horoscope ['hɒrəskəʊp] *n* horoscope *m*.

horror ['hɒrər] *n* horreur *f*; (*little*) **h.** (*child*) *Fam* petit monstre *m*; – *a* (*film etc*) d'épouvante, d'horreur. ◆**ho'rrendous** *a* horrible. ◆**horrible** *a* horrible, affreux. ◆**horribly** *adv* horriblement. ◆**horrid** *a* horrible; (*child*) épouvantable, méchant. ◆**ho'rrific** *a* horrible, horrifiant. ◆**horrify** *vt* horrifier.

hors-d'œuvre [ɔːˈdɜːv] *n* hors-d'œuvre *m inv*.

horse [hɔːs] *n* **1** cheval *m*; **to go h. riding** faire du cheval; **h. show** concours *m* hippique. **2 h. chestnut** marron *m* (d'Inde). ◆**horseback** *n* **on h.** à cheval. ◆**horseman** *n* (*pl* **-men**) cavalier *m*. ◆**horseplay** *n* jeux *mpl* brutaux. ◆**horsepower** *n* cheval *m* (vapeur). ◆**horseracing** *n* courses *fpl*. ◆**horseradish** *n* radis *m* noir, raifort *m*. ◆**horseshoe** *n* fer *m* à cheval. ◆**horsewoman** *n* (*pl* **-women**) cavalière *f*.

horticulture ['hɔːtɪkʌltʃər] *n* horticulture *f*. ◆**horti'cultural** *a* horticole.

hose [həʊz] *n* (*tube*) tuyau *m*; – *vt* (*garden etc*) arroser. ◆**hosepipe** *n* tuyau *m*.

hosiery ['həʊzɪərɪ, *Am* 'həʊʒərɪ] *n* bonneterie *f*.

hospice ['hɒspɪs] *n* (*for dying people*) hospice *m* (*pour incurables*).

hospitable [hɒˈspɪtəb(ə)l] *a* hospitalier. ◆**hospitably** *adv* avec hospitalité. ◆**hospi'tality** *n* hospitalité *f*.

hospital ['hɒspɪt(ə)l] *n* hôpital *m*; **in h.,** *Am*

in the h. à l'hôpital; – *a* (*bed etc*) d'hôpital; (*staff, services*) hospitalier. ◆**hospitalize** *vt* hospitaliser.

host [həʊst] *n* **1** (*man who receives guests*) hôte *m*. **2 a h. of** (*many*) une foule de. **3** *Rel* hostie *f*. ◆**hostess** *n* (*in house, aircraft, nightclub*) hôtesse *f*.

hostage ['hɒstɪdʒ] *n* otage *m*; **to take s.o. h.** prendre qn en otage.

hostel ['hɒst(ə)l] *n* foyer *m*; **youth h.** auberge *f* de jeunesse.

hostile ['hɒstaɪl, *Am* 'hɒst(ə)l] *a* hostile (**to, towards** à). ◆**ho'stility** *n* hostilité *f* (**to, towards** envers); *pl Mil* hostilités *fpl*.

hot ¹ [hɒt] *a* (**hotter, hottest**) chaud; (*spice*) fort; (*temperament*) passionné; (*news*) *Fam* dernier; (*favourite*) *Sp* grand; **to be** or **feel h.** avoir chaud; **it's h.** il fait chaud; **not so h.** **at** (*good at*) *Fam* pas très calé en; **not so h.** (*bad*) *Fam* pas fameux; **h. dog** (*sausage*) hot-dog *m*. ◆**hotbed** *n Pej* foyer *m* (**of** de). ◆**hot-'blooded** *a* ardent. ◆**hothead** *n* tête *f* brûlée. ◆**hot-'headed** *a* impétueux. ◆**hothouse** *n* serre *f* (chaude). ◆**hotplate** *n* chauffe-plats *m* inv; (*on stove*) plaque *f* chauffante. ◆**hot-'tempered** *a* emporté. ◆**hot-'water bottle** *n* bouillotte *f*.

hot ² [hɒt] *vi* (**-tt-**) **to h. up** (*increase*) s'intensifier; (*become dangerous or excited*) chauffer.

hotchpotch ['hɒtʃpɒtʃ] *n* fatras *m*.

hotel [həʊˈtel] *n* hôtel *m*; – *a* (*industry*) hôtelier. ◆**hotelier** [həʊˈteliər] *n* hôtelier, -ière *mf*.

hotly ['hɒtlɪ] *adv* passionnément.

hound [haʊnd] **1** *n* (*dog*) chien *m* courant. **2** *vt* (*pursue*) poursuivre avec acharnement; (*worry*) harceler.

hour ['aʊər] *n* heure *f*; **half an h.**, **a half-h.** une demi-heure; **a quarter of an h.** un quart d'heure; **paid ten francs an h.** payé dix francs (de) l'heure; **ten miles an h.** dix miles à l'heure; **open all hours** ouvert à toute heure; **h. hand** (*of watch, clock*) petite aiguille *f*. ◆**—ly** *a* (*rate, pay*) horaire; **an h. bus/train/etc** un bus/train/etc toutes les heures; – *adv* toutes les heures; **h. paid, paid h.** payé à l'heure.

house ¹, *pl* **-ses** [haʊs, -zɪz] *n* maison *f*; (*audience*) *Th* salle *f*, auditoire *m*; (*performance*) *Th* séance *f*; **the H.** *Pol* la Chambre; **the Houses of Parliament** le Parlement; **at** or **to my h.** chez moi; **on the h.** (*free of charge*) aux frais de la maison; **h. prices** prix *mpl* immobiliers. ◆**housebound** *a* confiné chez soi. ◆**house-**

breaking n Jur cambriolage m. ◆**house-broken** a (dog etc) Am propre.

◆**household** n ménage m, maison f, famille f; **h. duties** soins mpl du ménage; **a h. name** un nom très connu. ◆**householder** n (owner) propriétaire mf; (family head) chef m de famille. ◆**housekeeper** n (employee) gouvernante f; (housewife) ménagère f. ◆**housekeeping** n ménage m. ◆**houseman** n (pl -men) interne mf (des hôpitaux). ◆**houseproud** a qui s'occupe méticuleusement de sa maison. ◆**housetrained** a (dog etc) propre. ◆**housewarming** n & a **to have a h.-warming (party)** pendre la crémaillère. ◆**housewife** n (pl -wives) ménagère f. ◆**housework** n (travaux mpl du) ménage m.

hous/e² [hauz] vt loger, (of building) abriter; **it is housed in** (kept) on le garde dans. ◆**-ing** n logement m, (houses) logements mpl; – a (crisis etc) du logement.

hovel ['hɒv(ə)l] n (slum) taudis m.

hover ['hɒvər] vi (of bird, aircraft, danger etc) planer; (of person) rôder, traîner. ◆**hovercraft** n aéroglisseur m.

how [hau] adv comment; **h.'s that?, h. so?, h. come?** Fam comment ça?; **h. kind!** comme c'est gentil!; **h. do you do?** (greeting) bonjour; **h. long/high is . . . ?** quelle est la longueur/hauteur de . . . ?; **h. much?, h. many?** combien?; **h. much time/etc?** combien de temps/etc?; **h. many apples/etc?** combien de pommes/etc?; **h. about a walk?** si on faisait une promenade?; **h. about some coffee?** (si on prenait) du café?; **h. about me?** et moi?

howdy! ['haudɪ] int Am Fam salut!

however [hau'evər] **1** adv **h. big he may be** quelque or si grand qu'il soit; **h. she may do it** de quelque manière qu'elle le fasse; **h. that may be** quoi qu'il en soit. **2** conj cependant.

howl [haul] vi hurler; (of baby) brailler; (of wind) mugir; – n hurlement m; braillement m; mugissement m; (of laughter) éclat m.

howler ['haulər] n (mistake) Fam gaffe f.

HP [eɪtʃ'piː] abbr = **hire purchase**.

hp abbr (horsepower) CV.

HQ [eɪtʃ'kjuː] abbr = **headquarters**.

hub [hʌb] n (of wheel) moyeu m; Fig centre m. ◆**hubcap** n Aut enjoliveur m.

hubbub ['hʌbʌb] n vacarme m.

huckleberry ['hʌk(ə)lbəri] n Bot Am myrtille f.

huddle ['hʌd(ə)l] vi **to h. (together)** se blottir (les uns contre les autres).

hue [hjuː] n (colour) teinte f.

huff [hʌf] n **in a h.** (offended) Fam fâché.

hug [hʌg] vt (-gg-) (person) serrer dans les bras, étreindre; **to h. the kerb/coast** (stay near) serrer le trottoir/la côte; – n (embrace) étreinte f.

huge [hjuːdʒ] a énorme. ◆**-ly** adv énormément. ◆**-ness** n énormité f.

hulk [hʌlk] n (person) lourdaud, -aude mf.

hull [hʌl] n (of ship) coque f.

hullabaloo [hʌləbə'luː] n Fam (noise) vacarme m; (fuss) histoire(s) f(pl).

hullo! [hʌ'ləu] int = **hallo**.

hum [hʌm] vi (-mm-) (of insect) bourdonner; (of person) fredonner; (of top, radio) ronfler; (of engine) vrombir; – vt (tune) fredonner; – n (of insect) bourdonnement m.

human ['hjuːmən] a humain; **h. being** être m humain; – npl humains mpl. ◆**hu'mane** a (kind) humain. ◆**hu'manely** adv humainement. ◆**humani'tarian** a & n humanitaire (mf). ◆**hu'manity** n (human beings, kindness) humanité f. ◆**humanly** adv (possible etc) humainement.

humble ['hʌmb(ə)l] a humble; – vt humilier. ◆**humbly** adv humblement.

humbug ['hʌmbʌg] n (talk) fumisterie f; (person) fumiste mf.

humdrum ['hʌmdrʌm] a monotone.

humid ['hjuːmɪd] a humide. ◆**hu'midify** vt humidifier. ◆**hu'midity** n humidité f.

humiliate [hjuː'mɪlɪeɪt] vt humilier. ◆**humili'ation** n humiliation f. ◆**humility** n humilité f.

humour ['hjuːmər] **1** n (fun) humour m; (temper) humeur f; **to have a sense of h.** avoir le sens de l'humour; **in a good h.** de bonne humeur. **2** vt **to h. s.o.** faire plaisir à qn, ménager qn. ◆**humorist** n humoriste mf. ◆**humorous** a (book etc) humoristique; (person) plein d'humour. ◆**humorously** adv avec humour.

hump [hʌmp] **1** n (lump, mound) bosse f; – vt (one's back) voûter. **2** n **to have the h.** Fam (depression) avoir le cafard; (bad temper) être en rogne. ◆**humpback** a **h. bridge** Aut pont m en dos d'âne.

hunch [hʌntʃ] **1** vt (one's shoulders) voûter. **2** n (idea) Fam intuition f, idée f. ◆**hunchback** n bossu, -ue mf.

hundred ['hʌndrəd] a & n cent (m); **a h. pages** cent pages; **two h. pages** deux cents pages; **hundreds of** des centaines de.

◆**hundredfold** a centuple; – adv au centuple. ◆**hundredth** a & n centième (mf). ◆**hundredweight** n 112 livres (= 50,8 kg); Am 100 livres (= 45,3 kg).

hung [hʌŋ] see **hang**[1].

Hungary ['hʌŋgəri] n Hongrie f. ◆**Hungarian** a & n hongrois, -oise (mf); – n (language) hongrois m.

hunger ['hʌŋgər] n faim f. ◆**hungry** a (-ier, -iest) to be or feel h. avoir faim; to go h. souffrir de la faim; to make h. donner faim à; h. for (news etc) avide de. ◆**hungrily** adv avidement.

hunk [hʌŋk] n (gros) morceau m.

hunt [hʌnt] n Sp chasse f; (search) recherche f (for de); – vt chasser; (pursue) poursuivre; (seek) chercher; to h. down (fugitive etc) traquer; to h. out (information etc) dénicher; – vi chasser; to h. for sth (re)chercher qch. ◆–**ing** n Sp chasse f. ◆–**er** n (person) chasseur m.

hurdle ['hɜːd(ə)l] n (fence) Sp haie f; Fig obstacle m.

hurl [hɜːl] vt (throw) jeter, lancer; (abuse) lancer; to h. oneself at s.o. se ruer sur qn.

hurly-burly ['hɜːlibɜːli] n tumulte m.

hurray! [hʊ'rei] int hourra!

hurricane ['hʌrikən, Am 'hʌrikein] n ouragan m.

hurry ['hʌri] n hâte f; in a h. à la hâte, en hâte; to be in a h. être pressé; to be in a h. to do avoir hâte de faire; there's no h. rien ne presse; – vi se dépêcher, se presser (to do de faire); to h. out sortir à la hâte; to h. along or on or up se dépêcher; – vt (person) bousculer, presser; (pace) presser; to h. one's meal manger à toute vitesse; to h. s.o. out faire sortir qn à la hâte. ◆**hurried** a (steps, decision etc) précipité; (travail) fait à la hâte; (visit) éclair inv; to be h. (in a hurry) être pressé.

hurt [hɜːt] vt (pt & pp hurt) (physically) faire du mal à, blesser; (emotionally) faire de la peine à; (offend) blesser; (prejudice, damage) nuire à; to h. s.o.'s feelings blesser qn; his arm hurts (him) son bras lui fait mal; – vi faire mal; – n mal m; – a (injured) blessé. ◆**hurtful** a (remark) blessant.

hurtle ['hɜːt(ə)l] vi to h. along aller à toute vitesse; to h. down dégringoler.

husband ['hʌzbənd] n mari m.

hush [hʌʃ] int chut!; – n silence m; – vt (person) faire taire; (baby) calmer; to h. up (scandal) Fig étouffer. ◆–**ed** a (voice)

étouffé; (silence) profond. ◆**hush-hush** a Fam ultra-secret.

husk [hʌsk] n (of rice, grain) enveloppe f.

husky ['hʌski] a (-ier, -iest) (voice) enroué, voilé.

hussy ['hʌsi] n Pej friponne f, coquine f.

hustings ['hʌstiŋz] npl campagne f électorale, élections fpl.

hustle ['hʌs(ə)l] **1** vt (shove, rush) bousculer (qn); – vi (work busily) Am se démener (to get sth pour avoir qch. **2** n h. and bustle agitation f, activité f, tourbillon m.

hut [hʌt] n cabane f, hutte f.

hutch [hʌtʃ] n (for rabbit) clapier m.

hyacinth ['haiəsinθ] n jacinthe f.

hybrid ['haibrid] a & n hybride (m).

hydrangea [hai'dreindʒə] n (shrub) hortensia m.

hydrant ['haidrənt] n (fire) h. bouche f d'incendie.

hydraulic [hai'drɔːlik] a hydraulique.

hydroelectric [haidrəʊi'lektrik] a hydro-électrique.

hydrogen ['haidrədʒən] n Ch hydrogène m.

hyena [hai'iːnə] n (animal) hyène f.

hygiene ['haidʒiːn] n hygiène f. ◆**hy'gienic** a hygiénique.

hymn [him] n Rel cantique m, hymne m.

hyper- ['haipər] pref hyper-.

hypermarket ['haipəmɑːkit] n hypermarché m.

hyphen ['haif(ə)n] n trait m d'union. ◆**hyphenat/e** vt mettre un trait d'union à. ◆–**ed** a (word) à trait d'union.

hypnosis [hip'nəʊsis] n hypnose f. ◆**hypnotic** a hypnotique. ◆**'hypnotism** n hypnotisme m. ◆**'hypnotist** n hypnotiseur m. ◆**'hypnotize** vt hypnotiser.

hypochondriac [haipə'kɒndriæk] n malade mf imaginaire.

hypocrisy [hi'pɒkrisi] n hypocrisie f. ◆**'hypocrite** n hypocrite mf. ◆**hypo-'critical** a hypocrite.

hypodermic [haipə'dɜːmik] a hypodermique.

hypothesis, pl **-eses** [hai'pɒθisis, -isiːz] n hypothèse f. ◆**hypo'thetical** a hypothétique.

hysteria [hi'stiəriə] n hystérie f. ◆**hysterical** a hystérique; (funny) Fam désopilant; to be or become h. (wildly upset) avoir une crise de nerfs. ◆**hysterically** adv (to cry) sans pouvoir s'arrêter; to laugh h. rire aux larmes. ◆**hysterics** npl (tears etc) crise f de nerfs; (laughter) crise f de rire.

I

I, i [aɪ] n I, i m.

I [aɪ] pron je, j'; (stressed) moi; **I want** je veux; **she and I** elle et moi.

ic/e¹ [aɪs] n glace f; (on road) verglas m; **i. (cream)** glace f; **black i.** (on road) verglas m; **i. cube** glaçon m; — vi **to i. (over)** (of lake) geler; (of windscreen) givrer. ◆—**ed** a (tea) glacé. ◆**iceberg** n iceberg m ◆**icebox** n (box) Fig glacière f; Am réfrigérateur m. ◆**ice-'cold** a glacial; (drink) glacé. ◆**ice-skating** n patinage m (sur glace). ◆**icicle** n glaçon m.

ic/e² [aɪs] vt (cake) glacer. ◆—**ing** n (on cake etc) glaçage m.

Iceland ['aɪslənd] n Islande f. ◆**Ice'landic** a islandais.

icon ['aɪkɒn] n Rel icône f.

icy ['aɪsɪ] a (-ier, -iest) (water, hands, room) glacé; (manner, weather) glacial; (road etc) verglacé.

idea [aɪ'dɪə] n idée f (of de); **I have an i. that** … j'ai l'impression que … ; **that's my i. of rest** c'est ce que j'appelle du repos; **that's the i.!** Fam c'est ça!; **not the slightest or foggiest i.** pas la moindre idée.

ideal [aɪ'dɪəl] a idéal; — n (aspiration) idéal m; pl (spiritual etc) idéal m. ◆**idealism** n idéalisme m. ◆**idealist** n idéaliste mf. ◆**idea'listic** a idéaliste. ◆**idealize** vt idéaliser. ◆**ideally** adv idéalement; **i. we should stay** l'idéal, ce serait de rester or que nous restions.

identical [aɪ'dentɪk(ə)l] a identique (**to, with** à). ◆**identifi'cation** n identification f; **I have (some) i.** j'ai une pièce d'identité. ◆**identify** vt identifier; **to i. (oneself) with** s'identifier avec. ◆**identikit** n portrait-robot m. ◆**identity** n identité f; **i. card** carte f d'identité.

ideology [aɪdɪ'ɒlədʒɪ] n idéologie f. ◆**ideo'logical** a idéologique.

idiom ['ɪdɪəm] n expression f idiomatique; (language) idiome m. ◆**idio'matic** a idiomatique.

idiosyncrasy [ɪdɪə'sɪŋkrəsɪ] n particularité f.

idiot ['ɪdɪət] n idiot, -ote mf. ◆**idiocy** n idiotie f. ◆**idi'otic** a idiot, bête. ◆**idi'otically** adv idiotement.

idle ['aɪd(ə)l] a (unoccupied) désœuvré, oisif; (lazy) paresseux; (unemployed) en chômage; (moment) de loisir; (machine) au repos; (promise) vain; (pleasure, question) futile; (rumour) sans fondement; — vi (laze about) paresser; (of machine, engine) tourner au ralenti; — vt **to i. away** (time) gaspiller. ◆—**ness** n oisiveté f; (laziness) paresse f. ◆**idler** n paresseux, -euse mf. ◆**idly** adv paresseusement; (to suggest, say) négligemment.

idol ['aɪd(ə)l] n idole f. ◆**idolize** vt idolâtrer.

idyllic [aɪ'dɪlɪk] a idyllique.

i.e. [aɪ'iː] abbr (id est) c'est-à-dire.

if [ɪf] conj si; **if he comes** s'il vient; **even if** même si; **if so** dans ce cas, si c'est le cas; **if not for pleasure** sinon pour le plaisir; **if only I were rich** si seulement j'étais riche; **if only to look** ne serait-ce que pour regarder; **as if** comme si; **as if nothing had happened** comme si de rien n'était; **as if to say** comme pour dire; **if necessary** s'il le faut.

igloo ['ɪgluː] n igloo m.

ignite [ɪg'naɪt] vt mettre le feu à; — vi prendre feu. ◆**ignition** n Aut allumage m; **to switch on the i.** mettre le contact.

ignominious [ɪgnə'mɪnɪəs] a déshonorant, ignominieux.

ignoramus [ɪgnə'reɪməs] n ignare mf.

ignorance ['ɪgnərəns] n ignorance f (of de). ◆**ignorant** a ignorant (of de). ◆**ignorantly** adv par ignorance.

ignore [ɪg'nɔːr] vt ne prêter aucune attention à, ne tenir aucun compte de; (duty) méconnaître; (pretend not to recognize) faire semblant de ne pas reconnaître.

ilk [ɪlk] n of that i. (kind) de cet acabit.

ill [ɪl] a (sick) malade; (bad) mauvais; **i. will** malveillance f; — npl (misfortunes) maux mpl, malheurs mpl; — adv mal; **to speak i. of** dire du mal de. ◆**ill-ad'vised** a malavisé, peu judicieux. ◆**ill-'fated** a malheureux. ◆**ill-'gotten** a mal acquis. ◆**ill-in'formed** a mal renseigné. ◆**ill-'mannered** a mal élevé. ◆**ill-'natured** a (mean, unkind) désagréable. ◆**ill-'timed** a inopportun. ◆**ill-'treat** vt maltraiter.

illegal [ɪ'liːg(ə)l] a illégal. ◆**ille'gality** n illégalité f.

illegible [ɪ'ledʒəb(ə)l] a illisible.

illegitimate [ɪlɪ'dʒɪtɪmət] a (child, claim) illégitime. ◆**illegitimacy** n illégitimité f.

illicit [ɪ'lɪsɪt] a illicite.

illiterate [ɪ'lɪtərət] a & n illettré, -ée (mf), analphabète (mf). ◆**illiteracy** n analphabétisme m.

illness ['ɪlnɪs] n maladie f.

illogical [ɪ'lɒdʒɪk(ə)l] a illogique.

illuminate [ɪ'luːmɪneɪt] vt (street, question etc) éclairer; (monument etc for special occasion) illuminer. ◆**illumi'nation** n éclairage m; illumination f.

illusion [ɪ'luːʒ(ə)n] n illusion f (about sur); I'm not under any i. je ne me fais aucune illusion (about sur, quant à). ◆**illusive** a, ◆**illusory** a illusoire.

illustrate ['ɪləstreɪt] vt (with pictures, examples) illustrer (with de). ◆**illu'stration** n illustration f. ◆**illustrative** a (example) explicatif.

illustrious [ɪ'lʌstrɪəs] a illustre.

image ['ɪmɪdʒ] n image f; (public) i. (of firm etc) image f de marque; he's the (living or spitting or very) i. of his brother c'est (tout) le portrait de son frère. ◆**imagery** n images fpl.

imagin/e [ɪ'mædʒɪn] vt (picture to oneself) (s')imaginer, se figurer (that que); (suppose) imaginer (that que); i. that . . . imaginez que . . . ; you're imagining (things)! tu te fais des illusions! ◆—**ings** npl (dreams) imaginations fpl. ◆—**able** a imaginable; the worst thing i. le pire que l'on puisse imaginer. ◆**imaginary** a imaginaire. ◆**imagi'nation** n imagination f. ◆**imaginative** a plein d'imagination, imaginatif.

imbalance [ɪm'bæləns] n déséquilibre m.

imbecile ['ɪmbəsiːl, Am 'ɪmbəs(ə)l] a & n imbécile (mf). ◆**imbe'cility** n imbécillité f.

imbibe [ɪm'baɪb] vt absorber.

imbued [ɪm'bjuːd] a i. with (ideas) imprégné de; (feelings) pénétré de, imbu de.

imitate ['ɪmɪteɪt] vt imiter. ◆**imi'tation** n imitation f; – a (jewels) artificiel; **i. leather** imitation f cuir. ◆**imitative** a imitateur. ◆**imitator** n imitateur, -trice mf.

immaculate [ɪ'mækjʊlət] a (person, appearance, shirt etc) impeccable.

immaterial [ɪmə'tɪərɪəl] a peu important (to pour).

immature [ɪmə'tʃʊər] a (fruit) vert; (animal) jeune; (person) qui manque de maturité.

immeasurable [ɪ'meʒərəb(ə)l] a incommensurable.

immediate [ɪ'miːdɪət] a immédiat. ◆**immediacy** n caractère m immédiat. ◆**immediately** adv (at once) tout de suite, immédiatement; (to concern, affect) directement; – conj (as soon as) dès que.

immense [ɪ'mens] a immense. ◆**immensely** adv (rich etc) immensément; to enjoy oneself i. s'amuser énormément. ◆**immensity** n immensité f.

immerse [ɪ'mɜːs] vt plonger, immerger; **immersed in work** plongé dans le travail. ◆**immersion** n immersion f; **i. heater** chauffe-eau m inv électrique.

immigrate ['ɪmɪgreɪt] vi immigrer. ◆**immigrant** n immigrant, -ante mf; (long-established) immigré, -ée mf; – a immigré. ◆**immi'gration** n immigration f.

imminent ['ɪmɪnənt] a imminent. ◆**imminence** n imminence f.

immobile [ɪ'məʊbaɪl, Am ɪ'məʊb(ə)l] a immobile. ◆**immo'bility** n immobilité f. ◆**immobilize** vt immobiliser.

immoderate [ɪ'mɒdərət] a immodéré.

immodest [ɪ'mɒdɪst] a impudique.

immoral [ɪ'mɒrəl] a immoral. ◆**immo'rality** n immoralité f.

immortal [ɪ'mɔːt(ə)l] a immortel. ◆**immor'tality** n immortalité f. ◆**immortalize** vt immortaliser.

immune [ɪ'mjuːn] a Med & Fig immunisé (to, from contre). ◆**immunity** n immunité f. ◆'**immunize** vt immuniser (against contre).

immutable [ɪ'mjuːtəb(ə)l] a immuable.

imp [ɪmp] n diablotin m, lutin m.

impact ['ɪmpækt] n impact m (on sur).

impair [ɪm'peər] vt détériorer; (hearing, health) abîmer.

impale [ɪm'peɪl] vt empaler.

impart [ɪm'pɑːt] vt communiquer (to à).

impartial [ɪm'pɑːʃ(ə)l] a impartial. ◆**imparti'ality** n impartialité f.

impassable [ɪm'pɑːsəb(ə)l] a (road) impraticable; (river) infranchissable.

impasse ['æmpɑːs, Am 'ɪmpæs] n (situation) impasse f.

impassioned [ɪm'pæʃ(ə)nd] a (speech etc) enflammé, passionné.

impassive [ɪm'pæsɪv] a impassible. ◆—**ness** n impassibilité f.

impatient [ɪm'peɪʃ(ə)nt] a impatient (to do de faire); **i. of or with** intolérant à l'égard de. ◆**impatience** n impatience f. ◆**impatiently** adv impatiemment.

impeccab/le [ɪm'pekəb(ə)l] a impeccable. ◆—**ly** adv impeccablement.

impecunious [ımpı'kjuːnıəs] *a Hum* sans le sou, impécunieux.

impede [ım'piːd] *vt* (*hamper*) gêner; **to i. s.o. from doing** (*prevent*) empêcher qn de faire.

impediment [ım'pedımənt] *n* obstacle *m*; (*of speech*) défaut *m* d'élocution.

impel [ım'pel] *vt* (**-ll-**) (*drive*) pousser; (*force*) obliger (**to do** à faire).

impending [ım'pendıŋ] *a* imminent.

impenetrable [ım'penıtrəb(ə)l] *a* (*forest, mystery etc*) impénétrable.

imperative [ım'perətıv] *a* (*need, tone*) impérieux; (*necessary*) essentiel; **it is i. that you come** il faut absolument que *or* il est indispensable que tu viennes; – *n Gram* impératif *m*.

imperceptible [ımpə'septəb(ə)l] *a* imperceptible (**to** à).

imperfect [ım'pɜːfıkt] **1** *a* imparfait; (*goods*) défectueux. **2** *n* (*tense*) *Gram* imparfait *m*. ◆**imper'fection** *n* imperfection *f*.

imperial [ım'pıərıəl] *a* impérial; (*majestic*) majestueux; (*measure*) *Br* légal. ◆**imperialism** *n* impérialisme *m*.

imperil [ım'perıl] *vt* (**-ll-**, *Am* **-l-**) mettre en péril.

imperious [ım'pıərıəs] *a* impérieux.

impersonal [ım'pɜːsən(ə)l] *a* impersonnel.

impersonate [ım'pɜːsəneıt] *vt* (*mimic*) imiter; (*pretend to be*) se faire passer pour. ◆**imperso'nation** *n* imitation *f*. ◆**impersonator** *n* imitateur, -trice *mf*.

impertinent [ım'pɜːtınənt] *a* impertinent (**to** envers). ◆**impertinence** *n* impertinence *f*. ◆**impertinently** *adv* avec impertinence.

impervious [ım'pɜːvıəs] *a* imperméable (**to** à).

impetuous [ım'petjʊəs] *a* impétueux. ◆**impetu'osity** *n* impétuosité *f*.

impetus [ım'pıtəs] *n* impulsion *f*.

impinge [ım'pındʒ] *vi* **to i. on** (*affect*) affecter; (*encroach upon*) empiéter sur.

impish ['ımpıʃ] *a* (*naughty*) espiègle.

implacable [ım'plækəb(ə)l] *a* implacable.

implant [ım'plɑːnt] *vt* (*ideas*) inculquer (**in** à).

implement¹ ['ımplımənt] *n* (*tool*) instrument *m*; (*utensil*) *Culin* ustensile *m*; *pl Agr* matériel *m*.

implement² ['ımplıment] *vt* (*carry out*) mettre en œuvre, exécuter. ◆**implemen-'tation** *n* mise *f* en œuvre, exécution *f*.

implicate ['ımplıkeıt] *vt* impliquer (**in** dans). ◆**impli'cation** *n* (*consequence, involvement*) implication *f*; (*innuendo*) insinuation *f*; (*impact*) portée *f*; **by i.** implicitement.

implicit [ım'plısıt] *a* (*implied*) implicite;

(*belief, obedience etc*) absolu. ◆**—ly** *adv* implicitement.

implore [ım'plɔːr] *vt* implorer (**s.o. to do** de faire).

imply [ım'plaı] *vt* (*assume*) impliquer, supposer (**that** que); (*suggest*) laisser entendre (**that** que); (*insinuate*) *Pej* insinuer (**that** que). ◆**implied** *a* implicite.

impolite [ımpə'laıt] *a* impoli. ◆**—ness** *n* impolitesse *f*.

import 1 [ım'pɔːt] *vt* (*goods etc*) importer (**from** de); – ['ımpɔːt] *n* (*object, action*) importation *f*. **2** ['ımpɔːt] *n* (*meaning*) sens *m*. ◆**im'porter** *n* importateur, -trice *mf*.

importance [ım'pɔːtəns] *n* importance *f*; **to be of i.** avoir de l'importance; **of no i.** sans importance. ◆**important** *a* (*significant*) important. ◆**importantly** *adv* **more i.** ce qui est plus important.

impose [ım'pəʊz] *vt* imposer (**on** à); (*fine, punishment*) infliger (**on** à); **to i. (oneself) on s.o.** s'imposer à qn; – *vi* s'imposer. ◆**impo'sition** *n* imposition *f* (**of** de); (*inconvenience*) dérangement *m*.

impossible [ım'pɒsəb(ə)l] *a* impossible (**to do** à faire); **it is i. (for us) to do** il (nous) est impossible de faire; **it is i. that** il est impossible que (+ *sub*); **to make it i. for s.o. to do** mettre qn dans l'impossibilité de faire; – *n* **to do the i.** faire l'impossible. ◆**impossi'bility** *n* impossibilité *f*. ◆**impossibly** *adv* (*late, hard*) incroyablement.

impostor [ım'pɒstər] *n* imposteur *m*.

impotent ['ımpətənt] *a Med* impuissant. ◆**impotence** *n Med* impuissance *f*.

impound [ım'paʊnd] *vt* (*of police*) saisir, confisquer; (*vehicle*) emmener à la fourrière.

impoverish [ım'pɒvərıʃ] *vt* appauvrir.

impracticable [ım'præktıkəb(ə)l] *a* irréalisable, impraticable.

impractical [ım'præktık(ə)l] *a* peu réaliste.

imprecise [ımprı'saıs] *a* imprécis.

impregnable [ım'pregnəb(ə)l] *a Mil* imprenable; (*argument*) *Fig* inattaquable.

impregnate ['ımpregneıt] *vt* (*imbue*) imprégner (**with** de); (*fertilize*) féconder.

impresario [ımprı'sɑːrıəʊ] *n* (*pl* **-os**) impresario *m*.

impress [ım'pres] *vt* impressionner (*qn*); (*mark*) imprimer; **to i. sth on s.o.** faire comprendre qch à qn. ◆**impression** *n* impression *f*; **to be under** *or* **have the i. that** avoir l'impression que; **to make a good i. on s.o.** faire une bonne impression à qn. ◆**impressionable** *a* (*person*) impression-

nable; (age) où l'on est impressionnable.
◆**impressive** a impressionnant.

imprint [ɪm'prɪnt] vt imprimer; – ['ɪmprɪnt] n empreinte f.

imprison [ɪm'prɪz(ə)n] vt emprisonner. ◆**—ment** n emprisonnement m; life i. la prison à vie.

improbable [ɪm'prɒbəb(ə)l] a improbable; (story, excuse) invraisemblable. ◆**improba'bility** n improbabilité f; invraisemblance f.

impromptu [ɪm'prɒmptjuː] a & adv impromptu.

improper [ɪm'prɒpər] a (indecent) inconvenant, indécent; (wrong) incorrect. ◆**impropriety** [ɪmprə'praɪətɪ] n inconvenance f; (wrong use) Ling impropriété f.

improve [ɪm'pruːv] vt améliorer; (mind) cultiver, développer; to i. one's English se perfectionner en anglais; to i. s.o.'s looks embellir qn; vi s'améliorer; (of business) aller de mieux en mieux, reprendre; to i. on (do better than) faire mieux que. ◆**—ment** n amélioration f; (of mind) développement m; (progress) progrès m(pl); there has been some or an i. il y a du mieux.

improvise ['ɪmprəvaɪz] vti improviser. ◆**improvi'sation** n improvisation f.

impudent ['ɪmpjudənt] a impudent. ◆**impudence** n impudence f.

impulse ['ɪmpʌls] n impulsion f; on i. sur un coup de tête. ◆**im'pulsive** a (person, act) impulsif, irréfléchi; (remark) irréfléchi. ◆**im'pulsively** adv de manière impulsive.

impunity [ɪm'pjuːnɪtɪ] n with i. impunément.

impure [ɪm'pjʊər] a impur. ◆**impurity** n impureté f.

in [ɪn] prep **1** dans; in the box/the school/etc dans la boîte/l'école/etc; in an hour's (time) dans une heure; in so far as dans la mesure où. **2** à; in school à l'école; in the garden dans le jardin, au jardin; in Paris à Paris; in the USA aux USA; in Portugal au Portugal; in fashion à la mode; in pencil au crayon; in my opinion à mon avis. **3** en; in summer/secret/French en été/secret/français; in Spain en Espagne; in May en mai, au mois de mai; in season en saison; in an hour (during the period of an hour) en une heure; in doing en faisant. **4** de; in a soft voice d'une voix douce; the best in the class le meilleur de la classe. **5** in the rain sous la pluie; in the morning le matin; he hasn't done it in years ça fait des années qu'il ne l'a pas fait; in an hour (at the end of

an hour) au bout d'une heure; one in ten un sur dix; in thousands par milliers; in here ici; in there là-dedans. **6** adv to be in (home) être là, être à la maison; (of train) être arrivé; (in fashion) être en vogue; (in season) être en saison; (in power) Pol être au pouvoir; day in day out jour après jour; in on (a secret) au courant de; we're in for some rain/trouble/etc on va avoir de la pluie/des ennuis/etc; it's the in thing Fam c'est dans le vent. **7** npl the ins and outs of les moindres détails de.

inability [ɪnə'bɪlɪtɪ] n incapacité f (to do de faire).

inaccessible [ɪnək'sesəb(ə)l] a inaccessible.

inaccurate [ɪn'ækjurət] a inexact. ◆**inaccuracy** n inexactitude f.

inaction [ɪn'ækʃ(ə)n] n inaction f.

inactive [ɪn'æktɪv] a inactif; (mind) inerte. ◆**inac'tivity** n inactivité f, inaction f.

inadequate [ɪn'ædɪkwət] a (quantity) insuffisant; (person) pas à la hauteur, insuffisant; (work) médiocre. ◆**inadequacy** n insuffisance f. ◆**inadequately** adv insuffisamment.

inadmissible [ɪnəd'mɪsəb(ə)l] a inadmissible.

inadvertently [ɪnəd'vɜːtəntlɪ] adv par inadvertance.

inadvisable [ɪnəd'vaɪzəb(ə)l] a (action) à déconseiller; it is i. to il est déconseillé de.

inane [ɪ'neɪn] a (absurd) inepte.

inanimate [ɪn'ænɪmət] a inanimé.

inappropriate [ɪnə'prəuprɪət] a (unsuitable) peu approprié, inadéquat; (untimely) inopportun.

inarticulate [ɪnɑː'tɪkjulət] a (person) incapable de s'exprimer; (sound) inarticulé.

inasmuch as [ɪnəz'mʌtʃəz] adv (because) vu que; (to the extent that) en ce sens que.

inattentive [ɪnə'tentɪv] a inattentif (to à).

inaudible [ɪn'ɔːdəb(ə)l] a inaudible.

inaugural [ɪ'nɔːgjurəl] a inaugural. ◆**inaugurate** vt (policy, building) inaugurer; (official) installer (dans ses fonctions). ◆**inaugu'ration** n inauguration f; investiture f.

inauspicious [ɪnɔː'spɪʃəs] a peu propice.

inborn [ɪn'bɔːn] a inné.

inbred [ɪn'bred] a (quality etc) inné.

Inc abbr (Incorporated) Am Com SA, SARL.

incalculable [ɪn'kælkjuləb(ə)l] a incalculable.

incandescent [ɪnkæn'des(ə)nt] a incandescent.

incapable [ɪn'keɪpəb(ə)l] a incapable (of

doing de faire); **i. of** (*pity etc*) inaccessible à.

incapacitate [ɪnkə'pæsɪteɪt] *vt Med* rendre incapable (*de travailler etc*). ◆**incapacity** *n* (*inability*) *Med* incapacité *f*.

incarcerate [ɪn'kɑːsəreɪt] *vt* incarcérer. ◆**incarce'ration** *n* incarcération *f*.

incarnate [ɪn'kɑːnət] *a* incarné; − [ɪn'kɑːneɪt] *vt* incarner. ◆**incar'nation** *n* incarnation *f*.

incendiary [ɪn'sendɪərɪ] *a* (*bomb*) incendiaire.

incense 1 [ɪn'sens] *vt* mettre en colère. **2** ['ɪnsens] *n* (*substance*) encens *m*.

incentive [ɪn'sentɪv] *n* encouragement *m*, motivation *f*; **to give s.o. an i. to work**/*etc* encourager qn à travailler/*etc*.

inception [ɪn'sepʃ(ə)n] *n* début *m*.

incessant [ɪn'ses(ə)nt] *a* incessant. ◆**−ly** *adv* sans cesse.

incest ['ɪnsest] *n* inceste *m*. ◆**in'cestuous** *a* incestueux.

inch [ɪntʃ] *n* pouce *m* (= 2,54 cm); (*loosely*) *Fig* centimètre *m*; **within an i. of** (*success*) à deux doigts de; **i. by i.** petit à petit; − *vti* **to i. (one's way) forward** avancer petit à petit.

incidence ['ɪnsɪdəns] *n* fréquence *f*.

incident ['ɪnsɪdənt] *n* incident *m*; (*in book, film etc*) épisode *m*.

incidental [ɪnsɪ'dent(ə)l] *a* accessoire, secondaire; (*music*) de fond; **i. expenses** frais *mpl* accessoires. ◆**−ly** *adv* accessoirement; (*by the way*) à propos.

incinerate [ɪn'sɪnəreɪt] *vt* (*refuse, leaves etc*) incinérer. ◆**incinerator** *n* incinérateur *m*.

incipient [ɪn'sɪpɪənt] *a* naissant.

incision [ɪn'sɪʒ(ə)n] *n* incision *f*.

incisive [ɪn'saɪsɪv] *a* incisif.

incisor [ɪn'saɪzər] *n* (*tooth*) incisive *f*.

incite [ɪn'saɪt] *vt* inciter (**to do** à faire). ◆**−ment** *n* incitation *f* (**to do** à faire).

incline 1 [ɪn'klaɪn] *vt* (*tilt, bend*) incliner; **to i. s.o. to do** incliner qn à faire; **to be inclined to do** (*feel a wish to*) être enclin à faire; (*tend to*) avoir tendance à faire; − *vi* **to i. or be inclined towards** (*indulgence etc*) incliner à. **2** ['ɪnklaɪn] *n* (*slope*) inclinaison *f*. ◆**incli'nation** *n* inclination *f*; **to have no i. to do** n'avoir aucune envie de faire.

includ/e [ɪn'kluːd] *vt* (*contain*) comprendre, englober; (*refer to*) s'appliquer à; **my invitation includes you** mon invitation s'adresse aussi à vous; **to be included** (*on list*) être inclus; (*in price*) être compris. ◆**−ing** *prep* y compris; **i. service** service *m* compris. ◆**inclusion** *n* inclusion *f*. ◆**inclusive** *a* inclus; **from the fourth to the tenth of May**

i. du quatre jusqu'au dix mai inclus(ivement); **to be i.** comprendre; **i. charge** prix *m* global.

incognito [ɪnkɒg'niːtəʊ] *adv* incognito.

incoherent [ɪnkəʊ'hɪərənt] *a* incohérent. ◆**−ly** *adv* sans cohérence.

income ['ɪnkʌm] *n* revenu *m*; **private i.** rentes *fpl*; **i. tax** impôt *m* sur le revenu.

incoming ['ɪnkʌmɪŋ] *a* (*tenant, president*) nouveau; **i. tide** marée *f* montante; **i. calls** *Tel* appels *mpl* de l'extérieur.

incommunicado [ɪnkəmjuːnɪ'kɑːdəʊ] *a* (*tenu*) au secret.

incomparable [ɪn'kɒmpərəb(ə)l] *a* incomparable.

incompatible [ɪnkəm'pætɪb(ə)l] *a* incompatible (**with** avec). ◆**incompati'bility** *n* incompatibilité *f*.

incompetent [ɪn'kɒmpɪtənt] *a* incompétent. ◆**incompetence** *n* incompétence *f*.

incomplete [ɪnkəm'pliːt] *a* incomplet.

incomprehensible [ɪnkɒmprɪ'hensəb(ə)l] *a* incompréhensible.

inconceivable [ɪnkən'siːvəb(ə)l] *a* inconcevable.

inconclusive [ɪnkən'kluːsɪv] *a* peu concluant.

incongruous [ɪn'kɒŋgruəs] *a* (*building, colours*) qui jure(nt) (**with** avec); (*remark, attitude*) incongru; (*absurd*) absurde.

inconsequential [ɪnkɒnsɪ'kwenʃ(ə)l] *a* sans importance.

inconsiderate [ɪnkən'sɪdərət] *a* (*action, remark*) irréfléchi, inconsidéré; **to be i.** (*of person*) manquer d'égards (**towards** envers).

inconsistent [ɪnkən'sɪstənt] *a* inconséquent, incohérent; (*reports etc at variance*) contradictoire; **i. with** incompatible avec. ◆**inconsistency** *n* inconséquence *f*, incohérence *f*.

inconsolable [ɪnkən'səʊləb(ə)l] *a* inconsolable.

inconspicuous [ɪnkən'spɪkjʊəs] *a* peu en évidence, qui passe inaperçu. ◆**−ly** *adv* discrètement.

incontinent [ɪn'kɒntɪnənt] *a* incontinent.

inconvenient [ɪnkən'viːnɪənt] *a* (*room, situation*) incommode; (*time*) inopportun; **it's i. (for me) to...** ça me dérange de...; **that's very i.** c'est très gênant. ◆**inconvenience** *n* (*bother*) dérangement *m*; (*disadvantage*) inconvénient *m*; − *vt* déranger, gêner.

incorporate [ɪn'kɔːpəreɪt] *vt* (*introduce*) incorporer (**into** dans); (*contain*) contenir;

incorporated society *Am* société *f* anonyme, société *f* à responsabilité limitée.

incorrect [ɪnkəˈrekt] *a* incorrect, inexact; **you're i.** vous avez tort.

incorrigible [ɪnˈkɒrɪdʒəb(ə)l] *a* incorrigible.

incorruptible [ɪnkəˈrʌptəb(ə)l] *a* incorruptible.

increas/e [ɪnˈkriːs] *vi* augmenter; (*of effort, noise*) s'intensifier; **to i. in weight** prendre du poids; – *vt* augmenter; intensifier; – [ˈɪnkriːs] *n* augmentation *f* (**in, of** de); intensification *f* (**in, of** de); **on the i.** en hausse. ◆**—ing** *a* (*amount etc*) croissant. ◆**—ingly** *adv* de plus en plus.

incredib/le [ɪnˈkredəb(ə)l] *a* incroyable. ◆**—ly** *adv* incroyablement.

incredulous [ɪnˈkredjʊləs] *a* incrédule. ◆**incre'dulity** *n* incrédulité *f*.

increment [ˈɪŋkrəmənt] *n* augmentation *f*.

incriminat/e [ɪnˈkrɪmɪneɪt] *vt* incriminer. ◆**—ing** *a* compromettant.

incubate [ˈɪŋkjʊbeɪt] *vt* (*eggs*) couver. ◆**incu'bation** *n* incubation *f*. ◆**incubator** *n* (*for baby, eggs*) couveuse *f*.

inculcate [ˈɪnkʌlkeɪt] *vt* inculquer (**in** à).

incumbent [ɪnˈkʌmbənt] *a* **it is i. upon him** or **her** to il lui incombe de; – *n Rel Pol* titulaire *mf*.

incur [ɪnˈkɜːr] *vt* (**-rr-**) (*debt*) contracter; (*expenses*) faire; (*criticism, danger*) s'attirer.

incurable [ɪnˈkjʊərəb(ə)l] *a* incurable.

incursion [ɪnˈkɜːʃ(ə)n] *n* incursion *f* (**into** dans).

indebted [ɪnˈdetɪd] *a* **i. to s.o. for sth/for doing sth** redevable à qn de qch/d'avoir fait qch. ◆**—ness** *n* dette *f*.

indecent [ɪnˈdiːs(ə)nt] *a* (*offensive*) indécent; (*unsuitable*) peu approprié. ◆**indecency** *n* indécence *f*; (*crime*) *Jur* outrage *m* à la pudeur. ◆**indecently** *adv* indécemment.

indecisive [ɪndɪˈsaɪsɪv] *a* (*person, answer*) indécis. ◆**indecision, i ◆indecisiveness** *n* indécision *f*.

indeed [ɪnˈdiːd] *adv* en effet; **very good/etc i.** vraiment très bon/*etc*; **yes i.!** bien sûr!; **thank you very much i.!** merci mille fois!

indefensible [ɪndɪˈfensəb(ə)l] *a* indéfendable.

indefinable [ɪndɪˈfaɪnəb(ə)l] *a* indéfinissable.

indefinite [ɪnˈdefɪnət] *a* (*feeling, duration etc*) indéfini; (*plan*) mal déterminé. ◆**—ly** *adv* indéfiniment.

indelible [ɪnˈdeləb(ə)l] *a* (*ink, memory*) indélébile; **i. pencil** crayon *m* à marquer.

indelicate [ɪnˈdelɪkət] *a* (*coarse*) indélicat.

indemnify [ɪnˈdemnɪfaɪ] *vt* indemniser (**for** de). ◆**indemnity** *n* indemnité *f*.

indented [ɪnˈdentɪd] *a* (*edge*) dentelé, découpé; (*line*) *Typ* renfoncé. ◆**inden-'tation** *n* dentelure *f*, découpure *f*; *Typ* renfoncement *m*.

independent [ɪndɪˈpendənt] *a* indépendant (**of** de); (*opinions, reports*) de sources différentes. ◆**independence** *n* indépendance *f*. ◆**independently** *adv* de façon indépendante; **i. of** indépendamment de.

indescribable [ɪndɪˈskraɪbəb(ə)l] *a* indescriptible.

indestructible [ɪndɪˈstrʌktəb(ə)l] *a* indestructible.

indeterminate [ɪndɪˈtɜːmɪnət] *a* indéterminé.

index [ˈɪndeks] *n* (*in book etc*) index *m*; (*in library*) catalogue *m*; (*number, sign*) indice *m*; **i. card** fiche *f*; **i. finger** index *m*; – *vt* (*classify*) classer. ◆**i.-'linked** *a Econ* indexé (**to** sur).

India [ˈɪndɪə] *n* Inde *f*. ◆**indian** *a & n* indien, -ienne (*mf*).

indicate [ˈɪndɪkeɪt] *vt* indiquer (**that** que); **I was indicating right** *Aut* j'avais mis mon clignotant droit. ◆**indi'cation** *n* (*sign*) indice *m*, indication *f*; (*idea*) idée *f*. ◆**indicative** *a* indicatif (**of** de); – *n* (*mood*) *Gram* indicatif *m*. ◆**indicator** *n* (*instrument*) indicateur *m*; (*sign*) indication *f* (**of** de); *Aut* clignotant *m*; (*display board*) tableau *m* (indicateur).

indict [ɪnˈdaɪt] *vt* inculper (**for** de). ◆**—ment** *n* inculpation *f*.

Indies [ˈɪndɪz] *npl* **the West I.** les Antilles *fpl*.

indifferent [ɪnˈdɪf(ə)rənt] *a* indifférent (**to** à); (*mediocre*) *Pej* médiocre. ◆**indifference** *n* indifférence *f* (**to** à). ◆**indifferently** *adv* indifféremment.

indigenous [ɪnˈdɪdʒɪnəs] *a* indigène.

indigestion [ɪndɪˈdʒestʃ(ə)n] *n* dyspepsie *f*; **(an attack of) i.** une indigestion, une crise de foie. ◆**indigestible** *a* indigeste.

indignant [ɪnˈdɪɡnənt] *a* indigné (**at de, with** contre); **to become i.** s'indigner. ◆**indignantly** *adv* avec indignation. ◆**indig'nation** *n* indignation *f*.

indignity [ɪnˈdɪɡnɪtɪ] *n* indignité *f*.

indigo [ˈɪndɪɡəʊ] *n & a* (*colour*) indigo *m & a inv*.

indirect [ɪndaɪˈrekt] *a* indirect. ◆**—ly** *adv* indirectement.

indiscreet [ɪndɪˈskriːt] *a* indiscret. ◆**indiscretion** *n* indiscrétion *f*.

indiscriminate [ɪndɪˈskrɪmɪnət] *a* (*person*)

qui manque de discernement; *(random)* fait, donné *etc* au hasard. ◆**—ly** *adv (at random)* au hasard; *(without discrimination)* sans discernement.

indispensable [ɪndɪ'spensəb(ə)l] *a* indispensable **(to** à).

indisposed [ɪndɪ'spəʊzd] *a (unwell)* indisposé. ◆**indispo'sition** *n* indisposition *f*.

indisputable [ɪndɪ'spjuːtəb(ə)l] *a* incontestable.

indistinct [ɪndɪ'stɪŋkt] *a* indistinct.

indistinguishable [ɪndɪ'stɪŋgwɪʃəb(ə)l] *a* indifférenciable **(from** de).

individual [ɪndɪ'vɪdʒʊəl] *a* individuel; *(unusual, striking)* singulier, particulier; – *n (person)* individu *m*. ◆**individualist** *n* individualiste. ◆**individua'listic** *a* individualiste. ◆**individu'ality** *n (distinctiveness)* individualité *f*. ◆**individually** *adv (separately)* individuellement; *(unusually)* de façon (très) personnelle.

indivisible [ɪndɪ'vɪzəb(ə)l] *a* indivisible.

Indo-China [ɪndəʊ'tʃaɪnə] *n* Indochine *f*.

indoctrinate [ɪn'dɒktrɪneɪt] *vt Pej* endoctriner. ◆**indoctri'nation** *n* endoctrinement *m*.

indolent ['ɪndələnt] *a* indolent. ◆**indolence** *n* indolence *f*.

indomitable [ɪn'dɒmɪtəb(ə)l] *a (will, energy)* indomptable.

Indonesia [ɪndəʊ'niːʒə] *n* Indonésie *f*.

indoor ['ɪndɔːr] *a (games, shoes etc)* d'intérieur; *(swimming pool etc)* couvert. ◆**in'doors** *adv* à l'intérieur; **to go** *or* **come i.** rentrer.

induce [ɪn'djuːs] *vt (persuade)* persuader **(to do** de faire); *(cause)* provoquer; **to i.** labour *Med* déclencher le travail. ◆**—ment** *n* encouragement *m* **(to do** à faire).

indulge [ɪn'dʌldʒ] *vt (s.o.'s desires)* satisfaire; *(child etc)* gâter, tout passer à; **to i. oneself** se gâter; – *vi* **to i. in** *(action)* s'adonner à; *(ice cream etc)* se permettre. ◆**indulgence** *n* indulgence *f*. ◆**indulgent** *a* indulgent **(to** envers, **with** avec).

industrial [ɪn'dʌstrɪəl] *a* industriel; *(conflict, legislation)* du travail; **i. action** action *f* revendicative; **i. park** *Am* complexe *m* industriel. ◆**industrialist** *n* industriel, -ielle *mf*. ◆**industrialized** *a* industrialisé.

industrious [ɪn'dʌstrɪəs] *a* travailleur.

industry ['ɪndəstrɪ] *n* industrie *f*; *(hard work)* application *f*.

inedible [ɪn'edəb(ə)l] *a* immangeable.

ineffective [ɪnɪ'fektɪv] *a (measure etc)* sans effet, inefficace; *(person)* incapable. ◆**—ness** *n* inefficacité *f*.

ineffectual [ɪnɪ'fektʃʊəl] *a (measure etc)* inefficace; *(person)* incompétent.

inefficient [ɪnɪ'fɪʃ(ə)nt] *a (person, measure etc)* inefficace; *(machine)* peu performant. ◆**inefficiency** *n* inefficacité *f*.

ineligible [ɪn'elɪdʒəb(ə)l] *a (candidate)* inéligible; **to be i. for** ne pas avoir droit à.

inept [ɪ'nept] *a (foolish)* inepte; *(unskilled)* peu habile **(at sth** à qch); *(incompetent)* incapable, inapte. ◆**ineptitude** *n (incapacity)* inaptitude *f*.

inequality [ɪnɪ'kwɒlətɪ] *n* inégalité *f*.

inert [ɪ'nɜːt] *a* inerte. ◆**inertia** [ɪ'nɜːʃə] *n* inertie *f*.

inescapable [ɪnɪ'skeɪpəb(ə)l] *a* inéluctable.

inevitable [ɪn'evɪtəb(ə)l] *a* inévitable. ◆**inevitably** *adv* inévitablement.

inexcusable [ɪnɪk'skjuːzəb(ə)l] *a* inexcusable.

inexhaustible [ɪnɪg'zɔːstəb(ə)l] *a* inépuisable.

inexorable [ɪn'eksərəb(ə)l] *a* inexorable.

inexpensive [ɪnɪk'spensɪv] *a* bon marché *inv*.

inexperience [ɪnɪk'spɪərɪəns] *n* inexpérience *f*. ◆**inexperienced** *a* inexpérimenté.

inexplicable [ɪnɪk'splɪkəb(ə)l] *a* inexplicable.

inexpressible [ɪnɪk'spresəb(ə)l] *a* inexprimable.

inextricable [ɪnɪk'strɪkəb(ə)l] *a* inextricable.

infallible [ɪn'fæləb(ə)l] *a* infaillible. ◆**infalli'bility** *n* infaillibilité *f*.

infamous ['ɪnfəməs] *a (evil)* infâme. ◆**infamy** *n* infamie *f*.

infant ['ɪnfənt] *n (child)* petit(e) enfant *mf*; *(baby)* nourrisson *m*; **i. school** classes *fpl* préparatoires. ◆**infancy** *n* petite enfance *f*; **to be in its i.** *(of art, technique etc)* en être à ses premiers balbutiements. ◆**infantile** *a (illness, reaction etc)* infantile.

infantry ['ɪnfəntrɪ] *n* infanterie *f*.

infatuated [ɪn'fætʃʊeɪtɪd] *a* amoureux; **i. with** *(person)* amoureux de; engoué de; *(sport etc)* engoué de. ◆**infatu'ation** *n* engouement *m* **(for, with** pour).

infect [ɪn'fekt] *vt (contaminate)* *Med* infecter; **to become infected** s'infecter; **to i. s.o. with sth** communiquer qch à qn. ◆**infection** *n* infection *f*. ◆**infectious** *a (disease)* infectieux, contagieux; *(person, laughter etc)* contagieux.

infer [ɪn'fɜːr] *vt* **(-rr-)** déduire **(from** de, **that** que). ◆**inference** *n* déduction *f*, conclusion *f*.

inferior [in'fiəriər] *a* inférieur (**to** à); (*goods, work*) de qualité inférieure; – *n* (*person*) Pej inférieur, -eure *mf*. ◆**inferi'ority** *n* infériorité *f*.

infernal [in'fɜːn(ə)l] *a* infernal. ◆**—ly** *adv* Fam épouvantablement.

inferno [in'fɜːnəu] *n* (*pl* **-os**) (*blaze*) brasier *m*, incendie *m*; (*hell*) enfer *m*.

infertile [in'fɜːtail, *Am* in'fɜːt(ə)l] *a* (*person, land*) stérile.

infest [in'fest] *vt* infester (**with** de).

infidelity [infi'deliti] *n* infidélité *f*.

infighting ['infaitiŋ] *n* (*within group*) luttes *fpl* intestines.

infiltrate ['infiltreit] *vi* s'infiltrer (**into** dans); – *vt* (*group etc*) s'infiltrer dans. ◆**infil'tration** *n* infiltration *f*; *Pol* noyautage *m*.

infinite ['infinit] *a* & *n* infini (*m*). ◆**infinitely** *adv* infiniment. ◆**in'finity** *n* Math Phot infini *m*; **to i.** Math à l'infini.

infinitive [in'finitiv] *n* Gram infinitif *m*.

infirm [in'fɜːm] *a* infirme. ◆**infirmary** *n* (*sickbay*) infirmerie *f*; (*hospital*) hôpital *m*. ◆**infirmity** *n* (*disability*) infirmité *f*.

inflame [in'fleim] *vt* enflammer. ◆**inflammable** *a* inflammable. ◆**infla'mmation** *n* Med inflammation *f*. ◆**inflammatory** *a* (*remark*) incendiaire.

inflate [in'fleit] *vt* (*tyre, prices etc*) gonfler. ◆**inflatable** *a* gonflable. ◆**inflation** *n* Econ inflation *f*. ◆**inflationary** *a* Econ inflationniste.

inflection [in'flekʃ(ə)n] *n* Gram flexion *f*; (*of voice*) inflexion *f*.

inflexible [in'fleksəb(ə)l] *a* inflexible.

inflexion [in'flekʃ(ə)n] *n* = **inflection**.

inflict [in'flikt] *vt* infliger (**on** à); (*wound*) occasionner (**on** à).

influence ['influəns] *n* influence *f*; **under the i.** of (*anger, drugs*) sous l'effet de; **under the i.** of drink *or* alcohol *Jur* en état d'ébriété; – *vt* influencer. ◆**influ'ential** *a* influent.

influenza [influ'enzə] *n* Med grippe *f*.

influx ['inflaks] *n* flot *m*, afflux *m*.

info ['infəu] *n* Sl tuyaux *mpl*, renseignements *mpl* (**on** sur).

inform [in'fɔːm] *vt* informer (**of** de, **that** que); – *vi* **to i. on** dénoncer. ◆**—ed** *a* informé; **to keep s.o. i.** of tenir qn au courant de. ◆**informant** *n* informateur, -trice *mf*. ◆**informative** *a* instructif. ◆**informer** *n* (*police*) i. indicateur, -trice *mf*.

informal [in'fɔːm(ə)l] *a* (*without fuss*) simple, sans façon; (*occasion*) dénué de formalité; (*tone, expression*) familier; (*announcement*) officieux; (*meeting*) non-officiel. ◆**infor-**

'mality *n* simplicité *f*; (*of tone etc*) familiarité *f*. ◆**informally** *adv* (*without fuss*) sans cérémonie; (*to meet*) officieusement; (*to dress*) simplement.

information [infə'meiʃ(ə)n] *n* (*facts*) renseignements *mpl* (**about**, **on** sur); (*knowledge*) & Math information *f*; **a piece of i.** un renseignement, une information; **to get some i.** se renseigner.

infrared [infrə'red] *a* infrarouge.

infrequent [in'friːkwənt] *a* peu fréquent.

infringe [in'frindʒ] *vt* (*rule*) contrevenir à; – *vi* **to i. upon** (*encroach on*) empiéter sur. ◆**—ment** *n* infraction *f* (**of** à).

infuriate [in'fjuərieit] *vt* exaspérer. ◆**—ing** *a* exaspérant.

infuse [in'fjuːz] *vt* (*tea*) (faire) infuser. ◆**infusion** *n* infusion *f*.

ingenious [in'dʒiːniəs] *a* ingénieux. ◆**inge'nuity** *n* ingéniosité *f*.

ingot ['iŋgət] *n* lingot *m*.

ingrained [in'greind] *a* (*prejudice*) enraciné; **i. dirt** crasse *f*.

ingratiat/e [in'greiʃieit] *vt* **to i. oneself with** s'insinuer dans les bonnes grâces de. ◆**—ing** *a* (*person, smile*) insinuant.

ingratitude [in'grætitjuːd] *n* ingratitude *f*.

ingredient [in'griːdiənt] *n* ingrédient *m*.

ingrown [in'grəun] *a* (*nail*) incarné.

inhabit [in'hæbit] *vt* habiter. ◆**—able** *a* habitable. ◆**inhabitant** *n* habitant, -ante *mf*.

inhale [in'heil] *vt* aspirer; **to i. the smoke** (*of smoker*) avaler la fumée. ◆**inha'lation** *n* inhalation *f*. ◆**inhaler** *n* Med inhalateur *m*.

inherent [in'hiərənt] *a* inhérent (**in** à). ◆**—ly** *adv* intrinsèquement, en soi.

inherit [in'herit] *vt* hériter (de); (*title*) succéder à. ◆**inheritance** *n* héritage *m*; (*process*) Jur succession *f*; (*cultural*) patrimoine *m*.

inhibit [in'hibit] *vt* (*hinder*) gêner; (*control*) maîtriser; (*prevent*) empêcher (**from** de); **to be inhibited** être inhibé, avoir des inhibitions. ◆**inhi'bition** *n* inhibition *f*.

inhospitable [inhɒ'spitəb(ə)l] *a* inhospitalier.

inhuman [in'hjuːmən] *a* (*not human, cruel*) inhumain. ◆**inhu'mane** *a* (*not kind*) inhumain. ◆**inhu'manity** *n* brutalité *f*, cruauté *f*.

inimitable ['inimitəb(ə)l] *a* inimitable.

iniquitous [i'nikwitəs] *a* inique. ◆**iniquity** *n* iniquité *f*.

initial [i'niʃ(ə)l] *a* initial, premier; – *n* (*letter*) initiale *f*; (*signature*) paraphe *m*; –

vt (**-ll-**, *Am* **-l-**) parapher. **◆—ly** *adv* initialement, au début.

initiate [ɪˈnɪʃɪeɪt] *vt* (*reforms*) amorcer; (*schemes*) inaugurer; **to i. s.o. into** initier qn à; **the initiated** les initiés *mpl*. **◆initi'ation** *n* amorce *f*; inauguration *f*; initiation *f*. **◆initiator** *n* initiateur, -trice *mf*.

initiative [ɪˈnɪʃɪətɪv] *n* initiative *f*.

inject [ɪnˈdʒekt] *vt* injecter (**into** à); (*new life etc*) *Fig* insuffler (**into** à). **◆injection** *n* *Med* injection *f*, piqûre *f*.

injunction [ɪnˈdʒʌŋkʃ(ə)n] *n* *Jur* ordonnance *f*.

injur/e [ˈɪndʒər] *vt* (*physically*) blesser; (*prejudice, damage*) nuire à; (*one's chances*) compromettre; **to i. one's foot**/*etc* se blesser au pied/*etc*. **◆—ed** *a* blessé; – *n* **the i.** les blessés *mpl*. **◆injury** *n* (*to flesh*) blessure *f*; (*fracture*) fracture *f*; (*sprain*) foulure *f*; (*bruise*) contusion *f*; (*wrong*) *Fig* préjudice *m*.

injurious [ɪnˈdʒʊərɪəs] *a* préjudiciable (**to** à).

injustice [ɪnˈdʒʌstɪs] *n* injustice *f*.

ink [ɪŋk] *n* encre *f*; **Indian i.** encre *f* de Chine. **◆inkpot** *n*, **◆inkwell** *n* encrier *m*. **◆inky** *a* couvert d'encre.

inkling [ˈɪŋklɪŋ] *n* (petite) idée *f*; **to have some** *or* **an i. of** sth soupçonner qch, avoir une (petite) idée de qch.

inlaid [ɪnˈleɪd] *a* (*marble etc*) incrusté (**with** de); (*wood*) marqueté.

inland [ˈɪnlənd, ˈɪnlænd] *a* intérieur; **the I. Revenue** le fisc; – [ɪnˈlænd] *adv* à l'intérieur (*des terres*).

in-laws [ˈɪnlɔːz] *npl* belle-famille *f*.

inlet [ˈɪnlet] *n* (*of sea*) crique *f*; **i. pipe** tuyau *m* d'arrivée.

inmate [ˈɪnmeɪt] *n* résident, -ente *mf*; (*of asylum*) interné, -ée *mf*; (*of prison*) détenu, -ue *mf*.

inmost [ˈɪnməʊst] *a* le plus profond.

inn [ɪn] *n* auberge *f*. **◆innkeeper** *n* aubergiste *mf*.

innards [ˈɪnədz] *npl* *Fam* entrailles *fpl*.

innate [ɪˈneɪt] *a* inné.

inner [ˈɪnər] *a* intérieur; (*ear*) interne; (*feelings*) intime, profond; **the i. city** le cœur de la ville; **an i. circle** (*group of people*) un cercle restreint; **the i. circle** le saint des saints; **i. tube** (*of tyre*) chambre *f* à air. **◆innermost** *a* le plus profond.

inning [ˈɪnɪŋ] *n* *Baseball* tour *m* de batte. **◆innings** *n inv* *Cricket* tour *m* de batte; **a good i.** *Fig* une vie longue.

innocent [ˈɪnəs(ə)nt] *a* innocent. **◆inno-**

cence *n* innocence *f*. **◆innocently** *adv* innocemment.

innocuous [ɪˈnɒkjʊəs] *a* inoffensif.

innovate [ˈɪnəveɪt] *vi* innover. **◆inno-'vation** *n* innovation *f*. **◆innovator** *n* innovateur, -trice *mf*.

innuendo [ɪnjuːˈendəʊ] *n* (*pl* **-oes** *or* **-os**) insinuation *f*.

innumerable [ɪˈnjuːmərəb(ə)l] *a* innombrable.

inoculate [ɪˈnɒkjʊleɪt] *vt* vacciner (**against** contre). **◆inocu'lation** *n* inoculation *f*.

inoffensive [ɪnəˈfensɪv] *a* inoffensif.

inoperative [ɪnˈɒpərətɪv] *a* (*without effect*) inopérant.

inopportune [ɪnˈɒpətjuːn] *a* inopportun.

inordinate [ɪˈnɔːdɪnət] *a* excessif. **◆—ly** *adv* excessivement.

in-patient [ˈɪnpeɪʃ(ə)nt] *n* malade *mf* hospitalisé(e).

input [ˈɪnpʊt] *n* (*computer operation*) entrée *f*; (*data*) données *fpl*; (*current*) *El* énergie *f*.

inquest [ˈɪnkwest] *n* enquête *f*.

inquir/e [ɪnˈkwaɪər] *vi* se renseigner (**about** sur); **to i. after** s'informer de; **to i. into** examiner, faire une enquête sur; – *vt* demander, **to i. how to get to** demander le chemin de. **◆—ing** *a* (*mind, look*) curieux. **◆inquiry** *n* (*question*) question *f*; (*request for information*) demande *f* de renseignements; (*information*) renseignements *mpl*; *Jur* enquête *f*; **to make inquiries** demander des renseignements; (*of police*) enquêter.

inquisitive [ɪnˈkwɪzɪtɪv] *a* curieux. **◆inquisitively** *adv* avec curiosité. **◆inqui'sition** *n* (*inquiry*) & *Rel* inquisition *f*.

inroads [ˈɪnrəʊdz] *npl* (*attacks*) incursions *fpl* (**into** dans); **to make i. into** *Fig* entamer.

insane [ɪnˈseɪn] *a* fou, dément. **◆insanely** *adv* comme un fou. **◆insanity** *n* folie *f*, démence *f*.

insanitary [ɪnˈsænɪt(ə)rɪ] *a* insalubre.

insatiable [ɪnˈseɪʃəb(ə)l] *a* insatiable.

inscribe [ɪnˈskraɪb] *vt* inscrire; (*book*) dédicacer (**to** à). **◆inscription** *n* inscription *f*; dédicace *f*.

inscrutable [ɪnˈskruːtəb(ə)l] *a* impénétrable.

insect [ˈɪnsekt] *n* insecte *m*; – *a* (*powder, spray*) insecticide; **i. repellant** crème *f* anti-insecte. **◆in'secticide** *n* insecticide *m*.

insecure [ɪnsɪˈkjʊər] *a* (*not fixed*) peu solide; (*furniture, ladder*) branlant, bancal; (*window*) mal fermé; (*uncertain*) incertain;

(unsafe) peu sûr; *(person)* qui manque d'assurance. ◆**insecurity** n *(of person, situation)* insécurité f.

insemination [ɪnsemɪ'neɪʃ(ə)n] n Med insémination f.

insensible [ɪn'sensəb(ə)l] a Med inconscient.

insensitive [ɪn'sensɪtɪv] a insensible **(to** à). ◆**insensi'tivity** n insensibilité f.

inseparable [ɪn'sep(ə)rəb(ə)l] a inséparable **(from** de).

insert [ɪn'sɜːt] vt insérer **(in, into** dans). ◆**insertion** n insertion f.

inshore ['ɪnʃɔːr] a côtier.

inside [ɪn'saɪd] adv dedans, à l'intérieur; **come i.!** entrez!; − prep à l'intérieur de, dans; *(time)* en moins de; − n dedans m, intérieur m; pl *(stomach)* Fam ventre m; **on the i.** à l'intérieur **(of** de); **i. out** *(coat, socks etc)* à l'envers; *(to know, study etc)* à fond; **to turn everything i. out** Fig tout chambouler; − a intérieur; *(information)* obtenu à la source; **the i. lane** Aut la voie de gauche, Am la voie de droite.

insidious [ɪn'sɪdɪəs] a insidieux.

insight ['ɪnsaɪt] n perspicacité f; **to give an i. into** *(s.o.'s character)* permettre de comprendre, *(question)* donner un aperçu de.

insignia [ɪn'sɪgnɪə] npl *(of important person)* insignes mpl.

insignificant [ɪnsɪg'nɪfɪkənt] a insignifiant. ◆**insignificance** n insignifiance f.

insincere [ɪnsɪn'sɪər] a peu sincère. ◆**insincerity** n manque m de sincérité.

insinuate [ɪn'sɪnjʊeɪt] vt **1** Pej insinuer **(that** que). **2 to i. oneself into** s'insinuer dans. ◆**insinu'ation** n insinuation f.

insipid [ɪn'sɪpɪd] a insipide.

insist [ɪn'sɪst] vi insister **(on doing** pour faire); **to i. on sth** *(demand)* exiger qch; *(assert)* affirmer qch; − vt *(order)* insister **(that** pour que); *(declare firmly)* affirmer **(that** que); **I i. that you come** or **on your coming** j'insiste pour que tu viennes. ◆**insistence** n insistance f; **her i. on seeing me** l'insistance qu'elle met à vouloir me voir. ◆**insistent** a insistant; **I was i. (about it)** j'ai été pressant. ◆**insistently** adv avec insistance.

insolent ['ɪnsələnt] a insolent. ◆**insolence** n insolence f. ◆**insolently** adv insolemment.

insoluble [ɪn'sɒljʊb(ə)l] a insoluble.

insolvent [ɪn'sɒlvənt] a Fin insolvable.

insomnia [ɪn'sɒmnɪə] n insomnie f. ◆**insomniac** n insomniaque mf.

insomuch as [ɪnsəʊ'mʌtʃəz] adv = **inasmuch as**.

inspect [ɪn'spekt] vt inspecter; *(tickets)* contrôler; *(troops)* passer en revue. ◆**inspection** n inspection f; contrôle m; revue f. ◆**inspector** n inspecteur, -trice mf; *(on bus)* contrôleur, -euse mf.

inspir/e [ɪn'spaɪər] vt inspirer **(s.o. with sth** qch à qn); **to be inspired to do** avoir l'inspiration de faire. ◆**−ed** a inspiré. ◆**−ing** a qui inspire. ◆**inspi'ration** n inspiration f; *(person)* source f d'inspiration.

instability [ɪnstə'bɪlɪtɪ] n instabilité f.

install [ɪn'stɔːl] vt installer. ◆**insta'llation** n installation f.

instalment [ɪn'stɔːlmənt] *(Am* **installment**) n *(of money)* acompte m, versement m (partiel); *(of serial)* épisode m; *(of publication)* fascicule m; **to buy on the i. plan** Am acheter à crédit.

instance ['ɪnstəns] n *(example)* exemple m; *(case)* cas m; *(occasion)* circonstance f; **for i.** par exemple; **in the first i.** en premier lieu.

instant ['ɪnstənt] a immédiat; **i. coffee** m soluble or instantané, nescafé® m; **of the 3rd i.** *(in letter)* Com du 3 courant; − n *(moment)* instant m; **this (very) i.** *(at once)* à l'instant; **the i. that** *(as soon as)* dès que. ◆**instan'taneous** a instantané. ◆**instantly** adv immédiatement.

instead [ɪn'sted] adv *(as alternative)* au lieu de cela, plutôt; **i. of** au lieu de; **i. of s.o.** à la place de qn; **i. (of him** or **her)** à sa place.

instep ['ɪnstep] n *(of foot)* cou-de-pied m; *(of shoe)* cambrure f.

instigate ['ɪnstɪgeɪt] vt provoquer. ◆**insti'gation** n instigation f. ◆**instigator** n instigateur, -trice mf.

instil [ɪn'stɪl] vt (**-ll-**) *(idea)* inculquer **(into** à); *(courage)* insuffler **(into** à).

instinct ['ɪnstɪŋkt] n instinct m; **by i.** d'instinct. ◆**in'stinctive** a instinctif. ◆**in'stinctively** adv instinctivement.

institute ['ɪnstɪtjuːt] **1** vt *(rule, practice)* instituer; *(inquiry, proceedings)* Jur entamer, intenter. **2** n institut m. ◆**insti'tution** n *(custom, private or charitable organization etc)* institution f; *(school, hospital)* établissement m; *(home)* Med asile m. ◆**insti'tutional** a institutionnel.

instruct [ɪn'strʌkt] vt *(teach)* enseigner **(s.o. in sth** qch à qn); **to i. s.o. about sth** *(inform)* instruire qn de qch; **to i. s.o. to do** *(order)* charger qn de faire. ◆**instruction** n *(teaching)* instruction f; pl *(orders)* instructions fpl; **instructions (for use)** mode m

d'emploi. ◆**instructive** a instructif.
◆**instructor** n professeur m; Sp moniteur,
-trice mf; Mil instructeur m; Univ Am
maître-assistant, -ante mf; **driving i.**
moniteur, -trice mf de conduite.

instrument ['ɪnstrʊmənt] n instrument m.
◆**instru'mental** a Mus instrumental; **to
be i. in sth/in doing sth** contribuer à qch/à
faire qch. ◆**instru'mentalist** n Mus
instrumentaliste mf. ◆**instrumen'tation**
n Mus orchestration f.

insubordinate [ɪnsə'bɔːdɪnət] a indiscipliné. ◆**insubordi'nation** n indiscipline f.

insubstantial [ɪnsəb'stænʃ(ə)l] a (argument,
evidence) peu solide.

insufferable [ɪn'sʌfərəb(ə)l] a intolérable.

insufficient [ɪnsə'fɪʃənt] a insuffisant.
◆**-ly** adv insuffisamment.

insular ['ɪnsjʊlər] a (climate) insulaire;
(views) Pej étroit, borné.

insulate ['ɪnsjʊleɪt] vt (against cold etc) & El
isoler; (against sound) insonoriser; **to i. s.o.
from** Fig protéger qn de; **insulating tape**
chatterton m. ◆**insu'lation** n isolation f;
insonorisation f; (material) isolant m.

insulin ['ɪnsjʊlɪn] n Med insuline f.

insult [ɪn'sʌlt] vt insulter; – ['ɪnsʌlt] n insulte
f (to à).

insuperable [ɪn'suːpərəb(ə)l] a insurmontable.

insure [ɪn'ʃʊər] vt **1** (protect against damage
etc) assurer (**against** contre). **2** Am =
ensure. ◆**insurance** n assurance f; **i.
company** compagnie f d'assurances; **i.
policy** police f d'assurance.

insurgent [ɪn'sɜːdʒənt] a & n insurgé, -ée
(mf).

insurmountable [ɪnsə'maʊntəb(ə)l] a
insurmontable.

insurrection [ɪnsə'rekʃ(ə)n] n insurrection f.

intact [ɪn'tækt] a intact.

intake ['ɪnteɪk] n (of food) consommation f;
Sch Univ admissions fpl; Tech admission f.

intangible [ɪn'tændʒəb(ə)l] a intangible.

integral ['ɪntɪgrəl] a intégral; **to be an i. part**
of faire partie intégrante de.

integrate ['ɪntɪgreɪt] vt intégrer (**into** dans);
– vi s'intégrer (**into** dans); (racially) integrated (school etc) Am où se pratique la
déségrégation raciale. ◆**integration** n
intégration f; (racial) i. déségrégation f
raciale.

integrity [ɪn'tegrɪtɪ] n intégrité f.

intellect ['ɪntɪlekt] n (faculty) intellect m,
intelligence f; (cleverness, person) intelli-

gence f. ◆**inte'llectual** a & n intellectuel,
-elle (mf).

intelligence [ɪn'telɪdʒəns] n intelligence f;
Mil renseignements mpl. ◆**intelligent** a
intelligent. ◆**intelligently** adv intelligemment. ◆**intelli'gentsia** n intelligentsia f.

intelligible [ɪn'telɪdʒəb(ə)l] a intelligible.
◆**intelligi'bility** n intelligibilité f.

intemperance [ɪn'tempərəns] n intempérance f.

intend [ɪn'tend] vt (gift, remark etc) destiner
(**for** à); **to i. to do** avoir l'intention de faire;
I i. you to stay mon intention est que vous
restiez. ◆**-ed** a (deliberate) intentionnel,
voulu; (planned) projeté; **i. to be** (meant)
destiné à être. ◆**intention** n intention f (of
doing de faire). ◆**intentional** a intentionnel; **it wasn't i.** ce n'était pas fait exprès.
◆**intentionally** adv intentionnellement,
exprès.

intense [ɪn'tens] a intense; (interest) vif;
(person) passionné. ◆**intensely** adv intensément; Fig extrêmement. ◆**intensi-
'cation** n intensification f. ◆**intensify** vt
intensifier; – vi s'intensifier. ◆**intensity** n
intensité f. ◆**intensive** a intensif; **in i.
care** Med en réanimation.

intent [ɪn'tent] **1** a (look) attentif; **i. on**
(task) absorbé par; **i. on doing** résolu à faire. **2** n
intention f; **to all intents and purposes** en
fait, essentiellement.

inter [ɪn'tɜːr] vt (-rr-) enterrer.

inter- ['ɪntə(r)] pref inter-.

interact [ɪntə'rækt] vi (of ideas etc) être
interdépendants; (of people) agir conjointement; Ch interagir. ◆**interaction** n
interaction f.

intercede [ɪntə'siːd] vi intercéder (**with**
auprès de).

intercept [ɪntə'sept] vt intercepter. ◆**interception** n interception f.

interchange ['ɪntəʃeɪndʒ] n Aut échangeur
m. ◆**inter'changeable** a interchangeable.

intercom ['ɪntəkɒm] n interphone m.

interconnect/ed [ɪntəkə'nektɪd] a (facts
etc) liés. ◆**-ing** a **i. rooms** pièces fpl
communicantes.

intercontinental [ɪntəkɒntɪ'nent(ə)l] a
intercontinental.

intercourse ['ɪntəkɔːs] n (sexual, social)
rapports mpl.

interdependent [ɪntədɪ'pendənt] a interdépendant; (parts of machine) solidaire.

interest ['ɪnt(ə)rɪst, 'ɪntrəst] n intérêt m; Fin
intérêts mpl; **an i. in** (stake) Com des intérêts dans; **his or her i. is** (hobby etc) ce qui

l'intéresse c'est; **to take an i.** in s'intéresser
à; **to be of i. to s.o.** intéresser qn; – *vt* intéresser. **◆–ed** *a* (*involved*) intéressé; (*look*)
d'intérêt; **to seem i.** sembler intéressé (in
par); **to be i. in sth/s.o.** s'intéresser à
qch/qn; **I'm i. in doing** ça m'intéresse de
faire; **are you i.?** ça vous intéresse? **◆–ing**
a intéressant. **◆–ingly** *adv* **i. (enough),**
she . . . curieusement, elle . . . .

interface ['ɪntəfeɪs] *n* Tech interface *f*.

interfer/e [ɪntə'fɪər] *vi* se mêler des affaires
d'autrui; **to i.** s'ingérer dans; **to i. with**
(*upset*) déranger; (*touch*) toucher (à).
◆–ing (*a person*) importun. **◆interfer-
ence** *n* ingérence *f*; *Rad* parasites *mpl*.

interim ['ɪntərɪm] *n* intérim *m*; **in the i.**
pendant l'intérim; – *a* (*measure etc*)
provisoire; (*post*) intérimaire.

interior [ɪn'tɪərɪər] *a* intérieur; – *n* intérieur
m; **Department of the I.** *Am* ministère *m* de
l'Intérieur.

interjection [ɪntə'dʒekʃ(ə)n] *n* interjection *f*.
interlock [ɪntə'lɒk] *vi* Tech s'emboîter.
interloper ['ɪntələʊpər] *n* intrus, -use *mf*.
interlude ['ɪntəluːd] *n* intervalle *m*; Th
intermède *m*; *Mus* TV interlude *m*.

intermarry [ɪntə'mærɪ] *vi* se marier (entre
eux). **◆intermarriage** *n* mariage *m* (*entre
personnes de races etc différentes*).

intermediary [ɪntə'miːdɪərɪ] *a* & *n*
intermédiaire (*mf*).

intermediate [ɪntə'miːdɪət] *a* intermédiaire;
(*course*) Sch moyen.

interminable [ɪn'tɜːmɪnəb(ə)l] *a* interminable.

intermingle [ɪntə'mɪŋg(ə)l] *vi* se mélanger.

intermission [ɪntə'mɪʃ(ə)n] *n* Cin Th
entracte *m*.

intermittent [ɪntə'mɪtənt] *a* intermittent.
◆–ly *adv* par intermittence.

intern 1 [ɪn'tɜːn] *vt* Pol interner. **2** ['ɪntɜːn] *n*
Med Am interne *mf* (des hôpitaux).
◆inter'nee *n* interné, -ée *mf*.
◆in'ternment *n* Pol internement *m*.

internal [ɪn'tɜːn(ə)l] *a* interne; (*policy,
flight*) intérieur; **i. combustion engine**
moteur *m* à explosion; **the I. Revenue
Service** *Am* le fisc. **◆–ly** *adv* intérieurement.

international [ɪntə'næʃ(ə)nəl] *a* international; (*fame, reputation*) mondial; – *n*
(*match*) rencontre *f* internationale;
(*player*) international *m*. **◆–ly** *adv*
(*renowned etc*) mondialement.

interplanetary [ɪntə'plænɪt(ə)rɪ] *a* interplanétaire.

interplay ['ɪntəpleɪ] *n* interaction *f*, jeu *m*.

interpolate [ɪn'tɜːpəleɪt] *vt* interpoler.

interpret [ɪn'tɜːprɪt] *vt* interpréter; – *vi* Ling
faire l'interprète. **◆interpre'tation** *n*
interprétation *f*. **◆interpreter** *n* interprète
mf.

interrelated [ɪntərɪ'leɪtɪd] *a* en corrélation.
◆interrelation *n* corrélation *f*.

interrogate [ɪn'terəgeɪt] *vt* (*question closely*)
interroger. **◆interro'gation** *n* interrogation *f*; *Jur* interrogatoire *m*. **◆interro-
gator** *n* (*questioner*) interrogateur, -trice
mf.

interrogative [ɪntə'rɒgətɪv] *a* & *n* Gram
interrogatif (*m*).

interrupt [ɪntə'rʌpt] *vt* interrompre.
◆interruption *n* interruption *f*.

intersect [ɪntə'sekt] *vt* couper; – *vi*
s'entrecouper, se couper. **◆intersection** *n*
(*crossroads*) croisement *m*; (*of lines etc*)
intersection *f*.

intersperse [ɪntə'spɜːs] *vt* parsemer (with
de).

intertwine [ɪntə'twaɪn] *vt* entrelacer.

interval ['ɪntəv(ə)l] *n* intervalle *m*; *Th*
entracte *m*; **at intervals** (*time*) de temps à
autre; (*space*) par intervalles; **bright intervals** Met éclaircies *fpl*.

intervene [ɪntə'viːn] *vi* intervenir; (*of event*)
survenir; **ten years intervened** dix années
s'écoulèrent; **if nothing intervenes** s'il
n'arrive rien entre-temps. **◆intervention**
n intervention *f*.

interview ['ɪntəvjuː] *n* entrevue *f*, entretien
m (with avec); *Journ* TV interview *f*; **to call
for (an) i.** convoquer; – *vt* avoir une
entrevue avec; *Journ* TV interviewer.
◆–er *n Journ* TV interviewer *m*; *Com* Pol
enquêteur, -euse *mf*.

intestine [ɪn'testɪn] *n* intestin *m*.

intimate 1 ['ɪntɪmət] *a* intime; (*friendship*)
profond; (*knowledge, analysis*) approfondi.
◆intimacy *n* intimité *f*. **◆intimately** *adv*
intimement.

intimate 2 ['ɪntɪmeɪt] *vt* (*hint*) suggérer (that
que). **◆inti'mation** *n* (*announcement*)
annonce *f*; (*hint*) suggestion *f*; (*sign*) indication *f*.

intimidate [ɪn'tɪmɪdeɪt] *vt* intimider.
◆intimi'dation *n* intimidation *f*.

into ['ɪntuː, *unstressed* 'ɪntə] *prep* **1** dans; **to
put i.** mettre dans; **to go i.** (*room, detail*)
entrer dans. **2** en; **to translate i.** traduire
en; **to change i.** transformer *ou* changer en;
to go i. town aller en ville; **i. pieces** (*to break
etc*) en morceaux. **3** to be **i.** yoga/*etc* Fam
être à fond dans le yoga/*etc*.

intolerable [ɪn'tɒlərəb(ə)l] *a* intolérable

(that que (+ *sub*)). ◆**intolerably** *adv* insupportablement. ◆**intolerance** *n* intolérance *f*. ◆**intolerant** *a* intolérant (**of** de). ◆**intolerantly** *adv* avec intolérance.

intonation [ɪntəˈneɪʃ(ə)n] *n Ling* intonation *f*.

intoxicate [ɪnˈtɒksɪkeɪt] *vt* enivrer. ◆**intoxicated** *a* ivre. ◆**intoxi'cation** *n* ivresse *f*.

intra- ['ɪntrə] *pref* intra-.

intransigent [ɪnˈtrænsɪdʒənt] *a* intransigeant. ◆**intransigence** *n* intransigeance *f*.

intransitive [ɪnˈtrænsɪtɪv] *a & n Gram* intransitif (*m*).

intravenous [ɪntrəˈviːnəs] *a Med* intraveineux.

intrepid [ɪnˈtrepɪd] *a* intrépide.

intricate ['ɪntrɪkət] *a* complexe, compliqué. ◆**intricacy** *n* complexité *f*. ◆**intricately** *adv* de façon complexe.

intrigue 1 [ɪnˈtriːg] *vt* (*interest*) intriguer; **I'm intrigued to know . . .** je suis curieux de savoir . . . . **2** ['ɪntriːg] *n* (*plot*) intrigue *f*. ◆**-ing** (*a news etc*) curieux.

intrinsic [ɪnˈtrɪnsɪk] *a* intrinsèque. ◆**intrinsically** *adv* intrinsèquement.

introduce [ɪntrəˈdjuːs] *vt* (*insert, bring in*) introduire (**into** dans); (*programme, subject*) présenter; **to i. s.o. to s.o.** présenter qn à qn; **to i. s.o. to Dickens/geography/***etc* faire découvrir Dickens/la géographie/*etc* à qn. ◆**introduction** *n* introduction *f*; présentation *f*; (*book title*) initiation *f*; **her i. to** (*life abroad etc*) son premier contact avec. ◆**introductory** *a* (*words*) d'introduction; (*speech*) de présentation; (*course*) d'initiation.

introspective [ɪntrəˈspektɪv] *a* introspectif. ◆**introspection** *n* introspection *f*.

introvert ['ɪntrəvɜːt] *n* introverti, -ie *mf*.

intrude [ɪnˈtruːd] *vi* (*of person*) s'imposer (**on s.o.** à qn), déranger (**on s.o.** qn); **to i. on** (*s.o.'s time etc*) abuser de. ◆**intruder** *n* intrus, -use *mf*. ◆**intrusion** *n* intrusion *f* (**into** dans); **forgive my i.** pardonnez-moi de vous avoir dérangé.

intuition [ɪntjuːˈɪʃ(ə)n] *n* intuition *f*. ◆**in'tuitive** *a* intuitif.

inundate ['ɪnʌndeɪt] *vt* inonder (**with** de); **inundated with work** submergé de travail. ◆**inun'dation** *n* inondation *f*.

invade [ɪnˈveɪd] *vt* envahir; (*privacy*) violer. ◆**-er** *n* envahisseur, -euse *mf*.

invalid¹ ['ɪnvəlɪd] *a & n* malade (*mf*); (*through injury*) infirme (*mf*); **i. car** voiture *f* d'infirme.

invalid² [ɪnˈvælɪd] *a* non valable. ◆**invalidate** *vt* invalider, annuler.

invaluable [ɪnˈvæljʊəb(ə)l] *a* (*help etc*) inestimable.

invariab/le [ɪnˈveərɪəb(ə)l] *a* invariable. ◆**-ly** *adv* invariablement.

invasion [ɪnˈveɪʒ(ə)n] *n* invasion *f*; **i. of s.o.'s privacy** intrusion *f* dans la vie privée de qn.

invective [ɪnˈvektɪv] *n* invective *f*.

inveigh [ɪnˈveɪ] *vi* **to i. against** invectiver contre.

inveigle [ɪnˈveɪg(ə)l] *vt* **to i. s.o. into doing** amener qn à faire par la ruse.

invent [ɪnˈvent] *vt* inventer. ◆**invention** *n* invention *f*. ◆**inventive** *a* inventif. ◆**inventiveness** *n* esprit *m* d'invention. ◆**inventor** *n* inventeur, -trice *mf*.

inventory ['ɪnvənt(ə)rɪ] *n* inventaire *m*.

inverse [ɪnˈvɜːs] *a & n Math* inverse (*m*).

invert [ɪnˈvɜːt] *vt* intervertir; **inverted commas** guillemets *mpl*. ◆**inversion** *n* interversion *f*; *Gram Anat etc* inversion *f*.

invest [ɪnˈvest] *vt* (*funds*) investir (**in** dans); (*money*) placer, investir; (*time, effort*) consacrer (**in** à); **to i. s.o. with** (*endow*) investir qn de; **–** *vi* **to i. in** (*project*) placer son argent dans; (*firm*) investir dans; (*house, radio etc*) *Fig* se payer. ◆**investiture** *n* (*of bishop etc*) investiture *f*. ◆**investment** *n* investissement *m*, placement *m*. ◆**investor** *n* (*shareholder*) actionnaire *mf*; (*saver*) épargnant, -ante *mf*.

investigate [ɪnˈvestɪgeɪt] *vt* (*examine*) examiner, étudier; (*crime*) enquêter sur. ◆**investi'gation** *n* examen *m*, étude *f*; (*by police*) enquête *f* (**of** sur); (*inquiry*) enquête *f*, investigation *f*. ◆**investigator** *n* (*detective*) enquêteur, -euse *mf*.

inveterate [ɪnˈvetərət] *a* invétéré.

invidious [ɪnˈvɪdɪəs] *a* qui suscite la jalousie; (*hurtful*) blessant; (*odious*) odieux.

invigilate [ɪnˈvɪdʒɪleɪt] *vi* être de surveillance (**à un examen**). ◆**invigilator** *n* surveillant, -ante *mf*.

invigorat/e [ɪnˈvɪgəreɪt] *vt* revigorer. ◆**-ing** *a* stimulant.

invincible [ɪnˈvɪnsəb(ə)l] *a* invincible.

invisible [ɪnˈvɪzəb(ə)l] *a* invisible; **i. ink** encre *f* sympathique.

invit/e [ɪnˈvaɪt] *vt* inviter (**to do** à faire); (*ask for*) demander; (*lead to, give occasion for*) appeler; (*trouble*) chercher; **to i. out** inviter (à sortir); **to i. over** inviter (à venir); **–** ['ɪnvaɪt] *n Fam* invitation *f*. ◆**-ing** *a* engageant, invitant; (*food*) appétissant. ◆**invi'tation** *n* invitation *f*.

invoice ['ɪnvɔɪs] *n* facture *f*; **–** *vt* facturer.

invoke [ɪn'vəʊk] vt invoquer.

involuntar/y [ɪn'vɒləntərɪ] a involontaire. ◆**—ily** adv involontairement.

involv/e [ɪn'vɒlv] vt (include) mêler (qn) (in à), impliquer (qn) (in dans); (associate) associer (qn) (in à); (entail) entraîner; **to i. oneself, get involved** (commit oneself) s'engager (in dans); **to i. s.o. in expense** entraîner qn à des dépenses; **the job involves going abroad** le poste nécessite des déplacements à l'étranger. ◆**—ed** a (complicated) compliqué; (factors/etc i. (at stake) les facteurs/etc en jeu; **the person i. la** personne en question; **i. with s.o.** mêlé aux affaires de qn; **personally i.** concerné; **emotionally i. with** amoureux de; **to become i.** (of police) intervenir. ◆**—ement** n participation f (in à), implication f (in dans); (commitment) engagement m (in dans); (problem) difficulté f; **emotional i.** liaison f.

invulnerable [ɪn'vʌln(ə)rəb(ə)l] a invulnérable.

inward ['ɪnwəd] a & adv (movement, to move) vers l'intérieur; – a (inner) intérieur. ◆**i.-looking** a replié sur soi. ◆**inwardly** adv (inside) à l'intérieur; (to laugh, curse etc) intérieurement. ◆**inwards** adv vers l'intérieur.

iodine ['aɪədiːn, Am 'aɪədaɪn] n Med teinture f d'iode.

iota [aɪ'əʊtə] n (of truth etc) grain m; (in text) iota m.

IOU [aɪəʊ'juː] n abbr (I owe you) reconnaissance f de dette.

IQ [aɪ'kjuː] n abbr (intelligence quotient) QI m inv.

Iran [ɪ'rɑːn] n Iran m. ◆**Iranian** [ɪ'reɪnɪən] a & n iranien, -ienne (mf).

Iraq [ɪ'rɑːk] n Irak m. ◆**Iraqi** a & n irakien, -ienne (mf).

irascible [ɪ'ræsɪb(ə)l] a irascible.

ire [aɪər] n Lit courroux m. ◆**i'rate** a furieux.

Ireland ['aɪələnd] n Irlande f. ◆**Irish** a irlandais; – n (language) irlandais m. ◆**Irishman** n (pl -men) Irlandais m. ◆**Irishwoman** n (pl -women) Irlandaise f.

iris ['aɪərɪs] n Anat Bot iris m.

irk [ɜːk] vt ennuyer. ◆**irksome** a ennuyeux.

iron ['aɪən] n fer m; (for clothes) fer (à repasser); **old i., scrap i.** ferraille f; **i. and steel industry** sidérurgie f; **the I. Curtain** Pol le rideau de fer; – vt (clothes) repasser; **to i. out** (difficulties) Fig aplanir. ◆**—ing** n repassage m; **i. board** planche f à repasser. ◆**ironmonger** n quincailler m. ◆**iron-**

mongery n quincaillerie f. ◆**ironwork** n ferronnerie f.

irony ['aɪərənɪ] n ironie f. ◆**i'ronic(al)** a ironique.

irradiate [ɪ'reɪdɪeɪt] vt irradier.

irrational [ɪ'ræʃən(ə)l] a (act) irrationnel; (fear) irraisonné; (person) peu rationnel, illogique.

irreconcilable [ɪrekən'saɪləb(ə)l] a irréconciliable, inconciliable; (views, laws etc) inconciliable.

irrefutable [ɪrɪ'fjuːtəb(ə)l] a irréfutable.

irregular [ɪ'regjʊlər] a irrégulier. ◆**irregu-'larity** n irrégularité f.

irrelevant [ɪ'reləvənt] a (remark) non pertinent; (course) peu utile; **i. to** sans rapport avec; **that's i.** ça n'a rien à voir. ◆**irrelevance** n manque m de rapport.

irreparable [ɪ'rep(ə)rəb(ə)l] a (harm, loss) irréparable.

irreplaceable [ɪrɪ'pleɪsəb(ə)l] a irremplaçable.

irrepressible [ɪrɪ'presəb(ə)l] a (laughter etc) irrépressible.

irresistible [ɪrɪ'zɪstəb(ə)l] a (person, charm etc) irrésistible.

irresolute [ɪ'rezəluːt] a irrésolu, indécis.

irrespective of [ɪrɪ'spektɪvəv] prep sans tenir compte de.

irresponsible [ɪrɪ'spɒnsəb(ə)l] a (act) irréfléchi; (person) irresponsable.

irretrievable [ɪrɪ'triːvəb(ə)l] a irréparable.

irreverent [ɪ'revərənt] a irrévérencieux.

irreversible [ɪrɪ'vɜːsəb(ə)l] a (process) irréversible; (decision) irrévocable.

irrevocable [ɪ'revəkəb(ə)l] a irrévocable.

irrigate ['ɪrɪgeɪt] vt irriguer. ◆**irri'gation** n irrigation f.

irritate ['ɪrɪteɪt] vt irriter. ◆**—ing** a irritant. ◆**irritable** a (easily annoyed) irritable. ◆**irritant** n irritant m. ◆**irri'tation** n (anger) & Med irritation f.

is [ɪz] see be.

Islam ['ɪzlɑːm] n islam m. ◆**Islamic** [ɪz'læmɪk] a islamique.

island ['aɪlənd] n île f; **traffic i.** refuge m; – a insulaire. ◆**islander** n insulaire mf. ◆**isle** [aɪl] n île f; **the British Isles** les îles Britanniques.

isolate ['aɪsəleɪt] vt isoler (from de). ◆**isolated** a (remote, unique) isolé. ◆**iso'lation** n isolement m; **in i.** isolément.

Israel ['ɪzreɪl] n Israël m. ◆**is'raeli** a & n israélien, -ienne (mf).

issue ['ɪʃuː] vt (book etc) publier; (an order) donner; (tickets) distribuer; (passport) délivrer; (stamps, banknotes) émettre;

(*warning*) lancer; (*supply*) fournir (**with de,** **to à**); – *vi* **to i. from** (*of smell*) se dégager de; (*stem from*) provenir de; – *n* (*matter*) question *f*; (*problem*) problème *m*; (*outcome*) résultat *m*; (*of text*) publication *f*; (*of stamps etc*) émission *f*; (*newspaper*) numéro *m*; **at i.** (*at stake*) en cause; **to make an i. of** faire toute une affaire de.

isthmus ['ɪsməs] *n Geog* isthme *m*.

it [ɪt] *pron* **1** (*subject*) il, elle; (*object*) le, l'; (**to**) **it** (*indirect object*) lui; **it bites** (*dog*) il mord; **I've done it** je l'ai fait. **2** (*impersonal*) il; **it's snowing** il neige; **it's hot** il fait chaud. **3** (*non specific*) ce, cela, ça; **it's good** c'est bon; **it was pleasant** c'était agréable; **who is it?** qui est-ce?; **that's it!** (*I agree*) c'est ça!; (*it's done*) ça y est!; **to consider it wise to do** juger prudent de faire; **it was Paul who ...** c'est Paul qui ... ; **she's got it in her to succeed** elle est capable de réussir; **to have it in for s.o.** en vouloir à qn. **4 of it, from it, about it, on it,** en; **in it, to it, at it, y; on it** dessus; **under it** dessous.

italic [ɪ'tælɪk] *a Typ* italique; – *npl* italique *m*.

Italy ['ɪtəlɪ] *n* Italie *f*. ◆**I'talian** *a & n* italien, -ienne (*mf*); – *n* (*language*) italien *m*.

itch [ɪtʃ] *n* démangeaison(s) *f(pl)*; **to have an i. to do** avoir une envie folle de faire; – *vi* démanger; **my arm itches** son bras le *or* lui démange; **I'm itching to do** *Fig* ça me démange de faire. ◆**—ing** *n* démangeaison(s) *f(pl)*. ◆**itchy** *a* **an i. hand** une main qui me démange.

item ['aɪtəm] *n Com Journ* article *m*; (*matter*) question *f*; (*on entertainment programme*) numéro *m*; **a news i.** une information. ◆**itemize** *vt* détailler.

itinerant [aɪ'tɪnərənt] *a* (*musician, actor*) ambulant; (*judge, preacher*) itinérant.

itinerary [aɪ'tɪnərərɪ] *n* itinéraire *m*.

its [ɪts] *poss a* son, sa, *pl* ses. ◆**it'self** *pron* lui-même, elle-même; (*reflexive*) se, s'; **goodness i.** la bonté même; **by i.** tout seul.

IUD [aɪjuː'diː] *n abbr* (*intrauterine device*) stérilet *m*.

ivory ['aɪvərɪ] *n* ivoire *m*.

ivy ['aɪvɪ] *n* lierre *m*.

J

J, j [dʒeɪ] *n* J, j *m*.

jab [dʒæb] *vt* (**-bb-**) (*thrust*) enfoncer (**into** dans); (*prick*) piquer (*qn*) (**with sth** du bout de qch); – *n* coup *m* (sec); (*injection*) *Med Fam* piqûre *f*.

jabber ['dʒæbər] *vi* bavarder, jaser; – *vt* bredouiller. ◆**—ing** *n* bavardage *m*.

jack [dʒæk] **1** *n Aut* cric *m*; – *vt* **to j. up** soulever (*avec un cric*); (*price*) *Fig* augmenter. **2** *n Cards* valet *m*. **3** *vt* **to j. (in)** (*job etc*) *Fam* plaquer. **4** *n* **j. of all trades** homme *m* à tout faire. ◆**j.-in-the-box** *n* diable *m* (à ressort).

jackal ['dʒæk(ə)l] *n* (*animal*) chacal *m*.

jackass ['dʒækæs] *n* (*fool*) idiot, -ote *mf*.

jackdaw ['dʒækdɔː] *n* (*bird*) choucas *m*.

jacket ['dʒækɪt] *n* (*short coat*) veste *f*; (*of man's suit*) veston *m*; (*of woman*) veste *f*, jaquette *f*; (*bulletproof*) gilet *m*; (*of book*) jaquette *f*; **in their jackets** (*potatoes*) en robe des champs.

jack-knife ['dʒæknaɪf] **1** *n* couteau *m* de poche. **2** *vi* (*of lorry, truck*) se mettre en travers de la route.

jackpot ['dʒækpɒt] *n* gros lot *m*.

jacks [dʒæks] *npl* (*jeu m* d')osselets *mpl*.

jacuzzi [dʒə'kuːzɪ] *n* (*bath, pool*) jacousi *m*.

jade [dʒeɪd] *n* **1** (*stone*) jade *m*. **2** (*horse*) rosse *f*, canasson *m*.

jaded ['dʒeɪdɪd] *a* blasé.

jagged ['dʒægɪd] *a* déchiqueté.

jaguar ['dʒægjuər] *n* (*animal*) jaguar *m*.

jail [dʒeɪl] *n* prison *f*; – *vt* emprisonner (**for theft/etc** pour vol/etc); **to j. for life** condamner à perpétuité. ◆**jailbreak** *n* évasion *f* (de prison). ◆**jailer** *n* geôlier, -ière *mf*.

jalopy [dʒə'lɒpɪ] *n* (*car*) *Fam* vieux tacot *m*.

jam¹ [dʒæm] *n Culin* confiture *f*. ◆**jamjar** *n* pot *m* à confiture.

jam² [dʒæm] **1** *n* (*traffic*) **j.** embouteillage *m*; **in a j.** (*trouble*) *Fig Fam* dans le pétrin. **2** *vt* (**-mm-**) (*squeeze, make stuck*) coincer, bloquer; (*gun*) enrayer; (*street, corridor etc*) encombrer; (*building*) envahir; *Rad* brouiller; **to j. sth into** (*pack, cram*) (en)tasser qch dans; (*thrust, put*) enfoncer *or* fourrer qch dans; **to j. on** (*brakes*) bloquer; – *vi* (*get stuck*) se coincer, se bloquer; (*of gun*) s'enrayer; **to j. into** (*of crowd*) s'entasser dans. ◆**jammed** a (machine etc) coincé, bloqué; (street etc) encombré. ◆**jam-'packed** a (hall etc) bourré de monde.

Jamaica [dʒə'meɪkə] n Jamaïque f.

jangl/e ['dʒæŋg(ə)l] vi cliqueter; – n cliquetis m. ◆**–ing** a (noise) discordant.

janitor ['dʒænɪtər] n concierge m.

January ['dʒænjʊərɪ] n janvier m.

Japan [dʒə'pæn] n Japon m. ◆**Japa'nese** a & n japonais, -aise (mf); – n (language) japonais m.

jar [dʒɑːr] 1 n (vessel) pot m; (large, glass) bocal m. 2 n (jolt) choc m; – vt (-rr-) (shake) ébranler. 3 vi (-rr-) (of noise) grincer; (of note) Mus détonner; (of colours, words) jurer (with avec); to j. on (s.o.'s nerves) porter sur; (s.o.'s ears) écorcher. ◆**jarring** a (note) discordant.

jargon ['dʒɑːɡən] n jargon m.

jasmine ['dʒæzmɪn] n Bot jasmin m.

jaundice ['dʒɔːndɪs] n Med jaunisse f. ◆**jaundiced** a (bitter) Fig aigri; to take a j. view of voir d'un mauvais œil.

jaunt [dʒɔːnt] n (journey) balade f.

jaunt/y ['dʒɔːntɪ] a (-ier, -iest) (carefree) insouciant; (cheerful, lively) allègre; (hat etc) coquet, chic. ◆**–ily** adv avec insouciance; allègrement.

javelin ['dʒævlɪn] n javelot m.

jaw [dʒɔː] 1 n Anat mâchoire f. 2 vi (talk) Pej Fam papoter; – n to have a j. Fam tailler une bavette.

jay [dʒeɪ] n (bird) geai m.

jaywalker ['dʒeɪwɔːkər] n piéton m imprudent.

jazz [dʒæz] n jazz m; – vt to j. up Fam (music) jazzifier; (enliven) animer; (clothes, room) égayer.

jealous ['dʒeləs] a jaloux (of de). ◆**jealousy** n jalousie f.

jeans [dʒiːnz] npl (blue-)jean m.

jeep [dʒiːp] n jeep f.

jeer [dʒɪər] vti to j. (at) (mock) railler; (boo) huer; – n raillerie f; pl (boos) huées fpl. ◆**–ing** a railleur; – n railleries fpl; (of crowd) huées fpl.

jell [dʒel] vi (of ideas etc) Fam prendre tournure.

jello® ['dʒeləʊ] n inv Culin Am gelée f. ◆**jellied** a Culin en gelée. ◆**jelly** n Culin gelée f. ◆**jellyfish** n méduse f.

jeopardy ['dʒepədɪ] n danger m, péril m. ◆**jeopardize** vt mettre en danger or en péril.

jerk [dʒɜːk] 1 vt to give a j. donner une secousse à (pour tirer, pousser etc); – n secousse f, saccade f. 2 n (person) Pej Fam pauvre type m;

(stupid) j. crétin, -ine mf. ◆**jerk/y** a (-ier, -iest) 1 saccadé. 2 (stupid) Am Fam stupide, bête. ◆**–ily** adv par saccades.

jersey ['dʒɜːzɪ] n (cloth) jersey m; (garment) & Fb maillot m.

Jersey ['dʒɜːzɪ] n Jersey f.

jest [dʒest] n plaisanterie f; in j. pour rire; – vi plaisanter. ◆**–er** n Hist bouffon m.

Jesus ['dʒiːzəs] n Jésus m; J. Christ Jésus-Christ m.

jet [dʒet] 1 n (of liquid, steam etc) jet m. 2 n Av avion m à réaction; – a (engine) à réaction; j. lag fatigue f (due au décalage horaire). ◆**jet-lagged** a Fam qui souffre du décalage horaire.

jet-black [dʒet'blæk] a noir comme (du) jais, (noir) de jais.

jettison ['dʒetɪs(ə)n] vt Nau jeter à la mer; (fuel) Av larguer; Fig abandonner.

jetty ['dʒetɪ] n jetée f; (landing-place) embarcadère m.

Jew [dʒuː] n (man) Juif m; (woman) Juive f. ◆**Jewess** n Juive f. ◆**Jewish** a juif.

jewel ['dʒuːəl] n bijou m; (in watch) rubis m. ◆**jewelled** a orné de bijoux. ◆**jeweller** n bijoutier, -ière mf. ◆**jewellery** n, Am ◆**jewelry** n bijoux mpl.

jib [dʒɪb] vi (-bb-) regimber (at devant); to j. at doing se refuser à faire.

jibe [dʒaɪb] vi & n = gibe.

jiffy ['dʒɪfɪ] n Fam instant m.

jig [dʒɪɡ] n (dance, music) gigue f.

jigsaw ['dʒɪɡsɔː] n j. (puzzle) puzzle m.

jilt [dʒɪlt] vt (lover) laisser tomber.

jingle ['dʒɪŋɡ(ə)l] vi (of keys, bell etc) tinter; – vt faire tinter; – n tintement m.

jinx [dʒɪŋks] n (person, object) porte-malheur m inv; (spell, curse) (mauvais) sort m, poisse f.

jitters ['dʒɪtəz] npl to have the j. Fam avoir la frousse. ◆**jittery** a to be j. Fam avoir la frousse.

job [dʒɒb] n (task) travail m; (post) poste m, situation f; (crime) Fam coup m; to have a j. doing or to do (much trouble) avoir du mal à faire; to have the j. of doing (unpleasant task) être obligé de faire; (for a living etc) être chargé de faire; it's a good j. (that) Fam heureusement que; that's just the j. Fam c'est juste ce qu'il faut; out of a j. au chômage. ◆**jobcentre** n agence f nationale pour l'emploi. ◆**jobless** a au chômage.

jockey ['dʒɒkɪ] n jockey m; – vi to j. for (position, job) manœuvrer pour obtenir.

jocular ['dʒɒkjʊlər] a jovial, amusant.

jog [dʒɒɡ] 1 n (jolt) secousse f; (nudge) coup

m de coude; – *vt* (**-gg-**) (*shake*) secouer; (*elbow*) pousser; (*memory*) *Fig* rafraîchir. **2** *vi* (**-gg-**) **to j. along** (*of vehicle*) cahoter; (*of work*) aller tant bien que mal; (*of person*) faire son petit bonhomme de chemin. **3** *vi* (**-gg-**) *Sp* faire du jogging. ◆**jogging** *n Sp* jogging *m*.

john [dʒɒn] *n* (*toilet*) *Am Sl* cabinets *mpl*.

join [dʒɔɪn] **1** *vt* (*unite*) joindre, réunir; (*link*) relier; (*wires, pipes*) raccorder; **to j. s.o.** (*catch up with, meet*) rejoindre qn; (*associate oneself with, go with*) se joindre à qn (**in doing** pour faire); **to j. the sea** (*of river*) rejoindre la mer; **to j. hands** se donner la main; **to j. together** *or* **up** (*objects*) joindre; – *vi* (*of roads, rivers etc*) se rejoindre; **to j. (together** *or* **up)** (*of objects*) se joindre (**with** à); **to j.** in participer; (*in a game*) prendre part à un jeu; – *n* raccord *m*, joint *m*. **2** *vt* (*become a member of*) s'inscrire à (*club, parti*); (*army*) s'engager dans; (*queue, line*) se mettre à; – *vi* (*become a member*) devenir membre; **to j. up** *Mil* s'engager.

joiner [dʒɔɪnər] *n* menuisier *m*.

joint [dʒɔɪnt] **1** *n Anat* articulation *f*; *Culin* rôti *m*; *Tech* joint *m*; **out of j.** *Med* démis. **2** *n* (*nightclub etc*) *Sl* boîte *f*. **3** *a* (*account, statement etc*) commun; (*effort*) conjugé; **j. author** coauteur *m*. ◆**-ly** *adv* conjointement.

jok/e [dʒəʊk] *n* plaisanterie *f*; (*trick*) tour *m*; **it's no j.** (*it's unpleasant*) ce n'est pas drôle (**doing** de faire); – *vi* plaisanter (**about** sur). ◆**-er** *n* plaisantin *m*; (*fellow*) *Fam* type *m*; *Cards* joker *m*. ◆**-ingly** *adv* en plaisantant.

jolly [dʒɒlɪ] **1** *a* (**-ier, -iest**) (*happy*) gai; (*drunk*) *Fam* éméché. **2** *adv* (*very*) *Fam* rudement. ◆**jollifi'cation** *n* (*merry-making*) réjouissances *fpl*. ◆**jollity** *n* jovialité *f*; (*merry-making*) réjouissances *fpl*.

jolt [dʒəʊlt] *vt* **to j. s.o.** (*of vehicle*) cahoter qn; (*shake*) *Fig* secouer qn; – *vi* **to j. (along)** (*of vehicle*) cahoter; – *n* cahot *m*, secousse *f*; (*shock*) *Fig* secousse *f*.

Jordan [dʒɔːd(ə)n] *n* Jordanie *f*.

jostle [dʒɒs(ə)l] *vt* (*push*) bousculer; – *vi* (*push each other*) se bousculer (**for** pour obtenir); **don't j.!** ne bousculez pas!

jot [dʒɒt] *vt* (**-tt-**) **to j. down** noter. ◆**jotter** *n* (*notepad*) bloc-notes *m*.

journal [dʒɜːn(ə)l] *n* (*periodical*) revue *f*, journal *m*. ◆**journa'lese** *n* jargon *m* journalistique. ◆**journalism** *n* journalisme *m*. ◆**journalist** *n* journaliste *mf*.

journey [dʒɜːnɪ] *n* (*trip*) voyage *m*;

(*distance*) trajet *m*; **to go on a j.** partir en voyage; – *vi* voyager.

jovial [dʒəʊvɪəl] *a* jovial.

joy [dʒɔɪ] *n* joie *f*; **j.** (*of countryside, motherhood etc*) plaisirs *mpl* (**of** de). ◆**joyful** *a*, ◆**joyous** *a* joyeux. ◆**joyride** *n* virée *f* (*dans une voiture volée*).

joystick [dʒɔɪstɪk] *n* (*of aircraft, computer*) manche *m* à balai.

JP [dʒeɪˈpiː] *abbr* = **Justice of the Peace.**

jubilant [dʒuːbɪlənt] *a* **to be j.** jubiler. ◆**jubi'lation** *n* jubilation *f*.

jubilee [dʒuːbɪliː] *n* (*golden*) **j.** jubilé *m*.

Judaism [dʒuːdeɪ(ə)m] *n* judaïsme *m*.

judder [dʒʌdər] *vi* (*shake*) vibrer; – *n* vibration *f*.

judg/e [dʒʌdʒ] *n* juge *m*; – *vti* juger; **judging by** à en juger par. ◆**-(e)ment** *n* jugement *m*.

judicial [dʒuːˈdɪʃ(ə)l] *a* judiciaire. ◆**judiciary** *n* magistrature *f*. ◆**judicious** *a* judicieux.

judo [dʒuːdəʊ] *n* judo *m*.

jug [dʒʌg] *n* cruche *f*; (*for milk*) pot *m*.

juggernaut [dʒʌgənɔːt] *n* (*truck*) poids *m* lourd, mastodonte *m*.

juggl/e [dʒʌg(ə)l] *vi* jongler; – *vt* jongler avec. ◆**-er** *n* jongleur, -euse *mf*.

Jugoslavia [juːgəʊˈslɑːvɪə] *n* Yougoslavie *f*. ◆**Jugoslav** *a* & *n* yougoslave (*mf*).

juice [dʒuːs] *n* jus *m*; (*in stomach*) suc *m*. ◆**juicy** *a* (**-ier, -iest**) (*fruit*) juteux; (*meat*) succulent; (*story*) *Fig* savoureux.

jukebox [dʒuːkbɒks] *n* juke-box *m*.

July [dʒuːˈlaɪ] *n* juillet *m*.

jumble [dʒʌmb(ə)l] *vt* **to j. (up)** (*objects, facts etc*) brouiller, mélanger; – *n* fouillis *m*; **j. sale** (*used clothes etc*) vente *f* de charité.

jumbo [dʒʌmbəʊ] *a* géant; – *a* & *n* (*pl* **-os**) **j. (jet)** jumbo-jet *m*, gros-porteur *m*.

jump [dʒʌmp] *n* (*leap*) saut *m*, bond *m*; (*start*) sursaut *m*; (*increase*) hausse *f*; – *vi* sauter (**at** sur); (*start*) sursauter; (*of price, heart*) faire un bond; **to j. about** sautiller; **to j. across sth** traverser qch d'un bond; **to j. to conclusions** tirer des conclusions hâtives; **j. in** *or* **on!** *Aut* montez!; **to j. on** (*bus*) sauter dans; **to j. off** *or* **out** sauter; **to j. off sth, j. out of sth** sauter de qch; **to j. out of the window** sauter par la fenêtre; **to j. up** se lever d'un bond; – *vt* sauter; **to j. the lights** *Aut* griller un feu rouge; **to j. the rails** (*of train*) dérailler; **to j. the queue** resquiller.

jumper [dʒʌmpər] *n* pull(-over) *m*; (*dress*) *Am* robe *f* chasuble.

jumpy [dʒʌmpɪ] *a* (**-ier, -iest**) nerveux.

junction ['dʒʌŋkʃ(ə)n] n (joining) jonction f; (crossroads) carrefour m.

juncture ['dʒʌŋktʃər] n at this j. (critical point in time) en ce moment même.

June [dʒuːn] n juin m.

jungle ['dʒʌŋg(ə)l] n jungle f.

junior ['dʒuːnɪər] a (younger) plus jeune; (in rank, status etc) subalterne; (teacher, doctor) jeune; **to be j. to s.o.**, **be s.o.'s j.** être plus jeune que qn; (in rank, status) être au-dessous de qn; **Smith j.** Smith fils or junior; **j. school** école f primaire; **j. high school** Am = collège m d'enseignement secondaire; – n cadet, -ette mf; Sch petit, -ite mf, petit(e) élève mf; Sp junior mf, cadet, -ette mf.

junk [dʒʌŋk] **1** n (objects) bric-à-brac m inv; (metal) ferraille f; (goods) Pej camelote f; (film, book etc) Pej idiotie f; (nonsense) idioties fpl; **j. shop** (boutique f de) brocanteur m. **2** vt (get rid of) Am Fam balancer.

junkie ['dʒʌŋkɪ] n Fam drogué, -ée mf.

junta ['dʒʌntə] n Pol junte f.

jurisdiction [dʒuərɪs'dɪkʃ(ə)n] n juridiction f.

jury ['dʒuərɪ] n (in competition) & Jur jury m. **◆juror** n Jur juré m.

just [dʒʌst] **1** adv (exactly, slightly) juste; (only) juste, seulement; (simply) (tout) simplement; **it's j. as I thought** c'est bien ce que je pensais; **j. at that time** à cet instant

même; **she has/had j. left** elle vient/venait de partir; **I've j. come from** j'arrive de; **I'm j. coming!** j'arrive!; **he'll j. catch the bus** il aura son bus de justesse; **he missed it** il l'a manqué de peu; **j. as big/light/etc** tout aussi grand/léger/etc (as que); **j. listen!** écoute donc!; **j. a moment!** un instant!; **j. over ten** un peu plus de dix; **j. one** un(e) seul(e) (of de); **j. about** (approximately) à peu près; (almost) presque; **j. about to do** sur le point de faire. **2** a (fair) juste (to envers). **◆-ly** adv avec justice. **◆-ness** n (of cause etc) justice f.

justice ['dʒʌstɪs] n justice f; (judge) juge m; **to do j. to** (meal) faire honneur à; **it doesn't do you j.** (hat, photo) cela ne vous avantage pas; (attitude) cela ne vous fait pas honneur; **J. of the Peace** juge m de paix.

justify ['dʒʌstɪfaɪ] vt justifier; **to be justified in doing** (have right) être en droit de faire; (have reason) avoir toutes les bonnes raisons de faire. **◆justi'fiable** a justifiable. **◆justi'fiably** adv légitimement. **◆justifi'cation** n justification f.

jut [dʒʌt] vi (-tt-) **to j. out** faire saillie; **j. out over sth** (overhang) surplomber qch.

jute [dʒuːt] n (fibre) jute m.

juvenile ['dʒuːvənaɪl] n adolescent, -ente mf; – a (court, book etc) pour enfants; (delinquent, zone) juvénile; (behaviour) Pej puéril. **◆juxtapose** [dʒʌkstə'pəʊz] vt juxtaposer. **◆juxtapo'sition** n juxtaposition f.

K

K, k [keɪ] n K, k m.

kaleidoscope [kə'laɪdəskəʊp] n kaléidoscope m.

kangaroo [kæŋgə'ruː] n kangourou m.

kaput [kə'pʊt] a (broken, ruined) Sl fichu.

karate [kə'rɑːtɪ] n Sp karaté m.

keel [kiːl] n Nau quille f; – vi **to k. over** (of boat) chavirer.

keen [kiːn] a (edge, appetite) aiguisé; (interest, feeling) vif; (mind) pénétrant; (wind) coupant, piquant; (enthusiastic) enthousiaste; **a k. sportsman** un passionné de sport; **to be k. to do** or **on doing** tenir (beaucoup) à faire; **to be k. on** (music, sport etc) être passionné de; **he is k. on her/the idea** elle/l'idée lui plaît beaucoup. **◆-ly** adv (to work etc) avec enthousiasme; (to feel, interest) vivement. **◆-ness** n

enthousiasme m; (of mind) pénétration f; (of interest) intensité f; **k. to do** empressement m à faire.

keep¹ [kiːp] vt (pt & pp kept) garder; (shop, car) avoir; (diary, promise) tenir; (family) entretenir; (rule) observer, respecter; (feast day) célébrer; (birthday) fêter; (detain, delay) retenir; (put) mettre; **to k. (on) doing** (continue) continuer à faire; **to k. clean** tenir or garder propre; **to k. from** (conceal) cacher à; **to k. s.o. from doing** (prevent) empêcher qn de faire; **to k. s.o. waiting/working** faire attendre/travailler qn; **to k. sth going** (engine, machine) laisser qch en marche; **to k. s.o. in whisky/etc** fournir qn en whisky/etc; **to k. an appointment** se rendre à un rendez-vous; **to k. back** (withhold, delay) retenir; (conceal) cacher (from à); **to k. down** (control) maîtriser; (restrict) limiter; (costs, price) maintenir bas; **to k. in** empêcher de sortir; (pupil) Sch consigner; **to k. off** or **away** (person) éloigner (from de); **'k. off the grass'** 'ne pas marcher sur les pelouses'; **k. your hands off!** n'y touche(z) pas!; **to k. on** (hat, employee) garder; **to k. out** empêcher d'entrer; **to k. up** (continue, maintain) continuer (**doing sth** à faire qch); (road, building) entretenir; − vi (continue) continuer; (remain) rester; (of food) se garder, se conserver; (wait) attendre; **how is he keeping?** comment va-t-il?; **to k. still** rester or se tenir tranquille; **to k. from doing** (refrain) s'abstenir de faire; **to k. going** (continue) continuer; **to k. at it** (keep doing it) continuer à le faire; **to k. away** or **off** or **back** ne pas s'approcher (from de); **if the rain keeps off** s'il ne pleut pas; **to k. on at s.o.** harceler qn; **to k. out** rester en dehors (of de); **to k. to** (subject, path) ne pas s'écarter de; (room) garder; **to k. to the left** tenir la gauche; **to k. to oneself** se tenir à l'écart; **to k. up** (continue) continuer; (follow) suivre qn; **to k. up with s.o** (follow) se maintenir à la hauteur de qn; − n (food) subsistance f; **to have one's k.** être logé et nourri; **for keeps** Fam pour toujours. **◆−ing** n (care) garde f; **in k.** with en rapport avec. **◆−er** n gardien, -ienne mf.

keep² [kiːp] n (tower) Hist donjon m.

keepsake ['kiːpseɪk] n (object) souvenir m.

keg [keg] n tonnelet m.

kennel ['ken(ə)l] n niche f; (for boarding) chenil m.

Kenya ['kiːnjə, 'kenjə] n Kenya m.

kept [kept] see keep¹; − a **well** or **nicely k.** (house etc) bien tenu.

kerb [kɜːb] n bord m du trottoir.

kernel ['kɜːn(ə)l] n (of nut) amande f.

kerosene ['kerəsiːn] n (aviation fuel) kérosène m; (paraffin) Am pétrole m (lampant).

ketchup ['ketʃəp] n (sauce) ketchup m.

kettle ['ket(ə)l] n bouilloire f; **the k. is boiling** l'eau bout.

key [kiː] n clef f, clé f; (of piano, typewriter, computer) touche f; − a (industry, post etc) clef (f inv), clé (f inv); **k. man** pivot m; **k. ring** porte-clefs m inv. **◆keyboard** n clavier m. **◆keyhole** n trou m de (la) serrure. **◆keynote** n (of speech) note f dominante. **◆keystone** n (of policy etc) & Archit clef f de voûte.

keyed [kiːd] a **to be k. up** avoir les nerfs tendus.

khaki ['kɑːkɪ] a & n kaki a inv & m.

kibbutz [kɪˈbuts] n kibboutz m.

kick [kik] n coup m de pied; (of horse) ruade f; **to get a k. out of doing** (thrill) Fam prendre un malin plaisir à faire; **for kicks** Pej Fam pour le plaisir; − vt donner un coup de pied à; (of horse) lancer une ruade à; **to k. back** (ball) renvoyer (du pied); **to k. down** or **in** démolir à coups de pied; **to k. out** (eject) Fam flanquer dehors; **to k. up** (fuss, row) Fam faire; − vi donner des coups de pied; (of horse) ruer; **to k. off** Fb donner le coup d'envoi; (start) Fig démarrer. **◆k.-off** n Fb coup m d'envoi.

kid [kid] **1** n (goat) chevreau m. **2** n (child) Fam gosse mf; **his** or **her k. brother** Am Fam son petit frère. **3** vti (-dd-) (joke, tease) Fam blaguer; **to k. oneself** se faire des illusions.

kidnap ['kidnæp] vt (-pp-) kidnapper. **◆kidnapping** n enlèvement m. **◆kidnapper** n kidnappeur, -euse mf.

kidney ['kidni] n Anat rein m; Culin rognon m; **on a k. machine** sous rein artificiel; **k. bean** haricot m rouge.

kill [kil] vt tuer; (bill) Pol repousser, faire échouer; (chances) détruire; (rumour) étouffer; (story) étouffer; (engine) Fam arrêter; **my feet are killing me** Fam je ne sens plus mes pieds, j'ai les pieds en compote; **to k. off** (person etc) & Fig détruire; − vi tuer; − n mise f à mort; (prey) animaux mpl tués. **◆−ing 1** n (of person) meurtre m; (of group) massacre m; (of animal) mise f à mort; **to make a k.** Fin réussir un beau coup. **2** a (tiring) Fam tuant. **◆−er** n tueur, -euse mf. **◆killjoy** n rabat-joie m inv.

kiln [kiln] n (for pottery) four m.

kilo ['kiːləʊ] n (pl -os) kilo m. **◆kilogramme** ['kiːləʊgræm] n kilogramme m. **◆kilometre** [kɪˈlɒmɪtər] n kilomètre m. **◆kilowatt** ['kiːləʊwɒt] n kilowatt m.

kilt [kilt] n kilt m.

kimono [kɪˈməʊnəʊ] n (pl -os) kimono m.

kin [kin] n (relatives) parents mpl; **one's next of k.** son plus proche parent.

kind [kaɪnd] **1** n (sort, type) genre m; **a k.** of une sorte or une espèce de; **to pay in k.** payer en nature; **what k. of drink/etc is it?** qu'est-ce que c'est comme boisson/etc?; **that's the k. of man he is** il est comme ça; **nothing of the k.!** absolument pas!; **k. of worried/sad/etc** (somewhat) plutôt inquiet/triste/etc; **k. of fascinated** (as if) Fam comme fasciné; **in a k. of way** d'une certaine façon; **it's the only one of its k.**, it's **one of a k.** c'est unique en son genre; **we are**

two of a k. nous nous ressemblons. **2** a (-er, -est) (*helpful, pleasant*) gentil (**to** avec, pour), bon (**to** pour); **that's k. of you** c'est gentil or aimable à vous. ◆**k.-'hearted** a qui a bon cœur. ◆**kindly** adv avec bonté; **k. wait**/etc ayez la bonté d'attendre/etc; **not to take k. to sth** ne pas apprécier qch; – a (*person*) bienveillant. ◆**kindness** n bonté f, gentillesse f.

kindergarten ['kɪndəgɑːt(ə)n] n jardin m d'enfants.

kindle ['kɪnd(ə)l] vt allumer; – vi s'allumer.

kindred ['kɪndrɪd] n (*relationship*) parenté f; (*relatives*) parents mpl; **k. spirit** semblable mf, âme f sœur.

king [kɪŋ] n roi m. ◆**k.-size(d)** a géant; (*cigarette*) long. ◆**kingdom** n royaume m; **animal/plant k.** règne m animal/végétal. ◆**kingly** a royal.

kingfisher ['kɪŋfɪʃər] n (*bird*) martin-pêcheur m.

kink [kɪŋk] n (*in rope*) entortillement m.

kinky ['kɪŋkɪ] a (-ier, -iest) (*person*) Psy Pej vicieux; (*clothes etc*) bizarre.

kinship ['kɪnʃɪp] n parenté f.

kiosk ['kiːɒsk] n kiosque m; (**telephone**) **k.** cabine f (téléphonique).

kip [kɪp] vi (**-pp-**) (*sleep*) Sl roupiller.

kipper ['kɪpər] n (*herring*) kipper m.

kiss [kɪs] n baiser m, bise f; **the k. of life** le bouche-à-bouche; – vt (*person*) embrasser; **to k. s.o.'s hand** baiser la main de qn; – vi s'embrasser.

kit [kɪt] n équipement m, matériel m; (*set of articles*) trousse f; **gym k.** (*belongings*) affaires fpl de gym; **tool k.** trousse f à outils; (**do-it-yourself**) **k.** kit m; **in k. form** en kit; **k. bag** sac m (de soldat etc); – vt (**-tt-**) **to k. out** équiper (**with** de).

kitchen ['kɪtʃɪn] n cuisine f; **k. cabinet** buffet m de cuisine; **k. garden** jardin m potager; **k. sink** évier m. ◆**kitche'nette** n kitchenette f, coin-cuisine m.

kite [kaɪt] n (*toy*) cerf-volant m.

kith [kɪθ] n **k. and kin** amis mpl et parents mpl.

kitten ['kɪt(ə)n] n chaton m, petit chat m.

kitty ['kɪtɪ] n (*fund*) cagnotte f.

km abbr (*kilometre*).

knack [næk] n (*skill*) coup m (de main), truc m (of doing pour faire); **to have** a or **the k. of doing** (*aptitude, tendency*) avoir le don de faire.

knackered ['nækəd] a (*tired*) Sl vanné.

knapsack ['næpsæk] n sac m à dos.

knead [niːd] vt (*dough*) pétrir.

knee [niː] n genou m; **to go down on one's**

knees se mettre à genoux; **k. pad** Sp genouillère f. ◆**kneecap** n Anat rotule f. ◆**knees-up** n Sl soirée f dansante, sauterie f.

kneel [niːl] vi (pt & pp **knelt** or **kneeled**) **to k. (down)** s'agenouiller; **to be kneeling (down)** être à genoux.

knell [nel] n glas m.

knew [njuː] see **know**.

knickers ['nɪkəz] npl (*woman's undergarment*) culotte f, slip m.

knick-knack ['nɪknæk] n babiole f.

knife [naɪf] n (pl **knives**) couteau m; (*penknife*) canif m; – vt poignarder.

knight [naɪt] n Hist & Br Pol chevalier m; Chess cavalier m; – vt (of monarch) Br Pol faire (qn) chevalier. ◆**knighthood** n titre m de chevalier.

knit [nɪt] vt (**-tt-**) tricoter; **to k. together** Fig souder; **to k. one's brow** froncer les sourcils; – vi tricoter; **to k. (together)** (of bones) se souder. ◆**knitting** n tricot m; **k. needle** aiguille f à tricoter. ◆**knitwear** n tricots mpl.

knob [nɒb] n (*on door etc*) bouton m; (*on stick*) pommeau m; (*of butter*) noix f.

knock [nɒk] vt (*strike*) frapper; (*collide with*) heurter; (*criticize*) Fam critiquer; **to k. one's head on** se cogner la tête contre; **to k. senseless** (*stun*) assommer; **to k. to the ground** jeter à terre; **to k. about** (*ill-treat*) malmener; **to k. back** (*drink, glass etc*) Fam s'envoyer (*derrière la cravate*), siffler; **to k. down** (*vase, pedestrian etc*) renverser; (*house, tree, wall etc*) abattre; (*price*) baisser, casser; **to k. in** (*nail*) enfoncer; **to k. off** (*person, object*) faire tomber (**from** de); (*do quickly*) Fam expédier; (*steal*) Fam piquer; **to k. £5 off** (*the price*) Fam piquer; to k. £5 off (the price) faire le prix de cinq livres, faire cinq livres sur le prix; **to k. out** (*stun*) assommer; (*beat in competition*) éliminer; **to k. oneself out** (*tire*) Fam s'esquinter (**doing** à faire); **to k. over** (*pedestrian, vase*) renverser; **to k. up** (*meal*) Fam préparer à la hâte; – vi (*strike*) frapper; **to k. against** or **into** (*bump into*) heurter; **to k. about** (*travel*) Fam bourlinguer; (*lie around, stand around*) traîner; **to k. off** (*stop work*) Fam s'arrêter de travailler; – n (*blow*) coup m; (*collision*) heurt m; **there's a k. at the door** quelqu'un frappe; **I heard a k.** j'ai entendu frapper. ◆**knockdown** a **k. price** prix m imbattable. ◆**knock-'kneed** a cagneux. ◆**knock-out** n Boxing knock-out m; **to be a k.-out** (*of person, film etc*) Fam être formidable.

knocker ['nɒkər] n (for door) marteau m.

knot [nɒt] **1** n (in rope etc) nœud m; − vt (-tt-) nouer. **2** n (unit of speed) Nau nœud m. ◆**knotty** a (-ier, -iest) (wood etc) noueux; (problem) Fig épineux.

know [nəʊ] vt (pt knew, pp known) (facts, language etc) savoir; (person, place etc) connaître; (recognize) reconnaître (by à); **to k. that** savoir que; **to k. how to do** savoir faire; **for all I k.** (autant) que je sache; **I'll let you k.** je te le ferai savoir; **I'll have you k. that** . . . sachez que . . . ; **to k.** (a lot) **about** (person, event) en savoir long sur; (cars, sewing etc) s'y connaître en; **I've never known him to complain** je ne l'ai jamais vu se plaindre; **to get to k.** (about) sth apprendre qch; **to get to k. s.o.** (meet) faire la connaissance de qn; − vi savoir; **I k.** je (le) sais; **I wouldn't k., I k. nothing about it** je n'en sais rien; **I k. about that** je sais ça, je suis au courant; **to k. of** (have heard of) avoir entendu parler de; **do you k. of?** (a good tailor etc) connais-tu?; **you (should) k. better than to do that** tu es trop intelligent pour faire ça; **you should have known better** tu aurais dû réfléchir; − n **in the k.** Fam au courant. ◆**-ing** a (smile, look) entendu. ◆**-ingly** adv (consciously) sciemment. ◆**known** a connu; **a k. expert** un expert reconnu; **well k.** (bien) connu (that que); **she is k. to be** . . . on sait qu'elle est . . . . ◆**know-all** n, Am **know-it-all** n je-sais-tout mf inv. ◆**know-how** n (skill) compétence f (**to do** pour faire), savoir-faire m inv.

knowledge ['nɒlidʒ] n connaissance f (of de); (learning) connaissances fpl, savoir m; **to (the best of) my k.** à ma connaissance; **without the k. of** à l'insu de; **to have no k. of** ignorer; **general k.** culture f générale. ◆**knowledgeable** a bien informé (about sur).

knuckle ['nʌk(ə)l] **1** n articulation f du doigt. **2** vi **to k. down to** (task) Fam s'atteler à; **to k. under** céder.

Koran [kə'rɑːn] n Rel Coran m.

kosher ['kəʊʃər] a Rel kascher inv.

kowtow [kaʊ'taʊ] vi se prosterner (**to** devant).

kudos ['kjuːdɒs] n (glory) gloire f.

L

L, l [el] L, l m.

lab [læb] n Fam labo m. ◆**laboratory** [lə'bɒrɪt(ə)rɪ, Am 'læbrətərɪ] n laboratoire m; **language l.** laboratoire m de langues.

label ['leɪb(ə)l] n étiquette f; − vt (-ll-, Am -l-) (goods, person) étiqueter (as comme).

laborious [lə'bɔːrɪəs] a laborieux.

labour ['leɪbər] n (work, childbirth) travail m; (workers) main-d'œuvre f; **L.** Br Pol les travaillistes mpl; **in l.** Med au travail; − a (market, situation) du travail; (conflict, dispute) ouvrier; (relations) ouvriers-patronat m; **l. force** main-d'œuvre f; **l. union** Am syndicat m; − vi (toil) peiner; − vt **to l. a point** insister sur un point. ◆**-ed** a (style) laborieux. ◆**-er** n (on roads etc) manœuvre m; Agr ouvrier m agricole.

laburnum [lə'bɜːnəm] n Bot cytise m.

labyrinth ['læbɪrɪnθ] n labyrinthe m.

lace [leɪs] **1** n (cloth) dentelle f. **2** n (of shoe) lacet m; − vt **to l. (up)** (tie up) lacer. **3** vt (drink) additionner, arroser (with de).

lack [læk] n manque m; **for l. of** à défaut de; − vt manquer de; − vi **to be lacking** manquer (**in, for** de).

lackey ['lækɪ] n Hist & Fig laquais m.

laconic [lə'kɒnɪk] a laconique.

lacquer ['lækər] n laque f; − vt laquer.

lad [læd] n gars m, garçon m; **when I was a l.** quand j'étais gosse.

ladder ['lædər] n échelle f; (in stocking) maille f filée; − vti (stocking) filer.

laden ['leɪd(ə)n] a chargé (**with** de).

ladle ['leɪd(ə)l] n louche f.

lady ['leɪdɪ] n dame f; **a young l.** une jeune fille; (married) une jeune femme; **the l. of the house** la maîtresse de maison; **Ladies and Gentlemen!** Mesdames, Mesdemoiselles, Messieurs!; **l. doctor** femme f médecin; **l. friend** amie f; **ladies' room** Fig toilettes fpl. ◆**l.-in-'waiting** n (pl ladies-in-waiting) dame f d'honneur. ◆**ladybird** n, Am ◆**ladybug** n coccinelle f. ◆**ladylike** a (manner) distingué; **she's (very) l.** elle est très grande dame.

lag [læg] **1** vi (-gg-) **to l. behind** (in progress, work) avoir du retard; (dawdle) traîner; **to l. behind s.o.** avoir du retard sur qn; − n

time l. (*between events*) décalage *m*; (*between countries*) décalage *m* horaire. **2** *vt* (-gg-) (*pipe*) calorifuger.

lager ['lɑːgər] *n* bière *f* blonde.

lagoon [lə'guːn] *n* lagune *f*; (*small, coral*) lagon *m*.

laid [leɪd] *see* **lay**². ◆**l.-'back** *a Fam* relax.

lain [leɪn] *see* **lie**¹.

lair [leər] *n* tanière *f*.

laity ['leɪɪtɪ] *n* **the l.** les laïcs *mpl*.

lake [leɪk] *n* lac *m*.

lamb [læm] *n* agneau *m*. ◆**lambswool** *n* laine *f* d'agneau.

lame [leɪm] *a* (-er, -est) (*person, argument*) boiteux; (*excuse*) piètre; **to be l.** boiter. ◆—**ness** *n Med* claudication *f*; (*of excuse*) Fig faiblesse *f*.

lament [lə'ment] *n* lamentation *f*; – *vt* to **l.** (**over**) se lamenter sur. ◆**lamentable** *a* lamentable. ◆**lamen'tation** *n* lamentation *f*.

laminated ['læmɪneɪtɪd] *a* (*metal*) laminé.

lamp [læmp] *n* lampe *f*; (*bulb*) ampoule *f*; *Aut* feu *m*. ◆**lamppost** *n* réverbère *m*. ◆**lampshade** *n* abat-jour *m inv*.

lance [lɑːns] **1** *n* (*weapon*) lance *f*. **2** *vt Med* inciser.

land [lænd] **1** *n* terre *f*; (*country*) pays *m*; (*plot of*) **l.** terrain *m*; **on dry l.** sur la terre ferme; **no man's l.** *Mil & Fig* no man's land *m inv*; – *a* (*flora, transport etc*) terrestre; (*reform, law*) agraire; (*owner, tax*) foncier. **2** *vi* (*of aircraft*) atterrir, se poser; (*of ship*) mouiller, relâcher; (*of passengers, cargo*) débarquer; (*of bomb etc*) (re)tomber; **to l. up** (*end up*) se retrouver; – *vt* (*passengers, cargo*) débarquer; (*aircraft*) poser; (*blow*) *Fig* flanquer (on à); (*job, prize etc*) *Fam* décrocher; **to l. s.o. in trouble** *Fam* mettre-qn dans le pétrin; **to be landed with** *Fam* (*person*) avoir sur les bras; (*fine*) ramasser, écoper de. ◆—**ed** *a* (*owning land*) terrien. ◆—**ing** *n* **1** *Av* atterrissage *m*; *Nau* débarquement *m*; **forced l.** atterrissage *m* forcé; **l. stage** débarcadère *m*. **2** *n* (*at top of stairs*) palier *m*; (*floor*) étage *m*. ◆**landlady** *n* logeuse *f*, propriétaire *f*. ◆**landlocked** *a* sans accès à la mer. ◆**landlord** *n* propriétaire *m*; (*of pub*) patron *m*. ◆**landmark** *n* point *m* de repère. ◆**landslide** *n Geol* glissement *m* de terrain, éboulement *m*; *Pol* raz-de-marée *m inv* électoral.

landscape ['lændskeɪp] *n* paysage *m*.

lane [leɪn] *n* (*in country*) chemin *m*; (*in town*) ruelle *f*; (*division of road*) voie *f*; (*line of

traffic) file *f*; *Av Nau Sp* couloir *m*; **bus l.** couloir *m* (*réservé aux autobus*).

language ['læŋgwɪdʒ] *n* (*faculty, style*) langage *m*; (*national tongue*) langue *f*; **computer l.** langage *m* machine; – *a* (*laboratory*) de langues; (*teacher, studies*) de langue(s).

languid ['læŋgwɪd] *a* languissant. ◆**languish** *vi* languir (**for, after** après).

lank [læŋk] *a* (*hair*) plat et terne.

lanky ['læŋkɪ] *a* (-ier, -iest) dégingandé.

lantern ['læntən] *n* lanterne *f*; **Chinese l.** lampion *m*.

lap [læp] **1** *n* (*of person*) genoux *mpl*; **the l. of luxury** le plus grand luxe. **2** *n Sp* tour *m* (*de piste*). **3** *vt* (-pp-) **to l. up** (*drink*) laper; (*like very much*) *Fam* adorer; (*believe*) *Fam* gober; – *vi* (*of waves*) clapoter. **4** *vi* (-pp-) **to l. over** (*overlap*) se chevaucher.

lapel [lə'pel] *n* (*of jacket etc*) revers *m*.

lapse [læps] **1** *n* (*fault*) faute *f*; (*weakness*) défaillance *f*; **a l. of memory** un trou de mémoire; **a l. in behaviour** un écart de conduite; – *vi* (*err*) commettre une faute; **to l. into** retomber dans. **2** *n* (*interval*) intervalle *m*; **a l. of time** un intervalle (**between** entre). **3** *vi* (*expire*) se périmer, expirer; (*of subscription*) prendre fin.

larceny ['lɑːsənɪ] *n* vol *m* simple.

lard [lɑːd] *n* saindoux *m*.

larder ['lɑːdər] *n* (*cupboard*) garde-manger *m inv*.

large [lɑːdʒ] *a* (-er, -est) (*in size or extent*) grand; (*in volume, bulkiness*) gros; (*quantity*) grand, important; **to become** *or* **grow** *or* **get l.** grossir, grandir; **to a l. extent** en grande mesure; **at l.** (*of prisoner, animal*) en liberté; (*as a whole*) en général; **by and l.** dans l'ensemble, généralement. ◆**l.-scale** *a* (*reform*) (fait) sur une grande échelle. ◆**largely** *adv* (*to a great extent*) en grande mesure. ◆**largeness** *n* grandeur *f*; grosseur *f*.

largesse [lɑː'ʒes] *n* largesse *f*.

lark [lɑːk] **1** *n* (*bird*) alouette *f*. **2** *n* (*joke*) *Fam* rigolade *f*, blague *f*; – *vi* **to l. about** *Fam* s'amuser.

larva, *pl* **-vae** ['lɑːvə, -viː] *n* (*of insect*) larve *f*.

larynx ['lærɪŋks] *n Anat* larynx *m*. ◆**laryn-'gitis** *n Med* laryngite *f*.

lascivious [lə'sɪvɪəs] *a* lascif.

laser ['leɪzər] *n* laser *m*.

lash [læʃ] **1** *n* (*with whip*) coup *m* de fouet; – *vt* (*strike*) fouetter; (*tie*) attacher (**to** à); **the dog lashed its tail** le chien donna un coup de queue; – *vi* **to l. out** (*spend wildly*) *Fam* claquer son argent; **to l. out at** envoyer des coups à; (*abuse*) *Fig* invectiver; (*criticize*) *Fig* fustiger. **◆—ings** *npl* **l. of** *Culin Fam* des masses de, une montagne de.

lash² [læʃ] *n* (*eyelash*) cil *m*.

lass [læs] *n* jeune fille *f*.

lassitude [ˈlæsɪtjuːd] *n* lassitude *f*.

lasso [ˈlæsəʊ] *n* (*pl* **-os**) lasso *m*; − *vt* attraper au lasso.

last¹ [lɑːst] *a* dernier; **in ten lines** les dix dernières lignes; **l. but one** avant-dernier; **l. night** (*evening*) hier soir; (*during night*) cette nuit; **the day before l.** avant-hier; − *adv* (*lastly*) en dernier lieu, enfin; (*on the last occasion*) (pour) la dernière fois; **to leave l.** sortir le dernier *or* en dernier; − *n* (*person, object*) dernier, -ière *mf*; (*end*) fin *f*; **the l. of the beer/***etc* (*remainder*) le reste de la bière/*etc*; **at (long) l.** enfin. **◆l.-ditch** *a* désespéré. **◆l.-minute** *a* de dernière minute. **◆lastly** *adv* en dernier lieu, enfin.

last² [lɑːst] *vi* durer; **to l. (out)** (*endure, resist*) tenir; (*of money, supplies*) durer; **it lasted me ten years** ça m'a duré *or* fait dix ans. **◆—ing** *a* durable.

latch [lætʃ] **1** *n* loquet *m*; **the door is on the l.** la porte n'est pas fermée à clef. **2** *vi* **to l. on to** *Fam* (*grab*) s'accrocher à; (*understand*) saisir.

late¹ [leɪt] *a* (**-er, -est**) (*not on time*) en retard (**for** à); (*former*) ancien; (*meal, fruit, season, hour*) tardif; (*stage*) avancé; (*edition*) dernier; **to be l.** (*of person, train etc*) être en retard, avoir du retard; **to be l. (in) coming** arriver en retard; **he's an hour l.** il a une heure de retard; **it's l.** il est tard; **Easter/***etc* **is l.** Pâques/*etc* est tard; **in l. June/***etc* fin juin/*etc*; **a later edition/***etc* (*more recent*) une édition/*etc* plus récente; **the latest edition/***etc* (*last*) la dernière édition/*etc*; **in later life** plus tard dans la vie; **to take a later train** prendre un train plus tard; **at a later date** à une date ultérieure; **the latest date** la date limite; **at the latest** au plus tard; **of l.** dernièrement; − *adv* (*in the day, season etc*) tard; (*not on time*) en retard; **it's getting l.** il se fait tard; **later (on)** plus tard; **not** *or* **no later than** plus tard que. **◆latecomer** *n* retardataire *mf*. **◆lately** *adv* dernièrement. **◆lateness** *n* (*of person, train etc*) retard *m*; **constant l.** des retards continuels; **the l. of the hour** l'heure tardive.

late² [leɪt] *a* **the l. Mr Smith/***etc* (*deceased*) feu Monsieur Smith/*etc*; **our l. friend** notre regretté ami.

latent [ˈleɪtənt] *a* latent.

lateral [ˈlætərəl] *a* latéral.

lathe [leɪð] *n* *Tech* tour *m*.

lather [ˈlɑːðər] *n* mousse *f*; − *vt* savonner; − *vi* mousser.

Latin [ˈlætɪn] *a* latin; **L. America** Amérique *f* latine; **L. American** d'Amérique latine; − *n* (*person*) Latin, -ine *mf*; (*language*) latin *m*.

latitude [ˈlætɪtjuːd] *n* *Geog* & *Fig* latitude *f*.

latrines [ləˈtriːnz] *npl* latrines *fpl*.

latter [ˈlætər] *a* (*later, last-named*) dernier; (*second*) deuxième; − *n* dernier, -ière *mf*; second, -onde *mf*. **◆-ly** *adv* dernièrement; (*late in life*) sur le tard.

lattice [ˈlætɪs] *n* treillis *m*.

laudable [ˈlɔːdəb(ə)l] *a* louable.

laugh [lɑːf] *n* rire *m*; **to have a good l.** bien rire; − *vi* rire (**at, about** de); **to l. to oneself** rire en soi-même; − *vt* **to l. off** tourner en plaisanterie. **◆—ing** *a* riant; **it's no l. matter** il n'y a pas de quoi rire; **to be the l.-stock of** être la risée de. **◆—able** *a* ridicule. **◆laughter** *n* rire(s) *m*(*pl*); **to roar with l.** rire aux éclats.

launch [lɔːntʃ] **1** *n* (*motor boat*) vedette *f*; (*pleasure boat*) bateau *m* de plaisance. **2** *vt* (*rocket, boat, fashion etc*) lancer; − *vi* **to l. (out) into** (*begin*) se lancer dans; − *n* lancement *m*. **◆—ing** *n* lancement *m*.

launder [ˈlɔːndər] *vt* (*clothes*) blanchir; (*money from drugs etc*) *Fig* blanchir. **◆—ing** *n* blanchissage *m*. **◆launde'rette** *n, Am* **laundromat** *n* laverie *f* automatique. **◆laundry** *n* (*place*) blanchisserie *f*; (*clothes*) linge *m*.

laurel [ˈlɒrəl] *n* *Bot* laurier *m*.

lava [ˈlɑːvə] *n* *Geol* lave *f*.

lavatory [ˈlævətrɪ] *n* cabinets *mpl*.

lavender [ˈlævɪndər] *n* lavande *f*.

lavish [ˈlævɪʃ] *a* prodigue (**with** de); (*helping, meal*) généreux; (*decor, house etc*) somptueux; (*expenditure*) excessif; − *vt* prodiguer (**sth on s.o.** qch à qn). **◆-ly** *adv* (*to give*) généreusement; (*to furnish*) somptueusement.

law [lɔː] *n* (*rule, rules*) loi *f*; (*study, profession, system*) droit *m*; **court of l.,** **l. court** cour *f* de justice; **l. and order** l'ordre public. **◆l.-abiding** *a* respectueux des lois. **◆lawful** *a* (*action*) légal; (*child, wife etc*) légitime. **◆lawfully** *adv* légalement. **◆lawless** *a* (*country*) anarchique. **◆lawlessness** *n* anarchie *f*. **◆lawsuit** *n* procès *m*.

lawn [lɔːn] *n* pelouse *f*, gazon *m*; **l. mower** tondeuse *f* (à gazon); **l. tennis** tennis *m* (sur gazon).

lawyer [ˈlɔːjər] *n* (*in court*) avocat *m*; (*author,* *legal expert*) juriste *m*; (*for wills, sales*) notaire *m*.

lax [læks] *a* (*person*) négligent; (*discipline, behaviour*) relâché; **to be l. in doing** faire avec négligence. ◆**laxity** *n*, ◆**laxness** *n* négligence *f*; relâchement *m*.

laxative [ˈlæksətɪv] *n & a Med* laxatif (*m*).

lay¹ [leɪ] *a* (*non-religious*) laïque; (*non-specialized*) d'un profane *m*. ◆**layman** *n* (*pl* **-men**) (*non-specialist*) profane *mf*.

lay² [leɪ] (*pt & pp* **laid**) **1** *vt* (*put down, place*) poser; (*table*) mettre; (*blanket*) étendre (**over** sur); (*trap*) tendre; (*money*) miser (**on** sur); (*accusation*) porter; (*ghost*) exorciser; **to l. a bet** parier; **to l. bare** mettre à nu; **to l. waste** ravager; **to l. s.o. open to** exposer qn à; **to l. one's hands on** mettre la main sur; **to l. a hand** *or* **a finger on s.o.** lever la main sur qn; **to l. down** poser; (*arms*) déposer; (*condition*) (im)poser; **to l. down the law** faire la loi (**to** à); **to l. s.o. off** (*worker*) licencier qn; **to l. on** (*install*) mettre, installer; (*supply*) fournir; **to l. it on** (**thick**) *Fam* y aller un peu fort; **to l. out** (*garden*) dessiner; (*house*) concevoir; (*prepare*) préparer; (*display*) disposer; (*money*) *Fam* dépenser (**on** pour); **to be laid up** (*in bed*) *Med* être alité; – *vi* **to l. into** *Fam* attaquer; **to l. off** (*stop*) *Fam* arrêter; **to l. off s.o.** (*leave alone*) *Fam* laisser qn tranquille; **l. off!** (*don't touch*) *Fam* pas touche!; **to l. out** *Fam* payer. **2** *vt* (*egg*) pondre; – *vi* (*of bird etc*) pondre. ◆**layabout** *n Fam* fainéant, -ante *mf*. ◆**lay-by** *n* (*pl* **-bys**) *Aut* aire *f* de stationnement *or* de repos. ◆**lay-off** *n* (*of worker*) licenciement *m*. ◆**layout** *n* disposition *f*; *Typ* mise *f* en pages. ◆**lay-over** *n Am* halte *f*.

lay³ [leɪ] *see* **lie¹**.

layer [ˈleɪər] *n* couche *f*.

laze [leɪz] *vi* **to l.** (**about** *or* **around**) paresser. ◆**lazy** *a* (**-ier, -iest**) (*person etc*) paresseux; (*holiday*) passé à ne rien faire. ◆**lazybones** *n Fam* paresseux, -euse *mf*.

lb *abbr* (*libra* = **pound** (*weight*).

lead¹ [liːd] *vt* (*pt & pp* **led**) (*conduct*) mener, conduire (**to** à); (*team, government etc*) diriger; (*regiment*) commander; (*life*) mener; **to l. s.o. in/out/etc** faire entrer/sortir/*etc* qn; **to l. s.o. to do** (*induce*) amener qn à faire; **to l. the way** montrer le chemin; **to l. the world** tenir le premier rang mondial; **easily led** influençable; **to l. away** *or* **off** emmener; **to l. back** ramener; **to l. on** (*tease*) faire marcher; – *vi* (*of street etc*) mener, conduire (**to** à); (*in match*) mener;

(*in race*) être en tête; (*go ahead*) aller devant; **to l. to** (*result in*) aboutir à; (*cause*) causer, amener; **to l. up to** (*of street*) conduire à, mener à; (*precede*) précéder; (*approach gradually*) en venir à; – *n* (*distance or time ahead*) *Sp* avance *f* (**over** sur); (*example*) exemple *m*, initiative *f*; (*clue*) piste *f*, indice *m*; (*star part*) *Th* rôle *m* principal; (*leash*) laisse *f*; (*wire*) *El* fil *m*; **to take the l.** *Sp* prendre la tête; **to be in the l.** (*in race*) être en tête; (*in match*) mener. ◆**leading** *a* (*main*) principal; (*important*) important; (*front*) de tête; **the l. author** l'auteur principal *or* le plus important; **a l. figure** un personnage marquant; **the l. lady** *Cin* la vedette féminine; **l. article** *Journ* éditorial *m*. ◆**leader** *n* chef *m*; *Pol* dirigeant, -ante *mf*; (*of strike, riot*) meneur, -euse *mf*; (*guide*) guide *m*; (*article*) *Journ* éditorial *m*. ◆**leadership** *n* direction *f*; (*qualities*) qualités *fpl* de chef; (*leaders*) *Pol* dirigeants *mpl*.

lead² [led] *n* (*metal*) plomb *m*; (*of pencil*) mine *f*; **l. pencil** crayon *m* à mine de plomb. ◆**leaden** *a* (*sky*) de plomb.

leaf [liːf] **1** *n* (*pl* **leaves**) *Bot* feuille *f*; (*of book*) feuillet *m*; (*of table*) rallonge *f*. **2** *vi* **to l. through** (*book*) feuilleter. ◆**leaflet** *n* prospectus *m*; (*containing instructions*) notice *f*. ◆**leafy** *a* (**-ier, -iest**) (*tree*) feuillu.

league [liːg] *n* **1** (*alliance*) ligue *f*; *Sp* championnat *m*; **in l. with** *Pej* de connivence avec. **2** (*measure*) *Hist* lieue *f*.

leak [liːk] *n* (*in pipe, information etc*) fuite *f*; (*in boat*) voie *f* d'eau; – *vi* (*of liquid, pipe, tap etc*) fuir; (*of ship*) faire eau; **to l. out** (*of information*) *Fig* être divulgué; – *vt* (*liquid*) répandre; (*information*) *Fig* divulguer. ◆**-age** *n* fuite *f*; (*amount lost*) perte *f*. ◆**leaky** *a* (**-ier, -iest**) (*kettle etc*) qui fuit.

lean¹ [liːn] *a* (**-er, -est**) (*thin*) maigre; (*year*) difficile. ◆**-ness** *n* maigreur *f*.

lean² [liːn] *vi* (*pt & pp* **leaned** *or* **leant** [lent]) (*of object*) pencher; (*of person*) se pencher; **to l. against/on** (*of person*) s'appuyer contre/sur; **to l. back against** s'adosser à; **to l. on s.o.** (*influence*) *Fam* faire pression sur qn (**to do** pour faire); **to l. forward** *or* **over** (*of person*) se pencher (en avant); **to l. over** (*of object*) pencher; – *vt* appuyer (**against** contre); **to l. one's head on/out of** pencher la tête sur/par. ◆**-ing 1** *a* (*wall*) penché; (*resting*) appuyé contre. **2** *npl* tendances *fpl* (**towards** à). ◆**lean-to** *n* (*pl* **-tos**) (*building*) appentis *m*.

leap [liːp] *n* (*jump*) bond *m*, saut *m*; (*change, increase etc*) *Fig* bond *m*; **l. year** année *f* bissextile; **in leaps and bounds** à pas de géant; – *vi* (*pt & pp* **leaped** *or* **leapt** [lept]) bondir, sauter; (*of flames*) jaillir; (*of profits*) faire un bond; **to l. to one's feet, l. up** se lever d'un bond. ◆**leapfrog** *n* saute-mouton *m inv*.

learn [lɜːn] *vt* (*pt & pp* **learned** *or* **learnt**) apprendre (**that** que); **to l. (how) to do** apprendre à faire; – *vi* apprendre; **to l. about** (*study*) étudier; (*hear about*) apprendre. ◆**–ed** [-ɪd] *a* savant. ◆**–ing** *n* érudition *f*, savoir *m*; (*of language*) apprentissage *m* (**of** de). ◆**–er** *n* débutant, -ante *mf*.

lease [liːs] *n Jur* bail *m*; **a new l. of life** *or Am* **on life** un regain de vie, une nouvelle vie; – *vt* (*house etc*) louer à bail. ◆**leasehold** *n* propriété *f* louée à bail.

leash [liːʃ] *n* laisse *f*; **on a l.** en laisse.

least [liːst] *a* **the l.** (*smallest amount of*) le moins de; (*slightest*) le *or* la moindre; **he has (the) l. talent** il a le moins de talent (**of all** de tous); **the l. effort/noise/etc** le moindre effort/bruit/*etc*; – *n* **the l.** le moins; **at l.** (*with quantity*) au moins; **at l. that's what she says** du moins c'est ce qu'elle dit; **not in the l.** pas du tout; – *adv* (*to work, eat etc*) le moins; (*with adjective*) le *or* la moins; **l. of all** (*especially not*) surtout pas.

leather ['leðər] *n* cuir *m*; (*wash*) **l.** peau *f* de chamois.

leave [liːv] **1** *n* (*holiday*) congé *m*; (*consent*) & *Mil* permission *f*; **l. of absence** congé *m* exceptionnel; **to take (one's) l.** of prendre congé de. **2** *vt* (*pt & pp* **left**) (*allow to remain, forget*) laisser; (*depart from*) quitter; (*room*) sortir de, quitter; **to l. the table** sortir de table; **to l. s.o. in charge of** laisser à qn la garde de qn/qch; **to l. sth with s.o.** (*entrust, give*) laisser qch à qn; **to be left (over)** rester; **there's no hope/bread/etc left** il ne reste plus d'espoir/de pain/*etc*; **l. it to me!** laisse-moi faire!; **I'll l. it (up) to you** je m'en remets à toi; **to l. go (of)** (*release*) lâcher; **to l. behind** laisser; (*surpass*) dépasser; (*in race*) *Sp* distancer; **to l. off** (*lid*) ne pas (re)mettre; **to l. off doing** (*stop*) *Fam* arrêter de faire; **to l. on** (*hat, gloves*) garder; **to l. out** (*forget*) omettre; (*exclude*) exclure; – *vi* (*depart*) partir (**from** de, **for** pour); **to l. off** (*stop*) *Fam* s'arrêter. ◆**leavings** *npl* restes *mpl*.

Lebanon ['lebənən] *n* Liban *m*. ◆**Lebanese** *a & n* libanais, -aise (*mf*).

lecher ['letʃər] *n* débauché *m*. ◆**lecherous** *a* lubrique, luxurieux.

lectern ['lektən] *n* (*for giving speeches*) pupitre *m*; *Rel* lutrin *m*.

lecture ['lektʃər] **1** *n* (*public speech*) conférence *f*; (*as part of series*) *Univ* cours *m* (*magistral*); – *vi* faire une conférence *or* un cours; **l l. in chemistry** je suis professeur de chimie. **2** *vt* (*scold*) *Fig* faire la morale à, sermonner; – *n* (*scolding*) sermon *m*. ◆**lecturer** *n* conférencier, -ière *mf*; *Univ* enseignant, -ante *mf*. ◆**lectureship** *n* poste *m* à l'université.

led [led] *see* **lead**[1].

ledge [ledʒ] *n* rebord *m*; (*on mountain*) saillie *f*.

ledger ['ledʒər] *n Com* registre *m*, grand livre *m*.

leech [liːtʃ] *n* (*worm, person*) sangsue *f*.

leek [liːk] *n* poireau *m*.

leer [liər] *vi* **l. (at)** lorgner; – *n* regard *m* sournois.

leeway ['liːweɪ] *n* (*freedom*) liberté *f* d'action; (*safety margin*) marge *f* de sécurité.

left[1] [left] *see* **leave 2**; – *a* **l.** luggage office consigne *f*. ◆**leftovers** *npl* restes *mpl*.

left[2] [left] *a* (*side, hand etc*) gauche; – *adv* à gauche; – *n* gauche *f*; **on** *or* **to the l.** à gauche (**of** de). ◆**l.-hand** *a* à *or* to gauche; **on the l.-hand side** à gauche (**of** de). ◆**l.-'handed** *a* (*person*) gaucher. ◆**l.-wing** *a Pol* de gauche. ◆**leftist** *n* & *a Pol* gauchiste (*mf*).

leg [leg] *n* jambe *f*; (*of bird, dog etc*) patte *f*; (*of lamb*) *Culin* gigot *m*; (*of chicken*) *Culin* cuisse *f*; (*of table*) pied *m*; (*of journey*) étape *f*; **to pull s.o.'s l.** (*make fun of*) mettre qn en boîte; **on its last legs** (*machine etc*) *Fam* prêt à claquer; **to be on one's last legs** *Fam* avoir un pied dans la tombe. ◆**l.-room** *n* place *f* pour les jambes. ◆**leggy** *a* (**-ier, -iest**) (*person*) aux longues jambes, tout en jambes.

legacy ['legəsɪ] *n Jur* & *Fig* legs *m*.

legal ['liːg(ə)l] *a* (*lawful*) légal; (*mind, affairs, adviser*) juridique; (*aid, error*) judiciaire; **l. expert** juriste *m*; **l. proceedings** procès *m*. ◆**le'gality** *n* légalité *f*. ◆**legalize** *vt* légaliser. ◆**legally** *adv* légalement.

legation [lɪ'geɪʃ(ə)n] *n Pol* légation *f*.

legend ['ledʒənd] *n* (*story, inscription etc*) légende *f*. ◆**legendary** *a* légendaire.

leggings ['legɪnz] *npl* jambières *fpl*.

legible ['ledʒəb(ə)l] *a* lisible. ◆**legi'bility** *n* lisibilité *f*. ◆**legibly** *adv* lisiblement.

legion ['liːdʒən] *n Mil* & *Fig* légion *f*.

legislate ['ledʒɪsleɪt] *vi* légiférer. ◆**legis-**

'lation *n* (*laws*) législation *f*; (*action*) élaboration *f* des lois; (*piece of*) l. loi *f*. ◆**legislative** *a* législatif.

legitimate [lɪˈdʒɪtɪmət] *a* (*reason, child etc*) légitime. ◆**legitimacy** *n* légitimité *f*.

legless [ˈleglɪs] *a* (*drunk*) *Fam* (complètement) bourré.

leisure [ˈleʒər, *Am* ˈliːʒər] *n* l. (**time**) loisirs *mpl*; l. **activities** loisirs *mpl*; moment *m* de loisir; **at** (**one's**) l. à tête reposée. ◆**-ly** *a* (*walk, occupation*) peu fatigant; (*meal, life*) calme; **at a l. pace,** in a l. way sans se presser.

lemon [ˈlemən] *n* citron *m*; l. **drink,** l. **squash** citronnade *f*; l. **tea** thé *m* au citron. ◆**lemo'nade** *n* (*fizzy*) limonade *f*; (*still*) *Am* citronnade *f*.

lend [lend] *vt* (*pt & pp* **lent**) prêter (**to** à); (*charm, colour etc*) *Fig* donner (**to** à); **to l. credence to** ajouter foi à. ◆**-ing** *n* prêt *m*. ◆**-er** *n* prêteur, -euse *mf*.

length [leŋθ] *n* longueur *f*; (*section of pipe etc*) morceau *m*; (*of road*) tronçon *m*; (*of cloth*) métrage *m*; (*of horse, swimming pool*) *Sp* longueur *f*; (*duration*) durée *f*; l. **of time** temps *m*; **at l.** (*at last*) enfin; **at** (**great**) l. (*in detail*) dans le détail; (*for a long time*) longuement; **to go to great lengths** se donner beaucoup de mal (**to do** pour faire). ◆**lengthen** *vt* allonger; (*in time*) prolonger. ◆**lengthwise** *adv* dans le sens de la longueur. ◆**lengthy** *a* (-ier, -iest) long.

lenient [ˈliːnɪənt] *a* indulgent (**to** envers). ◆**leniency** *n* indulgence *f*. ◆**leniently** *adv* avec indulgence.

lens [lenz] *n* lentille *f*; (*in spectacles*) verre *m*; *Phot* objectif *m*.

Lent [lent] *n* *Rel* Carême *m*.

lentil [ˈlentɪl] *n* *Bot Culin* lentille *f*.

leopard [ˈlepəd] *n* léopard *m*.

leotard [ˈliːətɑːd] *n* collant *m* (*de danse*).

leper [ˈlepər] *n* lépreux, -euse *mf*. ◆**leprosy** *n* lèpre *f*.

lesbian [ˈlezbɪən] *n & a* lesbienne (*f*).

lesion [ˈliːʒ(ə)n] *n* *Med* lésion *f*.

less [les] *a* & *n* moins (**than** que); l. **time/etc** moins de temps/*etc*; **she has l.** (**than you**) elle en a moins (que toi); l. **than a kilo/ten/etc** (*with quantity, number*) moins d'un kilo/de dix/*etc*; − *adv* (*to sleep, know etc*) moins (**than** que); l. (**often**) moins souvent; l. **and l.** de moins en moins; **one** un(e) de moins; − *prep* (*minus*) l. **six francs** moins six francs. ◆**lessen** *vti* diminuer. ◆**lessening** *n* diminution *f*. ◆**lesser** *a* moindre; − *n* **the l.** of le *or* la moindre de.

-less [ləs] *suffix* sans; **childless** sans enfants.

lesson [ˈles(ə)n] *n* leçon *f*; **an English l.** une leçon *or* un cours d'anglais; **I have lessons now** j'ai cours maintenant.

lest [lest] *conj* *Lit* de peur que (+ *ne* + *sub*).

let[1] [let] **1** *vt* (*pt & pp* **let,** *pres p* **letting**) (*allow*) laisser (**s.o. do** qn faire); **to l. s.o. have sth** donner qch à qn; **to l. away** (*allow to leave*) laisser partir; **to l. down** (*lower*) baisser; (*hair*) dénouer; (*dress*) rallonger; (*tyre*) dégonfler; **to l. s.o. down** (*disappoint*) décevoir qn; **don't l. me down** je compte sur toi; **the car l. me down** la voiture est tombée en panne. ◆**letdown** *n* déception *f*; **to l. in** (*person, dog*) faire entrer; (*noise, light*) laisser entrer; **to l. in the clutch** *Aut* embrayer; **to l. s.o. in on** *Fig* mettre qn au courant de; **to l. oneself in for** (*expense*) se laisser entraîner à; (*trouble*) s'attirer; **to l. off** (*bomb*) faire éclater; (*firework, gun*) faire partir; **to l. s.o. off** laisser partir qn; (*not punish*) ne pas punir qn; (*clear*) *Jur* disculper qn; **to be l. off with** (*a fine etc*) s'en tirer avec; **to l. s.o. off doing** dispenser qn de faire; **to l. on that** *Fam* (*admit*) avouer que; (*reveal*) dire que; **to l. out** faire *or* laisser sortir; (*prisoner*) relâcher; (*cry, secret*) laisser échapper; (*skirt*) élargir; **to l. s.o. out of** (*the house*) ouvrir la porte à qn; **to l. out the clutch** *Aut* débrayer; − *vi* **not to l. on** *Fam* ne rien dire, garder la bouche cousue; **to l. up** (*of rain, person etc*) s'arrêter. ◆**letup** *n* arrêt *m*, répit *m*. **2** *v aux* l. **us eat/go/etc,** l.'s **eat/go/etc** mangeons/partons/*etc*; l.'s **go for a stroll** allons nous promener; l. **him come** qu'il vienne.

let[2] [let] *vt* (*pt & pp* **let,** *pres p* **letting**) **to l.** (**off** *or* **out**) (*house, room etc*) louer. ◆**letting** *n* (*renting*) location *f*.

lethal [ˈliːθ(ə)l] *a* mortel; (*weapon*) meurtrier.

lethargy [ˈleθədʒɪ] *n* léthargie *f*. ◆**le'thargic** *a* léthargique.

letter [ˈletər] *n* (*missive, character*) lettre *f*; **man of letters** homme *m* de lettres; l. **bomb** lettre *f* piégée; l. **writer** correspondant, -ante *mf*. ◆**letterbox** *n* boîte *f* aux *or* à lettres. ◆**letterhead** *n* en-tête *m*. ◆**lettering** *n* (*letters*) lettres *fpl*; (*on tomb*) inscription *f*.

lettuce [ˈletɪs] *n* laitue *f*, salade *f*.

leuk(a)emia [luːˈkiːmɪə] *n* leucémie *f*.

level [ˈlev(ə)l] **1** *n* niveau *m*; **on the l.** (*speed*) en palier; − *a* (*surface*) plat, uni; (*object on surface*) horizontal; (*spoonful*) ras; (*equal in score*) à égalité (**with** avec); (*in height*) au même niveau, à la même hauteur (**with** que); l. **crossing** Rail passage m à niveau; − vt (**-ll-,** Am **-l-**) (surface, differences) niveler, aplanir; (plane down) raboter; (building) raser; (gun) braquer; (accusation) lancer (at contre); − vi **to l. off** or **out** (stabilize) Fig se stabiliser. **2** n **on the l.** Fam (honest) honnête, franc; (frankly) honnêtement, franchement; − vi (**-ll-,** Am **-l-**) **to l. with** Fam être franc avec. ◆**l.-'headed** a équilibré.

lever ['liːvər, Am 'levər] n levier m. ◆**leverage** n (power) influence f.

levity ['levɪtɪ] n légèreté f.

levy ['levɪ] vt (tax, troops) lever; − n (tax) impôt m.

lewd [luːd] a (**-er, -est**) obscène.

liable ['laɪəb(ə)l] a **l. to** (dizziness etc) sujet à; (fine, tax) passible de; **he's l. to do** il est susceptible de faire, il pourrait faire; **l. for** (responsible) responsable de. ◆**lia'bility** n responsabilité f (**for** de); (disadvantage) handicap m; pl (debts) dettes fpl.

liaise [lɪ'eɪz] vi travailler en liaison (**with** avec). ◆**liaison** n (association) & Mil liaison f.

liar ['laɪər] n menteur, -euse mf.

libel ['laɪb(ə)l] vt (**-ll-,** Am **-l-**) diffamer (par écrit); − n diffamation f.

liberal ['lɪbərəl] a (open-minded) & Pol libéral; (generous) généreux (**with** de); − n Pol libéral, -ale mf. ◆**liberalism** n libéralisme m.

liberate ['lɪbəreɪt] vt libérer. ◆**libe'ration** n libération f. ◆**liberator** n libérateur, -trice mf.

liberty ['lɪbətɪ] n liberté f; **at l. to do** libre de faire; **what a l.!** (cheek) Fam quel culot!; **to take liberties with s.o.** se permettre des familiarités avec qn.

Libra ['liːbrə] n (sign) la Balance.

library ['laɪbrərɪ] n bibliothèque f. ◆**li'brarian** n bibliothécaire mf.

libretto [lɪ'bretəu] n (pl **-os**) Mus livret m.

Libya ['lɪbjə] n Libye f. ◆**Libyan** a & n libyen, -enne (mf).

lice [laɪs] see louse.

licence, Am **license** ['laɪsəns] n **1** permis m, autorisation f; (for driving) permis m; Com licence f; **pilot's l.** brevet m de pilote; **l. fee** Rad TV redevance f; **l. plate/number** Aut plaque f/numéro m d'immatriculation. **2** (freedom) licence f.

license ['laɪsəns] vt accorder une licence à, autoriser; **licensed premises** établissement m qui a une licence de débit de boissons.

licit ['lɪsɪt] a licite.

lick [lɪk] vt lécher; (defeat) Fam écraser; (beat physically) Fam rosser; **to be licked** (by problem etc) Fam être dépassé; − n coup m de langue; **a l. of paint** un coup de peinture. ◆**-ing** n Fam (defeat) déculottée f; (beating) rossée f.

licorice ['lɪkərɪʃ, -rɪs] n Am réglisse f.

lid [lɪd] n **1** (of box etc) couvercle m. **2** (of eye) paupière f.

lido ['liːdəu] n (pl **-os**) piscine f (découverte).

lie ¹ [laɪ] vi (pt **lay,** pp **lain,** pres p **lying**) (in flat position) s'allonger, s'étendre; (remain) rester; (be) être; (in grave) reposer; **to be lying** (on the grass etc) être allongé ou étendu; **he lay asleep** il dormait; **here lies** (on tomb) ci-gît; **the problem lies in** le problème réside dans; **to l. heavy on** (of meal etc) & Fig peser sur; **to l. low** (hide) se cacher; (be inconspicuous) se faire tout petit; **to l. about** or **around** (of objects, person) traîner; **to l. down, to have a l.-down** s'allonger, se coucher; **lying down** (resting) allongé, couché; **to l. in, to have a l.-in** Fam faire la grasse matinée.

lie ² [laɪ] vi (pt & pp **lied,** pres p **lying**) (tell lies) mentir; − n mensonge m; **to give the l. to** (show as untrue) démentir.

lieu [luː] n **in l. of** au lieu de.

lieutenant [lef'tenənt, Am lu:'tenənt] n lieutenant m.

life [laɪf] n (pl **lives**) vie f; (of battery, machine) durée f (de vie); **to come to l.** (of street, party etc) s'animer; **at your time of l.** à ton âge; **loss of l.** perte f en vies humaines; **true to l.** conforme à la réalité; **to take one's (own)** l. se donner la mort; **bird's l.** les oiseaux mpl; − a (cycle, style de) vie; (belt, raft) de sauvetage; (force) vital; **l. annuity** rente f viagère; **l. blood** Fig âme f; **l. insurance** assurance-vie f; **l. jacket** gilet m de sauvetage; **l. peer** pair m à vie. ◆**lifeboat** n canot m de sauvetage. ◆**lifebuoy** n bouée f de sauvetage. ◆**lifeguard** n maître-nageur m sauveteur. ◆**lifeless** a sans vie. ◆**lifelike** a qui semble vivant. ◆**lifelong** a de toute une vie; (friend) de toujours. ◆**lifesaving** n sauvetage m. ◆**lifesize(d)** a grandeur nature inv. ◆**lifetime** n Fig éternité f; **in my l.** de mon vivant; **a once-in-a-l. experience/etc** l'expérience/etc de votre vie.

lift [lɪft] vt (sth heavy) lever, soulever; (ban, siege) Fig lever; (idea etc) Fig voler, prendre (**from** à); **to l. down** or **off** (take down) descendre (**from** de); **to l. out** (take out) sortir; **to l. up** (arm, eyes) lever; (object) (sou)lever; – *vi (of fog)* se lever; **to l. off** *(of space vehicle)* décoller; – *n (elevator)* ascenseur *m*; **to give s.o. a l.** emmener *or* accompagner qn (en voiture) (**to** à). ◆**l.-off** *n Av* décollage *m*.

ligament ['lɪɡəmənt] *n* ligament *m*.

light¹ [laɪt] **1** *n* lumière *f*, (*daylight*) jour *m*, lumière *f*; (*on vehicle*) feu *m*, (*headlight*) phare *m*; **by the l. of** à la lumière de; **in the l. of** (*considering*) sous le jour *or* cet éclairage; **against the l.** à contre-jour; **to bring to l.** mettre en lumière; **to come to l.** être découvert; **to throw l. on** (*matter*) éclaircir; **do you have a l.?** (*for cigarette*) est-ce que vous avez du feu?; **to set l. to** mettre le feu à; **leading l.** (*person*) *Fig* phare *m*, sommité *f*, lumière *f*; **l. bulb** ampoule *f* (électrique); – *vt* (*pt & pp* **lit** *or* **lighted**) (*candle etc*) allumer; (*match*) gratter; **to l. (up)** (*room*) éclairer; – *vi* **to l. up** (*of window*) s'allumer. **2** *a* (*bright, not dark*) clair; **a l. green jacket** une veste vert clair. ◆—**ing** *n El* éclairage *m*; **the l. of** (*candle etc*) l'allumage *m* de. ◆**lighten¹** *vt* (*light up*) éclairer; (*colour, hair*) éclaircir. ◆**lighter** *n* (*for cigarettes etc*) briquet *m*; *Culin* allume-gaz *m inv.* ◆**lighthouse** *n* phare *m*. ◆**lightness¹** *n* clarté *f*.

light² [laɪt] *a* (*in weight, quantity, strength etc*) léger; (*task*) facile; **l. rain** pluie *f* fine; **to travel l.** voyager avec peu de bagages. ◆**l.-'fingered** *a* chapardeur. ◆**l.-'headed** *a* (*giddy, foolish*) étourdi. ◆**l.-'hearted** *a* gai. ◆**lighten²** *vt* (*a load*) alléger. ◆**lightly** *adv* légèrement. ◆**lightness²** *n* légèreté *f*.

light³ [laɪt] *vi* (*pt & pp* **lit** *or* **lighted**) **to l. upon** trouver par hasard.

lightning ['laɪtnɪŋ] *n Met* (*light*) éclair *m*; (*charge*) foudre *f*; (*flash of*) **l.** éclair *m*; – *a* (*speed*) foudroyant; (*visit*) éclair *inv*; **l. conductor** paratonnerre *m*.

lightweight ['laɪtweɪt] *a* (*cloth etc*) léger; (*not serious*) pas sérieux, léger.

like¹ [laɪk] *a* (*alike*) semblable, pareil; – *prep* comme; **l. this** comme ça; **what's he l.?** (*physically, as character*) comment est-il?; **to be** *or* **look l.** ressembler à; **what was the book l.?** comment as-tu trouvé le livre?; **I have one l. it** j'en ai un pareil; – *adv* **nothing l. as big** loin d'être aussi grand/*etc*; – *conj* (*as*) *Fam* comme; **it's l. I say** c'est comme je vous le dis; – *n* ... and **l.** ... et ainsi de suite; **l. of which** we **shan't see again** comme on n'en reverra plus; **the likes of you** des gens de ton acabit.

lik/e² [laɪk] *vt* aimer (bien) (**to do, doing** faire); **I l. him** je l'aime bien, il me plaît; **she likes it here** elle se plaît ici; **to l. best** préférer; **I'd l. to come** (*want*) je voudrais (bien) *or* j'aimerais (bien) venir; **I'd l. a kilo of apples** je voudrais un kilo de pommes; **would you l. a cigar?** voulez-vous un cigare?; **if you l.** si vous voulez; (**how**) **would you l. to come?** ça te plairait *or* te dirait de venir?; – *npl* **one's likes** nos goûts *mpl*. ◆—**ing** *n* **a l. for** (*person*) de la sympathie pour; (*thing*) du goût pour; **to my l.** à mon goût. ◆**likeable** *a* sympathique.

likely ['laɪklɪ] *a* (**-ier, -iest**) (*event, result etc*) probable; (*excuse*) vraisemblable; (*place*) propice; (*candidate*) prometteur; **a l. excuse!** *Iron* belle excuse!; **it's l.** (**that**) **she'll come** il est probable qu'elle viendra; **he's l. to come** il viendra probablement; **he's not l. to come** il ne risque pas de venir; – *adv* **very l.** très probablement; **not l.!** pas question! ◆**likelihood** *n* probabilité *f*; **there's little l.** that il y a peu de chances que (+ *sub*).

liken ['laɪkən] *vt* comparer (**to** à). ◆**likeness** ['laɪknɪs] *n* ressemblance *f*; **a family l.** un air de famille; **it's a good l.** c'est ressemblant.

likewise ['laɪkwaɪz] *adv* (*similarly*) de même, pareillement.

lilac ['laɪlək] *n* lilas *m*; – *a* (*colour*) lilas *inv*.

Lilo® ['laɪləʊ] *n* (*pl* **-os**) matelas *m* pneumatique.

lilt [lɪlt] *n Mus* cadence *f*.

lily ['lɪlɪ] *n* lis *m*, lys *m*; **l. of the valley** muguet *m*.

limb [lɪm] *n Anat* membre *m*; **to be out on a l.** *Fig* être le seul de son opinion.

limber ['lɪmbər] *vi* **to l. up** faire les exercices d'assouplissement.

limbo (in) [lɪmbəʊ] *adv* (*uncertain, waiting*) dans l'expectative.

lime [laɪm] *n* **1** (*tree*) tilleul *m*. **2** (*substance*) chaux *f*. **3** (*fruit*) lime *f*, citron *m* vert; **l. juice** jus *m* de citron vert.

limelight ['laɪmlaɪt] *n* **in the l.** (*glare of publicity*) en vedette.

limit ['lɪmɪt] *n* limite *f*; (*restriction*) limitation *f* (**of** de); **that's the l.!** *Fam* c'est le comble!; **within limits** dans une certaine limite; – *vt* limiter (**to** à); **to l. oneself to doing** se borner à faire. ◆—**ed** *a* (*restricted*) limité; (*mind*) borné; (*edition*) à tirage limité; **l. company** *Com* société *f* à responsabilité limitée; (*public*) **l. company** (*with shareholders*) société *f* anonyme; **to a**

l. degree jusqu'à un certain point. ◆**limi-'tation** n limitation f. ◆**limitless** a illimité.

limousine [lɪmə'ziːn] n (car) limousine f; (airport etc shuttle) Am voiture-navette f.

limp [lɪmp] 1 vi (of person) boiter; (of vehicle etc) Fig avancer tant bien que mal; – **to have a l.** boiter. 2 a (-er, -est) (soft) mou; (flabby) flasque; (person, hat) avachi.

limpid ['lɪmpɪd] a (liquid) Lit limpide.

linchpin ['lɪntʃpɪn] n (person) pivot m.

linctus ['lɪŋktəs] n Med sirop m (contre la toux).

line[1] [laɪn] n ligne f; (stroke) trait m, ligne f; (of poem) vers m; (wrinkle) ride f; (track) voie f; (rope) corde f; (row) rangée f, ligne f; (of vehicles) file f; (queue) Am file f, queue f; (family) lignée f; (business) métier m, rayon m; (article) Com article m; **one's lines** (of actor) son texte m; **on the l.** Tel (speaking) au téléphone; (at other end of line) au bout du fil; **to be on the l.** (at risk) être en danger; **hold the l.!** Tel ne quittez pas!; **the hot l.** Tel le téléphone rouge; **to stand in l.** Am faire la queue; **to step** ou **get out of l.** Fig refuser de se conformer; (misbehave) faire une incartade; **out of l. with** (ideas etc) en désaccord avec; **in l. with** conforme à; **he's in l. for** (promotion etc) il doit recevoir; **to take a hard l.** adopter une attitude ferme; **along the same lines** (to work, think) de la même façon; **sth along those lines** qch dans ce genre-là; **to drop a l.** Fam envoyer un mot (**to** à); **where do we draw the l.?** où fixer les limites?; – vt (paper) régler; (face) rider; **to l. the street** (of trees) border la rue; (of people) faire la haie le long de la rue; **to l. up** (children, objects) aligner; (arrange) organiser; (get ready) préparer; **to have sth lined up** (in mind) avoir qch en vue; – vi **to l. up** s'aligner; (queue) Am faire la queue. ◆**l.-up** n (row) file f; Pol front m; TV programme(s) m(pl).

line[2] [laɪn] vt (clothes) doubler; (pockets) Fig se remplir. ◆**lining** n (of clothes) doublure f; (of brakes) garniture f.

lineage ['lɪnɪɪdʒ] n lignée f.

linear ['lɪnɪər] a linéaire.

linen ['lɪnɪn] n (sheets etc) linge m; (material) (toile f de) lin m, fil m.

liner ['laɪnər] n 1 (ship) paquebot m. 2 (dust)bin l. sac n poubelle.

linesman ['laɪnzmən] n (pl -men) Fb etc juge m de touche.

linger ['lɪŋɡər] vi **to l.** (on) (of person) s'attarder; (of smell, memory) persister; (of doubt) subsister. ◆**-ing** a (death) lent.

lingo ['lɪŋɡəu] n (pl -os) Hum Fam jargon m.

linguist ['lɪŋɡwɪst] n linguiste mf. ◆**lin-'guistic** a linguistique. ◆**lin'guistics** n linguistique f.

liniment ['lɪnɪmənt] n onguent m, pommade f.

link [lɪŋk] vt (connect) relier (**to** à); (relate, associate) lier (**to** à); **to l. up** Tel relier; – vi **to l. up** (of roads) se rejoindre; – n (connection) lien m; (of chain) maillon m; (by road, rail) liaison f. ◆**l.-up** n TV Rad liaison f; (of spacecraft) jonction f.

lino ['laɪnəu] n (pl -os) lino m. ◆**linoleum** [lɪ'nəuliəm] n linoléum m.

linseed ['lɪnsiːd] n **l. oil** huile f de lin.

lint [lɪnt] n Med tissu m ouaté; (fluff) peluche(s) f(pl).

lion ['laɪən] n lion m; **l. cub** lionceau m. ◆**lioness** n lionne f.

lip [lɪp] n Anat lèvre f; (rim) bord m; (cheek) Sl culot m. ◆**l.-read** vi (pt & pp -read [red]) lire sur les lèvres. ◆**lipstick** n (material) rouge m à lèvres; (stick) tube m de rouge.

liqueur [lɪ'kjuər] n liqueur f.

liquid ['lɪkwɪd] n & a liquide (m). ◆**liquefy** vt liquéfier; – vi se liquéfier. ◆**liquidizer** n Culin (for fruit juices) centrifugeuse f; (for purées etc) robot m, moulinette® f.

liquidate ['lɪkwɪdeɪt] vt (debt, person) liquider. ◆**liqui'dation** n liquidation f.

liquor ['lɪkər] n alcool m, spiritueux m; **l. store** Am magasin m de vins et de spiritueux.

liquorice ['lɪkərɪʃ, -rɪs] n réglisse f.

lira, pl lire ['lɪərə, 'lɪəreɪ] n (currency) lire f.

lisp [lɪsp] vi zézayer; – n **to have a l.** zézayer.

list [lɪst] 1 n liste f; – vt (one's possessions etc) faire la liste de; (names) mettre sur la liste; (enumerate) énumérer; (catalogue) cataloguer. 2 vi (of ship) gîter. ◆**-ed** a (monument) classé.

listen ['lɪsən] vi écouter; **to l.** to écouter; **to l.** (out) for (telephone, person etc) tendre l'oreille pour, guetter; **to l. in** (to) Rad écouter. ◆**-ing** n écoute f (to de). ◆**-er** n Rad auditeur, -trice mf; **to be a good l.** (pay attention) savoir écouter.

listless ['lɪstləs] a apathique, indolent. ◆**-ness** n apathie f.

lit [lɪt] see **light 1** 1.

litany ['lɪtənɪ] n Rel litanies fpl.

literal ['lɪtərəl] a littéral; (not exaggerated) réel. ◆**-ly** adv littéralement; (really) réellement; **he took it l.** il l'a pris au pied de la lettre.

literate ['lɪtərət] a qui sait lire et écrire;

highly l. (*person*) très instruit. ◆**literacy** *n* capacité *f* de lire et d'écrire; (*of country*) degré *m* d'alphabétisation.

literature ['lɪt(ə)rɪtʃər] *n* littérature *f*; (*pamphlets etc*) documentation *f*. ◆**literary** *a* littéraire.

lithe [laɪð] *a* agile, souple.

litigation [lɪtɪˈgeɪʃ(ə)n] *n Jur* litige *m*.

litre ['liːtər] *n* litre *m*.

litter ['lɪtər] **1** *n* (*rubbish*) détritus *m*; (*papers*) papiers *mpl*; (*bedding for animals*) litière *f*; (*confusion*) *Fig* fouillis *m*; **l. basket** *or* **bin** boîte *f* à ordures; – *vt* **to l. (with papers** *or* **rubbish)** (*street etc*) laisser traîner des papiers *or* des détritus dans; **a street littered with** une rue jonchée de. **2** *n* (*young animals*) portée *f*.

little ['lɪt(ə)l] **1** *a* (*small*) petit; **the l. ones** les petits. **2** *a & n* (*not much*) peu (de); **l. time/money/***etc* peu de temps/d'argent/*etc*; **I've l. left** il m'en reste peu; **she eats l.** elle mange peu; **to have l. to say** avoir peu de chose à dire; **as l. as possible** le moins possible; **l. money/time/***etc* (*some*) un peu d'argent/de temps/*etc*; **I have a l.** (*some*) j'en ai un peu; **the l. that I have** le peu que j'ai; – *adv* (*somewhat, rather*) peu; **a l. heavy/***etc* un peu lourd/*etc*; **to work/***etc* **a l.** travailler/*etc* un peu; **it's l. better** (*hardly*) ce n'est guère mieux; **l. by l.** peu à peu.

liturgy ['lɪtədʒɪ] *n* liturgie *f*.

live¹ [lɪv] *vi* vivre; (*reside*) habiter, vivre; **where do you l.?** où habitez-vous? **to l. in Paris** habiter *or* vivre à Paris; **to l. off** *or* **on** (*eat*) vivre de; (*sponge on*) *Pej* vivre aux crochets *or* aux dépens de (*qn*); **to l. on** (*of memory etc*) survivre, se perpétuer; **to l. through** (*experience*) vivre; (*survive*) survivre à; **to l. up to** (*one's principles*) vivre selon; (*s.o.'s expectations*) se montrer à la hauteur de; – *vt* (*life*) vivre, mener; (*one's faith etc*) vivre pleinement; **to l. down** faire oublier (avec le temps); **to l. it up** *Fam* mener la grande vie.

live² [laɪv] **1** *a* (*alive, lively*) vivant; (*coal*) ardent; (*bomb*) non explosé; (*ammunition*) réel, de combat; (*wire*) *El* sous tension; (*switch*) *El* mal isolé; (*plugged in*) *El* branché; **a real l. king/***etc* un roi/*etc* en chair et en os. **2** *a & adv* *Rad TV* en direct; **a l. broadcast** une émission en direct; **a l. audience** le *or* un public; **a l. recording** un enregistrement public.

livelihood ['laɪvlɪhʊd] *n* moyens *mpl* de subsistance; **my l.** mon gagne-pain; **to earn one's** *or* **a l.** gagner sa vie.

lively ['laɪvlɪ] *a* (**-ier, -iest**) (*person, style*)

vif, vivant; (*street, story*) vivant; (*interest, mind, colour*) vif; (*day*) mouvementé; (*forceful*) vigoureux; (*conversation, discussion*) animé. ◆**—iness** *n* vivacité *f*.

liven ['laɪv(ə)n] *vt* **to l. up** (*person*) égayer; (*party*) animer; – *vi* **to l. up** (*of person, party*) s'animer.

liver ['lɪvər] *n* foie *m*.

livery ['lɪvərɪ] *n* (*uniform*) livrée *f*.

livestock ['laɪvstɒk] *n* bétail *m*.

livid ['lɪvɪd] *a* (*blue-grey*) livide; (*angry*) *Fig* furieux; **l. with cold** blême de froid.

living ['lɪvɪŋ] *a* (*alive*) vivant; **not a l. soul** (*nobody*) personne, pas âme qui vive; **within l. memory** de mémoire d'homme; **l. or dead** mort ou vif; **the l.** les vivants *mpl*. **2** *n* (*livelihood*) vie *f*; **to make a** *or* **one's l.** gagner sa vie; **to work for a l.** travailler pour vivre; **the cost of l.** le coût de la vie; – *a* (*standard, conditions*) de vie; (*wage*) qui permet de vivre; **l. room** salle *f* de séjour.

lizard ['lɪzəd] *n* lézard *m*.

llama ['lɑːmə] *n* (*animal*) lama *m*.

load [ləʊd] *n* (*object carried, burden*) charge *f*; (*freight*) chargement *m*, charge *f*; (*strain, weight*) poids *m*; **a l. of**, **loads of** (*people, money etc*) *Fam* un tas de, énormément de; **to take a l. off s.o.'s mind** ôter un grand poids à qn; – *vt* charger; **to l. down** *or* **up** charger (**with** de); – *vi* **to l. (up)** charger la voiture, le navire etc. ◆**—ed** *a* (*gun, vehicle etc*) chargé; (*dice*) pipé; (*rich*) *Fam* plein aux as; **a l. question** une question piège; **l. (down) with** (*debts*) accablé de.

loaf [ləʊf] **1** *n* (*pl* **loaves**) pain *m*; **French l.** baguette *f*. **2** *vi* **to l. (about)** fainéanter. ◆**—er** *n* fainéant, -ante *mf*.

loam [ləʊm] *n* (*soil*) terreau *m*.

loan [ləʊn] *n* (*money lent*) prêt *m*; (*money borrowed*) emprunt *m*; **on l. from** prêté par; (**out) on l.** (*book*) sorti; **may I have the l. of . . . ?** puis-je emprunter . . . ?; – *vt* (*lend*) prêter (**to** à).

loath [ləʊθ] *a* **to do** *Lit* peu disposé à faire.

loath/e [ləʊð] *vt* détester (**doing** faire). ◆**—ing** *n* dégoût *m*. ◆**loathsome** *a* détestable.

lobby ['lɒbɪ] **1** *n* (*of hotel*) vestibule *m*, hall *m*; *Th* foyer *m*. **2** *n Pol* groupe *m* de pression, lobby *m*; – *vt* faire pression sur.

lobe [ləʊb] *n Anat* lobe *m*.

lobster ['lɒbstər] *n* homard *m*; (*spiny*) langouste *f*.

local ['ləʊk(ə)l] *a* local; (*of the neighbourhood*) du *or* de quartier; (*regional*) du pays; **are you l.?** êtes-vous du coin *or* d'ici?; **the doctor is l.** le médecin est tout près d'ici; **a l. phone call** (*within town*) une communication urbaine; – *n* (*pub*) *Fam* bistrot *m* du coin, pub *m*; **she's a l.** elle est du coin; **the locals** (*people*) les gens du coin. ◆**lo'cality** *n* (*neighbourhood*) environs *mpl*; (*region*) région *f*; (*place*) lieu *m*; (*site*) emplacement *m*. ◆**localize** *vt* (*confine*) localiser. ◆**locally** *adv* dans les environs, dans le coin; (*around here*) par ici; (*in precise place*) localement.

locate [ləʊ'keɪt] *vt* (*find*) repérer; (*pain, noise, leak*) localiser; (*situate*) situer; (*build*) construire. ◆**location** *n* (*site*) emplacement *m*; (*act*) repérage *m*; localisation *f*; **on l.** *Cin* en extérieur.

lock [lɒk] **1** *vt* **to l. (up)** fermer à clef; **to l. the wheels** *Aut* bloquer les roues; **to l. s.o.** enfermer qn; **to l. s.o. in sth** enfermer qn dans qch; **to l. s.o. out** (*accidentally*) enfermer qn dehors; **to l. away** *or* **up** (*prisoner*) enfermer; (*jewels etc*) mettre sous clef, enfermer; – *vi* **to l. (up)** fermer à clef; – *n* (*on door, chest etc*) serrure *f*; (*of gun*) cran *m* de sûreté; (*turning circle*) *Aut* rayon *m* de braquage; (**anti-theft**) *Aut* antivol *m*; **under l. and key** sous clef. **2** *n* (*on canal*) écluse *f*. **3** *n* (*of hair*) mèche *f*. ◆**locker** *n* casier *m*; (*for luggage*) *Rail* casier *m* de consigne automatique; (*for clothes*) vestiaire *m* (métallique); **l. room** *Sp Am* vestiaire *m*. ◆**lockout** *n* (*industrial*) lock-out *m inv*. ◆**locksmith** *n* serrurier *m*.

locket ['lɒkɪt] *n* (*jewel*) médaillon *m*.

loco ['ləʊkəʊ] *a Sl* cinglé, fou.

locomotion [ləʊkə'məʊʃ(ə)n] *n* locomotion *f*. ◆**locomotive** *n* locomotive *f*.

locum ['ləʊkəm] *n* (*doctor*) remplaçant, -ante *f*.

locust ['ləʊkəst] *n* criquet *m*, sauterelle *f*.

lodg/e [lɒdʒ] **1** *vt* (*person*) loger; (*valuables*) déposer (**with** chez); **to l. a complaint** porter plainte; – *vi* (*of bullet*) se loger (**in** dans); **to be lodging** (*accommodated*) être logé (**with** chez). **2** *n* (*house*) pavillon *m* de gardien *or* de chasse; (*of porter*) loge *f*. ◆—**ing** *n* (*accommodation*) logement *m*; *pl* (*flat*) logement *m*; (*room*) chambre *f*; **in lodgings** en meublé. ◆—**er** *n* (*room and meals*) pensionnaire *mf*; (*room only*) locataire *mf*.

loft [lɒft] *n* (*attic*) grenier *m*.

loft/y ['lɒftɪ] *a* (**-ier, -iest**) (*high, noble*) élevé; (*haughty*) hautain. ◆—**iness** *n* hauteur *f*.

log [lɒg] **1** *n* (*tree trunk*) rondin *m*; (*for fire*) bûche *f*, rondin *m*; **l. fire** feu *m* de bois. **2** *vt* (**-gg-**) (*facts*) noter; **to l. (up)** (*distance*) faire, couvrir. ◆**logbook** *n Nau Av* journal *m* de bord.

logarithm ['lɒgərɪðm] *n* logarithme *m*.

loggerheads (at) [æt'lɒgəhedz] *adv* en désaccord (**with** avec).

logic ['lɒdʒɪk] *n* logique *f*. ◆**logical** *a* logique. ◆**logically** *adv* logiquement.

logistics [lə'dʒɪstɪks] *n* logistique *f*.

logo ['ləʊgəʊ] *n* (*pl* **-os**) logo *m*.

loin [lɒɪn] *n* (*meat*) filet *m*.

loins [lɒɪnz] *npl Anat* reins *mpl*.

loiter ['lɒɪtər] *vi* traîner.

loll [lɒl] *vi* (*in armchair etc*) se prélasser.

lollipop ['lɒlɪpɒp] *n* (*sweet on stick*) sucette *f*; (*ice on stick*) esquimau *m*. ◆**lolly** *n Fam* sucette *f*; (*money*) *Sl* fric *m*; (*ice*) **l.** *Fam* esquimau *m*.

London ['lʌndən] *n* Londres *m or f*; – *a* (*taxi etc*) londonien. ◆**Londoner** *n* Londonien, -ienne *mf*.

lone [ləʊn] *a* solitaire; **l. wolf** *Fig* solitaire *mf*. ◆**loneliness** *n* solitude *f*. ◆**lonely** *a* (**-ier, -iest**) (*road, house, life etc*) solitaire; (*person*) seul, solitaire. ◆**loner** *n* solitaire *mf*. ◆**lonesome** *a* solitaire.

long¹ [lɒŋ] **1** *a* (**-er, -est**) long; **to be ten metres l.** être long de dix mètres, avoir dix mètres de long; **to be six weeks l.** durer six semaines; **how l. is...** quelle est la longueur de...?; (*time*) quelle est la durée de...?; **a l. time** longtemps; **in the l. run** à la longue; **a l. face** une grimace; **a l. memory** une bonne mémoire; **l. jump** *Sp* saut *m* en longueur. **2** *adv* (*a long time*) longtemps; **l. before** longtemps avant; **has he been here l.?** il y a longtemps qu'il est ici?, il est ici depuis longtemps?; **l. ago** (*ago*?) (il y a) combien de temps?; **not l. ago** il y a peu de temps; **before l.** sous *or* avant peu; **no longer** ne plus; **she no longer swims** elle ne nage plus; **a bit longer** (*to wait etc*) encore un peu; **I won't be l.** je n'en ai pas pour longtemps; **at the longest** (*tout*) au plus; **all summer l.** tout l'été; **l. live the queen/etc** vive la reine/etc; **as l. as, so l. as** (*provided that*) pourvu que (+ *sub*); **as l. as I live** tant que je vivrai.

long² [lɒŋ] *vi* **to l. for sth** avoir très envie de qch; **to l. for s.o.** languir après qn; **to l. to do** avoir très envie de faire. ◆—**ing** *n* désir *m*, envie *f*.

long-distance [lɒŋ'dɪstəns] *a* (*race*) de fond; (*phone call*) interurbain; (*flight*) long-courrier. ◆**long-drawn-'out** *a* interminable. ◆**long'haired** *a* aux cheveux longs. ◆**longhand** *n* écriture *f* normale. ◆**long-'playing** *a* **l.-playing record** 33 tours *m inv*. ◆**long-range** *a* (*forecast*) à long terme. ◆**long'sighted** *a* *Med* presbyte. ◆**long'standing** a de longue date. ◆**long'suffering** a très patient. ◆**long-'term** a à long terme. ◆**long-'winded** a (speech, speaker) verbeux.

longevity [lɒn'dʒevɪtɪ] n longévité f.

longitude ['lɒndʒɪtjuːd] n longitude f.

longways ['lɒŋweɪz] adv en longueur.

loo [luː] n (toilet) Fam cabinets mpl.

look [lʊk] n regard m; (appearance) air m, allure f; (good) looks la beauté, une belle physique; **to have a l. (at)** jeter un coup d'œil (à), regarder; **to have a l. (for)** chercher; **to have a l. (a)round** regarder; (walk) faire un tour; **let me have a l.** fais voir; **I like the l. of him** il me fait bonne impression, il me plaît; — vti regarder; **to l. s.o. in the face** regarder qn dans les yeux; **to l. tired/happy/etc** (seem) sembler ou avoir l'air fatigué/heureux/etc; **to l. pretty/ugly** (be) être joli/laid; **so here!** dites donc!; **you l. like ou as if you're tired** tu as l'air fatigué, on dirait que tu es fatigué; **it looks like ou as if she won't leave** elle n'a pas l'air de vouloir partir; **it looks like it!** c'est probable; **to l. like a child** avoir l'air d'un enfant; **to l. like an apple** avoir l'air d'être une pomme; **you l. like my brother** tu ressembles à mon frère; **it looks like rain (to me)** il me semble ou on dirait qu'il va pleuvoir; **what does he l. like?** (describe him) comment est-il?; **to l. well ou good** (of person) avoir bonne mine; **you l. good in that hat/etc** ce chapeau/etc te va très bien; **that looks bad** (action etc) ça fait mauvais effet. ■ **to l. after** vt (deal with) s'occuper de; (patient, hair) soigner; (keep safely) garder (for s.o. pour qn); **to l. after oneself** (keep healthy) faire bien attention à soi; **I can l. after myself** (cope) je suis assez grand pour me débrouiller; **to l. around** vt (visit) visiter; — vi (have a look) regarder; (walk round) faire un tour; **to l. at** vt regarder; (consider) considérer, voir; (check) vérifier; **to l. away** vi détourner les yeux; **to l. back** vi regarder derrière soi; (in time) regarder en arrière; **to l. down** vi baisser les yeux; (from height) regarder en bas; **to l. down on** (consider scornfully) mépriser, regarder de haut; **to l. for** vt (seek) chercher; **to l. forward to** vt (event) attendre avec impatience; **to l. in** vi regarder (à l'intérieur); **to l. in on s.o.** Fam passer voir qn; **to l. into** vt (examine) examiner; (find out about) se renseigner sur; **to l. on** vi regarder; — vt (consider) considérer; **to l. out** vi (be careful) faire attention (for à); **to l. out for** (seek) chercher; (watch) guetter; **to l. (out) on to** (of window, house etc) donner sur; **to l. over ou through** vt (examine fully) examiner, regarder de près; (briefly) parcourir; (region, town) parcourir, visiter; **to l. round** vt (visit) visiter; — vi (have a look) regarder; (walk round) faire un tour; (look back) se retourner; **to l. round for** (seek) chercher; **to l. up** vi (of person) lever les yeux; (into the air ou sky) regarder en l'air; (improve) s'améliorer; **to l. up to s.o.** Fig respecter qn; — vt (word) chercher; **to l. s.o. up** (visit) passer voir qn. ◆**-looking** suffix pleasant-/tired-/etc **l.** à l'air agréable/fatigué/etc. ◆**looking-glass** n glace f, miroir m.

lookout ['lʊkaʊt] n (soldier) guetteur m; (sailor) vigie f; **l. (post)** poste m de guet; (on ship) vigie f; **to be on the l.** faire le guet; **to be on the l. for** guetter.

loom [luːm] **1** vi **to l. (up)** (of mountain etc) apparaître indistinctement; Fig paraître imminent. **2** n Tex métier m à tisser.

loony ['luːnɪ] n & a Sl imbécile (mf).

loop [luːp] n (in river etc) & Av boucle f; (contraceptive device) stérilet m; — vt **to l. the loop** Av boucler la boucle. ◆**loophole** n (in rules) point m faible, lacune f; (way out) échappatoire f.

loose [luːs] a (-er, -est) (screw, belt, knot) desserré; (tooth, stone) branlant; (page) détaché; (animal) libre, (set loose) lâché; (clothes) flottant; (hair) dénoué; (flesh) flasque; (wording, translation) approximatif, vague; (link) vague; (discipline) relâché; (articles) Com en vrac; (cheese, tea etc) Com au poids; (woman) Pej facile; **l. change** petite monnaie f; **l. covers** housses fpl; **l. living** vie f dissolue; **to get l.** (of dog, page) se détacher; **to set ou turn l.** (dog etc) libérer, lâcher; **he's at a l. end ou Am at l. ends** il ne sait pas trop quoi faire; — **n on the l.** (prisoner etc) en liberté; — vt (animal) lâcher. ◆**loosely** adv (to hang) lâchement; (to hold, tie) sans serrer; (to translate) librement; (to link) vaguement. ◆**loosen** vt (knot, belt, screw) desserrer; (rope) détendre; (grip) relâcher; — vi **to l. up** Sp faire des exercices d'assouplissement. ◆**looseness** n (of screw, machine parts) jeu m.

loot [luːt] n butin m; (money) Sl fric m; — vt piller. ◆**-ing** n pillage m. ◆**-er** n pillard, -arde mf.

lop [lɒp] vt (-pp-) **to l. (off)** couper.

lop-sided [lɒp'saɪdɪd] a (crooked) de travers; **to walk l.-sided** (limp) se déhancher.

loquacious [ləʊ'kweɪʃəs] a loquace.

lord [lɔːd] n seigneur m; (title) Br lord m; **good L.!** Fam bon sang!; **oh L.!** Fam mince!; **the House of Lords** Pol la Chambre des Lords; – vt **to l. it over s.o.** Fam dominer qn. ◆**lordly** a digne d'un grand seigneur; (arrogant) hautain. ◆**lordship** n Your L. (to judge) Monsieur le juge.

lore [lɔːr] n traditions fpl.

lorry ['lɒrɪ] n camion m; (heavy) poids m lourd; **l. driver** camionneur m; **long-distance l. driver** routier m.

los/e [luːz] vt (pt & pp lost) perdre; **to get lost** (of person) se perdre; **the ticket/etc got lost** on a perdu le billet/etc; **get lost!** Fam fiche le camp!; **to l. s.o. sth** faire perdre qch à qn; **to l. interest in** se désintéresser de; **I've lost my bearings** je suis désorienté; **the clock loses six minutes a day** la pendule retarde de six minutes par jour; **to l. one's life** trouver la mort (in dans); – vi perdre; **to l. out** être perdant; **to l. to** Sp être battu par. ◆**-ing** a perdant; **a l. battle** Fig une bataille perdue d'avance. ◆**-er** n perdant, -ante mf; (failure in life) Fam paumé, -ée mf; **to be a good l.** être bon or beau joueur.

loss [lɒs] n perte f; **at a l.** (confused) perplexe; **to sell at a l.** Com vendre à perte; **at a l. to do** incapable de faire. ◆**lost** a perdu; **l. property**, Am **l. and found** objets mpl trouvés.

lot [lɒt] n **1** (destiny) sort m; (batch, land) lot m; **to draw lots** tirer au sort; **parking l.** Am parking m; **a bad l.** (person) Fam un mauvais sujet. **2** the **l.** (everything) le tout; **the l. of you** vous tous; **a l. of, lots of** beaucoup de; **a l.** beaucoup; **quite a l.** pas mal (of de); **such a l.** tellement (of de), tant (of de); **what a l. of flowers/water/etc!** que de fleurs/d'eau/etc!; **what a l.!** quelle quantité!; **what a l. of flowers/etc you have!** que vous avez (beaucoup de fleurs/etc!

lotion ['ləʊʃ(ə)n] n lotion f.

lottery ['lɒtərɪ] n loterie f.

lotto ['lɒtəʊ] n (game) loto m.

loud [laʊd] a (-er, -est) bruyant; (voice, radio) fort; (noise, cry) grand; (gaudy) voyant; – adv (to shout etc) fort; **out l.** tout haut. ◆**-ly** adv (to speak, laugh etc) bruyamment, fort; (to shout) fort. ◆**-ness** n (of voice etc) force f; (noise) bruit m. ◆**loud'hailer** n mégaphone m. ◆**loud'speaker** n haut-parleur m; (of hi-fi unit) enceinte f.

lounge [laʊndʒ] n **1** salon m; **l. suit** complet

m veston. **2** vi (loll) se prélasser; **to l. about** (idle) paresser; (stroll) flâner.

louse, pl **lice** [laʊs, laɪs] **1** n (insect) pou m. **2** n (person) Pej Sl salaud m. **3** vt **to l. up** (mess up) Sl gâcher.

lousy ['laʊzɪ] a (-ier, -iest) (bad) Fam infect; **l. with** (crammed, loaded) Sl bourré de.

lout [laʊt] n rustre m. ◆**loutish** a (attitude) de rustre.

lov/e [lʌv] n amour m; Tennis zéro m; **in l.** amoureux (with de); **they're in l.** ils s'aiment; **art is his** or **her l.** l'art est sa passion; **yes, my l.** oui mon amour; – vt aimer; (like very much) aimer (beaucoup) (to do, doing faire); **give him** or **her my l.** (greeting) dis-lui bien des choses de ma part; **l. affair** liaison f (amoureuse). ◆**-ing** a affectueux, aimant. ◆**-able** a adorable. ◆**-er** n (man) amant m; (woman) maîtresse f; **a l. of** (art, music etc) un amateur de; **a nature l.** un amoureux de la nature. ◆**lovesick** a amoureux.

lovely ['lʌvlɪ] a (-ier, -iest) (pleasing) agréable, bon; (excellent) excellent; (pretty) joli; (charming) charmant; (kind) gentil; **the weather's l.** il fait beau; **l. to see you!** je suis ravi de te voir; **l. and hot/dry/etc** bien chaud/sec/etc.

low¹ [ləʊ] a (-er, -est) bas; (speed, income, intelligence) faible; (opinion, quality) mauvais; **she's l. on** (money etc) elle n'a plus beaucoup de; **to feel l.** (depressed) être déprimé; **in a l. voice** à voix basse; **lower** inférieur; – adv (-er, -est) bas; **to turn (down) l.** mettre plus bas; **to run l.** (of supplies) s'épuiser; – n Met dépression f; **to reach a new l.** or **an all-time l.** (of prices etc) atteindre leur niveau le plus bas. ◆**low-'calorie** a (diet) (à) basses calories. ◆**low-'cost** a bon marché inv. ◆**low-cut** a décolleté. ◆**low-down** a méprisable. ◆**lowdown** n (facts) Fam tuyaux mpl. ◆**low-'fat** a (milk) écrémé; (cheese) de régime. ◆**low-'key** a (discreet) discret. ◆**lowland(s)** n plaine f. ◆**low-level** a bas. ◆**low-paid** a mal payé. ◆**low-'salt** a (food) à faible teneur en sel.

low² [ləʊ] vi (of cattle) meugler.

lower ['ləʊər] vt baisser; **to l. s.o./sth** (by rope) descendre qn/qch; **to l. oneself** Fig s'abaisser. ◆**-ing** n (drop) baisse f.

lowly ['ləʊlɪ] a (-ier, -iest) humble.

loyal ['lɔɪəl] a loyal (to envers), fidèle (to à). ◆**loyalty** n loyauté f, fidélité f.

lozenge ['lɒzɪndʒ] n (sweet) Med pastille f; (shape) Geom losange m.

L-plates ['elpleɪts] *npl Aut* plaques *fpl* d'apprenti conducteur.

Ltd *abbr* (*Limited*) *Com* SARL.

lubricate ['luːbrɪkeɪt] *vt* lubrifier; *Aut* graisser. ◆**lubricant** *n* lubrifiant *m*. ◆**lubri'cation** *n Aut* graissage *m*.

lucid ['luːsɪd] *a* lucide. ◆**lu'cidity** *n* lucidité *f*.

luck [lʌk] *n* (*chance*) chance *f*; (*good fortune*) (*bonne*) chance *f*, bonheur *m*; (*fate*) hasard *m*, fortune *f*; **bad l.** malchance *f*, malheur *m*; **hard l.!**, **tough l.!** pas de chance!; **worse l.** (*unfortunately*) malheureusement. ◆**luckily** *adv* heureusement. ◆**lucky** *a* (**-ier, -iest**) (*person*) chanceux, heureux; (*guess, day*) heureux; **to be l.** (*of person*) avoir de la chance (**to do** faire); **I've had a l. day** j'ai eu de la chance aujourd'hui; **l. charm** porte-bonheur *m inv*; **l. number/etc** chiffre *m/etc* porte-bonheur; **how l.!** quelle chance!

lucrative ['luːkrətɪv] *a* lucratif.

ludicrous ['luːdɪkrəs] *a* ridicule.

ludo ['luːdəʊ] *n* jeu *m* des petits chevaux.

lug [lʌg] *vt* (**-gg-**) (*pull*) traîner; **to l. around** trimbaler.

luggage ['lʌgɪdʒ] *n* bagages *mpl*.

lugubrious [luːˈguːbrɪəs] *a* lugubre.

lukewarm ['luːkwɔːm] *a* tiède.

lull [lʌl] **1** *n* arrêt *m*; (*in storm*) accalmie *f*. **2** *vt* (**-ll-**) apaiser; **to l. to sleep** endormir.

lullaby ['lʌləbaɪ] *n* berceuse *f*.

lumbago [lʌmˈbeɪgəʊ] *n* lumbago *m*.

lumber[1] ['lʌmbər] *n* (*timber*) bois *m* de charpente; (*junk*) bric-à-brac *m inv*. ◆**lumberjack** *n Am Can* bûcheron *m*. ◆**lumberjacket** *n* blouson *m*. ◆**lumber-room** *n* débarras *m*.

lumber[2] ['lʌmbər] *vt* **l. s.o. with sth/s.o.** *Fam* coller qch/qn à qn; **he got lumbered with the chore** il s'est appuyé la corvée.

luminous ['luːmɪnəs] *a* (*dial etc*) lumineux.

lump [lʌmp] *n* morceau *m*; (*in soup*) grumeau *m*; (*bump*) bosse *f*; (*swelling*) Med grosseur *f*; **l. sum** somme *f* forfaitaire; – *vt* **to l. together** réunir; *Fig Pej* mettre dans le même sac. ◆**lumpy** *a* (**-ier, -iest**) (*soup etc*) grumeleux; (*surface*) bosselé.

lunar ['luːnər] *a* lunaire.

lunatic ['luːnətɪk] *a* fou, dément; – *n* fou *m*, folle *f*. ◆**lunacy** *n* folie *f*, démence *f*.

lunch [lʌntʃ] *n* déjeuner *m*; **to have l.** déjeuner; **l. break, l. hour, l. time** heure *f* du déjeuner; – *vi* déjeuner (**on, off** de). ◆**luncheon** *n* déjeuner *m*; **l. meat** mortadelle *f*, saucisson *m*; **l. voucher** chèque-déjeuner *m*.

lung [lʌŋ] *n* poumon *m*; **l. cancer** cancer *m* du poumon.

lunge [lʌndʒ] *n* coup *m* en avant; – *vi* **to l. at s.o.** se ruer sur qn.

lurch [lɜːtʃ] **1** *vi* (*of person*) tituber; (*of ship*) faire une embardée. **2** *n* **to leave s.o. in the l.** *Fam* laisser qn en plan, laisser tomber qn.

lure [lʊər] *vt* attirer (par la ruse) (**into** dans); – *n* (*attraction*) attrait *m*.

lurid ['lʊərɪd] *a* (*horrifying*) horrible, affreux; (*sensational*) à sensation; (*gaudy*) voyant; (*colour, sunset*) sanglant.

lurk [lɜːk] *vi* (*hide*) se cacher (**in** dans); (*prowl*) rôder; (*of suspicion, fear etc*) persister.

luscious ['lʌʃəs] *a* (*food etc*) appétissant.

lush [lʌʃ] **1** *a* (*vegetation*) luxuriant; (*wealthy*) *Fam* opulent. **2** *n Am Sl* ivrogne *mf*.

lust [lʌst] *n* (*for person, object*) convoitise *f* (**for** de); (*for power, knowledge*) soif *f* (**for** de); – *vi* **to l. after** (*object, person*) convoiter; (*power, knowledge*) avoir soif de.

lustre ['lʌstər] *n* (*gloss*) lustre *m*.

lusty ['lʌstɪ] *a* (**-ier, -iest**) vigoureux.

lute [luːt] *n Mus* luth *m*.

Luxembourg ['lʌksəmbɜːg] *n* Luxembourg *m*.

luxuriant [lʌgˈʒʊərɪənt] *a* luxuriant. ◆**luxuriate** *vi* (*laze about*) paresser (**in** bed/*etc* au lit/*etc*).

luxury ['lʌkʃərɪ] *n* luxe *m*; – *a* (*goods, flat etc*) de luxe. ◆**luxurious** [lʌgˈʒʊərɪəs] *a* luxueux.

lying ['laɪɪŋ] *see* lie[1,2]; – *n* le mensonge; – *a* (*account*) mensonger; (*person*) menteur.

lynch [lɪntʃ] *vt* lyncher. ◆**—ing** *n* lynchage *m*.

lynx [lɪŋks] *n* (*animal*) lynx *m*.

lyre ['laɪər] *n Mus Hist* lyre *f*.

lyric ['lɪrɪk] *a* lyrique; – *npl* (*of song*) paroles *fpl*. ◆**lyrical** *a* (*effusive*) lyrique. ◆**lyricism** *n* lyrisme *m*.

M

M, m [ɛm] n M, m m.

m abbr **1** (metre) mètre m. **2** (mile) mile m.

MA abbr = Master of Arts.

ma'am [mæm] n madame f.

mac [mæk] n (raincoat) Fam imper m.

macabre [mə'kɑːbrə] a macabre.

macaroni [mækə'rəʊnɪ] n macaroni(s) m(pl).

macaroon [mækə'ruːn] n (cake) macaron m.

mace [meɪs] n (staff, rod) masse f.

Machiavellian [mækɪə'velɪən] a machiavélique.

machination [mækɪ'neɪʃ(ə)n] n machination f.

machine [mə'ʃiːn] n (apparatus, car, system etc) machine f. **◆machinegun** n mitrailleuse f; – vt (-nn-) mitrailler. **◆machinery** n (machines) machines fpl; (works) mécanisme m; Fig rouages mpl. **◆machinist** n (on sewing machine) piqueur, -euse mf.

macho ['mætʃəʊ] n (pl -os) macho m; – a (attitude etc) macho (f inv).

mackerel ['mækrəl] n inv (fish) maquereau m.

mackintosh ['mækɪntɒʃ] n imperméable m.

mad [mæd] a (madder, maddest) fou; (dog) enragé; (bull) furieux; **m. (at)** (angry) Fam furieux (contre); **to be m. (keen) on Fam** (person) être fou de; (films etc) se passionner or s'emballer pour; **to drive m.** rendre fou; (irritate) énerver; **he drove me m. to go** Fam il m'a cassé les pieds pour que j'y aille; **like m.** comme un fou. **◆maddening** a exaspérant. **◆madhouse** n Fam maison f de fous. **◆madly** adv (in love, to spend money etc) follement; (desperately) désespérément. **◆madman** n (pl -men) fou m. **◆madness** n folie f.

Madagascar [mædə'gæskər] n Madagascar f.

madam ['mædəm] n (married) madame f; (unmarried) mademoiselle f.

made [meɪd] see make.

Madeira [mə'dɪərə] n (wine) madère m.

madonna [mə'dɒnə] n Rel madone f.

maestro ['maɪstrəʊ] n (pl -os) Mus maestro m.

Mafia ['mæfɪə] n maf(f)ia f.

magazine [mægə'ziːn] n (periodical) magazine m, revue f; (of gun, camera) magasin m.

maggot ['mægət] n ver m, asticot m. **◆maggoty** a véreux.

magic ['mædʒɪk] n magie f; – a (word, wand) magique. **◆magical** a (evening etc) magique. **◆ma'gician** n magicien, -ienne mf.

magistrate ['mædʒɪstreɪt] n magistrat m.

magnanimous [mæg'nænɪməs] a magnanime.

magnate ['mægneɪt] n (tycoon) magnat m.

magnesium [mæg'niːzɪəm] n magnésium m.

magnet ['mægnɪt] n aimant m. **◆mag'netic** a magnétique. **◆magnetism** n magnétisme m. **◆magnetize** vt magnétiser.

magnificent [mæg'nɪfɪsənt] a magnifique. **◆magnificence** n magnificence f. **◆magnificently** adv magnifiquement.

magnify ['mægnɪfaɪ] vt (image) & Fig grossir; (sound) amplifier; **magnifying glass** loupe f. **◆magnifi'cation** n grossissement m; amplification f. **◆magnitude** n ampleur f.

magnolia [mæg'nəʊlɪə] n (tree) magnolia m.

magpie ['mægpaɪ] n (bird) pie f.

mahogany [mə'hɒgənɪ] n acajou m.

maid [meɪd] n (servant) bonne f; **old m.** Pej vieille fille f. **◆maiden** n Old-fashioned jeune fille f; – a (speech etc) premier; (flight) inaugural; **m. name** nom m de jeune fille. **◆maidenly** a virginal.

mail [meɪl] n (system) poste f; (letters) courrier m; – a (van, bag etc) postal; **m. order** vente f par correspondance; – vt mettre à la poste; **mailing list** liste f d'adresses. **◆mailbox** n Am boîte f à or aux lettres. **◆mailman** n (pl -men) Am facteur m.

maim [meɪm] vt mutiler, estropier.

main [meɪn] a principal; **the m. thing is to ...** l'essentiel est de ...; **m. line** Rail grande ligne f; **m. road** grande route f; **in the m.** (mostly) en gros, dans l'ensemble. **2** n water/gas m. conduite f d'eau/de gaz; **the mains** El le secteur; **a mains radio** une radio secteur. **◆—ly** adv principalement, surtout. **◆mainland** n continent m. **◆main-**

stay n (of family etc) soutien m; (of organization, policy) pilier m. ◆**mainstream** n tendance f dominante.

maintain [meɪnˈteɪn] vt (continue, assert) maintenir (that que); (vehicle, family etc) entretenir; (silence) garder. ◆**maintenance** n (of vehicle, road etc) entretien m; (of prices, order, position etc) maintien m; (alimony) pension f alimentaire.

maisonette [meɪzəˈnet] n duplex m.

maize [meɪz] n (cereal) maïs m.

majesty [ˈmædʒəstɪ] n majesté f; Your M. (title) Votre Majesté. ◆**maˈjestic** a majestueux.

major [ˈmeɪdʒər] 1 a (main, great) & Mus majeur; a m. road une grande route. 2 n Mil commandant m. 3 n (subject) Univ Am dominante f; – vi to m. in se spécialiser en. ◆**majoˈrette** n (drum) majorette f.

Majorca [məˈjɔːkə] n Majorque f.

majority [məˈdʒɒrɪtɪ] n majorité f (of de); in the or a m. en majorité, majoritaire; the m. of people la plupart des gens; – a (vote etc) majoritaire.

make [meɪk] vt (pt & pp made) faire; (tool, vehicle etc) fabriquer; (decision) prendre; (friends, wage) se faire; (points) Sp marquer; (destination) arriver à; to m. happy/tired/etc rendre heureux/fatigué/etc; he made ten francs on it Com ça lui a rapporté dix francs; she made the train (did not miss) elle a eu le train; to m. s.o. do sth faire faire qch à qn, obliger qn à faire qch; to m. oneself heard se faire entendre; to m. oneself at home se mettre à l'aise; to m. ready préparer; to m. yellow jaunir; she made him her husband elle en a fait son mari; to m. do (manage) se débrouiller (with avec); to m. do with (be satisfied with) se contenter de; to m. it (arrive) arriver; (succeed) réussir; (say) dire; I m. it five o'clock j'ai cinq heures; what do you m. of it? qu'en penses-tu?; I can't m. anything of it je n'y comprends rien; to m. a living gagner sa vie; you're made (for life) ton avenir est assuré; to m. believe (pretend) faire semblant (that one is d'être); (n) it's m.-believe c'est pure invention; to live in a world of m.-believe se bercer d'illusions; – vi to m. as if to (appear to) faire mine de; to m. for (go towards) aller vers; – n (brand) marque f; of French/etc m. de fabrication française/etc. ■ to m. out vt (see) distinguer; (understand) comprendre; (decipher) déchiffrer; (draw up) faire (chèque, liste); (claim) prétendre (that que);

you made me out to be silly tu m'as fait passer pour un idiot; – vi (manage) Fam se débrouiller; to m. over vt (transfer) céder; (change) transformer (into en); to m. up vt (story) inventer; (put together) faire (collection, liste, lit etc); (prepare) préparer; (form) former, composer; (loss) compenser; (quantity) compléter; (quarrel) régler; (one's face) maquiller; – vi (of friends) se réconcilier; to m. up for (loss, damage, fault) compenser; (lost time, mistake) rattraper. ◆**m.-up** n (of object etc) constitution f; (of person) caractère m; (for face) maquillage m. ◆**making** n (manufacture) fabrication f; (of dress) confection f; history in the m. l'histoire en train de se faire; the makings of les éléments mpl (essentiels) de; to have the makings of a pianist/etc avoir l'étoffe d'un pianiste/etc. ◆**maker** n Com fabricant m. ◆**makeshift** n expédient m; – a (arrangement etc) de fortune, provisoire.

maladjusted [mæləˈdʒʌstɪd] a inadapté.

malaise [mæˈleɪz] n malaise m.

malaria [məˈleərɪə] n malaria f.

Malaysia [məˈleɪzɪə] n Malaisie f.

male [meɪl] a Biol Bot etc mâle; (clothes, sex) masculin; – n (man, animal) mâle m.

malevolent [məˈlevələnt] a malveillant. ◆**malevolence** n malveillance f.

malfunction [mælˈfʌŋkʃ(ə)n] n mauvais fonctionnement m; – vi fonctionner mal.

malice [ˈmælɪs] n méchanceté f; to bear s.o. m. vouloir du mal à qn. ◆**maˈlicious** a malveillant. ◆**maˈliciously** adv avec malveillance.

malign [məˈlaɪn] vt (slander) calomnier.

malignant [məˈlɪɡnənt] a (person etc) malfaisant; m. tumour Med tumeur f maligne. ◆**malignancy** n Med malignité f.

malingerer [məˈlɪŋɡərər] n (pretending illness) simulateur, -euse mf.

mall [mɔːl] n (shopping m.) (covered) galerie f marchande; (street) rue f piétonnière.

malleable [ˈmælɪəb(ə)l] a malléable.

mallet [ˈmælɪt] n (tool) maillet m.

malnutrition [mælnjuːˈtrɪʃ(ə)n] n malnutrition f, sous-alimentation f.

malpractice [mælˈpræktɪs] n Med Jur faute f professionnelle.

malt [mɔːlt] n malt m.

Malta [ˈmɔːltə] n Malte f. ◆**Malˈtese** a & n maltais, -aise (mf).

mammal [ˈmæm(ə)l] n mammifère m.

mammoth [ˈmæməθ] a (large) immense; – n (extinct animal) mammouth m.

man [mæn] n (pl **men** [men]) homme m;
(player) Sp joueur m; (chess piece) pièce f;
a golf m. (enthusiast) un amateur de golf;
he's a Bristol m. (by birth) il est de Bristol;
to be m. and wife être mari et femme; my
old m. Fam (father) mon père; (husband)
mon homme; yes old m.! Fam oui mon
vieux!; the m. in the street l'homme de la
rue; – vt (-nn-) (ship) pourvoir d'un équipage; (fortress) armer; (guns) servir; (be on
duty at) être de service à; manned spacecraft engin m spatial habité. ◆manhood
n (period) âge m d'homme. ◆manhunt
n chasse f à l'homme. ◆manlike a (quality)
d'homme viril. ◆manly a (-ier, -iest) viril.
◆man-'made a artificiel; (fibre) synthétique. ◆manservant n (pl menservants)
domestique m. ◆man-to-'man a & adv
d'homme à homme.

manacle ['mænɪk(ə)l] n menotte f.

manag/e ['mænɪdʒ] vt (run) diriger; (affairs
etc) Com gérer; (handle) manier; (take)
Fam prendre; (eat) Fam manger; (contribute) Fam donner; to m. to do (succeed)
réussir or arriver à faire; (contrive) se
débrouiller pour faire; I'll m. it j'y
arriverai; – vi (succeed) y arriver; (make
do) se débrouiller (with avec); to m. without
sth se passer de qch. ◆–ing a m. director
directeur m général; the m. director le
PDG. ◆–eable a (parcel, person etc)
maniable; (feasible) faisable. ◆–ement n
direction f; (of property etc) gestion f;
(executive staff) cadres mpl. ◆–er n
directeur m, (of shop, café) gérant m; (business) m. (of actor, boxer etc) manager m.
◆manage'ress n directrice f; gérante f.
◆managerial [mænə'dʒɪərɪəl] a directo-
rial; the m. class or staff les cadres mpl.

mandarin ['mændərɪn] 1 n (high-ranking
official) haut fonctionnaire m; (in political
party) bonze m; (in university) Pej mandarin m. 2 a & n m. (orange) mandarine f.

mandate ['mændeɪt] n mandat m.
◆mandatory a obligatoire.

mane [meɪn] n crinière f.

maneuver [mə'nuːvər] n & vti Am =
manoeuvre.

mangle ['mæŋg(ə)l] 1 n (for wringing)
essoreuse f; – vt (clothes) essorer. 2 vt
(damage) mutiler.

mango ['mæŋgəʊ] n (pl -oes or -os) (fruit)
mangue f.

mangy ['meɪndʒɪ] a (animal) galeux.

manhandle [mæn'hænd(ə)l] vt maltraiter.

manhole ['mænhəʊl] n trou m d'homme; m.
cover plaque f d'égout.

mania ['meɪnɪə] n manie f. ◆maniac n fou
m, folle f; Psy Med maniaque mf; sex m.
obsédé m sexuel.

manicure ['mænɪkjʊər] n soin m des mains;
– vt (person) manucurer; (s.o.'s nails) faire.
◆manicurist n manucure mf.

manifest ['mænɪfest] 1 a (plain) manifeste.
2 vt (show) manifester.

manifesto [mænɪ'festəʊ] n (pl -os or -oes)
Pol manifeste m.

manifold ['mænɪfəʊld] a multiple.

manipulate [mə'nɪpjʊleɪt] vt manœuvrer;
(facts, electors etc) Pej manipuler.
◆manipu'lation n manœuvre f; Pej
manipulation f (of de).

mankind [mæn'kaɪnd] n (humanity) le genre
humain.

manner ['mænər] n (way) manière f; (behaviour) attitude f, comportement m; pl
(social habits) manières fpl; in this m. (like
this) de cette manière; all m. of toutes
sortes de. ◆mannered a (affected)
maniéré; well-/bad-m. bien/mal élevé.
◆mannerism n Pej tic m.

manoeuvre [mə'nuːvər] n manœuvre f; –
vti manœuvrer. ◆manoeuvra'bility n (of
vehicle etc) maniabilité f.

manor ['mænər] n m. (house) manoir m.

manpower ['mænpaʊər] n (labour)
main-d'œuvre f; Mil effectifs mpl; (effort)
force f.

mansion ['mænʃ(ə)n] n hôtel m particulier;
(in country) manoir m.

manslaughter ['mænslɔːtər] n Jur homicide
m involontaire.

mantelpiece ['mænt(ə)lpiːs] n (shelf)
cheminée f.

mantle ['mænt(ə)l] n (cloak) cape f.

manual ['mænjʊəl] 1 a (work) manuel. 2
n (book) manuel m.

manufactur/e [mænjʊ'fæktʃər] vt fabriquer; – n fabrication f. ◆–er n fabricant,
-ante mf.

manure [mə'njʊər] n fumier m, engrais m.

manuscript ['mænjʊskrɪpt] n manuscrit m.

many ['menɪ] a & n beaucoup (de); m. things
beaucoup de choses; m. came beaucoup
sont venus; very m., a good or great m. un
très grand nombre (de); (a good or great)
m. of un (très) grand nombre de; m. of
them un grand nombre d'entre eux; m.
times, m. a time bien des fois; m. kinds
toutes sortes (of de); how m.? combien
(de)?; too m. trop (de); one too m. un de
trop; there are too m. of them ils sont trop
nombreux; so m. tant (de); as m. books/etc

map 500 Marxism

as autant de livres/*etc* que; **as m. as** (*up to*) jusqu'à.

map [mæp] *n* (*of country etc*) carte *f*; (*plan*) plan *m*; − *vt* (**-pp-**) faire la carte *or* le plan de; **to m. out** (*road*) faire le tracé de; (*one's day etc*) Fig organiser.

maple ['meip(ə)l] *n* (*tree, wood*) érable *m*.

mar [mɑːr] *vt* (**-rr-**) gâter.

marathon ['mærəθən] *n* marathon *m*.

maraud [mə'rɔːd] *vi* piller. ◆**-ing** *a* pillard. ◆**-er** *n* pillard, -arde *mf*.

marble ['mɑːb(ə)l] *n* (*substance*) marbre *m*; (*toy ball*) bille *f*.

march [mɑːtʃ] *n* Mil marche *f*; − *vi* Mil marcher (*au pas*); **to m. in/out/***etc* Fig entrer/sortir/*etc* d'un pas décidé; **to m. past** defiler; − *vt* **to m. s.o. off** *or* **away** emmener qn. ◆**m.-past** *n* défilé *m*.

March [mɑːtʃ] *n* mars *m*.

mare [meər] *n* jument *f*.

margarine [mɑːdʒə'riːn] *n* margarine *f*.

margin ['mɑːdʒin] *n* (*of page etc*) marge *f*; **by a narrow m.** (*to win*) de justesse. ◆**marginal** *a* marginal; **m. seat** *Pol* siège *m* disputé. ◆**marginally** *adv* très légèrement.

marguerite [mɑːgə'riːt] *n* (*daisy*) marguerite *f*.

marigold ['mærigəuld] *n* (*flower*) souci *m*.

marijuana [mærɪ'wɑːnə] *n* marijuana *f*.

marina [mə'riːnə] *n* marina *f*.

marinate ['mærineit] *vti* Culin mariner.

marine [mə'riːn] **1** *a* (*life, flora etc*) marin. **2** *n* (*soldier*) fusilier *m* marin, *Am* marine *m*.

marionette [mæriə'net] *n* marionnette *f*.

marital ['mærit(ə)l] *a* matrimonial; (*relations*) conjugal; **m. status** situation *f* de famille.

maritime ['mæritaim] *a* (*province, climate etc*) maritime.

marjoram ['mɑːdʒərəm] *n* (*spice*) marjolaine *f*.

mark¹ [mɑːk] *n* (*symbol*) marque *f*; (*stain, trace*) trace *f*, tache *f*, marque *f*; (*token, sign*) Fig signe *m*; (*for exercise etc*) Sch note *f*; (*target*) but *m*; (*model*) Tech série *f*; **to make one's m.** Fig s'imposer; **up to the m.** (*person, work*) à la hauteur; − *vt* marquer; (*exam etc*) Sch corriger, noter; (*pay attention to*) faire attention à; **to m. time** Mil marquer le pas; Fig piétiner; **m. you . . . !** remarquez que . . . ; **to m. down** (*price*) baisser; **to m. off** (*separate*) séparer; (*on list*) cocher; **to m. out** (*area*) délimiter; **to m. s.o. out for** désigner qn pour; **to m. up** (*increase*) augmenter. ◆**-ed** *a* (*noticeable*) marqué. ◆**-edly** [-ɪdlɪ] *adv* visiblement.

◆**-ing** *n*(*pl*) (*on animal etc*) marques *fpl*; (*on road*) signalisation *f* horizontale. ◆**-er** *n* (*flag etc*) marque *f*; (*pen*) feutre *m*, marqueur *m*.

mark² [mɑːk] *n* (*currency*) mark *m*.

market ['mɑːkit] *n* marché *m*; **on the open m.** en vente libre; **on the black m.** au marché noir; **the Common M.** le Marché commun; **m. value** valeur *f* marchande; **m. price** prix *m* courant; **m. gardener** maraîcher, -ère *mf*; − *vt* (*sell*) vendre; (*launch*) commercialiser. ◆**-ing** *n* marketing *m*, vente *f*. ◆**-able** *a* vendable.

marksman ['mɑːksmən] *n* (*pl* -**men**) tireur *m* d'élite.

marmalade ['mɑːməleid] *n* confiture *f* d'oranges.

maroon [mə'ruːn] *a* (*colour*) bordeaux *inv*.

marooned [mə'ruːnd] *a* abandonné; (*in snowstorm etc*) bloqué (**by** par).

marquee [mɑː'kiː] *n* (*for concerts, garden parties etc*) chapiteau *m*; (*awning*) *Am* marquise *f*.

marquis ['mɑːkwis] *n* marquis *m*.

marrow ['mærəu] *n* **1** (*of bone*) moelle *f*. **2** (*vegetable*) courge *f*.

marr/y ['mæri] *vt* épouser, se marier avec; **to m.** (**off**) (*of priest etc*) marier; − *vi* se marier. ◆**-ied** *a* marié; (*life, state*) conjugal; **m. name** nom *m* de femme mariée; **to get m.** se marier. ◆**marriage** *n* mariage *m*; **to be related by m.** to être parent par alliance de; − *a* (*bond*) conjugal; (*certificate*) de mariage; **m. bureau** agence *f* matrimoniale. ◆**marriageable** *a* en état de se marier.

marsh [mɑːʃ] *n* marais *m*, marécage *m*. ◆**marshland** *n* marécages *mpl*. ◆**marshmallow** *n* Bot Culin guimauve *f*.

marshal ['mɑːʃ(ə)l] **1** *n* (*in army*) maréchal *m*; (*in airforce*) général *m*; (*at public event*) membre *m* du service d'ordre; *Jur Am* shérif *m*. **2** *vt* (**-ll-**, *Am* **-l-**) (*gather*) rassembler; (*lead*) mener cérémonieusement.

martial ['mɑːʃ(ə)l] *a* martial; **m. law** loi *f* martiale.

Martian ['mɑːʃ(ə)n] *n & a* martien, -ienne (*mf*).

martyr ['mɑːtər] *n* martyr, -yre *mf*; − *vt* Rel martyriser. ◆**martyrdom** *n* martyre *m*.

marvel ['mɑːv(ə)l] *n* (*wonder*) merveille *f*; (*miracle*) miracle *m*; − *vi* (**-ll-**, *Am* **-l-**) s'émerveiller (**at** de); − *vt* **to m. that** s'étonner de ce que (+ *sub or indic*). ◆**marvellous** *a* merveilleux.

Marxism ['mɑːksiz(ə)m] *n* marxisme *m*. ◆**Marxist** *a & n* marxiste (*mf*).

marzipan ['maːzɪpæn] n pâte f d'amandes.

mascara [mæ'skɑːrə] n mascara m.

mascot ['mæskɒt] n mascotte f.

masculine ['mæskjʊlɪn] a masculin. ◆**mascu'linity** n masculinité f.

mash [mæʃ] n (for poultry etc) pâtée f; (potatoes) Culin purée f; – vt to m. (up) (crush) & Culin écraser; **mashed potatoes** purée f (de pommes de terre).

mask [mɑːsk] n masque m; – vt (cover, hide) masquer (**from** à).

masochism ['mæsəkɪz(ə)m] n masochisme m. ◆**masochist** n masochiste mf. ◆**maso'chistic** a masochiste.

mason ['meɪs(ə)n] n maçon m. ◆**masonry** n maçonnerie f.

masquerade [mɑːskə'reɪd] n (gathering, disguise) mascarade f; – vi to m. **as** se faire passer pour.

mass¹ [mæs] n masse f; **a m. of** (many) une multitude de; (pile) un tas de, une masse de; **to be a m. of bruises** Fam être couvert de bleus; **masses of** Fam des masses de; **the masses** (people) les masses fpl; – a (education) des masses; (culture, demonstration) de masse; (protests, departure) en masse; (production) en série, en masse; (hysteria) collectif; **m. grave** fosse f commune; **m. media** mass media mpl; – vi (of troops, people) se masser. ◆**m.-pro'duce** vt fabriquer en série.

mass² [mæs] n Rel messe f.

massacre ['mæsəkər] n massacre m; – vt massacrer.

massage ['mæsɑːʒ] n massage m; – vt masser. ◆**ma'sseur** n masseur m. ◆**ma'sseuse** n masseuse f.

massive ['mæsɪv] a (solid) massif; (huge) énorme, considérable. ◆**-ly** adv (to increase, reduce etc) considérablement.

mast [mɑːst] n Nau mât m; Rad TV pylône m.

master ['mɑːstər] n maître m; (in secondary school) professeur m; **a m.'s degree** une maîtrise (in de); **M. of Arts/Sciences** (person) Univ Maître ès lettres/sciences; **m. of ceremonies** (presenter) Am animateur, -trice mf; **m. card** carte f maîtresse; **m. stroke** coup m de maître; **m. key** passe-partout m inv; **old m.** (painting) tableau m de maître; **I'm my own m.** je ne dépends que de moi; – vt (control) maîtriser; (subject, situation) dominer; **she has mastered Latin** elle possède le latin. ◆**masterly** a magistral. ◆**mastery** n maîtrise f (**of** de).

mastermind ['mɑːstəmaɪnd] n (person) cerveau m; – vt organiser.

masterpiece ['mɑːstəpiːs] n chef-d'œuvre m.

mastic ['mæstɪk] n mastic m (silicone).

masturbate ['mæstəbeɪt] vi se masturber. ◆**mastur'bation** n masturbation f.

mat [mæt] n tapis m, natte f; (at door) paillasson m; **(table) m.** (of fabric) napperon m; (hard) dessous-de-plat m inv; **(place) m.** set m (de table). **2** a (paint, paper) mat.

match¹ [mætʃ] n allumette f; **book of matches** pochette f d'allumettes. ◆**match-box** n boîte f à allumettes. ◆**matchstick** n allumette f.

match² [mætʃ] n (game) Sp match m; (equal) égal, -ale mf; (marriage) mariage m; **to be a good m.** (of colours, people etc) être bien assortis; **he's a good m.** (man to marry) c'est un bon parti; – vt (of clothes) aller (bien) avec; **to m. (up to)** (equal) égaler; **to m. (up)** (plates etc) assortir; **to be well-matched** (of colours, people etc) être (bien) assortis, aller (bien) ensemble; – vi (go with each other) être assortis, aller (bien) ensemble. ◆**-ing** a (dress etc) assorti.

mate [meɪt] **1** n (friend) camarade mf; (of animal) mâle m, femelle f; (builder's/ electrician's/etc **m.** aide-maçon/-électricien/etc m. **2** vi (of animals) s'accoupler (**with** avec). **3** n Chess mat m; – vt faire or mettre mat.

material [mə'tɪərɪəl] **1** a matériel; (important) important. **2** n (substance) matière f; (cloth) tissu m; (for book) matériaux mpl; **material(s)** (equipment) matériel m; **building material(s)** matériaux mpl de construction. ◆**materialism** n matérialisme m. ◆**materialist** n matérialiste mf. ◆**materia'listic** a matérialiste. ◆**materialize** vi se matérialiser. ◆**materially** adv matériellement; (well-off etc) sur le plan matériel.

maternal [mə'tɜːn(ə)l] a maternel. ◆**maternity** n maternité f; **m. hospital, m. unit** maternité f; – a (clothes) de grossesse; (allowance, leave) de maternité.

mathematical [mæθə'mætɪk(ə)l] a mathématique; **to have a m. brain** être doué pour les maths. ◆**mathema'tician** n mathématicien, -ienne mf. ◆**mathematics** n mathématiques fpl. ◆**maths** n, Am ◆**math** n Fam maths fpl.

matinée ['mætɪneɪ] n Th matinée f.

matriculation [mətrikjʊ'leɪʃ(ə)n] n *Univ* inscription f.

matrimony ['mætriməni] n mariage m. ◆**matri'monial** a matrimonial.

matrix, pl **-ices** ['meɪtrɪks, -ɪsiz] n *Tech* matrice f.

matron ['meɪtrən] n *Lit* mère f de famille, dame f âgée; (*nurse*) infirmière f (en) chef. ◆**matronly** a (*air etc*) de mère de famille; (*mature*) mûr; (*portly*) corpulent.

matt [mæt] a (*paint, paper*) mat.

matted ['mætɪd] a **m. hair** cheveux mpl emmêlés.

matter¹ ['mætər] n matière f; (*affair*) affaire f, question f; (*thing*) chose f; **no m.!** (*no importance*) peu importe!; **no m. what she does** quoi qu'elle fasse; **no m. where you go** où que tu ailles; **no m. who you are** qui que vous soyez; **no m. when** quel que soit le moment; **what's the m.?** qu'est-ce qu'il y a?; **what's the m. with you?** qu'est-ce que tu as?; **there's sth the m.** il y a qch qui ne va pas; **there's sth the m. with my leg** j'ai qch à la jambe; **there's nothing the m. with him** il n'a rien; – vi (*be important*) importer (**to** à); **it doesn't m. if/when/who/etc** peu importe si/quand/qui/etc; **it doesn't m.!** ça ne fait rien!, peu importe! ◆**m.-of-'fact** a (*person, manner*) terre à terre; (*voice*) neutre.

matter² ['mætər] n (*pus*) *Med* pus m.

matting ['mætɪŋ] n (*material*) nattage m; **a piece of m.**, **some m.** une natte.

mattress ['mætrɪs] n matelas m.

mature [mə'tʃʊər] a mûr; (*cheese*) fait; – vt (*person, plan*) (faire) mûrir; – vi mûrir; (*of cheese*) se faire. ◆**maturity** n maturité f.

maul [mɔːl] vt (*of animal*) mutiler; (*of person*) *Fig* malmener.

mausoleum [mɔːsə'lɪəm] n mausolée m.

mauve [məʊv] a & n (*colour*) mauve m.

maverick ['mævərɪk] n & a *Pol* dissident, -ente (mf).

mawkish ['mɔːkɪʃ] a d'une sensiblerie excessive, mièvre.

maxim ['mæksɪm] n maxime f.

maximum ['mæksɪməm] n (pl **-ima** [-ɪmə] or **-imums**) maximum m; – a maximum (f inv), maximal. ◆**maximize** vt porter au maximum.

may [meɪ] v aux (pt might) **1** (*possibility*) he **m. come** il peut arriver; he **might come** il pourrait arriver; **I m. or might be wrong** il se peut que je me trompe, je me trompe peut-être; **you m. or might have to** tu aurais pu; **I m. or might have forgotten it** je l'ai peut-être oublié; **we m. or might as well go**

nous ferions aussi bien de partir; **she fears I m. or might get lost** elle a peur que je ne me perde. **2** (*permission*) **m. I stay?** puis-je rester?; **m. I?** vous permettez?; **you m. go** tu peux partir. **3** (*wish*) **m. you be happy** (que tu) sois heureux. ◆**maybe** adv peut-être.

May [meɪ] n mai m.

mayhem ['meɪhem] n (*chaos*) pagaïe f; (*havoc*) ravages mpl.

mayonnaise [meɪə'neɪz] n mayonnaise f.

mayor [meər] n (*man, woman*) maire m. ◆**mayoress** n femme f du maire.

maze [meɪz] n labyrinthe m.

MC [em'siː] abbr = master of ceremonies.

me [miː] pron me, m'; (*after prep etc*) moi; (*to*) **me** (*indirect*) me, m'; **she knows me** elle me connaît; **he helps me** il m'aide; **he gives (to) me** il me donne; **with me** avec moi.

meadow ['medəʊ] n pré m, prairie f.

meagre ['miːgər] a maigre.

meal [miːl] n **1** (*food*) repas m. **2** (*flour*) farine f.

mealy-mouthed [miːlɪ'maʊðd] a mielleux.

mean¹ [miːn] vt (pt & pp **meant** [ment]) (*signify*) vouloir dire, signifier; (*destine*) destiner (**for** à); (*entail*) entraîner; (*represent*) représenter; (*refer to*) faire allusion à; **to m. to do** (*intend*) avoir l'intention de faire, vouloir faire; **I m. it, I m. what I say** je suis sérieux; **to m. sth to s.o.** (*matter*) avoir de l'importance pour qn; **it means sth to me** (*name, face*) ça me dit qch; **I didn't m. to!** je ne l'ai pas fait exprès!; **you were meant to come** vous étiez censé venir. ◆**-ing** n sens m, signification f. ◆**meaningful** a significatif. ◆**meaningless** a qui n'a pas de sens; (*absurd*) *Fig* insensé.

mean² [miːn] a (-er, -est) (*stingy*) avare, mesquin; (*petty*) mesquin; (*nasty*) méchant; (*inferior*) misérable. ◆**-ness** n (*greed*) avarice f; (*nastiness*) méchanceté f.

mean³ [miːn] a (*distance*) moyen; – n (*middle position*) milieu m; (*average*) *Math* moyenne f; **the happy m.** le juste milieu.

meander [mi'ændər] vi (*of river*) faire des méandres.

means [miːnz] n(pl) (*method*) moyen(s) m(pl) (**to do, of doing** de faire); (*wealth*) moyens mpl; **by m. of** (*stick etc*) au moyen de; (*work, concentration*) à force de; **by all m.!** très certainement!; **by no m.** nullement; **independent** or **private m.** fortune f personnelle.

meant [ment] see **mean**¹.

meantime ['miːntaɪm] adv & n (**in the) m.** entre-temps. ◆**meanwhile** adv entre-temps.

measles ['miːz(ə)lz] n rougeole f.

measly ['miːzlɪ] a (contemptible) Fam minable.

measur/e ['meʒər] n mesure f; (ruler) règle f; **made to m.** fait sur mesure; – vt mesurer; (strength etc) Fig estimer, mesurer; (adjust, adapt) adapter (**to** à); **to m. up** mesurer; – vi **to m. up to** être à la hauteur de. ◆**–ed** a (careful) mesuré. ◆**–ement** n (of chest, waist etc) tour m; pl (dimensions) mesures fpl; **your hip m.** ton tour de hanches.

meat [miːt] n viande f; (of crab, lobster etc) chair f; Fig substance f; **m. diet** régime m carné. ◆**meaty** a (-ier, -iest) (fleshy) charnu; (flavour) de viande; Fig substantiel.

mechanic [mɪ'kænɪk] n mécanicien, -ienne mf. ◆**mechanical** a mécanique; (reply etc) Fig machinal. ◆**mechanics** n (science) mécanique f; pl (workings) mécanisme m. ◆'**mechanism** n mécanisme m. ◆'**mechanize** vt mécaniser.

medal ['med(ə)l] n médaille f. ◆**me-'dallion** n (ornament, jewel) médaillon m. ◆**medallist** n médaillé, -ée mf; **to be a gold/silver m.** Sp être médaille d'or/ d'argent.

meddle ['med(ə)l] vi (interfere) se mêler (**in** de); (tamper) toucher (**with** à). ◆**meddlesome** a qui se mêle de tout.

media ['miːdɪə] npl 1 **the (mass) m.** les médias. 2 see **medium** 2.

mediaeval [medɪ'iːv(ə)l] a médiéval.

median ['miːdɪən] a **m. strip** Aut Am bande f médiane.

mediate ['miːdɪeɪt] vi servir d'intermédiaire (**between** entre). ◆**medi'ation** n médiation f. ◆**mediator** n médiateur, -trice mf.

medical ['medɪk(ə)l] a médical; (school, studies) de médecine; (student) en médecine; – n (in school, army) visite f médicale; (private) examen m médical. ◆**medicated** a (shampoo) médical. ◆**medi'cation** n médicaments mpl. ◆**me'dicinal** a médicinal. ◆**medicine** n médecine f; (substance) médicament m; **m. cabinet, m. chest** pharmacie f.

medieval [medɪ'iːv(ə)l] a médiéval.

mediocre [miːdɪ'əʊkər] a médiocre. ◆**mediocrity** n médiocrité f.

meditate ['medɪteɪt] vi méditer (**on** sur). ◆**medi'tation** n méditation f. ◆**meditative** a méditatif.

Mediterranean [medɪtə'reɪnɪən] a méditerranéen; – n **the M.** la Méditerranée.

medium ['miːdɪəm] 1 a (average, middle) moyen. 2 n (pl **media** ['miːdɪə]) Phys

véhicule m; Biol milieu m; (for conveying data or publicity) support m; **through the m. of** par l'intermédiaire de; **the happy m.** le juste milieu. 3 n (person) médium m. ◆**m.-sized** a moyen, de taille moyenne.

medley ['medlɪ] n mélange m; Mus pot-pourri m.

meek [miːk] a (-er, -est) doux.

meet [miːt] vt (pt & pp **met**) (encounter) rencontrer; (see again, join) retrouver; (pass in street, road etc) croiser; (fetch) (aller or venir) chercher; (wait for) attendre; (debt, enemy, danger) faire face à; (need) combler; (be introduced to) faire la connaissance de; **to arrange to m. s.o.** donner rendez-vous à qn; – vi (of people, teams, rivers, looks) se rencontrer; (of people by arrangement) se retrouver; (be introduced) se connaître; (of society) se réunir; (of trains, vehicles) se croiser; **to m. up** rencontrer; (by arrangement) retrouver; **to m. up to** se rencontrer; se retrouver; **to m. with** (accident, problem) avoir; (loss, refusal) essuyer; (obstacle, difficulty) rencontrer; **to m. with s.o.** Am rencontrer qn; retrouver qn; – n Sp Am réunion f; **to make a m. with** Fam donner rendez-vous à. ◆**–ing** n réunion f; (large) assemblée f; (between two people) rencontre f, (prearranged) rendez-vous m inv; **in a m.** en conférence.

megalomania [megələʊ'meɪnɪə] n mégalomanie f. ◆**megalomaniac** n mégalomane mf.

megaphone ['megəfəʊn] n porte-voix m inv.

melancholy ['melənkəlɪ] n mélancolie f; – a mélancolique.

mellow ['meləʊ] a (-er, -est) (fruit) mûr; (colour, voice, wine) moelleux; (character) mûri par l'expérience; – vi (of person) s'adoucir.

melodrama ['melədrɑːmə] n mélodrame m. ◆**melodra'matic** a mélodramatique.

melody ['melədɪ] n mélodie f. ◆**me'lodic** a mélodique. ◆**me'lodious** a mélodieux.

melon ['melən] n (fruit) melon m.

melt [melt] vi fondre; **to m. into** (merge) Fig se fondre dans; – vt (faire) fondre; **to m. down** (metal object) fondre; **melting point** point m de fusion; **melting pot** Fig creuset m.

member ['membər] n membre m; **M. of Parliament** député m. ◆**membership** n adhésion f (**of** à); (number) nombre m de(s) membres; (members) membres mpl; **m. (fee)** cotisation f.

membrane ['membreɪn] n membrane f.
memento [mə'mentəʊ] n (pl -os or -oes) (object) souvenir m.
memo ['meməʊ] n (pl -os) note f; **m. pad** bloc-notes m. ◆**memo'randum** n note f; Pol Com mémorandum m.
memoirs ['memwɑːz] npl (essays) mémoires mpl.
memory ['memərɪ] n mémoire f; (recollection) souvenir m; **to the** or **in m. of** à la mémoire de. ◆**memorable** a mémorable. ◆**me'morial** a (plaque etc) commémoratif; – n monument m, mémorial m. ◆**memorize** vt apprendre par cœur.
men [men] see **man**. ◆**menfolk** n Fam hommes mpl.
menac/e ['menɪs] n danger m; (nuisance) Fam plaie f; (threat) menace f; – vt menacer. ◆**-ingly** adv (to say) d'un ton menaçant; (to do) d'une manière menaçante.
menagerie [mɪ'nædʒərɪ] n ménagerie f.
mend [mend] vt (repair) réparer; (clothes) raccommoder; **to m. one's ways** se corriger, s'amender; – n raccommodage m; **to be on the m.** (after illness) aller mieux.
menial ['miːnɪəl] a inférieur.
meningitis [menɪn'dʒaɪtɪs] n Med méningite f.
menopause ['menəʊpɔːz] n ménopause f.
menstruation [menstru'eɪʃ(ə)n] n menstruation f.
mental ['ment(ə)l] a mental; (hospital) psychiatrique; (mad) Sl fou; **m. strain** tension f nerveuse. ◆**men'tality** n mentalité f. ◆**mentally** adv mentalement; **he's m. handicapped** c'est un handicapé mental; **she's m. ill** c'est une malade mentale.
mention ['menʃ(ə)n] vt mentionner, faire mention de; **not to m . . .** sans parler de . . . , sans compter . . . ; **don't m. it!** il n'y a pas de quoi!; **no savings/etc worth mentioning** pratiquement pas d'économies/etc; – n mention f.
mentor ['mentɔːr] n (adviser) mentor m.
menu ['menjuː] n menu m.
mercantile ['mɜːkəntaɪl] a (activity etc) commercial; (ship) marchand; (nation) commerçant.
mercenary ['mɜːsɪnərɪ] a n mercenaire (m).
merchandise ['mɜːtʃəndaɪz] n (articles) marchandises fpl; (total stock) marchandise f.
merchant ['mɜːtʃ(ə)nt] n (trader) Fin négociant, -ante mf; (retail) m. commer-çant m (en détail); **wine m.** négociant, -ante mf en vins; (shopkeeper) marchand m de

vins; – a (vessel, navy) marchand; (seaman) de la marine marchande; **m. bank** banque f de commerce.
mercury ['mɜːkjʊrɪ] n mercure m.
mercy ['mɜːsɪ] n pitié f; Rel miséricorde f; **to beg for m.** demander grâce; **at the m. of** à la merci de; **it's a m. that . . .** (stroke of luck) c'est une chance que . . . . ◆**merciful** a miséricordieux. ◆**mercifully** adv (fortunately) Fam heureusement. ◆**merciless** a impitoyable.
mere [mɪər] a simple; (only) ne . . . que; **she's a m. child** ce n'est qu'une enfant; **it's a m. kilometre** ça ne fait qu'un kilomètre; **by m. chance** par pur hasard; **the m. sight of her** or **him** sa seule vue. ◆**-ly** adv (tout) simplement.
merg/e [mɜːdʒ] vi (blend) se mêler (with à); (of roads) se (re)joindre; (of firms) Com fusionner; – vt (unify) Pol unifier; Com fusionner. ◆**-er** n Com fusion f.
meridian [mə'rɪdɪən] n méridien m.
meringue [mə'ræŋ] n (cake) meringue f.
merit ['merɪt] n mérite m; **on its merits** (to consider sth etc) objectivement; – vt mériter.
mermaid ['mɜːmeɪd] n (woman) sirène f.
merry ['merɪ] a (-ier, -iest) gai; (drunk) Fam éméché. ◆**m.-go-round** n (at funfair etc) manège m. ◆**m.-making** n réjouissances fpl. ◆**merrily** adv gaiement. ◆**merriment** n gaieté f, rires mpl.
mesh [meʃ] n (of net etc) maille f; (fabric) tissu m à mailles; (of intrigue etc) Fig réseau m; (of circumstances) Fig engrenage m; **wire m.** grillage m.
mesmerize ['mezməraɪz] vt hypnotiser.
mess [mes] n 1 (confusion) désordre m, pagaïe f; (muddle) gâchis m; (dirt) saleté f; **in a m.** en désordre; (trouble) Fam dans le pétrin; (pitiful state) dans un triste état; **to make a m. of** (spoil) gâcher. 2 vt **to m. s.o. about** (bother, treat badly) Fam déranger qn, embêter qn; **to m. up** (spoil) gâcher; (dirty) salir; (room) mettre en désordre; – vi **to m. about** (have fun, idle) s'amuser; (play the fool) faire l'idiot; **to m. about with** (fiddle with) s'amuser avec. ◆**m.-up** n (disorder) Fam gâchis m. ◆**messy** a (-ier, -iest) (untidy) en désordre; (dirty) sale; (confused) Fig embrouillé, confus.
mess 2 [mes] n Mil mess m inv.
message ['mesɪdʒ] n message m. ◆**messenger** n messager, -ère mf; (in office, hotel) coursier, -ière mf.
Messiah [mɪ'saɪə] n Messie m.

Messrs ['mesəz] npl **M. Brown** Messieurs or MM Brown.

met [met] see **meet**.

metal ['met(ə)l] n métal m. ◆**me'tallic** a métallique; (paint) métallisé. ◆**metalwork** n (objects) ferronnerie f; (study, craft) travail m des métaux.

metamorphosis, pl **-oses** [metə'mɔːfəsɪs, -əsiːz] n métamorphose f.

metaphor ['metəfər] n métaphore f. ◆**meta'phorical** a métaphorique.

metaphysical [metə'fɪzɪk(ə)l] a métaphysique.

mete [miːt] vt to m. out (justice) rendre; (punishment) infliger.

meteor ['miːtɪər] n météore m. ◆**mete'oric** a m. rise Fig ascension f fulgurante. ◆**meteorite** n météorite m.

meteorological [miːtɪərə'lɒdʒɪk(ə)l] a météorologique. ◆**meteo'rology** n météorologie f.

meter ['miːtər] n (device) compteur m; (parking) m. parcmètre m; m. maid Aut Fam contractuelle f.

method ['meθəd] n méthode f. ◆**me'thodical** a méthodique.

Methodist ['meθədɪst] a & n Rel méthodiste (mf).

methylated ['meθɪleɪtɪd] a m. spirit(s) alcool m à brûler. ◆**meths** n Fam = methylated spirits.

meticulous [mɪ'tɪkjʊləs] a méticuleux. ◆**—ness** n soin m méticuleux.

metre ['miːtər] n mètre m. ◆**metric** ['metrɪk] a métrique.

metropolis [mə'trɒpəlɪs] n (chief city) métropole f. ◆**metro'politan** a métropolitain.

mettle ['met(ə)l] n courage m, fougue f.

mew [mjuː] vi (of cat) miauler.

mews [mjuːz] n (street) ruelle f; m. flat appartement m chic (aménagé dans une ancienne écurie).

Mexico ['meksɪkəʊ] n Mexique m. ◆**Mexican** a & n mexicain, -aine (mf).

mezzanine ['mezəniːn] n m. (floor) entresol m.

miaow [miːˈaʊ] vi (of cat) miauler; n miaulement m; int miaou.

mice [maɪs] see **mouse**.

mickey ['mɪkɪ] n to take the m. out of s.o. Sl charrier qn.

micro- ['maɪkrəʊ] pref micro-.

microbe ['maɪkrəʊb] n microbe m.

microchip ['maɪkrəʊtʃɪp] n puce f.

microcosm ['maɪkrəʊkɒz(ə)m] n microcosme m.

microfilm ['maɪkrəʊfɪlm] n microfilm m.

microphone ['maɪkrəfəʊn] n microphone m.

microscope ['maɪkrəskəʊp] n microscope m. ◆**micro'scopic** a microscopique.

microwave ['maɪkrəʊweɪv] n micro-onde f; m. oven four m à micro-ondes.

mid [mɪd] a (in) m.-June (à) la mi-juin; (in) m. morning au milieu de la matinée; (in) air en plein ciel; to be in one's m.-twenties avoir environ vingt-cinq ans.

midday [mɪd'deɪ] n midi m; — a de midi.

middle ['mɪd(ə)l] n milieu m; (waist) Fam taille f; (right) in the m. of au (beau) milieu de; in the m. of work en plein travail; in the m. of saying/working/etc en train de dire/travailler/etc; — a (central) du milieu; (class, ear, quality) moyen; (name) deuxième. ◆**m.-'aged** a d'un certain âge. ◆**m.-'class** a bourgeois. ◆**m.-of-the-'road** a (politics, views) modéré; (music, tastes) sage.

middling ['mɪdlɪŋ] a moyen, passable.

midge [mɪdʒ] n (fly) moucheron m.

midget ['mɪdʒɪt] n nain m, naine f; — a minuscule.

Midlands ['mɪdləndz] npl the M. les comtés mpl du centre de l'Angleterre.

midnight ['mɪdnaɪt] n minuit f.

midriff ['mɪdrɪf] n Anat diaphragme m; (belly) Fam ventre m.

midst [mɪdst] n in the m. of (middle) au milieu de; in our/their m. parmi nous/eux.

midsummer [mɪd'sʌmər] n milieu m de l'été; (solstice) solstice m d'été. ◆**midwinter** n milieu m de l'hiver; solstice m d'hiver.

midterm ['mɪdtɜːm] a m. holidays Sch petites vacances fpl.

midway [mɪd'weɪ] a & adv à mi-chemin.

midweek [mɪd'wiːk] n milieu m de la semaine.

midwife ['mɪdwaɪf] n (pl -wives) sage-femme f.

might [maɪt] **1** see **may**. **2** n (strength) force f. ◆**mighty** a (-ier, -iest) puissant; (ocean) vaste; (very great) Fam sacré; — adv (very) Fam rudement.

migraine ['miːgreɪn, 'maɪgreɪn] n Med migraine f.

migrate [maɪ'greɪt] vi émigrer. ◆**'migrant** a & n m. (worker) migrant, -ante (mf). ◆**migration** n migration f.

mike [maɪk] n Fam micro m.

mild [maɪld] a (-er, -iest) (person, weather, taste) doux; (beer, punishment) léger; (medicine, illness) bénin. ◆**—ly** adv doucement; (*slightly*) légèrement; **to put it m.** pour ne pas dire plus. ◆**—ness** *n* douceur *f*; légèreté *f*; caractère *m* bénin.

mildew ['mıldjuː] *n* (*on cheese etc*) moisissure *f*.

mile [maıl] *n* mile *m*, mille *m* (= 1,6 *km*); *pl* (*loosely*) = kilomètres *mpl*; **to walk for miles** marcher pendant des kilomètres; **miles better** (*much*) *Fam* bien mieux. ◆**mileage** *n* = kilométrage *m*, (*per gallon*) = consommation *f* aux cent kilomètres. ◆**milestone** *n* = borne *f* kilométrique; *Fig* jalon *m*.

militant ['mılıtənt] *a & n* militant, -ante (*mf*). ◆**military** *a* militaire; — *n* **the m.** (*soldiers*) les militaires *mpl*; (*army*) l'armée *f*. ◆**militate** *vi* (*of arguments etc*) militer (**in favour of** pour).

militia [mə'lıʃə] *n* milice *f*. ◆**militiaman** *n* (*pl* -**men**) milicien *m*.

milk [mılk] *n* lait *m*; (*evaporated*) **m.** lait *m* concentré; – *a* (*chocolate*) au lait; (*bottle, can*) à lait; (*diet*) lacté; (*produce*) laitier; **m. float** voiture *f* de laitier; **m. shake** milk-shake *m*; – *vt* (*cow*) traire; (*extract*) *Fig* soutirer (**s.o. of sth** qch à qn); (*exploit*) *Fig* exploiter. ◆**—ing** *n* traite *f*. ◆**milkman** *n* (*pl* -**men**) laitier *m*. ◆**milky** *a* (-**ier**, -**iest**) (*diet*) lacté; (*coffee, tea*) au lait; (*colour*) laiteux; **the M. Way** la Voie lactée.

mill [mıl] *n* **1** moulin *m*; (*factory*) usine *f*; **cotton m.** filature *f* de coton; **paper m.** papeterie *f*; – *vt* (*grind*) moudre. **2** *vi* **to m. around** (*of crowd*) grouiller. ◆**miller** *n* meunier, -ière *m*. ◆**millstone** *n* (*burden*) boulet *m* (**round one's neck** qu'on traîne).

millennium, *pl* -**nia** [mı'lenıəm, -nıə] *n* millénium *m*.

millet ['mılıt] *n Bot* millet *m*.

milli- ['mılı] *pref* milli-.

millimetre ['mılımiːtər] *n* millimètre *m*.

million ['mıljən] *n* million *m*; **a m. men/etc** un million d'hommes/*etc*; **two m.** deux millions. ◆**millio'naire** *n* millionnaire *mf*. ◆**millionth** *a & n* millionième (*mf*).

mime [maım] *n* (*actor*) mime *mf*; (*art*) mime *m*; – *vti* mimer.

mimeograph® ['mımıəgrɑːf] *vt* polycopier.

mimic ['mımık] *vt* (-**ck**-) imiter; – *n* imitateur, -trice *mf*. ◆**mimicking** *n*, ◆**mimicry** *n* imitation *f*.

mimosa [mı'məuzə] *n Bot* mimosa *m*.

minaret [mınə'ret] *n* (*of mosque*) minaret *m*.

mince [mıns] *n* (*meat*) hachis *m* (de viande); *Am* = mincemeat; – *vt* hacher; **not to m. matters** *or* **one's words** ne pas mâcher ses

mots. ◆**mincemeat** *n* (*dried fruit*) mélange *m* de fruits secs. ◆**mincer** *n* (*machine*) hachoir *m*.

mind [maınd] **1** *n* esprit *m*; (*sanity*) raison *f*; (*memory*) mémoire *f*; (*opinion*) avis *m*, idée *f*; (*thought*) pensée *f*; (*head*) tête *f*; **to change one's m.** changer d'avis; **to my m.** à mon avis; **in two minds** (*undecided*) irrésolu; **to make up one's m.** se décider; **to be on s.o.'s m.** (*worry*) préoccuper qn; **out of one's m.** (*mad*) fou; **to bring to m.** (*recall*) rappeler; **to bear** *or* **keep in m.** (*remember*) se souvenir de; **to have in m.** (*person, plan*) avoir en vue; **to have a good m. to do** avoir bien envie de faire. **2** *vti* (*heed*) faire attention à; (*look after*) garder, s'occuper de; (*noise, dirt etc*) être gêné par; (*one's language*) surveiller; **m. you don't fall** (*beware*) prends garde de ne pas tomber; **m. you do it** n'oublie pas de le faire; **do you m. if?** (*I smoke etc*) ça vous gêne si?; (*I leave, help etc*) ça ne vous fait rien si?; **I don't m. the sun** le soleil ne me gêne pas, je ne suis pas gêné par le soleil; **I wouldn't m. a cup of tea** (*would like*) j'aimerais bien une tasse de thé; **I m. that . . .** ça m'ennuie *or* me gêne que . . . ; **never m.!** (*it doesn't matter*) ça ne fait rien!, tant pis!; (*don't worry*) ne vous en faites pas!; **m. (out)!** (*watch out*) attention!; **m. you . . .** remarquez (que) . . . ; **m. your own business!, never you m.!** mêlez-vous de ce qui vous regarde! ◆**-ed** *suffix* **fair-m.** impartial; **like-m.** *a* de même opinion. ◆**-er** *n* (*for children*) gardien, -ienne *mf*, (*nurse*) nourrice *f*; (*bodyguard*) *Fam* gorille *m*. ◆**mind-boggling** *a* stupéfiant, qui confond l'imagination. ◆**mindful** *a*, **m. of sth/doing** attentif à qch/à faire. ◆**mindless** *a* stupide.

mine¹ [maın] *poss pron* **le mien, la mienne**, *pl* **les mien(ne)s**; **this hat is m.** ce chapeau est à moi *or* est le mien; **a friend of m.** un ami à moi.

mine² [maın] **1** *n* (*for coal, gold etc*) & *Fig* mine *f*; – *vt* **to m. (for)** (*coal etc*) extraire. **2** *n* (*explosive*) mine *f*; – *vt* (*beach, bridge etc*) miner. ◆**-ing** *n* exploitation *f* minière; – *a* (*industry*) minier. ◆**-er** *n* mineur *m*.

mineral ['mınərəl] *a & n* minéral (*m*).

mingle ['mıŋg(ə)l] *vi* se mêler (**with** à); **to m. with** (*socially*) fréquenter.

mingy ['mındʒı] *a* (-**ier**, -**iest**) (*mean*) *Fam* radin.

mini ['mını] *pref* mini-.

miniature ['mınıtʃər] *n* miniature *f*; – *a* (*train etc*) miniature *inv*; (*tiny*) minuscule.

minibus ['mɪnɪbʌs] n minibus m. ◆**mini-cab** n (radio-)taxi m.

minim ['mɪnɪm] n Mus blanche f.

minimum ['mɪnɪməm] n (pl -ima [-ɪmə] or -imums) minimum m; – a minimum (f inv), minimal. ◆**minimal** a minimal. ◆**minimize** vt minimiser.

minister ['mɪnɪstər] n Pol Rel ministre m. ◆**mini'sterial** a ministériel. ◆**ministry** n ministère m.

mink [mɪŋk] n (animal, fur) vison m.

minor ['maɪnər] a (small) Jur Mus mineur; (detail, operation) petit; – n Jur mineur, -eure mf.

Minorca [mɪ'nɔːkə] n Minorque f.

minority [maɪ'nɒrɪtɪ] n minorité f; **in the** of a m. en minorité, minoritaire; – a minoritaire.

mint [mɪnt] **1** n (place) Hôtel m de la Monnaie; **a m. (of money)** Fig une petite fortune; – vt (money) frapper; – a (stamp) neuf; **in m. condition** à l'état neuf. **2** n Bot Culin menthe f; (sweet) pastille f de menthe; – a à la menthe.

minus ['maɪnəs] prep Math moins; (without) Fam sans; **it's m. ten** (degrees) il fait moins dix (degrés); – n m. (sign) (signe m) moins m.

minute[1] ['mɪnɪt] **1** n minute f; **this (very) m.** (now) à la minute; **any m.** (now) d'une minute à l'autre; **m. hand** (of clock) grande aiguille f. **2** npl (of meeting) procès-verbal m.

minute[2] [maɪ'njuːt] a (tiny) minuscule; (careful, exact) minutieux.

minx [mɪŋks] n (girl) Pej diablesse f, chipie f.

miracle ['mɪrək(ə)l] n miracle m. ◆**mi'raculous** a miraculeux.

mirage ['mɪrɑːʒ] n mirage m.

mire [maɪər] n Lit fange f.

mirror ['mɪrər] n miroir m, glace f; Fig miroir m; **(rear view) m.** Aut rétroviseur m; – vt refléter.

mirth [mɜːθ] n Lit gaieté f, hilarité f.

misadventure [mɪsəd'ventʃər] n mésaventure f.

misanthropist [mɪ'zænθrəpɪst] n misanthrope m.

misapprehend [mɪsæprɪ'hend] vt mal comprendre. ◆**misapprehension** n malentendu m.

misappropriate [mɪsə'prəʊprɪeɪt] vt (money) détourner.

misbehave [mɪsbɪ'heɪv] vi se conduire mal; (of child) faire des sottises.

miscalculate [mɪs'kælkjʊleɪt] vt mal

calculer; – vi Fig se tromper. ◆**miscalcu-'lation** n erreur f de calcul.

miscarriage [mɪs'kærɪdʒ] n **to have a m.** Med faire une fausse couche; **m. of justice** erreur f judiciaire. ◆**miscarry** vi Med faire une fausse couche; (of plan) Fig échouer.

miscellaneous [mɪsɪ'leɪnɪəs] a divers.

mischief ['mɪstʃɪf] n espièglerie f; (maliciousness) méchanceté f; **to get into m.** faire des bêtises; **full of m.** = mischievous; **to make m. for** (trouble) créer des ennuis à; **to do s.o. a m.** (harm) faire mal à qn; **a little m.** (child) un petit démon. ◆**mischievous** a (playful, naughty) espiègle, malicieux; (malicious) méchant.

misconception [mɪskən'sepʃ(ə)n] n idée f fausse.

misconduct [mɪs'kɒndʌkt] n mauvaise conduite f; Com mauvaise gestion f.

misconstrue [mɪskən'struː] vt mal interpréter.

misdeed [mɪs'diːd] n méfait m.

misdemeanor [mɪsdɪ'miːnər] n Jur délit m.

misdirect [mɪsdɪ'rekt] vt (letter) mal adresser; (energies) mal diriger; (person) mal renseigner.

miser ['maɪzər] n avare mf. ◆**-ly** a avare.

misery ['mɪzərɪ] n (suffering) supplice m; (sadness) tristesse f; (sad person) Fam grincheux, -euse mf; pl (troubles) misères fpl; **his life is a m.** il est malheureux. ◆**miserable** a (wretched) misérable; (unhappy) malheureux; (awful) affreux; (derisory) dérisoire. ◆**miserably** adv misérablement; (to fail) lamentablement.

misfire [mɪs'faɪər] vi (of engine) avoir des ratés; (of plan) Fig rater.

misfit ['mɪsfɪt] n Pej inadapté, -ée mf.

misfortune [mɪs'fɔːtʃuːn] n malheur m, infortune f.

misgivings [mɪs'gɪvɪŋz] npl (doubts) doutes mpl; (fears) craintes fpl.

misguided [mɪs'gaɪdɪd] a (action etc) imprudent; **to be m.** (of person) se tromper.

mishandle [mɪs'hænd(ə)l] vt (affair, situation) traiter avec maladresse; (person) s'y prendre mal avec.

mishap ['mɪshæp] n (accident) mésaventure f; (hitch) contretemps m.

misinform [mɪsɪn'fɔːm] vt mal renseigner.

misinterpret [mɪsɪn'tɜːprɪt] vt mal interpréter.

misjudge [mɪs'dʒʌdʒ] vt (person, distance etc) mal juger.

mislay [mɪs'leɪ] vt (pt & pp mislaid) égarer.

mislead [mɪs'liːd] vt (pt & pp misled) tromper. ◆**-ing** a trompeur.

mismanage [mis'mænidʒ] *vt* mal administrer. ◆**—ment** *n* mauvaise administration *f*.

misnomer [mis'nəumər] *n* (*name*) nom *m* or terme *m* impropre.

misogynist [mi'sodʒinist] *n* misogyne *mf*.

misplac/e [mis'pleis] *vt* (*trust etc*) mal placer; (*lose*) égarer. ◆**—ed** *a* (*remark etc*) déplacé.

misprint ['misprint] *n* faute *f* d'impression, coquille *f*.

mispronounce [mispra'nauns] *vt* mal prononcer.

misquote [mis'kwəut] *vt* citer inexactement.

misrepresent [misrepri'zent] *vt* présenter sous un faux jour.

miss¹ [mis] *vt* (*train, target, opportunity etc*) manquer, rater; (*not see*) ne pas voir; (*not understand*) ne pas comprendre; (*one's youth, deceased person etc*) regretter; (*sth just lost*) remarquer l'absence de; **he misses Paris/her** Paris/elle lui manque; **I m. you** tu me manques; **don't m. seeing this play** (*don't fail to*) ne manque pas de voir cette pièce; **to m. out** (*omit*) sauter; – *vi* manquer, rater; **to m. out** (*lose a chance*) rater l'occasion; **to m. out on** (*opportunity etc*) rater, laisser passer; – *n* coup *m* manqué; **that was** *or* **we had a near m.** on l'a échappé belle; **I'll give it a m.** *Fam* (*not go*) je n'y irai pas; (*not take or drink or eat*) je n'en prendrai pas. ◆**—ing** *a* (*absent*) absent; (*in war, after disaster*) disparu; (*object*) manquant; **there are two cups/students m.** il manque deux tasses/des étudiants.

miss² [mis] *n* mademoiselle *f*; **Miss Brown** Mademoiselle *or* Mlle Brown.

misshapen [mis'ʃeip(ə)n] *a* difforme.

missile ['misail, *Am* 'mis(ə)l] *n* (*rocket*) *Mil* missile *m*; (*object thrown*) projectile *m*.

mission ['miʃ(ə)n] *n* mission *f*. ◆**missionary** *n* missionnaire *m*.

missive ['misiv] *n* (*letter*) missive *f*.

misspell [mis'spel] *vt* (*pt & pp* **-ed** *or* **misspelt**) mal écrire.

mist [mist] *n* (*fog*) brume *f*; (*on glass*) buée *f*; – *vi* **to m. over** *or* **up** s'embuer.

mistake [mi'steik] *n* erreur *f*, faute *f*; **to make a m.** se tromper, faire (une) erreur; **by m.** par erreur; – *vt* (*pt* **mistook**, *pp* **mistaken**) (*meaning, intention etc*) se tromper sur; **to m. the date/place/***etc* se tromper de date/de lieu/*etc*; **you can't m., there's no mistaking** (*his face, my car etc*) il est impossible de ne pas reconnaître; **to m.**

s.o./sth for prendre qn/qch pour. ◆**mistaken** *a* (*idea etc*) erroné; **to be m.** se tromper. ◆**mistakenly** *adv* par erreur.

mister ['mistər] *n Fam* monsieur *m*.

mistletoe ['mis(ə)ltəu] *n Bot* gui *m*.

mistreat [mis'triːt] *vt* maltraiter.

mistress ['mistris] *n* maîtresse *f*; (*in secondary school*) professeur *m*.

mistrust [mis'trʌst] *n* méfiance *f*; – *vt* se méfier de. ◆**mistrustful** *a* méfiant.

misty ['misti] *a* (*-ier, -iest*) (*foggy*) brumeux; (*glass*) embué.

misunderstand [misʌndə'stænd] *vt* (*pt & pp* **misunderstood**) mal comprendre. ◆**misunderstanding** *n* (*disagreement*) malentendu *m*; (*mistake*) erreur *f*. ◆**misunderstood** *a* (*person*) incompris.

misuse [mis'juːz] *vt* (*word, tool*) mal employer; (*power etc*) abuser de; – [mis'juːs] *n* (*of word*) emploi *m* abusif; (*of tool*) usage *m* abusif; (*of power etc*) abus *m*.

mite [mait] *n* **1** (*insect*) mite *f*. **2** (*poor*) m. (*child*) (*pauvre*) petit, *-ite* mf. **3 a m.** (*somewhat*) *Fam* un petit peu.

mitigate ['mitigeit] *vt* atténuer.

mitt(en) [mit, 'mit(ə)n] *n* (*glove*) moufle *f*.

mix [miks] *vt* mélanger, mêler; (*cement, cake*) préparer; (*salad*) remuer; **to m. up** mélanger; (*perplex*) embrouiller (*qn*); (*confuse, mistake*) confondre (**with** avec); **to be mixed up with s.o.** (*involved*) être mêlé aux affaires de qn; **to m. up in** (*involve*) mêler à; – *vi* se mêler; (*of colours*) s'allier; **to m. with** (*socially*) fréquenter; **she doesn't m. (in)** elle n'est pas sociable; – *n* (*mixture*) mélange *m*. ◆**—ed** *a* (*school, marriage*) mixte; (*society*) mêlé; (*feelings*) mitigés, mêlés; (*results*) divers; (*nuts, chocolates etc*) assortis; **to be (all) m. up** (*of person*) être désorienté; (*of facts, account etc*) être embrouillé. ◆**—ing** *n* mélange *m*. ◆**—er** *n Culin El* mixe(u)r *m*; (*for mortar*) *Tech* malaxeur *m*; **to be a good m.** (*of person*) être sociable. ◆**mixture** *n* mélange *m*; (*for cough*) sirop *m*. ◆**mix-up** *n Fam* confusion *f*.

mm *abbr* (*millimetre*) mm.

moan [məun] *vi* (*groan*) gémir; (*complain*) se plaindre (**to** à, **about** de, **that** que); – *n* gémissement *m*; plainte *f*.

moat [məut] *n* douve(s) *f(pl)*.

mob [mbb] *n* (*crowd*) cohue *f*, foule *f*; (*gang*) bande *f*; **the m.** (*masses*) la populace; (*Mafia*) *Am Sl* la mafia; – *vt* (*-bb-*) assiéger. ◆**mobster** *n Am Sl* gangster *m*.

mobile ['məubail, *Am* 'məub(ə)l] *a* mobile; (*having a car etc*) *Fam* motorisé; **m. home**

mobil-home *m*; **m. library** bibliobus *m*; − *n* (*Am* ['məubɪl]) (*ornament*) mobile *m*. **◆mo'bility** *n* mobilité *f*. **◆mobili'zation** *n* mobilisation *f*. **◆mobilize** *vti* mobiliser.

moccasin ['mɒkəsɪn] *n* (*shoe*) mocassin *m*.

mocha ['məukə] *n* (*coffee*) moka *m*.

mock [mɒk] **1** *vt* se moquer de; (*mimic*) singer; − *vi* se moquer (**at** de). **2** *a* (*false*) simulé; (*exam*) blanc. **◆—ing** *n* moquerie *f*; − *a* moqueur. **◆mockery** *n* (*act*) moquerie *f*; (*parody*) parodie *f*; **to make a m.** of tourner en ridicule.

mock-up ['mɒkʌp] *n* (*model*) maquette *f*.

mod cons [mɒd'kɒnz] *abbr Fam* = **modern conveniences**.

mode [məud] *n* (*manner, way*) mode *m*; (*fashion, vogue*) mode *f*.

model ['mɒd(ə)l] *n* (*example, person etc*) modèle *m*; (*fashion*) mannequin *m*; (*scale*) **m.** modèle *m* (réduit); − *a* (*behaviour, factory etc*) modèle; (*car, plane*) modèle réduit *inv*; **m. railway** train *n* miniature; − *vt* modeler (**on** sur); (*hats*) présenter (les modèles de); − *vi* (*for fashion*) être mannequin; (*pose for artist*) poser. **◆modelling** *n* (*of statues etc*) modelage *m*.

moderate¹ ['mɒdərət] *a* modéré; (*in speech*) mesuré; (*result*) passable; − *n Pol* modéré, -ée *mf*. **◆—ly** *adv* (*in moderation*) modérément; (*averagely*) moyennement.

moderate² ['mɒdəreɪt] *vt* (*diminish, tone down*) modérer. **◆mode'ration** *n* modération *f*; **in m.** avec modération.

modern ['mɒd(ə)n] *a* moderne; **m. languages** langues *fpl* vivantes; **m. conveniences** tout le confort moderne. **◆modernism** *n* modernisme *m*. **◆moderni'zation** *n* modernisation *f*. **◆modernize** *vt* moderniser.

modest ['mɒdɪst] *a* modeste. **◆modesty** *n* (*quality*) modestie *f*; (*moderation*) modération *f*; (*of salary etc*) modicité *f*.

modicum ['mɒdɪkəm] *n* **a m. of** un soupçon de, un petit peu de.

modify ['mɒdɪfaɪ] *vt* (*alter*) modifier; (*tone down*) modérer. **◆modifi'cation** *n* modification *f*.

modulate ['mɒdjuleɪt] *vt* moduler. **◆modu'lation** *n* modulation *f*.

module ['mɒdjuːl] *n* module *m*.

mogul ['məug(ə)l] *n* magnat *m*, manitou *m*.

mohair ['məuheər] *n* mohair *m*.

moist [mɔɪst] *a* (**-er, -est**) humide; (*clammy, sticky*) moite. **◆moisten** *vt* humecter. **◆moisture** *n* humidité *f*; (*on glass*) buée *f*.

◆moisturiz/e *vt* (*skin*) hydrater. **◆—er** *n* (*cream*) crème *f* hydratante.

molar ['məulər] *n* (*tooth*) molaire *f*.

molasses [mə'læsɪz] *n* (*treacle*) *Am* mélasse *f*.

mold [məuld] *Am* = **mould**.

mole [məul] *n* **1** (*on skin*) grain *m* de beauté. **2** (*animal, spy*) taupe *f*.

molecule ['mɒlɪkjuːl] *n* molécule *f*.

molest [mə'lest] *vt* (*annoy*) importuner; (*child, woman*) *Jur* attenter à la pudeur de.

mollusc ['mɒləsk] *n* mollusque *m*.

mollycoddle ['mɒlɪkɒd(ə)l] *vt* dorloter.

molt [məult] *Am* = **moult**.

molten ['məult(ə)n] *a* (*metal*) en fusion.

mom [mɒm] *n Am Fam* maman *f*.

moment ['məumənt] *n* moment *m*, instant *m*; **this (very) m.** (*now*) à l'instant; **the m.** **she leaves** dès qu'elle partira; **any m. (now)** d'un moment ou d'un instant à l'autre. **◆momentarily** (*Am* [məumən'terɪlɪ]) *adv* (*temporarily*) momentanément; (*soon*) *Am* tout à l'heure. **◆momentary** *a* momentané.

momentous [məu'mentəs] *a* important.

momentum [məu'mentəm] *n* (*speed*) élan *m*; **to gather** *or* **gain m.** (*of ideas etc*) *Fig* gagner du terrain.

mommy ['mɒmɪ] *n Am Fam* maman *f*.

Monaco ['mɒnəkəu] *n* Monaco *f*.

monarch ['mɒnək] *n* monarque *m*. **◆monarchy** *n* monarchie *f*.

monastery ['mɒnəst(ə)rɪ] *n* monastère *m*.

Monday ['mʌndɪ] *n* lundi *m*.

monetary ['mʌnɪt(ə)rɪ] *a* monétaire.

money ['mʌnɪ] *n* argent *m*; **paper m.** papier-monnaie *m*, billets *mpl*; **to get one's m.'s worth** en avoir pour son argent; **he gets** *or* **earns good m.** il gagne bien (sa vie); **to be in the m.** *Fam* rouler sur l'or; **m. order** mandat *m*. **◆moneybags** *n Pej Fam* richard, -arde *mf*. **◆moneybox** *n* tirelire *f*. **◆moneychanger** *n* changeur *m*. **◆moneylender** *n* prêteur, -euse *mf* sur gages. **◆moneymaking** *a* lucratif. **◆money-spinner** *n* (*source of wealth*) *Fam* mine *f* d'or.

mongol ['mɒŋg(ə)l] *n & a Med* mongolien, -ienne (*mf*).

mongrel ['mʌŋgrəl] *n* (*dog*) bâtard *m*.

monitor ['mɒnɪtər] **1** *n* (*pupil*) chef *m* de classe. **2** *n* (*screen*) *Tech* moniteur *m*. **3** *vt* (*a broadcast*) *Rad* écouter; (*check*) *Fig* contrôler.

monk [mʌŋk] *n* moine *m*, religieux *m*.

monkey ['mʌŋkɪ] *n* singe *m*; **little m.** (*child*) *Fam* polisson, -onne *mf*; **m. business** *Fam* singeries *fpl*; – *vi* to m. about *Fam* faire l'idiot.

mono ['mɒnəʊ] *a* (record etc) mono *inv*.

mono- ['mɒnəʊ] *pref* mono-.

monocle ['mɒnək(ə)l] *n* monocle *m*.

monogram ['mɒnəgræm] *n* monogramme *m*.

monologue ['mɒnəlɒg] *n* monologue *m*.

monopoly [mə'nɒpəlɪ] *n* monopole *m*. ◆**monopolize** *vt* monopoliser.

monosyllable ['mɒnəsɪləb(ə)l] *n* monosyllabe *m*. ◆**monosy'llabic** *a* monosyllabique.

monotone ['mɒnətəʊn] *n* in a m. sur un ton monocorde.

monotony [mə'nɒtənɪ] *n* monotonie *f*. ◆**monotonous** *a* monotone.

monsoon [mɒn'suːn] *n* (wind, rain) mousson *f*.

monster ['mɒnstər] *n* monstre *m*. ◆**mon'strosity** *n* (horror) monstruosité *f*. ◆**monstrous** *a* (abominable, enormous) monstrueux.

month [mʌnθ] *n* mois *m*. ◆**monthly** *a* mensuel; **m. payment** mensualité *f*; – *n* (periodical) mensuel *m*; – *adv* (every month) mensuellement.

Montreal [mɒntrɪ'ɔːl] *n* Montréal *m* or *f*.

monument ['mɒnjʊmənt] *n* monument *m*. ◆**monu'mental** *a* monumental; **m. mason** marbrier *m*.

moo [muː] *vi* meugler; – *n* meuglement *m*.

mooch [muːtʃ] **1** *vi* to m. around *Fam* flâner. **2** *vt* to m. sth off s.o. (cadge) *Am Sl* taper qch à qn.

mood [muːd] *n* (of person) humeur *f*; (of country) état *m* d'esprit; *Gram* mode *m*; in a **good/bad m.** de bonne/mauvaise humeur; to be in the m. to do or for doing être d'humeur à faire, avoir envie de faire. ◆**moody** *a* (-ier, -iest) (changeable) d'humeur changeante; (bad-tempered) de mauvaise humeur.

moon [muːn] *n* lune *f*; **once in a blue m.** (rarely) *Fam* tous les trente-six du mois; **over the m.** (delighted) *Fam* ravi (about de). ◆**moonlight 1** *n* clair *m* de lune. **2** *vi Fam* travailler au noir. ◆**moonshine** *n* (talk) *Fam* balivernes *fpl*.

moor [mʊər] **1** *vt Nau* amarrer; – *vi* mouiller. **2** *n* (open land) lande *f*. ◆**-ings** *npl Nau* (ropes etc) amarres *fpl*; (place) mouillage *m*.

moose [muːs] *n inv* (animal) orignac *m*, élan *m*.

moot [muːt] **1** *a* (point) discutable. **2** *vt* (question) soulever, suggérer.

mop [mɒp] **1** *n* balai *m* (à laver), balai *m* éponge; **dish m.** lavette *f*; **m. of hair** tignasse *f*. **2** *vt* (-pp-) (wipe) essuyer; **to m. one's brow** s'essuyer le front.

mope [məʊp] *vi* to m. (about) être déprimé, avoir le cafard.

moped ['məʊped] *n* cyclomoteur *m*, mobylette® *f*.

moral ['mɒrəl] *a* moral; – *n* (of story etc) morale *f*; *pl* (standards) moralité *f*, morale *f*. ◆**morale** [mə'rɑːl, *Am* mə'ræl] *n* moral *m*. ◆**moralist** *n* moraliste *mf*. ◆**mo'rality** *n* (morals) moralité *f*. ◆**moralize** *vi* moraliser. ◆**morally** *adv* moralement.

morass [mə'ræs] *n* (land) marais *m*; (mess) *Fig* bourbier *m*.

moratorium [mɒrə'tɔːrɪəm] *n* moratoire *m*.

morbid ['mɔːbɪd] *a* morbide.

more [mɔːr] *a & n* plus (de) (than que); (other) d'autres; **m. cars/etc** plus de voitures/etc; **he has m.** (than you) il en a plus (que toi); **a few m. months** encore quelques mois, quelques mois de plus; (some) **m. tea/etc** encore du thé/etc; (some) **m. details** d'autres détails; **m. than a kilo/ten/etc** (with quantity, number) plus d'un kilo/de dix/etc; – *adv* (tired, rapidly etc) plus (than que); **m. and m.** de plus en plus; **m. or less** plus ou moins; **the m. he shouts the m.** he gets plus il crie plus il s'enroue; **she hasn't any m.** elle n'en a plus. ◆**mo'reover** *adv* de plus, d'ailleurs.

moreish ['mɔːrɪʃ] *a Fam* qui a un goût de revenez-y.

mores ['mɔːreɪz] *npl* mœurs *fpl*.

morgue [mɔːg] *n* (mortuary) morgue *f*.

moribund ['mɒrɪbʌnd] *a* moribond.

morning ['mɔːnɪŋ] *n* matin *m*; (duration of morning) matinée *f*; **in the m.** (every morning) le matin; (during the morning) pendant la matinée; (tomorrow) demain matin; **at seven in the m.** à sept heures du matin; **every Tuesday m.** tous les mardis matin; **in the early m.** au petit matin; – *a* du matin, matinal. ◆**mornings** *adv Am* le matin.

Morocco [mə'rɒkəʊ] *n* Maroc *m*. ◆**Moroccan** *a & n* marocain, -aine (*mf*).

moron ['mɔːrɒn] *n* crétin, -ine *f*.

morose [mə'rəʊs] *a* morose.

morphine ['mɔːfiːn] *n* morphine *f*.

Morse [mɔːs] *n & a* M. (code) morse *m*.

morsel ['mɔːs(ə)l] *n* (of food) petite bouchée *f*.

mortal ['mɔːt(ə)l] *a & n* mortel, -elle (*mf*). ◆**mor'tality** *n* (death rate) mortalité *f*.

mortar ['mɔːtər] *n* mortier *m*.

mortgage ['mɔːgɪdʒ] n prêt-logement m; – vt (house, future) hypothéquer.

mortician [mɔː'tɪʃ(ə)n] n Am entrepreneur m de pompes funèbres.

mortify ['mɔːtɪfaɪ] vt mortifier.

mortuary ['mɔːtjuərɪ] n morgue f.

mosaic [məʊ'zeɪɪk] n mosaïque f.

Moscow ['mɒskəʊ, Am 'mɒskaʊ] n Moscou m or f.

Moses ['məʊzɪz] a M. basket couffin m.

Moslem ['mɒzlɪm] a & n musulman, -ane (mf).

mosque [mɒsk] n mosquée f.

mosquito [mɒs'kiːtəʊ] n (pl -oes) moustique m; m. net moustiquaire f.

moss [mɒs] n Bot mousse f. ◆**mossy** a moussu.

most [məʊst] a & n the m. (greatest in amount etc) le plus (de); **I have (the) m. books** j'ai le plus de livres; **I have (the) m.** j'en ai le plus; **m. (of the) books/etc** la plupart des livres/etc; **m. of the cake/etc** la plus grande partie du gâteau/etc; **m. of them** la plupart d'entre eux; **m. of it** la plus grande partie; **at (the very) m.** tout au plus; **to make the m. of** profiter (au maximum) de; – adv (le) plus; (very) fort, très; **the m. beautiful** le plus beau, la plus belle (**in**, de); **to talk (the) m.** parler le plus; **m.** (especially) surtout. ◆**—ly** adv surtout, pour la plupart.

motel [məʊ'tel] n motel m.

moth [mɒθ] n papillon m de nuit; (clothes) m. mite f. ◆**m.-eaten** a mité. ◆**mothball** n boule f de naphtaline.

mother ['mʌðər] n mère f; **M.'s Day** la fête des Mères; **m. tongue** langue f maternelle; – vt (care for) materner. ◆**motherhood** n maternité f. ◆**motherly** a maternel.

mother-in-law ['mʌðərɪnlɔː] n (pl mothers-in-law) belle-mère f. ◆**m.-of-pearl** n (substance) nacre f. ◆**m.-to-be** n (pl mothers-to-be) future mère f.

motion ['məʊʃ(ə)n] n mouvement m; Pol motion f; **m. picture** film m; – vti **to m. (to) s.o. to do** faire signe à qn de faire. ◆**—less** a immobile.

motive ['məʊtɪv] n motif m (**for, of** de); Jur mobile m (**for** de). ◆**motivate** vt (person, decision etc) motiver. ◆**moti'vation** n motivation f; (incentive) encouragement m.

motley ['mɒtlɪ] a (coloured) bigarré; (collection) hétéroclite.

motor ['məʊtər] n (engine) moteur m; (car) Fam auto f; – a (industry, vehicle etc) automobile; (accident) d'auto; **m. boat** canot m automobile; **m. mechanic** mécanicien-auto

m; **m. mower** tondeuse f à moteur; – vi (drive) rouler en auto. ◆**—ing** n Sp automobilisme m; **school of m.** auto-école f. ◆**motorbike** n Fam moto f. ◆**motorcade** n cortège m (officiel) (de voitures). ◆**motorcar** n automobile f. ◆**motorcycle** n moto f, motocyclette f. ◆**motorcyclist** n motocycliste mf. ◆**motorist** n automobiliste mf. ◆**motorized** a motorisé. ◆**motorway** n autoroute f.

mottled ['mɒt(ə)ld] a tacheté.

motto ['mɒtəʊ] n (pl -oes) devise f.

mould [məʊld] **1** n (shape) moule m; – vt (clay etc) mouler; (statue, character) modeler. **2** n (growth, mildew) moisissure f. ◆**mouldy** a (-ier, -iest) moisi; **to go m.** moisir.

moult [məʊlt] vi muer. ◆**—ing** n mue f.

mound [maʊnd] n (of earth) tertre m; (pile) Fig monceau m.

mount [maʊnt] **1** n (mountain) Lit mont m. **2** n (horse) monture f; (frame for photo or slide) cadre m; (stamp hinge) charnière f; – vt (horse, hill, jewel, photo, demonstration etc) monter; (ladder, tree etc) monter sur, grimper à; (stamp) coller (dans un album); – vi **to m. (up)** (on horse) se mettre en selle. **3** vi (increase) monter; **to m. up** (add up) chiffrer (**to** à); (accumulate) s'accumuler.

mountain ['maʊntɪn] n montagne f; – a (people, life) montagnard. ◆**mountaineer** n alpiniste mf. ◆**mountaineering** n alpinisme m. ◆**mountainous** a montagneux.

mourn [mɔːn] vti **to m. (for)** pleurer. ◆**—ing** n deuil m; **in m.** en deuil. ◆**—er** n parent, -ente mf or ami, -ie mf du défunt or de la défunte. ◆**mournful** a triste.

mouse, pl **mice** [maʊs, maɪs] n souris f. ◆**mousetrap** n souricière f.

mousse [muːs] n Culin mousse f.

moustache [mə'stɑːʃ, Am 'mʌstæʃ] n moustache f.

mousy ['maʊsɪ] a (-ier, -iest) (hair) Pej châtain terne; (shy) Fig timide.

mouth [maʊθ] n (pl -s [maʊðz]) bouche f; (of dog, lion etc) gueule f; (of river) embouchure f; (of cave, harbour) entrée f; – [maʊð] vt Pej dire. ◆**mouthful** n (of food) bouchée f; (of liquid) gorgée f. ◆**mouthorgan** n harmonica m. ◆**mouthpiece** n Mus embouchure f; (spokesman) Fig porte-parole m inv. ◆**mouthwash** n bain m de bouche. ◆**mouth-watering** a appétissant.

mov/e [muːv] n mouvement m; (change of

house etc) déménagement *m*; (*change of job*) changement *m* d'emploi; (*transfer of employee*) mutation *f*; (*in game*) coup *m*, (*one's turn*) tour *m*; (*act*) Fig démarche *f*; (*step*) pas *m*; (*attempt*) tentative *f*; **to make a m.** (*leave*) se préparer à partir; (*act*) Fig passer à l'action; **to get a m. on** Fam se dépêcher; **on the m.** en marche; – *vt* déplacer, remuer, bouger; (*arm, leg*) remuer; (*crowd*) faire partir; (*put*) mettre; (*transport*) transporter; (*piece in game*) jouer; (*propose*) Pol proposer; **to m. s.o.** (*incite*) pousser qn (**to do** à faire); (*emotionally*) émouvoir qn; (*transfer in job*) muter qn; **to m. house** déménager; **to m. sth back** reculer qch; **to m. sth down** descendre qch; **to m. sth forward** avancer qch; **to m. sth over** pousser qch; – *vi* bouger, remuer; (*go*) aller (**to** à); (*pass*) passer (**to** à); (*leave*) partir; (*change seats*) changer de place; (*progress*) avancer; (*act*) agir; (*play*) jouer; **to m. (out)** (*of house etc*) déménager; **to m. (to** (*a new region etc*) aller habiter; **to m. about** or **away** (*fidget*) remuer; **to m. along** or **forward** or **on** avancer; **to m. away** or **off** (*go away*) s'éloigner; **to m. back** (*withdraw*) reculer; (*return*) retourner; **to m. in** (*to house*) emménager; **to m. in** (*house*) emménager dans; **m. on!** circulez!; **to m. over** or **up** se pousser. ◆**—ing** *a* en mouvement; (*part*) Tech mobile; (*stairs*) mécanique; (*touching*) émouvant. ◆**mov(e)able** *a* mobile. ◆**movement** *n* (*action, group etc*) & *Mus* mouvement *m*.

movie ['muːvɪ] *n* Fam film *m*; **the movies** (*cinema*) le cinéma; **m. camera** caméra *f*. ◆**moviegoer** *n* cinéphile *mf*.

mow [məʊ] *vt* (*pp* **mown** or **mowed**) (*field*) faucher; **to m. the lawn** tondre le gazon; **to m. down** (*kill etc*) Fig faucher. ◆**—er** *n* (*lawn*) **m.** tondeuse *f* (à gazon).

MP [em'piː] *n abbr* (*Member of Parliament*) député *m*.

Mrs ['mɪsɪz] *n* (*married woman*) **Mrs Brown** Madame or Mme Brown.

Ms [mɪz] *n* (*married or unmarried woman*) **Ms Brown** Madame or Mme Brown.

MSc, *Am* **MS** *abbr* = Master of Science.

much [mʌtʃ] *a & n* beaucoup (**de**); **not m. time/money/etc** pas beaucoup de temps/ d'argent/*etc*; **not m.** pas beaucoup; **m.** *of* (*a good deal of*) une bonne partie de; **as m.** as (*to do, know etc*) autant que; **as m. wine/etc** as autant de vin/*etc* que; **as m. as you like** autant que tu veux; **twice as m.** deux fois plus (**de**); **how m.?** combien (**de**)?; **too m.**

trop (**de**); **so m.** tant (**de**), tellement (**de**); **I know/I shall do this m.** je sais/je ferai ceci (du moins); **this m. wine** ça de vin; **it's not m. of a garden** ce n'est pas merveilleux comme jardin; **m. the same** presque le même; – *adv* very **m.** beaucoup; **not (very) m.** pas beaucoup; **she doesn't say very m.** elle ne dit pas grand-chose.

muck [mʌk] **1** *n* (*manure*) fumier *m*; (*filth*) Fig saleté *f*. **2** *vi* **to m. about** Fam (*have fun, idle*) s'amuser; (*play the fool*) faire l'idiot; **to m. about with** Fam (*fiddle with*) s'amuser avec; (*alter*) changer (*texte etc*); **to m. in** (*join in*) Fam participer, contribuer; – *vt* **to m. s.o. about** Fam embêter qn, déranger qn; **to m. up** (*spoil*) Fam gâcher, ruiner. ◆**m.-up** *n* Fam gâchis *m*. ◆**mucky** *a* (**-ier, -iest**) sale.

mucus ['mjuːkəs] *n* mucosités *fpl*.

mud [mʌd] *n* boue *f*. ◆**muddy** *a* (**-ier, -iest**) (*water*) boueux; (*hands etc*) couvert de boue. ◆**mudguard** *n* garde-boue *m inv*.

muddle ['mʌd(ə)l] *n* (*mess*) désordre *m*; (*mix-up*) confusion *f*; **in a m.** (*room etc*) sens dessus dessous, en désordre; (*person*) désorienté; (*mind, ideas*) embrouillé; – *vt* (*person, facts etc*) embrouiller; (*papers*) mélanger; – *vi* **to m. through** Fam se débrouiller tant bien que mal.

muff [mʌf] *n* (*for hands*) manchon *m*.

muffin ['mʌfɪn] *n* petit pain *m* brioché.

muffl/e ['mʌf(ə)l] *vt* (*noise*) assourdir. ◆**—ed** *a* (*noise*) sourd. ◆**—er** *n* (*scarf*) cache-col *m inv*; *Aut Am* silencieux *m*.

mug [mʌg] **1** *n* grande tasse *f*; (*of metal or plastic*) gobelet *m*; (*beer*) **m.** chope *f*. **2** *n* (*face*) Sl gueule *f*; **m. shot** Pej photo *f* (d'identité). **3** *n* (*fool*) Fam niais, -aise *mf*. **4** *vt* (**-gg-**) (*attack*) agresser. ◆**mugger** *n* agresseur *m*. ◆**mugging** *n* agression *f*.

muggy ['mʌgɪ] *a* (**-ier, -iest**) (*weather*) lourd.

mulberry ['mʌlbərɪ] *n* (*fruit*) mûre *f*.

mule [mjuːl] *n* (*male*) mulet *m*; (*female*) mule *f*.

mull [mʌl] **1** *vt* (*wine*) chauffer. **2** *vi* **to m. over** (*think over*) ruminer.

mullet ['mʌlɪt] *n* (*fish*) mulet *m*; (*red*) **m.** rouget *m*.

multi- ['mʌltɪ] *pref* multi-.

multicoloured ['mʌltɪkʌləd] *a* multicolore.

multifarious [mʌltɪ'feərɪəs] *a* divers.

multimillionaire [mʌltɪmɪljə'neər] *n* milliardaire *mf*.

multinational [mʌltɪ'næʃ(ə)nəl] *n* multinationale *f*.

multiple ['mʌltɪp(ə)l] *a* multiple; – *n Math* multiple *m.* ◆**multipli'cation** *n* multiplication *f.* ◆**multi'plicity** *n* multiplicité *f.* ◆**multiply** *vt* multiplier; – *vi* (*reproduce*) se multiplier.

multistorey [mʌltɪ'stɔːrɪ] (*Am* **multistoried**) *a* à étages.

multitude ['mʌltɪtjuːd] *n* multitude *f.*

mum [mʌm] **1** *n Fam* maman *f.* **2** *a* **to keep m.** garder le silence.

mumble ['mʌmb(ə)l] *vti* marmotter.

mumbo-jumbo [mʌmbəʊ'dʒʌmbəʊ] *n* (*words*) charabia *m.*

mummy ['mʌmɪ] *n* **1** *Fam* maman *f.* **2** (*body*) momie *f.*

mumps [mʌmps] *n* oreillons *mpl.*

munch [mʌntʃ] *vti* (*chew*) mastiquer; **to m.** (**on**) (*eat*) *Fam* bouffer.

mundane [mʌn'deɪn] *a* banal.

municipal [mjuː'nɪsɪp(ə)l] *a* municipal. ◆**munici'pality** *n* municipalité *f.*

munitions [mjuː'nɪʃ(ə)nz] *npl* munitions *fpl.*

mural ['mjʊərəl] *a* mural; – *n* fresque *f,* peinture *f* murale.

murder ['mɜːdər] *n* meurtre *m,* assassinat *m;* **it's m.** (*dreadful*) *Fam* c'est affreux; – *vt* (*kill*) assassiner; (*spoil*) *Fig* massacrer. ◆**—er** *n* meurtrier, assassin *m;* ◆**murderous** *a* meurtrier.

murky ['mɜːkɪ] *a* (**-ier, -iest**) obscur; (*water, business, past*) trouble; (*weather*) nuageux.

murmur ['mɜːmər] *n* murmure *m;* (*of traffic*) bourdonnement *m;* – *vti* murmurer.

muscle ['mʌs(ə)l] *n* muscle *m;* – *vi* **to m. in on** (*group*) *Sl* s'introduire par la force à. ◆**muscular** *a* (*tissue etc*) musculaire; (*brawny*) musclé.

muse [mjuːz] *vi* méditer (**on** sur).

museum [mjuː'zɪəm] *n* musée *m.*

mush [mʌʃ] *n* (*soft mass*) bouillie *f; Fig* sentimentalité *f.* ◆**mushy** *a* (**-ier, -iest**) (*food etc*) en bouillie; *Fig* sentimental.

mushroom ['mʌʃrʊm] **1** *n* champignon *m.* **2** *vi* (*grow*) pousser comme des champignons; (*spread*) se multiplier.

music ['mjuːzɪk] *n* musique *f;* **m. centre** chaîne *f* stéréo compacte; **m. critic** critique *m* musical; **m. hall** music-hall *m;* **m. lover** mélomane *mf;* **canned m.** musique *f* (de fond) enregistrée. ◆**musical** *a* musical; (*instrument*) de musique; **to be (very) m.** être (très) musicien; – *n* (*film, play*) comédie *f* musicale. ◆**mu'sician** *n* musicien, -ienne *mf.*

musk [mʌsk] *n* (*scent*) musc *m.*

Muslim ['mʊzlɪm] *a* & *n* musulman, -ane (*mf*).

muslin ['mʌzlɪn] *n* (*cotton*) mousseline *f.*

mussel ['mʌs(ə)l] *n* (*mollusc*) moule *f.*

must [mʌst] *v aux* **1** (*necessity*) **you m. obey** tu dois obéir, il faut que tu obéisses. **2** (*certainty*) **she m. be clever** elle doit être intelligente; **I m. have seen it** j'ai dû le voir; – *n* **this is a m.** ceci est (absolument) indispensable.

mustache ['mʌstæʃ] *n Am* moustache *f.*

mustard ['mʌstəd] *n* moutarde *f.*

muster ['mʌstər] *vt* (*gather*) rassembler; (*sum*) réunir; – *vi* se rassembler.

musty ['mʌstɪ] *a* (**-ier, -iest**) (*smell*) de moisi; **it smells m.,** it's m. ça sent le moisi.

mutation [mjuː'teɪʃ(ə)n] *n Biol* mutation *f.*

mute [mjuːt] *a* (*silent*) & *Gram* muet; – *vt* (*sound, colour*) assourdir. ◆**-ed** *a* (*criticism*) voilé.

mutilate ['mjuːtɪleɪt] *vt* mutiler. ◆**muti'lation** *n* mutilation *f.*

mutiny ['mjuːtɪnɪ] *n* mutinerie *f;* – *vi* se mutiner. ◆**mutinous** *a* (*troops*) mutiné.

mutter ['mʌtər] *vti* marmonner.

mutton ['mʌt(ə)n] *n* (*meat*) mouton *m.*

mutual ['mjuːtʃʊəl] *a* (*help, love etc*) mutuel, réciproque; (*common, shared*) commun; **m. fund** *Am* fonds *m* commun de placement. ◆**-ly** *adv* mutuellement.

muzzle ['mʌz(ə)l] *n* (*snout*) museau *m;* (*device*) muselière *f;* (*of gun*) gueule *f;* – *vt* (*animal, press etc*) museler.

my [maɪ] *poss a* mon, ma, *pl* mes. ◆**my'self** *pron* moi-même; (*reflexive*) me, m'; (*after prep*) moi; **I wash m.** je me lave; **I think of m.** je pense à moi.

mystery ['mɪstərɪ] *n* mystère *m.* ◆**my'sterious** *a* mystérieux.

mystic ['mɪstɪk] *a* & *n* mystique (*mf*). ◆**mystical** *a* mystique. ◆**mysticism** *n* mysticisme *m.* ◆**my'stique** *n* (*mystery, power*) mystique *f* (of de).

mystify ['mɪstɪfaɪ] *vt* (*bewilder*) laisser perplexe; (*fool*) mystifier. ◆**mystifi'cation** *n* (*bewilderment*) perplexité *f.*

myth [mɪθ] *n* mythe *m.* ◆**mythical** *a* mythique. ◆**mytho'logical** *a* mythologique. ◆**my'thology** *n* mythologie *f.*

N

N, n [en] *n* N, n *m*; **the nth time** la énième fois.

nab [næb] *vt* (**-bb-**) (*catch, arrest*) *Fam* épingler.

nag [næg] *vti* (**-gg-**) (*criticize*) critiquer; **to n. (at) s.o.** (*pester*) harceler *or* embêter qn (**to do** pour qu'il fasse). ◆**nagging** *a* (*doubt, headache*) qui subsiste; *n* critiques *fpl*.

nail [neɪl] **1** *n* (*of finger, toe*) ongle *m*; *a* (*polish, file etc*) à ongles. **2** *n* (*metal*) clou *m*; *vt* clouer; **to n. s.o.** (*nab*) *Fam* épingler qn; **to n. down** (*lid etc*) clouer.

naïve [naɪˈiːv] *a* naïf. ◆**naïveté** *n* naïveté *f*.

naked [ˈneɪkɪd] *a* (*person*) nu; (*eye, flame*) nu; **to see with the n. eye** voir à l'œil nu. ◆**-ness** *n* nudité *f*.

name [neɪm] *n* nom *m*; (*reputation*) *Fig* réputation *f*; **my n. is . . .** je m'appelle . . . ; **in the n. of** au nom de; **to put one's n. down for** (*school, course*) s'inscrire à; (*job, house*) demander, faire une demande pour avoir; **to call s.o. names** injurier qn; **first n., given n.** prénom *m*; **last n.** nom de famille; **a good/bad n.** *Fig* une bonne/mauvaise réputation; **n. plate** plaque *f*; *vt* nommer; (*ship, street*) baptiser; (*designate*) désigner, nommer; (*date, price*) fixer; **he was named after** *or* *Am* **for . . .** il a reçu le nom de . . . ◆**-less** *a* sans nom, anonyme. ◆**-ly** *adv* (*that is*) à savoir. ◆**namesake** *n* (*person*) homonyme *m*.

nanny [ˈnænɪ] *n* nurse *f*, bonne *f* d'enfants; (*grandmother*) *Fam* mamie *f*.

nanny-goat [ˈnænɪɡəʊt] *n* chèvre *f*.

nap [næp] *n* (*sleep*) petit somme *m*; **to have** *or* **take a n.** faire un petit somme; (*after lunch*) faire la sieste; *vi* (**-pp-**) **to be napping** sommeiller; **to catch napping** *Fig* prendre au dépourvu.

nape [neɪp] *n* **n.** (**of the neck**) nuque *f*.

napkin [ˈnæpkɪn] *n* (*at table*) serviette *f*; (*for baby*) couche *f*. ◆**nappy** *n* (*for baby*) couche *f*. ◆**nappy-liner** *n* protège-couche *m*.

narcotic [nɑːˈkɒtɪk] *a & n* narcotique (*m*).

narrate [nəˈreɪt] *vt* raconter. ◆**narration** *n*, ◆**'narrative** (*story*) récit *m*, narration *f*; (*art, act*) narration *f*. ◆**narrator** *n* narrateur, -trice *mf*.

narrow [ˈnærəʊ] *a* (**-er, -est**) étroit; (*major-*ity) faible, petit; *vi* (*of path*) se rétrécir; **to n. down** (*of choice etc*) se limiter (**to** à); *vt* **to n. (down)** (*limit*) limiter. ◆**-ly** *adv* (*to miss etc*) de justesse; (*strictly*) strictement; **he n. escaped** *or* **missed being killed/etc** il a failli être tué/*etc*. ◆**-ness** *n* étroitesse *f*.

narrow-minded [nærəʊˈmaɪndɪd] *a* borné. ◆**-ness** *n* étroitesse *f* (d'esprit).

nasal [ˈneɪz(ə)l] *a* nasal; (*voice*) nasillard.

nasty [ˈnɑːstɪ] *a* (**-ier, -iest**) (*bad*) mauvais, vilain; (*spiteful*) méchant, désagréable (**to, towards** avec); **a n. mess** *or* **muddle** un gâchis. ◆**nastily** *adv* (*to act*) méchamment; (*to rain*) horriblement. ◆**nastiness** *n* (*malice*) méchanceté *f*; **the n. of the weather/taste/etc** le mauvais temps/goût/*etc*.

nation [ˈneɪʃ(ə)n] *n* nation *f*; **the United Nations** les Nations Unies. ◆**n.-wide** *a* & *adv* dans le pays (tout) entier. ◆**national** *a* national; **n. anthem** hymne *m* national; **N. Health Service** = Sécurité *f* Sociale; **n. insurance** = assurances *fpl* sociales; *n* (*citizen*) ressortissant, -ante *mf*. ◆**nationalist** *n* nationaliste *mf*. ◆**nationa'listic** *a* *Pej* nationaliste. ◆**natio'nality** *n* nationalité *f*. ◆**nationalize** *vt* nationaliser. ◆**nationally** *adv* (*to travel, be known etc*) dans le pays (tout) entier.

native [ˈneɪtɪv] *a* (*country*) natal; (*habits, costume*) du pays; (*tribe, plant*) indigène; (*charm, ability*) inné; **n. language** langue *f* maternelle; **to be an English n. speaker** parler l'anglais comme langue maternelle; *n* (*person*) autochtone *mf*; (*non-European in colony*) indigène *mf*; **to be a n.** **of** être originaire *or* natif de.

nativity [nəˈtɪvɪtɪ] *n Rel* nativité *f*.

NATO [ˈneɪtəʊ] *n abbr* (*North Atlantic Treaty Organization*) OTAN *f*.

natter [ˈnætər] *vi Fam* bavarder; *n Fam* **to have a n.** bavarder.

natural [ˈnætʃ(ə)rəl] *a* naturel; (*actor, gardener etc*) né; *n* **to be a n. for** (*job etc*) *Fam* être celui qu'il faut pour, être fait pour. ◆**naturalist** *n* naturaliste *mf*. ◆**naturally** *adv* (*as normal, of course*) naturellement; (*by nature*) de nature; (*with naturalness*) avec naturel. ◆**naturalness** *n* naturel *m*.

naturalize ['nætʃ(ə)rəlaız] vt (person) Pol naturaliser. **◆naturali'zation** n naturalisation f.

nature ['neɪtʃər] n (natural world, basic quality) nature f; (disposition) naturel m; by n. de nature; **n. study** sciences fpl naturelles.

naught [nɔːt] n 1 Math zéro m. 2 (nothing) Lit rien m.

naught/y ['nɔːtɪ] a (-ier, -iest) (child) vilain, malicieux; (joke, story) osé, grivois. **◆—ily** adv (to behave) mal; (to say) avec malice. **◆—iness** n mauvaise conduite f.

nausea ['nɔːzɪə] n nausée f. **◆nauseate** vt écœurer. **◆nauseous** a (smell etc) nauséabond; **to feel n.** Am (sick) avoir envie de vomir; (disgusted) Fig être écœuré.

nautical ['nɔːtɪk(ə)l] a nautique.

naval ['neɪv(ə)l] a naval; (power, hospital) maritime; (officer) de marine.

nave [neɪv] n (of church) nef f.

navel ['neɪv(ə)l] n Anat nombril m.

navigate ['nævɪgeɪt] vi naviguer; – vt (boat) diriger, piloter; (river) naviguer sur. **◆navigable** a (river) navigable; (seaworthy) en état de naviguer. **◆navi'gation** n navigation f. **◆navigator** n Av navigateur m.

navvy ['nævɪ] n (labourer) terrassier m.

navy ['neɪvɪ] n marine f; – a n. (blue) bleu marine inv.

Nazi ['nɑːtsɪ] a & n Pol Hist nazi, -ie (mf).

near [nɪər] adv (-er, -est) près; **quite n., n.** at hand tout près; **to draw n.** (s.)approcher (to de); (of date) approcher; **n.** to près de; **to come n. to being killed/etc** faillir être tué/etc; **n. enough** (more or less) Fam plus ou moins; – prep (-er, -est) **n.** (to) près de; **n. the bed** près du lit; **to be n.** (to) **victory/death** frôler la victoire/la mort; **the end** vers la fin; **to come n. to** s.'approcher de qn; – a (-er, -est) proche; (likeness) fidèle; **the nearest hospital** l'hôpital le plus proche; **the nearest way** la route la plus directe; **in the n. future** dans un avenir proche; **to the nearest franc** (to calculate) à un franc près; (to round up or down) au franc supérieur ou inférieur; **n. side** Aut côté m gauche, Am côté m droit; – vt (approach) approcher de; **nearing completion** près d'être achevé. **◆near'by** adv tout près; – ['nɪəbaɪ] a proche. **◆nearness** n (in space, time) proximité f.

nearly ['nɪəlɪ] adv presque; **she (very) n. fell** elle a failli tomber; **not n. as clever/etc as** loin d'être aussi intelligent/etc que.

neat [niːt] a (-er, -est) (clothes, work) soigné,

propre, net; (room) ordonné, bien rangé; (style) élégant; (pretty) Fam joli, beau; (pleasant) Fam agréable; **to drink one's whisky/etc n.** prendre son whisky/etc sec. **◆—ly** adv avec soin; (skilfully) habilement. **◆—ness** n netteté f; (of room) ordre m.

necessary ['nesɪs(ə)rɪ] a nécessaire; **it's n. to do** il est nécessaire de faire, il faut faire; **to make it n. for s.o. to do** mettre qn dans la nécessité de faire; **to do what's n.** or **the n.** Fam faire le nécessaire (for pour); – npl **the necessaries** (food etc) l'indispensable m. **◆nece'ssarily** adv nécessairement.

necessity [nɪ'sesɪtɪ] n (obligation, need) nécessité f; (poverty) indigence f; **there's no n. for you to do that** tu n'es pas obligé de faire cela; **of n.** nécessairement; **to be a n.** être indispensable; **the (bare) necessities** les (strict) nécessaire m. **◆necessitate** vt nécessiter.

neck [nek] n Anat cou m; (of dress, horse) encolure f; (of bottle) col m; **low n.** (of dress) décolleté m; **n. and n.** Sp à égalité. **◆necklace** n collier m. **◆neckline** n encolure f. **◆necktie** n cravate f.

neck [nek] vi (kiss etc) Fam se peloter.

nectarine ['nektərɪn] n (fruit) nectarine f, brugnon m.

née [neɪ] adv n. Dupont née Dupont.

need [niːd] 1 n (necessity, want, poverty) besoin m; **in n.** dans le besoin; **to be in n. of** avoir besoin de; **there's no n. (for you) to do** tu n'as pas besoin de faire; **if n. be** si besoin est, s'il le faut; – vt avoir besoin de; **you n. it** tu en as besoin, il te le faut; **it needs an army to do, an army is needed to do** il faut une armée pour faire; **this sport needs patience** ce sport demande de la patience; **her hair needs cutting** il faut qu'elle se fasse couper les cheveux. 2 v aux **n. he wait?** est-il obligé d'attendre?, a-t-il besoin d'attendre?; **I needn't have rushed** ce n'était pas la peine de me presser; **I n. hardly say that . . .** je n'ai guère besoin de dire que . . . . **◆needless** a inutile. **◆needlessly** adv inutilement. **◆needy** a (-ier, -iest) nécessiteux.

needle ['niːd(ə)l] 1 n aiguille f; (of record player) saphir m. 2 vt (irritate) Fam agacer. **◆needlework** n couture f, travaux mpl d'aiguille; (object) ouvrage m.

negate [nɪ'geɪt] vt (nullify) annuler; (deny) nier. **◆negation** n (denial) & Gram négation f.

negative ['negətɪv] a négatif; – n Phot négatif m; (word) Gram négation f; (form)

Gram forme *f* négative; **to answer in the n.** répondre par la négative.

neglect [nɪ'glekt] *vt* (*person, health, work etc*) négliger; (*garden, car etc*) ne pas s'occuper de; (*duty*) manquer à; (*rule*) désobéir à, méconnaître; **to n. to do** négliger de faire; – *n* (*of person*) manque *m* de soins (*of* envers); (*of rule*) désobéissance *f* (*of* à); (*of duty*) manquement *m* (*of* à); (*carelessness*) négligence *f*; **in a state of n.** (*garden, house etc*) mal tenu. ◆**neglected** *a* (*appearance, person*) négligé; (*garden, house etc*) mal tenu; **to feel n.** sentir qu'on vous néglige. ◆**neglectful** *a* négligent; **to be n. of** négliger.

negligent ['neglɪdʒənt] *a* négligent. ◆**negligence** *n* négligence *f*. ◆**negligently** *adv* négligemment.

negligible ['neglɪdʒəb(ə)l] *a* négligeable.

negotiate [nɪ'gəʊʃɪeɪt] **1** *vti* Fin Pol négocier. **2** *vt* (*fence, obstacle*) franchir; (*bend*) Aut négocier. ◆**negotiable** *a* Fin négociable. ◆**negoti'ation** *n* négociation *f*; **in n.** in pourparlers avec. ◆**negotiator** *n* négociateur, -trice *mf*.

Negro ['niːgrəʊ] *a* (*pl* -**oes**) (*man*) Noir *m*; (*woman*) Noire *f*; – *a* noir; (*art, sculpture etc*) nègre. ◆**Negress** *n* Noire *f*.

neigh [neɪ] *vi* (*of horse*) hennir; – *n* hennissement *m*.

neighbour ['neɪbər] *n* voisin, -ine *mf*. ◆**neighbourhood** *n* (*neighbours*) voisinage *m*; (*district*) quartier *m*, voisinage *m*; (*region*) région *f*; **in the n. of ten pounds** dans les dix livres. ◆**neighbouring** *a* avoisinant. ◆**neighbourly** *a* (*feeling etc*) de bon voisinage, amical; **they're n. (people)** ils sont bons voisins.

neither ['naɪðər, Am 'niːðər] *adv* ni; **n. ... nor** ni ... ni; **you nor me** ni toi ni moi; **he n. sings nor dances** il ne chante ni ne danse; – *conj* (*not either*) ni ... non plus; **n. shall I go** je n'y irai pas non plus; **do I, n. can I etc** (ni) moi non plus; – *a* **n. boy (came)** aucun des deux garçons (n'est venu); **on n. side** ni d'un côté ni de l'autre; – *pron* **n. (of them)** ni l'un(e) ni l'autre, aucun(e) (des deux).

neo- ['niːəʊ] *pref* néo-.

neon ['niːɒn] *n* (*gas*) néon *m*; – *a* (*lighting etc*) au néon.

nephew ['nevjuː, 'nefjuː] *n* neveu *m*.

nepotism ['nepətɪz(ə)m] *n* népotisme *m*.

nerve [nɜːv] *n* nerf *m*; (*courage*) Fig courage *m* (**to do** de faire); (*confidence*) assurance *f*; (*calm*) sang-froid *m*; (*cheek*) Fam culot *m* (**to do** de faire); **you get on my nerves** Fam

tu me portes *or* me tapes sur les nerfs; **to have (an attack of) nerves** (*fear, anxiety*) avoir le trac; **to have a bundle** *or* **mass** *or* **bag of nerves** (*person*) Fam un paquet de nerfs; **to have bad nerves** être nerveux; – *a* (*cell, centre*) nerveux. ◆**n.-racking** *a* éprouvant pour les nerfs. ◆**nervous** *a* (*tense*) & Anat nerveux; (*worried*) inquiet (**about** de); **to be** *or* **feel n.** (*ill-at-ease*) se sentir mal à l'aise; (*before exam etc*) avoir le trac. ◆**nervously** *adv* nerveusement; (*worriedly*) avec inquiétude. ◆**nervousness** *n* nervosité *f*; (*fear*) trac *m*. ◆**nervy** *a* (*-ier, -iest*) Fam (*anxious*) nerveux; (*brash*) Am culotté.

nest [nest] *n* nid *m*; **n. egg** (*money saved*) pécule *m*; **n. of tables** (*pile*) *m*; – *vi* (*of bird*) (se) nicher.

nestle ['nes(ə)l] *vi* se pelotonner (**up to** contre); **a village nestling in** (*forest, valley etc*) un village niché dans.

net [net] **1** *n* filet *m*; **n. curtain** voilage *m*; – *vt* (**-tt-**) (*fish*) prendre au filet. **2** *a* (*profit, weight etc*) net *inv*; – *vt* (**-tt-**) (*of person, firm etc*) gagner net; **this venture netted him** *or* **her ...** cette entreprise lui a rapporté ... ◆**netting** *n* (*nets*) filets *mpl*; (*mesh*) mailles *fpl*; (*fabric*) voile *m*; (*wire*) **n.** treillis *m*.

Netherlands (the) [ðə'neðələndz] *npl* les Pays-Bas *mpl*.

nettle ['net(ə)l] *n* Bot ortie *f*.

network ['netwɜːk] *n* réseau *m*.

neurosis, *pl* -**oses** [njʊə'rəʊsɪs, -əʊsiːz] *n* névrose *f*. ◆**neurotic** *a* & *n* névrosé, -ée (*mf*).

neuter ['njuːtər] **1** *a* & *n* Gram neutre (*m*). **2** *vt* (*cat etc*) châtrer.

neutral ['njuːtrəl] *a* neutre; (*policy*) de neutralité; – *n* El neutre *m*; **in n. (gear)** Aut au point mort. ◆**neu'trality** *n* neutralité *f*. ◆**neutralize** *vt* neutraliser.

never ['nevər] *adv* **1** (*not ever*) (ne) ... jamais; **she n. lies** elle ne ment jamais; **n. in (all) my life** jamais de ma vie; **n. again** plus jamais. **2** (*certainly not*) Fam **I n. did it** je ne l'ai pas fait. ◆**n.-ending** *a* interminable.

nevertheless [nevəðə'les] *adv* néanmoins, quand même.

new [njuː] *a* (*-er, -est*) nouveau; (*brand-new*) neuf; **to be n. to** (*job*) être nouveau dans; (*city*) être un nouveau-venu dans, être fraîchement installé dans; **a n. boy** Sch un nouveau; **what's n.?** Fam quoi de neuf?; **a n. glass/pen/etc** (*different*) un autre verre/stylo/etc; **to break n. ground** innover; **n. look** style *m* nouveau; **as good as**

n. comme neuf; **a n.-laid egg** un œuf du jour; **a n.-born baby** un nouveau-né, une nouveau-née. ◆**newcomer** n nouveau-venu m, nouvelle-venue f. ◆**new-'fangled** a Pej moderne. ◆**new-found** a nouveau. ◆**newly** adv (recently) nouvellement, fraîchement; **the n.-weds** les nouveaux mariés. ◆**newness** n (condition) état m neuf; (novelty) nouveauté f.

news [njuːz] n nouvelle(s) f(pl); Journ Rad TV informations fpl, actualités fpl; sports/etc n. (newspaper column) chronique f or rubrique f sportive/etc; **a piece of n.,** some n. une nouvelle; Journ Rad TV une information; **n. headlines** titres mpl de l'actualité; **n. flash** flash m. ◆**newsagent** n marchand, -ande mf de journaux. ◆**newsboy** n vendeur m de journaux. ◆**newscaster** n présentateur, -trice mf. ◆**newsletter** n (of club, group etc) bulletin m. ◆**newspaper** n journal m. ◆**newsreader** n présentateur, -trice mf. ◆**newsreel** n Cin actualités fpl. ◆**newsworthy** a digne de faire l'objet d'un reportage. ◆**newsy** a (-ier, -iest) Fam plein de nouvelles.

newt [njuːt] n (animal) triton m.

New Zealand [njuːˈziːlənd] n Nouvelle-Zélande f; – a néo-zélandais. ◆**New Zealander** n Néo-Zélandais, -aise mf.

next [nekst] a prochain; (room, house) d'à-côté, voisin; (following) suivant; **n. month** (in the future) le mois prochain; **he returned the n. month** (in the past) il revint le mois suivant; **the n. day** le lendemain; **the n. morning** le lendemain matin; **within the n. ten days** d'ici (à) dix jours, dans un délai de dix jours; **(by) this time n. week** d'ici (à) la semaine prochaine; **from one year to the n.** d'une année à l'autre; **you're n.** c'est ton tour; **n. (please)!** (au) suivant!; **the n. thing to do is ...** ce qu'il faut faire ensuite c'est ...; **the n. size (up)** la taille au-dessus; **to live/etc n. door** habiter/etc à côté (**to** de); **n.-door neighbour/room** voisin m/pièce f d'à-côté; – n (in series etc) suivant, -ante mf; – adv (afterwards) ensuite, après; (now) maintenant; **when you come in.** la prochaine fois que tu viendras; **the n. best solution** la seconde solution; – prep n. **to** (beside) à côté de; **n. to nothing** presque rien.

NHS [eneɪtʃˈes] abbr = National Health Service.

nib [nɪb] n (of pen) plume f, bec m.

nibble ['nɪb(ə)l] vti (eat) grignoter; (bite) mordiller.

nice [naɪs] a (-er, -est) (pleasant) agréable; (charming) charmant, gentil; (good) bon; (fine) beau; (pretty) joli; (kind) gentil (**to** avec); (respectable) bien inv; (subtle) délicat; **it's n. here** c'est bien ici; **n. and easy/warm/etc** (very) bien facile/chaud/etc. ◆**n.-'looking** a beau, joli. ◆**nicely** adv agréablement; (kindly) gentiment; (well) bien. ◆**niceties** ['naɪsətɪz] npl (pleasant things) agréments mpl; (subtleties) subtilités fpl.

niche [niːʃ, nɪtʃ] n **1** (recess) niche f. **2** (job) (bonne) situation f; (direction) voie f; **to make a n. for oneself** faire son trou.

nick [nɪk] n **1** (on skin, wood) entaille f; (in blade, crockery) brèche f. **2** n (prison) Sl taule f; – vt (steal, arrest) Sl piquer. **3** n in **the n. of time** juste à temps; **in good n.** Sl en bon état.

nickel ['nɪk(ə)l] n (metal) nickel m; (coin) Am pièce f de cinq cents.

nickname ['nɪkneɪm] n (informal name) surnom m; (short form) diminutif m; – vt surnommer.

nicotine ['nɪkətiːn] n nicotine f.

niece [niːs] n nièce f.

nifty ['nɪftɪ] a (-ier, -iest) (stylish) chic inv; (skilful) habile; (fast) rapide.

Nigeria [naɪˈdʒɪərɪə] n Nigéria m or f. ◆**Nigerian** a & n nigérian, -ane (mf).

niggardly ['nɪgədlɪ] a (person) avare; (amount) mesquin.

niggling ['nɪglɪŋ] a (trifling) insignifiant; (irksome) irritant; (doubt) persistant.

night [naɪt] n nuit f; (evening) soir m; Th soirée f; **last n.** (evening) hier soir; (night) la nuit dernière; **to have an early/late n.** se coucher tôt/tard; **to have a good n.** (sleep well) bien dormir; **first n.** Th première f; – a (work etc) de nuit; (life) nocturne; **n. school** cours mpl du soir; **n. watchman** veilleur m de nuit. ◆**nightcap** n (drink) boisson f (alcoolisée ou chaude prise avant de se coucher). ◆**nightclub** n boîte f de nuit. ◆**nightdress** n, ◆**nightgown** n, Fam ◆**nightie** n (woman's) chemise f de nuit. ◆**nightfall** n at **n.** à la tombée de la nuit. ◆**nightlight** n veilleuse f. ◆**nighttime** n nuit f.

nightingale ['naɪtɪŋgeɪl] n rossignol m.

nightly ['naɪtlɪ] adv chaque nuit or soir; – a de chaque nuit or soir.

nil [nɪl] n (nothing) & Sp zéro m; **the risk/result/etc is n.** le risque/résultat/etc est nul.

nimble ['nɪmb(ə)l] a (-er, -est) agile.

nincompoop ['nɪŋkəmpuːp] *n Fam* imbécile *mf*.

nine [naɪn] *a & n* neuf (*m*). ◆**nine'teen** *a & n* dix-neuf (*m*). ◆**nine'teenth** *a & n* dix-neuvième (*mf*). ◆**ninetieth** *a & n* quatre-vingt-dixième (*mf*). ◆**ninety** *a & n* quatre-vingt-dix (*m*). ◆**ninth** *a & n* neuvième (*mf*); **a n. une neuvième**.

nip [nɪp] **1** *vt* (-pp-) (*pinch, bite*) pincer; **to n. in the bud** *Fig* étouffer dans l'œuf; − *n* pinçon *m*; **there's a n. in the air** ça pince. **2** *vi* (-pp-) (*dash*) **to n. round** courir ou faire un saut chez qn; **to n. in/out** entrer/sortir un instant.

nipper ['nɪpər] *n* (*child*) *Fam* gosse *mf*.

nipple ['nɪp(ə)l] *n* bout *m* de sein, mamelon *m*; (*teat on bottle*) *Am* tétine *f*.

nippy ['nɪpɪ] *a* **1** (-ier, -iest) (*chilly*) frais; **it's n.** (*weather*) ça pince. **2 to be n.** (*about it*) (*quick*) *Fam* faire vite.

nit [nɪt] *n* **1** (*fool*) *Fam* idiot, -ote *mf*. **2** (*of louse*) lente *f*. ◆**nitwit** *n* (*fool*) *Fam* idiot, -ote *mf*.

nitrogen ['naɪtrədʒən] *n* azote *m*.

nitty-gritty [nɪtɪ'grɪtɪ] *n* **to get down to the n.-gritty** *Fam* en venir au fond du problème.

no [nəʊ] *adv & n* non (*m inv*); **no! non!; no more than** *or* **ten/a kilo/etc** pas plus de dix/d'un kilo/*etc*; **no more time/***etc* plus de temps/*etc*; **I have no more time** je n'ai plus de temps; **no more than you** pas plus que vous; **you can do no better** tu ne peux pas faire mieux; **the noes** *Pol* les non; − *a* aucun(e); pas de; **I've (got)** *or* **I have no idea** je n'ai aucune idée; **no child came** aucun enfant n'est venu; **I've (got)** *or* **I have no time/***etc* je n'ai pas de temps/*etc*; **of no importance/value/***etc* sans importance/valeur/*etc*; **with no gloves/***etc* on sans gants/*etc*; **there's no knowing** . . . impossible de savoir . . . ; **'no smoking'** 'défense de fumer'; **no way!** *Am Fam* pas question!; **no one = nobody**.

noble ['nəʊb(ə)l] *a* (-er, -est) noble; (*building*) majestueux. ◆**nobleman** *n* (*pl* -men) noble *m*. ◆**noblewoman** *n* (*pl* -women) noble *f*. ◆**no'bility** *n* (*character, class*) noblesse *f*.

nobody ['nəʊbɒdɪ] *pron* (ne) . . . personne; **n. came** personne n'est venu; **he knows n.** il ne connaît personne; **n.!** personne!; − *n a* **n.** une nullité.

nocturnal [nɒk'tɜːn(ə)l] *a* nocturne.

nod [nɒd] **1** *vti* (-dd-) **to n. (one's head)** incliner la tête, faire un signe de tête; − *n*

inclination *f* ou signe *m* de tête. **2** *vi* (-dd-) **to n. off** (*go to sleep*) s'assoupir.

noise [nɔɪz] *n* bruit *m*; (*of bell, drum*) son *m*; **to make a n.** faire du bruit. ◆**noisily** *adv* bruyamment. ◆**noisy** *a* (-ier, -iest) (*person, street etc*) bruyant.

nomad ['nəʊmæd] *n* nomade *mf*. ◆**no'madic** *a* nomade.

nominal ['nɒmɪn(ə)l] *a* (*value, fee etc*) nominal; (*head, ruler*) de nom.

nominate ['nɒmɪneɪt] *vt Pol* désigner, proposer (**for** comme candidat à); (*appoint*) désigner, nommer. ◆**nomi'nation** *n* désignation *f* ou proposition *f* de candidat; (*appointment*) nomination *f*. ◆**nomi'nee** *n* (*candidate*) candidat *m*.

non- [nɒn] *pref* non-.

nonchalant ['nɒnʃələnt] *a* nonchalant.

noncommissioned [nɒnkə'mɪʃ(ə)nd] *a* **n. officer** *Mil* sous-officier *m*.

non-committal [nɒnkə'mɪt(ə)l] *a* (*answer, person*) évasif.

nonconformist [nɒnkən'fɔːmɪst] *a & n* non-conformiste (*mf*).

nondescript ['nɒndɪskrɪpt] *a* indéfinissable; *Pej* médiocre.

none [nʌn] *pron* aucun(e) *mf*; (*in filling a form*) néant; **n. of them** aucun d'eux; **she has n.** (**at all**) elle n'en a pas (du tout); **n.** (**at all**) **came** pas une(e) seul(e) n'est venu(e); **n. can tell** personne ne peut le dire; **n. of the cake/***etc* pas une seule partie du gâteau/*etc*; **n. of the trees/***etc* aucun arbre/*etc*, aucun des arbres/*etc*; **n. of it** *or* **this** rien (de ceci); − *adv* **n. too hot/***etc* pas tellement chaud/*etc*; **he's n. the happier/wiser/***etc* il n'en est pas plus heureux/sage/*etc*; **n. the less** néanmoins. ◆**nonethe'less** *adv* néanmoins.

nonentity [nɒ'nentɪtɪ] *n* (*person*) nullité *f*.

non-existent [nɒnɪg'zɪstənt] *a* inexistant.

non-fiction [nɒn'fɪkʃ(ə)n] *n* littérature *f* non-romanesque; (*in library*) ouvrages *mpl* généraux.

non-flammable [nɒn'flæməb(ə)l] *a* ininflammable.

nonplus [nɒn'plʌs] *vt* (-ss-) dérouter.

nonsense ['nɒnsəns] *n* absurdités *fpl*; **that's n.** c'est absurde. ◆**non'sensical** *a* absurde.

non-smoker [nɒn'sməʊkər] *n* (*person*) non-fumeur, -euse *mf*; (*compartment*) *Rail* compartiment *m* non-fumeurs.

non-stick [nɒn'stɪk] *a* (*pan*) anti-adhésif, qui n'attache pas.

non-stop [nɒn'stɒp] *a* sans arrêt; (*train,*

flight) direct; – *adv* (*to work etc*) sans arrêt; (*to fly*) sans escale.

noodles ['nuːd(ə)lz] *npl* nouilles *fpl*; (*in soup*) vermicelle(s) *m(pl)*.

nook [nʊk] *n* coin *m*; **in every n. and cranny** dans tous les coins (et recoins).

noon [nuːn] *n* midi *m*; **at n.** à midi; – *a* (*sun etc*) de midi.

noose [nuːs] *n* (*loop*) nœud *m* coulant; (*of hangman*) corde *f*.

nor [nɔːr] *conj* ni; **neither you n. me** ni toi ni moi; **she neither drinks n. smokes** elle ne fume ni ne boit; **n. do I, n. can I** *etc* (ni) moi non plus; **n. will I (go)** je n'y irai pas non plus.

norm [nɔːm] *n* norme *f*.

normal ['nɔːm(ə)l] *a* normal; – *n* **above n.** au-dessus de la normale. ◆**nor'mality** *n* normalité *f*. ◆**normalize** *vt* normaliser. ◆**normally** *adv* normalement.

Norman ['nɔːmən] *a* normand.

north [nɔːθ] *n* nord *m*; – *a* (*coast*) nord *inv*; (*wind*) du nord; **to be n. of** être au nord de; **N. America/Africa** Amérique *f*/Afrique *f* du Nord; **N. American,** -aine (*mf*); – *adv* au nord, vers le nord. ◆**northbound** *a* (*carriageway*) nord *inv*; (*traffic*) en direction du nord. ◆**north-'east** *n* & *a* nord-est *m* & *a inv*. ◆**northerly** *a* (*point*) nord *inv*; (*direction, wind*) du nord. ◆**northern** *a* (*coast*) nord *inv*; (*town*) du nord; **N. France** le Nord de la France; **N. Europe** Europe *f* du Nord; **N. Ireland** Irlande *f* du Nord. ◆**northerner** *n* habitant, -ante *mf* du nord. ◆**northward(s)** *a* & *adv* vers le nord. ◆**north-'west** *n* & *a* nord-ouest *m* & *a inv*.

Norway ['nɔːweɪ] *n* Norvège *f*. ◆**Nor'wegian** *a* & *n* norvégien, -ienne (*mf*); – *n* (*language*) norvégien *m*.

nose [nəuz] *n* nez *m*; **her n. is bleeding** elle saigne du nez; **to turn one's n. up** *Fig* faire le dégoûté (**at** devant); – *vi* **to n. about** (*pry*) *Fam* fouiner. ◆**nosebleed** *n* saignement *m* de nez. ◆**nosedive** *n* *Av* piqué *m*; (*in prices*) chute *f*.

nos(e)y ['nəuzɪ] *a* (**-ier, -iest**) fouineur, indiscret; **n. parker** fouineur, -euse *mf*.

nosh [nɒʃ] *vi* *Fam* (*eat heavily*) bouffer; (*nibble*) grignoter (**entre les repas**); – *n* (*food*) *Fam* bouffe *f*.

nostalgia [nɒ'stældʒɪə] *n* nostalgie *f*. ◆**nostalgic** *a* nostalgique.

nostril ['nɒstr(ə)l] *n* (*of person*) narine *f*; (*of horse*) naseau *m*.

not [nɒt] *adv* **1** (ne) . . . pas; **he's n. there, he**

isn't there il n'est pas là; **n. yet** pas encore; **why n.?** pourquoi pas?; **n. one reply/etc** pas une seule réponse/*etc*; **n. at all** pas du tout; (*after 'thank you'*) je vous en prie. **2** non; **I think/hope n.** je pense/j'espère que non; **n. guilty** non coupable; **isn't she?, don't you?** *etc* non?

notable ['nəutəb(ə)l] *a* (*remarkable*) notable; – *n* (*person*) notable *m*. ◆**notably** *adv* (*noticeably*) notablement; (*particularly*) notamment.

notary ['nəutərɪ] *n* notaire *m*.

notation [nəu'teɪʃ(ə)n] *n* notation *f*.

notch [nɒtʃ] **1** *n* (*in wood etc*) entaille *f*, encoche *f*; (*in belt, wheel*) cran *m*. **2** *vt* **to n. up** (*a score*) marquer; (*a victory*) enregistrer.

note [nəut] *n* (*written comment, tone etc*) & *Mus* note *f*; (*summary, preface*) notice *f*; (*banknote*) billet *m*; (*piano key*) touche *f*; (*message, letter*) petit mot *m*; **to take (a) n. of, make a n. of** prendre note de; **of n.** (*athlete, book etc*) éminent; – *vt* (*take note of*) noter; (*notice*) remarquer, noter; **to n. down** noter. ◆**notebook** *n* carnet *m*; *Sch* cahier *m*; (*pad*) bloc-notes *m*. ◆**notepad** *n* bloc-notes *m*. ◆**notepaper** *n* papier *m* à lettres.

noted ['nəutɪd] *a* (*author etc*) éminent; **to be n. for** être connu pour.

noteworthy ['nəutwɜːðɪ] *a* notable.

nothing ['nʌθɪŋ] *pron* (ne) . . . rien; **he knows n.** il ne sait rien; **n. to do/eat/etc** rien à faire/manger/*etc*; **n. big/etc** rien de grand/*etc*; **n. much** pas grand-chose; **I've got n. to do with it** je n'y suis pour rien; **I can do n. (about it)** je n'y peux rien; **to come to n.** (*of effort etc*) ne rien donner; **there's n. like it** il n'y a rien de tel; **for n.** (*in vain, free of charge*) pour rien; – *adv* **to look n. like s.o.** ne ressembler nullement à qn; **n. like as large/etc** loin d'être aussi grand/*etc*; – *n* *a* (*mere*) **n.** (*person*) une nullité; (*thing*) un rien. ◆**-ness** *n* (*void*) néant *m*.

notice ['nəutɪs] *n* (*notification*) avis *m*; *Journ* annonce *f*; (*sign*) pancarte *f*, écriteau *m*; (*poster*) affiche *f*; (*review of film etc*) critique *f*; (*attention*) attention *f*; (*knowledge*) connaissance *f*; (*advance*) **n.** (*of departure etc*) préavis *m*; **to n. (to quit), n.** (*of dismissal*) congé *m*; **to give (in) one's n.** (*resignation*) donner sa démission; **to give s.o. n. of** (*inform of*) avertir qn de; **to take n.** faire attention (**of** à); **to bring sth to s.o.'s n.** porter qch à la connaissance de qn; **until further n.** jusqu'à nouvel ordre; **at short n.** à bref délai; **n. board** tableau *m* d'affichage; – *vt* (*perceive*) remarquer (*qn*); (*fact, trick, danger*) s'apercevoir de; **I n. that** je m'aperçois que. ◆**-able** *a* visible, perceptible; **that's n.** ça se voit; **she's n.** elle se fait remarquer.

notify ['nəʊtɪfaɪ] *vt* (*inform*) aviser (*s.o. of sth* qn de qch); (*announce*) notifier (**to** à). ◆**notifi'cation** *n* annonce *f*, avis *m*.

notion ['nəʊʃ(ə)n] **1** *n* (*thought*) idée *f*; (*awareness*) notion *f*; **some n. of** (*knowledge*) quelques notions de. **2** *npl* (*sewing articles*) *Am* mercerie *f*.

notorious [nəʊ'tɔːrɪəs] *a* (*event, person etc*) tristement célèbre; (*stupidity, criminal*) notoire. ◆**notoriety** [-ə'raɪətɪ] *n* (triste) notoriété *f*.

notwithstanding [nɒtwɪð'stændɪŋ] *prep* malgré; – *adv* tout de même.

nougat ['nuːɡɑː, 'nʌɡət] *n* nougat *m*.

nought [nɔːt] *n Math* zéro *m*.

noun [naʊn] *n Gram* nom *m*.

nourish ['nʌrɪʃ] *vt* nourrir. ◆**-ing** *a* nourrissant. ◆**-ment** *n* nourriture *f*.

novel ['nɒv(ə)l] **1** *n Liter* roman *m*. **2** *a* (*new*) nouveau, original. ◆**novelist** *n* romancier, -ière *mf*. ◆**novelty** *n* (*newness, object, idea*) nouveauté *f*.

November [nəʊ'vembər] *n* novembre *m*.

novice ['nɒvɪs] *n* novice *mf* (**at** en).

now [naʊ] *adv* maintenant; **just n., right n.** en ce moment; **I saw her just n.** je l'ai vue à l'instant; **for n.** pour le moment; **even n.** encore maintenant; **from n. on** désormais, à partir de maintenant; **until n., up to n.** jusqu'ici; **before n.** avant; **n. and then** de temps à autre; **n. hot, n. cold** tantôt chaud, tantôt froid; **n. (then)!** bon!, alors!; (*telling s.o. off*) allons!; **n. it happened that . . .** or il advint que . . . ; – *conj* **n. (that)** maintenant que. ◆**nowadays** *adv Am* aujourd'hui, de nos jours.

noway ['nəʊweɪ] *adv Am* nullement.

nowhere ['nəʊweər] *adv* nulle part; **n. else** nulle part ailleurs; **it's n. I know** ce n'est pas un endroit que je connais; **n. near the house** loin de la maison; **n. near enough** loin d'être assez.

nozzle ['nɒz(ə)l] *n* (*of hose*) jet *m*, lance *f* (à eau); (*of syringe, tube*) embout *m*.

nth [enθ] *a* nième.

nuance ['njuːɑːns] *n* (*of meaning, colour etc*) nuance *f*.

nub [nʌb] *n* (*of problem*) cœur *m*.

nuclear ['njuːklɪər] *a* nucléaire; **n. scientist** spécialiste *mf* du nucléaire, atomiste *mf*.

nucleus, *pl* **-clei** ['njuːklɪəs, -klɪaɪ] *n* noyau *m*.

nude [njuːd] *a* nu; – *n* (*female or male figure*) nu *m*; **in the n.** (tout) nu. ◆**nudism** *n* nudisme *m*, naturisme *m*. ◆**nudist** *n* nudiste *mf*, naturiste *mf*; – *a* (*camp*) de nudistes, de naturistes. ◆**nudity** *n* nudité *f*.

nudge [nʌdʒ] *vt* pousser du coude; – *n* coup *m* de coude.

nugget ['nʌɡɪt] *n* (*of gold etc*) pépite *f*.

nuisance ['njuːs(ə)ns] *n* (*annoyance*) embêtement *m*; (*person*) peste *f*; **that's a n.** c'est embêtant; **he's being a n., he's making a n. of himself** il nous embête, il m'embête *etc*.

null [nʌl] *a* **n. (and void)** nul (et non avenu). ◆**nullify** *vt* infirmer.

numb [nʌm] *a* (*stiff*) engourdi; *Fig* paralysé; – *vt* engourdir; *Fig* paralyser.

number ['nʌmbər] *n* nombre *m*; (*of page, house, newspaper etc*) numéro *m*; **a dance/song n.** un numéro de danse/de chant; **a/any n. of** un certain/grand nombre de; **n. plate** (*of vehicle*) plaque *f* d'immatriculation; – *vt* (*page etc*) numéroter; (*include, count*) compter; **they're eight in n.** ils sont au nombre de huit. ◆**-ing** *n* numérotage *m*.

numeral ['njuːm(ə)rəl] *n* chiffre *m*; – *a* numéral. ◆**nu'merical** *a* numérique. ◆**numerous** *a* nombreux.

numerate ['njuːm(ə)rət] *a* (*person*) qui sait compter.

nun [nʌn] *n* religieuse *f*.

nurs/e [nɜːs] **1** *n* infirmière *f*; (*nanny*) nurse *f*; (*male*) **n.** infirmier *m*. **2** *vt* (*look after*) soigner; (*cradle*) bercer; (*suckle*) nourrir; (*a grudge etc*) *Fig* nourrir; (*support, encourage*) *Fig* épauler (*qn*). ◆**-ing** *a* (*mother*) qui allaite; (*staff*) soignant; – *n* (*care*) soins *mpl*; (*job*) profession *f* d'infirmière or d'infirmier; **home nursing** clinique *f*. ◆**nursemaid** *n* bonne *f* d'enfants.

nursery ['nɜːsərɪ] *n* (*room*) chambre *f* d'enfants; (*for plants, trees*) pépinière *f*; **(day) n.** (*school etc*) crèche *f*, garderie *f*; **n. rhyme** chanson *f* enfantine; **n. school** école *f* maternelle.

nurture ['nɜːtʃər] *vt* (*educate*) éduquer.

nut¹ [nʌt] *n* (*fruit*) fruit *m* à coque; (*walnut*) noix *f*; (*hazelnut*) noisette *f*; (*peanut*) cacah(o)uète *f*; **Brazil/cashew n.** noix *f* du Brésil/de cajou. ◆**nutcracker(s)** *n(pl)* casse-noix *m inv*. ◆**nutshell** *n* coquille *f* de noix; **in a n.** *Fig* en un mot.

nut² [nʌt] *n* **1** (*for bolt*) *Tech* écrou *m*. **2**

(head) *Sl* caboche *f.* **3** *(person)* *Sl* cinglé, -ée *mf*; **to be nuts** *Sl* être cinglé. ◆**nutcase** *n* cinglé, -ée *mf.* ◆**nutty** *a* (**-ier, -iest**) *Sl* cinglé.

nutmeg ['nʌtmeg] *n* muscade *f.*

nutritious [njuːˈtrɪʃəs] *a* nutritif. ◆**'nutri-**

ent *n* élément *m* nutritif. ◆**nutrition** *n* nutrition *f.*

nylon ['naɪlɒn] *n* nylon *m*; *pl* (*stockings*) bas *mpl* nylon.

nymph [nɪmf] *n* nymphe *f.* ◆**nympho-**
'maniac *n* Pej nymphomane *f.*

O

O, o [əu] *n* O, o *m.*

oaf [əuf] *n* rustre *m.* ◆**oafish** *a* (*behaviour*) de rustre.

oak [əuk] *n* (*tree, wood*) chêne *m.*

OAP [əueɪˈpiː] *n abbr* (*old age pensioner*) retraité, -ée *mf.*

oar [ɔːr] *n* aviron *m*, rame *f.*

oasis, *pl* **oases** [əuˈeɪsɪs, əuˈeɪsiːz] *n* oasis *f.*

oath [əuθ] *n* (*pl* **-s** [əuðz]) (*promise*) serment *m*; (*profanity*) juron *m*; **to take an o. to do** faire le serment de faire.

oats [əuts] *npl* avoine *f.* ◆**oatmeal** *n* flocons *mpl* d'avoine.

obedient [əˈbiːdɪənt] *a* obéissant. ◆**obe-**
dience *n* obéissance *f* (to à). ◆**obediently** *adv* docilement.

obelisk ['ɒbəlɪsk] *n* (*monument*) obélisque *m.*

obese [əuˈbiːs] *a* obèse. ◆**obesity** *n* obésité *f.*

obey [əˈbeɪ] *vt* obéir à; **to be obeyed** être obéi; *– vi* obéir.

obituary [əˈbɪtjuərɪ] *n* nécrologie *f.*

object¹ ['ɒbdʒɪkt] *n* (*thing*) objet *m*; (*aim*) but *m*, objet *m*; *Gram* complément *m* (d'objet); **with the o. of** dans le but de; **that's no o.** (*no problem*) ça ne pose pas de problème; **price no o.** prix *m* indifférent.

object² [əbˈdʒekt] *vt* **to o. to sth/s.o.** désap-prouver qch/qn; **I o. to you(r) doing that** ça me gêne que tu fasses ça; **I o.!** je proteste!; **she didn't o. when . . .** elle n'a fait aucune objection quand . . . ; *– vt* **to o. that** objecter que. ◆**objection** *n* objection *f*; **I've got no o.** ça ne me gêne pas, je n'y vois pas d'objection *or* d'inconvénient. ◆**objectionable** *a* très désagréable. ◆**objector** *n* opposant, -ante *mf* (to à); **conscientious o.** objecteur *m* de conscience. **objective** [əbˈdʒektɪv] **1** *a* (*opinion etc*) objectif. **2** *n* (*aim, target*) objectif *m.* ◆**objectively** *adv* objectivement. ◆**ob-**
jec'tivity *n* objectivité *f.*

obligate ['ɒblɪgeɪt] *vt* contraindre (**to do** à faire). ◆**obli'gation** *n* obligation *f*; (*debt*) dette *f*; **under an o. to do** dans l'obligation de faire; **under an o. to s.o.** redevable à qn (**for** de). ◆**o'bligatory** *a* (*compulsory*) obligatoire; (*imposed by custom*) de rigueur.

oblig/e [əˈblaɪdʒ] *vt* **1** (*compel*) obliger (**s.o. to do** qn à faire); **obliged to do** obligé de faire. **2** (*help*) rendre service à, faire plaisir à; **obliged to s.o.** reconnaissant à qn (**for** de); **much obliged!** merci infiniment! *—ing* *a* (*kind*) obligeant. ◆**—ingly** *adv* obligeamment.

oblique [əˈbliːk] *a* oblique; (*reference*) Fig indirect.

obliterate [əˈblɪtəreɪt] *vt* effacer. ◆**oblite-**
'ration *n* effacement *m.*

oblivion [əˈblɪvɪən] *n* oubli *m.* ◆**oblivious** *a* inconscient (**to, of** de).

oblong ['ɒblɒŋ] *a* (*elongated*) oblong; (*rectangular*) rectangulaire; *– n* rectangle *m.*

obnoxious [əbˈnɒkʃəs] *a* odieux; (*smell*) nauséabond.

oboe ['əubəu] *n* Mus hautbois *m.*

obscene [əbˈsiːn] *a* obscène. ◆**obscenity** *n* obscénité *f.*

obscure [əbˈskjuər] *a* (*reason, word, actor, life etc*) obscur; *– vt* (*hide*) cacher; (*confuse*) embrouiller, obscurcir. ◆**obscurely** *adv* obscurément. ◆**obscurity** *n* obscurité *f.*

obsequious [əbˈsiːkwɪəs] *a* obséquieux.

observe [əbˈzɜːv] *vt* (*notice, watch, respect*) observer; (*say*) (faire) remarquer (**that** que); **to o. the speed limit** respecter la limi-tation de vitesse. ◆**observance** *n* (*of rule etc*) observation *f.* ◆**observant** *a* observateur. ◆**obser'vation** *n* (*observing, remark*) observation *f*; (*by police*) surveil-lance *f*; **under o.** (*hospital patient*) en obser-

vation. ◆**observatory** n observatoire m.
◆**observer** n observateur, -trice mf.

obsess [əb'ses] vt obséder. ◆**obsession** n obsession f; **to have an o. with** or **about** avoir l'obsession de. ◆**obsessive** a (memory, idea) obsédant; (fear) obsessif; (neurotic) Psy obsessionnel; **to be o. about** avoir l'obsession de.

obsolete ['ɒbsəliːt] a (out of date, super-seded) désuet, dépassé; (ticket) périmé; (machinery) archaïque. ◆**obso'lescent** a quelque peu désuet; (word) vieilli.

obstacle ['ɒbstək(ə)l] n obstacle m.

obstetrics [əb'stetrɪks] n Med obstétrique f. ◆**obste'trician** n médecin m accoucheur.

obstinate ['ɒbstɪnət] a (person, resistance etc) obstiné, opiniâtre; (disease, pain) rebelle, opiniâtre. ◆**obstinacy** n obstination f. ◆**obstinately** adv obstinément.

obstreperous [əb'strepərəs] a turbulent.

obstruct [əb'strʌkt] vt (block) boucher; (hinder) entraver; (traffic) entraver, bloquer. ◆**obstruction** n (act, state) & Med Pol Sp obstruction f; (obstacle) obstacle m; (in pipe) bouchon m; (traffic jam) embouteillage m. ◆**obstructive** a to be o. faire de l'obstruction.

obtain [əb'teɪn] 1 vt obtenir. 2 vi (of practice etc) avoir cours. ◆—**able** a (available) disponible; (on sale) en vente.

obtrusive [əb'truːsɪv] a (person) importun; (building etc) trop en évidence.

obtuse [əb'tjuːs] a (angle, mind) obtus.

obviate ['ɒbvɪeɪt] vt (necessity) éviter.

obvious ['ɒbvɪəs] a évident; **he's the o. man to see** c'est évidemment l'homme qu'il faut voir. ◆—**ly** adv (evidently, of course) évidemment; (conspicuously) visiblement.

occasion [ə'keɪʒ(ə)n] **1** n (time, opportunity) occasion f; (event, ceremony) événement m; **on the o. of** à l'occasion de; **on o.** à l'occasion; **on several occasions** à plusieurs reprises or occasions. **2** n (cause) raison f, occasion f; – vt occasionner. ◆**occasional** a (event) qui a lieu de temps en temps; (rain, showers) intermittent; **she drinks the o. whisky** elle boit un whisky de temps en temps. ◆**occasionally** adv de temps en temps; **very o.** très peu souvent, rarement.

occult [ə'kʌlt] a occulte.

occupy ['ɒkjʊpaɪ] vt (house, time, space, post etc) occuper; **to keep oneself occupied** s'occuper (doing à faire). ◆**occupant** n (inhabitant) occupant, -ante mf. ◆**occu-'pation** n (activity) occupation f; (job) emploi m; (trade) métier m; (profession)

profession f; **the o. of** (action) l'occupation f de; **fit for o.** (house) habitable. ◆**occu-'pational** a (hazard) du métier; (disease) du travail. ◆**occupier** n (of house) occupant, -ante mf; Mil occupant m.

occur [ə'kɜːr] vi (-rr-) (happen) avoir lieu; (be found) se rencontrer; (arise) se présenter; **it occurs to me that...** il me vient à l'esprit que...; **the idea occurred to her to...** l'idée lui est venue de.... ◆**occurrence** [ə'kʌrəns] n (event) événement m; (existence) existence f; (of word) Ling occurrence f.

ocean ['əʊʃ(ə)n] n océan m. ◆**oce'anic** a océanique.

o'clock [ə'klɒk] adv (it's) three **o'c.**/etc (il est) trois heures/etc.

octagon ['ɒktəgən] n octogone m. ◆**oc'tagonal** a octogonal.

octave ['ɒktɪv, 'ɒkteɪv] n Mus octave f.

October [ɒk'təʊbər] n octobre m.

octogenarian [ɒktəʊdʒɪneərɪən] n octogé-naire mf.

octopus ['ɒktəpəs] n pieuvre f.

odd [ɒd] a **1** (strange) bizarre, curieux; **an o. size** une taille peu courante. **2** (number) impair. **3** (left over) **I have an o. penny** il me reste un penny; **a few o. stamps** quelques timbres (qui restent); **the o. man out, the o. one out** l'exception f; **sixty o.** soixante et quelques; **an o. glove/book**/etc un gant/livre/etc dépareillé. **4** (occasional) qu'on fait, voit etc de temps en temps; **to find the o. mistake** trouver de temps en temps une (petite) erreur; **at o. moments** de temps en temps; **o. jobs** (around house) menus travaux mpl; **o. job man** homme m à tout faire. ◆**oddity** n (person) personne f bizarre; (object) curiosité f; pl (of language, situation) bizarreries fpl. ◆**oddly** adv bizarrement; **o. (enough), he was...** chose curieuse, il était.... ◆**oddment** n Com fin f de série. ◆**oddness** n bizarrerie f.

odds [ɒdz] npl **1** (in betting) cote f; (chances) chances fpl; **we have heavy o. against us** nous avons très peu de chances de réussir. **2 it makes no o.** (no difference) Fam ça ne fait rien. **3 at o.** (in disagreement) en désac-cord (with avec). **4 o. and ends** des petites choses.

ode [əʊd] n (poem) ode f.

odious ['əʊdɪəs] a détestable, odieux.

odour ['əʊdər] n odeur f. ◆—**less** a inodore.

oecumenical [iːkjʊ'menɪk(ə)l] a Rel œcuménique.

of [əv, stressed ɒv] prep de; **of the table** de la

table; **of the boy** du garçon; **of the boys** des garçons; **of a book** d'un livre; **of it, of them** en; **she has a lot of it** *or* **of them** elle en a beaucoup; **a friend of his** un ami à lui; **there are ten of us** nous sommes dix; **that's nice of you** c'est gentil de ta part; **of no value/interest/***etc* sans valeur/intérêt/*etc*; **of late** ces derniers temps; **a man of fifty** un homme de cinquante ans; **the fifth of June** le cinq juin.

off [ɒf] **1** *adv* (*absent*) absent, parti; (*light, gas, radio etc*) éteint, fermé; (*tap*) fermé; (*switched off at mains*) coupé; (*detached*) détaché, (*removed*) enlevé; (*cancelled*) annulé; (*not fit to eat or drink*) mauvais; (*milk, meat*) tourné; **2 km** à 2 km (*d'ici or* de là), éloigné de 2 km; **to be** ou **go o.** (*leave*) partir; **where are you o. to?** où vas-tu?; **he has his hat o.** il a enlevé son chapeau; **with his, my** *etc* **gloves o.** sans gants; **a day o.** (*holiday*) un jour de congé; **I'm o. today, I have today o.** j'ai congé aujourd'hui; **the strike's o.** il n'y aura pas de grève, la grève est annulée; **5% o.** une réduction de 5%; **on and o., o. and on** (*sometimes*) de temps à autre; **to be better o.** (*wealthier, in a better position*) être mieux. **2** *prep* (*from*) de; (*distant*) éloigné de; **to fall/***etc* **the wall/ladder/***etc* tomber/*etc* du mur/de l'échelle/*etc*; **to get o. the bus/***etc* descendre du bus/*etc*; **to take sth o. the table/***etc* prendre qch sur la table/*etc*; **to eat o. a plate** manger dans une assiette; **to keep** *or* **stay o. the grass** ne pas marcher sur les pelouses; **she's o. her food** elle ne mange plus rien; **o. Dover** Nau au large de Douvres/*etc*; **o. limits** interdit; **the o. side** Aut le côté droit, Am le côté gauche. ◆**off'beat** a excentrique. ◆**off-'colour** a (*ill*) patraque; (*indecent*) scabreux. ◆**off'hand** a désinvolte; – *adv* impromptu. ◆**off'handedness** n désinvolture f. ◆**off-licence** n magasin m de vins et de spiritueux. ◆**off-'load** vt (*vehicle etc*) décharger; **to o.-load sth onto s.o.** (*task etc*) se décharger de qch sur qn. ◆**off-'peak** a (*crowds, traffic*) aux heures creuses; (*rate, price*) heures creuses *inv*; **o.-peak hours** heures *fpl* creuses. ◆**off-putting** a Fam rebutant. ◆**off'side** a to be o. Fb être hors jeu. ◆**off-'stage** a & adv dans les coulisses. ◆**off-'white** a blanc cassé *inv*.

offal ['ɒf(ə)l] n Culin abats *mpl*.

offence [ə'fens] (Am **offense**) n Jur délit m; **to take o.** s'offenser (at de); **to give o.** offenser.

offend [ə'fend] vt froisser, offenser; (*eye*) Fig

choquer; **to be offended (at)** se froisser (de), s'offenser (de). ◆**—ing** a (*object, remark*) incriminé. ◆**offender** n Jur délinquant, -ante *mf*; (*habitual*) récidiviste *mf*.

offensive [ə'fensiv] **1** a (*unpleasant*) choquant, repoussant; (*insulting*) insultant, offensant; (*weapon*) offensif. **2** n Mil offensive f.

offer ['ɒfər] n offre f; **on** (*special*) **o.** Com en promotion, en réclame; **o. of marriage** demande f en mariage; – vt offrir; (*opinion, remark*) proposer; **to o. to do** offrir *or* proposer de faire. ◆**—ing** n (*gift*) offrande f; (*act*) offre f; **peace o.** cadeau m de réconciliation.

office ['ɒfɪs] n **1** bureau m; (*of doctor*) Am cabinet m; (*of lawyer*) étude f; **head o.** siège m central; **o. block** immeuble m de bureaux; **o. worker** employé, -ée *mf* de bureau. **2** (*post*) fonction f; (*duty*) fonctions *fpl*; **in o.** (*of party etc*) Pol au pouvoir. **3** one's good offices (*help*) ses bons offices *mpl*. ◆**officer** n (*in army, navy etc*) officier m; (*of company*) Com directeur, -trice *mf*; (*police*) **o.** agent m (de police).

official [ə'fɪʃ(ə)l] a (*uniform*) règlementaire; – n (*person of authority*) officiel m; (*civil servant*) fonctionnaire *mf*; (*employee*) employé, -ée *mf*. ◆**officialdom** n bureaucratie f. ◆**officially** adv officiellement. ◆**officiate** vi faire fonction d'officiel (at à); (*preside*) présider; Rel officier.

officious [ə'fɪʃəs] a Pej empressé.

offing ['ɒfɪŋ] n **in the o.** en perspective.

offset ['ɒfset, ɒf'set] vt (*pt & pp* offset, *pres p* offsetting) (*compensate for*) compenser; (*s.o.'s beauty etc by contrast*) faire ressortir.

offshoot ['ɒfʃuɪt] n (*of firm*) ramification f; (*consequence*) conséquence f.

offspring ['ɒfsprɪŋ] n progéniture f.

often ['ɒf(t)ən] adv souvent; **how o.?** combien de fois?; **how o. do they run?** (*trains, buses etc*) il y en a tous les combien?; **once too o.** une fois de trop; **every so o.** de temps en temps.

ogle ['əʊg(ə)l] vt Pej reluquer.

ogre ['əʊgər] n ogre m.

oh! [əʊ] int oh!, ah!; (*pain*) aïe!; **oh yes?** ah oui?, ah bon?

oil [ɔɪl] n (*for machine, in cooking etc*) huile f; (*mineral*) pétrole m; (*fuel oil*) mazout m; **to paint in oils** faire de la peinture à l'huile; – a (*industry, product*) pétrolier; (*painting, paints*) à l'huile; **o. lamp** lampe f à pétrole *or* à huile; **o. change** Aut vidange f; – vt

graisser, huiler. ◆**oilcan** n burette f.
◆**oilfield** n gisement m pétrolifère. ◆**oil-
fired** a au mazout. ◆**oilskin(s)** n(pl)
(garment) ciré m. ◆**oily** a (-ier, -iest)
(substance, skin) huileux; (hands) graisseux; (food) gras.

ointment ['ɔɪntmənt] n pommade f.

OK [əʊ'keɪ] int (approval, exasperation) ça
va!; (agreement) d'accord!, entendu!; OK!;
– a (satisfactory) bien inv; (unharmed) sain
et sauf; (undamaged) intact; (without
worries) tranquille; **it's OK now** (fixed) ça
marche maintenant; **I'm OK** (healthy) je
vais bien; – adv (to work etc) bien; – vt (pt
& pp **OKed**, pres p **OKing**) approuver.

okay [əʊ'keɪ] = **OK**.

old [əʊld] a (-er, -est) vieux; (former)
ancien; **how o. is he?** quel âge a-t-il?; **he's
ten years o.** il a dix ans, il est âgé de dix
ans; **he's older than** il est plus âgé que; **an
older son** un fils aîné; **the oldest son** le fils
aîné; **o. enough to** assez grand pour
faire; **o. enough to marry/vote** en âge de se
marier/de voter; **an o. man** un vieillard, un
vieil homme; **an o. woman** une vieille
(femme); **to get** or **grow old(er)** vieillir; **o.
age** vieillesse f; **the O. Testament** l'Ancien
Testament; **the O. World** l'Ancien Monde;
any o. how Fam n'importe comment; – n
the o. (people) les vieux mpl. ◆**o.-
'fashioned** a (customs etc) d'autrefois;
(idea, attitude) Pej vieux jeu inv; (person)
de la vieille école, Pej vieux jeu inv.
◆**o.-'timer** n (old man) Fam vieillard m.

olden ['əʊld(ə)n] a in o. days jadis.

olive ['ɒlɪv] n (fruit) olive f; – a (green)
(vert) olive inv; **o. oil** huile f d'olive; **o. tree**
olivier m.

Olympic [ə'lɪmpɪk] a olympique.

ombudsman ['ɒmbʊdzmən] n (pl -men)
Pol médiateur m.

omelet(te) ['ɒmlɪt] n omelette f; **cheese/etc
o.** omelette au fromage/etc.

omen ['əʊmən] n augure m. ◆**ominous** a
de mauvais augure; (tone) menaçant;
(noise) sinistre.

omit [əʊ'mɪt] vt (-tt-) omettre (**to do** de
faire). ◆**omission** n omission f.

omni- ['ɒmnɪ] pref omni-. ◆**om'nipotent**
a omnipotent.

on [ɒn] prep 1 (position) sur; **on the chair** sur
la chaise; **to put on (to)** mettre sur; **to look
out on to** donner sur. 2 (concerning, about)
sur; **an article on** un article sur; **to speak** or
talk on Dickens/etc parler sur Dickens/etc.
3 (manner, means) à; **on foot** à pied; **on the
blackboard** au tableau; **on the radio** à la

radio; **on the train/plane/etc** dans le
train/avion/etc; **on holiday**, Am **on vacation** en vacances; **to be on** (course) suivre;
(project) travailler à; (salary) toucher;
(team, committee) être membre de, faire
partie de; **to keep** or **stay on** (road, path etc)
suivre; **it's on me!** (I'll pay) Fam c'est moi
qui paie! 4 (time) on Monday lundi; **on
Mondays** le lundi; **on May 3rd** le 3 mai; **on
the evening of May 3rd** le 3 mai au soir; **on
my arrival** à mon arrivée. 5 (+ present
participle) en; **on learning that...** en
apprenant que...; **on seeing this** en
voyant ceci. 6 adv (ahead) en avant; (in
progress) en cours; (started) commencé;
(lid, brake) mis; (light, radio) allumé; (gas,
tap) ouvert; (machine) en marche; **on** (and
on) sans cesse; **to play/etc** on continuer à
jouer/etc; **she has her hat on** elle a mis or
elle porte son chapeau; **he has sth/nothing
on** il est habillé/tout nu; **I've got sth on**
(I'm busy) je suis pris; **the strike's on** la
grève aura lieu; **what's on?** TV qu'y a-t-il à
la télé?; Cin Th qu'est-ce qu'on joue?;
there's a film on on passe un film; **to be on
at s.o.** (pester) Fam être après qn; **I've been
on to him** Tel je l'ai eu au bout du fil; **to be
on to s.o.** (of police etc) être sur la piste de
qn; **from then on** à partir de là. ◆**on-
coming** a (vehicle) qui vient en sens
inverse. ◆**on-going** a en cours.

once [wʌns] adv (on one occasion) une fois;
(formerly) autrefois; **o. a month/etc** une
fois par mois/etc; **o. again, o. more** encore
une fois; **at o.** (immediately) tout de suite;
all at o. (suddenly) tout à coup; (at the same
time) à la fois; **o. and for all** une fois pour
toutes; – conj une fois que. ◆**o.-over** n **to
give sth the o.-over** (quick look) Fam
regarder qch d'un coup d'œil.

one [wʌn] a 1 un, une; **o. man** un homme; **o.
woman** une femme; **twenty-o., thirty-o.**
vingt et un, trente et un. 2 (sole) seul; **my o.
(and only) aim** mon seul (et unique) but. 3
(same) même; **in the o. bus** dans le même
bus; – pron 1 un, une; **do you want o.?** en
veux-tu (un)?; **he's o. of us** il est des nôtres;
o. of them l'un d'eux, l'une d'elles; **a
big/small/etc o.** un grand/petit/etc; **this
book is o.** that I've read ce livre est parmi
ceux que j'ai lus; **she's o.** (a teacher,
gardener etc) elle l'est; **this o.** celui-ci,
celle-ci; **that o.** celui-là, celle-là; **the o. who**
or **which** celui or celle qui; **it's Paul's o.**
Fam c'est celui de Paul; **it's my o.** Fam c'est à
moi; **another o.** un(e) autre; **I for o.** pour
ma part. 2 (impersonal) on; **o. knows** on
sait; **it helps o.** ça nous or vous aide; **one's**

family sa famille. ◆one-'armed a (*person*) manchot. ◆one-'eyed a borgne. ◆one-'off a, Am one-of-a-'kind a Fam unique, exceptionnel. ◆one-'sided a (*judgement etc*) partial; (*contest*) inégal; (*decision*) unilatéral. ◆one-time a (*former*) ancien. ◆one-'way a (*street*) à sens unique; (*traffic*) en sens unique; (*ticket*) Am simple.

oneself [wʌn'self] pron soi-même; (*reflexive*) se, s'; **to cut o.** se couper.

onion ['ʌnjən] n oignon m.

onlooker ['ɒnlʊkər] n spectateur, -trice mf.

only ['əʊnlɪ] a seul; **the o. house/etc** la seule maison/etc; **the o. one** le seul, la seule; **an o. son** son fils unique; – adv seulement, ne … que; **I have ten, I have ten o.** je n'en ai que dix, j'en ai dix seulement; **if o.** si seulement; **not o.** non seulement; **I have o. just seen it** je viens tout juste de le voir; **o. he knows** lui seul le sait; – conj (but) Fam seulement; **o. I can't** seulement je ne peux pas.

onset ['ɒnset] n (*of disease*) début m; (*of old age*) approche m.

onslaught ['ɒnslɔːt] n attaque f.

onto ['ɒntuː] prep = on to.

onus ['əʊnəs] n inv **the o. is on you/etc** c'est votre/etc responsabilité (**to do** de faire).

onward(s) ['ɒnwəd(z)] adv en avant; **from that time o.** à partir de là.

onyx ['ɒnɪks] n (*precious stone*) onyx m.

ooze [uːz] vi **to o.** (**out**) suinter; – vt (*blood etc*) laisser couler.

opal ['əʊp(ə)l] n (*precious stone*) opale f.

opaque [əʊ'peɪk] a opaque; (*unclear*) Fig obscur.

open ['əʊpən] a ouvert; (*site, view, road*) dégagé; (*car*) décapoté, découvert; (*meeting*) public; (*competition*) ouvert à tous; (*post*) vacant; (*attempt, envy*) manifeste; (*question*) non résolu; (*result*) indécis; (*ticket*) Av open inv; **wide o.** grand ouvert; **in the o. air** en plein air; **in (the) o.** country en rase campagne; **it's o. to doubt** c'est douteux; **it's o. to you to** il ne tient qu'à vous de; **to** (*criticism, attack*) exposé à; (*ideas, suggestions*) ouvert à; **I've got an o. mind on it** je n'ai pas d'opinion arrêtée là-dessus; **to leave o.** (*date*) ne pas préciser; – n (**out**) **in the o.** (*outside*) en plein air; **to sleep** (**out**) **in the o.** dormir à la belle étoile; **to bring** (**out**) **into the o.** (*reveal*) divulguer; – vt ouvrir; (*conversation*) entamer; (*legs*) écarter; **to o.** **out** or **up** ouvrir; – vi (*of flower, eyes etc*) s'ouvrir; (*of shop, office etc*) ouvrir; (*of play*) débuter; (*of film*) sortir; **the door opens** (*is*

opened) la porte s'ouvre; (*can open*) la porte ouvre; **to o. on to** (*of window etc*) donner sur; **to o.** **out** or **up** s'ouvrir; **to o.** **out** (*widen*) s'élargir; **to o. up** (*open a or the door*) ouvrir. ◆**—ing** n ouverture f; (*of flower*) éclosion f; (*career prospect, trade outlet*) débouché m; – a (*time, speech*) d'ouverture; **o. night** Th première f. ◆**—ly** adv (*not secretly, frankly*) ouvertement; (*publicly*) publiquement. ◆**—ness** n (*frankness*) franchise f; **o. of mind** ouverture f d'esprit.

open-air [əʊpən'eər] a (*pool etc*) en plein air. ◆**o.-'heart** a (*operation*) Med à cœur ouvert. ◆**o.-'necked** a (*shirt*) sans cravate. ◆**o.-'plan** a Archit sans cloisons.

opera ['ɒprə] n opéra m; **o. glasses** jumelles fpl de théâtre. ◆**ope'ratic** a d'opéra. ◆**ope'retta** n opérette f.

operat/e ['ɒpəreɪt] 1 vi (*of machine etc*) fonctionner; (*proceed*) opérer; – vt faire fonctionner; (*business*) gérer. 2 vi (*of surgeon*) opérer (**on s.o.** qn, **for** de). ◆**—ing** a **o. costs** frais mpl d'exploitation; **o. thea-tre**, Am **o. room** Med salle f d'opération; **o. wing** Med bloc m opératoire. ◆**ope'ration** n (*working*) fonctionnement m; Med Mil Math etc opération f; **in o.** (*machine*) en service; (*plan*) Fig en vigueur. ◆**ope-'rational** a opérationnel. ◆**operative** a Med opératoire; (*law, measure etc*) en vigueur; – n ouvrier, -ière mf. ◆**operator** n Tel standardiste mf; (*on machine*) opéra-teur, -trice mf; (*criminal*) escroc m; **tour o.** organisateur, -trice mf de voyages, voyagiste m.

opinion [ə'pɪnjən] n opinion f, avis m; **in my o.** à mon avis. ◆**opinionated** a dogma-tique.

opium ['əʊpɪəm] n opium m.

opponent [ə'pəʊnənt] n adversaire mf.

opportune ['ɒpətjuːn] a opportun. ◆**oppor'tunism** n opportunisme m.

opportunity [ɒpə'tjuːnɪtɪ] n occasion f (**to do** or **of doing** de faire); pl (*prospects*) perspectives fpl; **equal opportunities** des chances fpl égales.

oppos/e [ə'pəʊz] vt (*person, measure etc*) s'opposer à; (*law, motion*) Pol faire opposi-tion à. ◆**—ed** a opposé (**to** à); **as o. to** par opposition à. ◆**—ing** a (*team, interests*) opposé. ◆**oppo'sition** n opposition f (**to** à); **the o.** (*rival camp*) Fam l'adversaire m.

opposite ['ɒpəzɪt] a (*side etc*) opposé; (*house*) en face; **one's o. number** (*counter-part*) son homologue mf; – adv (*to sit etc*) en face; – prep **o.** (**to**) en face de; – n **the o.** le contraire, l'opposé m.

oppress [ə'pres] vt (tyrannize) opprimer; (of heat, anguish) oppresser; **the oppressed** les opprimés mpl. ◆**oppression** n oppression f. ◆**oppressive** a (ruler etc) oppressif; (heat) oppressant; (régime) tyrannique. ◆**oppressor** n oppresseur m.

opt [ɒpt] vi **to o. for** opter pour; **to o. to do** choisir de faire; **to o. out** Fam refuser de participer (**of** à). ◆**option** n option f; (subject) Sch matière f à option; **she has no o.** elle n'a pas le choix. ◆**optional** a facultatif; **o. extra** (on car etc) option f, accessoire m en option.

optical ['ɒptɪk(ə)l] a (glass) optique; (illusion, instrument etc) d'optique. ◆**op'tician** n opticien, -ienne mf.

optimism ['ɒptɪmɪz(ə)m] n optimisme m. ◆**optimist** n optimiste mf. ◆**opti'mistic** a optimiste. ◆**opti'mistically** adv avec optimisme.

optimum ['ɒptɪməm] a & n optimum (m); **the o. temperature** la température optimum. ◆**optimal** a optimal.

opulent ['ɒpjʊlənt] a opulent. ◆**opulence** n opulence f.

or [ɔːr] conj ou; **one or two** un ou deux; **he doesn't drink or smoke** il ne boit ni ne fume; **ten or so** environ dix.

oracle ['ɒrək(ə)l] n oracle m.

oral ['ɔːrəl] a oral; – n (examination) Sch oral m.

orange ['ɒrɪndʒ] **1** n (fruit) orange f; – a (drink) à l'orange; **o. tree** oranger m. **2** a & n (colour) orange a & m inv. ◆**orangeade** n orangeade f.

orang-outang [ɔːræŋʊ'tæŋ] n orang-outan(g) m.

oration [ɔː'reɪʃ(ə)n] n funeral **o.** oraison f funèbre.

oratory ['ɒrətərɪ] n (words) Pej rhétorique f.

orbit ['ɔːbɪt] n (of planet etc) & Fig orbite f; – vt (sun etc) graviter autour de.

orchard ['ɔːtʃəd] n verger m.

orchestra ['ɔːkɪstrə] n (classical) orchestre m. ◆**or'chestral** a (music) orchestral; (concert) symphonique. ◆**orchestrate** vt (organize) & Mus orchestrer.

orchid ['ɔːkɪd] n orchidée f.

ordain [ɔː'deɪn] vt (priest) ordonner; **to o. that** décréter que.

ordeal [ɔː'diːl] n épreuve f, supplice m.

order ['ɔːdər] n (command, structure, association etc) ordre m; (purchase) Com commande f; **in o.** (drawer, room etc) en ordre; (passport etc) en règle; **in (numerical) o.** dans l'ordre numérique; **in working o.** en état de marche; **in o. of age** par ordre

d'âge; **in o. to do** pour faire; **in o. that** pour que (+ sub); **it's in o. to smoke**/etc (allowed) il est permis de fumer/etc; **out of o.** (machine) en panne; (telephone) en dérangement; **to make** or **place an o.** Com passer une commande; **on o.** Com commandé; **money o.** mandat m; **postal o.** mandat m postal; – vt (command) ordonner (**s.o. to do** à qn de faire); (meal, goods etc) commander; (taxi) appeler; **to o. s.o. around** commander qn, régenter qn; – vi (in café etc) commander. ◆—**ly 1** a (tidy) ordonné; (mind) méthodique; (crowd) discipliné. **2** n Mil planton m; (in hospital) garçon m de salle.

ordinal ['ɔːdɪnəl] a (number) ordinal.

ordinary ['ɔːd(ə)nrɪ] a (usual) ordinaire; (average) moyen; (mediocre) médiocre, ordinaire; **an o. individual** un simple particulier; **in o. use** d'usage courant; **in the o. course of events** en temps normal; **in the o. way** normalement; **it's out of the o.** ça sort de l'ordinaire.

ordination [ɔːdɪ'neɪʃ(ə)n] n Rel ordination f.

ordnance ['ɔːdnəns] n (guns) Mil artillerie f.

ore [ɔːr] n minerai m.

organ ['ɔːgən] n **1** Anat & Fig organe m. **2** Mus orgue m, orgues fpl; **barrel o.** orgue m de Barbarie. ◆**organist** n organiste mf.

organic [ɔː'gænɪk] a organique. ◆**organism** n organisme m.

organization [ɔːgənaɪ'zeɪʃ(ə)n] n (arrangement, association) organisation f.

organiz/e ['ɔːgənaɪz] vt organiser. ◆—**ed** a (mind, group etc) organisé. ◆—**er** n organisateur, -trice mf.

orgasm ['ɔːgæz(ə)m] n orgasme m.

orgy ['ɔːdʒɪ] n orgie f.

orient ['ɔːrɪənt] vt Am = **orientate**. ◆**orientate** vt orienter.

Orient ['ɔːrɪənt] n **the O.** l'Orient m. ◆**ori'ental** a & n oriental, -ale (mf).

orifice ['ɒrɪfɪs] n orifice m.

origin ['ɒrɪdʒɪn] n origine f.

original [ə'rɪdʒɪn(ə)l] a (first) premier, originel, primitif; (novel, unusual) original; (sin) originel; (copy, version) original; – n (document etc) original m. ◆**origi'nality** n originalité f. ◆**originally** adv (at first) à l'origine; (in a novel way) originalement; **she comes o. from** elle est originaire de. ◆**originate** vi (begin) prendre naissance (**in** dans); **to o. from** (of idea etc) émaner de; (of person) être originaire de; – vt être l'auteur de. ◆**originator** n auteur m (**of** de).

ornament ['ɔːnəmənt] n (decoration) ornement *m*; *pl* (*vases etc*) bibelots *mpl.* ◆**orna'mental** *a* ornemental. ◆**orna-men'tation** *n* ornementation *f.* ◆**or'nate** *a* (*style etc*) (très) orné. ◆**or'nately** *adv* (*decorated etc*) de façon surchargée, à outrance.

orphan ['ɔːf(ə)n] *n* orphelin, -ine *mf*; – *a* orphelin. ◆**orphaned** *a* orphelin; **he was o. by the accident** l'accident l'a rendu orphelin. ◆**orphanage** *n* orphelinat *m.*

orthodox ['ɔːθədɒks] *a* orthodoxe. ◆**orthodoxy** *n* orthodoxie *f.*

orthop(a)edics [ɔːθə'piːdɪks] *n* orthopédie *f.*

Oscar ['ɒskər] *n* Cin oscar *m.*

oscillate ['ɒsɪleɪt] *vi* osciller.

ostensibly [ɒ'stensɪblɪ] *adv* apparemment, en apparence.

ostentation [ɒsten'teɪʃ(ə)n] *n* ostentation *f.* ◆**ostentatious** *a* plein d'ostentation, prétentieux.

ostracism ['ɒstrəsɪz(ə)m] *n* ostracisme *m.* ◆**ostracize** *vt* proscrire, frapper d'ostracisme.

ostrich ['ɒstrɪtʃ] *n* autruche *f.*

other ['ʌðər] *a* autre; **o. people** d'autres; **the o. one** l'autre *mf*; **I have no o. gloves than these** je n'ai pas d'autres gants que ceux-ci; – *pron* autre; (*some*) **others** d'autres; **some do, others don't** les uns le font, les autres ne le font pas; **none o. than, no o. than** nul autre que; – *adv* **o. than** autrement que. ◆**otherwise** *adv* autrement; – *a* (*different*) (tout) autre.

otter ['ɒtər] *n* loutre *f.*

ouch! [aʊtʃ] *int* aïe!, ouille!

ought [ɔːt] *v aux* **1** (*obligation, desirability*) **you o.** to leave tu devrais partir; **I o. to have done it** j'aurais dû le faire; **he said he o. to stay** il a dit qu'il devrait rester. **2** (*probability*) **it o. to be ready** ça devrait être prêt.

ounce [aʊns] *n* (*measure*) once *f*, & *Fig* once *f* (= 28,35 g).

our [aʊər] *poss a* notre, *pl* nos. ◆**ours** *pron* le nôtre, la nôtre, *pl* les nôtres; **this book is o.** ce livre est à nous *or* est le nôtre; **a friend of o.** un ami à nous. ◆**our'selves** *pron* nous-mêmes; (*reflexive* & *after prep etc*) nous; **we wash o.** nous nous lavons.

oust [aʊst] *vt* évincer (**from** de).

out [aʊt] *adv* (*outside*) dehors; (*not at home etc*) sorti; (*light, fire*) éteint; (*news, secret*) connu, révélé; (*flower*) ouvert; (*book*) publié, sorti; (*finished*) fini; **to be** *or* **go o. a lot** sortir beaucoup; **he's o. in Italy** il est (parti) en Italie; **o. there** là-bas; **to have a**

day o. sortir pour la journée; **5 km o.** Nau à 5 km du rivage; **the sun's o.** il fait (du) soleil; **the tide's o.** la marée est basse; **you're o.** (*wrong*) tu es trompé; (*in game etc*) tu es éliminé (**of** de); **the trip** *or* **journey o.** l'aller *m*; **to be o. to win** être résolu à gagner; – *prep* **o.** (*outside*) en dehors de; (*danger, breath, reach, water*) hors de; (*without*) sans; **o. of pity/love/etc** par pitié/amour/*etc*; **to look/jump/etc o.** (*window etc*) regarder/sauter/*etc* par; **to drink/take/copy o.** boire/prendre/copier dans; **made o. of** (*created from*) fait en; **to make sth o. of a box/rag/etc** faire qch avec une boîte/un chiffon/*etc*; **a page o. of** une page de; **she's o. of town** elle n'est pas en ville; **5 km o. of** (*away from*) à 5 km de; **four o. of five** quatre sur cinq; **o. of the blue** de manière inattendue; **to feel o. of it** *or* **of things** se sentir hors du coup. ◆**'out-and-out** *a* (*cheat, liar etc*) achevé; (*believer*) à tout crin. ◆**o.-of-'date** *a* (*expired*) périmé; (*old-fashioned*) démodé. ◆**o.-of-'doors** *adv* dehors. ◆**o.-of-the-'way** *a* (*place*) écarté.

outbid [aʊt'bɪd] *vt* (*pt* & *pp* **outbid**, *pres p* **outbidding**) **to o. s.o.** (*at auction*) surenchérir sur qn.

outboard ['aʊtbɔːd] *a* **o. motor** Nau moteur *m* hors-bord *inv.*

outbreak ['aʊtbreɪk] *n* (*of war*) début *m*; (*of violence, pimples*) éruption *f*; (*of fever*) accès *m*; (*of hostilities*) ouverture *f.*

outbuilding ['aʊtbɪldɪŋ] *n* (*of mansion, farm*) dépendance *f.*

outburst ['aʊtbɜːst] *n* (*of anger, joy*) explosion *f*; (*of violence*) flambée *f*; (*of laughter*) éclat *m.*

outcast ['aʊtkɑːst] *n* (*social*) *o.* paria *m.*

outcome ['aʊtkʌm] *n* résultat *m*, issue *f.*

outcry ['aʊtkraɪ] *n* tollé *m.*

outdated [aʊt'deɪtɪd] *a* démodé.

outdistance [aʊt'dɪstəns] *vt* distancer.

outdo [aʊt'duː] *vt* (*pt* **outdid**, *pp* **outdone**) surpasser (**in** en).

outdoor ['aʊtdɔːr] *a* (*game*) de plein air; (*pool, life*) en plein air; **o. clothes** tenue *f* pour sortir. ◆**out'doors** *adv* dehors.

outer ['aʊtər] *a* extérieur; **o. space** l'espace *m* (cosmique); **the o. suburbs** la grande banlieue.

outfit ['aʊtfɪt] *n* équipement *m*; (*kit*) trousse *f*; (*toy*) panoplie *f* (*de pompier, cow-boy etc*); (*clothes*) costume *m*; (*for woman*) toilette *f*; (*group, gang*) Fam bande *f*; (*firm*) Fam boîte *f*; **o. sports/ski** *o.* tenue *f* de sport/de ski. ◆**outfitter** *n* chemisier *m.*

outgoing ['aʊtgəʊɪŋ] **1** *a* (*minister etc*)

sortant; (*mail, ship*) en partance. **2** *a* (*sociable*) liant, ouvert. **3** *npl* (*expenses*) dépenses *fpl*.

outgrow [aʊt'grəʊ] *vt* (*pt* **outgrew**, *pp* **outgrown**) (*clothes*) devenir trop grand pour; (*habit*) perdre (en grandissant); **to o. s.o.** (*grow more than*) grandir plus vite que qn.

outhouse [aʊthaʊs] *n* (*of mansion, farm*) dépendance *f*; (*lavatory*) *Am* cabinets *mpl* extérieurs.

outing [aʊtɪŋ] *n* sortie *f*, excursion *f*.

outlandish [aʊt'lændɪʃ] *a* (*weird*) bizarre; (*barbaric*) barbare.

outlast [aʊt'lɑːst] *vt* durer plus longtemps que; (*survive*) survivre à.

outlaw [aʊtlɔː] *n* hors-la-loi *m inv*; – *vt* (*ban*) proscrire.

outlay [aʊtleɪ] *n* (*money*) dépense(s) *f*(*pl*).

outlet [aʊtlet] *n* (*for liquid, of tunnel etc*) sortie *f*; *El* prise *f* de courant; (*market for goods*) *Com* débouché *m*; (*for feelings, energy*) moyen *m* d'exprimer, exutoire *m*; **retail o.** *Com* point *m* de vente, magasin *m*.

outline [aʊtlaɪn] *n* (*shape*) contour *m*, profil *m*; (*rough*). (*of article, plan etc*) esquisse *f*; **the broad or general or main outline(s)** (*chief features*) les grandes lignes; – *vt* (*plan, situation*) décrire à grands traits, esquisser; (*book, speech*) résumer; **to be outlined against** (*of tree etc*) se profiler sur.

outlive [aʊt'lɪv] *vt* survivre à.

outlook [aʊtlʊk] *n inv* (*for future*) perspective(s) *f*(*pl*); (*point of view*) perspective *f* (**on** sur), attitude *f* (**on** à l'égard de); *Met* prévisions *fpl*.

outlying [aʊtlaɪɪŋ] *a* (*remote*) isolé; (*neighbourhood*) périphérique.

outmoded [aʊt'məʊdɪd] *a* démodé.

outnumber [aʊt'nʌmbər] *vt* être plus nombreux que.

outpatient [aʊtpeɪʃ(ə)nt] *n* malade *mf* en consultation externe.

outpost [aʊtpəʊst] *n* avant-poste *m*.

output [aʊtpʊt] *n* rendement *m*, production *f*; (*computer process*) sortie *f*; (*computer data*) donnée(s) *f*(*pl*) de sortie.

outrage [aʊtreɪdʒ] *n* atrocité *f*, crime *m*; (*indignity*) indignité *f*; (*scandal*) scandale *m*; (*indignation*) indignation *f*; **bomb o.** attentat *m* à la bombe; – *vt* (*morals*) outrager; **outraged by** sth indigné de qch. ◆**out'rageous** *a* (*atrocious*) atroce; (*shocking*) scandaleux; (*dress, hat etc*) grotesque.

outright [aʊtraɪt] *adv* (*completely*) complètement; (*to say, tell*) franchement; (*to be*

killed) sur le coup; **to buy o.** (*for cash*) acheter au comptant; – [aʊtraɪt] *a* (*complete*) complet; (*lie, folly*) pur; (*refusal, rejection etc*) catégorique, net; (*winner*) incontesté.

outset [aʊtset] *n* **at the o.** au début; **from the o.** dès le départ.

outside [aʊt'saɪd] *adv* (au) dehors, à l'extérieur; **to go o.** sortir; – *prep* à l'extérieur de, en dehors de; (*beyond*) *Fig* en dehors de; **o. my room** *or* **door** à la porte de ma chambre; – *n* extérieur *m*, dehors *m*; – [aʊtsaɪd] *a* extérieur; (*bus or train seat etc*) côté couloir *inv*; (*maximum*) *Fig* maximum; **the o. lane** *Aut* la voie de droite, *Am* la voie de gauche; **an o. chance** une faible chance. ◆**out'sider** *n* (*stranger*) étranger, -ère *mf*; *Sp* outsider *m*.

outsize [aʊtsaɪz] *a* (*clothes*) grande taille *inv*.

outskirts [aʊtskɜːts] *npl* banlieue *f*.

outsmart [aʊt'smɑːt] *vt* être plus malin que.

outspoken [aʊt'spəʊk(ə)n] *a* (*frank*) franc.

outstanding [aʊt'stændɪŋ] *a* remarquable, exceptionnel; (*problem, business*) non réglé, en suspens; (*debt*) impayé; **work o.** travail *m* à faire.

outstay [aʊt'steɪ] *vt* **to o. one's welcome** abuser de l'hospitalité de son hôte, s'incruster.

outstretched [aʊt'stretʃt] *a* (*arm*) tendu.

outstrip [aʊt'strɪp] *vt* (**-pp-**) devancer.

outward [aʊtwəd] *a* (*look, movement*) vers l'extérieur; (*sign, appearance*) extérieur; **o. journey** *or* **trip** aller *m*. ◆**outward(s)** *adv* vers l'extérieur.

outweigh [aʊt'weɪ] *vt* (*be more important than*) l'emporter sur.

outwit [aʊt'wɪt] *vt* (**-tt-**) être plus malin que.

oval [ˈəʊv(ə)l] *a* & *n* ovale (*m*).

ovary [ˈəʊvərɪ] *n* *Anat* ovaire *m*.

ovation [əʊˈveɪʃ(ə)n] *n* (*standing*) **o.** ovation *f*.

oven [ˈʌv(ə)n] *n* four *m*; (*hot place*) *Fig* fournaise *f*; **o. glove** gant *m* isolant.

over [ˈəʊvər] *prep* (*on*) sur; (*above*) au-dessus de; (*on the other side of*) de l'autre côté de; **bridge o. the river** pont *m* sur le fleuve; **to jump/look/etc o. sth** sauter/regarder/etc par-dessus qch; **to fall o. the balcony**/*etc* tomber du balcon/*etc*; **she fell o.** il elle en est tombée; **o. it** (*on*) dessus; (*above*) au-dessus; (*to jump over*) par-dessus; **to criticize**/*etc* **o. sth** (*about*) critiquer/*etc* à propos de qch; **an advantage o.** un avantage sur *or* par rapport à; **the radio** (*on*) à la radio; **o. the phone** au téléphone; **o. the holidays** (*during*) pendant les vacances; – **ten days** (*more than*) plus de dix jours; **men o. sixty** les hommes de plus de soixante ans; – and **above o.** (*on the*) au-dessus; **he's o. his flu** (*recovered from*) il est remis de sa grippe; **all o.** Spain (*everywhere in*) dans toute l'Espagne, partout en Espagne; **all o. the carpet** (*everywhere on*) partout sur le tapis; – *adv* (*above*) (par-)dessus; (*finished*) fini; (*danger*) passé; (*again*) encore; (*too*) trop; **jump o.!** sauter par-dessus!; **o. here** ici; **o. there** là-bas; **to be** *or* **come** *or* **go o.** (*visit*) passer; **he's o. in Italy** il est (parti) en Italie; **she's o. from Paris** elle est venue de Paris; **all o.** (*everywhere*) partout; **wet all o.** tout mouillé; **it's (all) o.!** (*finished*) c'est fini!; **she's o.** (*fallen*) elle est tombée; **a kilo or o.** (*more*) un kilo ou plus; **I have ten o.** (*left*) il m'en reste dix; **there's some bread o.** il reste du pain; – **o. and o.** (*again*) (*often*) à plusieurs reprises; **to start all o. (again)** recommencer à zéro; **o. pleased/etc** trop content/*etc*. ◆**o.-a'bundant** *a* surabondant. ◆**o.-de'veloped** *a* trop développé. ◆**o.-fa'miliar** *a* trop familier. ◆**o.-in'dulge** *vt* (*one's desires etc*) céder trop facilement à; (*person*) trop gâter. ◆**o.-sub'scribed** *a* (*course*) ayant trop d'inscrits.

overall 1 [əʊvərɔːl] *a* (*measurement, length, etc*) total; (*result, effort etc*) global; – *adv* globalement. **2** [ˈəʊvərɔːl] *n* blouse *f* (de travail); *pl* bleus *mpl* de travail.

overawe [əʊvərˈɔː] *vt* intimider.

overbalance [əʊvəˈbæləns] *vi* basculer.

overbearing [əʊvəˈbeərɪŋ] *a* autoritaire.

overboard [ˈəʊvəbɔːd] *adv* à la mer.

overburden [əʊvəˈbɜːd(ə)n] *vt* surcharger.

overcast [əʊvəˈkɑːst] *a* (*sky*) couvert.

overcharge [əʊvəˈtʃɑːdʒ] *vt* **to o. s.o. for sth** faire payer qch trop cher à qn.

overcoat [ˈəʊvəkəʊt] *n* pardessus *m*.

overcome [əʊvəˈkʌm] *vt* (*pt* **overcame**, *pp* **overcome**) (*enemy, shyness etc*) vaincre; (*disgust, problem*) surmonter; **to be o. by** (*fatigue, grief etc*) être accablé par; (*fumes, temptation*) succomber à; **he was o. by emotion** l'émotion eut raison de lui.

overcrowded [əʊvəˈkraʊdɪd] *a* (*house, country*) surpeuplé; (*bus, train*) bondé. ◆**overcrowding** *n* surpeuplement *m*.

overdo [əʊvəˈduː] *vt* (*pt* **overdid**, *pp* **overdone**) exagérer; *Culin* cuire trop. **to o. it** (*exaggerate*) exagérer; (*work too much*) se surmener; *Iron* se fatiguer.

overdose [ˈəʊvədəʊs] *n* overdose *f*, dose *f* excessive (de barbituriques *etc*).

overdraft [ˈəʊvədrɑːft] *n* *Fin* découvert *m*. ◆**over'draw** *vt* (*pt* **overdrew**, *pp* **overdrawn**) (*account*) mettre à découvert.

overdress [əʊvəˈdres] *vi* s'habiller avec trop de recherche.

overdue [əʊvəˈdjuː] *a* (*train etc*) en retard; (*debt*) arriéré; (*apology, thanks*) tardif.

overeat [əʊvərˈiːt] *vi* manger trop.

overestimate [əʊvərˈestɪmeɪt] *vt* surestimer.

overexcited [əʊvərɪkˈsaɪtɪd] *a* surexcité.

overfeed [əʊvəˈfiːd] *vt* (*pt & pp* **overfed**) suralimenter.

overflow 1 [ˈəʊvəfləʊ] *n* (*outlet*) trop-plein *m*; (*of people, abstract*) *Fig* excédent *m*. **2** [əʊvəˈfləʊ] *vi* déborder (**with** de); **to be overflowing with** (*of town, shop, house etc*) regorger de (*visiteurs, livres etc*).

overgrown [əʊvəˈɡrəʊn] *a* envahi par la végétation; **o. with** (*weeds etc*) envahi par; **you're an o. schoolgirl** *Fig Pej* tu as la mentalité d'une écolière.

overhang [əʊvəˈhæŋ] *vi* (*pt & pp* **overhung**) faire saillie; – *vt* surplomber.

overhaul [əʊvəˈhɔːl] *vt* (*vehicle, doctrine etc*) réviser; – [ˈəʊvəhɔːl] *n* révision *f*.

overhead [əʊvəˈhed] *adv* au-dessus; – [ˈəʊvəhed] **1** *a* (*railway etc*) aérien. **2** *npl* (*expenses*) frais *mpl* généraux.

overhear [əʊvəˈhɪər] *vt* (*pt & pp* **overheard**) surprendre, entendre.

overheat [əʊvəˈhiːt] *vt* surchauffer; – *vi* (*of engine*) chauffer.

overjoyed [əʊvəˈdʒɔɪd] *a* ravi, enchanté.

overland [ˈəʊvəlænd] *a & adv* par voie de terre.

overlap [əʊvəˈlæp] *vi* (**-pp-**) se chevaucher; – *vt* chevaucher; – [ˈəʊvəlæp] *n* chevauchement *m*.

overleaf [əʊvəˈliːf] *adv* au verso.

overload [əʊvəˈləʊd] *vt* surcharger.

overlook [əʊvəˈlʊk] *vt* **1** (*not notice*) ne pas remarquer; (*forget*) oublier; (*disregard, ignore*) fermer les yeux sur. **2** (*of window, house etc*) donner sur; (*of tower, fort*) dominer.

overly [ˈəʊvəlɪ] *adv* excessivement.

overmuch [əʊvəˈmʌtʃ] *adv* trop, excessivement.

overnight [əʊvəˈnaɪt] *adv* (*during the night*) (pendant) la nuit; (*all night*) toute la nuit; (*suddenly*) *Fig* du jour au lendemain; **to stay o.** passer la nuit; – [ˈəʊvənaɪt] *a* (*stay*) d'une nuit; (*clothes*) pour une nuit; (*trip*) de nuit.

overpass [ˈəʊvəpæs] *n* (*bridge*) *Am* toboggan *m*.

overpopulated [əuvə'pɒpuleɪtɪd] *a* surpeuplé.

overpower [əuvə'pauər] *vt* (*physically*) maîtriser; (*defeat*) vaincre; *Fig* accabler. **◆—ing** *a* (*charm etc*) irrésistible; (*heat etc*) accablant.

overrat/e [əuvə'reɪt] *vt* surestimer. **◆—ed** *a* surfait.

overreach [əuvə'riːtʃ] *vt* to o. oneself trop entreprendre.

overreact [əuvərɪ'ækt] *vi* réagir excessivement.

overrid/e [əuvə'raɪd] *vt* (*pt* overrode, *pp* overridden) (*invalidate*) annuler; (*take no notice of*) passer outre à; (*be more important than*) l'emporter sur. **◆—ing** *a* (*passion*) prédominant; (*importance*) primordial.

overrule [əuvə'ruːl] *vt* (*reject*) rejeter.

overrun [əuvə'rʌn] *vt* (*pt* overran, *pp* overrun, *pres p* overrunning) 1 (*invade*) envahir. 2 (*go beyond*) aller au-delà de.

overseas [əuvə'siːz] *adv* (*Africa etc*) outre-mer; (*abroad*) à l'étranger; – ['əuvəsiːz] *a* (*visitor, market etc*) d'outre-mer; étranger; (*trade*) extérieur.

overse/e [əuvə'siː] *vt* (*pt* oversaw, *pp* overseen) surveiller. **◆—er** ['əuvəsiːər] *n* (*foreman*) contremaître *m*.

overshadow [əuvə'ʃædəu] *vt* (*make less important*) éclipser; (*make gloomy*) assombrir.

overshoot [əuvə'ʃuːt] *vt* (*pt & pp* overshot) (*of aircraft*) & *Fig* dépasser.

oversight ['əuvəsaɪt] *n* omission *f*, oubli *m*; (*mistake*) erreur *f*.

oversimplify [əuvə'sɪmplɪfaɪ] *vti* trop simplifier.

oversize(d) ['əuvəsaɪz(d)] *a* trop grand.

oversleep [əuvə'sliːp] *vi* (*pt & pp* overslept) dormir trop longtemps, oublier de se réveiller.

overspend [əuvə'spend] *vi* dépenser trop.

overstaffed [əuvə'stɑːft] *a* au personnel pléthorique.

overstay [əuvə'steɪ] *vt* to o. one's welcome abuser de l'hospitalité de son hôte, s'incruster.

overstep [əuvə'step] *vt* (**-pp-**) dépasser.

overt ['əuvɜːt] *a* manifeste.

overtake [əuvə'teɪk] *vt* (*pt* overtook, *pp* overtaken) dépasser; (*vehicle*) doubler, dépasser; **overtaken by** (*nightfall, storm*) surpris par; – *vi* Aut doubler, dépasser.

overtax [əuvə'tæks] *vt* 1 (*strength*) excéder; (*brain*) fatiguer. 2 (*taxpayer*) surimposer.

overthrow [əuvə'θrəu] *vt* (*pt* overthrew, *pp* overthrown) *Pol* renverser; – ['əuvəθrəu] *n* renversement *m*.

overtime ['əuvətaɪm] *n* heures *fpl* supplémentaires; – *adv* to work o. faire des heures supplémentaires.

overtones ['əuvətəunz] *npl* Fig note *f*, nuance *f* (of de).

overture ['əuvətʃuər] *n* Mus & Fig ouverture *f*.

overturn [əuvə'tɜːn] *vt* (*chair, table etc*) renverser; (*car, boat*) retourner; (*decision etc*) *Fig* annuler; – *vi* (*of car, boat*) se retourner.

overweight [əuvə'weɪt] *a* to be o. (*of suitcase etc*) peser trop; (*of person*) avoir des kilos en trop.

overwhelm [əuvə'welm] *vt* (*of feelings, heat etc*) accabler; (*defeat*) écraser; (*amaze*) bouleverser. **◆—ed** *a* (*overjoyed*) ravi (**by, with** de); o. **with** (*grief, work etc*) accablé de; (*offers*) submergé par; **o. by** (*kindness, gift etc*) vivement touché par. **◆—ing** *a* (*heat, grief etc*) accablant; (*majority*) écrasant; (*desire*) irrésistible; (*impression*) dominant. **◆—ingly** *adv* (*to vote, reject etc*) en masse; (*utterly*) carrément.

overwork [əuvə'wɜːk] *n* surmenage *m*; – *vi* se surmener; – *vt* surmener.

overwrought [əuvə'rɔːt] *a* (*tense*) tendu.

owe [əu] *vt* devoir (to à); **I'll o. it (to) you, I'll o. you (for) it** (*money*) je te le devrai; **to o. it to oneself to** se devoir de faire. **◆owing** 1 *a* (*money etc*) dû, qu'on doit. 2 *prep* **o. to** à cause de.

owl [aul] *n* hibou *m*.

own [əun] 1 *a* propre; **my o. house** ma propre maison; – *pron* **it's my (very) o.** c'est à moi (tout seul); **a house of his o.** sa propre maison, sa maison à lui; **(all) on one's o.** (*alone*) tout seul; **to get one's o. back** prendre sa revanche (**on sur, for** de); **to come into one's o.** (*fulfil oneself*) s'épanouir. 2 *vt* (*possess*) posséder; **who owns this ball/etc?** à qui appartient cette balle/*etc*? 3 *vi* **to o. up** (*confess*) avouer; **to o. up to sth** s'avouer qch. **◆owner** *n* propriétaire *mf*. **◆ownership** *n* possession *f*; **home o.** accession *f* à la propriété; **public o.** *Econ* nationalisation *f*.

ox, *pl* oxen [ɒks, 'ɒks(ə)n] *n* bœuf *m*.

oxide ['ɒksaɪd] *n Ch* oxyde *m*. **◆oxidize** *vi* s'oxyder; – *vt* oxyder.

oxygen ['ɒksɪdʒ(ə)n] *n* oxygène *m*; – *a* (*mask, tent*) à oxygène.

oyster ['ɔɪstər] *n* huître *f*.

P

P, p [piː] n P, p m.

p [piː] abbr = **penny, pence**.

pa [pɑː] n (father) Fam papa m.

pace [peɪs] n (speed) pas m, allure f; (measure) pas m; **to keep p. with** (follow) suivre; (in work, progress) se maintenir à la hauteur de; – vi **to p. up and down** faire les cent pas; – vt (room etc) arpenter. ◆**pacemaker** n (device) stimulateur m cardiaque.

Pacific [pəˈsɪfɪk] a (coast etc) pacifique; – n **the P.** le Pacifique.

pacify [ˈpæsɪfaɪ] vt (country) pacifier; (calm, soothe) apaiser. ◆**pacifier** n (dummy) Am sucette f, tétine f. ◆**pacifist** n & a pacifiste (mf).

pack [pæk] **1** n (bundle, packet) paquet m; (bale) balle f; (of animal) charge f; (ruck-sack) sac m (à dos); Mil paquetage m; (of hounds, wolves) meute f; (of runners) Sp peloton m; (of thieves) bande f; (of cards) jeu m; (of lies) tissu m. **2** vt (fill) remplir (**with** de); (excessively) bourrer; (suitcase) faire; (object into box etc) emballer; (object into suitcase) mettre dans sa valise; (make into package) empaqueter; **to p. into** (cram) entasser dans; (put) mettre dans; **to p. away** (tidy away) ranger; **to p. (down)** (compress, crush) tasser; **to p. off** (person) Fam expédier; **to p. up** (put into box) emballer; (put into case) mettre dans sa valise; (give up) Fam laisser tomber; – vi (fill one's bags) faire ses valises; **to p. into** (of people) s'entasser dans; **to p. in** or up (of machine, vehicle) Fam tomber en panne; **to p. up** (stop) Fam s'arrêter; (leave) plier bagage. ◆**—ed** a (bus, cinema etc) bourré; **p. lunch** panier-repas m; **p. out** (crowded) Fam bourré. ◆**—ing** n (material, action) emballage m; **p. case** caisse f d'emballage.

packag/e [ˈpækɪdʒ] n paquet m; (computer programs) progiciel m; **p. deal** Com contrat m global, train m de propositions; **p. tour** voyage m organisé; – vt emballer, empaqueter. ◆**—ing** n (material, action) emballage m.

packet [ˈpækɪt] n paquet m; (of sweets) sachet m, paquet m; (of money) Fam **to make/cost a p.** Fam faire/coûter beaucoup d'argent.

pact [pækt] n pacte m.

pad [pæd] n (wad, plug) tampon m; (for writing, notes etc) bloc m; (on leg) Sp jambière f; (on knee) Sp genouillère f; (room) Sl piaule f; **launch(ing) p.** rampe f de lancement; **ink(ing) p.** tampon m encreur; – vt (**-dd-**) (stuff) rembourrer, matelasser; **to p. out** (speech, text) délayer. ◆**padding** n rembourrage m; (of speech, text) délayage m.

paddle [ˈpæd(ə)l] **1** vi (splash about) bar-boter; (dip one's feet) se mouiller les pieds; – n **to have a (little) p.** se mouiller les pieds. **2** n (pole) pagaie f; **p. boat, p. steamer** bateau m à roues; – vt **to p. a canoe** pagayer.

paddock [ˈpædək] n enclos m; (at race-course) paddock m.

paddy [ˈpædɪ] n **p. (field)** rizière f.

padlock [ˈpædlɒk] n (on door etc) cadenas m; (on bicycle, moped) antivol m; – vt (door etc) cadenasser.

p(a)ediatrician [piːdɪəˈtrɪʃ(ə)n] n Med pédiatre mf.

pagan [ˈpeɪgən] a & n païen, -enne (mf). ◆**paganism** n paganisme m.

page [peɪdʒ] **1** n (of book etc) page f. **2** n (boy) (in hotel etc) chasseur m; (at court) Hist page m; – vt **to p. s.o.** faire appeler qn.

pageant [ˈpædʒənt] n grand spectacle m historique. ◆**pageantry** n pompe f, apparat m.

pagoda [pəˈgəʊdə] n pagode f.

paid [peɪd] see **pay**; – a (assassin etc) à gages; **to put to** (hopes, plans) anéantir; **to put p. to s.o.** (ruin) couler qn.

pail [peɪl] n seau m.

pain [peɪn] n (physical) douleur f; (grief) peine f; pl (efforts) efforts mpl; **to have a p. in one's arm** avoir mal or une douleur au bras; **to be in p.** souffrir; **to go to** or **take (great) pains to do** (exert oneself) se donner du mal à faire; **to go to** or **take (great) pains not to do** (be careful) prendre bien soin de ne pas faire; **to be a p. (in the neck)** (of person) Fam être casse-pieds; – vt (grieve) peiner. ◆**p.-killer** n analgésique m, calmant m. ◆**painful** a (illness, operation) douloureux; (arm, leg) qui fait mal, douloureux; (distressing) douloureux, pénible; (difficult) pénible; (bad) Fam affreux. ◆**painless** a sans douleur; (*illness, operation*) indolore; (*easy*) Fam facile. ◆**painstaking** a (*a person*) soigneux; (*work*) soigné.

paint [peɪnt] n peinture f; pl (*in box, tube*) couleurs fpl; – vt (*colour, describe*) peindre; **to p. blue**/*etc* peindre en bleu/*etc*; – vi peindre. ◆—**ing** n (*activity*) peinture f; (*picture*) tableau m, peinture f. ◆—**er** n peintre m. ◆**paintbrush** n pinceau m. ◆**paintwork** n peinture(s) f(pl).

pair [peər] n paire f; (*man and woman*) couple m; **a p. of shorts** un short; **the p. of you** Fam vous deux; – vi **to p. off** (*of people*) former un couple; – vt (*marry*) marier.

pajama(s) [pəˈdʒɑːmə(z)] a & npl Am = pyjama(s).

Pakistan [pɑːkɪˈstɑːn] n Pakistan m. ◆**Pakistani** a & n pakistanais, -aise (mf).

pal [pæl] n Fam copain, copine f; – vi (-ll-) **to p. up** devenir copains; **to p. up with** devenir copain avec.

palace [ˈpælɪs] n (*building*) palais m. ◆**palatial** [pəˈleɪʃ(ə)l] a comme un palais.

palatable [ˈpælətəb(ə)l] a (*food*) agréable; (*fact, idea etc*) acceptable.

palate [ˈpælɪt] n Anat palais m.

palaver [pəˈlɑːvər] n Fam (*fuss*) histoire(s) f(pl); (*talk*) palabres mpl.

pale [peɪl] a (-er, -est) (*face, colour etc*) pâle; **p. blue** bleu/blonde; – vi pâlir. ◆**-ness** n pâleur f.

palette [ˈpælɪt] n (*of artist*) palette f.

paling [ˈpeɪlɪŋ] n (*fence*) palissade f.

pall [pɔːl] **1** vi devenir insipide or ennuyeux (**on** pour). **2** n (*of smoke*) voile m.

pallbearer [ˈpɔːlbeərər] n personne f qui aide à porter un cercueil.

pallid [ˈpælɪd] a pâle. ◆**pallor** n pâleur f.

pally [ˈpælɪ] a (-ier, -iest) Fam copain am, copine af (**with** avec).

palm [pɑːm] n **1** n (*of hand*) paume f. **2** n (*symbol*) palme f; **p. (tree)** palmier m; **p. (leaf)** palme f; **P. Sunday** les Rameaux mpl. **3** vt Fam **to p. sth off** (*pass off*) refiler qch (**on** à); **to p. s.o. off on s.o.** coller qn à qn.

palmist [ˈpɑːmɪst] n chiromancien, -ienne mf. ◆**palmistry** n chiromancie f.

palpable [ˈpælpəb(ə)l] a (*obvious*) manifeste.

palpitate [ˈpælpɪteɪt] vi (*of heart*) palpiter. ◆**palpitation** n palpitation f.

paltry [ˈpɔːltrɪ] a (-ier, -iest) misérable, dérisoire.

pamper [ˈpæmpər] vt dorloter.

pamphlet [ˈpæmflɪt] n brochure f.

pan [pæn] **1** n casserole f; (*for frying*) poêle f (à frire); (*of lavatory*) cuvette f. **2** vt (-nn-) (*criticize*) Fam éreinter. **3** vi (-nn-) **to p. out** (*succeed*) aboutir.

Pan- [pæn] pref pan-.

panacea [pænəˈsɪə] n panacée f.

panache [pəˈnæʃ] n (*showy manner*) panache m.

pancake [ˈpænkeɪk] n crêpe f.

pancreas [ˈpæŋkrɪəs] n Anat pancréas m.

panda [ˈpændə] n (*animal*) panda m; **P. car** = voiture f pie inv (de la police).

pandemonium [pændɪˈməʊnɪəm] n (*chaos*) chaos m; (*uproar*) tumulte m; (*place*) bazar m.

pander [ˈpændər] vi **to p. to** (*tastes, fashion etc*) sacrifier à; **to p. to s.o.** or **s.o.'s desires** se plier aux désirs de qn.

pane [peɪn] n vitre f, carreau m.

panel [ˈpæn(ə)l] n **1** n (*of door etc*) panneau m; (*control*) Tech El console f; (*instrument*) **p.** Av Aut tableau m de bord. **2** n (*of judges*) jury m; (*of experts*) groupe m; (*of candidates*) équipe f; **a p. of guests** des invités; **a p. game** TV Rad un jeu par équipes. ◆**panelled** a (*room etc*) lambrissé. ◆**panelling** n lambris m. ◆**panellist** n TV Rad (*guest*) invité, -ée mf; (*expert*) expert m; (*candidate*) candidat, -ate mf.

pangs [pæŋz] npl **p. of conscience** remords mpl (*of conscience*); **p. of hunger/death** les affres fpl de la faim/de la mort.

panic [ˈpænɪk] n panique f; **to get into a p.** paniquer; – vi (-ck-) s'affoler, paniquer. ◆**p.-stricken** a affolé. ◆**panicky** a (*person*) a Fam qui s'affole facilement; **to get p.** s'affoler.

panorama [pænəˈrɑːmə] n panorama m. ◆**panoramic** a panoramique.

pansy [ˈpænzɪ] n Bot pensée f.

pant [pænt] vi (*gasp*) haleter.

panther [ˈpænθər] n (*animal*) panthère f.

panties [ˈpæntɪz] npl (*female underwear*) slip m.

pantomime [ˈpæntəmaɪm] n (*show*) spectacle m de Noël.

pantry [ˈpæntrɪ] n (*larder*) garde-manger m inv; (*storeroom in hotel etc*) office m or f.

pants [pænts] npl (*male underwear*) slip m; (*loose, long*) caleçon m; (*female underwear*) slip m; (*trousers*) Am pantalon m.

pantyhose [ˈpæntɪhəʊz] n (*tights*) Am collant(s) m(pl).

papacy [ˈpeɪpəsɪ] n papauté f. ◆**papal** a papal.

paper [ˈpeɪpər] n papier m; (*newspaper*) journal m; (*wallpaper*) papier m peint;

(*exam*) épreuve *f* (écrite); (*student's exercise*) *Sch* copie *f*; (*learned article*) exposé *m*, communication *f*; **brown p.** papier *m* d'emballage; **to put down on p.** mettre par écrit; – *a* (*bag etc*) en papier; (*cup, plate*) en carton; **p. clip** trombone *m*; **p. knife** coupe-papier *m inv*; **p. mill** papeterie *f*; **p. shop** marchand *m* de journaux; – *vt* (*room, wall*) tapisser. ◆**paperback** *n* (*book*) livre *m* de poche. ◆**paperboy** *n* livreur *m* de journaux. ◆**paperweight** *n* presse-papiers *m inv*. ◆**paperwork** *n* *Com* écritures *fpl*; (*red tape*) *Pej* paperasserie *f*.

paprika ['pæprɪkə] *n* paprika *m*.

par [pɑːr] *n* on a p. au même niveau (with que); **below p.** (*unwell*) *Fam* pas en forme.

para- ['pærə] *pref* para-.

parable ['pærəb(ə)l] *n* (*story*) parabole *f*.

parachute ['pærəʃuːt] *n* parachute *f*; **to drop by p.** (*men, supplies*) parachuter; – *vi* descendre en parachute; – *vt* parachuter. ◆**parachutist** *n* parachutiste *mf*.

parade [pə'reɪd] **1** *n* *Mil* (*ceremony*) parade *f*; (*procession*) défilé *m*; **fashion p.** défilé *m* de mode *or* de mannequins; **p. ground** *Mil* terrain *m* de manœuvres; **to make a p. of** faire étalage de; – *vi* *Mil* défiler; to **p. about** (*walk about*) se balader; – *vt* faire étalage de. **2** *n* (*street*) avenue *f*.

paradise ['pærədaɪs] *n* paradis *m*.

paradox ['pærədɒks] *n* paradoxe *m*. ◆**para'doxically** *adv* paradoxalement.

paraffin ['pærəfɪn] *n* pétrole *m* (lampant); (*wax*) *Am* paraffine *f*; **p. lamp** lampe *f* à pétrole.

paragon ['pærəg(ə)n] *n* **p. of virtue** modèle *m* de vertu.

paragraph ['pærəgrɑːf] *n* paragraphe *m*; **'new p.'** 'à la ligne'.

parakeet ['pærəkiːt] *n* perruche *f*.

parallel ['pærəlel] *a* (*comparable*) & *Math* parallèle (with, to à); **to run p. to** *or* **with** être parallèle à; – *n* (*comparison*) & *Geog* parallèle *m*; (*line*) *Math* parallèle *f*; – *vt* être semblable à.

paralysis [pə'rælɪsɪs] *n* paralysie *f*. ◆**'paralyse** *vt* (*Am* -lyze) paralyser. ◆**para'lytic** *a* & *n* paralytique (*mf*).

parameter [pə'ræmɪtər] *n* paramètre *m*.

paramount ['pærəmaunt] *a* **of p. importance** de la plus haute importance.

paranoia [pærə'nɔɪə] *n* paranoïa *f*. ◆**'paranoid** *a* & *n* paranoïaque (*mf*).

parapet ['pærəpɪt] *n* parapet *m*.

paraphernalia [pærəfə'neɪlɪə] *n* attirail *m*.

paraphrase ['pærəfreɪz] *n* paraphrase *f*; – *vt* paraphraser.

parasite ['pærəsaɪt] *n* (*person, organism*) parasite *m*.

parasol ['pærəsɒl] *n* (*over table, on beach*) parasol *m*; (*lady's*) ombrelle *f*.

paratrooper ['pærətruːpər] *n* *Mil* parachutiste *m*. ◆**paratroops** *npl* *Mil* parachutistes *mpl*.

parboil ['pɑːbɔɪl] *vt* *Culin* faire bouillir à demi.

parcel ['pɑːs(ə)l] **1** *n* colis *m*, paquet *m*; **to be part and p. of** faire partie intégrante de. **2** *vt* (**-ll-**, *Am* **-l-**) to **p. out** (*divide*) partager; **to p. up** faire un paquet de.

parch [pɑːtʃ] *vt* dessécher; **to be parched** (*thirsty*) être assoiffé; **to make parched** (*thirsty*) donner très soif à.

parchment ['pɑːtʃmənt] *n* parchemin *m*.

pardon ['pɑːd(ə)n] *n* pardon *m*; *Jur* grâce *f*; **general p.** amnistie *f*; **I beg your p.** (*apologize*) je vous prie de m'excuser; (*not hearing*) vous dites?; **p.?** (*not hearing*) comment?; **p. (me)!** (*sorry*) pardon!; – *vt* pardonner (**s.o. for sth** qch à qn; **s.o. to do** à qn de faire qch); *Jur* gracier qn.

pare [peər] *vt* (*trim*) rogner; (*peel*) éplucher; to **p. down** *Fig* réduire, rogner.

parent ['peərənt] *n* père *m*, mère *f*; **one's parents** ses parent *mpl*, son père et sa mère; **p. firm, p. company** *Com* maison *f* mère. ◆**parentage** *n* (*origin*) origine *f*. ◆**pa'rental** *a* des parents, parental. ◆**parenthood** *n* paternité *f*, maternité *f*.

parenthesis, *pl* **-eses** [pə'renθəsɪs, -əsiːz] *n* parenthèse *f*.

Paris ['pærɪs] *n* Paris *m or f*. ◆**Parisian** [pə'rɪzɪən, *Am* pə'riːʒən] *a* & *n* parisien, -ienne (*mf*).

parish ['pærɪʃ] *n* *Rel* paroisse *f*; (*civil*) commune *f*; – *a* (*church, register*) paroissial; **p. council** conseil *m* municipal. ◆**pa'rishioner** *n* paroissien, -ienne *mf*.

parity ['pærɪtɪ] *n* parité *f*.

park [pɑːk] **1** *n* (*garden*) parc *m*. **2** *vt* (*vehicle*) garer; (*put*) *Fam* mettre, poser; – *vi Aut* se garer; (*remain parked*) stationner. ◆**—ing** *n* stationnement *m*; **'no p.'** 'défense de stationner'; **p. bay** aire *f* de stationnement; **p. lot** *Am* parking *m*; **p. meter** parcmètre *m*; **p. place** endroit *m* pour se garer; **p. ticket** contravention *f*.

parka ['pɑːkə] *n* (*coat*) parka *m*.

parkway ['pɑːkweɪ] *n Am* avenue *f*.

parliament ['pɑːləmənt] *n* parlement *m*; **P.** *Br* Parlement *m*. ◆**parlia'mentary** *a* parlementaire. ◆**parliam'tarian** *n* parlementaire *mf* (expérimenté(e)).

parlour ['pɑːlər] *n* (*in mansion*) (petit) salon

m; **ice-cream p.** *Am* salon de glaces; **p. game** jeu *m* de société.

parochial [pə'rəʊkɪəl] *a* (*mentality, quarrel*) *Pej* de clocher; (*person*) *Pej* provincial, borné; *Rel* paroissial.

parody ['pærədɪ] *n* parodie *f*; – *vt* parodier.

parole [pə'rəʊl] *n* **on p.** *Jur* en liberté conditionnelle.

parquet ['pɑːkeɪ] *n* **p.** (**floor**) parquet *m*.

parrot ['pærət] *n* perroquet *m*; **p. fashion** *Pej* comme un perroquet.

parry ['pærɪ] *vt* (*blow*) parer; (*question*) éluder; – *n Sp* parade *f*.

parsimonious [pɑːsɪ'məʊnɪəs] *a* parcimonieux. **◆—ly** *adv* avec parcimonie.

parsley ['pɑːslɪ] *n* persil *m*.

parsnip ['pɑːsnɪp] *n* panais *m*.

parson ['pɑːs(ə)n] *n* pasteur *m*; **p.'s nose** (*of chicken*) croupion *m*.

part [pɑːt] **1** *n* partie *f*; (*of machine*) pièce *f*; (*of periodical*) livraison *f*; (*of serial*) épisode *m*; (*in play, film, activity*) rôle *m*; (*division*) Culin mesure *f*; (*in hair*) raie *f*; **to take p.** participer (**in** à); **to take s.o.'s p.** (*side*) prendre parti pour qn; **in p.** en partie; **for the most p.** dans l'ensemble; **to be a p. of** faire partie de; **on the p. of** (*on behalf of*) de la part de; **for my p.** pour ma part; **in these parts** dans ces parages; **p. exchange** reprise *f*; **to take in p. exchange** reprendre; **p. owner** copropriétaire *mf*; **payment** paiement *m* partiel; – *adv* en partie; **p. American** en partie américain. **2** *vt* (*separate*) séparer; (*crowd*) diviser; **to part one's hair** se faire une raie; **to p. company with** (*leave*) quitter; – *vi* (*of friends etc*) se quitter; (*of married couple*) se séparer; **to p. with** (*get rid of*) se séparer de. **◆—ing 1** *n* séparation *f*; – *a* (*gift, words*) d'adieu. **2** *n* (*in hair*) raie *f*.

partake [pɑː'teɪk] *vi* (*pt* **partook**, *pp* **partaken**) **to p. in** participer à; **to p. of** (*meal, food*) prendre, manger.

partial ['pɑːʃəl] *a* partiel; (*biased*) partial (**towards** envers); **to be p. to** (*fond of*) *Fam* avoir un faible pour. **◆parti'ality** *n* (*bias*) partialité *f*; (*liking*) prédilection *f*.

participate [pɑː'tɪspeɪt] *vi* participer (**in** à). **◆participant** *n* participant, -ante *mf*. **◆partici'pation** *n* participation *f*.

participle ['pɑːtɪsɪp(ə)l] *n* participe *m*.

particle ['pɑːtɪk(ə)l] *n* (*of atom, dust, name*) particule *f*; (*of truth*) grain *m*.

particular [pə'tɪkjʊlər] **1** *a* (*a specific, special*) particulier; (*fastidious, fussy*) difficile (**about** sur); (*meticulous*) méticuleux; **this p. book** ce livre-ci en particulier; **in p.** en

particulier; **to be p. about** faire très attention à. **2** *n* (*detail*) détail *m*; **s.o.'s particulars** le nom et l'adresse de qn; (*description*) le signalement de qn. **◆—ly** *adv* particulièrement.

partisan [pɑːtɪ'zæn, *Am* 'pɑːtɪz(ə)n] *n* partisan *m*.

partition [pɑː'tɪʃ(ə)n] **1** *n* (*of room*) cloison *f*; – *vt* **to p. off** cloisonner. **2** *n* (*of country*) Pol partition *f*, partage *m*; – *vt* Pol partager.

partly ['pɑːtlɪ] *adv* en partie; **p. English p. French** moitié anglais moitié français.

partner ['pɑːtnər] *n* Com associé, -ée *mf*; (*lover, spouse*) & *Sp* Pol partenaire *mf*; (*of racing driver etc*) coéquipier, -ière *mf*; (*dancing*) cavalier, -ière *mf*. **◆partnership** *n* association *f*; **to take into p.** prendre comme associé(e); **in p. with** en association avec.

partridge ['pɑːtrɪdʒ] *n* perdrix *f*.

part-time ['pɑːt'taɪm] *a & adv* à temps partiel; (*half-time*) à mi-temps.

party ['pɑːtɪ] *n* **1** (*group*) groupe *m*; Pol parti *m*; (*in contract, lawsuit*) Jur partie *f*; Mil détachement *m*; Tel correspondant, -ante *mf*; **rescue p.** équipe *f* de sauveteurs *or* de secours; **third p.** Jur tiers *m*; **innocent p.** innocent, -ente *mf*; **to be a p. to** (*crime*) être complice de; **p. line** Tel ligne *f* partagée; Pol ligne *f* du parti; **p. ticket** billet *m* collectif. **2** (*gathering*) réception *f*; (*informal*) surprise-partie *f*; – (*for birthday*) fête *f*; **cocktail p.** cocktail *m*; **dinner p.** dîner *m*; **tea p.** thé *m*.

pass [pɑːs] **1** *n* (*entry permit*) laissez-passer *m inv*; (*free ticket*) Th billet *m* de faveur; (*season ticket*) carte *f* d'abonnement; (*over mountains*) Geog col *m*; Fb etc passe *f*; (*in exam*) mention *f* passable (**in French/** *etc* en français/*etc*); **to make a p. at** faire des avances à; **p. mark** (*in exam*) moyenne *f*, barre *f* d'admissibilité; **p. key** passe-partout *m inv*. **2** *vi* (*go, come, disappear*) passer (**to** à, **through** par); (*overtake*) Aut dépasser; (*in exam*) être reçu (**in French/** *etc* en français/*etc*); (*take place*) se passer; **that'll p.** (*be acceptable*) ça ira; **he can p. for thirty** on lui donnerait trente ans; **to p. along** *or* **through** passer; **to p. away** *or* **on** (*die*) mourir; **to p. by** passer (à côté); **to p. off** (*happen*) se passer; **to p. on** (*to move on to*) passer à; **to p. out** (*faint*) s'évanouir; – *vt* (*move, spend, give etc*) passer (**to** à); (*go past*) passer devant (*immeuble etc*); (*vehicle*) dépasser; (*exam*) être reçu à; (*candidate*) recevoir; (*judgement, opinion*) prononcer (**on** sur); (*remark*) faire; (*allow*) autoriser; *(bill, law)* Pol voter; **to p. (by) s.o.** *(in street)* croiser qn; **to p. by** *(building)* passer devant; **to p. oneself off as** se faire passer pour; **to p. sth off on** *(fob off on)* refiler qch à; **to p. over** *(ignore)* passer sur, oublier; **to p. round** *(cigarettes, sweets etc)* faire passer; **to p. up** *(chance)* laisser passer. ◆**—ing** *a (vehicle etc)* qui passe; *(beauty)* passager; *— n (of visitor, vehicle etc)* passage m; *(of time)* écoulement m; *(death)* disparition f.

passable [ˈpɑːsəb(ə)l] *a (not bad)* passable; *(road)* praticable; *(river)* franchissable.

passage [ˈpæsɪdʒ] *n (passing, way through, of text, of speech etc)* passage m; *(of time)* écoulement m; *(corridor)* couloir m; Nau traversée f, passage m. ◆**passageway** *n (way through)* passage m; *(corridor)* couloir m.

passbook [ˈpɑːsbʊk] *n* livret m de caisse d'épargne.

passenger [ˈpæsɪndʒər] *n* passager, -ère mf; Rail voyageur, -euse mf.

passer-by [pɑːsəˈbaɪ] *n (pl passers-by)* passant, -ante mf.

passion [ˈpæʃ(ə)n] *n* passion f; **to have a p. for** *(cars etc)* avoir la passion de, adorer. ◆**passionate** *a* passionné. ◆**passionately** *adv* passionnément.

passive [ˈpæsɪv] *a (not active)* passif; *— n* Gram passif m. ◆**—ness** *n* passivité f.

Passover [ˈpɑːsəʊvər] *n* Rel Pâque f.

passport [ˈpɑːspɔːt] *n* passeport m.

password [ˈpɑːswɜːd] *n* mot m de passe.

past [pɑːst] **1** *n (time, history)* passé m; **in the p.** *(formerly)* dans le temps; **it's a thing of the p.** ça n'existe plus; *(a gone by)* passé; *(former)* ancien; **these p. months** ces derniers mois; **that's all p.** c'est du passé; **in the p. tense** Gram au passé. **2** *prep (in front of)* devant; *(after)* après; *(further than)* plus loin que; *(too old for)* Fig trop vieux pour; **p. four o'clock** quatre heures passées, plus de quatre heures; **to be p. fifty** avoir cinquante ans passés; **it's p. belief** c'est incroyable; **I wouldn't put it p. him** ça ne m'étonnerait pas de lui, il en est bien capable; *— adv* devant; **to go p.** passer.

pasta [ˈpæstə] *n* Culin pâtes fpl *(alimentaires)*.

paste [peɪst] **1** *n (of meat)* pâté m; *(of anchovy etc)* beurre m; *(dough)* pâte f. **2** *n (glue)* colle f *(blanche)*; *— vt* coller; **to p. up** *(notice etc)* afficher.

pastel [ˈpæstəl, *Am* pæˈstel] *n* pastel m; *— a (shade)* pastel inv; *(drawing)* au pastel.

pasteurized [ˈpæstəraɪzd] *a (milk)* pasteurisé.

pastiche [pæˈstiːʃ] *n* pastiche m.

pastille [ˈpæstɪl, *Am* pæˈstiːl] *n* pastille f.

pastime [ˈpɑːstaɪm] *n* passe-temps m inv.

pastor [ˈpɑːstər] *n* Rel pasteur m. ◆**pastoral** *a* pastoral.

pastry [ˈpeɪstrɪ] *n (dough)* pâte f; *(cake)* pâtisserie f; **puff p.** pâte f feuilletée. ◆**pastrycook** *n* pâtissier, -ière mf.

pasture [ˈpɑːstʃər] *n* pâturage m.

pasty 1 [ˈpeɪstɪ] *a (-ier, -iest) (complexion)* terreux. **2** [ˈpæstɪ] *n* Culin petit pâté m *(en croûte)*.

pat [pæt] **1** *vt (-tt-) (cheek, table etc)* tapoter; *(animal)* caresser; *— n* petite tape; caresse f. **2** *adv* **to answer p.** avoir la réponse toute prête; **to know sth off p.** savoir qch sur le bout du doigt.

patch [pætʃ] *n (for clothes)* pièce f; *(over eye)* bandeau m; *(for bicycle tyre)* rustine® f; *(of colour)* tache f; *(of sky)* morceau m; *(of fog)* nappe f; *(of land)* allée f; *(of cabbage/etc* p. un carré de choux/etc; **a bad p.** Fig une mauvaise passe; **not to be a p. on** *(not as good as)* Fam ne pas arriver à la cheville de; *— vt* **to p. (up)** *(clothing)* rapiécer; **to p. up** *(quarrel)* régler; *(marriage)* replâtrer. ◆**patchwork** *n* patchwork m. ◆**patchy** *a (-ier, -iest)* inégal.

patent 1 [ˈpeɪtənt] *a* patent, manifeste; **p. leather** cuir m verni. **2** [ˈpeɪtənt, ˈpætənt] *n* brevet m *(d'invention)*; *— vt (faire)* breveter. ◆**—ly** *adv* manifestement.

paternal [pəˈtɜːn(ə)l] *a* paternel. ◆**paternity** *n* paternité f.

path [pɑːθ] *n (pl -s [pɑːðz])* sentier m, chemin m; *(in park)* allée f; *(of river)* cours m; *(of bullet, planet)* trajectoire f. ◆**pathway** *n* sentier m, chemin m.

pathetic [pəˈθetɪk] *a* pitoyable.

pathology [pəˈθɒlədʒɪ] *n* pathologie f. ◆**patho'logical** *a* pathologique.

pathos [ˈpeɪθɒs] *n* pathétique m.

patient 1 [ˈpeɪʃ(ə)nt] *a* patient. **2** *n (in hospital)* malade mf, patient, -ente mf; *(on doctor's or dentist's list)* patient, -ente mf. ◆**patience** *n* patience f; **to have p.** prendre patience; **to lose p.** perdre patience; **to play p.** Cards faire des réussites. ◆**patiently** *adv* patiemment.

patio [ˈpætɪəʊ] *n (pl -os)* patio m.

patriarch [ˈpeɪtrɪɑːk] *n* patriarche m.

patriot ['pætrɪət, 'peɪtrɪət] n patriote mf. ◆**patri'otic** a (views, speech etc) patriotique; (person) patriote. ◆**patriotism** n patriotisme m.

patrol [pə'trəʊl] n patrouille f; **p. boat** patrouilleur m; **police p. car** voiture f de police; **p. wagon** Am fourgon m cellulaire; – vi (-ll-) patrouiller; – vt patrouiller dans. ◆**patrolman** n (pl -men) Am agent m de police; (repair man) Aut dépanneur m.

patron ['peɪtrən] n (of artist) protecteur, -trice mf; (customer) Com client, -ente mf; (of cinema, theatre) habitué, -ée mf; **p. saint** patron, -onne mf. ◆**patronage** n (support) patronage m; (of the arts) protection f; (custom) Com clientèle f. ◆**patronize** ['pætrənaɪz, Am 'peɪtrənaɪz] vt **1** Com accorder sa clientèle à. **2** (person) Pej traiter avec condescendance. ◆**-ing** a condescendant.

patter ['pætə(r)] **1** n (of footsteps) petit bruit m; (of rain, hail) crépitement m; – vi (of rain, hail) crépiter, tambouriner. **2** n (talk) baratin m.

pattern ['pæt(ə)n] n dessin m, motif m; (paper model for garment) patron m; (fabric sample) échantillon m; Fig modèle m; (plan) plan m; (method) formule f; (of a crime) scénario m. ◆**patterned** a (dress, cloth) à motifs.

paucity ['pɔːsɪtɪ] n pénurie f.

paunch [pɔːntʃ] n panse f, bedon m. ◆**paunchy** a (-ier, -iest) bedonnant.

pauper ['pɔːpər] n pauvre mf, indigent, -ente mf.

pause [pɔːz] n pause f; (in conversation) silence m; – vi (stop) faire une pause; (hesitate) hésiter.

pav/e [peɪv] vt paver; **to p. the way for** Fig ouvrir la voie à. ◆**-ing** n (surface) pavage m, dallage m; **p. stone** pavé m. ◆**pavement** n trottoir m; (roadway) Am chaussée f; (stone) pavé m.

pavilion [pə'vɪljən] n (building) pavillon m.

paw [pɔː] **1** n patte f; – vt (of animal) donner des coups de patte à. **2** vt (touch improperly) tripoter.

pawn [pɔːn] **1** n Chess pion m. **2** n mettre en gage; – **in p.** en gage. ◆**pawnbroker** n prêteur, -euse mf sur gages. ◆**pawnshop** n mont-de-piété m.

pay [peɪ] n salaire m; (of workman) paie f, salaire m; Mil solde f, paie f; **p. phone** téléphone m public; **p. day** jour m de paie; **p. slip** bulletin m or fiche f de paie; – vt (pt & pp **paid**) (person, sum) payer; (deposit) verser; (yield) Com rapporter; (compli-

ment, attention, visit) faire; **to p. s.o. to do** or **for doing** payer qn pour faire; **to p. s.o. for sth** payer qch à qn; **to p. money into one's account** or **the bank** verser de l'argent sur son compte; **it pays (one) to be cautious** on a intérêt à être prudent; **to p. homage** or **tribute to** rendre hommage à; **to p. back** (creditor, loan etc) rembourser; **I'll p. you back for this!** je te revaudrai ça!; **to p. in** (cheque) verser (**to one's account** sur son compte); **to p. off** (debt, creditor etc) rembourser; (in instalments) rembourser par acomptes; (staff, worker) licencier; **to p. off an old score** or **a grudge** Fig régler un vieux compte; **to p. out** (spend) dépenser; – vi **to p. up** payer; – vi payer; **to p. for sth** payer qch; **to p. a lot (for)** payer cher; **to p. off** (be successful) être payant; **to p. up** payer. ◆**-ing** a (guest) payant; (profitable) rentable. ◆**-able** a (due) payable; **a cheque p. to** un chèque à l'ordre de. ◆**-ment** n paiement m; (of deposit) versement m; (reward) récompense f; **on p. of 20 francs** moyennant 20 francs. ◆**payoff** n Fam (reward) récompense f; (revenge) règlement m de comptes. ◆**payroll** n **to be on the p. of** (firm, factory) être employé par; **to have twenty workers on the p.** employer vingt ouvriers.

pea [piː] n pois m; **garden** or **green peas** petits pois mpl; **p. soup** soupe f aux pois.

peace [piːs] n paix f; **p. of mind** tranquillité f d'esprit; **in p.** en paix; **at p.** en paix (**with** avec); **to have (some) p. and quiet** avoir la paix; **to disturb the p.** troubler l'ordre public; **to hold one's p.** garder le silence. ◆**p.-keeping** a (force) de maintien de la paix; (measure) de pacification. ◆**p.-loving** a pacifique. ◆**peaceable** a paisible, pacifique. ◆**peaceful** a paisible, calme; (coexistence, purpose, demonstration) pacifique. ◆**peacefulness** n paix f.

peach [piːtʃ] n (fruit) pêche f; (tree) pêcher m; – a (colour) pêche inv.

peacock ['piːkɒk] n paon m.

peak [piːk] n (mountain top) sommet m; (mountain itself) pic m; (of cap) visière f; (of fame etc) Fig sommet m, apogée m; **the traffic has reached** or **is at its p.** la circulation est à son maximum; – a (hours, period) de pointe; (demand, production) maximum; – vi (of sales etc) atteindre son maximum. ◆**peaked** a **p. cap** casquette f.

peaky ['piːkɪ] a (-ier, -iest) Fam (ill) patraque; (pale) pâlot.

peal [piːl] **1** n (of laughter) éclat m; (of thunder) roulement *m*. **2** *n* **p. of bells** carillon *m*; – *vi* **to p. (out)** (*of bells*) carillonner.

peanut ['piːnʌt] *n* cacah(o)uète *f*; (*plant*) arachide *f*; **to earn/etc peanuts** (*little money*) *Fam* gagner/etc des clopinettes.

pear [peər] *n* poire *f*; **p. tree** poirier *m*.

pearl [pɜːl] *n* perle *f*; (*mother-of-pearl*) nacre *f*. ◆**pearly** *a* (**-ier, -iest**) (*colour*) nacré.

peasant ['pezənt] *n* & *a* paysan, -anne (*mf*).

peashooter ['piːʃuːtər] *n* sarbacane *f*.

peat [piːt] *n* tourbe *f*.

pebble ['pebəl] *n* (*stone*) caillou *m*; (*on beach*) galet *m*. ◆**pebbly** *a* (*beach*) (couvert) de galets.

pecan ['piːkæn] *n* (*nut*) *Am* pacane *f*.

peck [pek] *vti* **to p. (at)** (*of bird*) picorer (*du pain etc*); (*person*) *Fig* donner un coup de bec à; **to p. at one's food** (*of person*) manger du bout des dents; – *n* coup *m* de bec; (*kiss*) *Fam* bécot *m*.

peckish ['pekif] *a* **to be p.** (*hungry*) *Fam* avoir un petit creux.

peculiar [pɪ'kjuːlɪər] *a* (*strange*) bizarre; (*characteristic, special*) particulier (**to** à). ◆**peculi'arity** *n* (*feature*) particularité *f*; (*oddity*) bizarrerie *f*. ◆**peculiarly** *adv* bizarrement; (*specially*) particulièrement.

pedal ['pedəl] *n* pédale *f*; **p. boat** pédalo *m*; – *vi* (**-ll-**, *Am* **-l-**) pédaler; – *vt* (*bicycle etc*) actionner les pédales de. ◆**pedalbin** *n* poubelle *f* à pédale.

pedant ['pedənt] *n* pédant, -ante *mf*. ◆**pe'dantic** *a* pédant. ◆**pedantry** *n* pédantisme *m*.

peddl/e ['pedəl] *vt* colporter; (*drugs*) faire le trafic de; – *vi* faire du colportage. ◆**-er** *n Am* (*door-to-door*) colporteur, -euse *mf*; (*in street*) camelot *m*; **drug p.** revendeur, -euse *mf* de drogues.

pedestal ['pedɪstəl] *n Archit & Fig* piédestal *m*.

pedestrian [pə'destrɪən] **1** *n* piéton *m*; **p. crossing** passage *m* pour piétons; **p. precinct** zone *f* piétonnière. **2** *a* (*speech, style*) prosaïque. ◆**pedestrianize** *vt* (*street etc*) rendre piétonnier.

pedigree ['pedɪgriː] *n* (*of dog, horse etc*) pedigree *m*; (*of person*) ascendance *f*; – *a* (*dog, horse etc*) de race.

pedlar ['pedlər] *n* (*door-to-door*) colporteur, -euse *mf*; (*in street*) camelot *m*.

pee [piː] *n* **to go for a p.** *Fam* faire pipi.

peek [piːk] *n* coup *m* d'œil furtif; – *vi* jeter un coup d'œil (**at** à).

peel [piːl] *n* (*of vegetable, fruit*) pelure(s) *f(pl)*, épluchure(s) *f(pl)*; (*of orange skin*) écorce *f*; (*in food, drink*) zeste *m*; **a piece of**

p. une pelure, une épluchure; – *vt* (*fruit, vegetable*) peler, éplucher; **to keep one's eyes peeled** *Fam* être vigilant; **to p. off** (*label etc*) décoller; – *vi* (*of sunburnt skin*) peler; (*of paint*) s'écailler; **to p. easily** (*of fruit*) se peler facilement. ◆**—ings** *npl* pelures *fpl*, épluchures *fpl*. ◆**—er** *n* (*knife etc*) éplucheur *m*.

peep [piːp] **1** *n* coup *m* d'œil (furtif); – *vi* **to p. (at)** regarder furtivement; **to p. out** se montrer; **peeping Tom** voyeur, -euse *mf*. **2** *vi* (*of bird*) pépier. ◆**peephole** *n* judas *m*.

peer [pɪər] **1** *n* (*equal*) pair *m*, égal, -ale *mf*; (*noble*) pair *m*. **2** *vi* **to p. (at)** regarder attentivement (*comme pour mieux voir*); **to p. into** (*darkness*) scruter. ◆**peerage** *n* (*rank*) pairie *f*.

peeved [piːvd] *a Fam* irrité.

peevish ['piːvɪʃ] *a* grincheux, irritable.

peg [peg] **1** *n* (*wooden*) *Tech* cheville *f*; (*metal*) *Tech* fiche *f*; (*for tent*) piquet *m*; (*for clothes*) pince *f* (à linge); (*for coat, hat etc*) patère *f*; **to buy off the p.** acheter en prêt-à-porter. **2** *vt* (**-gg-**) (*prices*) stabiliser.

pejorative [pɪ'dʒɒrətɪv] *a* péjoratif.

pekin(g)ese [piːkɪ'niːz] *n* (*dog*) pékinois *m*.

pelican ['pelɪkən] *n* (*bird*) pélican *m*.

pellet ['pelɪt] *n* (*of paper etc*) boulette *f*; (*for gun*) (grain *m* de) plomb *m*.

pelt [pelt] **1** *n* (*skin*) peau *f*; (*fur*) fourrure *f*. **2** *vt* **to p. s.o. with** (*stones etc*) bombarder qn de. **3** *vi* **it's pelting (down)** (*raining*) il pleut à verse. **4** *vi* **to p. along** (*run, dash*) *Fam* foncer, courir.

pelvis ['pelvɪs] *n Anat* bassin *m*.

pen [pen] **1** *n* (*dipped in ink*) porte-plume *m* inv; (*fountain pen*) stylo *m* (à encre *or* à plume); (*ballpoint*) stylo *m* à bille, stylo(-)bille *m*; **to live by one's p.** *Fig* vivre de sa plume; **p. friend, p. pal** correspondant, -ante *mf*; **p. name** pseudonyme *m*; **p. nib** (bec *m* de) plume *f*; **p. pusher** *Pej* gratte-papier *m* inv; – *vt* (**-nn-**) (*write*) écrire. **2** *n* (*enclosure for baby or sheep or cattle*) parc *m*.

penal ['piːnəl] *a* (*law, code etc*) pénal; (*colony*) pénal. ◆**penalize** *vt Sp Jur* pénaliser (**for** pour); (*handicap*) désavantager.

penalty ['penəltɪ] *n Jur* peine *f*; (*fine*) amende *f*; *Sp* pénalisation *f*; *Fb* penalty *m*; *Rugby* pénalité *f*; **to pay the p.** *Fig* subir les conséquences.

penance ['penəns] *n* pénitence *f*.

pence [pens] *see* **penny**.

pencil ['pensəl] *n* crayon *m*; **in p.** au crayon; **p. box** plumier *m*; **p. sharpener**

taille-crayon(s) *m inv*; – *vt* (**-ll-**, *Am* **-l-**) crayonner; **to p. in** *Fig* noter provisoirement.

pendant ['pendənt] *n* pendentif *m*; (*on earring, chandelier*) pendeloque *f*.

pending ['pendɪŋ] **1** *a* (*matter*) en suspens. **2** *prep* (*until*) en attendant.

pendulum ['pendjuləm] *n* (*of clock*) balancier *m*, pendule *m*; *Fig* pendule *f*.

penetrat/e ['penɪtreɪt] *vt* (*substance, mystery etc*) percer; (*plan, secret etc*) découvrir; – *vti* **to p. (into)** (*forest, group etc*) pénétrer dans. **◆—ing** *a* (*mind, cold etc*) pénétrant. **◆pene'tration** *n* pénétration *f*.

penguin ['peŋgwɪn] *n* manchot *m*, pingouin *m*.

penicillin [penɪ'sɪlɪn] *n* pénicilline *f*.

peninsula [pə'nɪnsjulə] *n* presqu'île *f*, péninsule *f*. **◆pensinsular** *a* péninsulaire.

penis ['piːnɪs] *n* pénis *m*.

penitent ['penɪtənt] *a & n* pénitent, -ente (*mf*). **◆penitence** *n* pénitence *f*.

penitentiary [penɪ'tenʃərɪ] *n Am* prison *f* (*centrale*).

penknife ['pennaɪf] *n* (*pl* **-knives**) canif *m*.

pennant ['penənt] *n* (*flag*) flamme *f*, banderole *f*.

penny ['penɪ] *n* **1** (*pl* **pennies**) (*coin*) penny *m*; *Am Can* cent *m*; **I don't have a p.** *Fig* je n'ai pas le sou. **2** (*pl* **pence** [pens]) (*value, currency*) penny *m*. **◆p.-pinching** *a* (*miserly*) *Fam* avare. **◆penniless** *a* sans le sou.

pension ['penʃ(ə)n] *n* pension *f*; **retirement p.** (pension *f* de) retraite *f*; (*private*) retraite *f* complémentaire; – *vt* **to p. off** mettre à la retraite. **◆—able** *a* (*age*) de la retraite; (*job*) qui donne droit à une retraite. **◆—er** *n* pensionné, -ée *mf*; (*old age*) p. retraité, -ée *mf*.

pensive ['pensɪv] *a* pensif.

pentagon ['pentəgən] *n* **the P.** *Am Pol* le Pentagone.

pentathlon [pen'tæθlən] *n Sp* pentathlon *m*.

Pentecost ['pentɪkɒst] *n* (*Whitsun*) *Am* Pentecôte *f*.

penthouse ['penthaʊs] *n* appartement *m* de luxe (*construit sur le toit d'un immeuble*).

pent-up [pent'ʌp] *a* (*feelings*) refoulé.

penultimate [pɪ'nʌltɪmət] *a* avant-dernier.

peony ['piːənɪ] *n Bot* pivoine *f*.

people ['piːp(ə)l] *npl* (*in general*) gens *mpl or fpl*; (*specific persons*) personnes *fpl*; (*of region, town*) habitants *mpl*, gens *mpl or fpl*; **the p.** (*citizens*) *Pol* le peuple; **old p.** les personnes *fpl* âgées; **old people's home**

hospice *m* de vieillards; (*private*) maison *f* de retraite; **two p.** deux personnes; **English p.** les Anglais *mpl*, le peuple anglais; **a lot of p.** beaucoup de monde *or* de gens; **p. think that . . .** on pense que . . . ; – *n* (*nation*) peuple *m*; – *vt* (*populate*) peupler (**with** de).

pep [pep] *n* entrain *m*; **p. talk** *Fam* petit laïus d'encouragement; – *vt* (**-pp-**) **to p. up** (*perk up*) ragaillardir.

pepper ['pepər] *n* poivre *m*; (*vegetable*) poivron *m*; – *vt* poivrer. **◆peppercorn** *n* grain *m* de poivre. **◆peppermint** *n* (*plant*) menthe *f* poivrée; (*sweet*) pastille *f* de menthe. **◆peppery** *a Culin* poivré.

per [pɜːr] *prep* par; **p. annum** par an; **p. head, p. person** par personne; **p. cent** pour cent; **50 pence p. kilo** 50 pence le kilo; **40 km p. hour** 40 km à l'heure. **◆per'centage** *n* pourcentage *m*.

perceive [pə'siːv] *vt* (*see, hear*) percevoir; (*notice*) remarquer (**that** que). **◆perceptible** *a* perceptible. **◆perception** *n* perception *f* (**of** de); (*intuition*) intuition *f*. **◆perceptive** *a* (*person*) perspicace; (*study, remark*) pénétrant.

perch [pɜːtʃ] **1** *n* perchoir *m*; – *vi* (*of bird*) (se) percher; (*of person*) *Fig* se percher, se jucher; – *vt* (*put*) percher. **2** *n* (*fish*) perche *f*.

percolate ['pɜːkəleɪt] *vi* (*of liquid*) filtrer, passer (**through** par); – *vt* (*coffee*) faire dans une cafetière; **percolated coffee** du vrai café. **◆percolator** *n* cafetière *f*; (*in café or restaurant*) percolateur *m*.

percussion [pə'kʌʃ(ə)n] *n Mus* percussion *f*.

peremptory [pə'remptərɪ] *a* péremptoire.

perennial [pə'renɪəl] **1** *a* (*complaint, subject etc*) perpétuel. **2** *a* (*plant*) vivace; – *n* plante *f* vivace.

perfect ['pɜːfɪkt] *a* parfait; – *a & n* **p. (tense)** *Gram* parfait *m*; – [pə'fekt] *vt* (*book, piece of work etc*) parachever, parfaire; (*process, technique*) mettre au point; (*one's French etc*) parfaire ses connaissances en. **◆per'fection** *n* perfection *f* (**of** de); (*act*) parachèvement *m* (**of** de); mise *f* au point (**of** de); **to p. à la perfection. ◆per'fectionist** *n* perfectionniste *mf*. **◆'perfectly** *adv* parfaitement.

perfidious [pə'fɪdɪəs] *a Lit* perfide.

perforate ['pɜːfəreɪt] *vt* perforer. **◆perfo'ration** *n* perforation *f*.

perform [pə'fɔːm] *vt* (*task, miracle*) accomplir; (*a function, one's duty*) remplir; (*rite*) célébrer; (*operation*) *Med* pratiquer (**on**

sur; (*a play, symphony*) jouer; (*sonata*) interpréter; – *vi* (*play*) jouer; (*sing*) chanter; (*dance*) danser; (*of circus animal*) faire un numéro; (*function*) fonctionner; (*behave*) se comporter; **you performed very well!** tu as très bien fait! ◆–**ing** *a* (*animal*) savant. ◆**performance** *n* 1 (*show*) Th représentation *f*, séance *f*; Cin Mus séance *f*. 2 (*of athlete, machine etc*) performance *f*; (*of actor, musician etc*) interprétation *f*; (*circus etc*) numéro *m*; (*fuss*) Fam histoire(s) *f*(*pl*) laissez-passer *m* **in the p. of one's duties** l'exercice *m* de ses fonctions. ◆**performer** *n* interprète *mf* (**of** de); (*entertainer*) artiste *mf*.

perfume ['pɜːfjuːm] *n* parfum *m*; – [pə'fjuːm] *vt* parfumer.

perfunctory [pə'fʌŋktərɪ] *a* (*action*) superficiel; (*smile etc*) de commande.

perhaps [pə'hæps] *adv* peut-être; **p. not** peut-être que non.

peril ['perɪl] *n* péril *m*, danger *m*; **at your p.** à vos risques et péril. ◆**perilous** *a* périlleux.

perimeter [pə'rɪmɪtər] *n* périmètre *m*.

period ['pɪərɪəd] 1 *n* (*length of time, moment in time*) période *f*; (*historical*) époque *f*; (*time limit*) délai *m*; (*lesson*) Sch leçon *f*; (*full stop*) Gram point *m*; **in the p. of a month** en l'espace d'un mois; **I refuse, p.!** Am je refuse, un point c'est tout!; – *a* (*furniture etc*) d'époque; (*costume*) de l'époque. 2 *n* (*menstruation*) règles *fpl*. ◆**peri'odic** *a* périodique. ◆**peri'odical** *n* (*magazine*) périodique *m*. ◆**peri'odically** *adv* périodiquement.

periphery [pə'rɪfərɪ] *n* périphérie *f*. ◆**peripheral** *a* (*question*) sans rapport direct (**to** avec); (*interest*) accessoire; (*neighbourhood*) périphérique.

periscope ['perɪskəʊp] *n* périscope *m*.

perish ['perɪʃ] *vi* (*die*) périr; (*of food, substance*) se détériorer; **to be perished** or **perishing** (*of person*) Fam être frigorifié. ◆–**ing** *a* (*cold, weather*) Fam glacial. ◆–**able** *a* (*food*) périssable; – *npl* denrées *fpl* périssables.

perjure ['pɜːdʒər] *vt* **to p. oneself** se parjurer. ◆**perjurer** *n* (*person*) parjure *mf*. ◆**perjury** *n* parjure *m*; **to commit p.** se parjurer.

perk [pɜːk] 1 *vi* **to p. up** (*buck up*) se ragaillardir; – *vt* **to p. s.o. up** remonter qn, ragaillardir qn. 2 *n* (*advantage*) avantage *m*; (*extra profit*) à-côté *m*. ◆**perky** *a* (-**ier**, -**iest**) (*cheerful*) guilleret, plein d'entrain.

perm [pɜːm] *n* (*of hair*) permanente *f*; – *vt to*

have one's hair permed se faire faire une permanente.

permanent ['pɜːmənənt] *a* permanent; (*address*) fixe; **she's p. here** elle est ici à titre permanent. ◆**permanence** *n* permanence *f*. ◆**permanently** *adv* à titre permanent.

permeate ['pɜːmɪeɪt] *vt* (*of ideas etc*) se répandre dans; **to p. (through)** (*of liquid etc*) pénétrer. ◆**permeable** *a* perméable.

permit [pə'mɪt] *vt* (-**tt**-) permettre (**s.o. to do** à qn de faire); **weather permitting** si le temps le permet; – ['pɜːmɪt] *n* (*licence*) permis *m*; (*entrance pass*) laissez-passer *m* *inv*. ◆**per'missible** *a* permis. ◆**per'mission** *n* permission *f*, autorisation *f* (**to do** de faire); **to ask (for)/give p.** demander/donner la permission. ◆**per'missive** *a* (*too tolerant*) tolérant, laxiste. ◆**per'missiveness** *n* laxisme *m*.

permutation [pɜːmjʊ'teɪʃ(ə)n] *n* permutation *f*.

pernicious [pə'nɪʃəs] *a* (*harmful*) & Med pernicieux.

pernickety [pə'nɪkɪtɪ] *a* Fam (*precise*) pointilleux; (*demanding*) difficile (**about** sur).

peroxide [pə'rɒksaɪd] *n* (*bleach*) eau *f* oxygénée; – *a* (*hair, blond*) oxygéné.

perpendicular [pɜːpən'dɪkjʊlər] *a* & *n* perpendiculaire (*f*).

perpetrate ['pɜːpɪtreɪt] *vt* (*crime*) perpétrer. ◆**perpetrator** *n* auteur *m*.

perpetual [pə'petʃʊəl] *a* perpétuel. ◆**perpetually** *adv* perpétuellement. ◆**perpetuate** *vt* perpétuer. ◆**perpetuity** [pɜːpɪ'tjuːɪtɪ] *n* perpétuité *f*.

perplex [pə'pleks] *vt* rendre perplexe, dérouter. ◆–**ed** *a* perplexe. ◆–**ing** *a* déroutant. ◆**perplexity** *n* perplexité *f*; (*complexity*) complexité *f*.

persecute ['pɜːsɪkjuːt] *vt* persécuter. ◆**perse'cution** *n* persécution *f*.

persevere [pɜːsɪ'vɪər] *vi* persévérer (**in** dans). ◆–**ing** *a* (*persistent*) persévérant. ◆**perseverance** *n* persévérance *f*.

Persian ['pɜːʃ(ə)n, 'pɜːʒ(ə)n] *a* (*language, cat, carpet*) persan; – *n* (*language*) persan *m*.

persist [pə'sɪst] *vi* persister (**in doing** à faire, **in sth** dans qch). ◆**persistence** *n* persistance *f*. ◆**persistent** *a* (*fever, smell etc*) persistant; (*person*) obstiné; (*attempts, noise etc*) continuel. ◆**persistently** *adv* (*stubbornly*) obstinément; (*continually*) continuellement.

person ['pɜːs(ə)n] *n* personne *f*; **in p.** en personne; **a p. to p. call** Tel une communication avec préavis. ◆**personable** *a* avenant, qui présente bien.

personal ['pɜːsən(ə)l] *a* personnel; *(application)* en personne; *(hygiene, friend)* intime; *(life)* privé; *(indiscreet)* indiscret; **p. assistant, p. secretary** secrétaire *m* particulier, secrétaire *f* particulière. ◆**perso'nality** *n (character, famous person)* personnalité *f*; **a television p.** une vedette de la télévision. ◆**personalize** *vt* personnaliser. ◆**personally** *adv* personnellement; *(in person)* en personne.

personify [pə'sɒnɪfaɪ] *vt* personnifier. ◆**personifi'cation** *n* personnification *f*.

personnel [pɜːsə'nel] *n (staff)* personnel *m*; *(department)* service *m* du personnel.

perspective [pə'spektɪv] *n (artistic & viewpoint)* perspective *f*; **in (its true) p.** *Fig* sous son vrai jour.

perspire [pə'spaɪər] *vi* transpirer. ◆**perspi'ration** *n* transpiration *f*, sueur *f*.

persuade [pə'sweɪd] *vt* persuader (**s.o. to do** qn de faire). ◆**persuasion** *n* persuasion *f*; *Rel* religion *f*. ◆**persuasive** *a (person, argument etc)* persuasif. ◆**persuasively** *adv* de façon persuasive.

pert [pɜːt] *a (impertinent)* impertinent; *(lively)* gai, plein d'entrain; *(hat etc)* coquet, chic. ◆**—ly** *adv* avec impertinence.

pertain [pə'teɪn] *vt* **to p. to** *(relate)* se rapporter à; *(belong)* appartenir à.

pertinent ['pɜːtɪnənt] *a* pertinent. ◆**—ly** *adv* pertinemment.

perturb [pə'tɜːb] *vt* troubler, perturber.

Peru [pə'ruː] *n* Pérou *m*. ◆**Peruvian** *a & n* péruvien, -ienne *(mf)*.

peruse [pə'ruːz] *vt* lire (attentivement); *(skim through)* parcourir. ◆**perusal** *n* lecture *f*.

pervade [pə'veɪd] *vi* se répandre dans. ◆**pervasive** *a* qui se répand partout, envahissant.

perverse [pə'vɜːs] *a (awkward)* contrariant; *(obstinate)* entêté; *(wicked)* pervers. ◆**perversion** *n* perversion *f*; *(of justice, truth)* travestissement *m*. ◆**perversity** *n* esprit *m* de contradiction; *(obstinacy)* entêtement *m*; *(wickedness)* perversité *f*.

pervert [pə'vɜːt] *vt* pervertir; *(mind)* corrompre; *(justice, truth)* travestir; — ['pɜːvɜːt] *n* perverti, -ie *mf*.

pesky ['peskɪ] *a* (-ier, -iest) *(troublesome)* *Am Fam* embêtant.

pessimism ['pesɪmɪz(ə)m] *n* pessimisme *m*. ◆**pessimist** *n* pessimiste *mf*. ◆**pessi'mistic** *a* pessimiste. ◆**pessi'mistically** *adv* avec pessimisme.

pest [pest] *n* animal *m* or insecte *m* nuisible; *(person)* *Fam* casse-pieds *mf inv*, peste *f*. ◆**pesticide** *n* pesticide *m*.

pester ['pestər] *vt (harass)* harceler (**with questions** de questions); **to p. s.o. to do sth/for sth** harceler *or* tarabuster qn pour qu'il fasse qch/jusqu'à ce qu'il donne qch.

pet [pet] **1** *n* animal *m* (domestique); *(favourite person)* chouchou, -oute *mf*; **yes (my) p.** *Fam* oui mon chou; **to have** *or* **keep a p.** avoir un animal chez soi; — *a (dog etc)* domestique; *(tiger etc)* apprivoisé; *(favourite)* favori; **p. shop** magasin *m* d'animaux; **p. hate** bête *f* noire; **p. name** petit nom *m* (d'amitié); **p. subject** dada *m*. **2** *vt* (-tt-) *(fondle)* caresser; *(sexually)* *Fam* peloter; — *vi* *Fam* se peloter.

petal ['pet(ə)l] *n* pétale *m*.

peter ['piːtər] *vi* **to p. out** *(run out)* s'épuiser; *(dry up)* se tarir; *(die out)* mourir; *(disappear)* disparaître.

petite [pə'tiːt] *a (woman)* petite et mince, menue.

petition [pə'tɪʃ(ə)n] *n (signatures)* pétition *f*; *(request)* *Jur* requête *f*; **p. for divorce** demande *f* en divorce; — *vt* adresser une pétition *or* une requête à (**for sth** pour demander qch).

petrify ['petrɪfaɪ] *vt (frighten)* pétrifier de terreur.

petrol ['petrəl] *n* essence *f*; **I've run out of p.** je suis tombé en panne d'essence; **p. engine** moteur *m* à essence; **p. station** poste *m* d'essence, station-service *f*.

petroleum [pə'trəʊlɪəm] *n* pétrole *m*.

petticoat ['petɪkəʊt] *n* jupon *m*.

petty ['petɪ] *a* (-ier, -iest) *(small)* petit; *(trivial)* insignifiant, menu, petit; *(mean)* mesquin; **p. cash** *Com* petite caisse *f*, menue monnaie *f*. ◆**pettiness** *n* petitesse *f*; insignifiance *f*; mesquinerie *f*.

petulant ['petjʊlənt] *a* irritable. ◆**petulance** *n* irritabilité *f*.

petunia [pɪ'tjuːnɪə] *n* *Bot* pétunia *m*.

pew [pjuː] *n* banc *m* d'église; **take a p.!** *Hum* assieds-toi!

pewter ['pjuːtər] *n* étain *m*.

phallic ['fælɪk] *a* phallique.

phantom ['fæntəm] *n* fantôme *m*.

pharmacy ['fɑːməsɪ] *n* pharmacie *f*. ◆**pharmaceutical** [-'sjuːtɪk(ə)l] *a* pharmaceutique. ◆**pharmacist** *n* pharmacien, -ienne *mf*.

pharynx ['færɪŋks] *n* *Anat* pharynx *m*. ◆**pharyn'gitis** *n* *Med* pharyngite *f*.

phase [feɪz] *n (stage)* phase *f*; — *vt* **to p.**

in/out introduire/supprimer progressivement. ◆**phased** a (*changes etc*) progressif.

PhD [piːeɪtʃˈdiː] n abbr (*Doctor of Philosophy*) (*degree*) Univ doctorat m.

pheasant [ˈfezənt] n (*bird*) faisan m.

phenomenon, pl -ena [fɪˈnɒmɪnən, -ɪnə] n phénomène m. ◆**phenomenal** a phénoménal.

phew! [fjuː] int (*relief*) ouf!

philanderer [fɪˈlændərər] n coureur m de jupons.

philanthropist [fɪˈlænθrəpɪst] n philanthrope m. ◆**philan'thropic** a philanthropique.

philately [fɪˈlætəlɪ] n philatélie. ◆**phila'telic** a philatélique. ◆**philatelist** n philatéliste m.

philharmonic [fɪləˈmɒnɪk] a philharmonique.

Philippines [ˈfɪlɪpiːnz] npl the P. les Philippines fpl.

philistine [ˈfɪlɪstaɪn] n béotien, -ienne m, philistin m.

philosophy [fɪˈlɒsəfɪ] n philosophie f. ◆**philosopher** n philosophe mf. ◆**philo'sophical** a philosophique; (*stoical, resigned*) Fig philosophe. ◆**philo'sophically** adv (*to say etc*) avec philosophie. ◆**philosophize** vi philosopher.

phlegm [flem] n Med glaires fpl; (*calmness*) Fig flegme m. ◆**phleg'matic** a flegmatique.

phobia [ˈfəʊbɪə] n phobie f.

phone [fəʊn] n téléphone m; on the p. (*speaking here*) au téléphone; (*at other end*) au bout du fil; to be on the p. (*as subscriber*) avoir le téléphone; p. call coup m de fil ou de téléphone; to make a p. call téléphoner (to à); p. book annuaire m; p. box, p. booth cabine f téléphonique; p. number numéro m de téléphone; – vt (*message*) téléphoner (to à); to p. s.o. (up) téléphoner à qn; – vi to p. (up) téléphoner; to p. back rappeler. ◆**phonecard** n télécarte f.

phonetic [fəˈnetɪk] a phonétique. ◆**phonetics** n (*science*) phonétique f.

phoney [ˈfəʊnɪ] a (-ier, -iest) Fam (*jewels, writer etc*) faux; (*attack, firm*) bidon inv; (*attitude*) fumiste; – n Fam (*impostor*) imposteur m; (*joker, shirker*) fumiste mf; it's a p. (*jewel, coin etc*) c'est du faux.

phonograph [ˈfəʊnəgræf] n Am électrophone m.

phosphate [ˈfɒsfeɪt] n Ch phosphate m.

phosphorus [ˈfɒsfərəs] n Ch phosphore m.

photo [ˈfəʊtəʊ] n (pl -os) photo f; to have one's p. taken se faire photographier.

◆**photocopier** n (*machine*) photocopieur m. ◆**photocopy** n photocopie f; – vt photocopier. ◆**photo'genic** a photogénique. ◆**photograph** n photographie f; – vt photographier; – vi to p. well être photogénique. ◆**photographer** [fəˈtɒgrəfər] n photographe mf. ◆**photo'graphic** a photographique. ◆**photography** [fəˈtɒgrəfɪ] n (*activity*) photographie f. ◆**photostat®** = photocopy.

phras/e [freɪz] n (*saying*) expression f; (*idiom*) & Gram locution f; – vt (*express*) exprimer; (*letter*) rédiger. ◆**—ing** n (*wording*) termes mpl. ◆**phrasebook** n (*for tourists*) manuel m de conversation.

physical [ˈfɪzɪk(ə)l] a physique; (*object, world*) matériel; p. examination Med examen m médical; p. education, p. training éducation f physique. ◆**physically** adv physiquement; p. impossible matériellement impossible.

physician [fɪˈzɪʃ(ə)n] n médecin m.

physics [ˈfɪzɪks] n (*science*) physique f. ◆**physicist** n physicien, -ienne mf.

physiology [fɪzɪˈɒlədʒɪ] n physiologie f. ◆**physio'logical** a physiologique.

physiotherapy [fɪzɪəˈθerəpɪ] n kinésithérapie f. ◆**physiotherapist** n kinésithérapeute mf.

physique [fɪˈziːk] n (*appearance*) physique m; (*constitution*) constitution f.

piano [pɪˈænəʊ] n (pl -os) piano m. ◆**'pianist** n pianiste mf.

piazza [pɪˈætsə] n (*square*) place f; (*covered*) passage m couvert.

picayune [pɪkəˈjuːn] a (*petty*) Am Fam mesquin.

pick [pɪk] n (*choice*) choix m; the p. of (*best*) le meilleur de; the p. of the bunch le dessus du panier; to take one's p. faire son choix, choisir; – vt (*choose*) choisir; (*flower, fruit etc*) cueillir; (*hole*) faire (in dans); (*lock*) crocheter; to p. one's nose se mettre les doigts dans le nez; to p. one's teeth se curer les dents; to p. a fight chercher la bagarre (with avec); to p. holes in Fig relever les défauts de; to p. (off) (*remove*) enlever; to p. out (*choose*) choisir; (*identify*) reconnaître, distinguer; to p. up (*sth dropped*) ramasser; (*fallen person or chair*) relever; (*person into air, weight*) soulever; (*cold, money*) Fig ramasser; (*habit, accent, speed*) prendre; (*fetch, collect*) (passer) prendre; (*find*) trouver; (*baby*) prendre dans ses bras; (*programme etc*) Rad capter; (*survivor*) recueillir; (*arrest*) arrêter, ramasser; (*learn*) apprendre; – vi to p. and choose choisir avec soin; **to p. on** (*nag*) harceler; (*blame*) accuser; **why p. on me?** pourquoi moi?; **to p. up** (*improve*) s'améliorer; (*of business, trade*) reprendre; *Med* aller mieux; (*resume*) continuer. ◆**—ing 1** *n* (*choosing*) choix *m* (of de); (*of flower, fruit etc*) cueillette *f*. **2** *npl* (*leftovers*) restes *mpl*; *Com* profits *mpl*. ◆**pick-me-up** *n* (*drink*) *Fam* remontant *m*. ◆**pick-up** *n* (*of record player*) (bras *m* de) pick-up *m*; (*person*) *Pej Fam* partenaire *mf* de rencontre; **p.-up** (**truck**) pick-up *m*.

pick(axe) (*Am* **-ax**) ['pɪk(æks)] *n* (*tool*) pioche *f*; **ice pick** pic *m* à glace.

picket ['pɪkɪt] **1** *n* (*striker*) gréviste *mf*; **p. (line)** piquet *m* (de grève); – *vt* (*factory*) installer des piquets de grève aux portes de. **2** *n* (*stake*) piquet *m*.

pickle ['pɪk(ə)l] **1** *n* (*brine*) saumure *f*; (*vinegar*) vinaigre *m*; *pl* (*vegetables*) pickles *mpl*; *Am* concombres *mpl*, cornichons *mpl*; – *vt* mariner. **2** *n* **in a p.** (*trouble*) *Fam* dans le pétrin.

pickpocket ['pɪkpɒkɪt] *n* (*thief*) pickpocket *m*.

picky ['pɪkɪ] *a* (**-ier, -iest**) (*choosey*) *Am* difficile.

picnic ['pɪknɪk] *n* pique-nique *m*; – *vi* (**-ck-**) pique-niquer.

pictorial [pɪk'tɔːrɪəl] *a* (*in pictures*) en images; (*periodical*) illustré.

picture ['pɪktʃər] **1** *n* image *f*; (*painting*) tableau *m*, peinture *f*; (*drawing*) dessin *m*; (*photo*) photo *f*; (*film*) film *m*; (*scene*) *Fig* tableau *m*; **the pictures** *Cin* le cinéma; **to put s.o. in the p.** *Fig* mettre qn au courant; **p. frame** cadre *m*. **2** *vt* (*imagine*) s'imaginer (**that** que); (*remember*) revoir; (*depict*) décrire.

picturesque [pɪktʃə'resk] *a* pittoresque.

piddling ['pɪdlɪŋ] *a* *Pej* dérisoire.

pidgin ['pɪdʒɪn] *n* **p. (English)** pidgin *m*.

pie [paɪ] *n* (*of meat, vegetable*) tourte *f*; (*of fruit*) tarte *f*, tourte *f*; (*compact filling*) pâté *m* en croûte; **cottage p.** hachis *m* Parmentier.

piebald ['paɪbɔːld] *a* pie *inv*.

piece [piːs] *n* morceau *m*; (*of bread, paper, chocolate, etc*) bout *m*, morceau *m*; (*of fabric, machine, game, artillery*) pièce *f*; (*coin*) pièce *f*; **bits and pieces** des petites choses; **in pieces** en morceaux, en pièces; **to smash to pieces** briser en morceaux; **to take to pieces** (*machine etc*) démonter; **to come to pieces** se démonter; **to go to pieces** (*of person*) *Fig* craquer; **a p.** (*of luck/news/etc*) une chance/nouvelle/*etc*; **in**

one p. (*object*) intact; (*person*) indemne; – *vt* **to p. together** (*facts*) reconstituer; (*one's life*) refaire. ◆**piecemeal** *adv* petit à petit; – *a* (*unsystematic*) peu méthodique.

◆**piecework** *n* travail *m* à la tâche *or* à la pièce.

pier [pɪər] *n* (*promenade*) jetée *f*; (*for landing*) appontement *m*.

pierc/e [pɪəs] *vt* percer; (*of cold, sword, bullet*) transpercer (*qn*). ◆**—ing** *a* (*voice, look etc*) perçant; (*wind etc*) glacial.

piety ['paɪətɪ] *n* piété *f*.

piffling ['pɪflɪŋ] *a* *Fam* insignifiant.

pig [pɪg] *n* cochon *m*, porc *m*; (*evil person*) *Pej* cochon *m*; (*glutton*) *Pej* goinfre *m*. ◆**piggish** *a* *Pej* (*dirty*) sale; (*greedy*) goinfre. ◆**piggy** *a* (*greedy*) *Fam* goinfre. ◆**piggybank** *n* tirelire *f* (en forme de cochon).

pigeon ['pɪdʒɪn] *n* pigeon *m*. ◆**pigeonhole** *n* casier *m*; – *vt* classer; (*shelve*) mettre en suspens.

piggyback ['pɪgɪbæk] *n* **to give s.o. a p.** porter qn sur le dos.

pigheaded [pɪg'hedɪd] *a* obstiné.

pigment ['pɪgmənt] *n* pigment *m*. ◆**pigmen'tation** *n* pigmentation *f*.

pigsty ['pɪgstaɪ] *n* porcherie *f*.

pigtail ['pɪgteɪl] *n* (*hair*) natte *f*.

pike [paɪk] *n* **1** (*fish*) brochet *m*. **2** (*weapon*) pique *f*.

pilchard ['pɪltʃəd] *n* pilchard *m*, sardine *f*.

pile¹ [paɪl] *n* pile *f*; (*fortune*) *Fam* fortune *f*; **piles of, a p. of** *Fam* beaucoup de, un tas de; – *vt* **to p. up** (*stack up*) empiler; – *vi* **to p. into** (*of people*) s'entasser dans; **to p. up** (*accumulate*) s'accumuler, s'amonceler. ◆**p.-up** *n* *Aut* collision *f* en chaîne, carambolage *m*.

pile² [paɪl] *n* (*of carpet*) poils *mpl*.

piles [paɪlz] *npl* *Med* hémorroïdes *fpl*.

pilfer ['pɪlfər] *vt* (*steal*) chaparder (**from s.o.** à qn). ◆**—ing** *n*, ◆**—age** *n* chapardage *m*.

pilgrim ['pɪlgrɪm] *n* pèlerin *m*. ◆**pilgrimage** *n* pèlerinage *m*.

pill [pɪl] *n* pilule *f*; **to be on the p.** (*of woman*) prendre la pilule; **to go on/off the p.** se mettre à/arrêter la pilule.

pillage ['pɪlɪdʒ] *vti* piller; – *n* pillage *m*.

pillar ['pɪlər] *n* pilier *m*; (*of smoke*) *Fig* colonne *f*. ◆**p.-box** *n* boîte *f* à *or* aux lettres (située sur le trottoir).

pillion ['pɪljən] *adv* **to ride p.** (*on motorbike*) monter derrière.

pillory ['pɪlərɪ] *vt* (*ridicule, scorn*) mettre au pilori.

pillow ['pɪləʊ] *n* oreiller *m*. ◆**pillowcase** *n*, ◆**pillowslip** *n* taie *f* d'oreiller.

pilot ['paɪlət] **1** *n* (*of aircraft, ship*) pilote *m*; – *vt* piloter; – *a* **p. light** (*on appliance*) voyant *m*. **2** *a* (*experimental*) (-)pilote; **p. scheme** projet(-)pilote *m*.

pimento [pɪ'mentəʊ] *n* (*pl* -os) piment *m*.

pimp [pɪmp] *n* souteneur *m*.

pimple ['pɪmp(ə)l] *n* bouton *m*. ◆**pimply** *a* (-ier, iest) boutonneux.

pin [pɪn] *n* épingle *f*; (*drawing pin*) punaise *f*; *Tech* goupille *f*, fiche *f*; **to have pins and needles** *Med Fam* avoir des fourmis (**in** dans); – *vt* (-nn-) **to p.** (**on**) (*attach*) épingler (**to** sur, à); (*to wall*) punaiser (**to, on** à); **to p. one's hopes on** mettre tous ses espoirs dans; **to p. on to** s.o. (*crime, action*) accuser qn de; **to p. down** (*immobilize*) immobiliser; (*fix*) fixer; (*enemy*) clouer; **to p. s.o. down** *Fig* forcer qn à préciser ses idées; **to p. up** (*notice*) afficher. ◆**pincushion** *n* pelote *f* (à épingles). ◆**pinhead** *n* tête *f* d'épingle.

pinafore ['pɪnəfɔːr] *n* (*apron*) tablier *m*; (*dress*) robe *f* chasuble.

pinball ['pɪnbɔːl] *a* **p. machine** flipper *m*.

pincers ['pɪnsəz] *npl* tenailles *fpl*.

pinch [pɪntʃ] **1** *n* (*mark*) pinçon *m*; (*of salt*) pincée *f*; **to give s.o. a p.** pincer qn; **at a p.**, *Am* **in a p.** (*if necessary*) au besoin; **to feel the p.** *Fig* souffrir (*du manque d'argent etc*); – *vt* pincer; – *vi* (*of shoes*) faire mal. **2** *vt Fam* (*steal*) piquer (**from** à); (*arrest*) pincer.

pine [paɪn] **1** *n* (*tree, wood*) pin *m*; **p. forest** pinède *f*. **2** *vi* **to p. for** désirer vivement (*retrouver*), languir après; **to p. away** dépérir.

pineapple ['paɪnæp(ə)l] *n* ananas *m*.

ping [pɪŋ] *n* bruit *m* métallique. ◆**pinger** *n* (*on appliance*) signal *m* sonore.

ping-pong ['pɪŋpɒŋ] *n* ping-pong *m*.

pink [pɪŋk] *a & n* (*colour*) rose (*m*).

pinkie ['pɪŋkɪ] *n Am* petit doigt *m*.

pinnacle ['pɪnək(ə)l] *n* (*highest point*) *Fig* apogée *m*.

pinpoint ['pɪnpɔɪnt] *vt* (*locate*) repérer; (*define*) définir.

pinstripe ['pɪnstraɪp] *a* (*suit*) rayé.

pint [paɪnt] *n* pinte *f* (*Br* = 0,57 litre, *Am* = 0,47 litre); **a p. of beer** = un demi.

pinup ['pɪnʌp] *n* (*girl*) pin-up *f inv*.

pioneer [paɪə'nɪər] *n* pionnier, -ière *mf*; – *vt* (*research, study*) entreprendre pour la première fois.

pious ['paɪəs] *a* (*person, deed*) pieux.

pip [pɪp] **1** *n* (*of fruit*) pépin *m*. **2** *n* (*on uniform*) *Mil* galon *m*, sardine *f*. **3** *npl* **the pips** (*sound*) *Tel* le bip-bip.

pip/e [paɪp] **1** *n* tuyau *m*; (*of smoker*) pipe *f*; (*instrument*) *Mus* pipeau *m*; **the pipes** (*bagpipes*) *Mus* la cornemuse; **(peace) p.** calumet *m* de la paix; **to smoke a p.** fumer la pipe; **p. cleaner** cure-pipe *m*; **p. dream** chimère *f*; – *vt* (*water etc*) transporter par tuyaux *or* par canalisation; **piped music** musique *f* (de fond) enregistrée. **2** *vi* **to p. down** (*shut up*) *Fam* la boucler, se taire. ◆**-ing** *n* (*system of pipes*) canalisations *fpl*, tuyaux *mpl*; **length of p.** tuyau *m*; – *adv* **it's p. hot** (*soup etc*) c'est très chaud. ◆**pipeline** *n* pipeline *m*; **it's in the p.** *Fig* c'est en route.

pirate ['paɪərət] *n* pirate *m*; – *a* (*radio, ship*) pirate. ◆**piracy** *n* piraterie *f*. ◆**pirated** *a* (*book, record etc*) pirate.

Pisces ['paɪsiːz] *npl* (*sign*) les Poissons *mpl*.

pistachio [pɪ'stɑːʃɪəʊ] *n* (*pl* -os) (*fruit, flavour*) pistache *f*.

pistol ['pɪstl] *n* pistolet *m*.

piston ['pɪst(ə)n] *n Aut* piston *m*.

pit [pɪt] **1** *n* (*hole*) trou *m*; (*mine*) mine *f*; (*quarry*) carrière *f*; (*of stomach*) creux *m*; *Th* orchestre *m*; *Sp Aut* stand *m* de ravitaillement. **2** *vt* (-tt-) **to p. oneself** *or* **one's wits against** se mesurer à. **3** *n* (*stone of fruit*) *Am* noyau *m*. ◆**pitted** *a* **1** (*face*) grêlé; **p. with rust** piqué de rouille. **2** (*fruit*) *Am* dénoyauté.

pitch¹ [pɪtʃ] **1** *n Sp* terrain *m*; (*in market*) place *f*; **2** *n* (*degree*) degré *m*; (*of voice*) hauteur *f*; *Mus* ton *m*. **3** *vt* (*ball*) lancer; (*camp*) établir; (*tent*) dresser; **a pitched battle** *Mil* une bataille rangée; *Fig* une belle bagarre. **4** *vi* (*of ship*) tanguer. **5** *vi* **to p. in** (*cooperate*) *Fam* se mettre de la partie; **to p. into s.o.** attaquer qn.

pitch² [pɪtʃ] *n* (*tar*) poix *f*. ◆**p.-'black** *a*, ◆**p.-'dark** *a* noir comme dans un four.

pitcher ['pɪtʃər] *n* cruche *f*, broc *m*.

pitchfork ['pɪtʃfɔːk] *n* fourche *f* (à foin).

pitfall ['pɪtfɔːl] *n* (*trap*) piège *m*.

pith [pɪθ] *n* (*of orange*) peau *f* blanche; (*essence*) *Fig* moelle *f*. ◆**pithy** *a* (-ier, -iest) (*remark etc*) piquant et concis.

pitiful ['pɪtɪfəl] *a* pitoyable. ◆**pitiless** *a* impitoyable.

pittance ['pɪtəns] *n* (*income*) revenu *m* or salaire *m* misérable; (*sum*) somme *f* dérisoire.

pitter-patter ['pɪtəpætər] *n* = **patter 1**.

pity ['pɪtɪ] *n* pitié *f*; (**what**) **a p.!** (quel) dommage!; **it's a p.** c'est dommage (**that**

que (+ *sub*), **to do** de faire); **to have** *or* **take p. on** avoir pitié de; – *vt* plaindre.

pivot ['pɪvət] *n* pivot *m*; – *vi* pivoter.

pixie ['pɪksɪ] *n* (*fairy*) lutin *m*.

pizza ['piːtsə] *n* pizza *f*.

placard ['plækɑːd] *n* (*notice*) affiche *f*.

placate [plə'keɪt, *Am* 'pleɪkeɪt] *vt* calmer.

place [pleɪs] *n* endroit *m*; (*specific*) lieu *m*; (*house*) maison *f*; (*premises*) locaux *mpl*; (*seat, position, rank*) place *f*; **in the first p.** (*firstly*) en premier lieu; **to take p.** (*happen*) avoir lieu; **p. of work** lieu *m* de travail; **market p.** (*square*) place *f* du marché; **at my p.,** *or* **to my p.** *Fam* chez moi; **some p.** (*somewhere*) *Am* quelque part; **no p.** (*nowhere*) *Am* nulle part; **all over the p.** partout; **to lose one's place** perdre sa place; (*in book etc*) perdre sa page; **to set p.** couvert *m*; **to lay three places** (*at the table*) mettre trois couverts; **to take the p. of** remplacer; **in p. of** à la place de; **out of p.** (*remark, object*) déplacé; (*person*) dépaysé; **to p. mat** set *m* (de table); – *vt* (*put, situate, invest*) & *Sp* placer; (*an order*) *Com* passer (**with** s.o. à qn); (*remember*) se rappeler; (*identify*) reconnaître. ◆**placing** *n* (*of money*) placement *m*.

placid ['plæsɪd] *a* placide.

plagiarize ['pleɪdʒəraɪz] *vt* plagier. ◆**plagiarism** *n* plagiat *m*.

plague [pleɪg] **1** *n* (*disease*) peste *f*; (*nuisance*) *Fam* plaie *f*. **2** *vt* (*harass, pester*) harceler (**with** de).

plaice [pleɪs] *n* (*fish*) carrelet *m*, plie *f*.

plaid [plæd] *n* (*fabric*) tissu *m* écossais.

plain[1] [pleɪn] **1** *a* (**-er, -est**) (*clear, obvious*) clair; (*outspoken*) franc; (*simple*) simple; (*not patterned*) uni; (*woman, man*) sans beauté; (*sheer*) pur; **in p. clothes** en civil; **to make it p. to s.o. that** faire comprendre à qn que; **p. speaking** franc-parler *m*; – *adv* (*tired etc*) tout bonnement. ◆**-ly** *adv* clairement; franchement. ◆**-ness** *n* clarté *f*; simplicité *f*; manque *m* de beauté.

plain[2] [pleɪn] *n Geog* plaine *f*.

plaintiff ['pleɪntɪf] *n Jur* plaignant, -ante *mf*.

plait [plæt] *n* tresse *f*, natte *f*; – *vt* tresser, natter.

plan [plæn] *n* projet *m*; (*elaborate*) plan *m*; (*of house, book etc*) & *Pol Econ* plan *m*; **the best p. would be to . . .** le mieux serait de . . .; **according to p.** comme prévu; **to have no plans** (*be free*) n'avoir rien de prévu; **to change one's plans** (*decide differently*) changer d'idée; **master p.** stratégie *f* d'ensemble; – *vt* (**-nn-**) (*envisage, decide on*) prévoir, projeter; (*organize*) organiser;

(*prepare*) préparer; (*design*) concevoir; *Econ* planifier; **to p. to do** (*intend*) avoir l'intention de faire; **as planned** comme prévu; – *vi* faire des projets; **to p. for** (*rain, disaster*) prévoir. ◆**planning** *n Econ* planification *f*; (*industrial, commercial*) planning *m*; **family p.** planning *m* familial; **town p.** urbanisme *m*. ◆**planner** *n* **town p.** urbaniste *mf*.

plane [pleɪn] *n* **1** (*aircraft*) avion *m*. **2** *Carp* rabot *m*. **3** (*tree*) platane *m*. **4** (*level*) & *Fig* plan *m*.

planet ['plænɪt] *n* planète *f*. ◆**planetarium** *n* planétarium *m*. ◆**planetary** *a* planétaire.

plank [plæŋk] *n* planche *f*.

plant [plɑːnt] **1** *n* plante *f*; **house p.** plante d'appartement; – *vt* planter (**with** en, de); (*bomb*) *Fig* (dé)poser; **to p. sth on s.o.** (*hide*) cacher qch sur qn. **2** *n* (*machinery*) matériel *m*; (*fixtures*) installation *f*; (*factory*) usine *f*. ◆**plan'tation** *n* (*land, trees etc*) plantation *f*.

plaque [plæk] *n* **1** (*commemorative plate*) plaque *f*. **2** (*on teeth*) plaque *f* dentaire.

plasma ['plæzmə] *n Med* plasma *m*.

plaster ['plɑːstər] *n* (*substance*) plâtre *m*; (*sticking*) sparadrap *m*; **p. of Paris** plâtre *m* à mouler; **in p.** *Med* dans le plâtre; **p. cast** *Med* plâtre *m*; – *vt* plâtrer; **to p. down** (*hair*) plaquer; **to p. with** (*cover*) couvrir de. ◆**-er** *n* plâtrier *m*.

plastic ['plæstɪk] *a* (*substance, art*) plastique; (*object*) en plastique; **p. explosive** plastic *m*; **p. surgery** chirurgie *f* esthétique; – *n* plastique *m*, matière *f* plastique.

plasticine® ['plæstɪsiːn] *n* pâte *f* à modeler.

plate [pleɪt] *n* (*dish*) assiette *f*; (*metal sheet on door, on vehicle etc*) plaque *f*; (*book illustration*) gravure *f*; (*dental*) dentier *m*; **gold/silver p.** vaisselle *f* d'or/d'argent; **a lot on one's p.** (*work*) *Fig* du pain sur la planche; **p. glass** verre *m* à vitre; – *vt* (*jewellery, metal*) plaquer (**with** de). ◆**plateful** *n* assiettée *f*, assiette *f*.

plateau ['plætəʊ] *n Geog* (*pl* **-s** *or* **-x**) plateau *m*.

platform ['plætfɔːm] *n* estrade *f*; (*for speaker*) tribune *f*; (*on bus*) & *Pol* plate-forme *f*; *Rail* quai *m*; **p. shoes** chaussures *fpl* à semelles compensées.

platinum ['plætɪnəm] *n* (*metal*) platine *m*; – *a* *p. or* **p.-blond(e) hair** cheveux *mpl* platinés.

platitude ['plætɪtjuːd] *n* platitude *f*.

platonic [plə'tɒnɪk] *a* (*love etc*) platonique.

platoon [plə'tuːn] *n Mil* section *f*.

platter ['plætər] n Culin plat m.

plaudits ['plɔːdɪts] npl applaudissements mpl.

plausible ['plɔːzəb(ə)l] a (argument etc) plausible; (speaker etc) convaincant.

play [pleɪ] n (amusement, looseness) jeu m; Th pièce f (de théâtre), spectacle m; **a p. on words** un jeu de mots; **to come into p.** entrer en jeu; **to call into p.** faire entrer en jeu; – vt (card, part, tune etc) jouer; (game) jouer à; (instrument) jouer de; (match) disputer (with avec); (team, opponent) jouer contre; (record) passer; (radio) faire marcher; **to p. ball with** Fig coopérer avec; **to p. the fool** faire l'idiot; **to p. a part in doing/in sth** contribuer à faire/à qch; **to p. it cool** Fam garder son sang-froid; **to p. back** (tape) réécouter; **to p. down** minimiser; **to p. s.o. up** Fam (of bad back etc) tracasser qn; (of child etc) faire enrager qn; **played out** Fam (tired) épuisé; (idea, method) périmé, vieux jeu inv; **to p. on** (with avec, at à); (of record player, tape recorder) marcher; **what are you playing at?** Fam qu'est-ce que tu fais?; **to p. about** or **around** jouer, s'amuser; **to p. on** (piano etc) jouer de; (s.o.'s emotions etc) jouer sur; **to p. up** (of child, machine etc) Fam faire des siennes; **to p. up to s.o.** faire de la lèche à qn. ◆**-ing** n jeu m; **p. card** carte f à jouer; **p. field** terrain m de jeu. ◆**-er** n Sp joueur, -euse mf; Th acteur m, actrice f, de clarinette/etc p. joueur, -euse mf de clarinette/etc; **cassette p.** lecteur m de cassettes.

play-act ['pleɪækt] vi jouer la comédie. ◆**playboy** n playboy m. ◆**playgoer** n amateur m de théâtre. ◆**playground** n Sch cour f de récréation. ◆**playgroup** n = playschool. ◆**playmate** n camarade mf. ◆**playpen** n parc m (pour enfants). ◆**playroom** n (in house) salle f de jeux. ◆**playschool** n garderie f (d'enfants). ◆**plaything** n (person) Fig jouet m. ◆**playtime** n Sch récréation f. ◆**playwright** n dramaturge mf.

playful ['pleɪfəl] a enjoué; (child) joueur. ◆**-ly** adv (to say) en badinant. ◆**-ness** n enjouement m.

plc [piːel'siː] abbr (public limited company) SA.

plea [pliː] n (request) appel m; (excuse) excuse f; **to make a p. of guilty** Jur plaider coupable. ◆**plead** vi Jur plaider; (for help etc) implorer; – vt Jur plaider; (as excuse) alléguer. ◆**pleading** n (requests) prières fpl.

pleasant ['plezənt] a agréable; (polite) aimable. ◆**-ly** adv agréablement. ◆**-ness** n (charm) charme m; (of person) amabilité f. ◆**pleasantries** npl (jokes) plaisanteries fpl; (polite remarks) civilités fpl.

pleas/e [pliːz] adv s'il vous plaît, s'il te plaît; **p. sit down** asseyez-vous, je vous prie; **p. do!** bien sûr!, je vous en prie!; **'no smoking.' 'prière de ne pas fumer';** – vt plaire à; (satisfy) contenter; **hard to p.** difficile (à contenter), exigeant; **p. yourself!** comme tu veux!; – vi plaire; **do as you p.** fais comme tu veux; **as much** or **as many as you p.** autant qu'il vous plaira. ◆**-ed** a content (with de, that que (+ sub), to do de); **p. to meet you!** enchanté!; **I'd be p. to!** avec plaisir! ◆**-ing** a agréable, plaisant.

pleasure ['pleʒər] n plaisir m; **p. boat** bateau m de plaisance. ◆**pleasurable** a très agréable.

pleat [pliːt] n (fold) pli m; – vt plisser.

plebiscite ['plebɪsɪt, -saɪt] n plébiscite m.

pledge [pledʒ] 1 n (promise) promesse f, engagement m (to do de faire); – vt promettre (to do de faire). 2 n (token, object) gage m; – vt (pawn) engager.

plenty ['plentɪ] n abondance f; **in p.** en abondance; **p. of** beaucoup de; **that's p.** (enough) c'est assez, ça suffit. ◆**plentiful** a abondant.

plethora ['pleθərə] n pléthore f.

pleurisy ['plʊərɪsɪ] n Med pleurésie f.

pliable ['plaɪəb(ə)l] a souple.

pliers ['plaɪəz] npl (tool) pince(s) f(pl).

plight [plaɪt] n (crisis) situation f critique; (sorry) p. triste situation f.

plimsoll ['plɪmsəl] n chaussure f de tennis, tennis f.

plinth [plɪnθ] n socle m.

plod [plɒd] vi (-dd-) **to p.** (along) avancer or travailler laborieusement; **to p. through** (book) lire laborieusement. ◆**plodding** a (slow) lent; (step) pesant. ◆**plodder** n (steady worker) bûcheur, -euse mf.

plonk [plɒŋk] 1 int (splash) plouf! 2 vt **to p.** (down) (drop) Fam poser (bruyamment). 3 n (wine) Pej Sl pinard m.

plot [plɒt] 1 n (conspiracy) complot m (against contre); Cin Th Liter intrigue f; – vti (-tt-) comploter (to do de faire). 2 n (of land) terrain m; (patch in garden) carré m de terre; building p. terrain m à bâtir. 3 vt (-tt-) **to p.** (out) déterminer; (graph, diagram) tracer; (s.o.'s position) relever. ◆**plotting** n (conspiracies) complots mpl.

plough [plaʊ] n charrue f; – vt labourer; **to**

p. back into (*money*) *Fig* réinvestir dans; – *vi* labourer; **to p. into** (*crash into*) percuter; **to p. through** (*snow etc*) avancer péniblement dans; (*fence, wall*) défoncer. ◆**ploughman** n (pl -**men**) laboureur m; **p.'s lunch** *Culin* assiette f composée (*de crudités et fromage*).

plow [plaʊ] *Am* = **plough**.

ploy [plɔɪ] n stratagème m.

pluck [plʌk] 1 n courage m; – vt **to p. up courage** s'armer de courage. 2 vt (*fowl*) plumer; (*eyebrows*) épiler; (*string*) *Mus* pincer; (*flower*) cueillir. ◆**plucky** a (-**ier**, -**iest**) courageux.

plug [plʌg] 1 n (*of cotton wool, wood etc*) tampon m, bouchon m; (*for sink etc drainage*) bonde f; (*for bath*) bonde f; – vt (-**gg-**) **to p. in** brancher. 3 n *Aut* bougie f. 4 n (*publicity*) *Fam* battage m publicitaire; – vt (-**gg-**) *Fam* faire du battage publicitaire pour. 5 vi (-**gg-**) **to p. away** (*work*) *Fam* bosser (**at** à). ◆**plughole** n trou m (du lavabo *etc*), vidange f.

plum [plʌm] n prune f; **a p. job** *Fam* un travail en or, un bon fromage.

plumage ['pluːmɪdʒ] n plumage m.

plumb [plʌm] 1 vt (*probe, understand*) sonder. 2 adv (*crazy etc*) *Am Fam* complètement; **p. in the middle** en plein milieu.

plumber ['plʌmər] n plombier m. ◆**plumbing** n plomberie f.

plume [pluːm] n (*feather*) plume f; (*on hat etc*) plumet m; **a p. of smoke** un panache de fumée.

plummet ['plʌmɪt] vi (*of aircraft etc*) plonger; (*of prices*) dégringoler.

plump [plʌmp] 1 a (-**er**, -**est**) (*person*) grassouillet; (*arm, chicken*) dodu; (*cushion, cheek*) rebondi. 2 vi **to p. for** (*choose*) se décider pour, choisir. ◆—**ness** n rondeur f.

plunder ['plʌndər] vt piller; – n (*act*) pillage m; (*goods*) butin m.

plunge [plʌndʒ] vt (*thrust*) plonger (**into** dans); – vi (*dive*) plonger (**into** dans); (*fall*) tomber (**from** de); (*rush*) se lancer; – n (*dive*) plongeon m; (*fall*) chute f; **to take the p.** *Fig* se jeter à l'eau. ◆—**ing** a (*neckline*) plongeant. ◆—**er** n ventouse f (*pour déboucher un tuyau*), débouchoir m.

plural ['plʊərəl] a (*form*) pluriel; (*noun*) au pluriel; – n pluriel m; **in the p.** au pluriel.

plus [plʌs] prep plus; – a (*factor etc*) *El* positif; **twenty p.** vingt et quelques; – n

(*sign*) *Math* (signe m) plus m; **it's a p.** c'est un (avantage en) plus.

plush [plʌʃ] a (-**er**, -**est**) (*splendid*) somptueux.

plutonium [pluːˈtəʊnɪəm] n plutonium m.

ply [plaɪ] 1 vt (*trade*) exercer; (*oar, tool*) *Lit* manier. 2 vi **to p. between** (*travel*) faire la navette entre. 3 vt **to p. s.o. with** (*whisky etc*) faire boire continuellement à qn; (*questions*) bombarder qn de.

p.m. [piːˈem] adv (*afternoon*) de l'après-midi; (*evening*) du soir.

PM [piːˈem] n abbr (*Prime Minister*) Premier ministre m.

pneumatic [njuːˈmætɪk] a **p. drill** marteau-piqueur m, marteau m pneumatique.

pneumonia [njuːˈməʊnɪə] n pneumonie f.

poach [pəʊtʃ] 1 vt (*egg*) pocher. 2 vi (*hunt, steal*) braconner; – vt (*employee from rival firm*) débaucher, piquer. ◆—**ing** n braconnage m. ◆—**er** n 1 (*person*) braconnier m. 2 (*egg*) pocheuse f.

PO Box [piːˈəʊˈbɒks] abbr (*Post Office Box*) BP.

pocket ['pɒkɪt] n poche f; (*area*) *Fig* petite zone f; (*of resistance*) poche f, îlot m; **I'm $5 out of p.** j'ai perdu 5 dollars; – a (*money, book etc*) de poche; – vt (*gain, steal*) empocher. ◆**pocketbook** n (*notebook*) carnet m; (*woman's handbag*) *Am* sac m à main. ◆**pocketful** n **a p. of** une pleine poche de.

pockmarked ['pɒkmɑːkt] a (*face*) grêlé.

pod [pɒd] n cosse f.

podgy ['pɒdʒɪ] a (-**ier**, -**iest**) (*arm etc*) dodu; (*person*) rondelet.

podium ['pəʊdɪəm] n podium m.

poem ['pəʊɪm] n poème m. ◆**poet** n poète m. ◆**po'etic** a poétique. ◆**poetry** n poésie f.

poignant ['pɔɪnjənt] a poignant.

point [pɔɪnt] 1 n (*of knife etc*) pointe f; pl *Rail* aiguillage m; (**power**) *El* prise f (de courant). 2 n (*dot, position, question, degree, score etc*) point m; (*decimal*) virgule f; (*meaning*) *Fig* sens m; (*importance*) intérêt m; (*remark*) remarque f; **p. of view** point de vue; **at this p. in time** en ce moment; on **the p. of doing** sur le point de faire; **what's the p.?** à quoi bon? (**of** waiting/*etc* attendre/*etc*); **there's no p. (in) staying**/*etc* ça ne sert à rien de rester/*etc*; **that's not the p.** il ne s'agit pas de ça; **it's beside the p.** c'est à côté de la question; **to make a p. of doing** prendre garde de faire; **his good**

points ses qualités *fpl*; **his bad points** ses défauts *mpl*. **3** *vt* (*aim*) pointer (**at** sur); (*vehicle*) tourner (**towards** vers); **to p. the way** indiquer le chemin (**to** à); *Fig* montrer la voie (**to** à); **to p. one's finger at** indiquer du doigt, pointer son doigt vers; **to p. out** (*show*) indiquer; (*mention*) signaler (**that** que); – *vi* **to p.** (**at** *or* **to s.o.**) indiquer (qn) du doigt. **to p. to, be pointing to** (*show*) indiquer; **to p. east** indiquer l'est; **to be pointing** (*of vehicle*) être tourné (**towards** vers); (*of gun*) être braqué (**at** sur). ◆**-ed** *a* pointu; (*beard*) en pointe; (*remark, criticism*) *Fig* pertinent; (*incisive*) mordant. ◆**-edly** *adv* (*to the point*) avec pertinence; (*incisively*) d'un ton mordant. ◆**-er** *n* (*on dial etc*) index *m*; (*advice*) conseil *m*; (*clue*) indice *m*; **to be a p.** (*possible solution etc*) laisser entrevoir. ◆**-less** *a* inutile, futile. ◆**-lessly** *adv* inutilement.

point-blank [pɔɪnt'blæŋk] *adv & a* (*to shoot, a shot*) à bout portant; (*to refuse, a refusal*) *Fig* (tout) net; (*to request, a request*) de but en blanc.

pois/e [pɔɪz] *n* (*balance*) équilibre *m*; (*of body*) port *m*; (*grace*) grâce *f*; (*confidence*) assurance *f*, calme *m*; – *vt* tenir en équilibre. ◆**-ed** *a* en équilibre; (*hanging*) suspendu; (*composed*) calme; **p. to attack/etc** (*ready*) prêt à attaquer/etc.

poison [pɔɪz(ə)n] *n* poison *m*; (*of snake*) venin *m*; **p. gas** gaz *m* toxique; – *vt* empoisonner; **to p. s.o.'s mind** corrompre qn. ◆**poisoning** *n* empoisonnement *m*. ◆**poisonous** *a* (*fumes, substance*) toxique; (*snake*) venimeux; (*plant*) vénéneux.

pok/e [pəʊk] *vt* (*push*) pousser (*avec un bâton etc*); (*touch*) toucher; (*fire*) tisonner; **to p. sth into** (*put, thrust*) fourrer *or* enfoncer qch dans; **to p. one's finger at** pointer son doigt vers; **to p. one's nose into** fourrer le nez dans; **to p. a hole in** faire un trou dans; **to p. one's head out of the window** passer la tête par la fenêtre; **to p. out s.o.'s eye** crever un œil à qn; – *vi* pousser; **to p. about** *or* **around** fouiner dans; – *n* (*jab*) (petit) coup *m*; (*shove*) poussée *f*, coup *m*. ◆**-er** *n* **1** (*for fire*) tisonnier *m*. **2** *Cards* poker *m*.

poky [pəʊkɪ] *a* (**-ier, -iest**) (*small*) exigu et misérable, rikiki; (*slow*) *Am* lent.

Poland [pəʊlənd] *n* Pologne *f*. ◆**Pole** *n* Polonais, -aise *mf*.

polarize [pəʊləraɪz] *vt* polariser.

pole [pəʊl] *n* **1** (*rod*) perche *f*; (*fixed*) poteau *m*; (*for flag*) mât *m*. **2** *Geog* pôle *m*;

North/South P. pôle Nord/Sud. ◆**polar** *a* polaire; **p. bear** ours *m* blanc.

polemic [pə'lemɪk] *n* polémique *f*. ◆**polemical** *a* polémique.

police [pə'liːs] *n* police *f*; **more** *or* **extra p.** des renforts *mpl* de police; (*inquiry etc*) de la police; (*state, dog*) policier; **p. cadet** agent *m* de police stagiaire; **p. car** voiture *f* de police; **p. force** police *f*; – *vt* (*city etc*) maintenir l'ordre *or* la paix dans; (*frontier*) contrôler. ◆**policeman** *n* (*pl* **-men**) agent *m* de police. ◆**policewoman** *n* (*pl* **-women**) femme-agent *f*.

policy [pɒlɪsɪ] *n* **1** *Pol Econ etc* politique *f*; (*individual course of action*) règle *f*, façon *f* d'agir; *pl* (*ways of governing*) *Pol* politique *f*; **matter of p.** question *f* de principe. **2** (*insurance*) **p.** police *f* (d'assurance); **p. holder** assuré, -ée *mf*.

polio(myelitis) [pəʊlɪəʊ(maɪə'laɪtɪs)] *n* polio(myélite) *f*; **p. victim** polio *mf*.

polish [pɒlɪʃ] *vt* (*floor, table, shoes etc*) cirer; (*metal*) astiquer; (*rough surface*) polir; (*manners*) *Fig* raffiner; (*style*) *Fig* polir; **to p. up** (*one's French etc*) travailler; **to p. off** (*food, work etc*) *Fam* terminer, finir (en vitesse); – *n* (*for shoes*) cirage *m*; (*for floor, furniture*) cire *f*; (*shine*) vernis *m*; *Fig* raffinement *m*; (**nail**) **p.** vernis *m* (à ongles); **to give sth a p.** faire briller qch.

Polish [pəʊlɪʃ] *a* polonais; – *n* (*language*) polonais *m*.

polite [pə'laɪt] *a* (**-er, -est**) poli (**to, with** avec); **in p. society** dans la bonne société. ◆**-ly** *adv* poliment. ◆**-ness** *n* politesse *f*.

political [pə'lɪtɪk(ə)l] *a* politique. ◆**politician** *n* homme *m* *or* femme *f* politique. ◆**politicize** *vt* politiser. ◆**politics** *n* politique *f*.

polka [pɒlkə, *Am* pəʊlkə] *n* (*dance*) polka *f*; **p. dot** pois *m*.

poll [pəʊl] *n* (*voting*) scrutin *m*, élection *f*; (*vote*) vote *m*; (*turnout*) participation *f* électorale; (*list*) liste *f* électorale; **to go to the polls** aller aux urnes; (*opinion*) **p.** sondage *m* (d'opinion); **50% of the p.** 50% des votants; – *vt* (*votes*) obtenir; (*people*) sonder l'opinion de. ◆**-ing** *n* (*election*) élections *fpl*; **p. booth** isoloir *m*; **p. station** bureau *m* de vote.

pollen [pɒlən] *n* pollen *m*.

pollute [pə'luːt] *vt* polluer. ◆**pollutant** *n* polluant *m*. ◆**pollution** *n* pollution *f*.

polo [pəʊləʊ] *n* *Sp* polo *m*; **p. neck** (*sweater, neckline*) col *m* roulé.

polyester [pɒlɪ'estər] *n* polyester *m*.

Polynesia [ˌpɒlɪˈniːʒə] n Polynésie f.

polytechnic [ˌpɒlɪˈteknɪk] n institut m universitaire de technologie.

polythene [ˈpɒlɪθiːn] n polyéthylène m; **p. bag** sac m en plastique.

pomegranate [ˈpɒmɪgrænɪt] n (fruit) grenade f.

pomp [pɒmp] n pompe f. ◆**pomˈposity** n emphase f, solennité f. ◆**pompous** a pompeux.

pompon [ˈpɒmpɒn] n (ornament) pompon m.

pond [pɒnd] n étang m; (stagnant) mare f; (artificial) bassin m.

ponder [ˈpɒndər] vt to p. (over) réfléchir à; – vi réfléchir.

ponderous [ˈpɒndərəs] a (heavy, slow) pesant.

pong [pɒŋ] n Sl mauvaise odeur f; – vi (stink) Sl schlinguer.

pontificate [pɒnˈtɪfɪkeɪt] vi (speak) Pej pontifier (about sur).

pony [ˈpəʊnɪ] n poney m. ◆**ponytail** n (hair) queue f de cheval.

poodle [ˈpuːd(ə)l] n caniche m.

poof [pʊf] n (homosexual) Pej Sl pédé m.

pooh! [puː] int bah!; (bad smell) ça pue!

pooh-pooh [puːˈpuː] vt (scorn) dédaigner; (dismiss) se moquer de.

pool [puːl] **1** n (puddle) flaque f; (of blood) mare f; (pond) étang m; (for swimming) piscine f. **2** n (of experience, talent) réservoir m; (of advisers etc) équipe f; (of typists) Com pool m; (kitty) cagnotte f; (football) **pools** prognostics mpl (sur les matchs de football); – vt (share) mettre en commun; (combine) unir. **3** n Sp billard m américain.

pooped [puːpt] a (exhausted) Am Fam vanné, crevé.

poor [pʊər] a (-er, -est) (not rich, deserving pity) pauvre; (bad) mauvais; (inferior) médiocre; (meagre) maigre; (weak) faible; **p. thing!** le or la pauvre!; – n the **p.** les pauvres mpl. ◆**-ly 1** adv (badly) mal; (clothed, furnished) pauvrement. **2** a (ill) malade.

pop¹ [pɒp] **1** int pan! – n (noise) bruit m sec; to **p.** faire pan; (of champagne bottle) faire pop; – vt (-pp-) (balloon etc) crever; (bottle top, button) faire sauter; – vi (burst) crever; (come off) sauter; (of ears) se déboucher. **2** vt (put) Fam mettre; – vi Fam to **p. in** (go in) entrer (en passant); to **p. off** (leave) partir; to **p. out** sortir (un instant); to **p. over** or **round** faire un saut (to chez); to **p. up** (of person) surgir, réapparaître; (of question etc) surgir.

◆**p.-'eyed** a aux yeux exorbités. ◆**p.-up book** n livre m en relief.

pop² [pɒp] **1** n (music) pop m; – a (concert, singer etc) pop inv. **2** n (father) Am Fam papa m. **3** n (soda) **p.** (drink) Am soda m.

popcorn [ˈpɒpkɔːn] n pop-corn m.

pope [pəʊp] n pape m; **p.'s nose** (of chicken) croupion m.

poplar [ˈpɒplər] n (tree, wood) peuplier m.

poppy [ˈpɒpɪ] n (cultivated) pavot m; (red, wild) coquelicot m.

poppycock [ˈpɒpɪkɒk] n Fam fadaises fpl.

popsicle® [ˈpɒpsɪk(ə)l] n (ice lolly) Am esquimau m.

popular [ˈpɒpjʊlər] a (a person, song, vote, science etc) populaire; (fashionable) à la mode; to be **p. with** plaire beaucoup à. ◆**popu'larity** n popularité f (with auprès de). ◆**popularize** vt populariser; (science, knowledge) vulgariser. ◆**popularly** adv communément.

populat/e [ˈpɒpjʊleɪt] vt peupler. ◆**-ed** a peuplé (with de). ◆**popu'lation** n population f. ◆**populous** a (crowded) populeux.

porcelain [ˈpɔːsəlɪn] n porcelaine f.

porch [pɔːtʃ] n porche m; (veranda) Am véranda f.

porcupine [ˈpɔːkjʊpaɪn] n (animal) porc-épic m.

pore [pɔːr] **1** n (of skin) pore m. **2** vi to **p. over** (book, question etc) etudier de près. ◆**porous** a poreux.

pork [pɔːk] n (meat) porc m; **p. butcher** charcutier, -ière mf.

pornography [pɔːˈnɒgrəfɪ] n (Fam porn) pornographie f. ◆**porno'graphic** a pornographique, porno (f inv).

porpoise [ˈpɔːpəs] n (sea animal) marsouin m.

porridge [ˈpɒrɪdʒ] n porridge m; **p. oats** flocons mpl d'avoine.

port [pɔːt] **1** n (harbour) port m; **p. of call** escale f; – a (authorities, installations etc) portuaire. **2** n **p. (side)** (left) Nau Av bâbord m; – a de bâbord. **3** n (wine) porto m.

portable [ˈpɔːtəb(ə)l] a portatif, portable.

portal [ˈpɔːt(ə)l] n portail m.

porter [ˈpɔːtər] n (for luggage) porteur m; (doorman) portier m; (caretaker) concierge m, (of public building) gardien, -ienne mf.

portfolio [pɔːtˈfəʊlɪəʊ] n (pl -os) Com Pol portefeuille m.

porthole [ˈpɔːthəʊl] n Nau Av hublot m.

portico [ˈpɔːtɪkəʊ] n (pl -oes or -os) Archit portique m; (of house) porche m.

portion [ˈpɔːʃ(ə)n] n (share, helping) portion

f; (of train, book etc) partie f; – vt **to p. out** répartir.

portly ['pɔːtli] a (-ier, -iest) corpulent.

portrait ['pɔːtrit, 'pɔːtreit] n portrait m; **p. painter** portraitiste mf.

portray [pɔː'trei] vt (describe) représenter. ◆**portrayal** n portrait m, représentation f.

Portugal ['pɔːtjug(ə)l] n Portugal m. ◆**Portuguese** a & n inv portugais, -aise (mf); – n (language) portugais m.

pose [pəuz] **1** n (in art or photography) & Fig pose f; – vi (of model etc) poser (for pour); **to p. as a lawyer**/etc se faire passer pour un avocat/etc. **2** vt (question) poser. ◆**poser** n **1** (question) Fam colle f. **2** = poseur. ◆**poseur** [-ˈzɜːr] n Pej poseur, -euse mf.

posh [pɔʃ] a (smart) Fam chic inv; (snobbish) snob (f inv).

position [pəˈzɪʃ(ə)n] n (place, posture, opinion etc) position f; (of building, town) emplacement m, position f; (job, circumstances) situation f; (customer window in bank etc) guichet m; **in a p. to do** en mesure or en position de faire; **in a good p. to do** bien placé pour faire; **in p.** en place, en position; – vt (camera, machine etc) mettre en position; (put) placer.

positive ['pɒzɪtɪv] a positif; (order) catégorique; (progress, change) réel; (sure) sûr, certain (of, that que); **a p. genius** Fam un vrai génie. ◆**-ly** adv (for certain) & El positivement; (undeniably) indéniablement; (completely) complètement; (categorically) catégoriquement.

possess [pəˈzes] vt posséder. ◆**possession** n possession f; **in p. of** en possession de; **to take p. of** prendre possession de. ◆**possessive** a (adjective, person etc) possessif; – n Gram possessif m. ◆**possessor** n possesseur m.

possible ['pɒsəb(ə)l] a possible (to do à faire); **it is p. (for us) to do it** il (nous) est possible de le faire; **it is p. that** il est possible que (+ sub); **as far as p.** dans la mesure du possible; **if p.** si possible; **as much or as many as p.** autant que possible; – n (person, object) Fam choix m possible. ◆**possi'bility** n possibilité f; **some p. of** quelques chances fpl de; **there's some p. that** il est (tout juste) possible que (+ sub); **she has possibilities** elle promet; **it's a distinct p.** c'est bien possible. ◆**possibly** adv **1** (with can, could etc) **if you p.** can si cela t'est possible; **to do all one p. can** faire tout son possible (**to do** pour faire); **he**

cannot p. stay il ne peut absolument pas rester. **2** (perhaps) peut-être.

post¹ [pəust] n (postal system) poste f; (letters) courrier m; **by p.** par la poste; **to catch/miss the p.** avoir/manquer la levée; – a (bag, code etc) postal; **p. office** (bureau m de) poste f; **P. Office** (administration) (service m des) postes (fpl); – vt (put in postbox) poster, mettre à la poste; (send) envoyer; **to keep s.o. posted** Fig tenir qn au courant. ◆**postage** n tarif m (postal), tarifs mpl (postaux) (**to** pour); **p. stamp** timbre-poste m. ◆**postal** a (district etc) postal; (inquiries) par la poste; (clerk) des postes; (vote) par correspondance. ◆**postbox** n boîte f à or aux lettres. ◆**postcard** n carte f postale. ◆**postcode** n code m postal. ◆**post-'free** adv, ◆**post'paid** adv franco.

post² [pəust] n (job, place) & Mil poste m; – vt (sentry, guard) poster; (employee) affecter (**to** à). ◆**-ing** n (appointment) affectation f.

post³ [pəust] n (pole) poteau m; (of bed, door) montant m; **finishing** or **winning p.** Sp poteau m d'arrivée; – vt **to p. (up)** (notice etc) afficher.

post- [pəust] pref post-; **p.-1800** après 1800.

postdate [pəust'deit] vt postdater.

poster ['pəustər] n affiche f; (for decoration) poster m.

posterior [pɒ'stiəriər] n (buttocks) Hum postérieur m.

posterity [pɒ'steriti] n postérité f.

postgraduate [pəust'grædʒuət] a (studies etc) Univ de troisième cycle; – n étudiant, -ante mf de troisième cycle.

posthumous ['pɒstjuməs] a posthume. ◆**-ly** adv à titre posthume.

postman ['pəustmən] n (pl -men) facteur m. ◆**postmark** n cachet m de la poste; – vt oblitérer. ◆**postmaster** n receveur m (des postes).

post-mortem [pəust'mɔːtəm] n p.-mortem (**examination**) autopsie f (**on** de).

postpone [pəu'spəun] vt remettre (**for** de), renvoyer (à plus tard). ◆**-ment** n remise f, renvoi m.

postscript ['pəustskript] n post-scriptum m inv.

postulate ['pɒstjuleit] vt postuler.

posture ['pɒstʃər] n posture f; – vi (for effect) Pej attitude f.

postwar ['pəustwɔːr] a d'après-guerre.

posy ['pəuzi] n petit bouquet m (de fleurs).

pot [pɒt] **1** n pot m; (for cooking) marmite f; **pots and pans** casseroles fpl; **jam p.** pot m à confiture; **to take p. luck** tenter sa chance; (with food) manger à la fortune du pot; **to go to p.** Fam aller à la ruine; **gone to p.** (person, plans etc) Fam fichu; − vt (**-tt-**) mettre en pot. **2** n (marijuana) Sl marie-jeanne f; (hashish) Sl haschisch m. ◆**potted** a **1** (plant) en pot; (jam, meat) en bocaux. **2** (version etc) abrégé, condensé.

potato [pə'teɪtəʊ] n (pl -**oes**) pomme f de terre; **p. peeler** (knife) couteau m à éplucher, éplucheur m; **p. crisps**, Am p. **chips** pommes fpl frites.

potbelly ['pɒtbelɪ] n bedaine f. ◆**potbellied** a ventru.

potent ['pəʊtənt] a puissant; (drink) fort; (man) viril. ◆**potency** n puissance f; (of man) virilité f.

potential [pə'tenʃ(ə)l] a (danger, resources) potentiel; (client, sales) éventuel; (leader, hero etc) en puissance; − n potentiel m; Fig (perspectives fpl d')avenir m; **to have p.** avoir de l'avenir. ◆**potenti'ality** n potentialité f; pl Fig (perspectives fpl d')avenir m. ◆**potentially** adv potentiellement.

pothole ['pɒthəʊl] n (in road) nid m de poules; (in rock) gouffre m; (cave) caverne f. ◆**potholing** n spéléologie f.

potion ['pəʊʃ(ə)n] n breuvage m magique; Med potion f.

potshot ['pɒtʃɒt] n **to take a p.** faire un carton (at sur).

potter ['pɒtər] **1** n (person) potier m. **2** vi **to p.** (about) bricoler. ◆**pottery** n (art) poterie f; (objects) poteries fpl; **a piece of p.** une poterie.

potty ['pɒtɪ] a (**-ier, -iest**) (mad) Fam toqué. **2** n pot m (de bébé).

pouch [paʊtʃ] n petit sac m; (of kangaroo, under eyes) poche f; (for tobacco) blague f.

pouf(fe) [puːf] n (seat) pouf m.

poultice ['pəʊltɪs] n Med cataplasme m.

poultry ['pəʊltrɪ] n volaille f. ◆**poulterer** n volailler m.

pounce [paʊns] vi (leap) bondir, sauter (on sur); **to p. on** (idea) Fig sauter sur; − n bond m.

pound [paʊnd] **1** n (weight) livre f (= 453,6 grammes); **p. (sterling)** livre f (sterling). **2** n (for cars, dogs) fourrière f. **3** vt (spices, nuts etc) piler; (meat) attendrir; (bombard) Mil pilonner; **to p. (on)** (thump) Fig taper sur, marteler; (of sea) battre; − vi (of heart) battre à tout rompre; (walk heavily) marcher à pas pesants.

pour [pɔːr] vt (liquid) verser; (wax) couler; **to p. money into** investir beaucoup d'argent

dans; **to p. away** or **off** (empty) vider; **to p. out** verser; (empty) vider; (feelings) épancher (**to** devant); − vi **to p. (out)** (of liquid) couler or sortir à flots; **to p. in** (of liquid, sunshine) entrer à flots; (of people, money) Fig affluer; **to p. out** (of people) sortir en masse (**from** de); (of smoke) s'échapper (**from** de); **it's pouring (down)** il pleut à verse; **pouring rain** pluie f torrentielle.

pout [paʊt] vti **to p.** (one's lips) faire la moue; − n moue f.

poverty ['pɒvətɪ] n pauvreté f; (grinding or extreme) **p.** misère f. ◆**p.-stricken** a (person) indigent; (conditions) misérable.

powder ['paʊdər] n poudre f; **p. keg** (place) Fig poudrière f; **p. puff** houppette f; **p. room** toilettes fpl (pour dames); − vt (hair, skin) poudrer; **to p. one's face** or **nose** se poudrer. ◆**-ed** a (milk, eggs) en poudre. ◆**powdery** a (snow) poudreux; (face) couvert de poudre.

power ['paʊər] n (ability, authority) pouvoir m; (strength, nation) & Math Tech puissance f; (energy) Phys Tech énergie f; (current) El courant m; **he's a p. within the firm** c'est un homme de poids au sein de l'entreprise; **in p.** Pol au pouvoir; **in one's p.** en son pouvoir; **the p. of speech** la faculté de la parole; **p. cut** coupure f de courant; **p. station**, Am p. **plant** El centrale f (électrique); − vt **to be powered by** être actionné or propulsé par; (gas, oil etc) fonctionner à. ◆**powerful** a puissant. ◆**powerfully** adv puissamment. ◆**powerless** a impuissant (**to do** à faire).

practicable ['præktɪkəb(ə)l] a (project, road etc) praticable.

practical ['præktɪk(ə)l] a (knowledge, person, tool etc) pratique; **p. joke** farce f. ◆**practi'cality** n (of scheme etc) aspect m pratique; (of person) sens m pratique; (detail) détail m pratique.

practically ['præktɪk(ə)lɪ] adv (almost) pratiquement.

practice ['præktɪs] n (exercise, proceeding) pratique f; (habit) habitude f; Sp entraînement m; (rehearsal) répétition f; (of profession) exercice m (**of** de); (clients) clientèle f; **to put into p.** mettre en pratique; **in p.** (in reality) en pratique; **to be in p.** (have skill etc) être en forme; (of doctor, lawyer) exercer; **to be in general p.** (of doctor) faire de la médecine générale; **to be out of p.** avoir perdu la pratique. ◆**practis/e** vt (put into practice) pratiquer; (medicine, law etc) exercer; (flute, *piano etc*) s'exercer à; (*language*) (s'exercer à) parler (**on** avec); (*work at*) travailler; (*do*) faire; – *vi Mus Sp* s'exercer; (*of doctor, lawyer*) exercer; – *n Am* = **practice**. ◆**–ed** *a* (*experienced*) chevronné; (*ear, eye*) exercé. ◆**–ing** *a Rel* pratiquant; (*doctor, lawyer*) exerçant.

practitioner [præk'tɪʃ(ə)nər] *n* praticien, -ienne *mf*; **general p.** (médecin *m*) généraliste *m*.

pragmatic [præg'mætɪk] *a* pragmatique.

prairie(s) ['preərɪ(z)] *n(pl)* (*in North America*) Prairies *fpl*.

praise [preɪz] *vt* louer (**for sth** de qch; **p. s.o. for doing** *or* **having done** louer qn d'avoir fait; – *n* louange(s) *f(pl)*, éloge(s) *m(pl)*; **in p. of** à la louange de. ◆**praiseworthy** *a* digne d'éloges.

pram [præm] *n* landau *m*, voiture *f* d'enfant.

prance [prɑːns] *vi* **to p. about** (*of dancer etc*) caracoler; (*strut*) se pavaner; (*go about*) *Fam* se balader.

prank [præŋk] *n* (*trick*) farce *f*, tour *m*; (*escape*) frasque *f*.

prattle ['præt(ə)l] *vi* jacasser.

prawn [prɔːn] *n* crevette *f* (rose), bouquet *m*.

pray [preɪ] *vt Lit* prier (**that** de (+ *sub*); **s.o. to do qn** de faire); – *vi Rel* prier (**to p. to God**) **for sth** prier Dieu pour qu'il nous accorde qch. ◆**prayer** [preər] *n* prière *f*.

pre- [priː] *pref* **p.-1800** avant 1800.

preach [priːtʃ] *vti* prêcher; (*sermon*) faire; **to p. to s.o.** *Rel & Fig* prêcher qn. ◆**–ing** *n* prédication *f*. ◆**–er** *n* prédicateur *m*.

preamble [priː'æmb(ə)l] *n* préambule *m*.

prearrange [priːə'reɪndʒ] *vt* arranger à l'avance.

precarious [prɪ'keərɪəs] *a* précaire.

precaution [prɪ'kɔːʃ(ə)n] *n* précaution *f* (**of doing** de faire); **as a p.** par précaution.

preced/e [prɪ'siːd] *vti* précéder; **to p. sth by sth** faire précéder qch de qch. ◆**–ing** *a* précédent.

precedence ['presɪdəns] *n* (*in rank*) préséance *f*; (*importance*) priorité *f*; **to take p. over** avoir la préséance sur; avoir la priorité sur. ◆**precedent** *n* précédent *m*.

precept ['priːsept] *n* précepte *m*.

precinct ['priːsɪŋkt] *n* (*of convent etc*) enceinte *f*; (*boundary*) limite *f*; (*of town*) *Am Pol* circonscription *f*; (*for shopping*) zone *f* (piétonnière).

precious ['preʃəs] **1** *a* précieux; **her p. little bike** *Iron* son cher petit vélo. **2** *adv* **p. few, p. little** *Fam* très peu (de).

precipice ['presɪpɪs] *n* (*sheer face*) *Geog* à-pic *m inv*; (*chasm*) *Fig* précipice *m*.

precipitate [prɪ'sɪpɪteɪt] *vt* (*hasten, throw*) & *Ch* précipiter; (*trouble, reaction etc*) provoquer, déclencher. ◆**precipi'tation** *n* (*haste*) & *Ch* précipitation *f*; (*rainfall*) précipitations *fpl*.

précis ['preɪsiː, *pl* 'preɪsiːz] *n inv* précis *m*.

precise [prɪ'saɪs] *a* précis; (*person*) minutieux. ◆**–ly** *adv* (*accurately, exactly*) précisément; **at 3 o'clock p.** à 3 heures précises; **p. nothing** absolument rien. ◆**precision** *n* précision *f*.

preclude [prɪ'kluːd] *vt* (*prevent*) empêcher (**from doing** de faire); (*possibility*) exclure.

precocious [prɪ'kəʊʃəs] *a* (*child etc*) précoce. ◆**–ness** *n* précocité *f*.

preconceived [priːkən'siːvd] *a* préconçu. ◆**preconception** *n* préconception *f*.

precondition [priːkən'dɪʃ(ə)n] *n* préalable *m*.

precursor [priː'kɜːsər] *n* précurseur *m*.

predate [priː'deɪt] *vt* (*precede*) précéder; (*cheque etc*) antidater.

predator ['predətər] *n* (*animal*) prédateur *m*. ◆**predatory** *a* (*animal, person*) rapace.

predecessor ['priːdɪsesər] *n* prédécesseur *m*.

predicament [prɪ'dɪkəmənt] *n* situation *f* fâcheuse.

predict [prɪ'dɪkt] *vt* prédire. ◆**predictable** *a* prévisible. ◆**prediction** *n* prédiction *f*.

predispose [priːdɪ'spəʊz] *vt* prédisposer (**to do** à faire). ◆**predispo'sition** *n* prédisposition *f*.

predominant [prɪ'dɒmɪnənt] *a* prédominant. ◆**predominance** *n* prédominance *f*. ◆**predominantly** *adv* (*almost all*) pour la plupart, en majorité. ◆**predominate** *vi* prédominer (**over** sur).

preeminent [priː'emɪnənt] *a* prééminent.

preempt [priː'empt] *vt* (*decision, plans etc*) devancer.

preen [priːn] *vt* (*feathers*) lisser; **she's preening herself** *Fig* elle se bichonne.

prefab ['priːfæb] *n Fam* maison *f* préfabriquée. ◆**pre'fabricate** *vt* préfabriquer.

preface ['prefɪs] *n* préface *f*; – *vt* (*speech etc*) faire précéder (**with** de).

prefect ['priːfekt] *n Sch* élève *mf* chargé(e) de la discipline; (*French official*) préfet *m*.

prefer [prɪ'fɜːr] *vt* (-rr-) préférer (**to** à), aimer mieux (**to** que); **to p. to do** préférer faire, aimer mieux faire; **to p. charges** *Jur* porter plainte (**against** contre). ◆**preferable** *a* préférable (**to** à). ◆**preferably** *adv* de préférence. ◆**preference** *n* préférence *f* (**for** pour); **in p. to** de préférence à. ◆**prefe'rential** *a* préférentiel.

prefix ['priːfiks] n préfixe m.

pregnant ['pregnant] a (woman) enceinte; (animal) pleine; **five months p.** enceinte de cinq mois. ◆**pregnancy** n (of woman) grossesse f.

prehistoric [priːhɪ'stɒrɪk] a préhistorique.

prejudge [priːˈdʒʌdʒ] vt (question) préjuger de; (person) juger d'avance.

prejudic/e ['predʒʊdɪs] n (bias) préjugé m, parti m pris; (attitude) préjugés mpl; Jur préjudice m; – vt (person) prévenir (against contre); (success, chances etc) porter préjudice à, nuire à. ◆**-ed** a (idea) partial; **she's p.** elle a des préjugés ou un préjugé (against contre); (on an issue) elle est de parti pris. ◆**preju'dicial** a Jur préjudiciable.

preliminary [prɪ'lɪmɪnərɪ] a (initial) initial; (speech, inquiry, exam) préliminaire; – npl préliminaires mpl.

prelude ['preljuːd] n prélude m; – vt préluder à.

premarital [priːˈmærɪt(ə)l] a avant le mariage.

premature ['premətʃʊər, Am priːmə'tʃʊər] a prématuré. ◆**-ly** adv prématurément; (born) avant terme.

premeditate [priːˈmedɪteɪt] vt préméditer. ◆**premedi'tation** n préméditation f.

premier ['premɪər, Am prɪ'mɪər] n Premier ministre m.

première ['premɪeər, Am prɪ'mjeər] n Th Cin première f.

premise ['premɪs] n Phil prémisse f.

premises ['premɪsɪz] npl locaux mpl; **on the p.** sur les lieux; **off the p.** hors des lieux.

premium ['priːmɪəm] n Fin prime f; (insurance) p. prime f (d'assurance); **to be at a p.** (rare) être (une) denrée rare, faire prime; **p. bond** bon m à lots.

premonition [premə'nɪʃ(ə)n, Am priːmə'nɪʃ(ə)n] n prémonition f, pressentiment m.

prenatal [priːˈneɪt(ə)l] a Am prénatal.

preoccupy [priːˈɒkjʊpaɪ] vt (worry) préoccuper (with de). ◆**preoccu'pation** n préoccupation f; **a p. with** (money etc) une obsession de.

prep [prep] a **p. school** école f primaire privée; Am école f secondaire privée; – n (homework) Sch devoirs mpl.

prepaid [priːˈpeɪd] a (reply) payé.

prepar/e [prɪ'peər] vt préparer (sth for s.o. qch à qn, **s.o.** for sth qn à qch); **to p.** to do se préparer à faire; – vi **to p.** for (journey, occasion) faire des préparatifs pour; (get dressed up for) se préparer pour; (exam) préparer. ◆**-ed** a (ready) prêt, disposé (to

do à faire); **to be p.** for (expect) s'attendre à. ◆**prepa'ration** n préparation f; pl préparatifs mpl (for de). ◆**pre'paratory** a préparatoire; **p. school** = prep school.

preposition [prepə'zɪʃ(ə)n] n préposition f.

prepossessing [priːpə'zesɪŋ] a avenant, sympathique.

preposterous [prɪ'pɒstərəs] a absurde.

prerecorded [priːrɪ'kɔːdɪd] a (message etc) enregistré à l'avance; **p. broadcast** Rad TV émission f en différé.

prerequisite [priːˈrekwɪzɪt] n (condition f) préalable m.

prerogative [prɪ'rɒgətɪv] n prérogative f.

Presbyterian [prezbɪ'tɪərɪən] a & n Rel presbytérien, -ienne (mf).

preschool ['priːskuːl] a (age etc) préscolaire.

prescrib/e [prɪ'skraɪb] vt prescrire. ◆**-ed** a (textbook) (inscrit) au programme. ◆**prescription** n (order) prescription f; Med ordonnance f; **on p.** sur ordonnance.

presence ['prezns] n présence f; **in the p. of** en présence de; **p. of mind** présence f d'esprit.

present¹ ['prez(ə)nt] **1** a (not absent) présent (at à, in dans); **those p.** les personnes présentes. **2** a (year, state etc) présent, actuel; (being considered) présent; (job, house etc) actuel; – n (time) présent m; **for the p.** pour le moment; **at p.** à présent. **3** n (gift) cadeau m. ◆**-ly** adv (soon) tout à l'heure; (now) à présent. ◆**present-'day** a actuel.

present² [prɪ'zent] vt (show, introduce, compere etc) présenter (to à); (concert etc) donner; (proof) fournir; **to p. s.o. with** (gift) offrir à qn; (prize) remettre à qn. ◆**-able** a présentable. ◆**-er** n présentateur, -trice mf. ◆**presen'tation** n présentation f; (of prize) remise f.

preserve [prɪ'zɜːv] **1** vt (keep, maintain) conserver; (fruit etc) Culin mettre en conserve; **to p. from** (protect) préserver de. **2** n (sphere) domaine m. **3** n & npl (fruit etc) Culin confiture f. ◆**preser'vation** n conservation f. ◆**preservative** n (in food) agent m de conservation. ◆**preserver** n **life p.** Am gilet m de sauvetage.

preside [prɪ'zaɪd] vi présider; **to p. over** or **at** (meeting) présider.

president ['prezɪdənt] n président, -ente mf. ◆**presidency** n présidence f. ◆**presi'dential** a présidentiel.

press¹ [pres] **1** n (newspapers) presse f; (printing firm) imprimerie f; (printing) presse f; – a (conference etc) de presse. **2** n (*machine for trousers, gluing etc*) presse *f*; (*for making wine*) pressoir *m*.

press² [pres] *vt* (*button, doorbell etc*) appuyer sur; (*tube, lemon, creditor*) presser; (*hand*) serrer; (*clothes*) repasser; (*demand, insist on*) insister sur; (*claim*) renouveler; **to p. s.o. to do** (*urge*) presser qn de faire; **to p. down** (*button etc*) appuyer sur; **to p. charges** *Jur* engager des poursuites (**against** contre); – *vi* (*with finger*) appuyer (**on** sur); (*of weight*) faire pression (**on** sur); (*of time*) presser; **to p. for sth** faire des démarches pour obtenir qch; (*insist*) insister pour obtenir qch; **to p. on** (*continue*) continuer (**with** qch); – *n* to give sth a p. (*trousers etc*) repasser qch. ◆**—ed** (*a hard*) **p.** (*busy*) débordé; **to be hard p.** (*in difficulties*) être en difficultés; **to be (hard) p. for** (*time, money*) être à court de. ◆**—ing** 1 *a* (*urgent*) pressant. 2 *n* (*ironing*) repassage *m*.

pressgang ['presgæn] *vt* **to p. s.o.** faire pression sur qn (**into doing** pour qu'il fasse). ◆**press-stud** *n* (bouton-)pression *m*. ◆**press-up** *n Sp* pompe *f*.

pressure ['preʃər] *n* pression *f*; **the p. of work** le surmenage; **p. cooker** cocotte-minute *f*; **p. group** groupe *m* de pression; **under p.** (*duress*) sous la contrainte; (*hurriedly, forcibly*) sous pression; – *vt* **to p. s.o.** faire pression sur qn (**into doing** pour qu'il fasse). ◆**pressurize** *vt Av* pressuriser; **to p. s.o.** faire pression sur qn (**into doing** pour qu'il fasse).

prestige [pre'stiːʒ] *n* prestige *m*. ◆**prestigious** [pre'stɪdʒəs, Am -'stiːdʒəs] *a* prestigieux.

presume [prɪ'zjuːm] *vt* (*suppose*) présumer (**that** que); **to p. to do** se permettre de faire. ◆**presumably** *adv* (*you'll come etc*) je présume que. ◆**presumption** *n* (*supposition, bold attitude*) présomption *f*. ◆**presumptuous** *a* présomptueux.

presuppose [priːsə'pəʊz] *vt* présupposer (**that** que).

pretence [prɪ'tens] *n* feinte *f*; (*claim, affectation*) prétention *f*; (*pretext*) prétexte *m*; **to make a p. of sth/of doing** feindre qch/de faire; **on** *or* **under false pretences** sous de faux prétextes fallacieux. ◆**pretend** *vt* (*make believe*) faire semblant (**to do** de faire, **that** que); (*claim, maintain*) prétendre (**to do** faire, **that** que); – *vi* faire semblant; **to p. to** (*throne, title*) prétendre à.

pretension [prɪ'tenʃ(ə)n] *n* (*claim, vanity*) prétention *f*; ◆**pre'tentious** *a* prétentieux.

pretext ['priːtekst] *n* prétexte *m*; **on the p. of/that** sous prétexte de/que.

pretty ['prɪtɪ] 1 *a* (**-ier, -iest**) joli. 2 *adv Fam* (*rather, quite*) assez; **p. well, p. much, p. nearly** (*almost*) pratiquement, à peu de chose près.

prevail [prɪ'veɪl] *vi* (*be prevalent*) prédominer; (*win*) prévaloir (**against** contre); **to p. (up)on s.o.** (*persuade*) persuader qn (**to do** de faire). ◆**—ing** *a* (*most common*) courant; (*most important*) prédominant; (*situation*) actuel; (*wind*) dominant.

prevalent ['prevələnt] *a* courant, répandu. ◆**prevalence** *n* fréquence *f*; (*predominance*) prédominance *f*.

prevaricate [prɪ'værɪkeɪt] *vi* user de faux-fuyants.

prevent [prɪ'vent] *vt* empêcher (**from doing** de faire). ◆**preventable** *a* évitable. ◆**prevention** *n* prévention *f*. ◆**preventive** *a* préventif.

preview ['priːvjuː] *n* (*of film, painting*) avant-première *f*; (*survey*) Fig aperçu *m*.

previous ['priːvɪəs] *a* précédent, antérieur; (*experience*) préalable; **she's had a p. job** elle a déjà eu un emploi; **p. to** avant. ◆**—ly** *adv* avant, précédemment.

prewar ['priːwɔːr] *a* d'avant-guerre.

prey [preɪ] *n* proie *f*; **to be (a) p. to** être en proie à; **bird of p.** rapace *m*, oiseau *m* de proie; – *vi* **to p. on** faire sa proie de; **to p. on s.o.** *or* **s.o.'s mind** Fig tracasser qn.

price [praɪs] *n* (*of object, success etc*) prix *m*; **to pay a high p. for sth** payer cher qch; Fig payer chèrement qch; **he wouldn't do it at any p.** il ne le ferait à aucun prix; – *a* (*control, war, rise etc*) des prix; **p. list** tarif *m*; – *vt* mettre un prix à; **it's priced at £5** ça coûte cinq livres. ◆**priceless** *a* (*jewel, help etc*) inestimable; (*amusing*) Fam impayable. ◆**pricey** *a* (**-ier, -iest**) Fam coûteux.

prick [prɪk] *vt* piquer (**with** avec); (*burst*) crever; **to p. up one's ears** dresser l'oreille; – *n* (*act, mark, pain*) piqûre *f*.

prickle ['prɪk(ə)l] *n* (*of animal*) piquant *m*; (*of plant*) épine *f*, piquant *m*. ◆**prickly** *a* (**-ier, -iest**) (*plant*) épineux; (*animal*) hérissé; (*subject*) Fig épineux; (*person*) Fig irritable.

pride [praɪd] *n* (*satisfaction*) fierté *f*; (*self-esteem*) amour-propre *m*, orgueil *m*; (*arrogance*) orgueil *m*; **to take p. in** (*person, work etc*) être fier de; (*look after*) prendre soin de; **to take p. in doing** mettre (toute) sa fierté à faire; **to be s.o.'s p. and joy** être la fierté de qn; **to have p. of place** avoir la place d'honneur; – *vt* **to p. oneself on** s'enorgueillir de.

priest [priːst] *n* prêtre *m*. ◆**priesthood** *n* (*function*) sacerdoce *m*. ◆**priestly** *a* sacerdotal.

prig [prɪg] *n* hypocrite *mf*, pharisien, -ienne *mf*. ◆**priggish** *a* hypocrite, suffisant.

prim [prɪm] *a* (*primmer, primmest*) **p. (and proper)** (*affected*) guindé; (*seemly*) convenable; (*near*) impeccable.

primacy ['praɪməsɪ] *n* primauté *f*.

primary ['praɪmərɪ] *a* Sch Pol Geol etc primaire; (*main, basic*) principal, premier; **of p. importance** de première importance; – *n* (*election*) Am primaire *f*. ◆**primarily** [Am praɪ'merɪlɪ] *adv* essentiellement.

prime [praɪm] **1** *a* (*reason etc*) principal; (*importance*) primordial; (*quality, number*) premier; (*meat*) de premier choix; (*example, condition*) excellent, parfait; **P. Minister** Premier ministre *m*. **2** *n* **the p. of life** la force de l'âge. **3** *vt* (*gun, pump*) amorcer; (*surface*) apprêter. ◆**primer** *n* **1** (*book*) Sch premier livre *m*. **2** (*paint*) apprêt *m*.

primeval [praɪ'miːv(ə)l] *a* primitif.

primitive ['prɪmɪtɪv] *a* (*art, society, conditions etc*) primitif. ◆**-ly** *adv* (*to live*) dans des conditions primitives.

primrose ['prɪmrəʊz] *n* Bot primevère *f* (jaune).

prince [prɪns] *n* prince *m*. ◆**princely** *a* princier. ◆**prin'cess** *n* princesse *f*. ◆**princi'pality** *n* principauté *f*.

principal ['prɪnsɪp(ə)l] **1** *a* (*main*) principal. **2** *n* (*of school*) directeur, -trice *mf*. ◆**-ly** *adv* principalement.

principle ['prɪnsɪp(ə)l] *n* principe *m*; **in p.** en principe; **on p.** par principe.

print [prɪnt] *n* (*of finger, foot etc*) empreinte *f*; (*letters*) caractères *mpl*; (*engraving*) estampe *f*, gravure *f*; (*fabric, textile design*) imprimé *m*; Phot épreuve *f*; (*ink*) encre *m*; **in p.** (*book*) disponible (en librairie); **out of p.** (*book*) épuisé; – *vt* Typ imprimer; Phot tirer; (*write*) écrire en caractères d'imprimerie; **to p. 100 copies of** (*book etc*) tirer à 100 exemplaires; **to p. out** (*of computer*) imprimer. ◆**-ed** *a* imprimé; **p. matter** *or* **papers** imprimés *mpl*; **to have a book p.** publier un livre. ◆**-ing** *n* (*action*) Typ impression *f*; (*technique, art*) Typ imprimerie *f*; Phot tirage *m*; **p. press** Typ presse *f*. ◆**-able** *a* Fig (*word etc*) Fig obscène. ◆**-er** *n* (*person*) imprimeur *m*; (*of computer*) imprimante *f*. ◆**print-out** *n* (*of computer*) sortie *f* sur imprimante.

prior ['praɪər] *a* précédent, antérieur; (*expe-*

rience) préalable; **p. to sth/to doing** avant qch/de faire.

priority [praɪ'ɒrɪtɪ] *n* priorité *f* (*over* sur).

priory ['praɪərɪ] *n* Rel prieuré *m*.

prise [praɪz] *vt* **to p. open/off** (*box, lid*) ouvrir/enlever (en faisant levier).

prism ['prɪz(ə)m] *n* prisme *m*.

prison ['prɪz(ə)n] *n* prison *f*; **in p.** en prison; – *a* (*system, life etc*) pénitentiaire; (*camp*) de prisonniers; **p. officer** gardien, -ienne *mf* de prison. ◆**prisoner** *n* prisonnier, -ière *mf*; **to take s.o. p.** faire qn prisonnier.

prissy ['prɪsɪ] *a* (*-ier, -iest*) bégueule.

pristine ['prɪstiːn] *a* (*condition*) parfait; (*primitive*) primitif.

privacy ['praɪvəsɪ, 'prɪvəsɪ] *n* intimité *f*, solitude *f*; (*quiet place*) coin *m* retiré; (*secrecy*) secret *m*; **to give s.o. some p.** laisser qn seul. ◆**private 1** *a* (*life, lesson, car etc*) particulier; (*confidential*) confidentiel; (*personal*) personnel; (*wedding etc*) intime; **p. citizen** un simple particulier; **p. detective, p. investigator,** Am Fam **p. eye** détective *m* privé; **p. parts** parties *fpl* génitales; **p. place** coin *m* retiré; **p. tutor** précepteur *m*; **to be a very p. person** aimer la solitude; – *n* **in p.** (*not publicly*) en privé; (*ceremony*) dans l'intimité. **2** *n* Mil (*simple*) soldat *m*. ◆**privately** *adv* en privé; (*inwardly*) intérieurement; (*personally*) à titre personnel; (*to marry, dine etc*) dans l'intimité; **p. owned** appartenant à un particulier.

privet ['prɪvɪt] *n* (*bush*) troène *m*.

privilege ['prɪvɪlɪdʒ] *n* privilège *m*. ◆**privileged** *a* privilégié; **to be p. to do** avoir le privilège de faire.

privy ['prɪvɪ] *a* **p. to** (*knowledge etc*) au courant de.

prize[1] [praɪz] *n* prix *m*; (*in lottery*) lot *m*; **the first p.** (*in lottery*) le gros lot; – *a* (*essay, animal etc*) primé; **a p. fool**/*etc* Fig Hum un parfait idiot/*etc*. ◆**p.-giving** *n* distribution *f* des prix. ◆**p.-winner** *n* lauréat, -ate *mf*; (*in lottery*) gagnant, -ante *mf*. ◆**p.-winning** *a* (*essay, animal etc*) primé; (*ticket*) gagnant.

prize[2] [praɪz] *vt* (*value*) priser. ◆**-ed** *a* (*possession etc*) précieux.

prize[3] [praɪz] *vt* = **prise.**

pro [prəʊ] *n* (*professional*) Fam pro *mf*.

pro- [prəʊ] *pref* pro-.

probable ['prɒbəb(ə)l] *a* probable (**that** que); (*plausible*) vraisemblable. ◆**proba'bility** *n* probabilité *f*; **in all p.** selon toute probabilité. ◆**probably** *adv* probablement, vraisemblablement.

probation [prə'beɪʃ(ə)n] *n* **on p.** Jur en

liberté surveillée, sous contrôle judiciaire; (*in job*) à l'essai; **p. officer** responsable *mf* des délinquants mis en liberté surveillée. ◆**probationary** *a* (*period*) d'essai, Jur de liberté surveillée.

prob/e [prəʊb] *n* (*device*) sonde *f*; Journ enquête *f* (**into** dans); – *vt* (*investigate*) & Med sonder; (*examine*) examiner; – *vi* (*investigate*) faire des recherches; Pej fouiner; **to p. into** (*origins etc*) sonder. ◆**-ing** *a* (*question etc*) pénétrant.

problem [ˈprɒbləm] *n* problème *m*; **he's got a drug/a drink p.** c'est un drogué/un alcoolique; **you've got a smoking p.** tu fumes beaucoup trop; **no p.!** *Am Fam* pas de problème!; **to have a p. doing** avoir du mal à faire; – *a* (*child*) difficile, caractériel. ◆**proble'matic** *a* problématique; **it's p. whether** il est douteux que (+ *sub*).

procedure [prəˈsiːdʒər] *n* procédure *f*.

proceed [prəˈsiːd] *vi* (*go*) avancer, aller; (*act*) procéder; (*continue*) continuer; (*of debate*) se poursuivre; **to p. to** (*next question etc*) passer à; **to p. with** (*task etc*) continuer; **to p. to do** (*start*) se mettre à faire. ◆**-ing** *n* (*course of action*) procédé *m*; *pl* (*events*) évènements *mpl*; (*meeting*) séance *f*; (*discussions*) débats *mpl*; (*minutes*) actes *mpl*; **to take** (*legal*) **proceedings** intenter un procès (**against** contre).

proceeds [ˈprəʊsiːdz] *npl* (*profits*) produit *m*, bénéfices *mpl*.

process [ˈprəʊses] **1** *n* (*operation, action*) processus *m*; (*method*) procédé *m* (**for** *or* **of doing** pour faire); **in p.** (*work etc*) en cours; **in the p. of doing** en train de faire. **2** *vt* (*food, data etc*) traiter; (*examine*) examiner; *Phot* développer; **processed cheese** fromage *m* fondu. ◆**-ing** *n* traitement *m*; *Phot* développement *m*; **data** *or* **information p.** informatique *f*. ◆**-or** *n* (*in computer*) processeur *m*; **food p.** robot *m* (ménager); **word p.** machine *f* de traitement de texte.

procession [prəˈseʃ(ə)n] *n* cortège *m*, défilé *m*.

proclaim [prəˈkleɪm] *vt* proclamer (**that** que); **to p. king** proclamer roi. ◆**procla'mation** *n* proclamation *f*.

procrastinate [prəʊˈkræstɪneɪt] *vi* temporiser, tergiverser.

procreate [ˈprəʊkrɪeɪt] *vt* procréer. ◆**procre'ation** *n* procréation *f*.

procure [prəˈkjʊər] *vt* obtenir; **to p. sth for oneself** se procurer qch; **to p. sth for s.o.** procurer qch à qn.

prod [prɒd] *vti* (**-dd-**) **to p. (at)** pousser (*du*

coude, avec un bâton etc); **to p. s.o. into doing** *Fig* pousser qn à faire; – *n* (*petit*) *coup m*; (*shove*) poussée *f*.

prodigal [ˈprɒdɪg(ə)l] *a* (*son etc*) prodigue.

prodigious [prəˈdɪdʒəs] *a* prodigieux.

prodigy [ˈprɒdɪdʒɪ] *n* prodige *m*; **infant p., child p.** enfant *mf* prodige.

produce [prəˈdjuːs] *vt* (*manufacture, yield etc*) produire; (*bring out, show*) sortir (*pistolet, mouchoir etc*); (*passport, proof*) présenter; (*profit*) rapporter; (*cause*) provoquer, produire; (*publish*) publier; (*play*) *Th TV* mettre en scène; (*film*) *Cin* produire; *Rad* réaliser; (*baby*) donner naissance à; **oil-producing country** pays *m* producteur de pétrole; – *vi* (*of factory etc*) produire; – [ˈprɒdjuːs] *n* (*agricultural etc*) produits *mpl*. ◆**pro'ducer** *n* (*of goods*) & *Cin* producteur, -trice *mf*; *Th TV* metteur *m* en scène; *Rad* réalisateur, -trice *mf*.

product [ˈprɒdʌkt] *n* produit *m*.

production [prəˈdʌkʃ(ə)n] *n* production *f*; *Th TV* mise *f* en scène; *Rad* réalisation *f*; **to work on the p. line** travailler à la chaîne. ◆**productive** *a* (*land, meeting, efforts*) productif. ◆**produc'tivity** *n* productivité *f*.

profane [prəˈfeɪn] *a* (*sacrilegious*) sacrilège; (*secular*) profane; – *vt* (*dishonour*) profaner. ◆**profanities** *npl* (*oaths*) blasphèmes *mpl*.

profess [prəˈfes] *vt* professer; **to p. to be** prétendre être. ◆**-ed** *a* (*anarchist etc*) déclaré.

profession [prəˈfeʃ(ə)n] *n* profession *f*; **by p.** de profession. ◆**professional** *a* professionnel; (*man, woman*) qui exerce une profession libérale; (*army*) de métier; (*diplomat*) de carrière; (*piece of work*) de professionnel; – *n* professionnel, -elle *mf*; (*executive, lawyer etc*) membre *m* des professions libérales. ◆**professionalism** *n* professionnalisme *m*. ◆**professionally** *adv* professionnellement; (*to perform, play*) en professionnel; (*to meet s.o.*) dans le cadre de son travail.

professor [prəˈfesər] *n* Univ professeur *m* (titulaire d'une chaire). ◆**profe'ssorial** *a* professoral.

proffer [ˈprɒfər] *vt* offrir.

proficient [prəˈfɪʃ(ə)nt] *a* compétent (**in** en). ◆**proficiency** *n* compétence *f*.

profile [ˈprəʊfaɪl] *n* (*of person, object*) profil *m*; **in p.** de profil; **to keep a low p.** *Fig* garder un profil bas. ◆**profiled** *a* **to be p. against** se profiler sur.

profit [ˈprɒfɪt] *n* profit *m*, bénéfice *m*; **to sell**

at a p. vendre à profit; **p. margin** marge *f* bénéficiaire; **p. motive** recherche *f* du profit; – *vi* **to b. by** *or* **from** tirer profit de. ◆**p.-making** *a* à but lucratif. ◆**profita'bility** *n* Com rentabilité *f*. ◆**profitable** *a* Com rentable; (*worthwhile*) Fig rentable, profitable. ◆**profitably** *adv* avec profit. ◆**profi'teer** *n Pej* profiteur, -euse *mf*; – *vi Pej* faire des profits malhonnêtes.

profound [prə'faund] *a* (*silence, remark etc*) profond. ◆**profoundly** *adv* profondément. ◆**profundity** *n* profondeur *f*.

profuse [prə'fjuːs] *a* abondant; **p. in** (*praise etc*) prodigue de. ◆**profusely** *adv* (*to flow, grow*) à profusion; (*to bleed*) abondamment; (*to thank*) avec effusion; **to apologize p.** se répandre en excuses. ◆**profusion** *n* profusion *f*; **in p.** à profusion.

progeny ['prɒdʒɪnɪ] *n* progéniture *f*.

program¹ ['prəʊɡræm] *n* (*of computer*) programme *m*; – *vt* (**-mm-**) (*computer*) programmer. ◆**programming** *n* programmation *f*. ◆**programmer** *n* (**computer**) *p.* programmeur, -euse *mf*.

programme, *Am* **program²** ['prəʊɡræm] *n* programme *m*; (*broadcast*) émission *f*; – *vt* (*arrange*) programmer.

progress ['prəʊɡres] *n* progrès *m*(*pl*); **to make (good) p.** faire des progrès; (*in walking, driving etc*) bien avancer; **in p.** en cours; – [prə'ɡres] *vi* (*advance, improve*) progresser; (*of story, meeting*) se dérouler. ◆**pro'gression** *n* progression *f*. ◆**pro'gressive** *a* (*gradual*) progressif; (*party*) *Pol* progressiste; (*firm, ideas*) moderniste. ◆**pro'gressively** *adv* progressivement.

prohibit [prə'hɪbɪt] *vt* interdire (**s.o. from doing** à qn de faire); **we're prohibited from leaving/etc** il nous est interdit de partir/*etc*. ◆**prohi'bition** *n* prohibition *f*. ◆**prohibitive** *a* (*price, measure etc*) prohibitif.

project 1 ['prɒdʒekt] *n* (*plan*) projet *m* (**for sth** pour qch, **to do, for doing** pour faire); (*undertaking*) entreprise *f*; (*study*) étude *f*; (*housing*) **p.** (*for workers*) *Am* cité *f* (ouvrière). **2** [prə'dʒekt] *vt* (*throw, show etc*) projeter; – *vi* (*jut out*) faire saillie. ◆**-ed** *a* (*planned*) prévu. ◆**pro'jection** *n* projection *f*; (*projecting object*) saillie *f*. ◆**pro'jectionist** *n Cin* projectionniste *mf*. ◆**pro'jector** *n Cin* projecteur *m*.

proletarian [prəʊlə'teərɪən] *n* prolétaire *mf*; – *a* (*class*) prolétarien; (*outlook*) de prolétaire. ◆**prole'tariat** *n* prolétariat *m*.

proliferate [prə'lɪfəreɪt] *vi* proliférer. ◆**prolife'ration** *n* prolifération *f*.

prolific [prə'lɪfɪk] *a* prolifique.

prologue ['prəʊlɒɡ] *n* prologue *m* (**to, à**).

prolong [prə'lɒŋ] *vt* prolonger.

promenade [prɒmə'nɑːd] *n* (*place, walk*) promenade *f*; (*gallery*) *Th* promenoir *m*.

prominent ['prɒmɪnənt] *a* (*nose*) proéminent; (*chin, tooth*) saillant; (*striking*) Fig frappant, remarquable; (*role*) majeur; (*politician*) marquant; (*conspicuous*) (bien) en vue. ◆**prominence** *n* (*importance*) importance *f*. ◆**prominently** *adv* (*displayed, placed*) bien en vue.

promiscuous [prə'mɪskjʊəs] *a* (*person*) de mœurs faciles; (*behaviour*) immoral. ◆**promis'cuity** *n* liberté *f* de mœurs; immoralité *f*.

promis/e ['prɒmɪs] *n* promesse *f*; **to show great p., be full of p.** (*hope*) être très prometteur; – *vt* promettre (**s.o. sth, sth to s.o.** qch à qn; **to do** de faire; **that** que); – *vi* **I p.!** je te le promets!; **p.?** promis? ◆**-ing** *a* (*start etc*) prometteur; (*person*) qui promet; **that looks p.** ça s'annonce bien.

promote [prə'məʊt] *vt* (*product, research*) promouvoir; (*good health, awareness*) favoriser; **to p. s.o.** promouvoir qn (**à**); **promoted to manager/general/etc** promu directeur/général/*etc*. ◆**promoter** *n Sp* organisateur, -trice *mf*; (*instigator*) promoteur, -trice *mf*. ◆**promotion** *n* (*of person*) avancement *m*, promotion *f*; (*of sales, research etc*) promotion *f*.

prompt [prɒmpt] **1** *a* (*speedy*) rapide; (*punctual*) à l'heure, ponctuel; **p. to act** prompt à agir; – *adv* **at 8 o'clock p.** à 8 heures pile. **2** *vt* (*urge*) inciter, pousser (**to do** à faire); (*cause*) provoquer. **3** *vt* (*person*) *Th* souffler (son rôle) à. ◆**-ing** *n* (*urging*) incitation *f*. ◆**-er** *n Th* souffleur, -euse *mf*. ◆**-ness** *n* rapidité *f*; (*readiness to act*) promptitude *f*.

prone [prəʊn] *a* **1 p. to sth** (*liable*) prédisposé à qch; **to be p. to do** avoir tendance à faire. **2** (*lying flat*) sur le ventre.

prong [prɒŋ] *n* (*of fork*) dent *f*.

pronoun ['prəʊnaʊn] *n Gram* pronom *m*. ◆**pro'nominal** *a* pronominal.

pronounce [prə'naʊns] *vt* (*articulate, declare*) prononcer; – *vi* (*articulate*) prononcer; (*give judgment*) se prononcer (**on** sur). ◆**-d** *a* (*noticeable*) prononcé. ◆**pronounce'ment** *n* déclaration *f*. ◆**pronunci'ation** *n* prononciation *f*.

pronto ['prɒntəʊ] *adv* (*at once*) *Fam* illico.

proof [pruːf] **1** *n* (*evidence*) preuve *f*; (*of book, photo*) épreuve *f*; (*of drink*) teneur *f* en alcool. **2** *a* **p. against** (*material*) à l'épreuve de (*feu, acide etc*). ◆**proof-reader** n Typ correcteur, -trice mf.

prop [prɒp] **1** n Archit support m, étai m; (*for clothes line*) perche f; (*person*) Fig soutien m; – vt (**-pp-**) **to p. up** (*ladder etc*) appuyer (**against** contre); (*one's head*) caler; (*wall*) étayer; (*help*) Fig soutenir. **2** n prop(s) Th accessoire(s) m (pl).

propaganda [prɒpə'gændə] n propagande f. ◆**propagandist** n propagandiste mf.

propagate ['prɒpəgeɪt] vt propager; – vi se propager.

propel [prə'pel] vt (**-ll-**) (*drive, hurl*) propulser. ◆**propeller** n Av Nau hélice f.

propensity [prə'pensɪtɪ] n propension f (**for** sth à qch, **to do** à faire).

proper ['prɒpər] a (*suitable, seemly*) convenable; (*correct*) correct; (*right*) bon; (*real, downright*) véritable; (*noun, meaning*) propre; **in the p. way** comme il faut; **the** *village/etc* **p.** le *village/etc* proprement dit. ◆**-ly** adv comme il faut, convenablement, correctement; (*completely*) Fam vraiment; **very p.** (*quite rightly*) à juste titre.

property ['prɒpətɪ] **1** n (*building etc*) propriété f; (*possessions*) biens mpl, propriété f; – a (*crisis, market etc*) immobilier; (*owner, tax*) foncier. **2** n (*of substance etc*) propriété f. ◆**propertied** a possédant.

prophecy ['prɒfɪsɪ] n prophétie f. ◆**prophesy** [-saɪ] vti prophétiser; **to p. that** prédire que.

prophet ['prɒfɪt] n prophète m. ◆**pro-'phetic** a prophétique.

proponent [prə'pəʊnənt] n (*of cause etc*) défenseur m, partisan, -ane mf.

proportion [prə'pɔːʃ(ə)n] n (*ratio*) proportion f; (*portion*) partie f; (*amount*) pourcentage m; pl (*size*) proportions fpl; **in p.** en proportion (**to** de); **out of p.** hors de proportion (**to** avec); – vt proportionner (**to** à); **well** or **nicely proportioned** bien proportionné. ◆**proportional** a, ◆**proportionate** a proportionnel (**to** à).

propose [prə'pəʊz] vt (*suggest*) proposer (**to** à, **that** que (+ *sub*)); **to p. to do, p. doing** (*intend*) se proposer de faire; – vi faire une demande (en mariage) (**to** à). ◆**proposal** n proposition f; (*of marriage*) demande f (en mariage). ◆**propo'sition** n proposition f; (*matter*) Fig affaire f.

propound [prə'paʊnd] vt proposer.

proprietor [prə'praɪətər] n propriétaire mf. ◆**proprietary** a (*article*) Com de marque déposée; **p. name** marque f déposée.

propriety [prə'praɪətɪ] n (*behaviour*) bienséance f; (*of conduct, remark*) justesse f.

propulsion [prə'pʌlʃ(ə)n] n propulsion f.

pros [prəʊz] npl **the p. and cons** le pour et le contre.

prosaic [prəʊ'zeɪɪk] a prosaïque.

proscribe [prəʊ'skraɪb] vt proscrire.

prose [prəʊz] n prose f; (*translation*) Sch thème m.

prosecute ['prɒsɪkjuːt] vt poursuivre (en justice); (*for stealing/etc* pour vol/etc). ◆**prose'cution** n Jur poursuites fpl; **the p.** (*lawyers*) = le ministère public. ◆**prosecutor** n (**public**) **p.** Jur procureur m.

prospect[1] ['prɒspekt] n (*idea, outlook*) perspective f (**of doing** de faire); (*possibility*) possibilité f (**of sth** de qch); (*future*) **prospects** perspectives fpl d'avenir; **it has prospects** c'est prometteur; **she has prospects** elle a de l'avenir. ◆**pro'spective** a (*possible*) éventuel; (*future*) futur.

prospect[2] [prə'spekt] vt (*land*) prospecter; – vi **to p. for** (*gold etc*) chercher. ◆**-ing** n prospection f. ◆**prospector** n prospecteur, -trice mf.

prospectus [prə'spektəs] n (*publicity leaflet*) prospectus m; Univ guide m (de l'étudiant).

prosper ['prɒspər] vi prospérer. ◆**pro-'sperity** n prospérité f. ◆**prosperous** a (*thriving*) prospère; (*wealthy*) riche, prospère.

prostate ['prɒsteɪt] n **p. (gland)** Anat prostate f.

prostitute ['prɒstɪtjuːt] n (*woman*) prostituée f; – vt prostituer. ◆**prosti'tution** n prostitution f.

prostrate ['prɒstreɪt] a (*prone*) sur le ventre; (*worshipper*) prosterné; (*submissive*) soumis; (*exhausted*) prostré; – [prɒ'streɪt] vt **to p. oneself** se prosterner (**before** devant).

protagonist [prəʊ'tægənɪst] n protagoniste mf.

protect [prə'tekt] vt protéger (**from** de, **against** contre); (*interests*) sauvegarder. ◆**protection** n protection f. ◆**protective** a (*tone etc*) & Econ protecteur; (*screen, clothes etc*) de protection. ◆**protector** n protecteur, -trice mf.

protein ['prəʊtiːn] n protéine f.

protest ['prəʊtest] n protestation f (**against** contre); **under p.** contre son gré; – [prə'test] vt protester (**that** que); (*one's innocence*) protester de; – vi protester (**against** contre); (*in the streets etc*) Pol contester. ◆**-er** n Pol contestataire mf.

Protestant ['prɒtɪstənt] a & n protestant,

-ante (mf). ◆**Protestantism** n protestantisme m.

protocol ['prəutəkɒl] n protocole m.

prototype ['prəutəutaip] n prototype m.

protract [prə'trækt] vt prolonger.

protractor [prə'træktər] n (instrument) Geom rapporteur m.

protrud/e [prə'trud] vi dépasser; (of balcony, cliff etc) faire saillie; (of tooth) avancer. ◆**-ing** a saillant; (of tooth) qui avance.

proud [praud] a (-er, -est) (honoured, pleased) fier (of de, to de de faire); (arrogant) orgueilleux. ◆**-ly** adv fièrement; orgueilleusement.

prove [pruv] vt prouver (that que); to p. oneself faire ses preuves; – vi to p. (to be) difficult/etc s'avérer difficile/etc. ◆**proven** a (method etc) éprouvé.

proverb ['prɒvɜːb] n proverbe m. ◆**pro-verbial** a proverbial.

provid/e [prə'vaid] vt (supply) fournir (s.o. with sth qch à qn); (give) donner, offrir (to à); to p. s.o. with (equip) pourvoir qn de; to p. that Jur stipuler que; – vi to p. for s.o. (s.o.'s needs) pourvoir aux besoins de qn; (s.o.'s future) assurer l'avenir de qn; to p. for sth (make allowance for) prévoir qch. ◆**-ed** conj p. (that) pourvu que (+ sub). ◆**-ing** conj p. (that) pourvu que (+ sub).

providence ['prɒvidəns] n providence f.

provident ['prɒvidənt] a (society) de prévoyance; (person) prévoyant.

province ['prɒvins] n province f; Fig domaine m, compétence f; the provinces la province; in the provinces en province. ◆**pro'vincial** a & n provincial, -ale (mf).

provision [prə'viʒ(ə)n] n (supply) provision f; (clause) disposition f; the p. of (supplying) la fourniture de; to make p. for = to provide for.

provisional [prə'viʒən(ə)l] a provisoire. ◆**-ly** adv provisoirement.

proviso [prə'vaizəu] n (pl -os) stipulation f.

provok/e [prə'vauk] vt (rouse, challenge) provoquer (to do, into doing à faire); (annoy) agacer; (cause) provoquer (accident, réaction etc). ◆**-ing** a (annoying) agaçant. ◆**provo'cation** n provocation f. ◆**provocative** a (person, remark etc) provocant; (thought-provoking) qui donne à penser.

prow [prau] n Nau proue f.

prowess ['praues] n (bravery) courage m; (skill) talent m.

prowl [praul] vi to p. (around) rôder; – n to be on the p. rôder. ◆**-er** n rôdeur, -euse mf.

proximity [prɒk'simiti] n proximité f.

proxy ['prɒksi] n by p. par procuration.

prude [prud] n prude f. ◆**prudery** n pruderie f. ◆**prudish** a prude.

prudent ['prudənt] a prudent. ◆**prudence** n prudence f. ◆**prudently** adv prudemment.

prun/e [prun] 1 n (dried plum) pruneau m. 2 vt (cut) Bot tailler, élaguer; (speech etc) Fig élaguer. ◆**-ing** n Bot taille f.

pry [prai] 1 vi être indiscret; to p. into (meddle) se mêler de; (s.o.'s reasons etc) chercher à découvrir. 2 vt to p. open Am forcer (en faisant levier). ◆**-ing** a indiscret.

PS [piː'es] abbr (postscript) P.-S.

psalm [saːm] n psaume m.

pseud [sjuːd] n Fam bêcheur, -euse mf.

pseudo- ['sjuːdəu] pref pseudo-.

pseudonym ['sjuːdənim] n pseudonyme m.

psychiatry [sai'kaiətri] n psychiatrie f. ◆**psychi'atric** a psychiatrique. ◆**psychiatrist** n psychiatre mf.

psychic ['saikik] a (méta)psychique; I'm not p. Fam je ne suis pas devin; – n (person) médium m.

psycho- ['saikəu] pref psycho-. ◆**psycho-'analysis** n psychanalyse f. ◆**psycho-'analyst** n psychanalyste mf.

psychology [sai'kɒlədʒi] n psychologie f. ◆**psycho'logical** a psychologique. ◆**psychologist** n psychologue mf.

psychopath ['saikəupæθ] n psychopathe mf.

psychosis, pl **-oses** [sai'kəusis, -əusiːz] n psychose f.

PTO [piːtiː'əu] abbr (please turn over) TSVP f.

pub [pʌb] n pub m.

puberty ['pjuːbəti] n puberté f.

public ['pʌblik] a public; (baths, library) municipal; to make a p. protest protester publiquement; in the p. eye très en vue; p. building édifice m public; p. company société f par actions; p. corporation société f nationalisée; p. figure personnalité f connue; p. house pub m; p. life les affaires fpl publiques; to be p.-spirited avoir le sens civique; – n public m; in p. en public; a member of the p. un simple particulier; the sporting/etc p. les amateurs mpl de sport/etc. ◆**-ly** adv publiquement; p. owned (nationalized) Com nationalisé.

publican ['pʌblik(ə)n] n patron, -onne mf d'un pub.

publication [pʌblɪ'keɪʃ(ə)n] n (*publishing, book etc*) publication f.

publicity [pʌb'lɪsɪtɪ] n publicité f. ◆'**publicize** vt rendre public; (*advertise* Com) faire de la publicité pour.

publish ['pʌblɪʃ] vt publier; (*book*) éditer, publier; to p. s.o. éditer qn; '**published weekly**' 'paraît toutes les semaines'. ◆—**ing** n publication f (**of** de); (*profession*) édition f. ◆—**er** n éditeur, -trice mf.

puck [pʌk] n (*in ice hockey*) palet m.

pucker ['pʌkər] vt to p. (**up**) (*brow, lips*) plisser; — vi to p. (**up**) se plisser.

pudding ['pʊdɪŋ] n dessert m, gâteau m; (**plum**) p. pudding m; **rice p.** riz m au lait.

puddle ['pʌd(ə)l] n flaque f (d'eau).

pudgy ['pʌdʒɪ] a (**-ier, -iest**) = **podgy**.

puerile ['pjʊəraɪl] a puérile.

puff [pʌf] n (*of smoke*) bouffée f; (*of wind, air*) bouffée f, souffle m; **to have run out of p.** Fam être à bout de souffle; — vi (*blow, pant*) souffler; **to p. at** (*cigar*) tirer sur; — vt (*smoke etc*) souffler (**into** dans); **to p. out** (*cheeks etc*) gonfler. ◆**puffy** a (**-ier, -iest**) (*swollen*) gonflé.

puke [pjuːk] vi (*vomit*) Sl dégueuler.

pukka ['pʌkə] a Fam authentique.

pull [pʊl] n (*attraction*) attraction f; (*force*) force f; (*influence*) influence f; **to give sth a p.** tirer qch; — vt (*draw, tug*) tirer; (*tooth*) arracher; (*stopper*) enlever; (*trigger*) appuyer sur; (*muscle*) se claquer; **to p. apart** *or* **to bits** *or* **to pieces** mettre en pièces; **to p. a face** faire la moue; **to (get s.o. to) p. strings** Fig se faire pistonner; — vi (*tug*) tirer; (*go, move*) aller; **to p. at** *or* **on** tirer (sur). ■ **to p. along** vt (*drag*) traîner (**to** jusqu'à); **to p. away** vt (*move*) éloigner; (*snatch*) arracher (**from** à); — vi Aut démarrer; **to p. away from** s'éloigner de; **to p. back** vi (*withdraw*) Mil se retirer; — vt retirer; (*curtains*) ouvrir; **to p. down** vt (*lower*) baisser; (*knock down*) faire tomber; (*demolish*) démolir, abattre; **to p. in** vt (*rope*) ramener; (*drag into room etc*) faire entrer; (*stomach*) rentrer; (*crowd*) attirer; — vi (*arrive*) Aut arriver; (*stop*) Aut se garer; **to p. into the station** (*of train*) entrer en gare; **to p. off** vt enlever; (*plan, deal*) Fig mener à bien; **to p. it off** Fig réussir son coup; **to p. on** vt (*boots etc*) mettre; **to p. out** vt (*extract*) arracher (**from** à); (*remove*) enlever (**from** de); (*from pocket, bag etc*) tirer, sortir (**from** de); (*troops*) retirer; — vi (*depart*) Aut démarrer; (*move out*) Aut se déboîter; **to p. out from** (*negotiations etc*) se retirer de; **to p. over** vt (*drag*) traîner (**to** jusqu'à); (*knock down*) faire tomber; — vi Aut se ranger (sur le côté); **to p. round** vi Med se remettre; **to p. through** vi s'en tirer; **to p. oneself together** vt se ressaisir; **to p. up** vt (*socks, bucket etc*) remonter; (*haul up*) hisser; (*uproot*) arracher; (*stop*) arrêter; — vi Aut s'arrêter. ◆**p.-up** n Sp traction f.

pulley ['pʊlɪ] n poulie f.

pullout ['pʊlaʊt] n (*in newspaper etc*) supplément m détachable.

pullover ['pʊləʊvər] n pull-(over) m.

pulp [pʌlp] n (*of fruit etc*) pulpe f; (*for paper*) pâte f à papier; **in a p.** Fig en bouillie.

pulpit ['pʊlpɪt] n Rel chaire f.

pulsate [pʌl'seɪt] vi produire des pulsations, battre. ◆**pulsation** n (*heartbeat etc*) pulsation f.

pulse [pʌls] n Med pouls m.

pulverize ['pʌlvəraɪz] vt (*grind, defeat*) pulvériser.

pumice ['pʌmɪs] n **p. (stone)** pierre f ponce.

pump [pʌmp] **1** n pompe f; (**petrol**) **p. attendant** pompiste mf; — vt pomper; (*blood*) Med faire circuler; (*money*) Fig injecter (**into** dans); **to p. s.o.** (*for information*) tirer les vers du nez à qn; **to p. in** refouler (*à l'aide d'une pompe*); **to p. out** pomper (**of** de); **to p. air into, to p.** (**up**) (*tyre*) gonfler; — vi pomper; (*of heart*) battre. **2** n (*for dancing*) escarpin m; (*plimsoll*) tennis f.

pumpkin ['pʌmpkɪn] n potiron m.

pun [pʌn] n calembour m.

punch¹ [pʌntʃ] n (*blow*) coup m de poing; (*force*) Fig punch m; **to pack a p.** Boxing & Fig avoir du punch; **p. line** (*of joke*) astuce f finale; — vt (*person*) donner un coup de poing à; (*ball etc*) frapper d'un coup de poing. ◆**p.-up** n Fam bagarre f.

punch² [pʌntʃ] **1** n (*for tickets*) poinçonneuse f; (*for paper*) perforeuse f; **p. card** carte f perforée; — vt (*ticket*) poinçonner, (*with date*) composter; (*card, paper*) perforer; **to p. a hole in** faire un trou dans. **2** n (*drink*) punch m.

punctilious [pʌŋk'tɪlɪəs] a pointilleux.

punctual ['pʌŋktʃʊəl] a (*arriving on time*) à l'heure; (*regularly on time*) ponctuel, exact. ◆**punctu'ality** n ponctualité f, exactitude f. ◆**punctually** adv à l'heure; (*habitually*) ponctuellement.

punctuate ['pʌŋktʃʊeɪt] vt ponctuer (**with** de). ◆**punctu'ation** n ponctuation f; **p. mark** signe m de ponctuation.

puncture ['pʌŋktʃər] n (*in tyre*) crevaison f;

to have a p. crever; - *vt* (*burst*) crever; (*pierce*) piquer; - *vi* (*of tyre*) crever.

pundit ['pʌndɪt] *n* expert *m*, ponte *m*.

pungent ['pʌndʒənt] *a* âcre, piquant. ◆**pungency** *n* âcreté *f*.

punish ['pʌnɪʃ] *vt* punir (**for sth** de qch, **for doing** *or* **having done** pour avoir fait); (*treat roughly*) Fig malmener. ◆**-ing** *a* (*tiring*) éreintant. ◆**-able** *a* punissable (**by** de). ◆**-ment** *n* punition *f*; châtiment *m*; **capital p.** peine *f* capitale; **to take a** (**lot of**) **p.** (*damage*) Fig en encaisser.

punitive ['pjuːnɪtɪv] *a* (*measure etc*) punitif.

punk [pʌŋk] **1** *n* (*in music*) punk *m*; (*fan*) punk *mf*; - **a punk** (*person*). **2** *n* (*hoodlum*) Am Fam voyou *m*.

punt [pʌnt] **1** *n* barque *f* (à fond plat). **2** *vi* (*bet*) Fam parier. ◆**-ing** *n* canotage *m*. ◆**-er** *n* **1** (*gambler*) parieur, -euse *mf*. **2** (*customer*) Sl client, -ente *mf*.

puny ['pjuːnɪ] *a* (**-ier, -iest**) (*sickly*) chétif; (*small*) petit; (*effort*) faible.

pup ['pʌp] *n* (*dog*) chiot *m*.

pupil ['pjuːpɪl] *n* **1** (*person*) élève *mf*. **2** (*of eye*) pupille *f*.

puppet ['pʌpɪt] *n* marionnette *f*; - *a* (*government, leader*) fantoche.

puppy ['pʌpɪ] *n* (*dog*) chiot *m*.

purchas/e ['pɜːtʃɪs] *n* (*bought article, buying*) achat *m*; - *vt* acheter (**from s.o.** à qn, **for s.o.** à *or* pour qn). ◆**-er** *n* acheteur, -euse *mf*.

pure [pjʊər] *a* (**-er, -est**) pur. ◆**purely** *adv* purement. ◆**purifi'cation** *n* purification *f*. ◆**purify** *vt* purifier. ◆**purity** *n* pureté *f*.

purée ['pjʊəreɪ] *n* purée *f*.

purgatory ['pɜːgətrɪ] *n* purgatoire *m*.

purge [pɜːdʒ] *n* Pol Med purge *f*; - *vt* (*rid*) purger (**of** de); (*group*) Pol épurer.

purist ['pjʊərɪst] *n* puriste *m*.

puritan ['pjʊərɪt(ə)n] *n & a* puritain, -aine (*mf*). ◆**puri'tanical** *a* puritain.

purl [pɜːl] *n* (*knitting stitch*) maille *f* à l'envers.

purple ['pɜːp(ə)l] *a & n* violet (*m*); **to go p.** (*with anger*) devenir pourpre; (*with shame*) devenir cramoisi.

purport [pɜː'pɔːt] *vt* **to p. to be** (*claim*) prétendre être.

purpose ['pɜːpəs] *n* **1** (*aim*) but *m*; **for this p.** dans ce but; **on p.** exprès; **to no p.** inutilement; **to serve no p.** ne servir à rien; **for** (**the**) **purposes of** pour les besoins de. **2** (*determination, willpower*) résolution *f*; **to have a sense of p.** être résolu. ◆**p.-'built** *a* construit spécialement. ◆**purposeful** *a* (*determined*) résolu. ◆**purposefully** *adv*

dans un but précis; (*resolutely*) résolument. ◆**purposely** *adv* exprès.

purr [pɜːr] *vi* ronronner; - *n* ronron(nement) *m*.

purse [pɜːs] **1** *n* (*for coins*) porte-monnaie *m inv*; (*handbag*) Am sac *m* à main. **2** *vt* **to p. one's lips** pincer les lèvres.

purser ['pɜːsər] *n* Nau commissaire *m* du bord.

pursue [pə'sjuː] *vt* (*chase, hound, seek, continue*) poursuivre; (*fame, pleasure*) rechercher; (*course of action*) suivre. ◆**pursuer** *n* poursuivant, -ante *mf*. ◆**pursuit** *n* (*of person, glory etc*) poursuite *f*; (*activity, pastime*) occupation *f*; **to go in p. of** se mettre à la poursuite de.

purveyor [pə'veɪər] *n* Com fournisseur *m*.

pus [pʌs] *n* pus *m*.

push [pʊʃ] *n* (*shove*) poussée *f*; (*energy*) Fig dynamisme *m*; (*help*) coup *m* de pouce; (*campaign*) campagne *f*; **to give s.o./sth a p.** pousser qn/qch; **to give s.o. the p.** (*dismiss*) Fam flanquer qn à la porte; - *vt* pousser (**to, as far as** jusqu'à); (*product*) Com pousser la vente de; (*drugs*) Fam revendre; **to p.** (**down**) (*button*) appuyer sur; (*lever*) abaisser; **to p.** (**forward**) (*views etc*) mettre en avant; **to p. sth into/between** (*thrust*) enfoncer *or* fourrer qch dans/entre; **to p. s.o. into doing** (*urge*) pousser qn à faire; **to p. sth off the table** faire tomber qch de la table (en le poussant); **to p. s.o. off a cliff** pousser qn du haut d'une falaise; **to be pushing forty/etc** Fam friser la quarantaine/etc; - *vi* pousser; **to p. for** faire pression pour obtenir. ■ **to p. about** *or* **around** *vt* (*bully*) Fam marcher sur les pieds à; **to p. aside** *vt* (*person, objection etc*) écarter; **to p. away** *or* **back** *vt* repousser; (*curtains*) ouvrir; **to p. in** *vi* (*in queue*) Fam resquiller; **to p. off** *vi* (*leave*) Fam filer; **p. off!** Fam fiche le camp!; **to p. on** *vi* continuer (**with** sth qch); (*in journey*) poursuivre sa route; **to p. over** *vt* (*topple*) renverser; **to p. through** *vt* (*law*) faire adopter; - *vti* **to p.** (**one's way**) **through** se frayer un chemin (**a crowd**/etc à travers une foule/etc); **to p. up** *vt* (*lever etc*) relever; (*increase*) Fam augmenter, relever. ◆**pushed** *a* **to be p.** (**for time**) (*rushed, busy*) être très bousculé. ◆**pusher** *n* (*of drugs*) revendeur, -euse *mf* (de drogue).

pushbike ['pʊʃbaɪk] *n* Fam vélo *m*. ◆**push-button** *n* poussoir *m*; - *a* (*radio etc*) à poussoir. ◆**pushchair** *n* poussette *f* (*pliante*). ◆**pushover** *n* **to be p.** (*easy*)

Fam être facile, être du gâteau. ◆**push-up** *n Sp Am* pompe *f*.

pushy ['pʊʃɪ] *a* (**-ier, -iest**) *Pej* entreprenant; (*in job*) arriviste.

puss(y) ['pʊs(ɪ)] *n* (*cat*) minet *m*, minou *m*.

put [pʊt] *vt* (*pt & pp* **put**, *pres p* **putting**) mettre; (*savings, money*) placer (**into** dans); (*pressure, mark*) faire (**on** sur); (*problem, argument*) présenter (**to** à); (*question*) poser (**to** à); (*say*) dire; (*estimate*) évaluer (**at** à); **to p. it bluntly** pour parler franc. ■ **to p. across** *vt* (*idea etc*) communiquer (**to** à); **to p. away** *vt* (*in its place*) ranger (*livre, voiture etc*); (*criminal*) mettre qn en prison; (*insane person*) enfermer qn; **to p. back** *vt* remettre; (*receiver*) *Tel* raccrocher; (*progress, clock*) retarder; **to p. by** *vt* (*money*) mettre de côté; **to p. down** *vt* (*on floor, table etc*) poser; (*passenger*) déposer; (*deposit*) *Fin* verser; (*revolt*) réprimer; (*write down*) inscrire; (*assign*) attribuer (**to** à); (*kill*) faire piquer (*chien etc*); **to p. forward** *vt* (*argument, clock, meeting*) avancer; (*opinion*) exprimer; (*candidate*) proposer (**for** à); **to p. in** *vt* (*insert*) introduire; (*add*) ajouter; (*present*) présenter; (*request, application*) faire; (*enrol*) inscrire (**for** à); – *vi* **to p. in for** (*job etc*) faire une demande de; **to p. in at** (*of ship etc*) faire escale à; **to p. off** *vt* (*postpone*) renvoyer (à plus tard); (*passenger*) déposer; (*gas, radio*) fermer; (*dismay*) déconcerter; **to p. s.o. off** (*dissuade*) dissuader qn (**doing** de faire); (*disgust*) dégoûter qn (**sth** de qch); **to p. s.o. off doing** (*disgust*) ôter à qn l'envie de faire; **to p. on** *vt* (*clothes, shoe etc*) mettre; (*weight, accent*) prendre; (*film*) jouer; (*gas, radio*) mettre, allumer; (*record, cassette*) passer; (*clock*) avancer; **to p. s.o. on** (*tease*) *Am* faire marcher qn; **she p. me on to you** elle m'a donné votre adresse; **p. me on to him!** *Tel* passez-le-moi!; **to p. out** *vt* (*take*

outside) sortir; (*arm, leg*) étendre; (*hand*) tendre; (*tongue*) tirer; (*gas, light*) éteindre, fermer; (*inconvenience*) déranger; (*upset*) déconcerter; (*issue*) publier; (*dislocate*) démettre; **to p. through** *vt Tel* passer (**to** à); **to p. together** *vt* (*assemble*) assembler; (*compose*) composer; (*prepare*) préparer; (*collection*) faire; **to p. up** *vi* (*lodge*) descendre (**at a hotel** dans un hôtel); **to p. up with** (*tolerate*) supporter; – *vt* (*lift*) lever; (*window*) remonter; (*tent, statue, barrier, ladder*) dresser; (*flag*) hisser; (*building*) construire; (*umbrella*) ouvrir; (*picture, poster*) mettre; (*price, sales, numbers*) augmenter; (*resistance, plea, suggestion*) offrir; (*candidate*) proposer (**for** à); (*guest*) loger; **p.-up job** *Fam* coup *m* monté. ◆**p.-you-up** *n* canapé-lit *m*, convertible *m*.

putrid ['pjuːtrɪd] *a* putride. ◆**putrify** *vi* se putréfier.

putt [pʌt] *n Golf* putt *m*. ◆**putting** *n Golf* putting *m*; **p. green** green *m*.

putter ['pʌtər] *vi* **to p. around** *Am* bricoler.

putty ['pʌtɪ] *n* (*pour fixer une vitre*) mastic *m*.

puzzl/e ['pʌz(ə)l] *n* mystère *m*, énigme *f*; (*game*) casse-tête *m inv*; (*jigsaw*) puzzle *m*; – *vt* laisser perplexe; **to p. out why/when/** *etc* essayer de comprendre pourquoi/quand/*etc*; – *vi* **to p. over** (*problem, event*) se creuser la tête sur. ◆**—ed** *a* perplexe. ◆**—ing** *a* mystérieux, surprenant.

PVC [piːviːsiː] *n* (*plastic*) PVC *m*.

pygmy ['pɪgmɪ] *n* pygmée *m*.

pyjama [pɪ'dʒɑːmə] *a* (*jacket etc*) de pyjama. ◆**pyjamas** *npl* pyjama *m*; **a pair of p.** un pyjama.

pylon ['paɪlən] *n* pylône *m*.

pyramid ['pɪrəmɪd] *n* pyramide *f*.

Pyrenees [pɪrə'niːz] *npl* **the P.** les Pyrénées *fpl*.

python ['paɪθən] *n* (*snake*) python *m*.

Q

Q, q [kjuː] *n* Q, q *m*.

quack [kwæk] **1** *n* (*of duck*) coin-coin *m inv*. **2** *a & n* **q.** (*doctor*) charlatan *m*.

quad(rangle) ['kwɒd(ræŋg(ə)l)] *n* (*of college*) cour *f*.

quadruped ['kwɒdrʊped] *n* quadrupède *m*.

quadruple [kwɒ'druːp(ə)l] *vt* quadrupler.

quadruplets [kwɒ'druːplɪts] (*Fam* **quads** [kwɒdz]) *npl* quadruplés. -ées *mfpl*.

quaff [kwɒf] *vt* (*drink*) avaler.

quagmire ['kwægmaɪər] *n* bourbier *m*.

quail [kweɪl] *n* (*bird*) caille *f*.

quaint [kweɪnt] *a* (**-er, -est**) *(picturesque)* pittoresque; *(antiquated)* vieillot; *(odd)* bizarre. **◆-ness** *n* pittoresque *m*; caractère *m* vieillot; bizarrerie *f*.

quake [kweɪk] *vi* trembler (**with** de); *– n Fam* tremblement *m* de terre.

Quaker ['kweɪkər] *n* quaker, -eresse *mf*.

qualification [kwɒlɪfɪ'keɪʃ(ə)n] *n* 1 *(competence)* compétence *f* (**for** pour, **to do** pour faire); *(diploma)* diplôme *m*; *pl (requirements)* conditions *fpl* requises. 2 *(reservation)* réserve *f*.

qualify ['kwɒlɪfaɪ] 1 *vt (make competent)* & *Sp* qualifier (**for sth** pour qch, **to do** pour faire); *– vi* obtenir son diplôme (**as a doctor**/*etc* de médecin/*etc*); *Sp* se qualifier (**for** pour); **to q. for** *(post)* remplir les conditions requises pour. 2 *vt (modify)* faire des réserves à; *(opinion)* nuancer; *Gram* qualifier. **◆qualified** *a (able)* qualifié (**to do** pour faire); *(doctor etc)* diplômé; *(success)* limité; *(opinion)* nuancé; *(support)* conditionnel. **◆qualifying** *a (exam)* d'entrée; **q. round** *Sp* (épreuve *f*) éliminatoire *f*.

quality ['kwɒlɪtɪ] *n* qualité *f*; *– a (product)* de qualité. **◆qualitative** *a* qualitatif.

qualms [kwɑːmz] *npl (scruples)* scrupules *mpl*; *(anxieties)* inquiétudes *fpl*.

quandary ['kwɒndrɪ] *n* **in a q.** bien embarrassé; **to be in a q. about what to do** ne pas savoir quoi faire.

quantity ['kwɒntɪtɪ] *n* quantité *f*; **in q.** (**to** *purchase etc*) en grande(s) quantité(s). **◆quantify** *vt* quantifier. **◆quantitative** *a* quantitatif.

quarantine ['kwɒrəntiːn] *n Med* quarantaine *f*; *– vt* mettre en quarantaine.

quarrel ['kwɒrəl] *n* querelle *f*, dispute *f*; **to pick a q.** chercher querelle (**with s.o.** à qn); *– vi* (**-ll-**, *Am* **-l-**) se disputer, se quereller (**with** avec); **to q. with sth** trouver à redire à qch. **◆quarrelling** *n*, *Am* **quarreling** *n* (*quarrels*) querelles *fpl*. **◆quarrelsome** *a* querelleur.

quarry ['kwɒrɪ] *n* 1 *(excavation)* carrière *f*. 2 *(prey)* proie *f*.

quart [kwɔːt] *n* litre *m* (*mesure approximative*) (*Br* = 1,14 *litres*, *Am* = 0,95 *litre*).

quarter ['kwɔːtər] *n* 1 quart *m*; *(of year)* trimestre *m*; *(money)* *Am* quart *m* de dollar; *(of moon, fruit)* quartier *m*; **to divide into quarters** diviser en quatre; **q. (of a) pound** quart *m* de livre; **a q. past nine**, *Am* **a q. after nine** neuf heures et *or* un quart; **a q. to nine** neuf heures moins le quart; **from all quarters** de toutes parts. 2 *n (district)*

quartier *m*; *pl (circles)* milieux *mpl*; *(living)* **quarters** logement(s) *m(pl)*; *Mil* quartier(s) *m(pl)*; *(of troops)* *Mil* cantonner. **◆-ly** *a* trimestriel; *– adv* trimestriellement; *– n* publication *f* trimestrielle.

quarterfinal [kwɔːtə'faɪn(ə)l] *n Sp* quart *m* de finale.

quartet(te) [kwɔː'tet] *n Mus* quatuor *m*; (**jazz**) **q.** quartette *m*.

quartz [kwɔːts] *n* quartz *m*; *– a (clock etc)* à quartz.

quash [kwɒʃ] *vt (rebellion etc)* réprimer; *(verdict)* *Jur* casser.

quaver ['kweɪvər] 1 *vi* chevroter; *– n* chevrotement *m*. 2 *n Mus* croche *f*.

quay [kiː] *n Nau* quai *m*. **◆quayside** *n* on the **q.** sur les quais.

queas/y ['kwiːzɪ] *a* (**-ier, -iest**) **to feel** *or* **be q.** avoir mal au cœur. **◆-iness** *n* mal *m* au cœur.

Quebec [kwɪ'bek] *n* le Québec.

queen [kwiːn] *n* reine *f*; *Chess Cards* dame *f*; **the q. mother** la reine mère.

queer ['kwɪər] *a* (**-er, -est**) *(odd)* bizarre; *(dubious)* louche; *(ill)* *Fam* patraque; *– n (homosexual)* *Pej Fam* pédé *m*.

quell [kwel] *vt (revolt etc)* réprimer.

quench [kwentʃ] *vt (fire)* éteindre; **to q. one's thirst** se désaltérer.

querulous ['kweruləs] *a (complaining)* grognon.

query ['kwɪərɪ] *n* question *f*; *(doubt)* doute *m*; *– vt* mettre en question.

quest [kwest] *n* quête *f* (**for** de); **in q. of** en quête de.

question ['kwestʃ(ə)n] *n* question *f*; **there's some q. of it** il en est question; **there's no q. of it, it's out of the q.** il n'en est pas question, c'est hors de question; **without q.** incontestable(ment); **in q.** en question, dont il s'agit; **q. mark** point *m* d'interrogation; **q.** *master* *TV Rad* animateur, -trice *mf*; *– vt* interroger (**about** sur); *(doubt)* mettre en question; **to q. whether** douter que (**+** *sub*). **◆-ing** *a (look etc)* interrogateur; *– n* interrogation *f*. **◆-able** *a* douteux. **◆questio'nnaire** *n* questionnaire *m*.

queue [kjuː] *n (of people)* queue *f*; *(of cars)* file *f*; **to stand in a q.**, **form a q.** faire la queue; *– vi* **to q.** (**up**) faire la queue.

quibbl/e ['kwɪb(ə)l] *vi* ergoter, discuter (**over** sur). **◆-ing** *n* ergotage *m*.

quiche [kiːʃ] *n (tart)* quiche *f*.

quick [kwɪk] *a* (**-er, -est**) rapide; **q. to react** prompt à réagir; **to be q.** faire vite; **to have a q. shave/meal**/*etc* se raser/manger/*etc* en vitesse; **to be a q. worker** travailler vite; − *adv* (**-er, -est**) vite; **as q. as a flash** en un clin d'œil. **2** *n* to cut to the q. blesser au vif. ◆**q.-'tempered** *a* irascible. ◆**q.-'witted** *a* à l'esprit vif. ◆**quicken** *vt* accélérer; − *vi* s'accélérer. ◆**quickie** *n* (*drink*) *Fam* pot *m* (*pris en vitesse*). ◆**quickly** *adv* vite. ◆**quicksands** *npl* sables *mpl* mouvants.

quid [kwɪd] *n inv Fam* livre *f* (sterling).

quiet [kwaɪət] *a* (**-er, -est**) (*silent, still, peaceful*) tranquille, calme; (*machine, vehicle, temperament*) silencieux; (*gentle*) doux; (*voice*) bas, doux; (*sound*) léger, doux; (*private*) intime; (*colour*) discret; **to be** *or* **keep q.** (*shut up*) se taire; (*make no noise*) ne pas faire de bruit; **q.!** silence!; **to keep q. about sth, keep sth q.** ne pas parler de qch; **on the q.** (*secretly*) *Fam* en cachette; − *vt* = **quieten.** ◆**quieten** *vti* **to q. (down)** (*se*) calmer. ◆**quietly** *adv* tranquillement; (*gently, not loudly*) doucement; (*silently*) silencieusement; (*secretly*) en cachette; (*discreetly*) discrètement. ◆**quietness** *n* tranquillité *f*.

quill [kwɪl] *n* (*pen*) plume *f* (d'oie).

quilt [kwɪlt] *n* édredon *m*; (**continental**) **q.** couette *f*; − *vt* (*stitch*) piquer; (*pad*) matelasser.

quintessence [kwɪn'tesəns] *n* quintessence *f*.

quintet(te) [kwɪn'tet] *n* quintette *m*.

quintuplets [kwɪn'tjuːplɪts] (*Fam* **quins** [kwɪnz]) *npl* quintuplés, -ées *mfpl*.

quip [kwɪp] *n* (*remark*) boutade *f*; − *vi* (**-pp-**) faire des boutades; − *vt* dire sur le ton de la boutade.

quirk [kwɜːk] *n* bizarrerie *f*; (*of fate*) caprice *m*.

quit [kwɪt] *vt* (*pt & pp* quit *or* quitted, *pres p* quitting) (*leave*) quitter; **to q. doing** arrêter de faire; − *vi* (*give up*) abandonner; (*resign*) démissionner.

quite [kwaɪt] *adv* (*entirely*) tout à fait; (*really*) vraiment; (*rather*) assez; **q. another matter** une tout autre affaire *or* question; **q. a genius** un véritable génie; **q. good** (*not bad*) pas mal (du tout); **q. (so!)** exactement!; **I q. understand** je comprends très bien; **q. a lot** pas mal (**of** de); **q. a (long) time ago** il y a pas mal de temps.

quits [kwɪts] *a* quitte (**with** envers); **to call it q.** en rester là.

quiver [ˈkwɪvər] *vi* frémir (**with** de); (*of voice*) trembler, frémir; (*of flame*) vaciller, trembler.

quiz [kwɪz] *n* (*pl* quizzes) (*riddle*) devinette *f*; (*test*) test *m*; **q.** (**programme**) *TV Rad* jeu(-concours) *m*; − *vt* (**-zz-**) questionner. ◆**quizmaster** *n TV Rad* animateur, -trice *mf*.

quizzical [ˈkwɪzɪk(ə)l] *a* (*mocking*) narquois; (*perplexed*) perplexe.

quorum [ˈkwɔːrəm] *n* quorum *m*.

quota [ˈkwəʊtə] *n* quota *m*.

quote [kwəʊt] *vt* citer; (*reference number*) *Com* rappeler; (*price*) indiquer; (*price on Stock Exchange*) coter; − *vi* **to q. from** (*author, book*) citer; − *n Fam* = quotation; **in quotes** entre guillemets. ◆**quo'tation** *n* citation *f*; (*estimate*) *Com* devis *m*; (*on Stock Exchange*) cote *f*; **q. marks** guillemets *mpl*; **in q. marks** entre guillemets.

quotient [ˈkwəʊʃ(ə)nt] *n* quotient *m*.

R

R, r [ɑːr] *n* R, r *m*.

rabbi [ˈræbaɪ] *n* rabbin *m*; **chief r.** grand rabbin.

rabbit [ˈræbɪt] *n* lapin *m*.

rabble [ˈræb(ə)l] *n* (*crowd*) cohue *f*; **the r.** *Pej* la populace.

rabies [ˈreɪbiːz] *n Med* rage *f*. ◆**rabid** [ˈræbɪd] *a* (*dog*) enragé; (*person*) *Fig* fanatique.

raccoon [rəˈkuːn] *n* (*animal*) raton *m* laveur.

rac/e¹ [reɪs] *n Sp & Fig* course *f*; − *vt*

(*horse*) faire courir; (*engine*) emballer; **to r.** (**against** *or* **with**) **s.o.** faire une course avec qn; − *vi* (*run*) courir; (*of engine*) s'emballer; (*of pulse*) battre à tout rompre. ◆**-ing** *n* courses *fpl*; − *a* (*car, bicycle etc*) de course; **r. driver** coureur *m* automobile. ◆**racecourse** *n* champ *m* de courses. ◆**racegoer** *n* turfiste *m*. ◆**racehorse** *n* cheval *m* de course. ◆**racetrack** *n* piste *f*; (*for horses*) *Am* champ *m* de courses.

race² [reɪs] *n* (*group*) race *f*; − *a* (*prejudice etc*) racial; **r. relations** rapports *mpl* entre les races. ◆**racial** a racial. ◆**racialism** n racisme m. ◆**racism** n racisme m. ◆**racist** a & n raciste (mf).

rack [ræk] **1** n (shelf) étagère f; (for bottles etc) casier m; (for drying dishes) égouttoir m; (luggage) r. (on bicycle) porte-bagages m inv; (on bus, train etc) filet m à bagages; (roof) r. (of car) galerie f. **2** vt to r. one's brains se creuser la cervelle. **3** n to go to r. and ruin (of person) aller à la ruine; (of building) tomber en ruine; (of health) se délabrer.

racket [rækɪt] n **1** (for tennis etc) raquette f. **2** (din) vacarme m. **3** (crime) racket m; (scheme) combine f; the drug(s) r. le trafic m de (la) drogue. ◆**racke'teer** n racketteur m. ◆**racke'teering** n racket m.

racoon [rə'ku:n] n (animal) raton m laveur.

racy ['reɪsɪ] a (-ier, -iest) piquant; (suggestive) osé.

radar ['reɪdɑːr] n radar m; – a (control, trap etc) radar inv; r. operator opérateur m radar.

radiant ['reɪdɪənt] a (person) rayonnant (with de), radieux. ◆**radiance** n éclat m, rayonnement m. ◆**radiantly** adv (to shine) avec éclat; r. happy rayonnant de joie.

radiate ['reɪdɪeɪt] vt (emit) dégager; (joy) Fig rayonner de; – vi (of heat, lines) rayonner (from de). ◆**radia'tion** n (of heat etc) rayonnement m (of de); (radioactivity) Phys radiation f; (rays) irradiation f; r. sickness mal m des rayons.

radiator ['reɪdɪeɪtər] n radiateur m.

radical ['rædɪk(ə)l] a radical; – n (person) Pol radical, -ale mf.

radio ['reɪdɪəʊ] n (pl -os) radio f; on the r. à la radio; car r. autoradio m; r. set poste m (de) radio; r. operator radio m; r. wave onde f hertzienne; – vt (message) transmettre (par radio) (to à); to r. s.o. appeler qn par radio. ◆**r.-con'trolled** a radioguidé. ◆**radio'active** a radioactif. ◆**radio'activity** n radioactivité f.

radiographer [reɪdɪ'ɒɡrəfər] n (technician) radiologue mf. ◆**radiography** n radiographie f. ◆**radiologist** n (doctor) radiologue mf. ◆**radiology** n radiologie f.

radish ['rædɪʃ] n radis m.

radius [pl -dii ['reɪdɪəs, -dɪaɪ] n (of circle) rayon m; within a r. of dans un rayon de.

RAF [ɑːrɪ'ɛf] n abbr (Royal Air Force) armée f de l'air (britannique).

raffia ['ræfɪə] n raphia m.

raffle ['ræf(ə)l] n tombola f.

raft [rɑːft] n (boat) radeau m.

rafter ['rɑːftər] n (beam) chevron m.

rag [ræɡ] n **1** (old garment) loque f, haillon

m; (for dusting etc) chiffon m; in rags (clothes) en loques; (person) en haillons; r.-and-bone man chiffonnier m. **2** (newspaper) torchon m. **3** (procession) Univ carnaval m (au profit d'œuvres de charité). ◆**ragged** ['ræɡɪd] a (clothes) en loques; (person) en haillons; (edge) irrégulier. ◆**ragman** n (pl -men) chiffonnier m.

ragamuffin ['ræɡəmʌfɪn] n va-nu-pieds m inv.

rag/e [reɪdʒ] n rage f; (of sea) furie f; to fly into a r. se mettre en rage; to be all the r. (of fashion etc) faire fureur; – vi (be angry) rager; (of storm, battle) faire rage. ◆**-ing** a (storm, fever) violent; a r. fire un grand incendie; in a r. temper furieux.

raid [reɪd] n Mil raid m; (by police) descente f; (by thieves) hold-up m; air r. raid m aérien, attaque f aérienne; – vt faire un raid ou une descente ou un hold-up dans; Av attaquer; (larder, fridge etc) Fam dévaliser. ◆**raider** n (criminal) malfaiteur m; pl Mil commando m.

rail [reɪl] n **1** (for train) rail m; by r. (to travel) par le train; (to send) par chemin de fer; to go off the rails (of train) dérailler; – a ferroviaire; (strike) des cheminots. **2** n (rod on balcony) balustrade f; (on stairs, for spotlight) rampe f; (for curtain) tringle f; (towel) r. porte-serviettes m inv. ◆**railing** n (of balcony) balustrade f; pl (fence) grille f. ◆**railroad** n Am = railway; r. track voie f ferrée. ◆**railway** n (system) chemin m de fer; (track) voie f ferrée; – a (ticket) de chemin de fer; (network) ferroviaire; r. line (route) ligne f de chemin de fer; (track) voie f ferrée; r. station gare f. ◆**railwayman** n (pl -men) cheminot m.

rain [reɪn] n pluie f; in the r. sous la pluie; I'll give you a r. check (for invitation) Am Fam j'accepterai volontiers à une date ultérieure; – vi pleuvoir; to r. (down) (of blows, bullets) pleuvoir; it's raining il pleut. ◆**rainbow** n arc-en-ciel m. ◆**raincoat** n imper(méable) m. ◆**raindrop** n goutte f de pluie. ◆**rainfall** n (shower) chute f de pluie; (amount) précipitations fpl. ◆**rainstorm** n trombe f d'eau. ◆**rainwater** n eau f de pluie. ◆**rainy** a (-ier, -iest) pluvieux; the r. season la saison des pluies.

raise [reɪz] vt (lift) lever; (sth heavy) (sou)lever; (child, animal, voice, statue) élever; (crops) cultiver; (salary, price) augmenter, relever; (temperature) faire monter; (question, protest) soulever; (taxes, blockade) lever; to r. a smile/a laugh (in others) faire sourire/rire; to r. s.o.'s hopes faire naître les espérances de qn; **to r. money** réunir des fonds; – *n* (*pay rise*) *Am* augmentation *f* (de salaire).

raisin ['reɪz(ə)n] *n* raisin *m* sec.

rake [reɪk] **1** *n* râteau *m*; – *vt* (*garden*) ratisser; (*search*) fouiller dans; **to r. (up)** (*leaves*) ramasser (avec un râteau); **to r. in** (*money*) *Fam* ramasser à la pelle; **to r. up** (*the past*) remuer. ◆**r.-off** *n Fam* pot-de-vin *m*, ristourne *f*.

rally ['rælɪ] *vt* (*unite, win over*) rallier (**to** à); (*one's strength*) *Fig* reprendre; – *vi* se rallier (**to** à); (*recover*) se remettre (**from** de); **to r. round** (*help*) venir en aide (**s.o.** à qn); – *n Mil* ralliement *m*; *Pol* rassemblement *m*; *Sp Aut* rallye *m*.

ram [ræm] **1** *n* (*animal*) bélier *m*. **2** *vt* (-**mm**-) (*ship*) heurter; (*vehicle*) emboutir; **to r. sth into** (*thrust*) enfoncer qch dans.

rambl/e ['ræmb(ə)l] **1** *n* (*hike*) randonnée *f*; – *vi* faire une randonnée *or* des randonnées. **2** *vi* **to r. on** (*talk*) *Pej* discourir. ◆**—ing 1** *a* (*house*) construit sans plan; (*spread out*) vaste; (*rose etc*) grimpant. **2** *a* (*speech*) décousu; – *npl* divagations *fpl*. ◆**—er** *n* promeneur, -euse *mf*.

ramification [ræmɪfɪ'keɪʃ(ə)n] *n* ramification *f*.

ramp [ræmp] *n* (*slope*) rampe *f*; (*in garage*) *Tech* pont *m* (de graissage); *Av* passerelle *f*; **'r.'** *Aut* 'dénivellation'.

rampage ['ræmpeɪdʒ] *n* **to go on the r.** (*of crowd*) se déchaîner; (*loot*) se livrer au pillage.

rampant ['ræmpənt] *a* **to be r.** (*of crime, disease etc*) sévir.

rampart ['ræmpɑːt] *n* rempart *m*.

ramshackle ['ræmʃæk(ə)l] *a* délabré.

ran [ræn] *see* **run**.

ranch [rɑːntʃ] *n Am* ranch *m*; **r. house** maison *f* genre bungalow (sur sous-sol).

rancid ['rænsɪd] *a* rance.

rancour ['ræŋkər] *n* rancœur *f*.

random ['rændəm] *n* **at r.** au hasard; – *a* (*choice*) fait au hasard; (*sample*) prélevé au hasard; (*pattern*) irrégulier.

randy ['rændɪ] *a* (**-ier, -iest**) *Fam* sensuel, lascif.

rang [ræŋ] *see* **ring²**.

range [reɪndʒ] **1** *n* (*of gun, voice etc*) portée *f*; (*of aircraft, ship*) rayon *m* d'action; (*series*) gamme *f*; (*choice*) choix *m*; (*of prices*) éventail *m*; (*of voice*) *Mus* étendue *f*; (*of temperature*) variations *fpl*; (*sphere*) *Fig* champ *m*, étendue *f*; – *vi* (*vary*) varier; (*extend*) s'étendre; (*roam*) errer, rôder. **2** *n* (*of mountains*) chaîne *f*; (*grassland*) *Am*

prairie. **3** *n* (*stove*) *Am* cuisinière *f*. **4** *n* (*shooting or rifle*) **r.** (*at funfair*) stand *m* de tir; (*outdoors*) champ *m* de tir.

ranger ['reɪndʒər] *n* (*forest*) **r.** *Am* garde *m* forestier.

rank [ræŋk] **1** *n* (*position, class*) rang *m*; (*grade*) *Mil* grade *m*, rang *m*; **the r. and file** (*workers etc*) *Pol* la base; **the ranks** (*men in army, numbers*) les rangs *mpl* (**of** de); **taxi r. station** *f* de taxi; – *vti* **to r.** among compter parmi. **2** *a* (-**er, -est**) (*smell*) fétide; (*vegetation*) luxuriant; *Fig* absolu.

rankle ['ræŋk(ə)l] *vi* **it rankles (with me)** je l'ai sur le cœur.

ransack ['rænsæk] *vt* (*search*) fouiller; (*plunder*) saccager.

ransom ['ræns(ə)m] *n* rançon *f*; **to hold to r.** rançonner; – *vt* (*redeem*) racheter.

rant [rænt] *vi* **to r. (and rave)** tempêter (**at** contre).

rap [ræp] *n* petit coup *m* sec; – *vi* (-**pp**-) frapper (**at** à); – *vt* **to r. s.o. over the knuckles** taper sur les doigts de qn.

rapacious [rə'peɪʃəs] *a* (*greedy*) rapace.

rape [reɪp] *vt* violer; – *n* viol *m*. ◆**rapist** *n* violeur *m*.

rapid ['ræpɪd] **1** *a* rapide. **2** *n & npl* (*of river*) rapide(s) *m(pl)*. ◆**ra'pidity** *n* rapidité *f*. ◆**rapidly** *adv* rapidement.

rapport [ræ'pɔːr] *n* (*understanding*) rapport *m*.

rapt [ræpt] *a* (*attention*) profond.

rapture ['ræptʃər] *n* extase *f*; **to go into raptures** s'extasier (**about** sur). ◆**rapturous** *a* (*welcome, applause*) enthousiaste.

rare [reər] *a* (-**er, -est**) rare; (*meat*) *Culin* saignant; (*first-rate*) *Fam* fameux; **it's r. for her to do it** il est rare qu'elle le fasse. ◆**—ly** *adv* rarement. ◆**—ness** *n* rareté *f*. ◆**rarity** *n* (*quality, object*) rareté *f*.

rarefied ['reərɪfaɪd] *a* raréfié.

raring ['reərɪŋ] *a* **r. to start/etc** impatient de commencer/*etc*.

rascal ['rɑːsk(ə)l] *n* coquin, -ine *mf*. ◆**rascally** *a* (*child etc*) coquin; (*habit, trick etc*) de coquin.

rash [ræʃ] **1** *n Med* éruption *f*. **2** *a* (-**er, -est**) irréfléchi. ◆**—ly** *adv* sans réflexion. ◆**—ness** *n* irréflexion *f*.

rasher ['ræʃər] *n* tranche *f* de lard.

rasp [rɑːsp] *n* (*file*) râpe *f*.

raspberry ['rɑːzbərɪ] *n* (*fruit*) framboise *f*; (*bush*) framboisier *m*.

rasping ['rɑːspɪŋ] *a* (*voice*) âpre.

rat [ræt] **1** *n* rat *m*; **r. poison** mort-aux-rats *f*; **the r. race** *Fig* la course au bifteck, la jungle. **2** *vi* (-**tt**-) **to r. on** (*desert*) lâcher;

(denounce) cafarder sur; (promise etc)
manquer à.

rate [reɪt] **1** n (percentage, level) taux m;
(speed) vitesse f; (price) tarif m; pl (on
housing) impôts mpl locaux; **insurance
rates** primes fpl d'assurance; **r. of flow**
débit m; **postage** or **postal r.** tarif m postal;
at the r. of à une vitesse de; (amount) à
raison de; **at this r.** (slow speed) à ce
train-là; **at any r.** en tout cas; **the success r.**
(chances) les chances fpl de succès; (candidates) le pourcentage de reçus. **2** vt (evaluate) évaluer; (regard) considérer (**as**
comme); (deserve) mériter; **to r. highly**
apprécier (beaucoup); **to be highly rated**
être très apprécié. ◆**rateable** a r. value
valeur f locative nette. ◆**ratepayer** n
contribuable mf.

rather [ˈrɑːðər] adv (preferably, instead)
plutôt; **I'd r. stay** j'aimerais mieux or je
préférerais rester (**than** que); **I'd r. you
came** je préférerais que vous veniez; **a than
leave**/etc plutôt que de partir/etc; **r. more
tired**/etc un peu plus fatigué/etc (**than**
que); **it's r. nice** c'est bien.

ratify [ˈrætɪfaɪ] vt ratifier. ◆**ratifi'cation** n
ratification f.

rating [ˈreɪtɪŋ] n (classification) classement
m; (wage etc level) indice m; **credit r.** Fin
réputation f de solvabilité; **the ratings** TV
l'indice m d'écoute.

ratio [ˈreɪʃɪəʊ] n (pl -os) proportion f.

ration [ˈræʃ(ə)n, Am ˈreɪʃ(ə)n] n ration f; pl
(food) vivres mpl; – vt rationner; **I was
rationed to** . . . ma ration était . . . .

rational [ˈræʃ(ə)n(ə)l] a (method, thought etc)
rationnel; (person) raisonnable. ◆**rationalize** vt (organize) rationaliser; (explain)
justifier. ◆**rationally** adv raisonnablement.

rattle [ˈræt(ə)l] **1** n (baby's toy) hochet m; (of
sports fan) crécelle f. **2** n petit bruit m (sec);
cliquetis m; crépitement m; – vi faire du
bruit; (of bottles) cliqueter; (of gunfire)
crépiter; (of window) trembler; – vt (shake)
agiter; (window) faire trembler; (keys) faire
cliqueter. **3** vt **to r. s.o.** (make nervous) Fam
ébranler qn; **to r. off** (poem etc) Fam
débiter (à toute vitesse). ◆**rattlesnake** n
serpent m à sonnette.

ratty [ˈrætɪ] a (-ier, -iest) **1** (shabby) Am Fam
minable. **2 to get r.** (annoyed) Fam prendre
la mouche.

raucous [ˈrɔːkəs] a rauque.

raunchy [ˈrɔːntʃɪ] a (-ier, -iest) (joke etc) Am
Fam grivois.

ravage [ˈrævɪdʒ] vt ravager; – npl ravages
mpl.

rav/e [reɪv] vi (talk nonsense) divaguer;
(rage) tempêter (**at contre**); **to r. about**
(enthuse) ne pas se tarir d'éloges sur; – a **r.
review** Fam critique f dithyrambique.
◆**-ing** a **to be r. mad** être fou furieux; –
npl (wild talk) divagations fpl.

raven [ˈreɪv(ə)n] n corbeau m.

ravenous [ˈrævənəs] a vorace; **I'm r.** Fam
j'ai une faim de loup.

ravine [rəˈviːn] n ravin m.

ravioli [rævɪˈəʊlɪ] n ravioli mpl.

ravish [ˈrævɪʃ] vt (rape) Lit violenter.
◆**-ing** a (beautiful) ravissant. ◆**-ingly**
adv **r. beautiful** d'une beauté ravissante.

raw [rɔː] a (-er, -est) (vegetable etc) cru;
(sugar) brut; (immature) inexpérimenté;
(wound) à vif; (skin) écorché; (weather)
rigoureux; **r. edge** bord m coupé; **r. material** matière f première; **to get a r. deal** Fam
être mal traité.

Rawlplug® [ˈrɔːlplʌɡ] n cheville f, tampon
m.

ray [reɪ] n (of light, sun etc) & Phys rayon m;
(of hope) lueur f.

raze [reɪz] vt **to r. (to the ground)** (destroy)
raser.

razor [ˈreɪzər] n rasoir m.

re [riː] prep Com en référence à.

re- [riː] pref ré-, re-, r-.

reach [riːtʃ] vt (place, aim etc) atteindre,
arriver à; (gain access to) accéder à; (of
letter) parvenir à (qn); (contact) joindre
(qn); **to r. s.o. (over) sth** (hand over) passer
qch à qn; **to r. out** (one's arm) (é)tendre; –
vi (extend) s'étendre (**to** à); (of voice)
porter; **to r. (out)** (é)tendre le bras (**for**
pour prendre); – n portée f; Boxing
allonge f; **within r. of** à portée de; (near) à
proximité de; **within easy r.** (object) à
portée de main; (shops) facilement accessible.

react [rɪˈækt] vi réagir. ◆**reaction** n réaction f. ◆**reactionary** a & n réactionnaire
(mf).

reactor [rɪˈæktər] n réacteur m.

read [riːd] vt (pt & pp **read** [red]) lire; (study)
Univ faire des études de; (meter) relever;
(of instrument) indiquer; **to r. back** or **over**
relire; **to r. out** lire (à haute voix); **to r.
through** (skim) parcourir; **to r. up (on)**
(study) étudier; – vi lire; **to r. well** (of text)
se lire bien; **to r. to s.o.** faire la lecture à qn;
to r. about (s.o., sth) lire qch sur; **to r. for**
(degree) Univ préparer; – n **to have a r.**
Fam faire un peu de lecture; **this book's a**

good r. *Fam* ce livre est agréable à lire. ◆**—ing** *n* lecture *f*; *(of meter)* relevé *m*; *(by instrument)* indication *f*; *(variant)* variante *f*; *– a (room)* de lecture; **r. matter** choses *fpl* à lire; **r. lamp** lampe *f* de bureau *or* de chevet. ◆**—able** *a* lisible. ◆**—er** *n* lecteur, -trice *mf*; *(book)* livre *m* de lecture. ◆**readership** *n* lecteurs *mpl*, public *m*.

readdress [riːəˈdres] *vt (letter)* faire suivre.

readjust [riːəˈdʒʌst] *vt (instrument)* régler; *(salary)* réajuster; *– vi* se réadapter **(to** à). ◆**—ment** *n* réglage *m*; réajustement *m*; réadaptation *f*.

readily [ˈredɪlɪ] *adv (willingly)* volontiers; *(easily)* facilement. ◆**readiness** *n* empressement *m* **(to do** à faire); **in r.** for prêt pour.

ready [ˈredɪ] *a* **(-ier, -iest)** prêt **(to do** à faire, **for sth** à *or* pour qch); *(quick)* prompt **(to do** à faire); **to get sth r.** préparer qch; **to get r.** se préparer **(for sth** à qch, **to do** à faire); **r. cash, r. money** argent *m* liquide; *– n* argent *m* tout prêt. ◆**r.-'cooked** *a* tout cuit. ◆**r.-'made** *a* tout fait; **r.-made clothes** prêt-à-porter *m* *inv*.

real [rɪəl] *a* vrai, véritable; *(life, world etc)* réel; **it's the r. thing** *Fam* c'est du vrai de vrai; **r. estate** *Am* immobilier *m*; *– adv Fam* vraiment; **r. stupid** vraiment bête; *– n* **for r.** *Fam* pour de vrai. ◆**realism** *n* réalisme *m*. ◆**realist** *n* réaliste *mf*. ◆**rea'listic** *a* réaliste. ◆**rea'listically** *adv* avec réalisme.

reality [rɪˈælɪtɪ] *n* réalité *f*; **in r.** en réalité.

realize [ˈrɪəlaɪz] *vt* **1** *(know)* se rendre compte de, réaliser; *(understand)* comprendre **(that** que); **to r. that** *(know)* se rendre compte que. **2** *(carry out, convert into cash)* réaliser; *(price)* atteindre. ◆**reali'zation** *n* **1** *(prise f de)* conscience *f*. **2** *(of aim, assets)* réalisation *f*.

really [ˈrɪəlɪ] *adv* vraiment; **is it r. true?** est-ce bien vrai?

realm [relm] *n (kingdom)* royaume *m*; *(of dreams etc)* *Fig* monde *m*.

realtor [ˈrɪəltər] *n Am* agent *m* immobilier.

reap [riːp] *vt (field, crop)* moissonner; *Fig* récolter.

reappear [riːəˈpɪər] *vi* réapparaître.

reappraisal [riːəˈpreɪz(ə)l] *n* réévaluation *f*.

rear [rɪər] **1** *n (back part)* arrière *m*; *(of column)* queue *f*; **in** *or* **at the r.** à l'arrière **(of** de); **from the r.** par derrière; *– a* arrière *inv*, de derrière; **r.-view mirror** rétroviseur *m*. **2** *vt (family, animals etc)* élever; *(one's head)* relever. **3** *vi* **r. (up)** *(of horse)* se cabrer. ◆**rearguard** *n* arrière-garde *f*.

rearrange [riːəˈreɪndʒ] *vt* réarranger.

reason [ˈriːz(ə)n] *n (cause, sense)* raison *f*; **the r. for/why** *or* **that . . .** la raison de/pour laquelle . . .; **for no r.** sans raison; **that stands to r.** cela va sans dire, c'est logique; **within r.** avec modération; **to do everything within r. to . . .** faire tout ce qu'il est raisonnable de faire pour . . .; **to have every r. to believe/etc** avoir tout lieu de croire/etc; *– vi* raisonner; **to r. with s.o.** raisonner qn; *– vt* **to r. that** calculer que. ◆**—ing** *n* raisonnement *m*. ◆**—able** *a* raisonnable. ◆**—ably** *adv* raisonnablement; *(fairly, rather)* assez; **r. fit** en assez bonne forme.

reassur/e [riːəˈʃʊər] *vt* rassurer. ◆**—ing** *a* rassurant. ◆**reassurance** *n* réconfort *m*.

reawaken [riːəˈweɪk(ə)n] *vt (interest etc)* réveiller. ◆**—ing** *n* réveil *m*.

rebate [ˈriːbeɪt] *n (discount on purchase)* ristourne *f*; *(refund)* remboursement *m* *(partiel)*.

rebel [ˈreb(ə)l] *a & n* rebelle *(mf)*; *–* [rɪˈbel] *vi* **(-ll-)** se rebeller **(against** contre). ◆**re'bellion** *n* rébellion *f*. ◆**re'bellious** *a* rebelle.

rebirth [ˈriːbɜːθ] *n* renaissance *f*.

rebound [rɪˈbaʊnd] *vi (of ball)* rebondir; *(of stone)* ricocher; *(of lies, action etc)* *Fig* retomber *(on* sur); *–* [ˈriːbaʊnd] *n* rebond *m*; ricochet *m*; **on the r.** *(to marry s.o. etc)* par dépit.

rebuff [rɪˈbʌf] *vt* repousser; *– n* rebuffade *f*.

rebuild [riːˈbɪld] *vt (pt & pp* rebuilt*)* reconstruire.

rebuke [rɪˈbjuːk] *vt* réprimander; *– n* réprimande *f*.

rebuttal [rɪˈbʌt(ə)l] *n* réfutation *f*.

recalcitrant [rɪˈkælsɪtrənt] *a* récalcitrant.

recall [rɪˈkɔːl] *vt (call back)* rappeler; *(remember)* se rappeler **(that** que, **doing** avoir fait); **to r. sth to s.o.** rappeler qch à qn; *– n* rappel *m*; **beyond r.** irrévocable.

recant [rɪˈkænt] *vi* se rétracter.

recap [riːˈkæp] *vti* **(-pp-)** récapituler; *– n* récapitulation *f*. ◆**reca'pitulate** *vti* récapituler. ◆**recapitu'iation** *n* récapitulation *f*.

recapture [riːˈkæptʃər] *vt (prisoner etc)* reprendre; *(rediscover)* retrouver; *(recreate)* recréer; *– n (of prisoner)* arrestation *f*.

reced/e [rɪˈsiːd] *vi (into the distance)* s'éloigner; *(of floods)* baisser. ◆**—ing** *a (forehead)* fuyant; **his hair(line) is r.** son front se dégarnit.

receipt [rɪˈsiːt] *n (for payment)* reçu *m* **(for** de); *(for letter, parcel)* récépissé *m*, accusé *m* de réception; *pl* (*takings*) recettes *fpl*; **to acknowledge r.** accuser réception (**of** de); **on r. of** dès réception de.

receiv/e [rɪ'siːv] *vt* recevoir; (*stolen goods*) *Jur* receler. ◆**—ing** *n Jur* recel *m*. ◆**—er** *n Tel* combiné *m*; *Rad* récepteur *m*; (*of stolen goods*) *Jur* receleur, -euse *mf*; **to pick up or lift the r.** *Tel* décrocher.

recent ['riːsənt] *a* récent; **in r. months** ces mois-ci. ◆**—ly** *adv* récemment; **as r. as** pas plus tard que.

receptacle [rɪ'septək(ə)l] *n* récipient *m*.

reception [rɪ'sep∫(ə)n] *n* (*receiving, welcome, party etc*) & *Rad* réception *f*; **r. desk** réception *f*; **r. room** salle *f* de séjour. ◆**receptionist** *n* réceptionniste *mf*. ◆**receptive** *a* réceptif (**to an idea/etc** à une idée/*etc*); **r. to s.o.** compréhensif envers qn.

recess [rɪ'ses, 'riːses] *n* **1** (*holiday*) vacances *fpl*; *Sch Am* récréation *f*. **2** (*alcove*) renfoncement *m*; (*nook*) & *Fig* recoin *m*.

recession [rɪ'se∫(ə)n] *n Econ* récession *f*.

recharge [riː't∫ɑːdʒ] *vt* (*battery*) recharger.

recipe ['resɪpɪ] *n Culin* & *Fig* recette *f* (**for** de).

recipient [rɪ'sɪpɪənt] *n* (*of award, honour*) récipiendaire *m*.

reciprocal [rɪ'sɪprək(ə)l] *a* réciproque. ◆**reciprocate** *vt* (*compliment*) retourner; (*gesture*) faire à son tour; – *vi* (*do the same*) en faire autant.

recital [rɪ'saɪt(ə)l] *n Mus* récital *m*.

recite [rɪ'saɪt] *vt* (*poem etc*) réciter; (*list*) énumérer. ◆**reci'tation** *n* récitation *f*.

reckless ['rekləs] *a* (*rash*) imprudent. ◆**—ly** *adv* imprudemment.

reckon ['rek(ə)n] *vt* (*count*) compter; (*calculate*) calculer; (*consider*) considérer; (*think*) *Fam* penser (**that** que); – *vi* compter; calculer; **to r. with** (*take into account*) compter avec; (*deal with*) avoir affaire à; **to r. on/without** compter sur/sans; **to r. on doing** *Fam* compter or penser faire. ◆**—ing** *n* calcul(s) *m*(*pl*).

reclaim [rɪ'kleɪm] *vt* **1** (*land*) mettre en valeur; (*from sea*) assécher. **2** (*ask for back*) réclamer; (*luggage at airport*) récupérer.

recline [rɪ'klaɪn] *vi* (*of person*) être allongé; (*of head*) être appuyé; – *vt* (*head*) appuyer (**on** sur). ◆**—ing** *a* (*seat*) à dossier inclinable or réglable.

recluse [rɪ'kluːs] *n* reclus, -use *mf*.

recognize ['rekəgnaɪz] *vt* reconnaître (**by** à, **that** que). ◆**recog'nition** *n* reconnaissance *f*; **to change beyond** or **out of all r.** devenir méconnaissable; **to gain r.** être

reconnu. ◆**recognizable** *a* reconnaissable.

recoil [rɪ'kɔɪl] *vi* reculer (**from doing** à l'idée de faire).

recollect [rekə'lekt] *vt* se souvenir de; **to r. that** se souvenir que; – *vi* se souvenir. ◆**recollection** *n* souvenir *m*.

recommend [rekə'mend] *vt* (*praise, support, advise*) recommander (**to** à, **for** pour); **to r. s.o. to do** recommander à qn de faire. ◆**recommen'dation** *n* recommandation *f*.

recompense ['rekəmpens] *vt* (*reward*) récompenser; – *n* récompense *f*.

reconcile ['rekənsaɪl] *vt* (*person*) réconcilier (**with, to** avec); (*opinion*) concilier (**with** avec); **to r. oneself to sth** se résigner à qch. ◆**reconcili'ation** *n* réconciliation *f*.

reconditioned [riːkən'dɪ∫(ə)nd] *a* (*engine*) refait (à neuf).

reconnaissance [rɪ'kɒnɪsəns] *n Mil* reconnaissance *f*. ◆**reconnoitre** [rekə'nɔɪtər] *vt Mil* reconnaître.

reconsider [riːkən'sɪdər] *vt* reconsidérer; – *vi* revenir sur sa décision.

reconstruct [riːkən'strʌkt] *vt* (*crime*) reconstituer.

record 1 ['rekɔːd] *n* (*disc*) disque *m*; **r. library** discothèque *f*; **r. player** électrophone *m*. **2** *n Sp* & *Fig* record *m*; – *a* (*attendance, time etc*) record *inv*. **3** *n* (*report*) rapport *m*; (*register*) registre *m*; (*recording on tape etc*) enregistrement *m*; (*mention*) mention *f*; (*note*) note *f*; (*background*) antécédents *mpl*; (*case history*) dossier *m*; (*police*) **r.** casier *m* judiciaire; (**public**) **records** archives *fpl*; **to make** or **keep a r. of** noter; **on r.** (*fact, event*) attesté; **off the r.** à titre confidentiel; **their safety r.** leurs résultats *mpl* en matière de sécurité. **4** [rɪ'kɔːd] *vt* (*on tape etc, in register etc*) enregistrer; (*in diary*) noter; (*relate*) rapporter (**that** que); – *vi* (*on tape etc*) enregistrer. ◆**—ed** *a* enregistré; (*prerecorded*) *TV* en différé; (*fact*) attesté; **letter sent** (**by**) **r. delivery** = lettre *f* avec avis de réception. ◆**—ing** *n* enregistrement *m*. ◆**—er** *n Mus* flûte *f* à bec; (*tape*) **r.** magnétophone *m*.

recount 1 [rɪ'kaʊnt] *vt* (*relate*) raconter. **2** ['riːkaʊnt] *n Pol* nouveau dépouillement *m* du scrutin.

recoup [rɪ'kuːp] *vt* (*loss*) récupérer.

recourse ['riːkɔːs] *n* recours *m*; **to have r. to** avoir recours à.

recover [rɪ'kʌvər] **1** *vt* (*get back*) retrouver, récupérer. **2** *vi* (*from shock etc*) se remettre; (*get better*) *Med* se remettre (**from** de); (*of* *economy, country*) se redresser; (*of currency*) remonter. ◆**recovery** n 1 Econ redressement m. **2 the r. of sth** (*getting back*) la récupération de qch.

recreate [riːkri'eɪt] vt recréer.

recreation [rekri'eɪʃ(ə)n] n récréation f. ◆**recreational** a (*activity etc*) de loisir.

recrimination [rɪkrɪmɪ'neɪʃ(ə)n] n Jur contre-accusation f.

recruit [rɪ'kruːt] n recrue f; – vt recruter; **to r. s.o. to do** (*persuade*) Fig embaucher qn pour faire. ◆**-ment** n recrutement m.

rectangle ['rektæŋg(ə)l] n rectangle m. ◆**rec'tangular** a rectangulaire.

rectify ['rektɪfaɪ] vt rectifier. ◆**rectifi'cation** n rectification f.

rector ['rektər] n Rel curé m; Univ président m.

recuperate [rɪ'kuːpəreɪt] vi récupérer (ses forces); – vt récupérer.

recur [rɪ'kɜːr] vi (-rr-) (*of theme*) revenir; (*of event*) se reproduire; (*of illness*) réapparaître. ◆**recurrence** [rɪ'kʌrəns] n répétition f; (*of illness*) réapparition f. ◆**recurrent** a fréquent.

recycle [riː'saɪk(ə)l] vt (*material*) recycler.

red [red] a (**redder, reddest**) rouge; (*hair*) roux; **to turn** or **go r.** rougir; (*traffic light*) feu m rouge; **R. Cross** Croix-Rouge f; **R. Indian** Peau-Rouge mf; **r. tape** bureaucratie f; – n (*colour*) rouge m; **R.** (*person*) Pol rouge mf; **in the r.** (*firm, account*) en déficit; (*person*) à découvert. ◆**r.-'faced** a Fig rouge de confusion. ◆**r.-'handed** adv **caught r.-handed** pris en flagrant délit. ◆**r.-'hot** a brûlant. ◆**redden** vti rougir. ◆**reddish** a rougeâtre; (*hair*) carotte. ◆**redness** n rougeur f; (*of hair*) rousseur f.

redcurrant [red'kʌrənt] n groseille f.

redecorate [riː'dekəreɪt] vt (*room etc*) refaire; – vi refaire la peinture et les papiers.

redeem [rɪ'diːm] vt (*restore to favour, free, pay off*) racheter; (*convert into cash*) réaliser; **redeeming feature** point m favorable. ◆**redemption** n rachat m; réalisation f; Rel rédemption f.

redeploy [riːdɪ'plɔɪ] vt (*staff*) réorganiser; (*troops*) redéployer.

redhead ['redhed] n roux m, rousse f.

redirect [riːdaɪ'rekt] vt (*mail*) faire suivre.

redo [riː'duː] vt (*pt* **redid**, *pp* **redone**) refaire.

redress [rɪ'dres] n **to seek r.** demander réparation (**for** de).

reduce [rɪ'djuːs] vt réduire (**to** à, **by** de); (*temperature*) faire baisser; **at a reduced** price (*ticket*) à prix réduit; (*goods*) au rabais. ◆**reduction** n réduction f; (*of temperature*) baisse f; (*discount*) rabais m.

redundant [rɪ'dʌndənt] a (*not needed*) superflu, de trop; **to make r.** (*workers*) mettre en chômage, licencier. ◆**redundancy** n (*of workers*) licenciement m; **r. pay(ment)** indemnité f de licenciement.

re-echo [riː'ekəʊ] vi résonner; – vt (*sound*) répercuter; Fig répéter.

reed [riːd] n 1 Bot roseau m. 2 Mus anche f; – a (*instrument*) à anche.

re-educate [riː'edjʊkeɪt] vt (*criminal, limb*) rééduquer.

reef [riːf] n récif m, écueil m.

reek [riːk] vi puer; **to r. of** (*smell*) & Fig puer; – n puanteur f.

reel [riːl] n 1 (*of thread, film*) bobine f; (*film itself*) Cin bande f; (*of hose*) dévidoir m; (*for fishing line*) moulinet m. 2 (*stagger*) chanceler; (*of mind*) chavirer; (*of head*) tourner. 3 vt **to r. off** (*rattle off*) débiter à toute vitesse.

re-elect [riːɪ'lekt] vt réélire.

re-entry [riː'entrɪ] n (*of spacecraft*) rentrée f.

re-establish [riːɪ'stæblɪʃ] vt rétablir.

ref [ref] n Sp Fam arbitre m.

refectory [rɪ'fektərɪ] n réfectoire m.

refer [rɪ'fɜːr] vi (-rr-) **to r. to** (*allude to*) faire allusion à; (*speak of*) parler de; (*apply to*) s'appliquer à; (*consult*) se reporter à; – vt **to r. sth to** (*submit*) soumettre qch à; **to r. s.o. to** (*office, article etc*) renvoyer qn à. ◆**refe'ree** n Sp arbitre m; (*for job etc*) répondant, -ante mf; – vt Sp arbitrer. ◆'**reference** n (*in book, recommendation*) référence f; (*allusion*) allusion f (**to** à); (*mention*) mention f (**to** de); (*connection*) rapport m (**to** avec); **in** or **with r. to** concernant; Com suite à; **terms of r.** (*of person, investigating body*) compétence f; (*of law*) étendue f; **r. book** livre m de référence.

referendum [refə'rendəm] n référendum m.

refill [riː'fɪl] vt remplir (à nouveau); (*lighter, pen etc*) recharger; – ['riːfɪl] n recharge f; **a r.** (*drink*) Fam un autre verre.

refine [rɪ'faɪn] vt (*oil, sugar, manners*) raffiner; (*metal, ore*) affiner; (*technique, machine*) perfectionner; – vi **to r. upon** raffiner sur. ◆**refinement** n (*of person*) raffinement m; (*of sugar, oil*) raffinage m; (*of technique*) perfectionnement m; *pl* (*improvements*) Tech améliorations fpl. ◆**refinery** n raffinerie f.

refit [riː'fɪt] vt (-tt-) (*ship*) remettre en état.

reflate [riː'fleɪt] vt (*economy*) relancer.

reflect [rɪ'flekt] **1** vt (light) & Fig refléter; (of mirror) réfléchir, refléter; **to r. sth on s.o.** (credit, honour) faire rejaillir qch sur qn; — vi **to r. on s.o.** (rebound) rejaillir sur qn. **2** vi (think) réfléchir (on à); — vt **to r. that** penser que. ◆**reflection** n **1** (thought, criticism) réflexion (on sur); **on r.** tout bien réfléchi. **2** (image) & Fig reflet m; (reflecting) réflexion f (of de). ◆**reflector** n réflecteur m. ◆**reflexion** n = reflection. ◆**reflexive** a (verb) Gram réfléchi.

reflex ['riːfleks] n & a réflexe (m); **r. action** réflexe m.

refloat [riː'fləʊt] vt (ship) & Com renflouer.

reform [rɪ'fɔːm] n réforme f; — vt réformer; (person, conduct) corriger; — vi (of person) se réformer. ◆—**er** n réformateur, -trice mf.

refrain [rɪ'freɪn] **1** vi s'abstenir (from doing de faire). **2** n Mus & Fig refrain m.

refresh [rɪ'freʃ] vt (of bath, drink) rafraîchir; (of sleep, rest) délasser; **to r. oneself** (drink) se rafraîchir; **to r. one's memory** se rafraîchir la mémoire. ◆—**ing** a rafraîchissant; (sleep) réparateur; (pleasant) agréable; (original) nouveau. ◆—**er** a (course) de recyclage. ◆—**ments** npl (drinks) rafraîchissements mpl; (snacks) collation f.

refrigerate [rɪ'frɪdʒəreɪt] vt réfrigérer. ◆**refrigerator** n réfrigérateur m.

refuel [riː'fjuːəl] vi (**-ll-**, Am **-l-**) Av se ravitailler; — vt Av ravitailler.

refuge ['refjuːdʒ] n refuge m; **to take r.** se réfugier (in dans). ◆**refu'gee** n réfugié, -ée mf.

refund [rɪ'fʌnd] vt rembourser; — ['riːfʌnd] n remboursement m.

refurbish [riː'fɜːbɪʃ] vt remettre à neuf.

refuse¹ [rɪ'fjuːz] vt refuser (**s.o. sth** qch à qn, **to do** de faire); — vi refuser. ◆**refusal** n refus m.

refuse² ['refjuːs] n (rubbish) ordures fpl, détritus m; (waste materials) déchets mpl; **r. collector** éboueur m; **r. dump** dépôt m d'ordures.

refute [rɪ'fjuːt] vt réfuter.

regain [rɪ'geɪn] vt (favour, lost ground) regagner; (strength) récupérer, retrouver, reprendre; (health, sight) retrouver; (consciousness) reprendre.

regal ['riːg(ə)l] a royal, majestueux.

regalia [rɪ'geɪlɪə] npl insignes mpl (royaux).

regard [rɪ'gaːd] vt (consider) considérer, regarder; (concern) regarder; **as regards** en ce qui concerne; — n considération f (for pour); **to have (a) great r. for** avoir de l'estime pour; **without r. to** sans égard

pour; **with r. to** en ce qui concerne; **to give** or **send one's regards to** (greetings) faire ses hommages à. ◆—**ing** prep en ce qui concerne. ◆—**less 1** a **r. of** sans tenir compte de. **2** adv (all the same) Fam quand même.

regatta [rɪ'gætə] n régates fpl.

regency ['riːdʒənsɪ] n régence f.

regenerate [rɪ'dʒenəreɪt] vt régénérer.

reggae ['regeɪ] n (music) reggae m; — a (group etc) reggae inv.

régime [reɪ'ʒiːm] n Pol régime m.

regiment ['redʒɪmənt] n régiment m. ◆**regi'mental** a régimentaire, du régiment. ◆**regimen'tation** n discipline f excessive.

region ['riːdʒ(ə)n] n région f; **in the r. of** (about) Fig environ; **in the r. of £500** dans les 500 livres. ◆**regional** a régional.

register ['redʒɪstər] n registre m; Sch cahier m d'appel; **electoral r.** liste f électorale; — vt (record, note) enregistrer; (birth, death) déclarer; (vehicle) immatriculer; (express) exprimer; (indicate) indiquer; (letter) recommander; (realize) Fam réaliser; — vi (enrol) s'inscrire; (in hotel) signer le registre; **it hasn't registered (with me)** Fam je n'ai pas encore réalisé ça. ◆—**ed** a (member) inscrit; (letter) recommandé; **r. trademark** marque f déposée. ◆**regi'strar** n officier m de l'état civil; Univ secrétaire m général. ◆**regi'stration** n enregistrement m; (enrolment) inscription f; **r. number** Aut numéro m d'immatriculation; **r. document** Aut = carte f grise. ◆**registry** a & n **r. (office)** bureau m de l'état civil.

regress [rɪ'gres] vi régresser.

regret [rɪ'gret] vt (**-tt-**) regretter (**doing, to do** de faire; **that** que (+ sub)); **I r. to hear that . . .** je suis désolé d'apprendre que . . . ; — n regret m. ◆**regretfully** adv **r., I . . .** à mon grand regret, je . . . . ◆**regrettable** a regrettable (**that** que (+ sub)). ◆**regrettably** adv malheureusement; (poor, ill etc) fâcheusement.

regroup [riː'gruːp] vi se regrouper; — vt regrouper.

regular ['regjʊlər] a (steady, even) régulier; (surface) uni; (usual) habituel; (price, size) normal; (reader, listener) fidèle; (staff) permanent; (fool, slave etc) Fam vrai; **a r. guy** Am Fam un chic type; — n (in bar etc) habitué, -ée mf; Mil régulier m. ◆**regu'larity** n régularité f. ◆**regularly** adv régulièrement.

regulate ['regjʊleɪt] vt régler. ◆**regu-**

'lation 1 n (rule) règlement m; – a (uniform etc) réglementaire. **2** n (regulating) réglage m.

rehabilitate [riːhəˈbɪlɪteɪt] vt (in public esteem) réhabiliter; (wounded soldier etc) réadapter.

rehash [riːˈhæʃ] vt (text) Pej remanier; Culin réchauffer; – ['riːhæʃ] n a r. Culin & Fig du réchauffé.

rehearse [rɪˈhɜːs] vt Th répéter; (prepare) Fig préparer; – vi Th répéter. ◆**rehearsal** n Th répétition f.

reign [reɪn] n règne m; **in** or **during the r. of** sous le règne de; – vi régner (over sur).

reimburse [riːɪmˈbɜːs] vt rembourser (for de). ◆—ment n remboursement m.

rein [reɪn] n rênes rênes fpl; **to give free r. to** Fig donner libre cours à.

reindeer ['reɪndɪər] n inv renne m.

reinforce [riːɪnˈfɔːs] vt renforcer (with de); **reinforced concrete** béton m armé. ◆—ment n renforcement m (of de); pl Mil renforts mpl.

reinstate [riːɪnˈsteɪt] vt réintégrer. ◆—ment n réintégration f.

reissue [riːˈɪʃuː] vt (book) rééditer.

reiterate [riːˈɪtəreɪt] vt (say again) réitérer.

reject [rɪˈdʒekt] vt (refuse to accept) rejeter; (as useless) rejeter; – ['riːdʒekt] n Com article m de rebut; – a (article) de deuxième choix; **r. shop** solderie f. ◆**re'jection** n rejet m; (of candidate etc) refus m.

rejoice [rɪˈdʒɔɪs] vi se réjouir (over or **at sth** de qch, **in doing** de faire). ◆—ing(s) n(pl) réjouissance(s) f(pl).

rejoin [rɪˈdʒɔɪn] **1** vt (join up with) rejoindre. **2** vi (retort) répliquer.

rejuvenate [rɪˈdʒuːvəneɪt] vt rajeunir.

rekindle [riːˈkɪnd(ə)l] vt rallumer.

relapse [rɪˈlæps] n Med rechute f; – vi Med rechuter; **to r. into** Fig retomber dans.

relat/e [rɪˈleɪt] **1** vt (narrate) raconter (that que); (report) rapporter (that que). **2** vt (connect) établir un rapport entre (faits etc); **to r. sth to** (link) rattacher qch à; – vi **to r. to** (apply to) se rapporter à; (get on with) communiquer or s'entendre avec. ◆—ed a (linked) lié (to à); (languages, styles) apparentés; **to be r. to** (by family) être parent de.

relation [rɪˈleɪʃ(ə)n] n (relative) parent, -ente mf; (relationship) rapport m, relation f (between entre, with avec); **what r. are you to him?** quel est ton lien de parenté avec lui?; **international/etc relations** relations fpl internationales/etc. ◆**relationship** n (kinship) lien(s) m(pl) de parenté; (rela-

tions) relations fpl, rapports mpl; (connection) rapport m; **in r. to** relativement à.

relative ['relətɪv] n (person) parent, -ente mf; – a relatif (to à); (respective) respectif; **r. to** (compared to) relativement à; **to be r. to** (depend on) être fonction de. ◆**relatively** adv relativement.

relax [rɪˈlæks] **1** vt (person, mind) détendre; – vi se détendre; **r.!** (calm down) Fam du calme! **2** vt (grip, pressure etc) relâcher; (restrictions, principles, control) assouplir. ◆—ed a (person, atmosphere) décontracté, détendu. ◆—ing a (bath) délassant. ◆**rela'xation** n **1** (rest, recreation) détente f; (of body) décontraction f. **2** (of grip etc) relâchement m; (of restrictions etc) assouplissement m.

relay ['riːleɪ] n relais m; **by r. race** course f de relais; – vt (message etc) Rad retransmettre, Fig transmettre (to à).

release [rɪˈliːs] vt (free) libérer (from de); (bomb, s.o.'s hand) lâcher; (spring) déclencher; (brake) desserrer; (film, record) sortir; (news, facts) publier; (smoke, trapped person) dégager; (tension) éliminer; – n libération f; (of film, book) sortie f (of de); (record) nouveau disque m; (film) nouveau film m; (relief) Fig délivrance f; Psy défoulement m; **press r.** communiqué m de presse; **to be on general r.** (of film) passer dans toutes les salles.

relegate ['relɪgeɪt] vt reléguer (to à).

relent [rɪˈlent] vi (be swayed) se laisser fléchir; (change one's mind) revenir sur sa décision. ◆—less a implacable.

relevant ['relɪvənt] a (apt) pertinent (to à); (fitting) approprié; (useful) utile; (significant) important; **that's not r.** ça n'a rien à voir. ◆**relevance** n pertinence f (to à); (significance) intérêt m; (connection) rapport m (to avec).

reliable [rɪˈlaɪəb(ə)l] a (person, information, firm) sérieux, sûr, fiable; (machine) fiable. ◆**relia'bility** n (of person) sérieux m, fiabilité f; (of machine, information, firm) fiabilité f. ◆**reliably** adv **to be r. informed that** apprendre de source sûre que.

reliance [rɪˈlaɪəns] n (trust) confiance f (on en); (dependence) dépendance f (on de). ◆**reliant** a **to be r. on** (dependent) dépendre de; (trusting) avoir confiance en.

relic ['relɪk] n relique f; pl (of the past) vestiges mpl.

relief [rɪˈliːf] n (from pain etc) soulagement m (from de); (help, supplies) secours m; (in art) & Geog relief m; **tax r.** dégrèvement m; **to be on r.** Am recevoir l'aide sociale; – a

(*train etc*) supplémentaire; (*work etc*) de secours; **r. road** route *f* de délestage.
◆**relieve** *vt* (*pain etc*) soulager; (*boredom*) dissiper; (*situation*) remédier à; (*take over from*) relayer (qn); (*help*) secourir, soulager; **to r. s.o. of** (*rid*) débarrasser qn de; **to r. s.o. of his post** relever qn de ses fonctions; **to r. congestion in** *Aut* décongestionner; **to r. oneself** (*go to the lavatory*) *Hum Fam* se soulager.

religion [rɪ'lɪdʒ(ə)n] *n* religion *f*. ◆**religious** *a* religieux; (*war, book*) de religion. ◆**religiously** *adv* religieusement.

relinquish [rɪ'lɪŋkwɪʃ] *vt* (*give up*) abandonner; (*let go*) lâcher.

relish ['relɪʃ] *n* (*liking, taste*) goût *m* (*for* pour); (*pleasure*) plaisir *m*; (*seasoning*) assaisonnement *m*; **to eat with r.** manger de bon appétit; – *vt* (*food etc*) savourer; (*like*) aimer (*doing* faire).

relocate [riːləʊ'keɪt] *vi* (*move to new place*) déménager; **to r. in** *or* **to** s'installer à.

reluctant [rɪ'lʌktənt] *a* (*greeting, gift, promise*) accordé à contrecœur; **to be r.** to do être peu disposé à faire; **a r. teacher/etc** un professeur/*etc* malgré lui. ◆**reluctance** *n* répugnance *f* (*to do* à faire). ◆**reluctantly** *adv* à contrecœur.

rely [rɪ'laɪ] *vi* **to r. on** (*count on*) compter sur; (*be dependent upon*) dépendre de.

remain [rɪ'meɪn] *vi* rester. 2 *npl* restes *mpl*; **mortal r.** dépouille *f* mortelle. ◆**-ing** *a* qui reste(nt). ◆**remainder** *n* 1 reste *m*; **the r.** (*remaining people*) les autres *mfpl*; **the r. of the girls** les autres filles. 2 (*book*) invendu *m* soldé.

remand [rɪ'mɑːnd] *vt* **to r. (in custody)** *Jur* placer en détention préventive; – *n* **on r.** en détention préventive.

remark [rɪ'mɑːk] *n* remarque *f*; – *vt* (*say*) (faire) remarquer (*that* que); – *vi* **to r.** on faire des remarques sur. ◆**-able** *a* remarquable (*for* par). ◆**-ably** *adv* remarquablement.

remarry [riː'mærɪ] *vi* se remarier.

remedial [rɪ'miːdɪəl] *a* (*class*) *Sch* de rattrapage; (*measure*) de redressement; (*treatment*) *Med* thérapeutique.

remedy ['remɪdɪ] *vt* remédier à; – *n* remède *m* (*for* contre, à, de).

remember [rɪ'membər] *vt* se souvenir de, se rappeler; (*commemorate*) commémorer; **to r. that/doing** se rappeler que/d'avoir fait; **to r. to do** (*not forget to do*) penser à faire; **r. me to him** *or* **her!** rappelle-moi à son bon souvenir!; – *vi* se souvenir, se rappeler. ◆**remembrance** *n* (*memory*) souvenir *m*; **in r. of** en souvenir de.

remind [rɪ'maɪnd] *vt* rappeler (s.o. of sth qch à qn, s.o. that à qn que); **to r. s.o. to do** faire penser à qn à faire; **that** *or* **which reminds me!** à propos! ◆**-er** *n* (*of event & letter*) rappel *m*; (*note to do sth*) pense-bête *m*; **it's a r.** (for him *or* her) that . . . c'est pour lui rappeler que. . . .

reminisce [remɪ'nɪs] *vi* raconter *or* se rappeler ses souvenirs (*about* de). ◆**reminiscences** *npl* réminiscences *fpl*. ◆**reminiscent** *a* **r. of** qui rappelle.

remiss [rɪ'mɪs] *a* négligent.

remit [rɪ'mɪt] *vt* (**-tt-**) (*money*) envoyer. ◆**remission** *n* *Jur* remise *f* (*de peine*); *Med Rel* rémission *f*. ◆**remittance** *n* (*sum*) paiement *m*.

remnant ['remnənt] *n* (*remaining part*) reste *m*; (*trace*) vestige *m*; (*of fabric*) coupon *m*; (*oddment*) fin *f* de série.

remodel [riː'mɒd(ə)l] *vt* (**-ll-,** *Am* **-l-**) remodeler.

remonstrate ['remənstreɪt] *vi* **to r. with s.o.** faire des remontrances à qn.

remorse [rɪ'mɔːs] *n* remords *m(pl)* (*for* pour); **without r.** sans pitié. ◆**-less** *a* implacable. ◆**-lessly** *adv* (*to hit etc*) implacablement.

remote [rɪ'məʊt] *a* (**-er, -est**) 1 (*far-off*) lointain, éloigné; (*isolated*) isolé; (*aloof*) distant; **r. from** loin de; **r. control** télécommande *f*. 2 (*slight*) petit, vague; **not the remotest idea** pas la moindre idée. ◆**-ly** *adv* (*slightly*) vaguement, un peu; (*situated*) au loin; **not r. aware/etc** nullement conscient/*etc*. ◆**-ness** *n* éloignement *m*; isolement *m*; *Fig* attitude *f* distante.

remould ['riːməʊld] *n* pneu *m* rechapé.

remove [rɪ'muːv] *vt* (*clothes, stain etc*) enlever (*from s.o.* à qn, *from sth* de qch); (*withdraw*) retirer; (*lead away*) emmener (*to* à); (*furniture*) déménager; (*obstacle, threat, word*) supprimer; (*fear, doubt*) dissiper; (*employee*) renvoyer; (*far*) **removed from** loin de. ◆**removable** *a* (*lining etc*) amovible. ◆**removal** *n* enlèvement *m*; déménagement *m*; suppression *f*; **r. man** déménageur *m*; **r. van** camion *m* de déménagement. ◆**remover** *n* (*for make-up*) démaquillant *m*; (*for nail polish*) dissolvant *m*; (*for paint*) décapant *m*; (*for stains*) détachant *m*.

remunerate [rɪ'mjuːnəreɪt] *vt* rémunérer. ◆**remune'ration** *n* rémunération *f*.

renaissance [rə'neɪsəns] *n* (*in art etc*) renaissance *f*.

rename [riː'neɪm] *vt* (*street etc*) rebaptiser.

render ['rendər] *vt* (*give, make*) rendre; *Mus*

interpréter; *(help)* prêter. ◆**—ing** *n Mus*
interprétation *f*; *(translation)* traduction *f*.

rendez-vous ['rɒndɪvu:, *pl* -vu:z] *n inv*
rendez-vous *m inv*.

renegade ['renɪgeɪd] *n* renégat, -ate *mf*.

reneg(u)e [rɪ'niːg] *vi* **to r. on** *(promise etc)*
revenir sur.

renew [rɪ'njuː] *vt* renouveler; *(resume)*
reprendre; *(library book)* renouveler le prêt
de. ◆**—ed** *a (efforts)* renouvelés; *(attempt)*
nouveau; **with r. vigour**/*etc* avec un regain
de vigueur/*etc.* ◆**renewable** *a* renouvelable. ◆**renewal** *n* renouvellement *m*;
(resumption) reprise *f*; *(of strength etc)*
regain *m*.

renounce [rɪ'naʊns] *vt (give up)* renoncer à;
(disown) renier.

renovate ['renəveɪt] *vt (house)* rénover,
restaurer; *(painting)* restaurer. ◆**reno-
'vation** *n* rénovation *f*; restauration *f*.

renown [rɪ'naʊn] *n* renommée *f*.
◆**renowned** *a* renommé (**for** pour).

rent [rent] *n* loyer *m*; *(of television)* (prix *m*
de) location *f*; **r. collector** encaisseur *m* de
loyers; – *vt* louer; **to r. out** louer; – *vi (of
house etc)* se louer. ◆**r.-'free** *adv* sans
payer de loyer; – *a* gratuit. ◆**rental** *n (of
television)* (prix *m* de) location *f*; *(of telephone)* abonnement *m*.

renunciation [rɪnʌnsɪ'eɪʃ(ə)n] *n (giving up)*
renonciation *f* (**of** à); *(disowning)* reniement *m* (**of** de).

reopen [riː'əʊpən] *vti* rouvrir. ◆**—ing**
n réouverture *f*.

reorganize [riː'ɔːgənaɪz] *vt* réorganiser.

rep [rep] *n Fam* représentant, -ante *mf* de
commerce.

repaid [rɪ'peɪd] *see* **repay.**

repair [rɪ'peər] *vt* réparer; – *n* réparation *f*;
beyond r. irréparable; **in** bon/mauvais état; **'road under r.'** *Aut*
'travaux'; **r. man** réparateur *m*; **r. woman**
réparatrice *f*.

reparation [repə'reɪʃ(ə)n] *n* réparation *f* (**for**
de); *pl Mil Hist* réparations *fpl*.

repartee [repɑː'tiː] *n (sharp reply)* repartie *f*.

repatriate [riː'pætrɪeɪt] *vt* rapatrier.

repay [riː'peɪ] *vt (pt & pp* **repaid)** *(pay back)*
rembourser; *(kindness)* payer de retour;
(reward) récompenser (**for** de). ◆**—ment** *n*
remboursement *m*; récompense *f*.

repeal [rɪ'piːl] *vt (law)* abroger; – *n* abroga-
tion *f*.

repeat [rɪ'piːt] *vt* répéter **(that** que); *(promise, threat)* réitérer; *(class)* *Sch* redoubler;
to r. oneself *or* **itself** se répéter; – *vi*
répéter; **to r. on s.o.** *(of food)* *Fam* revenir à

qn; – *n TV Rad* rediffusion *f*; – *a (performance)* deuxième. ◆**—ed** *a* répété;
(efforts) renouvelés. ◆**—edly** *adv* à
maintes reprises.

repel [rɪ'pel] *vt* **(-ll-)** repousser. ◆**repellent**
a repoussant; **insect r.** insectifuge *m*.

repent [rɪ'pent] *vi* se repentir **(of** de).
◆**repentance** *n* repentir *m*. ◆**repentant**
a repentant.

repercussion [riːpə'kʌʃ(ə)n] *n* répercussion
f.

repertoire ['repətwɑːr] *n Th & Fig* répertoire *m*. ◆**repertory** *n Th & Fig* répertoire
m; **r. (theatre)** théâtre *m* de répertoire.

repetition [repɪ'tɪʃ(ə)n] *n* répétition *f*.
◆**repetitious** *a*, ◆**re'petitive** *a (speech
etc)* répétitif.

replace [rɪ'pleɪs] *vt (take the place of)*
remplacer (**by, with** par); *(put back)* remettre, replacer; *(receiver)* *Tel* raccrocher.
◆**—ment** *n* remplacement *m* (**of** de);
(person) remplaçant, -ante *mf*; *(machine
part)* pièce *f* de rechange.

replay ['riːpleɪ] *n Sp* match *m* rejoué;
(instant or action) **r.** *TV* répétition *f* immé-
diate (au ralenti).

replenish [rɪ'plenɪʃ] *vt (refill)* remplir (de
nouveau; **with** de); *(renew)* renouveler.

replete [rɪ'pliːt] *a* **r. with** rempli de; **r. (with
food)** rassasié.

replica ['replɪkə] *n* copie *f* exacte.

reply [rɪ'plaɪ] *vti* répondre; – *n* réponse *f*; **in
r.** en réponse **(to** à).

report [rɪ'pɔːt] *n (account)* rapport *m*; *(of
meeting)* compte rendu *m*; *Journ TV Rad*
reportage *m*; *Pol* enquête *f*; *Sch* Met bulletin *m*; *(rumour)* rumeur *f*; *(of gun)* détonation *f*; – *vt (give account of)* rapporter,
rendre compte de; *(announce)* annoncer
(that que); *(notify)* signaler **(to** à);
(denounce) dénoncer **(to** à); *(event)* *Journ*
faire un reportage sur; – *vi* faire un
rapport *or Journ* un reportage **(on** sur); *(go)*
se présenter **(to** à, **to s.o.** chez qn, **for** work
au travail). ◆**—ed** *a (speech)* *Gram* indirect; **it is r.** that on dit que; **r. missing** porté
disparu. ◆**—edly** *adv* à ce qu'on dit.
◆**—ing** *n Journ* reportage *m*. ◆**—er** *n*
reporter *m*.

repose [rɪ'pəʊz] *n Lit* repos *m*.

repossess [riːpə'zes] *vt Jur* reprendre
possession de.

reprehensible [reprɪ'hensəb(ə)l] *a* répréhensible.

represent [reprɪ'zent] *vt* représenter.
◆**represen'tation** *n* représentation *f*; *pl
(complaints)* remontrances *fpl*. ◆**repre-**

sentative *a* représentatif (**of** de); – *n* représentant, -ante *mf*; *Pol Am* député *m*.

repress [rɪ'pres] *vt* réprimer; *(feeling)* refouler. ◆**repressive** *a* répressif.

reprieve [rɪ'priːv] *n* *Jur* sursis *m*; *Fig* répit *m*, sursis *m*; – *vt* accorder un sursis *or Fig* un répit à.

reprimand ['reprɪmɑːnd] *n* réprimande *f*; – *vt* réprimander.

reprint ['riːprɪnt] *n* *(reissue)* réimpression *f*; – *vt* réimprimer.

reprisal [rɪ'praɪz(ə)l] *n* **reprisals** représailles *fpl*; **in r.** en représailles de.

reproach [rɪ'prəʊtʃ] *n* *(blame)* reproche *m*; *(shame)* honte *f*; **beyond r.** sans reproche; – *vt* reprocher (**s.o. for sth** qch à qn). ◆**reproachful** *a* réprobateur. ◆**reproachfully** *adv* d'un ton *or* d'un air réprobateur.

reproduce [riːprə'djuːs] *vt* reproduire; – *vi* *Biol Bot* se reproduire. ◆**reproduction** *(of sound etc)* & *Biol Bot* reproduction *f*. ◆**reproductive** *a* reproducteur.

reptile ['reptaɪl] *n* reptile *m*.

republic [rɪ'pʌblɪk] *n* république *f*. ◆**republican** *a* & *n* républicain, -aine *(mf)*.

repudiate [rɪ'pjuːdɪeɪt] *vt* *(offer)* repousser; *(accusation)* rejeter; *(spouse, idea)* répudier.

repugnant [rɪ'pʌgnənt] *a* répugnant; **he's r. to me** il me répugne. ◆**repugnance** *n* répugnance *f* (**for** pour).

repulse [rɪ'pʌls] *vt* repousser. ◆**repulsion** *n* répulsion *f*. ◆**repulsive** *a* repoussant.

reputable ['repjʊtəb(ə)l] *a* de bonne réputation. ◆**re'pute** *n* réputation *f*; **of r.** de bonne réputation. ◆**re'puted** *a* réputé (**to be** pour être). ◆**re'putedly** *adv* à ce qu'on dit.

reputation [repjʊ'teɪʃ(ə)n] *n* réputation *f*; **to have a r. for frankness/***etc* avoir la réputation d'être franc/*etc*.

request [rɪ'kwest] *n* demande *f* (**for** de); **on r.** sur demande; **on s.o.'s r.** à la demande de qn; **by popular r.** à la demande générale; **r. stop** *(for bus)* arrêt *m* facultatif; – *vt* demander (**from** *or* **of s.o.** à qn, **s.o. to do** à qn de faire).

requiem ['rekwɪəm] *n* requiem *m inv*.

requir/e [rɪ'kwaɪər] *vt* *(necessitate)* demander; *(demand)* exiger; *(of person)* avoir besoin de *(qch, qn)*; *(staff)* rechercher; **to r. sth of s.o.** *(order)* exiger qch de qn; **to r. s.o. to do** exiger de qn qu'il fasse; *(ask)* demander à qn de faire; **if required** s'il le faut. ◆**—ed** *a* requis, exigé. ◆**—ement** *n*

(need) exigence *f*; *(condition)* condition *f* *(requise)*.

requisite ['rekwɪzɪt] **1** *a* nécessaire. **2** *n* *(for travel etc)* article *m*; **toilet requisites** articles *mpl or* nécessaire *m* de toilette.

requisition [rekwɪ'zɪʃ(ə)n] *vt* réquisitionner; – *n* réquisition *f*.

reroute [riː'ruːt] *vt* *(aircraft etc)* dérouter.

rerun ['riːrʌn] *n* *Cin* reprise *f*; *TV* rediffusion *f*.

resale ['riːseɪl] *n* revente *f*.

resat [riː'sæt] *see* **resit**.

rescind [rɪ'sɪnd] *vt* *Jur* annuler; *(law)* abroger.

rescu/e ['reskjuː] *vt* *(save)* sauver; *(set free)* délivrer *(from* de); – *n* *(action)* sauvetage *m* *(of* de); *(help, troops etc)* secours *mpl*; **to go/***etc* **to s.o.'s r.** aller/*etc* au secours de qn; **to the r.** à la rescousse; – *a* *(team, operation)* de sauvetage. ◆**—er** *n* sauveteur *m*.

research [rɪ'sɜːtʃ] *n* recherches *fpl* (**on, into** sur); **some r.** de la recherche; **a piece of r.** *(work)* un travail de recherche; – *vi* faire des recherches (**on, into** sur). ◆**—er** *n* chercheur, -euse *mf*.

resemble [rɪ'zemb(ə)l] *vt* ressembler à. ◆**resemblance** *n* ressemblance *f* (**to** avec).

resent [rɪ'zent] *vt* *(anger)* s'indigner de, ne pas aimer; *(bitterness)* éprouver de l'amertume à l'égard de; **I r. that** ça m'indigne. ◆**resentful** *a* **to be r.** éprouver de l'amertume. ◆**resentment** *n* amertume *f*, ressentiment *m*.

reserv/e [rɪ'zɜːv] **1** *vt* *(room, decision etc)* réserver; *(right)* se réserver; *(one's strength)* ménager; – *n* *(reticence)* réserve *f*. **2** *n* *(stock, land)* réserve *f*; **r.** *(player)* *Sp* remplaçant, -ante *mf*; **the r.** *Mil* la réserve; **the reserves** *(troops)* *Mil* les réserves *fpl*; **nature r.** réserve *f* naturelle; **in r.** en réserve; **r. tank** *Av Aut* réservoir *m* de secours. ◆**—ed** *a* *(person, room)* réservé. ◆**reser'vation** *n* **1** *(doubt etc)* réserve *f*; *(booking)* réservation *f*. **2** *(land)* *Am* réserve *f*; **central r.** *(on road)* terre-plein *m*.

reservoir ['rezəvwɑːr] *n* réservoir *m*.

resettle [riː'set(ə)l] *vt* *(refugees)* implanter.

reshape [riː'ʃeɪp] *vt* *(industry etc)* réorganiser.

reshuffle [riː'ʃʌf(ə)l] *n* *(cabinet)* **r.** *Pol* remaniement *m* *(ministériel)*; – *vt* *Pol* remanier.

reside [rɪ'zaɪd] *vi* résider. ◆**residence** *n* *(home)* résidence *f*; *(of students)* foyer *m*; **in r.** *(doctor)* sur place; *(students on campus)* sur le campus, *(in halls of residence)* rentrés. ◆**'resident** n habitant, -ante mf; (of hotel) pensionnaire mf; (foreigner) résident, -ente mf; – a résidant, qui habite sur place; (population) fixe; (correspondent) permanent; **to be r. in London** résider à Londres. ◆**resi'dential** a (neighbourhood) résidentiel.

residue ['rezɪdjuː] n résidu m. ◆**re'sidual** a résiduel.

resign [rɪ'zaɪn] vt (right, claim) abandonner; **to r. (from) one's job** démissionner; **to r. oneself to sth/to doing** se résigner à qch/à faire; – vi démissionner (**from** de). ◆**—ed** a résigné. ◆**resig'nation** n (from job) démission f; (attitude) résignation f.

resilient [rɪ'zɪliənt] a élastique; (person) Fig résistant. ◆**resilience** n élasticité f; Fig résistance f.

resin ['rezɪn] n résine f.

resist [rɪ'zɪst] vt (attack etc) résister à; **to r. doing sth** s'empêcher de faire qch; **she can't r. cakes** elle ne peut pas résister devant les gâteaux; **he can't r. her** (indulgence) il ne peut rien lui refuser; (charm) il ne peut pas résister à son charme; – vi résister. ◆**resistance** n résistance f (**to** à). ◆**resistant** a résistant (**to** à); **r. to** Med rebelle à.

resit [riː'sɪt] vt (pt & pp resat, pres p resitting) (exam) repasser.

resolute ['rezəluːt] a résolu. ◆**—ly** adv résolument. ◆**reso'lution** n résolution f.

resolv/e [rɪ'zɒlv] vt résoudre (**to do** de faire, **that** que); – n résolution f. ◆**—ed** a résolu (**to do** à faire).

resonant ['rezənənt] a (voice) résonnant; **to be r. with** résonner de. ◆**resonance** n résonance f.

resort [rɪ'zɔːt] **1** n (recourse) recours m (**to** à); **as a last r.** en dernier ressort; – vi **to r. to s.o.** avoir recours à qn; **to r. to doing** en venir à faire; **to r. to drink** se rabattre sur la boisson. **2** n (holiday) r. station f de vacances; **seaside/ski r.** station f balnéaire/de ski.

resound [rɪ'zaʊnd] vi résonner (**with** de); Fig avoir du retentissement. ◆**—ing** a (success, noise) retentissant.

resource [rɪ'sɔːs, rɪ'zɔːs] n (expedient, recourse) ressource f; pl (wealth etc) ressources fpl. ◆**resourceful** a (person, scheme) ingénieux. ◆**resourcefulness** n ingéniosité f, ressource f.

respect [rɪ'spekt] n respect m (**for** pour, de); (aspect) égard m; **in r. of, with r. to** en ce qui concerne; **with all due r.** sans vouloir vous vexer; – vt respecter. ◆**respecta'bility** n

respectabilité f. ◆**respectable** a (honourable, sizeable) respectable; (satisfying) honnête; (clothes, behaviour) convenable. ◆**respectably** adv (to dress etc) convenablement; (rather well) passablement. ◆**respectful** a respectueux (**to** envers, de). ◆**respectfully** adv respectueusement.

respective [rɪ'spektɪv] a respectif. ◆**—ly** adv respectivement.

respiration [respɪ'reɪʃ(ə)n] n respiration f.

respite ['respaɪt] n répit m.

respond [rɪ'spɒnd] vi répondre (**to** à); **to r. to treatment** Med réagir positivement au traitement. ◆**response** n réponse f; **in p. to** en réponse à.

responsible [rɪ'spɒnsəb(ə)l] a responsable (**for** de, **to s.o.** devant qn); (job) à responsabilités; **who's r. for . . . ?** qui est (le) responsable de . . . ? ◆**responsi'bility** n responsabilité f. ◆**responsibly** adv de façon responsable.

responsive [rɪ'spɒnsɪv] a (reacting) qui réagit bien; (alert) éveillé; (attentive) qui fait attention; (to kindness) sensible à; (suggestion) réceptif à. ◆**—ness** n (bonne) réaction f.

rest¹ [rest] n (repose) repos m; (support) support m; **to have or take a r.** se reposer; **to set or put s.o.'s mind at r.** tranquilliser qn; **to come to r.** (of ball etc) s'immobiliser; (of bird, eyes) se poser (**on** sur); **r. home** maison f de repos; **r. room** Am toilettes fpl; – vi (relax) se reposer; (be buried) reposer; **to r. on** (of roof, argument) reposer sur; **I won't r. till** je n'aurai de repos que (+ sub); **to be resting on** (of hand etc) être posé sur; **a resting place** un lieu de repos; – vt (eyes etc) reposer; (horse etc) laisser reposer; (lean) poser, appuyer (**on** sur); (base) fonder. ◆**restful** a reposant.

rest² [rest] n (remainder) reste m (**of** de); **the r.** (others) les autres mfpl; **the r. of the men/etc** les autres hommes/etc; – vi (remain) **it rests with you to do** il vous incombe de faire; **r. assured** soyez assuré (**that** que).

restaurant ['restərɒnt] n restaurant m.

restitution [restɪ'tjuːʃ(ə)n] n (for damage) Jur réparation f; **to make r.** of restituer.

restive ['restɪv] a (person, horse) rétif.

restless ['restləs] a agité. ◆**—ly** adv avec agitation. ◆**—ness** n agitation f.

restore [rɪ'stɔːr] vt (give back) rendre (**to** à); (order, right) Jur rétablir; (building, painting) restaurer; (to life or power) ramener (qn) (**to** à).

restrain [rɪ'streɪn] vt (person, emotions) retenir, maîtriser; (crowd) contenir; (limit) limiter; **to r. s.o. from doing** retenir qn de faire; **to r. oneself** se maîtriser. ◆**—ed** a (feelings) contenu; (tone) mesuré. ◆**restraint** n (moderation) retenue f, mesure f; (restriction) contrainte f.

restrict [rɪ'strɪkt] vt limiter, restreindre (to à). ◆**—ed** a (space, use) restreint; (sale) contrôlé. ◆**restriction** n restriction f, limitation f. ◆**restrictive** a restrictif.

result [rɪ'zʌlt] n (outcome, success) résultat m; **as a r.** en conséquence; **as a r. of** par suite de; − vi résulter (**from** de); **to r.** aboutir à.

resume [rɪ'zjuːm] vti (begin or take again) reprendre; **to r. doing** se remettre à faire. ◆**resumption** n reprise f.

résumé ['rezjʊmeɪ] n (summary) résumé m; Am curriculum vitae m inv.

resurface [riː'sɜːfɪs] vt (road) refaire le revêtement de.

resurgence [rɪ'sɜːdʒəns] n réapparition f.

resurrect [rezə'rekt] vt (custom, hero) Pej ressusciter. ◆**resurrection** n résurrection f.

resuscitate [rɪ'sʌsɪteɪt] vt Med réanimer.

retail ['riːteɪl] n (vente f au) détail m; − a (price, shop etc) de détail; − vi se vendre (au détail); − vt vendre (au détail); − adv (to sell) au détail. ◆**—er** n détaillant, -ante f.

retain [rɪ'teɪn] vt (hold back, remember) retenir; (freshness, hope etc) conserver. ◆**retainer** n (fee) avance f, acompte m. ◆**retention** n (memory) mémoire f. ◆**retentive** a (memory) fidèle.

retaliate [rɪ'tælɪeɪt] vi riposter (**against s.o.** contre qn, **against an attack** à une attaque). ◆**retali'ation** n riposte f, représailles fpl; **in r. for** en représailles de.

retarded [rɪ'tɑːdɪd] a (mentally) r. arriéré.

retch [retʃ] vi avoir un or des haut-le-cœur.

rethink [riː'θɪŋk] vt (pt & pp rethought) repenser.

reticent ['retɪsənt] a réticent. ◆**reticence** n réticence f.

retina ['retɪnə] n Anat rétine f.

retir/e [rɪ'taɪər] **1** vi (from work) prendre sa retraite; − vt mettre à la retraite. **2** vi (withdraw) se retirer (**from** de, **to** à); (go to bed) aller se coucher. ◆**—ed** a (having stopped working) retraité. ◆**—ing** a **1** (age) de la retraite. **2** (reserved) réservé. ◆**retirement** n retraite f; **r. age** âge m de la retraite.

retort [rɪ'tɔːt] vt rétorquer; − n réplique f.

retrace [riː'treɪs] vt (past event) se

remémorer, reconstituer; **to r. one's steps** revenir sur ses pas, rebrousser chemin.

retract [rɪ'trækt] vt (statement etc) rétracter; − vi (of person) se rétracter. ◆**retraction** n (of statement) rétractation f.

retrain [riː'treɪn] vi se recycler; − vt recycler. ◆**—ing** n recyclage m.

retread ['riːtred] n pneu m rechapé.

retreat [rɪ'triːt] n (withdrawal) retraite f; (place) refuge m; − vi se retirer (**from** de); Mil battre en retraite.

retrial [riː'traɪəl] n Jur nouveau procès m.

retribution [retrɪ'bjuːʃ(ə)n] n châtiment m.

retrieve [rɪ'triːv] vt (recover) récupérer; (rescue) sauver (**from** de); (loss, error) réparer; (honour) rétablir. ◆**retrieval** n récupération f; **information r.** recherche f documentaire. ◆**retriever** n (dog) chien m d'arrêt.

retro- ['retrəʊ] pref rétro-. ◆**retro'active** a rétroactif.

retrograde ['retrəgreɪd] a rétrograde.

retrospect ['retrəspekt] n **in r.** rétrospectivement. ◆**retro'spective 1** a (law, effect) rétroactif. **2** n (of film director, artist) rétrospective f.

return [rɪ'tɜːn] vi (come back) revenir; (go back) retourner; (go back home) rentrer; **to r. to** (subject) revenir à; − vt (give back) rendre; (put back) remettre; (bring back) & Fin rapporter; (send back) renvoyer; (greeting) répondre à; (candidate) Pol élire; − n retour m; (yield) Fin rapport m; pl (profits) Fin bénéfices mpl; **the r. to school** la rentrée (des classes); **r. (ticket)** (billet m d')aller et retour m; **tax r.** déclaration f de revenus; **many happy returns (of the day)!** bon anniversaire!; **in r.** (exchange) en échange (**for** de); − a (trip, flight etc) de retour; **r. match** match m retour. ◆**—able** a (bottle) consigné.

reunion [riː'juːnɪən] n réunion f. ◆**reu'nite** vt réunir.

rev [rev] n Aut Fam tour m; **r. counter** compte-tours m inv; − vt (-vv-) **to r. (up)** (engine) Fam faire ronfler.

revamp [riː'væmp] vt (method, play etc) Fam remanier.

reveal [rɪ'viːl] vt (make known) révéler (**that** que); (make visible) laisser voir. ◆**—ing** a (sign etc) révélateur.

revel ['rev(ə)l] vi (-ll-) faire la fête; **to r. in sth** se délecter de qch. ◆**revelling** n, ◆**revelry** n festivités fpl. ◆**reveller** n noceur, -euse mf.

revenge [rɪ'vendʒ] n vengeance f; Sp revanche f; **to have** or **get one's r.** se venger (on s.o. de qn, **on s.o. for sth** de qch sur qn); **in r.** pour se venger; - *vt* venger.

revenue ['revənjuː] *n* revenu *m*.

reverberate [rɪ'vɜːbəreɪt] *vi* (*of sound*) se répercuter.

revere [rɪ'vɪər] *vt* révérer. ◆'**reverence** *n* révérence *f*. ◆'**reverend** *a* (*father*) Rel révérend; - *n* **R.** Smith (*Anglican*) le révérend Smith; (*Catholic*) l'abbé *m* Smith; (*Jewish*) le rabbin Smith. ◆'**reverent** *a* respectueux.

reverse [rɪ'vɜːs] *a* contraire; (*order, image*) inverse; **r. side** (*of coin etc*) revers *m*; (*of paper*) verso *m*; - *n* contraire *m*; (*of coin, fabric etc*) revers *m*; (*of paper*) verso *m*; **in r.** (*gear*) *Aut* en marche arrière; - *vt* (*situation*) renverser; (*order, policy*) inverser; (*decision*) annuler; (*bucket etc*) retourner; **to r. the charges** *Tel* téléphoner en PCV; - *vti* **to r. (the car)** faire marche arrière; **to r. in/out** rentrer/sortir en marche arrière; **reversing light** phare *m* de recul. ◆**reversal** *n* renversement *m*; (*of policy, situation, opinion*) revirement *m*; (*of fortune*) revers *m*. ◆**reversible** *a* (*fabric etc*) réversible.

revert [rɪ'vɜːt] *vi* **to r.** to revenir à.

review [rɪ'vjuː] **1** *vt* (*troops, one's life*) passer en revue; (*situation*) réexaminer; (*book*) faire la critique de; - *n* revue *f*; (*of book*) critique *f*. **2** *n* (*magazine*) revue *f*. ◆-**er** *n* critique *m*.

revile [rɪ'vaɪl] *vt* injurier.

revise [rɪ'vaɪz] *vt* (*opinion, notes, text*) réviser; - *vi* (*for exam*) réviser (**for** pour). ◆**revision** *n* révision *f*.

revitalize [riː'vaɪt(ə)laɪz] *vt* revitaliser.

revive [rɪ'vaɪv] *vt* (*unconscious person, memory, conversation*) ranimer; (*dying person*) réanimer; (*custom, plan, fashion*) ressusciter; (*hope, interest*) faire renaître; - *vi* (*of unconscious person*) reprendre connaissance; (*of country, dying person*) ressusciter; (*of hope, interest*) renaître. ◆**revival** *n* (*of custom, business, play*) reprise *f*; (*of country*) essor *m*; (*of faith, fashion, theatre*) renouveau *m*.

revoke [rɪ'vəʊk] *vt* (*decision*) annuler; (*contract*) *Jur* révoquer.

revolt [rɪ'vəʊlt] *n* révolte *f*; - *vt* (*disgust*) révolter; - *vi* (*rebel*) se révolter (**against** contre). ◆-**ing** *a* dégoûtant; (*injustice*) révoltant.

revolution [revə'luːʃ(ə)n] *n* révolution *f*. ◆**revolutionary** *a & n* révolutionnaire (*mf*). ◆**revolutionize** *vt* révolutionner.

revolv/e [rɪ'vɒlv] *vi* tourner (**around** autour

de). ◆-**ing** *a* **r. chair** fauteuil *m* pivotant; **r. door(s)** (*porte f à*) tambour *m*.

revolver [rɪ'vɒlvər] *n* revolver *m*.

revue [rɪ'vjuː] *n* (*satirical*) *Th* revue *f*.

revulsion [rɪ'vʌlʃ(ə)n] *n* **1** (*disgust*) dégoût *m*. **2** (*change*) revirement *m*.

reward [rɪ'wɔːd] *n* récompense *f* (**for** de); - *vt* récompenser (**s.o. for sth** qn de *or* pour qch). ◆-**ing** *a* qui (en) vaut la peine; (*satisfying*) satisfaisant; (*financially*) rémunérateur.

rewind [riː'waɪnd] *vt* (*pt & pp* **rewound**) (*tape*) réembobiner.

rewire [riː'waɪər] *vt* (*house*) refaire l'installation électrique de.

rewrite [riː'raɪt] *vt* (*pt* **rewrote**, *pp* **rewritten**) récrire; (*edit*) réécrire.

rhapsody ['ræpsədɪ] *n* rhapsodie *f*.

rhetoric ['retərɪk] *n* rhétorique *f*. ◆**rhe-'torical** *a* (*question*) de pure forme.

rheumatism ['ruːmətɪz(ə)m] *n* Med rhumatisme *m*; **to have r.** avoir des rhumatismes. ◆**rheu'matic** *a* (*pain*) rhumatismal; (*person*) rhumatisant.

rhinoceros [raɪ'nɒsərəs] *n* rhinocéros *m*.

rhubarb ['ruːbɑːb] *n* rhubarbe *f*.

rhyme [raɪm] *n* rime *f*; (*poem*) vers *mpl*; - *vi* rimer.

rhythm ['rɪð(ə)m] *n* rythme *m*. ◆**rhythmic(al)** *a* rythmique.

rib [rɪb] *n* Anat côte *f*.

ribald ['rɪb(ə)ld] *a* Lit grivois.

ribbon ['rɪbən] *n* ruban *m*; **to tear to ribbons** mettre en lambeaux.

rice [raɪs] *n* riz *m*. ◆**ricefield** *n* rizière *f*.

rich [rɪtʃ] *a* (-**er**, -**est**) riche (**in** en); (*profits*) gros; - *n* **the r.** les riches *mpl*. ◆**riches** *npl* richesses *fpl*. ◆**richly** *adv* (*dressed, illustrated etc*) richement; (*deserved*) amplement. ◆**richness** *n* richesse *f*.

rick [rɪk] *vt* **to r. one's back** se tordre le dos.

rickety ['rɪkɪtɪ] *a* (*furniture*) branlant.

ricochet ['rɪkəʃeɪ] *vi* ricocher; - *n* ricochet *m*.

rid [rɪd] *vt* (*pt & pp* **rid**, *pres p* **ridding**) débarrasser (**of** de); **to get r. of, to r. oneself of** se débarrasser de. ◆**riddance** *n* **good r.!** *Fam* bon débarras!

ridden ['rɪd(ə)n] *see* **ride**.

-**ridden** ['rɪd(ə)n] *suffix* **debt-r.** criblé de dettes; **disease-r.** en proie à la maladie.

riddle ['rɪd(ə)l] **1** *n* (*puzzle*) énigme *f*. **2** *vt* cribler (**with** de); **riddled with** (*bullets, holes, mistakes*) criblé de; (*criminals*) plein de; (*corruption*) en proie à.

rid/e [raɪd] *n* (*on bicycle, by car etc*) promenade *f*; (*distance*) trajet *m*; (*in taxi*) course *f*; (*on merry-go-round*) tour *m*; **to go for a (car) r.** faire une promenade (en voiture); **to give s.o. a r.** Aut emmener qn en voiture; **to have a r. on** (*bicycle*) monter sur; **to take s.o. for a r.** (*deceive*) Fam mener qn en bateau; – *vi* (*pt* **rode,** *pp* **ridden**) aller (à bicyclette, à cheval *etc*) (**to** à); (*on horse*) Sp monter (à cheval); **to be riding in a car** être en voiture; – *vt* **r. up** (*of skirt*) remonter; – *vt* (*a particular horse*) monter; (*distance*) faire (à cheval *etc*); **to r. a horse** *or* **horses** (*go riding*) Sp monter à cheval; **I was riding** (*on*) **a bike/donkey** j'étais à bicyclette/à dos d'âne; **to know how to r. a bike** savoir faire de la bicyclette; **to r. a bike** aller à bicyclette à; **may I r. your bike?** puis-je monter sur ta bicyclette?; **to r. s.o.** (*annoy*) Am Fam harceler qn. ◆**—ing** *n* (*horse*) équitation *f*; **r. boots** bottes *fpl* de cheval. ◆**—er** *n* **1** (*on horse*) cavalier, -ière *mf*; (*cyclist*) cycliste *mf*. **2** (*to document*) Jur annexe *f*.

ridge [rɪdʒ] *n* (*of roof, mountain*) arête *f*, crête *f*.

ridicule ['rɪdɪkjuːl] *n* ridicule *m*; **to hold up to r.** tourner en ridicule; **object of r.** objet *m* de risée; – *vt* tourner en ridicule, ridiculiser. ◆**ri'diculous** *a* ridicule.

rife [raɪf] *a* (*widespread*) répandu.

riffraff ['rɪfræf] *n* racaille *f*.

rifle ['raɪf(ə)l] **1** *n* fusil *m*, carabine *f*. **2** *vt* (*drawers, pockets etc*) vider.

rift [rɪft] *n* (*crack*) fissure *f*; (*in party*) Pol scission *f*; (*disagreement*) désaccord *m*.

rig [rɪg] *n* **1** (*oil*) **r.** derrick *m*; (*at sea*) plate-forme *f* pétrolière. **2** *vt* (-gg-) (*result, election etc*) Pej truquer; (*equipment*) installer; (*meeting etc*) Fam arranger. **3** *vt* (-gg-) **to r. out** (*dress*) Fam habiller. ◆**r.-out** *n* Fam tenue *f*.

right¹ [raɪt] *a* (*correct*) bon, exact, juste; (*fair*) juste; (*angle*) droit; **to be r.** (*of person*) avoir raison (**to do** de faire); **it's the r. road** c'est la bonne route, c'est bien la route; **the r. time** l'heure exacte; **the clock's r.** la pendule est à l'heure; **at the r. time** au bon moment; **he's the r. man** c'est l'homme qu'il faut; **the r. thing to do** la meilleure chose à faire; **it's not r. to steal** ce n'est pas bien de voler; **it doesn't look r.** ça ne va pas; **to put r.** (*error*) rectifier; (*fix*) arranger; **to put s.o. r.** (*inform*) éclairer qn, détromper qn; **r.!** bien!; **that's r.** c'est ça, c'est bien, c'est exact; – *adv* (*straight*) (tout) droit; (*completely*) tout à fait; (*correctly*) juste; (*well*) bien; **she did r.** elle a bien fait; **r. round** tout autour (**sth** de qch);

r. behind juste derrière; **r. here** ici même; **r. away, r. now** tout de suite; **R. Honourable** Pol Très Honorable; – *n* **to be in the r.** avoir raison; **r. and wrong** le bien et le mal; – *vt* (*error, wrong, car*) redresser. **2** all **r.** *a* (*satisfactory*) bien *inv*; (*unharmed*) sain et sauf; (*undamaged*) intact; (*without worries*) tranquille; **it's all r.** ça va; **it's all r. now** (*fixed*) ça marche maintenant; **I'm all r.** (*healthy*) je vais bien, ça va; – *adv* (*well*) bien; **all r.!, r.!, r. you are!** (*yes*) d'accord!; **I got your letter all r.** j'ai bien reçu ta lettre. ◆**rightly** *adv* bien, correctement; (*justifiably*) à juste titre; **r. or wrongly** à tort ou à raison.

right² [raɪt] *a* (*hand, side etc*) droit; – *adv* à droite; – *n* droite *f*; **on** *or* **to the r.** à droite (**of** de). ◆**r.-hand** *a* à droite; **on the r.-hand side** à droite (**of** de); **r.-hand man** bras *m* droit. ◆**r.-'handed** *a* (*person*) droitier. ◆**r.-wing** *a* Pol de droite.

right³ [raɪt] *n* (*claim, entitlement*) droit *m* (**to do** de faire); **to have a r. to sth** avoir droit à qch; **he's famous in his own r.** il est lui-même célèbre; **r. of way** priorité *f*; **human rights** les droits de l'homme.

righteous ['raɪtʃəs] *a* (*person*) vertueux; (*cause, indignation*) juste.

rightful ['raɪtfəl] *a* légitime. ◆**—ly** *adv* légitimement.

rigid ['rɪdʒɪd] *a* rigide. ◆**ri'gidity** *n* rigidité *f*. ◆**rigidly** *adv* (*opposed*) rigoureusement (**to** à).

rigmarole ['rɪgmərəʊl] *n* (*process*) procédure *f* compliquée.

rigour ['rɪgər] *n* rigueur *f*. ◆**rigorous** *a* rigoureux.

rile [raɪl] *vt* (*annoy*) Fam agacer.

rim [rɪm] *n* (*of cup etc*) bord *m*; (*of wheel*) jante *f*.

rind [raɪnd] *n* (*of cheese*) croûte *f*; (*of melon, lemon*) écorce *f*; (*of bacon*) couenne *f*.

ring¹ [rɪŋ] *n* anneau *m*; (*on finger*) anneau *m*, (*with stone*) bague *f*; (*of people, chairs*) cercle *m*; (*of smoke, for napkin*) rond *m*; (*gang*) bande *f*; (*at circus*) piste *f*; Boxing ring *m*; (*burner on stove*) brûleur *m*; **diamond r.** bague *f* de diamants; **to have rings under one's eyes** avoir les yeux cernés; **r. road** route *f* de ceinture; (*motorway*) périphérique *m*; – *vt* **to r. (round)** (*surround*) entourer (**with** de); (*item on list etc*) entourer d'un cercle. ◆**ringleader** *n* Pej (*of gang*) chef *m* de bande; (*of rebellion etc*) meneur, -euse *mf*.

ring² [rɪŋ] *n* (*sound*) sonnerie *f*; **there's a r. on sonne; to give s.o. a r.** (*phone call*) passer un coup de fil à qn; **a r. of** (*truth*) Fig l'accent *m* de; – *vi* (*pt* **rang**, *pp* **rung**) (*of bell, person etc*) sonner; (*of sound, words*) retentir; **to r. (up)** *Tel* téléphoner; **to r. back** *Tel* rappeler; **to r. for s.o.** sonner qn; **to r. off** *Tel* raccrocher; **to r. out** (*of bell*) sonner; (*of sound*) retentir; – *vt* sonner; **r. s.o. (up)** *Tel* téléphoner à qn; **to r. s.o. back** *Tel* rappeler qn; **to r. the bell** sonner; **to r. the doorbell** sonner à la porte; **that rings a bell** *Fam* ça me rappelle quelque chose; **to r. in** (*the New Year*) carillonner. ◆**-ing** *n* (*of bell*) sonnerie *f*; (*of ears*) bourdonnement *m*.

ringlet ['rɪŋlɪt] *n* (*curl*) anglaise *f*.

rink [rɪŋk] *n* (*ice-skating*) patinoire *f*; (*roller-skating*) skating *m*.

rinse [rɪns] *vt* rincer; **to r. one's hands** se passer les mains à l'eau; (*remove soap*) se rincer les mains; **to r. out** rincer; – *n* rinçage *m*; (*hair colouring*) shampooing *m* colorant; **to give sth a r.** rincer qch.

riot ['raɪət] *n* (*uprising*) émeute *f*; (*demonstration*) manifestation *f* violente; **a r. of colour** *Fig* une orgie de couleurs; **to run r.** (*of crowd*) se déchaîner; **the r. police** = les CRS *mpl*; – *vi* (*rise up*) faire une émeute; (*fight*) se bagarrer. ◆**-ing** *n* émeutes *fpl*; bagarres *fpl*. ◆**-er** *n* émeutier, -ière *mf*; (*demonstrator*) manifestant, -ante *mf*. ◆**riotous** *a* (*crowd etc*) tapageur; **r. living** vie *f* dissolue.

rip [rɪp] *vt* (**-pp-**) déchirer; **to r. off** or **out** arracher; **to r. off** *Fam* (*deceive*) rouler; (*steal*) *Am* voler; **to r. up** déchirer; – *vi* (*of fabric*) se déchirer; – *n* déchirure *f*; **it's a r.-off** *Fam* c'est du vol manifeste.

ripe [raɪp] *a* (**-er, -est**) mûr; (*cheese*) fait. ◆**ripen** *vti* mûrir. ◆**ripeness** *n* maturité *f*.

ripple ['rɪp(ə)l] *n* (*on water*) ride *f*; (*of laughter*) *Fig* cascade *f*; – *vi* (*of water*) se rider.

ris/e [raɪz] *vi* (*pt* **rose**, *pp* **risen**) (*get up from chair or bed*) se lever; (*of temperature, balloon, price etc*) monter, s'élever; (*in society*) s'élever; (*of hope*) grandir; (*of sun, curtain, wind*) se lever; (*of dough*) lever; **to r. in price** augmenter de prix; **to r. to the surface** remonter à la surface; **the river rises in ...**; the fleuve prend sa source dans ...; **to r. (up)** (*rebel*) se soulever (**against** contre); **to r. to power** accéder au pouvoir; **to r. from the dead** ressusciter; – *n* (*of land, curtain*) lever *m*; (*in pressure, price etc*) hausse *f* (**in** de); (*in river*) crue *f*; (*of leader*) *Fig* ascension *f*; (*of industry, technology*)

essor *m*; (*to power*) accession *f*; (*slope in ground*) éminence *f*; (**pay**) **r.** augmentation *f* (de salaire); **to give r. to** donner lieu à. ◆**-ing** *n* (*of curtain*) lever *m*; (*of river*) crue *f*; (*revolt*) soulèvement *m*; – *a* (*sun*) levant; (*number*) croissant; (*tide*) montant; (*artist etc*) d'avenir; **the r. generation** la nouvelle génération; **r. prices** la hausse des prix. ◆**-er** *n* **early r.** lève-tôt *mf inv*; **late r.** lève-tard *mf inv*.

risk [rɪsk] *n* risque *m* (**of doing** de faire); **at r.** (*person*) en danger; (*job*) menacé; **at your own r.** à tes risques et périls; (**at one's life, an accident etc**) risquer; **she won't r. leaving** (*take the risk*) elle ne se risquera pas à partir; **let's r. it** risquons le coup. ◆**riskiness** *n* risques *mpl*. ◆**risky** *a* (**-ier, -iest**) (*full of risk*) risqué.

rissole ['rɪsəʊl] *n Culin* croquette *f*.

rite [raɪt] *n* rite *m*; **the last rites** *Rel* les derniers sacrements *mpl*. ◆**ritual** *a* & *n* rituel (*m*).

ritzy ['rɪtsɪ] *a* (**-ier, -iest**) *Fam* luxueux, classe *inv*.

rival ['raɪv(ə)l] *a* (*firm etc*) rival; (*forces, claim etc*) opposé; – *n* rival, -ale *mf*; – *vt* (**-ll-**, *Am* **-l-**) (*compete with*) rivaliser avec (**in** de); (*equal*) égaler (**in** en). ◆**rivalry** *n* rivalité *f* (**between** entre).

river ['rɪvər] *n* (*small*) rivière *f*; (*major, flowing into sea*) *Fig* fleuve *m*; **the R. Thames** la Tamise; – *a* (*port etc*) fluvial; **r. bank** rive *f*. ◆**riverside** *a* & *n* (**by the**) **r.** au bord de l'eau.

rivet ['rɪvɪt] *n* (*pin*) rivet *m*; – *vt* (*metal*) river, riveter; (*eyes*) *Fig* fixer. ◆**-ing** *a* (*story etc*) fascinant.

Riviera [rɪvɪ'eərə] *n* **the (French) R.** la Côte d'Azur.

road [rəʊd] *n* route *f* (**to** qui va à); (*small*) chemin *m*; (*in town*) rue *f*; (*roadway*) chaussée *f*; (*path*) *Fig* voie *f*, chemin *m*, route *f* (**to** de); **the Paris r.** la route de Paris; **across** *or* **over the r.** (*building etc*) en face; **by r.** par la route; **get out of the r.!** ne reste pas sur la chaussée!; – *a* (*map, safety*) routier; (*accident*) de la route; (*sense*) de la signalisation; **r. hog** *Fam* chauffard *m*; **r. sign** panneau *m* (routier *or* de signalisation); **r. works** travaux *mpl*. ◆**roadblock** *n* barrage *m* routier. ◆**roadside** *a* & *n* (**by the**) **r.** au bord de la route. ◆**roadway** *n* chaussée *f*. ◆**roadworthy** *a* (*vehicle*) en état de marche.

roam [rəʊm] *vt* parcourir; – *vi* errer, rôder; **to r. (about) the streets** (*of child etc*) traîner dans les rues.

roar [rɔːr] vi hurler; (of lion, wind, engine) rugir; (of thunder) gronder; **to r. with laughter** éclater de rire; **to r. past** (of truck etc) passer dans un bruit de tonnerre; – vt **to r. (out)** hurler; – n hurlement m; rugissement m; grondement m. ◆—ing n = roar n; – a **a r. fire** une belle flambée; **a r. success** un succès fou; **to do a r. trade** vendre beaucoup (**in** de).

roast [rəʊst] vt rôtir; (coffee) griller; – vi (of meat) rôtir; **we're roasting here** Fam on rôtit ici; – n (meat) rôti m; – a (chicken etc) rôti; **r. beef** rosbif m.

rob [rɒb] vt (-bb-) (person) voler; (bank, house) dévaliser; **to r. s.o. of sth** voler qch à qn; (deprive) priver qn de qch. ◆**robber** n voleur, -euse mf. ◆**robbery** n vol m; **it's daylight r.!** c'est du vol organisé; **armed r.** vol m à main armée.

robe [rəʊb] n (of priest, judge etc) robe f; (dressing gown) peignoir m.

robin ['rɒbɪn] n (bird) rouge-gorge m.

robot ['rəʊbɒt] n robot m.

robust [rəʊ'bʌst] a robuste.

rock[1] [rɒk] **1** vt (baby, boat) bercer, balancer; (cradle, branch) balancer; (violently) secouer; – vi (sway) se balancer; (of building, ground) trembler. **2** n Mus rock m. ◆—ing n (of horse, chair) à bascule. ◆**rocky**[1] a (-ier, -iest) (furniture etc) branlant.

rock[2] [rɒk] n (substance) roche f; (boulder, rock face) rocher m; (stone) Am pierre f; **a stick of r.** (sweet) un bâton de sucre d'orge; **r. face** paroi f rocheuse; **on the rocks** (whisky) avec des glaçons; (marriage) en pleine débâcle. ◆**r.-'bottom** n point m le plus bas; – a (prices) les plus bas, très bas. ◆**r.-climbing** n varappe f. ◆**rockery** n (in garden) rocaille f. ◆**rocky**[2] a (-ier, -iest) (road) rocailleux; (hill) rocheux.

rocket ['rɒkɪt] n fusée f; – vi (of prices) Fig monter en flèche.

rod [rɒd] n (wooden) baguette f; (metal) tige f; (of curtain) tringle f; (for fishing) canne f à pêche.

rode [rəʊd] see **ride**.

rodent ['rəʊdənt] n (animal) rongeur m.

rodeo ['rəʊdɪəʊ] n (pl -os) rodéo m.

roe [rəʊ] n **1** (eggs) œufs mpl de poisson. **2** r. (deer) chevreuil m.

rogue [rəʊg] n (dishonest) crapule f; (mischievous) coquin, -ine mf. ◆**roguish** a (smile etc) coquin.

role [rəʊl] n rôle m.

roll [rəʊl] n (of paper, film etc) rouleau m; (of bread) petit pain m; (of fat, flesh) bourrelet

m; (of drum, thunder) roulement m; (of ship) roulis m; (list) liste f; **to have a r. call** faire l'appel; **r. neck** (neckline, sweater) col m roulé; – vi (of ball, ship etc) rouler; (of person, animal) se rouler; **to be rolling in money or in it** Fam rouler sur l'or; **r. on tonight!** Fam vivement ce soir!; – vt **to r. in** Fam (flow in) affluer; (of person) s'amener; **to r. over** (many times) se rouler; (once) se retourner; **to r. up** (arrive) Fam s'amener; **to r. (up) into a ball** (of animal) se rouler en boule; – vt rouler; **to r. down** (blind) baisser; (slope) descendre (en roulant); **to r. on** (paint, stocking) mettre; **to r. out** (dough) étaler; **to r. up** (map, cloth) rouler; (sleeve, trousers) retrousser. ◆—ing n (ground, gait) onduleux; **r. pin** rouleau m à pâtisserie. ◆—er n (for hair, painting etc) rouleau m; **r. coaster** (at funfair) montagnes fpl russes. ◆**roller-skate** n patin m à roulettes; – vi faire du patin à roulettes.

rollicking ['rɒlɪkɪŋ] a joyeux (et bruyant).

roly-poly [rəʊlɪ'pəʊlɪ] a Fam grassouillet.

Roman ['rəʊmən] **1** a & n romain, -aine mf. **2 R. Catholic** a & n catholique (mf).

romance [rəʊ'mæns] **1** n (story) histoire f or roman m d'amour; (love) amour m; (affair) aventure f amoureuse; (charm) poésie f. **2** a **R. language** langue f romane. ◆**romantic** a (of love, tenderness etc) romantique; (fanciful, imaginary) romanesque; – n (person) romantique mf. ◆**romantically** adv (to behave) de façon romantique. ◆**romanticism** n romantisme m.

Romania [rəʊ'meɪnɪə] n Roumanie f. ◆**Romanian** a & n roumain, -aine mf; – n (language) roumain m.

romp [rɒmp] vi s'ébattre (bruyamment); **to r. through** (exam) Fig avoir les doigts dans le nez; – n ébats mpl.

rompers ['rɒmpəz] npl (for baby) barboteuse f.

roof [ruːf] n (of building, vehicle) toit m; (of tunnel, cave) plafond m; **r. of the mouth** voûte f du palais; **r. rack** (of car) galerie f. ◆—ing n toiture f. ◆**rooftop** n toit m.

rook [rʊk] n **1** (bird) corneille f. **2** Chess tour f.

rookie ['rʊkɪ] n (new recruit) Mil Fam bleu m.

room [ruːm, rʊm] n **1** (in house etc) pièce f; (bedroom) chambre f; (large, public) salle f; **one's rooms** son appartement m; **in rooms** en meublé; **men's r., ladies' r.** Am toilettes fpl. **2** (space) place f (**for** pour); (some) **r.** de la place; **there's r. for doubt** le doute est permis; **no r. for** doubt aucun doute possible. ◆**rooming house** n Am maison f de rapport. ◆**roommate** n camarade m de chambre. ◆**roomy** a (-ier, -iest) spacieux; (clothes) ample.

roost [ruːst] vi (of bird) percher; – n perchoir m.

rooster ['ruːstər] n coq m.

root [ruːt] **1** n (of plant, person etc) & Math racine f; Fig cause f, origine f; **to pull up by the root(s)** déraciner; **to take r.** (of plant) & Fig prendre racine; **to put down (new) roots** Fig s'enraciner; **r. cause** cause f première; – vt to **r. out** (destroy) extirper. **2** vi (of plant cutting) s'enraciner; **to r. about for** fouiller pour trouver. **3** vi to **r. for** (cheer, support) Fam encourager. ◆**—ed** a deeply r. bien enraciné (in dans); **r. to the spot** (immobile) cloué sur place. ◆**—less** a sans racines.

rope [rəʊp] n corde f; Nau cordage m; **to know the ropes** Fam être au courant; – vt (tie) lier; **to r. s.o. in** (force to help) Fam embrigader qn (**to do** pour faire); **to r. off** séparer (avec une corde).

rop(e)y ['rəʊpɪ] a (-ier, -iest) Fam (thing) minable; (person) patraque.

rosary ['rəʊzərɪ] n Rel chapelet m.

rose¹ [rəʊz] **1** n (flower) rose f; (colour) rose m; **r. bush** rosier m. **2** n (of watering can) pomme f. ◆**ro'sette** n Sp cocarde f; (rose-shaped) rosette f. ◆**rosy** a (-ier, -iest) (pink) rose; (future) Fig tout en rose.

rose² [rəʊz] see **rise**.

rosé ['rəʊzeɪ] n (wine) rosé m.

rosemary ['rəʊzmərɪ] n Bot Culin romarin m.

roster ['rɒstər] n (duty) r. liste f (de service).

rostrum ['rɒstrəm] n tribune f; Sp podium m.

rot [rɒt] n pourriture f; (nonsense) Fam inepties fpl; – vti (-tt-) to **r. (away)** pourrir.

rota ['rəʊtə] n liste f (de service).

rotate [rəʊ'teɪt] vi tourner; – vt faire tourner; (crops) alterner. ◆**'rotary** a rotatif; **r. airer** (washing line) séchoir m parapluie; – n (roundabout) Aut Am sens m giratoire. ◆**rotation** n rotation f; **in r.** à tour de rôle.

rote [rəʊt] n **by r.** machinalement.

rotten ['rɒt(ə)n] a (decayed, corrupt) pourri; (bad) Fam moche; (filthy) Fam sale; **to feel r.** (ill) être mal fichu. ◆**rottenness** n pourriture f. ◆**rotting** a (meat, fruit etc) qui pourrit.

rotund [rəʊ'tʌnd] a (round) rond; (plump) rondelet.

rouble ['ruːb(ə)l] n (currency) rouble m.

rouge [ruːʒ] n rouge m (à joues).

rough¹ [rʌf] a (-er, -est) (surface, task, manners) rude; (ground) inégal, accidenté; (rocky) rocailleux; (plank, bark) rugueux; (sound) âpre, rude; (coarse) grossier; (brutal) brutal; (weather, neighbourhood) mauvais; (sea) agité; (diamond) brut; **a r. child** (unruly) un enfant dur; **to feel r.** (ill) Fam être mal fichu; **r. and ready** (conditions, solution) grossier (mais adéquat); – adv (to sleep, live) à la dure; (to play) brutalement; – n (violent man) Fam voyou m; – vt **to r. it** Fam vivre à la dure; **to r. up** (hair) ébouriffer; (person) Fam malmener. ◆**r.-and-'tumble** n (fight) mêlée f; (of s.o.'s life) remue-ménage m inv. ◆**roughen** vt rendre rude. ◆**roughly¹** adv (not gently) rudement; (coarsely) grossièrement; (brutally) brutalement. ◆**roughness** n rudesse f; inégalité f; grossièreté f; brutalité f.

rough² [rʌf] a (-er, -est) (calculation, figure, terms etc) approximatif; **r. copy, r. draft** brouillon m; **r. paper** du papier brouillon; **r. guess, r. estimate** approximation f; **a r. plan** l'ébauche f d'un projet; – vt to **r. out** (plan) ébaucher. ◆**—ly²** adv (approximately) à peu de choses près.

roughage ['rʌfɪdʒ] n (in food) fibres fpl (alimentaires).

roulette [ruː'let] n roulette f.

round [raʊnd] **1** adv autour; **all r., right r.** tout autour; **to go r. to s.o.** passer chez qn; **to ask r.** inviter chez soi; **he'll be r.** il passera; **r. here** par ici; **the long way r.** le chemin le plus long; – prep autour de; **r. about** (house etc) autour de; (approximately) environ; **r. (about) midday** vers midi; **to go r.** (world) faire le tour de; (corner) tourner. **2** a (-er, -est) rond; **a r. trip** Am un (voyage) aller et retour. **3** n (slice) Culin tranche f; Sp Pol manche f; (of golf) partie f; Boxing round m; (of talks) série f; (of drinks, visits) tournée f; **one's round(s)** (of milkman etc) sa tournée; (of doctor) ses visites fpl; (of policeman) sa ronde; **delivery r.** livraisons fpl, tournée f; **r. of applause** salve f d'applaudissements; **r. of ammunition** cartouche f, balle f; – vt **to r. a corner** (in car) prendre un virage; **to r. off** (finish) terminer; **to r. up** (gather) rassembler; (figure) arrondir au chiffre supérieur. ◆**r.-'shouldered** a voûté, aux épaules rondes. ◆**rounded** a arrondi. ◆**rounders** npl Sp sorte de baseball. ◆**roundness** n rondeur f. ◆**roundup** n (of criminals) rafle f.

roundabout ['raʊndəbaʊt] **1** *a* indirect, détourné. **2** *n* (*at funfair*) manège *m*; (*junction*) Aut rond-point *m* (à sens giratoire).

rous/e [raʊz] *vt* éveiller; **roused (to anger)** en colère; **to r. to action** inciter à agir. ◆**—ing** *a* (*welcome*) enthousiaste; (*speech*) vibrant; (*music*) allègre.

rout [raʊt] *n* (*defeat*) dēen déroute *f*; – *vt* mettre route.

route 1 [ruːt] *n* itinéraire *m*; (*of aircraft*) route *f*; **sea r.** route *f* maritime; **bus r.** ligne *f* d'autobus; – *vt* (*train etc*) fixer l'itinéraire de. **2** [raʊt] *n* (*delivery round*) Am tournée *f*.

routine [ruːˈtiːn] *n* routine *f*; **one's daily r.** (*in office etc*) son travail journalier; **the daily r.** (*monotony*) la train-train quotidien; – *a* (*inquiry, work etc*) de routine, *Pej* routinier.

rov/e [raʊv] *vi* errer; – *vt* parcourir. ◆**—ing** *a* (*life*) nomade; (*ambassador*) itinérant.

row¹ [raʊ] *n* (*line*) rang *m*, rangée *f*; (*of cars*) file *f*; **two days in a r.** deux jours de suite ou d'affilée. **2** *vi* (*in boat*) ramer; – *vt* (*boat*) faire aller à la rame; (*person*) transporter en canot; – *n* **to go for a r.** canoter; **r. boat** Am bateau *m* à rames. ◆**—ing** *n* canotage *m*; *Sp* aviron *m*; **r. boat** bateau *m* à rames.

row² [raʊ] *n* Fam (*noise*) vacarme *m*; (*quarrel*) querelle *f*; – *vi* Fam se quereller (**with** avec).

rowdy ['raʊdɪ] *a* (**-ier, -iest**) chahuteur (et brutal); – *n* (*person*) Fam voyou *m*.

royal ['rɔɪəl] *a* royal; – *npl* **the royals** Fam la famille royale. ◆**royalist** *a & n* royaliste (*mf*). ◆**royally** *adv* (*to treat*) royalement. ◆**royalty 1** *n* (*persons*) personnages *mpl* royaux. **2** *npl* (*from book*) droits *mpl* d'auteur; (*on oil, from patent*) royalties *fpl*.

rub [rʌb] *vt* (**-bb-**) frotter; (*polish*) astiquer; **to r. shoulders with** Fig coudoyer, côtoyer; **to r. away** (*mark*) effacer; (*tears*) essuyer; **to r. down** (*person*) frictionner; (*wood, with sandpaper*) poncer; **to r. in** (*cream*) Med faire pénétrer en massant; **to r. it in** Fig Fam retourner le couteau dans la plaie; **to r. off** *ou* **out** (*mark*) effacer; **rubbing alcohol** Am alcool *m* à 90°; – *vi* frotter; **to r. off** (*of mark*) partir; (*of manners etc*) déteindre (**on s.o.** sur qn); – *n* (*massage*) friction *f*; **to give sth a r.** frotter qch; (*polish*) astiquer qch.

rubber ['rʌbər] *n* (*substance*) caoutchouc *m*; (*eraser*) gomme *f*; (*contraceptive*) Am Sl capote *f*; **r. stamp** tampon *m*. ◆**r.-'stamp** *vt* Pej approuver (sans discuter). ◆**rubbery** *a* caoutchouteux.

rubbish ['rʌbɪʃ] **1** *n* (*refuse*) ordures *fpl*, détritus *mpl*; (*waste*) déchets *mpl*; (*junk*) saleté(s) *f(pl)*; (*nonsense*) Fig absurdités *fpl*; **that's r.** (*absurd*) c'est absurde; (*worthless*) ça ne vaut rien; **r. bin** poubelle *f*; **r. dump** dépôt *m* d'ordures, décharge *f* (publique); (*in garden*) tas *m* d'ordures. **2** *vt* **to r. s.o./sth** (*criticize*) Fam dénigrer qn/qch. ◆**rubbishy** *a* (*book etc*) sans valeur; (*goods*) de mauvaise qualité.

rubble ['rʌb(ə)l] *n* décombres *mpl*.

ruble ['ruːb(ə)l] *n* (*currency*) rouble *m*.

ruby ['ruːbɪ] *n* (*gem*) rubis *m*.

rucksack ['rʌksæk] *n* sac *m* à dos.

ruckus ['rʌkəs] *n* (*uproar*) Fam chahut *m*.

rudder ['rʌdər] *n* gouvernail *m*.

ruddy ['rʌdɪ] *a* (**-ier, -iest**) **1** (*complexion*) coloré. **2** (*bloody*) Sl fichu.

rude [ruːd] *a* (**-er, -est**) (*impolite*) impoli (**to** envers); (*coarse*) grossier; (*indecent*) indécent, obscène; (*shock*) violent. ◆**—ly** *adv* impoliment; grossièrement. ◆**—ness** *n* impolitesse *f*; grossièreté *f*.

rudiments ['ruːdɪmənts] *npl* rudiments *mpl*. ◆**rudi'mentary** *a* rudimentaire.

ruffian ['rʌfɪən] *n* voyou *m*.

ruffle ['rʌf(ə)l] **1** *vt* (*hair*) ébouriffer; (*water*) troubler; **to r. s.o.** (*offend*) froisser qn. **2** *n* (*frill*) ruche *f*.

rug [rʌg] *n* carpette *f*, petit tapis *m*; (*over knees*) plaid *m*; (*bedside*) r. descente *f* de lit.

rugby ['rʌgbɪ] *n* **r.** (**football**) rugby *m*. ◆**rugger** *n* Fam rugby *m*.

rugged ['rʌgɪd] *a* (*surface*) rugueux, rude; (*terrain, coast*) accidenté; (*person, features, manners*) rude; (*determination*) Fig farouche.

ruin ['ruːɪn] *n* (*destruction, rubble, person etc*) ruine *f*; **in ruins** (*building*) en ruine; – *vt* (*health, country, person etc*) ruiner; (*clothes*) abîmer; (*spoil*) gâter. ◆**—ed** *a* (*person, country etc*) ruiné; (*building*) en ruine. ◆**ruinous** *a* ruineux.

rul/e [ruːl] **1** *n* (*principle*) règle *f*; (*regulation*) règlement *m*; (*custom*) coutume *f*; (*authority*) autorité *f*; *Pol* gouvernement *m*; **against the rules** contraire à la règle; **as a** (**general) r.** en règle générale; **it's the** *or* **a r. that** il est de règle de (+ *sub*); – *vt* (*country*) *Pol* gouverner; (*decide*) *Jur* Sp décider (**that** que); **to r. s.o.** (*dominate*) mener qn; **to r. out** (*exclude*) exclure; – *vi* (*of monarch*) régner (**over** sur); (*of judge*) statuer (**against** contre, **on** sur). **2** *n* (*for measuring*) règle *f*. ◆**—ed** *a* (*paper*) réglé, ligné. ◆**—ing** *a* (*passion*) dominant;

(class) dirigeant; (party) Pol au pouvoir; − n Jur Sp décision f. ◆**ruler** n 1 (of country) Pol dirigeant, -ante mf; (sovereign) souverain, -aine mf. 2 (measure) règle f.

rum [rʌm] n rhum m.

Rumania [ruːˈmeɪnɪə] see **Romania**.

rumble [ˈrʌmb(ə)l] vi (of train, thunder, gun) gronder; (of stomach) gargouiller; − n grondement m; gargouillement m.

ruminate [ˈruːmɪneɪt] vi to r. over (scheme etc) ruminer.

rummage [ˈrʌmɪdʒ] vi to r. (about) farfouiller; **r. sale** (used clothes etc) Am vente f de charité.

rumour [ˈruːmər] n rumeur f, bruit m. ◆**rumoured** a it is r. that on dit que.

rump [rʌmp] n (of horse) croupe f; (of fowl) croupion m; **r. steak** rumsteck m.

rumple [ˈrʌmp(ə)l] vt (clothes) chiffonner.

run [rʌn] n (running) course f; (outing) tour m; (journey) parcours m, trajet m; (series) série f; (period) période f; Cards suite f; (rush) ruée f (on sur); (trend) tendance f; (for skiing) piste f; (in cricket) point m; to go for a r. courir, faire une course à pied; on the r. (prisoner etc) en fuite; to have the r. of (house etc) avoir à sa disposition; in the long r. avec le temps, à la longue; the runs Med Fam la diarrhée; − vi (pt ran, pp run, pres p running) courir; (flee) fuir; (of curtain) glisser; (of river, nose, pen, tap) couler; (of colour in washing) déteindre; (of ink) baver; (melt) fondre; (of play, film) se jouer; (of contract) être valide; (last) durer; (pass) passer; (function) marcher; (tick over) Aut tourner; (of stocking) filer; to r. down/in/etc descendre/entrer/etc en courant; **r. for president** être candidat à la présidence; to r. with blood ruisseler de sang; to r. between (of bus) faire le service entre; to go running Sp faire du jogging; the road runs to . . . la route va à . . . ; the river runs into the sea le fleuve se jette dans la mer; it runs into a hundred pounds ça va chercher dans les cent livres; it runs in the family ça tient de famille; − vt (race, risk) courir; (horse) faire courir; (temperature, errand) faire; (blockade) forcer; (machine) faire fonctionner; (engine) Aut faire tourner; (drive) Aut conduire; (furniture, goods) transporter (to à); (business, country etc) diriger; (courses, events) organiser; (film, play) présenter; (house) tenir; (article) publier (on sur); (bath) faire couler; to **r. one's hand over** passer la main sur; to **r. one's eye over** jeter un coup d'œil à or sur; to **r. its course** (of illness etc) suivre son

cours; **to r. 5 km** Sp faire 5 km de course à pied; **to r. a car** avoir une voiture. ■ r. **about** vi courir çà et là; (gallivant) se balader; **to r. across** vt (meet) tomber sur; **to r. along** vi **r. along!** filez!; **to r. away** vi (flee) s'enfuir, se sauver (from de); **to r. back** vt (person) Aut ramener (to à); **to r. down** vt (pedestrian) Aut renverser; (belittle) dénigrer; (restrict) limiter peu à peu. ◆**r.-'down** a (weak, tired) Med à plat; (district etc) miteux; **to r. in** vt (vehicle) roder; **to r. s.o. in** (of police) Fam arrêter qn; **to r. into** vt (meet) tomber sur; (crash into) Aut percuter; **to r. into debt** s'endetter; **to r. off** vt (print) tirer; − vi (flee) s'enfuir; **to r. out** vi (of stocks) s'épuiser; (of lease) expirer; (of time) manquer; **to r. out of** (time, money) manquer de; **we've r. out of coffee** on n'a plus de café; − vt **to r. s.o. out of** (chase) chasser qn de qc; **to r. over** vi (of liquid) déborder; − vt (kill pedestrian) Aut écraser; (knock down pedestrian) Aut renverser; (notes, text) revoir; **to r. round** vt (surround) entourer; **to r. through** vt (recap) revoir; **to r. up** vt (bill, debts) laisser s'accumuler. ◆**r.-up** n the r.-up to (elections etc) la période qui précède. ◆**running** n course f; (of machine) fonctionnement m; (of firm, country) direction f; to be in/out of the r. être/ne plus être dans la course; − a (commentary) suivi; (battle) continuel; **r. water** eau f courante; **six days**/etc de suite; **r. costs** (of factory) frais mpl d'exploitation; − a (commentary) suivi; (battle) continuel; **r. water** eau f courante; **six days/**etc **de suite**; **r. costs** (of factory) frais mpl d'exploitation; **r. costs** dépenses fpl courantes. ◆**runner** n Sp etc coureur m; **r. bean** haricot m (grimpant). ◆**runner-'up** n Sp second, -onde mf. ◆**runny** a (-ier, -iest) a liquide; (nose) qui coule.

runaway [ˈrʌnəweɪ] n fugitif, -ive mf; − a (car, horse) emballé; (lorry) fou; (wedding) clandestin; (victory) qu'on remporte haut la main; (inflation) galopant.

rung[1] [rʌŋ] n (of ladder) barreau m.

rung[2] [rʌŋ] see **ring**[2].

run-of-the-mill [rʌnəvðəˈmɪl] a ordinaire.

runway [ˈrʌnweɪ] n Av piste f.

rupture [ˈrʌptʃər] n Med hernie f; the r. of (breaking) la rupture de; − vt rompre; **to r. oneself** se donner une hernie.

rural [ˈruərəl] a rural.

ruse [ruːz] n (trick) ruse f.

rush[1] [rʌʃ] vi (move fast, throw oneself) se précipiter, se ruer (at sur, towards vers); (of blood) affluer (to à); (hurry) se dépêcher (to do de faire); (of vehicle) foncer; to r. out partir en vitesse; − vt (attack) Mil foncer sur; **to r. s.o.** bousculer qn; **to r. s.o. to hospital** transporter qn d'urgence à l'hôpital; **to r. (through) sth** *(job, meal, order etc)* faire, manger, envoyer *etc* qch en vitesse; **to be rushed into** *(decision, answer etc)* être forcé à prendre, donner *etc*; – *n* ruée *f* (**for** vers, **on** sur); *(confusion)* bousculade *f*; *(hurry)* hâte *f*; *(of orders)* avalanche *f*; **to be in a r.** être pressé *(to do* de faire); **to leave**/*etc* **in a r.** partir/*etc* en vitesse; **the gold r.** la ruée vers l'or; **the r. hour** l'heure *f* d'affluence; **a r. job** un travail d'urgence.

rush² [rʌʃ] *n (plant)* jonc *m*.

rusk [rʌsk] *n* biscotte *f*.

russet ['rʌsɪt] *a* roux, roussâtre.

Russia ['rʌʃə] *n* Russie *f*. ◆**Russian** *a & n* russe (*mf*); – *n (language)* russe *m*.

rust [rʌst] *n* rouille *f*; – *vi* (se) rouiller. ◆**rustproof** *a* inoxydable. ◆**rusty** *a* (**-ier**, **-iest**) *(metal, athlete, memory etc)* rouillé.

rustic ['rʌstɪk] *a* rustique.

rustle ['rʌs(ə)l] **1** *vi (of leaves)* bruire; *(of skirt)* froufrouter; – *n* bruissement *m*; frou-frou *m*. **2** *vt* **to r. up** *Fam (prepare)* préparer; *(find)* trouver.

rut [rʌt] *n* ornière *f*; **to be in a r.** *Fig* être encroûté.

rutabaga [ruːtəˈbeɪɡə] *n (swede) Am* rutabaga *m*.

ruthless ['ruːθləs] *a (attack, person etc)* impitoyable, cruel; *(in taking decisions)* très ferme. ◆**—ness** *n* cruauté *f*.

rye [raɪ] *n* seigle *m*; **r. bread** pain *m* de

S

S, s [es] *n* S, s *m*.

Sabbath ['sæbəθ] *n (Jewish)* sabbat *m*; *(Christian)* dimanche *m*. ◆**sa'bbatical** *a (year etc) Univ* sabbatique.

sabotage ['sæbətɑːʒ] *n* sabotage *m*; – *vt* saboter. ◆**saboteur** [-'tɜːr] *n* saboteur, -euse *mf*.

sabre ['seɪbər] *n (sword)* sabre *m*.

saccharin ['sækərɪn] *n* saccharine *f*.

sachet ['sæʃeɪ] *n (of lavender etc)* sachet *m*; *(of shampoo)* dosette *f*.

sack [sæk] **1** *n (bag)* sac *m*. **2** *vt (dismiss) Fam* renvoyer; **to get the s.** se faire virer; **to give s.o. the s.** virer qn. **3** *vt (town etc)* saccager, mettre à sac. ◆**—ing** *n* **1** *(cloth)* toile *f* à sac. **2** *(dismissal) Fam* renvoi *m*.

sacrament ['sækrəmənt] *n Rel* sacrement *m*.

sacred ['seɪkrɪd] *a (holy)* sacré.

sacrifice ['sækrɪfaɪs] *n* sacrifice *m*; – *vt* sacrifier *(to* à, *for* sth/s.o. pour qch/qn).

sacrilege ['sækrɪlɪdʒ] *n* sacrilège *n*. ◆**sacri'legious** *a* sacrilège.

sacrosanct ['sækrəʊsæŋkt] *a Iron* sacro-saint.

sad [sæd] *a (sadder, saddest)* triste. ◆**sadden** *vt* attrister. ◆**sadly** *adv* tristement; *(unfortunately)* malheureusement; *(very)* très. ◆**sadness** *n* tristesse *f*.

saddle ['sæd(ə)l] *n* selle *f*; **to be in the s.** *(in*

control) Fig tenir les rênes; – *vt (horse)* seller; **to s. s.o. with** *(chore, person) Fam* coller à qn.

sadism ['seɪdɪz(ə)m] *n* sadisme *m*. ◆**sadist** *n* sadique *mf*. ◆**sa'distic** *a* sadique.

sae [eseɪˈiː] *abbr* = **stamped addressed envelope**.

safari [səˈfɑːrɪ] *n* safari *m*; **to be** *or* **go on s.** faire un safari.

safe¹ [seɪf] *a (-er, -est) (person)* en sécurité; *(equipment, toy, animal)* sans danger; *(place, investment, method)* sûr; *(bridge, ladder)* solide; *(prudent)* prudent; *(winner)* assuré, garanti; **s. (and sound)** sain et sauf; **it's s. to go out** on peut sortir sans danger; **the safest thing (to do) is ...** le plus sûr est de ...; **s. from** à l'abri de; **to be on the s. side** pour plus de sûreté; **in s. hands** en mains sûres; **s. journey!** bon voyage! ◆**s.'conduct** *n* sauf-conduit *m*. ◆**safe-'keeping** *n* **for s.** à garder en sécurité. ◆**safely** *adv (without mishap)* sans accident; *(securely)* en sûreté; *(without risk)* sans risque, sans danger. ◆**safety** *n* sécurité *f*; *(solidity)* solidité *f*; *(salvation)* salut *m*; – *a (belt, device, screen, margin)* de sécurité; *(pin, razor, chain, valve)* de sûreté; **s. precaution** mesure *f* de sécurité.

safe² [seɪf] *n (for money etc)* coffre-fort *m*.

safeguard ['seɪfɡɑːd] *n* sauvegarde *f* *(against* contre); – *vt* sauvegarder.

saffron ['sæfrən] *n* safran *m*.

sag [sæg] *vi* (**-gg-**) (*of roof, ground*) s'affaisser; (*of cheeks*) pendre; (*of prices, knees*) fléchir. ◆**sagging** *a* (*roof, breasts*) affaissé.

saga ['sɑːɡə] *n* Liter saga *f*; (*bad sequence of events*) Fig feuilleton *m*.

sage [seɪdʒ] *n* **1** Bot Culin sauge *f*. **2** (*wise man*) sage *m*.

Sagittarius [sædʒɪ'teərɪəs] *n* (*sign*) le Sagittaire.

sago ['seɪɡəʊ] *n* (*cereal*) sagou *m*.

Sahara [sə'hɑːrə] *n* **the S.** (*desert*) le Sahara.

said [sed] *see* **say**.

sail [seɪl] *vi* (*navigate*) naviguer; (*leave*) partir; Sp faire de la voile; (*glide*) Fig glisser; **to s. into port** entrer au port; **to s. round** (*world, island etc*) faire le tour de en bateau; **to s. through** (*exam etc*) Fig réussir haut la main; − *vt* (*boat*) piloter; (*seas*) parcourir; − *n* voile *f*; (*trip*) tour *m* en bateau; **to set s.** (*of boat*) partir (**for** à destination de). ◆**-ing** *n* navigation *f*; Sp voile *f*; (*departure*) départ *m*; (*crossing*) traversée *f*; **s. boat** voilier *m*. ◆**sailboard** *n* planche *f* (à voile). ◆**sailboat** *n Am* voilier *m*. ◆**sailor** *n* marin *m*, matelot *m*.

saint [seɪnt] *n* saint *m*, sainte *f*; **S. John** saint Jean; **s.'s day** Rel fête *f* (de saint). ◆**saintly** *a* (**-ier, -iest**) saint.

sake [seɪk] *n* **for my/your s.** pour moi/toi; **for your father's s.** pour (l'amour de) ton père; (**just**) **for the s. of eating**/*etc* simplement pour manger/*etc*; **for heaven's** *or* **God's s.** pour l'amour de Dieu.

salacious [sə'leɪʃəs] *a* obscène.

salad ['sæləd] *n* (*dish of vegetables, fruit etc*) salade *f*; **s. bowl** saladier *m*; **s. cream** mayonnaise *f*; **s. dressing** vinaigrette *f*.

salamander ['sæləmændər] *n* (*lizard*) salamandre *f*.

salami [sə'lɑːmɪ] *n* salami *m*.

salary ['sælərɪ] *n* (*professional*) traitement *m*; (*wage*) salaire *m*. ◆**salaried** *a* (*person*) qui perçoit un traitement.

sale [seɪl] *n* vente *f*; **sale(s)** (*at reduced prices*) Com soldes *mpl*; **in a** *or* **the s.,** *Am* **on s.** (*cheaply*) en solde; (*available*) en vente; (**up**) **for s.** à vendre; **to put up for s.** mettre en vente; **s. price** Com prix *m* de solde; **sales check** *or* **slip** *Am* reçu *m*. ◆**saleable** *a* Com vendable. ◆**salesclerk** *n Am* vendeur, -euse *mf*. ◆**salesman** *n* (*pl* **-men**) (*in shop*) vendeur *m*; (*travelling*) représentant *m* (de commerce). ◆**saleswoman** *n* (*pl* **-women**) vendeuse *f*; représentante *f* (de commerce).

salient ['seɪlɪənt] *a* (*point, fact*) marquant.

saliva [sə'laɪvə] *n* salive *f*. ◆**'salivate** *vi* saliver.

sallow ['sæləʊ] *a* (**-er, -est**) jaunâtre.

sally ['sælɪ] *n* Mil sortie *f*; − *vi* **to s. forth** Fig sortir allègrement.

salmon ['sæmən] *n* saumon *m*.

salmonella [sælmə'nelə] *n* (*poisoning*) salmonellose *f*.

salon ['sælɒn] *n* **beauty/hairdressing s.** salon *m* de beauté/de coiffure.

saloon [sə'luːn] *n* Nau salon *m*; (*car*) berline *f*; (*bar*) *Am* bar *m*; **s. bar** (*of pub*) salle *f* chic.

salt [sɔːlt] *n* sel *m*; **bath salts** sels *mpl* de bain; − *a* (*water, beef etc*) salé; (*mine*) de sel; **s. free** sans sel; − *vt* saler. ◆**saltcellar** *n, Am* ◆**saltshaker** *n* salière *f*. ◆**salty** *a* (**-ier, -iest**) *a* salé.

salubrious [sə'luːbrɪəs] *a* salubre.

salutary ['sæljʊtərɪ] *a* salutaire.

salute [sə'luːt] *n* Mil salut *m*; (*of guns*) salve *f*; − *vt* (*greet*) & Mil saluer; − *vi* Mil faire un salut.

salvage ['sælvɪdʒ] *n* sauvetage *m* (**of** de); récupération *f* (**of** de); (*saved goods*) objets *mpl* sauvés; − *vt* (*save*) sauver (**from** de); (*old iron etc to be used again*) récupérer.

salvation [sæl'veɪʃ(ə)n] *n* salut *m*.

same [seɪm] *a* même; **the (very) s. house as** (exactement) la même maison que; − *pron* **the s.** le même, la même; **the s.** (**thing**) la même chose; **it's all the s. to me** ça m'est égal; **all** *or* **just the s.** tout de même; **to do the s.** en faire autant. ◆**-ness** *n* identité *f*; Pej monotonie *f*.

sampl/e ['sɑːmp(ə)l] *n* échantillon *m*; (*of blood*) prélèvement *m*; − *vt* (*wine, cheese etc*) déguster, goûter; (*product, recipe etc*) essayer; (*army life etc*) goûter de. ◆**-ing** *n* (*of wine*) dégustation *f*.

sanatorium [sænə'tɔːrɪəm] *n* sanatorium *m*.

sanctify ['sæŋktɪfaɪ] *vt* sanctifier. ◆**sanctity** *n* sainteté *f*. ◆**sanctuary** *n* Rel sanctuaire *m*; (*refuge*) & Pol asile *m*; (*for animals*) réserve *f*.

sanctimonious [sæŋktɪ'məʊnɪəs] *a* (*person, manner*) tartuffe.

sanction ['sæŋkʃ(ə)n] *n* (*approval, punishment*) sanction *f*; − *vt* (*approve*) sanctionner.

sand [sænd] *n* sable *m*; **the sands** (*beach*) la plage; − *vt* (*road*) sabler; **s.** (**down**) (*wood etc*) poncer. ◆**sandbag** *n* sac *m* de sable. ◆**sandcastle** *n* château *m* de sable. ◆**sander** *n* (*machine*) ponceuse *f*. ◆**sandpaper** *n* papier *m* de verre; − *vt*

poncer. ◆**sandstone** n (rock) grès m.
◆**sandy** a (-ier, -iest) (beach) de sable;
(road, ground) sablonneux; (water)
sableux. 2 (hair) blond roux inv.

sandal ['sænd(ə)l] n sandale f.

sandwich ['sænwɪdʒ] 1 n sandwich m;
cheese/etc s. sandwich au fromage/etc. 2 vt
to s. (in) (fit in) intercaler; **sandwiched in
between** (caught) coincé entre.

sane [seɪn] a (-er, -est) (person) sain
(d'esprit); (idea, attitude) raisonnable.

sang [sæŋ] see **sing**.

sanguine ['sæŋgwɪn] a (hopeful) optimiste.

sanitarium [sænɪ'teərɪəm] n Am sanatorium
m.

sanitary ['sænɪtərɪ] a (fittings, conditions)
sanitaire; (clean) hygiénique. ◆**sani-
'tation** n hygiène f (publique); (plumbing
etc) installations fpl sanitaires.

sanity ['sænɪtɪ] n santé f mentale; (reason)
raison f.

sank [sæŋk] see **sink**².

Santa Claus ['sæntəklɔːz] n le père Noël.

sap [sæp] 1 n Bot & Fig sève f. 2 vt (-pp-)
(weaken) miner (énergie etc).

sapphire ['sæfaɪər] n (jewel, needle) saphir
m.

sarcasm ['sɑːkæz(ə)m] n sarcasme m.
◆**sar'castic** a sarcastique.

sardine [sɑː'diːn] n sardine f.

Sardinia [sɑː'dɪnɪə] n Sardaigne f.

sardonic [sɑː'dɒnɪk] a sardonique.

sash [sæʃ] n 1 (on dress) ceinture f; (of
mayor etc) écharpe f. 2 s. window fenêtre f à
guillotine.

sat [sæt] see **sit**.

Satan ['seɪt(ə)n] n Satan m. ◆**sa'tanic** a
satanique.

satchel ['sætʃ(ə)l] n cartable m.

satellite ['sætəlaɪt] n satellite m; s. (country)
Pol pays m satellite.

satiate ['seɪʃɪeɪt] vt rassasier.

satin ['sætɪn] n satin m.

satire ['sætaɪər] n satire f (on contre).
◆**sa'tirical** a satirique. ◆**satirist** n
écrivain m satirique. ◆**satirize** vt faire la
satire de.

satisfaction [sætɪs'fækʃ(ə)n] n satisfaction
f. ◆**satisfactory** a satisfaisant. ◆'**satisfy**
vt satisfaire; (persuade, convince)
persuader (that que); (demand, condition)
satisfaire à; **to s. oneself as to/that**
s'assurer de que; **satisfied with** satisfait de;
– vi donner satisfaction. ◆'**satisfying** a
satisfaisant; (food, meal) substantiel.

satsuma [sæt'suːmə] n (fruit) mandarine f.

saturate ['sætʃəreɪt] vt (fill) saturer (with

de); (soak) tremper. ◆**satu'ration** n saturation f.

Saturday ['sætədɪ] n samedi m.

sauce [sɔːs] n 1 sauce f; tomato s. sauce
tomate; s. boat saucière f. 2 (cheek) Fam
toupet m. ◆**saucy** a (-ier, -iest) (cheeky)
impertinent; (smart) Fam coquet.

saucepan ['sɔːspən] n casserole f.

saucer ['sɔːsər] n soucoupe f.

Saudi Arabia [saʊdɪ'reɪbɪə, Am sɔːdɪə-
'reɪbɪə] n Arabie f Séoudite.

sauna ['sɔːnə] n sauna m.

saunter ['sɔːntər] vi flâner.

sausage ['sɒsɪdʒ] n (cooked, for cooking)
saucisse f; (precooked, dried) saucisson m.

sauté ['səʊteɪ] a Culin sauté.

savage ['sævɪdʒ] a (primitive) sauvage;
(fierce) féroce; (brutal, cruel) brutal, sauvage; – n (brute) sauvage mf; – vt (of
animal, critic etc) attaquer (férocement).
◆**savagery** n (cruelty) sauvagerie f.

sav/e [seɪv] 1 vt sauver (from de); (keep)
garder, réserver; (money, time) économiser,
épargner; (stamps) collectionner; (prevent)
empêcher (from de); (problems, trouble)
éviter; **that will s. him or her** (the bother of)
going ça lui évitera d'y aller; **to s. up**
(money) économiser; – vi to s. (up) faire
des économies (for sth, to buy sth pour
(s')acheter qch); – vi to s. up arrêt m. 2 prep
(except) sauf. ◆**-ing** n (of time, money)
économie f, épargne f (of de); (rescue)
sauvetage m; (thrifty habit) l'épargne f; (money) économies fpl; **savings bank** caisse
f d'épargne. ◆**saviour** n sauveur m.

saveloy ['sævəlɔɪ] n cervelas m.

savour ['seɪvər] n (taste, interest) saveur f; –
vt savourer. ◆**savoury** a (tasty)
savoureux; (not sweet) Culin salé; **not very
s.** (neighbourhood) Fig peu recommandable.

saw¹ [sɔː] n scie f; – vt (pt sawed, pp sawn or
sawed) scier; to s. off scier; a sawn-off or
Am sawed-off shotgun un fusil à canon scié.
◆**sawdust** n sciure f. ◆**sawmill** n scierie
f.

saw² [sɔː] see **see**¹.

saxophone ['sæksəfəʊn] n saxophone m.

say [seɪ] vt (pt & pp said [sed]) dire (to à, that
que); (prayer) faire, dire; (of dial etc)
marquer; to s. again répéter; it is said that
... on dit que...; **what do you s. to a
walk?** que dirais-tu d'une promenade?;
(let's) s. tomorrow disons demain; to s. the
least c'est le moins que l'on puisse dire; to
s. nothing of ... sans parler de ...; **that's
to s.** c'est-à-dire; – vi dire; **you don't s.!**

Fam sans blague!; **I s.**! dites donc!; **s.!** *Am Fam* dis donc!; − **n to have one's s.** dire ce que l'on a à dire, s'exprimer; **to have a lot of s.** avoir beaucoup d'influence; **to have no s.** ne pas avoir voix au chapitre (in pour).
◆**—ing** *n* proverbe *m*.

scab [skæb] *n* **1** *Med* croûte *f*. **2** *(blackleg) Fam* jaune *m*.

scaffold ['skæfəld] *n* échafaudage *m*; *(gallows)* échafaud *m*. ◆**—ing** *n* échafaudage *m*.

scald [skɔːld] *vt (burn, cleanse)* ébouillanter; *(sterilize)* stériliser; − *n* brûlure *f*.

scale [skeɪl] **1** *n (of map, wages etc)* échelle *f*; *(of numbers)* série *f*; *Mus* gamme *f*; **on a small/large s.** sur une petite/grande échelle; − *a (drawing)* à l'échelle; **s. model** modèle *m* réduit; − *vt* **to s. down** réduire (proportionnellement). **2** *n (on fish)* écaille *f*; *(dead skin) Med* squame *f*; *(on teeth)* tartre *m*; − *vt (teeth)* détartrer. **3** *vt (wall)* escalader.

scales [skeɪlz] *npl (for weighing)* balance *f*; *(bathroom)* **s.** pèse-personne *m*; *(baby's)* **s.** pèse-bébé *m*.

scallion ['skæljən] *n (onion) Am* ciboule *f*.

scallop ['skɒləp] *n* coquille *f* Saint-Jacques.

scalp [skælp] *n Med* cuir *m* chevelu; − *vt (cut off too much hair from) Fig Hum* tondre *(qn)*.

scalpel ['skælp(ə)l] *n* bistouri *m*, scalpel *m*.

scam [skæm] *n (swindle) Am Fam* escroquerie *f*.

scamp [skæmp] *n* coquin, -ine *mf*.

scamper ['skæmpər] *vi* **to s. off** *or* **away** détaler.

scampi ['skæmpɪ] *npl* gambas *fpl*.

scan [skæn] **1** *vt (-nn-) (look at briefly)* parcourir (des yeux); *(scrutinize)* scruter; *(poetry)* scander; *(of radar)* balayer. − *n* **to have a s.** *(of pregnant woman)* passer une échographie.

scandal ['skænd(ə)l] *n (disgrace)* scandale *m*; *(gossip)* médisances *fpl*; **to cause a s.** *(of film, book etc)* causer un scandale; *(of attitude, conduct)* faire (du) scandale. ◆**scandalize** *vt* scandaliser. ◆**scandalous** *a* scandaleux.

Scandinavia [skændɪ'neɪvɪə] *n* Scandinavie *f*. ◆**Scandinavian** *a* & *n* scandinave *(mf)*.

scanner ['skænər] *n (device) Med* scanner *m*.

scant [skænt] *a (meal, amount)* insuffisant; **s. attention/regard** peu d'attention/de cas. ◆**scantily** *adv* insuffisamment; **s. clad** à peine vêtu. ◆**scanty** *a (-ier, -iest)* insuffisant; *(bikini)* minuscule.

scapegoat ['skeɪpgəʊt] *n* bouc *m* émissaire.

scar [skɑːr] *n* cicatrice *f*; − *vt (-rr-)* marquer d'une cicatrice; *Fig* marquer.

scarce [skeəs] *a (-er, -est) (food, people, book etc)* rare; **to make oneself s.** se tenir à l'écart. ◆**scarcely** *adv* à peine. ◆**scarceness** *n*, ◆**scarcity** *n (shortage)* pénurie *f*; *(rarity)* rareté *f*.

scare [skeər] *n* peur *f*; **to give s.o. a s.** faire peur à qn; **bomb s.** alerte *f* à la bombe; − *vt* faire peur à; **to s. off** *(person)* faire fuir; *(animal)* effaroucher. ◆**scared** *a* effrayé; **to be s. (stiff)** avoir (très) peur. ◆**scarecrow** *n* épouvantail *m*. ◆**scaremonger** *n* alarmiste *mf*. ◆**scary** *a (-ier, -iest) Fam* qui fait peur.

scarf [skɑːf] *n (pl scarves) (long)* écharpe *f*; *(square, for women)* foulard *m*.

scarlet ['skɑːlət] *a* écarlate; **s. fever** scarlatine *f*.

scathing ['skeɪðɪŋ] *a (remark etc)* acerbe; **to be s. about** critiquer de façon acerbe.

scatter ['skætər] *vt (disperse)* disperser *(foule, nuages etc)*; *(dot or throw about)* éparpiller; *(spread)* répandre; − *vi (of crowd)* se disperser. ◆**—ing** *n* **a s. of houses**/*etc* quelques maisons/*etc* dispersées. ◆**scatterbrain** *n* écervelé *m*. ◆**scatty** *a (-ier, -iest) Fam* écervelé, farfelu.

scaveng/e ['skævɪndʒ] *vi* fouiller dans les ordures *(for* pour trouver). ◆**—er** *n Pej* clochard, -arde *mf* (qui fait les poubelles).

scenario [sɪ'nɑːrɪəʊ] *n (pl -os) Cin & Fig* scénario *m*.

scene [siːn] *n (setting, fuss)* & *Th* scène *f*; *(of crime, accident etc)* lieu *m*; *(situation)* situation *f*; *(incident)* incident *m*; *(view)* vue *f*; **behind the scenes** *Th & Fig* dans les coulisses; **on the s.** sur les lieux; **to make** *or* **create a s.** faire une scène (à qn). ◆**scenery** *n* paysage *m*, décor *m*; *Th* décor(s) *m(pl)*. ◆**scenic** *a (beauty etc)* pittoresque.

scent [sent] *n (fragrance, perfume)* parfum *m*; *(animal's track) & Fig* piste *f*; − *vt* parfumer *(with* de); *(smell, sense)* flairer.

sceptic ['skeptɪk] *a* & *n* sceptique *(mf)*. ◆**sceptical** *a* sceptique. ◆**scepticism** *n* scepticisme *m*.

sceptre ['septər] *n* sceptre *m*.

schedul/e ['ʃedjuːl, *Am* 'skedʒuːl] *n (of work etc)* programme *m*; *(timetable)* horaire *m*; *(list)* liste *f*; **to be behind s.** *(of person, train)* avoir du retard; **to be on s.** *(on time)* être à l'heure; *(up to date)* être à jour; **ahead of s.** en avance; **according to s.** comme prévu; −

scheme 588 scout

vt (plan) prévoir; (event) fixer le programme or l'horaire de. **◆—ed** a (planned) prévu; (service, flight) régulier; **she's s. to leave at 8** elle doit partir à 8 h.

schem/e ['skiːm] n plan m (**to do** pour faire); (idea) idée f; (dishonest trick) combine f, manœuvre f; (arrangement) arrangement m; — vi manœuvrer. **◆—ing** a intrigant; — npl Pej machinations fpl. **◆—er** n intrigant, -ante mf.

schizophrenic [skɪtsəʊ'frɛnɪk] a & n schizophrène (mf).

scholar ['skɒlər] n érudit, -ite mf; (specialist) spécialiste mf; (grant holder) boursier, -ière mf. **◆scholarly** a érudit. **◆scholarship** n érudition f; (grant) bourse f (d'études). **◆scho'lastic** a scolaire.

school [skuːl] n école f; (teaching, lessons) classe f; Univ Am faculté f; (within university) institut m, département m; **in** or **at s.** à l'école; **secondary s.,** Am **high s.** collège m, lycée m; **public s.** école f privée; Am école publique; **s. of motoring** auto-école f; **summer s.** cours mpl d'été or de vacances; — a (year, equipment etc) scolaire; (hours) de classe; **s. fees** frais mpl de scolarité. **◆—ing** n (learning) instruction f; (attendance) scolarité f. **◆schoolboy** n écolier m. **◆schooldays** npl années fpl d'école. **◆schoolgirl** n écolière f. **◆schoolhouse** n école f. **◆school-'leaver** n jeune mf qui a terminé ses études secondaires. **◆schoolmaster** n (primary) instituteur m; (secondary) professeur m. **◆schoolmate** n camarade mf de classe. **◆schoolmistress** n institutrice f; professeur m. **◆schoolteacher** n (primary) instituteur, -trice mf; (secondary) professeur m.

schooner ['skuːnər] n Nau goélette f.

science ['saɪəns] n science f; **to study s.** étudier les sciences; — a (subject) scientifique; (teacher) de sciences; **s. fiction** science-fiction f. **◆scien'tific** a scientifique. **◆scientist** n scientifique mf.

scintillating ['sɪntɪleɪtɪŋ] a (conversation, wit) brillant.

scissors ['sɪzəz] npl ciseaux mpl; **a pair of s.** une paire de ciseaux.

sclerosis [sklɪ'rəʊsɪs] n Med sclérose f; **multiple s.** sclérose en plaques.

scoff [skɒf] **1** vt **to s. at** se moquer de. **2** vti (eat) Fam bouffer.

scold [skəʊld] vt gronder, réprimander (**for doing** pour avoir fait). **◆—ing** n réprimande f.

scone [skəʊn, skɒn] n petit pain m au lait.

scoop [skuːp] n (shovel) pelle f (à main);

(spoon-shaped) Culin cuiller f; Journ exclusivité f; **at one's.** d'un seul coup; — vt (prizes) rafler; **to s. out** (hollow out) (é)vider; **to s. up** ramasser (avec une pelle or une cuiller).

scoot [skuːt] vi (rush, leave) Fam filer.

scooter ['skuːtər] n (child's) trottinette f; (motorcycle) scooter m.

scope [skəʊp] n (range) étendue f; (of mind) envergure f; (competence) compétence(s) f(pl); (limits) limites fpl; **s. for sth/for doing** possibilités fpl de qch/de faire; **the s. of one's activity** le champ de ses activités.

scorch [skɔːtʃ] vt (linen, grass etc) roussir; — n **s.** (mark) brûlure f légère. **◆—ing** a (day) torride; (sun, sand) brûlant. **◆—er** n Fam journée f torride.

score [skɔːr] n Sp score m; Cards marque f; Mus partition f; (of film) musique f; **a s. to settle** Fig un compte à régler; **on that s.** (in that respect) à cet égard; — vt (point, goal) marquer; (exam mark) avoir; (success) remporter; Mus orchestrer; — vi marquer un point or un but; (keep score) marquer les points. **◆scoreboard** n Sp tableau m d'affichage. **◆scorer** n Sp marqueur m.

score² [skɔːr] n (twenty) vingt; **a s. of** une vingtaine de; **scores of** Fig un grand nombre de.

score³ [skɔːr] vt (cut) rayer; (paper) marquer.

scorn [skɔːn] vt mépriser; — n mépris m. **◆scornful** a méprisant; **to be s. of** mépriser. **◆scornfully** adv avec mépris.

Scorpio ['skɔːpɪəʊ] n (sign) le Scorpion.

scorpion ['skɔːpɪən] n scorpion m.

Scot [skɒt] n Écossais, -aise mf. **◆Scotland** n Écosse f. **◆Scotsman** n (pl -men) Écossais m. **◆Scotswoman** n (pl -women) Écossaise f. **◆Scottish** a écossais.

scotch [skɒtʃ] **1** a **s. tape®** Am scotch® m. **2** vt (rumour) étouffer; (attempt) faire échouer.

Scotch [skɒtʃ] n (whisky) scotch m.

scot-free [skɒt'friː] adv sans être puni.

scoundrel ['skaʊndr(ə)l] n vaurien m.

scour [skaʊər] vt (pan) récurer; (streets etc) Fig parcourir (**for** à la recherche de). **◆—er** n tampon m à récurer.

scourge [skɜːdʒ] n fléau m.

scout [skaʊt] n **1** (soldier) éclaireur m; (boy) **s.** scout m, éclaireur m; **girl s.** Am éclaireuse f; **s. camp** camp m scout. **2** vi to

s. round for (*look for*) chercher. ◆—**ing** *n* scoutisme *m*.

scowl [skaʊl] *vi* se refrogner; **to s. at s.o.** regarder qn d'un air mauvais. ◆—**ing** *a* renfrogné.

scraggy ['skrægɪ] *a* (-ier, -iest) (*bony*) osseux, maigrichon; (*unkempt*) débraillé.

scram [skræm] *vi* (-mm-) Fam filer.

scramble ['skræmb(ə)l] **1** *vi* **to s. for** se ruer vers; **to s. up** (*climb*) grimper; **to s. through** traverser avec difficulté; – *n* ruée *f* (**for** vers). **2** *vt* (*egg, message*) brouiller.

scrap [skræp] **1** *n* (*piece*) petit morceau *m* (**of** de); (*of information, news*) fragment *m*; *pl* (*food*) restes *mpl*; **not a s. of** (*truth etc*) pas un brin de; **s. paper** (papier *m*) brouillon *m*. **2** *n* (*metal*) ferraille *f*; **to sell for s.** vendre à la casse; – *a* (*yard, heap*) de ferraille; **s. dealer, s. merchant** marchand *m* de ferraille; **s. iron** ferraille *f*; **on the s. heap** *Fig* au rebut; – *vt* (-pp-) envoyer à la ferraille; (*unwanted object, idea, plan*) *Fig* mettre au rancart. **3** *n* (*fight*) *Fam* bagarre *f*. ◆**scrapbook** *n* album *m* (*pour collages etc*).

scrap/e [skreɪp] *vt* racler, gratter; (*skin*) *Med* érafler; **to s. away** or **off** (*mud etc*) racler; **to s. together** (*money, people*) réunir (difficilement); – *vi* **to s. against** frotter contre; **to s. along** *Fig* se débrouiller; **to s. through** (*in exam*) réussir de justesse; – *n* raclement *m*; éraflure *f*; **to get into a s.** *Fam* s'attirer des ennuis. ◆—**ings** *npl* raclures *fpl*. ◆—**er** *n* racloir *m*.

scratch [skrætʃ] *n* (*mark, injury*) éraflure *f*; (*on glass*) rayure *f*; **to have a s.** (*scratch oneself*) *Fam* se gratter; **to start from s.** (re)partir de zéro; **to be/come up to s.** être/se montrer à la hauteur; – *vt* (*to relieve an itch*) gratter; (*skin, wall etc*) érafler; (*glass*) rayer; (*with claw*) griffer; (*one's name*) graver (**on** sur); – *vi* (*relieve an itch*) se gratter; (*of cat etc*) griffer; (*of pen*) gratter, accrocher.

scrawl [skrɔːl] *vt* gribouiller; – *n* gribouillis *m*.

scrawny ['skrɔːnɪ] *a* (-ier, -iest) (*bony*) osseux, maigrichon.

scream [skriːm] *vti* crier, hurler; **to s. at s.o.** crier après qn; **to s. with pain**/*etc* hurler de douleur/*etc*; – *n* cri *m* (perçant).

screech [skriːtʃ] *vi* crier, hurler; (*of brakes*) hurler; – *n* cri *m*; hurlement *m*.

screen [skriːn] **1** *n* écran *m*; *Fig* masque *m*; (*folding*) **s.** paravent *m*. **2** *vt* (*hide*) cacher (**from s.o.** à qn); (*protect*) protéger (**from** de); (*a film*) projeter; (*visitors, documents*) filtrer; (*for cancer etc*) *Med* faire subir un test de dépistage à (qn) (**for** pour). ◆—**ing** *n* (*of film*) projection *f*; (*selection*) tri *m*; (*medical examination*) (test *m* de) dépistage *m*. ◆**screenplay** *n* Cin scénario *m*.

screw [skruː] *n* vis *f*; – *vt* visser (**to** à); **to s. down** or **on** visser; **to s. off** dévisser; **to s. up** (*paper*) chiffonner; (*eyes*) plisser; (*mess up*) *Sl* gâcher; **to s. one's face up** grimacer. ◆**screwball** *n* & *a* Am Fam cinglé, -ée (*mf*). ◆**screwdriver** *n* tournevis *m*. ◆**screwy** *a* (-ier, -iest) (*idea, person etc*) farfelu.

scribble ['skrɪb(ə)l] *vti* griffonner; – *n* griffonnage *m*.

scribe [skraɪb] *n* scribe *m*.

scrimmage ['skrɪmɪdʒ] *n* Fb Am mêlée *f*.

script [skrɪpt] *n* (*of film*) scénario *m*; (*of play*) texte *m*; (*in exam*) copie *f*. ◆**scriptwriter** *n* Cin scénariste *mf*, dialoguiste *mf*; TV Rad dialoguiste *mf*.

Scripture ['skrɪptʃər] *n* Rel Écriture *f* (sainte).

scroll [skrəʊl] *n* rouleau *m* (de parchemin); (*book*) manuscrit *m*.

scrooge [skruːdʒ] *n* (*miser*) harpagon *m*.

scroung/e [skraʊndʒ] *vt* (*meal*) se faire payer (**off** or **from s.o.** par qn); (*steal*) piquer (**off** or **from s.o.** à qn); **to s. money off** or **from** (*beg*) quémander à qn; – *vi* vivre en parasite; **to s. around for** *Pej* chercher. ◆—**er** *n* parasite *m*.

scrub [skrʌb] **1** *vt* (-bb-) frotter, nettoyer (à la brosse); (*pan*) récurer; (*cancel*) *Fig* annuler; **to s. out** (*erase*) *Fig* effacer; – *n* (*scrub floors*) frotter les planchers; **scrubbing brush** brosse *f* dure; – *n* **to give sth a s.** frotter qch; **s. brush** *Am* brosse *f* dure. **2** *n* (*land*) broussailles *fpl*.

scruff [skrʌf] *n* **1** **by the s. of the neck** par la peau du cou. **2** (*person*) *Fam* individu *m* débraillé. ◆**scruffy** *a* (-ier, -iest) (*untidy*) négligé; (*dirty*) malpropre.

scrum [skrʌm] *n* Rugby mêlée *f*.

scrumptious ['skrʌmpʃəs] *a* Fam super bon, succulent.

scruple ['skruːp(ə)l] *n* scrupule *m*. ◆**scrupulous** *a* scrupuleux. ◆**scrupulously** *adv* (*conscientiously*) scrupuleusement; (*completely*) absolument.

scrutinize ['skruːtɪnaɪz] *vt* scruter. ◆**scrutiny** *n* examen *m* minutieux.

scuba ['skjuːbə, Am 'skuːbə] *n* scaphandre *m* autonome; **s. diving** la plongée sous-marine.

scuff [skʌf] *vt* **to s.** (**up**) (*scrape*) érafler.

scuffle ['skʌf(ə)l] *n* bagarre *f*.

scullery ['skʌlərɪ] n arrière-cuisine f.

sculpt [skʌlpt] vti sculpter. ◆**sculptor** n sculpteur m. ◆**sculpture** n (art, object) sculpture f; – vti sculpter.

scum [skʌm] n 1 (on liquid) écume f. 2 Fam (people) racaille f; (person) salaud m; **the s. of** (society etc) la lie de.

scupper ['skʌpər] vt (plan) Fam saboter.

scurf [skɜːf] n pellicules fpl.

scurrilous ['skʌrɪləs] a (criticism, attack) haineux, violent et grossier.

scurry ['skʌrɪ] vi (rush) se précipiter, courir; **to s. off** décamper.

scuttle ['skʌt(ə)l] 1 vt (ship) saborder. 2 vi to **s. off** filer.

scythe [saɪð] n faux f.

sea [siː] n mer f; (out) **at s.** en mer; **by s.** par mer; **by** or **beside the s.** au bord de la mer; **to be all at s.** Fig nager complètement; – a (level, breeze) de la mer; (water, fish) de mer; (air, salt) marin; (battle, power) naval; (route) maritime; **s. bed, s. floor** fond m de la mer; **s. lion** (animal) otarie f. ◆**seaboard** n littoral m. ◆**seafarer** n marin m. ◆**seafood** n fruits mpl de mer. ◆**seafront** n front m de mer. ◆**seagull** n mouette f. ◆**seaman** n (pl -men) marin m. ◆**seaplane** n hydravion m. ◆**seaport** n port m de mer. ◆**seashell** n coquillage m. ◆**seashore** n bord m de la mer. ◆**seasick** a to be **s.** avoir le mal de mer. ◆**seasickness** n mal m de mer. ◆**seaside** n bord m de la mer; – a (town, holiday) au bord de la mer. ◆**seaway** n route f maritime. ◆**seaweed** n algue(s) f(pl). ◆**seaworthy** a (ship) en état de naviguer.

seal [siːl] 1 n (animal) phoque m. 2 n (mark, design) sceau m; (on letter) cachet m (de cire); (putty for sealing) joint m; – vt (document, container) sceller; (with wax) cacheter; (stick down) coller; (with putty) boucher; (s.o.'s fate) Fig décider de; **to s. off** (room etc) interdire l'accès de; **to s. off a house/district** (of police, troops) boucler une maison/un quartier.

seam [siːm] n (in cloth etc) couture f; (of coal, quartz etc) veine f.

seamy ['siːmɪ] a (-ier, -iest) **the s. side** le côté peu reluisant (of de).

séance ['seɪɑːns] n séance f de spiritisme.

search [sɜːtʃ] n (quest) recherche f (for de); (of person, place) fouille f; **in s. of** à la recherche de; **s. party** équipe f de secours; – vt (person, place) fouiller (for pour trouver); (study) examiner (documents etc); **to s. (through) one's papers**/etc **for sth** chercher qch dans ses papiers/etc; – vi

chercher; **to s. for sth** chercher qch. ◆**—ing** a (look) pénétrant; (examination) minutieux. ◆**searchlight** n projecteur m.

season ['siːz(ə)n] 1 n saison f; **the festive s.** la période des fêtes; **in the peak s., in (the) high s.** en pleine or haute saison; **in the low** or **off s.** en basse saison; **a Truffaut s.** Cin une rétrospective Truffaut; **s. ticket** carte f d'abonnement. 2 vt (food) assaisonner; **highly seasoned** (dish) relevé. ◆**—ed** a (worker) expérimenté; (soldier) aguerri. ◆**—ing** n Culin assaisonnement m. ◆**seasonable** a (weather) de saison. ◆**seasonal** a saisonnier.

seat [siːt] n (for sitting, centre) & Pol siège m; (on train, bus) banquette f; Cin Th fauteuil m; (place) place f; (of trousers) fond m; **to take** or **have a s.** s'asseoir; **in the hot s.** (in difficult position) Fig sur la sellette; **s. belt** ceinture f de sécurité; – vt (at table) placer (qn); (on one's lap) asseoir (qn); **the room seats 50** la salle a 50 places (assises); **be seated!** asseyez-vous! ◆**—ed** a (sitting) assis. ◆**—ing** n **s.** (room) (seats) places fpl assises; **the s. arrangements** la disposition des places; **s. capacity** nombre m de places assises. ◆**—er** a in two**-s.** (car) voiture f à deux places.

secateurs [sekə'tɜːz] npl sécateur m.

secede [sɪ'siːd] vi faire sécession. ◆**secession** n sécession f.

secluded [sɪ'kluːdɪd] a (remote) isolé. ◆**seclusion** n solitude f.

second¹ ['sekənd] a deuxième, second; **every s. week** une semaine sur deux; **in s.** (gear) Aut en seconde; **s. to none** sans pareil; **s. in command** second m; Mil commandant m en second; – adv (to say) deuxièmement; **to come s.** Sp se classer deuxième; **the s. biggest** la deuxième en ordre de grandeur; **the s. richest country** le deuxième pays le plus riche; **my s. best** (choice) mon deuxième choix; – n (person, object) deuxième mf, second, -onde mf; **Louis the S.** Louis Deux; **s.** (of goods) Com articles mpl de second choix; – vt (motion) appuyer. ◆**s.-'class** a (product) de qualité inférieure; (ticket) Rail de seconde (classe); (mail) non urgent. ◆**s.-'rate** a médiocre. ◆**secondly** adv deuxièmement.

second² ['sekənd] n (unit of time) seconde f; **s. hand** (of clock, watch) trotteuse f.

second³ [sɪ'kɒnd] vt (employee) détacher (to à). ◆**—ment** n détachement m; **on s.** en (position de) détachement (to à).

secondary ['sekəndərɪ] a secondaire.

secondhand [sekənd'hænd] **1** a & adv (not

new) d'occasion. **2** *a* (*report, news*) de seconde main.

secret ['siːkrɪt] *a* secret; – *n* secret *m*; **in s.** en secret; **an open s.** le secret de Polichinelle. ◆**secrecy** *n* (*discretion, silence*) secret *m*; **in s.** en secret. ◆**secretive** *a* (*person*) cachottier; (*organization*) qui a le goût du secret; **to be s. about** faire un mystère de; (*organization*) être très discret sur. ◆**secretively** *adv* en catimini.

secretary ['sekrət(ə)rɪ] *n* secrétaire *mf*; **Foreign S.,** *Am* **S. of State** = ministre *m* des Affaires étrangères. ◆**secre'tarial** *a* (*work*) de secrétaire, de secrétariat; (*school*) de secrétariat. ◆**secre'tariat** *n* (*in international organization*) secrétariat *m*.

secrete [sɪ'kriːt] *vt Med Biol* sécréter. ◆**se'cretion** *n* sécrétion *f*.

sect [sekt] *n* secte *f*. ◆**sec'tarian** *a & n Pej* sectaire (*mf*).

section ['sekʃ(ə)n] *n* (*of road, book, wood etc*) section *f*; (*of town, country*) partie *f*; (*of machine, furniture*) élément *m*; (*department*) section *f*; (*in store*) rayon *m*; **the sports/etc s.** (*of newspaper*) la page des sports/etc; – *vt* **to s. off** (*separate*) séparer.

sector ['sektər] *n* secteur *m*.

secular ['sekjələr] *a* (*teaching etc*) laïque; (*music, art*) profane.

secure [sɪ'kjʊər] **1** *a* (*person, valuables*) en sûreté, en sécurité; (*in one's mind*) tranquille; (*place*) sûr; (*solid, firm*) solide; (*door, window*) bien fermé; (*certain*) assuré; **s. from** à l'abri de; (*emotionally*) sécurisé; – *vt* (*fasten*) attacher; (*window etc*) bien fermer; (*success, future etc*) assurer; **to s. against** protéger de. **2** *vt* (*obtain*) procurer (**s.th for s.o.** qch à qn); **to s. sth** (*for oneself*) se procurer qch. ◆**securely** *adv* (*firmly*) solidement; (*safely*) en sûreté. ◆**security** *n* sécurité *f*; (*for loan, bail*) caution *f*; **s. firm** société *f* de surveillance; **s. guard** agent *m* de sécurité; (*transferring money*) convoyeur *m* de fonds.

sedan [sɪ'dæn] *n* (*saloon*) *Aut Am* berline *f*.

sedate [sɪ'deɪt] **1** *a* calme. **2** *vt* mettre sous calmants. ◆**sedation** *n* **under s.** sous calmants. ◆**'sedative** *n* calmant *m*.

sedentary ['sedəntərɪ] *a* sédentaire.

sediment ['sedɪmənt] *n* sédiment *m*.

sedition [sə'dɪʃ(ə)n] *n* sédition *f*. ◆**seditious** *a* séditieux.

seduce [sɪ'djuːs] *vt* séduire. ◆**seducer** *n* séducteur, -trice *mf*. ◆**seduction** *n* séduc-

tion *f*. ◆**seductive** *a* (*person, offer*) séduisant.

see [1] [siː] *vti* (*pt* **saw,** *pp* **seen**) voir; **we'll s. on verra** (**bien**); **I s.!** je vois!; **I can s. (clearly)** j'y vois clair; **I saw him run(ning)** je l'ai vu courir; **to s. reason** entendre raison; **to s. the joke** comprendre la plaisanterie; **s. who it is** va voir qui c'est; **s. you (later)!** à tout à l'heure!; **s. you (soon)!** à bientôt!; **to s. about** (*deal with*) s'occuper de; (*consider*) songer à; **to s. in the New Year** fêter la Nouvelle Année; **to s. s.o. off** accompagner qn (*à la gare etc*); **to s. s.o. out** raccompagner qn; **to s. through** (*task*) mener à bonne fin; **to s. s.o. through** (*be enough for*) suffire à qn; **to s. through s.o.** deviner le jeu de qn; **to s. to** (*deal with*) s'occuper de; (*mend*) réparer; **to s. (to it) that** (*attend*) veiller à ce que (+ *sub*); (*check*) s'assurer que; **to s. s.o. to** (*accompany*) raccompagner qn à. ◆**s.-through** *a* (*dress etc*) transparent.

see [2] [siː] *n* (*of bishop*) siège *m* (épiscopal).

seed [siːd] *n Agr* graine *f*; (*in grape*) pépin *m*; (*source*) *Fig* germe; *Tennis* tête *f* de série; **seed(s)** (*for sowing*) *Agr* graines *fpl*; **to go to s.** (*of lettuce etc*) monter en graine. ◆**seedbed** *n Bot* semis *m*; (*of rebellion etc*) *Fig* foyer *m* (of de). ◆**seedling** *n* (*plant*) semis *m*.

seedy ['siːdɪ] *a* (**-ier, -iest**) miteux. ◆**seediness** *n* aspect *m* miteux.

seeing ['siːɪŋ] *conj* **s. (that)** vu que.

seek [siːk] *vt* (*pt & pp* **sought**) chercher (**to do** à faire); (*ask for*) demander (**from** à); **to s. (after)** rechercher; **to s. out** aller trouver.

seem [siːm] *vi* sembler (**to do** faire); **it seems that . . .** (*impression*) il semble que . . . (+ *sub or indic*); (*rumour*) il paraît que . . . ; **it seems to me that . . .** il me semble que . . . ; **we s. to know each other** il me semble qu'on se connaît; **I can't s. to do it** je n'arrive pas à le faire. ◆**-ing** *a* apparent. ◆**-ingly** *adv* apparemment.

seemly ['siːmlɪ] *a* convenable.

seen [siːn] *see* **see** [1].

seep [siːp] *vi* (*ooze*) suinter; **to s. into** s'infiltrer dans. ◆**-age** *n* suintement *m*; infiltration(s) *f(pl)* (**into** dans); (*leak*) fuite *f*.

seesaw ['siːsɔː] *n* (*jeu m de*) bascule *f*.

seethe [siːð] *vi* **to s. with anger** bouillir de colère; **to s. with people** grouiller de monde.

segment ['segmənt] *n* segment *m*; (*of orange*) quartier *m*.

segregate ['segrɪgeɪt] *vt* séparer; (**racially**)

segregated (*school*) où se pratique la ségrégation raciale. ◆**segre'gation** n ségrégation f.

seize [siːz] 1 vt saisir; (*power, land*) s'emparer de; – vi to s. on (*offer etc*) saisir. 2 vi to s. up (*of engine*) (se) gripper. ◆**seizure** [-ʒər] n (*of goods etc*) saisie f; Mil prise f; Med crise f.

seldom ['seldəm] adv rarement.

select [sɪ'lekt] vt choisir (**from** parmi); (*candidates, pupils etc*) & Sp sélectionner; – a (*chosen*) choisi; (*exclusive*) select; (*club*) inv. ◆**selection** n sélection f. ◆**selective** a (*memory, recruitment etc*) sélectif; (*person*) qui opère un choix; (*choosey*) difficile.

self [self] n (pl selves) the s. Phil le moi; he's back to his old s. Fam il est redevenu lui-même. ◆**s.-a'ssurance** n assurance f. ◆**s.-a'ssured** a sûr de soi. ◆**s.-'catering** a où l'on fait la cuisine soi-même. ◆**s.-'centred** a égocentrique. ◆**s.-'cleaning** a (*oven*) autonettoyant. ◆**s.-con'fessed** a (*liar*) de son propre aveu. ◆**s.-'confident** a sûr de soi. ◆**s.-'conscious** a gêné. ◆**s.-'consciousness** n gêne f. ◆**s.-con'tained** a (*flat*) indépendant. ◆**s.-con'trol** n maîtrise f de soi. ◆**s.-de'feating** a qui a un effet contraire à celui qui est recherché. ◆**s.-de'fence** n Jur légitime défense f. ◆**s.-de'nial** n abnégation f. ◆**s.-determi'nation** n autodétermination f. ◆**s.-'discipline** n autodiscipline f. ◆**s.-em'ployed** a qui travaille à son compte. ◆**s.-es'teem** n amour-propre m. ◆**s.-'evident** a évident, qui va de soi. ◆**s.-ex'planatory** a qui tombe sous le sens, qui se passe d'explication. ◆**s.-'governing** a autonome. ◆**s.-im'portant** a suffisant. ◆**s.-in'dulgent** a qui ne se refuse rien. ◆**s.-'interest** n intérêt m (personnel). ◆**s.-o'pinionated** a entêté. ◆**s.-'pity** n to feel s.-pity s'apitoyer sur son propre sort. ◆**s.-'portrait** n autoportrait m. ◆**s.-po'ssessed** a assuré. ◆**s.-'raising** or Am **s.-rising 'flour** n farine f à levure. ◆**s.-re'liant** a indépendant. ◆**s.-re'spect** n amour-propre m. ◆**s.-re'specting** a qui se respecte. ◆**s.-'righteous** a pharisaïque. ◆**s.-'sacrifice** n abnégation f. ◆**s.-'satisfied** a content de soi. ◆**s.-'service** n & a libre-service (m inv). ◆**s.-'styled** a soi-disant. ◆**s.-su'fficient** a indépendant, qui a son indépendance. ◆**s.-su'pporting** a financièrement indépendant. ◆**s.-'taught** a autodidacte.

selfish ['selfɪʃ] a égoïste; (*motive*) intéressé. ◆**selfless** a désintéressé. ◆**selfishness** n égoïsme m.

selfsame ['selfseɪm] a même.

sell [sel] vt (pt & pp sold) vendre; (*idea etc*) Fig faire accepter; she sold me it for twenty pounds elle me l'a vendu vingt livres; to s. back revendre; to s. off liquider; to have or be sold out of (*cheese etc*) n'avoir plus de; this book is sold out ce livre est épuisé; – vi se vendre; (*of idea etc*) Fig être accepté; to s. up vendre sa maison; Com vendre son affaire; selling price prix m de vente. ◆**seller** n vendeur, -euse mf. ◆**sellout** n 1 (*betrayal*) trahison f. 2 it was a s. Th Cin tous les billets ont été vendus.

sellotape® ['seləteɪp] n scotch® m; – vt scotcher.

semantic [sɪ'mæntɪk] a sémantique. ◆**semantics** n sémantique f.

semaphore ['seməfɔːr] n (*device*) Rail Nau sémaphore m; (*system*) signaux mpl à bras.

semblance ['sembləns] n semblant m.

semen ['siːmən] n sperme m.

semester [sɪ'mestər] n Univ semestre m.

semi- ['semɪ] pref demi-, semi-. ◆**semiauto'matic** a semi-automatique. ◆**semibreve** [-briːv] n Mus ronde f. ◆**semicircle** n demi-cercle m. ◆**semi'circular** a semi-circulaire. ◆**semi'colon** n point-virgule m. ◆**semi'conscious** a à demi conscient. ◆**semide'tached** a s. house maison f jumelle. ◆**semi'final** n Sp demi-finale f.

seminar ['semɪnɑːr] n Univ séminaire m.

seminary ['semɪnərɪ] n Rel séminaire m.

Semite ['siːmaɪt, Am 'semaɪt] n Sémite mf. ◆**Se'mitic** a sémite; (*language*) sémitique.

semolina [seməˈliːnə] n semoule f.

senate ['senɪt] n Pol sénat m. ◆**senator** ['senətər] n Pol sénateur m.

send [send] vt (pt & pp sent) envoyer (to à); to s. s.o. for sth/s.o. envoyer qn chercher qch/qn; to s. s.o. crazy or mad rendre qn fou; to s. s.o. packing Fam envoyer promener qn; to s. away or off envoyer (to à); (*dismiss*) renvoyer; to s. back renvoyer; to s. in (*form*) envoyer; (*person*) faire entrer; to s. on (*letter, luggage*) faire suivre; to s. out (*invitation etc*) envoyer; (*heat*) émettre; (*from room etc*) faire sortir (qn); to s. up (*balloon, rocket*) lancer; (*price, luggage*) faire monter; (*mock*) Fam parodier; – vi to s. away or off for commander (par courrier); **to s. for** (doctor etc) faire venir, envoyer chercher; **to s. (out) for** (meal, groceries) envoyer chercher. ◆**s.-off** n to give s.o. a s.-off Fam faire des adieux chaleureux à qn. ◆**s.-up** n Fam parodie f. ◆**sender** n expéditeur, -trice mf.

senile ['siːnaɪl] a gâteux, sénile. ◆**se'nility** n gâtisme m, sénilité f.

senior ['siːnɪər] a (older) plus âgé; (position, executive, rank) supérieur; (teacher, partner) principal; **to be s. to s.o., be s.o.'s s.** être plus âgé que qn; (in rank) être au-dessus de qn; **Brown s.** Brown père; **s. citizen** personne f âgée; **s. year** Sch Univ Am dernière année f; – n aîné, -ée mf; Sch grand, -ande mf; Sch Univ Am étudiant, -ante mf de dernière année; Sp senior mf. ◆**seni'ority** n priorité f d'âge; (in service) ancienneté f; (in rank) supériorité f.

sensation [sen'seɪʃ(ə)n] n sensation f. ◆**sensational** a (event) qui fait sensation; (newspaper, film) à sensation; (terrific) Fam sensationnel.

sense [sens] n (faculty, awareness, meaning) sens m; **a s. of hearing** (le sens de) l'ouïe f; **to have (good) s.** avoir du bon sens; **a s. of** (physical) une sensation de (chaleur etc); (mental) un sentiment de (honte etc); **a s. of humour/direction** le sens de l'humour/de l'orientation; **a s. of time** la notion de l'heure; **to bring s.o. to his senses** ramener qn à la raison; **to make s.** (of story, action etc) avoir du sens; **to make s. of** comprendre; – vt sentir (intuitivement) (that que); (have a foreboding of) pressentir. ◆**—less** a (stupid, meaningless) insensé; (unconscious) sans connaissance. ◆**—lessness** n stupidité f.

sensibility [sensɪ'bɪlɪtɪ] n sensibilité f; pl (touchiness) susceptibilité f.

sensible ['sensəb(ə)l] a (wise) raisonnable, sensé; (clothes) pratique.

sensitive ['sensɪtɪv] a (responsive, painful) sensible (to à); (delicate) délicat (peau, question etc); (touchy) susceptible (about à propos de etc). ◆**sensi'tivity** n sensibilité f; (touchiness) susceptibilité f.

sensory ['sensərɪ] a sensoriel.

sensual ['senʃʊəl] a (bodily, sexual) sensuel. ◆**sensu'ality** n sensualité f. ◆**sensuous** a (pleasing, refined) sensuel. ◆**sensuously** adv avec sensualité. ◆**sensuousness** n sensualité f.

sent [sent] see **send**.

sentence ['sentəns] 1 n Gram phrase f. 2 n Jur condamnation f; (punishment) peine f;

to pass s. prononcer une condamnation (**on s.o.** contre qn); **to serve a s.** purger une peine; – vt Jur prononcer une condamnation contre; **to s. to** condamner à.

sentiment ['sentɪmənt] n sentiment m. ◆**senti'mental** a sentimental. ◆**sentimen'tality** n sentimentalité f.

sentry ['sentrɪ] n sentinelle f; **s. box** guérite f.

separate a ['sepərət] (distinct) séparé; (independent) indépendant; (different) différent; (individual) particulier; – ['sepəreɪt] vt séparer (**from** de); – vi se séparer (**from** de). ◆**'separately** adv séparément. ◆**sepa'ration** n séparation f.

separates ['sepərəts] npl (garments) coordonnés mpl.

September [sep'tembər] n septembre m.

septic ['septɪk] a (wound) infecté; **s. tank** fosse f septique.

sequel ['siːkwəl] n suite f.

sequence ['siːkwəns] n (order) ordre m; (series) succession f; Mus Cards séquence f; **film s.** séquence de film; **in s.** dans l'ordre, successivement.

sequin ['siːkwɪn] n paillette f.

serenade [serə'neɪd] n sérénade f; – vt donner une or la sérénade à. ◆**serenity** n sérénité f.

serene [sə'riːn] a serein. ◆**serenity** n sérénité f.

sergeant ['sɑːdʒənt] n Mil sergent m; (in police force) brigadier m.

serial ['sɪərɪəl] n (story, film) feuilleton m; **s. number** (of banknote, TV set etc) numéro de série. ◆**serialize** vt publier en feuilleton; TV Rad adapter en feuilleton.

series ['sɪəriːz] n inv série f; (book collection) collection f.

serious ['sɪərɪəs] a sérieux; (illness, mistake, tone) grave, sérieux; (damage) important. ◆**—ly** adv sérieusement; (ill, damaged) gravement; **to take s.** prendre au sérieux. ◆**—ness** n sérieux m; (of illness etc) gravité f; (of damage) importance f; **in all s.** sérieusement.

sermon ['sɜːmən] n sermon m.

serpent ['sɜːpənt] n serpent m.

serrated [sə'reɪtɪd] a (knife) à dents (de scie).

serum ['sɪərəm] n sérum m.

servant ['sɜːvənt] n (in house etc) domestique mf; (person who serves) serviteur m; **public s.** fonctionnaire mf.

serve [sɜːv] vt servir (**to s.o.** à qn, **s.o. with sth** qch à qn); (of train, bus etc) desservir (un village, un quartier etc); (supply) El alimenter; (apprenticeship) faire; (summons) Jur remettre (**on** à); **it serves its**

purpose ça fait l'affaire; **(it) serves you right!** *Fam* ça t'apprendra!; – *vi* or *out* servir; – *vi* servir **(as de); to s. on** *(jury, committee)* être membre de; **to s. to show**/*etc* servir à montrer/*etc*; – *n Tennis* service *m*.

servic/e ['sɜːvɪs] *n* (*serving*) & *Mil Rel Tennis* service *m*; *(machine or vehicle repair)* révision *f*; **to be of s.** to être utile à, rendre service à; **the (armed) services** les forces *fpl* armées; **s. (charge)** *(tip)* service *m*; **s. department** *(workshop)* atelier *m*; **s. area** *(on motorway)* aire *f* de service; **s. station** station-service *f*; – *vt* (*machine, vehicle*) réviser. ◆—**ing** *n Tech Aut* révision *f*. ◆**serviceable** *a* (*usable*) utilisable; (*useful*) commode; (*durable*) solide. ◆**serviceman** *n* (*pl* -men) *n* militaire *m*.

serviette [sɜːvɪˈet] *n* serviette *f* (de table).

servile ['sɜːvaɪl] *a* servile.

session ['seʃ(ə)n] *n* séance *f*; *Jur Pol* session *f*, séance *f*; *Univ* année *f* or trimestre *m* universitaire; *Univ Am* semestre *m* universitaire.

set [set] **1** *n* (*of keys, needles, tools*) jeu *m*; (*of stamps, numbers*) série *f*; (*of people*) groupe *m*; (*of facts*) & *Math* ensemble *m*; (*of books*) collection *f*; (*of plates*) service *m*; (*of tyres*) train *m*; (*kit*) trousse *f*; (*stage*) *Th Cin* plateau *m*; (*scenery*) *Th Cin* décor *m*, scène *f*; (*hairstyle*) mise *f* en plis; *Tennis* set *m*; **television s.** téléviseur *m*; **radio s.** poste *m* de radio; **tea s.** service *m* à thé; **chess s.** (*box*) jeu *m* d'échecs; **a s. of teeth** une rangée de dents, une denture; **the skiing/racing s.** le monde du ski/des courses. **2** *a* (*time etc*) fixe; (*lunch*) à prix fixe; (*book etc*) *Sch* au programme; (*speech*) préparé à l'avance; (*in one's habits*) régulier; (*situated*) situé; **s. phrase** expression *f* consacrée; **a purpose** un but déterminé; **the s. menu** le plat du jour; **dead s. against** absolument opposé à; **s. on doing** résolu à faire; **to be s. on sth** vouloir qch à tout prix; **all s.** (*ready*) prêt **(to do** pour faire); **to be s. back from** (*of house etc*) être en retrait de (*route etc*). **3** *vt* (*pt* & *pp* **set**, *pres p.* **setting**) (*put*) mettre, poser; (*date, limit etc*) fixer; (*record*) *Sp* établir; (*adjust*) *Tech* régler; (*arm etc in plaster*) *Med* plâtrer; (*task*) donner (**for s.o.** à qn); (*problem*) poser; (*diamond*) monter; (*precedent*) créer; **to have one's hair s.** se faire faire une mise en plis; **s. (loose)** (*dog*) lâcher (**on** contre); **to s. s.o. off/** *crying*/*etc* faire pleurer/*etc* qn; **to s. back** (*in time*) retarder; (*cost*) *Fam* coûter; **to s.**

down déposer; **to s. off** (*bomb*) faire exploser; (*activity, mechanism*) déclencher; (*complexion, beauty*) rehausser; **to s. out** (*display, explain*) exposer (**to** à); (*arrange*) disposer; **to s. up** (*furniture*) installer; (*statue, tent*) dresser; (*school*) fonder; (*government*) établir; (*business*) créer; (*inquiry*) ouvrir; **to s. s.o. up in business** lancer qn dans les affaires; – *vi* (*of sun*) se coucher; (*of jelly*) prendre; (*of bone*) *Med* se ressouder; **to s. about** (*job*) se mettre à; **to s. about doing** se mettre à faire; **to s. in** (*start*) commencer; (*arise*) surgir; **to s. off** or **out** (*leave*) partir; **to s. out do do** entreprendre de faire; **to s. up in business** monter une affaire; **to s. upon** (*attack*) attaquer (*qn*). ◆**setting** *n* (*surroundings*) cadre *m*; (*of sun*) coucher *m*; (*of diamond*) monture *f*. ◆**setter** *n* chien *m* couchant.

setback ['setbæk] *n* revers *m*; *Med* rechute *f*.

setsquare ['setskweər] *n Math* équerre *f*.

settee [se'tiː] *n* canapé *m*.

settle ['set(ə)l] *vt* (*decide, arrange, pay*) régler; (*date*) fixer; (*place in position*) placer; (*person*) installer (*dans son lit etc*); (*nerves*) calmer; (*land*) coloniser; **let's s. things** arrangeons les choses; **let's (all) settled** (*decided*) c'est décidé; – *vi* (*live*) s'installer, s'établir; (*of dust*) se déposer; (*of bird*) se poser; (*of snow*) tenir; **to s. (down) into** (*armchair*) s'installer dans; (*job*) s'habituer à; **to s. (up) with s.o.** régler qn; **to s. for** se contenter de, accepter; **to s. down** (*in chair or house*) s'installer; (*of nerves*) se calmer; (*in one's lifestyle*) se ranger; (*marry*) se caser; **to s. down to** (*get used to*) s'habituer à; (*work, task*) se mettre à. ◆**settled** *a* (*weather, period*) stable; (*habits*) régulier. ◆**settlement** *n* (*of account etc*) règlement *m*; (*agreement*) accord *m*; (*colony*) colonie *f*. ◆**settler** *n* colon *m*.

set-to [set'tuː] *n* (*quarrel*) *Fam* prise *f* de bec.

setup ['setʌp] *n Fam* situation *f*.

seven ['sev(ə)n] *a* & *n* sept (*m*). ◆**seven-'teen** *a* & *n* dix-sept (*m*). ◆**seven'teenth** *a* & *n* dix-septième (*mf*). ◆**seventh** *a* & *n* septième (*mf*). ◆**seventieth** *a* & *n* soixante-dixième (*mf*). ◆**seventy** *a* & *n* soixante-dix (*m*); **s.-one** soixante et onze.

sever ['sevər] *vt* sectionner, couper; (*relations*) *Fig* rompre. ◆**severing** *n*, ◆**severance** *n* (*of relations*) rupture *f*.

several ['sev(ə)rəl] *a* & *pron* plusieurs (**of** d'entre).

severe [sə'vɪər] a (judge, tone etc) sévère; (winter, training) rigoureux; (test) dur; (injury) grave; (blow, setback) violent; (cold, frost) intense; (overwork) excessif; **a s. cold** Med un gros rhume; **s. to** or **with s.o.** sévère envers qn. ◆**severely** adv sévèrement; (wounded) gravement. ◆**se'verity** n sévérité f; rigueur f; gravité f; violence f.

sew [səʊ] vti (pt **sewed**, pp **sewn** [səʊn] or **sewed**) coudre; **to s. on** (button) (re)coudre; **to s. up** (tear) (re)coudre. ◆**-ing** n couture f; **s. machine** machine f à coudre.

sewage ['suːɪdʒ] n eaux fpl usées or d'égout. ◆**sewer** n égout m.

sewn [səʊn] see **sew**.

sex [seks] n (gender, sexuality) sexe m; (activity) relations fpl sexuelles; **the opposite s.** l'autre sexe; **to have s. with** coucher avec; – a (education, act etc) sexuel; **s. maniac** obsédé, -ée mf sexuel(le). ◆**sexist** a & n sexiste (mf). ◆**sexual** a sexuel. ◆**sexu'ality** n sexualité f. ◆**sexy** a (-ier, -iest) (book, garment, person) sexy inv; (aroused) qui a envie (de faire l'amour).

sextet [sek'stet] n sextuor m.

sh! [ʃ] int chut!

shabby ['ʃæbɪ] a (-ier, -iest) (town, room etc) miteux; (person) pauvrement vêtu; (mean) Fig mesquin. ◆**shabbily** adv (dressed) pauvrement. ◆**shabbiness** n aspect m miteux; mesquinerie f.

shack [ʃæk] **1** n cabane f. **2** vi **to s. up with** Pej Fam se coller avec.

shackles ['ʃæk(ə)lz] npl chaînes fpl.

shade [ʃeɪd] n ombre f; (of colour) ton m, nuance f; (of opinion, meaning) nuance f; (of lamp) abat-jour m inv; (blind) store m; **in the s.** à l'ombre; **a s. faster/taller/etc** (slightly) un rien plus vite/plus grand/etc; – vt (of tree) ombrager; (protect) abriter (from de); **to s. in** (drawing) ombrer. ◆**shady** a (-ier, -iest) (place) ombragé; (person etc) Fig louche.

shadow ['ʃædəʊ] **1** n ombre f. **2** a (cabinet) Pol fantôme. **3** vt **to s. s.o.** (follow) filer qn. ◆**shadowy** a (-ier, -iest) (form etc) obscur, vague.

shaft [ʃɑːft] n **1** (of tool) manche m; (in machine) arbre m; **s. of light** trait m de lumière. **2** (of mine) puits m; (of lift) cage f.

shaggy ['ʃægɪ] a (-ier, -iest) (hair, beard) broussailleux; (dog etc) à longs poils.

shake [ʃeɪk] vt (pt **shook**, pp **shaken**) (move up and down) secouer; (bottle) agiter; (belief, resolution etc) Fig ébranler; (upset) bouleverser, secouer; **to s. the windows** (of shock) ébranler les vitres; **to s. one's head**

(say no) secouer la tête; **to s. hands with** serrer la main à; **we shook hands** nous nous sommes serré la main; **to s. off** (dust etc) secouer; (cough, infection, pursuer) Fig se débarrasser de; **to s. s.o. up** (disturb, rouse) secouer qn; **to s. sth out of sth** (remove) secouer qch de qch; **s. yourself out of it!** secoue-toi!; – vi trembler (**with** de); – n secousse f; **to give sth a s.** secouer qch; **with a s. of his** or **her head** en secouant la tête; **in two shakes** (soon) Fam dans une minute. ◆**s.-up** n Fig réorganisation f.

shaky ['ʃeɪkɪ] a (-ier, -iest) (trembling) tremblant; (ladder etc) branlant; (memory, health) chancelant; (on one's legs, in a language) mal assuré.

shall [ʃæl, unstressed ʃəl] v aux **1** (future) **I s. come, I'll come** je viendrai; **we s. not come, we shan't come** nous ne viendrons pas. **2** (question) **s. I leave?** veux-tu que je parte?; **s. we leave?** on part? **3** (order) **he s. do it if I order it** il le devra le faire si je le ordonne.

shallot [ʃə'lɒt] n (onion) échalote f.

shallow ['ʃæləʊ] a (-er, -est) peu profond; Fig Pej superficiel; – npl (of river) bas-fond m. ◆**-ness** n manque m de profondeur; Fig Pej caractère m superficiel.

sham [ʃæm] n (pretence) comédie f, feinte f; (person) imposteur m; (jewels) imitation f; – a (false) faux; (illness, emotion) feint; – vt (**-mm-**) feindre.

shambles ['ʃæmb(ə)lz] n désordre m, pagaïe f; **to be a s.** être en pagaïe; **to make a s. of** gâcher.

shame [ʃeɪm] n (feeling, disgrace) honte f; **it's a s.** c'est dommage (**to do** de faire); **it's a s. (that)** c'est dommage que (+ sub); **what a s.!** (quel) dommage!; **to put to s.** faire honte à; – vt (disgrace, make ashamed) faire honte à. ◆**shamefaced** a honteux; (bashful) timide. ◆**shameful** a honteux. ◆**shamefully** adv honteusement. ◆**shameless** a (brazen) effronté; (indecent) impudique.

shammy ['ʃæmɪ] n **s. (leather)** Fam peau f de chamois.

shampoo [ʃæm'puː] n shampooing m; – vt (carpet) shampooiner; **to s. s.o.'s hair** faire un shampooing à qn.

shandy ['ʃændɪ] n (beer) panaché m.

shan't [ʃɑːnt] = **shall not**.

shanty¹ ['ʃæntɪ] n (hut) baraque f. ◆**shantytown** n bidonville f.

shanty² ['ʃæntɪ] n **sea s.** chanson f de marins.

shape [ʃeɪp] n forme f; **in (good) s.** (fit) en forme; **to be in good/bad s.** (of vehicle, *house etc*) être en bon/mauvais état; (*of business*) marcher bien/mal; **to take s.** prendre forme; **in the s. of a pear** en forme de poire; – *vt* (*fashion*) façonner (**into** en); (*one's life*) Fig déterminer; – *vi* **to s. up** (*of plans*) prendre (bonne) tournure, s'annoncer bien; (*of pupil, wrongdoer*) s'y mettre, s'appliquer; (*of patient*) faire des progrès. ◆**-ed** *suffix* pear-s./etc en forme de poire/etc. ◆**shapeless** *a* informe. ◆**shapely** *a* (**-ier, -iest**) (*woman, legs*) bien tourné.

share [ʃeər] *n* part *f* (**of,** in de); (*in company*) Fin action *f*; **one's (fair) s.** de sa part de; **to do one's (fair) s.** fournir sa part d'efforts; **stocks and shares** Fin valeurs *fpl* (boursières); – *vt* (*meal, joy, opinion etc*) partager (**with** avec); (*characteristic*) avoir en commun; **to s. out** (*distribute*) partager; – *vi* **to s. (in)** partager. ◆**shareholder** *n* Fin actionnaire *mf*.

shark [ʃɑːk] *n* (*fish*) & Fig requin *m*.

sharp [ʃɑːp] **1** *a* (**-er, -est**) (*knife, blade etc*) tranchant; (*pointed*) pointu; (*point, voice*) aigu; (*pace, mind*) vif; (*pain*) aigu, vif; (*change, bend*) brusque; (*taste*) piquant; (*words, wind, tone*) âpre; (*eyesight, cry*) perçant; (*distinct*) net; (*lawyer etc*) Pej peu scrupuleux; **s. practice** Pej procédé(s) *m*(*pl*) malhonnête(s); – *adv* (*to stop*) net; **five o'clock**/etc **s.** cinq heures/etc pile; **right/left** tout de suite à droite/à gauche. **2** *n* Mus dièse *m*. ◆**sharpen** *vt* (*knife*) aiguiser; (*pencil*) tailler. ◆**sharpener** *n* (*for pencils*) taille-crayon(s) *m* inv; (*for blades*) aiguisoir *m*. ◆**sharply** *adv* (*suddenly*) brusquement; (*harshly*) vivement; (*clearly*) nettement. ◆**sharpness** *n* (*of blade*) tranchant *m*; (*of picture*) netteté *f*. ◆**sharpshooter** *n* tireur *m* d'élite.

shatter [ʃætər] *vt* (*smash*) fracasser; (*glass*) faire voler en éclats; (*career, health*) briser; (*person, hopes*) anéantir; – *vi* (*smash*) se fracasser; (*of glass*) voler en éclats. ◆**-ed** *a* (*exhausted*) anéanti. ◆**-ing** *a* (*defeat*) accablant; (*news, experience*) bouleversant.

shav-e [ʃeɪv] *vt* (*person, head*) raser; **to s. off one's beard**/etc se raser la barbe/etc; – *vi* se raser; – *n* **to have a s.** se raser, se faire la barbe; **to have a close s.** Fig Fam l'échapper belle. ◆**-ing** *n* rasage *m*; (*strip of wood*) copeau *m*; **s. brush** blaireau *m*; **s. cream, s. foam** crème *f* à raser; (*after shaving*) rasé (de près). ◆**shaven** *a* rasé (de près). ◆**shaver** *n* rasoir *m* électrique.

shawl [ʃɔːl] *n* châle *m*.

she [ʃiː] *pron* elle; **s. wants** elle veut; **she's a**

happy woman c'est une femme heureuse; **if I were s.** si j'étais elle; – *n* femelle *f*; **s.-bear** ourse *f*.

sheaf [ʃiːf] *n* (*pl* **sheaves**) (*of corn*) gerbe *f*.

shear [ʃɪər] *vt* tondre; – *npl* cisaille(s) *f*(*pl*); **pruning shears** sécateur *m*. ◆**-ing** *n* tonte *f*.

sheath [ʃiːθ] *n* (*pl* **-s** [ʃiːðz]) (*container*) gaine *f*, fourreau *m*; (*contraceptive*) préservatif *m*.

shed [ʃed] **1** *n* (*in garden etc*) remise *f*; (*for goods or machines*) hangar *m*. **2** *vt* (*pt & pp* **shed,** *pres p* **shedding**) (*lose*) perdre; (*tears, warmth etc*) répandre; (*get rid of*) se défaire de; (*clothes*) enlever; **to s. light on** Fig éclairer.

sheen [ʃiːn] *n* lustre *m*.

sheep [ʃiːp] *n* inv mouton *m*. ◆**sheepdog** *n* chien *m* de berger. ◆**sheepskin** *n* peau *f* de mouton.

sheepish [ʃiːpɪʃ] *a* penaud. ◆**-ly** *adv* d'un air penaud.

sheer [ʃɪər] **1** *a* (*luck, madness etc*) pur; (*impossibility etc*) absolu; **it's s. hard work** ça demande du travail; **by s. determination/hard work** à force de détermination/de travail. **2** *a* (*cliff*) à pic; – *adv* (*to rise*) à pic. **3** *a* (*fabric*) très fin.

sheet [ʃiːt] *n* (*on bed*) drap *m*; (*of paper, wood etc*) feuille *f*; (*of glass, ice*) plaque *f*; (*dust cover*) housse *f*; (*canvas*) bâche *f*; **s. metal** tôle *f*.

sheikh [ʃeɪk] *n* scheik *m*, cheik *m*.

shelf [ʃelf] *n* (*pl* **shelves**) rayon *m*, étagère *f*; (*in shop*) rayon *m*; (*on cliff*) saillie *f*; **to be (left) on the s.** (*not married*) Fam être toujours célibataire.

shell [ʃel] **1** *n* coquille *f* (*of tortoise*) carapace *f*; (*seashell*) coquillage *m*; (*of peas*) cosse *f*; (*of building*) carcasse *f*; – *vt* (*peas*) écosser; (*nut, shrimp*) décortiquer. **2** *n* (*explosive*) Mil obus *m*; – *vt* (*town etc*) Mil bombarder. ◆**-ing** *n* bombardement *m*. ◆**shellfish** *n* inv Culin (*oysters etc*) fruits *mpl* de mer.

shelter [ʃeltər] *n* (*place, protection*) abri *m*; **to take s.** se mettre à l'abri (**from** de); **to seek s.** chercher un abri (**from** de); – *vt* abriter (**from** de); (*criminal*) protéger; – *vi* s'abriter. ◆**-ed** *a* (*place*) abrité; (*life*) très protégé.

shelve [ʃelv] *vt* (*postpone*) laisser en suspens.

shelving [ʃelvɪŋ] *n* (*shelves*) rayonnage(s) *m*(*pl*); **s. unit** (*set of shelves*) étagère *f*.

shepherd [ʃepəd] **1** *n* berger *m*; **s.'s pie** hachis *m* Parmentier. **2** *vt* **to s. in** faire entrer; **to s. s.o. around** piloter qn. ◆**shepherdess** n bergère f.

sherbet ['ʃɜːbət] n (powder) poudre f acidulée; (water ice) Am sorbet m.

sheriff ['ʃerɪf] n Am shérif m.

sherry ['ʃerɪ] n xérès m, sherry m.

shh! [ʃ] int chut!

shield [ʃiːld] n bouclier m; (on coat of arms) écu m; (screen) Tech écran m; – vt protéger (**from** de).

shift [ʃɪft] n (change) changement m (**of, in** de); (period of work) poste m; (workers) équipe f; gear**s.** Aut Am levier m de vitesse; **s. work** travail m en équipe; – vt (move) déplacer, bouger; (limb) bouger; (employee) muter (**to** à); (scenery) Th changer; (blame) rejeter (**on to** sur); **to s. places** changer de place; **to s. gear(s)** Aut Am changer de vitesse; – vi bouger; (of heavy object) se déplacer; (of views) changer; (pass) passer (**to** à); (go) aller (**to** à); **to s. to** (new town) déménager à; **to s. along** avancer; **to s. over** or **up** se pousser. ◆**–ing** a (views) changeant.

shiftless ['ʃɪftləs] a velléitaire, paresseux.

shifty ['ʃɪftɪ] a (-ier, -iest) (sly) sournois; (dubious) louche.

shilling ['ʃɪlɪŋ] n shilling m.

shilly-shally ['ʃɪlɪʃælɪ] vi hésiter, tergiverser.

shimmer ['ʃɪmər] vi chatoyer, miroiter; – n chatoiement m, miroitement m.

shin [ʃɪn] n tibia m; **s. pad** n Sp jambière f.

shindig ['ʃɪndɪg] n Fam réunion f bruyante.

shin/e [ʃaɪn] vi (pt & pp shone [ʃɒn, Am ʃəʊn]) briller; **to s. with** (happiness etc) rayonner de; – vt (polish) faire briller; **to s. a light** or **a torch** éclairer (**on sth** qch); – n éclat m; (on shoes, cloth) brillant m. ◆**–ing** a (bright, polished) brillant; **a shining example** of un bel exemple de. ◆**shiny** a (-ier, -iest) (bright, polished) brillant; (clothes, through wear) lustré.

shingle ['ʃɪŋg(ə)l] n (on beach) galets mpl; (on roof) bardeau m.

shingles ['ʃɪŋg(ə)lz] n Med zona m.

ship [ʃɪp] n navire m, bateau m; **by s.** en bateau; **s. owner** armateur m; – vt (-pp-) (send) expédier; (transport) transporter; (load up) embarquer (**on to** sur). ◆**shipping** n (traffic) navigation f; (ships) navires mpl; – a (agent) maritime; **s. line** compagnie f de navigation. ◆**shipbuilding** n construction f navale. ◆**shipmate** n camarade m de bord. ◆**shipment** n (goods) chargement m, cargaison f. ◆**shipshape** a & adv en ordre. ◆**shipwreck** n naufrage m. ◆**shipwrecked** a

naufragé; **to be s.** faire naufrage. ◆**shipyard** n chantier m naval.

shirk [ʃɜːk] vt (duty) se dérober à; (work) éviter de faire; – vi tirer au flanc. ◆**–er** n tire-au-flanc m inv.

shirt [ʃɜːt] n chemise f; (of woman) chemisier m. ◆**shirtfront** n plastron m. ◆**shirtsleeves** npl **in (one's) s.** en bras de chemise.

shiver ['ʃɪvər] vi frissonner (**with** de); – n frisson m.

shoal [ʃəʊl] n (of fish) banc m.

shock [ʃɒk] n (moral blow) choc m; (impact) & Med choc m; (of explosion) secousse f; (electric) **s.** décharge f (électrique) (**from sth** en touchant qch); **a feeling of s.** un sentiment d'horreur; **suffering from s., in a state of s.** en état de choc; **to come as a s. to s.o.** stupéfier qn; – a (tactics, wave) de choc; (effect, image etc) -choc inv; **s. absorber** amortisseur m; – vt (offend) choquer; (surprise) stupéfier; (disgust) dégoûter. ◆**–ing** a affreux; (outrageous) scandaleux; (indecent) choquant. ◆**–ingly** adv affreusement. ◆**–er** n **to be a s.** Fam être affreux or horrible. ◆**shockproof** a résistant au choc.

shoddy ['ʃɒdɪ] a (-ier, -iest) (goods etc) de mauvaise qualité. ◆**shoddily** adv (made, done) mal.

shoe [ʃuː] n chaussure f, soulier m; (for horse) fer m; Aut sabot m (de frein); **in your shoes** Fig à ta place; **s. polish** cirage m; – vt (pt & pp shod) (horse) ferrer. ◆**shoehorn** n chausse-pied m. ◆**shoelace** n lacet m. ◆**shoemaker** n fabricant m de chaussures; (cobbler) cordonnier m. ◆**shoestring** n **on a s.** Fig avec peu d'argent (en poche).

shone [ʃɒn, Am ʃəʊn] see shine.

shoo [ʃuː] vt **to s.** (away) chasser; – int ouste!

shook [ʃʊk] see shake.

shoot¹ [ʃuːt] vt (pt & pp shot) (kill) tuer (d'un coup de feu), abattre; (wound) blesser (d'un coup de feu); (execute) fusiller; (hunt) chasser; (gun) tirer un coup de; (bullet) tirer; (missile, glance, questions) lancer (**at** à); (film) tourner; (person) Phot prendre; **to s. down** (aircraft) abattre; – vi (with gun, bow etc) tirer (**at** sur); **to s. ahead/off** avancer/partir à toute vitesse; **to s. up** (grow) pousser vite; (rise, spurt) jaillir; (of price) monter en flèche. ◆**–ing** n (gunfire, execution) fusillade f; (shots) coups mpl de feu; (murder) meurtre m; (of *film*) tournage *m*; (*hunting*) chasse *f*. ◆**shoot-out** *n Fam* fusillade *f*.

shoot² [ʃuːt] *n* (*on plant*) pousse *f*.

shop [ʃɒp] **1** *n* magasin *m*; (*small*) boutique *f*; (*workshop*) atelier *m*; **at the baker's s.** à la boulangerie, chez le boulanger; **s. assistant** vendeur, -euse *mf*; **s. floor** (*workers*) ouvriers *mpl*; **s. steward** délégué, -ée *mf* syndical(e); **s. window** vitrine *f*; − *vi* (**-pp-**) faire ses courses (**at** chez); **to s. around** comparer les prix. **2** *vt* (**-pp-**) **to s. s.o.** *Fam* dénoncer qn (*à la police etc*). ◆**shopping** *n* (*goods*) achats *mpl*; **to go s.** faire des courses; **to do one's s.** faire ses courses; − *a* (*street, district*) commerçant; (*bag*) à provisions; **s. centre** centre *m* commercial. ◆**shopper** *n* (*buyer*) acheteur, -euse *mf*; (*customer*) client, -ente *mf*; (*bag*) sac *m* à provisions.

shopkeeper [ˈʃɒpkiːpər] *n* commerçant, -ante *mf*. ◆**shoplifter** *n* voleur, -euse *mf* à l'étalage. ◆**shoplifting** *n* vol *m* à l'étalage. ◆**shopsoiled** *a*, *Am* ◆**shopworn** *a* abîmé.

shore [ʃɔːr] **1** *n* (*of sea, lake*) rivage *m*; (*coast*) côte *f*, bord *m* de (la) mer; (*beach*) plage *f*; **on s.** (*passenger*) *Nau* à terre. **2** *vt* **to s. up** (*prop up*) étayer.

shorn [ʃɔːn] *a* (*head*) tondu; **s. of** (*stripped of*) *Lit* dénué de.

short [ʃɔːt] *a* (**-er, -est**) court; (*person, distance*) petit; (*syllable*) bref; (*curt, impatient*) brusque; **a s. time** *or* **while ago** il y a peu de temps; **s. cut** raccourci *m*; **to be s. of money/time** être à court d'argent/de temps; **we're s. of ten men** il nous manque dix hommes; **money/time is** il l'argent/le temps manque; **not far s.** of pas loin de; **s. of** (*except*) sauf; **to be s. for** (*of name*) être l'abréviation *or* le diminutif de; **in s.** bref; **s. circuit** *El* court-circuit *m*; **s. list** liste *f* de candidats choisis; − *adv* **to cut s.** (*visit etc*) abréger; (*person*) couper la parole à; **to go** *or* **get** *or* **run s. of** manquer de; **to get** *or* **run s.** manquer; **to stop s.** s'arrêter net; − *El* court-circuit *m*; (**a pair of**) **shorts** un short. ◆**shorten** *vt* (*visit, time, line, dress etc*) raccourcir. ◆**shortly** *adv* (*soon*) bientôt; **s. after** peu après. ◆**shortness** *n* (*of person*) petitesse *f*; (*of hair, stick, legs*) manque *m* de longueur.

shortage [ˈʃɔːtɪdʒ] *n* manque *m*, pénurie *f*; (*crisis*) crise *f*.

shortbread [ˈʃɔːtbred] *n* sablé *m*. ◆**short-ˈchange** *vt* (*buyer*) ne pas rendre juste à. ◆**short-ˈcircuit** *vt El & Fig* court-circuiter. ◆**shortcoming** *n* défaut *m*.

◆**shortfall** *n* manque *m*. ◆**shorthand** *n* sténo *f*; **s. typist** sténodactylo *f*. ◆**short-ˈhanded** *a* à court de personnel. ◆**short-ˈlived** *a* éphémère. ◆**short-ˈsighted** *a* myope; *Fig* imprévoyant. ◆**short-ˈsightedness** *n* myopie *f*; imprévoyance *f*. ◆**short-ˈsleeved** *a* à manches courtes. ◆**short-ˈstaffed** *a* à court de personnel. ◆**short-ˈterm** *a* à court terme.

shortening [ˈʃɔːt(ə)nɪŋ] *n Culin* matière *f* grasse.

shot [ʃɒt] *see* **shoot¹**; − *n* coup *m*; (*bullet*) balle *f*; *Cin Phot* prise *f* de vues; (*injection*) *Med* piqûre *f*; **a good s.** (*person*) un bon tireur; **to have a s. at (doing)** sth essayer de faire qch; **a long s.** (*attempt*) un coup à tenter; **big s.** *Fam* gros bonnet *m*; **like a s.** (*at once*) tout de suite; **to be s. of** (*rid of*) *Fam* être débarrassé de. ◆**shotgun** *n* fusil *m* de chasse.

should [ʃud, *unstressed* ʃəd] *v aux* **1** (= *ought to*) **you s. do it** vous devriez le faire; **I s. have stayed** j'aurais dû rester; **that s. be Pauline** ça doit être Pauline. **2** (= *would*) **I s. like to** j'aimerais bien; **it's strange she s. say no** il est étrange qu'elle dise non. **3** (*possibility*) **if he s. come** s'il vient; **s. I be free** si je suis libre.

shoulder [ˈʃəʊldər] **1** *n* épaule *f*; **to have round shoulders** avoir le dos voûté, être voûté; (**hard**) **s.** (*of motorway*) accotement *m* stabilisé; **s. bag** sac *m* à bandoulière; **s. blade** omoplate *f*; **s.-length hair** cheveux *mpl* mi-longs. **2** *vt* (*responsibility*) endosser, assumer.

shout [ʃaʊt] *n* cri *m*; **to give s.o. a s.** appeler qn; − *vi* (**out**) crier; **to s. to** *or* **at s.o.** **to do** crier à qn de faire; **to s. at s.o.** (*scold*) crier après qn; − *vt* **to s.** (**out**) (*insult etc*) crier; **to s. down** (*speaker*) huer. ◆−**ing** *n* (*shouts*) cris *mpl*.

shove [ʃʌv] *n* poussée *f*; **to give a s. (to)** pousser; − *vt* pousser; (*put*) *Fam* fourrer; **to s. sth into** (*thrust*) enfoncer *or* fourrer qch dans; **to s. s.o. around** *Fam* régenter qn; − *vi* pousser; **to s. off** (*leave*) *Fam* ficher le camp, filer; **to s. over** (*move over*) *Fam* se pousser.

shovel [ˈʃʌv(ə)l] *n* pelle *f*; − *vt* (*-ll-*, *Am* *-l-*) (*grain etc*) pelleter; **to s. up** *or* **away** (*remove*) enlever à la pelle; **to s. sth into** (*thrust*) *Fam* fourrer qch dans.

show [ʃəʊ] *n* (*of joy, force*) démonstration *f* (*of de*); (*semblance*) semblant *m* (*of de*); (*ostentation*) parade *f*; (*sight*) & *Th* spectacle *m*; (*performance*) *Cin* séance *f*; (*exhibition*) exposition *f*; **the Boat/Motor S.**

Salon de la Navigation/de l'Automobile; **horse** s. concours *m* hippique; **to give a good s.** *Sp Mus Th* jouer bien; **good s.!** bravo!; **(just) for s.** pour l'effet; **on s.** (*painting etc*) exposé; **s. business** le monde du spectacle; **s. flat** appartement *m* témoin; – *vt* (*pt* showed, *pp* shown) montrer (**to à, that que**); (*exhibit*) exposer; (*film*) passer, donner; (*indicate*) indiquer, montrer; **to s.o. to the door** reconduire qn; **it** (*just*) **goes to s. that**... ça (dé)montre (bien) que...; **I'll s. him** *or* **her!** *Fam* je lui apprendrai!; – *vi* (*be visible*) se voir; (*of film*) passer; **'now showing'** *Cin* 'à l'affiche' (**at à**). ▪ **s.** (**a)round** *vt* faire visiter; **he** *or* **she was shown a)round the house** on lui a fait visiter la maison; **to s. in** *vt* faire entrer; **to s. off** *vt Pej* étaler; (*highlight*) faire valoir; – *vi Pej* crâner. ◆**s.-off** *n Pej* crâneur, -euse *mf*; **to s. out** *vt* (*visitor*) reconduire; **to s. up** *vt* (*fault*) faire ressortir; (*humiliate*) faire honte à; – *vi* ressortir (**against** sur); (*of error*) être visible; (*of person*) *Fam* arriver, s'amener. ◆**showing** *n* (*of film*) projection *f* (**of** de); (*performance*) *Cin* séance *f*; (*of team, player*) performance *f*.

showcase ['ʃəʊkeɪs] *n* vitrine *f*. ◆**showdown** *n* confrontation *f*, conflit *m*. ◆**showgirl** *n* (*in chorus etc*) girl *f*. ◆**showjumping** *n Sp* jumping *m*. ◆**showmanship** *n* art *m* de la mise en scène. ◆**showpiece** *n* modèle du genre. ◆**showroom** *n* (*for cars etc*) salle *f* d'exposition.

shower ['ʃaʊər] *n* (*of rain*) averse *f*; (*of blows*) déluge *m*; (*bath*) douche *f*; (*party*) *Am* réception *f* (*pour la remise de cadeaux*); – *vt* **to s. s.o. with** (*gifts, abuse*) couvrir qn de. ◆**showery** *a* pluvieux.

shown [ʃəʊn] *see* show.

showy ['ʃəʊɪ] *a* (*-ier, -iest*) (*colour, hat*) voyant; (*person*) prétentieux.

shrank [ʃræŋk] *see* shrink 1.

shrapnel ['ʃræpnəl] *n* éclats *mpl* d'obus.

shred [ʃred] *n* lambeau *m*; (*of truth*) *Fig* grain *m*; **not a s. of evidence** pas la moindre preuve; – *vt* (*-dd-*) mettre en lambeaux; (*cabbage, carrots*) râper. ◆**shredder** *n Culin* râpe *f*.

shrew [ʃruː] *n* (*woman*) *Pej* mégère *f*.

shrewd [ʃruːd] *a* (*-er, -est*) (*person, plan*) astucieux. ◆**-ly** *adv* astucieusement. ◆**-ness** *n* astuce *f*.

shriek [ʃriːk] *n* cri *m* (aigu); – *vti* crier; **to s. with pain/laughter** hurler de douleur/de rire.

shrift [ʃrɪft] *n* **to get short s.** être traité sans ménagement.

shrill [ʃrɪl] *a* (*-er, -est*) aigu, strident.

shrimp [ʃrɪmp] *n* crevette *f*; (*person*) *Pej* nabot, -ote *mf*; (*child*) *Fam* puce *f*.

shrine [ʃraɪn] *n* lieu *m* saint; (*tomb*) châsse *f*.

shrink [ʃrɪŋk] **1** *vi* (*pt* shrank, *pp* shrunk *or* shrunken) (*of clothes*) rétrécir; (*of aging person*) se tasser; (*of amount, audience etc*) diminuer; **to s. from** reculer devant (**doing** l'idée de faire); – *vt* rétrécir. **2** *n* (*person*) *Am Hum* psy(chiatre) *m*. ◆**-age** *n* rétrécissement *m*; diminution *f*.

shrivel ['ʃrɪv(ə)l] *vi* (*-ll-*, *Am* **-l-**) **to s. (up)** se ratatiner; – *vt* **to s. (up)** ratatiner.

shroud [ʃraʊd] *n* linceul *m*; (*of mystery*) *Fig* voile *m*; – *vt* **shrouded in mist** enseveli *or* enveloppé sous la brume; **shrouded in mystery** enveloppé de mystère.

Shrove Tuesday [ʃrəʊv'tjuːzdɪ] *n* Mardi *m* gras.

shrub [ʃrʌb] *n* arbrisseau *m*.

shrug [ʃrʌg] *vt* (*-gg-*) **to s. one's shoulders** hausser les épaules; **to s. off** (*dismiss*) écarter (dédaigneusement); – *n* haussement *m* d'épaules.

shrunk(en) ['ʃrʌŋk(ən)] *see* shrink 1.

shudder ['ʃʌdər] *vi* frémir (**with** de); (*of machine etc*) vibrer; – *n* frémissement *m*; vibration *f*.

shuffle ['ʃʌf(ə)l] **1** *vti* **to s. one's feet** traîner les pieds. **2** *vti* (*cards*) battre.

shun [ʃʌn] *vt* (*-nn-*) fuir, éviter; **to s. doing** éviter de faire.

shunt [ʃʌnt] *vt* (*train, conversation*) aiguiller (**on to** sur); **we were shunted (to and fro)** *Fam* on nous a baladés (**from office to office/etc** de bureau en bureau/etc).

shush! [ʃʊʃ] *int* chut!

shut [ʃʌt] *vt* (*pt & pp* shut, *pp* shutting) fermer; **to s. one's finger in** (*door etc*) se prendre le doigt dans; **to s. away** *or* **in** (*lock away or in*) enfermer; **to s. down** fermer; **to s. off** fermer; (*engine*) arrêter; (*isolate*) isoler; **to s. out** (*light*) empêcher d'entrer; (*view*) boucher; (*exclude*) exclure (**of, from** de); **to s. s.o. out** (*lock out accidentally*) enfermer qn dehors; **to s. up** fermer; (*lock up*) enfermer (*person, objet précieux etc*); (*silence*) *Fam* faire taire; – *vi* (*of door etc*) se fermer; (*of shop, museum etc*) fermer; **the door doesn't s.** la porte ne ferme pas; **to s. down** fermer (*définitivement*); **to s. up** (*be quiet*) *Fam* se taire. ◆**shutdown** *n* fermeture *f*.

shutter ['ʃʌtər] *n* volet *m*; (*of camera*) obturateur *m*.

shuttle ['ʃʌt(ə)l] n (bus, spacecraft etc) navette f; **s. service** navette f; − vi **faire la navette**; − vt (in vehicle etc) transporter. ◆**shuttlecock** n (in badminton) volant m.

shy [ʃaɪ] a (-er, -est) timide; **to be s.** avoir peur de faire; − vi **to s. away** reculer (**from** s.o. devant qn, **from doing** à l'idée de faire). ◆**-ness** n timidité f.

Siamese [saɪəˈmiːz] a siamois; **S. twins** frères mpl siamois, sœurs fpl siamoises.

sibling ['sɪblɪŋ] n frère m, sœur f.

Sicily ['sɪsɪlɪ] n Sicile f.

sick [sɪk] a (-er, -est) (ill) malade; (mind) malsain; (humour) noir; (cruel) sadique; **to be s.** (vomit) vomir; **to be off or away s., to be on s. leave** être en congé de maladie; **to feel s.** avoir mal au cœur; **to be s. (and tired) of** Fam en avoir marre de; **he makes me s.** Fam il m'écœure; − n **the s.** les malades mpl; − vi (vomit) Fam vomir; − vt **to s. sth up** Fam vomir qch. ◆**sickbay** n infirmerie f. ◆**sickbed** n lit m de malade. ◆**sickly** a (-ier, -iest) maladif; (pale, faint) pâle; (taste) écœurant. ◆**sickness** n maladie f; (vomiting) vomissement(s) m(pl); **motion s.** Aut mal m de la route.

sicken ['sɪkən] 1 vt écœurer. 2 vi **to be sickening for** (illness) couver. ◆**-ing** a écœurant.

side [saɪd] n côté m; (of hill, animal) flanc m; (of road, river) bord m; (of beef) quartier m; (of question) aspect m; (of character) facette f, aspect m; Sp équipe f; Pol parti m; **the right s.** (of fabric) l'endroit m, **the wrong s.** (of fabric) l'envers m; **by the s. of** (nearby) à côté de; **at or by my s.** à côté de moi, à mes côtés; **s. by s.** l'un à côté de l'autre; **to move to one s.** s'écarter; **on this s.** de ce côté; **on the other s.** de l'autre côté; **the other s.** TV Fam l'autre chaîne f; **on the big/etc s.** Fam plutôt grand/etc; **to take sides with** se ranger du côté de; **on our s.** de notre côté, avec nous; **on the s.** Fam (secretly) en catimini; (to make money) en plus; − a (lateral) latéral; (glance, view) de côté; (street) transversal; − vi **to s. with** se ranger du côté de. ◆**-sided** suffix **ten-s.** à dix côtés. ◆**sideboard 1** n buffet m. **2** npl (hair) pattes fpl. ◆**sideburns** npl (hair) pattes fpl. ◆**sidecar** n side-car m. ◆**sidekick** n Fam associé, -ée mf. ◆**sidelight** n Aut feu m de position. ◆**sideline** n activité f secondaire. ◆**sidesaddle** adv (to ride) en amazone. ◆**sidestep** vt (-pp-) éviter. ◆**sidetrack** vt **to get sidetracked**

s'écarter du sujet. ◆**sidewalk** n Am trottoir m. ◆**sideways** adv & a de côté.

siding ['saɪdɪŋ] n Rail voie f de garage.

sidle ['saɪd(ə)l] vi **to s. up to s.o.** s'approcher furtivement de qn.

siege [siːdʒ] n Mil siège m.

siesta [sɪˈestə] n sieste f.

sieve [sɪv] n tamis m; (for liquids) Culin passoire f; − vt tamiser. ◆**sift** vt tamiser; **to s. out** (truth) Fig dégager; − vi **to s. through** (papers etc) examiner (à la loupe).

sigh [saɪ] n soupir m; − vi soupirer.

sight [saɪt] n vue f; (spectacle) spectacle m; (on gun) mire f; **to lose s. of** perdre de vue; **to catch s. of** apercevoir; **to come into s.** apparaître; **at first s.** à première vue; **by s.** de vue; **on or at s.** à vue; **in s.** (target, end, date etc) en vue; **keep out of s.!** ne te montre pas!; **he hates the s. of me** il ne peut pas me voir; **it's a lovely s.** c'est beau à voir; **the (tourist) sights** les attractions fpl touristiques; **to set one's sights on** (job etc) viser; **a s. longer/etc** Fam bien plus long/etc; − vt (land) apercevoir. ◆**-ed** a qui voit, clairvoyant. ◆**-ing** n **to make a s. of** voir. ◆**sightseer** n touriste mf. ◆**sightseeing** n tourisme m.

slightly ['saɪtlɪ] a not very s. laid.

sign [saɪn] **1** n signe m; (notice) panneau m; (over shop, inn) enseigne f; **no s. of** aucune trace de; **to use s. language** parler par signes. **2** vt (put signature to) signer; **to s. away or over** céder (**to** à); **to s. on or up** (worker, soldier) engager; − vi signer; **to s. for** (letter) signer le reçu de; **to s. in** signer le registre; **to s. off** dire au revoir; **to s. on** (on the dole) s'inscrire au chômage; **to s. on or up** (of soldier, worker) s'engager; (for course) s'inscrire. ◆**signpost** n poteau m indicateur; − vt flécher.

signal ['sɪgnəl] n signal m; **traffic signals** feux mpl de circulation; **s. box**, Am **s. tower** Rail poste m d'aiguillage; − vt (-ll-, Am -l-) (message) communiquer (**to** à); (arrival etc) signaler (**to** à); − vi **faire des signaux**; **to s. (to) s.o. to do** faire signe à qn de faire. ◆**signalman** n (pl -men) Rail aiguilleur m.

signature ['sɪgnətʃər] n signature f; **s. tune** indicatif m (musical). ◆**signatory** n signataire mf.

signet ring ['sɪgnɪtrɪŋ] n chevalière f.

significant [sɪgˈnɪfɪkənt] a (meaningful) significatif; (important, large) important. ◆**significance** n (meaning) signification f; (importance) importance f. ◆**significantly** adv (appreciably) sensiblement; **s.,**

he . . . fait significatif, il . . . . ◆'signify vt (mean) signifier (that que); (make known) indiquer, signifier (to à).

silence ['saɪləns] n silence m; in s. en silence; – vt faire taire. ◆silencer n (on car, gun) silencieux m. ◆silent a silencieux; (film, anger) muet; to keep or be s. garder le silence (about sur). ◆silently adv silencieusement.

silhouette [sɪluː'et] n silhouette f. ◆silhouetted a to be s. against se profiler contre.

silicon ['sɪlɪkən] n silicium m; s. chip puce f de silicium. ◆silicone ['sɪlɪkəʊn] n silicone f.

silk [sɪlk] n soie f. ◆silky a (-ier, -iest) soyeux.

sill [sɪl] n (of window etc) rebord m.

silly ['sɪlɪ] a (-ier, -iest) idiot, bête; to do sth s. faire une bêtise; s. fool, Fam s. billy idiot, -ote mf; – adv (to act, behave) bêtement.

silo ['saɪləʊ] n (pl -os) silo m.

silt [sɪlt] n vase f.

silver ['sɪlvər] n argent m; (silverware) argenterie f; £5 in s. 5 livres en pièces d'argent; – a (spoon etc) en argent, d'argent; (hair, colour) argenté; s. jubilee vingt-cinquième anniversaire m (d'un événement); s. paper papier m d'argent; s. plate argenterie f. ◆s.-'plated a plaqué argent. ◆silversmith n orfèvre m. ◆silverware n argenterie f. ◆silvery a (colour) argenté.

similar ['sɪmɪlər] a semblable (to à). ◆simi'larity n ressemblance f (between entre, to avec). ◆similarly adv de la même façon; (likewise) de même.

simile ['sɪmɪlɪ] n Liter comparaison f.

simmer ['sɪmər] vi Culin mijoter, cuire à feu doux; (of water) frémir; (of revolt, hatred etc) couver; to s. with (rage) bouillir de; to s. down (calm down) Fam se calmer; – vt faire cuire à feu doux; (water) laisser frémir.

simper ['sɪmpər] vi minauder.

simple ['sɪmp(ə)l] a (-er, -est) (plain, uncomplicated, basic etc) simple; s. 'minded a simple d'esprit. ◆s.-'mindedness n simplicité f d'esprit. ◆simpleton n nigaud, -aude mf. ◆sim'plicity n simplicité f. ◆simpli'fication n simplification f. ◆simplify vt simplifier. ◆sim'plistic a simpliste. ◆simply adv (plainly, merely) simplement; (absolutely) absolument.

simulate ['sɪmjʊleɪt] vt simuler.

simultaneous [sɪməl'teɪnɪəs, Am saɪməl-

'teɪnɪəs] a simultané. ◆-ly adv simultané- ment.

sin [sɪn] n péché m; – vi (-nn-) pécher.

since [sɪns] 1 prep (in time) depuis; s. my departure depuis mon départ; – conj depuis que; s. she's been here depuis qu'elle est ici; it's a year s. I saw him ça fait un an que je ne l'ai pas vu; – adv (ever) s. depuis. 2 conj (because) puisque.

sincere [sɪn'sɪər] a sincère. ◆sincerely adv sincèrement; yours s. (in letter) Com veuil- lez croire à mes sentiments dévoués. ◆sin'cerity n sincérité f.

sinew ['sɪnjuː] n Anat tendon m.

sinful ['sɪnfəl] a (guilt-provoking) coupable; (shocking) scandaleux; he's s. c'est un pécheur; that's s. c'est un péché.

sing [sɪŋ] vti (pt sang, pp sung) chanter; to s. up chanter plus fort. ◆-ing n (of bird & musical technique) chant m; (way of sing- ing) façon f de chanter; – a (lesson, teacher) de chant. ◆-er n chanteur, -euse mf.

singe [sɪndʒ] vt (cloth) roussir; (hair) brûler; to s. s.o.'s hair (at hairdresser's) faire un brûlage à qn.

single ['sɪŋg(ə)l] a (only one) seul; (room, bed) pour une personne; (unmarried) célibataire; s. ticket billet m simple; every s. day tous les jours sans exception; s. party Pol parti m unique; – n (ticket) aller m (simple); (record) 45 tours m inv; pl Tennis simples mpl; singles bar bar m pour célibataires; – vt to s. out (choose) choisir. ◆s.-'breasted a (jacket) droit. ◆s.-'decker n (bus) autobus m sans impériale. ◆s.-'handed a sans aide. ◆s.-'minded a (person) résolu, qui n'a qu'une idée en tête. ◆singly adv (one by one) un à un.

singlet ['sɪŋglɪt] n (garment) maillot m de corps.

singsong ['sɪŋsɒŋ] n to get together for a s. se réunir pour chanter.

singular ['sɪŋgjʊlər] 1 a (unusual) singulier. 2 a Gram (form) singulier; (noun) au singu- lier; – n Gram singulier m; in the s. au singulier.

sinister ['sɪnɪstər] a sinistre.

sink¹ [sɪŋk] n (in kitchen) évier m; (washba- sin) lavabo m.

sink² [sɪŋk] vi (pt sank, pp sunk) (of ship, person etc) couler; (of sun, price, water level) baisser; (collapse, subside) s'affaisser; to s. (down) into (mud etc) s'enfoncer dans; (armchair etc) s'affaler dans; to s. in (of ink etc) pénétrer; (of fact etc) Fam rentrer (dans le crâne); **has that sunk in?** *Fam* as-tu compris ça?; – *vt* (*ship*) couler; (*well*) creuser; **to s. into** (*thrust*) enfoncer dans; (*money*) *Com* investir dans; **a sinking feeling** un serrement de cœur.

sinner ['sɪnər] *n* pêcheur *m*, pêcheresse *f*.

sinuous ['sɪnjʊəs] *a* sinueux.

sinus ['saɪnəs] *n Anat* sinus *m inv*.

sip [sɪp] *vt* (**-pp-**) boire à petites gorgées; – *n* (*mouthful*) petite gorgée *f*; (*drop*) goutte *f*.

siphon ['saɪfən] *n* siphon *m*; – *vt* **to s. off** (*petrol*) siphonner; (*money*) *Fig* détourner.

sir [sɜːr] *n* monsieur *m*; **S. Walter Raleigh** (*title*) sir Walter Raleigh.

siren ['saɪərən] *n* (*of factory etc*) sirène *f*.

sirloin ['sɜːlɔɪn] *n* (*steak*) faux-filet *m*; (*joint*) aloyau *m*.

sissy ['sɪsɪ] *n* (*boy, man*) *Fam* femmelette *f*.

sister ['sɪstər] *n* sœur *f*; (*nurse*) infirmière *f* en chef. **◆s.-in-law** *n* (*pl* **sisters-in-law**) belle-sœur *f*. **◆sisterly** *a* fraternel.

sit [sɪt] *vi* (*pp & pp* **sat**, *pres p* **sitting**) s'asseoir; (*for artist*) poser (**for** pour); (*remain*) rester; (*of assembly etc*) siéger, être en séance; **to be sitting** (*of person, cat etc*) être assis; (*of bird*) être perché; **she sat** *or* **was sitting reading** elle était assise à lire; **to s. around** (*do nothing*) ne rien faire; **to s. back** (*in chair*) se caler; (*rest*) se reposer; (*do nothing*) ne rien faire; **to s. down** s'asseoir; **s.-down strike** grève *f* sur le tas; **to s. in on** (*lecture etc*) assister à; **to s. on** (*jury etc*) être membre de; (*fact etc*) *Fam* garder pour soi; **to s. through** *or* **out** (*film etc*) rester jusqu'au bout de; **to s. up** (*straight*) s'asseoir (bien droit); **to s. up waiting for s.o.** (*at night*) ne pas se coucher en attendant qn; – *vt* ne pas asseoir; **to s. s.o. (down)** asseoir qn; **to s. out** (*event, dance*) ne pas prendre part à. **◆sitting** *n* séance *f*; (*for one's portrait*) séance *f* de pose; (*in restaurant*) service *m*; – *a* (*committee etc*) en séance; **s. duck** *Fam* victime *f* facile; **s. tenant** locataire *m*ƒ en possession des lieux. **◆sitting room** *n* salon *m*.

site [saɪt] *n* emplacement *m*; (*archaeological*) site *m*; (*building*) chantier *m*; **launching s.** aire *f* de lancement; – *vt* (*building*) placer.

sit-in [sɪtɪn] *n Pol* sit-in *m inv*.

sitter ['sɪtər] *n* (*for child*) baby-sitter *m*ƒ.

situate ['sɪtʃʊeɪt] *vt* situer; **to be situated** être situé. **◆situ'ation** *n* situation *f*.

six [sɪks] *a & n* six (*m*). **◆six'teen** *a & n* seize (*m*). **◆six'teenth** *a & n* seizième (*m*ƒ). **◆sixth** *a & n* sixième (*m*ƒ); (*lower*) **s.**

form *Sch* = classe *f* de première; (**upper**) **s.**

form *Sch* = classe *f* terminale; (*fraction*) un sixième. **◆sixtieth** *a & n* soixantième (*m*ƒ). **◆sixty** *a & n* soixante (*m*).

size [saɪz] **1** *n* (*of person, animal, garment etc*) taille *f*; (*measurements*) dimensions *f*pl; (*of egg, packet*) grosseur *f*; (*of book*) grandeur *f*, format *m*; (*of problem, town, damage*) importance *f*, étendue *f*; (*of sum*) montant *m*, importance *f*; (*of shoes, gloves*) pointure *f*; (*of shirt*) encolure *f*; **hip/chest s.** tour *m* de hanches/de poitrine; **it's the s. of** ... c'est grand comme ... **2** *n* (*glue*) colle *f*. **3** *vt* **to s. up** (*person*) jauger; (*situation*) évaluer. **◆sizeable** *a* assez grand *or* gros.

sizzle ['sɪz(ə)l] *vi* grésiller. **◆—ing** *a* **s.** (**hot**) brûlant.

skat/e[1] [skeɪt] *n* patin *m*; – *vi* patiner. **◆—ing** *n* patinage *m*; **to go s.** faire du patinage; **s. rink** (*ice*) patinoire *f*; (*roller*) skating *m*. **◆skateboard** *n* skateboard *m*. **◆skater** *n* patineur, -euse *m*ƒ.

skate[2] [skeɪt] *n* (*fish*) raie *f*.

skedaddle [skɪ'dæd(ə)l] *vi Fam* déguerpir.

skein [skeɪn] *n* (*of yarn*) écheveau *m*.

skeleton ['skelɪt(ə)n] *n* squelette *m*; – *a* (*crew, staff*) (réduit au) minimum; **s. key** passe-partout *m inv*.

skeptic ['skeptɪk] *Am* = **sceptic.**

sketch [sketʃ] *n* (*drawing*) croquis *m*, esquisse *f*; *Th* sketch *m*; **a rough s. of** (*plan*) *Fig* une esquisse de; – *vt* **to s. (out)** (*view, idea etc*) esquisser; **to s. in** (*details*) ajouter; – *vi* faire un *or* des croquis. **◆sketchy** *a* (**-ier, -iest**) incomplet, superficiel.

skew [skjuː] *n* **on the s.** de travers.

skewer ['skjʊər] *n* (*for meat etc*) broche *f*; (*for kebab*) brochette *f*.

ski [skiː] *n* (*pl* **skis**) ski *m*; **s. lift** télésiège *m*; **s. pants** fuseau *m*; **s. run** piste *f* de ski; **s. tow** téléski *m*; – *vi* (*pt* **skied** [skiːd], *pres p* **skiing**) faire du ski. **◆—ing** *n Sp* ski *m*; – *a* (*school, clothes*) de ski. **◆—er** *n* skieur, -euse *m*ƒ.

skid [skɪd] **1** *vi* (**-dd-**) *Aut* déraper; **to s. into** déraper et heurter; – *n* dérapage *m*. **2** *n* **s. row** *Am* quartier *m* de clochards *or* de squats.

skill [skɪl] *n* habileté *f*, adresse *f* (**at** à); (*technique*) technique *f*; **one's skills** (*aptitudes*) ses compétences *f*pl. **◆skilful** *a*, *Am* **◆skillful** *a* habile (**at doing** à faire, **at sth** à qch). **◆skilled** *a* habile (**at doing** à faire, **at sth** à qch); (*worker*) qualifié; (*work*) de spécialiste, de professionnel.

skillet ['skɪlɪt] *n Am* poêle *f* (à frire).

skim [skɪm] **1** *vt* (**-mm-**) (*milk*) écrémer;

skimp [skɪmp] *vi* (*on fabric, food etc*) lésiner (**on** sur). ◆**skimpy** *a* (**-ier, -iest**) (*clothes*) étriqué; (*meal*) insuffisant.

skin [skɪn] *n* peau *f*; **he has thick s.** *Fig* c'est un dur; **s. diving** plongée *f* sous-marine; **s. test** cuti(-réaction) *f*; – *vt* (**-nn-**) (*animal*) écorcher; (*fruit*) peler. ◆**s.-'deep** *a* superficiel. ◆**s.-'tight** *a* moulant, collant.

skinflint ['skɪnflɪnt] *n* avare *mf*.

skinhead ['skɪnhed] *n* skinhead *m*, jeune voyou *m*.

skinny ['skɪnɪ] *a* (**-ier, -iest**) maigre.

skint [skɪnt] *a* (*penniless*) *Fam* fauché.

skip¹ [skɪp] **1** *vi* (**-pp-**) (*jump*) sauter; (*hop about*) sautiller; (*with rope*) sauter à la corde; **to s. off** (*leave*) *Fam* filer; **skipping rope** corde *f* à sauter; – *n* petit saut *m*. **2** *vt* (**-pp-**) (*omit, miss*) sauter; **to s. classes** sécher les cours; **s. it!** (*forget it*) *Fam* laisse tomber!

skip² [skɪp] *n* (*container for debris*) benne *f*.

skipper ['skɪpər] *n Nau Sp* capitaine *m*.

skirmish ['skɜːmɪʃ] *n* accrochage *m*.

skirt [skɜːt] **1** *n* jupe *f*. **2** *vt* **to s. round** contourner; **skirting board** (*on wall*) plinthe *f*.

skit [skɪt] *n Th* pièce *f* satirique; **a s. on** une parodie de.

skittle ['skɪt(ə)l] *n* quille *f*; *pl* (*game*) jeu *m* de quilles.

skiv/e [skaɪv] *vi* (*skirk*) *Fam* tirer au flanc; **to s. off** (*slip away*) *Fam* se défiler. ◆**-er** *n Fam* tire-au-flanc *m inv*.

skivvy ['skɪvɪ] *n Pej Fam* bonne *f* à tout faire, bon(n)iche *f*.

skulk [skʌlk] *vi* rôder (furtivement).

skull [skʌl] *n* crâne *m*. ◆**skullcap** *n* calotte *f*.

skunk [skʌŋk] *n* (*animal*) mouffette *f*; (*person*) *Pej* salaud *m*.

sky [skaɪ] *n* ciel *m*. ◆**skydiving** *n* parachutisme *m* en chute libre. ◆**sky-'high** *a* (*prices*) exorbitant. ◆**skylight** *n* lucarne *f*. ◆**skyline** *n* (*outline of buildings*) ligne *f* d'horizon. ◆**skyrocket** *vi* (*of prices*) *Fam* monter en flèche. ◆**skyscraper** *n* gratte-ciel *m inv*.

slab [slæb] *n* (*of concrete etc*) bloc *m*; (*thin, flat*) plaque *f*; (*of chocolate*) tablette *f*, plaque *f*; (*paving stone*) dalle *f*.

slack [slæk] *a* (**-er, -est**) (*knot, spring*) lâche; (*discipline, security*) relâché, lâche; (*trade, grip*) faible, mou; (*negligent*) négligent; (*worker, student*) peu sérieux; **s. periods**

(*weeks etc*) périodes *fpl* creuses; (*hours*) heures *fpl* creuses; **to be s.** (*of rope*) avoir du mou; – *vi* **to s. off** (*in effort*) se relâcher. ◆**slacken** *vi* **to s. (off)** (*in effort*) se relâcher; (*of production, speed, zeal*) diminuer; – *vt* **to s. (off)** (*rope*) relâcher; (*pace, effort*) ralentir. ◆**slacker** *n* (*person*) *Fam* flemmard, -arde *mf*. ◆**slackly** *adv* (*loosely*) lâchement. ◆**slackness** *n* négligence *f*; (*of dealings*) relâchement *m*; (*of rope*) mou *m*; *Com* stagnation *f*.

slacks [slæks] *npl* pantalon *m*.

slag [slæg] *n* (*immoral woman*) *Sl* salope *f*, traînée *f*.

slagheap ['slæghiːp] *n* terril *m*.

slake [sleɪk] *vt* (*thirst*) *Lit* étancher.

slalom ['slɑːləm] *n Sp* slalom *m*.

slam [slæm] **1** *vt* (**-mm-**) (*door, lid*) claquer; (*hit*) frapper violemment; **to s. (down)** (*put down*) poser violemment; **to s. on the brakes** écraser le frein, freiner à bloc; – *vi* (*of door*) claquer; – *n* claquement *m*. **2** *vt* (**-mm-**) (*criticize*) *Fam* critiquer (avec virulence).

slander ['slɑːndər] *n* diffamation *f*, calomnie *f*; – *vt* diffamer, calomnier.

slang [slæŋ] *n* argot *m*; – *a* (*word etc*) d'argot, argotique. ◆**slanging match** *n Fam* engueulade *f*.

slant [slɑːnt] *n* inclinaison *f*; (*point of view*) *Fig* angle *m* (**on** sur); (*bias*) *Fig* parti-pris *m*; **on a s.** penché; (*roof*) en pente; – *vi* (*of writing*) pencher; (*of roof*) être en pente; – *vt* (*writing*) faire pencher; (*news*) *Fig* présenter de façon partiale. ◆**-ed**, ◆**-ing** *a* penché; (*roof*) en pente.

slap [slæp] *n* tape *f*, claque *f*; (*on face*) gifle *f*; – *vt* (**-pp-**) donner une tape à; **to s. s.o.'s face** gifler qn; **to s. s.o.'s bottom** donner une fessée à qn. **2** *vt* (**-pp-**) (*put*) mettre, flanquer; **to s.** (*on*) (*apply*) appliquer à la va-vite; (*add*) ajouter. **3** *adv* **s. in the middle** *Fam* en plein milieu. ◆**slapdash** *a* (*person*) négligent; (*task*) fait à la va-vite; – *adv* à la va-vite. ◆**slaphappy** *a Fam* (*carefree*) insouciant; (*negligent*) négligent. ◆**slapstick** *a* & *n* **s.** (*comedy*) grosse farce *f*. ◆**slap-up 'meal** *n Fam* gueuleton *m*.

slash [slæʃ] **1** *vt* (*cut with blade etc*) entailler, taillader; (*sever*) trancher; – *n* entaille *f*, taillade *f*. **2** *vt* (*reduce*) réduire radicalement; (*prices*) *Com* écraser.

slat [slæt] *n* (*in blind*) lamelle *f*.

slate [sleɪt] **1** *n* ardoise *f*. **2** *vt* (*book etc*) *Fam* critiquer, démolir.

slaughter ['slɔːtər] *vt* (*people*) massacrer;

(*animal*) abattre; – *n* massacre *m*; abattage *m*. ◆**slaughterhouse** *n* abattoir *m*.

Slav [slɑːv] *a* & *n* slave (*mf*). ◆**Sla′vonic** *a* (*language*) slave.

slave [sleɪv] *n* esclave *mf*; **the s. trade** *Hist* la traite des noirs; **s. driver** *Fig Pej* négrier *m*; – *vi* **to s. (away)** se crever (au travail), bosser comme une bête; **to s. away doing** s'escrimer à faire. ◆**slavery** *n* esclavage *m*. ◆**slavish** *a* servile.

slaver ['slævər] *vi* (*dribble*) baver (**over** sur); – *n* bave *f*.

slay [sleɪ] *vt* (*pt* **slew**, *pp* **slain**) *Lit* tuer.

sleazy ['sliːzɪ] *a* (**-ier, -iest**) *Fam* sordide, immonde.

sledge [sledʒ] (*Am* **sled** [sled]) *n* luge *f*; (*horse-drawn*) traîneau *m*.

sledgehammer ['sledʒhæmər] *n* masse *f*.

sleek [sliːk] *a* (**-er, -est**) lisse, brillant; (*manner*) onctueux.

sleep [sliːp] *n* sommeil *m*; **to have a s., get some s.** dormir; **to send to s.** endormir; **to go** *or* **get to s.** s'endormir; **to go to s.** (*of arm, foot*) *Fam* s'engourdir; – *vi* (*pt* & *pp* **slept**) dormir; (*spend the night*) coucher; **to s. tight** *or* **well!** dors bien!; **I'll s. on it** *Fig* je déciderai demain, la nuit portera conseil; – *vt* **this room sleeps six** on peut coucher *or* loger six personnes dans cette chambre; **to s. it off** *Fam*, **s. off a hangover** cuver son vin. ◆**-ing** *a* (*asleep*) endormi; **s. bag** sac *m* de couchage; **s. car** wagon-lit *m*; **s. pill** somnifère *m*; **s. quarters** chambre(s) *f*(*pl*); dortoir *m*. ◆**sleeper** *n* **1** **to be a light/sound s.** avoir le sommeil léger/lourd. **2** *Rail* (*on track*) traverse *f*; (*berth*) couchette *f*; (*train*) train *m* couchettes. ◆**sleepiness** *n* torpeur *f*. ◆**sleepless** *a* (*hours*) sans sommeil; (*night*) d'insomnie. ◆**sleepwalker** *n* somnambule *mf*. ◆**sleepwalking** *n* somnambulisme *m*. ◆**sleepy** *a* (**-ier, -iest**) (*town, voice*) endormi; **to be s.** (*of person*) avoir sommeil.

sleet [sliːt] *n* neige *f* fondue; (*sheet of ice*) *Am* verglas *m*; – *vi* **it's sleeting** il tombe de la neige fondue.

sleeve [sliːv] *n* (*of shirt etc*) manche *f*; (*of record*) pochette *f*; **up one's s.** (*surprise, idea etc*) *Fig* en réserve; **long-/short-sleeved** à manches longues/courtes.

sleigh [sleɪ] *n* traîneau *m*.

sleight [slaɪt] *n* **s. of hand** prestidigitation *f*.

slender ['slendər] *a* (*person*) mince, svelte; (*neck, hand*) fin; (*feeble, small*) *Fig* faible.

slept [slept] *see* **sleep.**

sleuth [sluːθ] *n* (*detective*) *Hum* (fin) limier *m*.

slew [sluː] *n* **a s. of** *Am Fam* un tas de, une tapée de.

slice [slaɪs] *n* tranche *f*; (*portion*) *Fig* partie *f*, part *f*; – *vt* **to s. (up)** couper (en tranches); **to s. off** (*cut off*) couper.

slick [slɪk] *a* **1** (**-er, -est**) (*glib*) qui a la parole facile; (*manner*) mielleux; (*cunning*) astucieux; (*smooth, slippery*) lisse. **2** *n* **oil s.** nappe *f* de pétrole; (*large*) marée *f* noire.

slid/e [slaɪd] *n* (*act*) glissade *f*; (*in value etc*) *Fig* (légère) baisse *f*; (*in playground*) toboggan *m*; (*on ice*) glissoire *f*; (*for hair*) barrette *f*; *Phot* diapositive *f*; (*of microscope*) lamelle *f*, lame *f*; **s. rule** règle *f* à calcul; – *vi* (*pt* & *pp* **slid**) glisser; **to s. into** (*room etc*) se glisser dans; – *vt* (*letter etc*) glisser (**into** dans); (*table etc*) faire glisser. ◆**-ing** *a* (*door, panel*) à glissière; (*roof*) ouvrant; **s. scale** *Com* échelle *f* mobile.

slight [slaɪt] *a* **1** (**-er, -est**) (*slim*) mince, (*frail*) frêle; (*intelligence*) faible; **the slightest thing** la moindre chose; **not in the slightest** pas le moins du monde. **2** *vt* (*offend*) offenser; (*ignore*) bouder; – *n* affront *m* (**on** à). ◆**-ly** *adv* légèrement, un peu; **s. built** fluet.

slim [slɪm] *a* (**slimmer, slimmest**) mince; – *vi* (**-mm-**) maigrir. ◆**slimming** *a* (*diet*) amaigrissant; (*food*) qui ne fait pas grossir. ◆**slimness** *n* minceur *f*.

slime [slaɪm] *n* boue *f* (visqueuse); (*of snail*) bave *f*. ◆**slimy** *a* (**-ier, -iest**) (*muddy*) boueux; (*sticky, smarmy*) visqueux.

sling [slɪŋ] **1** *n* (*weapon*) fronde *f*; (*toy*) lance-pierres *m* inv; (*for arm*) *Med* écharpe *f*; **in a s.** en écharpe. **2** *vt* (*pt* & *pp* **slung**) (*throw*) jeter, lancer; (*hang*) suspendre; **to s. away** *or* **out** (*throw out*) *Fam* balancer. ◆**slingshot** *n Am* lance-pierres *m* inv.

slip [slɪp] **1** *n* (*mistake*) erreur *f*; (*woman's undergarment*) combinaison *f*; (*of paper for filing*) fiche *f*; **a s. of paper** (*bit*) un bout de papier; **a s. (of the tongue)** un lapsus; **to give s.o. the s.** fausser compagnie à qn; **s. road** *Aut* bretelle *f*. **2** *vi* (**-pp-**) glisser; **to s. into** (*go, put*) se glisser dans; (*habit*) prendre; (*garment*) mettre; **to let s.** (*chance, oath, secret*) laisser échapper; **to s. through** (*crowd*) se faufiler parmi; **to s. along** *or* **over to** faire un saut chez; **to s. away** (*escape*) s'esquiver; **to s. back/in** retourner/entrer furtivement; **to s. out** sortir furtivement; (*pop out*) sortir (un instant); (*of secret*) s'éventer; **to s. past** (*guards*) passer sans être vu de; **to s. up** (*make a* *mistake*) *Fam* gaffer; – *vt* (*slide*) glisser (**to à**, **into** dans); **it slipped his** *or* **her notice** ça lui a échappé; **it slipped his** *or* **her mind** ça lui est sorti de l'esprit; **to s. off** (*garment etc*) enlever; **to s. on** (*garment etc*) mettre. ◆**s.-up** *n Fam* gaffe *f*, erreur *f*.

slipcover ['slɪpkʌvər] *n Am* housse *f*.

slipper ['slɪpər] *n* pantoufle *f*.

slippery ['slɪpərɪ] *a* glissant.

slipshod ['slɪpʃɒd] *a* (*negligent*) négligent; (*slovenly*) négligé.

slit [slɪt] *n* (*opening*) fente *f*; (*cut*) coupure *f*; – *vt* (*pt & pp* **slit**, *pres p* **slitting**) (*cut*) couper; (*tear*) déchirer; **to s. open** (*sack*) éventrer.

slither ['slɪðər] *vi* glisser; (*of snake*) se couler.

sliver ['slɪvər] *n* (*of apple etc*) lichette *f*; (*of wood*) éclat *m*.

slob [slɒb] *n Fam* malotru *m*, goujat *m*.

slobber ['slɒbər] *vi* (*of dog etc*) baver (**over** sur); – *n* bave *f*.

slog [slɒg] **1** *n* a (*hard*) **s.** (*effort*) un gros effort; (*work*) un travail dur; – *vi* (**-gg-**) **to s.** (**away**) bosser, trimer. **2** *vt* (**-gg-**) (*hit*) donner un grand coup à.

slogan ['slaʊgən] *n* slogan *m*.

slop [slɒp] *n* **slops** eaux *fpl* sales; – *vi* (**-pp-**) **to s.** (**over**) (*spill*) se répandre; – *vt* répandre.

slop/e [slaʊp] *n* pente *f*; (*of mountain*) flanc *m*; (*slant*) inclinaison *f*; – *vi* être en pente; (*of handwriting*) pencher; **to s. down** descendre en pente. ◆**—ing** *a* en pente; (*handwriting*) penché.

sloppy ['slɒpɪ] *a* (**-ier, -iest**) (*work, appearance*) négligé; (*person*) négligent; (*mawkish*) sentimental; (*wet*) détrempé; (*watery*) liquide.

slosh [slɒʃ] *vt* (*pour*) *Fam* répandre. ◆**—ed** *a* (*drunk*) *Fam* bourré.

slot [slɒt] *n* (*slit*) fente *f*; (*groove*) rainure *f*; (*in programme*) *Rad TV* créneau *m*; **s. machine** (*vending*) distributeur *m* automatique; (*gambling*) machine *f* à sous; – *vt* (**-tt-**) (*insert*) insérer (**into** dans); – *vi* s'insérer (**into** dans).

sloth [slaʊθ] *n Lit* paresse *f*.

slouch [slaʊtʃ] **1** *vi* ne pas se tenir droit; (*have stoop*) avoir le dos voûté; (*in chair*) se vautrer (**in** dans); **slouching over** (*desk etc*) penché sur; – *vi* à mauvaise tenue *f*; **with a s.** (*to walk*) en se tenant mal; le dos voûté. **2** *n Fam* (*person*) lourdaud, -aude *mf*; (*lazy*) paresseux, -euse *mf*.

slovenly ['slʌvənlɪ] *a* négligé. ◆**slovenli-**

ness *n* (*of dress*) négligé *m*; (*carelessness*) négligence *f*.

slow [slaʊ] *a* (**-er, -est**) lent; (*business*) calme; (*party, event*) ennuyeux; **at (a) s. speed** à vitesse réduite; **to be a s. walker** marcher lentement; **to be s.** (*of clock, watch*) retarder; **to be five minutes s.** retarder de cinq minutes; **to be s. to act** *or* **in acting** être lent à agir; **in s. motion** au ralenti; – *adv* lentement; – *vt* **to s. down** *or* **up** ralentir; (*delay*) retarder; – *vi* **to s. down** *or* **up** ralentir. ◆**—ly** *adv* lentement; (*bit by bit*) peu à peu. ◆**—ness** *n* lenteur *f*.

slowcoach ['slaʊkaʊtʃ] *n Fam* lambin, -ine *mf*. ◆**slow-down** *n* ralentissement *m*; **s.-down** (*strike*) *Am* grève *f* perlée. ◆**slow-'moving** *a* (*vehicle etc*) lent.

sludge [slʌdʒ] *n* gadoue *f*.

slue [slu:] *n Am Fam* = **slew**.

slug [slʌg] **1** *n* (*mollusc*) limace *f*. **2** *n* (*bullet*) *Am Sl* pruneau *m*. **3** *vt* (**-gg-**) (*hit*) *Am Fam* frapper; – *n* coup *m*, marron *m*.

sluggish ['slʌgɪʃ] *a* lent, mou.

sluice [slu:s] *n* **s.** (**gate**) vanne *f*.

slum [slʌm] *n* (*house*) taudis *m*; **the slums** les quartiers *mpl* pauvres; – *a* (*district*) pauvre; – *vt* (**-mm-**) **to s. it** *Fam* manger de la vache enragée. ◆**slummy** *a* (**-ier, -iest**) sordide, pauvre.

slumber ['slʌmbər] *n Lit* sommeil *m*.

slump [slʌmp] *n* baisse *f* soudaine (**in** de); (*in prices*) effondrement *m*; *Econ* crise *f*; – *vi* (*decrease*) baisser; (*of prices*) s'effondrer; **to s. into** (*armchair etc*) s'affaisser dans.

slung [slʌŋ] *see* **sling 2**.

slur [slɜːr] *vt* (**-rr-**) prononcer indistinctement; **to s. one's words** manger ses mots. **2** *n* **to cast a s. on** (*reputation etc*) porter atteinte à. ◆**slurred** *a* (*speech*) indistinct.

slush [slʌʃ] *n* (*snow*) neige *f* fondue; (*mud*) gadoue *f*. ◆**slushy** *a* (**-ier, -iest**) (*road*) couvert de neige fondue.

slut [slʌt] *n Pej* (*immoral*) salope *f*, traînée *f*; (*untidy*) souillon *f*.

sly [slaɪ] *a* (**-er, -est**) (*deceitful*) sournois; (*crafty*) rusé; – *n* **on the s.** en cachette. ◆**—ly** *adv* sournoisement; (*in secret*) en cachette.

smack [smæk] **1** *n* claque *f*; gifle *f*; fessée *f*; – *vt* donner une claque à; **to s. s.o.'s face** gifler qn; **to s. s.o.('s bottom)** donner une fessée à qn. **2** *adv* **s. in the middle** *Fam* en plein milieu. **3** *vi* **to s. of** (*be suggestive of*) avoir des relents de. ◆**—ing** *n* fessée *f*.

small [smɔːl] *a* (**-er, -est**) petit; **in the s. hours** au petit matin; **s. talk** menus propos mpl; – adv (to cut, chop) menu; – n **the s. of the back** le creux m des reins. ◆**-ness** n petitesse f. ◆**smallholding** n petite ferme f. ◆**small-scale** a Fig peu important. ◆**small-time** a (crook, dealer etc) petit, sans grande envergure.

smallpox ['smɔːlpɒks] n petite vérole f.

smarmy ['smɑːmɪ] a (-ier, -iest) Pej Fam visqueux, obséquieux.

smart¹ [smɑːt] a (-er, -est) (in appearance) élégant; (astute) astucieux; (clever) intelligent; (quick) rapide; **s. aleck** Fam je-sais-tout mf inv. ◆**smarten** vt **s. up** (room etc) embellir; – vti **to s. (oneself) up** (make oneself spruce) se faire beau, s'arranger. ◆**smartly** adv élégamment; (quickly) en vitesse; (astutely) astucieusement. ◆**smartness** n élégance f.

smart² [smɑːt] vi (sting) brûler, faire mal.

smash [smæʃ] vt (break) briser; (shatter) fracasser; (enemy) écraser; (record) pulvériser; **to s. s.o.'s face (in)** Fam casser la gueule à qn; **to s. down** or **in** (door) fracasser; **to s. up** (car) esquinter; (room) démolir; – vi se briser; **to s. into** (of car) se fracasser contre; – n (noise) fracas m; (blow) coup m; (accident) collision f; **s. hit** Fam succès m fou. ◆**s.-up** n collision f.

smashing ['smæʃɪŋ] a (wonderful) Fam formidable. ◆**smasher** n **to be a (real) s.** Fam être formidable.

smattering ['smætərɪŋ] n **a s. of** (French etc) quelques notions fpl de.

smear [smɪər] vt (coat) enduire (with de); (stain) tacher (with de); (smudge) faire une trace sur; – n (mark) trace f; (stain) tache f; Med frottis m; **a s. on** (attack) Fig une atteinte à; **s. campaign** campagne f de diffamation.

smell [smel] n odeur f; (sense of) **s.** odorat m; – vt (pt & pp smelled or smelt) sentir; (of animal) flairer; – vi (stink) sentir (mauvais); (have smell) avoir une odeur; **to s. of smoke/etc** sentir la fumée/etc; **smelling salts** sels mpl. ◆**smelly** a (-ier, -iest) **to be s.** sentir (mauvais).

smelt¹ [smelt] see smell.

smelt² [smelt] vt (ore) fondre; **smelting works** fonderie f.

smidgen ['smɪdʒən] n **a s.** (a little) Am Fam un brin (of de).

smile [smaɪl] n sourire m; – vi sourire (at s.o. à qn; at sth de qch). ◆**-ing** a souriant.

smirk [smɜːk] n (smug) sourire m suffisant; (scornful) sourire m goguenard.

smith [smɪθ] n (blacksmith) forgeron m.

smithereens [smɪðəˈriːnz] npl **to smash to s.** briser en mille morceaux f.

smitten ['smɪt(ə)n] a **s. with** Hum (desire, remorse) pris de; (in love with) épris de.

smock [smɒk] n blouse f.

smog [smɒg] n brouillard m épais, smog m.

smoke [sməʊk] n fumée f; **to have a s.** fumer une cigarette etc; – vt (cigarette, salmon etc) fumer; **to s. out** (room etc) enfumer; – vi fumer; **'no smoking'** 'défense de fumer'; **smoking compartment** Rail compartiment m fumeurs. ◆**smokeless** a **s. fuel** combustible m non polluant. ◆**smoker** n fumeur, -euse mf; Rail compartiment m fumeurs. ◆**smoky** a (-ier, -iest) (air) enfumé; (wall) noirci de fumée; **it's s. here** il y a de la fumée ici.

smooth [smuːð] a (-er, -est) (surface, skin etc) lisse; (road) à la surface égale; (movement) régulier, sans à-coups; (flight) agréable; (cream, manners) onctueux; (person) doucereux; (sea) calme; **the s. running** (of de); – vt **to s. down** or **out** lisser; **to s. out** or **over** (problems etc) Fig aplanir. ◆**-ly** adv (to land, pass off) en douceur. ◆**-ness** n aspect m lisse; (of road) surface f égale.

smother ['smʌðər] vt (stifle) étouffer; **to s. with** (kisses etc) Fig couvrir de.

smoulder ['sməʊldər] vi (of fire, passion etc) couver.

smudge [smʌdʒ] n tache f, bavure f; – vt (paper etc) faire des taches sur, salir.

smug [smʌg] a (smugger, smuggest) (smile etc) béat; (person) content de soi, suffisant. ◆**-ly** adv avec suffisance.

smuggl/e ['smʌg(ə)l] vt passer (en fraude); **smuggled goods** contrebande f. ◆**-ing** n contrebande f. ◆**-er** n contrebandier, -ière mf.

smut [smʌt] n inv (obscenity) saleté(s) f(pl). ◆**smutty** a (-ier, -iest) (joke etc) cochon.

snack [snæk] n casse-croûte m inv; **s. bar** snack(-bar) m.

snafu [snæˈfuː] n Sl embrouillamini m.

snag [snæg] n **1** (hitch) inconvénient m, os m. **2** (in cloth) accroc m.

snail [sneɪl] n escargot m; **at a s.'s pace** comme une tortue.

snake [sneɪk] n (reptile) serpent m; – vi (of river) serpenter.

snap [snæp] **1** vt (-pp-) casser (avec un bruit sec); (fingers, whip) faire claquer; **to s. up a bargain** sauter sur une occasion; – vi se casser net; (of whip) claquer; (of person) Fig parler sèchement (at à); **s. out of it!** Fam secoue-toi!; – n claquement m, bruit *m sec*; *Phot* photo *f*; (*fastener*) *Am* bouton-pression *m*; **cold s.** Met coup *m* de froid. **2 a** soudain, brusque; **to make a s. decision** décider sans réfléchir. ◆**snapshot** *n* photo *f*, instantané *m*.

snappy ['snæpɪ] *a* (**-ier, -iest**) (*pace*) vif; **make it s.!** Fam dépêche-toi!

snare [sneər] *n* piège *m*.

snarl [snɑːl] *vi* gronder (en montrant les dents); – *n* grondement *m*. ◆**s.-up** *n Aut Fam* embouteillage *m*.

snatch [snætʃ] *vt* saisir (*d'un geste vif*); (*some rest etc*) *Fig* (réussir à) prendre; **to s. sth from s.o.** arracher qch à qn; – *n* (*theft*) vol *m* (à l'arraché).

snatches ['snætʃɪz] *npl* (*bits*) fragments *mpl* (of de).

snazzy ['snæzɪ] *a* (**-ier, -iest**) *Fam* (*flashy*) tapageur; (*smart*) élégant.

sneak [sniːk] **1** *vi* **to s. in/out** entrer/sortir furtivement; **to s. off** s'esquiver; – *a* (*attack, visit*) furtif. **2** *n* (*telltale*) *Sch Fam* rapporteur, -euse *mf*; – *vi* **to s. on s.o.** *Sch Fam* dénoncer. ◆**sneaking** *a* (*suspicion*) vague; (*desire*) secret. ◆**sneaky** *a* (**-ier, -iest**) (*sly*) *Fam* sournois.

sneaker ['sniːkər] *n* (*shoe*) tennis *f*.

sneer [snɪər] *n* ricanement *m*; – *vi* ricaner; **to s. at** se moquer de.

sneeze [sniːz] *n* éternuement *m*; – *vi* éternuer.

snicker ['snɪkər] *n & vi Am* = **snigger**.

snide [snaɪd] *a* (*remark etc*) sarcastique.

sniff [snɪf] *n* reniflement *m*; – *vt* renifler; (*of dog*) flairer, renifler; **to s. out** (*bargain*) *Fig* renifler; – *vi* **to s. (at)** renifler. ◆**sniffle** *vi* renifler; – *n* **s., the sniffles** *Fam* un petit rhume.

snigger ['snɪgər] *n* (petit) ricanement *m*; – *vi* ricaner. ◆**-ing** *n* ricanement(s) *m(pl)*.

snip [snɪp] *n* (*piece*) petit bout *m* (coupé); (*bargain*) *Fam* bonne affaire *f*; **to make a s.** couper; – *vt* (**-pp-**) couper.

sniper ['snaɪpər] *n Mil* tireur *m* embusqué.

snippet ['snɪpɪt] *n* (*of conversation etc*) bribe *f*.

snivel ['snɪv(ə)l] *vi* (**-ll-, Am -l-**) pleurnicher. ◆**snivelling** *a* pleurnicheur.

snob [snɒb] *n* snob *mf*. ◆**snobbery** *n* snobisme *m*. ◆**snobbish** *a* snob *inv*.

snook [snuːk] *n* **to cock a s.** faire un pied de nez (**at** à).

snooker ['snuːkər] *n* snooker *m*, sorte de jeu de billard.

snoop [snuːp] *vi* fouiner son nez partout; **to s. on s.o.** (*spy on*) espionner qn.

snooty ['snuːtɪ] *a* (**-ier, -iest**) *Fam* snob *inv*.

snooze [snuːz] *n* petit somme *m*; – *vi* faire un petit somme.

snor/e [snɔːr] *vi* ronfler; – *n* ronflement *m*. ◆**-ing** *n* ronflements *mpl*.

snorkel ['snɔːk(ə)l] *n Sp Nau* tuba *m*.

snort [snɔːt] *vi* (*grunt*) grogner; (*sniff*) renifler; (*of horse*) renâcler; – *n* (*grunt*) grognement *m*.

snot [snɒt] *n Pej Fam* morve *f*. ◆**snotty** *a* (**-ier, -iest**) *Fam* (*nose*) qui coule; (*child*) morveux. ◆**snotty-nosed** *a Fam* morveux.

snout [snaʊt] *n* museau *m*.

snow [snəʊ] *n* neige *f*; – *vi* neiger; – *vt* **to be snowed in** être bloqué par la neige; **to be s. under with** (*work etc*) être submergé de. ◆**snowball** *n* boule *f* de neige; – *vi* (*increase*) faire boule de neige. ◆**snowbound** *a* bloqué par la neige. ◆**snow-capped** *a* (*mountain*) enneigé. ◆**snowdrift** *n* congère *f*. ◆**snowdrop** *n Bot* perce-neige *m or f inv*. ◆**snowfall** *n* chute *f* de neige. ◆**snowflake** *n* flocon *m* de neige. ◆**snowman** *n* (*pl* **-men**) bonhomme *m* de neige. ◆**snowmobile** *n* motoneige *f*. ◆**snowplough** *n*, *Am* ◆**snowplow** *n* chasse-neige *m inv*. ◆**snowstorm** *n* tempête *f* de neige. ◆**snowy** *a* (**-ier, -iest**) (*weather, hills, day etc*) neigeux.

snub [snʌb] **1** *n* rebuffade *f*; – *vt* (**-bb-**) (*offer etc*) rejeter; **to s. s.o.** snober qn. **2** *a* (*nose*) retroussé.

snuff [snʌf] **1** *n* tabac *m* à priser. **2** *vt* **to s. (out)** (*candle*) moucher. ◆**snuffbox** *n* tabatière *f*.

snuffle ['snʌf(ə)l] *vi & n* = **sniffle**.

snug [snʌg] *a* (**snugger, snuggest**) (*house etc*) confortable, douillet; (*garment*) bien ajusté; **we're s.** (*in chair etc*) on est bien; **s. in bed** bien au chaud dans son lit.

snuggle ['snʌg(ə)l] *vi* **to s. up to** se pelotonner contre.

so [səʊ] **1** *adv* (*to such a degree*) si, tellement (*that* que); (*thus*) ainsi, comme ça; **so that** (*purpose*) pour que (+ *sub*); (*result*) si bien que; **so as to do** pour faire; **I think so** je le pense, je pense que oui; **do so!** faites-le!; **if so si** si oui; **is that so?** c'est vrai?; **so am I, so do I** *etc* moi aussi; **so much** (*to work etc*) tant, tellement (**that** que); (*such courage/etc*) tant *or* tellement de courage/*etc* (**that** que); **so many** tant, tellement; **so many books**/*etc* tant *or* tellement de livres/*etc* (**that** que); **so very fast**/*etc* vraiment si vite/*etc*; **ten or so** environ dix; **so long!** *Fam* au revoir!; **and so on et** ainsi de suite. **2** *conj (therefore)* donc; *(in that case)* alors; so what? et alors? ◆**So-and-so** *n* Mr So-and-so Monsieur Un tel. ◆**so-'called** *a* soi-disant *inv.* ◆**so-so** *a Fam* comme ci comme ça.

soak [səʊk] *vt (drench)* tremper; *(washing, food)* faire tremper; *(of liquid)* absorber; – *vi (of washing etc)* tremper; **to s. up** absorber; – *vi (of washing etc)* tremper; **to s. in** *(of liquid)* s'infiltrer; – *vt* **to give sth a s.** faire tremper qch. ◆**–ed** *a* **s. (through)** trempé (jusqu'aux os). ◆**–ing** *a* & *adv* **s. (wet)** trempé; – *n* trempage *m.*

soap [səʊp] *n* savon *m*; **s. opera** téléroman *m*; **s. powder** lessive *f*; – *vt* savonner. ◆**soapflakes** *npl* savon *m* en paillettes. ◆**soapsuds** *npl* mousse *f* de savon. ◆**soapy** *a* (**-ier, -iest**) savonneux.

soar [sɔːr] *vi (of bird etc)* s'élever; *(of price)* monter (en flèche); *(of hope)* Fig grandir.

sob [sɒb] *n* sanglot *m*; – *vi* (**-bb-**) sangloter. ◆**sobbing** *n (sobs)* sanglots *mpl.*

sober ['səʊbər] **1** *a* he's **s.** *(not drunk)* il n'est pas ivre; – *vti* **to s. up** dessoûler. **2** *a (serious)* sérieux, sensé; *(meal, style)* sobre. ◆**–ly** *adv* sobrement.

soccer ['sɒkər] *n* football *m.*

sociable ['səʊʃəb(ə)l] *a (person)* sociable; *(evening)* amical. ◆**sociably** *adv (to act, reply)* aimablement.

social ['səʊʃəl] *a* social; *(life, gathering)* mondain; **s. club** foyer *m*; **s. science(s)** sciences *fpl* humaines; **s. security** *(aid)* aide *f* sociale; *(retirement pension) Am* pension *f* de retraite; **s. services** = sécurité *f* sociale; **s. worker** assistant *m* social; – *n (gathering)* réunion *f* (amicale). ◆**socialism** *n* socialisme *m.* ◆**socialist** *a* & *n* socialiste *(mf).* ◆**socialite** *n* mondain, -aine *mf.* ◆**socialize** *vi (mix)* se mêler aux autres; *(talk)* bavarder (with avec). ◆**socially** *adv* socialement; *(to meet s.o., behave)* en société.

society [sə'saɪətɪ] *n (community, club, companionship etc)* société *f*; *Univ Sch* club *m*; – *a (wedding etc)* mondain.

sociology [səʊsɪ'ɒlədʒɪ] *n* sociologie *f.* ◆**socio'logical** *a* sociologique. ◆**sociologist** *n* sociologue *mf.*

sock [sɒk] **1** *n* chaussette *f.* **2** *vt (hit) Sl* flanquer un marron à.

socket ['sɒkɪt] *n (of bone)* cavité *f*; *(of eye)* orbite *f*; *(power point) El* prise *f* de courant; *(of lamp)* douille *f.*

sod [sɒd] *n (turf) Am* gazon *m.*

soda ['səʊdə] *n* **1** *Ch* soude *f*; **washing s.** cristaux *mpl* de soude. **2** *(water)* eau *f* de Seltz; **s. (pop)** *Am* soda *m.*

sodden ['sɒd(ə)n] *a (ground)* détrempé.

sodium ['səʊdɪəm] *n Ch* sodium *m.*

sofa ['səʊfə] *n* canapé *m*, divan *m*; **s. bed** canapé-lit *m.*

soft [sɒft] *a* (**-er, -est**) *(smooth, gentle, supple)* doux; *(butter, ground, snow)* mou; *(wood, heart, paste, colour)* tendre; *(flabby)* flasque, mou; *(easy)* facile; *(indulgent)* indulgent; *(cowardly) Fam* poltron; *(stupid) Fam* ramolli; **it's too s.** *(radio etc)* ce n'est pas assez fort; **s. drink** boisson *f* non alcoolisée. ◆**s.-'boiled** *a (egg)* à la coque. ◆**soften** ['sɒf(ə)n] *vt (object)* ramollir; *(voice, pain, colour)* adoucir; – *vi* se ramollir; s'adoucir. ◆**softie** *n Fam* sentimental, -ale *mf*; *(weakling)* mauviette *f.* ◆**softly** *adv* doucement. ◆**softness** *n* douceur *f*; *(of butter, ground, snow)* mollesse *f.*

software ['sɒftweər] *n inv (of computer)* logiciel *m.*

soggy ['sɒgɪ] *a* (**-ier, -iest**) *(ground)* détrempé; *(biscuit, bread)* ramolli.

soil [sɔɪl] **1** *n (earth)* sol *m*, terre *f.* **2** *vt (dirty)* salir; – *vi* se salir.

solar ['səʊlər] *a* solaire.

sold [səʊld] *see* sell.

solder ['sɒldər, *Am* 'sɒdər] *vt* souder; – *n* soudure *f.*

soldier ['səʊldʒər] **1** *n* soldat *m*, militaire *m.* **2** *vi* **to s. on** persévérer.

sole [səʊl] **1** *n (of shoe)* semelle *f*; *(of foot)* plante *f*; – *vt* ressemeler. **2** *a (only)* seul, unique; *(rights, representative) Com* exclusif. **3** *n (fish)* sole *f.* ◆**–ly** *adv* uniquement; **you're s. to blame** tu es seul coupable.

solemn ['sɒləm] *a (formal)* solennel; *(serious)* grave. ◆**so'lemnity** *n* solennité *f*; gravité *f.* ◆**solemnly** *adv (to promise)* solennellement; *(to say)* gravement.

solicit [sə'lɪsɪt] *vt (seek)* solliciter; – *vi (of prostitute)* racoler. ◆**solicitor** *n (for wills etc)* notaire *m.*

solid ['sɒlɪd] *a (car, character, meal etc)* & *Ch* solide; *(wall, line, ball)* plein; *(gold, rock)* massif; *(crowd, mass)* compact; **frozen s.** entièrement gelé; **ten days s.** dix jours d'affilée; – *n Ch* solide *m*; *pl Culin* aliments *mpl* solides. ◆**so'lidify** *vi* se solidifier. ◆**so'lidity** *n* solidité *f.* ◆**solidly** *adv (built etc)* solidement; *(to support, vote)* en masse.

solidarity [sɒlɪ'dærətɪ] *n* solidarité *f* (with avec).

soliloquy [sə'lɪləkwɪ] *n* monologue *m.*

solitary ['sɒlɪtərɪ] *a (lonely, alone)* solitaire;

(*only*) seul; **s. confinement** *Jur* isolement *m* (cellulaire). ◆**solitude** *n* solitude *f*.

solo ['səʊləʊ] *n* (*pl* -os) *Mus* solo *m*; – *a* solo *inv*; – *adv Mus* en solo; (*to fly*) en solitaire. ◆**soloist** *n Mus* soliste *mf*.

solstice ['sɒlstɪs] *n* solstice *m*.

soluble ['sɒljʊb(ə)l] *a* (*substance, problem*) soluble.

solution [sə'luːʃ(ə)n] *n* (*to problem etc*) & *Ch* solution *f* (*to* de).

solv/e [sɒlv] *vt* (*problem etc*) résoudre. ◆**–able** *a* soluble.

solvent ['sɒlvənt] **1** *a* (*financially*) solvable. **2** *n Ch* (dis)solvant *m*. ◆**solvency** *f Fin* solvabilité *f*.

sombre ['sɒmbər] *a* sombre, triste.

some [sʌm] *a* **1** (*amount, number*) **s. wine** du vin; **s. glue** de la colle; **s. water** de l'eau; **s. dogs** des chiens; **s. pretty flowers** de jolies fleurs. **2** (*unspecified*) un, une; **s. man** (*or other*) un homme (quelconque); **s. charm** (*a certain amount of*) un certain charme; **s. other way** quelque autre *or* un autre moyen; **that's s. book!** *Fam* ça, c'est un livre! **3** (*a few*) quelques, certains; (*a little*) un peu de; – *pron* **1** (*number*) quelques-un(e)s, certain(e)s (*of* de, d'entre). **2** (*a certain quantity*) en; **I want s.** j'en veux; **do you have s.?** en as-tu?; **s. of it is over** il en reste un peu *or* une partie; – *adv* (*about*) quelque; **s. ten years** quelque dix ans.

somebody ['sʌmbədɪ] *pron* = **someone**. ◆**someday** *adv* un jour. ◆**somehow** *adv* (*in some way*) d'une manière ou d'une autre; (*for some reason*) on ne sait pourquoi. ◆**someone** *pron* quelqu'un; **at s.'s house** chez qn; **s. small/etc** quelqu'un de petit/*etc*. ◆**someplace** *adv Am* quelque part. ◆**something** *pron* quelque chose; **s. awful/etc** quelque chose d'affreux/*etc*; **s. of a liar/etc** un menteur/*etc*; – *adv* **she plays s. like . . .** elle joue un peu comme . . . ; **it was s. awful** c'était vraiment affreux. ◆**sometime 1** *adv* un jour; **s. in May/etc** au cours du mois de mai/*etc*; **s. before his departure** avant son départ. **2** *a* (*former*) ancien. ◆**sometimes** *adv* quelquefois, parfois. ◆**somewhat** *adv* quelque peu, assez. ◆**somewhere** *adv* quelque part; **s. about fifteen** (*approximately*) environ quinze.

somersault ['sʌməsɔːlt] *n* culbute *f*; (*in air*) saut *m* périlleux; – *vi* faire la *or* une culbute.

son [sʌn] *n* fils *m*. ◆**s.-in-law** *n* (*pl* **sons-in-law**) beau-fils *m*, gendre *m*.

sonar ['səʊnɑːr] *n* sonar *m*.

sonata [sə'nɑːtə] *n Mus* sonate *f*.

song [sɒŋ] *n* chanson *f*; (*of bird*) chant *m*. ◆**songbook** *n* recueil *m* de chansons.

sonic ['sɒnɪk] *a* **s. boom** bang *m* (supersonique).

sonnet ['sɒnɪt] *n* (*poem*) sonnet *m*.

soon [suːn] *adv* (-**er**, -**est**) (*in a short time*) bientôt; (*quickly*) vite; (*early*) tôt; **s. after** peu après; **as s. as she leaves** aussitôt qu'elle partira; **no sooner had he spoken than** à peine avait-il parlé que; **I'd sooner leave** je préférerais partir; **I'd just as s. leave** j'aimerais autant partir; **sooner or later** tôt ou tard.

soot [sʊt] *n* suie *f*. ◆**sooty** *a* (-**ier**, -**iest**) couvert de suie.

sooth/e [suːð] *vt* (*pain, nerves*) calmer; *Fig* rassurer. ◆**–ing** *a* (*ointment, words*) calmant.

sophisticated [sə'fɪstɪkeɪtɪd] *a* (*person, taste*) raffiné; (*machine, method, beauty*) sophistiqué.

sophomore ['sɒfəmɔːr] *n Am* étudiant, -ante *mf* de seconde année.

soporific [sɒpə'rɪfɪk] *a* (*substance, speech etc*) soporifique.

sopping ['sɒpɪŋ] *a* (*wet*) trempé.

soppy ['sɒpɪ] *a* (-**ier**, -**iest**) *Fam* (*silly*) idiot, bête; (*sentimental*) sentimental.

soprano [sə'prɑːnəʊ] *n* (*pl* -os) *Mus* (*singer*) soprano *mf*; (*voice*) soprano *m*.

sorbet ['sɔːbeɪ] *n* (*water ice*) sorbet *m*.

sorcerer ['sɔːsərər] *n* sorcier *m*.

sordid ['sɔːdɪd] *a* (*act, street etc*) sordide.

sore [sɔːr] *a* (-**er**, -**est**) (*painful*) douloureux; (*angry*) *Am* fâché (at contre); **a s. point** *Fig* un sujet délicat; **she has a s. thumb** elle a mal au pouce; **he's still s.** *Med* il a encore mal; – *n Med* plaie *f*. ◆**–ly** *adv* (*tempted, regretted*) très; **s. needed** dont on a grand besoin. ◆**–ness** *n* (*pain*) douleur *f*.

sorrow ['sɒrəʊ] *n* chagrin *m*, peine *f*. ◆**sorrowful** *a* triste.

sorry ['sɒrɪ] *a* (-**ier**, -**iest**) (*sight, state etc*) triste; **to be s.** (*regret*) être désolé, regretter (**to do** de faire); **I'm s. she can't come** je regrette qu'elle ne puisse pas venir; **I'm s. about the delay** je m'excuse pour ce retard; **s.!** pardon!; **to say s.** demander pardon (**to** à); **to feel** *or* **be s. for** plaindre.

sort [sɔːt] **1** *n* genre *m*, espèce *f*, sorte *f*; **a s. of** une sorte *or* espèce de; **a good s.** (*person*) *Fam* un brave type; **s. of sad**/*etc* plutôt triste/*etc*. **2** *vt* (*letters*) trier; **to s. out** (*classify, select*) trier; (*separate*) séparer (**from** de); (*arrange*) arranger; (*tidy*) ranger; (*problem*) régler; **to s. s.o. out** (*punish*) *Fam* faire voir à qn; – *vi* **to s. through** (*letters etc*) trier; **sorting office** centre *m* de tri. **◆—er** *n* (*person*) trieur, -euse *mf*.

soufflé ['suːfleɪ] *n Culin* soufflé *m*.

sought [sɔːt] *see* **seek**.

soul [soʊl] *n* âme *f*; **not a living s.** (*nobody*) personne, pas âme qui vive; **a good s.** *Fig* un brave type; **s. mate** âme *f* sœur. **◆s.-destroying** *a* abrutissant. **◆s.-searching** *n* examen *m* de conscience.

sound[1] [saʊnd] *n* son *m*; (*noise*) bruit *m*; **I don't like the s. of it** ça ne me plaît pas du tout; – *a* (*wave, film*) sonore; (*engineer*) du son; **s. archives** phonothèque *f*; **s. barrier** mur *m* du son; **s. effects** bruitage *m*; – *vt* (*bell, alarm etc*) sonner; (*bugle*) sonner de; (*letter*) *Gram* prononcer; **to s. one's horn** *Aut* klaxonner; – *vi* retentir, sonner; (*seem*) sembler; **to s. like** sembler être; (*resemble*) ressembler à; **it sounds like or as if** il semble que (+ *sub or indic*); **to s. off about** *Fig* (*boast*) se vanter de; (*complain*) rouspéter à propos de. **◆soundproof** *a* insonorisé; – *vt* insonoriser. **◆soundtrack** *n* (*of film etc*) bande *f* sonore.

sound[2] [saʊnd] *a* (**-er, -est**) (*healthy*) sain; (*sturdy, reliable*) solide; (*instinct*) sûr; (*advice*) sensé; (*beating, sense*) bon; – *adv* **s. asleep** profondément endormi. **◆—ly** *adv* (*asleep*) profondément; (*reasoned*) solidement; (*beaten*) complètement. **◆—ness** *n* (*of mind*) santé *f*; (*of argument*) solidité *f*.

sound[3] [saʊnd] *vt* (*test, measure*) sonder; **to s. s.o. out** sonder qn (**about** sur).

soup [suːp] *n* soupe *f*, potage *m*; **in the s.** (*in trouble*) *Fam* dans le pétrin.

sour ['saʊər] *a* (**-er, -est**) aigre; **to turn s.** (*of wine*) s'aigrir; (*of milk*) tourner; (*of friendship*) se détériorer; (*of conversation*) tourner au vinaigre; – *vi* (*of temper*) s'aigrir.

source [sɔːs] *n* (*origin*) source *f*; **s. of energy** source d'énergie.

south [saʊθ] *n* sud *m*; – *a* (*coast*) sud *inv*; (*wind*) du sud; **to be s. of** être au sud de; **S. America/Africa** Amérique *f*/Afrique *f* du Sud; **S. American** *a* & *n* sud-américain, -aine (*mf*); **S. African** *a* & *n* sud-africain, -aine (*mf*); – *adv* au sud, vers le sud. **◆southbound** *a* (*carriageway*) sud *inv*; (*traffic*) en direction du sud. **◆south-'east** *n* & *a* sud-est *m* & *a inv*. **◆southerly** ['saʊðəlɪ] *a* (*point*) sud *inv*; (*direction, wind*) du sud. **◆southern** ['saʊðən] *a* (*town*) du sud; (*coast*) sud *inv*; **S. Italy** le Sud de

l'Italie; **S. Africa** Afrique *f* australe. **◆southerner** ['saʊðənər] *n* habitant, -ante *mf* du Sud. **◆southward(s)** *a* & *adv* vers le sud. **◆south-'west** *n* & *a* sud-ouest *m* & *a inv*.

souvenir [suːvəˈnɪər] *n* (*object*) souvenir *m*.

sovereign ['sɒvrɪn] *n* souverain, -aine *mf*; – *a* (*State, authority*) souverain; (*rights*) de souveraineté. **◆sovereignty** *n* souveraineté *f*.

Soviet ['saʊvɪət] *a* soviétique; **the S. Union** l'Union *f* soviétique.

sow[1] [saʊ] *n* (*pig*) truie *f*.

sow[2] [saʊ] *vt* (*pt sowed, pp sowed or sown*) (*seeds, doubt etc*) semer; (*land*) ensemencer (**with** de).

soya ['sɔɪə] *n* **s.** (**bean**) graine *f* de soja. **◆soybean** *n Am* graine *f* de soja.

sozzled ['sɒz(ə)ld] *a* (*drunk*) *Sl* bourré.

spa [spɑː] *n* (*town*) station *f* thermale; (*spring*) source *f* minérale.

space [speɪs] *n* (*gap, emptiness*) espace *m*; (*period*) période *f*; **blank s.** espace *m*, blanc *m*; (*outer*) **s.** l'espace (cosmique); **to take up s.** (*room*) prendre de la place; **in the s. of** en l'espace de; **s. heater** (*electric*) radiateur *m*; – *a* (*voyage etc*) spatial; – *vt* **to s. out** espacer; **double/single spacing** (*on typewriter*) double/simple interligne *f*. **◆spaceman** *n* (*pl* **-men**) astronaute *m*. **◆spaceship** *n* **◆spacecraft** *n inv* engin *m* spatial. **◆spacesuit** *n* scaphandre *m* (de cosmonaute).

spacious ['speɪʃəs] *a* spacieux, grand. **◆—ness** *n* grandeur *f*.

spade [speɪd] *n* **1** (*for garden*) bêche *f*; (*of child*) pelle *f*. **2** *Cards* pique *m*. **◆spadework** *n Fig* travail *m* préparatoire; (*around problem or case*) débroussaillage *m*.

spaghetti [spəˈgetɪ] *n* spaghetti(s) *mpl*.

Spain [speɪn] *n* Espagne *f*.

span [spæn] *n* (*of arch*) portée *f*; (*of wings*) envergure *f*; (*of life*) *Fig* durée *f*; – *vt* (**-nn-**) (*of bridge etc*) enjamber (*rivière etc*); *Fig* couvrir, embrasser.

Spaniard ['spænjəd] *n* Espagnol, -ole *mf*. **◆Spanish** *a* espagnol; – *n* (*language*) espagnol *m*. **◆Spanish-A'merican** *a* hispano-américain.

spaniel ['spænjəl] *n* épagneul *m*.

spank [spæŋk] *vt* fesser, donner une fessée à; – *n* **to give s.o. a s.** fesser qn. **◆—ing** *n* fessée *f*.

spanner ['spænər] *n* (*tool*) clé *f* (à écrous); **adjustable s.** clé *f* à molette.

spar/e[1] [speər] **1** *a* (*extra, surplus*) de or en

trop; (*clothes, tyre*) de rechange; (*wheel*) de secours; (*available*) disponible; (*bed, room*) d'ami; **s. time** loisirs *mpl*; **– s.** (**part**) *Tech Aut* pièce *f* détachée. **2** *vt* (*do without*) se passer de; (*s.o.'s life*) épargner; (*efforts, s.o.'s feelings*) ménager; **to s. s.o.** (*not kill*) épargner qn; (*grief, details etc*) épargner à qn; (*time*) accorder à qn; (*money*) donner à qn; **I can't s. the time** je n'ai pas le temps; **five to s.** cinq de trop. ◆**–ing** *a* (*use*) modéré; **to be s. with** (*butter etc*) ménager.

spare² [spɛər] *a* (*lean*) maigre.

spark [spɑːk] **1** *n* étincelle *f*. **2** *vt* **to s. off** (*cause*) provoquer. ◆**spark(ing) plug** *n* Aut bougie *f*.

sparkl/e [spɑːk(ə)l] *vi* étinceler, scintiller; **– n** éclat *m*. ◆**–ing** *a* (*wine, water*) pétillant.

sparrow [spærəʊ] *n* moineau *m*.

sparse [spɑːs] *a* clairsemé. ◆**–ly** *adv* (*populated etc*) peu.

spartan [spɑːtən] *a* spartiate, austère.

spasm [spæz(ə)m] *n* (*of muscle*) spasme *m*; (*of coughing etc*) *Fig* accès *m*. ◆**spas-'modic** *a* (*pain etc*) spasmodique; *Fig* irrégulier.

spastic [spæstɪk] *n* handicapé, -ée *mf* moteur.

spat [spæt] *see* **spit 1**.

spate [speɪt] *n* **a s. of** (*orders etc*) une avalanche de.

spatter [spætər] *vt* (*clothes, person etc*) éclabousser (**with** de); **– vi to s. over s.o.** (*of mud etc*) éclabousser qn.

spatula [spætjʊlə] *n* spatule *f*.

spawn [spɔːn] *n* (*of fish etc*) frai *m*; **– vi** frayer; **– vt** pondre; *Fig* engendrer.

speak [spiːk] *vi* (*pt* **spoke**, *pp* **spoken**) parler; (*formally, in assembly*) prendre la parole; **so to s.** pour ainsi dire; **that speaks for itself** c'est évident; **to s. well of** doit du bien de; **nothing to s. of** pas grand-chose; **Bob speaking** *Tel* Bob à l'appareil; **that's spoken for** c'est pris or réservé; **to s. out** or **up** (*boldly*) parler (franchement); **to s. up** (*more loudly*) parler plus fort; **– vt** (*language*) parler; (*say*) dire; **to s. one's mind** dire ce que l'on pense. ◆**–ing** *n* **in public s.** art *m* oratoire; **– a to be on s. terms with** parler à; **English-/French-speaking** anglophone/francophone. ◆**–er** *n* (*public*) orateur *m*; (*in dialogue*) interlocuteur, -trice *mf*; (*loudspeaker*) haut-parleur *m*; (*of hi-fi*) enceinte *f*; **to be a Spanish/a bad/etc s.** parler espagnol/mal/*etc*.

spear [spɪər] *n* lance *f*. ◆**spearhead** *vt*

(*attack*) être le fer de lance de; (*campaign*) mener.

spearmint [spɪəmɪnt] *n Bot* menthe *f* (verte); **– a** à la menthe; (*chewing-gum*) mentholé.

spec [spek] *n* **on s.** (*as a gamble*) *Fam* à tout hasard.

special [speʃ(ə)l] *a* spécial; (*care, attention*) (tout) particulier; (*measures*) *Pol* extraordinaire; (*favourite*) préféré; **by s. delivery** (*letter etc*) par exprès; **– n today's s.** (*in restaurant*) le plat du jour. ◆**specialist** *n* spécialiste *mf* (**in** de); **– a** (*dictionary, knowledge*) spécialisé. ◆**speci'ality** *n* spécialité *f*. ◆**specialize** *vi* se spécialiser (**in** dans). ◆**specialized** *a* spécialisé. ◆**specially** *adv* (*specifically*) spécialement; (*on purpose*) (tout) spécialement. ◆**specialty** *n Am* spécialité *f*.

species [spiːʃiːz] *n inv* espèce *f*.

specific [spəsɪfɪk] *a* précis, explicite; *Phys Ch* spécifique. ◆**specifically** *adv* (*expressly*) expressément; (*exactly*) précisément.

specify [spesɪfaɪ] *vt* spécifier (**that** que). ◆**specifi'cation** *n* spécification *f*; *pl* (*of car, machine etc*) caractéristiques *fpl*.

specimen [spesɪmən] *n* (*example, person*) spécimen *m*; (*of blood*) prélèvement *m*; (*of urine*) échantillon *m*; **s. signature** spécimen *m* de signature; **s. copy** (*of book etc*) spécimen *m*.

specious [spiːʃəs] *a* spécieux.

speck [spek] *n* (*stain*) petite tache *f*; (*of dust*) grain *m*; (*dot*) point *m*.

speckled [spek(ə)ld] *a* tacheté.

specs [speks] *npl Fam* lunettes *fpl*.

spectacle [spektək(ə)l] **1** *n* (*sight*) spectacle *m*. **2** *npl* (*glasses*) lunettes *fpl*. ◆**spec-'tacular** *a* spectaculaire. ◆**spec'tator** *n Sp etc* spectateur, -trice *mf*.

spectre [spektər] *n* (*menacing image*) spectre *m* (**of** de).

spectrum, *pl* **-tra** [spektrəm, -trə] *n Phys* spectre *m*; (*range*) *Fig* gamme *f*.

speculate [spekjʊleɪt] *vi Fin Phil* spéculer; **to s. about** (*s.o.'s motives etc*) s'interroger sur; **– vt to s. that** (*guess*) conjecturer que. ◆**specu'lation** *n Fin Phil* spéculation *f*; (*guessing*) conjectures *fpl* (**about** sur). ◆**speculator** *n* spéculateur, -trice *mf*. ◆**speculative** *a Fin Phil* spéculatif; **that's s.** (*guesswork*) c'est (très) hypothétique.

sped [sped] *see* **speed 1**.

speech [spiːtʃ] *n* (*talk, address*) & *Gram* discours *m* (**on** sur); (*faculty*) parole *f*;

(*diction*) élocution *f*; (*of group*) langage *m*; **a short s.** une allocution *f*; **freedom of s.** liberté *f* d'expression; **part of s.** Gram catégorie *f* grammaticale. ◆**–less** *a* muet (with de).

speed [spiːd] **1** *n* (*rate of movement*) vitesse *f*; (*swiftness*) rapidité *f*; **s. limit** Aut limitation *f* de vitesse; – *vt* (*pt & pp* sped) **to s. up** accélérer; – *vi* **to s. up** (*of person*) aller plus vite; (*of pace*) s'accélérer; **to s. past** passer à toute vitesse (**sth** devant qch). **2** *vi* (*pt & pp* speeded) (*drive too fast*) aller trop vite. ◆**–ing** *n* Jur excès *m* de vitesse. ◆**speedboat** *n* vedette *f*. ◆**spee'd-ometer** *n* Aut compteur *m* (de vitesse). ◆**speedway** *n* Sp piste *f* de vitesse pour motos; *Sp Aut Am* autodrome *m*.

speed/y ['spiːdɪ] *a* (**-ier, -iest**) rapide. ◆**–ily** *adv* rapidement.

spell [spel] *n* (*magic*) charme *m*, sortilège *m*; (*curse*) sort *m*; Fig charme *m*; **under a s.** envoûté. ◆**spellbound** *a* (*audience etc*) captivé.

spell [spel] *n* (*period*) (courte) période *f*; (*moment, while*) moment *m*; **s. of duty** tour *m* de service.

spell [spel] *vt* (*pt & pp* spelled *or* spelt) (*write*) écrire; (*say aloud*) épeler; (*of letters*) former (*mot*); (*mean*) Fig signifier; **to be able to s.** savoir l'orthographe; **how is it spelt?** comment cela s'écrit-il?; **to s. out** (*aloud*) épeler; Fig expliquer très clairement. ◆**–ing** *n* orthographe *f*.

spend [spend] **1** *vt* (*pt & pp* spent) (*money*) dépenser (**on** pour); – *vi* dépenser. **2** *vt* (*pt & pp* spent) (*time, holiday etc*) passer (**on** sth sur qch, **doing** à faire); (*energy, care etc*) consacrer (**on** sth à qch, **doing** à faire). ◆**–ing** *n* dépenses *fpl*; – *a* (*money*) de poche. ◆**–er** *n* **to be a big s.** dépenser beaucoup. ◆**spendthrift** *n* **to be a s.** être dépensier.

spent [spent] *see* spend; – *a* (*used*) utilisé; (*energy*) épuisé.

sperm [spɜːm] *n* (*pl* sperm *or* sperms) sperme *m*.

spew [spjuː] *vt* vomir.

sphere [sfɪər] *n* (*of influence, action etc*) & Geom Pol sphère *f*; (*of music, poetry etc*) domaine *m*; **the social s.** le domaine social. ◆**spherical** ['sferɪk(ə)l] *a* sphérique.

sphinx [sfɪŋks] *n* sphinx *m*.

spice [spaɪs] *n* Culin épice *f*; (*interest etc*) Fig piment *m*; – *vt* épicer. ◆**spicy** *a* (**-ier, -iest**) épicé; (*story*) Fig pimenté.

spick-and-span [spɪkən'spæn] *a* (*clean*) impeccable.

spider ['spaɪdər] *n* araignée *f*.

spiel [ʃpiːl] *n* Fam baratin *m*.

spike [spaɪk] *n* (*of metal*) pointe *f*; – *vt* (*pierce*) transpercer. ◆**spiky** *a* (**-ier, -iest**) à garni de pointes.

spill [spɪl] *vt* (*pt & pp* spilled *or* spilt) (*liquid*) répandre, renverser (**on, over** sur); **to s. the beans** Fam vendre la mèche; – *vi* **to s. (out)** se répandre; **to s. over** déborder.

spin [spɪn] *n* (*motion*) tour *m*; (*car ride*) petit tour *m*; (*on washing machine*) essorage *m*; **s. dryer** essoreuse *f*; – *vt* (*pt & pp* spun, *pres p* spinning) (*web, yarn, wool etc*) filer (**into** en); (*wheel, top*) faire tourner; (*washing*) essorer; (*story*) Fig débiter; **to s. out** (*speech etc*) faire durer; – *vi* (*of spinner, spider*) filer; **to s. (round)** (*of dancer, top, planet etc*) tourner; (*of head, room*) Fig tourner; (*of vehicle*) faire un tête-à-queue. ◆**spinning** *n* (*by hand*) filage *m*; (*process*) Tech filature *f*; **s. top** toupie *f*; **s. wheel** rouet *m*. ◆**spin-dry** *vt* essorer. ◆**spin-off** *n* avantage *m* inattendu; (*of process, book etc*) dérivé *m*.

spinach ['spɪnɪdʒ] *n* (*plant*) épinard *m*; (*leaves*) Culin épinards *mpl*.

spindle ['spɪnd(ə)l] *n* Tex fuseau *m*. ◆**spindly** *a* (**-ier, -iest**) (*legs, arms*) grêle.

spine [spaɪn] *n* Anat colonne *f* vertébrale; (*spike of animal or plant*) épine *f*. ◆**spinal** *a* (*column*) vertébral; **s. cord** moelle *f* épinière. ◆**spineless** *a* Fig mou, faible.

spinster ['spɪnstər] *n* célibataire *f*, Pej vieille fille *f*.

spiral ['spaɪərəl] **1** *n* spirale *f*; – *a* en spirale; (*staircase*) en colimaçon. **2** *vi* (**-ll-**, *Am* **-l-**) (*of prices*) monter en flèche.

spire ['spaɪər] *n* (*of church*) flèche *f*.

spirit ['spɪrɪt] **1** *n* (*soul, ghost etc*) esprit *m*; (*courage*) Fig courage *m*, vigueur *f*; *pl* (*drink*) alcool *m*, spiritueux *mpl*; **spirit(s)** (*morale*) moral *m*; Ch alcool *m*; **in good spirits** de bonne humeur; **the right s.** l'attitude *f* qu'il faut; – *a* (*lamp*) à alcool; **s. level** niveau *m* à bulle (d'air). **2** *vt* **to s. away** (*person*) faire disparaître mystérieusement; (*steal*) Hum subtiliser. ◆**–ed** *a* (*person, remark*) fougueux; (*campaign*) vigoureux.

spiritual ['spɪrɪtʃʊəl] *a* Phil Rel spirituel; – *n* (*Negro*) (negro-)spiritual *m*. ◆**spiritualism** *n* spiritisme *m*. ◆**spiritualist** *n* spirite *mf*.

spit [spɪt] **1** *n* crachat *m*; – *vi* (*pt & pp* spat *or* spit, *pres p* spitting) cracher; (*splutter*) Fig crépiter; – *vt* cracher; **to s. out** (re)cracher; **the spitting image of s.o.** le portrait (tout craché) de qn. **2** n (for meat) broche f.

spite [spaɪt] **1** n en s. of malgré; **in s. of the fact that** (although) bien que (+ sub). **2** n (dislike) rancune f; – vt (annoy) contrarier. ◆**spiteful** a méchant. ◆**spitefully** adv méchamment.

spittle ['spɪt(ə)l] n salive f, crachat(s) m(pl).

splash [splæʃ] n (spatter) éclabousser (with de, over sur); (spill) répandre; – vi (of mud, ink etc) faire des éclaboussures; (of waves) clapoter, déferler; **to s. over** sth/s.o. éclabousser qch/qn; **to s. (about)** (in river, mud) patauger; (in bath) barboter; **to s. out** (spend money) Fam claquer de l'argent; – n (splashing) éclaboussement m; (of colour) Fig tache f; **s. (mark)** éclaboussure f; **s.!** plouf!

spleen [spli:n] n Anat rate f.

splendid ['splendɪd] a (wonderful, rich, beautiful) splendide. ◆**splendour** n splendeur f.

splint [splɪnt] n Med éclisse f.

splinter ['splɪntər] n (of wood etc) éclat m; (in finger) écharde f; **s. group** Pol groupe m dissident.

split [splɪt] n fente f; (tear) déchirure f; (of couple) rupture f; Pol scission f; **to do the splits** (in gymnastics) faire le grand écart; **one's s.** (share) Fam sa part; – vt (pt & pp split, pres p splitting) (break apart) fendre; (tear) déchirer; **to s. (up)** (group) diviser; (money, work) partager (**between** entre); **to s. one's head open** s'ouvrir la tête; **to s. one's sides** (laughing) se tordre (de rire); **to s. hairs** Fig couper les cheveux en quatre; **s.-level apartment** duplex m; – vi se fendre; (tear) se déchirer; **to s. (up)** (of group) éclater; (of couple) rompre, se séparer; **to s.** (become loose) se détacher (**from** de); **to s. up** (of crowd) se disperser. ◆**splitting** a (headache) atroce. ◆**split-up** n (of couple) rupture f.

splodge [splɒdʒ] n, **splotch** [splɒtʃ] n (mark) tache f.

splurge [splɜ:dʒ] vi (spend money) Fam claquer de l'argent.

splutter ['splʌtər] vi (of sparks, fat) crépiter; (stammer) bredouiller.

spoil [spɔɪl] vt (pt & pp spoilt or spoiled) (pamper, make unpleasant or less good) gâter; (damage, ruin) abîmer; (pleasure, life) gâcher, gâter. ◆**spoilsport** n rabat-joie m inv.

spoils [spɔɪlz] npl (rewards) butin m.

spoke[1] [spəʊk] n (of wheel) rayon m.

spoke[2] [spəʊk] see speak. ◆**spoken** see speak; – a (language etc) parlé; **softly s.** (person) à la voix douce. ◆**spokesman** n (pl -men) porte-parole m inv (**for**, de).

sponge [spʌndʒ] **1** n éponge f; **s. bag** trousse f de toilette; **s. cake** gâteau m de Savoie; – vt **to s. down/off** laver/enlever à l'éponge. **2** vi **to s. off** or **on s.o.** Fam vivre aux crochets de qn; – vt **to s. sth off s.o.** Fam taper qn de qch. ◆**sponger** n Fam parasite m. ◆**spongy** a (-ier, -iest) spongieux.

sponsor ['spɒnsər] n (of appeal, advertiser etc) personne f assurant le patronage (**of** de); (for membership) parrain m, marraine f; Jur garant, -ante mf; Sp sponsor m; – vt (appeal etc) patronner; (member, firm) parrainer. ◆**sponsorship** n patronage m; parrainage m.

spontaneous [spɒn'teɪnɪəs] a spontané. ◆**spontaneity** [spɒntə'neɪtɪ] n spontanéité f. ◆**spontaneously** adv spontanément.

spoof [spu:f] n Fam parodie f (**on** de).

spooky ['spu:kɪ] a (-ier, -iest) Fam qui donne le frisson.

spool [spu:l] n bobine f.

spoon [spu:n] n cuiller f. ◆**spoonfeed** vt (pt & pp spoonfed) (help) Fig mâcher le travail à. ◆**spoonful** n cuillerée f.

sporadic [spə'rædɪk] a sporadique; **s. fighting** échauffourées fpl. ◆**sporadically** adv sporadiquement.

sport [spɔ:t] **1** n sport m; **a (good) s.** (person) Fam un chic type; **to play s.** or Am **sports** faire du sport; **sports club** club m sportif; **sports car/jacket** voiture f/veste f de sport; **sports results** résultats mpl sportifs. **2** vt (wear) arborer. ◆**-ing** a (conduct, attitude, person etc) sportif; **that's s. of you** Fig c'est chic de ta part. ◆**sportsman** n (pl -men) sportif m. ◆**sportsmanlike** a sportif. ◆**sportsmanship** n sportivité f. ◆**sportswear** n vêtements mpl de sport. ◆**sportswoman** n (pl -women) sportive f. ◆**sporty** a (-ier, -iest) sportif.

spot[1] [spɒt] n (stain, mark) tache f; (dot) point m; (polka dot) pois m; (pimple) bouton m; (place) endroit m, coin m; (act) Th numéro m; (drop) goutte f; **a s. of** (bit) Fam un peu de; **a soft s. for** un faible pour; **on the s.** sur place, sur les lieux; (at once) sur le coup; **in a (tight)** s. (difficulty) dans le pétrin; (accident) black s. Aut point m noir; **s. cash** argent m comptant; **s. check** contrôle m au hasard or à l'improviste. ◆**spotless** a (clean) impeccable. ◆**spot-**

lessly adv s. clean impeccable. ◆**spotlight** n (lamp) Th projecteur m; (for photography etc) spot m; **in the s.** Th sous le feu des projecteurs. ◆**spot-'on** a Fam tout à fait exact. ◆**spotted** a (fur) tacheté; (dress etc) à pois; (stained) taché. ◆**spotty** a (-ier, -iest) 1 (face etc) boutonneux. 2 (patchy) Am inégal.

spot² [spɒt] vt (-tt-) (notice) apercevoir, remarquer.

spouse [spaus, spauz] n époux m, épouse f.

spout [spaut] 1 n (of jug etc) bec m; **up the s.** (hope etc) Sl fichu. 2 vi (gush out, s. out) jaillir. 3 vt (say) Pej débiter.

sprain [sprein] n entorse f, foulure f; **to s. one's ankle/wrist** se fouler la cheville/le poignet.

sprang [spræŋ] see spring¹.

sprawl [sprɔːl] vi (of town, person) s'étaler; **to be sprawling** être étalé; — n the urban s. les banlieues fpl tentaculaires. ◆**-ing** a (city) tentaculaire.

spray [sprei] 1 n (water drops) (nuage m de) gouttelettes fpl; (can, device) bombe f, vaporisateur m; **hair s.** laque f à cheveux; — vt (liquid, surface) vaporiser; (crops, plant) arroser, traiter; (car etc) peindre à la bombe. 2 n (of flowers) petit bouquet m.

spread [spred] vt (pt & pp spread) (stretch, open out) étendre; (legs, fingers) écarter; (strew) répandre, étaler (over sur); (paint, payment, cards, visits) étaler; (people) disperser; (fear, news) répandre; (illness) propager; **to s. out** étendre; écarter; étaler; — vi (of fire, town, fog) s'étendre; (of news, fear) se répandre; **to s. out** (of people) se disperser; — n (of fire, illness, ideas) propagation f; (of wealth) répartition f; (paste) Culin pâte f (à tartiner); (meal) festin m; **cheese s.** fromage m à tartiner. ◆**s.-'eagled** a bras et jambes écartés.

spree [spriː] n **to go on a spending s.** faire des achats extravagants.

sprig [sprig] n (branch of heather etc) brin m; (of parsley) bouquet m.

sprightl/y [spraitli] a (-ier, -iest) alerte. ◆**-iness** n vivacité f.

spring¹ [spriŋ] n (metal device) ressort m; (leap) bond m; — vi (pt sprang, pp sprung) (leap) bondir; **to s. to mind** venir à l'esprit; **to s. into action** passer à l'action; **to s. from** (stem from) provenir de; **to s. up** (appear) surgir; — vt (news) annoncer brusquement (on à); (surprise) faire (on à); **to s. a leak** (of boat) commencer à faire eau. ◆**spring-**

board n tremplin m. ◆**springy** a (-ier, -iest) élastique.

spring² [spriŋ] n (season) printemps m; **in (the) s.** au printemps; **s. onion** ciboule f. ◆**s.-'cleaning** n nettoyage m de printemps. ◆**springlike** a printanier. ◆**springtime** n printemps m.

spring³ [spriŋ] n (of water) source f; **s. water** eau f de source.

sprinkl/e [spriŋk(ə)l] vt (sand etc) répandre (on, over sur); **to s. with water, s. water on** asperger d'eau, arroser; **to s. with** (sugar, salt, flour) saupoudrer de. ◆**-ing** n a (of a few) quelques. ◆**-er** n (in garden) arroseur m.

sprint [sprint] n Sp sprint m; — vi sprinter. ◆**-er** n sprinter m, sprinteuse f.

sprite [sprait] n (fairy) lutin m.

sprout [spraut] 1 vi (of seed, bulb etc) germer, pousser; **to s. up** (grow) pousser vite; (appear) surgir; — vt (leaves) pousser; (beard) Fig laisser pousser. 2 n (Brussels) s. chou m de Bruxelles.

spruce [spruːs] a (-er, -est) (neat) pimpant, net; — vt **to s. oneself up** se faire beau.

sprung [sprʌŋ] see spring¹; — a (mattress, seat) à ressorts.

spry [sprai] a (spryer, spryest) (old person etc) alerte.

spud [spʌd] n (potato) Fam patate f.

spun [spʌn] see spin.

spur [spɜːr] n (of horse rider etc) éperon m; (stimulus) Fig aiguillon m; **on the s. of the moment** sur un coup de tête; — vt (-rr-) **to s. (on)** (urge on) éperonner.

spurious ['spjuəriəs] a faux.

spurn [spɜːn] vt rejeter (avec mépris).

spurt [spɜːt] vi (gush out) jaillir; (rush) foncer; **to s. out** jaillir; — n jaillissement m; (of energy) sursaut m; **to put on a s.** foncer.

spy [spai] n espion, -onne mf; — a (story etc) d'espionnage; **s. hole** (peephole) judas m; **s. ring** réseau m d'espionnage; — vi espionner; **to s. on s.o.** espionner qn; — vt (notice) Lit apercevoir. ◆**-ing** n espionnage m.

squabbl/e ['skwɒb(ə)l] vi se chamailler (over à propos de); — n chamaillerie f. ◆**-ing** n chamailleries fpl.

squad [skwɒd] n (group) & Mil escouade f; (team) Sp équipe f; **s. car** voiture f de police.

squadron ['skwɒdrən] n Mil escadron m; Nau Av escadrille f.

squalid ['skwɒlid] a sordide. ◆**squalor** n conditions fpl sordides.

squall [skwɔːl] n (of wind) rafale f.

squander ['skwɒndər] vt (money, time etc) gaspiller (**on** en).

square ['skweər] n carré m; (on chessboard, graph paper) case f; (in town) place f; (drawing implement) Tech équerre f; **to be back to s. one** repartir à zéro; – a carré; (in order, settled) Fig en ordre; (honest) honnête; (meal) solide; (**all**) **s.** (quits) quitte (**with** envers); – vt (settle) mettre en ordre, régler; (arrange) arranger; Math carrer; (reconcile) faire cadrer; – vi (tally) cadrer (**with** avec); **to s. up to** faire face à. ◆**—ly** adv (honestly) honnêtement; (exactly) tout à fait; **s. in the face** en face.

squash [skwɒʃ] **1** vt (crush) écraser; (squeeze) serrer; – n **lemon/orange s.** (concentrated) sirop m de citron/d'orange; (diluted) citronnade f/orangeade f. **2** n (game) squash m. **3** n (vegetable) Am courge f. ◆**squashy** a (-ier, -iest) (soft) mou.

squat [skwɒt] a (short and thick) trapu. **2** vi (-tt-) **to s. (down)** s'accroupir. **3** n (house) squat m. ◆**squatting** a accroupi. ◆**squatter** n squatter m.

squawk [skwɔːk] vi pousser des cris rauques; – n cri m rauque.

squeak [skwiːk] vi (of door) grincer; (of shoe) craquer; (of mouse) faire couic; – n grincement m; craquement m; couic m. ◆**squeaky** a (-ier, -iest) (door) grinçant; (shoe) qui craque.

squeal [skwiːl] vi pousser des cris aigus; (of tyres) crisser; – n cri m aigu; crissement m. **2** vi **to s. on s.o.** (inform on) Fam balancer qn.

squeamish ['skwiːmiʃ] a bien délicat, facilement dégoûté.

squeegee ['skwiːdʒiː] n raclette f (à vitres).

squeeze/e [skwiːz] vt (press) presser; (hand, arm) serrer; **to s. sth out of s.o.** (information) soutirer qch à qn; **to s. sth into** faire rentrer qch dans; **to s. (out)** (extract) exprimer (**from** de); – vi **to s. through/into/etc** (force oneself) se glisser par/dans/etc; **to s. in** trouver un peu de place; – n pression f; to give sth a s. presser qch; **it's a tight s.** il y a peu de place; **credit s.** Fin restrictions fpl de crédit. ◆**—er** n **lemon s.** presse-citron m inv.

squelch [skweltʃ] **1** vi patauger (en faisant floc-floc). **2** vt (silence) Fam réduire au silence.

squid [skwɪd] n (mollusc) calmar m.

squiggle ['skwɪg(ə)l] n ligne f onduleuse, gribouillis m.

squint [skwɪnt] n Med strabisme m; **to have a s.** loucher; – vi loucher; (in the sunlight etc) plisser les yeux.

squire ['skwaɪər] n propriétaire m terrien.

squirm [skwɜːm] vi (wriggle) se tortiller; **to s. in pain** se tordre de douleur.

squirrel ['skwɪrəl, Am 'skwɜːrəl] n écureuil m.

squirt [skwɜːt] **1** vt (liquid) faire gicler; – vi gicler; – n giclée f, jet m. **2** n **little s.** (person) Fam petit morveux m.

stab [stæb] vt (-bb-) (with knife etc) poignarder; – n coup m (de couteau or de poignard). ◆**stabbing** n **there was a s.** quelqu'un a été poignardé; – a (pain) lancinant.

stable[1] ['steɪb(ə)l] a (-er, -est) stable; **mentally s.** (person) bien équilibré. ◆**stability** n stabilité f; **mental s.** équilibre m. ◆**stabilize** vt stabiliser; – vi se stabiliser. ◆**stabilizer** n stabilisateur m.

stable[2] ['steɪb(ə)l] n écurie f; **s. boy** lad m.

stack [stæk] n (heap) tas m; **stacks of** (lots of) Fam un or des tas de; – vt **to s. (up)** entasser. **2** npl (in library) réserve f.

stadium ['steɪdɪəm] n Sp stade m.

staff [stɑːf] n **1** personnel m; Sch professeurs mpl; Mil état-major m; **s. meeting** Sch Univ conseil m des professeurs; **s. room** Sch Univ salle f des professeurs; – vt pourvoir en personnel. **2** n (stick) Lit bâton m.

stag [stæg] n cerf m; **s. party** réunion f entre hommes.

stage[1] [steɪdʒ] n (platform) Th scène f; **the s.** (profession) le théâtre; **on s.** sur (la) scène; **s. door** entrée f des artistes; **s. fright** le trac; – vt (play) Th monter; Fig organiser, effectuer; **it was staged** (not real) c'était un coup monté. ◆**s.-hand** n machiniste m. ◆**s.-manager** n régisseur m.

stage[2] [steɪdʒ] n (phase) stade m, étape f; (of journey) étape f; (of track, road) section f; **in (easy) stages** par étapes; **at an early s.** au début.

stagecoach ['steɪdʒkəʊtʃ] n Hist diligence f.

stagger ['stægər] **1** vi (reel) chanceler. **2** vt (holidays etc) étaler, échelonner. **3** vt **to s. s.o.** (shock, amaze) stupéfier qn. ◆**—ing** a stupéfiant.

stagnant ['stægnənt] a stagnant. ◆**stag'nate** vi stagner. ◆**stag'nation** n stagnation f.

staid [steɪd] a posé, sérieux.

stain [steɪn] vt **1** (mark, dirty) tacher (**with**

de); − n tache f. **2** vt (colour) teinter (du bois); **stained glass window** vitrail m; − n (colouring for wood) teinture f. **◆−less** a (steel) inoxydable; **s.-steel knife/etc** couteau m/etc inoxydable.

stair [stear] n a s. (step) une marche; **the stairs** (staircase) l'escalier m; − a (carpet etc) d'escalier. **◆staircase** n, **◆stairway** n escalier m.

stake [steik] **1** n (post) pieu m; (for plant) tuteur m; Hist bûcher m; − vt to s. out (land) jalonner, délimiter; **to s. one's claim** to revendiquer. **2** n (betting) enjeu m; (investment) Fin investissement m; (interest) Fin intérêts mpl; **at s.** en jeu; − vt (bet) jouer (on sur).

stale [steil] a (-er, -est) (food) pas frais; (bread) rassis; (beer) éventé; (air) vicié; (smell) de renfermé; (news) Fig vieux; (joke) usé, vieux; (artist) manquant d'invention. **◆−ness** n (of food) manque m de fraîcheur.

stalemate [ˈsteɪlmeɪt] n Chess pat m; Fig impasse f.

stalk [stɔːk] **1** n (of plant) tige f, queue f; (of fruit) queue f. **2** vt (animal, criminal) traquer. **3** vi to s. out (walk) partir avec raideur or en marchant à grands pas.

stall [stɔːl] **1** n (in market) étal m, éventaire m; (for newspapers, flowers) kiosque m; (in stable) stalle f; **the stalls** Cin l'orchestre m. **2** vti Aut caler. **3** vi to s. (for time) chercher à gagner du temps.

stallion [ˈstæljən] n (horse) étalon m.

stalwart [ˈstɔːlwət] a (supporter) brave, fidèle; − n (follower) fidèle mf.

stamina [ˈstæmɪnə] n vigueur f, résistance f.

stammer [ˈstæmər] vti bégayer; − n bégaiement m; **to have a s.** être bègue.

stamp [stæmp] **1** n (for postage, implement) timbre m; (mark) cachet m, timbre m; **the s.** of Fig la marque de; **men of your s.** les hommes de votre trempe; **s. collecting** philatélie f; − vt (mark) tamponner, timbrer; (letter) timbrer; (metal) estamper; **to s. sth on sth** (affix) apposer qch sur qch; **to s. out** (rebellion, evil) écraser; (disease) supprimer; **stamped addressed envelope** enveloppe f timbrée à votre adresse. **2** vti to s. (one's feet) taper or frapper des pieds; **stamping ground** Fam lieu m favori.

stampede [stæmˈpiːd] n fuite f précipitée; (rush) ruée f; − vi fuir en désordre; (rush) se ruer.

stance [stɑːns] n position f.

stand [stænd] n (position) position f; (support) support m; (at exhibition) stand m; (for spectators) Sp tribune f; (witness) s. Jur Am barre f; **to make a s., take one's s.** prendre position (against contre); **news/flower s.** (in street) kiosque m à journaux/à fleurs; **hat s.** porte-chapeaux m inv; **music s.** pupitre m à musique; − vt (pt & pp **stood**) (pain, journey, person etc) supporter; **to s.** (up) (put straight) mettre (debout); **to s. s.o. sth** (pay for) payer qch à qn; **to s. a chance** avoir une chance; **to s. s.o. up** Fam poser un lapin à qn; − vi être or se tenir (debout); (rise) se lever; (remain) rester (debout); (be situated) se trouver; (be) être; (put up, argument) reposer (on sur); **to leave to s.** (liquid) laisser reposer; **to s. to lose** risquer de perdre; **to s. around** (in street etc) traîner; **to s. aside** s'écarter; **to s. back** reculer; **to s. by** (do nothing) rester là (sans rien faire); (be ready) être prêt (à partir or à intervenir); (one's opinion etc) s'en tenir à; (friend etc) rester fidèle à; **to s. down** (withdraw) se désister; **to s. for** (represent) représenter; Pol être candidat à; (put up with) supporter; **to s. in for** (replace) remplacer; **to s. out** (be visible or conspicuous) ressortir (against sur); **to s. over s.o.** (watch closely) surveiller qn; **to s. up** (rise) se lever; **to s. up for** (defend) défendre; **to s. up to** (resist) résister à. **◆−ing** a debout inv; (committee, offer, army) permanent; **s. room** places fpl debout; **s. joke** plaisanterie f classique; − n (reputation) réputation f; (social, professional) rang m; (financial) situation f; **of six years'** (duration) qui dure depuis six ans; **of long s.** de longue date. **◆standby** n (pl -bys) on s. prêt à partir or à intervenir; − a (battery etc) de réserve; (ticket) Av sans garantie. **◆stand-in** n remplaçant, -ante mf (for de); Th doublure f (for de).

standard [ˈstændəd] **1** n (norm) norme f, critère m; (level) niveau m; (of weight, gold) étalon m; pl (morals) principes mpl; **s. of living** niveau m de vie; **to be** or **come up to s.** (of person) être à la hauteur; (of work etc) être au niveau; − a (average) ordinaire, courant; (model, size) Com standard inv; (weight) étalon inv; (dictionary, book) classique; **s. lamp** lampadaire m. **2** n (flag) étendard m. **◆standardize** vt standardiser.

stand-offish [stændˈɒfɪʃ] a (person) distant, froid.

standpoint [ˈstændpɔɪnt] n point m de vue.

standstill [ˈstændstɪl] n **to bring to a s.** immobiliser; **to come to a s.** s'immobiliser;

at a s. immobile; (*industry, negotiations*) paralysé.

stank [stæŋk] *see* **stink**.

stanza ['stænzə] *n* strophe *f*.

stapl/e ['steɪp(ə)l] **1** *a* (*basic*) de base; **s. food** *or* **diet** nourriture *f* de base. **2** *n* (*for paper etc*) agrafe *f*; – *vt* agrafer. ◆**-er** *n* (*for paper etc*) agrafeuse *f*.

star [stɑːr] *n* étoile *f*; (*person*) Cin vedette *f*; **shooting s.** étoile *f* filante; **s. part** rôle *m* principal; **the Stars and Stripes, the S.-Spangled Banner** *Am* la bannière étoilée; **two-s.** (*petrol*) de l'ordinaire *m*; **four-s.** (*petrol*) du super; – *vi* (**-rr-**) (*of actor*) être la vedette (**in** de); – *vt* (*of film*) avoir pour vedette. ◆**stardom** *n* célébrité *f*. ◆**starfish** *n* étoile *f* de mer. ◆**starlit** *a* (*night*) étoilé.

starboard ['stɑːbəd] *n Nau Av* tribord *m*.

starch [stɑːtʃ] *n* (*for stiffening*) amidon *m*; *pl* (*foods*) féculents *mpl*; – *vt* amidonner. ◆**starchy** *a* (**-ier, -iest**) (*food*) féculent; (*formal*) Fig guindé.

stare [steər] *n* regard *m* (fixe); – *vi* to s. at fixer (du regard); – *vt* to s. s.o. in the face dévisager qn.

stark [stɑːk] *a* (**-er, -est**) (*place*) désolé; (*austere*) austère; (*fact, reality*) brutal; **the s. truth** la vérité toute nue; – *adv* **s. naked** complètement nu. ◆**starkers** *a Sl* complètement nu, à poil.

starling ['stɑːlɪŋ] *n* étourneau *m*.

starry ['stɑːrɪ] *a* (**-ier, -iest**) (*sky*) étoilé. ◆**s.-eyed** *a* (*naïve*) ingénu, naïf.

start¹ [stɑːt] *n* commencement *m*, début *m*; (*of race*) départ *m*; Sp & Fig avance *f* (**on** sur); **to make a s.** commencer; **for a s.** pour commencer; **from the s.** dès le début; – *vt* commencer; (*bottle*) entamer, commencer; (*fashion*) lancer; **to s. a war** provoquer une guerre; **to s. a fire** (*in grate*) allumer un feu; (*accidentally*) provoquer un incendie; **to s. s.o. (off)** **on** (*career*) lancer qn dans; **to s. (up)** (*engine, vehicle*) mettre en marche; **to s. doing** *or* **to do** commencer *or* se mettre à faire; – *vi* commencer (**with sth** par qch, **by doing** sth par faire); **to s. on sth** commencer qch; **to s. (up)** (*of vehicle*) démarrer; **to s. off** *or* **out** (*leave*) partir (**for** pour); (*in job*) débuter; **to s. back** (*return*) repartir; **to s. with** (*firstly*) pour commencer. ◆**-ing** *n* (*point, line*) de départ; **s. post** Sp ligne *f* de départ; **s. from** à partir de. ◆**-er** *n* (*runner*) partant *m*; (*official*) Sp starter *m*; (*device*) Aut démarreur *m*; *pl* Culin

hors-d'œuvre *m inv*; **for starters** (*first*) pour commencer.

start² [stɑːt] *vi* (*be startled, jump*) sursauter; – *n* sursaut *m*; **to give s.o. a s.** faire sursauter qn.

startle ['stɑːt(ə)l] *vt* (*make jump*) faire sursauter; (*alarm*) Fig alarmer; (*surprise*) surprendre.

starve [stɑːv] *vi* (*die*) mourir de faim; (*suffer*) souffrir de la faim; **I'm starving** Fig je meurs de faim; – *vt* (*kill*) laisser mourir de faim; (*make suffer*) faire souffrir de la faim; (*deprive*) Fig priver (**of** de). ◆**star'vation** *n* faim *f*; – *a* (*wage, ration*) de famine; **on a s. diet** à la diète.

stash [stæʃ] *vt* **to s. away** (*hide*) cacher; (*save up*) mettre de côté.

state¹ [steɪt] **1** *n* (*condition*) état *m*; (*pomp*) apparat *m*; **not in a (fit) s. to, in no (fit) s. to** hors d'état de; **to lie in s.** (*of body*) être exposé. **2** *n* S. (*nation etc*) État *m*; **the States** Geog Fam les États-Unis *mpl*; – *a* (*secret, document*) d'État; (*control, security*) de l'État; (*school, education*) public; **s. visit** voyage *m* officiel; **S. Department** Pol Am Département *m* d'État. ◆**stateless** *a* apatride; **s. person** apatride *mf*. ◆**state-'owned** *a* étatisé. ◆**statesman** *n* (*pl* **-men**) homme *m* d'État. ◆**statesmanship** *n* diplomatie *f*.

state² [steɪt] *vt* déclarer (**that** que); (*opinion*) formuler; (*problem*) exposer; (*time, date*) fixer. ◆**statement** *n* déclaration *f*; Jur déposition *f*; **bank s., s. of account** Fin relevé *m* de compte.

stately ['steɪtlɪ] *a* (**-ier, -iest**) majestueux; **s. home** château *m*.

static ['stætɪk] *a* statique; – *n* (*noise*) Rad parasites *mpl*.

station ['steɪʃ(ə)n] *n* Rail gare *f*; (*underground*) station *f*; (*position*) & Mil poste *m*; (*social*) rang *m*; (*police*) **s.** commissariat *m* *or* poste *m* (de police); **space/observation/radio/etc s.** station *f* spatiale/d'observation/de radio/etc; **bus** *or* **coach s.** gare *f* routière; **s. wagon** Aut Am break *m*; – *vt* (*position*) placer, poster. ◆**stationmaster** *n* Rail chef *m* de gare.

stationary ['steɪʃən(ə)rɪ] *a* (*motionless*) stationnaire; (*vehicle*) à l'arrêt.

stationer ['steɪʃənər] *n* papetier, -ière *mf*; **s.'s (shop)** papeterie *f*. ◆**stationery** *n* (*paper*) papier *m*; (*articles*) papeterie *f*.

statistic [stə'tɪstɪk] *n* (*fact*) statistique *f*; *pl* (*science*) la statistique. ◆**statistical** *a* statistique.

statue ['stætʃuː] n statue f. ◆**statu'esque** a (beauty etc) sculptural.

stature ['stætʃər] n stature f.

status ['steɪtəs] n (position) situation f; Jur statut m; (prestige) standing m, prestige m; **s. symbol** marque f de standing; **s. quo** statu quo m inv.

statute ['stætʃuːt] n (law) loi f; pl (of club, institution) statuts mpl. ◆**statutory** a (right etc) statutaire; **s. holiday** fête f légale.

staunch [stɔːntʃ] a (-er, -est) loyal, fidèle. ◆**-ly** adv loyalement.

stave [steɪv] **1** vt to **s. off** (danger, disaster) conjurer; (hunger) tromper. **2** n Mus portée f.

stay [steɪ] **1** n (visit) séjour m; — vi (remain) rester; (reside) loger; (of person) Nau tenir le gouvernail, gouverner; to **s. put** ne pas bouger; to **s. with** (plan, idea) ne pas lâcher; to **s. away** (keep one's distance) ne pas s'approcher (from de); to **s. away from** (school, meeting etc) ne pas aller à; to **s. in** (at home) rester à la maison; (of nail, tooth etc) tenir; to **s. out** (outside) rester dehors; (not come home) ne pas rentrer; to **s. out of sth** (not interfere in) ne pas se mêler de qch; (avoid) éviter qch; to **s. up** (at night) ne pas se coucher; (of fence etc) tenir; to **s. up late** se coucher tard; **staying power** endurance f. **2** vt (hunger) tromper. ◆**s.-at-home** n & a Pej casanier, -ière (mf).

St Bernard [sənt'bɜːnəd, Am seıntbə'naːd] n (dog) saint-bernard m.

stead [sted] n to **stand s.o. in good s.** être bien utile à qn; **in s.o.'s s.** à la place de qn.

steadfast ['stedfɑːst] a (intention etc) ferme.

steady ['stedɪ] a (-ier, -iest) (firm, stable) stable; (hand) sûr, assuré; (progress, speed, demand) régulier, constant; (nerves) solide; (staid) sérieux; **a s. boyfriend** un petit ami; **s. (on one's feet)** solide sur ses jambes; — adv to **go s. with** Fam sortir avec; — vt (chair etc) maintenir (en place); (hand) assurer; (nerves) calmer; (wedge, prop up) caler; to **s. oneself** (stop oneself falling) reprendre son aplomb. ◆**steadily** adv (to walk) d'un pas assuré; (regularly) régulièrement; (gradually) progressivement; (continuously) sans arrêt. ◆**steadiness** n stabilité f, régularité f.

steak [steɪk] n steak m, bifteck m. ◆**steakhouse** n grill(-room) m.

steal¹ [stiːl] vti (pt stole, pp stolen) voler (from s.o. à qn).

steal² [stiːl] vi (pt stole, pp stolen) to **s. in/ out** entrer/sortir furtivement. ◆**stealth**

[stelθ] n by **s.** furtivement. ◆**stealthy** a (-ier, -iest) furtif.

steam [stiːm] n vapeur f; (on glass) buée f; to **let off s.** (unwind) Fam se défouler, décompresser; **s. engine/iron** locomotive f/fer m à vapeur; — vt Culin cuire à la vapeur; to **get steamed up** (of glass) se couvrir de buée; Fig Fam s'énerver; — vi (of kettle etc) fumer; to **s. up** (of glass) se couvrir de buée. ◆**steamer** n, ◆**steamship** n (bateau m à) vapeur m; (liner) paquebot m. ◆**steamroller** n rouleau m compresseur. ◆**steamy** a (-ier, -iest) humide; (window) embué; (love affair etc) brûlant.

steel [stiːl] **1** n acier m; **s. industry** sidérurgie f. **2** vt to **s. oneself** s'endurcir (against contre). ◆**steelworks** n aciérie f.

steep [stiːp] **1** a (-er, -est) (stairs, slope etc) raide; (hill) escarpé; (price) Fig excessif. **2** vt (soak) tremper (in dans); **steeped in** Fig imprégné de. ◆**-ly** adv (to rise) en pente raide, (of prices) Fig excessivement.

steeple ['stiːp(ə)l] n clocher m.

steeplechase ['stiːp(ə)ltʃeɪs] n (race) steeple(-chase) m.

steer [stɪər] vt (vehicle, person) diriger, piloter; (ship) diriger, gouverner; — vi (of person) Nau tenir le gouvernail, gouverner; to **s. towards** faire route vers; to **s. clear of** éviter. ◆**-ing** n Aut direction f; **s. wheel** volant m.

stem [stem] **1** n (of plant etc) tige f; (of glass) pied m. **2** vt (-mm-) to **s. (the flow of)** (stop) arrêter, contenir. **3** vi (-mm-) to **s. from** provenir de.

stench [stentʃ] n puanteur f.

stencil ['stens(ə)l] n (metal, plastic) pochoir m; (paper, for typing) stencil m; — vt (-ll-, Am -l-) (notes etc) polycopier.

stenographer [stə'nɒɡrəfər] n Am sténo-dactylo f.

step [step] n (movement, sound) pas m; (stair) marche f; (on train, bus) marchepied m; (doorstep) pas m de la porte; (action) Fig mesure f; (flight of) steps (indoors) escalier m; (outdoors) perron m; (pair of) steps (ladder) escabeau m; **s. by s.** pas à pas; to **keep in s.** marcher au pas; **in s. with** Fig en accord avec; — vi (-pp-) (walk) marcher (on sur); **s. this way!** (venez) par ici!; to **s. aside** s'écarter; to **s. back** reculer; to **s. down** descendre (from de); (withdraw) Fig se retirer; to **s. forward** faire un pas en avant; to **s. in** (enter; intervene) Fig intervenir; **s. into** (car etc) monter dans; to **s. off** (chair etc) descendre de; to **s. out of** (car etc) descende de; **to s. over** (*obstacle*) enjamber; − *vt* **to s. up** (*increase*) augmenter, intensifier; (*speed up*) activer. ◆**stepladder** *n* escabeau *m*. ◆**stepping-stone** *n Fig* tremplin *m* (**to** pour arriver à).

stepbrother ['stepbrʌðər] *n* demi-frère *m*. ◆**stepdaughter** *n* belle-fille *f*. ◆**stepfather** *n* beau-père *m*. ◆**stepmother** *n* belle-mère *f*. ◆**stepsister** *n* demi-sœur *f*. ◆**stepson** *n* beau-fils *m*.

stereo ['steriəʊ] *n* (*pl* -os) (*sound*) stéréo(phonie) *f*; (*record player*) chaîne *f* (stéréo *inv*); − *a* (*record player*) stéréo *inv*; (*broadcast*) en stéréo. ◆**stereo'phonic** *a* stéréophonique.

stereotype ['steriətaip] *n* stéréotype *m*. ◆**stereotyped** *a* stéréotypé.

sterile ['sterail, *Am* 'sterəl] *a* stérile. ◆**ste'rility** *n* stérilité *f*. ◆**sterili'zation** *n* stérilisation *f*. ◆**sterilize** *vt* stériliser.

sterling ['stɜːlɪŋ] *n* (*currency*) livre(s *f*)(*pl*) sterling *inv*; − *a* (*pound*) sterling *inv*; (*silver*) fin; (*quality, person*) *Fig* sûr.

stern [stɜːn] **1** *a* (-er, -est) sévère. **2** *n* (of *ship*) arrière *m*.

stethoscope ['steθəskəʊp] *n* stéthoscope *m*.

stetson ['stetsən] *n Am* chapeau *m* à larges bords.

stevedore ['stiːvədɔːr] *n* docker *m*.

stew [stjuː] *n* ragoût *m*; **in a s.** *Fig* dans le pétrin; **s. pan, s. pot** cocotte *f*; − *vt* (*meat*) faire *or* cuire en ragoût; (*fruit*) faire cuire; **stewed fruit** compote *f*; − *vi* cuire. ◆**—ing** *a* (*pears etc*) à cuire.

steward ['stjuːəd] *n Av Nau* steward *m*; (*in college, club etc*) intendant *m* (*préposé au ravitaillement*); **shop s.** délégué, -ée *mf* syndical(e). ◆**stewar'dess** *n Av* hôtesse *f*.

stick¹ [stɪk] *n* (*piece of wood, chalk, dynamite*) bâton *m*; (*branch*) branche *f*; (*for walking*) canne *f*; **the sticks** *Pej Fam* la campagne, la cambrousse; **to give s.o. some s.** (*scold*) *Fam* engueuler qn.

stick² [stɪk] *vt* (*pt & pp* **stuck**) (*glue*) coller; (*put*) *Fam* mettre, planter; (*tolerate*) *Fam* supporter; **to s. sth into** (*thrust*) planter *or* enfoncer qch dans; **to s. down** (*envelope*) coller; (*put down*) *Fam* poser; **to s. on** (*stamp*) coller; (*hat etc*) mettre, planter; **to s. out** (*tongue*) tirer; (*head*) *Fam* sortir; **to s. it out** (*resist*) *Fam* tenir le coup; **to s. up** (*notice*) afficher; (*hand*) *Fam* lever; − *vi* coller, adhérer (**to** à); (*of food in pan*) attacher; (*remain*) *Fam* rester; (*of drawer etc*) être bloqué *or* coincé; **to s. by s.o.** rester fidèle à qn; **to s. to the facts** (*confine oneself to*) s'en tenir aux faits; **to s. around** *Fam*

rester dans les parages; **to s. out** (*of petticoat etc*) dépasser; (*of tooth*) avancer; **to s. up for** (*defend*) défendre; **sticking plaster** sparadrap *m*. ◆**sticker** *n* (*label*) autocollant *m*. ◆**stick-on** *a* (*label*) adhésif. ◆**stick-up** *n Fam* hold-up *m inv*.

stickler ['stɪklər] *n* **a s. for** (*rules, discipline, details*) intransigeant sur.

sticky ['stɪkɪ] *a* (-ier, -iest) collant, poisseux; (*label*) adhésif; (*problem*) *Fig* difficile.

stiff [stɪf] *a* (-er, -est) raide; (*joint, leg etc*) ankylosé; (*brush, paste*) dur; (*person*) *Fig* froid, guindé; (*difficult*) difficile; (*price*) élevé; (*whisky*) bien tassé; **to have a s. neck** avoir le torticolis; **to be bored s.** *Fam* s'ennuyer à mourir; **frozen s.** *Fam* complètement gelé. ◆**stiffen** *vt* raidir; − *vi* se raidir. ◆**stiffly** *adv* (*coldly*) *Fig* froidement. ◆**stiffness** *n* raideur *f*; (*hardness*) dureté *f*.

stifle ['staif(ə)l] *vt* (*feeling, person etc*) étouffer; − *vi* **it's stifling** on étouffe.

stigma ['stɪgmə] *n* (*moral stain*) flétrissure *f*. ◆**stigmatize** *vt* (*denounce*) stigmatiser.

stile [stail] *n* (*between fields etc*) échalier *m*.

stiletto [stɪ'letəʊ] *a* **s. heel** talon *m* aiguille.

still¹ [stɪl] *adv* encore, toujours; (*even*) encore; (*nevertheless*) tout de même; **better s., s. better** encore mieux.

still² [stɪl] *a* (-er, -est) (*motionless*) immobile; (*calm*) calme, tranquille; (*drink*) non gazeux; **to keep** *or* **lie** *or* **stand s.** rester tranquille; **s. life** nature *f* morte; − *n* (of *night*) silence *m*; *Cin* photo *f*. ◆**stillborn** *a* mort-né. ◆**stillness** *n* immobilité *f*; calme *m*.

still³ [stɪl] *n* (*for making alcohol*) alambic *m*.

stilt [stɪlt] *n* (*pole*) échasse *f*.

stilted ['stɪltɪd] *a* guindé.

stimulate ['stɪmjʊleɪt] *vt* stimuler. ◆**stimulant** *n Med* stimulant *m*. ◆**stimu'lation** *n* stimulation *f*. ◆**stimulus**, *pl* **-li** [-laɪ] *n* (*encouragement*) stimulant *m*; (*physiological*) stimulus *m*.

sting [stɪŋ] *vt* (*pt & pp* **stung**) (*of insect, ointment, wind etc*) piquer; (*of remark*) *Fig* blesser; − *vi* piquer; − *n* piqûre *f*; (*insect's organ*) dard *m*. ◆**—ing** *a* (*pain, remark*) cuisant.

sting/y ['stɪndʒɪ] *a* (-ier, -iest) avare, mesquin; **s. with** (*money, praise*) avare de; (*food, wine*) mesquin sur. ◆**—iness** *n* avarice *f*.

stink [stɪŋk] *n* puanteur *f*; **to cause** *or* **make a s.** (*trouble*) *Fam* faire du foin; − *vi* (*pt* **stank** *or* **stunk**, *pp* **stunk**) puer; (of *book, film etc*)

Fam être infect; **to s.** *of* smoke/*etc* empester la fumée/*etc*; – *vt* **to s. out** (*room etc*) empester. ◆**—er** *n Fam* (*person*) sale type *m*; (*question, task etc*) vacherie *f*.

stint [stint] **1** *n* (*share*) part *f* de travail; (*period*) période *f* de travail. **2** *vi* **to s. on** lésiner sur.

stipend ['staɪpend] *n Rel* traitement *m*.

stipulate ['stɪpjʊleɪt] *vt* stipuler (*that* que). ◆**stipu'lation** *n* stipulation *f*.

stir [stɜːr] *n* agitation *f*; **to give sth a s.** remuer qch; **to cause a s.** *Fig* faire du bruit; – *vt* (**-rr-**) (*coffee, leaves etc*) remuer; (*excite*) *Fig* exciter; (*incite*) inciter (**to do** à faire); **to s. oneself** (*make an effort*) se secouer; **to s. up** (*trouble*) provoquer; (*memory*) réveiller; – *vi* remuer, bouger. ◆**stirring** *a* (*speech etc*) excitant, émouvant.

stirrup ['stɪrəp] *n* étrier *m*.

stitch [stɪtʃ] *n* point *m*; (*in knitting*) maille *f*; *Med* point de suture; **a s.** (*in one's side*) (*pain*) un point de côté; **to be in stitches** *Fam* se tordre (de rire); – *vt* **to s.** (**up**) (*sew up*) coudre; *Med* suturer.

stoat [stəʊt] *n* (*animal*) hermine *f*.

stock [stɒk] *n* (*supply*) provision *f*, stock *m*, réserve *f*; (*of knowledge, ideas*) fonds *m*, mine *f*; *Fin* valeurs *fpl*, titres *mpl*; (*descent, family*) souche *f*; (*soup*) bouillon *m*; (*cattle*) bétail *m*; **the stocks** *Hist* le pilori; **in s.** (*goods*) en magasin, disponible; **out of s.** (*goods*) épuisé, non disponible; **to take s.** *Fig* faire le point (*of* de); **s. reply/size** réponse *f*/taille *f* courante; **s. phrase** expression *f* toute faite; **the S. Exchange** *or* **Market** la Bourse; – *vt* (*sell*) vendre; (*keep in store*) stocker; **to s.** (**up**) (*shop, larder*) approvisionner; **well-stocked** bien approvisionné; – *vi* **to s. up** s'approvisionner (**with** de, en). ◆**stockbroker** *n* agent *m* de change. ◆**stockcar** *n* stock-car *m*. ◆**stockholder** *n Fin* actionnaire *mf*. ◆**stockist** *n* dépositaire *mf*, stockiste *m*. ◆**stockpile** *vt* stocker, amasser. ◆**stockroom** *n* réserve *f*, magasin *m*. ◆**stocktaking** *n Com* inventaire *m*.

stocking ['stɒkɪŋ] *n* (*garment*) bas *m*.

stocky ['stɒkɪ] *a* (**-ier, -iest**) trapu.

stodge [stɒdʒ] *n* (*food*) *Fam* étouffe-chrétien *m inv.* ◆**stodgy** *a* (**-ier, -iest**) lourd, indigeste; (*person, style*) compassé.

stoic ['stəʊɪk] *a & n* stoïque (*mf*). ◆**stoical** *a* stoïque. ◆**stoicism** *n* stoïcisme *m*.

---

stok/e [stəʊk] *vt* (*fire*) entretenir; (*engine*) chauffer. ◆**—er** *n Rail* chauffeur *m*.

stole¹ [stəʊl] *n* (*shawl*) étole *f*.

stole², **stolen** [stəʊl, 'stəʊl(ə)n] *see* **steal¹,²**.

stolid ['stɒlɪd] *a* (*manner, person*) impassible.

stomach ['stʌmək] *n* **1** *Anat* estomac *m*; (*abdomen*) ventre *m*; – *vt* (*put up with*) *Fig* supporter. ◆**stomachache** *n* mal *m* de ventre; **to have a s.** avoir mal au ventre.

stone [stəʊn] *n* pierre *f*; (*pebble*) caillou *m*; (*in fruit*) noyau *m*; (*in kidney*) *Med* calcul *m*; (*weight*) = 6,348 kg; **a stone's throw away** *Fig* à deux pas d'ici; – *vt* lancer des pierres sur, lapider; (*fruit*) dénoyauter. ◆**stonemason** *n* tailleur *m* de pierre, maçon *m*. ◆**stony** *a* **1** (**-ier, -iest**) (*path etc*) pierreux, caillouteux. **2 s. broke** (*penniless*) *Sl* fauché.

stone- [stəʊn] *pref* complètement. ◆**s.-'broke** *a Am Sl* fauché. ◆**s.-'cold** *a* complètement froid. ◆**s.-'dead** *a* raide mort. ◆**s.-'deaf** *a* sourd comme un pot.

stoned [stəʊnd] *a* (*high on drugs*) *Fam* camé.

stooge [stuːdʒ] *n* (*actor*) comparse *mf*; (*flunkey*) *Pej* larbin *m*; (*dupe*) *Pej* pigeon *m*.

stood [stʊd] *see* **stand**.

stool [stuːl] *n* tabouret *m*.

stoop [stuːp] **1** *n* **to have a s.** être voûté; – *vi* se baisser; **to s. to doing/to sth** *Fig* s'abaisser à faire/à qch. **2** *n* (*in front of house*) *Am* perron *m*.

stop [stɒp] *n* (*place, halt*) arrêt *m*, halte *f*; *Av Nau* escale *f*; *Gram* point *m*; **bus s.** arrêt *m* d'autobus; **to put a s. to** mettre fin à; **to bring to a s.** arrêter; **to come to a s.** s'arrêter; **without a s.** sans arrêt; **s. light** (*on vehicle*) stop *m*; **s. sign** (*road sign*) stop *m*; – *vt* (**-pp-**) arrêter; (*end*) mettre fin à; (*prevent*) empêcher (**from doing** de faire); (*cheque*) faire opposition à; **to s. up** (*sink, pipe, leak etc*) boucher; – *vi* s'arrêter; (*of pain, conversation etc*) cesser; (*stay*) rester; **to s. eating/***etc* s'arrêter de manger/*etc*; **to s. snowing/***etc* cesser de neiger/*etc*; **to s. by** passer (*s.o.'s* chez qn); **to s. off** *or* **over** (*on journey*) s'arrêter. ◆**stoppage** *n* arrêt *m*; (*in pay*) retenue *f*; (*in work*) arrêt *m* de travail; (*strike*) débrayage *m*; (*blockage*) obstruction *f*. ◆**stopper** *n* bouchon *m*.

stopcock ['stɒpkɒk] *n* robinet *m* d'arrêt. ◆**stopgap** *n* bouche-trou *m*; – *a* intérimaire. ◆**stopoff** *n*, ◆**stopover** *n* halte *f*. ◆**stopwatch** *n* chronomètre *m*.

store [stɔːr] n (*supply*) provision f; (*of information, jokes etc*) Fig fonds m; (*dépôt, warehouse*) entrepôt m; (*shop*) grand magasin m, Am magasin m; (*computer memory*) mémoire f; **to have sth in s. for s.o.** (*surprise*) réserver qch à qn; **to keep in s.** garder en réserve; **to set great s. by** attacher une grande importance à; − vt **to s. (up)** (*in warehouse etc*) emmagasiner; (*for future use*) mettre en réserve; **to s. (away)** (*in furniture*) entreposer. ◆**storage** n emmagasinage m; (*for future use*) mise f en réserve; **s. space** or **room** espace m de rangement. ◆**storekeeper** n magasinier m; (*shopkeeper*) Am commerçant, -ante mf. ◆**storeroom** n réserve f.

storey [stɔːrɪ] n étage m.

stork [stɔːk] n cigogne f.

storm [stɔːm] n 1 (*in weather*) and Fig tempête f; (*thunderstorm*) orage m; **s. cloud** nuage m orageux. 2 vt (*attack*) Mil prendre d'assaut. 3 vi **to s. out** (*angrily*) sortir comme une furie. ◆**stormy** a (**-ier, -iest**) (*weather, meeting etc*) orageux; (*wind*) d'orage.

story [stɔːrɪ] n 1 histoire f; (*newspaper article*) article m; **s. (line)** Cin Th intrigue f; **short s.** Liter nouvelle f, conte m; **fairy s.** conte m de fées. 2 (*storey*) Am étage m. ◆**storyteller** n conteur, -euse mf; (*liar*) Fam menteur, -euse mf.

stout [staʊt] 1 a (**-er, -est**) (*person*) gros, corpulent; (*stick, volume*) gros, épais; (*shoes*) solide. 2 n (*beer*) bière f brune. ◆**-ness** n corpulence f.

stove [stəʊv] n (*for cooking*) cuisinière f; (*solid fuel*) fourneau m; (*small*) réchaud m; (*for heating*) poêle m.

stow [stəʊ] 1 vt (*cargo*) arrimer; **to s. away** (*put away*) ranger. 2 vi **to s. away** Nau voyager clandestinement. ◆**stowaway** n Nau passager, -ère mf clandestin(e).

straddle [strædə(ə)l] vt (*chair, fence*) se mettre or être à califourchon sur; (*step over, span*) enjamber; (*line in road*) Aut chevaucher.

straggl/e [strægə(ə)l] vi (*stretch*) s'étendre (en désordre); (*trail*) traîner (en désordre); **to s. in** entrer par petits groupes. ◆**-er** n traînard, -arde mf.

straight [streɪt] a (**-er, -est**) droit; (*hair*) raide; (*route*) direct; (*tidy*) en ordre; (*frank*) franc; (*refusal*) net; (*actor, role*) sérieux; **I want to get this s.** comprenons-nous bien; **to keep a s. face** garder son sérieux; **to put** or **set s.** (*tidy*) ranger; − n the s. Sp la ligne droite; − adv (*to walk etc*) droit; (*directly*) tout droit, directe-

ment; (*to drink gin, whisky etc*) sec; **s. away** (*at once*) tout de suite; **s. out, s. off** sans hésiter; **s. opposite** juste en face; **s. ahead** or **on** (*to walk etc*) tout droit; **s. ahead** (*to look*) droit devant soi. ◆**straighta'way** adv tout de suite. ◆**straighten** vt **to s. (up)** redresser; (*tie, room*) arranger; **to s. things out** Fig arranger les choses. ◆**straight-'forward** a (*frank*) franc; (*easy*) simple.

strain [streɪn] n 1 tension f; (*tiredness*) fatigue f; (*stress*) Med tension f nerveuse; (*effort*) effort m; − vt (*rope, wire*) tendre excessivement; (*muscle*) Med froisser; (*ankle, wrist*) fouler; (*eyes*) fatiguer; (*voice*) forcer; Fig mettre à l'épreuve; **to s. one's ears** (*to hear*) tendre l'oreille; **to s. oneself** (*hurt oneself*) se faire mal; (*tire oneself*) se fatiguer; − vi fournir un effort (**to do** pour faire). 2 vt (*soup etc*) passer; (*vegetables*) égoutter. 3 n (*breed*) lignée f; (*of virus*) souche f; (*streak*) tendance f. 4 npl Mus accents mpl (**of** de). ◆**-ed** a (*relations*) tendu; (*laugh*) forcé; (*ankle, wrist*) foulé. ◆**-er** n passoire f.

strait [streɪt] 1 n & npl Geog détroit m. 2 npl **in financial straits** dans l'embarras. ◆**straitjacket** n camisole f de force. ◆**strait'laced** a collet monté inv.

strand [strænd] n (*of wool etc*) brin m; (*of hair*) mèche f; (*of story*) Fig fil m.

stranded [strændɪd] a (*person, vehicle*) en rade.

strange [streɪndʒ] a (**-er, -est**) (*odd*) étrange, bizarre; (*unknown*) inconnu; (*new*) nouveau; **to feel s.** (*in a new place*) se sentir dépaysé. ◆**strangely** adv étrangement; **s. (enough) she ... chose étrange, elle ....** ◆**strangeness** n étrangeté f. ◆**stranger** n (*unknown*) inconnu, -ue mf; (*outsider*) étranger, -ère mf; **he's a s. here** il n'est pas d'ici; **she's a s. to me** elle m'est inconnue.

strangle [strængə(ə)l] vt étrangler. ◆**strangler** n étrangleur, -euse mf. ◆**stranglehold** n emprise f totale (**on** sur).

strap [stræp] n courroie f, sangle f; (*on dress*) bretelle f; (*on watch*) bracelet m; (*on sandal*) lanière f; − vt (**-pp-**) **to s. (down** or **in)** attacher (avec une courroie).

strapping [stræpɪŋ] a (*well-built*) robuste.

stratagem [strætədʒəm] n stratagème m.

strategy [strætədʒɪ] n stratégie f. ◆**stra'tegic** a stratégique.

stratum, pl **-ta** [strɑːtəm, -tə] n couche f.

straw [strɔː] n paille f; **a (drinking) s.** une paille; **that's the last s.!** c'est le comble!

strawberry [strɔːbərɪ] n fraise f; − a

(*flavour, ice cream*) à la fraise; (*jam*) de fraises; (*tart*) aux fraises.

stray [streɪ] *a* (*lost*) perdu; **a s. car**/*etc* une voiture/*etc* isolée; **a few s. cars**/*etc* quelques rares voitures/*etc*; – *n* animal *m* perdu; – *vi* s'égarer; **to s. from** (*subject, path*) s'écarter de.

streak [striːk] *n* (*line*) raie *f*; (*of light*) filet *m*; (*of colour*) strie *f*; (*trace*) Fig trace *f*; (*tendency*) tendance *f*; **grey**/*etc* **streaks** (*in hair*) mèches *fpl* grises/*etc*; **a mad s.** une tendance à la folie; **my literary s.** ma fibre littéraire. ◆**streaked** *a* (*marked*) strié, zébré; (*stained*) taché (**with** de). ◆**streaky** *a* (**-ier, -iest**) strié; (*bacon*) pas trop maigre.

stream [striːm] *n* (*brook*) ruisseau *m*; (*current*) courant *m*; (*flow*) & Fig flot *m*; Sch classe *f* (de niveau); – *vi* ruisseler (**with** de); **to s. in** (*of sunlight, people etc*) Fig entrer à flots.

streamer ['striːmər] *n* (*paper*) serpentin *m*; (*banner*) banderole *f*.

streamlin/e ['striːmlaɪn] *vt* (*work, method etc*) rationaliser. ◆**-ed** *a* (*shape*) aérodynamique.

street [striːt] *n* rue *f*; **s. door** porte *f* d'entrée; **s. lamp, s. light** réverbère *m*; **s. map, s. plan** plan *m* des rues; **up my s.** Fig Fam dans mes cordes; **streets ahead** Fam très en avance (**of** sur). ◆**streetcar** *n* (*tram*) Am tramway *m*.

strength [streŋθ] *n* force *f*; (*health, energy*) forces *fpl*; (*of wood, fabric*) solidité *f*; **on the s. of** Fig en vertu de; **in full s.** au (grand) complet. ◆**strengthen** *vt* (*building, position etc*) renforcer, consolider; (*body, soul, limb*) fortifier.

strenuous ['strenjʊəs] *a* (*effort etc*) vigoureux, énergique; (*work*) ardu; (*active*) actif; (*tiring*) fatigant. ◆**-ly** *adv* énergiquement.

strep [strep] *a* **s. throat** Med Am angine *f*.

stress [stres] *n* (*pressure*) pression *f*; Med Psy tension *f* (nerveuse), stress *m*; (*emphasis*) & Gram accent *m*; Tech tension *f*; **under s.** Med Psy sous pression, stressé; – *vt* insister sur; (*word*) accentuer; **to s. that** souligner que. ◆**stressful** *a* stressant.

stretch [stretʃ] *vt* (*rope, neck*) tendre; (*shoe, rubber*) étirer; (*meaning*) Fig forcer; **to s.** (**out**) (*arm, leg*) étendre, allonger; **to s.** (**out**) **one's arm** (*reach out*) tendre le bras (**to take** pour prendre); **to s. one's legs** Fig se dégourdir les jambes; **to s. s.o.** Fig exiger un effort de qn; **to be** (**fully**) **stretched** (*of budget etc*) être tiré au maximum; **to s. out** (*visit*) prolonger; – *vi* (*of person, elastic*)

s'étirer; (*of influence etc*) s'étendre; **to s.** (**out**) (*of rope, plain*) s'étendre; – *n* (*area, duration*) étendue *f*; (*of road etc*) tronçon *m*, partie *f*; (*route, trip*) trajet *m*; **at a s.** d'une (seule) traite; **ten**/*etc* **hours at a s.** dix/*etc* heures d'affilée; **s. socks**/*etc* chaussettes *fpl*/*etc* extensibles; **s. nylon** nylon *m* stretch *inv*. ◆**stretchmarks** *npl* (*on body*) vergetures *fpl*.

stretcher ['stretʃər] *n* brancard *m*.

strew [struː] *vt* (*pt* strewed, *pp* strewed *or* strewn) (*scatter*) répandre; **strewn with** (*covered*) jonché de.

stricken ['strɪk(ə)n] *a* **s. with** (*illness*) atteint de; (*panic*) frappé de.

strict [strɪkt] *a* (**-er, -est**) (*severe, absolute*) strict. ◆**-ly** *adv* strictement; **s. forbidden** formellement interdit. ◆**-ness** *n* sévérité *f*.

stride [straɪd] *n* (grand) pas *m*, enjambée *f*; **to make great strides** Fig faire de grands progrès; – *vi* (*pt* strode) **to s. across** *or* **over** enjamber; **to s. up and down a room** arpenter une pièce.

strident ['straɪdənt] *a* strident.

strife [straɪf] *n inv* conflit(s) *m*(*pl*).

strik/e [straɪk] **1** *n* (*attack*) Mil raid *m* (aérien); (*of oil etc*) découverte *f*; – *vt* (*pt* & *pp* struck) (*hit, impress*) frapper; (*collide with*) heurter; (*beat*) battre; (*a blow*) donner; (*a match*) frotter; (*gold, problem*) trouver; (*coin*) frapper; (*of clock*) sonner; **to s. a bargain** conclure un accord; **to s. a balance** trouver l'équilibre; **to s.** (**off**) (*from list*) rayer (**from** de); **to be struck off** (*of doctor*) être radié; **it strikes me as/that** il me semble que/que; **how did it s. you?** quelle impression ça t'a fait?; **to s. s.o.** (*of illness etc*) terrasser (qn); **to s. up a friendship** lier amitié (**with** avec); – *vi* **to s.** (**at**) (*attack*) attaquer; **to s. back** (*retaliate*) riposter; **to s. out** donner des coups. **2** *n* (*of workers*) grève *f*; **to go** (**out**) **on s.** se mettre en grève (**for** pour obtenir, **against** pour protester contre); – *vi* (*pt* & *pp* struck) (*of workers*) faire grève. ◆**-ing** *a* (*impressive*) frappant. ◆**-ingly** *adv* (*beautiful etc*) extraordinairement. ◆**-er** *n* gréviste *mf*; Fb buteur *m*.

string [strɪŋ] *n* ficelle *f*; (*of anorak, apron*) cordon *m*; (*of violin, racket etc*) corde *f*; (*of pearls, beads*) rang *m*; (*of onions, insults*) chapelet *m*; (*of people, vehicles*) file *f*; (*of questions etc*) série *f*; **to pull strings** Fig faire jouer ses relations; – *a* (*instrument, quartet*) Mus à cordes; **s. bean** haricot *m* vert; – *vt* (*pt* & *pp* strung) (*beads*) enfiler; **to s. up**

(*hang up*) suspendre; – *vi* **to s. along** (**with**) *Fam* suivre; – **-ed** *a* (*instrument*) *Mus* à cordes. ◆**stringy** *a* (-ier, -iest) (*meat etc*) filandreux.

stringent ['strɪndʒənt] *a* rigoureux. ◆**stringency** *n* rigueur *f*.

strip [strɪp] **1** *n* (*piece*) bande *f*; (*of water*) bras *m*; (*thin*) **s.** (*of metal etc*) lamelle *f*; **landing s.** (*for plane*) piste *f* d'atterrissage; **s. cartoon, comic s.** bande *f* dessinée. **2** *vt* (-pp-) (*undress*) déshabiller; (*bed*) défaire; (*deprive*) dépouiller (**of** de); (**s. down**) (*machine*) démonter; **to s. off** (*remove*) enlever; – *vi* (**s. off**) (*undress*) se déshabiller. ◆**stripper** *n* (*woman*) strip-teaseuse *f*; (*paint*) **s.** décapant *m*. ◆**strip-'tease** *n* strip-tease *m*.

stripe [straɪp] *n* rayure *f*; *Mil* galon *m*. ◆**striped** *a* rayé (**with** de). ◆**stripy** *a* rayé.

strive [straɪv] *vi* (*pt* **strove**, *pp* **striven**) s'efforcer (**to do** de faire, **for** d'obtenir).

strode [strəud] *see* **stride**.

stroke [strəuk] *n* (*movement*) coup *m*; (*of pen, genius*) trait *m*; (*of brush*) touche *f*; (*on clock*) coup *m*; (*caress*) caresse *f*; *Med* coup *m* de sang; (*swimming style*) nage *f*; **at a s.** d'un coup; **a s. of luck** un coup de chance; **you haven't done a s.** tu n'as rien fait; **heat s.** (*sunstroke*) insolation *f*; **four-s.-engine** moteur *m* à quatre temps; – *vt* (*beard, cat etc*) caresser.

stroll [strəul] *n* promenade *f*; – *vi* se promener, flâner; **to s. in/etc** entrer/*etc* sans se presser. ◆**-ing** *a* (*musician etc*) ambulant.

stroller ['strəulər] *n* (*pushchair*) *Am* poussette *f*.

strong [strɒŋ] *a* (-er, -est) fort; (*shoes, nerves*) solide; (*interest*) vif; (*measures*) énergique; (*supporter*) ardent; **sixty s.** au nombre de soixante; – *adv* **to be going s.** aller toujours bien. ◆**-ly** *adv* (*to protest, defend*) énergiquement; (*to desire, advise, remind*) fortement; (*to feel*) profondément; **s. built** solide. ◆**strongarm** *a* brutal. ◆**strongbox** *n* coffre-fort *m*. ◆**stronghold** *n* bastion *m*. ◆**strong-'willed** *a* résolu.

strove [strəuv] *see* **strive**.

struck [strʌk] *see* **strike** 1,2.

structure ['strʌktʃər] *n* structure *f*; (*of building*) armature *f*; (*building itself*) construction *f*. ◆**structural** *a* structural; (*fault*) *Archit* de structure.

struggle ['strʌg(ə)l] *n* (*fight*) lutte *f* (**to do** pour faire); (*effort*) effort *m*; **to put up a s.**

résister; **to have a s. doing** *or* **to do** avoir du mal à faire; – *vi* (*fight*) lutter, se battre (**with** avec); (*resist*) résister; (*thrash about wildly*) se débattre; **to s. to do** (*try hard*) s'efforcer de faire; **to s. out of** sortir péniblement de; **to s. along** *or* **on** se débrouiller; **a struggling lawyer**/*etc* un avocat/*etc* qui a du mal à débuter.

strum [strʌm] *vt* (-mm-) (*guitar etc*) gratter de.

strung [strʌŋ] *see* **string**; – **a s. out** (*things, people*) espacés; (*washing*) étendu.

strut [strʌt] **1** *vi* (-tt-) (**to s.** (**about** *or* **around**) se pavaner. **2** *n* (*support*) *Tech* étai *m*.

stub [stʌb] **1** *n* (*of pencil, cigarette etc*) bout *m*; (*counterfoil of cheque etc*) talon *m*; – *vt* (-bb-) **to s. out** (*cigarette*) écraser. **2** *vt* (-bb-) **to s. one's toe** se cogner le doigt de pied (**on, against** contre).

stubble ['stʌb(ə)l] *n* barbe *f* de plusieurs jours.

stubborn ['stʌbən] *a* (*person*) entêté, opiniâtre; (*cough, efforts, manner etc*) opiniâtre. ◆**-ly** *adv* opiniâtrement. ◆**-ness** *n* entêtement *m*; opiniâtreté *f*.

stubby ['stʌbɪ] *a* (-ier, -iest) (*finger etc*) gros et court, épais; (*person*) trapu.

stuck [stʌk] *see* **stick** [2]; – *a* (*caught, jammed*) coincé; **s. in bed/indoors** cloué au lit/chez soi; **to be s.** (*unable to do sth*) ne pas savoir quoi faire; **I'm s.** (**for an answer**) je ne sais que répondre; **to be s. with** **sth/s.o.** se farcir qch/qn. ◆**s.-'up** *a* *Fam* prétentieux, snob *inv*.

stud [stʌd] *n* **1** (*nail*) clou *m* (à grosse tête); (*for collar*) bouton *m* de col. **2** (*farm*) haras *m*; (*horses*) écurie *f*; (*stallion*) étalon *m*; (*virile man*) *Sl* mâle *m*. ◆**studded** *a* (*boots, tyres*) clouté; **s. with** (*covered*) *Fig* constellé de, parsemé de.

student ['stju:dənt] *n* *Univ* étudiant, -ante *mf*; *Sch* *Am* élève *mf*; **music**/*etc* **s.** étudiant, -ante en musique/*etc*; – *a* (*life, protest*) étudiant; (*restaurant, residence, grant*) universitaire.

studio ['stju:dɪəu] *n* (*pl* -os) (*of painter etc*) & *Cin* *TV* studio *m*; **s. flat** *or* *Am* **apartment** studio *m*.

studious ['stju:dɪəs] *a* (*person*) studieux. ◆**-ly** *adv* (*carefully*) avec soin. ◆**-ness** *n* application *f*.

study ['stʌdɪ] *n* étude *f*; (*office*) bureau *m*; – *vt* (*learn, observe*) étudier; – *vi* étudier; **to s. to be a doctor**/*etc* faire des études pour devenir médecin/*etc*; **to s. for** (*exam*) préparer. ◆**studied** *a* (*deliberate*) étudié.

stuff [stʌf] **1** *n* (*thing*) truc *m*, chose *f*;

(substance) substance *f*; *(things)* trucs *mpl*, choses *fpl*; *(possessions)* affaires *fpl*; *(nonsense)* sottises *fpl*; **this s.'s good, it's good s.** c'est bon (ça). **2** *vt* *(chair, cushion etc)* rembourrer **(with** avec); *(animal)* empailler; *(cram, fill)* bourrer **(with** de); *(put, thrust)* fourrer **(into** dans); *(chicken etc)* Culin farcir; **to s. (up)** *(hole etc)* colmater; **my nose is stuffed (up)** j'ai le nez bouché. ◆**-ing** *n* *(padding)* bourre *f*; Culin farce *f*.

stuffy ['stʌfɪ] *a* (**-ier, -iest**) *(room etc)* mal aéré; *(formal)* Fig compassé; *(old-fashioned)* vieux jeu *inv*; **it smells s.** ça sent le renfermé.

stumble ['stʌmb(ə)l] *vi* trébucher **(over** sur, **against** contre); **to s. across** *or* **on** *(find)* tomber sur; **stumbling block** pierre *f* d'achoppement.

stump [stʌmp] *n* *(of tree)* souche *f*; *(of limb)* moignon *m*; *(of pencil)* bout *m*; Cricket piquet *m*.

stumped [stʌmpt] *a* **to be s.** **by sth** *(baffled)* ne pas savoir que penser de qch.

stun [stʌn] *vt* (**-nn-**) *(daze)* étourdir; *(animal)* assommer; *(amaze)* Fig stupéfier. ◆**stunned** *a* Fig stupéfait (**by** par). ◆**stunning** *a* *(blow)* étourdissant; *(news)* stupéfiant; *(terrific)* Fam sensationnel.

stung [stʌŋ] *see* **sting**.

stunk [stʌŋk] *see* **stink**.

stunt [stʌnt] **1** *n* *(feat)* tour *m* (de force); Cin cascade *f*; *(ruse, trick)* truc *m*; **s. man** Cin cascadeur *m*; **s. woman** Cin cascadeuse *f*. **2** *vt* *(growth)* retarder. ◆**-ed** *a* *(person)* rabougri.

stupefy ['stjuːpɪfaɪ] *vt* *(of drink etc)* abrutir; *(amaze)* Fig stupéfier.

stupendous [stjuː'pendəs] *a* prodigieux.

stupid ['stjuːpɪd] *a* stupide, bête; **a s. thing** une sottise; **s. fool, s. idiot** idiot, -ote *mf*. ◆**stu'pidity** *n* stupidité *f*. ◆**stupidly** *adv* stupidement, bêtement.

stupor ['stjuːpər] *n* *(daze)* stupeur *f*.

sturdy ['stɜːdɪ] *a* (**-ier, -iest**) *(person, shoe etc)* robuste. ◆**sturdiness** *n* robustesse *f*.

sturgeon ['stɜːdʒ(ə)n] *n* *(fish)* esturgeon *m*.

stutter ['stʌtər] *n* bégaiement *m*; **to have a s.** être bègue; — *vi* bégayer.

sty [staɪ] *n* *(pigsty)* porcherie *f*.

stye [staɪ] *n* *(on eye)* orgelet *m*.

style [staɪl] *n* style *m*; *(fashion)* mode *f*; *(design of dress etc)* modèle *m*; *(of hair)* coiffure *f*; *(sort)* genre *m*; **to have s.** avoir de la classe; **in s.** *(in superior manner)* de la meilleure façon possible; *(to live, travel)* dans le luxe; — *vt* *(design)* créer; **he styles**

---

himself . . . *Pej* il se fait appeler . . . ; **to s.** **s.o.'s hair** coiffer qn. ◆**styling** *n* *(cutting of hair)* coupe *f*. ◆**stylish** *a* chic, élégant. ◆**stylishly** *adv* élégamment. ◆**stylist** *n* *(hair)* **s.** coiffeur, -euse *mf*. ◆**sty'listic** *a* de style, stylistique. ◆**stylized** *a* stylisé.

stylus ['staɪləs] *n* *(of record player)* pointe *f* de lecture.

suave [swɑːv] *a* (**-er, -est**) *(urbane)* courtois; *Pej* doucereux.

sub- [sʌb] *pref* sous-, sub-.

subconscious [sʌb'kɒnʃəs] *a* & *n* subconscient (*m*). ◆**-ly** *adv* inconsciemment.

subcontract [sʌbkən'trækt] *vt* sous-traiter. ◆**subcontractor** *n* sous-traitant *m*.

subdivide [sʌbdɪ'vaɪd] *vt* subdiviser **(into** en). ◆**subdivision** *n* subdivision *f*.

subdu/e [səb'djuː] *vt* *(country)* asservir; *(feelings)* maîtriser. ◆**-ed** *a* *(light)* atténué; *(voice)* bas; *(reaction)* faible; *(person)* qui manque d'entrain.

subheading ['sʌbhedɪŋ] *n* sous-titre *m*.

subject¹ ['sʌbdʒɪkt] *n* **1** *(matter)* & *Gram* sujet *m*; *Sch Univ* matière *f*; **s. matter** *(topic)* sujet; *(content)* contenu *m*. **2** *(citizen)* ressortissant, -ante *mf*; *(of monarch, monarchy)* sujet, -ette *mf*; *(person etc in experiment)* sujet *m*.

subject² ['sʌbdʒɪkt] *a* *(tribe etc)* soumis; **s. to** *(prone to)* sujet à *(maladie etc)*; *(ruled by)* soumis à *(loi, règle etc)*; *(conditional upon)* sous réserve de; **prices are s. to change** les prix peuvent être modifiés; — [səb'dʒekt] *vt* soumettre **(to** à); *(expose)* exposer **(to** à). ◆**sub'jection** *n* soumission *f* **(to** à).

subjective [səb'dʒektɪv] *a* subjectif. ◆**-ly** *adv* subjectivement. ◆**subjec'tivity** *n* subjectivité *f*.

subjugate ['sʌbdʒʊgeɪt] *vt* subjuguer.

subjunctive [səb'dʒʌŋktɪv] *n* Gram subjonctif *m*.

sublet [sʌb'let] *vt* (*pt* & *pp* **sublet**, *pres p* **subletting**) sous-louer.

sublimate ['sʌblɪmeɪt] *vt* Psy sublimer.

sublime [sə'blaɪm] *a* sublime; *(indifference, stupidity)* suprême; — *n* sublime *m*.

submachine-gun [sʌbmə'ʃiːngʌn] *n* mitraillette *f*.

submarine ['sʌbməriːn] *n* sous-marin *m*.

submerge [səb'mɜːdʒ] *vt* *(flood, overwhelm)* submerger; *(immerse)* immerger **(in** dans); — *vi* *(of submarine)* s'immerger.

submit [səb'mɪt] *vt* (**-tt-**) soumettre **(to** à); **to s. that** *Jur* suggérer que; — *vi* se soumettre **(to** à). ◆**submission** *n* soumission *f* **(to** à). ◆**submissive** *a* soumis. ◆**submissively** *adv* avec soumission.

subnormal [sʌb'nɔːm(ə)l] *a* au-dessous de la normale; (*mentally*) arriéré.

subordinate [sə'bɔːdɪnət] *a* subalterne; *Gram* subordonné; – *n* subordonné, -ée *mf*; – [sə'bɔːdɪneɪt] *vt* subordonner (**to** à). ◆**subordi'nation** *n* subordination *f* (**to** à).

subpoena [səb'piːnə] *vt Jur* citer; – *n Jur* citation *f*.

subscribe [səb'skraɪb] *vt* (*money*) donner (**to** à); – *vi* cotiser; **to s.** (*take out subscription*) s'abonner à (*journal etc*); (*be a subscriber*) être abonné à (*journal etc*); (*fund, idea*) souscrire à. ◆**subscriber** *n Journ Tel* abonné, -ée *mf*. ◆**subscription** *n* (*to newspaper etc*) abonnement *m*; (*to fund, idea*) & *Fin* souscription *f*; (*to club etc*) cotisation *f*.

subsequent ['sʌbsɪkwənt] *a* postérieur (**to** à); **our s. problems** les problèmes que nous avons eus par la suite; **s. to** (*as a result of*) consécutif à. ◆**-ly** *adv* par la suite.

subservient [səb'sɜːvɪənt] *a* obséquieux; **to be s.** (*a slave to*) être asservi à.

subside [səb'saɪd] *vi* (*of building, land*) s'affaisser; (*of wind, flood*) baisser. ◆**'subsidence** *n* affaissement *m*.

subsidiary [səb'sɪdɪərɪ] *a* accessoire; (*subject*) *Univ* secondaire; – *n* (*company*) *Com* filiale *f*.

subsidize ['sʌbsɪdaɪz] *vt* subventionner. ◆**subsidy** *n* subvention *f*.

subsist [səb'sɪst] *vi* (*of person, doubts etc*) subsister. ◆**subsistence** *n* subsistance *f*.

substance ['sʌbstəns] *n* substance *f*; (*firmness*) solidité *f*; **a man of s.** un homme riche. ◆**substantial** [səb'stænʃ(ə)l] *a* important, considérable; (*meal*) substantiel. ◆**substantially** *adv* considérablement, beaucoup; **s. true**/*etc* (*to a great extent*) en grande partie vrai/*etc*; **s. different** très différent.

substandard [sʌb'stændəd] *a* de qualité inférieure.

substantiate [səb'stænʃɪeɪt] *vt* prouver, justifier.

substitute ['sʌbstɪtjuːt] *n* (*thing*) produit *m* de remplacement; (*person*) remplaçant, -ante *mf* (**for** de); **there's no s. for . . .** rien ne peut remplacer . . .; – *vt* substituer (**for** à); – *vi* **to s. for** remplacer; (*deputize for in job*) se substituer à. ◆**substi'tution** *n* substitution *f*.

subtitle ['sʌbtaɪt(ə)l] *n* sous-titre *m*; – *vt* sous-titrer.

subtle ['sʌt(ə)l] *a* (**-er, -est**) subtil. ◆**sub-**

tlety *n* subtilité *f*. ◆**subtly** *adv* subtilement.

subtotal [sʌb'təʊt(ə)l] *n* total *m* partiel, sous-total *m*.

subtract [səb'trækt] *vt* soustraire (**from** de). ◆**subtraction** *n* soustraction *f*.

suburb ['sʌbɜːb] *n* banlieue *f*; **the suburbs** la banlieue; **in the suburbs** en banlieue. ◆**su'burban** *a* (*train*) de banlieue; (*accent*) de la banlieue. ◆**su'burbia** *n* la banlieue.

subversive [səb'vɜːsɪv] *a* subversif. ◆**subversion** *n* subversion *f*. ◆**subvert** *vt* (*system etc*) bouleverser; (*person*) corrompre.

subway ['sʌbweɪ] *n* passage *m* souterrain; *Rail Am* métro *m*.

succeed [sək'siːd] **1** *vi* réussir (**in doing** à faire, **in sth** dans qch). **2** *vt* **to s. s.o.** (*follow*) succéder à qn; – *vi* **to s. to the throne** succéder à la couronne. ◆**-ing** *a* (*in past*) suivant; (*in future*) futur; (*consecutive*) suivant.

success [sək'ses] *n* succès *m*, réussite *f*; **to make a s. of sth** réussir qch; **he was a s.** il a eu du succès; **his** *or* **her s. in the exam** sa réussite à l'examen; **s. story** réussite *f* complète *ou* exemplaire. ◆**successful** *a* (*venture etc*) couronné de succès, réussi; (*outcome*) heureux; (*firm*) prospère; (*candidate in exam*) admis, reçu; (*in election*) élu; (*writer, film etc*) à succès; **to be s.** réussir (**in dans, in an exam** à un examen, **in doing** à faire). ◆**successfully** *adv* avec succès.

succession [sək'seʃ(ə)n] *n* succession *f*; **in s.** successivement; **ten days in s.** dix jours consécutifs; **in rapid s.** coup sur coup. ◆**successive** *a* successif; **ten s. days** dix jours consécutifs. ◆**successor** *n* successeur *m* (**of, to** de).

succinct [sək'sɪŋkt] *a* succinct.

succulent ['sʌkjʊlənt] *a* succulent.

succumb [sə'kʌm] *vi* (*yield*) succomber (**to** à).

such [sʌtʃ] *a* tel; **s. a car**/*etc* une telle voiture/*etc*; **s. happiness**/*etc* (*so much*) tant *ou* tellement de bonheur/*etc*; **there's no s. thing** ça n'existe pas; **I said no s. thing** je n'ai rien dit de tel; – *as* comme, tel que; **s. and s.** tel ou tel; – *adv* (*so very*) si; (*in comparisons*) aussi; **s. a kind woman as you** une femme aussi gentille que vous; **s. long trips** de si longs voyages; **s. a large helping** une si grosse portion; – *pron* **happiness**/*etc* **as s.** le bonheur/*etc* en tant que tel; **s. was**

my idea telle était mon idée. ◆**suchlike** n . . . and s. *Fam* . . . et autres.

suck [sʌk] vt sucer; (*of baby*) téter (*lait, biberon etc*); **to s. (up)** (*with straw, pump*) aspirer; **to s. up** or **in** (*absorb*) absorber; — vi (*of baby*) téter; **to s. at** sucer. ◆**—er** n **1** (*fool*) *Fam* dupe f. **2** (*pad*) ventouse f.

suckle ['sʌk(ə)l] vt (*of woman*) allaiter; (*of baby*) téter.

suction ['sʌkʃ(ə)n] n succion f; **s. disc, s. pad** ventouse f.

Sudan [suːˈdɑːn] n Soudan m.

sudden ['sʌd(ə)n] a soudain, subit; **all of a s.** tout à coup. ◆**—ly** adv subitement. ◆**—ness** n soudaineté f.

suds [sʌdz] npl mousse f de savon.

sue [suː] vt poursuivre (en justice); — vi engager des poursuites (judiciaires).

suede [sweɪd] n daim m; — a de daim.

suet ['suːɪt] n graisse f de rognon.

suffer ['sʌfər] vi souffrir (**from** de); **to s. from** pimples/the flu avoir des boutons/la grippe; **your work/etc will s.** ton travail/etc s'en ressentira; — vt (*attack, loss etc*) subir; (*pain*) ressentir; (*tolerate*) souffrir. ◆**—ing** n souffrance(s) f(pl). ◆**—er** n *Med* malade mf; (*from misfortune*) victime f.

suffice [səˈfaɪs] vi suffire.

sufficient [səˈfɪʃ(ə)nt] a (*quantity, number*) suffisant; **s. money/etc** (*enough*) suffisamment d'argent/etc; **to have s.** en avoir suffisamment. ◆**—ly** adv suffisamment.

suffix ['sʌfɪks] n *Gram* suffixe m.

suffocate ['sʌfəkeɪt] vti étouffer, suffoquer. ◆**suffo'cation** n (*of industry, mind etc*) & *Med* étouffement m, asphyxie f.

suffrage ['sʌfrɪdʒ] n (*right to vote*) *Pol* suffrage m.

suffused [səˈfjuːzd] a **s. with** (*light, tears*) baigné de.

sugar ['ʃʊgər] n sucre m; — a (*cane, tongs*) à sucre; (*industry*) sucrier; **s. bowl** sucrier m; — vt sucrer. ◆**sugary** a (*taste, tone*) sucré.

suggest [səˈdʒest] vt (*propose*) proposer, suggérer (**to** à, **that que** (+ *sub*)); (*evoke, imply*) suggérer; (*hint*) *Pej* insinuer. ◆**suggestion** n suggestion f, proposition f; (*evocation*) suggestion f; *Pej* insinuation f. ◆**suggestive** a suggestif; **to be s. of** suggérer.

suicide ['suːɪsaɪd] n suicide m; **to commit s.** se suicider. ◆**sui'cidal** a suicidaire.

suit [suːt] **1** n (*man's*) complet m, costume m; (*woman's*) tailleur m; (*of pilot, diver etc*) combinaison f. **2** n (*lawsuit*) *Jur* procès m. **3** n *Cards* couleur f. **4** vt (*satisfy, be appropri-*ate to) convenir à; (*of dress, colour etc*) aller (bien) à; (*adapt*) adapter (**to** à); **it suits me to stay** ça m'arrange de rester; **s. yourself!** comme tu voudras! (*appropriate for*) fait pour; (*appropriate to*) approprié à; **well suited** (*couple etc*) bien assorti. ◆**suita-'bility** n (*of remark etc*) à-propos m; (*of person*) aptitudes fpl (**for** pour); **I'm not sure of the s.** (*of date etc*) je ne sais pas si ça convient. ◆**suitable** a qui convient (**for** à); (*dress, colour*) qui va (bien); (*example*) approprié; (*socially*) convenable. ◆**suitably** adv convenablement.

suitcase ['suːtkeɪs] n valise f.

suite [swiːt] n (*rooms*) suite f; (*furniture*) mobilier m; **bedroom s.** (*furniture*) chambre f à coucher.

suitor ['suːtər] n soupirant m.

sulfur ['sʌlfər] n *Am* soufre m.

sulk [sʌlk] vi bouder. ◆**sulky** a (-ier, -iest) boudeur.

sullen ['sʌlən] a maussade. ◆**—ly** adv d'un air maussade.

sully ['sʌlɪ] vt *Lit* souiller.

sulphur ['sʌlfər] n soufre m.

sultan ['sʌltən] n sultan m.

sultana [sʌlˈtɑːnə] n raisin m de Smyrne.

sultry ['sʌltrɪ] a (-ier, -iest) (*heat*) étouffant, *Fig* sensuel.

sum [sʌm] n **1** (*amount, total*) somme f; *Math* calcul m; pl (*arithmetic*) le calcul; **s. total** résultat m. **2** vt (-mm-) **to s. up** (*facts etc*) récapituler, résumer; (*text*) résumer; (*situation*) évaluer; (*person*) jauger; — vi **to s. up** récapituler. ◆**summing-'up** n (pl summings-up) résumé m.

summarize ['sʌməraɪz] vt résumer. ◆**summary** n résumé m; — a (*brief*) sommaire.

summer ['sʌmər] n été m; **in (the) s.** en été; **Indian s.** été indien or de la Saint-Martin; — a d'été; **s. holidays** grandes vacances fpl. ◆**summerhouse** n pavillon m (de gardin). ◆**summertime** n été m; **in (the) s.** en été. ◆**summery** a (*weather etc*) estival; (*dress*) d'été.

summit ['sʌmɪt] n (*of mountain, power etc*) sommet m; **s. conference/meeting** *Pol* conférence f/rencontre f au sommet.

summon ['sʌmən] vt (*call*) appeler; (*meeting, s.o. to meeting*) convoquer (**to** à); **s. s.o. to do** sommer qn de faire; **to s. up** (*courage, strength*) rassembler.

summons ['sʌmənz] n *Jur* assignation f; — vt *Jur* assigner.

sumptuous ['sʌmptʃʊəs] a somptueux. ◆**—ness** n somptuosité f.

sun [sʌn] n soleil m; **in the s.** au soleil; **the**

sun's shining il fait (du) soleil; – a (*cream, filter etc*) solaire; **s. lounge** solarium m; – vt (**-nn-**) **to s. oneself** se chauffer au soleil. ◆**sunbaked** a brûlé par le soleil. ◆**sunbathe** vi prendre un bain de soleil. ◆**sunbeam** n rayon m de soleil. ◆**sunburn** n (*tan*) bronzage m; *Med* coup m de soleil. ◆**sunburnt** a bronzé; *Med* brûlé par le soleil. ◆**sundial** n cadran m solaire. ◆**sundown** n coucher m du soleil. ◆**sundrenched** a brûlé par le soleil. ◆**sunflower** n tournesol m. ◆**sunglasses** npl lunettes fpl de soleil. ◆**sunlamp** n lampe f à rayons ultraviolets. ◆**sunlight** n (lumière f du) soleil m. ◆**sunlit** a ensoleillé. ◆**sunrise** n lever m du soleil. ◆**sunroof** n Aut toit m ouvrant. ◆**sunset** n coucher m du soleil. ◆**sunshade** n (on table) parasol m; (portable) ombrelle f. ◆**sunshine** n soleil m. ◆**sunstroke** n insolation f. ◆**suntan** n bronzage m; – a (lotion, oil) solaire. ◆**suntanned** a bronzé. ◆**sunup** n Am lever m du soleil.

sundae ['sʌndeɪ] n glace f aux fruits.

Sunday ['sʌndɪ] n dimanche m.

sundry ['sʌndrɪ] a divers; **all and s.** tout le monde; – npl Com articles mpl divers.

sung [sʌŋ] see **sing**.

sunk [sʌŋk] see **sink**[2]; – a **I'm s.** Fam je suis fichu. ◆**sunken** a (rock etc) submergé; (eyes) cave.

sunny ['sʌnɪ] a (-ier, -iest) ensoleillé; **it's s.** il fait (du) soleil; **s. period** Met éclaircie f.

super ['suːpər] a Fam sensationnel.

super- ['suːpər] pref super-.

superannuation [suːpərænjuː'eɪʃ(ə)n] n (amount) cotisations fpl (pour la) retraite.

superb [suː'pɜːb] a superbe.

supercilious [suːpə'sɪlɪəs] a hautain.

superficial [suːpə'fɪʃ(ə)l] a superficiel. ◆**-ly** adv superficiellement.

superfluous [suː'pɜːfluəs] a superflu.

superhuman [suːpə'hjuːmən] a surhumain.

superimpose [suːpərɪm'pəuz] vt superposer (on à).

superintendent [suːpərɪn'tendənt] n directeur, -trice mf; (police) **s.** commissaire m (de police).

superior [suː'pɪərɪər] a supérieur (**to** à); (goods) de qualité supérieure; – n (person) supérieur, -eure mf. ◆**superi'ority** n supériorité f.

superlative [suː'pɜːlətɪv] a sans pareil; – a & n Gram superlatif (m).

superman ['suːpəmæn] n (pl -men) surhomme m.

supermarket ['suːpəmɑːkɪt] n supermarché m.

supernatural [suːpə'nætʃ(ə)rəl] a & n surnaturel (m).

superpower ['suːpəpauər] n Pol superpuissance f.

supersede [suːpə'siːd] vt remplacer, supplanter.

supersonic [suːpə'sɒnɪk] a supersonique.

superstition [suːpə'stɪʃ(ə)n] n superstition f. ◆**superstitious** a superstitieux.

supertanker ['suːpətæŋkər] n pétrolier m géant.

supervise ['suːpəvaɪz] vt (person, work) surveiller; (office, research) diriger. ◆**super'vision** n surveillance f; direction f. ◆**supervisor** n surveillant, -ante mf; (in office) chef m de service; (shop) chef m de rayon. ◆**super'visory** a (post) de surveillant(e).

supper ['sʌpər] n dîner m; (late-night) souper m.

supple ['sʌp(ə)l] a souple. ◆**-ness** n souplesse f.

supplement ['sʌplɪmənt] n (addition) & Journ supplément m (**to** à); – ['sʌplɪment] vt compléter; **to s. one's income** arrondir ses fins de mois. ◆**supple'mentary** a supplémentaire.

supply [sə'plaɪ] vt (provide) fournir; (feed) alimenter (with en); (equip) équiper, pourvoir (with de); **to s. a need** subvenir à un besoin; **to s. s.o. with sth, s. sth to s.o.** (facts etc) fournir qch à qn; – n (stock) provision f, réserve f; (equipment) matériel m; **the s. of** (act) la fourniture de; **the s. of gas/electricity** l'alimentation f en gaz/électricité de; (food) **supplies** vivres mpl; (office) **supplies** fournitures fpl (de bureau); **s. and demand** l'offre f et la demande; **to be in short s.** manquer; – a (ship, train) ravitailleur; **s. teacher** suppléant, -ante mf. ◆**-ing** n (provision) fourniture f; (feeding) alimentation f. ◆**supplier** n Com fournisseur m.

support [sə'pɔːt] vt (bear weight of) soutenir, supporter; (help, encourage) soutenir, appuyer; (theory, idea) appuyer; (be in favour of) être en faveur de; (family, wife etc) assurer la subsistance de; (endure) supporter; – n (help, encouragement) appui m, soutien m; Tech support m; **means of s.** moyens mpl de subsistance; **in s. of** en faveur de; (evidence, theory) à l'appui de. ◆**-ing** a (role) Th Cin secondaire; (actor) qui a un rôle secondaire. ◆**supporter** n partisan, -ane *mf*; *Fb* supporter *m*. ◆**supportive** *a* to be s. prêter son appui (**of**, to à).

suppos/e [sə'pəʊz] *vti* supposer (**that** que); **I'm supposed to work** *or* **be working** (*ought*) je suis censé travailler; **he's s. to be rich** on le dit riche; **I s. (so)** je pense; **I don't s. so, I s. not** je ne pense pas; **you're tired, I s.** vous êtes fatigué, je suppose; **s.** *or* **supposing we go** (*suggestion*) si nous partions; **s.** *or* **supposing (that) you're right** supposons que tu aies raison. ◆**—ed** *a* soi-disant. ◆**—edly** [-idli] *adv* soi-disant. ◆**supposition** *n* supposition *f*.

suppository [sə'pɒzɪtərɪ] *n Med* suppositoire *m*.

suppress [sə'pres] *vt* (*put an end to*) supprimer; (*feelings*) réprimer; (*scandal, yawn etc*) étouffer. ◆**suppression** *n* suppression *f*; répression *f*. ◆**suppressor** *n El* dispositif *m* antiparasite.

supreme [suː'priːm] *a* suprême. ◆**supremacy** *n* suprématie *f* (**over** sur).

supremo [suː'priːməʊ] *n* (*pl* -os) *Fam* grand chef *m*.

surcharge ['sɜːtʃɑːdʒ] *n* (*extra charge*) supplément *m*; (*on stamp*) surcharge *f*; (*tax*) surtaxe *f*.

sure [ʃʊər] *a* (-er, -est) sûr (**of** de, **that** que); **she's s. to accept** il est sûr qu'elle acceptera; **it's s. to snow** il va sûrement neiger; **to make s. of** s'assurer de; **for s.** à coup sûr, pour sûr; **s.!, Fam s. thing!** bien sûr!; **s. enough** (*in effect*) en effet; **it s. is cold** *Am* il fait vraiment froid; **be s. to do it!** ne manquez pas de le faire! ◆**surefire** *a* infaillible. ◆**surely** *adv* (*certainly*) sûrement; **s. he didn't refuse?** (*I think, I hope*) il n'a tout de même pas refusé.

surety ['ʃʊərətɪ] *n* caution *f*.

surf [sɜːf] *n* (*foam*) ressac *m*. ◆**surfboard** *n* planche *f* (de surf). ◆**surfing** *n Sp* surf *m*.

surface ['sɜːfɪs] *n* surface *f*; **s. area** superficie *f*; **s. mail** courrier *m* par voie(s) de surface; **on the s.** (*to all appearances*) *Fig* en apparence; **–** *vt* (*road*) revêtir; **–** *vi* (*of swimmer etc*) remonter à la surface; (*of ideas, person etc*) *Fam* apparaître.

surfeit ['sɜːfɪt] *n* (*excess*) excès *m* (**of** de).

surge [sɜːdʒ] *n* (*of sea, enthusiasm*) vague *f*; (*rise*) montée *f*; **–** *vi* (*of crowd, hatred*) déferler; (*rise*) monter; **to s. forward** se lancer en avant.

surgeon ['sɜːdʒ(ə)n] *n* chirurgien *m*. ◆**surgery** *n* (*science*) chirurgie *f*; (*doctor's office*) cabinet *m*; (*sitting, period*) consultation *f*; **to undergo s.** subir une intervention.

◆**surgical** *a* chirurgical; (*appliance*) orthopédique; **s. spirit** alcool *m* à 90°.

surly ['sɜːlɪ] *a* (-ier, -iest) bourru. ◆**surliness** *n* air *m* bourru.

surmise [sə'maɪz] *vt* conjecturer (**that** que).

surmount [sə'maʊnt] *vt* (*overcome, be on top of*) surmonter.

surname ['sɜːneɪm] *n* nom *m* de famille.

surpass [sə'pɑːs] *vt* surpasser (**in** en).

surplus ['sɜːpləs] *n* surplus *m*; **–** *a* (*goods*) en surplus; **some s. material**/*etc* (*left over*) un surplus de tissu/*etc*; **s. stock** surplus *mpl*.

surpris/e [sə'praɪz] *n* surprise *f*; **to give s.o. a s.** faire une surprise à qn; **to take s.o. by s.** prendre qn au dépourvu; **–** *a* (*visit, result etc*) inattendu; **–** *vt* (*astonish*) étonner, surprendre; (*come upon*) surprendre. ◆**—ed** *a* surpris (**that** que **+** *sub*, **at** de qch, **at seeing**/*etc* de voir/*etc*); **I'm s. at his** *or* **her stupidity** sa bêtise m'étonne *or* me surprend. ◆**—ing** *a* surprenant. ◆**—ingly** *adv* étonnamment; **s. (enough) he ...** chose étonnante, il . . . .

surrealistic [sərɪə'lɪstɪk] *a* (*strange*) *Fig* surréaliste.

surrender [sə'rendər] **1** *vi* (*give oneself up*) se rendre (**to** à); **to s. to** (*police*) se livrer à; **–** *n Mil* reddition *f*, capitulation *f*. **2** *vt* (*hand over*) remettre, rendre (**to** à); (*right, claim*) renoncer à.

surreptitious [sʌrəp'tɪʃəs] *a* subreptice.

surrogate ['sʌrəgət] *n* substitut *m*; **s. mother** mère *f* porteuse.

surround [sə'raʊnd] *vt* entourer (**with** de); *Mil* encercler; **surrounded by** entouré de. ◆**—ing** *a* environnant. ◆**—ings** *npl* environs *mpl*; (*setting*) cadre *m*.

surveillance [sɜː'veɪləns] *n* (*of prisoner etc*) surveillance *f*.

survey [sə'veɪ] *vt* (*look at*) regarder; (*review*) passer en revue; (*house etc*) inspecter; (*land*) arpenter; **–** ['sɜːveɪ] *n* (*investigation*) enquête *f*; (*of house etc*) inspection *f*; (*of opinion*) sondage *m*; **a (general) s.** of une vue générale de. ◆**sur'veying** *n* arpentage *m*. ◆**sur'veyor** *n* (*arpenteur m*) géomètre *m*; (*of house etc*) expert *m*.

survive [sə'vaɪv] *vt* (*of person, custom etc*) survivre; **–** *vt* survivre à. ◆**survival** *n* (*act*) survie *f*; (*relic*) vestige *m*. ◆**survivor** *n* survivant, -ante *f*.

susceptible [sə'septəb(ə)l] *a* (*sensitive*) sensible (**to** à); **s. to colds**/*etc* (*prone to*) prédisposé aux rhumes/*etc*. ◆**suscepti'bility** *n* sensibilité *f*; prédisposition *f*; *pl* susceptibilité *f*.

suspect ['sʌspekt] *n* & *a* suspect, -ecte (*mf*); − [sə'spekt] *vt* soupçonner (**that** que, **of sth** de qch, **of doing** d'avoir fait); (*think questionable*) suspecter, douter de; **yes, I s.** oui, j'imagine.

suspend [sə'spend] *vt* **1** (*hang*) suspendre (**from à**). **2** (*stop, postpone, dismiss*) suspendre; (*passport etc*) retirer (provisoirement); (*pupil*) *Sch* renvoyer; **suspended sentence** *Jur* condamnation *f* avec sursis. ◆**suspender** *n* (*for stocking*) jarretelle *f*; *pl* (*braces*) *Am* bretelles *fpl*; **s. belt** porte-jarretelles *m inv.* ◆**suspension** *n* **1** (*stopping*) suspension *f*; (*of passport etc*) retrait *m* (provisoire). **2** (*of vehicle etc*) suspension *f*; **s. bridge** pont *m* suspendu.

suspense [sə'spens] *n* attente *f* (angoissée); (*in film, book etc*) suspense *m*; **in s.** (*person, matter*) en suspens.

suspicion [sə'spɪʃ(ə)n] *n* soupçon *m*; **to arouse s.** éveiller les soupçons; **with s.** (*distrust*) avec méfiance; **under s.** considéré comme suspect. ◆**suspicious** *a* (*person*) soupçonneux, méfiant; (*behaviour*) suspect; **s.(-looking)** (*suspect*) suspect; **to be s. of** *or* **about** (*distrust*) se méfier de. ◆**suspiciously** *adv* (*to behave etc*) d'une manière suspecte; (*to consider etc*) avec méfiance.

sustain [sə'steɪn] *vt* (*effort, theory*) soutenir; (*weight*) supporter; (*with food*) nourrir; (*life*) maintenir; (*damage, attack*) subir; (*injury*) recevoir. ◆**sustenance** *n* (*food*) nourriture *f*; (*quality*) valeur *f* nutritive.

swab [swɒb] *n* (*pad*) *Med* tampon *m*; (*specimen*) *Med* prélèvement *m*.

swagger ['swægər] *vi* (*walk*) parader; − *n* démarche *f* fanfaronne.

swallow ['swɒləʊ] **1** *vt* avaler; **to s. down** *or* **up** avaler; **to s. up** *Fig* engloutir; − *vi* avaler. **2** *n* (*bird*) hirondelle *f*.

swam [swæm] *see* **swim**.

swamp [swɒmp] *n* marais *m*, marécage *m*; − *vt* (*flood, overwhelm*) submerger (**with** de). ◆**swampy** *a* (**-ier, -iest**) marécageux.

swan [swɒn] *n* cygne *m*.

swank [swæŋk] *vi* (*show off*) *Fam* crâner, fanfaronner.

swap [swɒp] *n* échange *m*; *pl* (*stamps etc*) doubles *mpl*; − *vt* (**-pp-**) échanger (**for** contre); **to s. seats** changer de place; − *vi* échanger.

swarm [swɔːm] *n* (*of bees, people etc*) essaim *m*; − *vi* (*of bees, insects, people etc*) fourmiller (**with** de); **to s. in** (*of people*) entrer en foule.

swarthy ['swɔːðɪ] *a* (**-ier, -iest**) (*dark*) basané.

swastika ['swɒstɪkə] *n* (*Nazi emblem*) croix *f* gammée.

swat [swɒt] *vt* (**-tt-**) (*fly etc*) écraser.

sway [sweɪ] *vi* se balancer, osciller; − *vt* balancer; *Fig* influencer; − *n* balancement *m*; *Fig* influence *f*.

swear [sweər] *vt* (*pt* **swore**, *pp* **sworn**) jurer (**to do** faire, **that** que); **to s. an oath** prêter serment; **to s. s.o. to secrecy** faire jurer le silence à qn; **sworn enemies** ennemis *mpl* jurés; − *vi* (*take an oath*) jurer (**to sth** de qch); (*curse*) jurer, pester (**at** contre); **she swears by this lotion** elle ne jure que par cette lotion. ◆**swearword** *n* gros mot *m*, juron *m*.

sweat [swet] *n* sueur *f*; **s. shirt** sweat-shirt *m*; − *vi* (*of person, wall etc*) suer (**with** de); − *vt* **to s. out** (*cold*) *Med* se débarrasser de (*en transpirant*). ◆**sweater** *n* (*garment*) pull *m*. ◆**sweaty** *a* (**-ier, -iest**) (*shirt etc*) plein de sueur; (*hand*) moite; (*person*) (tout) en sueur, (tout) en nage.

swede [swiːd] *n* (*vegetable*) rutabaga *m*.

Swede [swiːd] *n* Suédois, -oise *mf.* ◆**Sweden** *n* Suède *f.* ◆**Swedish** *a* suédois; − *n* (*language*) suédois *m*.

sweep [swiːp] *n* coup *m* de balai; (*movement*) *Fig* (*large*) mouvement *m*; (*curve*) courbe *f*; **to make a clean s.** (*removal*) faire table rase de (*of*); (*victory*) remporter une victoire totale; − *vt* (*pt* & *pp* **swept**) (*with broom*) balayer; (*chimney*) ramoner; (*river*) draguer; **to s. away** *or* **out** *or* **up** balayer; **to s. away** *or* **along** (*carry off*) emporter; **to s. aside** (*dismiss*) écarter; − *vi* **to s. (up)** balayer; **to s. in** (*of person*) *Fig* entrer rapidement *or* majestueusement; **to s. through** (*of fear etc*) saisir (*groupe etc*); (*of disease etc*) ravager (*pays etc*). ◆**-ing** *a* (*gesture*) large; (*change*) radical; (*statement*) trop général. ◆**sweepstake** *n* (*lottery*) sweepstake *m*.

sweet [swiːt] *a* (**-er, -est**) (*not sour*) doux; (*agreeable*) agréable, doux; (*tea, coffee etc*) sucré; (*person, house, kitchen*) mignon, gentil; **to have a s. tooth** aimer les sucreries; **to be s.-smelling** sentir bon; **s. corn** maïs *m*; **s. pea** *Bot* pois *m* de senteur; **s. potato** patate *f* douce; **s. shop** confiserie *f*; **s. talk** *Fam* cajoleries *fpl*, douceurs *fpl*; − *n* (*candy*) bonbon *m*; (*dessert*) dessert *m*; **my s.!** (*darling*) mon ange! ◆**sweeten** *vt* (*tea etc*) sucrer; *Fig* adoucir. ◆**sweetener** *n* saccharine *f*. ◆**sweetie** *n* (*darling*) *Fam* chéri, -ie *mf.* ◆**sweetly** *adv* (*kindly*) genti-

ment; (softly) doucement. ◆**sweetness** n
douceur f; (taste) goût m sucré.

sweetbread ['switbred] n ris m de veau or
d'agneau.

sweetheart ['swithɑːt] n (lover) ami, -ie mf;
my s.! (darling) mon ange!

swell [swel] **1** n (of sea) houle f. **2** a (very
good) Am Fam formidable. **3** vi (pt swelled,
pp swollen or swelled) se gonfler; (of river,
numbers) grossir; **to s. (up)** Med enfler,
gonfler; – vt (river, numbers) grossir.
◆**—ing** n Med enflure f.

swelter ['sweltər] vi étouffer. ◆**—ing** a
étouffant; **it's s.** on étouffe.

swept [swept] see sweep.

swerve [swɜːv] vi (while running etc) faire un
écart; (of vehicle) faire une embardée.

swift [swift] **1** a (-er, -est) rapide; **to s. act**
prompt à agir. **2** n (bird) martinet m.
◆**—ly** adv rapidement. ◆**—ness** n rapidité f.

swig [swig] n (of beer etc) lampée f.

swill [swil] vt **to s. (out or down)** laver (à
grande eau).

swim [swim] n baignade f; **to go for a s.** se
baigner, nager; – vi (pt swam, pp swum,
pres p swimming) nager; Sp faire de la natation; (of head, room) Fig tourner; **to go
swimming** aller nager; **to s. away** se sauver
(à la nage); – vt (river) traverser à la nage;
(length, crawl etc) nager. ◆**swimming**
natation f; s. **costume** maillot m de bain; s.
pool, s. **baths** piscine f; s. **trunks** slip m or
caleçon m de bain. ◆**swimmer** n nageur,
-euse mf. ◆**swimsuit** n maillot m de bain.

swindl/e ['swindl] n escroquerie f; – vt
escroquer; **to s. s.o. out of money** escroquer
de l'argent à qn. ◆**—er** n escroc m.

swine [swain] n inv (person) Pej salaud m.

swing [swiŋ] n (seat) balançoire f; (movement) balancement m; (of pendulum) oscillation f; (in opinion) revirement m;
(rhythm) rythme m; **to be in full s.** battre
son plein; **to be in the s. of things** Fam être
dans le bain; s. **door** porte f de saloon; – vi
(pt & pp swung) (sway) se balancer; (of
pendulum) osciller; (turn) virer; **to s. round**
(turn suddenly) virer, tourner; (of person) se
retourner (vivement); (of vehicle in collision
etc) faire un tête-à-queue; **to s. into action**
passer à l'action; – vt (arms etc) balancer;
(axe) brandir; (influence) Fam influencer;
to s. round (car etc) faire tourner. ◆**—ing** a
Fam (trendy) dans le vent; (lively) plein de
vie; (music) entraînant.

swingeing ['swindʒiŋ] a s. **cuts** des réduc-
tions fpl draconiennes.

swipe [swaip] vt Fam (hit) frapper dur;
(steal) piquer (from s.o. à qn); – n Fam
grand coup m.

swirl [swɜːl] n tourbillon m; – vi tourbillonner.

swish [swiʃ] **1** a (posh) Fam rupin, chic. **2** vi
(of whip etc) siffler; (of fabric) froufrouter;
– n sifflement m; froufrou m.

Swiss [swis] a suisse; – n inv Suisse m, Suissesse f; **the S.** les Suisses mpl.

switch [switʃ] n El bouton m (électrique),
interrupteur m; (change) changement m (in
de); (reversal) revirement m (in de); – vt
(money, employee etc) transférer (to à);
(affection, support) reporter (to sur, from
de); (exchange) échanger (for contre); **to s.
buses/etc** changer de bus/etc; **to s. places**
or seats changer de place; **to s. off** (lamp,
gas, radio etc) éteindre; (engine) arrêter; **to
s. itself off** (of heating etc) s'éteindre tout
seul; **to s. on** (lamp, gas, radio etc) mettre,
allumer; (engine) mettre en marche; – vi **to
s. (over) to** passer à; **to s. off** (switch off
light, radio etc) éteindre; **to s. on** (switch on
light, radio etc) allumer. ◆**switchback** n
(at funfair) montagnes fpl russes.
◆**switchblade** n Am couteau m à cran
d'arrêt. ◆**switchboard** n Tel standard m;
s. **operator** standardiste mf.

Switzerland ['switsələnd] n Suisse f.

swivel ['swivl] vi (-ll-, Am -l-) **to s. (round)**
(of chair etc) pivoter; – a s. **chair** fauteuil m
pivotant.

swollen ['swəul(ə)n] see swell 3; – a (leg etc)
enflé.

swoon [swuːn] vi Lit se pâmer.

swoop [swuːp] **1** vi **to s. (down) on** (of bird)
fondre sur. **2** n (of police) descente f; – vi
faire une descente (on dans).

swop [swɒp] n, vt & vi = swap.

sword [sɔːd] n épée f. ◆**swordfish** n
espadon m.

swore, sworn [swɔːr, swɔːn] see swear.

swot [swɒt] vti (-tt-) **to s. (up)** (study) Fam
potasser; **to s. (up) for** (exam), **to s. up on**
(subject) Fam potasser; – n Pej Fam
bûcheur, -euse mf.

swum [swʌm] see swim.

swung [swʌŋ] see swing.

sycamore ['sikəmɔːr] n (maple) sycomore
m; (plane) Am platane m.

sycophant ['sikəfænt] n flagorneur, -euse
mf.

syllable ['siləb(ə)l] n syllabe f.

syllabus ['siləbəs] n Sch Univ programme
m.

symbol ['simb(ə)l] n symbole m. ◆**sym-**

'**bolic** a symbolique. ◆**symbolism** n symbolisme m. ◆**symbolize** vt symboliser.

symmetry ['sɪmətrɪ] n symétrie f. ◆**sy'mmetrical** a symétrique.

sympathy ['sɪmpəθɪ] n (pity) compassion f; (understanding) compréhension f; (condolences) condoléances fpl; (solidarity) solidarité f (for avec); **to be in s. with** (workers in dispute) être du côté de; (s.o.'s opinion etc) comprendre, être en accord avec. ◆**sympa'thetic** a (showing pity) compatissant; (understanding) compréhensif; **s. to** (favourable) bien disposé à l'égard de. ◆**sympa'thetically** adv avec compassion; avec compréhension. ◆**sympathize** vi **I s. (with you)** (pity) je compatis (à votre sort); (understanding) je vous comprends. ◆**sympathizer** n Pol sympathisant, -ante mf.

symphony ['sɪmfənɪ] n symphonie f; – a (orchestra, concert) symphonique. ◆**sym'phonic** a symphonique.

symposium [sɪm'pəʊzɪəm] n symposium m.

symptom ['sɪmptəm] n symptôme m. ◆**sympto'matic** a symptomatique (of de).

synagogue ['sɪnəgɒg] n synagogue f.

synchronize ['sɪŋkrənaɪz] vt synchroniser.

syndicate ['sɪndɪkət] n (of businessmen, criminals) syndicat m.

syndrome ['sɪndrəʊm] n Med & Fig syndrome m.

synod ['sɪnəd] n Rel synode m.

synonym ['sɪnənɪm] n synonyme m. ◆**sy'nonymous** a synonyme (**with** de).

synopsis, pl **-opses** [sɪ'nɒpsɪs, -ɒpsiːz] n résumé m, synopsis m; (of film) synopsis m.

syntax ['sɪntæks] n Gram syntaxe f.

synthesis, pl **-theses** ['sɪnθəsɪs, -θəsiːz] n synthèse f.

synthetic [sɪn'θetɪk] a synthétique.

syphilis ['sɪfɪlɪs] n syphilis f.

Syria ['sɪrɪə] n Syrie f. ◆**Syrian** a & n syrien, -ienne (mf).

syringe [sɪ'rɪndʒ] n seringue f.

syrup ['sɪrəp] n sirop m; (golden) **s.** (treacle) mélasse f (raffinée). ◆**syrupy** a sirupeux.

system ['sɪstəm] n (structure, plan, network etc) & Anat système m; (human body) organisme m; (order) méthode f; **systems analyst** analyste-programmeur mf. ◆**syste'matic** a systématique. ◆**syste'matically** adv systématiquement.

T

T, t [tiː] n T, t m. ◆**T-junction** n Aut intersection f en T. ◆**T-shirt** n tee-shirt m, T-shirt m.

ta! [tɑː] int Sl merci!

tab [tæb] n (label) étiquette f; (tongue) patte f; (loop) attache f; (bill) Am addition f; **to keep tabs on** Fam surveiller (de près).

tabby ['tæbɪ] a **t. cat** chat, chatte mf tigré(e).

table¹ ['teɪb(ə)l] n **1** (furniture) table f; **bedside/card/operating t.** table de nuit/de jeu/d'opération; **to lay** or **set/clear the t.** mettre/débarrasser la table; (sitting) **at the t.** à table; **t. top** dessus m de table. **2** (list) table f; **t. of contents** table des matières. ◆**tablecloth** n nappe f. ◆**tablemat** n (of fabric) napperon m; (hard) dessous-de-plat m inv. ◆**tablespoon** n = cuiller f à soupe. ◆**tablespoonful** n = cuillerée f à soupe.

table² ['teɪb(ə)l] vt (motion etc) Pol présenter; (postpone) Am ajourner.

tablet ['tæblɪt] n **1** (pill) Med comprimé m. **2** (inscribed stone) plaque f.

tabloid ['tæblɔɪd] n (newspaper) quotidien m populaire.

taboo [tə'buː] a & n tabou (m).

tabulator ['tæbjʊleɪtər] n (of typewriter) tabulateur m.

tacit ['tæsɪt] a tacite. ◆**—ly** adv tacitement.

taciturn ['tæsɪtɜːn] a taciturne.

tack [tæk] n **1** (nail) semence f; (thumbtack) Am punaise f; **to get down to brass tacks** Fig en venir aux faits; – vt **to t. (down)** clouer. **2** n (stitch) Tex point m de bâti; – vt **to t. (down** or **on) bâtir; to t. on (add)** Fig r)ajouter. **3** vi (of ship) louvoyer; – n (course of action) Fig voie f.

tackle ['tæk(ə)l] n **1** (gear) matériel m, équipement m. **2** vt (task, problem etc) s'attaquer à; (thief etc) saisir; Sp plaquer; – n Sp plaquage m.

tacky ['tækɪ] a (-ier, -iest) **1** (wet, sticky) collant, pas sec. **2** (clothes, attitude etc) Am Fam moche.

tact [tækt] n tact m. ◆**tactful** a (remark etc) plein de tact, diplomatique; **she's t.** elle a du tact. ◆**tactfully** adv avec tact. ◆**tact-less** a qui manque de tact. ◆**tactlessly** adv sans tact.

tactic ['tæktɪk] n a t. une tactique; **tactics** n la tactique. ◆**tactical** a tactique.

tactile ['tæktaɪl] a tactile.

tadpole ['tædpəʊl] n têtard m.

taffy ['tæfɪ] n (toffee) Am caramel m (dur).

tag [tæg] **1** n (label) étiquette f; (end piece) bout m; – vt (-gg-) **to t. on** (add) Fam rajouter (to à). **2** n (-gg-) **to t. along** (follow) suivre.

Tahiti [taː'hiːtɪ] n Tahiti m.

tail [teɪl] **1** n (of animal) queue f; (of shirt) pan m; pl (outfit) habit m, queue-de-pie f; **t. end** fin f, bout m; **heads or tails** pile ou face? **2** vt (follow) suivre, filer. **3** vi **to t. off** (lessen) diminuer. ◆**tailback** n (of traffic) bouchon m. ◆**tailcoat** n queue-de-pie f. ◆**taillight** n Aut Am feu m arrière inv.

tailor ['teɪlər] n (person) tailleur m; – vt (garment) façonner; Fig adapter (**to, to suit** à). ◆**t.-'made** a fait sur mesure; **t.-made for** (specially designed) conçu pour; (suited) fait pour.

tainted ['teɪntɪd] a (air) pollué; (food) gâté; Fig souillé.

take [teɪk] vt (pt took, pp taken) prendre; (choice) faire; (prize) remporter; (exam) passer; (contain) Math soustraire (**from** de); (tolerate) supporter; (bring) apporter (qch) (**to** à); (person) amener (**to** à), (person by car) conduire (**to** à); (escort) accompagner (**to** à); (lead away) emmener; (of road) mener (qn); **to t. sth to s.o.** (ap)porter qch à qn; **to t. s.o. (out) to** (theatre etc) emmener qn à; **to t. sth with one** emporter qch; **to t. over or round or along** (object) apporter; (person) amener; **to t. s.o. home** (on foot, by car etc) ramener qn; **it takes an army/courage/etc** (requires) il faut une armée/du courage/etc (**to do** pour faire); **I took an hour to do it or over it** j'ai mis une heure à le faire, ça m'a pris une heure pour le faire; **I t. it that** je présume que; – n Cin prise f de vue(s); – vi (of glue) prendre. ■ **to t. after** (be like) ressembler à; **to t. apart** vt (machine) démonter; **to t. away** vt (thing) emporter; (person) emmener; (remove) enlever (**from** à); Math soustraire (**from** de). ◆**t.-away** (meal) a à emporter; – n café m or restaurant m qui fait des plats à emporter; (meal) plat m à emporter; **to t. back** vt reprendre; (return) rapporter; (statement) retirer; **to t. down** vt (object) descendre; (notes) prendre; **to t. in**

lir; (skirt) reprendre; (include) englober; (distance) couvrir; (understand) comprendre; (deceive) Fam rouler; **to t. off** vt (remove) enlever; (train, bus) supprimer; (lead away) emmener; (mimic) imiter; Math déduire (**from** de); – vi (of aircraft) décoller. ◆**takeoff** n (of aircraft) décollage m; **to t. on** vt (work, employee, passenger, shape) prendre (**to** à); **to t. out** vt (from pocket etc) sortir; (stain) enlever; (tooth) arracher; (licence, insurance) prendre; **to t. it out on** Fam passer sa colère sur. ◆**t.-out** a & n Am = **t.-away; to t. over** vt (be responsible for the running of) prendre la direction de; (overrun) envahir; (buy out) Com racheter (compagnie); **to t. over s.o.'s job** remplacer qn; – vi Mil Pol prendre le pouvoir; (relieve) prendre la relève (**from** de); (succeed) prendre la succession (**from** de). ◆**t.-over** n Com rachat m; Pol prise f de pouvoir; **to t. round** vt (distribute) distribuer; (visitor) faire visiter; **to t. to** vi **to t. to doing** se mettre à faire; **I didn't t. to him/it** il/ça ne m'a pas plu; **to t. up** vt (carry up) monter; (hem) raccourcir; (continue) reprendre; (occupy) prendre; (hobby) se mettre à; – vi **to t. up with** se lier avec. ◆**taken** a (seat) pris; (impressed) impressionné (**with, by** par); **to be t. ill** tomber malade. ◆**taking** n (capture) Mil prise f; pl (money) Com recette f.

talcum ['tælkəm] n **t. powder** talc m.

tale [teɪl] n (story) conte m; (account, report) récit m; (lie) histoire f; **to tell tales** rapporter (**on** sur).

talent ['tælənt] n talent m; (talented people) talents mpl; **to have a t. for** avoir du talent pour. ◆**talented** a doué, talentueux.

talk [tɔːk] n (words) propos mpl; (gossip) bavardage(s) m(pl); (conversation) conversation f (**about** à propos de); (interview) entretien m; (lecture) exposé m (**on** sur); (informal) causerie f (**on** sur); pl (negotiations) pourparlers mpl; **to have a t. with** parler avec; **there's t. of** on parle de; – vi parler (**to** à; **with** avec; **about, of** de); (chat) bavarder; **to t. down to s.o.** parler à qn comme à un inférieur; – vt (nonsense) dire; **to t. politics** parler politique; **to t. s.o. into doing/out of doing** persuader qn de faire/de ne pas faire; **to t. over** discuter (de); **to t. s.o. round** persuader qn. ◆**—ing** a (film) parlant; **to give s.o. a talking-to** Fam passer un savon à qn. ◆**talkative** a bavard. ◆**talker** n causeur, -euse mf; **she's a good t.** elle parle bien.

tall [tɔːl] a (-er, -est) (person) grand; (tree,

house etc) haut; **how t. are you?** combien mesures-tu?; **a t. story** *Fig* une histoire invraisemblable *or* à dormir debout. ◆**tallboy** *n* grande commode *f*. ◆**tallness** *n (of person)* grande taille *f*; *(of building etc)* hauteur *f*.

tally ['tælɪ] *vi* correspondre **(with** à).

tambourine [tæmbə'riːn] *n* tambourin *m*.

tame [teɪm] *a* **(-er, -est)** *(animal, bird)* apprivoisé; *(person)* Fig docile; *(book, play)* fade. − *vt (animal, bird)* apprivoiser; *(lion, passion)* dompter.

tamper ['tæmpər] *vi* **to t. with** *(lock, car etc)* toucher à; *(text)* altérer.

tampon ['tæmpɒn] *n* tampon *m* hygiénique.

tan [tæn] **1** *n (suntan)* bronzage *m*; − *vti* **(-nn-)** bronzer. **2** *a (colour)* marron clair *inv*. **3** *vt* **(-nn-)** *(hide)* tanner.

tandem ['tændəm] *n* **1** *(bicycle)* tandem *m*. **2 in t.** *(to work etc)* en tandem.

tang [tæŋ] *n (taste)* saveur *f* piquante; *(smell)* odeur *f* piquante. ◆**tangy** *a* **(-ier, -iest)** piquant.

tangerine [tændʒə'riːn] *n* mandarine *f*.

tangible ['tændʒəb(ə)l] *a* tangible.

tangl/e ['tæŋg(ə)l] *n* enchevêtrement *m*; **to get into a t.** *(of rope)* s'enchevêtrer; *(of hair)* s'emmêler; *(of person)* Fig se mettre dans une situation sans espoir possible. ◆**−ed** *a* enchevêtré; *(hair)* emmêlé; **to get t. =** **to get into a tangle**.

tank [tæŋk] *n* **1** *(for storage of water, fuel etc)* réservoir *m*; *(vat)* cuve *f*; *(fish)* aquarium *m*. **2** *(vehicle)* Mil char *m*, tank *m*.

tankard ['tæŋkəd] *n (beer mug)* chope *f*.

tanker ['tæŋkər] *n (truck)* Aut camion-citerne *m*; *(oil)* t. *(ship)* pétrolier *m*.

tantalizing ['tæntəlaɪzɪŋ] *a (irrésistiblement)* tentant. ◆**−ly** *adv* d'une manière tentante.

tantamount ['tæntəmaʊnt] *a* **it's t. to** cela équivaut à.

tantrum ['tæntrəm] *n* accès *m* de colère.

tap [tæp] **1** *n (for water)* robinet *m*; **on t.** *Fig* disponible. **2** *vti* **(-pp-)** frapper légèrement, tapoter; − *n* petit coup *m*; **t. dancing** claquettes *fpl*. **3** *vt* **(-pp-)** *(phone)* placer sur table d'écoute. **4** *vt* **(-pp-)** *(resources)* exploiter.

tape [teɪp] **1** *n* ruban *m*; **(sticky) t.** ruban adhésif; **t. measure** mètre *m* à) ruban; − *vt (stick)* coller *(avec du ruban adhésif)*. **2** *n (for sound recording)* bande *f (magnétique)*; *(video)* bande *f (vidéo)*; **t. recorder** magnétophone *m*; − *vt* enregistrer.

taper ['teɪpər] **1** *vi (of fingers etc)* s'effiler; **to t. off** *Fig* diminuer. **2** *n (candle)* Rel cierge

m. ◆**−ed** *a*, ◆**−ing** *a (fingers)* fuselé; *(trousers)* à bas étroits.

tapestry ['tæpəstrɪ] *n* tapisserie *f*.

tapioca [tæpɪ'əʊkə] *n* tapioca *m*.

tar [tɑːr] *n* goudron *m*; − *vt* **(-rr-)** goudronner.

tardy ['tɑːdɪ] *a* **(-ier, -iest)** *(belated)* tardif; *(slow)* lent.

target ['tɑːgɪt] *n* cible *f*; Fig objectif *m*; **t. date** date *f* fixée; − *vt (aim)* Fig destiner (at à); *(aim at)* Fig viser.

tariff ['tærɪf] *n (tax)* tarif *m* douanier; *(prices)* tarif *m*.

tarmac ['tɑːmæk] *n* macadam *m (goudronné)*; *(runway)* piste *f*.

tarnish ['tɑːnɪʃ] *vt* ternir.

tarpaulin [tɑː'pɔːlɪn] *n* bâche *f (goudronnée)*.

tarragon ['tærəgən] *n* Bot Culin estragon *m*.

tarry ['tærɪ] *vi (remain)* Lit rester.

tart [tɑːt] **1** *n (pie)* tarte *f*. **2** *a* **(-er, -est)** *(taste, remark)* aigre. **3** *n (prostitute)* Pej Fam poule *f*. **4** *vt* **to t. up** Pej Fam *(decorate)* embellir; *(dress)* attifer. ◆**−ness** *n* aigreur *f*.

tartan ['tɑːt(ə)n] *n* tartan *m*; − *a* écossais.

tartar ['tɑːtər] **1** *n (on teeth)* tartre *m*. **2** *a* **t. sauce** sauce *f* tartare.

task [tɑːsk] *n* tâche *f*; **to take to t.** prendre à partie; **t. force** Mil détachement *m* spécial; Pol commission *f* spéciale.

tassel ['tæs(ə)l] *n (on clothes etc)* gland *m*.

taste [teɪst] *n* goût *m*; **to get a t. for** prendre goût à; **in good/bad t.** de bon/mauvais goût; **to have a t. of** goûter; goûter à; goûter de; − *vt (eat, enjoy)* goûter; *(try, sample)* goûter à; *(make out the taste of)* sentir (le goût de); *(experience)* goûter de; − *vi* **to t. of** *or* **like** avoir un goût de; **to t. delicious/etc** avoir un goût délicieux/etc; **how does it t.?** comment le trouves-tu?; − *a* **t. bud** papille *f* gustative. ◆**tasteful** *a* de bon goût. ◆**tastefully** *adv* avec goût. ◆**tasteless** *a (a food etc)* sans goût; *(joke etc)* Fig de mauvais goût. ◆**tasty** *a* **(-ier, -iest)** savoureux.

tat [tæt] *see* **tit 2**.

ta-ta! [tæ'tɑː] *int* Sl au revoir!

tattered ['tætəd] *a (clothes)* en lambeaux; *(person)* déguenillé. ◆**tatters** *npl* **in t.** en lambeaux.

tattoo [tæ'tuː] **1** *n (pl -oos)* (on body) tatouage *m*; − *vt* tatouer. **2** *n (pl -oos)* Mil spectacle *m* militaire.

tatty ['tætɪ] *a* **(-ier, -iest)** *(clothes etc)* Fam miteux.

taught [tɔːt] *see* **teach**.

taunt [tɔ:nt] *vt* railler; – *n* raillerie *f.*
◆**–ing** *a* railleur.

Taurus ['tɔ:rəs] *n* (*sign*) le Taureau.

taut [tɔ:t] *a* (*rope, person etc*) tendu.

tavern ['tævən] *n* taverne *f.*

tawdry ['tɔ:drɪ] *a* (-ier, -iest) *Pej* tape-à-l'œil *inv.*

tawny ['tɔ:nɪ] *a* (*colour*) fauve; (*port*) ambré.

tax[1] [tæks] *n* taxe *f*, impôt *m*; (**income**) **t.** impôts *mpl* (sur le revenu); – *a* fiscal; **t. collector** percepteur *m*; **t. relief** dégrèvement *m* (d'impôt); – *vt* (*person, goods*) imposer. ◆**taxable** *a* imposable. ◆**tax-'ation** *n* (*act*) imposition *f*; (*taxes*) impôts *mpl.* ◆**tax-free** *a* exempt d'impôts. ◆**taxman** *n* (*pl* **-men**) *Fam* percepteur *m.* ◆**taxpayer** *n* contribuable *mf.*

tax[2] [tæks] *vt* (*patience etc*) mettre à l'épreuve; (*tire*) fatiguer. ◆**–ing** *a* (*journey etc*) éprouvant.

taxi ['tæksɪ] **1** *n* taxi *m*; **t. cab** taxi *m*; **t. rank**, *Am* **t. stand** station *f* de taxis. **2** *vi* (*of aircraft*) rouler au sol.

tea [ti:] *n* thé *m*; (*snack*) goûter *m*; **high t.** goûter *m* (dînatoire); **to have t.** prendre le thé; (*afternoon snack*) goûter; **t. break** pause-thé *f*; **t. chest** caisse *f* (à thé); **t. cloth** (*for drying dishes*) torchon *m*; **t. set** service *m* à thé; **t. towel** torchon *m.* ◆**teabag** *n* sachet *m* de thé. ◆**teacup** *n* tasse *f* à thé. ◆**tealeaf** *n* (*pl* **-leaves**) feuille *f* de thé. ◆**teapot** *n* théière *f.* ◆**tearoom** *n* salon *m* de thé. ◆**teaspoon** *n* petite cuiller *f.* ◆**teaspoonful** *n* cuillerée *f* à café. ◆**teatime** *n* l'heure *f* du thé.

teach [ti:tʃ] *vt* (*pt* & *pp* **taught**) apprendre (s.o. sth qch à qn, that que); (*in school etc*) enseigner (s.o. sth qch à qn); **to t. s.o. (how) to do** apprendre à qn à faire; **to t. school** *Am* enseigner; **to t. oneself sth** apprendre qch tout seul; – *vi* enseigner. ◆**–ing** *n* enseignement *m*; – *a* (*staff*) enseignant; (*method, material*) pédagogique; **t. profession** enseignement *m*; (*teachers*) enseignants *mpl*; **t. qualification** diplôme *m* permettant d'enseigner. ◆**–er** *n* professeur *m*; (*in primary school*) instituteur, -trice *mf.*

teak [ti:k] *n* (*wood*) teck *m.*

team [ti:m] *n Sp* équipe *f*; (*of oxen*) attelage *m*; **t. mate** coéquipier, -ière *mf*; – *vi* **to t. up** faire équipe (with avec). ◆**teamster** *n Am* routier *m.* ◆**teamwork** *n* collaboration *f.*

tear[1] [teər] *n* déchirure *f*; – *vt* (*pt* **tore**, *pp* **torn**) (*rip*) déchirer; (*snatch*) arracher (**from** s.o. à qn); **torn between** *Fig* tiraillé entre; **to t. down** (*house etc*) démolir; **to t. away** *or* **off**

or **out** (*forcefully*) arracher; (*stub, receipt, stamp etc*) détacher; **to t. up** déchirer; – *vi* (*of cloth etc*) se déchirer. **2** *vi* (*pt* **tore**, *pp* **torn**) **to t. along** (*rush*) aller à toute vitesse.

tear[2] [tɪər] *n* larme *f*; **in tears** en larmes; **close to** *or* **near** (**to**) **tears** au bord des larmes. ◆**tearful** *a* (*eyes, voice*) larmoyant; (*person*) en larmes. ◆**tearfully** *adv* en pleurant. ◆**teargas** *n* gaz *m* lacrymogène.

tearaway ['teərəweɪ] *n Fam* petit voyou *m.*

tease [ti:z] *vt* taquiner; (*harshly*) tourmenter; – *n* (*person*) taquin, -ine *mf.* ◆**–ing** *a* (*remark etc*) taquin. ◆**–er** *n* **1** (*person*) taquin, -ine *mf.* **2** (*question*) *Fam* colle *f.*

teat [ti:t] *n* (*of bottle, animal*) tétine *f.*

technical ['teknɪk(ə)l] *a* technique. ◆**techni'cality** *n* (*detail*) détail *m* technique. ◆**technically** *adv* techniquement; *Fig* théoriquement. ◆**tech'nician** *n* technicien, -ienne *mf.* ◆**tech'nique** *n* technique *f.* ◆**technocrat** *n* technocrate *m.* ◆**techno'logical** *a* technologique. ◆**tech'nology** *n* technologie *f.*

teddy ['tedɪ] *n* **t. (bear)** ours *m* (en peluche).

tedious ['ti:dɪəs] *a* fastidieux. ◆**tediousness** *n*, ◆**tedium** *n* ennui *m.*

teem [ti:m] *vi* **1** (*swarm*) grouiller (with de). **2 to t. (with rain)** pleuvoir à torrents. ◆**–ing** *a* **1** (*crowd, street etc*) grouillant. **2 t. rain** pluie *f* torrentielle.

teenage ['ti:neɪdʒ] *a* (*person, behaviour*) adolescent; (*fashion*) pour adolescents. ◆**teenager** *n* adolescent, -ente *mf.* ◆**teens** *npl* **in one's t.** adolescent.

teeny (weeny) ['ti:nɪ('wi:nɪ)] *a* (*tiny*) *Fam* minuscule.

tee-shirt ['ti:ʃɜ:t] *n* tee-shirt *m.*

teeter ['ti:tər] *vi* chanceler.

teeth [ti:θ] *see* **tooth.** ◆**teeth/e** [ti:ð] *vi* faire ses dents. ◆**–ing** *n* dentition *f*; **t. ring** anneau *m* de dentition; **t. troubles** *Fig* difficultés *fpl* de mise en route.

teetotal [ti:'təʊt(ə)l] *a*, ◆**teetotaller** *n* (*personne f*) qui ne boit pas d'alcool.

tele- ['telɪ] *pref* télé-.

telecommunications [telɪkəmju:nɪ'keɪ-ʃ(ə)nz] *npl* télécommunications *fpl.*

telegram ['telɪgræm] *n* télégramme *m.*

telegraph ['telɪgrɑ:f] *n* télégraphe *m*; – *a* (*wire etc*) télégraphique; **t. pole** poteau *m* télégraphique.

telepathy [tə'lepəθɪ] *n* télépathie *f.*

telephone ['telɪfəʊn] *n* téléphone *m*; **on the t.** (*speaking*) au téléphone; – *a* (*call, line etc*) téléphonique; (*directory*) du téléphone; (*number*) de téléphone; **t. booth, t. box** cabine *f* téléphonique; – *vi* téléphoner; – *vt* (*message*) téléphoner (to à); **to t. s.o.** téléphoner à qn. ◆**te'lephonist** *n* téléphoniste *mf*.

teleprinter ['telɪprɪntər] *n* téléscripteur *m*.

telescope ['telɪskəup] *n* télescope *m*. ◆**tele'scopic** *a* (*pictures, aerial, umbrella*) télescopique.

teletypewriter [telɪ'taɪpraɪtər] *n Am* téléscripteur *m*.

televise ['telɪvaɪz] *vt* téléviser. ◆**tele'vision** *n* télévision *f*; **on (the) t.** à la télévision; **to watch (the) t.** regarder la télévision; – *a* (*programme etc*) de télévision; (*serial, report*) télévisé.

telex ['teleks] *n* (*service, message*) télex *m*; – *vt* envoyer par télex.

tell [tel] *vt* (*pt & pp* told) dire (**s.o. sth** qch à qn, **that** que); (*story*) raconter; (*future*) prédire; (*distinguish*) distinguer (**from** de); (*know*) savoir; **to t. s.o. to do** dire à qn de faire; **to know how to t. the time** savoir lire l'heure; **to t. the difference** voir la différence (**between** entre); **to t. off** (*scold*) *Fam* gronder; – *vi* dire; (*have an effect*) avoir un effet; (*know*) savoir; **to t. of** *or* **about sth** parler de qch; **to t. on s.o.** *Fam* rapporter sur qn. ◆**-ing** (*smile etc*) révélateur; (*blow*) efficace. ◆**telltale** *n Fam* rapporteur, -euse *mf*.

teller ['telər] *n* (*bank*) **t.** caissier, -ière *mf*.

telly ['telɪ] *n Fam* télé *f*.

temerity [tə'merɪtɪ] *n* témérité *f*.

temp [temp] *n* (*secretary etc*) *Fam* intérimaire *mf*.

temper ['tempər] **1** *n* (*mood, nature*) humeur *f*; (*anger*) colère *f*; **to lose one's t.** se mettre en colère; **in a bad t.** de mauvaise humeur; **to have a (bad** *or* **awful) t.** avoir un caractère de cochon. **2** *vt* (*steel*) tremper; *Fig* tempérer.

temperament ['temprəmənt] *n* tempérament *m*. ◆**tempera'mental** *a* (*person, machine etc*) capricieux; (*inborn*) inné.

temperance ['tempərəns] *n* (*in drink*) tempérance *f*.

temperate ['tempərət] *a* (*climate etc*) tempéré.

temperature ['temp(ə)rətʃər] *n* température *f*; **to have a t.** *Med* avoir *or* faire de la température.

tempest ['tempɪst] *n Lit* tempête *f*. ◆**tem'pestuous** *a* (*meeting etc*) orageux.

template ['templət] *n* (*of plastic, metal etc*) *Tex* patron *m*; *Math* trace-courbes *m inv*.

temple ['temp(ə)l] *n* **1** *Rel* temple *m*. **2** *Anat* tempe *f*.

tempo ['tempəu] *n* (*pl* -os) tempo *m*.

temporal ['tempərəl] *a* temporel.

temporary ['tempərərɪ] *a* provisoire; (*job, worker*) temporaire; (*secretary*) intérimaire.

tempt [tempt] *vt* tenter; **tempted to do** tenté de faire; **to t. s.o. to do** persuader qn de faire. ◆**-ing** *a* tentant. ◆**-ingly** *adv* d'une manière tentante. ◆**temp'tation** *n* tentation *f*.

ten [ten] *a & n* dix (*m*). ◆**tenfold** *a* **t. increase** augmentation *f* par dix; – *adv* **to increase t.** (se) multiplier par dix.

tenable ['tenəb(ə)l] *a* (*argument*) défendable; (*post*) qui peut être occupé.

tenacious [tə'neɪʃəs] *a* tenace. ◆**tenacity** *n* ténacité *f*.

tenant ['tenənt] *n* locataire *nmf*. ◆**tenancy** *n* (*lease*) location *f*; (*period*) occupation *f*.

tend [tend] **1** *vt* (*look after*) s'occuper de. **2** *vi* **to t. to do** avoir tendance à faire; **to t. towards** incliner vers. ◆**tendency** *n* tendance *f* (**to do** à faire).

tendentious [ten'denʃəs] *a Pej* tendancieux.

tender[1] ['tendər] *a* (*delicate, soft, loving*) tendre; (*painful, sore*) sensible. ◆**-ly** *adv* tendrement. ◆**-ness** *n* tendresse *f*; (*soreness*) sensibilité *f*; (*of meat*) tendreté *f*.

tender[2] ['tendər] **1** *vt* (*offer*) offrir; **to t. one's resignation** donner sa démission. **2** *n* **to be legal t.** (*of money*) avoir cours. **3** *n* (*for services etc*) *Com* soumission *f* (**for** pour).

tendon ['tendən] *n Anat* tendon *m*.

tenement ['tenəmənt] *n* immeuble *m* (de rapport) (*Am* dans un quartier pauvre).

tenet ['tenɪt] *n* principe *m*.

tenner ['tenər] *n Fam* billet *m* de dix livres.

tennis ['tenɪs] *n* tennis *m*; **table t.** tennis de table; **t. court** court *m* (de tennis), tennis *m*.

tenor ['tenər] *n* **1** (*sense, course*) sens *m* général. **2** *Mus* ténor *m*.

tenpin ['tenpɪn] *a* **t. bowling** bowling *m*. ◆**tenpins** *n Am* bowling *m*.

tense [tens] **1** *a* (**-er, -est**) (*person, muscle, situation*) tendu; – *vt* tendre, crisper; – *vi* **to t. (up)** (*of person, face*) se crisper. **2** *n Gram* temps *m*. ◆**tenseness** *n* tension *f*. ◆**tension** *n* tension *f*.

tent [tent] *n* tente *f*.

tentacle ['tentək(ə)l] *n* tentacule *m*.

tentative ['tentətɪv] *a* (*not definite*) provisoire; (*hesitant*) timide. ◆**-ly** *adv* provisoirement; timidement.

tenterhooks ['tentəhuks] *npl* **on t.** (*anxious*) sur des charbons ardents.

tenth [tenθ] *a* & *n* dixième (*mf*); **a t.** un dixième.

tenuous ['tenjʊəs] *a* (*link, suspicion etc*) ténu.

tenure ['tenjər] *n* (*in job*) période *f* de jouissance; (*job security*) *Am* titularisation *f*.

tepid ['tepɪd] *a* (*liquid*) & *Fig* tiède.

term [tɜːm] *n* (*word, limit*) terme *m*; (*period*) période *f*; *Sch Univ* trimestre *m*; (*semester*) *Am* semestre *m*; *pl* (*conditions*) conditions *fpl*; (*prices*) *Com* prix *mpl*; **t. (of office)** *Pol* mandat *m*; **easy terms** *Fin* facilités *fpl* de paiement; **on good/bad terms** en bons/mauvais termes (**with s.o.** avec qn); **to be on close terms** être intime (**with** avec); **in terms** *of* (*speaking of*) sur le plan de; **in real terms** dans la pratique; **to come to terms with** (*person*) tomber d'accord avec; (*situation etc*) *Fig* faire face à; **in the long/short t.** à long/court terme; **at (full) t.** (*baby*) à terme; – *vt* (*name, call*) appeler.

terminal ['tɜːmɪn(ə)l] **1** *n* (*of computer*) terminal *m*; *El* borne *f*; (*air*) aérogare *f*; (*oil*) t. terminal *m* (pétrolier). **2** *a* (*patient, illness*) incurable; (*stage*) terminal. ◆**—ly** *adv* **t. ill** (*patient*) incurable.

terminate ['tɜːmɪneɪt] *vt* mettre fin à; (*contract*) résilier; (*pregnancy*) interrompre; – *vi* se terminer. ◆**termi'nation** *n* fin *f*; résiliation *f*; interruption *f*.

terminology [tɜːmɪ'nɒlədʒɪ] *n* terminologie *f*.

terminus ['tɜːmɪnəs] *n* terminus *m*.

termite ['tɜːmaɪt] *n* (*insect*) termite *m*.

terrace ['terɪs] *n* terrace *f*; (*houses*) maisons *fpl* en bande; **the terraces** *Sp* les gradins *mpl*. ◆**terraced** *a* **t. house** maison *f* attenante aux maisons voisines.

terracota [terə'kɒtə] *n* terre *f* cuite.

terrain [tə'reɪn] *n* *Mil Geol* terrain *m*.

terrestrial [tə'restrɪəl] *a* terrestre.

terrible ['terəb(ə)l] *a* affreux, terrible. ◆**terribly** *adv* (*badly*) affreusement; (*very*) terriblement.

terrier ['terɪər] *n* (*dog*) terrier *m*.

terrific [tə'rɪfɪk] *a* *Fam* (*extreme*) terrible; (*excellent*) formidable, terrible. ◆**terrifically** *adv* *Fam* (*extremely*) terriblement; (*extremely well*) terriblement bien.

terrify ['terɪfaɪ] *vt* terrifier; **to be terrified of** avoir très peur de. ◆**—ing** *a* terrifiant. ◆**—ingly** *adv* épouvantablement.

territory ['terɪtərɪ] *n* territoire *m*. ◆**territorial** *a* territorial.

terror ['terər] *n* terreur *f*; (*child*) *Fam* polisson, -onne *mf*. ◆**terrorism** *n* terrorisme

m. ◆**terrorist** *n* & *a* terroriste (*mf*). ◆**terrorize** *vt* terroriser.

terry(cloth) ['terɪ(klɒθ)] *n* tissu-éponge *m*.

terse [tɜːs] *a* laconique.

tertiary ['tɜːʃərɪ] *a* tertiaire.

Terylene® ['terɪliːn] *n* tergal® *m*.

test [test] *vt* (*try*) essayer; (*examine*) examiner; (*analyse*) analyser; (*product, intelligence*) tester; (*pupil*) *Sch* faire subir une interrogation à; (*nerves, courage etc*) *Fig* éprouver; – *n* (*trial*) test *m*, essai *m*; examen *m*; analyse *f*; *Sch* interrogation *f*; test *m*; (*of courage etc*) *Fig* épreuve *f*; **driving t.** (*examen m du*) permis *m* de conduire; – *a* (*pilot, flight*) d'essai; **t. case** *Jur* affaire-test *f*; **t. match** *Sp* match *m* international; **t. tube** éprouvette *f*; **t. tube baby** bébé *m* éprouvette.

testament ['testəmənt] *n* testament *m*; (*proof, tribute*) témoignage *m*; **Old/New T.** *Rel* Ancien/Nouveau Testament.

testicle ['testɪk(ə)l] *n* *Anat* testicule *m*.

testify ['testɪfaɪ] *vi* *Jur* témoigner (**against** contre); **to t. to sth** (*of person, event etc*) témoigner de qch; – *vt* **to t. that** *Jur* témoigner que. ◆**testi'monial** *n* références *fpl*, recommandation *f*. ◆**testimony** *n* témoignage *m*.

testy ['testɪ] *a* (*-ier, -iest*) irritable.

tetanus ['tetənəs] *n* *Med* tétanos *m*.

tête-à-tête [teɪtɑː'teɪt] *n* tête-à-tête *m inv*.

tether ['teðər] **1** *vt* (*fasten*) attacher. **2** *n* **at the end of one's t.** à bout de nerfs.

text [tekst] *n* texte *m*. ◆**textbook** *n* manuel *m*.

textile ['tekstaɪl] *a* & *n* textile (*m*).

texture ['tekstʃər] *n* (*of fabric, cake etc*) texture *f*; (*of paper, wood*) grain *m*.

Thames [temz] *n* the T. la Tamise *f*.

than [ðən, *stressed* ðæn] *conj* **1** que; **happier t. he** plus heureux que; **he has more t. you** il en a plus que toi; **fewer oranges t. plums** moins d'oranges que de prunes. **2** (*with numbers*) de; **more t. six** plus de six.

thank [θæŋk] *vt* remercier (**for sth** de qch, **for doing** d'avoir fait); **t. you** merci (**for sth** pour *or* de qch, **for doing** d'avoir fait); **no, t. you** (non) merci; **t. God, t. heavens, t. goodness** Dieu merci; – *npl* remerciements *mpl*; **thanks to** (*because of*) grâce à; (**many**) **thanks!** merci (beaucoup)! ◆**thankful** *a* reconnaissant (**for** de); **t. that** bien heureux que (+ *sub*). ◆**thankfully** *adv* (*gratefully*) avec reconnaissance; (*happily*) heureusement. ◆**thankless** *a* ingrat. ◆**Thanksgiving** *n* **T. (day)** (*holiday*) *Am* jour *m* d'action de grâce(s).

that [ðət, stressed ðæt] **1** conj que; **to say t.** dire que. **2** rel pron (subject) qui; (object) que; **the boy t. left** le garçon qui est parti; **the book t. I read** le livre que j'ai lu; **the carpet t. I put it on** (with prep) sur lequel je l'ai mis; **the house t. she told me about** la maison dont elle m'a parlé; **the day/morning t. she arrived** le jour/matin où elle est arrivée. **3** dem a (pl see those) ce, cet (before vowel or mute h) masc; (opposed to 'this') . . . -là; **t. day** ce jour; **t. man** cet homme; **t. girl** cette fille; cette fille-là. **4** dem pron (pl see those) ça, cela; ce; **t. (one)** celui-là masc, celle-là f; **give me t.** donne-moi ça or cela; **I prefer t. (one)** je préfère celui-là; **before t.** avant ça or cela; **t.'s right** c'est juste; **who's t.?** qui est-ce?; **t.'s the house** c'est la maison; (pointing) voilà la maison; **what do you mean by t.?** qu'entends-tu par là; **t. is (to say)** . . . c'est-à-dire . . . **5** adv (so) Fam si; **not t. good** pas si bon; **t. high** (pointing) haut comme ça; **t. much** (to cost, earn etc) (au)tant que ça.

thatch [θætʃ] n chaume m. ◆**thatched** a (roof) de chaume; **t. cottage** chaumière f.

thaw [θɔː] n dégel m; − vi dégeler; (of snow) fondre; **it's thawing** Met ça dégèle; **to t. (out)** (of person) Fig se dégeler; − vt (ice) dégeler, faire fondre; (food) faire dégeler; (snow) faire fondre.

the [ðə, before vowel ðɪ, stressed ðiː] def art le, l', la, pl les; **t. roof** le toit; **t. man** l'homme; **t. moon** la lune; **t. orange** l'orange; **t. boxes** les boîtes; **the smallest** le plus petit; **of t., from t.** du, de l', de la, pl des; **to t., at t.** au, à l', à la, pl aux; **Elizabeth t. Second** Élisabeth deux; **all t. better** d'autant mieux.

theatre [ˈθɪətər] n (place, art) & Mil théâtre m. ◆**theatregoer** n amateur m de théâtre. ◆**the'atrical** a théâtral; **t. company** troupe f de théâtre.

theft [θeft] n vol m.

their [ðeər] poss a leur, pl leurs; **t. house** leur maison f. ◆**theirs** [ðeəz] poss pron le leur, la leur, pl les leurs; **this book is t.** ce livre est à eux or leur est le leur; **a friend of t.** un ami à eux.

them [ðəm, stressed ðem] pron les; (after prep etc) eux mpl, elles fpl; (to) **t.** (indirect) leur; **I see t.** je les vois; **I give (to) t.** je leur donne; **with t.** avec eux, avec elles; **ten of t.** dix d'entre eux, dix d'entre elles; **all of t.** tous, toutes. ◆**them'selves** pron eux-mêmes mpl, elles-mêmes fpl; (reflexive) se, s'; (after prep etc) eux mpl, elles fpl;

they wash t. ils se lavent, elles se lavent; **they think of t.** ils pensent à eux, elles pensent à elles.

theme [θiːm] n thème m; **t. song** or **tune** Cin TV chanson f principale.

then [ðen] **1** adv (at that time) alors, à ce moment-là; (next) ensuite, puis; **from t. on** dès lors; **before t.** avant cela; **until t.** jusque-là, jusqu'alors; − **a t. mayor**/etc le maire/etc d'alors. **2** conj (therefore) donc, alors.

theology [θɪˈɒlədʒɪ] n théologie f. ◆**theo'logical** a théologique. ◆**theo'logian** n théologien m.

theorem [ˈθɪərəm] n théorème m.

theory [ˈθɪərɪ] n théorie f; **in t.** en théorie. ◆**theo'retical** a théorique. ◆**theo'retically** adv théoriquement. ◆**theorist** n théoricien, -ienne mf.

therapy [ˈθerəpɪ] n thérapeutique f. ◆**thera'peutic** a thérapeutique.

there [ðeər] adv là; (down or over) **t.** là-bas; **on t.** là-dessus; **she'll be t.** elle sera là, elle y sera; **t. is, t. are** il y a; (pointing) voilà; **t. he is** le voilà; **t. she is** la voilà; **t. they are** voilà; **that man t.** cet homme-là; **t. (you are)!** (take this) tenez!; **t., (t.,) don't cry!** allons, allons, ne pleure pas! ◆**therea'bout(s)** adv par là; (in amount) à peu près. ◆**there'after** adv après cela. ◆**thereby** adv de ce fait. ◆**therefore** adv donc. ◆**thereu'pon** adv sur ce.

thermal [ˈθɜːm(ə)l] a (energy, unit) thermique; (springs) thermal; (underwear) tribo-électrique, en thermolactyl®.

thermometer [θəˈmɒmɪtər] n thermomètre m.

thermonuclear [θɜːməʊˈnjuːklɪər] a thermonucléaire.

Thermos® [ˈθɜːməs] n **T. (flask)** thermos® m or f.

thermostat [ˈθɜːməstæt] n thermostat m.

thesaurus [θɪˈsɔːrəs] n dictionnaire m de synonymes.

these [ðiːz] **1** dem a (sing see **this**) ces; (opposed to 'those') . . . + -ci; **t. men** ces hommes; ces hommes-ci. **2** dem pron (sing see **this**) **t. (ones)** celles-ci mpl, celles-ci fpl; **t. are my friends** ce sont mes amis.

thesis, pl theses [ˈθiːsɪs, ˈθiːsiːz] n thèse f.

they [ðeɪ] pron **1** ils mpl, elles fpl; (stressed) eux mpl, elles fpl; **t. go** ils vont, elles vont; **t. are doctors** ce sont des médecins. **2** (people in general) on; **t. say** on dit.

thick [θɪk] a (-er, -est) épais (f épaisse); (stupid) Fam lourd; **to be t.** (of friends) Fam être très liés; − adv (to grow) dru; (to spread) en couche épaisse; − n **in the t. of** (battle etc) au plus gros de. ◆**thicken** vt épaissir; – vi s'épaissir. ◆**thickly** adv (to grow, fall) dru; (to spread) en couche épaisse; (populated, wooded) très. ◆**thickness** n épaisseur f.

thicket ['θɪkɪt] n (trees) fourré m.

thickset [θɪk'set] a (person) trapu. ◆**thick-skinned** a (person) dur, peu sensible.

thief [θiːf] n (pl **thieves**) voleur, -euse f. ◆**thiev/e** vti voler. ◆**—ing** a voleur; – n vol m.

thigh [θaɪ] n cuisse f. ◆**thighbone** n fémur m.

thimble ['θɪmb(ə)l] n dé m (à coudre).

thin [θɪn] a (**thinner**, **thinnest**) (slice, paper etc) mince; (person, leg) mince, mince; (soup) peu épais; (hair, audience) clairsemé; (excuse, profit) Fig maigre, mince; – adv (to spread) en couche mince; – vt (-**nn-**) to t. (**down**) (paint etc) délayer; – vi to t. **out** (of crowd, mist) s'éclaircir. ◆**—ly** adv (to spread) en couche mince; (populated, wooded) peu; (disguised) à peine. ◆**—ness** n minceur f; maigreur f.

thing [θɪŋ] n chose f; **one's things** (belongings, clothes) ses affaires fpl; **it's a funny t.** c'est drôle; **poor little t.!** pauvre petit!; **that's (just) the t.** voilà (exactement) ce qu'il faut; **how are things?**, Fam **how's things?** comment (ça) va?; **I'll think things over** j'y réfléchirai; **for one t. . . . , and for another t.** d'abord . . . et ensuite; **tea things** (set) service m à thé; (dishes) vaisselle f. ◆**thingummy** n Fam truc m, machin m.

think [θɪŋk] vi (pt & pp **thought**) penser (about, of à); **to t.** (carefully) réfléchir (about, of à); **to t. of doing** penser or songer à faire; **to t. highly of**, **to t. a lot of** penser beaucoup de bien de; **she doesn't t. much of it** ça ne lui dit pas grand-chose; **to t. better of it** se raviser; **I can't t. of it** je n'arrive pas à m'en souvenir; – vt **to t. that** (believe) penser (que); **I t. so** je pense or crois que oui; **what do you t. of him?** que penses-tu de lui?; **I thought it difficult** je l'ai trouvé difficile; **to t. out** or **through** (reply etc) réfléchir sérieusement à, peser; **to t. over** réfléchir à; **to t. up** (invent) inventer, avoir l'idée de; – n **to have a t.** Fam réfléchir (about à); – a **t. tank** comité m d'experts. ◆**—ing** a (person) intelligent; – n (opinion) opinion f; **to my t.** à mon avis. ◆**—er** n penseur, -euse f.

thin-skinned [θɪn'skɪnd] a (person) susceptible.

third [θɜːd] a troisième; **t. person** or **party** tiers m; **t.-party insurance** assurance f au tiers; **T. World** Tiers-Monde m; – n

troisième mf; **a t.** (fraction) un tiers; – adv (in race) troisième. ◆**—ly** adv troisièmement.

third-class [θɜːd'klɑːs] a de troisième classe. ◆**t.-rate** a (très) inférieur.

thirst [θɜːst] n soif f (for de). ◆**thirsty** a (-ier, -iest) **to be** or **feel t.** avoir soif; **to make t.** donner soif à; **t. for** (power etc) Fig assoiffé de.

thirteen [θɜː'tiːn] a & n treize (m). ◆**thirteenth** a & n treizième (mf). ◆**'thirtieth** a & n trentième (mf). ◆**'thirty** a & n trente (m).

this [ðɪs] 1 dem a (pl see **these**) ce, cet (before vowel or mute h), cette; (opposed to 'that') . . . + -ci; **t. book** ce livre; ce livre-ci; **t. man** cet homme; cet homme-ci; **t. photo** cette photo; cette photo-ci. 2 dem pron (pl see **these**) ceci; ce; **t.** (one) celui-ci m, celle-ci f; **give me t.** donne-moi ceci; **I prefer t.** (one) je préfère celui-ci; **before t.** avant ceci; **who's t.?** qui est-ce?; **t. is Paul** c'est Paul; **t. is the house** voici la maison. 3 adv (so) Fam si; **t. high** (pointing) haut comme ceci; **t. far** (until now) jusqu'ici.

thistle ['θɪs(ə)l] n chardon m.

thorn [θɔːn] n épine f. ◆**thorny** a (-ier, -iest) (bush, problem etc) épineux.

thorough ['θʌrə] a (painstaking, careful) minutieux, consciencieux; (knowledge, examination) approfondi; (rogue, liar) fieffé; (disaster) complet; **to give sth a t. washing** laver qch à fond. ◆**—ly** adv (completely) tout à fait; (painstakingly) avec minutie; (to know, clean, wash) à fond. ◆**—ness** n minutie f; (depth) profondeur f.

thoroughbred ['θʌrəbred] n (horse) pur-sang m inv.

thoroughfare ['θʌrəfeər] n (street) rue f; **'no t.'** 'passage interdit'.

those [ðəʊz] 1 dem a (sing see **that**) ces; (opposed to 'these') . . . + -là; **t. men** ces hommes; ces hommes-là. 2 dem pron (sing see **that**) **t.** (**ones**) ceux-là mpl, celles-là fpl; **t. are my friends** ce sont mes amis.

though [ðəʊ] 1 conj (even) bien que (+ sub); **as t.** comme si; **strange t. it may seem** si étrange que cela puisse paraître. 2 adv (nevertheless) cependant, quand même.

thought [θɔːt] see **think**; – n pensée f; (idea) idée f, pensée f; (careful) t. réflexion f; **without (a) t. for** sans penser à; **to have second thoughts** changer d'avis; **on second thoughts**, Am **on second** t. à la réflexion. ◆**thoughtful** a (pensive) pensif; (serious) sérieux; (considerate, kind) gentil, prèvenant. ◆**thoughtfully** adv (considerately) gentiment. ◆**thoughtfulness** n gentillesse f, prévenance f. ◆**thoughtless** a (towards others) désinvolte; (careless) étourdi. ◆**thoughtlessly** adv (carelessly) étourdiment; (inconsiderately) avec désinvolture.

thousand ['θauzənd] a & n mille a & m inv; **a t. pages** mille pages; **two t. pages** deux mille pages; **thousands of** des milliers de.

thrash [θræʃ] **1** vt **to t. s.o.** rouer qn de coups; (defeat) écraser qn; **to t. out** (plan etc) élaborer (à force de discussions). **2** vi **to t. about** (struggle) se débattre. ◆**—ing** n (beating) correction f.

thread [θred] n (yarn) & Fig fil m; (of screw) pas m; – vt (needle, beads) enfiler; **to t. one's way** Fig se faufiler (**through** the crowd/etc parmi la foule/etc). ◆**threadbare** a élimé, râpé.

threat [θret] n menace f (**to** à). ◆**threaten** vi menacer; – vt menacer (**to do** de faire, **with** sth de qch). ◆**threatening** a menaçant. ◆**threateningly** adv (to say) d'un ton menaçant.

three [θriː] a & n trois (m); **t.-piece suite** canapé m et deux fauteuils. ◆**threefold** a triple; – adv **to increase t.** tripler. ◆**three-'wheeler** n (tricycle) tricycle m; (car) voiture f à trois roues.

thresh [θreʃ] vt Agr battre.

threshold ['θreʃhəuld] n seuil m.

threw [θruː] see throw.

thrift [θrɪft] n (virtue) économie f. ◆**thrifty** a (-ier, -iest) économe.

thrill [θrɪl] n émotion f, frisson m; **to get a t. out of doing** prendre plaisir à faire; – vt (delight) réjouir; (excite) faire frissonner. ◆**—ed** a ravi (**with** sth de qch, **to do** de faire). ◆**—ing** n a passionnant. ◆**—er** n film m ou roman m à suspense.

thriv/e [θraɪv] vi (of business, person, plant etc) prospérer; **he or she thrives on hard work** le travail lui profite. ◆**—ing** a prospère, florissant.

throat [θrəut] n gorge f; **to have a sore t.** avoir mal à la gorge. ◆**throaty** a (voice) rauque; (person) à la voix rauque.

throb [θrɒb] vi (-bb-) (of heart) palpiter; (of engine) vrombir; Fig vibrer; **my finger is throbbing** mon doigt me fait des élancements; – n palpitation f; vrombissement m; élancement m.

throes [θrəuz] npl **in the t. of** au milieu de; (illness, crisis) en proie à; **in the t. of doing** en train de faire.

thrombosis [θrɒm'bəusɪs] n (coronary) Med infarctus m.

throne [θrəun] n trône m.

throng [θrɒŋ] n foule f; – vi (rush) affluer; – vt (street, station etc) se presser dans; **thronged with people** noir de monde.

throttle ['θrɒt(ə)l] **1** n Aut accélérateur m. **2** vt (strangle) étrangler.

through [θruː] prep (place) à travers; (time) pendant; (means) par; (thanks to) grâce à; **to go or get t.** (forest etc) traverser; (hole etc) passer par; **the window/door** par la fenêtre/porte; **to speak t. one's nose** parler du nez; **Tuesday t. Saturday** Am de mardi à samedi; – adv à travers; **to go t.** (cross) traverser; (pass) passer; **to let t.** laisser passer; **all or right t.** (to the end) jusqu'au bout; **French t. and t.** français jusqu'au bout des ongles; **to be t.** (finished) Am Fam avoir fini; **we're t.** Am Fam c'est fini entre nous; **I'm t. with the book** Am Fam je n'ai plus besoin du livre; **t. to or till** jusqu'à; **I'll put you t. (to him)** Tel je vous le passe; – a (train, traffic, ticket) direct; **'no t. road'** (no exit) 'voie sans issue'. ◆**through'out** prep **t. the neighbourhood/etc** dans tout le quartier/etc; **t. the day/etc** (time) pendant toute la journée/etc; – adv (everywhere) partout; (all the time) tout le temps. ◆**throughway** n Am autoroute f.

throw [θrəu] n (of stone etc) jet m; Sp lancer m; (of dice) coup m; (turn) tour m; – vt (pt threw, pp thrown) jeter (**to, at** à); (stone, ball) lancer, jeter; (hurl) projeter; (of horse) désarçonner (qn); (party, reception) donner; (baffle) Fam dérouter; **to t. away** (discard) jeter; (ruin, waste) Fig gâcher; **to t. back** (ball) renvoyer (**to** à); (one's head) rejeter en arrière; **to t. in** (include as extra) Fam donner en prime; **to t. off** (get rid of) se débarrasser de; **to t. out** (discard) jeter; (suggestion) repousser; (expel) mettre (qn) à la porte; (distort) fausser (calcul etc); **to t. over** abandonner; **to t. up** (job) Fam laisser tomber; – vi **to t. up** (vomit) Sl dégobiller. ◆**throwaway** a (disposable) à jeter, jetable.

thrush [θrʌʃ] n (bird) grive f.

thrust [θrʌst] n (push) poussée f; (stab) coup m; (of argument) poids m; (dynamism) allant m; – vt (pt & pp thrust) (push) pousser; (pui) mettre (**into** dans); **to t. sth into sth** (stick, knife, pin) enfoncer qch dans qch; **to t. sth/s.o. upon s.o.** Fig imposer qch/qn à qn.

thud [θʌd] n bruit m sourd.

thug [θʌg] n voyou m.

thumb [θʌm] n pouce m; **with a t. index** (*book*) à onglets; – vt to t. (**through**) feuilleter; **to t. a lift** or **a ride** Fam faire du stop. ◆**thumbtack** n Am punaise f.

thump [θʌmp] vt (*person*) frapper, cogner sur; (*table*) taper sur; **to t. one's head** (*on door etc*) se cogner la tête (**on** contre); – vi frapper, cogner (**on** sur); (*of heart*) battre à grands coups; – n (*grand*) coup m; (*noise*) bruit m sourd. ◆**—ing** a (*huge, great*) Fam énorme.

thunder [θʌndər] n tonnerre m; – vi (*of weather, person, guns*) tonner; **it's thundering** Met il tonne; **to t. past** passer (vite) dans un bruit de tonnerre. ◆**thunderbolt** n (*event*) Fig coup m de tonnerre. ◆**thunderclap** n coup m de tonnerre. ◆**thunderstorm** n orage m. ◆**thunderstruck** a abasourdi.

Thursday [θɜːzdɪ] n jeudi m.

thus [ðʌs] adv ainsi.

thwart [θwɔːt] vt (*plan, person*) contrecarrer.

thyme [taɪm] n Bot Culin thym m.

thyroid [θaɪrɔɪd] a & n Anat thyroïde (*f*).

tiara [tɪˈɑːrə] n (*of woman*) diadème m.

tic [tɪk] n (*in face, limbs*) tic m.

tick [tɪk] **1** n (*of clock*) tic-tac m; – vi faire tic-tac; **to t. over** (*of engine, factory, business*) tourner au ralenti. **2** n (*on list*) coche f, trait m; – vt **to t.** (**off**) cocher; **to t. off** (*reprimand*) Fam passer un savon à. **3** n (*moment*) Fam instant m. **4** n (*insect*) tique f. **5** adv **on t.** (*on credit*) Fam à crédit. ◆**—ing** n (*of clock*) tic-tac m; **to give s.o. a t.-off** Fam passer un savon à qn.

ticket [tɪkɪt] n billet m; (*for tube, bus, cloakroom*) ticket m; (*for library*) carte f; (*fine*) Aut Fam contravention f, contredanse f; Pol Am liste f; (*price*) t. étiquette f; **t. collector** contrôleur, -euse mf; **t. holder** personne f munie d'un billet; **t. office** guichet m.

tickle [tɪk(ə)l] vt chatouiller; (*amuse*) Fig amuser; – n chatouillement m. ◆**ticklish** a (*person*) chatouilleux; (*fabric*) qui chatouille; (*problem*) Fig délicat.

tidbit [tɪdbɪt] n (*food*) Am bon morceau m.

tiddlywinks [tɪdlɪwɪŋks] n jeu m de puce.

tide [taɪd] **1** n marée f; **against the t.** Nau & Fig à contre-courant; **the rising t. of discontent** le mécontentement grandissant. **2** vt **to t. s.o. over** (*help out*) dépanner qn. ◆**tidal** a (*river*) qui a une marée; **t. wave** raz-de-marée m inv; (*in public opinion etc*) Fig vague f de fond. ◆**tidemark** n Fig Hum ligne f de crasse.

tidings [taɪdɪŋz] npl Lit nouvelles fpl.

tidy [taɪdɪ] a (**-ier, -iest**) (*place, toys etc*) bien rangé; (*clothes, looks*) soigné; (*methodical*) ordonné; (*amount, sum*) Fam joli, bon; **to make t.** ranger; – vt **to t.** (**up** or **away**) ranger; **to t. oneself** (**up**) s'arranger; **to t. out** (*cupboard etc*) vider; – vi **to t. up** ranger. ◆**tidily** adv avec soin. ◆**tidiness** n (*bon*) ordre m; (*care*) soin m.

tie [taɪ] n (*string, strap etc*) & Fig lien m, attache f; (*necktie*) cravate f; (*sleeper*) Rail Am traverse f; Sp égalité f de points; (*match*) match m nul; – vt (*fasten*) attacher, lier (**to** à); (*a knot*) faire (**to** à); (*shoe*) lacer; (*link*) lier (**to** à); **to t. down** attacher; **to t. s.o. down to** (*date, place etc*) obliger qn à accepter; **to t. up** attacher; (*money*) Fig immobiliser; **to be tied up** (*linked*) être lié (**with** avec); (*busy*) Fam être occupé; – vi Sp finir à égalité de points; Fb faire match nul; (*in race*) être ex aequo; **to t. in with** (*tally with*) se rapporter à. ◆**t.-up** n (*link*) lien m; (*traffic jam*) Am Fam bouchon m.

tier [tɪər] n (*seats*) Sp Th gradin m; (*of cake*) étage m.

tiff [tɪf] n petite querelle f.

tiger [taɪgər] n tigre m. ◆**tigress** n tigresse f.

tight [taɪt] a (**-er, -est**) (*rope etc*) raide; (*closely-fitting clothing*) ajusté, (*fitting too closely*) (trop) étroit, (trop) serré; (*drawer, lid*) dur; (*control*) strict; (*schedule, credit*) serré; (*drunk*) Fam gris; (*with money*) Fam avare; **a t. spot** or **corner** Fam une situation difficile; **it's a t. squeeze** il y a juste la place; – adv (*to hold, shut, sleep*) bien; (*to squeeze*) fort; **to sit t.** ne pas bouger. ◆**tighten** vt **to t. (up)** (*rope*) tendre; (*bolt etc*) (res)serrer; (*security*) Fig renforcer; – vi **to t. up on** se montrer plus strict à l'égard de. ◆**tightly** adv (*to hold*) bien; (*to squeeze*) fort; **t. knit** (*close*) très uni. ◆**tightness** n (*of garment*) étroitesse f; (*of control*) rigueur f; (*of rope*) tension f.

tight-fitting [taɪtfɪtɪŋ] a (*garment*) ajusté. ◆**tightfisted** a avare. ◆**tightrope** n corde f raide. ◆**tightwad** n (*miser*) Am Fam grippe-sou m.

tights [taɪts] npl (*garment*) collant m; (*for dancer etc*) justaucorps m.

til/e [taɪl] n (*on roof*) tuile f; (*on wall or floor*) carreau m; – vt (*wall, floor*) carreler. ◆**—ed** a (*roof*) de tuiles; (*wall, floor*) carrelé.

till [tɪl] **1** prep & conj = **until**. **2** n (*for money*) caisse f (enregistreuse). **3** vt (*land*) Agr cultiver.

tilt [tɪlt] *vti* pencher; – *n* inclinaison *f*; **(at) full t.** à toute vitesse.

timber ['tɪmbər] *n* bois *m* (de construction); *(epoch)* arbres *mpl*; – *a* de ou en bois. ◆**timberyard** *n* entrepôt *m* de bois.

time [taɪm] *n* temps *m*; *(point in time)* moment *m*; *(epoch)* époque *f*; *(on clock)* heure *f*; *(occasion)* fois *f*; *Mus* mesure *f*; **in (the course of) t.**, **with (the passage of) t.** avec le temps; **some of the t.** *(not always)* une partie du temps; **most of the t.** la plupart du temps; **in a year's t.** dans un an; **a long t.** longtemps; **a short t.** peu de temps, un petit moment; **full-t.** à plein temps; **part-t.** à temps partiel; **to have a good** ou **a nice t.** *(fun)* s'amuser (bien); **to have a hard t. doing** avoir du mal à faire; **t. off** du temps libre; **in no t. (at all)** en un rien de temps; **(just) in t.** *(to arrive)* à temps *(for sth pour qch, to do pour faire)*; **in my t.** *(formerly)* de mon temps; **from t. to t.** de temps en temps; **what t. is it?** quelle heure est-il?; **the right** ou **exact t.** l'heure *f* exacte; **on t.** à l'heure; **at the same t.** en même temps (**as** que); *(simultaneously)* à la fois; **for the t. being** pour le moment; **at the t.** à ce moment-là; **at the present t.** à l'heure actuelle; **at times** par moments, parfois; **at one t.** à un moment donné; **this t. tomorrow** demain à cette heure-ci; **(the) next t. you come** la prochaine fois que tu viendras; **(the) last t.** la dernière fois; **t. and again** maintes fois; **ten times ten** dix fois dix; **t. bomb** bombe *f* à retardement; **t. lag** décalage *m*; **t. limit** délai *m*; **t. zone** fuseau *m* horaire; – *vt (sportsman, worker etc)* chronométrer; *(programme, operation)* minuter; *(choose the time of)* choisir le moment de; *(to plan)* prévoir. ◆**timing** *n* chronométrage *m*; minutage *m*; *(judgement of artist etc)* rythme *m*; **the t. of** *(time)* le moment choisi pour. ◆**time-consuming** *a* qui prend du temps. ◆**time-honoured** *a* consacré *(par l'usage).*

timeless ['taɪmləs] *a* éternel.

timely ['taɪmlɪ] *a* à propos. ◆**timeliness** *n* à-propos *m*.

timer ['taɪmər] *n* Culin minuteur *m*, compte-minutes *m inv*; *(sand-filled)* sablier *m*; *(on machine)* minuteur *m*; *(to control lighting)* minuterie *f*.

timetable ['taɪmteɪb(ə)l] *n* horaire *m*; *(in school)* emploi *m* du temps.

timid ['tɪmɪd] *a (shy)* timide; *(fearful)* timoré. ◆**–ly** *adv* timidement.

tin [tɪn] *n* étain *m*; *(tinplate)* fer-blanc *m*; *(can)* boîte *f*; *(for baking)* moule *m*; **t. can** boîte *f* (en fer-blanc); **t. opener** ouvre-boîtes *m inv*; **t. soldier** soldat *m* de plomb. ◆**tinfoil** *n* papier *m* d'aluminium, papier alu. ◆**tinned** *a* en boîte. ◆**tinplate** *n* fer-blanc *m*.

tinge [tɪndʒ] *n* teinte *f*. ◆**tinged** *a* **t. with** *(pink etc)* teinté de; *(jealousy etc)* Fig empreint de.

tingle ['tɪŋg(ə)l] *vi* picoter; **it's tingling** ça me picote. ◆**tingly** *a (feeling)* de picotement.

tinker ['tɪŋkər] *vi* **to t. (about) with** bricoler.

tinkle ['tɪŋk(ə)l] *vi* tinter; – *n* tintement *m*; **to give s.o. a t.** *(phone s.o.)* Fam passer un coup de fil à qn.

tinny ['tɪnɪ] *a (-ier, -iest) (sound)* métallique; *(vehicle, machine)* de mauvaise qualité.

tinsel ['tɪns(ə)l] *n* clinquant *m*, guirlandes *fpl* de Noël.

tint [tɪnt] *n* teinte *f*; *(for hair)* shampooing *m* colorant; – *vt (paper, glass)* teinter.

tiny ['taɪnɪ] *a (-ier, -iest)* tout petit.

tip [tɪp] **1** *n (end)* bout *m*; *(pointed)* pointe *f*. **2** *n (money)* pourboire *m*; – *vt (-pp-)* donner un pourboire à. **3** *n (advice)* conseil *m*; *(information)* & *Sp* tuyau *m*; **to get a t.-off** se faire tuyauter; – *vt (-pp-)* **to t. a horse/etc** donner un cheval/etc gagnant; **to t. off** *(police)* prévenir. **4** *n (for rubbish)* décharge *f*; – *vt (-pp-)* **to t. (up** ou **over)** *(tilt)* incliner, pencher; *(overturn)* faire basculer; **to t. (out)** *(liquid, load)* déverser *(into* dans); – *vi* **to t. (up** ou **over)** *(tilt)* pencher; *(overturn)* basculer.

tipped [tɪpt] *a* **t. cigarette** cigarette *f* (à bout) filtre.

tipple ['tɪp(ə)l] *vi (drink)* Fam picoler.

tipsy ['tɪpsɪ] *a (-ier, -iest) (drunk)* gai, pompette.

tiptoe ['tɪptəʊ] *n* **on t.** sur la pointe des pieds; – *vi* marcher sur la pointe des pieds.

tiptop ['tɪptɒp] *a* Fam excellent.

tirade [taɪ'reɪd] *n* diatribe *f*.

tir/e[1] [taɪər] *vt* fatiguer; **to t. out** *(exhaust)* épuiser; – *vi* se fatiguer. ◆**–ed** *a* fatigué; **to be t. of sth/s.o./doing** en avoir assez de qch/de qn/de faire; **to get t. of doing** se lasser de faire. ◆**–ing** *a* fatigant. ◆**tiredness** *n* fatigue *f*. ◆**tireless** *a* infatigable. ◆**tiresome** *a* ennuyeux.

tire[2] [taɪər] *n* Am pneu *m*.

tissue ['tɪʃuː] *n* Biol tissu *m*; *(handkerchief)* mouchoir *m* en papier, kleenex® *m*; **t. (paper)** papier *m* de soie.

tit [tɪt] *n* **1** *(bird)* mésange *f*. **2** **to give t. for tat** rendre coup pour coup.

titbit ['tɪtbɪt] *n (food)* bon morceau *m*.

titillate ['tɪtɪleɪt] *vt* exciter.

titl/e ['taɪt(ə)l] *n* (*name, claim*) & *Sp* titre *m*; **t. deed** titre *m* de propriété; **t. role** *Th Cin* rôle *m* principal; – *vt* (*film*) intituler, titrer. ◆**-ed** *a* (*person*) titré.

titter ['tɪtər] *vi* rire bêtement.

tittle-tattle ['tɪt(ə)ltæt(ə)l] *n Fam* commérages *mpl*.

to [tə, *stressed* tuː] **1** *prep* à; (*towards*) vers; (*of feelings, attitude*) envers; (*right up to*) jusqu'à; (*of*) de; **give it to him** *or* **her** donne-le-lui; **to town** en ville; **to France** en France; **to Portugal** au Portugal; **the butcher('s)** chez le boucher/*etc*; **the road to** la route de; **the train to** le train pour; **well-disposed to** bien disposé envers; **kind to** gentil envers *or* avec *or* pour; **from bad to worse** de mal en pis; **ten to one** (*proportion*) dix contre un; **it's ten (minutes) to one** il est une heure moins dix; **one person to a room** une personne par chambre; **to say/to remember/**etc (*with inf*) dire/se souvenir/*etc*; **she tried to rob a** (*door*) fermer; **to go** *or* **walk to and fro** aller et venir. ◆**to-do** [tə'duː] *n* (*fuss*) *Fam* histoire *f*.

toad [təud] *n* crapaud *m*.

toadstool ['təudstuːl] *n* champignon *m* (vénéneux).

toast [təust] **1** *n Culin* pain *m* grillé, toast *m*; – *vt* (*bread*) (faire) griller. **2** *n* (*drink*) toast *m*; – *vt* (*person*) porter un toast à; (*success, event*) arroser. ◆**toaster** *n* grille-pain *m inv*.

tobacco [tə'bækəu] *n* (*pl* **-os**) tabac *m*. ◆**tobacconist** *n* buraliste *mf*; **t., tobacconist's (shop)** bureau *m* de) tabac *m*.

toboggan [tə'bɒgən] *n* luge *f*, toboggan *m*.

today [tə'deɪ] *adv* & *n* aujourd'hui (*m*).

toddle ['tɒd(ə)l] *vi* **t. off** (*leave*) *Hum Fam* se sauver.

toddler ['tɒdlər] *n* petit(e) enfant *mf*.

toddy ['tɒdɪ] *n* (**hot**) **t.** grog *m*.

toe [təu] **1** *n* orteil *m*; **on one's toes** *Fig* vigilant. **2** *vt* to **t. the line** se conformer; **to t. the party line** respecter la ligne du parti. ◆**toenail** *n* ongle *m* du pied.

toffee ['tɒfɪ] *n* (*sweet*) caramel *m* (*dur*); **t. apple** pomme *f* d'amour.

together [tə'geðər] *adv* ensemble; (*at the same time*) en même temps; **t. with** avec. ◆**-ness** *n* (*of group*) camaraderie *f*; (*of husband and wife*) intimité *f*.

togs [tɒgz] *npl* (*clothes*) *Sl* nippes *fpl*.

toil [tɔɪl] *n* labeur *m*; – *vi* travailler dur.

toilet ['tɔɪlɪt] *n* (*room*) toilettes *fpl*, cabinets

mpl; (*bowl, seat*) cuvette *f or* siège *m* des cabinets; **to go to the t.** aller aux toilettes; – *a* (*articles*) de toilette; **t. paper** papier *m* hygiénique; **t. roll** rouleau *m* de papier hygiénique; **t. water** (*perfume*) eau *f* de toilette. ◆**toiletries** *npl* articles *mpl* de toilette.

token ['təukən] *n* (*symbol, sign*) témoignage *m*; (*metal disc*) jeton *m*; (*voucher*) bon *m*; **gift t.** chèque-cadeau *m*; **book t.** chèque-livre *m*; **record t.** chèque-disque *m*; – *a* symbolique.

told [təuld] *see* **tell**; – *adv* **all t.** (*taken together*) en tout.

tolerable ['tɒlərəb(ə)l] *a* (*bearable*) tolérable; (*fairly good*) passable. ◆**tolerably** *adv* (*fairly, fairly well*) passablement. ◆**tolerance** *n* tolérance *f*. ◆**tolerant** *a* tolérant (**of** à l'égard de). ◆**tolerantly** *adv* avec tolérance. ◆**tolerate** *vt* tolérer.

toll [təul] *n* péage *m*; – *a* (*road*) à péage. **2** *n* **the death t.** le nombre de morts, le bilan en vies humaines; **to take a heavy t.** (*of accident etc*) faire beaucoup de victimes. **3** *vi* (*of bell*) sonner. ◆**tollfree** *a* **t. number** *Tel Am* numéro *m* vert.

tomato [tə'mɑːtəu, *Am* tə'meɪtəu] *n* (*pl* **-oes**) tomate *f*.

tomb [tuːm] *n* tombeau *m*. ◆**tombstone** *n* pierre *f* tombale.

tomboy ['tɒmbɔɪ] *n* (*girl*) garçon *m* manqué.

tomcat ['tɒmkæt] *n* matou *m*.

tome [təum] *n* (*book*) tome *m*.

tomfoolery [tɒm'fuːlərɪ] *n* niaiserie(s) *f(pl)*.

tomorrow [tə'mɒrəu] *adv* & *n* demain (*m*); **t. morning/evening** demain matin/soir; **the day after t.** après-demain.

ton [tʌn] *n* tonne *f* (*Br* = 1016 *kg, Am* = 907 *kg*); **metric t.** tonne *f* (= 1000 *kg*); **tons of** (*lots of*) *Fam* des tonnes de.

tone [təun] *n* ton *m*; (*of radio, telephone*) tonalité *f*; **in that t.** sur ce ton; **to set the t.** donner le ton; **she's t.-deaf** elle n'a pas d'oreille; – *vt* **to t. down** atténuer; **to t. up** (*muscles, skin*) tonifier; – *vi* **to t. in** s'harmoniser (**with** avec).

tongs [tɒŋz] *npl* pinces *fpl*; (*for sugar*) pince *f*; (*curling*) **t.** fer *m* à friser.

tongue [tʌŋ] *n* langue *f*; **t. in cheek** ironique(ment). ◆**t.-tied** *a* muet (et gêné).

tonic ['tɒnɪk] *a* & *n* tonique (*m*); **gin and t.** gin-tonic *m*.

tonight [tə'naɪt] *adv* & *n* (*this evening*) ce soir (*m*); (*during the night*) cette nuit (*f*).

tonne [tʌn] *n* (*metric*) tonne *f*. ◆**tonnage** *n* tonnage *m*.

tonsil ['tɒns(ə)l] *n* amygdale *f*. ◆**tonsi'l-**

lectomy n opération f des amygdales. ◆**tonsillitis** [tɒnsə'laɪtɪs] n **to have t.** avoir une angine.

too [tuː] adv **1** (excessively) trop; **t. tired to play** trop fatigué pour jouer; **t. hard to solve** trop difficile à résoudre; **it's only t. true** ce n'est que trop vrai. **2** (also) aussi; (moreover) en plus.

took [tʊk] see take.

tool [tuːl] n outil m; **t. bag, t. kit** trousse f à outils.

toot [tuːt] vti **to t. (the horn)** Aut klaxonner.

tooth, pl **teeth** [tuːθ, tiːθ] n dent f; **front t.** dent de devant; **back t.** molaire f; **milk/wisdom t.** dent de lait/de sagesse; **t. decay** carie f dentaire; **to have a sweet t.** aimer les sucreries; **long in the t.** (old) Hum chenu, vieux. ◆**toothache** n mal m de dents. ◆**toothbrush** n brosse f à dents. ◆**toothcomb** n peigne m fin. ◆**toothpaste** n dentifrice m. ◆**toothpick** n cure-dent m.

top¹ [tɒp] n (of mountain, tower, tree) sommet m; (of wall, dress, ladder, page) haut m; (of box, table, surface) dessus m; (of list) tête f; (of water) surface f; (of car) toit m; (of bottle, tube) bouchon m; (of bottle cap) capsule f; (of saucepan) couvercle m; (of pen) capuchon m; **pyjama t.** veste f de pyjama; **(at the) t. of the class** le premier de la classe; **on t. of** sur; (in addition to) Fig en plus de; **on t.** (in bus etc) en haut; **from t. to bottom** de fond en comble; **the big t.** (circus) le chapiteau; – a (drawer, shelf) du haut, premier; (step, layer, storey) dernier; (upper) supérieur; (in rank, exam) premier; (chief) principal; (best) meilleur; (great, distinguished) éminent; (maximum) maximum; **in t. gear** Aut en quatrième vitesse; **at t. speed** à toute vitesse; **t. hat** (chapeau m) haut-de-forme m. ◆**t.-'flight** a Fam excellent. ◆**t.-'heavy** a trop lourd du haut. ◆**t.-level** a (talks etc) au sommet. ◆**t.-'notch** a Fam excellent. ◆**t.-'ranking** a (official) haut placé. ◆**t.-'secret** a ultra-secret.

top² [tɒp] vt (-pp-) (exceed) dépasser; **to t. up** (glass etc) remplir (de nouveau); (coffee, oil etc) rajouter; **and to t. it all . . .** et pour comble . . . ; **topped with** Culin nappé de.

top³ [tɒp] n (toy) toupie f.

topaz ['təʊpæz] n (gem) topaze f.

topic ['tɒpɪk] n sujet m. ◆**topical** a d'actualité. ◆**topi'cality** n actualité f.

topless ['tɒpləs] a (woman) aux seins nus.

topography [tə'pɒɡrəfɪ] n topographie f.

topple ['tɒp(ə)l] vi **to t. (over)** tomber; – vt **to t. (over)** faire tomber.

topsy-turvy [tɒpsɪ'tɜːvɪ] a & adv sens dessus dessous.

torch [tɔːtʃ] n (burning) torche f, flambeau m; (electric) lampe f électrique. ◆**torchlight** n & a **by t.** à la lumière des flambeaux; **t. procession** retraite f aux flambeaux.

tore [tɔːr] see tear¹.

torment [tɔː'ment] vt (make suffer) tourmenter; (annoy) agacer; – ['tɔːment] n tourment m.

tornado [tɔː'neɪdəʊ] n (pl -oes) tornade f.

torpedo [tɔː'piːdəʊ] n (pl -oes) torpille f; **t. boat** torpilleur m; – vt torpiller.

torrent ['tɒrənt] n torrent m. ◆**torrential** [tə'renʃ(ə)l] a torrentiel.

torrid ['tɒrɪd] a (love affair etc) brûlant, passionné; (climate, weather) torride.

torso ['tɔːsəʊ] n (pl -os) torse m.

tortoise ['tɔːtəs] n tortue f. ◆**tortoiseshell** a (comb etc) en écaille; (spectacles) à monture d'écaille.

tortuous ['tɔːtʃʊəs] a tortueux.

tortur/e ['tɔːtʃər] n torture f; – vt torturer. ◆**-er** n tortionnaire m.

Tory ['tɔːrɪ] n tory m; – a a tory inv.

toss [tɒs] vt (throw) jeter, lancer (**to** à); **to t. s.o. (about)** (of boat, vehicle) ballotter qn, faire tressauter qn; **to t. a coin** jouer à pile ou à face; **to t. back** (one's head) rejeter en arrière; – vi **to t. (about), t. and turn** (in one's sleep etc) se tourner et se retourner; **we'll t. (up) for it, we'll t. up** on va jouer à pile ou à face; **t. up** with the head of d'un mouvement brusque de la tête. ◆**t.-up** n **it's a t.-up whether he leaves or stays** Sl il y a autant de chances pour qu'il parte ou pour qu'il reste.

tot [tɒt] **1** n (tiny) **t.** petit(e) enfant mf. **2** vt (-tt-) **to t. up** (add) Fam additionner.

total ['təʊt(ə)l] a total; **the t. sales** le total des ventes; – n total m; **in t.** au total; – vt (-ll-, Am -l-) (of debt, invoice) s'élever à; **to t. (up)** (find the total of) totaliser; **that totals $9** ça fait neuf dollars en tout. ◆**-ly** adv totalement.

totalitarian [təʊtælɪ'teərɪən] a Pol totalitaire.

tote [təʊt] **1** n Sp Fam pari m mutuel. **2** vt (gun) porter.

totter ['tɒtər] vi chanceler.

touch [tʌtʃ] n (contact) contact m, toucher m; (sense) toucher m; (of painter) & Fb Rugby touche f; **a t. of** (small amount) un petit peu de, un soupçon de; **the finishing**

touches la dernière touche; **in t. with** (*person*) en contact avec; (*events*) au courant de; **to be out of t.** ne plus être en contact avec; (*events*) ne plus être au courant de; **to get in t.** se mettre en contact (**with** avec); **we lost t.** on s'est perdu de vue; – *vt* toucher; (*lay a finger on, tamper with, eat*) toucher à; (*move emotionally*) toucher; (*equal*) *Fig* égaler; **to t. up** retoucher; **I don't t. the stuff** (*beer etc*) je n'en bois jamais; – *vi* (*of lines, ends etc*) se toucher; **don't t.!** n'y *or* ne touche pas!; **he's always touching** c'est un touche-à-tout; **to t. down** (*of aircraft*) atterrir; **to t. on** (*subject*) toucher à. ◆**—ed** (*emotionally*) touché (**by** de); (*crazy*) *Fam* cinglé. ◆**—ing** (*story etc*) touchant. ◆**touch-and-'go** *a* (*uncertain*) *Fam* douteux. ◆**touchdown** *n Av* atterrissage *m*. ◆**touchline** *n Fb Rugby* (ligne *f* de) touche *f*.

touchy ['tʌtʃi] *a* (**-ier, -iest**) (*sensitive*) susceptible (**about** à propos de).

tough [tʌf] *a* (**-er, -est**) (*hard*) dur; (*meat, businessman*) coriace; (*sturdy*) solide; (*strong*) fort; (*relentless*) acharné; (*difficult*) difficile, dur; **t. guy** dur *m*; **t. luck!** pas de chance!, quelle déveine! – *n* (*tough guy*) *Fam* dur *m*. ◆**toughen** *vt* (*body, person*) endurcir; (*reinforce*) renforcer. ◆**toughness** *n* dureté *f*; solidité *f*; force *f*.

toupee ['tuːpeɪ] *n* postiche *m*.

tour [tuər] *n* (*journey*) voyage *m*; (*visit*) visite *f*; (*by artist, team etc*) tournée *f*; (*on bicycle, on foot*) randonnée *f*; **on t.** en voyage; en tournée; **a t. of** (*France*) un voyage en; une tournée en; une randonnée en; – *vt* visiter; (*of artist etc*) être en tournée en *or* dans etc. ◆**—ing** *n* tourisme *m*; **to go t.** faire du tourisme. ◆**tourism** *n* tourisme *m*. ◆**tourist** *n* touriste *mf*; – *a* touristique; (*class*) touriste *inv*; **t. office** syndicat *m* d'initiative. ◆**touristy** *a Pej Fam* (*trop*) touristique.

tournament ['tuənəmənt] *n Sp & Hist* tournoi *m*.

tousled ['tauz(ə)ld] *a* (*hair*) ébouriffé.

tout [taut] *vi* racoler; **to t. for** (*customers*) racoler; – *n* racoleur, -euse *mf*; **ticket t.** revendeur, -euse *mf* (en fraude) de billets.

tow [tau] *vt* (*car, boat*) remorquer; (*caravan, trailer*) tracter; **to t. away** (*vehicle*) *Jur* emmener à la fourrière; – *n* **'on t.'** 'en remorque'; **t. truck** (*breakdown lorry*) *Am* dépanneuse *f*. ◆**towpath** *n* chemin *m* de halage. ◆**towrope** *n* (*câble m* de) remorque *f*.

toward(s) [təˈwɔːd(z), *Am* tɔːd(z)] *prep* vers;

(*of feelings*) envers; **money t.** de l'argent pour (acheter).

towel ['tauəl] *n* serviette *f* (de toilette); (*for dishes*) torchon *m*; **t. rail** porte-serviettes *m inv*. ◆**towelling**, *Am* ◆**toweling** *n* tissu-éponge *m*; (**kitchen**) *Am* essuie-tout *m inv*.

tower ['tauər] *n* tour *f*; **t. block** tour *f*, immeuble *m*; **ivory t.** *Fig* tour *f* d'ivoire; – *vi* **to t. above** *or* **over** dominer. ◆**—ing** *a* très haut.

town [taun] *n* ville *f*; **in t.,** (**in**)**to t.** en ville; **out of t.** en province; **country t.** bourg *m*; **t. centre** centre-ville *m*; **t. clerk** secrétaire *mf* de mairie; **t. council** conseil *m* municipal; **t. hall** mairie *f*; **t. planner** urbaniste *mf*; **t. planning** urbanisme *m*. ◆**township** *n* (*in South Africa*) commune *f* (noire).

toxic ['tɒksik] *a* toxique. ◆**toxin** *n* toxine *f*.

toy [tɔɪ] *n* jouet *m*; **soft t.** (*jouet m* en) peluche *f*; – *a* (*gun*) d'enfant; (*house, car, train*) miniature; – *vi* **to t. with** jouer avec. ◆**toyshop** *n* magasin *m* de jouets.

trac/e [treɪs] *n* trace *f* (**of** de); **to vanish** *or* **disappear without (a) t.** disparaître sans laisser de traces; – *vt* (*draw*) tracer; (*with tracing paper*) (dé)calquer; (*locate*) retrouver (la trace de), dépister; (*follow*) suivre (la piste de) (**to** à); (*relate*) retracer; **to t.** (**back**) **to** (*one's family*) faire remonter jusqu'à. ◆**—ing** *n* (*drawing*) calque *m*; **t. paper** papier-calque *m inv*.

track [træk] *n* trace *f*, (*of bullet, rocket*) trajectoire *f*; (*of person, animal, tape recorder*) *Sp* piste *f*; (*of record*) plage *f*; *Rail* voie *f*; (*path*) piste *f*, chemin *m*; *Sch Am* classe *f* (de niveau); **to keep t. of** suivre; **to lose t. of** (*friend*) perdre de vue; (*argument*) perdre le fil de; **to make tracks** *Fam* se sauver; **the right t.** la bonne voie *or* piste; **t. event** *Sp* épreuve *f* sur piste; **t. record** (*of person, firm etc*) *Fig* antécédents *mpl*; – *vt* **to t.** (**down**) (*locate*) retrouver, dépister; (*pursue*) traquer. ◆**—er** *a* **t. dog** chien *m* policier. ◆**tracksuit** *n Sp* survêtement *m*.

tract [trækt] *n* (*stretch of land*) étendue *f*.

traction ['trækʃ(ə)n] *n Tech* traction *f*.

tractor ['træktər] *n* tracteur *m*.

trade [treɪd] *n* commerce *m*; (*job*) métier *m*; (*exchange*) échange *m*; – *a* (*fair, balance, route*) commercial; (*price*) de (demi-)gros; (*secret*) de fabrication; (*barrier*) douanier; **t. union** syndicat *m*; **t. unionist** syndicaliste *mf*; – *vi* faire du commerce (**with** avec); **to t. in** (*sugar etc*) faire le commerce de; – *vt* (*exchange*) échanger (**for** contre); **to t. sth in** (*old article*) faire reprendre qch. ◆**t. in** *n*

Com reprise *f*. **◆t.-off** *n* échange *m*. **◆trading** *n* commerce *m*; – *a* (*activity*, *port etc*) commercial; (*nation*) commerçant; **t. estate** zone *f* industrielle. **◆trader** *n* commerçant, -ante *mf*; (*street*) *t*. vendeur, -euse *mf* de rue. **◆tradesman** *n* (*pl* **-men**) commerçant *m*.

trademark ['treidmɑːk] *n* marque *f* de fabrique; (*registered*) *t*. marque déposée.

tradition [trə'dɪʃ(ə)n] *n* tradition *f*. **◆tra-'ditional** *a* traditionnel. **◆traditionally** *adv* traditionnellement.

traffic ['træfik] **1** *n* (*on road*) circulation *f*; *Av Nau Rail* trafic *m*; **busy** or **heavy t.** beaucoup de circulation; **heavy t.** (*vehicles*) poids *mpl* lourds; **t. circle** *Am* rond-point *m*; **t. cone** cône *m* de chantier; **t. jam** embouteillage *m*; **t. lights** feux *mpl* (de signalisation); (*when red*) feu *m* rouge; **t. sign** panneau *m* de signalisation. **2** (*trade*) *Pej* trafic *m* (**in** de); – *vi* (*-ck-*) trafiquer (**in** de). **◆trafficker** *n Pej* trafiquant, -ante *mf*.

tragedy ['trædʒədɪ] *n Th & Fig* tragédie *f*. **◆tragic** *a* tragique. **◆tragically** *adv* tragiquement.

trail [treɪl] *n* (*of powder, smoke, blood etc*) traînée *f*; (*track*) piste *f*, trace *f*; (*path*) sentier *m*; **in its** *t*. (*wake*) dans son sillage; – *vt* (*drag*) traîner; (*caravan*) tracter; (*follow*) suivre (la piste de); – *vi* (*on the ground etc*) traîner; (*of plant*) ramper; **to t. behind** (*lag behind*) traîner. **◆—er** *n* **1** *Aut* remorque *f*; *Am* caravane *f*. **2** *Cin* bande *f* annonce.

train [treɪn] **1** *n* (*engine, transport, game*) train *m*; (*underground*) rame *f*; (*procession*) *Fig* file *f*; (*of events*) suite *f*; (*of dress*) traîne *f*; **my t. of thought** le fil de ma pensée; **t. set** train *m* électrique. **2** *vt* (*teach, develop*) former (**to do** à faire); *Sp* entraîner; (*animal, child*) dresser (**to do** à faire); (*ear*) exercer; **to t. oneself to do** s'entraîner à faire; **to t. sth on** (*aim*) braquer qch sur; – *vi* recevoir une formation (**as a doctor**/*etc* de médecin/*etc*); *Sp* s'entraîner. **◆—ed** *a* (*having professional skill*) qualifié; (*nurse etc*) diplômé; (*animal*) dressé; (*ear*) exercé. **◆—ing** *n* formation *f*; *Sp* entraînement *m*; (*of animal*) dressage *m*; **to be in t.** *Sp* s'entraîner; (*teachers'*) **t. college** école *f* normale. **◆trai'nee** *n* & *a* stagiaire (*mf*). **◆trainer** *n* (*of athlete, racehorse*) entraîneur *m*; (*of dog, lion etc*) dresseur *m*; (*running shoe*) jogging *m*, chaussure *f* de sport.

traipse [treɪps] *vi Fam* (*tiredly*) traîner les pieds; **to t.** (**about**) (*wander*) se balader.

trait [treɪt] *n* (*of character*) trait *m*.

traitor ['treɪtər] *n* traître *m*.

trajectory [trə'dʒektərɪ] *n* trajectoire *f*.

tram [træm] *n* tram(way) *m*.

tramp [træmp] **1** *n* (*vagrant*) clochard, -arde *mf*; (*woman*) *Pej Am* traînée *f*. **2** *vi* (*walk*) marcher d'un pas lourd; (*hike*) marcher à pied; – *vt* (*streets etc*) parcourir; – *n* (*sound*) pas lourds *mpl*; (*hike*) randonnée *f*.

trample ['træmp(ə)l] *vti* **to t. sth** (**underfoot**), **t. on sth** piétiner qch.

trampoline ['træmpəliːn] *n* trampoline *m*.

trance [trɑːns] *n* **in a t.** (*mystic*) en transe.

tranquil ['træŋkwɪl] *a* tranquille. **◆tran-'quillity** *n* tranquillité *f*. **◆tranquillizer** *n Med* tranquillisant *m*.

trans- [træns, trænz] *pref* trans-.

transact [træn'zækt] *vt* (*business*) traiter. **◆transaction** *n* (*in bank etc*) opération *f*; (*on Stock Market*) transaction *f*; **the t. of** (*business*) la conduite de.

transatlantic [trænzət'læntɪk] *a* transatlantique.

transcend [træn'send] *vt* transcender. **◆transcendent** *a* transcendant.

transcribe [træn'skraɪb] *vt* transcrire. **◆'transcript** *n* (*document*) transcription *f*. **◆transcription** *n* transcription *f*.

transfer [træns'fɜːr] *vt* (*-rr-*) (*person, goods etc*) transférer (**to** à); (*power*) *Pol* faire passer (**to** à); **to t. the charges** téléphoner en PCV; – *vi* être transféré (**to** à); – ['trænsfɜːr] *n* transfert *m* (**to** à); (*of power*) *Pol* passation *f*; (*image*) décalcomanie *f*; **bank** or **credit t.** virement *m* (bancaire). **◆trans'ferable** *a* **not t.** (*on ticket*) strictement personnel.

transform [træns'fɔːm] *vt* transformer (**into** en). **◆transfor'mation** *n* transformation *f*. **◆transformer** *n El* transformateur *m*.

transfusion [træns'fjuːʒ(ə)n] *n* (*blood*) *t*. transfusion *f* (sanguine).

transient ['trænzɪənt] *a* (*ephemeral*) transitoire.

transistor [træn'zɪstər] *n* (*device*) transistor *m*; **t.** (**radio**) transistor *m*.

transit ['trænzɪt] *n* transit *m*; **in t.** en transit.

transition [træn'zɪʃ(ə)n] *n* transition *f*. **◆transitional** *a* de transition, transitoire.

transitive ['trænsɪtɪv] *a Gram* transitif.

transitory ['trænzɪtərɪ] *a* transitoire.

translate [træns'leɪt] *vt* traduire (**from** de, **into** en). **◆translation** *n* traduction *f*; (*into mother tongue*) *Sch* version *f*; (*from mother tongue*) *Sch* thème *m*. **◆translator** *n* traducteur, -trice *mf*.

transmit [trænz'mɪt] *vt* (*-tt-*) (*send, pass*)

transmettre; – *vti* (*broadcast*) émettre. ◆**transmission** *n* transmission *f*; (*broadcast*) émission *f*. ◆**transmitter** *n* Rad TV émetteur *m*.

transparent [træns'pærənt] *a* transparent. ◆**transparency** *n* transparence *f*; (*slide*) Phot diapositive *f*.

transpire [træn'spaɪər] *vi* (*of secret etc*) s'ébruiter; (*happen*) Fam arriver; **it transpired that . . .** il s'est avéré que . . .

transplant [træns'plɑːnt] *vt* (*plant*) transplanter; (*organ*) Med greffer, transplanter; – ['trænsplɑːnt] *n* Med greffe *f*, transplantation *f*.

transport [træn'spɔːt] *vt* transporter; – ['trænspɔːt] *n* transport *m*; **public t.** les transports en commun; **do you have t.?** es-tu motorisé?; **t. café** routier *m*. ◆**transpor'tation** *n* transport *m*.

transpose [træns'pəʊz] *vt* transposer.

transvestite [trænz'vestaɪt] *n* travesti *m*.

trap [træp] *n* piège *m*; (*mouth*) Pej Sl gueule *f*; **t. door** trappe *f*; – *vt* (**-pp-**) (*snare*) prendre (au piège); (*jam, corner*) coincer, bloquer; (*cut off by snow etc*) bloquer (by par); **to t. one's finger** se coincer le doigt. ◆**trapper** *n* (*hunter*) trappeur *m*.

trapeze [trə'piːz] *n* (*in circus*) trapèze *m*; **t. artist** trapéziste *mf*.

trappings ['træpɪŋz] *npl* signes *mpl* extérieurs.

trash [træʃ] *n* (*nonsense*) sottises *fpl*; (*junk*) saleté(s) *f(pl)*; (*waste*) Am ordures *fpl*; (*riffraff*) Am racaille *f*. ◆**trashcan** *n* Am poubelle *f*. ◆**trashy** *a* (**-ier, -iest**) (*book etc*) moche, sans valeur; (*goods*) de camelote.

trauma ['trɔːmə, 'traʊmə] *n* (*shock*) traumatisme *m*. ◆**trau'matic** *a* traumatisant. ◆**traumatize** *vt* traumatiser.

travel ['trævəl] *vi* (**-ll-**, Am **-l-**) voyager; (*move*) aller, se déplacer; – *vt* (*country, distance, road*) parcourir; – *n* & *npl* voyages *mpl*; **on one's travels** en voyage; – *a* (*agency, book*) de voyages; **t. brochure** dépliant *m* touristique. ◆**travelled** *a* to be **well** *or* **widely t.** avoir beaucoup voyagé. ◆**travelling** *n* voyages *mpl*; – *a* (*bag etc*) de voyage; (*expenses*) de déplacement; (*circus, musician*) ambulant. ◆**traveller** *n* voyageur, -euse *mf*; **traveller's cheque**, Am **traveler's check** chèque *m* de voyage. ◆**travelogue** *n*, Am **travelog** (*book*) récit *m* de voyages. ◆**travelsickness** *n* (*in car*) mal *m* de la route; (*in aircraft*) mal *m* de l'air.

travesty ['trævəstɪ] *n* parodie *f*.

travolator ['trævəleɪtər] *n* trottoir *m* roulant.

trawler ['trɔːlər] *n* (*ship*) chalutier *m*.

tray [treɪ] *n* plateau *m*; (*for office correspondence etc*) corbeille *f*.

treacherous ['tretʃərəs] *a* (*person, action, road, journey etc*) traître. ◆**treacherously** *adv* traîtreusement; (*dangerously*) dangereusement. ◆**treachery** *n* traîtrise *f*.

treacle ['triːk(ə)l] *n* mélasse *f*.

tread [tred] *vi* (*pt* trod, *pp* trodden) (*walk*) marcher (on sur); (*proceed*) Fig avancer; – *vt* (*path*) parcourir; (*soil*) Fig fouler; **to t. sth into a carpet** étaler qch (avec les pieds) sur un tapis; – *n* (*step*) pas *m*; (*of tyre*) chape *f*. ◆**treadmill** *n* Pej Fig routine *f*.

treason ['triːz(ə)n] *n* trahison *f*.

treasure ['treʒər] *n* trésor *m*; **a real t.** (*person*) Fig une vraie perle; **t. hunt** chasse *f* au trésor; – *vt* (*value*) tenir à, priser; (*keep*) conserver (précieusement). ◆**treasurer** *n* trésorier, -ière *mf*. ◆**Treasury** *n* the T. Pol = le ministère des Finances.

treat [triːt] **1** *vt* (*person, product etc*) & Med traiter; (*consider*) considérer (**as** comme); **to t. with care** prendre soin de; **to t. s.o. to sth** offrir qch à qn. **2** *n* (*pleasure*) plaisir *m* (*special*); (*present*) cadeau-surprise *m*; (*meal*) régal *m*; **it was a t. (for me) to do it** ça m'a fait plaisir de le faire. ◆**treatment** *n* (*behaviour*) & Med traitement *m*; **his t. of her** la façon dont il la traite; **rough t.** mauvais traitements *mpl*.

treatise ['triːtɪz] *n* (*book*) traité *m* (on de).

treaty ['triːtɪ] *n* Pol traité *m*.

treble ['treb(ə)l] *a* triple; – *vti* tripler; – *n* le triple; **it's t. the price** c'est le triple du prix.

tree [triː] *n* arbre *m*; **Christmas t.** sapin *m* de Noël; **family t.** arbre *m* généalogique. ◆**t.-lined** *a* bordé d'arbres. ◆**t.-top** *n* cime *f* (d'un arbre). ◆**t.-trunk** *n* tronc *m* d'arbre.

trek [trek] *vi* (**-kk-**) cheminer *or* voyager (*péniblement*); Sp marcher à pied; (*go*) Fam traîner; – *n* voyage *m* (*pénible*); Sp randonnée *f*; (*distance*) Fam tirée *f*.

trellis ['trelɪs] *n* treillage *m*.

tremble ['tremb(ə)l] *vi* trembler (**with** de). ◆**tremor** *n* tremblement *m*; (**earth**) **t.** secousse *f* (sismique).

tremendous [trə'mendəs] *a* (*huge*) énorme; (*dreadful*) terrible; (*wonderful*) formidable, terrible. ◆**-ly** *adv* terriblement.

trench [trentʃ] *n* tranchée *f*.

trend [trend] *n* tendance *f* (**towards** à); **the t.** (*fashion*) la mode; **to set a** *or* **the t.** donner le ton, lancer une *or* la mode. ◆**trendy** *a* (-**ier**, -**iest**) (*person, clothes, topic etc*) *Fam* à la mode, dans le vent.

trepidation [trepɪ'deɪʃ(ə)n] *n* inquiétude *f*.

trespass ['trespəs] *vi* s'introduire sans autorisation (**on, upon** dans); '**no trespassing**' 'entrée interdite'.

tresses ['tresɪz] *npl Lit* chevelure *f*.

trestle ['tres(ə)l] *n* tréteau *m*.

trial ['traɪəl] *n Jur* procès *m*; (*test*) essai *m*; (*ordeal*) épreuve *f*; **t. of strength** épreuve *f* de force; **to go** *or* **be on t., stand t.** passer en jugement; **to put s.o. on t.** juger qn; **by t. and error** par tâtonnements; – *a* (*period, flight etc*) d'essai; (*offer*) à l'essai; **t. run** (*of new product etc*) période *f* d'essai.

triangle ['traɪæŋg(ə)l] *n* triangle *m*; (*setsquare*) *Math Am* équerre *f*. ◆**triangular** *a* triangulaire.

tribe [traɪb] *n* tribu *f*. ◆**tribal** *a* tribal.

tribulations [trɪbjʊ'leɪʃ(ə)nz] *npl* (**trials and**) **t. tribulations** *fpl*.

tribunal [traɪ'bjuːn(ə)l] *n* commission *f*, tribunal *m*; *Mil* tribunal *m*.

tributary ['trɪbjʊtərɪ] *n* affluent *m*.

tribute ['trɪbjuːt] *n* hommage *m*, tribut *m*; **to pay t. to** rendre hommage à.

trick [trɪk] *n* (*joke, deception & of conjurer etc*) tour *m*; (*ruse*) astuce *f*; (*habit*) manie *f*; **to play a t. on** s.o. jouer un tour à qn; *cards* **t.** tour *m* de cartes; **that will do the t.** *Fam* ça fera l'affaire; **t. photo** photo *f* truquée; **t. question** question-piège *f*; – *vt* (*deceive*) tromper, attraper; **to t. s.o. into doing sth** amener qn à faire qch par la ruse. ◆**trickery** *n* ruse *f*. ◆**tricky** *a* (-**ier**, -**iest**) (*problem etc*) difficile, délicat; (*person*) rusé.

trickle ['trɪk(ə)l] *n* (*of liquid*) filet *m*; **a t.** (*of letters, people etc*) *Fig* un petit nombre de; – *vi* (*flow*) dégouliner, couler (lentement); **to t. in** (*of letters, people etc*) *Fig* arriver en petit nombre.

tricycle ['traɪsɪk(ə)l] *n* tricycle *m*.

trier ['traɪər] *n* **to be a t.** être persévérant.

trifl/e ['traɪf(ə)l] *n* (*article, money*) bagatelle *f*; (*dessert*) diplomate *m*; – *a & adv* **a t. small/too much/**etc un tantinet petit/trop/etc; – *vi* **to t. with** (*s.o.'s feelings*) jouer avec; (*person*) plaisanter avec. ◆—**ing** *a* insignifiant.

trigger ['trɪgər] *n* (*of gun*) gâchette *f*; – *vt* **to t. (off)** (*start, cause*) déclencher.

trilogy ['trɪlədʒɪ] *n* trilogie *f*.

trim [trɪm] **1** *a* (**trimmer, trimmest**) (*neat*) soigné, net; (*slim*) svelte; – *n* **in t.** (*fit*) en (bonne) forme. **2** *n* (*cut*) légère coupe *f*; (*haircut*) coupe *f* de rafraîchissement; – *vt*

(-**mm**-) couper (légèrement); (*finger nail, edge*) rogner; (*hair*) rafraîchir. **3** *n* (*on garment*) garniture *f*; (*on car*) garnitures *fpl*; – *vt* (-**mm**-) **to t. with** (*lace etc*) orner de. ◆**trimmings** *npl* garniture(s) *f*(*pl*); (*extras*) *Fig* accessoires *mpl*.

Trinity ['trɪnɪtɪ] *n* **the T.** (*union*) *Rel* la Trinité.

trinket ['trɪŋkɪt] *n* colifichet *m*.

trio ['triːəʊ] *n* (*pl* -**os**) (*group*) & *Mus* trio *m*.

trip [trɪp] **1** *n* (*journey*) voyage *m*; (*outing*) excursion *f*; **to take a t. to** (*cinema, shops etc*) aller à. **2** *n* (*stumble*) faux pas *m*; – *vi* (-**pp**-) **to t. (over** *or* **up)** trébucher; **to t. over sth** trébucher contre qch; – *vt* **to t. s.o. up** faire trébucher qn. **3** *vi* (-**pp**-) (*walk gently*) marcher d'un pas léger. ◆**tripper** *n Br* excursionniste *f*.

tripe [traɪp] *n Culin* tripes *fpl*; (*nonsense*) *Fam* bêtises *fpl*.

triple ['trɪp(ə)l] *a* triple; – *vti* tripler. ◆**triplets** *npl* (*children*) triplés, -ées *mfpl*.

triplicate ['trɪplɪkət] *n* **in t.** en trois exemplaires.

tripod ['traɪpɒd] *n* trépied *m*.

trite [traɪt] *a* banal. ◆—**ness** *n* banalité *f*.

triumph ['traɪʌmf] *n* triomphe *m* (**over** sur); – *vi* triompher (**over** de). ◆**triumphal** *a* triomphal. ◆**triumphant** *a* (*team, army, gesture*) triomphant; (*success, welcome, return*) triomphal. ◆**triumphantly** *adv* triomphalement.

trivia ['trɪvɪə] *npl* vétilles *fpl*. ◆**trivial** *a* (*unimportant*) insignifiant; (*trite*) banal. ◆**triviality** *n* insignifiance *f*; banalité *f*; *pl* banalités *fpl*.

trod, trodden [trɒd, 'trɒd(ə)n] *see* tread.

trolley ['trɒlɪ] *n* (*for luggage*) chariot *m*; (*for shopping*) poussette *f* (de marché); (*in supermarket*) caddie® *m*; (*trolleybus*) trolley *m*; (**tea**) **t.** table *f* roulante; (*for tea urn*) chariot *m*; **t.** (**car**) *Am* tramway *m*. ◆**trolleybus** *n* trolleybus *m*.

trombone [trɒm'bəʊn] *n Mus* trombone *m*.

troop [truːp] *n* bande *f*; *Mil* troupe *f*; **the troops** (*army, soldiers*) les troupes, la troupe; – *vi* **to t. in/out/**etc entrer/sortir/etc en masse. ◆—**ing** *n* **t. the colour** le salut du drapeau. ◆—**er** *n* (*state*) **t.** *Am* membre *m* de la police montée.

trophy ['trəʊfɪ] *n* trophée *m*.

tropic ['trɒpɪk] *n* tropique *m*. ◆**tropical** *a* tropical.

trot [trɒt] *n* (*of horse*) trot *m*; **on the t.** (*one after another*) *Fam* de suite; – *vi* (-**tt**-) trotter; **to t. off** or **along** (leave) Hum Fam se sauver; − vt **to t. out** (say) Fam débiter.

troubl/e ['trʌb(ə)l] n (difficulty) ennui(s) m(pl); (bother, effort) peine f, mal m; **trouble(s)** (social unrest etc) & Med troubles mpl; **to be in t.** avoir des ennuis; **to get into t.** s'attirer des ennuis (with avec); **the t. (with you) is** . . . l'ennui (avec toi) c'est que . . . ; **to go to the t. of doing, take the t. to do** se donner la peine ou le mal de faire; **I didn't put her to any t.** je ne l'ai pas dérangée; **to find the t.** trouver le problème; **a spot of t.** un petit problème; **a t. spot** Pol un point chaud; − vt (inconvenience) déranger, ennuyer; (worry, annoy) ennuyer; (hurt) faire mal à; (grieve) peiner; **to t. to do** se donner la peine de faire; − vi **to t. (oneself)** se déranger. **◆−ed** a (worried) inquiet; (period) agité. **◆trouble-free** a (machine, vehicle) qui ne tombe jamais en panne, fiable. **◆troublemaker** n fauteur m de troubles. **◆troubleshooter** n Tech dépanneur m, expert m; Pol conciliateur, -trice mf. **◆troublesome** ['trʌb(ə)ls(ə)m] a ennuyeux, gênant; (leg etc) qui fait mal.

trough [trɒf] n (for drinking) abreuvoir m; (for feeding) auge f; **t. of low pressure** Met dépression f.

trounce [traʊns] vt (defeat) écraser.

troupe [truːp] n Th troupe f.

trousers ['traʊzəz] npl pantalon m; **a pair of t., some t.** un pantalon; **(short) t.** culottes fpl courtes.

trousseau ['truːsəʊ] n (of bride) trousseau m.

trout [traʊt] n truite f.

trowel ['traʊəl] n (for cement or plaster) truelle f; (for plants) déplantoir m.

truant ['truːənt] n (pupil, shirker) absentéiste mf; **to play t.** faire l'école buissonnière. **◆truancy** n Sch absentéisme m scolaire.

truce [truːs] n Mil trêve f.

truck [trʌk] n 1 (lorry) camion m; Rail wagon m plat; **t. driver** camionneur m; (long-distance) routier m; **t. stop** (restaurant) routier m. 2 **t. farmer** Am maraîcher, -ère mf. **◆trucker** n Am (haulier) transporteur m routier; (driver) camionneur m, routier m.

truculent ['trʌkjʊlənt] a agressif.

trudge [trʌdʒ] vi marcher d'un pas pesant.

true [truː] a (-er, -est) vrai; (accurate) exact; (genuine) vrai, véritable; (friend, promise etc) fidèle (to à); **t. to life** conforme à la réalité; **to come t.** se réaliser; **to hold t.** (of argument etc) valoir (for pour); **too t.!** Fam

ah, ça oui! **◆truly** adv vraiment; (faithfully) fidèlement; **well and t.** bel et bien.

truffle ['trʌf(ə)l] n (mushroom) truffe f.

truism ['truːɪz(ə)m] n lapalissade f.

trump [trʌmp] 1 n Cards atout m; **t. card** (advantage) Fig atout m. 2 vt **to t. up** (charge, reason) inventer.

trumpet ['trʌmpɪt] n trompette f; **t. player** trompettiste mf.

truncate [trʌŋ'keɪt] vt tronquer.

truncheon ['trʌntʃ(ə)n] n matraque f.

trundle ['trʌnd(ə)l] vti **to t. along** rouler bruyamment.

trunk [trʌŋk] n (of tree, body) tronc m; (of elephant) trompe f; (case) malle f; (of vehicle) Am coffre m; pl (for swimming) slip m ou caleçon m de bain; **t. call** Tel communication f interurbaine; **t. road** route f nationale.

truss [trʌs] vt **to t. (up)** (prisoner) ligoter.

trust [trʌst] n (faith) confiance f (in en); (group) Fin trust m; Jur fidéicommis m; **to take on t.** accepter de confiance; − vt (person, judgement) avoir confiance en, se fier à; (instinct, promise) se fier à; **to t. s.o. with sth, to t. sth to s.o.** confier qch à qn; **to t. s.o. to do** (rely on, expect) compter sur qn pour faire; **I t. that** (hope) j'espère que; − vi **to t. in s.o.** se fier à qn; **to t. to luck** ou **chance** se fier au hasard. **◆−ed** a (friend, method etc) éprouvé. **◆−ing** a confiant. **◆trus'tee** n (of school) administrateur -trice mf. **◆trustworthy** a sûr, digne de confiance.

truth [truːθ] n (pl -s [truːðz]) vérité f; **there's some t. in** . . . il y a du vrai dans . . . . **◆truthful** a (statement etc) véridique, vrai; (person) sincère. **◆truthfully** adv sincèrement.

try [traɪ] 1 vt essayer (**to do, doing** de faire); (s.o.'s patience etc) mettre à l'épreuve; **to t. one's hand at** s'essayer à; **to t. one's luck** tenter sa chance; **to t. (out)** (car, method etc) essayer; (employee etc) mettre à l'essai; **to t. on** (clothes, shoes) essayer; − vi essayer (**for** qch); **to t. hard** faire un gros effort; **t. and come!** essaie de venir!; − n (attempt) & Rugby essai m; **to have a t.** essayer; **at (the) first t.** du premier coup. 2 vt (person) Jur juger (**for theft**/etc pour vol/etc). **◆−ing** a pénible, éprouvant.

tsar [zɑːr] n tsar m.

tub [tʌb] n (for washing clothes etc) baquet m; (bath) baignoire f; (for ice cream etc) pot m.

tuba ['tjuːbə] n Mus tuba m.

tubby ['tʌbɪ] a (-ier, -iest) Fam dodu.

tube [tjuːb] n tube m; Rail Fam métro m; (of tyre) chambre f à air. ◆**tubing** n (tubes) tubes mpl. ◆**tubular** a tubulaire.

tuberculosis [tjuːbɜːkjuˈləʊsɪs] n tuberculose f.

tuck [tʌk] 1 n (fold in garment) rempli m; – vt (put) mettre; **to t. away** ranger; (hide) cacher; **to t. in** (shirt) rentrer; (person in bed, a blanket) border; **to t. up** (skirt) remonter. 2 vi **to t. in** (eat) Fam manger; **to t. into** (meal) Fam attaquer; – n **t. shop** Sch boutique f à provisions.

Tuesday [ˈtjuːzdɪ] n mardi m.

tuft [tʌft] n (of hair, grass) touffe f.

tug [tʌg] 1 vt (-gg-) (pull) tirer; – vi tirer (at, on sur); – n **to give sth a t.** tirer (sur) qch. 2 n (boat) remorqueur m.

tuition [tjuːˈɪʃ(ə)n] n (teaching) enseignement m; (lessons) leçons fpl; (fee) frais mpl de scolarité.

tulip [ˈtjuːlɪp] n tulipe f.

tumble [ˈtʌmb(ə)l] vi **to t. (over)** (fall) dégringoler; (backwards) tomber à la renverse; **to t. to sth** (understand) Sl réaliser qch; – n (fall) dégringolade f. **t. drier** sèche-linge m inv. ◆**tumbledown** a délabré. ◆**tumbler** [ˈtʌmblər] n (drinking glass) gobelet m.

tummy [ˈtʌmɪ] n Fam ventre m.

tumour [ˈtjuːmər] n tumeur f.

tumult [ˈtjuːmʌlt] n tumulte m. ◆tu'**multuous** a tumultueux.

tuna [ˈtjuːnə] n **t. (fish)** thon m.

tun/e [tjuːn] n (melody) air m; **to be** or **sing in t./out of t.** chanter juste/faux; **in t.** (instrument) accordé; **out of t.** (instrument) désaccordé; **t. with** (harmony) Fig en accord avec; **to the t. of £50** d'un montant de 50 livres, dans les 50 livres; – vt **to t. (up)** Mus accorder; Aut régler; – vi **to t. in (to)** Rad TV se mettre à l'écoute (de), écouter. ◆**-ing** n Aut réglage m. **t. fork** Mus diapason m. ◆**tuneful** a mélodieux.

tunic [ˈtjuːnɪk] n tunique f.

Tunisia [tjuːˈnɪzɪə] n Tunisie f. ◆**Tunisian** a & n tunisien, -ienne (mf).

tunnel [ˈtʌn(ə)l] n tunnel m; (in mine) galerie f; – vi (-ll-, Am -l-) percer un tunnel (into dans).

turban [ˈtɜːbən] n turban m.

turbine [ˈtɜːbaɪn, Am ˈtɜːbɪn] n turbine f.

turbulence [ˈtɜːbjʊləns] n Phys Av turbulences fpl.

turbulent [ˈtɜːbjʊlənt] a (person etc) turbulent.

tureen [tjuːˈriːn, təˈriːn] n (soup) **t.** soupière f.

turf [tɜːf] 1 n (grass) gazon m; **the t.** Sp le turf; **t. accountant** bookmaker m. 2 vt **to t. out** (get rid of) Fam jeter dehors.

turgid [ˈtɜːdʒɪd] a (style, language) boursouflé.

turkey [ˈtɜːkɪ] n dindon m, dinde f; (as food) dinde f.

Turkey [ˈtɜːkɪ] n Turquie f. ◆**Turk** n Turc m, Turque f. ◆**Turkish** a turc; **T. delight** (sweet) loukoum m; – n (language) turc m.

turmoil [ˈtɜːmɔɪl] n confusion f, trouble m; **in t.** en ébullition.

turn [tɜːn] n (movement, action & in game etc) tour m; (in road) tournant m; (of events, mind) tournure f; Med crise f; Psy choc m; (act) Th numéro m; **t. of phrase** tour m or tournure f (de phrase); **to take turns** se relayer; **in t.** à tour de rôle; **by turns** tour à tour; **in (one's) t.** à son tour; **it's your t. to play** c'est à toi de jouer; **to do s.o. a good t.** rendre service à qn; **the t. of the century** le début du siècle; – vt tourner; (mechanically) faire tourner; (mattress, pancake) retourner; **to turn s.o./sth into** (change) changer or transformer qn/qch en; **to t. sth red/yellow** rougir/jaunir qch; **to t. sth on s.o.** (aim) braquer qch sur qn; **she's turned twenty** elle a vingt ans passés; **it's turned seven** il est sept heures passées; **it turns my stomach** cela me soulève le cœur; – vi (of wheel, driver etc) tourner; (turn head and body) se (re)tourner (towards vers); (become) devenir; **to t. to** (question, adviser etc) se tourner vers; **to t. against** se retourner contre; **to t. into** (change) se changer or se transformer en. ■ **to t. around** vi (of person) se retourner; **to t. away** vt (avert) détourner (from de); (refuse) renvoyer (qn); – vi (stop facing) détourner les yeux, se détourner; **to t. back** vt (bed sheet, corner of page) replier; (person) renvoyer; (clock) reculer (to jusqu'à); – vi (return) retourner (sur ses pas); **to t. down** vt (fold down) rabattre; (gas, radio etc) baisser; (refuse) refuser (qn, offre etc); **to t. in** vt (hand in) rendre (to à); (prisoner etc) Fam livrer (à la police); – vi (go to bed) Fam se coucher; **to t. off** vt (light, radio etc) éteindre; (tap) fermer; (machine) arrêter; – vi (in vehicle) tourner; **to t. on** vt (light, radio etc) mettre, allumer; (tap) ouvrir; (machine) mettre en marche; **to t. s.o. on** (sexually) Fam exciter qn; – vi tel; **to t. out** vt (light) éteindre; (contents of box etc) vider (from de); (produce) produire; – vi (of crowds) venir; (happen) se passer; **it turns out that il**

s'avère que; **she turned out to be** ... elle s'est révélée être ... ; **to t. over** vt (page) tourner; – vi (of vehicle, person etc) se retourner; (of car engine) tourner au ralenti; **to t. round** vt (head, object) tourner; (vehicle) faire faire demi-tour à; – vi (of person) se retourner; **to t. up** vt (radio, light etc) mettre plus fort; (collar) remonter; (unearth, find) déterrer; **a turned-up nose** un nez retroussé; – vi (arrive) arriver; (be found) être (re)trouvé. ◆**turning** n (street) petite rue f; (bend in road) tournant m; **t. circle** Aut rayon m de braquage; **t. point** (in time) tournant m. ◆**turner** n (workman) tourneur m.

turncoat ['tɜːnkəʊt] n renégat, -ate mf. ◆**turn-off** n (in road) embranchement m. ◆**turnout** n (people) assistance f; (at polls) participation f. ◆**turnover** n (money) Com chiffre m d'affaires; (of stock) Com rotation f; **staff t.** (starting and leaving) la rotation du personnel; **apple t.** chausson m (aux pommes). ◆**turnup** n (on trousers) revers m.

turnip ['tɜːnɪp] n navet m.

turnpike ['tɜːnpaɪk] n Am autoroute f à péage.

turnstile ['tɜːnstaɪl] n (gate) tourniquet m.

turntable ['tɜːnteɪb(ə)l] n (of record player) platine f.

turpentine ['tɜːpəntaɪn] n (Fam **turps** [tɜːps]) n térébenthine f.

turquoise ['tɜːkwɔɪz] a turquoise inv.

turret ['tʌrɪt] n tourelle f.

turtle ['tɜːt(ə)l] n tortue f de mer; Am tortue f. ◆**turtleneck** a (sweater) à col roulé; – n col m roulé.

tusk [tʌsk] n (of elephant) défense f.

tussle ['tʌs(ə)l] n bagarre f.

tutor ['tjuːtər] n précepteur, -trice mf; Univ directeur, -trice mf d'études; Univ Am assistant, -ante mf; – vt donner des cours particuliers à. ◆**tu'torial** n Univ travaux mpl dirigés.

tut-tut! ['tʌt'tʌt] int allons donc!

tuxedo [tʌk'siːdəʊ] n (pl -os) Am smoking m.

TV [tiː'viː] n télé f.

twaddle ['twɒd(ə)l] n fadaises fpl.

twang [twæŋ] n son m vibrant; (nasal) t. nasillement m; – vi (of wire etc) vibrer.

twee [twiː] a (fussy) maniéré.

tweed [twiːd] n tweed m.

tweezers ['twiːzəz] npl pince f (à épiler).

twelve [twelv] a & n douze (m). ◆**twelfth** a & n douzième (mf).

twenty ['twentɪ] a & n vingt (m). ◆**twentieth** a & n vingtième (mf).

twerp [twɜːp] n Sl crétin, -ine mf.

twice [twaɪs] adv deux fois; **t. as heavy**/etc deux fois plus lourd/etc; **t. a month**/etc, **t. monthly**/etc deux fois par mois/etc.

twiddle ['twɪd(ə)l] vti **to t. (with) sth** (pencil, knob etc) tripoter qch; **to t. one's thumbs** se tourner les pouces.

twig [twɪg] **1** n (of branch) brindille f. **2** vti (-gg-) (understand) Sl piger.

twilight ['twaɪlaɪt] n crépuscule m; – a crépusculaire.

twin [twɪn] n jumeau m, jumelle f; **identical t.** vrai jumeau; **t. brother** frère m jumeau; **t. beds** lits mpl jumeaux; **t. town** ville f jumelée; – vt (-nn-) (town) jumeler. ◆**twinning** n jumelage m.

twine [twaɪn] **1** n (string) ficelle f. **2** vi (twist) s'enlacer (round autour de).

twinge [twɪndʒ] n a t. (of pain) un élancement; **a t. of remorse** un pincement de remords.

twinkle ['twɪŋk(ə)l] vi (of star) scintiller; (of eye) pétiller; – n scintillement m; pétillement m.

twinkie ['twɪŋk(ə)l] vi (of star) scintiller; (of eye) pétiller; – n scintillement m; pétillement m.

twirl [twɜːl] vi tournoyer; – vt faire tournoyer; (moustache) tortiller.

twist [twɪst] vt (wine, arm etc) tordre; (roll round) enrouler; (weave together) entortiller; (knob) tourner; (truth etc) Fig déformer; **to s.o.'s arm** Fig forcer la main à qn; – vi (wind) s'entortiller (round sth autour de qch); (of road, river) serpenter; – n torsion f; (turn) tour m; (in rope) entortillement m; (bend in road) tournant m; (in story) coup m de théâtre; (in event) tournure f; (of lemon) zeste m; **a road full of twists** une route qui fait des zigzags. ◆**-ed** a (ankle, wire, mind) tordu. ◆**-er** n **tongue t.** mot m or expression f imprononçable.

twit [twɪt] n Fam idiot, -ote mf.

twitch [twɪtʃ] **1** n (nervous) tic m; – vi (of person) avoir un tic; (of muscle) se convulser. **2** n (jerk) secousse f.

twitter ['twɪtər] vi (of bird) pépier.

two [tuː] a & n deux (m). ◆**t.-cycle** n Am = t.-stroke. ◆**t.-'faced** a Fig hypocrite. ◆**t.-'legged** a bipède. ◆**t.-piece** n (garment) deux-pièces m inv. ◆**t.-'seater** n Aut voiture f à deux places. ◆**t.-stroke** n (engine) deux-temps m inv. ◆**t.-way** a (traffic) dans les deux sens; **t.-way radio** émetteur-récepteur m.

twofold ['tuːfəʊld] *a* double; – *adv* **to increase t.** doubler.

twosome ['tuːsəm] *n* couple *m*.

tycoon [taɪ'kuːn] *n* magnat *m*.

type[1] [taɪp] *n* **1** (*example, person*) type *m*; (*sort*) genre *m*, sorte *f*, type *m*; **blood t.** groupe *m* sanguin. **2** (*print*) *Typ* caractères *mpl*; **in large t.** en gros caractères. ◆**typesetter** *n* compositeur, trice *mf*.

typ[2] [taɪp] *vti* (*write*) taper (à la machine). ◆**-ing** *n* dactylo(graphie) *f*; **a page of t.** une page dactylographiée; **t. error** faute *f* de frappe. ◆**typewriter** *n* machine *f* à écrire. ◆**typewritten** *a* dactylographié. ◆**typist** *n* dactylo *f*.

typhoid ['taɪfɔɪd] *n* **t. (fever)** *Med* typhoïde *f*.

typhoon [taɪ'fuːn] *n* *Met* typhon *m*.

typical ['tɪpɪk(ə)l] *a* typique (**of** de); (*customary*) habituel; **that's t. (of him)!** c'est bien lui! ◆**typically** *adv* typiquement; (*as usual*) comme d'habitude. ◆**typify** *vt* être typique de; (*symbolize*) représenter.

tyranny ['tɪrənɪ] *n* tyrannie *f*. ◆**tyrannical** [tɪ'rænɪk(ə)l] *a* tyrannique. ◆**tyrant** ['taɪrənt] *n* tyran *m*.

tyre ['taɪər] *n* pneu *m*.

U

U, u [juː] *n* U *m*, u *m*. ◆**U-turn** *n* *Aut* demi-tour *m*;*Fig Pej* volte-face *f inv*.

ubiquitous [juː'bɪkwɪtəs] *a* omniprésent.

udder ['ʌdər] *n* (*of cow etc*) pis *m*.

ugh! [ɜː(h)] *int* pouah!

ugly ['ʌglɪ] *a* (**-ier, -iest**) laid, vilain. ◆**ugliness** *n* laideur *f*.

UK [juː'keɪ] *abbr* = **United Kingdom.**

ulcer ['ʌlsər] *n* ulcère *m*.

ulterior [ʌl'tɪərɪər] *a* **u. motive** arrière-pensée *f*.

ultimate ['ʌltɪmət] *a* (*final, last*) ultime; (*definitive*) définitif; (*basic*) fondamental; (*authority*) suprême. ◆**-ly** *adv* (*finally*) à la fin; (*fundamentally*) en fin de compte; (*subsequently*) à une date ultérieure.

ultimatum [ʌltɪ'meɪtəm] *n* ultimatum *m*.

ultra- ['ʌltrə] *pref* ultra-.

ultramodern [ʌltrə'mɒdən] *a* ultra-moderne.

ultraviolet [ʌltrə'vaɪələt] *a* ultraviolet.

umbilical [ʌm'bɪlɪk(ə)l] *a* **u. cord** cordon *m* ombilical.

umbrage ['ʌmbrɪdʒ] *n* **to take u.** se froisser (**at** de).

umbrella [ʌm'brelə] *n* parapluie *m*; **u. stand** porte-parapluies *m inv*.

umpire ['ʌmpaɪər] *n* *Sp* arbitre *m*; – *vt* arbitrer.

umpteen [ʌmp'tiːn] *a* (*many*) *Fam* je ne sais combien de. ◆**umpteenth** *a Fam* énième.

un- [ʌn] *pref* in-, peu, non, sans.

UN [juː'en] *abbr* = **United Nations.**

unabashed [ʌnə'bæʃt] *a* nullement déconcerté.

unabated [ʌnə'beɪtɪd] *a* aussi fort qu'avant.

unable [ʌn'eɪb(ə)l] *a* **to be u. to do** être incapable de faire; **he's u. to swim** il ne sait pas nager.

unabridged [ʌnə'brɪdʒd] *a* intégral.

unacceptable [ʌnək'septəb(ə)l] *a* inacceptable.

unaccompanied [ʌnə'kʌmpənɪd] *a* (*person*) non accompagné; (*singing*) sans accompagnement.

unaccountable [ʌnə'kaʊntəb(ə)l] *a* inexplicable. ◆**-ly** *adv* inexplicablement.

unaccounted [ʌnə'kaʊntɪd] *a* **to be (still) u. for** rester introuvable.

unaccustomed [ʌnə'kʌstəmd] *a* inaccoutumé; **to be u. to sth/to doing** ne pas être habitué à qch/à faire.

unadulterated [ʌnə'dʌltəreɪtɪd] *a* pur.

unaided [ʌn'eɪdɪd] *a* sans aide.

unanimity [juːnə'nɪmɪtɪ] *n* unanimité *f*. ◆**u'nanimous** *a* unanime. ◆**u'nanimously** *adv* à l'unanimité.

unappetizing [ʌn'æpɪtaɪzɪŋ] *a* peu appétissant.

unapproachable [ʌnə'prəʊtʃəb(ə)l] *a* (*person*) inabordable.

unarmed [ʌn'ɑːmd] *a* (*person*) non armé; (*combat*) à mains nues.

unashamed [ʌnə'ʃeɪmd] *a* éhonté; **she's u. about it** elle n'en a pas honte. ◆**-ly** [-ɪdlɪ] *adv* sans vergogne.

unassailable [ʌnə'seɪləb(ə)l] *a* (*argument, reputation*) inattaquable.

unassuming [ʌnə'sjuːmɪŋ] *a* modeste.

unattached [ʌnə'tætʃt] *a* (*independent, not married*) libre.

unattainable [ʌnə'teɪnəb(ə)l] *a* (*goal, aim*) inaccessible.

unattended [ʌnə'tendɪd] *a* sans surveillance.

unattractive [ʌnə'træktɪv] *a* (*idea, appearance etc*) peu attrayant; (*character*) peu sympathique; (*ugly*) laid.

unauthorized [ʌn'ɔːθəraɪzd] *a* non autorisé.

unavailable [ʌnə'veɪləb(ə)l] *a* (*person, funds*) indisponible; (*article*) Com épuisé.

unavoidable [ʌnə'vɔɪdəb(ə)l] *a* inévitable.
◆—**ly** *adv* inévitablement (*delayed*) pour une raison indépendante de sa volonté.

unaware [ʌnə'weər] *a* to be u. of ignorer; to be u. that ignorer que. ◆**unawares** *adv* to catch s.o. u. prendre qn au dépourvu.

unbalanced [ʌn'bælənst] *a* (*mind, person*) déséquilibré.

unbearab/le [ʌn'beərəb(ə)l] *a* insupportable. ◆—**ly** *adv* insupportablement.

unbeatable [ʌn'biːtəb(ə)l] *a* imbattable. ◆**unbeaten** *a* (*player*) invaincu; (*record*) non battu.

unbeknown(st) [ʌnbɪ'nəʊn(st)] *a* u. to à l'insu de.

unbelievable [ʌnbɪ'liːvəb(ə)l] *a* incroyable. ◆**unbelieving** *a* incrédule.

unbend [ʌn'bend] *vi* (*pt & pp* unbent) (*relax*) se détendre. ◆—**ing** *a* inflexible.

unbias(s)ed [ʌn'baɪəst] *a* impartial.

unblock [ʌn'blɒk] *vt* (*sink etc*) déboucher.

unborn [ʌn'bɔːn] *a* (*child*) à naître.

unbounded [ʌn'baʊndɪd] *a* illimité.

unbreakable [ʌn'breɪkəb(ə)l] *a* incassable. ◆**unbroken** *a* (*continuous*) continu; (*intact*) intact; (*record*) non battu.

unbridled [ʌn'braɪd(ə)ld] *a* Fig débridé.

unburden [ʌn'bɜːd(ə)n] *vt* to u. oneself Fig s'épancher (to auprès de, avec).

unbutton [ʌn'bʌt(ə)n] *vt* déboutonner.

uncalled-for [ʌn'kɔːldfɔːr] *a* déplacé, injustifié.

uncanny [ʌn'kænɪ] *a* (-ier, -iest) étrange, mystérieux.

unceasing [ʌn'siːsɪŋ] *a* incessant. ◆—**ly** *adv* sans cesse.

unceremoniously [ʌnserɪ'məʊnɪəslɪ] *adv* (*to treat*) sans ménagement; (*to show out*) brusquement.

uncertain [ʌn'sɜːt(ə)n] *a* incertain (about, of de); it's *or* he's u. whether *or* that il n'est pas certain que (+ *sub*). ◆**uncertainty** *n* incertitude *f*.

unchanged [ʌn'tʃeɪndʒd] *a* inchangé. ◆**unchanging** *a* immuable.

uncharitable [ʌn'tʃærɪtəb(ə)l] *a* peu charitable.

unchecked [ʌn'tʃekt] *adv* sans opposition.

uncivil [ʌn'sɪv(ə)l] *a* impoli, incivil.

uncivilized [ʌn'sɪvɪlaɪzd] *a* barbare.

uncle ['ʌŋk(ə)l] *n* oncle *m*.

unclear [ʌn'klɪər] *a* (*meaning*) qui n'est pas clair; (*result*) incertain; it's u. whether ... on ne sait pas très bien si ....

uncomfortable [ʌn'kʌmftəb(ə)l] *a* (*house, chair etc*) inconfortable; (*heat, experience*) désagréable; (*feeling*) troublant; she is *or* feels u. (*uneasy*) elle est mal à l'aise.

uncommon [ʌn'kɒmən] *a* rare. ◆—**ly** *adv* (*very*) extraordinairement; not u. (*fairly often*) assez souvent.

uncommunicative [ʌnkə'mjuːnɪkətɪv] *a* peu communicatif.

uncomplicated [ʌn'kɒmplɪkeɪtɪd] *a* simple.

uncompromising [ʌn'kɒmprəmaɪzɪŋ] *a* intransigeant.

unconcerned [ʌnkən'sɜːnd] *a* (*not anxious*) imperturbable; (*indifferent*) indifférent (by, with à).

unconditional [ʌnkən'dɪʃ(ə)nəl] *a* inconditionnel; (*surrender*) sans condition.

unconfirmed [ʌnkən'fɜːmd] *a* non confirmé.

uncongenial [ʌnkən'dʒiːnɪəl] *a* peu agréable; (*person*) antipathique.

unconnected [ʌnkə'nektɪd] *a* (*events, facts etc*) sans rapport (with avec).

unconscious [ʌn'kɒnʃəs] *a* Med sans connaissance; (*desire*) inconscient; u. of (*unaware of*) inconscient de; – *n* Psy inconscient *m*. ◆—**ly** *adv* inconsciemment.

uncontrollable [ʌnkən'trəʊləb(ə)l] *a* (*emotion, laughter*) irrépressible.

unconventional [ʌnkən'venʃ(ə)nəl] *a* peu conventionnel.

unconvinced [ʌnkən'vɪnst] *a* to be *or* remain u. ne pas être convaincu (of de). ◆**unconvincing** *a* peu convaincant.

uncooperative [ʌnkəʊ'ɒp(ə)rətɪv] *a* peu coopératif.

uncork [ʌn'kɔːk] *vt* (*bottle*) déboucher.

uncouple [ʌn'kʌp(ə)l] *vt* (*carriages*) Rail dételer.

uncouth [ʌn'kuːθ] *a* grossier.

uncover [ʌn'kʌvər] *vt* (*saucepan, conspiracy etc*) découvrir.

unctuous ['ʌŋktjʊəs] *a* (*insincere*) onctueux.

uncut [ʌn'kʌt] *a* (*film, play*) intégral; (*diamond*) brut.

undamaged [ʌn'dæmɪdʒd] *a* (*goods*) en bon état.

undaunted [ʌn'dɔːntɪd] *a* nullement découragé.

undecided [ʌndɪ'saɪdɪd] *a* (*person*) indécis

(about sur); **I'm u.** whether to do it or not je n'ai pas décidé si je le ferai ou non.

undefeated [ʌndɪ'fiːtɪd] a invaincu.

undeniable [ʌndɪ'naɪəb(ə)l] a incontestable.

under ['ʌndər] prep sous; (*less than*) moins de; (*according to*) selon; **children u. nine** les enfants de moins de or enfants au-dessous de neuf ans; **u. the circumstances** dans les circonstances; **u. there** là-dessous; **u. it** dessous; **u. (the command of) s.o.** sous les ordres de qn; **u. age** mineur; **u. discussion/repair** en discussion/réparation; **u. way** (*in progress*) en cours; (*on the way*) en route; **to be u. the impression that** avoir l'impression que; – adv au-dessous.

under- ['ʌndər] pref sous-.

undercarriage ['ʌndəkærɪdʒ] n (*of aircraft*) train m d'atterrissage.

undercharge [ʌndə'tʃɑːdʒ] vt **I undercharged him (for it)** je ne (le) lui ai pas fait payer assez.

underclothes ['ʌndəkləʊðz] npl sous-vêtements mpl.

undercoat ['ʌndəkəʊt] n (*of paint*) couche f de fond.

undercooked [ʌndə'kʊkt] a pas assez cuit.

undercover [ʌndə'kʌvər] a (*agent, operation*) secret.

undercurrent [ʌndə'kʌrənt] n (*in sea*) courant m (sous-marin); **an u. of** Fig un courant profond de.

undercut [ʌndə'kʌt] vt (*pt & pp* undercut, *pres p* undercutting) Com vendre moins cher que.

underdeveloped [ʌndədɪ'veləpt] a (*country*) sous-développé.

underdog ['ʌndədɒg] n (*politically, socially*) opprimé, -ée mf; (*likely loser*) perdant, -ante mf probable.

underdone [ʌndə'dʌn] a Culin pas assez cuit; (*steak*) saignant.

underestimate [ʌndər'estɪmeɪt] vt sous-estimer.

underfed [ʌndə'fed] a sous-alimenté.

underfoot [ʌndə'fʊt] adv sous les pieds.

undergo [ʌndə'gəʊ] vt (*pt* underwent, *pp* undergone) subir.

undergraduate [ʌndə'grædʒʊət] n étudiant, -ante mf (qui prépare la licence).

underground ['ʌndəgraʊnd] a souterrain; (*secret*) Fig clandestin; – n Rail métro m; (*organization*) Pol résistance f; – [ʌndə'graʊnd] adv sous terre; **to go u.** (*of fugitive etc*) Fig passer dans la clandestinité.

undergrowth ['ʌndəgrəʊθ] n sous-bois m inv.

underhand [ʌndə'hænd] a (*dishonest*) sournois.

underlie [ʌndə'laɪ] vt (*pt* underlay, *pp* underlain, *pres p* underlying) sous-tendre. ◆**underlying** a (*basic*) fondamental; (*hidden*) profond.

underline [ʌndə'laɪn] vt (*text, idea etc*) souligner.

undermanned [ʌndə'mænd] a (*office etc*) à court de personnel.

undermine [ʌndə'maɪn] vt (*building, strength, society etc*) miner, saper.

underneath [ʌndə'niːθ] prep sous; – adv (en) dessous; **the book u.** le livre d'en dessous; – n dessous m.

undernourished [ʌndə'nʌrɪʃt] a sous-alimenté.

underpants ['ʌndəpænts] npl (*male underwear*) slip m; (*loose, long*) caleçon m.

underpass ['ʌndəpɑːs] n (*for cars or pedestrians*) passage m souterrain.

underpay [ʌndə'peɪ] vt sous-payer. ◆**underpaid** a sous-payé.

underpriced [ʌndə'praɪst] a **it's u.** le prix en est trop bas, c'est bradé.

underprivileged [ʌndə'prɪvɪlɪdʒd] a défavorisé.

underrate [ʌndə'reɪt] vt sous-estimer.

undershirt ['ʌndəʃɜːt] n Am tricot m or maillot m de corps.

underside ['ʌndəsaɪd] n dessous m.

undersigned ['ʌndəsaɪnd] a soussigné; **I the u.** je soussigné(e).

undersized [ʌndə'saɪzd] a trop petit.

underskirt ['ʌndəskɜːt] n jupon m.

understaffed [ʌndə'stɑːft] a à court de personnel.

understand [ʌndə'stænd] vti (*pt & pp* understood) comprendre; **I u. that** (*hear*) je crois comprendre que, il paraît que; **I've been given to u. that** on m'a fait comprendre que. ◆—**ing** n (*act, faculty*) compréhension f; (*agreement*) accord m, entente f; (*sympathy*) entente f; **on the u. that** à condition que (+ sub); – a (*person*) compréhensif. ◆**understood** a (*agreed*) entendu; (*implied*) sous-entendu. ◆**understandable** a compréhensible. ◆**understandably** adv naturellement.

understatement [ʌndə'steɪtmənt] n euphémisme m.

understudy ['ʌndəstʌdɪ] n Th doublure f.

undertak/e [ʌndə'teɪk] vt (*pt* undertook, *pp* undertaken) (*task*) entreprendre; (*responsibility*) assumer; **to u. to do** se charger de faire. ◆—**ing** n (*task*) entreprise f; (*prom-*

ise) promesse *f*; **to give an u.** promettre (**that** que).

undertaker ['ʌndəteɪkər] *n* entrepreneur *m* de pompes funèbres.

undertone ['ʌndətəʊn] *n* **in an u.** à mi-voix; **an u. of** (*criticism, sadness etc*) *Fig* une note de.

undervalue [ʌndə'væljuː] *vt* sous-évaluer; **it's undervalued at ten pounds** ça vaut plus que dix livres.

underwater [ʌndə'wɔːtər] *a* sous-marin; – *adv* sous l'eau.

underwear ['ʌndəweər] *n* sous-vêtements *mpl*.

underweight [ʌndə'weɪt] *a* (*person*) qui ne pèse pas assez; (*goods*) d'un poids insuffisant.

underworld ['ʌndəwɜːld] *n* **the u.** (*criminals*) le milieu, la pègre.

undesirable [ʌndɪ'zaɪərəb(ə)l] *a* peu souhaitable (**that** que (+ *sub*)); (*person*) indésirable; – *n* (*person*) indésirable *mf*.

undetected [ʌndɪ'tektɪd] *a* non découvert; **to go u.** passer inaperçu.

undies ['ʌndɪz] *npl* (*female underwear*) *Fam* dessous *mpl*.

undignified [ʌn'dɪgnɪfaɪd] *a* qui manque de dignité.

undisciplined [ʌn'dɪsɪplɪnd] *a* indiscipliné.

undiscovered [ʌndɪ'skʌvəd] *a* **to remain u.** ne pas être découvert.

undisputed [ʌndɪ'spjuːtɪd] *a* incontesté.

undistinguished [ʌndɪ'stɪŋgwɪʃt] *a* médiocre.

undivided [ʌndɪ'vaɪdɪd] *a* **my u. attention** toute mon attention.

undo [ʌn'duː] *vt* (*pt* **undid**, *pp* **undone**) défaire; (*bound person, hands*) détacher, délier; (*a wrong*) réparer. **—ing** *n* (*downfall*) perte *f*, ruine *f*. **—undone** *a* **to leave u.** (*work etc*) ne pas faire; **to come u.** (*of knot etc*) se défaire.

undoubted [ʌn'daʊtɪd] *a* indubitable. **—ly** *adv* indubitablement.

undreamt-of [ʌn'dremtɒv] *a* insoupçonné.

undress [ʌn'dres] *vi* se déshabiller; – *vt* déshabiller; **to get undressed** se déshabiller.

undue [ʌn'djuː] *a* excessif. **—unduly** *adv* excessivement.

undulating ['ʌndjʊleɪtɪŋ] *a* (*movement*) onduleux; (*countryside*) vallonné.

undying [ʌn'daɪɪŋ] *a* éternel.

unearned [ʌn'ɜːnd] *a* **u. income** rentes *fpl*.

unearth [ʌn'ɜːθ] *vt* (*from ground*) déterrer; (*discover*) *Fig* dénicher, déterrer.

unearthly [ʌn'ɜːθlɪ] *a* sinistre, mystérieux; **u. hour** *Fam* heure *f* indue.

uneasy [ʌn'iːzɪ] *a* (*peace, situation*) précaire; (*silence*) gêné; **to be** *or* **feel u.** (*ill at ease*) être mal à l'aise, être gêné; (*worried*) être inquiet.

uneconomic(al) [ʌniːkə'nɒmɪk((ə)l)] *a* peu économique.

uneducated [ʌn'edʒʊkeɪtɪd] *a* (*person*) inculte; (*accent*) populaire.

unemployed [ʌnɪm'plɔɪd] *a* sans travail, en chômage; – *n* **the u.** les chômeurs *mpl*. **—unemployment** *n* chômage *m*.

unending [ʌn'endɪŋ] *a* interminable.

unenthusiastic [ʌnɪnθjuːzɪ'æstɪk] *a* peu enthousiaste.

unenviable [ʌn'enviəb(ə)l] *a* peu enviable.

unequal [ʌn'iːkwəl] *a* inégal; **to be u. to** (*task*) ne pas être à la hauteur de. **—unequalled** *a* (*incomparable*) inégalé.

unequivocal [ʌnɪ'kwɪvək(ə)l] *a* sans équivoque.

unerring [ʌn'ɜːrɪŋ] *a* infaillible.

unethical [ʌn'eθɪk(ə)l] *a* immoral.

uneven [ʌn'iːv(ə)n] *a* inégal.

uneventful [ʌnɪ'ventfəl] *a* (*journey, life etc*) sans histoires.

unexceptionable [ʌnɪk'sepʃ(ə)nəb(ə)l] *a* irréprochable.

unexpected [ʌnɪk'spektɪd] *a* inattendu. **—ly** *adv* à l'improviste; (*suddenly*) subitement; (*unusually*) exceptionnellement.

unexplained [ʌnɪk'spleɪnd] *a* inexpliqué.

unfailing [ʌn'feɪlɪŋ] *a* (*optimism, courage, support etc*) inébranlable; (*supply*) inépuisable.

unfair [ʌn'feər] *a* injuste (**to s.o.** envers qn); (*competition*) déloyal. **—ly** *adv* injustement. **—ness** *n* injustice *f*.

unfaithful [ʌn'feɪθfəl] *a* infidèle (**to** à).

unfamiliar [ʌnfə'mɪlɪər] *a* inconnu; peu familier; **to be u. with** ne pas connaître.

unfashionable [ʌn'fæʃ(ə)nəb(ə)l] *a* (*subject etc*) démodé; (*district etc*) peu chic *inv*, ringard; **it's u. to do** il n'est pas de bon ton de faire.

unfasten [ʌn'fɑːs(ə)n] *vt* défaire.

unfavourable [ʌn'feɪv(ə)rəb(ə)l] *a* défavorable.

unfeeling [ʌn'fiːlɪŋ] *a* insensible.

unfinished [ʌn'fɪnɪʃt] *a* inachevé; **to have some u. business** avoir une affaire à régler.

unfit [ʌn'fɪt] *a* (*unwell*) mal fichu; (*unsuited*) inapte (**for sth** à qch, **to do** à faire); (*unworthy*) indigne (**for sth** de qch, **to do** de faire);

to be u. to do (*incapable*) ne pas être en état de faire.

unflagging [ʌnˈflægɪŋ] *a* (*zeal*) inlassable; (*interest*) soutenu.

unflappable [ʌnˈflæpəb(ə)l] *a Fam* imperturbable.

unflattering [ʌnˈflæt(ə)rɪŋ] *a* peu flatteur.

unflinching [ʌnˈflɪntʃɪŋ] *a* (*fearless*) intrépide.

unfold [ʌnˈfəuld] *vt* déplier; (*wings*) déployer; (*ideas, plan*) *Fig* exposer; – *vi* (*of story, view*) se dérouler.

unforeseeable [ʌnfɔːˈsiːəb(ə)l] *a* imprévisible. ◆**unforeseen** *a* imprévu.

unforgettable [ʌnfəˈgetəb(ə)l] *a* inoubliable.

unforgivable [ʌnfəˈgɪvəb(ə)l] *a* impardonnable.

unfortunate [ʌnˈfɔːtʃ(ə)nət] *a* malheureux; (*event*) fâcheux; **you were u.** tu n'as pas eu de chance. ◆**–ly** *adv* malheureusement.

unfounded [ʌnˈfaundɪd] *a* (*rumour etc*) sans fondement.

unfriendly [ʌnˈfrendlɪ] *a* peu amical, froid. ◆**unfriendliness** *n* froideur *f*.

unfulfilled [ʌnfulˈfɪld] *a* (*desire*) insatisfait; (*plan*) non réalisé; (*condition*) non rempli.

unfurl [ʌnˈfɜːl] *vt* (*flag etc*) déployer.

unfurnished [ʌnˈfɜːnɪʃt] *a* non meublé.

ungainly [ʌnˈgeɪnlɪ] *a* (*clumsy*) gauche.

ungodly [ʌnˈgɒdlɪ] *a* impie; **u. hour** *Fam* heure *f* indue.

ungrammatical [ʌngrəˈmætɪk(ə)l] *a* non grammatical.

ungrateful [ʌnˈgreɪtfəl] *a* ingrat.

unguarded [ʌnˈgɑːdɪd] *a* **in a u. moment** dans un moment d'inattention.

unhappy [ʌnˈhæpɪ] *a* (**-ier, -iest**) (*sad*) malheureux, triste; (*worried*) inquiet; **u. with** (*not pleased*) mécontent de; **he's u. about doing it** ça le dérange de le faire. ◆**unhappily** *adv* (*unfortunately*) malheureusement. ◆**unhappiness** *n* tristesse *f*.

unharmed [ʌnˈhɑːmd] *a* indemne, sain et sauf.

unhealthy [ʌnˈhelθɪ] *a* (**-ier, -iest**) (*person*) en mauvaise santé; (*climate, place, job*) malsain; (*lungs*) malade.

unheard-of [ʌnˈhɜːdɒv] *a* (*unprecedented*) inouï.

unheeded [ʌnˈhiːdɪd] *a* **it went u.** on n'en a pas tenu compte.

unhelpful [ʌnˈhelpfəl] *a* (*person*) peu obligeant *or* serviable; (*advice*) peu utile.

unhinge [ʌnˈhɪndʒ] *vt* (*person, mind*) déséquilibrer.

unholy [ʌnˈhəulɪ] *a* (**-ier, -iest**) impie; (*din*) *Fam* de tous les diables.

unhook [ʌnˈhuk] *vt* (*picture, curtain*) décrocher; (*dress*) dégrafer.

unhoped-for [ʌnˈhəuptfɔːr] *a* inespéré.

unhurried [ʌnˈhʌrɪd] *a* (*movement*) lent; (*stroll, journey*) fait sans hâte.

unhurt [ʌnˈhɜːt] *a* indemne, sain et sauf.

unhygienic [ʌnhaɪˈdʒiːnɪk] *a* pas très hygiénique.

unicorn [ˈjuːnɪkɔːn] *n* licorne *f*.

uniform [ˈjuːnɪfɔːm] **1** *n* uniforme *m*. **2** *a* (*regular*) uniforme; (*temperature*) constant. ◆**uniformed** *a* en uniforme. ◆**uniˈformity** *n* uniformité *f*. ◆**uniformly** *adv* uniformément.

unify [ˈjuːnɪfaɪ] *vt* unifier. ◆**unifiˈcation** *n* unification *f*.

unilateral [juːnɪˈlæt(ə)rəl] *a* unilatéral.

unimaginable [ʌnɪˈmædʒɪnəb(ə)l] *a* inimaginable. ◆**unimaginative** *a* (*person, plan etc*) qui manque d'imagination.

unimpaired [ʌnɪmˈpeəd] *a* intact.

unimportant [ʌnɪmˈpɔːtənt] *a* peu important.

uninhabitable [ʌnɪnˈhæbɪtəb(ə)l] *a* inhabitable. ◆**uninhabited** *a* inhabité.

uninhibited [ʌnɪnˈhɪbɪtɪd] *a* (*person*) sans complexes.

uninitiated [ʌnɪˈnɪʃɪeɪtɪd] *n* **the u.** les profanes *mpl*, les non-initiés.

uninjured [ʌnˈɪndʒəd] *a* indemne.

uninspiring [ʌnɪnˈspaɪərɪŋ] *a* (*subject etc*) pas très inspirant.

unintelligible [ʌnɪnˈtelɪdʒəb(ə)l] *a* inintelligible.

unintentional [ʌnɪnˈtenʃ(ə)nəl] *a* involontaire.

uninterested [ʌnˈɪntrɪstɪd] *a* indifférent (**in** à). ◆**uninteresting** *a* (*book etc*) inintéressant; (*person*) fastidieux.

uninterrupted [ʌnɪntəˈrʌptɪd] *a* ininterrompu.

uninvited [ʌnɪnˈvaɪtɪd] *a* (*to arrive*) sans invitation. ◆**uninviting** *a* peu attrayant.

union [ˈjuːnjən] *n* union *f*; (*trade union*) syndicat *m*; – *a* syndical; (*trade*) **u. member** syndiqué, -ée *mf*; **U. Jack** drapeau *m* britannique. ◆**unionist** *n* **trade u.** syndicaliste *mf*. ◆**unionize** *vt* syndiquer.

unique [juːˈniːk] *a* unique. ◆**–ly** *adv* exceptionnellement.

unisex [ˈjuːnɪseks] *a* (*clothes etc*) unisexe *inv*.

unison [ˈjuːnɪs(ə)n] *n* **in u.** à l'unisson (**with** de).

unit [ˈjuːnɪt] *n* unité *f*; (*of furniture etc*) élément *m*; (*system*) bloc *m*; (*group, team*)

groupe *m*; **u. trust** *Fin* fonds *m* commun de placement.

unite [juː'naɪt] *vt* unir; *(country, party)* unifier; **United Kingdom** Royaume-Uni *m*; **United Nations** (Organisation *f* des) Nations unies *fpl*; **United States (of America)** États-Unis *mpl* (d'Amérique); – *vi* s'unir. ◆**unity** *n (cohesion)* unité *f*; *(harmony) Fig* harmonie *f*.

universal [juːnɪ'vɜːs(ə)l] *a* universel. ◆**—ly** *adv* universellement.

universe ['juːnɪvɜːs] *n* univers *m*.

university [juːnɪ'vɜːsɪtɪ] *n* université *f*; **at u.** à l'université; – *a* universitaire; *(student, teacher)* d'université.

unjust [ʌn'dʒʌst] *a* injuste.

unjustified [ʌn'dʒʌstɪfaɪd] *a* injustifié.

unkempt [ʌn'kempt] *a (appearance)* négligé; *(hair)* mal peigné.

unkind [ʌn'kaɪnd] *a* peu aimable **(to s.o.** avec qn); *(nasty)* méchant **(to s.o.** avec qn). ◆**—ly** *adv* méchamment.

unknowingly [ʌn'nəʊɪŋlɪ] *adv* inconsciemment.

unknown [ʌn'nəʊn] *a* inconnu; **u. to me,** he'd left il était parti, ce que j'ignorais; – *n (person)* inconnu, -ue *mf*; **the u.** *Phil* l'inconnu *m*; *(quantity) Math & Fig* inconnue *f*.

unlawful [ʌn'lɔːf(ə)l] *a* illégal.

unleaded [ʌn'ledɪd] *a (gasoline) Am* sans plomb.

unleash [ʌn'liːʃ] *vt (force etc)* déchaîner.

unless [ʌn'les] *conj* à moins que; **u. she comes** à moins qu'elle ne vienne; **u. you work harder, you'll fail** à moins de travailler plus dur, vous échouerez.

unlike [ʌn'laɪk] *a* différent; – *prep* **u. me, she ...** à la différence de moi ou contrairement à moi, elle ...; **he's very u. his father** il n'est pas du tout comme son père; **that's u. him** ça ne lui ressemble pas.

unlikely [ʌn'laɪklɪ] *a* improbable; *(implausible)* invraisemblable; **she's u. to win** il est peu probable qu'elle gagne. ◆**unlikelihood** *n* improbabilité *f*.

unlimited [ʌn'lɪmɪtɪd] *a* illimité.

unlisted [ʌn'lɪstɪd] *a (phone number) Am* qui ne figure pas à l'annuaire.

unload [ʌn'ləʊd] *vt* décharger.

unlock [ʌn'lɒk] *vt* ouvrir *(avec une clef)*.

unlucky [ʌn'lʌkɪ] *a* (-ier, -iest) *(person)* malchanceux; *(colour, number etc)* qui porte malheur; **you're u.** tu n'as pas de chance. ◆**unluckily** *adv* malheureusement.

unmade [ʌn'meɪd] *a (bed)* défait.

unmanageable [ʌn'mænɪdʒəb(ə)l] *a (child)* difficile; *(hair)* difficile à coiffer; *(packet, size)* peu maniable.

unmanned [ʌn'mænd] *a (ship)* sans équipage; *(spacecraft)* inhabité.

unmarked [ʌn'mɑːkt] *a (not blemished)* sans marque; **u. police car** voiture *f* banalisée.

unmarried [ʌn'mærɪd] *a* célibataire.

unmask [ʌn'mɑːsk] *vt* démasquer.

unmentionable [ʌn'menʃ(ə)nəb(ə)l] *a* dont il ne faut pas parler; *(unpleasant)* innommable.

unmercifully [ʌn'mɜːsɪf(ə)lɪ] *adv* sans pitié.

unmistakable [ʌnmɪ'steɪkəb(ə)l] *a (obvious)* indubitable; *(face, voice etc)* facilement reconnaissable.

unmitigated [ʌn'mɪtɪgeɪtɪd] *a (disaster)* absolu; *(folly)* pur.

unmoved [ʌn'muːvd] *a* **to be u.** *(feel no emotion)* ne pas être ému **(by** par); *(be unconcerned)* être indifférent **(by** à).

unnatural [ʌn'nætʃ(ə)rəl] *a (not normal)* pas naturel; *(crime)* contre nature; *(affected)* qui manque de naturel. ◆**—ly** *adv* **not u.** naturellement.

unnecessary [ʌn'nesəs(ə)rɪ] *a* inutile; *(superfluous)* superflu.

unnerve [ʌn'nɜːv] *vt* désarçonner, déconcerter.

unnoticed [ʌn'nəʊtɪst] *a* inaperçu.

unobstructed [ʌnəb'strʌktɪd] *a (road, view)* dégagé.

unobtainable [ʌnəb'teɪnəb(ə)l] *a* impossible à obtenir.

unobtrusive [ʌnəb'truːsɪv] *a* discret.

unoccupied [ʌn'ɒkjʊpaɪd] *a (person, house)* inoccupé; *(seat)* libre.

unofficial [ʌnə'fɪʃ(ə)l] *a* officieux; *(visit)* privé; *(strike)* sauvage. ◆**—ly** *adv* à titre officieux.

unorthodox [ʌn'ɔːθədɒks] *a* peu orthodoxe.

unpack [ʌn'pæk] *vt (case)* défaire; *(goods, belongings, contents)* déballer; **u. a comb/etc from** sortir un peigne/etc de; – *vi* défaire sa valise; *(take out goods)* déballer.

unpaid [ʌn'peɪd] *a (bill, sum)* impayé; *(work, worker)* bénévole; *(leave)* non payé.

unpalatable [ʌn'pælətəb(ə)l] *a* désagréable, déplaisant.

unparalleled [ʌn'pærəleld] *a* sans égal.

unperturbed [ʌnpə'tɜːbd] *a* nullement déconcerté.

unplanned [ʌn'plænd] *a (visit, baby etc)* imprévu.

unpleasant [ʌn'plezənt] *a* désagréable **(to s.o.** avec qn). ◆**—ness** *n* caractère *m* désagréable (**of** de); (*quarrel*) petite querelle *f*.

unplug [ʌn'plʌg] *vt* (**-gg-**) *El* débrancher; (*unblock*) déboucher.

unpopular [ʌn'pɒpjʊlər] *a* impopulaire; **to be u. with** ne pas plaire à.

unprecedented [ʌn'presɪdentɪd] *a* sans précédent.

unpredictable [ʌnprɪ'dɪktəb(ə)l] *a* imprévisible; (*weather*) indécis.

unprepared [ʌnprɪ'peəd] *a* non préparé; (*speech*) improvisé; **to be u. for** (*not expect*) ne pas s'attendre à.

unprepossessing [ʌnpriːpə'zesɪŋ] *a* peu avenant.

unpretentious [ʌnprɪ'tenʃəs] *a* sans prétention.

unprincipled [ʌn'prɪnsɪp(ə)ld] *a* sans scrupules.

unprofessional [ʌnprə'feʃ(ə)nəl] *a* (*unethical*) contraire aux règles de sa profession.

unpublished [ʌn'pʌblɪʃt] *a* (*text, writer*) inédit.

unpunished [ʌn'pʌnɪʃt] *a* **to go u.** rester impuni.

unqualified [ʌn'kwɒlɪfaɪd] *a* **1** (*teacher etc*) non diplômé; **he's u. to do** il n'est pas qualifié pour faire. **2** (*support*) sans réserve; (*success, rogue*) parfait.

unquestionab/le [ʌn'kwestʃ(ə)nəb(ə)l] *a* incontestable. ◆**-ly** *adv* incontestablement.

unravel [ʌn'ræv(ə)l] *vt* (**-ll-**, *Am* **-l-**) (*threads etc*) démêler; (*mystery*) *Fig* éclaircir.

unreal [ʌn'rɪəl] *a* irréel. ◆**unrea'listic** *a* peu réaliste.

unreasonable [ʌn'riːz(ə)nəb(ə)l] *a* qui n'est pas raisonnable; (*price*) excessif.

unrecognizable [ʌnrekəg'naɪzəb(ə)l] *a* méconnaissable.

unrelated [ʌnrɪ'leɪtɪd] *a* (*facts etc*) sans rapport (**to** avec); (*mystery*) inexpliqué; (*crime*) dont l'auteur n'est pas connu.

unrelenting [ʌnrɪ'lentɪŋ] *a* (*person*) implacable; (*effort*) acharné.

unreliable [ʌnrɪ'laɪəb(ə)l] *a* (*person*) peu sérieux, peu sûr; (*machine*) peu fiable.

unrelieved [ʌnrɪ'liːvd] *a* (*constant*) constant; (*colour*) uniforme.

unremarkable [ʌnrɪ'mɑːkəb(ə)l] *a* médiocre.

unrepeatable [ʌnrɪ'piːtəb(ə)l] *a* (*offer*) unique.

unrepentant [ʌnrɪ'pentənt] *a* impénitent.

unreservedly [ʌnrɪ'zɜːvɪdlɪ] *adv* sans réserve.

unrest [ʌn'rest] *n* troubles *mpl*, agitation *f*.

unrestricted [ʌnrɪ'strɪktɪd] *a* illimité; (*access*) libre.

unrewarding [ʌnrɪ'wɔːdɪŋ] *a* ingrat; (*financially*) peu rémunérateur.

unripe [ʌn'raɪp] *a* (*fruit*) vert, pas mûr.

unroll [ʌn'rəʊl] *vt* dérouler; – *vi* se dérouler.

unruffled [ʌn'rʌf(ə)ld] *a* (*person*) calme.

unruly [ʌn'ruːlɪ] *a* (**-ier, -iest**) indiscipliné.

unsafe [ʌn'seɪf] *a* (*place, machine etc*) dangereux; (*person*) en danger.

unsaid [ʌn'sed] *a* **to leave sth u.** passer qch sous silence.

unsaleable [ʌn'seɪləb(ə)l] *a* invendable.

unsatisfactory [ʌnsætɪs'fæktərɪ] *a* peu satisfaisant. ◆**un'satisfied** *a* insatisfait; **u. with** peu satisfait de.

unsavoury [ʌn'seɪvərɪ] *a* (*person, place etc*) répugnant.

unscathed [ʌn'skeɪðd] *a* indemne.

unscrew [ʌn'skruː] *vt* dévisser.

unscrupulous [ʌn'skruːpjʊləs] *a* (*person, act*) peu scrupuleux.

unseemly [ʌn'siːmlɪ] *a* inconvenant.

unseen [ʌn'siːn] **1** *a* inaperçu. **2** *n* (*translation*) *Sch* version *f*.

unselfish [ʌn'selfɪʃ] *a* (*person, motive etc*) désintéressé.

unsettl/e [ʌn'set(ə)l] *vt* (*person*) troubler. ◆**-ed** *a* (*weather, situation*) instable; (*in one's mind*) troublé; (*in a job*) mal à l'aise.

unshakeable [ʌn'ʃeɪkəb(ə)l] *a* (*person, faith*) inébranlable.

unshaven [ʌn'ʃeɪv(ə)n] *a* pas rasé.

unsightly [ʌn'saɪtlɪ] *a* laid, disgracieux.

unskilled [ʌn'skɪld] *a* inexpert; (*work*) de manœuvre; **u. worker** manœuvre *m*, ouvrier, -ière *mf* non qualifié(e).

unsociable [ʌn'səʊʃəb(ə)l] *a* insociable.

unsocial [ʌn'səʊʃəl] *a* **to work u. hours** travailler en dehors des heures de bureau.

unsolved [ʌn'sɒlvd] *a* (*problem*) non résolu; (*mystery*) inexpliqué; (*crime*) dont l'auteur n'est pas connu.

unsophisticated [ʌnsə'fɪstɪkeɪtɪd] *a* simple.

unsound [ʌn'saʊnd] *a* (*construction etc*) peu solide; (*method*) peu sûr; (*decision*) peu judicieux; **he is of u. mind** il n'a pas toute sa raison.

unspeakable [ʌn'spiːkəb(ə)l] *a* (*horrible*) innommable.

unspecified [ʌn'spesɪfaɪd] *a* indéterminé.

unsporting [ʌn'spɔːtɪŋ] *a* déloyal.

unstable [ʌn'steɪb(ə)l] *a* instable.

unsteady [ʌn'stedɪ] *a* (*hand, voice, step etc*) mal assuré; (*table, ladder etc*) instable. ◆**unsteadily** *adv* (*to walk*) d'un pas mal assuré.

unstinting [ʌnˈstɪntɪŋ] a (generosity) sans bornes.

unstoppable [ʌnˈstɒpəb(ə)l] a qu'on ne peut (pas) arrêter.

unstuck [ʌnˈstʌk] a to come u. (of stamp etc) se décoller; (fail) Fam se planter.

unsuccessful [ʌnsəkˈsesfəl] a (attempt etc) infructueux; (outcome, candidate) malheureux; (application) non retenu; to be u. ne pas réussir (in doing à faire); (of book, artist) ne pas avoir de succès. ◆**-ly** adv en vain, sans succès.

unsuitable [ʌnˈsuːtəb(ə)l] a qui ne convient pas (for à); (example) peu approprié; (manners, clothes) peu convenable. ◆**unsuited** a u. to impropre à; they're u. ils ne sont pas compatibles.

unsure [ʌnˈʃʊər] a incertain (of, about de).

unsuspecting [ʌnsəˈspektɪŋ] a qui ne se doute de rien.

unswerving [ʌnˈswɜːvɪŋ] a (loyalty etc) inébranlable.

unsympathetic [ʌnsɪmpəˈθetɪk] a incompréhensif; u. to indifférent à.

untangle [ʌnˈtæŋɡ(ə)l] vt (rope etc) démêler.

untapped [ʌnˈtæpt] a inexploité.

untenable [ʌnˈtenəb(ə)l] a (position) intenable.

unthinkable [ʌnˈθɪŋkəb(ə)l] a impensable, inconcevable.

untidy [ʌnˈtaɪdɪ] a (-ier, -iest) (appearance, hair) peu soigné; (room) en désordre; (unmethodical) désordonné. ◆**untidily** adv sans soin.

untie [ʌnˈtaɪ] vt (person, hands) détacher; (knot, parcel) défaire.

until [ʌnˈtɪl] prep jusqu'à; u. then jusque-là; not u. tomorrow/etc (in the future) pas avant demain/etc; I didn't come u. Monday (in the past) je ne suis venu que lundi; – conj u. she comes jusqu'à ce qu'elle vienne, en attendant qu'elle vienne; do nothing u. I come (before) ne fais rien avant que j'arrive.

untimely [ʌnˈtaɪmlɪ] a inopportun; (death) prématuré.

untiring [ʌnˈtaɪ(ə)rɪŋ] a infatigable.

untold [ʌnˈtəʊld] a (quantity, wealth) incalculable.

untoward [ʌntəˈwɔːd] a malencontreux.

untranslatable [ʌntrænˈsleɪtəb(ə)l] a intraduisible.

untroubled [ʌnˈtrʌb(ə)ld] a (calm) calme.

untrue [ʌnˈtruː] a faux. ◆**untruth** n contre-vérité f. ◆**untruthful** a (person) menteur; (statement) mensonger.

unused 1 [ʌnˈjuːzd] a (new) neuf; (not in

use) inutilisé. **2** [ʌnˈjuːst] a u. to sth/to doing peu habitué à qch/à faire.

unusual [ʌnˈjuːʒʊəl] a exceptionnel, rare; (strange) étrange. ◆**-ly** adv exceptionnellement.

unveil [ʌnˈveɪl] vt dévoiler. ◆**-ing** n (ceremony) inauguration f.

unwanted [ʌnˈwɒntɪd] a (useless) superflu, dont on n'a pas besoin; (child) non désiré.

unwarranted [ʌnˈwɒrəntɪd] a injustifié.

unwavering [ʌnˈweɪv(ə)rɪŋ] a (belief etc) inébranlable.

unwelcome [ʌnˈwelkəm] a (news, fact) fâcheux; (gift, visit) inopportun; (person) importun.

unwell [ʌnˈwel] a indisposé.

unwieldy [ʌnˈwiːldɪ] a (package etc) encombrant.

unwilling [ʌnˈwɪlɪŋ] a he's u. to do il ne neut pas faire, il est peu disposé à faire. ◆**-ly** adv à contrecœur.

unwind [ʌnˈwaɪnd] **1** vt (thread etc) dérouler; – vi se dérouler. **2** vi (relax) Fam décompresser.

unwise [ʌnˈwaɪz] a imprudent. ◆**-ly** adv imprudemment.

unwitting [ʌnˈwɪtɪŋ] a involontaire. ◆**-ly** adv involontairement.

unworkable [ʌnˈwɜːkəb(ə)l] a (idea etc) impraticable.

unworthy [ʌnˈwɜːðɪ] a indigne (of de).

unwrap [ʌnˈræp] vt (-pp-) ouvrir, défaire.

unwritten [ʌnˈrɪt(ə)n] a (agreement) verbal, tacite.

unyielding [ʌnˈjiːldɪŋ] a (person) inflexible.

unzip [ʌnˈzɪp] vt (-pp-) ouvrir (la fermeture éclair® de).

up [ʌp] adv en haut; (in the air) en l'air; (of sun, hand) levé; (out of bed) levé, debout; (of road) en travaux; (of building) construit; (finished) fini; to come or go up monter; to be up (of price, level etc) être monté (by de); up there là-haut; up above au-dessus; up on (roof etc) sur; further or higher up plus haut; up to (as far as) jusqu'à; (task) Fig à la hauteur de; to be up to doing (capable) être de taille à faire; (in a position to) être à même de faire; it's up to you to do it c'est à toi de le faire; it's up to you ça dépend de toi; where are you up to? (in book etc) où en es-tu?; what are you up to? Fam que fais-tu?; what's up? (what's the matter?) Fam qu'est-ce qu'il y a?; time's up c'est l'heure; halfway up (on hill etc) à mi-chemin; to walk up and down marcher de long en large; to be well up in (versed in) Fam s'y connaître en; to be up against

(*confront*) être confronté à; **up (with) the workers/***etc*! *Fam* vive(nt) les travailleurs/*etc*! – *prep* (*a hill*) en haut de; (*a tree*) dans; (*a ladder*) sur; **to go up** (*hill, stairs*) monter; **to live up the street** habiter plus loin dans la rue; – *npl* **to have ups and downs** avoir des hauts et des bas; – *vt* (*-pp-*) (*increase*) *Fam* augmenter.
◆**up-and-'coming** a plein d'avenir.
◆**upbeat** a (*cheerful*) *Am Fam* optimiste.
◆**upbringing** n éducation f. ◆**upcoming** a *Am* imminent. ◆**up'date** vt mettre à jour. ◆**up'grade** vt (*job*) revaloriser; (*person*) promouvoir. ◆**up'hill 1** adv le go up u. monter. **2** [ʌphil] a (*struggle, task*) pénible. ◆**up'hold** vt (*pt & pp* upheld) maintenir. ◆**upkeep** n entretien m. ◆**uplift** [ʌp'lift] vt élever; – ['ʌplift] n élévation f spirituelle. ◆**upmarket** a *Com* haut de gamme. ◆**upright 1** a & adv (*erect, honest*) droit; – n (*post*) montant m. **2** a (*honest*) droit. ◆**uprising** n insurrection f. ◆**up'root** vt (*plant, person*) déraciner. ◆**upside 'down** adv à l'envers; **to turn u. down** (*room, plans etc*) *Fig* chambouler. ◆**up'stairs** adv (*to*) en haut; **to go u.** monter (l'escalier); – ['ʌpsteəz] a (*people, room*) du dessus. ◆**up'stream** adv en amont. ◆**upsurge** n (*of interest*) recrudescence f; (*of anger*) accès m. ◆**uptake** n **to be quick on the u.** comprendre vite. ◆**up'tight** a *Fam* (*tense*) crispé; (*angry*) en colère. ◆**up-to-'date** a moderne; (*information*) à jour; (*well-informed*) au courant (**on** de). ◆**upturn** n (*improvement*) amélioration f (**in** de); (*rise*) hausse f (**in** de). ◆**up'turned** a (*nose*) retroussé. ◆**upward** a (*movement*) ascendant; (*path*) qui monte; (*trend*) à la hausse. ◆**upwards** adv vers le haut; **from five francs u.** à partir de cinq francs; **u. of fifty** cinquante et plus.

upheaval [ʌp'hiːv(ə)l] n bouleversement m.
uphold [ʌp'həʊldər] vt (*pad*) rembourrer; (*cover*) recouvrir. ◆**upholsterer** n tapissier m. ◆**upholstery** n (*activity*) réfection f de sièges; (*in car*) sièges mpl.
upon [ə'pɒn] prep sur.
upper ['ʌpər] **1** a supérieur; **u. class** aristocratie f; **to have/get the u.** hand avoir/prendre le dessus. **2** n (*of shoe*) empeigne f, dessus m. ◆**u.-'class** a aristocratique. ◆**uppermost** a (*highest*) le plus haut; **to be u.** (*on top*) être en dessus.
uproar ['ʌprɔːr] n tumulte m.
upset [ʌp'set] vt (*pt & pp* upset, *pres p* upsetting) (*knock over*) renverser; (*plans, stomach, routine etc*) déranger; **to u. s.o.** (*grieve,*

peiner qn; (*offend*) vexer qn; (*annoy*) contrarier qn; – a vexé; contrarié; (*stomach*) dérangé; – ['ʌpset] n (*in plans etc*) dérangement m (**in** de); (*grief*) peine f; **to have a stomach u.** avoir l'estomac dérangé.
upshot ['ʌpʃɒt] n résultat m.
upstart ['ʌpstɑːt] n *Pej* parvenu, -ue mf.
uranium [jʊ'reɪnɪəm] n uranium m.
urban ['ɜːbən] a urbain.
urbane [ɜː'beɪn] a courtois, urbain.
urchin ['ɜːtʃɪn] n polisson, -onne mf.
urge [ɜːdʒ] vt **to u. s.o. to do** (*advise*) conseiller vivement à qn de faire; **to u. on** (*person, team*) encourager; – n forte envie f, besoin m.
urgency ['ɜːdʒənsɪ] n urgence f; (*of request, tone*) insistance f. ◆**urgent** a urgent, pressant; (*tone*) insistant; (*letter*) urgent. ◆**urgently** adv d'urgence; (*insistently*) avec insistance.
urinal [jʊ'raɪn(ə)l] n urinoir m.
urine [jʊ(ə)rɪn] n urine f. ◆**urinate** vi uriner.
urn [ɜːn] n urne f; (*for coffee or tea*) fontaine f.
us [əs, *stressed* ʌs] pron nous; (**to**) **us** (*indirect*) nous; **she sees us** elle nous voit; **he gives (to) us** il nous donne; **with us** avec nous; **all of us** nous tous; **let's** *or* **let us eat!** mangeons!
US [juːes] abbr = United States.
USA [juːes'eɪ] abbr = United States of America.
usage ['juːsɪdʒ] n (*custom*) & *Ling* usage m.
use [juːs] n emploi m, emploi m; (*way of using*) emploi m; **to have the u. of** avoir l'usage de; **to make u. of** se servir de; **in u.** en usage; **out of u.** hors d'usage; **ready for u.** prêt à l'emploi; **to be of u.** servir, être utile; **it's no u. crying/***etc* ça ne sert à rien de pleurer/*etc*; **what's the u. of worrying/***etc*? à quoi bon s'inquiéter/*etc*?; **I have no u. for** it je n'en ai pas l'usage, qu'est-ce que je ferais de ça?; **he's no u.** (*hopeless*) il est nul; – [juːz] vt se servir de, utiliser, employer (**as** comme; **to do, for doing** pour faire); **it's used to do** *or* **for doing** ça sert à faire; **it's used as** ça sert de; **I u. it to clean** je m'en sers pour nettoyer, me m'en sert à nettoyer; **to u. (up)** (*fuel etc*) consommer; (*supplies*) épuiser; (*money*) dépenser. ◆**used 1** [juːzd] a (*second-hand*) d'occasion; (*stamp*) oblitéré. **2** [juːst] v aux **I u. to do** souvent, je faisais; – a **u. to sth/to doing** (*accustomed*) habitué à qch/à faire; **to get u. to** s'habituer à. ◆**useful** ['juːsfəl] a utile; **to**

come in u. être utile; **to make oneself u.** se rendre utile. ◆**usefulness** n utilité f. ◆**useless** ['juːsləs] a inutile; (*unusable*) inutilisable; (*person*) nul, incompétent. ◆**user** ['juːzər] n (*of road, dictionary etc*) usager m; (*of machine*) utilisateur, -trice mf.

usher ['ʌʃər] n (*in church or theatre*) placeur m; (*in law court*) huissier m; – vt **to u. in** faire entrer; (*period etc*) Fig inaugurer. ◆**ushe'rette** n Cin ouvreuse f.

USSR [juːesesˈɑːr] n abbr (*Union of Soviet Socialist Republics*) URSS f.

usual ['juːʒʊəl] a habituel, normal; **as u.** comme d'habitude; **it's her u. practice** c'est son habitude; – n **the u.** (*food, excuse etc*) Fam la même chose que d'habitude. ◆**—ly** adv d'habitude.

usurer ['juːʒərər] n usurier, -ière mf.

usurp [juːˈzɜːp] vt usurper.

utensil [juːˈtens(ə)l] n ustensile m.

uterus ['juːt(ə)rəs] n Anat utérus m.

utilitarian [juːtɪlɪˈteərɪən] a utilitaire. ◆**u'tility** n (*public*) u. service m public; – a (*goods vehicle*) utilitaire.

utilize ['juːtɪlaɪz] vt utiliser. ◆**utili'zation** n utilisation f.

utmost ['ʌtməʊst] a **the u. ease**/*etc* (*greatest*) la plus grande facilité/*etc*; **the u. danger**/*limit*/*etc* (*extreme*) un danger/une limite/*etc* extrême; – n **to do one's u.** faire tout son possible (**to do** pour faire).

utopia [juːˈtəʊpɪə] n (*perfect state*) utopie f. ◆**utopian** a utopique.

utter ['ʌtər] **1** a complet, total; (*folly*) pur; (*idiot*) parfait; **it's u. nonsense** c'est complètement absurde. **2** vt (*say, express*) proférer; (*a cry, sigh*) pousser. ◆**utterance** n (*remark etc*) déclaration f; **to give u. to** exprimer. ◆**utterly** adv complètement.

V

V, v [viː] n V, v m. ◆**V.-neck(ed)** a (*pullover etc*) à col en V.

vacant ['veɪkənt] a (*post*) vacant; (*room, seat*) libre; (*look*) vague, dans le vide. ◆**vacancy** n (*post*) poste m vacant; (*room*) chambre f disponible; **'no vacancies'** (*in hotel*) 'complet'. ◆**vacantly** adv **to gaze v.** regarder dans le vide.

vacate [vəˈkeɪt, Am ˈveɪkeɪt] vt quitter.

vacation [veˈkeɪʃ(ə)n] n Am vacances fpl; **on v.** en vacances. ◆**—er** n Am vacancier, -ière mf.

vaccinate ['væksɪneɪt] vt vacciner. ◆**vacci'nation** n vaccination f. ◆**vaccine** [-iːn] n vaccin m.

vacillate ['væsɪleɪt] vi (*hesitate*) hésiter.

vacuum ['vækjʊ(ə)m] n vide m; **v. cleaner** aspirateur m; **v. flask** thermos® m or f; – vt (*carpet etc*) passer à l'aspirateur. ◆**v.-packed** a emballé sous vide.

vagabond ['vægəbɒnd] n vagabond, -onde mf.

vagary ['veɪgərɪ] n caprice m.

vagina [vəˈdʒaɪnə] n vagin m.

vagrant ['veɪgrənt] n Jur vagabond, -onde mf.

vague [veɪg] a (-er, -est) vague; (*memory, outline, photo*) flou; **the vaguest idea** la moindre idée; **he was v.** (*about it*) il est resté vague. ◆**—ly** adv vaguement.

vain [veɪn] a (-er, -est) **1** (*attempt, hope*) vain; **in v.** en vain; **his** or **her efforts were in v.** ses efforts ont été inutiles. **2** (*conceited*) vaniteux. ◆**—ly** adv (*in vain*) vainement.

valentine ['væləntaɪn] n (*card*) carte f de la Saint-Valentin.

valet ['vælɪt, 'væleɪ] n valet m de chambre.

valiant ['væljənt] a courageux. ◆**valour** n bravoure f.

valid ['vælɪd] a (*ticket, motive etc*) valable. ◆**validate** vt valider. ◆**va'lidity** n validité f; (*of argument*) justesse f.

valley ['vælɪ] n vallée f.

valuable ['væljʊəb(ə)l] a (*object*) de (grande) valeur; (*help, time etc*) Fig précieux; – npl objets mpl de valeur. ◆**value** ['væljuː] n valeur f; **to be of great/little v.** (*of object*) valoir cher/peu (*etc*); **it's good v.** c'est très avantageux; **v. added tax** taxe f à la valeur ajoutée; – vt (*appraise*) évaluer; (*appreciate*) attacher de la valeur à. ◆**valu'ation** n évaluation f; (*by expert*) expertise f. ◆**valuer** n expert m.

valve [vælv] n (*of machine*) soupape f; (*in radio*) lampe f; (*of tyre*) valve f; (*of heart*) valvule f.

vampire ['væmpaɪər] n vampire m.

van [væn] n (*small*) camionnette f; (*large*) camion m; Rail fourgon m.

vandal ['vænd(ə)l] n vandale mf. ◆**vandal-**

ism n vandalisme m. ◆**vandalize** vt saccager, détériorer.

vanguard ['vænga:d] n (of army, progress etc) avant-garde f.

vanilla [və'nɪlə] n vanille f; – a (ice cream) à la vanille.

vanish ['vænɪʃ] vi disparaître.

vanity ['vænɪtɪ] n vanité f; v. case vanity m inv.

vanquish ['væŋkwɪʃ] vt vaincre.

vantage point ['vɑːntɪdʒpɔɪnt] n (place, point of view) (bon) point m de vue.

vapour ['veɪpər] n vapeur f; (on glass) buée f.

variable ['veərɪəb(ə)l] a variable. ◆**variance** n at v. en désaccord (with avec). ◆**variant** a différent; – n variante f. ◆**variation** n variation f.

varicose ['værɪkəʊs] a v. veins varices fpl.

variety [və'raɪətɪ] n 1 (diversity) variété f; a v. of opinions/reasons/etc (many) diverses opinions/raisons/etc; a v. of (articles) Com une gamme de. 2 Th variétés fpl; v. show spectacle m de variétés.

various ['veərɪəs] a divers. ◆—ly adv diversement.

varnish ['vɑːnɪʃ] vt vernir; – n vernis m.

vary ['veərɪ] vti varier (from de). ◆**varied** a varié. ◆**varying** a variable.

vase [vɑːz, Am veɪs] n vase m.

Vaseline ['væsəliːn] n vaseline f.

vast [vɑːst] a vaste, immense. ◆—ly adv (very) infiniment, extrêmement. ◆—ness n immensité f.

vat [væt] n cuve f.

VAT [viːeɪ'tiː, væt] n abbr (value added tax) TVA f.

Vatican ['vætɪkən] n Vatican m.

vaudeville ['vɔːdəvɪl] n Th Am variétés fpl.

vault [vɔːlt] 1 n (cellar) cave f; (tomb) caveau m; (in bank) chambre f forte, coffres mpl; (roof) voûte f. 2 vti (jump) sauter.

veal [viːl] n (meat) veau m.

veer [vɪər] vi (of wind) tourner; (of car, road) virer; to v. off the road quitter la route.

vegan ['viːgən] n végétaliste mf.

vegetable ['vedʒtəb(ə)l] n légume m; – a (kingdom, oil) végétal; v. garden (jardin m) potager m. ◆**vege'tarian** a & n végétarien, -ienne (mf). ◆**vege'tation** n végétation f.

vegetate ['vedʒɪteɪt] vi (of person) Pej végéter.

vehement ['viːəmənt] a (feeling, speech) véhément; (attack) violent. ◆—ly adv avec véhémence; violemment.

vehicle ['viːɪk(ə)l] n véhicule m; heavy goods v. (lorry) poids m lourd.

veil [veɪl] n (covering) & Fig voile m; – vt (face, truth etc) voiler.

vein [veɪn] n (in body or rock) veine f; (in leaf) nervure f; (mood) Fig esprit m.

vellum ['veləm] n (paper, skin) vélin m.

velocity [və'lɒsɪtɪ] n vélocité f.

velvet ['velvɪt] n velours m; – a de velours. ◆**velvety** a velouté.

vendetta [ven'detə] n vendetta f.

vending machine ['vendɪŋməʃiːn] n distributeur m automatique.

vendor ['vendər] n vendeur, -euse mf.

veneer [və'nɪər] n (in wood) placage m; (appearance) Fig vernis m.

venerable ['ven(ə)rəb(ə)l] a vénérable. ◆**venerate** vt vénérer.

venereal [və'nɪərɪəl] a (disease etc) vénérien m.

venetian [və'niːʃ(ə)n] a v. blind store m vénitien.

vengeance ['vendʒəns] n vengeance f; with a v. (to work, study etc) furieusement; (to rain, catch up etc) pour de bon.

venison ['venɪs(ə)n] n venaison f.

venom ['venəm] n (substance) & Fig venin m. ◆**venomous** a (speech, snake etc) venimeux.

vent [vent] 1 n (hole) orifice m; (for air) bouche f d'aération; (in jacket) fente f. 2 n to give v. to (feelings etc) donner libre cours à; – vt (anger) décharger (on sur).

ventilate ['ventɪleɪt] vt ventiler. ◆**ventilation** n ventilation f. ◆**ventilator** n (in wall etc) ventilateur m.

ventriloquist [ven'trɪləkwɪst] n ventriloque mf.

venture ['ventʃər] n entreprise f (risquée); my v. into mon incursion f dans; – vt (opinion, fortune) hasarder; to v. to do (dare) oser faire; – vi s'aventurer, se risquer (into dans).

venue ['venjuː] n lieu m de rencontre or de rendez-vous.

veranda(h) [və'rændə] n véranda f.

verb [vɜːb] n verbe m. ◆**verbal** a (promise, skill etc) verbal. ◆**verbatim** [vɜː'beɪtɪm] a & adv mot pour mot.

verbose [vɜː'bəʊs] a (wordy) verbeux.

verdict ['vɜːdɪkt] n verdict m.

verdigris ['vɜːdɪgrɪs] n vert-de-gris m inv.

verge [vɜːdʒ] n (of road) accotement m, bord m; on the v. of Fig (ruin, tears etc) au bord de; (discovery) à la veille de; on the v. of doing sur le point de faire; – vi to v. on friser, frôler; (of colour) tirer sur.

verger ['vɜːdʒər] n Rel bedeau m.

verify ['verɪfaɪ] *vt* vérifier. ◆**verifi'cation** *n* vérification *f*.

veritable ['verɪtəb(ə)l] *a* véritable.

vermicelli [vɜːmɪ'selɪ] *n* Culin vermicelle(s) *m(pl)*.

vermin ['vɜːmɪn] *n* (*animals*) animaux *mpl* nuisibles; (*insects, people*) vermine *f*.

vermouth ['vɜːməθ] *n* vermouth *m*.

vernacular [və'nækjʊlər] *n* (*of region*) dialecte *m*.

versatile ['vɜːsətaɪl, *Am* 'vɜːsət(ə)l] *a* (*mind*) souple; (*material, tool, computer*) polyvalent; **he's v.** il a des talents variés, il est polyvalent. ◆**versa'tility** *n* souplesse *f*; **his v.** la variété de ses talents.

verse [vɜːs] *n* (*stanza*) strophe *f*; (*poetry*) vers *mpl*; (*of Bible*) verset *m*.

versed [vɜːst] *a* (**well**) **v. in** versé dans.

version ['vɜːʃ(ə)n] *n* version *f*.

versus ['vɜːsəs] *prep* contre.

vertebra, *pl* **-ae** ['vɜːtɪbrə, -iː] *n* vertèbre *f*.

vertical ['vɜːtɪk(ə)l] *a* vertical; – *n* verticale *f*. ◆**-ly** *adv* verticalement.

vertigo ['vɜːtɪgəʊ] *n* (*fear of falling*) vertige *m*.

verve [vɜːv] *n* fougue *f*.

very ['verɪ] **1** *adv* très; **I'm v. hot** j'ai très chaud; **v. much** beaucoup; **the v. first** le tout premier; **at the v. least/most** tout au moins/plus; **at the v. latest** au plus tard. **2** *a* (*actual*) même; **his** *or* **her v. brother** son frère même; **at the v. end** (*of play etc*) tout à la fin; **to the v. end** jusqu'au bout.

vespers ['vespəz] *npl* Rel vêpres *fpl*.

vessel ['ves(ə)l] *n* Anat Bot Nau vaisseau *m*; (*receptacle*) récipient *m*.

vest [vest] *n* tricot *m or* maillot *m* de corps; (*woman's*) chemise *f* (américaine); (*waistcoat*) *Am* gilet *m*.

vested ['vestɪd] *a* **v. interests** Com droits *mpl* acquis; **she's got a v. interest in** Fig elle est directement intéressée dans.

vestige ['vestɪdʒ] *n* vestige *m*; **not a v. of truth/good sense** pas un grain de vérité/de bon sens.

vestry ['vestrɪ] *n* sacristie *f*.

vet [vet] **1** *n* vétérinaire *mf*. **2** *vt* (**-tt-**) (*document*) examiner de près; (*candidate*) se renseigner à fond sur. ◆**veteri'narian** *n Am* vétérinaire *mf*. ◆**veterinary** *a* vétérinaire; **v. surgeon** vétérinaire *mf*.

veteran ['vet(ə)rən] *n* vétéran *m*; (*war*) ancien combattant *m*; – *a* **v. golfer/etc** golfeur/etc expérimenté.

veto ['viːtəʊ] *n* (*pl* **-oes**) (*refusal*) veto *m inv*; (*power*) droit *m* de veto; – *vt* mettre *or* opposer son veto à.

vex [veks] *vt* contrarier, fâcher; **vexed question** question *f* controversée.

via ['vaɪə] *prep* via, par.

viable ['vaɪəb(ə)l] *a* (*baby, firm, plan etc*) viable. ◆**via'bility** *n* viabilité *f*.

viaduct ['vaɪədʌkt] *n* viaduc *m*.

vibrate [vaɪ'breɪt] *vi* vibrer. ◆**'vibrant** *a* vibrant. ◆**vibration** *n* vibration *f*. ◆**vibrator** *n* vibromasseur *m*.

vicar ['vɪkər] *n* (*in Church of England*) pasteur *m*. ◆**vicarage** *n* presbytère *m*.

vicarious [vɪ'keərɪəs] *a* (*emotion*) ressenti indirectement. ◆**-ly** *adv* (*to experience*) indirectement.

vice [vaɪs] *n* **1** (*depravity*) vice *m*; (*fault*) défaut *m*; **v. squad** brigade *f* des mœurs. **2** (*tool*) étau *m*.

vice- [vaɪs] *pref* vice-. ◆**v.-'chancellor** *n* Univ président *m*.

vice versa [vaɪs(ɪ)'vɜːsə] *adv* vice versa.

vicinity [və'sɪnɪtɪ] *n* environs *mpl*; **in the v. of** (*place, amount*) aux environs de.

vicious ['vɪʃəs] *a* (*spiteful*) méchant; (*violent*) brutal; **v. circle** cercle *m* vicieux. ◆**-ly** *adv* méchamment; brutalement. ◆**-ness** *n* méchanceté *f*; brutalité *f*.

vicissitudes [vɪ'sɪsɪtjuːdz] *npl* vicissitudes *fpl*.

victim ['vɪktɪm] *n* victime *f*; **to be the v. of** être victime de. ◆**victimize** *vt* persécuter. ◆**victimi'zation** *n* persécution *f*.

Victorian [vɪk'tɔːrɪən] *a* & *n* victorien, -ienne (*mf*).

victory ['vɪktərɪ] *n* victoire *f*. ◆**victor** *n* vainqueur *m*. ◆**vic'torious** *a* victorieux.

video ['vɪdɪəʊ] *a* **video** *inv*; – *n* **1** (**cassette**) vidéocassette *f*; **v.** (**recorder**) magnétoscope *m*; **on v.** sur cassette; **to make a v. of** faire une cassette de; – *vt* (*programme etc*) enregistrer au magnétoscope. ◆**videotape** *n* bande *f* vidéo.

vie [vaɪ] *vi* (*pres p* **vying**) rivaliser (**with** avec).

Vietnam [vjet'næm, *Am* -'nɑːm] *n* Viêt-nam *m*. ◆**Vietna'mese** *a* & *n* vietnamien, -ienne (*mf*).

view [vjuː] *n* vue *f*; **to come into v.** apparaître; **in full v. of everyone** à la vue de tous; **in my v.** (*opinion*) à mon avis; **on v.** (*exhibit*) exposé; **with a v. to** (*considering*) étant donné (**the fact that**); **with a v. to doing** afin de faire; – *vt* (*consider*) considérer; (*house*) visiter. ◆**-er** *n* **1** *TV* téléspectateur, -trice *mf*. **2** (*for slides*) visionneuse *f*. ◆**viewfinder** *n* Phot viseur *m*. ◆**viewpoint** *n* point *m* de vue.

vigil ['vɪdʒɪl] n veille f; (over sick person or corpse) veillée f.

vigilant ['vɪdʒɪlənt] a vigilant. ◆**vigilance** n vigilance f.

vigilante [vɪdʒɪ'læntɪ] n Pej membre m d'une milice privée.

vigour ['vɪgər] n vigueur f. ◆**vigorous** a (person, speech etc) vigoureux.

vile [vaɪl] a (-er, -est) (base) infâme, vil; (unpleasant) abominable.

vilify ['vɪlɪfaɪ] vt diffamer.

villa ['vɪlə] n (in country) grande maison f de campagne.

village ['vɪlɪdʒ] n village m. ◆**villager** n villageois, -oise mf.

villain ['vɪlən] n scélérat, -ate mf; (in story or play) traître m. ◆**villainy** n infamie f.

vindicate ['vɪndɪkeɪt] vt justifier. ◆**vindi-'cation** n justification f.

vindictive [vɪn'dɪktɪv] a vindicatif, rancunier.

vine [vaɪn] n (grapevine) vigne f; v. grower viticulteur m. ◆**vineyard** ['vɪnjəd] n vignoble m.

vinegar ['vɪnɪgər] n vinaigre m.

vintage ['vɪntɪdʒ] 1 n (year) année f. 2 a (wine) de grand cru; (car) d'époque; (film) classique; (good) Fig bon; v. Shaw/etc du meilleur Shaw/etc.

vinyl ['vaɪn(ə)l] n vinyle m.

viola [vɪ'əʊlə] n (instrument) Mus alto m.

violate ['vaɪəleɪt] vt violer. ◆**vio'lation** n violation f.

violence ['vaɪələns] n violence f. ◆**violent** a violent; a v. dislike une aversion vive. ◆**violently** adv violemment; to be v. sick (vomit) vomir.

violet ['vaɪələt] 1 a & n (colour) violet (m). 2 n (plant) violette f.

violin [vaɪə'lɪn] n violon m; – a (concerto etc) pour violon. ◆**violinist** n violoniste mf.

VIP [viːaɪ'piː] n abbr (very important person) personnage m de marque.

viper ['vaɪpər] n vipère f.

virgin ['vɜːdʒɪn] n vierge f; to be a v. (of woman, man) être vierge; – a (woman, snow etc) vierge. ◆**vir'ginity** n virginité f.

Virgo ['vɜːgəʊ] n (sign) la Vierge.

virile ['vɪraɪl, Am 'vɪrəl] a viril. ◆**vi'rility** n virilité f.

virtual ['vɜːtʃʊəl] a it was a v. failure/etc ce fut en fait un échec/etc. ◆**-ly** adv (in fact) en fait; (almost) pratiquement.

virtue ['vɜːtʃuː] n 1 (goodness, chastity) vertu f; (advantage) mérite m, avantage m. 2 by

or in v. of en raison de. ◆**virtuous** a vertueux.

virtuoso, pl **-si** [vɜːtʃʊ'əʊsəʊ, -siː] n virtuose mf. ◆**virtuosity** [-'ɒsɪtɪ] n virtuosité f.

virulent ['vɪrʊlənt] a virulent. ◆**virulence** n virulence f.

virus ['vaɪərəs] n virus m.

visa ['viːzə] n visa m.

vis-à-vis [viːzɑː'viː] prep vis-à-vis de.

viscount ['vaɪkaʊnt] n vicomte m. ◆**viscountess** n vicomtesse f.

viscous ['vɪskəs] a visqueux.

vise [vaɪs] n (tool) Am étau m.

visible ['vɪzəb(ə)l] a visible. ◆**visi'bility** n visibilité f. ◆**visibly** adv visiblement.

vision ['vɪʒ(ə)n] n vision f; a man/a woman of v. Fig un homme/une femme qui voit loin. ◆**visionary** a & n visionnaire (mf).

visit ['vɪzɪt] n (call, tour) visite f; (stay) séjour m; – vt (place) visiter; to visit s.o. (call on) rendre visite à qn; (stay with) faire un séjour chez qn; – vi être en visite (Am with chez). ◆**-ing** a (card, hours) de visite. ◆**visitor** n visiteur, -euse mf; (guest) invité, -ée mf; (in hotel) client, -ente mf.

visor ['vaɪzər] n (of helmet) visière f.

vista ['vɪstə] n (view of place etc) vue f; (of future) Fig perspective f.

visual ['vɪʒʊəl] a visuel; v. aid (in teaching) support m visuel. ◆**visualize** vt (imagine) se représenter; (foresee) envisager.

vital ['vaɪt(ə)l] a vital; of v. importance d'importance capitale; v. statistics (of woman) Fam mensurations fpl. ◆**-ly** adv extrêmement.

vitality [vaɪ'tælɪtɪ] n vitalité f.

vitamin ['vɪtəmɪn, Am 'vaɪtəmɪn] n vitamine f.

vitriol ['vɪtrɪəl] n Ch Fig vitriol m. ◆**vitri-'olic** a (attack, speech etc) au vitriol.

vivacious [vɪ'veɪʃəs] a plein d'entrain.

vivid ['vɪvɪd] a (imagination, recollection etc) vif; (description) vivant. ◆**-ly** adv (to describe) de façon vivante; to remember sth v. avoir un vif souvenir de qch.

vivisection [vɪvɪ'sekʃ(ə)n] n vivisection f.

vocabulary [və'kæbjʊlərɪ] n vocabulaire m.

vocal ['vəʊk(ə)l] a (cords, music) vocal; (outspoken, noisy, critical) qui se fait entendre. ◆**vocalist** n chanteur, -euse mf.

vocation [vəʊ'keɪʃ(ə)n] n vocation f. ◆**vocational** a professionnel.

vociferous [və'sɪf(ə)rəs] a bruyant.

vodka ['vɒdkə] n vodka f.

vogue [vəʊg] n vogue f; in v. en vogue.

voice [vɔɪs] n voix f; at the top of one's v. à

tue-tête; – vt (feeling, opinion etc) formuler, exprimer.

void [vɔɪd] **1** n vide m; – a **v. of** (lacking in) dépourvu de. **2** a (not valid) Jur nul.

volatile ['vɒlətaɪl, Am 'vɒlət(ə)l] a (person) versatile, changeant; (situation) explosif.

volcano [vɒl'keɪnəʊ] n (pl -oes) volcan m. ◆**volcanic** [-'kænɪk] a volcanique.

volition [və'lɪʃ(ə)n] n of one's own **v.** de son propre gré.

volley ['vɒlɪ] n (of blows) volée f; (gunfire) salve f; (of insults) Fig bordée f. ◆**volleyball** n Sp volley(-ball) m.

volt [vəʊlt] n El volt m. ◆**voltage** n voltage m.

volume ['vɒljuːm] n (book, capacity, loudness) volume m. ◆**voluminous** [və'luːmɪnəs] a volumineux.

voluntary ['vɒləntərɪ] a volontaire; (unpaid) bénévole. ◆**voluntarily** [Am vɒlən'terɪlɪ] adv volontairement; bénévolement. ◆**volun'teer** n volontaire mf; – vi se proposer (for sth pour qch, to do pour faire); Mil s'engager comme volontaire (for dans); – vt offrir (spontanément).

voluptuous [və'lʌptʃʊəs] a voluptueux, sensuel.

vomit ['vɒmɪt] vti vomir; – n (matter) vomi m.

voracious [və'reɪʃəs] a (appetite, reader etc) vorace.

vot/e [vəʊt] n vote m; (right to vote) droit m de vote; **to win votes** gagner des voix; **v. of censure** or **no confidence** motion f de censure; **v. of thanks** discours m de remerciement; – vt (bill, funds etc) voter; (person) élire; – vi voter; **to v. Conservative** voter conservateur or pour les conservateurs. ◆**–ing** n vote m (of de); (polling) scrutin m. ◆**–er** n Pol électeur, -trice mf.

vouch [vaʊtʃ] vi **to v. for** répondre de.

voucher ['vaʊtʃər] n (for meals etc) bon m, chèque m.

vow [vaʊ] n vœu m; – vt (obedience etc) jurer (to à); **to v. to do** jurer de faire, faire le vœu de faire.

vowel ['vaʊəl] n voyelle f.

voyage ['vɔɪdʒ] n voyage m (par mer).

vulgar ['vʌlɡər] a vulgaire. ◆**vul'garity** n vulgarité f.

vulnerable ['vʌln(ə)rəb(ə)l] a vulnérable. ◆**vulnera'bility** n vulnérabilité f.

vulture ['vʌltʃər] n vautour m.

W

W, w ['dʌb(ə)ljuː] n W, w m.

wacky ['wækɪ] a (-ier, -iest) Am Fam farfelu.

wad [wɒd] n (of banknotes, papers etc) liasse f; (of cotton wool, cloth) tampon m.

waddle ['wɒd(ə)l] vi se dandiner.

wade [weɪd] vi **to w. through** (mud, water etc) patauger dans; (book etc) Fig venir péniblement à bout de; **I'm wading through this book** j'avance péniblement dans ce livre.

wafer ['weɪfər] n (biscuit) gaufrette f; Rel hostie f.

waffle ['wɒf(ə)l] **1** n (talk) Fam verbiage m, blabla m; – vi Fam parler pour ne rien dire, blablater. **2** n (cake) gaufre f.

waft [wɒft] vi (of smell etc) flotter.

wag [wæɡ] **1** vt (-gg-) (tail, finger) agiter, remuer; – vi remuer; **tongues are wagging** Pej on en jase, les langues vont bon train. **2** n (joker) farceur, -euse mf.

wage [weɪdʒ] **1** n **wage(s)** salaire m, paie f; **w. claim** or **demand** revendication f salariale; **w. earner** salarié, -ée mf; (breadwin-ner) soutien m de famille; **w. freeze** blocage m des salaires; **w. increase** or **rise** augmentation f de salaire. **2** vt (campaign) mener; **to w. war** faire la guerre (on à).

wager ['weɪdʒər] n pari m; – vt parier (that que).

waggle ['wæɡ(ə)l] vti remuer.

wag(g)on ['wæɡən] n (cart) chariot m; Rail wagon m (de marchandises); **on the w.** (abstinent) Fam au régime sec.

waif [weɪf] n enfant mf abandonné(e).

wail [weɪl] vi (cry out, complain) gémir; (of siren) hurler; – n gémissement m; (of siren) hurlement m.

waist [weɪst] n taille f; **stripped to the w.** nu jusqu'à la ceinture. ◆**waistband** n (part of garment) ceinture f. ◆**waistcoat** ['weɪskəʊt] n gilet m. ◆**waistline** n taille f.

wait [weɪt] n attente f; **to lie in w.** (for) guetter; – vi attendre; **to w. for** attendre; **w. until I've gone, w. for me to go** attends que je sois parti; **to keep s.o. waiting** faire attendre qn; **w. and see!** attends voir!; **I can't w.**

to do it j'ai hâte de le faire; **to w. about (for)** attendre; **to w. behind** rester; **to w. up** veiller; **to w. up for s.o.** attendre le retour de qn avant de se coucher. **2** vt (serve) **to w. at table** servir à table; **to w. on s.o.** servir qn. ◆**-ing** n attente f; **'no w.'** Aut 'arrêt interdit'; - a w. list/room liste f/salle f d'attente. ◆**waiter** n garçon m (de café), serveur m; w.! garçon! ◆**waitress** n serveuse f; w.! mademoiselle!

waive [weɪv] vt renoncer à, abandonner.

wake¹ [weɪk] vi (pt woke, pp woken) **to w. (up)** se réveiller; **to w. up to** (fact etc) Fig prendre conscience de; - vt **to w. (up)** réveiller; **to spend one's waking hours working/etc** passer ses journées à travailler/etc. ◆**waken** vt éveiller, réveiller; - vi s'éveiller, se réveiller.

wake² [weɪk] n (of ship) & Fig sillage m; **in the w. of** Fig dans le sillage de, à la suite de.

Wales [weɪlz] n pays m de Galles.

walk [wɔːk] n promenade f; (short) (petit) tour m; (gait) démarche f; (pace) marche f, pas m; (path) allée f, chemin m; **to go for a w.** faire une promenade; (shorter) faire un (petit) tour; **to take for a w.** (child etc) emmener se promener; (baby, dog) promener; **five minutes' w. (away)** à cinq minutes à pied; **walks of life** Fig conditions sociales fpl; - vi (move, stroll) se promener; (go on foot) aller à pied; w.! (don't run) ne cours pas!; **to w. away or off** s'éloigner, partir (from de); **to w. away or off with** (steal) Fam faucher; **to w. in** entrer; **to w. into** (tree etc) rentrer dans; (trap) tomber dans; **to w. out** (leave) partir; (of workers) se mettre en grève; **to w. out on s.o.** (desert) Fam laisser tomber qn; **to w. over to** (go up to) s'approcher de; - vt (distance) faire à pied; (streets) (par)courir; (take for a walk) promener (bébé, chien); **to w. s.o. to** (station etc) accompagner qn à. ◆**-ing** n marche f (à pied); - a a **w.-corpse/dictionary** (person) Fig un cadavre/dictionnaire ambulant; **at a w. pace** au pas; w. stick canne f. ◆**walker** n marcheur, -euse mf; (for pleasure) promeneur, -euse mf. ◆**walkout** n (strike) grève f surprise; (from meeting) départ m (en signe de protestation). ◆**walkover** n (in contest etc) victoire f facile. ◆**walkway** n moving w. trottoir m roulant.

walkie-talkie [wɔːkɪˈtɔːkɪ] n talkie-walkie m.

Walkman® [ˈwɔːkmən] n (pl **Walkmans**) baladeur m.

wall [wɔːl] n mur m; (of cabin, tunnel, stomach etc) paroi f; (of ice) Fig muraille f; (of

smoke) Fig rideau m; **to go to the w.** (of firm) Fig faire faillite; – a (mural), – vt **to w. up** (door etc) murer; **walled city** ville f fortifiée. ◆**wallflower** n Bot giroflée f; **to be a w.** (at dance) faire tapisserie. ◆**wallpaper** n papier m peint; – vt tapisser. ◆**wall-to-wall 'carpet(ing)'** n moquette f.

wallet [ˈwɒlɪt] n portefeuille m.

wallop [ˈwɒləp] vt (hit) Fam taper sur; – n (blow) Fam grand coup m.

wallow [ˈwɒləʊ] vi **to w. in** (mud, vice etc) se vautrer dans.

wally [ˈwɒlɪ] n (idiot) Fam andouille f, imbécile mf.

walnut [ˈwɔːlnʌt] n (nut) noix f; (tree, wood) noyer m.

walrus [ˈwɔːlrəs] n (animal) morse m.

waltz [wɔːls, Am wɒlts] n valse f; – vi valser.

wan [wɒn] a (pale) Lit pâle.

wand [wɒnd] n baguette f (magique).

wander [ˈwɒndər] vi (of thoughts) vagabonder; **to w. (about or around)** (roam) errer, vagabonder; (stroll) flâner; **to w. from or off** (path, subject) s'écarter de; **to w. off** (go away) s'éloigner; **my mind's wandering** je suis distrait; – vt **to w. the streets** errer dans les rues. ◆**-ing** a (life, tribe) vagabond, nomade; – npl vagabondages mpl. ◆**-er** n vagabond, -onde mf.

wane [weɪn] vi (of moon, fame, strength etc) décroître; – n **to be on the w.** décroître, être en déclin.

wangle [ˈwæŋɡ(ə)l] vt Fam (obtain) se débrouiller pour obtenir; (avoiding payment) carotter (from à).

want [wɒnt] vt vouloir (to do faire); (ask for) demander; (need) avoir besoin de; **I w. him to go** je veux qu'il parte; **you w. to try** (should) tu devrais essayer; **you're wanted on the phone** on vous demande au téléphone; – vi **not to w. for** (not lack) ne pas manquer de; – n (lack) manque m (of de); (poverty) besoin m; **for w. of** par manque de; **for w. of money/time** faute d'argent/de temps; **for w. of anything better** faute de mieux; **your wants** (needs) tes besoins mpl. ◆**-ed** a (man, criminal) recherché par la police; **to feel w.** sentir qu'on vous aime. ◆**-ing** a (inadequate) insuffisant; **to be w.** manquer (in de).

wanton [ˈwɒntən] a (gratuitous) gratuit; (immoral) impudique.

war [wɔːr] n guerre f; **at w.** en guerre (with avec); **to go to w.** entrer en guerre (with avec); **to declare w.** déclarer la guerre (on à); – a (wound, criminal etc) de guerre; w.

memorial monument *m* aux morts.
◆**warfare** *n* guerre *f*. ◆**warhead** *n* (*of missile*) ogive *f*. ◆**warlike** *a* guerrier. ◆**warmonger** *n* fauteur *m* de guerre. ◆**warpath** *n* **to be on the w.** (*angry*) Fam être d'humeur massacrante. ◆**warring** *a* (*countries etc*) en guerre; (*ideologies etc*) Fig en conflit. ◆**warship** *n* navire *m* de guerre. ◆**wartime** *n* **in w.** en temps de guerre.

warble ['wɔːb(ə)l] *vi* (*of bird*) gazouiller.

ward¹ [wɔːd] *n* **1** (*in hospital*) salle *f*. **2** (*child*) *Jur* pupille *mf*. **3** (*electoral division*) circonscription *f* électorale.

ward² [wɔːd] *vt* **to w. off** (*blow, anger*) détourner; (*danger*) éviter.

warden ['wɔːd(ə)n] *n* (*of institution, Am of prison*) directeur, -trice *mf*; (*of park*) gardien, -ienne *mf*; (**traffic**) **w.** contractuel, -elle *mf*.

warder ['wɔːdər] *n* gardien *m* (de prison).

wardrobe ['wɔːdrəub] *n* (*cupboard*) penderie *f*; (*clothes*) garde-robe *f*.

warehouse, *pl* **-ses** ['weəhaus, -zɪz] *n* entrepôt *m*.

wares [weəz] *npl* marchandises *fpl*.

warily ['weərɪlɪ] *adv* avec précaution.

warm [wɔːm] *a* (**-er, -est**) chaud; (*iron, oven*) moyen; (*welcome, thanks etc*) chaleureux; **to be** *or* **feel w.** avoir chaud; **it's** (**nice and**) **w.** (*of weather*) il fait (agréablement) chaud; **to get w.** (*of person, room etc*) se réchauffer; (*of food, water*) chauffer; – *vt* **to w.** (**up**) (*person, food etc*) réchauffer; – *vi* **to w. up** (*of person, room, engine*) se réchauffer; (*of food, water*) chauffer; (*of discussion*) s'échauffer; **to w. to s.o.** Fig se prendre de sympathie pour qn. ◆**warm-'hearted** *a* chaleureux. ◆**warmly** *adv* (*to wrap up*) chaudement; (*to welcome, thank etc*) chaleureusement. ◆**warmth** *n* chaleur *f*.

warn [wɔːn] *vt* avertir, prévenir (**that** que); **to w. s.o. against** *or* **off sth** mettre qn en garde contre qch; **to w. s.o. against doing** conseiller à qn de ne pas faire. ◆**-ing** *n* avertissement *m*; (*advance notice*) (pré)avis *m*; *Met* avis *m*; (*alarm*) alerte *f*; **without w.** sans prévenir; **a note** *or* **word of w.** une mise en garde; **w. light** (*on appliance etc*) voyant *m* lumineux; **hazard w. lights** *Aut* feux *mpl* de détresse.

warp [wɔːp] **1** *vt* (*wood etc*) voiler; (*judgment, person etc*) Fig pervertir; **a warped mind** un esprit tordu; **a warped account** un récit déformé; – *vi* se voiler. **2** *n* *Tex* chaîne *f*.

warrant ['wɒrənt] **1** *n* *Jur* mandat *m*; **a w. for**

your arrest un mandat d'arrêt contre vous. **2** *vt* (*justify*) justifier; **I w. you that...** (*declare confidently*) je t'assure que.... ◆**warranty** *n* *Com* garantie *f*.

warren ['wɒrən] *n* (*rabbit*) w. garenne *f*.

warrior ['wɒrɪər] *n* guerrier, -ière *mf*.

wart [wɔːt] *n* verrue *f*.

wary ['weərɪ] *a* (**-ier, -iest**) prudent; **to be w. of s.o./sth** se méfier de qn/qch; **to be w. of doing** hésiter beaucoup à faire.

was [wɒz, *stressed* wɒz] *see* **be**.

wash [wɒʃ] *n* (*clothes*) lessive *f*; (*of ship*) sillage *m*; **to have a w.** se laver; **to give sth a w.** laver qch; **to do the w.** faire la lessive; **in the w.** à la lessive; – *vt* laver; (*flow over*) baigner; **to w. one's hands** se laver les mains (*Fig of sth* de qch); **to w.** (**away**) (*of sea etc*) emporter (*qch, qn*); **to w. away** *or* **off** *or* **out** (*stain*) faire partir (en lavant); **to w. down** (*vehicle, deck*) laver à grande eau; (*food*) arroser (**with** de); **to w. out** (*bowl etc*) laver; – *vi* se laver; (*do the dishes*) laver la vaisselle; **to w. away** *or* **off** *or* **out** (*of stain*) partir (au lavage); **to w. up** (*do the dishes*) faire la vaisselle; (*have a wash*) *Am* se laver. ◆**washed-'out** *a* (*tired*) lessivé. ◆**washed-'up** *a* (*all*) **w.-up** (*person, plan*) *Sl* fichu. ◆**washable** *a* lavable. ◆**washbasin** *n* lavabo *m*. ◆**washcloth** *n* *Am* gant *m* de toilette. ◆**washout** *n* *Sl* (*event etc*) fiasco *m*; (*person*) nullité *f*. ◆**washroom** *n* *Am* toilettes *fpl*.

washer ['wɒʃər] *n* (*ring*) rondelle *f*, joint *m*.

washing ['wɒʃɪŋ] *n* (*act*) lavage *m*; (*clothes*) lessive *f*, linge *m*; **to do the w.** faire la lessive; **w. line** corde *f* à linge; **w. machine** machine *f* à laver; **w. powder** lessive *f*. ◆**w.-'up** *n* vaisselle *f*; **to do the w.-up** faire la vaisselle; **w.-up liquid** produit *m* pour la vaisselle.

wasp [wɒsp] *n* guêpe *f*.

wast/e [weɪst] *n* gaspillage *m*; (*of time*) perte *f*; (*rubbish*) déchets *mpl*; *pl* (*land*) étendue *f* déserte; **w. disposal unit** broyeur *m* d'ordures; – *a* **w. material** *or* **products** déchets *mpl*; **w. land** (*uncultivated*) terres *fpl* incultes; (*in town*) terrain *m* vague; **w. paper** vieux papiers *mpl*; **w. pipe** tuyau *m* d'évacuation; – *vt* (*money, food etc*) gaspiller; (*time, opportunity*) perdre; **to w. one's time on frivolities/***etc* gaspiller son temps en frivolités/*etc*, perdre son temps à des frivolités/*etc*; **to w. one's life** gâcher sa vie; – *vi* **to w. away** dépérir. ◆**-ed** *a* (*effort*) inutile; (*body etc*) émacié. ◆**wastage** *n* gaspillage *m*; (*losses*) pertes *fpl*; **some w.** (*of goods, staff etc*) du déchet. ◆**wastebin** *n* *(in kitchen)* poubelle f. ◆**wastepaper basket** n corbeille f (à papier).

wasteful ['weɪstfəl] a *(person)* gaspilleur; *(process)* peu économique.

watch [wɒtʃ] **1** n *(small clock)* montre f. **2** n *(over suspect, baby etc)* surveillance f; *Nau* quart m; **to keep (a) w. on** or **over** surveiller; **to keep w.** faire le guet; **to be on the w. (for)** guetter; – vt regarder; *(observe)* observer; *(suspect, baby etc)* surveiller; *(be careful of)* faire attention à; – vi regarder; **to w. (out) for** *(be on the lookout for)* guetter; **to w. out** *(take care)* faire attention *(for* à); **w. out!** attention!; **to w. over** surveiller. ◆**watchdog** n chien m de garde. ◆**watchmaker** n horloger, -ère mf. ◆**watchman** n *(pl -men)* **night w.** veilleur m de nuit. ◆**watchstrap** n bracelet m de montre. ◆**watchtower** n tour f de guet. ◆**watchful** ['wɒtʃfəl] a vigilant.

water ['wɔːtər] n eau f; **by w.** en bateau; **under w.** *(road, field etc)* inondé; *(to swim)* sous l'eau; **at high w.** à marée haute; **it doesn't hold w.** *(of theory etc)* Fig ne tient pas debout; **in hot w.** Fig dans le pétrin; **w. cannon** lance f à eau; **w. ice** sorbet m; **w. lily** nénuphar m; **w. pistol** pistolet m à eau; **w. polo** Sp water-polo m; **w. power** énergie f hydraulique; **w. rates** taxes fpl sur l'eau; **w. skiing** ski m nautique; **w. tank** réservoir m d'eau; **w. tower** château m d'eau; – vt *(plant etc)* arroser; **to w. down** *(wine etc)* couper; *(text etc)* édulcorer; – vi *(of eyes)* larmoyer; **it makes his** or **her mouth w.** ça lui fait venir l'eau à la bouche. ◆**-ing** n *(of plant etc)* arrosage m; **w. can** arrosoir m. ◆**watery** a *(colour)* délavé; *(soup)* Pej trop liquide; *(eyes)* larmoyant; **w. tea** or **coffee** de la lavasse.

watercolour ['wɔːtəkʌlər] n *(picture)* aquarelle f; *(paint)* couleur f pour aquarelle. ◆**watercress** n cresson m de fontaine. ◆**waterfall** n chute f d'eau. ◆**waterhole** n *(in desert)* point m d'eau. ◆**waterline** n *(on ship)* ligne f de flottaison. ◆**waterlogged** a délavé. ◆**watermark** n *(in paper)* filigrane m. ◆**watermelon** n pastèque f. ◆**waterproof** a *(material)* imperméable. ◆**watershed** n *(turning point)* tournant m *(décisif)*. ◆**watertight** a *(container etc)* étanche. ◆**waterway** n voie f navigable. ◆**waterworks** n *(place)* station f hydraulique.

watt [wɒt] n El watt m.

wave [weɪv] n *(of sea)* & Fig vague f; *(in hair)* ondulation f; Rad onde f; *(sign)* signe m *(de la main)*; **long/medium/short w.** Rad ondes fpl longues/moyennes/ courtes; – vi *(with hand)* faire signe *(de la main)*; *(of flag)* flotter; – vt *(greet)* saluer de la main; – vt *(arm, flag etc)* agiter; *(hair)* onduler; **to w. s.o. on** faire signe à qn d'avancer; **to w. aside** *(objection etc)* écarter. ◆**waveband** n Rad bande f de fréquence. ◆**wavelength** n Rad & Fig longueur f d'ondes.

waver ['weɪvər] vi *(of flame, person etc)* vaciller.

wavy ['weɪvɪ] a *(-ier, -iest)* *(line)* onduleux; *(hair)* ondulé.

wax [wæks] **1** n cire f; *(for ski)* fart m; – vt cirer; *(ski)* farter; *(car)* lustrer; – a *(candle, doll etc)* de cire; **w. paper** Culin Am papier m paraffiné. **2** vi *(of moon)* croître. **3** vi **to w. lyrical/merry** devenir l'un faire lyrique/gai. ◆**waxworks** npl *(place)* musée m de cire; *(dummies)* figures fpl de cire.

way [weɪ] **1** n *(path, road)* chemin m *(to* de); *(direction)* sens m, direction f; *(distance)* distance f; **all the w., the whole w.** *(to talk etc)* pendant tout le chemin; **this w.** par ici; **that w.** par là; **which w.?** par où?; **to lose one's w.** se perdre; **I'm on my w.** *(coming)* j'arrive; *(going)* je pars; **he made his w. out/home** il est sorti/rentré; **to w. there** l'aller m; **the w. back** le retour; **the w. in** l'entrée f; **the w. out** la sortie; **a w. out of a problem etc)** Fig une solution à; **the w. is clear** Fig la voie est libre; **across the w.** en face; **on the w.** en route *(to* pour); **by w. of** *(via)* par; *(as)* Fig comme; **out of the w.** *(isolated)* isolé; **to go out of one's w. to do** se donner du mal pour faire; **by the w. . . . .** Fig à propos; **to be** or **stand in the w.** barrer le passage; **she's in my w.** *(hindrance)* Fig elle me gêne; **to get out of the w., make w.** s'écarter; **to give w.** céder; Aut céder le passage or la priorité; **a long w. (away** or **off)** très loin; **it's the wrong w. up** c'est dans le mauvais sens; **do it the other w. round** fais le contraire; **to get under w.** *(of campaign etc)* démarrer; – adv *(behind etc)* très loin; **w. ahead** très en avance *(of* sur). **2** n *(manner)* façon f; *(means)* moyen m; *(condition)* état m; *(habit)* habitude f; *(particular)* égard m; **one's ways** *(behaviour)* ses manières fpl; **to get one's own w.** obtenir ce qu'on veut; **(in) this w.** de cette façon; **in a way** *(to some extent)* dans un certain sens; **a w. of life** façon f de vivre, mode m de vie; **no w.!** *(certainly not)* Fam pas question! ◆**wayfarer** n voyageur, -euse mf. ◆**way-'out** a Fam extraordinaire. ◆**wayside** n by the w. au bord de la route.

waylay [wer'leɪ] vt (pt & pp -**laid**) (attack) attaquer par surprise; (stop) Fig arrêter au passage.

wayward ['weɪwəd] a rebelle, capricieux.

WC [dʌb(ə)lju:'si:] n w-c mpl, waters mpl.

we [wi:] pron nous; **we go** nous allons; **we teachers** nous autres professeurs; **we never know** (indefinite) on ne sait jamais.

weak [wi:k] a (-er, -est) faible; (tea, coffee) léger; (health, stomach) fragile. ◆**w.-'willed** a faible. ◆**weaken** vt affaiblir; – vi faiblir. ◆**weakling** n (in body) mauviette f; (in character) faible mf. ◆**weakly** adv faiblement. ◆**weakness** n faiblesse f; (of health, stomach) fragilité f; (fault) point m faible; **a w. for** (liking) un faible pour.

weal [wi:l] n (wound on skin) marque f, zébrure f.

wealth [welθ] n (money, natural resources) richesse(s) f(pl); **a w. of** (abundance) Fig une profusion de. ◆**wealthy** a (-ier, -iest) riche; – n the w. les riches mpl.

wean [wi:n] vt (baby) sevrer.

weapon ['wepən] n arme f. ◆**weaponry** n armements mpl.

wear [weər] **1** vt (pt **wore**, pp **worn**) (have on body) porter; (look, smile) avoir; (put on) mettre; **to have nothing to w.** n'avoir rien à se mettre; – n men's/sports w. vêtements mpl pour hommes/de sport; **evening w.** tenue f de soirée. **2** vt (pt **wore**, pp **worn**) **to w.** (away or down or out) (material, patience etc) user; **to w. s.o. out** (exhaust) épuiser qn; **to w. oneself out** s'épuiser (doing à faire); – vi (last) faire de l'usage, durer; **to w.** (out) (of clothes etc) s'user; **to w. off** (of colour, pain etc) passer, disparaître; **to w. on** (of time) passer; **to w. out** (of patience) s'épuiser; – n (use) usage m; **w.** (and tear) usure f. ◆**-ing** a (tiring) épuisant. ◆**-er** n the w. (of hat, glasses etc) la personne qui porte.

weary ['wɪərɪ] a (-ier, -iest) (tired) fatigué, las (of doing de faire); (tiring) fatigant; (look, smile) las; – vi to w. of se lasser de. ◆**wearily** adv avec lassitude. ◆**weariness** n lassitude f.

weasel ['wi:z(ə)l] n belette f.

weather ['weðər] n temps m; what's the w. like? quel temps fait-il?; (in the) hot w. par temps chaud; **under the w.** (not well) Fig patraque; – a (chart etc) météorologique; **w. forecast, w. report** prévisions fpl météorologiques, météo f; **w. vane** girouette f; –

vt (storm, hurricane) essuyer; (crisis) Fig surmonter. ◆**weather-beaten** a (face, person) tanné, hâlé. ◆**weathercock** n girouette f. ◆**weatherman** n (pl -men) TV Rad Fam monsieur m météo.

weav/e [wi:v] vt (pt **wove**, pp **woven**) (cloth, plot) tisser; (basket, garland) tresser; – vi Tex tisser; **to w. in and out of** (crowd, cars etc) Fig se faufiler entre; – n (style) tissage m. ◆**-ing** n tissage m. ◆**-er** n tisserand, -ande mf.

web [web] n (of spider) toile f; (of lies) Fig tissu m. ◆**webbed** a (foot) palmé. ◆**webbing** n (in chair) sangles fpl.

wed [wed] vt (-dd-) (marry) épouser; (qualities etc) Fig allier (to à); – vi se marier. ◆**wedded** a (bliss, life) conjugal. ◆**wedding** n mariage m; **golden/silver w.** noces fpl d'or/d'argent; – a (cake) de noces; (anniversary, present) de mariage; (dress) de mariée; **his** or **her w. day** le jour de son mariage; **w. ring**, Am **w. band** alliance f. ◆**wedlock** n born out of w. illégitime.

wedge [wedʒ] n (for splitting) coin m; (under wheel, table etc) cale f; **w. heel** (of shoe) semelle f compensée; – vt (wheel, table etc) caler; (push) enfoncer (into dans); **wedged (in) between** (caught, trapped) coincé entre.

Wednesday ['wenzdɪ] n mercredi m.

wee [wi:] a (tiny) Fam tout petit.

weed [wi:d] n (plant) mauvaise herbe f; (weak person) Fam mauviette f; **w. killer** désherbant m; – vti désherber; **to w. out** Fig éliminer (from de). ◆**weedy** a (-ier, -iest) (person) Fam maigre et chétif.

week [wi:k] n semaine f; **the w. before last** pas la semaine dernière, celle d'avant; **the w. after next** pas la semaine prochaine, celle d'après; **tomorrow w., a w. tomorrow** demain en huit. ◆**weekday** n jour m de semaine. ◆**week'end** n week-end m; **at** or **on** or **over the w.** ce week-end, pendant le week-end. ◆**weekly** a hebdomadaire; – adv toutes les semaines; – n (magazine) hebdomadaire m.

weep [wi:p] vi (pt pp **wept**) pleurer; (of wound) suinter; **to w. for s.o.** pleurer qn; – vt (tears) pleurer; **weeping willow** saule m pleureur.

weft [weft] n Tex trame f.

weigh [weɪ] vt peser; **to w. down** (with load etc) surcharger (with de); (bend) faire plier; **to w. up** (goods, chances etc) peser; – vi peser; **it's weighing on my mind** ça me tracasse; **to w. down on s.o.** (of worries etc)

accabler qn. ◆**weighing-machine** n
balance f.

weight [weɪt] n poids m; **to put on w.** grossir;
to lose w. maigrir; **to carry w.** (of argument
etc) Fig avoir du poids (with pour); **to pull
one's w.** (do one's share) Fig faire sa part du
travail; **w. lifter** haltérophile mf; **w. lifting**
haltérophilie f; – int (heavy object) maintenir
avec un poids; **to w. down** (weigh down
with (overload) surcharger de.
◆**weightlessness** n apesanteur f.
◆**weighty** a (-ier, -iest) lourd; (argument,
subject) Fig de poids.

weighting ['weɪtɪŋ] n (on salary) indemnité f
de résidence.

weir [wɪər] n (across river) barrage m.

weird [wɪəd] a (-er, -est) (odd) bizarre;
(eerie) mystérieux.

welcome ['welkəm] a (pleasant) agréable;
(timely) opportun; **w.** (of person,
people) être le bienvenu or la bienvenue or
les bienvenu(e)s; **w.!** soyez le bienvenu or
la bienvenue or les bienvenu(e)s!; **to make
s.o. (feel) w.** faire bon accueil à qn; **you're
w.!** (after 'thank you') il n'y a pas de quoi!;
w. to do (free) libre de faire; **you're w. to
(take or use) my bike** mon vélo est à ta
disposition; **you're w. to it!** Iron grand bien
vous fasse!; – n accueil m; **to extend a w. to
(greet)** souhaiter la bienvenue à; – vt
accueillir; (warmly) faire bon accueil à; (be
glad of) se réjouir de; **I w. you!** je vous
souhaite la bienvenue! ◆**welcoming** a
(smile etc) accueillant; (speech, words)
d'accueil.

weld [weld] vt **to w. (together)** souder;
(groups etc) Fig unir; – n (joint) soudure f.
◆**–ing** n soudure f. ◆**–er** n soudeur m.

welfare ['welfeər] n (physical, material)
bien-être m; (spiritual) santé f; (public aid)
aide f sociale; **public w.** (good) le bien
public; **the w. state** (in Great Britain)
l'État-providence m; **w. work** assistance f
sociale.

well¹ [wel] **1** n (for water) puits m; (of stairs,
lift) cage f; (oil) **w.** puits de pétrole. **2** vi **to
w. up** (rise) monter.

well² [wel] adv (better, best) bien; **to do w.**
(succeed) réussir; **you'd do w. to refuse** tu
ferais bien de refuser; **w. done!** bravo!; **I,
you, she etc might (just) as w. have left** il
valait mieux partir, autant valait partir; **it's
just as w. that** (lucky) heureusement que
. . . ; **as w.** (also) aussi; **as w. as** aussi bien
que; **as w. as two cats, he has . . .** en plus de
deux chats, il a . . . ; – a bien inv; **she's w.**
(healthy) elle va bien; **not a w. man** un

homme malade; **to get w.** se remettre;
that's all very w., but . . . tout ça c'est très
joli, mais . . . ; – int (surprise) tiens, tiens!;
(resignation) enfin, assez grand. **w. , w.!**
(surprise) tiens, tiens!; **enormous!, w. , quite
big** énorme, enfin, assez grand.

well-behaved [welbɪ'heɪvd] a sage.
◆**w.-'being** n bien-être m. ◆**w.-'built** a
(person, car) solide. ◆**w.-'founded** a bien
fondé. ◆**w.-'heeled** a (rich) Fam nanti.
◆**w.-in'formed** a (person, newspaper)
bien informé. ◆**w.-'known** a (bien)
connu. ◆**w.-'meaning** a bien intentionné. ◆**'w.-nigh** adv presque. ◆**w.-'off**
a aisé, riche. ◆**w.-'read** a instruit.
◆**w.-'spoken** a (person) qui a un accent
cultivé, qui parle bien. ◆**w.-'thought-of** a
hautement considéré. ◆**w.-'timed** a
opportun. ◆**w.-to-'do** a aisé, riche.
◆**w.-'tried** a (method) éprouvé. ◆**w.-
'trodden** a (path) battu. ◆**'w.-wish-
ers** npl admirateurs, -trices mfpl.
◆**w.-'worn** a (clothes, carpet) usagé.

wellington ['welɪŋtən] n botte f de caoutchouc.

welsh [welʃ] vi **to w. on** (debt, promise) ne
pas honorer.

Welsh [welʃ] a gallois; **W. rabbit** Culin toast
m au fromage; – n (language) gallois m.
◆**Welshman** n (pl -men) Gallois m.
◆**Welshwoman** n (pl -women) Galloise f.

wench [wentʃ] n Hum jeune fille f.

wend [wend] vt **to w. one's way** s'acheminer
(to vers).

went [went] see **go 1**.

wept [wept] see **weep**.

were [wər, stressed wɜːr] see **be**.

werewolf ['weəwulf] n (pl -wolves)
loup-garou m.

west [west] n ouest m; – a (coast) ouest inv;
(wind) d'ouest; **W. Africa** Afrique f
occidentale; **W. Indian** a & n antillais, -aise
(mf); **the W. Indies** les Antilles fpl; – adv à
l'ouest, vers l'ouest. ◆**westbound** a
(carriageway) ouest inv; (traffic) en direction de l'ouest. ◆**westerly** a (point) ouest
inv; (direction) de l'ouest; (wind) d'ouest.
◆**western** a (coast) ouest inv; (culture) Pol
occidental; **W. Europe** Europe f de l'Ouest;
– n (film) western m. ◆**westerner** n habitant, -ante mf de l'Ouest; Pol occidental.
-ale mf. ◆**westernize** vt occidentaliser.
◆**westward(s)** a & adv vers l'ouest.

wet [wet] a (wetter, wettest) mouillé; (damp,
rainy) humide; (day, month) de pluie; **w.
paint/ink** peinture f/encre f fraîche; **w.
through** trempé; **to get w.** se mouiller; **it's
w.** (raining) il pleut; **he's w.** (weak-willed)

Fam c'est une lavette; **w. blanket** *Fig* rabat-joie *m inv*; **w. nurse** nourrice *f*; **w. suit** combinaison *f* de plongée; – **n the w.** (*rain*) la pluie; (*damp*) l'humidité *f*; – *vt* (**-tt-**) mouiller. ◆**-ness** *n* humidité *f*.

whack [wæk] *n* (*blow*) grand coup *m*; – *vt* donner un grand coup à. ◆**-ed** *a* **w.** (**out**) (*tired*) *Fam* claqué. ◆**-ing** *a* (*big*) *Fam* énorme.

whale [weil] *n* baleine *f*. ◆**whaling** *n* pêche *f* à la baleine.

wham! [wæm] *int* vlan!

wharf [wɔːf] *n* (*pl* **wharfs** *or* **wharves**) (*for ships*) quai *m*.

what [wɒt] **1** *a* quel, quelle, *pl* quel(le)s; **w. book?** quel livre?; **w. one?** *Fam* lequel?, laquelle?; **w. a fool/etc** quel idiot/*etc*!; **I know w. book it is** je sais quel livre c'est; **w.** (*little*) **she has** le peu qu'elle a. **2** *pron* (*in questions*) qu'est-ce qui; (*object*) qu'est-ce que; (*after prep*) quoi; **w.'s happening?** qu'est-ce qui se passe?; **w. does he do?** qu'est-ce qu'il fait?, que fait-il?; **w. is it?** qu'est-ce que c'est?; **w.'s that book?** quel est ce livre?; **w.!** (*surprise*) quoi!, comment!; **w.'s it called?** comment ça s'appelle?; **w. for?** pourquoi?; **w. about me/etc?** et moi/*etc*?; **w. about leaving/etc?** si on partait/*etc*? **3** *pron* (*indirect, relative*) ce qui; (*object*) ce que; **I know w. will happen/w. she'll do** je sais ce qui arrivera/ce qu'elle fera; **w. happens is . . .** ce qui arrive c'est que . . . ; **w. I need ce** dont j'ai besoin. ◆**what'ever** *a* **w.** (**the**) **mistake/etc** (*no matter what*) quelle que soit l'erreur/*etc*; **of w. size de** n'importe quelle taille; **no chance w.** pas la moindre chance; **nothing w.** rien du tout; – *pron* (*no matter what*) quoi que (+ *sub*); **w. happens** quoi qu'il arrive; **w. you do** quoi que tu fasses; **w. is important** tout ce qui est important; **w. you want** tout ce que tu veux. ◆**what's-it** *n* (*thing*) *Fam* machin *m*. ◆**whatso'ever** *a* & *pron* = **whatever**.

wheat [wiːt] *n* blé *m*, froment *m*. ◆**wheatgerm** *n* germes *mpl* de blé.

wheedle ['wiːd(ə)l] *vt* **to w. s.o.** enjôler qn (*into doing pour qu'il fasse*); **to w. sth out of s.o.** obtenir qch de qn par la flatterie.

wheel [wiːl] **1** *n* roue *f*; **at the w.** *Aut* au volant; *Nau* au gouvernail; – *vt* (*push*) pousser; – *vi* (*turn*) tourner. **2** *vi* **to w. and deal** *Fam* faire des combines. ◆**wheelbarrow** *n* brouette *f*. ◆**wheelchair** *n* fauteuil *m* roulant.

wheeze [wiːz] **1** *vi* respirer bruyamment. **2** *n*

(*scheme*) *Fam* combine *f*. ◆**wheezy** *a* (**-ier, -iest**) poussif.

whelk [welk] *n* (*mollusc*) buccin *m*.

when [wen] *adv* quand; – *conj* quand, lorsque; (*whereas*) alors que; **I've finished** quand j'aurai fini; **w. I saw him** *or* **w. I'd seen him,** I left après l'avoir vu, je suis parti; **the day/moment w.** le jour/moment où; **I talked about w. . . .** j'ai parlé de l'époque où . . . . ◆**when'ever** *conj* (*at whatever time*) quand; (*each time that*) chaque fois que.

where [weər] *adv* où; **w. are you from?** d'où êtes-vous?; – *conj* où; (*whereas*) alors que; **that's w. you'll find it** c'est là que tu le trouveras; **I found it w.** she'd left it je l'ai trouvé là où elle l'avait laissé; **I went to w. he was** je suis allé à l'endroit où il était. ◆**whereabouts** *adv* où (*donc*); – *n* **his w.** l'endroit *m* où il est. ◆**where'as** *conj* alors que. ◆**where'by** *adv* par quoi. ◆**where'upon** *adv* sur quoi. ◆**wher'ever** *conj* **w. you go** (*everywhere*) partout où tu iras, où que tu ailles; **I'll go w. you like** (*anywhere*) j'irai (là) où vous voudrez.

whet [wet] *vt* (**-tt-**) (*appetite, desire etc*) aiguiser.

whether ['weðər] *conj* si; **I don't know w. to leave** je ne sais pas si je dois partir; **w. she does it or not** qu'elle le fasse ou non; **w. now or tomorrow** que ce soit maintenant ou demain; **it's doubtful w.** il est douteux que (+ *sub*).

which [witʃ] **1** *a* (*in questions etc*) quel, quelle, *pl* quel(le)s; **w. hat?** quel chapeau?; **in w. case** auquel cas. **2** *rel pron* qui; (*object*) que; (*after prep*) lequel, laquelle, *pl* lesquel(le)s; **the house w. is . . .** la maison qui est . . . ; **the book w.** I like le livre que j'aime; **the film of w. . . .** le film dont *or* duquel . . . ; **she's ill, w. is sad** elle est malade, ce qui est triste; **he lies, w.** I don't like il ment, ce que je n'aime pas; **after w.** (*whereupon*) après quoi. **3** *pron* **w.** (**one**) (*in questions*) lequel, laquelle, *pl* lesquel(le)s; **w.** (**one**) **of us?** lequel *or* laquelle d'entre nous?; **w.** (**ones**) **are the best of these books** quels sont les meilleurs de ces livres? **4** *pron* **w.** (**one**) (*the one that*) celui qui, celle qui, *pl* ceux qui, celles qui; (*object*) celui *et* ceux; **show me w.** (**one**) **is red** montrez-moi celui *or* celle qui est rouge; **I know w.** (**ones**) **you want** je sais ceux *or* celles que vous désirez. ◆**which'ever** *a* & *pron* **w.** book/*etc or* **w. of the books/etc you buy** quel que soit le livre/*etc* que tu achètes; **take w. books or w. of the books interest you** prenez les livres qui vous intéressent; **take w. (one) you like** prends celui or celle qui te veux; **w. (ones) remain** ceux or celles qui restent.

whiff [wɪf] n (*puff*) bouffée f; (*smell*) odeur f.

while [waɪl] conj (*when*) pendant que; (*although*) bien que (+ sub); (*as long as*) tant que; (*whereas*) tandis que; **w. doing** (*in the course of*) en faisant; − n **a w.** un moment, quelque temps; **all the w.** tout le temps; − vt **to w. away** (*time*) passer. ◆**whilst** [waɪlst] conj = **while**.

whim [wɪm] n caprice m.

whimper ['wɪmpər] vi (*of dog, person*) gémir faiblement; (*snivel*) Pej pleurnicher; − n faible gémissement m; **without a w.** (*complaint*) Fig sans se plaindre.

whimsical ['wɪmzɪk(ə)l] a (*look, idea*) bizarre; (*person*) fantasque, capricieux.

whine [waɪn] vi gémir; (*complain*) Fig se plaindre; − n gémissement m, plainte f.

whip [wɪp] n fouet m; − vt (-pp-) (*person, cream etc*) fouetter; (*defeat*) Fam dérouiller; **to w. off** (*take off*) enlever brusquement; **to w. out** (*from pocket etc*) sortir brusquement (**from** de); **to w. up** (*interest*) susciter; (*meal*) Fam préparer rapidement; − vi (*move*) aller à toute vitesse; **to w. round to s.o.'s** faire un saut chez qn. ◆**whip-round** n Fam collecte f.

whirl [wɜːl] vi tourbillonner, tournoyer; − vt faire tourbillonner; − n tourbillon m. ◆**whirlpool** n tourbillon m; **w. bath** Am bain m à remous. ◆**whirlwind** n tourbillon m (de vent).

whirr [wɜːr] vi (*of engine*) vrombir; (*of top*) ronronner.

whisk [wɪsk] **1** n Culin fouet m; − vt fouetter. **2** vt **to w. away** or **off** (*tablecloth etc*) enlever rapidement; (*person*) emmener rapidement; (*chase away*) chasser.

whiskers ['wɪskəz] npl (*of animal*) moustaches fpl; (*beard*) barbe f; (*moustache*) moustache f; (*side*) w. favoris mpl.

whisky, Am **whiskey** ['wɪskɪ] n whisky m.

whisper ['wɪspər] vti chuchoter; **w. to me!** chuchote à mon oreille!; − n chuchotement m; (*rumour*) Fig rumeur f, bruit m.

whistle ['wɪs(ə)l] n sifflement m; (*object*) sifflet m; **to blow** or **give a w.** siffler; − vti siffler; **to w. at** (*girl*) siffler; **to w. for** (*dog, taxi*) siffler.

Whit [wɪt] a **W. Sunday** dimanche m de Pentecôte.

white [waɪt] a (*-er, -est*) blanc; **to go** or **turn w.** blanchir; **w. coffee** café m au lait; **w. elephant** Fig objet m or projet m etc inutile;

w. lie pieux mensonge m; **w. man** blanc m; **w. woman** blanche f; − n (*colour, of egg, of eye*) blanc m; (*person*) blanc m, blanche f. ◆**white-collar 'worker** n employé, -ée mf de bureau. ◆**whiten** vti blanchir. ◆**whiteness** n blancheur f. ◆**whitewash** n (*for walls etc*) blanc m de chaux; − vt blanchir à la chaux; (*person*) Fig blanchir; (*faults*) justifier.

whiting ['waɪtɪŋ] n (*fish*) merlan m.

Whitsun ['wɪts(ə)n] n la Pentecôte.

whittle ['wɪt(ə)l] vt **to w. down** (*wood*) tailler; (*price etc*) Fig rogner.

whizz [wɪz] **1** vi (*rush*) aller à toute vitesse; **to w. past** passer à toute vitesse; **to w. through the air** fendre l'air. **2** a **w. kid** Fam petit prodige m.

who [huː] pron qui; **w. did it?** qui (est-ce qui) a fait ça?; **the woman w.** la femme qui; **w. did you see** tu as vu qui? ◆**who'ever** pron (*no matter who*) qui que ce soit qui; (*object*) qui que ce soit que; **w. has travelled** (*anyone who*) quiconque a or celui qui a voyagé; **w. you are** qui que vous soyez; **this man, w. he is** cet homme, quel qu'il soit; **w. did that?** qui donc a fait ça?

whodunit [huː'dʌnɪt] n (*detective story*) Fam polar m.

whole [həʊl] a entier; (*intact*) intact; **the w. time** tout le temps; **the w. apple** toute la pomme, la pomme (tout) entière; **the w. truth** toute la vérité; **the w. world** le monde entier; **the w. lot** le tout; **to swallow sth w.** avaler qch tout rond; − n (*unit*) tout m; (*total*) totalité f; **the w. of the village** le village (tout) entier, tout le village; **the w. of the night** toute la nuit; **on the w., as a w.** dans l'ensemble. ◆**whole-'hearted** a, ◆**whole-'heartedly** adv sans réserve. ◆**wholemeal** a, Am ◆**wholewheat** a (*bread*) complet. ◆**wholly** adv entièrement.

wholesale ['həʊlseɪl] n Com gros m; − a (*firm*) de gros; (*destruction etc*) Fig en masse; − adv (*in bulk*) en gros; (*to buy or sell one article*) au prix de gros; (*to destroy etc*) Fig en masse. ◆**wholesaler** n grossiste mf.

wholesome ['həʊlsəm] a (*food, climate etc*) sain.

whom [huːm] pron (*object*) que; (*in questions and after prep*) qui; **w. did she see?** qui a-t-elle vu?; **the man w. you know** l'homme que tu connais; **with w.** avec qui; **of w.** dont.

whooping cough ['huːpɪŋkɒf] n coqueluche f.

whoops! [wʊps] int (apology etc) oups!
whopping ['wɒpɪŋ] a (big) Fam énorme.
◆**whopper** n Fam chose f énorme.
whore [hɔːr] n (prostitute) putain f.
whose [huːz] poss pron & a à qui, de qui; **w. book is this?, w. is this book?** à qui est ce livre?; **w. daughter are you?** de qui es-tu la fille?; **the woman w. book I have** la femme dont or de qui j'ai le livre; **the man w. mother I spoke to** l'homme à la mère de qui j'ai parlé.
why [waɪ] 1 adv pourquoi; **w. not?** pourquoi pas?; – conj **the reason w. they . . .** la raison pour laquelle ils . . . ; – npl **the whys and wherefores** le pourquoi et le comment. 2 int (surprise) eh bien!, tiens!
wick [wɪk] n (of candle, lamp) mèche f.
wicked ['wɪkɪd] a (evil) méchant, vilain; (mischievous) malicieux. ◆**—ly** adv méchamment; malicieusement. ◆**—ness** n méchanceté f.
wicker ['wɪkər] n osier m; – a (chair etc) en osier, d'osier. ◆**wickerwork** n (objects) vannerie f.
wicket ['wɪkɪt] n (cricket stumps) guichet m.
wide [waɪd] a (-er, -est) large; (desert, ocean) vaste; (choice, knowledge, variety) grand; **to be three metres w.** avoir trois mètres de large; – adv (to fall, shoot) loin du but; (to open) tout grand. ◆**wide-'awake** a (alert, not sleeping) éveillé. ◆**widely** adv (to broadcast, spread) largement; (to travel) beaucoup; **w. different** très différent; **it's w. thought** or **believed that . . .** on pense généralement que . . . . ◆**widen** vt élargir; – vi s'élargir. ◆**wideness** n largeur f.
widespread ['waɪdspred] a (très) répandu.
widow ['wɪdəʊ] n veuve f. ◆**widowed** a (man) veuf; (woman) veuve; **to be w.** (become a widower or widow) devenir veuf or veuve. ◆**widower** n veuf m.
width [wɪdθ] n largeur f.
wield [wiːld] vt (handle) manier; (brandish) brandir; (power) Fig exercer.
wife [waɪf] n (pl wives) femme f, épouse f.
wig [wɪg] n perruque f.
wiggle ['wɪg(ə)l] vt agiter; **to w. one's hips** tortiller des hanches; – vi (of worm etc) se tortiller; (of tail) remuer.
wild [waɪld] a (-er, -est) (animal, flower, region etc) sauvage; (enthusiasm, sea) déchaîné; (idea, life) fou; (look) farouche; (angry) furieux (with contre); **w. with** (joy, anger etc) fou de; **I'm not w. about it** (plan etc) Fam ça ne m'emballe pas; **to be w. about s.o.** (very fond of) être dingue de qn; **to grow w.** (of plant) pousser à l'état sau-

vage; **to run w.** (of animals) courir en liberté; (of crowd) se déchaîner; **the W. West** Am le Far West; – npl régions fpl sauvages. ◆**wildcat 'strike** n grève f sauvage. ◆**wild-'goose chase** n fausse piste f. ◆**wildlife** n animaux mpl sauvages, faune f.
wilderness ['wɪldənəs] n désert m.
wildly ['waɪldlɪ] adv (madly) follement; (violently) violemment.
wile [waɪl] n ruse f, artifice m.
wilful ['wɪlfəl] a (Am willful) (intentional, obstinate) volontaire. ◆**—ly** adv volontairement.
will[1] [wɪl] v aux **he will come, he'll come** (future tense) il viendra (**won't he?** n'est-ce pas?); **you will not come, you won't come** tu ne viendras pas (**will you?** n'est-ce pas?); **w. you have a tea?** veux-tu prendre un thé?; **w. you be quiet!** veux-tu te taire!; **I w.!** (yes) oui!; **it won't open** ça ne s'ouvre pas, ça ne veut pas s'ouvrir.
will[2] [wɪl] 1 vt (wish, intend) vouloir (that que (+ sub)); **to w. oneself to do** faire un effort de volonté pour faire; – n volonté f; **against one's w.** à contrecœur; **at w.** (to depart etc) quand on veut; (to choose) à volonté. 2 n (legal document) testament m. ◆**willpower** n volonté f.
willing ['wɪlɪŋ] a (helper, worker) de bonne volonté; (help etc) spontané; **to be w. to do** être disposé or prêt à faire, vouloir bien faire; – n **to show w.** faire preuve de bonne volonté. ◆**—ly** adv (with pleasure) volontiers; (voluntarily) volontairement. ◆**—ness** n (goodwill) bonne volonté f; **his** or **her w. to do** (enthusiasm) son empressement m à faire.
willow ['wɪləʊ] n (tree, wood) saule m. ◆**willowy** a (person) svelte.
willy-nilly [wɪlɪ'nɪlɪ] adv bon gré mal gré, de gré ou de force.
wilt [wɪlt] vi (of plant) dépérir; (of enthusiasm etc) Fig décliner.
wily ['waɪlɪ] a (-ier, -iest) rusé.
wimp [wɪmp] n (weakling) Fam mauviette f.
win [wɪn] n (victory) victoire f; – vi (pt & pp won, pres p winning) gagner; – vt (money, race etc) gagner; (victory, prize) remporter; (fame) acquérir; (friends) se faire; **to w. s.o. over** gagner qn (to à). ◆**winning** a (number, horse etc) gagnant; (team) victorieux; (goal) décisif; (smile) engageant; – npl gains mpl.
wince [wɪns] vi (flinch) tressaillir; (pull a face) grimacer; **without wincing** sans sourciller.

winch [wintʃ] n treuil m; – vt to w. (up) hisser au treuil.

wind[1] [wind] n vent m; (breath) souffle m; **to have w.** Med avoir des gaz; **to get w. of** Fig avoir vent de; **in the w.** Fig dans l'air; **w. instrument** Mus instrument m à vent; – vt to w. s.o. couper le souffle à qn. ◆**windbreak** n (fence, trees) brise-vent m inv. ◆**windcheater** n, Am ◆**windbreaker** n blouson m, coupe-vent m inv. ◆**windfall** n (piece of fruit) fruit m abattu par le vent; (unexpected money) Fig aubaine f. ◆**windmill** n moulin m à vent. ◆**windpipe** n Anat trachée f. ◆**windscreen** n, Am ◆**windshield** n Aut pare-brise m inv; **w. wiper** essuie-glace m inv. ◆**windsurfing** n to go w. faire de la planche à voile. ◆**windswept** a (street etc) balayé par les vents. ◆**windy** a (-ier, -iest) venteux, venté; **it's w.** (of weather) il y a du vent.

wind[2] [waind] vt (pt & pp wound) (roll) enrouler; (clock) remonter; **to w. up** (meeting) terminer; (firm) liquider; – vi (of river, road) serpenter; **to w. down** (relax) se détendre; **to w. up** (end up) finir (doing par faire); **to w. up with sth** se retrouver avec qch. ◆**–ing** n (of road etc) sinueux; (staircase) tournant. ◆**–er** n (of watch) remontoir m.

window [windəu] n fenêtre f; (pane) vitre f, carreau m; (in vehicle or train) vitre f; (in shop) vitrine f; (counter) guichet m; **French w.** porte-fenêtre f; **w. box** jardinière f; **w. cleaner** or Am **washer** laveur, -euse mf de carreaux; **w. dresser** étalagiste mf; **w. ledge** = windowsill; **to go w. shopping** faire du lèche-vitrines. ◆**windowpane** n vitre f, carreau m. ◆**windowsill** n (inside) appui m de (la) fenêtre; (outside) rebord m de (la) fenêtre.

wine [wain] n vin m; – a (bottle, cask) à vin: **w. cellar** cave f (à vin); **w. grower** viticulteur m; **w. list** carte f des vins; **w. taster** dégustateur, -trice mf de vins; **w. tasting** dégustation f de vins; **w. waiter** sommelier m; – vt **to w. and dine s.o.** offrir à dîner et à boire à qn. ◆**wineglass** n verre m à vin. ◆**wine-growing** a viticole.

wing [wiŋ] n aile f; **the wings** Th les coulisses fpl; **under one's w.** Fig sous son aile. ◆**winged** a ailé. ◆**winger** n Sp ailier m. ◆**wingspan** n envergure f.

wink [wiŋk] vi faire un clin d'œil (at, à); (of light) clignoter; – n clin m d'œil.

winkle [wiŋk(ə)l] n (sea animal) bigorneau m.

winner [winər] n (of contest etc) gagnant, -ante mf; (of argument, fight) vainqueur m; **that idea/etc is a w.** Fam c'est une idée/etc en or.

winter [wintər] n hiver m; – a d'hiver; **in (the) w.** en hiver. ◆**wintertime** n hiver m. ◆**wintry** a hivernal.

wip/e [waip] vt essuyer; **to w. one's feet/hands** s'essuyer les pieds/les mains; **to w. away** or **off** or **up** (liquid) essuyer; **to w. out** (clean) essuyer; (erase) effacer; (destroy) anéantir; – vi **to w. up** (dry the dishes) essuyer la vaisselle; – n coup m de torchon or d'éponge. ◆**–er** n Aut essuie-glace m inv.

wir/e [waiər] n fil m; (telegram) télégramme m; **w. netting** grillage m; – vt **to w. (up)** (house) El faire l'installation électrique de; **to w. s.o.** (telegraph) télégraphier à qn. ◆**–ing** n El installation f électrique. ◆**wirecutters** npl pince f coupante.

wireless [waiələs] n (set) TSF f, radio f; **by w.** (to send a message) par sans-fil.

wiry [waiəri] a (-ier, -iest) maigre et nerveux.

wisdom [wizdəm] n sagesse f.

wise [waiz] a (-er, -est) (prudent) sage, prudent; (learned) savant; **to put s.o. w./be w. to** Fam mettre qn/être au courant de qch. **w. guy** Fam gros malin m. ◆**wisecrack** n Fam (joke) astuce f; (sarcastic remark) sarcasme m. ◆**wisely** adv prudemment.

-wise [waiz] suffix (with regard to) money/etc-wise question argent/etc.

wish [wiʃ] vt souhaiter, vouloir (to do faire); **I w. (that) you could help me/could have helped me** je voudrais que/j'aurais voulu que vous m'aidiez; **I w. I hadn't done that** je regrette d'avoir fait ça; **if you w.** si tu veux; **I w. you well** or **luck** je vous souhaite bonne chance; **I wished him** or **her (a) happy birthday** je lui ai souhaité bon anniversaire; **I could** si seulement je pouvais; – vi **to w. for sth** souhaiter qch; – n (specific) souhait m, vœu m; (general) désir m; **the w. for sth/to do** le désir de qch/de faire; **best wishes** (on greeting card) meilleurs vœux mpl; (in letter) amitiés fpl, bien amicalement; **send him** or **her my best wishes** fais-lui mes amitiés. ◆**wishbone** n bréchet m. ◆**wishful** a **it's w. thinking (on your part)** tu te fais des illusions, tu prends tes désirs pour la réalité.

wishy-washy [wiʃiwɒʃi] a (taste, colour) fade.

wisp [wisp] n (of smoke) volute f; (of hair)

fine mèche f; **a (mere) w. of a girl** une fillette toute menue.

wisteria [wɪˈstɪərɪə] n Bot glycine f.

wistful [ˈwɪstfəl] a mélancolique et rêveur. ◆**—ly** adv avec mélancolie.

wit [wɪt] n **1** (humour) esprit m; (person) homme m or femme f d'esprit. **2** wit(s) (intelligence) intelligence f (**to do** de faire); **to be at one's wits'** or **wit's end** ne plus savoir que faire.

witch [wɪtʃ] n sorcière f. ◆**witchcraft** n sorcellerie f. ◆**witch-hunt** n Pol chasse f aux sorcières.

with [wɪð] prep **1** avec; **come w. me** viens avec moi; **w. no hat** sans chapeau; **I'll be right w. you** je suis à vous dans une minute; **I'm w. you** (I understand) Fam je te suis; **w. it** (up-to-date) Fam dans le vent. **2** (at the house, flat etc) of chez; **she's staying w. me** elle loge chez moi; **it's a habit w. me** c'est une habitude chez moi. **3** (cause) de; **to jump w. joy** sauter de joie. **4** (instrument, means) avec; **to write w. a pen** écrire avec un stylo; **to fill w.** remplir de; **satisfied w.** satisfait de; **w. my own eyes** de mes propres yeux. **5** (description) à; **w. blue eyes** aux yeux bleus. **6** (despite) malgré.

withdraw [wɪðˈdrɔː] vt (pt **withdrew**, pp **withdrawn**) retirer (**from** de); – vi se retirer (**from** de). ◆**withdrawn** a (person) renfermé. ◆**withdrawal** n retrait m; **to suffer from w. symptoms** (of drug addict etc) être en manque.

wither [ˈwɪðər] vi (of plant etc) se flétrir; – vt flétrir. ◆**—ed** a (limb) atrophié. ◆**—ing** a (look) foudroyant; (remark) cinglant.

withhold [wɪðˈhəʊld] vt (pt & pp **withheld**) (help, permission etc) refuser (**from** à); (decision) différer; (money) retenir (**from** de); (information etc) cacher (**from** à).

within [wɪˈðɪn] adv à l'intérieur; – prep (place, container etc) à l'intérieur de, dans; **w. a kilometre of** à moins d'un kilomètre de; **w. a month** (to return etc) avant un mois; (to finish sth) en moins d'un mois; (to pay) sous un mois; **w. my means** dans (les limites de) mes moyens; **w. sight** en vue.

without [wɪˈðaʊt] prep sans; **w. a tie/etc** sans cravate/etc; **w. doing** sans faire.

withstand [wɪðˈstænd] vt (pt & pp **withstood**) résister à.

witness [ˈwɪtnɪs] n (person) témoin m; (evidence) Jur témoignage m; **to bear w. to** témoigner de; – vt être (le) témoin de, voir; (document) signer (pour attester l'authenticité de).

witty [ˈwɪtɪ] a (-ier, -iest) spirituel. ◆**witti-**

-cism n bon mot m, mot m d'esprit. ◆**wittiness** n esprit m.

wives [waɪvz] see **wife**.

wizard [ˈwɪzəd] n magicien m; (genius) Fig génie m, as m.

wizened [ˈwɪz(ə)nd] a ratatiné.

wobble [ˈwɒb(ə)l] vi (of chair etc) branler, boiter; (of cyclist, pile etc) osciller; (of jelly, leg) trembler; (of wheel) tourner de façon irrégulière. ◆**wobbly** a (table etc) bancal, boiteux; **to be w. =** to **wobble**.

woe [wəʊ] n malheur m. ◆**woeful** a triste.

woke, woken [wəʊk, ˈwəʊkən] see **wake**[1].

wolf [wʊlf] **1** n (pl **wolves**) loup m; **w. whistle** sifflement m admiratif. **2** vt **to w. (down)** (food) engloutir.

woman, pl **women** [ˈwʊmən, ˈwɪmɪn] n femme f; **she's a London w.** c'est une Londonienne; **w. doctor** femme f médecin; **women drivers** les femmes fpl au volant; **w. friend** amie f; **w. teacher** professeur m femme; **women's** (attitudes, clothes etc) féminin. ◆**womanhood** n (quality) féminité f; **to reach w.** devenir femme. ◆**womanizer** n Pej coureur m (de femmes or de jupons). ◆**womanly** a féminin.

womb [wuːm] n utérus m.

women [ˈwɪmɪn] see **woman**.

won [wʌn] see **win**.

wonder [ˈwʌndər] **1** n (marvel) merveille f, miracle m; (sense, feeling) émerveillement m; **in w.** (to watch etc) émerveillé; **(it's) no w.** ce n'est pas étonnant (**that** que (+ sub)); – vi (marvel) s'étonner (**at** de); – vt **I w. that** je or ça m'étonne que (+ sub). **2** vt (ask oneself) se demander (**if** si, **why** pourquoi); – vi (reflect) songer (**about** à). ◆**wonderful** a (excellent, astonishing) merveilleux. ◆**wonderfully** adv (beautiful, hot etc) merveilleusement; (to do, work etc) à merveille.

wonky [ˈwɒŋkɪ] a (-ier, -iest) Fam (table etc) bancal; (hat, picture) de travers.

won't [wəʊnt] = **will not**.

woo [wuː] vt (woman) faire la cour à, courtiser; (try to please) Fig chercher à plaire à.

wood [wʊd] n (material, forest) bois m. ◆**woodcut** n gravure f sur bois. ◆**wooded** a (valley etc) boisé. ◆**wooden** a de or en bois; (manner, dancer etc) Fig raide. ◆**woodland** n région f boisée. ◆**woodpecker** n (bird) pic m. ◆**woodwind** n (instruments) Mus bois mpl. ◆**woodwork** n (craft, objects) menuiserie f. ◆**woodworm** n (larvae) vers mpl (du bois); **it has w.** c'est vermoulu. ◆**woody** a

(**-ier, -iest**) (*hill etc*) boisé; (*stem etc*) ligneux.

wool [wʊl] *n* laine *f*; – *a* de laine; (*industry*) lainier. ◆**woollen** *a* de laine; (*industry*) lainier; – *npl* (*garments*) lainages *mpl*. ◆**woolly** *a* (**-ier, -iest**) laineux; (*unclear*) *Fig* nébuleux; – *n* (*garment*) *Fam* lainage *m*.

word [wɜːd] *n* mot *m*; (*spoken*) parole *f*, mot *m*; (*promise*) parole *f*; (*command*) ordre *m*; *pl* (*of song etc*) paroles *fpl*; **by w. of mouth** de vive voix; **to have a w. with s.o.** (*speak to*) parler à qn; (*advise, lecture*) avoir un mot avec qn; **in other words** autrement dit; **I have no w. from** (*news*) je suis sans nouvelles de; **to send w. that . . .** faire savoir que . . . ; **to leave w. that . . .** dire que . . . ; **the last w. in** (*latest development*) le dernier cri en matière de; **w. processing** traitement *m* de texte; – *vt* (*express*) rédiger, formuler. ◆**wording** *n* termes *mpl*. ◆**wordy** *a* (**-ier, -iest**) verbeux.

wore [wɔːr] *see* **wear** 1,2.

work [wɜːk] *n* travail *m*; (*product*) & *Liter* œuvre *f*, ouvrage *m*; (*building or repair work*) travaux *mpl*; **to be at w.** travailler; **farm w.** travaux *mpl* agricoles; **out of w.** au *or* en chômage; **a day off w.** un jour de congé *or* de repos; **he's off w.** il n'est pas allé travailler; **the works** (*mechanism*) le mécanisme; **a gas works** (*factory*) une usine à gaz; **w. force** main-d'œuvre *f*; **a heavy w. load** beaucoup de travail; – *vi* travailler; (*of machine etc*) marcher, fonctionner; (*of drug*) agir; **to w. on** (*book etc*) travailler à; (*principle*) se baser sur; **to w. at** *or* **on sth** (*improve*) travailler qch; **to w. loose** (*of knot, screw*) se desserrer; (*of tooth*) se mettre à branler; **to w. towards** (*result, agreement, aim*) travailler à; **to w. out** (*succeed*) marcher; (*train*) *Sp* s'entraîner; **it works out at £5** ça fait cinq livres; **it works up to** (*climax*) ça tend vers; **to w. up to sth** (*in speech etc*) en venir à qch; – *vt* (*person*) faire travailler; (*machine*) faire marcher; (*mine*) exploiter; (*miracle*) faire; (*metal, wood etc*) travailler; **to get worked up** s'exciter; **to w. in** (*reference, bolt*) introduire; **to w. off** (*debt*) payer en travaillant; (*excess fat*) se débarrasser de (par l'exercice); (*anger*) passer, assouvir; **to w. out** (*solve*) résoudre; (*calculate*) calculer; (*scheme, plan*) élaborer; **to w. up an appetite** s'ouvrir l'appétit; **to w. up enthusiasm** s'enthousiasmer; **to w. one's way up** (*rise socially etc*) faire du chemin. ◆**working** *a* (*day, clothes etc*) de travail; (*population*)

actif; **Monday's a w. day** on travaille le lundi, lundi est un jour ouvré; **w. class** classe *f* ouvrière; **in w. order** en état de marche; – *npl* (*mechanism*) mécanisme *m*. ◆**workable** *a* (*plan*) praticable. ◆**worker** *n* travailleur, -euse *mf*; (*manual*) ouvrier, -ière *mf*; (*employee, clerk*) employé, -ée *mf*; **blue-collar w.** col *m* bleu.

workaholic [wɜːkəˈhɒlɪk] *n Fam* bourreau *m* de travail. ◆**workbench** *n* établi *m*. ◆**working-'class** *a* ouvrier. ◆**workman** *n* (*pl* **-men**) ouvrier *m*. ◆**workmanship** *n* maîtrise *f*, travail *m*. ◆**workmate** *n* camarade *mf* de travail. ◆**workout** *n Sp* (*séance f*) d'entraînement *m*. ◆**workroom** *n* salle *f* de travail. ◆**workshop** *n* atelier *m*. ◆**work-shy** *a* peu enclin au travail. ◆**work-to-'rule** *n* grève *f* du zèle.

world [wɜːld] *n* monde *m*; **all over the w.** dans le monde entier; **the richest/etc in the world** le *or* la plus riche/*etc* du monde; **a w. of** (*a lot of*) énormément de; **to think the w. of** penser énormément de bien de; **why in the w. . . . ?** pourquoi diable . . . ?; **out of this w.** (*wonderful*) *Fam* formidable; – *a* (*war etc*) mondial; (*champion, cup, record*) du monde. ◆**world-'famous** *a* de renommée mondiale. ◆**worldly** *a* (*pleasures*) de ce monde; (*person*) qui a l'expérience du monde. ◆**world'wide** *a* universel.

worm [wɜːm] **1** *n* ver *m*. **2** *vt* **to w. one's way into** s'insinuer dans; **to w. sth out of s.o.** soutirer qch à qn. ◆**worm-eaten** *a* (*wood*) vermoulu; (*fruit*) véreux.

worn [wɔːn] *see* **wear** 1,2; – *a* (*tyre etc*) usé. ◆**worn-'out** *a* (*object*) complètement usé; (*person*) épuisé.

worry ['wʌrɪ] *n* souci *m*; – *vi* s'inquiéter (*about sth* de qch, *about s.o.* pour qn); – *vt* inquiéter; **to be worried** être inquiet; **to be worried sick** se ronger les sangs. ◆**-ing** *a* (*news etc*) inquiétant. ◆**worrier** *n* anxieux, -euse *mf*. ◆**worryguts** *n*, *Am* **worrywart** *n Fam* anxieux, -euse *mf*.

worse [wɜːs] *a* pire, plus mauvais (**than** que); **to get w.** se détériorer; **he's getting w.** (*in health*) il va de plus en plus mal; (*in behaviour*) il se conduit de plus en plus mal; – *adv* plus mal (**than** que); **I could do w.** je pourrais faire pire; **to hate/etc w.** than détester/*etc* plus que; **to be w. off** (*financially*) aller moins bien financièrement; – *n* **there's w. (to come)** il y a pire encore; **a change for the w.** une détérioration. ◆**worsen** *vti* empirer.

worship ['wɜːʃɪp] *n* culte *m*; **his W. the Mayor** Monsieur le Maire; – *vt* (**-pp-**)

(*person*) & *Rel* adorer; (*money etc*) *Pej* avoir le culte de; – *vi Rel* faire ses dévotions (**at** à). **◆worshipper** *n* adorateur, -trice *mf*; (*in church*) fidèle *mf*.

worst [wɜːst] *a* pire, plus mauvais; – *adv* (**the**) le plus mal; **to come off w.** (*in struggle etc*) avoir le dessous; – *n* **the w.** (**one**) (*object, person*) le *or* la pire, le *or* la plus mauvais(e); **the w. (thing) is that . . .** le pire c'est que . . . ; **at (the) w.** au pis aller; **at its w.** (*crisis*) à son plus mauvais point *or* moment; **to get the w. of it** (*in struggle etc*) avoir le dessous; **the w. is yet to come** on n'a pas encore vu le pire.

worsted ['wustid] *n* laine *f* peignée.

worth [wɜːθ] *n* valeur *f*; **to buy 50 pence w. of chocolates** acheter pour cinquante pence de chocolats; – *a* **to be w.** valoir; **how much** *or* **what is it w.?** ça vaut combien?; **the film's w. seeing** le film vaut la peine *or* le coup d'être vu; **it's w. (one's) while** ça (en) vaut la peine *or* le coup; **it's w. (while) waiting** ça vaut la peine d'attendre. **◆worthless** *a* qui ne vaut rien. **◆worth'while** *a* (*book, film etc*) qui vaut la peine d'être lu, vu *etc*; (*activity*) qui (en) vaut la peine; (*contribution, plan*) valable; (*cause*) louable; (*satisfying*) qui donne des satisfactions.

worthy ['wɜːði] *a* (**-ier, -iest**) digne (**of** de); (*laudable*) louable; – *n* (*person*) notable *m*.

would [wud, *unstressed* wəd] *v aux* **I w. stay, I'd stay** (*conditional tense*) je resterais; **he w. have done it** il l'aurait fait; **w. you help me, please?** voulez-vous m'aider, s'il vous plaît?; **w. you like some tea?** voudriez-vous (prendre) du thé?; **I w. see her every day** (*used to*) je la voyais chaque jour. **◆would-be** *a* (*musician etc*) soi-disant.

wound¹ [wuːnd] *vt* (*hurt*) blesser; **the wounded** les blessés *mpl*; – *n* blessure *f*.

wound² [waund] *see* **wind²**.

wove, woven [wəuv, 'wəuv(ə)n] *see* **weave**.

wow! [wau] *int Fam* (c'est) formidable!

wrangle ['ræŋg(ə)l] *n* dispute *f*; – *vi* se disputer.

wrap [ræp] *vt* (**-pp-**) **to w. (up)** envelopper; **to w. (oneself) up** (*dress warmly*) se couvrir; **wrapped up in** (*engrossed*) *Fig* absorbé par; – *n* (*shawl*) châle *m*; (*cape*) pèlerine *f*; **plastic w.** *Am* scel-o-frais® *m*. **◆wrapping** *n* (*action, material*) emballage *m*; **w. paper** papier *m* d'emballage. **◆wrapper** *n* (*of sweet*) papier *m*; (*of book*) jaquette *f*.

wrath [rɒθ] *n Lit* courroux *m*.

wreak [riːk] *vt* **to w. vengeance on** se venger de; **to w. havoc on** ravager.

wreath [riːθ] *n* (*pl* **-s** [riːðz]) (*on head, for funeral*) couronne *f*.

wreck [rek] *n* (*ship*) épave *f*; (*sinking*) naufrage *m*; (*train etc*) train *m etc* accidenté; (*person*) épave *f* (humaine); **to be a nervous w.** être à bout de nerfs; – *vt* détruire; (*ship*) provoquer le naufrage de; (*career, hopes etc*) *Fig* briser, détruire. **◆—age** *n* (*fragments*) débris *mpl*. **◆—er** *n* (*breakdown truck*) *Am* dépanneuse *f*.

wren [ren] *n* (*bird*) roitelet *m*.

wrench [rentʃ] *vt* (*tug at*) tirer sur; (*twist*) tordre; **to w. sth from s.o.** arracher qch à qn; – *n* mouvement *m* de torsion; (*tool*) clé *f* (à écrous), *Am* clé *f* à mollette; (*distress*) *Fig* déchirement *m*.

wrest [rest] *vt* **to w. sth from s.o.** arracher qch à qn.

wrestl|e ['res(ə)l] *vi* lutter (**with s.o.** contre qn); **to w. with** (*problem etc*) *Fig* se débattre avec. **◆—ing** *n Sp* lutte *f*; (**all-in**) w. catch *m*. **◆—er** *n* lutteur, -euse *mf*; catcheur, -euse *mf*.

wretch [retʃ] *n* (*unfortunate person*) malheureux, -euse *mf*; (*rascal*) misérable *mf*. **◆wretched** [-ɪd] *a* (*poor, pitiful*) misérable; (*dreadful*) affreux; (*annoying*) maudit.

wriggle ['rɪg(ə)l] *vi* **to w. (about)** se tortiller; (*of fish*) frétiller; **to w. out of** (*difficulty, task etc*) esquiver; – *vt* (*fingers, toes*) tortiller.

wring [rɪŋ] *vt* (*pt & pp* **wrung**) (*neck*) tordre; **to w. (out)** (*clothes*) essorer; (*water*) faire sortir; **to w. sth out of s.o.** *Fig* arracher qch à qn; **wringing wet** (*trempé*) à tordre.

wrinkle ['rɪŋk(ə)l] *n* (*on skin*) ride *f*; (*in cloth or paper*) pli *m*; – *vt* (*skin*) rider; (*cloth, paper*) plisser; – *vi* se rider; faire des plis.

wrist [rɪst] *n* poignet *m*. **◆wristwatch** *n* montre-bracelet *f*.

writ [rɪt] *n* acte *m* judiciaire; **to issue a w. against s.o.** assigner qn (en justice).

write [raɪt] *vt* (*pt* **wrote**, *pp* **written**) écrire; **to w. down** noter; **to w. off** (*debt*) passer aux profits et pertes; **to w. out** écrire; (*copy*) recopier; **to w. up** (*from notes*) rédiger; (*diary, notes*) mettre à jour; – *vi* écrire; **to w. away** *or* **off** *or* **up for** (*details etc*) écrire pour demander; **to w. back** répondre; **to w. in** *Rad TV* écrire (**for information/***etc* pour demander des renseignements/*etc*). **◆w.-off** *n a* (**complete**) **w.-off** (*car*) une véritable épave. **◆w.-up** *n* (*report*) *Journ* compte rendu *m*. **◆writing** *n* (*handwriting*) écriture *f*; (*literature*) littérature *f*; **to put (down) in w.** mettre par écrit; **some w.** (*on page*) quelque chose d'écrit; **his** *or* **her**

writing(s) (*works*) ses écrits *mpl;* **w. desk** secrétaire *m;* **w. pad** bloc *m* de papier à lettres; **w. paper** papier *m* à lettres. ◆**writer** *n* auteur *m* (**of** de); (*literary*) écrivain *m.*

writhe [raɪð] *vi* (*in pain etc*) se tordre.

written ['rɪt(ə)n] *see* write.

wrong [rɒŋ] *a* (*sum, idea etc*) faux, erroné; (*direction, time etc*) mauvais; (*unfair*) injuste; **to be w.** (*of person*) avoir tort (**to do** de faire); (*mistaken*) se tromper; **it's w. to swear/etc** (*morally*) c'est mal de jurer/*etc;* **it's the w. road** ce n'est pas la bonne route; **you're the w. man** (*for job etc*) tu n'es pas l'homme qu'il faut; **the clock's w.** la pendule n'est pas à l'heure; **something's w.** quelque chose ne va pas; **something's w. with the phone** le téléphone ne marche pas bien; **something's w. with her arm** elle a quelque chose au bras; **nothing's w.** tout va bien; **what's w. with you?** qu'est-ce tu as?; **the w. way round** *or* **up** à l'envers; – *adv* mal; **to go w.** (*err*) se tromper; (*of plan*) mal tourner; (*of vehicle, machine*) tomber en panne; – *n* (*injustice*) injustice *f;* (*evil*) mal *m;* **to be in the w.** avoir tort; **right and w.** le bien et le mal; – *vt* faire (du) tort à. ◆**wrongdoer** *n* (*criminal*) malfaiteur *m.* ◆**wrongful** *a* injustifié; (*arrest*) arbitraire. ◆**wrongfully** *adv* à tort. ◆**wrongly** *adv* incorrectement; (*to inform, translate*) mal; (*to suspect etc*) à tort.

wrote [rəʊt] *see* write.

wrought [rɔːt] *a* **w. iron** fer *m* forgé. ◆**w.-'iron** *a* en fer forgé.

wrung [rʌŋ] *see* wring.

wry [raɪ] *a* (**wryer, wryest**) (*comment*) ironique; (*smile*) forcé; **to pull a w. face** grimacer.

X

X, x [eks] *n* X, x *m.* ◆**X-ray** *n* (*beam*) rayon *m* X; (*photo*) radio(graphie) *f;* **to have an X-ray** passer une radio; **X-ray examination** examen *m* radioscopique; – *vt* radiographier.

xenophobia [zenə'fəʊbɪə] *n* xénophobie *f.*
Xerox® ['zɪərɒks] *n* photocopie *f;* – *vt* photocopier.
Xmas ['krɪsməs] *n Fam* Noël *m.*
xylophone ['zaɪləfəʊn] *n* xylophone *m.*

Y

Y, y [waɪ] *n* Y, y *m.*
yacht [jɒt] *n* yacht *m.* ◆**—ing** *n* yachting *m.*
yank [jæŋk] *vt Fam* tirer d'un coup sec; **to y. off** *or* **out** arracher; – *n* coup *m* sec.
Yank(ee) ['jæŋk(ɪ)] *n Fam* Ricain, -aine *mf, Pej* Amerloque *mf.*
yap [jæp] *vi* (**-pp-**) (*of dog*) japper; (*jabber*) *Fam* jacasser.
yard [jɑːd] *n* **1** (*of house etc*) cour *f;* (*for storage*) dépôt *m,* chantier *m;* (*garden*) *Am* jardin *m* (à l'arrière de la maison); **builder's y.** chantier *m* de construction. **2** (*measure*) yard *m* (= 91,44 cm). ◆**yardstick** *n* (*criterion*) mesure *f.*
yarn [jɑːn] *n* **1** (*thread*) fil *m.* **2** (*tale*) *Fam* longue histoire *f.*
yawn [jɔːn] *vi* bâiller; – *n* bâillement *m.* ◆**—ing** *a* (*gulf etc*) béant.

yeah [jeə] *adv* (*yes*) *Fam* ouais.
year [jɪər] *n* an *m,* année *f;* (*of wine*) année *f; school/tax/etc* **y.** année *f* scolaire/fiscale/*etc;* **this y.** cette année; **in the y. 1990** en (l'an) 1990; **he's ten years old** il a dix ans; **New Y.** Nouvel An, Nouvelle Année; **New Year's Day** le jour de l'An; **New Year's Eve** la Saint-Sylvestre. ◆**yearbook** *n* annuaire *m.* ◆**yearly** *a* annuel; – *adv* annuellement.
yearn [jɜːn] *vi* **to y.** for s.o. languir après qn; **to y. for sth** avoir très envie de qch; **to y. to do** avoir très envie de faire. ◆**—ing** *n* grande envie *f* (**for** de, **to do** de faire); (*nostalgia*) nostalgie *f.*
yeast [jiːst] *n* levure *f.*
yell [jel] *vti* **to y.** (**out**) hurler; **to y. at s.o.** (*scold*) crier après qn; – *n* hurlement *m.*

yellow ['jelǝʊ] **1** *a* & *n* (*colour*) jaune (*m*); −
vi jaunir. **2** *a* (*cowardly*) *Fam* froussard.
◆**yellowish** *a* jaunâtre.

yelp [jelp] *vi* (*of dog*) japper; − *n* jappement
m.

yen [jen] *n* (*desire*) grande envie *f* (**for** de, **to**
do de faire).

yes [jes] *adv* oui; (*contradicting negative
question*) si; − *n* oui *m* inv.

yesterday ['jestǝdɪ] *adv* & *n* hier (*m*); **y.
morning/evening** hier matin/soir; **the day
before y.** avant-hier.

yet [jet] **1** *adv* encore; (*already*) déjà; **she
hasn't come (as) y.** elle n'est pas encore
venue; **has he come y.?** est-il déjà arrivé?;
the best y. le meilleur jusqu'ici; **y. more
complicated** (*even more*) encore plus
compliqué; **not** (*just*) **y., not y. awhile** pas
pour l'instant. **2** *conj* (*nevertheless*)
pourtant.

yew [juː] *n* (*tree, wood*) if *m*.

Yiddish ['jɪdɪʃ] *n* & *a* yiddish (*m*).

yield [jiːld] *n* rendement *m*; (*profit*) rapport
m; − *vt* (*produce*) produire, rendre; (*profit*)
rapporter; (*give up*) céder (**to** à); − *vi*
(*surrender, give way*) céder (**to** à); (*of tree,
land etc*) rendre; **'y.'** (*road sign*) *Am* 'cédez
la priorité'.

yob(bo) ['jɒb(ǝʊ)] *n* (*pl* **yob(bo)s** *Sl*
loubar(d) *m*.

yoga ['jǝʊgǝ] *n* yoga *m*.

yog(h)urt ['jɒgǝt, *Am* 'jǝʊgǝt] *n* yaourt *m*.

yoke [jǝʊk] *n* (*for oxen*) & *Fig* joug *m*.

yokel ['jǝʊk(ǝ)l] *n Pej* plouc *m*.

yolk [jǝʊk] *n* jaune *m* (d'œuf).

yonder ['jɒndǝr] *adv Lit* là-bas.

you [juː] *pron* **1** (*polite form singular*) vous;
(*familiar form singular*) tu; (*polite and
familiar form plural*) vous; (*object*) vous, te,
t'; *pl* vous; (*after prep & stressed*) vous; toi;
pl vous; (**to**) **y.** (*indirect*) vous, te, t'; *pl*

vous; **y. are** vous êtes; tu es; **I see y.** je vous
vois; je te vois; **I give it to y.** je vous le
donne; je te le donne; **with y.** avec vous;
avec toi; **y. teachers** vous autres professeurs; **y. idiot!** espèce d'imbécile! **2** (*indefinite*) on; (*object*) vous; te, t'; *pl* vous; **y.
never know** on ne sait jamais.

young [jʌŋ] *a* (**-er**, **-est**) jeune; **my young(er)
brother** mon (frère) cadet; **his** *or* **her youngest brother** le cadet de ses frères; **the
youngest son** le cadet; − *n* (*of animals*)
petits *mpl*; **the y.** (*people*) les jeunes *mpl*.
◆**young-looking** *a* qui a l'air jeune.
◆**youngster** *n* jeune *m/f*.

your [jɔːr] *poss a* (*polite form singular, polite
and familiar form plural*) votre, *pl* vos;
(*familiar form singular*) ton, ta, *pl* tes;
(*one's*) son, sa, *pl* ses. ◆**yours** *poss pron* le
vôtre, la vôtre, *pl* les vôtres; (*familiar form
singular*) le tien, la tienne, *pl* les tien(ne)s;
this book is y. ce livre est à vous *or* est le
vôtre; ce livre est à toi *or* est le tien; **a friend
of y.** un ami à vous; un ami à toi. ◆**your-
'self** *pron* (*polite form*) vous-même;
(*familiar form*) toi-même; (*reflexive*) vous;
te, t'; (*after prep*) vous; toi; **you wash y.**
vous vous lavez; tu te laves. ◆**your-
'selves** *pron pl* vous-mêmes; (*reflexive &
after prep*) vous.

youth [juːθ] *n* (*pl* **-s** [juːðz]) (*age, young
people*) jeunesse *f*; (*young man*) jeune *m*; **y.
club** maison *f* des jeunes. ◆**youthful** *a*
(*person*) jeune; (*quality, smile etc*) juvénile,
jeune. ◆**youthfulness** *n* jeunesse *f*.

yoyo ['jǝʊjǝʊ] *n* (*pl* **-os**) yo-yo *m* inv.

yucky ['jʌkɪ] *a Sl* dégueulasse.

Yugoslav ['juːgǝʊslɑːv] *a* & *n* yougoslave
(*m/f*). ◆**Yugo'slavia** *n* Yougoslavie *f*.

yummy ['jʌmɪ] *a* (**-ier**, **-iest**) *Sl* délicieux.

yuppie ['jʌpɪ] *n* jeune cadre *m* ambitieux,
jeune loup *m*, NAP *m/f*.

Z

Z, z [zed, *Am* ziː] *n* Z, z *m*.

zany ['zeɪnɪ] *a* (**-ier**, **-iest**) farfelu.

zeal [ziːl] *n* zèle *m*. ◆**zealous** ['zelǝs] *a* zélé.
◆**zealously** *adv* avec zèle.

zebra ['ziːbrǝ, 'zebrǝ] *n* zèbre *m*; **z. crossing**
passage *m* pour piétons.

zenith ['zenɪθ] *n* zénith *m*.

zero ['zɪǝrǝʊ] *n* (*pl* **-os**) zéro *m*; **z. hour** *Mil*
& *Fig* l'heure H.

zest [zest] *n* **1** (*gusto*) entrain *m*; (*spice*) *Fig*
piquant *m*; **z. for living** appétit *m* de vivre.
2 (*of lemon, orange*) zeste *m*.

zigzag ['zɪgzæg] *n* zigzag *m*; − *a* & *adv* en
zigzag; − *vi* (**-gg-**) zigzaguer.

zinc [zɪŋk] *n* (*metal*) zinc *m*.

zip [zɪp] **1** *n* **z.** (**fastener**) fermeture *f*
éclair®; − *vt* (**-pp-**) **to z.** (**up**) fermer (avec
une fermeture éclair®). **2** *n* (*vigour*) *Fam*

entrain *m*; – *vi* (-pp-) (*go quickly*) aller comme l'éclair. **3** *a* **z. code** *Am* code *m* postal. ◆**zipper** *n Am* fermeture *f* éclair®.

zit [zɪt] *n* (*pimple*) *Am Fam* bouton *m*.

zither ['zɪðər] *n* cithare *f*.

zodiac ['zəudɪæk] *n* zodiaque *m*.

zombie ['zɒmbɪ] *n* (*spiritless person*) *Fam* robot *m*, zombie *m*.

zone [zəun] *n* zone *f*; (*division of city*) secteur *m*.

zoo [zuː] *n* zoo *m*. ◆**zoological** [zuːə-'lɒdʒɪk(ə)l] *a* zoologique. ◆**zoology** [zuː-'ɒlədʒɪ] *n* zoologie *f*.

zoom [zuːm] **1** *vi* (*rush*) se précipiter; **to z. past** passer comme un éclair. **2** *n* **z. lens** zoom *m*; – *vi* **to z. in** *Cin* faire un zoom, zoomer (**on** sur).

zucchini [zuːˈkiːnɪ] *n* (*pl* **-ni** *or* **-nis**) *Am* courgette *f*.

zwieback ['zwiːbæk] *n* (*rusk*) *Am* biscotte *f*.